PUBLISHER'S FOREWORD

An Expository Dictionary of Biblical Words combines in one volume W. E. Vine's *An Expository Dictionary of New Testament Words* and *Nelson's Expository Dictionary of the Old Testament* by Merrill Unger and William White, Jr. The lasting popularity of these works has provided a convincing indication that serious students of the Bible would find this one-volume edition a useful and welcome addition to any reference library.

The publication of this volume provides a resource that will facilitate the study of biblical word meanings for those who may or may not have had formal training in Greek or Hebrew. At no other time has there been available a more complete language aid or study tool.

An Expository Dictionary of Biblical Words allows the reader easy access to the alphabetized English equivalents of the Greek or Hebrew words from which they are translated. Throughout the text the most significant biblical words are illustrated by Scripture passages, comments, cross-references, ancient and modern meanings, precise etymologies, historical notes, and clearly defined technical information. Each original language is indexed, making this volume's format especially practical.

It is a pleasure to introduce a versatile reference work of this importance that will service the needs of beginning lay students and scholars alike.

February, 1984   The Publisher

Nelson's Expository Dictionary
of the
Old Testament

Edited by
Merrill F. Unger, Th.M., Th.D., Ph.D.
William White, Jr., Th.M., Ph.D.

CONTRIBUTORS

Gleason Archer
E. Clark Copeland
Leonard Coppes
Louis Goldberg
R. K. Harrison
Horace Hummel
George Kufeldt
Eugene H. Merrill
Walter Roehrs
Raymond Surburg
Willem van Gemeren
Donald Wold

FOREWORD

THE *Expository Dictionary of the Old Testament* will be a useful tool in the hands of the student who has little or no formal training in the Hebrew language. It will open up the treasures of truth that often lie buried in the original language of the Old Testament, sometimes close to the surface and sometimes deeply imbedded far beneath the surface.

The student trained in Hebrew will find the *Expository Dictionary* to be a handy reference source. But the student without Hebrew training will experience a special thrill in being able to use this study tool in digging out truths from the Hebrew Bible not otherwise accessible to him.

It is, of course, possible to be a serious student of the Old Testament without having a knowledge of the Hebrew language. English translations and commentaries are of inestimable value and have their proper place. But a reference book that opens up the language in which the Scriptures were originally revealed and recorded, and which makes them available to readers unacquainted with the original tongue, has a value that at once becomes apparent.

As the language divinely chosen to record the prophecies of Christ, Hebrew possesses admirable qualities for the task assigned it. The language has a singularly rhythmic and musical quality. In poetic form, it especially has a noble dignity of style, combined with a vividness that makes it an effective vehicle for expression of sacred truth. The ideas behind its vocabulary give Hebrew a lively, picturesque nature.

Most Hebrew words are built upon verbal roots consisting of three consonants called *radicals*. There are approximately 1850 such roots in the Old Testament, from which various nouns and other parts of speech have been derived. Many of these roots represent theological, moral, and ceremonial concepts that have been obscured by the passage of time; recent archaeological and linguistic research is shedding new light on many of these concepts. Old Testament scholars find that biblical Hebrew can be compared with other Semitic languages such as Arabic, Assyrian, Ugaritic, Ethiopic, and Aramaic to discover the basic meaning of many heretofore obscure terms.

But it is not enough merely to have clarified the meaning of each root word. Each word can take on different shades of meaning as it is employed in various contexts, so one must study the various biblical occurrences of the word to arrive at an accurate understanding of its intended use.

This type of research has introduced students of Hebrew to a new world of understanding the Old Testament. But how can this material be made available to those who do not know Hebrew? That is the purpose of the present work.

Now the lay student can have before him the Hebrew root, or a Hebrew word based on that root, and can trace its development to its use in the passage before him. Moreover, he can acquire some appreciation of the richness and variety of the Hebrew vocabulary. For example, Hebrew synonyms often have pivotal doctrinal repercussions, as with the word *virgin* in Isaiah 7:14, compared with similar words meaning "young woman." In some cases, a play on words is virtually impossible to reflect in the English translation (e.g., Zeph. 2:4-7). Some Hebrew words can have quite different—sometimes exactly

vii

opposite—meanings in different contexts; thus the word *bārak* can mean "to bless" or "to curse," and *gā'al* can mean "to redeem" or "to pollute."

The lay student, of course, will suffer some disadvantage in not knowing Hebrew. Yet it is fair to say that an up-to-date expository dictionary that makes a happy selection of the more meaningful Hebrew words of the Old Testament will open up a treasure house of truth contained in the Hebrew Bible. It can offer a tremendous boon to the meaningful study of Scripture. It cannot fail to become an essential reference work for all serious students of the Bible.

MERRILL F. UNGER

INTRODUCTION

THE writings of the New Testament are based to a large measure on God's revelation in the Old Testament. To understand the New Testament themes of Creation, Fall, and Restoration, it is necessary to read of their origin in the Old Testament.

The New Testament was written in a popular dialect of an Indo-European language, Greek. The Old Testament was written in the Semitic languages of Hebrew and Aramaic. For centuries, lay students of the Bible have found it very difficult to understand the structure of biblical Hebrew. Study guides to biblical Hebrew are designed for people who can read Hebrew—and many of them are written in German, which only compounds the difficulty.

This *Expository Dictionary* seeks to present about 500 significant terms of the Old Testament for lay readers who are not familiar with Hebrew. It describes the frequency, usage, and meaning of these terms as fully as possible. No source has been ignored in seeking to bring the latest Hebrew scholarship to the student who seeks it. It is hoped that this small reference book will enlighten Bible students to the riches of God's truth in the Old Testament.

A. The Place of Hebrew in History. Hebrew language and literature hold a unique place in the course of Western civilization. It emerged sometime after 1500 B.C. in the area of Palestine, along the eastern shore of the Mediterranean Sea. The Jewish people have used Hebrew continuously in one location or another to the present day. A modernized dialect of Hebrew (with spelling modifications) is the official language of the State of Israel.

When Alexander the Great came to power, he united the Greek city-states under the influence of Macedonia from about 330 B.C. to 323 B.C. Alexander and his generals virtually annihilated the social structures and languages of the ancient societies that their empire had absorbed. The Babylonians, Aramaeans, Persians, and Egyptians ceased to exist as distinct civilizations; only the Greek (Hellenistic) culture remained. Judaism was the only ancient religion and Hebrew the only ancient language that survived this onslaught.

The Hebrew Bible contains the continuous history of civilization from Creation to Roman times. It is the only record of God's dealings with humanity through His prophets, priests, and kings. In addition, it is the only ancient religious document that has survived completely intact.

Hebrew is related to Aramaic, Syriac, and such modern languages as Amharic and Arabic (both ancient and modern). It belongs to a group of languages known as the *Semitic* languages (so called because Scripture says that they were spoken by the descendants of Noah's son, Shem). The oldest known Semitic language is Akkadian, which was written in the "wedge-shaped" or *cuneiform* system of signs. The earliest Akkadian texts were written on clay tablets in about 2400 B.C. Babylonian and Assyrian are later dialects of Akkadian; both influenced the development of Hebrew. Because the Akkadian, Babylonian, and Assyrian languages were all used in Mesopotamia, they are classified as "East Semitic" languages.

The earliest evidence for the origins of "West Semitic" languages appears to be an inscription from the ancient city of Ebla. This was a little-known capital of a Semitic state in what is now Northern Syria. The tablets of Ebla are bilingual, written in both Sumerian and Eblaite. The team of Italian archaeologists excavating Ebla have reported that these tablets contain a number of personal and place names mentioned in the Book of Genesis. Some of the tablets have been dated as early as 2400 B.C. Since Hebrew was also a West Semitic language, the publication of Ebla's texts may cast new light on many older Hebrew words and phrases.

The earliest complete series of pre-Hebrew texts comes from the ancient Canaanite city of Ugarit. Located on a cluster of hills in southern Lebanon, Ugarit has yielded texts that contain detailed information about the religion, poetry, and trade of the Canaanite people. The texts are dated between 1800 and 1200 B.C. These tablets contain many words and phrases that are almost identical to words found in the Hebrew Bible. The Ugaritic dialect illuminates the development of Old Hebrew (or Paleo-Hebrew). The poetic structure of the Ugaritic language is mirrored in many passages of the Old Testament, such as the "Song of Deborah" in Judges 5. The scribes of Ugarit wrote in a modified cuneiform script that was virtually alphabetic; this script prepared the way for using the simpler Phoenician writing system.

A number of texts from various parts of the Near East contain West Semitic words and phrases. The most important of these are the tablets from the ancient Egyptian city of Amarna. These tablets were written by the petty rulers of the Egyptian colonies of Syria-Palestine and by their overlord, the pharaoh. The tablets from the minor princes were written in Babylonian; but when the correspondent's scribe did not know the proper Babylonian word to express a certain idea, he substituted a Canaanite "gloss." These glosses tell us much about the words and spellings that were used in Palestine during the time when Paleo-Hebrew emerged as a distinct language.

The Hebrew language probably came into existence during the patriarchal period, about 2000 B.C.. The language was reduced to writing in about 1250 B.C., and the earliest extant Hebrew inscription dates from about 1000 B.C. These early inscriptions were carved on stone; the oldest known Hebrew scrolls were found in the Qumran caves near the Dead Sea, and they date from the third century B.C. While some secular Hebrew texts have survived, the primary source for our knowledge of classical Hebrew is the Old Testament itself.

B. The Origin of the Hebrew Writing System. Greek tradition claims that Phoenicians invented the alphabet. Actually, this is only partially true, since the Phoenician writing system was not an alphabet as we know it today. It was a simplified *syllabary* system—in other words, its various symbols represent syllables rather than separate vocal components. The Hebrew writing system grew out of the Phoenician system.

The Hebrew writing system gradually changed over the centuries. From 1000 to 200 B.C., a rounded script (Old Phoenician style) was used. This script was last used for copying the biblical text and may be seen in the Dead Sea Scrolls. But after the Jews returned from their Babylonian Captivity, they began to use the square script of the Aramaic language, which was the official language of the Persian Empire. Jewish scribes adopted the Aramaic book hand, a more precise form of the script. When Jesus mentioned the "jot" and "tittle" of the Mosaic Law, He was referring to manuscripts in the square script. The book hand is used in all printed editions of the Hebrew Bible.

C. A Concise History of the Hebrew Bible. Undoubtedly the text of the Hebrew Bible was updated and revised several times in antiquity, and there was more than one textual tradition. Many archaic words in the Pentateuch suggest that Moses used early cuneiform documents in compiling his account of history. Scribes of the royal court under David and Solomon probably revised the text and updated obscure expressions. Apparently certain historical books, such as 1 and 2 Kings and 1 and 2 Chronicles, represent the official annals of the kingdom. These books represent the historical tradition of the priestly class.

The message of the prophets was probably written down sometime after the prophets delivered their message. There is a variety of writing styles among the prophetic books; and several, such as Amos and Hosea, seem to be closer to colloquial speech.

The text of the Old Testament was probably revised again during the time of King Josiah after the Book of Law was rediscovered (2 Kings 22–27; 2 Chronicles 24–35). This would have taken place about 620 B.C. The next two centuries, which brought the Babylonian Captivity, were the most momentous times in the history of Israel. When the Jews began to rebuild Jerusalem under Ezra and Nehemiah in 450 B.C., their common speech was the Aramaic language of the Persian court. This language became more popular among the Jews until it displaced Hebrew as the dominant language of Judaism in the Christian era. There is evidence that the Old Testament text was revised again at that time.

After the Greeks came to power under Alexander the Great, the preservation of Hebrew became a political issue; the conservative Jewish parties wanted to retain it. But the Jews of the *Diaspora*—those living outside of Palestine—depended upon versions of the biblical text in Aramaic (called the *Targums*) or Greek (called the *Septuagint*).

Both the Targums and Septuagint were translated from Hebrew manuscripts. There were substantial differences between these versions, and the Jewish rabbis went to great efforts to explain these differences.

After Jerusalem fell to the armies of the Roman general Titus, Jewish biblical scholars were scattered throughout the ancient world and the knowledge of Hebrew began to decline. From A.D. 200 to nearly A.D. 900, groups of scholars attempted to devise systems of vowel markings (later called *points*) to aid Jewish readers who no longer spoke Hebrew. The scholars who did this work are called *Masoretes,* and their markings are called the *Masora.* The Masoretic text that they produced represents the *consonants* that had been preserved from about 100 B.C. (as proven by the Dead Sea scrolls); but the *vowel markings* reflect the understanding of the Hebrew language in about A.D. 300. The Masoretic text dominated Old Testament studies in the Middle Ages, and it has served as the basis for virtually all printed versions of the Hebrew Bible.

Unfortunately, we have no complete text of the Hebrew Bible older than the tenth century A.D. The earliest complete segment of the Old Testament (the Prophets) is a copy dating from A.D. 895. While the Dead Sea scrolls yield entire books such as Isaiah, they do not contain a complete copy of the Old Testament text. Therefore, we must still depend upon the long tradition of Hebrew scholarship used in the printed editions of the Hebrew Bible.

The first complete printed edition of the Hebrew Bible was prepared by Felix Pratensis and published by Daniel Bomberg in Venice in 1516. A more extensive edition of the Hebrew Bible was edited by the Jewish-Christian scholar Jacob ben Chayyim in 1524. Scholars continue to use the ben Chayyim text as the basic printed Hebrew Bible.

D. The Hebrew of the Old Testament. The Hebrew of the Old Testament does not have one neat and concise structure; the Old Testament was written over such a long span of time that we cannot expect to have one uniform linguistic tradition. In fact, the Hebrew of the three major sections of the Old Testament varies considerably. These three sections are known as the *Torah* (The Law), *Nevi'im* (The Prophets), and *Kethuvim* (The Writings). In addition to the linguistic differences between the major sections, certain books of the Old Testament have their own peculiarities. For example, Job and Psalms have very ancient words and phrases similar to Ugaritic; Ruth preserves some archaic forms of Moabite speech; and First and Second Samuel reveal the rough, warlike nature of the colloquial idiom of the era of Solomon and David.

As Israel changed from being a confederation of tribes to a dynastic kingdom, the language changed from the speech of herdsmen and caravan traders to the literary language of a settled population. While the books of the New Testament reflect a Greek dialect as it was used over a span of about 75 years, the Old Testament draws upon various forms of the Hebrew language as it evolved over nearly 2,000 years. Therefore, certain texts—such as the early narrative of the Book of Exodus and the last of the Psalms—are virtually written in two different dialects and should be studied with this in mind.

E. Characteristics of the Hebrew Language. Because Hebrew is a Semitic language, its structure and function are quite different from Indo-European languages such as French, German, Spanish, and English. A number of Hebrew consonants cannot be transformed exactly into English letters. Therefore, our English transliterations of Hebrew words suggest that the language sounded very harsh and rough, but it probably was very melodious and beautiful.

Most Hebrew words are built upon a three-consonant root. The same root may appear in a noun, a verb, an adjective and an adverb—all with the same basic meaning. For example, *kəthāb* is a Hebrew noun meaning "book." A verbal form, *kāthab,* means to "write." There is also the Hebrew noun *kəthōbeth,* which means "decoration" or "tattoo." Each of these words repeats the basic set of three consonants, giving them a similarity of sound that would seem awkward in English. It would seem ludicrous for an English writer to compose a sentence like, "The writer wrote the written writing of the writ." But this kind of repetition would be very common in biblical Hebrew. Many Old Testament texts, such as Genesis 49 and Numbers 23, use this type of repetition to play upon the meaning of words.

Hebrew also differs from English and other Indo-European languages in varying the form of a single part of speech. English has only one form of a particular noun or verb, while Hebrew may have two or more forms of the same basic part of speech. Scholars have studied these less common forms of Hebrew words for many centuries, and they have developed a vast literature about these words. Any study of the more important theological terms of the Old Testament must take these studies into consideration.

F. The Form of Words (Morphology). In principle, the basic Hebrew word consists of a three-consonant root and three vowels—two internal and one final (though the final vowel is often not pronounced). We might diagram the typical Hebrew word in his manner:

$$C_1 + V_1 + C_2 + V_2 + C_3 + V_3$$

Using the word *kāthab* as an example, the diagram would look like this:

$$K + A + TH + A + B + \underline{\quad}$$

The different forms of Hebrew words always keep the three consonants in the same relative positions, but they change the vowels inserted between the consonants. For example, *kōthēb* is the participle of *kāthab*, while *kāthôb* is the infinitive.

By extending the verbal forms of their words, Hebrew writers were able to develop very extensive and complex meanings. For example, they could do this by adding syllables at the beginning of the three-consonant root, like this:

Root = *KTHB*
yi + *kǝtōb*—"let him write"
we + *kāthab*—"and he will write"

Sometimes, a writer would double a consonant while keeping the three basic consonants in the same position. For example, he could take the root of KTHB and make the word *wayyikǝtōb*, meaning "and he caused to write."

The Hebrew writer could also add several different endings or *suffixes* to a basic verb to produce an entire clause. For example, using the verb *qātal* (meaning "to kill"), he could develop the word *qǝtaltî-hû* (meaning "I have killed him").

These examples emphasize the fact that Hebrew is a syllabic language. There are no unique consonantal combinations such as diphthongs (or glides) like *cl*, *gr*, *bl*, as in English.

G. Hebrew Word Order. The normal word order of a verbal sentence in Hebrew narrative or prose passage is:

Verb—Object—Indirect Object or Pronoun—Subject

However, it is interesting to note that the Hebrew word order for a nominal sentence may parallel that of English:

Subject—Verb—Predicate Nominative/Adjective

Hebrew writers frequently departed from the verbal arrangement for the sake of emphasis. Yet a Hebrew sentence can seldom be translated into English word-for-word, because the result would be meaningless. Over the centuries, translators have developed standard ways to express these peculiar Semitic thought forms in Indo-European speech.

H. Foreign Words in Hebrew. The Old Testament uses foreign words in various ways, depending upon the context. Akkadian proper names often appear in the patriarchal narratives of Genesis. Here are some examples:

(Sumero-Akkadian) *Sumer* = *Shinar* (Hebrew)
(Akkadian) *Sharrukin* = *Nimrod* (Hebrew)

Several Egyptian terms appear in the narrative of Joseph, just as Babylonian terms appear in the writings of Isaiah and Jeremiah, and Persian words in the Book of Daniel. None of these words have theological significance, however. There is little linguistic evidence that the religious concepts of Israel were borrowed from foreign sources.

The greatest inroad of a foreign idiom is the case of the Aramaic language, which appears in several isolated verses and some entire chapters of the Book of Daniel. As we have already noted, Aramaic became the primary religious language of the Jews living outside of Palestine after the Babylonian Captivity.

I. The Written Text of the Hebrew Bible. The Hebrew text of the Old Testament offers two immediate problems to the uninitiated reader. First is the fact that Hebrew is read from right to left, unlike Indo-European languages; each character of the text and its attendant symbols are read from top to bottom, as well as from right to left. Second is the fact that written Hebrew is a complicated system of syllable symbols, each of which has three components.

The first component is the sign for the consonant itself. Some of the less frequent consonantal signs stand for vowel sounds. (These letters are *aleph* [indicating the long *a* sound], *waw* [to indicate the long *u* sound], and *yod* [to indicate the "ee" sound—as in "see"].) The second component is the pattern of vowel points. The third component is the pattern of *cantellations,* which were added during the Middle Ages to aid cantors in singing the text. Some practice is required before a person is able to read the Hebrew text using all of the three components. The accompanying illustration shows the direction and sequence for reading the text. (Cantellations are omitted.)

ENGLISH TRANSLITERATION: *'ashərê hā'îsh 'asher*

The specific vowel points and their sequence within the word indicate the weight or accentuation to be given to each syllable of the word. Different traditions within Judaism indicate different ways of pronouncing the same Hebrew word, and the vowel points of a particular manuscript will reflect the pronunciation used by the scribes who copied the manuscript. Many Slavic and Spanish speech patterns crept into the medieval Hebrew manuscripts, due to the Jews' association with Slavic and Spanish cultures during the Middle Ages. However, the use of Hebrew speech in modern Israel is tending to standardize the pronunciation of Hebrew.

J. The Meaning of Hebrew Words. Christians have studied the Hebrew language with varying degrees of intensity as long as the church has existed. During the apostolic and early church age (A.D. 40–150), Christians had a great deal of interest in the Hebrew language. Eventually, they depended more heavily upon the Greek Septuagint for reading the Old Testament. In the early Middle Ages, Jerome had to employ Jewish scholars to help him in translating the official Latin Vulgate version of the Old Testament. There was little Christian interest in the Hebrew language in medieval times.

In the sixteenth century, a German Roman Catholic scholar named Johannes Reuchlin studied Hebrew with a Jewish rabbi and began to write introductory books in Latin about Hebrew for Christian students. He also compiled a small Hebrew-Latin dictionary. Reuchlin's work awakened an interest in Hebrew among Christian scholars that has continued to our own day. (The Jewish synagogues had passed on the meaning of the text for centuries, giving little attention to the mechanics of the Hebrew language itself. These traditional meanings are reflected in the King James Version, published after Reuchlin's studies.)

By comparing Akkadian, Ugaritic, Aramaic, and Hebrew languages, modern scholars have been able to understand the meaning of Hebrew words. Here are some of the keys that they have discovered:

1. Cognate Words. Foreign words that have sounds or constructions similar to Hebrew words are called *cognates*. Because words of different Semitic languages are based upon the same three-consonant root, cognates abound. In times past, these cognates gave rise to "folk etymology"—an unscholarly interpretation of words based upon folklore and tradition. Often these folk etymologies were used in interpreting the Old Testament. However, words that are *philological cognates* (form-related) are not necessarily *semantic cognates* (meaning-related). A good example is the Hebrew word *shar,* which means "prince." This same word is used in other Semitic languages, where it means "king."

For centuries, European students of Hebrew used Arabic philological cognates to decipher the meaning of obscure Hebrew words. This unreliable method is used by many of the older English dictionaries and lexicons.

2. Meaning from Context. It has often been said that the best commentary on Scripture is Scripture itself. Nowhere is this more true than in Hebrew word studies. The best method for determining the meaning of any Hebrew word is to study the context in which it appears. If it appears in many different contexts, then the meaning of the word can be found with greater accuracy. For the words that appear with very low frequency (four times or less), non-biblical Hebrew texts or other Semitic texts can help us locate the meaning of the word.

However, there is one caution: It is never wise to use one obscure word to try to determine the meaning of another obscure word. The most difficult words are those that occur only once in the Old Testament text; these are called *hapax legomena* (Greek, "read once"). Fortunately, all the Hebrew words of theological significance occur fairly frequently.

3. Poetic Parallelism. Fully one-third of the Old Testament is poetry. This amount of text is equal to the entire New Testament. English translators have tended to ignore the poetic structure of lengthy Old Testament passages, such as Isaiah 40–66 and the entire Book of Job; but the complexities of Hebrew poetry are vital to our understanding of the Old Testament. This can be seen by studying a modern English version of the Bible that prints poetic passages as such. Several verses from the Psalms in the RSV will illustrate the underlying structure of Hebrew poetry.

Note there is neither rhythm nor meter in Hebrew poetry, unlike most English poetry. Hebrew poetry repeats ideas or the relation of ideas in successive lines. Here is an example:

> (I) "O magnify the Lord with me,
> (II) And let us exalt his name together!"

Notice that virtually every part of speech in Line I can be substituted for its equal in Line II. Scholars designate the individual words in Line I (or Hemistich I) as "A" words and those in Line II (or Hemistich II) as "B" words. Thus we see the pattern in these lines from Psalm 34:

> Hemistich I: O magnify$_A$ the Lord$_A$ with me,$_A$
> Hemistich II: Let us exalt$_B$ His name$_B$ together!"$_B$

As one can readily see, the "A" words can be substituted for the "B" words without changing the meaning of the line, and the reverse is also true. This characteristic of Hebrew poetry is called *parallelism*. In scholarly studies of Hebrew poetry, paired words in a parallel structure are often marked with slanting parallel bars to show (a) which word usually occurs first—that is, the "A" word, (b) the fact that the two words form a parallel pair, and (c) which word is usually the second or "B." We can show this for the third verse of Psalm 34 in this manner:

> O magnify / / exalt; the Lord / / His name; with me / / together.

This *Expository Dictionary* cites such pairs because they indicate important relationships in meaning. Many pairs are used over and over again, almost as synonyms. Thus the usage of Hebrew words in poetry becomes a very valuable tool for our understanding of their meaning. Most of the significant theological terms, including the names and titles of God, are found in such poetic pairs.

K. Theories of Translation. Theories of translation greatly affect our interpretation of our Hebrew words. We may describe the current dominant theories of translation as follows:

1. The Direct Equivalence Method. This method assumes that one will find only one English word to represent each Hebrew word that appears in the Old Testament text. Since some Hebrew words have no one-word equivalent in

English, they are simply *transliterated* (turned into English letters). In this case, the reader must be taught what the transliterated term really meant. This method was used in the earliest translations of the New Testament, which attempted to bring the Latin equivalents of Greek words directly into English. This is how our early English versions adopted a large amount of Latin theological terminology, such as *justification, sanctification,* and *concupiscence.*

2. The Historico-Linguistic Method. This method attempts to find a limited number of English terms that will adequately express the meaning of a particular Hebrew term. A scholar using this method studies the historical record of how the word has been used and gives preference to its most frequent meaning in context. This method has been used in preparing the *Expository Dictionary.*

3. The Dynamic Equivalence Method. This method does not attempt to make any consistent use of an English word for a specific Hebrew word. Instead it endeavors to show the thrust or emphasis of a Hebrew word in each specific context. Thus it allows a very free, colloquial rendering of Old Testament passages. This enables lay readers to get the real kernel of meaning from a particular passage, but it makes Bible word study virtually impossible. For example, a comparison of the concordance for *The Living Bible* and the concordance for the RSV will show the difference in methods of translation. The RSV actually uses fewer different words than the KJV to translate the Hebrew Old Testament. *The Living Bible* uses many more specific words to reflect the subtle shades of meaning in the Hebrew text, thus making it impossible to trace how a particular Hebrew word has been used in different contexts.

This *Expository Dictionary* attempts to show the different methods of translation by indicating the different meanings of a Hebrew word given by various English versions.

L. How to Use This Book. When beginning a word study of a particular Hebrew term, you should obtain good editions of at least three English versions of the Old Testament. Always have a King James Version, a more scholarly version such as the RSV or NASB, and a colloquial version such as the TEV. You should also have a good concordance to the KJV or the RSV.

The *Expository Dictionary* gives wide ranges of meanings for most Hebrew words. They should not be substituted for each other without carefully reviewing the usage of the term in its different contexts. All Hebrew words have different meanings—sometimes even opposite meanings—so they should be studied in all of their occurrences, and not just one.

Strive for consistency in rendering a particular Hebrew word in different contexts. Seek the smallest number of equivalent English words. The contributors to this book have already done extensive research in the original languages and in modern scholarly literature. You can make the best use of their work by looking up the various usages of each word in order to get a balanced view.

Comparison and *frequency* are two fundamental factors in Bible word study. Write down the passages that you are comparing. Do not be afraid to look up all of the occurrences of a particular word. The time you spend will open up your Bible as it has never been opened before.

WILLIAM WHITE, JR.

A

ABOMINATION

A. Noun.

to'ēbāh (תּוֹעֵבָה), "abomination; loathsome, detestable thing." Cognates of this word appear only in Phoenician and Targumic Aramaic. The word appears 117 times and in all periods.

First, *to'ēbāh* defines something or someone as essentially unique in the sense of being "dangerous," "sinister," and "repulsive" to another individual. This meaning appears in Gen. 43:32 (the first occurrence): ". . . The Egyptians might not eat bread with the Hebrews; for that is an abomination unto the Egyptians." To the Egyptians, eating bread with foreigners was repulsive because of their cultural or social differences (cf. Gen. 46:34; Ps. 88:8). Another clear illustration of this essential clash of disposition appears in Prov. 29:27: "An unjust man is an abomination to the just: and he that is upright in the way is abomination to the wicked." When used with reference to God, this nuance of the word describes people, things, acts, relationships, and characteristics that are "detestable" to Him because they are contrary to His nature. Things related to death and idolatry are loathsome to God: "Thou shalt not eat any abominable thing" (Deut. 14:3). People with habits loathsome to God are themselves detestable to Him: "The woman shall not wear that which pertaineth unto a man, neither shall a man put on a woman's garment: for all that do so are abomination unto the Lord thy God" (Deut. 22:5). Directly opposed to *to'ēbāh* are such reactions as "delight" and "loveth" (Prov. 15:8-9).

Second, *to'ēbāh* is used in some contexts to describe pagan practices and objects: "The graven images of their gods shall ye burn with fire; thou shalt not desire the silver or gold that is on them, nor take it unto thee, lest thou be snared therein: for it is an abomination to the Lord thy God. Neither shalt thou bring an abomination into thine house . . ." (Deut. 7:25-26). In other contexts, *to'ēbāh* describes the repeated failures to observe divine regulations: "Because ye multiplied more than the nations that are round about you, and have not walked in my statutes, neither have kept my judgments, neither have done according to the judgments of the nations that are round about you; . . . because of all thine abominations" (Ezek. 5:7, 9). *To'ēbāh* may represent the pagan cultic practices themselves, as in Deut. 12:31, or the people who perpetrate such practices: "For all that do these things are an abomination unto the Lord: and because of these abominations the Lord thy God doth

1

drive them out from before thee'' (Deut. 18:12). If Israelites are guilty of such idolatry, however, their fate will be worse than exile: death by stoning (Deut. 17:2-5).

Third, *to'ēbāh* is used in the sphere of jurisprudence and of family or tribal relationships. Certain acts or characteristics are destructive of societal and familial harmony; both such things and the people who do them are described by *to'ēbāh*: "These six things doth the Lord hate; yea, seven are an abomination unto him: . . . a proud look, a lying tongue, and hands that shed innocent blood, a heart that deviseth wicked imaginations, . . . and he that soweth discord among brethren" (Prov. 6:16-19). God says, "The scorner is an abomination to men" (Prov. 24:9) because he spreads his bitterness among God's people, disrupting unity and harmony.

B. Verb.

tā'ab (תָּעַב), "to abhor; treat as abhorrent; cause to be an abomination; act abominably." This verb occurs 21 times, and the first occurrence is in Deut. 7:26: "Neither shalt thou bring an abomination into thine house. . . ."

TO ACCEPT

rātsāh (רָצָה), "to be pleased, be pleased with, accept favorably, satisfy." This is a common term in both biblical and modern Hebrew. Found approximately 60 times in the text of the Old Testament, one of its first appearances is in Gen. 33:10: "Thou wast pleased with me." In the RSV rendering of this verse, "favor" appears twice, the first time being a translation of *chen*.

When *rātsāh* expresses God's being pleased with someone, the English versions often translate it as "be delighted," which seems to reflect a sense of greater pleasure: ". . . mine elect, in whom my soul delighteth" (Isa. 42:1); ". . . thou hadst a favor unto them" (Ps. 44:3). This nuance is reflected also in Prov. 3:12, where *rātsāh* is paralleled with *'āhab*, "to love": ". . . for whom the Lord loveth he correcteth; even as a father the son in whom he delighteth."

On the other hand, when one must meet a certain requirement to merit *rātsāh*, it seems more logical to translate it with "to please" or "to accept." For example: "Will the Lord be pleased with thousands of rams . . .?" (Mic. 6:7); ". . . burnt offerings and your meat offerings, I will not accept them . . ." (Amos 5:22).

Rātsāh can be used in the sense of "to pay for" or "to satisfy a debt," especially as it relates to land lying fallow in the sabbath years: "Then shall the land enjoy her sabbaths, as long as it lieth desolate . . ., even then shall the land rest, and enjoy her sabbaths" (Lev. 26:34). Here the RSV, NASB, and NEB also translate *rātsāh* as "enjoy." However, the context seems to require something like "the land shall repay (satisfy) its sabbaths." Similarly, the phrase, ". . . her iniquity is pardoned" (Isa. 40:2), must mean "her iniquity is paid for" or "her punishment is accepted as satisfactory."

TO ADD

yāsaph (יָסַף), "to add, continue, do again, increase, surpass." This verb occurs in the northwest Semitic dialects and Aramaic. It occurs in biblical Hebrew (around 210 times), post-biblical Hebrew, and in biblical Aramaic (once).

Basically, *yāsaph* signifies increasing the number of something. It may also be used to indicate adding one thing to another, e.g., "And if a man eat of the holy thing unwittingly, then he shall put the fifth part thereof unto it, and shall give it unto the priest . . ." (Lev. 22:14).

This verb may be used to signify the repetition of an act stipulated by another verb. For example, the dove that Noah sent out "returned not again" (Gen. 8:12). Usually the repeated action is indicated by an infinitive absolute, preceded by the preposition *lə*—"And he did not have relations with her again." Literally, this reads "And he did not add again (*'ad*) to knowing her [intimately]" (Gen. 38:26).

In some contexts *yāsaph* means "to heighten," but with no suggestion of numerical increase. God says, "The meek also shall increase (*yāsaph*) their joy in the Lord . . ." (Isa. 29:19). This same emphasis appears in Ps. 71:14: ". . . and will yet praise thee more and more (*yāsaph*)," or literally, "And I will add to all Thy praises." In such cases, more than an additional quantity of joy or praise is meant. The author is referring to a new quality of joy or praise—i.e., a heightening of them.

Another meaning of *yāsaph* is "to surpass." The Queen of Sheba told Solomon, "Thy wisdom and prosperity exceedeth the fame which I heard," or literally, "You add [with respect to] wisdom and prosperity to the report which I heard" (1 Kings 10:7).

This verb may also be used in covenantal formulas, e.g., Ruth summoned God's curse upon herself by saying, "The Lord do so to me, and more also (*yāsaph*), if ought but death part thee and me," or literally, "Thus may the Lord do to me, and thus may he add, if . . ." (Ruth 1:17; cf. Lev. 26; Deut. 27–28).

ALL

A. Nouns.

kōl (כֹּל), "all; the whole." The noun *kōl*, derived from *kālal,* has cognates in Ugaritic, Akkadian, Phoenician, and Moabite. *Kōl* appears in biblical Hebrew about 5,404 times and in all periods. Biblical Aramaic attests it about 82 times.

The word can be used alone, meaning "the entirety," "whole," or "all," as in: "And thou shalt put all [*kōl*] in the hands of Aaron, and in the hands of his sons . . ." (Exod. 29:24).

Kōl can signify everything in a given unit whose members have been selected from others of their kind: "That the sons of God saw the daughters of men that they were fair; and they took them wives of all which they chose" (Gen. 6:2).

kālîl (כָּלִיל), "whole offering." This word represents the "whole offering" from which the worshiper does not partake: "It is a statute for ever unto the Lord; it shall be wholly burnt" (Lev. 6:22).

B. Adjectives.

kōl (כֹּל), "all; whole; entirety; every; each." When *kōl* precedes a noun, it expresses a unit and signifies the whole: "These are the three sons of Noah: and of them was the whole earth overspread" (Gen. 9:19). *Kōl* may also signify the entirety of a noun that does not necessarily represent a unit: "All the people, both small and great" entered into the covenant (2 Kings 23:2). The use of the word in such instances tends to unify what is not otherwise a unit.

Kōl can precede a word that is only part of a larger unit or not part of a given unit at all. In this case, the prominent idea is that of "plurality," a heterogeneous unit: "And it came to pass from the time that he had made him overseer in his house, and over all that he had, that the Lord blessed the Egyptian's house for Joseph's sake; and the blessing of the Lord was upon all that he had in the house, and in the field" (Gen. 39:5).

Related to the preceding nuance is the use of *kōl* to express comprehensiveness. Not only does it indicate that the noun modified is a plurality, but also that the unit formed by the addition of *kōl* includes everything in the category indicated by the noun: "All the cities were ten with their suburbs for the families of the children of Kohath that remained" (Josh. 21:26). In Gen. 1:21 (its first occurrence), the word precedes a collective noun and may be translated "every": "And God created great whales, and every living creature that moveth, . . ."

When used to refer to the individual members of a group, *kōl* means "every": "His hand will be against every man, and every man's hand against him" (Gen. 16:12). Another example: "Thy princes are rebellious, and companions of thieves: every one loveth gifts, and followeth after rewards" (Isa. 1:23). Related to this use is the meaning "none but."

In Deut. 19:15, *kōl* means "every kind of" or "any"; the word focuses on each and every member of a given unit: "One witness shall not rise up against a man for any iniquity, or for any sin, in any sin that he sinneth . . ." A related nuance appears in Gen. 24:10, but here the emphasis is upon "all sorts": "And the servant took ten camels of the camels of his master, and departed; for all [i.e., a variety of] the goods of his master were in his hand."

kālîl (כָּלִיל), "the entire; whole." In Num. 4:6, *kālîl* refers to the "cloth wholly of blue." In other words, it indicates "the entire" cloth.

C. Verb.

kālal (כָּלַל), "to perfect." This common Semitic root appears in biblical Hebrew only 3 times. Ezek 27:11 is a good example: ". . . They have made thy beauty perfect [*kālal*]."

ALTAR

mizəbēach (מִזְבֵּחַ), "altar." This noun has cognates in Aramaic, Syriac, and Arabic. In each of these languages the consonantal root is *mdbh*. *Mizəbēach* occurs about 396 times in the Old Testament.

This word signifies a raised place where a sacrifice was made, as in Gen. 8:20 (its first biblical appearance): "And Noah builded an altar unto the Lord; and took of every clean beast, and of every clean fowl, and offered burnt offerings on the altar." In later references, this word may refer to a table upon which incense was burned: "And thou shalt make an altar to burn incense upon: of shittim wood shalt thou make it" (Exod. 30:1).

From the dawn of human history, offerings were made on a raised table of stone or ground (Gen. 4:3). At first, Israel's altars were to be made of earth— i.e., they were fashioned of material that was strictly the work of God's hands. If the Jews were to hew stone for altars in the wilderness, they would have been compelled to use war weapons to do the work. (Notice that in Exod. 20:25 the word for "tool" is *chereb*, "sword.")

At Sinai, God directed Israel to fashion altars of valuable woods and metals. This taught them that true worship required man's best and that it was to conform exactly to God's directives; God, not man, initiated and controlled worship. The altar that stood before the holy place (Exod. 27:1-8) and the altar of incense within the holy place (Exod. 30:1-10) had "horns." These horns had a vital function in some offerings (Lev. 4:30; 16:18). For example, the sacrificial animal may have been bound to these horns in order to allow its blood to drain away completely (Ps. 118:27).

Mizəbēach is also used of pagan altars: "But ye shall destroy their *altars*, break their images, and cut down their groves" (Exod. 34:13).

This noun is derived from the Hebrew verb *zabah*, which literally means "to slaughter for food" or "to slaughter for sacrifice." *Zabah* has cognates in Ugaritic and Arabic (*dbh*), Akkadian (*zibu*), and Phoenician (*zbh*). Another Old Testament noun derived from *zabah* is *zebach* (162 times), which usually refers to a sacrifice that establishes communion between God and those who eat the thing offered.

AMONG

A. Preposition.

qereb (קֶרֶב), "among." The first usage of this preposition is in Genesis: "Abram dwelled in the land of Canaan, and Lot dwelled in [among] the cities of the plain, and pitched his tent toward Sodom" (13:12). This word is used 222 times in the Old Testament; it is predominant in the Pentateuch (especially Deuteronomy) but is rare in the historical books (apart from the early books, Joshua and Judges). In the poetical books, *qereb* is used most often in the Book of Psalms. It occurs only once in Job and three times in Proverbs. It is fairly well represented in the prophetical books.

B. Noun.

qereb (קֶרֶב), "inward part; midst." As a noun, this word is related to the Akkadian root *qarab,* which means "midst." In Mishnaic and modern Hebrew, *qereb* generally means "midst" rather than "inward part" or "entrails."

One idiomatic usage of *qereb* denotes an inward part of the body that is the seat of laughter (Gen. 18:12) and of thoughts (Jer. 4:14). The Bible limits another idiomatic usage, meaning "inner parts," to animals: "Eat not of it raw, nor sodden at all with water, but roast with fire—his head with his legs, and with the purtenance thereof" (Exod. 12:9).

The noun approximates the prepositional use with the meaning of "midst" or "in." Something may be "in the midst of" a place: "Peradventure there be fifty righteous within [*qereb*] the city: wilt thou also destroy and not spare the place for the fifty righteous that are therein?" (Gen. 18:24). It may be in the midst of people: "Then Samuel took the horn of oil, and anointed him in the midst [*qereb*] of his brethren: and the Spirit of the Lord came upon David from that day forward" (1 Sam. 16:13).

God is said to be in the midst of the land (Exod. 8:22), the city of God (Ps. 46:4), and Israel (Num. 11:20). Even when He is close to His people, God is nevertheless holy: "Cry out and shout, thou inhabitant of Zion: for great is the Holy One of Israel in the midst [*qereb*] of thee" (Isa. 12:6; cf. Hos. 11:9).

The idiomatic use of *qereb* in Psalm 103:1—"Bless the Lord, O my soul: and all that is within me, bless his holy name"—is more difficult to discern because the noun is in the plural. It seems best to take "all that is within me" as a reference to the Psalmist's whole being, rather than to a distinct part of the body that is within him.

The Septuagint gives the following Greek translations of *qereb: kardia,* "heart [as seat of physical, spiritual, and mental life]" or "heart [figurative in the sense of being interior or central]"; *koilia,* "body cavity, belly"; and *mesos,* "middle" or "in the midst." The KJV gives these senses: "midst" and "inwards."

ANGEL

malǝ'āk (מַלְאָךְ), "messenger; angel." In Ugaritic, Arabic, and Ethiopic, the verb *Lǝ'ak* means "to send." Even though *lǝ'ak* does not exist in the Hebrew Old Testament, it is possible to recognize its etymological relationship to *malǝ'āk.* In addition, the Old Testament uses the word "message" in Hag. 1:13; this word incorporates the meaning of the root *lǝ'ak,* "to send." Another noun form of the root is *malā'kāh,* "work," which appears 167 times. The name *Malachi*—literally, "my messenger"—is based on the noun *malǝ'āk.*

The noun *malǝ'āk* appears 213 times in the Hebrew Old Testament. Its frequency is especially great in the historical books, where it usually means "messenger": Judges (31 times), 2 Kings (20 times), 1 Samuel (19 times), and 2 Samuel (18 times). The prophetical works are very moderate in their usage of *malə'āk,* with the outstanding exception of the Book of Zechariah, where the angel of the Lord communicates God's message to Zechariah. For example: "Then I answered and said unto the angel that talked to me, 'What are these, my lord?' And the angel answered and said unto me, 'These are the four spirits [pl. of *malə'āk*] of the heavens, which go forth from standing before the Lord of all the earth' " (Zech. 6:4-5).

The word *malə'āk* denotes someone sent over a great distance by an individual (Gen. 32:3) or by a community (Num. 21:21), in order to communicate a message. Often several messengers are sent together: "And Ahaziah fell down through a lattice in his upper chamber that was in Samaria, and was sick: and he sent messengers [pl. of *malə'āk*] and said unto them, Go, inquire of Baal-zebub the god of Ekron whether I shall recover of this disease" (2 Kings 1:2). The introductory formula of the message borne by the *malə'āk* often contains the phrase "Thus says . . .," or "This is what . . . says," signifying the authority of the messenger in giving the message of his master: "Thus saith Jephthah, Israel took not away the land of Moab, nor the land of the children of Ammon" (Judg. 11:15).

As a representative of a king, the *malə'āk* might have performed the function of a diplomat. In 1 Kings 20:1ff., we read that Ben-hadad sent messengers with the terms of surrender: "He sent messengers to Ahab king of Israel into the city, and said unto him, Thus saith Ben-hadad . . ." (1 Kings 20:2).

These passages confirm the important place of the *malə'āk*. Honor to the messenger signified honor to the sender, and the opposite was also true. David took personally the insult of Nabal (1 Sam. 25:14ff.); and when Hanun, king of Ammon, humiliated David's servants (2 Sam 10:4ff.), David was quick to dispatch his forces against the Ammonites.

God also sent messengers. First, there are the prophetic messengers: "And the Lord God of their fathers sent to them by his messengers, rising up betimes, and sending; because he had compassion on his people, and on his dwelling place: But they mocked the messengers of God, and despised his words, and misused his prophets, until the wrath of the Lord arose against his people, till there was no remedy" (2 Chron. 36:15-16). Haggai called himself "the messenger of the Lord," *malə'āk Yahweh.*

There were also angelic messengers. The English word *angel* is etymologically related to the Greek word *angelos,* whose translation is similar to the Hebrew: "messenger" or "angel." The angel is a supernatural messenger of the Lord sent with a particular message. Two angels came to Lot at Sodom: "And there came two angels to Sodom at even; and Lot sat in the gate of Sodom: and Lot seeing them rose up to meet them; and he bowed himself with his face toward the ground . . ." (Gen. 19:1). The angels were also commissioned to protect God's people: "For he shall give his angels charge over thee, to keep thee in all thy ways" (Ps. 91:11).

Third, and most significant, are the phrases *malə'āk Yahweh,* "the angel of the Lord," and *malə'āk elōhîm,* "the angel of God." The phrase is always used in the singular. It denotes an angel who had mainly a saving and protective function: "For mine angel shall go before thee, and bring thee in unto the Amorites, and the Hittites, and the Perizzites, and the Canaanites, the Hivites, and the Jebusites: and I will cut them off'' (Exod. 23:23). He might also bring about destruction: ''And David lifted up his eyes, and saw the angel of the Lord stand between the earth and the heaven, having a drawn sword in his hand stretched out over Jerusalem. Then David and the elders of Israel, who were clothed in sackcloth, fell upon their faces'' (1 Chron. 21:16).

The relation between the Lord and the ''angel of the Lord'' is often so close that it is difficult to separate the two (Gen. 16:7 ff.; 21:17 ff.; 22:11 ff.; 31:11 ff.; Exod. 3:2 ff.; Judg. 6:11 ff.; 13:21 f.). This identification has led some interpreters to conclude that the ''angel of the Lord'' was the pre-incarnate Christ.

In the Septuagint the word *malə'āk* is usually translated by *angelos* and the phrase ''angel of the Lord'' by *angelos kuriou*. The English versions follow this twofold distinction by translating *malə'āk* as simply ''angel'' or ''messenger'' (KJV, RSV, NASB, NIV).

ANGER, BURNING

A. Verb.

chārāh (חָרָה), ''to get angry, be angry.'' This verb appears in the Bible 92 times. In the basic stem, the word refers to the ''burning of anger'' as in Jonah 4:1. In the causative stem, *chārāh* means ''to become heated with work'' or ''with zeal for work'' (Neh. 3:20).

B. Noun.

chārôn (חָרוֹן), ''burning anger.'' The 41 occurrences of this word cover every period of the Bible. This word refers exclusively to divine anger as that which is ''burning.'' *Chārôn* first appears in Exod. 32:12: ''Turn from thy fierce wrath [*chārôn*], and repent of this evil against thy people.''

TO ANOINT

A. Verb.

māshach (מָשַׁח), ''to anoint, smear, consecrate.'' A common word in both ancient and modern Hebrew, *māshach* is also found in ancient Ugaritic. It occurs approximately 70 times in the Hebrew Old Testament.

The word is found for the first time in the Old Testament in Gen. 31:13: ''. . . where thou anointedst the pillar, and . . . vowedst a vow unto me . . .'' This use illustrates the idea of anointing something or someone as an act of consecration. The basic meaning of the word, however, is simply to ''smear'' something on an object. Usually oil is involved, but it could be other substances, such as paint or dye (cf. Jer. 22:14). The expression ''anoint the shield'' in Isa. 21:5 probably has more to do with lubrication than consecration in that context. When unleavened bread is ''tempered with oil'' in Exod. 29:2, it is basically equivalent to our act of buttering bread.

The Old Testament most commonly uses *māshach* to indicate "anointing" in the sense of a special setting apart for an office or function. Thus, Elisha was "anointed" to be a prophet (1 Kings 19:16). More typically, kings were "anointed" for their office (1 Sam. 16:12; 1 Kings 1:39). Vessels used in the worship at the sacred shrine (both tabernacle and temple) were consecrated for use by "anointing" them (Exod. 29:36; 30:26; 40:9-10). In fact, the recipe for the formulation of this "holy anointing oil" is given in detail in Exod. 30:22-25.

B. Noun.

māshîach (מָשִׁיחַ), "anointed one." A word that is important both to Old Testament and New Testament understandings is the noun *māshîach,* which gives us the term *messiah.* As is true of the verb, *māshîach* implies an anointing for a special office or function. Thus, David refused to harm Saul because Saul was "the Lord's anointed" (1 Sam. 24:6). The Psalms often express the messianic ideals attached to the Davidic line by using the phrase "the Lord's anointed" (Ps. 2:2; 18:50; 89:38, 51).

Interestingly enough, the only person named "messiah" in the Old Testament was Cyrus, the pagan king of Persia, who was commissioned by God to restore Judah to her homeland after the Exile (Isa. 45:1). The anointing in this instance was more figurative than literal, since Cyrus was not aware that he was being set apart for such a divine purpose.

The New Testament title of *Christ* is derived from the Greek *Christos* which is exactly equivalent to the Hebrew *māshîach,* for it is also rooted in the idea of "to smear with oil." So the term *Christ* emphasizes the special anointing of Jesus of Nazareth for His role as God's chosen one.

TO ANSWER

'ānāh (עָנָה), "to respond, answer, reply." This root occurs in most Semitic languages, although it bears many meanings. With the meaning that undergirds *'ānāh,* it appears in Ugaritic, Akkadian, Arabic, post-biblical Hebrew, and biblical Aramaic. It should be contrasted to *'ānāh,* meaning "oppress, subdue."

Biblical Hebrew attests the verb *'ānāh* about 320 times. One of the two meanings of *'ānāh* is "to respond," but not necessarily with a verbal response. For example, in Gen. 35:3 Jacob tells his household, "And let us arise, and go up to Bethel; and I will make there an altar unto God, who answered me in the day of my distress. . . ." In Gen. 28:10 ff., where this "answering" is recorded, it is quite clear that God initiated the encounter and that, although He spoke with Jacob, the emphasis is on the vision of the ladder and the relationship with God that it represented. This meaning is even clearer in Exod. 19:18, where we read that God reacted to the situation at Sinai with a sound (of thunder).

A nonverbal reaction is also indicated in Deut. 20:11. God tells Israel that before they besiege a city they should demand its surrender. Its inhabitants are to live as Israel's slaves "if it [the city] make thee answer of peace [literally, responds peaceably], and open unto thee. . . ." In Job 30:20, Job says he cried out to God, who did not "respond" to him (i.e., did not pay any attention to him). In Isaiah 49:8 the Lord tells the Messiah, "In an acceptable time have I heard thee, and in a day of salvation have I helped thee. . . ." Here responding ("hearing") is synonymously parallel to helping—i.e., it is an action (cf. Ps. 69:17; Isa. 41:17).

The second major meaning of 'ānāh is "to respond with words," as when one engages in dialogue. In Gen. 18:27 (the first occurrence of 'ānāh), we read: "Abraham answered and said" to the Lord, who had just spoken. In this formula, the two verbs represent one idea (i.e., they form an *hendiadys*). A simpler translation might be "respond," since God had asked no question and required no reply. On the other hand, when the sons of Heth "answer and say" (Gen. 23:5), they are responding verbally to the implied inquiry made by Abraham (v. 4). Therefore, they really do answer.

'Ānāh may mean "respond" in the special sense of verbally reacting to a truth discovered: "Then answered the five men that went to spy out the country of Laish, and said . . ." (Judg. 18:14). Since no inquiry was addressed to them, this word implies that they gave a report; they responded to what they had discovered. In Deut. 21:7, the children of Israel are told how to respond to the rite of the heifer—viz., "They shall answer and say, Our hands have not shed this blood, neither have our eyes seen it."

'Ānāh can also be used in the legal sense of "testify": "Thou shalt not bear false witness against thy neighbor" (Exod. 20:16). Or we read in Exod. 23:2: "Thou shalt not follow a multitude to do evil. . . ." In a similar sense, Jacob proposed that Laban give him all the spotted and speckled sheep of the flock, so that "my righteousness [will] answer [i.e., testify] for me in time to come, when it shall come [to make an investigation] for my hire before thy face . . ." (Gen. 30:33).

TO ARISE

A. Verb.

qûm (‎‏קוּם‎), "to arise, stand up, come about." This word occurs in nearly every Semitic language, including biblical Hebrew and Aramaic. It occurs about 630 times in biblical Hebrew and 39 times in biblical Aramaic.

It may denote any movement to an erect position, such as getting up out of a bed (Gen. 19:33), or it can be used as the opposite of sitting or kneeling, as when Abraham "stood up from before his dead" (Gen. 23:3). It can also refer to the *result* of arising, as when Joseph saw his sheaf *arise* and remain erect (Gen. 37:7).

Qûm may be used by itself, with no direct object to refer to the origin of something, as when Isaiah says, "It shall not stand . . ." (Isa. 7:7). Sometimes *qûm* is used in an intensive mood to signify empowering or strengthening: "Strengthen thou me according unto thy word" (Ps. 119:28). It is also used to denote the inevitable occurrence of something predicted or prearranged (Ezek. 13:6).

In a military context, *qûm* may mean "to engage in battle." In Ps. 18:38, for instance, God says, "I have wounded them that were not able to rise . . ." (cf. 2 Sam. 23:10).

Qûm may also be used very much like *'āmad* to indicate the continuation of something—e.g., "Thy kingdom shall not continue" (1 Sam. 13:14). Sometimes it indicates validity, as when a woman's vow shall not "stand" (be valid) if her father forbids it (Num. 30:5). Also see Deut. 19:15, which states that a matter may be "confirmed" only by the testimony of two or more witnesses. In some passages, *qûm* means "immovable"; so Eli's eyes were "set" (1 Sam. 4:15).

Another special use of *qûm* is "rise up again," as when a childless widow complains to the elders, "My husband's brother refuseth to raise up unto his brother a name in Israel . . ." (Deut. 25:7). In other words, the brother refuses to continue that name or "raise it up again."

When used with another verb, *qûm* may suggest simply the beginning of an action. When Scripture says that "[Jacob] rose up, and passed over the [Euphrates] river" (Gen. 31:21), it does not mean that he literally stood up— merely that he began to cross the river.

Sometimes *qûm* is part of a compound verb and carries no special meaning of its own. This is especially true in commands. Thus Gen. 28:2 could simply be rendered, "Go to Padan-aram," rather than, "Arise, go . . ." (KJV). Other special meanings emerge when *qûm* is used with certain particles. With *'al*, "against," it often means "to fight against or attack": "A man riseth against his neighbor, and slayeth him . . ." (Deut. 22:26). This is its meaning in Gen. 4:8, the first biblical occurrence. With the particle *bə* ("against"), *qûm* means "make a formal charge against": "One witness shall not rise up against a man . . ." (Deut. 19:15). With *lə* ("for"), *qûm* means "to testify in behalf of": "Who will rise up for me against the evildoers?" (Ps. 94:16). The same construction can mean "to deed over," as when Ephron's field was deeded over (KJV, "made sure"—Gen. 23:17).

B. Noun.

māqôm (מָקוֹם), "place; height; stature; standing." The Old Testament contains three nouns related to *qûm*. The most important of these is *māqôm*, which occurs 401 times in the Old Testament. It refers to the place where something stands (1 Sam. 5:3), sits (1 Kings 10:19), dwells (2 Kings 8:21), or is (Gen. 1:9). It may also refer to a larger location, such as a country (Exod. 3:8) or to an undetermined "space between" (1 Sam. 26:13). A "place" is sometimes a task or office (Eccl. 10:4). This noun is used to signify a sanctuary—i.e., a "place" of worship (Gen. 22:3).

ARK

'ārôn (אָרוֹן), "ark; coffin; chest; box." This word has cognates in Phoenician, Aramaic, Akkadian, and Arabic. It appears about 203 times in biblical Hebrew and in all periods.

In Gen. 50:26, this word represents a coffin or sarcophagus (as the same word does in Phoenician): "So Joseph died, being a hundred and ten years old: and they embalmed him, and he was put in a coffin in Egypt." This coffin was probably quite elaborate and similar to those found in ancient Egyptian tombs.

During the reign of Joash (or Jehoash), when the temple was repaired, money for the work was deposited in a "chest" with a hole in its lid. The high priest Jehoida prepared this chest and put it at the threshold to the temple (2 Kings 12:9).

In most occurrences, '*ārôn* refers to the "ark of the covenant." This piece of furniture functioned primarily as a container. As such the word is often modified by divine names or attributes. The divine name first modifies '*ārôn* in 1 Sam. 3:3: "And ere the lamp of God went out in the temple of the Lord, where the ark of God was, and Samuel was laid down to sleep. . . ." '*Ārôn* is first modified by God's covenant name, *Yahweh,* in Josh. 4:5. Judg. 20:27 is the first appearance of the "ark" as the ark of the covenant of *Elōhîm.* 1 Sam. 5:11 uses the phrase "the ark of the God [*Elōhîm*] of Israel," and 1 Chron. 15:12 employs "the ark of the Lord [*Yahweh*] God [*Elōhîm*] of Israel."

Sometimes divine attributes replace the divine name: "Arise, O Lord, into thy rest; thou, and the ark of thy strength" (Ps. 132:8). Another group of modifiers focuses on divine redemption (cf. Heb. 8:5). Thus '*ārôn* is often described as the "ark of the covenant" (Josh. 3:6) or "the ark of the covenant of the Lord" (Num. 10:33). As such, the ark contained the memorials of God's great redemptive acts—the tablets upon which were inscribed the Ten Commandments, an omer, or two quarts, of manna, and Aaron's rod. By Solomon's day, only the stone tablets remained in the ark (1 Kings 8:9). This chest was also called "the ark of the testimony" (Exod. 25:22), which indicates that the two tablets were evidence of divine redemption.

Exod. 25:10-22 tells us that this ark was made of acacia wood and measured 3¾ feet by 2¼ feet by 2¼ feet. It was gold-plated inside and outside, with a molding of gold. Each of its four feet had a golden ring at its top, through which passed unremovable golden carrying poles. The golden cover or mercy seat (place of propitiatory atonement) had the same dimensions as the top of the ark. Two golden cherubim sat on this cover facing each other, representing the heavenly majesty (Ezek. 1:10) that surrounds the living God.

In addition to containing memorials of divine redemption, the ark represented the presence of God. To be before it was to be in God's presence (Num. 10:35), although His presence was not limited to the ark (cf. 1 Sam. 4:3-11; 7:2, 6). The ark ceased to have this sacramental function when Israel began to regard it as a magical box with sacred power (a *palladium*).

God promised to meet Moses at the ark (Exod. 25:22). Thus, the ark functioned as a place where divine revelation was received (Lev. 1:1; 16:2; Num. 7:89). The ark served as an instrument through which God guided and defended Israel during the wilderness wandering (Num. 10:11). Finally, it was upon this ark that the highest of Israel's sacraments, the blood of atonement, was presented and received (Lev. 16:2 ff).

ARM

zərô'a (זְרוֹעַ), "arm; power; strength; help." Cognates of *zərô'a* occur both in Northwest and South Semitic languages. *Zərô'a* is attested 92 times in biblical Hebrew and in all periods. The related word *'ezərô'a* appears twice (Job 31:22; Jer. 32:21). Biblical Aramaic attests *dəra'* once and *'edərā* once.

Zərô'a means "arm," a part of the body: "Blessed be he that enlargeth Gad: he dwelleth as a lion, and teareth the arm with the crown of the head" (Deut. 33:20). The word refers to arms in Gen. 49:24 (the first occurrence): "But his bow abode in strength, and the arms of his hands were made strong . . ." The strength of his arms enabled him to draw the bow. In some passages, *zərô'a* refers especially to the forearm: "It shall be as when the harvestman gathereth the corn, and reapeth the ears with his arm . . ." (Isa. 17:5). Elsewhere, the word represents the shoulder: "And Jehu drew a bow with his full strength, and smote Jehoram between his arms . . ." (2 Kings 9:24).

Zərô'a connotes the "seat of strength": "He teacheth my hands to war, so that a bow of steel is broken by mine arms" (Ps. 18:34). In Job 26:2, the poor are described as the arm that hath no strength.

God's strength is figured by anthropomorphisms (attributing to Him human bodily parts), such as His "stretched out arm" (Deut. 4:34) or His "strong arm" (Jer. 21:5). In Isa. 30:30, the word seems to represent lightning bolts: "And the Lord shall cause his glorious voice to be heard, and shall show the lighting down of his arm, with the indignation of his anger, and with the flame of a devouring fire, with scattering, and tempest, and hailstones" (cf. Job 40:9).

The arm is frequently a symbol of strength, both of man (1 Sam. 2:31) and of God (Ps. 71:18): "Now also when I am old and gray-headed, O God, forsake me not; until I have showed thy strength unto this generation, and thy power to every one that is to come." In Ezek. 22:6 *zərô'a* may be translated "power": "Behold, the princes of Israel, every one were in thee to their power to shed blood." A third nuance is "help": "Assur also is joined with them: they have helped the children of Lot" (Ps. 83:8).

The word can represent political or military forces: "And the arms of the south shall not withstand, neither his chosen people, neither shall there be any strength to withstand" (Dan. 11:15; cf. Ezek. 17:9).

In Num. 6:19 *zərô'a* is used of an animal's shoulder: "And the priest shall take the sodden shoulder of the ram . . ." (cf. Deut. 18:3).

ASHERAH

'Ashērāh (אֲשֵׁרָה), "Asherah; Asherim (pl.)." This noun, which has an Ugaritic cognate, first appears in the Bible in passages anticipating the settlement in Palestine. The word's most frequent appearances, however, are usually in historical literature. Of its 40 appearances, 4 are in Israel's law code, 4 in Judges, 4 in prophetic books, and the rest are in 1 Kings and 2 Chronicles.

'Ashērāh refers to a cultic object representing the presence of the Canaanite goddess Asherah. When the people of Israel entered Palestine, they were to have nothing to do with the idolatrous religions of its inhabitants. Rather, God said, "But ye shall destroy their altars, break their images, and cut down their groves [Ashērîm] . . ." (Exod. 34:13). This cult object was manufactured from wood (Judg. 6:26; 1 Kings 14:15) and it could be burned (Deut. 12:3). Some scholars conclude that it was a sacred pole set up near an altar to Baal. Since there was only one goddess with this name, the plural (Ashērîm) probably represents her several "poles."

'Ashērāh signifies the name of the goddess herself: "Now therefore send, and gather to me all Israel unto mount Carmel, and the prophets of Baal four hundred and fifty, and the prophets of the groves ['Ashērāh] four hundred, which eat at Jezebel's table" (1 Kings 18:19) of the high god El. The Canaanites believed that 'Ashērāh ruled the sea, was the mother of all the gods including Baal, and sometimes was his deadly enemy. Apparently, the mythology of Canaan maintained that 'Ashērāh was the consort of Baal, who had displaced El as their highest god. Thus her sacred objects (poles) were immediately beside altars to Baal, and she was worshiped along with him.

TO ASK

A. Verb.

shā'al (שָׁאַל), "to ask, inquire, consult." This word is found in many Semitic languages, including ancient Akkadian and Ugaritic. It is found throughout the various periods of Hebrew and is used approximately 170 times in the Hebrew Bible. The first occurrence is found in Gen. 24:47, where the servant of Abraham asks Rebekah, "Whose daughter art thou?" It is commonly used for simple requests, as when Sisera asked for water from Jael (Judg. 5:25).

Since prayer often includes petition, shā'al is sometimes used in the sense of "praying for" something: "Pray for the peace of Jerusalem" (Ps. 122:6). In the idiomatic phrase, "to ask another of his welfare," it carries the sense of a greeting (cf. Exod. 18:7; Judg. 18:15; 1 Sam. 10:4). Frequently, it is used to indicate someone's asking for God's direction or counsel (Josh. 9:14; Isa. 30:2). In Ps. 109:10 it is used to indicate a begging: "Let his children be continually vagabonds, and beg."

B. Noun.

shə'ôl (שְׁאוֹל), "place of the dead." Shā'al seems to be the basis for an important noun in the Old Testament, shə'ôl. Found 65 times in the Hebrew Bible, shə'ôl refers to the netherworld or the underground cavern to which all buried dead go. Often incorrectly translated "hell" in the KJV, shə'ôl was not understood to be a place of punishment, but simply the ultimate resting place of all mankind (Gen. 37:35). Thus, it was thought to be the land of no return (Job 16:22; 17:14-16). It was a place to be dreaded, not only because it meant the end of physical life on earth, but also because there was no praise of God there (Ps. 6:5). Deliverance from it was a blessing (Ps. 30:3).

In some instances, it may be a symbol of distress or even plague; it is often used in parallel with "the Pit," another symbol of destruction. Everything about *shə'ôl* was negative, so it is little wonder that the concept of hell developed from it in the intertestamental and New Testament literature.

Shə'ôl is translated variously in the English versions: "hell, pit, grave" (KJV); "netherworld" (NAB). Some versions simply give the transliteration, "Sheol" (RSV, JB, NASB).

ASSEMBLY

A. Noun.

qāhāl (קָהָל), "assembly; company." Cognates derived from this Hebrew noun appear in late Aramaic and Syriac. *Qāhāl* occurs 123 times and in all periods of biblical Hebrew.

In many contexts, the word means an assembly gathered to plan or execute war. One of the first of these is Gen. 49:6. In 1 Kings 12:3 (RSV), "all the assembly of Israel" asked Rehoboam to ease the tax burden imposed by Solomon. When Rehoboam refused, they withdrew from him and rejected their feudal (military) allegiance to him. For the application of *qāhāl* to an army, see Ezek. 17:17: "Neither shall Pharaoh with his mighty army and great company make for him in the war. . . ."

Quite often, *qāhāl* is used to denote a gathering to judge or deliberate. This emphasis first appears in Ezek. 23:45-47, where the "company" judges and executes judgment. In many passages, the word signifies an assembly representing a larger group: "David consulted with the commanders of thousands and of hundreds, with every leader. And David said to all the assembly of Israel . . ." (1 Chron. 13:1-2, RSV). Here, "the whole assembly" of Israel refers to the assembled leaders (cf. 2 Chron. 1:2). Thus, in Lev. 4:13 we find that the sin of the whole congregation of Israel can escape the notice of the "assembly" (the judges or elders who represent the congregation).

Sometimes *qāhāl* represents all the males of Israel who were eligible to bring sacrifices to the Lord: "He whose testicles are crushed or whose male member is cut off shall not enter the assembly of the Lord" (Deut. 23:1, RSV). The only eligible members of the assembly were men who were religiously bound together under the covenant, who were neither strangers (living in Israel temporarily) nor sojourners (permanent non-Hebrew residents) (Num. 15:15). In Num. 16:3 and 33, it is clear that the "assembly" was the worshiping, voting community (cf. 18:4).

Elsewhere, the word *qāhāl* is used to signify all the people of Israel. The whole congregation of the sons of Israel complained that Moses had brought them forth into the wilderness to kill the whole assembly with hunger (Exod. 16:3). The first occurrence of the word also bears the connotation of a large group: "And God Almighty bless thee, and make thee fruitful, and multiply thee, that thou mayest be a multitude [*qāhāl*] of people . . ." (Gen. 28:3).

B. Verb.

qāhal (קָהַל), "to gather." The verb *qāhal,* which occurs 39 times, is derived from the noun *qāhāl.* Like the noun, this verb appears in all periods of biblical Hebrew. It means "to gather" as a *qāhāl* for conflict or war, for religious purposes, and for judgment: "Then Solomon assembled the elders [*qāhal*] of Israel . . ." (1 Kings 8:1).

TO ATONE

A. Verb.

kāphar (כָּפַר), "to cover over, atone, propitiate; pacify." This root is found in the Hebrew language at all periods of its history, and perhaps is best known from the term *Yom Kippur,* "Day of Atonement." Its verbal forms occur approximately 100 times in the Hebrew Bible. *Kāphar* is first found in Gen. 6:14, where it is used in its primary sense of "to cover over." Here God gives Noah instructions concerning the ark, including, "Cover it inside and out with pitch" (RSV). (The KJV translates, "Pitch it within and without with pitch.")

Most uses of the word, however, involve the theological meaning of "covering over," often with the blood of a sacrifice, in order to atone for some sin. It is not clear whether this means that the "covering over" hides the sin from God's sight or implies that the sin is wiped away in this process.

As might be expected, this word occurs more frequently in the Book of Leviticus than in any other book, since Leviticus deals with the ritual sacrifices that were made to atone for sin. For example, Lev. 4:13-21 gives instructions for bringing a young bull to the tent of meeting for a sin offering. After the elders laid their hands on the bull (to transfer the people's sin to the bull), the bull was killed. The priest then brought some of the blood of the bull into the tent of meeting and sprinkled it seven times before the veil. Some of the blood was put on the horns of the altar and the rest of the blood was poured at the base of the altar of burnt offering. The fat of the bull was then burned on the altar. The bull itself was to be burned outside the camp. By means of this ritual, "the priest shall make an atonement *(kāphar)* for them, and it shall be forgiven them" (Lev. 4:20).

The term "atonement" is found at least 16 times in Lev. 16, the great chapter concerning the Day of Atonement. Before anything else, the high priest had to "make atonement" for himself and his house by offering a bull as a sin offering. After lots were cast upon the two goats, one was sent away into the wilderness as an atonement (v. 10), while the other was sacrificed and its blood sprinkled on the mercy seat as an atonement for the people (vv. 15-20). The Day of Atonement was celebrated only once a year. Only on this day could the high priest enter the holy of holies of the tabernacle or temple on behalf of the people of Israel and make atonement for them.

Sometimes atonement for sin was made apart from or without blood offerings. During his vision-call experience, Isaiah's lips were touched with a coal of fire taken from the altar by one of the seraphim. With that, he was told,

"Thy sin is purged [*kāphar*]" (Isa. 6:7). The English versions translate the word variously as "purged" (KJV, JB); "forgiven" (RSV, NASB, TEV); and "wiped away" (NEB). In another passage, Scripture says that the guilt or iniquity of Israel would be "purged" (KJV, NEB) by the destruction of the implements of idolatrous worship (Isa. 27:9). In this case, the RSV renders *kāphar* as "expiated," while the NASB and TEV translate it as "forgiven."

B. Noun.

kappōreth (כַּפֹּרֶת), "mercy seat; throne of mercy." This noun form of *kāphar* has been variously interpreted by the English versions as "mercy seat" (KJV, RSV); "cover" (NEB); "lid" (TEV); "throne of mercy" (JB); and "throne" (Knox). It refers to a slab of gold that rested on top of the ark of the covenant. Images of two cherubims stood on this slab, facing each other. This slab of gold represented the throne of God and symbolized His real presence in the worship shrine. On the Day of Atonement, the high priest sprinkled the blood of the sin offering on it, apparently symbolizing the blood's reception by God. Thus the *kappōreth* was the central point at which Israel, through its high priest, could come into the presence of God.

This is further seen in the fact that the temple proper was distinguished from its porches and other accompanying structures by the name "place of the mercy seat *(kappōreth)*" (1 Chron. 28:11). The Septuagint refers to the mercy seat as a "propitiary" *(hilasteirion)*.

TO AVENGE

A. Verb.

nāqam (נָקַם), "to avenge, take vengeance, punish." This root and its derivatives occur 87 times in the Old Testament, most frequently in the Pentateuch, Isaiah, and Jeremiah; occasionally it occurs in the historical books and the Psalms. The root occurs also in Aramaic, Assyrian, Arabic, Ethiopic, and late Hebrew.

Lamech's sword song is a scornful challenge to his fellows and a blatant attack on the justice of God: ". . . for I have slain a man to my wounding, and a young man to my hurt. If Cain shall be avenged sevenfold, truly Lamech seventy and sevenfold" (Gen. 4:23-24).

The Lord reserves vengeance as the sphere of His own action: "To me belongeth vengeance, and recompense . . . for he will avenge the blood of his servants, and will render vengeance to his adversaries" (Deut. 32:35, 43). The law therefore forbad personal vengeance: "Thou shalt not avenge, nor bear any grudge against the children of thy people, but thou shalt love thy neighbor as thyself: I am the Lord" (Lev 19:18). Hence the Lord's people commit their case to Him, as David: "The Lord judge between me and thee [Saul], and the Lord avenge me of thee: but mine hand shall not be upon thee" (1 Sam. 24:12).

The Lord uses men to take vengeance, as He said to Moses: "Avenge the children of Israel of the Midianites. . . . And Moses spake unto the people, saying, Arm some of yourselves unto the war, and let them go against the Midianites, and avenge the Lord of Midian'' (Num. 31:2, 3). Vengeance for Israel is the Lord's vengeance.

The law stated, ''And if a man smite his servant, or his maid, with a rod, and he die under his hand; he shall be surely punished'' (Exod. 21:20). In Israel, this responsibility was given to the ''avenger of blood'' (Deut. 19:6). He was responsible to preserve the life and personal integrity of his nearest relative.

When a man was attacked because he was God's servant, he could rightly call for vengeance on his enemies, as Samson prayed for strength, ''. . . that I may be at once avenged of the Philistines for my two eyes'' (Judg. 16:28).

In the covenant, God warned that His vengeance may fall on His own people: ''And I will bring a sword upon you, that shall avenge the quarrel of my covenant . . .'' (Lev. 26:25). Isaiah thus says of Judah: ''Therefore saith the Lord, the Lord of hosts . . . Ah, I will ease me of mine adversaries, and avenge me of my enemies'' (1:24).

B. Noun.

nāqam (נָקָם), ''vengeance.'' The noun is first used in the Lord's promise to Cain: ''Therefore whosoever slayeth Cain, vengeance shall be taken on him sevenfold'' (Gen. 4:15).

In some instances a man may call for ''vengeance'' on his enemies, such as when another man has committed adultery with his wife: ''For jealousy is the rage of a man: therefore he will not spare in the day of vengeance'' (Prov. 6:34).

The prophets frequently speak of God's ''vengeance'' on His enemies: Isa. 59:17; Mic. 5:15; Nah. 1:2. It will come at a set time: ''For it is the day of the Lord's vengeance, and the year of recompenses for the controversy of Zion'' (Isa. 34:8).

Isaiah brings God's ''vengeance'' and redemption together in the promise of messianic salvation: ''The spirit of the Lord God is upon me; . . . he hath sent me . . . to proclaim the acceptable year of the Lord, and the day of vengeance of our God . . .'' (61:1-2). When Jesus announced that this was fulfilled in Himself, He stopped short of reading the last clause; but His sermon clearly anticipated that ''vengeance'' that would come on Israel for rejecting Him. Isaiah also said: ''For the day of vengeance is in mine heart, and the year of my redeemed is come'' (63:4).

TO AWAKE

'ûr (עוּר), ''to awake, stir up, rouse oneself, rouse.'' This word is found in both ancient and modern Hebrew, as well as in ancient Ugaritic. It occurs approximately 80 times in the Hebrew Old Testament. Its first use in the Old Testament has the sense of ''rousing'' someone to action: ''Awake, awake, Deborah'' (Judg. 5:12). This same meaning is reflected in Ps. 7:6, where it is used in parallelism with ''arise'': ''Arise, O Lord, in thine anger, . . . awake

for me to the judgment that thou hast commanded." The RSV translates this passage: ". . . Awake, O my God; thou hast appointed a judgment." This probably is more in harmony with the total parallelism involved (arise/awake; Lord/God) than the KJ version. Also, the RSV's change from "for me" to "O my God" involves only a very slight change of one vowel in the word. (Remember that Hebrew vowels were not part of the alphabet. They were added after the consonantal text was written down.)

'Ûr commonly signifies awakening out of ordinary sleep (Zech. 4:1) or out of the sleep of death (Job 14:12). In Job 31:29, it expresses the idea of "being excited" or "stirred up": "If I . . . lifted up myself when evil found him. . . ." This verb is found several times in the Song of Solomon, for instance, in contrast with *sleep:* "I sleep, but my heart waketh . . ." (5:2). It is found three times in an identical phrase: ". . . that you stir not up, nor awake my love, till he please" (Song of Sol. 2:7; 3:5; 8:4).

B

BAAL, MASTER

ba'al (בַּעַל), "master; baal." In Akkadian, the noun *bēlu* ("lord") gave rise to the verb *bēlu* ("to rule"). In other northwest Semitic languages, the noun *ba'al* differs somewhat in meaning, as other words have taken over the meaning of "sir" or "lord." (Cf. Heb. *'adôn*.) The Hebrew word *ba'al* seems to have been related to these homonyms.

The word *ba'al* occurs 84 times in the Hebrew Old Testament, 15 times with the meaning of "husband" and 50 times as a reference to a deity. The first occurrence of the noun *ba'al* is in Gen. 14:13: "And there came one that had escaped, and told Abram the Hebrew; for he dwelt in the plain of Mamre the Amorite, brother of Eshcol, and brother of Aner: and these were confederate with [literally, *ba'als* of a covenant with] Abram."

The primary meaning of *ba'al* is "possessor." Isaiah's use of *ba'al* in parallel with *qānāh* clarifies this basic significance of *ba'al:* "The ox knoweth his owner [*qānāh*], and the ass his master's [*ba'al*] crib: but Israel does not know, my people doth not consider" (Isa. 1:3). Man may be the owner [*ba'al*] of an animal (Exod. 22:10), a house (Exod. 22:7), a cistern (Exod. 21:34), or even a wife (Exod. 21:3).

A secondary meaning, "husband," is clearly indicated by the phrase *ba'al ha-issha* (literally, "owner of the woman"). For example: "If men strive, and hurt a woman with child, so that her fruit depart from her, and yet no mischief follow: he shall be surely punished, according as the woman's husband (*ba'al ha-issha*) will lay upon him; and he shall pay as the judges determine" (Exod. 21:22). The meaning of *ba'al* is closely related to *îsh* ("man"), as is seen in the usage of these two words in one verse: "When the wife of Uriah heard that Uriah her husband [*îsh*] was dead, she mourned for her husband [*ba'al*]" (2 Sam. 11:26).

The word *ba'al* with another noun may signify a peculiar characteristic or quality: "And they said one to another, Behold, this dreamer cometh" (Gen. 37:19); the KJV offers a literal translation of the Hebrew—"master of dreams"—as an alternative.

Thirdly, the word *ba'al* may denote any deity other than the God of Israel. *Baal* was a common name given to the god of fertility in Canaan. In the Canaanite city of Ugarit, Baal was especially recognized as the god of fertility. The Old Testament records that Baal was "the god" of the Canaanites. The Israelites worshiped Baal during the time of the judges (Judg. 6:25-32) and of King Ahab. Elijah stood as the opponent of the Baal priests at Mount Carmel (1 Kings 18:21 ff.). Many cities made Baal a local god and honored him with special acts of worship: Baal-peor (Num. 25:5), Baal-berith at Shechem (Judg. 8:33), Baal-zebub (2 Kings 1:2-16) at Ekron, Baal-zephon (Num. 33:7), and Baal-hermon (Judg. 3:3).

Among the prophets, Jeremiah and Hosea mention Baal most frequently. Hosea pictured Israel as turning to the baals and only returning to the Lord after a time of despair (Hos. 2:13,17). He says that the name of *Ba'al* will no longer be used, not even with the meaning of "Lord" or "master," as the association was contaminated by the idolatrous practices: "And it shall be at that day, saith the Lord, that thou shalt call me Ishi; and shalt call me no more Ba-a-li [*ba'al*]. For I will take away the names of Ba-a-lim out of her mouth, and they shall no more be remembered by their name" (Hos. 2:16-17). In Hosea's and Jeremiah's time, the ba'al idols were still worshiped, as the peoples sacrificed, built high places, and made images of the ba'alim (plural).

In the Septuagint, the word *ba'al* is not uniformly translated: *kurios* ("lord, owner"); *aner* ("man, husband"); the simple transliteration; and *ba'al*. The KJV has these translations: "Baal, man, owner, husband, master."

BAND; ARMY

gədûd (גְּדוּד), "band (of raiders); marauding band; raiding party; army; units (of an army); troops; bandits; raid." The 33 occurrences of this noun are distributed throughout every period of biblical Hebrew.

Basically, this word represents individuals or a band of individuals who raid and plunder an enemy. The units that perform such raids may be a group of outlaws ("bandits"), a special unit of any army, or an entire army. Ancient peoples frequently suffered raids from their neighbors. When the Amalekites "raided" Ziklag, looting and burning it while taking captive the wives and families of the men who followed David, he inquired of God, "Shall I pursue after this troop? shall I overtake them?" (1 Sam. 30:8). In this case, the "raiding band" consisted of the entire army of Amalek. This meaning of *gədûd* occurs for the first time in Gen. 49:19: ". . . A troop shall overcome him." Here the word is a collective noun referring to all the "band of raiders" to come. When Job described the glory of days gone by, he said he "dwelt as a king in the army [NASB, troops]" (Job 29:25). When David and his followers were called a *gədûd*, they were being branded outlaws—men who lived by fighting and raiding (1 Kings 11:24).

In some passages, *gədûd* signifies a smaller detachment of troops or a military unit or division: "And Saul's son had two men that were captains of bands" (2 Sam. 4:2). God sent against Jehoiakim "units" from the Babylonian army—"bands of the Chaldees, and bands of the Syrians, and bands of the Moabites, and bands of the children of Ammon . . ." (2 Kings 24:2).

The word can also represent individuals who are members of such raiding or military bands. The individuals in the household of Izrahiah, the descendant of Issachar, formed a military unit, "and with them by their generations, after the house of their fathers, were bands of soldiers for war, six and thirty thousand men . . ." (1 Chron. 7:4). Bildad asks the rhetorical question concerning God, "Is there any number [numbering] of his armies?" (Job 25:3).

The verb *gādad* means "to gather together against" (Ps. 94:21), "to make incisions into oneself" as a religious act (Deut. 14:1), "to roam about" (Jer. 30:23), or "to muster troops" (Mic. 5:1).

TO BE

hāyāh (הָיָה), "to become, occur, come to pass, be." This verb occurs only in Hebrew and Aramaic. The Old Testament attests *hāyāh* about 3,560 times, in both Hebrew and Aramaic.

Often this verb indicates more than simple existence or identity (this may be indicated by omitting the verb altogether). Rather, the verb makes a strong statement about the being or presence of a person or thing. Yet the simple meaning "become" or "come to pass" appears often in the English versions.

The verb can be used to emphasize the presence of a person (e.g., God's Spirit—Judg. 3:10), an emotion (e.g., fear—Gen. 9:2), or a state of being (e.g., evil—Amos 3:6). In such cases, the verb indicates that their presence (or absence) is noticeable—it makes a real difference to what is happening.

On the other hand, in some instances *hāyāh* does simply mean "happen, occur." Here the focus is on the simple occurrence of the events—as seen, for example, in the statement following the first day of creation: "And so it happened" (Gen. 1:7). In this sense, *hāyāh* is frequently translated "it came to pass."

The use of this verb with various particles colors its emphasis accordingly. In passages setting forth blessing or cursing, for example, this verb not only is used to specify the *object* of the action but also the dynamic forces behind and within the action. Gen. 12:2, for example, records that God told Abram: ". . . I will bless thee, and make thy name great; and thou shalt be *(hāyāh)* a blessing." Abram was already blessed, so God's pronouncement conferred upon him a future blessedness. The use of *hāyāh* in such passages declares the actual release of power, so that the accomplishment is assured—Abram will be blessed because God has ordained it.

In another set of passages, *hāyāh* constitutes intent rather than accomplishment. Hence, the blessing becomes a promise and the curse a threat (cf. Gen. 15:5).

Finally, in a still weaker use of *hāyāh*, the blessing or curse constitutes a wish or desire (cf. Ps. 129:6). Even here the verb is somewhat dynamic, since the statement recognizes God's presence, man's faithfulness (or rebellion), and God's intent to accomplish the result pronounced.

In miracle accounts, *hāyāh* often appears at the climax of the story to confirm the occurrence of the event itself. Lot's wife looked back and "became" a pillar of salt (Gen. 19:26); the use of *hāyāh* emphasizes that the event really occurred. This is also the force of the verb in Gen. 1:3, in which God said, "Let there *be* light." He accomplished His word so that there *was* light.

The prophets use *hāyāh* to project God's intervention in the future. By using this verb, they emphasize not so much the occurrence of predicted events and circumstances as the underlying divine force that will effect them (cf. Isa. 2:2).

Legal passages use *hāyāh* in describing God's relationship to His covenant people, to set forth what is desired and intended (cf. Exod. 12:16). When covenants were made between two partners, the formulas usually included *hāyāh* (Deut. 26:17-18; Jer. 7:23).

One of the most debated uses of *hāyāh* occurs in Exod. 3:14, where God tells Moses His name. He says: "I am *(hāyāh)* that I am *(hāyāh)*." Since the divine name *Jehovah* or *Yahweh* was well-known long before (cf. Gen. 4:1), this revelation seems to emphasize that the God who made the covenant was the God who kept the covenant. So Exod. 3:14 is more than a simple statement of identity: "I am that I am"; it is a declaration of divine control of all things (cf. Hos. 1:9).

TO BEAR

A. Verb.

yālad (יָלַד), "to bear, bring forth, beget, be delivered." This verb occurs in all Semitic languages and in nearly all verbal forms. The noteworthy exception is biblical Aramaic. However, the Aramaic verb is well attested outside the Bible. The verb *yālad* occurs about 490 times in the Bible.

Essentially, the word refers to the action of "giving birth" and its result, "bearing children." God cursed woman by multiplying her pain in "bringing forth" children (cf. Gen. 3:16, the first occurrence of *yālad*). The second meaning is exemplified by Gen. 4:18, which reports that Irad "begat" ("became the father of") Mehujael. This verb can also be used in reference to animals; in Gen. 30:39, the strong among Laban's flocks "birthed" striped, speckled, and spotted offspring.

One recurring theme in biblical history is typified by Abram and Sarah. They had no heirs, but God made them a promise and gave them a son (Gen. 16:1, 16). This demonstrates that God controls the opening of the womb (Gen. 20:17-18) and bestows children as an indication of His blessing. The prophets use the image of childbirth to illustrate the terror to overcome men in the day of the Lord (Isa. 13:8). Hosea uses the image of marriage and childbearing to describe God's relationship to Israel (1:3, 6, 8). One of the most hotly debated passages of Scripture, Isa. 7:14, uses this verb to predict the "birth" of Immanuel. Finally, the prophets sometimes mourn the day of their "birth" (Jer. 15:10).

Yālad describes the relationship between God and Israel at other places in the Bible as well. This relationship is especially relevant to the king who typifies the Messiah, the Son whom God "begot" (Ps. 2:7). God also says He "begot" the nation of Israel as a whole (Deut. 32:18). This statement is in noticeable contrast to Moses' disclaimer that he did not "birth" them (Num. 11:12) and, therefore, does not want to be responsible for them any longer.

The motif that God "gave birth" to Israel is picked up by Jeremiah. In Jer. 31:20, God states that His heart yearns for Ephraim His son *(yeled)*. Ezekiel develops this motif in the form of an allegory, giving the names Aholah and Aholibah to Samaria and Jerusalem respectively, to those whom He "bore" (Ezek. 23:4, 37).

The Septuagint renders *yālad* with words connoting "giving birth" *(tinknein)* and "begetting" *(gennaō)*.

B. Noun.

yeled (יֶלֶד), "boy; child." The noun *yeled* differs from *bēn* ("son"), which more exactly specifies the parental relationship. For example, the child that Naomi nursed was a "boy" (Ruth 4:16).

Yeled, which appears 89 times in the Bible, is rendered by several different Greek words. Other nouns built on the verb *yālad* include *yalda* ("girl"; 3 times), *yālîd* ("son" or "slave"; 3 times), *yillôd* ("newborn"; 5 times), *wālād* ("child"; once), *lēdâ* ("bringing forth" or "birth"; 4 times), *môledeth* ("offspring, kindred, parentage"; 22 times), and *tôlēdôth* ("descendants, contemporaries, generation, genealogy, record of the family"; 39 times).

BEAST

bəhēmāh (בְּהֵמָה), "beast; animal; domesticated animal; cattle; riding beast; wild beast." A cognate of this word appears in Arabic. Biblical Hebrew uses *bəhēmāh* about 185 times and in all periods of history.

In Exod. 9:25, this word clearly embraces even the larger "animals," all the animals in Egypt: "And the hail smote throughout all the land of Egypt all that was in the field, both man and beast. . . ." This meaning is especially clear in Gen. 6:7: "I will destroy man whom I have created from the face of the earth; both man, and beast, and the creeping thing, and the fowls of the air. . . ." In 1 Kings 4:33, this word seems to exclude birds, fish, and reptiles: "He [Solomon] spake also of beasts, and of fowl, and of creeping things, and of fishes."

The word *bəhēmāh* can be used of all the domesticated beasts or animals other than man: "And God said, Let the earth bring forth the living creature after his kind, cattle, and creeping thing, and [wild] beast of the earth after his kind . . ." (Gen. 1:24, first occurrence). Ps. 8:7 uses *bəhēmāh* in synonymous parallelism with "oxen" and "sheep," as though it includes both: "All sheep and oxen, yea, and the beasts of the field." The word can, however, be used of cattle only: "Shall not their cattle and their substance and every beast of theirs [NASB, animals] be ours?" (Gen. 34:23).

In a rare use of the word, it signifies a "riding animal," such as a horse or mule: "And I arose in the night, I and some few men with me; neither told I any man what my God had put in my heart to do at Jerusalem: neither was there any beast with me, save the beast that I rode upon" (Neh. 2:12).

Infrequently, *bahēmāh* represents any wild, four-footed, undomesticated beast: "And thy carcase shall be meat unto all fowls of the air, and unto the beasts of the earth, and no man shall [frighten] them away" (Deut. 28:26).

BEHIND

A. Verb.

'achar (אַחַר), "behind; after(wards)." A cognate of this word occurs in Ugaritic. *'Achar* appears about 713 times in biblical Hebrew and in all periods.

One adverbial use of *'achar* has a local-spatial emphasis that means "behind": "The singers went before, the players on instruments followed after . . ." (Ps. 68:25). Another adverbial usage has a temporal emphasis that can mean "afterwards": "And I will fetch a morsel of bread, and comfort ye your hearts; after that ye shall pass on . . ." (Gen. 18:5).

B. Preposition.

'achar (אַחַר), "behind; after." *'Achar* as a preposition can have a local-spatial significance, such as "behind": "And the man said, They are departed hence; for I heard them say, Let us go to Dothan" (Gen. 37:17). As such, it can mean "follow after": "And also the king that reigneth over you [will] continue following the Lord your God" (1 Sam. 12:14). *'Achar* can signify "after" with a temporal emphasis: "And Noah lived after the flood three hundred and fifty years" (Gen. 9:28, the first biblical occurrence of the word). This same emphasis may occur when *'achar* appears in the plural (cf. Gen. 19:6—local-spatial; Gen. 17:8—temporal).

C. Conjunction.

'achar (אַחַר), "after." *'Achar* may be a conjunction, "after," with a temporal emphasis: "And the days of Adam after he had begotten Seth were eight hundred years . . ." (Gen. 5:4).

TO BELIEVE

A. Verb.

'āmēn (אָמֵן), "to be firm; endure; be faithful; be true; stand fast; trust; have belief; believe." Outside of Hebrew, this word appears in Aramaic (infrequently), Arabic, and Syriac. It appears in all periods of biblical Hebrew (about 96 times) and only in the causative and passive stems.

In the passive stem, *'āmēn* has several emphases. First, it indicates that a subject is "lasting" or "enduring," which is its meaning in Deut. 28:59: "Then the Lord will make thy plagues wonderful, and the plagues of thy seed, even great plagues, and of long continuance, and sore sicknesses, and of long continuance." It also signifies the element of being "firm" or "trustworthy." In Isa. 22:23, '*āmēn* refers to a "firm" place, a place into which a peg will be driven so that it will be immovable. The peg will remain firmly anchored, even though it is pushed so hard that it breaks off at the point of entry (Isa. 22:25). The Bible also speaks of "faithful" people who fulfill their obligations (cf. 1 Sam. 22:14; Prov. 25:13).

The nuance meaning "trustworthy" also occurs: "He that is of a faithful spirit concealeth the matter" (Prov. 11:13; cf. Isa. 8:2). An office-bearer may be conceived as an "entrusted one": "He removeth away the speech of the trusty [entrusted ones], and taketh away the understanding of the aged" (Job 12:20). In this passage, '*āmēn* is synonymously parallel (therefore equivalent in meaning) to "elders" or office-bearers. Thus, it should be rendered "entrusted ones" or "those who have been given a certain responsibility (trust)." Before receiving the trust, they are men "worthy of trust" or "trustworthy" (cf. Neh. 13:13; 1 Sam. 2:35).

In Gen. 42:20 (the first biblical appearance of this word in this stem), Joseph requests that his brothers bring Benjamin to him; "so shall your words be verified," or "be shown to be true" (cf. Hos. 5:9; 1 Kings 8:26). In Hos. 11:12, '*āmēn* contrasts Judah's actions ("faithful") with those of Ephraim and Israel ("deceit"). So here '*āmēn* represents both "truthfulness" and "faithfulness" (cf. Ps. 78:37; Jer 15:18). The word may be rendered "true" in several passages (1 Kings 8:26; 2 Chron. 1:9; 6:17).

A different nuance of '*āmēn* is seen in Deut. 7:9: ". . . the faithful God, which keepeth covenant and mercy. . . ." There is a good reason here to understand the word '*āmēn* as referring to what God has done ("faithfulness"), rather than what He will do ("trustworthy"), because He has already proved Himself faithful by keeping the covenant. Therefore, the translation would become, ". . . faithful God who has kept His covenant and faithfulness, those who love Him kept . . ." (cf. Isa. 47:7).

In the causative stem, '*āmēn* means "to stand fast," or "be fixed in one spot," which is demonstrated by Job 39:24: "He [a war horse] swalloweth the ground with fierceness and rage: neither believeth he that it is the sound of the trumpet."

Even more often, this stem connotes a psychological or mental certainty, as in Job 29:24: "If I laughed on them, they believed it not." Considering something to be trustworthy is an act of full trusting or believing. This is the emphasis in the first biblical occurrence of '*āmēn*: "And (Abram) believed in the Lord; and he counted it to him for righteousness" (Gen. 15:6). The meaning here is that Abram was full of trust and confidence in God, and that he did not fear Him (v. 1). It was not primarily in God's words that he believed, but in God Himself. Nor does the text tell us that Abram believed God so as to accept what He said as "true" and "trustworthy" (cf. Gen. 45:26), but simply that he believed in God. In other words, Abram came to experience a personal relationship to God rather than an impersonal relationship with His promises. Thus, in Exod. 4:9 the meaning is, "if they do not believe in view of the two signs," rather than, "if they do not believe these two signs." The focus is on the act of believing, not on the trustworthiness of the signs. When God is the subject or object of the verb, the Septuagint almost always renders this stem of *'āmēn* with *pisteuō* ("to believe") and its composites. The only exception to this is Prov. 26:25.

A more precise sense of *'āmēn* does appear sometimes: "That they may believe that the Lord . . . hath appeared unto thee" (Exod. 4:5; cf. 1 Kings 10:7).

In other instances, *'āmēn* has a cultic use, by which the worshiping community affirms its identity with what the worship leader says (1 Chron. 16:32). The "God of the *'āmēn*" (Isa. 65:16; 2 Chron. 20:20) is the God who always accomplishes what He says; He is a "God who is faithful."

B. Nouns.

'emûnāh (אֱמוּנָה), "firmness; faithfulness; truth; honesty; official obligation." In Exod. 17:12 (the first biblical occurrence), the word means "to remain in one place": "And his [Moses'] hands were steady until the going down of the sun." Closely related to this use is that in Isa. 33:6: "And wisdom and knowledge shall be the stability of thy times. . . ." In passages such as 1 Chron. 9:22, *'emûnāh* appears to function as a technical term meaning "a fixed position" or "enduring office": "All these which were chosen to be porters in the gates were two hundred and twelve. These were reckoned by their genealogy in their villages, whom David and Samuel the seer did ordain in their set [i.e., established] office."

The most frequent sense of *'emûnāh* is "faithfulness," as illustrated by 1 Sam. 26:23: "The Lord render to every man his righteousness and his faithfulness. . . ." The Lord repays the one who demonstrates that he does what God demands.

Quite often, this word means "truthfulness," as when it is contrasted to false swearing, lying, and so on: "Run ye to and fro through the streets of Jerusalem, and see now, and know, and seek in the broad places thereof, if ye can find a man, if there be any that executeth judgment, that seeketh the truth [i.e., honesty]" (Jer. 5:1; cf. Jer. 5:2). Here *'emûnāh* signifies the condition of being faithful to God's covenant, practicing truth, or doing righteousness. On the other hand, the word can represent the abstract idea of "truth": "This is a nation that obeyeth not the voice of the Lord their God, nor receiveth correction: truth [*'emûnāh*] is perished, and is cut off from their mouth" (Jer. 7:28). These quotations demonstrate the two senses in which *'emûnāh* means "true"—the personal sense, which identifies a subject as honest, trustworthy, faithful, truthful (Prov. 12:22); and the factual sense, which identifies a subject as being factually true (cf. Prov. 12:27), as opposed to that which is false.

The essential meaning of *'emûnāh* is "established" or "lasting," "continuing," "certain." So God says, "And in mercy shall the throne be established: and he shall sit upon it in truth in the tabernacle of David, judging, and seeking judgment, and hasting righteousness" (Isa. 16:5; cf. 2 Sam. 7:16). Thus, the phrase frequently rendered "with lovingkindness and truth" should be rendered "with perpetual (faithful) lovingkindness" (cf. Josh. 2:14). He who sows righteousness earns a "true" or "lasting" reward (Prov. 11:18), a reward on which he can rely.

In other contexts, *'emûnāh* embraces other aspects of the concept of truth:

"[The Lord] hath remembered his mercy and his truth toward the house of Israel . . ." (Ps. 98:3). Here the word does not describe the endurance of God but His "truthfulness"; that which He once said He has maintained. The emphasis here is on truth as a subjective quality, defined personally. In a similar sense, one can both practice (Gen. 47:29) and speak the "truth" (2 Sam. 7:28). In such cases, it is not a person's dependability (i.e., others can act on the basis of it) but his reliability (conformity to what is true) that is considered. The first emphasis is subjective and the second objective. It is not always possible to discern which emphasis is intended by a given passage.

'emeth (אֱמֶת), "truth; right; faithful." This word appears 127 times in the Bible. The Septuagint translates it in 100 occurrences as "truth" *(aletheia)* or some form using this basic root. In Zech. 8:3, Jerusalem is called "a city of truth." Elsewhere, *'emeth* is rendered as the word "right" *(dikaios):* "Howbeit thou art just in all that is brought upon us; for thou hast done right, but we have done wickedly . . ." (Neh. 9:33). Only infrequently (16 times) is *'emeth* translated "faithful" *(pistis),* as when Nehemiah is described as "a faithful man, and feared God above many" (Neh. 7:2).

C. Adverb.

'āmēn (אָמֵן), "truly; genuinely; amen; so be it." The term *'āmēn* is used 30 times as an adverb. The Septuagint renders it as "truly" *(lethinos)* once; transliterates it as "amen" three times; and translates it as "so be it" *(genoitō)* the rest of the time. This Hebrew word usually appears as a response to a curse that has been pronounced upon someone, as the one accursed accepts the curse upon himself. By so doing, he binds himself to fulfill certain conditions or else be subject to the terms of the curse (cf. Deut. 29:15-26).

Although signifying a voluntary acceptance of the conditions of a covenant, the *'āmēn* was sometimes pronounced with coercion. Even in these circumstances, the one who did not pronounce it received the punishment embodied in the curse. So the *'āmēn* was an affirmation of a covenant, which is the significance of the word in Num. 5:22, its first biblical occurrence. Later generations or individuals might reaffirm the covenant by voicing their *'āmēn* (Jer. 18:6; Neh. 5:1-13).

In 1 Kings 1:36, *'āmēn* is noncovenantal. It functions as an assertion of a person's agreement with the intent of a speech just delivered: "And Benaiah the son of Jehoiada answered the king, and said, Amen: the Lord God of my lord the king say so too." However, the context shows that Benaiah meant to give more than just verbal assent; his *'āmēn* committed him to carry out the wishes of King David. It was a statement whereby he obligated himself to do what David had indirectly requested of him (cf. Neh. 8:6).

BETWEEN

bên (בֵּין), "between; in the midst of; among; within; in the interval of." A cognate of this word is found in Arabic, Aramaic, and Ethiopic. The approximately 375 biblical appearances of this word occur in every period of biblical

Hebrew. Scholars believe that the pure form of this word is *bayin,* but this form never occurs in biblical Hebrew.

This word nearly always (except in 1 Sam. 17:4, 23) is a preposition meaning "in the interval of" or "between." The word may represent "the area between" in general: "And it shall be for a sign unto thee upon thine hand, and for a memorial between thine eyes . . ." (Exod. 13:9). Sometimes the word means "within," in the sense of a person's or a thing's "being in the area of": "The slothful man saith, There is a lion in the way; a lion is in the streets" (Prov. 26:13). In other places, *bên* means "among": "Shall the companions make a banquet of him [Leviathan]? Shall they part him among [give each a part] the merchants?" (Job 41:6). In Job 34:37, the word means "in the midst of," in the sense of "one among a group": "For he addeth rebellion unto his sin, he clappeth his hands among us. . . ."

The area separating two particular objects is indicated in several ways. First, by repeating *bên* before each object: "And God divided the light from the darkness" [literally, "between the light and between the darkness"] (Gen. 1:4); that is, He put an interval or space between them. In other places (more rarely), this concept is represented by putting *bên* before one object and the preposition *lə* before the second object: "Let there be a firmament in the midst [*bên*] of the waters, and let it divide the waters from [*lə*] the waters" (Gen. 1:6). In still other instances, this idea is represented by placing *bên* before the first object plus the phrase meaning "with reference to" before the second (Joel 2:17), or by *bên* before the first object and the phrase "with reference to the interval of" before the second (Isa. 59:2).

Bên is used in the sense of "distinguishing between" in many passages: "Let there be lights in the firmament of the heaven to divide the day from [*bên*] the night" (Gen. 1:14).

Sometimes *bên* signifies a metaphorical relationship. For example, "This is the token of the covenant which I make between [*bên*] me and you and every living creature . . ." (Gen. 9:12). The covenant is a contractual relationship. Similarly, the Bible speaks of an oath (Gen. 26:28) and of goodwill (Prov. 14:9) filling the metaphorical "space" between two parties.

This word is used to signify an "interval of days," or "a period of time": "Now that which was prepared for me was . . . once in ten days [literally, "at ten-day intervals"] store of all sorts of wine . . ." (Neh. 5:18).

In the dual form, *bên* represents "the space between two armies": "And there went out a champion [literally, "a man between the two armies"] out of the camp of the Philistines, named Goliath . . ." (1 Sam. 17:4). In ancient warfare, a battle or even an entire war could be decided by a contest between two champions.

TO BIND

'āsar (אָסַר), "to bind, imprison, tie, gird, to harness." This word is a common Semitic term, found in both ancient Akkadian and Ugaritic, as well as throughout the history of the Hebrew language. The word occurs around 70 times in its verbal forms in the Hebrew Old Testament. The first use of *'āsar*

in the Hebrew text is in Gen. 39:20, which tells how Joseph was "imprisoned" after being wrongfully accused by Potiphar's wife.

The common word for "tying up" for security and safety, *'āsar* is often used to indicate the tying up of horses and donkeys (2 Kings 7:10). Similarly, oxen are "harnessed" to carts (1 Sam. 6:7, 10). Frequently, *'āsar* is used to describe the "binding" of prisoners with cords and various fetters (Gen. 42:24; Judg. 15:10, 12-13). Samson misled Delilah as she probed for the secret of his strength, telling her to "bind" him with bowstrings (Judg. 16:7) and new ropes (Judg. 16:11), none of which could hold him.

Used in an abstract sense, *'āsar* refers to those who are spiritually "bound" (Ps. 146:7; Isa. 49:9; 61:1) or a man who is emotionally "captivated" by a woman's hair (Song of Sol. 7:5). Strangely, the figurative use of the term in the sense of obligation or "binding" to a vow or an oath is found only in Num. 30, but it is used there a number of times (vv. 3,5-6,8-9,11-12). This section also illustrates how such "binding" is variously rendered in the English versions: "bind" (RSV, KJV, NAB); "promises" (TEV); "puts himself under a binding obligation" (NEB, NASB); "takes a formal pledge under oath" (JB).

TO BLESS

A. Verb.

bārak (בָּרַךְ), "to kneel, bless, be blessed, curse." The root of this word is found in other Semitic languages which, like Hebrew, use it most frequently with a deity as subject. There are also parallels to this word in Egyptian.

Bārak occurs about 330 times in the Bible, first in Gen. 1:22: "And God blessed them, saying, Be fruitful and multiply, . . ." God's first word to man is introduced in the same way: "And God blessed them, and God said unto them, Be fruitful, and multiply . . ." (v. 28). Thus the whole creation is shown to depend upon God for its continued existence and function (cf. Ps. 104:27-30). *Bārak* is used again of man in Gen. 5:2, at the beginning of the history of believing men, and again after the Flood in Gen. 9:1: "And God blessed Noah and his sons. . . ." The central element of God's covenant with Abram is: "I will bless thee . . . and thou shalt be a blessing: And I will bless them that bless thee . . . and in thee shall all families of the earth be blessed" (Gen. 12:2-3). This "blessing" on the nations is repeated in Gen. 18:18; 22:18; and 28:14 (cf. Gen. 26:4; Jer. 4:2). In all of these instances, God's blessing goes out to the nations through Abraham or his seed. The Septuagint translates all of these occurrences of *bārak* in the passive, as do the KJV, NASB, and NIV. Paul quotes the Septuagint's rendering of Gen. 22:18 in Gal. 3:8.

The covenant promise called the nations to seek the "blessing" (cf. Isa. 2:2-4), but made it plain that the initiative in blessing rests with God, and that Abraham and his seed were the instruments of it. God, either directly or through His representatives, is the subject of this verb over 100 times. The Levitical benediction is based on this order: "On this wise ye shall bless the children of Israel . . . the Lord bless thee . . . and they shall put my name upon the children of Israel; and I will bless them" (Num. 6:23-27).

The passive form of *bārak* is used in pronouncing God's "blessing on men," as through Melchizedek: "Blessed be Abram of the most high God . . ." (Gen. 14:19). "Blessed be the Lord God of Shem . . ." (Gen. 9:26) is an expression of praise. "Blessed be the most high God, which hath delivered thine enemies into thy hand" (Gen. 14:20) is mingled praise and thanksgiving.

A common form of greeting was, "Blessed be thou of the Lord" (1 Sam. 15:13; cf. Ruth 2:4). "Saul went out to meet [Samuel], that he might salute him" (1 Sam. 13:10; "greet," NASB and NIV).

The simple form of the verb is used in 2 Chron. 6:13: "He . . . kneeled down . . . ." Six times the verb is used to denote profanity, as in Job 1:5: "It may be that my sons have sinned, and cursed God in their hearts."

B. Noun.

bərākāh (בְּרָכָה), "blessing." The root form of this word is found in north-west and south Semitic languages. It is used in conjunction with the verb *bārak* ("to bless") 71 times in the Old Testament. The word appears most frequently in Genesis and Deuteronomy. The first occurrence is God's blessing of Abram: "I will make of thee a great nation, and I will bless thee, and make thy name great; and thou shalt be a blessing [*bərākāh*]" (Gen. 12:2).

When expressed by men, a "blessing" was a wish or prayer for a blessing that is to come in the future: "And [God] give thee the blessing of Abraham, to thee, and to thy seed with thee; that thou mayest inherit the land wherein thou art a stranger, which God gave unto Abraham" (Gen. 28:4). This refers to a "blessing" that the patriarchs customarily extended upon their children before they died. Jacob's "blessings" on the tribes (Gen. 49) and Moses' "blessing" (Deut. 33:1 ff.) are other familiar examples of this.

Blessing was the opposite of a cursing (*qelālāh*): "My father peradventure will feel me, and I shall seem to him as a deceiver; and I shall bring a curse upon me, and not a blessing" (Gen. 27:12). The blessing might also be presented more concretely in the form of a gift. For example, "Take, I pray thee, my blessing that is brought to thee; because God hath dealt graciously with me, and because I have enough. And he urged him, and he took it" (Gen. 33:11). When a "blessing" was directed to God, it was a word of praise and thanksgiving, as in: "Stand up and bless the Lord your God for ever and ever: and blessed be thy glorious name, which is exalted above all blessing and praise" (Neh. 9:5).

The Lord's "blessing" rests on those who are faithful to Him: "A blessing, if ye obey the commandments of the Lord your God, which I command you this day . . ." (Deut. 11:27). His blessing brings righteousness (Ps. 24:5), life (Ps. 133:3), prosperity (2 Sam. 7:29), and salvation (Ps. 3:8). The "blessing" is portrayed as a rain or dew: "I will make them and the places round about my hill a blessing; and I will cause the shower to come down in his season; there shall be showers of blessing" (Ezek. 34:26; cf. Ps. 84:6). In the fellowship of the saints, the Lord commands His "blessing": "[It is] as the dew of Hermon, and as the dew that descended upon the mountains of Zion: for there the Lord commanded the blessing, even life for evermore" (Ps. 133:3).

In a few cases, the Lord made people to be a "blessing" to others. Abraham is a blessing to the nations (Gen. 12:2). His descendants are expected to become a blessing to the nations (Isa. 19:24; Zech. 8:13).

The Septuagint translates *bǝrākāh* as *eulogia* ("praise; blessing"). The KJV has these translations: "blessing; present (gift)."

BLESSED

ashǝrê (אַשְׁרֵי), "blessed; happy." All but 4 of the 44 biblical occurrences of this noun are in poetical passages, with 26 occurrences in the Psalms and 8 in Proverbs.

Basically, this word connotes the state of "prosperity" or "happiness" that comes when a superior bestows his favor (blessing) on one. In most passages, the one bestowing favor is God Himself: "Happy art thou, O Israel: who is like unto thee, O people saved by the Lord" (Deut. 33:29). The state that the blessed one enjoys does not always appear to be "happy": "Behold, blessed [KJV, "happy"] is the man whom God correcteth: therefore despise not thou the chastening of the Almighty: for he maketh sore, and bindeth up . . ." (Job 5:17-18). Eliphaz was not describing Job's condition as a happy one; it was "blessed," however, inasmuch as God was concerned about him. Because it was a blessed state and the outcome would be good, Job was expected to laugh at his adversity (Job 5:22).

God is not always the one who makes one "blessed." At least, the Queen of Sheba flatteringly told Solomon that this was the case (1 Kings 10:8).

One's status before God (being "blessed") is not always expressed in terms of the individual or social conditions that bring what moderns normally consider to be "happiness." So although it is appropriate to render *ashǝrê* as "blessed," the rendering of "happiness" does not always convey its emphasis to modern readers.

BLOOD

dām (דָּם), "blood." This is a common Semitic word with cognates in all the Semitic languages. Biblical Hebrew attests it about 360 times and in all periods.

Dām is used to denote the "blood" of animals, birds, and men (never of fish). In Gen. 9:4, "blood" is synonymous with "life": "But flesh with the life thereof, which is the blood thereof, shall ye not eat." The high value of life as a gift of God led to the prohibition against eating "blood": "It shall be a perpetual statute for your generations throughout all your dwellings, that ye eat neither fat nor blood" (Lev. 3:17). Only infrequently does this word mean "blood-red," a color: "And they rose up early in the morning, and the sun shone upon the water, and the Moabites saw the water on the other side as red as blood" (2 Kings 3:22). In two passages, *dām* represents "wine": "He washed his garments in wine, and his clothes in the blood of grapes" (Gen. 49:11; cf. Deut. 32:14).

Dām bears several nuances. First, it can mean "blood shed by violence":

"So ye shall not pollute the land wherein ye are: for blood it defileth the land: and the land cannot be cleansed of the blood that is shed therein . . ." (Num. 35:33). Thus it can mean "death": "So will I send upon you famine and evil beasts, and they shall bereave thee; and pestilence and blood shall pass through thee; and I will bring the sword upon thee" (Ezek. 5:17).

Next, *dām* may connote an act by which a human life is taken, or blood is shed: "If there arise a matter too hard for thee in judgment, between blood and blood [one kind of homicide or another] . . ." (Deut. 17:8). To "shed blood" is to commit murder: "Whoso sheddeth man's blood, by man shall his blood be shed . . ." (Gen. 9:6). The second occurrence here means that the murderer shall suffer capital punishment. In other places, the phrase "to shed blood" refers to a non-ritualistic slaughter of an animal: "What man soever there be of the house of Israel, that killeth an ox, or lamb . . . in the camp, or that killeth it out of the camp, and bringeth it not unto the door of the tabernacle of the congregation, to offer an offering unto the Lord before the tabernacle of the Lord; blood [guiltiness] shall be imputed unto that man" (Lev. 17:3-4).

In judicial language, "to stand against one's blood" means to stand before a court and against the accused as a plaintiff, witness, or judge: "Thou shalt not go up and down as a talebearer among thy people: neither shalt thou stand against the blood [i.e., act against the life] of thy neighbor . . ." (Lev. 19:16). The phrase, "his blood be on his head," signifies that the guilt and punishment for a violent act shall be on the perpetrator: "For everyone that curseth his father or his mother shall be surely put to death: he hath cursed his father or his mother; his blood [guiltiness] shall be upon him" (Lev. 20:9). This phrase bears the added overtone that those who execute the punishment by killing the guilty party are not guilty of murder. So here "blood" means responsibility for one's dead: "And it shall be, that whosoever shall go out of the doors of thy house into the street, his blood shall be upon his head, and we will be guiltless: and whosoever shall be with thee in the house, his blood shall be on our head, if any hand be upon him" (Josh. 2:19).

Animal blood could take the place of a sinner's blood in atoning (covering) for sin: "For it is the blood that maketh an atonement for the soul" (Lev. 17:11). Adam's sin merited death and brought death on all his posterity (Rom. 5:12); so the offering of an animal in substitution not only typified the payment of that penalty, but it symbolized that the perfect offering would bring life for Adam and all others represented by the sacrifice (Heb. 10:4). The animal sacrifice prefigured and typologically represented the blood of Christ, who made the great and only effective substitutionary atonement, and whose offering was the only offering that gained life for those whom He represented. The shedding of His "blood" seals the covenant of life between God and man (Matt. 26:28).

TO BLOW

tāqa' (תָּקַע), "to strike, give a blast, clap, blow, drive." Found in both ancient and modern Hebrew, this word occurs in the Hebrew Old Testament nearly 70 times. In the verse where *tāqa'* first occurs, it is found twice: "Jacob had pitched [*tāqa'*] his tent in the mount: and Laban with his brethren pitched in the mount of Gilead" (Gen. 31:25). The meaning here is that of "striking" or "driving" a tent peg, thus "pitching" a tent. The same word is used of Jael's "driving" the peg into Sisera's temple (Judg. 4:21). The Bible also uses *tāqa'* to describe the strong west wind that "drove" the locusts into the Red Sea (Exod. 10:19).

Tāqa' expresses the idea of "giving a blast" on a trumpet. It is found seven times with this meaning in the story of the conquest of Jericho (Josh. 6:4, 8-9, 13, 16, 20).

To "strike" one's hands in praise or triumph (Ps. 47:1) or "shake hands" on an agreement (Prov. 6:1; 17:18; 22:26) are described by this verb. To "strike" the hands in an agreement was a surety or guarantor of the agreement.

BONE

'etsem (עֶצֶם), "bone; body; substance; full; selfsame." Cognates of this word appear in Akkadian, Punic, Arabic, and Ethiopic. The word appears about 125 times in biblical Hebrew and in all periods.

This word commonly represents a human "bone." In Job 10:11, *'etsem* is used to denote the bone as one of the constituent parts of the human body: "Thou hast clothed me with skin and flesh, and hast fenced me with bones and sinews." When Adam remarked of Eve that she was "bone of his bone," and flesh of his flesh, he was referring to her creation from one of his rib bones (Gen. 2:23—the first biblical appearance). *'Etsem* used with "flesh" can indicate a blood relationship: "And Laban said to [Jacob], Surely thou art my bone and my flesh" (Gen. 29:14).

Another nuance of this meaning appears in Job 2:5 where, used with "flesh," *'etsem* represents one's body: "But put forth thine hand now, and touch his bone and his flesh [his "body"]." A similar use appears in Jer. 20:9, where the word used by itself (and in the plural form) probably represents the prophet's entire "bodily frame": "Then I said, I will not make mention of him, nor speak any more in his name. But his word was in mine heart as a burning fire shut up in my bones. . . ." Judg. 19:29 reports that a Levite cut his defiled and murdered concubine into twelve pieces "limb by limb" (according to her "bones" or bodily frame) and sent a part to each of the twelve tribes of Israel. In several passages, the plural form represents the "seat of vigor or sensation": "His bones are full of the sin of his youth . . ." (Job 20:11; cf. 4:14).

In another nuance, *'etsem* is used for the "seat of pain and disease": "My bones are pierced in me in the night season: and my sinews take no rest" (Job 30:17).

The plural of *'etsem* sometimes signifies one's "whole being": "Have mercy upon me, O Lord; for I am weak: O Lord, heal me; for my bones are vexed" (Ps. 6:2). Here the word is synonymously parallel to "I."

This word is frequently used of the "bones of the dead": "And whosoever toucheth one that is slain with a sword in the open fields, or a dead body, or a bone of a man, or a grave, shall be unclean seven days" (Num. 19:16). Closely related to this nuance is the use of *'etsem* for "human remains," probably including a mummified corpse: "And Joseph took an oath of the children of Israel, saying, God will surely visit you, and ye shall carry up my bones from hence" (Gen. 50:25).

'Etsem sometimes represents "animal bones." For example, the Passover lamb is to be eaten in a single house and "thou shalt not carry forth aught of the flesh abroad out of the house; neither shall ye break a bone thereof" (Exod. 12:46).

The word sometimes stands for the "substance of a thing": "And they saw the God of Israel: and there was under his feet as it were a paved work of a sapphire stone, and as it were the body of heaven in his clearness [as the bone of the sky]" (Exod. 24:10). In Job 21:23, the word means "full": "One dieth in his full strength. . . ." At other points, *'etsem* means "same" or "self-same": "In the selfsame day entered Noah, and Shem, and Ham and Japheth, the sons of Noah . . ." (Gen. 7:13).

BOOK

sēpher (סֵפֶר), "book; document; writing." *Sēpher* seems to be a loanword from the Akkadian *sipru* ("written message," "document"). The word appears 187 times in the Hebrew Old Testament, and the first occurrence is in Gen. 5:1: "This is the book of the generations of Adam. When God created man, he made him in the likeness of God" (RSV). The word is rare in the Pentateuch except for Deuteronomy (11 times). The usage increases in the later historical books (Kings 60 times but Chronicles 24 times; cf. Esther 11 times and Nehemiah 9 times).

The most common translation of *sēpher* is "book." A manuscript was written (Exod. 32:32; Deut. 17:18) and sealed (Isa. 29:11), to be read by the addressee (2 Kings 22:16). The sense of *sēpher* is similar to "scroll" *(məgil-lāh):* "Therefore go thou, and read in the roll [*sēpher*] which thou hast written from my mouth, the words of the Lord in the ears of the people in the Lord's house upon the fasting day: and also thou shalt read them in the ears of all Judah that come out of their cities" (Jer. 36:6). *Sēpher* is also closely related to "book" *(sifra)* (Ps. 56:8).

Many "books" are named in the Old Testament: the "book" of remembrance (Mal. 3:16), "book" of life (Ps. 69:28), "book" of Jasher (Josh. 10:13), "book" of the generations (Gen. 5:1), "book" of the Lord, "book" of the chronicles of the kings of Israel and of Judah, and the annotations on the "book" of the Kings (2 Chr. 24:27). Prophets wrote "books" in their lifetime. Nahum's prophecy begins with this introduction: "The burden of Nineveh. The book of the vision of Nahum the Elkoshite" (1:1).

Jeremiah had several "books" written in addition to his letters to the exiles. He wrote a "book" on the disasters that were to befall Jerusalem, but the "book" was torn up and burned in the fireplace of King Jehoiakim (Jer. 36). In this context, we learn about the nature of writing a "book." Jeremiah dictated to Baruch, who wrote with ink on the scroll (36:18). Baruch took the "book" to the Judeans who had come to the temple to fast. When the "book" had been confiscated and burned, Jeremiah wrote another scroll and had another "book" written with a strong condemnation of Jehoiakim and his family: "Then took Jeremiah another roll, and gave it to Baruch the scribe, the son of Neriah; who wrote therein from the mouth of Jeremiah all the words of the book which Jehoiakim king of Judah had burned in the fire: and there were added besides unto them many like words" (Jer. 36:32).

Ezekiel was commanded to eat a "book" (Ezek 2:8–3:1) as a symbolic act of God's judgment on and restoration of Judah.

Sēpher can also signify "letter." The prophet Jeremiah wrote a letter to the Babylonian exiles, instructing them to settle themselves, as they were to be in Babylon for 70 years: "Now these are the words of the letter for *(sēpher)* that Jeremiah the prophet sent from Jerusalem unto the residue of the elders which were carried away captives, and to the priests, and to the prophets, and to all the people whom Nebuchadnezzar had carried away captive from Jerusalem to Babylon . . ." (Jer. 29:1).

The contents of the *sēpher* varied. It might contain a written order, a commission, a request, or a decree, as in: "And [Mordecai] wrote in the king Ahasuerus' name, and sealed it [*sēpher*] with the king's ring, and sent letters by posts on horseback, and riders on mules, camels, and young dromedaries" (Esther 8:10). In divorcing his wife, a man gave her a legal document known as the *sēpher* of divorce (Deut. 24:1). Here *sēpher* meant a "certificate" or "legal document." Some other legal document might also be referred to as a *sēpher*. As a "legal document," the *sēpher* might be published or hidden for the appropriate time: "Thus saith the Lord of hosts, the God of Israel; Take these evidences [*sēpher*], this evidence of the purchase, both which is sealed, and this evidence which is open; and put them in an earthen vessel, that they may continue many days" (Jer. 32:14).

The Septuagint gives the following translations: *biblion* ("scroll; document") and *gramma* ("letter; document; writing; book"). The KJV gives these senses: "book; letter; evidence."

BOOTY

shālāl (שָׁלָל), "booty; prey; spoil; plunder; gain." This word occurs 75 times and in all periods of biblical Hebrew.

Shālāl literally means "prey," which an animal tracks down, kills, and eats: "Benjamin shall raven as a wolf: in the morning he shall devour the prey [*shālāl*], and at night he shall divide the spoil" (Gen. 49:27—the first occurrence).

The word may mean "booty" or "spoil of war," which includes anything and everything a soldier or army captures from an enemy and carries off: "But the women, and the little ones, . . . even all the spoil thereof, shalt thou take unto thyself . . ." (Deut. 20:14). An entire nation can be "plunder" or a "spoil of war" (Jer. 50:10). To "save one's own life as booty" is to have one's life spared (cf. Jer. 21:9).

Shālāl is used in a few passages of "private plunder": "Woe unto them that . . . turn aside the needy from judgment, and . . . take away the right from the poor of my people, that widows may be their prey, and that they may rob the fatherless!" (Isa. 10:1-2).

This word may also represent "private gain": "The heart of her husband doth safely trust in her, so that he shall have no need of spoil" (Prov. 31:11).

BOSOM

chêq (חֵיק), "bosom; lap; base." Cognates of this word appear in Akkadian, late Aramaic, and Arabic. The word appears 38 times throughout biblical literature.

The word represents the "outer front of one's body" where beloved ones, infants, and animals are pressed closely: "Have I conceived all this people? have I begotten them, that thou shouldest say unto me, Carry them in thy bosom, as a nursing father beareth the sucking child . . ." (Num. 11:12). In its first biblical appearance, *chêq* is used of a man's "bosom": "And Sarai said unto Abram, My wrong be upon thee: I have given my maid into thy bosom; and when she saw that she had conceived, I was despised in her eyes . . ." (Gen. 16:5). The "husband of one's bosom" is a husband who is "held close to one's heart" or "cherished" (Deut. 28:56). This figurative inward sense appears again in Ps. 35:13: ". . . My prayer returned into mine own bosom" (cf. Job 19:27). In 1 Kings 22:35, the word means the "inside" or "heart" of a war chariot.

Chêq represents a fold of one's garment above the belt where things are hidden: "And the Lord said furthermore unto him [Moses], Put now thine hand into thy bosom" (Exod. 4:6).

Various translations may render this word as "lap": "The lot is cast into the lap; but the whole disposing thereof is of the Lord" (Prov. 16:33). Yet "bosom" may be used, even where "lap" is clearly intended: "But the poor man had nothing, save one little ewe lamb, which he had bought and nourished up: and it grew up together with him, and with his children; it did eat of his own meat, and drank of his own cup, and lay in his bosom . . ." (2 Sam. 12:3).

Finally, *chêq* means the "base of the altar," as described in Ezek. 43:13 (cf. Ezek. 43:17).

BOUNDARY

gəbûl (גְּבוּל), "boundary; limit; territory; closed area." This word has cognates in Phoenician and Arabic. It occurs about 240 times in biblical Hebrew and in all periods.

Gəbûl literally means "boundary" or "border." This meaning appears in Num. 20:23, where it signifies the border or boundary of the entire land of Edom. Sometimes such an imaginary line was marked by a physical barrier: ". . . Arnon is the border of Moab, between Moab and the Amorites" (Num.

21:13). Sometimes *gəbûl* denoted ethnic boundaries, such as the borders of the tribes of Israel: "And unto the Reubenites and unto the Gadites I gave from Gilead even unto the river Arnon half the valley, and the border even unto the river Jabbok, which is the border of the children of Ammon . . ." (Deut. 3:16). In Gen. 23:17, *gəbûl* represents the "border" of an individual's field or piece of ground: "And the field of Ephron, which was in Machpelah, which was before Mamre, the field, and the cave which was therein, and all the trees that were in the field, that were in all the borders round about, were made sure." Fields were delineated by "boundary marks," whose removal was forbidden by law (Deut. 19:14; cf. Deut. 27:17).

Gəbûl can suggest the farthest extremity of a thing: "Thou hast set a bound that they may not pass over; that they turn not again to cover the earth" (Ps. 104:9).

This word sometimes represents the concrete object marking the border of a thing or area (cf. Ezek. 40:12). The "border" of Ezekiel's altar is signified by *gəbûl* (Ezek. 43:13) and Jerusalem's "surrounding wall" is represented by this word (Isa. 54:12).

Gəbûl represents the territory within certain boundaries: "And the border of the Canaanites was from Sidon, as thou comest to Gerar, unto Gaza; as thou goest, unto Sodom, and Gomorrah, and Admah, and Zeboim, even unto Lasha" (Gen. 10:19). In Exod. 34:24, Num. 21:22, 1 Chron. 21:12, and Ps. 105:31-32, *gəbûl* is paralleled to the "territory" surrounding and belonging to a city.

Gəbûlāh, the feminine form of *gəbûl*, occurs 9 times. *Gəbûlāh* means "boundary" in such passages as Isa. 10:13, and "territory" or "area" in other passages, such as Num. 34:2.

TO BOW, BEND

kāra' (כָּרַע), "to bow, bow down, bend the knee." This term is found in both ancient and modern Hebrew and in Ugaritic. It occurs in the Hebrew Old Testament approximately 35 times. *Kāra'* appears for the first time in the deathbed blessing of Jacob as he describes Judah: ". . . He stooped down, he couched as a lion" (Gen. 49:9).

The implication of *kāra'* seems to be the bending of one's legs or knees, since a noun meaning "leg" is derived from it. To "bow down" to drink was one of the tests for elimination from Gideon's army (Judg. 7:5-6). "Kneeling" was a common attitude for the worship of God (1 Kings 8:54; Ezra 9:5; Isa. 45:23; cf. Phil. 2:10).

"Bowing down" before Haman was required by the Persian king's command (Esther 3:2-5). To "bow down upon" a woman was a euphemism for sexual intercourse (Job 31:10). A woman in process of giving birth was said to "bow down" (1 Sam. 4:19). Tottering or feeble knees are those that "bend" from weakness or old age (Job 4:4).

BREAD

lechem (לֶחֶם), "bread; meal; food; fruit." This word has cognates in Ugaritic, Syriac, Aramaic, Phoenician, and Arabic. *Lechem* occurs about 297 times and at every period of biblical Hebrew.

This noun refers to "bread," as distinguished from meat. The diet of the early Hebrews ordinarily consisted of bread, meat, and liquids: "And he humbled thee, and suffered thee to hunger, and fed thee with manna, which thou knewest not, neither did thy fathers know; that he might make thee know that man doth not live by bread only, but by every word that proceedeth out of the mouth of the Lord . . ." (Deut. 8:3). "Bread" was baked in loaves: "And it shall come to pass, that every one that is left in thine house shall come and crouch to him for a piece of silver and a morsel of bread . . ." (1 Sam. 2:36). Even when used by itself, *lechem* can signify a "loaf of bread": ". . . They will salute thee, and give thee two loaves of bread . . ." (1 Sam. 10:4). In this usage, the word is always preceded by a number. "Bread" was also baked in cakes (2 Sam. 6:19).

A "bit of bread" is a term for a modest meal. So Abraham said to his three guests, "Let a little water, I pray you, be fetched . . . and I will fetch a morsel of bread, and comfort ye your hearts . . ." (Gen. 18:4-5). In 1 Sam. 20:27, *lechem* represents an entire meal: ". . . Saul said unto Jonathan his son, Wherefore cometh not the son of Jesse to meat, neither yesterday, nor to-day?" Thus, "to make bread" may actually mean "to prepare a meal": "A feast is made for laughter, and wine maketh merry . . ." (Eccles. 10:19). The "staff of bread" is the "support of life": "And when I have broken the staff of your bread, ten women shall bake your bread in one oven, and they shall deliver you your bread again by weight: and ye shall eat, and not be satisfied" (Lev. 26:26). The Bible refers to the "bread of the face" or "the bread of the Presence," which was the bread constantly set before God in the Holy Place of the tabernacle or temple: "And thou shalt set upon the table showbread before me always" (Exod. 25:30).

In several passages, *lechem* represents the grain from which "bread" is made: "And the seven years of dearth began to come, according as Joseph had said: and the dearth was in all the lands; but in all the land of Egypt there was bread" (Gen. 41:54). The meaning "grain" is very clear in 2 Kings 18:32: "Until I come and take you away to a land like your own land, a land of corn and wine, a land of bread and vineyards. . . ."

Lechem can represent food in general. In Gen. 3:19 (the first biblical occurrence), it signifies the entire diet: "In the sweat of thy face shalt thou eat bread. . . ." This nuance may include meat, as it does in Judg. 13:15-16: "And Manoah said unto the angel of the Lord, I pray thee, let us detain thee, until we shall have made ready a kid for thee. And the angel of the Lord said unto Manoah, Though thou detain me, I will not eat of thy bread. . . ." In 1 Sam. 14:24, 28, *lechem* includes honey, and in Prov. 27:27 goat's milk. *Lechem* may also represent "food" for animals: "He giveth to the beast his food, and to the young ravens which cry" (Ps. 147:9; cf. Prov. 6:8). Flesh and grain offered to God are called "the bread of God": ". . . For the offerings of the Lord made by fire, and the bread of their God, they do offer . . ." (Lev. 21:6; cf. 22:13).

There are several special or figurative uses of *lechem*. The "bread" of wickedness is "food" gained by wickedness: "For [evil men] eat the bread of wickedness, and drink the wine of violence" (Prov. 4:17). Compare the "bread" or "food" gained by deceit (Prov. 20:17) and lies (23:3). Thus, in Prov. 31:27 the good wife "looketh well to the ways of her household, and eateth not the bread of idleness"—i.e., unearned food. The "bread of my portion" is the food that one earns (Prov. 30:8).

Figuratively, men are the "food" or prey for their enemies: "Only rebel not ye against the Lord, neither fear ye the people of the land; for they are bread for us . . ." (Num. 14:9). The Psalmist in his grief says his tears are his "food" (Ps. 42:3). Evil deeds are likened to food: "[The evil man's] meat in his bowels is turned, it is the gall of asps within him" (Job 20:14). In Jer. 11:19, *lechem* represents "fruit from a tree" and is a figure of a man and his offspring: ". . . And I knew not that they had devised devices against me, saying, Let us destroy the tree with the fruit thereof, and let us cut him off from the land of the living, that his name may be no more remembered."

matstsāh (מַצָּה), "unleavened bread." This noun occurs 54 times, all but 14 of them in the Pentateuch. The rest of the occurrences are in prose narratives or in Ezekiel's discussion of the new temple (Ezek. 45:21).

In the ancient Orient, household bread was prepared by adding fermented dough to the kneading trough and working it through the fresh dough. Hastily made bread omitted the fermented (leavened) dough: Lot "made them a feast, and did bake unleavened bread, and they did eat" (Gen. 19:3). In this case, the word represents bread hastily prepared for unexpected guests. The feasts of Israel often involved the use of unleavened bread, perhaps because of the relationship between fermentation, rotting, and death (Lev. 2:4 f.), or because unleavened bread reminded Jews of the hasty departure from Egypt and the rigors of the wilderness march.

BREADTH

rōchab (רֹחַב), "breadth; width; expanse." The noun *rōchab* appears 101 times and in all periods of biblical Hebrew.

First, the word refers to how broad a flat expanse is. In Gen. 13:17, we read: "Arise, walk through the land in the length of it and in the breadth of it; for I will give it unto thee." *Rōchab* itself sometimes represents the concept length, breadth, or the total territory: ". . . And the stretching out of his wings shall fill the breadth of thy land, O Immanuel" (Isa. 8:8). The same usage appears in Job 37:10, where the NASB renders the word "expanse." This idea is used figuratively in 1 Kings 4:29, describing the dimensions of Solomon's discernment: "And God gave Solomon wisdom and understanding exceeding much, and largeness [*rōchab*] of heart, even as the sand that is on the seashore."

Second, *rōchab* is used to indicate the "thickness" or "width" of an object.

In its first biblical occurrence the word is used of Noah's ark: "The length of the ark shall be three hundred cubits, the breadth of it fifty cubits, and the height of it thirty cubits" (Gen. 6:15). In Ezek. 42:10, the word represents the "thickness" of a building's wall in which there were chambers (cf. Ezek. 41:9).

Rōchab is derived from the verb *rāhab*, as is the noun *rǝchôb* or *rǝchōb*.

rǝchôb (רְחוֹב) or *rǝchōb* (רְחֹב), "town square." *Rǝchôb* (or *rǝchōb*) occurs 43 times in the Bible. Cognates of this noun appear in Ugaritic, Akkadian, and Aramaic. *Rǝchôb* represents the "town square" immediately near the gate(s), as in Gen. 19:2 (the first occurrence). This "town square" often served for social functions such as assemblies, courts, and official proclamations.

TO BREAK

shābar (שָׁבַר), "to break, shatter, smash, crush." This word is frequently used in ancient Akkadian and Ugaritic, and is common throughout Hebrew. It is found almost 150 times in the Hebrew Bible. The first biblical occurrence of *shābar* is in Gen. 19:9, which tells how the men of Sodom threatened to "break" Lot's door to take his house guests.

The common word for "breaking" things, *shābar* describes the breaking of earthen vessels (Judg. 7:20; Jer. 19:10), of bows (Hos. 1:5), of swords (Hos. 2:18), of bones (Exod. 12:46), and of yokes or bonds (Jer. 28:10, 12-13). Sometimes it is used figuratively to describe a "shattered" heart or emotion (Ps. 69:20; Ezek. 6:9). In its intensive sense, *shābar* connotes "shattering" something, such as the tablets of the Law (Exod. 32:19) or idol images (2 Kings 11:18), or the "shattering" of trees by hail (Exod. 9:25).

BREATH

hebel (הֶבֶל), "breath; vanity; idol." Cognates of this noun occur in Syriac, late Aramaic, and Arabic. All but 4 of its 72 occurrences are in poetry (37 in Ecclesiastes).

First, the word represents human "breath" as a transitory thing: "I loathe it; I would not live always: let me alone; for my days are vanity [literally, but a breath]" (Job 7:16).

Second, *hebel* means something meaningless and purposeless: "Vanity of vanities, saith the Preacher, vanity of vanities; all is vanity" (Eccles. 1:2).

Third, this word signifies an "idol," which is unsubstantial, worthless, and vain: "They have moved me to jealousy with that which is not God; they have provoked me to anger with their vanities . . ." (Deut. 32:21—the first occurrence).

BROTHER

'ach (אָח), "brother." This word has cognates in Ugaritic and most other Semitic languages. Biblical Hebrew attests the word about 629 times and at all periods.

In its basic meaning, *'āch* represents a "male sibling," a "brother." This is its meaning in the first biblical appearance: "And she again bare his brother Abel" (Gen. 4:2). This word represents a full brother or a half-brother: "And he said to him, Go, I pray thee, see whether it be well with thy brethren . . ." (Gen. 37:14).

In another nuance, *'āch* can represent a "blood relative." Abram's nephew is termed his "brother": "And he brought back all the goods, and also brought again his brother Lot, and his goods, and the women also, and the people" (Gen. 14:16). This passage, however, might also reflect the covenantal use of the term whereby it connotes "ally" (cf. Gen. 13:8). In Gen. 9:25, *'āch* clearly signifies "relative": "Cursed be Canaan; a servant of servants shall he be unto his brethren." Laban called his cousin Jacob an *'āch*: "And Laban said unto Jacob, Because thou art my brother, shouldest thou therefore serve me for nought?" (Gen. 29:15). Just before this, Jacob described himself as an *'āch* of Rachel's father (Gen. 29:12).

Tribes may be called *'āchîm:* "And [the tribe of] Judah said unto [the tribe of] Simeon his brother, Come up with me into my lot . . ." (Judg. 1:3). The word *'āch* is used of a fellow tribesman: "With whomsoever thou findest thy gods, let him not live: before our brethren discern thou what is thine . . ." (Gen. 31:32). Elsewhere it describes a fellow countryman: "And it came to pass in those days, when Moses was grown, that he went out unto his brethren, and looked on their burdens . . ." (Exod. 2:11).

In several passages, the word *'āch* connotes "companion" or "colleague"—that is, a brother by choice. One example is found in 2 Kings 9:2: "And when thou comest thither, look out there Jehu the son of Jehoshaphat the son of Nimshi, and go in, and make him arise up from among his brethren, and carry him to an inner chamber" (cf. Isa. 41:6; Num. 8:26). Somewhat along this line is the covenantal use of the word as a synonym for "ally": "And Lot went out at the door unto them, and shut the door after him, and said, I pray you, brethren, do not so wickedly" (Gen. 19:6-7). Notice this same use in Num. 20:14 and 1 Kings 9:13.

'Āch can be a term of polite address, as it appears to be in Gen. 29:4: "And Jacob said unto them [shepherds, whose identity he did not know], My brethren, whence be ye?"

The word *'āch* sometimes represents someone or something that simply exists alongside a given person or thing: "And surely your blood of your lives will I require; at the hand of every beast will I require it, and at the hand of . . . every man's brother will I require the life of man" (Gen. 9:5-6).

TO BUILD

A. Verb.

bānāh (בָּנָה), "to build, establish, construct, rebuild." This root appears in all the Semitic languages except Ethiopic and in all periods of Hebrew. In biblical Hebrew, it occurs about 375 times and in biblical Aramaic 23 times.

In its basic meaning, *bānāh* appears in Gen. 8:20, where Noah is said to have "constructed" an ark. In Gen. 4:17, *bānāh* means not only that Enoch built a city, but that he "founded" or "established" it. This verb can also mean "to manufacture," as in Ezek. 27:5: "They have made all thy ship boards of fir trees. . . ." Somewhat in the same sense, we read that God "made" or "fashioned" Eve out of Adam's rib (Gen. 2:22—the first biblical occurrence). In like manner, Asa began with the cities of Geba and Mizpah and "fortified" them (1 Kings 15:22). In each case, the verb suggests adding to existing material to fashion a new object.

Bānāh can also refer to "rebuilding" something that is destroyed. Joshua cursed anyone who would rise up and rebuild Jericho, the city that God had utterly destroyed (Josh. 6:26).

Metaphorically or figuratively, the verb *bānāh* is used to mean "building one's house"—i.e., having children. Sarai said to Abram, "I pray thee, go in unto my maid; it may be that I may obtain children by her" (Gen. 16:2). It was the duty of the nearest male relative to conceive a child with the wife of a man who had died childless (Deut. 25:9); he thus helped "to build up the house" of his deceased relative. Used figuratively, "to build a house" may also mean "to found a dynasty" (2 Sam. 7:27).

B. Nouns.

bēn (בֵּן), "son." *bath* (בַּת), "daughter." These nouns are derived from the verb *bānāh*. They are actually different forms of the same noun, which occurs in nearly every Semitic language (except Ethiopic and Akkadian). Biblical occurrences number over 5,550 in the Hebrew and about 22 in Aramaic.

Basically, this noun represents one's immediate physical male or female offspring. For example, Adam "begat sons and daughters" (Gen. 5:4). The special emphasis here is on the physical tie binding a man to his offspring. The noun can also be used of an animal's offspring: "Binding his *foal* unto the vine, and his ass's *colt* unto the choice vine . . ." (Gen. 49:11). Sometimes the word *bēn*, which usually means "son," can mean "children" (both male and female). God told Eve that "in sorrow thou shalt bring forth children" (Gen. 3:16—the first occurrence of this noun). The words *bēn* and *bath* can signify "descendants" in general—daughters, sons, granddaughters, and grandsons. Laban complained to Jacob that he had not allowed him "to kiss my sons and my daughters" (Gen. 31:28; cf. v. 43).

The phrase, "my son," may be used by a superior to a subordinate as a term of familiar address. Joshua said to Achan, "My son, give, I pray thee, glory to the Lord God of Israel . . ." (Josh. 7:19). A special use of "my son" is a teacher's speaking to a disciple, referring to intellectual or spiritual son-ship: "My son, if sinners entice thee, consent thou not" (Prov. 1:10). On the lips of the subordinate, "son" signifies conscious submission. Ben-hadad's servant Hazael took gifts to Elisha, saying, "Thy son Ben-hadad king of Syria hath sent me to thee" (2 Kings 8:9).

Bēn can also be used in an adoption formula: "Thou art my Son; this day have I begotten thee" (Ps. 2:7). *Bēn* often is used in this sense of a king's relationship to God (i.e., he is God's adopted son). Sometimes the same word expresses Israel's relationship to God: "When Israel was a child, then I loved him, and called my son out of Egypt" (Hos. 11:1).

The Bible also refers to the heavenly court as the "sons of God" (Job 1:6). God called the elders of Israel the "sons [KJV, children] of the Most High" (Ps. 82:6). In Gen. 6:2, the phrase "sons of God" is variously understood as members of the heavenly court, the spiritual disciples of God (the sons of Seth), and the boastful among mankind.

Bēn may signify "young men" in general, regardless of any physical relationship to the speaker: "And [I] beheld among the simple ones, I discerned among the youths, a young man void of understanding" (Prov. 7:7). A city may be termed a "mother" and its inhabitants its "sons": "For he hath strengthened the bars of thy gates; he hath blessed thy children within thee" (Ps. 147:13).

Bēn is sometimes used to mean a single individual; thus Abraham ran to his flock and picked out a "son of a cow" (Gen. 18:7). The phrase "son of man" is used in this sense—God is asked to save the poor individuals, not the children of the poor (Ps. 72:4).

Bēn may also denote a member of a group. An example is a prophet who followed Elijah (1 Kings 20:35; cf. Amos 7:14).

This noun may also indicate someone worthy of a certain fate—e.g., "a stubborn and rebellious son" (Deut. 21:18).

Used figuratively, "son of" can mean "something belonging to"—e.g., "the arrow [literally, the son of a bow] cannot make him flee" (Job 41:28).

BULLOCK

pār (פַּר), "bullock." Cognates of this word appear in Ugaritic, Aramaic, Syriac, and Arabic. *Pār* appears about 132 times in the Bible and in every period, although most of its appearances are in prose contexts dealing with sacrifices to God.

Pār means "young bull," which is the significance in its first biblical appearance (Gen. 32:15), which tells us that among the gifts Jacob sent to placate Esau were "ten bulls." In Ps. 22:12, the word is used to describe "fierce, strong enemies": "Many bulls have compassed me: strong bulls of Bashan have beset me round." When God threatens the nations with judgment in Isa. 34:7, He describes their princes and warriors as "young bulls," which He will slaughter (cf. Jer. 50:27; Ezek. 39:18).

Pārāh is the feminine form of *pār*, and it is used disdainfully of women in Amos 4:1: "Hear this word, you cows [KJV, "kine"] of Bashan . . . ." (RSV). *Pārāh* occurs 25 times in the Old Testament, and its first appearance is in Gen. 32:15.

TO BURN

A. Verb.

sāraph (שָׂרַף), "to burn." A common Semitic term, this word is found in ancient Akkadian and Ugaritic, as well as throughout the history of the Hebrew language. It occurs in its verb form nearly 120 times in the Hebrew Old

Testament. *Sāraph* is found first in Gen. 11:3 in the Tower of Babel story: "Go to, let us make brick, and burn them thoroughly."

Since burning is the main characteristic of fire, the term *sāraph* is usually used to describe the destroying of objects of all kinds. Thus, the door of a city tower was "burned" (Judg. 9:52), as were various cities (Josh. 6:24; 1 Sam. 30:1), chariots (Josh. 11:6, 9), idols (Exod. 32:20; Deut. 9:21), and the scroll that Jeremiah had dictated to Baruch (Jer. 36:25, 27-28). The Moabites' "burning" of the bones of the king of Edom (Amos 2:1) was a terrible outrage to all ancient Semites. The "burning" of men's bodies on the sacred altar was a great act of desecration (1 Kings 13:2). Ezekiel "burned" a third of his hair as a symbol that part of the people of Judah would be destroyed (Ezek. 5:4).

Interestingly, *sāraph* is never used for the "burning" of a sacrifice on the altar, although a few times it designates the disposal of refuse, unused sacrificial parts, and some diseased parts. The "burning" of a red heifer was for the purpose of producing ashes for purification (Lev. 19:5, 8).

B. Noun.

sārāph (שָׂרָף), "burning one; fiery being." In Num. 21:6, 8, the term *sāraph* describes the serpents that attacked the Israelites in the wilderness. They are referred to as "fiery" serpents. A "fiery" flying serpent appears in Isa. 14:29, as well as in Isa. 30:6.

sǝraphîm (שְׂרָפִים), "burning, noble." *Sǝraphîm* refers to the ministering beings in Isa. 6:2, 6, and may imply either a serpentine form (albeit with wings, human hands, and voices) or beings that have a "glowing" quality about them. One of the *sǝraphîm* ministered to Isaiah by bringing a glowing coal from the altar.

TO BURN INCENSE

A. Verb.

qātar (קָטַר), "to burn incense, cause to rise up in smoke." The primary stem of this verb appears in Akkadian. Related forms appear in Ugaritic, Arabic, Phoenician, and post-biblical Hebrew. The use of this verb in biblical Hebrew is never in the primary stem, but only in the causative and intensive stems (and their passives).

The first biblical occurrence of *qātar* is in Exod. 29:13: "And thou shalt take all the fat that covereth the inwards, and caul that is above the liver, and the two kidneys, and the fat that is upon them, and *offer them up in smoke* on the altar." Technically this verb means "offering true offerings" every time it appears in the causative stem (cf. Hos. 4:13; 11:2), although it may refer only to the "burning of incense" (2 Chron. 13:11). Offerings are burned in order to change the thing offered into smoke (the ethereal essence of the offering), which would ascend to God as a pleasing or placating savor. The things sacrificed were mostly common foods, and in this way Israel offered up to God life itself, their labors, and the fruit of their labors.

Such offerings represent both the giving of the thing offered and a vicarious substitution of the offering for the offerer (cf. John 17:19; Eph. 5:2). Because of man's sinfulness (Gen. 8:21; Rom. 5:12), he was unable to initiate a relationship with God. Therefore, God Himself told man what was necessary in order to worship and serve Him. God specified that only the choicest of one's possessions could be offered, and the best of the offering belonged to Him (Lev. 4:10). Only His priests were to offer sacrifices (2 Kings 16:13). All offerings were to be made at the designated place; after the conquest, this was the central sanctuary (Lev. 17:6).

Some of Israel's kings tried to legitimatize their idolatrous offerings, although they were in open violation of God's directives. Thus the causative stem is used to describe, for example, Jeroboam's idolatrous worship: "So he offered upon the altar which he had made in Beth-el the fifteenth day of the eighth month, even in the month which he had devised of his own heart; and ordained a feast unto the children of Israel: and he offered upon the altar, and burnt incense" (1 Kings 12:33; cf. 2 Kings 16:13; 2 Chron. 28:4).

The intensive stem (occurring only after the Pentateuch) always represents "false worship." This form of *qātar* may represent the "total act of ritual" (2 Chron. 25:14). Such an act was usually a conscious act of idolatry, imitative of Canaanite worship (Isa. 65:7). Such worship was blasphemous and shameful (Jer. 11:17). Those who performed this "incense-burning" were guilty of forgetting God (Jer. 19:4), while the practice itself held no hope for those who were involved in it (Jer. 11:12). Amos ironically told Israelites to come to Gilgal and Bethel (idolatrous altars) and "offer" a thank offering. This irony is even clearer in the Hebrew, for Amos uses *qātar* in the intensive stem.

B. Nouns.

qᵊtōreth (קְטֹרֶת), "incense." The first biblical occurrence of *qᵊtōreth* is in Exod. 25:6, and the word is used about 60 times in all. The word represents "perfume" in Prov. 27:9.

Qitēr means "incense." This word appears once in the Old Testament, in Jer. 44:21. Another noun, *qᵊtōrah*, also means "incense." This word's only appearance is in Deut. 33:10. *Qîtôr* refers to "smoke; vapor." This word does not refer to the smoke of an offering, but to other kinds of smoke or vapor. The reference in Ps. 148:8 ("vapor") is one of its four biblical occurrences. *Muqᵊtar* means "the kindling of incense." The word is used only once, and that is in Mal. 1:11: ". . . And in every place incense shall be offered unto my name. . . ."

Miqᵊteret means "censer; incense." The word occurs twice. *Miqᵊteret* represents a "censer"—a utensil in which coals are carried—in 2 Chron. 26:19. The word refers to "incense" in Ezek. 8:11. *Mᵊqatērah* refers to "incense altar." The word occurs once (2 Chron. 26:19). *Miqᵊtār* means a "place of sacrificial smoke; altar." The word appears once (Exod. 30:1).

TO BURY

A. Verb.

qābar (קָבַר), "to bury." This verb is found in most Semitic languages including Ugaritic, Akkadian, Arabic, Aramaic, Phoenician, and post-biblical Aramaic. Biblical Hebrew attests it about 130 times and in all periods.

This root is used almost exclusively of human beings. (The only exception is Jer. 22:19; see below.) This verb generally represents the act of placing a dead body into a grave or tomb. In its first biblical appearance, *qābar* bears this meaning. God told Abraham, "And thou shalt go to thy fathers in peace; thou shalt be buried in a good old age" (Gen. 15:15).

A proper burial was a sign of special kindness and divine blessing. As such, it was an obligation of the responsible survivors. Abraham sought the cave of Machpelah so that he might bury his dead. David thanked the men of Jabesh-gilead for their daring reclamation of the bodies of Saul and Jonathan (1 Sam. 31:11-13), and for properly "burying" them. He said, "Blessed be ye of the Lord, that ye have showed this kindness unto your lord, even unto Saul, and have buried him" (2 Sam. 2:5). Later, David took the bones of Saul and Jonathan and buried them in their family tomb (2 Sam. 21:14); here the verb means both "bury" and "rebury." A proper burial was not only a kindness; it was a necessity. If the land were to be clean before God, all bodies had to be "buried" before nightfall: "His body shall not remain all night upon the tree, but thou shalt in any wise bury him that day; (for he that is hanged is accursed of God;) that thy land be not defiled, which the Lord thy God giveth thee for an inheritance" (Deut. 21:23). Thus, if a body was not buried, divine approval was withdrawn.

Not to be "buried" was a sign of divine disapproval, both on the surviving kinsmen and on the nation. Ahijah the prophet told Jeroboam's wife, "And all Israel shall mourn for him [Jeroboam's son], and bury him: for he only of Jeroboam shall come to the grave" (1 Kings 14:13). As for the rest of his family, they would be eaten by dogs and birds of prey (v. 11; cf. Jer. 8:2). Jeremiah prophesied that Jehoiakim would "be buried with the burial of an ass, drawn and cast forth beyond the gates of Jerusalem" (Jer. 22:19).

Bodies may be "buried" in caves (Gen. 25:9), sepulchers (Judg. 8:32), and graves (Gen. 50:5). In a few places, *qābar* is used elliptically of the entire act of dying. So in Job 27:15 we read: "Those that remain of him [his survivors] shall be buried in *death:* and his widows shall not weep."

B. Noun.

qeber (קֶבֶר), "grave; tomb; sepulcher." *Qeber* occurs 67 times, and in its first biblical appearance (Gen. 23:4) the word refers to a "tomb-grave" or "sepulcher." The word carries the meaning of "grave" in Jer. 5:16, and in Ps. 88:11 *qeber* is used of a "grave" that is the equivalent of the underworld. In Judg. 8:32, the word signifies a "family sepulcher." Jer. 26:23 uses the word for a "burial place," specifically an open pit.

TO BUY, ACQUIRE

qānāh (קָנָה), "to get, acquire, create, buy." A common Semitic word, *qānāh* is found in ancient and modern Hebrew and in ancient Akkadian and Ugaritic. It occurs in the text of the Hebrew Old Testament 84 times. The first occurrence of *qānāh* in the Old Testament is in Gen. 4:1: "I have gotten a man from the Lord." In this passage, *qānāh* expresses a basic meaning of God's "creating" or "bringing into being," so Eve is really saying, "I have created a man-child with the help of the Lord." This meaning is confirmed in Gen. 14:19, 22 where both verses refer to God as "creator of heaven and earth" (KJV, NASB, "possessor"; RSV, "maker").

In Deut. 32:6, God is called the "father" who "created" Israel; a father begets or "creates," rather than "acquires" children. In the Wisdom version of the Creation story (Prov. 8:22-36), Wisdom herself states that "the Lord created me at the beginning of his work" (RSV, NEB, JB, TEV). "Possessed" (KJV, NASB) is surely not as appropriate in such a context.

When the Psalmist says to God, "Thou didst form my inward parts" (Ps. 139:13, RSV) he surely meant "create" (JB).

Qānāh is used several times to express God's redeeming activity in behalf of Israel, again reflecting "creativity" rather than "purchase." Exod. 15:16 is better translated, ". . . Thy people . . . whom thou hast created," rather than "thou hast purchased" (RSV). See also Ps. 74:2; 78:54.

The meaning "to buy" is expressed by *qānāh* frequently in contexts where one person makes a purchase agreement with another. The word is used to refer to "buying" a slave (Exod. 21:2) and land (Gen. 47:20).

C

CALAMITY

'êd (אֵיד), "calamity; disaster." A possible cognate of this word appears in Arabic. Its 24 biblical appearances occur in every period of biblical Hebrew (12 in wisdom literature and only 1 in poetical literature, the Psalms).

This word signifies a "disaster" or "calamity" befalling a nation or individual. When used of a nation, it represents a "political or military event": "To me belongeth vengeance, and recompense; their foot shall slide in due time: for the day of their calamity is at hand, and the things that shall come upon them make haste" (Deut. 32:35—first occurrence). The prophets tend to use *'êd* in the sense of national "disaster," while Wisdom writers use it for "personal tragedy."

TO CALL

A. Verb.

qārā' (קָרָא), "to call, call out, recite." This root occurs in Old Aramaic, Canaanite, and Ugaritic, and other Semitic languages (except Ethiopic). The word appears in all periods of biblical Hebrew.

Qārā' may signify the "specification of a name." Naming a thing is frequently an assertion of sovereignty over it, which is the case in the first use of *qārā':* "And God called the light Day, and the darkness he called Night" (Gen. 1:5). God's act of creating, "naming," and numbering includes the stars (Ps. 147:4) and all other things (Isa. 40:26). He allowed Adam to "name" the animals as a concrete demonstration of man's relative sovereignty over them (Gen. 2:19). Divine sovereignty and election is extended over all generations, for God "called" them all from the beginning (Isa. 41:4; cf. Amos 5:8). "Calling" or "naming" an individual may specify the individual's primary characteristic (Gen. 27:36); it may consist of a confession or evaluation (Isa. 58:13; 60:14); and it may recognize an eternal truth (Isa. 7:14).

This verb also is used to indicate "calling to a specific task." In Exod. 2:7, Moses' sister Miriam asked Pharaoh's daughter if she should go and "call" (summon) a nurse. Israel was "called" (elected) by God to be His people (Isa. 65:12), as were the Gentiles in the messianic age (Isa. 55:5).

To "call" on God's name is to summon His aid. This emphasis appears in Gen. 4:26, where men began to "call" on the name of the Lord. Such a "calling" on God's name occurs against the background of the Fall and the murder of Abel. The "calling" on God's name is clearly not the beginning of prayer, since communication between God and man existed since the Garden of Eden; nor is it an indication of the beginning of formal worship, since formal worship began at least as early as the offerings of Cain and Abel (Gen. 4:7 ff.) The sense of "summoning" God to one's aid was surely in Abraham's mind when he "called upon" God's name (Gen. 12:8). "Calling" in this sense constitutes a prayer prompted by recognized need and directed to One who is able and willing to respond (Ps. 145:18; Isa. 55:6).

Basically, *qārā'* means "to call out loudly" in order to get someone's attention so that contact can be initiated. So Job is told: "Call now, if there be any that will answer thee; and to which of the saints wilt thou turn?" (Job 5:11). Often this verb represents sustained communication, paralleling "to say" *('amar),* as in Gen. 3:9: "And the Lord God called unto Adam, and said unto him. . . ." *Qārā'* can also mean "to call out a warning," so that direct contact may be avoided: "And the leper in whom the plague is, his clothes shall be rent, and his head bare, and he shall put a covering upon his upper lip, and shall cry, Unclean, unclean" (Lev. 13:45).

Qārā' may mean "to shout" or "to call out loudly." Goliath "shouted" toward the ranks of Israel (1 Sam. 17:8) and challenged them to individual combat (duel). Sometimes ancient peoples settled battles through such combatants. Before battling an enemy, Israel was directed to offer them peace: "When thou comest nigh unto a city to fight against it, then proclaim peace unto it [call out to it in terms of peace]" (Deut. 20:10).

Qārā' may also mean "to proclaim" or "to announce," as when Israel proclaimed peace to the sons of Benjamin (Judg. 21:13). This sense first occurs in Gen. 41:43, where we are told that Joseph rode in the second chariot; "and they cried before him, Bow the knee." Haman recommended to King Ahasuerus that he adorn the one to be honored and "proclaim" ("announce") before him, "Thus shall it be done to the man whom the king delighteth to honor" (Esther 6:9). This proclamation would tell everyone that the man so announced was honored by the king. The two emphases "proclamation" and "announce" occur in Exod. 32:5: ". . . Aaron made proclamation, and said, Tomorrow is a feast to the Lord.'' This instance implies ''summoning'' an official assemblage of the people. In prophetic literature, *qārā'* is a technical term for ''declaring'' a prophetic message: ''For the saying which he *cried* by the word of the Lord . . . shall surely come to pass'' (1 Kings 13:32).

Another major emphasis of *qārā'* is ''to summon.'' When Pharaoh discovered Abram's deceit concerning Sarai, he ''summoned'' (''called'') Abram so that he might correct the situation (Gen. 12:18). Often the summons is in the form of a friendly invitation, as when Reuel (or Jethro) told his daughters to ''invite him [Moses] to have something to eat'' (Exod. 2:20—KJV, ''that he may eat bread''). The participial form of *qārā'* is used to denote ''invited guests'': ''As soon as you enter the city you will find him before he goes up to the high place to eat . . . afterward *those who are invited* will eat'' (1 Sam. 9:13 NASB). This verb is also used in judicial contexts, to mean being ''summoned to court''; if a man is accused of not fulfilling his levirate responsibility, ''then the elders of his city shall call him, and speak unto him . . .'' (Deut. 25:8). *Qārā'* is used of ''summoning'' someone and/or ''mustering'' an army: ''Why hast thou served us thus, that thou calledst us not, when thou wentest to fight with the Midianites?'' (Judg. 8:1).

The meaning ''to read'' apparently arose from the meaning ''to announce'' and ''to declare,'' inasmuch as reading was done out loud so that others could hear. This sense appears in Exod. 24:7. In several prophetic passages, the Septuagint translates *qārā'* ''to read'' rather than ''to proclaim'' (cf. Jer. 3:12; 7:2, 27; 19:2). *Qārā'* means ''to read to oneself'' only in a few passages.

At least once, the verb *qārā'* means ''to dictate'': ''Then Baruch answered them, He (dictated) all these words unto me . . . and I wrote them with ink in the book'' (Jer. 36:18).

B. Noun.

miqərā' (מִקְרָא), ''public worship service; convocation.'' The word implies the product of an official summons to worship (''convocation''). In one of its 23 appearances, *miqərā'* refers to Sabbaths as ''convocation days'' (Lev. 23:2).

CAMP

machaneh (מַחֲנֶה), ''camp; encampment; host.'' This noun derived from the verb *chānāh* occurs 214 times in the Bible, most frequently in the Pentateuch and in the historical books. The word is rare in the poetical and prophetic literature.

Those who travel were called ''campers,'' or in most versions (KJV, RSV, NASB) a ''company'' or ''group'' (NIV), as in Gen. 32:8. Naaman stood before Elisha ''with all his company'' (2 Kings 5:15 NASB—NEB, ''retinue''). Travelers, tradesmen, and soldiers spent much time on the road. They all set up ''camp'' for the night.

Jacob ''encamped'' by the Jabbok with his retinue (Gen. 32:10). The name *Mahanaim* (''camps''—Gen. 32:2) owes its origin to Jacob's experience with the angels. He called the place *Mahanaim* in order to signify that it was God's "camp" (Gen. 32:2), as he had spent the night "in the camp" (Gen. 32:21) and wrestled with God (Gen. 32:24). Soldiers also established "camps" by the city to be conquered (Ezek. 4:2).

Usage of *machaneh* varies according to context. First, it signifies a nation set over against another (Exod. 14:20). Second, the word refers to a division concerning the Israelites; each of the tribes had a special "encampment" in relation to the tent of meeting (Num. 1:52). Third, the word "camp" is used to describe the whole people of Israel: "And it came to pass on the third day in the morning, that there were thunders and lightnings, and a thick cloud upon the mount, and the voice of the trumpet exceeding loud; so that all the people that was in the *camp* trembled" (Exod. 19:16).

God was present in the "camp" of Israel: "For the Lord thy God walketh in the midst of thy camp, to deliver thee, and to give up thine enemies before thee; therefore shall thy camp be holy: that he see no unclean thing in thee, and turn away from thee" (Deut. 23:14). As a result, sin could not be tolerated within the camp, and the sinner might have to be stoned outside the camp (Num. 15:35).

The Septuagint translated *machaneh* by the Greek *parembole* ("camp; barracks; army") 193 times. Compare these Old Testament occurrences with the use of "camp" in Hebrews 13:11: "For the bodies of those beasts, whose blood is brought into the sanctuary by the high priest for sin, are burned without the camp."

In the English versions, the word is variously translated "camp; company; army" (KJV, RSV, NASB, NIV), "host" (KJV), "attendances; forces" (NIV).

CAN, MAY

yākōl (יָכֹל), "can; may; to be able, prevail, endure." This word is used about 200 times in the Old Testament, from the earliest to the latest writings. It is also found in Assyrian and Aramaic. As in English, the Hebrew word usually requires another verb to make the meaning complete.

Yākōl first occurs in Gen. 13:6: "And the land was not *able* to bear them, that they might dwell together. . . ." God promised Abraham: "And I will make thy seed as the dust of the earth: so that if a man can number the dust of the earth, then shall thy seed also be numbered" (Gen. 13:16, NIV; cf. Gen. 15:5).

The most frequent use of this verb is in the sense of "can" or "to be able." The word may refer specifically to "physical ability," as in 1 Sam. 17:33: "You are not able to go against this Philistine to fight with him" (NASB). *Yākōl* may express "moral inability," as in Josh. 7:13: ". . . Thou canst not stand before thine enemies, until ye take away the accursed thing from among you." For a similar sense, see Jer. 6:10: "Behold, their ear is uncircumcised, and they cannot hearken. . . ." In the negative sense, it may be used to express "prohibition": "Thou mayest not eat within thy gates the tithe of thy corn . . ." (Deut. 12:17, NIV). Or the verb may indicate a "social barrier," as in Gen. 43:32: ". . . The Egyptians might not eat bread with the Hebrews; for that is an abomination unto the Egyptians" (KJV, RSV—NIV, NASB, "could not").

Yākōl is also used of God, as when Moses pleaded with God not to destroy Israel lest the nations say, "Because the Lord could not bring this people into the land . . . , therefore He slaughtered them . . ." (Num. 14:16, NASB). The word may indicate a positive sense: "If it be so, our God whom we serve is *able* to deliver us . . ." (Dan. 3:17). The word *yākōl* appears when God limits His patience with the insincere: "When the Lord could no longer *endure* your wicked actions . . . , your land became an object of cursing . . ." (Jer. 44:22, NIV).

When *yākōl* is used without another verb, the sense is "to prevail" or "to overcome," as in the words of the angel to Jacob: "Your name will no longer be Jacob, but Israel, because you have struggled with God, and with men and have overcome" (Gen. 32:28, NIV—KJV, NASB, "prevailed"). With the word *yākōl,* God rebukes Israel's insincerity: "I cannot endure iniquity and the solemn assembly" (Isa. 1:13, NASB—NIV, "bear"). ". . . How long will it be ere they attain to innocency?" (Hos. 8:5, KJV—NASB, "will they be capable of").

There is no distinction in Hebrew between "can" and "may," since *yākōl* expresses both "ability" and "permission," or prohibition with the negative. Both God and man can act. There is no limit to God's ability apart from His own freely determined limits of patience with continued disobedience and insincerity (Isa. 59:1-2) and will (Dan. 3:17-18).

The Septuagint translates *yākōl* by several words, *dunamai* being by far the most common. *Dunamai* means "to be able, powerful." It is first used in the New Testament in Matt. 3:9: ". . . God is able of these stones to raise up children unto Abraham."

CANAAN; CANAANITE

kəna'an (כְּנַעַן), "Canaan"; *kəna'anî* (כְּנַעֲנִי), "Canaanite; merchant." "Canaan" is used 9 times as the name of a person and 80 times as a place name. "Canaanite" occurs 72 times of the descendants of "Canaan," the inhabitants of the land of Canaan. Most occurrences of these words are in Genesis through Judges, but they are scattered throughout the Old Testament.

"Canaan" is first used of a person in Gen. 9:18: ". . . and Ham is the father of Canaan" (cf. Gen. 10:6). After a listing of the nations descended from "Canaan," Gen. 10:18-19 adds: ". . . and afterward were the families of the Canaanites spread abroad. And the border of the Canaanites was from Sidon, as thou comest to Gerar, unto Gaza; as thou goest, unto Sodom, and Gomorrah, ..." "Canaan" is the land west of the Jordan, as in Num. 33:51: "When ye are passed over Jordan into the land of Canaan" (cf. Josh. 22:9-11). At the call of God, Abram ". . . went forth to go into the land of Canaan; and into the land of Canaan they came. . . . And the Canaanite was then in the land" (Gen. 12:5, 6). Later God promised Abram: "Unto thy seed have I given this land, . . . [the land of] the Canaanites . . .'' (Gen. 15:18-20; cf. Exod. 3:8, 17; Josh. 3:10).

''Canaanite'' is a general term for all the descendants of ''Canaan'': ''When the Lord thy God shall bring thee into the land whither thou goest to possess it, and hath cast out many nations before thee . . . the Canaanites . . .'' (Deut. 7:1). It is interchanged with Amorite in Gen. 15:16: ''. . . for the iniquity of the Amorites is not yet full'' (cf. Josh. 24:15, 18).

''Canaanite'' is also used in the specific sense of one of the peoples of Canaan: ''. . . and the Canaanites dwell by the sea, and by the coast of Jordan'' (Num. 13:29; cf. Josh. 5:1; 2 Sam. 24:7). As these peoples were traders, ''Canaanite'' is a symbol for ''merchant'' in Prov. 31:24 and Job 41:6 and notably, in speaking of the sins of Israel, Hosea says, ''He is a merchant, the balances of deceit are in his hand . . .'' (Hos. 7:12; cf. Zeph. 1:11).

Gen. 9:25-27 stamps a theological significance on ''Canaan'' from the beginning: ''Cursed be Canaan; a servant of servants shall he be unto his brethren. . . . Blessed be the Lord God of Shem; and Canaan shall be his servant. And God shall enlarge Japheth . . . and Canaan shall be his servant.'' Noah prophetically placed this curse on ''Canaan'' because his father had stared at Noah's nakedness and reported it grossly to his brothers. Ham's sin, deeply rooted in his youngest son, is observable in the Canaanites in the succeeding history. Leviticus 18 gives a long list of sexual perversions that were forbidden to Israel prefaced by the statement: ''. . . and after the doings of the land of Canaan, whither I bring you, shall ye not do . . .'' (Lev. 18:3). The list is followed by a warning: ''Defile not ye yourselves in any of these things: for in all these the nations are defiled which I cast out before you'' (Lev. 18:24).

The command to destroy the ''Canaanites'' was very specific: ''. . . thou shalt smite them, and utterly destroy them. . . . ye shall destroy their altars, and break down their images. . . . For thou art a holy people unto the Lord thy God . . .'' (Deut. 7:2-6). But too often the house of David and Judah ''built them high places, and images, and groves, on every high hill, and under every green tree. And there were also sodomites in the land: and they did according to all the abominations of the nations which the Lord cast out before the children of Israel'' (1 Kings 14:23-24; cf. 2 Kings 16:3-4; 21:1-15). The nations were the ''Canaanites''; thus ''Canaanite'' became synonymous with religious and moral perversions of every kind.

This fact is reflected in Zech. 14:21: ''. . . and in that day there shall be no more the Canaanite in the house of the Lord of hosts.'' A ''Canaanite'' was not permitted to enter the tabernacle or temple; no longer would one of God's people who practiced the abominations of the ''Canaanites'' enter the house of the Lord.

This prophecy speaks of the last days and will be fulfilled in the New Jerusalem, according to Rev. 21:27: ''And there shall in no wise enter into it any thing that defileth, neither whatsoever worketh abomination, or maketh a lie . . .'' (cf. Rev. 22:15).

These two words occur in Acts 7:11 and 13:19 in the New Testament.

TO CAST DOWN

shālak (שָׁלַךְ), "to throw, fling, cast, overthrow." This root seems to be used primarily in Hebrew, including modern Hebrew. *Shālak* is found 125 times in the Hebrew Bible. Its first use in the Old Testament is in Gen. 21:15, which says that Hagar "cast the child [Ishmael] under one of the shrubs."

The word is used to describe the "throwing" or "casting" of anything tangible: Moses "threw" a tree into water to sweeten it (Exod. 15:25); Aaron claimed he "threw" gold into the fire and a golden calf walked out (Exod. 32:24). Trees "shed" or "cast off" wilted blossoms (Job 15:33).

Shālak indicates "rejection" in Lam. 2:1: "How hath the Lord . . . cast down from heaven unto the earth the beauty of Israel. . . ." The word is used figuratively in Ps. 55:22: "Cast thy burden upon the Lord. . . ."

CATTLE

'eleph (אֶלֶף), "cattle; thousand; group." The first word, "cattle," signifies the domesticated animal or the herd animal. It has cognates in Aramaic, Akkadian, Ugaritic, and Phoenician. It appears only 8 times in the Bible, first in Deut. 7:13: "He will also bless the fruit of thy womb, and the fruit of thy land, thy corn, and thy wine, and thine oil, the increase of thy kine [NASB, herd], and the flocks of thy sheep. . . ."

This noun is probably related to the verb *'lp*, "to get familiar with, teach, instruct." This verb occurs 4 times, only in Job and Proverbs.

The related noun *'allûph* usually means "familiar; confident." It, too, occurs only in biblical poetry. In Ps. 144:14, *'allûph* signifies a tame domesticated animal: "That our oxen may be strong to labor; that there be no breaking in, nor going out. . . ."

The second word, "thousand," occurs about 490 times and in all periods of biblical Hebrew. It first appears in Gen. 20:16: "Behold, I have given thy brother a thousand pieces of silver. . . ."

The third word, "group," first occurs in Num. 1:16: "These were the renowned of the congregation, princes of the tribes of their fathers, heads of thousands [divisions] in Israel." It appears to be related to the word *'ellûph,* "leader of a large group," which is applied almost exclusively to non-Israelite tribal leaders (exceptions: Zech. 9:7; 12:5-6). *'Ellûph* first occurs in Gen. 36:15: "These were [*chiefs*] of the sons of Esau. . . ."

TO CEASE

A. Verbs.

chādal (חָדַל), "to cease, come to an end, desist, forbear, lack." This word is found primarily in Hebrew, including modern Hebrew. In the Hebrew Old Testament, it is found fewer than 60 times. The first occurrence of *chādal* is in

Gen. 11:8 where, after man's language was confused, "they left off building the city" (RSV).

The basic meaning of *chādal* is "coming to an end." Thus, Sarah's capacity for childbearing had long since "ceased" before an angel informed her that she was to have a son (Gen. 18:11). The Mosaic law made provision for the poor, since they would "never cease out of the land" (Deut. 15:11; Matt. 26:11). In Exod. 14:12, this verb is better translated "let us alone" for the literal "cease from us."

shābath (שָׁבַת), "to rest, cease." This word occurs about 200 times throughout the Old Testament. The root also appears in Assyrian, Arabic, and Aramaic.

The verb first occurs in Gen. 2:2-3: "And on the seventh day God ended his work which he had made; and he *rested* on the seventh day from all his work which he had made. And God blessed the seventh day, and sanctified it: because that in it he had *rested* from all his work which God created and made."

The basic and most frequent meaning of *shābath* is shown in Gen. 8:22: "While the earth remaineth, seedtime and harvest, and cold and heat, and summer and winter, and day and night shall not cease." This promise became a prophetic sign of God's faithfulness: "If those ordinances depart from before me, saith the Lord, then the seed of Israel also shall cease from being a nation before me for ever" (Jer. 31:36).

We find a variety of senses: ". . . Even the first day ye shall *put away* leaven out of your houses . . ." (Exod. 12:15). "Neither shalt thou suffer the salt of the covenant of thy God to *be lacking* from thy meat offering" (Lev. 2:13 NASB, KJV—NIV, "do not leave out"). Josiah "put down the idolatrous priests . . ." (2 Kings 23:5). "I will also eliminate harmful beasts from the land" (Lev. 26:6 NASB—KJV, "rid"; RSV, NIV, "remove").

B. Noun.

shabbāth (שַׁבָּת), "the sabbath." The verb *shābath* is the root of *shabbāth:* "Six days you are to do your work, but on the seventh day you shall cease from labor . . ." (Exod. 23:12, NASB—KJV, "rest"). In Exod. 31:15, the seventh day is called the "sabbath rest" (NASB, "a sabbath of complete rest").

A man's "rest" was to include his animals and servants (Exod. 23:12): even "in earing time and in harvest thou shalt rest" (Exod. 34:21). "It is a sign between me and the children of Israel for ever: for in six days the Lord made heaven and earth, and on the seventh day he rested, and was refreshed" (Exod. 31:17).

". . . Then shall the land keep a sabbath unto the Lord" (Lev. 25:2). Six years' crops will be sown and harvested, but the seventh year "shall be a sabbath of rest unto the land, a sabbath for the Lord . . ." (Lev. 25:4). The feast of trumpets, the Day of Atonement, and the first and eighth days of the Feast of Tabernacles are also called "a sabbath observance" or "a sabbath of complete rest" (Lev. 23:24, 32, 39).

The "sabbath" was a "day of worship" (Lev. 23:3) as well as a "day of rest and refreshment'' for man (Exod. 23:12). God ''rested and was refreshed'' (Exod. 31:17). The ''sabbath'' was the covenant sign of God's lordship over the creation. By observing the ''sabbath,'' Israel confessed that they were God's redeemed people, subject to His lordship to obey the whole of His law. They were His stewards to show mercy with kindness and liberality to all (Exod. 23:12; Lev. 25).

By ''resting,'' man witnessed his trust in God to give fruit to his labor; he entered into God's ''rest.'' Thus ''rest'' and the ''sabbath'' were eschatological in perspective, looking to the accomplishment of God's ultimate purpose through the redemption of His people, to whom the ''sabbath'' was a covenant sign.

The prophets rebuked Israel for their neglect of the sabbath (Isa. 1:13; Jer. 17:21-27; Ezek. 20:12-24; Amos 8:5). They also proclaimed ''sabbath'' observance as a blessing in the messianic age and a sign of its fulness (Isa. 56:2-4; 58:13; 66:23; Ezek. 44:24; 45:17; 46:1, 3-4, 12). The length of the Babylonian Captivity was determined by the extent of Israel's abuse of the sabbatical year (2 Chron. 36:21; cf. Lev. 26:34-35).

CHARIOTRY

A. Nouns.

rekeb (רֶכֶב), ''chariotry; chariot units; chariot horse; chariot; train; upper millstone.'' The noun *rekeb* appears 119 times and in all periods of biblical Hebrew.

The word is used collectively of an entire force of ''military chariotry'': ''And he took six hundred chosen chariots, and all the [*chariotry*]'' (Exod. 14:7—KJV, NASB, ''chariots''). This use of *rekeb* might well be rendered ''chariot-units'' (the chariot, a driver, an offensive and a defensive man). The immediately preceding verse uses *rekeb* of a single ''war-chariot'' (or perhaps ''chariot unit''). The following translation might better represent Exod. 14:6-7: ''So he made his chariot ready and took his courtiers with him, and he took six hundred select chariot units, and all the chariotry of Egypt with defensive men.''

In its first biblical appearance, *rekeb* means ''chariotry'': ''And there went up with him both chariotry [KJV, chariots] and horsemen . . .'' (Gen. 50:9). In 2 Sam. 8:4, the word represents ''chariot-horse'': ''. . .And David hamstrung [KJV, houghed] all the chariot horses. . . .'' *Rekeb* also is used of the ''chariot'' itself: ''. . . And the king was propped [KJV, stayed] up in his chariot against the Syrians . . .'' (1 Kings 22:35).

Next, *rekeb* refers to a ''column'' or ''train of donkeys and camels'': ''And he saw a chariot with a couple of horsemen, a chariot of asses, and a chariot of camels . . .'' (Isa. 21:7).

Finally, *rekeb* sometimes signifies an ''upper millstone'': ''No man shall take the nether or the upper millstone to pledge . . .'' (Deut. 24:6; cf. Judg. 9:53; 2 Sam. 11:21).

merəkābāh (מֶרְכָּבָה), ''war chariot.'' This word occurs 44 times.

Merəkābāh has cognates in Ugaritic, Syriac, and Akkadian. Like *rekeb,* it is derived from *rākab.* The word represents a "war-chariot" (Exod. 14:25), which may have been used as a "chariot of honor" (Gen. 41:43—the first occurrence). It may also be translated "traveling coach" or "cart" (2 Kings 5:21).

B. Verb.

rākab (רָכַב), "to ride upon, drive, mount (an animal)." This verb, which has cognates in Ugaritic and several other Semitic languages, occurs 78 times in the Old Testament. The first occurrence is in Gen. 24:61: "And Rebekah arose, and her damsels, and they rode upon the camels. . . ."

TO CHOOSE

A. Verb.

bāchar (בָּחַר), "to choose." This verb is found 170 times throughout the Old Testament. It is also found in Aramaic, Syriac, and Assyrian. The word has parallels in Egyptian, Akkadian, and Canaanite languages.

Bāchar first occurs in the Bible in Gen. 6:2: ". . . They took them wives of all which they chose." It is often used with a man as the subject: "Lot chose [for himself] all the plain of Jordan . . ." (Gen. 13:11). In more than half of the occurrences, God is the subject of *bāchar,* as in Num. 16:5: ". . . The Lord will show who are his, and who is holy; . . . even him whom he hath chosen will he cause to come near unto him."

Neh. 9:7-8 describes God's "choosing" (election) of persons as far back as Abram: "You are the Lord God, who chose Abram . . . and you made a covenant with him" (NIV). *Bāchar* is used 30 times in Deuteronomy, all but twice referring to God's "choice" of Israel or something in Israel's life. "Because he loved thy fathers, therefore he chose their seed after them . . ." (Deut. 4:37). Being "chosen" by God brings people into an intimate relationship with Him: ". . . The children of the Lord your God: . . . the Lord hath chosen thee to be a peculiar people unto himself, above all the nations that are upon the earth" (Deut. 14:1-2).

God's "choices" shaped the history of Israel; His "choice" led to their redemption from Egypt (Deut. 7:7-8), sent Moses and Aaron to work miracles in Egypt (Ps. 105:26-27), and gave them the Levites "to bless in the name of the Lord" (Deut. 21:5). He "chose" their inheritance (Ps. 47:4), including Jerusalem, where He dwelt among them (Deut. 12:5; 2 Chron. 6:5, 21). But "they have chosen their own ways, and . . . I also will choose their delusions, and will bring their fears upon them . . ." (Isa. 66:3-4). The covenant called men to respond to God's election: ". . . I have set before you life and death . . .: therefore choose life . . ." (Deut. 30:19; cf. Josh. 24:22).

The Greek Septuagint version translated *bāchar* chiefly by *eklegein,* and through this word the important theological concept of God's "choosing" came into the New Testament. The verb is used of God's or Christ's "choice" of men for service, as in Luke 6:13 ("of them he chose twelve . . .") or of the objects of His grace: ". . . He hath chosen us in him before the foundation of the world . . ." (Eph. 1:4). John 15:16 expresses the central truth of election in both Testaments: "Ye have not chosen me, but I have chosen you, . . . that ye should go and bring forth fruit, and that your fruit should remain. . . ."

B. Noun.

bāchîr (בָּחִיר), "chosen ones." Another noun, *bāchîr,* is used 13 times, always of the Lord's "chosen ones": "Saul, whom the Lord did choose" (2 Sam. 21:6); "ye children of Jacob, his chosen ones" (1 Chron. 16:13).

TO CIRCUMCISE

mûl (מוּל), "to circumcise, cut off." This verb occurs more than 30 times in the Old Testament. Its usage is continued in rabbinic and modern Hebrew. However, the verb "to cut off" is not found in other Semitic languages.

Most of the occurrences in the Old Testament take place in the Pentateuch (20 times) and Joshua (8 times). *Mûl* occurs most frequently in Genesis (17 times, 11 of them in Genesis 17 alone) and Joshua (8 times). *Mûl* occurs in 3 of the 7 verb patterns and in several rare patterns. It has no derivatives other than the *hapax legomenon (môlot)* in Exod. 4:26: "At that time she said, 'bridegroom of blood,' referring to circumcision" (NIV).

The physical act of circumcision was introduced by God as a sign of the Abrahamic covenant: "This is my covenant with you and your descendants after you . . . Every male among you shall be circumcumcised. You are to undergo circumcision, and it will be the sign of the covenant between me and you" (Gen. 17:10-11, NIV). It was a permanent "cutting off" of the foreskin of the male organ, and as such was a reminder of the perpetuity of the covenantal relationship. Israel was enjoined to be faithful in "circumcising" all males; each male baby was to be "circumcised" on the eighth day (Gen. 17:12; Lev. 12:3). Not only were the physical descendants of Abraham "circumcised," but also those who were servants, slaves, and foreigners in the covenant community (Gen. 17:13-14).

The special act of circumcision was a sign of God's gracious promise. With the promise and covenantal relations, God expected that His people would joyously and willingly live up to His expectations, and thus demonstrate His rule on earth. To describe the "heart" attitude, several writers of Scripture use the verb "to circumcise." The "circumcision" of the flesh is a physical sign of commitment to God. Deuteronomy particularly is fond of the spiritual usage of the verb "to circumcise": "Circumcise your hearts, therefore, and do not be stiff-necked any longer" (Deut. 10:16, NIV; cf. 30:6). Jeremiah took over this usage: "Circumcise yourselves to the Lord, and take away the foreskins of your heart, ye men of Judah . . . , because of the evil of your doings" (Jer. 4:4).

Few occurrences of the verb differ from the physical and the spiritual usage of "to circumcise." *Mûl* in the Book of Psalms has the meaning of "to cut off, destroy": "All the nations surrounded me, but in the name of the Lord I cut them off" (Ps. 118:10, NIV; cf. vv. 11-12).

The verb is translated as *peritemnō* in the Septuagint. The verb and the noun *peritomē* are used in both the physical and the spiritual sense. In addition to this, it also is a figure for baptism: "In him you were also circumcised, . . . not with a circumcision alone by the hands of men but with the circumcision done by Christ, having been buried with him in baptism and raised with him through your faith in the power of God, who raised him from the dead" (Col. 2: 11-12, NIV).

In the English versions, the verb is rendered "to circumcise," "to destroy" (KJV), as well as "to cut off" and "to wither" (RSV, NASB, NIV).

CITY

'îr (עִיר), "city; town; village; quarter [of a city]." Cognates of this word appear in Ugaritic, Phoenician, Sumerian, and old Arabic. This noun occurs about 1,092 times and in every period of biblical Hebrew.

The word suggests a "village." An unwalled village is represented by the Hebrew word *chātsēr. Qirəyat*, a synonym of *'îr*, is an Aramaic loan word.

But *'îr* and its synonym do not necessarily suggest a walled city. This usage is seen in Deut. 3:5, where *'îr* may be a city standing in the open country (perhaps surrounded by dirt or stone ramparts for protection): "All these cities were fenced with high walls, gates, and bars; beside unwalled towns a great many." A comparison of Lev. 25:29 and Lev. 25:31 shows that *'îr* can be used as synonym of *chātsēr:* "And if a man sell a dwelling house in a walled city, then he may redeem it within a whole year after it is sold; . . . but the houses of the villages [*chātsēr*] which have no wall round about them shall be counted as the fields of the country. . . ."

'îr can signify not only a "village consisting of permanent houses" but also one in a permanent place, even though the dwellings are tents: "And Saul came to a *city* of Amalek, and laid wait in the valley" (1 Sam. 15:5).

In Gen. 4:17 (the first occurrence), the word *'îr* means a "permanent dwelling center" consisting of residences of stone and clay. As a rule, there are no political overtones to the word; *'îr* simply represents the "place where people dwell on a permanent basis." At some points, however, *'îr* represents a political entity (1 Sam. 15:5; 30:29).

This word can represent "those who live in a given town": "And when he came, lo, Eli sat upon a seat by the wayside watching: for his heart trembled for the ark of God. And when the man came into the city, and told it, *all the city* cried out" (1 Sam. 4:13).

'îr can also signify only "a part of a city," such as a part that is surrounded by a wall: "Nevertheless David took the stronghold of Zion: the same is the *city* of David" (2 Sam. 5:7). Ancient cities (especially larger ones) were sometimes divided into sections (quarters) by walls, in order to make it more difficult to capture them. This suggests that, by the time of the statement just cited, *'îr* normally implied a "walled city."

TO BE CLEAN

A. Verb.

tāhēr (טָהֵר), "to be clean, pure." The root of this word appears over 200 times in various forms—as a verb, adjective, or noun.

Since the fall of Adam and Eve, none of their offspring is clean in the sight of the holy God: "Who can say, I have made my heart clean, I am pure from my sin?" (Prov. 20:9). Reminding Job that protestations of innocence are of no avail, Eliphaz asked: "Shall mortal man be more just than God? Shall a man be more pure than his Maker?" (Job 4:17).

There is hope, however, because God promised penitent Israel: "And I will cleanse them from all their iniquity, whereby they have sinned against me . . ." (Jer. 33:8). He said: ". . . I will save them out of all their dwelling places, wherein they have sinned, and will cleanse them: so they shall be my people, and I will be their God" (Ezek. 37:23).

The baleful effect of sin was recognized when a person contracted the dread disease of leprosy. After the priest diagnosed the disease, he could declare a person "clean" only after cleansing ceremonies had been performed: ". . . And he shall wash his clothes, also he shall wash his flesh in water, and he shall be clean" (Lev. 14:9).

God required that His people observe purification rites when they came into His presence for worship. On the Day of Atonement, for example, prescribed ceremonies were performed to "cleanse" the altar from "the uncleanness of the children of Israel" and to "hallow it" (Lev. 16:17-19; cf. Exod. 29:36 ff.). The priests were to be purified before they performed their sacred tasks. Moses was directed to "take the Levites . . . and cleanse them" (Num. 8:6; cf. Lev. 8:5-13). After they had been held captive in the unclean land of Babylon, ". . . the priests and the Levites purified themselves, and purified the people, and the gates, and the wall [of the rebuilt city of Jerusalem]" (Neh. 12:30).

Cleansing might be achieved by physically removing the objects of defilement. During the reform of King Hezekiah, "the priests went into the inner part of the house of the Lord, to cleanse it, and brought out all the uncleanness that they found in the temple of the Lord . . ." (2 Chron. 29:16).

Some rites required blood as the purifying agent: "And he shall sprinkle of the blood upon it [the altar] with his finger seven times, and cleanse it, and hallow it from the uncleanness of the children of Israel" (Lev. 16:19). Sacrifices were offered to make atonement for a mother after childbirth: ". . . she shall bring . . . the one for the burnt offering, and the other for a sin offering: and the priest shall make an atonement for her, and she shall be clean" (Lev. 12:8).

B. Adjective.

tāhôr (טָהוֹר), "clean; pure." The word denotes the absence of impurity, filthiness, defilement, or imperfection. It is applied concretely to substances that are genuine or unadulterated, as well as describing an unstained condition of a spiritual or ceremonial nature.

Gold is a material frequently said to be free of baser ingredients. Thus the ark of the covenant, the incense altar, and the porch of the temple were "overlaid with pure gold" (Exod. 25:11; 37:11, 26; 2 Chron. 3:4). Some of the furnishings and utensils in the temple—such as the mercy seat, the lampstand, the dishes, pans, bowls, jars, snuffers, trays—were of "pure gold" (Exod. 37:6, 16-24). The high priest's vestment included "two chains of pure gold" and "a plate of pure gold" (Exod. 28:14, 22, 36).

God demands that His people have spiritual and moral purity, unsullied by sin. Anyone not clean of sin is subject to divine rejection and punishment. This contamination is never outgrown or overcome. Because sin pollutes one generation after another, Job asks: "Who can bring a clean thing out of an unclean?" (Job 14:4). All outward appearances to the contrary, it cannot be said that there is "one event . . . to the clean, and to the unclean" (Eccl. 9:2). Hope is available even to the chief of sinners, because any man can entreat the mercy of God and say: "Create in me a clean heart, O God; and renew a right spirit within me" (Ps. 51:10).

In sharp contrast with mankind's polluted nature and actions, "the words of the Lord are pure words . . ." (Ps. 12:6). The Lord is "of purer eyes than to behold evil" (Hab. 1:13).

"Clean" most frequently describes the purity maintained by avoiding contact with other human beings, abstaining from eating animals, and using things that are declared ceremonially clean. Conversely, cleansing results if ritual procedures symbolizing the removal of contamination are observed.

The people of the old covenant were told that "he that toucheth the dead body of any man shall be unclean seven days" (Num. 19:11). A priest was not to defile himself "for the dead among his people" except "for his kin, that is near unto him" (Lev. 21:1-2). This relaxation of the rule was even denied the high priest and a Nazarite during "all the days that he separateth himself unto the Lord" (Num. 6:6 ff.).

Cleansing rituals emphasized the fact that the people were conceived and born in sin. Though conception and birth were not branded immoral (just as dying itself was not sinful), a woman who had borne a child remained unclean until she submitted to the proper purification rites (Lev. 12). Chapter 15 of Leviticus prescribes ceremonial cleansing for a woman having her menstrual flow, for a man having seminal emissions, and for "the woman also with whom man shall lie with seed of copulation" (Lev. 15:18).

To be ceremonially "clean," the Israelite also had to abstain from eating certain animals and even from touching them (Lev. 11; Deut. 14:3-21). After the Israelites settled in the Promised Land, some modifications were made in the regulations (Deut. 12:15, 22; 15:22).

Purification rites frequently involved the use of water. The person to be cleansed was required to wash himself and his clothes (Lev. 15:27). Water was sprinkled on the individual, on his tent, and on all its furnishings: "And a clean person shall take hyssop, and dip it in the water, and sprinkle it upon the tent, and upon all the vessels, and upon the persons that were there, and upon him that touched a bone, or the slain, or one dead, or a grave" (Num. 19:18). Sometimes the person being cleansed also had to change garments (Lev. 6:11).

However, the rites were not meritorious deeds, earning God's favor and forgiveness. Nor did the ceremonies serve their intended purpose if performed mechanically. Unless the rites expressed a person's contrite and sincere desire to be cleansed from the defilement of sin, they were an abomination to God and only aggravated a person's guilt. Anyone who appeared before Him in ritual and ceremony with "hands . . . full of blood" (Isa. 1:15) and did not plead for cleansing of his crimes was judged to be as wicked as the people of Sodom and Gomorrah. Zion's hope lay in this cleansing by means of an offering: "And they shall bring all your brethren for an offering unto the Lord out of all nations upon horses . . . as the children of Israel bring an offering in a clean vessel into the house of the Lord" (Isa. 66:20).

TO CLEAVE, CLING

dābaq (דָּבַק), "to cling, cleave, keep close." Used in modern Hebrew in the sense of "to stick to, adhere to," *dābaq* yields the noun form for "glue" and also the more abstract ideas of "loyalty, devotion." Occurring just over 60 times in the Hebrew Old Testament, this term is found very early in the text, in Gen. 2:24: "Therefore shall a man leave his father and his mother, and shall *cleave* unto his wife: and they shall be one flesh." This usage reflects the basic meaning of one object's (person's) being joined to another. In this sense, Eleazar's hand "cleaved" to the sword as he struck down the Philistines (2 Sam. 23:10). Jeremiah's linen waistcloth "clung" to his loins, symbolic of Israel's "clinging" to God (Jer. 13:11). In time of war and siege, the resulting thirst and famine caused the tongue "to cleave" to the roof of the mouth of those who had been so afflicted.

The literal statement, "My soul cleaveth unto the dust" (Ps. 119:25; RSV, "cleaves"), is better understood as one consults the other English versions: "I lie prone in the dust" (NEB); "Down in the dust I lie prostrate" (JB); "I lie prostrate in the dust" (NAB); "I lie defeated in the dust" (TEV).

The figurative use of *dābaq* in the sense of "loyalty" and "affection" is based on the physical closeness of the persons involved, such as a husband's closeness to his wife (Gen. 2:24), Shechem's affection for Dinah (Gen. 34:3), or Ruth's staying with Naomi (Ruth 1:14). "Cleaving" to God is equivalent to "loving" God (Deut. 30:20).

TO CLEAVE, SPLIT

bāqa' (בָּקַע), "to cleave, split, break open, break through." This word occurs in all the periods of the Hebrew language and is also found in ancient Ugaritic or Canaanite. It is the origin of the name of the famous Beqa Valley (which means "valley" or "cleft") in Lebanon.

In its verbal forms, *bāqa'* is found some 50 times in the Hebrew Old Testament. The word is first used there in Gen. 7:11, which states that the "fountains of the great deep [were] broken up," resulting in the Flood. The everyday use of the verb is seen in references to "splitting" wood (Eccles. 10:9) and the ground "splitting" asunder (Num. 16:31). Serpents' eggs "split open" or "hatch out" their young (Isa. 59:5). City walls are "breached" or "broken into" in order to take them captive (Jer. 52:7). One of the horrors of war was the "ripping open" of pregnant women by the enemy (2 Kings 8:12; 15:16). Three times God is said "to split open" rocks or the ground in order to provide water for His people (Judg. 15:19; Ps. 74:15; Isa. 48:21).

In the figurative sense, it is said that the light of truth will "break forth as the morning" (Isa. 58:8). Using hyperbole or exaggeration, the historian who recorded the celebration for Solomon's coronation said that it was so loud "that the earth rent with the sound of them" (1 Kings 1:40). As here, the KJV often renders *bāqaʿ* by "rent." In other contexts, it may be translated "burst; clave (cleave); tear; divide; break."

TO CLOTHE

lābash (לָבַשׁ), "to put on (a garment), clothe, wear, be clothed." A common Semitic term, this word is found in ancient Akkadian and Ugaritic, in Aramaic, and throughout the history of the Hebrew language. The word occurs about 110 times in the text of the Hebrew Bible. *Lābash* is found very early in the Old Testament, in Gen. 3:21: "Unto Adam also and to his wife did the Lord God make coats of skin, and *clothed* them." As always, God provided something much better for man than man could do for himself—in this instance, fig-leaf garments (Gen. 3:7).

Lābash is regularly used for the "putting on" of ordinary clothing (Gen. 38:19; Exod. 29:30; 1 Sam. 28:8). The word also describes the "putting on" of armor (Jer. 46:4). Many times it is used in a figurative sense, as in Job 7:5: "My flesh is clothed [covered] with worms. . . ." Jerusalem is spoken of as "putting on" the Jews as they return after the Exile (Isa. 49:18). Often the figurative garment is an abstract quality: "For he put on righteousness as a breastplate, . . . he put on garments of vengeance for clothing . . ." (Isa. 59:17). God is spoken of as being "clothed with honor and majesty" (Ps. 104:1). Job says, "I put on righteousness, and it clothed me . . ." (Job 29:14).

These abstract qualities are sometimes negative: "The prince shall be clothed [RSV, "wrapped"] with desolation" (Ezek. 7:27). "They that hate thee shall be clothed with shame" (Job 8:22). "Let mine adversaries be clothed with shame" (Ps. 109:29). A very important figurative use of *lābash* is found in Judg. 6:34, where the stative form of the verb may be translated, "The spirit of the Lord clothed itself [was clothed] with Gideon." The idea seems to be that the Spirit of the Lord incarnated Himself in Gideon and thus empowered him from within. The English versions render it variously: "came upon" (KJV, NASB, JB); "took possession of" (NEB, RSV); "took control" (TEV); "wrapped round" (Knox).

CLOUD

'ānān ('ānān), "cloud; fog; storm cloud; smoke." Cognates of this word appear in Aramaic and Arabic. Its 87 appearances are scattered throughout the biblical material.

The word commonly means "cloud mass." *'Ānān* is used especially of the "cloud mass" that evidenced the special presence of God: "And the Lord went before them by day in a pillar of a cloud, to lead them the way . . ." (Exod. 13:21). In Exod. 34:5, this presence is represented by *'ānān* only: "And the Lord descended in the cloud, and stood with him [Moses] there, and proclaimed the name of the Lord."

When the ark of the covenant was brought into the holy place, "The cloud filled the house of the Lord, so that the priests could not stand to minister because of the cloud: for the glory of the Lord had filled the house of the Lord" (1 Kings 8:10-11). Thus the "cloud" evidenced the presence of God's glory. So the psalmist wrote that God was surrounded by "clouds and darkness" (Ps. 97:2); God appears as the controller and sovereign of nature. This description is somewhat parallel to the descriptions of Baal, the lord of the storm and god of nature set forth in Ugaritic mythology. The "cloud" is a sign and figure of "divine protection" (Isa. 4:5) and serves as a barrier hiding the fulness of divine holiness and glory, as well as barring sinful man's approach to God (Lam. 3:44). Man's relationship to God, therefore, is God-initiated and God-sustained, not humanly initiated or humanly sustained.

In its first biblical occurrence, *'ānān* is used in conjunction with God's sign that He would never again destroy the earth by a flood: "I do set my bow in the cloud, and it shall be for a token of a covenant between me and the earth" (Gen. 9:13). Elsewhere, the transitory quality of a cloud is used to symbolize the loyalty (Hos. 6:4) and existence of Israel (13:3). In Isa. 44:22, God says that after proper punishment He will wipe out, "as a thick cloud, thy transgressions, and, as a cloud, thy sins. . . ."

'Ānān can mean "storm cloud" and is used to symbolize "an invading force": "Thou shalt ascend and come like a storm, thou shalt be like a cloud to cover the land, thou, and all thy bands, and many people with thee" (Ezek. 38:9; cf. Jer. 4:13). In Job 26:8, the storm cloud is said to be God's: "He bindeth up the waters in his thick clouds; and the cloud is not rent under them." In several passages, the thick storm cloud and the darkness accompanying it are symbols of "gloom" (Ezek. 30:18) and/or "divine judgment" (Ezek. 30:3).

'Ānān can represent the "smoke" arising from burning incense: "And he shall put the incense upon the fire before the Lord, that the cloud of the incense may cover the mercy seat that is upon the testimony, that he die not . . ." (Lev. 16:13). This "cloud of smoke" may represent the covering between God's presence (above the mercy seat) and sinful man. If so, it probably also symbolizes the "divine glory." On the other hand, many scholars feel it represents the human prayers offered up to God.

TO COME

bô' (בּוֹא), "to go in, enter, come, go." This root appears in most Semitic languages, but with varying meanings. For example, the meaning "come" appears in the Babylonian letters of Mari (1750–1697 B.C.). The corresponding Ugaritic word (1550–1200 B.C.) has the same significance as its Hebrew counterpart, while the Phoenician root (starting around 900 B.C.) means "come forth." *Bô'* occurs about 2,570 times in Old Testament Hebrew.

First, this verb connotes movement in space from one place toward another. The meaning "go in" or "enter" appears in Gen. 7:7, where it is said that Noah and his family "entered" the ark. In the causative stem, this verb can signify "cause to enter" or "bring into" (Gen. 6:19) or "bring unto" (its meaning in its first biblical occurrence, Gen. 2:19). In Gen. 10:19, the verb is used more absolutely in the phrase "as thou goest unto Sodom." Interestingly, this verb can also mean "to come" and "to return." Abram and his family "came" to the land of Canaan (Gen. 12:5), while in Deut. 28:6 God blessed the godly who "go forth" (to work in the morning) and "return" (home in the evening).

Sometimes *bô'* refers to the "going down" or "setting" of the sun (Gen. 15:12). It can connote dying, in the sense of "going to one's fathers" (Gen. 15:15). Another special use is the "going into one's wife" or "cohabitation" (Gen. 6:4). *Bô'* can also be used of movement in time. For example, the prophets speak of the "coming" day of judgment (1 Sam. 2:31). Finally, the verb can be used of the "coming" of an event such as the sign predicted by a false prophet (Deut. 13:2).

There are three senses in which God is said "to come." God "comes" through an angel (Judg. 6:11) or other incarnated being (cf. Gen. 18:14). He "appears" and speaks to men in dreams (Gen. 20:3) and in other actual manifestations (Exod. 20:20). For example, during the Exodus, God "appeared" in the cloud and fire that went before the people (Exod. 19:9).

Secondly, God promises to "come" to the faithful wherever and whenever they properly worship Him (Exod. 20:24). The Philistines felt that God had "come" into the Israelite camp when the ark of the covenant arrived (1 Sam. 4:7). This usage associated with formal worship may appear in Ps. 24:7, where the gates of Zion are said to open as the King of glory "enters" Jerusalem. Also, the Lord is "to return" ("come back") to the new temple described in Ezek. 43:2.

Finally, there is a group of prophetic pictures of divine "comings." This theme may have originated in the hymns sung of God's "coming" to aid His people in war (cf. Deut. 33:2). In the Psalms (e.g., 50:3) and prophets (e.g., Isa. 30:27), the Lord "comes" in judgment and blessing—a poetic figure of speech borrowed from ancient Near Eastern mythology (cf. Ezek. 1:4).

Bô' also is used to refer to the "coming" of the Messiah. In Zech. 9:9, the messianic king is pictured as "coming" on a foal of a donkey. Some of the passages pose especially difficult problems, such as Gen. 49:10, which prophesies that the scepter will remain in Judah "until Shiloh come." Another difficult passage is Ezek. 21:27: "until he come whose right it is." A very well-known prophecy using the verb *bô'* is that concerning the "coming" of the Son of Man (Dan. 7:13). Finally, there is the "coming" of the last day (Amos 8:2) and the Day of the Lord (Isa. 13:6).

The Septuagint translates this verb with many Greek words paralleling the connotations of the Hebrew verb, but especially with words meaning "to come," "to enter," and "to go."

TO COME NEAR, APPROACH

nāgash (נָגַשׁ), "to approach, draw near, bring." Found primarily in biblical Hebrew, this word is also found in ancient Ugaritic. It occurs 125 times in the Hebrew text of the Old Testament. *Nāgash* is used for the first time in the biblical text in Gen. 18:23, where Abraham is said to "draw near" to God to plead that Sodom be spared.

The word is often used to describe ordinary "contact" of one person with another (Gen. 27:22; 43:19). Sometimes *nāgash* describes "contact" for the purpose of sexual intercourse (Exod. 19:15). More frequently, it is used to speak of the priests "coming into the presence of" God (Ezek. 44:13) or of the priests' "approach" to the altar (Exod. 30:20). Oppposing armies are said "to draw near" to battle each other (Judg. 20:23; KJV, "go up"). Inanimate objects, such as the close-fitting scales of the crocodile, are said to be so "near" to each other that no air can come between them (Job. 41:16). Sometimes the word is used to speak of "bringing" an offering to the altar (Mal. 1:7).

The English versions render *nāgash* variously, according to context: "went near" (RSV), "moved closer" (TEV), "came close" (JB, NEB, NASB).

TO COME UP, ASCEND

A. Verb.

'ālāh (עָלָה), "to go up, ascend, offer up." This word occurs in all Semitic languages, including biblical Hebrew. The Old Testament attests it about 890 times.

Basically, *'ālāh* suggests movement from a lower to a higher place. That is the emphasis in Gen. 2:6 (the first occurrence of the word), which reports that Eden was watered by a mist or stream that "went up" over the ground. *'Ālāh* may also mean "to rise up" or "ascend." The king of Babylon said in his heart, "I will ascend into heaven" (Isa. 14:13). This word may mean "to take a journey," as in traveling from Egypt (Gen. 13:1) toward Palestine or other points northward. The verb may be used in a special sense meaning "to extend, reach"—for example, the border of Benjamin "went up ["extended, reached"] through the mountains westward" (Josh. 18:12).

The use of *'ālāh* to describe the journey from Egypt to Palestine is such a standard phrase that it often appears without the geographical reference points. Joseph told his brothers to "go up" to their father in peace (Gen. 44:17). Even the return from the Exile, which was a journey from north to south (Palestine), is described as a "going up" (Ezra 2:1). Thus, the reference may be not so much to physically "going up," but to a figurative or spiritual "going up." This usage appears long before Ezra's time, when it is said that one "goes up" to the place where the sanctuary is located (cf. Deut. 17:8). The verb became a technical term for "making a pilgrimage" (Exod. 34:24) or "going up" before the Lord; in a secular context, compare Joseph's "going up" before Pharaoh (Gen. 46:31).

In instances where an enemy located himself in a superior position (frequently a higher place), one "goes up" to battle (Josh. 22:12). The verb can also refer merely to "going out" to make war against someone, even though there is no movement from a lower to a higher plane. So Israel "went up" to make war against the Moabites, who heard of the Israelites' approach while still dwelling in their cities (2 Kings 3:21). Even when '*ālāh* is used by itself, it can mean "to go to war"; the Lord told Phinehas, "Go up; for tomorrow I will deliver them into thine hand" (Judg. 20:28). On the other hand, if the enemy is recognized to be on a lower plane, one can "go down" (*yārad*) to fight (Judg. 1:9). The opposite of "going up" to war is not descending to battle, but "leaving off" ('*ālāh mē'al), literally, "going up from against."

Another special use of '*ālāh* is "to overpower" (literally, "to go up from"). For example, the Pharaoh feared the Israelites lest in a war they join the enemy, fight against Egypt, and "overpower" the land (Exod. 1:10). "To go up" may also be used of "increasing in strength," as the lion that becomes strong from his prey: The lion "goes up from his prey" (Gen. 49:9; cf. Deut. 28:43).

Not only physical things can "go up." '*Ālāh* can be used also of the "increasing" of wrath (2 Sam. 11:20), the "ascent" of an outcry before God (Exod. 2:23), and the "continual" sound of battle (although "sound of" is omitted; cf. 1 Kings 22:35). The word can also be used passively to denote mixing two kinds of garments together, causing one "to lie upon" or "be placed upon" the other (Lev. 19:19). Sometimes "go up" means "placed," even when the direction is downward, as when placing a yoke upon an ox (Num. 19:2) or going to one's grave (Job 5:26). This may be an illustration of how Hebrew verbs can sometimes mean their opposite. The verb is also used of "recording" a census (1 Chron. 27:24).

The verb '*ālāh* is used in a causative stem to signify "presenting an offering" to God. In 63 cases, the word is associated with the presentation of the whole burnt offering ('*ōlāh). '*Ālāh* is used of the general act of "presenting offerings" when the various offerings are mentioned in the same context (Lev. 14:20), or when the purpose of the offering is not specifically in mind (Isa. 57:6). Sometimes this verb means merely "to offer" (e.g., Num. 23:2).

B. Nouns.

'*elayôn* (עֶלְיוֹן), "the upper; the highest." This word occurs 53 times. The use of '*elayôn* in Gen. 40:17 means "the upper" as opposed to "the lower." Where referring to or naming God, '*elayôn* means "the highest" (Gen. 14:18).

ma'alāh (מַעֲלָה), "step; procession; pilgrimage." In some of its 47 biblical appearances, *ma'alāh* signifies a "step" or "stair" (cf. Exod. 20:26). The word can also mean "procession" (Ps. 84:6).

TO COMMAND

tsāwāh (צָוָה), "to command." This verb occurs only in biblical Hebrew (in all periods) and imperial Aramaic (starting from around 500 B.C.). Biblical occurrences number around 485.

Essentially, this verb refers to verbal communication by which a superior "orders" or "commands" a subordinate. The word implies the content of what was said. Pharaoh "ordered" ("commanded") his men concerning Abraham, and they escorted Abraham and his party out of Egypt (Gen. 12:20). This "order" defines an action relevant to a specific situation. *Tsāwāh* can also connote "command" in the sense of the establishment of a rule by which a subordinate is to act in every recurring similar situation. In the Garden of Eden (the first appearance of this word in the Bible), God "commanded" ("set down the rule"): "Of every tree of the garden thou mayest freely eat: . . ." (Gen. 2:16). In this case, the word does not contain the content of the action but focuses on the action itself.

One of the recurring formulas in the Bible is "X did all that Y commanded him"—e.g., Ruth "did according to all that her mother-in-law bade her" (Ruth 3:6). This means that she carried out Naomi's "orders." A similar formula, "X did just as Y commanded," is first found in Num. 32:25, where the sons of Reuben and Gad say to Moses that they "will do as my lord commandeth." These formulas indicate the accomplishment of, or the intention to accomplish, the "orders" of a superior.

The verb *tsāwāh* can be used of a commission or charge, such as the act of "commanding," "telling," or "sending" someone to do a particular task. In Gen. 32:4, Jacob "commissioned" his servants to deliver a particular message to his brother Esau. They acted as his emissaries. Jacob commissioned (literally, "commanded") his sons to bury him in the cave of Machpelah (Gen. 49:30), and then he died. This "command" constituted a last will and testament—an obligation or duty. The verb again indicates, therefore, appointing someone to be one's emissary.

The most frequent subject of this verb is God. However, He is not to be questioned or "commanded" to explain the work of His hands (Isa. 45:11). He tells Israel that His "commands" are unique, requiring an inner commitment and not just external obedience, as the commands of men do (Gen. 29:13). His "ordering" is given to Moses from above the mercy seat (Exod. 25:22) and from His "commands" at Sinai (Lev. 7:38; cf. 17:1 ff.). At other times when He "commands," the thing simply occurs; His word is active and powerful (Ps. 33:9). He also issues "orders" through and to the prophets (Jer. 27:4) who explain, apply, and speak His "commands" (Jer. 1:17).

COMMANDER

sar (שַׂר), "official; leader; commander; captain; chief; prince; ruler." This word, which has an Akkadian cognate, appears about 420 times in biblical Hebrew. The word is often applied to certain non-Israelite "officials or representatives of the king." This meaning appears in Gen. 12:15, its first biblical appearance: 'The *princes* also of Pharaoh saw her [Sarah], and commended her before Pharaoh. . . .'' In other contexts *sar* represents "men who clearly have responsibility over others"; they are "rulers or chieftains." *Sar* may mean simply a "leader" of a profession, a group, or a district, as Phichol was the "commander" of Abimelech's army (Gen. 21:22) and Potiphar was "an officer of Pharaoh's and captain of the [body]guard" (Gen. 37:36). In such usage, "chief" means "head official" (cf. Gen. 40:2). *Sarîm* (plural) were "honored men" (Isa. 23:8).

Sar is used of certain "notable men" within Israel. When Abner was killed by Joab, David said to his servants (palace officials), "Know ye not that there is a prince and a great man fallen this day in Israel?" (2 Sam. 3:38; cf. Num. 21:18). Joab, Abishai, and Ittai were "commanders" in David's army (cf. 2 Sam. 23:19). "Local leaders in Israel" are also called *sarîm:* "And the *princes* of Succoth said . . ." (Judg. 8:6).

In several passages, *sar* refers to the task of "ruling." Moses tried to break up a fight between two Hebrews and one of them asked him, "Who made thee a prince and a judge over us?" (Exod. 2:14). In such a context, *sar* means "leader," "ruler," and "judge": "Moreover thou shalt provide out of all the people able men, such as fear God, men of truth, hating covetousness; and place such over them, to be rulers of thousands, and rulers of hundreds, rulers of fifties, and rulers of tens . . ." (Exod. 18:21). The "commander" of Israel's army was called a *sar* (1 Sam. 17:55).

In Judg. 9:30, *sar* represents a "ruler" of a city. Any government official might be called a *sar* (Neh. 3:14). "Religious officiants" who served in the temple of God were also called *sarîm* (Jer. 35:4).

The "leaders" or "chiefs" of the Levites (1 Chron. 15:16) or priests (Ezra 8:24) are *sarîm.* In 1 Chron. 24:5, the word appears to be a title: "Thus were they divided by lot, one sort with another; for the governors of the sanctuary [*sarîm gōdesh*], and governors of the house of God [*sarîm ha'elōhîm*], were of the sons of Eleazar, and of the sons of Ithamar" (NASB, "officers of the sanctuary" and "officers of God").

In the Book of Daniel, *sar* is used of "superhuman beings" or "patron angels." Thus, Michael is the "prince" of Judah (Dan. 10:21; cf. Josʾ. 5:14). Daniel 8:25 speaks of a king who will arise and "stand up against the Prince of princes" (i.e., the Messiah).

COMMANDMENT

mitsəwāh (מִצְוָה), "commandment." This noun occurs 181 times in the Old Testament. Its first occurrence is in Gen. 26:5, where *mitsəwāh* is synonymous with *hōq* ("statute") and *tôrāh* ("law"): "Because that Abraham obeyed my voice, and kept my charge, my *commandments,* my statutes, and my laws."

In the Pentateuch, God is always the Giver of the *mitsəwāh:* "All the commandments which I command thee this day shall ye observe to do, that ye may live, and multiply, and go in and possess the land which the Lord sware unto your fathers. And thou shalt remember all the way which the Lord thy God led thee these forty years in the wilderness, to humble thee, and to prove thee, to know what was in thine heart, whether thou wouldest keep his commandments, or no" (Deut. 8:1-2). The "commandment" may be a prescription ("thou shalt do . . .") or a proscription ("thou shalt not do . . ."). The commandments were given in the hearing of the Israelites (Exod. 15:26; Deut. 11:13), who were to "do" (Lev. 4:2 ff.) and "keep" (Deut. 4:2; Ps. 78:7) them. Any failure to do so signified a covenantal breach (Num. 15:31), transgression (2 Chron. 24:20), and apostasy (1 Kings 18:18).

The plural of *mitsəwāh* often denotes a "body of laws" given by divine revelation. They are God's "word": "Wherewithal shall a young man cleanse his way? By taking heed thereto according to thy word" (Ps. 119:9). They are also known as "the commandments of God."

Outside the Pentateuch, "commandments" are given by kings (1 Kings 2:43), fathers (Jer. 35:14), people (Isa. 29:13), and teachers of wisdom (Prov. 6:20; cf. 5:13). Only about ten percent of all occurrences in the Old Testament fit this category.

The Septuagint translations are: *entolē* ("commandment; order") and *prostagma* ("order; commandment; injunction").

COMPANION

A. Nouns.

rēʿa (רֵעַ), "friend; companion." This noun is also represented in Akkadian, Ugaritic, and Aramaic. *Rēʿa* appears 187 times in the Hebrew Old Testament, and it has an extensive range of meaning.

The basic meaning of *rēʿa* is in the narrow usage of the word. A *rēʿa* is a "personal friend" with whom one shares confidences and to whom one feels very close: "And the Lord spake unto Moses face to face, as a man speaketh unto his friend" (Exod. 33:11). The closeness of relationship is best expressed by those texts where the *rēʿa* is like a brother or son, a part of the family: "For my brethren and companions' sakes . . ." (Ps. 122:8; cf. Deut. 13:6). For this reason, when Zimri became king over Israel he killed not only all relatives of Baasha, but also his "friends" (1 Kings 16:11). In this sense, the word is a synonym of *'ach* ("brother") and of *qārôb* ("kin"): ". . . Go in and out from gate to gate throughout the camp, and slay every man his brother, and every man his *companion,* and every man his neighbor" (Exod. 32:27).

Similar to the above is the sense of "marriage partner": "His mouth is most sweet: yea, he is altogether lovely. This is my beloved, and this is my *friend,* O daughters of Jerusalem" (Song of Sol. 5:16). However, *rēʿa* may also signify "illegitimate partners": ". . . If a man put away his wife, and she go from him, and become another man's, shall he return unto her again? shall not that land be greatly polluted? but thou has played the harlot with many lovers (*rēʿa*); yet return again to me, saith the Lord" (Jer. 3:1). The prophet Hosea was commanded to take back his wife from her "friend" (lover), as she had played the adulteress long enough.

The wider usage of *rēʿa* resembles the English word *neighbor,* the person with whom one associates regularly or casually without establishing close relations. One may borrow from his "neighbor" (Exod. 22:14), but not bear false witness (Exod. 20:16) or covet his neighbor's possessions (Exod. 20:17-18). The laws regulate how one must not take advantage of one's "neighbors." The second greatest commandment, which Jesus reiterated—"Love thy neighbor as thyself" (Lev. 19:18)—receives reinforcement in the laws of the Pentateuch. The prophets charged Israel with breaking the commandment: They oppressed each other (Isa. 3:5) and desired their neighbors' wives (Jer. 5:8); they committed adultery with these women (Ezek. 18:6); they did not pay wages to the worker (Jer. 22:13); and they improperly took advantage of their "neighbors" (Ezek. 22:12). According to Proverbs, not loving one's neighbor is a sign of foolishness (Prov. 11:12).

The wider meaning comes to expression in the proverb of the rich man and his "friends": "Wealth maketh many friends; but the poor is separated from his neighbor" (Prov. 19:4). Here the "friend" is a person whose association is not long-lasting, whose friendship is superficial.

The Septuagint gives the following translations: *plesion* ("near; close by"), *philos* ("friend"). The KJV gives these senses: "neighbor; friend; fellow; companion."

Rē'eh also means "friend." This noun appears in 1 Kings 4:5: ". . . Zabud the son of Nathan was principal officer, and the king's *friend*. . . ." *Re'āh* refers to a "female friend." See Judg. 11:37 for this usage: "And she said unto her father . . . let me alone two months, that I may go up and down upon the mountains, and bewail my virginity, I and my *fellows*" (cf. Judg. 11:38; Ps. 45:14). The noun *ra'ayāh* means "beloved companion; bride." *Ra'ayāh* occurs many times in the Song of Solomon: 1:9, 15; 2:2, 10, 13; 4:1, 7; 5:2; 6:4. *Ra'ûh* refers to a "fellow woman." This word is usually translated idiomatically in a reciprocal phrase of "one another," as in Zech 11:9: "Then said I, I will not feed you: that that dieth, let it die; and that that is to be cut off, let it be cut off; and let the rest eat every one the flesh of *another*."

B. Verb.

rā'āh (רָעָה), "to associate with." This word appears in Prov. 22:24: "Make no friendship with an angry man; and with a furious man thou shalt not go. . . ."

TO HAVE COMPASSION, BE MERCIFUL

A. Verb.

rācham (רָחַם), "to have compassion, be merciful, pity." The words from this root are found 125 times in all parts of the Old Testament. The root is also found in Assyrian, Ethiopic, and Aramaic.

The verb is translated "love" once: "I will love thee, O Lord. . ." (Ps. 18:1). *Rācham* is also used in God's promise to declare His name to Moses: "I will make all my goodness pass before thee, and I will proclaim the name of the Lord before thee; and will be gracious to whom I will be gracious, and will *show mercy* on whom I will show mercy" (Exod. 33:19). So men pray: "Remember, O Lord, thy tender mercies and thy loving-kindnesses" (Ps. 25:6);

and Isaiah prophesies messianic restoration: ". . . With great mercies will I gather thee. . . . But with everlasting kindness will I have mercy on thee, saith the Lord thy Redeemer" (Isa. 54:7-8). This is the heart of salvation by the suffering Servant-Messiah.

B. Nouns.

rechem (רֶחֶם), "bowels; womb; mercy." The first use of *rechem* is in its primary meaning of "womb": "The Lord had fast closed up all the wombs of the house of Abimelech" (Gen. 20:18). The word is personified in Judg. 5:30: "Have they not divided the prey; to every man a damsel or two . . . ?" In another figurative sense, the KJV reads in 1 Kings 3:26: "Her bowels yearned upon her son," which the NIV translates more idiomatically: "[She] was filled with compassion for her son." The greatest frequency is in this figurative sense of "tender love," such as a mother has for the child she has borne.

rachamîm (רַחֲמִים), "bowels; mercies; compassion." This noun, always used in the plural intensive, occurs in Gen. 43:14: "And God Almighty give you mercy [NASB, "compassion"]." In Gen. 43:30, it is used of Joseph's feelings toward Benjamin: "His bowels did yearn upon his brother." (NIV, "He was deeply moved at the sight of his brother.") *Rachamîm* is most often used of God, as by David in 2 Sam. 24:14: "Let us fall now into the hand of the Lord; for his mercies are great. . . ." We have the equivalent Aramaic word in Daniel's request to his friends: "That they would desire mercies of the God of heaven concerning this secret . . ." (Dan. 2:18).

The Greek version of the Old Testament *rācham* consists chiefly of three groups of words that come into the New Testament. *Eleos* is the most important, and it is used to translate several Hebrew words. Mary's song recalls the promise in Ps. 103:11, 17, where *eleos* translates both *rechem* and *chesed* as "mercy": "His mercy is on them that fear him from generation to generation" (Luke 1:50). *Rācham* is probably behind the often-heard plea: "Thou son of David, have mercy on us" (Matt. 9:27).

C. Adjective.

rachûm (רַחוּם), "compassionate; merciful." The adjective is used in that important proclamation of God's name to Moses: "The Lord, The Lord God, merciful and gracious . . ." (Exod. 34:6—NASB, NIV, "compassionate").

TO COMPLETE

A. Verb.

shālam (שָׁלַם) "to finish, complete, repay, reward." The Hebrew root denotes perfection in the sense that a condition or action is "complete." This concept emerges when a concrete object is described. When sufficient building materials were at hand and workmen had enough time to apply them, "the wall [of Jerusalem] was finished" at the time of Nehemiah (Neh. 6:15). However, this Hebrew root is also found in words with so many nuances and applications that at times its original and basic intent is all but obscured. In the NASB, for example, *shālam* is represented with such words as: "fulfill, make up, restore, pay, repay, full, whole, wholly, entire, without harm, friendly, peaceably, to be at peace, make peace, safe, reward, retribution, restitution, recompense, vengeance, bribe, peace offering."

Perfection and completeness is primarily attributed to God. He is deficient in nothing; His attributes are not marred by any shortcomings; His power is not limited by weakness. God reminded Job of His uninhibited independence and absolute self-sufficiency: "Who hath prevented me, that I should repay him? Whatsoever is under the whole heaven is mine" (Job 41:11). And Job himself admitted: "And who shall repay him what he hath done?" (Job 21:31).

Without any deficiency or flaw in executing justice, God is likewise never lacking in mercy and power to bestow benevolences of every kind. Job is told by his friend: "If thou wert pure . . . he would make the habitation of thy righteousness prosperous" (Job 8:6). He can make it happen that ". . . to the righteous good shall be repaid" (Prov. 13:21). Cyrus says of the Lord: "He . . . shall perform all my pleasure" (Isa. 44:28). The Lord will also ". . . restore comforts unto him and to his mourners" who wept in the Babylonian exile (Isa. 57:18).

The God of perfect justice and goodness expects total devotion from His creatures. Job, suspected of not rendering the required obedience to his Maker, is therefore urged to "be at peace [with God]" (Job 22:21).

The concept of meeting one's obligation in full is basic in human relationships. Israel's social law required that the person causing injury or loss ". . . shall surely make it good" (Exod. 22:14). "And he that killeth a beast shall make it good; beast for beast" (Lev. 24:18). In some instances, an offender ". . . shall pay double unto his neighbor" (Exod. 22:9). David declared that the rich man who slaughtered the poor man's only lamb ". . . shall restore the lamb fourfold . . ." (2 Sam. 12:6). Debts were not to be left unpaid. After providing the widow with the amount needed, Elisha directed her: "Go sell the oil, and pay [*shālam*] thy debt . . ." (2 Kings 4:7). "The wicked borroweth, and payeth not again . . ." (Ps. 37:21). A robber who has mended his ways ". . . give[s] again that he had robbed . . ." (Ezek. 33:15).

National relationships were established on the basis of "complete" negotiations. Thus cities and peoples "made peace with Israel" after they agreed to Joshua's stipulations (Josh. 10:1). War between the two kingdoms ended when Jehoshaphat ". . . made peace with the king of Israel" (1 Kings 22:44).

B. Adjective.

shālēm (שָׁלֵם), "perfect." God demanded total obedience from His people: "Let [their] heart therefore be perfect with the Lord our God, to walk in his statutes, and to keep his commandments . . ." (1 Kings 8:61). Solomon failed to meet this requirement because ". . . his heart was not perfect with the Lord his God" (1 Kings 11:4). Hezekiah, on the other hand, protested: ". . . I have walked before thee in truth and with a perfect heart" (2 Kings 20:3).

In business transactions, the Israelites were required to ". . . have a perfect and just weight, a perfect and just measure . . ." (Deut. 25:15).

TO CONFESS

yādāh (יָדָה), "to confess, praise, give thanks." The root, translated "confess" or "confession" about twenty times in the KJV, is also frequently rendered "praise" or "give thanks." At first glance, the meanings may appear unrelated. But upon closer inspection, it becomes evident that each sense profoundly illumines and interprets the other.

Yādah overlaps in meaning with a number of other Hebrew words implying "praise," such as *chālal* (whence *hallelujah*). Man is occasionally the object of *yādāh;* but far more commonly, God is the object.

The usual context seems to be public worship, where the worshipers affirm and renew their relationship with God. The subject is not primarily the isolated individual, but the congregation. Especially in the hymns and thanksgivings of the Psalter, it is evident that *yādāh* is a recital of, and thanksgiving for, Yahweh's mighty acts of salvation.

An affirmation or confession of God's undeserved kindness throws man's unworthiness into sharp relief. Hence, a confession of sin may be articulated in the same breath as a confession of faith or praise and thanksgiving. The confession is not a moralistic, autobiographical catalogue of sins—individual infractions of a legal code—but a confession of the underlying sinfulness that engulfs all mankind and separates us from the holy God. God is even to be praised for His judgments, by which He awakens repentance (e.g., Ps. 51:4). So one is not surprised to find praises in penitential contexts, and vice versa (1 Kings 8:33 ff.; Neh. 9:2 ff.; Dan. 9:4 ff.). If praise inevitably entails confession of sin, the reverse is also true: The sure word of forgiveness elicits praise and thanksgiving on the confessor's part. This wells up almost automatically from the new being of the repentant person.

Often the direct object of *yādāh* is the "name" of Yahweh (e.g., Ps. 105:1; Isa. 12:4; 1 Chron. 16:8). In one sense, this idiom is simply synonymous with praising Yahweh. In another sense, however, it introduces the entire dimension evoked by the "name" in biblical usage. It reminds us that the holy God cannot be directly approached by fallen man, but only through His "name"— i.e, His Word and reputation, an anticipation of the incarnation. God reveals Himself only in His "name," especially in the sanctuary where He "causes His name to dwell" (a phrase especially frequent in Deuteronomy).

The vista of *yādāh* expands both vertically and horizontally—vertically to include all creation, and horizontally stretching foward to that day when praise and thanksgiving shall be eternal (e.g., Ps. 29; 95:10; 96:7-9; 103:19-22).

TO CONFRONT

qādam (קָדַם), "to meet, confront, go before, be before." This verb occurs 27 times and in every period of biblical Hebrew. Most often, this verb is used in a martial context. Such confrontations may be peaceful, as in the meeting of allies: "For thou [dost meet] him with the blessings of goodness . . ." (Ps. 21:3). They may also be hostile: "The sorrows of hell compassed me about; the snares of death confronted (KJV, "prevented") me" (2 Sam. 22:6).

CONGREGATION

'ēdāh (עֵדָה), "congregation." This word may have etymologically signified a "company assembled together" for a certain purpose, similar to the Greek words *sunagoge* and *ekklesia,* from which our words "synagogue" and "church" are derived. In ordinary usage, *'ēdāh* refers to a "group of people." It occurs 149 times in the Old Testament, most frequently in the Book of Numbers. The first occurrence is in Exod. 12:3, where the word is a synonym for *qāhāl,* "assembly."

The most general meaning of *'ēdāh* is "group," whether of animals—such as a swarm of bees (Judg. 14:8), a herd of bulls (Ps. 68:30), and the flocking together of birds (Hos. 7:12)—or of people, such as the righteous (Ps. 1:5), the evildoers (Ps. 22:16), and the nations (Ps. 7:7).

The most frequent reference is to the "congregation of Israel" (9 times), "the congregation of the sons of Israel" (26 times), "the congregation" (24 times), or "all of the congregation" (30 times). Elders (Lev. 4:15), family heads (Num. 31:26), and princes (Num. 16:2; 31:13; 32:2) were placed in charge of the "congregation" in order to assist Moses in a just rule.

The Septuagint translation is *sunagoge* ("place of assembly"). The KJV has these translations: "congregation; company; assembly."

mô'ēd (מוֹעֵד), "appointed place of meeting; meeting." The noun *mô'ēd* appears in the Old Testament 223 times, of which 160 times are in the Pentateuch. The historical books are next in the frequency of usage (27 times).

The word *mô'ēd* keeps its basic meaning of "appointed," but varies as to what is agreed upon or appointed according to the context: the time, the place, or the meeting itself. The usage of the verb in Amos 3:3 is illuminating: "Can two walk together, except they be agreed?" Whether they have agreed on a time or a place of meeting, or on the meeting itself, is ambiguous.

The meaning of *mô'ēd* is fixed within the context of Israel's religion. First, the festivals came to be known as the "appointed times" or the set feasts. These festivals were clearly prescribed in the Pentateuch. The word refers to any "festival" or "pilgrimage festival," such as Passover (Lev. 23:15 ff.), the feast of first fruits (Lev. 23:15 ff.), the feast of tabernacles (Lev. 23:33 ff.), or the Day of Atonement (Lev. 23:27). God condemned the people for observing the *mô'ēd* ritualistically: "Your new moons and your appointed feasts my soul hateth . . ." (Isa. 1:14).

The word *mô'ēd* also signifies a "fixed place." This usage is not frequent: "For thou hast said in thine heart, I will ascend into heaven, I will exalt my throne above the stars of God: I will sit also upon the mount of the congregation [*mô'ēd*], in the sides of the north . . ." (Isa. 14:13). "For I know that thou wilt bring me to death, and to *the house appointed* for all living" (Job 30:23).

In both meanings of *mô'ēd*—"fixed time" and "fixed place"—a common denominator is the "meeting" of two or more parties at a certain place and time—hence the usage of *mô'ēd* as "meeting." However, in view of the similarity in meaning between "appointed place" or "appointed time" and "meeting," translators have a real difficulty in giving a proper translation in each context. For instance, "He hath called an assembly [*mô'ēd*] against me" (Lam. 1:15) could be read: "He has called an appointed time against me" (NASB) or "He summoned an army against me" (NIV).

The phrase, "tabernacle of the congregation," is a translation of the Hebrew *'ōhel mô'ēd* ("tent of meeting"). The phrase occurs 139 times—mainly in Exodus, Leviticus, and Numbers, rarely in Deuteronomy. It signifies that the Lord has an "appointed place" by which His presence is represented and through which Israel was assured that their God was with them. The fact that the tent was called the "tent of meeting" signifies that Israel's God was among His people and that He was to be approached at a certain time and place that were "fixed" (*yā'ad*) in the Pentateuch. In the KJV, this phrase is translated as "tabernacle of the congregation" (Exod. 28:43) because translators realized that the noun *'ēdāh* ("congregation") is derived from the same root as *mô'ēd*. The translators of the Septuagint had a similar difficulty. They noticed the relation of *mô'ēd* to the root *'ûd* ("to testify") and translated the phrase *'ōhel hamô'ed* as "tabernacle of the testimony." This phrase was picked up by the New Testament: "And after that I looked, and, behold, the temple of the tabernacle of the testimony in heaven was opened . . ." (Rev. 15:5).

Of the three meanings, the appointed "time" is most basic. The phrase "tent of meeting" lays stress on the "place of meeting." The "meeting" itself is generally associated with "time" or "place."

The Septuagint has the following translations of *mô'ēd: kairos* ("time"), *eorte* ("feast; festival"). The English translators give these senses: "congregation" (KJV, RSV, NASB, NIV); "appointed time" (NASB); "appointed feast" (RSV, NASB); "set time" (RSV, NASB, NIV).

TO CONSUME

A. Verb.

kālāh (כָּלָה), "to cease, be finished, perish, be completed." This verb occurs in most Semitic languages and in all periods. In Hebrew, it occurs both in the Bible (about 210 times) and in post-biblical literature. The word does not appear in biblical Aramaic.

Basically, the word means "to cease or stop." *Kālāh* may refer to the "end" of a process or action, such as the cessation of God's creating the universe: "And on the seventh day God ended his work which he had made . . ." (Gen. 2:2—the first occurrence of the word). The word can also refer to the "disappearance" of something: "And the water was *spent* in the bottle . . ." (Gen. 21:15). Finally, *kālāh* can be used of "coming to an end" or "the process of ending": "The barrel of meal shall not waste" (1 Kings 17:14).

Kālāh can have the more positive connotation of "successfully completing" something. First Kings 6:38 says that the house of the Lord was "finished throughout all the parts thereof, and according to all [its plans]." In this same sense, the word of the Lord "is fulfilled": "Now in the first year of Cyrus king of Persia, that the word of the Lord by the mouth of Jeremiah might be fulfilled, the Lord stirred up the spirit of Cyrus king of Persia, that he made a proclamation . . ." (Ezra 1:1).

Kālāh sometimes means "making a firm decision." David tells Jonathan that if Saul is very angry, "be sure that evil is determined by him" (1 Sam. 20:7).

Negatively, "to complete" something may mean "to make it vanish" or "go away." *Kālāh* is used in this sense in Deut. 32:23, when God says: "I will heap mischiefs upon them; I will spend mine arrows upon them." In other words, His arrows will "vanish" from His possession. This nuance is used especially of clouds: "As the cloud is consumed and vanisheth away . . ." (Job 7:9). Another negative nuance is to "destroy" something or someone: "the famine shall consume the land" (Gen. 41:30). Along this same line is the use of *kālāh* in Isa. 1:28: ". . . They that forsake the Lord shall be consumed"; here, however, the verb is a synonym for "dying" or "perishing." One's sight may also "vanish" and one may go blind: "But the eyes of the wicked shall fail, and they shall not escape . . ." (Job 11:20). An altogether different emphasis appears when one's heart comes "to an end" or "stops within": "My soul longeth, yea, even fainteth for the courts of the Lord" (Ps. 84:2); the psalmist probably meant that his desire for God's presence was so intense that nothing else had any meaning for him—he "died" to be there.

B. Noun.

kālāh (כָּלָה), "consumption; complete annihilation." *Kālāh* appears 15 times; one occurrence is Neh. 9:31: "Nevertheless for thy great mercies' sake thou didst not utterly consume them, nor forsake them;. . . ."

TO BE CONSUMED

A. Verb.

tāmam (תָּמַם), "to be complete, finished, perfect, spent, sound, used up, have integrity." Found in both ancient and modern Hebrew, this word also exists in ancient Ugaritic. *Tāmam* is found approximately 60 times in the Hebrew Old Testament in its verbal forms.

The basic meaning of this word is that of "being complete" or "finished," with nothing else expected or intended. When it was said that the temple was "finished" (1 Kings 6:22), this meant that the temple was "complete," with nothing else to add. Similarly, when the notation is made in Job 31:40, "The words of Job are ended [finished]," this indicates that the cycle of Job's speeches is "complete." *Tāmam* is sometimes used to express the fact that something is "completed" or "finished" with regard to its supply. Thus, money that is all spent is "finished" or "exhausted" (Gen. 47:15, 18). Jeremiah was given bread daily until "all the bread in the city [was] spent [exhausted]" (Jer. 37:21). When a people came "to a full end" (Num. 14:35, RSV), it meant that they were "consumed" or "completely destroyed." To "consume" the filthiness out of the people (Ezek. 22:15) meant "to destroy it" or "to make an end of it."

Tāmam sometimes expresses moral and ethical "soundness": "Then shall I be upright" (Ps. 19:13), says the psalmist, when God helps him to keep God's Law.

B. Adjective.

tām (תָּם), "perfect." When the adjectival form *tām* is used to describe Job (1:1), the meaning is not that he was really "perfect" in the ultimate sense, but rather that he was "blameless" (RSV) or "had integrity."

CONTINUALLY

A. Adverb.

tāmîd (תָּמִיד), "always; continually; regularly." This word comes from a root that means "to measure." The root is found in Assyrian, Aramaic, Arabic, and Phoenician. *Tāmîd* occurs 100 times in all parts of the Old Testament. It signifies what is to be done regularly or continuously without interruption.

Tāmîd is first used in Exod. 25:30: "And thou shalt set upon the table showbread before me always" (KJV; NASB, "at all times"). Sometimes the continuity is explained by what follows, as in Isa. 21:8: ". . . My lord, I stand continually upon the watchtower in the daytime, and I am set in my ward whole nights."

Because of his covenant with Jonathan, David said to Mephibosheth: ". . . And you shall eat at my table regularly" (2 Sam. 9:7; cf. 2 Sam. 9:10, NASB; KJV, "continually"; RSV, "always").

Tāmîd occurs most frequently of the daily rituals in the tabernacle and temple: "Now this is that which thou shalt offer upon the altar; two lambs of the first year day by day continually" (Exod. 29:38). The variety in the English versions indicates that both ideas—regularity and continuousness—are present in the Hebrew word. In this passage, *tāmîd* indicates that these rituals were to be performed regularly and without interruption for the duration of the old covenant.

The word is also used of God. It describes His visible presence at the tabernacle: "So it was always: the cloud covered it by day, and the appearance of fire by night" (Num. 9:16). It describes His care for His people: ". . . let thy loving-kindness and thy truth continually preserve me" (Ps. 40:11); "And the Lord shall guide thee continually . . ." (Isa. 58:11).

Tāmîd is also used of Jerusalem: ". . . thy walls are continually before me" (Isa. 49:16). The word describes man's response to God: "I have set the Lord always before me" (Ps. 16:8); ". . . his praise shall continually be in my mouth" (Ps. 34:1); "So I shall keep thy law continually, for ever and ever" (Ps. 119:44). In contrast, Israel is "a people that provoketh me to anger continually to my face" (Isa. 65:3). Finally, it is said of Zion eschatologically: "Therefore thy gates shall be open continually; they shall not be shut day nor night" (Isa. 60:11).

B. Adjective.

tāmîd (תָּמִיד), "continual." In Exod. 30:7-8, Aaron is commanded to burn incense morning and evening when he trims the lamps. He is told to offer

". . . a perpetual incense before the Lord throughout your generations" (KJV). The same Hebrew expression is used often of priestly functions (cf. Num. 28:6; Ezek. 46:15).

CONTINUITY

A. Noun.

tāmîd (תָּמִיד) "continuity." *Tāmîd* is often used as a noun. In Num. 4:7, the word is used with "bread," literally meaning "the bread of continuity" (NASB, "the continual bread") or the bread that is "always there." In other groups of passages, the word emphasizes "regular repetition": for example, Exod. 29:42 mentions, literally, "the burnt offering of continuity" (NASB, "continual burnt offering"), or the offering made every morning and evening. The "daily sacrifice" of Dan. 8:11 is also this continual burnt offering.

The nonreligious usage indicates that *tāmîd* describes "continuity in time," in the sense of a routine or habit. *Tāmîd* may also have the connotation of a routine that comes to an end when the job is completed: "And they shall sever out men of continual employment, passing through the land to bury with the passengers those that remain upon the face of the earth, to cleanse it: after the end of seven months shall they search" (Ezek. 39:14).

B. Adverb.

tāmîd (תָּמִיד), "continually; at all times; ever." A cognate of this word appears in Arabic. Biblical Hebrew attests it in all periods.

The word is used as an adverb meaning "continually." In its first occurrence, *tāmîd* represents "uninterrupted action": "And thou shalt set upon the table showbread before me always" (Exod. 25:30). In Jer. 6:7, we read: ". . . Before me continually is grief and wounds." In many passages, *tāmîd* bears the nuance of "regular repetition": "Now this is that which thou shalt offer upon the altar; two lambs of the first year day by day *continually*. The one lamb thou shalt offer in the morning; and the other lamb thou shalt offer at even . . ." (Exod. 29:38-39).

In poetic usage, *tāmîd* is found in the context of a fervent religious expression: "Mine eyes are ever toward the Lord; for he shall pluck my feet out of the net" (Ps. 25:15). It may express a firm belief in God's faithfulness: "Withhold not thou thy tender mercies from me, O Lord: let thy loving-kindness and thy truth continually preserve me" (Ps. 40:11).

COPPER

nachōsheth (נְחֹשֶׁת), "copper; bronze; bronze chains." Cognates of this word appear in Phoenician, Aramaic, Arabic, and Ethiopic. It is attested about 136 times in biblical Hebrew and in all periods.

Nachōsheth basically means "copper." This word refers to the metal ore: "A land wherein thou shalt eat bread without scarceness, thou shalt not lack any thing in it; a land whose stones are iron, and out of whose hills thou mayest dig [copper]'' (Deut. 8:9). The word can also represent the refined ore: ''And Zillah, she also bare Tubal-cain, an instructor of every artificer in copper [KJV, ''brass''; NASB, ''bronze''] and iron'' (Gen. 4:22).

Inasmuch as it was a semiprecious metal, *nachōsheth* is sometimes listed as a spoil of war (2 Sam. 8:8). In such passages, it is difficult to know whether the reference is to copper or to copper mixed with tin (i.e., bronze). Certainly, ''bronze'' is intended in 1 Sam. 17:5, where *nachōsheth* refers to the material from which armor is made. Bronze is the material from which utensils (Lev. 6:21), altars (Exod. 38:30), and other objects were fashioned. This material could be polished (1 Kings 7:45) or shined (Ezra 8:27). This metal was less valuable than gold and more valuable than wood (Isa. 60:17).

Still another meaning of *nachōsheth* appears in Judg. 16:21: ''But the Philistines took [Samson], and put out his eyes, and brought him down to Gaza, and bound him with fetters of [bronze]; and he did grind in the prison house.'' Usually, when the word has this meaning it appears in the dual form (in the singular form only in Lam. 3:7).

Deut. 28:23 uses *nachōsheth* to symbolize the cessation of life-giving rain and sunshine: ''And thy heaven that is over thy head shall be [bronze], and the earth that is under thee shall be iron.''

CORD

chebel (חֶבֶל), ''cord; rope; tackle; measuring line; measurement; allotment; portion; region.'' Cognates of this word appear in Aramaic, Syriac, Ethiopic, Arabic, and Akkadian. The word appears about 50 times in the Old Testament.

Chebel primarily means ''cord'' or ''rope.'' Rahab lowered the spies over the city wall with the use of a ''rope'': ''Then she let them down by a rope through the window, for her house was built into the city wall'' (Josh. 2:15, RSV). The word is used of ''tent ropes'' in Isa. 33:20: ''. . . A tabernacle that shall not be taken down . . . neither shall any of the cords thereof be broken.'' A ship's ''tackle'' is the meaning of *chebel* in Isa. 33:23.

Used figuratively, *chebel* emphasizes ''being bound.'' In 1 Kings 20:31, we read that the Syrians who fled into Aphek proposed to put sackcloth on their heads as a sign of repentance for attacking Israel, and to put ''ropes'' about their necks as a sign of submission to Israel's authority. Snares used ''cords'' or ''ropes,'' forming a web or a noose into which the prey stepped and was caught. In this manner, the wicked would be caught by God (Job 18:10). In many passages, death is pictured as a hunter whose trap has been sprung and whose quarry is captured by the ''cords'' of the trap: ''The cords of Sheol entangled me; the snares of death confronted me'' (2 Sam. 22:6, RSV).

In other cases, the thing that ''binds'' is good: ''I drew them with cords of a man, with bands of love . . .'' (Hos. 11:4). Eccl. 12:6 pictures human life as being held together by a silver ''cord.''

A ''cord'' could be used as a ''measuring line'': ''And he smote Moab, and measured them with a line, casting them down to the ground; even with two lines measured he to put to death, and with one full line to keep alive" (2 Sam. 8:2). This meaning of *chebel* also occurs in Ps. 78:55: ". . . And [He] divided them an inheritance by line." Compare Mic. 2:5: "Therefore thou shalt have none that shall cast a cord by lot in the congregation of the Lord." The act referred to by Micah appears in Ps. 16:6 as an image of one's life in general: "The lines are fallen unto me in pleasant places; yea, I have a goodly heritage."

Chebel also means "the thing measured or allotted": "For the Lord's portion is his people; Jacob is the lot of his inheritance" (Deut. 32:9). Here the use is clearly figurative, but in 1 Chron. 16:18 the "portion" of Israel's inheritance is a concrete "measured thing"; this nuance first appears in Josh. 17:5. In passages such as Deut. 3:4, the word is used of a "region" or "a measured area": ". . . Threescore cities, all the region of Argob, the kingdom of Og in Bashan."

The word may refer to a group of people, describing them as that which is tied together—"a band": ". . . Thou shalt meet a company of prophets coming down from the high place . . ." (1 Sam. 10:5).

TO COUNSEL

A. Verb.

yā'ats (יָעַץ), "to advise, counsel, consult." Used throughout the history of the Hebrew language, this verb occurs in the Hebrew Old Testament approximately 80 times. *Yā'ats* is found first in Exod. 18:19, where Jethro says to his son-in-law Moses: "I will give thee counsel, and God shall be with thee." The word is found only one other time in the Hexateuch, and that is in Num. 24:14: "I will advise you" (NASB—RSV, "I will let you know"; JB, "let me warn you"; NEB, "I will warn you").

While *yā'ats* most often describes the "giving of good advice," the opposite is sometimes true. A tragic example was the case of King Ahaziah of Judah, whose mother "was his counselor to do wickedly" (2 Chron. 22:3). The idea of "decision" is expressed in Isa. 23:9: "The Lord of hosts hath purposed it" (RSV, NEB, NASB, "planned it"; JB, "decision").

B. Nouns.

yō'ēts (יוֹעֵץ), "counselor." Perhaps the most familiar use of this root is the noun form found in the messianic passage, Isa. 9:6. On the basis of the syntax involved, it is probably better to translate the familiar "Wonderful Counselor" (NASB, TEV) as "Wonder-Counsellor" (JB, NAB) or "Wonder of a Counsellor." The NEB renders it "in purpose wonderful." Another possibility is that of separating the terms: "Wonderful, Counselor" (KJV).

yā'ats (יָעַץ), "those who give counsel." *Yā'ats* is frequently used in its participial form, "those who give counsel," especially in connection with political and military leaders (2 Sam. 15:12; 1 Chron. 13:1).

COURT

chātsēr (חָצֵר), "court; enclosure." This word is related to a common Semitic verb that has two meanings: "to be present," in the sense of living at a certain place (encampment, residence, court), and "to enclose, surround, press together." In the Hebrew Old Testament, *chātsēr* appears about 190 times; its usage is well-distributed throughout, except for the minor prophets.

In some Hebrew dictionaries, the usage of *chātsēr* as "settled abode," "settlement," or "village" is separated from the meaning "court." But most modern dictionaries identify only one root with two related meanings.

The first biblical occurrence of *chātsēr* is in Gen. 25:16: "These are the sons of Ishmael, and these are their names, by their *towns,* and by their castles; twelve princes according to their nations." Here *chātsēr* is related to the first meaning of the root; this occurs less frequently than the usage meaning "court." The *chātsēr* ("settlement") was a place where people lived without an enclosure to protect them. The word is explained in Lev. 25:31: "But the houses of the villages which have no wall round about them shall be counted as the fields of the country [*chātsēr*]: they may be redeemed, and they shall go out in the jubilee."

Chātsēr signifies the "settlements" of semi-nomadic peoples: the Ishmaelites (Gen. 25:16), the Avim (Deut. 2:23), and Kedar (Isa. 42:11). *Chātsēr* also denotes a "settlement" of people outside the city wall. The cities of Canaan were relatively small and could not contain the whole population. In times of peace, residents of the city might build homes and workshops for themselves outside the wall and establish a separate quarter. If the population grew, the king or governor often decided to enclose the new quarter by surrounding it with a wall and incorporating the section into the existing city, in order to protect the population from bandits and warriors. Jerusalem gradually extended its size westward; at the time of Hezekiah, it had grown into a large city. Huldah the prophetess lived in such a development, known in Hebrew as the *mishnah:* ". . . she dwelt in Jerusalem in the Second Quarter" (2 Kings 22:14, RSV).

The Book of Joshua includes Israel's victories in Canaan's major cities as well as the suburbs: "Ain, Remmon, and Ether, and Ashan; four cities and their villages . . ." (19:7; cf. 15:45, 47; 21:12).

The predominant usage of *chātsēr* is "court," whether of a house, a palace, or the temple. Each house generally had a courtyard surrounded by a wall or else one adjoined several homes: "Nevertheless a lad saw them, and told Absalom: but they went both of them away quickly, and came to a man's house in Bahurim, which had a well in his court; whither they went down" (2 Sam. 17:18). Solomon's palace had several "courts"—an outer "court," an "enclosed space" around the palace, and a "court" around which the palace was built. Similarly, the temple had various courts. The psalmist expressed his joy in being in the "courts" of the temple, where the birds built their nests (Ps. 84:3); "For a day in thy courts is better than a thousand. I had rather be a doorkeeper in the house of my God, than to dwell in the tents of wickedness" (Ps. 84:10). God's people looked forward to the thronging together of all the people in God's "courts": ". . . In the courts of the Lord's house, in the midst of thee, O Jerusalem" (Ps. 116:19).

The Septuagint translations are: *aulē* ("courtyard; farm; house; outer court; palace"), *epaulis* ("farm; homestead; residence"), and *komē* ("village; small town"). The KJV gives these translations: "court; village; town."

COVENANT

bərîth (בְּרִית), "covenant; league; confederacy." This word is most probably derived from an Akkadian root meaning "to fetter"; it has parallels in Hittite, Egyptian, Assyrian, and Aramaic. *Bərîth* is used over 280 times and in all parts of the Old Testament. The first occurrence of the word is in Gen. 6:18: "But with thee [Noah] will I establish my covenant."

The KJV translates *bərîth* fifteen times as "league": ". . . Now therefore make ye a league with us" (Josh. 9:6). These are all cases of political agreement within Israel (2 Sam. 3:12-13, 21; 5:3) or between nations (1 Kings 15:19). Later versions may use "covenant," "treaty," or "compact," but not consistently. In Judg. 2:2, the KJV has: "And ye shall make no league with the inhabitants of this land. . . ." The command had been also given in Exod. 23:32; 34:12-16; and Deut. 7:2-6, where the KJV has "covenant."

The KJV translates *bərîth* as "covenant" 260 times. The word is used of "agreements between men," as Abraham and Abimelech (Gen. 21:32): "Thus they made a covenant at Beer-sheba. . . ." David and Jonathan made a "covenant" of mutual protection that would be binding on David's descendants forever (1 Sam. 18:3; 20:8, 16-18, 42). In these cases, there was "mutual agreement confirmed by oath in the name of the Lord." Sometimes there were also material pledges (Gen. 21:28-31).

Ahab defeated the Syrians: "So he made a covenant with [Ben-hadad], and sent him away" (1 Kings 20:34). The king of Babylon "took of the king's seed [Zedekiah], and made a covenant with him, and hath taken an oath of him . . ." (Ezek. 17:13—NIV, "treaty"). In such "covenants," the terms were imposed by the superior military power; they were not mutual agreements.

In Israel, the kingship was based on "covenant": ". . . David made a covenant [KJV, "league"] with them [the elders of Israel] in Hebron before the Lord . . ." (2 Sam. 5:3). The "covenant" was based on their knowledge that God had appointed him (2 Sam. 5:2); thus they became David's subjects (cf. 2 Kings 11:4, 17).

The great majority of occurrences of *bərîth* are of God's "covenants" with men, as in Gen. 6:18 above. The verbs used are important: "I will *establish* my covenant" (Gen. 6:18)—literally, "cause to stand" or "confirm." "I will *make* my covenant" (Gen. 17:2, RSV). "He *declared* to you his covenant" (Deut. 4:13). "My covenant which I *commanded* them . . ." (Josh. 7:11). "I have *remembered* my covenant. Wherefore . . . I will bring you out from under the burdens of the Egyptians" (Exod. 6:5-6). God will not reject Israel for their disobedience so as "to destroy them utterly, and to *break* my covenant with them . . ." (Lev. 26:44). "He will not . . . forget the covenant . . .

which he *sware* unto them" (Deut. 4:31). The most common verb is "to cut [*kārath*] a covenant," which is always translated as in Gen. 15:18: "The Lord made a covenant with Abram." This use apparently comes from the ceremony described in Gen. 15:9-17 (cf. Jer. 34:18), in which God appeared as "a smoking furnace, and a burning lamp [flaming torch] that passed between those pieces" (Gen. 15:17). These verbs make it plain that God takes the sole initiative in covenant making and fulfillment.

"Covenant" is parallel or equivalent to the Hebrew words *dābār* ("word"), *hōq* ("statute") *piqûd* ("precepts"—Ps. 103:18, NASB), *'ēdāh* ("testimony"—Ps. 25:10), *tôrāh* ("law"—Ps. 78:10), and *chesed* ("lovingkindness"—Deut. 7:9, NASB). These words emphasize the authority and grace of God in making and keeping the "covenant," and the specific responsibility of man under the covenant. The words of the "covenant" were written in a book (Exod. 24:4, 7; Deut. 31:24-26) and on stone tablets (Exod. 34:28).

Men "enter into" (Deut. 29:12) or "join" (Jer. 50:5) God's "covenant." They are to obey (Gen. 12:4) and "observe carefully" all the commandments of the "covenant" (Deut. 4:6). But above all, the "covenant" calls Israel to "love the Lord thy God with all thine heart, and with all thy soul, and with all thy might" (Deut. 6:5). God's "covenant" is a relationship of love and loyalty between the Lord and His chosen people.

". . . If ye will obey my voice indeed, and keep my covenant, then ye shall be a peculiar treasure unto me above all people . . . and ye shall be unto me a kingdom of priests, and a holy nation" (Exod. 19:5-6). "All the commandments . . . shall ye observe to do, that ye may live, and multiply, and go in and possess the land which the Lord sware unto your fathers" (Deut. 8:1). In the "covenant," man's response contributes to covenant fulfillment; yet man's action is not causative. God's grace always goes before and produces man's response.

Occasionally, Israel "made a covenant before the Lord, to walk after the Lord, and to keep his commandments . . . , to perform the words of this covenant that were written in this book" (2 Kings 23:3). This is like their original promise: "All that the Lord hath spoken we will do" (Exod. 19:8; 24:7). Israel did not propose terms or a basis of union with God. They responded to God's "covenant."

The wholly gracious and effective character of God's "covenant" is confirmed in the Septuagint by the choice of *diatheke* to translate *bərith*. A *diatheke* is a will that distributes one's property after death according to the owner's wishes. It is completely unilateral. In the New Testament, *diatheke* occurs 33 times and is translated in the KJV 20 times as "covenant" and 13 times as "testament." In the RSV and the NASB, only "covenant" is used.

The use of "Old Testament" and "New Testament" as the names for the two sections of the Bible indicates that God's "covenant" is central to the entire book. The Bible relates God's "covenant" purpose, that man be joined to Him in loving service and know eternal fellowship with Him through the redemption that is in Jesus Christ.

TO CREATE

bārā' (אֶרֶב), "to create, make." This verb is of profound theological significance, since it has only God as its subject. Only God can "create" in the sense implied by *bārā'*. The verb expresses creation out of nothing, an idea seen clearly in passages having to do with creation on a cosmic scale: "In the beginning God created the heaven and the earth" (Gen. 1:1; cf. Gen. 2:3; Isa. 40:26; 42:5). All other verbs for "creating" allow a much broader range of meaning; they have both divine and human subjects, and are used in contexts where bringing something or someone into existence is not the issue.

Bārā' is frequently found in parallel to these other verbs, such as *'āsāh,* "to make" (Isa. 41:20; 43:7; 45:7, 12; Amos 4:13), *yātsar,* "to form" (Isa. 43:1, 7; 45:7; Amos 4:13), and *kûn,* "to establish." A verse that illustrates all of these words together is Isa. 45:18: "For thus saith the Lord that created [*bārā'*] the heavens; God himself that formed [*yātsar*] the earth and made [*'āsāh*] it; he hath established [*kûn*] it, he created [*bārā'*] it not in vain, he formed [*yātsar*] it to be inhabited: I am the Lord; and there is none else." The technical meaning of *bārā'* (to "create out of nothing") may not hold in these passages; perhaps the verb was popularized in these instances for the sake of providing a poetic synonym.

Objects of the verb include the heavens and earth (Gen. 1:1; Isa. 40:26; 42:5; 45:18; 65:17); man (Gen. 1:27; 5:2; 6:7; Deut. 4:32; Ps. 89:47; Isa. 43:7; 45:12); Israel (Isa. 43:1; Mal. 2:10); a new thing (Jer. 31:22); cloud and smoke (Isa. 4:5); north and south (Ps. 89:12); salvation and righteousness (Isa. 45:8); speech (Isa. 57:19); darkness (Isa. 45:7); wind (Amos 4:13); and a new heart (Ps. 51:10). A careful study of the passages where *bārā'* occurs shows that in the few nonpoetic uses (primarily in Genesis), the writer uses scientifically precise language to demonstrate that God brought the object or concept into being from previously nonexistent material.

Especially striking is the use of *bārā'* in Isaiah 40-65. Out of 49 occurrences of the verb in the Old Testament, 20 are in these chapters. Because Isaiah writes prophetically to the Jews in Exile, he speaks words of comfort based upon God's past benefits and blessings to His people. Isaiah especially wants to show that, since Yahweh is the Creator, He is able to deliver His people from captivity. The God of Israel has created all things: "I have made [*'āsāh*] the earth, and created [*bārā'*] man upon it: I, even my hands, have stretched out the heavens, and all their host have I commanded" (Isa. 45:12). The gods of Babylon are impotent nonentities (Isa. 44:12-20; 46:1-7), and so Israel can expect God to triumph by effecting a new creation (43:16-21; 65:17-25).

Though a precisely correct technical term to suggest cosmic, material creation from nothing, *bārā'* is a rich theological vehicle for communicating the sovereign power of God, who originates and regulates all things to His glory.

qānāh (קָנָה), "to get, acquire, earn." These basic meanings are dominant in the Old Testament, but certain poetic passages have long suggested that this verb means "create." In Gen. 14:19, Melchizedek blessed Abram and said: "Blessed be Abram by God Most High, maker [KJV, "possessor"] of heaven and earth" (RSV). Gen. 14:22 repeats this divine epithet. Deut. 32:6 makes this meaning certain in that *qānāh* is parallel to *'āsāh,* "to make": "Is

he not your father, who created *(qānāh)* you, // who made *('āsāh)* you and
established *(kûn)* you?'' (RSV). Ps. 78:54; 139:13; and Prov. 8:22-23 also
suggest the idea of creation.

The cognate languages usually follow the Hebrew in the basic meaning of
"to get, acquire." Ugaritic, however, attests the meaning "create." In fact,
qny is the primary Ugaritic term to express creation. The close relationship of
Hebrew and Ugaritic and the contextual meaning of *qānāh* as "create" in the
Old Testament passages cited above argue for the use of *qānāh* as a synonym
for "create" along with *bārā', 'āsāh,* and *yātsar.*

'āsāh (עָשָׂה), "to create, do, make." This verb, which occurs over 2600
times in the Old Testament, is used as a synonym for "create" only about 60
times. There is nothing inherent in the word to indicate the nature of the
creation involved; it is only when *'āsāh* is parallel to *bārā'* that we can be sure
that it implies creation.

Unfortunately, the word is not attested in cognate languages contemporary
with the Old Testament, and its etymology is unclear. Because *'āsāh* describes the most common of human (and divine) activities, it is ill-suited to
communicate theological meaning—except where it is used with *bārā'* or
other terms whose technical meanings are clearly established.

The most instructive occurrences of *'āsāh* are in the early chapters of
Genesis. Gen. 1:1 uses the verb *bārā'* to introduce the Creation account, and
Gen. 1:7 speaks of its detailed execution: "And God made ['*āsāh*] the firmament. . . ." Whether or not the firmament was made of existing material
cannot be determined, since the passage uses only *'āsāh.* But it is clear that
the verb expresses creation, since it is used in that context and follows the
technical word *bārā'.* The same can be said of other verses in Genesis: 1:16
(the lights of heaven); 1:25, 3:1 (the animals); 1:31; 2:2 (all his work); and 6:6
(man). In Gen. 1:26-27, however, *'āsāh* must mean creation from nothing,
since it is used as a synonym for *bārā'.* The text reads, "Let us make ['*āsāh*]
man in our image, after our likeness. . . . So God created [*bārā'*] man in his
own image. . . ." Similarly, Gen. 2:4 states: "These are the generations of the
heavens and of the earth when they were created [*bārā'*], in the day that the
Lord God made ['*āsāh*] the earth and the heavens." Finally, Gen. 5:1 equates
the two as follows: "In the day that God created [*bārā'*] man, in the likeness
of God made ['*āsāh*] he him." The unusual juxtaposition of *bārā'* and *'āsāh* in
Gen. 2:3 refers to the totality of creation, which God had "created" by "making."

It is unwarranted to overly refine the meaning of *'āsāh* to suggest that it
means creation from something, as opposed to creation from nothing. Only
context can determine its special nuance. It can mean either, depending upon
the situation.

TO CRY

tsā'aq (צָעַק), "to cry, cry out, call." Found in both biblical and modern
Hebrew, this word has the sense of "to shout, yell." The word is a close
parallel to the very similar sounding word, *zā'aq,* also translated "to cry."

The verb *tsā'aq* is found about 55 times in the Hebrew Old Testament. The word occurs for the first time in Gen. 4:10: "The voice of thy brother's blood *crieth* unto me from the ground."

This word is often used in the sense of "crying out" for help. Sometimes it is man "crying out" to man: ". . . The people cried to Pharaoh for bread . . ." (Gen. 41:55). More often it is man "crying" to God for help: ". . . And the children of Israel cried out unto the Lord" (Exod. 14:10). The prophets always spoke sarcastically of those who worship idols: ". . . One shall cry unto him, yet can he not answer . . ." (Isa. 46:7). This word is frequently used to express "distress" or "need": ". . . He cried with a great and exceeding bitter cry . . ." (Gen. 27:34).

zā'aq (צָעַק), "to cry, cry out, call." This term is found throughout the history of the Hebrew language, including modern Hebrew. The word occurs approximately 70 times in the Hebrew Old Testament. Its first occurrence is in the record of the suffering of the Israelite bondage in Egypt: ". . . And the children of Israel sighed by reason of the bondage, and they cried [for help] . . ." (Exod. 2:23).

Zā'aq is perhaps most frequently used to indicate the "crying out" for aid in time of emergency, especially "crying out" for divine aid. God often heard this "cry" for help in the time of the judges, as Israel found itself in trouble because of its backsliding (Judg. 3:9, 15; 6:7; 10:10). The word is used also in appeals to pagan gods (Judg. 10:14; Jer. 11:12; Jonah 1:5). That *zā'aq* means more than a normal speaking volume is indicated in appeals to the king (2 Sam. 19:28).

The word may imply a "crying out" in distress (1 Sam. 4:13), a "cry" of horror (1 Sam. 5:10), or a "cry" of sorrow (2 Sam. 13:19). Used figuratively, it is said that "the stone shall cry out of the wall" (Hab. 2:11) of a house that is built by means of evil gain.

CUBIT

'ammāh (אַמָּה), "cubit." This word has cognates in Akkadian, Ugaritic, and Aramaic. It appears about 245 times in biblical Hebrew and in all periods, but especially in Exod. 25–27; 37–38 (specifications of the tabernacle); 1 Kings 6–7 (the specifications of Solomon's temple and palace); and Ezek. 40–43 (the specifications of Ezekiel's temple).

In one passage, *'ammāh* means "pivot": "And the posts [literally, "sockets"] of the door moved at the voice of him that cried . . ." (Isa. 6:4).

In almost every other occurrence, the word means "cubit," the primary unit of linear measurement in the Old Testament. Some scholars maintain that Israel's system of linear measurement was primarily based on the Egyptian system. In view of the history of Israel, this is a reasonable position. A "cubit" ordinarily was the distance from one's elbow to the tip of the middle finger. Since this distance varied from individual to individual, the "cubit" was a rather imprecise measurement. Yet the first appearance of *'ammāh* (Gen. 6:15) refers to the measurement of Noah's ark, which implies that the word must refer to a more precise length than the ordinary "cubit."

There was an official "cubit" in Egypt. In fact, there were both a shorter "cubit" (17.6 inches) and a longer "cubit" (20.65 inches). The Siloam inscription states that the Siloam tunnel was 1,200 "cubits" long. This divided by its measurement in feet (1, 749) demonstrates that as late as Hezekiah's day (cf. 2 Chron. 32:4) the "cubit" was about 17.5 inches or the shorter Egyptian cubit. Ezekiel probably used the Babylonian "cubit" in describing the temple. The Egyptian shorter cubit is only about three inches shorter than the longer cubit; on the other hand, the Babylonian shorter cubit was about four-fifths the length of the official royal "cubit," about a handbreadth shorter: "And behold a wall on the outside of the house round about, and in the man's hand a measuring reed of six cubits long by the cubit and a handbreadth . . ." (Ezek. 40:5). In other words, it was the width of seven palms rather than six.

TO CURSE

A. Verbs.

qālal (קָלַל), "to be trifling, light, swift; to curse." This wide-ranging word is found in both ancient and modern Hebrew, in ancient Akkadian, and (according to some) in ancient Ugaritic. The word occurs about 82 times in the Hebrew Old Testament. As will be seen, its various nuances grow out of the basic idea of being "trifling" or "light," with somewhat negative connotations involved.

Qālal is found for the first time in Gen. 8:8: ". . . To see if the waters had subsided . . ." (RSV). Other English versions translate: "abated" (KJV, NASB), "dried up" (JB), "had lessened" (NEB), "had gone down" (TEV). All of these terms indicate a lessening of what had existed.

The idea of "to be swift" is expressed in the Hebrew comparative form. So, Saul and Jonathan "were swifter than eagles" (2 Sam. 1:23—literally, "more than eagles they were light"). A similar idea is expressed in 1 Sam. 18:23: "And David said, Seemeth it to you a light thing to a king's son-in-law . . . ?"

Qālal frequently includes the idea of "cursing" or "making little or contemptible": "And he that curseth [belittles] his father, or his mother, shall surely be put to death" (Exod. 21:17). "To curse" had the meaning of an "oath" when related to one's gods: "And the Philistine cursed David by his gods" (1 Sam. 17:43). The negative aspect of "non-blessing" was expressed by the passive form: ". . . The sinner being a hundred years old shall be accursed [by death]" (Isa. 65:20). Similar usage is reflected in: ". . . Their portion is cursed in the earth . . ." (Job 24:18).

The causative form of the verb sometimes expressed the idea of "lightening, lifting a weight": ". . . Peradventure he will lighten his hand from off you . . ." (1 Sam. 6:5); ". . . so shall it be easier for thyself . . ." (Exod. 18:22).

'ārar (אָרַר), "to curse." This root is found in South Arabic, Ethiopic, and Akkadian. The verb occurs 60 times in the Old Testament.

The first occurrence is in Gen. 3:14: "Thou [the serpent] art cursed above all cattle," and Gen. 3:17: "Cursed is the ground for thy [Adam's] sake." This form accounts for more than half of the occurrences. It is a pronouncement of judgment on those who break covenant, as: "Cursed is the man who . . ." (twelve times in Deut. 27:15-26).

"Curse" is usually parallel with "bless." The two "curses" in Gen. 3 are in bold contrast to the two blessings ("And God blessed them . . .") in Gen. 1. The covenant with Abraham includes: "I will bless them that bless thee, and curse [different root] him that curseth thee . . ." (Gen. 12:3). Compare Jeremiah's "Cursed be the man that trusteth in man" and "Blessed is the man that trusteth in the Lord" (17:5, 7).

Pagans used the power of "cursing" to deal with their enemies, as when Balak sent for Balaam: "Come . . . , curse me this people" (Num. 22:6). Israel had the ceremonial "water that causeth the curse" (Num. 5:18 ff.).

God alone truly "curses." It is a revelation of His justice, in support of His claim to absolute obedience. Men may claim God's "curses" by committing their grievances to God and trusting in His righteous judgment (cf. Ps. 109:26-31).

The Septuagint translates *'ārar* by *epikatarasthai,* its compounds and derivatives, by which it comes into the New Testament. "Curse" in the Old Testament is summed up in the statement: "Cursed be the man that obeyeth not the words of this covenant . . ." (Jer. 11:3). The New Testament responds: "Christ hath redeemed us from the curse of the law, being made a curse for us: for it is written, Cursed is every one that hangeth on a tree . . ." (Gal. 3:13).

B. Noun.

'ālāh (אָלָה), "curse; oath." Cognates of this word appear in Phoenician and Arabic. The 36 Old Testament occurrences of this noun appear in every period of biblical literature.

In distinction from *'ārar* ("to curse by laying an anathema on someone or something") and *qālal* ("to curse by abusing or by belittling"), *'ālāh* basically refers to "the execution of a proper oath to legalize a covenant or agreement." As a noun, *'ālāh* refers to the "oath" itself: "Then shalt thou be clear from this my oath, when thou comest to my kindred; and if they give not thee one, thou shalt be clear from my oath" (Gen. 24:41—the first occurrence). The "oath" was a "curse" on the head of the one who broke the agreement. This same sense appears in Lev. 5:1, referring to a general "curse" against anyone who would give false testimony in a court case.

So *'ālāh* functions as a "curse" sanctioning a pledge or commission, and it can close an agreement or covenant. On the other hand, the word sometimes represents a "curse" against someone else, whether his identity is known or not.

D

DAY

yôm (**ם׳**), "daylight; day; time; moment; year." This word also appears in Ugaritic, extrabiblical Hebrew or Canaanite (e.g., the Siloam inscription), Akkadian, Phoenician, and Arabic. It also appears in post-biblical Hebrew. Attested at every era of biblical Hebrew, *yôm* occurs about 2,304 times.

Yôm has several meanings. The word represents the period of "daylight" as contrasted with nighttime: "While the earth remaineth, seedtime and harvest, and cold and heat, and summer and winter, and day and night shall not cease" (Gen. 8:22). The word denotes a period of twenty-four hours: "And it came to pass, as she spake to Joseph day by day . . ." (Gen. 39:10). *Yôm* can also signify a period of time of unspecified duration: "And God blessed the seventh day, and sanctified it: because that in it he had rested from all his work which God created and made" (Gen. 2:3). In this verse, "day" refers to the entire period of God's resting from creating this universe. This "day" began after He completed the creative acts of the seventh day and extends at least to the return of Christ. Compare Gen. 2:4: "These are the generations of the heavens and of the earth when they were created, in the day [*bəyôm*] that the Lord God made the earth and the heavens. . . ." Here "day" refers to the entire period envisioned in the first six days of creation. Another nuance appears in Gen. 2:17, where the word represents a "point of time" or "a moment": "But of the tree of the knowledge of good and evil, thou shalt not eat of it: for in the day [*bəyôm*] that thou eatest thereof thou shalt surely die." Finally, when used in the plural, the word may represent "year": "Thou shalt therefore keep this ordinance in his season from year to year [*yāmîm*]" (Exod. 13:10).

There are several other special nuances of *yôm* when it is used with various prepositions. First, when used with *kə* ("as," "like"), it can connote "first": "And Jacob said, Sell me this day [first] thy birthright" (Gen. 25:31). It may also mean "one day," or "about this day": "And it came to pass about this time, that Joseph went into the house to do his business . . ." (Gen. 39:11). On Joseph's lips, the phrase connotes "this present result" (literally, "as it is this day"): "But as for you, ye thought evil against me; but God meant it unto good, to bring to pass, as it is this day, to save much people alive" (Gen. 50:20). Adonijah used this same phrase to represent "today": "Let king Solomon swear unto me today that he will not slay his servant . . ." (1 Kings 1:51). Yet another nuance appears in 1 Sam. 9:13: "Now therefore get you up; for about this time ye shall find him." When used with the definite article *lə*, the noun may mean "today" (as it does in Gen. 4:14) or refer to some particular "day" (1 Sam. 1:4) and the "daytime" (Neh. 4:16).

The first biblical occurrence of *yôm* is found in Gen. 1:5: "And God called the light Day, and the darkness he called Night. And the evening and the morning were the first day." The second use introduces one of the most debated occurrences of the word, which is the duration of the days of creation. Perhaps the most frequently heard explanations are that these "days" are 24 hours long, indefinitely long (i.e., eras of time), or logical rather than temporal categories (i.e., they depict theological categories rather than periods of time).

The "day of the Lord" is used to denote both the end of the age (eschatologically) or some occurrence during the present age (non-eschatologically). It may be a day of either judgment or blessing, or both (cf. Isa. 2).

It is noteworthy that Hebrew people did not divide the period of daylight into regular hourly periods, whereas nighttime was divided into three watches (Exod. 14:24; Judg. 7:19). The beginning of a "day" is sometimes said to be dusk (Esther 4:16) and sometimes dawn (Deut. 28:66-67).

TO DEAL OUT, DEAL WITH

gāmal (גָּמַל), "to deal out, deal with, wean, ripen." Found in both biblical and modern Hebrew, this word occurs 35 times in the Hebrew Old Testament. While the basic meaning of the word is "to deal out, with," the wide range of meaning can be seen in its first occurrence in the biblical text: "And the child grew, and was weaned . . ." (Gen. 21:8).

Gāmal is used most frequently in the sense of "to deal out to," such as in Prov. 31:12: "She will do him good and not evil. . . ." The word is used twice in 1 Sam. 24:17: ". . . Thou hast rewarded me good, whereas I have rewarded thee evil." The psalmist rejoices and sings to the Lord "because he hath dealt bountifully with me" (Ps. 13:6). This word can express ripening of grapes (Isa. 18:5) or bearing ripe almonds (Num. 17:8).

DEATH

māweth (מָוֶת), "death." This word appears 150 times in the Old Testament. The word *māweth* occurs frequently as an antonym of *chayyim* ("life"): "I call heaven and earth to record this day against you, that I have set before you life and death, blessing and cursing: therefore choose life, that both thou and thy seed may live . . ." (Deut. 30:19). In the poetic language, *māweth* is used more often than in the historical books: Job–Proverbs (about 60 times), Joshua–Esther (about 40 times); but in the major prophets only about 25 times.

"Death" is the natural end of human life on this earth; it is an aspect of God's judgment on man: "But of the tree of the knowledge of good and evil, thou shalt not eat of it: for in the day that thou eatest thereof thou shalt surely die" (Gen. 2:17). Hence all men die: "If these men die the common death of all men . . . then the Lord hath not sent me" (Num. 16:29). The Old Testament uses "death" in phrases such as "the day of death" (Gen. 27:2) and "the year of death" (Isa. 6:1), or to mark an event as occurring before (Gen. 27:7, 10) or after (Gen. 26:18) someone's passing away.

"Death" may also come upon someone in a violent manner, as an execution of justice: "And if a man have committed a sin worthy of death and he be to be put to death, and thou hang him on a tree: his body shall not remain all night upon the tree . . ." (Deut. 21:22-23). Saul declared David to be a "son of death" because he intended to have David killed (1 Sam. 20:31; cf. Prov. 16:14). In one of his experiences, David composed a psalm expressing how close an encounter he had had with death: "When the waves of death compassed me, the floods of ungodly men made me afraid; the sorrows of hell compassed me about; the snares of death prevented me" (2 Sam. 22:5-6; cf. Ps. 18:5-6). Isaiah predicted the Suffering Servant was to die a violent death: "And he made his grave with the wicked, and with the rich in his death; because he had done no violence, neither was any deceit in his mouth" (Isa. 53:9).

Associated with the meaning of "death" is the meaning of "death by a plague." In a besieged city with unsanitary conditions, pestilence would quickly reduce the weakened population. Jeremiah alludes to this type of death as God's judgment on Egypt (43:11); note that "death" refers here to "death of famine and pestilence." Lamentations describes the situation of Jerusalem before its fall: ". . . Abroad the sword bereaveth, at home there is as death" (Lam. 1.20; cf. also Jer. 21:8-9).

Finally, the word *māweth* denotes the "realm of the dead" or *shəʾōl*. This place of death has gates (Ps. 9:13; 107:18) and chambers (Prov. 7:27); the path of the wicked leads to this abode (Prov. 5:5).

Isaiah expected "death" to be ended when the Lord's full kingship would be established: "He will swallow up death in victory; and the Lord God will wipe away tears from off all faces; and the rebuke of his people shall he take away from off all the earth: for the Lord hath spoken it" (Isa. 25:8). Paul argued on the basis of Jesus' resurrection that this event had already taken place (1 Cor. 15:54), but John looked forward to the hope of the resurrection when God would wipe away our tears (Rev. 21:4).

Təmûthāh means "death." One occurrence is in Ps. 79:11: "Let the sighing of the prisoner come before thee; according to the greatness of thy power preserve thou those that are appointed to die [literally, sons of death]" (cf. Ps. 102:20).

Māmôth refers to "death." *Māmôth* appears in Jer. 16:4: "They shall die of grievous deaths . . ." (cf. Ezek. 28:8).

DECEIT

shāwə' (שָׁוְא), "deceit; deception; malice; falsity; vanity; emptiness." The 53 occurrences of *shāwə'* are primarily in poetry.

The basic meaning of this word is "deceit" or "deception," "malice," and "falsehood." This meaning emerges when *shāwə'* is used in a legal context: "Put not thine hand with the wicked to be an *unrighteous* witness" (Exod. 23:1). Used in cultic contexts, the word bears these same overtones but may be rendered variously. For example, in Ps. 31:6 the word may be rendered "vain" (KJV, "lying"), in the sense of "deceitful" (cf. Ezek. 12:24). Eliphaz described the ungodly as those who trust in "emptiness" or "deception," though they gain nothing but emptiness as a reward for that trust (Job 15:31).

TO DELIVER

A. Verbs.

nātan (נָתַן), "to deliver, give, place, set up, lay, make, do." This verb occurs in the different Semitic languages in somewhat different forms. The form *nātan* occurs not only in Aramaic (including in the Bible) and in Hebrew (in all periods). The related forms *nadānu* (Akkadian) and *yātan* (Phoenician) are also attested. These verbs occur about 2,010 times in the Bible.

First, *nātan* represents the action by which something is set going or actuated. Achsah asked her father Caleb to "give" her a blessing, such as a tract of land with abundant water, as her dowry; she wanted him to "transfer" it from his possession to hers (Josh. 15:19). There is a technical use of this verb without an object: Moses instructs Israel to "give" generously to the man in desperate need (Deut. 15:10). In some instances, *nātan* can mean to "send forth," as in "sending forth" a fragrance (Song of Sol. 1:12). When used of a liquid, the word means to "send forth" in the sense of "spilling," for example, to spill blood (Deut. 21:8).

Nātan also has a technical meaning in the area of jurisprudence, meaning to hand something over to someone—for example, "to pay" (Gen. 23:9) or "to loan" (Deut. 15:10). A girl's parent or someone else in a responsible position may "give" her to a man to be his wife (Gen. 16:3), as well as presenting a bride price (Gen. 34:12) and dowry (1 Kings 9:16). The verb also is used of "giving" or "granting" a request (Gen. 15:2).

Sometimes, *nātan* can be used to signify "putting" ("placing") someone into custody (2 Sam. 14:7) or into prison (Jer. 37:4), or even of "destroying" something (Judg. 6:30). This same basic sense may be applied to "dedicating" ("handing over") something or someone to God, such as the first-born son (Exod. 22:29). Levites are those who have been "handed over" in this way (Num. 3:9). This word is used of "bringing reprisal" upon someone or of "giving" him what he deserves; in some cases, the stress is on the act of reprisal (1 Kings 8:32), or bringing his punishment on his head.

Nātan can be used of "giving" or "ascribing" something to someone, such as "giving" glory and praise to God (Josh. 7:19). Obviously, nothing is passed from men to God; nothing is added to God, since He is perfect. This means, therefore, that a worshiper recognizes and confesses what is already His.

Another major emphasis of *nātan* is the action of "giving" or "effecting" a result. For example, the land will "give" ("yield") its fruit (Deut. 25:19). In some passages, this verb means "to procure" ("to set up"), as when God "gave" ("procured, set up") favor for Joseph (Gen. 39:21). The word can be used of sexual activity, too, emphasizing the act of intercourse or "one's lying down" with an animal (Lev. 18:23).

God "placed" (literally, "gave") the heavenly lights into the expanse of the heavens (Gen. 1:17—the first occurrence of the verb). A garland is "placed" (literally, "given") upon one's head (Prov. 4:9). The children of Israel are commanded not to "set up" idols in their land.

A third meaning of *nātan* is seen in Gen. 17:5: ". . . For a father of many nations have I made [literally, "given"] thee." There are several instances where the verb bears this significance.

Nātan has a number of special implications when used with bodily parts—for example, "to give" or "turn" a stubborn shoulder (Neh. 9:29). Similarly, compare expressions such as "turning [giving] one's face" (2 Chron. 29:6). To "turn [give] one's back" is to flee (Exod. 23:27). "Giving one's hand" may be no more than "putting it forth," as in the case of the unborn Zarah (Gen. 38:28). This word can also signify an act of friendship as when Jehonadab "gave his hand" (instead of a sword) to Jehu to help him into the chariot (2 Kings 10:15); an act of oathtaking, as when the priests "pledged" ("gave their hands") to put away their foreign wives (Ezra 10:19); and "making" or "renewing" a covenant, as when the leaders of Israel "pledged" themselves ("gave their hands") to follow Solomon (1 Chron. 29:24).

"To give something into someone's hand" is to "commit" it to his care. So after the Flood, God "gave" the earth into Noah's hand (Gen. 9:2). This phrase is used to express the "transfer of political power," such as the divine right to rule (2 Sam. 16:8). *Nātan* is used especially in a military and judicial sense, meaning "to give over one's power or control," or to grant victory to someone; so Moses said God would "give" the kings of Canaan into Israel's hands (Deut. 7:24). "To give one's heart" to something or someone is "to be concerned about it"; Pharaoh was not "concerned" about ("did not set his heart to") Moses' message from God (Exod. 7:23). "To put [give] something into one's heart" is to give one ability and concern to do something; thus God "put" it in the heart of the Hebrew craftsmen to teach others (Exod. 36:2).

"To give one's face to" is to focus one's attention on something, as when Jehoshaphat was afraid of the alliance of the Transjordanian kings and "set [his face] to seek the Lord" (2 Chron. 20:3). This same phrase can merely mean "to be facing someone or something" (cf. Gen. 30:40). "To give one's face against" is a hostile action (Lev. 17:10). Used with *laphəne* (literally, "before the face of"), this verb may mean "to place an object before" or to "set it down before" (Exod. 30:6). It may also mean "to put before" (Deut. 11:26), "to smite" (cf. Deut. 2:33), or "to give as one's possession" (Deut. 1:8).

yāshaʿ (יָשַׁע), "to deliver, help." Apart from Hebrew, this root occurs only in a Moabite inscription. The verb occurs over 200 times in the Bible. For example: "For thus saith the Lord God, the Holy One of Israel; In returning and rest shall ye be *saved;* in quietness and in confidence shall be your strength: and ye would not" (Isa. 30:15).

B. Nouns.

yəshûʿāh (יְשׁוּעָה), "deliverance." This noun appears 78 times in the Old Testament, predominantly in the Books of Psalms (45 times) and Isaiah (19 times). The first occurrence is in Jacob's last words: "I have waited for thy salvation, O Lord" (Gen. 49:18).

"Salvation" in the Old Testament is not understood as a salvation from sin, since the word denotes broadly anything from which "deliverance" must be sought: distress, war, servitude, or enemies. There are both human and divine deliverers, but the word *yəshûʿāh* rarely refers to human "deliverance." A couple of exceptions are when Jonathan brought respite to the Israelites from the Philistine pressure (1 Sam. 14:45), and when Joab and his men were to help one another in battle (2 Sam. 10:11). "Deliverance" is generally used with God as the subject. He is known as the salvation of His people: "But Jeshurun waxed fat, and kicked: thou art waxen fat, thou art grown thick, thou art covered with fatness; then he forsook God which made him, and lightly esteemed the Rock of his salvation" (Deut. 32:15; cf. Isa. 12:2). He worked many wonders in behalf of His people: "O sing unto the Lord a new song; for he hath done marvelous things: his right hand, and his holy arm, hath [worked salvation for him]" (Ps. 98:1).

Yəshû'āh occurs either in the context of rejoicing (Ps. 9:14) or in the context of a prayer for "deliverance": "But I am poor and sorrowful: let thy salvation, O God, set me up on high" (Ps. 69:29).

Habakkuk portrays the Lord's riding on chariots of salvation (3:8) to deliver His people from their oppressors. The worst reproach that could be made against a person was that God did not come to his rescue: "Many there be which say of my soul, there is no help for him in God [literally, "he has no deliverance in God"]" (Ps. 3:2).

Many personal names contain a form of the root, such as *Joshua* ("the Lord is help"), *Isaiah* ("the Lord is help"), and *Jesus* (a Greek form of *yəshû'āh*).

yēsha' (יֵשַׁע), "deliverance." This noun appears 36 times in the Old Testament. One appearance is in Ps. 50:23: "Whoso offereth praise glorifieth me: and to him that ordereth his conversation aright will I show the salvation of God."

təshû'āh (תְּשׁוּעָה), "deliverance." *Təshû'āh* occurs 34 times. One example is Isa. 45:17: "But Israel shall be saved in the Lord with an everlasting *salvation*: ye shall not be ashamed nor confounded world without end."

The Septuagint translations of *təshû'āh* are: *soteria* and *soterion* ("salvation; preservation; deliverance") and *soter* ("savior; deliverer"). The KJV gives these translations: "salvation; deliverance; help."

TO DEPART

nāsa' (נָסַע), "to journey, depart, set out, march." Found throughout the development of the Hebrew language, this root is also found in ancient Akkadian. The word is used nearly 150 times in the Hebrew Bible. It occurs for the first time in Gen. 11:2, where *nāsa'* refers to the "migration" (RSV) of people to the area of Babylon. It is probably the most common term in the Old Testament referring to the movement of clans and tribes. Indeed, the word is used almost 90 times in the Book of Numbers alone, since this book records the "journeying" of the people of Israel from Sinai to Canaan.

This word has the basic meaning of "pulling up" tent pegs (Isa. 33:20) in preparation for "moving" one's tent and property to another place; thus it lends itself naturally to the general term of "traveling" or "journeying." Samson is said to have "pulled up" the city gate and posts (Judg. 16:3), as well as the pin on the weaver's loom (Judg. 16:14). *Nāsa'* is used to describe the "movement" of the angel of God and the pillar of cloud as they came between Israel and the pursuing Egyptians at the Sea of Reeds (Exod. 14:19). In Num. 11:31, the word refers to the "springing up" (NEB) of the wind that brought the quail to feed the Israelites in the wilderness.

Nāsa' lends itself to a wide range of renderings, depending upon the context.

TO BE DESOLATE

shāmēm (שָׁמֵם), "to be desolate, astonished, appalled, devastated, ravaged." This verb is found in both biblical and modern Hebrew. It occurs approximately 90 times in the text of the Hebrew Old Testament. *Shāmēm* does not occur until Lev. 26:22: "Your high ways shall be desolate." Interestingly, the word occurs 25 times in the Book of Ezekiel alone, which may reflect either Ezekiel's times or (more likely) his personality.

Just how the meanings "be desolate," "be astonished," and "be appalled" are to be connected with each other is not clear. In some instances, the translator must make a subjective choice. For example, after being raped by her half-brother, Tamar is said to have remained in her brother Absalom's house, "desolate" (2 Sam. 13:20). However, she surely was "appalled" at what Amnon had done. Also, the traditional expression, "to be desolated," sometimes means much the same as "to be destroyed" (cf. Amos 7:9; Ezek. 6:4).

Shāmēm often expresses the idea of to "devastate" or "ravage": "I will destroy her vines" (Hos. 2:12). What one sees sometimes is so horrible that it "horrifies" or "appalls": "Mark me, and be astonished, and lay your hand upon your mouth [i.e., be speechless]" (Job 21:5).

TO DESPISE

mā'as (מָאַס), "to reject, refuse, despise." This verb is common in both biblical and modern Hebrew. It occurs about 75 times in the Hebrew Old Testament and is found for the first time in Lev. 26:15: ". . . If ye shall despise [RSV, "spurn"] my statutes. . . ."

God will not force man to do His will, so He sometimes must "reject" him: "Because thou hast rejected knowledge, I will also reject thee, that thou shalt be no priest to me . . ." (Hos. 4:6). Although God had chosen Saul to be king, Saul's response caused a change in God's attitude: "Because thou hast rejected the word of the Lord, he hath also rejected thee from being king" (1 Sam. 15:23).

As a creature of free choice, man may "reject" God: ". . . Ye have despised the Lord which is among you" (Num. 11:20). At the same time, man may "reject" evil (Isa. 7:15-16).

When the things that God requires are done with the wrong motives or attitudes, God "despises" such actions: "I hate, I despise your feast days . . ." (Amos 5:21). Purity of heart and attitude are more important to God than perfection and beauty of ritual.

TO DESTROY

shāmad (שָׁמַד), "to destroy, annihilate, exterminate." This biblical word occurs also in modern Hebrew, with the root having the connotation of "religious persecution" or "forced conversion." *Shāmad* is found 90 times in the Hebrew Old Testament, the first time in Gen. 34:30: "I shall be destroyed."

This word always expresses complete "destruction" or "annihilation." While the word is often used to express literal "destruction" of people (Deut. 2:12; Judg. 21:16), *shāmad* frequently is part of an open threat or warning given to the people of Israel, promising "destruction" if they forsake God for idols (cf. Deut. 4:25-26). This word also expresses the complete "destruction" of the pagan high places (Hos. 10:8) of Baal and his images (2 Kings 10:28). When God wants to completely "destroy," He will sweep "with the [broom] of destruction" (Isa. 14:23).

shāchath (שָׁחַת), "to corrupt, spoil, ruin, mar, destroy." Used primarily in biblical Hebrew, this word has cognate forms in a few other Semitic languages such as Aramaic and Ethiopic. It is used about 150 times in the Hebrew Bible and is found first in Gen. 6, where it is used 4 times in reference to the "corruption" that prompted God to bring the Flood upon the earth (Gen. 6:11-12, 17).

Anything that is good can be "corrupted" or "spoiled," such as Jeremiah's loincloth (Jer. 13:7), a vineyard (Jer. 12:10), cities (Gen. 13:10), and a temple (Lam. 2:6). *Shāchath* has the meaning of "to waste" when used of words that are inappropriately spoken (Prov. 23:8). In its participial form, the word is used to describe a "ravening lion" (Jer. 2:30, RSV) and the "destroying angel" (1 Chron. 21:15). The word is used as a symbol for a trap in Jer. 5:26. *Shāchath* is used frequently by the prophets in the sense of "to corrupt morally" (Isa. 1:4; Ezek. 23:11; Zeph. 3:7).

TO DEVISE

chāshab (חָשַׁב), "to think, account, reckon, devise, plan." This word is found throughout the historical development of Hebrew and Aramaic. Found at least 120 times in the Hebrew Bible, *chāshab* occurs in the text for the first time in Gen. 15:6, where it was said of Abraham: "He believed the Lord; and he reckoned it to him as righteousness" (RSV). Here the term has the meaning of "to be imputed."

Frequently used in the ordinary sense of "thinking," or the normal thought processes (Isa. 10:7; 53:4; Mal. 3:16), *chāshab* also is used in the sense of "devising evil plans" (Gen. 50:20; Jer. 48:2). The word refers to craftsmen "inventing" instruments of music, artistic objects, and weapons of war (Exod. 31:4; 2 Chron. 26:15; Amos 6:5).

TO DIE

mûth (מוּת), "to die, kill." This verb occurs in all Semitic languages (including biblical Aramaic) from the earliest times, and in Egyptian. The verb occurs about 850 times in biblical Hebrew and in all periods.

Essentially, *mûth* means to "lose one's life." The word is used of physical "death," with reference to both man and beast. Gen. 5:5 records that Adam lived "nine hundred and thirty years: and he died." Jacob explains to Esau that, were his livestock to be driven too hard (fast), the young among them would "die" (Gen. 33:13). At one point, this verb is also used to refer to the stump of a plant (Job 14:8). Occasionally, *mûth* is used figuratively of land (Gen. 47:19) or wisdom (Job 12:2). Then, too, there is the unique hyperbolic expression that Nabal's heart had "died" within him, indicating that he was overcome with great fear (1 Sam. 25:37).

In an intensive stem, this root is used of the last act inflicted upon one who is already near death. Thus Abimelech, his head having been cracked by a millstone, asked his armor-bearer to "kill" him (Judg. 9:54). In the usual causative stem, this verb can mean "to cause to die" or "to kill"; God is the one who "puts to death" and gives life (Deut. 32:39). Usually, both the subject and object of this usage are personal, although there are exceptions—as when the Philistines personified the ark of the covenant, urging its removal so it would not "kill" them (1 Sam. 5:11). Death in this sense may also be inflicted by animals (Exod. 21:29). This word describes "putting to death" in the broadest sense, including war and judicial sentences of execution (Josh. 10:26).

God is clearly the ultimate Ruler of life and death (cf. Deut. 32:39). This idea is especially clear in the Creation account, in which God tells man that he will surely die if he eats of the forbidden fruit (Gen. 2:17—the first occurrence of the verb). Apparently there was no death before this time. When the serpent questioned Eve, she associated disobedience with death (Gen. 3:3). The serpent repeated God's words, but negated them (Gen. 3:4). When Adam and Eve ate of the fruit, both spiritual and physical death came upon Adam and Eve and their descendants (cf. Rom. 5:12). They experienced spiritual death immediately, resulting in their shame and their attempt to cover their nakedness (Gen. 3:7). Sin and/or the presence of spiritual death required a covering, but man's provision was inadequate; so God made a perfect covering in the form of a promised redeemer (Gen. 3:15) and a typological covering of animal skins (Gen. 3:21).

TO DISCERN

nākar (נָכַר), "to discern, regard, recognize, pay attention to, be acquainted with." This verb is found in both ancient and modern Hebrew. It occurs approximately 50 times in the Hebrew Old Testament. The first time *nākar* is used is in Gen. 27:23.

The basic meaning of the term is a "physical apprehension," whether through sight, touch, or hearing. Darkness sometimes makes "recognition" impossible (Ruth 3:14). People are often "recognized" by their voices (Judg. 18:3). *Nākar* sometimes has the meaning of "pay attention to," a special kind of "recognition": "Blessed be the man who took notice of you" (Ruth 2:19, RSV—KJV, "did take knowledge of"). This verb can mean "to be acquainted with," a kind of intellectual awareness: ". . . Neither shall his place know him any more" (Job 7:10; cf. Ps. 103:16). The sense of "to distinguish" is seen in Ezra 3:13: ". . . The people could not discern the noise of the shout of joy from the noise of the weeping of the people. . . ."

TO BE DISMAYED

chāthath (חָתַת), "to be dismayed, shattered, broken, terrified." Used primarily in the Hebrew Old Testament, this verb has been identified in ancient Akkadian and Ugaritic texts by some scholars. The word is used approximately 50 times in the Hebrew Old Testament and occurs for the first time in Deut. 1:21 as Moses challenged Israel: "Do not fear or be dismayed" (RSV—NEB, "afraid"; KJV, JB, "discouraged"). As here, *chāthath* is often used in parallelism with the Hebrew term for "fear" (cf. Deut. 31:8; Josh. 8:1; 1 Sam. 17:11). Similarly, *chāthath* is frequently used in parallelism with "to be ashamed" (Isa. 20:5; Jer. 8:9).

An interesting figurative use of the word is found in Jer. 14:4, where the ground "is dismayed [KJV, "chapt"], for there was no rain." The meaning "to be shattered" is usually employed in a figurative sense, as with reference to the nations coming under God's judgment (Isa. 7:8; 30:31). The coming Messiah is to "shatter" or "break" the power of all His enemies (Isa. 9:4).

DISTRESS

A. Nouns.

tsārāh (צָרָה), "distress; straits." The 70 appearances of *tsārāh* occur in all periods of biblical literature, although most occurrences are in poetry (poetical, prophetical, and wisdom literature).

Tsārāh means "straits" or "distress" in a psychological or spiritual sense, which is its meaning in Gen. 42:21 (the first occurrence): "We are verily guilty concerning our brother, in that we saw the anguish of his soul, when he besought us, and we would not hear. . . ."

tsar (צַר), "distress." This word also occurs mostly in poetry. In Prov. 24:10, *tsar* means "scarcity" or the "distress" caused by scarcity. The emphasis of the noun is sometimes on the feeling of "dismay" arising from a distressful situation (Job 7:11). In this usage the word *tsar* represents a psychological or spiritual status. In Isa. 5:30, the word describes conditions that cause distress: ". . . If one look unto the land, behold darkness and *sorrow* . . ." (cf. Isa. 30:20). This nuance appears to be the most frequent use represented by *tsar*.

B. Verb.

tsārar (צָרַר), "to wrap, tie up, be narrow, be distressed, be in pangs of birth." This verb, which appears in the Old Testament 54 times, has cognates in Aramaic, Syriac, Akkadian, and Arabic. In Judg. 11:7, the word carries the meaning of "to be in distress."

C. Adjective.

tsar (צַר), "narrow." *Tsar* describes a space as "narrow" and easily blocked by a single person (Num. 22:26).

TO DIVIDE
A. Verb.

chālaq (חָלַק), "to divide, share, plunder, assign, distribute." Used throughout the history of Hebrew, this verb is probably reflected in the ancient Akkadian term for "field" i.e., that which is divided. The word is found approximately 60 times in the Hebrew Old Testament; it appears for the first time in Gen. 14:15, where it is said that Abram "divided his forces" (RSV) as he rescued his nephew Lot from the enemy. Apparently, Abram was "assigning" different responsibilities to his troops as part of his strategy. The sense of "dividing" or "allotting" is found in Deut. 4:19, where the sun, moon, and stars are said to have been "allotted" to all peoples by God. A similar use is seen in Deut. 29:26, where God is said not to have "allotted" false gods to His people.

Chālaq is used in the legal sense of "sharing" an inheritance in Prov. 17:2. The word is used three times in reference to "sharing" the spoils of war in 1 Sam. 30:24.

This verb describes the "division" of the people of Israel, as one half followed Tibni and the other half followed Omri (1 Kings 16:21). The word *chālaq* is also important in the description of the "dividing" of the land of Canaan among the various tribes and clans (Num. 26:52-55).

B. Noun.

chēleq (חֵלֶק), "portion; territory." The noun form of *chālaq* is used often in the biblical text. It has a variety of meanings, such as "booty" of war (Gen. 14:24), a "portion" of food (Lev. 6:17), a "tract" of land (Josh. 18:5), a spiritual "possession" or blessing (Ps. 73:26), and a chosen "pattern" or "life-style" (Ps. 50:18).

TO DIVINE, PRACTICE DIVINATION

qāsam (קָסַם), "to divine, practice divination." Cognates of this word appear in late Aramaic, Coptic, Syriac, Mandean, Ethiopic, Palmyran, and Arabic. This root appears 31 times in biblical Hebrew: 11 times as a verb, 9 times as a participle, and 11 times as a noun.

Divination was a pagan parallel to prophesying: "There shall not be found among you anyone who makes his son or daughter pass through the fire, one who uses divination. . . . For those nations, which you shall dispossess, listen to those who practice witchcraft and to diviners, but as for you the Lord your God has not allowed you to do so. The Lord your God will raise up for you a prophet like me from among you, from your countrymen; you shall listen to him'' (Deut. 18:10, 14-15, NASB—first occurrence.)

Qāsam is a seeking after the will of the gods, in an effort to learn their future action or divine blessing on some proposed future action (Josh. 13:22). It seems probable that the diviners conversed with demons (1 Cor. 10:20).

The practice of divination might involve offering sacrifices to the deity on an altar (Num. 23:1 f.). It might also involve the use of a hole in the ground, through which the diviner spoke to the spirits of the dead (1 Sam. 28:8). At other times, a diviner might shake arrows, consult with household idols, or study the livers of dead animals (Ezek. 21:21).

Divination was one of man's attempts to know and control the world and the future, apart from the true God. It was the opposite of true prophecy, which essentially is submission to God's sovereignty (Deut. 18:14).

Perhaps the most perplexing uses of this word occur in Num. 22–23 and Prov. 16:10, where it seems to be an equivalent of prophecy. Balaam was well-known among the pagans as a diviner; at the same time, he recognized Yahweh as his God (Num. 22:18). He accepted money for his services and probably was not beyond adjusting the message to please his clients. This would explain why God, being angry, confronted him (Num. 22:22 ff.), even though God had told him to accept the commission and go with his escort (22:20). It appears that Balaam was resolved to please his clients. Once that resolve was changed to submission, God sent him on his journey (22:35).

TO DO GOOD

A. Verb.

yātab (יָטַב), ''to be good, do well, be glad, please, do good.'' This word is found in various Semitic languages, and is very common in Hebrew, both ancient and modern. *Yātab* is found approximately 100 times in biblical Hebrew. This verbal form is found first in the story of Cain and Abel, where it is used twice in one verse: ''If you *do well*, will not your countenance be lifted up? And if you do not *do well*, sin is crouching at the door'' (Gen. 4:7, NASB).

Among other nuances of the verb are ''to deal well'' (Exod. 1:20), ''to play [a musical instrument] well'' (1 Sam. 16:17), ''to adorn, make beautiful'' (2 Kings 9:30), and ''to inquire diligently'' (Deut. 17:4).

B. Adjective.

tôb (טוֹב), ''good.'' This word occurs some 500 times in the Bible. Its first occurrence is in Gen. 1:4: ''God saw that the light was good'' (NASB). God appraises each day's creative work as being ''good,'' climaxing it with a ''very good'' on the sixth day (Gen. 1:31).

As a positive term, the word is used to express many nuances of that which is ''good,'' such as a ''glad'' heart (Judg. 18:20), ''pleasing'' words (Gen. 34:18), and a ''cheerful'' face (Prov. 15:13).

DOORWAY

A. Noun.

petach (פֶּתַח), "doorway; opening; entrance; gate." This word appears 164 times in biblical Hebrew and in all periods.

Petach basically represents the "opening through which one enters a building, tent, tower (fortress), or city." Abraham was sitting at the "doorway" of his tent in the heat of the day when his three heavenly visitors appeared (Gen. 18:1). Lot met the men of Sodom at the "doorway" of his home, having shut the door behind him (Gen. 19:6). Larger buildings had larger entryways, so in Gen. 43:19 *petach* may be rendered by the more general word, "entrance." In Gen. 38:14, *petach* may be translated "gateway": Tamar "sat in the gateway [KJV, "open place"]." Thus a *petach* was both a place to sit (a location) and an opening for entry (a passageway): ". . . And the incense altar, and his staves, and the anointing oil, and the sweet incense, and the hanging for the *door* at the *entering in* of the tabernacle . . ." (Exod. 35:15).

There are a few notable special uses of *petach*. The word normally refers to a part of the intended construction plans of a dwelling, housing, or building; but in Ezek. 8:8 it represents an "entrance" not included in the original design of the building: ". . . When I had digged in the wall, behold a door." This is clearly not a doorway. This word may be used of a cave's "opening," as when Elijah heard the gentle blowing that signified the end of a violent natural phenomenon: ". . . He wrapped his face in his mantle, and went out, and stood in the entering in of the cave" (1 Kings 19:13). In the plural form, *petach* sometimes represents the "city gates" themselves: "And her [Zion's] gates shall lament and mourn . . ." (Isa. 3:26). This form of the word is used as a figure for one's lips; in Mic. 7:5, for example, the prophet mourns the low morality of his people and advises his hearers to trust no one, telling them to guard their lips (literally, the "openings" of their mouths).

In its first biblical occurrence, *petach* is used figuratively. The heart of men is depicted as a house or building with the Devil crouching at the "entrance," ready to subdue it utterly and destroy its occupant (Gen. 4:7).

B. Verb.

pātach (פָּתַח), "to open." This verb, which appears 132 times in the Old Testament, has attested cognates in Ugaritic, Akkadian, Arabic, and Ethiopic. The first occurrence is in Gen. 7:11.

Although the basic meaning of *pātach* is "to open," the word is extended to mean "to cause to flow," "to offer for sale," "to conquer," "to surrender," "to draw a sword," "to solve [a riddle]," "to free." In association with *min*, the word becomes "to deprive of."

DREAM

A. Noun.

chalôm (חֲלוֹם), "dream." This noun appears about 65 times and in all periods of biblical Hebrew.

The word means "dream." It is used of the ordinary dreams of sleep: "Then thou scarest me with dreams, and terrifiest me through visions . . ." (Job 7:14). The most significant use of this word, however, is with reference to prophetic "dreams" and/or "visions." Both true and false prophets claimed to communicate with God by these dreams and visions. Perhaps the classical passage using the word in this sense is Deut. 13:1 ff.: "If there arise among you a prophet, or a dreamer of dreams, and giveth thee a sign or a wonder, and the sign or the wonder come to pass. . . ." This sense, that a dream is a means of revelation, appears in the first biblical occurrence of *chalôm* (or *chalōm*): "But God came to Abimelech in a dream by night. . ." (Gen. 20:3).

B. Verb.

chālam (חָלַם), "to become healthy or strong; to dream." This verb, which appears 27 times in the Old Testament, has cognates in Ugaritic, Aramaic, Syriac, Coptic, Arabic, and Ethiopic. The meaning, "to become healthy," applies only to animals though "to dream" is used of human dreams. Gen. 28:12, the first occurrence, tells how Jacob "dreamed" that he beheld a ladder to heaven.

TO DRINK

shāthāh (שָׁתָה), "to drink." This verb appears in nearly every Semitic language, although in biblical Aramaic it is not attested as a verb (the noun form *mishotteh* does appear). Biblical Hebrew attests *shāthāh* at every period and about 215 times.

This verb primarily means "to drink" or "to consume a liquid," and is used of inanimate subjects, as well as of persons or animals. The verb *shāqah*, which is closely related to *shāthāh* in meaning, often appears both with animate and inanimate subjects. The first occurrence of *shāthāh* reports that Noah "drank of the wine, and was drunken" (Gen. 9:21). Animals also "drink": "I will draw water for thy camels also, until they have done drinking" (Gen. 24:19). God says He does not "drink the blood of goats" (Ps. 50:13).

"To drink a cup" is a metaphor for consuming all that a cup may contain (Isa. 51:17). Not only liquids may be drunk, since *shāthāh* is used figuratively of "drinking" iniquity: "How much more abominable and filthy is man, which drinketh iniquity like water?" (Job 15:16). Only infrequently is this verb used of inanimate subjects, as in Deut. 11:11: "But the land, whither ye go to possess it . . . drinketh water of the rain of heaven. . . ."

Shāthāh may also be used of the initial act of "taking in" a liquid: "Is not this it in which my lord drinketh. . . ?" (Gen. 44:5). "To drink" from a cup does not necessarily involve consuming what is drunk. Therefore, this passage uses *shāthāh* of "drinking in," and not of the entire process of consuming a liquid.

This word may be used of a communal activity: "And they went out into . . . the house of their god, and did eat and drink, and cursed Abimelech" (Judg. 9:27). The phrase "eat and drink" may mean "to eat a meal": "And they did

eat and drink, he and the men that were with him, and tarried all night . . .''
(Gen. 24:54). This verb sometimes means "to banquet" (which included many
activities in addition to just eating and drinking), or "participating in a feast":
". . . Behold, they eat and drink before him, and say, God save king
Adonijah" (1 Kings 1:25). In one case, *shāthāh* by itself means "to participate
in a feast": "So the king and Haman came to the banquet that Esther had
prepared" (Esther 5:5).

The phrase, "eating and drinking," may signify a religious meal—i.e., a
communion meal with God. The seventy elders on Mt. Sinai "saw God, and
did eat and drink" (Exod. 24:11). By this act, they were sacramentally united
with God (cf. 1 Cor. 10:19). In contrast to this communion with the true God,
the people at the foot of the mountain communed with a false god—they "sat
down to eat and to drink, and rose up to play" (Exod. 32:6). When Moses
stood before God, however, he ate nothing during the entire forty days and
nights (Exod. 34:28). His communion was face-to-face rather than through a
common meal.

Priests were commanded to practice a partial fast when they served before
God—they were not to drink wine or strong drink (Lev. 10:9). They and all
Israel were to eat no unclean thing. These conditions were stricter for Nazi-
rites, who lived constantly before God. They were commanded not to eat any
product of the vine (Num. 6:3; cf. Judg. 13:4; 1 Sam. 1:15). Thus, God laid
claim to the ordinary and necessary processes of human living. In all that man
does, he is obligated to recognize God's control of his existence. Man is to
recognize that he eats and drinks only as he lives under God's rule; and the
faithful are to acknowledge God in all their ways.

The phrase, "eating and drinking," may also signify life in general; "Judah
and Israel were many, as the sand which is by the sea in multitude, eating and
drinking, and making merry" (1 Kings 4:20; cf. Eccles. 2:24; 5:18; Jer. 22:15).
In close conjunction with the verb "to be drunk [intoxicated]," *shāthāh* means
"to drink freely" or "to drink so much that one becomes drunk." When
Joseph hosted his brothers, they "drank, and were merry with him" (Gen.
43:34).

TO DRIVE OUT

nādach (נָדַח), "to drive out, banish, thrust, move." This word is found
primarily in biblical Hebrew, although in late Hebrew it is used in the sense of
"to beguile." *Nādach* occurs approximately 50 times in the Hebrew Old
Testament, and its first use is in the passive form: "And lest thou . . . shouldest be driven to worship them. . ." (Deut. 4:19). The implication seems to be
that an inner "drivenness" or "drawing away," as well as an external force,
was involved in Israel's potential turning toward idolatry.

Nādach expresses the idea of "being scattered" in exile, as in Jer. 40:12:
"Even all the Jews returned out of all places whither they were driven. . . ."
Job complained that any resource he once possessed no longer existed, for it
"is . . . driven quite from me" (Job 6:13). Evil "shepherds" or leaders did not
lead but rather "drove away" and scattered Israel (Jer. 23:2). The enemies of

a good man plot against him "to thrust him down from his eminence" (Ps. 62:4, RSV).

DUST

'*āphār* (עָפָר), "dust; clods; plaster; ashes." Cognates of this word appear in Ugaritic, Akkadian, Aramaic, Syriac, and Arabic. It appears about 110 times in biblical Hebrew and in all periods.

This noun represents the "porous loose earth on the ground," or "dust." In its first biblical occurrence, '*āphār* appears to mean this porous loose earth: "And the Lord God formed man of the *dust* of the ground, and breathed into his nostrils the breath of life . . ." (Gen. 2:7). In Gen. 13:16, the word means the "fine particles of the soil": "And I will make thy [descendants] as the dust of the earth. . . ." In the plural, the noun can mean "dust masses" or "clods" of earth: ". . . While as yet he had not made the earth, nor the fields, nor the first clods [KJV, "highest part of the dust"; NASB, "dust"] of the world" (Prov. 8:26).

'*Āphār* can signify "dry crumbled mortar or plaster": "And he shall cause the house to be scraped within round about, and they shall pour out the dust that they scrape off without the city into an unclean place. . ." (Lev. 14:41). In Lev. 14:42, the word means "wet plaster": "And they shall take other stones, and put them in the place of those stones; and he shall take other mortar, and shall plaster the house." '*Āphār* represents "finely ground material" in Deut. 9:21: "And I took your sin, the calf which ye had made, and burnt it with fire, and stamped it, and ground it very small, even until it was as small as dust: and I cast the dust thereof into the brook that descended out of the mount." '*Āphār* can represent the "ashes" of something that has been burned: "And the king commanded Hilkiah the high priest, and the priests of the second order, and the keepers of the door, to bring forth out of the temple of the Lord all the vessels that were made for Baal, and for the grove, and for all the host of heaven: and he burned them [outside] Jerusalem . . . and carried the ashes of them unto Bethel" (2 Kings 23:4). In a similar use, the word represents the "ashes" of a burnt offering (Num. 19:17).

The "rubble" of a destroyed city sometimes is called "dust": "And Ben-hadad sent unto him, and said, The gods do so unto me, and more also, if the *dust* of Samaria shall suffice for handfuls for all the people that follow me" (1 Kings 20:10). In Gen. 3:14 the serpent was cursed with "dust" as his perpetual food (cf. Isa. 65:25; Mic. 7:17). Another nuance arising from the characteristics of dust appears in Job 28:6, where the word parallels "stones." Here the word seems to represent "the ground": "The stones of it are the place of sapphires: and it hath dust of gold."

'*Āphār* may be used as a symbol of a "large mass" or "superabundance" of something. This use, already cited (Gen. 13:16), appears again in its fulfillment in Num. 23:10: "Who can count the dust of Jacob, and the number of the fourth part of Israel?" "Complete destruction" is represented by '*āphār* in 2 Sam. 22:43: "Then did I beat them as small as the dust of the earth: I did stamp them as the mire of the street. . . ." In Ps. 7:5, the word is used of "valuelessness" and "futility": "Let the enemy persecute my soul, and take it; yea, let him tread down my life upon the earth, and lay mine honor in the dust." To experience defeat is "to lick the dust" (Ps. 72:9), and to be restored from defeat is "to shake oneself from the dust" (Isa. 52:2). To throw "dust" ("dirt") at someone is a sign of shame and humiliation (2 Sam. 16:13), while mourning is expressed by various acts of self-abasement, which may include throwing "dust" or "dirt" on one's own head (Josh. 7:6). Abraham says he is but "dust and ashes," not really important (Gen. 18:27).

In Job 7:21 and similar passages, *'āphār* represents "the earth" of the grave: "For now shall I sleep in the dust; and thou shalt seek me in the morning, but I shall not be." This word is also used as a simile for a "widely scattered army": ". . . For the king of Syria had destroyed them, and had made them like the dust by threshing" (2 Kings 13:7).

TO DWELL
A. Verbs.

yāshab (יָשַׁב), "to dwell, sit, abide, inhabit, remain." The word occurs over 1,100 times throughout the Old Testament, and this root is widespread in other ancient Semitic languages.

Yāshab is first used in Gen. 4:16, in its most common connotation of "to dwell": "Cain went out . . . and dwelt [NASB, "settled"; NIV, "lived"] in the land of Nod. . . ." The word appears again in Gen. 18:1: "He [Abraham] *sat* in the tent door." In Gen. 22:5, *yāshab* is translated: "*Abide* ye here [NIV, "stay here"] with the ass; and I and the lad will go yonder and worship. . . ." The word has the sense of "to remain": "Remain a widow at thy father's house . . ." (Gen. 38:11), and it is used of God in a similar sense: "Thou, O Lord, remainest for ever; thy throne from generation to generation . . ." (Lam. 5:19). The promise of restoration from captivity was: "And they shall build houses and inhabit them. . ." (Isa. 65:21).

Yāshab is sometimes combined with other words to form expressions in common usage. For example, "When he sitteth upon the throne of his kingdom" (Deut. 17:18; cf. 1 Kings 1:13, 17, 24) carries the meaning "begins to reign." "To sit in the gate" means "to hold court" or "to decide a case," as in Ruth 4:1-2 and 1 Kings 22:10. "Sit thou at my right hand" (Ps. 110:1) means to assume a ruling position as deputy. "There will I sit to judge all the heathen" (Joel 3:12) was a promise of eschatological judgment. "To sit in the dust" or "to sit on the ground" (Isa. 47:1) was a sign of humiliation and grief.

Yāshab is often used figuratively of God. The sentences, "I saw the Lord sitting on his throne" (1 Kings 22:19); "He that sitteth in the heavens shall laugh" (Ps. 2:4); and "God sitteth upon the throne of his holiness" (Ps. 47:8) all describe God as the exalted Ruler over the universe. The idea that God also "dwells" among men is expressed by this verb: "Shalt thou [David] build me a house for me to dwell in?" (2 Sam. 7:5; cf. Ps. 132:14). The usage of *yāshab* in such verses as 1 Sam. 4:4: ". . . The Lord of hosts, which dwelleth between the cherubim," describes His presence at the ark of the covenant in the tabernacle and the temple.

The word is also used to describe man's being in God's presence: "One thing have I desired of the Lord, . . . that I may dwell in the house of the Lord all the days of my life. . ." (Ps. 27:4; cf. Ps. 23:6). "Thou shalt bring them in, and plant them in the mountain of thine inheritance, in the place, O Lord, which thou hast made for thee to dwell in. . ." (Exod. 15:17).

shākēn (שָׁכֵן), "to dwell, inhabit, settle down, abide." This word is common to many Semitic languages, including ancient Akkadian and Ugaritic, and it is found throughout all levels of Hebrew history. *Shākēn* occurs nearly 130 times in Old Testament Hebrew.

Shākēn is first used in the sense of "to dwell" in Gen. 9:27: ". . . And he shall dwell in the tents of Shem." Moses was commanded: "And let them make me a sanctuary, that I may dwell among them" (Exod. 25:8).

Shākēn is a word from nomadic life, meaning "to live in a tent." Thus, Balaam "saw Israel abiding in his tents according to their tribes" (Num. 24:2). In that verse, *shākēn* refers to temporary "camping," but it can also refer to being permanently "settled" (Ps. 102:28). God promised to give Israel security, "that they may dwell in a place of their own, and move no more . . ." (2 Sam. 7:10).

The Septuagint version of the Old Testament uses a great number of Greek words to translate *yāshab* and *shākēn*. But one word, *katoikein,* is used by far more often than any other. This word also expresses in the New Testament the "dwelling" of the Holy Spirit in the church: "That Christ may dwell in your hearts by faith" (Eph. 3:17). The Greek word *skenein* ("to live in a tent") shares in this also, being the more direct translation of *shākēn*. John 1:14 says of Jesus, "The Word was made flesh, and dwelt among us." The Book of Hebrews compares the tabernacle sacrifices of Israel in the wilderness with the sacrifice of Jesus at the true tabernacle: "Behold, the tabernacle of God is with men, and he will dwell [*skenein*] with them, and they shall be his people, and God himself shall be with them and be their God" (Rev. 21:3).

B. Noun.

mishəkān (מִשְׁכָּן), "dwelling place; tent." This word occurs nearly 140 times, and often refers to the wilderness "tabernacle" (Exod. 25:9). *Mishəkān* was also used later to refer to the "temple." This usage probably prepared the way for the familiar term *shəkînāh,* which was widely used in later Judaism to refer to the "presence" of God.

C. Participle.

yāshab (יָשַׁב), "remaining; inhabitant." This participle is sometimes used as a simple adjective: ". . . Jacob was a plain man, *dwelling* in tents" (Gen. 25:27). But the word is more often used as in Gen. 19:25: ". . . All the *inhabitants* of the cities."

E

EAR

A. Noun.

'ōzen (אֹזֶן), "ear." The noun *'ōzen* is common to Semitic languages. It appears 187 times in the Old Testament, mainly to designate a part of the body. The first occurrence is in Gen. 20:8: "Abimelech rose early in the morning, and called all his servants, and told all these things in their ears: and the men were sore afraid."

The "ear" was the place for earrings (Gen. 35:4); thus it might be pierced as a token of perpetual servitude (Exod. 21:6).

Several verbs are found in relation to "ear": "to inform" (Ezek. 24:26), "to pay attention" (Ps. 10:17), "to listen" (Ps. 78:1), "to stop up" (Isa. 33:15), "to make deaf" (Isa. 6:10), and "to tingle" (1 Sam. 3:11).

Animals are also said to have "ears" (Prov. 26:17). God is idiomatically said to have "ears": "Hide not thy face from me in the day when I am in trouble; incline thine ear unto me; . . . when I call answer me speedily" (Ps. 102:2). In this particular passage, the NEB prefers a more idiomatic rendering: "Hide not thy face from me when I am in distress. Listen to my prayer and, when I call, answer me soon." Elsewhere, the KJV reads: "And Samuel heard all the words of the people, and he rehearsed them in the ears of the Lord" (1 Sam. 8:21); here the NIV renders "in the ears of" idiomatically as "before." The Lord "pierces" (i.e., opens up) ears (Ps. 40:6), implants ears (Ps. 94:9), and fashions ears (Prov. 20:12) in order to allow man to receive direction from his Creator. As the Creator, He also is able to hear and respond to the needs of His people (Ps. 94:9). The Lord reveals His words to the "ears" of his prophets: "Now the Lord had told Samuel in his ear a day before Saul came, saying . . ." (1 Sam. 9:15). Since the Israelites had not responded to the prophetic message, they had made themselves spiritually deaf: "Hear now this, O foolish people, and without understanding; which have eyes, and see not; which have ears, and hear not" (Jer. 5:21). After the Exile, the people of God were to experience a spiritual awakening and new sensitivity to God's Word which, in the words of Isaiah, is to be compared to the opening of the "ears" (Isa. 50:5).

The KJV gives these renderings: "ear; audience; hearing."

EARTH

'erets (אֶרֶץ), "earth; land." This is one of the most common Hebrew nouns, occurring more than 2,500 times in the Old Testament. It expresses a world view contrary to ancient myths, as well as many modern theories seeking to explain the origin of the universe and the forces which sustain it.

'Erets may be translated "earth," the temporal scene of human activity, experience, and history. The material world had a beginning when God

"made the earth by His power," "formed it," and "spread it out" (Isa. 40:28; 42:5; 45:12, 18; Jer. 27:5; 51:15). Because He did so, it follows that "the earth is the Lord's" (Ps. 24:1; Deut. 10:1; Ex. 9:29; Neh. 9:6). No part of it is independent of Him, for "the very ends of the earth are His possession," including "the mountains," "the seas," "the dry land," "the depths of the earth" (Ps. 2:8; 95:4,5; Amos 4:13; Jonah 1:9).

God formed the earth to be inhabited (Isa. 45:18). Having "authority over the earth" by virture of being its Maker, He decreed to "let the earth sprout vegetation: of every kind" (Job 34:13; Gen. 1:11). It was never to stop its productivity, for "while the earth stands, seedtime and harvest, and cold and heat, and summer and winter, and day and night shall not cease" (Gen. 8:22). "The earth is full of God's riches" and mankind can "multiply and fill the earth and subdue it" (Ps. 104:24; Gen. 1:28; 9:1). Let no one think that the earth is an independent, self-contained mechanism, for "the Lord reigns" as He "sits on the vault of the earth" from where "He sends rain on the earth" (Ps. 97:1; Isa. 40:22; 1 Kings 17:14; Ps. 104:4).

As "the eyes of the Lord run to and fro throughout the earth," He sees that "there is not a just man on earth" (Eccles. 7:20). At an early stage, God endeavored to "blot out man . . . from the face of the earth" (Gen. 6:5-7). Though He relented and promised to "destroy never again all flesh on the earth," we can be sure that "He is coming to judge the earth" (Gen. 7:16 f.; Ps. 96:13). At that time, "the earth shall be completely laid waste" so that "the exalted people of the earth fade away" (Jer. 10:10; Joel 2:10; Isa. 33:3-6; Ps. 75:8). But He also provides a way of escape for all who heed His promise: "Turn to me and be saved, all the ends of the earth" (Isa. 45:22).

What the Creator formed "in the beginning" is also to have an end, for He will "create a new heaven and a new earth" (Isa. 65:17; 66:22).

The Hebrew word 'erets also occurs frequently in the phrase "heaven and earth" or "earth and heaven." In other words, the Scriptures teach that our terrestrial planet is a part of an all-embracing cosmological framework which we call the universe. Not the result of accident or innate forces, the un-fathomed reaches of space and its uncounted components owe their origin to the Lord "who made heaven and earth" (Ps. 121:2; 124:8; 134:3).

Because God is "the possessor of heaven and earth," the whole universe is to reverberate in the praise of His glory, which is "above heaven and earth" (Gen. 14:19,22; Ps. 148:13). "Shout, O heavens and rejoice, O earth": "let the heavens be glad and let the earth rejoice" (Ps. 49:13; 96:11). Such adoration is always appropriate, for "whatever the Lord pleases, He does, In heaven and in earth, in the seas and in all deeps" (Ps. 135:6, NASB).

'Erets does not only denote the entire terrestrial planet, but is also used of some of the earth's component parts. English words like land, country, ground, and soil transfer its meaning into our language. Quite frequently, it refers to an area occupied by a nation or tribe. So we read of "the land of Egypt," "the land of the Philistines," "the land of Israel," "the land of Benjamin," and so on (Gen. 47:13; Zech. 2:5; 2 Kings 5:2,4; Judg. 21:21). Israel is said to live "in the land of the Lord" (Lev. 25:33 f.; Hos. 9:13). When the people arrived at its border, Moses reminded them that it would be theirs only because the Lord drove out other nations to "give you their land for an inheritance" (Deut. 4:38). Moses promised that God would make its soil productive, for "He will give rain for your land" so that it would be "a fruitful land," "a land flowing with milk and honey, a land of wheat and barley" (Deut. 11:13-15; 8:7-9; Jer. 2:7).

The Hebrew noun may also be translated "the ground" (Job 2:13; Amos 3:5; Gen. 24:52; Ezek. 43:14). When God executes judgment, "He brings down the wicked to the ground" (Ps. 147:6, NASB).

TO EAT

A. Verb.

'ākal (אָכַל), "to eat, feed, consume, devour." This verb occurs in all Semitic languages (except Ethiopic) and in all periods, from the early Akkadian to the latest Hebrew. The word occurs about 810 times in Old Testament Hebrew and 9 times in Aramaic.

Essentially, this root refers to the "consumption of food by man or animals." In Gen. 3:6, we read that Eve took of the fruit of the tree of the knowledge of good and evil and "ate" it.

The function of eating is presented along with seeing, hearing, and smelling as one of the basic functions of living (Deut. 4:28). "Eating," as every other act of life, is under God's control; He stipulates what may or may not be eaten (Gen. 1:29). After the Flood, man was allowed to "eat" meat (Gen. 9:3). But under the Mosaic covenant, God stipulated that certain foods were not to be "eaten" (Lev. 11; Deut. 14), while others were permissible. This distinction is certainly not new, inasmuch as it is mentioned prior to the Flood (Gen. 7:2; cf. Gen. 6:19). A comparison of these two passages demonstrates how the Bible can speak in general terms, with the understanding that certain limitations are included. Hence, Noah was commanded to bring into the ark two of every kind (Gen. 6:19), while the Bible tells us that this meant two of every unclean and fourteen of every clean animal (Gen. 7:2). Thus, Gen. 9:3 implies that man could "eat" only the clean animals.

This verb is often used figuratively with overtones of destroying something or someone. So the sword, fire, and forest are said to "consume" men. The things "consumed" may include such various things as land (Gen. 3:17), fields (Isa. 1:7), offerings (Deut. 18:1), and a bride's purchase price (Gen. 31:15). 'Ākal might also connote bearing the results of an action (Isa. 3:10).

The word can refer not only to "eating" but to the entire concept "room and board" (2 Sam. 9:11, 13), the special act of "feasting" (Eccles. 10:16), or the entire activity of "earning a living" (Amos 7:12; cf. Gen. 3:19). In Dan. 3:8 and 6:24, "to eat one's pieces" is to charge someone maliciously. "To eat another's flesh," used figuratively, refers to tearing him to pieces or "killing him" (Ps. 27:2), although 'ākal may also be used literally, as when one "eats" human beings in times of serious famine (Lev. 26:29). Eccles. 4:5 uses the expression, "eat one's own flesh," for allowing oneself to waste away.

Abstinence from eating may indicate deep emotional upset, like that which overcame Hannah before the birth of Samuel (1 Sam. 1:7). It may also indicate the religious self-denial seen in fasting.

Unlike the pagan deities (Deut. 32: 37-38), God "eats" no food (Ps. 50:13); although as a "consuming" fire (Deut. 4:24), He is ready to defend His own honor and glory. He "consumes" evil and the sinner. He will also "consume" the wicked like a lion (Hos. 13:8). There is one case in which God literally "consumed" food—when He appeared to Abraham in the form of three "strangers" (Gen. 18:8).

God provides many good things to eat, such as manna to the Israelites (Exod. 16:32) and all manner of food to those who delight in the Lord (Isa. 58:14), even the finest food (Ps. 81:16). He puts the Word of God into one's mouth; by "consuming" it, it is taken into one's very being (Ezek. 3:2).

B. Nouns.

'ōkel (אֹכֶל), "food." This word occurs 44 times in the Old Testament. *'ōkel* appears twice in Gen. 41:35 with the sense of "food supply": "And let them gather all the food of those good years that come, and lay up corn under the hand of Pharaoh, and let them keep food in the cities." The word refers to the "food" of wild animals in Ps. 104:21: "The young lions roar after their prey, and seek their meat from God." *'Ōkel* is used for "food" given by God in Ps. 145:15. The word may also be used for "food" as an offering, as in Mal. 1:12. A related noun, *'ăkəlāh*, also means "food." This noun has 18 occurrences in the Old Testament.

ELDER; AGED

zāqēn (זָקֵן), "old man; old woman; elder; old." *Zāqēn* occurs 174 times in the Hebrew Old Testament as a noun or as an adjective. The first occurrence is in Gen. 18:11: "Now Abraham and Sarah were old and well stricken in age; and it ceased to be with Sarah after the manner of women." In Gen. 19:4, the word "old" is used as an antonym of "young": "But before they lay down, the men of the city, even the men of Sodom, compassed the house round, both old and young [*na'ar*, "young man"], all the people from every quarter" (cf. Josh. 6:21). A similar usage of *zāqēn* and "young" appears in other Bible references: "But [Rehoboam] forsook the counsel of the old men, which they had given him, and consulted with the young men [*yeled*, "boy; child"] that were grown up with him . . ." (1 Kings 12:8). "Then shall the virgin rejoice in the dance, both young men [*bāchûr*] and old together: for I will turn their mourning into joy, and will comfort them, and make them rejoice from their sorrow" (Jer. 31:13). The "old man" is described as being advanced in days (Gen. 18:11), as being satisfied with life or full of years. A feminine form of *zāqēn* refers to an "old woman" (*zəqēnāh*).

The word *zāqēn* has a more specialized use with the sense of "elder" (more than 100 times). The "elder" was recognized by the people for his gifts of leadership, wisdom, and justice. He was set apart to administer justice, settle disputes, and guide the people of his charge. Elders are also known as officers *(shōthərîm),* heads of the tribes, and judges; notice the parallel usage: "Joshua called for all Israel, and for their *elders,* and for their heads, and for their judges, and for their officers, and said unto them; I am old and stricken in age . . ." (Josh. 23:2). The "elders" were consulted by the king, but the king could determine his own course of action (1 Kings 12:8). In a given city, the governing council was made up of the "elders," who were charged with the well-being of the town: "And Samuel did that which the Lord spake, and came to Bethlehem. And the elders of the town trembled at his coming, and said, Comest thou peaceably?" (1 Sam. 16:4). The elders met in session by the city gate (Ezek. 8:1). The place of meeting became known as the "seat" or "council" (KJV, "assembly") of the elders (Ps. 107:32).

The Septuagint gives the following translations: *presbutera* ("man of old; elder; presbyter"), *presbutes* ("old man; aged man"), *gerousia* ("council of elders"). The KJV gives various translations of *zāqēn:* "old; elder; old man; ancient." Note that the KJV distinguishes between "elder" and "ancient"; whenever the word *zāqēn* does not apply to age or to rule, the KJV uses the word "ancient."

Zāqān means "beard." The word *zāqān* refers to a "beard" in Ps. 133:2: "It is like the precious ointment upon the head, that ran down upon the beard, even Aaron's beard: that went down to the skirts of his garments. . . ." The association of "old age" with a "beard" can be made, but should not be stressed. The verb *zāqēn* ("to be old") comes from this noun.

ENCHANTER

'ashshāph (אַשָּׁף), "enchanter." Cognates of this word appear in Akkadian, Syriac, and biblical Aramaic (6 times). The noun appears only twice in biblical Hebrew, and only in the Book of Daniel.

The vocation of *ashipu* is known from earliest times in the Akkadian (Old Babylonian) society. It is not clear whether the *ashipu* was an assistant to a particular order of Babylonian priests *(mashmashu)* or an order parallel in function to the *mashmashu* order. In either case, the *ashipu* offered incantations to deliver a person from evil magical forces (demons). The sick often underwent actual surgery while the incantations were spoken.

In the Bible, *'ashshāph* first occurs in Dan. 1:20: "And as for every matter of wisdom and understanding about which the king consulted them, he found them ten times better than all the magicians and enchanters (NASB, "conjurers") who were in his realm."

TO ENCOUNTER, BEFALL

qārā' (קָרָא), "to encounter, befall." *Qārā'* represents an intentional confrontation, whereby one person is immediately before another person. This might be a friendly confrontation, in which friend intentionally "meets" friend; so the kings of the valley came out to "meet" Abram upon his return from defeating the marauding army of Chedorlaomer (Gen. 14:17). A host may go forth to "meet" a prospective ally (Josh. 9:11; 2 Sam. 19:15). In cultic contexts, one "meets" God or "is met" by God (Exod. 5:3).

Qārā' may also be used of hostile "confrontation." In military contexts, the word often represents the "confrontation" of two forces to do battle (Josh. 8:5); so Israel is told: "Prepare to meet thy God, O Israel" (Amos 4:12). This verb infrequently may represent an "accidental meeting," so it is sometimes translated "befall" (Gen. 42:4).

END

A. Nouns.

'ephes (אֶפֶס), "end; not; nothing; only." The 42 occurrences of this word appear in every period of biblical literature. It has a cognate in Ugaritic. Basically, the noun indicates that a thing "comes to an end" and "is no more."

Some scholars suggest that this word is related to the Akkadian *apsu* (Gk. *abussos*), the chasm of fresh water at the edge of the earth (the earth was viewed as a flat surface with four corners and surrounded by fresh water). But this relationship is highly unlikely, since none of the biblical uses refers to an area beyond the edge of the earth. The idea of the "far reaches" of a thing is seen in passages such as Prov. 30:4: "Who hath gathered the wind in his fists? Who hath bound the waters in a garment? Who hath established all the ends [boundaries] of the earth?" (cf. Ps. 72:8). In other contexts, *'ephes* means the "territory" of the nations other than Israel: ". . . With them he shall push the people together to the ends of the earth . . ." (Deut. 33:17). More often, this word represents the peoples who live outside the territory of Israel: "Ask of me, and I shall give thee the heathen for thine inheritance, and the [very ends] of the earth for thy possession" (Ps. 2:8). In Ps. 22:27, the phrase, "the ends of the world," is synonymously parallel to "all the [families] of the nations." Therefore, "the ends of the earth" in such contexts represents all the peoples of the earth besides Israel.

'Ephes is used to express "non-existence" primarily in poetry, where it appears chiefly as a synonym of *'ayin* ("none, nothing"). In one instance, *'ephes* is used expressing the "non-existence"of a person or thing and is translated "not" or "no": "Is there not yet any of the house of Saul, that I may show the kindness of God unto him?" (2 Sam. 9:3). In Isa. 45:6, the word means "none" or "no one": "That they may know from the rising of the sun, and from the west, that there is none beside me" (cf. v. 9).

In a few passages, *'ephes* used as a particle of negation means "at an end" or "nothing": "And all her princes shall be nothing," or "unimportant" and "not exalted" to kingship (Isa. 34:12). The force of this word in Isa. 41:12 is on the "non-existence" of those so described: ". . . They that war against thee shall be as nothing, and as a thing of nought."

This word can also mean "nothing" in the sense of "powerlessness" and "worthlessness": "All nations before him are as nothing; and they are counted to him less than nothing, and [meaningless]" (Isa. 40:17).

In Num. 22:35, *'ephes* means "nothing other than" or "only": "Go with the men: but only the word that I shall speak unto thee, that thou shall speak" (cf. Num. 23:13). In such passages, *'ephes* (with the Hebrew particle *kî*) qualifies the preceding phrase. In 2 Sam. 12:14, a special nuance of the word is represented by the English "howbeit."

In Isa. 52:4, *'ephes* preceded by the preposition *bə* ("by; because of") means "without cause": ". . . And the Assyrian oppressed them without cause."

qēts (קֵץ), "end." A cognate of this word occurs in Ugaritic. Biblical Hebrew attests *qēts* about 66 times and in every period.

First, the word is used to denote the "end of a person" or "death": "And God said unto Noah, The end of all flesh is come before me . . ." (Gen. 6:13). In Ps. 39:4, *qēts* speaks of the "farthest extremity of human life," in the sense of how short it is: "Lord, make me to know mine end, and the measure of my days, what it is; that I may know how frail I am."

Second, *qēts* means "end" as the state of "being annihilated": "He setteth an end to darkness, and searcheth out all perfection . . ." (Job 28:3).

Third, related to the previous meaning but quite distinct, is the connotation "farthest extremity of," such as the "end of a given period of time": "And after certain years [literally, "at the end of years"] he went down to Ahab to Samaria . . ." (2 Chron. 18:2; cf. Gen. 4:3—the first biblical appearance).

A fourth nuance emphasizes a "designated goal," not simply the extremity but a conclusion toward which something proceeds: "For the vision is yet for an appointed time, but at the end it shall speak, and not lie . . ." (Hab. 2:3).

In another emphasis, *qēts* represents the "boundary" or "limit" of something: "I have seen an end of all perfection" (Ps. 119:96).

In 2 Kings 19:23, the word (with the preposition *lə*) means "farthest": ". . . And I will enter into the lodgings of his borders, and into the forest of his Carmel."

qātseh (קָצֶה), "end; border; extremity." The noun *qātseh* appears 92 times and in all periods of biblical Hebrew.

In Gen. 23:9, *qātseh* means "end" in the sense of "extremity": "That he may give me the cave of Machpelah, which he hath, which is in the end of his field. . . ." The word means "[nearest] edge or border" in Exod. 13:20: "And they took their journey from Succoth, and encamped in the Etham, in the edge of the wilderness." At other points, the word clearly indicates the "farthest extremity": "If any of thine be driven out unto the outmost parts of heaven, from thence will the Lord thy God gather thee, and from thence will he fetch thee" (Deut. 30:4).

Second, *qātseh* can signify a "temporal end," such as the "end of a period of time"; that is the use in Gen. 8:3, the first biblical occurrence of the word: ". . . After the end of the hundred and fifty days the waters were abated."

One special use of *qātseh* occurs in Gen. 47:2, where the word is used with the preposition *min* ("from"): "And from among his brothers he took five men and presented them to Pharaoh" (RSV; cf. Ezek. 33:2). In Gen. 19:4, the same construction means "from every quarter (or "part") of a city": ". . . The men of the city, even the men of Sodom, compassed the house round, both old and young, all the people from every quarter." A similar usage occurs in Gen. 47:21, except that the phrase is repeated twice and is rendered "from one end of the borders of Egypt to the other." In Jer. 51:31, the phrase means "in every quarter" or "completely."

qātsāh (קָצֶה), "end; border; edge; extremity." The noun *qātsāh* appears in the Bible 28 times and also appears in Phoenician. This word refers primarily to concrete objects. In a few instances, however, *qātsāh* is used of abstract objects; one example is of God's way (Job 26:14): "These are but the *fringe* of his power; and how faint the whisper that we hear of him!" (NEB).

'acharîth (אַחֲרִית), "hind-part; end; issue; outcome; posterity." Akkadian, Aramaic, and Ugaritic also attest this word. It occurs about 61 times in biblical Hebrew and in all periods; most of its occurrences are in poetry.

Used spatially, the word identifies the "remotest and most distant part of something": "If I take the wings of the morning, and dwell in the *uttermost* parts of the sea . . ." (Ps. 139:9).

The most frequent emphasis of the word is "end," "issue," or "outcome." This nuance is applied to time in a superlative or final sense: ". . . The eyes of the Lord thy God are always upon it, from the beginning of the year even unto the end of the year" (Deut. 11:12). A slight shift of meaning occurs in Dan. 8:23, where *'acharîth* is applied to time in a relative or comparative sense: "And in the latter time of their kingdom, when the transgressors are come to the full, a king of fierce countenance, and understanding dark sentences, shall stand up." Here the word refers to a "last period," but not necessarily the "end" of history. In a different nuance, the word can mean "latter" or "what comes afterward": "O that they were wise, that they understood this, that they would consider their latter end!" (Deut. 32:29). In some passages, *'acharîth* represents the "ultimate outcome" of a person's life. Num. 23:10 speaks thus of death: "Who can count the dust of Jacob, and the number of the fourth part of Israel? Let me die the death of the righteous, and let my last end be like his!"

In other passages, *'acharîth* refers to "all that comes afterwards." Passages such as Jer. 31:17 use the word of one's "descendants" or "posterity" (KJV, "children"). In view of the parallelism suggested in this passage, the first line should be translated "and there is hope for your posterity." In Amos 9:1, *'acharîth* is used of the "rest" (remainder) of one's fellows. Both conclusion and result are apparent in passages such as Isa. 41:22, where the word represents the "end" or "result" of a matter: "Let them bring them forth, and show us what shall happen: let them show the former things what they be, that we may consider them, and know the latter end of them; or declare us things for to come."

A third nuance of *'acharîth* indicates the "last" or the "least in importance": "Your mother shall be sore confounded; she that bare you shall be ashamed: behold, the hindermost of the nations shall be a wilderness, a dry land, and a desert" (Jer. 50:12).

The fact that *'acharîth* used with "day" or "years" may signify either "a point at the end of time" or "a period of the end time" has created considerable debate on fourteen Old Testament passages. Some scholars view this use of the word as non-eschatological—that it merely means "in the day which follows" or "in the future." This seems to be its meaning in Gen. 49:1 (its first occurrence in the Bible): "Gather yourselves together, that I may tell you that which shall befall you in the last days." Here the word refers to the entire period to follow. On the other hand, Isa. 2:2 uses the word more absolutely of the "last period of time": "In the last days, . . . the mountain of the Lord's house shall be established [as the chief of the mountains] . . . ." Some scholars believe the phrase sometimes is used of the "very end of time": "Now I am come to make thee understand what shall befall thy people in the latter days: for yet the vision is for many days" (Dan. 10:14). This point, however, is much debated.

B. Adverb.

'ephes (אֶפֶס), "howbeit; notwithstanding; however; without cause." This word's first occurrence is in Num. 13:28: "*Nevertheless* the people be strong that dwell in the land . . . ."

ENEMY

'ōyēb (אֹיֵב), "enemy." *'Ōyēb* has an Ugaritic cognate. It appears about 282 times in biblical Hebrew and in all periods. In form, the word is an active infinitive (or more precisely, a verbal noun).

This word means "enemy," and is used in at least one reference to both individuals and nations: ". . . In blessing I will bless thee, and in multiplying I will multiply thy seed as the stars of the heaven, and as the sand which is upon the sea shore; and thy seed shall possess the gate of his enemies" (Gen. 22:17—the first occurrence). "Personal foes" may be represented by this word: "If thou meet thine enemey's ox or his ass going astray, thou shalt surely bring it back to him again" (Exod. 23:4). This idea includes "those who show hostility toward me": "But mine enemies are lively, and they are strong; and they that hate me wrongfully are multiplied" (Ps. 38:19).

One might be an "enemy" of God: ". . . The Lord will take vengeance on his adversaries, and he reserveth wrath for his enemies" (Nah. 1:2). God is the "enemy" of all who refuse to submit to His lordship: "But they rebelled, and vexed his holy Spirit: therefore he was turned to be their enemy . . ." (Isa. 63:10).

tsar (צַר), "adversary; enemy; foe." This noun occurs 70 times in the Hebrew Old Testament, mainly in the Psalms (26 times) and Lamentations (9 times). The first use of the noun is in Gen. 14:20: "And blessed be the most high God, which hath delivered thine enemies into thy hand."

Tsar is a general designation for "enemy." The "enemy" may be a nation (2 Sam. 24:13) or, more rarely, the "opponent" of an individual (cf. Gen. 14:20; Ps. 3:1). The Lord may also be the "enemy" of His sinful people as His judgment comes upon them (cf. Deut. 32:41-43). Hence, the Book of Lamentations describes God as an "adversary" of His people: "He hath bent his bow like an enemy ['*ōyēb*]: he stood with his right hand as an adversary [*tsar*], and slew all that were pleasant to the eye in the tabernacle of the daughter of Zion: he poured out his fury like fire'' (Lam. 2:4).

The word *tsar* has several synonyms: *'ōyēb,* ''enemy'' (cf. Lam. 2:5); *sōneh,* ''hater'' (Ps. 44:7); *rōdēph,* ''persecutor'' (Ps. 119:157); *'ārîts,* ''tyrant; oppressor'' (Job 6:23).

In the Septuagint, *tsar* is generally translated by *echthros* (''enemy''). The KJV gives these translations: ''enemy; adversary; foe.''

EPHOD

'ēphôd (אֵפוֹד), ''ephod.'' This word, which appears in Assyrian and (perhaps) Ugaritic, occurs 49 times in the biblical Hebrew, 31 times in the legal prescriptions of Exodus—Leviticus and only once in biblical poetry (Hos. 3:4).

This word represents a close-fitting outer garment associated with worship. It was a kind of long vest, generally reaching to the thighs. The ''ephod'' of the high priest was fastened with a beautifully woven girdle (Exod. 28:27-28) and had shoulder straps set in onyx stones, on which were engraved the names of the twelve tribes. Over the chest of the high priest was the breastplate, also containing twelve stones engraved with the tribal names. Rings attached it to the ''ephod.'' The Urim and Thummin were also linked to the breastplate.

Apparently, this ''ephod'' and attachments were prominently displayed in the sanctuary. David consulted the ''ephod'' to learn whether the people of Keilah would betray him to Saul (1 Sam. 23:9-12); no doubt the Urim and Thummim were used. The first biblical occurrence of the word refers to this high priestly ephod: ''Onyx stones, and stones to be set in the ephod, and in the breastplate'' (Exod. 25:7). So venerated was this ''ephod'' that replicas were sometimes made (Judg. 8:27; 17:1-5) and even worshiped. Lesser priests (1 Sam. 2:28) and priestly trainees wore less elaborate ''ephods'' made of linen whenever they appeared before the altar.

'Aphuddāh means ''ephod; covering.'' This word is a feminine form of *'ēphôd* (or *'ēphōd*). The word occurs 3 times, first in Exod. 28:8: ''And the curious girdle of the ephod, which is upon it, shall be of . . . gold, of blue, and purple, and scarlet, and fine twined linen.''

TO ESCAPE

mālat (מָלַט), ''to escape, slip away, deliver, give birth.'' This word is found in both ancient and modern Hebrew. *Mālat* occurs approximately 95 times in the Hebrew Old Testament. The word appears twice in the first verse in which it is found: ''Flee for your life; . . . flee to the hills, lest you be consumed'' (Gen. 19:17, RSV). Sometimes *mālat* is used in parallelism with *nûs,* ''to flee'' (1 Sam. 19:10), or with *bārach,* ''to flee'' (1 Sam. 19:12).

The most common use of this word is to express the ''escaping'' from any kind of danger, such as an enemy (Isa. 20:6), a trap (2 Kings 10:24), or a temptress (Eccles. 7:26). When Josiah's reform called for burning the bones of false prophets, a special directive was issued to spare the bones of a true prophet buried at the same place: ". . . So they let his bones alone. . ." (2 Kings 23:18; literally, "they let his bones escape"). *Mālat* is used once in the sense of "delivering a child" (Isa. 66:7).

EVENING

'ereb (עֶרֶב), "evening, night." The noun *'ereb* appears about 130 times and in all periods. This word represents the time of the day immediately preceding and following the setting of the sun. During this period, the dove returned to Noah's ark (Gen. 8:11). Since it was cool, women went to the wells for water in the "evening" (Gen. 24:11). It was at "evening" that David walked around on top of his roof to refresh himself and cool off, and observed Bathsheba taking a bath (2 Sam. 11:2). In its first biblical appearance, *'ereb* marks the "opening of a day": "And the evening and the morning were the first day" (Gen. 1:5). The phrase "between the evenings" means the period between sunset and darkness, "twilight" (Exod. 12:6; KJV, "in the evening").

Second, in a late poetical use, the word can mean "night": "When I lie down, I say, When shall I arise, and the *night* be gone? And I am full of tossings to and fro unto the dawning of the day" (Job 7:4).

EVER; EVERLASTING

'ôlām (עוֹלָם), "eternity; remotest time; perpetuity." This word has cognates in Ugaritic, Moabite, Phoenician, Aramaic, Arabic, and Akkadian. It appears about 440 times in biblical Hebrew and in all periods.

First, in a few passages the word means "eternity" in the sense of not being limited to the present. Thus, in Eccles. 3:11 we read that God had bound man to time and given him the capacity to live "above time" (i.e., to remember yesterday, plan for tomorrow, and consider abstract principles); yet He has not given him divine knowledge: "He hath made every thing beautiful in his time: also he hath set the world in their heart, so that no man can find out the work that God maketh from the beginning to the end."

Second, the word signifies "remotest time" or "remote time." In 1 Chron. 16:36, God is described as blessed "from everlasting to everlasting" (KJV, "for ever and ever"), or from the most distant past time to the most distant future time. In passages where God is viewed as the One Who existed before the creation was brought into existence, *'ôlām* (or *'ōlām*) may mean: (1) "at the very beginning": "Remember the former things [the beginning things at the very beginning] of old: for I am God, and there is none else . . ." (Isa. 46:9); or (2) "from eternity, from the pre-creation, till now": "Remember, O Lord, thy tender mercies and thy loving-kindnesses; for they have been ever of old [from eternity]" (Ps. 25:6). In other passages, the word means "from (in) olden times": ". . . Mighty men which were of old, men of renown" (Gen. 6:4). In Isa. 42:14, the word is used hyperbolically meaning "for a long time": "I have long time holden my peace; I have been still, and refrained myself. . . ." This word may include all the time between the ancient beginning and the present: "The prophets that have been before me and before thee of old prophesied . . ." (Jer. 28:8). The word can mean "long ago" (from long ago): "For [long ago] I have broken thy yoke, and burst thy bands . . ." (Jer. 2:20). In Josh. 24:2, the word means "formerly; in ancient times." The word is used in Jer. 5:15, where it means "ancient": "Lo, I will bring a nation upon you from far, O house of Israel, saith the Lord: it is a mighty nation, it is an ancient nation. . . ." When used with the negative, *'ôlām* (or *'ōlām*) can mean "never": "We are thine: thou never barest rule [literally, "not ruled from the most distant past"] over them . . ." (Isa. 63:19). Similar meanings emerge when the word is used without a preposition and in a genitive relationship to some other noun.

With the preposition *'ad,* the word can mean "into the indefinite future": "An Ammonite or Moabite shall not enter into the congregation of the Lord; even to their tenth generation shall they not enter into the congregation of the Lord for ever" (Deut. 23:3). The same construction can signify "as long as one lives": "I will not go up until the child be weaned, and then I will bring him, that he may appear before the Lord, and there abide *for ever*" (1 Sam. 1:22). This construction then sets forth an extension into the indefinite future, beginning from the time of the speaker.

In the largest number of its occurrences, *'ôlām* (or *'ōlām*) appears with the preposition *lə*. This construction is weaker and less dynamic in emphasis than the previous phrase, insofar as it envisions a "simple duration." This difference emerges in 1 Kings 2:33, where both phrases occur. *Lə ôlām* is applied to the curse set upon the dead Joab and his descendants. The other, more dynamic phrase *('ad 'ôlām),* applied to David and his descendants, emphasizes the ever-continued, ever-acting presence of the blessing extended into the "indefinite future": "Their blood shall therefore return upon the head of Joab, and upon the head of his seed for ever [*lə 'ôlām*]: but upon David, and upon his seed, and upon his house, and upon his throne, shall there be peace for ever [*'ad 'ôlām*] from the Lord." In Exod. 21:6 the phrase *lə 'ôlām* means "as long as one lives": ". . . And his master shall bore his ear through with an awl; and he shall serve him for ever." This phrase emphasizes "continuity," "definiteness," and "unchangeability." This is its emphasis in Gen. 3:22, the first biblical occurrence of *'ôlām* (or *'ōlām*): ". . . And now, lest he put forth his hand, and take also of the tree of life, and eat, and live for ever. . . ."

The same emphasis on "simple duration" pertains when *'ôlām* (or *'ōlām*) is used in passages such as Ps. 61:8, where it appears by itself: "So will I sing praise unto thy name for ever, that I may daily perform my vows." The parallelism demonstrates that *'ôlām* (or *'ōlām*) means "day by day," or "continually." In Gen. 9:16, the word (used absolutely) means the "most distant future": "And the bow shall be in the cloud; and I will look upon it, that I may remember the everlasting covenant between God and every living creature. . . ." In other places, the word means "without beginning, without end, and ever-continuing": "Trust ye in the Lord for ever: for in the Lord Jehovah is everlasting strength" (Isa. 26:4).

The plural of this word is an intensive form.

TO BE EXALTED

A. Verb.

rûm (רוּם), "to be high, exalted." This root also appears in Ugaritic (with the radicals *r-m*), Phoenician, Aramaic (including biblical Aramaic, 4 times), Arabic, and Ethiopic. In extra-biblical Aramaic, it appears as *r'm*. The word occurs in all periods of biblical Hebrew and about 190 times. Closely related is the rather rare (4 times) *rmm,* "to rise, go away from."

Basically, *rûm* represents either the "state of being on a higher plane" or "movement in an upward direction." The former meaning appears in the first biblical occurrence of the word: "And the flood was forty days upon the earth; and the waters increased, and bare up the ark, and it was lifted [rose] up above the earth" (Gen. 7:17). Used of men, this verb may refer to their "physical stature"; For example, the spies sent into Canaan reported that "the people is greater and taller than we; the cities are great and walled up to heaven . . ." (Deut. 1:28).

The second emphasis, representing what is done to the subject or what it does to itself, appears in Ps. 12:8: "The wicked walk on every side, when the vilest men are exalted." The psalmist confesses that the Lord will "set me up upon a rock" so as to be out of all danger (Ps. 27:5). A stormy wind (Ps. 107:25) "lifts up" the waves of the sea. *Rûm* is used of the building of an edifice. Ezra confessed that God had renewed the people of Israel, allowing them "to set up the house of our God, and to repair the desolations thereof, and to give us a wall in Judah and Jerusalem" (Ezra 9:9; cf. Gen. 31:45). In Ezek. 31:4, this verb is used of "making a plant grow larger": "The waters made him [the cedar in Lebanon] great, the deep set him up on high. . . ." Since in Deut. 1:28 *gādal* ("larger") and *rûm* ("taller") are used in close connection, Ezek. 31:4 could be translated: "The waters made it grow bigger, the deep made it grow taller." Closely related to this nuance is the use of *rûm* to represent the process of child-rearing. God says through Isaiah: ". . . I have nourished [*gādal*] and brought up children, and they have rebelled against me" (Isa. 1:2).

Rûm sometimes means "to take up away from," as in Isa. 57:14: "Cast ye up, cast ye up, prepare the way, take up the stumbling block out of the way of my people." When used in reference to offerings, the word signifies the "removal of a certain portion" (Lev. 2:9). The presentation of the entire offering is also referred to as an "offering up" (Num. 15:19).

In extended applications, *rûm* has both negative and positive uses. Positively, this word can signify "to bring to a position of honor." So God says: "Behold, my servant shall deal prudently, he shall be exalted and extolled, and be very high" (Isa. 52:13). This same meaning occurs in 1 Sam. 2:7, where Hannah confessed: "The Lord maketh poor, and maketh rich: he bringeth low, and lifteth up." Used in a negative sense, *rûm* means "to be haughty": "And the afflicted people thou wilt save: but thine eyes are upon the haughty, that thou mayest bring them down" (2 Sam. 22:28).

Rûm is often used with other words in special senses. For example, to lift one's voice is "to cry aloud." Potiphar's wife reported that when Joseph attacked her, she "raised" her voice screaming. These two words (*rûm* and "voice") are used together to mean "with a loud voice" (Deut. 27:14).

The raising of the hand serves as a symbol of power and strength and signifies being "mighty" or "triumphant": "Were it not that I feared the wrath of the enemy, lest their adversaries should behave themselves strangely, and lest they should say, Our hand is high [literally, "is raised"] . . ." (Deut. 32:27). To raise one's hand against someone is to rebel against him. Thus, "Jeroboam . . . lifted up his hand against the king" (1 Kings 11:26).

The raising of one's horn suggests the picture of a wild ox standing in all its strength. This is a picture of "triumph" over one's enemies: "My heart rejoiceth in the Lord, mine horn is exalted in the Lord; my mouth is enlarged over mine enemies . . ." (1 Sam. 2:1). Moreover, horns symbolized the focus of one's power. Thus, when one's horn is "exalted," one's power is exalted. When one exalts another's horn, he gives him "strength": ". . . He [the Lord] shall give strength unto his king, and exalt the horn of his anointed" (1 Sam. 2:10).

Raising one's head may be a public gesture of "triumph and supremacy," as in Ps. 110:7, where it is said that after defeating all His enemies the Lord will "lift up the head." This nuance is sometimes used transitively, as when someone else lifts a person's head. Some scholars suggest that in such cases the verb signifies the action of a judge who has pronounced an accused person innocent by raising the accused's head. This phrase also came to signify "to mark with distinction," "to give honor to," or "to place in a position of strength": "But thou, O Lord, art a shield for me; my glory, and the lifter up of mine head" (Ps. 3:3).

To raise one's eyes or heart is to be "proud" and "arrogant": "Then thine heart be lifted up, and thou forget the Lord thy God, which brought thee forth out of the land of Egypt" (Deut. 8:14).

B. Nouns.

rûm (רוּם), "height; haughtiness." This word occurs 6 times, and it means "height" in Prov. 25:3. *Rûm* signifies "haughtiness" in Isa. 2:11.

mārôm (מָרוֹם), "higher plane; height; high social position." *Mārôm* appears about 54 times in biblical Hebrew. It also is attested in Ugaritic and Old South Arabic. In its first biblical occurrence (Judg. 5:18), *mārôm* means "a higher plane on the surface of the earth." Job 16:19 and Isa. 33:5 contain the word with the meaning of "the height" as the abode of God. Job 5:11 uses the word to refer to "a high social position." *Mārôm* can also signify "self-exaltation" (2 Kings 19:22; Ps. 73:8).

EXCEEDINGLY

A. Adverb.

mə'ōd (מְאֹד), "exceedingly; very; greatly; highly." This word occurs about 300 times and in all periods of biblical Hebrew. A verb with a similar basic semantic range appears in Akkadian, Ugaritic, and Arabic.

Mə'ōd functions adverbially, meaning "very." The more superlative emphasis appears in Gen. 7:18, where the word is applied to the "amount (quantity)" of a thing: "And the waters prevailed, and were increased greatly upon the earth. . . ." In Ps. 47:9, *mə'ōd* is used of "magnifying" and "exaltation": ". . . For the shields of the earth belong unto God; he is greatly exalted." The doubling of the word is a means of emphasizing its basic meaning, which is "very much": "And the waters prevailed exceedingly (NASB, "more and more") upon the earth . . ." (Gen. 7:19).

B. Noun.

mə'ōd (מְאֹד), "might." This word is used substantively in the sequence "heart . . . soul . . . might": "And thou shalt love the Lord thy God with all thine heart, and with all thy soul, and with all thy might" (Deut. 6:5).

EYE

'ayin (עַיִן), "eye; well; surface; appearance; spring." *'Ayin* has cognates in Ugaritic, Akkadian, Aramaic, and other Semitic languages. It occurs about 866 times and in all periods of biblical Hebrew (5 times in biblical Aramaic).

First, the word represents the bodily part, "eye." In Gen. 13:10, *'ayin* is used of the "human eye": "And Lot lifted up his eyes, and beheld all the plain of Jordan. . . ." It is also used of the "eyes" of animals (Gen. 30:41), idols (Ps. 115:5), and God (Deut. 11:12—anthropomorphism). The expression "between the eyes" means "on the forehead": "And it shall be for a sign unto thee upon thine hand, and for a memorial between thine eyes, that the Lord's law may be in thy mouth . . ." (Exod. 13:9). "Eyes" are used as typical of one's "weakness" or "hurt": "And it came to pass, that when Isaac was old, and his eyes were dim, so that he could not see, he called Esau his eldest son, and said . . ." (Gen. 27:1). The "apple of the eye" is the central component, the iris: "Keep me as the apple of the eye" (Ps. 17:8). "Eyes" might be a special feature of "beauty": "Now he was ruddy, and withal [fair of eyes], and goodly to look to" (1 Sam. 16:12).

'Ayin is often used in connection with expressions of "seeing": "And, behold, your eyes see, and the eyes of my brother Benjamin, that it is my mouth that speaketh unto you" (Gen. 45:12). The expression "to lift up one's eyes" is explained by a verb following it: one lifts up his eyes to do something—whatever the verb stipulates (cf. Gen. 13:10). "Lifting up one's eyes" may also be an act expressing "desire," "longing," "devotion": "And it came to pass after these things, that his master's wife [looked with desire at] Joseph . . ." (Gen. 39:7). The "eyes" may be used in gaining or seeking a judgment, in the sense of "seeing intellectually," "making an evaluation," or "seeking an evaluation or proof of faithfulness": "And thou saidst unto thy servants, Bring him down unto me, that I may set mine eyes upon him" (Gen. 44:21).

"Eyes" sometimes show mental qualities, such as regret: "Also regard not [literally, "do not let your eye look with regret upon"] your stuff; for the good of all the land of Egypt is yours" (Gen. 45:20).

"Eyes" are used figuratively of mental and spiritual abilities, acts and states. So the "opening of the eyes" in Gen. 3:5 (the first occurrence) means to become autonomous by setting standards of good and evil for oneself. In passages such as Prov. 4:25, "eye" represents a moral faculty: "Let thine eyes look right on, and let thine eyelids look straight before thee." Prov. 23:6 uses the word of a moral state (literally, "evil eye"): "Eat thou not the bread of [a selfish man], neither desire thou his dainty meats." An individual may serve as a guide, or one's "eyes": "And he said, Leave us not, I pray thee; forasmuch as thou knowest how we are to encamp in the wilderness, and thou mayest be to us instead of eyes" (Num. 10:31).

The phrase, "in the eye of," means "in one's view or opinion": "And he went in unto Hagar, and she conceived: and when she saw that she had conceived, her mistress was despised in her eyes" (Gen. 16:4).

Another phrase, "from the eyes of," may signify that a thing or matter is "hidden" from one's knowledge: "And a man lie with her carnally, and it be hid from the eyes of her husband, and [she be undetected] . . ." (Num. 5:13).

In Exod. 10:5, the word represents the "visible surface of the earth": "And they shall cover the face of the earth, that one cannot be able to see the earth. . . ." Lev. 13:5 uses *'ayin* to represent "one's appearance": "And the priest shall look on him the seventh day: and behold, if the plague in his sight be at a stay [NASB, "if in his eyes the infection has not changed"] . . . ." A "gleam or sparkle" is described in the phrase, "to give its eyes," in passages such as Prov. 23:31: "Look not thou upon the wine when it is red, when it giveth his color [gives its eyes] in the cup. . . ."

'Ayin also represents a "spring" (literally, an "eye of the water"): "And the angel of the Lord found her by a spring [KJV, "fountain"] of water in the wilderness, by the spring [KJV, "fountain"] on the way to Shur" (Gen. 16:7).

ma'ăyān (מַעְיָן), "spring." This word appears 23 times in the Old Testament. In Lev. 11:36, *ma'ăyān* means "spring": "Nevertheless a fountain or pit, wherein there is plenty of water, shall be clean: but that which toucheth their carcase shall be unclean." Another example is found in Gen. 7:11: "In the six hundredth year of Noah's life, in the second month, . . . the same day were all the fountains of the great deep broken up, and the windows of heaven were opened."

F

FACE

pānîm (פָּנִים), "face." This noun appears in biblical Hebrew about 2,100 times and in all periods, except when it occurs with the names of persons and places, it always appears in the plural. It is also attested in Ugaritic, Akkadian, Phoenician, Moabite, and Ethiopic.

In its most basic meaning, this noun refers to the "face" of something. First, it refers to the "face" of a human being: "And Abram fell on his face: and God talked with him . . ." (Gen. 17:3). In a more specific application, the word represents the look on one's face, or one's "countenance": "And Cain was very [angry], and his countenance fell" (Gen. 4:5). To pay something to someone's "face" is to pay it to him personally (Deut. 7:10); in such contexts, the word connotes the person himself. *Pānîm* can also be used of the surface or visible side of a thing, as in Gen. 1:2: "The Spirit of God moved upon the *face* of the waters." In other contexts, the word represents the "front side" of something: "And thou shalt couple five curtains by themselves, and six curtains by themselves, and shalt double the sixth curtain in the forefront of the tabernacle" (Exod. 26:9). When applied to time, the word (preceded by the preposition *lə*) means "formerly": "The Horim also dwelt in Seir [formerly] . . ." (Deut. 2:12).

This noun is sometimes used anthropomorphically of God; the Bible speaks of God as though He had a "face": ". . . For therefore I have seen thy face, as though I had seen the face of God" (Gen. 33:10). The Bible clearly teaches that God is a spiritual being and ought not to be depicted by an image or any likeness whatever (Exod. 20:4). Therefore, there was no image or likeness of God in the innermost sanctuary—only the ark of the covenant was there, and God spoke from above it (Exod. 25:22). The word *pānîm*, then, is used to identify the bread that was kept in the holy place. The KJV translates it as "the showbread," while the NASB renders "the bread of the Presence" (Num. 4:7). This bread was always kept in the presence of God.

FAITHFULNESS

A. Noun.

'emûnāh (אֱמוּנָה), "faithfulness." This word occurs in Punic as *emanethi* ("certainty"). In the Hebrew Old Testament, the noun occurs 49 times, mainly in the Book of Psalms (22 times). The first occurrence of the word refers to Moses' hands: "But Moses' hands were heavy; and they took a stone, and put it under him, and he sat thereon; and Aaron and Hur stayed up his hands, the one on the one side, and the other on the other side; and his hands were *steady* until the going down of the sun" (Exod. 17:12).

The basic meaning of *'emûnāh* is "certainty" and "faithfulness." Man may show himself "faithful" in his relations with his fellow men (1 Sam. 26:23).

But generally, the Person to whom one is "faithful" is the Lord Himself: "And he charged them, saying, Thus shall ye do in the fear of the Lord, faithfully, and with a perfect heart" (2 Chron. 19:9). The Lord has manifested His "faithfulness" to His people: "He is the Rock, his work is perfect: for all his ways are judgment: a God of truth and without iniquity, just and right is he" (Deut. 32:4). All his works reveal his "faithfulness" (Ps. 33:4). His commandments are an expression of his "faithfulness" (Ps. 119:86); those who seek them are found on the road of "faithfulness": "I have chosen the way of *truth:* thy judgments have I laid before me" (Ps. 119:30). The Lord looks for those who seek to do His will with all their hearts. Their ways are established and His blessing rests on them: "A faithful man shall abound with blessings: but he that maketh haste to be rich shall not be innocent" (Prov. 28:20). The assurance of the abundance of life is in the expression quoted in the New Testament (Rom. 1:17; Gal. 3:11) from Hab. 2:4: "Behold, his soul which is lifted up is not upright in him: but the just shall live by his faith."

The word *'emûnāh* is synonymous with *tsedeq* ("righteousness"—cf. Isa. 11:5), with *chesed* ("lovingkindness"—cf. Ps. 98:3, NASB), and with *mishəpāt* ("justice"—cf. Jer. 5:1).

The relationship between God and Israel is best described by the word *chesed* ("love"); but as a synonym, *'emûnāh* fits very well. Hosea portrays God's relation to Israel as a marriage and states God's promise of "faithfulness" to Israel: "And I will betroth thee unto me for ever; yea, I will betroth thee unto me in righteousness, and in judgment, and in loving-kindness, and in mercies. I will even betroth thee unto me in *faithfulness:* and thou shalt [acknowledge] the Lord" (Hos. 2:19-20). In these verses, the words "righteousness," "judgment" ("justice"), "loving-kindness," "mercies," and "faithfulness" bear out the conclusion that the synonyms for *'emûnāh* are covenantal terms expressive of God's "faithfulness" and "love." The assurance of the covenant and the promises is established by God's nature; He is "faithful."

Man's acts (Prov. 12:22) and speech (12:17) must reflect his favored status with God. As in the marriage relationship, "faithfulness" is not optional. For the relation to be established, the two parties are required to respond to each other in "faithfulness." Isaiah and Jeremiah condemn the people for not being "faithful" to God: "Run ye to and fro through the streets of Jerusalem, and see now, and know, and seek in the broad places thereof, if ye can find a man, if there be any that executeth judgment, that seeketh the *truth;* and I will pardon [this city]" (Jer. 5:1; cf. Isa. 59:4; Jer. 7:28; 9:3).

Faithfulness will be established in the messianic era (Isa. 11:5). The prophetic expectation was fulfilled in Jesus Christ, as his contemporaries witnessed in Him God's grace (cf. *chesed*) and truth (cf. *'emûnāh*): "No man hath seen God at any time; the only begotten Son, which is in the bosom of the Father, he hath declared him" (John 1:18). It is significant that John puts these two terms side by side, even as they are found together in the Old Testament.

The Septuagint translations are: *aletheia* ("truthfulness; dependability; uprightness; truth; reality") and *pistos* ("trustworthy; faithfulness; reliability; rest; confidence; faith"). The KJV gives these translations: "faithfulness; truth; set office; faithfully; faithful."

B. Verb.

'āman (אָמַן), to be certain, enduring; to trust, believe." This root is found in Akkadian, Ugaritic, and Phoenician. In the Old Testament, the word occurs fewer than 100 times.

Three words are derived from this verb: *'āmēn* ("amen"—30 times; e.g., Ps. 106:48), *'emeth* ("true"—127 times; e.g., Isa. 38:18), and *'emûnāh* ("faithfulness").

FALSEHOOD

sheqer (שֶׁקֶר), "falsehood; lie." The presence of this root is limited to Hebrew and Old Aramaic. The word *sheqer* occurs 113 times in the Old Testament. It is rare in all but the poetic and prophetic books, and even in these books its usage is concentrated in Psalms (24 times), Proverbs (20 times), and Jeremiah (37 times). The first occurrence is in Exod. 5:9: "Let there more work be laid upon the men, that they may labor therein: and let them not regard vain words [lies]."

In about thirty-five passages, *sheqer* describes the nature of "deceptive speech": "to speak" (Isa. 59:3), "to teach" (Isa. 9:15), "to prophesy" (Jer. 14:14), and "to lie" (Mic. 2:11). It may also indicate a "deceptive character," as expressed in one's acts: "to deal treacherously" (2 Sam. 18:13) and "to deal falsely" (Hos. 7:1).

Thus *sheqer* defines a way of life that goes contrary to the law of God. The psalmist, desirous of following God, prayed: "Remove from me the way of lying: and grant me thy law graciously. I have chosen the way of truth: thy judgments have I laid before me" (Ps. 119:29-30; cf. vv. 104, 118, 128). Here we see the opposites: "falsehood" and "faithfulness." As "faithfulness" is a relational term, "falsehood" denotes "one's inability to keep faith" with what one has said or to respond positively to the faithfulness of another being.

The Old Testament saint was instructed to avoid "deception" and the liar: "Keep thee far from a false matter; and the innocent and righteous slay thou not: for I will not justify the wicked" (Exod. 23:7; cf. Prov. 13:5).

The Septuagint has these translations: *adikos/adikia* ("unjust; unrighteous; wrongdoing; wickedness") and *pseudes* ("falsehood; lie"). The KJV gives these meanings: "lie; falsehood; false; falsely."

FAMILY

mishəpāchāh (מִשְׁפָּחָה), "family; clan." A form of this Hebrew word occurs in Ugaritic and Punic, also with the meaning of "family" or "clan." The word is found in the Dead Sea Scrolls, as well as in Mishnaic and modern Hebrew. *Mishəpāchāh* occurs 300 times in the Hebrew Old Testament. The word is first used in Gen. 8:19: "Every beast, every creeping thing, and every fowl, and whatsoever creepeth upon the earth, after their *kinds,* went forth out of the ark."

The word is related to the verbal root *shipəchāh,* but the verbal form is absent from the Old Testament. Another noun form is *phəchah* ("maidservant"), as in Gen. 16:2: "And Sarai said unto Abram . . . I pray thee, go in unto my maid. . . ."

The noun *mishəpāchāh* is used predominantly in the Pentateuch (as many as 154 times in Numbers) and in the historical books, but rarely in the poetical literature (5 times) and the prophetical writings.

All members of a group who were related by blood and who still felt a sense of consanguinity belonged to the "clan" or "the extended family." Saul argued that since he belonged to the least of the "clans," he had no right to the kingship (1 Sam. 9:21). This meaning determined the extent of Rahab's family that was spared from Jericho: ". . . And they brought out all her *kindred,* and left them without the camp of Israel" (Josh. 6:23). So the "clan" was an important division within the "tribe." The Book of Numbers gives a census of the leaders and the numbers of the tribes according to the "families" (Num. 1–4; 26). In capital cases, where revenge was desired, the entire clan might be taken: "And, behold, the whole family is risen against thine handmaid, and they said, Deliver him that smote his brother, that we may kill him, for the life of his brother whom he slew; and we will destroy the heir also: and so they shall quench my coal which is left, and shall not leave to my husband neither name nor remainder upon the earth" (2 Sam. 14:7).

A further extension of the meaning "division" or "clan" is the idiomatic usage of "class" or "group," such as "the families" of the animals that left the ark (Gen. 8:19) or the "families" of the nations (Ps. 22:28; 96:7; cf. Gen. 10:5). Even God's promise to Abraham had reference to all the nations: "And I will bless them that bless thee, and curse him that curseth thee: and in thee shall all families of the earth be blessed" (Gen. 12:3).

The narrow meaning of *mishəpāchāh* is similar to our usage of "family" and similar to the meaning of the word in modern Hebrew. Abraham sent his servant to his relatives in Padan-aram to seek a wife for Isaac (Gen. 24:38). The law of redemption applied to the "close relatives in a family": "After that he is sold he may be redeemed again; one of his brethren may redeem him: Either his uncle, or his uncle's son, may redeem him, or any that is nigh of kin unto him of his family may redeem him; or if he be able, he may redeem himself" (Lev. 25:48-49).

In the Septuagint, several words are given as a translation: *demos* ("people; populace; crowd"), *phule* ("tribe; nation; people"), and *patria* ("family; clan"). The KJV translates *mishəpāchāh* with "family; kindred; kind." Most versions keep the translation "family"; but instead of "kindred" and "kind," some read "relative" (NASB) or "clan."

FAMINE

A. Noun.

rā'āb (רָעָב), "famine; hunger." This word appears about 101 times and in all periods of biblical Hebrew. *Rā'āb* means "hunger" as opposed to "thirst": "Therefore shalt thou serve thine enemies which the Lord shall send against thee, in hunger, and in thirst, and in nakedness, and in want of all things . . ." (Deut. 28:48).

Another meaning of the word is "famine," or the lack of food in an entire geographical area: "And there was a famine in the land: and Abram went down into Egypt . . ." (Gen. 12:10—the first occurrence). God used a "famine" as a means of judgment (Jer. 5:12), of warning (1 Kings 17:1), of correction (2 Sam. 21:1), or of punishment (Jer. 14:12), and the "famine" was always under divine control, being planned and used by Him. *Rā'āb* was also used to picture the "lack of God's word" (Amos 8:11; cf. Deut. 8:3).

B. Verb.

rā'ēb (רָעֵב), "to be hungry, suffer famine." This verb, which appears in the Old Testament 14 times, has cognates in Ugaritic *(rgb)*, Arabic, and Ethiopic. The first biblical occurrence is in Gen. 41:55: "And when all the land of Egypt was famished. . . ."

C. Adjective.

rā'ēb (רָעֵב), "hungry." This word appears as an adjective 19 times. The first biblical occurrence is in 1 Sam. 2:5: ". . . And they that were hungry ceased: . . ."

FAR

rāchaq (רָחַק), "far." A common Semitic term, this word was known in ancient Akkadian and Ugaritic long before the Hebrew of the Old Testament. *Rāchaq* is a common word in modern Hebrew as well. The word is used about 55 times in the Hebrew Old Testament and it occurs for the first time in Gen. 21:16.

Rāchaq is used to express "distance" of various types. It may be "distance" from a place (Deut. 12:21), as when Job felt that his friends kept themselves "aloof" from him (Job 30:10). Sometimes the word expresses "absence" altogether: ". . . The comforter that should relieve my soul is far from me . . ." (Lam. 1:16). "To be distant" was also "to abstain": "Keep thee far from a false matter" (Exod. 23:7).

Sometimes *rāchaq* implies the idea of "exile": ". . . The Lord [removes] men far away" (Isa. 6:12). "To make the ends of the land distant" is "to extend the boundaries": ". . . thou hast increased the [borders of the land]" (Isa. 26:15).

FATHER

'āb (אָב), "father; grandfather; forefather; ancestor." Cognates of this word occur in Ugaritic, Akkadian, Phoenician, and other Semitic languages. Biblical Hebrew attests it about 1,120 times and in all periods.

Basically, *'āb* relates to the familial relationship represented by the word "father." This is the word's significance in its first biblical appearance: "Therefore shall a man leave his father and his mother, and shall cleave unto his wife . . ." (Gen. 2:24). In poetical passages, the word is sometimes paralleled to *'ēm*, "mother": "I have said to corruption, Thou art my father: to the worm, Thou art my mother, and my sister" (Job 17:14). The word is also used in conjunction with "mother" to represent one's parents (Lev. 19:3). But unlike the word *'ēm*, *'āb* is never used of animals.

'Āb also means "grandfather" and/or "great-grandfather," as in Gen. 28:13: "I am the Lord God of Abraham thy [grand]father, and the God of Isaac. . . ." Such progenitors on one's mother's side were called "thy mother's father" (Gen. 28:2). This noun may be used of any one of the entire line of men from whom a given individual is descended: "But he [Elijah] himself went a day's journey into the wilderness, and came and sat down under a juniper tree: and he requested for himself that he might die; and said, It is enough; now, O Lord, take away my life; for I am not better than my fathers" (1 Kings 19:4). In such use, the word may refer to the first man, a "forefather," a clan (Jer. 35:6), a tribe (Josh. 19:47), a group with a special calling (1 Chron. 24:19), a dynasty (1 Kings 15:3), or a nation (Josh. 24:3). Thus, "father" does not necessarily mean the man who directly sired a given individual.

This noun sometimes describes the adoptive relationship, especially when it is used of the "founder of a class or station," such as a trade: "And Adah bare Jabal: he was the *father* of such as dwell in tents, and of such as have cattle" (Gen. 4:20).

'Āb can be a title of respect, usually applied to an older person, as when David said to Saul: "Moreover, my father, see, yea, see the skirt of thy robe in my hand . . ." (1 Sam. 24:11). The word is also applied to teachers: "And Elisha saw it, and he cried, My father, my father, the chariot of Israel, and the horsemen thereof . . ." (2 Kings 2:12). In 2 Kings 6:21, the word is applied to the prophet Elisha and in Judg. 17:10, to a priest; this word is also a title of respect when used of "one's husband": "Wilt thou not from this time cry unto me, My father, thou art the guide of my youth?" (Jer. 3:4). In Gen. 45:8, the noun is used of an "advisor": "So now it was not you that sent me hither, but God: and he hath made me a father [advisor] to Pharaoh, and lord of all his house, and a ruler throughout all the land of Egypt." In each case, the one described as "father" occupied a position or status and received the honor due to a "father."

In conjunction with *bayith* ("house"), the word *'āb* may mean "family": "In the tenth day of this month they shall take to them every man a lamb, according to the house of their fathers . . ." (Exod. 12:3). Sometimes the plural of the word used by itself can represent "family": ". . . These are the heads of the fathers [households] of the Levites according to their families'' (Exod. 6:25).

God is described as the "father" of Israel (Deut. 32:6). He is the One who begot and protected them, the One they should revere and obey. Mal. 2:10 tells us that God is the "father" of all people. He is especially the "protector" or "father" of the fatherless: "A father of the fatherless, and a judge of the widows, is God in his holy habitation" (Ps. 68:5). As the "father" of a king, God especially aligns Himself to that man and his kingdom: "I will be his father, and he shall be my son. If he commit iniquity, I will chasten him with the rod of men, and with the stripes of the children of men" (2 Sam. 7:14). Not every king was a son of God—only those whom He adopted. In a special sense, the perfect King was God's adopted Son: "I will declare the decree: the Lord hath said unto me, Thou art my Son; this day have I begotten thee" (Ps. 2:7). The extent, power, and duration of His kingdom are guaranteed by the Father's sovereignty (cf. Ps.2:8-9). On the other hand, one of the Messiah's enthronement names is "Eternal Father": ". . . And his name shall be called Wonderful, Counselor, The mighty God, The everlasting Father, The Prince of Peace" (Isa. 9:6).

FAVOR

A. Noun.

rātsôn (רָצוֹן), "favor; goodwill; acceptance; will; desire; pleasure." The 56 occurrences of this word are scattered throughout Old Testament literature.

Rātsôn represents a concrete reaction of the superior to an inferior. When used of God, *rātsôn* may represent that which is shown in His blessings: "And for the precious things of the earth and fulness thereof, and for the *good will* of him that dwelt in the bush" (Deut. 33: 16). Thus Isaiah speaks of the day, year, or time of divine "favor"—in other words, the day of the Lord when all the blessings of the covenant shall be heaped upon God's people (Isa. 49:8; 58:5; 61:2). In wisdom literature, this word is used in the sense of "what men can bestow": "He that diligently seeketh good procureth favor: but he that seeketh mischief, it shall come unto him" (Prov. 11:27). In Prov. 14:35, *rātsôn* refers to what a king can or will do for someone he likes.

This word represents the position one enjoys before a superior who is favorably disposed toward him. This nuance is used only of God and frequently in a cultic context: ". . . And it [the plate engraved with "holy to the Lord"] shall be always upon his [the high priest's] forehead, that they may be accepted before the Lord" (Exod. 28:38). Being "accepted" means that God subjectively feels well disposed toward the petitioner.

Rātsôn also signifies a voluntary or arbitrary decision. Ezra told the people of Israel to do the "will" of God, to repent and observe the law of Moses (Ezra 10:11). This law was dictated by God's own nature; His nature led Him to be concerned for the physical well-being of His people. Ultimately, His laws were highly personal; they were simply what God wanted His people to be and do. Thus the psalmist confessed his delight in doing God's "will," or His law (Ps. 40:8).

When a man does according to his own "will," he does "what he desires": "I saw the ram pushing westward, and northward, and southward; so that no beasts might stand before him, neither was there any that could deliver out of his hand; but he did according to his will, and became great" (Dan. 8:4). In Ps. 145:16, the word *rātsôn* means "one's desire" or "what one wants" (cf. Esther 1:8). This emphasis is found in Gen. 49:6 (the first occurrence): ". . . And in their self-will they [brought disaster upon themselves]."

B. Verb.

rātsāh (רָצָה), "to be pleased with or favorable to, be delighted with, be pleased to, make friends with; be graciously received; make oneself favored." This verb, which occurs 50 times in the Old Testament, has cognates in Ugaritic, Aramaic, Syriac, and Arabic. Gen. 33:10 contains one appearance of this word: ". . . thou wast pleased with me."

TO FEAR

A. Verb.

yārē' (יָרֵא), "to be afraid, stand in awe, fear." This verb occurs in Ugaritic and Hebrew (both biblical and post-biblical). The Bible attests it approximately 330 times and in all periods.

Basically, this verb connotes the psychological reaction of "fear." *Yārē'* may indicate being afraid of something or someone. Jacob prayed: "Deliver me, I pray thee, from the hand of my brother, from the hand of Esau: for I fear him, lest he will come and smite me, and the mother with the children" (Gen. 32:11).

Used of a person in an exalted position, *yārē'* connotes "standing in awe." This is not simple fear, but reverence, whereby an individual recognizes the power and position of the individual revered and renders him proper respect. In this sense, the word may imply submission to a proper ethical relationship to God; the angel of the Lord told Abraham: ". . . I know that thou fearest God, seeing thou hast not withheld thy son, thine only son from me" (Gen. 22:12). The verb can be used absolutely to refer to the heavenly and holy attributes of something or someone. So Jacob said of Bethel: "How [awesome] is this place! this is none other but the house of God, and this is the gate of heaven" (Gen. 28:17). The people who were delivered from Egypt saw God's great power, "feared the Lord, and believed the Lord, and his servant Moses" (Exod. 14:31). There is more involved here than mere psychological fear. The people also showed proper "honor" ("reverence") for God and "stood in awe of" Him and of His servant, as their song demonstrates (Exod. 15). After experiencing the thunder, lightning flashes, sound of the trumpet, and smoking mountain, they were "afraid" and drew back; but Moses told them not to be afraid, "for God is come to prove you, and that his fear may be before your faces, that ye sin not" (Exod. 20:20). In this passage, the word represents "fear" or "dread" of the Lord. This sense is also found when God says, "fear not" (Gen. 15:1).

Yārē' can be used absolutely (with no direct object), meaning "to be afraid." Adam told God: ". . . I was afraid, because I was naked; and I hid myself" (Gen. 3:10—the first occurrence). One may be "afraid" to do something, as when Lot "feared to dwell in Zoar" (Gen. 19:30).

B. Nouns.

môrā' (מוֹרָא), "fear." The noun *môrā'*, which appears 12 times, is used exclusively of the fear of being before a superior kind of being. Usually it is used to describe the reaction evoked in men by God's mighty works of destruction and sovereignty (Deut. 4:24). Hence, the word represents a very strong "fear" or "terror." In the singular, this word emphasizes the divine acts themselves. *Môrā'* may suggest the reaction of animals to men (Gen. 9:2) and of the nations to conquering Israel (Deut. 11:25).

yirə'āh (יִרְאָה), "fear; reverence." The noun *yirə'āh* appears 45 times in the Old Testament. It may mean "fear" of men (Deut. 2:25), of things (Isa. 7:25), of situations (Jonah 1:10), and of God (Jonah 1:12); it may also mean "reverence" of God (Gen. 20:11).

FEAST

chag (חַג), "feast; festal sacrifice." Cognates of this noun appear in Aramaic, Syriac, and Arabic. Biblical Hebrew attests it about 62 times and in all periods, except in the wisdom literature.

This word refers especially to a "feast observed by a pilgrimage." That is its meaning in its first biblical occurrence, when Moses said to Pharaoh: "We will go with our young and with our old, with our sons and with our daughters, with our flocks and with our herds will we go; for we must hold a feast unto the Lord" (Exod. 10:9). *Chag* (or *chāg*) usually represents Israel's three annual "pilgrimage feasts," which were celebrated with processions and dances. These special feasts are distinguished from the sacred seasons ("festal assemblies"—Ezek. 45:17), the new moon festivals, and the Sabbaths (Hos. 2:11).

There are two unique uses of *chag*. First, Aaron proclaimed a "feast to the Lord" at the foot of Mt. Sinai. This "feast" involved no pilgrimage but was celebrated with burnt offerings, communal meals, singing, and dancing. The whole matter was displeasing to God (Exod. 32:5-7).

In two passages, *chag* represents the "victim sacrificed to God" (perhaps during one of the three annual sacrifices): ". . . Bind the [festal] sacrifice with cords, even unto the horns of the altar" (Ps. 118:27; cf. Exod. 23:18).

FIELD

sādeh (שָׂדֶה), "field; country; domain [of a town]." *Sādeh* has cognates in Akkadian, Phoenician, Ugaritic, and Arabic. It appears in biblical Hebrew about 320 times and in all periods.

This word often represents the "open field" where the animals roam wild. That is its meaning in its first biblical appearance: "And every plant of the field before it was in the earth, and every herb of the field before it grew: for the Lord God had not caused it to rain upon the earth . . ." (Gen. 2:5). Thus, "Esau was a cunning hunter, a man of the field; and Jacob was a plain man, dwelling in tents" (Gen. 25:27). A city in the "open field" was unfortified; David wisely asked Achish for such a city, showing that he did not intend to be hostile (1 Sam. 27:5). Dwelling in an unfortified city meant exposure to attack.

Sādeh represents the "fields surrounding a town" (Josh. 21:12; cf. Neh. 11:25). "Arable land," land that is either cultivated or to be cultivated, is also signified by *sādeh:* "If it be your mind that I should bury my dead out of my sight; hear me, and entreat for me to Ephron the son of Zohar, that he may give me the cave of Machpelah, which he hath, which is in the end of his field . . ." (Gen. 23:8-9). The entirety of one's cultivated or pasture land is called his "field": "And the king [David] said unto him [Mephibosheth], Why speakest thou any more of thy matters? I have said, Thou and Ziba divide the land [previously owned by Saul]" (2 Sam. 19:29).

Sometimes particular sections of land are identified by name: "And after this, Abraham buried Sarah his wife in the cave of the field of Machpelah before Mamre . . ." (Gen. 23:19).

sāday (שָׂדַי), "open field." *Sāday* occurs 12 times, only in poetical passages. Deut. 32:13 is the first biblical appearance: "He made him ride on the high places of the earth, that he might eat the increase of the fields; . . ."

TO FIGHT

A. Verb.

lācham (לָחַם), "to fight, do battle, engage in combat." This word is found in all periods of Hebrew, as well as in ancient Ugaritic. It occurs in the text of the Hebrew Bible more than 170 times. *Lācham* appears first in Exod. 1:10, where the Egyptian pharaoh expresses his fears that the Israelite slaves will multiply and join an enemy "to fight" against the Egyptians.

While the word is commonly used in the context of "armies engaged in pitched battle" against each other (Num. 21:23; Josh. 10:5; Judg. 11:5), it is also used to describe "single, hand-to-hand combat" (1 Sam. 17:32-33). Frequently, God "fights" the battle for Israel (Deut. 20:4). Instead of swords, words spoken by a lying tongue are often used "to fight" against God's servants (Ps. 109:2).

In folk etymology, *lācham* is often connected with *lechem,* the Hebrew term for "bread," on the contention that wars are fought for bread. There is, however, no good basis for such etymology.

B. Noun.

miləchāmāh (מִלְחָמָה), "battle; war." This noun occurs more than 300 times in the Old Testament, indicating how large a part military experience and terminology played in the life of the ancient Israelites. Gen. 14:8 is an early occurrence of *milachāmāh*: "And there went out the king of Sodom, and the king of Gomorrah, . . . and they joined battle with them in the vale of Siddim."

TO FILL

A. Verb.

mālē' (מָלֵא), "to fill, fulfill, overflow, ordain, endow." This verb occurs in all Semitic languages (including biblical Aramaic) and in all periods. Biblical Hebrew attests it about 250 times.

Basically, *mālē'* means "to be full" in the sense of having something done to one. In 2 Kings 4:6, the word implies "to fill up": "And it came to pass, when the vessels were full, that she said. . . ." The verb is sometimes used figuratively as in Gen. 6:13, when God noted that "the earth is filled with violence."

Used transitively, this verb means the act or state of "filling something." In Gen. 1:22 (the first occurrence of the word), God told the sea creatures to "penetrate" the waters thoroughly but not exhaustively: "Be fruitful, and multiply, and fill the waters in the seas." *Mālē'* can also mean "to fill up" in an exhaustive sense: ". . . And the glory of the Lord filled the tabernacle" (Exod. 40:34). In this sense an appetite can be "filled up," "satiated," or "satisfied."

Mālē' is sometimes used in the sense "coming to an end" or "to be filled up," to the full extent of what is expected. For example, in 1 Kings 2:27 we read: "So Solomon thrust out Abiathar from being priest unto the Lord; that he might *fulfill* the word of the Lord, which he spake concerning the house of Eli in Shiloh." This constitutes a proof of the authority of the divine Word.

In a different but related nuance, the verb signifies "to confirm" someone's word. Nathan told Bathsheba: "Behold, while thou yet talkest there with the king, I also will come in after thee, and confirm thy words" (1 Kings 1:14). This verb is used to signify filling something to the full extent of what is necessary, in the sense of being "successfully completed": "When her days to be delivered were fulfilled . . ." (Gen. 25:24). This may also mean "to bring to an end"; so God tells Isaiah: "Speak ye comfortably to Jerusalem, and cry unto her, that her warfare is *accomplished* . . ." (Isa. 40:2).

Mālē' is used of "filling to overflowing"—not just filling up to the limits of something, but filling so as to go beyond its limits: "For Jordan overfloweth all his banks all the time of harvest" (Josh. 3:15).

A special nuance appears when the verb is used with "heart"; in such cases, it means "to presume." King Ahasuerus asked Esther: "Who is he, and where is he, that durst presume [literally, "fill his heart"] to do so?" (Esther 7:5). To call out "fully" is to cry aloud, as in Jer. 4:5.

The word often has a special meaning in conjunction with "hand." *Mālē'* can connote "endow" ("fill one's hand"), as in Exod. 28:3: "And thou shalt speak unto all that are wisehearted, whom I have [endowed] with the spirit of wisdom. . . ." In Judg. 17:5, "to fill one's hand" is "to consecrate" someone to priestly service. A similar idea appears in Ezek. 43:26, where no literal hand is filled with anything, but the phrase is a technical term for "consecration": "Seven days shall they [make atonement for] the altar and purify it; and they shall consecrate themselves." This phrase is used not only of setting someone or something aside for special religious or cultic use, but of formally installing someone with the authority and responsibility to fulfill a cultic function (i.e., to be a priest). So God commands concerning Aaron and his sons: "And thou . . . shalt anoint them, and consecrate them, and sanctify them, that they may minister unto me in the priest's office" (Exod. 28:41).

In military contexts, "to fill one's hand" is to prepare for battle. This phrase may be used of "becoming armed," as in Jer. 51:11: "Sharpen the arrows, fill the quivers." (KJV, "Make bright the arrows; gather the shields.") In a fuller sense, the phrase may signify the step immediately before shooting arrows: "And Jehu drew [literally, "filled his hand with"] a bow with his full strength . . ." (2 Kings 9:24). It can also signify "being armed," or having weapons on one's person: "But the man that shall touch them must be [armed] with iron and the staff of a spear . . ." (2 Sam. 23:7).

B. Adjective.

mālē' (מָלֵא), "full." The adjective *mālē'* appears 67 times. The basic meaning of the word is "full" or "full of" (Ruth 1:21; Deut. 6:11).

TO FIND

mātsā' (מָצָא), "to find, meet, get." This word is found in every branch of the Semitic languages (including biblical Aramaic) and in all periods. It is attested both in biblical (about 455 times) and post-biblical Hebrew.

Mātsā' refers to "finding" someone or something that is lost or misplaced, or "finding" where it is. The thing may be found as the result of a purposeful search, as when the Sodomites were temporarily blinded by Lot's visitors and were not able to "find" the door to his house (Gen. 19:11). In a very similar usage, the dove sent forth by Noah searched for a spot to land and was unable to "find" it (Gen. 8:9). On other occasions, the location of something or someone may be found without an intentional search, as when Cain said: "[Whoever] findeth me shall slay me" (Gen. 4:14).

Mātsā' may connote not only "finding" a subject in a location, but "finding something" in an abstract sense. This idea is demonstrated clearly by Gen. 6:8: "But Noah found grace in the eyes of the Lord." He found— "received"—something he did not seek. This sense also includes "finding" something one has sought in a spiritual or mental sense: "Mine hand had gotten much . . ." (Job 31:25). Laban tells Jacob: ". . . If I have found favor in thine eyes [stay with me], . . ." (Gen. 30:27). Laban is asking Jacob for a favor that he is seeking in an abstract sense.

Mātsā' can also mean "to discover." God told Abraham: "If I find in Sodom fifty righteous within the city, then I will spare all the place for their sakes'' (Gen. 18:26). This same emphasis appears in the first biblical occurrence of the word: ''. . . But for Adam there was not found a help meet for him'' (Gen. 2:20). As noted earlier, there can be a connotation of the unintentional here, as when the Israelites ''found'' a man gathering wood on the Sabbath (Num. 15:32). Another special nuance is ''to find out,'' in the sense of ''gaining knowledge about.'' For example, Joseph's brothers said: ''God hath found out the iniquity of thy servants . . .'' (Gen. 44:16).

Mātsā' sometimes suggests ''being under the power'' of something, in a concrete sense. David told Abishai: ''. . . Take thou thy lord's servants, and pursue after him, lest he get him fenced cities, and escape us'' (2 Sam. 20:6). The idea is that Sheba would ''find,'' enter, and defend himself in fortified cities. So to ''find'' them could be to ''take them over.'' This usage appears also in an abstract sense. Judah told Joseph: ''For how shall I go up to my father, and the lad be not with me? lest peradventure I see the evil that shall come on my father'' (Gen. 44:34). The word *mātsā'*, therefore, can mean not only to ''find'' something, but to ''obtain'' it as one's own: ''Then Isaac sowed in that land, and received in the same year . . .'' (Gen. 26:12).

Infrequently, the word implies movement in a direction until one arrives at a destination; thus it is related to the Ugaritic root meaning ''reach'' or ''arrive'' *(ms')*. This sense is found in Job 11:7: ''Canst thou by searching find out God?'' (cf. 1 Sam. 23:17). In a somewhat different nuance, this meaning appears in Num. 11:22: ''Shall the flocks and the herds be slain for them, to *suffice* them?''

FIRE

'ēsh (אֵשׁ), ''fire.'' Cognates of this word occur in Ugaritic, Akkadian, Aramaic, and Ethiopic. The 378 occurrences of this word in biblical Hebrew are scattered throughout its periods.

In its first biblical appearance this word, *'ēsh,* represents God's presence as ''a torch of fire'': ''And it came to pass, that, when the sun went down, and it was dark, behold a smoking furnace, and a [flaming torch] . . .'' (Gen. 15:17). ''Fire'' was the instrument by which an offering was transformed into smoke, whose ascending heavenward symbolized God's reception of the offering (Lev. 9:24). God also consumed people with the ''fire of judgment'' (Num. 11:1; Ps. 89:46). Various things were to be burnt as a sign of total destruction and divine judgment (Exod. 32:20).

''Fire'' often attended God's presence in theophanies (Exod. 3:2). Thus He is sometimes called a ''consuming fire'' (Exod. 24:17).

The noun *'ishsheh,* meaning ''an offering made by fire,'' is derived from *'ēsh.*

FIRSTBORN

bəkôr (בְּכוֹר), ''firstborn.'' *Bəkôr* appears about 122 times in biblical Hebrew and in all periods. The word represents the ''firstborn'' individual in a family (Gen. 25:13); the word can also represent the "firstborn" of a nation, collectively (Num. 3:46). The plural form of the word appears occasionally (Neh. 10:36); in this passage, the word is applied to animals. In other passages, the singular form of *bəkôr* signifies a single "firstborn" animal (Lev. 27:26; KJV, "firstling") or collectively the "firstborn" of a herd (Exod. 11:5).

The "oldest" or "firstborn" son (Exod. 6:14) had special privileges within the family. He received the special family blessing, which meant spiritual and social leadership and a double portion of the father's possessions—or twice what all the other sons received (Deut. 21:17). He could lose this blessing through misdeeds (Gen. 35:22) or by selling it (Gen. 25:29-34). God claimed all Israel and all their possessions as His own. As a token of this claim, Israel was to give Him all its "firstborn" (Exod. 13:1-16). The animals were to be sacrificed, redeemed, or killed, while the male children were redeemed either by being replaced with Levites or by the payment of a redemption price (Num. 3:40 ff.).

Israel was God's "firstborn"; it enjoyed a privileged position and blessings over all other nations (Exod. 4:22; Jer. 31:9).

The "first-born of death" is an idiom meaning a deadly disease (Job 18:13); the "first-born of the poor" is the poorest class of people (Isa. 14:30).

bikkûrîm (בִּכּוּרִים), "first fruits." This noun appears 16 times. The "first grain and fruit" harvested was to be offered to God (Num. 28:26) in recognition of God's ownership of the land and His sovereignty over nature. Bread of the "first fruits" was bread made of the first harvest grain, presented to God at Pentecost (Lev. 23:20). The "day of the first fruits" was Pentecost (Num. 28:26).

TO FLEE

bārach (בָּרַח), "to flee, pass through." Some scholars see this word, which is used throughout the history of the Hebrew language, reflected in ancient Ugaritic as well. *Bārach* occurs about 60 times in the Hebrew Bible. The word first appears in Gen. 16:6, where it is said that Hagar "fled from her [Sarah's] face" as a result of Sarah's harsh treatment.

Men may "flee" from many things or situations. David "fled" from Naioth in Ramah in order to come to Jonathan (1 Sam. 20:1). Sometimes it is necessary to "flee" from weapons (Job 20:24). In describing flight from a person, the Hebrew idiom "from the presence of" (literally, "from the face of") is often used (Gen. 16:6, 8; 31:27; 35:1, 7).

In its figurative use, the word describes days "fleeing" away (Job 9:25) or frail man "fleeing" like a shadow (Job. 14:2). A rather paradoxical use is found in Song of Sol. 8:14, in which "flee" must mean "come quickly": "Make haste [literally, "flee"], my beloved, and be thou like to a gazelle. . . ."

nûs (נוּס), "to flee, escape, take flight, depart." This term is found primarily in biblical Hebrew, where it occurs some 160 times. *Nûs* occurs for the first time in Gen. 14:10, where it is used twice to describe the "fleeing" of the kings of Sodom and Gomorrah. *Nûs* is the common word for "fleeing" from an enemy or danger (Gen. 39:12; Num. 16:34; Josh. 10:6). The word is also used to describe "escape," as in Jer. 46:6 and Amos 9:1. In a figurative use, the word describes the "disappearance" of physical strength (Deut. 34:7), the "fleeing" of evening shadows (Song of Sol. 2:17), and the "fleeing away" of sorrow (Isa. 35:10).

FLESH

bāsār (בָּשָׂר), "flesh; meat; male sex organ." Cognates of this word appear in Ugaritic, Arabic, and Aramaic. Biblical Hebrew attests it about 270 times and in all periods.

The word means the "meaty part plus the skin" of men: "And the Lord God caused a deep sleep to fall upon Adam, and he slept: and he took one of his ribs, and closed up the flesh instead thereof" (Gen. 2:21—the first occurrence). This word can also be applied to the "meaty part" of animals (Deut. 14:8). Gen. 41:2 speaks of seven cows, sleek and "fat of flesh." In Num. 11:33, *bāsār* means the meat or "flesh" of the quail that Israel was still chewing. Thus the word means "flesh," whether living or dead.

Bāsār often means the "edible part" of animals. Eli's sons did not know God's law concerning the priests' portion, so "when any man offered sacrifice, the priest's [Eli's] servant came, while the flesh was [boiling], with a [three-pronged fork] in his hand" (1 Sam. 2:13). However, they insisted that "before they burnt the fat . . ., Give flesh to roast for the priest; for he will not have [boiled] flesh of thee, but raw" (literally, "living"—1 Sam. 2:15). *Bāsār*, then, represents edible animal "flesh" or "meat," whether cooked (Dan. 10:3) or uncooked. The word sometimes refers to "meat" that one is forbidden to eat (cf. Exod. 21:28).

This word may represent a part of the body. At some points, the body is viewed as consisting of two components, "flesh" and bones: "This is now bone of my bones, and flesh of my flesh: she shall be called Woman, because she was taken out of Man" (Gen. 2:23). That part of the "fleshly" element known as the foreskin was to be removed by circumcision (Gen. 17:11). In other passages, the elements of the body are the "flesh," the skin, and the bones (Lam. 3:4). Num. 19:5 mentions the "flesh," hide, blood, and refuse of a heifer. In Job 10:11, we read: "Thou hast clothed me with skin and flesh, and hast [knit] me with bones and sinews."

Flesh sometimes means "blood relative": "And Laban said to him [Jacob], Surely thou art my bone and my flesh" (Gen. 29:14). The phrase "your flesh" or "our flesh" standing alone may bear the same meaning: "Come, and let us sell him to the Ishmaelites, and let not our hand be upon him; for he is our brother and our flesh" (Gen. 37:27). The phrase *shə'ēr bāsār* is rendered "blood relative" (Lev. 18:6; KJV, "near of kin").

About 50 times, "flesh" represents the "physical aspect" of man or animals as contrasted with the spirit, soul, or heart (the nonphysical aspect). In the case of men, this usage appears in Num. 16:22: "O God, the God of the spirits of all flesh, shall one man sin, and wilt thou be wroth with all the congregation?" In such passages, then, *bāsār* emphasizes the "visible and structural part" of man or animal.

In a few passages, the word appears to mean "skin," or the part of the body that is seen: "By reason of the voice of my groaning my bones cleave to my skin" (Ps. 102:5; 119:120). In passages such as Lev. 13:2, the ideas "flesh" and "skin" are clearly distinguished.

Bāsār sometimes represents the "male sex organ": "Speak unto the children of Israel, and say unto them, When any man hath a running issue out of his flesh [NASB, "body"], because of his issue he is unclean" (Lev. 15:2).

The term "all flesh" has several meanings. It means "all mankind" in Deut. 5:26: "For who is there of all flesh, that hath heard the voice of the living God. . . ?" In another place, this phrase refers to "all living creatures within the cosmos," or all men and animals (Gen. 6:17).

FLOCK

tsō'n (**צֹאן**), "flock; small cattle; sheep; goats." A similar word is found in Akkadian, Aramaic, and Syriac, and in the Tel Amarna tablets. In Hebrew, *tsō'n* kept its meaning in all stages of the development of the language. The word occurs 273 times in the Hebrew Old Testament, with its first occurrence in Gen. 4:2. The word is not limited to any period of Hebrew history or to any type of literature. The Book of Genesis, with the narratives on the patriarchs in their pastoral setting, has the greatest frequency of usage (about 60 times).

The primary meaning of *tsō'n* is "small cattle," to be distinguished from *bāqār* ("herd"). The word may refer to "sheep" only (1 Sam. 25:2) or to both "sheep and goats": "So shall my righteousness answer for me in time to come, when it shall come for my hire before thy face: every one that is not speckled and spotted among the goats, and brown among the sheep, that shall be counted stolen with me" (Gen. 30:33). The "flock" was an important economic factor in the ancient Near East. The animals were eaten (1 Sam. 14:32; cf. Ps. 44:11), shorn for their wool (Gen. 31:19), and milked (Deut. 32:14). They were also offered as a sacrifice, as when Abel sacrificed a firstling of his "flock" (Gen. 4:4).

In the metaphorical usage of *tsō'n*, the imagery of a "multitude" may apply to people: "As the holy flock, as the flock of Jerusalem in her solemn feasts; so shall the waste cities be filled with flocks of men: and they shall know that I am the Lord" (Ezek. 36:38). God is viewed as the shepherd of His "flock," God's people: "Know ye that the Lord he is God: it is he that hath made us, and not we ourselves; we are his people, and the sheep of his pasture" (Ps. 100:3; cf. Ps. 23; 79:13; Mic. 7:14). In a period of oppression, the psalmist compared God's people to "sheep for the slaughter" (Ps. 44:22) and prayed for God's deliverance.

People without a leader were compared to a "flock" without a shepherd (1 Kings 22:17; cf. Zech. 10:2; 13:7). Jeremiah viewed the Judeans as having been guided astray by their shepherds, or leaders (Jer. 50:6). Similarly, Isaiah wrote: "All we like sheep have gone astray; we have turned every one to his own way; and the Lord hath laid on him the iniquity of us all" (Isa. 53:6).

The prophetic promise pertains to God's renewed blessing on the remnant of the "flock": "And I will gather the remnant of my flock out of all countries whither I have driven them, and will bring them again to their folds; and they shall be fruitful and increase" (Jer. 23:3). This would come to pass as the Messiah ("the Branch of David") will establish His rule over the people (vv. 5-6). This idea is also expressed by Ezekiel: "And I will set up one shepherd over them, and he shall feed them, even my servant David; he shall feed them, and he shall be their shepherd. And I the Lord will be their God, and my servant David a prince among them; I the Lord have spoken it" (Ezek. 34:23-24).

The Septuagint gives the following translations: *probaton* ("sheep") and *poimnion* ("flock"). The KJV gives these senses: "flocks; sheep; cattle."

FOLLOWING

'achēr (אַחֵר), "following; different; other." This word occurs about 166 times and in all periods of biblical Hebrew.

The first meaning of this word is temporal, and is seen in Gen. 17:21: "But my covenant will I establish with Isaac, which Sarah shall bear unto thee at this set time in the *next* year" (i.e., the year "following"). The first biblical occurrence of the word is in Gen. 4:25: "And Adam [had relations with] his wife again; and she bare a son, and called his name Seth: For God, said she, hath appointed me *another* seed instead of Abel. . . ."

This meaning of "different" or "another" also appears in Lev. 27:20: "And if he will not redeem the field, or if he have sold the field to another man, it shall not be redeemed any more." In Isa. 28:11, *'achēr* defines tongue or language; hence it should be understood as "foreign": "For with stammering lips and *another* tongue will he speak to this people." Since this verse is quoted in 1 Cor. 14:21 as an Old Testament prophecy of tongues-speaking, *'achēr* figures prominently in the debate on that subject.

Finally, *'achēr* can mean "other." In this usage, the word distinguishes one thing from another without emphasizing any contrast. This is its meaning in Exod. 20:3: "Thou shalt have no other gods before me."

FOOL

'ewîl (אֱוִיל), "fool." This word appears primarily in the wisdom literature. A person described by *'ewîl* generally lacks wisdom; indeed, wisdom is beyond his grasp (Prov. 24:7). In another nuance, "fool" is a morally undesirable individual who despises wisdom and discipline (Prov. 1:7; 15:5). He mocks guilt (Prov. 14:9), and is quarrelsome (Prov. 20:3) and licentious (Prov. 7:22). Trying to give him instruction is futile (Prov. 16:22).

FOOLISHNESS

'iwweleth (אִוֶּלֶת), "foolishness; stupidity." This noun appears 25 times in the Old Testament. It can mean "foolishness" in the sense of violating God's law, or "sin" (Ps. 38:5). The word also describes the activities and life-style of the man who ignores the instructions of wisdom (Prov. 5:23). In another

nuance, the noun means "thoughtless." Hence *'iwweleth* describes the way a young person is prone to act (Prov. 22:15) and the way any fool or stupid person chatters (Prov. 15:2).

nəbālāh (נְבָלָה), "foolishness; senselessness; impropriety; stupidity." This abstract noun appears 13 times in the Old Testament. Its use in 1 Sam. 25:25 signifies "disregarding God's will." *Nəbālāh* is most often used as a word for a serious sin (Gen. 34:7—the first occurrence).

FOOT

regel (רֶגֶל), "foot; leg." *Regel* is a word found in many Semitic languages, referring to a part of the body. In the Old Testament, the word is used a total of 245 times, with its first occurrence in Gen. 8:9.

Regel may refer to the "foot" of a human (Gen. 18:4), an animal (Ezek. 29:11), a bird (Gen. 8:9), or even a table (a rare usage; Exod. 25:26, KJV). The word's usage is also extended to signify the "leg": "And he had greaves of brass upon his legs, and a target of brass between his shoulders" (1 Sam. 17:6). *Regel* is used euphemistically for the genital area; thus urine is "water of the legs" (2 Kings 18:27) and pubic hair is "hair of the legs" (Isa. 7:20). The foot's low place gave rise to an idiom: "From the sole of the foot to the crown of the head" (cf. Deut. 28:35), signifying the "total extent of the body."

"Foot" may be a metaphor of "arrogance": "Let not the foot of pride come against me, and let not the hand of the wicked remove me" (Ps. 36:11). It is used to represent Israel: "Neither will I make the feet of Israel move any more out of the land which I gave their fathers; only if they will observe to do according to all that I have commanded them, and according to all the law that my servant Moses commanded them" (2 Kings 21:8).

In anthropomorphic expressions, God has "feet." Thus God revealed Himself with a pavement of sapphire as clear as the sky under His "feet" (Exod. 24:10). The authors of Scripture portray God as having darkness (Ps. 18:9) and clouds of dust beneath His "feet" (Nah. 1:3), and sending a plague out from His "feet" (Hab. 3:5). His "feet" are said to rest on the earth (Isa. 66:1); the temple is also the resting place of His "feet": ". . . And I will make the place of my feet glorious" (Isa. 60:13). Similarly, the seraphim had "feet," which they covered with a pair of wings as they stood in the presence of God (Isa. 6:2); the cherubim had "feet" that Ezekiel described (Ezek. 1:7).

The Septuagint gives the following translations: *pous* ("foot") and *skelos* ("leg").

TO FORGET

shākach (שָׁכַח), "to forget." The common word meaning "to forget" appears in all periods of the Hebrew language; this term is also found in Aramaic. It occurs just over 100 times in the Hebrew Bible. *Shākach* is found for the first time in the Old Testament in Gen. 27:45, when Rebekah urges Jacob to flee his home until Esau "forget that which thou hast done to him."

As the people worshiped strange gods, Jeremiah reminded Judah that "all thy lovers have forgotten thee; they seek thee not" (Jer. 30:14). But God does not "forget" His people: "Can a woman forget her suckling child, that she should not have compassion on the son of her womb? yea, they may forget, yet will I not forget thee" (Isa. 49:15). In spite of this, when destruction came, Judah complained: "Wherefore dost thou forget us for ever . . .?" (Lam. 5:20). Israel would often "forget" God's law (Hos. 4:6) and God's name (Jer. 23:27).

TO FORGIVE

sālach (סָלַח), "to forgive." This verb appears 46 times in the Old Testament. The meaning "to forgive" is limited to biblical and rabbinic Hebrew; in Akkadian, the word means "to sprinkle," and in Aramaic and Syriac signifies "to pour out." The meaning of *sālach* in Ugaritic is debatable.

The first biblical occurrence is in Moses' prayer of intercession on behalf of the Israelites: ". . . It is a stiffnecked people; and [forgive] our iniquity and our sin, and take us for thine inheritance" (Exod. 34:9). The basic meaning undergoes no change throughout the Old Testament. God is always the subject of "forgiveness." No other Old Testament verb means "to forgive," although several verbs include "forgiveness" in the range of meanings given a particular context (e.g., *nāsa'* and *'āwōn* in Exod. 32:32; *kāphar* in Ezek. 16:63).

The verb occurs throughout the Old Testament. Most occurrences of *sālach* are in the sacrificial laws of Leviticus and Numbers. In the typology of the Old Testament, sacrifices foreshadowed the accomplished work of Jesus Christ, and the Old Testament believer was assured of "forgiveness" based on sacrifice: "And the priest shall make an atonement [for him in regard to his sin]" (Num. 15:25, 28), "And it shall be forgiven him" (Lev. 4:26; cf. vv. 20, 31, 35; 5:10, 13, 16, 18). The mediators of the atonement were the priests who offered the sacrifice. The sacrifice was ordained by God to promise ultimate "forgiveness" in God's sacrifice of His own Son. Moreover, sacrifice was appropriately connected to atonement, as there is no forgiveness without the shedding of blood (Lev. 4:20; cf. Heb. 9:22).

Out of His grace, God alone "forgives" sin. The Israelites experienced God's "forgiveness" in the wilderness and in the Promised Land. As long as the temple stood, sacrificial atonement continued and the Israelites were assured of God's "forgiveness." When the temple was destroyed and sacrifices ceased, God sent the prophetic word that He graciously would restore Israel out of exile and "forgive" its sins (Jer. 31:34).

The psalmist appealed to God's great name in his request for "forgiveness": "For thy name's sake, O Lord, pardon mine iniquity; for it is great" (Ps. 25:11). David praised God for the assurance of "forgiveness" of sins: "Bless the Lord, O my soul . . ., who forgiveth all thine iniquities . . ." (Ps. 103:2-3). The Old Testament saints, while involved in sacrificial rites, put their faith in God.

In the Septuagint, *sālach* is most frequently translated by *hileos einai* ("to be gracious; be merciful''), *hilaskesthai* (''to propitiate, expiate'') and *apievai* (''to forgive, pardon, leave, cancel''). The translation ''to forgive'' is found in most English versions (KJV, RSV, NASB, NIV), and at times also ''to pardon'' (KJV, RSV).

TO FORM

yātsar (יָצַר), ''to form, mold, fashion.'' A word common to Hebrew in all its periods, *yātsar* is used in modern Hebrew in the sense of ''to produce,'' or ''to create.'' The word is found just over 60 times in the Hebrew Old Testament. The first occurrence in the Old Testament is in Gen. 2:7: ''. . . God formed man of the dust of the ground,'' reflecting the basic meaning of ''molding'' something to a desired shape.

Yātsar is a technical potter's word, and it is often used in connection with the potter at work (Isa. 29:16; Jer. 18:4, 6). The word is sometimes used as a general term of ''craftsmanship or handiwork,'' whether molding, carving, or casting (Isa. 44:9-10, 12).

The word may be used to express the ''forming'' of plans in one's mind (Ps. 94:20; KJV, ''frameth''). *Yātsar* is frequently used to describe God's creative activity, whether literally or figuratively. Thus, God ''formed'' not only man (Gen. 2:7-8) but the animals (Gen. 2:19). God also ''formed'' the nation of Israel (Isa. 27:11; 45:9, 11); Israel was ''formed'' as God's special servant, even from the womb (Isa. 44:2, 24; 49:5). While yet in the womb, Jeremiah was ''formed'' to be a prophet (Jer. 1:5). God ''formed'' locusts as a special visual lesson for Amos (Amos 7:1); the great sea monster, Leviathan, was ''formed'' to play in the seas (Ps. 104:26).

The concreteness of ancient Hebrew thinking is vividly seen in a statement such as this: ''I form the light, and create darkness . . . .'' (Isa. 45:7). Similarly, the psalmist confessed to God: ''. . . Thou hast made summer and winter'' (Ps. 74:17). God ''formed'' the spirit of man (Zech. 12:1), as well as the heart or mind of man (Ps. 33:15). *Yātsar* is used to express God's ''planning'' or ''preordaining'' according to His divine purpose (Isa. 22:11; 46:11).

Almost one half of the uses of this word in the Old Testament are found in the Book of Isaiah, with God as the subject of most of them.

FORMER

ri'shôn (רִאשׁוֹן), ''former; chief; first.'' This word comes from a common Semitic root that also yields *rō'sh* (''head'') and *rē'shîth* (''beginning''). *Ri'shôn,* which appears 182 times (first in Gen. 8:13), is well represented throughout the entire Old Testament, with the exception of the poetic books and the minor prophets.

The basic meaning of *ri'shôn* is ''first'' in a series. The word is the antonym of *'acharôn* (''last''). On the one hand, *ri'shôn* may refer to the ''first month'' (Exod. 40:2), the ''first day'' (Exod. 12:15), the ''former temple'' (Ezra 3:12), or the ''firstborn'' (Gen. 25:25 ff.).

On the other hand, the word may denote the "most prominent" in a series. Thus God is "the first" as well as "the last": "Who hath wrought and done it, calling the generations from the beginning? I the Lord, the first, and with the last; I am he" (Isa. 41:4). The most prominent people at a banquet sat in the "first place" (Esth. 1:14). The use of *ri'shôn* with "father" in "Thy first father hath sinned, and thy teachers have transgressed against me" (Isa. 43:27) expresses how Israel's beginnings started with sin and rebellion.

As a reference to time, *ri'shôn* signifies what has been—i.e., the "former." This usage appears in phrases meaning a "former position" (Gen. 40:13) and a "deceased husband" (Hos. 2:7). The "prophets of the past" (Zech. 1:4) and "ancestors" (Lev. 26:45) are both best understood as expressions referring to the past. The prophetic phrase "former days" (unlike "latter days") expresses Israel's past sin and God's judgment on Israel: "Behold, the former things are come to pass, and new things do I declare: before they spring forth I tell you of them" (Isa. 42:9).

The Septuagint translations are: *proteros* ("earlier; former; superior"), *protos* ("first; earlier; earliest"), *emprosthen* ("ahead; in front"), *archē* ("beginning; first cause; ruler; rule"). The KJV gives these translations: "first; former; before; beginning."

TO FORSAKE

'āzab (עָזַב), "to leave, forsake, abandon, leave behind, be left over, let go." This word occurs in Akkadian and post-biblical Hebrew and Aramaic. Similar words appear in Arabic and Ethiopic. The word occurs in biblical Hebrew about 215 times and in all periods.

Basically *'āzab* means "to depart from something," or "to leave." This is the meaning of the word in its first biblical appearance: "[For this cause] shall a man leave his father and his mother, and shall cleave unto his wife . . ." (Gen. 2:24). A special nuance of the word is "to leave in the lurch," or to leave someone who is depending upon one's services. So Moses said to Hobab the Midianite (Kenite): "Leave us not [in the lurch] I pray thee; forasmuch as thou knowest how we are to encamp in the wilderness, and thou mayest be to us instead of eyes" (Num. 10:31).

The word also carries the meaning "forsake," or "leave entirely." Such passages convey a note of finality or completeness. So Isaiah is to preach that ". . . the land that thou abhorrest shall be forsaken of both her kings" (Isa. 7:16). In other places, the abandonment is complete but not necessarily permanent. God says that Israel is "as a woman forsaken and grieved in spirit. . . . For a small moment have I forsaken thee; but with great mercies will I gather thee" (Isa. 54:6–7). In Akkadian, this word carries a technical sense of "completely and permanently abandoned" or "divorced." Isaiah employs this sense in 62:4: "Thou shalt no more be termed Forsaken; . . . but thou shalt be called [My delight is in her], and thy land [Married]. . . ."

Another special use of the word is "to disregard advice": "But he forsook the counsel of the old men which they had given him . . ." (1 Kings 12:8).

A second emphasis of *'āzab* is "to leave behind," meaning to allow something to remain while one leaves the scene. In Gen. 39:12, Joseph "left" his garment in the hand of Potiphar's wife and fled. The word may also refer to an intentional "turning over one's possessions to another's trust," or "leaving something in one's control." Potiphar "left all that he had in Joseph's hand" (Gen. 39:6).

In a somewhat different nuance, the word means to "let someone or something alone with a problem": "If thou see the ass of him that hateth thee lying under his burden, and wouldest forbear to help him . . ." (Exod. 23:5). Used figuratively, *'āzab* means to "put distance between" in a spiritual or intellectual sense: "Cease from anger, and forsake wrath . . ." (Ps. 37:8).

The third emphasis of the word is "to be left over," or "to take most of something and leave the rest behind": "And thou shalt not glean thy vineyard, neither shalt thou gather every grape of thy vineyard; thou shalt leave them [over] for the poor and stranger: I am the Lord your God" (Lev. 19:10).

Finally, *'āzab* can mean "to let go" or "allow to leave." The "stupid and senseless men" are those who make no provision for the future; they die leaving ("allowing it to go") their wealth to others (Ps. 49:10). A different nuance occurs in Ruth 2:16, where the verb means "to let something lie" on the ground. *'Āzab* can also mean "to give up": "He that covereth his sins shall not prosper: but whoso confesseth and forsaketh them [gives them up] shall have mercy" (Prov. 28:13), and the word can mean "to set free," as in 2 Chron. 28:14: "So the armed men left the captives and the spoil before the princes and all the congregation." *'Āzab* can signify "let go," or "make it leave." Concerning evil, Zophar remarks, ". . . [The wicked] forsake it not, but keep it still within his mouth" (Job 20:13).

'Āzab can mean to "allow someone to do something," as in 2 Chron. 32:31, where "God left [Hezekiah], to try him, that he might know all that was in his heart"; God "let" Hezekiah do whatever he wanted. "Letting an activity go" may also signify its discontinuance: "I pray you, let us leave off this usury" (Neh. 5:10).

'Āzab is sometimes used in a judicial technical sense of "being free," which is the opposite of being in bondage. The Lord will vindicate His people, and will have compassion on His servants "when he seeth that their power is gone, and there is none shut up, or left" (Deut. 32:36).

FRIEND

rē'a (ﬠﬧ), "friend; companion; fellow." This noun appears about 187 times in the Bible. The word refers to a "friend" in 2 Sam. 13:3: "But Amnon had a friend, whose name was Jonadab." The word may be used of a husband (Jer. 3:20) or a lover (Song of Sol. 5:16).

In another sense, *rē'a* may be used of any person with whom one has reciprocal relations: "And they said every one to his fellow, Come, and let us cast lots . . ." (Jonah 1:7). The word also appears in such phrases as "one another," found in Gen. 11:3: "And they said one to another . . ." (cf. Gen. 31:49).

Other related nouns that appear less frequently are *rē'eh,* which means "friend" about 5 times (e.g., 1 Kings 4:5); and *rē'āh,* which means "companion or attendant" (Judg. 11:38; Ps. 45:14).

FRUIT

A. Noun.

pərî (פְּרִי), "fruit; reward; price; earnings; product; result." Cognates of this word appear in Ugaritic and Egyptian. *Pərî* appears about 120 times in biblical Hebrew and in every period.

First, *pərî* represents the mature edible product of a plant, which is its "fruit." This broad meaning is evident in Deut. 7:13: "He will also bless the fruit of thy womb, and the fruit of thy land, thy corn, and thy wine, and thine oil, the increase of thy kine and the flocks of thy sheep. . . ." In its first biblical appearance, the word is used to signify both "trees" and the "fruit" of trees: "And God said, Let the earth bring forth grass, the herb yielding seed, and the fruit tree yielding fruit after his kind . . ." (Gen. 1:11). In Ps. 107:34, the word is used as a modifier of land. The resulting term is "a fruitful land" in the sense of a "land of fruit."

Second, *pərî* means "offspring," or the "fruit of a womb." In Deut. 7:13, the word represents "human offspring," but it can also be used of animal "offspring" (Gen. 1:22).

Third, the "product" or "result" of an action is, in poetry, sometimes called its "fruit": "A man shall say, Verily there is a reward for the righteous: verily he is a God that judgeth in the earth" (Ps. 58:11). Isa. 27:9 speaks of "the full price of the pardoning of his sin" (KJV, "all the fruit to take away his sin"), i.e., the result of God's purifying acts toward Israel. The wise woman buys and plants a field with her earnings or the "fruit of her hands" (Prov. 31:16). In other words, she is to be rewarded by receiving the "product" of her hands (Prov. 31:31). The righteous will be rewarded "according to his ways, according to the results of his deeds" (Jer. 17:10, NASB; cf. 21:14). In most passages similar to these, the NASB renders *pərî* "fruit" (cf. Prov. 18:21).

B. Verb.

pārāh (פָּרָה), "to be fruitful, bear fruit." This verb appears 29 times in the Old Testament. Its first occurrence is in Gen. 1:22: "And God blessed them, saying, Be fruitful, and multiply, . . ."

G

GARMENT

beged (בֶּגֶד), "garment; covering; cloth; blanket; saddlecloth." This word appears in biblical Hebrew about 200 times and in all periods.

The word signifies any kind of "garment" or "covering," usually for human wear. *Beged* first appears in Gen. 24:53: "And the servant brought forth jewels of silver, and jewels of gold, and garments [KJV, "raiment"], and gave them to Rebekah. . . ." Here the word represents "garments made of precious materials." The "garments" of widows, on the other hand, must have been quite common and valueless (Gen. 38:14). Certainly mourners' "garments" must have been very plain, if not torn (2 Sam. 14:2).

Beged sometimes refers to "outer garments." Thus in 2 Kings 7:15, the Syrian soldiers who fled from Jerusalem left behind their "clothes" and equipment; they left behind everything that would hinder their escape. Surely this did not include their essential "clothing." In Judg. 14:12, however, the word is distinguished from linen wrappings ("outer garments")—Samson promised the Philistines that if they would solve his riddle, he would give them "thirty linen wraps [KJV, "sheets"] and thirty change of garments" (cf. Judg. 17:10). The "holy garments" Moses was commanded to make for Aaron included everything he was to wear while officiating before the Lord: ". . . A breastplate, and an ephod, and a robe, and an embroidered coat, a mitre, and a [sash]; and they shall make holy garments for Aaron . . ." (Exod. 28:4).

In passages such as Num. 4:6, *beged* means "covering," in the sense of a large flat piece of cloth material to be laid over something: "And [they] shall put thereon the covering of badgers' skins, and shall spread over it a cloth wholly of blue. . . ." When put over people, such clothes were probably "blankets": "Now king David was old and stricken in years; and they covered him with blankets [KJV and NASB, "clothes"], but he gat no heat" (1 Kings 1:1). When put over beasts, such coverings were "saddlecloths" (Ezek. 27:20).

GATE

sha'ar (שַׁעַר), "gate." This word has cognates in Ugaritic, Arabic, Moabite, Aramaic, and Phoenician. Biblical Hebrew attests it about 370 times and in all periods.

Basically, this word represents a structure closing and enclosing a large opening through a wall, or a barrier through which people and things pass to an enclosed area. The "gate" of a city often was a fortified structure deeper than the wall. This is especially true of strong, well-fortified cities, as in the case of the first biblical appearance of the word: "And there came two angels to Sodom at even; and Lot sat in the gate of Sodom . . ." (Gen. 19:1). Within major cities there were usually strongly fortified citadels with "gates" (Neh.

2:8). Certain "gates" were only the thickness of a curtain: "And for the gate of the court [of the tabernacle] shall be a hanging of twenty cubits . . ." (Exod. 27:16). Later, the temple had large openings between its various courts: "Stand in the gate of the Lord's house, and proclaim there this word, and say, Hear the word of the Lord, all ye of Judah, that enter in at these gates to worship the Lord" (Jer. 7:2).

Exod. 32:26 speaks of an opening ("gate") in the barrier surrounding Israel's temporary camp at the foot of Sinai. Such camps often were enclosed with barriers of earth and/or rock. Ancient fortified cities had to find a source of water for periods of siege, and sometimes dams were built. Nah. 2:6 apparently refers to such a dam when it says: "The gates of the rivers shall be opened, and the palace shall be dissolved" (i.e., swept away). Both the underworld (Job 38:17) and heaven, the domain of God (Gen. 28:17), are pictured as cities with "gates."

The "gates" of ancient cities sometimes enclosed city squares or were immediately in front of squares (2 Chron. 32:6). The entry way (2 Chron. 23:15) could be secured with heavy doors that were attached to firmly embedded pillars and reinforced by bars (Judg. 16:3; cf. Ps. 147:13; Neh. 3:3). Palaces could be citadels with strongly fortified "gates" large enough to have rooms over them. During siege, such rooms housed warriors. It was such a room into which David climbed and wept over the death of his son Absalom (2 Sam. 18:33). "Gates" had rooms to house guards (Ezek. 40:7). The rooms bordering the "gates" could also be used to store siege supplies (Neh. 12:25).

The "gates" were the place where local courts convened: "And if the man like not to take his brother's wife, then let his brother's wife go up to the gate unto the elders, and say, My husband's brother refuseth . . ." (Deut. 25:7). The sentence sometimes was executed at the city "gates": "And I will fan them with a fan in the gates of the land; I will bereave them of children, I will destroy my people . . ." (Jer. 15:7). In this passage, all of the land of Israel is envisioned as a city at whose "gates" God gathers the offenders for trial, judgment, sentence, and punishment.

The phrase, "within the gates," means "within the area enclosed." Thus the sojourner who is "in your gates" is the foreigner who permanently lives in one of Israel's towns (Exod. 20:10). In passages such as Deut. 12:15, this phrase means "wherever you live": "Notwithstanding thou mayest kill and eat flesh in all thy gates. . . ."

TO GATHER

qābats (קָבַץ), "to collect, gather, assemble." This verb also appears in Ugaritic, Arabic, Aramaic, and post–biblical Hebrew; a similar word (having the same radicals but a different meaning) occurs in Ethiopic. *Qābats* appears in all periods of Hebrew and about 130 times in the Bible. The verb *'āsaph* is a near synonym to *qābats*, differing from it only by having a more extensive range of meanings. *'Āsaph* duplicates, however, all the meanings of *qābats*.

First, *qābats* means "to gather" things together into a single location. The word may focus on the process of "gathering," as in Gen. 41:35 (the first occurrence): Joseph advised Pharaoh to appoint overseers to "gather all the food of those good years that come, and lay up corn under the hand of Pharaoh. . . ." The verb may also focus on the result of the process, as in Gen. 41:48: "And he gathered up all the food of the seven years, which were in the land of Egypt. . . ." Only in one passage does qābats mean "to harvest" (Isa. 62:9): "But they that have gathered [harvested] it [grain] shall eat it, and praise the Lord; and they that have brought it [wine] together shall drink it in the courts of my holiness."

This verb is used metaphorically of things that can be "gathered" only in a figurative sense. So in Ps. 41:6, the enemy's "heart gathereth iniquity to itself" while visiting—i.e., the enemy considers how he can use everything he hears and sees against his host.

Qābats is often used of "gathering" people or "assembling" them. This "gathering" is usually a response to a summons, but not always. In 1 Kings 11:24, David "gathered men unto him, and became captain over a [marauding] band." This action was not the result of a summons David issued, but resulted from reports that circulated about him. The entire story makes it quite clear that David was not seeking to set up a force rivalling Saul's. But when men came to him, he marshalled them.

Quite often this verb is used of "summoning" people to a central location. When Jacob blessed his sons, for example, he "summoned" them to him and then told them to gather around closer (Gen. 49:2). This same word is used of "summoning" the militia. All able-bodied men in Israel between the ages of 20 and 40 were members of the militia. In times of peace they were farmers and tradesmen; but when danger threatened, a leader would "assemble" them or "summon" them to a common location and organize them into an army (cf. Judg. 12:4). All Israel could be "summoned" or "gathered" for battle (as a militia); thus ". . . Saul gathered all Israel together, and they pitched in Gilboa" (1 Sam. 28:4). This military use may also signify "marshalling" a standing army in the sense of "setting them up" for battle. The men of Gibeon said: "All the kings of the Amorites that dwell in the mountains are gathered together against us" (Josh. 10:6). In 1 Kings 20:1, qābats carries this sense in addition to overtones of "concentrating" an entire army against a particular point: "And Ben-hadad the king of Syria gathered all his host together: and there were thirty and two kings with him, and horses, and chariots: and he went up and besieged Samaria, and warred against it."

Ordered assemblies may include assemblies for covenant-making: "And Abner said unto David, I will arise and go, and will gather all Israel unto my lord the king, that they may make a league with thee . . ." (2 Sam. 3:21). In several instances, assemblies are "convened" for public worship activities: "Samuel said, Gather all Israel to Mizpeh. . . . And they gathered together to Mizpeh, and drew water, and poured it out before the Lord, and fasted on that day . . ." (1 Sam. 7:5-6; cf. Joel 2:16).

When qābats appears in the intensive stem, God is often the subject. This usage connotes that something will result that would not result if things were left to themselves. The verb is used in this sense to refer to "divine judgment'': ''As they gathered silver, and brass . . . into the midst of the furnace, to blow the fire upon it, to melt it; so will I gather you in mine anger and in my fury (Ezek. 22:20). *Qābats* is also applied to ''divine deliverance'': ''. . . The Lord thy God will turn thy captivity, and have compassion upon thee, and will return and gather thee from all the nations, whither the Lord thy God hath scattered thee'' (Deut. 30:3).

A special use of the verb *qābats* appears in Joel 2:6, namely ''to glow'' or ''glow with excitement'' or ''become pale [white]'': ''Before their face the people shall be much pained: all faces shall gather blackness.''

'āsaph (אָסַף), ''to gather, gather in, take away.'' This verb also occurs in Akkadian, Ugaritic, Phoenician, and Aramaic. It is attested at all periods of biblical literature, and it appears about 200 times.

Basically, *'āsaph* refers to ''bringing objects to a common point.'' This may mean to ''gather'' or ''collect'' something such as food. The first occurrence is when God told Noah to ''gather'' food to himself (Gen. 6:21). Eventually, the food was to go into the ark. This verb can also refer to ''gathering'' food at harvest time, or ''harvesting'': ''And six years thou shalt sow thy land, and shalt gather in the fruits thereof'' (Exod. 23:10). Second Kings 22:4 refers not to a process of going out and getting something together, but to standing still as someone brings money to one. Also notice Gen. 29:22: ''And Laban gathered together all the men of the place, and made a feast''; this verse similarly focuses on the end product of gathering. But here the ''gatherer'' does not physically handle what is ''gathered.'' He is simply the impetus or active cause for a congregating of all those men. God may ''gather'' a man to his fathers—i.e., cause him to die (2 Kings 22:20). Here the emphasis is on the end product, and God as the agent who ''gathers.''

'Āsaph may represent not only the process of bringing things to a common location; the word may also represent ''bringing'' things to oneself. After the harvest is brought (''gathered'') in from the threshing floor and wine vat, the Feast of Booths is to be celebrated (Deut. 16:13). In Deut. 22:2, a man is to ''gather'' into his home (bring home and care for) a lost animal whose owner cannot be found. In this manner, God ''gathers'' to Himself those abandoned by their family (Ps. 27:10). A special application of this nuance is to ''receive hospitality'': ''. . . When he went in he sat him down in a street of the city: for there was no man that took them into his house to lodging'' (Judg. 19:15). ''To gather in'' also may mean ''to be consumed by''—God promises that His people ''shall be no more consumed with hunger'' (Ezek. 34:29). Finally, used in this way the verb can mean ''to bring into,'' as when Jacob ''gathered up his feet into the bed'' (Gen. 49:33).

The third emphasis is the ''withdrawal'' or ''removal'' of something; the action is viewed from the perspective of one who loses something because someone has taken it (''gathered it in''). In Ps. 85:3, the ''gathering'' represents this sort of ''withdrawal away from'' the speaker. Thus, anger ''disappears'': ''Thou hast taken away all thy wrath.'' Compare also Rachel's statement at the birth of Joseph: ''God hath taken away my reproach'' (Gen. 30:23). In this case, Sarah speaks of the ''destruction'' of her reproach. ''To gather one's soul'' is ''to lose'' one's life (Judg. 18:25). God can also be the agent who "gathers" or "takes away" a soul: "Gather not my soul with sinners . . ." (Ps. 26:9). In this sense, *'āsaph* can mean "being cured" of a disease; "Would God my lord were with the prophet that is in Samaria! for he would recover him of his leprosy" (2 Kings 5:3).

GENERATION

dôr (דּוֹר), "generation." This noun belongs to a common Semitic root, which signifies "duration" in East Semitic and "generation" in West Semitic. The Akkadian words *daru* ("long duration") and *duru* ("circle") seem by form to be related to the root for the Hebrew word *dôr*.

In the Old Testament, the word *dôr* occurs about 166 times; as many as 74 of these are in the repetition "*dôr* plus *dôr*," meaning "alway." The first occurrence of the word is in Gen. 6:9: "These are the generations of Noah [the account of Noah]: Noah was a just man and perfect in his generations, and Noah walked with God."

First the concrete meaning of "generation" is the "period during which people live": "And the Lord said unto Noah, Come thou and all thy house into the ark; for thee have I seen righteous before me in this generation" (Gen. 7:1). A "generation" may be described as "stubborn" (Deut. 32:5—KJV, "perverse") or "righteous" (Ps. 14:5). Close to this meaning is the temporal element of *dôr*: A *dôr* is roughly the period of time from one's birth to one's maturity, which in the Old Testament corresponds to a period of about 40 years (Num. 14:33). Abraham received the promise that four "generations" of his descendants were to be in Egypt before the Promised Land would be inherited. Israel was warned to be faithful to the Lord, as the punishment for disobedience would extend to the fourth "generation" (Exod. 20:5); but the Lord's love extends to a thousand "generations" of those who love Him (Deut. 7:9).

The lasting element of God's covenantal faithfulness is variously expressed with the word *dôr*: "Thy faithfulness is unto all generations: thou hast established the earth, and it abideth" (Ps. 119:90).

The use of *dôr* in Isa. 51 teaches the twofold perspective of "generation," with reference to the future as well as to the past. Isaiah spoke about the Lord's lasting righteousness and said that His deliverance is everlasting (literally, "generation of generations"—v. 8); but in view of Israel's situation, Isaiah petitioned the Lord to manifest His loving strength on behalf of Israel as in the past (literally, "generations forever"—v. 9). Thus, depending on the context, *dôr* may refer to the past, the present, or the future.

The psalmist recognized the obligation of one "generation" to the "generations" to come: "One generation shall praise thy works to another, and shall declare thy mighty acts" (Ps. 145:4). Even the gray-haired man has the opportunity to instruct the youth (Ps. 71:17-18).

In the Septuagint, *dôr* is nearly always translated by *genea* ("generation"). The KJV translates it by "generation; age."

TO GIVE DRINK

shāqāh (שָׁקָה), "to give drink, irrigate, water." This verb is found in ancient Akkadian and Ugaritic, as well as in biblical and modern Hebrew. The word usually occurs in the causative sense, while its much more common counterpart, *shāthāh,* is used primarily in the simple active form, "to drink." In its first occurrence in the biblical text, *shāqāh* expresses the idea of "to irrigate," or "to water": "But there went up a mist from the earth, and watered the whole face of the ground" (Gen. 2:6). In view of the Mesopotamian background of this passage, both linguistic and agricultural, the Hebrew word for "mist" probably is to be connected with the idea of an irrigation canal or system.

The dry climate of the Middle East makes *shāqāh* a most important word, since it expresses the act of "irrigating" or "watering" crops (Deut. 11:10). God "waters" the earth and causes plants to grow (Ps. 104:13-14). Figuratively, He "irrigates" His vineyard, Israel (Isa. 27:3).

A frequent use of *shāqāh* is to express the "giving of water to drink" to animals (Gen. 24:14, 46; 29:2-3, 7-8, 10). Men are given a variety of things to drink, such as water (Gen. 24:43), wine (Gen. 19:32; Amos 2:12), milk (Judg. 4:19), and vinegar (Ps. 69:21). In a symbol of divine judgment, God is said to give "poisoned water [KJV, "water of gall"] to drink" to Israel (Jer. 8:14; 9:15; 23:15). In this time of judgment and mourning, Israel was not to be given "the cup of consolation to drink" (Jer. 16:7).

A healthy person is one whose bones "are moistened" with marrow (Job 21:24; literally, whose bones "are watered" or "irrigated" with marrow).

GLORY

A. Noun.

tipha'ereth (תִּפְאָרֶת), "glory; beauty; ornament; distinction; pride." This word appears about 51 times and in all periods of biblical Hebrew.

The word represents "beauty," in the sense of the characteristic enhancing one's appearance: "And thou shalt make holy garments for Aaron thy brother for glory and for beauty" (Exod. 28:2—the first occurrence). In Isa. 4:2, the word identifies the fruit of the earth as the "beauty" or "adornment" of the survivors of Israel.

Tipha'ereth (or *tipha'arāh*) means "glory" in several instances. The word is used of one's rank. A crown of "glory" is a crown which, by its richness, indicates high rank—Wisdom will "[present you with] a crown of glory (NASB, "beauty")" (Prov. 4:9). "The hoary head is a crown of glory" (Prov. 16:31), a reward for righteous living. In Isa. 62:3, the phrase "crown of glory (NASB, "beauty")" is paralleled by "royal diadem." This word also modifies the greatness of a king (Esther 1:4) and the greatness of the inhabitants of Jerusalem (Zech. 12:7). In each of these instances, this word emphasizes the rank of the persons or things so modified. The word is used of one's renown:

". . . And to make thee high above all nations which he hath made, in praise, and in name, and in honor [distinction]" (Deut. 26:19).

In another related nuance, *tiphə'ereth* (or *tiphə'arāh*) is used of God, to emphasize His rank, renown, and inherent "beauty": "Thine, O Lord, is the greatness, and the power, and the glory, and the victory, and the majesty . . ." (1 Chron. 29:11).

This word represents the "honor" of a nation, in the sense of its position before God: "[He has] cast down from heaven unto the earth the beauty [honor or pride] of Israel . . ." (Lam. 2:1). This nuance is especially clear in passages such as Judg. 4:9: "I will surely go with thee: notwithstanding the journey that thou takest shall not be for thine honor [i.e., distinction]; for the Lord shall sell Sisera into the hand of a woman."

In Isa. 10:12, *tiphə'ereth* (or *tiphə'arāh*) represents a raising of oneself to a high rank in one's own eyes: ". . . I will punish the fruit of the stout heart of the king of Assyria, and the glory of his high looks."

B. Verb.

pā'ar (פָּאַר), "to glorify." This verb occurs 13 times in biblical Hebrew. One appearance of this verb is in Isa. 60:9: ". . . And to the Holy One of Israel, because he hath gloried thee."

TO GO AWAY, LEAVE

A. Verb.

gālāh (גָּלָה), "to leave, depart, uncover, reveal." This verb occurs in Ugaritic, Phoenician, Arabic, imperial Aramaic, biblical Aramaic, and Ethiopic. Biblical Hebrew attests it in all periods and about 190 times. Some scholars divide this verb into two homonyms (two separate words spelled the same). If this division is accepted, *gālāh* (1) appears about 112 times and *gālāh* (2) about 75 times. Other scholars consider this one verb with an intransitive emphasis and a transitive emphasis. This seems more likely.

Intransitively, *gālāh* signifies "depart" or "leave." This meaning is seen clearly in 1 Sam. 4:21: "And she named the child Ichabod, saying, The glory is departed from Israel. . . ." Thus Isaiah 24:11 could be translated: "The gaiety of the earth departs." One special use of this sense of the verb is "to go into exile." The first biblical occurrence of *gālāh* carries this nuance: "And the children of Dan set up the graven image: and Jonathan . . . and his sons were priests to the tribe of Dan until the day of the *captivity* of the land" (Judg. 18:30), or until they lost control of the land and were forced to serve other gods.

The best-known Old Testament captivity was the one brought by God through the kings of Assyria and Babylon (1 Chron. 5:26; cf. Jer. 29:1).

Although *gālāh* is not used in this sense in the law of Moses, the idea is clearly present. If Israel does not "observe to do all the words of this law that are written in this book, that thou mayest fear this glorious and fearful name, The Lord Thy God; . . . ye shall be plucked from off the land whither thou goest to possess it. And the Lord shall scatter thee among all people . . ." (Deut. 28:58, 63-64; cf. Lev. 26:27, 33). This verb can also be used of the "exile of individuals," such as David (2 Sam. 15:19).

This word may signify "making oneself naked." Noah "drank of the wine, and was drunken; and he was uncovered within his tent" (Gen. 9:21).

The transitive form occurs less frequently, but has a greater variety of meanings. "To uncover" another person may mean "to have sexual relations with" him or her: "None of you shall approach to any [blood relative of his] to uncover their nakedness: I am the Lord" (Lev. 18:6). Uncovering one's nakedness does not always, however, refer to sexual relations (cf. Exod. 20:26). Another phrase, "to uncover someone's skirts," means to have sexual relations with a person (Deut. 22:30).

In Isaiah 16:3, *gālāh* (2) (in the intensive stem) signifies "betray": ". . . Hide the outcasts [do not betray the fugitive]. . . ." This verb may also be used of "uncovering" (KJV "discovering") things, of "laying them bare" so that they become visible: ". . . The foundations of the world were discovered at the rebuking of the Lord . . ." (2 Sam. 22:16). In a related sense Ezek. 23:18 speaks of "uncovering" harlotries, of "exposing" them constantly or leading a life of harlotry.

God's "uncovering" of Himself means that He "revealed" Himself (Gen. 35:7). "To uncover someone's ears" is to tell him something: "Now the day before Saul came, the Lord had revealed [literally, "had uncovered the ear"] to Samuel . . ." (1 Sam. 9:15, RSV). In this case, the verb means not simply "to tell," but "to tell someone something that was not known." Used in this sense, *gālāh* is applied to the "revealing" of secrets (Prov. 11:13) and of one's innermost feelings. Hence, Jer. 11:20 should be translated: "For unto thee have I revealed my case."

Thus *gālāh* can be used of "making something" openly known, or of "publicizing" it: "The copy of the writing for a commandment to be given in every province was published unto all people, that they should be ready against that day" (Esth. 3:14). Another nuance appears in Jer. 32:11, where *gālāh*, in connection with a deed of purchase, means "not sealed or closed up."

B. Noun.

gôlāh (גּוֹלָה), "exile; people exiled." This word makes 42 Old Testament appearances. Ezra 2:1 uses the word of "people returning from the exile." In other references, the word means "people in exile" (2 Kings 24:15). In 1 Chron. 5:22, *gôlāh* refers to the era of the "exile."

TO GO DOWN

yārad (יָרַד), "to descend, go down, come down." This verb occurs in most Semitic languages (including post-biblical Hebrew) and in all periods. In biblical Hebrew, the word appears about 380 times and in all periods.

Basically, this verb connotes "movement" from a higher to a lower location. In Gen. 28:12, Jacob saw a "ladder set up on the earth, and the top of it reached to heaven: and behold the angels of God ascending and descending on it." In such a use, the speaker or observer speaks from the point of destination, and the movement is "downward" toward him. Thus one may "go down" below or under the ground's surface (Gen. 24:16). The speaker may also speak as though he stands at the point of departure and the movement is away from him and "downward."

Interestingly, one may "go down" to a lower spot in order to reach a city's gates (Judg. 5:11) or to get to a city located on a lower level than the access road (1 Sam. 10:8)—usually one goes up to a city and "goes down" to leave a city (1 Sam. 9:27). The journey from Palestine to Egypt is referred to as "going down" (Gen. 12:10). This reference is not to a movement in space from a higher to a lower spot; it is a more technical use of the verb.

Yārad is used frequently of "dying." One "goes down" to his grave. Here the idea of spatial movement is present, but in the background. This "going down" is much more of a removal from the world of conscious existence: "For the grave cannot praise thee, death cannot celebrate thee: they that go down into the pit cannot hope for thy truth. The living, the living, he shall praise thee . . ." (Isa. 38:18-19). On the other hand, "going down to the dust" implies a return to the soil—i.e., a return of the body to the soil from which it came (Gen. 3:19). "All they that go down to the dust shall bow before him . . ." (Ps. 22:29). There is also the idea of the "descent" of the human soul into the realm of the dead. When Jacob mourned over Joseph, whom he thought to be dead, he said: "For I will go down into the grave unto my son mourning" (Gen. 37:35). Since one can "descend" into Sheol alive as a form of punishment (Num. 16:30), this phrase means more than the end of human life. This meaning is further established because Enoch was rewarded by being taken off the earth: "And Enoch walked with God: and he was not; for God took him" (Gen. 5:24); he was rewarded by not having "to descend" into Sheol.

Yārad may also be used of "coming down," when the emphasis is on "moving downward" toward the speaker: "And the Lord came down to see the city and the tower" of Babel (Gen. 11:5—the first biblical occurrence). This verb may also be used to express coming down from the top of a mountain, as Moses did when he "descended" from Sinai (Exod. 19:14). The word may be used of "dismounting" from a donkey: "And when Abigail saw David, she hasted, and lighted off the ass . . ." (1 Sam. 25:23). Abigail's entire body was not necessarily lower than before, so movement from a higher to a lower location is not indicated. However, she was no longer on the animal's back. So the verb here indicates "getting off" rather than getting down or descending. In a somewhat related nuance, one may "get out" of bed. Elijah told Ahaziah: "Thou shalt not come down from that bed on which thou art gone up . . ." (2 Kings 1:4). Again, the idea is not of descending *from* something. When one comes down from a bed, he stands up; he is higher than he was while yet in the bed. Therefore, the meaning here is "get out of" rather than "descend." This verb is used also to describe what a beard does—it "hangs down" (Ps. 133:2).

Yārad is used to indicate "coming away from" the altar: "And Aaron lifted up his hand toward the people, and blessed them, and came down from offering of the sin offering . . .'' (Lev. 9:22). This special use is best seen as the opposite of "ascending to" the altar, which is not just a physical movement from a lower to a higher plane but a spiritual ascent to a higher realm of reality. For example, to "ascend" before a king is to go into the presence of someone who is on a higher social level. "To ascend" before God (represented by the altar) is to go before Someone on a higher spiritual plane. To stand before God is to stand in His presence, before His throne, on a higher spiritual plane. *Yārad* may thus be used of the humbled approach before God. God tells Moses that all the Egyptians shall "come down" to Him and bow themselves before Him (Exod. 11:8). Equally interesting is the occasional use of the verb to represent "descending" to a known sanctuary (cf. 2 Kings 2:2).

Figuratively, the verb has many uses. The "going down" of a city is its destruction (Deut. 20:20). When a day "descends," it comes to an end (Judg. 19:11). The "descent" of a shadow is its lengthening (2 Kings 20:11). Tears "flow down" the cheeks when one weeps bitterly (Jer. 13:17). *Yārad* is also used figuratively of a "descent in social position": "The stranger that is within thee shall get up above thee very high; and thou shalt come down very low" (Deut. 28:43).

At least once the word means "to go up." Jephthah's daughter said: "Let me alone two months, that I may go up and down upon the mountains, and bewail my virginity . . ." (Judg. 11:37).

TO GO OUT, GO FORTH

A. Verb.

yātsā' (יָצָא), "to come forth, go out, proceed, go forth, bring out, come out." This verb occurs in all Semitic languages, including biblical Aramaic and Hebrew. It occurs in every period of Hebrew; the Old Testament attests the word about 1,070 times.

Basically, this word means "movement away" from some point, even as *bô'* ("come") means movement toward some point. *Yātsa'* is the word used of "coming forth"—the observer is outside the point of departure but also speaks from the perspective of that departing point. For example, Gen. 2:10 (the first occurrence of the word) reports that a river "came forth" or "flowed out" from the garden of Eden.

In comparison to this continuing "going out," there is the one-time (punctiliar) "coming forth," as seen when all the animals "came out" of the ark (Gen. 9:10). Thus, Goliath the champion of the Philistines "went forward" from the camp to challenge the Israelites to a duel (1 Sam. 17:4). In the art of ancient warfare, a battle was sometimes decided on the basis of two duelers.

This verb may be used with "come" (*bô'*) as an expression for "constant activity." The raven Noah sent out "went forth to and fro" (literally, "in and out") until the water had abated (Gen. 8:7). Various aspects of a man's personality may "go forth," indicating that they "leave" him. When one's soul "departs" the body, the person dies (Gen. 35:18). When one's heart "departs," he loses all inner strength and confidence (Gen. 42:28).

Yātsa' has a number of special uses. It can be used of "giving birth" (Exod. 21:22) or of "begetting" descendants (Gen. 17:6). The "going forth" of a year is its close, as in the harvest season (Exod. 23:16). Another special use of this verb has to do with "moving out" a camp for either a military campaign (1 Sam. 8:20) or some other purpose (Deut. 23:10). "Going and coming" may also be used of "fighting" in wars. Toward the end of his life Moses said he was unable to "come and go" (Deut. 31:2; cf. Josh. 14:11). He probably meant that he could not engage in war (Deut. 31:3). On the other hand, this phrase can refer to the normal activities of life (1 Kings. 3:7). *Yātsa'* also has a cultic use, describing the "movement" of the priest in the tabernacle; bells were attached to the hem of the priest's robe so the people could follow his actions (Exod. 28:35).

When applied to God, the action of "going out" only infrequently refers to His "abandoning" a certain location. In Ezek. 10:18, the glory of the Lord "left" the "threshhold of the [temple], and stood over the cherubim," and eventually departed the temple altogether (Ezek 10:19). Often this verb pictures the Lord as "going forth" to aid His people, especially in texts suggesting or depicting His appearances among men (theophanies; cf. Judg. 5:4). In Egypt, the Lord "went out" into the midst of the Egyptians to smite their first born (Exod. 11:4). The Lord's departure-point in such cases is variously represented as Seir (Judg. 5:4) and His heavenly dwelling place (Mic. 1:3), although it is often unexpressed.

The messenger of God also "goes forth" to accomplish specific tasks (Num. 22:32). God's providential work in history is described by Laban and Bethuel as "the thing proceedeth from the Lord" (Gen. 24:50). Also, "going out" from the Lord are His hand (Ruth 1:13), His Word (Isa. 55:11), His salvation (Isa. 51:5), His justice (Isa. 45:23), and His wisdom (Isa. 51:4).

Yātsa' is not used of God's initial creative act, but only of His using what already exists to accomplish His purposes, such as His causing water to "come out" of the rock (Deut. 8:15). Because *yātsa'* can mean "to bring forth," it is often used of "divine deliverance," as the One who "bringeth me forth from mine enemies" (2 Sam. 22:49) "into a large place" (2 Sam. 22:20). One of the most important formulas in the Old Testament uses the verb *yātsa'*: "the Lord [who] brought [Israel] out of [Egypt]"; He brought them from slavery into freedom (Exod. 13:3).

B. Nouns.

môtsā' (מוֹצָא), "place of going forth; that which comes forth; going forth." The word occurs 23 times. *Môtsā'* is a word for "east" (cf. Ps. 19:6), where the sun rises ("goes forth"). The word also represents the "place of departure" or "exit" from the temple in Ezekiel's vision (Ezek. 42:11), and the "starting point" of a journey (Num. 33:2). *Môtsā'* may also refer to that which "comes forth," for example, an "utterance" (Num. 30:13), and the "going forth" of the morning and evening, the dawn and dusk (Ps. 65:8). Finally, the word can represent the "actual going forth" itself. So Hosea says that the Lord's "going forth" to redeem His people is as certain as the sunrise (6:3).

tôtsā'ôth (תּוֹצָאוֹת), "departure; place of departure." The word *tôtsā'ôth* can connote both the source or place of "departure" (Prov. 4:23) and the actual "departure" itself ("escape," Ps. 68:20). However, the word may also represent the extremity of a territory or its "border"—the place where one departs a given territory (Josh. 15:7).

GOAT-DEMONS

sā'îr (שָׂעִיר), "goat-demons; goat-idols." This word occurs 4 times in biblical Hebrew. In its first biblical appearance, the word represents "goat-demons" (some scholars translate it "goat-idols"): "And they shall no more offer their sacrifices unto devils [NASB, "goat demons"], after whom they have gone a whoring" (Lev. 17:7). This passage demonstrates that the word represents beings that were objects of pagan worship. Worship of these "demons" persisted long in the history of Israel, appearing under Jeroboam I (929–909 B.C.), who ". . . ordained him priests for the high places, and for the devils [RSV, "satyrs"], and for the calves which he had made" (2 Chron. 11:15). In this instance, *sā'îr* represents idols that Jeroboam had manufactured. Josiah's revival probably involved the breaking down of the high places of the goat demons (2 Kings 23:8).

GOD

'ēl (אֵל), "god." This term was the most common general designation of deity in the ancient Near East. While it frequently occurred alone, *'ēl* was also combined with other words to constitute a compound term for deity, or to identify the nature and functions of the "god" in some manner. Thus the expression "God, the God of Israel" (Gen. 33:20) identified the specific activities of Israel's God.

In the ancient world, knowledge of a person's name was believed to give one power over that person. A knowledge of the character and attributes of pagan "gods" was thought to enable the worshipers to manipulate or influence the deities in a more effective way than they could have if the deity's name remained unknown. To that extent, the vagueness of the term *'ēl* frustrated persons who hoped to obtain some sort of power over the deity, since the name gave little or no indication of the god's character. This was particularly true for El, the chief Canaanite god. The ancient Semites stood in mortal dread of the superior powers exercised by the gods and attempted to propitiate them accordingly. They commonly associated deity with the manifestation and use of enormous power. Perhaps this is reflected in the curious Hebrew phrase, "the power ['ēl] of my hand" (Gen. 31:29, KJV; RSV, "It is in my power"; cf. Deut. 28:32). Some Hebrew phrases in the Psalms associated *'ēl* with impressive natural features, such as the cedar trees of Lebanon (Ps. 80:10) or mountains (Ps. 36:6). In these instances, *'ēl* conveys a clear impression of grandeur or majesty.

Names with *'ēl* as one of their components were common in the Near East in the second millennium B.C. The names Methusael (Gen. 4:18) and Ishmael (Gen. 16:11) come from a very early period. In the Mosaic period, *'ēl* was synonymous with the Lord who delivered the Israelites from bondage in Egypt and made them victorious in battle (Num. 24:8). This tradition of the Hebrew *'ēl* as a "God" who revealed Himself in power and entered into a covenant relationship with His people was prominent in both poetry (Ps. 7:11; 85:8) and prophecy (Isa. 43:12; 46:9). The name of *'ēl* was commonly used by the Israelites to denote supernatural provision or power. This was both normal and legitimate, since the covenant between "God" and Israel assured an obedient and holy people that the creative forces of the universe would sustain and protect at all times. Equally, if they became disobedient and apostate, these same forces would punish them severely.

'elāh (אֱלָהּ), "god." This Aramaic word is the equivalent of the Hebrew *'elôah*. It is a general term for "God" in the Aramaic passages of the Old Testament, and it is a cognate form of the word *'allāh,* the designation of deity used by the Arabs. The word was used widely in the Book of Ezra, occurring no fewer than 43 times between Ezra 4:24 and 7:26. On each occasion, the reference is to the "God" of the Jewish people, whether the speaker or writer was himself Jewish or not. Thus the governor of the province "Beyond the River" (i.e., west of the river Euphrates) spoke to king Darius of the "house of the great God" (Ezra 5:8). So also Cyrus instructed Sheshbazzar, the governor, that the "house of God be builded" in Jerusalem (Ezra 5:15).

While the Persians were certainly not worshipers of the "God" of Israel, they accorded Him the dignity that befitted a "God of heaven" (Ezra 6:10). This was done partly through superstition; but the pluralistic nature of the newly-won Persian empire also required them to honor the gods of conquered peoples, in the interests of peace and social harmony. When Ezra himself used the word *'elāh,* he frequently specified the God of the Jews. Thus he spoke of the "God of Israel" (5:1; 6:14), the "God of heaven" (5:12; 6:9), and "God of Jerusalem" (7:19); he also associated "God" with His house in Jerusalem (5:17; 6:3). In the decree of Artaxerxes, Ezra was described as "the priest, the scribe of the God of heaven" (7:12, 21). This designation would have sounded strange coming from a pagan Persian ruler, had it not been for the policy of religious toleration exercised by the Achaemenid regime. Elsewhere in Ezra, *'elāh* is associated with the temple, both when it was about to be rebuilt (5:2, 13) and as a finished edifice, consecrated for divine worship (6:16).

In the only verse in the Book of Jeremiah that was written in Aramaic (10:11), the word *'elāh* appears in plural form to describe "gods" that had not participated in the creation of the universe. Although such false "gods" were being worshiped by pagan nations (and perhaps worshiped by some of the Hebrews who were in exile in Babylonia), these deities would ultimately perish because they were not eternal in nature.

In the Book of Daniel, *'elāh* was used both of heathen "gods" and the one true "God" of heaven. The Chaldean priests told Nebuchadnezzar: "And it is a rare thing that the king requireth, and there is none other that can show it before the king, except the gods, whose dwelling is not with flesh" (Dan.

2:11). The Chaldeans referred to such "gods" when reporting that Shadrach, Meshach, and Abed-nego refused to participate in idol worship on the plain of Dura (Dan. 3:12). The "gods" were enumerated by Daniel when he condemned Nebuchadnezzar's neglect of the worship of Israel's one true "God" (Dan. 5:23). In Dan. 3:25, the word refers to a divine being or messenger sent to protect the three Hebrews (Dan. 3:28). In Dan. 4:8-9, 18; and 5:11, the phrase "the spirit of the holy gods" appears (KJV, RSV, NEB, NIV). Elsewhere the references to *'elāh* are to the living "God" whom Daniel worshiped.

'elôah (אֱלוֹהַ), "god." This Hebrew name for "God" corresponds to the Aramaic *'elāh* and the Ugaritic *il* (or, if denoting a goddess, *ilt*). The origin of the term is unknown, and it is used rarely in Scripture as a designation of deity. Indeed, its distribution throughout the various books of the Bible is curiously uneven. *'Elôah* occurs 40 times in the Book of Job between 3:4 and 40:2, while in the remainder of the Old Testament it is used no more than 15 times.

Certain scholars regard the word as being a singular version of the common plural form *'elōhîm,* a plural of majesty. *'Elôah* is commonly thought to be vocative in nature, meaning "O God." But it is not clear why a special form for the vocative in an address to God should be needed, since the plural *'elōhîm* is frequently translated as a vocative when the worshiper is speaking directly to God, as in Ps. 79:1. There is an obvious general linguistic relationship between *'elôah* and *'elōhîm,* but determining its precise nature is difficult.

The word *'elôah* is predominant in poetry rather than prose literature, and this is especially true of the Book of Job. Some scholars have suggested that the author of Job deliberately chose a description for godhead that avoided the historical associations found in a phrase such as "the God of Bethel" (Gen. 31:13) or "God of Israel" (Exod. 24:10). But even the Book of Job is by no means historically neutral, since places and peoples are mentioned in introducing the narrative (cf. Job 1:1, 15, 17). Perhaps the author considered *'elôah* a suitable term for poetry and used it accordingly with consistency. This is also apparently the case in Ps. 18:31, where *'elôah* is found instead of *'ēl,* as in the parallel passage of 2 Sam. 22:32. *'Elôah* also appears as a term for God in Ps. 50:22; 139:19; and Prov. 30:5. Although *'elôah* as a divine name is rarely used outside Job, its literary history extends from at least the second millennium B.C. (as in Deut. 32:15) to the fifth century B.C. (as in Neh. 9:17).

'Ēl Shaddai (אֵל שַׁדַּי), "God Almighty." This combination of *'ēl* with a qualifying term represents a religious tradition among the Israelites that was probably in existence by the third millennium B.C. A few centuries later, *Shaddai* appeared in Hebrew personal names such as Zurishaddai (Num. 1:6) and Ammishaddai (Num. 1:12). The earliest Old Testament appearance of the appellation as a title of deity ("God Almighty") is in Gen. 17:1, where "God" identifies Himself in this way to Abraham.

Unfortunately, the name is not explained in any manner; and even the directions "walk before me, and be thou perfect" throw no light on the meaning of *Shaddai.* Scholars have attempted to understand the word relating it to the Akkadian *shadū* ("mountain"), as though "God" had either revealed His mighty power in association with mountain phenomena such as volcanic eruptions, or that He was regarded strong and immutable, like the "everlasting hills" of the blessing of Jacob (Gen. 49:26). Certainly the associating of deity with mountains was an important part of Mesopotamian religion. The "gods" were believed to favor mountaintop dwellings, and the Sumerians constructed their staged temple-towers or ziggurats as artificial mountains for worship. It was customary to erect a small shrine on the uppermost stage of the ziggurat so that the patron deity could descend from heaven and inhabit the temple. The Hebrews began their own tradition of mountain revelation just after the Exodus, but by this time the name *'Ēl Shaddai* had been replaced by the tetragrammaton of Yahweh (Exod. 3:15; 6:3).

'Ēl Shaddai served as the patriarchs' covenant name for "God," and continued as such until the time of Moses, when a further revelation took place (Exod. 6:3). The Abrahamic covenant was marked by a degree of closeness between "God" and the human participants that was distinctive in Hebrew history. "God Almighty" revealed Himself as a powerful deity who was able to perform whatever He asserted. But the degree of intimacy between *'Ēl Shaddai* and the patriarchs at various stages shows that the covenant involved God's care and love for this growing family that He had chosen, protected, and prospered. He led the covenant family from place to place, being obviously present with them at all times. His covenant formulations show that He was not preoccupied with cultic rites or orgiastic celebrations. Instead, He demanded a degree of obedience that would enable Abraham and his descendants to walk in His presence, and live blameless moral and spiritual lives (Gen. 17:1). The true covenantal service of *'Ēl Shaddai*, therefore, was not cultic or ritualistic, but moral and ethical in character.

In the early Mosaic era, the new redemptive name of "God" and the formulation of the Sinai covenant made *'Ēl Shaddai* largely obsolete as a designation of deity. Subsequently, the name occurs about 35 times in the Old Testament, most of which are in the Book of Job. Occasionally, the name is used synonymously with the tetragrammaton of Yahweh (Ruth 1:21; Ps. 91:1-2), to emphasize the power and might of "God" in characteristic fashion.

'Ēl 'Ôlām (אֵל עוֹלָם), "God of eternity; God the everlasting; God for ever." The word *'ôlām* has related forms in various ancient Near Eastern languages, all of which describe lengthy duration or distant time. The idea seems to be quantitative rather than metaphysical. Thus in Ugaritic literature, a person described as *'bd'lm* was a "permanent slave," the term *'lm* (the same as the Hebrew *'ôlām*) expressing a period of time that could not be measured other than as lengthy duration.

Only in rare poetic passages such as Ps. 90:2 are temporal categories regarded inadequate to describe the nature of God's existence as *'Ēl 'Ôlām*. In such an instance, the Creator is deemed to have been "from everlasting to everlasting"; but even this use of *'ôlām* expresses the idea of continued, measurable existence rather than a state of being independent of temporal considerations.

The name *'Ēl 'Ôlām* was associated predominantly with Beer-sheba (Gen.

21:25-34). The settlement of Beer-sheba was probably founded during the Early Bronze Age, and the Genesis narrative explains that the name means "well of the oath" (Gen. 21:31). But it could also mean "well of the seven"— i.e., the seven lambs that were set apart as witnesses of the oath.

Abraham planted a commemorative tree in Beer-sheba and invoked the name of the Lord as 'Ēl 'Ôlām. The fact that Abraham subsequently stayed many days in the land of the Philistines seems to imply that he associated continuity and stability with 'Ēl 'Ôlām, who was not touched by the vicissitudes of time. Although Beer-sheba may have been a place where the Canaanites worshiped originally, the area later became associated with the veneration of the God of Abraham.

At a subsequent period, Jacob journeyed to Beer-sheba and offered sacrifices to the God of Isaac his father. He did not offer sacrifices to 'Ēl 'Ôlām by name, however; and although he saw a visionary manifestation of God, he received no revelation that this was the God Abraham had venerated at Beer-sheba. Indeed, God omitted any mention of Abraham, stating that He was the God of Jacob's father.

Gen. 21:33 is the only place in the Old Testament where the title 'Ēl 'Ôlām occurs. Isa. 40:28 is the only other instance where 'ôlām is used in conjunction with a noun meaning "God." *See also* LORD.

GOLD

zāhāb (זָהָב), "gold." This word has cognates in Arabic and Aramaic. It occurs about 385 times in biblical Hebrew and in every period.

Zāhāb can refer to "gold ore," or "gold in its raw state." This is its meaning in its first biblical appearance: "The name of the first is Pison: that is it which compasseth the whole land of Havilah, where there is gold" (Gen. 2:11). The word can also be used of "gold" which has already been refined: "But he knoweth the way that I take: when he hath tried me, I shall come forth as gold" (Job 23:10). "Gold" could be beaten (1 Kings 10:16) and purified (Exod. 25:11). One can also speak of the best "gold" (2 Chron. 3:5).

Zāhāb can be conceived of as an "object of wealth": "And Abram was very rich in cattle, in silver, and in gold" (Gen. 13:2). As such, the emphasis is on "gold" as a valuable or precious commodity. Consequently, the word is used in comparisons: "The gold and the crystal cannot equal it: and the exchange of it shall not be for jewels of fine gold" (Job 28:17).

"Gold" was often one of the spoils of war: "But all the silver, and gold, and vessels of brass and iron, are consecrated unto the Lord: they shall come into the treasury of the Lord" (Josh. 6:19).

"Gold" was bought and sold as an object of merchandise: "The merchants of Sheba and Raamah, they were thy merchants: they [paid for your wares] with chief of all spices, and with all precious stones, and gold" (Ezek. 27:22).

Zāhāb was used as a costly gift: "And Balaam answered and said unto the servants of Balak, If Balak would give me his house full of silver and gold, I [could not do anything] . . ." (Num. 22:18).

This metal was used as a material to make jewelry and other valuable items: "And it came to pass, as the camels had done drinking, that the man took a golden earring of half a shekel weight, and two bracelets for her hands of ten shekels weight of gold . . ." (Gen. 24:22). Solomon's temple was adorned with "gold" (1 Kings 6:20-28).

Gold was used as money, being exchanged in various weights and values (according to its weight): "And he made three hundred shields of beaten gold; three pound of gold went to one shield . . ." (1 Kings 10:17; cf. 2 Sam. 12:30). "Gold" even existed in the form of "coins" (Ezra 2:69).

Zāhāb is used for the color "gold": "What be these two olive branches which through the two golden pipes empty the golden oil out of themselves?" (Zech. 4:12).

GOOD

A. Adjective.

tôb (טוֹב), "good; favorable; festive; pleasing; pleasant; well; better; right; best." This word appears in Akkadian, Aramaic, Arabic, Ugaritic, and Old South Arabic. Occurring in all periods of biblical Hebrew, it appears about 559 times.

This adjective denotes "good" in every sense of that word. For example, *tôb* is used in the sense "pleasant" or "delightful": "And he saw that [a resting place] was good, and the land that it was pleasant; and bowed his shoulder to bear [burdens] . . ." (Gen. 49:15). An extension of this sense appears in Gen. 40:16, where *tôb* means "favorable" or "in one's favor": "When the chief baker saw that the interpretation was *good,* he said unto Joseph. . . ." In 1 Sam. 25:8, the emphasis is on the nuance "delightful" or "festal": ". . . Let the young men find favor in thine eyes: for we come in a *good* day. . . ." God is described as One who is "good," or One who gives "delight" and "pleasure": "But it is good for me to draw near to God: I have put my trust in the Lord God, that I may declare all thy works" (Ps. 73:28).

In 1 Sam. 29:6, this word describes human activities: ". . . As the Lord liveth, thou hast been upright, and thy going out and thy coming in with me in the [army] is good in my sight. . . ." *Tôb* can be applied to scenic beauty, as in 2 Kings 2:19: "Behold, I pray thee, the situation of this city is pleasant, as my lord seeth:but the water is naught, and the ground barren." Second Chron. 12:12 employs a related nuance when it applies the word to the conditions in Judah under King Rehoboam, after he humbled himself before God: ". . . Things went well."

Tôb often qualifies a common object or activity. When the word is used in this sense, no ethical overtones are intended. In 1 Sam. 19:4, *tôb* describes the way Jonathan spoke about David: "And Jonathan spake good of David unto Saul his father, and said unto him, Let not the king sin against his servant, against David; because he hath not sinned against thee, and because his works have been [toward thee] very good." First Sam. 25:15 characterizes a people as "friendly" or "useful": "But the men were very good unto us, and we were not hurt, neither missed we any thing, as long as we were conversant with them, when we were in the fields. . . .'' Often this word bears an even stronger emphasis, as in 1 Kings 12:7, where the ''good word'' is not only friendly but eases the life of one's servants. God's ''good word'' promises life in the face of oppression and uncertainty: ''. . . There hath not failed one word of all his good promise, which he promised by the hand of Moses his servant'' (1 Kings 8:56). *Tôb* often characterizes a statement as an important assertion for salvation and prosperity (real or imagined): ''Is not this the word that we did tell thee in Egypt, saying, Let us alone, that we may serve the Egyptians? For it had been *better* for us to serve the Egyptians, than that we should die in the wilderness'' (Exod. 14:12). God judged that man's circumstance without a wife or helpmeet was not ''good'' (Gen. 2:18). Elsewhere *tôb* is applied to an evaluation of one's well-being or of the well-being of a situation or thing: ''And God saw the light, that it was good: and God divided the light from the darkness'' (Gen. 1:4—the first occurrence).

Tôb is used to describe land and agriculture: ''And I am come down to deliver them out of the [power] of the Egyptians, and to bring them up out of that land unto a good [fertile] land and a large, unto a land flowing with milk and honey . . .'' (Exod. 3:8). This suggests its potential of supporting life (Deut. 11:17). Thus the expression ''the good land'' is a comment about not only its existing, but its potential, productivity. In such contexts the land is viewed as one aspect of the blessings of salvation promised by God; thus the Lord did not permit Moses to cross the Jordan and enter the land which His people were to inherit (Deut. 3:26-28). This aspect of the ''good land'' includes overtones of its fruitfulness and ''pleasantness'': ''And he will take your fields, and your vineyards, and your oliveyards, even the best of them . . .'' (1 Sam. 8:14).

Tôb is used to describe men or women. Sometimes it is used of an ''elite corps'' of people: ''And he will take your menservants, and your maidservants, and your goodliest young men, and your asses . . .'' (1 Sam. 8:16). In 2 Sam. 18:27, Ahimaaz is described as a ''good'' man because he comes with ''good'' military news. In 1 Sam. 15:28, the word has ethical overtones: ''The Lord hath rent the kingdom of Israel from thee this day, and hath given it to a neighbor of thine, that is better than thou'' (cf. 1 Kings 2:32). In other passages, *tôb* describes physical appearance: ''And the damsel was very fair to look upon [literally, ''good of appearance''] . . .'' (Gen. 24:16). When applied to one's heart, the word describes ''well-being'' rather than ethical status. Therefore, the parallel idea is ''joyous and happy'': ''. . . And they . . . went unto their tents joyful and glad of heart for all the goodness that the Lord had done for David . . .'' (1 Kings 8:66). Dying ''at a good old age'' describes ''advanced age,'' rather than moral accomplishment, but a time when due to divine blessings one is fulfilled and satisfied (Gen. 15:15).

Tôb indicates that a given word, act, or circumstance contributes positively to the condition of a situation. Often this judgment does not mean that the thing is actually ''good,'' only that it is so evaluated: ''When the chief baker saw that the interpretation was good . . .'' (Gen. 40:16). The judgment may be ethical: ''It is not good that ye do: ought ye not to walk in the fear of our God because of the reproach of the heathen. . .?'' (Neh. 5:9). The word may also represent "agreement" or "concurrence": "The thing proceedeth from the Lord: we cannot speak unto thee bad or good" (Gen. 24:50).

Tôb is often used in conjunction with the Hebrew word *rā'ah* ("bad; evil"). Sometimes this is intended as a contrast; but in other contexts it may mean "everything from good [friendly] to bad [unfriendly]," which is a way of saying "nothing at all." In other contexts, more contrast is suggested: "And what the land is that they dwell in, whether it be good or bad . . ." (Num. 13:19). In this case, the evaluation would determine whether the land could support the people well or not.

In Gen. 2:9, *tôb* contrasted with evil has moral overtones: ". . . The tree of life also in the midst of the garden, and the tree of knowledge of good and evil." The fruit of this tree, if consumed, would reveal the difference between moral evil and moral "good." This reference also suggests that, by eating this fruit, man attempted to determine for himself what "good" and evil are.

B. Verbs.

yātab (יָטַב), "to go well, be pleasing, be delighted, be happy." This verb appears 117 times in the Old Testament. The meaning of the word, as expressed in Neh. 2:6, is "pleased."

tôb (טוֹב), "to be joyful, glad, pleasant, lovely, appropriate, becoming, good, precious." *Tôb* has cognates in Akkadian and Arabic. The verb occurs 21 times in the Old Testament. Job 13:9 is one example of the word's meaning, "to be good": "Is it good that he should search you out?"

TO BE GRACIOUS, SHOW FAVOR

A. Verb.

chānan (חָנַן), "to be gracious, considerate; to show favor." This word is found in ancient Ugaritic with much the same meaning as in biblical Hebrew. But in modern Hebrew *chānan* seems to stress the stronger meaning of "to pardon or to show mercy." The word occurs around 80 times in the Hebrew Old Testament, the first time in Gen. 33:5: "The children which God hath graciously given thy servant." Generally, this word implies the extending of "favor," often when it is neither expected nor deserved. *Chānan* may express "generosity," a gift from the heart (Ps. 37:21). God especially is the source of undeserved "favor" (Gen. 33:11), and He is asked repeatedly for such "gracious" acts as only He can do (Num. 6:25; Gen. 43:29). The psalmist prays: ". . . Grant me thy law graciously" (Ps. 119:29).

God's "favor" is especially seen in His deliverance from one's enemies or surrounding evils (Ps. 77:9; Amos 5:15). However, God extends His "graciousness" in His own sovereign way and will to whomever He chooses (Exod. 33:19).

In many ways, *chānan* combines the meaning of the Greek *charis* (with the general classical Greek sense of "charm" or "graciousness") and the New Testament sense of "undeserved favor" or "mercy."

B. Noun.

chēn (חֵן), "favor; grace." The root with the meaning "to favor someone" is a common Semitic term. In Akkadian, the verb *enēnu* ("to have compassion") is related to *hinnu* ("favor"), which occurs only as a proper noun. The Hebrew noun *chēn* occurs 69 times, mainly in the Pentateuch and in the historical books through Samuel. The word's frequency increases in the poetic books, but it is rare in the prophetic books. The first occurrence is in Gen. 6:8: "But Noah found grace in the eyes of the Lord."

The basic meaning of *chēn* is "favor." Whatever is "pleasant and agreeable" can be described by this word. When a woman is said to have *chēn*, she is a "gracious" woman (Prov. 11:16); or the word may have the negative association of being "beautiful without sense" (Prov. 31:30). A person's speech may be characterized by "graciousness": "He that loveth pureness of heart, for the grace of his lips the king shall be his friend" (Prov. 22:11; cf. Ps. 45:2).

Chēn also denotes the response to whatever is "agreeable." The verbs used with "favor" are: "give favor" (Gen. 39:21), "obtain favor" (Exod. 3:21), and "find favor" (Gen. 6:8, RSV). The idioms are equivalent to the English verbs "to like" or "to love": "[She] said to him, Why have I found favor in your eyes, that you should take notice of me, when I am a foreigner?" (Ruth 2:10, RSV).

The Septuagint translations are: *charis* ("grace; favor; graciousness; attractiveness") and *eleos* ("mercy; compassion; pity").

C. Adjective.

channûn (חַנּוּן), "gracious." One of the word's 13 occurrences is in Exod. 34:6: "And the Lord passed by before him [Moses], and proclaimed, The Lord, The Lord God, merciful and gracious, long-suffering, and abundant in goodness and truth. . . ."

TO BE GREAT, HEAVY

A. Verbs.

kābēd (כָּבֵד), "to be heavy, weighty, burdensome, dull, honored, glorious." This word is a common Semitic term, one that is found frequently in ancient Akkadian and Ugaritic, as well as in Hebrew of all periods. *Kābēd* occurs more than 150 times in the Hebrew Bible. The verb's first occurrence is in Gen. 13:2 in the sense of "being rich": "And Abram was very rich. . . ." This usage vividly illustrates the basic implications of the word. Whenever *kābēd* is used, it reflects the idea of "weightiness," or that which is added to something else. Thus, to be "very rich" means that Abram was heavily "weighted down" with wealth. This idea also explains how the word can be used to indicate the state of "being honored" or "glorious," for honor and glory are additional qualities that are added to a person or thing.

"To be heavy" includes negative as well as positive aspects. Thus, calamity is "heavier than the sand of the sea" (Job. 6:3), and the hand of God is "very heavy" in punishing the Philistines (1 Sam. 5:11). Bondage and heavy work are "heavy" on the people (Exod. 5:9; Neh. 5:18). Eyes (Gen. 48:10) and ears (Isa. 59:1) that have become insensitive, or "dull," have had debilitating conditions added to them, whether through age or other causes. The heart of a man may become excessively "weighted" with stubbornness and thus become "hardened" (Exod. 9:7).

"To honor" or "glorify" anything is to add something which it does not have in itself, or that which others can give. Children are commanded to "honor" their parents (Exod. 20:12; Deut. 5:16); Balak promised "honor" to Balaam (Num. 22:17); Jerusalem (Lam. 1:8) and the Sabbath (Isa. 58:13) are "honored" or "made glorious." Above all, "honor" and "glory" are due to God, as repeatedly commanded in the biblical text: "Honor the Lord with thy substance" (Prov. 3:9); "Let the Lord be glorified" (Isa. 66:5); "Glorify ye the Lord" (Isa. 24:15).

Kābēd is also the Hebrew word for "liver," apparently reflecting the sense that the liver is the heaviest of the organs of the body.

rābab (רָבַב), "to be numerous, great, large, powerful." This verb, which occurs 24 times in biblical Hebrew, appears in most other Semitic languages as well. The first occurrence means "to be (or become) numerous" (Gen. 6:1). *Rābab* can also mean "to be great" in size, prestige, or power (cf. Gen. 18:20; Job 33:12; Ps. 49:16). With a subject indicating time, this verb implies "lengthening" (Gen. 38:12), and with special subjects the word may imply "extension of space" (Deut. 14:24).

B. Nouns.

rōb (רֹב), "multitude; abundance." This noun occurs about 150 times in biblical Hebrew. The word basically means "multitude" or "abundance"; it has numerical implications apparent in its first biblical appearance: "I will multiply thy seed exceedingly, that it shall not be numbered for multitude" (Gen. 16:10).

When applied to time or distance, *rōb* indicates a "large amount" or "long": "And these bottles of wine, which we filled, were new; and, behold, they be rent: and these our garments and our shoes are become old by reason of the very long journey" (Josh. 9:13). In several passages, the word is applied to abstract ideas or qualities. In such cases, *rōb* means "great" or "greatness": ". . . This that is glorious in his apparel, traveling in the greatness of his strength" (Isa. 63:1).

The preposition *lə* when prefixed to the noun *rōb* sometimes forms an adverbial phrase meaning "abundantly": "For it was little which thou hadst before I came, and it is now increased unto a multitude . . ." (Gen. 30:30). The same phrase bears a different sense in 1 Kings 10:10, where it seems to be almost a substantive: "There came no more such abundance of spices as these which the queen of Sheba gave to king Solomon." The phrase literally appears to mean "great" with respect to "multitude." This phrase is applied to Uzziah's building activities: ". . . And on the wall of Ophel he built much" (2 Chron. 27:3), where it means "much." This phrase is extended by the addition of *'ad*. Thus we have *'ad lərōb,* meaning "exceeding much": "Since the people began to bring the offerings into the house of the Lord, we have had enough to eat, and have left plenty [literally, "the remainder is exceeding much"] . . ." (2 Chron. 31:10).

rab (רב), "chief." This word is a transliteration of the Akkadian *rab,* an indication of "military rank" similar to our word *general.* The first appearance: "And it came to pass, that at midnight [literally, "the middle of the *officers* of his house. . . ."] One should especially note the titles in Jeremiah: "And all the princes [officials] of the king of Babylon came in, and sat in the middle gate, even Nergal-shar-ezer, Samgar-nebo, Sarsechim, Rab-saris, Nergal-sharezer, Rab-mag, with all the residue of the princes of the king of Babylon" (39:3). Verses 9, 10, 11, and 13 of Jeremiah 39 mention Nebuzaradan as the "captain" of the bodyguard.

C. Adjective.

rab (רב), "many; great; large; prestigious; powerful." This adjective has a cognate in biblical Aramaic. The Hebrew word appears about 474 times in the Old Testament and in all periods.

First, this word represents plurality in number or amount, whether applied to people or to things. *Rab* is applied to people in Gen. 26:14: "For he [Isaac] had possession of flocks, and possession of herds, and great store of servants. . . ." In Gen. 13:6, the word is applied to things: "And the land was not able to bear them, that they might dwell together: for their substance was great, so that they could not dwell together." This word is sometimes used of "large groups of people" (Exod. 5:5). This basic idea of "numerical multiplicity" is also applied to amounts of liquids or masses of non-liquids: "And Moses lifted up his hand, and with his rod he smote the rock twice: and the water came out abundantly . . ." (Num. 20:11); a "great" amount of water came forth. Rebekah told Abraham's servant that her father had "straw and provender enough, and room to lodge in" (Gen. 24:25).

The phrase "many waters" is a fixed phrase meaning the "sea": ". . . Thou whom the merchants of Zidon, that pass over the sea, have replenished. And by great waters the seed of Sihor, the harvest of the river, is her revenue . . ." (Isa. 23:2-3). "And the channels of the sea appeared, the foundations of the world were discovered, at the rebuking of the Lord, at the blast of the breath of his nostrils. He sent from above, he took me; he drew me out of many waters . . ." (2 Sam. 22:16-17). This imagery is used in several Old Testament poetical passages; it would be wrong to conclude that this view of the world was true or actual. On the other hand, Gen. 7:11 uses a related phrase as a figure of the "sources of all water": ". . . The same day were all the fountains of the great deep broken up. . . ."

Used in conjunction with "days" or "years," *rab* means "long," and the resulting phrase means "a long time": "And Abraham sojourned in the Philistines' land many days" (Gen. 21:34).

The word can be used metaphorically, describing an abstract concept: "And God saw that the wickedness of man was great in the earth, and that every imagination of the thoughts of his heart was only evil continually"

(Gen. 6:5—the first biblical occurrence). This use of *rab* does not describe the relative *value* of the thing modified, but its numerical recurrence. The statement implies, however, that man's constant sinning was more reprehensible than the more occasional sinning previously committed.

When *rab* is applied to land areas, it means "large" (1 Sam. 26:13). This usage is related to the usual meaning of the Semitic cognates, which represent "size" rather than numerical multiplicity (also cf. *gādal*): "And the Lord delivered them into the hand of Israel, who smote them, and chased them unto great Zidon . . ." (Josh. 11:8). When God is called the "great King" (Ps. 48:2), the adjective refers to His superior power and sovereignty over all kings (vv. 4 ff.). This meaning emerges in Job 32:9: "The great may not be wise, nor may elders understand justice" (cf. Job 35:9). Uses such as these in Job emphasize "greatness in prestige," whereas passages such as 2 Chron. 14:11 emphasize "strength and might": "Lord, there is none like thee to help [in battle], between the mighty and the weak" (RSV).

TO BE GUILTLESS

A. Verb.

nāqāh (נָקָה), "to be pure, innocent." Only in Hebrew does this verb mean being "innocent." In Aramaic and Arabic it occurs with the meaning of being "clean." The verb is found 44 times in the Old Testament.

Isaiah described the future of Jerusalem as an empty ("cleaned out") city: "The gates of Zion will lament and mourn; destitute [*nāqāh*], she will sit on the ground" (Isa. 3:26, NIV). On the more positive side, a land may also be "cleansed" of robbers: ". . . Every thief will be banished [KJV, "cut off"] and everyone who swears falsely will be banished" (Zech. 5:3, NIV).

The verb is more often used to mean being "free" (with the preposition *min*). The first occurrence in the Old Testament is in Gen. 24:8, and is illustrative of this usage. Abraham ordered his servant to find a wife for Isaac. The servant pledged that he would fulfill his commission; however, if he did not succeed—that is, in case the woman was unwilling to make the long journey with him—Abraham would free him: ". . . Then thou shalt be clear from this my oath. . . ." The freedom may be from an oath (cf. Gen. 24:8, 41), from wrongdoing (Num. 5:31), or from punishment (Exod. 21:19; Num. 5:28). The translations vary in these contexts.

The verb *nāqāh* also appears with the legal connotation of "innocence." First, a person may be declared "innocent," or "acquitted." David prayed: "Keep your servant also from willful sins. . . . Then will I be blameless, innocent of great transgression" (Ps. 19:13, NIV). On the other hand, the sinner is not "acquitted" by God: "I still dread all my sufferings, for I know you will not hold me innocent" (Job 9:28, NIV). The punishment of the person who is not "acquitted" is also expressed by a negation of the verb *nāqāh:* "The Lord will not hold anyone guiltless who misuses his name" (Exod. 20:7, NIV; "The Lord will not leave unpunished," NEB). "I will discipline you but only with justice; I will not let you go entirely unpunished" (Jer. 30:11, NIV). The fate of the wicked is the judgment of God: ". . . the wicked shall not be unpunished [*nāqāh*]: but the seed of the righteous shall be delivered [*mālath*]'' (Prov. 11:21).

The verb is translated in the Septuagint generally as *athos* (''to be innocent, guiltless''). However, the range of the meaning of the Hebrew word is wider. It extends from ''to be emptied [cleaned out]'' to the legal jargon of ''acquittal.'' In English versions, there is no uniformity of translation: ''to be innocent, unpunished, acquitted, cleansed, held innocent'' (KJV, RSV, NIV); ''to be guiltless, free, cut off'' (RSV); ''to be deserted, purged'' (NASB); ''to be released, banished'' (NIV).

B. Adjective.

nāqî (נָקִי), ''innocent.'' This adjective appears 43 times in the Old Testament. One occurrence is in Ps. 15:5, which says of the righteous man, ''. . . Nor does he take a bribe against the innocent'' (NASB).

H

HALF

A. Noun.

chatsî (חֲצִי), ''half; halfway; middle.'' This word appears about 123 times and in all periods of biblical Hebrew.

First, the word is used to indicate ''half'' of anything. This meaning first occurs in Exod. 24:6: ''And Moses took half of the blood, and put it in basins; and half of the blood he sprinkled on the altar.''

Second, *chatsî* can mean ''middle,'' as it does in its first biblical appearance: ''And it came to pass, that at midnight [literally, ''the middle of the night''] the Lord smote all the first-born in the land of Egypt . . . '' (Exod. 12:29). In Exod. 27:5, the word means ''halfway'': ''And thou shalt put it under the compass of the altar beneath, that the net may be even to the midst [i.e., up to the middle] of the altar.''

B. Verb.

chātsāh (חָצָה), ''to divide, reach unto.'' This verb appears about 15 times in biblical Hebrew and has cognates in Phoenician, Moabite, and Arabic. The word most commonly means ''to divide,'' as in Exod. 21:35: ''. . . Then they shall sell the live ox, and divide the money of it. . . .''

HAND

yād (יָד), ''hand; side; border; alongside; hand-measure; portion; arm (rest); monument; manhood (male sex organ); power; rule.'' This word has cognates in most of the other Semitic languages. Biblical Hebrew attests it about 1,618 times and in every period.

The primary sense of this word is ''hand'': ''And the Lord God said, Behold, the man is become as one of us, to know good and evil: and now, lest he put forth his hand, and take also of the tree of life . . ." (Gen. 3:22—the first biblical occurrence). Sometimes the word is used in conjunction with an object that can be grasped by the "hand": "And if he smite him with throwing a stone [literally, "hand stone"] . . ." (Num. 35:17). In a similar usage, the word means "human": ". . . He shall also stand up against the Prince of princes; but he shall be broken without hand [i.e., human agency]" (Dan. 8:25; cf. Job 34:20).

In Isa. 49:2, "hand" is used of God; God tells Moses that He will put His "hand" over the mouth of the cave and protect him. This is a figure of speech, an anthropomorphism, by which God promises His protection. God's "hand" is another term for God's "power" (cf. Jer. 16:21). The phrase "between your hands" may mean "upon your chest": "And one shall say unto him, What are these wounds in thine hands [upon your chest]?" (Zech. 13:6).

Yād is employed in several other noteworthy phrases. The "lifting of the hand" may be involved in "taking an oath" (Gen. 14:22). "Shaking" [literally, "giving one's hand"] is another oath-taking gesture (cf. Prov. 11:21). For "one's hands to be on another" (Gen. 37:27) or "laid upon another" (Exod. 7:4) is to do harm to someone. "Placing one's hands with" signifies "making common cause with someone" (Exod. 23:1). If one's hand does not "reach" something, he is "unable to pay" for it (Lev. 5:7, RSV). When one's countryman is "unable to stretch out his hand to you," he is not able to support himself (Lev. 25:35).

"Putting one's hand on one's mouth" is a gesture of silence (Prov. 30:32). "Placing one's hands under someone" means submitting to him (1 Chron. 29:24). "Giving something into one's hand" is entrusting it to him (Gen. 42:37).

A second major group of passages uses *yād* to represent the location and uses of the hand. First, the word can mean "side," where the hand is located: "And Absalom rose up early, and stood *beside* the way of the gate . . ." (2 Sam. 15:2). In 2 Chron. 21:16, the word means "border": "Moreover the Lord stirred up against Jehoram the spirit of the Philistines, and of the Arabians, that were near [literally, "by the hand of"] the Ethiopians." A similar use in Exod. 25 applies this word to the "banks" of the Nile River: "And the daughter of Pharaoh came down to wash herself at the river; and her maidens walked *along by* the [Nile]. . . ." In this sense, *yād* can represent "length and breadth." In Gen. 34:21 we read that the land was (literally) "broad of hands": "These men are peaceable with us; therefore let them dwell in the land, and trade therein; for the land, behold, it is large enough for them. . . ."

Second, since the hand can receive only a part or fraction of something, the word can signify a "part" or "fraction": "And he took and sent [portions] unto them from before him: but Benjamin's [portion] was five times so much as any of theirs" (Gen. 43:34).

Third, *yād* comes to mean that which upholds something, a "support" (1 Kings 7:35 ff.) or an "arm rest" (1 Kings 10:19).

Fourth, since a hand may be held up as a "sign," *yād* can signify a "monument" or "stele": ". . . Saul came to Carmel, and, behold, he set him up a place [monument], and is gone about, and passed on, and gone down to Gilgal" (1 Sam. 15:12).

Fifth, *yād* sometimes represents the "male sex organ": ". . . And art gone up; thou hast enlarged thy bed, and made thee a covenant with them; thou lovedst their bed where thou sawest it [you have looked on their *manhood*]" (Isa. 57:8; cf v. 10; 6:2; 7:20).

In several passages, *yād* is used in the sense of "power" or "rule": "And David smote Hadarezer king of Zobah unto Hamath, as he went to stablish his dominion by the river Euphrates" (1 Chron. 18:3). "To be delivered into one's hands" means to be "given into one's power": "God hath delivered him into mine hand; for he is shut in, by entering into a town that hath gates and bars" (1 Sam. 23:7; cf. Prov. 18:21).

"To fill someone's hand" may be a technical term for "installing him" in office: "And thou shalt put them upon Aaron thy brother, and his sons with him; and shalt anoint them, and consecrate them [literally, "fill their hands"], and sanctify them, that they may minister unto me in the priest's office" (Exod. 28:41).

Yād is frequently joined to the preposition *bə* and other prepositions as an extension; there is no change in meaning, only a longer form: "For what have I done? or what evil is in mine hand?" (1 Sam. 26:18).

TO HASTEN, MAKE HASTE

māhar (מָהַר), "to hasten, make haste." This verb and various derivatives are common to both ancient and modern Hebrew. *Māhar* occurs approximately 70 times in the Hebrew Bible; it appears twice in the first verse in which it is found: "And Abraham *hastened* into the tent unto Sarah, and said, *Make ready quickly* three measures of fine meal . . ." (Gen. 18:6). *Māhar* often has an adverbial use when it appears with another verb, such as in Gen. 18:7: ". . . hasted to dress it" (or "quickly prepared it").

TO HATE

A. Verb.

sānē' (שָׂנֵא) "to hate, set against." This verb appears in Ugaritic, Moabite, Aramaic, and Arabic. It appears in all periods of Hebrew and about 145 times in the Bible.

Sānē' represents an emotion ranging from intense "hatred" to the much weaker "set against" and is used of persons and things (including ideas, words, inanimate objects).

The strong sense of the word typifies the emotion of jealousy; and therefore, *sānē'* is the feeling Joseph's brothers experienced because their father preferred him (Gen. 37:4; cf. v. 11). This "hatred" increased when Joseph reported his dreams (Gen. 37:8). Obviously, the word covers emotion ranging from "bitter disdain" to outright "hatred," for in Gen. 37:18 ff. the brothers plotted Joseph's death and achieved his removal.

This emphasis can be further heightened by a double use of the root. Delilah's father told Samson: "I verily thought that thou hadst utterly hated her [literally, "hating, you hated her"] . . ." (Judg. 15:2).

One special use of *sānē'* is ingressive, indicating the initiation of the emotion. So "Amnon hated [literally, "began to hate"] her exceedingly; so that the hatred wherewith he hated ["began to hate"] her was greater than the love wherewith he had loved her" (2 Sam. 13:15). This emphasis appears again in Jer. 12:8: "Mine heritage is unto me as a lion in the forest; it crieth out against me: therefore have I [come to hate] it" (also cf. Hos. 9:15).

In a weaker sense, *sānē'* signifies "being set against" something. Jethro advised Moses to select men who hated ["were set against"] covetousness to be secondary judges over Israel (Exod. 18:21). A very frequent but special use of the verb means "to be unloved." For example, *sānē* may indicate that someone is "untrustworthy," therefore an enemy to be ejected from one's territory. This sense is found in an early biblical occurrence, in which Isaac said to Abimelech and his army: "Wherefore come ye to me, seeing ye hate me, and have sent me away from you?" (Gen. 26:27). The word may mean "unloved" in the sense of deteriorating marital relations: "And the damsel's father shall say unto the elders, I gave my daughter unto this man to wife, and he hateth [i.e., turned against] her" (Deut. 22:16). This nuance is especially clear in Ezek. 23:28, where the verb is in synonymous parallelism to "alienated": "Behold, I will deliver thee into the hand of them whom thou hatest, into the hand of them from whom thy mind is alienated." In the case of two wives in a family, in which one was preferred over the other, it may be said that one was loved and the other "hated" (Deut. 21:15). This emphasis is found in Gen. 29:31: "And when the Lord saw that Leah was hated, he opened her womb; but Rachel was barren." The word, used as a passive participle, represents a spurned woman: ". . . An odious [unloved] woman when she is married . . ." (Prov. 30:23).

B. Noun.

sinə'āh (שִׂנְאָה), "hatred." This noun occurs 17 times in the Old Testament. Num 35:20 is one occurrence: "And if he stabbed him from hatred, or hurled at him, lying in wait . . ." (RSV).

HEAD

A. Nouns.

rō'sh (רֹאשׁ), "head; top; first; sum." Cognates of *rō'sh* appear in Ugaritic, Akkadian, Phoenician, biblical Aramaic, Arabic, and Ethiopic. *Rō'sh* and its alternate form *rē'sh* appear about 596 times in biblical Hebrew.

This word often represents a "head," a bodily part (Gen. 40:20). *Rō'sh* is also used of a decapitated "head" (2 Sam. 4:8), an animal "head" (Gen. 3:15), and a statue "head" (Dan. 2:32). In Dan. 7:9, where God is pictured in human form, His "head" is crowned with hair like pure wool (i.e., white).

To "lift up one's own head" may be a sign of declaring one's innocence: "If I be wicked, woe unto me; and if I be righteous, yet will I not lift up my head. I am full of confusion; therefore see thou mine affliction" (Job 10:15). This same figure of speech may indicate an intention to begin a war, the most violent form of self-assertion: "For, lo, thine enemies make a tumult: and they that hate thee have lifted up the head" (Ps. 83:2). With a negation, this phrase may symbolize submission to another power: "Thus was Midian subdued before the children of Israel, so that they lifted up their heads no more" (Judg. 8:28). Used transitively (i.e., to lift up someone else's "head"), this word may connote restoring someone to a previous position: "Yet within three days shall Pharaoh lift up thine head, and restore thee unto thy place . . ." (Gen. 40:13). It can also denote the release of someone from prison: ". . . Evil-merodach king of Babylon in the year that he began to reign did lift up the head of Jehoiachin king of Judah out of prison" (2 Kings 25:27).

With the verb *rûm* ("to raise"), *rō'sh* can signify the victory and power of an enthroned king—God will "lift up [His] head," or exert His rule (Ps. 110:7). When God lifts up (*rûm*) one's "head," He fills one with hope and confidence: "But thou, O Lord, art a shield for me; my glory, and the lifter up of mine head" (Ps. 3:3).

There are many secondary nuances of *rō'sh*. First, the word can represent the "hair on one's head": "And on the seventh day, he shall shave all his hair off his head [*rō'sh*]; he shall shave off his beard and his eyebrows, all his hair" (Lev. 14:9, RSV).

The word can connote unity, representing every individual in a given group: "Have they not sped? have they not divided the prey; to every man a damsel or two . . ." (Judg. 5:30). This word may be used numerically, meaning the total number of persons or individuals in a group: "Take ye the sum of all the congregation of the children of Israel, after their families, by the house of their fathers, with the number of their names, every male by their polls" (Num. 1:2).

Rō'sh can also emphasize the individual: "And there was a great famine in Samaria: and, behold, they besieged it, until an ass's head [i.e., an individual donkey] was sold for fourscore pieces of silver . . ." (2 Kings 6:25). It is upon the "head" (upon the person himself) that curses and blessings fall: "The blessings of thy father have prevailed above the blessings of my progenitors . . . : they shall be on the head of Joseph . . ." (Gen. 49:26).

Rō'sh sometimes means "leader," whether appointed, elected, or self-appointed. The word can be used of the tribal fathers, who are the leaders of a group of people: "And Moses chose able men out of all Israel, and made them heads over the people . . ." (Exod. 18:25). Military leaders are also called "heads": "These be the names of the mighty men whom David had: The Tachmonite that sat in the seat, chief among the captains . . ." (2 Sam. 23:8). In Num. 1:16, the princes are called "heads" (cf. Judg. 10:18). This word is used of those who represent or lead the people in worship (2 Kings 25:18—the chief priest).

When used of things, *rō'sh* means "point" or "beginning." With a local emphasis, the word refers to the "top" or summit of a mountain or hill: ". . . Tomorrow I will stand on the top of the hill with the rod of God in mine hand" (Exod. 17:9). Elsewhere the word represents the topmost end of a natural or constructed object: "Go to, let us build us a city and a tower, whose top may reach unto heaven . . ." (Gen. 11:4).

In Gen. 47:31, the word denotes the "head" of a bed, or where one lays his "head." In 1 Kings 8:8, *rō'sh* refers to the ends of poles. The word may be used of the place where a journey begins: "Thou hast built thy high place at every head of the way . . ." (Ezek. 16:25); cf. Dan. 7:1: "the sum of the matters. . . ." This sense of the place of beginning appears in Gen. 2:10 (the first occurrence): "And a river went out of Eden to water the garden; and from thence it was parted, and became [the source of four rivers]." This nuance identifies a thing as being placed spatially in front of a group; it stands in front or at the "head" (Deut. 20:9; cf. 1 Kings 21:9). The "head" of the stars is a star located at the zenith of the sky (Job 22:12). The "head" cornerstone occupies a place of primary importance. It is the stone by which all the other stones are measured; it is the chief cornerstone (Ps. 118:22).

This word may have a temporal significance, meaning "beginning" or "first." The second sense is seen in Exod. 12:2: "This month shall be unto you the beginning of months. . . ." In 1 Chron. 16:7 the word describes the "first" in a whole series of acts: "Then on that day David delivered first this psalm to thank the Lord into the hand of Asaph and his brethren."

Rō'sh may also have an estimative connotation: "Take thou also unto thee [the finest of] spices . . ." (Exod. 30:23).

rē'shîth (רֵאשִׁית), "beginning; first; choicest." The abstract word *rē'shîth* corresponds to the temporal and estimative sense of *rō'sh*. *Rē'shîth* connotes the "beginning" of a fixed period of time: ". . . The eyes of the Lord thy God are always upon it, from the beginning of the year even unto the end of the year" (Deut. 11:12). The "beginning" of one's period of life is intended in Job 42:12: "So the Lord blessed the latter end of Job more than his beginning. . . ." This word can represent a point of departure, as it does in Gen. 1:1 (the first occurrence): "In the beginning God created the heaven and the earth." Estimatively, this word can mean the "first" or "choicest": "The first of the first fruits of thy land thou shalt bring into the house of the Lord thy God" (Exod. 23:19). This nuance of *rēshîth* may appear in the comparative sense, meaning "choicest" or "best." Dan. 11:41 exhibits the nuance of "some": ". . . But these shall escape out of his hand, even Edom, and Moab, and the chief [NASB, foremost] of the children of Ammon" (Dan. 11:41).

Used substantively, the word can mean "first fruits": "As for the oblation of the first fruits, ye shall offer them unto the Lord: but they shall not be burnt on the altar for a sweet savor" (Lev. 2:12). ". . . The first fruits of them which they shall offer unto the Lord, them have I given thee" (Num. 18:12). Sometimes this word represents the "first part" of an offering: "Ye shall offer up a cake of the first of your dough for a heave offering . . ." (Num. 15:20).

B. Adjective.

ri'shôn (רִאשׁוֹן), "first; foremost; preceding; former." This word occurs about 182 times in biblical Hebrew. It denotes the "first" in a temporal sequence: "And it came to pass in the six hundredth and first year, in the first month, the first day of the month . . ." (Gen. 8:13). In Ezra 9:2, *ri'shôn* is used both of precedence in time and of leadership: ". . . The holy seed have mingled themselves with the people of those lands: yea, the hand of the princes and rulers hath been chief in this trespass."

A second meaning of this adjective is "preceding" or "former": ". . . Unto the place of the altar, which he had made there at the first . . ." (Gen. 13:4). Gen. 33:2 uses this word locally: "And he put the handmaids and their children foremost, and Leah and her children after, and Rachel and Joseph hindermost." The "former ones" are "ancestors": "But I will for their sakes remember the covenant of their ancestors, whom I brought forth out of the land of Egypt in the sight of the heathen . . ." (Lev. 26:45). But in most cases, this adjective has a temporal emphasis.

TO HEAL

rāphā' (רָפָא), "to heal." This word is common to both ancient and modern Hebrew. It occurs approximately 65 times in the Hebrew Old Testament, appearing first in Gen. 20:17: ". . . God healed Abimelech."

"To heal" may be described as "restoring to normal," an act which God typically performs. Thus, appeals to God for healing are common: ". . . O Lord, heal me; for my bones are vexed" (Ps. 6:2); "Heal me, O Lord, and I shall be healed . . ." (Jer. 17:14). Not only are human diseases "healed," but bad water is restored to normal or "healed" (2 Kings 2:22); salt water is "healed" or made fresh (Ezek. 47:8); even pottery is "healed" or restored (Jer. 19:11).

A large number of the uses of *rāphā'* express the "healing" of the nation—such "healing" not only involves God's grace and forgiveness, but also the nation's repentance. Divine discipline leads to repentance and "healing": "Come, and let us return unto the Lord: for he hath torn, and he will heal us . . ." (Hos. 6:1). God promises: "For I will restore health unto thee, and I will heal thee of thy wounds, saith the Lord . . ." (Jer. 30:17). Even foreign cities and powers can know God's "healing" if they repent (Jer. 51:8-9).

False prophets are condemned because they deal only with the symptoms and not with the deep spiritual hurts of the people: "They have healed also the hurt of the daughter of my people slightly, saying, Peace, peace; when there is no peace" (Jer. 6:14; also 8:11).

TO HEAR

A. Verb.

shāma' (שָׁמַע), "to hear, hearken, listen, obey, publish." This word occurs throughout the Semitic languages including biblical Hebrew and Aramaic. *Shāma'* occurs in all historical layers of Hebrew, and about 1,160 times in the Bible. The word is attested 9 times in biblical Aramaic.

Basically, this verb means to "hear" something with one's ears, but there are several other nuances. In Gen. 37:17, a man told Joseph that he "heard" Joseph's brothers say, "Let us go to Dothan"; in other words, he unintentionally "overheard" them say it. *Shāma'* can also be used of "eavesdropping," or intentionally listening in on a conversation; so Sarah "overheard" what the three men said to Abram (Gen. 18:10).

Joseph asked his brothers to "listen" as he recounted what he had dreamed (Gen. 37:6). In 1 Chron. 28:2, David told his audience to "listen" as he spoke; they were to give him their undivided attention.

To "hear" something may imply to "have knowledge," as when Abimelech told Abraham that he did not know about the controversy over the wills because no one had told him and neither had he "heard" it (Gen. 21:26). *Shāma'* may also imply to "gain knowledge" or to "get knowledge": ". . . The Chaldeans that besieged Jerusalem heard [the report] . . ." (Jer. 37:5).

Again, the word may mean to "come into knowledge about." Moses told the unclean men to wait while he "listened" to what the Lord would command regarding them (Num. 9:8). His intent clearly was more than just to "hear" something; he intended to "gain some knowledge" from the Lord.

The verb can represent the mere "hearing" of something, as when Adam and Eve "heard" the sound of God walking in the garden (Gen. 3:8—first biblical occurrence). To "make someone hear" something (without any specification of what was heard) suggests "summoning" the person (1 Kings 15:22).

"Hearing" can be both intellectual and spiritual. Spiritually, one may "hear" God's Word (Num. 24:4), or "learn" it from God. Conversely, God told Abraham that He had "heard" his prayer and would act accordingly (Gen. 17:20). In this context, to "hear" means not only to hear what is said, but to agree with its intention or petition (cf. Gen. 16:11). In the case of hearing and hearkening to a higher authority, *shāma'* can mean to "obey." In Abraham's seed, all nations would be blessed because he "heard" (obeyed) God's voice (Gen. 22:18).

Another nuance of intellectual "hearing" appears in Gen. 11:7, in which we are told that God planned to confuse human language, "that they may not understand one another's speech."

To have a "hearing heart" is to have "discernment" or "understanding" (1 Kings 3:9). Certainly when Moses told Israel's judges to "hear" cases, he meant more than listening with one's ear. He meant for them to examine the merits of a case, so as to render a just decision (Deut. 1:16).

B. Nouns.

Shôma' means "things heard by accident; hearsay." This word appears infrequently in the Old Testament, as in Josh. 6:27: "So the Lord was with Joshua; and his fame [*shôma'*] was noised throughout all the country."

shēma' (שֵׁמַע), "something heard by design; report." The Old Testament attests this word 17 times. Gen 29:13 contains one occurrence: "And it came to pass, when Laban heard the tidings [*shēma'*] of Jacob his sister's son. . . ."

shəmû'āh (שְׁמוּעָה), "revelation; something heard." This word appears 27 times. One appearance is in Isa. 28:9: "Whom shall he teach knowledge? and whom shall he make to understand doctrine [*shəmû'āh*]?"

HEART

A. Noun.

lēb (לֵב), "heart; mind; midst." *Lēb* and its synonym *lēbāb* appear 860 times in the Old Testament. The law, prophets, and Psalms often speak of the "heart." The root occurs also in Akkadian, Assyrian, Egyptian, Ugaritic, Aramaic, Arabic, and post-biblical Hebrew. The corresponding Aramaic nouns occur seven times in the Book of Daniel.

"Heart" is used first of man in Gen. 6:5: "And God saw that the wickedness of man was great in the earth, and that every imagination of the thoughts of his heart was only evil continually." In Gen. 6:6 *lēb* is used of God: "And it repented the Lord that he had made man on the earth, and it grieved him at his heart."

"Heart" may refer to the organ of the body: "And Aaron shall bear the names of the children of Israel in the breastplate of judgment upon his heart, when he goeth in unto the holy place . . ." (Exod. 28:29); ". . . [Joab] took three darts in his hand, and thrust them through the heart of Absalom . . ." (2 Sam. 18:14); "My heart panteth . . ." (Ps. 38:10).

Lēb may also refer to the inner part or middle of a thing: ". . . and the depths were congealed in the heart of the sea" (Exod. 15:8); ". . . and the mountain burned with fire in the midst [RSV, "to the heart"] of heaven . . ." (Deut. 4:11, KJV); "Yea, thou shalt be as he that lieth down in the midst of the sea . . ." (Prov. 23:34).

Lēbāb can be used of the inner man, contrasted to the outer man, as in Deut. 30:14: "But the word is very nigh unto thee, in thy mouth, and in thy heart, that thou mayest do it" (cf. Joel 2:13); ". . . man looketh on the outward appearance, but the Lord looketh on the heart" (1 Sam. 16:7). *Lēbāb* is often compounded with "soul" for emphasis, as in 2 Chron. 15:12; "And they entered into a covenant to seek the Lord God of their fathers with all their heart and with all their soul" (cf. 2 Chron. 15:15). *Nephesh* ("soul; life; self") is translated "heart" fifteen times in the KJV. Each time, it connotes the "inner man": "For as he thinketh in his heart [*nephesh*], so is he" (Prov. 23:7).

Lēb can be used of the man himself or his personality: "Then Abraham fell upon his face and laughed, and said in his heart, . . ." (Gen. 17:17); ". . . my heart had great experience . . ." (Eccl. 1:16). *Lēb* is also used of God in this sense: "And I will give you pastors according to mine heart" (Jer. 3:15).

The seat of desire, inclination, or will can be indicated by "heart": "Pharaoh's heart is hardened . . ." (Exod. 7:14); ". . . whosoever is of a willing heart, let him bring it . . ." (Exod. 35:5; cf. vv. 21, 29); "I will praise thee, O Lord my God, with all my heart . . ." (Ps. 86:12). *Lēb* is also used of God in this sense: ". . . and I will plant them in this land assuredly with my whole heart and with my whole soul" (Jer. 32:41). Two people are said to be in agreement when their "hearts" are right with each other: "Is thine heart right, as my heart is with thy heart?" (2 Kings 10:15). In 2 Chron. 24:4, ". . . Joash was minded to repair the house of the Lord" (Heb. "had in his heart").

The "heart" is regarded as the seat of emotions: "And thou shalt love the

Lord thy God with all thine heart, . . ." (Deut. 6:5); ". . . and when he [Aaron] seeth thee, he will be glad in his heart" (Exod. 4:14; cf. 1 Sam. 2:1). So there are "merry" hearts (Judg. 16:25), "fearful" hearts (Isa. 35:4), and hearts that "trembled" (1 Sam. 4:13).

The "heart" could be regarded as the seat of knowledge and wisdom and as a synonym of "mind." This meaning often occurs when "heart" appears with the verb "to know": "Thus you are to know in your heart . . ." (Deut. 8:5, NASB); and "Yet the Lord hath not given you a heart to perceive [know] . . ." (Deut. 29:4, KJV; RSV, "mind"). Solomon prayed, "Give therefore thy servant an understanding heart to judge thy people, that I may discern between good and bad . . ." (1 Kings 3:9; cf. 4:29). Memory is the activity of the "heart," as in Job 22:22: ". . . lay up his [God's] words in thine heart."

The "heart" may be the seat of conscience and moral character. How does one respond to the revelation of God and of the world around him? Job answers: ". . . my heart shall not reproach me as long as I live" (27:6). On the contrary, "David's heart smote him . . ." (2 Sam. 24:10). The "heart" is the fountain of man's deeds: ". . . in the integrity of my heart and innocency of my hands I have done this" (Gen. 20:5; cf. v. 6). David walked "in uprightness of heart" (1 Kings 3:6) and Hezekiah "with a perfect heart" (Isa. 38:3) before God. Only the man with "clean hands, and a pure heart" (Ps. 24:4) can stand in God's presence.

Lēb may refer to the seat of rebellion and pride. God said: ". . . for the imagination of man's heart is evil from his youth" (Gen. 8:21). Tyre is like all men: "Because thine heart is lifted up, and thou hast said, I am a God" (Ezek. 28:2). They all become like Judah, whose "sin . . . is graven upon the table of their heart" (Jer. 17:1).

God controls the "heart." Because of his natural "heart," man's only hope is in the promise of God: "A new heart also will I give you, . . . and I will take away the stony heart out of your flesh, and I will give you a heart of flesh" (Ezek. 36:26). So the sinner prays: "Create in me a clean heart, O God" (Ps. 51:10); and ". . . unite my heart [give me an undivided heart] to fear thy name" (Ps. 86:11). Also, as David says, "I know also, my God, that thou triest the heart, and hast pleasure in uprightness" (1 Chron. 29:17). Hence God's people seek His approval: ". . . try my reins and my heart" (Ps. 26:2).

The "heart" stands for the inner being of man, the man himself. As such, it is the fountain of all he does (Prov. 4:4). All his thoughts, desires, words, and actions flow from deep within him. Yet a man cannot understand his own "heart" (Jer. 17:9). As a man goes on in his own way, his "heart" becomes harder and harder. But God will circumcise (cut away the uncleanness of) the "heart" of His people, so that they will love and obey Him with their whole being (Deut. 30:6).

B. Adverb.

lēb (לֵב), "tenderly; friendly; comfortably." *Lēb* is used as an adverb in Gen. 34:3: "And his soul clave unto Dinah . . . and he loved the damsel, and spake kindly unto the damsel." In Ruth 4:13, the word means "friendly":

". . . thou hast spoken friendly unto thine handmaid. . . ." The word means "comfortably" in 2 Chron. 30:22 and in Isa. 40:2.

HEAVENS

shāmayim (שָׁמַיִם), "heavens; heaven; sky." This general Semitic word appears in languages such as Ugaritic, Akkadian, Aramaic, and Arabic. It occurs 420 times and in all periods of biblical Hebrew.

First, *shāmayim* is the usual Hebrew word for the "sky" and the "realm of the sky." This realm is where birds fly. God forbids Israel to make any "likeness of any winged fowl that flieth in the air" (Deut. 4:17). When Absalom's hair caught in the branches of a tree, he hung suspended between the "heaven" and the earth (2 Sam. 18:9). This area, high above the ground but below the stars and heavenly bodies, is often the locus of visions: "And David lifted up his eyes, and saw the angel of the Lord stand between the earth and the heaven, having a drawn sword in his hand stretched out over Jerusalem" (1 Chron. 21:16).

Second, this word represents an area farther removed from the earth's surface. From this area come such things as frost (Job 38:29), snow (Isa. 55:10), fire (Gen. 19:24), dust (Deut. 28:24), hail (Josh. 10:11), and rain: "The fountains also of the deep and the windows of heaven were stopped, and the rain from heaven was restrained" (Gen. 8:2). This realm is God's storehouse; God is the dispenser of the stores and Lord of the realm (Deut. 28:12). This meaning of *shāmayim* occurs in Gen. 1:7-8: "And God made the firmament, and divided the waters which were under the firmament from the waters which were above the firmament: and it was so. And God called the firmament Heaven."

Third, *shāmayim* also represents the realm in which the sun, moon, and stars are located: "And God said, Let there be lights in the firmament of the heaven to divide the day from the night . . ." (Gen. 1:14). This imagery is often repeated in the Creation account and in poetical passages. Thus the "heavens" can be stretched out like a curtain (Ps. 104:2) or rolled up as a scroll (Isa. 34:4).

Fourth, the phrase "heaven and earth" may denote the entire creation. This use of the word appears in Gen. 1:1: "In the beginning God created the heaven and the earth."

Fifth, "heaven" is the dwelling place of God: "He that sitteth in the heavens shall laugh: the Lord shall have them in derision" (Ps. 2:4; cf. Deut. 4:39). Again, note Deut. 26:15: "Look down from thy holy habitation, from heaven, and bless thy people Israel. . . ." Another expression representing the dwelling place of God is "the highest heaven [literally, the heaven of heavens]." This does not indicate height, but an absolute—i.e., God's abode is a unique realm not to be identified with the physical creation: "Behold the heaven and the heaven of heavens is the Lord's thy God, the earth also, with all that therein is" (Deut. 10:14).

TO HELP

'āzar (עָזַר), "to help, assist, aid." This word and its derivatives are common in both ancient and modern Hebrew. The verb occurs about 80 times in the biblical text. *'Āzar* is first found in the Old Testament in Jacob's deathbed blessing of Joseph: ". . . The God of thy father, who shall help thee . . ." (Gen. 49:25).

Help or aid comes from a variety of sources: Thirty-two kings "helped" Ben-hadad (1 Kings 20:6); one city "helps" another (Josh. 10:33); even false gods are believed to be of "help" (2 Chron. 28:23). Of course, the greatest source of help is God Himself; He is "the helper of the fatherless" (Ps. 10:14). God promises: "I will help thee" (Isa. 41:10); "and the Lord shall help them, and deliver them . . ." (Ps. 37:40).

HERD

bāqār (בָּקָר), "herd; cattle." This noun has cognates in Arabic and Aramaic. It appears about 180 times in biblical Hebrew and in all periods.

One meaning of the word is "cattle." Such beasts were slaughtered for food, and their hides were presented as offerings to God (Num. 15:8). This meaning of *bāqār* is in Gen. 12:16 (the first biblical occurrence): "And he [Pharaoh] entreated Abram well for her [Sarah's] sake: and he had sheep, and oxen, and he asses. . . ." These were grazing beasts (1 Chron. 27:29) and were eaten (1 Kings 4:23). These animals pulled carts (2 Sam. 6:6) and plows (Job 1:14), and carried burdens on their backs (1 Chron. 12:40).

Bāqār often refers to a group of cattle or "herd" (both sexes), as it does in Gen. 13:5: "And Lot also, which went with Abram, had flocks, and herds [in the Hebrew, this word appears in a singular form] and tents." The word can represent a "small group of cattle" (not a herd; cf. Gen. 47:17; Exod. 22:1) or even a pair of oxen (Num. 7:17). A single ox is indicated either by some other Hebrew word or called an offspring of oxen (Gen. 18:7).

Bāqār also refers to statues of oxen: "It [the altar of burnt offerings] stood upon twelve oxen, three looking toward the north, and three looking toward the west, and three looking toward the south, and three looking toward the east . . ." (1 Kings 7:25).

Some scholars believe this noun is related to the verb *bāqār* ("to seek out") and to the noun *bōqer* ("morning").

HERO

A. Nouns.

gibbôr (גִּבּוֹר), "hero." This word appears 159 times in the Old Testament. The first occurrence of *gibbôr* is in Gen. 6:4: "There were giants in the earth in those days; and also after that, when the sons of God came in unto the daughters of men, and they bare children to them, the same became mighty men [*gibbôr*] which were of old, men of renown."

In the context of battle, the word is better understood to refer to the category of warriors. The *gibbôr* is the proven warrior; especially is this true when *gibbôr* is used in combination with *chayil* ("strength"). The KJV gives a literal translation, "mighty men [*gibbôr*] of valor [*chayil*]," whereas the NIV renders the phrase idiomatically, "fighting men" (cf. Josh. 1:14). David, who had proven himself as a warrior, attracted "heroes" to his band while he was being pursued by Saul (2 Sam. 23). When David was enthroned as king, these men became a part of the elite military corps. The phrase *gibbôr chayil* may also refer to a man of a high social class, the landed man who had military responsibilities. Saul came from such a family (1 Sam. 9:1); so also Jeroboam (1 Kings 11:28).

The king symbolized the strength of his kingdom. He had to lead his troops in battle, and as commander he was expected to be a "hero." Early in David's life, he was recognized as a "hero" (1 Sam. 18:7). The king is described as a "hero": "Gird thy sword upon thy thigh, O most Mighty *(gibbôr)*, with thy glory and thy majesty" (Ps. 45:3). The messianic expectation included the hope that the Messiah would be "mighty": "For unto us a child is born, unto us a son is given: and the government shall be upon his shoulder; and his name shall be called Wonderful, Counselor, The mighty [*gibbôr*] God, The everlasting Father, The Prince of Peace" (Isa. 9:6).

Israel's God was a mighty God (Isa. 10:21). He had the power to deliver: "The Lord thy God in the midst of thee is mighty [*gibbôr*]; he will save, he will rejoice over thee with joy; he will rest in his love, he will joy over thee with singing" (Zeph. 3:17). Jeremiah's moving confession (32:17 ff.) bears out the might of God in creation (v. 17) and in redemption (vv. 18 ff.). The answer to the emphatic question, "Who is this King of glory?" in Psalm 24 is: "The Lord strong and mighty, the Lord mighty in battle" (v. 8).

The Septuagint gives the following translations: *dunatos* ("powerful; strong; mighty; able ruler") and *ischuros* ("strong; mighty; powerful"). The KJV gives these senses: "mighty men; mighty one; strong; violent."

geber (גֶּבֶר), "man." This word occurs 66 times in the Old Testament, once in 1 Chron. 23:3: "Now the Levites were numbered from the age of thirty years and upward: and their number by their polls, man by man, was thirty and eight thousand."

B. Verb.

gābar (גָּבַר), "to be strong." The root meaning "to be strong" appears in all Semitic languages as a verb or a noun, but the verb occurs only 25 times in the Old Testament. Job 21:7 contains an occurrence of *gābar:* "Wherefore do the wicked live, become old, yea, are mighty in power?"

C. Adjective.

gibbôr (גִּבּוֹר), "strong." *Gibbôr* may be translated by the adjective "strong" in the following contexts: a "strong" man (1 Sam. 14:52), a "strong" lion (Prov. 30:30), a mighty hunter (Gen. 10:9), and the mighty ones (Gen. 6:1-4).

TO HIDE

sātar (סָתַר), "to conceal, hide, shelter." This verb and various derivatives are found in modern Hebrew as well as in biblical Hebrew. *Sātar* occurs approximately 80 times in the Old Testament. The word is found for the first time in Gen. 4:14 as Cain discovers that because of his sin, he will be "hidden" from the presence of God, which implies a separation.

In the so-called Mizpah Benediction (which is really a warning), *sātar* again has the sense of "separation": "The Lord watch between me and thee, when we are absent one from another" (Gen. 31:49). To "hide oneself" is to take refuge: "Doth not David hide himself with us . . . ?" (1 Sam. 23:19). Similarly, to "hide" someone is to "shelter" him from his enemy: ". . . The Lord hid them" (Jer. 36:26).

To pray, "Hide thy face from my sins" (Ps. 51:9), is to ask God to ignore them. But when the prophet says, "And I will wait upon the Lord, that hideth his face from the house of Jacob . . ." (Isa. 8:17), he means that God's favor has been withdrawn. Similarly, Judah's sins have "hidden" God's face from her (Isa. 59:2).

HIGH

A. Adjective.

gābōah (גָּבֹהַּ), "high; exalted." This adjective occurs about 24 times. The root seen in this adjective, in the verb *gābah* and in the noun *gōbah,* occurs in every period of biblical Hebrew.

This word means "high, lofty, tall in dimension": "And the waters [of the flood] prevailed exceedingly upon the earth; and all the high hills, that were under the whole heaven, were covered" (Gen. 7:19—the first occurrence). When used of a man, *gābōah* means "tall": Saul was "higher than any of the people" (1 Sam. 9:2; cf. 16:7). In Dan. 8:2, *gābōah* describes the length of a ram's horns: ". . . And the two horns were high; but one was higher than the other, and the higher came up last."

The word means "high or exalted in station": "Thus saith the Lord God; Remove the diadem, and take off the crown: this shall not be the same: exalt him that is low, and abase him that is high" (Ezek. 21:26). In Eccles. 5:8, this connotation of "one of high rank" may be expressed in the translation "official" (RSV).

Gābōah may be used of a psychological state, such as "haughtiness": "Talk no more so exceeding proudly [this double appearance of the word emphasizes it]; let not arrogancy come out of your mouth . . ." (1 Sam. 2:3).

'elyôn (עֶלְיוֹן), "high; top; uppermost; highest; upper; height." The 53 occurrences of this word are scattered throughout biblical literature.

This word indicates the "uppermost" (as opposed to the lower): ". . . I had three white baskets on my head: And in the uppermost basket there was of all manner of bakemeats . . ." (Gen. 40:16-17). In Ezek. 42:5, *'elyôn* describes the "uppermost" of three stories: "Now the upper chambers were shorter: for the galleries were higher than these, than the lower, and than the middlemost of the building." A figurative use of the word appears in 2 Chron.

7:21, where it modifies the dynasty (house) of Solomon. The messianic Davidic king will be God's firstborn, "higher than the kings of the earth" (Ps. 89:27).

In many passages, *'elǝyôn* means "upper," in the sense of the top or higher of two things: ". . . the border of their inheritance on the east side was Ataroth-addar, unto Beth-horon the upper" (Josh. 16:5; cf. 2 Chron. 8:5).

This word is frequently used in a name (*El 'Elǝyôn*) of God; it describes Him as the Most High, the "highest" and only Supreme Being. The emphasis here is on divine supremacy rather than divine exclusiveness: "And Melchizedek king of Salem brought forth bread and wine: and he was the priest of the most high God [*El 'Elǝyôn*]" (Gen. 14:18—the first occurrence). This name for a god also appears in extra-biblical Palestinian documents.

Also the figurative use of *'elǝyôn* to describe the "house" or dynasty of Israel takes an unusual turn in 1 Kings 9:8, where the kingdom is said to be the "height" of astonishment: "And at this house, which [will be a heap of ruins], every one that passeth by it shall be astonished, and shall hiss; and they shall say, Why hath the Lord done thus unto this land, and to this house?"

B. Verb.

gābāh (גָּבַהּ), "to be high, exalted, lofty." This verb, which occurs 38 times in the Bible, has cognates in Akkadian, Aramaic, and Arabic. Its meanings parallel those of the adjective. It may mean "to be high, lofty." In this sense, it is used of trees (Ezek. 19:11), the heavens (Job 35:5), and a man (1 Sam. 10:23). It may mean "to be exalted" in dignity and honor (Job 36:7). Or it may simply mean "to be lofty," used in the positive sense of "being encouraged" (2 Chron. 17:6) or in the negative sense of "being haughty or proud" (2 Chron. 26:16).

C. Noun.

gōbah (גֹּבַהּ), "height; exaltation; grandeur; haughtiness; pride." This noun, which occurs 17 times in biblical Hebrew, refers to the "height" of things (2 Chron. 3:4) and of men (1 Sam. 17:4). It may also refer to "exaltation" or "grandeur" (Job 40:10), and to "haughtiness" or "pride" (2 Chron. 32:26).

HIGH PLACE

bāmāh (בָּמָה), "high place." This noun occurs in other Semitic languages, meaning the "back" of an animal or of a man (Ugaritic), the incline or "back" of a mountain (Akkadian), and the "block" (of stone) or grave of a saint (Arabic). *Bāmāh* is used about 100 times in biblical Hebrew, and the first occurrence is in Lev. 26:30: "And I will destroy your high places, and cut down your images, and cast your carcases upon the carcases of your idols, and my soul shall abhor you." Most of the uses are in the Books of Kings and Chronicles, with the sense of "cultic high place." The word is rarely used in the Pentateuch or in the poetic or prophetic literature.

Bāmāh with the sense of "back" is still to be found in the Hebrew Old

Testament: "So your enemies shall cringe before you, and you shall tread upon their high places" (Deut. 33:29, NASB). Compare this with the NEB "Your enemies come crying to you, and you shall trample their bodies [*bāmāh*] underfoot."

The Bible's metaphorical use of the "backs" of the clouds and the waves of the sea gives problems to translators: "I will ascend above the heights [*bāmāh*] of the clouds; I will be like the most High" (Isa. 14:14), and "[He] alone spreadeth out the heavens, and treadeth upon the waves [literally, "high places"] of the sea" (Job 9:8). A similar problem is found in Ps. 18:33 (cf. 2 Sam. 22:34; Hab. 3:19): "He maketh my feet like hinds' feet, and setteth me upon my high places." In these passages, *bāmāh* must be understood idiomatically, meaning "authority."

The word is used metaphorically to portray the Lord as providing for His people: "He made him ride on the high places of the earth, that he might eat the increase of the fields; and he made him to suck honey out of the rock, and oil out of the flinty rock" (Deut. 32:13; cf. Isa. 58:14). The idiom, "to ride upon the high places of the earth," is a Hebraic way of expressing God's protection of His people. It expresses the exalted nature of Israel, whose God is the Lord.

Not every literal *bāmāh* was a cultic high place; the word may simply refer to a geographical unit; "Therefore shall Zion for your sake be plowed as a field, and Jerusalem shall become heaps, and the mountain of the [temple] as the high places of the forest" (Mic. 3:12; cf. Amos. 4:13). The Canaanites served their gods on these hills, where pagan priests presented the sacrifices to the gods; Israel imitated this practice (1 Kings 3:2), even when they sacrificed to the Lord. The surrounding nations had high places dedicated to Chemosh (1 Kings 11:7), Baal (Jer. 19:5), and other deities. On the "high place," a temple was built and dedicated to a god: "[Jeroboam] made a house of high places, and made priests of the lowest of the people, which were not of the sons of Levi" (1 Kings 12:31). Cultic symbols were added as decoration; thus, the sacred pillars (*'ashērāh*) and sacred trees or poles (*matstsēbāh*) were associated with a temple: "For they also built them high places, and [sacred stones], and groves, on every high hill [*gibə'āh*], and under every green tree" (1 Kings 14:23; cf. 2 Kings 16:4).

Before the temple was built, Solomon worshiped the Lord at the great *bāmāh* of Gideon (1 Kings 3:4). This was permissible until the temple was constructed; however, history demonstrates that Israel soon adopted these "high places" for pagan customs. The *bāmāh* was found in the cities of Samaria (2 Kings 23:19), in the cities of Judah (2 Chron. 21:11), and even in Jerusalem (2 Kings 23:13). The *bāmāh* was a place of cult prostitution: "[They] pant after the dust of the earth on the head of the poor, and turn aside the way of the meek: and a man and his father will go in unto the same maid, to profane my holy name: And they lay themselves down upon clothes laid to pledge by every altar, and they drink the wine of the condemned in the house of their god" (Amos 2:7-8).

The Septuagint gives the following translations: *hupselos* ("high; lofty; elevated''), *bama* (a transliteration of the Hebrew), *bomos* (''altar''), *stele* (''pillar'') and *hupsos* (''height; high place'').

HOLY

A. Adjective.

qādôsh (קָדוֹשׁ), ''holy.'' The Semitic languages have two separate original forms of the root. The one signifies ''pure'' and ''devoted,'' as in Akkadian *qadistu* and in Hebrew *qades*, ''holy.'' The word describes something or someone. The other signifies ''holiness'' as a situation or as an abstract, as in Arabic *al-qaddus* ''the most holy or most pure.'' In Hebrew the verb *qādash* and the word *qādēsh* combine both elements: the descriptive and the static. The traditional understanding of ''separated'' is only a derived meaning, and not the primary.

Qādôsh is prominent in the Pentateuch, poetic and prophetic writings, and rare in the historical books. The first of its 116 occurrences is in Exod. 19:16: ''And ye shall be unto me a kingdom of priests, and a holy nation. These are the words which thou shalt speak unto the children of Israel.''

In the Old Testament *qādôsh* has a strongly religious connotation. In one sense the word describes an object or place or day to be ''holy'' with the meaning of ''devoted'' or ''dedicated'' to a particular purpose: ''And the priest shall take holy water in an earthen vessel . . .'' (Num. 5:17). Particularly the sabbath day is ''devoted'' as a day of rest: ''If thou turn away thy foot from the sabbath, from doing thy pleasure on my holy day; and call the sabbath a delight, the holy of the Lord, honorable; and shalt honor him, not doing thine own ways, nor finding thine own pleasure, nor speaking thine own words: Then shalt thou delight thyself in the Lord . . .'' (Isa. 58:13, 14). The prescription is based on Gen. 2:3 where the Lord ''sanctified,'' or ''dedicated,'' the sabbath.

God has dedicated Israel as His people. They are ''holy'' by their relationship to the ''holy'' God. All of the people are in a sense ''holy,'' as members of the covenant community, irrespective of their faith and obedience: ''And they gathered themselves together against Moses and against Aaron, and said unto them, Ye take too much upon you, seeing all the congregation are holy, every one of them, and the Lord is among them: wherefore then lift ye up yourselves above the congregation of the Lord?'' (Num. 16:3). God's intent was to use this ''holy'' nation as a ''holy,'' royal priesthood amongst the nations (Exod. 19:6). Based on the intimate nature of the relationship, God expected His people to live up to His ''holy'' expectations and, thus, to demonstrate that they were a ''holy nation'': ''And ye shall be holy unto me: for I the Lord am holy, and have severed you from other people, that ye should be mine'' (Lev. 20:26).

The priests were chosen to officiate at the Holy Place of the tabernacle/temple. Because of their function as intermediaries between God and Israel and because of their proximity to the temple, they were dedicated by God to the office of priest: "They shall be holy unto their God, and not profane the name of their God: for the offerings of the Lord made by fire, and the bread of their God, they do offer: therefore they shall be holy. They shall not take a wife that is a whore, or profane; neither shall they take a woman put away from her husband: for he is holy unto his God. Thou shalt sanctify him therefore; for he offereth the bread of thy God: he shall be holy unto thee: for I the Lord, which sanctify you, am holy" (Lev. 21:6-8). Aaron as the high priest was "the holy one of the Lord" (Ps. 106:16, NASB).

The Old Testament clearly and emphatically teaches that God is "holy." He is "the Holy One of Israel" (Isa. 1:4), the "holy God" (Isa. 5:16), and "the Holy One" (Isa. 40:25). His name is "Holy": "For thus saith the high and lofty One that inhabiteth eternity, whose name is Holy; I dwell in the high and holy place, with him also that is of a contrite and humble spirit, to revive the spirit of the humble, and to revive the heart of the contrite ones" (Isa. 57:15). The negative statement, "There is none holy as the Lord: for there is none besides thee: neither is there any rock like our God" (1 Sam. 2:2), explains that He is most "holy" and that no one is as "holy" as He is. Also the angels in the heavenly entourage are "holy": "And the valley of my mountains shall be stopped up, for the valley of the mountains shall touch the side of it; and you shall flee as you fled from the earthquake in the days of Uzziah king of Judah. Then the Lord your God will come, and all the holy ones [KJV, "saints"] with him" (Zech. 14:5 RSV). The seraphim proclaimed to each other the holiness of God: "And one cried unto another, and said, "Holy, holy, holy, is the Lord of hosts: the whole earth is full of his glory" (Isa. 6:3).

In the Septuagint the word *hagios* ("holy") stands for the Hebrew *qādôsh*.

B. Verb.

qādēsh (קָדֵשׁ) or *qādash* (קָדַשׁ), "to be holy; to sanctify." This verb, which occurs 175 times, can mean "to be holy" (Exod. 29:37; Lev. 6:18) or "to sanctify": "Hear me, ye Levites, sanctify now yourselves, and sanctify the house of the Lord God of your fathers, and carry forth the filthiness out of the holy place" (2 Chron. 29:5).

C. Nouns.

qōdesh (קֹדֶשׁ), "holiness; holy thing; sanctuary." This noun occurs 469 times with the meanings: "holiness" (Exod. 15:11); "holy thing" (Num. 4:15); and "sanctuary" (Exod. 36:4).

Another noun, *qādēsh*, means "temple-prostitute" or "sodomite": "There shall be no whore of the daughters of Israel, nor a sodomite of the sons of Israel" (Deut. 23:17). The noun is found 11 times.

TO HONOR

A. Verbs.

kābēd (כָּבֵד), "to honor." This verb occurs about 114 times and in all periods of biblical Hebrew. Its cognates appear in the same languages as those of the noun *kābôd*. One occurrence of *kābēd* is in Deut. 5:16: "Honor thy father and thy mother, as the Lord thy God hath commanded thee. . . ."

hādar (הָדַר), "to honor, prefer, exalt oneself, behave arrogantly." This verb, which appears 8 times in biblical Hebrew, has cognates only in Aramaic although some scholars suggest cognates in Egyptian and Syriac.

The word means "to honor" or "to prefer" in Exod. 23:3: "Neither shalt thou countenance a poor man in his cause." In Prov. 25:6 *hādar* means "to exalt oneself" or "to behave arrogantly."

B. Nouns.

kābôd (כָּבוֹד), "honor; glory; great quantity; multitude; wealth; reputation [majesty]; splendor." Cognates of this word appear in Ugaritic, Phoenician, Arabic, Ethiopic, and Akkadian. It appears about 200 times in biblical Hebrew and in all periods.

Kābôd refers to the great physical weight or "quantity" of a thing. In Nah. 2:9 one should read: "For there is no limit to the treasure—a great quantity of every kind of desirable object." Isa. 22:24 likens Eliakim to a peg firmly anchored in a wall upon which is hung "all the [weighty things] of his father's house." This meaning is required in Hos. 9:11, where *kābôd* represents a great crowd of people or "multitude": "As for Ephraim, their [multitude] shall fly away. . . ." The word does not mean simply "heavy," but a heavy or imposing quantity of things.

Kābôd often refers to both "wealth" and significant and positive "reputation" (in a concrete sense). Laban's sons complained that "Jacob hath taken away all that was our father's; and of that which was our father's hath he gotten all this [wealth]" (Gen. 31:1—the first biblical occurrence). The second emphasis appears in Gen. 45:13, where Joseph told his brothers to report to his "father . . . all my [majesty] in Egypt." Here this word includes a report of his position and the assurance that if the family came to Egypt, Joseph would be able to provide for them. Trees, forests, and wooded hills have an imposing quality, a richness or "splendor." God will punish the king of Assyria by destroying most of the trees in his forests, "and shall consume the glory of his forest, . . . and the rest of the trees of his forest shall be few, that a child may write them" (Isa. 10:18-19). In Ps. 85:9 the idea of richness or abundance predominates: "Surely his salvation is nigh them that fear him; that glory [or abundance] may dwell in our land." This idea is repeated in Ps. 85:12: "Yea, the Lord shall give that which is good; and our land shall yield her increase."

Kābôd can also have an abstract emphasis of "glory," imposing presence or position. Phinehas' wife named their son Ichabod, "saying, The glory is departed from Israel: because the ark of God was taken, and because of her father-in-law and her husband" (they, the high priests, had died; 1 Sam. 4:21). In Isa. 17:3 *kābôd* represents the more concrete idea of a fullness of things including fortified cities, sovereignty (self-rule), and people. Among such qualities is "honor," or respect and position. In Isa. 5:13 this idea of "honor" is represented by *kābôd*: ". . . And their [my people's] honorable men are famished, and their multitude dried up with thirst." Thus the word *kābôd* and its parallel (the multitude) represent all the people of Israel: the upper classes and the common people. In many passages the word represents a future rather than a present reality: "In that day shall the branch of the Lord be beautiful and glorious . . ." (Isa. 4:2).

When used in the sense of "honor" or "importance" (cf. Gen. 45:13) there are two nuances of the word. First, *kābôd* can emphasize the position of an individual within the sphere in which he lives (Prov. 11:16). This "honor" can be lost through wrong actions or attitudes (Prov. 26:1, 8) and evidenced in proper actions (Prov. 20:3; 25:2). This emphasis then is on a relationship between personalities. Second, there is a suggestion of nobility in many uses of the word, such as "honor" that belongs to a royal family (1 Kings 3:13). Thus, *kābôd* can be used of the social distinction and position of respect enjoyed by nobility.

When applied to God, the word represents a quality corresponding to Him and by which He is recognized. Joshua commanded Achan to give glory to God, to recognize His importance, worth, and significance (Josh. 7:19). In this and similar instances "giving honor" refers to doing something; what Achan was to do was to tell the truth. In other passages giving honor to God is a cultic recognition and confession of God as God (Ps. 29:1). Some have suggested that such passages celebrate the sovereignty of God over nature wherein the celebrant sees His "glory" and confesses it in worship. In other places the word is said to point to God's sovereignty over history and specifically to a future manifestation of that "glory" (Isa. 40:5). Still other passages relate the manifestation of divine "glory" to past demonstrations of His sovereignty over history and peoples (Exod. 16:7; 24:16).

hādār (הָדָר), "honor; splendor." Cognates of this word appear only in Aramaic. Its 31 appearances in the Bible are exclusively in poetic passages and in all periods.

First, *hādār* refers to "splendor" in nature: "And ye shall take you on the first day the boughs of goodly trees [literally, trees of splendor or beauty] . . ." (Lev. 23:40—the first occurrence).

Second, this word is a counterpart to Hebrew words for "glory" and "dignity." Thus *hādār* means not so much overwhelming beauty as a combination of physical attractiveness and social position. The Messiah is said to have "no form nor [majesty]; and when we shall see him, there is no beauty that we should desire him" (Isa. 53:2). Mankind is crowned with "glory and honor" in the sense of superior desirability (for God) and rank (Ps. 8:5). In Prov. 20:29 *hādār* focuses on the same idea—an aged man's mark of rank and privilege is his gray hair. This reflects the theme present throughout the Bible that long life is a mark of divine blessing and results (often) when one is faithful to God, whereas premature death is a result of divine judgment. The ideas of glorious brilliance, pre-eminence, and lordship are included in *hādār* when it is applied to God: "Glory and honor are in his presence; strength and gladness are in his place" (1 Chron. 16:27). Not only are these characteristics of His sanctuary (Ps. 96:6) but He is clothed with them (Ps. 104:1). This use of *hādār* is rooted in the ancient concept of a king or of a royal city. God gave David all good things: a crown of gold on his head, long life, and glory or "splendor" and majesty (Ps. 21:3-5). In the case of earthly kings their beauty or brilliance usually arises from their surroundings. So God says of Tyre: "They of Persia and of Lud and of Phut were in thine army, thy men of war: they hanged the shield and helmet in thee; they set forth thy comeliness [honor]. The men of Arvad with thine army were upon thy walls round about, and the Gammadim were in thy towers: they hanged their shields upon thy walls round about; they have made thy beauty perfect" (Ezek. 27:10-11). God, however, manifests the characteristic of "honor or splendor" in Himself.

The noun *hadārāh* means "majesty; splendor; exaltation; adornment." This noun appears 5 times in the Bible. The word implies "majesty or exaltation" in Prov. 14:28: "In a multitude of people is the glory of a King, but without people a prince is ruined" (RSV). *Hadārāh* refers to "adornment" in Ps. 29:2.

C. Adjective.

kābēd (כָּבֵד), "heavy; numerous; severe; rich." The adjective *kābēd* occurs about 40 times. Basically this adjective connotes "heavy." In Exod. 17:12 the word is used of physical weight: "But Moses' hands were heavy; and they took a stone, and put it under him, and he sat thereon; and Aaron and Hur stayed up his hands. . . ." This adjective bears the connotation of heaviness as an enduring, ever-present quality, a lasting thing. Used in a negative but extended sense, the word depicts sin as a yoke ever pressing down upon one: "For mine iniquities are gone over mine head: as a heavy burden they are too heavy for me" (Ps. 38:4). A task can be described as "heavy" (Exod. 18:18). Moses argued his inability to lead God's people out of Egypt because he was "slow of speech, and of a slow tongue"; his speech or tongue was not smooth-flowing but halting (heavy; Exod. 4:10). This use of *kābēd* appears with an explanation in Ezek. 3:6, where God is describing the people to whom Ezekiel is to minister: ". . . not to many people of a strange speech and of a hard language, whose words thou canst not understand." Another nuance of this word appears in Exod. 7:14, where it is applied to Pharaoh's heart: "Pharaoh's heart is hardened, he refuseth to let the people go." In all such contexts *kābēd* depicts a burden which weighs down one's body (or some part of it) so that one is either disabled or unable to function successfully.

A second series of passages uses this word of something that falls upon or overcomes one. So God sent upon Egypt a "heavy" hail (Exod. 9:18), a "great" swarm of insects (8:24), "numerous" locusts, and a "severe" pestilence (9:3). The first appearance of the word belongs to this category: ". . . The famine was [severe] in the land" of Egypt (Gen. 12:10).

Used with a positive connotation, *kābēd* can describe the amount of "riches" one has: "And Abram was very rich in cattle, in silver, and in gold" (Gen. 13:2). In Gen. 50:9 the word is used to modify a group of people, "a very great company." The next verse uses *kābēd* in the sense of "imposing" or "ponderous": ". . . They mourned with a great and very sore lamentation. . . ."

This adjective is never used of God.

HORSE

sûs (םוּס), "horse." Cognates of this word appear in Ugaritic, Akkadian, Egyptian, and Syriac. It appears in biblical Hebrew about 138 times and in all periods.

The first biblical appearance of *sûs* is in Gen. 47:17: "And they brought their cattle unto Joseph: and Joseph gave them bread in exchange for horses, and for the flocks, and for the cattle of the herds, and for the asses. . . ." In the second quarter of the second millennium the chariot became a major military weapon and "horses" a very desirable commodity. This was the time of Joseph. It was not until the end of the second millennium that a rudimentary cavalry appeared on the battlefield. In the period of the eighth-century prophets and following, "horses" became a sign of luxury and apostasy (Isa. 2:7; Amos 4:10) inasmuch as Israel's hope for freedom and security was to be the Lord: "But he [the king] shall not multiply horses to himself, nor cause the people to return to Egypt, to . . . multiply horses . . ." (Deut. 17:16).

The "horses" of God are the storm clouds with which he treads upon the sea (Hab. 3:15).

HOST

A. Noun.

tsābā' (אָבָצ), "host; military service; war; army; service; labor; forced labor; conflict." This word has cognates in either a verbal or noun form in Akkadian, Ugaritic, Arabic, and Ethiopic. The noun form occurs 486 times in biblical Hebrew and in all periods of the language.

This word involves several interrelated ideas: a group; impetus; difficulty; and force. These ideas undergird the general concept of "service" which one does for or under a superior rather than for himself. *Tsābā'* is usually applied to "military service" but is sometimes used of "work" in general (under or for a superior). In Num. 1:2-3 the word means "military service": "Take ye the sum of all the congregation of the children of Israel . . . from twenty years old and upward, all that are able to go forth to war in Israel. . . ." The idea is more concrete in Josh. 22:12, where the word represents serving in a military campaign: "And when the children of Israel heard of it, the whole congregation of the children of Israel gathered themselves together at Shiloh, to go to war against them." Num. 31:14 uses *tsābā'* of the actual battling itself: "And Moses was wroth with the officers of the [army], . . . which came from the battle."

The word can also represent an "army host": "And Eleazer the priest said unto the men of war which went to the battle . . ." (Num. 31:21). Even clearer is Num. 31:48: "And the officers which were over thousands of the host, the captains of thousands, and captains of hundreds, came near unto Moses." This meaning first appears in Gen. 21:22, which mentions Phichol, the captain of Abimelech's "army." At several points this is the meaning of the feminine plural: "And it shall be, when the officers have made an end of speaking unto the people, that they shall make captains of the armies to lead the people"

(Deut. 20:9). In Num. 1, 2, and 10, where *tsābā'* occurs with regard to a census of Israel, it is suggested that this was a military census by which God organized His "army" to march through the wilderness. Some scholars have noted that the plan of the march, or the positioning of the tribes, recalls the way ancient armies were positioned during military campaigns. On the other hand, groupings of people might be indicated regardless of military implications, as seems to be the case in passages such as Exod. 6:26: "These are that Aaron and Moses, to whom the Lord said, Bring out the children of Israel from the land of Egypt according to their armies."

That *tsābā'* can refer to a "nonmilitary host" is especially clear in Ps. 68:11: "The Lord gave the word: great was the company of those that published it." The phrase "hosts of heaven" signifies the stars as visual indications of the gods of the heathen: "And them that worship the host of heaven upon the housetops; and them that worship and that swear by the Lord, and that swear by Malcham . . ." (Zeph. 1:5). This meaning first appears in Deut. 4:19. Sometimes this phrase refers to the "host of heaven," or the angels: "And [Micaiah] said, Hear thou therefore the word of the Lord: I saw the Lord sitting on his throne, and all the host of heaven [the angels] standing by him on his right hand and on his left" (1 Kings 22:19). God Himself is the commander of this "host" (Dan. 8:10-11). In Josh. 6:14 the commander of the "host" of God confronted Joshua. This heavenly "host" not only worships God but serves to do all His will: "Bless ye the Lord, all ye his hosts; ye ministers of his, that do his pleasure" (Ps. 103:21).

Another meaning of the phrase "the host(s) of heaven" is simply "the numberless stars": "As the host of heaven cannot be numbered, neither the sand of the sea measured: so will I multiply the seed of David my servant, and the Levites that minister unto me" (Jer. 33:22). This phrase can include all the heavenly bodies, as it does in Ps. 33:6: "By the word of the Lord were the heavens made; and all the host of them by the breath of his mouth." In Gen. 2:1 *tsābā'* includes the heavens, the earth, and everything in the creation: "Thus the heavens and the earth were finished, and all the host of them."

The meaning "nonmilitary service in behalf of a superior" emerges in Num. 4:2-3: "Take the sum of the sons of Kohath . . . from thirty years old and upward even until fifty years old, all that enter [the service], to do the work in the tabernacle of the congregation." In Job 7:1 the word represents the burdensome everyday "toil" of mankind: "Is there not an appointed time to man upon earth? Are not his days also like the days of a hireling?" In Job 14:14 *tsābā'* seems to represent "forced labor." In Dan. 10:1 the word is used for "conflict": "In the third year of Cyrus king of Persia a word was revealed to Daniel, who was named Belteshazzar. And the word was true, and it was a great conflict" [RSV; KJV, "time appointed"].

B. Verb.

tsābā' (צָבָא), "to wage war; to muster an army; to serve in worship." This verb appears 14 times in biblical Hebrew. *Tsābā'* means "to wage war" in Num. 31:7: "And they warred against the Midianites, as the Lord commanded Moses. . . ." The word is used in 2 Kings 25:19 to refer to "mustering an army." Another sense of *tsābā'* appears in Num. 4:23 with the meaning of "serving in worship": ". . . all that enter in to perform the service, to do the work in the tabernacle of the congregation."

HOUSE

bayith (בַּיִת), " house or building; home; household; land." The noun has cognates in most other Semitic languages including biblical Aramaic. *Bayith* appears about 2,048 times in biblical Hebrew (44 times in Aramaic) and in all periods.

First, this noun denotes a fixed, established structure made from some kind of material. As a "permanent dwelling place" it is usually distinguished from a tent (2 Sam. 16:21, cf. v. 22). This word can even be applied to a one-room dwelling: "And he [Lot] said [to the two angels], Behold now, my lords, turn in, I pray you, into your servant's house . . ." (Gen. 19:2). *Bayith* is also distinguished from temporary booths or huts: "And Jacob journeyed to Succoth, and built him a house, and made booths for his cattle . . ." (Gen. 33:17). In Ps. 132:3 the word means "dwelling-living-place" and is used in direct conjunction with "tent," (literally, "tent of my house"): "Surely I will not come into the tabernacle of my house, nor go up into my bed." A similar usage appears in 1 Chron. 9:23 (literally, "the tent house"): "So they and their children had the oversight of the gates of the house of the Lord, namely, the house of the tabernacle, by wards."

Second, in many passages (especially when the word is joined to the word God") *bayith* represents a place of worship or "sanctuary": "The first of the first fruits of thy land thou shalt bring into the house of the Lord thy God" (Exod. 23:19). Elsewhere this noun signifies God's temple in Jerusalem: "And against the wall of the house he built chambers round about, against the walls of the house round about, both of the temple and of the oracle . . ." (1 Kings 6:5). Sometimes the word has this meaning although it is not further defined (cf. Ezek. 41:7).

Third, *bayith* can signify rooms and/or wings of a house: "And let the king appoint officers in all the provinces of his kingdom, that they may gather together all the fair young virgins unto Shushan the palace, to the [harem] (literally, to the house of the women; Esth. 2:3). . . ." In this connection *bayith* can also represent the inside of a building or some other structure as opposed to the outside: "Make thee an ark of gopher wood; rooms shalt thou make in the ark, and shalt pitch it within and without with pitch" (Gen. 6:14—the first biblical occurrence).

Fourth, *bayith* sometimes refers to the place where something or someone dwells or rests. So the underworld (Sheol) is termed a "home": "If I wait, the grave is mine house: I have made my bed in the darkness" (Job 17:13). An "eternal home" is one's grave: ". . . Man goeth to his long home, and the mourners go about the streets" (Eccl. 12:5). "House" can also mean "place" when used with "grave," as in Neh. 2:3: "Let the king live for ever: why should not my countenance be sad, when the city, the place of my fathers' sepulchers. . . ." *Bayith* means a receptacle (NASB, "box") in Isa. 3:20. In 1 Kings 18:32 the "house of two seeds" is a container for seed: "And with the stones he built an altar in the name of the Lord: and he made a trench about the altar, as great as would contain [literally, a house of] two measures of seed." Houses for bars are supports: "And thou shalt overlay the boards with gold, and make their rings of gold for places [literally, houses] for the bars" (Exod. 26:29). Similarly, see "the places [house] of the two paths," a crossing of two paths, in Prov. 8:2. The steppe is termed the "house of beasts": ". . . whose house I have made the wilderness, and the barren land his dwellings [house of beasts]" (Job 39:6).

Fifth, *bayith* is often used of those who live in a house, i.e., a "household": "Come thou and all thy house into the ark . . ." (Gen. 7:1). In passages such as Josh. 7:14 this word means "family": ". . . And it shall be, that the tribe which the Lord taketh shall come according to the families thereof; and the family which the Lord shall take shall come by households [literally, by house or by those who live in a single dwelling]. . . ." In a similar nuance this noun means "descendants": "And there went a man of the house of Levi, and took to wife a daughter of Levi" (Exod. 2:1). This word can be used of one's extended family and even of everyone who lives in a given area: "And the men of Judah came, and there they anointed David king over the house of Judah" (2 Sam. 2:4). Gen. 50:4, however, uses *bayith* in the sense of "a royal court" or all the people in a king's court: "And when the days of his mourning were past, Joseph spake unto the house of Pharaoh. . . ." The ideas "royal court" and "descendant" are joined in 1 Sam. 20:16: "So Jonathan made a covenant with the house of David. . . ."

In a few passages *bayith* means "territory" or "country": "Set the trumpet to thy mouth. He shall come as an eagle against the house of the Lord . . ." (Hos. 8:1; 9:15; Jer. 12:7; Zech. 9:8).

TO HUMBLE (SELF)

A. Verbs.

kāna‘ (כָּנַע), "to be humble; to humble, subdue." This biblical Hebrew word is also found in modern Hebrew. The word can mean "to humble, to subdue," and it can have a passive or reflexive use, "to be humble" or "to humble oneself." While *kāna‘* occurs some 35 times in the Hebrew Old Testament, the word is not found until Deut. 9:3: ". . . The Lord thy God . . . shall destroy them, and he shall bring them down. . . ." *Kāna‘* is frequently used in this sense of "subduing, humbling," enemies (2 Sam. 8:1; 1 Chron. 17:10; Ps. 81:14). "To humble oneself" before God in repentance is a common theme and need in the life of ancient Israel (Lev. 26:41; 2 Chron. 7:14; 12:6-7, 12).

shāphēl (שָׁפֵל), "to be low, become low; sink down; be humiliated; be abased." This root appears in most Semitic languages (except Ethiopic) with the basic meaning "to be low" and "to become low." *Shāphēl* occurs about twenty-five times in the Old Testament. It is a poetic term.

The verb, as can be expected in poetic usage, is generally used in a figurative sense. *Shāphēl* rarely denotes a literal lowness. Even in passages where the meaning may be taken literally, the prophet communicates a spiritual truth: ". . . The high [trees] of stature shall be hewn down, and the haughty shall be humbled" (Isa. 10:33), or "Every valley shall be exalted, and every mountain and hill shall be made low . . ." (Isa. 40:4). Isaiah particularly presented Judah's sin as one of rebellion, self-exaltation, and pride (2:17; 3:16-17). In the second chapter he repeated God's indictment on human pride. When the Lord comes in judgment, He will not tolerate pride: ". . . The Lord alone shall be exalted in that day" (Isa. 2:11); then "the Lord of hosts shall be upon every one that is proud and lofty, and upon every one that is lifted up; and he shall be brought low" (Isa. 2:12). Isaiah applied to Judah the principle found in Proverbs: "A man's pride shall bring him low: but honor shall uphold the humble in spirit" (Prov. 29:23).

Pride and self-exaltation have no place in the life of the godly, as the Lord "brings low" a person, a city, and a nation: "The Lord maketh poor, and maketh rich: he bringeth low, and lifteth up" (1 Sam. 2:7).

The prophets called the people to repent and to demonstrate their return to God by lowliness. Their call was generally unheeded. Ultimately the Exile came, and the people were humbled by the Babylonians. Nevertheless, the promise came that, regardless of the obstacles, God would initiate the redemption of His people. Isaiah expressed the greatness of the redemption in this way: "Prepare ye the way of the Lord. . . . Every valley shall be exalted, and every mountain and hill shall be made low. . . . And the glory of the Lord shall be revealed. . . ." (Isa. 40:3-5).

In the Septuagint *shāphēl* is represented by *tapeinō* ("to level, be humble, humiliate"). It is translated in English versions as "to be low" (KJV, RSV, NASB, NIV); "to bring low" (KJV, RSV); "to bring down" (NASB, NIV); "to be humble" (KJV, RSV, NASB, NIV).

B. Nouns.

Some nouns related to this verb occur infrequently. *Shēphel* refers to a "low condition, low estate." This word appears twice (Ps. 136:23; Eccl. 10:6). The noun *shiphəlah* means a "humiliated state." This noun occurs once: "When it shall hail, coming down on the forest; and the city shall be low in a low place" (Isa. 32:19); the city is leveled completely. *Shəphēlah* means "lowland." This word is used most often as a technical designation for the low-lying hills of the Judean hill country (cf. Deut. 1:7; Josh. 9:1). *Shiphəlût* refers to a "sinking." This noun's single appearance is in Eccl. 10:18: "By much slothfulness the building decayeth; and through idleness [*shiphəlût*] of the hands the house droppeth through." The word implies a negligence or "sinking" of the hands.

C. Adjective.

Shāphāl means "low; humble." This word means "low" in Ezek. 17:24: "And all the trees of the field shall know that I the Lord have brought down the high tree, have exalted the low tree. . . ." In Isa. 57:15 *shāphāl* refers to "humble": ". . . I dwell in the high and holy place, with him also that is of a contrite and humble spirit, to revive the spirit of the humble, and to revive the heart of the contrite ones."

TO BE HUMBLED, AFFLICTED

A. Verb.

'ānāh (עָנָה), "to be afflicted, be bowed down, be humbled, be meek." This word, common to both ancient and modern Hebrew, is the source of several important words in the history and experience of Judaism: "humble, meek, poor, and affliction." *'Ānāh* occurs approximately 80 times in the Hebrew Old Testament. It is found for the first time in Gen. 15:13: ". . . they shall afflict them four hundred years."

'Ānāh often expresses harsh and painful treatment. Sarai "dealt hardly" with Hagar (Gen. 16:6). When Joseph was sold as a slave, his feet were hurt with fetters (Ps. 105:18). Frequently the verb expresses the idea that God sends affliction for disciplinary purposes: ". . . the Lord thy God led thee these forty years in the wilderness, to humble thee, and to prove thee, to know what was in thine heart . . ." (Deut. 8:2; see also 1 Kings 11:39; Ps. 90:15). To take a woman sexually by force may be "to humble" her (Gen. 34:2 KJV, RSV), but the word is more appropriately translated "dishonor" (JB, NEB).

In the Day of Atonement observance, "to humble oneself" is probably connected with the requirement for fasting on that day (Lev. 23:28-29).

B. Noun.

'ānî (עָנִי), "poor; humble; meek." Especially in later Israelite history, just before the Exile and following, this noun came to have a special connection with those faithful ones who were being abused, taken advantage of, by the rich (Isa. 29:19; 32:7; Amos 2:7). The prophet Zephaniah's reference to them as the "meek of the earth" (Zeph. 2:3) set the stage for Jesus' concern and ministry to the "poor" and the "meek" (Matt. 5:3, 5; Luke 4:18; cf. Isa. 61:1). By New Testament times, "the poor of the land" were more commonly known as *'am ha'ārets*, "the people of the land."

I

IDOL

tərāphîm (תְּרָפִים), "idol; household idol; cultic mask; divine symbol." This word is a loanword from Hittite-Hurrian (*tarpish*) which in West Semitic assumes the basic form *tarpi*. Its basic meaning is "spirit" or "demon." Biblical Hebrew attests this word 15 times.

Tərāphîm first appears in Gen. 31:19: "And Laban went to shear his sheep: and Rachel had stolen the [household gods] that were her father's." Hurrian law of this period recognized "household idols" as deeds to the family's succession and goods. This makes these *tərāphîm* (possibly a plural of majesty as is *'elōhîm* when used of false gods; cf. 1 Kings 11:5, 33) extremely important to Laban in every way.

In 1 Sam. 19:13 we read that "Michal took the *tərāphîm* [here a plural of "majesty"] and laid it on the bed, and put a quilt of goat's hair at its head, and covered it with blankets" (author's translation). In view of 1 Sam. 19:11, where it is said that they were in David's private quarters, supposing that this *tərāphîm* was a "household idol" is difficult, although not impossible. Some scholars suggest that this was a "cultic" mask used in worshiping God.

Either of the former suggestions is the possible meaning of the word in the Micah incident recorded in Judg. 17-18. Notice in Judg. 17:5: ". . . Micah had a house of gods, and made an ephod, and *tərāphîm*, and consecrated one of his sons, who became his priest." In Judg. 18:14 *tərāphîm* appears to be distinguished from idols: ". . . there is in these houses an ephod, and *tərāphîm*, and a graven image, and a molten image?" The verses that follow suggest that the graven image and the molten image may have been the same thing: Judg. 18:17 uses all four words in describing what the Danites stole; Judg. 18:20 omits "molten image" from the list; and Judg. 18:31 reports that only the graven image was set up for worship. We know that the ephod was a special priestly garment. Could it be that *tərāphîm* was a "cultic mask" or some other symbol of the divine presence?

Thus *tərāphîm* may signify an "idol," a "cultic mask," or perhaps a "symbol of the divine presence." In any case the item is associated with pagan worship and perhaps with worship of God.

'elîl (אֱלִיל), "idol; gods; nought; vain." The 20 occurrences of this noun are primarily in Israel's legal code and the prophetic writings (especially Isaiah). Cognates of this word appear in Akkadian, Syriac, and Arabic.

This disdainful word signifies an "idol" or "false god." *'Elîl* first appears in Lev. 19:4: "Turn ye not unto idols, nor make to yourselves molten gods. . . ." In Lev. 26:1 the *'elîlîm* are what Israel is forbidden to make: "Ye shall make you no idols. . . ." The irony of this is biting not only with respect to the usual meaning of this word but also in view of its similarity to the usual word for God (*'elōhîm*; cf. Ps. 96:5): "For all the gods [*'elōhîm*] of the people are idols [*'elîlîm*] . . . " (1 Chron. 16:26).

Second, this word can mean "nought" or "vain." 1 Chron. 16:26 might well be rendered: "For all the gods of the people are nought." This nuance appears clearly in Job 13:4: "But ye are forgers of lies; ye are all physicians of no value [physicians of vanity]." Jeremiah told Israel that their prophets were "prophesy [ing] unto you a false vision and divination, and a thing of nought . . ." (14:14).

gillûlîm (גִּלּוּלִים), "idols." Of the 48 occurrences of this word, all but 9 appear in Ezekiel. This word for "idols" is a disdainful word and may originally have meant "dung pellets": "And I will destroy your high places, and cut down your images, and cast your carcases upon the carcases of your idols, and my soul shall abhor you" (Lev. 26:30).

This word and others for "idol" exhibit the horror and scorn that biblical writers felt toward them. In passages such as Isa. 66:3 the word for "idol," *'awen*, means "uncanny or wickedness." Jer. 50:38 evidences the word *'ēmîm*, which means "fright or horror." The word *'elîl* appears for "idol" in Lev. 19:4; it means "nothingness or feeble." 1 Kings 15:13 uses the Hebrew word, *miphəletset*, meaning a "horrible thing, a cause of trembling." A root signifying to make an image or to shape something, *'tsb* (a homonym of the root meaning "sorrow and grief") is used in several passages (cf. 1 Sam. 31:9).

TO INHERIT

A. Verb.

nāchal (נָחַל), "to inherit, get possession of, take as a possession." This term is found in both ancient and modern Hebrew, as well as in ancient Ugaritic. It is found around 60 times in the Hebrew Old Testament. The first time *nāchal* is used in the Old Testament text is in Exod. 23:30: "inherit the land." The RSV "possess" translates more appropriately here, since the land of Canaan was not literally an inheritance in the usual sense of the word, but a possession, that which was due her, through God's direct intervention. In fact, in most cases of the use of *nāchal* in the Old Testament, the word has the basic sense of "to possess" rather than "to inherit" by means of a last will and testament. One of the few instances of "to inherit" by last will and testament is in Deut. 21:16: ". . . when he maketh his sons to inherit that which he hath. . . ." This clause is more literally translated "in the day he causes his sons to inherit that which is his."

When Moses prayed: ". . . O Lord, . . . take us for thine inheritance" (Exod. 34:9), he did not mean that God should "inherit" through a will, but that He should "take possession of" Israel. The meaning "to get as a possession" is seen in its figurative use. Thus, "the wise shall inherit [possess as their due] glory" (Prov. 3:35); "the upright shall have good things in possession" (Prov. 28:10); "our fathers have inherited lies" (Jer. 16:19); "he that troubleth his own house shall inherit the wind" (Prov. 11:29).

B. Noun.

nachalāh (נַחֲלָה), "possession; property; inheritance." This noun is used frequently (220 times), but mainly in the Pentateuch and Joshua. It is rare in the historical books. The first occurrence of the word is in Gen. 31:14: "And Rachel and Leah answered and said unto him, Is there yet any portion or inheritance for us in our father's house?"

The basic translation of *nachalāh* is "inheritance": "And Naboth said to Ahab, The Lord forbid it me, that I should give the inheritance of my fathers unto thee" (1 Kings 21:3). The word more appropriately refers to a "possession" to which one has received the legal claim. The usage of *nachalāh* in the Pentateuch and Joshua indicates that the word often denotes that "possession" which all of Israel or a tribe or a clan received as their share in the Promised Land. The share was determined by lot (Num. 26:56) shortly before Moses' death, and it fell upon Joshua to execute the division of the "possession": "So Joshua took the whole land, according to all that the Lord said unto Moses; and Joshua gave it for an inheritance unto Israel according to their divisions by their tribes" (Josh. 11:23). After the Conquest the term "inheritance" is no longer used to refer to newly gained territory by warfare. Once "possession" had been taken of the land, the legal process came into operation by which the hereditary property was supposed to stay within the family. For this reason Naboth could not give his rights over to Ahab (1 Kings 21:3-4). One could redeem the property, whenever it had come into other hands, as did Boaz, in order to maintain the name of the deceased: "Moreover Ruth the Moabitess, the wife of Mahlon, have I purchased to be my wife, to raise up the name of the dead upon his inheritance, that the name of the dead be not cut off from among his brethren, and from the gate of his place" (Ruth 4:10).

Metaphorically, Israel is said to be God's "possession": "But the Lord hath taken you, and brought you forth out of the iron furnace, even out of Egypt, to be unto him a people of inheritance, as ye are this day" (Deut. 4:20).

Within the special covenantal status Israel experienced the blessing that its children were a special gift from the Lord (Ps. 127:3). However, the Lord abandoned Israel as His "possession" to the nations (cf. Isa. 47:6), and permitted a remnant of the "possession" to return: "Who is a God like unto thee, that pardoneth iniquity, and passeth by the transgression of the remnant of his heritage? he retaineth not his anger for ever, because he delighteth in mercy" (Mic. 7:18).

On the other hand, it can even be said that the Lord is the "possession" of His people. The priests and the Levites, whose earthly "possessions" were limited, were assured that their "possession" is the Lord: "Wherefore Levi hath no part nor inheritance with his brethren; the Lord is his inheritance, according as the Lord thy God promised him" (Deut. 10:9; cf. 12:22; Num. 18:23).

The Septuagint gives the following translations: *kleronomia* ("inheritance; possession; property"), and *kleros* ("lot; position; share"). The KJV gives these senses: "inheritance, heritage."

INIQUITY

A. Verb.

'āwāh (עָוָה), "to do iniquity." This verb appears in the Bible 17 times. In Arabic this verb appears with the meaning "to bend" or "to deviate from the way." 'Āwāh is often used as a synonym of chātā', "to sin," as in Ps. 106:6: "We have sinned [chātā'] with our fathers, we have committed iniquity ['āwāh), we have done wickedly [rāsha']."

B. Nouns.

'āwōn (עָוֹן), "iniquity; guilt; punishment." This noun, which appears 231 times in the Old Testament, is limited to Hebrew and biblical Aramaic. The prophetic and poetic books employ 'āwōn with frequency. The Pentateuch as a whole employs the word about 50 times. In addition to these, the historical books infrequently use 'āwōn. The first use of 'āwōn comes from Cain's lips, where the word takes the special meaning of "punishment": "And Cain said unto the Lord, My punishment is greater than I can bear" (Gen. 4:13).

The most basic meaning of 'āwōn is "iniquity." The word signifies an offense, intentional or not, against God's law. This meaning is also most basic to the word chattā'th, "sin," in the Old Testament, and for this reason the words chattā'th and 'āwōn are virtually synonymous; cf. "Lo, this [the live coal] hath touched thy [Isaiah's] lips; and thine iniquity ['āwōn] is taken away, and thy sin [chattā'th] purged" (Isa. 6:7).

"Iniquity" as an offense to God's holiness is punishable. The individual is warned that the Lord punishes man's transgression: "But every one shall die for his own iniquity: every man that eateth the sour grape, his teeth shall be set on edge" (Jer. 31:30). There is also a collective sense in that the one is responsible for the many: "Thou shalt not bow down thyself to them, nor serve them: for I the Lord thy God am a jealous God, visiting the iniquity of the fathers upon the children unto the third and fourth generation of them that hate me" (Exod. 20:5). No generation, however, was to think that it bore God's judgment for the "iniquity" of another generation: "Yet say ye, Why? doth not the son bear the iniquity of the father? When the son hath done that which is lawful and right, and hath kept all my statutes, and hath done them, he shall surely live. The soul that sinneth, it shall die. The son shall not bear the iniquity of the father, neither shall the father bear the iniquity of the son: the righteousness of the righteous shall be upon him, and the wickedness of the wicked shall be upon him" (Ezek. 18:19-20).

Israel went into captivity for the sin of their fathers and for their own sins: "And the heathen shall know that the house of Israel went into captivity for their iniquity; because they trespassed against me, therefore hid I my face from them, and gave them into the hand of their enemies: so fell they all by the sword" (Ezek. 39:23).

Serious as "iniquity" is in the covenantal relationship between the Lord and His people, the people are reminded that He is a living God who willingly forgives "iniquity": "Keeping mercy for thousands, forgiving iniquity and transgression and sin, and that will by no means clear the guilty; visiting the iniquity of the fathers upon the children, and upon the children's children, unto the third and to the fourth generation" (Exod. 34:7). God expects confession of sin: "I acknowledged my sin unto thee, and mine iniquity have I not hid. I said, I will confess my transgressions unto the Lord; and thou forgavest the iniquity of my sin" (Ps. 32:5), and a trusting, believing heart which expresses the humble prayer: "Wash me thoroughly from mine iniquity, and cleanse me from my sin" (Ps. 51:2).

Isaiah 53 teaches that God put upon Jesus Christ our "iniquities" (v. 6), that He having been bruised for our "iniquities" (v. 5) might justify those who believe on Him: "He shall see of the travail of his soul, and shall be satisfied: by his knowledge shall my righteous servant justify many; for he shall bear their iniquities" (Isa. 53:11).

The usage of '*āwōn* includes the whole area of sin, judgment, and "punishment" for sin. The Old Testament teaches that God's forgiveness of "iniquity" extends to the actual sin, the guilt of sin, God's judgment upon that sin, and God's punishment of the sin. "Blessed is the man unto whom the Lord imputeth not iniquity, and in whose spirit there is no guile" (Ps. 32:2).

In the Septuagint the word has the following renderings: *adikia* ("wrongdoing; unrighteousness; wickedness"); *hamartia* ("sin; error"); and *anomia* ("lawlessness"). In the English versions the translation "iniquity" is fairly uniform. The RSV and NIV give at a few places the more specialized rendering "guilt" or the more general translation "sin."

'*āwen* (אָוֶן), "iniquity; misfortune." This noun is derived from a root meaning "to be strong," found only in the Northwest Semitic languages. The word occurs about 80 times and almost exclusively in poetic-prophetic language. The usage is particularly frequent in the poetical books. Isaiah's use stands out among the prophets. The first occurrence is in Num. 23:21: "He hath not beheld iniquity in Jacob, neither hath he seen perverseness in Israel: the Lord his God is with him, and the shout of a king is among them."

The meaning of "misfortune" comes to expression in the devices of the wicked against the righteous. The psalmist expected "misfortune" to come upon him: "And if he come to see me, he speaketh vanity: his heart gathereth iniquity to itself; when he goeth abroad, he telleth it" (Ps. 41:6). '*Āwen* in this sense is synonymous with '*êd*, "disaster" (Job 18:12). In a real sense '*āwen* is part of human existence, and as such the word is identical with '*āmāl*, "toil," as in Ps. 90:10: "The days of our years are threescore years and ten; and if by reason of strength they be fourscore years, yet is their strength labor and sorrow; for it is soon cut off, and we fly away."

'*Āwen* in a deeper sense characterizes the way of life of those who are without God: "For the vile person will speak villany, and his heart will work iniquity, to practice hypocrisy, and to utter error against the Lord, to make empty the soul of the hungry, and he will cause the drink of the thirsty to fail" (Isa. 32:6). The being of man is corrupted by "iniquity." Though all of mankind is subject to '*āwen* ("toil"), there are those who delight in causing difficulties and "misfortunes" for others by scheming, lying, and acting deceptively. The psalmist puts internalized wickedness this way: "Behold, he travaileth with iniquity, and hath conceived mischief, and brought forth falsehood" (Ps. 7:14; cf. Job 15:35).

Those who are involved in the ways of darkness are the "workers of iniquity," the doers of evil or the creators of "misfortune" and disaster. Synonyms for *'āwen* with this sense are *ra‘*, "evil," and *rashā‘*, "wicked," opposed to "righteousness" and "justice." They seek the downfall of the just (Ps. 141:9). Between Ps. 5:5 and 141:9 there are as many as 16 references to the workers of evil (cf. "The foolish shall not stand in thy sight: thou hatest all workers of iniquity"—Ps. 5:5). In the context of Ps. 5, the evil spoken of is falsehood, bloodshed, and deceit (v. 6). The qualitative aspect of the word comes to the best expression in the verbs with *'āwen*. The wicked work, speak, beget, think, devise, gather, reap, and plow *'āwen*, and it is revealed ("comes forth") by the misfortune that comes upon the righteous. Ultimately when Israel's religious festivals (Isa. 1:13) and legislation (Isa. 10:1) were affected by their apostate way of life, they had reduced themselves to the Gentile practices and way of life. The prophetic hope lay in the period after the purification of Israel, when the messianic king would introduce a period of justice and righteousness (Isa. 32) and the evil men would be shown up for their folly and ungodliness.

The Septuagint has several translations: *anomia* ("lawlessness"); *kopos* ("work; labor; toil"); *mataios* ("empty; fruitless; useless; powerless"); *poneria* ("wickedness; maliciousness; sinfulness"); and *adikia* ("unrighteousness; wickedness; injustice"). The KJV has these translations: "iniquity; vanity; wickedness."

INSTRUCTION

A. Noun.

mûsār (מוּסָר), "instruction; chastisement; warning." This noun occurs 50 times, mainly in Proverbs. The first occurrence is in Deut. 11:2: ". . . I speak not with your children which have not known, and which have not seen the chastisement of the Lord your God, his greatness, his mighty hand, and his stretched out arm."

One of the major purposes of the wisdom literature was to teach wisdom and *mûsār* (Prov. 1:2). *Mûsār* is discipline, but more. As "discipline" it teaches how to live correctly in the fear of the Lord, so that the wise man learns his lesson before temptation and testing: "Then I saw, and considered it well: I looked upon it, and received instruction" (Prov. 24:32). This "discipline" is training for life; hence, paying attention to *mûsār* is important. Many verbs bear out the need for a correct response: "hear, obey, love, receive, obtain, take hold of, guard, keep." Moreover, the rejection is borne out by many verbs connected with *mûsār*: "reject, hate, ignore, not love, despise, forsake." When *mûsār* as "instruction" has been given, but was not observed, the *mûsār* as "chastisement" or "discipline" may be the next step: "Foolishness is bound in the heart of a child; but the rod of correction shall drive it far from him" (Prov. 22:15).

Careful attention to "instruction" brings honor (Prov. 1:9), life (Prov. 4:13), and wisdom (Prov. 8:33), and above all it pleases God: "For whoso findeth me findeth life, and shall obtain favor of the Lord" (Prov. 8:35). The lack of observance of "instruction" brings its own results: death (Prov. 5:23), poverty, and shame (Prov. 13:18), and is ultimately a sign that one has no regard for one's own life (Prov. 15:32).

The receptivity for "instruction" from one's parents, teacher, the wise, or the king is directly corollary to one's subjugation to God's discipline. The prophets charged Israel with not receiving God's discipline: "O Lord, are not thine eyes upon the truth? thou hast stricken them, but they have not grieved; thou hast consumed them, but they have refused to receive correction: they have made their faces harder than a rock; they have refused to return" (Jer. 5:3). Jeremiah asked the men of Judah and the inhabitants in the besieged Jerusalem to pay attention to what was happening around them, that they still might subject themselves to "instruction" (35:13). Isaiah predicted that God's chastisement on man was carried by the Suffering Servant, bringing peace to those who believe in Him: "But he was wounded for our transgressions, he was bruised for our iniquities: the chastisement of our peace was upon him; and with his stripes we are healed" (53:5).

The Septuagint has the translation of *paideia* ("upbringing; training; instruction"). The Greek word is the basis for our English word *pedagogy*, "training of a child." The KJV has the translations: "instruction; correction; chastisement; chastening."

B. Verb.

yāsar (יָסַר), "to discipline." This verb occurs in Hebrew and Ugaritic with the sense of "to discipline." Outside of these languages the root is not represented. The verb appears 42 times in the Old Testament; cf. Prov. 19:18: "Chasten thy son while there is hope, and let not thy soul spare for his crying."

J

TO BE JEALOUS, ZEALOUS

A. Verb.

qānā' (קָנָא), "to be jealous; to be zealous." This verb, derived from the noun *qinə'āh*, occurs 34 times in the Old Testament. The root appears in several Semitic languages with the meaning "to be zealous" (Aramaic and Ethiopic). In Ugaritic and Arabic the root occurs, but it is questionable if the root is related to the meaning "to be zealous"; the meaning in Ugaritic text is uncertain, and the meaning in Arabic, "became intensely red," is not to be explained etymologically. The verb *qānā'* appears in rabbinic Hebrew.

At the interhuman level *qānā'* has a strongly competitive sense. In its most positive sense the word means "to be filled with righteous zeal or jealousy." The law provides that a husband who suspects his wife of adultery can bring her to a priest, who will administer a test of adultery. Whether his accusation turns out to be grounded or not, the suspicious man has a legitimate means of ascertaining the truth. In his case a spirit of jealousy has come over him, as he "is jealous" of his wife (Num. 5:30). However, even in this context (Num. 5:12-31), the jealousy has arisen out of a spirit of rivalry which cannot be tolerated in a marriage relationship. The jealousy must be cleared by a means ordained by the law and administered by the priests. *Qānā'*, then, in its most basic sense is the act of advancing one's rights to the exclusion of the rights of others: ". . . Ephraim shall not envy Judah, and Judah shall not vex Ephraim" (Isa. 11:13). Saul sought to murder the Gibeonite enclave "in his zeal to the children of Israel and Judah" (2 Sam. 21:2). Next, the word signifies the attitude of envy toward an opponent. Rachel in her barren state "envied her sister" (Gen. 30:1) and in the state of envy approached Jacob: "Give me children, or else I die." The Philistines envied Isaac because of the multitude of his flocks and herds (Gen. 26:14).

The Bible contains a strong warning against being envious of sinners, who might prosper and be powerful today, but will be no more tomorrow: "Do not envy a violent man or choose any of his ways" (Prov. 3:31, NIV; cf. Ps. 37:1).

In man's relation to God, the act of zeal is more positively viewed as the act of the advancement of God and His glory over against substitutes. The tribe of Levi received the right to service because "he was zealous for his God" (Num. 25:13). Elijah viewed himself as the only faithful servant left in Israel: "I have been very jealous for the Lord God of hosts: for the children of Israel have forsaken thy covenant . . . And I, even I only, am left . . ." (1 Kings 19:10). However, the sense of *qānā'* is "to make jealous," that is, "to provoke to anger": "They provoked him to jealousy with strange gods, with abominations provoked they him to anger" (Deut. 32:16).

God is not tainted with the negative connotation of the verb. His holiness does not tolerate competitors or those who sin against Him. In no single passage in the whole Old Testament is God described as envious. Even in those texts where the adjective "jealous" is used, it might be more appropriate to understand it as "zealous." When God is the subject of the verb *qānā'*, the meaning is "be zealous," and the preposition *lə* ("to, for") is used before the object: His holy name (Ezek. 39:25); His land (Joel 2:18); and His inheritance (Zech. 1:14). Cf. Zech. 8:2: "This is what the Lord Almighty says: I am very jealous for Zion; I am burning with jealousy for her" (NIV), where we must interpret "jealous[y]" as "zealous" and "zeal."

In the Septuagint the word *zelos* ("zeal; ardor; jealousy") brings out the Hebrew usage. In the English versions similar translations are given: "to be jealous" or "to be zealous" (KJV, RSV, NASB, NIV) and "to be envious" (KJV and NIV).

B. Noun.

qinə'āh (קִנְאָה), "ardor; zeal; jealousy." This noun occurs 43 times in biblical Hebrew. One occurrence is in Deut. 29:20: "The Lord will not spare him, but then the anger of the Lord and his jealousy shall smoke against that man. . . ."

C. Adjectives.

qannā' (קַנָּא), "jealous." This adjective occurs 6 times in the Old Testament. The word refers directly to the attributes of God's justice and holiness, as He is the sole object of human worship and does not tolerate man's sin. One appearance is in Exod. 20:5: ". . . For I the Lord thy God am a jealous God, visiting the iniquity of the fathers upon the children unto the third and fourth generation of them that hate me."

The adjective *qannô'* also means "jealous." This word appears only twice, with implications similar to *qannā'*. Josh. 24:19 is one example: "And Joshua said unto the people, Ye cannot serve the Lord: for he is a holy God; he is a jealous God; he will not forgive your transgressions nor your sins." Nah. 1:2 contains the other occurrence of *qannô'*.

TO JUDGE

A. Verb.

shāphat (שָׁפַט), "to judge, deliver, rule." This verb also occurs in Ugaritic, Phoenician, Arabic, Akkadian, and post–biblical Hebrew. Biblical Hebrew attests *shāphat* around 125 times and in all periods.

In many contexts this root has a judicial sense. *Shāphat* refers to the activity of a third party who sits over two parties at odds with one another. This third party hears their cases against one another and decides where the right is and what to do about it (he functions as both judge and jury). So Sarai said to Abram: "My wrong [outrage done me] be upon thee [in your lap]: I have given my maid into thy bosom; and when she saw that she had conceived, I was despised in her eyes: the Lord judge between me and thee" (Gen. 16:5—the first occurrence of the word). Sarai had given Hagar to Abram in her stead. This act was in keeping with ancient Nuzi law, which Abram apparently knew and followed. The legal rights to the child would be Sarai's. This would mean that Hagar "did all the work" and received none of the privileges. Consequently she made things miserable for Sarai. As the tribal and family head Abram was responsible for keeping things in order. This he did not do. Thus Sarai declares that she is innocent of wrongdoing; she has done nothing to earn Hagar's mistreatment, and Abram is at fault in not getting the household in order. Her appeal is: since Abram has not done his duty (normally he would be the judge of tribal matters), "the Lord decide" between us, that is, in a judicial sense, as to who is in the right. Abram granted the legitimacy of her case and handed Hagar over to her to be brought into line (Gen. 16:6).

Shāphat also speaks of the accomplishing of a sentence. Both this concept and those of hearing the case and rendering a decision are seen in Gen. 18:25, where Abraham speaks of "the Judge [literally, "One who judges"] of all the earth." In 1 Sam. 3:13 the emphasis is solely on "delivering" the sentence: "For I have told him that I will judge his house for ever for the iniquity which he knoweth. . . ."

In some cases "judging" really means delivering from injustice or oppression. David says to Saul: "The Lord therefore be judge and judge between me and thee, and see, and plead my cause, and deliver me out of thine hand" (1 Sam. 24:15). This sense (in addition to the judicial sense), "to deliver," is to be understood when one speaks of the judges of Israel (Judg. 2:16): "Nevertheless the Lord raised up judges, which delivered them out of the hand of those that [plundered] them."

Shāphat can be used not only of an act of deliverance, but of a process whereby order and law are maintained within a group. This idea also is included in the concept of the judges of Israel: "And Deborah, a prophetess, the wife of Lapidoth, she judged Israel at that time" (Judg. 4:4). This activity was judicial and constituted a kind of ruling over Israel. Certainly ruling is in mind in Num. 25:5: "And Moses said unto the judges of Israel, 'Slay ye every one his men that were joined unto Baal–Peor" (1 Sam. 8:1).

The military deliverer was the head over a volunteer army summoned when danger threatened (militia). In the time of Samuel this procedure proved inadequate for Israel. They wanted a leader who would organize and lead a standing army. They asked Samuel, therefore, for a king such as the other nations had, one who was apt and trained in warfare, and whose successor (son) would be carefully trained, too. There would be more continuity in leadership as a result. Included in this idea of a king who would "judge" them like the other nations was the idea of a ruler; in order to sustain a permanent army and its training, the people had to be organized for taxation and conscription. This is what is in view in 1 Sam. 8:6–18 as Samuel explains.

B. Nouns.

mishəpāt (מִשְׁפָּט), "judgment; rights." This noun, which appears around 420 times, also appears in Ugaritic.

This word has two main senses; the first deals with the act of sitting as a judge, hearing a case, and rendering a proper verdict. Eccl. 12:14 is one such occurrence: "For God shall bring every work into judgment, with every secret thing, whether it be good, or whether it be evil."

Mishəpāt can also refer to the "rights" belonging to someone (Exod. 23:6). This second sense carries several nuances: the sphere in which things are in proper relationship to one's claims (Gen. 18:19—the first occurrence); a judicial verdict (Deut. 17:9); the statement of the case for the accused (Num. 27:5); and an established ordinance (Exod. 21:1).

The noun *shəphātîm* refers to "acts of judgment." One of the 16 occurrences is in Num. 33:4: "For the Egyptians buried all their firstborn, which the Lord had smitten among them: upon their gods also the Lord executed judgments."

K

TO KEEP, OVERSEE

A. Verb.

nātsach (נָצַח), "to keep, oversee, have charge over." The word appears as "to set forward" in the sense of "to oversee or to lead" in 1 Chron. 23:4, 2 Chron. 34:12, Ezra 3:8, and Ezra 3:9: "Then stood Jeshua with his sons and his brethren, Kadmiel and his sons, the sons of Judah, together, to set forward the workmen in the house of God. . . ." The word appears as "to oversee" in 2 Chron. 2:2: "And Solomon told out threescore and ten thousand men to bear burdens . . . and three thousand and six hundred to oversee them."

B. Participle.

nātsach (נָצַח), "overseer; director." Used throughout the history of the Hebrew language, this root is used in the noun sense in modern Hebrew to mean "eternity, perpetuity." While this word is used approximately 65 times in the Hebrew Old Testament, almost all of them (except for 5 or 6) are participles, used as verbal-nouns. The participial form has the meaning of "overseer, director," reflecting the idea that one who is pre-eminent or conspicuous is an "overseer." Thus, *nātsach* is found in the Book of Psalms a total of 55 times in the titles of various psalms (Ps. 5, 6, 9, et al.) with the meaning, "To the choirmaster" (JB, RSV). Other versions render it "choir director" (NASB); "chief musician" (KJV); and "leader" (NAB). The significance of this title is not clear. Of the 55 psalms involved, 39 are connected with the name of David, 9 with Korah, and 5 with Asaph, leaving only two anonymous psalms. The Hebrew preposition meaning "to" or 'for" which is used with this participle could mean assignment to the person named, or perhaps more reasonably, an indication of a collection of psalms known by the person's name. This title is found also at the end of Hab. 3, showing that this psalm was part of a director's collection.

The word refers to "overseers" in 2 Chron. 2:18: ". . . and three thousand and six hundred overseers to set the people a work."

C. Adjective.

Nātsach is used only in Jer. 8:5 in the sense of "enduring": "Why then is this people of Jerusalem slidden back by a perpetual backsliding?"

TO KEEP, WATCH, GUARD

A. Verb.

nātsar (נָצַר), "to watch; to guard; to keep." Common to both ancient and modern Hebrew, this verb is found also in ancient Ugaritic. It occurs some 60 times in the Hebrew Old Testament. *Nātsar* is found for the first time in the biblical text in Exod. 34:7, where it has the sense of "keeping with faithfulness." This meaning is usually found when man is the subject: "keeping" the covenant (Deut. 33:9); "keeping" the law (Ps. 105:45 and 10 times in Ps. 119); "keeping" the rules of parents (Prov. 6:20).

Nātsar is frequently used to express the idea of "guarding" something, such as a vineyard (Isa. 27:3) or a fortification (Nah. 2:1). "To watch" one's speech is a frequent concern, so advice is given "to watch" one's mouth (Prov. 13:3), the tongue (Ps. 34:13), and the lips (Ps. 141:3). Many references are made to God as the one who "preserves" His people from dangers of all kinds (Deut. 32:10; Ps. 31:23). Generally, *nātsar* is a close synonym to the much more common verb, *shāmar*, "to keep, tend."

Sometimes "to keep" has the meaning of "to besiege," as in Isa. 1:8, ". . . as a besieged city."

shāmar (שָׁמַר), "to keep, tend, watch over, retain." This verb occurs in most Semitic languages (biblical Aramaic attests only a noun formed from this verb). Biblical Hebrew attests it about 470 times and in every period.

Shāmar means "to keep" in the sense of "tending" and taking care of. So God put Adam "into the garden of Eden to dress it and to keep it" (Gen. 2:15—the first occurrence). In 2 Kings 22:14 Harhas is called "keeper of the wardrobe" (the priest's garments). Satan was directed "to keep," or "to tend" (so as not to allow it to be destroyed) Job's life: "Behold, he is in thine hand; but save his life" (Job. 2:6). In this same sense God is described as the keeper of Israel (Ps. 121:4).

The word also means "to keep" in the sense of "watching over" or giving attention to. David, ironically chiding Abner for not protecting Saul, says: "Art not thou a valiant man? and who is like to thee in Israel? wherefore then hast thou not kept thy lord the king?" (1 Sam. 26:15). In extended application this emphasis comes to mean "to watch, observe": "And it came to pass, as she continued praying before the Lord, that Eli [was watching] her mouth" (1 Sam. 1:12). Another extended use of the verb related to this emphasis appears in covenantal contexts. In such cases "keep" means "to watch over" in the sense of seeing that one observes the covenant, keeping one to a covenant. God says of Abraham: "For I know him, that he will command his children and his household after him, and they shall keep the way of the Lord, to do justice and judgment . . ." (Gen. 18:19). As God had said earlier, "Thou shalt keep my covenant therefore, thou, and thy seed after thee in their generations" (Gen. 17:9). When used in close connection with another verb, *shāmar* can signify carefully or watchfully doing that action: "And he answered and said, Must I not take heed to speak that which the Lord hath put in my mouth?" (Num. 23:12). Not only does *shāmar* signify watching, but it signifies doing it *as a watchman* in the sense of fulfilling a responsibility: "And the spies saw a man come forth out of the city . . ." (Judg. 1:24).

In a third group of passages this verb means "to keep" in the sense of saving or "retaining." When Jacob told his family about his dream, "his brethren envied him; but his father observed the saying" (Gen. 37:11); he "retained" it mentally. Joseph tells Pharaoh to appoint overseers to gather food: "And let them . . . lay up corn under the hand of Pharaoh, and let them keep food in the cities" (Gen. 41:35); let them not give it out but see that it is "retained" in storage.

In three passages *shāmar* seems to have the same meaning as the Akkadian root, "to revere." So the psalmist says: "I have hated them that regard [revere] lying vanities: but I trust in the Lord" (Ps. 31:6).

B. Nouns.

mishəmār (מִשְׁמָר), "guard; guardpost." In the first of its 22 occurrences *mishəmār* means "guard": "And he put them in ward [*mishəmār*] in the house of the captain of the guard, into the prison . . ." (Gen. 40:3). The word implies "guardpost" in Neh. 7:3. The word also refers to men on "guard" (Neh. 4:23) and to groups of attendants (Neh. 12:24).

mishəmereth (מִשְׁמֶרֶת), "those who guard; obligation." This noun appears 78 times. The word refers to "those who guard" in 2 Kings 11:5: ". . . A third part of you that enter in on the sabbath shall even be keepers of the watch of the king's house." In Gen. 26:5 the word refers to an "obligation": "Because that Abraham obeyed my voice, and kept my charge [*mishəmereth*], my commandments, my statutes, and my laws."

Some other nouns are related to the verb *shāmar*. *Shəmarîm* refers to "dregs of wine, lees." One of the 4 appearances of this word is in Isa. 25:6: ". . . shall the Lord of hosts make unto all people a feast of fat things, a feast of wines on the lees, of fat things full of marrow, of wines on the lees well refined." The noun *shāmərāh* means "guard, watch." The single appearance of this word is in Ps. 141:3. *Shimmurîm* means a "night vigil." In Exod. 12:42 this word carries the meaning of "night vigil" in the sense of "night of watching": "It is a night to be much observed unto the Lord for bringing them out from the land of Egypt: this is that night of the Lord to be observed of all the children of Israel in their generations." This noun occurs twice in this entry and in no other verse. *'Ashəmûrāh* (or *'ashəmōret*) refers to "watch." This noun occurs 7 times and in Exod. 14:24 refers to "morning watch": ". . . that in the morning watch the Lord looked unto the host of the Egyptians. . . ."

TO KILL

shāchat (שָׁחַט), "to slaughter, kill." This word is common to both ancient and modern Hebrew, as well as ancient Ugaritic. The idea that the ancient Akkadian term *shachatsu* ("to flay") may be related appears to have some support in the special use of *shāchat* in 1 Kings 10:16-17: "beaten gold" (see also 2 Chron. 9:15-16). *Shāchat* occurs in the Hebrew Bible approximately 80 times. It first appears in Gen. 22:10: "And Abraham . . . took the knife to slay his son." Expressing "slaying" for sacrifice is the most frequent use of *shāchat* (51 times); and as might be expected, the word is found some 30 times in the Book of Leviticus alone.

Shāchat sometimes implies the "slaughtering" of animals for food (1 Sam. 14:32, 34; Isa. 22:13). The word is used of the "killing" of people a number of times (Judg. 12:6; 1 Kings 18:40; 2 Kings 10:7, 14). Sometimes God is said "to slay'' people (Num. 14:16). Backslidden Judah went so far as "to slaughter" children as sacrifices to false gods (Ezek. 16:21; 23:39; Isa. 57:5).

hārag (הָרַג), "to kill, slay, destroy." This term is commonly used in modern Hebrew in its verb and noun forms to express the idea of "killing, slaughter." The fact that it is found in the Old Testament some 170 times reflects how commonly this verb was used to indicate the taking of life, whether animal or human. *Hārag* is found for the first time in the Old Testament in the Cain and Abel story (Gen. 4:8; also vv. 14–15).

Rarely suggesting premeditated killing or murder, this term generally is used for the "killing" of animals, including sacrificially, and for ruthless personal violence of man against man. *Hārag* is not the term used in the sixth commandment (Exod. 20:13; Deut. 5:17). The word there is *rātsach,* and since it implies premeditated killing, the commandment is better translated: "Do not murder," as most modern versions have it.

The word *hārag* often means wholesale slaughter, both in battle and after battle (Num. 31:7-8; Josh. 8:24; 2 Sam. 10:18). The word is only infrequently used of men's killing at the command of God. In such instances, the causative form of the common Hebrew verb for "to die" is commonly found. In general, *hārag* refers to violent "killing" and destruction, sometimes even referring to the "killing" of vines by hail (Ps. 78:47).

rātsach (רָצַח), "to kill, murder, slay." This verb occurs more than 40 times in the Old Testament, and its concentration is in the Pentateuch. *Rātsach* is rare in rabbinic Hebrew, and its usage has been increased in modern Hebrew with the exclusive meaning of "to murder." Apart from Hebrew, the verb appears in Arabic with the meaning of "to bruise, to crush."

Rātsach occurs primarily in the legal material of the Old Testament. This is not a surprise, as God's law included regulations on life and provisions for dealing with the murderer. The Decalogue gives the general principle in a simple statement, which contains the first occurrence of the verb: "Thou shalt not kill [murder]" (Exod. 20:13). Another provision pertains to the penalty: "Whoso killeth any person, the murderer shall be put to death by the mouth of witnesses . . ." (Num. 35:30). However, before a person is put to death, he is assured of a trial.

The Old Testament recognizes the distinction between premeditated murder and unintentional killing. In order to assure the rights of the manslayer, who unintentionally killed someone, the law provided for three cities of refuge (Num. 35; Deut. 19; Josh. 20; 21) on either side of the Jordan, to which a manslayer might flee and seek asylum: ". . . that the slayer may flee thither, which killeth any person at unawares" (Num. 35:11). The provision gave the manslayer access to the court system, for he might be "killed" by the blood avenger if he stayed within his own community (Num. 35:21). He is to be tried (Num. 35:12), and if he is found to be guilty of unintentional manslaughter, he is required to stay in the city of refuge until the death of the high priest (Num. 35:28). The severity of the act of murder is stressed in the requirement of exile even in the case of unintentional murder. The man guilty of manslaughter is to be turned over to the avenger of blood, who keeps the right of killing the manslayer if the manslayer goes outside the territory of the city of refuge before the death of the high priest. On the other hand, if the manslayer is chargeable with premeditated murder (examples of which are given in Num. 35:16-21), the blood avenger may execute the murderer without a trial. In this way the Old Testament underscores the principles of the sanctity of life and of retribution; only in the cities of refuge is the principle of retribution suspended.

The prophets use *rātsach* to describe the effect of injustice and lawlessness in Israel: ". . . because there is no truth, nor mercy, nor knowledge of God in the land. By swearing, and lying, and killing, and stealing, and committing adultery . . ." (Hos. 4:1-2; cf. Isa. 1:21; Jer. 7:9). The psalmist, too, metaphorically expresses the deprivation of the rights of helpless murder victims: "They slay the widow and the stranger, and murder the fatherless" (Ps. 94:6).

The Septuagint gives the following translation: *phoneuein* ("murder; kill; put to death"). The KJV gives these senses: "kill; murder; be put to death; be slain."

KINGDOM

maləkûth (מַלְכוּת), "kingdom; reign; rule." The word *maləkûth* occurs 91 times in the Hebrew Old Testament and apparently belongs to late biblical Hebrew. The first occurrence is in Num. 24:7: "He shall pour the water out of his buckets, and his seed shall be in many waters, and his king shall be higher than Agag, and his kingdom shall be exalted."

The word *maləkûth* denotes: (1) the territory of the kingdom: "When he showed the riches of his glorious kingdom and the honor of his excellent majesty many days, even a hundred and fourscore days" (Esth. 1:4); (2) the accession to the throne: "For if thou altogether holdest thy peace at this time, then shall there enlargement and deliverance arise to the Jews from another place; but thou and thy father's house shall be destroyed: and who knoweth whether thou art come to the kingdom for such a time as this?" (Esth. 4:14); (3) the year of rule: "So Esther was taken unto king Ahasuerus into his house royal in the tenth month, which is the month Tebeth, in the seventh year of his reign" (Esth. 2:16); and (4) anything "royal" or "kingly": throne (Esth. 1:2), wine (Esth. 1:7), crown (Esth. 1:11), word (Esth. 1:19), garment (Esth. 6:8), palace (Esth. 1:9), scepter (Ps. 45:6), and glory (Ps. 145:11-12).

The Septuagint translations of *maləkûth* are: *basileia* ("kingship; kingdom; royal power") and *basileus* ("king").

maməlākāh (מַמְלָכָה), "kingdom; sovereignty; dominion; reign." The word appears about 115 times throughout the Old Testament. *Maməlākāh* occurs first in Gen. 10:10: "And the beginning of his kingdom was Babel, and Erech, and Accad, and Calneh, in the land of Shinar" in the sense of the "realm" of the kingdom.

The basic meaning of *maməlākāh* is the area and people that constitute a "kingdom." The word refers to non-Israelite nations who are ruled by a *melek*, "king": "And it shall come to pass after the end of seventy years, that the Lord will visit Tyre, and she shall turn to her hire, and shall commit fornication with all the kingdoms of the world upon the face of the earth'' (Isa. 23:17). *Maməlākāh* is a synonym for *'am,* ''people,'' and *gôy,* ''nation'': ''. . . they went from one nation to another, from one kingdom to another people'' (Ps. 105:13). *Maməlākāh* also denotes Israel as God's ''kingdom'': ''And ye shall be unto me a kingdom of priests, and a holy nation'' (Exod. 19:6). The Davidic king was the theocratic agent by whom God ruled over and blessed His people: ''And thine house and thy kingdom shall be established for ever before thee: thy throne shall be established for ever'' (2 Sam. 7:16). Nevertheless, the one *maməlākāh* after Solomon was divided into two kingdoms which Ezekiel predicted would be reunited: ''And I will make them one nation in the land upon the mountains of Israel; and one king shall be king to them all: and they shall be no more two nations, neither shall they be divided into two kingdoms . . .'' (Ezek. 37:22).

Close to the basic meaning is the usage of *maməlākāh* to denote ''king,'' as the king was considered to be the embodiment of the ''kingdom.'' He was viewed as a symbol of the kingdom proper: ''Thus saith the Lord God of Israel, I brought up Israel out of Egypt, and delivered you out of the hand of the Egyptians, and out of the hand of all kingdoms, and of them that oppressed you'' (1 Sam. 10:18; in Hebrew the noun ''kingdoms'' is feminine and the verb ''oppress'' has a masculine form, signifying that we must understand ''kingdoms'' as ''kings'').

The function and place of the king is important in the development of the concept ''kingdom.'' ''Kingdom'' may signify the head of the kingdom. The word further has the meaning of the royal ''rule,'' the royal ''sovereignty,'' and the ''dominion.'' The royal ''sovereignty'' was taken from Saul because of his disobedience (1 Sam. 28:17). ''Royal sovereignty'' is also the sense in Jer. 27:1: ''In the beginning of the reign of Jehoiakim. . . .'' The Old Testament further defines as expressions of the royal ''rule'' all things associated with the king: (1) the throne: ''And it shall be, when he sitteth upon the throne of his kingdom, that he shall write him a copy of this law in a book out of that which is before the priests the Levites'' (Deut. 17:18); (2) the pagan sanctuary supported by the throne: ''But prophesy not again any more at Beth–el: for it is the king's chapel, and it is the king's court'' (Amos 7:13); and (3) a royal city: ''And David said unto Achish, If I have now found grace in thine eyes, let them give me a place in some town in the country, that I may dwell there: for why should thy servant dwell in the royal city with thee?'' (1 Sam. 27:5).

All human rule is under God's control. Consequently the Old Testament fully recognizes the kingship of God. The Lord ruled as king over His people Israel (1 Chron. 29:11). He graciously ruled over His people through David and his followers until the Exile (2 Chron. 13:5).

In the New Testament usage all the above meanings are to be associated with the Greek word *basileia* (''kingdom''). This is the major translation of *maməlākāh* in the Septuagint, and as such it is small wonder that the New Testament authors used this word to refer to God's ''kingdom'': the realm, the king, the sovereignty, and the relationship to God Himself.

melek (מֶ֫לֶךְ), ''king.'' This word occurs about 2,513 times in the Old

Testament. It is found several times in Gen. 14:1: "And it came to pass in the days of Amraphel king of Shinar, Arioch king of Ellasar, Chedorlaomer king of Elam, and Tidal king of nations."

TO KNOW

A. Verb.

nākar (נָכַר), "to know, regard, recognize, pay attention to, be acquainted with." This verb, which is found in both ancient and modern Hebrew, occurs approximately 50 times in the Hebrew Old Testament. The first time is in Gen. 27:23: ". . . he did not recognize him" (RSV).

The basic meaning of the term is a physical apprehension, whether through sight, touch, or hearing. Darkness sometimes makes recognition impossible (Ruth 3:14). People are often "recognized" by their voices (Judg. 18:3). *Nākar* sometimes has the meaning "pay attention to," a special kind of recognition: "Blessed be the man who took notice of [KJV, "took knowledge of"] you" (Ruth 2:19 RSV).

This verb can mean "to be acquainted with," a kind of intellectual awareness: ". . . neither shall his place know him any more" (Job 7:10; cf. Ps. 103:16).

The sense of "to distinguish" is seen in Ezra 3:13: ". . . The people could not discern the noise of the shout of joy from the noise of the weeping of the people. . . ."

yāda' (יָדַע), "to know." This verb occurs in Ugaritic, Akkadian, Phoenician, Arabic (infrequently), biblical Aramaic, and in Hebrew in all periods. This verb occurs about 1,040 times (995 in Hebrew and 47 in Aramaic) in the Bible.

Essentially *yāda'* means: (1) to know by observing and reflecting (thinking), and (2) to know by experiencing. The first sense appears in Gen. 8:11, where Noah "knew" the waters had abated as a result of seeing the freshly picked olive leaf in the dove's mouth; he "knew" it after observing and thinking about what he had seen. He did not actually see or experience the abatement himself.

In contrast to this knowing through reflection is the knowing which comes through experience with the senses, by investigation and proving, by reflection and consideration (firsthand knowing). Consequently *yāda'* is used in synonymous parallelism with "hear" (Exod. 3:7), "see" (Gen. 18:21), and "perceive, see" (Job. 28:7). Joseph told his brothers that were they to leave one of their number with him in Egypt then he would "know," by experience, that they were honest men (Gen. 42:33). In the Garden of Eden, Adam and Eve were forbidden to eat of the tree whose fruit if eaten would give them the experience of evil and, therefore, the knowledge of both good and evil. Somewhat characteristically the heart plays an important role in knowing. Because they experienced the sustaining presence of God during the wilderness wandering, the Israelites "knew" in their hearts that God was disciplining or caring for them as a father cares for a son (Deut. 8:5). Such knowing can be hindered by a wrongly disposed heart (Ps. 95:10).

Thirdly, this verb can represent that kind of knowing which one learns and can give back. So Cain said that he did not "know" he was Abel's keeper (Gen. 4:9), and Abram told Sarai that he "knew" she was a beautiful woman (Gen. 12:11). One can also "know" by being told—in Lev. 5:1 a witness either sees or otherwise "knows" (by being told) pertinent information. In this sense "know" is paralleled by "acknowledge" (Deut. 33:9) and "learn" (Deut. 31:12-13). Thus, little children not yet able to speak do not "know" good and evil (Deut. 1:39); they have not learned it so as to tell another what it is. In other words, their knowledge is not such that they can distinguish between good and evil.

In addition to the essentially cognitive knowing already presented, this verb has a purely experiential side. The "knower" has actual involvement with or in the object of the knowing. So Potiphar was unconcerned about (literally, "did not know about") what was in his house (Gen. 39:6)—he had no actual contact with it. In Gen. 4:1 Adam's knowing Eve also refers to direct contact with her—in a sexual relationship. In Gen. 18:19 God says He "knows" Abraham; He cared for him in the sense that He chose him from among other men and saw to it that certain things happened to him. The emphasis is on the fact that God "knew" him intimately and personally. In fact, it is parallel in concept to "sanctified" (cf. Jer. 1:5). A similar use of this word relates to God's relationship to Israel as a chosen or elect nation (Amos 3:2).

Yāda' in the intensive and causative stems is used to express a particular concept of revelation. God did not make Himself known by His name Jehovah to Abraham, Isaac, and Jacob. He did reveal that name to them, that He was the God of the covenant. Nevertheless, the covenant was not fulfilled (they did not possess the Promised Land) until the time of Moses. The statement in Exod. 6:3 implies that now God was going to make Himself known "by His name"; He was going to lead them to possess the land. God makes Himself known through revelatory acts such as bringing judgment on the wicked (Ps. 9:16) and deliverance to His people (Isa. 66:14). He also reveals Himself through the spoken word—for example, by the commands given through Moses (Ezek. 20:11), by promises like those given to David (2 Sam. 7:21). Thus, God reveals Himself in law and promise.

"To know" God is to have an intimate experiential knowledge of Him. So Pharaoh denies that he knows Jehovah (Exod. 5:2) or that he recognizes His authority over him. Positively "to know" God is paralleled to fear Him (1 Kings 8:43), to serve (1 Chron. 28:9), and to trust (Isa. 43:10).

B. Noun.

da'ath (דַּעַת), "knowledge." Several nouns are formed from *yāda'*, and the most frequently occurring is *da'ath*, which appears 90 times in the Old Testament. One appearance is in Gen. 2:9: ". . . and the tree of knowledge of good and evil." The word also appears in Exod. 31:3.

C. Particle.

maddû'a (מַדּוּעַ), "why." This word, which occurs 72 times, is related to the verb *yāda'*. The word is found in Exod. 1:18: ". . . Why have ye done this thing, and have saved the men children alive?"

L

LABOR

A. Noun.

'āmāl (עָמָל), "labor; toil; anguish; troublesome work; trouble; misery." Cognates of this noun and the verb from which it is derived occur in Aramaic, Arabic, and Akkadian. The 55 occurrences of the noun are mostly in later poetic and prophetic literature (Gen. 41:51; Deut. 26:7; Judg. 10:16).

First, the word means "labor" in the sense of toil: ". . . The Lord heard our voice, and looked on our affliction, and our labor, and our oppression" (Deut. 26:7). In Isa. 53:11 *'āmāl* is used of the toilsome "labor" of the Messiah's soul: "He shall see of the travail of his soul. . . ."

Second, something gained by toil or labor is *'āmāl:* "[He] gave them the lands of the heathen: and they inherited the labor of the people [i.e., of the land of Palestine]" (Ps. 105:44).

Third, *'āmāl* means "troublesome work"; the emphasis is on the difficulty involved in a task or work as troublesome and burdensome: "What profit hath a man of all his labor [troublesome labor] which he taketh under the sun?" (Eccl. 1:3). All 17 appearances of the word in Ecclesiastes bear this meaning.

Fourth, sometimes the emphasis shifts to the area of trouble so that an enterprise or situation is exclusively troublesome or unfortunate: ". . . For God, said he, hath made me forget all my toil, and all my father's house" (Gen. 41:51—the first occurrence). In Judg. 10:16 we read that God "was grieved for the misery of Israel."

Fifth, *'āmāl* can have an ethical connotation and is used as a word for sin. The wicked man "travaileth with iniquity, and hath conceived mischief, and brought forth falsehood" (Ps. 7:14; cf. Job 4:8).

Another noun *'āmēl* means "laborer, sufferer." This word appears infrequently in biblical Hebrew. In Prov. 16:26 the word refers to "laborer": "He that laboreth, laboreth for himself; for his mouth craveth it of him." In Job 3:20 *'āmēl* refers to a "sufferer": "Wherefore is light given to him that is in misery. . . ."

B. Verbs.

'āmal (עָמַל), "to labor." This verb occurs 11 times in biblical Hebrew and only in poetry. *'Āmal* appears several times in Ecclesiastes (2:11, 19, 21; 5:16). The verb is also found in Ps. 127:1: "Except the Lord build the house, they labor in vain that build it. . . ."

'Āmel means "toiling." This verb occurs only in a few instances in Ecclesiastes. One occurrence is in Eccl. 3:9: "What profit hath he that worketh in that wherein he laboreth?"

LAMB (MALE)

kebes (כֶּבֶשׂ), "lamb (male); kid." The Akkadian cognate of this noun means "lamb," whereas the Arabic cognate signifies "a young ram." The word occurs 107 times in the Hebrew Old Testament, and especially in the Pentateuch.

The *kebes* is a "young lamb" which is nearly always used for sacrificial purposes. The first usage in Exodus pertains to the Passover: "Your lamb shall be without blemish, a male of the first year: ye shall take it out from the sheep, or from the goats" (12:5). The word *gədî*, "kid," is a synonym for *kebes:* "The wolf also shall dwell with the lamb [*kebes*], and the leopard shall lie down with the kid [*gədî*]; and the calf and the young lion and the fatling together; and a little child shall lead them" (Isa. 11:6). The traditional translation "lamb" leaves the gender uncertain. In Hebrew the word *kebes* is masculine, whereas the *kibəsah*, "young ewe lamb," is feminine; cf. "And Abraham set seven ewe lambs of the flock by themselves" (Gen. 21:28).

The Septuagint gives the following translations: *amnos* ("lamb"); *probaton* ("sheep"); and *arnos* ("lamb"). The KJV gives these senses: "lamb; sheep."

LAND

'adāmāh (אֲדָמָה), "ground; land; earth." This noun also occurs in Arabic. Hebrew occurrences number about 224 and cover every period of biblical Hebrew.

Initially this noun represents arable "ground" (probably red in color). As such it supports water and plants: "But there went up a mist from the earth, and watered the whole face of the ground" (Gen. 2:6). This meaning is in Gen. 1:25, where it first appears: ". . . every thing that creepeth upon the earth. . . ." The word is contrasted to unproductive soil, or "waste land," and the generic word for the surface of the planet "earth," which may represent either or both of the preceding words. The body of the first man, Adam, was formed exclusively from the *'adāmāh* (cf. Gen. 2:9): "And the Lord God formed man ['*ādām*] of the dust of the ground ['*adāmāh*] . . ." (Gen. 2:7).

'Adāmāh may be used specifically to describe what has been and will be cultivated by a given group of people, or what they possess to this end: "Look down from thy holy habitation, from heaven, and bless thy people Israel, and the land which thou hast given us, as thou swarest unto our fathers, a land that floweth with milk and honey "(Deut. 26:15). A further variation of this nuance refers to the actual soil itself: "Shall there not then, I pray thee, be given to thy servant two mules' burden of earth [with which to build an altar to the true God]?" (2 Kings 5:17).

In Exod. 3:5 *'adāmāh* is used more in the sense "ground," what is below one's feet irrespective of its cultivable properties: ". . . Put off thy shoes from off thy feet, for the place whereon thou standest is holy *ground*."

The nuance "property" or "possession" comes more clearly to the fore in passages such as Zech. 2:12: "And the Lord shall inherit Judah his portion in the holy land . . ." (cf. Ps. 49:11). Although '*adāmāh* is never used politically, its use as "landed property" or "home country" sometimes approaches that sense (cf. Isa. 14:2; 19:17; and especially Ezek. 7:2). Isa. 15:9, ". . . For I will bring more upon Dimon, lions upon him that escapeth of Moab, and upon the remnant of the land," further illustrates this usage.

Throughout the Old Testament there is a relationship between '*ādām*, "man," and the '*adāmāh*. The two words have an etymological affinity inasmuch as they both appear to be derived from the verb '*ādōm*, "to be red." If Adam were to remain obedient to God, the "ground" would give forth its fruit. Hence, the "ground" was God's possession and under His command (Gen. 2:6). He made it respond to His servant. The entry of sin disrupted the harmony between man and the "ground," and the "ground" no longer responded to man's care. His life moved in and toward death rather than upward and toward life. Increased human rebellion caused decreased fruitfulness of the "ground" (Gen. 4:12, 14; cf. 8:21). In Abraham the promised redemption (Gen. 3:15) took the form of the restoration of a proper relation between God and man and between man and the "ground" (Gen. 28:14-15). Under Moses the fruitfulness of the "ground" depended on the obedience of God's people (cf. Deut. 11:17).

'*erets* (אֶרֶץ), "land (the whole earth); dry land; ground; land (political); underworld." This word has cognates in Ugaritic, Phoenician-Punic, Moabite, Akkadian, Aramaic (here the radicals are '*rq* or '*r*'), and Arabic ('*rd*). '*Erets* occurs in biblical Hebrew about 2,504 times (22 times in biblical Aramaic) and in all periods.

The word often represents the whole surface of this planet and, together with the word "heavens," describes the entire physical creation and everything in it. This meaning is in its first biblical occurrence: "In the beginning God created the heaven and the earth" (Gen. 1:1).

'*Erets* sometimes means "land" as contrasted to sea or water. This use, for example, is in Exod. 20:11: "For in six days the Lord made heaven and earth, the sea, and all that in them is, and rested the seventh day. . . ." This more narrow meaning first appears in Gen. 1:10, where God called the dry ground "land." Here "land" includes desert and arable land, valleys and mountains—everything that we know today as continents and islands.

'*Erets* refers to the physical "ground" under the feet of men and animals. Upon the "ground" creep all creeping things: "Let us make man in our image, after our likeness: and let them have dominion . . . over every creeping thing that creepeth upon the earth" (Gen. 1:26). Dust lies upon the '*erets* (Exod. 8:16), and rain and dew fall on it (Gen. 2:5).

'*Erets* may be used geographically, i.e., to identify a territory: "And Haran died before his father Terah in the land of his nativity" (Gen. 11:28).

'*Erets* sometimes bears a political connotation and represents both a given political territory and the people who live there: "And there was no bread in all the land; for the famine was very sore, so that the land of Egypt and all the land of Canaan fainted by reason of the famine" (Gen. 47:13). Not only the "land" languished, but (and especially) the people suffered.

Next, in several passages this noun has both geographical and political overtones and identifies the possession or inheritance of a tribe. This emphasis is in Num. 32:1: "Now the children of Reuben and the children of Gad had a very great multitude of cattle: and when they saw the land of Jazer, and the land of Gilead, that, behold, the place was a place for cattle. . . ."

In a seldom used, but interesting, nuance 'erets represents the "underworld": "But those that seek my soul, to destroy it, shall go into the lower parts of the earth" (Ps. 63:9). Sometimes even used by itself (absolutely) this noun represents the "underworld": "I went down to the bottoms of the mountains; the earth with her bars was about me for ever . . ." (Jonah 2:6). The Akkadian cognates sometimes bear this same meaning. Other Old Testament passages where some scholars find this meaning are Exod. 15:12; Ps. 71:20; and Jer. 17:13.

LAST

A. Adjective.

'acharôn (אַחֲרוֹן), "at the back; western; later; last; future." This word occurs about 51 times in biblical Hebrew.

'Acharôn has a local-spatial meaning. Basically, it means "at the back": "And he put the handmaids and their children foremost, and Leah and her children after, and Rachel and Joseph hindermost" (Gen. 33:2—the first biblical appearance). When applied elsewhere, the word means "western": "Every place whereon the soles of your feet shall tread shall be yours: from the wilderness and Lebanon, from the river, the river Euphrates, even unto the uttermost [western] sea shall your coast be" (Deut. 11:24).

Used temporally, *'acharôn* has several nuances. First, it means "last" as contrasted to the first of two things: "And it shall come to pass, if they will not believe thee, neither hearken to the voice of the first sign, that they will believe the voice of the latter sign" (Exod. 4:8). Second, it can represent the "last" in a series of things or people: "Ye are my brethren, ye are my bones and my flesh: wherefore then are ye the last to bring back the king?" (2 Sam. 19:12). The word also connotes "later on" and/or "afterwards": "But thou shalt surely kill him; thine hand shall be first upon him to put him to death, and afterwards the hand of all the people" (Deut. 13:9). Next the emphasis can be on the finality or concluding characteristic of a given thing: "Now these be the last words of David" (2 Sam. 23:1).

'Acharôn connotes "future," or something that is yet to come: ". . . So that the generation to come of your children that shall rise up after you, and the stranger that shall come from a far land, shall say, when they see the plagues of that land . . ." (Deut. 29:22).

The combination of "first" and "last" is an idiom of completeness: "Now the rest of the acts of Solomon, first and last, are they not written in the book of Nathan the prophet, and in the prophecy of Ahijah the Shilonite, and in the visions of Iddo the seer against Jeroboam the son of Nebat?'' (2 Chron. 9:29). Likewise the phrase expresses the sufficiency of the Lord, since He is said to include within Himself the ''first'' as well as the ''last'': ''Thus saith the Lord the King of Israel, and his Redeemer the Lord of hosts; I am the first, and I am the last; and beside me there is no God'' (Isa. 44:6; cf. 48:12). These verses affirm that there is no other God, because all exists in Him.

B. Verb.

'āchar (אָחַר), ''to tarry, remain behind, delay.'' Other words derived from this verb are: ''other,'' ''after (wards),'' ''backwards.'' *'Āchar* appears in Exod. 22:29 with the meaning ''delay'': ''Thou shalt not delay to offer the first of thy ripe fruits, and of thy liquors: the first-born of thy sons shalt thou give unto me.''

LAW

A. Noun.

tôrāh (תּוֹרָה), ''law; direction; instruction.'' This noun occurs 220 times in the Hebrew Old Testament.

In the wisdom literature, where the noun does not appear with a definite article, *tôrāh* signifies primarily ''direction, teaching, instruction'': ''The law of the wise is a fountain of life, to depart from the snares of death'' (Prov. 13:14), and ''Receive, I pray thee, the law from his mouth, and lay up his words in thine heart'' (Job 22:22). The ''instruction'' of the sages of Israel, who were charged with the education of the young, was intended to cultivate in the young a fear of the Lord so that they might live in accordance with God's expectations. The sage was a father to his pupils: ''Whoso keepeth the law is a wise son: but he that is a companion of riotous men shameth his father'' (Prov. 28:7; cf. 3:1; 4:2; 7:2). The natural father might also instruct his son in wise living, even as a God-fearing woman was an example of kind ''instruction'': ''She openeth her mouth with wisdom; and in her tongue is the law of kindness'' (Prov. 31:26).

The ''instruction'' given by God to Moses and the Israelites became known as ''the law'' or ''the direction'' *(ha-tôrāh),* and quite frequently as ''the Law of the Lord'': ''Blessed are the undefiled in the way, who walk in the law of the Lord'' (Ps. 119:1), or ''the Law of God'': ''Also day by day, from the first day unto the last day, [Ezra] read in the book of the law of God'' (Neh. 8:18), and also as ''the Law of [given through] Moses'': ''Remember ye the law of Moses my servant, which I commanded unto him in Horeb for all Israel . . .'' (Mal. 4:4). The word can refer to the whole of the ''law'': ''For he established a testimony in Jacob, and appointed a law in Israel, which he commanded our fathers, that they should make them known to their children'' (Ps. 78:5), or to particulars: ''And this is the law which Moses set before the children of Israel . . .'' (Deut. 4:44).

God had communicated the "law" that Israel might observe and live: "And what nation is there so great, that hath statutes and judgments so righteous as all this law, which I set before you this day?" (Deut. 4:8). The king was instructed to have a copy of the "law" prepared for him at his coronation (Deut. 17:18). The priests were charged with the study and teaching of, as well as the jurisprudence based upon, the "law" (Jer. 18:18). Because of rampant apostasy the last days of Judah were times when there were no teaching priests (2 Chron. 15:3); in fact, in Josiah's days the "law" (whether the whole Torah, or a book or a part) was recovered: "And Hilkiah . . . said to Shaphan the scribe, I have found the book of the law in the house of the Lord" (2 Chron. 34:15).

The prophets called Israel to repent by returning to the *tôrāh* ("instruction") of God (Isa. 1:10). Jeremiah prophesied concerning God's new dealing with His people in terms of the New Covenant, in which God's law is to be internalized, God's people would willingly obey Him: "But this shall be the covenant that I will make with the house of Israel; After those days, saith the Lord, I will put my law in their inward parts, and write it in their hearts; and will be their God, and they shall be my people" (Jer. 31:33). The last prophet of the Old Testament reminded the priests of their obligations (Mal. 2) and challenged God's people to remember the "law" of Moses in preparation for the coming Messiah (Mal. 4:4).

The Septuagint gives the following translations: *nomos* ("law; rule"); *nomimos* ("comformable to law; lawful"); *entole* ("command[ment]; order"); and *prostagma* ("order; commandment; injunction").

B. Verb.

yārāh (יָרָה), "to throw, cast, direct, teach, instruct." The noun *tôrāh* is derived from this root. The meaning "to cast" appears in Gen. 31:51: "And Laban said to Jacob, Behold this heap, and behold this pillar, which I have cast betwixt me and thee." *Yārāh* means "to teach" in 1 Sam. 12:23: ". . . but I will teach you the good and the right way."

TO BE LEFT, REMAIN

A. Verb.

yāthar (יָתַר), "to be left; remain over; excel; show excess." This word is found in various Semitic languages, ranging from ancient Akkadian to modern Hebrew. In its verb forms, the word is found just over 100 times in the Hebrew Bible. *Yāthar* occurs for the first time in the biblical text in Gen. 30:36, where it is stated that "Jacob fed the rest of Laban's flocks." This statement reflects the word's frequent use to show separation from a primary group. Thus, Jacob "was left alone" (Gen. 32:24) when his family and flocks went on beyond the brook Jabbok.

Sometimes the word indicates survivors, as in 2 Sam. 9:1: "Is there yet any that is left of the house of Saul . . . ?" The remnant idea is reflected in Ezek. 6:8: "Yet will I leave a remnant, that ye may have some that shall escape the sword. . . ."

B. Noun.

yēther (יֶתֶר), "remainder; excess." This noun occurs nearly 100 times. As "remainder, excess," it is used especially in the sense of a lesser number or quality as compared to something of primary importance. So, *yēther* is used to refer to "the rest of the vessels" left in Jerusalem by Nebuchadnezzar (Jer. 27:19-20 RSV), and the men who were left after Joab had assigned his picked men in the battle lines (2 Sam. 10:10). Occasionally *yēther* is used to indicate "excess" in a negative way, so the literal "lip of excess" has the meaning of "false speech" (Prov. 17:7 RSV).

A few times this noun implies "superiority" or "pre-eminence," as in Gen. 49:3, where Jacob describes his son Reuben as being "pre-eminent in pride and pre-eminent in power" (RSV). The name of Jethro, Moses' father-in-law, is derived from this word.

TO LIE

A. Verb.

shākab (שָׁכַב), "to lie down; lie; have sexual intercourse with." This word also occurs in Ugaritic, Akkadian, Ethiopic, post-biblical Aramaic, and post-biblical Hebrew. Biblical Hebrew attests it about 160 times and in all periods.

Basically this verb signifies a person's lying down—though in Job 30:17 and Eccl. 2:23 it refers to something other than a human being. *Shākab* is used of the state of reclining as opposed to sitting: "And every thing that she lieth upon in her [menstruation] shall be unclean: every thing also that she sitteth upon . . ." (Lev. 15:20). This general sense appears in several nuances. First, there is the meaning "to lie down to rest." Elisha "came thither, and he turned into the chamber [which the Shunammite had prepared for his use], and lay there" (2 Kings 4:11). Job remarks that his gnawing pains "take no rest" (Job 30:17; cf. Eccl. 2:23).

Shākab can also be used of lying down on a bed, for example, when one is sick. Jonadab told Amnon: "Lay thee down on thy bed, and make thyself [pretend to be] sick . . ." (2 Sam. 13:5). The word can be used as an equivalent of the phrase "to go to bed": "But before they [Lot's visitors] lay down, the men of the city, even the men of Sodom, compassed the house round . . ." (Gen. 19:4—the first occurrence of the verb). *Shākab* also signifies "lying down asleep." The Lord told Jacob: ". . . The land whereon thou liest, to thee will I give it, and to thy seed" (Gen. 28:13).

In Exod. 22:26-27 the verb denotes the act of sleeping more than the lying down: "If thou at all take thy neighbor's raiment to pledge, thou shalt deliver it unto him by that the sun goeth down . . . [In what else] shall he sleep?"

Shākab can also be used to mean "lodge" and thus refers to sleeping and eating. Israel's spies lodged with Rahab: "And they went, and came into a harlot's house, named Rahab, and lodged there" (Josh. 2:1; cf. 2 Kings 4:11).

This verb can mean "to lie down" in a figurative sense of to be humbled or to be robbed of power. The trees of Lebanon are personified and say concerning the king of Babylon: "Since thou art laid down, no feller [tree cutter] is come up against us" (Isa. 14:8).

Used reflexively, *shākab* means "to humble oneself, to submit oneself": "We lie down in our shame . . ." (Jer. 3:25).

Another special nuance is "to put something on its side": "Who can number the clouds in wisdom? Or who can [tip] the bottles of heaven, when the dust groweth into hardness, and the clods cleave fast together?" (Job 38:37-38).

A second emphasis of *shākab* is "to die," to lie down in death. Jacob instructed his sons as follows: "But I will lie with my fathers, and thou shalt carry me out of Egypt, and bury me in their burying place" (Gen. 47:30). This phrase ("lie down with one's fathers") does not necessarily refer to being buried or to dying an honorable death (cf. 1 Kings 22:40) but is a synonym for a human's dying. (It is never used of animals or inanimate things.) The idea is that when one dies he no longer stands upright. Therefore, to "lie with one's fathers" parallels the concept of "lying down" in death. *Shākab,* as 1 Kings 22:40 suggests, can refer to the state of being dead ("so Ahab slept with his fathers"), since v. 37 already reports that he had died and was buried in Samaria. The verb used by itself may mean "to die," or "to lie dead"; cf. "At her feet he bowed, he fell, he lay [dead]: at her feet he bowed, he fell: where he bowed, there he fell down dead" (Judg. 5:27).

A third major use of *shākab* is "to have sexual relations with." The first occurrence of this use is in Gen. 19:32, where Lot's daughters say: "Come, let us make our father drink wine, and we will lie with him, that we may preserve seed of our father." Even when a physical "lying down" is not necessarily in view, the word is used of having sexual relations: "Whosoever lieth with a beast shall surely be put to death" (Exod. 22:19). The word is also used of homosexual activities (Lev. 18:22).

B. Nouns.

mishəkāb (מִשְׁכָּב), "place to lie; couch; bed; act of lying." This noun appears 46 times in the Old Testament. In Gen. 49:4 *mishəkāb* is used to mean a "place to lie" or "bed": ". . . because thou wentest up to thy father's bed. . . ." The word refers to the "act of lying" in Num. 31:17: ". . . kill every woman that hath known man by lying with him."

Shəkābāh means "layer of dew." In one of its 9 appearances, *shəkābāh* refers to a "layer of dew": ". . . and in the morning the dew lay round about the host" (Exod. 16:13).

Shəkōbeth refers to "copulation." This noun occurs rarely (4 times), as in Lev. 18:20: "Moreover thou shalt not lie carnally with thy neighbor's wife, to defile thyself with her."

TO LIGHT

A. Verb.

'ôr (אוֹר), "to become light; become lighted up (of daybreak); give light; cause light to shine." This verb is found also in Akkadian and Canaanite. The Akkadian word *urru* means "light," but generally "day."

'Ôr means "to become light" in Gen. 44:3: "As soon as the morning was

light, the men were sent away, they and their asses." The word means "to give light" in Num. 8:2: ". . . the seven lamps shall give light over against the candlestick."

B. Nouns.

'ôr (אוֹר), "light." This noun appears about 120 times and is clearly a poetic term.

The first occurrence of 'ôr is in the Creation account: "And God said, Let there be light: and there was light" (Gen. 1:3). Here "light" is the opposite of "darkness." The opposition of "light" and "darkness" is not a unique phenomenon. It occurs frequently as a literary device: "Woe unto them that call evil good, and good evil; that put darkness for light, and light for darkness; that put bitter for sweet, and sweet for bitter!" (Isa. 5:20); and "In that day they shall roar against them like the roaring of the sea: and if one look unto the land, behold darkness and sorrow, and the light is darkened in the heavens thereof" (Isa. 5:30). In Hebrew various antonyms of 'ôr are used in parallel constructions: "The people that walked in darkness have seen a great light: they that dwell in the land of the shadow of death, upon them hath the light shined" (Isa. 9:2).

The basic meaning of 'ôr is "daylight" (cf. Gen. 1:3). In the Hebrew mind the "day" began at the rising of the sun: "And he shall be as the light of the morning, when the sun riseth, even a morning without clouds; as the tender grass springeth out of the earth by clear shining after rain" (2 Sam. 23:4). The "light" given by the heavenly bodies was also known as 'ôr: "Moreover the light of the moon shall be as the light of the sun, and the light of the sun shall be sevenfold, as the light of seven days, in the day that the Lord bindeth up the breach of his people, and healeth the stroke of their wound" (Isa. 30:26).

In the metaphorical use 'ôr signifies life over against death: "For thou hast delivered my soul from death: wilt not thou deliver my feet from falling, that I may walk before God in the light of the living?" (Ps. 56:13). To walk in the "light" of the face of a superior (Prov. 16:15), or of God (Ps. 89:15), is an expression of a joyful, blessed life in which the quality of life is enhanced. The believer is assured of God's "light," even in a period of difficulty; cf. "Rejoice not against me, O mine enemy: when I fall, I shall arise; when I sit in darkness, the Lord shall be a light unto me" (Mic. 7:8; cf. Ps. 23:4).

In the Septuagint 'ôr has many translations, of which phos ("light") is most frequent.

The noun 'ûr means "shine; light-giving." This word occurs infrequently, once in Isa. 50:11: "Behold, all ye that kindle a fire, that compass yourselves about with sparks: walk in the light ['ûr] of your fire, and in the sparks that ye have kindled."

'Ôrāh refers to "light." This noun means "light" in Ps. 139:12: "Yea, the darkness hideth not from thee; but the night shineth as the day: the darkness and the light are both alike to thee."

Ma'ôr also means "light." This noun appears about 20 times. Ma'ôr occurs more than once in Gen. 1:16: "And God made two great lights; the greater light to rule the day, and the lesser light to rule the night: he made the stars also.''

LIKENESS

A. Verb.

dāmāh (דָּמָה), "to be like; resemble; be or act like; liken or compare; devise; balance or ponder.'' This verb appears in biblical Hebrew about 28 times. Cognates of this word appear in biblical Aramaic, Akkadian, and Arabic. *Dāmāh* means "to be like" in Ps. 102:6: "I am like a pelican of the wilderness: I am like an owl of the desert.''

B. Noun.

dəmûth (דְּמוּת), "likeness; shape; figure; form; pattern.'' All but 5 of the 25 appearances of this word are in poetical or prophetical books of the Bible.

First, the word means "pattern," in the sense of the specifications from which an actual item is made: "Now King Ahaz went to Damascus . . . and saw the altar which was at Damascus; and King Ahaz sent to Urijah the priest the pattern of the altar and its model, according to all its workmanship'' (2 Kings 16:10 NASB).

Second, *dəmûth* means "shape" or "form," the thing(s) made after a given pattern. In 2 Chron. 4:3 the word represents the "shape" of a bronze statue: "And under it was the similitude of oxen, which did compass it round about: ten in a cubit, compassing the sea round about.'' In such passages *dəmûth* means more than just "shape" in general; it indicates the "shape" in particular. In Ezek. 1:10, for example, the word represents the "form" or "likeness" of the faces of the living creatures Ezekiel describes. In Ezek. 1:26 the word refers to what something seemed to be rather than what it was: "And above the firmament that was over their heads was the likeness of a throne. . . .''

Third, *dəmûth* signifies the original after which a thing is patterned: "To whom then will ye liken God? or what likeness will ye compare unto him?'' (Isa. 40:18). This significance is in its first biblical appearance: "And God said, Let us make man in our image, after our likeness . . .'' (Gen. 1:26).

Fourth, in Ps. 58:4 the word appears to function merely to extend the form but not the meaning of the preposition *kə:* "Their poison is like the poison of a serpent. . . .''

LION

'arî (אֲרִי), "lion." This apparently Aramaic loan word finds a cognate only in Aramaic. Occurring in all periods of biblical Hebrew, it is attested 83 times.

The word represents a "full-grown lion." This word should be compared to: (1) *gûr* (Gen. 49:9), a suckling lion; (2) *shāchal* (Hos. 5:14), a young lion which no longer is a suckling; and (3) *kəphîr* (Judg. 14:5), a young lion which no longer is a suckling and which hunts for its food independently.

The "lion" was a much-feared beast (Amos 3:12) found mostly in the Trans-jordan (Jer. 49:19) and in the mountainous areas (Song of Sol. 4:8). The various characteristics of the "lion" make it a frequent figure of strength and power (Judg. 14:18), of plundering (Gen. 49:9), and of malicious scheming (Ps. 10:9).

LIP

sāphāh (שָׂפָה), "lip; edge." This Hebrew word is related to cognate lan-guages where a similar word signifies "lip" or "edge" (cf. Akkadian *saptu*). *Sāphāh* has undergone little change in the history of the Hebrew language. It occurs about 175 times in the Old Testament, mainly in the poetic literature. The word is most frequent in the prophetical books, except for Isaiah (13 times) and Ezekiel (7 times).

"Lip" is first a part of the body. Isaiah's "lips" were ritually cleansed by the burning coal (Isa. 6:7). The compression of the "lips" was an indication of evil thoughts or motivation: "He shutteth his eyes to devise froward things: moving his lips he bringeth evil to pass" (Prov. 16:30).

The use of "lip" as an organ of speech is more frequent. With the lips, or human speech, one may flatter (Ps. 12:3), lie (Ps. 31:18), speak mischief (Ps. 140:9), and speak perversity (Prov. 4:24). On the other hand, the "lip" (speech) of the people of God is described as not sinful (Job 2:10), rejoicing (Job 8:21), prayerful (Ps. 17:1), God's word (Ps. 119:13), truthful (Prov. 12:19), wise (Prov. 14:7; 15:7), righteous (Prov. 16:13), and excellent (Prov. 17:7). In all these examples "the lip" signifies a manner of speech; cf. "Excel-lent speech becometh not a fool: much less do lying lips a prince" (Prov. 17:7).

The use of *sāphāh* is similar to that of *lāshôn*, "tongue," in that both words denote speech and also human language. *Sāphāh* with the meaning of human language occurs in the phrase "the language of Canaan" (Isa. 19:18). Isaiah described foreign language as "deeper speech than thou canst perceive" (lit-erally, "depths of lip"; 33:19).

The metaphorical use of *sāphāh* ("edge") appears mainly in the narrative literature. The word denotes the shore of a sea (Gen. 22:17) or of a river (Gen. 41:3), or the edge of material (Exod. 26:4), or the brim of a vessel (1 Kings 7:23).

The Septuagint translation is *cheilos* ("lip; shore; bank"); and the KJV has these translations: "lip; bank; brim; edge; language; shore; and speech."

TO LIVE

A. Verb.

chāyāh (חָיָה), "to live." This verb, which has cognates in most other Semitic languages (except Akkadian), occurs 284 times in biblical Hebrew and in all periods. In the ground stem this verb connotes "having life": "And Adam lived a hundred and thirty years . . ." (Gen. 5:3). A similar meaning appears in Num. 14:38 and Josh 9:21.

The intensive form of *chāyāh* means "to preserve alive": ". . . Two of every sort shalt thou bring into the ark, to keep them alive with thee . . ." (Gen. 6:19). This word may also mean "to bring to life" or "to cause to live": ". . . I dwell . . . with him also that is of a contrite and humble spirit, to revive the spirit of the humble, and to revive the heart of the contrite ones" (Isa. 57:15).

"To live" is more than physical existence. According to Deut. 8:3, "man doth not live by bread only, but by every word that proceedeth out of the mouth of the Lord doth man live." Moses said to Israel: ". . . Love the Lord thy God . . . that thou mayest live and multiply" (Deut. 30:16).

B. Noun.

chay (חַי), "living thing; life." The use of this word occurs only in the oath formula "as X lives," literally, "by the life of X": "And he said, They were my brethren, even the sons of my mother: as the Lord liveth, if ye had saved them alive, I would not slay you" (Judg. 8:19). This formula summons the power of a superior to sanction the statement asserted. In Judg. 8:19 God is the witness to Gideon's pledge to kill his enemies and this statement that they brought the penalty on themselves. A similar use appears in Gen. 42:15 except that the power summoned is Pharaoh's: "Hereby ye shall be proved: By the life of Pharaoh ye shall not go forth hence, except your youngest brother come hither." In 1 Sam. 1:26 Hannah employs a similar phrase summoning Eli himself to attest the truthfulness of her statement: "And she said, Oh my lord, as thy soul liveth, my lord, I am the woman that stood by thee here, praying unto the Lord." Only God swears by His own power: "And the Lord said, I have pardoned according to thy word: But as truly as I live, all the earth shall be filled with the glory of the Lord" (Num. 14:20-21).

The feminine form of the word, *chayyāh*, means "living being" and is especially used of animals. When so used, it usually distinguishes wild and undomesticated from domesticated animals; the word connotes that the animals described are untamed: "And God remembered Noah, and every living thing, and all the cattle that was with him in the ark . . ." (Gen. 8:1). Job 37:8 uses *chayyāh* of rapacious beasts: "Then the beasts go into dens, and remain in their places." This same word may also connote "evil beast": "Come now therefore, and let us slay him, and cast him into some pit, and we will say, Some evil beast hath devoured him . . ." (Gen. 37:20). In another nuance the word describes land animals as distinct from birds and fish: "Be fruitful, and multiply, and replenish the earth, and subdue it: and have dominion over the fish of the sea, and over the fowl of the air, and over every living thing that moveth upon the earth" (Gen. 1:28).

Infrequently *chayyāh* represents a domesticated animal: "And the cities shall they have to dwell in; and the suburbs of them shall be for their cattle, and for their goods, and for all their beasts" (Num. 35:3). Sometimes this word is used of "living beings" in general: "Also out of the midst thereof came the likeness of four living creatures" (Ezek. 1:5). In such passages the word is synonymous with the Hebrew word *nephesh*.

The plural of the noun *chay*, *chayyîm*, is a general word for the state of living as opposed to that of death. This meaning is in Deut. 30:15: "See, I have set before thee this day life and good, and death and evil." Notice also Gen. 27:46: "And Rebekah said to Isaac, I am weary of my life because of the daughters of Heth. . . ." In a second nuance the plural signifies "lifetime," or the days of one's life: ". . . And dust shalt thou eat all the days of thy life" (Gen. 3:14). The phrase "the years of one's life" represents the same idea: "And Sarah was a hundred and seven and twenty years old: these were the years of the life of Sarah" (Gen. 23:1). The "breath of life" in Gen. 2:7 is the breath that brings "life": "And the Lord God formed man of the dust of the ground, and breathed into his nostrils the breath of life; and man became a living soul" (cf. Gen. 6:17).

The "tree of life" is the tree which gives one eternal, everlasting "life." Therefore, it is the tree whose fruit brings "life": "And out of the ground made the Lord God to grow every tree that is pleasant to the sight, and good for food; the tree of life also in the midst of the garden . . ." (Gen. 2:9). In another nuance this word suggests a special quality of "life," life as a special gift from God (a gift of salvation): "I call heaven and earth to record this day against you, that I have set before you life and death, blessing and cursing: therefore choose life, that both thou and thy seed may live" (Deut. 30:19). The plural of the word can represent "persons who are alive," or living persons: "And he stood between the dead and the living; and the plague was stayed" (Num. 16:48).

C. Adjective.

chay (חַי), "alive; living." This word has cognates in Ugaritic, Canaanite, Phoenician, Punic, and Aramaic. It occurs about 481 times in biblical Hebrew and in all periods.

The word *chay* is used both as an adjective and as a noun. Used adjectivally it modifies men, animals, and God, but never plants. In Gen. 2:7 the word used with the noun *nephesh* ("soul, person, being") means a "living" person: "And the Lord God formed man of the dust of the ground, and breathed into his nostrils the breath of life; and man became a living soul." The same two words are used in Gen. 1:21 but with a slightly different meaning: "And God created . . . every living creature that moveth, which the waters brought forth abundantly, after their kind. . . ." Here a living *nephesh* ("creature") is an animal. Deut. 5:26 refers to God as the "living" God, distinguishing Him from the lifeless gods/idols of the heathen.

In a related nuance *chay* describes flesh (animal meat or human flesh) under the skin, or "raw flesh." In Lev. 13:10 one reads that leprosy involved seeing quick (alive), raw *(chay)* flesh: "And the priest shall see him: and, behold, if the rising be white in the skin, and it have turned the hair white, and there be quick raw flesh in the rising. . . ." The same words *(bāsār chay)* are applied to dead, raw (skinned) animal flesh: "Give flesh to roast for the priest; for he will not have [boiled] flesh of thee, but raw" (1 Sam. 2:15).

Applied to liquids, *chay* means "running"; it is used metaphorically describing something that moves: "And Isaac's servants digged in the valley, and found there a well of springing water" (Gen. 26:19). In Jer. 2:13 the NASB translates "living" waters, or waters that give life (cf. Jer. 17:13; Zech.

14:8). The Song of Solomon uses the word in a figure of speech describing one's wife; she is "a well of living waters" (4:15). The emphasis is not on the fact that the water flows but on its freshness; it is not stagnant, and therefore is refreshing and pleasant when consumed.

LOAD

massā' (מַשָּׂא), "load; burden; tribute; delight." The 43 occurrences of this word are scattered throughout the periods of biblical Hebrew.

The word means that which is borne by a man, an ass, a mule, or a camel: "If thou see the ass of him that hateth thee lying under his burden, and wouldest forbear to help him . . ." (Exod. 23:5—the first occurrence). A "load" may be hung on a peg (Isa. 22:25). This word is used figuratively of spiritual "loads" one is carrying: "For mine iniquities are gone over mine head: as a heavy burden they are too heavy for me" (Ps. 38:4).

Massā' means "burden" in the sense of something burdensome, a hardship. Moses asked God: ". . . Wherefore have I not found favor in thy sight, that thou layest the burden of all this people upon me?" (Num. 11:11).

Once the word represents that which is borne to a lord, a "tribute": "Also some of the Philistines brought Jehoshaphat presents, and tribute silver . . ." (2 Chron. 17:11).

In Ezek. 24:25 *massā'* bears a unique meaning: "Will it not be on the day when I take from them their stronghold, the joy of their pride, the desire of their eyes, and their heart's delight [or, the longing of their soul], their sons and their daughters . . ." (NASB).

massā' (מַשָּׂא), "utterance; oracle." This noun, closely related to the above noun, is used 21 times. *Massā'* means "utterance" or "oracle": "For remember, when you and I rode side by side behind Ahab his father, how the Lord uttered this oracle against him" (2 Kings 9:25 RSV). In Jer. 23:33-38 the word appears to connote both a burden and an oracle.

TO LOOK

nābat (נָבַט), "to look, regard, behold." This verb is found in both ancient and modern Hebrew. It occurs approximately 70 times in the Old Testament. The first use of this term is in Gen. 15:5, where it is used in the sense of "take a good look," as God commands Abraham: "Look now toward heaven, and [number] the stars. . . ."

While *nābat* is commonly used of physical "looking" (Exod. 3:6), the word is frequently used in a figurative sense to mean a spiritual and inner apprehension. Thus, Samuel is told by God: "Look not on his countenance. . . ." (1 Sam. 16:7) as he searched for a king among Jesse's sons. The sense of "consider" (with insight) is expressed in Isa. 51:1-2: ". . . Look unto the rock whence ye are hewn. . . . Look unto Abraham your father. . . ." "Pay attention to" seems to be the meaning in Isa. 5:12: ". . . they regard not the work of the Lord. . . ."

LOOSE CONDUCT

A. Noun.

zimmāh (זִמָּה), "loose conduct; lewdness." The 28 occurrences of this noun are all in legal and poetical books of the Bible, except for a single occurrence in Judges.

This noun signifies "loose or infamous conduct" and is used most often with regard to illicit sexual conduct: "Thou shalt not uncover the nakedness of a woman and her daughter, . . . or her daughter's daughter, to uncover her nakedness; for they are her near kinswomen: it is wickedness" (Lev. 18:17—the first occurrence). Rejection of God's law or spiritual adultery may be represented by *zimmāh* (Ps. 119:150; cf. Ezek. 16:12-28). A plan or scheme identified by the word is, therefore, a "harlotrous" plan (Ps. 26:10).

məzimmāh (מְזִמָּה), "purpose; evil device; evil thoughts; discretion." This noun occurs 19 times. The word means "purpose" in Job 42:2: "I know that thou canst do all things, and that no purpose of time can be thwarted" (RSV). *Məzimmāh* refers to "evil device" in Jer. 11:15: "What hath my beloved to do in mine house, seeing she hath wrought lewdness with many. . . ." In Job 21:27 the word is used to mean "evil thoughts," and in Prov. 1:4 the word is used for "discretion."

B. Verb.

zāmam (זָמַם), "to ponder; to cogitate." The noun *məzimmāh* is derived from this verb that occurs 13 times. In Zech. 8:14-15 the word appears to carry the sense of "to ponder": "For thus saith the Lord of hosts; As I thought to punish you, when your fathers provoked me to wrath . . . and I repented not: So again have I thought in these days to do well unto Jerusalem and to the house of Judah: fear ye not."

LORD

'ādôn (אָדוֹן), or *'adōnāy* (אֲדֹנָי), "lord; master; Lord." Cognates of this word appear in Ugaritic and Phoenician. The form *'ādôn* appears 334 times, while the form *'adōnāy* (used exclusively as a divine name) appears 439 times.

Basically, *'ādôn* means "lord" or "master." It is distinguished from the Hebrew word *ba'al*, which signifies "possessor" or "owner." *'Ādôn* basically describes the one who occupies the position of a "master" or "lord" over a slave or servant: "And the servant put his hand under the thigh of Abraham his master . . ." (Gen. 24:9). It is used of kings and their most powerful aides. Joseph told his brothers: "So now it was not you that sent me hither, but God: and he hath made me a father [i.e., an adviser] to Pharaoh, and lord of all his house, and a ruler throughout all the land of Egypt" (Gen. 45:8; cf. 42:30). Only once is this word used in the sense of "owner" or "possessor" (1 Kings 16:24).

'Ādôn is often used as a term of polite address. In some cases, the one so named really occupies a position of authority. In Gen. 18:12 (the first occur-

rence) Sarah called Abraham her "lord." On the other hand, this may be a purely honorary title by which the speaker intends to indicate his submission to the one so addressed. Jacob instructed his slaves to speak to "my lord Esau" (Gen. 32:18); i.e., Jacob called his brother Esau "lord." In places where the speaker is addressing someone calling him "lord," the word virtually means "you."

When applied to God, 'ādôn is used in several senses. It signifies His position as the one who has authority (like a master) over His people to reward the obedient and punish the disobedient: "Ephraim provoked him to anger most bitterly: therefore shall he leave his blood upon him, and his reproach shall his Lord return unto him" (Hos. 12:14). In such contexts God is conceived as a Being who is sovereign ruler and almighty master. The word is often a title of respect, a term of direct address usually assuming a specific concrete lord-vassal or master-servant relationship (Ps. 8:1). In some cases the word appears to be a title suggesting God's relationship to and position over Israel: "Three times in the year all thy males shall appear before the Lord God" (Exod. 23:17). In such contexts 'ādôn is a formal divine name and should probably be transliterated if the proper emphasis is to be retained. In the form 'adōnāy the word means "Lord" par excellence or "Lord over all," even as it sometimes does in the form 'ādôn (cf. Deut. 10:17, where God is called the "God of gods, and Lord of lords"; Josh. 3:11, where He is called the "Lord of all the earth").

The word 'adōnāy appears in Gen. 15:2: "And Abram said, Lord God, what wilt thou give me, seeing I go childless, ..." This word frequently appears in Psalms (Ps. 68:17; 86:3) and Isaiah (Isa. 29:13; 40:10).

yǝhôwāh (יְהוָֹה), "Lord." The Tetragrammaton YHWH appears without its own vowels, and its exact pronunciation is debated (Jehovah, Yehovah, Jahweh, Yahweh). The Hebrew text does insert the vowels for 'adōnāy, and Jewish students and scholars read 'adōnāy whenever they see the Tetragrammaton. This use of the word occurs 6,828 times. The word appears in every period of biblical Hebrew.

The divine name YHWH appears only in the Bible. Its precise meaning is much debated. God chose it as His personal name by which He related specifically to His chosen or covenant people. Its first appearance in the biblical record is Gen. 2:4: "These are the generations of the heavens and of the earth when they were created, in the day that the Lord God made the earth and the heavens." Apparently Adam knew Him by this personal or covenantal name from the beginning, since Seth both called his son Enosh (i.e., man as a weak and dependent creature) and began (along with all other pious persons) to call upon (formally worship) the name of YHWH, "the Lord" (Gen. 4:26). The covenant found a fuller expression and application when God revealed Himself to Abraham (Gen. 12:8), promising redemption in the form of national existence. This promise became reality through Moses, to whom God explained that He was not only the "God who exists" but the "God who effects His will": "Thus shalt thou say unto the children of Israel, The Lord [YHWH] God of your fathers, the God of Abraham, the God of Isaac, and the God of Jacob, hath sent me unto you: this is my name for ever, and this is my memorial unto all generations. Go, and gather the elders of Israel together, and say unto them, The Lord [*YHWH*] God of your fathers, the God of Abraham, of Isaac, and of Jacob, appeared unto me, saying, I have surely visited you, and seen that which is done to you in Egypt: And I have said, I will bring you up out of the affliction of Egypt unto the land of the Canaanites. . ." (Exod. 3:15-17). So God explained the meaning of "I am who I am" (Exod. 3:14). He spoke to the fathers as *YHWH*, but the promised deliverance and, therefore, the fuller significance or experienced meaning of His name were unknown to them (Exod. 6:2-8).

LOT

gôrāl (גּוֹרָל), "lot." This word is attested 77 times and in all periods of the language (if a traditional view of the formation of the canon is accepted).

Gôrāl represents the "lot" which was cast to discover the will of God in a given situation: "And Aaron shall cast lots upon the two goats; one lot for the Lord, and the other lot for the scapegoat" (Lev. 16:8—the first occurrence). Exactly what casting the "lot" involved is not known.

Since the land of Palestine was allocated among the tribes by the casting of the "lot," these allotments came to be known as their lots: "This then was the lot of the tribe of the children of Judah by their families; even to the border of Edom. . ." (Josh. 15:1).

In an extended use the word *gôrāl* represents the idea "fate" or "destiny": "And behold at eveningtide trouble; and before the morning he is not. This is the portion of them that spoil us, and the lot of them that rob us" (Isa. 17:14). Since God is viewed as controlling all things absolutely, the result of the casting of the "lot" is divinely controlled: "The lot is cast into the lap; but the whole disposing thereof is of the Lord" (Prov. 16:33). Thus, Providence (divine control of history) is frequently figured as one's "lot."

TO LOVE

A. Verb.

'āhab (אָהַב) or *'āhēb* (אָהֵב), "to love; like." This verb occurs in Moabite and Ugaritic. It appears in all periods of Hebrew and around 250 times in the Bible.

Basically this verb is equivalent to the English "to love" in the sense of having a strong emotional attachment to and desire either to possess or to be in the presence of the object. First, the word refers to the love a man has for a woman and a woman for a man. Such love is rooted in sexual desire, although as a rule it is desire within the bounds of lawful relationships: "And Isaac brought her into his mother Sarah's tent, and took Rebekah, and she became his wife; and he loved her. . ." (Gen. 24:67). This word may refer to an erotic but legal love outside marriage. Such an emotion may be a desire to marry and care for the object of that love, as in the case of Shechem's love for Dinah (Gen. 34:3). In a very few instances *'āhab* (or *'āhēb*) may signify no more than pure lust—an inordinate desire to have sexual relations with its object (cf. 2 Sam. 13:1). Marriage may be consummated without the presence of love for one's marriage partner (Gen. 29:30).

'*Āhab* (or '*āhēb*) seldom refers to making love (usually this is represented by *yāda'*, "to know," or by *shākab*, "to lie with"). The word does seem to have this added meaning, however, in 1 Kings 11:1: "But King Solomon loved many strange women, together with the daughter of Pharaoh. . ." (cf. Jer. 2:25). Hosea appears to use this nuance when he writes that God told him to "go yet, love a woman beloved of her friend, yet an adulteress. . ." (3:1). This is the predominant meaning of the verb when it appears in the causative stem (as a participle). In every instance except one (Zech. 13:6) '*āhab* (or '*āhēb*) signifies those with whom one has made or intends to make love: "Go up to Lebanon, and cry; and lift up thy voice in Bashan, and cry from the passages: for all thy lovers are destroyed" (Jer. 22:20; cf. Ezek. 16:33).

'*Āhab* (or '*āhēb*) is also used of the love between parents and their children. In its first biblical appearance, the word represents Abraham's special attachment to his son Isaac: "And he said, Take now thy son, thine only son Isaac, whom thou lovest. . ." (Gen. 22:2). '*Āhab* (or '*āhēb*) may refer to the family love experienced by a daughter-in-law toward her mother-in-law (Ruth 4:15). This kind of love is also represented by the word *rācham*.

'*Āhab* (or '*āhēb*) sometimes depicts a special strong attachment a servant may have toward a master under whose dominance he wishes to remain: "And if the servant shall plainly say, I love my master, my wife, and my children; I will not go out free. . ." (Exod. 21:5). Perhaps there is an overtone here of family love; he "loves" his master as a son "loves" his father (cf. Deut. 15:16). This emphasis may be in 1 Sam. 16:21, where we read that Saul "loved [David] greatly." Israel came "to love" and deeply admire David so that they watched his every move with admiration (1 Sam. 18:16).

A special use of this word relates to an especially close attachment of friends: ". . . The soul of Jonathan was knit with the soul of David, and Jonathan loved him as his own soul" (1 Sam. 18:1). In Lev. 19:18: ". . . Thou shalt love thy neighbor as thyself. . ." (cf. Lev. 19:34; Deut. 10:19) '*āhab* (or '*āhēb*) signifies this brotherly or friendly kind of love. The word suggests, furthermore, that one seek to relate to his brother and all men according to what is specified in the law structure God gave to Israel. This was to be the normal state of affairs between men.

This verb is used politically to describe the loyalty of a vassal or a subordinate to his lord—so Hiram of Tyre "loved" David in the sense that he was completely loyal (1 Kings 5:1).

The strong emotional attachment and desire suggested by '*āhab* (or '*āhēb*) may also be fixed on objects, circumstances, actions, and relationships.

B. Noun.

'*ahabāh* (אַהֲבָה), "love." This word appears about 55 times, and it represents several kinds of "love." The first biblical occurrence of '*ahabāh* is in Gen. 29:20; there the word deals with the "love" between man and wife as a general concept. In Hos. 3:1 the word is used of "love" as a sexual activity.

'*Ahabāh* means "love" between friends in 1 Sam. 18:3: "Then Jonathan and David made a covenant because he loved him as his own soul." The word refers to Solomon's "love" in 1 Kings 11:2 and to God's "love" in Deut. 7:8.

C. Participle.

'*āhab* (אָהַב), "friend." This word used as a participle may mean "friend": ". . . The rich hath many friends" (Prov. 14:20).

LOVING-KINDNESS

A. Noun.

chesed (חֶסֶד), "loving-kindness; steadfast love; grace; mercy; faithfulness; goodness; devotion." This word is used 240 times in the Old Testament, and is especially frequent in the Psalter. The term is one of the most important in the vocabulary of Old Testament theology and ethics.

The Septuagint nearly always renders *chesed* with *eleos* ("mercy"), and that usage is reflected in the New Testament. Modern translations, in contrast, generally prefer renditions close to the word "grace." KJV usually has "mercy," although "loving-kindness" (following Coverdale), "favor," and other translations also occur. RSV generally prefers "steadfast love." NIV often offers simply "love."

In general, one may identify three basic meanings of the word, which always interact: "strength," "steadfastness," and "love." Any understanding of the word that fails to suggest all three inevitably loses some of its richness. "Love" by itself easily becomes sentimentalized or universalized apart from the covenant. Yet "strength" or "steadfastness" suggest only the fulfillment of a legal or other obligation.

The word refers primarily to mutual and reciprocal rights and obligations between the parties of a relationship (especially Yahweh and Israel). But *chesed* is not only a matter of obligation; it is also of generosity. It is not only a matter of loyalty, but also of mercy. The weaker party seeks the protection and blessing of the patron and protector, but he may not lay absolute claim to it. The stronger party remains committed to his promise, but retains his freedom, especially with regard to the manner in which he will implement those promises. *Chesed* implies personal involvement and commitment in a relationship beyond the rule of law.

Marital love is often related to *chesed*. Marriage certainly is a legal matter, and there are legal sanctions for infractions. Yet the relationship, if sound, far transcends mere legalities. The prophet Hosea applies the analogy to Yahweh's *chesed* to Israel within the covenant (e.g., 2:21). Hence, "devotion" is sometimes the single English word best capable of capturing the nuance of the original. The RSV attempts to bring this out by its translation, "steadfast love." Hebrew writers often underscored the element of steadfastness (or strength) by pairing *chesed* with '*emeth* ("truth, reliability") and '*emûnāh* ("faithfulness").

Biblical usage frequently speaks of someone "doing," "showing," or "keeping" *chesed*. The concrete content of the word is especially evident when it is used in the plural. God's "mercies," "kindnesses," or "faithfulnesses" are His specific, concrete acts of redemption in fulfillment of His promise. An example appears in Isa. 55:3: ". . . And I will make an everlasting covenant with you, even the sure mercies of David."

Chesed has both God and man as its subject. When man is the subject of *chesed,* the word usually describes the person's kindness or loyalty to another; cf. 2 Sam. 9:7: "And David said . . . I will surely show thee [Mephibosheth] kindness for Jonathan thy father's sake. . . ." Only rarely is the term applied explicitly to man's affection or fidelity toward God; the clearest example is probably Jer. 2:2: "Go and cry in the ears of Jerusalem, saying, thus saith the Lord; I remember thee, the kindness of thy youth, the love of thine espousals, when thou wentest after me in the wilderness. . . ."

Man exercises *chesed* toward various units within the community—toward family and relatives, but also to friends, guests, masters, and servants. *Chesed* toward the lowly and needy is often specified. The Bible prominently uses the term *chesed* to summarize and characterize a life of sanctification within, and in response to, the covenant. Thus, Hos. 6:6 states that God desires "mercy [RSV, "steadfast love"] and not sacrifice" (i.e., faithful living in addition to worship). Similarly, Mic. 6:8 features *chesed* in the prophets' summary of biblical ethics: ". . . and what doth the Lord require of thee, but . . . to love *mercy*. . . ?"

Behind all these uses with man as subject, however, stand the repeated references to God's *chesed*. It is one of His most central characteristics. God's loving-kindness is offered to His people, who need redemption from sin, enemies, and troubles. A recurrent refrain describing God's nature is "abounding/plenteous in *chesed*" (Exod. 34:6; Neh. 9:17; Ps. 103:8; Jonah 4:2). The entire history of Yahweh's covenantal relationship with Israel can be summarized in terms of *chesed*. It is the one permanent element in the flux of covenantal history. Even the Creation is the result of God's *chesed* (Ps. 136:5-9). His love lasts for a "thousand generations" (Deut. 7:9; cf. Deut. 5:10 and Exod. 20:6), indeed "forever" (especially in the refrains of certain psalms, such as Ps. 136).

Words used in synonymous parallelism with *chesed* help to define and explain it. The word most commonly associated with *chesed* is *'emet* ("fidelity; reliability"): ". . . Let thy loving-kindness [*chesed*] and thy truth [*'emeth*] continually preserve me." *'Emûnāh* with a similar meaning is also common: "He hath remembered his mercy [*chesed*] and his truth [*'emûnāh*] toward the house of Israel. . . ." This emphasis is especially appropriate when God is the subject, because His *chesed* is stronger and more enduring than man's. Etymological investigation suggests that *chesed*'s primitive significance may have been "strength" or "permanence." If so, a puzzling use of *chesed* in Isa. 40:6 would be explained: "All flesh is grass, and all the goodliness thereof is as the flower of the field."

The association of *chesed* with "covenant" keeps it from being misunderstood as mere providence or love for all creatures; it applies primarily to God's particular love for His chosen and covenanted people. "Covenant" also stresses the reciprocity of the relationship; but since God's *chesed* is ultimately beyond the covenant, it will not ultimately be abandoned, even when the human partner is unfaithful and must be disciplined (Isa. 54:8, 10). Since its final triumph and implementation is eschatological, *chesed* can imply the goal and end of all salvation-history (Ps. 85:7, 10; 130:7; Mic. 7:20).

The proper noun *Hasdiah* (1 Chron. 3:20) is related to *chesed*. The name of Zerubbabel's son means "Yahweh is faithful/gracious," a fitting summary of the prophet's message.

B. Adjective.

chāsîd (חָסִיד), "pious; devout; faithful; godly." The adjective *chāsîd,* derived from *chesed,* is often used to describe the faithful Israelite. God's *chesed* provides the pattern, model, and strength by which the life of the *chāsîd* is to be directed. One reference to the "godly" man appears in Ps. 12:1: "Help, Lord; for the godly man ceaseth; for the faithful fail from among the children of men." Usually a suffix or possessive pronoun referring to God is attached to the word, indicating His special attachment to those who pattern their lives after His: "O love the Lord, all ye his saints [literally, "His pious ones"; NASB, "His godly ones"]: for the Lord preserveth the faithful, and plentifully rewardeth the proud doer" (Ps. 31:23).

Following the Greek *hosios* and Latin *sanctus,* the KJV often renders the word "saint"—which must be understood in the sense of sanctification [dependent upon grace], not moralistically [of native goodness].

M

TO MAGNIFY

A. Verb.

gādal (גָּדַל), "to become strong; grow up; be great or wealthy; evidence oneself as great (magnified); be powerful, significant, or valuable." This verb occurs elsewhere only in Ugaritic and Arabic; it is not attested in biblical Aramaic or post-biblical Hebrew. In other Semitic languages the meaning of the word is generally represented by roots with the radicals *rbh,* and such a root exists in biblical Hebrew as a synonym of *gādal.* These two synonyms differ, however, inasmuch as *gādal* does not refer to numerical increase (except perhaps in Gen. 48:19). The Bible attests *gādal* about 120 times and in every period.

This verb can signify the increasing of size and age as with the maturing process of human life: "And the child grew, and was weaned . . ." (Gen. 21:8). The word also depicts the "growing up" of animals (2 Sam. 12:3) and plants (Isa. 44:14) and the maturing of animal horns (Dan. 8:9) and other growing things. In the intensive stem *gādal* indicates that this rearing has occurred: ". . . I have nourished and brought up children . . ." (Isa. 1:2). This stem may also imply permission: ". . . [He] shall let the locks of the hair of his head grow" (Num. 6:5).

Gādal can represent the status of "being great or wealthy." Abraham's servant reported: "And the Lord hath blessed my master greatly; and he is become great . . ."(Gen. 24:35)—here the word represents the conclusion of a process. In the intensive stem the verb sets forth a fact, as when God said: "And I will make of thee a great nation, and I will bless thee, and make thy name great . . ." (Gen. 12:2—the first biblical occurrence of the verb).

This word is sometimes used with the meaning "to be great, to evidence oneself as great": "And now, I beseech thee, let the power of my Lord be great, according as thou hast spoken . . ." (Num. 14:17). Moses is praying that God will demonstrate that He is truly great, even as He has said, and do so not by destroying His people. Such an act (destroying Israel) would make onlookers conclude that God was not able to accomplish what He had promised. If, however, He would bring Israel into Palestine, this would exhibit His greatness before the nations. This same sense appears in 2 Sam. 7:22, except with the added overtone of "magnified," "praised as great": "Wherefore thou art great, O Lord God: for there is none like thee, neither is there any God besides thee, according to all that we have heard with our ears."

Another emphasis of *gādal* is "to be great, powerful, important, or valuable." This nuance arises when the word is applied to kings. Pharaoh said to Joseph: "Thou shalt be over my house, and according unto thy word shall all my people be ruled: only in the throne will I be greater [more powerful and honored] than thou" (Gen. 41:40). The Messiah "shall stand and feed in the strength of the Lord, in the majesty of the name of the Lord his God; and they shall abide: for now shall he be great unto the ends of the earth" (Mic. 5:4); He will be powerful to the ends of the earth. The nuance "to be valuable" appears in 1 Sam. 26:24 when David said to Saul: "And, behold, as thy life was much set by this day in mine eyes, so let my life be much set by in the eyes of the Lord, and let him deliver me out of all tribulation." In this statement the second use of the verb is in the intensive stem. Perhaps the force of this could be expressed if one were to translate: "So may my life be very highly valued. . . ."

In the reflexive stem *gādal* may signify "to magnify oneself." God says: "Thus will I magnify myself, and sanctify myself; and I will be known in the eyes of many nations . . ." (Ezek. 38:23). The context shows that He will bring judgment. In this way He "magnifies Himself," or shows Himself to be great and powerful. On the other hand, a false statement of greatness and power is an empty boast. So *gādal* can mean "to boast": "Shall the axe boast itself against him that heweth therewith? or shall the saw magnify itself against him that shaketh it?" (Isa. 10:15). In the causative stem the verb may signify "to assume great airs": "If indeed ye will magnify yourselves against me, and plead against me my reproach . . ." (Job 19:5). A nuance appears in Job 7:17, where *gādal* is in the intensive stem, suggesting an estimation of greatness: "What is man, that thou shouldest magnify him? and that thou shouldest set thine heart upon him?" (Ps. 8:4). When man is so insignificant, why then does God esteem him so important?

B. Nouns.

gədûllāh (גְּדוּלָה), "greatness; great dignity; great things." This noun occurs 12 times. It means "greatness" in Ps. 71:21: "Thou shalt increase my greatness, and comfort me on every side." *Gədûllāh* may refer also to "great dignity" (Esth. 6:3) and to "great things" (2 Sam. 7:21).

gōdel (גֹּדֶל), "greatness." This noun appears 13 times. *Gōdel* means "greatness" in terms of size (Ezek. 31:7), of divine power (Ps. 79:11), of divine dignity (Deut. 32:3), of divine majesty (Deut. 3:24), of divine mercy (Num. 14:19), or of the false greatness of one's heart (insolence; Isa. 9:9).

migədāl (מִגְדָּל), "strong place; wooden podium." This noun, which occurs 49 times, usually refers to a tower or a "strong place" (Gen. 11:4-5), but it also occurs once to refer to a "wooden podium": "And Ezra the scribe stood upon a pulpit of wood . . ." (Neh. 8:4).

C. Adjectives.

gādôl (גָּדוֹל), "great." The adjective *gādôl* is the most frequently appearing word related to the verb *gādal* (about 525 times). *Gādôl* is used of extended dimension (Gen. 1:21), of number (Gen. 12:2), of power (Deut. 4:37), of punishment (Gen. 4:13), and of value or importance (Gen. 39:9).

The verb *gādal* and the related adjective *gādôl* may each be used to make distinctive statements. In Hebrew one may say "he is great" both by using the verb alone and by using the pronoun and the adjective *gādôl*. The first sets forth a standing and existing condition—so Mal. 1:5 could be rendered: "The Lord is magnified beyond the borders of Israel." The second construction announces newly experienced information to the recipient, as in Isa. 12:6: ". . . Great is the Holy One of Israel in the midst of thee." This information was known previously, but recent divine acts have made it to be experienced anew. The emphasis is on the freshness of the experience.

Another adjective *gādēl* means "becoming great; growing up." This verbal adjective occurs 4 times, once in Gen. 26:13: "And the man waxed great, and went forward, and grew until he became very great."

MAIDEN; VIRGIN

bəthûlāh (בְּתוּלָה), "maiden; virgin." Cognates of this word appear in Ugaritic and Akkadian. Its 50 biblical occurrences are distributed throughout every period of Old Testament literature.

This word can mean "virgin," as is clear in Deut. 22:17, where if a man has charged that "I found not thy daughter a maid," the father is to say, "And yet these are the tokens of my daughter's virginity [*bəthûlîm*]." The text continues: "And they shall spread the cloth before the elders of the city." The husband was to be chastised and fined (which was given to the girl's father), "because he hath brought up an evil name upon a virgin of Israel" (Deut. 22:19). If she was found not to be a "virgin," she was to be stoned to death "because she hath wrought folly in Israel, to play the whore in her father's house" (Deut. 22:21).

In several passages this word merely means a grown-up girl or a "maiden"; it identifies her age and marital status. The prophets who denounce Israel for playing the harlot also called her the *bəthûlāh* of Yahweh, or the *bəthûlāh* (daughter) of Israel (Jer. 31:4, 21). The other nations are also called *bəthûlôth:* Isa. 23:12—Zidon; Isa. 47:1—Babylon; Jer. 46:11—Egypt. These nations are hardly being commended for their purity! In Ugaritic literature the word is used frequently of the goddess Anat, the sister of Baal and hardly a virgin. What was true of her and figuratively of these nations (including Israel) was that she was a vigorous young woman at the height of her powers and not married. Thus *bəthûlāh* is often used in parallelism with the Hebrew *bāchûr,* which signifies a young man, regardless of his virginity, who is at the height of his powers (Deut. 32:25). In such contexts virility and not virginity is in view. Because of this ambiguity Moses described Rebekah as a young girl (*naʿarāh*) who was "very fair to look upon, a virgin [*bəthûlāh*], neither had any man known her" (Gen. 24:16—the first occurrence of the word).

Both the masculine and feminine forms appear in Isa. 23:4: ". . . I travail not, nor bring forth children, neither do I nourish up young men (*bəthûlîm*), nor bring up virgins (*bəthûlôth*)." A similar occurrence is found in Lam. 1:18: ". . . Behold my sorrow: my *virgins* and my *young* men are gone into captivity" (cf. Lam. 2:21; Zech. 9:17).

The standard edition of William Gesenius' lexicon by Brown, Driver, and Briggs (BDB) observes that the Assyrian word *batultu* (masc. *batulu*) is a cognate of *bəthûlāh*. This Assyrian word means "maiden" or "young man."

Most scholars agree that *bəthûlāh* and *batultu* are phonetically related; yet they disagree as to whether they are true cognates. Various Old Testament contexts indicate that *bəthûlāh* should be translated "maiden" more often than "virgin." If this is true, the BDB etymology is probably correct.

TO MAKE (CUT) A COVENANT

A. Verb.

kārath (כָּרַת), "to cut off, cut down, fell, cut or make (a covenant or agreement)." This verb also occurs in Akkadian, Moabite, and post-biblical Hebrew. In biblical Hebrew it is attested about 290 times and in all periods.

Basically *kārath* means "to sever" something from something else by cutting it with a blade. The nuance depends upon the thing being cut off. In the case of a branch, one "cuts it down" (Num. 13:23), and one "[swings] the axe to cut down the tree" (Deut. 19:5). The word is also used of "chopping down" wooden idols (Exod. 34:13). *Kārath* can signify "chopping off" a man's head and feet (1 Sam. 5:4). In Jer. 34:18 this verb means "to cut into two pieces." "Cut off" may also imply cutting off in the sense of circumcision. In Exod. 4:25 Zipporah took a flint knife and "cut off" her son's foreskin. In a related but different usage this word appears in Num. 11:33, where it means "to chew" meat.

"To cut off" can mean "to exterminate or destroy." God told Noah that "all flesh [shall never again] be cut off . . . by the waters of a flood . . ." (Gen. 9:11—the first occurrence of the word). *Kārath* can be used of spiritual and social extermination. A person "cut off" in this manner is not necessarily killed but may be driven out of the family and removed from the blessings of the covenant. God told Abraham that "the uncircumcised man child whose flesh of his foreskin is not circumcised, that soul shall be cut off from his people; he hath broken my covenant" (Gen. 17:14).

One of the best known uses of this verb is "to make" a covenant. The process by which God made a covenant with Abraham is called "cutting": "In the same day the Lord made a covenant with Abram . . ." (Gen. 15:18). The word "covenant" appears nine times before this in Genesis, but it is not connected with *kārath*. A synonym to this verb appears in this immediate context (Gen. 15:10) and is directly related to the process of making the covenant. Furthermore, hereafter in Genesis and throughout the Bible *kārath* is frequently associated with making a covenant. This verb, therefore, constitutes a rather technical term for making a covenant. In Genesis it often alludes to an act by which animals were cut in two and the party taking the oath passed between the pieces. This act was not created by God especially to deal with Abraham but was a well-known practice at that time among many men.

Later, "cutting" a covenant did not necessarily include this act but seems to be an allusion to the Abrahamic covenantal process (cf. Jer. 34:18). In such a covenant the one passing through the pieces pledged his faithfulness to the covenant. If that faithfulness was broken, he called death upon himself, or the same fate which befell the animals. In some cases it is quite clear that no literal cutting took place and that *kārath* is used in a technical sense of "making an agreement in writing" (Neh. 9:38).

B. Nouns.

Kərîthûth refers to a "bill of divorcement." This word implies the cutting off of a marriage by means of a "bill of divorcement": "When a man hath taken a wife, and married her, and it come to pass that she find no favor in his eyes, because he hath found some uncleanness in her: then let him write her a bill of divorcement, and give it in her hand, and send her out of his house" (Deut. 24:1). *Kərîthûth* appears 4 times.

Kərûthôth means "beams." This noun, which occurs only 3 times, refers to "beams" in the sense of things "cut off" in 1 Kings 6:36: "And he built the inner court with three rows of hewed stone, and a row of cedar beams."

TO MAKE HASTE, HASTEN

māhar (מָהַר), "to hasten; make haste." This verb, along with various derivatives, is common to both ancient and modern Hebrew. It occurs approximately 70 times in the Hebrew Bible. *Māhar* occurs twice in the first verse in which it is found: "And Abraham hastened into the tent unto Sarah, and said, Make ready quickly three measures of fine meal . . ." (Gen. 18:6).

Māhar often has an adverbial use when it is used with another verb, such as in Gen. 18:7: ". . . hasted to prepare it" (or, "quickly prepared it"). Anyone who yields to seduction is likened by the wise man to a bird that rushes into a snare (Prov. 7:23).

MALE

A. Noun.

zākār (זָכָר), "male." Cognates of this word appear in Akkadian, Aramaic, and Arabic. It occurs 82 times and usually in early prose (Genesis through Deuteronomy), only 5 times in the biblical prophets, and never in biblical wisdom or poetical literature.

Zākār emphasizes "maleness" as over against "femaleness"; this word focuses on the sex of the one so named. Thus, "God created man in his own image, in the image of God created he him; male and female created he them" (Gen. 1:27). The word can be used not only of an "adult male" but also of a "male child" (Lev. 12:7). *Zākār* is used collectively in many passages—in singular form, with a plural reference (Judg. 21:11).

In some contexts the word represents a "male animal": "And of every living thing of all flesh, two of every sort shalt thou bring into the ark, to keep them alive with thee; they shall be male and female" (Gen. 6:19).

B. Adjective.

zākār (זָכָר), "male." Sometimes *zākār* is used as an adjective: "Number all the first-born of the males of the children of Israel from a month old and upward . . ." (Num. 3:40). The word appears in Jer. 20:15: "A man child is born unto thee; making him very glad."

MAN

A. Nouns.

'ādām (אָדָם), "man; mankind; people; someone (indefinite); Adam (the first man)." This noun appears in Ugaritic, Phoenician, and Punic. A word with the same radicals occurs in old South Arabic meaning "serf." In late Arabic the same radicals mean not only "mankind" but "all creation." Akkadian *admu* signifies "child." The Hebrew word appears about 562 times and in all periods of biblical Hebrew.

This noun is related to the verb *'adōm*, "to be red," and therefore probably relates to the original ruddiness of human skin. The noun connotes "man" as the creature created in God's image, the crown of all creation. In its first appearance *'ādām* is used for mankind, or generic man: "And God said, Let us make man in our image, after our likeness . . ." (Gen. 1:26). In Gen. 2:7 the word refers to the first "man," Adam: "And the Lord God formed man of the dust of the ground, and breathed into his nostrils the breath of life; and man became a living soul.''

Throughout Gen. 2:5–5:5 there is a constant shifting and interrelationship between the generic and the individual uses. ''Man'' is distinguished from the rest of the creation insofar as he was created by a special and immediate act of God: he alone was created in the image of God (Gen. 1:27). He consisted of two elements, the material and the nonmaterial (Gen. 2:7). From the outset he occupied an exalted position over the rest of the earthly creation and was promised an even higher position (eternal life) if he obeyed God: ''And God blessed them, and God said unto them, Be fruitful, and multiply, and replenish the earth, and subdue it: and have dominion over the fish of the sea, and over the fowl of the air, and over every living thing that moveth upon the earth'' (Gen. 1:28; cf. 2:16-17). In Gen. 1 ''man'' is depicted as the goal and crown of creation, while in Gen. 2 the world is shown to have been created as the scene of human activity. ''Man'' was in God's image with reference to his soul and/or spirit. (He is essentially spiritual; he has an invisible and immortal aspect which is simple or indivisible.) Other elements of this image are his mind and will, intellectual and moral integrity (he was created with true knowledge, righteousness, and holiness), his body (this was seen as a fit organ to share immortality with man's soul and the means by which dominion over the creation was exercised), and dominion over the rest of the creation.

The Fall greatly affected the nature of ''man,'' but he did not cease to be in God's image (Gen. 9:6). Fallen ''man'' occupies a new and lower position before God: ''And God saw that the wickedness of man was great in the earth, and that every imagination of the thoughts of his heart was only evil continually'' (Gen. 6:5; cf. 8:21). No longer does ''man'' have perfect communion with the Creator; he is now under the curse of sin and death. Original knowledge, righteousness, and holiness are destroyed. Restoration to his proper place in the creation and relationship to the Creator comes only through spiritual union with the Christ, the second Adam (Rom. 5:12-21). In some later passages of Scripture 'ādām is difficult to distinguish from 'îsh—man as the counterpart of woman and/or as distinguished in his maleness.

Sometimes 'ādām identifies a limited and particular ''group of men'': ''Behold, waters rise up out of the north, and shall be an overflowing flood, and shall overflow the land [of the Philistines], and all that is therein; the city, and them that dwell therein: then the men [used in the singular] shall cry, and all the inhabitants of the land shall howl'' (Jer. 47:2). When used of a particular group of individual ''men,'' the noun appears in the phrase ''sons of men'': ''And the Lord came down to see the city and the tower, which the children of men builded'' (Gen. 11:5). The phrase ''son of man'' usually connotes a particular individual: '';God is not a man ['îsh], that he should lie; neither the son of man, that he should repent . . .'' (Num. 23:19; cf. Ezek. 2:1). The one notable exception is the use of this term in Dan. 7:13-14: ''I saw in the night visions, and, behold, one like the Son of man ['enôsh] came with the clouds of heaven. . . . His dominion is an everlasting dominion, which shall not pass away . . .'' Here the phrase represents a divine being.

'Ādām is also used in reference to any given man, or to anyone male or female: "When a man [anyone] shall have in the skin of his flesh a rising, a scab, or bright spot, and it be in the skin of his flesh like the plague of leprosy; then he shall be brought unto Aaron . . ." (Lev. 13:2).

The noun *'ōdem* means "ruby." This word occurs 3 times and in Hebrew only. It refers to the red stone, the "ruby" in Exod. 28:17: ". . . the first row shall be a sardius ['*ōdem*], a topaz, and a carbuncle. . . ."

geber (גֶּבֶר), "man." This word occurs 60 times in the Hebrew Old Testament, and its frequency of usage is higher (32 times, nearly half of all the occurrences) in the poetical books. The word occurs first in Exod. 10:11: "Not so: go now ye that are men [*geber*], and serve the Lord; for that ye did desire."

The root meaning "to be strong" is no longer obvious in the usage of *geber*, since it is a synonym of *'îsh:* "Thus saith the Lord, Write ye this man ['*îsh*] childless, a man [*geber*] that shall not prosper in his days: for no man of his seed shall prosper, sitting upon the throne of David . . ." (Jer. 22:30). Other synonyms are *zākār*, "male" (Jer. 30:6); *'enôsh*, "man" (Job 4:17); and *'ādām*, "man" (Job 14:10). A *geber* denotes a "male," as an antonym of a "woman"; cf. "The woman ['*ishshāh*] shall not wear that which pertaineth unto a man, neither shall a man [*geber*] put on a woman's ['*ishshāh*] garment: for all that do so are abomination unto the Lord thy God" (Deut. 22:5).

In standardized expressions of curse and blessing *geber* also functions as a synonym for *'îsh*, "man." The expression may begin with "Cursed be the man" (*geber;* Jer. 17:5) or "Blessed is the man" (*geber;* Ps. 34:8), but these same expressions also occur with *'îsh* (Ps. 1:1; Deut. 27:15).

The Septuagint gives the following translations: *aner* ("man"); *anthropos* ("human being; man"); and *dunatos* ("powerful or strong ones").

'îsh (אִישׁ), "man; husband; mate; human being; human; somebody; each; every." Cognates of this word appear in Phoenician, Punic, old Aramaic, and old South Arabic. This noun occurs about 2,183 times and in all periods of biblical Hebrew. The plural of this noun is usually *'anāshîm*, but 3 times it is *'îshîm* (Ps. 53:3).

Basically, this word signifies "man" in correspondence to woman; a "man" is a person who is distinguished by maleness. This emphasis is in Gen. 2:24 (the first biblical occurrence): "Therefore shall a man leave his father and his mother, and shall cleave unto his wife. . . ." Sometimes the phrase "man and woman" signifies anyone whatsoever, including children: "If an ox gore a man or a woman, that they die: then the ox shall be surely stoned . . ." (Exod. 21:28). This phrase can also connote an inclusive group, including children: "And they utterly destroyed all that was in the city, both man and woman, young and old, and ox, and sheep, and ass, with the edge of the sword" (Josh. 6:21). This idea is sometimes more explicitly expressed by the word series "men, women, and children": "Gather the people together, men, and women, and children, and thy stranger that is within thy gates . . ." (Deut. 31:12).

'îsh is often used in marriage contexts (cf. Gen. 2:24) meaning "husband" or "mate": "Take ye wives, and beget sons and daughters; and take wives for your sons, and give your daughters to husbands, that they may bear sons and

daughters . . ." (Jer. 29:6). A virgin is described as a lass who has not known a "man" ("husband"): ". . . And she went with her companions, and bewailed her virginity upon the mountains. And it came to pass at the end of two months, that she returned unto her father, who did with her according to his vow which he had vowed: and she knew no man" (Judg. 11:38-39). The sense "mate" appears in Gen. 7:2, where the word represents male animals: "Of every clean beast thou shalt take to thee by sevens, the male and his female. . . ."

One special nuance of *'îsh* appears in passages such as Gen. 3:6, where it means "husband," or one responsible for a wife or woman and revered by her: "[And she] gave also unto her husband with her: and he did eat." This emphasis is in Hos. 2:16 where it is applied to God (cf. the Hebrew word *ba'al*).

Sometimes this word connotes that the one so identified is a "man" *par excellence*. As such he is strong, influential, and knowledgeable in battle: "Be strong, and quit yourselves like men, O ye Philistines, that ye be not servants unto the Hebrews . . ." (1 Sam. 4:9).

In a few places *'îsh* is used as a synonym of "father": "We are all sons of one man . . ." (Gen. 42:11, RSV). In other passages the word is applied to a son (cf. Gen. 2:24).

In the plural the word can be applied to groups of men who serve or obey a superior. Pharaoh's men escorted Abraham: "And Pharaoh commanded his men concerning him: and they sent him away . . ." (Gen. 12:20). In a similar but more general sense, the word may identify people who belong to someone or something: "For all these abominations have the men of the land done, which were before you, and the land is defiled" (Lev. 18:27).

Infrequently (and in later historical literature) this word is used as a collective noun referring to an entire group: "And his servant said, . . . Should I set this before a hundred men?" (2 Kings 4:43).

Many passages use *'îsh* in the more general or generic sense of "man" (*'ādām*), a human being: "He that smiteth a man, so that he die, shall be surely put to death" (Exod. 21:12). Even if one strikes a woman or child and he or she dies, the attacker should be put to death. Again, notice Deut. 27:15: "Cursed be the man that maketh any graven or molten image. . . ." This is the sense of the word when it is contrasted with animals: "But against any of the children of Israel shall not a dog move his tongue, against man or beast . . ." (Exod. 11:7). The same nuance appears when man over against God is in view: "God is not a man, that he should lie . . ." (Num. 23:19).

Sometimes *'îsh* is indefinite, meaning "somebody" or "someone" ("they"): "And I will make thy seed as the dust of the earth: so that if a man can number the dust of the earth, then shall thy seed also be numbered" (Gen. 13:16). In other passages the word suggests the meaning "each" (Gen. 40:5). Closely related to the previous nuance is the connotation "every" (Jer. 23:35).

The word *'îshôn* means "little man." This diminutive form of the noun, which appears 3 times, has a cognate in Arabic. Although it literally means "little man," it signifies the pupil of the eye and is so translated (cf. Deut. 32:10 NASB; RSV and KJV, "apple of his eye").

'enôsh (אֱנוֹשׁ), "man." This common Semitic word is the usual word for "man" (generic) in biblical Aramaic (This meaning is served by Hebrew *'ādām*). It occurs 25 times in biblical Aramaic and 42 times in biblical Hebrew. Hebrew uses *'enôsh* exclusively in poetical passages. The only apparent exception is 2 Chron. 14:11, but this is a prayer and, therefore, uses poetical words.

'Enôsh never appears with the definite article and at all times except once (Ps. 144:3) sets forth a collective idea, "man." In most cases where the word occurs in Job and the Psalms it suggests the frailty, vulnerability, and finitude of "man" as contrasted to God: "As for man, his days are as grass: as a flower of the field, so he flourisheth" (Ps. 103:15). As such "man" cannot be righteous or holy before God: "Shall mortal man be more just than God? Shall a man be more pure than his Maker?" (Job 4:17). In the Psalms this word is used to indicate the enemy: "Arise, O Lord; let not man prevail: let the heathen be judged in thy sight" (Ps. 9:19). Here the parallelism shows that *'enôsh* is synonymous with "nations," or the enemy. They are, therefore, presented as weak, vulnerable, and finite: "Put them in fear, O Lord: that the nations may know themselves to be but men" (Ps. 9:20).

'Enôsh may connote "men" as weak but not necessarily morally weak: Blessed is the man that doeth this, and the son of man that layeth hold of it" (Isa. 56:2). In this passage the *'enôsh* is blessed because he has been morally strong.

In a few places the word bears no moral overtones and represents "man" in a sense parallel to Hebrew *'ādām*. He is finite as contrasted to the infinite God: "I said, I would scatter them into corners, I would make the remembrance of them to cease from among men" (Deut. 32:26—the first biblical occurrence).

bāchûr (בָּחוּר), "young man." The 44 occurrences of this word are scattered throughout every period of biblical Hebrew.

This word signifies the fully developed, vigorous, unmarried man. In its first occurrence *bāchûr* is contrasted to *bəthûlāh*, "maiden": "The sword without, and terror within, shall destroy both the young man and the virgin, the suckling also with the man of gray hairs" (Deut. 32:25). The strength of the "young man" is contrasted with the gray hair (crown of honor) of old men (Prov. 20.29).

The period during which a "young man" is in his prime (could this be the period during which he is eligible for the draft—i.e., age 20-50?) is represented by the two nouns, *bachûrîm* and *bəchûrôth*, both of which occur only once. *Bəchûrîm* is found in Num. 11:28.

B. Verb.

bāchar (בָּחַר), "to examine; choose; select; choose out; elect; prefer." This verb, which occurs 146 times in biblical Hebrew, has cognates in late Aramaic and Coptic. The poetic noun *bāchîr*, "chosen or elect one(s)," is also derived from this verb. Not all scholars agree that these words are related to the noun *bāchûr*. They would relate it to the first sense of *bchr*, whose cognate in Akkadian has to do with fighting men. The word means "choose or select" in Gen. 6:2: ". . . and they took them wives of all which they chose."

TO BE MARVELOUS

A. Verb.

pālā' (אְלָפָ), "to be marvelous, be extraordinary; be beyond one's power to do, do wonderful acts." As can be seen from the suggested meanings, this verb is not easy to define. As a denominative verb, it is based on the noun for "wonder, marvel," so it expresses the idea of doing or making a wondrous thing. Found in both biblical and modern Hebrew, *pālā'* occurs some 70 times in the Hebrew Old Testament. The verb is found for the first time in Gen. 18:14: "Is any thing too hard for the Lord?"

Pālā' is used primarily with God as its subject, expressing actions that are beyond the bounds of human powers or expectations. This idea is well expressed by the psalmist: "This is the Lord's doing; it is marvelous in our eyes" (Ps. 118:23). Deliverance from Egypt was the result of God's wondrous acts: "And I will stretch out my hand, and smite Egypt with all my wonders which I will do in [it] . . ." (Exod. 3:20). Praise is constantly due God for all His wonderful deeds (Ps. 9:1). At the same time, God does not require anything of His people that is too hard for them (Deut. 30:11). Although something may appear impossible to man, it still is within God's power: "If it be marvelous in the eyes of the remnant of this people in these days, should it also be marvelous in mine eyes? saith the Lord of hosts" (Zech. 8:6).

B. Noun.

pele' (אְלֶפֶ), "wonder; marvel." This noun frequently expresses the "wonder," the extraordinary aspects, of God's dealings with His people (Exod. 15:11; Ps. 77:11; Isa. 29:14). The messianic title, "marvel of a counselor" (Isa. 9:6, KJV; RSV, "wonderful counselor"), points toward God's Anointed continuing the marvelous acts of God.

TO MEASURE

A. Verb.

mādad (דדַמָ), "to measure, measure off, extend." Found in both ancient and modern Hebrew, in modern usage this word has the nuance of "to survey." The word has cognates in Akkadian, Phoenician, and Arabic. It occurs 53 times in the text of the Hebrew Old Testament. The basic meaning of the verb is illustrated in its first occurrence in the Old Testament: ". . . they did mete it with an omer . . ." (Exod. 16:18). *Mādad* is used not only of "measuring" volume but also of "measuring" distance (Deut. 21:2) and length (Num. 35:5).

A rather gruesome use is found in 2 Sam. 8:2, where, after defeating the Moabites, David "measured them with a line, casting them down to the ground; even with two lines measured he to put to death, and with one full line to keep alive."

The greatness of the creator God is expressed in the question, "Who hath measured the waters in the hollow of his hand . . . ?" (Isa. 40:12). Also, God "stood, and measured [NASB, "surveyed"] the earth" (Hab. 3:6).

Mādad can express the idea of extending, stretching: "And he stretched himself upon the child three times . . ." (1 Kings 17:21).

B. Noun.

middāh (מִדָּה), "measure; measurement; extent; size; stature; section; area." Of the 53 times this noun appears, 25 appearances are in Ezekiel. The rest of the word's occurrences are scattered throughout every period of biblical Hebrew.

This noun refers to the act of "measurement": "You shall do no wrong in judgment, in measures of length or weight or quantity" (Lev. 19:35 RSV). In Ezek. 41:17 this word is used of length "measurement," and in Job 28:25 of liquid "measurement."

Second, *middāh* means the thing measured, or the "size." Exod. 26:2 (the first occurrence) specifies: ". . . Every one of the curtains shall have one measure [the same size]." The word can also refer to the duration of one's life: "Lord, make me to know [realize] mine end, and the measure of my days [how short my life really is] . . ." (Ps. 39:4). A "man of measure" is one of great "stature or size": "And he [Benaiah] slew an Egyptian, a man of great stature, five cubits [about 7½ feet] high . . ." (1 Chron. 11:23).

Third, *middāh* sometimes represents a "measured portion" of a thing: "Malchijah the son of Harim, and Hashub the son of Pahath–moab, repaired the other piece, and the tower of the furnaces" (Neh. 3:11). In Ezek. 45:3 the word appears to represent a "measured area."

TO MEDITATE

hāgāh (הָגָה), "to meditate; moan, growl, utter, speak." This word is common to both ancient and modern Hebrew. Found only 25 times in the Hebrew Old Testament, it seems to be an onomatopoetic term, reflecting the sighing and low sounds one may make while musing, at least as the ancients practiced it. This meaning is seen in its first occurrence in the text: "This book of the law shall not depart out of thy mouth; but thou shalt meditate therein day and night . . ." (Josh. 1:8). Perhaps the most famous reference "to meditating" on the law day and night is Ps. 1:2.

Hāgāh also expresses the "growl" of lions (Isa. 31:4) and the "mourning" of doves (Isa. 38:14). When the word is used in the sense of "to mourn," it apparently emphasizes the sorrowful sounds of mourning, as seen in this parallelism: "Therefore will I howl for Moab, and I will cry out for all Moab; mine heart shall mourn for the men of Kir-heres" (Jer. 48:31). The idea that mental exercise, planning, often is accompanied by low talking seems to be reflected by Prov. 24:1-2: "Be not thou envious against evil men, . . . for their heart studieth destruction, and their lips talk of mischief."

MESSIAH

A. Nouns.

māshîach (מָשִׁיחַ), "anointed one; Messiah." Of the 39 occurrences of *māshîach*, none occurs in the wisdom literature. They are scattered throughout the rest of biblical literary types and periods.

First, *māshîach* refers to one who is anointed with oil, symbolizing the reception of the Holy Spirit, enabling him to do an assigned task. Kings (1 Sam. 24:6), high priests, and some prophets (1 Kings 19:16) were so anointed: "If the priest that is anointed do sin according to the sin of the people . . ." (Lev. 4:3—the first biblical appearance). In the case of Cyrus, he was anointed with God's Spirit only and commissioned an "anointed deliverer" of Israel (Isa. 45:1). The patriarchs, too, are called "anointed ones": "Touch not mine anointed, and do my prophets no harm" (Ps. 105:15).

Second, the word is sometimes transliterated "Messiah." After the promise to David (2 Sam. 7:13) *māshîach* refers immediately to the Davidic dynasty, but ultimately it points to the "Messiah," Jesus the Christ: "The kings of the earth [take their stand], and the rulers take counsel together, against the Lord, and against his Anointed . . ." (Ps. 2:2). In Dan. 9:25 the word is transliterated: "Know therefore and understand, that from the going forth of the commandment to restore and to build Jerusalem unto the Messiah the Prince. . . ." The New Testament also attests the word in this latter meaning (John 1:41). Most frequently in the New Testament the word is translated ("Christ") rather than transliterated ("Messiah"). *See also* ANOINT.

mishǝchāh (מָשְׁחָה), "anointment." This noun occurs 21 times and only in Exodus, Leviticus, and Numbers. It always follows the Hebrew word for oil. The first occurrence is Exod. 25:6: "Oil for the light, spices for anointing oil, and for sweet incense."

B. Verb.

māshach (מָשַׁח), "to smear with oil or paint; anoint." This verb, which appears 69 times in biblical Hebrew, has cognates in Ugaritic, Akkadian, Aramaic, and Arabic. The objects of this verb are people, sacrificial victims, and objects of worship. Aaron and his sons are the objects of this verb in Exod. 30:30: "And thou shalt anoint Aaron and his sons, and consecrate them, that they may minister unto me in the priest's office."

MIDST

tāwek (תָּוֶךְ), "midst; middle." This word, which also appears in Ugaritic, occurs about 418 times in biblical Hebrew and in all periods.

Tāwek indicates the part of a space, place, number of people, things, or line which is not on the end or outside edge. This emphasis is in Gen. 9:21: "And he [Noah] drank of the wine, and was drunken; and he was uncovered within [literally, in the midst of] his tent." In many contexts the word means "among," not necessarily in the middle: ". . . And he [Pharaoh] lifted up the head of the chief butler and of the chief baker among [literally, in the midst of] his servants" (Gen. 40:20). Exod. 14:29 uses *tāwek* as an extension of the word "through": "But the children of Israel walked upon dry land in the midst of the sea. . . ." The idea "within" can be emphasized with the addition of words like *me'îm*, "belly, inwards," or *lēb*, "heart": ". . . My heart is like wax; it is melted in the midst of my bowels" (Ps. 22:14). This word also sometimes means simply "in" in the sense of "mixed into something": "And they did beat the gold into thin plates, and cut it into wires, to work it in the blue . . ." (Exod. 39:3).

Tāwek can mean "middle" when applied to an object or person between two others: "And they made bells of pure gold, and put the bells between the pomegranates upon the hem of the robe . . ." (Exod. 39:25). The same sense but a different translation is required in Judg. 15:4: "And Samson went and caught three hundred foxes, and took firebrands, and turned tail to tail, and put a firebrand in the midst between two tails." This appears to be the meaning of the word in its first biblical occurrence: "And God said, Let there be a firmament in the midst of the waters, and let it divide the waters from the waters" (Gen. 1:6). In Num. 35:5 the word means "in the center": "And ye shall measure from without the city on the east side two thousand cubits, and on the south side two thousand cubits, and on the west side two thousand cubits, and on the north side two thousand cubits; and the city shall be in the midst. . . ." In other passages this word signifies the hypothetical center line dividing something into two equal parts: "And he [Abraham] took unto him all these, and divided them in the midst, and laid each piece one against another . . ." (Gen. 15:10; cf. Ezek. 15:4).

In a few instances *tāwek* is used substantively, meaning "the middle or the center part of a thing": "Sihon king of the Amorites . . . ruled from Aroer, which is upon the bank of the river Arnon, and from the middle of the river . . ." (Josh. 12:2).

The word occurs only 7 times without a preceding preposition.

MIGHT

gəbûrāh (גְּבוּרָה), "might." This noun is found 61 times in the Hebrew Old Testament, predominantly in poetic books and in Isaiah and Jeremiah. The first occurrence is in Exod. 32:18: "And he said, It is not the voice of them that shout for mastery [*gəbûrāh*], neither is it the voice of them that cry for being overcome: but the noise of them that sing do I hear."

The primary meaning of *gəbûrāh* is "power" or "strength." Certain animals are known for their "strength," such as horses (Ps. 147:10) and crocodiles (Job 41:4). Man also demonstrates "might" in heroic acts (Judg. 8:21) and in war (Isa. 3:25). David's powerful regime is expressed as a "kingship of *gəbûrāh*" (1 Chron. 29:30; KJV, "his reign and his might"). Since both physical strength and wisdom were necessary for leadership, these two qualities are joined together: "Counsel is mine, and sound wisdom: I am understanding; I have strength" (Prov. 8:14). Also Micah, being filled with the Holy Spirit, said: "But truly I am full of power by the spirit of the Lord, and of judgment, and of might, to declare unto Jacob his transgression, and to Israel his sin" (Mic. 3:8). In messianic expectations the prophets projected the Messiah's special role as a demonstration of "might" and counsel: "And the spirit of the Lord shall rest upon him, the spirit of wisdom and understanding, the spirit of counsel and might, the spirit of knowledge and of the fear of the Lord" (Isa. 11:2).

The Psalms ascribe "might" to God. These characterizations are found either in the context of "praise": ". . . which by his strength setteth fast the mountains; being girded with power" (Ps. 65:6), or in the context of prayer: "Save me, O God, by thy name, and judge me by thy strength" (Ps. 54:1). The Lord's "might" is a manifestation of His wisdom: "With him is wisdom and strength, he hath counsel and understanding" (Job 12:13). In the plural *gəbûrāh* denotes God's mighty deeds of the past: "O Lord God, thou hast begun to show thy servant thy greatness, and thy mighty hand: for what God is there in heaven or in earth, that can do according to thy works, and according to thy might?" (Deut. 3:24).

The Septuagint gives the following translations: *dunasteis* ("ruler, sovereign; court official"); *ischus* ("strength; power; might"); and *dunamis* ("power; strength; might; ability; capability"). The KJV gives these senses: "might; strength; power; mighty acts."

TO MINISTER, SERVE

A. Verb.

shārath (שָׁרַת), "to minister, serve, officiate." This word is a common term in Hebrew usage, ancient and modern, in various verbal and noun forms. It occurs in ancient Phoenician, and some see it in ancient Ugaritic as well. *Shārath* is found just under 100 times in the Hebrew Old Testament. The first time it is used in the Hebrew Bible is in the story of Joseph as he becomes the slave of Potiphar: "And Joseph found grace in his sight, and he served [RSV, "attended"] him. . ." (Gen. 39:4).

As a term for serving or ministering, *shārath* is to be distinguished from the term for more menial serving, *'ābad,* from which the word meaning "slave" or "servant" is derived. *Shārath* is characteristically used of "serving" done by royal household workers (2 Sam. 13:17; 1 Kings 10:5). In the manner of the modern "public servant" idea, the word is used in reference to court officials and royal servants (1 Chron. 27:1; 28:1; Esther 1:10).

Elisha "ministered" to Elijah (1 Kings 19:21). Foreign kings are "to minister" to God's people (Isa. 60:10).

This term is used most frequently as the special term for service in worship. The Levitical priests "stand before the Lord to minister unto him" (Deut.

10:8). They also are "to stand before the congregation to minister unto them" (Num. 16:9). In the post-exilic temple, the Levites who had earlier "ministered" in idolatry will not be allowed "to serve" as priests but rather as maintenance workers in the temple (Ezek. 44:11-14).

B. Noun.

shārath (שָׁרַת), "minister; servant." The noun form of the verb appears several times meaning "minister" or "servant." As Moses' right-hand man Joshua is referred to as "minister" (KJV), "servant" (RSV, JB, NASB), "assistant" (NEB), or "aide" (NAB) in Exod. 24:13. Angels are God's "ministers . . . that do his pleasure" (Ps. 103:21; cf. Ps. 104:4).

MORNING
A. Noun.

bōqer (בֹּקֶר), "morning." This word occurs about 214 times and in every period of biblical Hebrew.

This word means "morning," though not the period of time before noon. Rather it indicates the point of time at which night is changing to day or that time at the end of night: "And Moses stretched forth his rod over the land of Egypt, and the Lord brought an east wind upon the land all that day, and all that night; and when it was morning, the east wind brought the locusts" (Exod. 10:13).

Bōqer can represent the time just before the rising of the sun. In Judg. 19:25 we read that the men of Gibeah raped and abused the Levite's concubine "all the night until the morning: and when the day began to spring, they let her go" (cf. Ruth 3:13). In the ancient Near East the night was divided into three watches. The last period of the night was called the morning watch (Exod. 14:24). It lasted from 2:00 A.M. until sunrise, and in such a context the word indicates this period of time.

Bōqer can mean "daybreak" or "dawn." In Exod. 14:27 it is reported that the water of the Red Sea "returned to his [normal state] when the morning appeared [literally, at the turning of the morning]." *Bōqer* is used as a synonym of "dawn" in Job 38:12: "Hast thou commanded the morning since thy days; and caused the dayspring to know his place . . . ?"

Sometimes *bōqer* appears to mean "early morning," or shortly after daybreak: "And Joseph came in unto them in the morning, and looked upon them and, behold, they were sad" (Gen. 40:6). Thus, Moses "rose up early in the morning" and went up to Mount Sinai; he arose before daybreak so he could appear before God in the "morning" as God had commanded (Exod. 34:2, 4). In the "morning" Jacob saw that his bride was Leah rather than Rachel (Gen. 29:25; cf. 1 Sam. 29:10).

As the opposite of night the word represents the entire period of daylight. The psalmist prays that it is good "to show forth thy loving-kindness in the morning, and thy faithfulness every night" (Ps. 92:2), in other words, to always be praising God (cf. Amos 5:8).

In Ps. 65:8 *bōqer* represents a place, specifically, the place where the sun rises: "They also that dwell in the uttermost parts are afraid at thy tokens: thou makest the outgoings of the morning and evening to rejoice."

At least once the word appears to represent the resurrection: "Like sheep they [the ungodly] are laid in the grave; death shall feed on them; and the upright shall have dominion over them in the morning . . ." (Ps. 49:14).

Bōqer can mean "morrow" or "next day." This meaning first appears in Exod. 12:10, where God tells Israel not to leave any of the Passover "until the morning; and that which remaineth of it until the morning ye shall burn with fire" (cf. Lev. 22:30).

B. Verb.

bāqar (בָּקַר), "to attend, bestow care on, seek with pleasure." Although this verb is found only 7 times in biblical Hebrew, it occurs in early, middle, and late periods and in both prose and poetry. The word has cognates in Arabic and Nabataean. Some scholars relate to this verb the noun *bāqār*, "herd, cattle, ox."

In Lev. 13:36 *bāqar* means "to attend to": ". . . If the scall be spread in the skin, the priest shall not seek for yellow hair. . . ." The word implies "to seek with pleasure or delight" in Ps. 27:4: ". . . to behold the beauty of the Lord, and to inquire [*bāqar*] in his temple."

MOTHER

'ēm (אֵם), "mother; grandmother; stepmother." Cognates of this word appear in nearly all Semitic languages including Ugaritic and Aramaic. Biblical Hebrew attests it 220 times and in all periods.

The basic meaning of the word has to do with the physical relationship of the individual called "mother." This emphasis of the word is in Gen. 2:24 (the first biblical appearance): "Therefore shall a man leave his father and his mother, and shall cleave unto his wife. . . ." *'Ēm* sometimes represents an animal "mother": "Likewise shalt thou do with thine oxen, and with thy sheep: seven days it shall be with its [mother]; on the eighth day thou shalt give it me" (Exod. 22:30). The phrase "father and mother" is the biblical phrase for parents: "And he brought up Hadassah, that is, Esther, his uncle's daughter: for she had neither father nor mother [living]" (Esth. 2:7). The "son of one's mother" is his brother (Gen. 43:29), just as the "daughter of one's mother" is his sister (Gen. 20:12). These phrases usually emphasize that the persons so represented are whole brothers or sisters, whereas the Hebrew words *'āch*, "brother," and *'achôth*, "sister," meaning both whole and half siblings, leave the issue unclear. On the other hand, in Gen. 27:29 this phrase appears to mean peoples more distantly related: "Let people serve thee, and nations bow down to thee: be lord over thy brethren, and let thy mother's sons bow down to thee: cursed be every one that curseth thee, and blessed be he that blesseth thee."

'Ēm can represent blood relatives further removed than one's mother. In 1 Kings 15:10 the word means "grandmother": "And forty and one years

reigned he in Jerusalem. And his [grand]mother's name was Maachah, the daughter of Abishalom." This word can also mean "stepmother." When Joseph told his dream to his family, "his father rebuked him, and said unto him, What is this dream that thou hast dreamed? Shall I and thy [step]mother and thy brethren indeed come to bow down ourselves to thee to the earth?" (Gen. 37:10; cf. 35:16 ff., where we read that Rachel died). The word can signify a mother-in-law, or the mother of one's wife: "And if a man take a wife and her mother, it is wickedness . . ." (Lev. 20:14). The woman through whom a nation originated is called its "mother"; she is the first or tribal "mother," an ancestress: "Thus saith the Lord God unto Jerusalem; Thy birth and thy nativity is of the land of Canaan; thy father was an Amorite, and thy mother a Hittite" (Ezek. 16:3). Even further removed physically is Eve, "the mother of all living" (Gen. 3:20).

'Ēm can represent all one's female forebears: "Let the iniquity of his fathers be remembered with the Lord; and let not the sin of his mother be blotted out" (Ps. 109:14).

A group of people, a people, or a city may be personified and called a "mother." Hosea calls the priests (probably) the "mother" of Israel: ". . . And the prophet also shall fall with thee in the night, and I will destroy thy mother" (Hos. 4:5). The people of Israel, the northern kingdom, are the "mother" of Judah: "Where is the bill of your mother's divorcement, whom I have put away? or which of my creditors is it to whom I have sold you? Behold, for your iniquities have ye sold yourselves, and for your transgressions is your mother put away" (Isa. 50:1; cf. Hos. 2:4, 7).

An important city may be called a "mother" of its citizens: ". . . Thou seekest to destroy a city and a mother in Israel. . ." (2 Sam. 20:19).

The title "mother in Israel" was a title of respect in Deborah's day (Judg. 5:7).

"The mother of a way" is the starting point for roads: "For the king of Babylon stood at the parting of the way, at the head of the two ways, to use divination . . ." (Ezek. 21:21).

MOUNTAIN RANGE

har (הַר), "mountain range; mountainous region; mount." This word also appears in Ugaritic, Phoenician, and Punic. Biblical Hebrew attests it about 558 times and in all periods.

In its first biblical appearance *har* refers to the "mountain range" upon which Noah's ark came to rest (Gen. 8:4). In the singular form the word can mean a "mountain range" or the "mountains" of a given area: ". . . And [he] set his face toward the mount [NASB, "hill country"] Gilead" (Gen. 31:21). Jacob was fleeing from Laban toward the "mountains" where he thought to find protection. A further extension of this meaning applies this word to an area which is primarily mountainous; the word focuses on the territory in general rather than on the mountains in particular: "And they gave them the city of Arba the father of Anak, which city is Hebron, in the hill country of Judah, with the suburbs thereof round about it" (Josh. 21:11).

The word can be used of particular "mountains": ". . . And he led the flock to the backside of the desert, and came to the mountain of God, even to Horeb'' (Exod. 3:1). In this particular instance "the mountain of God" refers to Horeb. Elsewhere it is Jerusalem: "Why leap ye, ye high hills? This is the hill which God desireth to dwell in; yea, the Lord will dwell in it for ever'' (Ps. 68:16).

Har signifies inhabitable sites situated on hills and/or mountainsides: "And at that time came Joshua, and cut off the Anakim from the mountains, from Hebron, from Debir, from Anab, and from all the mountains of Judah, and from all the mountains of Israel: Joshua destroyed them utterly with their cities" (Josh. 11:21). In this regard, compare Deut. 2:37: "Only unto the land of the children of Ammon thou camest not, nor unto any place of the river Jabbok, nor unto the cities in the mountains, nor unto whatsoever the Lord our God forbade us." A comparison of Judg. 1:35 and Josh. 19:41 shows that Mount Heres is the same as the city of Heres.

In the poetical literature of the Old Testament, the view of the world held by men of that era finds its reflection. One can speak of the foundations of the mountains as rooted in the underworld (Deut. 32:22), serving to support the earth as the "bars" of the earth (Jonah 2:6). Mountain peaks may be said to reach into the heavens where God dwells (Isa. 24:21; in Gen. 11:4, the men who built the tower at Babel erroneously thought they were going to reach God's dwelling place). Although it would be wrong to conclude that God is setting forth this understanding of creation, yet He used it in explaining His word to men just as He used other contemporaneous ideas. Since "mountains" were associated with deity (Isa. 14:13), God chose to make great revelations on "mountains," concretely impressing the recipients with the solemnity and authority of the message (Deut. 27; Josh. 8:30-35). At the same time such locations provided for better audibility and visibility (Judg. 9:7; 2 Chron. 13:4). "Mountains" often serve as a symbol of strength (Zech. 4:7) inasmuch as they carried mythological significance since many people thought of them as sacred areas (Jer. 3:22-23), and they were the locations of strong fortresses (Josh. 10:6). Even the "mountains" tremble before the Lord; He is mightier than they are (Job 14:18).

TO MOURN

'ābal (אָבַל), "to mourn, lament." This word is common to both ancient and modern Hebrew. Found in the Hebrew Old Testament 39 times, *'ābal* is used in the simple, active verbal form primarily in poetry, and usually in a figurative sense. When it is used of mourning for the dead in a literal sense, the word is found in prose sections and in the reflexive form, indicating action back on the subject. It first occurs in Gen. 37:34: "And Jacob . . . mourned for his son many days."

When used in the figurative sense, *'ābal* expresses "mourning" by gates (Isa. 3:26), by the land (Isa. 24:4), and by pastures (Amos 1:2). In addition to mourning for the dead, "mourning" may be over Jerusalem (Isa. 66:10), over sin (Ezra 10:6), or over God's judgment (Exod. 33:4). One may pretend to be a mourner (2 Sam. 14:2) simply by putting on mourning clothes.

MOUTH

peh (פֶּה), "mouth; edge; opening; entrance; collar; utterance; order; command; evidence." This word has cognates in Ugaritic, Akkadian, Arabic, Aramaic, and Amorite. It appears about 500 times and in every period of biblical Hebrew.

First, the word means "mouth." It is often used of a human "mouth": "And he shall be thy spokesman unto the people: and he shall be, even he shall be to thee instead of a mouth . . ." (Exod. 4:16). In passages such as Num. 22:28 this word represents an animal's "mouth": "And the Lord opened the mouth of the ass, and she said unto Balaam. . . ." When used of a bird's "mouth" it refers to its beak: "And the dove came in to him in the evening; and, lo, in her mouth was an olive leaf plucked off . . ." (Gen. 8:11). This word may be used figuratively of "the mouth of the ground," referring to the fact that liquid went into the ground—the ground drank it: "And now art thou cursed from the earth, which hath opened her mouth to receive thy brother's blood from thy hand" (Gen. 4:11—the first biblical occurrence). A similar use appears in Ps. 141:7: "Our bones are scattered at the grave's mouth. . . ." In this case Sheol is perhaps conceived as a pit and then personified with its "mouth" consuming men once they die.

Second, this word can be used in an impersonal, nonpersonified sense of an "opening": "And he looked, and behold a well in the field, and, lo, there were three flocks of sheep lying by it; for out of that well they watered the flocks: and a great stone was upon the well's mouth" (Gen. 29:2). In Isa. 19:7 this word represents the "edge" of a river: "The paper reeds by the brooks, by the mouth of the brooks, and every thing sown by the brooks, shall wither, be driven away. . . ." Gen. 42:27 uses *peh* to refer to an orifice, or the area within the edges of a sack's opening: ". . . He espied his money; for, behold, it was in his sack's mouth." A similar use appears in Josh. 10:18, where the word is used of a cave "entrance" or "opening." *Peh* can mean not only an opening which is closed in on all sides but a city gate, an opening opened at the top: ". . . at the gates, at the entry of the city, at the coming in at the doors" (Prov. 8:3). Exod. 28:32 uses this word to mean an "opening" in a tunic around which a collar would be woven: "And there shall be a hole in the top of it, in the midst thereof: it shall have a binding of woven work round about the hole of it, as it were the hole of a habergeon, that it be not rent." Job 30:18 uses the word of the "collar" itself: "By the great force of my disease is my garment changed: it bindeth me about as the collar of my coat" (cf. Ps. 133:2).

In several passages *peh* represents the edge of a sword, perhaps in the sense of the part that consumes and/or bites: "And they slew Hamor and Shechem his son with the edge of the sword . . ." (Gen. 34:26).

Several noteworthy idioms employ *peh*. In Josh. 9:2 "with one mouth" means "with one accord": ". . . That they gathered themselves together, to fight with Joshua and with Israel, with one accord." In Num. 12:8 God described His unique communication as "mouth to mouth" or person to person. A similar construction appears in Jer. 32:4 (cf. 34:3, which has the same force): "And Zedekiah king of Judah shall not escape out of the hand of the Chaldeans, but shall surely be delivered into the hand of the king of Babylon, and shall speak with him mouth to mouth, and his eyes shall behold his eyes." The phrase "from mouth to mouth" or "mouth to mouth" can mean "from end to end": "And they came into the house of Baal; and the house of Baal was full from one end to another" (2 Kings 10:21). "With open mouth" is a phrase which emphasizes greedy consumption: "The Syrians before, and the Philistines behind; and they shall devour Israel with open mouth" (Isa. 9:12). Placing one's hands on one's mouth is a gesture of silence (Job 29:9). "To ask someone's mouth" is to ask him personally: "We will call the damsel, and inquire at her mouth [NASB, "consult her wishes"]" (Gen. 24:57).

This word can also stand for "utterance" or "order": "Thou shalt be over my house, and according unto thy word shall all my people be ruled . . ." (Gen. 41:40). "The mouth of two witnesses" means their testimony: "Whoso killeth any person, the murderer shall be put to death by the mouth of witnesses. . ." (Num. 35:30). In Jer. 36:4 "from the mouth of Jeremiah" means "by dictation": ". . . And Baruch wrote from the mouth of Jeremiah all words of the Lord . . . upon a [scroll]."

Peh used with various prepositions has special meanings. (1) Used with *kə*, it means "according to." In Lev. 25:52 this construction has the special nuance "in proportion to": "And if there remain but few years unto the year of jubilee, then he shall count with him, and according unto [in proportion to] his years shall he give him again the price of his redemption." The meaning "according to" appears in passages such as Num. 7:5: "Take it of them, that they may be to do the service of the tabernacle of the congregation; and thou shalt give them unto the Levites, to every man according to his service." The phrase means "as much as" in Exod. 16:21. A different nuance appears in Job 33:6: "Behold, I am according to thy wish in God's stead. . . ." (2) When the word is preceded by *lə*, its meanings are quite similar to those just discussed. In Lev. 25:51 it means "in proportion to." Jer. 29:10 uses the word in the sense "according to": "After seventy years be accomplished at Babylon," which can be read literally, "according to the fullness of the seventy years of Babylon." (3) With *'al* the word also means "according to" or "in proportion to" (cf. Lev. 27:18).

The phrase *pî shənayim* (literally, "two mouths") has two different meanings. In Deut. 21:17 it means "double portion" (two parts): "But he shall acknowledge the son of the hated for the first-born, by giving him a double portion of all that he hath. . . ." This same phrase, however, also means "two thirds": "And it shall come to pass, that in all the land, saith the Lord, two parts therein shall be cut off and die; but the third shall be left therein" (Zech. 13:8).

TO MULTIPLY, INCREASE

A. Verb.

rābāh (רָבָה), "to multiply, become numerous, become great." This verb also occurs in Akkadian, Arabic, Amorite, and biblical Aramaic. Biblical Hebrew attests it about 220 times and in all periods. This word should be compared to *gādal* and *rābab*.

Basically this word connotes numerical increase. It can refer to the process of increasing numerically: God told the sea and air creatures to "be fruitful, and multiply" (Gen. 1:22—the first occurrence). In Gen. 38:12 the word refers to the end result in the sense that a great many of something existed: "And in process of time the daughter of Shuah Judah's wife died [literally, and the days became multiplied]. . . ." When used with "days," the word may also signify "long life": ". . . I shall multiply my days as the sand" (Job 29:18: cf. Prov. 4:10). *Rābāh* sometimes refers to increasing in wealth, although in such cases the material is clearly specified (cf. Deut. 8:13: ". . . and thy silver and thy gold is multiplied").

This verb can be used of being quantitatively large. In Gen. 7:17 the waters are said to have "increased, and bare up the ark, and it was lifted up above the earth." So here the verb means "to increase in quantity." A similar use occurs in Gen. 15:1, where God tells Abram: "I am . . . thy exceeding great reward." The first instance speaks of the process of increasing and the latter of the end product (something that is larger).

In a special nuance this verb signifies the process of growing up: "Their young ones are in good liking, they grow up [in the open field]" (Job 39:4). *Rābāh* can also be used of the end product: "I have caused thee to multiply as the bud of the field, and thou hast increased and waxen great, and thou art come to excellent ornaments: thy breasts are fashioned, and thine hair is grown . . ." (Ezek. 16:7). A somewhat different nuance occurs in Ezek. 19:2, where the verb speaks of a parent's care for an offspring: ". . . She nourished her whelps."

Rābāh is sometimes used with another verb to signify its increase in occurrence or frequency. In some passages it signifies that a process is continuing: "The people bring much more than enough for the service of the work. . ." (Exod. 36:5), literally, "the people continue to bring." It can also signify a great number of times with the sense of "repeatedly." The sinner is urged to return to God, "for he will abundantly pardon" (Isa. 55:7). This sense appears clearly in Amos 4:4: "Come to Beth-el, and transgress; at Gilgal multiply transgression. . . ."

B. Nouns.

'arəbeh (אַרְבֶּה), "locust." This noun, which occurs 24 times, refers to a kind of swarming "locust": "Stretch out thine hand over the land of Egypt for the locusts, that they may come up upon the land of Egypt, and eat every herb of the land . . ." (Exod. 10:12).

Several other nouns related to this verb appear infrequently. *Marəbeh*, which appears once, means "abundance" (Isa. 33:23). *Marəbîth*, which is found 5 times, refers to a "greater number" (1 Sam. 2:33) or the "greater half" (2 Chron. 9:6). *Tarəbûth* has a single appearance to mean "increase" (Num. 32:14). *Tarəbîth*, which occurs 6 times, can mean "interest, increment, usury" (Lev. 25:36).

MULTITUDE

A. Noun.

hāmôn (הָמוֹן), ''multitude; lively commotion; agitation; tumult; uproar; commotion; turmoil; noise; crowd; abundance.'' This noun appears 85 times in biblical Hebrew and in all periods.

The word represents a ''lively commotion or agitation'': ''Look down from heaven, and behold from the habitation of thy holiness and of thy glory: where is thy zeal and thy strength, the sounding of thy bowels and of thy mercies toward me?'' (Isa. 63:15).

Hāmôn represents the stirring or agitation of a crowd of people: ''When Joab sent the king's servant, and me thy servant, I saw a great tumult, but I knew not what it was'' (2 Sam. 18:29). In Isa. 17:12 the word is synonymously parallel to *shā'ôn*, ''rumbling'': ''Woe to the multitude of many people, which make a noise like the noise of the seas; and to the rushing of nations, that make a rushing like the rushing of mighty waters!''

Sometimes *hāmôn* represents the noise raised by an agitated crowd of people (a ''tumult''): ''And when Eli heard the noise of the crying, he said, What meaneth the noise of this tumult [raised by the report that the battle was lost]?'' (1 Sam. 4:14). In Isa. 13:4 the word represents the mighty sound of a gathering army rather than the confused outcry of a mourning city: ''The noise of a multitude in the mountains, like as of a great people; a tumultuous noise of the kingdoms of nations gathered together: the Lord of hosts mustereth the host of the battle.'' A young lion eating his prey is not disturbed by the noise of a band of shepherds trying to scare him off (Isa. 31:4). There are exceptions to the rule that the word represents the sound of a large number of people. In 1 Kings 18:41 *hāmôn* signifies the roar of a heavy downpour of rain (cf. Jer. 10:13), and in Jer 47:3 it represents the tumult of chariots.

Hāmôn sometimes means a ''multitude or crowd'' from which a tumult may arise. Frequently the word represents a large army: ''And I will draw unto thee, to the river Kishon, Sisera, the captain of Jabin's army, with his chariots and his multitude [NASB, ''many troops''] . . .'' (Judg. 4:7; cf. 1 Sam. 14:16). Elsewhere *hāmôn* represents a whole people: ''And he dealt among all the people, even among the whole multitude of Israel . . .'' (2 Sam. 6:19). Finally, any great throng, or a great number of people (Gen. 17:4—the first occurrence) may be represented by this word.

A great number of things can be indicated by *hāmôn:* ''O Lord our God, all this store that we have prepared to build thee a house for thine holy name . . .'' (1 Chron. 29:16).

Abundance of possessions or wealth is indicated by *hāmôn,* as in: ''A little that a righteous man hath is better than the riches of many wicked'' (Ps. 37:16; cf. Eccl. 5:10—parallel to ''silver [money]''; Isa. 60:5).

Finally, *hāmôn* refers to a group of people organized around a king, specifically, his courtiers: ''Son of man, speak unto Pharaoh king of Egypt, and to his multitude [his train or royal retinue]; Whom art thou like in thy greatness?'' (Ezek. 31:2). Thus in Ps. 42:4 the word can represent a festival procession, a kind of train.

B. Verb.

hāmāh (הָמָה), "to make a noise, be tumultuous, roar, groan, bark, sound, moan." This verb, which occurs 33 times in biblical Hebrew, has cognates in Aramaic and Arabic. Psalm 83:2 contains one appearance: "For, lo, thine enemies make a tumult: and they that hate thee have lifted up the head."

N

NAKEDNESS

A. Nouns.

'erəwāh (עֶרְוָה), "nakedness; indecent thing." Thirty-two of the 53 occurrences of this noun are in the social laws of Lev. 18, 20. The rest of its appearances are scattered throughout the various periods of Old Testament literature with the notable exception of poetical literature.

This word represents male or female sexual organs. In its first biblical appearance *'erəwāh* implies shameful exposure: "And Ham, the father of Canaan, saw the nakedness of his father. . . . And Shem and Japheth took a garment, and laid it upon both their shoulders, and went backward, and covered the nakedness of their father; and their faces were backward, and they saw not their father's nakedness" (Gen. 9:22-23). This word is often used of female nakedness (the uncovered sex organs) and is symbolical of shame. In Lam. 1:8 plundered, devastated Jerusalem is pictured as a woman whose nakedness is exposed. To uncover one's nakedness is a frequent euphemism for cohabitation: "None of you shall approach to any that is near of kin to him, to uncover their nakedness: I am the Lord" (Lev. 18:6).

The phrase "indecent thing" represents any uncleanness in a military camp or any violation of the laws of sexual abstinence—nocturnal emission not properly cleansed, sexual cohabitation and other laws of purity (for example, excrement buried in the camp): "For the Lord thy God walketh in the midst of thy camp, to deliver thee, and to give up thine enemies before thee; therefore shall thy camp be holy: that he see no unclean thing [literally, a matter of an indecent thing] in thee, and turn away from thee" (Deut. 23:14). In Deut. 24:1 *'erəwāh* appears to bear this emphasis on any violation of the laws of purity— if a groom is dissatisfied with his bride "because he hath found some *uncleanness* in her," he may divorce her. Obviously this evidence is not of previous cohabitation, since such a sin merits death (Deut. 22:13 ff.).

The "undefended parts" or nakedness of a land is represented by *'erəwāh* in Gen. 42:9: "Ye are spies; to see the nakedness of the land ye are come."

Other nouns related to this word appear less often. *Ma'ar*, which refers to "sexual nakedness," appears in a figurative sense in Nah. 3:5. *'Êrōm* appears as a noun abstract in several instances. This word represents the more general idea of being without clothes, with no necessary suggestion of shamefulness; it means the "state of being unclothed." In Ezek. 16:7,39 the word *'êrōm* appears as "naked," but it can literally be translated as "nakedness" or one being in his "nakedness."

Two nouns, *ta'ar* and *môrāh*, have a different significance. *Ta'ar*, which occurs 13 times, means "razor" (Num. 6:5) or a "knife" to sharpen scribal pens (Jer. 36:23). The word's meaning of a "sword sheath" (1 Sam. 17:51) has a cognate in Ugaritic. *Môrāh* also means "razor" (1 Sam. 1:11).

B. Adjectives.

'ārôm (עָרוֹם), or *'ārōm* (עָרֹם), "naked." This word occurs 16 times. The first occurrence is in Gen. 2:25: "And they were both naked, the man and his wife, and were not ashamed."

Another adjective, found 6 times in biblical poetry, is *'erəyāh*. It appears to be a variant spelling of *'erəwāh*. One appearance is in Ezek. 16:22: ". . . When thou wast naked and bare. . . ."

C. Verb.

'ārāh (עָרָה), "to pour out, make bare, destroy, spread oneself out." This verb, which appears 14 times in biblical Hebrew, has cognates in Akkadian, Phoenician, Egyptian, and Syriac. The word means "to pour out" in Isa. 32:15: "Until the spirit be poured upon us from on high. . . ." The verb implies "to make bare" in Lev. 20:19. *'Ārāh* is used in the sense of "to destroy" in Isa. 3:17: "Therefore the Lord will smite with a scab the crown of the head of the daughters of Zion, and the Lord will discover their secret parts." In Ps. 37:35 the word means "to spread oneself out."

NAME

shēm (שֵׁם), "name; reputation; memory; renown." Cognates of this word appear in Akkadian, Ugaritic, Phoenician, Aramaic, and Arabic. This word appears about 864 times and in all periods of biblical Hebrew.

It is not always true that an individual's "name" reveals his essence. Names using foreign loan words and ancient words were probably often not understood. Of course, names such as "dog" (Caleb) and "bee" (Deborah) were not indicative of the persons who bore them. Perhaps some names indicated a single decisive characteristic of their bearer. In other cases, a "name" recalls an event or mood which the parent(s) experienced at or shortly before the child's birth and/or naming. Other names make a statement about an individual. This sense of a name as an identification appears in Gen. 2:19 (an early occurrence of this word): ". . . And whatsoever Adam called every living creature, that was the name thereof." On the other hand, the names by which God revealed Himself (*'Adōnāy, 'El, 'Elōhîm*) do reflect something of His person and work.

Shēm can be a synonym for "reputation" or "fame": "Go to, let us build us a city and a tower, whose top may reach unto heaven; and let us make us a name; lest we be scattered abroad upon the face of the whole earth" (Gen. 11:4). To "give a name for one" is to make him famous: "And what one nation in the earth is like thy people, even like Israel, whom God went to redeem for a people to himself, and to make a name, and to do for you great things and terrible, for thy land . . ." (2 Sam. 7:23). If a name goes forth for one, his "reputation" of fame is made known: "And thy renown went forth among the heathen for thy beauty . . ." (Ezek. 16:14). Fame may include power: "And he lifted up his spear against three hundred, and slew them, and had the name among three" (2 Sam. 23:18). This sense, "men of reputation," appears in Gen. 6:4: ". . . mighty men which were of old, men of renown."

This word is sometimes a synonym for "memory" or "reputation" (that which remains): ". . . And so they shall quench my coal which is left, and shall not leave to my husband neither name nor remainder upon the earth" (2 Sam. 14:7). In this respect "name" may include property, or an inheritance: "Why should the name of our father be done away from among his family, because he hath no son? Give unto us therefore a possession among the brethren of our father" (Num. 27:4).

Shēm can connote "renown" and "continuance" (in those remaining after one): "And they rose up before Moses, with certain of the children of Israel, two hundred and fifty princes of the assembly, famous in the congregation, men of renown" (Num. 16:2). This significance is in the phrase "to raise up his name after him": "What day thou buyest the field of the hand of Naomi, thou must buy it also of Ruth the Moabitess, the wife of the dead, to raise up the name of the dead upon his inheritance" (Ruth 4:5; cf. Deut. 9:14; 25:6).

NATION

gôy (גּוֹי), "nation; people; heathen." Outside the Bible, this noun appears only in the Mari texts (Akkadian) and perhaps in Phoenician-Punic. This word occurs about 56 times and in all periods of biblical Hebrew.

Gôy refers to a "people or nation," usually with overtones of territorial or governmental unity/identity. This emphasis is in the promise formulas where God promised to make someone a great, powerful, numerous "nation" (Gen. 12:2). Certainly these adjectives described the future characteristics of the individual's descendants as compared to other peoples (cf. Num. 14:12). So *gôy* represents a group of individuals who are considered as a unit with respect to origin, language, land, jurisprudence, and government. This emphasis is in Gen. 10:5 (the first occurrence): "By these were the isles of the Gentiles divided in their lands; every one after his tongue, after their families, in their nations." Deut. 4:6 deals not with political and national identity but with religious unity, its wisdom, insight, righteous jurisprudence, and especially its nearness to God: "Keep therefore and do them; for this is your wisdom and your understanding in the sight of the nations, which shall hear all these statutes, and say, Surely this great nation is a wise and understanding people." Certainly all this is viewed as the result of divine election (Deut. 4:32 ff.). Israel's greatness is due to the greatness of her God and the great acts He has accomplished in and for her.

The word *'am,* "people, nation," suggests subjective personal interrelationships based on common familial ancestry and/or a covenantal union, while *gôy* suggests a political entity with a land of its own: "Now therefore, I pray thee, if I have found grace in thy sight, show me thy way, that I may know thee, that I may find grace in thy sight: and consider that this nation is thy people" (Exod. 33:13). *Gôy* may be used of a people, however, apart from its territorial identity: "And ye shall be unto me a kingdom of priests, and a holy nation" (Exod. 19:6).

Gôy is sometimes almost a derogatory name for non-Israelite groups, or the "heathen": "And I will scatter you among the heathen, and will draw out a sword . . ." (Lev. 26:33). This negative connotation is not always present, however, when the word is used of the heathen: "For from the top of the rocks I see him, and from the hills I behold him: lo, the people shall dwell alone, and shall not be reckoned among the nations" (Num. 23:9). Certainly in contexts dealing with worship the *gôyim* are the non-Israelites: "They feared the Lord, and served their own gods, after the manner of the nations whom they carried away from thence" (2 Kings 17:33). In passages such as Deut. 4:38 *gôyim* specifically describes the early inhabitants of Canaan prior to the Israelite conquest. Israel was to keep herself apart from and distinct from the "heathen" (Deut. 7:1) and was an example of true godliness before them (Deut. 4:6). On the other hand, as a blessing to all the nations (Gen. 12:2) and as a holy "nation" and kingdom of priests (Exod. 19:6), Israel was to be the means by which salvation was declared to the nations (heathen) and they came to recognize God's sovereignty (Isa. 60). So the Messiah is the light of the nations (Isa. 49:6).

NEEDY (PERSON)

A. Noun.

'ebəyôn (אֶבְיוֹן), "needy (person)." This word also occurs in Ugaritic and Ethiopic. Biblical Hebrew attests it about 60 times (33 times in the Psalms alone) and in all periods.

This noun refers, first, to someone who is poor in a material sense. Such a one may have lost the land of his inheritance: "But the seventh year thou shalt let it rest and lie still; that the poor of thy people may eat: and what they leave the beasts of the field shall eat" (Exod. 23:11). He has come into difficult financial straits (Job 30:25) and perhaps lacks clothing (Job 31:19) or food (Ps. 132:15).

Secondly, *'ebəyôn* may refer to the lack of social standing which causes a need for protection. The first biblical occurrence bears this emphasis. God guarantees protection for such a one: "Thou shalt not wrest the judgment of thy poor in his cause" (Exod. 23:6). The godly man defends the needy and defenseless: "I was a father to the poor: and the cause which I knew not I searched out" (Job 29:16; cf. Prov. 31:9; Rom. 3:14–15). Divine provisions are encased in the Mosaic stipulations such as the seventh-year reversion of ancestral hereditary lands (Exod. 23:11), cancellation of loans (Deut. 15:4), and special extension of loans (Deut. 15:7, 9, 11).

Thirdly, this noun sometimes describes one's spiritual condition before

God: "Thus saith the Lord; For three transgressions of Israel, and for four, I will not turn away the punishment thereof; because they sold the righteous for silver, and the poor for a pair of shoes" (Amos 2:6). In this verse 'ebəyôn is in synonymous parallelism to "righteous," which means that it describes a moral quality.

B. Verb.

'ābāh (אָבָה), "to accede, accept, consent." This verb, which occurs about 52 times and in all periods of biblical Hebrew, is sometimes associated with the noun 'ebəyôn, "needy (person)." The same radicals appear in Akkadian ("to wish"), Arabic ("to refuse"), Aramaic ("to want"), and Egyptian ("to desire"). This verb means "to consent to" in Deut. 13:8: "Thou shalt not consent unto him, nor hearken unto him. . . ."

NEW; NEW MOON

A. Verb.

chādash (חָדַשׁ), "to renew." This verb occurs in post-Mosaic literature (with the exception of Job 10:17). The root is found in all the Semitic languages with the same sense; usually the radicals are h-d-th. The first appearance of chādash in the Bible is in 1 Sam. 11:14: "Then said Samuel to the people, Come, and let us go to Gilgal, and renew the kingdom there."

B. Noun.

chōdesh (חֹדֶשׁ), "new moon; month." This noun occurs about 283 times in biblical Hebrew and in all periods.

The word refers to the day on which the crescent reappears: "So David hid himself in the field: and when the new moon was come, the king sat him down to eat meat" (1 Sam. 20:24). Isa. 1:14 uses this word of the feast which occurred on that day: "Your new moons [festivals] and your appointed feasts my soul hateth . . ." (cf. Num. 28:14; 29:6).

Chōdesh can refer to a "month," or the period from one new moon to another. The sense of a measure of time during which something happens occurs in Gen. 38:24: "And it came to pass about three months after, that it was told Judah. . . ." In a related nuance the word refers not so much to a measure of time as to a period of time, or a calendar month. These "months" are sometimes named (Exod. 13:4) and sometimes numbered (Gen. 7:11).

C. Adjective.

chādāsh (חָדָשׁ), "new; renewed." This adjective appears 53 times in biblical Hebrew.

Chādāsh means "new" both in the sense of recent or fresh (as the opposite of old) and in the sense of something not previously existing. The first nuance appears in Lev. 23:16: "Even unto the morrow after the seventh sabbath shall ye number fifty days; and ye shall offer a new meat offering unto the Lord." The first biblical occurrence of *chādāsh* (Exod. 1:8) demonstrates the second meaning: "Now there arose up a new king over Egypt, which knew not Joseph." This second nuance occurs in Isaiah's discussion of the future salvation. For example, in Isa. 42:10 a new saving act of God will bring forth a new song of praise to Him: "Sing unto the Lord a new song, and his praise from the end of the earth. . . ." The Psalter uses the phrase "a new song" in this sense; a new saving act of God has occurred and a song responding to that act celebrates it. The "new" is often contrasted to the former: "Behold, the former things are come to pass, and new things do I declare: before they spring forth I tell you of them" (Isa. 42:9). Jer. 31:31-34 employs this same nuance speaking of the new covenant (cf. Ezek. 11:19; 18:31).

A unique meaning appears in Lam. 3:23, where *chādāsh* appears to mean "renewed"; just as God's creation is renewed and refreshed, so is His compassion and lovingkindness: "They are new every morning: great is thy faithfulness." This nuance is more closely related to the verb from which this word is derived.

NIGHT

layəlāh (לַיְלָה), "night." Cognates of this noun appear in Ugaritic, Moabite, Akkadian, Aramaic, Syrian, Arabic, and Ethiopic. The word appears about 227 times in biblical Hebrew and in all periods.

Layəlāh means "night," the period of time during which it is dark: "And God called the light Day, and the darkness he called Night" (Gen. 1:5—the first biblical appearance). In Exod. 13:21 and similar passages the word means "by night," or "during the night": "And the Lord went before them by day in a pillar of cloud . . . and by night in a pillar of fire, to give them light; to go by day and night." This word is used figuratively of protection: "Take counsel, execute judgment; make thy shadow as the night in the midst of the noonday; hide the outcasts; [betray] not him that wandereth" (Isa. 16:3). *Layəlāh* also figures deep calamity without the comforting presence and guidance of God, and/or other kinds of distress: "Where is God my maker, who giveth songs in the night . . .?" (Job 35:10).

During Old Testament times the "night" was divided into three watches: (1) from sunset to 10 P.M. (Lam. 2:19), (2) from 10 P.M. to 2 A.M. (Judg. 7:19), and (3) from 2 A.M. to sunrise (Exod. 14:24).

NO

'ayin (אַיִן), "no, not; nothing; or else; nor." Cognates of this word appear in Akkadian, Ugaritic, and Phoenician (Punic). The word appears 789 times in biblical Hebrew and in all periods.

'Ayin may be used absolutely, with no suffixes and not in a construct chain. When so used the word signifies nonexistence. This is its use and significance in Gen. 2:5 (the first occurrence): ". . . And there was not a man to till the

ground." Preceded by the particle *'im,* the word may mean "not": "Is the Lord among us, or not?" (Exod. 17:7). In Gen. 30:1 this construction means "or else." In other contexts the word means "nothing": ". . . Mine age is as nothing before thee . . ." (Ps. 39:5).

In the construct state *'ayin* has the same basic meaning. In one special nuance the word is virtually a predicate meaning "there is not" or "we do not have" (Num. 14:42; cf. Gen. 31:50). In several contexts the word might be translated "without": "Without counsel purposes are disappointed . . ." (Prov. 15:22). Preceded by the preposition *min, 'ayin* can mean "because" (Jer. 7:32). Elsewhere the word expresses simple negation: "They have ears, but they hear not; neither is there any breath in their mouths" (Ps. 135:17).

With a suffixed pronoun *'ayin* negates the existence of the one or thing so represented; with the suffixed pronoun "he," the word means "he was no longer": "And Enoch walked with God: and he was [no longer]; for God took him" (Gen. 5:24).

This word should be distinguished from another *'ayin* meaning "whence," or "from where."

NOBLE

A. Nouns.

'addîr (אַדִּיר), "noble; principal; stately one." As a noun, *'addîr* is paralleled to "mighty" in Judg. 5:13: "Then he made him that remaineth have dominion over the nobles among the people: the Lord made me have dominion over the mighty." The word also occurs in Jer. 14:3 and Jer. 30:21. In 2 Chron. 23:20 *'addîr* is paralleled to "captains and governors." The word is applied to the Messiah; the Messiah is none other than God Himself: "But there the glorious Lord will be unto us a place of broad rivers . . ." (Isa. 33:21).

Two less frequently occurring nouns are *'addereth* and *'eder.* *'Addereth* may mean "luxurious outer garment, mantle, cloak." This word appears in Gen. 25:25 to mean "mantle." *'Eder* may refer to a "luxurious outer garment" (Mic. 2:8).

B. Adjectives.

'addîr (אַדִּיר), "mighty; majestic." The word *'addîr* (adjective or noun) occurs about 26 times in biblical Hebrew and mostly in poetical passages (of all periods). Ugaritic and Phoenician attest cognates of the word.

In its first appearance the adjective *'addîr* describes God's superior (majestic) holiness which was demonstrated by His delivering Israel from Egyptian bondage: "Who is like unto thee, O Lord, among the gods? Who is like thee, glorious in holiness, fearful in praises, doing wonders?" (Exod. 15:11). The idea of superior power is also suggested here (cf. Exod. 15:6; 1 Sam. 4:8). It is God's eternal and sovereign might which overcame His enemies: "and [he] slew famous kings" (Ps. 136:18)—He was/is mightier than mighty kings. Hence, His name (His person) is lauded as sovereign in power and majesty:

"O Lord, our Lord, how majestic is thy name in all the earth" (Ps. 8:1 NASB). The word, therefore, has two implications: might and splendor. Only God is Lord (exercises '*addîr*) over the oceans (Ps. 93:4) and the mountains (Ps. 76:4).

God also exalts other things; He makes them majestic. Israel's exaltation is described in the figure of a cedar (Ezek. 17:23).

Two other adjectives are related to this word. '*Addereth* used as an adjective and a noun appears 12 times. In Ezek. 17:8 the word implies "noble or majestic": "It was planted in a good soil by great waters . . . that it might be a goodly ['*addereth*] vine." '*Eder* occurs once as an adjective (Zech. 11:13); there it modifies the value of an amount of money.

C. Verb.

'*ādar* (אָדַר), "to be majestic." This verb occurs only twice and in a poetical usage. The word appears in Isa. 42:21: "The Lord is well pleased for his righteousness' sake; he will magnify the law, and make it honorable ['*ādar*]." The word also appears in Exod. 15:11.

NOSE

A. Noun.

'*aph* (אַף), "nose; nostrils; face; wrath; anger." This general Semitic word has cognates in Akkadian, Ugaritic, Phoenician, Aramaic, and Arabic. This word appears in every period of biblical Hebrew and about 277 times.

The fundamental meaning of the word is "nose," as a literal part of the body. '*Aph* bears this meaning in the singular, while the dual refers to the "nostrils" through which air passes in and out: "And the Lord God formed man of the dust of the ground, and breathed into his nostrils the breath of life" (Gen. 2:7—the first biblical occurrence).

In other contexts '*aph* in the dual represents the "entire face." God cursed Adam saying: "In the sweat of thy face shalt thou eat bread, till thou return unto the ground . . ." (Gen. 3:19). This emphasis appears often with the phrase "to bow one's face to the ground": ". . . And Joseph's brethren came, and bowed down themselves before him with their faces to the earth" (Gen. 42:6).

The words "length of face or nostrils" constitute an idiom meaning "longsuffering" or "slow to anger." It is used both of God and of man: "The Lord, The Lord God, merciful and gracious, long-suffering, and abundant in goodness and truth" (Exod. 34:6). The contrasting idiom, meaning "quick to anger," might literally mean "short of face/nostrils." It implies a changeable countenance, a capricious disposition. Prov. 14:17 uses this idiom with a little stronger emphasis: "He that is soon angry dealeth foolishly: and a man of wicked devices is hated." The accuracy of this translation is supported by the parallelism of the phrase and "a man of evil devices." Clearly '*aph* must mean something evil in God's sight.

Finally, the dual form can mean "wrath" (only in 4 passages): "Surely the churning of milk bringeth forth butter, and the wringing of the nose bringeth forth blood: so the forcing of wrath bringeth forth strife" (Prov. 30:33; cf. Exod. 15:8).

The singular form means "nose" about 25 times. In Num. 11:19-20 the word represents a human nose: "You [Israel] shall . . . eat [the meat God will supply] . . . a whole month, until it comes out of your nostrils and becomes loathsome to you" (NASB). Isa. 2:22 makes it clear that the word represents the place where the breath is: "Stop regarding man, whose breath of life is in his nostrils" (NASB). Perhaps the NASB translation in such passages is acceptable. The first passage, however, refers to the two holes or nostrils, while the second passage appears to refer to the entire frontal part of the nasal passages (where one is aware of breath being present). This word may be used of the structure protruding from one's face: ". . . They shall take away thy nose and thine ears; and thy remnant shall fall by the sword . . ." (Ezek. 23:25; cf. Song of Sol. 7:4). 'Aph is applied also to the "nose" of animals. In Job 40:24, God speaks of a large water animal: "He taketh it with his eyes: his nose pierceth through snares."

The word can be used anthropomorphically of God. Certainly passages such as Deut. 4:15-19 make it clear that God is a Spirit (John 4:24) and has not a body like men. Yet, speaking figuratively, it may be said: "They shall teach Jacob thy judgments, and Israel thy law: they shall put incense before thee [literally, "in thy nostrils"], and whole burnt sacrifice upon thine altar" (Deut. 33:10; cf. Ps. 18:8, 15). The idiom "high of nose" means "haughty" (cf. the English idiom "to have one's nose in the air"): "The wicked, through the pride of his countenance, will not seek after God . . ." (Ps. 10:4).

The singular form often means "anger" or "wrath." This meaning first appears in Gen. 30:2: "And Jacob's anger was kindled against Rachel. . . ." This meaning is applied to God as a figure of speech (anthropopathism) whereby He is attributed human emotions. Since God is infinite, eternal, and unchangeable and since anger is an emotion representing a change in one's reaction (cf. Num. 25:4), God does not really become angry, He only appears to do so in the eyes of men (cf. Prov. 29:8). The Spirit of God can seize a man and move him to a holy "anger" (Judg. 14:19; 1 Sam. 11:6).

B. Verb.

'ānaph (אָנַף), "to be angry." This verb, which has cognates in most of the Semitic languages, occurs 39 times in biblical Hebrew and in all periods. The verb appears in Isa. 12:1: "O Lord, I will praise thee: though thou wast angry with me. . . ."

FOR NOTHING

chinnām (חִנָּם), "for nothing; for no purpose; useless; without a cause; for no reason." The 32 appearances of this word are scattered throughout every period of biblical Hebrew.

This substantive is used chiefly as an adverb. Chinnām means "for nought": "And Laban said unto Jacob, Because thou art my brother, shouldest thou therefore serve me for nought? tell me, what shall thy wages be?" (Gen. 29:15—the first occurrence). The word means "in vain," or "for no purpose": "Surely in vain the net is spread in the sight of any bird" (Prov. 1:17). Finally, *chinnām* means "for no cause": ". . . Wherefore then wilt thou sin against innocent blood, to slay David without a cause?" (1 Sam. 19:5).

The verb *chānan* and the noun *chēn* are related to this word.

TO NUMBER, COUNT

A. Verb.

sāphar (סָפַר), "to number, count, proclaim, declare." The relationship of this verb to similar verbs in other languages is greatly debated, but it does occur in Ugaritic, Ethiopic, and Old South Arabic. Attested in all periods of biblical Hebrew, it appears about 110 times.

In the basic verbal form this verb signifies "to number or count." This meaning is in its first biblical appearance, Gen. 15:5: "Look now toward heaven, and tell the stars, if thou be able to number them. . . ." Here the counting is a process which has no completion in view. In Lev. 15:13 the emphasis is on a completed task: "And when [the man with the discharge becomes cleansed]; then he shall number to himself seven days for his cleansing, and wash his clothes, and bathe his flesh. . . ." Another nuance of this usage is "to count up" or "to take a census": "And David's heart smote him after that he had numbered the people" (2 Sam. 24:10). The verb is also used of assigning persons to particular jobs: "And Solomon told out threescore and ten thousand men to bear burdens . . ." (2 Chron. 2:2). Another special use appears in Ezra 1:8, where *sāphar* means "to count out according to a list" as the recipient listens: "Even those [the temple furnishings] did Cyrus king of Persia bring forth by the hand of Mithredath the treasurer, and numbered them unto Sheshbazzar, the prince of Judah." In Ps. 56:8 the word signifies "taking account of," or being aware and concerned about each detail of: "Thou tellest my wanderings. . . ." This verb can also mean "to measure," in the sense of what one does with grain: "And Joseph gathered corn as the sand of the sea, very much, until he left numbering; for it was without number" (Gen. 41:49). Finally, the verb *sāphar* can represent recording something in writing, or enumerating. So, "the Lord shall count, when he writeth up the people, that this man was born there" (Ps. 87:6).

In about 90 instances this verb appears in an intensive form. For the most part the verb in this form means "to recount," to orally list in detail. The one exception to this significance is Job 38:37: "Who can number the clouds in wisdom? Or who can stay the bottles of heaven . . . ?" In every other instance the verb signifies a vocal statement (listing or enumeration) of a series of given facts. In Gen. 24:66 Eliezer, Abraham's servant, "told Isaac all things that he had done"; he gave him a summarized but complete account of his activities. Thus Isaac knew who Rebekah was, and why she was there, so he took her to be his wife. In a similar but somewhat different sense Jacob "told Laban" who he was, that he was from the same family (Gen. 29:13). In this case the word represents something other than a report; it represents an account of Jacob's genealogy and perhaps of the events of his parents' lives. This emphasis on accurate recounting is especially prominent in Num. 13:27, where the spies report back to Moses concerning what they saw in Palestine. Even more emphatic is Exod. 24:3, where one word represents a detailed repetition of what Moses heard from God: "And Moses came and told the people all the words of the Lord, and all the judgments. . . ." Again, in Isa. 43:26 a detailed and accurate recounting is clearly in view. In this case the prophet has in mind the presentation of a law case: "Put me in remembrance: let us plead together: declare thou, that thou mayest be justified." Because of the predominant meaning presented above, Ps. 40:5 could be translated: "If I would declare and speak of them, they would be too numerous to recount" (instead of "to count").

In at least one case the verb in the intensive stem means "to exhibit," to recount or list in detail by being a living example. This meaning first appears in Exod. 9:16, where God tells Moses to say to Pharaoh: "And in very deed for this cause have I raised thee up, for to show in thee my power; and that my name may be declared throughout all the earth."

B. Nouns.

misəpār (מִסְפָּר), "measure; (a certain) number; account." This noun occurs about 132 times. *Misəpār* can mean "measure" (quantity) as in Gen. 41:49. In Gen. 34:30, the first biblical occurrence, the word refers to "a certain number" in the sense of the sum total of individuals that are counted: ". . . and I being few in number, they shall gather themselves together against me, and slay me. . . ." The word means "account" (what is set forth in a detailed report) in Judg. 7:15.

sēpher (סֵפֶר), "book; tablet." This noun occurs in Akkadian, Phoenician, and Aramaic (including biblical Aramaic), and in all periods of biblical Hebrew. It occurs 187 times in the Old Testament. Basically this word represents something one writes upon. So in Exod. 17:14 "the Lord said unto Moses, Write this for a memorial in a book." In Isa. 30:8 *sēpher* represents a tablet. In Gen. 5:1 (the first biblical occurrence of this word) it signifies something that has been written upon, or a written record: "This is the book of the generations of Adam." Such a written document may be a summary of God's law (Exod. 24:7). During the monarchy *sēpher* came to represent a letter (2 Sam. 11:14). Even later it means a king's written decree sent throughout his empire (Esther 1:22). Usually the word means "book" (Exod. 32:32)—a complete record of whatever one wants to preserve accurately. Often this word can signify the way a people writes, the written language or script (Isa. 29:11).

sōphēr (סֹפֵר), "scribe." *Sōphēr,* which occurs about 50 times in biblical Hebrew, appears also in Akkadian, Ugaritic, and Aramaic. In the early monarchy the chief "scribe" was the highest court official next to the king (2 Sam. 8:17). His job was to receive and evaluate all royal correspondence— to answer the unimportant and give the rest to the proper officer or to the king himself. He also wrote and/or composed royal communications to those within the kingdom. There was probably an entire corps of lesser scribes under his direction. As a highly trusted official he was sometimes involved in counting and managing great influxes of royal revenue (2 Kings 12:10) and in certain diplomatic jobs (2 Kings 19:2). Later *sōphēr* represented the Jewish official in the Persian court who was responsible for Jewish belongings (Ezra 7:11). In the post-exilic community this word came to mean someone who was learned in the Old Testament Scripture and especially the Mosaic Law (the Pentateuch; Ezra 7:6). The word first occurs in Judg. 5:14, where its meaning is debated. The NASB translates it "office"; some scholars translate it "scribe" (KJV, "they that handle the pen of the writer").

Some other nouns are related to the verb *sāphar*. Three of them occur only once: *saphār*, "numbering or census" (2 Chron. 2:17); *sipharāh*, "book" (Ps. 56:8); *saphōrāh*, "number or sum" (Ps. 71:15).

TO NUMBER, VISIT, PUNISH

A. Verb.

pāqad (פָּקַד), "to number, visit, be concerned with, look after, make a search for, punish." This very ancient Semitic word is found in both Akkadian and Ugaritic long before it appears in Hebrew. It is used over 285 times in the Old Testament. The first occurrence is in Gen. 21:1 ("The Lord visited Sarah") in the special sense of "to intervene on behalf of," so as to demonstrate the divine intervention in the normal course of events to bring about or fulfil a divine intent. Often this intervention is by miraculous means.

The verb is used in an expression which is unique to Hebrew and which shows great intensity of meaning. Such an occurrence appears in Exod. 3:16 ff., in which it is used twice in two different grammatical forms to portray the intensity of the action; the text reads (literally): "Looking after, I have looked after" (KJV, "I have surely visited"). The usage refers to God's intervention in His saving the children of Israel from their bondage in Egypt. The same verb in a similar expression can also be used for divine intervention for punishment: "Shall I not visit them for these things?" (Jer. 9:9), which means literally: "Shall I not punish them for these things?"

Hebrew usage also allows a use which applies to the speaker in a nearly passive sense. This is termed the reflexive, since it turns back upon the speaker. *Pāqad* is used in such a sense meaning "be missed, be lacking," as in 1 Sam. 25:7: ". . . Neither was there aught missing. . . ."

However, the most common usage of the verb in the whole of the Old Testament is in the sense of "drawing up, mustering, or numbering," as of troops for marching or battle (Exod. 30:12 and very frequently in Numbers; less so in 1 and 2 Samuel). Recent English versions have tended to use the meaning "take a census," but this equivalent seems to encompass only part of the actual meaning. The verb is used in this sense fully 100 times in the historical books.

The term has such a wide application of meanings on the whole that the Greek Septuagint and the Latin Vulgate versions use a number of terms to translate the single Hebrew word. The usage in the English versions also varies: "number, visit, punish" (KJV, RSV); "take a census, take note of, visit, punish" (NASB); "did as promised, to see, visit, punish," and other variations (LB); "blessed, seen, to take a census" (TEV); "take note of, to witness, visit, punish" (NAB); "take a census, be gracious, punish," and other variations (NIV).

B. Noun.

pāqîd (פָּקִיד), "one who looks after." This noun, derived from *pāqad* in the sense "to number, muster, draw up (troops)," possibly means "one who draws up troops," hence "officer" (2 Chron. 24:11). Another example of this meaning occurs in Jer. 20:1: "Now Pashur the son of Immer the priest, who was also chief governor in the house of the Lord. . . ."

O

TO OFFER

A. Verb.

qārab (קָרַב), "to offer, come near, approach." This word appears in nearly all branches of the Semitic languages from the earliest times and at all periods. Hebrew also attests the verb at all periods and about 295 times. (It appears 9 times in biblical Aramaic.)

In general *qārab* signifies "approach or coming near someone or something" apart from any sense of intimacy. In Gen. 12:11 (the first biblical occurrence) the word is used of spatial proximity, of being spatially close to something: "And it came to pass, when he was come near to enter into Egypt, that he said unto Sarai his wife. . . ." Usually the word represents being so close to something (or someone) that the subject can see (Exod. 32:19), speak to (Num. 9:6), or even touch (Exod. 36:2) the object or person in question.

This verb also is used of temporal nearness, in the sense that something is about to occur. *Qārab* can be used of the imminence of joyous occasions, such as religious feasts: "Beware that there be not a thought in thy wicked heart, saying, The seventh year, the year of release, is at hand . . ." (Deut. 15:9). The word is also used of the imminence of foreboding events: ". . . Esau said in his heart, The days of mourning for my father are at hand [literally, my father will soon die] . . ." (Gen. 27:41).

Qārab is used in a number of technical senses. In all these instances personal involvement is suggested; the idea is not simply being close to something (someone) but being actively and personally involved with it (him). In military contexts the word signifies armed conflict. In Deut. 2:37 the Lord commended Israel because "unto the land of the children of Ammon thou camest not." Yet in Deut. 2:19 He allowed them to "come nigh" that land: "And when thou comest nigh over against the children of Ammon, distress them not, nor meddle with them. . . ." The later passage (Deut. 2:37) uses the word technically, to close in battle. Therefore, Israel did not come close to the land of Ammon; they did not close in battle with them (cf. Josh. 8:5). In some passages this martial coloring is not immediately obvious to the casual reader but is nonetheless present: "When the wicked . . . came upon me to eat up my flesh . . ." (Ps. 27:2). Ps. 27:3 ("though a host should encamp against me") substantiates that this use of the verb is "to close in battle" (cf. Ps. 91:10; 119:150).

Qārab is used technically of having sexual relations. In Gen. 20:4 before Abimelech states his innocence with regard to Sarah we read he "had not come near her" (cf. Deut. 22:14; Isa. 8:3).

In another technical use the word represents every step one performs in presenting his offering and worship to God. This idea first appears in Exod. 3:5 where God tells Moses not to "draw near" before removing his sandals. Later Israel's meeting with God's representative was a drawing near to God (Exod. 16:9). At Sinai they drew near to receive God's law (Deut. 5:23, 27). In the causative stem the verb often represents the sacrificial presentation of offerings (Lev. 1:14) through the priests (Lev. 1:5) to the Lord (Lev. 1:13).

Israel also came near the Lord's representative in serious legal cases so that God the great King and Judge could render a decision (Josh. 7:14). In the eschaton all peoples are to gather before God; they are "to come near" Him to hear and receive His judgment (Isa. 41:1; 48:16).

B. Nouns.

qorəbān (קָרְבָּן), "offering; oblation." This noun occurs about 80 times in biblical Hebrew. The word is also found in Ethiopic and old South Arabic. The first occurrence of the word is used of an "offering" presented as a sacrifice: "If any man of you bring an offering unto the Lord, ye shall bring your offering of the cattle, even of the herd, and of the flock" (Lev. 1:2).

Some other related nouns appear less frequently: *qārôb*, "neighbor" (Exod. 32:27); *qirəbāh* occurs twice with the meaning of drawing near to worship God and offer sacrifice (Ps. 73:28; Isa. 58:2); *qurəbān*, which appears twice, means "supply, offering" (Neh. 10:35; 13:31)—it appears to be a late pronunciation of *qorəbān*. The word *qərāb*, which appears 8 times, is an Aramaic loan word; it means "war, battle," or the actual engaging in battle (Ps. 55:18).

C. Adjectives.

qārôb (קָרוֹב), "near." This word occurs about 77 times. *Qārôb* can represent nearness in space (Gen. 19:20—the first biblical occurrence) and an epistemological nearness (Deut. 30:14). The adjective also appears in Ezek. 6:12: "He that is far off shall die of the pestilence; and he that is near shall fall by the sword. . . ."

The adjective *qārēb* parallels *qārôb* in meaning. *Qārēb*, which occurs 11 times, means "near"; it represents intimate proximity (usually in a cultic context referring to cultic activity). One appearance is in Ezek. 45:4: "The holy portion of the land shall be for the priests the ministers of the sanctuary, which shall come near to minister unto the Lord. . . .''

OFFERING

minəchāh (מִנְחָה), ''meat [cereal] offering; offering; tribute; present; gift; sacrifice; oblation.'' The KJV characteristically translates the word as ''meat offering,'' using it some 40 times in this way in both Leviticus and Numbers alone. The word ''meat'' in this KJV use really means ''food''; the RSV's rendering, ''cereal offering,'' generally is much more accurate. *Minəchāh* is found some 200 times in the Old Testament.

Minəchāh is found in all periods of Hebrew, although in modern Hebrew while it is commonly used in the sense of ''gift,'' it also is used to refer to ''afternoon prayers.'' This latter use is an obvious echo of the Old Testament liturgy connected with sacrifices. It appears in other Semitic languages such as Arabic and Phoenician, and seems to be used in ancient Ugaritic in the sense of ''tribute/gift.'' *Minəchāh* occurs for the first time in the Old Testament in Gen. 4:3: ''. . . Cain brought of the fruit of the ground an offering unto the Lord.'' This use reflects the most common connotation of *minəchāh* as a ''vegetable or cereal offering.''

Minəchāh is used many times in the Old Testament to designate a ''gift'' or ''present'' which is given by one person to another. For example, when Jacob was on his way back home after twenty years, his long-standing guilt and fear of Esau prompted him to send a rather large ''present'' (bribe) of goats, camels, and other animals (Gen. 32:13-15). Similarly, Jacob directed his sons to ''carry down the man a present'' (Gen. 43:11) to appease the Egyptian ruler that later turned out to be his lost son Joseph. Those who came to hear Solomon's great wisdom all brought to him an appropriate ''present'' (1 Kings 10:25), doing so on a yearly basis.

Frequently *minəchāh* is used in the sense of ''tribute'' paid to a king or overlord. The delivering of the ''tribute'' of the people of Israel to the king of Moab by their judge-deliverer became the occasion for the deliverance of Israel from Moabite control as Ehud assassinated Eglon by a rather sly maneuver (Judges 3:15-23). Years later when David conquered the Moabites, they ''became servants to David and brought gifts [tribute]'' (2 Sam. 8:2). Hosea proclaimed to Israel that its pagan bull-god would ''be carried unto Assyria for a present [tribute]'' (Hosea 10:6). Other passages where *minəchāh* has the meaning of ''tribute'' are: Ps. 72:10; 1 Kings 4:21; 2 Kings 17:3, 4.

Minəchāh is often used to refer to any ''offering'' or ''gift'' made to God, whether it was a ''vegetable offering'' or a ''blood sacrifice.'' The story of Cain and Abel vividly illustrates this general usage: ''. . . Cain brought of the fruit of the ground an offering unto the Lord. And Abel, he also brought of the firstlings of his flock and of the fat thereof. And the Lord had respect unto Abel and to his offering: But unto Cain and to his offering he had not respect'' (Gen. 4:3-5). The animal sacrifices which were misappropriated by the wicked sons of Eli were simply designated as ''the offering of the Lord'' (1 Sam. 2:17). In each case ''offering'' is the translation of *minəchāh*.

A common use of *minəchāh,* especially in later Old Testament texts, is to designate "meat [grain/cereal] offerings." Sometimes it referred to the "meat [cereal] offering" of first fruits, "green ears of corn, dried by the fire. . . ." (Lev. 2:14). Such offerings included oil and frankincense which were burned with the grain. Similarly, the "meat [grain] offering" could be in the form of finely ground flour upon which oil and frankincense had been poured also. Sometimes the oil was mixed with the "meat [cereal] offering" (Lev. 14:10, 21; 23:13; Num. 7:13), again in the form of fine flour. The priest would take a handful of this fine flour, burn it as a memorial portion, and the remainder would belong to the priest (Lev. 2:9-10). The "meat [cereal] offering" frequently was in the form of fine flour which was mixed with oil and then formed into cakes and baked, either in a pan or on a griddle (Lev. 2:4-5). Other descriptions of this type of baked "meat [cereal] offering" are found in Num. 6:15 and Lev. 7:9. These baked "meat [cereal] offerings" were always to be made without leaven, but were to be mixed with salt and oil (Lev. 2:11,13).

The *minəchāh* was prescribed as a "meat offering" of flour kneaded with oil to be given along with the whole burnt offering. A libation of wine was to be given as well. This particular rule applied especially to the Feast of Weeks or Pentecost (Lev. 23:18), to the daily "continual offering" (Exod. 29:38-42), and to all the whole burnt offerings or general sacrifices (Num. 15:1-16). The "meat [cereal] offering" was to be burned, while the wine seems to have been poured out at the foot of the altar like blood of the sacrificial animal.

The regular daily morning and evening sacrifices included the *minəchāh* and were specifically referred to as "meat [cereal] offering of the morning" (Exod. 29:41; cf. Num. 28:8) and as "the evening meat [cereal] offering" (2 Kings 16:15; cf. Ps. 141:2 and Ezra 9:4, 5, "evening sacrifice").

Minəchāh provides an interesting symbolism for the prophet when he refers to the restoration of the Jews: "And they shall bring all your brethren for an offering unto the Lord out of all nations upon horses, and in chariots . . . to my holy mountain Jerusalem, saith the Lord, as the children of Israel bring an offering in a clean vessel into the house of the Lord" (Isa. 66:20). In his vision of the universal worship of God, even in Gentile lands, Malachi saw the *minəchāh* given as "a pure offering" to God by believers everywhere (Mal. 1:11).

tərûmāh (תְּרוּמָה), "heave offering; offering; oblation." This word is found in the literature of ancient Ugarit in the term, "bread of offering," as well as in all periods of Hebrew. In modern Hebrew it is often used in the sense of "contribution," quite like the use found in Ezek. 45:13, 16, where it refers to a contribution to be given to the prince. *Tərûmāh* is found approximately 70 times in the Old Testament, being used for the first time in the Old Testament text in Exod. 25:2: "Speak unto the children of Israel, that they bring me an offering: of every man that giveth it willingly with the heart ye shall take my offering."

In more than a third of its occurrences in the text, the KJV translates *tərûmāh* as "heave offering," all of these instances being found in Exodus, Leviticus, Numbers (where the majority are found), and Deuteronomy. This translation apparently is derived from the fact that the word is based on the common Semitic root, "to be high, exalted." The inference seems to be that such "offerings" were raised high by the priest in some sort of motion as it was placed on the altar. This is clearly illustrated in Num. 15:20: "Ye shall offer up a cake of the first of your dough for a heave offering: as ye do the heave offering of the threshing floor, so shall ye heave it." From texts like this, it appears that *tərûmāh* was used in the early period to refer to "contributions" or "gifts" which consisted of the produce of the ground, reflecting the agricultural character of early Israel. See Deut. 12:6, 11, 17 for other examples.

Tərûmāh often is used to designate those gifts or contributions to God, but which were set apart specifically for the priests: "And every offering of all the holy things of the children of Israel, which they bring unto the priest, shall be his" (Num. 5:9). Such "offerings" were to go to the priests because of a special covenant God had made: "All the holy offerings which the people of Israel present to the Lord I give to you [Aaron], and to your sons and daughters with you, as a perpetual due; it is a covenant of salt for ever before the Lord for you and for your offspring with you" (Num. 18:19 RSV). Such offerings, or contributions, sometimes were of grain or grain products: "Besides the cakes, he shall offer for his offering leavened bread with the sacrifice of thanksgiving of his peace offerings. And of it he shall offer one out of the whole oblation for a heave offering unto the Lord, and it shall be the priest's that sprinkleth the blood of the peace offerings" (Lev. 7:13-14). Part of the animal sacrifices was also designated as a *tərûmāh* for the priests: "And the right shoulder shall ye give unto the priest for a heave offering of the sacrifices of your peace offerings" (Lev. 7:32; cf. Lev. 10:14, 15; Num. 6:20). Such contributions to the priests obviously were given to provide the needed foodstuffs for the priests and their families since their tribe, Levi, was given no land on which to raise their own food.

While all the priests had to be from the tribe of Levi, inheriting their office through their fathers, not all Levites could function as priests. For one thing, there were too many of them. Also, some were needed to work in the tabernacle, and later the temple, as maintenance and clean-up people, something that is readily understandable when one thinks of all that was involved in the sacrificial system. The Levites actually lived in various parts of Israel, and they were the welfare responsibility of the Israelites among whom they lived. They, like the widow, the orphan, and the resident alien, were to be given the tithe of all farm produce every third year (Deut. 14:28-29). The Levites, then, were to tithe the tithe they received, giving their own tithe from what they received from the people to the Lord. Part of that tithe was to be a *tərûmāh* or "heave offering" to the priests, the descendants of Aaron (see Num. 18:25-32).

In order to provide for the materials necessary for the construction of the wilderness tabernacle, Moses was instructed to receive an "offering" or *tərûmāh*. The "offering" was to consist of all kinds of precious metals and stones, as well as the usual building materials such as wood and skins (Exod. 25:3-9). When Moses announced this to the people of Israel, he said: "Take ye from among you an offering unto the Lord; whosoever is of a willing heart, let him bring it, an offering of the Lord . . ." (Exod. 35:5), following this with a list of the needed materials (Exod. 35:6-8). The implication here is twofold: the *tərûmāh* is really the Lord's, and it is best given freely, willing, from a generous heart. In the Second Temple Period, following the Exile, the silver and gold and the vessels for the temple are called "the offering for the house of our God" (Ezra 8:25), also signifying a contribution.

The *tərûmāh* sometimes was an "offering" which had the meaning of a tax, an obligatory assessment which was made against every Israelite male who was twenty years old or older, to be paid for the support of the tabernacle and, later, the temple (Exod. 30:11-16). This tax was levied on all males without any allowance for their financial situation: "The rich shall not give more, and the poor shall not give less than half a shekel, when they give an offering unto the Lord, to make an atonement for your souls" (Exod. 30:15). This tax actually had its basis in the census or count of the male population, the tax then being required as a ransom or atonement from the wrath of God because such a census was taken (2 Sam. 24:1). The practical aspect of it was that it provided needed financial support for the sanctuary. Another example of *tərûmāh* in the sense of taxes may be seen in Prov. 29:4: "The king by judgment establisheth the land; but he that receiveth gifts overthroweth it." Solomon's heavy taxation which led to the split of the kingdom may be a case in point (1 Kings 12).

A very different use of *tərûmāh* is found in Ezek. 45:1; 48:9, 20, 21, where it refers to an "oblation" which was that portion of land on which the post-exilic temple was to be built, as well as accommodations for the priests and Levites. This tract of land is referred to as "the holy oblation" (Ezek. 48:20; RSV, "holy portion"), since it belongs to God just as much as the *tərûmāh* which was given to him as a sacrifice.

qorəbān (קָרְבָּן), "offering; oblation; sacrifice." *Qorəbān* is found in various Semitic languages and is derived from the verb "to come/bring near." It is found in ancient Akkadian in the sense of "a present," while a form of the verb is found in Ugaritic to refer to the offering of a sacrifice. Found throughout the history of Hebrew, in late or modern Hebrew it is used in the sense of "offering" and "consecration." In the Septuagint, it is often rendered as "gift."

While the root, "to come/bring near," is found literally hundreds of times in the Old Testament, the derived noun *qorəbañ* occurs only about 80 times. All but two of the occurrences in the Old Testament are found in the books of Numbers and Leviticus. The two exceptions are in Ezekiel (20:28; 40:43), a book which has a great concern for ritual. The word occurs for the first time in Lev. 1:2.

Qorəbān may be translated as "that which one brings near to God or the altar." It is not surprising, then, that the word is used as a general term for all sacrifices, whether animal or vegetable. The very first reference to "sacrifice" in Leviticus is to the *qorəbān* as a burnt "offering": "If any man of you bring an offering unto the Lord, ye shall bring your offering of the cattle, even of the herd, and of the flock. If his offering be a burnt sacrifice . . ."

(Lev. 1:2-3; cf. Lev. 1:10; 3:2, 6; 4:23). The first reference to *qorəbān* as a "meat [cereal] offering" is in Lev. 2:1: "And when any will offer a meat offering unto the Lord, his offering shall be of fine flour. . . ."

What is perhaps the best concentration of examples of the use of *qorəbān* is Numbers 7. In this one chapter, the word is used some 28 times, referring to all kinds of animal and meat [cereal] offerings, but with special attention to the various silver and gold vessels which were offered to the sanctuary. For example, Eliab's "offering was one silver charger, the weight whereof was a hundred and thirty shekels, one silver bowl of seventy shekels, . . . both of them full of fine flour mingled with oil for a meat offering; One golden spoon of ten shekels, full of incense; One young bullock, one ram, one lamb of the first year, for a burnt offering" (Num. 7:25-27).

In the two uses found in Ezekiel, both are in the general sense of "offering." In Ezek. 20:28 the word refers to the pagan "provocation of their offering" which apostate Israel gave to other gods, while in Ezek. 40:43, *qorəbān* refers to regular animal sacrifices.

qurəbān (קֻרְבָּן), "wood offering." *Qurəbān* is closely related to *qārəbān*, and it is found in Neh. 10:34; 13:31. Here it refers to the "wood offering" which was to be provided for the burning of the sacrifices in the Second Temple. Lots were to be cast among the people, priests, and Levites to determine who would bring in the "wood offering" or fuel at the scheduled times throughout the year.

'ōlāh (עוֹלָה), "whole burnt offering." This word has cognates in late and biblical Aramaic. It occurs about 280 times in biblical Hebrew and at all periods.

In its first biblical occurrence *'ōlāh* identifies a kind of "offering" presented to God: "And Noah builded an altar unto the Lord; and took of every clean beast, and of every clean fowl, and offered burnt offerings on the altar" (Gen. 8:20). Its second nuance appears in Lev. 1:4, where it represents the "thing being offered": "And he shall put his hand upon the head of the burnt offering; and it shall be accepted for him to make atonement for him."

This kind of "offering" could be made with a bull (Lev. 1:3-5), a sheep, a goat (Lev. 1:10), or a bird (Lev. 1:14). The offerer laid his hands on the sacrificial victim, symbolically transferring his sin and guilt to it. After he slew the animal (on the north side of the altar), the priest took its blood, which was presented before the Lord prior to being sprinkled around the altar. A bird was simply given to the priest, but he wrung its neck and allowed its blood to drain beside the altar (Lev. 1:15). This sacrifice effected an atonement, a covering for sin necessary before the essence of the sacrifice could be presented to God. Next, the "offering" was divided into sections. They were carefully purified (except those parts which could not be purified) and arranged on the altar (Lev. 1:6-9, 12-13). The entire sacrifice was then consumed by the fire and its essence sent up to God as a placating (pleasing) odor. The animal skin was given to the priest as his portion (Lev. 7:8).

The word *'ōlāh* was listed first in Old Testament administrative prescriptions and descriptions as the most frequent offering. Every day required the presentation of a male lamb morning and evening—the continual "whole burnt offering'' (Exod. 29:38-42). Each month was consecrated by a ''whole burnt offering,'' of two young bulls, one ram, and seven male lambs (Num. 28:11-14). The same sacrifice was mandated, for each day of the Passover-Unleavened Bread feast (Num. 28:19-24), and the Feast of Weeks (Num. 28:26-29). Other stated feasts required ''burnt offerings'' as well. The various purification rites mandated both ''burnt'' and sin ''offerings.''

The central significance of '*ōlāh* as the ''whole burnt offering'' was the total surrender of the heart and life of the offerer to God. Sin offerings could accompany them when the offerer was especially concerned with a covering or expiation for sin (2 Chron. 29:27). When peace offerings accompanied ''burnt offerings,'' the offerer's concern focused on fellowship with God (2 Chron. 29:31-35). Before the Mosaic legislation, it appears, the ''whole burnt offering'' served the full range of meanings expressed in all the various Mosaic sacrifices.

'*ishsheh* (אִשֶּׁה), ''fire offering.'' Sixty-two of the 64 appearances of this word occur in the sacramental prescriptions of Exodus-Deuteronomy. The other two occurrences (Josh. 13:14; 1 Sam. 2:28) bear the same meaning and sacramental context.

All legitimate sacrifices had to be presented before God at His altar, and all of them involved burning to some degree. Thus they may all be called fire offerings. The word '*ishsheh* first occurs in Exod. 29:18: ''And thou shalt burn the whole ram upon the altar: it is a burnt offering unto the Lord: it is a sweet savor, an offering made by fire unto the Lord.''

'*āshām* (אָשָׁם), ''guilt offering; offense; guilt; gift of restitution; gift of atonement.'' The noun '*āshām* occurs 46 times in biblical Hebrew; 33 of its occurrences are in the Pentateuch.

The most frequent meaning of the word is ''guilt offering'': ''And he shall bring his trepass [guilt] offering unto the Lord for his sin which he hath sinned . . .'' (Lev. 5:6). This specialized kind of sin offering (Lev. 5:7) was to be offered when someone had been denied what was due to him. The valued amount defrauded was to be repaid plus 20 percent (Lev. 5:16; 6:5). Ritual infractions and periods of leprosy and defilement took from God a commodity or service rightfully belonging to Him and required repayment plus restitution. Every violation of property rights required paying full reparation and the restitution price (20 percent) to the one violated as well as presenting the guilt offering to God as the Lord of all (i.e., as a feudal lord over all). If the offended party was dead, reparation and restitution were made to God (i.e., given to the priests; Num. 5:5-10). Usually the ''guilt offering'' consisted of a ram (Lev. 5:15) or a male lamb. The offerer presented the victim, laying his hands on it. The priest sprinkled its blood around the altar, burned the choice parts on the altar, and received the rest as food (Lev. 7:2-7). When a cleansed leper made this offering, blood from the sacrifice was applied to the man's right ear, right thumb, and right big toe (Lev. 14:14).

In some passages, '*āshām* is used of an offense against God and the guilt incurred by it: ''And Abimelech said, What is this thou hast done unto us? one of the people might lightly have lain with thy wife, and thou shouldest have brought guiltiness upon us'' (Gen. 26:10—the first occurrence). There is an added sense here that the party offended would punish the perpetrator of the crime.

In two verses (Num. 5:7-8), 'āshām represents the repayment made to one who has been wronged: "Then they shall confess their sin which they have done: and he shall recompense his trespass with the principal thereof, and add unto it the fifth part thereof, and give it unto him against whom he hath trespassed." In the Hebrew the word is the value of the initial thing taken from the injured party, which value is to be returned to him, i.e., the reparation or restitution itself. This basic idea is extended so that the word comes to mean a gift made to God to remove guilt (1 Sam. 6:3), or atone for sin (Isa. 53:10) other than the specified offerings to be presented at the altar.

(OLIVE) OIL

A. Nouns.

shemen (שֶׁמֶן), "(olive) oil; olive; perfume; olivewood." Cognates of this word appear in Ugaritic, Akkadian, Phoenician, Syriac, Arabic, and Aramaic. This word appears about 190 times and in all periods of biblical Hebrew.

Shemen means olive "oil": "And Jacob rose up early in the morning, and took the stone that he had put for his pillows, and set it up for a pillar, and poured oil upon the top of it" (Gen. 28:18). Olive "oil" was also used to anoint a future office bearer (Exod. 25:6; 2 Kings 9:6); one's head as a sign of mourning (2 Sam. 14:2); one's head as a sign of rejoicing (Ps. 23:5); and one's ear lobe, thumb, and toe as a ritual cleansing (Lev. 14:17). *Shemen* is used as a preservative on shield-leather (2 Sam. 1:21) and in baking (Exod. 29:2) and as a medication (Ezek. 16:9). This "oil" is burned for light (Exod. 25:6). Its many uses made olive oil a valuable trade item (Ezek. 27:17).

In many contexts *shemen* perhaps means the "olive" itself: ". . . But ye, gather ye wine, and summer fruits, and oil, and put them in your vessels . . ." (Jer. 40:10).

Once the word appears to mean lavish dishes, or dishes mixed with much oil: "And in this mountain shall the Lord of hosts make unto all people a feast of fat things [NASB, "lavish banquet"]" (Isa. 25:6).

Shemen is "a kind of perfume," or olive oil mixed with certain odors to make a perfume, in passages such as Song of Sol. 1:3: "Because of the savor of thy good ointments [NASB, "oils"] thy name is as ointment poured forth. . . ."

Shemen sometimes modifies "wood": "In the inner sanctuary he made two cherubim of olivewood, each ten cubits high" (1 Kings 6:23 RSV).

A related noun *mishəmān* appears 4 times. It means "stout or vigorous ones" (Isa. 10:16) and "fertile spots" (Dan. 11:24).

B. Verb.

The verb *shāman,* which appears 5 times, has cognates in Aramaic, Syriac, and Arabic. The word means "to grow or be fat" (Neh. 9:25; Jer. 5:28).

C. Adjective.

The adjective *shāmēn*, which occurs 10 times, in Ugaritic cognates means: "fat" (Ezek. 34:16); "rich" in the sense of fattening (Gen. 49:20—the first occurrence); "fertile" (Num. 13:20); "robust or muscular" (Judg. 3:29); and "large" (Hab. 1:16).

TO OVERLAY, SPY

A. Verb.

tsāphāh (צָפָה), "to overlay, spy, keep watch." This word is found in both biblical and modern Hebrew, and some scholars suggest that it exists in Ugaritic. *Tsāphāh* is found in the text of the Hebrew Bible about 37 times. It occurs for the first time in the Old Testament in the so-called Mizpah Benediction: "The Lord watch between me and thee . . ." (Gen. 31:49). The meaning in this context is "to watch" with a purpose, that of seeing that the covenant between Laban and Jacob was kept. Thus, the statement by Laban is more of a threat than a benediction. Similarly, when God's "eyes behold the nations" (Ps. 66:7), it is much more than a casual look. Perhaps in most uses, the connotation of "to spy" would be the most accurate.

B. Participle.

The participial form of *tsāphāh* is often used as a noun, *tsōpeh*, meaning "watchman," or one whose task it is "to keep close watch" (2 Sam. 13:34).

TO OVERTAKE

nāsag (נָשַׂג), "to reach, overtake, attain." This verb is found in both ancient and modern Hebrew. It is used in the text of the Hebrew Old Testament approximately 50 times, the first time being Gen. 31:25: "Then Laban overtook Jacob." Often it is used in connection with the verb, "to pursue, follow," as in Gen. 44:4: ". . . follow after the men; and when thou dost overtake them. . . ." *Nāsag* is sometimes used in the figurative sense to describe "being overtaken" by something undesirable or unwanted, such as war (Hos. 10:9), the sword (Jer. 42:16), or curses (Deut. 28:15, 45). Fortunately, blessings may "overtake" those who are obedient (Deut. 28:2). *Nāsag* may mean "to attain to" something, "to come into contact" with it: "The sword of him that layeth at him [Leviathan] . . ." (Job 41:26). Used figuratively, "The ransomed of the Lord . . . shall obtain joy and gladness . . ." (Isa. 35:10). Jacob complained: ". . . the days of the years of my pilgrimage . . . have not attained unto the days of the years of the life of my fathers . . ." (Gen. 47:9).

P

PALM (OF HAND)

A. Noun.

kaph (כַּף), "palm (of hand)." Cognates of this noun are attested in Akkadian, Ugaritic, Aramaic, Arabic, Ethiopic, and Egyptian. It appears about 193 times in biblical Hebrew and at all periods.

Basically, *kaph* represents the "palm," the hollow part of the hand as distinguished from its fingers, thumbs, and back. Thus we read that part of the ritual for cleansing a leper is that a "priest shall take some of the log of oil, and pour it into the palm of his own left hand" (Lev. 14:15).

The word represents the entire inside of the hand when it is cupped, or the "hollow of the hand." God told Moses: ". . . While my glory passeth by, that I will put thee in a clift of the rock, and will cover thee with my hand while I pass by" (Exod. 33:22; cf. Ps. 139:5).

This word means fist, specifically the inside of a fist. The woman of Zarephath told Elijah: ". . . I have not a cake, but a handful of meal in a barrel, and a little oil in a cruse . . ." (1 Kings 17:12). This was, indeed, a very small amount of flour—enough for only one little biscuit.

Kaph also refers to the flat of the hand, including the fingers and the thumb. These are what one claps together in joy and applause: "And he brought forth the king's son, and put the crown upon him, and gave him the testimony; and they made him king, and anointed him; and they clapped their hands, and said, God save the king" (2 Kings 11:12). Clapping the hands may also be an expression of scorn and contempt (Num. 24:10). The flat of the hands may be raised heavenward in prayer to symbolize one's longing to receive. Moses told Pharaoh: "As soon as I am gone out of the city, I will spread abroad my hands unto the Lord . . ." (Exod. 9:29).

This word can suggest the inside part of a hand grasp as distinguished from the hand as a whole :"And the Lord said unto Moses, Put forth thine hand, and take it by the tail. And he put forth his hand, and caught it, and it became a rod in his hand" (Exod. 4:4). A mutual hand grasp may signify entrance into a pledge (Prov. 6:1). To take one's life (*nephesh*) into one's own hands is to put oneself into danger (Judg. 12:3).

In many passages *kaph* is synonymous with the entire hand. Jacob tells Laban that "God hath seen . . . the labor of my hands . . ." (Gen. 31:42). Perhaps the same nuance occurs in passages such as Gen. 20:5: ". . . In the integrity of my heart and innocency of my hands have I done this."

The word may be used symbolically and figuratively meaning "power." Gideon complained to the Angel of the Lord that "now the Lord hath forsaken us, and delivered us into the hands [the power] of the Midianites" (Judg. 6:13). Israel was not literally in the Midianites' hands but was dominated by them and under their control.

Once the word represents animal paws: "And whatsoever goeth upon his paws, among all manner of beasts that go on all four, those are unclean unto you . . ." (Lev. 11:27).

In many passages *kaph* signifies the sole of the foot, the hollow part. This meaning appears in Gen. 8:9 (first biblical appearance): "But the dove found no rest for the sole of her foot . . ." (cf. Josh. 3:13 where the word is used of the sole of a human foot).

Various hollow, bending, or beaten objects are represented by *kaph*. First, it is used of a thigh joint: "And when he [the Angel of the Lord] saw that he prevailed not against him [Jacob], he touched the hollow of his thigh; and the hollow of Jacob's thigh was out of joint, as he wrestled with him" (Gen. 32:25). Second, a certain shaped pan or vessel is called a *kaph:* "And thou shalt make the dishes thereof, and spoons thereof, and covers thereof, and bowls thereof, to cover withal: of pure gold shalt thou make them" (Exod. 25:29). Third, the word is used of the hollow of a sling: ". . . And the souls of thine enemies, them shall he sling out, as out of the middle of a sling" (1 Sam. 25:29). Next, the huge hand-shaped branches of palm trees are represented by the word: "And ye shall take you on the first day the boughs of goodly trees, branches of palm trees, and the boughs of thick trees . . ." (Lev. 23:40). Finally, in Song of Sol. 5:5 this word represents the bent piece of metal or wood which forms a door handle.

B. Verb.

kāphaph (כָּפַף), "to bend, bow down." This word appears 5 times in biblical poetry and has cognates in Akkadian and Arabic. The verb occurs in Isa. 58:5: ". . . is it to bow down his head as a bulrush, and to spread sackcloth and ashes under him?"

PART

A. Particle.

bad (בַּד), "part; portion; limbs; piece of cloth; pole; shoot; alone; by themselves; only; apart from; besides; aside from." This word occurs about 219 times and in all periods of biblical Hebrew.

First, *bad* means a "part or portion" of something. In Exod. 30:34 it refers to the portion or amount of spices mixed together to make incense for the worship of God. In Job 18:13 the word represents the members or parts of the wicked (cf. Job 41:12—"limbs" of a crocodile).

Second, the word means a piece of cloth: "And thou shalt make them linen breeches to cover their nakedness . . ." (Exod. 28:42—first occurrence of this nuance). This word is always used of a priestly garment or at least of a garment worn by one who appears before God or His altar.

Third, *bad* can mean a long piece of wood or woody material. The ark, altars, and table of the Bread of the Presence were carried by staves passed through rings attached to these articles: "And thou shalt put the staves into the rings by the sides of the ark, that the ark may be borne with them" (Exod. 25:14—first occurrence of this nuance). In Ezek. 19:14 *bad* is used of the "shoots" or limbs of a vine; "And fire is gone out of a rod of her branches . . ." (cf. Ezek. 17:6). The gates of a city are *badîm* (Job 17:16).

Fourth, in most of its appearances (152 times) this word is preceded by the preposition *lə*. This use means "alone" (89 times): "And the Lord God said, It is not good that the man should be alone; I will make him a help meet for him" (Gen. 2:18—first occurrence of the word). In a second nuance the phrase identifies a unit by itself, a single unit: "And thou shalt couple five curtains by themselves, and six curtains by themselves . . ." (Exod. 26:9). Twice the word is used as an adverb of limitation meaning "only": "Lo, this only have I found, that God hath made man upright; but they have sought out many inventions" (Eccl. 7:29). When followed by the preposition *min* (or *'al*) the word functions as an adverb meaning "apart from" or "besides": "And the children of Israel journeyed from Rameses to Succoth, about six hundred thousand on foot that were men, beside children" (Exod. 12:37). In Num. 29:39 the translation "besides" is appropriate: "These things ye shall do unto the Lord in your set feasts, beside your vows, and your freewill offerings. . . ." In 33 passages the word is preceded by the preposition *min* but still means "besides."

B. Verb.

bādad (בָּדַד), "to be isolated, be alone." This verb has an Arabic cognate. One of its 3 appearances is in Ps. 102:7: "I watch, and am as a sparrow alone upon the housetop."

TO PASS ON, PASS AWAY

chālaph (חָלַף), "to pass on, pass away, change, overstep, transgress." Common to both biblical and modern Hebrew, this term appears approximately 30 times in the Hebrew Old Testament. When used in the simple active form, *chālaph* occurs only in poetry (except for 1 Sam. 10:3), and it has the meaning of "to pass on, through." The word is typically used in narrative or prose with the meaning of "to change." With this meaning *chālaph* first occurs in the Old Testament in Gen. 31:7: ". . . Your father hath deceived me, and changed my wages ten times . . ." (cf. Gen. 31:41). *Chālaph* expresses the "sweeping on" of a flood (Isa. 8:8), of a whirlwind (Isa. 21:1), and of God Himself (Job 9:11). The word has the meaning of "to pass away or to vanish," with reference to days (Job 9:26), the rain (Song of Sol. 2:11), and idols (Isa. 2:18). Not only wages, but garments are "changed" (Gen. 35:2; Ps. 102:26). "To change" is "to renew" strength (Isa. 40:31; 41:1); a tree appears "to be renewed" when it sprouts again (Job 14:7).

TO PASS OVER

A. Verb.

'ābar (עָבַר), "to pass away, pass over." This verb occurs in all Semitic languages and at all periods of those languages, including biblical Hebrew and Aramaic. The Bible attests about 550 uses of this verb in Hebrew.

The verb refers primarily to spatial movement, to "moving over, through, or away from." This basic meaning can be used of "going over or through" a particular location to get to the other side, as when Jacob "crossed over" the Euphrates to escape Laban (Gen. 31:21). Another specific use of this general meaning is to pass through something; Ps. 8:8 speaks of whatever "passes through" the sea as being under Adam's control. *'Ābar* can also merely mean "to go as far as"—Amos tells his audience not to "cross over" to Beer-sheba (Amos 5:5). "To go as far as" an individual is to overtake him (2 Sam. 18:23). Abram "passed through" Canaan as far as Mamre; he did not go out of the land (cf. Gen. 12:6). The word can also be used of "passing by" something; Abraham begged the three men not "to pass by" him but to stop and refresh themselves (Gen. 18:3). *'Ābar* is sometimes used of "passing over" a law, order, or covenant as if it were not binding. When the people decided to enter Palestine against the command of God, Moses said, "Wherefore now do ye transgress the commandment of the Lord?" (Num. 14:41).

This verb first occurs in Gen. 8:1 where it means "pass over on top of." God caused the wind "to pass over" the flood waters and to carry them away.

The word can also mean "to pass away," "to cease to be," as in Gen. 50:4 where the days of mourning over Jacob "were past."

A number of technical phrases where this root has a regular and specialized meaning appear. For example, one who "passes over" the sea is a seafarer or sailor (Isa. 23:2—a similar technical usage appears in Akkadian). *'Ābar* is used in business affairs with silver or money in the sense of reckoning money according to the "going" (passing) rate (Gen. 23:16 ff.). In Song of Sol. 5:5 (RSV) the verb is used to mean "flow" as what a liquid does ("flowing" or "liquid" myrrh). The phrase "pass over to be numbered" is a phrase meaning to move from one status to another (to move into the ranks of the militia) in Exod. 30:13, 14.

The intensive stem of *'ābar* is used in two special senses: of "overlaying" with precious metals (1 Kings 6:21) and of the ox's act of making a cow pregnant (Job 21:10). The verb also has special meanings in the causative stem: "to devote" the firstborn to the Lord (Exod. 13:12); "to offer" a child by burning him in fire (Deut. 18:10); "to make" a sound "come forth" (Lev. 25:9); "to sovereignly transfer" a kingdom or cause it to pass over to another's leadership (2 Sam. 3:10); "to put away or cause to cease" (1 Kings 15:12); and "to turn" something "away" (Ps. 119:37).

B. Nouns.

'ibərî (עִבְרִי), "Hebrew." The origin and meaning of this word, which appears 34 times, is much debated. The word is an early generic term for a variety of Semitic peoples and is somewhat akin to our word *barbarian*. So Abram is identified as a "Hebrew" (Gen. 14:13). This ethnic term indicates family origin whereas the term "sons of Israel" is a political and religious term. Unquestionably in the ancient Near East "Hebrew" was applied to a far larger group than the Israelites. The word occurs in Ugaritic, Egyptian, and Babylonian writings describing a diverse mixture of nomadic wanderers or at least those who appear to have at one time been nomadic. Sometimes the word seems to be a term of derision. Such usage recalls 1 Sam. 29:3, where the Philistine leaders asked Achish, "What do these Hebrews here?" There is

considerable debate about identifying Hebrew with the well-known Habiru (Semitic warlords) who occupied Egypt in the first half of the second millennium B.C.

Several other nouns are derived from the verb '*ābar*. '*Ēber*, which occurs 89 times, refers to the "side" (1 Sam. 14:1) or "edge" (Exod. 28:26) of something. When speaking of rivers or seas, '*ēber* means the "edge or side opposite the speaker" or "the other side" (Josh. 2:10). *Ma'ǝbārāh*, which appears 8 times, means "ford" (Josh. 2:7) and "ravine" or "passage" (1 Sam. 14:4). *Ma'abār* appears 3 times to mean: "sweep" (of a staff, Isa. 30:32); "ford" (Gen. 32:22); and "ravine" or "passage" (1 Sam. 13:23). '*Abārāh*, which occurs twice, means "crossing or ford" (2 Sam. 19:18 RSV).

PEACE

A. Nouns.

shālôm (שָׁלוֹם), "peace; completeness; welfare; health." The root is a common Semitic root with the meaning "peace" in Akkadian, Ugaritic, Phoenician, Aramaic, Syriac, Arabic, and Ethiopic.

Shālôm is a very important term in the Old Testament and has maintained its place in Mishnaic, rabbinic, and modern Hebrew. In Israel today, people greet the newcomer and each other with the words *mah shlomkha*, "what is your peace," "how are you doing," and they ask about the "peace" ("well-being") of one's family.

The use of *shālôm* is frequent (237 times) and varied in its semantic range. The first two occurrences in Genesis already indicate the changes in meaning: "And thou shalt go to thy fathers in peace [*shālôm* in the sense of "in tranquility," "at ease," "unconcerned"]; thou shalt be buried in a good old age" (Gen. 15:15); and "that thou wilt do us no hurt, as we have not touched thee, and as we have done unto thee nothing but good, and have sent thee away in peace [*shālôm* with the meaning of "unharmed" and "unhurt"] . . ." (Gen. 26:29). Yet, both uses are essentially the same, as they express the root meaning of "to be whole." The phrase *ish shlomi* ("friend of my peace") in Ps. 41:9, "Yea, mine own familiar friend [literally, "friend of my peace"], in whom I trusted, which did eat of my bread, hath lifted up his heel against me" (cf. Jer. 20:10), signifies a state in which one can feel at ease, comfortable with someone. The relationship is one of harmony and wholeness, which is the opposite of the state of strife and war: "I am for peace: but when I speak, they are for war" (Ps. 120:7). *Shālôm* as a harmonious state of the soul and mind encourages the development of the faculties and powers. The state of being at ease is experienced both externally and internally. In Hebrew it finds expression in the phrase *be-shālôm* ("in peace"): "I will both lay me down in peace [*be-shālôm*], and sleep: for thou, Lord, only makest me dwell in safety" (Ps. 4:8).

Closely associated to the above is the meaning "welfare," specifically personal "welfare" or "health." This meaning is found in questions: "And Joab said to Amasa, Art thou in health, my brother? And Joab took Amasa by the beard with the right hand to kiss him" (2 Sam. 20:9), or in the prepositional phrase *le-shalôm* with the verb "to ask": "And he asked them of their welfare, and said, Is your father well, the old man of whom ye spake? Is he yet alive?" (Gen. 43:27).

Shalôm also signifies "peace," indicative of a prosperous relationship between two or more parties. *Shalôm* in this sense finds expression in speech: "Their tongue is as an arrow shot out; it speaketh deceit: one speaketh peaceably [literally, "in peace"] to his neighbor with his mouth, but in heart he layeth his wait" (Jer. 9:8); in diplomacy: "Howbeit Sisera fled away on his feet to the tent of Jael the wife of Heber the Kenite: for there was peace between Jabin the king of Hazor and the house of Heber the Kenite" (Judg. 4:17); and in warfare: ". . . If it make thee answer of peace, and open unto thee, then it shall be, that all the people that is found therein shall be tributaries unto thee, and they shall serve thee" (Deut. 20:11).

Isaiah prophesied concerning the "prince of peace" (Isa. 9:6), whose kingdom was to introduce a government of "peace" (Isa. 9:7). Ezekiel spoke about the new covenant as one of "peace": "Moreover I will make a covenant of peace with them; it shall be an everlasting covenant with them: and I will place them, and multiply them, and will set my sanctuary in the midst of them for evermore" (Ezek. 37:26). Psalm 122 is one of those great psalms in celebration of and in prayer for the "peace of Jerusalem": "Pray for the peace of Jerusalem: they shall prosper that love thee" (Ps. 122:6). In benedictions God's peace was granted to His people: ". . . Peace shall be upon Israel" (Ps. 125:5).

The Septuagint gives the following translations: *eirene* ("peace; welfare; health"); *eirenikos* ("peaceable; peaceful"); *soteria* ("deliverance; preservation; salvation"); and *hugiainein* ("be in good health; sound").

Another related noun is *shelem,* which occurs 87 times, and means "peace offering": "And he sent young men of the children of Israel, which offered burnt offerings, and sacrificed peace offerings of oxen unto the Lord" (Exod. 24:5).

B. Verbs.

shalēm (שָׁלֵם), "to be complete, be sound." This verb occurs 103 times. The word signifies "to be complete" in 1 Kings 9:25: "So he finished the house."

Another verb, *shalam,* means "to make peace": "When a man's ways please the Lord, he maketh even his enemies to be at peace with him" (Prov. 16:7).

C. Adjective.

shalēm (שָׁלֵם), "complete; perfect." This word is found in Gen. 15:16 with the meaning of not quite "complete": "But in the fourth generation they shall come hither again: for the iniquity of the Amorites is not yet full." The word means "perfect" in Deut. 25:15.

PEOPLE

'am (עַם), "people; relative." This common Semitic word has cognates in Akkadian, Amorite, Phoenician, Ugaritic, Punic, Moabite, Aramaic, and Arabic. This word occurs about 1,868 times and at all periods of biblical Hebrew.

The word bears subjective and personal overtones. First, *'am* represents a familial relationship. In Ruth 3:11 the word means "male kinsmen" with special emphasis on the paternal relationship: "And now, my daughter, fear not; I will do to thee all that thou requirest: for all the city of my people doth know that thou art a virtuous woman." Here the word is a collective noun insofar as it occurs in the singular; indeed, it is almost an abstract noun. In the plural the word refers to all the individuals who are related to a person through his father: "But he shall not defile himself, being a chief man among his people, to profane himself" (Lev. 21:4). This emphasis of the word is related to the meaning of its cognates in Ugaritic (clan), Arabic (uncle on one's father's side), and Nabataean (uncle on one's father's side). The word is quite often combined with divine names and titles in people's names (theophoric names) where God is set forth as the God of a particular tribe, clan, or family—for example, Jekameam (God has raised up a clan or family, 1 Chron. 23:19) and Jokneam (God has created a clan or family, Josh. 12:22).

Second, *'am* may signify those relatives (including women and children) who are grouped together locally whether or not they permanently inhabit a given location: "Then Jacob was greatly afraid and distressed: and he divided the people that was with him, and the flocks, and herds, and the camels, into two bands" (Gen. 32:7).

Third, this word may refer to the whole of a nation formed and united primarily by their descent from a common ancestor. Such a group has strong blood ties and social interrelationships and interactions. Often they live and work together in a society in a common location. This is the significance of the word in its first biblical appearance: "And the Lord said, Behold, the people is one, and they have all one language . . ." (Gen. 11:6). Hence, in this usage *'am* refers not simply to male relatives but to men, women, and children.

'Am may also include those who enter by religious adoption and marriage. The people of Israel initially were the descendants of Jacob (Israel) and their families: "And he said unto his people [Egyptians], Behold, the people of the children of Israel are more and mightier than we" (Exod. 1:9). Later the basic unity in a common covenant relationship with God becomes the unifying factor underlying *'am*. When they left Egypt, the people of Israel were joined by many others: "And a mixed multitude went up also with them; and flocks, and herds, even very much cattle" (Exod. 12:38). Such individuals and their families were taken into Israel before they observed the Passover: "And when a stranger shall sojourn with thee, and will keep the passover to the Lord, let all his males be circumcised, and then let him come near and keep it; and he shall be as one that is born in the land . . ." (Exod. 12:48). There is another mention of this group (perhaps) in Num. 11:4: "And the mixed multitude that

was among them fell a lusting: and the children of Israel also wept again, and said. . . ."

After that, however, we read of them no more. By the time of the conquest we read only of the "people" (*'am*) of Israel entering the land of Canaan and inheriting it (Judg. 5:11). Passages such as Deut. 32:9 clearly focus on this covenantal relationship as the basis of unity: "For the Lord's portion is his people; Jacob is the lot of his inheritance." This sense certainly emerges in the concept "to be cut off from one's people": "And the uncircumcised man child whose flesh of his foreskin is not circumcised, that soul shall be cut off from his people; he hath broken my covenant" (Gen. 17:14).

'Am can mean all those physical ancestors who lived previously and are now dead. So Abraham was gathered to his people: "Then Abraham gave up the ghost, and died in a good old age, an old man, and full of years; and was gathered to his people" (Gen. 25:8). There might be covenantal overtones here in the sense that Abraham was gathered to all those who were true believers. Jesus argued that such texts taught the reality of life after death (Matt. 22:32).

'Am can represent the individuals who together form a familial (and covenantal) group within a larger group: "Zebulun and Naphtali were a people that jeoparded their lives unto the death in the high places of the field [on the battlefield]" (Judg. 5:18). Some scholars have suggested that the reference here is to a fighting unit with the idea of blood relationship in the background. One must never forget, however, that among nomadic and semi-nomadic tribes there is no distinction between the concepts "militia" and "kinsmen": "And the Lord said unto Joshua, Fear not, neither be thou dismayed: take all the people of war with thee, and arise . . ." (Josh. 8:1). Compare Josh. 8:5 where *'am* by itself means fighting unit: "And I, and all the people that are with me, will approach unto the city . . ." (cf. Gen. 32:7).

'Am may signify the inhabitants of a city regardless of their familial or covenantal relationship; it is a territorial or political term: "And Boaz said unto the elders, and unto all the people, Ye are witnesses . . ." (Ruth 4:9).

This noun can be used of those who are privileged. In the phrase "people of the land" *'am* may signify those who have feudal rights, or those who may own land and are especially protected under the law: "And Abraham stood up, and bowed himself to the people of the land, even to the children of Heth" (Gen. 23:7). This sense of a full citizen appears when the phrase is used of Israel, too (cf. 2 Kings 11:14 ff.). In some contexts this phrase excludes those of high office such as the king, his ministers, and priests; "For, behold, I have made thee this day a defenced city, and an iron pillar, and brazen walls against the whole land, against the kings of Judah, against the princes thereof, against the priests thereof, and against the people of the land" (Jer. 1:18). In Lev. 4:27 this same phrase signifies the entire worshiping community of Israel: "And if any one of the common people [people of the land] sin through ignorance. . . ." The sense of privileged people with a proper relationship to and unique knowledge of God appears in Job 12:2: "No doubt but ye are the people, and wisdom shall die with you." Could it be that in Isa. 42:5 all mankind are conceived to be the privileged recipients of divine revelation and blessing: "Thus saith God the Lord, he that created the heavens, and stretched them out; he that spread forth the earth, and that which cometh out of it; he that giveth breath unto the people upon it, and spirit to them that walk therein."

Finally, sometimes *'am* used of an entire nation has political and territorial overtones. As such it may be paralleled to the Hebrew word with such overtones *(gôy):* "For thou art a holy people unto the Lord thy God, and the Lord hath chosen thee to be a peculiar people unto himself, above all the nations that are upon the earth" (Deut. 14:2; cf. Exod. 19:5,6).

PERADVENTURE

'ûlay (אוּלַי), "peradventure; perhaps; suppose; if; less." The 43 occurrences of this word appear in every period of biblical Hebrew.

This word meaning "peradventure or perhaps" usually expresses a hope: "Behold now, the Lord hath restrained me from bearing: I pray thee, go in unto my maid; it may be that I may obtain children by her" (Gen. 16:2—the first occurrence). Elsewhere *'ûlay* expresses fear or doubt: "Peradventure the woman will not be willing to follow me unto this land; must I needs bring thy son again unto the land from whence thou camest?" (Gen. 24:5).

If followed by another clause the word almost functions to introduce a protasis: "Peradventure there be fifty righteous within the city: wilt thou also destroy . . ." (Gen. 18:24).

In Num. 22:33 the word has a different force: "And the ass saw me, and turned from me these three times: unless she had turned from me, surely now also I had slain thee, and saved her alive."

PERFECT

A. Adjectives.

tāmîm (תָּמִים), "perfect; blameless; sincerity; entire; whole; complete; full." The 91 occurrences of this word are scattered throughout biblical literature with 51 of them in passages dealing with cultic offerings.

Tāmîm means "complete," in the sense of the entire or whole thing: "And he shall offer of the sacrifice of the peace offering an offering made by fire unto the Lord; the fat thereof, and the whole rump, it shall he take off hard by the backbone . . ." (Lev. 3:9). The sun stood still for the "whole" day while Joshua fought the Gibeonites (Josh. 10:13). In Lev. 23:15 God commands that there be seven "complete" sabbaths after the first fruit feast plus fifty days and then that the new grain offering be presented. A house within a walled city must be purchased back within a "full" year if it is to remain the permanent property of the seller (Lev. 25:30).

This word may mean "intact," or not cut up into pieces: "Behold, when it was whole, it [a piece of wood] was meet for no work . . ." (Ezek. 15:5).

Tāmîm may mean incontestable or free from objection. In Deut. 32:4 the word modifies God's work: "His work is perfect." The people of God are to avoid the idolatrous practices of the Canaanites. They are to "be perfect with the Lord thy God" (Deut. 18:13). Used in such contexts the word means the one so described externally meets all the requirements of God's law (cf. Ps. 18:23). This word modifies the victim to be offered to God (51 times). It means that the victim has no blemish (Lev. 22:18-21) as "blemish" is defined by God: "Ye shall offer at your own will a male without blemish, of the beeves, of the sheep, or of the goats" (Lev. 22:19).

In several contexts the word has a wider background. When one is described by it, there is nothing in his outward activities or internal disposition that is odious to God; ". . . Noah was a just man and perfect in his generations, and Noah walked with God" (Gen. 6:9). This word describes his entire relationship to God. In Judg. 9:16, where *tāmîm* describes a relationship between men, it is clear that more than mere external activity is meant: "Now therefore, if ye have done truly and sincerely [literally, in a sincere manner], in that ye have made Abimelech king. . . ." This extended connotation of this nuance is also evidenced when one compares Gen. 17:1 with Rom. 4 where Paul argues that Abraham fulfilled God's condition but that he did so only through faith.

Another adjective, *tām,* appears 15 times. With a cognate in Ugaritic the word means "complete or perfect" (Song of Sol. 5:2 RSV), "sound or wholesome" (Gen. 25:27), and "complete, morally innocent, having integrity" (Job 1:8).

B. Noun.

tōm (םֹת), "completeness." This noun, which occurs 25 times, signifies "completeness" in the following senses: fullness (Job 21:23), innocency or simplicity (2 Sam. 15:11), integrity (Gen. 20:5).

C. Verb.

tāmam (םַמָּת), "to be complete, be finished, be consumed, be without blame." This verb, which appears 64 times, has cognates in Aramaic, Syriac, and Arabic. The word means "to be finished or completed" in Gen. 47:18: "When that year was ended, they came unto him. . . ."

TO PERISH

A. Verb.

'ābad (דַבָא), "to perish, die, be lost, go astray, go to ruin, succumb, be carried off, fail." The word occurs in all the branches of the Semitic languages including biblical Aramaic. Biblical Hebrew attests this verb at every time period and about 120 times.

Basically *'ābad* represents the disappearance of someone or something. In its strongest sense the word means "to die or to cease to exist." The Lord warned Israel that disobedience and godlessness would be punished by their removal from the Promised Land and death in a foreign land: "And ye shall perish among the heathen, and the land of your enemies shall eat you up" (Lev. 26:38). This sense may be further heightened by the use of the intensive stem so that the verb comes to mean "utterly destroy." The stem also changes the force of the verb from intransitive to transitive. So God told Israel "to utterly destroy" ("bring to non-existence") the false gods of Canaan: ". . . [Utterly] destroy all their pictures and [utterly] destroy all their molten images . . ." (Num. 33:52). The force of this command was further heightened when He said: "Ye shall utterly destroy all the places, wherein the nations which ye shall possess served their gods . . . and destroy the names of them out of that place" (Deut. 12:2-3). This intensified sense is used of the destruction of peoples (armies), too; as for Pharaoh's army, "the Lord hath destroyed them unto this day" (Deut. 11:4).

A somewhat different emphasis of 'ābad is "to go to ruin" or "to be ruined." After the second plague Pharaoh's counsellors told him to grant Israel's request to leave because the nation was in ruins: ". . . knowest thou not yet that Egypt is destroyed [ruined]?" (Exod. 10:7—the first biblical occurrence). In a similar sense Moab is said "to be ruined" or laid waste: "Woe to thee, Moab! Thou art undone [NASB, "ruined"], O people of Chemosh . . . We have shot at them; Heshbon is perished even unto Dibon, and we have laid them waste even unto Nophah . . ." (Num. 21:29, 30).

Closely related to the immediately preceding emphasis is that of "to succumb." This use of 'ābad focuses on the process rather than the conclusion. The sons of Israel spoke to Moses about the disastrous effects of everyone drawing near to God. They needed some mediators (priests) who could focus on keeping ritualistically prepared so they would not die when they approached God. They used the verb, therefore, in the sense of the nation gradually perishing, or "succumbing" to death: "Behold, we die, we perish, we all perish. Whosoever cometh any thing near unto the tabernacle of the Lord shall die: shall we be consumed with dying?" (Num. 17:12, 13). God responds by establishing the priesthood so "that there be no wrath any more upon the children of Israel" (Num. 18:5).

'Ābad can also speak of being carried off to death or destruction by some means. The leaders of the rebellion against the Aaronic priesthood (Korah, Dathan, and Abiram) and their families were swallowed up by the ground: ". . . and the earth closed upon them: and they perished from among the congregation" (Num. 16:33). This same nuance appears when God says the people will "perish" from off the land if they do not keep the covenant: ". . . Ye shall soon utterly perish from off the land whereunto ye go over Jordan to possess it; ye shall not prolong your days upon it, but shall utterly be destroyed" (Deut. 4:26). As a nation they will be destroyed as far as the land is concerned.

The verb may mean to disappear but not be destroyed, in other words "to be lost." God instructs Israel concerning lost possessions: "In like manner shalt thou do with his ass; and so shalt thou do with his raiment; and with all lost things of thy brother's, which he hath lost, and thou hast found, shalt thou do likewise: thou mayest not hide thyself" (Deut. 22:3). Israel is called "lost sheep" whose "shepherds have caused them to go astray" (Jer. 50:6).

Another nuance of the verb is "to go astray" in the sense of wandering. At the dedication of the first fruits Israel is to recognize God's rights to the land, that He is the landowner and they are the temporary tenants, by confessing "a Syrian ready to perish was my father" (Deut. 26:5; NASB, "my father was a wandering Aramean").

Finally, *'ābad* can be applied to human qualities which are lessening or have lessened: "For they are a nation void of counsel, neither is there any understanding in them" (Deut. 32:28). The word can also be used of the failure of human wisdom as in Ps. 146:4: as for man "his breath goeth forth, he returneth to his earth; in that very day his thoughts perish."

B. Nouns.

There are four nouns related to the verb. *'Abēdāh,* which is found 4 times, refers to a "thing which has been lost" (Exod. 22:9). The noun *'abaddôn* occurs 6 times and means "the place of destruction" (Job 26:6). *'Abədān* occurs once with the meaning "destruction" (Esth. 9:5). *'Ābədān* also occurs twice with the meaning "destruction" (Esth. 8:6; 9:5).

PESTILENCE

deber (דֶּבֶר), "pestilence." The meaning of the cognate word varies in other Semitic languages from the Hebrew. In Ugaritic, *dbr* probably signifies "death." The Arabic word *dabrat* means "misfortune," similar to the Akkadian *dibiru,* "misfortune." The word occurs fewer than 60 times in the Old Testament, and mainly in the prophets Jeremiah and Ezekiel.

The meaning of *deber* is best denoted by the English word "pestilence" or "plague." A country might be quickly reduced in population by the "plague" (cf. 2 Sam. 24:13 ff.). The nature of the "plague" (bubonic or other) is often difficult to determine from the contexts, as the details of medical interest are not given or are scanty. In the prophetical writings, the "plague" occurs with other disasters: famine, flood, and the sword: "When they fast, I will not hear their cry; and when they offer burnt offering and an oblation, I will not accept them: but I will consume them by the sword, and by the famine, and by the pestilence" (Jer. 14:12).

The Septuagint gives the following translation: *thanatos* ("death").

PILLAR

'ayil (אַיִל), "pillar." This word appears 22 times and only once outside Ezek. 40–41: "And for the entering of the oracle he made doors of olive tree: the lintel [pillar] and side posts were a fifth part of the wall" (1 Kings 6:31).

matstsēbāh (מַצֵּבָה), "pillar; monument; sacred stone." This word is derived from the verb *nātsab,* and it is found about 35 times.

This word refers to a "pillar" as a personal memorial in 2 Sam. 18:18: "Now Absalom in his lifetime had taken and reared up for himself a pillar . . . and he called the pillar after his own name: and it is called unto this day,

Absalom's place." In Gen. 28:18 the "monument" is a memorial of the Lord's appearance. *Matstsēbāh* is used in connection with the altar built by Moses in Exod. 24:4, and it refers to "sacred stones or pillars."

PIOUS

chāsîd (חָסִיד), "one who is pious, godly." Psalms contains 25 of the 32 appearances of this word.

Basically, *chāsîd* means one who practices *chesed* ("loving-kindness"), so it is to be translated the "pious" or "godly one." The word's first biblical occurrence is in Deut. 33:8 where it represents a human being: "Give to Levi thy Thummim, and thy Urim to thy godly one" (RSV). The word appears in Ps. 32:6: "For this shall every one that is godly pray unto thee in a time when thou mayest be found. . . ." The word is applied to God in Ps. 145:17: "The Lord is righteous in all his ways, and holy in all his works."

This noun is derived from the noun *chesed*.

PIT

bə'ēr (בְּאֵר), "pit; well." Cognates of this noun appear in Ugaritic, Akkadian, Arabic, Phoenician, Aramaic, and Ethiopic. This word appears 37 times in the Bible with no occurrences in the Old Testament prophetic books.

Bə'ēr means a "well" in which there may be water. (By itself the word does not always infer the presence of water.) The word refers to the "pit" itself whether dug or natural: "And Abraham reproved Abimelech because of a well of water, which Abimelech's servants had violently taken away" (Gen. 21:25). Such a "well" may have a narrow enough mouth that it can be blocked with a stone which a single strong man could move (Gen. 29:2, 10). In the desert country of the ancient Near East a "well" was an important place and its water the source of deep satisfaction for the thirsty. This concept pictures the role of a wife for a faithful husband (Prov. 5:15).

A "pit" may contain something other than water. In its first biblical appearance *bə'ēr* is used of tar pits: "And the vale of Siddim was full of slimepits . . ." (Gen. 14:10). A "pit" may contain nothing as does the "pit" which becomes one's grave (Ps. 55:23, "pit of the grave"). In some passages the word was to represent more than a depository for the body but a place where one exists after death (Ps. 69:15). Since Babylonian mythology knows of such a place with gates that shut over the deceased, it is not at all unreasonable to see such a place alluded to (minus the erroneous ideas of the pagans) in the Bible.

TO PLANT

nāta' (נָטַע), "to plant." Common in both ancient and modern Hebrew, this word is also found in ancient Ugaritic. It occurs approximately 60 times in the Hebrew Old Testament. The word is used for the first time in the text in Gen.

2:8: "And the Lord God planted a garden eastward in Eden. . . ." The regular word for planting trees and vineyards, *nāta'* is used figuratively of planting people: "Yet I had planted thee [Judah] a noble vine . . ." (Jer. 2:21). This use is a close parallel to the famous "Song of the Vineyard" (Isa. 5:1-10) where Israel and Judah are called God's "pleasant planting" (Isa. 5:7 RSV). *Nāta'* is used in Isa. 17:10 in an unusual description of idolatry: ". . . Therefore shalt thou plant pleasant plants, and shalt set it with strange slips." The NEB (much like the JB) translates more specifically: "Plant them, if you will, your gardens in honor of Adonis" (Adonis was the god of vegetation). "To plant" sometimes has the meaning of "to establish." Thus, God promises in the latter days, "I will plant them upon their land" (Amos 9:15).

TO PLEAD

A. Verb.

rîb (רִיב), "to plead, strive, conduct a legal case, make a charge." Found in both biblical and modern Hebrew, this term occurs as a verb some 70 times. It appears in the text for the first time in Gen. 26:20: "And the herdmen of Gerar did strive with Isaac's herdmen. . . ." Such "striving" with words is found frequently in the biblical text (Gen. 31:36; Exod. 17:2). Sometimes contentious words lead to bodily struggle and injury: "And if men strive together, and one smite another . . ." (Exod. 21:18). The prophets use *rîb* frequently to indicate that God has an indictment, a legal case, against Israel: "The Lord standeth up to plead, and standeth to judge the people" (Isa. 3:13). In one of his visions, Amos noted: ". . . the Lord God called to contend by fire . . ." (Amos 7:4 KJV; RSV, "calling for a judgment"). Micah 6 is a classic example of such a legal case against Judah, calling on the people "to plead" their case (6:1) and progressively showing how only God has a valid case (6:8).

B. Noun.

rîb (רִיב), "strife; dispute." This word appears as a noun 60 times. The word appears twice in Mic. 6:2: "Hear ye, O mountains, the Lord's controversy, and ye strong foundations of the earth: for the Lord hath a controversy with his people, and he will plead with Israel."

PLEASURE

A. Noun.

chēphets (חֵפֶץ), "pleasure; delight; desire; request; affair; thing." None of the 39 occurrences of this word appear before First Samuel. All its occurrences are scattered through the rest of biblical literature.

This word often means "pleasure" or "delight": "Hath the Lord as great delight in burnt offerings and sacrifices, as in obeying the voice of the Lord?" (1 Sam. 15:22—the first occurrence). Thus "the preacher [writer of Ecclesiastes] sought to find out acceptable [*chēphets*] words: and that which was written was upright, even words of truth" (Eccl. 12:10), words that were both true and aesthetically pleasing. A good wife works with "hands of delight," or hands which delight in her work because of her love for her family; "she seeketh wool, and flax, and worketh willingly [in delight] with her hands" (Prov. 31:13).

Chēphets can mean not simply what one takes pleasure in or what gives someone delight but one's wish or desire: "Although my house be not so with God; yet he hath made with me an everlasting covenant, ordered in all things, and sure: for this is all my salvation, and all my desire, although he make it not to grow" (2 Sam. 23:5). "To do one's desire" is to grant a request (1 Kings 5:8). "Stones of desire" are precious stones (Isa. 54:12).

Third, *chēphets* sometimes represents one's affairs as that in which one takes delight: ". . . There is . . . a time to every purpose [literally, delight] under the heaven" (Eccl. 3:1). In Isa. 58:13 the first occurrence of this word means "pleasure" or "delight," while the last occurrence indicates an affair or matter in which one delights: "If thou turn away thy foot from the sabbath, from doing thy pleasure on my holy day; and call the sabbath a delight, the holy of the Lord, honorable; and shalt honor him, not doing thine own ways, nor finding thine own pleasure, nor speaking thine own words."

Finally, in one passage this word means "affair" in the sense of a "thing" or "situation": "If thou seest the oppression of the poor, and violent perverting of judgment and justice in a province, marvel not at the matter [NASB, "sight"] . . ." (Eccl. 5:8).

B. Verb.

chāphets (חָפֵץ), "to take pleasure in; take care of; desire; delight in; have delight in." This verb, which occurs 72 times in biblical Hebrew, has cognates in Arabic, Phoenician, Syriac, and Arabic. *Chāphets* means not "to delight in" in 2 Sam. 15:26: "But if he thus say, I have no delight in thee; behold, here am I, let him do to me as seemeth good unto him."

C. Adjective.

chāphets (חָפֵץ), "delighting in; having pleasure in." This adjective appears 12 times in biblical Hebrew. The word is found in Ps. 35:27: "Let the Lord be magnified, which hath pleasure in the prosperity of his servant."

TO PLOW

A. Verb.

chārash (חָרַשׁ), "to plow, engrave, work in metals." This word occurs in ancient Ugaritic, as well as in modern Hebrew where it has the primary sense of "to plow." It is found approximately 50 times in the Hebrew Old Testament. A fitting word for the agricultural nature of Israelite culture, *chārash* is frequently used of "plowing" a field, usually with animals such as oxen (1 Kings 19:19). The imagery of cutting up or tearing up a field with a plow easily lent itself to the figurative use of the word to mean mistreatment by others: "The plowers plowed upon my back: they made long their furrows" (Ps. 129:3). The word is used to express the plotting of evil against a friend in Prov. 3:29: "Devise not evil against thy neighbor, seeing he dwelleth securely by thee [literally, "do not plow evil"]."

The use of *chārash* in the sense of "working or engraving" metals is not used in the Old Testament as much as it might have been if Israel had been as given to such craftsmanship as her neighbors, or perhaps because of the commandment against images (Exod. 20:4). The word is used in 1 Kings 7:14: ". . . His father was a man of Tyre, a worker in brass [literally, "a man who works in brass"]. . . ." The first occurrence of *chārash* is in Gen. 4:22 where it is used of the "artificer in brass and iron." The figurative use of "engraving" is vividly seen in the expression describing the extent of Israel's sin: "The sin of Judah is written with a pen of iron, and with the point of a diamond: it is graven upon the table of their heart . . ." (Jer. 17:1).

An updating or correction of the KJV is called for in 1 Sam. 8:12 where *chārash* is translated by the old English term, "to ear the ground"!

B. Noun.

chārāsh (חָרָשׁ), "engraver; artificer." The prophets denounced the craftsmanship of these workers in metals when they made images (Isa. 40:20; Hos. 8:6). A more positive approach to the word is conveyed in 1 Chron. 29:5: "The gold for things of gold . . . and for all manner of work to be made by the hands of artificers. And who then is willing to consecrate his service this day unto the Lord?"

TO POLLUTE

chālal (חָלַל), "to pollute, defile, profane, begin." This word is used more than 225 times in the Old Testament. As a verb, *chālal* is used in what seem to be two quite different ways. In one sense, the word means "to pollute" or "to profane." In the second usage the word has the sense of "to begin."

The most frequent use of this Hebrew root is in the sense of "to pollute, defile." This may be a ritual defilement, such as that resulting from contact with a dead body (Lev. 21:4), or the ceremonial profaning of the sacred altar by the use of tools in order to shape the stones (Exod. 20:25). Holy places may be profaned (Ezek. 7:24); the name of God (Ezek. 20:9) and even God Himself (Ezek. 22:26) may be profaned. The word is often used to describe the defilement which results from illicit sexual acts, such as harlotry (Lev. 21:9) or violation of one's father's bed (Gen. 49:4—the first occurrence).

In more than 50 instances, this root is used in the sense of "to begin." Perhaps the most important of such uses is found in Gen. 4:26. There it is stated that after the birth of Seth, who was born to Adam and Eve after the murder of Abel by Cain, "men began to call upon the name of the Lord" (RSV). The Septuagint translates it something like this: "he hoped [trusted] to call on the name of the Lord God." The Jerusalem Bible says: "This man was the first to invoke the name of Yahweh." One must ask whether the writer meant to say that it was not until the birth of Enosh, the son of Seth, that people "began" to call on the name of the Lord altogether, or whether he meant that this was the first time the name Yahweh was used. In view of the accounts in Gen. 1-3, neither of these seems likely. Perhaps the writer is simply saying that in contrast to the apparent non-God-fearing attitude expressed by Cain, the generation beginning with Seth and his son Enosh was known for its God-fearing way of life. Perhaps, in view of the passive intensive verb form used here, the meaning is something like this: "Then it was begun again to call on the name of the Lord."

POOR (PERSON), WEAK (PERSON)

A. Nouns.

'ānî (עָנִי), "poor; weak; afflicted; humble." This word, which also appears in early Aramaic and post-biblical Hebrew, occurs in biblical Hebrew about 76 times and in all periods.

This noun is frequently used in synonymous parallelism with 'ebəyôn ("needy") and/or dal ("poor"). It differs from both in emphasizing some kind of disability or distress. A hired servant as one who is in a lower (oppressive) social and material condition is described both as an 'ebəyôn and 'ānî: "Thou shalt not oppress a hired servant that is poor and needy, whether he be of thy brethren, or of thy strangers that are in thy land within thy gates: At his day thou shalt give him his hire, neither shall the sun go down upon it; for he is poor, and setteth his heart upon it: lest he cry against thee unto the Lord, and it be sin unto thee" (Deut. 24:14–15). If wrongly oppressed, he can call on God for defense. Financially, the 'ānî lives from day to day and is socially defenseless, being subject to oppression. In its first biblical occurrence the 'ānî is guaranteed (if men obey God's law) his outer garment for warmth at night even though that garment might be held as collateral during the day: "If thou lend money to any of my people that is poor by thee, thou shall not be to him as a usurer, neither shalt thou lay upon him usury" (Exod. 22:25). The godly protect and deliver the "afflicted" (Isa. 10:2; Ezek. 18:17), while the ungodly take advantage of them, increasing their oppressed condition (Isa. 58:7). The king is especially charged to protect the 'ānî: "Open thy mouth, judge righteously, and plead the cause of the poor and needy" (Prov. 31:9).

'Ānî can refer to one who is physically oppressed: "Therefore hear now this, thou afflicted, and drunken, but not with wine" (Isa. 51:21).

Physical oppression is sometimes related to spiritual oppression as in Ps. 22:24: "For he hath not despised nor abhorred the affliction of the afflicted; neither hath he hid his face from him. . . ." Outward affliction frequently leads to inner spiritual affliction and results in an outcry to God: "Turn thee unto me, and have mercy upon me; for I am desolate and afflicted" (Ps. 25:16). Even apart from outward affliction, the pious are frequently described as the "afflicted" or "poor" for whom God provides: "Thy congregation hath dwelt therein: thou, O God, hast prepared of thy goodness for the poor" (Ps. 68:10). In such cases spiritual poverty and want are clearly in view.

Sometimes the word means "humble" or "lowly," as it does in Zech. 9:9, where it describes the Messiah: "Behold, thy King cometh unto thee: he is just, and having salvation; lowly, and riding upon an ass . . ." (cf. Ps. 18:27; Prov. 3:34; Isa. 66:2).

Related to '*ānî* is the noun '*onî*, "affliction." It appears about 36 times and in all periods of biblical Hebrew. '*Onî* represents the state of pain and/or punishment resulting from affliction. In Deut. 16:3 the shewbread is termed the bread of "affliction" because it is a physical reminder of sin, the cause of "affliction" (Ps. 25:18), the hardship involved in sin (especially the Egyptian bondage), and divine deliverance from sin (Ps. 119:50).

'*Ānî* is also related to the word '*anāwāh*, "humility, gentleness." This word occurs only 5 times, setting forth the two characteristics gained from affliction. Applied to God, it represents His submission to His own nature (Ps. 45:4).

dal (לַד), "one who is low, poor, reduced, helpless, weak." This noun also appears in Ugaritic. It occurs in biblical Hebrew about 47 times and in all periods.

Dal is related to, but differs from, '*ānî* (which suggests affliction of some kind), '*ebəyôn* (which emphasizes need), and *rāsh* (which suggests destitution). The *dallîm* constituted the middle class of Israel—those who were physically deprived (in the ancient world the majority of people were poor). For example, the *dallîm* may be viewed as the opposite of the rich (Exod. 30:15; cf. Ruth 3:10; Prov. 10:15).

In addition, the word may connote social poverty or lowliness. As such, *dal* describes those who are the counterparts of the great: "Ye shall do no unrighteousness in judgment: thou shalt not respect the person of the poor, nor honor the person of the mighty: but in righteousness shalt thou judge thy neighbor" (Lev. 19:15; cf. Amos 2:7).

When Gideon challenged the Lord's summoning him to deliver Israel, he emphasized that his clan was too weak to do the job: "And he said unto him, Oh my Lord, wherewith shall I save Israel? behold, my family is poor in Manasseh . . ." (Judg. 6:15; cf. 2 Sam. 3:1). God commands that society protect the poor, the lowly, and the weak: "Thou shalt not follow a multitude to do evil; neither shalt thou speak in a cause to decline after many to wrest judgment: neither shalt thou countenance a poor man in his cause" (Exod. 23:2-3; cf. Lev. 14:21; Isa. 10:2). He also warns that if men fail to provide justice, He will do so (Isa. 11:4).

A fourth emphasis appears in Gen. 41:19 (the first biblical appearance of the word), where *dal* is contrasted to "healthy" or "fat": "And behold, seven other kine came up after them, poor and very ill-favored and lean-fleshed. . . ." Thus, *dal* indicates a physical condition and appearance of sickliness. It is used in this sense to describe Amnon's appearance as he longed for Tamar (2 Sam. 13:4).

Dal is used (very infrequently) of spiritual poverty (in such cases it is sometimes paralleled to '*ebəyôn*): "Therefore I said, Surely these are poor; they are foolish: for they know not the way of the Lord, nor the judgment of their God" (Jer. 5:4). Some scholars argue that here the word means "ignorance"; and as the context shows, this is ignorance in the knowledge of God's word.

Another noun, *dallah*, is related to *dal*. *Dallah*, which appears about 8 times, means "poverty; dishevelled hair." The word appears in 2 Kings 24:14: ". . . none remained, save the poorest sort of the people of the land," where *dallah* emphasizes the social lowliness and "poverty" of those people whom it describes. In Song of Sol. 7:5 the word refers to "dishevelled hair" in the sense of something that hangs down.

B. Verbs.

dālal (דָּלַל), "to be low, hang down." This verb appears only 8 times in the Bible and always in poetical passages. It has cognates or near cognates in Arabic, Ethiopic, Akkadian, and extra-biblical Hebrew. The word appears in Ps. 79:8: "O remember not against us former iniquities: let thy tender mercies speedily prevent us; for we are brought very low."

'ānāh (עָנָה), "to afflict; oppress; humble." This verb, which also appears in Arabic, occurs about 74 times in biblical Hebrew and in every period. The first occurrence is in Gen. 15:13: "Know of a surety that thy seed shall be a stranger in a land that is not theirs, and shall serve them; and they shall afflict them four hundred years."

C. Adjective.

'ānāw (עָנָו), "humble; poor; meek." This adjective, which appears about 21 times in biblical Hebrew, is closely related to *'ānî* and derived from the same verb. Sometimes this word is synonymous with *'ānî*. Perhaps this is due to the well-known *waw-yodh* interchange. *'Ānāw* appears almost exclusively in poetical passages and describes the intended outcome of affliction from God, namely "humility." In its first appearance the word depicts the objective condition as well as the subjective stance of Moses. He was entirely dependent on God and saw that he was: "Now the man Moses was very meek, above all the men which were upon the face of the earth" (Num. 12:3).

TO POSSESS

A. Verb.

yārash (יָרַשׁ), "to inherit; subdue; take possession; dispossess; impoverish." This word is attested in all Semitic languages except Akkadian, Phoenician, and biblical Aramaic. The word appears in all periods of Hebrew; the Bible attests it about 260 times.

Basically *yārash* means "to inherit." The verb can connote the state of being designated as an heir. Abram said to God: "Behold, to me thou hast given no [offspring]: and, lo, one born in my house is mine heir [literally, is the one who is inheriting me]" (Gen. 15:3—the first biblical occurrence of the word). Whatever Abram had to be passed on to his legal descendants was destined to be given to his servant. Hence his servant was his legally designated heir.

This root can also represent the status of having something as one's permanent possession, as a possession which may be passed on to one's legal descendants. God told Abram: ''I am the Lord that brought thee out of Ur of the Chaldees, to give thee this land to inherit it'' (Gen. 15:7). *Yārash* can mean ''to take over as a permanent possession'': ''And if his father have no brethren, then ye shall give his inheritance unto his kinsman that is next to him of his family, and he shall possess it . . .'' (Num. 27:11). The verb sometimes means to take something over (in the case of the Promised Land) by conquest as a permanent possession: ''The Lord shall make the pestilence cleave unto thee, until he have consumed thee from off the land, whither thou goest to possess it'' (Deut. 28:21).

When people are the object, *yārash* sometimes means ''to dispossess'' in the sense of taking away their inheritable goods and putting them in such a social position that they cannot hold possessions or inherit permanent possessions: ''The Horim also dwelt in Seir beforetime; but the children of Esau succeeded them, when they had destroyed them from before them, and dwelt in their stead . . .'' (Deut. 2:12). To cause someone to be dispossessed is ''to impoverish'' him: ''The Lord maketh poor, and maketh rich . . .'' (1 Sam. 2:7), the Lord makes one to be without permanent inheritable possessions.

B. Nouns.

Several nouns related to *yārash* occur infrequently in biblical Hebrew. *Yərēshāh*, which appears twice, means ''something given as a permanent possession; to be taken over by conquest'' (Num. 24:18). *Yərushshāh* occurs 14 times; it means ''to have as a possession'' (Deut. 2:5), ''to be designated as a possession, to receive as a possession'' (Deut. 2:9). The noun *môrāsh* means ''a place one has as a permanent possession'' in its 2 appearances (Isa. 14:23; Obad. 17). *Môrāshāh*, which occurs 9 times, can refer to ''a place one has as a permanent possession'' (Exod. 6:8), ''a thing one has as a permanent possession'' (Deut. 33:4), and ''people to be dispossessed'' (Ezek. 25:4).

Some scholars associate *resheth*, ''net,'' with *yārash*. Hence, a ''net'' is conceived as a thing which receives and holds (possesses) something or someone (Job 18:8). Others suggest that *resheth* can also mean ''pit'' (cf. Ps. 9:15; 35:7-8).

POSSESSION

səgullāh (סְגֻלָּה), ''possession.'' Cognates of this word appear in late Aramaic and Akkadian. This word occurs only 8 times.

Səgullāh signifies ''property'' in the special sense of a private possession one personally acquired and carefully preserves. Six times this word is used of Israel as God's personally acquired (elected, delivered from Egyptian bondage, and formed into what He wanted them to be), carefully preserved, and privately possessed people: ''Now therefore, if ye will obey my voice indeed, and keep my covenant, then ye shall be a peculiar treasure [NASB, ''possession''] unto me above all people: for all the earth is mine'' (Exod. 19:5—first occurrence).

TO POUR, FLOW

yātsaq (יָצַק), "to pour, pour out, cast, flow." Commonly used throughout
the history of the Hebrew language, this word occurs in ancient Ugaritic with
the same nuances as in the Old Testament. *Yātsaq* occurs in the Hebrew Bible
just over 50 times. The word is used first in Gen. 28:18, where it is said that
after Jacob had slept at Bethel with his head resting on a stone, he "poured oil
upon the top of it." He again "poured" oil on a stone pillar at Bethel while on
his return trip home twenty years later (Gen. 35:14). The idea expressed in
these two instances and others (Lev. 8:12; 21:10) is that of anointing with oil;
it is not the ordinary term for "to anoint." (The regular term for "to anoint" is
māshach, which gives us the word "messiah.")

Many things may "be poured out," such as oil in sacrifice (Lev. 2:1), water
for washing purposes (2 Kings 3:11), and pottage for eating (2 Kings 4:41).
This verb is used to express the idea of "pouring out" or "casting" molten
metals (Exod. 25:12; 26:37; 1 Kings 7:46). The idea of "pouring upon or
infusing" someone is found in Ps. 41:8: "A wicked thing is poured out upon
him" (NASB). The context seems to imply the infusion of a sickness, as
interpreted by the JB: "This sickness is fatal that has overtaken him."

shāphak (שָׁפַךְ), "to pour out, pour, shed." A common Semitic word, this
verb is found in both ancient Akkadian and Ugaritic, as well as throughout
Hebrew. *Shāphak* occurs just over 100 times in the text of the Hebrew Bible.
In its first use in the Old Testament, the word is part of the general principle
concerning the taking of human life: "Whoso sheddeth man's blood, by man
shall his blood be shed . . ." (Gen. 9:6). While it is frequently used in this
sense of "shedding" or "pouring out" blood, the word is commonly used of
the "pouring out" of the contents of a vessel, such as water (Exod. 4:9;
1 Sam. 7:6), plaster or dust (Lev. 14:41), and drink offerings to false gods (Isa.
57:6).

In its figurative use, *shāphak* indicates the "pouring out" of God's wrath
(Hos. 5:10), of contempt (Job 12:21), of wickedness (Jer. 14:16), and of the
Spirit of God (Ezek. 39:29). The psalmist describes his helpless condition in
this picturesque phrase: "I am poured out like water" (Ps. 22:14 KJV; NEB,
"My strength drains away like water"; JB, "I am like water draining away").

POWER

kōach (כֹּחַ), "strength; power; force; ability." This Hebrew word is used
in biblical, rabbinic, and modern Hebrew with little change in meaning. The
root is uncertain in Hebrew, but the verb is found in Arabic (*wakaha,* "batter
down," and *kwh,* "defeat"). *Kōach,* which occurs 124 times, is a poetic word
as it is used most frequently in the poetic and prophetical literature.

The basic meaning of *kōach* is an ability to do something. Samson's
"strength" lay in his hair (Judg. 16:5), and we must keep in mind that his
"strength" had been demonstrated against the Philistines. Nations and kings
exert their "powers" (Josh. 17:17; Dan. 8:24). It is even possible to say that a
field has *kōach,* as it does or does not have vital "powers" to produce and

harvest: "When thou tillest the ground, it shall not henceforth yield unto thee her strength [i.e., crops] . . ." (Gen. 4:12—the first occurrence). In the Old Testament it is recognized that by eating one gains "strength" (1 Sam. 28:22), whereas one loses one's "abilities" in fasting (1 Sam. 28:20); "And he arose, and did eat and drink, and went in the strength of that meat forty days and forty nights unto Horeb the mount of God" (1 Kings 19:8).

The above definition of *kōach* fits well in the description of Daniel and his friends: "Children in whom was no blemish, but well-favored, and skillful in all wisdom, and cunning in knowledge, and understanding science, and such as had ability [*kōach*] in them to stand in the king's palace, and whom they might teach the learning and the tongue of the Chaldeans" (Dan. 1:4). The "ability" is here not physical but mental. They were talented in having the intellectual acumen of learning the skills of the Babylonians and thus training for being counselors to the king. The internal fortitude was best demonstrated by the difficulties and frustrations of life. A strong man withstood hard times. The proverb bears out this important teaching: "If thou faint in the day of adversity, thy strength is small" (Prov. 24:10).

A special sense of *kōach* is the meaning "property." The results of native "abilities," the development of special gifts, and the manifestation of one's "strength" led often to prosperity and riches. Those who returned from the Exile gave willingly out of their riches *(kōach)* to the building fund of the temple (Ezra 2:69). A proverb warns against adultery, because one's "strength," or one's wealth, may be taken by others: "Lest strangers be filled with thy wealth [*kōach*]; and thy labors be in the house of a stranger" (Prov. 5:10).

In the Old Testament, God had demonstrated His "strength" to Israel. The language of God's "strength" is highly metaphorical. God's right hand gloriously manifests His "power" (Exod. 15:6). His voice is loud: "The voice of the Lord is powerful; the voice of the Lord is full of majesty" (Ps. 29:4). In His "power," He delivered Israel from Egypt (Exod. 32:11) and brought them through the Red Sea (Exod. 15:6; cf. Num. 14:13). Even as He advances the rights of the poor and needy (Isa. 50:2), He brought the Israelites as a needy people into the Promised Land with His "power": "He hath showed his people the power of his works, that he may give them the heritage of the heathen" (Ps. 111:6). He delights in helping His people; however, the Lord does not tolerate self-sufficiency on man's part. Isaiah rebuked the king of Assyria for his arrogance in claiming to have been successful in his conquests (10:12-14), and he remarked that the axe (Assyria) should not boast over the one who chops (God) with it (v. 15). Likewise God had warned His people against pride in taking the land of Canaan: "And thou say in thine heart, My power [*kōach*] and the might of mine hand hath gotten me this wealth. But thou shalt remember the Lord thy God: for it is he that giveth thee power [*kōach*] to get wealth, that he may establish his covenant which he sware unto thy fathers, as it is this day" (Deut. 8:17-18). The believer must learn to depend upon God and trust in Him: "This is the word of the Lord unto Zerubbabel, saying, Not by might, nor by power, but by my spirit, saith the Lord of hosts" (Zech. 4:6).

The Septuagint gives the following translations: *ischus* ("strength; power; might") and *dunamis* ("power; might; strength; force; ability; capability").

TO PRAISE

A. Verb.

hālal (הָלַל), "to praise, celebrate, glory, sing (praise), boast." The meaning "to praise" is actually the meaning of the intensive form of the Hebrew verb *hālal*, which in its simple active form means "to boast." In this latter sense *hālal* is found in its cognate forms in ancient Akkadian, of which Babylonian and Assyrian are dialects. The word is found in Ugaritic in the sense of "shouting," and perhaps "jubilation." Found more than 160 times in the Old Testament, *hālal* is used for the first time in Gen. 12:15, where it is noted that because of Sarah's great beauty, the princes of Pharaoh "praised" (KJV, "commended") her to Pharaoh.

While *hālal* is often used simply to indicate "praise" of people, including the king (2 Chron. 23:12) or the beauty of Absalom (2 Sam. 14:25), the word is usually used in reference to the "praise" of God. Indeed, not only all living things but all created things, including the sun and moon, are called upon "to praise" God (Ps. 148:2-5, 13; 150:1). Typically, such "praise" is called for and expressed in the sanctuary, especially in times of special festivals (Isa. 62:9).

The Hebrew name for the Book of Psalms is simply the equivalent for the word "praises" and is a bit more appropriate than "Psalms," which comes from the Greek and has to do with the accompaniment of singing with a stringed instrument of some sort. It is little wonder that the Book of Psalms contains more than half the occurrences of *hālal* in its various forms. Psalms 113–118 are traditionally referred to as the "Hallel Psalms," because they have to do with praise to God for deliverance from Egyptian bondage under Moses. Because of this, they are an important part of the traditional Passover service. There is no reason to doubt that these were the hymns sung by Jesus and His disciples on Maundy Thursday when He instituted the Lord's Supper (Matt. 26:30).

The word *hālal* is the source of "Hallelujah," a Hebrew expression of "praise" to God which has been taken over into virtually every language of mankind. The Hebrew "Hallelujah" is generally translated "Praise the Lord!" The Hebrew term is more technically translated "Let us praise Yah," the term "Yah" being a shortened form of "Yahweh," the unique Israelite name for God. The term "Yah" is found in the KJV rendering of Ps. 68:4, reflecting the Hebrew text; however, the Jerusalem Bible (JB) translates it with "Yahweh." Most versions follow the traditional translation "Lord," a practice begun in Judaism before New Testament times when the Hebrew term for "Lord" was substituted for "Yahweh," although it probably means something like "He who causes to be." The Greek approximation of "Hallelujah" is found 4 times in the New Testament in the form "Alleluia" (Rev. 19:1, 3-4, 6). Christian hymnody certainly would be greatly impoverished if the term "Hallelujah" were suddenly removed from our language of praise.

yādāh (יָדָה), "to give thanks; laud; praise." A common Hebrew word in all its periods, this verb is an important word in the language of worship. *Yādāh* is found nearly 120 times in the Hebrew Bible, the first time being in the story of the birth of Judah, Jacob's son who was born to Leah: "And she conceived again and bore a son, and said, This time I will praise the Lord; therefore she called his name Judah" (Gen. 29:35 RSV).

As is to be expected, this word is found most frequently in the Book of Psalms (some 70 times). As an expression of thanks or praise, it is a natural part of ritual or public worship as well as personal praise to God (Ps. 30:9, 12; 35:18). Thanks often are directed to the name of the Lord (Ps. 106:47; 122:4).

The variation in translation may be seen in 1 Kings 8:33: "confess" thy name (KJV, NEB, NASB); "acknowledge" (RSV); "praise" (JB, NAB).

B. Nouns.

təhillāh (תְּהִלָּה), "glory; praise; song of praise; praiseworthy deeds." *Təhillāh* occurs 57 times and in all periods of biblical Hebrew.

First, this word denotes a quality or attribute of some person or thing, "glory or praiseworthiness": "He is thy praise, and he is thy God, that hath done for thee these great and terrible things, which thine eyes have seen" (Deut. 10:21). Israel is God's "glory" when she exists in a divinely exalted and blessed state: "And give him no rest, till he establish, and till he make Jerusalem a praise in the earth" (Isa. 62:7; cf. Jer. 13:11).

Second, in some cases *təhillāh* represents the words or song by which God is publicly lauded, or by which His "glory" is publicly declared: "My praise [the Messiah is speaking here] shall be of thee in the great congregation. . ." (Ps. 22:25). Ps. 22:22 is even clearer: "I will declare thy name unto my brethren: in the midst of the congregation will I praise thee."

In a third nuance *təhillāh* is a technical-musical term for a song *(shîr)* which exalts or praises God: "David's psalm of praise" (heading for Ps. 145; v. 1 in the Hebrew). Perhaps Neh. 11:17 refers to a choirmaster or one who conducts such singing of "praises": "And Mattaniah . . . , the son of Asaph, was the principal to begin the thanksgiving in prayer [who at the beginning was the leader of praise at prayer]. . . ."

Finally, *təhillāh* may represent deeds which are worthy of "praise," or deeds for which the doer deserves "praise and glory." This meaning is in the word's first biblical appearance: "Who is like unto thee, O Lord, among the gods? Who is like thee, glorious in holiness, fearful in praises [in praiseworthy deeds], doing wonders [miracles]?" (Exod. 15:11).

Two other related nouns are *mahalāl* and *hillûlîm*. *Mahalāl* occurs once (Prov. 27:21) and denotes the degree of "praise" or its lack. *Hillûlîm*, which occurs twice, means "festal jubilation" in the fourth year at harvest time (Lev. 19:24, RSV; Judg. 9:27, NASB).

tôdāh (תּוֹדָה), "thanksgiving." This important noun form, found some 30 times in the Old Testament, is used there in the sense of "thanksgiving." The word is preserved in modern Hebrew as the regular word for "thanks." In the Hebrew text *tôdāh* is used to indicate "thanksgiving" in songs of worship (Ps. 26:7; 42:4). Sometimes the word is used to refer to the thanksgiving choir or procession (Neh. 12:31, 38). One of the peace offerings, or "sacrings," was designated the thanksgiving offering (Lev. 7:12).

TO PRAY

A. Verb.

pālal (פָּלַל), "to pray, intervene, mediate, judge." Found in both biblical and modern Hebrew, this word occurs 84 times in the Hebrew Old Testament. The word is used 4 times in the intensive verbal form; the remaining 80 times are found in the reflexive or reciprocal form, in which the action generally points back to the subject. In the intensive form *pālal* expresses the idea of "to mediate, to come between two parties," always between human beings. Thus, "if a man sins against a man, God will mediate for him. . ." (1 Sam. 2:25 RSV). "To mediate" requires "making a judgment," as in Ezek. 16:52: "Thou also, which hast judged thy sisters. . . ." In the remaining 2 references in which the intensive form is used, *pālal* expresses "making a judgment" in Gen. 48:11 and "coming between" in Ps. 106:30.

The first occurrence of *pālal* in the Old Testament is in Gen. 20:7, where the reflexive or reciprocal form of the verb expresses the idea of "interceding for, prayer in behalf of": ". . . He shall pray for thee. . . ." Such intercessory praying is frequent in the Old Testament: Moses "prays" for the people's deliverance from the fiery serpents (Num. 21:7); he "prays" for Aaron (Deut. 9:20); and Samuel "intercedes" continually for Israel (1 Sam. 12:23). Prayer is directed not only toward Yahweh but toward pagan idols as well (Isa. 44:17). Sometimes prayer is made to Yahweh that He would act against an enemy: "That which thou hast prayed to me against Sennacherib king of Assyria I have heard" (2 Kings 19:20).

Just why this verb form is used to express the act of praying is not completely clear. Since this verb form points back to the subject, in a reflexive sense, perhaps it emphasizes the part which the person praying has in his prayers. Also, since the verb form can have a reciprocal meaning between subject and object, it may emphasize the fact that prayer is basically communication, which always has to be two-way in order to be real.

B. Noun.

təphillāh (תְּפִלָּה), "prayer." This word, which appears 77 times in biblical Hebrew, is the most general Hebrew word for "prayer." It first appears in 1 Kings 8:28: "Yet have thou respect unto the prayer of thy servant, and to his supplication. . . ." In the eschaton God's house will be a house of "prayer" for all peoples (Isa. 56:7); it will be to this house that all nations will come to worship God. The word can mean both a non-liturgical non-poetical "prayer" and a liturgical poetical "prayer." In the latter special meaning *təphillāh* is used as a psalm title in 5 psalms and as the title of Habakkuk's prayer (Hab. 3:1). In these uses *təphillāh* means a prayer set to music and sung in the formal worship service. In Ps. 72:20 the word describes all the psalms or "prayers" of Psalms 1–72, only one of which is specifically called a "prayer" (17:1).

PRECIOUS

A. Adjective.

yāqār (יָקָר), "precious; rare; excellent; weighty; noble." Although none of the 35 biblical appearances of this word occurs before First Samuel, they are scattered throughout the rest of the Bible.

First, *yāqār* means "precious" in the sense of being rare and valuable: "And he took their king's crown from off his head, the weight whereof was a talent of gold with the precious stones: and it was set on David's head" (2 Sam. 12:30). The emphasis is on the nuance "rare" in 1 Sam. 3:1: "And the word of the Lord was precious in those days; there was no open vision."

Second, the word can focus on the value of a thing: "How excellent is thy loving-kindness, O God!" (Ps. 36:7).

Third, this word means "weighty" or "noble": "A little foolishness is weightier than wisdom and honor" (Eccl. 10:1 NASB); like dead flies which make perfume stink, so a little foolishness spoils wisdom and honor—it is worth more in a negative sense (cf. Lam. 4:2).

B. Verb.

yāqar (יָקַר), "to be difficult; be valued from; be valued or honored; be precious." This verb, which occurs 11 times in biblical Hebrew, has cognates in Ugaritic, Arabic, and Akkadian. The word means "to be precious" in 1 Sam. 26:21: "Then said Saul, I have sinned: return, my son David: for I will no more do thee harm, because my soul was precious in thine eyes this day. . . ."

C. Noun.

yǝqār (יְקָר), "precious thing; value; price; splendor; honor." This noun, which appears 16 times in biblical Hebrew, is Aramaic in form. The word signifies "value or price" (Zech. 11:13), "splendor" (Esth. 1:4), and "honor" (Esth. 8:16). In Jer. 20:5 the word refers to "precious things": "Moreover I will deliver all the strength of this city, and all the labors thereof, and all the precious things thereof. . . ."

TO PREPARE

A. Verb.

kûn (כוּן), "to be established, be readied, be prepared, be certain, be admissible." This verb occurs in nearly every Semitic language (not in biblical Aramaic). *Kûn* appears in the Bible about 220 times and in all periods of Hebrew.

This root used concretely connotes being firmly established, being firmly anchored, and being firm. The first meaning is applied to a roof which is "firmly established" on pillars. So Samson said to the lad who was leading him: "Suffer me that I may feel the pillars whereupon the house standeth, that I may lean upon them" (Judg. 16:26). In a similar sense the inhabited earth "is firmly established or anchored"; it is immovable: ". . . The world also is stablished, that it cannot be moved" (Ps. 93:1). In Ps. 75:3 the image shifts to the earth "firmly established" upon pillars. In Ps. 65:6 the divine establishing of the mountains is synonymous with divine creating. The verb also means "to be firm": "And you grew up and became tall and arrived at [the age for fine ornaments]; your breasts were formed, and your hair had grown" (Ezek. 16:7 RSV).

Used abstractly, *kûn* can refer to a concept as "established," or "fixed" so as to be unchanging and unchangeable: "And for that the dream was doubled unto Pharaoh twice; it is because the thing is established by God, and God will shortly bring it to pass" (Gen. 41:32–the first occurrence of the word). In somewhat the same sense one can speak of the light of day "being firmly established," or having fully arrived: "But the path of the just is as the shining light, that shineth more and more unto the perfect day" (Prov. 4:18). *Kûn* can be used of the "establishing" of one's descendants, of seeing them prosperous (Job 21:8).

Something can be "fixed" in the sense of "being prepared or completed": "Now all the work of Solomon was prepared unto the day of the foundation of the house of the Lord. . ." (2 Chron. 8:16).

An "established" thing can be something that is enduring. In 1 Sam. 20:31 Saul tells Jonathan: "For as long as the son of Jesse liveth upon the ground, thou shalt not be established, nor thy kingdom." Truthful lips (what they say) "shall be established," or will endure forever (Prov. 12:19). One's plans "will endure" (be established) if he commits his works to the Lord (Prov. 16:3).

Kûn can also mean "to be established" in the sense of "being ready." So Josiah told the people "to prepare" themselves for the Passover (2 Chron. 35:4). This same sense appears in Exod. 19:11: "And be ready against the third day: for the third day the Lord will come down in the sight of all the people upon mount Sinai." A somewhat different nuance appears in Job 18:12; Bildad says that wherever godlessness breaks out, there is judgment: ". . . Destruction shall be ready at his side." That is, calamity is "fixed or prepared" so that it exists potentially even before godlessness breaks out.

Something "fixed" or "established" can "be certain": "Then shalt thou inquire, and make search, and ask diligently; and, behold, if it be truth, and the thing certain. . ." (Deut. 13:14). In a somewhat different nuance the thing can be trustworthy or true. The psalmist says of the wicked that "there is no faithfulness in their mouth" (Ps. 5:9). A further development of this emphasis is that a matter "may be admissible"—so Moses said to Pharaoh: "It is not meet so to do; for we shall sacrifice the abomination of the Egyptians to the Lord our God. . ." (Exod. 8:26).

When one "fixes" an arrow on the bow, he takes aim or "prepares" to shoot his bow (cf. Ps. 7:12).

B. Nouns.

məkônāh (מְכוֹנָה), "proper place; base." This noun occurs 25 times; it means "proper place" in Ezra 3:3: "And they set the altar upon his bases. . . ." The word refers to "bases" in 1 Kings 7:27.

Two other nouns are related to the verb *kûn. Mākôn*, which appears 17 times, means "an established place or site" (Exod. 15:17). *Təkûnāh*, which makes 3 appearances, means "fixed place" as in Job 23:3 or "fixed matter" as in Ezek. 43:11: ". . . Show them the form of the house, and the fashion [*təkûnāh*] thereof. . . ."

C. Adjective.

kēn (כֵּן), "right; veritable; honest." This adjective occurs 24 times in biblical Hebrew. The word implies "honest or righteous" in Gen. 42:11: "We are all one man's sons; we are true men, thy servants are no spies." The word means not "right" in 2 Kings 17:9.

PRIDE

A. Verb.

gā'āh (גָּאָה), "to be proud, be exalted." This verb appears 7 times in biblical Hebrew. The word appears in Exod. 15:1 in the sense of "to be exalted": "I will sing to the Lord, for He is highly exalted [KJV, "he hath triumphed"]; The horse and its rider He has hurled into the sea" (NASB).

B. Nouns.

gā'ôn (גָּאוֹן), "pride." This root occurs only in northwest Semitic languages, as in Ugaritic: *gan*, "pride." This noun is a poetic word, which is found only in poetic books, the prophets (12 times in Isaiah), Moses' song (Exod. 15:7), and Leviticus (26:19). In rabbinic Hebrew, *gā'ôn* signifies a man of great learning. A *gā'ôn* was the head of the rabbinic academies of Susa and Pumpedita in Babylonia. Saadiah Gaon was one of the most outstanding.

In a positive sense *gā'ôn*, like the verb, signifies "excellence" or "majesty." God's "majesty" was expressed in Israel's deliverance through the Red Sea (Exod. 15:7). Israel as the redeemed people, then, is considered to be an expression of God's "majesty": "He shall choose our inheritance for us, the excellency of Jacob whom he loved" (Ps. 47:4). The meaning of *gā'ôn* is here close to that of *kābôd*, "glory."

Related to "majesty" is the word *gā'ôn* attributed to nature as something mighty, luxuriant, rich, and thick. The poets use the word to refer to the proud waves (Job 38:11) or the thick shrubbery by the Jordan; cf. "If thou hast run with the footmen, and they have wearied thee, then how canst thou contend with horses? and if in the land of peace, wherein thou trustedst, they wearied thee, then how wilt thou do in the swelling [literally, majesty] of Jordan?" (Jer. 12:5; cf. 49:19; 50:44).

The majority of the uses of *gā'ôn* are negative in that they connote human "pride" as an antonym for humility (Prov. 16:18). Proverbs puts *gā'ôn* together with arrogance, evil behavior, and perverse speech. In her independence from the Lord, Israel as a majestic nation, having been set apart by a majestic God, had turned aside and claimed its excellence as a prerogative earned by herself. The new attitude of insolence was not tolerated by God: "The Lord God hath sworn by himself, saith the Lord the God of hosts, I abhor the excellency of Jacob, and hate his palaces: therefore will I deliver up the city with all that is therein" (Amos 6:8).

The Septuagint translations are: *hubris* ("insolence; arrogance") and *huperephania* ("arrogance; haughtiness; pride").

Some other nouns are related to *gā'ôn*. *Gē'āh* occurs once to mean "pride" (Prov. 8:13). The noun *ga'awāh*, which is found 19 times, also means "pride": "And all the people shall know, even Ephraim and the inhabitant of Samaria, that say in the pride and stoutness of heart. . ." (Isa. 9:9). *Gē'ûth* appears 8 times and refers to "majesty": "Let favor be showed to the wicked, yet will he not learn righteousness: in the land of uprightness will he deal unjustly, and will not behold the majesty of the Lord" (Isa. 26:10).

C. Adjectives.

The adjective *gē'*, which is thought to be a scribal error for *gē'eh*, appears only once as "proud" (Isa. 16:6). *Gē'eh* also means "proud" in its 8 occurrences, once in Isa. 2:12: "For the day of the Lord of hosts shall be upon every one that is proud and lofty. . . ."

Ga'ayôn, which means "pride," appears once in biblical Hebrew (Ps. 123:4).

PRIEST; PRIESTHOOD

A. Noun.

kōhēn (כֹּהֵן), "priest." This word is found 741 times in the Old Testament. More than one-third of the references to the "priests" are found in the Pentateuch. Leviticus, which has about 185 references, is called the "manual of the priests."

The term *kōhēn* was used to refer not only to the Hebrew priesthood but to Egyptian "priests" (Gen. 41:50; 46:20; 47:26), the Philistine "priests" (1 Sam. 6:2), the "priests" of Dagon (1 Sam. 5:5), "priests" of Baal (2 Kings 10:19), "priests" of Chemosh (Jer. 48:7), and "priests" of the Baalim and Asherim (2 Chron. 34:5).

Joseph married the daughter of the "priest" of On (Gen. 41:45), and she bore him two sons, Ephraim and Manasseh (Gen. 46:20). Joseph did not purchase the land of the "priests" of Egypt, because the Egyptian "priests" received regular allotments from Pharaoh (Gen. 47:22).

A "priest" is an authorized minister of deity who officiates at the altar and in other cultic rites. A "priest" performs sacrificial, ritualistic, and mediatorial duties; he represents the people before God. By contrast, a "prophet" is an intermediary between God and the people.

The Jewish priestly office was established by the Lord in the days of Moses. But prior to the institution of the high priesthood and the priestly office, we read of the priesthood of Melchizedek (Gen. 14:18) and of Midianite "priests" (Exod. 2:16; 3:1; 18:1). In Exod. 19:24, other "priests" are mentioned: these may have been either Midianite "priests" or "priests" in Israel prior to the official establishment of the Levitical priesthood. No doubt priestly functions were performed in pre-Mosaic times by the head of the family, such as Noah, Abraham, and Job. After the Flood, for example, Noah built an altar to the Lord (Gen. 8:20-21). At Bethel, Mamre, and Moriah, Abraham built altars. In Gen. 22:12-13, we read that Abraham was willing to offer his son as a sacrifice. Job offered up sacrifices for his sinning children (Job 1:5).

The priesthood constituted one of the central characteristics of Old Testament religion. A passage showing the importance of the priesthood is Num. 16:5-7: "And he spake unto Korah and unto all his company, saying, Even tomorrow the Lord will show who are his, and who is holy; and will cause him to come near unto him: even him whom he hath chosen will he cause to come near unto him. This do; Take you censers, Korah, and all his company; And put fire therein, and put incense in them before the Lord . . . the man whom the Lord doth choose, he shall be holy. . . ."

God established Moses, Aaron, and Aaron's sons Nadab, Abihu, Eleazer, and Ithamar as "priests" in Israel (Exod. 28:1, 41; 29:9, 29-30). Because Nadab and Abihu were killed when they "offered strange fire before the Lord," the priesthood was limited to the lines of Eleazar and Ithamar (Lev. 10:1-2; Num. 3:4; 1 Chron. 24:2).

However, not all individuals born in the family of Aaron could serve as "priest." Certain physical deformities excluded a man from that perfection of holiness which a "priest" should manifest before Yahweh (Lev. 21:17-23). A "priest" who was ceremonially unclean was not permitted to perform his priestly duties. Lev. 21:1-15 gives a list of ceremonial prohibitions that forbade a "priest" from carrying out his duties.

Exod. 29:1-37 and Lev. 8 describe the seven-day consecration ceremony of Aaron and his sons. Both the high priest *(kohēn haggadōl)* and his sons were washed with water (Exod. 29:4). Then Aaron the high priest dressed in holy garments with a breastplate over his heart, and there was placed on his head a holy crown—the mitre or turban (Exod. 29:5-6). After that, Aaron was anointed with oil on his head (Exod. 29:7; cf. Ps. 133:2). Finally, the blood of a sacrificial offering was applied to Aaron and his sons (Exod. 29:20-21). The consecrating bloodmark was placed upon the tip of the right ear, on the thumb of the right hand, and on the great toe of the right foot.

The duties of the priesthood were very clearly defined by the Mosaic law. These duties were assumed on the eighth day of the service of consecration (Lev. 9:1). The Lord told Aaron: "Therefore thou and thy sons with thee shall keep your priest's office for every thing of the altar, and within the veil; and ye shall serve. . ." (Num. 18:7).

The "priests" were to act as teachers of the Law (Lev. 10:10-11; Deut. 33:10; 2 Chron. 5:3; 17:7-9; Ezek. 44:23; Mal. 2:6-9), a duty they did not always carry out (Mic. 3:11; Mal. 2:8). In certain areas of health and jurisprudence, "priests" served as limited revelators of God's will. For example, it was the duty of the "priest" to discern the existence of leprosy and to perform the rites of cleansing (Lev. 13-14). Priests determined punishments for murder and other civil matters (Deut. 21:5; 2 Chron. 19:8-11).

B. Verb.

kāhan (כָּהַן), "to act as a priest." This verb, which appears 23 times in biblical Hebrew, is derived from the noun *kōhēn*. The verb appears only in the intensive stem. One occurrence is in Exod. 28:1: "And take thou unto thee Aaron thy brother, and his sons with him, from among the children of Israel, that he may minister unto me in the priest's office. . . ."

PRINCE

A. Nouns.

nāsî' (נָשִׂיא), "prince; chief; leader." This noun appears 129 times in biblical Hebrew. An early occurrence of *nāsî'* is in Gen. 23:6: "Hear us, my lord: thou art a mighty prince among us. . . ." The books of Numbers and Ezekiel use the word most frequently. Elsewhere it rarely occurs.

Though the origin and meaning of *nāsî'* are controversial, it is clearly associated with leadership, both Israelite and non-Israelite. M. Noth proposed the idea that the *nāsî'* was originally a tribal representative or a "deputy, chief." Ishmael was promised to give rise to twelve "princes" (Gen. 17:20; cf. 25:16); the Midianites had "princes" (Num. 25:18), as well as the Amorites (Josh. 13:21), the peoples of the sea (Ezek. 26:16), Kedar (Ezek. 27:21), Egypt (Ezek. 30:13), and Edom (Ezek. 32:29). Also Israel had her "princes" ("rulers"): ". . . On the sixth day they gathered twice as much bread, two omers for one man: and all the rulers of the congregation came and told Moses" (Exod. 16:22). The "princes" ("leaders") of Israel did not only participate in the civil leadership; they were also regarded as pillars in Israelite religious life, the upholders of the covenantal way of life: "And Moses called unto them; and Aaron and all the rulers of the congregation returned unto him: and Moses talked with them" (Exod. 34:31; cf. Josh. 22:30). Hence, Israel was to obey her "leaders": "Thou shalt not revile the gods, nor curse the ruler of thy people" (Exod. 22:28).

The Septuagint translation is *arxon* ("ruler; lord; prince; authority; official"), and the KJV has these translations: "prince; captain; chief; ruler."

Another noun, *nəsî'îm*, is related to *nāsî'*. The word, which is found 4 times, means "clouds": "Whoso boasteth himself of a false gift is like clouds and wind without rain" (Prov. 25:14; cf. Ps. 135:7; Jer. 10:13; 51:16).

B. Verb.

nāsā' (נָשָׂא), "to lift up, carry." This verb appears 654 times in the Old Testament; once in Gen. 44:1: "Fill the men's sacks with food, as much as they can carry. . . ."

PROPERTY

A. Noun.

'achuzzāh (אֲחֻזָּה), "property; possession." This word appears 66 times, with most of its appearances being in Genesis–Joshua and Ezekiel.

Essentially *'achuzzāh* is a legal term usually used of land, especially family holdings to be passed down to one's heirs. In Gen. 17:13 (an early occurrence of the word) Abram is promised the territory of Palestine as a familial or tribal possession until the indiscriminate future. In Gen. 23:20 (cf. vv. 4, 9) the word bears a similar meaning. The difference appears to be that here no feudal responsibilities were attached to this "possession." However, the rather small lot belonged to Abraham and his descendants as a burial site: "And the field, and the cave that is therein, were made sure unto Abraham for a possession of a burying place by the sons of Heth" (Gen. 23:20).

In Lev. 25:45-46 non-Israelites could also be inheritable property, but a fellow Israelite could not. The "inheritable property" of the Levites was not fields but the Lord Himself (Ezek. 44:28).

B. Verb.

'āchaz (אָחַז), "to seize, grasp, hold fast, bolt (a door)." This verb, which occurs 64 times in biblical Hebrew, occurs also in most other Semitic languages. The verb appears in Gen. 25:26: ". . . And his hand took hold on Esau's heel. . . ." The meaning of "to bolt" (a door) appears in Neh. 7:3: ". . . Let them shut and bolt [KJV, "bar"] the doors" (NASB). In 2 Chron. 9:18, *'āchaz* means "fastened."

TO PROPHESY

A. Verb.

nābā' (נָבָא), "to prophesy." This word appears in all periods of the Hebrew language. It seems to be related to the ancient Akkadian word *nabû*, which in its passive form means "to be called." The word is found in the biblical Hebrew text about 115 times. Its first appearance is in 1 Sam. 10:6, where Saul is told by Samuel that when he meets a certain band of ecstatic prophets, he too will "prophesy with them, and . . . be turned into another man." This incident points up the fact that there is a certain amount of ambiguity in the biblical use of both the verb and the noun forms, just as there is in the English "to prophesy" and "prophet." Thus, there is a wide range of meanings reflected in the term in the Old Testament.

Most frequently *nābā'* is used to describe the function of the true prophet as he speaks God's message to the people, under the influence of the divine spirit (1 Kings 22:8; Jer. 29:27; Ezek. 37:10). "To prophesy" was a task that the prophet could not avoid: "The Lord God hath spoken, who can but prophesy?" (Amos 3:8; cf. Jer. 20:7, where Jeremiah says that he was both attracted to and forced into being a prophet). While the formula "The word of the Lord came [to the prophet]" is used literally hundreds of times in the Old

Testament, there is no real indication as to the manner in which it came—whether it came through the thought-processes, through a vision, or in some other way. Sometimes, especially in the earlier prophets, it seems that some kind of ecstatic experience may have been involved, as in 1 Sam. 10:6, 11; 19:20. Music is sometimes spoken of as a means of prophesying, as in 1 Chron. 25:1–3.

The false prophets, although not empowered by the divine spirit, are spoken of as prophesying also: ". . . I have not spoken to them, yet they prophesied" (Jer. 23:21). The false prophet is roundly condemned because he speaks a non–authentic word: ". . . Prophesy against the prophets of Israel that prophesy, and say thou unto them that prophesy out of their own hearts, Hear ye the word of the Lord; . . . Woe unto the foolish prophets, that follow their own spirit, and have seen nothing!" (Ezek. 13:2-3). The false prophet especially is subject to frenzied states of mind which give rise to his prophesying, although the content of such activity is not clearly spelled out (1 Kings 22:10). The point is that in the biblical context "to prophesy" can refer to anything from the frenzied ecstaticism of a false prophet to the cold sober proclamation of God's judgment by an Amos or an Isaiah.

"To prophesy" is much more than the prediction of future events. Indeed, the first concern of the prophet is to speak God's word to the people of his own time, calling them to covenant faithfulness. The prophet's message is conditional, dependent upon the response of the people. Thus, by their response to this word, the people determine in large part what the future holds, as is well illustrated by the response of the Ninevites to Jonah's preaching. Of course, prediction does enter the picture at times, such as in Nahum's prediction of the fall of Nineveh (Nah. 2:13) and in the various messianic passages (Isa. 9:1-6; 11:1-9; 52:13–53:12).

B. Noun.

nābî' (נָבִיא), "prophet." The word has a possible cognate in Akkadian. It occurs about 309 times in biblical Hebrew and in all periods.

Nābî' represents "prophet," whether a true or false prophet (cf. Deut. 13:1-5). True prophets were mouthpieces of the true God. In 1 Chron. 29:29 three words are used for "prophet": "Now the acts of David the king, first and last, behold, they are written in the Book of Samuel the Seer [*rō'eh*] and in the Book of Nathan the Prophet [*nābî'*], and in the Book of Gad the Seer [*chōzēh*]." The words translated "seer" emphasize the means by which the "prophet" communicated with God but do not identify the men as anything different from prophets (cf. 1 Sam. 9:9). The first occurrence of *nābî'* does not help to clearly define it either: "Now therefore restore the man [Abraham] his wife; for he is a prophet, and he shall pray for thee, and thou shalt live . . ." (Gen. 20:7).

The second occurrence of *nābî'* establishes its meaning: "And the Lord said unto Moses, See, I have made thee a god to Pharaoh: and Aaron thy brother shall be thy prophet" (Exod. 7:1). The background of this statement is Exod. 4:10-16, where Moses argued his inability to speak clearly. Hence, he could not go before Pharaoh as God's spokesman. God promised to appoint

Aaron (Moses' brother) to be the speaker: "And he shall be thy spokesman unto the people: and he shall be, even he shall be to thee instead of a mouth, and thou shalt be to him instead of God" (Exod. 4:16). Exod. 7:1 expresses the same idea in different words. It is clear that the word "prophet" is equal to one who speaks for another, or his mouth.

This basic meaning of *nābî'* is supported by other passages. In the classical passage Deut. 18:14-22, God promised to raise up another "prophet" like Moses who would be God's spokesman (v. 18). They were held responsible for what he told them and were admonished to obey him (Deut. 18:19). However, if what the "prophet" said proved to be wrong, he was to be killed (Deut. 18:20). Immediately, this constitutes a promise and definition of the long succession of Israel's prophets. Ultimately, it is a promise of the Great Prophet, Jesus Christ (cf. Acts 3:22-23). The "prophet" or dreamer of dreams might perform miracles to demonstrate that he was God's man, but the people were to look to the message rather than the miracle before they heeded his message (Deut. 13:1-5).

In the plural *nābî'* is used of some who do not function as God's mouth-pieces. In the time of Samuel there were men who followed him. They went about praising God (frequently with song) and trying to stir the people to return to God (1 Sam. 10:5, 10; 19:20). Followers of Elijah and Elisha formed into groups to assist and/or to learn from these masters. They were called sons of the prophets (1 Kings 20:35). Used in this sense, the word *nābî'* means a companion and/or follower of a prophet.

The word is also used of "heathen prophets": "Now therefore send, and gather to me all Israel unto mount Carmel, and the prophets of Baal four hundred and fifty, and the prophets of the groves four hundred, which eat at Jezebel's table" (1 Kings 18:19).

This word has a feminine form, "prophetess" *(nəbî'āh),* which appears 6 times. In Exod. 15:20 Miriam is called a "prophetess." Isaiah's wife, too, is called a "prophetess" (Isa. 8:3). This usage may be related to the meaning "a companion and/or follower of a prophet."

TO PROSPER

tsālēach (צָלֵחַ), "to succeed, prosper." This word is found in both ancient and modern Hebrew. Occurring some 65 times in the text of the Hebrew Old Testament, the word is first found in Gen. 24:21: ". . . whether the Lord had made his journey prosperous [literally, to prosper] or not." This word generally expresses the idea of a successful venture, as contrasted with failure. The source of such success is God: ". . . as long as he sought the Lord, God made him to prosper" (2 Chron. 26:5). In spite of that, the circumstances of life often raise the question, "Wherefore doth the way of the wicked prosper?" (Jer. 12:1).

Tsāleach is sometimes used in such a way as to indicate "victory": "In your majesty ride forth victoriously" (Ps. 45:4 RSV; the KJV rendering, "ride prosperously," is not nearly so appropriate).

TO PROVOKE (ANGER)

kā'as (כָּעַס), "to provoke, vex, make angry." This word is common throughout the history of Hebrew and is used in modern Hebrew in the sense of "to be angry, to rage." It occurs some 55 times in the Hebrew Old Testament.

A word that is characteristic of the Book of Deuteronomy, it seems fitting that *kā'as* is found for the first time in the Old Testament in that book: ". . . To provoke him to anger" (Deut. 4:25). The word is characteristic also of the books of Jeremiah and Kings. A review of the uses of this verb shows that around 80 percent of them involve Yahweh's "being provoked to anger" by Israel's sin, especially its worship of other gods. One such example is in 2 Kings 23:19: "And all the houses also of the high places that were in the cities of Samaria, which the kings of Israel had made to provoke the Lord to anger, Josiah took away. . . ."

TO PURSUE

rādaph (רָדַף), "to pursue; follow after; pass away; persecute." This verb also appears in Coptic, Syriac, Mandaean, Arabic, and post-biblical Aramaic. It appears in the Bible about 135 times and in all periods.

The basic meaning of this verb is "to pursue after" an enemy with the intent of overtaking and defeating him. In most of its occurrences *rādaph* is a military term. It first occurs in Gen. 14:14, where it is reported that Abram mustered his men (318 men) and "pursued them [men who took his brother] unto Dan." A nuance of this verb is "to pursue" a defeated enemy with the intent of killing him: "And he divided himself against them, he and his servants, by night, and smote them, and pursued them unto Hobah, which is on the left hand of Damascus" (Gen. 14:15). The one pursued is not always a hostile force—so Laban "took his brethren [army] with him, and pursued after him [Jacob] seven days' journey; and they overtook him in the mount Gilead" (Gen. 31:23). At times *rādaph* signifies pursuing without having a specific location or direction in mind, as in hunting for someone. This meaning is in 1 Sam. 26:20—David asked Saul why he was exerting so much effort on such an unimportant task (namely, pursuing him), "as when one doth hunt a partridge in the mountains." The word occurs in Josh. 2:5, where Rahab tells the soldiers of Jericho: ". . . Whither the men [Israelite spies] went I wot not: pursue after them quickly; for ye shall overtake them." This verse embodies the meaning first mentioned, but by Josh. 2:22 the emphasis has shifted to hunting, not intentional pursuit after an enemy whose location is known but a searching for an enemy in order to kill him: "And they went, and came unto the mountain, and abode there three days, until the pursuers were returned: and the pursuers sought them throughout all the way, but found them not."

In another nuance *rādaph* can signify "to put to flight" or to confront and cause to flee. Moses reminded the Israelites that "the Amorites . . . came out against you, and chased you, as bees do, and destroyed you in Seir, even unto Hormah" (Deut. 1:44). Bees do not pursue their victims, but they certainly do put them to flight, or cause them to flee. In Josh. 23:10 Israel is reminded: "One man of you shall chase a thousand: for the Lord your God he it is that fighteth for you, as he hath promised you" (cf. Lev. 26:8).

Used in another sense, *rādaph* signifies the successful accomplishment of a pursuit; the pursuer overtakes the pursued but does not utterly destroy him (in the case of an army) and, therefore, continues the pursuit until the enemy is utterly destroyed. So Israel is warned of the penalty of disobedience to God: "The Lord shall smite thee with a consumption, and with a fever . . .; and they shall pursue thee until thou perish" (Deut. 28:22; cf. v. 45). This is the emphasis when God admonishes Israel: "That which is altogether just shalt thou follow, that thou mayest live, and inherit the land . . ." (Deut. 16:20); Israel is "to pursue" justice and only justice, as a goal always achieved but never perfected. They are to always have justice in their midst, and always "to pursue" it. This same sense appears in other figurative uses of the word: "Surely goodness and mercy shall follow me all the days of my life . . ." (Ps. 23:6; cf. Isa. 1:23; 5:11; Hos. 6:3).

In a related meaning *rādaph* can signify "follow after." This is not with any intention to do harm to the one pursued but merely "to overtake" him. So Gehazi "pursued" (followed after) Naaman, overtook him, and asked him for a talent of silver and two changes of clothes (2 Kings 5:21-22). The word also means "to follow after" in the sense of "practicing," or following a leader: "They also that render evil for good are mine adversaries; because I follow the thing that good is" (Ps. 38:20; cf. 119:150; Prov. 21:21).

The third meaning of *rādaph,* "to persecute," represents the constant infliction of pain or trouble upon one's enemies. This meaning is seen in Deut. 30:7: "And the Lord thy God will put all these curses upon thine enemies, and on them that hate thee, which persecuted thee" (cf. Job 19:22, 28).

A special use of *rādaph* appears in Eccl. 3:15: ". . . God requireth [holds men accountable for] that which is past." Men should serve God (literally, fear him) because God controls all things. Men should be on His side, since He is totally sovereign. The intensive stem sometimes means to pursue relentlessly and passionately as a harlot "pursues" her lovers (Prov. 11:19).

R

RAM

'ayil (אַיִל), "ram." This word, which has cognates in Ugaritic, Egyptian, and Coptic, occurs in biblical Hebrew about 164 times and in all periods.

'Ayil represents a male sheep or "ram." The word first appears in Gen. 15:9, where God told Abram: "Take me a heifer of three years old, and a she goat of three years old, and a ram of three years old, and a turtledove, and a young pigeon." These animals were often used in sacrificing (cf. Gen. 22:13). They were eaten (Gen. 31:38), and the wool used to make clothing (cf. 2 Kings

3:4). Consequently as highly valuable animals such "rams" were selected by Jacob to be part of a peace present sent to Esau (Gen. 32:14).

Many passages use *'ayil* as a figure of despots or mighty men: "Then the dukes of Edom shall be amazed; the mighty men of Moab, trembling shall take hold upon them . . ." (Exod. 15:15). The king of Babylon deported Judah's kings, princes, and the "mighty of the land" (Ezek. 17:13). In the first instance the word represents chiefs in the sense of head political figures, whereas in the second use it appears to signify lesser figures. An even more powerful figure is in view in Ezek. 31:11, where *'ayil* represents a central powerful earthly figure who will ruthlessly destroy Assyria: "I have therefore delivered him into the hand of the mighty one of the heathen; he shall surely deal with him: I have driven him out for his wickedness."

yôbēl (יוֹבֵל), "ram; ram's horn; jubilee year." Cognates of this word appear in late Aramaic, Phoenician, and Arabic. The 27 biblical appearances of the noun all occur before the Book of Judges.

First, this word means "ram's horn": "When the ram's horn [KJV, "trumpet"] sounds a long blast, they shall come up to the mountain" (Exod. 19:13—the first occurrence). In Josh. 6:5 the word is preceded by the Hebrew word for "horn," which is modified by *yôbēl*, "horn of a ram."

Second, this word signifies "jubilee year." The law concerning this institution is recorded in Lev. 25:8-15; 27:16-25. In the fiftieth year on the Day of Atonement jubilee was to be declared. All land was to return to the individual or family to whom it had originally belonged by inheritance, even if he (or she) were in bondservice. When land was valued in anticipation of selling it or devoting it to God, it was to be valued in terms of anticipated productivity prior to the year of jubilee. Between jubilees land might be redeemed for its productivity value. City property, however, must be redeemed within a year of its sale or loss. Levitical property was not subject to these rules. Israelites who fell into bondage were to be released in the jubilee year, or redeemed in the interim period.

TO REBEL

A. Verb.

mārāh (מָרָה), "to rebel, be contentious." The meaning of "being rebellious" is limited to the Hebrew language, as the meaning of this verb in other Semitic languages differs: "to make angry" (Aramaic), "to contend with" (Syriac), and "to dispute with" (Arabic). *Mārāh* occurs some 50 times in the Old Testament, and its usage is scattered throughout the Old Testament (historical, prophetic, poetic, and legal literature). Some personal names are partly composed of the verb: *Meraiah* ("stubborn headed"; Neh. 12:12) and *Miriam* ("stubborn headed," if actually derived from the verb).

Mārāh signifies an opposition to someone motivated by pride: "If a man have a stubborn [*sārar*] and rebellious [*mārāh*] son, which will not obey the voice of his father . . ." (Deut. 21:18). The sense comes out more clearly in Isa. 3:8 (NASB): "For Jerusalem has stumbled, and Judah has fallen, Because their speech and their actions are against the Lord, To rebel against His glorious presence."

More particularly, the word generally connotes a rebellious attitude against God. Several prepositions are used to indicate the object of rebellion (*im, et,* generally translated as "against"): ". . . Ye have been rebellious against [*im*] the Lord" (Deut. 9:7); ". . . She hath been rebellious against [*et*] me . . ." (Jer. 4:17).

The primary meaning of *mārāh* is "to disobey." Several passages attest to this: ". . . Forasmuch as thou hast disobeyed the mouth of the Lord, and hast not kept the commandment which the Lord thy God commanded thee" (1 Kings 13:21); cf. 1 Kings 13:26: "It is the man of God, who was disobedient unto the word of the Lord. . . ."

The Old Testament sometimes specifically states that someone "rebelled" against the Lord; at other times it may refer to a rebelling against the word of the Lord (Ps. 105:28; 107:11), or against the mouth of God (KJV, "word"; NIV, "command"; cf. Num. 20:24; Deut. 1:26, 43; 9:23; 1 Sam. 12:14-15). The intent of the Hebrew is to signify the act of defying the command of God: "The Lord is righteous; for I have rebelled against his commandment . . ." (Lam. 1:18).

The verb *mārāh* is at times strengthened by a form of the verb *sārar* ("to be stubborn"): "[They] might not be as their fathers, a stubborn [*sārar*] and rebellious [*mārāh*] generation; a generation that set not their heart aright . . ." (Ps. 78:8; cf. Deut. 21:18, 20; Jer. 5:23).

An individual (Deut. 21:18, 20), a nation (Num. 20:24), and a city (Zeph. 3:1) may be described as "being rebellious." Zephaniah gave a vivid image of the nature of the rebellious spirit: "Woe to her that is rebellious and defiled, the oppressing city! She listens to no voice, she accepts no correction. She does not trust in the Lord, she does not draw near to her God" (Zeph. 3:1-2 RSV).

The Septuagint translates *mārāh* by *parəpikraino* ("make bitter; make angry; provoke; be rebellious") and by *atheteo* ("to reject; not to recognize"). The English versions give the meanings "rebel; provoke" (KJV, RSV, NIV).

B. Nouns.

mərî (מְרִי), "rebellion." This word occurs infrequently: "For I know thy rebellion, and thy stiff neck . . ." (Deut. 31:27; cf. Prov. 17:11).

The noun *mərātayim* means "double rebellion." This reference to Babylon (Jer. 50:21) is generally not translated (KJV, RSV, and NIV, "Merathaim").

C. Adjective.

mərî (מְרִי), "rebellious." This word occurs 23 times, mainly in Ezekiel. The word modifies "house" (referring to Israel) in Ezek. 2:8: ". . . Be not thou rebellious like that rebellious house. . . ."

TO RECKON

A. Verb.

yāchas (יָחַשׂ), "to reckon (according to race or family)." In Aramaic, *yāchas* appears in the Targumim for the Hebrew *mishəpāchāh* ("family") and *tôlədôth* ("genealogy or generations"). This word occurs about 20 times in the Old Testament.

In 1 Chron. 5:17 *yāchas* means "reckoned by genealogies": "All these were reckoned by genealogies in the days of Jotham King of Judah . . ." (cf. 1 Chron. 7:5). A similar use is found in Ezra 2:62: "These sought their register among those that were reckoned by genealogy, but they were not found . . ." (NASB, "searched among their ancestral registration").

The Septuagint renders *yāchas* variously: *ogdoēkonta* ("genealogy . . . to be reckoned"); *arithmos* ("member of them; father their genealogy"); *paratoxin* ("member throughout the genealogy"); *sunodias* ("reckoned by genealogy").

B. Noun.

yachas (יַחַשׂ), "genealogy." This word appears in the infinitive form as a noun to indicate a register or table of genealogy: "And the number throughout the genealogy of them that were apt to the war, and to battle was twenty and six thousand men" (1 Chron. 7:40; cf. 2 Chron. 31:18). Another rendering concerns the acts of Rehoboam, recorded in the histories of Shemaiah (2 Chron. 12:15), meant that the particulars were related in a genealogical table.

TO RECOMPENSE, REWARD

shālam (שָׁלַם), "to recompense, reward, be whole, be complete, sound." A common Semitic term, this verb is found in ancient Akkadian and Ugaritic and in all periods of Hebrew. The root is familiar to most people in the word *shālôm,* which is the common Jewish greeting. The verb *shālam* occurs just over 100 times in the Hebrew Bible.

In its first occurrence in the Old Testament, the word has the sense of "repaying" or "restoring": "Why have you returned evil for good?" (Gen. 44:4, RSV). Sometimes it means "to complete or finish"—for example, completing the temple (1 Kings 9:25). In Lev. 24:18, *shālam* describes compensation for injury: "And he that killeth a beast shall make it good [life for life]."

Perhaps it should be noted that the Arabic terms *Muslim* and *Islam* are derived from the Arabic cognate to *shālam* and imply "submission to Allah."

TO REDEEM

A. Verbs.

gā'al (גָּאַל), "to redeem, deliver, avenge, act as a kinsman." This word group is used 90 times, chiefly in the Pentateuch, Psalms, Isaiah, and Ruth.

The root appears to be almost exclusively Hebrew, the only cognate being an Amorite proper name.

The first occurrence of *gā'al* is in Gen. 48:16: "The angel which redeemed me [Jacob] from all evil . . ." (KJV), means as in the NIV, "delivered me from all harm." Its basic use had to do with the deliverance of persons or property that had been sold for debt, as in Lev. 25:25: "If thy brother be waxen poor, and hath sold away some of his possession, and if any of his kin come to redeem it, then shall he redeem that which his brother sold." If he prospers, the man himself may "redeem" it (Lev. 25:26). A poor man may sell himself to a fellow Israelite (Lev. 25:39) or to an alien living in Israel (Lev. 25:47). The responsibility "to redeem" belonged to the nearest relative— brother, uncle, uncle's son, or a blood relative from his family (Lev. 25:25, 48, 49). The person (kinsman) who "redeemed" the one in financial difficulties was known as a kinsman-redeemer, as the NIV translates the word in Ruth 2:20. In Deut. 19:6 the redeemer is called the "avenger of blood" whose duty it was to execute the murderer of his relative. The verb occurs in this sense 12 times and is translated "revenger" in KJV (Num. 35:19, 21, 24, 27) or "avenger" (Num. 35:12; always so in NASB and NIV).

The Book of Ruth is a beautiful account of the kinsman-redeemer. His responsibility is summed up in Ruth 4:5: "What day thou buyest the field of the hand of Naomi, thou must buy it also of Ruth the Moabitess, the wife of the dead, to raise up the name of the dead upon his inheritance." Thus the kinsman-redeemer was responsible for preserving the integrity, life, property, and family name of his close relative or for executing justice upon his murderer.

The greater usage of this word group is of God who promised: ". . . I am the Lord . . . I will redeem you with a stretched out arm and with great judgments" (Exod. 6:6; cf. Ps. 77:15). Israel confessed; "Thou in thy mercy hast led forth the people which thou hast *redeemed* . . ." (Exod. 15:13). "And they remembered that God was their rock, and the high God their redeemer" (Ps. 78:35).

The Book of Isaiah evidences the word "Redeemer" used of God 13 times, all in chapters 41–63, and *gā'al* is used 9 times of God, first in 43:1, "Fear not; for I have redeemed thee, I have called thee by thy name; thou art mine." *Gā'al* is used of deliverance from Egypt (51:10; 63:9) and from captivity in Babylon (48:20; 52:3,9; 62:12). Israel's "Redeemer" is "the Holy One of Israel" (41:14), "the creator of Israel, your King" (43:14-15), "the Lord of hosts" (44:6), and "the mighty One of Jacob" (49:26). Those who share His salvation are "the redeemed" (35:9).

The Book of Psalms often places spiritual redemption in parallel with physical redemption. For example: "Draw nigh unto my soul, and redeem it: // deliver me because of mine enemies" (Ps. 69:18). "Bless the Lord, O my soul, and forget not all his benefits: . . . who redeemeth thy life from destruction; who crowneth thee with loving-kindness and tender mercies" (Ps. 103:2, 4).

pādāh (פָּדָה), "to redeem, ransom." Originally, the usage of this word overlapped with that of *kāphar;* both meant "to ransom." In theological usage, however, each root tended to develop in different directions, so that they can often be considered synonymous only in a very broad sense.

Pādāh indicates that some intervening or substitutionary action effects a release from an undesirable condition. In more secular contexts, it implies a payment of some sort. But 1 Sam. 14:45 indicates that money is not intrinsic in the word; Saul is determined to execute Jonathan for his involuntary transgression, but "... the people rescued Jonathan, that he died not." Slavery appears as a condition from which one may be "ransomed" (Exod. 21:8; Lev. 19:20).

The word is connected with the laws of the firstborn. As a reminder of slaying all the Egyptian firstborn but sparing the Israelites, God retained an eternal claim on the life of all Israelite firstborn males, both of men and of cattle. The latter were often sacrificed, "but all the firstborn of my children I redeem" (Exod. 13:15). God accepted the separation of the tribe of Levi for liturgical service in lieu of all Israelite firstborn (Num. 3:40 ff.). However, the Israelite males still had to be "redeemed" *(pādāh)* from this service by payment of specified "redemption money" (Num. 3:44-51).

When God is the subject of *pādāh,* the word emphasizes His complete, sovereign freedom to liberate human beings. Sometimes God is said to "redeem" individuals (Abraham, Isa. 29:22; David, 1 Kings 1:29; and often in the Psalter, e.g., 26:11; 21:5; 71:23); but usually Israel, the elect people, is the beneficiary. Sometimes the redemption or deliverance is proclaimed absolutely (Hos. 7:13; 2 Sam. 7:23; Ps. 44:26); but the subject is said to be "ransomed" from a specific oppression. At other times, the reference is less explicit—e.g., from "troubles" (Ps. 25:22) and from "wicked" men (Jer. 15:21). Only once is *pādāh* used to describe liberation from sin or iniquity: "And he shall redeem Israel from all his iniquity" (Ps. 130:8).

kāphar (כָּפַר), "to ransom, atone, expiate, propitiate." *Kāphar* has an initial secular and non-theological range quite parallel to *pādāh.* In addition, however, *kāphar* became a technical term in Israel's sacrificial rituals. On its most basic level of meaning, *kāphar* denotes a material transaction or "ransom."

Sometimes man is the subject of *kāphar.* In 2 Sam. 21:3, David asks the Gibeonites, "... And wherewith shall I make the atonement, that ye may bless the inheritance of the Lord?" He receives in answer the advice to hang seven of Saul's sons in compensation. In Exod. 32:30, Moses ascends the mountain yet a third time in an effort to "make an atonement" for the people's sin (apparently merely by intercession, although this is not explicitly stated). Isa. 27:9 speaks of "purging" Israel's guilt by banishing idolatrous objects. In Num. 25:13, Phinehas is said to have "made an atonement for the children of Israel" by spearing a couple during orgiastic worship of Baal.

God is often the subject of *kāphar* in this general sense, too. In 2 Chron. 30:18, Hezekiah prays for God to "pardon" those who were not ritually prepared for the Passover. At the conclusion of the Song of Moses, Yahweh is praised because He "will atone for His land and His people" (Deut. 32:43, NASB). Similar general uses of the word appear in Ps. 65:3; 78:38; and Dan. 9:24. Jeremiah once uses *kāphar* to pray bitterly that Yahweh not "forgive" the iniquity of those plotting to slay him (Jer. 18:23), and in Ps. 79:9 the word means "to purge" sin.

Most often *kāphar* is used in connection with specific rites, and the immediate subject is a priest. All types of ritual sacrifice are explained in terms of *kāphar*. We find the priests' smearing of blood on the altar during the "sin offering" *(chattā'th)* described as "atonement" (Exod. 29:36-37; Lev. 4:20, 31; 10:17; Num. 28:22; 29:5; Neh. 10:33). The use of blood is not quite so prominent in sacrifices, but the relation to "atonement" still holds. It is clearly true of the "guilt offering" (Lev. 5:16, 18; 6:7; 7:7; 14:21; 19:22; Num. 5:8). The principle holds even when the poor cannot afford an animal or birds, and they sacrifice only a little flour—i.e., where obviously no blood is involved (Lev. 5:11-13). Making "atonement" *(kāphar)* is also part of the purpose of the "burnt offering" (Lev. 1:4; Num. 15:25). The only major type of sacrifice not classified an "atonement" in Leviticus is the "cereal offering" *(minǝchāh)* of chapter 2; but Ezek. 45:15, 17 does include it under that heading. First Chron. 6:49 applies the concept to the priestly ministry in general. The connection of all of the rituals with *kāphar* peaks in the complex ceremony of the annual "Day of Atonement" *(Yom Kippur),* as described in detail in Lev. 16.

Most English versions prefer to render *kāphar* with the more neutral term "atone" or even "ransom." But various translations often have "expiate" or "propitiate" as well. The terms are partly synonymous. In any sacrifice, the action is directed both toward God *(propitiation)* and toward the offense *(expiation).* "Expiate," "atone," and even "forgive" (if related to sacrifice) all have God as their primary subject, while "propitiation" addresses God as object.

All the sacrifices in the world would not satisfy God's righteousness (e.g., Mic. 6:7; Ps. 50:7-15). Hence God alone can provide an atonement or expiation for sin, by which His wrath is assuaged. The righteous God is neither implacable nor capricious, but provides Himself the "ransom" or substitute sacrifice that would satisfy Him. The priest at the altar represents God Himself, bringing the requisite offering before God; sacrifice is not essentially man's action, but God's own act of pardoning mercy.

B. Noun.

gǝ'ullāh (גְּאֻלָּה), "(right of) redemption." This word is used in regard to deliverance of persons or property that had been sold for debt. The law required that the "right of redemption" of land and of persons be protected (Lev. 25:24, 48). The redemption price was determined by the number of years remaining until the release of debts in the year of jubilee (Lev. 25:27, 28). The word *gǝ'ullāh* also occurs in Jer. 32:7: "Behold, Hanameel the son of Shallum thine uncle shall come unto thee, saying, Buy thee my field that is in Anathoth: for the right of redemption is thine to buy it."

The noun related to *pādāh* is *pǝdûth.* It occurs about 5 times and means "ransom or redemption": "He sent redemption unto his people: he hath commanded his covenant for ever . . ." (Ps. 111:9).

TO REIGN

mālak (מָלַךְ), "to reign, be king (or queen)." This root appears in most Semitic languages, although it means "advice" and "counsel" in Akkadian (and biblical Aramaic) and "own" exclusively in Ethiopic (and old South Arabic). In the Northwest Semitic dialects the root has a common meaning. The verbal form occurs in every period of Hebrew and about 350 times in the Bible.

Basically the word means to fill the functions of ruler over someone. To hold such a position was to function as the commander-in-chief of the army, the chief executive of the group, and to be an important, if not central, religious figure. The king was the head of his people and, therefore, in battle were the king to be killed, his army would disperse until a new king could be chosen. The first appearance of *mālak* is in Gen. 36:31: "And these are the kings that reigned in the land of Edom, before there reigned any king over the children of Israel." The king "reigned" as the earthly representative of the god (or God) who was recognized as the real king. Thus, he was considered to be god's (God's) son. This same idea recurs in Israel (Ps. 2:6). In Israel, too, God was the King: "The Lord shall reign for ever and ever" (Exod. 15:18). That the word can also be used of what a queen does when she "reigns" proves that it refers to the function of anyone in the office of king: "And he was with her hid in the house of the Lord six years. And Athaliah did reign over the land" (2 Kings 11:3).

Mālak can also be used of the idea "to become king"—someone was made, or made himself, a king: "And Bela died, and Jobab the son of Zerah of Bozrah reigned in his stead" (Gen. 36:33). This verb can be used of the assumption of a kingly reign, or of "beginning to reign": "Saul reigned one year; and when he had reigned two years over Israel . . ." (1 Sam. 13:1; cf. Prov. 30:22). Finally, the verb is used of receiving the title of queen (or king) whether or not one receives any political or military power. So it was said: "And let the maiden which pleaseth the king be queen instead of Vashti" (Esth. 2:4).

TO REJOICE

A. Verb.

sāmach (שָׂמַח), "to rejoice, be joyful." This verb also occurs in Ugaritic (where its radicals are *sh-m-ḫ*) and perhaps in Aramaic-Syriac. It appears in all periods of Hebrew and about 155 times in the Bible.

Sāmach usually refers to a spontaneous emotion or extreme happiness which is expressed in some visible and/or external manner. It does not normally represent an abiding state of well-being or feeling. This emotion arises at festivals, circumcision feasts, wedding feasts, harvest feasts, the overthrow of one's enemies, and other such events. The men of Jabesh broke out joyously when they were told that they would be delivered from the Philistines (1 Sam. 11:9).

The emotion expressed in the verb *sāmach* usually finds a visible expression. In Jer. 50:11 the Babylonians are denounced as being glad and "jubilant" over the pillage of Israel. Their emotion is expressed externally by their skipping about like a threshing heifer and neighing like stallions. The emotion represented in the verb (and concretized in the noun *simᵊchāh*) is sometimes accompanied by dancing, singing, and playing musical instruments. This was the sense when David was heralded by the women of Jerusalem as he returned victorious over the Philistines (1 Sam. 18:6). This emotion is usually described as the product of some external situation, circumstance, or experience, such as found in the first biblical appearance of *sāmach:* God told Moses that Aaron was coming to meet him and "when he seeth thee, he will be glad in his heart" (Exod. 4:14). This passage speaks of inner feeling which is visibly expressed. When Aaron saw Moses, he was overcome with joy and kissed him (v. 27).

Therefore, the verb *sāmach* suggests three elements: (1) a spontaneous, unsustained feeling of jubilance, (2) a feeling so strong that it finds expression in some external act, and (3) a feeling prompted by some external and unsustained stimulus.

This verb is used intransitively signifying that the action is focused on the subject (cf. 1 Sam. 11:9). God is sometimes the subject, the one who "rejoices and is jubilant": "The glory of the Lord shall endure for ever: the Lord shall rejoice in his works" (Ps. 104:31). The godly are to "be glad in the Lord, and rejoice . . . and shout for joy . . ." (Ps. 32:11). *Sāmach* can also mean "to be joyful or glad." In the place the Lord chooses, Israel is "to be joyful" in all in which the Lord blesses them (Deut. 12:7). Used thus the verb describes a state into which one places himself under given circumstances. It has a further and technical sense describing all that one does in making a feast before God: "And ye shall take you on the first day the boughs of goodly trees, branches of palm trees, and the boughs of thick trees, and willows of the brook; and ye shall rejoice before the Lord your God seven days" (Lev. 23:40).

In a few cases the verb describes an ongoing state. In 1 Kings 4:20 the reign of Solomon is summarized as follows: "Judah and Israel were many, as the sand which is by the sea in multitude, eating and drinking, and making merry."

B. Noun.

simᵊchāh (שִׂמְחָה), "joy." This noun, which also occurs in Ugaritic, is found 94 times in biblical Hebrew. *Simᵊchāh* is both a technical term for the external expression of "joy" (Gen. 31:27—the first biblical occurrence; cf. 1 Sam. 18:6; Jer. 50:11) and (usually) a representation of the abstract feeling or concept "joy" (Deut. 28:47). In another technical use this noun signifies the entire activity of making a feast before God: "And all the people went their way to eat, and to drink, and to send portions, and to make great mirth [literally, "to make a great rejoicing"] . . ." (Neh. 8:12).

The noun catches the concrete coloring of the verb, as in Isa. 55:12: "For ye shall go out with joy . . .: the mountains and the hills shall break forth before you into singing, and all the trees of the field shall clap their hands."

C. Adjective.

sāmēach (שָׂמֵחַ), "joyful; glad." This adjective occurs 21 times in the Old Testament. The first biblical occurrence is in Deut. 16:15: "Seven days shalt thou keep a solemn feast unto the Lord thy God in the place which the Lord shall choose: because the Lord thy God shall bless thee . . . therefore thou shalt surely rejoice."

TO REMAIN

lûn (לוּן), "to remain, lodge, spend the night, abide." Found also in ancient Ugaritic, this word continues in use from biblical Hebrew until now. The modern Hebrew term for "hotel" is derived from this term. *Lûn* is used approximately 60 times in the Hebrew Old Testament. Its first occurrence is in Gen. 19:2, where it is used twice: "Behold now, my lords, turn in, I pray you, into your servant's house, and tarry all night. . . . And they said, Nay; but we will abide in the street all night."

While it is usually used concerning human beings spending the night, *lûn* is sometimes used of animals, such as the wild ox (Job 39:9 NASB; KJV, "unicorn"), the pelican and the hedgehog (Zeph. 2:14 NASB; KJV, "the cormorant and the bittern"). The word does not necessarily mean sleeping through the night, but may be used to indicate being located in one place for the night: "Thou shalt not . . . [let] the fat of my sacrifice remain until the morning [literally, "pass the night until morning"] (Exod. 23:18). In a similar way, the figurative use of the word often has the connotation of "abiding, remaining": ". . . Mine error remaineth [NASB, "lodges"] with myself" (Job 19:4); ". . . Righteousness lodged in it . . ." (Isa. 1:21); "His soul shall dwell at ease . . ." (Ps. 25:13); ". . . [He] shall abide satisfied . . ." (Prov. 19:23).

REMAINDER; REMNANT

A. Nouns.

yether (יֶתֶר), "remainder; remnant." *Yether* appears 94 times in the Hebrew Old Testament. The word occurs mainly (about 45 times) in the historical books in the stereotype phrase "the rest of the acts," as in "And the rest of the acts of Solomon [the events of Solomon's reign], and all that he did, and his wisdom, are they not written in the Book of the Acts of Solomon?" (1 Kings 11:41). In these verses, *yether* is used to refer to those events which have not been included in the works of the biblical historiographers.

The more general meaning of *yether* is "whatever remains": the prey (Num. 31:32); the giants (Deut. 3:11); the kingdom (Josh. 13:27); and the people (Judg. 7:6). A good illustration is found in Joel's teaching on the locusts: "That which the palmerworm hath left hath the locust eaten; and that which the locust hath left hath the cankerworm eaten; and that which the cankerworm hath left hath the caterpillar eaten" (Joel 1:4).

The prophets used *shə'ērîth* as a technical term for "the remnant of Israel."

They predicted that after the Exile a "remnant" of God-fearing people would return to the land (cf. Hag. 2:2-3). Few prophets (Micah; Zeph. 2:9) employ *yether* for this purpose: "Therefore will he give them up, until the time that she which travaileth hath brought forth: then the remnant [*yether*] of his brethren shall return unto the children of Israel" (Mic. 5:3).

The Septuagint translations are: *loipos* ("remaining; rest; remainder") and *kataloipos* ("what is left; remaining").

Several other nouns which appear infrequently are related to *yether*. *Yôthēr* ("advantage; excess; over,") can be found in Eccl. 6:8: "For what advantage does the wise man have over the fool?" (NASB). *Yithərāh* means "abundance" or "riches" and occurs only in Jer. 48:36. *Yithərôn* can refer to "advantage, gain, profit," and this word appears only in Ecclesiastes (cf. Eccl. 1:3; 2:11). *Yōthereth*, "appendage of the liver," occurs about 10 times (cf. Exod. 29:13, 22; Lev. 3:4, 10, 15). *Môthār*, which means "abundance, superiority, profit," is found in Prov. 14:23. *See also* REMNANT.

B. Verb.

yāthar (יָתַר), "to be superfluous." This verb is related to other Semitic languages, where the root *yāthar/watar* signifies the state of abundance (Ugaritic, Phoenician, Arabic). In Hebrew many forms are derived from the verb *yāthar*. The word occurs about 107 times, once in Dan. 10:13: "But the prince of the kingdom of Persia withstood me one and twenty days: but, lo, Michael, one of the chief princes, came to help me; and I remained there with the kings of Persia."

TO REMEMBER

A. Verb.

zākar (זָכַר), "to remember, think of, mention." This root is found in Assyrian, Aramaic, Arabic, and Ethiopic. The group of words (the verb and the three nouns derived from it) is found throughout the Old Testament. The first occurrence of *zākar* is in Gen. 8:1 with God as the subject: "God remembered Noah . . . : and God made a wind to pass over the earth, and the waters assuaged." In Gen. 9:15 God said to Noah: "And I will remember my covenant . . . ; and the waters shall no more become a flood to destroy all flesh." As in these two cases (cf. Gen. 6:18), "remember" is used of God in respect to His covenant promises and is followed by an action to fulfill His covenant. God delivered Lot from Sodom because of His covenant with Abraham to bless all the nations through him (Gen. 18:17-33): "God remembered Abraham, and brought Lot out of the catastrophe . . ." (Gen. 19:29, NIV). This marks the history of Israel at every major point: "And I have also heard the groaning of the children of Israel, . . . and I have remembered my covenant. . . . and I will bring you out from under the burdens of the Egyptians . . ." (Exod. 6:5-6). The promise "to remember" was repeated in the covenant at Sinai (Lev. 26:40-45), God's remembrance was sung in the Psalms (98:3; 105:8, 42; 106:45), and the promise was repeated by the prophets in regard to restoration from captivity (Ezek. 16:60). The new covenant promise is: ". . . I will forgive their iniquity, and I will remember their sin no more" (Jer. 31:34).

Because of this God's people pray, as Moses: "Turn from thy fierce wrath. . . . Remember Abraham, Isaac, and Israel, thy servants, to whom thou swarest . . ." (Exod. 32:12–13); or Nehemiah: "Remember . . . the word that thou commandedst thy servant Moses . . ." (Neh. 1:8, quoting Lev. 26:33); or the psalmist: "Remember not the sins of my youth, nor my transgressions: according to thy mercy remember thou me . . ." (Ps. 25:7); or Jeremiah: ". . . Remember, break not thy covenant with us" (Jer. 14:21).

Men also "remember." Joseph said to Pharaoh's butler: "But think on me . . . , and make mention of me unto Pharaoh . . ." (Gen. 40:14; NIV, "remember . . . and mention"). Again, "to remember" means more than "to recall"; it means "to retain in thought" so as to tell someone who can take action (cf. Ps. 20:7). *Zākar* may have more specific connotations in certain circumstances: "Hear ye this, O house of Jacob, . . . which swear by the name of the Lord, . . . and make mention of the God of Israel. . . ." (Isa. 48:1). The NASB and the NIV translate the last clause "and invoke the God of Israel"; and the RSV has "confess." All point to the mention of God's name in worship. David appointed "Levites as ministers before the ark of the Lord, to invoke . . . the Lord . . ." (1 Chron. 16:4 RSV; NASB, "to celebrate"; NIV, "to make petition").

The covenant commanded Israel to "remember this day, in which ye came out from Egypt . . ." (Exod. 13:3); to "remember the sabbath day . . ." (Exod. 20:8); to "remember that thou wast a servant in the land of Egypt, and that the Lord thy God brought thee out thence through a mighty hand . . ." (Deut. 5:15 and often); and to "remember his marvelous works . . ." (Ps. 105:5; cf. 1 Chron. 16:15). But "the children of Israel remembered not the Lord their God, who had delivered them out of the hands of all their enemies . . ." (Judg. 8:34; cf. Ps. 78:42).

B. Nouns.

zēker (זֵכֶר) or *zeker* (זֶכֶר), "remembrance; memorial." Of His covenant name, *YHWH* ("Lord"), God said: ". . . This is my memorial unto all generations" (Exod. 3:15; cf. Ps. 30:4; 135:13). The name would recall His acts of covenant fulfillment. Moses was told to write an account of the war with Amalek "for a memorial [*zikkārôn*] in a book, and rehearse it in the ears of Joshua: for I will utterly put out the remembrance [*zēker* or *zeker*] of Amalek from under heaven" (Exod. 17:14).

The noun *zikkārôn* has similar meanings. God gave the bronze plates covering the altar (Num. 16:40) and the heap of stones at the Jordan (Josh. 4:7, 20-24) as perpetual "memorials" for the sons of Israel. The names of the twelve tribes of Israel were engraved on two stones that were attached to the ephod as "stones of memorial unto the children of Israel: and Aaron shall bear their names before the Lord . . ." (Exod. 28:12; cf. v. 29). When Israel went into battle, and when they offered sacrifice, they were to blow trumpets "that they may be to you for a memorial before your God" (Num. 10:9-10).

The noun *'azəkārāh* means "memorial offering," and it occurs primarily in

Leviticus. "Memorials" were directed toward God. A "memorial" portion of each meal offering was burnt on the altar (Lev. 2:2, 9, 16), in other words a small portion in place of the whole amount.

The Septuagint translates these words by several derivatives from one root, *mimneskō*, by which the idea comes into the New Testament. Zechariah praised the Lord God that He had "raised up a horn of salvation for us in the house of his servant David . . . and to remember his holy covenant . . ." (Luke 1:69-73). Our need for a reminder is met in "This do in remembrance of me" (1 Cor. 11:24-25).

REMNANT

A. Nouns.

shə'erîth (שְׁאֵרִית), "rest; remnant; residue." The idea of the "remnant" plays a prominent part in the divine economy of salvation throughout the Old Testament. The "remnant" concept is applied especially to the Israelites who survived such calamities as war, pestilence, and famine—people whom the Lord in His mercy spared to be His chosen people: "For out of Jerusalem shall go forth a remnant, and they that escape out of mount Zion: the zeal of the Lord of hosts shall do this" (2 Kings 19:31; cf. Ezra 9:14).

The Israelites repeatedly suffered major catastrophes that brought them to the brink of extinction. So they often prayed as in Jer. 42:2: "Let, we beseech thee, our supplication be accepted before thee, and pray for us unto the Lord thy God, even for all this remnant (for we are left but a few of many, as thine eyes do behold us:)."

Isaiah used the word *shə'erîth* 5 times to denote those who would be left after the Assyrian invasions: "For out of Jerusalem shall go forth a remnant, and they that escape out of mount Zion: the zeal of the Lord of hosts shall do this" (Isa. 37:32).

Micah also announced the regathering of the Jewish people after the Exile. Thus Micah prophesied: "I will surely assemble them together, O Jacob, all of thee; I will surely gather the remnant of Israel . . ." (2:12). In Mic. 4:7 he predicted: "And I will make her that halted a remnant and her that was cast far off a strong nation: and the Lord shall reign over them in mount Zion from henceforth, even for ever." In 5:7-8 and 7:18, Micah announces a similar idea.

Jeremiah discussed the plight of the Jews who fled to Egypt after Jerusalem's capture by Nebuchadnezzar: "Likewise when all the Jews that were in Moab, and among the Ammonites, and in Edom, and that were in all the countries, heard that the King of Babylon had left a remnant of Judah. . . . Then Johanan the son of Kareah spake to Gedaliah in Mizpah secretly, saying, Let me go, I pray thee, and I will slay Ishmael . . . wherefore should he slay thee, that all the Jews which are gathered unto thee should be scattered, and the remnant in Judah perish?" (Jer. 40:11, 15).

Zephaniah, a seventh-century prophet, identified the "remnant" with the poor and humble (2:3, 7; 3:12-13). Zechariah announced that a "remnant" would be present at the time of the coming of the Messiah's kingdom (12:10–13:1; 13:8-9).

shə'ār (שְׁאָר), "rest; remnant; residue." Isaiah describes the "remnant" of Israel: "And it shall come to pass in that day, that the remnant of Israel, and such as are escaped of the house of Jacob, shall no more again stay upon him that smote them; but shall stay upon the Lord, the Holy One of Israel, in truth" (Isa. 10:20).

Notice that a twofold theme emerges from most prophetic passages concerning the "remnant": (1) A "remnant" will survive when the people are subjected to punishment, and (2) the fact that a "remnant" does survive and does remain contains a note of hope for the future. Isa. 10:21 announces: "The remnant shall return, even the remnant of Jacob, unto the mighty God." In Isa. 11:11, the prophet proclaims: "And it shall come to pass in that day, that the Lord shall set his hand again the second time to recover the remnant of his people, which shall be left from Assyria, and from Egypt, and from Pathros, and from Cush, and from Elam, and from Shinar, and from Hamath, and from the islands of the sea." *See also* REMAINDER.

B. Verb.

shā'ar (שָׁאַר), "to remain, be left over." This verb and its noun derivatives occur about 220 times in the Old Testament.

Noah and his family were a "remnant" delivered by the Flood: ". . . And Noah only remained alive, and they that were with him in the ark" (Gen. 7:23). In the days of Elijah, when God's chosen people in the northern kingdom had fallen into apostasy, the Lord announced: "Yet I have left me seven thousand in Israel, all the knees which have not bowed unto Baal . . ." (1 Kings 19:18).

In the pre-exilic period, this remnant idea is stressed by Isaiah. Isaiah tells of the judgment on the earth from which a remnant will "remain": "Therefore hath the curse devoured the earth, and they that dwell therein are desolate: therefore the inhabitants of the earth are burned, and few men left" (Isa. 24:6). Isa. 4:3 refers to a "remnant" which shares holiness: "And it shall come to pass, that he that is left [*shā'ar*], and he that remaineth in Jerusalem, shall be called holy. . . ."

In the writing prophets, the idea of the "remnant" acquired a growing significance. Yet the idea may be found as early as the Pentateuch. The idea of "those being left" or "having escaped," especially a portion of the Israelite people, may be traced back to Deut. 4:27: "And the Lord shall scatter you among the nations, and ye shall be left few in number among the heathen, whither the Lord shall lead you" (cf. Deut. 28:62). In these passages, Moses warns that if Israel failed to live up to the stipulations of the Mosaic covenant, the Lord would scatter them among the nations, and then He would regather a "remnant."

In Neh. 1:2-3, the condition of the "remnant" of Israel is described: ". . . And I asked them concerning the Jews that had escaped, which were left of the captivity, and concerning Jerusalem. And they said unto me, the remnant that are left of the captivity there in the province are in great affliction and reproach. . . ."

TO REMOVE, DEPART

A. Verb.

nāsā' (נָשָׂא), "to remove, depart, carry away." This verb occurs in all Semitic languages including biblical Aramaic and in all periods of Hebrew. The Bible attests this Hebrew word about 650 times.

The meaning "to lift up" or "to bear" is seen, for example, in Gen. 7:17 (the first occurrence of this word), where it is reported that the waters "lifted up" the ark. A special use of this emphasis occurs in Job 6:2, where Job prays that his trouble be laid ("lifted up") in the balances because he believes his trouble far outweighs his sin. Then there is the sense "to bear up" or "to support," as a loaded donkey "bears up" his load (Gen. 45:23). Then, too, *nāsā'* can be used of bearing something away—David and his men "took away" the abandoned Philistine idols; they lifted them up, bore them, and carried them away (2 Sam. 5:21, RSV). This same nuance is applied to marriage, or taking a wife (Ruth 1:4). The same expression means to steal (or plunder) a wife (Judg. 21:23). The phrase "lift up . . . heads" sometimes means "to take a census" (KJV, "to number")—the Lord told Moses to "lift up" the heads of the sons of Israel (Exod. 30:12). This latest phrase may well be an evidence of direct influence from the Akkadian language.

Often *nāsā'* is used as a part of a gesture—for example, "to lift up" one's hand. This gesture can be hostile (2 Sam. 20:21), a part of taking an oath (Exod. 6:8), something done while praying (Ps. 28:9) and signaling (Isa. 49:22). "To lift up the head" can mean to be or declare independence in power and control (Judg. 8:28). The same phrase can be used of being free (2 Kings 25:27; cf. Gen. 40:13), while losing one's head can mean dying (cf. Gen. 40:19). To "lift one's face" means to be able to look someone straight in the eye, to have a clear conscience toward someone or with reference to something (2 Sam. 2:22), or to anticipate that things will go well (Job 22:26). God says He will "accept" Lot's request; He reassures Lot that things will go the way he wants them to (Gen. 19:21). This phrase can mean "to be well disposed toward" or "to respect" (2 Kings 3:14), and "to be biased in favor of" (Job 13:8). God's "raising His face on one" means that He will show one His favor (Num. 6:26). To raise one's eyes is to see (Gen. 13:10) and to lust for someone (Gen. 39:7).

Nāsā' can also be used with words for sounds and verbal communication. "To lift" one's voice often means to wail (Gen. 21:16). It can also mean to call out loudly (Judg. 9:7), to speak (a proverb; Num. 23:7), to declare (an oracle; 2 Kings 9:25), to slander (Ps. 15:3), to carry (a false rumor; Exod. 23:1), and to speak a name (Exod. 20:7).

This verb can be used with "soul," in the sense "to lift up" one's soul. This means "to hand oneself over to" or "to be dependent on" something—the poor man "lifts up his soul" to his wages (Deut. 24:15).

Sometimes *nāsā'* means "to support"—Gen. 13:6 says the land could not support, or provide enough sustenance for, Abraham's and Lot's parties.

The Bible speaks of bearing sin and iniquity in Exod. 28:38, where it is said that Aaron "may bear the iniquity of the holy things"; the sin of the holy things will be on Aaron, who is "holy to the Lord" (v. 36). In Gen. 18:24 Abraham pleads with God to spare Sodom and Gomorrah and to bear away the sin of the place.

B. Nouns.

nāsî' (נָשִׂיא), "(elected) chief." This noun appears 130 times, and it refers to one lifted up publicly: ". . . Twelve princes shall he beget, and I will make him a great nation" (Gen. 17:20; cf. Num. 1:44).

Several other related nouns occur less frequently. *Massā'* appears 45 times as "load" or "bearing" (Num. 11:11) and 21 times as "utterance" (2 Kings 9:25). *Masə'ēth,* which occurs 16 times, refers to the "action of lifting up" (cf. Ps. 141:2) and to "something lifted up" (Gen. 43:34). *Sə'ēt* occurs 14 times, with 2 senses: (1) a "lifting up," such as an "uprising" (Job 41:25), and "dignity" (Gen. 49:3); and (2) something that is "lifted up," such as a swelling or blotch (Lev. 13:2). *Nəsi'îm* occurs 4 times with the meaning "damp, fog, hovering clouds" (Jer. 10:13). Both *massā'āh* (Isa. 30:27) and *sî'* (Job 20:6) occur only once.

TO REND, TEAR

qāra' (קָרַע), "to rend, tear, tear away." This word is common to both ancient and modern Hebrew. Used some 63 times in the Hebrew Old Testament, it is found for the first time in Gen. 37:29: ". . . He rent his clothes." In the expression, "to tear one's clothes," *qāra'* is used 39 times. Usually such "rending" of clothes is an expression of grief (Gen. 37:34; 44:13; 2 Sam. 13:19).

Sometimes the word is used in a symbolic act, such as Ahijah's "tearing" a new garment into twelve pieces and sending them to the twelve tribes as a symbol of coming division (1 Kings 11:30). Samuel used *qāra'* figuratively when he said to Saul: "The Lord hath rent the kingdom of Israel from thee this day . . ." (1 Sam. 15:28). Wild animals "rend" or "tear" their prey (Hos. 13:8).

TO REPENT

nācham (נָחַם), "to repent, comfort." *Nācham* apparently means "to repent" about 40 times and "to comfort" about 65 times in the Old Testament. Scholars assert several views in trying to ascertain *nācham*'s meaning by connecting the word to a change of the heart or disposition, a change of mind, a change of purpose, or an emphasis upon the change of one's conduct.

Most uses of the term in the Old Testament are connected with God's repentance: ". . . It repented the Lord that he had made man. . ." (Gen. 6:6); "And the Lord repented [NASB, "changed his mind"] of the evil which he thought to do unto his people" (Exod. 32:14, KJV). Sometimes the Lord "repented" of the discipline He had planned to carry out concerning His people: "If that nation, against whom I have pronounced, turn from their evil,

I will repent of the evil that I thought to do unto them'' (Jer. 18:8); "If it do evil in my sight, that it obey not my voice, then I will repent of the good. . ." (Jer. 18:10); "And rend your heart, and not your garments, and turn unto the Lord your God: for he is gracious and merciful, slow to anger . . . and repenteth him of evil" (Joel 2:13). In other instances, the Lord changed His mind; obviously, He changed when man changed to make the right choices, but He could not change His attitude toward evil when man continued on the wrong course. As God changed His actions, He always remained faithful to His own righteousness.

In some situations, God was weary of "repenting" (Jer. 15:6), suggesting that there might be a point beyond which He had no choice but to implement His discipline. An instance of this action was in Samuel's word to Saul, that God took the kingdom from Israel's first king and intended to give it to another; Samuel declared, "And also the Strength of Israel will not lie nor repent; for he is not a man, that he should repent" (NASB, "change His mind"; 1 Sam. 15:29).

God usually changed His mind and "repented" of His actions because of man's intercession and repentance of his evil deeds. Moses pleaded with God as the intercessor for Israel: "Turn from thy fierce wrath, and repent of this evil against thy people" (Exod. 32:12). The Lord did that when He ". . . repented [changed His mind] of the evil which he thought to do unto his people" (Exod. 32:14). As God's prophet preached to Nineveh, ". . . God saw their works, that they turned from their evil way; and God repented of the evil, that he had said that he would do unto them . . ." (Jonah 3:10). In such instances, God "repented," or changed His mind, to bring about a change of plan. Again, however, God remained faithful to His absolutes of righteousness in His relation to and with man.

Other passages refer to a change (or lack of it) in man's attitude. When man did not "repent" of his wickedness, he chose rebellion (Jer. 8:6). In the eschatological sense, when Ephraim (as a representative of the northern branch of Israel) will "repent" (Jer. 31:19), God then will have mercy (Jer. 31:20).

Man also expressed repentance to other men. Benjamin suffered greatly from the crime of immorality (Judg. 19-20): "And the children of Israel [eleven tribes] repented them from Benjamin their brother, and said, There is one tribe cut off from Israel this day" (Judg. 21:6; cf. v. 15).

Nācham may also mean "to comfort." The refugees in Babylon would be "comforted" when survivors arrived from Jerusalem (Ezek. 14:23); the connection between "comfort" and "repent" here resulted from the calamity God brought upon Jerusalem as a testimony to the truth of His Word. David "comforted" Bathsheba after the death of her child born in sin (2 Sam. 12:24); this probably indicates his repentance of what had happened in their indiscretion.

On the other hand, the word was used in the human sense of "comfort." Job asked his three companions, "How then comfort ye me in vain, seeing in your answers there remaineth falsehood?" (Job 21:34; he meant that their attitude seemed cruel and unfeeling. The psalmist looked to God for "comfort'': ''Thou shalt increase my greatness, and comfort me on every side'' (Ps. 71:21). In an eschatological sense, God indicated that He would ''comfort'' Jerusalem with the restoration of Israel, as a mother comforts her offspring (Isa. 66:13).

REPROACH

A. Noun.

cherapāh (חֶרְפָּה), ''reproach.'' This noun occurs in the Old Testament and in rabbinic Hebrew. Its use in modern Hebrew has been taken over by other nouns. *Cherapāh* occurs 70 times in the Hebrew Old Testament. It is rare in the Pentateuch and in the historical books. The noun appears most frequently in the Book of Psalms, in the major prophets, and in Daniel. The first occurrence is in Gen. 30:23: ''And she conceived, and bare a son; and said, God hath taken away my reproach.''

''Reproach'' has a twofold usage. On the one hand, the word denotes the state in which one finds himself. The unmarried woman (Isa. 4:1) or the woman without children (Gen. 30:23) carried a sense of disgrace in a society where marriage and fertility were highly spoken of. The destruction of Jerusalem and the Exile brought Judah to the state of ''reproach'': ''O Lord, according to all thy righteousness, I beseech thee, let thine anger and thy fury be turned away from thy city Jerusalem, thy holy mountain: because for our sins, and for the iniquities of our fathers, Jerusalem and thy people are become a reproach to all that are about us'' (Dan. 9:16). On the other hand, the disgrace found in a person or a nation became the occasion for taunting the oppressed. The disgraced received abuse by the words spoken against them and by the rumors which were spread about them.

Whatever the occasion of the disgrace was, whether defeat in battle, exile, or enmity, the psalmist prayed for deliverance from the ''reproach'': ''Remove from me reproach and contempt; for I have kept thy testimonies'' (Ps. 119:22—see context; cf. Ps. 109:25). The verbal abuse that could be heaped upon the unfortunate is best evidenced by the synonyms found with *cherapāh* in Jer. 24:9: ''And I will deliver them to be removed into all the kingdoms of the earth for their hurt, to be a reproach and a proverb, a taunt and a curse, in all places whither I shall drive them.'' Several prophets predicted that Israel's judgment was partly to be experienced by the humiliating ''reproach'' of the nations: ''And I will persecute them with the sword, with the famine, and with the pestilence, and will deliver them to be removed to all the kingdoms of the earth, to be a curse, and an astonishment, and a hissing, and a reproach, among all the nations whither I have driven them'' (Jer. 29:18; cf. Ezek. 5:14). However, the Lord graciously promised to remove the ''reproach'' at the accomplishment of His purpose: ''He will swallow up death in victory; and the Lord God will wipe away tears from off all faces; and the rebuke of his people shall he take away from off all the earth . . .'' (Isa. 25:8).

The Septuagint translations are: *oneidismos* (''reproach; reviling; disgrace; insult'') and *oneidos* (''disgrace; reproach; insult''). The KJV gives these translations: ''reproach; shame; rebuke.''

B. Verb.

chãraph (חָרַף), "to say sharp things, reproach." The root with the meaning "to be sharp" is found in Northwest and South Semitic languages. In Hebrew the verb refers to a manner of speech, i.e., to reproach someone. The word appears about 50 times in the Old Testament, once in Ps. 42:10: "As with a sword in my bones, mine enemies reproach me; while they say daily unto me, Where is thy God?"

TO REPROVE

yãkach (יָכַח), "to decide, prove, convince, judge." As in biblical Hebrew, this verb is found in modern Hebrew primarily in the causative forms. It occurs some 60 times in the text of the Hebrew Bible. The first occurrence of the word is in Gen. 20:16, where the KJV translates: ". . . She was reproved." The context indicates, however, that Abraham, Sarah's husband, deserved being "reproved" in our modern meaning of the word, but that Sarah actually was "cleared" (NASB).

It is evident in most of the uses of *yãkach* that there is a value judgment involved, as in Ps. 50:21: ". . . I will reprove thee, and [lay the charge before thee]." Negative judgments may lead to reproof, especially by God (Job 5:17). Such divine reproof may be physical: ". . . I will chasten him with the rod of men . . ." (2 Sam. 7:14). But it is the conviction of the wise man that "the Lord reproves him whom he loves" (Prov. 3:12 RSV).

TO REST, REMAIN

nûach (נוּחַ), "to rest, remain, be quiet." This word is common to ancient and modern Hebrew, as well as ancient Akkadian and Ugaritic. It occurs in the text of the Old Testament approximately 65 times; the first occurrence is in Gen. 8:4: "And the ark [came to rest] . . . upon the mountains of Ararat." This illustrates the frequent use of this word to show a physical settling down of something at some particular place. Other examples are birds (2 Sam. 21:10), insects (Exod. 10:14), and soles of feet in the waters of the Jordan (Josh. 3:13).

"To rest" sometimes indicates a complete envelopment and thus permeation, as in the spirit of Elijah "resting" on Elisha (2 Kings 2:15), the hand of God "resting" on the mountain (Isa. 25:10), and when Wisdom "resteth in the heart of him that hath understanding" (Prov. 14:33). Frequently *nûach* means "to be quiet" or "to rest" after hard work (Exod. 20:11), from onslaught of one's enemies (Esth. 9:16), from trouble (Job 3:26), and in death (Job 3:17). The word may mean "to set one's mind at rest," as when a child receives the discipline of his parent (Prov. 29:17). Sometimes *nûach* means "to leave at rest" or "to allow to remain." Thus, God "allowed" the pagan nations "to remain" in Canaan during Joshua's lifetime (Judg. 2:23). God threatened to abandon the Israelites in the wilderness (Num. 32:15).

It should be noted that while *nûach* is used sometimes as a synonym for *shābath,* "to cease, to rest" (Exod. 20:11), *shābath* really is basically "to cease" from work which may imply rest, but not necessarily so. The writer of Gen. 2:3 is not stressing rest from work but rather God's ceasing from His creative work since it was complete.

TO RETURN

A. Verb.

shûb (שׁוּב), "to return or go back, bring back." This verb occurs in several Semitic languages (not in Phoenician–Punic and Ethiopic) including Ugaritic (1550-1200 B.C.) and in all periods of Hebrew. It occurs about 1,060 times in biblical Hebrew and about 8 times in biblical Aramaic (in the form *tûb*).

The basic meaning of the verb is movement back to the point of departure (unless there is evidence to the contrary). In the first occurrence of this verb God told Adam that he and Eve would "eat bread, till thou return unto the ground; for out of it wast thou taken: for dust thou art, and unto dust shalt thou return" (Gen. 3:19).

Used in this emphasis, *shûb* can be applied specifically of returning along a path already traversed: "So Esau returned that day on his way unto Seir" (Gen. 33:16). The word can mean "turn away from," as in Ps. 9:3: "When mine enemies are turned back . . . ," or "reverse a direction," as in 2 Kings 20:10: ". . . Let the shadow return backward ten degrees." It can mean the opposite of going out, as when the raven Noah sent forth was constantly going "to and fro" (Gen. 8:7)—this phrase, however, may also mean merely constant movement; the raven went about constantly "here and there" (cf. NASB). In Gen. 8:3 the word is used of the receding of the flood water; the water went *(hālak)* down *(shûb,* "returned") steadily.

The verb can also mean "to follow after": "Behold, thy sister-in-law is gone back unto her people, and unto her gods: return thou after thy sister-in-law" (Ruth 1:15).

Shûb can imply the cessation of something. In this sense, the word can imply "to go away or disappear": "And tarry with him a few days, until thy brother's fury turn away" (Gen. 27:44). It can refer to the initiation of the cessation of something. In some cases violence is the means of bringing something to cease: "How then wilt thou turn away the face of one captain of the least of my master's servants . . ." (2 Kings 18:24). In Isa. 47:10 the verb implies both turning away and destroying: "Thy wisdom and thy knowledge, it hath perverted thee. . . ."

In the case of spiritually returning (metaphorically) to the Lord, *shûb* can mean "turning away from" following Him (Num. 14:43), "turning from" pursuing evil (1 Kings 8:35), and "to return" to Him and obey Him (Deut. 30:2). The verb can also be used in close relation to another verb to indicate the repetition of an action presented by the other verb: ". . . I will again feed and keep thy flock" (Gen. 30:31).

B. Nouns.

məshûbāh (מְשׁוּבָה), "backturning; apostasy." This noun occurs 12 times, and it refers to "backsliding" in Hos. 14:4: "I will heal their backsliding, I will love them freely: for mine anger is turned away from him."

Other nouns related to the verb *shûb* occur less frequently. *Təshûbāh* is found 8 times, and it may mean "return" or "beginning" (1 Sam. 7:17) and "answer" (Job 21:34). *Shûbāh* occurs once to mean "coming back" or "turning back" (Isa. 30:15).

RIGHT HAND

yāmîn (יָמִין), "right hand." This word has cognates attested in Ugaritic, Arabic, Syriac, Aramaic, and Ethiopic. It appears about 137 times and in all periods of biblical Hebrew.

First, the word represents the bodily part called the "right hand": "And Joseph took them both, Ephraim in his right hand toward Israel's left hand, and Manasseh in his left hand toward Israel's right hand . . ." (Gen. 48:13). Ehud was "bound as to his right hand"; he was left-handed: "But when the children of Israel cried unto the Lord, the Lord raised them up a deliverer, Ehud the son of Gera, a Benjamite, a man lefthanded . . ." (Judg. 3:15). *Yāmîn* may be used in a figurative sense. God's taking one's "right hand" means that He strengthens him: "For I the Lord thy God will hold thy right hand, saying unto thee, Fear not: I will help thee" (Isa. 41:13). The Bible speaks anthropomorphically, attributing to God human parts and, in particular, a "right hand" (Exod. 15:6). The Bible teaches that God is a spirit and has no body or bodily parts (cf. Exod. 20:4; Deut. 4:15-19). This figure is used of God's effecting His will among men and of His working in their behalf (showing His favor): "And I said, This is my infirmity: but I will remember the years of the right hand of the Most High" (Ps. 77:10).

Second, *yāmîn* represents the direction, to the "right." In this use the word can specify the location of someone or something: "But the children of Israel walked upon dry land in the midst of the sea; and the waters were a wall unto them on their right hand, and on their left" (Exod. 14:29). In other contexts *yāmîn* signifies "direction toward": "Is not the whole land before thee? Separate thyself, I pray thee, from me: if thou wilt take the left hand, then I will go to the right; or if thou depart to the right hand, then I will go to the left" (Gen. 13:9—the first biblical appearance).

Third, *yāmîn* can be used of bodily parts other than the right hand. In Judg. 3:16 the word is used of one's thigh (literally, "thigh of the right hand"): "But Ehud made him a dagger which had two edges, of a cubit length; and he did gird it under his raiment upon his right thigh." The word is used in 1 Sam. 11:2 in conjunction with one's eye and in Exod. 29:22 with a thigh.

Fourth, this word is used to mean "south," since the south is on one's "right" when he faces eastward: "Then came up the Ziphites to Saul to Gibeah, saying, Doth not David hide himself with us in strongholds in the wood, in the hill of Hachilah, which is on the south of Jeshimon?" (1 Sam. 23:19).

Yəmānî (יְמָנִי), "right hand; on the right side; the right side (of one's body); southern." This noun appears 25 times in the Old Testament. *Yəmānî* means "right hand" in Exod. 29:20, the first biblical occurrence. In 1 Kings 7:21 the word refers to the "right side" in regard to a location. *Yəmānî* appears in Ezek. 4:6 with the meaning of the "right side" of the body. The word implies "southern" in 1 Kings 6:8: "The door for the middle chamber was in the right side [southern side] of the house. . . ."

têmān (תֵּימָן), "south; southern quarter; southwards." This noun makes 22 biblical appearances. In its first biblical occurrence (Exod. 26:18), the word refers to the direction "southward." *Têmān* can mean "south" or "southern quarter" as in Josh. 15:1.

TO BE RIGHTEOUS

A. Verb.

tsādaq (צָדַק), "to be righteous, be in the right, be justified, be just." This verb, which occurs fewer than 40 times in biblical Hebrew, is derived from the noun *tsedeq*. Nowhere is the issue of righteousness more appropriate than in the problem of the suffering of the righteous presented to us in Job, where the verb occurs 17 times. Apart from the Book of Job the frequency of *tsādaq* in the various books is small. The first occurrence of the verb is in Gen. 38:26, where Judah admits that Tamar was just in her demands: "She hath been more righteous than I; because that I gave her not to Shelah my son."

The basic meaning of *tsādaq* is "to be righteous." It is a legal term which involves the whole process of justice. God "is righteous" in all of His relations, and in comparison with Him man is not righteous: "Shall mortal man be more just [righteous] than God?" (Job 4:17). In a derived sense, the case presented may be characterized as a just cause in that all facts indicate that the person is to be cleared of all charges. Isaiah called upon the nations to produce witnesses who might testify that their case was right: "Let them bring forth their witnesses, that they may be justified: or let them hear, and say, It is truth" (43:9). Job was concerned about his case and defended it before his friends: ". . . Though I were righteous, yet would I not answer, but I would make supplication to my judge" (9:15). *Tsādaq* may also be used to signify the outcome of the verdict, when a man is pronounced "just" and is judicially cleared of all charges. Job believed that the Lord would ultimately vindicate him against his opponents (Job 13:18).

In its causative pattern, the meaning of the verb brings out more clearly the sense of a judicial pronouncement of innocence: "If there be a controversy between men, and they come unto judgment, that the judges may judge them; then they shall justify [*tsādaq*] the righteous [*tsaddîq*], and condemn the wicked" (Deut. 25:1). The Israelites were charged with upholding righteousness in all areas of life. When the court system failed because of corruption, the wicked were falsely "justified" and the poor were robbed of justice because of trumped-up charges. Absalom, thus, gained a large following by promising justice to the landowner (2 Sam. 15:4). God, however, assured

Israel that justice would be done in the end: "Thou shalt not wrest the judgment of thy poor in his cause. Keep thee far from a false matter; and the innocent and righteous slay thou not: for I will not justify the wicked" (Exod. 23:6-7). The righteous person followed God's example. The psalmist exhorts his people to change their judicial system: "Defend the poor and fatherless: do justice to the afflicted and needy" (Ps. 82:3).

Job's ultimate hope was in God's declaration of justification. The Old Testament is in agreement with this hope. When injustice prevails, God is the One who "justifies."

The Septuagint translates the verb by *dikaiaō* ("to do justice, justly; to vindicate"). In the English versions a frequent translation is "to justify" (KJV, RSV, NASB, NIV); modern versions also give the additional translations "to be vindicated" (RSV, NASB, NIV) and "to acquit" (RSV, NIV).

B. Nouns.

tsedeq (צֶדֶק); *tsədāqāh* (צְדָקָה), "righteousness." These nouns come from a Semitic root which occurs in Hebrew, Phoenician, and Aramaic with a juristic sense. In Phoenician and Old Aramaic it carries the sense of "loyalty" demonstrated by a king or priest as a servant of his own god. In these languages a form of the root is combined with other words or names, particularly with the name of a deity, in royal names. In the Old Testament we meet the name Melchizedek ("king of righteousness"). A more limited meaning of the root is found in Arabic (a South Semitic language): "truthfulness" (of propositions). In rabbinic Hebrew the noun *tsədāqāh* signifies "alms" or "demonstrations of mercy."

The word *tsədāqāh*, which occurs 157 times, is found throughout the Old Testament (except for Exodus, Leviticus, 2 Kings, Ecclesiastes, Lamentations, Habbakuk, and Zephaniah). *Tsedeq,* which occurs 119 times, is found mainly in poetic literature. The first usage of *tsedeq* is: "Ye shall do no unrighteousness in judgment: thou shalt not respect the person of the poor, nor honor the person of the mighty: but in righteousness shalt thou judge thy neighbor" (Lev. 19:15); and of *tsədāqāh* is: "[Abram] believed in the Lord; and he counted it to him for righteousness" (Gen. 15:6).

Translators have found it difficult to translate these two words. The older translations base their understanding on the Septuagint with the translation *dikaiosune* ("righteousness") and on the Vulgate *iustitia* ("justice"). In these translations the legal relationship of humans is transferred to God in an absolute sense as the Lawgiver and with the perfections of justice and "righteousness."

Exegetes have spilled much ink in an attempt to understand contextually the words *tsedeq* and *tsədāqāh*. The conclusions of the researchers indicate a twofold significance. On the one hand, the relationships among people and of a man to his God can be described as *tsedeq,* supposing the parties are faithful to each other's expectations. It is a relational word. In Jacob's proposal to Laban, Jacob used the word *tsədāqāh* to indicate the relationship. The KJV gives the following translation of *tsədāqāh:* "So shall my righteousness an-

swer for me in time to come, when it shall come for my hire before thy face
. . ." (Gen. 30:33). The NASB gives the word "righteousness" in a marginal
note, but prefers the word "honesty" in the text itself. The NEB reads "fair
offer" instead. Finally, the NIV has: "And my honesty [tsədāqāh] will testify
for me in the future, whenever you check on the wages you have paid me."
On the other hand, "righteousness" as an abstract or as the legal status of a
relationship is also present in the Old Testament. The *locus classicus* is Gen.
15:6: ". . . And he [the Lord] counted it to him [Abraham] for righteousness."

Regrettably, in a discussion of the dynamic versus the static sense of the
word, one or the other wins out, though both elements are present. The books
of Psalms and of the prophets particularly use the sense of "righteousness" as
a state; cf. "Hearken to me, ye that follow after righteousness, ye that seek
the Lord: look unto the rock whence ye are hewn, and to the hole of the pit
whence ye are digged" (Isa. 51:1); and "My righteousness is near; my salvation is gone forth, and mine arms shall judge the people; the isles shall wait
upon me, and on mine arm shall they trust" (Isa. 51:5). The NEB exhibits this
tension between dynamic and static in the translation of *tsedeq:* "My victory
[instead of righteousness] is near, my deliverance has gone forth and my arm
shall rule the nations; for me coasts and islands shall wait and they shall look
to me for protection" (Isa. 51:5). Thus, in the discussion of the two nouns
below, the meanings lie between the dynamic and the static.

Tsedeq and *tsədāqāh* are legal terms signifying justice in conformity with
the legal corpus (the Law; Deut. 16:20), the judicial process (Jer. 22:3), the
justice of the king as judge (1 Kings 10:9; Ps. 119:121; Prov. 8:15), and also the
source of justice, God Himself: "Judge me, O Lord my God, according to thy
righteousness; and let them not rejoice over me. . . . And my tongue shall
speak of thy righteousness and of thy praise all the day long" (Ps. 35:24, 28).

The word "righteousness" also embodies all that God expects of His
people. The verbs associated with "righteousness" indicate the practicality of
this concept. One judges, deals, sacrifices, and speaks righteously; and one
learns, teaches, and pursues after righteousness. Based upon a special relationship with God, the Old Testament saint asked God to deal righteously with
him: "Give the king thy judgments, O God, and thy righteousness unto the
king's son" (Ps. 72:1).

The Septuagint gives the following translations: *dikaios* ("those who are
upright, just, righteous, conforming to God's laws"); *dikalosunē* ("righteousness; uprightness"); and *eleemosunē* ("land deed; alms; charitable giving").
The KJV gives the senses "righteousness; justice."

C. Adjective.

tsaddîq (צַדִּיק), "righteous; just." This adjectival form occurs 206 times in
biblical Hebrew. In Old Aramaic the adjective signifies "loyalty" of a king or
high priest to his personal god, often represented by a gift to the god. Similarly
in Phoenician, the noun and adjective apply to the loyal relationship of the
king before the gods. The word is used of God in Exod. 9:27: "I have sinned
this time: the Lord is righteous, and I and my people are wicked." *Tsaddîq* is

used of a nation in Gen. 20:4: ". . . And he said, Lord, wilt thou slay also a righteous nation?"

TO RIDE

rākab (רָכַב), "to ride, cause to ride." Already found in ancient Akkadian and Ugaritic, this word is also common to both ancient and modern Hebrew. It occurs approximately 70 times in the text of the Hebrew Bible and is found for the first time in Gen. 24:61: "And Rebekah arose, and her damsels, and they rode upon the camels. . . ." In addition to camels, the biblical account records the riding of mules (2 Sam. 13:29), asses (1 Sam. 25:42), horses (Zech. 1:8), and chariots (2 Kings 9:16). "To ride" upon horses is symbolic of an alliance with Assyria (Hos. 14:3).

Isaiah's statement that "the Lord rideth upon a swift cloud" (Isa. 19:1) is an interesting parallel to the Ugaritic text's reference to the god Baal as "a rider on the clouds." This is not to equate Baal with God, but simply to note the similar imagery which is used, and the apparent influence of one literature on another.

TO RISE EARLY

shākam (שָׁכַם), "to rise early, start early." Found in both biblical and modern Hebrew, this verb occurs some 65 times in the Hebrew Old Testament. It is found for the first time in Gen. 19:2: ". . . And ye shall rise up early, and go on your ways." As in this instance, many of the instances of the use of *shākam* are in connection with traveling. Thus, it may be used with verbs of going (as above) or encamping (Judg. 7:1). The word is used some 30 times in reference to rising early in the morning, as in 1 Sam. 29:10, in which this phrase appears twice: "Wherefore now rise up early in the morning with thy master's servants that are come with thee: and as soon as ye be up early in the morning, and have light, depart."

A number of times in the Book of Jeremiah, "rising up early" is used with "speaking" (7:13; 25:3; 35:14), "sending" (7:25; 25:4; 29:19; 35:15; 44:4), "protesting" (11:7), or "teaching" (32:33). Ps. 127:2 gives some interesting advice while using this word: "It is vain for you to rise up early, to sit up late, to eat the bread of sorrows: for so he giveth his beloved sleep."

RIVER; WADI

A. Nouns.

nachal (נַחַל), "wadi (or wady); torrent-valley; torrent; river; shaft." This root also occurs in Akkadian, post-biblical Hebrew, and Syriac. In Arabic these same radicals mean "palm tree." *Nachal* occurs about 139 times in biblical Hebrew and in all periods.

This noun represents a dry valley in which water runs during the rainy season: "And Isaac departed thence, and pitched his tent in the valley of Gerar, and dwelt there" (Gen. 26:17—the first biblical appearance). The word can signify the "wady" when it is full of rushing water. Indeed, it appears to describe the rushing water itself: "And he took them, and sent them over the brook . . ." (Gen. 32:23). Sometimes *nachal* means a permanent stream or "river": "These shall ye eat of all that are in the waters: whatsoever hath fins and scales in the waters, in the seas, and in the rivers, them shall ye eat" (Lev. 11:9). Finally, the word represents a miner's shaft (only once in the Scripture): "They open shafts in a valley away from where men live" (Job 28:4 RSV).

The Pentateuch consistently distinguishes between extra-Egyptian waterways (calling them *nachal,* 13 times, and *nāhār,* 13 times) and inter-Egyptian waterways (calling them *yə'ôr*). This distinction demonstrates the kind of firsthand knowledge and historical concern expected from a mature eyewitness.

Nachal is used figuratively of many things that emerge and disappear suddenly or that have extreme onrushing power such as the pride of nations (Isa. 66:12), the strength of the invader (Jer. 47:2), and the power of the foe (Ps. 18:4). Torrents of oil do not please God if the offerer's heart is wrongly disposed (Mic. 6:7). God overfloods the godly with torrents of His good pleasure (Ps. 36:8). The eschaton is typified by streams, or torrents, in the desert (Ezek. 47:5-19; cf. Exod. 17:3 ff.).

nāhār (נָהָר), "river; stream; canal; current." Cognates of this word are attested in Ugaritic, Akkadian, Aramaic, and Arabic. The word appears about 120 times in biblical Hebrew and in all periods.

First, this word usually refers to permanent natural watercourses. In its first biblical appearance *nāhār* represents the primeval "rivers" of Eden: "And a river went out of Eden to water the garden; and from thence it was parted, and became into four heads" (Gen. 2:10).

In some passages *nāhār* may represent a "canal(s)": "Say unto Aaron, Take thy rod, and stretch out thine hand upon the waters of Egypt, upon their streams [the branches of the Nile], upon their rivers [canals], and upon their ponds . . ." (Exod. 7:19; cf. Ezek. 1:1).

Third, this word is used of "ocean currents": "For thou hadst cast me into the deep, in the midst of the seas; and the floods compassed me about: all thy billows and thy waves passed over me" (Jonah 2:3).

Fourth, *nāhār* is used of underground streams: "For he hath founded it [the earth] upon the seas, and established it upon the floods" (Ps. 24:2). This passage appears to be a literary allusion to the pagan concept of the creation and structure of the world—the next verse is "Who shall ascend into the hill of the Lord?" (Ps. 24:3).

This word plays a prominent role in the figure of divine blessing set forth in Ps. 46:4: "There is a river, the streams whereof shall make glad the city of God. . . ." This may be an allusion to the primeval "river" in Eden whose water gave life to the garden. In Isa. 33:21 the same Jerusalem is depicted as having "rivers" of blessing: ". . . A place of broad rivers and streams; wherein shall go no galley with oars, neither shall gallant ship pass thereby" (cf. Isa. 48:18). In other passages a "river" is a figure of trouble and difficulty: "When thou passest through the waters, I will be with thee; and through the rivers, they shall not overflow thee . . ." (Isa. 43:2). This is in marked contrast to the use of the same idea in Isa. 66:12, where an "overflowing stream" depicts respectively the onrush of God's glory and divine peace.

B. Verb.

nāhar (נָהַר), "to flow." This verb, derived from the noun *nāhār,* occurs 3 times in biblical Hebrew. The first occurrence is in Isa. 2:2: "And it shall come to pass in the last days, that the mountain of the Lord's house shall be established in the top of the mountains, and shall be exalted above the hills; and all nations shall flow unto it."

ROCK

tsûr (צוּר), "rock; rocky wall; cliff; rocky hill; mountain; rocky surface; boulder." Cognates of this word appear in Amorite, Phoenician, Ugaritic, and Aramaic. Other than in names of places and persons, the word appears 70 times in biblical Hebrew and in all periods.

First, *tsûr* means "rocky wall" or "cliff." This is probably what Moses struck in Exod. 17:6: "Behold, I will stand before thee there upon the rock in Horeb; and thou shalt smite the rock, and there shall come water out of it. . . ." Thus God hid Moses in a cleft of the "rocky cliff" (Exod. 33:21-22).

Second, the word frequently means "rocky hill" or "mountains." This emphasis clearly emerges in Isa. 2:10, 19: "Enter into the rock, and hide thee in the dust. . . . And [men] shall go into the holes of the rocks, and into the caves of the earth. . . ." Thus "rock" is an abbreviation for "caves of the rocks." A lookout sees someone "from the top of the rocks [hills] . . . , from the hills" (Num. 23:9). The "rock" (mountains or hills) flowing with honey and oil figures the abundant overflowing blessing of God (Deut. 32:13). The "rock" (or mountain) serves as a figure of security (Ps. 61:2), firmness (Job 14:18), and something that endures (Job 19:24).

Third, *tsûr* can mean "rocky ground" or perhaps a large flat "rock": "And Rizpah the daughter of Aiah took sackcloth, and spread it for her upon the rock . . ." (2 Sam. 21:10; cf. Prov. 30:19).

Fourth, in some passages the word means "boulder," in the sense of a rock large enough to serve as an altar: ". . . There rose up fire out of the rock, and consumed the flesh and the unleavened cakes . . ." (Judg. 6:21).

"Rock" is frequently used to picture God's support and defense of His people (Deut. 32:15). In some cases this noun is an epithet, or meaningful name, of God (Deut. 32:4), or of heathen gods: "For their rock [god] is not as our Rock [God] . . ." (Deut. 32:31).

Finally, Abraham is the source (rock) from which Israel was hewn (Isa. 51:1).

TO RULE

māshal (מָשַׁל), "to rule, reign, have dominion." This term is common in both ancient and modern Hebrew. It is found approximately 100 times in the text of the Hebrew Old Testament. The word is used for the first time in the Old Testament in Gen. 1:18, where the sun, moon, and stars are designated "to rule over the day and over the night. . . ."

Māshal is used most frequently in the text to express the "ruling or dominion" of one person over another (Gen. 3:16; 24:2). Cain is advised "to rule over" or "master" sin (Gen. 4:7). Joseph's brothers respond to his dreams with the angry question: "Shalt thou indeed reign over us?" (Gen. 37:8; the Hebrew verb here is literally "ruling will you rule," the repetition of the same root giving the needed emphasis).

As Creator and Sovereign over His world, God "ruleth by his power for ever" (Ps. 66:7). When God allowed Israel to have a king, it was with the condition that God was still the ultimate King and that first loyalty belonged to Him (Deut. 17:14-20). This theocratic ideal is perhaps best expressed by Gideon: "I will not rule over you, neither shall my son rule over you: the Lord shall rule over you" (Judg. 8:23). With the possible exception of David, no king of Israel fully lived up to the theocratic ideal, and David himself had some problems with it.

TO RUN

A. Verb.

rûts (רוּץ), "to hasten, run." This verb also appears in Ethiopic, Aramaic (where it is spelled *rəhats*), and Akkadian (where it means "hasten to one's aid"). It appears about 80 times in the Bible and in all periods of the language.

In some contexts *rûts* signifies moving very quickly or "hastening" rather than running. This appears to be the emphasis in its first occurrence, where we are told that "when [Abraham] saw them [the three men], he ran to meet them from the tent door . . ." (Gen. 18:2). Abraham did not run to meet the three men but instead moved very quickly to meet them. So, also, Abraham probably did not run but "hastened" to his herd to choose the animal for the meal (cf. Gen. 18:7). This meaning is confirmed by Isa. 59:7, where the verb is in synonymous parallelism with *māhar* ("to hasten"): "Their [the wicked's] feet run to evil, and they make haste to shed innocent blood. . . ." The sense "hasten" or "move quickly" also appears in Gen. 41:14, where we are told that "Pharaoh sent and called Joseph, and they brought him hastily out of the dungeon. . . ." It appears again in the sense "quickly" in Ps. 68:31: ". . . Let Ethiopia hasten to stretch out her hands to God" (RSV).

Usually this word means "to run." This significance is quite clear in Josh. 8:19, where it is reported that the Israelites in ambush (against Ai) "arose quickly out of their place, and they ran as soon as he [Joshua] had stretched out his hand: and they entered into the city, and took it. . . ." This is a military picture. It describes the height of battle when a troop rushes/runs headlong into the enemy or their camp. Samuel told Israel that God would give them a king after their own hearts (one that met their standards) but that he would make their sons "run" before his chariots, or "run" headlong into battle (1 Sam. 8:11). It was not having a king that was evil, for God had provided for a king in the Mosaic law (cf. Deut. 17:14 ff.). The people sinned because they wanted a king who would be like the kings over other peoples. He would be primarily a military leader. Therefore, God responded that He would give them the kind of king they wanted but that their battles would be won at the cost of their sons' lives. David, the man after God's own heart (the man of God's choosing), was an imperfect king, but when he repented and obeyed God, battles were won without the loss of Israelite lives. This military sense of charging into battle appears metaphorically, describing the lifestyle of the wicked—they "rush" headlong at God (Job 15:26). This emphasis also explains the rather difficult passage 2 Sam. 22:30: "For by thee I have run through a troop . . . ," which means to charge at the enemy (cf. NASB, "margin").

Rûts is also used of "running away from" something or someone. In the battle against Midian when Gideon and his band routed the unsuspecting enemy, "all the host [Midianites] ran, and cried, and fled" (Judg. 7:21). But as with the previous emphasis, so this nuance of "to run away from" may be used in non-military contexts. In 1 Sam. 20:36 the verb signifies running away from someone in search of something, in the sense of not fleeing but pursuing. Jonathan told his aide: "Run, find out now the arrows which I shoot."

Rûts can signify "running" into somewhere not only in a hostile sense but in order to be united with or hidden by it. For example, the sage confesses that "the name of the Lord is a strong tower: the righteous runneth into it, and is safe" (Prov. 18:10). The goal of "running" may be unspecified while the direction or path is emphasized. So used, *rûts* means to pursue a particular course of action: "I will run the way of thy commandments . . ." (Ps. 119:32).

The word is used in several technical senses. Kings and pretenders to the throne demonstrate their exalted position by having runners precede their chariots (2 Sam. 15:1). Perhaps this was in direct response to Samuel's description in 1 Sam. 8:11. Runners also served as official messengers; so Ahimaaz son of Zadok said: "Let me now run, and bear the king [David] tidings, how that the Lord hath avenged him of his enemies [Absalom]" (2 Sam. 18:19).

There are a few additional special nuances of *rûts*. In Song of Sol. 1:4 the word has something to do with love-making, so the translation "let us run together" (NASB) is probably misleading. Perhaps one might translate: "Draw me after you and let us hasten [to make love]; the king has brought me into his bed chambers." In Hag. 1:9 the word means "to busy oneself": "Because of mine house that is waste, and ye run every man unto his own house." Finally, Hab. 2:2 uses this verb to mean "to read quickly," or fluently: "Write the vision, and make it plain upon tables, that he may run that readeth it."

B. Noun.

Mērûts means "running; course." This noun, which occurs only 4 times in biblical Hebrew, represents both the mode of running (2 Sam. 18:27) and the course one runs (Jer. 23:10).

SACRIFICE

zebach (זֶבַח), "sacrifice." This root with the meaning "to sacrifice" is represented in other Semitic languages: Akkadian, Ugaritic, Phoenician, Aramaic, and Arabic. *Zebach* continued to be used in Mishnaic Hebrew, and its use is greatly reduced in modern Hebrew, since there is no temple. The word is used 162 times in the Hebrew Old Testament and in all periods. The first occurrence is in Gen. 31:54: "Then Jacob offered sacrifice upon the mount, and called his brethren to eat bread: and they did eat bread, and tarried all night in the mount."

The basic meaning of *zebach* is "sacrifice." When a "sacrifice" had been slaughtered by the priest, he then offered it to God. The purpose was not just to create communion between God and man; rather, the "sacrifice" represented the principle that, without the shedding of blood, there is no forgiveness of sins (Lev. 17:11; cf. Heb. 9:22). In the act of "sacrifice" the faithful Israelite submitted himself to the priest, who, in keeping with the various detailed regulations (see Leviticus), offered the "sacrifice" in accordance with God's expectations. The "sacrifices" are the Passover "sacrifice" (Exod. 12:27), "sacrifice" of the peace offering (Lev. 3:1 ff.), "sacrifice" of thanksgiving (Lev. 7:12), and "sacrifice" of the priest's offering (*qārəban;* Lev. 7:16). The *zebach* was not like the burnt offering (*'ōlāh),* which was completely burnt on the altar; and it was unlike the sin offering (*chattā'th),* where the meat was given to the priest, for most of the meat of the *zebach* was returned to the person who made the "sacrifice." The fat was burned on the altar (Lev. 3:4-5), and the blood was poured out around the altar (3:2). The person who made the *zebach* had to share the meat with the officiating priest (Exod. 29:28; Lev. 7:31-35; Deut. 18:3).

In view of the fact that the people shared in the eating of the *zebach,* the "sacrifice" became a communal meal in which the Lord hosted His people. Zephaniah's message of judgment is based on this conception of "sacrifice": "Hold thy peace at the presence of the Lord God: for the day of the Lord is at hand: for the Lord hath prepared a sacrifice, he hath bid his guests" (Zeph. 1:7). The Israelite came to the temple with the animal to be sacrificed. It was butchered, boiled, and eaten in the area of the sanctuary (1 Sam. 2:13). Apart from the sanctuaries, the Israelites also celebrated God's goodness together in their native villages. The story of Samuel gives several good illustrations of this custom (cf. 1 Sam. 9:13; 16:2-3).

The prophets looked with condemnation on apostate Israel's "sacrifices": "To what purpose is the multitude of your sacrifices unto me? saith the Lord: I am full of the burnt offerings of rams, and the fat of fed beasts; and I delight not in the blood of bullocks, or of lambs, or of he goats" (Isa. 1:11). Hosea spoke about the necessity of Israel's love for God: "For I desired mercy, and not sacrifice; and the knowledge of God more than burnt offerings" (Hos. 6:6). Samuel the prophet rebuked Saul with the familiar words: "Hath the Lord as great delight in burnt offerings and sacrifices, as in obeying the voice of the Lord? Behold, to obey is better than sacrifice, and to hearken than the fat of rams" (1 Sam. 15:22). David knew the proper response to God when he had sinned: "For thou desirest not sacrifice; else would I give it: thou delightest not in burnt offering. The sacrifices of God are a broken spirit: a broken and a contrite heart, O God, thou wilt not despise" (Ps. 51:16-17).

The Septuagint gives the following translation: *thusia* ("sacrifice; offering"). The KJV gives these senses: "sacrifice; offering."

TO SANCTIFY

A. Verb.

qādash (קָדַשׁ), "to sanctify, be holy." This verb also appears in Phoenician, biblical Aramaic, and Ethiopic. In Ugaritic *q-d-sh* signifies "sanctuary," and in Babylonian *qadāshu* means "shine." *Qādash* appears about 170 times in biblical Hebrew and in all periods of the language.

In the primary stem the verb signifies an act whereby, or a state wherein, people or things are set aside for use in the worship of God: they are consecrated or "made sacred." By this act and in this state the thing or person consecrated is to be withheld from workaday use (or profane use) and to be treated with special care as a possession of God. The first use of *qādash* in this stem focuses on the act: "And thou shalt take of the blood that is upon the altar, and of the anointing oil, and sprinkle it upon Aaron, and upon his garments, and upon his sons, and upon the garments of his sons with him: and he shall be hallowed, and his garments, and his sons, and his sons' garments with him" (Exod. 29:21). There are also overtones of ethical-moral (spiritual) holiness here since the atoning blood was applied to the people involved. The state appears to be emphasized when the word is used in Exod. 29:37: "Seven days thou shalt make an atonement for the altar, and sanctify it; and it shall be an altar most holy: whatsoever toucheth the altar shall be holy." Thus, whatever touches the altar enters into a new state. Now it belongs to God to be used solely by Him in the way He sees fit. In some cases this means destruction (2 Sam. 6:6 ff.), while in others it means such things are to be used only by those who are ritualistically pure (Num. 4:15; 1 Sam. 21:6). It might mean that such things are to be used in the sanctuary itself (Num. 16:37 ff.).

In some passages *qādash* seems to mean the opposite of "holy," defiled so as not to be usable to Israel (God's consecrated people): "Thou shalt not sow thy vineyard with [two kinds of] seeds: lest the fruit of thy seed which thou hast sown, and the fruit of thy vineyard, be defiled" (Deut. 22:9; cf. Ezek. 44:19; 46:20, etc.).

In the passive stem the verb means "to prove oneself holy." So Moses wrote: "This is the water of Meribah; because the children of Israel strove with the Lord, and he was sanctified in them" (Num. 20:13). This proving refers not to an act of judgment against sin (an ethical-moral holiness) but a miraculous act of deliverance. Some scholars see an emphasis here on divine power, arguing that at this stage of their history Israel's concept of holiness was similar to that of the pagans, namely, that "holy" signified the presence of extraordinary power. A similar use of the word occurs in the prophet's promise of the future restoration of Israel: "When I . . . am sanctified in them in the sight of many nations . . ." (Ezek. 39:27).

Another emphasis of this stem appears in Lev. 10:3 (its first biblical appearance), "to be treated as holy": ". . . I will be sanctified in them that come nigh me [approach me in formal worship], and before all the people I will be glorified." Again, the emphasis appears to be on divine power; God will have people obey Him and view Him as a powerful (holy) God. There is an ethical-moral overtone here, too, for God desires His people to obey Him, to hate sin and love righteousness (cf. Isa. 5:16). It is love not fear that lies at the root of Israel's relationship to their God (Deut. 6:3, 5 ff.).

Finally, this stem may be used as a true passive of the primary stem in the sense of to be consecrated or set aside for God's use: "And there [the tent of meeting] I will meet with the children of Israel, and the tabernacle shall be sanctified by my glory" (Exod. 29:43).

Qādash has several emphases in the intensive stem. First, it can mean "to declare something holy" or to declare it to be used exclusively for celebrating God's glory. In Gen. 2:3 (the first biblical occurrence of the word) "God blessed the seventh day, and sanctified it: because that in it he had rested from all his work which God created and made." A related meaning of the word appears in the Ten Commandments: "Remember the sabbath day, to keep it holy" (Exod. 20:8). Israel is to remember the Sabbath by keeping it holy, by celebrating God's person or worshiping Him in the way He specifies. In a still different nuance, "to sanctify" a holy day means to proclaim it, to bind oneself and one's fellows to keep it holy when it comes. This sense can be applied to pagan holy days: "Proclaim a solemn assembly for Baal. And they proclaimed it" (2 Kings 10:20). In Joel 1:14 the verb is applied to Israel's holy days: "Sanctify ye a fast, call a solemn assembly. . . ." Thus, the word comes to mean "to declare" and "to make proper preparations for." In this sense it is sometimes applied to warfare: "Prepare ye war against her; arise, and let us go up at noon" (Jer. 6:4; cf. Mic. 3:5). Even pagans declare holy war: "Set ye up a standard in the land, blow the trumpet among the nations, prepare the nations against her, call together against her the kingdoms of Ararat, Minni . . ." (Jer. 51:27).

This stem may also be used of putting something or someone into a state reserved exclusively for God's use: "Sanctify unto me all the first-born, whatsoever openeth the womb among the children of Israel, both of man and of beast: it is mine" (Exod. 13:2). The first-born of every beast is to be offered up to God by being given to the temple or killed (Exod. 13:12-13). The first son may be redeemed (bought back from the Lord; Num. 18:15-16) or given to the temple (1 Sam. 1:24).

Qādash may also be used in the sense of making something or someone cultically pure and meeting all God's requirements for purity in persons or things used in the formal worship of Him. This act appears in Exod. 19:10, where God told Moses to "go unto the people, and sanctify them today and tomorrow, and let them wash their clothes." Thus consecrated, the people could come into God's presence. In a related sense, the verb means to set someone aside for divine service. Although the primary emphasis here is ritualistic, there are ethical-moral overtones. Thus, God directed Moses to have the artisans make special clothing for Aaron: ". . . And they shall make holy garments for Aaron thy brother, . . . that he may minister unto me in the priest's office" (Exod. 28:4). When the consecration occurred, Aaron and his sons were sprinkled with the blood of the atonement. Such an offering necessitated their confessing their sin and submitting to a substitutionary (albeit typological) sacrifice. Used in this sense the word describes the necessary step preceding ordination to the priestly office.

Qādash is also applied to the consecration of things by placing them into a state of ritualistic or cultic purity and dedicating them solely to God's use (cultic use; cf. Exod. 29:36; Lev. 16:19). In some cases consecrating something to God requires no act upon the object, but leaving it entirely alone. Moses acknowledges to God that "the people cannot come up to mount Sinai: for thou chargedst us, saying, Set bounds about the mount, and sanctify it" (Exod. 19:23). In Isa. 29:23-24 the verb means "to recognize God as holy," as the only real source of truth, and to live according to His laws: "But when he [the house of Jacob] seeth his children, the work of mine hands, in the midst of him, they shall sanctify my name, and sanctify the Holy One of Jacob, and shall fear the God of Israel. They also that erred in spirit shall come to understanding, and they that murmured shall learn doctrine." In Ezek. 36:23 *qādash* means to prove oneself to be holy, or to demonstrate and vindicate one's holiness.

In the causative stem the word means "to give for God's use": "And it shall be upon Aaron's forehead, that Aaron may bear the iniquity of the holy things, which the children of Israel shall hallow . . ." (Exod. 28:38). The act whereby someone gives things to God is also described by the word *qādash*. The priests performed the actual consecration ceremony while an individual decided that something he owned was to be given to God: ". . . King David did dedicate [these vessels] unto the Lord . . ." (2 Sam. 8:11). In Lev. 27:14 ff. several objects are listed which may be given to God as a gift and which may be redeemed by substitutionary payments. In Num. 8:17 God identified "sanctifying" the first-born and killing them. Thus, they were removed from profane use and taken over completely by God: ". . . On the day that I smote every first-born in the land of Egypt I sanctified them for myself."

God's consecrating something or someone may also mean that He accepts that person or thing as in His service: ". . . I have hallowed this house, which thou hast built, to put my name there for ever; and mine eyes and mine heart shall be there perpetually" (1 Kings 9:3). In a more emphatic nuance the word is a correlative of election, signifying God's appointing someone to His service: ". . . Before thou camest forth out of the womb I sanctified thee, and I ordained thee a prophet unto the nations" (Jer. 1:5; cf. 12:3). This verb also means to prepare to approach God: ". . . For the Lord hath prepared a sacrifice, he hath bid his guests'' (Zeph. 1:7). Here, since the word is synonymously parallel to the concept "prepare," or "make ready," it, too, refers to making ready. In Num. 20:12 the stem presents the word in the meaning "trust as holy"; Moses did not follow God's orders recognizing His demand for perfect obedience (cf. Isa. 8:13).

B. Nouns.

qōdesh (קֹדֶשׁ), "holy thing." This noun, which occurs about 470 times in biblical Hebrew, also appears in Ugaritic. Appearing in all periods of biblical Hebrew, it reflects several of the verbal meanings just presented. First, *qōdesh* is used of things or people belonging to God. All Israel is holy (Exod. 30:31), separated to God's service, and therefore should keep itself separated to that service by observing the distinction between things holy (allowed by God) and things unclean (Lev. 10:10).

The word also describes things set aside for exclusive use by God's people (Isa. 35:8). It is used of a more narrow sense of "sacred," or something set aside for use in the temple (cultic use). So the word describes the priestly (sacred) garments (Exod. 28:2). It can be used of sacred things given to the Lord (to be used in the sanctuary and/or by the priests and Levites; Exod. 28:38) and sacred things to be used only by the priests and/or Levites (Exod. 29:32-33). In some cases such dedicated (sacred) gifts may be given to others—at the Lord's direction (Deut. 26:13). In a similar sense *qōdesh* describes sacred things appointed for sacrifice and ritualistic-cultic worship (Exod. 30:25; Lev. 27:10). Israel is to set aside certain sacred days (Sabbaths) exclusively for divine service—for rest from labor (Exod. 20:10), rest in the Lord (Deut. 5:14), and holy convocation (Exod. 12:16).

Qōdesh can also be used of what God makes a person, place, or thing to be. He designates a place to be His (Exod. 3:5—the first biblical appearance of the word), that is, separate and unique. Even more, God designates His sanctuary a holy place (Exod. 36:1). The outer part of the sanctuary is *the* holy place, the inner part the holy of holies (Exod. 26:33), and the altar a most holy place. This means that to varying degrees these places are identified with the holy God (2 Sam. 6:10-11), the God who is separate from and hates all that is death and/or associated with death and idolatry (Ezek. 39:25). This word is also used (infrequently) to describe God's majestic holiness, in that He is without equal and without imperfection (Exod. 15:11). In at least one place the emphasis is on God's holiness as power (Jer. 23:9).

The noun *miqədāsh*, which occurs in biblical Hebrew about 74 times, appears in Aramaic and post-biblical Hebrew. The word represents a "sacred place" or "sanctuary," a place set aside by men upon God's direction and acceptance as the place where He meets them and they worship Him (Exod. 15:17—the first biblical occurrence of the word).

The noun *qādēsh*, which occurs about 11 times in biblical Hebrew, indicates a "cult prostitute," whether female (Gen. 38:21—the first biblical appearance) or male. Male cultic prostitutes were homosexuals (1 Kings 22:46). This noun appears in the Pentateuch, all periods of historical writings, and Hosea and Job.

C. Adjective.

qādôsh (קָדוֹשׁ), "holy." The adjective *qādôsh* occurs about 116 times in biblical Hebrew and in all periods. This adjective is more focused in emphasis than the noun *qōdesh*. *Qādôsh* can refer (infrequently) to cultic holiness, or ritualistic ceremonial holiness (Num. 5:17). Its most frequent use, however, represents God's majestic (1 Sam. 2:2), moral (Lev. 11:44), and dynamistic holiness (holiness as power; 1 Sam. 6:20). The word is also used of what God claims for Himself, what is consecrated to His service (Exod. 29:31). When applied to people, the word may mean "set apart for God" (Ps. 16:3), ritualistically separated to Him (Exod. 19:6—the first biblical occurrence of the word), and thoroughly purified and perfected by Him from all moral evil (Isa. 4:3). Infrequently *qādôsh* is used of non-human beings, separate from this world and endued with great power (Job 5:1; Dan. 8:13).

SATAN

sātān (שָׂטָן), "adversary; Satan." This word appears 24 times in the Old Testament. Most uses of the term relate to the cosmic struggle in the unseen world between God and the opposing forces of darkness.

In Ps. 38:20, David cried out because he was the target of attack by his "adversaries." Possibly David suffered because of mistakes he made, and within the permissive will of God, He used David's enemies to discipline His servant.

In another psalm of distress by an individual, a godly man expressed his deep faith in the Lord. The writer prayed concerning those who were "adversaries" to his soul: "Let them be confounded and consumed that are adversaries to my soul; let them be covered with reproach and dishonor that seek my hurt" (Ps. 71:13). He expressed the reality of the powers of darkness against an individual who sought to live for God.

Imprecatory psalms call for judgment upon one's enemies, reflecting the battle in the unseen world between darkness and light. David's enemies became his "adversaries," but he continued to pray for them (Ps. 109:4). Because those enemies repaid him evil for good and hatred for his love, the king prayed: "Set thou a wicked man over him: and let Satan stand at his right hand" (Ps. 109:6). When they spoke evil against his soul, David called for the Lord's reward against his "adversaries" (Ps. 109:20), and finally, because David's accusers had intended him so much harm, he asked that his accusers be clothed with shame and dishonor (Ps. 109:29). In all of these passages, God worked indirectly by permitting individuals to act as "adversaries" of His people.

In another instance, David was merciful with members of Saul's family who cursed him and wished him harm when he fled from Absalom (2 Sam. 16:5 ff.). David restrained his army commanders from killing Saul's family who had repented of their misdeeds. The king did not want his officers to be his "adversaries" on the day of victory and joy (2 Sam. 19:22).

God can also be the "adversary." When Balaam went to curse the sons of

Israel, God warned him not to do so. When the prophet persisted, God disciplined him: ''And God's anger was kindled because he went: and the angel of the Lord stood in the way for an adversary against him'' (Num. 22:22). God stood as an ''adversary'' because no curse could undo the covenants and agreements already made with Israel.

God took up a controversy with Solomon. When Solomon added more and more pagan wives to his harem, God was greatly displeased (Deut. 17:17). But when the king built pagan shrines for his wives, God raised up ''adversaries'' against him (1 Kings 11:14), a direct action which caused the Edomites and Syrians to revolt against Israel.

Another special instance of intervention was the occasion when ''. . . Satan [lit., ''an adversary''] stood up against Israel, and provoked David to number Israel'' (1 Chron. 21:1). (No definite article is here in Hebrew and, therefore, ''an adversary'' is in mind.) In a parallel passage the Lord moved David to number Israel and Judah (2 Sam. 24:1). Even as the Lord stirred up an ''adversary'' against Solomon, so here God took a direct action to test David to help him learn a vital lesson. God tests believers to help them make the right choices and not depend upon their own human strength.

In the Book of Job, the word *Satan* always has the definite article preceding it (Job 1:6-12; 2:1-7), so the term emphasizes Satan's role as ''the adversary.'' God permitted Satan to test Job's faith, and the adversary inflicted the patriarch with many evils and sorrows. Satan was not all-powerful because he indicated that he could not get beyond God's protection of Job (Job 1:10). He penetrated the ''hedge'' only with God's permission and only for specific instances that would demonstrate God's righteousness. Job became the battleground between the forces of darkness and light. He learned that Satan could be defeated by making the right choices and that God can be glorified in every circumstance.

Zechariah recorded a vision of ''. . . Joshua the high priest standing before the angel of the Lord, and Satan standing at his right hand to resist him'' (lit., ''be his adversary''; Zech. 3:1). The Lord rebuked ''the adversary'' (Zech. 3:2). Satan was once again in conflict with God's purposes and the angels of God, but ''the adversary'' was not all-powerful and was subject to rebuke by God Himself.

A general usage of *sātān* (''adversary'') appears in 1 Kings 5:4: ''But now the Lord my God hath given me rest on every side, so that there is neither adversary or evil occurrent.'' In another instance, David went over to the side of the Philistines; in attempting to fight with them against Israel, some of the Philistine leaders doubted David's sincerity and felt that he would be ''an adversary'' in any battle between the two armies (1 Sam. 29:4).

In the Septuagint, the word is *diabolos*.

TO BE SATISFIED

sāba' (שָׂבַע), ''to be satisfied, sated, surfeited.'' This word is found in Akkadian and Ugaritic, as well as in all periods of Hebrew. It occurs some 96 times in the Hebrew Old Testament. In its first occurrence in the Old Testament text, *sāba‘* expresses the idea of "being filled, sated": ". . . When the Lord shall give you in the evening flesh to eat, and in the morning bread to the full . . ." (Exod. 16:8). As here, the word is frequently used in parallelism with "to eat," or "to graze" when used with cattle or sheep (Jer. 50:19). The earth too "can be sated, have its fill," of rain (Job 38:27).

In a notoriously difficult verse (Hab. 2:5), wine seems to be referred to as never "being satisfied, never having enough." Instead of "wine," the Habakkuk Dead Sea Scroll reads "wealth," which seems more appropriate in the context which points to Assyria as the concern of Habakkuk's complaint.

Sāba‘ sometimes expresses "being surfeited with," as in Prov. 25:16: "Hast thou found honey? Eat so much as is sufficient for thee, lest thou be filled therewith, and vomit it." God too can "become surfeited," especially when men offer sacrifices with the wrong motives: ". . . I am full of the burnt offerings of rams . . ." (Isa. 1:11). The wise man noted that the lazy man "that followeth after vain persons shall have poverty enough [be surfeited with poverty]" (Prov. 28:19; to translate "will have plenty of poverty," as does the RSV, is not quite strong enough).

Sāba‘ often expresses God's "satisfying, supplying," man with his material needs: ". . . Who satisfieth thy mouth with good things; so that thy youth is renewed like the eagle's" (Ps. 103:5). But even when God "fed them to the full," Israel was not satisfied and went after strange gods (Jer. 5:7). Used in parallelism with "to enrich" in Ezek. 27:33, *sāba‘* implies something of enriching as well: ". . . Thou filledst many people; . . . thou didst enrich the kings of the earth. . . ."

TO SAVE

A. Verb.

yāsha‘ (יָשַׁע), "to help, deliver, save." Outside Hebrew this word is attested only in Moabite. It appears in all periods of Hebrew (including post-biblical Hebrew) and in biblical Hebrew about 205 times. The verb occurs only in the causative and passive stems.

Essentially the word means to remove or seek to remove someone from a burden, oppression, or danger. In Exod. 2:17 (the first appearance of this verb) *yāsha‘* signifies to remove someone from a burden or job: ". . . Moses stood up and helped them, and watered their flock." The word is frequently used of removing or seeking to remove someone from the danger of defeat: "And the men of Gibeon sent unto Joshua . . . saying, slack not thy hand from thy servants; come up to us quickly, and save us, and help us . . ." (Josh. 10:6). This is a request to preserve them from possible death. The real danger is not yet upon them but soon will be. The Gibeonites see in Israel their only help.

Yāsha‘ is used in other situations as when Jephthah tells the Ephraimites that they had been summoned to the war at a crucial time but did not respond and "delivered me not out of their [children of Ammon] hands" (Judg. 12:2).

Here the emphasis is "set free," or "liberate," in other words, to remove someone from a condition already upon him. Militarily the word can also be used of "helping," emphasizing the union of forces so as to forge a single and stronger fighting unit. This is no last-ditch stand for the unit being helped. So Joab told Abishai: "If the Syrians be too strong for me, then thou shalt help me . . ." (2 Sam. 10:11). Also, compare: "So the Syrians feared to help [to serve as an ally] the children of Ammon any more" (2 Sam. 10:19).

In the realm of justice and civil law *yāsha‘* represents an obligation on the part of anyone who hears an outcry of one being mistreated: "For he [the rapist] found her [the one he was about to rape] in the field, and the betrothed damsel cried, and there was none to save her" (Deut. 22:27; cf. 28:29). There-fore, one may appeal especially to the king as the one obligated to help maintain one's rights: "And when the woman of Tekoah spake to the king, she fell on her face to the ground, and did obeisance, and said, Help, O king" (2 Sam. 14:4; cf. 2 Kings 6:26). The king also "delivered" his people from subjection to their enemies (1 Sam. 10:27; Hos. 13:10). Jeremiah says of the messianic king: "In his days Judah shall be saved, and Israel shall dwell safely . . ." (23:6). Here *yāsha‘* is paralleled by "dwell safely," a phrase which identifies the meaning of *yāsha‘* as "to be preserved from danger." Ulti-mately, God is the Great King who "goeth with you, to fight for you against your enemies, to save you [deliver you from danger]" (Deut. 20:4), and the Judge of all Israel.

The word appears in many prayer petitions: "Arise, O Lord; save me, O my God . . ." (Ps. 3:7). This is a combination, therefore, of military emphasis (a prayer for deliverance from some enemy by forceful interference) and judicial emphasis (a prayer for that which is the petitioner's due and the obligation of the one petitioned—in God's case the obligation is self-imposed through the establishment of the covenantal relationship; cf. Ps. 20:9). In other instances the judicial obligation is in view: "He [the Lord's anointed king] shall judge the poor of the people, he shall save the children of the needy, and shall break in pieces the oppressor" (Ps. 72:4). In this passage the word in synonymous parallelism to *yāsha‘* is *shāphath*, "to see that legal justice is executed." Very often the psalmist has in view the spiritual aspect of God's eternal covenant. This is clear in passages such as Ps. 86, where David confesses that, although the ruler of Israel, he is humbled (godly), and that, although enjoying kingly wealth, he is needy (trusting in God). On the basis of these spiritual conditions he prays for God's covenantal response: "Preserve my soul; for I am holy: O thou my God, save thy servant that trusteth in thee " (Ps. 86:2). The blessings sought here are both eternal (Ps. 86:11-13) and temporal (Ps. 86:14-17).

B. Nouns.

yəshû‘āh (יְשׁוּעָה), "salvation." This word appears about 78 times and refers primarily to God's acts of help which have already occurred and been experienced. In Gen. 49:18 (the first biblical occurrence), the word includes the idea of "salvation" through divinely appointed means and from inequity. In 1 Sam. 14:45 *yəshû‘āh* is used of a human act: "And the people said unto Saul, Shall Jonathan die, who hath wrought this great salvation in Israel?"

The word is used infrequently of deliverance and/or help effected by things (Isa. 12:3).

The noun *təshû'āh* also means "salvation." It occurs about 34 times. The word is frequently joined with responses of thanksgiving and rejoicing (Judg. 15:18—the first occurrence; 1 Sam. 11:13). *Təshû'āh*, therefore, is sometimes rendered "deliverance" (Judg. 15:18), "victory" (2 Sam. 19:2), as well as "salvation" (Isa. 45:17). The idea of "salvation" is that of preservation from threatened, impending, and perhaps deserved danger and suffering. *Təshû'āh* is used in a few instances of a human act: "Where no counsel is, the people fall: but in the multitude of counselors there is safety" (Prov. 11:14).

The noun *yēsha'*, which occurs 36 times, signifies that which God will do in man's behalf (2 Sam. 22:3), or that which has been done by Him for man (2 Sam. 22:36). In two instances this word means simply the general absence of oppression and need (Job 5:4, 11). The word may be translated as "salvation" or "safety."

The noun *mōshā'ôth* occurs only once to mean "saving acts" (Ps. 68:20).

SAVOR

A. Noun.

rêach (רֵיחַ), "savor; smell; fragrance; aroma." Of the 61 appearances of this word, 43 refer specifically to sacrifices made to God and appear in Genesis–Numbers and Ezekiel.

This word refers to the "scent or smell" of a person or thing: "And he [Jacob] came near, . . . and he [Isaac] smelled the smell of his raiment . . ." (Gen. 27:27). In Song of Sol. 1:12 *rêach* signifies the "fragrance" of perfume and in Song of Sol. 2:3 the "fragrance" of a flower. This word is used of a bad "smell" in Exod. 5:21: ". . . Because ye have made our savor to be abhorred [have made us odious] in the eyes of Pharaoh. . . ."

Most frequently *rêach* is used of the "odor" of a sacrifice being offered up to God. The sacrifice, or the essence of the thing it represents, ascends to God as a placating "odor": "And the Lord smelled a sweet [NASB, "soothing"] savor . . ." (Gen. 8:21—the first occurrence of the word).

B. Verb.

rûach (רוּחַ), "to perceive, enjoy, smell." Gen. 8:21 is the first occurrence: "And the Lord smelled a sweet savor. . . ." The word appears about 14 times.

TO SAY, SPEAK, ANSWER

A. Verb.

'āmar (אָמַר), "to say, speak, tell, command, answer." This verb occurs in all Semitic languages and in all periods of those languages although it has the meaning "to say, speak" only in the so-called Northwest Semitic dialects

(except in Ugaritic) and in Aramaic. Elsewhere the word means "to say" or "to see." This verb is used about 5,280 times in Old Testament Hebrew.

'Āmar refers to the simple act of communicating with the spoken word. Usually the word is used of direct speech ("say"), although it may be used of indirect speech as well ("speak").

The usual subject of this verb is some self-conscious personality—man (Gen. 2:23) or God (Gen. 1:3—the first occurrence of the word). Infrequently animals (Gen. 3:1) or, in figures of speech such as personification, inanimate objects "say" something (Judg. 9:8 ff.). This verb bears many connotations and in some passages is better translated accordingly. The KJV renders this verb "answer" 98 times ("say as a response"), while the NASB translates such passages "said." In Gen. 9:8 we read: "God spoke to Noah" (NASB); the specific content of the communication is not immediately detailed. In Gen. 22:2 Abraham is to offer Isaac on the "mountain of which" God "tells [says to] him" (NASB). Moses requests Pharaoh to let Israel go and sacrifice to God as He "commands" them (Exod. 8:27); the force of God's speaking is more than merely making a statement: It is authoritative.

In addition to these frequently occurring connotations, 'āmar is rendered with many words representing various aspects of spoken communication, such as "appoint" or "assign" (1 Kings 11:18), "mention" or "name" (Gen. 43:27), "call" (Isa. 5:20), and "promise" (2 Kings 8:19). Although not always so translated, this word can imply the act of thinking within oneself (Gen. 44:28) and the intention to do something (Exod. 2:14).

When used of divine speaking, this verb may refer to simple communication (Gen. 1:26). Often, however, there is a much fuller sense where God's saying effects the thing spoken (cf. Gen. 1). The phrase "thus says the Lord," so frequent in the prophets, has been analyzed as a message-formula. Ancient Near Eastern letters from, for example, Mari (1750-1697 B.C.) and Amarna (1400-1360 B.C.) contain a similar formula. One might compare our letters which open with "Dear sir." Divine messages are often concluded with the words "says the Lord." The Bible recognizes that behind the divine speaking is divine authority and power.

The Septuagint renders this verb by over 40 different Greek words and most often by *legō* ("to say") and *eipen* ("he said").

B. Nouns.

'ēmer (אֶמֶר), "word; speech." This noun appears 48 times. 'Ēmer refers to "words" in Prov. 2:1: "My son, if thou wilt receive my words, and hide my commandments with thee."

Several other nouns are related to the verb 'āmar. 'Imārāh also means "word, speech," and it occurs 37 times. One occurrence of 'imərāh is in 2 Sam. 22:31 (cf. Ps. 18:30). The noun 'ōmer is found 6 times and means "word, speech, promise" (Ps. 68:11; Hab. 3:9). Ma'amār and mē'mar mean "word, command." Ma'amār occurs 3 times (Esth. 1:15; 2:22; 9:32), and mē'mar occurs twice (Ezra 6:9; Dan. 4:17).

TO SAY, UTTER, AFFIRM

A. Verb.

nə'um (נְאֻם), "to say; utter an affirmation; speak." The word is a verbal form of the verb *nā'am,* which occurs only once in the entire Old Testament: "Behold, I am against the prophets, saith [*nə'um*] the Lord, that use their tongues, and say [*nā'am*], He saith [*nə'um*]" (Jer. 23:31). The word *nə'um* appears as many as 361 times and, because of the frequency in the prophetical books, it is characteristic of prophetic speech.

Nə'um is an indicator which generally appears at the end of the quotation: "What mean ye that ye beat my people to pieces, and grind the faces of the poor? saith [*nə'um*] the Lord God of hosts" (Isa. 3:15). The word may also be found in the middle of an argument: "And I raised up of your sons for prophets, and of your young men for Nazarites. Is it not even thus, O ye children of Israel? saith [*nə'um*] the Lord. But ye gave the Nazarites wine to drink; and commanded the prophets, saying, Prophesy not" (Amos 2:11-12).

B. Noun.

nə'um (נְאֻם), "utterance; saying." The use of *nə'um* is rare at the beginning of a statement: "The Lord said unto my Lord [literally, "a statement of Jehovah to my Lord"], Sit thou at my right hand, until I make thine enemies thy footstool" (Ps. 110:1).

The usage throughout the Old Testament is virtually limited to a word from God. In Numbers the utterances of Balaam are introduced with the formula "and he uttered his oracle": "The oracle [*nə'um*] of Balaam the son of Beor, the oracle [*nə'um*] of the man whose eye is opened" (Num. 24:3 RSV; cf. v. 15). David's concluding words begin with these words: "Now these are the last words of David: The oracle [*nə'um*] of David, the son of Jesse, the oracle [*nə'um*] of the man who was raised on high, the anointed of the God of Jacob, the sweet psalmist of Israel" (2 Sam. 23:1 RSV). Apart from these instances there are a few more examples, but as a rule *nə'um* is a prophetic term, which even beyond the prophetical literature is associated with a word from God.

The Septuagint gives the following translation(s): *legein* ("utterance in words") and *hode* (used with reference to what follows, e.g., "this is what . . . says").

TO SCATTER

pûts (פּוּץ), "to scatter, disperse, be scattered." This term is found in both ancient and modern Hebrew. Occurring some 65 times in the Hebrew Old Testament, the word is found for the first time in Gen. 10:18: ". . . The families of the Canaanites spread abroad." The word is used 3 times in the story of the tower of Babel (Gen. 11:4, 8–9), apparently to emphasize how men and their languages "were spread" throughout the world.

Pûts, in the sense of "scattering," often has an almost violent connotation to it. Thus, when Saul defeated the Ammonites, "they which remained were scattered, so that two of them were not left together" (1 Sam. 11:11). Such "scattering" of forces seems to have been a common thing after defeats in battle (1 Kings 22:17; 2 Kings 25:5). Many references are made to Israel as a people and nation "being scattered" among the nations, especially in the imagery of a scattered flock of sheep (Ezek. 34:5–6; Zech. 13:7). Ezekiel also promises the gathering together of this scattered flock: ". . . I will even gather you from the people, . . . where ye have been scattered . . ." (Ezek. 11:17; 20:34, 41).

In a figurative sense, this word is used to refer to lightning as arrows which God "scatters" (2 Sam. 22:15). According to Job, "the clouds scatter his lightning" (Job. 37:11 RSV). No harvest is possible unless first the seeds "are scattered" in rows (Isa. 28:25).

SEA

yām (◻ׇ), "sea; ocean." This word has cognates in Aramaic, Akkadian, Ugaritic, Phoenician, and Ethiopic. It occurs about 390 times and in all periods of biblical Hebrew.

This word refers to the body of water as distinct from the land bodies (continents and islands) and the sky (heavens): "For in six days the Lord made heaven and earth, the sea and all that in them is . . ." (Exod. 20:11). Used in this sense *yām* means "ocean." This is its meaning in Gen. 1:10, its first biblical appearance; unlike the use in the singular, where the word is a collective noun, it appears here in the plural: "And God called the dry land Earth; and the gathering together of the waters called he Seas. . . ."

Yām may be used of "seas," whether they are salty or fresh. The Great Sea is the Mediterranean: "From the wilderness and this Lebanon even unto the great river, the river Euphrates, all the land of the Hittites, and unto the Great Sea toward the going down of the sun, shall be your coast" (Josh. 1:4). This sea is also called the sea of the Philistines (Exod. 23:31) and the hinter or western sea (Deut. 11:24; KJV, "uttermost sea"). The Dead Sea is called the Salt Sea (Gen. 14:3), the Arabah (Deut. 3:17; KJV, "plain"), and the east sea (Ezek. 47:18). Thus, *yām* can be used of an inland salty "sea." It can also be used of a fresh water "sea" such as the Sea of Galilee: ". . . And the border shall descend, and shall reach unto the side of the Sea of Chinnereth eastward" (Num. 34:11).

The word is sometimes used of the direction west or westward, in the sense of toward the (Great) Sea: "Lift up now thine eyes, and look from the place where thou art northward, and southward, and eastward, and westward" (Gen. 13:14). In Gen. 12:8 *yām* means "on the west side": "And he removed from thence unto a mountain on the east of Beth–el, and pitched his tent, having Beth–el on the west, and Hai on the east. . . ." This word can also refer to a side of something and not just a direction, but it is the side that faces westward: "He turned about to the west side . . ." (Ezek. 42:19). Exod. 10:19 uses *yām* as an adjective modifying "wind": "And the Lord turned a mighty strong west wind, which took away the locusts. . . ."

Yām is used of the great basin immediately in front of the Holy Place: "And the pillars of brass that were in the house of the Lord, and the bases, and the brazen sea that was in the house of the Lord, did the Chaldees break in pieces, and carried the brass of them to Babylon" (2 Kings 25:13). This is also called the "sea" of cast metal (1 Kings 7:23; KJV, "molten sea") or simply the "sea" (Jer. 27:19).

Yām is used of mighty rivers such as the Nile: "And the waters shall fail from the sea, and the river shall be wasted and dried up" (Isa. 19:5). This statement occurs in the middle of a prophecy against Egypt. Therefore, "the river" is the Nile. But since the term "river" is in synonymous parallelism to "the sea," this latter term also refers to the Nile. Ezek. 32:2 uses *yām* of the branches of the Nile: ". . . And thou art as a whale in the seas: and thou camest forth with thy rivers, and troubledst the waters with thy feet, and fouledst their rivers." This word can also be used of the Euphrates River (Jer. 51:36).

In some instances the word *yām* may represent the Canaanite god Yamm, "which alone spreadeth out the heavens, and treadeth upon the waves of the sea" (Job 9:8). If understood as a statement about Yamm, this passage would read: "and tramples upon the back of Yamm." The parallelism between "heavens" and "seas," however, would lead us to conclude that the reference here is to the literal "sea." Ps. 89:9-10 is a more likely place to see a mention of Yamm, for there the word is identified as one of God's enemies in immediate proximity to the goddess Rahab: "Thou rulest the raging of the sea [Yamm]: when the waves thereof arise, thou stillest them. Thou hast broken Rahab in pieces, as one that is slain; thou hast scattered thine enemies with thy strong arm." Especially note Job 7:12: "Am I a sea [Yamm], or a whale, that thou settest a watch over me?" (cf. Job 26:12; Ps. 74:13).

SECRET

sôd (סוֹד), "secret or confidential plan(s); secret or confidential talk; secret; council; gathering; circle." This noun occurs 21 times in biblical Hebrew.

Sôd means, first, "confidential talk": "Hide me from the secret counsel of the wicked . . ." (Ps. 64:2). In Prov. 15:22 the word refers to plans which one makes on one's own and before they are shared by others: "Without counsel [self-made] purposes are disappointed: but in the multitude of counselors they [succeed]." Sometimes the word signifies simply a talk about something that should be kept confidential: "Debate thy cause with thy neighbor himself; and discover not a secret to another" (Prov. 25:9).

Second, the word represents a group of intimates with whom one shares confidential matters: "O my soul, come not thou into their [Simeon's and Levi's] secret; unto their assembly, mine honor, be not thou united . . ." (Gen. 49:6—the first occurrence of the word). Jer. 6:11 speaks of the "assembly [informal but still sharing confidential matters] of young men together." To "have sweet counsel" is to be in a group where everyone both shares and rejoices in what is being discussed and/or done (Ps. 55:14).

SECURITY

A. Nouns.

mibətāch (מִבְטָח), "the act of confiding; the object of confidence; the state of confidence or security." This word occurs 15 times. The word refers to "the act of confiding" in Prov. 21:22: "A wise man scaleth the city of the mighty, and casteth down the strength of the confidence thereof." *Mibətāch* means the "object of confidence" in Job 8:14 and the "state of confidence or security" in Prov. 14:26.

Betach is a noun meaning "security, trust." One occurrence is in Isa. 32:17: ". . . And the effect of righteousness quietness and assurance [*betach*] for ever."

B. Verb.

bātach (בָּטַח), "to be reliant, trust, be unsuspecting." This verb, which occurs 118 times in biblical Hebrew, has a possible Arabic cognate and a cognate in late Aramaic. The word means "to trust" in Deut. 28:52: "And he shall besiege thee in all thy gates, until thy high and fenced walls come down, wherein thou trustedst, throughout all thy land. . . ."

C. Adjective.

betach (בֶּטַח), "secure." In two passages this word is used as an adjective suggesting trust and security: "And Gideon went up . . . and smote the host: for the host was secure [unsuspecting]" (Judg. 8:11; cf. Isa. 32:17).

D. Adverb.

betach (בֶּטַח), "securely." The occurrences of this word appear in all periods of biblical Hebrew.

In its first occurrence *betach* emphasizes the status of a city which was certain of not being attacked: ". . . Two of the sons . . . took each man his sword, and came upon the city boldly, and slew all the males" (Gen. 34:25). Thus the city was unsuspecting regarding the impending attack. In passages such as Prov. 10:9 (cf. Prov. 1:33) *betach* emphasizes a confidence and the absence of impending doom: "He that walketh uprightly walketh surely: but he that perverteth his ways shall be known [faces certain judgment]." Israel dwells in security apart from any possible doom or danger because God keeps her completely safe (Deut. 33:12, 28; cf. 12:10). This condition is contingent on their faithfulness to God (Lev. 25:18-19). In the eschaton, however, such absence of danger is guaranteed by the Messiah's presence (Jer. 23:5-6).

TO SEE, PERCEIVE

A. Verb.

rā'āh (רָאָה), "to see, observe, perceive, get acquainted with, gain understanding, examine, look after (see to), choose, discover." This verb occurs only in Moabite and all periods of Hebrew. It appears in the Bible about 1,300 times.

Basically *rā'āh* connotes seeing with one's eyes: Isaac's "eyes were dim, so that he could not see" (Gen. 27:1). This is its meaning in Gen. 1:4, its first biblical appearance. The word can be used in the sense of seeing only what is obvious: ". . . For the Lord seeth not as man seeth . . ." (1 Sam. 16:7). This verb can also mean "to observe": ". . . And there were upon the roof about three thousand men and women, that beheld while Samson made sport" (Judg. 16:27). The second primary meaning is "to perceive," or to be consciously aware of—so idols "neither see, nor hear" (Deut. 4:28). Third, *rā'āh* can represent perception in the sense of hearing something—God brought the animals before Adam "to see what he would call them" (Gen. 2:19). In Isa. 44:16 the verb means "to enjoy": ". . . I am warm, I have seen the fire." It can also mean "to realize" or "to get acquainted with": "When I applied mine heart to know wisdom, and to see the business that is done upon the earth . . ." (Eccl. 8:16). The rebellious men of Jerusalem tell God they will not "see sword nor famine"; they will not experience it (Jer. 5:12).

This verb has several further extended meanings. For example, *rā'āh* can refer to "perceiving or ascertaining" something apart from seeing it with one's eyes, as when Hagar saw that she had conceived (Gen. 16:4). It can represent mentally recognizing that something is true: "We saw certainly that the Lord was with thee . . ." (Gen. 26:28). Seeing and hearing together can mean "to gain understanding": ". . . Kings shall shut their mouths at him: for that which had not been told them shall they see; and that which they had not heard shall they consider" (Isa. 52:15). In Mal. 3:18 the verb means "to distinguish": "Then shall ye return, and discern between the righteous and the wicked. . . ." The word can mean to consider the fact that Israel is God's people (Exod. 33:13).

In addition to these uses of *rā'āh* referring to intellectual seeing, there is seeing used in the sense of living. "To see the light" is to live life (Job 3:16; cf. 33:28). It can mean experience in the sense of what one is aware of as he lives: "Even as I have seen, they that plow iniquity . . . reap the same" (Job 4:8). In 2 Kings 25:19 the verb is used in the unique sense of "having trusted concourse with" when it speaks of the five advisors of the king.

A fourth idea of seeing is "to examine": "And the Lord came down to see the city and the tower . . ." (Gen. 11:5). This examining can have to do with more than looking something over; it can refer to looking after or supervising something (Gen. 39:23). Used in this sense *rā'āh* can imply looking upon with joy or pain. Hagar asked that she not be allowed to look on the death of Ishmael (Gen. 21:16). This verb may be used of attending to or visiting—so Jonadab said to Amnon: ". . . When thy father cometh to see thee, say unto him . . ." (2 Sam. 13:5). When Joseph advised Pharaoh "to look out a man discreet and wise," he was telling him to choose or select such a man (Gen. 41:33). "To examine" may also be "to observe" someone in order to imitate what he does (Judg. 7:17), or "to discover" something (find it out; Judg. 16:5).

B. Nouns.

rō'eh (רֹאֶה), "seer; vision." *Rō'eh*, which occurs 11 times, refers to a "prophet" (emphasizing the means by which revelation was received; 1 Sam. 9:9) and to "vision" (Isa. 28:7).

Several other nouns are related to the verb *rā'āh*. *Rə'î* appears once to mean "looking-glass" (Job 37:18). *Rō'î*, which occurs 4 times, means "looking, appearance" (1 Sam. 16:12 NASB). *Rə'ûth* occurs once, and it means "look" (Eccl. 5:11). *Marə'āh* means "visionary appearance" or "(prophetic) vision" (Gen. 46:2) and "looking glasses" (Exod. 38:8); this word appears 12 times. Of its 15 occurrences the noun *tō'ar* means "form, shape" in 1 Sam. 28:14 and "stately appearance" in 1 Sam. 25:3. *Marə'eh* occurs 103 times; this word and *tō'ar* are descriptive of blessing in Gen. 39:6: "Now Joseph was handsome in form [*tō'ar*] and appearance [*marə'eh*]" (NASB). *Marə'eh* refers more to external "appearance" (Gen. 2:9), and the word can also connote "sight" as in a range of vision (Lev. 13:3) and "sight" in the sense of a supernatural "sight" or manifestation (Exod. 3:3).

TO SEEK

A. Verbs.

bāqash (בָּקַשׁ), "to seek, search, consult." This verb occurs only in Ugaritic, Phoenician, and Hebrew (both biblical and post-biblical). It appears in the Bible about 220 times and in all periods.

Basically *bāqash* means "to seek" to find something that is lost or missing, or, at least, whose location is unknown. In Gen. 37:15 a man asks Joseph: "What seekest thou?" A special nuance of this sense is "to seek out of a group; to choose, select" something or someone yet undesignated, as in 1 Sam. 13:14: ". . . The Lord hath sought him a man after his own heart. . . ." To seek one's face is "to seek" to come before him, or to have a favorable audience with him; all the world "was seeking" the presence of Solomon (1 Kings 10:24). In a similar sense one may "seek" God's face by standing before Him in the temple praying (2 Sam. 21:1).

The sense "seek to secure" emphasizes the pursuit of a wish or the accomplishing of a plan. Moses asked the Levites who rebelled against the unique position of Aaron and his sons: ". . . Seek ye the priesthood also?" (Num. 16:10). This usage may have an emotional coloring, such as, "to aim at, devote oneself to, and be concerned about." So God asks the sons of men (mankind): ". . . How long will ye turn my glory into shame? How long will ye love vanity, and seek after [sin]?" (Ps. 4:2). Cultically one may "seek" to secure God's favor or help: "And Judah gathered themselves together, to ask help of the Lord . . ." (2 Chron. 20:4). In such usages the intellectual element usually is in the background; there is no seeking after information. An exception to this is Judg. 6:29: "And when they inquired [*dārash*] and asked [*bāqash*], they said, Gideon the son of Joash hath done this thing." Infrequently this verb is used of seeking information from God (Exod. 33:7). In a

similar sense one may "seek" God's face (2 Sam. 21:1). Here *bāqash* is
clearly used of searching for information (a cognitive pursuit). Also, compare
the pursuit of wisdom (Prov. 2:4).

This sense of "seeking to secure" may also be used of seeking one's life
(nephesh). God told Moses to "go, return into Egypt: for all the men are dead
which sought thy life" (Exod. 4:19). *Bāqash* may be used with this same
nuance but without *nephesh*—so Pharaoh "sought to slay Moses" (Exod.
2:15). Only twice is this nuance applied to seeking to procure one's good as in
Ps. 122:9: "Because of the house of the Lord our God I will seek thy good"
(usually *dārash* is used of seeking one's good).

About 20 times *bāqash* means to hold someone responsible for something
because the speaker has a (real or supposed) legal right to it. In Gen. 31:39
(the first biblical occurrence of the verb) Jacob points out to Laban that
regarding animals lost to wild beasts, "of my hand didst thou require it."

Only infrequently is *bāqash* used of seeking out a place, or as a verb of
movement toward a place. So Joseph "sought [a place] to weep; and he entered
into his chamber, and wept there" (Gen. 43:30).

Theologically, this verb can be used not only "to seek" a location before
the Lord (to stand before Him in the temple and seek to secure His blessing),
but it may also be used of a state of mind: "But if from thence thou shalt seek
the Lord thy God, thou shalt find him, if thou seek him [*dārash*] with all thy
heart and with all thy soul" (Deut. 4:29). In instances such as this where the
verb is used in synonymous parallelism with *dārash,* the two verbs have the
same meaning.

dārash (דָּרַשׁ), "to seek, inquire, consult, ask, require, frequent." This
word is a common Semitic word, being found in Ugaritic and Syriac as well as
in Hebrew in its various periods. It is commonly used in modern Hebrew in its
verbal form for "to interpret, expound" and then in its derived noun forms for
"sermon, preacher." Occurring more than 160 times in the Old Testament,
dārash is first used in Gen. 9:5: "And surely your blood of your lives will I
require. . . ." It often has the idea of avenging an offense against God or the
shedding of blood (see Ezek. 33:6).

One of the most frequent uses of this word is in the expression "to inquire
of God," which sometimes indicates a private seeking of God in prayer for
direction (Gen. 25:22), and often it refers to the contacting of a prophet who
would be the instrument of God's revelation (1 Sam. 9:9; 1 Kings 22:8). At
other times this expression is found in connection with the use of the Urim
and Thummim by the high priest as he sought to discover the will of God by
the throwing of these sacred stones (Num. 27:21). Just what was involved is
not clear, but it may be presumed that only yes-or-no questions could be
answered by the manner in which these stones fell. Pagan people and sometimes even apostate Israelites "inquired of" heathen gods. Thus, Ahaziah
instructed messengers: "Go, inquire of Baal-zebub the god of Ekron whether
I shall recover of this disease" (2 Kings 1:2). In gross violation of the Mosaic
law (Deut. 18:10–11), Saul went to the witch of Endor "to inquire of" her,
which in this instance meant that she was to call up the spirit of the dead
prophet Samuel (1 Sam. 28:3 ff.). Saul went to the witch of Endor as a last

resort, saying, "Seek out for me a woman who is a medium, that I may go to her and *inquire* of her" (1 Sam. 28:7, RSV).

This word is often used to describe the "seeking of" the Lord in the sense of entering into covenantal relationship with Him. The prophets often used *dārash* as they called on the people to make an about-face in living and instead "seek ye the Lord while he may be found . . ." (Isa. 55:6).

B. Noun.

Midərash can mean "study; commentary; story." This noun occurs a few times in late biblical Hebrew (2 Chron. 13:22); it is commonly used in post-biblical Judaism to refer to the various traditional commentaries by the Jewish sages. One occurrence of the word is in 2 Chron. 24:27: "Now concerning his sons, and the greatness of the burdens laid upon him . . . they are written in the story [commentary] of the Book of the Kings."

TO SELL

mākar (מָכַר), "to sell." Common in both ancient and modern Hebrew, this word is also found in ancient Akkadian and Ugaritic. It occurs approximately 70 times in the text of the Hebrew Old Testament and is found for the first time in the Old Testament in Gen. 25:31: "And Jacob said, Sell me this day thy birthright."

Anything tangible may be "sold," such as land (Gen. 47:20), houses (Lev. 25:29), animals (Exod. 21:35), and human beings as slaves (Gen. 37:27–28). Daughters were usually "sold" for an agreed bride price (Exod. 21:7).

Mākar is often used in the figurative sense to express various actions. Nineveh is accused of "selling" or "betraying" other nations (Nah. 3:4). Frequently it is said that God "sold" Israel into the power of her enemies, meaning that He gave them over entirely into their hands (Judg. 2:14). Similarly, it was said that "the Lord shall sell Sisera into the hand of a woman" (Judg. 4:9). "To be sold" sometimes means to be given over to death (Esth. 7:4).

TO SEND

A. Verb.

shālach (שָׁלַח), "to send, stretch forth, get rid of." This verb occurs in the Northwest Semitic languages (Hebrew, Phoenician, and Aramaic). It occurs in all periods of Hebrew and in the Bible about 850 times. Biblical Aramaic uses this word 14 times.

Basically this verb means "to send," in the sense of (1) to initiate and to see that such movement occurs or (2) to successfully conclude such an action. In Gen. 32:18 the second emphasis is in view—these animals are "a present sent unto my lord Esau." In Gen. 38:20 the first idea is in view: When "Judah sent the kid by the hand of his friend . . ., he found her not''; it never reached its goal. In 1 Sam. 15:20 Saul told Samuel about the ''way which the Lord sent'' him; here, too, the emphasis is on the initiation of the action.

The most frequent use of *shālach* suggests the sending of someone or something as a messenger to a particular place: ''. . . He shall send his angel before thee, and thou shalt take a wife unto my son from thence'' (Gen. 24:7); God's angel (messenger) will be sent to Nahor to prepare things for the successful accomplishment of the servant's task. One may also ''send a word'' by the hand of a messenger (fool); one may send a message (Prov. 26:6), send a letter (2 Sam. 11:14), and send instructions (Gen. 20:2).

Shālach can refer to shooting arrows by sending them to hit a particular target: ''And he sent out arrows, and scattered them . . .'' (2 Sam. 22:15). In Exod. 9:14 God ''sends'' His plague into the midst of the Egyptians; He ''sends'' them forth and turns them loose among them. Other special meanings of this verb include letting something go freely or without control: ''Thou givest thy mouth to evil . . .'' (Ps. 50:19).

Quite often this verb means ''to stretch out.'' God was concerned lest after the fall Adam ''put forth his hand, and take also of the tree of life'' (Gen. 3:22). One may stretch forth a staff (1 Sam. 14:27) or a sickle (Joel 3:13).

For the most part the intensive stems merely intensify the meanings already set forth, but the meaning ''to send away'' is especially frequent: '' . . . Abner was no longer with David in Hebron, for David had sent him away . . .'' (2 Sam. 3:22, NIV). That is, David ''let him go'' (v. 24, NIV). God sent man out of the garden of Eden; He made man leave (Gen. 3:23—the first occurrence of the verb). Noah sent forth a raven (Gen. 8:7). *Shālach* can also mean to give someone a send off, or ''to send'' someone on his way in a friendly manner: ''. . . And Abraham went with them to bring them on the way [send them off]'' (Gen. 18:16). In Deut. 22:19 the word is used of divorcing a wife, or sending her away.

This verb can signify ''to get rid of'' something: ''They bow themselves, they bring forth their young ones, they cast out their [labor pains]'' (Job 39:3). It can also be used of setting a bondservant free: ''And when thou sendest him out free from thee, thou shalt not let him go away empty'' (Deut. 15:13). In a less technical sense *shālach* can mean to release someone held by force. The angel with whom Jacob wrestled said: ''Let me go, for the day breaketh'' (Gen. 32:26). Yet another nuance is ''to hand someone over,'' as in Ps. 81:12: ''So I gave them up unto their own hearts' lust. . . .'' *Shālach* can also mean to set something afire, as in ''set the city on fire'' (Judg. 1:8).

In the passive sense the verb has some additional special meanings; in Prov. 29:15 it means ''to be left to oneself'': ''. . . But a child left to himself [who gets his own way] bringeth his mother to shame.''

B. Nouns.

Mishəlach means ''outstretching; undertaking.'' This noun occurs 7 times. The word refers to an ''undertaking'' in Deut. 28:8: ''The Lord shall command the blessing upon thee in thy storehouses, and in all that thou settest thine hand unto; and he shall bless thee. . . .'' The phrase ''that thou settest'' embodies the meaning of *mishəlach* here (cf. Deut. 28:20).

Other nouns are related to *shālach*. *Shillûchîm* occurs 3 times and means "presents" in the sense of something sent out to or with someone (1 Kings 9:16). *Mishəlôach* is found 3 times and refers to "the act of sending" (Esth. 9:19, 22) or "the place hands reach when stretched forth" (Isa. 11:14 RSV). *Shelach* means "something sent forth as a missile," and it can refer to a sword or a weapon. *Shelach* occurs 8 times (2 Chron. 32:5; Job 33:18; Neh. 4:17). The proper noun *Shiloāh* appears in Isa. 8:6 and refers to a channel through which water is sent forth.

TO SEPARATE

A. Verbs.

pārad (פָּרַד), "to divide, separate." This word and its derivatives are common to both ancient and modern Hebrew. It is found in the text of the Hebrew Old Testament only about 25 times. *Pārad* occurs for the first time in the text in Gen. 2:10: "And a river went out of Eden . . . and from thence it was parted, and became into four heads." The meaning here must be "dividing into four branches."

This word often expresses separation of people from each other, sometimes with hostility: "Separate thyself . . . from me . . ." (Gen. 13:9). A reciprocal separation seems to be implied in the birth of Jacob and Esau: "Two nations are in thy womb, and two manner of people shall be separated from thy bowels . . ." (Gen. 25:23). Sometimes economic status brings about separation: ". . . The poor is separated from his neighbor" (Prov. 19:4). Generally speaking, *pārad* has more negative than positive connotations.

nāzar (נָזַר), "to separate, be separated." This verb occurs about 10 times in the Old Testament. The root *nāzar* is a common Semitic verb. In Akkadian, *nazāru* meant "to curse," but in West Semitic it connoted "to dedicate." Students of Semitic languages often relate Hebrew *nāzar* to *nadhar* ("to vow").

"To separate" and "to consecrate" are not distinguished from one another in the early Old Testament books. For example, the earliest use of *nāzar* in the Pentateuch is in Lev. 15:31: "Thus shall ye *separate* the children of Israel from their uncleanness; that they die not in their uncleanness, when they defile my tabernacle that is among them." Here Moses uses the word in a cultic sense, meaning a kind of "consecration." A comparison of various twentieth-century translations will show that *nāzar* in Lev. 22:2 is sometimes rendered "to separate," and sometimes "to dedicate." The NIV translates this verse: "Tell Aaron and his sons to treat with respect the sacred offerings the Israelites *consecrated* to me, so that they will not profane my holy name. I am the Lord."

In the days of the prophet Zechariah, Jews asked the Lord whether certain fasts which they had voluntarily adopted were to be continued and observed. "When they had sent unto the house of God Sherezer and Regemmelech, and their men, to pray before the Lord, And to speak unto the priests which were in the house of the Lord of hosts, and to the prophets, saying, Should I weep in the fifth month, separating myself [NASB, "abstain"], as I have done these so many years?" (Zech. 7:2, 3). The Lord's response stated that it was no longer necessary and therefore needed not to be continued.

In prophetic literature, the verb *nāzar* indicates Israel's deliberate separation from Jehovah to dedication of foreign gods or idols. In Hos. 9:10, the various versions differ in their rendering of *nāzar:* "I found Israel like grapes in the wilderness; I saw your fathers as the firstripe in the fig tree at her first time: but they went to Baal-peor, and separated [NASB, "devoted"; NEB, RSV, "consecrated"] themselves unto that shame; and their abominations were according as they loved." The prophet Ezekiel employed *nāzar:* "For every one of the house of Israel, or of the stranger that sojourneth in Israel, which separateth himself from me, and setteth up his idols in his heart, and putteth the stumbling block of his iniquity before his face, and cometh to a prophet to inquire of him concerning me; I the Lord will answer him by myself" (Ezek. 14:7).

B. Noun.

nāzîr (נָזִיר), "one who is separated; Nazarite." There are 16 occurrences of the word in the Old Testament. The earliest use of *nāzîr* is found in Gen. 49:26: "The blessings of thy father . . . shall be on the head of Joseph . . . that was *separate* from his brethren" (cf. Deut. 33:16). Some modern-speech translators have translated *nāzîr* in these two verses as "prince" (NIV, NEB, NAB). The KJV and RSV render the phrase "separate from his brethren." This interpretation might be justified by assuming that Joseph was separated from his brethren to become the savior of his father, his brethren, and their families.

Most frequently in Old Testament usage, *nāzîr* is an appellation for one who vowed to refrain from certain things for a period of time: "And this is the law of the Nazarite, when the days of his separation are fulfilled: he shall be brought unto the door of the tabernacle of the congregation" (Num. 6:13).

According to Num. 6, a lay person of either sex could take a special vow of consecration to God's service for a certain period of time. A "Nazarite" usually made a vow voluntarily; however, in the case of Samson (Judg. 13:5, 7) his parents dedicated him for life. Whether or not this idea of separation to God was distinctive alone to Israel has been debated. Num. 6:1-23 laid down regulatory laws pertaining to Nazaritism. There were two kinds of "Nazarites": the temporary and the perpetual. The first class was much more common than the latter kind. From the Bible we have knowledge only of Samson, Samuel, and John the Baptist as persons who were lifelong "Nazarites."

According to the Mishna, the normal time for keeping a Nazarite vow was thirty days; but sometimes a double vow was taken, lasting sixty days. In fact, a vow was sometimes undertaken for a hundred days.

During the time of his vow, a "Nazarite" was required to abstain from wine and every kind of intoxicating drink. He was also forbidden to cut the hair of his head or to approach a dead body, even that of his nearest relative. If a "Nazarite" accidently defiled himself, he had to undergo certain rites of purification and then had to begin the full period of consecration over again.

The "Nazarite" was "holy unto the Lord," and he wore upon his head a diadem of his consecration.

There is but one reference in the prophetic literature to "Nazarites": The prophet Amos complained that the Lord had given the Israelites Nazarites and prophets as spiritual leaders, but that the people "gave the Nazarites wine to drink; and commanded the prophets, saying, Prophesy not" (Amos 2:11-12).

The New Testament occasionally refers to what appear to have been Nazarite vows. For example, Acts 18:18 says that Paul sailed with Priscilla and Aquila, "having shorn his head . . . for he had a vow" (cf. Acts 21:23-24).

TO SERVE

A. Verbs.

shārath (שָׁרַת), "to serve, minister." This word occurs less than 100 times in the Old Testament. In the vast majority of instances, *shārath* appears in the form of an infinitive or participle. When the participle is translated as a verbal noun, such as "servant" or "minister," it loses the connotation of duration or repetition. Another grammatical feature of *shārath* is its usage exclusively in the intensive form.

The reader of a modern English version can no longer be aware of the distinctive meaning of *shārath* because it and its synonym, *'ābad* (or *'ebed*), are both rendered "serve" or "servant."

Shārath often denotes "service" rendered in connection with Israel's worship; about 60 of its 97 occurrences have this meaning. When Samuel was still a boy, he ". . . did minister unto the Lord before Eli the priest" (1 Sam. 2:11), and the Lord called to him while he ". . . ministered unto the Lord before Eli" (1 Sam. 3:1). This kind of "service" was to honor only the Lord, for Israel was not to be "as the heathen, as the families of the countries; to serve wood and stone" (Ezek. 20:32). In the temple of Ezekiel's vision, those Levites who had ". . . ministered unto them [the people] before their idols . . ." were forbidden by the Lord to serve as priests (Ezek. 44:12). Furthermore, ". . . the Lord separated the tribe of Levi . . . to minister unto him, and to bless in his name . . ." (Deut. 10:8). From the tribe of Levi, Moses was to anoint Aaron and his sons and consecrate them, that they may "minister" as priests (Exod. 29:30). Those not of the family of Aaron, though chosen "to minister unto him forever," acted as assistants to the priests, performing such physical tasks as keeping the gates, slaughtering the burnt offering, caring for the altars and the utensils of the sanctuary (1 Chron. 15:2; Ezek. 44:11). But Isaiah foresees the time when ". . . the sons of strangers . . . shall minister unto thee" (Isa. 60:10).

In a number of situations, the word is used to denote "service" rendered to a fellow human being. Though the person "served" usually is of a higher rank or station in life, this word never describes a slave's servitude to his master. Moses was instructed: "Bring the tribe of Levi near, and present them before Aaron, the priest, that they may minister [NASB, "serve"] unto him" (Num.

3:6; cf. 8:26). Elisha "ministered" to Elijah (1 Kings 19:21). Abishag is said to have "ministered" unto David (1 Kings 1:15). Various kinds of officials "ministered" to David (1 Chron. 28:1). David's son Amnon had a "servant that ministered unto him" (2 Sam. 13:17). There were seven eunuchs that "served in the presence of Ahasuerus the king . . ." (Esth. 1:10). He also had "servants that ministered unto him . . ." (Esth. 2:2).

'ābad (עָבַד), "to serve, cultivate, enslave, work." This root is used widely in Semitic and Canaanite languages. This verb appears about 290 times in all parts of the Old Testament.

The verb is first used in Gen. 2:5: ". . . And there was not a man to till the ground." God gave to man the task "to dress [the ground]" (Gen. 2:15; 3:23; cf. 1:28 NASB). In Gen. 14:4 "they served Chedorlaomer . . ." means that they were his vassals. God told Abraham that his descendants would "serve" the people of a strange land 400 years (Gen. 15:13), meaning, as in the NIV, "to be enslaved by."

'Ābad is often used toward God: ". . . Ye shall serve God upon this mountain" (Exod. 3:12), meaning "to worship" as in the NASB and the NIV. The word is frequently used with another verb: "Thou shalt fear the Lord thy God, and serve him . . ." (Deut. 6:13), or ". . . hearken diligently unto my commandments which I command you this day, to love the Lord your God, and to serve him . . ." (Deut. 11:13). All nations are commanded: "Serve the Lord with gladness . . ." (Ps. 100:2). In the reign of Messiah, "all nations shall serve him" (Ps. 72:11). The verb and the noun may be used together as in Num. 8:11: "And Aaron shall offer the Levites before the Lord . . . that they may execute the service of the Lord."

B. Nouns.

'abôdāh (עֲבוֹדָה), "work; labors; service." This noun appears 145 times in the Hebrew Old Testament, and the occurrences are concentrated in Numbers and Chronicles. *'Abôdāh* is first used in Gen. 29:27: ". . . We will give thee this also for the service which thou shalt serve with me. . . ."

The more general meaning of *'abôdāh* is close to our English word for "work." "Labor" in the field (1 Chron. 27:26), daily "work" from morning till evening (Ps. 104:23), and "work" in the linen industry (1 Chron. 4:21) indicate a use with which we are familiar. To this, it must be added that *'abôdāh* may also be "hard labor," such as that of a slave (Lev. 25:39) or of Israel while in Egypt: "Go ye, get you straw where ye can find it: yet not aught of your work shall be diminished" (Exod. 5:11).

The more limited meaning of the word is "service." Israel was in the "service" of the Lord: "But that it may be a witness between us, and you, and our generations after us, that we might do the service ['abôdāh] of the Lord before him with our burnt offerings, and with our sacrifices, and with our peace offerings; that your children may not say to our children in time to come, Ye have no part in the Lord" (Josh. 22:27). Whenever God's people were not fully dependent on Him, they had to choose to serve the Lord God or human kings with their requirements of forced "labor" and tribute:

"Nevertheless they shall be his servants; that they may know my service, and the service of the kingdoms of the countries" (2 Chron. 12:8).

Further specialization of the usage is in association with the tabernacle and the temple. The priests were chosen for the "service" of the Lord: "And they shall keep his charge, and the charge of the whole congregation before the tabernacle of the congregation, to do the service of the tabernacle" (Num. 3:7). The Levites also had many important functions in and around the temple; they sang, played musical instruments, and were secretaries, scribes, and doorkeepers (2 Chron. 34:13; cf. 8:14). Thus anything, people and objects (1 Chron. 28:13), associated with the temple was considered to be in the "service" of the Lord. Our understanding of "worship," with all its components, comes close to the Hebrew meaning of '*abôdāh* as "service"; cf. "So all the service of the Lord was prepared the same day, to keep the passover, and to offer burnt offerings upon the altar of the Lord, according to the commandment of King Josiah" (2 Chron. 35:16).

The Septuagint translations are: *leitourgia* ("service"); *doulia* ("slavery"); *ergon* ("work; deed; occupation"); and *ergasia* ("pursuit; practice; working; profit; gain"). The KJV gives these senses: "service; bondage; work."

'*ebed* (עֶבֶד), "servant." This noun appears over 750 times in the Old Testament. '*Ebed* first appears in Gen. 9:25: ". . . A servant of servants shall he [Canaan] be unto his brethren," meaning "the lowest of slaves" (NIV). A "servant" may be bought with money (Exod. 12:44) or hired (1 Kings 5:6). The often repeated statement of God's redemption of Israel is: "I brought you out of the house of slaves" (Exod. 13:3, Heb.; KJV, RSV, "bondage"; NASB, NIV, "slavery"). '*Ebed* was used as a mark of humility and courtesy, as in Gen. 18:3: ". . . Pass not away, I pray thee, from thy servant" (cf. Gen. 42:10). Moses addressed God: "O my Lord, I am not eloquent, neither heretofore, nor since thou hast spoken unto thy servant . . ." (Exod. 4:10). It is the mark of those called by God, as in Exod. 14:31: ". . . [They] believed the Lord, and his servant Moses." God claimed: "For unto me the children of Israel are servants . . ." (Lev. 25:55; cf. Isa. 49:3). "And the Lord spake by his servants the prophets . . ." (2 Kings 21:10). The psalmist said: "I am thy servant" (116:16), indicating the appropriateness of the title to all believers.

Of prime significance is the use of "my servant" for the Messiah in Isaiah (42:1-7; 49:1-7; 50:4-10; 52:13–53:12). Israel was a blind and deaf "servant" (Isa. 42:18-22). So the Lord called "my righteous servant" (Isa. 53:11; cf. 42:6) "[to bear] the sin of many" (Isa. 53:12), "that thou mayest be my salvation unto the end of the earth" (Isa. 49:6).

The "servant" was not a free man. He was subject to the will and command of his master. But one might willingly and lovingly submit to his master (Exod. 21:5), remaining in his service when he was not obliged to do so. Hence it is a very fitting description of the relationship of man to God.

The Septuagint translates '*ābad* and its nouns by 7 different Greek roots that give more specific meanings to the term. Through these the basic uses of '*ābad* come into the New Testament. Notable is Jesus' fulfilment of the Servant of the Lord in Isaiah: "That signs and wonders may be done by the name of thy holy child Jesus" (Acts 4:30; RSV, NASB, NIV, "servant Jesus"); and another important use is Paul's personal use of "a servant of Jesus Christ" (Rom 1:1 KJV, RSV, NIV; but more precisely, "bond servant" in NASB).

C. Participle.

shārath (שָׁרַת), "servant; minister." This word is most regularly translated "minister"; Josh. 1:1 is one example: "Now after the death of Moses the servant ['*ebed*] of the Lord it came to pass, that the Lord spake unto Joshua, the son of Nun, Moses' minister [*shārath*], . . ." Ezek. 46:24 refers to a place in the temple complex which is reserved for ". . . the ministers of the house. . . ."

The privilege of serving the Lord is not restricted to human beings: "Bless ye the Lord, all ye his hosts [angels]; ye ministers of his, that do his pleasure" (Ps. 103:21). Fire and wind, conceived poetically as persons, are also God's "ministers" (Ps. 104:3-4).

Joshua was the "minister" of Moses (Exod. 24:13), and Elisha had a "servitor" (2 Kings 4:43; NASB, "attendant").

TO SET, PLACE

shîth (שִׁית), "to put, place, set, station, fix." In addition to biblical Hebrew, this verb is found frequently in ancient Ugaritic. It occurs more than 80 times in the Hebrew Old Testament, for the first time in Gen. 3:15: "And I will put enmity between thee and the woman. . . ."

Generally speaking, this word is a term of physical action, typically expressing movement from one place to another. Often it expresses "putting" hands on someone or something: ". . . Joseph shall put his hand upon thine eyes [close your eyes]" (Gen. 46:4). One may "put on" ornaments (Exod. 33:4); Naomi laid her "grandchild" Obed in her bosom (Ruth 4:16); a fine may be "laid" on someone for injury (Exod. 21:22). Sheep may be "set," or stationed, at a particular place (Gen. 30:40).

"To set" one's heart to something is to give heed to, to pay attention (Exod. 7:23; RSV, "he did not lay even this to heart"). To set one's heart may also be to reflect: "Then I saw, and considered it [set my heart to it] . . ." (Prov. 24:32). "To set" boundaries is "to set," or "fix," limits: "And I will set thy bounds from the Red Sea even unto the sea of the Philistines . . ." (Exod. 23:31). When Job cries: "Oh . . . that thou wouldest appoint me a set time, and remember me!" (Job 14:13), he wants limits "set" for him.

Shîth is sometimes used to express the making of something: ". . . I will make him prince . . ." (1 Kings 11:34); "And I will lay it waste . . ." (Isa. 5:6); ". . . I will make thee a wilderness . . ." (Jer. 22:6).

TO SET IN ORDER

'ārak (עָרַךְ), "to arrange, set in order, compare." While it occurs some 75 times in the Hebrew Old Testament, this root is also found in modern Hebrew, being connected with "editing" and "dictionary." The word is first

found in the Old Testament in Gen. 14:8: ". . . They joined battle [literally, "they arranged," referring to opposing battle lines]. . . ." It is used in this way many times in the record of the battles of Israel.

A common word in everyday life, 'ārak often refers to "arranging" a table (Isa. 21:5; Ezek. 23:41). The word is used several times in the Book of Job with reference to "arranging" or "setting" words "in order," as in an argument or rebuttal (Job 32:14; 33:5; 37:19). In Job 13:18, Job declares: "Behold now, I have ordered my cause [literally, "I have set my judgment in order"]. . . ." "To arrange in order" makes it possible "to compare" one thing with another. So, to show the superiority of God over the idols, the prophet asks: "To whom then will ye liken God? or what likeness will ye compare unto him?" (Isa. 40:18).

TO SET ON, SET UP

A. Verb.

sîm (שִׂים), "to put, place, set, fix." This word also appears in Akkadian (as *shamu*), Aramaic (including biblical Aramaic), Arabic, and Ethiopic. It appears about 580 times in biblical Hebrew, in all periods, and almost exclusively in the primary stem.

In its first biblical appearance *sîm* means "to put or place someone somewhere": "And the Lord God planted a garden eastward in Eden; and there he put the man whom he had formed" (Gen. 2:8). In Exod. 40:8 the verb means "to set up," in the sense of to place or put something so that it is perpendicular or vertical: "And thou shalt set up the court round about, and hang up the hanging at the court gate." Other things are "set up" in a figurative sense, like a wall. So Micah speaks of "setting up" a siege, a wall, around a city: ". . . He hath laid siege against us . . ." (Mic. 5:1; cf. 1 Kings 20:12). This image is also used figuratively of a human wall in one's path: "I remember that which Amalek did to Israel, how he laid wait for him in the way, when he came up from Egypt" (1 Sam. 15:2).

Sîm is used sometimes in the sense "to set over, impose on" (negatively): "Therefore they did set [imposed] over them taskmasters to afflict them with their burdens" (Exod. 1:11). A more positive use of the word in the sense "to appoint" (where the appointment is pleasing to the wards) appears in 1 Sam. 8:5—the elders of Israel asked the aged Samuel: ". . . Now make us a king to judge us like all the nations." In such usages one in authority determines or is asked to determine something. This is the focus of the word in Num. 24:23, where Balaam said: "Alas, who shall live when God doeth this!"

This verb means "to make," as it does in Zeph. 3:19: ". . . And I will get them praise and fame [make their shame into praise and fame] in every land where they have been put to shame."

In some passages *sîm* is used in the figurative sense of setting something or putting it before one's mind: ". . . They have not set God before them" (Ps. 54:3). The same phrase is used in a literal sense in Ezek. 14:4 (cf. NIV).

Sîm also means "to put down" in the sense of literally setting something on the ground, on a chair, or a flat surface: ". . . Abraham built an altar there, and laid the wood in order, and bound Isaac his son, and laid him on the altar upon the wood" (Gen. 22:9). In a related sense one "puts down" a distance or space between himself and someone else: "And he set three days' journey betwixt himself and Jacob . . ." (Gen. 30:36). In Job 4:18 the word means to charge someone with an error, or "to put it down" against or to him. Closely related to this legal use of *sîm* is 1 Sam. 22:15, where it means "to impute" (lay to one's charge), and Deut. 22:8, where it means "to bring guilt upon oneself." Other passages use this verb of putting clothing on, in the sense of setting it down upon one's body (Ruth 3:3). So, too, one may obligate someone with a task: one may impose it upon him (Exod. 5:8).

When used with "hand," *sîm* may signify putting (Exod. 4:21) or taking something (Judg. 4:21) into one's grasp. Closely related is the phrase "putting hands on," or "arresting" (2 Kings 11:16).

This verb may be used in the sense of "giving for" (in behalf of). So Job says: "Lay down now, put me in a surety with thee . . . ," or give a pledge for me (Job 17:3). In a related sense the Servant of the Lord would "make his soul an offering for sin" (Isa. 53:10).

In Dan. 1:7 *sîm* signifies "to assign something to, or give to"; the commander of the officials assigned new names to them. In Job 5:8 this giving constitutes handing over one's cause to another, while in Exod. 21:1 it represents fully stating God's word in the presence of His people so as to make it possible for them to receive it fully.

To place or put something on one's heart means to consider it (Isa. 47:7) or to pay heed to it (1 Sam. 21:12).

The meaning "to fix," as to fix something in a particular place, appears in Gen. 24:47: ". . . And I put the earring upon her face, and the bracelets upon her hands." So, too, in Deut. 14:1 God commands Israel not "to fix" a bald spot on their foreheads for the sake of the dead. Other things may be so "fixed," such as plants (Isa. 28:25) and ashes (Lev. 6:10).

The word means "to make" in Exod. 4:11: "Who hath made man's mouth? or who maketh the dumb, or deaf . . . ?" The first nuance here signifies the creation of the thing (fixing its nature) and the second its disposition (fixing its use; cf. Gen. 13:16). Closely related is the use of the verb to represent "to state, to appoint, or to assign"; in Exod. 21:13, God will appoint a place for the manslayer to flee. In an extended sense *sîm* signifies "to assign to continue," or "to preserve": "And God sent me before you to preserve you a posterity in the earth, and to save your lives by a great deliverance" (Gen. 45:7). Thus, to set a remnant is to keep it alive. Therefore, *sîm* means "to preserve." To set glory and praise to the Lord is to establish it by stating it (Josh. 7:19). God's establishing the plagues on Pharaoh is also an appointing (Exod. 8:12).

B. Noun.

Təsûmeth (תְּשׂוּמֶת), means "something laid down; a deposit or joint property." This noun occurs only once in biblical Hebrew: "If a soul sin, and commit a trespass against the Lord, and lie unto his neighbor in that which was delivered him to keep, or in fellowship [*təsûmeth*] . . ." (Lev. 6:2).

SHAME

A. Verb.

bôsh (בּוֹשׁ), "to be ashamed, feel ashamed." This verb, which occurs 129 times in biblical Hebrew, has cognates in Ugaritic, Akkadian, and Arabic. The word has overtones of being or feeling worthless. *Bôsh* means "to be ashamed" in Isa. 1:29: "For they shall be ashamed of the oaks which ye have desired, and ye shall be confounded for the gardens that ye have chosen."

B. Noun.

bōsheth (בֹּשֶׁת), "shame; shameful thing." The 30 appearances of this noun are mostly in poetic materials—only 5 appearances are in historical literature.

This word means a "shameful thing" as a substitute for the name Baal: "For shame hath devoured the labor of our fathers from our youth . . ." (Jer. 3:24; cf. Jer. 11:13; Hos. 9:10). This substitution also occurs in proper names: Ish-bosheth (2 Sam. 2:8), the "man of shame," was originally Esh-baal (cf. 1 Chron. 8:33), the "man of Baal."

This word represents both "shame and worthlessness": "Thou son of the perverse rebellious woman, do not I know that thou hast chosen the son of Jesse . . . unto the confusion of thy mother's nakedness" (1 Sam 20:30). The "shame of one's face" (2 Chron. 32:21) may well mean being red-faced or embarrassed.

———————

SHEOL

Shə'ôl (שְׁאוֹל), "Sheol." The 66 occurrences of this word are distributed throughout every period of biblical Hebrew.

First, the word means the state of death: "For in death there is no remembrance of thee: in the grave [*Shə'ôl*] who shall give thee thanks?" (Ps. 6:5; cf. 18:5). It is the final resting place of all men: "They spend their days in wealth, and in a moment go down to the grave [*Shə'ôl*]" (Job 21:13). Hannah confessed that it was the omnipotent God who brings men to *Shə'ôl* (death) or kills them (1 Sam. 2:6). "Sheol" is parallel to Hebrew words for "pit" or "hell" (Job 26:6), "corruption" or "decay" (Ps. 16:10), and "destruction" (Prov. 15:11).

Second, "Sheol" is used of a place of conscious existence after death. In the first biblical appearance of the word Jacob said that he would "go down into the grave [*Shə'ôl*] unto my son mourning" (Gen. 37:35). All men go to "Sheol"—a place and state of consciousness after death (Ps. 16:10). The wicked receive punishment there (Num. 16:30; Deut. 32:22; Ps. 9:17). They are put to shame and silenced in "Sheol" (Ps. 31:17). Jesus alluded to Isaiah's use of *Shə'ôl* (14:13-15) in pronouncing judgment on Capernaum (Matt. 11:23), translating "Sheol" as "Hades" or "Hell," meaning the place of conscious existence and judgment. It is an undesirable place for the wicked (Job 24:19) and a refuge for the righteous (Job 14:13). Thus "Sheol" is also a place of reward for the righteous (Hos. 13:14; cf. 1 Cor. 15:55). Jesus' teaching in Luke 16:19-31 seems to reflect accurately the Old Testament concept of *Shə'ôl*; it is a place of conscious existence after death, one side of which is occupied by the suffering unrighteous dead separated by a great chasm from the other side peopled by the righteous dead enjoying their reward.

TO SHEPHERD

A. Verb.

rā'āh (רָעָה), "to pasture, shepherd." This common Semitic root appears in Akkadian, Phoenician, Ugaritic, Aramaic, and Arabic. It is attested in all periods of Hebrew and about 170 times in the Bible. (The word should be distinguished from the verb "to have dealings with or associate with.")

Rā'āh represents what a shepherd allows domestic animals to do when they feed on grasses in the fields. In its first appearance Jacob tells the shepherds: "Lo, it is yet high day, neither is it time that the cattle should be gathered together: water ye the sheep, and go and feed them" (Gen. 29:7). *Rā'āh* can also represent the entire job of a shepherd. So "Joseph, being seventeen years old, was feeding the flock with his brethren; and [he was still a youth]" (Gen. 37:2). Used metaphorically this verb represents a leader's or a ruler's relationship to his people. At Hebron the people said to David: "Also in time past, when Saul was king over us, thou wast he that leddest out and broughtest in Israel: and the Lord said to thee, Thou shalt feed my people Israel, and thou shalt be a captain over Israel" (2 Sam. 5:2). The verb is used figuratively in the sense "to provide with nourishment" or "to enliven": "The lips of the righteous feed many: but fools die for want of wisdom" (Prov. 10:21).

Rā'āh is used intransitively describing what cattle do when they feed on the grass of the field. So Pharaoh dreamed that "there came up out of the river seven well-favored kine and fat-fleshed; and they fed in a meadow" (Gen. 41:2). This usage is applied metaphorically to men in Isa. 14:30: "And [those who are most helpless] shall feed, and the needy shall lie down in safety. . . ." This word is used to describe destruction: "Also the children of Noph and Tahapanes have broken [literally, "consumed as a domestic animal utterly bares a pasture"] the crown of thy head" (Jer. 2:16).

B. Nouns.

rō'ēh (רֹעֶה), "shepherd." This noun occurs about 62 times in the Old Testament. It is applied to God, the Great Shepherd, who pastures or feeds His sheep (Ps. 23:1-4; cf. John 10:11). This concept of God, the Great Shepherd, is very old, having first appeared in the Bible on Jacob's lips in Gen. 49:24: ". . . From thence is the shepherd, the stone of Israel."

When applied to human kings, *rō'ēh* recalls its usage among non-Israelites. There it depicts the king as the head of the cultus (official public worship) and the mediator between the god(s) and men. It also suggests that he is the center of national unity, the supreme protector and leader of the nation, the bestower of every earthly blessing, and the dispenser of justice. Interestingly, no biblical king claimed the title *rō'ēh* for himself (cf. 2 Sam. 5:2). In later times leaders other than the kings were also called "shepherds" (cf. Isa. 44:28; Ezek. 34:2).

Other nouns derived from the verb *rā'āh* occur infrequently. *Mirə'eh*, which occurs 12 times, means "pasture or pasturage" in the sense of where animals graze, and/or what they graze on (Gen. 47:4). *Marə'îth* appears 10 times and refers to a "pasture" (Ps. 74:1). *Rə'î* is found once and means "pasture" (1 Kings 4:23).

TO SHUT

sāgar (סָגַר), "to shut, close, shut up or imprison." Found in ancient Ugaritic, this verb is common also in ancient and modern Hebrew. It is found some 80 times in the text of the Hebrew Old Testament. *Sāgar* is used for the first time in the Old Testament in the story of the creation of the woman from the rib of the man: "And the Lord God . . . closed up the flesh instead thereof" (Gen. 2:21).

The obvious use of this verb is to express the "shutting" of doors and gates, and it is used in this way many times in the text (Gen. 19:10; Josh. 2:7). More specialized uses are: fat closing over the blade of a sword (Judg. 3:22) and closing up a breach in city walls (1 Kings 11:27).

Figuratively, men may "close their hearts to pity" (Ps. 17:10 RSV; KJV, "They are inclosed in their own fat," with "fat" symbolizing an unresponsive heart). In the books of Samuel, *sāgar* is used in the special sense of "to deliver up," implying that all avenues of escape "are closed": "This day will the Lord deliver thee into mine hand . . ." (1 Sam. 17:46; cf. 1 Sam. 24:18; 26:8; 2 Sam. 18:28).

In Lev. 13–14, in which the priest functions as a medical inspector of contagious diseases, *sāgar* is used a number of times in the sense of "to isolate, to shut up" a sick person away from other people (see Lev. 13:5, 11, 21, 26). The more extreme sense of "to imprison" is found in Job 11:10: "If he cut off, and shut up, or gather together, then who can hinder him?"

TO BE SICK

A. Verb.

chālāh (חָלָה), "to be sick, weak." This verb is common in all periods of the Hebrew language and occurs approximately 60 times in the Hebrew Bible. It is found in the text for the first time near the end of the Book of Genesis when Joseph is told: "Behold, thy father is sick . . ." (Gen. 48:1).

A survey of the uses of *chālāh* shows that there was a certain lack of precision in many of its uses, and that the context would be the deciding factor in its meaning. When Samson told Delilah that if he were tied up with bowstrings he would "be weak, and be as another man" (Judg. 16:7), the verb obviously did not mean "become sick," unless being sick implied being less than normal for Samson. When Joram is described as being sick because of wounds suffered in battle (2 Kings 8:29 RSV), perhaps it would be better to say that he was weak. Sacrificial animals that are described as being lame or "sick" (Mal. 1:8) are actually imperfect or not acceptable for sacrifice.

This word is sometimes used in the figurative sense of overexerting oneself, thus becoming "weak." This is seen in the various renderings of Jer. 12:13: "They have put themselves to pain . . ." (KJV); "they have tired themselves out . . ." (RSV); "they have worn themselves out" (JB); "they sift but get no grain" (NEB). The versions are divided in the translation of Song of Sol. 2:5, which the KJV, RSV, and JB translate "sick of/with love," while the NEB and NAB make it "faint with love." The NASB renders it "lovesick," but the TEV is probably closest to the meaning when it says "weak with passion."

B. Noun.

cholî (חֳלִי), "sickness." This noun occurs about 23 times. The use of this word in the description of the Suffering Servant in Isa. 53:3-4 has resulted in various translations. The RSV, KJV, and NASB render it "grief." It is "sufferings" in the NEB, JB, TEV and "infirmity" in the NAB.

The meaning of "sickness" occurs in Deut. 7:15: "And the Lord will take away from thee all sickness [*cholî*], and will put none of the evil diseases [*madəweh*] of Egypt. . . ." *Cholî* is used metaphorically as a distress of the land in Hos. 5:13.

SIGN

'ôth (אוֹת), "sign; mark." Cognates of this word appear in Aramaic and Arabic. It occurs 78 times in biblical Hebrew and in all periods of the language.

This word represents something by which a person or group is characteristically marked. This is its emphasis in Gen. 4:15: "And the Lord set a mark [NASB, "sign"] upon Cain, lest any finding him should kill him." In Exod. 8:23 God promises to "put a division between my people and thy people: tomorrow shall this sign be" (cf. Exod. 12:13). Num. 2:2 uses *'ôth* to represent a military banner, while Job 21:29 uses the word of the identifying banners of nomadic tribes. Rahab asked her Israelite guests for a trustworthy "mark" (NASB, "pledge of truth"), which they stipulated to be the scarlet cord by which she lowered them out of her window and outside Jericho's walls (Josh. 2:12, 18).

The word means "sign" as a reminder of one's duty. This usage first appears in Gen. 9:12: "This [the rainbow] is the token of the covenant which I make between me and you and every living creature . . ." (cf. vv. 4-15).

A reminding token is represented by *'ôth:* "And it [the observance of the Feast of Unleavened Bread] shall be for a sign unto thee upon thine hand, and for a memorial between thine eyes, that the Lord's law may be in thy mouth . . ." (Exod. 13:9).

A "sign" eventually showing the truth of a statement is indicated by *'ôth:* "Certainly I will be with thee; and this shall be a token unto thee, that I have sent thee: When thou hast brought forth the people out of Egypt, ye shall serve God upon this mountain" (Exod. 3:12).

In passages such as Exod. 4:8 *'ôth* represents a miraculous "sign": "And it shall come to pass, if they will not believe thee, neither hearken to the voice of the first sign, that they will believe the voice of the latter sign." "Signs" are attestations of the validity of a prophetic message, but they are not the highest or final test of a prophet; he must speak in conformity to past revelation (cf. Deut. 13:1-5).

Several passages use *'ôth* of omens and/or indications of future events: "But if they say thus, Come up unto us; then we will go up: for the Lord hath delivered them into our hand: and this shall be a sign unto us" (1 Sam. 14:10).

An *'ôth* can be a "warning sign": "The censers of these sinners against their own souls, let them make them broad plates for a covering of the altar: for they offered them before the Lord, therefore they are hallowed: and they shall be a sign unto the children of Israel" (Num. 16:38).

The first occurrence of *'ôth* is in Gen. 1:14. Here it refers to the stars, indicators of the time of day and seasons.

SILVER

A. Noun.

keseph (כֶּסֶף), "silver; money; price; property." This word has cognates in Akkadian, Ugaritic, Phoenician, and Aramaic. It occurs about 402 times in biblical Hebrew and in all periods.

This word represents the "metal ore silver": "Take away the dross from the silver, and there shall come forth a vessel for the finer" (Prov. 25:4; cf. Job 28:1).

Keseph may signify the "metal silver," or what has been refined from silver ore: "And the servant brought forth jewels of silver, and jewels of gold . . ." (Gen. 24:53). As a precious metal "silver" was not as valuable as gold—probably because it is not so rare: "And all king Solomon's drinking vessels were of gold, and all the vessels of the house of the forest of Lebanon were of pure gold; none were of silver: it was nothing accounted of in the days of Solomon" (1 Kings 10:21).

"Silver" was often a form of wealth. This is the meaning of *keseph* in Gen. 13:2 (the first biblical occurrence): "And Abram was very rich in cattle, in silver, and in gold." Silver pieces (not coins) were used as money: "Then Joseph commanded to fill their sacks with corn, and to restore every man's money into his sack . . ." (Gen. 42:25). Frequently the word absolutely (by itself) and in the singular form means "pieces of silver": "Behold, I have given thy brother a thousand pieces of silver . . ." (Gen. 20:16). In Lev. 25:50 the word is used in the general sense of "money, value, price": "And he shall reckon with him that bought him from the year that he was sold to him unto the year of jubilee: and the price of his sale shall be according unto the number of years. . . ."

Since it was a form of wealth, "silver" often was one of the spoils of war: "The kings came, they fought; . . . they got no spoils of silver" (Judg. 5:19 RSV).

This word may be used in the sense of "valuable property": "Notwithstanding, if he [the slave who has been beaten] continue a day or two, he shall not be punished: for he is his money" (Exod. 21:21).

Keseph sometimes represents the color "silver": "Though ye have lain among the pots, yet shall ye be as the wings of a dove covered with silver, and her feathers with yellow gold'' (Ps. 68:13).

B. Verb.

Kāsaph means "to long for." Some scholars derive *keseph* from this verb which occurs 5 times in the biblical text. *Kāsaph* means "to long for" in the sense of to be pale by reason of longing: "And now, though thou wouldest needs be gone, because thou sore longedst after thy father's house, yet wherefore hast thou stolen my gods?" (Gen. 31:30).

SIN

A. Nouns.

'āwen (אָוֶן), "iniquity; vanity; sorrow." Some scholars believe that this term has cognates in the Arabic words *'āna,* ("to be fatigued, tired") and *'aynun* ("weakness; sorrow; trouble"), or with the Hebrew word *'ayin* ("nothingness"). This relationship would imply that *'āwen* means the absence of all that has true worth; hence, it would denote "moral worthlessness," as in the actions of wrongdoing, evil devising, or false speaking.

Other scholars believe that the term implies a "painful burden or difficulty"—i.e., that sin is a toilsome, exhausting load of "trouble and sorrow," which the offender causes for himself or others. This meaning is indicated in Ps. 90:10: "The days of our years are three score years and ten; and if by reason of strength they be fourscore years, yet is their strength labor and *sorrow* [RSV, "trouble"]. . . ." A similar meaning appears in Prov. 22:8: "He that soweth iniquity shall reap vanity [*'āwen*]: and the rod of his anger shall fail."

'Āwen may be a general term for a crime or offense, as in Micah 2:1: "Woe to them that devise iniquity . . ." (cf. Isa. 1:13). In some passages, the word refers to falsehood or deception: "The words of his mouth are *iniquity* and deceit: he hath left off to be wise, and to do good" (Ps. 36:3). "For the idols have spoken *vanity* [NASB, "iniquity"] . . ." (Zech. 10:2). Isa. 41:29 portrays idols deceiving their worshipers: "Behold, they are all *vanity;* their works are nothing: Their molten images are wind and confusion."

'āshām (אָשָׁם), "sin; guilt; guilt offering; trespass; trespass offering." Cognates appear in Arabic as *'ithmun* ("sin; offense; misdeed; crime"), *'athima* ("to sin, err, slip"), and *'āthimun* ("sinful; criminal; evil; wicked"); but the Arabic usage does not include the idea of restitution. In the Ugaritic texts of Ras Shamra, the word *atm* occurs in similar passages. Scholars believe this Ugaritic word may mean "offense" or "guilt offering," but this cannot be ascertained.

'Āshām implies the condition of "guilt" incurred through some wrong-doing, as in Gen. 26:10: "And Abimelech said, . . . one of the people might lightly have lain with thy wife, and thou shouldest have brought guiltiness upon us." The word may also refer to the offense itself which entails the guilt: "For Israel hath not been forsaken . . . though their land was filled with sin

against the Holy One of Israel'' (Jer. 51:5). A similar meaning of the word appears in Ps. 68:21: "But God shall wound the head of his enemies and the hairy scalp of such a one as goeth on still in his trespasses [RSV, "guilty ways"; NASB, "guilty deeds"]."

Most occurrences of *'āshām* refer to the compensation given to satisfy someone who has been injured, or to the "trespass offering" or "guilt offering" presented on the altar by the repentant offender after paying a compensation of six-fifths of the damage inflicted (Num. 5:7-8). The "trespass offering" was the blood sacrifice of a ram: "And he shall bring a ram without blemish out of the flock, with thy estimation, for a trespass offering, unto the priest: and the priest shall make an atonement for him concerning his ignorance wherein he erred and wist it not, and it shall be forgiven him" (Lev. 5:18; cf. Lev. 7:5, 7; 14:12-13). The most significant theological statement containing *'āshām* is in Isa. 53:10, which says that the servant of Yahweh was appointed as an *'āshām* for sinful mankind. This suggests that His death furnished a 120-percent compensation for the broken law of God.

'āmāl (עָמָל), "evil; trouble; misfortune; mischief; grievance; wickedness; labor." This noun is related to the Hebrew verb *'āmal* ("to labor, toil"). The Arabic cognate *'amila* means "to get tired from hard work." The Aramaic *'amal* means "make" or "do," with no necessary connotation of burdensome labor. The Phoenician Canaanite usage of this term was closer to the Arabic; the Book of Ecclesiastes (which shows considerable Phoenician influence) clearly represents this use: "Yea, I hated all my *labor* which I had taken under the sun . . ." (Eccl. 2:18). "And also that every man should eat and drink, and enjoy the good of all his *labor* . . ." (Eccl. 3:13). A related example appears in Ps. 107:12: "Therefore he brought down their heart with *labor;* they fell down and there was none to help."

In general, *'āmāl* refers either to the trouble and suffering which sin causes the sinner or to the trouble that he inflicts upon others. Jer. 20:18 depicts self-inflicted sorrow: "Wherefore came I forth out of the womb to see labor [*'āmāl*] and sorrow [*yāgôn*], that my days should be consumed with shame?" Another instance is found in Deut. 26:7: "And when we cried unto the Lord God of our fathers, the Lord heard our voice, and looked on our affliction [*'onî*], and our labor [*'āmāl*], and our oppression [*lachats*]."

Job 4:8 illustrates the sense of trouble as mischief inflicted on others: ". . . They that plow iniquity [*'āwen*], and sow wickedness [*'āmāl*] reap the same." The word appears in Ps. 140:9: "As for the head of those that compass me about, let the mischief of their own lips cover them." Hab. 1:3 also refers to the trouble inflicted on others: "Why dost thou show me iniquity [*'āwen*], and cause me to behold grievance [*'āmāl*]? For spoiling and violence are before me; and there are that raise up strife and contention."

'āwōn (עָוֹן), "iniquity." This word is derived from the root *'āwāh*, which means "to be bent, bowed down, twisted, perverted" or "to twist, pervert." The Arabic cognate *'awā* means "to twist, bend down"; some scholars regard the Arabic term *gharā* ("to err from the way") as the true cognate, but there is less justification for this interpretation.

'Āwōn portrays sin as a perversion of life (a twisting out of the right way), a

perversion of truth (a twisting into error), or a perversion of intent (a bending of rectitude into willful disobedience). The word "iniquity" is the best single-word equivalent, although the Latin root *iniquitas* really means "injustice; unfairness; hostile; adverse."

'Āwōn occurs frequently throughout the Old Testament in parallelism with other words related to sin, such as *chattā'th* ("sin") and *pesha'* ("transgression"). Some examples are 1 Sam. 20:1: "And David . . . said before Jonathan, what have I done? what is mine iniquity [*'āwōn*]? and what is my sin [*chattā'th*] before thy father, that he seeketh my life?" (cf. Isa. 43:24; Jer. 5:25). Also note Job 14:17: "My transgression [*pesha'*] is sealed up in a bag, and thou sewest up mine iniquity [*'āwōn*]" (cf. Ps. 107:17; Isa. 50:1).

The penitent wrongdoer recognized his "iniquity" in Isa. 59:12: "For our transgressions are multiplied before thee, and our sins testify against us: for our transgressions are with us; and as for our iniquities, we know them" (cf. 1 Sam. 3:13). "Iniquity" is something to be confessed: "And Aaron shall lay both his hands upon the head of the live goat, and confess over him all the iniquities of the children of Israel . . ." (Lev. 16:21). "And the seed of Israel . . . confessed their sins, and the iniquities of their fathers" (Neh. 9:2; cf. Ps. 38:18).

The grace of God may remove or forgive "iniquity": "And unto him he said, Behold, I have caused thine inquity to pass from thee . . ." (Zech. 3:4; cf. 2 Sam. 24:10). His atonement may cover over "iniquity": "By mercy and truth iniquity is purged; and by the fear of the Lord men depart from evil" (Prov. 16:6; cf. Ps. 78:38).

'Āwōn may refer to "the guilt of iniquity," as in Ezek. 36:31: "Then shall ye remember your own evil ways . . . and shall loathe yourselves in your own sight for your iniquities and for your abominations" (cf. Ezek. 9:9). The word may also refer to "punishment for iniquity": "And Saul sware to her by the Lord, saying, As the Lord liveth, there shall no punishment happen to thee for this thing" (1 Sam. 28:10). In Exod. 28:38, *'āwōn* is used as the object of *nātsā'* ("to bear, carry away, forgive"), to suggest bearing the punishment for the "iniquity" of others. In Isa. 53:11, we are told that the servant of Yahweh bears the consequences of the "iniquities" of sinful mankind, including Israel.

rāshā' (רָשָׁע), "wicked; criminal; guilty." Some scholars relate this word to the Arabic *rash'a* ("to be loose, out of joint"), although that term is not actively used in literary Arabic. The Aramaic cognate *rəsha'* means "to be wicked" and the Syriac *aphel* ("to do wickedly").

Rāshā' generally connotes a turbulence and restlessness (cf. Isa. 57:21) or something disjointed or ill-regulated. Thus Robert B. Girdlestone suggests that it refers to the tossing and confusion in which the wicked live, and to the perpetual agitation they cause to others.

In some instances, *rāshā'* carries the sense of being "guilty of crime": "Thou shalt not raise a false report: put not thine hand with the wicked to be an unrighteous witness" (Exod. 23:1); "Take away the wicked from before the king, and his throne shall be established in righteousness" (Prov. 25:5). "An ungodly witness scorneth judgment: and the mouth of the *wicked* [plural form] devoureth iniquity" (Prov. 19:28; cf. Prov. 20:26).

Justifying the "wicked" is classed as a heinous crime: "He that justifieth the wicked, and he that condemneth the just, even they both are abomination to the Lord" (Prov. 17:15; cf. Exod. 23:7).

The *rāshā'* is guilty of hostility to God and His people: "Arise, O Lord, disappoint him, cast him down: deliver my soul from the wicked, which is thy sword" (Ps. 17:13); "Oh let the wickedness of the *wicked* [plural form] come to an end; but establish the just . . ." (Ps. 7:9). The word is applied to the people of Babylon in Isa. 13:11 and to the Chaldeans in Hab. 1:13.

chattā'th (חַטָּאת), "sin; sin-guilt; sin-purification; sin offering." The noun *chattā'th* appears about 293 times and in all periods of biblical literature.

The basic nuance of this word is "sin" conceived as missing the road or mark (155 times). *Chattā'th* can refer to an offense against a man: "And Jacob was wroth, and chode with Laban: and Jacob answered and said to Laban, What is my trespass [*pesha'*]? what is my sin, that thou hast so hotly pursued after me?" (Gen. 31:36). It is such passages which prove that *chattā'th* is not simply a general word for "sin"; since Jacob used two different words, he probably intended two different nuances. In addition, a full word study shows basic differences between *chattā'th* and other words rendered "sin."

For the most part this word represents a sin against God (Lev. 4:14). Men are to return from "sin," which is a path, a life-style, or act deviating from that which God has marked out (1 Kings 8:35). They should depart from "sin" (2 Kings 10:31), be concerned about it (Ps. 38:18), and confess it (Num. 5:7). The noun first appears in Gen. 4:7, where Cain is warned that "sin lieth at the door." This citation may introduce a second nuance of the word—"sin" in general. Certainly such an emphasis appears in Ps. 25:7, where the noun represents rebellious sin (usually indicated by *pāsha'*): "Remember not the sins of my youth, nor my transgressions. . . ."

In a few passages the term connotes the guilt or condition of sin: ". . . The cry of Sodom and Gomorrah is great, and . . . their sin is very grievous" (Gen. 18:20).

The word means "purification from sin" in two passages: "And thus shalt thou do unto them, to cleanse them: Sprinkle water of purifying upon them . . ." (Num. 8:7; cf. 19:9).

Chattā'th means "sin offering" (135 times). The law of the "sin offering" is recorded in Lev. 4–5:13; 6:24-30. This was an offering for some specific "sin" committed unwittingly, without intending to do it and perhaps even without knowing it at the time (Lev. 4:2; 5:15).

Also derived from the verb *chātā'* is the noun *chētə'*, which occurs 33 times in biblical Hebrew. This word means "sin" in the sense of missing the mark or the path. This may be sin against either a man (Gen. 41:9—the first occurrence of the word) or God (Deut. 9:18). Second, it connotes the "guilt" of such an act (Num. 27:3). The psalmist confessed that his mother was in the condition of sin and guilt (cf. Rom. 5:12) when he was conceived (Ps. 51:5). Finally, several passages use this word for the idea of "punishment for sin" (Lev. 20:20).

The noun *chattā'th*, with the form reserved for those who are typified with the characteristic represented by the root, is used both as an adjective (emphatic) and as a noun. The word occurs 19 times. Men are described as "sinners" (1 Sam. 15:18) and as those who are liable to the penalty of an offense (1 Kings 1:21). The first occurrence of the word is in Gen. 13:13: "But the men of Sodom were wicked and sinners before the Lord exceedingly."

B. Adjective.

rāshā' (רָשָׁע), "wicked; guilty." In the typical example of Deut. 25:2, this word refers to a person "guilty of a crime": "And it shall be, if the wicked man be worthy to be beaten, that the judge shall cause him . . . to be beaten. . . ." A similar reference appears in Jer. 5:26: "For among my people are found *wicked* [plural form] men: they lay wait, as he that setteth snares; they set a trap, they catch men." *Rāshā'* is used specifically of murderers in 2 Sam. 4:11: "How much more, when wicked men have slain a righteous person in his own house upon his bed? . . ." The expression "guilty of death" *(rāshā' lāmûth)* occurs in Num. 35:31 and is applied to a murderer.

Pharaoh and his people are portrayed as "wicked" people guilty of hostility to God and His people (Exod. 9:27).

ra' (רַע), "bad; evil; wicked; sore." The root of this term is disputed. Some scholars believe that the Akkadian term *raggu* ("evil; bad") may be a cognate. Some scholars derive *ra'* from the Hebrew word *rā'a'* ("to break, smash, crush"), which is a cognate of the Hebrew *rātsats* ("to smash, break to pieces"); *rātsats* in turn is related to the Arabic *radda* ("to crush, bruise"). If this derivation were correct, it would imply that *ra'* connotes sin in the sense of destructive hurtfulness; but this connotation is not appropriate in some contexts in which *ra'* is found.

Ra' refers to that which is "bad" or "evil," in a wide variety of applications. A greater number of the word's occurrences signify something morally evil or hurtful, often referring to man or men: "Then answered all the wicked men and men of Belial, of those that went with David . . ." (1 Sam. 30:22). "And Esther said, the adversary and enemy is the wicked Haman" (Esth. 7:6). "There they cry, but none giveth answer, because of the pride of evil men" (Job 35:12; cf. Ps. 10:15). *Ra'* is also used to denote evil words (Prov. 15:26), evil thoughts (Gen. 6:5), or evil actions (Deut. 17:5, Neh. 13:17). Ezek. 6:11 depicts grim consequences for Israel as a result of its actions: "Thus saith the Lord God; smite with thine hand, and stamp with thy foot, and say, Alas for all the evil abominations of the house of Israel! For they shall fall by the sword, by the famine, and by the pestilence."

Ra' may mean "bad" or unpleasant in the sense of giving pain or causing unhappiness: "And Jacob said unto Pharaoh, . . . Few and evil have the days of the years of my life been . . ." (Gen. 47:9). "And when the people heard these evil tidings, they mourned . . ." (Exod. 33:4; cf. Gen. 37:2). "Correction is grievous [*ra'*] unto him that forsaketh the way: and he that hateth reproof shall die" (Prov. 15:10).

Ra' may also connote a fierceness or wildness: "He cast upon them the fierceness of his anger, wrath, and indignation, and trouble, by sending evil [*ra'*] angels among them" (Ps. 78:49). "Some evil beast hath devoured him . . ." (Gen. 37:20; cf. Gen. 37:33; Lev. 26:6).

In less frequent uses, *ra'* implies severity: "For thus saith the Lord God;
How much more when I send my four sore [*ra'*] judgments upon Israel . . ."
(Ezek. 14:21; cf. Deut. 6:22); unpleasantness: "And the Lord will take away
from thee all sickness, and will put more of the evil diseases of Egypt . . .
upon thee . . ." (Deut. 7:15; cf. Deut. 28:59); deadliness: "When I shall send
upon them the evil arrows of famine, which shall be for their destruction . . ."
(Ezek. 5:16; cf. "hurtful sword," Ps. 144:10); or sadness: "Wherefore the
king said unto me, why is thy countenance sad . . ." (Neh. 2:2).

The word may also refer to something of poor or inferior quality, such as
"bad" land (Num. 13:19), "naughty" figs (Jer. 24:2), "ill-favored" cattle
(Gen. 41:3, 19), or a "bad" sacrificial animal (Lev. 27:10, 12, 14).

In Isa. 45:7 Yahweh describes His actions by saying, ". . . I make peace,
and create evil [*ra'*] . . ."; moral "evil" is not intended in this context, but
rather the antithesis of *shalom* ("peace; welfare; well-being"). The whole
verse affirms that as absolute Sovereign, the Lord creates a universe governed by a moral order. Calamity and misfortune will surely ensue from the
wickedness of ungodly men.

C. Verbs.

'ābar (עָבַר), "to transgress, cross over, pass over." This word occurs as a
verb only when it refers to sin. *'Ābar* often carries the sense of "transgressing" a covenant or commandment—i.e., the offender "passes beyond" the
limits set by God's law and falls into transgression and guilt. This meaning
appears in Num. 14:41: "And Moses said, wherefore now do ye transgress the
commandment of the Lord? but it shall not prosper." Another example is in
Judg. 2:20: "And the anger of the Lord was hot against Israel; and he said,
Because that this people hath transgressed my covenant which I commanded
their fathers, and have not hearkened unto my voice" (cf. 1 Sam. 15:24; Hos.
8:1).

Most frequently, *'ābar* illustrates the motion of "crossing over" or "passing over." (The Latin *transgredior,* from which we get our English word
transgress, has the similar meaning of "go beyond" or "cross over.") This
word refers to crossing a stream or boundage ("pass through," Num. 21:22),
invading a country ("passed over," Judg. 11:32), crossing a boundary against
a hostile army ("go over," 1 Sam. 14:4), marching over ("go over," Isa.
51:23), overflowing the banks of a river or other natural barriers ("pass
through," Isa. 23:10), passing a razor over one's head ("come upon," Num.
6:5), and the passing of time ("went over," 1 Chron. 29:30).

chātā' (חָטָא), "to miss, sin, be guilty, forfeit, purify." This verb occurs
238 times and in all parts of the Old Testament. It is found also in Assyrian,
Aramaic, Ethiopic, Sabean, and Arabic.

The basic meaning of this verb is illustrated in Judg. 20:16: There were 700
left-handed Benjamite soldiers who "could sling stones at a hair breadth, and
not *miss.*" The meaning is extended in Prov. 19:2: "He who makes haste with
his feet *misses* the way" (RSV, NIV, KJV, NASB, "sinneth"). The intensive
form is used in Gen. 31:39: "That which was torn of beasts I brought not unto
thee; I bare the *loss* of it. . . ."

From this basic meaning comes the word's chief usage to indicate moral failure toward both God and men, and certain results of such wrongs. The first occurrence of the verb is in Gen. 20:6, God's word to Abimelech after he had taken Sarah: "Yes, I know that in the integrity of your heart you have done this, and also I have kept you from sinning against Me" (NASB; cf. Gen. 39:9).

Sin against God is defined in Josh. 7:11: "Israel hath sinned, and they have also transgressed my covenant which I commanded them. . . ." Also note Lev. 4:27: "And if any one of the common people sin through ignorance, while he doeth somewhat against any of the commandments of the Lord concerning things which ought not to be done, and be guilty." The verb may also refer to the result of wrongdoing, as in Gen. 43:9: ". . . Then let me bear the blame for ever." Deut. 24:1-4, after forbidding adulterous marriage practices, concludes: ". . . For that is abomination before the Lord: and thou shalt not cause the land to sin . . ." (KJV); the RSV renders this passage: "You shall not bring guilt upon the land." Similarly, those who pervert justice are described as "those who by a word make a man out to be guilty" (Isa. 29:21, NIV). This leads to the meaning in Lev. 9:15: "And he . . . took the goat . . . and slew it, and offered it for sin. . . ." The effect of the offerings for sin is described in Ps. 51:7: "Purge me with hyssop, and I shall be clean . . ." (cf. Num. 19:1-13). Another effect is seen in the word of the prophet to evil Babylon: "You have forfeited your life" (Hab. 2:10, RSV, NIV; KJV, NASB, "sinned against").

The word is used concerning acts committed against men, as in Gen. 42:22: "Spake I not unto you, saying, Do not sin against the child . . .?" and 1 Sam. 19:4: "Do not let the king sin against his servant David, since he has not sinned against you . . ." (NASB; NIV, "wrong, wronged").

The Septuagint translates the group of words with the verb *hamartanō* and derived nouns 540 times. They occur 265 times in the New Testament. The fact that all "have sinned" continues to be emphasized in the New Testament (Rom. 3:10-18, 23; cf. 1 Kings 8:46; Ps. 14:1-3; Eccl. 7:20). The New Testament development is that Christ, "having made one sacrifice for sins for all time sat down at the right hand of God. . . . For by one offering he has perfected for all time those who are being sanctified" (Heb. 10:12-14, NASB).

TO SING

A. Verbs.

rānan (רָנַן), "to sing, shout, cry out." Found in both ancient and modern Hebrew, this word is used in modern Hebrew in the sense of "to chant, sing." It occurs approximately 50 times in the Hebrew Old Testament, with about half of these uses being in the Book of Psalms, where there is special emphasis on "singing" and "shouting" praises to God. *Rānan* is found for the first time in Lev. 9:24 at the conclusion of the consecration of Aaron and his sons to the priesthood. When the fire fell and consumed the sacrifice, the people "shouted, and fell on their faces."

Rānan is often used to express joy, exultation, which seems to demand loud singing, especially when it is praise to God: "Cry out and shout, thou inhabitant of Zion: for great is the Holy One of Israel in the midst of thee" (Isa. 12:6). When Wisdom calls, she cries aloud to all who will hear (Prov. 8:3). To shout for joy (Ps. 32:11) is to let joy ring out!

shîr (שִׁיר), "to sing." This word appears frequently in ancient and modern Hebrew, as well as in ancient Ugaritic. While it occurs almost 90 times in the Hebrew Old Testament, it is not used until Exod. 15:1: "Then sang Moses and the children of Israel this song unto the Lord. . . ." One might wonder if it took the miracle of the Exodus from Egypt to give the Israelites something "to sing" about!

Over one quarter of the instances of *shîr* are found in the Book of Psalms, often in the imperative form, calling the people to express their praise to God in singing. One such example is found in Ps. 96:1: "O sing unto the Lord a new song: sing unto the Lord, all the earth." Frequently *shîr* is found in parallelism with *zamar*, "to sing" (Ps. 68:4, 32).

B. Participle.

shîr (שִׁיר), "singers." In the Books of Chronicles, *shîr* is used in the participial form some 33 times to designate the Levitical "singers" (1 Chron. 15:16). "Female singers" are referred to occasionally (2 Sam. 19:35; 2 Chron. 35:25; Eccl. 2:8).

C. Noun.

shîr (שִׁיר), "song." This noun is found about 30 times in the titles of various psalms as well as elsewhere in the Old Testament. *Shîr* is used of a joyous "song" in Gen. 31:27: ". . . And didst not tell me, that I might have sent thee away with mirth, and with songs, with tabret, and with harp?" In Judg. 5:12 the word refers to a triumphal "song," and in Neh. 12:46 the word is used of a religious "song" for worship.

The book that is commonly designated "The Song of Solomon" actually has the title "The Song of Songs" in Hebrew. While this love "song" continues to create questions in the minds of many regarding its inclusion in the biblical canon, it must have had some special meaning to have earned the title it has. Rather than rationalize its place in the canon by stating that it is an allegory of the love between God and Israel, and then Christ and the church, perhaps one should simply recognize that it is a love "song," pure and simple, and that love has its rightful place in the divine plan for mature men and women.

SISTER

'āchôth (אָחוֹת), "sister." Like the words for "brother" and "father," this noun is common to many Semitic languages. Whereas "brother" appears 629 times, "sister" occurs only 114 times. The usage is rare in the poetic literature

with the exception of the Song of Solomon (7 times). The first occurrence is in Gen. 4:22: "And Zillah, she also bare Tubal–cain, an instructor of every artificer in brass and iron: and the sister of Tubal–cain was Naamah."

The translation of "sister" for *'āchôth* is only the beginning. In Hebrew custom the word was a term employed to refer to the daughter of one's father and mother (Gen. 4:22) or one's half-sister (Gen. 20:12). It may also refer to one's aunt on the father's side (Lev. 18:12; 20:19) or on the mother's side (Lev. 18:13; 20:19).

The use of *'āchôth* more generally denotes female relatives: "And they blessed Rebekah, and said unto her, Thou art our sister, be thou the mother of thousands of millions, and let thy seed possess the gate of those which hate them" (Gen. 24:60). This meaning lies behind the metaphorical use, where two divisions of a nation (Judah and Israel; Jer. 3:7) and two cities (Sodom and Samaria; Ezek. 16:46) are portrayed as sisters—Hebrew names of geographical entities are feminine.

The more specialized meaning "beloved" is found only in Song of Sol. 4:9: "Thou hast ravished my heart, my sister [or beloved], my spouse; thou hast ravished my heart with one of thine eyes, with one chain of thy neck." Here *'āchôth* is used as a term of endearment rather than a term for a blood relative.

The Septuagint translates the word *adelphe* ("sister").

TO SLAUGHTER

A. Verb.

zābach (זָבַח), "to slaughter, sacrifice." This word is a common Semitic term for sacrifice in general, although there are a number of other terms used in the Old Testament for specific sacrificial rituals. There is no question that this is one of the most important terms in the Old Testament; *zābach* is found more than 130 times in its verbal forms and its noun forms occur over 500 times. The first time the verb occurs is in Gen. 31:54, where "Jacob offered sacrifice upon the mount." In Exod. 20:24 the word is used in relation to the kinds of sacrifices to be made.

While there were grain and incense offerings prescribed as part of the Mosaic laws dealing with sacrifice (see Lev. 2), the primary kind of sacrifice was the blood offering which required the slaughter of an animal (cf. Deut. 17:1; 1 Chron. 15:26). This blood was poured around the altar, for the blood contained the life, as stated in Lev. 17:11: "For the life of the flesh is in the blood; and I have given it for you upon the altar to make atonement for your souls; for it is the blood that makes atonement, by reason of the life" (RSV). Since the blood was the vehicle of life, it belonged to God alone. Because the blood is the life, and because it is given to God in the process of pouring it about the altar, it becomes the means of expiating sin, as an offering for sin and not because it becomes a substitute for the sinner.

Zābach is also used as a term for "slaughter for eating." This usage is closely linked with "slaughter for sacrifice" since all eating of flesh was sacrificial among ancient Hebrews. The word carries this meaning in 1 Kings

19:21: "And he returned back from him, and took a yoke of oxen, and slew them, and boiled their flesh . . . and gave unto the people, and they did eat."

B. Nouns.

zebach (זֶבַח), "sacrifice." This noun occurs more than 160 times in biblical Hebrew. The "sacrifice" which was part of a covenant ritual involved the sprinkling of the blood on the people and upon the altar, which presumably symbolized God as the covenant partner (see Exod. 24:6-8). Another special "sacrifice" was "the sacrifice of the feast of the passover" (Exod. 34:25). In this case the sacrificial lamb provided the main food for the passover meal, and its blood was sprinkled on the doorposts of the Israelite homes as a sign to the death angel.

The "sacrifice" of animals was in no way unique to Israelite religion, for sacrificial rituals generally are part of all ancient religious cults. Indeed, the mechanics of the ritual were quite similar, especially between Israelite and Canaanite religions. However, the differences are very clear in the meanings which the rituals had as they were performed either to capricious Canaanite gods or for the one true God who kept His covenant with Israel.

The noun *zebach* is used of "sacrifices" to the one true God in Gen. 46:1: "And Israel took his journey with all that he had . . . and offered sacrifices unto the God of his father Isaac" (cf. Exod. 10:25; Neh. 12:43). The noun refers to "sacrifices" to other deities in Exod. 34:15: "Lest thou make a covenant with the inhabitants of the land, and they go a whoring after their gods, and do sacrifice unto their gods, and one call thee, and thou eat of his sacrifice" (cf. Num. 25:2; 2 Kings 10:19).

The idea of "sacrifice" certainly is taken over into the New Testament, for Christ became "the Lamb of God, who takes away the sin of the world" (John 1:29, RSV). The writer of Hebrews makes much of the fact that with the "sacrifice" of Christ, no more sacrifices are necessary (Heb. 9).

mizǝbēach (מִזְבֵּחַ), "altar." This word is used more than 400 times in the Old Testament. This frequent use is obviously another direct evidence of the centrality of the sacrificial system in Israel. The first appearance of *mizǝbēach* is in Gen. 8:20, where Noah built an "altar" after the Flood.

Countless "altars" are referred to as the story of Israel progresses on the pages of the Old Testament: that of Noah (Gen. 8:20); of Abram at Sichem (Gen. 12:7), at Beth–el (Gen. 12:8), and at Moriah (Gen. 22:9); of Isaac at Beer–sheba (Gen. 26:25); of Jacob at Shechem (Gen. 33:20); of Moses at Horeb (Exod. 24:4); of Samuel at Ramah (1 Sam. 7:17); of the temple in Jerusalem (1 Kings 6:20; 8:64); and of the two "altars" planned by Ezekiel for the restored temple (Ezek. 41:22; 43:13-17).

SMALL

A. Adjectives.

qātān (קָטָן), "small; youngest"; *qātōn* (קָטֹן), "small; young; insignificant." These adjectives are synonymous. Both occur in all periods of biblical Hebrew—*qātān*, 47 times; *qātōn*, 56 times.

Qātōn in its first appearance means "small and insignificant": "And God made two great lights; the greater light to rule the day, and the lesser light to rule the night . . ." (Gen. 1:16). The first appearance of *qātān* bears the sense "youngest": "And Noah awoke from his wine, and knew what his younger son had done unto him" (Gen. 9:24).

In their first nuance, "small," the words are often contrasted to *gādôl*, "great": "And all the vessels of the house of God, great and small, and the treasures of the house of the Lord . . ." (2 Chron. 36:18). Other uses of the words to mean "small" include their application to the size of a set of weights (Deut. 25:13), to the size of the smallest finger of one's hand (1 Kings 12:10), and to the degree of seriousness of a given sin (Num. 22:18).

In the sense "young" these words refer to the relative age of an individual: "And the Syrians had gone out by companies, and had brought away captive out of the land of Israel a little maid . . ." (2 Kings 5:2). Notice 2 Kings 5:14: "Then went he down, and dipped himself seven times in Jordan, according to the saying of the man of God: and his flesh came again like unto the flesh of a little child. . . ." In a related use the word is comparative, contrasting the age of a given individual with that of his sibling(s): "Hereby ye shall be proved: By the life of Pharaoh ye shall not go forth hence, except your youngest brother come hither" (Gen. 42:15).

Finally, these adjectives can represent the idea "insignificant," or small in importance or strength: "Ye shall not respect persons in judgment; but ye shall hear the small as well as the great . . ." (Deut. 1:17). In a related nuance *qātōn* signifies "low in social standing": "When thou wast little in thine own sight, wast thou not made the head of the tribes of Israel . . . ?" (1 Sam. 15:17). In Exod. 18:22 the word suggests triviality: "And let them judge the people at all seasons: and it shall be, that every great matter they shall bring unto thee, but every small matter they shall judge. . . ."

B. Verb.

Qātōn means "to be small, insignificant." This verb occurs 4 times in biblical Hebrew and emphasizes smallness in quality or quantity. The word refers to "being insignificant" in Gen. 32:10: "I am not worthy of the least of all the mercies, and of all the truth, which thou hast showed unto thy servant . . ." (cf. 2 Sam. 7:19, NASB). In Amos 8:5, *qātōn* refers to "making small."

TO SOJOURN, DWELL

A. Verb.

gûr (גּוּר), "to dwell as a client, sojourn." This verb occurs only in Northwest Semitic and outside Hebrew only as a noun. In biblical Hebrew the verb *gûr* occurs 84 times and in every period of the language. This sense of *gûr* should be distinguished from one that means "to be afraid of" (Num. 22:3).

This verb means "to dwell in a land as a client." The first occurrence of the word is in Gen. 12:10, where it is reported that Abram journeyed to Egypt and dwelt there as a client. In Gen. 21:23, Abraham makes a covenant with

Abimelech, saying, "... According to the kindness that I have done unto thee, thou shalt do unto me, and to the land wherein thou hast sojourned."

B. Nouns.

gēr (רֵגּ), "client; stranger." *Gēr* occurs about 92 times and in every period of biblical Hebrew.

A "client" was not simply a foreigner *(nākərî)* or a stranger *(zār)*. He was a permanent resident, once a citizen of another land, who had moved into his new residence. Frequently he left his homeland under some distress, as when Moses fled to Midian (Exod. 2:22). Whether the reason for his journey was to escape some difficulty or merely to seek a new place to dwell, he was one who sought acceptance and refuge. Consequently he might also call himself a *tôshāb*, a settler. Neither the settler nor the "client" could possess land. In the land of Canaan the possession of land was limited to members or descendants of the original tribal members. Only they were full citizens who enjoyed all the rights of citizenry, which meant sharing fully in the inheritance of the gods and forefathers—the feudal privileges and responsibilities (cf. Ezek. 47:22).

In Israel a *gēr*, like a priest, could possess no land and enjoyed the special privileges of the third tithe. Every third year the tithe of the harvest was to be deposited at the city gate with the elders and distributed among "the Levite, (because he hath no part nor inheritance with thee,) and the stranger, and the fatherless, and the widow, which are within thy gates . . ." (Deut. 14:29). In the eschaton such "clients" were to be treated as full citizens: "And it shall come to pass, that ye shall divide it [the land] by lot for an inheritance unto you, and to the strangers that sojourn among you, which shall beget children among you: and they shall be unto you as born in the country among the children of Israel; they shall have inheritance with you among the tribes of Israel" (Ezek. 47:22). Under the Mosaic law aliens were not slaves but were usually in the service of some Israelite whose protection they enjoyed (Deut. 24:14). This, however, was not always the case. Sometimes a "client" was rich and an Israelite would be in his service (Lev. 25:47).

The *gēr* was to be treated (except for feudal privileges and responsibilities) as an Israelite, being responsible to and protected by the law: "Hear the causes between your brethren, and judge righteously between every man and his brother, and the stranger that is with him" (Deut. 1:16); "ye shall therefore keep my statutes and my judgments, and shall not commit any of these abominations; neither any of your own nation, nor any stranger that sojourneth among you" (Lev. 18:26); "ye shall have one manner of law, as well for the stranger, as for one of your own country: for I am the Lord your God" (Lev. 24:22). The *gēr* also enjoyed the Sabbath rest (Lev. 25:6) and divine protection (Deut. 10:18). God commanded Israel to love the "client" as himself (Lev. 19:34).

The *gēr* could also be circumcised (Exod. 12:48) and enjoy all the privileges of the true religion: the Passover (Exod. 12:48–49), the Atonement feast (Lev. 16:29), presenting offerings (Lev. 17:8), and all the feasts (Deut. 16:11). He was also obligated to keep the purity laws (Lev. 17:15).

Israel is told that God is the true owner of all the land and its people are but "clients" owing Him feudal obedience (Lev. 19:34; Deut. 10:19). They are admonished to treat the client with justice, righteousness, and love because like Abraham (Gen. 23:4) they were "clients" in Egypt (Exod. 22:21). In legal cases the "client" could appeal directly to God the great feudal Lord (Lev. 24:22).

Two other nouns related to *gûr* are *məgûrîm* and *gērûth*. *Məgûrîm* occurs 11 times and refers to the "status or condition of being a client" (Gen. 17:8) and to a "dwelling where one is a client" (Job 18:19). *Gērûth* appears once to refer to a "place where clients dwell" (Jer. 41:17). Some scholars think this word is a proper name, a part of a place name.

SOUL; SELF; LIFE

A. Noun.

nephesh (נֶפֶשׁ), "soul; self; life; person; heart." This is a very common term in both ancient and modern Semitic languages. It occurs over 780 times in the Old Testament and is evenly distributed in all periods of the text with a particularly high frequency in poetic passages.

The basic meaning is apparently related to the rare verbal form, *nāphash*. The noun refers to the essence of life, the act of breathing, taking breath. However, from that concrete concept, a number of more abstract meanings were developed. In its primary sense the noun appears in its first occurrence in Gen. 1:20: "the moving creature that hath life," and in its second occurrence in Gen. 2:7: "living soul."

However, in over 400 later occurrences it is translated "soul." While this serves to make sense in most passages, it is an unfortunate mistranslation of the term. The real difficulty of the term is seen in the inability of almost all English translations to find a consistent equivalent or even a small group of high-frequency equivalents for the term. The KJV alone uses over 28 different English terms for this one Hebrew word. The problem with the English term "soul" is that no actual equivalent of the term or the idea behind it is represented in the Hebrew language. The Hebrew system of thought does not include the combination or opposition of the terms "body" and "soul," which are really Greek and Latin in origin. The Hebrew contrasts two other concepts which are not found in the Greek and Latin tradition: "the inner self" and "the outer appearance" or, as viewed in a different context, "what one is to oneself" as opposed to "what one appears to be to one's observers." The inner person is *nephesh,* while the outer person, or reputation, is *shēm,* most commonly translated "name." In narrative or historical passages of the Old Testament, *nephesh* can be translated as "life" or "self," as in Lev. 17:11: "For the life of the flesh is in the blood: and I have given it to you upon the altar to make an atonement for [yourselves]. . . ." Needless to say, the reading "soul" is meaningless in such a text.

But the situation in the numerous parallel poetic passages in which the term appears is much more difficult. The Greek Septuagint and the Latin Vulgate both simply use the Greek and Latin equivalent "soul," especially in the Psalms. The first occurrence is in Ps. 3:2: "Many are saying of my soul, / / There is no deliverance for him in God" (NASB). The next occurrence is in Ps. 6:3: "And my soul is greatly dismayed; / / But Thou, O Lord—how long?" (NASB). In both passages the parallel contrast is between *nephesh* and some aspect of the self, expressed as "him" in Ps. 3:2 and not expressed but understood in Ps. 6:3. There is no distinction as to whether it appears as an "A" or "B" word in the parallelism. However, since Hebrew rejects repeating the same noun in both halves of a poetic line, *nephesh* is often used as the parallel for the speaker, primary personal subject, and even for God, as in Ps. 11:5: "The Lord trieth the righteous: but the wicked / / and him that loveth violence [he himself] hateth." Such passages are frequent, and a proper understanding of the word enlightens many well-known passages, such as Ps. 119:109: "My life is continually in my hand, / / Yet I do not forget Thy law" (NASB).

The versions vary widely in their readings of *nephesh*, with the more contemporary versions casting widely for meanings.

B. Verb.

Nāphash means "to breathe; respire; be refreshed." This verb, which is apparently related to the noun *nephesh*, appears 3 times in the Old Testament (Exod. 23:12; 31:17). The other appearance is in 2 Sam. 16:14: "And the king, and all the people that were with him, came weary, and refreshed themselves there."

TO SOW

A. Verb.

zāra' (זָרַע), "to sow, scatter seed, make pregnant." Common throughout the history of the Hebrew language, this root is found in various Semitic languages, including ancient Akkadian. The verb is found approximately 60 times in the Hebrew Old Testament. It occurs first in Gen. 1:29 in the summary of the blessings of creation which God has given to mankind: ". . . In the which is the fruit of a tree yielding seed . . ."

In an agricultural society such as ancient Israel, *zāra'* would be most important and very commonly used, especially to describe the annual sowing of crops (Judg. 6:3; Gen. 26:12.) Used in the figurative sense, it is said that Yahweh "will sow" Israel in the land (Hos. 2:23); in the latter days, Yahweh promises: ". . . I will sow the house of Israel and the house of Judah with the seed of man, and with the seed of beast" (Jer. 31:27). Of great continuing comfort are the words, "They that sow in tears shall reap in joy" (Ps. 126:5). The universal law of the harvest, sowing and reaping, applies to all areas of life and experience.

A good example of the need for free translation of the inherent meaning rather than a strictly literal rendering involves *zāra'*, in both its verb and noun forms. This is found in Num. 5, which describes the law of trial by ordeal in the case of a wife accused of infidelity. If she was found innocent, it was declared: ". . . She shall be free, and shall conceive [zāra‘] seed [zera‘]" (Num. 5:28). This phrase is literally: "She shall be acquitted and shall be seeded seed," or "She shall be made pregnant with seed."

An Old Testament name, Jezreel, has been connected with this root. Jezreel ("God sows") refers both to a city and valley near Mt. Gilboa (Josh. 17:16; 2 Sam. 2:9) and to the symbolically named son of Hosea (Hos. 1:4).

B. Noun.

zera‘ (זֶרַע), "seed; sowing; seedtime; harvest; offspring; descendant(s); posterity." This word occurs about 228 times in biblical Hebrew and in all periods. It has cognates in Aramaic, Phoenician, Arabic, Ethiopic, and Akkadian.

Zera‘ refers to the process of scattering seed, or "sowing." This is the emphasis in Gen. 47:24: "And it shall come to pass in the increase, that ye shall give the fifth part unto Pharaoh, and four parts shall be your own, for seed of the field, and for your food . . . ." Num. 20:5 should be rendered: "It [the wilderness] is not a place of sowing [NASB, "grain"] or figs or vines or pomegranates, nor is there water to drink." Ezek. 17:5 should be rendered: "He also took some of the seed of the land and planted it in a field [suitable for] sowing" (NASB, "in a fertile field"). A closely related emphasis occurs in passages such as Gen. 8:22, where the word represents "sowing" as a regularly recurring activity: "While the earth remaineth, seedtime and harvest, and cold and heat . . . shall not cease."

Zera‘ frequently means "seed." There are several nuances under this emphasis, the first being what is sown to raise crops for food. The Egyptians told Joseph: "Buy us and our land for bread, and we and our land will be servants unto Pharaoh: and give us seed, that we may live, and not die, that the land be not desolate" (Gen. 47:19). The word represents the product of a plant: "Let the earth bring forth grass, the herb yielding seed [food], and the fruit tree yielding fruit after his kind, whose seed is in itself . . ." (Gen. 1:11—the first biblical appearance). In this and other contexts zera‘ specifically refers to "grain seed," or "edible seed" (cf. Lev. 27:30). This may be the meaning of the word in 1 Sam. 8:15: "And he will take the tenth of your seed, and of your vineyards . . . ." However, it is possible that here the word refers to arable land, as does its Akkadian cognate. In other contexts the word represents an entire "crop or harvest": "For the seed [harvest] shall be prosperous; the vine shall give her fruit, and the ground shall give her increase, and the heavens shall give their dew . . ." (Zech. 8:12). In Isa. 23:3 zera‘ and the usual Hebrew word for "harvest" (qātsîr) are in synonymous parallelism.

Zera‘ sometimes means "semen," or a man's "seed": "And if any man's seed of copulation go out from him [if he has a seminal emission] . . ." (Lev. 15:16). A beast's "semen" can also be indicated by this word (Jer. 31:27).

Zera‘ often means "offspring." Only rarely is this nuance applied to animals: "And I will put enmity between thee [the devil] and the woman [Eve], and between thy seed and her seed . . ." (Gen. 3:15). This verse uses the word in several senses. The first appearance means both the descendants of the snake and those of the spiritual being who used the snake (evil men). The second appearance of the word refers to all the descendants of the woman and ultimately to a particular descendant (Christ). In Gen. 4:25 *zera'* appears not as a collective noun but refers to a particular and immediate "offspring"; upon the birth of Seth, Eve said: "God . . . hath appointed me another seed [offspring] . . . ." Gen. 46:6 uses the word (in the singular) of one's entire family including children and grandchildren (cf. Gen. 17:12). One's larger family, including all immediate relatives, is included in the word in passages such as 1 Kings 11:14. The word is used of an entire nation of people in Esth. 10:3.

Zera' is used of groups and individuals marked by a common moral quality. This usage was already seen in Gen. 3:15. Isa. 65:23 mentions the "seed" of the blessed of God. The Messiah or Suffering Servant will see His "offspring," or those who believe in and follow Him (Isa. 53:10). We also read about the followers of the righteous (Prov. 11:21), the faithful "seed" (Jer. 2:21), and godly "offspring." In each case this word represents those who are united by being typified by the modifier of *zera'*. Several other passages exhibit the same nuance except that *zera'* is modified by an undesirable quality.

TO SPEAK

A. Verb.

dābar (דָּבַר), "to speak, say." This verb occurs in all periods of Hebrew, in Phoenician (starting from around 900 B.C.), and in imperial Aramaic (starting from about 500 B.C.). In Old Testament Hebrew it occurs about 1,125 times.

This verb focuses not only on the content of spoken verbal communication but also and especially on the time and circumstances of what is said. Unlike *'āmar,* "to say," *dābar* often appears without any specification of what was communicated. Those who "speak" are primarily persons (God or men) or organs of speech. In Gen. 8:15 (the first occurrence of this verb) God "spoke" to Noah, while in Gen. 18:5 one of the three men "spoke" to Abraham. Exceptions to this generalization occur, for example, in Job 32:7, where Elihu personifies "days" (a person's age) as that which has the right "to speak" first. In 2 Sam. 23:2 David says that the Spirit of the Lord "spoke" to him; contrary to many (especially liberal) scholars, this is probably a reference to the Holy Spirit (cf. NASB).

Among the special meanings of this verb are "to say" (Dan. 9:21), "to command" (2 Kings 1:9), "to promise" (Deut. 6:3), "to commission" (Exod. 1:17), "to announce" (Jer. 36:31), "to order or command" (Deut. 1:14), and "to utter a song" (Judg. 5:12). Such secondary meanings are, however, quite infrequent.

B. Nouns.

dābār (דָּבָר), "word; matter; something." This noun occurs 1,440 times. The noun *dābār* refers, first, to what is said, to the actual "word" itself;

whereas *'emer* is essentially oral communication (the act of speaking). Before the dispersion from the tower of Babel all men spoke the same "words" or language (Gen. 11:1). This noun can also be used of the content of speaking. When God "did according to the word of Moses" (Exod. 8:13), He granted his request. The noun can connote "matter" or "affair," as in Gen. 12:17, where it is reported that God struck Pharaoh's household with plagues because of the "matter of Sarah" (KJV, "because of Sarai"). A rather specialized occurrence of this sense appears in references to records of the "events of a period" (cf. 1 Kings 14:19) or the activities of a particular person (1 Kings 11:41; cf. Gen. 15:1). *Dābār* can be used as a more general term in the sense of "something"—so in Gen. 24:66 the "everything" (KJV, "all things") is literally "all of something(s)"; it is an indefinite generalized concept rather than a reference to everything in particular. This noun also appears to have had almost a technical status in Israel's law procedures. Anyone who had a "matter" before Moses had a law case (Exod. 18:16).

As a biblical phrase "the word of the Lord" is quite important; it occurs about 242 times. Against the background just presented it is important to note that "word" here may focus on the content (meaning) of what was said, but it also carries overtones of the actual "words" themselves. It was the "word of the Lord" that came to Abram in a vision after his victory over the kings who had captured Lot (Gen. 15:1). In most cases this is a technical phrase referring expressly to prophetic revelation (about 225 times). It has been suggested that this phrase has judicial overtones although there are only 7 passages where this is certain (cf. Num. 15:31). This noun is used twice of God's "affairs" in the sense of the care of the temple (1 Chron. 26:32).

The "word" of God indicates God's thoughts and will. This should be contrasted with His name, which indicates His person and presence. Therefore, God's "word" is called "holy" only once (cf. Ps. 105:42), while His name is frequently called "holy."

There is much discussion regarding the "word" as a hypostatization of divine reality and attributes as seen, for example, in John 1:1: "In the beginning was the Word." This theme is rooted in such Old Testament passages as Isa. 9:8: "The Lord sent a word into Jacob . . ." (cf. 55:10–11; Ps. 107:20; 147:15). Some scholars argue that this is no more than the poetical device of personification and does not foreshadow John's usage. Their evidence is that human attributes are frequently separated from a man and objectivized as if they had a separate existence (cf. Ps. 85:11–12).

The Septuagint translates the noun *dābār* with two words respectively carrying overtones of the (1) content and (2) form of speaking: (1) *logos* and (2) *rēma*.

Several other nouns related to the verb *dābar* occur infrequently. *Dibərāh*, which occurs 5 times, means "cause, manner" (Job 5:8). *Dabbereth* means "word" once (Deut. 33:3). *Dəbôrāh* appears 5 times and refers to "honey bee" (Deut. 1:44; Ps. 118:12). *Midəbār* refers to "speaking" once (Song of Sol. 4:3).

SPIRIT; BREATH

rûach (רוּחַ), "breath; air; strength; wind; breeze; spirit; courage; temper; Spirit." This noun has cognates in Ugaritic, Aramaic, and Arabic. The word occurs about 378 times and in all periods of biblical Hebrew.

First, this word means "breath," air for breathing, air that is being breathed. This meaning is especially evident in Jer. 14:6: "And the wild asses did stand in the high places, they snuffed up the wind like dragons. . . ." When one's "breath" returns, he is revived: ". . . When he [Samson] had drunk [the water], his spirit [literally, "breath"] came again, and he revived . . ." (Judg. 15:19). Astonishment may take away one's "breath": "And when the queen of Sheba had seen all Solomon's wisdom, and the house that he had built, And the meat of his table, . . . there was no more spirit in her [she was overwhelmed and breathless]" (1 Kings 10:4-5). *Rûach* may also represent speaking, or the breath of one's mouth: "By the word of the Lord were the heavens made; and all the host of them by the breath of his mouth" (Ps. 33:6; cf. Exod. 15:8; Job 4:9; 19:17).

Second, this word can be used with emphasis on the invisible, intangible, fleeting quality of "air": "O remember that my life is wind: mine eyes shall no more see good" (Job 7:7). There may be a suggestion of purposelessness, uselessness, or even vanity (emptiness) when *rûach* is used with this significance: "And the prophets shall become wind, and the word is not in them . . ." (Jer. 5:13). "Windy words" are really "empty words" (Job 16:3), just as "windy knowledge" is "empty knowledge" (Job 15:2; cf. Eccl. 1:14, 17—"meaningless striving"). In Prov. 11:29 *rûach* means "nothing": "He that troubleth his own house shall inherit the wind. . . ." This nuance is especially prominent in Eccl. 5:15-16: "And he came forth of his mother's womb, naked shall he return to go as he came, and shall take nothing of his labor, which he may carry away in his hand. And this also is a sore evil, that in all points as he came, so shall he go: and what profit hath he that hath labored for the wind?"

Third, *rûach* can mean "wind." In Gen. 3:8 it seems to mean the gentle, refreshing evening breeze so well known in the Near East: "And they heard the voice of the Lord God walking in the garden in the cool [literally, breeze] of the day. . . ." It can mean a strong, constant wind: ". . . And the Lord brought an east wind upon the land all that day, and all that night . . ." (Exod. 10:13). It can also signify an extremely strong wind: "And the Lord turned a mighty strong west wind . . ." (Exod. 10:19). In Jer. 4:11 the word appears to represent a gale or tornado (cf. Hos. 8:7). God is the Creator (Amos 4:13) and sovereign Controller of the winds (Gen. 8:1; Num. 11:31; Jer. 10:13).

Fourth, the wind represents direction. In Jer. 49:36 the four winds represent the four ends of the earth, which in turn represent every quarter: "And upon Elam will I bring the four winds [peoples from every quarter of the earth] from the four quarters of heaven, and will scatter them toward all those winds; and there shall be no nation whither the outcasts of Elam shall not come." Akkadian attests the same phrase with the same meaning, and this phrase begins to appear in Hebrew at a time when contact with Akkadian-speaking peoples was frequent.

Fifth, *rûach* frequently represents the element of life in a man, his natural "spirit": "And all flesh died that moved upon the earth, . . . All in whose nostrils was the breath of life . . ." (Gen. 7:21-22). In these verses the animals have a "spirit" (cf. Ps. 104:29). On the other hand, in Prov. 16:2 the word appears to mean more than just the element of life; it seems to mean "soul": "All the ways of a man are clean in his own eyes; but the Lord weigheth the spirits [NASB, "motives"]." Thus, Isaiah can put *nephesh*, "soul," and *rûach* in synonymous parallelism: "With my soul have I desired thee in the night; yea, with my spirit within me will I seek thee early . . ." (26:9). It is the "spirit" of a man that returns to God (Eccl. 12:7).

Sixth, *rûach* is often used of a man's mind-set, disposition, or "temper": "Blessed is the man unto whom the Lord imputeth not iniquity, and in whose spirit there is no guile" (Ps. 32:2). In Ezek. 13:3 the word is used of one's mind or thinking: "Woe unto the foolish prophets, that follow their own spirits, and have seen nothing" (cf. Prov. 29:11). *Rûach* can represent particular dispositions, as it does in Josh. 2:11: "And as soon as we had heard these things, our hearts did melt, neither did there remain any more courage in any man, because of you . . ." (cf. Josh. 5:1; Job 15:13). Another disposition represented by this word is "temper": "If the spirit [temper] of the ruler rise up against thee, leave not thy place . . ." (Eccl. 10:4). David prayed that God would "restore unto me the joy of thy salvation; and uphold me with thy free Spirit" (Ps. 51:12). In this verse "joy of salvation" and "free Spirit" are parallel and, therefore, synonymous terms. Therefore, "spirit" refers to one's inner disposition, just as "joy" refers to an inner emotion.

Seventh, the Bible often speaks of God's "Spirit," the third person of the Trinity. This is the use of the word in its first biblical occurrence: "And the earth was without form, and void; and darkness was upon the face of the deep. And the Spirit of God moved upon the face of the waters" (Gen. 1:2). Isa. 63:10-11 and Ps. 51:12 specifically speak of the "holy or free Spirit."

Eighth, the non-material beings (angels) in heaven are sometimes called "spirits": "And there came forth a spirit, and stood before the Lord, and said, I will persuade him" (1 Kings 22:21; cf. 1 Sam. 16:14).

Ninth, the "spirit" may also be used of that which enables a man to do a particular job or that which represents the essence of a quality of man: "And Joshua the son of Nun was full of the spirit of wisdom; for Moses had laid his hands upon him . . ." (Deut. 34:9). Elisha asked Elijah for a double portion of his "spirit" (2 Kings 2:9) and received it.

SPIRIT (OF THE DEAD); NECROMANCER

'ôb (אוֹב), "spirit (of the dead); necromancer; pit." This word has cognates in Sumerian, Akkadian, and Ugaritic, where the meanings "pit" and "spirit of one who has died" occur. In its earliest appearances (Sumerian), *'ôb* refers to a pit out of which a departed spirit may be summoned. Later Assyrian texts use this word to denote simply a pit in the ground. Akkadian texts describe a deity that is the personification of the pit, to whom a particular exorcism ritual was addressed. Biblical Hebrew attests this word 16 times.

The word usually represents the troubled spirit (or spirits) of the dead. This meaning appears unquestionably in Isa. 29:4: ". . . Thy voice shall be, as of one that hath a familiar spirit, out of the ground, and thy speech shall whisper out of the dust."

Its second meaning, "necromancer," refers to a professional who claims to summon forth such spirits when requested (or hired) to do so: "Regard not them that have familiar spirits, neither seek after wizards" (Lev. 19:31—first occurrence). These mediums summoned their "guides" from a hole in the ground. Saul asked the medium (witch) of Endor, "Divine for me from the hole ['ôb]" (1 Sam. 28:8, author's translation).

God forbade Israel to seek information by this means, which was so common among the pagans (Lev. 19:31; Deut. 18:11). Perhaps the pagan belief in manipulating one's basic relationship to a god (or gods) explains the relative silence of the Old Testament regarding life after death. Yet God's people believed in life after death, from early times (e.g., Gen. 37:35; Isa. 14:15 ff.).

Necromancy was so contrary to God's commands that its practitioners were under the death penalty (Deut. 13). Necromancers' unusual experiences do not prove that they truly had power to summon the dead. For example, the medium of Endor could not snatch Samuel out of God's hands against His wishes. But in this particular incident, it seems that God rebuked Saul's apostasy, either through a revived Samuel or through a vision of Samuel. Mediums do not have power to summon the spirits of the dead, since this is reprehensible to God and contrary to His will.

SPLENDOR

hôd (הוֹד), "splendor; majesty; authority." A possible cognate of this word appears in Arabic. All but 4 of its 24 biblical appearances occur in poetry.

The basic significance of "splendor and majesty" with overtones of superior power and position is attested in the application of this word to kings: "Therefore thus saith the Lord concerning Jehoiakim the son of Josiah king of Judah; They shall not lament for him, saying, Ah my brother! or, Ah sister! they shall not lament for him, saying, Ah lord! or, Ah his glory!" (Jer. 22:18). This concept is equally prominent when the word is used of God: "Fair weather cometh out of the north: with God is terrible majesty" (Job 37:22).

In many cases *hôd* focuses on "dignity and splendor" with overtones of superior power and position but not to the degree seen in oriental kings: "And thou shalt put some of thine honor upon him, that all the congregation of the children of Israel may be obedient" (Num. 27:20—the first occurrence of the word). When used of the olive tree (Hos. 14:6), *hôd* focuses on its "splendor and dignity" as the most desired and desirable of the trees (cf. Judg. 9:9-15). The proud carriage of a war horse and seeming bravery in the face of battle lead God to say, "The glory of his nostrils is terrible" (Job 39:20). In every use of the word the one so described evokes a sense of amazement and satisfaction in the mind of the beholder.

TO SPREAD OUT

pāras (פָּרַשׂ), "to spread out, scatter, display." Found in both ancient and modern Hebrew, this word occurs approximately 65 times in the Hebrew Old Testament. It is found for the first time in Exod. 9:29: ". . . I will spread abroad my hands unto the Lord. . . ." Such stretching of the hands probably reflected the characteristic posture of prayer in the Bible (cf. Ps. 143:6; Isa. 1:15).

Pāras sometimes expresses the "spreading out" of a garment to its widest extent (Judg. 8:25). It is commonly used of wings' "being spread," opened fully (Deut. 32:11; 1 Kings 6:27). "To spread out" a net is to set a snare or trap (Hos. 7:12). Sometimes "to spread out" is "to display": ". . . A fool layeth open his folly" (Prov. 13:16). "To spread" may mean "to cover over" and thus to hide from vision: "And the woman took and spread a covering over the well's mouth, and spread ground corn thereon; and the thing was not known" (2 Sam. 17:19). In some instances, "to spread" may have a more violent meaning of "to scatter": ". . . They that remain shall be scattered toward all winds . . ." (Ezek. 17:21).

TO SPRINKLE

zāraq (זָרַק), "to throw; sprinkle; strew; toss; scatter abundantly." This word is found in both ancient and modern Hebrew and is used in ancient Akkadian in the sense of "to spray." Used 35 times in the text of the Hebrew Old Testament, in 26 of those times it expresses the "throwing" or "sprinkling" of blood against the sacrificial altar or on the people. Thus, it appears very often in Leviticus (1:5, 11; 3:2, 8, 13 et al.).

Ezekiel's version of "the New Covenant" includes the "sprinkling" of the water of purification (Ezek. 36:25). In the first use of *zāraq* in the Old Testament, it describes the "throwing" of handfuls of dust into the air which would settle down on the Egyptians and cause boils (Exod. 9:8, 10). In his reform, Josiah ground up the Canaanite idol images and "scattered, strewed," the dust over the graves of idol-worshipers (2 Chron. 34:4). In Ezekiel's vision of the departure of God's glory from the temple, the man in linen takes burning coals and "scatters" them over Jerusalem (Ezek. 10:2).

TO STAND

A. Verbs.

nātsab (נָצַב), "to stand, station, set up, erect." Found in both ancient and modern Hebrew, this word goes back at least to ancient Ugaritic. It is found approximately 75 times in the Hebrew Bible. Its first occurrence in the Old Testament is in Gen. 18:2: ". . . Three men stood by him. . . ."

There are various ways of standing. One may "stand" for a definite purpose at a particular spot: ". . . Wait for him by the river's brink . . ." (Exod. 7:15 RSV; literally, "stand by the river's bank"). One often stands upright:

". . . And stood every man at his tent door . . ." (Exod. 33:8); ". . . my sheaf arose, and also stood upright . . ." (Gen. 37:7). One who is "stationed" in a position is usually over someone else: "And Azariah the son of Nathan was over the officers [lit., "those standing over"] . . ." (1 Kings 4:5). "To stand" something may be "to erect" something: "And Jacob set up a pillar . . ." (Gen. 35:14). The waters of the Sea of Reeds were said to "stand as a heap" (Ps. 78:13). To fix a boundary is "to establish or erect" a boundary marker (Deut. 32:8).

'Āmad (עָמַד), "to take one's stand; stand here or be there; stand still." Outside biblical Hebrew, where it occurs about 520 times and in all periods, this verb is attested only in Akkadian ("to stand, lean on"). A word spelled the same way appears in Arabic, but it means "to strive after."

The basic meaning of this verb is "to stand upright." This is its meaning in Gen. 18:8, its first biblical occurrence. It is what a soldier does while on watch (2 Sam. 18:30). From this basic meaning comes the meaning "to be established, immovable, and standing upright" on a single spot; the soles of the priests' feet "rested" (stood still, unmoving) in the waters of the Jordan (Josh. 3:13). Also, the sun and the moon "stood still" at Joshua's command (Josh. 10:13). Idols "stand upright" in one spot, never moving. The suggestion here is that they never do anything that is expected of living things (Isa. 46:7). 'Āmad may be used of the existence of a particular experience. In 2 Sam. 21:18 there "was" (hāyah) war again, while in 1 Chron. 20:4 war "existed" or "arose" ('āmad) again. Cultically (with reference to the formal worship activities) this verb is used of approaching the altar to make a sacrifice. It describes the last stage of this approaching, "to stand finally and officially" before the altar (before God; cf. Deut. 4:11). Such standing is not just a standing still doing nothing but includes all that one does in ministering before God (Num. 16:9).

In other contexts 'āmad is used as the opposite of verbs indicating various kinds of movement. The psalmist praises the man who does not walk (behave according to) in the counsel of the ungodly or "stand" (serve) in the path of the sinful (Ps. 1:1). Laban told Abraham not "to stand" (remain stationary, not entering) outside his dwelling but to come in (Gen. 24:31). The verb can suggest "immovable," or not being able to be moved. So the "house of the righteous shall stand" (Prov. 12:7). Yet another nuance appears in Ps. 102:26, which teaches the indestructibility and/or eternity of God—the creation perishes but He "shalt endure [will ever stand]." This is not the changelessness of doing nothing or standing physically upright, but the changelessness of ever-existing being, a quality that only God has in Himself. All other existing depends upon Him; the creation and all creatures are perishable. In a more limited sense the man who does not die as the result of a blow "stands," or remains alive (Exod. 21:21). In a military context "to stand" refers to gaining a victory: "Behold, two kings stood not before him: how then shall we stand?" (2 Kings 10:4; cf. Judg. 2:14).

'Āmad can be used of the ever unchanged content and/or existence of a document (Jer. 32:14), a city (1 Kings 15:4), a people (Isa. 66:22), and a divine worship (Ps. 19:9).

Certain prepositions sometimes give this verb special meanings. Jeroboam "ordained" (made to stand, to minister) priests in Bethel (1 Kings 12:32). With "to" the verb can signify being in a certain place to accomplish a predesignated task—so Moses said that certain tribes should "stand upon mount Gerizim to bless the people" (Deut. 27:12). With this same preposition this verb can be used judicially of (1) the act of being in court, or standing before a judge (1 Kings 3:16), and (2) the position (whether literal or figurative) assumed by a judge when pronouncing the sentence (Ezek. 44:24) or delivering judgment (Isa. 3:13; cf. Exod. 17:6). With the preposition "before" 'āmad is used to describe the service of a servant before a master—so Joshua "stood" before Moses (Deut. 1:38). This is not inactivity but activity.

In Neh. 8:5 the verb means "to stand up or rise up"; when Ezra opened the book, all the people "stood up" (cf. Dan. 12:13).

The Septuagint renders 'āmad usually with a verb meaning "to stand" and, where the contexts show it refers to temporal standing, with verbs meaning "to abide or remain."

B. Nouns.

'ammûd (עַמּוּד), "pillar; standing place." The noun 'ammûd occurs 111 times and usually signifies something that stands upright like or as a "pillar" (Exod. 26:32; Judg. 16:25). It may occasionally refer to a "standing place" (2 Kings 11:14).

Several other nouns are derived from the verb 'āmad. 'Ōmed occurs 9 times and refers to "standing places" (2 Chron. 30:16). 'Emədāh means "standing ground" once (Mic. 1:11). Ma'amād, which occurs 5 times, refers to "service" in 2 Chron. 9:4 and to "office or function" (in someone's service) in 1 Chron. 23:28. Mā'omād occurs once to mean "standing place" or "foothold" (Ps. 69:2).

STATUE

tselem (צֶלֶם), "statue; image; copy." Cognates of this word appear in Ugaritic and Phoenician (perhaps), Akkadian, Aramaic, and Arabic. Old Testament Hebrew attests it 17 times.

This word means "statue": "And all the people of the land went into the house of Baal, and brake it down; his altars and his images brake they in pieces thoroughly . . ." (2 Kings 11:18; cf. Num. 33:52).

This word signifies an "image or copy" of something in the sense of a replica: "Wherefore ye shall make images of your emerods, and images of your mice that mar the land; and ye shall give glory unto the God of Israel . . ." (1 Sam. 6:5). In Ezek. 23:14 tselem represents a wall painting of some Chaldeans.

The word also means "image" in the sense of essential nature. So Adam "begat a son in his own likeness, after his image; and called his name Seth" (Gen. 5:3). Human nature in its internal and external characteristics is what is meant here rather than an exact duplicate. So, too, God made man in His own "image," reflecting some of His own perfections: perfect in knowledge, righteousness, and holiness, and with dominion over the creatures (Gen. 1:26). Being created in God's "image" meant being created male and female, in a loving unity of more than one person (Gen. 1:27). It is noteworthy that in Gen. 1:26 (the first occurrence of the word) the "image" of God is represented by two Hebrew words (*tselem* and *dəmûth*); by *tselem* alone in Gen. 1:27 and 9:6; and by *dəmûth* alone in Gen. 5:1. This plus the fact that in other contexts the words are used exactly the same leads to the conclusion that the use of both in passages such as Gen. 1:26 is for literary effect.

In Ps. 39:6 *tselem* means "shadow" of a thing which represents the original very imprecisely, or it means merely a phantom (ghost?), a thing which represents the original more closely but lacks its essential characteristic (reality): "Surely every man walketh in a vain show [*tselem*]; surely they are disquieted in vain: he heapeth up riches, and knoweth not who shall gather them" (cf. Ps. 73:20—the word represents a "dream image").

STATUTE; ORDINANCE

A. Nouns.

chōq (חֹק), "statute; prescription; rule; law; regulation." This noun is derived from the verb *chāqaq*, "to cut in, determine, decree." *Chōq* occurs 127 times in biblical Hebrew.

The first usage of *chōq* is in Gen. 47:22: "Only the land of the priests bought he not; for the priests had a portion [*chōq*] assigned them of Pharaoh. . . ." This word is frequent in Deuteronomy and Psalms and rare in the historical books and in the prophets.

The meaning of *chōq* in the first occurrence (Gen. 47:22) differs from the basic meaning of "statute." It has the sense of something allotted or apportioned. A proverb speaks about "the food that is my portion" (Prov. 30:8, NASB; KJV, "food convenient for me"; literally, "food of my prescription or portion"). Job recognized in his suffering that God does what is appointed for him: "For he performeth the thing that is appointed for me [literally, "he will perform my Law"] . . ." (23:14). The "portion" may be something that is due to a person as an allowance or payment. The Egyptian priests received their income from Pharaoh (Gen. 47:22), even as God permitted a part of the sacrifice to be enjoyed by the priests: "And it shall be Aaron's and his sons' [as their portion] for ever from the children of Israel: for it is a heave offering . . ." (Exod. 29:28).

The word *chōq* also signifies "law," or "statute." In a general sense it refers to the "laws" of nature like rain: "When he made a decree for the rain, and a way for the lightning of the thunder" (Job 28:26; cf. Jer. 5:22); and the celestial bodies: "He hath also stablished them for ever and ever: he hath made a decree which shall not pass" (Ps. 148:6). Cf. "Thus saith the Lord, which giveth the sun for a light by day, and the ordinances of the moon and of the stars for a light by night, which divideth the sea when the waves thereof roar; The Lord of hosts is his name: If those ordinances depart from before me, saith the Lord, then the seed of Israel also shall cease from being a nation before me for ever" (Jer. 31:35-36). Moreover, the word *chōq* denotes a "law" promulgated in a country: "And Joseph made it a law over the land of Egypt unto this day, that Pharaoh should have the fifth part; except the land of the priests only, which became not Pharaoh's" (Gen. 47:26).

Finally, and most important, the "law" given by God is also referred to as a *chōq*: "When they have a matter, they come unto me; and I judge between one and another, and I do make them know the statutes [*chōq*] of God, and his laws [*tôrāh*]" (Exod. 18:16). The word's synonyms are *mitsəwāh*, "commandment"; *mishəpāt*, "judgment"; *bərîth*, "covenant"; *tôrāh*, "law"; and *'ēdûth*, "testimony." It is not easy to distinguish between these synonyms, as they are often found in conjunction with each other: "Ye shall diligently keep the commandments [*mitsəwāh*] of the Lord your God, and his testimonies [*'edāh*], and his statutes [*chōq*], which he hath commanded thee" (Deut. 6:17).

chuqqāh (חֻקָּה), "statute; regulation; prescription; term." This noun occurs about 104 times.

Chuqqāh is found for the first time in God's words of commendation about Abraham to Isaac: "Because that Abraham obeyed my voice, and kept my charge, my commandments [*mitsəwāh*], my statutes [*chuqqāh*], and my laws [*tôrāh*]" (Gen. 26:5), together with its synonyms *mishəmereth, mitsəwāh,* and *tôrāh*. The primary use of *chuqqāh* is in the Pentateuch, especially in Leviticus and Numbers. It is extremely rare in the poetical books and in the prophetic writings (except for Jeremiah and Ezekiel).

The meaning of "fixed" is similar to the usage of *chōq*, in the sense of the laws of nature: "Thus saith the Lord; If my covenant be not with day and night, and if I have not appointed the ordinances of heaven and earth" (Jer. 33:25; cf. Job 38:33). Even as the Israelites had a period of rainfall from October to April, there was a fixed period of harvest (from April to June): "Neither say they in their heart, Let us now fear the Lord our God, that giveth rain, both the former and the latter, in his season: he reserveth unto us the appointed weeks of the harvest" (Jer. 5:24). In addition to regularity of nature, the word *chuqqāh* signifies regular payment to the priests: "Which the Lord commanded to be given them of the children of Israel, in the day that he anointed them, by a statute for ever throughout their generations" (Lev. 7:36).

In non-religious usage, the word *chuqqāh* refers to the customs of the nations: "After the doings of the land of Egypt, wherein ye dwelt, shall ye not do: and after the doings of the land of Canaan, whither I bring you, shall ye not do: neither shall ye walk in their ordinances" (Lev. 18:3; cf. 20:23). The reason for the requirement to abstain from the pagan practices is that they were considered to be degenerate (Lev. 18:30).

The most significant usage of *chuqqāh* is God's "law." It is more specific in meaning than *chōq*. Whereas *chōq* is a general word for "law," *chuqqāh* denotes the "law" of a particular festival or ritual. There is the "law" of the Passover (Exod. 12:14), Unleavened Bread (Exod. 12:17), Feast of Tabernacles (Lev. 23:41), the Day of Atonement (Lev. 16:29 ff.), the priesthood (Exod. 29:9), and the blood and fat (Lev. 3:17).

The word *chuqqāh* has many synonyms. At times it forms a part of a series of three: "Beware that thou forget not the Lord thy God, in not keeping his commandments [*mitsəwāh*], and his judgments [*mishəpāt*], and his statutes [*chuqqāh*], which I command thee this day" (Deut. 8:11), and at other times of a series of four: "Therefore thou shalt love the Lord thy God, and keep his charge [*mishəmereth*], and his statutes [*chuqqāh*] and his judgments [*mishəpāt*], and his commandments [*mitsəwāh*], always" (Deut. 11:1; cf. Gen. 26:5 with *tôrāh* instead of *mishəpāt*).

The "statutes" of people are to be understood as the practices contrary to God's expectations: "For the statutes of Omri are kept, and all the works of the house of Ahab, and ye walk in their counsels; that I should make thee a desolation, and the inhabitants thereof a hissing: therefore ye shall bear the reproach of my people" (Mic. 6:16). The prophet Ezekiel condemned Judah for rejecting God's holy "statutes": "And she hath changed my judgments into wickedness more than the nations, and my statutes [*chuqqāh*] more than the countries that are round about her: for they have refused my judgments and my statutes [*chuqqāh*], they have not walked in them" (Ezek. 5:6). He also challenged God's people to repent and return to God's "statutes" that they might live: "If the wicked restore the pledge, give again that he had robbed, walk in the statutes of life, without committing iniquity; he shall surely live, he shall not die" (Ezek. 33:15).

The Septuagint gives the following translations of both *chōq* and *chuqqāh*: *prostagma* ("order; command; injunction"); *dikaioma* ("regulation; require-ment; commandment"); and *nomimos* ("lawful; conformable to law"). A translation of *chōq* is *diatheke* ("last will; testament; covenant"). A transla-tion of *chuqqāh* is *nomos* ("law").

B. Verb.

chāqaq (חָקַק), "to cut in; determine; decree." This root is found in Semi-tic languages with the above meaning or with the sense "to be true" (Arabic), "to be just" (Akkadian). This verb occurs less than 20 times in the Old Testament.

Chāqaq is used in Isa. 22:16 with the meaning "to cut in": ". . . That graveth a habitation for himself in a rock." In Isa. 10:1 the verb is used of "enacting a decree": "Woe unto them that decree unrighteous decrees, and that write grievousness which they have prescribed."

STEP

A. Noun.

pa'am (פַּעַם), "step; foot; hoofbeats; pedestal; stroke; anvil." This noun's attested cognates appear in Ugaritic (*p'n*) and Phoenician. Biblical occur-rences of this word number about 117 and appear in every period of the language.

The nuances of this word are related to the basic meaning "a human foot." The psalmist uses this meaning in Ps. 58:10: "The righteous shall rejoice when he seeth the vengeance: he shall wash his feet in the blood of the wicked." In

Exod. 25:12 the word is applied to the "pedestals or feet" of the ark of the covenant: "And thou shalt cast four rings of gold for it, and put them in the four [feet] thereof; and two rings shall be in the one side of it, and two rings in the other side of it." Elsewhere the word signifies the "steps" one takes, or "footsteps": "Hold up my goings in thy paths, that my footsteps slip not" (Ps. 17:5). Judg. 5:28 applies the word to the "steps" of a galloping horse, or its hoofbeats. This focus on the falling of a foot once is extended to the "stroke" of a spear: "Then said Abishai to David, . . . let me pin him to the earth with one stroke of the spear . . ." (1 Sam. 26:8 RSV). Finally, *pa'am* represents a foot-shaped object, an "anvil" (Isa. 41:7).

B. Adverb.

pa'am (**פַּעַם**), "once; now; anymore." This word functions as an adverb with the focus on an occurrence or time. In Exod. 10:17 the word bears this emphasis: "Now therefore forgive, I pray thee, my sin *only this once,* and entreat the Lord your God. . . ." The first biblical appearance of the word focuses on the finality, the absoluteness, of an event: "This is now bone of my bones . . ." (Gen. 2:23). The thrust of this meaning appears clearly in the translation of Gen. 18:32—Abraham said to God: "Oh, let not the Lord be angry, and I will speak yet but this once [only one more time]. . . ."

STONE

'eben (**אֶבֶן**), "stone." A comparison of Semitic languages shows that *'eben* was the common word for "stone" among the ancients. Exact philological and semantic cognates are found in Akkadian, Ugaritic, Phoenician, Aramaic, Old South Arabic, and several Ethiopic dialects. The Greek Old Testament usually has *lithos* (λιδος) for *'eben.* Used almost exclusively for movable stone(s), *'eben* is to be distinguished from *sela',* "rock," and *tsûr,* "cliff."

The noun *'eben* occurs in the Old Testament 260 times, with almost equal frequency in the singular (and collective) as in the plural. It appears more frequently in prose than in poetry.

Palestine was (and is) famous for its ubiquitous "stone." So much was "stone" a part of the ancient writer's consciousness that it served the literary interests of simile (Exod. 15:5), metaphor (Ezek. 11:19), and hyperbole (1 Kings 10:27; 2 Chron. 1:15; 9:27). That building with "stone" was the rule rather than the exception in Palestine is suggested by the biblical writer's allusion to the Mesopotamian custom of using clay bricks (Gen. 11:3). Yet it seems that Israelite craftsmen at the time of David lagged behind somewhat in the art of stonework, for stonemasons from Tyre were employed in constructing the royal residence (2 Sam. 5:11).

Beyond their use as a construction material, "stones" served as covers for wells (Gen. 29:3 ff.), storage containers (Exod. 7:19), weights (Deut. 25:13; Prov. 11:1), and slingstones (1 Sam. 17:49). Plumblines were suspended stones (Isa. 34:11); pavement was sometimes made of "stone" (2 Kings

16:17); and the Bible speaks of hailstones (Josh. 10:11; Ezek. 13:11 ff.). The Israelite custom of cave burials presumes stone tombs (Isa. 14:19); on 3 occasions when bodies were not interred, they were heaped with "stones" (Josh. 7:26; 8:29; 2 Sam. 18:17).

Pentateuchal laws relating to purity–impurity concepts stipulated that certain crimes were punishable by stoning. The standard formula employed either the verb *rāgam* or *sāqal* followed by a preposition and the noun *'eben*. Included under this penalty were the crimes of blasphemy (Lev. 24:23; Num. 15:35-36), Molech worship (Lev. 20:2), idolatry (Deut. 13:10), and prostitution (Deut. 22:21, 24). Originally, stoning was a means of merely expelling the lawbreaker from the community; however, in ancient Israel it was a means of capital punishment whereby the community could rid itself of the impure offender without coming into direct contact with him.

As for the cult, the carved "stone" figurines commonly worshiped throughout the ancient Near East were strictly forbidden to Israel (Lev. 26:1). To carve "stone" which was to be used in the cult was to profane it (Exod. 20:25). Altars and memorials especially common to the patriarchal age and the period of the Conquest were all made of unhewn "stones" (Gen. 28:18 ff.; 31:45; Josh. 4:5; 24:26-27). Of the cult objects in Israel's wilderness shrine, only the tablets of the Decalogue were made of "stone" (Exod. 24:12; 34:1, 4; Deut. 4:13; Ezek. 40:42—the stone tables of Ezekiel's temple served only utilitarian purposes).

Precious "stones" such as onyx (Gen. 2:12) and sapphire (Ezek. 1:26) are mentioned frequently in the Bible, especially with regard to the high priest's ephod and breastplate (Exod. 39:6 ff.). The expensiveness of the high priest's garments corresponded to the special workmanship of the most holy place where Aaron served.

In certain texts, *'eben* has been given theological interpretations. God is called the "stone of Israel" in Gen. 49:24. And several occurrences of *'eben* in the Old Testament have been viewed as messianic, as evidenced by the Greek Old Testament, rabbinic writings, and the New Testament; among them: Gen. 28:18; Ps. 118:22; Isa. 8:14; 28:16; Dan. 2:34; Zech. 4:7.

STREET

A. Noun.

chûts (חוּץ), "street." This word, of uncertain origin, appears in biblical, mishnaic, and modern Hebrew. In the Old Testament the total number of occurrences of the noun and adverb is about 160.

A particular use of *chûts* denotes the place outside the houses in a city, or the "street." The "street" was the place for setting up bazaars: "The cities, which my father took from thy father, I will restore; and thou shalt make streets for thee in Damascus, as my father made in Samaria" (1 Kings 20:34). Craftsmen plied their trade on certain "streets" named after the guild—for example, the Bakers Street: "Then Zedekiah the king commanded that they should commit Jeremiah into the court of the prison, and that they should give him daily a piece of bread out of the bakers' street, until all the bread in the city were spent" (Jer. 37:21). The absence of justice in the marketplace was an indication of the wickedness of the whole population of Jerusalem. Jeremiah was called to check in the "streets" to find an honest man: "Run ye to and fro through the streets of Jerusalem, and see now, and know, and seek in the broad places thereof, if ye can find a man, if there be any that executeth judgment, that seeketh the truth; and I will pardon it" (5:1).

Other descriptions of the "streets" are given by the prophets. Several mention that the "streets" were muddy: ". . . And to tread them down like the mire of the streets" (Isa. 10:6; cf. Mic. 7:10; Zech. 10:5). Others make reference to the blood (Ezek. 28:23), the famished (Lam. 2:19), and the dead (Nah. 3:10) which filled the "streets" in times of war.

The area outside a city was also known as the *chûts*. In this case it is better translated as "open country" or "field"; cf. "That our garners may be full, affording all manner of store; that sheep may bring forth thousands and ten thousands in our streets" (Ps. 144:13 KJV; RSV, "fields"; cf. Job 5:10; Prov. 8:26).

B. Adverb.

chûts (ווֹן), "outside." The first occurrence of this word is in Gen. 6:14: "Make thee an ark of gopher wood; rooms shalt thou make in the ark, and shalt pitch it within and without [*chûts*] with pitch."

By *chûts* the general idea of "the outside" is intimated. It is sometimes indeterminate where "outside" is, especially when connected with a verb: "You shall also have a place outside the camp; he may not reenter the camp" (Deut. 23:12 NASB). The area could be "outside" a house, tent, city, or camp—hence the adverbial usage of "outside." The word is also connected with a preposition with the sense of "in, to, on, toward the outside": "If he rise again, and walk abroad upon his staff, then shall he that smote him be quit: only he shall pay for the loss of his time, and shall cause him to be thoroughly healed" (Exod. 21:19).

STRENGTH

chayil (חַיִל), "strength; power; wealth; property; capable; valiant; army; troops; influential; upper-class people (courtiers)." The cognates of this word have been found in Aramaic, Akkadian, Syriac, Arabic, and Ethiopic. Biblical Hebrew attests it about 245 times and in all periods.

First, this word signifies a faculty or "power," the ability to effect or produce something. The word is used of physical "strength" in the sense of power that can be exerted: "If the iron be blunt, and he do not whet the edge, then must he put to more strength . . ." (Eccl. 10:10). Quite often this word appears in a military context. Here it is the physical strength, power, and ability to perform in battle that is in view. This idea is used of men in 1 Sam. 2:4: "The bows of the mighty men are broken, and they that stumbled are girded with strength" (cf. Ps. 18:32, 39). Ps. 33:17 applies the word to a war horse. An interesting use of *chayil* appears in Num. 24:17-18, where Balaam prophesied the destruction of Moab and Edom at the hands of Israel: "And Edom shall be a possession, Seir also shall be a possession for his enemies; and Israel shall do valiantly" (v. 18). The idea here is dynamic; something is happening. One might also render this phrase: "Israel performs mightily." This translation of the word is somewhat inexact; a noun is translated as an adverb.

Second, *chayil* means "wealth, property." This nuance of the word focuses on that which demonstrates one's ability, his wealth or goods; Levi, Simeon, and their cohorts attacked the Shechemites: "And all their wealth, and all their little ones, and their wives took they captive, and spoiled even all that was in the house" (Gen. 34:29—the first biblical occurrence of the word). In Num. 31:9 *chayil* includes all the possessions of the Midianites except the women, children, cattle, and flocks. Thus it seems to be a little narrower in meaning. When this nuance is used with the Hebrew word "to do or make," the resulting phrase means "to become wealthy or make wealth" (cf. Deut. 8:18; Ruth 4:11). This is in marked contrast to the emphasis of the same construction in Num. 24:18. Joel 2:22 uses *chayil* in the sense of "wealth" or products of the ability of a tree to produce fruit.

Third, several passages use the word in the sense of "able." In Gen. 47:6 the ability to do a job well is in view. Pharaoh told Joseph: "The land of Egypt is before thee; in the best of the land make thy father and brethren to dwell; in the land of Goshen let them dwell: and if thou knowest any men of activity [capable men] among them, then make them rulers over my cattle." This word can also represent the domestic skills of a woman—Ruth is described as a woman of ability and, therefore, either potentially or actually a good wife (Ruth 3:11; Prov. 12:4). When applied to men, *chayil* sometimes focuses on their ability to conduct themselves well in battle as well as being loyal to their commanders (1 Sam. 14:52; 1 Kings 1:42). When used in such contexts, the word may be translated "valiant": "And there was sore war against the Philistines all the days of Saul: and when Saul saw any strong man, or any valiant man, he took him unto him" (1 Sam. 14:52; cf. Num. 24:18; 1 Sam. 14:48).

Fourth, this word sometimes means "army"; "And I will harden Pharaoh's heart, that he shall follow after them; and I will be honored upon Pharaoh, and upon all his host [army] . . ." (Exod. 14:4). The word can also refer to the army as troops in the sense of a combination of a lot of individuals. Under such an idea the word can represent the members of an army distributed to perform certain functions. Jehoshaphat "placed forces in all the fenced cities of Judah, and set garrisons in the land of Judah . . ." (2 Chron. 17:2). This is also the emphasis in 1 Kings 15:20: "Ben-hadad . . . sent the captains of the hosts which he had [NASB, "commanders of his armies"] against the cities of Israel. . . ."

Fifth, *chayil* sometimes represents the "upper class," who, as in all feudal systems, were at once soldiers, wealthy, and influential; Sanballat "spake before his brethren and the army of Samaria," i.e., in the royal court (NASB, "wealthy men"; Neh. 4:2). The Queen of Sheba was accompanied by a large escort of upper-class people from her homeland: "And she came to Jerusalem with a very great train . . ." (1 Kings 10:2).

TO STRETCH OUT

A. Verb.

nātāh (נָטָה), "to stretch forth, spread out, stretch down, turn aside." This verb also occurs in Arabic, late Aramaic, and post-biblical Hebrew. The Bible attests it in all periods and about 215 times.

Nātāh connotes "extending something outward and toward" something or someone. So God told Moses: ". . . I will redeem you with a stretched out arm, and with great judgments" (Exod. 6:6). This is a figure of God's active, sovereign, and mighty involvement in the affairs of men. So this phrase means "to stretch out" something until it reaches a goal. The verb can also mean "to stretch out toward" but not to touch or reach anything. God told Moses to tell Aaron to take his staff in hand (cf. Exod. 9:23) and "stretch it out." This act was to be done as a sign. The pointed staff was a visible sign that God's power was directly related to God's messengers: ". . . Take thy rod, and stretch out thine hand upon the waters of Egypt, upon their streams, upon their rivers, and upon their ponds . . . ," over all the water in Egypt (Exod. 7:19). God "stretched out" (offered) 3 things to David (1 Chron. 21:10); this is a related sense with the absence of anything physical being "stretched out."

This verb may connote "stretch out" but not toward anything. When a shadow "stretches out," it lengthens. Hezekiah remarked: "It is a light thing for the shadow to go down ten degrees . . ." (2 Kings 20:10), to grow longer. *Nātāh* may be used in this sense without an object and referring to a day. The Levite was asked to "comfort thine heart, I pray thee. And they tarried until afternoon [literally, the "stretching" (of the day, or of the shadows)] . . ." (Judg. 19:8). "To stretch out" one's limbs full length is to recline: "And they lay themselves down upon clothes laid to pledge by every altar . . ." (Amos 2:8). This is a figure of temple prostitution. This verb may also mean "to extend" in every direction. It represents what one does in pitching a tent by unrolling the canvas (or skins sewn together) and "stretching it out." The end product is that the canvas is properly "spread out." Abram "pitched his tent, having Beth-el on the west, and Hai on the east . . ." (Gen. 12:8—the first appearance of the word). This act and its result is used as a figure of God's creating the heavens: ". . . Which alone spreadeth out the heavens . . ." (Job 9:8).

This verb also implies "stretching down toward" so as to reach something. Earlier in the Bible Rebekah was asked to "let down thy pitcher, . . . that I may drink" (Gen. 24:14); she was asked to "stretch it down" into the water. This is the nuance when God is said to have "inclined [stretched down] unto me, and heard my cry" (Ps. 40:1). Issachar is described as a donkey which "bowed his shoulder to bear [burdens]" (Gen. 49:15). In somewhat the same sense the heavens are bowed; the heavens are made to come closer to the earth. This is a figure of the presence of thick clouds: "He bowed the heavens also, and came down: and darkness was under his feet" (Ps. 18:9). The somewhat new element here is that the heavens do not touch the speaker but only "stretch downward" toward him.

This verb may mean "to turn aside" in the sense of "to visit": ". . . Judah went down from his brethren, and turned in to [visited] a certain Adullamite . . ." (Gen. 38:1). Another special nuance appears in Num. 22:23, where it means "to go off the way": "And the ass saw the angel of the Lord standing in the way . . ., and the ass turned aside out of the way. . . ." Applied to human relationships, this may connote seduction: "With her much fair speech she caused him to yield . . ." (Prov. 7:21).

B. Nouns.

matteh (מַטֶּה), "rod; staff; tribe." This noun occurs about 250 times. In Gen. 38:18 the word refers to a shepherd's "staff": "And he said, What pledge shall I give thee? And she said, Thy signet, and thy bracelets, and thy staff that is in thine hand." The word is used to refer to a number of kinds of "rods": A "rod" which symbolizes spiritual power, such as Moses' rod (Exod. 4:2), Aaron's rod (Exod. 7:9), and the sorcerers' rods (Exod. 7:12), and rods symbolizing authority (Num. 17:7). This noun is often used elliptically instead of "the rod of the tribe of"; the word signifies "tribe" (cf. Exod. 31:2). *Matteh* is also used in the phrase "the staff of bread," of staves around which loaves are suspended to keep them from mice (Lev. 26:26).

Some other nouns are related to the verb *nātāh. Muttôth* occurs once (Isa. 8:8) and refers to the "stretching out" of wings. *Mittāh* occurs about 29 times and means something which is stretched out. *Mittāh* is used of a couch (Song of Sol. 3:7) and of a metal framework (Esth. 1:6). *Mittāh* may also refer to a room, a bedchamber (2 Kings 11:2).

C. Adverb.

mattāh (מַטָּה), "downwards; beneath." This word occurs about 17 times. It means "beneath" (Deut. 28:13), "downward" (2 Kings 19:30), and "underneath" (Exod. 28:27).

STRIFE

A. Verb.

rîb (רִיב), "to strive, contend." This verb occurs 65 times and in all periods of biblical Hebrew.

In Exod. 21:18 *rîb* is used in connection with a physical struggle: "And if men strive together, and one smite another with a stone, or with his fist, and he die not. . . ." *Rîb* appears in Judg. 6:32 with the meaning of "to contend against" through words.

B. Nouns.

rîb (רִיב), "strife; quarrel; dispute; case; contentions; cause." This noun has a cognate only in Aramaic. Its 60 occurrences appear in all periods of biblical Hebrew.

The noun *rîb* is used of conflicts outside the realm of law cases and courts. This conflict between individuals may break out into a quarrel, as in Prov. 17:14: "The beginning of strife is as when one letteth out water: therefore leave off contention, before it be meddled with." In Gen. 13:7-8 (the first occurrence of *rîb*) the word is used of "contention" prior to open fighting between two groups: "And there was a strife between the herdmen of Abram's cattle and the herdmen of Lot's cattle. . . ." In such a case the one with the "strife" is clearly the guilty party.

Rîb sometimes represents a "dispute" between two parties. This "dispute" is set in the context of a mutual law structure binding both parties and a court which is empowered to decide and execute justice. This may involve "contention" between two unequal parties (an individual and a group), as when all Israel quarreled with Moses, asserting that he had not kept his end of the bargain by adequately providing for them. Moses appealed to the Judge, who vindicated him by sending water from a rock (cliff?) smitten by Moses: "And he called the name of the place Massah, and Meribah, because of the chiding [quarrel] of the children of Israel . . ." (Exod. 17:7). God decided who was the guilty party, Moses or Israel. The "contention" may be between two individuals as in Deut. 25:1, where the two disputants go to court (having a "case or dispute" does not mean one is a wrongdoer): "If there be a controversy between men, and they come unto judgment, that the judges may judge them; then they shall justify the righteous, and condemn the wicked." So in Isa. 1:23 the unjust judge accepts a bribe and does not allow the widow's just "cause" (NASB, "widow's plea") to come before him. Prov. 25:8-9 admonishes the wise to "debate thy cause with thy neighbor" when that neighbor has "put thee to shame."

Rîb may represent what goes on in an actual court situation. It is used of the entire process of adjudication: "Neither shalt thou [be partial to] a poor man in his cause" (Exod. 23:3; cf. Deut. 19:17). It is also used of the various parts of a lawsuit. In Job 29:16 Job defends his righteousness by asserting that he became an advocate for the defenseless: "I was a father to the poor: and the cause which I knew not I searched out." Here, then, the word means the false charge brought against a defendant. Earlier in the Book of Job (13:6), *rîb* represents the argument for the defense: "Hear now my reasoning, and hearken to the pleadings of my lips." Elsewhere the word represents the argument for the prosecution: "Give heed to me, O Lord, and hearken to the voice of them that contend with me [literally, "the men presenting the case for the prosecution"]" (Jer. 18:19). Finally, in Isa. 34:8 *rîb* signifies a "case" already argued and won and awaiting justice: "For it is the day of the Lord's vengeance, and the year of recompenses for the controversy of Zion."

Two other related nouns occur rarely. *Mərîbāh* occurs twice, and it means "strife." The word refers to an extra-legal (Gen. 13:8) and to a legal confrontation (Num. 27:14). *Yārîb* appears 3 times to mean "disputant; opponent; adversary" (Ps. 35:1; Isa. 49:25; Jer. 18:19).

TO BE STRONG

A. Verb.

chāzaq (חָזַק), "to be strong, strengthen, harden, take hold of." This verb is found 290 times in the Old Testament. The root also exists in Aramaic and Arabic.

The word first occurs in Gen. 41:56: ". . . And the famine waxed sore in the land of Egypt" (NASB, NIV, "was severe"). The strong form of the verb is used in Exod. 4:21: ". . . I will harden his [Pharaoh's] heart. . . ." This statement is found 8 times. Four times we read: "Pharaoh's heart was hard" (Exod. 7:13, 22; 8:19; 9:35 NIV; KJV, RSV, NASB, "was hardened"). In Exod. 9:34 Pharaoh's responsibility is made clear by the statement "he sinned yet more, and hardened his heart. . . ."

In the sense of personal strength *chāzaq* is first used in Deut. 11:8 in the context of the covenant: "Therefore shall ye keep all the commandments which I command you this day, that ye may be strong, and go in and possess the land. . . ." Moses was commanded to "charge Joshua, and encourage him" (Deut. 3:28). The covenant promise accompanies the injunction to "be strong and of a good courage": ". . . For the Lord thy God, he it is that doth go with thee; he will not fail thee, nor forsake thee" (Deut. 31:6). The same encouragement was given to the returned captives as they renewed the work of rebuilding the temple (Zech. 8:9, 13; cf. Hag. 2:4).

If in the above examples there is moral strength combined with physical, the latter is the sense of Judg. 1:28: "And it came to pass, when Israel was strong, that they put the Canaanites to [forced labor]. . . ." Israel sinned and the Lord "strengthened Eglon the king of Moab against Israel" (Judg. 3:12). The word is used in reference to a building: ". . . The priests had not repaired the breaches of the house" (2 Kings 12:6), or to a city: "Moreover Uzziah built towers in Jerusalem . . . and fortified them" (2 Chron. 26:9). In battle *chāzaq* means: "So David prevailed over the Philistine . . ." (1 Sam. 17:50).

As the prophet said, "For the eyes of the Lord run to and fro throughout the whole earth, to show himself strong in the behalf of them [NASB, "to strongly support them"] whose heart is perfect toward him" (2 Chron. 16:9). To His Servant, the Messiah, God said: "I . . . will hold thine hand . . ." (Isa. 42:6); and to Cyrus He said: ". . . Whose right hand I have holden . . ." (Isa. 45:1).

Other noteworthy uses of the word are: ". . . Thou shalt relieve him [a poor Israelite] . . ." (Lev. 25:35); and ". . . [Saul] laid hold upon the skirt of his mantle, and it rent" (1 Sam. 15:27).

In summary, this word group describes the physical and moral strength of man and society. God communicates strength to men, even to the enemies of His people as chastisement for His own. Men may turn their strength into stubbornness against God.

B. Adjective.

chāzāq (חָזָק), "strong; mighty; heavy; severe; firm; hard." This adjective occurs about 56 times and in all periods of biblical Hebrew.

First, the word means "firm" or "hard" in the sense that something is impenetrable. In Ezek. 3:8-9 the prophet's face is compared to rock; God has made him determined to his task just as Israel is determined not to listen to him: "Behold, I have made thy face [hard] against their faces, and thy forehead [hard] against their foreheads. As an adamant harder than flint have I made thy forehead. . . ." Job 37:18 uses *chāzāq* of molten solidified metal.

Second, this word means "strong." In its basic meaning it refers to physical strength. God's hand (an anthropomorphism; cf. Deut. 4:15, 19) as a symbol of His effecting His will among men is "strong": "And I am sure that the king of Egypt will not let you go, no, not by a mighty hand" (Exod. 3:19—the first biblical occurrence). This word modifies a noun, specifying that it is the opposite of weak, or unable to effect anything (Num. 13:18). Isaiah speaks of God's "sore and great and strong sword" (27:1). When Ezekiel wrote of "fat and strong" animals, he probably meant that they were well fed and healthy (34:16).

Third, *chāzāq* means "heavy." When applied to a battle or war, it describes the event(s) as severe (1 Sam. 14:52). The word is also used to indicate a severe sickness (1 Kings 17:17) and famine (1 Kings 18:2).

TO STUMBLE, BE WEAK

kāshal (כָּשַׁל), "to stumble, stagger, totter, be thrown down." As in biblical Hebrew, this word is used in modern Hebrew in the sense of "to stumble, fail." It occurs in the text of the Hebrew Old Testament approximately 60 times, the first time being in Lev. 26:37: "And they shall fall one upon another. . . ." This use illustrates the basic idea that one "stumbles" because of something or over something. Heavy physical burdens cause one "to stagger": ". . . The children fell under the [loads of] wood" (Lam. 5:13).

This word is often used figuratively to describe the consequences of divine judgment on sin: "Behold, I will lay stumblingblocks before this people, and the fathers and the sons together shall fall upon them . . ." (Jer. 6:21). Babylon, too, will know God's judgment: "And the most proud shall stumble and fall . . ." (Jer. 50:32). When the psalmist says: "My knees totter from my fasting" (Ps. 109:24 NAB), he means: "My knees are weak" (as translated by KJV, NASB, RSV, JB, NEB, TEV).

STUPID FELLOW

kəsîl (כְּסִיל), "stupid fellow; dull person; fool." This word occurs in the Old Testament 70 times. All of its occurrences are in wisdom literature except 3 in the Psalms.

The *kəsîl* is "insolent" in religion and "stupid or dull" in wise living (living out a religion he professes). In Ps. 92:6 the first emphasis is especially prominent: "A brutish man knoweth not; neither doth a fool understand this." The psalmist is describing an enemy of God who knew God and His word but, seeing the wicked flourishing, reasoned that they have the right life-style (Ps.

92:7). They have knowledge of God but do not properly evaluate or understand what they know. The second emphasis is especially prominent in wisdom contexts: "How long, ye simple ones, will ye love simplicity? and the scorners delight in their scorning, and fools hate knowledge?" (Prov. 1:22). In such contexts the person so described rejects the claims and teachings of wisdom. However, in the Bible wisdom is the practical outworking of one's religion. Therefore, even in these contexts there is a clear connotation of insolence in religion.

Kesel means "stupidity; imperturbability; confidence." This noun occurs 6 times. It means "stupidity" in Eccl. 7:25 and "confidence" in Prov. 3:26. The meaning of "confidence" also appears in Job 31:24: "If I have made gold my *hope. . . .*"

SUBURBS

A. Noun.

migərāsh (מִגְרָשׁ), "suburbs; pasture land; open land." This noun occurs about 100 times, mainly in Joshua and First Chronicles. It denotes the untilled ground outside a city or the "pasture land" belonging to the cities: "For the children of Joseph were two tribes, Manasseh and Ephraim: therefore they gave no part unto the Levites in the land, save cities to dwell in, with their suburbs for their cattle and for their substance" (Josh. 14:4).

Ezekiel describes a strip of land for the Levites around the city. Part of the land was to be used for houses and part to be left: "And the five thousand, that are left in the breadth over against the five and twenty thousand, shall be a profane place for the city, for dwelling, and for suburbs: and the city shall be in the midst thereof" (Ezek. 48:15).

The Septuagint translates the word *perisporia* ("suburb").

B. Verb.

gārash (גָּרַשׁ), "to drive out, cast out." This verb occurs about 45 times. An early occurrence in the Old Testament is in Exod. 34:11: ". . . Behold, I drive out before thee the Amorite, and the Canaanite. . . ." The word may be used of a divorced woman as in Lev. 21:7—a woman that is "put away from her husband."

SUFFICIENCY

day (דַּי), "sufficiency; the required; enough." Cognates of this word appear in late Aramaic, Syriac, and Phoenician. Its 42 biblical occurrences appear in all periods of biblical Hebrew.

The word is translated variously according to the needs of a given passage. The meaning "sufficiency" is clearly manifested in Exod. 36:7: "For the stuff they had was sufficient for all the work to make it, and too much." A different translation is warranted in Jer. 49:9: "If thieves [come] by night, they will destroy till they have enough'' (cf. Obad. 5). In Prov. 25:16 the word means only what one's digestive system can handle: "Hast thou found honey? Eat so much as is sufficient for thee, lest thou be filled therewith, and vomit it." Other passages use this word of money (Deut. 15:8). In Jer. 51:58 *day* preceded by the preposition *bә* means "only for": ". . . The people shall labor in vain [only for nothing], and the folk in the fire [only for fire], and they shall be weary." The phrase "as long as there is need" signifies until there is no more required (Mal. 3:10, NEB; KJV, "that there shall not be room enough to receive it"). The word first appears in Exod. 36:5 and is preceded by the preposition *min:* "The people bring much more than enough for the service of the work, which the Lord commanded to make."

There are many special uses of *day* where the basic meaning is in the background and the context dictates a different nuance. In Job 39:25 the word preceded by the preposition *bә* may be rendered "as often as": "As often as the trumpet sounds he says, Aha!" (NASB). When preceded by the preposition *kә*, "as," the word usually means "according to": ". . . The judge shall cause him to lie down, and to be beaten before his face, according to his fault, by a certain number" (Deut. 25:2). Preceded by *min,* "from," the word sometimes means "regarding the need." This illuminates passages such as 1 Sam. 7:16: "And he [Samuel] went from year to year [according to the need of each year; NASB, "annually"] in circuit to Beth-el . . ." (cf. Isa. 66:23). In other places this phrase (*day* preceded by *min*) signifies "as often as": "Then the princes of the Philistines went forth: and it came to pass, after [NASB, "as often as"] they went forth, that David behaved himself more wisely than all the servants of Saul . . ." (1 Sam. 18:30).

SUN

shemesh (שֶׁמֶשׁ), "sun; Shamshu (?); sunshield; battlement." Cognates of this word occur in Ugaritic *(sh-p-sh),* Akkadian, Aramaic, Phoenician, and Arabic. It appears 134 times in biblical Hebrew and in all periods.

This word means "sun": "And when the sun was going down, a deep sleep fell upon Abram . . ." (Gen. 15:12—the first occurrence of the word). The "wings of the sun" are probably its rays (Mal. 4:2). The "sun" and especially its regularity supported by divine sovereignty (Gen. 8:22) figures the security of God's allies: "So let all thine enemies perish, O Lord: but let them that love him be as the sun when he goeth forth in his might" (Judg. 5:31). God can also make the "sun" stand still when He wishes (Josh. 10:12–13) or darken as an indication of His judgment upon His enemies and salvation for His people (Joel 2:31-32). The "sun" and all the heavenly bodies were created by God (Gen. 1:16) and are summoned to praise Him (Ps. 148:3). The Canaanites and other people worshiped the "sun" as a god, and this paganism appeared among Israelites in times of spiritual decline (Deut. 4:19). In 2 Kings 23:5 perhaps one could translate: "Those who burned incense to Shamshu" (cf. v. 11). Perhaps passages like Ps. 148:3 are allusions to the sun god (although this is questionable).

Shemesh is used in phrases indicating direction. The east is "the rising of the sun'': ''And they journeyed from Oboth, . . . toward the sunrising'' (Num. 21:11). The west is ''the setting of the sun'': ''Are they not on the other side of Jordan, by the way where the sun goeth down . . . ?'' (Deut. 11:30).

In Ps. 84:11 the word represents a sun-shaped shield: ''For the Lord God is a sun and shield. . . .''

Shemesh may be a structural term: ''And I will make thy windows [NASB, ''battlements''] of agates, and thy gates of carbuncles . . .'' (Isa. 54:12).

There are a few noteworthy phrases related to *shemesh*. To be ''before the sun'' or ''before the eyes of the sun'' is to be openly exposed: ''Take all the heads of the people, and hang them up before the Lord against the sun [NASB, ''in broad daylight'']. . .'' (Num. 25:4). To ''see the sun'' is ''to live'': ''. . . Like the untimely birth of a woman, that they may not see the sun'' (Ps. 58:8). Something ''under the sun'' is life lived on the earth apart from God in contrast to life lived on earth with a proper relationship with God (Eccl. 1:3).

TO SWALLOW

bāla‘ (בָּלַע), ''to swallow, engulf.'' Commonly used throughout the history of the Hebrew language, this word is also found in ancient Akkadian, as well as several other Semitic languages. It occurs about 50 times in the Hebrew Old Testament. *Bāla‘* is first used in Gen. 41:7 in Pharaoh's dream of seven lean ears of grain ''swallowing up'' the seven plump ears.

While it is used of the normal physical swallowing of something quite frequently, such as Jonah's ''being swallowed'' by the great fish (Jon. 1:17), the word is used more often in the figurative sense, often implying destruction. Thus, the violent ''overwhelm'' the innocent (Prov. 1:11-12); an enemy ''swallows'' those he conquers ''like a dragon'' (Jer. 51:34); and the false prophet and priest ''are swallowed up of wine'' (Isa. 28:7; RSV, ''confused with'').

TO SWEAR

shāba‘ (שָׁבַע), ''to swear; take an oath.'' This is a common word throughout the history of the Hebrew language. The fact that it occurs more than 180 times in the Hebrew Bible attests to its importance there also. *Shāba‘* occurs for the first time in the Hebrew Bible in Gen. 21:23-24, where Abimelech requests Abraham to ''. . . swear unto me here by God that thou wilt not deal falsely with me, nor with my son. . . . And Abraham said, I will swear.''

Often ''to swear or to take an oath'' is to strongly affirm a promise. Thus, Joshua instructs the spies concerning Rahab of Jericho: ''Go into the harlot's house, and bring out thence the woman, and all that she hath, as ye sware unto her'' (Josh. 6:22). David and Jonathan strongly affirmed their love for each other with an oath (1 Sam. 20:17). Allegiance to God is pledged by an oath (Isa. 19:18). Zephaniah condemns the idolatrous priests ''that worship and that swear by the Lord, and that swear by Malcham [the Ammonite god]''

(Zeph. 1:5). In making and upholding His promises to men, God often "swears" by Himself. To Abraham after his test involving His command to sacrifice his son Isaac, God said: "By myself have I sworn, saith the Lord, for because thou hast done this thing, and hast not withheld thy son, thine only son: That in blessing I will bless thee . . ." (Gen. 22:16-17; cf. Isa. 45:23; Jer. 22:5). God also "swears" by His holiness (Amos 4:2).

The root for "to swear" and the root for "seven" are the same in Hebrew, and since the number seven is the "perfect number," some have conjectured that "to swear" is to somehow "seven oneself," thus to bind oneself with seven things. Perhaps this is paralleled by the use of "seven" in Samson's allowing himself to be bound by seven fresh bowstrings (Judg. 16:7) and weaving the seven locks of his head (Judg. 16:13). The relationship between "to swear" and "seven" is inconclusive.

SWORD

A. Noun.

chereb (חֶרֶב), "sword; dagger; flint knife; chisel." This noun has cognates in several other Semitic languages including Ugaritic, Aramaic, Syriac, Akkadian, and Arabic. The word occurs about 410 times and in all periods of biblical Hebrew.

Usually *chereb* represents an implement that can be or is being used in war, such as a "sword." The exact shape of that implement, however, is not specified by this word. Present-day archaeology has unearthed various sickle swords and daggers from the earliest periods. Sickle swords are so named because they are shaped somewhat like a sickle with the outer edge of the arc being the cutting edge. These were long one-edged "swords." This is what *chereb* refers to when one reads of someone's being slain with the edge of the "sword": "And they slew Hamor and Shechem his son with the edge of the sword, and took Dinah out of Shechem's house . . ." (Gen. 34:26). The first biblical occurrence of the word (Gen. 3:24) probably also represents such an implement: ". . . And he placed at the east of the garden of Eden cherubim, and a flaming sword which turned every way. . . ."

The precise meaning of *chereb* is confused, however, by its application to what we know as a "dagger," a short two-edged sword: "But Ehud made him a dagger which had two edges, of a cubit [eighteen to twenty-four inches] length . . ." (Judg. 3:16).

The sickle sword was probably the implement used up to and during the conquest of Palestine. About the same time the Sea Peoples (among whom were the Philistines) were invading the ancient Near East. They brought with them a new weapon—the long two-edged "sword." The first clear mention of such a "sword" in the biblical record appears in 1 Sam. 17:51: "Therefore David ran, and stood upon the Philistine [Goliath], and took his sword, and drew it out of the sheath thereof, and slew him. . . ." Perhaps Saul also used the highly superior Philistine armor and "sword" (1 Sam. 17:39), but this is not clear. It is also possible that the angel who confronted Balaam with a drawn "sword" wielded a long two-edged "sword" (Num. 22:23). Certainly this would have made him (humanly speaking) a much more formidable sight. By the time of David, with his expertise and concern for warfare, the large two-edged "sword" was much more prominent if not the primary kind of "sword" used by Israel's heavy infantry.

This two-edged "sword" can be compared to a tongue: ". . . Even the sons of men, whose teeth are spears and arrows, and their tongue a sharp sword" (Ps. 57:4). This usage tells us not only about the shape of the "sword" but that such a tongue is a violent, merciless, attacking weapon. In Gen. 27:40 "sword" is symbolic of violence: "And by thy sword shalt thou live. . . ." Prov. 5:4 uses *chereb* (of a long two-edged "sword") to depict the grievous result of dealing with an adulteress; it is certain death: "But her end is bitter as wormwood, sharp as a two-edged sword."

The "sword" is frequently depicted as an agent of God. It is not only used to safeguard the garden of Eden, but figures the judgment of God executed upon His enemies: "For my sword shall be bathed in heaven: behold, it shall come down upon Idumea . . ." (Isa. 34:5; cf. Deut. 28:22).

Chereb may be used of various other cutting implements. In Josh. 5:2 it means "knife": "Make thee sharp knives, and circumcise again the children of Israel the second time." Ezek. 5:1 uses *chereb* of a barber's "razor": "And thou, son of man, take thee a sharp knife, take thee a barber's razor, and cause it to pass upon thine head and upon thy beard. . . ." The exact size and shape of this tool cannot be determined, but it is clear that it was used as a razor.

This word can also be used of tools ("chisels") for hewing stone: "And if thou wilt make me an altar of stone, thou shalt not build it of hewn stone: for if thou lift up thy tool upon it, thou hast polluted it" (Exod. 20:25). The fact that a "sword," an implement of death, would be used to cut the stone for an altar, the instrument of life, explains why this action would profane the altar.

B. Verb.

Chārab means "to smite down; slaughter." This verb, which appears 3 times in biblical Hebrew, has cognates in Arabic. The word appears in 2 Kings 3:23: "This is blood: the kings are surely slain. . . ."

TABERNACLE

A. Noun.

mishəkān (מִשְׁכָּן), "dwelling place; tabernacle; shrine." This word appears 139 times and refers in its first occurrence to the "tabernacle": "According to all that I show thee, after the pattern of the tabernacle, and the pattern of all the instruments thereof, even so shall ye make it" (Exod. 25:9). *Mishəkān* is found primarily in Exodus and Numbers, and it always designates the sanctuary. With this meaning it is a synonym for the phrase "tent of meeting." In total, 100 out of the 139 uses of *mishəkān* throughout the Old Testament signify the tabernacle as "dwelling place." God dwelt amidst His people in the wilderness, and His presence was symbolically manifest in the tent of meeting. The word *mishəkān* places the emphasis on the representative presence of God: "And I will set my tabernacle among you: and my soul shall not abhor you. And I will walk among you, and will be your God, and ye shall be my people. I am the Lord your God, which brought you forth out of the land of Egypt, that ye should not be their bondmen; and I have broken the bands of your yoke, and made you go upright" (Lev. 26:11-13). Hence, sin among the Israelites defiled God's "dwelling-place" (Lev. 15:31; cf. Num. 19:13).

Whereas the "tabernacle" was mobile, the temple was built for the particular purpose of religious worship: ". . . I have not dwelt in any house since the time that I brought up the children of Israel out of Egypt, even to this day, but have walked in a tent and in a tabernacle" (2 Sam. 7:6). Solomon built it and the finished structure was known as "the house," the temple, instead of the dwelling place *(mishəkān)*. In later literature *mishəkān* is a poetic synonym for "temple": "I will not give sleep . . . until I find out a place for the Lord, a *habitation* for the mighty God of Jacob" (Ps. 132:4-5). The meaning of *mishəkān* was also extended to include the whole area surrounding the temple, as much as the city Jerusalem: "There is a river, the streams whereof shall make glad the city of God, the holy place of the tabernacles of the Most High" (Ps. 46:4), "the Lord loveth the gates of Zion more than all the dwellings of Jacob" (Ps. 87:2).

The defilement of the city and the temple area was sufficient reason for God to leave the temple (Ezek. 10) and to permit the destruction of His "dwelling place" by the brutish Babylonians: "They have cast fire into thy sanctuary, they have defiled by casting down the dwelling place of thy name to the ground" (Ps. 74:7). In the Lord's providence He had planned to restore His people and the temple so as to assure them of His continued presence: "My tabernacle also shall be with them: yea, I will be their God, and they shall be my people. And the heathen shall know that I the Lord do sanctify Israel, when my sanctuary shall be in the midst of them for evermore" (Ezek. 37:27-28). John comments that Jesus Christ was God's "tabernacle": "And the Word was made flesh, and dwelt among us, (and we beheld his glory, the glory as of the only begotten of the Father,) full of grace and truth" (John 1:14), and Jesus later referred to Himself as the temple: "But He spake of the temple of his body" (John 2:21).

In non-religious use *mishəkān* is "the dwelling place" of an individual (Num. 16:24), of Israel (Num. 24:5), and of strangers (Hab. 1:6).

The usual translation of *mishəkān* in the Septuagint is *skene* ("dwelling; booth"), which is also the translation for *'ōhel*, "tent." It has been suggested that the similarity in sound of the Hebrew *shākan* and the Greek *skene* influenced the translation. Another translation is *skenoma* ("tent; dwelling; lodging"). The translations in the KJV are: "tabernacle; dwelling place; dwelling; habitation."

B. Verb.

shākēn (שָׁכֵן), "to dwell, inhabit." This verb, which occurs about 129 times in biblical Hebrew, is found also in other Semitic languages. In Akkadian *śakānu,* "to lay, to set up, to be situated," has many forms, such as the noun *maskana,* "dwelling place." One occurrence of the verb is in Ps. 37:27: "Depart from evil, and do good; and dwell for evermore."

TO TAKE, HANDLE

tāphas (תָּפַשׂ), "to catch, seize, lay hold of, grasp, play." This verb is found in both biblical and modern Hebrew. It occurs approximately 60 times in the Hebrew Old Testament. The word is found for the first time in Gen. 4:21, where it expresses the idea of grasping something in one's hand in order to use it: ". . . He was the father of all such as handle the harp and organ." Other things that are "seized" with the hand, or "handled," are: swords (Ezek. 21:11), shields (Jer. 46:9), bows (Amos 2:15), and sickles (Jer. 50:16). The expert in *tôrāh,* "law," is one who "handles" the law, but he sometimes mishandles it also: ". . .They that handle the law knew me not. . ." (Jer. 2:8).

"To seize" someone may be to arrest him: ". . . Irijah took [NASB, "arrested"] Jeremiah, and brought him to the princes" (Jer. 37:14). Frequently, *tāphas* is used in the sense of "to capture": "And the king of Ai they took alive, and brought him to Joshua" (Josh. 8:23). "To lay hold of," or "seize," hearts is to terrorize: "That I may take the house of Israel in their own heart, because they are all estranged from me through their idols" (Ezek. 14:5).

'āchaz (אָחַז), "to seize, grasp, take hold, take possession." Found in various Semitic languages, including ancient Akkadian, this word is a common one throughout the stages of the Hebrew language. It occurs almost 70 times in the Hebrew Old Testament. It is used for the first time in the Old Testament in the passive sense with reference to the ram "caught in a thicket by his horns" (Gen. 22:13) and thus became a substitute for Isaac.

While *'āchaz* is a common term for taking hold of things physically, such as Jacob's "taking hold" of Esau's heel (Gen. 25:26), *'āchaz* is frequently used in a metaphorical or figurative sense. In His wrath, God "seized" Job by the neck (Job 16:12). On the other hand, the psalmist testifies that in His grace, God "holds" his right hand (Ps. 73:23). Pain and trembling "seize" the enemies of Israel (Exod. 15:14-15). Horror "seizes" the people of the east (Job 18:20).

This word gives us the name of Ahaz, king of Judah (2 Kings 16).

TO TAKE AWAY

A. Verb.

lāqach (לָקַח), "to take; receive; take away." This word occurs in all Semitic languages and in all periods of Hebrew. It occurs about 965 times in the Old Testament.

Primarily this word means "to take, grasp, take hold of," as when Noah reached out and "took hold of" the dove to bring it back into the ark (Gen. 8:9). A secondary meaning is "to take away, remove, take to oneself," as when the invading kings "took away" and "took to themselves" all the movable goods of the cities of the plain (Gen. 14:11). Sometimes this verb implies "to receive something from someone." So Abraham asks Ephron the Hittite to "receive from" his hand payment for the field which contained the sepulchre (Gen. 23:13). With the particle "for" *lāqach* means "to take someone or something," as when Joseph's brothers remarked that they were afraid he was scheming "to take" them to be slaves, mentioned in Gen. 43:18. Another secondary use of this word is "to transfer" a thing, concept, or emotion, such as "take vengeance" (Isa. 47:3), "receive reproach" (Ezek. 36:30), and "receive a [whisper]" (Job 4:12). In other passages this verb is virtually a helping verb serving to prepare for an action stipulated in a subsequent verb; God "took" Adam and put him into the garden of Eden (Gen. 2:15—the first occurrence of the verb). Finally, this word can be used elliptically, suggesting the phrase "take and bring," but only "taken" is written. Noah is told to "take" (and bring) clean animals by sevens into the ark (Gen. 7:2).

This verb is used of God in several connections. Sometimes God is pictured as having bodily parts (anthropomorphically). This is the implication of Gen. 2:15, where the Lord "took" Adam and put him into Eden. God's taking sometimes connotes election, as when He "took" Abraham from his father's house (Gen. 24:7). He also "takes" in the sense of taking to Himself or accepting. Thus, He "accepts" offerings (Judg. 13:23) and prayers (Ps. 6:9). God "takes away" in judgment David's wives (2 Sam. 12:11) and the kingdom (1 Kings 11:34).

Of special interest is the use of the verb in the absolute sense: God "took away" Enoch so that he was not found on earth (Gen. 5:24). This meaning of receiving one into heaven to Himself seems to be the force of Ps. 73:24 and perhaps of Ps. 49:15.

lākad (לָכַד), "to capture; seize; take captive." This term is found in both ancient and modern Hebrew. It occurs about 120 times in biblical Hebrew and is found for the first time in the text in Num. 21:32, where the Israelites are said to have taken the villages of the Amorites.

The act of "capturing, seizing" is usually connected with fighting wars or battles, so a variety of objects may be taken. Cities are often "captured" in war (Josh. 8:21; 10:1; Judg. 1:8, 12). Land or territory also is taken as booty of war (Josh. 10:42; Dan. 11:18). Strategic geographic areas such as watercourses "are captured" (Judg. 3:28). Sometimes kings and princes "are seized" in battle (Judg. 7:25; 8:12, 14), as well as fighting men and horses (2 Sam. 8:4). Saul is spoken of as actually taking the kingdom, apparently by force of arms (1 Sam. 14:47). In establishing the source of Israel's defeat by Ai, lots were used "to take or separate" the guilty party, Achan and his family (Josh. 7:14).

Occasionally *lākad* is used in the figurative sense, especially in terms of men "being caught" in the trap of divine judgment (Ps. 9:15; Isa. 8:15; 24:18).

B. Nouns.

leqach (לֶקַח), "teaching; instruction; persuasiveness; understanding." The word is used in the sense of something taken in. This noun occurs 9 times in the Old Testament, several times in Proverbs. One occurrence is in Prov. 1:5: "A wise man will hear, and will increase learning. . . ." The word refers to "persuasiveness" in Prov. 7:21.

Several other nouns are related to *lāqach*. *Maləqôach* refers to "things taken in warfare," and it appears 7 times (Num. 31:32). *Maləqôach* also means "jaws" once (Ps. 22:15). *Meləqāchayim* refers to "snuffers" (Exod. 37:23), and it is found 6 times. *Miqqāch* occurs once to mean "taking" (2 Chron. 19:7). *Maqqāchôth* means "wares" once (Neh. 10:31).

TO TEACH

A. Verbs.

lāmad (לָמַד), "to teach, learn, cause to learn." This common Semitic term is found throughout the history of the Hebrew language and in ancient Akkadian and Ugaritic. *Lāmad* is found approximately 85 times in the text of the Hebrew Old Testament. In its simple, active form, this verb has the meaning "to learn," but it is also found in a form giving the causative sense, "to teach." This word is first used in the Hebrew Old Testament in Deut. 4:1: ". . . Hearken, O Israel, unto the statutes and unto the judgments, which I teach you. . . ."

In Deut. 5:1 *lāmad* is used of learning God's laws: "Hear, O Israel, the statutes and judgments which I speak in your ears this day, that ye may learn them, and keep, and do them." A similar meaning occurs in Ps. 119:7. The word may be used of learning other things: works of the heathen (Ps. 106:35); wisdom (Prov. 30:3); and war (Mic. 4:3).

About half the occurrences of *lāmad* are found in the books of Deuteronomy and Psalms, underlining the teaching emphasis found in these books. Judaism's traditional emphasis on teaching and thus preserving its faith clearly has its basis in the stress on teaching the faith found in the Old Testament, specifically Deut. 6:4-9. Following the Shema', the "watchword of Judaism" that declares that Yahweh is One (Deut. 6:4), is the "first great commandment" (Deut. 6:5; Mark 12:28–29). When Moses delivered the Law to his people, he said, ". . . The Lord commanded me at that time to teach you statutes and judgments . . ." (Deut. 4:14).

The later Jewish term *talmud*, "instruction," is derived from this verb.

yārāh (יָרָה), "to throw, teach, shoot, point out." Found in all periods of the Hebrew language, this root is also found in ancient Ugaritic with the sense of "to shoot"; modern Hebrew uses the word to express the firing of a gun. *Yārāh* occurs approximately 80 times in the Hebrew Old Testament.

The first use of this verb in the Old Testament is in Gen. 31:51: ". . . Behold this pillar, which I have cast betwixt me and thee." This basic meaning, "to throw or cast," is expressed in "casting" lots (Josh. 18:6) and by Pharaoh's army "being cast" into the sea (Exod. 15:4).

The idea of "to throw" is easily extended to mean the shooting of arrows (1 Sam. 20:36-37). "To throw" seems to be further extended to mean "to point," by which fingers are thrown in a certain direction (Gen. 46:28; Prov. 6:13).

From this meaning it is only a short step to the concept of teaching as the "pointing out" of fact and truth. Thus, Bezaleel was inspired by God "to teach" others his craftsmanship (Exod. 35:34); the false prophets "teach" lies (Isa. 9:15); and the father "taught" his son (Prov. 4:4). It was the responsibility of the priests to interpret and "to teach" those things that had to do with ceremonial requirements and God's judgments: "They shall teach Jacob thy judgments, and Israel thy law . . ." (Deut. 33:10; cf. Deut. 17:10-11). Interestingly, priests at a later time were said "to teach" for hire, presumably "to teach" what was wanted rather than true interpretation of God's word (Mic. 3:11).

B. Noun.

tôrāh (תּוֹרָה), "direction; instruction; guideline." From *yārāh* is derived *tôrāh,* one of the most important words in the Old Testament. Seen against the background of the verb *yārāh,* it becomes clear that *tôrāh* is much more than law or a set of rules. *Tôrāh* is not restriction or hindrance, but instead the means whereby one can reach a goal or ideal. In the truest sense, *tôrāh* was given to Israel to enable her to truly become and remain God's special people. One might say that in keeping *tôrāh,* Israel was kept. Unfortunately, Israel fell into the trap of keeping *tôrāh* as something imposed, and for itself, rather than as a means of becoming what God intended for her. The means became the end. Instead of seeing *tôrāh* as a guideline, it became an external body of rules, and thus a weight rather than a freeing and guiding power. This burden, plus the legalism of Roman law, forms the background of the New Testament tradition of law, especially as Paul struggles with it in his Letter to the church at Rome.

C. Adjective.

Limmûd means "taught." This adjective forms an exact equivalent to the New Testament idea of "disciple, one who is taught." This is well expressed in Isa. 8:16: ". . . Seal the law among my disciples." The word also occurs in Isa. 54:13: "And all thy children shall be taught of the Lord. . . ."

TO TELL

A. Verb.

nāgad (נָגַד), "to tell, explain, inform." An exact equivalent to this verb is not known outside biblical Hebrew except in late Aramaic. The verb occurs around 335 times and in all periods of biblical Hebrew.

The first emphasis of the word is "to tell." This especially means that A (frequently a messenger or some other person who has witnessed something) "tells" B (the one to whom the report is made) C (the report). In such instances B (the one told) is spatially separated from the original source of the information. So, in Gen. 9:22, Ham (A) saw his father naked and went outside the tent and "told" his brothers (B) what he had seen (C).

In another group of passages *nāgad* represents the reporting of a messenger about a matter of life-or-death importance for the recipient. So a fugitive "came . . . and told Abram" that Lot had been captured and led away captive (Gen. 14:13). A note of this emotionally charged situation is seen in Jacob's message to Esau: ". . . I have sent to tell my lord, that I may find grace in thy sight" (Gen. 32:5). Although not a report from a messenger from afar, Gen. 12:18 uses the verb of a report that is of crucial importance to the one addressed. Pharaoh asked Abram: "Why didst thou not tell me that she was thy wife?" Gen. 12:17 reports that because Pharaoh had taken Sarai into his harem to become his wife, God had smitten his household with great plagues.

Finally, *nāgad* means "to explain or reveal" something one does not otherwise know. In Gen. 3:11 (the first biblical occurrence of the word) God asked Adam: "Who told thee that thou wast naked?" This was information immediately before them but not previously grasped by them. This usage appears in Gen. 41:24, where Pharaoh said of his dream: ". . . I told this unto the magicians; but there was none that could declare it to me." Similarly, David made certain there were no survivors from the Philistine cities he looted so no one would "tell" it to Achish (1 Sam. 27:11). This word sometimes has a more forceful significance—God told the prophet to "show my people their transgression" (Isa. 58:1).

B. Noun.

nāgîd (נָגִיד), "chief leader." This noun occurs 44 times in biblical Hebrew. In 1 Sam. 9:16 the word is used as a "chief leader" that is equivalent to a king: "Tomorrow about this time I will send thee a man out of the land of Benjamin, and thou shalt anoint him to be captain over my people Israel. . . ." *Nāgîd* appears in 1 Chron. 9:11 to refer to a "chief leader" (ruler) of a smaller region. The word may also be used of a head of a family (1 Chron. 9:20).

C. Preposition.

neged (נֶגֶד), "before; in the presence of; in the sight of; in front of; in one's estimation; straight ahead." This word occurs 156 times in biblical Hebrew as a preposition and an adverb. Basically the word indicates that its object is immediately "before" something or someone. It is used in Gen. 2:18, where God said He would make Adam "a help meet for him," or someone to correspond to him, just as the males and females of the animals corresponded to (matched) one another. To be immediately "before" the sun is to be fully in the sunlight (Num. 25:4). In Exod. 10:10 Pharaoh told Moses that evil was immediately "before" his face, or was in his mind. *Neged* signifies "in front of" (Exod. 19:2), "before" in the sense of "in one's estimation" (Isa. 40:17), and "straight ahead (before)" (Josh 6:5). In combination with other particles *neged* means "contrary to" (Num. 22:32).

D. Adverb.

neged (נֶגֶד), "opposite; over against." This meaning of *neged* appears in Gen. 21:16: "And she went, and sat her down over against him a good way off. . . ."

TEMPLE

hêkāl (הֵיכָל), "palace; temple." This word is indirectly derived from the Sumerian *é-gal*, "large house, palace," and more directly from the Akkadian *ēkallu*, "large house." The influence of the Akkadian *ēkallu* spread to the Northwest Semitic languages. In post-biblical Hebrew the meaning became limited to "temple." The *Hekhal Shlomo* ("Temple of Solomon") in modern Jerusalem signifies the building of Israel's chief rabbinate, in absence of the temple. The word occurs 78 times from First Samuel to Malachi, most frequently in Ezekiel. The first usage pertains to the tabernacle at Shiloh (1 Sam. 1:9).

The word "palace" in English versions may have one of three Hebrew words behind it: *hêkāl, bayîth,* or *'arəmôn*. The Sumero-Akkadian meaning "palace" for *hêkāl* is still to be found in biblical Hebrew. The *hêkāl* with its 15 usages as "palace" refers to the palaces of Ahab (1 Kings 21:1), of the king of Babylon (2 Kings 20:18), and of Nineveh (Nah. 2:6). The "palace" was luxuriously decorated and the residents enjoyed the fulfilment of their pleasures; cf.: "And the wild beasts of the islands shall cry in their desolate houses, and dragons in their pleasant palaces: and her time is near to come, and her days shall not be prolonged" (Isa. 13:22). The psalmist compared beautiful girls to fine pillars in an ornate "palace": ". . . That our sons may be as plants grown up in their youth; that our daughters may be as corner stones, polished after the similitude of a palace" (Ps. 144:12). Amos prophesied that the "songs of the palace" (KJV, "temple") were to turn to wailing at the destruction of the northern kingdom (Amos 8:3 NASB).

Hêkāl with the meaning "temple" is generally clarified in the context by two markers that follow. The first marker is the addition "of the Lord": "And when the builders laid the foundation of the temple of the Lord, they set the priests in their apparel with trumpets, and the Levites the sons of Asaph with cymbals, to praise the Lord, after the ordinance of David king of Israel" (Ezra 3:10). The second marker is a form of the word *qōdesh*, "holy": "O God, the heathen are come into thine inheritance; thy holy temple have they defiled; they have laid Jerusalem on heaps" (Ps. 79:1). Sometimes the definite article suffices to identify the "temple in Jerusalem": "In the year that King Uzziah died I saw also the Lord sitting upon a throne, high and lifted up, and his train filled the temple" (Isa. 6:1), especially in a section dealing with the "temple" (Ezek. 41).

The Old Testament also speaks about the heavenly *hêkāl*, the *hêkāl* of God. It is difficult to decide on a translation, whether "palace" or "temple." Most versions opt in favor of the "temple" idea: "Hear, all ye people; hearken, O earth, and all that therein is: and let the Lord God be witness against you, the

Lord from his holy temple'' (Mic. 1:2; cf. Ps. 5:7; 11:4; Hab. 2:20). ''In my distress I called upon the Lord, and cried to my God: and he did hear my voice out of his temple, and my cry did enter into his ears'' (2 Sam. 22:7). However, since Scripture portrays the presence of the royal judgment throne in heaven, it is not altogether impossible that the original authors had a royal ''palace'' in mind. The imagery of the throne, the ''palace,'' and judgment seems to lie behind Ps. 11:4-5. ''The Lord is in his holy temple, the Lord's throne is in heaven: his eyes behold, his eyelids try, the children of men. The Lord trieth the righteous: but the wicked and him that loveth violence his soul hateth.''

The Septuagint has the words *naos* (''temple'') and *oikos* (''house; palace; dwelling; household'').

TENT

'ōhel (אֹהֶל), ''tent; home; dwelling; habitation.'' Cognates of this word appear in Ugaritic, Phoenician, and Arabic. It appears about 343 times in biblical Hebrew and in all periods.

First, this word refers to the mobile structure called a ''tent.'' This is its meaning in Gen. 4:20: ''And Adah bare Jabal: he was the father of such as dwell in tents, and of such as have cattle.'' These are what nomadic Bedouins normally live in. ''Tents'' can also be used as housing for animals: ''They smote also the tents of cattle [NASB, ''those who owned''], and carried away sheep and camels in abundance . . .'' (2 Chron. 14:15). Soldiers lived in ''tents'' during military campaigns (1 Sam. 17:54). A ''tent'' was pitched on top of a house so everyone could see that Absalom went in to his father's concubines (2 Sam. 16:22). This constituted an open rejection of David's dominion and a declaration that he (Absalom) was claiming the throne.

Second, the word is a synonym for ''home, dwelling,'' and ''habitation.'' This emphasis is especially evident in Judg. 19:9: ''. . . Behold, the day groweth to an end, lodge here, that thine heart may be merry; and tomorrow get you early on your way, that thou mayest go home.'' This meaning appears in the phrase ''to your tents'': ''We have no part in David, neither have we inheritance in the son of Jesse: every man to his tents, O Israel'' (2 Sam. 20:1). The ''tabernacle'' (''tent'') of David, therefore, is his dwelling place or palace (Isa. 16:5). Similarly, the ''tabernacle (''tent'') of the daughter of Zion is Israel's capital, or what Israel inhabits—Jerusalem (Lam. 2:4).

Third, *'ōhel* may represent those who dwell in the dwellings of a given area or who form a unit of people. Thus the ''tents'' of Judah are her inhabitants: ''The Lord also shall save the tents of Judah first, that the glory of the house of David and the glory of the inhabitants of Jerusalem do not magnify themselves against Judah'' (Zech. 12:7; cf. Ps. 83:6).

Bedouin ''tents'' today (as in the past) are constructed of strong black cloth of woven goat's hair. They are shaped variously. The women pitch them by stretching the cloth over poles and tying it down with cords of goat's hair or hemp. Wooden mallets are used to drive the tent pegs into the ground (Judg. 4:21). Sometimes the structure is divided in order to separate families or to separate animals from people (2 Chron. 14:15). The back of the ''tent'' is closed and the front open. The door is made by turning back the fold where the two ends of the cloth meet (Gen. 18:1). The "tent" and all its contents are transported on the back of a single pack animal. Richer people cover the floor with mats of various materials. A chief or sheikh may have several "tents"—one for himself and his guest(s), another for his wives and other females in his immediate family, and still another for the animals (Gen. 31:33).

Before the construction of the tabernacle Moses pitched a "tent" outside the camp (Exod. 33:7). There he met with God. The "tent" outside the camp persisted as a living institution for only a short period after the construction of the tabernacle and before the departure from Sinai (Num. 11:16 ff.; 12:4 ff.). Eventually the ark of the covenant was moved into the tabernacle (Exod. 40:21) where the Lord met with Moses and spoke to Israel (Exod. 29:42). This structure is called the tent of meeting inasmuch as it contained the ark of the covenant and the tables of testimony (Num. 9:15). As the tent of meeting it was the place where God met with His people through Moses (or the high priest) and revealed His will to them (1 Sam. 2:22).

TO TEST

A. Verb.

tsāraph (צָרַף), "to refine; try; smelt; test." This root with the basic meaning of smelting and refining is found outside the Old Testament in Akkadian, Phoenician, and Syriac. In Arabic an adjective derived from the verb means "pure, unmixed," describing the quality of wine. *Tsāraph* has maintained the meaning "to refine" in rabbinic and modern Hebrew, but lost the primary significance of "to smelt" in modern Hebrew.

The verb occurs fewer than 35 times in the Old Testament, mainly in the prophets and in the Book of Psalms. The first occurrence is in the story of Gideon, where 10,000 are "being tested" and only 300 are chosen to fight with Gideon against the Midianites: "And the Lord said unto Gideon, The people are yet too many; bring them down unto the water, and I will try them for thee there . . ." (Judg. 7:4). The meaning in this context is "to test," to find out who is qualified for battle. The only other occurrence of the verb in Judges is equivalent to a noun in English: "smith," in this context a silversmith (17:4).

Jeremiah describes the process of smelting and refining: "The bellows [blow fiercely], the lead is consumed of the fire; the founder melteth in vain: for the wicked are not plucked away" (Jer. 6:29), and the failure of refining the silver leads to rejection (Jer. 6:30). The process (smelting) and the result (refining) are often considered together. It is difficult to separate them in biblical usage. Hence, the work of the smith involves smelting, refining, and particularly the use of the refined metals in making the final product: "The workman melteth a graven image, and the goldsmith spreadeth it over with gold, and casteth silver chains" (Isa. 40:19). He used a hammer and anvil in making fine layers of gold used in plating the form (Isa. 41:7).

Tsāraph is also used metaphorically with the sense "to refine by means of suffering." The psalmist describes the experience of Israel in this way: "For thou, O God, hast proved us: thou hast tried us, as silver is tried. Thou . . . laidst affliction upon our loins. . . . We went through fire and through water: but thou broughtest us out into a wealthy place'' (Ps. 66:10-12). God's judgment is also described as a process of refining: ''And I will . . . purely purge away thy dross, and take away all thy tin'' (Isa. 1:25). Those who were thus purified are those who call on the name of the Lord and receive the gracious benefits of the covenant (Zech. 13:9). The coming of the messenger of the covenant (Jesus Christ) is compared to the work of a smith: ''But who may abide the day of his coming? and who shall stand when he appeareth? for he is like a refiner's fire. . . . And he shall sit as a refiner and purifier of silver: and he shall purify the sons of Levi, and purge them as gold and silver . . .'' (Mal. 3:2-3). The believer can take comfort in the Word of God which alone on earth is tried and purified and by which we can be purified: ''Thy promise is well tried, and thy servant loves it'' (Ps. 119:140 RSV; cf. Ps. 18:30; Prov. 30:5).

Tsāraph has the following translations in the Septuagint: *purao* (''to burn; to make red hot'') and *chruso-o* (''to gild; to overlay with gold''). The KJV gives the following translations: ''to refine; try; melt; founder; goldsmith.'' In the RSV, NASB, and NIV the verb ''to test'' is given instead of ''to try.''

B. Nouns.

Two nouns derived from the verb *tsāraph* occur rarely. *Tsōrəphî* occurs once to mean ''goldsmith'' (Neh. 3:31). *Matsərēph* occurs twice and refers to a ''crucible'': ''The fining pot is for silver, and the furnace is for gold: but the Lord trieth the hearts'' (Prov. 17:3; cf. Prov. 27:21).

TESTIMONY

'ēdûth (עֵדוּת), ''testimony; ordinance.'' The 83 occurrences of this word are scattered throughout all types of biblical literature and all periods (although not before the giving of the law at Mount Sinai).

This word refers to the Ten Commandments as a solemn divine charge or duty. In particular, it represents those commandments as written on the tablets and existing as a reminder and ''testimony'' of Israel's relationship and responsibility to God: ''And he gave unto Moses, when he had made an end of communing with him upon mount Sinai, two tables of testimony, tables of stone, written with the finger of God'' (Exod. 31:18). Elsewhere these tablets are called simply ''the testimony'' (Exod. 25:16). Since they were kept in the ark, it became known as the ''ark of the testimony'' (Exod. 25:22) or simply ''the testimony'': ''As the Lord commanded Moses, so Aaron laid it up before the Testimony, to be kept'' (Exod. 16:34—the first biblical occurrence of the word). The tabernacle as the housing for the ark containing these tablets was sometimes called the ''tabernacle of testimony'' (Exod. 38:21) or the ''tent of the testimony'' (Num. 9:15).

The word sometimes refers to the entire law of God: ''The law of the Lord is perfect, converting the soul: the testimony of the Lord is sure, making wise the simple'' (Ps. 19:7). Here *'ēdûth* is synonymously parallel to ''law,'' making it a synonym to that larger concept. Special or particular laws are sometimes called "testimonies": "And keep the charge of the Lord thy God, to walk in his ways, to keep his statutes, and his commandments, and his judgments, and his testimonies . . ." (1 Kings 2:3). In Ps. 122:4 the annual pilgrimage feasts are called "the testimony of Israel."

THERE IS

yēsh (יֵשׁ), "there is; substance; he/she/it is/are." Cognates of this word are attested in Ugaritic, Aramaic, Akkadian, Amorite, and Arabic. It appears about 137 times and in all periods of biblical Hebrew.

This particle is used substantively only in Prov. 8:21: ". . . That I may cause those that love me to inherit substance; and I will fill their treasures."

In all other appearances the word asserts existence with emphasis. Sometimes *yēsh* appears with a predicate following, as it does in Gen. 28:16: "And Jacob awaked out of his sleep, and he said, Surely the Lord is in this place; and I knew it not." In a few passages the word is used as a response to an inquiry: "Is the seer here? And they [the young maidens] answered them, and said, He is; behold, he is before you . . ." (1 Sam. 9:11-12). Used absolutely the word can mean "there is/are/was/were," as it does in Gen. 18:24 (the first biblical appearance): "Peradventure there be fifty righteous within the city . . . ?" In many contexts *yēsh* used in framing questions or protestations suggests doubt that the matter queried exists or is to be found: "As the Lord thy God liveth, there is no nation or kingdom, whither my lord hath not sent to seek thee: and when they said, He is not there; he took an oath of the kingdom and nation, that they found thee not" (1 Kings 18:10). This is especially clear in Jer. 5:1, where God commands the prophet to go and seek "if ye can find a man, if there be any that executeth judgment, that seeketh the truth. . . ."

There are several other special uses of *yēsh*. Used with the particle *'im* and a participle, it emphasizes abiding intention: "And I came this day unto the well, and said, O Lord God of my master Abraham, if now thou do prosper my way which I go [literally, if there surely is a prospering of my way; or if it surely is that you intend to prosper] . . ." (Gen. 24:42). Possession is sometimes indicated by *yēsh* plus the preposition *lə:* "And Esau said, I have enough, my brother . . ." (Gen. 33:9). Used with the infinitive and the preposition *lə*, *yēsh* signifies possibility—Elisha told the Shunammite woman: ". . . Behold, thou hast been careful for us with all this care; what is to be done for thee? *wouldest* thou be spoken for ɔ the king, or to the captain of the host [is it possible that you want me to speak a word in your behalf to]?" (2 Kings 4:13).

TO THINK, DEVISE

A. Verb.

chāshab (חָשַׁב), "to think, devise, purpose, esteem, count, imagine, impute." This word appears 123 times in the Old Testament, and it implies any mental process involved in planning or conceiving.

Chāshab can be translated as "devise" in association with the sense of "to think and reckon." A gifted person of God "devises" excellent works in gold and other choice objects (Exod. 35:35). The word may deal with evil, as when Haman "devised" an evil plot against the Jewish people (Esth. 8:3). David issued his prayer against those who "devise" evil toward him as a servant of the Lord (Ps. 35:4), and the scoundrel "devises" perverse things in Prov. 16:30. Other verses indicating an immoral intent behind the action of "devising" are Jer. 18:11; 18:18; Ezek. 11:2.

The word may mean "think." Some "thought" to do away with David by sending him against the Philistines (1 Sam. 18:25); Judah "thought" Tamar to be a harlot (Gen. 38:15); and Eli "thought" Hannah was drunk (1 Sam. 1:13). God repented of the evil concerning the judgment he "thought" to bring upon Israel (Jer. 18:8). Those who fear the Lord may also "think" upon His name (Mal. 3:16).

Chāshab may be rendered "to purpose" or "esteem." God asked Job if he could tame the Leviathan, who ". . . esteemeth him as straw, and brass as rotten wood" (Job 41:27). A classic usage of "esteem" appears in Isa. 53:3-4: "He [the Messiah] is despised and rejected of men; a man of sorrows, and acquainted with grief; and we hid as it were our faces from him; he was despised, and we esteemed him not. Surely he hath borne our griefs. . . . Yet we did esteem him stricken, smitten of God, and afflicted." Some uses of "to purpose" have a malevolent intent. David's enemies have "purpose" to overthrow him (Ps. 140:4). God repented of the evil He "purposed" to do concerning Israel (Jer. 26:3), and perhaps the people will repent when they hear the evil God has "purposed" against the nation (Jer. 36:3). On the other hand, God "purposes" evil against the land of the Chaldeans in His judgment after using them for the purification of His people, Israel (Jer. 50:45).

Translated as "count," the word is used in a number of ways. It had a commercial connotation, as when land was being redeemed and the price was established, based on the value of crops until the next year of Jubilee: "Then let him count the years of the sale thereof, and restore the overplus . . ." (Lev. 25:27). The same idea concerns the provisions for the Levites when Israel offered their gifts to the Lord (Num. 18:30). "Count" may imply "to be thought or reckoned." Bildad declared to Job, "Wherefore are we counted as beasts, and reputed vile in your sight?" (Job 18:3). Those who seek to live for the Lord are "counted" as sheep for the slaughter (Ps. 44:22). The foolish person, when he holds his peace, is "counted" as wise (Prov. 17:28). A theological emphasis exists in God's reward of Abraham, when the patriarch believed God and His word: "And he believed in the Lord; and he counted it to him for righteousness" (Gen. 15:6).

Most uses of *chāshab* translated as "imagine" bear an evil connotation. Job chided his friends: "Do ye imagine to reprove words, and the speeches of one that is desperate . . ." (Job 6:26); David's enemies "imagined" a mischievous device (Ps. 21:11); and Nahum complained of those who "imagine" evil against the Lord (Nah. 1:11).

Other unique translations of *chāshab* occur. In order to approach God, Asaph had to remember and "consider" the days of old (Ps. 77:5). God had a controversy with Nebuchadnezzar, king of Babylon, because he "conceived" a plan against Him and His people (Jer. 49:30). The prophet Amos cites people who "invent" instruments of music and enjoy it (Amos 6:5). Huram of Tyre sent a man to help Solomon in the building of the temple, who knew how to "find out" all the works of art—i.e., he could work in various metals and fabrics to design a work of beauty (2 Chron. 2:14). Joseph had to remind his brethren that he did not seek to do them harm because they had sold him into slavery, since God "meant" it for the good of the preservation of Jacob's sons (Gen. 50:20).

Infrequently, *chāshab* is translated as "impute": "And if any of the flesh of the sacrifice of his peace offerings be eaten at all on the third day, it shall not be accepted, neither shall it be imputed unto him that offereth it; it shall be an abomination" (Lev. 7:18). When an Israelite killed a sacrifice in any place except an appointed altar, the blood was "imputed" to that man; the substitute sacrifice would not atone for the offerer at all, and the offerer would bear his own guilt (Lev. 17:4). David could praise God for forgiveness because the Lord will not "impute" iniquity after he had confessed his sin (Ps. 32:2).

B. Adjective.

chāshab (חָשֵׁב), "cunning." This word is applied to those who performed "cunning" work with parts of the tabernacle: "And with him was Aholiab, son of Ahisamach, . . . an engraver, and a cunning workman . . ." (Exod. 38:23). This meaning of *chāshab* as "cunning" appears 11 times in Exodus. But this skill was more than human invention—it indicated how the Spirit of God imparts wisdom, understanding, and knowledge (cf. Exod. 36:8; 39:3).

THRONE

kissē' (כִּסֵּא), "throne; seat." This word, with the basic meaning "seat of honor," occurs in many Semitic languages (Ugaritic, Phoenician, Aramaic, Syriac, Arabic) and in ancient Egyptian.

Kissē' occurs 130 times in the Hebrew Old Testament and, as is to be expected, the frequency is greater in the historical books and the prophetical works. It is rare in the Pentateuch. The first usage of *kissē'* is in Gen. 41:40: "Thou shalt be over my house, and according unto thy word shall all my people be ruled: only in the throne will I be greater than thou." In modern Hebrew the word mainly denotes a "chair," and "throne" is further described as a "royal chair."

In the Old Testament the basic meaning of *kissē'* is "seat" or "chair." Visitors were seated on a chair (1 Kings 2:19), as well as guests (2 Kings 4:10) and older men (1 Sam. 1:9). When the king or elders assembled to administer justice, they sat on the throne of justice (Prov. 20:8; cf. Ps. 9:4). In these contexts *kissē'* is associated with honor. However, in the case of the prostitute (Prov. 9:14) and soldiers who set up their chairs (Jer. 1:15—*kissē'* may mean "throne" here; cf. KJV, NASB, NIV), *kissē'* signifies a place and nothing more.

The more frequent sense of *kissē'* is "throne" or "seat of honor," also known as the "royal seat": "And it shall be, when he sitteth upon the throne of his kingdom, that he shall write him a copy of this law in a book out of that which is before the priests the Levites" (Deut. 17:18; cf. 1 Kings 1:46). Since the Davidic dynasty received the blessing of God, the Old Testament has a number of references to "the throne of David" (2 Sam. 3:10; Jer. 22:2, 30; 36:30): "Of the increase of his government and peace there shall be no end, upon the throne of David, and upon his kingdom, to order it, and to establish it with judgment and with justice from henceforth even for ever" (Isa. 9:7). The "throne of Israel" is a synonymous phrase for "throne of David" (1 Kings 2:4; cf. 8:20, 25; 9:5; 10:9; 2 Kings 10:30; 15:12, etc.).

The physical appearance of the "throne" manifested the glory of the king. Solomon's "throne" was an artistic product with ivory inlays, the wood covered with a layer of fine gold (1 Kings 10:18).

The word *kissē'* was also used to represent "kingship" and the succession to the throne. David had sworn that Solomon would sit on his "throne" (1 Kings 1:13; cf. 2 Kings 10:3).

Above all human kingship and "thrones" was the God of Israel: "God reigneth over the heathen: God sitteth upon the throne of his holiness" (Ps. 47:8). The Israelites viewed God as the ruler who was seated on a "throne." Micaiah said in the presence of Ahab and Jehoshaphat: "Hear thou therefore the word of the Lord: I saw the Lord sitting on his throne, and all the host of heaven standing by him on his right hand and on his left" (1 Kings 22:19). Isaiah received a vision of God's glory revealed in the temple (Isa. 6:1). The presence of the Lord in Jerusalem also gave rise to the conception that Jerusalem was the throne of God (Jer. 3:17).

The Septuagint translation is *thronos* ("throne; dominion; sovereignty").

TIME

A. Noun.

'ēth (עֵת), "time; period of time; appointed time; proper time; season." This word also appears in Phoenician, post-biblical Hebrew, Arabic (where the same radicals constitute a verb signifying "to appear"), and Akkadian (where these radicals form an adverb signifying "at the time when"). *'Ēth* appears about 290 times in the Bible and in all periods.

Basically this noun connotes "time" conceived as an opportunity or season. First, the word signifies an appointed, fixed, and set time or period. This is what astrologers claimed to discern: "Then the king said to the wise men, which knew the times . . ." (Esth. 1:13). God alone, however, knows and reveals such "appointed times": ". . . In the time of their visitation they shall be cast down, saith the Lord" (Jer. 8:12).

This noun also is used of the concept "proper or appropriate time." This nuance is applied to the "time" God has appointed for one to die: "Be not over much wicked, neither be thou foolish: why shouldest thou die before thy time?" (Eccl. 7:17). It is used of the "appropriate or suitable time" for a given activity in life: "He hath made every thing beautiful in his time . . ." (Eccl. 3:11; cf. Ps. 104:27). Finally, the "appropriate time" for divine judgment is represented by *'ēth:* "It is time for thee, Lord, to work: for they have made void thy law" (Ps. 119:126).

A third use connotes "season," or a regular fixed period of time such as springtime: "And he said, I will certainly return unto thee according to the time of life; and, lo, Sarah thy wife shall have a son" (Gen. 18:10). Similarly, the word is used of the rainy "season" (Ezra 10:13), the harvest "time" (Jer. 50:16), the migratory "period" (Jer. 8:7), and the mating "season" (Gen. 31:10).

This noun also is applied to differing "extensions of time." In its first biblical appearance, for example, *'ēth* represents the "time" (period of the day) when the sun is setting: "And the dove came in to him in the evening [literally, time of the evening] . . ." (Gen. 8:11). The word is used of special occasions such as the birth of a child (Mic. 5:3) and of periods during which certain conditions persist (Exod. 18:22; Dan. 12:11).

B. Verb.

'Ānāh means "to be exercised." The noun *'ēth* may be derived from this verb which occurs only 3 times in Hebrew poetry (cf. Eccl. 1:13). It may be related to an Arabic root meaning "to be disquieted or disturbed about something," an Ethiopic root and old South Arabic root meaning "to be concerned about." In later Hebrew this root means "to worry."

TOGETHER

A. Adverbs.

yachad (יַחַד), "together; alike; all at once; all together." *Yachad* appears about 46 times and in all periods of biblical Hebrew.

Used as an adverb, the word emphasizes a plurality in unity. In some contexts the connotation is on community in action. Goliath challenged the Israelites, saying: "I defy the armies of Israel this day; give me a man, that we may fight together" (1 Sam. 17:10). Sometimes the emphasis is on commonality of place: ". . . And it came to pass, that they which remained were scattered, so that two of them were not left together" (1 Sam. 11:11). The word can be used of being in the same place at the same time: "And he delivered them into the hands of the Gibeonites, and they hanged them in the hill before the Lord: and they fell all seven together . . ." (2 Sam. 21:9). In other passages *yachad* means "at the same time": "O that my grief were thoroughly weighed, and my calamity laid in the balances together!" (Job 6:2).

In many poetic contexts *yachad* is a near synonym of *kullām*, "altogether." *Yachad*, however, is more emphatic, meaning "all at once, all together." In Deut. 33:5 (the first biblical occurrence) the word is used emphatically, meaning "all together," or "all of them together": "And he was king in Jeshurun, when the heads of the people and the tribes of Israel were gathered together." Cf.: "Surely men of low degree are vanity, and men of high degree are a lie: to be laid in the balance, they are altogether lighter than vanity'' (Ps. 62:9). In such contexts *yachad* emphasizes the totality of a given group (cf. Ps. 33:15).

Yachad also sometimes emphasizes that things are "alike" or that the same thing will happen to all of them: "The fool and the stupid alike must perish" (Ps. 49:10 RSV).

yachədāw (יַחְדָּו), "all alike; equally; all at once; all together." The second adverbial form, *yachədāw,* appears about 92 times. It, too, speaks of community in action (Deut. 25:11), in place (Gen. 13:6—the first biblical appearance of this form), and in time (Ps. 4:8). In other places it, too, is synonymous with *kullām,* "altogether." In Isa. 10:8 *yachədāw* means "all alike," or "equally": "Are not my princes altogether kings?" In Exod. 19:8 this word implies "all at once" as well as "all together": "And all the people answered together, and said. . . ." The sense "alike" appears in Deut. 12:22: "Even as the roebuck and the hart is eaten, so thou shalt eat them: the unclean and the clean shall eat of them alike."

B. Verb.

Yāchad means "to be united, meet." This verb appears in the Bible 4 times and has cognates in Aramaic, Ugaritic, Arabic, Ethiopic, and Akkadian. One occurrence is in Gen. 49:6: "O my soul, come not thou into their secret; unto their assembly, mine honor, be not thou united. . . .''

C. Nouns.

yāchîd (יָחִיד), "very self." This word appears 12 times as a noun or as an adjective. *Yāchîd* has cognates in Ugaritic, Aramaic, and Syriac. The word can be used meaning "self, my soul": "Deliver my soul from the sword, my life [NASB, "only life"; KJV, "darling"] from the power of the dog" (Ps. 22:20 RSV; cf. Ps. 35:17).

The noun *yāchad* occurs only once to mean "unitedness." David said to the Benjaminites: "If ye be come peaceably unto me to help me, mine heart shall be knit unto you [I am ready to become one (or united) with you] . . ." (1 Chron. 12:17). This usage of the word as a substantive is unusual.

D. Adjective.

yāchîd (יָחִיד), "only; solitary; lonely." This word means "only": "Take now thy son, thine only son Isaac, whom thou lovest . . ." (Gen. 22:2—the first biblical occurrence of the word). In 2 passages this word means "solitary" or "lonely": "Turn thee unto me, and have mercy upon me; for I am desolate [RSV, "lonely"] and afflicted" (Ps. 25:16; cf. Ps. 68:6).

TOMORROW

A. Noun.

māchār (מָחָר), "tomorrow." This word has cognates in late Aramaic, Egyptian, Syriac, Phoenician, and Akkadian (here it appears with the word for "day"). *Māchār* appears as a noun or an adverb about 52 times in biblical Hebrew and in all periods of the language.

The word means the day following the present day: ". . . Tomorrow is the rest of the holy sabbath unto the Lord: bake that which ye will bake today . . ." (Exod. 16:23). *Māchār* also occurs as a noun in Prov. 27:1: "Boast not thyself of tomorrow; for thou knowest not what a day may bring forth."

B. Adverbs.

māchār (מָחָר), "tomorrow." The basic meaning of this word is clearly set forth in Exod. 19:10: "And the Lord said unto Moses, Go unto the people, and sanctify them today and tomorrow, and let them wash their clothes." In a few passages the Akkadian idiom is closely paralleled—the phrase *yôm māchār* is used: "So shall my righteousness answer for me in time to come [later] . . ." (Gen. 30:33). In most passages *māchār* by itself (used absolutely) means "tomorrow": "Behold, I go out from thee, and I will entreat the Lord that the swarms of flies may depart from Pharaoh, from his servants, and from his people, tomorrow . . ." (Exod. 8:29). Interestingly, in Exod. 8:10 the phrase *ləmāchār* (which appears 5 times in the Bible) is used: "And he said, Tomorrow." Used with the preposition *kə*, the word means "tomorrow about this time": "Behold, tomorrow about this time I will cause it to rain a very grievous hail . . ." (Exod. 9:18).

māchorāth (מָחֳרָת), "the next day." Closely related to the noun *māchār* is this adverb, which occurs about 32 times and in all periods of biblical Hebrew. About 28 times *māchorāth* is joined to the preposition *min* to mean "on the next day." This is its form and meaning in its first biblical appearance: "And it came to pass on the morrow . . ." (Gen. 19:34). In 3 passages this adverb is preceded by the preposition *lə*, but the meaning is the same: "And David smote them from the twilight even unto the evening of the next day . . ." (1 Sam. 30:17). In Num. 11:32 *māchorāth* appears after *yôm*, "day," and is preceded by the definite article: "And the people stood up all that day, and all that night, and all the next day, and they gathered the quails. . . ." First Chron. 29:21 displays yet another construction, with the same meaning: ". . . On the morrow after that day. . . ."

C. Verb.

'Āchar means "to be behind, tarry, defer." This verb, which occurs rarely in biblical Hebrew, is usually considered the root of *māchār*, "tomorrow." This verb appears in Prov. 23:30: "They that tarry long at the wine; they that go to seek mixed wine." The meaning of "to tarry" also occurs in Judg. 5:28: "Why tarry the wheels of his chariots?"

TONGUE

lāshôn (לָשׁוֹן), "tongue; language; speech." This word is thought to have the root meaning "to lick," but this is a conjecture. The noun occurs in Ugaritic, Akkadian *(Lišānu)*, Phoenician, and Arabic. In the Hebrew Old

Testament it appears 115 times, mainly in the poetic and, to a lesser extent, in the prophetical books. The first occurrence is in Gen. 10:5: "By these were the isles of the Gentiles divided in their lands; every one after his tongue, after their families, in their nations."

The basic meaning of *lāshôn* is "tongue," which as an organ of the body refers to humans (Lam. 4:4) and animals (Exod. 11:7; Job 41:1) The extended meaning of the word as an organ of speech occurs more frequently. A person may be "heavy" or "slow" of tongue or have a stammering "tongue" (Exod. 4:10); or he may be fluent and clear: "The heart also of the rash shall understand knowledge, and the tongue of the stammerers shall be ready to speak plainly" (Isa. 32:4). And see the description of the "tongue" in Ps. 45:1: "My heart is inditing a good matter: I speak of the things which I have made touching the King: my tongue is the pen of a ready writer." The word is often better translated as "speech," because of the negative and positive associations of *lāshôn*. Especially in the wisdom literature the manner of one's "speech" is considered to be the external expression of the character of the speaker. The fool's "speech" is unreliable (Ps. 5:9), deceitful (Ps. 109:2; 120:2-3; Prov. 6:17), boastful (Ps. 140:11), flattering (Prov. 26:28), slanderous (Ps. 15:3), and subversive (Prov. 10:31). The "tongue" of the righteous man heals (Prov. 15:4). While the "tongue" may be as sharp as a sword (Ps. 57:4), it is a means of giving life to the righteous and death to the wicked: "Death and life are in the power of the tongue: and they that love it shall eat the fruit thereof" (Prov. 18:21; cf. 21:23; 25:15). The biblical authors speak of divine inspiration as the Lord's enabling them to speak: "The Spirit of the Lord spake by me, and his word was in my tongue" (2 Sam. 23:2; cf. Prov. 16:1). "Tongue" with the meaning "speech" has as a synonym *peh*, "mouth" (Ps. 66:17), and more rarely *sāphāh*, "lip" (Job 27:4).

A further extension of meaning is "language." In Hebrew both *sāphāh* and *lāshôn* denote a foreign "language": "For with stammering lips and another tongue will he speak to this people" (Isa. 28:11). The foreigners to the "language" are well described in these words: "Thou shalt not see a fierce people, a people of a deeper speech than thou canst perceive; of a stammering tongue, that thou canst not understand" (Isa. 33:19).

Lāshôn also refers to objects that are shaped in the form of a tongue. Most important is the "tongue of fire," which even takes the character of "eating" or "devouring": "Therefore as the [tongues of fire] devoureth the stubble, and the flame consumeth the chaff . . ." (Isa. 5:24). The association in Isaiah of God's appearance in judgment with smoke and fire gave rise to a fine literary description of the Lord's anger: "Behold, the name of the Lord cometh from far, burning with his anger, and the burden thereof is heavy: his lips are full of indignation, and his tongue as a devouring fire" (Isa. 30:27). Notice the words "lips" and "tongue" here with the meaning of "flames of fire," even though the language evokes the representation of a tongue (as an organ of the body) together with a tongue (of fire). Also a bar of gold (Josh. 7:21) and a bay of the sea (Isa. 11:15) shaped in the form of a tongue were called *lāshôn*.

The Septuagint translation is *glossa* ("tongue; language").

TO TOUCH

A. Verb.

nāga' (נָגַע), "to touch, strike, reach, smite." Common throughout the history of the Hebrew language, this word is also found in Aramaic. It is used some 150 times in the Hebrew Old Testament. *Nāga'* first occurs in Gen. 3:3 in the Garden of Eden story, where the woman reminds the serpent that God had said: "Ye shall not eat of [the fruit of the tree which is in the midst of the garden], neither shall ye touch it. . . ." This illustrates the common meaning of physical touch involving various kinds of objects: Jacob's thigh was "touched" by the man at Jabbok (Gen. 32:25, 32); the Israelites were commanded not "to touch" Mount Horeb under pain of death (Exod. 19:12); and unclean things were not "to be touched" (Lev. 5:2–3).

Sometimes *nāga'* is used figuratively in the sense of emotional involvement: "And Saul also went home to Gibeah; and there went with him a band of men, whose hearts God had touched" (1 Sam. 10:26; NEB, "had moved"). The word is used to refer to sexual contact with another person, such as in Gen. 20:6, where God tells Abimelech that He did not allow him "to touch" Sarah, Abraham's wife (cf. Prov. 6:29). To refer to the touch of God's hand means that divine chastisement has been received: ". . . Have pity upon me, O ye my friends; for the hand of God hath touched me" (Job 19:21).

The word is commonly used also to describe "being stricken" with a disease: King Uzziah "was smitten" with leprosy (2 Chron. 26:20).

B. Noun.

nega' (נֶגַע), "plague; stroke; wound." This noun formed from *nāga'* occurs about 76 times in the Old Testament. The word refers to a "plague" most frequently (Gen. 12:17; Exod. 11:1). *Nega'* can also mean "stroke" (Deut. 17:8; 21:5) or "wound" (Prov. 6:33). Each meaning carries with it the sense of a person "being stricken or smitten in some way."

TOWER

migədāl (מִגְדָּל), "tower; small fortress; watchtower; podium." Cognates of this word appear in Ugaritic, Aramaic, Syriac, and Akkadian. The word occurs about 50 times in biblical Hebrew.

Migədāl means "tower." This is its use in Gen. 11:4 (the first occurrence of the word): "And they said, Go to, let us build us a city and a tower, whose top may reach unto heaven. . . ."

The word often refers to a "small fortress": "And he went up thence to Penuel, and spake unto them likewise: and the men of Penuel answered him as the men of Succoth had answered him. And he spake also unto the men of Penuel, saying, When I come again in peace, I will break down this tower" (Judg. 8:8-9).

Migədāl sometimes means "watchtower," one of the specially fortified towers safeguarding the gates of a city and spaced along city walls: "Moreover Uzziah built towers in Jerusalem at the corner gate, and at the valley gate, and at the [corner buttress], and fortified them" (2 Chron. 26:9).

In Neh. 8:4 the word is used of a wooden "podium": "And Ezra the scribe stood upon a pulpit of wood, which they had made for the purpose. . . ."

TO TRANSGRESS

A. Verb.

pasha' (פָּשַׁע), "to transgress, rebel." Apart from biblical Hebrew, this verb occurs in post-biblical Hebrew, in Palestinian Aramaic, and in Syriac, where it has the significance of "to be terrified" or "to be tepid, to be insipid." It does not appear in any other Semitic languages. The verb occurs 41 times in the Old Testament. It is not found in the Pentateuch. The first occurrence is in Solomon's prayer at the occasion of the dedication of the temple: "And forgive Thy people who have sinned against Thee and all their transgressions which they have transgressed against Thee . . ." (1 Kings 8:50 NASB).

The basic sense of *pasha'* is "to rebel." There are two stages of rebellion. First, the whole process of rebellion has independence in view: "Then Moab rebelled against Israel after the death of Ahab" (2 Kings 1:1). Second, the final result of the rebellion is the state of independence: "In his days Edom revolted from under the hand of Judah, and made a king over themselves" (2 Kings 8:20 NASB). A more radical meaning is the state of rebellion in which there is no end of the rebellion in view. The process is no longer goal-oriented. The state thus described refers to a *status quo:* "So Israel rebelled against the house of David unto this day" (1 Kings 12:19). The prepositions used (*bə,* "against," and more rarely *mittahat yād,* "from under the hand") indicate the object of revolt. The usage of *mittahat yād* with *pasha'* fits into the category of rebellion with no goal in view (2 Chron. 21:8, 10). It is best translated as an absolute, radical act ("to break away from").

Thus far, the usage has a king or a nation as the object of the revolt. Translations generally give the rendering "transgress" for *pasha'* when the act is committed against the Lord: "Woe unto them! for they have fled from me: destruction unto them! because they have transgressed against me . . ." (Hos. 7:13). This meaning also appears in Isa. 66:24: "And they shall go forth, and look upon the carcases of the men that have transgressed against me. . . ." The preposition *bə,* "against," before the name of God occurs about 10 times. In each case the act is an expression of an apostate way of life: "In transgressing and lying against the Lord, and departing away from our God, speaking oppression and revolt, conceiving and uttering from the heart words of falsehood" (Isa. 59:13).

The Septuagint translators are not consistent in the translation of *pasha'.* The most common translations are: *asebeo* ("to act unpiously"); *aphistemi* ("to go away, withdraw"); *anomos* ("lawless"); and *hamartia* ("sin"). The KJV gives these senses: "transgress; revolt; rebel."

B. Noun.

pesha' (פֶּשַׁע), "transgression; guilt; punishment; offering." A cognate of this word appears in Ugaritic. *Pesha'* appears 93 times and in all periods of biblical Hebrew.

Basically, this noun signifies wilful deviation from, and therefore rebellion against, the path of godly living. This emphasis is especially prominent in Amos 2:4: "For three transgressions of Judah, and for four, I will not turn away the punishment thereof; because they have despised the law of the Lord, and have not kept his commandments, and their lies caused them to err, after the which their fathers have walked." Such a wilful rebellion from a prescribed or agreed-upon path may be perpetrated against another man: ". . . Jacob answered and said to Laban, What is my trespass? what is my sin, that thou hast so hotly pursued after me?" (Gen. 31:36—the first occurrence of the word). Jacob is asking what he has done by way of violating or not keeping his responsibility (contract) with Laban. A nation can sin in this sense against another nation: "For three transgressions of Damascus, and for four . . . because they have threshed Gilead with threshing instruments of iron" (Amos 1:3). Usually, however, *pesha'* has immediate reference to one's relationship to God.

This word sometimes represents the guilt of such a transgression: "I am clean, without [guilt of] transgression, I am innocent; neither is there iniquity in me" (Job 33:9).

Pesha' can signify the punishment for transgression: "And a host was given him against the daily sacrifice by reason of transgression . . ." (Dan. 8:12); "How long shall be the vision concerning the daily sacrifice, and [punishment for] the transgression of desolation, to give both the sanctuary and the host to be trodden under foot?" (Dan. 8:13).

Finally, in Mic. 6:7 *pesha'* signifies an offering for "transgression": "Shall I give my first-born for my transgression [NASB, "for my rebellious acts"] . . . ?"

TREE

'ēts (עֵץ), "tree; wood; timber; stick; stalk." This word has cognates in Ugaritic, Akkadian, Phoenician, Aramaic *('ē'),* and Arabic. It occurs about 325 times in biblical Hebrew and in all periods.

In its first biblical appearance *'ēts* is used as a collective noun representing all trees bearing fruit (Gen. 1:11). In Exod. 9:25 the word means "tree" indiscriminately: ". . . And the hail smote every herb of the field, and brake every tree of the field." God forbids Israel to destroy the orchards around besieged cities: "When thou shalt besiege a city a long time, in making war against it to take it, thou shalt not destroy the trees . . . : for thou mayest eat of them [literally, ". . . its tree or orchard . . . for you may eat from it . . ."] . . ." (Deut. 20:19).

This word may signify a single "tree," as it does in Gen. 2:9: ". . . The tree of life also in the midst of the garden, and the tree of knowledge of good and evil."

This word may be used of the genus "tree." So Isa. 41:19 lists the olive "tree" and the box "tree" in the midst of a long list of various species of trees.

'Ēts can mean "wood." Thus, Deut. 16:21 should read: "You shall not plant for yourself an Asherah of any kind of wood" (NASB, "any kind of tree"). This word can represent "wood" as a material from which things are constructed, as a raw material to be carved: ". . . And in carving of timber, to work in all manner of workmanship" (Exod. 31:5). Large unprocessed pieces of "wood or timber" are also signified by *'ēts:* "Go up to the mountain, and bring wood [timber], and build the house . . ." (Hag. 1:8). The end product of wood already processed and fashioned into something may be indicated by *'ēts:* "And upon whatsoever any of them, when they are dead, doth fall, it shall be unclean; whether it be any vessel of wood . . ." (Lev. 11:32). This word means "stick" or "piece of wood" in Ezek. 37:16: ". . . Thou son of man, take thee one stick, and write upon it. . . ." This may also refer to a "pole" or "gallows": ". . . Within three days shall Pharaoh lift up thy head from off thee, and shall hang thee on a tree [gallows or pole] . . ." (Gen. 40:19).

'Ēts once means "stalk": "But she had brought them up to the roof of the house, and hid them with the stalks of flax, which she had laid in order upon the roof" (Josh. 2:6).

'ayil (אַיִל), "large, mighty tree." This word occurs 4 times and only in poetical passages. This does not mean a particular genus or species of tree but merely a large, mighty tree: "For they shall be ashamed of the [mighty trees] [KJV, RSV, NASB, "oaks"] which ye have desired . . ." (Isa. 1:29—the first biblical occurrence).

'ēlôn (אֵלוֹן), "large tree." This noun is probably related to *'ayil,* "large tree." *'Ēlôn* occurs 10 times and only in relation to places of worship. It may well be that these were all ancient cultic sites. The word does not represent a particular genus or species of tree but, like the noun to which it is related, simply a "big tree": "Gaal spoke again and said, Look, men are coming down from the center of the land, and one company is coming from the direction of the Diviners' oak [KJV, "Meonenim"; NASB, "oak"]" (Judg. 9:37 RSV). Judg. 9:6 speaks of the "tree of the pillar" (KJV, "plain of the pillar") in Shechem where the men of Shechem and Beth-millo made Abimelech king.

TO TRESPASS

A. Verb.

mā'al (מָעַל), "to trespass, act unfaithfully." This verb is not very common in Hebrew, biblical or rabbinic. It occurs 35 times in the Hebrew Old Testament, particularly in late Hebrew. Translations may give a separate translation of the verb and the noun *ma'al,* but most combine them into one phrase in which the verb takes the meaning of "to act" or "to commit"—e.g., Josh. 7:1: "But the children of Israel committed [*mā'al*] a trespass [*ma'al*] in the accursed thing . . ." (KJV); "But the Israelites acted unfaithfully" (NIV). Some versions give the sense more freely: "But the people of Israel broke faith" (RSV); "But the Israelites defied the ban" (NEB).

The first occurrence of the verb (together with the noun) is found in Lev. 5:15: "If a soul commit a trespass, and sin through ignorance. . . ." The sense of the verb is similar to the verb "to sin." In fact, in the next chapter the verb for "to sin" and *mā'al* are used together: "If a soul sin, and commit a trespass against the Lord, and lie unto his neighbor . . ." (Lev. 6:2). The combining of these two usages in Leviticus is significant. First, it shows that the verb may be a synonym for "to sin." *Mā'al* has basically this meaning in Lev. 5:15, since the sin is here out of ignorance instead of a deliberate act of treachery. Second, the meaning of *mā'al* is further expressed by a verb indicating the intent of being unfaithful to one's neighbor for personal profit ("commit a trespass against the Lord, and lie unto his neighbor . . .").

The offense is against God, even when one acts unfaithfully against one's neighbor. In 2 Chron. 29:6 we read: "For our fathers have trespassed, and done that which was evil in the eyes of the Lord our God, and have forsaken him . . ."; and Daniel prayed: ". . . Because of their trespass that they have trespassed against thee" (Dan. 9:7; cf. NIV, ". . . because of our unfaithfulness to you").

In view of the additional significance of "treachery," many versions translate the verb "to act unfaithfully" or "to act treacherously" instead of "to transgress" or "to commit a trespass." Both the verb and the noun have strongly negative overtones, which the translator must convey in English. When God spoke to Ezekiel: "Son of man, when the land sinneth against me by trespassing grievously, then will I stretch out mine hand upon it, and . . . cut off man and beast from it" (Ezek. 14:13), He communicated also His displeasure with Israel's rebellious, treacherous attitude. This is communicated in other versions: "Son of man, if a country sins against me by being unfaithful . . ." (NIV); "Son of man, if a country sins against Me by committing unfaithfulness . . ." (NASB).

The verb *mā'al* generally expresses man's unfaithfulness to God (Lev. 26:40; Deut. 32:51; 2 Chron. 12:2; Ezra 10:2; Ezek. 14:13). The word further signifies man's unfaithfulness to his fellow man; particularly it is illustrative of unfaithfulness in marriage: "If any man's wife go aside, and commit a trespass against him, And a man lie with her carnally . . . " (Num. 5:12-13). In this sense also must Lev. 6:2 be understood: "If anyone sins and is unfaithful to the Lord by deceiving his neighbor about something entrusted to him . . ." (NIV).

In the Septuagint we find these translations: *athetein* ("to nullify; reject; commit an offense"); *asunthetein* ("to be faithless"); and *aphistaveiv* ("to mislead; withdraw"). Modern versions set forth more explicitly the overt nature of the sin than the KJV ("trespass; transgress"): RSV, NASB, NIV, "act or be unfaithful"; RSV, NASB, "to break faith."

B. Noun.

ma'al (מַעַל), "trespass; unfaithful, treacherous act." This noun is used 29 times in biblical Hebrew. In addition to the primary sense of "trespass," given in KJV, there may be an indication of the motivation through which the sin was committed. Most of the usages support the idea of "faithlessness, treachery." It is an act committed by a person who knows better but who, for selfish motives, acts in bad faith. The story of Achan bears out the attitude of treachery (Josh. 7:1). Joshua challenged Israel not to follow the example of Achan: "Did not Achan the son of Zerah commit [*mā'al*] a trespass [*ma'al*] in the accursed thing, and wrath fell on all the congregation of Israel?" (Josh. 22:20).

In 2 Chron. 29:19 the "faithlessness" was committed against God: "Moreover all the vessels which king Ahaz in his reign did cast away in his transgression. . . ." *Ma'al* also appears in Ezra 9:2: ". . . Yea, the hand of the princes and rulers hath been chief in this trespass."

TRIBE

A. Nouns.

matteh (מַטֶּה), "staff; rod; shaft; branch; tribe." This noun is a distinctively Hebrew word. It occurs 251 times; the first usage is in Gen. 38:18: "And he said, What pledge shall I give thee? And she said, Thy signet, and thy bracelets, and thy staff that is in thine hand." The word appears most frequently in Numbers and Joshua, generally with the meaning "tribe" in these books.

The basic meaning of *matteh* is "staff." The use of the "staff" was in shepherding. Judah was a shepherd and gave his "staff" to his daughter-in-law, Tamar, as a pledge of sending her a kid of the flock (Gen. 38:17-18). Moses was a shepherd when he saw the vision of the burning bush and when the Lord turned his "staff" into a snake as a sign of His presence and power with Moses' mission (Exod. 4:2 ff.). His "staff" figured prominently throughout the wilderness journeys and was known as "the staff of God" because of the miraculous power connected with it: "And Moses said unto Joshua, Choose us out men, and go out, fight with Amalek: tomorrow I will stand on the top of the hill with the rod of God in mine hand" (Exod. 17:9). The "staff" was also a token of authority. The Egyptian magicians had "staffs" as symbols of their authority over the magical realm by which they duplicated several miracles (Exod. 7:12). Aaron had a "rod," which alone sprouted and put forth buds, whereas eleven rods "from all their leaders according to their father's household" (Num. 17:2 NASB) did not put forth buds.

The "staff" further signifies authority or power over another nation: "For thou hast broken the yoke of his burden, and the staff of his shoulder, the rod of his oppressor, as in the day of Midian" (Isa. 9:4). God gave to Assyria His "staff"; they received His authority, divine permission, to wield the sword, to plunder, and to destroy: "O Assyrian, the rod of mine anger, and the staff in their hand is mine indignation. I will send him against a hypocritical nation, and against the people of my wrath will I give him a charge, to take the spoil, and to take the prey, and to tread them down like the mire of the streets" (Isa. 10:5-6). The psalmist, in his expectation that the messianic rule included God's authority and judgment over the Gentiles, views the messianic rule as a strong "staff": "The Lord shall send the rod of thy strength out of Zion: rule thou in the midst of thine enemies'' (Ps. 110:2). Similarly, the prophet Ezekiel said, ''Fire is gone out of a *rod* of her branches, which hath devoured her fruit, so that she hath no strong *rod* to be a scepter to rule'' (Ezek. 19:14). The figurative usage of *matteh* occurs in the idiom *matteh-lechem,* ''staff of bread.'' This poetic idiom refers to the food supply, and it is found mainly in Ezekiel: ''Moreover he said unto me, Son of man, behold, I will break the staff of bread in Jerusalem: and they shall eat [rationed food in anxiety and drink rationed water in despair]'' (Ezek. 4:16; cf. 14:13).

A derived sense of *matteh* is ''tribe,'' which is used as many as 183 times. The ''tribes'' of Israel are each designated as *matteh:* ''And these are the countries which the children of Israel inherited in the land of Canaan, which Eleazar the priest, and Joshua the son of Nun, and the heads of the fathers of the tribes of the children of Israel, distributed for inheritance to them'' (Josh. 14:1). It is possible that the *matteh* (''staff''), as a symbol of authority, first applied to the tribal leader and thereafter by extension to the whole ''tribe.''

The several meanings of *matteh* are reflected in the Septuagint: *phule* (''tribe; nation; people'') and *rhabdos* (''rod; staff; scepter'').

shēbet (שֵׁבֶט), ''tribe; rod.'' In modern Hebrew this word mainly denotes ''tribe'' as a technical term. In Akkadian the related verb *šabatu* signifies ''to smite,'' and the noun *shabbitu* means ''rod'' or ''scepter.'' A synonym of the Hebrew *shēbet* is *matteh,* also ''rod'' or ''tribe,'' and what is applicable to *matteh* is also relevant to *shēbet.*

The ''rod'' as a tool is used by the shepherd (Lev. 27:32) and the teacher (2 Sam. 7:14). It is a symbol of authority in the hands of a ruler, whether it is the scepter (Amos 1:5, 8) or an instrument of warfare and oppression: ''Thou shalt break them with a rod of iron; thou shalt dash them in pieces like a potter's vessel'' (Ps. 2:9; cf. Zech. 10:11). The symbolic element comes to expression in a description of the messianic rule: ''But with righteousness shall he judge the poor, and reprove with equity for the meek of the earth: and he shall smite the earth with the rod of his mouth . . .'' (Isa. 11:4).

The word *shēbet* is most frequently used (143 times) to denote a ''tribe,'' a division in a nation. It is the preferred term for the twelve ''tribes'' of Israel (Gen. 49:16; Exod. 28:21). Jeremiah referred to all of Israel as the ''tribe'': ''The portion of Jacob is not like them; for he is the former of all things: and Israel is the rod of his inheritance: the Lord of hosts is his name'' (51:19).

The Septuagint translations are: *phule* (''tribe; nation; people''); *rhabdos* (''rod; staff''); and *skeptron* (''scepter; tribe'').

B. Verb.

nātāh (נָטָה), ''to stretch out, spread out, extend.'' This root occurs in biblical, mishnaic, and modern Hebrew and in Arabic with the same meaning. One occurrence of *nātāh* is in Exod. 9:22: ''Stretch forth thine hand toward heaven. . . .''

TO TURN

A. Verbs.

hāphak (הָפַךְ), "to turn, overturn, change, transform, turn back." A common word throughout the various periods of Hebrew, this term occurs in other Semitic languages, including ancient Akkadian. It is found almost 100 times in biblical Hebrew. Used for the first time in the biblical text in Gen. 3:24, the Hebrew verb form there indicates reflexive action: ". . . A flaming sword which turned every way [NAB, "revolving"; NEB, "whirling"] . . ."

In its simplest meaning, *hāphak* expresses the turning from one side to another, such as "turning" one's back (Josh. 7:8), or "as a man wipeth a dish, wiping it, and turning it upside down" (2 Kings 21:13). Similarly, Hosea refers to Israel as being "a cake not turned" (Hos. 7:8). The meaning of "transformation" or "change" is vividly illustrated in the story of Saul's encounter with the Spirit of God. Samuel promised that Saul would "be changed into another man" (1 Sam. 10:6 JB), and when the Spirit came on him, "God changed his heart" (1 Sam. 10:9 JB). Other examples of change are the "changing" of Pharaoh's mind (Exod. 14:5; literally, "the heart of Pharaoh . . . was turned"); the "turning" of Aaron's rod into a serpent (Exod. 7:15); dancing "turned" to mourning (Lam. 5:14); water "turned" into blood (Exod. 7:17); and the sun "turned" to darkness and the moon to blood (Joel 2:31). Ps. 41:3 presents a difficult translation problem in its use of *hāphak*. Literally, it reads: "All his bed you [Yahweh] change in his sickness." In view of the poetic parallelism involved, restoration of health must be meant. Thus, the RSV translates: "In his sickness thou healest all his infirmities." Perhaps only a refreshing of the bed is meant, so the NEB translates: "He turns his bed when he is ill."

The KJV rendering of Isa. 60:5 sounds strange to our modern ears: "The abundance of the sea shall be converted unto thee. . . ." A slight improvement is given by the RSV, which reads: "The abundance of the sea shall be turned to you." The meaning is best captured by the JB: "The riches of the sea shall be lavished upon you."

sābab (סָבַב), "to turn, go around, turn around (change direction)." This verb occurs only in Hebrew (including post-biblical Hebrew) and Ugaritic. Nouns using these radicals appear in Arabic and Akkadian. Biblical Hebrew attests the word in all periods and about 160 times.

Basically this verb represents a circular movement—"to take a turning." First, it refers to such movement in general. The first occurrence of *sābab* having this emphasis is in Gen. 42:24, where Joseph "turned himself about" from his brothers and wept. Here the verb does not tell the precise direction of his departure, only that he left their presence. Similarly, when Samuel was told that Saul went to Carmel and "is gone about, and passed on, and gone down to Gilgal" (1 Sam. 15:12), we are not told that he reversed direction in order to get from his origin to Carmel and Gilgal. God led Israel out of the way (by an out-of-the-way route) when He took them into the Promised Land. He wanted to avoid having them face war with the Philistines, an event that was unavoidable if they proceeded directly north from Egypt to Palestine. Therefore, He led them through the wilderness—a back route into the land: "But God led the people about, through the way of the wilderness of the Red Sea . . ." (Exod. 13:18). Perhaps one of the passages where this meaning is clearest is Prov. 26:14, which speaks of the "turning" of a door on its hinges. An extension of this meaning occurs in 1 Sam. 5:8-9, "to remove, to take away": "And they answered, Let the ark of the God of Israel be carried about [taken away] unto Gath. And they carried the ark of the God of Israel about thither" (cf. 2 Kings 16:18).

A second emphasis of *sābab* is "to go around," in the sense of to proceed or be arranged in a circle. Joseph tells his family: ". . . Lo, my sheaf arose, and also stood upright; and, behold, your sheaves stood round about, and made obeisance to my sheaf" (Gen. 37:7). They moved so as to surround his sheaf. This is the action pictured when Israel besieged Jericho, except with the further nuance of encircling in a processional and religious march: "And ye shall compass the city, all ye men of war, and go round about the city once" (Josh. 6:3). "To travel" and "to return" are used together to represent traveling a circuit. It is said of Samuel that he used to go annually "in circuit" (1 Sam. 7:16). Another variation of this emphasis is "to go around" a territory in order to avoid crossing through it: "And they journeyed from mount Hor by the way of the Red Sea, to compass [go around] the land of Edom: and the soul of the people was much discouraged because of the way" (Num. 21:4).

Sābab is also used of the completion of this movement, the state of literally or figuratively surrounding something or someone. The very first biblical occurrence of the word carries this force (according to many scholars): "The name of the first is Pison: that is it which compasseth [flows around] the whole land of Havilah . . ." (Gen. 2:11). Judg. 16:2, where the Gazites "compassed [Samson] in, and laid wait for him all night in the gate of the city," represents another occurrence of this nuance. When David spoke of the cords (as a trap) of Sheol "surrounding" him (2 Sam. 22:6), he meant that they actually touched him and held him fast. *Sābab* can be used of sitting down around a table. So Samuel told Jesse to fetch David, "for we will not sit down till he come hither" (1 Sam. 16:11).

A third use of this verb is "to change direction." This can be a change of direction *toward:* "Neither shall the inheritance remove from one tribe to another tribe . . ." (Num. 36:9); the usual direction of passing on an inheritance is down family lines, and God's commandment that the daughters of Zelophehad marry within their father's families would make certain that this movement of things not be interrupted. This emphasis appears more clearly in 1 Sam. 18:11: "And David [escaped] out of his presence twice"; it is certain that David is putting as much space between himself and Saul as possible. He is "running away or turning away" (cf. 1 Sam. 22:17). *Sābab* may also refer to a change of direction, as in Num. 34:4: "And your border shall turn. . . ."

There are three special nuances under this emphasis. First, the verb may mean "to roam through" as a scout looking for water: ". . . And they fetched a compass [made a circuit] of seven days' journey: and there was no water for the host, and for the cattle that followed them" (2 Kings 3:9). Some scholars suggest that this is the idea expressed in Gen. 2:11—that the Pison meandered through Havilah rather than flowed around it. Second, *sābab* may be used of "turning something over" to someone. So Adonijah said of Solomon: ". . . The kingdom was mine, . . . howbeit the kingdom is turned about, and is become my brother's . . ." (1 Kings 2:15). Third, *sābab* may be used of "changing or turning one thing into another": "And the land shall be turned as a plain from Geba to Rimmon south of Jerusalem . . ." (Zech. 14:10).

B. Nouns.

sābîb (סָבִיב), "area round about; circuit." This word appears about 336 times in biblical Hebrew. The word can be used as a noun, but it usually occurs as an adverb or preposition. In 1 Chron. 11:8 *sābîb* refers to the "parts round about": "And he built the city round about, even from Millo round about. . . ." The word may also be used for "circuits": ". . . And the wind returneth again according to his circuits" (Eccl. 1:6).

Other nouns are related to the verb *sābab*. *Sibbāh* and *nəsibbāh* both refer to "turn of affairs"; *sibbāh* is found in 1 Kings 12:15 and *nəsibbāh* in 2 Chron. 10:15. *Mûsab* occurs once with the meaning of "circular passage": ". . . For the winding about of the house went still upward round about the house . . ." (Ezek. 41:7). *Mēsab* occurs 4 times, and it refers to "that which surrounds or is round." *Mēsab* refers to a "round table" (Song of Sol. 1:12) and to "places round about" Jerusalem (2 Kings 23:5).

C. Adverb.

sābîb (סָבִיב), "round about; within the circuit of." In Exod. 25:11 *sābîb* appears as "round about": ". . . And shalt make upon it a crown of gold round about." The first biblical appearance of the word is in Gen. 23:17, and it refers to "within the circuit of."

D. Preposition.

sābîb (סָבִיב), "from every side; from round about." The word implies "from every side" in Exod. 16:13. The word refers to "round about" in 1 Kings 18:35: "And the water ran round about the altar. . . ."

TO TURN TOWARDS, TURN BACK

A. Verb.

pānāh (פָּנָה), "to turn towards, turn back, turn around, attach to, pass away, make clear." This verb also appears in Syriac and post-biblical Hebrew and post-biblical Aramaic. Related verbs which have the same radicals with a somewhat different meaning occur in Arabic and Ethiopic. The Bible attests *pānāh* about 155 times and in all periods.

Most occurrences of this verb carry the sense "to turn in another direction"; this is a verb of either physical or mental motion. Used of physical motion, the word signifies turning so as to move in another direction: "Ye have compassed this mountain long enough: turn you northward" (Deut. 2:3). *Pānāh* can also mean to turn so as to face or look at something or someone: "And it came to pass, as Aaron spake unto the whole congregation of the children of Israel, that they looked toward the wilderness . . ." (Exod. 16:10). "Turning toward" something may also signify looking at, or seeing it: "Remember thy servants, Abraham, Isaac, and Jacob; look not unto [do not see] the stubbornness of this people, nor to their wickedness, nor to their sin" (Deut. 9:27). A further extension in meaning is seen in Hag. 1:9, where *pānāh* means "to look for," or to expect: "Ye looked for much, and, lo, it came to little. . . ."

Another focus of meaning is "to turn back" so as to see. This is found in Josh. 8:20: "When the men of Ai turned back and looked, behold . . ." (NASB). In other passages the verb means "to turn around," in the sense of to look in every direction. So Moses "looked this way and that way, and when he saw there was no man, he slew the Egyptian, and hid him in the sand" (Exod. 2:12).

In the sense of "to turn around" *pānāh* is used of changing one's direction so as to leave the scene. So "the men turned their faces from thence, and went toward Sodom . . ." (Gen. 18:22—the first biblical occurrence of the verb).

Used of intellectual and spiritual turning, this verb signifies attaching oneself to something. God commanded Israel: "Turn ye not unto idols, nor make to yourselves molten gods . . ." (Lev. 19:4); they should not shift their attention to and attach themselves to idols. In an even stronger use this verb represents dependence on someone: ". . . Which bringeth their iniquity to remembrance, when they shall look after [depend on] them . . ." (Ezek. 29:16). "To turn towards" sometimes means to pay attention to someone. Job tells his friends: "Now . . . look upon me; for it is evident unto you if I lie" (Job 6:28).

In a still different emphasis the word connotes the "passing away" of something, such as the turning away of a day: "And Isaac went out to meditate in the field at the eventide . . ."—he went out "at the turning of the evening" (Gen. 24:63). Similarly the Bible speaks of the dawn as the "turning of the morning" (Exod. 14:27). The "turning of the day" is the end of the day (Jer. 6:4).

Used in a military context, *pānāh* can signify giving up fighting or fleeing before one's enemies. Because of Achan's sin the Lord was not with Israel at the battle of Ai: "Therefore the children of Israel could not stand before their enemies, but turned their backs before their enemies, because they were accursed . . ." (Josh. 7:12).

In the intensive stem the verb means "to remove," to take away: "The Lord hath taken away thy judgments, he hath cast out thine enemy . . ." (Zeph. 3:15). "To clear a house" (to set things in order) is often the means by which conditions are prepared for guests: "Come in, thou blessed of the Lord; wherefore standest thou without? for I have prepared the house . . ." (Gen. 24:31). Another nuance is "to prepare" a road for a victory march; Isaiah says: "Prepare ye the way of the Lord, make straight in the desert a highway for our God" (Isa. 40:3; cf. Matt. 3:3).

B. Nouns.

pinnāh (פִּנָּה), "corner." This noun occurs 30 times in the Old Testament. The word refers to "corners" in Exod. 27:2: "And thou shalt make the horns of it upon the four corners thereof. . . ." In 2 Kings 14:13 the word refers to a corner-tower, and in Judg. 20:2 *pinnāh* is used figuratively of a "chief" as the "corner" or defense of the people.

The noun *pānîm* is also related to the verb *pānāh*. It occurs 2,100 times to refer to the "face" of something. An early occurrence of the word is in Gen. 17:3.

C. Adjective.

pənîmî (פְּנִימִי), "inner." This adjective occurs about 33 times, and it refers to a part of a building, usually a temple. One occurrence is in 1 Kings 6:27: "And he set the cherubim within the inner house. . . ."

D. Adverb.

pənîmāh (פְּנִימָה), "within." This word occurs about 12 times. One appearance is in 1 Kings 6:18: "And the cedar of the house within was carved with knobs and open flowers. . . ." Here the word refers to the inside of the house.

TO BE UNCLEAN

A. Verb.

tāmē' (טָמֵא), "to be unclean." This root is limited to Hebrew, Aramaic, and Arabic. The verb occurs 160 times in biblical Hebrew and mainly in Leviticus, as in Lev. 11:26: "The carcases of every beast which divideth the hoof, and is not clovenfooted, nor cheweth the cud, are unclean unto you: every one that toucheth them shall be unclean." *Tāmē'* is the opposite of *tāhēr,* "to be pure."

B. Noun.

tumə'āh (טֻמְאָה), "uncleanness." This noun is derived from *tāmē'*. *Tumə'āh* occurs 37 times in biblical Hebrew. The word occurs in Num. 5:19: "And the priest shall charge her by an oath, and say unto the woman, If no man have lain with thee, and if thou hast not gone aside to uncleanliness with another instead of thine husband, be thou free from this bitter water that causeth the curse." Here the word refers to sexual "uncleanness." *Tumə'āh* occurs twice in Lev. 16:16 and refers to ethical and religious "uncleanness."

C. Adjective.

tāmē' (טָמֵא), "unclean." This adjective occurs 89 times in the Old Testament. The frequency of the word is high in Leviticus. Its first occurrence is also in Leviticus: "Or if a soul touch any unclean thing, whether it be a carcase of an unclean beast, or a carcase of unclean cattle, or the carcase of unclean creeping things, and if it be hidden from him; he also shall be unclean, and guilty'' (5:2).

The usage of *tāmē'* in the Old Testament resembles that of *tāhôr,* "pure." First, uncleanness is a state of being. The leper was compelled to announce his uncleanness wherever he went (Lev. 13:45); however, even here there is a religious overtone, in that his uncleanness was ritual. Hence, it is more appropriate to recognize that the second usage is most basic. *Tāmē'* in the religio-cultic sense is a technical term denoting a state of being ceremonially unfit. Animals, carcases, unclean people, and objects conveyed the impurity to those who touched them: "And whatsoever the unclean person toucheth shall be unclean; and the soul that toucheth it shall be unclean until even'' (Num. 19:22). The impurity could also be brought about by a seminal issue (Lev. 15:2) or a menstrual period (Lev. 15:25), and whatever the unclean touched was also rendered "unclean."

The Septuagint translations are: *akathartos* ("impure; unclean") and *miaino* ("stain; defile"). The KJV gives these translations: "unclean; defiled; polluted."

TO UNDERSTAND

A. Verbs.

sākal (שָׂכַל), "to be prudent, act wisely, give attention to, ponder, prosper." This word, which is common to both ancient and modern Hebrew, is found approximately 75 times in the text of the Hebrew Bible. Its first use in the text, in Gen. 3:6, contributes to an interesting paradox, for while the forbidden fruit was "to be desired to make one wise," it was a very unwise thing to take it!

The basic meaning of *sākal* seems to be "to look at, to give attention to," as illustrated in this parallelism: "That they may see, and know, and consider, and understand . . ." (Isa. 41:20). From this develops the connotation of insight, intellectual comprehension: "Let not the wise man glory in his wisdom . . . But let him that glorieth glory in this, that he understandeth and knoweth me . . ." (Jer. 9:23-24). As here, it is frequently used along with and in parallelism to the Hebrew *yāda'*, "to know" (primarily experientially). As is true of *chākam,* "to be wise," *sākal* never concerns abstract prudence, but acting prudently: "Therefore the prudent shall keep silence . . ." (Amos 5:13); ". . . He hath left off to be wise . . ." (Ps. 36:3).

bîn (בִּין), "to understand, be able, deal wisely, consider, pay attention to, regard, notice, discern, perceive, inquire." This verb, which occurs 126 times in biblical Hebrew, has cognates in Ugaritic, Arabic, Ethiopic, late Aramaic, and Syriac. *Bîn* appears in all periods of biblical Hebrew.

Bîn appears in Jer. 9:12 with the meaning "to understand": "Who is the wise man, that may understand this?" In Job 6:30 the word means "to discern," and in Deut. 32:7 it means "to consider."

B. Nouns.

bînāh (בִּינָה), "understanding." *Bînāh* appears 37 times and in all periods of biblical Hebrew even though it belongs primarily to the sphere of wisdom and wisdom literature.

This noun represents the "act of understanding": "And in all matters of wisdom and understanding, that the king inquired of them, he found them ten times better than all the magicians . . ." (Dan. 1:20).

Elsewhere *bînāh* signifies the faculty "understanding": ". . . The spirit of my understanding causeth me to answer" (Job 20:3).

In other passages the object of knowledge, in the sense of what one desires to know, is indicated by *bînāh:* "Keep therefore and do them [God's laws]: for this is your wisdom and your understanding in the sight of the nations, which shall hear all these statutes . . ." (Deut. 4:6; cf. 1 Chron. 22:12). God's law, therefore, is wisdom and "understanding"—what one should know.

This word is sometimes personified: "Yea, if thou criest after knowledge, and liftest up thy voice for understanding; if thou seekest her as silver, and searchest for her as for hid treasures . . ." (Prov. 2:3-4).

təbûnāh (תְּבוּנָה), "understanding." This word, which occurs 42 times, is also a wisdom term. Like *bînāh*, it represents the act (Job 26:12), faculty (Exod. 31:3), object (Prov. 2:3), and personification of wisdom (Prov. 8:1).

masəkîl (מַשְׂכִּיל), "didactic psalm(?)." This noun form, derived from *sākal*, is found in the title of 13 psalms and also in Ps. 47:7. Scholars are not agreed on the significance of this term, but on the basis of the general meaning of *sākal*, such psalms must have been considered didactic or teaching psalms.

UPRIGHT

A. Adjective.

yāshār (יָשָׁר), "upright; right; righteous; just." This adjective occurs first in Exodus in the idiom "right in his eyes": "[He] said, If thou wilt diligently hearken to the voice of the Lord thy God, and wilt do that which is right in his sight, and wilt give ear to his commandments, and keep all his statutes, I will put none of these diseases upon thee, which I have brought upon the Egyptians: for I am the Lord that healeth thee" (Exod. 15:26). Its usage is infrequent in the Pentateuch and in the prophetical writings. Predominantly a poetic term, *yāshār* also occurs idiomatically ("to do what is right") in the historical books; cf. 1 Kings 15:5: "Because David did that which was right in the eyes of the Lord, and turned not aside from any thing that he commanded him all the days of his life, save only in the matter of Uriah the Hittite."

The basic meaning is the root meaning "to be straight" in the sense of "to be level." The legs of the creatures in Ezekiel's vision were straight (Ezek. 1:7). The Israelites designated an easy road for traveling as a "level road." It had few inclines and declines compared to the mountain roads (cf. Jer. 31:9: "They shall come with weeping, and with supplications will I lead them: I will cause them to walk by the rivers of water in a straight way, wherein they shall not stumble: for I am a father to Israel, and Ephraim is my first-born").

Yāshār with the meaning "right" pertains to things and to abstracts. Samuel promised himself to instruct God's people in "the good and the right way" (1 Sam. 12:23). Nehemiah thanked God for having given just ordinances: "Thou camest down also upon mount Sinai, and spakest with them from heaven, and gavest them right judgments, and true laws, good statutes and commandments" (Neh. 9:13). Based on His revelation God expected His people to please Him in being obedient to Him: "And thou shalt do that which is right and good in the sight of the Lord: that it may be well with thee, and that thou mayest go in and possess the good land which the Lord sware unto thy fathers" (Deut. 6:18).

When *yāshār* pertains to people, it is best translated "just" or "upright." God is the standard of uprightness for His people: "Good and upright is the Lord: therefore will he teach sinners in the way" (Ps. 25:8). His word (Ps. 33:4), judgments (Ps. 19:9), and ways (Hos. 14:9) reveal His uprightness and are a blessing to His people. The believer follows Him in being "upright" in heart: "Be glad in the Lord, and rejoice, ye righteous; and shout for joy, all ye that are upright in heart" (Ps. 32:11; cf. 7:10; 11:2). In their daily walk they manifest that they are walking on the narrow road: "The wicked have drawn out the sword, and have bent their bow, to cast down the poor and needy, and to slay such as be of upright conversation" (Ps. 37:14). The "just" are promised God's blessing upon their lives (Prov. 11:10-11).

Finally, *yāshār* is also the abstract "rightness," especially when the Hebrew word has the definite article (*hayyāshār*, "the right"): "Hear this, I pray you, ye heads of the house of Jacob, and princes of the house of Israel, that abhor judgment, and pervert all equity [all that is right]" (Mic. 3:9).

The Septuagint translations are: *arestos* ("pleasing"); *dikaios* ("upright; just; righteous"); *euthes* ("upright"); and *euthus* ("straight").

B. Verb.

yāshar (יָשַׁר), "to be straight, be smooth, be right." This verb, which occurs rarely, has many derivatives in the Bible.

In Akkadian the verb *isaru* signifies "to be straight, bring in order," and the noun *misarum* denotes justice and an upright way of life. The Hebrew word has many related words in other Semitic languages (Phoenician, Ugaritic) and even in Egyptian.

One occurrence of the verb is in 1 Chron. 13:4: "And all the congregation said that they would do so: for the thing was right in the eyes of all the people." In this usage *yāshar* has the sense of being pleasing or agreeable. In Hab. 2:4 the word implies an ethical uprightness.

C. Nouns.

yosher (יֹשֶׁר), "straightness." This noun occurs about 15 times. One occurrence is in Prov. 2:13: "Who leave the paths of uprightness, to walk in the ways of darkness."

Other nouns occur less frequently. *Yishərāh* means "uprightness" and occurs once (1 Kings 3:6). The noun *yəshurûn* is an honorific title for Israel (Deut. 32:15; 33:5). *Mîshôr* means "level place, uprightness." In 1 Kings 20:23 *mîshôr* refers to "level country"; in Isa. 11:4 the word refers to "uprightness": ". . . And reprove with equity for the meek of the earth. . . ."

VESSEL

kəlî (כְּלִי), "vessel; receptacle; stuff; clothing; utensil; tool; instrument; ornament or jewelry; armor or weapon; male sex organ." A cognate to this word appears in Akkadian. *Kəlî* appears in biblical Hebrew about 320 times and in all periods.

This word is used of "receptacles" of various kinds used for storing and transporting. Thus, Jacob said to Laban: "Whereas thou hast searched through all my stuff [literally, receptacles], what hast thou found of all thy household stuff [literally, from all the receptacles of thy house]?" (Gen. 31:37). Such "receptacles" may be made of wood (Lev. 11:32) or potsherd or clay (Lev. 6:28). They may be used to hold documents (Jer. 32:14), wine, oil, fruits (Jer. 40:10), food (Ezek. 4:9), beverage (Ruth 2:9), or bread (1 Sam. 9:7). Even a shepherd's bag is a *kəlî* (1 Sam. 17:40). In 1 Sam. 17:22 the word is used of baggage, or "receptacles" (his shepherd's bag?) and what is in them: "And David left his carriage in the hand of the [baggage keeper]. . . ." The sailors on the ship in which Jonah sailed "cast forth the wares [cargo] . . . into the sea, to lighten it of them" (Jon. 1:5).

Ships are called "receptacles," presumably because they can hold people: "That sendeth ambassadors by the sea, even in vessels of bulrushes upon the waters . . ." (Isa. 18:2).

Kəlî can mean "clothing": "The woman shall not wear that which pertaineth unto a man, neither shall a man put on a woman's garment: for all that do so are abomination unto the Lord thy God" (Deut. 22:5).

The word may be used of various "vessels and utensils": "And the four tables were of hewn stone for the burnt offering . . .: whereupon also they laid the instruments wherewith they slew the burnt offering and the sacrifice" (Ezek. 40:42). In Gen. 45:20 this word refers to movable but large possessions: Pharaoh told Joseph to tell his brothers to take wagons and bring their family to Egypt, and "regard not your stuff; for the good of all the land of Egypt is yours." Thus in Exod. 27:19 the word represents all the furniture and utensils of the tabernacle (cf. Num. 3:8). Samuel warned Israel that the king on whom they insisted would organize them into levees (work crews) "to [plow] his ground, and to reap his harvest, and to make his instruments of war, and instruments of his chariots" (1 Sam. 8:12). More narrowly, *kəlî* may be used of oxen harnesses: ". . . Behold, here be oxen for burnt sacrifice, and threshing instruments and other instruments of the oxen for wood" (2 Sam. 24:22).

This word may be used of various "implements or tools": "Simeon and Levi are brethren; instruments of cruelty are in their habitations" (Gen. 49:5). In Jer. 22:7 the word represents "tools" with which trees may be cut down: "And I will prepare destroyers against thee, every one with his weapons: and they shall cut down thy choice cedars, and cast them into the fire." Isaac told Esau to take his gear, his quiver, and his bow, "and go out to the field, and take me some venison" (Gen. 27:3).

Weapons for war are called "implements": "And they [the Israelites] went after them unto Jordan: and, lo, all the way was full of garments and vessels, which the Syrians had cast away in their haste" (2 Kings 7:15). A bearer of implements is an armor-bearer (Judg. 9:54). A house of arms or an armory is referred to in 2 Kings 20:13.

In Amos 6:5 and such passages (2 Chron. 5:13; 7:6; 23:13; cf. Ps. 71:22) "musical instruments" are called *kelîm:* "That chant to the sound of the viol, and invent to themselves instruments of music. . . ."

Kelî stands for various kinds of "precious ornaments": "And the servant brought forth jewels of silver, and jewels of gold, and raiment, and gave them to Rebekah . . ." (Gen. 24:53—the first biblical appearance of the word). Such "precious ornaments" adorned the typical bride: "I will greatly rejoice in the Lord, my soul shall be joyful in my God; for he hath clothed me with the garments of salvation, he hath covered me with the robe of righteousness, as a bridegroom decketh himself with ornaments, and as a bride adorneth herself with her jewels" (Isa. 61:10).

In 1 Sam. 21:5 *kelî* may refer to the "male sex organ." This certainly makes more sense than if the word is rendered "vessels," since the matter under discussion is the ritualistic purity of David's men: "Of a truth women have been kept from us about these three days, since I came out, and the vessels [sex organs] of the young men are holy. . . ."

VINEYARD

kerem (כֶּרֶם), "vineyard." This Hebrew word is related to other Semitic languages (Akkadian, *karmu;* Arabic, *karm*). The word is evenly distributed throughout the Old Testament and is used 92 times. The first occurrence is in Gen. 9:20.

Isaiah gives a vivid description of the work involved in the preparation, planting, and cultivation of a "vineyard" (Isa. 5:1-7). The "vineyard" was located on the slopes of a hill (Isa. 5:1). The soil was cleared of stones before the tender vines were planted (Isa. 5:2). A watchtower provided visibility over the "vineyard" (Isa. 5:2), and a winevat and place for crushing the grapes were hewn out of the rock (Isa. 5:2). When all the preparations were finished, the "vineyard" was ready and in a few years it was expected to produce crops. In the meantime the *kerem* required regular pruning (Lev. 25:3-4). The time between planting and the first crop was of sufficient import as to free the owner from military duty: "And what man is he that hath planted a vineyard, and hath not yet eaten of it?" (Deut. 20:6).

The harvest time was a period of hard work and great rejoicing. The enjoyment of the "vineyard" was a blessing of God: "And they shall build houses, and inhabit them; and they shall plant vineyards, and eat the fruit of them" (Isa. 65:21). The failure of the "vineyard" to produce or the transfer of ownership of one's "vineyard" was viewed as God's judgment: "Forasmuch therefore as your treading is upon the poor, and ye take from him burdens of wheat: ye have built houses of hewn stone, but ye shall not dwell in them; ye have planted pleasant vineyards, but ye shall not drink wine of them" (Amos 5:11; cf. Deut. 28:30).

The words "vineyard" and "olive grove" (*zayith*) are often found together in the biblical text. These furnished the two major permanent agricultural activities in ancient Israel, as both required much work and time before the crops came in. God promised that the ownership of the "vineyards" and orchards of the Canaanites was to go to His people as a blessing from Him (Deut. 6:11-12). God's judgment to Israel extended to the "vineyards." The rejoicing in the "vineyard" would cease (Isa. 16:10) and the carefully cultivated "vineyard" would be turned into a thicket with thorns and briers (cf. Isa. 32:12-13). The "vineyard" would be reduced to a hiding place of wild animals and a grazing place for goats and wild donkeys (Isa. 32:14). The postexilic hope lay in God's blessings on the agricultural activity of His people: "And I will bring again the captivity of my people of Israel, and they shall build the waste cities, and inhabit them; and they shall plant vineyards, and drink the wine thereof; they shall also make gardens, and eat the fruit of them" (Amos 9:14).

The "vineyards" were located mainly in the hill country and in the low-lying hill country. The Bible mentions the "vineyard" at Timnath (Judg. 14:5), Jezreel (1 Kings 21:1), the hill country of Samaria (Jer. 31:5), and even at En-gedi (Song of Sol. 1:14).

The metaphorical use of *kerem* allows the prophet Isaiah to draw an analogy between the "vineyard" and Israel: "For the vineyard of the Lord of hosts is the house of Israel . . ." (Isa. 5:7). It has also been suggested that the "vineyard" in the Song of Solomon is better understood metaphorically as "person": "Look not upon me, because I am black, because the sun hath looked upon me: my mother's children were angry with me; they made me the keeper of the vineyards; but mine own vineyard have I not kept" (Song of Sol. 1:6).

VIOLENCE

A. Noun.

chāmās (חָמָס), "violence; wrong; maliciousness." This word appears about 60 times and in all periods of biblical Hebrew.

Basically *chāmās* connotes the disruption of the divinely established order of things. It has a wide range of nuances within this legal sphere. The expression "a witness in the case of violent wrongdoing" means someone who bears witness in a case having to do with such an offense (cf. Deut. 19:16). In this context the truthfulness of the witness is not established except upon further investigation (Deut. 19:18). Once he was established as a false witness, the penalty for the crime concerning which he bore false witness was to be executed against the liar (cf. Deut. 19:19). In Exod. 23:1 Israel is admonished: ". . . Put not thine hand with the wicked to be an unrighteous witness," i.e., a witness who in accusing someone of a violent crime intends to see the accused punished severely.

Chāmās perhaps connotes a "violent wrongdoing" which has not been righted, the guilt of which lies on an entire area (its inhabitants) disrupting their relationship with God and thereby interfering with His blessings.

It is this latter sense which appears in the phrase "the earth was full of violent wrongdoing": "The earth also was corrupt before God, and the earth was filled with violence" (Gen. 6:11—the first occurrence of the word). Thus, in Gen. 16:5 Sarai summons God to judge between Abram and herself because he has not acted properly toward her keeping Hagar in submission: "My wrong[done me] be upon thee: I have given my maid into thy bosom; and when she saw that she had conceived, I was despised in her eyes: the Lord judge between me and thee." Abram as God's judge (in God's stead) accepts the correctness of her case and commits Hagar to Sarai's care to be dealt with properly.

B. Verb.

Chāmās means "to treat violently." This verb, which occurs 7 times in biblical Hebrew, has cognates in Aramaic, Akkadian, and Arabic. This verb appears in Jer. 22:3 with the meaning of "to do no violence": ". . . And do no wrong, do no violence to the stranger, the fatherless, nor the widow, neither shed innocent blood in this place."

VIRGIN

'aləmāh (עַלְמָה), "virgin; maiden." This noun has an Ugaritic cognate, although the masculine form also appears in Aramaic, Syriac, and Arabic. The feminine form of the root appears 9 times; the only 2 appearances of the masculine form *('alam)* are in First Samuel. This suggests that this word was used rarely, perhaps because other words bore a similar meaning.

That *'aləmāh* can mean "virgin" is quite clear in Song of Sol. 6:8: "There are threescore queens, and fourscore concubines, and virgins [NASB, "maidens"] without number." Thus all the women in the court are described. The word *'aləmāh* represents those who are eligible for marriage but are neither wives (queens) nor concubines. These "virgins" all loved the king and longed to be chosen to be with him (to be his bride), even as did the Shulamite who became his bride (1:3-4). In Gen. 24:43 the word describes Rebekah, of whom it is said in Gen. 24:16 that she was a "maiden" with whom no man had had relations. Solomon wrote that the process of wooing a woman was mysterious to him (Prov. 30:19). Certainly in that day a man ordinarily wooed one whom he considered to be a "virgin." There are several contexts, therefore, in which a young girl's virginity is expressly in view.

Thus *'aləmāh* appears to be used more of the concept "virgin" than that of "maiden," yet always of a woman who had not borne a child. This makes it the ideal word to be used in Isa. 7:14, since the word *bəthûlāh* emphasizes virility more than virginity (although it is used with both emphases, too). The reader of Isa. 7:14 in the days preceding the birth of Jesus would read that a "virgin who is a maiden" would conceive a child. This was a possible, but irregular, use of the word since the word can refer merely to the unmarried status of the one so described. The child immediately in view was the son of the prophet and his wife (cf. Isa. 8:3) who served as a sign to Ahaz that his enemies would be defeated by God. On the other hand, the reader of that day must have been extremely uncomfortable with this use of the word, since its primary connotation is "virgin" rather than "maiden." Thus the clear translation of the Greek in Matt. 1:23 whereby this word is rendered "virgin" satisfies its fullest implication. Therefore, there was no embarrassment to Isaiah when his wife conceived a son by him, since the word *'aləmāh* allowed for this. Neither is there any embarrassment in Matthew's understanding of the word.

VISION

A. Nouns.

chāzôn (חָזוֹן), "vision." None of the 34 appearances of this word appear before First Samuel, and most of them are in the prophetic books.

Chāzôn almost always signifies a means of divine revelation. First, it refers to the means itself, to a prophetic "vision" by which divine messages are communicated: "The days are prolonged, and every vision faileth" (Ezek. 12:22). Second, this word represents the message received by prophetic "vision": "Where there is no vision, the people perish: but he that keepeth the law, happy is he" (Prov. 29:18). Finally, *chāzôn* can represent the entirety of a prophetic or prophet's message as it is written down: "The vision of Isaiah the son of Amoz . . ." (Isa. 1:1). Thus the word inseparably related to the content of a divine communication focuses on the means by which that message is received: "And the word of the Lord was precious in those days; there was no open vision" (1 Sam. 3:1—the first occurrence of the word). In Isa. 29:7 this word signifies a non-prophetic dream.

chizzāyôn (חִזָּיוֹן), "vision." This noun, which occurs 9 times, refers to a prophetic "vision" in Joel 2:28: "And it shall come to pass afterward, that I will pour out my spirit upon all flesh; and your sons and your daughters shall prophesy, your old men shall dream dreams, your young men shall see visions." *Chizzāyôn* refers to divine communication in 2 Sam. 7:17 (the first biblical occurrence) and to an ordinary dream in Job 4:13.

B. Verb.

chāzāh (חָזָה), "to see, behold, select for oneself." This verb appears 54 times and in every period of biblical Hebrew. Cognates of this word appear in Ugaritic, Aramaic, and Arabic. It means "to see or behold" in general (Prov. 22:29), "to see" in a prophetic vision (Num. 24:4), and "to select for oneself" (Exod. 18:21—the first occurrence of the word).

In Lam. 2:14 the word means "to see" in relation to prophets' vision: "Thy prophets have seen vain and foolish things for thee: and they have not discovered thine iniquity. . . ."

VOICE

qôl (קוֹל), "voice; sound; noise." This word also appears in Ugaritic ("sound"), Akkadian ("call"), Arabic ("say"), and in Phoenician, Ethiopic, and old South Arabic ("voice"). *Qôl* appears about 506 times in the Bible and in all periods.

In its first meaning the word denotes a "sound" produced by vocal cords. This includes the human "voice": "And there was no day like that before it or after it, that the Lord hearkened unto the voice of a man: for the Lord fought for Israel" (Josh. 10:14). The word also includes vocal "sounds" produced by animals: "And Samuel said, What meaneth then this bleating [literally, sound] of the sheep in mine ears, and the lowing [literally, sound] of the oxen which I hear?" (1 Sam. 15:14). In this regard *qôl* is used of the "voice" of personified inanimate objects or things: "And he said, What hast thou done? the voice of thy brother's blood crieth unto me from the ground" (Gen. 4:10).

The second meaning, "sound" or "noise," appears especially in poetical passages and covers a great variety of "noises and sounds," such as the "noise or sound" of battle: "And when Joshua heard the noise of the people as they shouted, he said unto Moses, There is a noise of war in the camp" (Exod. 32:17). It can be used of the "sound" of words (Deut. 1:34), water (Ezek. 1:24), weeping (Isa. 65:19), and thunder (Exod. 9:23).

The word can also represent the thing that is spoken: "And unto Adam he said, Because thou hast hearkened unto the voice of thy wife, and hast eaten of the tree of which I commanded thee . . ." (Gen. 3:17). In an extended nuance *qôl* signifies the thing said, even though it is written down: "Then he wrote a letter the second time to them, saying, If ye be mine, and if ye will hearken unto my voice . . ." (2 Kings 10:6).

There are several special phrases related to *qôl*. "To lift up one's *voice* and weep" signifies many things including crying out for help (Gen. 39:14), mourning for present or anticipated tragedy (Gen. 21:16), and the "sound" of disaster (Num. 16:34) or joy (Gen. 29:11).

"To hearken to one's voice" means such things as taking note of something and believing it (Gen. 4:23), following another's suggestions (Gen. 3:17), complying with another's request (Gen. 21:12), obeying another's command (Gen. 22:18), and answering a prayer (2 Sam. 22:7).

Theologically the word is crucial in contexts relating to prophecy. The prophet's "voice" is God's "voice" (Exod. 3:18; cf. 7:1; Deut. 18:18-19). God's "voice" is sometimes the roar of thunder (Exod. 9:23, 29) or a "still small voice" (1 Kings 19:12). Thunder demonstrated God's tremendous power and evoked fear and submission. In covenantal contexts God stipulates that His "voice," heard in both the roar of thunder and the prophetic message, is authoritative and when obeyed brings reward (Exod. 19:5; 1 Sam. 12:14-18). The blast ("sound") of a trumpet is used to signify divine power (Josh. 6:5) and presence (2 Sam. 6:15).

Interestingly the first biblical appearance of *qôl* (Gen. 3:8) is a highly debated passage. Exactly what did Adam and Eve hear in the garden? Was it the sound of God walking (cf. 1 Kings 14:6)?

VOW

A. Verb.

nādar (נָדַר), "to vow." This verb occurs in Semitic languages (Ugaritic, Phoenician, and Aramaic). In Phoenician-Punic inscriptions the verb and also the noun derived from it frequently denote human sacrifices and in a more general sense signify a gift. In the Old Testament *nādar* occurs 31 times.

The distribution of the verb is over the entire Old Testament (narrative, legal, poetic, but more rarely in the prophetic books). Beyond the Old Testament the verb occurs in the Dead Sea Scrolls, rabbinic Hebrew, medieval and modern Hebrew. However, its usage declined from post-Exilic times onward.

Both men and women could "vow" a vow. Numbers 30 deals with the law concerning vows; cf. Num. 30:2: "If a man vow a vow unto the Lord, or swear an oath to bind his soul with a bond . . ."; and Num. 30:3: "If a woman also vow a vow unto the Lord, and bind herself by a bond. . . ."

The Septuagint has *euchomai* ("to wish").

B. Noun.

neder (נֶדֶר), "vow; votive offering." This noun occurs 60 times in biblical Hebrew and is often used in conjunction with the verb (19 times): ". . . Any of thy vows which thou vowest . . ." (Deut. 12:17). Modern versions compress the noun and verb into one idiom: "Or whatever you have vowed to give" (NIV), or give a technical usage to the noun: "Or any of your votive offerings which you vow" (RSV).

The vow has two basic forms, the unconditional and the conditional. The unconditional is an "oath" where someone binds himself without expecting anything in return: "I will pay my vows unto the Lord now in the presence of all his people" (Ps. 116:14). The obligation is binding upon the person who has made a "vow." The word spoken has the force of an oath which generally could not be broken: "If a man vow a vow unto the Lord, or swear an oath to bind his soul with a bond; he shall not break his word, he shall do [everything he said]" (Num. 30:2). The conditional "vow" generally had a preceding clause before the oath giving the conditions which had to come to pass before the "vow" became valid: "And Jacob vowed a vow, saying, If God will be with me, and will [watch over me] . . . , so that I come again to my father's house in peace; then shall the Lord be my God . . . and of all that thou shalt give me I will surely give the tenth unto thee" (Gen. 28:20-22).

"Vows" usually occurred in serious situations. Jacob needed the assurance of God's presence before setting out for Padan-aram (Gen. 28:20-22); Jephthah made a rash "vow" before battle (Judg. 11:30; cf. Num. 21:1-3); Hannah greatly desired a child (1 Sam. 1:11), when she made a "vow." Though conditional "vows" were often made out of desperation, there is no question of the binding force of the "vow." Ecclesiastes amplifies the Old Testament teaching on "vowing": "When thou vowest a vow unto God, defer not to pay it. . . . Better is it that thou shouldest not vow, than that thou shouldest vow and not pay. . . . Neither say thou before the angel, that it was an error" (5:4-6). First, a "vow" is always made to God. Even non-Israelites made "vows" to Him (Jon. 1:16). Second, a "vow" is made voluntarily. It is never associated with a life of piety or given the status of religious requirement in the Old Testament. Third, a "vow" once made must be kept. One cannot annul the "vow." However, the Old Testament allows for "redeeming" the "vow"; by payment of an equal amount in silver, a person, a field, or a house dedicated by "vow" to the Lord could be redeemed (Lev. 27:1-25).

This practice, however, declined in Jesus' time, and therefore the Talmud frowns upon the practice of "vowing" and refers to those who vow as "sinners."

Neder signifies a kind of offering: "And thither ye shall bring your burnt offerings, and your sacrifices, and your tithes, and [contributions] of your hand, and your vows, and your freewill offerings . . ." (Deut. 12:6). In particular the word represents a kind of peace or "votive offering" (Ezra 7:16). It also is a kind of thank offering: "Behold upon the mountains the feet of him that bringeth good tidings, that publisheth peace! . . . Perform thy vows . . ." (Nah. 1:15). Here even Gentiles expressed their thanks to God presumably with a gift promised upon condition of deliverance (cf. Num. 21:1-3). Such offerings may also be expressions of zeal for God (Ps. 22:25). One can give to God anything not abominable to Him (Lev. 27:9 ff.; Deut. 23:18), including one's services (Lev. 27:2). Pagans were thought to feed and/or tend their gods, while God denied that "vows" paid to Him were to be so conceived (Ps. 50:9-13). In paganism the god rewarded the devotee because of and in proportion to his offering. It was a contractual relationship whereby the god was obligated to pay a debt thus incurred. In Israel no such contractual relationship was in view.

The Israelites' unique and concrete demonstrations of love for God show that under Moses love (Deut. 6:4) was more than pure legalism; it was spiritual devotion. God's Messiah was pledged to offer Himself as a sacrifice for sin (Ps. 22:25; cf. Lev. 27:2 ff.). This was the only sacrifice absolutely and unconditionally acceptable to God. Every man is obliged to pay the "vow" before God: "Praise waiteth for thee, O God in Zion: and unto thee shall the vow be performed. . . . Unto thee shall all flesh come" (Ps. 65:1-2).

The Septuagint has *euche* ("prayer; oath; vow").

TO WALK

A. Verb.

hālak (הָלַךְ), "to go, walk, behave." This verb appears in most Semitic languages (although it has a different meaning in Arabic). It is attested in all periods of Hebrew. Old Testament Hebrew attests it about 1,550 times, while the Aramaic uses it a few times.

Essentially, this root refers to movement without any suggestion of direction in the sense of going, whether of man (Gen. 9:23), beasts (Gen. 3:14), or inanimate objects (Gen. 2:14—the first occurrence of the word). In cases other than men (where it means "to walk") *hālak* may be translated "to go." It is used sometimes with a special emphasis on the end or goal of the action in mind; men are but flesh, "a wind that passeth [goes] away, and cometh not again"

(Ps. 78:39). Applied to human existence the word suggests "going to one's death," as in Gen. 15:2, when Abraham says: "O Lord God, what wilt thou give me, since I am [going to my death] childless . . . ?" (NASB). This verb can also be used of one's behavior, or the way one "walks in life." So he who "walks" uprightly shall be blessed of God (Isa. 33:15). This does not refer to walking upright on one's feet but to living a righteous life.

This root is used in various other special ways. It may be used to emphasize that a certain thing occurred; Jacob went and got the kid his mother requested, in other words, he actually did the action (Gen. 27:14). In Gen. 8:3 the waters of the flood steadily receded from the surface of the earth. Sometimes this verb implies movement away from, as in Gen. 18:33, when the Lord "departed" from Abraham.

God is said to "walk" or "go" in three senses. First, there are certain cases where He assumed some kind of physical form. For example, Adam and Eve heard the sound of God "walking" to and fro in the garden of Eden (Gen. 3:8). He "walks" on the clouds (Ps. 104:3) or in the heavens (Job 22:14); these are probably anthropomorphisms (God is spoken of as if He had bodily parts). Even more often God is said to accompany His people (Exod. 33:14), to go to redeem (deliver) them from Egypt (2 Sam. 7:23), and to come to save them (Ps. 80:2). The idea of God's "going" ("walking") before His people in the pillars of fire and cloud (Exod. 13:21) leads to the idea that His people must "walk" behind Him (Deut. 13:5). Quite often the people are said to have "walked" or to be warned against "walking behind" foreign gods (Deut. 4:3). Thus, the rather concrete idea of following God through the wilderness moves to "walking behind" Him spiritually. Some scholars suggest that "walking behind" pagan gods (or even the true God) arose from the pagan worship where the god was carried before the people as they entered the sanctuary. Men may also "walk . . . after the imagination of their evil heart," or act stubbornly (Jer. 3:17). The pious followed or practiced God's commands; they "walked" in righteousness (Isa. 33:15), in humility (Mic. 6:8), and in integrity (Ps. 15:2). They also "walk with God" (Gen. 5:22), and they live in His presence, and "walk before" Him (Gen. 17:1), in the sense of living responsibly before Him.

B. Nouns.

halîkāh (הֲלִיכָה), "course; doings; traveling company; caravan; procession." This noun occurs 6 times in the Old Testament.

This word conveys several nuances. In Nah. 2:5 *halîkāh* refers to a "course": "He shall recount his worthies: they shall stumble in their walk. . . ." The word means "doings" in Prov. 31:27. It may also mean "traveling-company" or "caravan" as in Job 6:19 or a "procession" as in Ps. 68:24.

Several other related nouns occur infrequently. *Mahalāk,* which appears 5 times, means "passage" (Ezek. 42:4) and "journey" (Neh. 2:6). *Hēlek* occurs twice and means a "visitor" (2 Sam. 12:4). *Hālîk* appears once with the meaning "steps" (Job 29:6). *Tahalukāh* occurs once to mean "procession," specifically a thanksgiving procession (Neh. 12:31).

WALL

chômāh (חוֹמָה), "wall." This word is found in several Semitic languages and even in Egyptian. In Phoenician, it has the more restricted significance of "fortifications." It is thought that the root meaning is "to protect," as in the Arabic *chama*, "to protect."

Chômāh occurs about 120 times in the Hebrew Bible. Its first occurrence is in Exod. 14:22: "And the children of Israel went into the midst of the sea upon the dry ground: and the waters were a wall unto them on their right hand, and on their left." It is rare in the Pentateuch, in the historical books, and in the poetical books. The most frequent use is in Nehemiah, where Nehemiah is in charge of the rebuilding of the "wall" of Jerusalem.

The primary meaning of *chômāh* is a "wall" around a city, since in ancient Israel people had to protect themselves by constructing such a well-fortified "wall" (cf. Lev. 25:29-30). Stones were used in the construction of the "wall": "Now Tobiah the Ammonite was by him, and he said, Even that which they build, if a fox go up, he shall even break down their stone wall" (Neh. 4:3). The "wall" was also strengthened by thickness and other devices. From Solomonic times double walls (casemate) served a strategic purpose in that they were easy to construct and could be filled in with rocks and dirt in the case of a siege. There was also another possibility during a siege: "And the city was broken up, and all the men of war fled by night by the way of the gate between two walls, which is by the king's garden: (now the Chaldees were against the city round about:) . . ." (2 Kings 25:4).

In the case of war the enemy besieged a city and made efforts to breach the "wall" with a battering ram. The goal was to force a breach wide enough for the troops to enter into the city; "And Jehoash king of Israel took Amaziah king of Judah, the son of Jehoash the son of Ahaziah, at Beth–shemesh, and came to Jerusalem, and brake down the wall of Jerusalem from the gate of Ephraim unto the corner gate, four hundred cubits [about six hundred feet]" (2 Kings 14:13). At the time of Nebuchadnezzar's invasion and victory over Jerusalem, he had the "walls" of the city demolished: "And they burnt the house of God, and brake down the wall of Jerusalem, and burnt all the palaces thereof with fire, and destroyed all the goodly vessels thereof" (2 Chron. 36:19). For this reason Nehemiah had to help his unsuccessful compatriots to rebuild the "wall" about 135 years later: "Then said I unto them, Ye see the distress that we are in, how Jerusalem lieth waste, and the gates thereof are burned with fire: come, and let us build up the wall of Jerusalem, that we be no more a reproach" (Neh. 2:17).

Chômāh also referred to any "wall," whether around buildings or parts of the city such as the temple precincts: "And behold a wall on the outside of the house round about, and in the man's hand a measuring reed of six cubits long by the cubit and a handbreadth: so he measured the breadth of the building, one reed; and the height, one reed" (Ezek. 40:5).

The Septuagint gives the following translation: *teichos* ("wall").

WAR

A. Noun.

miləchāmāh (מִלְחָמָה), ''war; battle; skirmish; combat.'' This word has a cognate only in Ugaritic. Biblical Hebrew attests it 315 times and in all periods.

This word means ''war,'' the over-all confrontation of two forces (Gen. 14:2). It can refer to the engagement in hostilities considered as a whole, the ''battle'': ''. . . And they joined battle with them in the vale of Siddim'' (Gen. 14:8). This word is used not only of what is intended but of the hand-to-hand fighting which takes place: ''And when Joshua heard the noise of the people as they shouted, he said unto Moses, There is a noise of war in the camp'' (Exod. 32:17). *Miləchāmāh* sometimes represents the art of soldiering, or ''combat'': ''The Lord is a man of war . . .'' (Exod. 15:3).

There are several principles which were supposed to govern ''war'' in the Old Testament. Unjust violence was prohibited, but ''war'' as a part of ancient life was led (Judg. 4:13) and used by God (Num. 21:14). If it was preceded by sacrifices recognizing His leadership and sovereignty (1 Sam. 7:9) and if He was consulted and obeyed (Judg. 20:23), Israel was promised divine protection (Deut. 20:1-4). Not one life would be lost (Josh. 10:11). God's presence in ''battle'' was symbolized by the ark of the covenant (1 Sam. 4:3-11). His presence necessitated spiritual and ritualistic cleanliness (Deut. 23:9-14). Before and during ''battle,'' trumpets were blown placing the cause before God in anticipation of the victory and gratitude for it (Num. 10:9-10), as well as to relay the orders of the commanders. A war cry accompanied the initiation of ''battle'' (Josh. 6:5). At the beginning Israel's army consisted of every man over twenty and under fifty (Num. 1:2-3). Sometimes only certain segments of this potential citizens' army were summoned (Num. 31:3-6). There were several circumstances which could exempt one from ''war'' (Num. 1:48-49; Deut. 20:5-8). Under David and Solomon there grew a professional army. It was especially prominent under Solomon, whose army was renowned for its chariotry. Cities outside Palestine were to be offered terms of surrender before being attacked. Compliance meant subjugation to slavery (Deut. 20:10-11). Cities and peoples within the Promised Land were to be utterly wiped out. They were under the ban (Deut. 2:34; 3:6; 20:16-18). This made these battles uniquely holy battles (a holy war) where everything was especially devoted and sacrificed to God. Israel's kings were admonished to trust in God as their strength rather than in a great many horses and chariots (Deut. 17:16). Her armies were forbidden to cut down fruit trees in order to build siege equipment (Deut. 20:19-20). Soldiers were paid by keeping booty won in ''battle'' (Num. 31:21-31). The entire army divided the spoil—even those in the rear guard (Num. 31:26-47; Judg. 5:30). God, too, was appointed a share (Num. 31:28-30).

B. Verb.

lācham (לָחַם), ''to engage in battle, fight, wage war.'' This verb occurs 171 times in biblical Hebrew. The first appearance is in Exod. 1:10: ''Come on, let us deal wisely with them; lest they multiply, and it come to pass, that, when there falleth out any war, they join also unto our enemies, and fight against us, and so get them up out of the land.''

TO WASH

rāchats (רָחַץ), "to wash, bathe." This word is common to both ancient and modern Hebrew and is found in ancient Ugaritic as well. It is used some 72 times in the text of the Hebrew Old Testament. The first occurrence of the word in the text illustrates one of its most common uses: "Let a little water . . . be fetched, and wash your feet . . ." (Gen. 18:4).

When the word is used figuratively to express vengeance, the imagery is a bit more gruesome: ". . . He shall wash his feet in the blood of the wicked" (Ps. 58:10). Pilate's action in Matt. 27:24 is reminiscent of the psalmist's statement "I will wash mine hands in innocency" (Ps. 26:6). The parts of a sacrificial animal usually "were washed" before they were burned on the altar (Exod. 29:17). *Rāchats* is frequently used in the sense of "bathing" or "washing" oneself (Exod. 2:5; 2 Sam. 11:2). Beautiful eyes are figuratively described as "washed with milk" (Song of Sol. 5:12).

kābas (כָּבַס), "to wash." A common term throughout the history of Hebrew for the "washing" of clothes, this word is found also in ancient Ugaritic and Akkadian, reflecting the treading aspect. *Kābas* occurs in the Hebrew Old Testament 51 times. It is found for the first time in the Old Testament in Gen. 49:11 as part of Jacob's blessing on Judah: ". . . He washed his garments in wine. . . ."

The word is used in the Old Testament primarily in the sense of "washing" clothes, both for ordinary cleansing (2 Sam. 19:24) and for ritual cleansing (Exod. 19:10, 14; Lev. 11:25). It is often used in parallelism with the expression "to wash oneself," as in Lev. 14:8-9. *Kābas* is used in the sense of "washing" or "bathing" oneself only in the figurative sense and in poetic usage, as in Jer. 4:14: "O Jerusalem, wash thine heart from wickedness, that thou mayest be saved."

WATCH

A. Noun.

mishəmereth (מִשְׁמֶרֶת); *mishəmār* (מִשְׁמָר), "watch; guard; post; confinement; prison; custody; division." The first or feminine form of this word appears 78 times, while the masculine form is attested 22 times. These forms are scattered through biblical literature.

The noun *mishəmār* means a "military watch" over a city: "Nevertheless we made our prayer unto our God, and set a watch against them day and night because of them [our enemies]" (Neh. 4:9). This word represents the place where a guard or watchman fulfills his task: ". . . And appoint watches of the inhabitants of Jerusalem, every one in his watch, and every one to be over against his house" (Neh. 7:3). Someone who guards something keeps "watch" over it: "Mattaniah, and Bakbukiah, . . . were porters keeping the ward at the thresholds of the gates" (Neh. 12:25). In Job 7:12 *mishəmār* means "watch" or "guard" in general (over a potentially dangerous criminal): "Am I a sea, or a whale, that thou settest a watch over me?"

Mishəmār can also represent a "place of confinement," such as a jail: "And he put them in ward in the house of the captain of the guard, into the prison, the place where Joseph was bound" (Gen. 40:3—the first occurrence of the word). Joseph put his brothers "into ward three days" (Gen. 42:17) and thereafter allowed 9 of them to return to Palestine to get Benjamin (an act supposedly proving they were not spies) while 1 of them remained in the Egyptian "prison" (Gen. 42:19). Under Mosaic law there were to be no prisons where people were held for extended periods after being convicted of a crime. Instead, those charged were held for a very short time (sometimes) immediately preceding trial until the trial could be arranged (Lev. 24:12). After the trial the guilty party was killed, punished, fined, or indentured until he worked out his fine.

Mishəmār sometimes represents a group of attendants, especially in the temple. In this nuance the word may represent the temple guard-units: "To Shuppim and Hosah the lot came forth westward, with the gate Shallecheth, by the causeway of the going up, ward against ward" (1 Chron. 26:16). However, in Neh. 12:24 the service rendered is the Levitical service in general, therefore, "division corresponding to division." All these Levitical "divisions" constituted the full services of the temple (Neh. 13:14).

The noun *mishəmereth* appears with the same meanings as those just set forth. It can mean a "military watchman or guard" (cf. Neh. 7:3). In Isa. 21:8 the word signifies the place where one keeps watch: ". . . I am set in my *wards* whole nights. . . ." The phrase "to keep watch," in the sense of to fulfill the function of a watchman or guard, appears with *mishəmereth* in 2 Kings 11:5: "A third part of you that enter in on the sabbath shall even be keepers of the watch of the king's house." *Mishəmereth* represents a place of confinement in 2 Sam. 20:3: David put 10 of his concubines who had been defiled by Absalom into a house of confinement (NASB, "under guard").

Mishəmereth often is used to represent a more abstract idea than *mishəmār,* whereas *mishəmār* means the units of Levites who served the Lord (perhaps with the exception of Neh. 13:30, where *mishəmereth* may mean "service-unit"). *Mishəmereth* refers to the priestly or Levitical service itself: "Therefore shall ye abide at the door of the tabernacle of the congregation day and night seven days, and keep the charge of the Lord . . ." (Lev. 8:35). Num. 3:25 speaks of the duties of the Levites in the tent of meeting. The Levites were to "keep the charge of the tabernacle of testimony" (Num. 1:53). The word, therefore, suggests both regularly prescribed act and obligation. The latter idea alone appears in Num. 8:26, where God allows Levites over 50 to serve in extraordinary circumstances, to keep an obligation.

This word often refers to divine obligation or service in general, a non-cultic obligation: "Because that Abraham obeyed my voice, and kept my charge, my commandments, my statutes, and my laws" (Gen. 26:5—the first occurrence of *mishəmereth;* cf. Deut. 11:1).

B. Verb.

shāmar (שָׁמַר), "to keep, watch." This verb occurs 468 times in the Old Testament. The word means "to watch" in Job 14:16: "For now thou numberest my steps: dost thou not watch over my sin?"

WATER

mayim (מַיִם), "water; flood." This word has cognates in Ugaritic and old South Arabic. It occurs about 580 times and in every period of biblical Hebrew.

First, "water" is one of the original basic substances. This is its significance in Gen. 1:2 (the first occurrence of the word): "And the Spirit of God moved upon the face of the waters." In Gen. 1:7 God separated the "waters" above and the "waters" below (cf. Exod. 20:4) the expanse of the heavens.

Second, the word represents that which is in a well, "water" to be drunk (Gen. 21:19). "Living water" is "water" that flows: "And Isaac's servants digged in the valley, and found there a well of springing [living] water . . . ." (Gen. 26:19). "Water" of oppression or affliction is so designated because it is drunk in prison: "Put this fellow in the prison, and feed him with bread of affliction and with water of affliction, until I come in peace" (1 Kings 22:27). Job 9:30 speaks of slush or snow water: "If I wash myself with snow water, and make my hands never so clean. . . ."

Third, *mayim* can represent liquid in general: ". . . For the Lord our God hath put us to silence, and given us water of gall to drink, because we have sinned against the Lord" (Jer. 8:14). The phrase, *me raglayim* ("water of one's feet") is urine: "Hath my master sent me to thy master, and to thee, to speak these words? hath he not sent me to the men which sit on the wall, that they may eat their own dung, and drink their own piss [water of their feet] with you?" (2 Kings 18:27; cf. Isa. 25:10).

Fourth, in Israel's cultus "water" was poured or sprinkled (no one was ever immersed into water), symbolizing purification. So Aaron and his sons were to be washed with "water" as a part of the rite consecrating them to the priesthood: "And Aaron and his sons thou shalt bring unto the door of the tabernacle of the congregation, and shalt wash them with water" (Exod. 29:4). Parts of the sacrificial animal were to be ritually cleansed with "water" during the sacrifice: "But his inwards and his legs shall he wash in water . . ." (Lev. 1:9). Israel's rites sometimes include consecrated "water": "And the priest shall take holy water in an earthen vessel; and of the dust that is in the floor of the tabernacle the priest shall take, and put it into the water" (Num. 5:17). "Bitter water" was used in Israel's rituals, too: "And the priest shall set the woman before the Lord, and uncover the woman's head, and put the offering of memorial in her hands, which is the jealousy offering: and the priest shall have in his hand the bitter water that causeth the curse" (Num. 5:18). It was "water" which when drunk brought a curse and caused bitterness (Num. 5:24).

Fifth, in proper names this word is used of springs, streams, or seas and/or the area in the immediate vicinity of such bodies of water: "Say unto Aaron,

Take thy rod, and stretch out thine hand upon the waters of Egypt, upon their streams, upon their rivers, and upon their ponds, and upon all their pools of water, that they may become blood . . .'' (Exod. 7:19).

Sixth, this word is used figuratively in many senses. *Mayim* symbolizes danger or distress: "He sent from above, he took me; he drew me out of many waters" (2 Sam. 22:17). Outbursting force is represented by *mayim* in 2 Sam. 5:20: "The Lord hath broken forth upon mine enemies before me, as the [break-through] of waters." "Mighty waters" describes the onrush of the godless nations against God: "The nations shall rush like the rushing of many waters . . ." (Isa. 17:13). Thus the word is used to picture something impetuous, violent, and overwhelming: "Terrors take hold on him as waters, a tempest stealeth him away in the night" (Job 27:20). In other passages "water" is used to represent timidity: ". . . Wherefore the hearts of the people melted, and became as water" (Josh. 7:5). Related to this nuance is the connotation "transitory": ". . . Because thou shalt forget thy misery, and remember it as waters that pass away" (Job 11:16). In Isa. 32:2 "water" represents that which is refreshing: "And a man shall be as a hiding place from the wind, and a covert from the tempest; as rivers of water in a dry place, as the shadow of a great rock in a weary land." Rest and peace are figured by waters of rest, or quiet waters: ". . . He leadeth me beside the still waters" (Ps. 23:2). Similar ideas are involved when one's wife's charms are termed "water of life" or "water which enlivens": "Drink waters out of thine own cistern, and running waters out of thine own well" (Prov. 5:15). Outpoured "water" represents bloodshed (Deut. 12:16), wrath (Hos. 5:10), justice (Amos 5:24; KJV, "judgment"), and strong feelings (Job 3:24).

təhôm (תְּהוֹם), "deep water; ocean; water table; waters; flood of waters." Cognates of this word appear in Ugaritic, Akkadian (as early as Ebla, around 2400-2250 B.C.), and Arabic. The 36 occurrences of this word appear almost exclusively in poetical passages but in all historical periods.

The word represents the "deep water" whose surface freezes when cold: "The waters are hid as with a stone, and the face of the deep is frozen" (Job 38:30). In Ps. 135:6 *təhôm* is used of the "ocean" in contrast to the seas: "Whatsoever the Lord pleased, that did he in heaven, and in earth, in the seas, and all deep places [in the entire ocean]" (cf. Ps. 148:7 et al.).

The word has special reference to the deep floods or sources of water. Sailors in the midst of a violent storm "mount up to the heaven, they go down again to the depths (Ps. 107:26). This is hyperbolic or exaggerated poetical talk, but it presents the "depths" as the opposite of the heavens or skies. This emphasis is especially prominent in the song of Moses, where the word represents the ever-existing (but not eternal), ever-threatening, and perilous "deep," not simply an element of nature but a dangerous element: "The depths have covered them: they sank into the bottom as a stone" (Exod. 15:5). On the other hand, in such contexts *təhôm* may mean no more than "deep water" into which heavy objects quickly sink.

Təhôm can represent an inexhaustible source of water or, by way of poetic comparison, of blessing: ". . . With blessings of heaven above, blessings of the deep that lieth under . . ." (Gen. 49:25). In such contexts the word represents the "water table" always available below the surface of the earth—what was tapped by digging wells, out of which flowed springs, and what was one with the waters beneath the surface of oceans, lakes, seas, and rivers. This was what God opened together with the waters above the expanse (Gen. 7:11; cf. 1:7) and what later was closed to cause and terminate the great Flood (Gen. 8:2; cf. Ps. 33:6; 104:6; Ezek. 26:19). In such contexts the word represents a "flood of waters" (Ps. 33:6).

In Gen. 1:2 (the first occurrence of the word) *təhôm* is used of "all waters" which initially covered the surface of the entire earth: ". . . And darkness was upon the face of the *deep*" (cf. Prov. 3:20; 8:24, 27–28).

WAY

A. Nouns.

derek (דֶּרֶךְ), "way (path, road, highway); distance; journey; manner, conduct; condition; destiny." This noun has cognates in Akkadian, Ugaritic (where it sometimes means "power" or "rule"), Phoenician, Punic, Arabic, and Aramaic. It occurs about 706 times in biblical Hebrew and in all periods.

First, this word refers to a path, a road, or a highway. In Gen. 3:24 (the first occurrence of the word) it means "path" or "route": ". . . And he placed at the east of the garden of Eden cherubim, and a flaming sword which turned every [direction], to [guard] the way of the tree of life." Sometimes, as in Gen. 16:7, the word represents a pathway, road, or route: "And the angel of the Lord found her by a fountain of water in the wilderness, by the fountain in the way to Shur." The actual road itself is represented in Gen. 38:21: "Where is the [temple prostitute], that was openly by the wayside?" In Num. 20:17 the word means "highway," a well-known and well-traveled road: ". . . We will go by the king's highway, we will not turn to the right hand nor to the left, until we have passed thy borders."

Second, this noun represents a "distance" (how far or how long) between two points: "And he set three days' journey [a distance of three days] betwixt himself and Jacob . . ." (Gen. 30:36).

In other passages *derek* refers to the action or process of "taking a journey": "And to his father he sent after this manner; ten asses laden with the good things of Egypt, and ten she asses laden with corn and bread and meat for his father by the way [on the journey]" (Gen. 45:23). In an extended nuance *derek* means "undertaking": "If thou turn away thy foot from the sabbath, from doing thy pleasure on my holy day; and call the sabbath a delight, the holy of the Lord, honorable; and shalt honor him, not doing thine own ways, nor finding thine own pleasure . . ." (Isa. 58:13). Cf. Gen. 24:21: "And the man wondering at her held his peace, to wit whether the Lord had made his journey prosperous or not" (cf. Deut. 28:29).

In another emphasis this word connotes how and what one does, a "manner, custom, behavior, mode of life": "Our father is old, and there is not a man in the earth to come in unto us after the manner of all the earth" (Gen. 19:31). In 1 Kings 2:4 *derek* is applied to an activity that controls one, one's life-style: "If thy children take heed to their way, to walk before me in truth with all their heart and with all their soul, there shall not fail thee . . . a man on the throne of Israel.'' In 1 Kings 16:26 *derek* is used of Jeroboam's attitude: "For he walked in all the way of Jeroboam the son of Nebat, and in his sin wherewith he made Israel to sin. . . .'' Deeds, or specific acts, may be connoted by this noun: "Lo, these are parts of his ways; but how little a portion is heard of him? But the thunder of his power who can understand?" (Job 26:14).

Derek refers to a "condition" in the sense of what has happened to someone. This is clear by the parallelism of Isa. 40:27: "Why sayest thou, O Jacob, and speakest, O Israel, My way is hid from the Lord, and [the justice due to me is passed away] from my God?" In one passage *derek* signifies the overall course and fixed path of one's life, or his "destiny": "O Lord, I know that the way of man is not in himself: it is not in man that walketh to direct his steps" (Jer. 10:23).

Finally, this word sometimes seems to bear the meaning of its Ugaritic cognate, "power" or "rulership": "Only acknowledge thine iniquity, that thou hast transgressed against the Lord thy God, and hast scattered thy ways [NASB, "favors"] to the strangers under every green tree . . .'' (Jer. 3:13; cf. Job 26:14; 36:23; 40:19; Ps. 67:2; 110:7; 119:37; 138:5; Prov. 8:22; 19:16; 31:3; Hos. 10:13; Amos 8:14). Some scholars, however, contest this explanation of these passages.

'ōrach (אֹרַח), "way; path; course; conduct; manner.'' Cognates of this word appear in Akkadian, Arabic, and Aramaic. Its 57 occurrences in biblical Hebrew are all in poetry except Gen. 18:11.

In meaning this word parallels Hebrew *derek,* which it often synonymously parallels. First, *'ōrach* means "path" or "way" conceived as a marked-out, well-traveled course: "Dan shall be a serpent by the way, an adder in the path, that biteth the horse heels . . .'' (Gen. 49:17). In Judg. 5:6 the word means "highway": "In the days of Shamgar . . . the highways were unoccupied, and the travelers walked through byways.'' When the sun is likened to a "strong man" who rejoices "to run a race" (Ps. 19:5), *'ōrach* represents a race course rather than a highway or a primitive snake-laden path. The man who makes his path straight goes directly on his journey, not turning aside for the beckoning harlot (Prov. 9:15). So here the word represents the "course" one follows between his departure and arrival conceived in terms of small units, almost step by step. In Ps. 8:8 the word represents the ocean currents: ". . . The fowl of the air and the fish of the sea, and whatsoever passeth through the paths of the seas.''

'Ōrach signifies the ground itself as the path upon which one treads: "He pursued them, and passed safely; even by the way that he had not gone with his feet" (Isa. 41:3).

In Job 30:12 the word seems to represent an obstruction or dam: ". . . They push away my feet, and they raise up against me the ways of their destruction.''

The word can refer to a recurring life event typical of an individual or a group. In its first biblical occurrence (Gen. 18:11) it is used of "the manner of women" (menstruation). Job 16:22 mentions the "way whence I shall not return," or death, while other passages speak of life actions (Job 34:11; literally, "conduct") or life-style (Prov. 15:10: "Correction is grievous unto him that forsaketh the way . . ."—prescribed life-style; Prov. 5:6: "Lest thou shouldest ponder the path [which is typified by] life . . ."). Thus, 'ōrach sometimes figures a proper course of action or proceeding within a given realm—"the path of judgment" (Isa. 40:14).

The noun 'ōrəchāh, which occurs 3 times, represents a "wandering company" or a "caravan" (Gen. 37:25).

B. Verb.

'Ārach means "to go, wander." This word, which occurs 6 times in biblical Hebrew, has cognates in Phoenician, Ethiopic, Aramaic, and Syriac. One example of this verb's usage is found in Job 34:7-8: "What man is like Job . . . which goeth in company with the workers of iniquity, and walketh with wicked men."

WEAKER ONE; LITTLE ONE

taph (רַף), "weaker one; child; little one." Cognates of this noun appear in Arabic and Ethiopic. All but 4 of the 42 occurrences of this word are in prose literature and mostly in early (pre-monarchy) prose narrative.

Basically this word signifies those members of a nomadic tribe who are not able to march or who can only march to a limited extent. The word implies the "weaker ones." Thus we read of the men and the *tāphîm*, or the men and those who were unable to move quickly over long stretches: "And Judah said unto Israel, his father, Send the lad with me, and we will arise and go; that we may live, and not die, both we, and thou, and also our little ones" (Gen. 43:8). This nuance is clearer in Gen. 50:7-8: "And Joseph went up to bury his father; and with him went up all the servants of Pharaoh, the elders of his house, and all the elders of the land of Egypt, and all the house of Joseph, and his brethren and his father's house: only their little ones, and their flocks, and their herds, they left in the land of Goshen." They left the women and the aged to take care of the beasts and babies. These verses certainly make it clear that only men went along.

In several passages *taph* represents only the children and old ones: "And all their wealth, and all their little ones, and their wives took they captive, and spoiled even all that was in the house" (Gen. 34:29, first occurrence). All the able-bodied men of Shechem were killed (Gen. 34:26).

Sometimes the word means "children": "But all the women children [NASB, "girls"], that have not known a man by lying with him, keep alive for yourselves" (Num. 31:18; cf. v. 17).

WEALTH

hôn (הוֹן), "wealth; substance; riches; possessions; enough." The 26 occurrences of this word are almost wholly in wisdom literature, with 17 of them in the Book of Proverbs. This word appears only in the singular form.

Hôn usually refers to movable goods considered as "wealth": "But if he [the thief] be found, he shall restore seven-fold; he shall give all the substance of his house" (Prov. 6:31; cf. Ezek. 27:12). "Wealth" can be good and a sign of blessing: "Wealth and riches shall be in his [the righteous man's] house: and his righteousness endureth for ever" (Ps. 112:3). The creation is God's wealth: "I have rejoiced in the way of thy testimonies, as much as in all riches" (Ps. 119:14). In the Proverbs "wealth" is usually an indication of ungodliness: "The rich man's wealth is his strong city: the destruction of the poor is their poverty" (Prov. 10:15).

This word can also represent any kind of concrete "wealth": ". . . If a man would give all the substance of his house for love, it would utterly be contemned" (Song of Sol. 8:7). This is the significance of the word in its first occurrence: "Thou sellest thy people for nought and dost not increase thy wealth by their price" (Ps. 44:12). "Wealth" in general is meant in Prov. 12:27: "The slothful man roasteth not that which he took in hunting: but the substance of a diligent man is precious."

Finally, *hôn* means "enough" (only in Prov. 30:15-16): "The horseleech hath two daughters, crying, Give, Give. There are three things that are never satisfied, yea, four things say not, It is enough: the grave; and the barren womb; the earth that is not filled with water; and the fire that saith not, It is enough."

WEEK

shəbû'a (שָׁבוּעַ), "week." This noun appears about 20 times in biblical Hebrew. In Gen. 29:27 it refers to an entire "week" of feasting. Exod. 34:22 speaks of a special feast in Israel's religious calendar: "And thou shalt observe the feast of weeks, of the first fruits of wheat harvest, and the feast of ingathering at the year's end." In Lev. 12:5 the word appears with the dual suffix and signifies a period of two weeks: "But if she bear a maid child, then she shall be unclean two weeks. . . ."

TO GO A WHORING, BE A HARLOT

zānāh (זָנָה), "to go a whoring, commit fornication, be a harlot, serve other gods." This is the regular term denoting prostitution throughout the history of Hebrew, with special nuances coming out of the religious experience of ancient Israel. The word occurs approximately 90 times in the Hebrew Old Testament. It is used for the first time in the text at the conclusion of the story of the rape of Dinah by Shechem, as her brothers excuse their revenge by asking: "Should he deal with our sister as with a harlot?" (Gen. 34:31).

While the term means "to commit fornication," whether by male or by female, it is to be noted that it is almost never used to describe sexual misconduct on the part of a male in the Old Testament. Part of the reason lies in the differing attitude in ancient Israel concerning sexual activity by men and women. The main reason, however, is the fact that this term is used most frequently to describe "spiritual prostitution" in which Israel turned from

God to strange gods. Deut. 31:16 illustrates this meaning: "And the Lord said unto Moses, Behold, thou shalt sleep with thy fathers; and this people will rise up, and go a whoring after the gods of the strangers of the land, whither they go to be among them, and will forsake me, and break my covenant which I have made with them."

Zānāh became, then, the common term for spiritual backsliding. The act of harloting after strange gods was more than changing gods, however. This was especially true when Israel went after the Canaanite gods, for the worship of these pagan deities involved actual prostitution with cult prostitutes connected with the Canaanite shrines. In the Old Testament sometimes the use of the phrase "go a whoring after" gods implies an individual's involvement with cult prostitutes. An example might be in Exod. 34:15-16: "Lest thou make a covenant with the inhabitants of the land, and they go a whoring after their gods, and do sacrifice unto their gods. . . . And thou take of their daughters unto thy sons, and their daughters go a whoring after their gods, and make thy sons go a whoring after their gods."

The religious theory behind such activity at the Canaanite shrine was that such sexual activity with cult prostitutes, both male and female, who represented the gods and goddesses of the Canaanite fertility cult, would stimulate fertility in their crops and flocks. Such cult prostitutes were not designated as prostitutes but rather "holy ones" or "set-apart ones," since the Semitic term for "holy" means, first of all, to be set apart for a special use. This is illustrated in Deut. 23:17: "There shall be no cult prostitute [set-apart one] of the daughters of Israel, neither shall there be a cult prostitute of the sons of Israel" (RSV; KJV, "whore of the daughters of Israel" and "sodomite of the sons of Israel"). This theme of religious harlotry looms large in the prophets who denounce this backsliding in no uncertain terms. Ezekiel minces no words as he openly calls both Judah and Israel "harlots" and vividly describes their backsliding in sexual terms (Ezek. 16:6-63; 23).

The Book of Hosea, in which Hosea's wife Gomer became unfaithful and most likely was involved in such cult prostitution, again illustrates not only Hosea's heartbreak but also God's own heartbreak because of the unfaithfulness of his wife, Israel. Israel's unfaithfulness appears in Hos. 9:1: "Rejoice not, O Israel, for joy, as other people: for thou hast gone a whoring from thy God, thou hast loved a reward upon every cornfloor."

WICKED

A. Nouns.

rāshā' (רָשָׁע), "wicked; ungodly; guilty." *Rāshā'* occurs only in Hebrew and late Aramaic. The word occurs about 260 times as a noun or an adjective and especially in the poetic literature of the Old Testament. It is rare in the Pentateuch and in the historical books. Its frequency increases in the prophetical books.

The narrow meaning of *rāshā'* lies in the concept of "wrongdoing" or "being in the wrong." It is a legal term. The person who has sinned against the law is guilty: "They that forsake the law praise the wicked: but such as keep the law contend with them" (Prov. 28:4). When in Israel's history justice did not prevail, the "guilty" were acquitted: ". . . When the wicked beareth rule, the people mourn" (Prov. 29:2; cf. 2 Chron. 6:23).

Rāshā‘ also denotes the category of people who have done wrong, are still living in sin, and are intent on continuing with wrongdoing. This is the more general meaning of the word. The first psalm exhorts the godly not to imitate the deeds and behavior of the ungodly, wicked people. The "wicked" does not seek God (Ps. 10:4); he challenges God (Ps. 10:13). In his way of life the "wicked" loves violence (Ps. 11:5), oppresses the righteous (Ps. 17:9), does not repay his debts (Ps. 37:21), and lays a snare to trap the righteous (Ps. 119:110). Ps. 37 gives a vivid description of the acts of the "wicked" and also of God's judgment upon them. Facing the terrible force of the "wicked," the righteous prayed for God's deliverance and for His judgment upon them. This theme of judgment has already been anticipated in Ps. 1:6: "For the Lord knoweth the way of the righteous: but the way of the ungodly shall perish." The expectation of the righteous includes God's judgment on the "wicked" in this life that they might be ashamed (Ps. 31:17), be overcome by sorrows (Ps. 32:10), fall by their devices (Ps. 141:10), and die a premature death (Prov. 10:27), and that their remembrance will be no more (Prov. 10:7). It is expected that at the time of their death there will be great shouting: "When it goeth well with the righteous, the city rejoiceth: when the wicked perish, there is shouting" (Prov. 11:10).

The judgment upon the "wicked" is particularly strong in Proverbs, where the authors contrast the advantages of wisdom and righteousness and the disadvantages of the "wicked" (cf. 2:22: "But the wicked shall be cut off from the earth, and the transgressors shall be rooted out of it"). In Job another theme finds expression: why are the "wicked" not cut off? "Wherefore do the wicked live, become old, yea, are mighty in power?" (21:7). There is no clear answer to this question in the Old Testament. Malachi predicts a new age in which the distinction of the righteous and the "wicked" will be clear and where the righteous will triumph: "Then shall ye return, and discern between the righteous and the wicked, between him that serveth God and him that serveth him not" (Mal 3:18).

The Septuagint has three translations of *rāshā‘: asebes* ("godless; impious"); *hamartolos* ("sinner; sinful"), and *anomos* ("lawless").

Two other related nouns occur in the Old Testament. *Rēsha‘*, which is found about 30 times, usually means "wickedness": "Remember thy servants, Abraham, Isaac, and Jacob; look not unto the stubbornness of this people, nor to their wickedness, nor to their sin" (Deut. 9:27). *Rishə‘āh*, which appears about 15 times, refers to "wickedness or guilt": "For my righteousness the Lord hath brought me in to possess this land: but for the wickedness of these nations the Lord doth drive them out from before thee" (Deut. 9:4).

B. Adjective.

rāshā‘ (רָשָׁע), "wicked; guilty." This word may also be used as an adjective. In some cases a person is so guilty that he deserves death: ". . . If the wicked man be worthy to be beaten, that the judge shall cause him to lie down, and to be beaten before his face . . . by a certain number'' (Deut. 25:2). The characteristics of a ''wicked'' person qualify him as a godless, impious man: ''How much more, when wicked men have slain a righteous person in his own house upon his bed? shall I not therefore now require his blood of your hand, and take you away from the earth?'' (2 Sam. 4:11; cf. Ezek. 3:18-19).

C. Verb.

rāsha' (רָשַׁע), ''to be wicked, act wickedly.'' This verb is derived from the noun *rāshā'*. There is a similar root in Ethiopic and Arabic, with the respective meanings ''to forget'' and ''to be loose.'' This verb appears in 2 Chron. 6:37: ''Yet if they bethink themselves in the land whither they are carried captive, and turn and pray unto thee in the land of their captivity, saying, We have sinned, we have done amiss, and have dealt wickedly.''

WICKEDNESS

bəlîya'al (בְּלִיַּעַל), ''wickedness; wicked; destruction.'' The 27 occurrences of this noun are scattered throughout the periods of biblical Hebrew.

The basic meaning of this word appears in a passage such as Judg. 20:13, where the sons of *bəlîya'al* are perpetrators of wickedness (they raped and murdered a man's concubine): ''Now therefore deliver us the men, the children of Belial [NASB, ''worthless fellows''] which are in Gibeah, that we may put them to death, and put away evil from Israel.'' In its first appearance the word represents men who lead others into idolatry: ''Certain men, the children of Belial, are gone out from among you, and have [seduced] the inhabitants of their city . . .'' (Deut. 13:13). In Deut. 15:9 the word modifies Hebrew *dābār*, ''word'' or ''matter.'' Israel is warned to avoid ''wicked'' words (thoughts) in their hearts. *Bəlîya'al* is a synonym for *rāshā'* (''wicked rebellious one'') in Job 34:18. In Nah. 1:11 the wicked counselor plots evil against God. The psalmist uses *bəlîya'al* as a synonym of death: ''The cords of death encompassed me, and the torrents of ungodliness [KJV, ''floods of ungodly men''] terrified me'' (Ps. 18:4 NASB).

WIDOW

'aləmānāh (אַלְמָנָה), ''widow.'' Cognates of this word appear in Aramaic, Arabic, Akkadian, Phoenician, and Ugaritic. Biblical Hebrew attests it 55 times and in all periods.

The word represents a woman who, because of the death of her husband, has lost her social and economic position. The gravity of her situation was increased if she had no children. In such a circumstance she returned to her father's home and was subjected to the levirate rule whereby a close male relative surviving her husband was to produce a child through her in her husband's behalf: ''Then said Judah to Tamar his daughter-in-law, Remain a widow at thy father's house, till Shelah my son be grown . . .'' (Gen. 38:11—the first occurrence of the word). These words constitute a promise to Tamar that the disgrace of being without both husband and child would be removed when Shelah was old enough to marry. Even if children had been born before her husband's death, a widow's lot was not a happy one (2 Sam. 14:5). Israel was admonished to treat "widows" and other socially disadvantaged people with justice, God Himself standing as their protector (Exod. 22:21-24).

Wives whose husbands shut them away from themselves are sometimes called "widows": "And David came to his house at Jerusalem; and the king took the ten women his concubines, whom he had left to keep the house, and put them in ward, and fed them, but went not in unto them. So they were shut up unto the day of their death, living in widowhood" (2 Sam. 20:3).

Destroyed, plundered Jerusalem is called a "widow" (Lam. 1:1).

TO WILL, BE WILLING

'ābāh (אָבָה), "to will, be willing, consent." Common throughout the history of the Hebrew language, this word occurs in the Hebrew Bible just over 50 times. It is found for the first time in Gen. 24:5, where Abraham's servant who is about to be sent to find a wife for Isaac says: "Peradventure the woman will not be willing to follow me unto this land . . . ?"

It is to be noted that in all but 2 instances of its use in the Old Testament (Job 39:9; Isa. 1:19), the word is used with a negation, to indicate lack of willingness or consent. Even in these two positive uses, there seems to be a negative aspect or expectation implied. Job asks: "Will the unicorn be willing to serve thee. . . ?" (Job 39:9); and Isaiah seems almost hopeless as he says to Judah: "If ye be willing and obedient, ye shall eat the good of the land" (Isa. 1:19).

WINE

yayin (יַיִן), "wine." Cognates of this word appear in Akkadian, Ugaritic, Aramaic, Arabic, and Ethiopic. It appears about 141 times and in all periods of biblical Hebrew.

This is the usual Hebrew word for fermented grape. It is usually rendered "wine." Such "wine" was commonly drunk for refreshment: "And Melchizedek king of Salem brought forth bread and wine . . ." (Gen. 14:18; cf. 27:25). Passages such as Ezek. 27:18 inform us that "wine" was an article of commerce: "Damascus was thy merchant in the multitude of the wares of thy making, for the multitude of all riches; in the wine of Helbon, and white wool." Strongholds were supplied with "wine" in case of siege (2 Chron. 11:11). Proverbs recommends that kings avoid "wine" and strong drink but that it be given to those troubled with problems that they might drink and forget their problems (Prov. 31:4-7). "Wine" was used to make merry, to make one feel good without being intoxicated (2 Sam. 13:28).

Second, "wine" was used in rejoicing before the Lord. Once a year all Israel is to gather in Jerusalem. The money realized from the sale of a tithe of all their harvest was to be spent "for whatsoever thy soul lusteth after, for oxen, or for sheep, or for wine, or for strong drink, or for whatsoever thy soul desireth: and thou shalt eat there before the Lord thy God, and thou shalt rejoice . . ." (Deut. 14:26). "Wine" was offered to God at His command as part of the prescribed ritual (Exod. 29:40). Thus it was part of the temple supplies available for purchase by pilgrims so that they could offer it to God (1 Chron. 9:29). Pagans used "wine" in their worship, but "their wine is the poison of dragons, and the cruel venom of asps" (Deut. 32:33).

Yayin clearly represents an intoxicating beverage. This is evident in its first biblical appearance: "And Noah began to be a husbandman, and he planted a vineyard: and he drank of the wine, and was drunken . . ." (Gen. 9:20-21). The word is used as a synonym of *tîrôsh*, "new wine," in Hos. 4:11, where it is evident that both can be intoxicating. *Tîrôsh* is distinguished from *yayin* by referring only to new wine not fully fermented; *yayin* includes "wine" at any stage. In Gen. 27:28 (the first biblical occurrence of the word) Jacob's blessing includes the divine bestowal of an abundance of new wine. In 1 Sam. 1:15 *yayin* parallels *shēkār*, "strong drink." *Shēkār* in early times included wine (Num. 28:7) but meant strong drink made from any fruit or grain (Num. 6:3). People in special states of holiness were forbidden to drink "wine," such as the Nazarites (Num. 6:3), Samson's mother (Judg. 13:4), and priests approaching God (Lev. 10:9).

In Gen. 9:24 *yayin* means drunkenness: "And Noah awoke from his wine. . . ."

WING

kānāph (כָּנָף), "wing." The Hebrew word is represented in Semitic languages (Ugaritic, Akkadian, Aramaic, Syriac, and Arabic) and in Egyptian. *Kānāph* has maintained its meaning in rabbinic and modern Hebrew.

In the Old Testament *kānāph* occurs first in the Creation account: "And God created great whales, and every living creature that moveth, which the waters brought forth abundantly, after their kind, and every winged fowl after his kind: and God saw that it was good" (Gen. 1:21; cf. Ps. 78:27). In the biblical usage the idiom "every bird wing" denotes the class of birds; cf. "They, and every beast after his kind, and all the cattle after their kind, and every creeping thing that creepeth upon the earth after his kind, and every fowl after his kind, every bird of every sort" (Gen. 7:14). This phrase is translated in the KJV, "any winged fowl" (Deut. 4:17; cf. NASB, "any winged bird that flies in the sky").

The word "wing" appears 109 times in the Hebrew Old Testament, with particular concentration in the description of the 2 cherubim of wood in Solomon's temple and in Ezekiel's vision of the "creatures," or cherubim. Elsewhere the Bible speaks of "wings" of the cherubim (Exod. 25:20; 37:9) and of the seraphim (Isa. 6:2).

As an extension of the usage "wing," *kānāph* signifies "extremity." The seam or lower part of a garment was known as the *kānāph*. In the "fold" (*kānāph;* KJV, "skirt") of the garment one could carry things (Hag. 2:12).

Saul tore the edge (*kānāph;* KJV "skirt") of Samuel's robe (1 Sam. 15:27). The extremity of a land on the world was also known by the word *kānāph* and is translated by "corner" in English: "And he shall set up an ensign for the nations, and shall assemble the outcasts of Israel, and gather together the dispersed of Judah from the four corners of the earth" (Isa. 11:12; cf. Job 37:3; 38:13; Ezek. 7:2).

In the metaphorical use God is said to protect His people as a bird protects her young with her "wings" (Deut. 32:11). The psalmist expressed God's care and protection as a "shadow" of the "wings" (Ps. 17:8; cf. 36:7; 57:1; 61:4; 63:7; 91:45). In keeping with this usage Malachi looked forward to a new age, when "the Sun of righteousness [will] arise with healing in his wings; and ye shall go forth, and grow up as calves of the stall" (4:2).

When the nations are compared to birds, the association is that of terror and conquest. This is best expressed in Ezekiel's parable of the two eagles and the vine: "And say, Thus saith the Lord God; A great eagle with great wings, longwinged, full of feathers, which had divers colors, came unto Lebanon, and took the highest branch of the cedar: he cropped off the top of his young twigs, and carried it into a land of traffic; he set it in a city of merchants" (Ezek. 17:3-4). The believer is enjoined to seek refuge with God when adversity strikes him or adversaries surround him: "He shall cover thee with his feathers, and under his wings shall thou trust: his truth shall be thy shield and buckler" (Ps. 91:4).

The Septuagint gives the following translations: *pteruks* ("wing; pinion"); *pterugion* ("end; edge"); and *pteroros* ("feathered; winged") The KJV gives these senses: "wing; skirt; border; corner."

WISE; SKILLED

A. Adjective.

chākām (חָכָם), "wise; skillful; practical." This word plus the noun *chakəmāh* and the verb "to be wise" signify an important element of the Old Testament religious point of view. Religious experience was not a routine, a ritual, or faith experience. It was viewed as a mastery of the art of living in accordance with God's expectations. In their definition, the words "mastery" and "art" signify that wisdom was a process of attainment and not an accomplishment. The secular usage bears out the importance of these observations.

Chākām appears 132 times in the Hebrew Old Testament. It occurs most frequently in Job, Proverbs, and Ecclesiastes, for which reason these books are known as wisdom literature. The first occurrence of *chākām* is in Gen. 41:8: "And it came to pass in the morning that his spirit was troubled; and he sent and called for all the magicians of Egypt, and all the wise men thereof: and Pharaoh told them his dream; but there was none that could interpret them unto Pharaoh."

The *chākām* in secular usage signified a man who was a "skillful" craftsman. The manufacturers of the objects belonging to the tabernacle were known to be wise, or experienced in their crafts (Exod. 36:4). Even the man who was skillful in making idols was recognized as a craftsman (Isa. 40:20; cf. Jer. 10:9). The reason for this is to be found in the man's skill, craftsmanship, and not in the object which was being manufactured. Those who were experienced in life were known as "wise," but their wisdom is not to be confused with the religious usage. Cleverness and shrewdness characterized this type of wisdom. Amnon consulted Jonadab, who was known as a shrewd man (2 Sam. 13:3), and followed his plan of seducing his sister Tamar. Joab hired a "wise" woman to make David change his mind about Absalom (2 Sam. 14:2).

Based on the characterization of wisdom as a skill, a class of counselors known as "wise men" arose. They were to be found in Egypt (Gen. 41:8), in Babylon (Jer. 50:35), in Tyre (Ezek. 27:9), in Edom (Obad. 8), and in Israel. In pagan cultures the "wise" man practiced magic and divination: "Then Pharaoh also called the wise men and the sorcerers: now the magicians of Egypt, they also did in like manner with their enchantments" (Exod. 7:11); and ". . . that frustrateth the tokens of the liars, and maketh diviners mad; that turneth wise men backward, and maketh their knowledge foolish" (Isa. 44:25).

The religious sense of *chākām* excludes delusion, craftiness, shrewdness, and magic. God is the source of wisdom, as He is "wise": "Yet he also is wise, and will bring evil, and will not call back his words: but will arise against the house of the evildoers, and against the help of them that work iniquity" (Isa. 31:2). The man or woman who, fearing God, lives in accordance with what God expects and what is expected of him in a God-fearing society is viewed as an integrated person. He is "wise" in that his manner of life projects the fear of God and the blessing of God rests upon him. Even as the craftsman is said to be skillful in his trade, the Old Testament *chākām* was learning and applying wisdom to every situation in life, and the degree in which he succeeded was a barometer of his progress on the road of wisdom.

The opposite of the *chākām* is the "fool" or wicked person, who stubbornly refuses counsel and depends on his own understanding: "For the turning away of the simple shall slay them, and the prosperity of fools shall destroy them" (Prov. 1:32; cf. Deut. 32:5-6; Prov. 3:35).

B. Noun.

chokəmāh (חָכְמָה), "wisdom; experience; shrewdness." This word appears 141 times in the Old Testament. Like *chākām*, most occurrences of this word are in Job, Proverbs, and Ecclesiastes.

The *chākām* seeks after *chokəmāh* "wisdom." Like *chākām,* the word *chokəmāh* can refer to technical skills or special abilities in fashioning something. The first occurrence of *chokəmāh* is in Exod. 28:3: "And thou shalt speak unto all that are wisehearted, whom I have filled with the spirit of wisdom, that they may make Aaron's garments to consecrate him, that he may minister unto me in the priest's office." This first occurrence of the word in the Hebrew Bible bears this out as well as the description of the workers on the tabernacle. The artisan was considered to be endowed with special abilities given to him by God: "And he hath filled him with the spirit of God, in wisdom, in understanding, and in knowledge, and in all manner of workmanship" (Exod. 35:31).

Chokəmāh is the knowledge and the ability to make the right choices at the opportune time. The consistency of making the right choice is an indication of maturity and development. The prerequisite for "wisdom" is the fear of the Lord: "The fear of the Lord is the beginning of knowledge: but fools despise wisdom and instruction" (Prov 1:7). "Wisdom" is viewed as crying out for disciples who will do everything to pursue her (Prov. 1:20). The person who seeks *chokəmāh* diligently will receive understanding: "For the Lord giveth wisdom: out of his mouth cometh knowledge and understanding" (Prov. 2:6); he will benefit in his life by walking with God: "That thou mayest walk in the way of good men, and keep the paths of the righteous" (Prov. 2:20). The advantages of "wisdom" are many: "For length of days, and long life, and peace, shall they add to thee. Let not mercy and truth forsake thee: bind them about thy neck; write them upon the table of thine heart: so shalt "thou find favor and good understanding in the sight of God and man" (Prov. 3:2-4). The prerequisite is a desire to follow and imitate God as He has revealed Himself in Jesus Christ, without self-reliance and especially *not* in a spirit of pride: "A wise man will hear, and will increase learning; and a man of understanding shall attain unto wise counsels: to understand a proverb, and the interpretation; the words of the wise, and their dark sayings. The fear of the Lord is the beginning of knowledge: but fools despise wisdom and instruction" (Prov. 1:5-7). The fruits of *chokəmāh* are many, and the Book of Proverbs describes the characters of the *chākām* and *chokəmāh*. In New Testament terms the fruits of "wisdom" are the same as the fruits of the Holy Spirit; cf. "But the fruit of the Spirit is love, joy, peace, long-suffering, gentleness, goodness, faith, meekness, temperance: against such there is no law" (Gal. 5:22-23); "But the wisdom that is from above is first pure, then peaceable, gentle, and easy to be entreated, full of mercy and good fruits, without partiality, and without hypocrisy. And the fruit of righteousness is sown in peace of them that make peace" (James 3:17-18).

The importance of "wisdom" explains why books were written about it. Songs were composed in celebration of "wisdom" (Job 28). Even "wisdom" is personified in Proverbs. *Chokəmāh* as a person stands for that divine perfection of "wisdom" which is manifest in God's creative acts. As a divine perfection it is visible in God's creative acts: "Doth not wisdom cry: and understanding put forth her voice? . . . I wisdom dwell with prudence, and find out knowledge of witty inventions. . . . The Lord possessed me in the beginning of his way, before his works of old. . . . Then I was by him, as one brought up with him: and I was daily his delight, rejoicing always before him. . . . Now therefore hearken unto me, O ye children: for blessed are they that keep my ways" (Prov. 8:1, 12, 22, 30, 32).

The Septuagint translations are: *sophos* ("clever; skillful; experienced; wise; learned"); *phronimos* ("sensible; thoughtful; prudent; wise"); and *sunetos* ("intelligent; sagacious; wise"). The KJV gives these translations: "wise; wise man; cunning."

C. Verb.

chākam (חָכַם), "to be wise, act wisely, make wise, show oneself wise." This root, which occurs 20 times in the Old Testament, appears in other

Semitic languages, such as in the Akkadian word *chakamu*. The word means "to be wise" in Prov. 23:15: "My son, if thine heart be wise, my heart shall rejoice, even mine." In Ps. 119:98 *chākam* means "to make wise": "Thou through thy commandments hast made me wiser than mine enemies: for they are ever with me."

TO WITHER

yābēsh (יָבֵשׁ), "to be dry, be dried up, be withered." This term is found throughout the development of the Hebrew language and a few other Semitic languages. It is found approximately 70 times in the Hebrew Old Testament. In its verbal form *yābēsh* is found for the first time in Gen. 8:7, when after the Flood, "the waters were dried up from the earth." However, the noun derivative, *yabbāshāh*, which means "dry ground," already occurs in Gen. 1:9.

Physical "drying up" can involve bread (Josh. 9:5), the ground in time of drought (Jer. 23:10; Amos 4:7), brooks and streams (1 Kings 17:7), and crops (Isa. 42:15). The shortness of man's life is compared to the "drying up" of grass (Ps. 90:6; 102:11; Isa. 40:7). Because of affliction, the heart too "withers" like the grass (Ps. 102:4). In his parable of the vine, Ezekiel likens God's judgment on Judah to the "withering" of a vine that is pulled up (Ezek. 17:9-10). Because of his disobedience, Jeroboam's hand "is dried up" as judgment from God (1 Kings 13:4). Psychosomatic awareness is clearly demonstrated in Prov. 17:22: ". . . A broken spirit drieth the bones."

WITNESS

A. Noun.

'ēd (עֵד), "witness." The 69 occurrences of this word are scattered throughout the various biblical literary genres and periods although it does not appear in historical literature outside the Pentateuch.

This word has to do with the legal or judicial sphere. First, in the area of civil affairs the word can mean someone who is present at a legal transaction and can confirm it if necessary. Such people worked as notaries, e.g., for an oral transfer of property: "Now this was the manner in former time in Israel concerning redeeming and concerning changing, for to confirm all things. . . . And Boaz said unto the elders, and unto all the people, Ye are witnesses this day, that I have bought all that was Elimelech's, and all that was Chilion's and Mahlon's, of the hand of Naomi" (Ruth 4:7, 9). At a later time the "witnesses" not only acted to attest the transaction and to confirm it orally, but they signed a document or deed of purchase. Thus "witness" takes on the new nuance of those able and willing to affirm the truth of a transaction by affixing their signatures: "And I gave the evidence of the purchase unto Baruch the son of Neriah . . . in the sight of Hanameel mine uncle's son, and in the presence of the witnesses that subscribed the book of the purchase . . ." (Jer. 32:12). An object or animal(s) can signify the truthfulness of an act or agreement. Its very existence or the acceptance of it by both parties (in the case of the animals given to Abimelech in Gen. 21:30) bears witness: "Now therefore come thou, let us make a covenant, I and thou; and let it be for a witness between me and thee [let it attest to our mutual relationship]" Gen. 31:44—the first biblical occurrence of the word). Jacob then set up a stone pillar or heap as a further "witness" (Gen. 31:48) calling upon God to effect judgment if the covenant were broken.

In Mosaic criminal law the accused has the right to be faced by his/her accuser and to give evidence of his/her innocence. In the case of a newly married woman charged by her own husband, his testimony is sufficient to prove her guilty of adultery unless her parents have clear evidence proving her virginity before her marriage (Deut. 22:14 ff.). Usually the accused is faced with someone who either saw or heard of his guilt: "And if a soul sin, and hear the voice of swearing, and is a witness, whether he hath seen or known of it . . ." (Lev. 5:1). Heavy penalties fell on anyone who lied to a court. The ninth commandment may well have immediate reference to such a concrete court situation (Exod. 20:16). If so, it serves to sanction proper judicial procedure, to safeguard individuals from secret accusation and condemnation and giving them the right and privilege of self-defense. In the exchange between Jacob and Laban mentioned above, Jacob also cites God as a "witness" (Gen. 31:50) between them, the one who will see violations; God, however, is also the Judge. Although human courts are (as a rule) to keep judge and "witness" separate, the "witnesses" do participate in executing the penalty upon the guilty party (Deut. 17:7), even as God does.

B. Verb.

'ûd (עוּד), "to take as witness, bear witness, repeat, admonish, warn, assure protection, relieve." This verb, which occurs 42 times in biblical Hebrew, has cognates in Ugaritic (perhaps), Arabic, Aramaic, Syriac, Phoenician, and Ethiopic.

In 1 Kings 21:10 'ûd means "to bear witness": "And set two men, sons of Belial, before him, to bear witness against him. . . ." The word means "to warn" in Jer. 6:10: "To whom shall I speak, and give warning, that they may hear?"

WOMAN

'ishshāh (אִשָּׁה), "woman; wife; betrothed one; bride; each." This word has cognates in Akkadian, Ugaritic, Aramaic, Arabic, and Ethiopic. It appears about 781 times in biblical Hebrew and in all periods of the language.

This noun connotes one who is a female human being regardless of her age or virginity. Therefore, it appears in correlation to "man" ('îsh): ". . . She shall be called Woman, because she was taken out of Man" (Gen. 2:23). This is its meaning in its first biblical usage: "And the rib, which the Lord God had taken from man ['ādām], made he a woman, and brought her unto the man" (Gen. 2:22). The stress here is on identification of womanhood rather than a family role.

The stress on the family role of a "wife" appears in passages such as Gen. 8:16: "Go forth of the ark, thou, and thy wife, and thy sons, and thy sons' wives with thee."

In one special nuance the word connotes "wife" in the sense of a woman who is under a man's authority and protection; the emphasis is on the family relationship considered as a legal and social entity: "And Abram took Sarai his wife and Lot his brother's son, and all their substance that they had gathered . . ." (Gen. 12:5).

In Lam. 2:20 'ishshāh is a synonym for "mother": "Shall the women eat their [offspring, the little ones who were born healthy]?" In Gen. 29:21 (cf. Deut. 22:24) it appears to connote "bride" or "betrothed one": "And Jacob said unto Laban, Give me my wife, for my days are fulfilled, that I may go in unto her." Eccl. 7:26 uses the word generically of "woman" conceived in general, or womanhood: "And I find more bitter than death the woman, whose heart is snares and nets . . ." (cf. Gen. 31:35).

This word is used only infrequently of animals: "Of every clean beast thou shalt take to thee by sevens, the male and his female: and of beasts that are not clean by two, the male and his female" (Gen. 7:2).

This word can also be used figuratively describing foreign warriors and/or heroes as "women," in other words as weak, unmanly, and cowardly: "In that day shall Egypt be like unto women: and it shall be afraid and fear because of the shaking of the hand of the Lord of hosts. . ." (Isa. 19:16).

In a few passages 'ishshāh means "each" or "every": "But every woman shall borrow of her neighbor, and of her that sojourneth in her house. . ." (Exod. 3:22; cf. Amos 4:3). A special use of this nuance occurs in passages such as Jer. 9:20, where in conjunction with rə'ûth ("neighbor") it means "one" (female): "Yet hear the word of the Lord, O ye women, and let your ear receive the word of his mouth, and teach your daughters wailing, and every one her neighbor lamentation."

WONDER

môphēth (מוֹפֵת), "wonder; sign; portent." The 36 appearances of this word are in all periods of biblical literature except wisdom literature. Poetical literature manifests it only 5 times and only in the Psalter.

First, this word signifies a divine act or a special display of divine power: "When thou goest to return into Egypt, see that thou do all those wonders before Pharaoh, which I have put in thine hand . . ." (Exod. 4:21—the first biblical occurrence of the word). Acts effecting the divine curses are called "wonders." Thus the word does not necessarily refer to a miraculous act, if "miracle" means something outside the realm of ordinary providence.

Second, the word can represent a "sign" from God or a token of a future event: "This is the sign which the Lord hath spoken: Behold, the altar shall be rent, and the ashes that are upon it shall be poured out" (1 Kings 13:3). This sense sometimes has the nuance "symbol": "Now listen, Joshua the high priest, you and your friends who are sitting in front of you—indeed they are men who are a symbol . . ." (Zech. 3:8 NASB; cf. Ps. 71:7).

TO WORK

A. Verbs.

pā'al (פָּעַל), "to do, work." Common to both ancient and modern Hebrew, this word is used in modern Hebrew in the sense of "to work, to act, to function." Found only 57 times in the Hebrew Old Testament, it is used primarily as a poetic synonym for the much more common verb *'āsāh*, "to do, to make." Thus, almost half the occurrences of this verb are in the Book of Psalms. *Pā'al* is used for the first time in the Old Testament in the Song of Moses: ". . . The place, O Lord, which thou hast made for thee to dwell in. . ." (Exod. 15:17). There is no distinction in the use of this verb, whether God or man is its subject. In Ps. 15:2 man is the subject: "He that walketh uprightly and worketh righteousness, and speaketh the truth in his heart."

'āsāh (עָשָׂה), "to make, do, create." This root also occurs in Moabite and Phoenician (only in a proper name). It occurs in early extra-biblical Hebrew, Hebrew, and about 2,625 times in the Bible (in all periods). It should be distinguished from the second sense of *'āsāh*, "to squeeze."

In its primary sense this verb represents the production of various objects. This includes making images and idols: "Thou shalt not make unto thee any graven image . . ." (Exod. 20:4). The verb can mean to make something into something: "And the residue thereof he maketh a god, even his graven image . . ." (Isa. 44:17). In an extended use this verb means to prepare a meal, a banquet, or even an offering: "And he [Abraham] took butter, and milk, and the calf which he had dressed, and set it before them [his three guests] . . ." (Gen. 18:8).

In Gen. 12:5 *'āsāh* means "to acquire" (as it often does): "And Abram took Sarai his wife, and Lot his brother's son, and all their substance that they had gathered, and the souls that they had gotten in Haran. . . ." The "souls that they had gotten" probably were slaves.

Used in association with "Sabbath" or the name of other holy days, this word signifies "keeping" or celebrating: "All the congregation of Israel shall keep it [the Passover]" (Exod. 12:47). In a related sense the word means "to spend" a day: "For who knoweth what is good for man in this life, all the days of his vain life which he spendeth as a shadow?" (Eccl. 6:12).

Depending upon its object, *'āsāh* has several other nuances within the general concept of producing some product. For example, with the object "book" the verb means "to write": ". . . Of making many books there is no end . . ." (Eccl. 12:12). The Bible also uses this word of the process of war: "These made war with Bera king of Sodom . . ." (Gen. 14:2). Sometimes the word represents an action: "And Joshua made peace with them, and made a league with them . . ." (Josh. 9:15). "To make a mourning" is to observe it: ". . . And he [Joseph] made a mourning for his father seven days" (Gen. 50:10). With "name" the verb means "to gain prominence and fame": "Go to, let us build us a city and a tower, whose top may reach unto heaven; and let us make us a name. . ." (Gen. 11:4). With the word "workmanship" the word signifies "to work": "And I have filled him with the spirit of God . . . , and in all manner of workmanship, . . . to work in gold, and in silver, and in brass" (Exod. 31:3-4).

'*Āsāh* may represent the relationship of an individual to another in his action or behavior, in the sense of what one does. So Pharaoh asks Abram: "What is this that thou hast done unto me?" (Gen. 12:18). Israel pledged: "All that the Lord hath said will we do, and be obedient" (Exod. 24:7). With the particle *la* the verb signifies inflicting upon another some act or behavior: "Then Abimelech called Abraham, and said unto him, What hast thou done unto us?" (Gen. 20:9). With the particle '*im* the word may mean "to show," or "to practice" something toward someone. The emphasis here is on an ongoing mutual relationship between two parties obligating them to a reciprocal act: "O Lord God of my master Abraham, I pray thee, send me good speed this day, and show kindness unto my master Abraham" (Gen. 24:12). In Gen. 26:29 '*āsāh* appears twice in the sense "to practice toward": "That thou wilt do us no harm, as we have not touched thee, and as we have done unto thee nothing but good. . . ."

Used absolutely this verb sometimes means "to take action": "Let Pharaoh do this, and let him appoint officers over the land . . ." (Gen. 41:34). In the Hebrew '*āsāh* has no object in this passage—it is used absolutely. Used in this manner it may also signify "to be active": "She seeketh wool, and flax, and worketh willingly with her hands" (Prov. 31:13). In 1 Chron. 28:10 the verb (used absolutely) means "to go to work," to go about doing a task: "Take heed now; for the Lord hath chosen thee to build a house for the sanctuary: be strong, and do it."

This verb used of plants signifies "bringing forth." In Gen. 1:11 it means "to bear" fruit: ". . . And the fruit tree [bearing] fruit after his kind. . . ." In another nuance this verb represents what a plant does in producing grain: ". . . It hath no stalk: the bud shall yield no meal . . ." (Hos. 8:7). The word signifies the production of branches, too: "It was planted in a good soil by great waters, that it might bring forth branches, and that it might bear fruit, that it might be a goodly vine" (Ezek. 17:8).

'*Āsāh* is used theologically of man's response to divine commands. God commanded Noah: "Make thee an ark of gopher wood. . ." (Gen. 6:14). Similarly Israel was commanded "to construct" a sanctuary for God (Exod. 25:8). The manipulation of the blood of the sacrifice is what the priest is to do (Lev. 4:20). The entire cultic activity is described by '*āsāh:* "As he hath done this day, so the Lord hath commanded to do. . ." (Lev. 8:34). Thus in his acts a man demonstrates his inward commitment and, therefore, his relationship to God (Deut. 4:13). Doing God's commands brings life upon a man (Lev. 18:5).

This verb is also applied specifically to all aspects of divine acts and actions. In the general sense of His actions toward His people Israel, the word first occurs in Gen. 12:2, where God promises "to make" Abram a great nation. '*Āsāh* is also the most general Old Testament expression for divine creating. Every aspect of this activity is described by this word: "For in six days the Lord made heaven and earth . . ." (Exod. 20:11). This is its meaning in its first biblical occurrence: "And God made the firmament, and divided the waters which were under the firmament from the waters which were above the firmament . . ." (Gen. 1:7). This word is used of God's acts effecting the entire created world and individual men (Exod. 20:6). God's acts and words perfectly correspond, so that what He says He does, and what He does is what He has said (Gen. 21:1; Ps. 115:3).

B. Noun.

ma'aseh (מַעֲשֶׂה), "work; deed; labor; behavior." This noun is used 235 times in biblical Hebrew. Lamech, Noah's father, in expressing his hope for a new world, used the noun for the first time in the Old Testament: "And he called his name Noah, saying, This same shall comfort us concerning our work and toil of our hands, because of the ground which the Lord hath cursed" (Gen. 5:29). The word is scattered throughout the Old Testament and all types of literature.

The basic meaning of *ma'aseh* is "work." Lamech used the word to signify agricultural labor (Gen. 5:29). The Israelites were commanded to celebrate the Festival of the Firstfruits, as it signified the blessing of God upon their "labors" (Exod. 23:16). It is not to be limited to this. As the word is the most general word for "work," it may be used to refer to the "work" of a skillful craftsman (Exod. 26:1), a weaver (26:36), a jeweler (28:11), and a perfumer (30:25). The finished product of the worker is also known as *ma'aseh:* "And in the uppermost basket there was of all manner of bakemeats [literally, work of a baker] for Pharaoh . . ." (Gen. 40:17); "And Moses and Eleazar the priest took the gold of them, even all wrought jewels [literally, articles of work]" (Num. 31:51). The artisan plied his craft during the work week, known in Hebrew as "the days of work," and rested on the Sabbath: "Thus saith the Lord God; The gate of the inner court that looketh toward the east shall be shut the six working days; but on the sabbath it shall be opened, and in the day of the new moon it shall be opened" (Ezek. 46:1; cf. Exod. 23:12).

The phrase "work of one's hands" signifies the worthlessness of the idols fashioned by human hands: "Asshur shall not save us; we will not ride upon horses: neither will we say any more to the work of our hands, Ye are our gods: for in thee the fatherless findeth mercy" (Hos. 14:3). However, the prayer of the psalmist includes the request that the "works" of God's people might be established: "And let the beauty of the Lord our God be upon us: and establish thou the work of our hands upon us; yea, the work of our hands establish thou it" (Ps. 90:17). Since the righteous work out God's work and are a cause of God's rejoicing, "the glory of the Lord shall endure for ever: the Lord shall rejoice in his works" (Ps. 104:31).

In addition to "work," *ma'aseh* also denotes "deed," "practice," or "behavior." Joseph asked his brothers, accused of having taken his cup of divination: "What deed is this that ye have done? wot ye not that such a man as I can certainly divine?" (Gen. 44:15). The Israelites were strongly commanded not to imitate the grossly immoral behavior of the Canaanites and the surrounding nations: "After the doings of the land of Egypt, wherein ye dwelt, shall ye not do: and after the doings of the land of Canaan, whither I bring you, shall ye not do: neither shall ye walk in their ordinances" (Lev. 18:3; cf. Exod. 23:24). However, the Israelites did not listen to the warning, and they "were mingled among the heathen, and learned their works. . . . Thus were they defiled with their own works, and went a whoring with their own inventions" (Ps. 106:35, 39).

Thus far, we have dealt with *ma'aseh* from man's perspective. The word may have a positive connotation ("work, deed") as well as a negative ("corrupt practice"). The Old Testament also calls us to celebrate the "work" of God. The psalmist was overwhelmed with the majesty of the Lord, as he looked at God's "work" of creation: "When I consider thy heavens, the work of thy fingers, the moon and the stars, which thou hast ordained" (Ps. 8:3; cf. 19:1; 102:25). The God of Israel demonstrated His love by His mighty acts of deliverance on behalf of Israel: "And Israel served the Lord all the days of Joshua, and all the days of the elders that [out] lived Joshua, and which had known all the works of the Lord, that he had done for Israel" (Josh. 24:31; cf. versions).

All of God's "works" are characterized by faithfulness to His promises and covenant: "For the word of the Lord is right; and all his works are done in truth" (Ps. 33:4).

Ma'aseh is translated in the Greek as *ergon* ("deed; action; manifestation") and *poiema* ("what is made; work; creation"). English translations are "work" (KJV, RSV, NASB, NIV), "doing" (KJV and RSV), "practice" (NASB, NIV).

TO WORSHIP

shāchāh (שָׁחָה), "to worship, prostrate oneself, bow down." This word is found in modern Hebrew in the sense of "to bow or stoop," but not in the general sense of "to worship." The fact that it is found more than 170 times in the Hebrew Bible shows something of its cultural significance. It is found for the first time in Gen. 18:2, where Abraham "bowed himself toward the ground" before the 3 messengers who announced that Sarah would have a son.

The act of bowing down in homage is generally done before a superior or a ruler. Thus, David "bowed" himself before Saul (1 Sam. 24:8). Sometimes it is a social or economic superior to whom one bows, as when Ruth "bowed" to the ground before Boaz (Ruth 2:10). In a dream, Joseph saw the sheaves of his brothers "bowing down" before his sheaf (Gen. 37:5, 9-10). *Shāchāh* is used as the common term for coming before God in worship, as in 1 Sam. 15:25 and Jer. 7:2. Sometimes it is in conjunction with another Hebrew verb for bowing down physically, followed by "worship," as in Exod. 34:8: "And Moses made haste, and bowed his head toward the earth, and worshiped." Other gods and idols are also the object of such worship by one's prostrating oneself before them (Isa. 2:20; 44:15, 17).

WRATH

A. Noun.

chēmāh (חֵמָה), "wrath; heat; rage; anger." This noun occurs in Semitic languages with the meanings "heat, wrath, poison, venom." The noun, as well as the verb *yācham*, denotes a strong emotional state. The noun is used 120 times, predominantly in the poetic and prophetic literature, especially Ezekiel.

The first usage of *chēmāh* takes place in the story of Esau and Jacob. Jacob is advised to go to Haran with the hope that Esau's "anger" will dissipate: "And tarry with him a few days, until thy brother's fury turn away" (Gen. 27:44).

The word indicates a state of anger. Most of the usage involves God's "anger." His "wrath" is expressed against Israel's sin in the wilderness: "For I was afraid of the anger and hot displeasure, wherewith the Lord was wroth against you to destroy you" (Deut. 9:19). The psalmist prayed for God's mercy in the hour of God's "anger": "O Lord, rebuke me not in thine anger, neither chasten me in thy hot displeasure" (Ps. 6:1). God's "anger" against Israel was ultimately expressed in the exile of the Judeans to Babylon: "The Lord hath accomplished his fury; he hath poured out his fierce anger, and hath kindled a fire in Zion, and it hath devoured the foundations thereof" (Lam. 4:11).

The metaphor "cup" denotes the judgment of God upon His people. His "wrath" is poured out: "Therefore he hath poured upon him the fury of his anger, and the strength of battle: and it hath set him on fire round about, yet he knew not; and it burned him, yet he laid it not to heart" (Isa. 42:25); and the "cup of wrath" is drunk: "Awake, awake, stand up, O Jerusalem, which hast drunk at the hand of the Lord the cup of his fury; thou hast drunken the dregs of the cup of trembling . . ." (Isa. 51:17).

Thus, God as the Almighty Potentate is angered by the sins and the pride of His people, as they are an insult to His holiness. In a derived sense, the rulers on earth are also described as those who are angered, but their "anger" is aroused from circumstances over which they have no control. Naaman was angry with Elisha's advice (2 Kings 5:11-12); Ahasuerus became enraged with Vashti's refusal to display her beauty before the men (Esth. 1:12).

Chēmāh also denotes man's reaction to everyday circumstances. Man's "rage" is a dangerous expression of his emotional state, as it inflames everybody who comes close to the person in rage. "Wrath" may arise for many reasons. Proverbs speaks strongly against *chēmāh*, as jealousy (6:34); cf. "Wrath is cruel, and anger is outrageous; but who is able to stand before envy?" (Prov. 27:4; cf. Ezek. 16:38). The man in rage may be culpable of crime and be condemned: "Be ye afraid of the sword: for wrath bringeth the punishments of the sword, that ye may know there is a judgment" (Job 19:29). The wise response to "rage" is a soft answer: "A soft answer turneth away wrath: but grievous words stir up anger" (Prov. 15:1).

Chēmāh is associated with *qinə'āh*, "jealousy," and also with *nāqām*, "vengeance," as the angered person intends to save his name or avenge himself on the person who provoked him. In God's dealing with Israel He was jealous of His Holy name, for which reason He had to deal justly with idolatrous Israel by avenging Himself: "That it might cause fury to come up to take vengeance; I have set her blood upon the top of a rock, that it should not be covered" (Ezek. 24:8); but He also avenges His people against their enemies: "God is jealous, and the Lord revengeth; the Lord revengeth, and is furious;

the Lord will take vengeance on his adversaries, and he reserveth wrath for his enemies'' (Nah. 1:2). Other synonyms of *chēmāh* are *'aph,* ''anger,'' and *qetseph,* ''wrath,'' as in Deut. 29:27 and Jer. 21:5.

There are two special meanings of *chēmāh.* One is ''heat,'' as in ''the Spirit lifted me up, and took me away, and I went in bitterness, in the heat of my spirit; but the hand of the Lord was strong upon me'' (Ezek. 3:14). The other is ''poison,'' or ''venom,'' as in Deut. 32:33: ''Their wine is the poison of dragons, and the cruel venom of asps.''

The Septuagint gives the following translations: *orge* (''anger; indignation; wrath'') and *thumos* (''passion; anger; wrath; rage''). The KJV gives these senses: ''fury; wrath; poison.''

B. Verb.

yācham (יָחַם), ''to be fiery, be hot.'' This verb, which occurs only 10 times in biblical Hebrew, is the root of the noun *chēmāh.*

In Deut. 19:6 *yācham* means ''to be hot'': ''Lest the avenger of the blood pursue the slayer, while his heart is hot, and overtake him. . . .''

TO WRITE

A. Verb.

kāthab (כָּתַב), ''to write, inscribe, describe, take dictation, engrave.'' This verb appears in most Semitic languages (not in Akkadian or Ugaritic). Biblical Hebrew attests around 203 occurrences (in all periods) and biblical Aramaic 7 occurrences.

Basically, this verb represents writing down a message. The judgment (ban) of God against the Amalekites was to be recorded in the book (scroll): ''And the Lord said unto Moses, Write this for a memorial in a book, and rehearse it in the ears of Joshua: for I will utterly put out the remembrance of Amalek from under heaven'' (Exod. 17:14—the first biblical occurrence of the word).

One may ''write'' upon a stone or ''write'' a message upon it. Moses told Israel that after crossing the Jordan ''thou shalt set thee up great stones, and plaster them with plaster: and thou shalt write upon them all the words of this law . . .'' (Deut. 27:2-3).

This use of the word implies something more than keeping a record of something so that it will be remembered. This is obvious in the first passage because the memory of Amalek is ''to be recorded'' and also blotted out. In such passages ''to be recorded,'' therefore, refers to the unchangeableness and binding nature of the Word of God. God has said it, it is fixed, and it will occur. An extended implication in the case of divine commands is that man must obey what God ''has recorded'' (Deut. 27:2-3). Thus, such uses of the word describe a fixed body of authoritative instruction, or a canon. These 2 passages also show that the word does not tell us anything specific about how the message was composed. In the first instance Moses seems not to have merely ''recorded'' as a secretary but ''to have written'' creatively what he heard and saw. Certainly in Exod. 32:32 the word is used of creative writing by the author; God was not receiving dictation from anyone when He "inscribed" the Ten Commandments. In Deut. 27:2-3 the writers must reproduce exactly what was previously given (as mere secretaries).

Sometimes *kāthab* appears to mean "to inscribe" and "to cover with inscription." The 2 tablets of the testimony which were given to Moses by God were "tables of stone, written [fully inscribed] with the finger of God" (Exod. 31:18). The verb means not only to write in a book but "to write a book," not just to record something in a few lines on a scroll but to complete the writing. Moses prays: "Yet now, if thou wilt forgive their sin—; and if not, blot me, I pray thee, out of thy book which thou hast written" (Exod. 32:32). Here "book" probably refers to a scroll rather than a book in the present-day sense.

Among the special uses of *kāthab* is the meaning "to record a survey." At Shiloh, Joshua told Israel to choose three men from each tribe "and they shall arise, and go through the land, and describe it . . ." (Josh. 18:4).

A second extended nuance of *kāthab* is "to receive dictation": "And Baruch wrote from the mouth of Jeremiah . . ." (Jer. 36:4). The word can also be used of signing one's signature: "And because of all this we make [are cutting] a sure covenant, and write it; and our princes, Levites, and priests, seal unto it" (Neh. 9:38). Thus they "cut," or completed, the agreement by having the representatives sign it. The cutting was the signing.

B. Nouns.

kəthāb (כְּתָב), "something written; register; scripture." This noun occurs 17 times in the Old Testament.

In 1 Chron. 28:19 *kəthāb* is used to mean "something written," such as an edict: "All this, said David, the Lord made me understand in writing by his hand upon me, even all the works of this pattern." The word also refers to a "register" (Ezra 2:62) and to "scripture" (Dan. 10:21).

Two other related nouns are *kəthōbeth* and *mikətāb*. *Kəthōbeth* occurs once to mean something inscribed, specifically a "tatooing" (Lev. 19:28). *Mikətāb* appears about 9 times and means "something written, a writing" (Exod. 32:16; Isa. 38:9).

TO BE WROTH, ANGRY

A. Verb.

qātsaph (קָצַף), "to be wroth, angry." This verb appears 34 times and is found mainly in the Pentateuch and in the prophets, and a few times in the historical books and the poetic literature. The word is used in rabbinic Hebrew, but its use in modern Hebrew has been displaced by other verbs. It is an ancient Canaanite word; as a gloss it appeared in the Amarna Tablets with the meaning "to become worried," or according to others, "to be embittered." The relation with the Arabic cognate *qasafa* is doubtful.

The general meaning of *qātsaph* is a strong emotional outburst of anger, especially when man is the subject of the reaction. The first usage of the word brings this out: "And Pharaoh was wroth against two of his officers . . . and he put them in [custody] . . ." (Gen. 40:2-3; cf. 41:10). Moses became bitterly angry with the disobedient Israelites (Exod. 16:20). The leaders of the Philistines "were wroth" with Achish (1 Sam. 29:4), and Naaman was strongly irritated by Elisha's lack of a sense of protocol (2 Kings 5:11). Elisha expressed his anger with Joash, king of Israel (2 Kings 13:19). King Ahasuerus deposed Vashti in his anger (Esth. 1:12). In these examples an exalted person (generally a king) demonstrated his royal anger in radical measures against his subjects. He was in a position "to be angered" by the response of his subjects. It is rarer for a person "to become angry" with an equal. It is even rarer for a subject "to be angry" with his superior: ". . . Two of the king's chamberlains . . . were wroth, and sought to lay hand on the king Ahasuerus" (Esth. 2:21).

The noun derived from *qātsaph* particularly refers to God's anger. The verb *qātsaph* is used 11 times to describe man's anger and 18 times to refer to God's anger. This fact, coupled with the observation that the verb generally is an expression of a superior against a subject, explains why the biblical text more frequently uses *qātsaph* to describe God's anger. The object of the anger is often indicated by the preposition *al* ("against"). "For I was afraid of the anger [*'aph*] and hot displeasure [*chēmāh*], wherewith the Lord was wroth [*qātsaph*] against [*al*] you to destroy you" (Deut. 9:19). The Lord's anger expresses itself against disobedience (Lev. 10:6) and sin (Eccl. 5:5 ff.). However, people themselves can be the cause for God's anger (Ps. 106:32). In the wilderness the Israelites provoked God to wrath by their disobedience and lack of faith: "Remember, and forget not, how thou provokedst the Lord thy God to wrath in the wilderness: from the day that thou didst depart out of the land of Egypt, until ye came unto this place, ye have been rebellious against the Lord" (Deut. 9:7; cf. vv. 8, 22). Moses spoke about God's wrath against Israel's disobedience which would in time be the occasion for the Exile (Deut. 29:27), and the prophets amplify Moses' warning of God's coming "wrath" (Jer. 21:5). After the Exile, God had compassion on Israel and turned His anger against Israel's enemies (Isa. 34:2).

In the Greek version we find the following translations: *orgizomai* ("to be angry") and *lupew* ("to grieve; to pain; to be sad").

B. Noun.

qetseph (קֶצֶף), "wrath." This noun occurs 28 times in biblical Hebrew and generally with reference to God. One occurrence of God's "wrath" is in 2 Chron. 29:8: "Wherefore the wrath of the Lord was upon Judah and Jerusalem. . . ." An example of man's "wrath" appears in Esth. 1:18: "Likewise shall the ladies of Persia and Media say this day unto all the king's princes, which have heard of the deed of the queen. Thus shall there arise too much contempt and wrath" (cf. Eccl. 5:17).

YEAR

shānāh (שָׁנָה), "year." This word has cognates in Ugaritic, Akaddian, Arabic, Aramaic, and Phoenician. Biblical Hebrew attests it about 877 times and in every period.

This Hebrew word signifies "year": "And God said, Let there be lights in the firmament of the heaven to divide the day from the night; and let them be for signs, and for seasons, and for days, and years" (Gen. 1:14—the first biblical occurrence of the word). There are several ways of determining what a "year" is. First, the "year" may be based on the relationship between the seasons and the sun, the solar year or agricultural year. Second, it can be based on a correlation of the seasons and the moon (lunar year). Third, the "year" may be decided on the basis of the correlation between the movement of the earth and the stars (stellar year). At many points the people of the Old Testament period set the seasons according to climatic or agricultural events; the year ended with the grape and fruit harvest in the month Elul: "[Thou shalt keep] the feast of harvest, the first fruits of thy labors, which thou hast sown in the field: and the feast of ingathering, which is in the end of the year, when thou hast gathered in thy labors out of the field" (Exod. 23:16).

The Gezer calendar shows that by the time it was written (about the tenth century B.C.) some in Palestine were using the lunar calendar, since it exhibits an attempt to correlate the agricultural and lunar systems. The lunar calendar began in the spring (the month Nisan, March-April) and had twelve lunations, or periods between new moons. It was necessary periodically to add a thirteenth month in order to synchronize the lunar calendar and the number of days in a solar year. The lunar calendar also seems to have underlain Israel's religious system with a special rite to celebrate the first day of each lunar month (Num. 28:11-15). The major feasts, however, seem to be based on the agricultural cycle, and the date on which they were celebrated varied from year to year according to work in the fields (e.g., Deut. 16:9-12). This solar-agricultural year beginning in the spring is similar to (if not derived from) the Babylonian calendar—the names of the months are Babylonian derivatives. These 2 systems, therefore, appear side by side at least from the time of Moses. An exact picture of the Old Testament "year" is difficult, if not impossible, to obtain.

YOUTH

na'ar (נַעַר), "youth; lad; young man." This word is found in Ugaritic, and it seems that the Egyptian word *na-arma* ("armed retainers") is also related to the West Semitic usage. The root with the meaning of "youth" occurs only as a noun and occurs in Hebrew in the feminine (*na'arāh*, "young girl") as well as the masculine form (e.g., Gen. 24:14).

Na'ar occurs 235 times in the Hebrew Old Testament. Its use is predominant in the Pentateuch and in the historical books. The first occurrence is in Gen. 14:23-24: ". . . I will not take any thing . . . save only that which the young men have eaten, and the portion of the men which went with me, Aner, Eshcol, and Mamre; let them take their portion."

The basic meaning of *na'ar* is "youth," over against an older man. At times it may signify a very young child: "For before the child shall know to refuse the evil, and choose the good, the land that thou abhorrest shall be forsaken of both her kings" (Isa. 7:16). Generally *na'ar* denotes a "young man" who is of marriageable age but is still a bachelor. We must keep in mind the opposition of youth and old age, so that we can better understand that Jeremiah, while claiming to be only a "youth," was not necessarily a youngster. In truth, he argued that he did not have the experience of the older men, when he said: "Ah, Lord God! behold, I cannot speak: for I am a child" (Jer. 1:6).

Absalom was considered a *na'ar,* even though he was old enough to lead the troups in rebellion against David: "And the king commanded Joab and Abishai and Ittai, saying, Deal gently for my sake with the young man, even with Absalom" (2 Sam. 18:5).

A derived meaning of *na'ar* is "servant." Jonathan used a "servant" as armorbearer: "Now it came to pass upon a day, that Jonathan the son of Saul said unto the young man that bare his armor, Come, and let us go over to the Philistines' garrison, that is on the other side" (1 Sam. 14:1). The *na'ar* ("servant") addressed his employer as "master": "And when they were by Jebus, the day was far spent; and the servant said unto his master, Come, I pray thee, and let us turn into this city of the Jebusites, and lodge in it" (Judg. 19:11). Kings and officials had "servants" who were referred to by the title *na'ar.* In this context the word is better translated as "attendant," as in the case of the attendants of King Ahasuerus, who gave counsel to the king: "Then said the king's servants [NASB, "attendants"] that ministered unto him, Let there be fair young virgins sought for the king" (Esth. 2:2). When a *na'ar* is commissioned to carry messages, he is a "messenger." Thus, we see that the meaning of the word *na'ar* as "servant" does not denote a "slave" or a performer of low duties. He carried important documents, was trained in the art of warfare, and even gave counsel to the king.

Another noun *nō'ar* means "youth." This noun appears only 4 times in the Bible, once in Ps. 88:15: "I am afflicted and ready to die from my youth up: while I suffer thy terrors I am distracted" (cf. Job 36:14).

The Septuagint gives the following translation(s): *paidarion* ("little boy; boy; child; young slave"); *neos* ("novice"); *neaniskos* ("youth; young man; servant"); *paidion* ("infant; child"); *pais* ("child"); and *neanias* ("youth; young man").

ENGLISH WORD

INDEX

A

abandon, to, 143–144
abased, to be, 193–194
abhor, to, 2
abhorrent, to treat as, 2
abide, to, 105–106, 323
ability, 299–301
able, to be, 51–52, 446
abominably, to act, 2
abomination, 1–2
abomination, to cause to be an, 2
abundance, 166–167, 256
accede, to, 261
accept, to, 261
accept favorably, to, 2
acceptance, 129–130
accident, things heard by, 176
account, 267
account, to, 96
acquainted with, to be (get), 97–98,
    212–213, 357–358
acquire, to, 46–47, 84–85
Adam (the first man), 239–241
add, to, 3
admissible, to be, 304–305
admonish, to, 477
adversary, 115–116, 348–349
advise, to, 80
affair, 292–293
affirmation, to utter an, 354
afflict, to, 297
afflicted, to be, 195, 295–297
afraid, to be, 130–131
after, 24
afterwards, 24
again, to do, 3
agitation, 256
aid, to, 180
air, 393–394
alike, 430–431
alive, 226–227
all, 3–4
all at once, 430–431
allotment, 79–80
all together, 430–431
alone, 280–281
alone, to be, 281
alongside, 169–171
altar, 5, 45
always, 77

amen, 27
among, 5, 27–28
ancestor, 128–129
angel, 6–8
anger, 264–265, 482–484
anger, burning, 8
angry, to be (get), 8, 265, 485–486
angry, to make, 313
anguish, 214
animal, 23–24; domesticated, 23–24
annihilate, to, 95–96
annihilation, complete, 76
anoint, to, 8–9, 246
anointed one, 9, 246
anointment, 246
answer, to, 9–10, 352–353
anvil, 401–402
anymore, 402
apart from, 280–281
apostasy, 334
appalled, to be, 95
appearance, 121–122
appointed time, 429–430
approach, to, 65, 269–270
appropriate, to be, 164
ardor, 203
area, 245
area, closed, 36–37
area round about, 443
arise, to, 10–11
ark, 11–12
arm, 13
armor, 449–450
arm(rest), 169–171
army, 20–21, 190–191, 404–406; to
    muster an, 191–192
aroma, 352
around, to go, 441–443
arrange, to, 368–369
arrogantly, to behave, 187
artificer, 294
ascend, to, 65–66
ashamed, to be, 371
ashamed, to feel, 371
asherah, 13–14
asherim, 13–14
ashes, 104–105
aside from, 280–281
ask, to, 14, 360–361
assemble, to, 147–150

assembly, 15
assign, to, 99
assist, to, 180
associate with, to, 70
astonished, to be, 95
astray, to go, 288–290
at all times, 78
atone, to, 16–17, 319–320
atonement, gift of, 276–277
attach to, 443–444
attain, to, 278
attend, to, 250
attention, to give (pay), 97–98,
    212–213, 446
authority, 395
avenge, to, 17–18, 317–318
awake, to, 18–19
away, to take, 417–418
awe, to stand in, 130–131

B

baal, 19–20
back, at the, 217–218
backturning, 334
balance, to, 223
band, marauding, 20–21
bandits, 20–21
band (of raiders), 20–21
banish, to, 103–104
bare, to make, 258
bark, to, 257
base, 36, 306
bathe, to, 460
battle, 132–133, 459
battle, to do, 132
battle, to engage in, 459–460
battlement, 412–413
be, to, 21–22
beams, 238
bear, to, 22–23
bear fruit, to, 145
beast, 23–24; riding, 23–24; wild,
    23–24
beauty, 151–152
become, to, 21–22
becoming, to be, 164
bed, 221
befall, to, 111–112
before, 421
before, to be, 73; to go, 73

beget, to, 22–23
begin, to, 294–295
beginning, 174
behave, to, 456–457
behavior, 481–482
behind, 24; to be, 432; to remain, 218
behold, to, 227, 453
belief, to have, 24–26
believe, to, 24–26, 125
bend, to, 280
bend the knee, to, 37
beneath, 407
besides, 280–281
best, 162–164
bestow care on, to, 250
betrothed one, 477–478
better, 162–164
between, 27–28
beyond one's power, to be, 244
bind, to, 28–29
birth, to be in pangs of, 98
birth, to give, 116–117
blame, to be without, 288
blameless, 287–288
blanket, 146
blast, to give a, 32–33
bless, to, 29–30
blessed, 31
blessed, to be, 29–30
blessing, 30–31
blood, 31–32
blow, to, 32–33
boast, to, 301
body, 33–34
bolt a door, to, 310
bone, 33–34
book, 34–35, 267
booty, 35–36
border, 113–114, 169–171
bosom, 36
boulder, 340
boundary, 36–37
bow, to, 37
bow down, to, 37, 280, 482
bowed down, to be, 195
bowels, 71
box, 11–12
boy, 23
branch, 439–440
bread, 38–39

HEBREW WORD
INDEX

INTRODUCTION TO THE HEBREW INDEX

This index lists the transliterated Hebrew words which are found in *Nelson's Expository Dictionary of Old Testament Words*. Immediately following each Hebrew word are two numbers set in brackets and set off from one another by a semicolon. The first is the reference number assigned to that word in the Hebrew and Chaldee Dictionary of *Strong's Exhaustive Concordance of the Bible*. By using a word's reference number, the student can then use *Strong's Concordance* to find every biblical reference where the indexed word may be found. The second number refers to the page in the *Hebrew and English Lexicon of the Old Testament* by Brown, Driver, and Briggs (BDB) where the word is listed. The lower case letter adjoining the BDB number refers to the quarter of the page on which the indexed word is found. Thus, *a* refers to the upper left, *b* the lower left, *c* the upper right, and *d* the lower right. The student can use the BDB number to discover the various forms and meanings the word takes in the Old Testament.

The page or pages on which an indexed word is found in *Nelson's Expository Dictionary of Old Testament Words* are listed immediately following the bracketed reference and BDB numbers.

A

'āb [1; 3a] 128

'ābad [5647; 712b] 248, 288, 289, 365, 366, 367

'abaddôn [11; 2b] 290

'ābāh [14; 2c] 261, 471

'ābal [56; 5b] 252

'ābar [5674; 716d] 281, 282, 283, 381

'abārāh [5679; 720b] 283

'abēdāh [9, 2b] 290

'abədān [13; 2b] 290

'abôdāh [5656; 715a] 366, 367

'āch [251; 26b] 40, 41, 69, 250

'āchar [309, 310; 29b, 29d] 24, 218, 432

'acharîth [319, 320; 31a, 1079d] 114

'acharôn [314; 30d] 142, 217

'āchaz [270; 28a] 310, 417

'achēr [312; 29c] 139

'āchîm [251; 26b] 41

'achôth [269; 27d] 250, 383, 384

'achuzzāh [272; 28c] 310

'ad [5703, 5705; 723c, 1105b] 3, 118, 167

'ādām [120; 9a] 215, 239, 240, 242, 243, 477

'adāmāh [127; 9c] 215, 216

'ādar [142; 12a] 264

'addereth [155; 12b] 263, 264

'addîr [117; 12b] 263, 264

'adōm [119; 10a] 216, 239

'ādôn [113; 10d] 19, 228, 229

adōnāy [136; 10d] 228, 229, 258

'āhab [158; 13b] 2, 230, 231, 232

'ahabāh [160; 13b] 231; 232

'āhēb [157; 12d] 230, 231

'ākal [398; 37a] 109

'ākəlāh [396; 38b] 110

'ālāh [423; 46d] 88

'ālāh [5927; 748a] 65, 66

'alam [5958; 761c] 452

'aləmāh [5959; 761c] 452, 453

'aləmānāh [490; 48b] 470

'allāh [427; 47c] 158

'allûph [441; 48d] 53

'am [5971; 766b] 211, 259, 285, 286, 287

'āmad [5975; 763c] 11, 397, 398

'āmāl [5999; 765d] 200, 214, 377

'āman [540; 1081a] 125

'āmar [559; 55c] 49, 352, 353, 391
'āmel [6001; 766a] 215
'āmēl [6001; 766a] 214
'āmēn [543; 53b] 24, 25, 26, 27, 125
'ammāh [520; 52a] 86
'ammûd [5982; 765a] 398
'ānāh [6030, 6031; 772c, 775d, 776a] 9, 10, 195, 297, 430
'ānān [6051; 777d] 63
'ānaph [599, 60a] 265
'anāshîm [376; 35d] 241
'ānāw [6035; 776c] 297
'anāwāh [6038; 776c] 296
'ānî [6041; 776d] 195, 295, 297
'aph [639; 60a] 264, 265, 484, 486
'āphār [6083; 779c] 104, 105
'aphuddāh [642; 65d] 116
'ārach [732; 72d] 466
'ārāh [6168; 788c] 258
'ārak [6186; 789b] 368, 369
'ārar [779; 76c] 87, 88
'arəbeh [697; 916a] 255
'arəmôn [759; 74d] 422
'arî [738, 71c] 223
'ārîts [6184; 792a] 116
'ārōm [5903; 735d] 258
'ārôn [727; 75b] 11, 12
'āsāh [6213; 796b] 84, 85, 479, 480
'āsaph [622; 62a] 147, 149, 150
'āshām [817; 79d] 276, 277, 376, 377
'ashəmōret [821; 1038a] 208
'ashəmûrāh [821; 1038a] 208
'ashērāh [842; 81b] 13, 14, 184
'ashərê [835; 80d] 31
'ashshāph [825; 80b] 111
'āwāh [5753; 730c, 731c] 199, 377
'āwēn [205; 19d] 197, 200, 201, 376, 377
'āwōn [5771; 730d] 141, 199, 200, 377, 378
'ayil [352; 17d, 18a,b] 290, 314, 315, 437
'ayin [369; 34a] 112, 262, 263, 376
'ayin [5869; 744a] 121, 122
'āzab [5800; 736d] 143, 144
'āzar [5826; 740b] 180
'azəkārāh [234; 272b] 325

B

ba'al [1167; 127b] 19, 20, 228, 242
bāchar [977; 103d] 56, 243
bāchîr [972; 104c] 57, 243
bāchûr [970; 104c] 110, 237, 243, 244
bad [905, 906; 94c, 94b] 280
bādad [910; 94d] 281
bāla' [1104; 108c] 413
bāmāh [1116; 119a] 183, 184
bānāh [1129; 124a] 41, 42
bāqa' [1234; 131d] 61, 62
bāqar [1239; 133a] 250
bāqār [1241; 133a] 138, 180
bāqash [1245; 134c] 359, 360
bārā' [1254; 135d] 84, 85
bārach [1272; 137d] 116, 136
bārak [1288; 138c] 29
bāsār [1320; 142b] 137, 138, 226
bātach [982; 105a] 357
bath [1323; 123a] 42
bayîth [1004; 108c] 128, 193, 422
bāchûr [970; 104c] 243
bəchûrôth [979; 104c] 243
bə'ēr [875; 91c] 291
beged [899; 93d] 146
bəhēmáh [929; 92d] 23, 24
bəkôr [1060; 114a] 135, 136
bəliya'al [1100; 116a] 470
bēn [1121; 119d] 23, 42, 43
bên [997; 1084b] 27, 28
bərākāh [1295; 140a] 30, 31
bərîth [1285; 136b] 82, 83, 400
betach [983; 105b] 357
bəthûlîm [1331; 144a] 236, 237
bəthûlôth [1330; 143d] 237
bikkûrîm [1061; 114c] 136
bîn [995; 106c] 446
bînāh [999; 1084b] 447
bô' [935; 97c] 64, 155
bōqer [1242; 133c] 180, 249, 250
bôsh [954; 101d] 371
bōsheth [1322; 102a] 371

C

chādal [2308; 292d] 53, 54
chādash [2318; 293d] 261

chādāsh [2319; 294a] 261, 262

chāg [2282; 290d] 131

chākam [2449; 314b] 446, 475, 476

chākām [2450; 314c] 473, 474, 475

chālāh [2470; 318c] 373

chālal [2490; 320a] 73, 294

chālam [2492; 321b] 102

chālaph [2498; 322a] 281

chālaq [2505; 323c] 99

chalôm [2472; 321c] 101, 102

chalōm [2492; 321b] 102

chāmās [2554, 2555; 329b, 329c] 451, 452

chānāh [2583; 333b] 51

chānan [2604; 1093b] 164, 266

channûn [2587; 337a] 165

chāphēts [2654, 2655; 342c, 343a] 293

chāqaq [2710; 349a] 401

chārab [2717; 352b] 415

chārāh [2734; 354a] 8

chāraph [2778; 357c] 332

chārash [2790; 361a] 293, 294

chārāsh [2796; 360d] 294

chārôn [2740; 354c] 8

chāshab [2803; 362d] 96, 426, 427, 428

chāsîd [2623; 339c] 234, 291

chātā' [2398; 306c] 199, 379, 381

chāthath [2865; 369a] 98

chātsāh [2673; 345b] 169

chātsēr [2691; 346d, 347b] 58, 81

chatsî [2677; 345c] 169

chattā'th [2403; 308b] 199, 320, 343, 378, 379

chay [2416; 311d] 225, 226

chāyāh [2421; 310d] 224, 225

chayil [2428; 298c] 404, 405

chayyāh [2421; 312c] 225

chayyîm [2416, 311d] 90, 225

chāzāh [2372; 302b] 453

chāzaq [2388; 304a] 409

chāzāq [2389; 305c] 409, 410

chāzôn [2377; 302d] 453

chebel [2256; 286c] 79, 80

chēleq [2506; 324a] 99

chēmāh [2534; 404b] 482, 483, 484, 486

chēn [2580; 336b] 2, 165, 266

chēphets [2656; 343a] 292, 293

chêq [2436; 300d] 36

chereb [2719; 352b] 5, 414, 415

cherəpāh [2781; 357d] 331

chesed [2617; 338c] 71, 83, 124, 232, 233, 234, 291

chētə' [2399; 307d] 379

chinnām [2600; 336c] 265, 266

chizzāyôn [2384; 303b] 453

chōdesh [2320; 294b] 261

chokəmāh [2451; 315b] 474, 475

cholî [2483; 318b] 374

chômāh [2346; 327b] 458

chōq [2706; 349b] 68, 83, 399, 400

chōzēh [2374; 302d] 311

chuqqāh [2708; 349d] 400, 401

chûts [2351; 299c] 403, 404

D

da'ath [1847; 395c] 213

dābaq [1692; 179c] 61

dabar [1696; 180b] 391, 392

dābār [1697; 182a] 83, 391, 392, 470

dabbereth [1703; 184c] 392

dal [1800; 195d] 295, 296

dālal [1809; 195c] 297

dallāh [1803; 195d] 297

dallîm [1800; 195d] 296

dām [1818; 196b] 31, 32

dāmāh [1819; 197d] 223

dārash [1875; 205a] 359, 360, 361

day [1767; 191b] 411, 412

deber [1698; 184a] 290

dəbôrāh [1682; 184b] 392

dəmûth [1823; 198b] 223, 399

derek [1870; 202c] 464, 465

dibərāh [1700; 184a] 392

dôr [1755; 189c] 150

E

'ebed [5650; 713d] 367

'eben [68; 6b] 402, 403

'ēber [5676; 719b] 283

'ebəyôn [34; 2d] 260, 261, 295, 296

'ēd [5707; 729c] 476
'êd [343; 15c] 48, 49, 200
'edāh [5713; 730a] 400
'ēdāh [5712; 417a] 74, 75, 83
'eder [145; 12a] 263, 264
'ēdûth [5715; 730b] 400, 425
'ēl [410; 41d] 157, 158, 159, 258
'elāh [426; 1080c] 158, 159
'eleph [504; 48c] 53
'eləyôn [5945; 751b] 66, 182, 183
'elîl [457; 47b] 196, 197
'ellûph [441; 48d] 53
'elôah [433; 43a] 158, 159
'elōhîm [430; 43b] 7, 12, 159, 196,
    258
'ēlôn [436; 18d] 437
'ēm [517; 51c] 128, 250, 251
'emədāh [5979; 765a] 398
'ēmer [561; 56d] 353, 392
'emeth [571; 54a] 27, 125, 232, 233
'ēmîm [367; 33d] 197
'emûnāh [530; 53c] 26, 123, 124,
    125, 232, 233
'enôsh [582; 60d] 240, 241, 243
'ephes [657; 67a] 112, 113, 115
'ēphôd [646; 65b] 116
'ereb [6153; 787d] 117
'erets [776; 75d] 107, 108, 216, 217
'erəwāh [6172; 788d] 257, 258
'erəyāh [6181; 789a] 258
'êrōm [5903; 735d] 257
'ēsh [784; 77b] 135
'ēth [6256; 773b] 429, 430
'ēts [6086; 781c] 436, 437
'etsem [6106; 782c] 33; 34
'ewîl [191; 17b] 139
'ezərô'a [248; 284b] 13

G

gā'āh [1342; 144b] 306
gā'al [1350; 146b] 317, 318
ga'awāh [1346; 144d] 307
ga'ayôn [1349; 145b] 307
gābah [1362; 147a] 182, 183
gābar [1396; 149c] 181
gābōah [1364; 147a] 182
gādad [1413; 151a] 21

gādal [1431; 152a] 119, 168, 234,
    235, 236, 254
gādēl [1432; 152d] 236
gādôl [1419; 152d] 236, 386
gālāh [1540; 162d] 152, 153
gāmal [1580; 168a] 90
gā'ôn [1347; 144d] 306, 307
gārash [1644; 176c] 411
gē' [1341; 144b] 307
gē'āh [1344; 144d] 307
geber [1397; 149d] 181, 241
gəbûl [1366; 147d] 36, 37
gəbûlāh [1367; 148b] 37
gəbûrāh [1369; 150b] 247, 248
gədî [1423; 152a] 215
gədûd [1416; 151b] 20, 21
gədûllāh [1420; 153c] 236
gē'eh [1343; 144b] 307
gēr [1616; 158a] 387
gērûth [1628; 158c] 388
gə'ullāh [1353; 145d] 320
gē'ûth [1348; 145a] 307
gibbôr [1368; 150a] 180, 181
gibə'āh [1389; 148d] 184
gillûlîm [1544; 165c] 197
gōbah [1363; 147b] 182, 183
gōdel [1433; 152d] 236
gôlāh [1473; 163c] 153
gôrāl [1486, 174a] 230
gôy [1471; 156c] 259, 260, 287
gôyim [1471; 156c] 260
gûr [1481, 1482; 157c, 158d] 223,
    386, 388

H

hādar [1921; 213d] 187
hādār [1926; 214a] 188
hadārah [1927; 214c] 189
hāgāh [1897; 211c] 245
hālak [1980; 229d] 333, 456
hālal [1984; 237d] 301
hālîk [1978; 237b] 457
halîkāh [1979; 237b] 457
hallelujah [1984; 238b] 73
hāmāh [1993; 242a] 257
hāmôn [1995; 242b] 256
hāphak [2015; 245b] 441

har [2022; 249a] 251, 252
hārag [2026; 246d] 209
hāyāh [1961; 224a] 21, 22, 397
hebel [1892; 210c] 40
hêkāl [1964; 228a] 422
hēlek [1982; 237a] 457
hillûlîm [1974; 239b] 302
hôn [1952; 223c] 466, 467
hôd [1935; 217a] 395

I

'ibərî [5680; 720a] 282
'im [518; 49c] 263, 426
'im [5973; 767a] 316, 480
'imərāh [565; 57a] 353
'îr [5892; 746b] 58
'îsh [376; 35d] 19, 240, 241, 242, 477
'îshîm [376; 35d] 241
'îshôn [380; 36b] 242
'ishshāh [802; 61a] 241, 477, 478
'ishsheh [801; 77d] 135, 276
'iwweleth [200; 17c] 139, 140

K

kā'as [3707; 494d] 313
kābas [3526; 460a] 460
kābēd [3515; 458a] 165, 166, 186, 187, 189
kābôd [3519; 458c] 187, 188, 306
kāhan [3547; 464c] 309
kālāh [3615; 477b] 75, 76
kālal [3634; 480d] 3, 4
kālîl [3632; 483a] 4
kāna' [3665; 488b] 193
kānāph [3671; 489b] 472, 473
kaph [3709; 496a] 279; 280
kāphaph [3721; 496a] 280
kaphar [3722; 497b] 16, 17, 141, 318, 319, 320
kappōreth [3727; 498c] 17
kāra' [3766; 502c] 37
kārath [3772; 503c] 83, 237, 238
kāsaph [3700; 493d] 376
kāshal [3782; 505b] 410

kāthab [3789; 507a] 484, 485
kebes [3532; 461a] 215
kəlî [3627; 479b] 449, 450
kēn [3651; 485d] 306
kəna'an [3667; 488d] 47
kəna'anî [3669; 489b] 47
kəphîr [3715; 498d] 223
kərîthûth [3748; 504d] 238
kərûthôth [3773; 503c] 238
kerem [3754, 501c] 450, 451
kesel [3689; 492d] 411
keseph [3701; 494a] 375
kəsîl [3685, 493a] 410
kəthāb [3791; 508b] 485
kəthōbeth [3793; 508b] 485
kibəsāh [3535; 461a] 215
kissē' [3678; 490c] 428, 429
kōach [3581; 470c] 299, 300
kōhēn [3548; 463a] 307, 309
kōl [3605; 481a] 3, 4
kûn [3559; 465c] 84, 85, 304, 305, 306

L

lābash [3847; 527d] 62
lācham [3898; 535b] 132, 459
lachats [3906; 537b] 377
lākad [3920; 539d] 418
lāmad [3925; 540c] 419
lāqach [3947; 542c] 417, 418
lāshôn [3956; 546a] 224, 432, 433
layəlāh [3915; 438c] 262
lēb [3820; 524b] 177, 178, 247
lēbāb [3824; 523b] 177
lechem [3899; 536d] 38, 39
leqach [3948; 544b] 418, 419
limmûd [3928; 541a] 420
lûn [3885; 533c] 323

M

ma'abār [4569; 721b] 283
mā'al [4603; 591a] 437, 438, 439
ma'alāh [4609, 752a] 66
ma'amād [4612; 765b] 398
ma'amār [3982; 57d] 353

ma'ar [4626; 789a] 257
mā'as [3988; 549b] 95
ma'aseh [4639; 795c] 481, 482
machaneh [4264; 334a] 51
māchār [4279; 563d] 431, 432
māchorāth [4283; 564a] 432
mādad [4058; 551a] 244, 245
maddû'a [4069; 396c] 214
madəweh [4064; 188c] 374
maəbārāh [4569; 721b] 283
ma'əyān [4599; 745d] 122
mahalāk [4109; 237b] 457
mahalāl [4110; 239c] 302
māhar [4116; 554d] 171, 238, 239, 341
mākar [4376; 569a] 361
mākôn [4349; 467c] 306
mālak [4427; 573d] 321
mālat [4422; 572b] 116, 117
malath [4422; 572b] 169
mālē' [4390; 569d] 133, 134
maləʾāk [4398; 1098d] 6, 7, 8
maləkûth [4438; 574d] 210
maməlākāh [4467; 575a] 210, 211
maləqôach [4455; 544c] 419
māmôth [4463; 560d] 91
ma'omād [4613; 765c] 398
ma'ôr [3974; 22c] 222
māqôm [4725; 879d] 11
maqqāchôth [4728; 544c] 419
mārāh [4784; 598a] 315, 316
marəʾāh [4759; 909c] 359
marəbeh [4766; 916a] 255
marəʾeh [4758; 909c] 359
marəbîth [4768; 916b] 255
marəʾîth [4830; 945c] 373
mārôm [4791; 928d] 120
masəʾēth [4864; 673a] 329
masəkîl [4905; 968d] 447
māshach [4886; 602d] 8, 9, 246, 299
māshal [4910; 605c] 341
māshîach [4899; 603c] 9, 246
massā' [4853; 672c] 227, 329
massā'āh [4858; 673a] 329
mātsā' [4672; 592c] 134, 135
matstsāh [4680; 594c] 39
matsərēph [4715; 864c] 425
matstsēbāh [4676; 663a] 184, 290, 291
mattāh [4295; 641c] 407

matteh [4295; 641c] 439, 440
māweth [4194; 560c] 90, 91
mayim [4325; 565b] 462, 463
magillāh [4039; 396c] 34
magurim [4033; 158c] 388
me'îm [4578; 588d] 247
makônāh [4350; 467d] 306
malāʾkāh [4399; 521d] 6
melek [4428; 572d] 210, 211
maləqāchayim [4457; 544c] 419
mē'mar [3983; 1081b] 353
maʾōd [3966; 547b] 120, 121
maqatērah [4729; 883b] 45
marəkabah [4818; 939d] 55, 56
marî [4805; 598b] 316
marîbāh [4808; 937b] 408
mērûts [4793, 930c] 343
mēsab [4524; 687b] 443
mashûbāh [4878; 1000b] 334
mazimmāh [4209; 273c] 228
mibətāch [4009; 105c] 357
middāh [4060; 551c] 245
midəbār [4057; 184c] 392
midərash [4097; 205d] 361
migədāl [4026; 153d] 236, 434, 435
migərāsh [4054; 177b] 411
mikətāb [4385; 508b] 485
miləchāmāh [4421; 536a] 132, 133, 459
min [4480; 577d] 113, 168, 263, 281
minəchāh [4503; 585a] 271, 272, 320
miphəletset [4656; 814a] 197
miqədāsh [4720; 874a] 347
miqərā' [4744; 896d] 50, 51
miqətār [4729; 883b] 45
miqəteret [4730; 883b] 45
miqqāch [4745; 899d] 419
mirəʾeh [4829; 945c] 373
misəpār [4557; 708d] 267
mishəchāh [4888; 603b] 246
mishəkāb [4904; 1012d] 221
mishəkān [4908; 1015c] 106, 415, 416
mishəlach [4916; 1020a] 362
mishəlôach [4916; 1020a] 363
mishəmān [4924; 1032d] 277
mishəmār [4929; 1038b] 208, 460, 461

mishəmereth [4931; 1038b] 208, 400, 460, 461

mishnəh [4932; 1041c] 81

mishəpāchāh [4940; 1046c] 125, 126, 317

mishəpāt [4941; 1048b] 124, 205, 400, 401

mîshôr [4334; 449d] 449

mitsəwāh [4687; 846b] 68, 69, 400, 401

mittāh [4296; 641d] 407

mizəbēach [4196; 258a] 5, 385

mô'ēd [4150; 417b] 74, 75

môledeth [4138; 409d] 23

môphēth [4159, 68d] 478

môrā' [4172; 432b] 131

môrāh [4177; 559a] 258

môrāsh [4180; 440c] 298

môrāshāh [4181; 440c] 298

mōshā'ôth [4190; 448a] 352

môthār [4195; 452d] 324

môtsā' [4161; 425d] 156

mûl [4135; 557d] 57

mûsab [4141; 687c] 443

mûsār [4148; 416b] 201

mûth [4191; 559b] 96, 97

muttôth [4298; 642a] 407

N

nā'am [5001; 610c] 354

na'ar [5287; 654c] 110, 487, 488

na'arāh [5291; 655a] 237, 487

nābā' [5012; 612a] 310

nābat [5027; 613c] 227

nābî' [5030; 611c] 311, 312

nāchal [5157; 635c] 197, 338, 339

nachalāh [5159; 635a] 197, 198

nacham [5162; 636d] 329, 330

nādach [5080; 623a] 103

nādar [5087; 623d] 455

nāga' [5060; 619a] 434

nāgad [5046; 616c] 420, 421

nāgash [5066; 620c] 65

nāgîd [5057; 617d] 421

nāhār [5104; 625c] 339

nāhar [5102; 625c] 340

nākar [5234; 647d] 97, 212

nākərî [5237; 648d] 387

nāqāh [5352; 667a] 168

nāqam [5358; 667d] 17, 18

nāqām [5359; 668b] 483

nāqî [5355; 667c] 169

nāphash [5314; 661c] 388, 389

nāsa' [5265; 652a] 94, 95, 141

nāsā' [5375; 669d] 309, 328

nāsag [5400; 969c] 278

nāsî' [5387; 672b] 309, 329

nāta' [5193; 642b] 291, 292

nātāh [5186; 639d] 406, 440

nātan [5414; 678a] 92, 93

nātsab [5324; 662a] 290, 396

nātsach [5329; 663d] 206

nātsar [5341; 665c] 206, 207

nāzar [5144; 634c] 363, 364

nāzîr [5139; 634c] 364

nəbālāh [5039; 615a] 140

nəbî'āh [5031; 612c] 312

nəchōsheth [5178; 638d] 78, 79

neder [5088; 623d] 455, 456

nega' [5061; 619c] 434

neged [5048; 617a] 421, 422

nephesh [5315; 659b] 177, 225, 226, 279, 360, 388, 389, 394

nəsibbāh [5252; 687c] 443

nəsî'îm [5387; 672b] 309, 329

nə'um [5002; 610b] 354

nō'ar [5290; 655a] 488

nûach [5117; 628a] 332, 333

nûs [5127; 630c] 116, 136

O

'ôb [178; 15b] 394, 395

'ōdem [124; 10b] 241

'ōhel [168; 13d] 75, 416, 432

'ōkel [400; 38a] 110

'ōlāh [5930; 750b] 66, 275, 276, 343

'ôlām [5769, 761d] 117, 118, 160, 161

'ōmed [5977; 765a] 398

'ōmer [562; 56d] 353

'onî [6040; 777a] 296, 377

'ôr [216; 21c] 221, 222

'ōrach [734; 73a] 465, 466

'ôrāh [219; 21d] 222

'ōrəchāh [736; 73c] 466

'ôth [226; 16d] 374, 375

'ōyēb [341; 33b] 115, 116
'ōzen [241; 23d] 107

P

pā'al [6466; 821b] 479
pa'am [6471; 821d] 401, 402
pā'ar [6286; 802b] 152
pādāh [6299; 804a] 318, 319, 320
pālā' [6381; 810c] 244
pālal [6419; 813a] 303
pānāh [6437; 815a] 443, 444, 445
pānîm [6440; 815d] 123; 445
pāqad [6485; 823b] 268, 269
pāqîd [6496; 824b] 269
pār [6499; 830d] 43
pārad [6504; 825b] 363
pārāh [6509; 6510; 826a, 831a] 43, 145
pāras [6566; 831a] 396
pāsha' [6586; 833b] 379, 435
pātach [6605; 834d] 101
pədûth [6304; 804b] 320
peh [6310; 804d] 253, 254, 433
pele' [6382; 810b] 244
pənîmāh [6441; 819b] 445
pənîmî [6442; 819b] 445
pərî [6529; 826b] 145
pesha' [6588; 833b] 378, 379, 436
petach [6607; 835d] 101
pinnāh [6438; 819c] 445
piqûd [6490; 824b] 83
puts [6327; 806d] 354

Q

qābar [6912; 868b] 45, 46
qābats [6908; 867c] 147, 148, 149
qādam [6923; 869d] 73
qādash [6942; 872d] 185, 186, 344, 345, 346
qādēsh [6942; 6945; 872d, 873c] 185, 186, 347.
qādôsh [6918; 872c] 185, 186, 348
qāhal [6950; 874d] 16
qāhāl [6951; 874c] 15, 74
qālal [7043; 886b] 87, 88
qānā' [7065; 888c] 202, 203

qānāh [7069, 888d] 19, 46, 47, 84, 85
qannā' [7067; 888b] 204
qāra' [7167; 902b] 329
qārā' [7121; 7122; 894d, 896d] 49, 50, 111, 112
qārēb [7127; 1111c] 270
qārəbān [7133; 898d] 275, 343
qārab [7126; 897b] 269, 270
qārôb [7138; 898b] 69, 270
qāsam [7080; 890c] 99, 100
qātān [6996; 881d] 385, 386
qātar [6999; 882d] 44, 45
qātōn [6996; 882b] 385, 386
qātsāh [7098; 892b] 114
qātsaph [7107; 893b] 485, 486
qātseh [7097; 892a] 113
qātsîr [7105; 894c] 390
qeber [6913; 868d] 46
qelālāh [7045; 887a] 30
qərāb [7128; 898b] 270
qereb [7130; 899a] 5, 6
qətōrah [6988; 882c] 45
qətoreth [7004; 882c] 45
qēts [7093; 893d] 113
qetseph [7110; 893c] 484, 486
qinə'āh [7068; 888b] 203, 483
qirəbāh [7132; 898b] 270
qirəyat [7149; 1111d] 58
qitēr [7002; 883b] 45
qîtōr [7008; 882c] 45
qōdesh [6944; 871c] 186, 347, 422
qôl [6963, 876d] 454
qorəbān [7133; 898d] 270, 274, 275
qûm [6965; 877c] 10, 11
qurəbān [7133; 898d] 270, 275

R

ra' [7451; 948a] 201, 380, 381
ra'a' [7489; 949b] 380
rā'āb [7458; 944b] 127
rā'āh [7200; 906b] 70, 357, 358, 359, 372, 373
rab [7227; 912d] 167, 168
rābab [7231; 912c] 166, 254
rābāh [7235; 915a] 254, 255
rācham [7355; 933c] 70, 71, 231
rachamîm [7356; 933b] 71

rāchaq [7368; 934d] 127
rāchats [7364; 934b] 460
rāchum [7349; 933d] 71
rādaph [7291; 922c] 313, 314
rā'ēb [7456, 7457; 944a, 944c] 127
ra'ayāh [7474; 946b] 70
rāgam [7275; 920c] 403
rāhab [7292; 923b] 40
rākab [7392; 938c] 56, 338
rānan [7442; 943b] 382, 383
rāphā' [7495; 950c] 175
rāsh [7567; 958b] 296
rāshā' [7563; 957b] 201, 378, 379,
   380, 468, 469
rāsha' [7561; 957d] 199, 470
rātsach [7523; 953d] 209, 210
rātsāh [7521; 953a] 2, 130
rātsats [7533; 954c] 380
rātsôn [7522; 953c] 129, 130
re'shîth [7225; 912a] 174
rē'a [7453; 945d] 69, 144
rêach [7381; 926a] 352
re'āh [7464; 946b] 70, 145
rechem [7358; 933a] 71
rachôb [7339; 932a] 40
rē'eh [7463; 946b] 70, 145
regel [7272; 919c] 140
ra'î [7209; 909b] 359, 373
rekeb [7393; 939a] 55, 56
rē'sh [7217; 1112a] 172
rēsha' [7562; 957c] 469
resheth [7568; 440b] 298
rē'shîth [7225; 912a] 142
ra'ûth [7468; 946b] 70, 359, 478
rîb [7378, 7379; 936b, 936d] 292,
   407, 408
risha'āh [7564; 958a] 469
ri'shōn [7223; 911c] 142, 174
rōb [7230; 913d] 166
rōchab [7341; 931d] 39, 40
rōdēph [7291; 922c] 116
rō'eh [7203; 909a] 311, 359
rō'ēh [7462; 944d] 372
rō'î [7210; 909b] 359
rō'sh [7218; 910c] 142, 172, 173, 174
rûach [7306, 7308; 926b, 1112d]
   352, 393, 394
rûm [7311, 7312, 926c, 927d] 119,
   120, 173
rûts [7323; 930a] 341, 342

S

sāba' [7646; 959b] 349, 350
sābab [5437; 685b] 441, 442, 443
sābîb [5439; 686d] 443
sāday [7706; 961a] 132
sādeh [7704; 961b] 131, 132
sāgar [5462; 688d] 373
sā'îr [8163, 972d] 157
sākal [7919; 968a] 446, 447
sālach [5545; 699b] 141
sāmach [8055; 970a] 321, 322
sāmēach [8056; 970c] 323
sānē' [8130, 971b] 171, 172
sāphāh [5595; 705a] 224
sāphar [5608; 707d] 266
saphār [5610; 708c] 268
sāqal [5619; 709c] 403
sar [8269; 978a] 67, 68
sārāph [8313; 8314; 976d, 977b] 43,
   44
sārar [5637; 710d] 315, 316
sātān [7853, 7854; 966c, 966b] 348,
   349
sātar [5642; 711b] 182
sa'ēt [7613; 673b] 329
sagullāh [5459; 688c] 298
sela' [5553; 700d] 402
saphār [5610; 708c] 268
sēpher [5612; 706d] 34, 35, 267
saphōrāh [5615; 708d] 268
saraphîm [8314; 977b] 44
shā'al [7592; 981b] 14
sha'ar [8179; 1044c] 146
shā'ar [7604; 983d] 327
shāba' [7650; 989a] 413
shābar [7665; 990c] 40
shābath [7673; 991d] 54, 333
shabbāth [7676; 992a] 54
shāchāh [7812; 1005b] 482
shāchal [7826; 1006c] 223
shāchat [7819; 1006a] 208
shāchath [7843; 1007d] 96
shaddai [7706; 994d] 159
shākab [7901; 1011d] 220, 221, 231
shākach [7911; 1013a] 140
shākam [7925; 1014c] 338
shākēn [7931; 1014d] 106, 416
shālach [7971; 1018a] 361, 362, 363
shālak [7993; 1020d] 53

shālāl [7998; 1021d] 35, 36
shālam [7999; 1022d] 71, 72, 284, 317
shālēm [8003; 1023d] 72, 284
shālôm [7965; 1022d] 283, 284, 381
shāma' [8085; 1033b] 175, 176
shāmad [8045; 1029b] 95, 96
shāman [8080; 1031d] 277
shāmar [8104; 1036b] 207, 208, 462
shāmayim [8064; 1029c] 179
shāmēm [8076; 1031b] 95
shāmēn [8082; 1032a] 278
shāmərāh [8108; 1037c] 208
shəmû'āh [8052; 1035b] 176
shānāh [8141; 1040a] 487
shā'ôn [7588; 981a] 256
shāphak [8210; 1049b] 299
shāphāl [8217; 1050c] 194, 195
shāphat [8199; 1047a] 204, 205
shāphath [8239; 1046b] 351
shāphēl [8213; 1050a] 193, 194
shāqāh [8248; 1052b] 102, 151
sharath [8334; 1058a] 248, 249, 365, 368
shāthāh [8354; 1059a] 102, 103, 151
shāwə' [7723; 996a] 91
shə'ār [7605; 984b] 327
shēbet [7626; 986d] 440
shəbû'a [7621; 989d] 467
shə'ērîth [7611; 984c] 323, 326
shəkābāh [7902; 1012c] 221
shēkār [7941; 1016b] 472
shəkōbeth [7903; 1012d] 221
shelach [7973; 1019c] 363
shēm [8034; 1027d] 258, 259, 388
shēma' [8088; 1034d] 176
shəmarîm [8105; 1038d] 208
shemen [8081; 1032a] 277
shemesh [8121; 1039a] 412, 413
shə'ôl [7585; 982d] 14, 15, 371
shəhphātîm [8201; 1048a] 205
shēphel [8216; 1050c] 194
sheqer [8267; 1055b] 125
shillûchim [7964; 1019d] 363
shimmurîm [8107; 1037d] 208
shipəchāh [8198; 1046c] 126
shipəlah [8218; 1050c] 194
shiphəlût [8220; 1050d] 194
shîr [7891; 1010c] 383
shîth [7896; 1011c] 368

shôma' [8089; 1035a] 176
shōthərîm [7860; 1009c] 111
shûb [7725; 996d] 333, 334
shûbāh [7729; 1000a] 334
sî' [7863; 673b] 329
sibbāh [5438; 686d] 443
sifra [5612; 706d] 34
sîm [7760; 962c] 369, 370
siməchāh [8057; 970d] 322
sinə'āh [8135; 971d] 172
ssiphərāh [5612; 706d] 268
sôd [5475; 691c] 356
sōneh [8130; 971b] 116
sōphēr [5613; 708b] 267, 268
sûs [5483; 692b] 190

T

tā'ab [8581; 1073a] 2
ta'ar [8593; 789b] 258
tahalukāh [8418; 237c] 457
tāhēr [2891; 372a] 59, 445
tāhôr [2889; 373a] 59, 446
tām [8535; 1070d] 77, 288
tāmam [8552; 1070b] 76, 288
tāmē' [2930, 2931; 379a, 379d] 445, 446
tāmîd [8548; 556b] 77, 78
tāmîm [8549; 1071a] 287, 288
taph [2945; 381b] 466
tāphas [8610; 1074c] 417
tāqa' [8628; 1075b] 32, 33
tarəbîth [8636; 916b] 255
tarəbûth [8635; 916b] 255
tāwek [8432; 1063c] 246, 247
təbûnāh [8394, 108b] 447
təhillāh [8416; 239d] 302
təhôm [8415; 1062d] 463, 464
təkûnāh [8498; 1067c] 306
têmān [8486; 412c] 335
təmûthāh [8546; 560d] 91
təphillāh [8605; 813c] 303
tərāphîm [8655; 1076c] 196
tərûmāh [8641; 929a] 272, 273, 274
təshû'āh [8668; 448b] 94, 352
təshûbāh [8666; 1000c] 334
təsûmeth [8667; 965a] 370
tipə'arath [8597; 802c] 151, 152
tîrôsh [8492; 440d] 472

tō'ar [8389; 1061b] 359
tôb [2895, 2896; 373b, 373c] 100,
162, 163, 164
tôdāh [8426; 392d] 302
to'ēbāh [8441; 1072d] 1, 2
tôlēdôth [8435; 410a] 23, 317
tōm [8537; 1070d] 288
tôrāh [8451; 435d] 68, 83, 218, 219,
400, 401, 417, 420
tôshāb [8453; 444c] 387
tôtsā'ôth [8444; 426a] 157
tsā'aq [6817; 858b] 85, 86
tsābā' [6633, 6635; 838c, 838d] 190,
191, 192
tsādaq [6663; 842c] 335
tsaddîq [6662; 843a] 335, 337
tsālēach [6743; 852b] 312
tsāphāh [6822; 859b] 278
tsar [6862; 865a, 865d] 98, 99, 115,
116
tsārāh [6869; 865b] 98
tsāraph [6884; 864a] 424, 425
tsārar [6887; 864c] 98
tsāwāh [6680; 845b] 67
tsədāqāh [6666; 842a] 336, 337
tsedeq [6664; 841c] 124, 336, 337
tselem [6754; 853d] 398, 399
tsō'n [6629; 838a] 138
tsōrəphî [6885; 864c] 425
tsûr [6697; 849c] 340, 402
tumə'āh [2932; 380a] 445

U

'ûd [5749; 729d] 75, 477
'ûlay [194; 19c] 287
'ûr [217; 22a] 222
'ûr [5782; 734d] 18, 19

W

wālād [3205; 408b] 23

Y

yā'ad [3259; 416d] 75
yā'ats [3289; 419c] 80

yabbāshāh [3004; 387a] 476
yābēsh [3001; 386b] 476
yachad [3162; 403a] 430, 431
yācham [3179; 404b] 483, 484
yāchas [3187; 405b] 317
yachas [3188; 405b] 317
yachədāw [3162; 403a] 431
yachîd [3173; 402d] 431
yād [3027; 388d] 169, 170, 171, 435
yāda' [3045; 393b] 212, 213, 214,
231, 446
yādāh [3034; 392a] 73, 301, 302
yāgôn [3015; 387b] 377
yahweh (YHWH) [3068; 217d] 7, 12,
22
yākach [3198; 406d] 332
yākōl [3201; 407b] 51, 52
yālad [3205; 408b] 22, 23
yalda [3207; 409c] 23
yālîd [3211; 409d] 23
yām [3220; 410d] 355, 356
yāmîn [3225; 411c] 334
yāqār [3365; 429c] 304
yāqar [3368; 429d] 304
yārad [3381; 432c] 66, 153, 154, 155
yārāh [3384; 434d] 219, 419, 420
yārash [3423; 439a] 297, 298
yārē' [3372; 431a] 130, 131
yārîb [3401; 937a] 408
yāsaph [3254; 414d] 3
yāsar [3256; 415d] 202
yāsha' [3467; 446b] 93, 350, 351
yāshab [3427; 442a] 105, 106
yāshār [3474, 3477; 448c, 449a]
447, 448
yātab [3190; 405c] 100, 164
yāthar [3498; 451b] 219, 324
yātsā' [3318; 422b] 155, 156
yātsaq [3332; 427a] 299
yātsar [3335; 427c] 84, 85, 142
yayin [3196; 406b] 471, 472
yəhôwāh (YHWH) [3068; 217d] 229
yeled [3206; 409b] 23, 110
yəmānî [3233; 412b] 335
yə'ôr [2975; 384b] 339
yəqār [3366; 430b] 304
yəreshāh [3424; 440b] 298
yərushshāh [3425; 440b] 298
yēsh [3426; 441b] 426
yēsha' [3468; 447a] 94, 352

Z

Notes

Notes

An Expository Dictionary

of

New Testament Words

An Expository Dictionary
of
New Testament Words

with their Precise Meanings
for English Readers

by
W. E. Vine, M.A.

FOREWORD

ANYONE who makes a serious and substantial contribution to the understanding of the New Testament, renders a public service, for if religion is the foundation of morality, by the knowledge of God is the welfare of the people. As a book the New Testament stands alone and supreme, simple in its profoundness, and profound in its simplicity. It is the record, in twenty-seven Writings, of the origin, nature and progress of Christianity, and in the quality of its influence it has done more for the world than all other books together.

We are more than fortunate to have this Book in a Version made immortal by William Tyndale, and we are grateful to have it also in the Revised Versions of 1611, and 1881-1885. But the fact remains that they who are entirely dependent upon a Version must miss very much of the glory and richness of these Writings. Provided there is spiritual appreciation, he who can read the New Testament in the language in which it was written stands to get the most out of it. But, of course, all cannot do this; although the accomplishment is by no means the preserve of the linguistic scholar. Yet the average reader is not wholly cut off from the treasures which lie in the Greek of the New Testament, for these have been put within our reach by means of Grammars and Lexicons, the special purpose of which has been to aid the English reader. So far as my acquaintance with these works goes, I do not hesitate to say that this Expository Dictionary more completely fulfills this design than any other such effort, in that it is at once a concordance, a dictionary, and a commentary, produced in the light of the best available scholarship.

Without encumbering this work with philological technicalities and extra-biblical references, Mr. Vine puts at the disposal of the English reader the labors of a lifetime bestowed devoutly upon the New Testament.

To several of the features of this Dictionary I would like to call attention.

First, it shows how rich is the language of the New Testament in words which present shades of the meaning of some common idea.

A good illustration of this is found on pages 195-199, under *Come*, and its related thoughts (e.g., *Appear*, pp. 56-59. Here, including the compounds, upwards of fifty words are employed to express one general thought, and the employment of any one of these, in any given passage, has precise historical or spiritual significance. If this root idea is followed out, for example, in its bearing on Christ's Second Advent, it is profoundly important to apprehend the significance respectively of *erchomai, heko, phaino, epiphaino, parousia, apokalupsis,* and *epiphaneia.*

Second, this Dictionary indicates the doctrinal bearing which the use of chosen words has. A case in point will be found on page 52, under *Another.* The use of *allos* and *heteros* in the New Testament should be carefully examined, for *another numerically* must not be confounded with *another generically.* Mr. Vine points this out in John 14:16. When Christ said, "I will make request of the Father, and He shall give you another

Helper (allon Parakleton)," He made a tremendous claim both for Himself and for the Spirit, for *allos* here implies the personality of the Spirit, and the equality of both Jesus and the Spirit with the Father. See also Mr. Vine's reference to the use of these words in Galatians 1:6 and 7. For an illustration of how one word can have a variety of meanings see pages 262–263 under *Day*. Unless such expressions as "man's day," "day of the Lord," and "day of Christ," are distinguished, one cannot understand the dispensational teaching of the New Testament. In this connection, the R.V. must be followed in 2 Thess. 2:2.

Third, this Dictionary shows how very many New Testament words are compounds, and how important are prepositional prefixes.

I think it was Bishop Westcott who said that New Testament doctrine is largely based on its prepositions; in any case the importance of them can scarely be exaggerated. These added to a word either emphasize or extend its meaning, and many such words have become Anglicized. For illustration take the three words *anabolism*, *katabolism*, and *metabolism*. These words are used in relation to biology and physiology. The root word in each is *ballo*, to cast, or throw, and each has a prepositional prefix; in the first, *ana*, up; in the second, *kata*, down; and in the third, *meta*, with. *Metabolism* tells of the chemical changes in living cells, by which the energy is provided for the vital processes and activities, and new material is assimilated to repair the waste; by a proper *metabolism* or *throwing-together* of the substances of the body, health is promoted. This building up of the nutritive substances into the more complex living protoplasm is *anabolism*, or *throwing-up*; and the want of this results in *katabolism*, or *throwing-down* of protoplasm. Now, two of the three words occur in the New Testament. For *metaballo* see p. 172; and for *kataballo*, p. 164, in both cases all the references are given (see Preface, p. xiv, par. 4).

For the possible range of prefixes to one word, see pages 195, 196; *Come*, with *eis*, and *ek*, and *epi*, and *dia*, and *kata*, and *para*, and *pros*, and *sun*; and two of the eleven compounds are double. No. 4 with *epi* and *ana*; and No. 8 with *para* and *eis*. These illustrations are sufficient to show the scope and simplicity of this work and consequently its immense usefulness to the English reader.

Fourth, this Dictionary is compiled in the light of the new knowledge which has come to us by the discovery of the papyri. During the last fifty years this light has been brought to bear upon the New Testament with precious and priceless results. In olden days in Egypt it was a custom not to burn waste paper, but to dump it outside the town, and the sands of the desert swept over it, and buried it, and for centuries a vast mass of such rubbish has lain there. However, in 1896-1897 Dr. Grenfell and Dr. Hunt began digging at Oxyrhynchus and discovered a number of papyri, among which was a crumpled leaf, written on both sides in uncial characters, which proved to be a collection of Sayings attributed to Jesus, Logia which Dr. J. Hope Moulton believed to be genuine. These and very many other papyri were classified and edited and one day when Dr. Deissmann was casually looking at a volume of these in the University Library at Heidelberg, he was impressed by the likeness of the language to that which he was familiar in his study of the Greek New Testament. By further study the great discovery was made that New Testament Greek is not the Attic of the Classics, nor is it "a language of the Holy Ghost" as one scholar called it, but it is the ordinary vernacular Greek of that period, the language of everyday life, as it was spoken and written by the ordinary men and women of the day, tradesmen, soldiers, schoolboys, lovers, clerks, and so on, that is, the *koine*, or "Common" Greek of the great Graeco-Roman world.

In illustration of this, look at Col. 2:14, which has several words which are found in the papyri; and take one of these, *Cheirographon*, handwriting. This means a memorandum of debt, "a writing by hand" used in public and private contracts, and it is a technical word in the Greek papyri. A large number of ancient notes of hand have been published and of these Dr. Deissmann says, "a stereotyped formula in these documents is the promise to pay back the borrowed money, 'I will repay'; and they all are in the debtor's own hand, or, if he could not write, in the handwriting of another acting for him, with the express remark, 'I have written for him.'" In such a note-of-hand, belonging to the first century, and with reference to a hundred silver drachmae, one named Papus wrote on behalf of two people who could not write, "which we will also repay, with any other that we owe, I Papus wrote for him who is not able to write."

Now, this expression occurs in the New Testament twice, in the parable of "The Lord and his Servants," "have patience with me, and I will pay thee all," and in Paul's note to Philemon concerning Onesimus, "if he hath wronged thee, or oweth thee ought, put that on mine account. I Paul have written it with mine own hand, I will repay it."

In the famous Florentine papyrus of A.D. 85, the governor of Egypt gives this order in the course of a trial,—"Let the hand-writing be crossed out," which corresponds to the "blotting out the hand-writing" of Col. 2:14. Many such illustrations might be given, from which we see that the papyri have a distinct expository value.

In Lexicons previous to this discovery are to be found lists of what are called *hapax legomena*, words which occur once only, and many of which, it was supposed, were created by the Holy Spirit for the conveyance of Christian truth, but now all or nearly all such words have been found in the papyri. The Holy Spirit did not create a special language for Christianity, but used the colloquial tongue of the time; He employed the cosmopolitan Greek. This fact has radically affected our approach to the New Testament, and although, in view of the magnitude of this Dictionary, it has been impossible to do more than make a reference here and there to this learning (e.g., pp. xiii–xiv, 51), yet the whole is produced in the light of it, and so represents present day scholarship.

I might have made reference also to etymological, cross-reference and other values in this work, but perhaps enough has been said to indicate its scope and usefulness. Mr. Vine has done a great service to the non-academic reader of the New Testament, and those also who are most familiar with the original tongue may learn much from these pages.

W. GRAHAM SCROGGIE, D.D.
(Edin.)

FOREWORD
TO NEW ONE-VOLUME EDITION

NEARLY twelve years have gone by since the first edition of this Expository Dictionary was completed. During these years the work has had ample opportunity to prove its worth as a handbook for serious students of the English Bible. And the high hopes with which the enterprise was launched have been justified not only by the warm welcome each volume of the first edition received as it appeared but also by the increasing sense of indebtness which Bible students all over the world have felt as they have come to know its value by daily use. Mr. Vine himself has passed from our midst in the meantime, but his biblical ministry survives in a wide range of published works, at the head of which stands his Expository Dictionary. It is a welcome token of its continued usefulness that the publishers have now decided to reissue it in a one-volume edition.

There is no work just like this. The English reader with little or no Greek has, of course, the standard concordances, notably Wigram's *Englishman's Greek Concordance;* the student of Greek has his Grimm-Thayer, Moulton-Milligan, and Bauer. These works provide the lexical skeleton; Mr. Vine's work clothes that skeleton with the flesh and sinews of living exposition, and makes available for the ordinary reader the expert knowledge contained in the more advanced works. In fact, this *Expository Dictionary* comes as near as possible to doing for the non-specialist what is being done for the specialist by Kittel's encyclopaedic *Theological Dictionary of the New Testament.*

A work of this kind, of course, cannot be expected to record every occurrence of each word in the New Testament. But all important and significant occurrences are mentioned, and many of the entries in fact are exhaustive, especially those dealing with words which do not occur very often. By the helpful system of cross-references the reader can see at a glance not only which Greek words are represented by one English word, but also which other English words, if any, are used to translate each Greek word. It is a further advantage that both A.V. and R.V. renderings are listed.

Mr. Vine's Greek scholarship was wide, accurate and up-to-date, and withal unobtrusive. Casual readers will hardly realize the wealth of ripe learning, the years of hard work, of which they may reap the fruit in this work. To his thorough mastery of the classical idiom the author added a close acquaintance with the Hellenistic vernacular, and used his knowledge of both to illustrate the meaning of New Testament words. And bearing in mind the New Testament writers' familiarity with the Septuagint and its influence on their language, he has enhanced the value of his work by giving select references to Septuagint usages.

There are few human pursuits more fascinating than the study of words. As vehicles for conveying the thoughts, feelings and desires of men, they have an abiding interest; how supremely interesting, then, should be the study of those "healthful words" in which the revelation of God Himself has been conveyed!

Yet words, divorced from their meanings, are but empty sounds; instead of being a vehicle of thought, they become a substitute for it. "Words," said Thomas Hobbes, "are wise men's counters; they do but reckon by them: but they are the money of fools." We must know what values to attach to them if we are to profit by them.

Words are not static things. They change their meanings with the passage of time. Many words used in the A.V. no longer possess in current English the meanings they had in 1611. We do not now use "prevent" in the sense of "precede", or "carriage" in the sense of "baggage." These changes of meaning may be inferred from the context, but there are other changes which might not be so readily noticed. An important example is the word "atonement," one of the great technical terms of theology. When this word retained its etymological sense of "at-one-ment," it was an appropriate rendering for Gk. *katallage,* and is so used in the A.V. of Rom. 5:11. But "atonement" has long since ceased to be an English equivalent of "reconciliation," and its continued use leads to confusion of thought on a theme of the utmost importance. A study of the articles on PROPITIATE, RANSOM, and RECONCILE in this work will greatly clarify the reader's understanding of the biblical presentation of what is commonly called "the doctrine of the atonement."

Not only in recent English, but in ancient Greek as well, we find words changing their meanings. Biblical exegetes of an earlier day were at a disadvantage in having to read New Testament words in the light of their classical usage of four or five centuries earlier. But they recognized certain marked differences between classical and New Testament Greek, and knowing no other Greek quite like that of the New Testament, they concluded that it must be a specially devised "language of the Holy Ghost." During the last seventy or eighty years, however, many documents have been found in the Near East written in this same Greek, from which we have learned the very salutary lesson that the "language of the Holy Ghost" is nothing other than the language of the common people. (One example of a change in the meaning of a Greek word between classical and New Testament times is pointed out in a note at the end of the entry on PUNISHMENT.)

There can be no true biblical theology unless it is based on sound biblical exegesis, and there can be no sound biblical exegesis unless a firm textual and grammatical foundation has been laid for it. Such a foundation is laid in this Expository Dictionary, but it provides much more than a foundation. The work is full of careful exegesis, and the student or teacher who makes it his constant companion in the study of Scripture will find that he can afford to dispense with a large number of lesser aids. In fact, it is so valuable a handbook to the study of the New Testament that many of us who have learned to use it regularly wonder how we ever got on without it. It has established a well-deserved reputation for itself and really needs no special commendation such as this, but it is a pleasure to commend it afresh, and to wish it a long term of service in its new format.

F. F. BRUCE,
Head of the Department of Biblical
History and Literature in the
September, 1952 *University of Sheffield.*

PREFACE

TO ascertain the exact meaning of the words and phraseology of the originals of the Holy Scriptures is of great importance, particularly those which have a variety of meanings in English. The research work of the past fifty years, with the discovery of a large number of inscriptions and documents, and especially of the non-literary writings in the tombs and dust heaps of Egypt, has yielded much light upon the use and meaning of the language of the originals. The importance of the Egyptian papyri writings etc. lies in the fact that they were written during the period in which the writers of the New Testament lived. Proof has thus been provided that the language of the New Testament was not a debased form of literary Greek corrupted by Hebrew idioms, but that in the main it was the vernacular, the speech of the everyday life of the people in the countries which came under Greek influence through the conquests of Alexander the Great. As the result of those conquests, the ancient Greek dialects became merged into one common speech, the *Koine* or "common" Greek. In one form this language became the literary *Koine,* or Hellenistic, of such writers as Josephus. In its spoken form it was the everyday speech of millions of people throughout the Graeco-Roman world, and in the providence of God it was under these conditions and in this world-language that the New Testament was written.

The fruit of these researchers has been provided in such volumes as the "Vocabulary of the Greek Testament," by J. H. Moulton and G. Milligan, the "Grammar of the New Testament Greek" by the former and the book entitled "New Testament Documents" by the latter, "Bible Studies" by G. A. Deissmann, "Light from the Ancient East" by A. Deissmann, and similarly well-known works by W. M. Ramsay. References will be found to some of these in the following pages.

The present volumes are produced especially for the help of those who do not study Greek, though it is hoped that those who are familiar with the original will find them useful.

The work is of an expository character, comments being given on various passages referred to under the different headings. The doctrines of Scripture are dealt with at some length, and notes are provided on matters historical, technical, and etymological.

In cases where an English word translates a variety of Greek words the latter are given in English form. Where there are no such variations, each word is dealt with according to its occurrences and usage in the New Testament, reference being made to the differences between the Authorized and Revised Versions.

The method of the Dictionary provides an exhaustive presentation of synonymous words. Where a word in the original has a variety of English renderings, a list is given of these at the close of the note on each word. The list provides in this way a comprehensive study of the use of any given word in the original. In cases where a list has already been given, only the first of these meanings is usually mentioned. There is thus a twofold presentation, firstly, of the different Greek words for one English word, secondly, of the different English meanings attached to a single Greek word.

The subject-matter is also analyzed under the various parts of speech. To take an example, DILIGENCE, DILIGENT, DILIGENTLY, are associated in one heading, and the forms in the original are divided respectively under the sections, Nouns, Verbs, Adjectives, Adverbs. The parts of speech are not given in the same order in every case. The order is largely dependent upon the greater prominence which a word receives in the original. Other considerations have made a variety in this respect advisable.

In many cases the student is referred to the occurrences in the Septuagint Version, especially where that Version presents a comparatively small number of occurrences or contains only one instance of the use. Reference to the Apocryphal books of the Old Testament is omitted.

The sign ¶ at the close of the treatment of a word indicates that all its occurrences in the original are mentioned. The Dictionary thus partakes to a considerable extent of the nature of a concordance.

In many instances all the occurrences and usages of a word are analyzed in a list, showing the different meanings as indicated by the context in each passage of the New Testament.

Considerable use has been made of the two commentaries, written jointly by Mr. C. F. Hogg of London and the present writer, upon the Epistle to the Galatians and the two Epistles to the Thessalonians. I have also made use of Hastings' Dictionary of the Bible, Abbott-Smith's Manual Greek Lexicon of the New Testament, the larger works by Cremer and by Thayer's Grimm, and of A.T. Robertson's Grammar of the Greek New Testament in the Light of Historical Research; also of such works as Trench's New Testament Synonyms.

A criticism may be raised in regard to a work like this that it would provide students who know little or nothing of the original with an opportunity of airing some knowledge of Greek. Even supposing that such a criticism were valid, the general advantage of the method adopted should outweigh the danger of such proclivities.

I wish to express my great indebtedness to, and appreciation of, the kind assistance of the Rev. H. E. Guillebaud, M.A., of Cambridge, and T. W. Rhodes, Esqre., M.A., recently of Madrid, who have made copious and useful suggestions and emendations, and have cooperated in going through the proofs.

It is with a sense of deep gratitude that I express my indebtedness to a friend Mr. F. F. Bruce, for his wholehearted assistance in going through the typescript and making corrections and valuable suggestions previous to its being printed, and in proofreading subsequently, whose efficiency, as a classical scholar, and whose knowledge of the originals, have enhanced the value of the work.

I trust that notwithstanding imperfections and limitations of treatment the work may afford assistance to Bible students in enabling them to increase in their knowledge of God and His Word and in helping to equip them in their use and ministry of the Holy Scriptures.

W. E. VINE.

Bath,
February, 1939

An Expository Dictionary

of

New Testament Words

A

ABASE

TAPEINOŌ (ταπεινόω) signifies to make low, bring low, (a) of bringing to the ground, making level, reducing to a plain, as in Luke 3 : 5 ; (b) metaphorically in the Active Voice, to bring to a humble condition, to abase, 2 Cor. 11 : 7, and in the Passive, to be abased, Phil. 4 : 12 ; in Matt. 23 : 12 ; Luke 14 : 11 ; 18 : 14, the A.V. has " shall be abased," the R.V. " shall be humbled." It is translated " humble yourselves " in the Middle Voice sense in Jas. 4 : 10 ; 1 Pet. 5 : 6 ; " humble," in Matt. 18 : 4 ; 2 Cor. 12 : 21 and Phil. 2 : 8. See HUMBLE, LOW.¶ Cp., tapeinos, lowly, tapeinōsis, humiliation, and tapeinophrosunē, humility.

ABBA

ABBA ('Aββâ) is an Aramaic word, found in Mark 14 : 36 ; Rom. 8 : 15 and Gal. 4 : 6. In the Gemara (a Rabbinical commentary on the Mishna, the traditional teaching of the Jews) it is stated that slaves were forbidden to address the head of the family by this title. It approximates to a personal name, in contrast to " Father," with which it is always joined in the N.T. This is probably due to the fact that, " Abba " having practically become a proper name, Greek-speaking Jews added the Greek word patēr, father, from the language they used. " Abba " is the word framed by the lips of infants, and betokens unreasoning trust ; " father " expresses an intelligent apprehension of the relationship. The two together express the love and intelligent confidence of the child.

ABHOR

1. APOSTUGEŌ (ἀποστυγέω) denotes to shudder (apo, from, here used intensively, stugeō, to hate) ; hence, to abhor, Rom. 12 : 9. ¶

2. BDELUSSŌ (βδελύσσω), to render foul (from bdeō, to stink), to cause to be abhorred (in the Sept. in Ex. 5 : 21 ; Lev. 11 : 43 ; 20 : 25 etc.), is used in the Middle Voice, signifying to turn oneself away from (as if from a stench) ; hence, to detest, Rom. 2 : 22. In Rev. 21 : 8 it denotes " to be abominable." See ABOMINABLE.¶

In the following pages † indicates that the word referred to (preposition, conjunction, or particle) is not dealt with in this volume.

¶ indicates that all the N.T. occurrences of the Greek word under consideration are mentioned under the heading or sub-heading.

ABIDE, ABODE
A. Verbs.

1. MENŌ (μένω), used (a) of place, e.g., Matt. 10 : 11, metaphorically 1 John 2 : 19, is said of God, 1 John 4 : 15 ; Christ, John 6 : 56 ; 15 : 4, etc. ; the Holy Spirit, John 1 : 32, 33 ; 14 : 17 ; believers, John 6 : 56 ; 15 : 4 ; 1 John 4 : 15, etc. ; the Word of God, 1 John 2 : 14 ; the truth, 2 John 2, etc. ; (b) of time ; it is said of believers, John 21 : 22, 23 ; Phil. 1 : 25 ; 1 John 2 : 17 ; Christ, John 12 : 34 ; Heb. 7 : 24 ; the Word of God, 1 Pet. 1 : 23 ; sin, John 9 : 41 ; cities, Matt. 11 : 23 ; Heb. 13 : 14 ; bonds and afflictions, Acts 20 : 23 ; (c) of qualities ; faith, hope, love, 1 Cor. 13 : 13 ; Christ's love, John 15 : 10 ; afflictions, Acts 20 : 23 ; brotherly love, Heb. 13 : 1 ; the love of God, 1 John 3 : 17 ; the truth, 2 John 2.

The R.V. usually translates it by " abide," but " continue " in 1 Tim. 2 : 15 ; in the following, the R.V. substitutes to abide for the A.V., to continue, John 2 : 12 ; 8 : 31 ; 15 : 9 ; 2 Tim. 3 : 14 ; Heb. 7 : 24 ; 13 : 14 ; 1 John 2 : 24. Cp. the noun monē, below. See CONTINUE, DWELL, ENDURE, REMAIN, STAND, TARRY.

2. EPIMENŌ (ἐπιμένω), to abide in, continue in, tarry, is a strengthened form of menō (epi, intensive), sometimes indicating perseverance in continuing, whether in evil, Rom. 6 : 1 ; 11 : 23, or good, Rom. 11 : 22 ; 1 Tim. 4 : 16. See CONTINUE, TARRY.

3. KATAMENŌ (καταμένω), kata, down (intensive), and No. 1, is used in Acts 1 : 13. The word may signify constant residence, but more probably indicates frequent resort. In 1 Cor. 16 : 6, it denotes to wait.¶

4. PARAMENŌ (παραμένω), to remain beside (para, beside), to continue near, came to signify simply to continue, e.g., negatively, of the Levitical priests, Heb. 7 : 23. In Phil. 1 : 25, the Apostle uses both the simple verb menō and the compound paramenō (some mss. have sumparamenō), to express his confidence that he will " abide," and " continue to abide," with the saints. In 1 Cor. 16 : 6 some mss. have this word. In Jas. 1 : 25, of stedfast continuance in the law of liberty. See CONTINUE.¶

5. HUPOMENŌ (ὑπομένω), lit., to abide under (hupo, under), signifies to remain in a place instead of leaving it, to stay behind, e.g., Luke 2 : 43 ; Acts 17 : 14 ; or to persevere, Matt. 10 : 22 ; 24 : 13 ; Mark 13 : 13 ; in each of which latter it is used with the phrase " unto the end ; " or to endure bravely and trustfully, e.g., Heb. 12 : 2, 3, 7, suggesting endurance under what would be burdensome. See also Jas. 1 : 12 ; 5 : 11 ; 1 Pet. 2 : 20. Cp., makrothumeō, to be longsuffering. See ENDURE, SUFFER, TAKE, Notes (12), TARRY.

6. PROSMENŌ (προσμένω), to abide still longer, continue with (pros, with) is used (a) of place, Matt. 15 : 32 ; Mark 8 : 2 ; Acts 18 : 18 ; 1 Tim. 1 : 3 ; (b) metaphorically, of cleaving unto a person, Acts 11 : 23, indicating persistent loyalty ; of continuing in a thing, Acts 13 : 43 ;

1 Tim. 5 : 5. See CLEAVE, CONTINUE, TARRY.¶ In the Sept., Judg. 3 : 25.¶

7. DIATRIBO (διατρίβω), lit., to wear through by rubbing, to wear away (dia, through, tribō, to rub), when used of time, to spend or pass time, to stay, is found twice in John's Gospel, 3 : 22 and 11 : 54, R.V., " tarried," instead of " continued ; " elsewhere only in the Acts, eight times, 12 : 19 ; 14 : 3, 28 ; 15 : 35 ; 16 : 12 ; 20 : 6 ; 25 : 6, 14. See CONTINUE, TARRY.¶

8. ANASTREPHO (ἀναστρέφω), used once in the sense of abiding, Matt. 17 : 22, frequently denotes to behave oneself, to live a certain manner of life ; here the most reliable mss. have sustrephomai, to travel about. See BEHAVE, CONVERSATION, LIVE, OVERTHROW, PASS, RETURN.

9. AULIZOMAI (αὐλίζομαι), to lodge, originally to lodge in the aulē, or courtyard, is said of shepherds and flocks ; hence, to pass the night in the open air, as did the Lord, Luke 21 : 37 ; to lodge in a house, as of His visit to Bethany, Matt. 21 : 17.¶

10. AGRAULEO (ἀγραυλέω), to lodge in a fold in a field (agros, a field, aulē, a fold), is used in Luke 2 : 8.¶ See LODGE.

11. HISTEMI (ἵστημι), to stand, to make to stand, is rendered " abode " in John 8 : 44, A.V. ; " continue," in Acts 26 : 22. In these places the R.V. corrects to " stood " and " stand." This word is suggestive of fidelity and stability. It is rendered " lay . . . to the charge " in Acts 7 : 60. See APPOINT, CHARGE, ESTABLISH, HOLDEN, PRESENT, SET, STANCH, STAND.

12. POIEO (ποιέω), to do, make, is used of spending a time or tarrying, in a place, Acts 15 : 33 ; 20 : 3 ; in 2 Cor. 11 : 25 it is rendered " I have been (a night and a day) ; " a preferable translation is ' I have spent,' as in Jas. 4 : 13, " spend a year " (R.V.). So in Matt. 20 : 12. Cp., the English idiom " did one hour ; " in Rev. 13 : 5 " continue " is perhaps the best rendering. See Do.

B. Noun.

MONE (μονή), an abode (akin to No. 1), is found in John 14 : 2, " mansions " (R.V. marg., " abiding places "), and 14 : 23, " abode."¶

ABILITY, ABLE
A. Nouns.

1. DUNAMIS (δύναμις) is (a) power, ability, physical or moral, as residing in a person or thing ; (b) power in action, as, e.g., when put forth in performing miracles. It occurs 118 times in the N.T. It is sometimes used of the miracle or sign itself, the effect being put for the cause, e.g., Mark 6 : 5, frequently in the Gospels and Acts. In 1 Cor. 14 : 11 it is rendered " meaning " ; " force " would be more accurate. Cp., the corresponding verbs, B. 1, 2, 3 and the adjective C. 1, below. See ABUNDANCE, DEED, MIGHT, POWER, STRENGTH, VIOLENCE, VIRTUE, WORK.

2. ISCHUS (ἰσχύς), connected with *ischō* and *echō*, to have, to hold (from the root *ech—*, signifying holding), denotes ability, force, strength ; " ability " in 1 Pet. 4 : 11, A.V. (R.V., " strength "). In Eph. 1 : 19 and 6 : 10, it is said of the strength of God bestowed upon believers, the phrase " the power of His might " indicating strength afforded by power. In 2 Thess. 1 : 9, " the glory of His might " signifies the visible expression of the inherent Personal power of the Lord Jesus. It is said of angels in 2 Pet. 2 : 11 (cp., Rev. 18 : 2, A.V., " mightily "). It is ascribed to God in Rev. 5 : 12 and 7 : 12. In Mark 12 : 30, 33, and Luke 10 : 27 it describes the full extent of the power wherewith we are to love God. See MIGHT, POWER, STRENGTH.¶

B. Verbs.

1. DUNAMAI (δύναμαι), to be able, to have power, whether by virtue of one's own ability and resources, e.g., Rom. 15 : 14 ; or through a state of mind, or through favourable circumstances, e.g., 1 Thess. 2 : 6 ; or by permission of law or custom, e.g., Acts 24 : 8, 11 ; or simply to be able, powerful, Matt. 3 : 9 ; 2 Tim. 3 : 15, etc. See CAN, MAY, POSSIBLE, POWER.

2. DUNAMOŌ (δυναμόω), to make strong, confirm, occurs in Col. 1 : 11 (some authorities have the 1st aorist or momentary tense, in Heb. 11 : 34 also). Cp. *endunamoō*, to enable, strengthen.¶

3. DUNATEŌ (δυνατέω) signifies to be mighty, to show oneself powerful, Rom. 4 : 14 ; 2 Cor. 9 : 8 ; 13 : 3. See A, No. 1.¶

4. ISCHUŌ (ἰσχύω), akin to A, No. 2, to be strong, to prevail, indicates a more forceful strength or ability than *dunamai*, e.g., Jas. 5 : 16, where it is rendered " availeth much " (i.e., " prevails greatly "). See AVAIL, CAN, DO, MAY, PREVAIL, STRENGTH, WORK.

Note : Still stronger forms are *exischuō*, to be thoroughly strong, Eph. 3 : 18, " may be strong " (not simply " may be able," A.V.).¶ ; *katischuō*, Matt. 16 : 18, and Luke 23 : 23, in the former, of the powerlessness of the gates of Hades to prevail against the Church ; in the latter, of the power of a fierce mob to prevail over a weak ruler (see Notes on Galatians, by Hogg and Vine, p. 251) ; also Luke 21 : 36. The prefixed prepositions are intensive in each case.¶

5. ECHŌ (ἔχω), to have, is translated " your ability " in 2 Cor. 8 : 11, and " ye may be able " in 2 Pet. 1 : 15, and is equivalent to the phrase ' to have the means of.' See CAN, HAVE.

6. EUPOREŌ (εὐπορέω), lit., to journey well (*eu*, well, *poreō*, to journey), hence, to prosper, is translated " according to (his) ability," in Acts 11 : 29.¶

Note : *Hikanoō*, corresponding to the adjective *hikanos* (see below) signifies to make competent, qualify, make sufficient ; in 2 Cor. 3 : 6, A.V., " hath made (us) able ; " R.V., " hath made us sufficient ; " in Col. 1 : 12, " hath made (us) meet." See ENOUGH, SUFFICIENT.¶

C. Adjectives.

1. DUNATOS (δυνατός), corresponding to A, No. 1, signifies powerful. See, e.g., Rom. 4:21; 9:22; 11:23; 12:18; 15:1; 1 Cor. 1:26; 2 Cor. 9:8. See MIGHTY, POSSIBLE, POWER, STRONG.

2. HIKANOS (ἱκανός), translated "able," is to be distinguished from *dunatos*. While *dunatos* means possessing power, *hikanos*, primarily, reaching to, has accordingly the meaning "sufficient." When said of things it signifies enough, e.g., Luke 22:38; when said of persons, it means "competent," "worthy," e.g., 2 Cor. 2:6, 16; 3:5; 2 Tim. 2:2. See CONTENT, ENOUGH, GOOD, GREAT, LARGE, LONG, MANY, MEET, MUCH, SECURITY, SUFFICIENT, WORTHY.

Note: Ischuros denotes strong, mighty; in an Active sense, mighty, in having inherent and moral power, e.g., Matt. 12:29; 1 Cor. 4:10; Heb. 6:18.

ABOARD

EPIBAINŌ (ἐπιβαινω), to go upon (*epi*, upon, *bainō*, to go), is once translated "we went aboard," Acts 21:2, the single verb being short for going aboard ship. In ver. 6 it is rendered "we went on board;" in 27:2 "embarking;" in Matt. 21:5, "riding upon." See COME, No. 16.

ABOLISH

KATARGEŌ (καταργέω), lit., to reduce to inactivity (*kata*, down, *argos*, inactive), is translated "abolish" in Eph. 2:15 and 2 Tim. 1:10, in the R.V. only in 1 Cor. 15:24, 26. It is rendered "is abolished" in the A.V. of 2 Cor. 3:13; the R.V. corrects to "was passing away" (marg., "was being done away"). In this and similar words not loss of being is implied, but loss of well being.

The barren tree was cumbering the ground, making it useless for the purpose of its existence, Luke 13:7; the unbelief of the Jews could not "make of none effect" the faithfulness of God, Rom. 3:3; the preaching of the Gospel could not make of none effect the moral enactments of the Law, 3:31; the Law could not make the promise of none effect, 4:14; Gal. 3:17; the effect of the identification of the believer with Christ in His death is to render inactive his body in regard to sin, Rom. 6:6; the death of a woman's first husband discharges her from the law of the husband, that is, it makes void her status as his wife in the eyes of the law, 7:2; in that sense the believer has been discharged from the Law, 7:6; God has chosen things that are not "to bring to nought things that are," i.e., to render them useless for practical purposes, 1 Cor. 1:28; the princes of this world are brought to nought, i.e., their wisdom becomes ineffective, 2:6; the use for which the human stomach exists ceases with man's death, 6:13; knowledge, prophesyings, and that which was in part were to be " done away," 1 Cor. 13 : 8, 10, i.e., they were to be rendered of no effect after their temporary use was fulfilled ; when the Apostle became a man he did away with the ways of a child, verse 11 ; God is going to abolish all rule and authority and power, i.e., He is going to render them inactive, 1 Cor. 15 : 24 ; the last enemy that shall be abolished, or reduced to inactivity, is death, ver. 26 ; the glory shining in the face of Moses, " was passing away," 2 Cor. 3 : 7, the transitoriness of its character being of a special significance ; so in verses 11, 13 ; the veil upon the heart of Israel is " done away " in Christ, ver. 14 ; those who seek justification by the Law are " severed " from Christ, they are rendered inactive in relation to Him, Gal. 5 ; 4 ; the essential effect of the preaching of the Cross would become inoperative by the preaching of circumcision, 5 : 11 ; by the death of Christ the barrier between Jew and Gentile is rendered inoperative as such, Eph. 2 : 15 ; the Man of Sin is to be reduced to inactivity by the manifestation of the Lord's Parousia with His people, 2 Thess. 2 : 8 ; Christ has rendered death inactive for the believer, 2 Tim. 1 : 10, death becoming the means of a more glorious life, with Christ ; the Devil is to be reduced to inactivity through the death of Christ, Heb. 2 : 14. See CEASE, CUMBER, DESTROY, DO, *Note* (7), OF NONE EFFECT, NOUGHT, PUT, No. 19, VOID.¶

ABOMINABLE, ABOMINATION

A. Adjectives.

1. ATHEMITOS (ἀθέμιτος) occurs in Acts 10 : 28, " unlawful," and 1 Pet. 4 : 3, " abominable " (*a*, negative, *themitos*, an adjective from *themis*, " law "), hence, unlawful. See UNLAWFUL.¶

2. BDELUKTOS (βδελυκτός), Tit. 1 : 16, is said of deceivers who profess to know God, but deny Him by their works.¶

B. Verb.

BDELUSSŌ (βδελύσσω) : See ABHOR, No. 2.

C. Noun.

BDELUGMA (βδέλυγμα), akin to A, No. 2 and B, denotes an object of disgust, an abomination. This is said of the image to be set up by Antichrist, Matt. 24 : 15 ; Mark 13 : 14 ; of that which is highly esteemed amongst men, in contrast to its real character in the sight of God, Luke 16 : 15. The constant association with idolatry suggests that what is highly esteemed among men constitutes an idol in the human heart. In Rev. 21 : 27, entrance is forbidden into the Holy City on the part of the unclean, or one who " maketh an abomination and a lie." It is also used of the contents of the golden cup in the hand of the evil woman described in Rev. 17 : 4, and of the name ascribed to her in the following verse.¶

For ABOUND see ABUNDANCE

ABOUT
A. Adverbs, etc.

Besides prepositions, the following signify " about " :—

1. KUKLOTHEN (κυκλόθεν), round about, or all round (from *kuklos*, a circle ; Eng., cycle), is found in the Apocalypse only, 4 : 3, 4, 8.¶

2. KUKLŌ (κύκλῳ), the dative case of *kuklos* (see above), means round about, lit., in a circle. It is used in the same way as No. 1, Mark 3 : 34 ; 6 : 6, 36 ; Luke 9 : 12 ; Rom. 15 : 19 ; Rev. 4 : 6 ; 5 : 11 ; 7 : 11.¶

3. POU (ποῦ), an indefinite particle, signifying " somewhere," somewhere about, nearly, has a limiting force, with numerals, e.g., Rom. 4 : 19. In referring to a passage in the O.T., it is translated " somewhere," in the R.V. of Heb. 2 : 6 and 4 : 4 (A.V., " in a certain place ") ; by not mentioning the actual passage referred to, the writer acknowledged the familiar acquaintance of his readers with the O.T. See PLACE.

4. HŌS (ὡς) usually means " as." Used with numerals it signifies " about," e.g. Mark 5 : 13 ; 8 : 9 ; John 1 : 40 ; 6 : 19 ; 11 : 18 ; Acts 1 : 15 ; Rev. 8 : 1.

5. HŌSEI (ὡσεί), " as if," before numerals, denotes about, nearly, something like, with perhaps an indication of greater indefiniteness than No. 4 ; e.g., Matt. 14 : 21 ; Luke 3 : 23 ; 9 : 14, 28 ; Acts 2 : 41 ; with a measure of space, Luke 22 : 41, " about a stone's cast." See LIKE.

B. Verb.

MELLŌ (μέλλω) signifies (*a*) of intention, to be about to do something, e.g., Acts 3 : 3 ; 18 : 14 ; 20 : 3 ; Heb. 8 : 5 ; (*b*) of certainty, compulsion or necessity, to be certain to act, e.g., John 6 : 71. See ALMOST, BEGIN, COME, INTEND, MEAN, MIND, POINT OF (at), READY, SHALL, SHOULD, TARRY.

Note : Zēteō, to seek, is translated " were about " in the A.V. of Acts 27 : 30 ; R.V., correctly, " were seeking to."

ABOVE

The following adverbs have this meaning (prepositions are omitted here) :—

1. ANŌ (ἄνω) denotes above, in a higher place, Acts 2 : 19 (the opposite to *katō*, below). With the article it means that which is above, Gal. 4 : 26 ; Phil. 3 : 14, " the high calling " (R.V. marg., " upward ") ; with the plural article, the things above, John 8 : 23, lit., ' from the things above ; ' Col. 3 : 1, 2. With *heōs*, as far as, it is translated " up to the brim," in John 2 : 7. It has the meaning " upwards " in John 11 : 41 and Heb. 12 : 15. See BRIM, HIGH, UP.¶

2. ANŌTERON (ἀνώτερον), the comparative degree of No. 1, is the neuter of the adjective *anōteros*. It is used (*a*) of motion to a higher place, ' higher," Luke 14 : 10 ; (*b*) of location in a higher place, i.e., in the preceding part of a passage, " above," Heb. 10 : 8. See HIGHER.¶

3. EPANŌ (ἐπάνω), *epi*, over, *anō*, above, is used frequently as a preposition with a noun; adverbially, of number, e.g., Mark 14:5, R.V.; 1 Cor. 15:6.

Note : In Acts 4:22, A.V., the adjective *pleion*, more, is translated " above," the R.V. corrects to " more than (forty years)."

4. ANŌTHEN (ἄνωθεν), from above, is used of place, (*a*) with the meaning " from the top," Matt. 27:51; Mark 15:38, of the temple veil; in John 19:23, of the garment of Christ, lit., ' from the upper parts ' (plural) ; (*b*) of things which come from heaven, or from God in Heaven, John 3:31; 19:11; Jas. 1:17; 3:15, 17. It is also used in the sense of " again." See AGAIN.

For ABROAD, see the verbs with which it is used, DISPERSE, NOISE, SCATTER, SHED, SPREAD.

ABSENCE, ABSENT
A. Noun.

APOUSIA (ἀπουσία), lit., a being away from, is used in Phil. 2:12, of the Apostle's absence from Philippi, in contrast to his *parousia*, his presence with the saints there (*parousia* does not signify merely a coming, it includes or suggests the presence which follows the arrival).¶

B. Verbs.

1. APEIMI (ἄπειμι), to be absent (*apo*, from, *eimi*, to be), is found in 1 Cor. 5:3; 2 Cor. 10:1, 11; 13:2, 10; Phil. 1:27; Col. 2:5. See GO.¶

2. EKDĒMEŌ (ἐκδημέω), lit., to be away from people (*ek*, from, or out of, *dēmos*, people), hence came to mean either (*a*) to go abroad, depart ; the Apostle Paul uses it to speak of departing from the body as the earthly abode of the spirit, 2 Cor. 5:8 ; or (*b*) to be away ; in the same passage, of being here in the body and absent from the Lord (ver. 6), or being absent from the body and present with the Lord (ver. 8). Its other occurrence is in ver. 9.¶

C. Preposition.

ATER (ἄτερ) means without, Luke 22:35, " without purse ; " in ver. 6, " in the absence (of the multitude)," marg., " without tumult." See WITHOUT.¶

ABSTAIN, ABSTINENCE

APECHŌ (ἀπέχω), to hold oneself from (*apo*, from, *echomai*, the Middle Voice of *echō*, to have, i.e., to keep oneself from), in the N.T., invariably refers to evil practices, moral and ceremonial, Acts 15:20, 29 ; 1 Thess. 4:3; 5:22 ; 1 Tim. 4:3 ; 1 Pet. 2:11 ; so in the Sept. in Job 1:1 ; 2:3. See ENOUGH, RECEIVE.¶

Note : The noun " abstinence " in Acts 27:21, A.V., translates *asitia*, " without food ", R.V. (*a*, negative, *sitos*, food). Cp. *asitos*, fasting, ver. 33.¶

ABUNDANCE, ABUNDANT, ABUNDANTLY, ABOUND
A. Nouns.

1. HADROTĒS (ἁδρότης), which, in 2 Cor. 8 : 20, in reference to the gifts from the church at Corinth for poor saints in Judæa, the R.V. renders " bounty " (A.V., " abundance "), is derived from *hadros*, thick, fat, full-grown, rich (in the Sept. it is used chiefly of rich and great men, e.g., Jer. 5 : 5). In regard, therefore, to the offering in 2 Cor. 8 : 20 the thought is that of bountiful giving, a fat offering, not mere abundance.¶

2. PERISSEIA (περισσεία), an exceeding measure, something above the ordinary, is used four times ; Rom. 5 : 17, of abundance of grace ; 2 Cor. 8 : 2, of abundance of joy ; 2 Cor. 10 : 15, of the extension of the Apostle's sphere of service through the practical fellowship of the saints at Corinth ; in Jas. 1 : 21 it is rendered, metaphorically, " overflowing," A.V. " superfluity ", with reference to wickedness. Some would render it " residuum," or what remains. See No. 3.¶

3. PERISSEUMA (περίσσευμα) denotes abundance in a slightly more concrete form, 2 Cor. 8 : 13, 14, where it stands for the gifts in kind supplied by the saints. In Matt. 12 : 34 and Luke 6 : 45 it is used of the abundance of the heart ; in Mark 8 : 8, of the broken pieces left after feeding the multitude " that remained over " (A.V. " that was left "). See REMAIN.¶ In the Sept., Eccl. 2 : 15.¶

4. HUPERBOLĒ (ὑπερβολή), lit., a throwing beyond (*huper*, over, *ballō*, to throw), denotes excellence, exceeding greatness, of the power of God in His servants, 2 Cor. 4 : 7 ; of the revelations given to Paul, 12 : 7 ; with the preposition *kata*, the phrase signifies " exceeding," Rom. 7 : 13 ; " still more excellent," 1 Cor. 12 : 31 ; " exceedingly," 2 Cor. 1 : 8 ; " beyond measure," Gal. 1 : 13 ; and, in a more extended phrase, " more and more exceedingly," 2 Cor. 4 : 17. See EXCELLENCY, EXCELLENT, MEASURE.¶

B. Verbs.

1. PERISSEUŌ (περισσεύω), akin to A, Nos. 2 and 3, is used intransitively (*a*) of exceeding a certain number, or measure, to be over, to remain, of the fragments after feeding the multitude (cp. *perisseuma*), Luke 9 : 17 ; John 6 : 12, 13 ; to exist in abundance ; as of wealth, Luke 12 : 15 ; 21 : 4 ; of food, 15 : 17. In this sense it is used also of consolation, 2 Cor. 1 : 5 ; of the effect of a gift sent to meet the need of saints, 2 Cor. 9 : 12 ; of rejoicing, Phil. 1 : 26 ; of what comes or falls to the lot of a person in large measure, as of the grace of God and the gift by the grace of Christ, Rom. 5 : 15 ; of the sufferings of Christ, 2 Cor. 1 : 5. In Mark 12 : 44 and Luke 21 : 4, the R.V. has " superfluity."

(*b*) to redound to, or to turn out abundantly for something, as of the liberal effects of poverty, 2 Cor. 8 : 2 ; in Rom. 3 : 7, argumentatively, of the effects of the truth of God, as to whether God's truthfulness becomes more conspicuous and His glory is increased through man's untruthfulness ; of numerical increase, Acts 16 : 5.

(c) to be abundantly furnished, to abound in a thing, as of material benefits, Luke 12 : 15 ; Phil. 4 : 18 of spiritual gifts, 1 Cor. 14 : 12, or to be pre-eminent, to excel, to be morally better off, as regards partaking of certain meats, 1 Cor. 8 : 8, " are we the better " ; to abound in hope, Rom. 15 : 13 ; the work of the Lord, 1 Cor. 15 : 58 ; faith and grace, 2 Cor. 8 : 7 ; thanksgiving, Col. 2 : 7 ; walking so as to please God, Phil. 1 : 9 ; 1 Thess. 4 : 1, 10 ; of righteousness, Matt. 5 : 20 ; of the Gospel, as the ministration of righteousness, 2 Cor. 3 : 9, " exceed."

It is used transitively, in the sense of to make to abound, e.g., to provide a person richly so that he has abundance, as of spiritual truth, Matt. 13 : 12 ; the right use of what God has entrusted to us, 25 : 29 ; the power of God in conferring grace, 2 Cor. 9 : 8 ; Eph. 1 : 8 ; to make abundant or to cause to excel, as of the effect of grace in regard to thanksgiving, 2 Cor. 4 : 15 ; His power to make us to abound in love, 1 Thess. 3 : 12. See BETTER, ENOUGH, EXCEED, EXCEL, INCREASE, REDOUND, REMAIN.¶

2. HUPERPERISSEUŌ (ὑπερπερισσεύω), a strengthened form of No. 1, signifies to abound exceedingly, Rom. 5 : 20, of the operation of grace ; 2 Cor. 7 : 4, in the Middle Voice, of the Apostle's joy in the saints. See JOYFUL.¶

3 PLEONAZŌ (πλεονάζω), from pleion, or pleon, " more " (greater in quantity), akin to pleō, to fill, signifies, (a) intransitively, to superabound, of a trespass or sin, Rom. 5 : 20 ; of grace, Rom. 6 : 1 ; 2 Cor. 4 : 15 ; of spiritual fruit, Phil. 4 : 17 ; of love, 2 Thess. 1 : 3 ; of various fruits, 2 Pet. 1 : 8 ; of the gathering of the manna, 2 Cor. 8 : 15, " had . . . over " ; (b) transitively, to make to increase, 1 Thess. 3 : 12. See INCREASE, OVER.¶

4. HUPERPLEONAZŌ (ὑπερπλεονάζω), a strengthened form of No. 3, signifying to abound exceedingly, is used in 1 Tim. 1 : 14, of the grace of God.¶

5. PLĒTHUNŌ (πληθύνω), a lengthened form of plēthō, to fill, akin to No. 3, and to plēthos, a multitude, signifies to increase, to multiply, and, in the Passive Voice, to be multiplied, e.g., of iniquity, Matt. 24 : 12, R.V. See MULTIPLY.

Note : Huperballō, akin to A, No. 4, to exceed, excel, is translated " passeth " in Eph. 3 : 19. See also 2 Cor. 3 : 10 (R.V., " surpasseth ; " A.V., " excelleth ") ; 9 : 14, " exceeding ; " Eph. 1 : 19 ; 2 : 7. See EXCEED, EXCEL.¶

C. Adjectives.

1. PERISSOS (περισσός), akin to B, No. 1, " abundant," is translated " advantage " in Rom. 3 : 1, " superfluous " in 2 Cor. 9 : 1. See ADVANTAGE, MORE, B, No. 2, SUPERFLUOUS.

2. PERISSOTEROS (περισσότερος), the comparative degree of No. 1, is translated as follows : in Matt. 11 : 9, and Luke 7 : 26, R.V., " much

more " (A.V., " more ") ; in Mark 12 : 40, " greater ; " in Luke 12 : 4, 48, " more ; " in 1 Cor. 12 : 23, 24, " more abundant ; " in 2 Cor. 2 : 7, " overmuch ; " in 2 Cor. 10 : 8, R.V., " abundantly," A.V., " more." See GREATER, MORE, OVERMUCH.

D. Adverbs.

1. PERISSŌS (περισσῶς), corresponding to Adjective No. 1 above, is found in Matt. 27 : 23, R.V., " exceedingly," A.V., " the more ; " Mark 10 : 26, R.V., " exceedingly," A.V., " out of measure ; " 15 : 14 ; Acts. 26 : 11, " exceedingly." See EXCEEDINGLY, B, No. 4, MEASURE, B, No. 2, MORE.¶

2. PERISSOTEROS (περισσοτέρως), the adverbial form of No. 2, above, means ' more abundantly ; ' in Heb. 2 : 1, lit., ' we ought to give heed more abundantly.' It is most frequent in 2 Cor. In 11 : 23, see the R.V. See EARNEST, EXCEEDINGLY, RATHER.

3. HUPERPERISSŌS (ὑπερπερισσῶς), a strengthened form of No. 1, signifies " exceeding abundantly," Mark 7 : 37.¶

4. HUPEREKPERISSOU (ὑπερεκπερισσοῦ), a still further strengthened form, is translated " exceeding abundantly " in Eph. 3 : 20 ; " exceedingly " in 1 Thess. 3 : 10 ; 5 : 13. See EXCEEDINGLY.¶

Note : *Huperballontōs*, akin to A, No. 4, denotes " above measure," 2 Cor. 11 : 23.¶

5. PLOUSIŌS (πλουσίως), connected with *ploutos*, riches, is rendered " abundantly," Tit. 3 : 6 and 2 Pet. 1 : 11 ; " richly," Col. 3 : 16 and 1 Tim. 6 : 17. It is used of (*a*) the gift of the Holy Spirit ; (*b*) entrance into the coming Kingdom ; (*c*) the indwelling of the Word of Christ ; (*d*) material benefits. See RICHLY.¶

Notes : (1) *Dunamis*, power, is translated " abundance " in the A.V. of Rev. 18 : 3 (R.V. and A.V. marg., " power ").

(2) *Polus*, much, many, is rendered " abundant " in 1 Pet. 1 : 3, A.V. (marg., " much "), R.V., " great."

(3) For the verbs *plouteō* and *ploutizō*, see RICH and ENRICH.

(4) For *ploutos*, wealth, riches, and *plousios*, rich, see RICH.

ABUSE, ABUSERS

A. Verb.

KATACHRAOMAI (καταχράομαι), lit., to use overmuch (*kata*, down, intensive, *chraomai*, to use), is found in 1 Cor. 7 : 31, with reference to the believer's use of the world (marg., " use to the full "), and 1 Cor. 9 : 18, A.V., " abuse," R.V., " use to the full." See USE.¶

B. Noun.

For the noun *arsenokoitēs*, see 1 Cor. 6 : 9, and 1 Tim. 1 : 10.¶

For ABYSS see BOTTOM.

ACCEPT, ACCEPTED, ACCEPTABLE
A. Verbs.

1. DECHOMAI (δέχομαι) signifies to accept, by a deliberate and ready reception of what is offered (cp. No. 4), e.g., 1 Thess. 2 : 13, R.V., " accepted ; " 2 Cor. 8 : 17 ; 11 : 4. See RECEIVE, TAKE.

2. APODECHOMAI (ἀποδέχομαι), consisting of *apo*, from, intensive, and No. 1, expresses *dechomai* more strongly, signifying to receive heartily, to welcome, Luke 8 : 40 (R.V., " welcomed," A.V., " gladly received ") ; Acts 2 : 41 ; 18 : 27 ; 24 : 3 ; 28 : 30. See RECEIVE, WELCOME.

3. PROSDECHOMAI (προσδέχομαι), *pros*, to, and No. 1, to accept favourably, or receive to oneself, is used of things future, in the sense of expecting ; with the meaning of accepting, it is used negatively in Heb. 11 : 35, " not accepting their deliverance ; " of receiving, e.g., Luke 15 : 2 ; Rom. 16 : 2 ; Phil. 2 : 29. See ALLOW, LOOK (for), RECEIVE, TAKE, WAIT.

4. LAMBANŌ (λαμβάνω), almost synonymous with *dechomai*, is distinct from it, in that it sometimes means to receive as merely a self-prompted action, without necessarily signifying a favourable reception, Gal. 2 : 6. See ATTAIN, CALL, CATCH, HAVE, HOLD, OBTAIN, RECEIVE, TAKE.

Note : The verb *charitoō*, to make acceptable, is translated " made accepted," in Eph. 1 : 6, A.V. ; R.V., " freely bestowed."

B. Adjectives.

The following adjectives are translated " acceptable," or in some cases " accepted." The R.V. more frequently adopts the former rendering.

1. DEKTOS (δεκτός), akin to No. 1, denotes a person or thing who has been regarded favourably, Luke 4 : 19, 24 ; Acts 10 : 35 ; 2 Cor. 6 : 2 (in this verse No. 3 is used in the second place) ; Phil. 4 : 18.¶

2. APODEKTOS (ἀποδεκτός), a strengthened form of No. 1 (*apo*, from, used intensively), signifies acceptable, in the sense of what is pleasing and welcome, 1 Tim. 2 : 3 ; 5 : 4.¶

3. EUPROSDEKTOS (εὐπρόσδεκτος), a still stronger form of No. 1, signifies a very favourable acceptance (*eu*, well, *pros*, towards, No. 1), Rom. 15 : 16, 31 ; 2 Cor. 6 : 2 ; 8 : 12 ; 1 Pet. 2 : 5.¶

4. EUARESTOS (εὐάρεστος), *eu*, well, *arestos*, pleasing, is rendered " acceptable," in the A.V. of Rom. 12 : 1, 2 ; 14 : 18 ; in 2 Cor. 5 : 9, " accepted " ; Eph. 5 : 10. The R.V. usually has " well-pleasing ; " so A.V. and R.V. in Phil. 4 : 18 ; Col. 3 : 20 ; in Tit. 2 : 9, " please well," A.V. ; Heb. 13 : 21. See PLEASING.¶

C. Adverb.

EUARESTŌS (εὐαρέστως), corresponding to B, No. 4, is used in Heb. 12 : 28, " so as to please." See PLEASE.¶

D. Nouns.

1. APODOCHĒ (ἀποδοχή), akin to B, No. 2, signifies worthy to be received with approbation, acceptation, 1 Tim. 1 : 15 ; 4 : 9. The phrase in 1 : 15 is found in a writing in the 1st century expressing appreciation of a gift from a princess.¶

2. CHARIS (χάρις), grace, indicating favour on the part of the giver, thanks on the part of the receiver, is rendered " acceptable " in 1 Pet. 2 : 19, 20. See margin.ˋ See BENEFIT, FAVOUR, GRACE, LIBERALITY, PLEASURE, THANK.

ACCESS

PROSAGŌGĒ (προσαγωγή), lit., a leading or bringing into the presence of (pros, to, agō, to lead), denotes access, with which is associated the thought of freedom to enter through the assistance or favour of another. It is used three times, (a) Rom. 5 : 2, of the access which we have by faith, through our Lord Jesus Christ, into grace ; (b) Eph. 2 : 18, of our access in one Spirit through Christ, unto the Father ; (c) Eph. 3 : 12, of the same access, there said to be " in Christ," and which we have " in confidence through our faith in Him." This access involves the acceptance which we have in Christ with God, and the privilege of His favour towards us. Some advocate the meaning " introduction."¶

ACCOMPANY

A. Verbs.

1. SUNEPOMAI (συνέπομαι), lit., to follow with (sun, with, hepomai, to follow), hence came to mean simply to accompany, Acts 20 : 4.¶

2. SUNERCHOMAI (συνέρχομαι), chiefly used of assembling together, signifies to accompany, in Luke 23 : 55 ; John 11 : 33 ; Acts 9 : 39 ; 10 : 45 ; 11 : 12 ; 15 : 38 ; 21 : 16. In Acts 1 : 21 it is said of men who had " companied with " the Apostles all the time the Lord Jesus was with them. See ASSEMBLE, COME, COMPANY, GO, RESORT.

3. ECHŌ (ἔχω), to have, is rendered " accompany," in Heb. 6 : 9, " things that accompany salvation." The margin gives perhaps the better sense, " things that are near to salvation."

4. PROPEMPŌ (προπέμπω), translated " accompanied," in Acts 20 : 38, A.V., lit. means " to send forward ; " hence, of assisting a person on a journey either (a) in the sense of fitting him out with the requisites for it, or (b) actually accompanying him for part of the way. The former seems to be indicated in Rom. 15 : 24 and 1 Cor. 16 : 6, and ver. 11, where the R.V. has " set him forward." So in 2 Cor. 1 : 16 and Tit. 3 : 13, and of John's exhortation to Gaius concerning travelling evangelists, " whom thou wilt do well to set forward on their journey worthily of God," 3 John 6, R.V. While personal accompaniment is not excluded, practical assistance seems to be generally in view, as indicated by Paul's word to Titus to set forward Zenas and Apollos on their journey and to see " that nothing

be wanting unto them." In regard to the parting of Paul from the elders of Ephesus at Miletus, personal accompaniment is especially in view, perhaps not without the suggestion of assistance, Acts 20 : 38, R.V., " brought him on his way ; " accompaniment is also indicated in 21 : 5 ; " they all with wives and children brought us on our way, till we were out of the city." In Acts 15 : 3, both ideas perhaps are suggested. See BRING, CONDUCT.¶

ACCOMPLISH, ACCOMPLISHMENT
A. Verbs.

1. EXARTIZŌ (ἐξαρτίζω), to fit out, (from ek, out, and a verb derived from artos, a joint), hence means to furnish completely, 2 Tim. 3 : 17, or to accomplish, Acts 21 : 5, there said of a number of days, as if to render the days complete by what was appointed for them. See FURNISH.¶ In the Sept., Ex. 28 : 7.¶

2. PLĒROŌ (πληρόω), to fulfil, to complete, carry out to the full (as well as to fill), is translated " perfect " in Rev. 3 : 2, A.V. ; R.V., " I have found no works of thine fulfilled before My God ; " " accomplish " in Luke 9 : 31. See COMPLETE, END, EXPIRE, FILL, FULFIL, FULL, PREACH.

Note : Its strengthened form, ekplēroō, to fulfil, lit., fill out, is used in Acts 13 : 33, of the fulfilment of a Divine promise of the resurrection of Christ.

3. TELEŌ (τελέω), to finish, to bring to an end (telos, an end), frequently signifies, not merely to terminate a thing, but to carry out a thing to the full. It is used especially in the Apocalypse, where it occurs eight times, and is rendered " finish " in 10 : 7 ; 11 : 7, and in the R.V. of 15 : 1, which rightly translates it " (in them) is finished (the wrath of God)." So in ver. 8 ; in 17 : 17, R.V., " accomplish," and " finish " in 20 : 3, 5, 7 ; in Luke 2 : 39, R.V., " accomplish," for A.V., " performed." See END, EXPIRE, FILL, FINISH, FULFIL, GO, No. 5, PAY, PERFORM.

4. EPITELEŌ (ἐπιτελέω), epi, up, intensive, and No. 3, is a strengthened form of that verb, in the sense of " accomplishing." The fuller meaning is to accomplish perfectly ; in Rom. 15 : 28, R.V., " accomplish ; " " perfecting " in 2 Cor. 7 : 1; " complete " in 8 : 6 and 11 ; " completion " in the latter part of this 11th verse, which is better than " performance ; " " perfected " in Gal. 3 : 3 ; " perfect " in Phil. 1 : 6. In Heb. 8 : 5 the margin rightly has " complete " instead of " make," with regard to the Tabernacle. In Heb. 9 : 6 it is translated " accomplish " and in 1 Pet. 5 : 9. See COMPLETE, DO, FINISH, MAKE, PERFECT, PERFORM.¶

5. TELEIOŌ (τελειόω), though distinct grammatically from teleō, has much the same meaning. The main distinction is that teleō more frequently signifies to fulfil, teleioō, more frequently, to make perfect, one of the chief features of the Epistle to the Hebrews, where it occurs

nine times. It is rendered "accomplish" in the R.V. of John 4 : 34 ; 5 : 36 ; 17 : 4, and Acts 20 : 24. See CONSECRATE, FINISH, FULFIL, PERFECT.

6. PLĒTHŌ (πλήθω), to fulfil, is translated "accomplished" in the A.V. of Luke 1 : 23 ; 2 : 6, 21, 22 (R.V., "fulfilled"). See FILL, No. 5, FURNISH, *Note.*

B. Noun.

EKPLĒRŌSIS (ἐκπλήρωσις), see A, No. 2, Note, means an entire fulfilment (*ek*, out, *plērosis*, a filling), Acts 21 : 26, of the fulfilment of days of purification.¶

ACCORD
A. Adverb.

HOMOTHUMADON (ὁμοθυμαδόν), of one accord (from *homos*, same, *thumos*, mind), occurs eleven times, ten in the Acts, 1 : 14 ; 2 : 46 ; 4 : 24 ; 5 : 12 ; 7 : 57 ; 8 : 6 ; 12 : 20 ; 15 : 25 ; 18 : 12 ; 19 : 29, and the other in Rom. 15 : 6, where, for A.V., "with one mind," the R.V. has "with one accord," as throughout the Acts. See MIND.¶

Note : In Acts 2 : 1, the adverb *homou*, "together," is so rendered in the R.V., for A.V., "of one accord."
B. Adjectives.
"*Of one's own accord.*"

1. AUTHAIRETOS (αὐτόματος), from *autos*, self, and *haireomai*, to choose, self-chosen, voluntary, of one's own accord, occurs in 2 Cor. 8 : 3, and 17, of the churches of Macedonia as to their gifts for the poor saints in Judæa, and of Titus in his willingness to go and exhort the church in Corinth concerning the matter. In 8 : 3 the R.V. translates it "(gave) of their own accord," consistently with the rendering in ver. 17. See WILLING.¶

2. AUTOMATOS (αὐτόματος), from *autos*, self, and a root *ma—*, signifying desire, denotes of oneself, moved by one's own impulse. It occurs in Mark 4 : 28, of the power of the earth to produce plants and fruits of itself ; Acts 12 : 10, of the door which opened of its own accord. See SELF.¶ In the Sept., Lev. 25 : 5, "spontaneous produce ;" ver. 11, "produce that comes of itself ;" Josh. 6 : 5 ; 2 Kings 19 : 29, "(that which groweth) of itself ;" Job 24 : 24, of an ear of corn "(falling off) of itself (from the stalk)."¶

3. SUMPSUCHOS (σύμψυχος), lit., fellow-souled or minded (*sun*, with, *psuchē*, the soul), occurs in Phil. 2 : 2, "of one accord."¶

ACCORDING AS
1. KATHOTI (καθότι), from *kata*, according to, and *hoti*, that, lit., because that, Luke 1 : 7 ; 19 : 9 ; Acts 2 : 24, is translated "according as" in Acts 2 : 45, R.V. (A.V., "as") and in 4 : 35 ; "inasmuch as" 17 : 31.¶

2. KATHŌS (καθώς), from *kata*, according to, and *hōs*, as, signifies " according as " or " even as," e.g., 1 Cor. 1 : 31 ; 2 Cor. 9 : 7.

3. HŌS (ὡς) is sometimes rendered " according as," e.g., Rev. 22 : 12 ; in 2 Pet. 1 : 3, the R.V. has " seeing that," for the A.V. " according as."

4. KATHO (καθό) : see INASMUCH AS.

ACCORDING TO : See Note † p. 9.

ACCOUNT (-ED) (Verbs and Noun)
A. Verbs.

1. DOKEŌ (δοκέω), primarily, to be of opinion, think, suppose, also signifies to seem, be accounted, reputed, translated " accounted " in Mark 10 : 42 ; Luke 22 : 24. It is not used ironically here, nor in Gal. 2 : 2, 6, 9, " those who were of repute." See REPUTE, SEEM, SUPPOSE, THINK.

2. ELLOGEŌ (or-AŌ) (ἐλλογέω), to put to a person's account, Philm. 18, is used of sin in Rom. 5 : 13, " reckon " (A.V., " impute "). See IMPUTE, No. 2.¶

3. HĒGEOMAI (ἡγέομαι) primarily signifies to lead ; then, to consider ; it is translated " accounting " in Heb. 11 : 26, R.V. (A.V., " esteeming ") ; 2 Pet. 3 : 15, " account." See CHIEF, COUNT, ESTEEM, GOVERNOR, JUDGE, RULE, SUPPOSE, THINK.

4. LOGIZOMAI (λογίζομαι) primarily signifies to reckon, whether by calculation or imputation, e.g., Gal. 3 : 6 (R.V., " reckoned ") ; then, to deliberate, and so to suppose, account, Rom. 8 : 36 ; 14 : 14 (A.V., " esteemeth ") ; 1 Cor. 4 : 1 ; Heb. 11 : 19 ; John 11 : 50 (A.V., " consider ") ; Acts 19 : 27 (" made of no account " ; A.V., " despised ") ; 1 Pet. 5 : 12 (A.V., " suppose "). It is used of love in 1 Cor. 13 : 5, as not taking account of evil, R.V. (A.V., " thinketh "). In 2 Cor. 3 : 5 the Apostle uses it in repudiation of the idea that he and fellow-servants of God are so self-sufficient as to " account anything " (R.V.) as from themselves (A.V., " think "), i.e., as to attribute anything to themselves. Cp. 12 : 6. In 2 Tim. 4 : 16 it is used of laying to a person's " account " (R.V.) as a charge against him (A.V., " charge ").

Note : In Phil. 4 : 8 it signifies to think upon a matter by way of taking account of its character (R.V. margin). See CONCLUDE, COUNT, CHARGE, ESTEEM, IMPUTE, NUMBER, REASON, RECKON, THINK, SUPPOSE.

5. KATAXIOŌ (καταξιόω) denotes to account worthy (*kata*, intensive, *axios*, worthy), to judge worthy, Luke 20 : 35 ; some mss. have it in 21 : 36 (so the A.V.) ; the most authentic mss. have the verb *katischuō*, to prevail ; Acts 5 : 41, " were counted worthy ; " so 2 Thess. 1 : 5.¶

6. EXOUTHENEŌ (ἐξουθενέω), to make of no account, frequently signifies to despise. In 1 Cor. 6 : 4, it is used, not in a contemptuous sense, but of Gentile judges, before whom the saints are not to go to law with one another, such magistrates having no place, and therefore being

" of no account " (R.V.), in the church. The Apostle is not speaking of any believers as " least esteemed " (A.V.). In 2 Cor. 10 : 10, for A.V., " contemptible," the R.V. suitably has " of no account." See DESPISE.

B. Noun.

LOGOS (λόγος), a word or saying, also means an account which one gives by word of mouth (cp. No. 4), Matt. 12 : 36 ; Matt. 18 : 23, R.V., " reckoning ; " 16 : 2 ; Acts 19 : 40 ; 20 : 24 (A.V., " count ") ; Rom. 14 : 12 ; Phil. 4 : 17 ; Heb. 13 : 17 ; 1 Pet. 4 : 5. See CAUSE, COMMUNICATION, DO, DOCTRINE, FAME, INTENT, MATTER, MOUTH, PREACHING, QUESTION, REASON, RECKONING, RUMOUR, SAYING, SHEW, SPEECH, TALK, THING, TIDINGS, TREATISE, UTTERANCE, WORD, WORK.

ACCURATELY

AKRIBŌS (ἀκριβῶς) is correctly translated in the R.V. of Luke 1 : 3, " having traced the course of all things accurately " (A.V., " having had perfect understanding "). It is used in Matt. 2 : 8, of Herod's command to the wise men as to searching for the young Child (R.V., " carefully," A.V., " diligently ") ; in Acts 18 : 25, of Apollos' teaching of " the things concerning Jesus " (R.V., " carefully," A.V., " diligently ") ; in Eph. 5 : 15, of the way in which believers are to walk (R.V., " carefully ; " A.V., " circumspectly ") ; in 1 Thess. 5 : 2, of the knowledge gained by the saints through the Apostle's teaching concerning the Day of the Lord (R.V. and A.V., " perfectly "). The word expresses that accuracy which is the outcome of carefulness. It is connected with *akros*, pointed.

This word and its other grammatical forms, *akribeia, akribēs, akribesteron* and *akriboō*, are used especially by Luke, who employs them eight times out of the thirteen in the N.T. ; Matthew uses them three times, Paul twice. See CAREFUL, DILIGENT, EXACTLY, PERFECT.¶

For ACCURSED see CURSE, A, No. 3

ACCUSATION, ACCUSE
A. Nouns.

1. AITIA (αἰτία) probably has the primary meaning of a cause, especially an· occasion of something evil, hence a charge, an accusation. It is used in a forensic sense, of (a) an accusation, Acts 25 : 18 (R.V., " charge "), 27 ; (b) a crime, Matt. 27 : 37 ; Mark 15 : 26 ; John 18 : 38 ; 19 : 4, 6 ; Acts 13 : 28 ; 23 : 28 ; 28 : 18. See CASE, CAUSE, CHARGE, CRIME, FAULT.

2. AITIŌMA (αἰτίωμα), an accusation, expressing No. 1 more concretely, is found in Acts 25 : 7, R.V., " charges," for A.V., " complaints." See COMPLAINT.¶

3. ENKLĒMA (ἔγκλημα) is an accusation made in public, but not necessarily before a tribunal. That is the case in Acts 23 : 29. " laid to

his charge." In 25 : 16 it signifies a matter of complaint ; hence the
R.V. has " the matter laid against him " (A.V., " crime "). See CHARGE,
CRIME.¶

4. KATĒGORIA (κατηγορία), an accusation, is found in John
18 : 29 ; 1 Tim. 5 : 19 and Tit. 1 : 6, lit., ' not under accusation.'
This and the verb katēgoreō, to accuse, and the noun katēgoros, an accuser
(see below), all have chiefly to do with judicial procedure, as distinct from
diaballō, to slander. It is derived from agora, a place of public speaking,
prefixed by kata, against ; hence it signifies a speaking against a
person before a public tribunal. It is the opposite to apologia, a defence.¶

Note : Krisis, which has been translated " accusation," in the A.V.
of 2 Pet. 2 : 11 and Jude 9 (R.V., " judgement "), does not come under
this category. It signifies a judgment, a decision given concerning
anything.

B. Verbs.

1. DIABALLŌ (διαβάλλω), used in Luke 16 : 1, in the Passive Voice,
lit. signifies to hurl across (dia, through, ballō, to throw), and hence
suggests a verbal assault. It stresses the act rather than the author, as
in the case of aitia and katēgoria. Diabolos is connected.¶

2. ENKALEŌ (ἐγκαλέω), — see A, No. 3, to bring a charge against,
or to come forward as an accuser against, lit. denotes to call in (en, in,
kaleō, to call), i.e., to call (something) in or against (someone) ; hence, to
call to account, to accuse, Acts 19 : 38, R.V. (A.V., " implead ") ; in ver.
40, " accused " (A.V., " call in question "). It is used in four other places
in the Acts, 23 : 28, 29 ; 26 : 2, 7, and elsewhere in Rom. 8 : 33, " shall
lay to the charge." See CALL, IMPLEAD.¶

3. EPĒREAZŌ (ἐπηρεάζω), besides its more ordinary meaning, to
insult, treat abusively, despitefully, Luke 6 : 28, has the forensic
significance to accuse falsely, and is used with this meaning in 1 Pet. 3 : 16,
R.V., " revile." See DESPITEFULLY, REVILE.¶

4. KATĒGOREŌ (κατηγορέω), to speak against, accuse (cp. A, No. 4),
is used (a) in a general way, to accuse, e.g., Luke 6 : 7, R.V., " how to
accuse ; " Rom. 2 : 15 ; Rev. 12 : 10 ; (b) before a judge, e.g., Matt.
12 : 10 ; Mark 15 : 4 (R.V., " witness against ") ; Acts 22 : 30 ; 25 : 16.
In Acts 24 : 19, R.V. renders it " make accusation," for the A.V.,
" object." See OBJECT, WITNESS.

5. SUKOPHANTEŌ (συκοφαντέω), Eng., sycophant, means (a) to
accuse wrongfully, Luke 3 : 14 (A.V. and R.V., margin) ; R.V., " exact
wrongfully ; " (b) to exact money wrongfully, to take anything by false
accusation, Luke 19 : 8, and the R.V. text of 3 : 14. It is more frequently
found in the Sept. ; see Gen. 43 : 18, to inform against ; Lev. 19 : 11,
" neither shall each falsely accuse his neighbour ; " Job. 35 : 9, " they
that are oppressed by false accusation ; " Psalm 119 : 122, " let not the
proud accuse me falsely ; " Prov. 14 : 31 and 22 : 16, " he that oppresses
the needy by false accusation."

The word is derived from *sukon*, a fig, and *phainō*, to show.   At Athens a man whose business it was to give information against anyone who might be detected exporting figs out of the province, is said to have been called a *sukophantēs* (see Note (2) below).   Probably, however, the word was used to denote one who brings figs to light by shaking the tree, and then in a metaphorical sense one who makes rich men yield up their fruit by false accusation.   Hence in general parlance it was used to designate a malignant informer, one who accused from love of gain. See EXACT.¶

Note : Proaitiaomai denotes to bring a previous charge against, Rom. 3 : 9, R.V.   See CHARGE.¶

ACCUSER

1. DIABOLOS (διάβολος), an accuser (cp. Accuse, B, No. 1), is used 34 times as a title of Satan, " the Devil " (the English word is derived from the Greek) ; once of Judas, John 6 : 70, who, in his opposition to God, acted the part of the Devil.   Apart from John 6 : 70, men are never spoken of as devils.   It is always to be distinguished from *daimōn*, a demon.   It is found three times, 1 Tim. 3 : 11 ; 2 Tim. 3 : 3 ; Tit. 2 : 3, of false accusers, slanderers.

2. KATĒGOROS (κατήγορος), an accuser (see p. 26), is used in John 8 : 10 ; Acts 23 : 30, 35 ; 24 : 8 ; 25 : 16, 18.   In Rev. 12 : 10, it is used of Satan.¶   In the Sept., Prov. 18 : 17.¶

Notes : (1) *Sukophantia*, a false accusation or oppression, is used in Eccl. 5 : 7 ; 7 : 8 ; Psa. 119 : 134 and Amos 2 : 8 (not in the N.T.).   See No. 5, above.

(2) *Sukophantēs*, a false accuser, or oppressor, occurs in Psa. 72 : 4 ; Prov. 28 : 16 (not in the N.T.).

ACKNOWLEDGE (-MENT)
A. Verb.

EPIGINŌSKŌ (ἐπιγινώσκω) signifies (*a*) to know thoroughly (*epi*, intensive, *ginōskō*, to know) ; (*b*) to recognize a thing to be what it really is, to acknowledge, 1 Cor. 14 : 37 (R.V., " take knowledge of ") ; 16 : 18 ; 2 Cor. 1 : 13, 14.   See KNOW, KNOWLEDGE, PERCEIVE.

Note : In 1 John 2 : 23, " acknowledgeth " translates the verb *homologeō*, to confess, R.V., " confesseth."

B. Noun.

EPIGNŌSIS (ἐπίγνωσις), akin to A, full, or thorough knowledge, discernment, recognition, is translated " acknowledging " in the A.V. of 2 Tim. 2 : 25 ; Tit. 1 : 1 and Philm. 6 (in all three, R.V., " knowledge," properly, " thorough knowledge ").   In Col. 2 : 2, A.V., " acknowledgement," R.V., " that they may know " (i.e., ' unto the full knowledge ').
See KNOWLEDGE.

ACQUAINTANCE

1. GNŌSTOS (γνωστός), from ginōskō, to know, signifies known, or knowable; hence, one's acquaintance; it is used in this sense, in the plural, in Luke 2 : 44 and 23 : 49. See KNOWN, NOTABLE.

2. IDIOS (ἴδιος), one's own, is translated "acquaintance" in the A.V. of Acts 24 : 23, "friends" (R.V.). See COMPANY.

For ACROSS (Acts 27 : 5, R.V.), see Note † p. 9.

ACT

1. EPAUTOPHŌRŌ (ἐπαυτοφώρῳ) primarily signifies caught in the act of theft (epi, upon, intensive, autos, self, phōr, a thief) ; then, caught in the act of any other crime, John 8 : 4. In some texts the preposition epi is detached from the remainder of the adjective, and appears as ep' autophōrō.¶

2. DIKAIŌMA (δικαίωμα) signifies an act of righteousness, a concrete expression of righteousness, as in the R.V. of Rom. 5 : 18, in reference to the Death of Christ ; the A.V. wrongly renders it " the righteousness of One." The contrast is between the one trespass by Adam and the one act of Christ in His atoning Death. In Rev. 15 : 4 and 19 : 8, the word is used in the plural to signify, as in the R.V., "righteous acts," respectively, of God, and of the saints. See JUDGMENT, JUSTIFICATION, ORDINANCE, RIGHTEOUSNESS.

3. PRASSŌ (πράσσω), to do, to practise, is translated " act " in the R.V. of Acts 17 : 7 (A.V., " do "). See COMMIT, DO, EXACT, KEEP, REQUIRE, USE.

ACTIVE

ENERGĒS (ἐνεργής), lit., ' in work ' (cp. Eng., energetic), is used (a) of the Word of God, Heb. 4 : 12 (R.V., " active," A.V., " powerful ") ; (b) of a door for the Gospel, 1 Cor. 16 : 9, " effectual ; " (c) of faith, Philm. 6, " effectual." See EFFECTUAL, POWERFUL. Cp. the synonymous words dunatos and ischuros (see ABLE).¶

ACTUALLY

HOLŌS (ὅλως), from holos, all, whole, is translated " actually " in 1 Cor. 5 : 1, R.V. (" it is actually reported ") ; the A.V. " commonly " does not convey the meaning. In 6 : 7 it is translated " altogether " (A.V. " utterly ") ; in 15 : 29, "at all," as in Matt. 5 : 34. See ALL, ALTOGETHER ¶

ADD

1. EPITITHĒMI (ἐπιτίθημι), lit., to put upon (epi, upon, tithēmi, to put), has a secondary and somewhat infrequent meaning, to add to, and is found in this sense in Mark 3 : 16, 17, lit., ' He added the name

Peter to Simon,' 'He added to them the name Boanerges,' and Rev. 22 : 18, where the word is set in contrast to " take away from " (ver. 19). See LADE, LAY, PUT, SET.

2. PROSTITHĒMI (προστίθημι), to put to (pros, to, tithēmi, to put), to add, or to place beside (the primary meaning), in Luke 17 : 5 is translated " increase," in the request " increase our faith ; " in Luke 20 : 11, 12, " he sent yet " (A.V. " again he sent "), lit., 'he added and sent,' as in 19 : 11, " He added and spake." In Acts 12 : 3, R.V., " proceeded," A.V., " proceeded further " (of repeating or continuing the action mentioned by the following verb) ; in Acts 13 : 36, " was laid unto " ; in Heb. 12 : 19, " more . . . be spoken," (lit., 'that no word should be added '). In Gal. 3 : 19, " What then is the law ? It was added because of transgressions," there is no contradiction of what is said in verse 15, where the word is epidiatassō (see No. 4), for there the latter word conveys the idea of supplementing an agreement already made ; here in ver. 19 the meaning is not that something had been added to the promise with a view to complete it, which the Apostle denies, but that something had been given in addition to the promise, as in Rom. 5 : 20, " The law came in beside." See GIVE, INCREASE, LAY, PROCEED, SPEAK.

3. PROSANATITHĒMI (προσανατίθημι), lit., to lay upon in addition, came to be used in the sense of putting oneself before another, for the purpose of consulting him ; hence simply to consult, to take one into counsel, to confer. With this meaning it is used only in Gal. 1 : 16. In Gal. 2 : 2, a shorter form, anatithēmi, is used, which means to lay before (A.V., " communicated unto "). This less intensive word may have been purposely used there by the Apostle to suggest that he described to his fellow-apostles the character of his teaching, not to obtain their approval or their advice concerning it, but simply that they might have the facts of the case before them on which they were shortly to adjudicate.

It was also used to signify to communicate, to impart. With this meaning it is used only in Gal. 2 : 6, in the Middle Voice, the suggestion being to add from one's store of things. In regard to his visit to Jerusalem the Apostle says " those who were of repute imparted nothing to me " (A.V., " in conference added "), that is to say, they neither modified his teaching nor added to his authority. See CONFER.¶

4. EPIDIATASSŌ (ἐπιδιατάσσω), lit., to arrange in addition (epi, upon, dia, through, tassō, to arrange), is used in Gal. 3 : 15 (" addeth," or rather, 'ordains something in addition '). If no one does such a thing in the matter of a human covenant, how much more is a covenant made by God inviolable ! The Judaizers by their addition violated this principle, and, by proclaiming the Divine authority for what they did, they virtually charged God with a breach of promise. He gave the Law, indeed, but neither in place of the promise nor to supplement it.¶

5. PAREISPHERŌ (παρεισφέρω), to bring in besides (para, besides, eis, in, pherō, to bring), means " to add," 2 Pet. 1 : 5, " adding on your

part " (R.V.) ; the words " on your part " represent the intensive force of the verb ; the A.V., " giving " does not provide an adequate meaning.¶

6. EPICHOREGEŌ (ἐπιχορηγέω) is translated " add " in the A.V. of 2 Pet. 1 : 5. Its meaning is to supply, to minister (*epi*, to, *chorēgeō*, to minister) ; R.V., " supply." See MINISTER.

7. DIDŌMI (δίδωμι), to give, is translated "add," in Rev. 8 : 3, R.V., for A.V., " offer " (marg., " add "). See GIVE.

Note : In Phil. 1: :17, R.V., *egeirō*, to raise, is translated " add " in the A.V. (R.V., " raise up "). See BRING, A, No. 6.

For ADDICTED (A.V. of 1 Cor. 16 : 15) see SET, No. 10.

ADJURE

1. HORKIZŌ (ὁρκίζω), to cause to swear, to lay under the obligation of an oath (*horkos*, Mark 5 : 7 ; Acts 19 : 13), is connected with the Heb. word for a thigh, cp. Gen. 24 : 2, 9 ; 47 : 29. Some mss. have this word in 1 Thess. 5 : 27. The most authentic have No. 3 (below). See CHARGE.¶

2. EXORKIZŌ (ἐξορκίζω), an intensive form of No. 1, signifies to appeal by an oath, to adjure, Matt. 26 : 63.¶ In the Sept., Gen. 24 : 3 ; Judg. 17 : 2 ; 1 Kings 22 : 16.¶

3. ENORKIZŌ (ἐνορκίζω), to put under (or bind by) an oath, is translated " adjure " in the R.V. of 1 Thess. 5 : 27 (A.V., " charge ").¶ In the Sept., Neh. 13 : 25.¶

Note : The synonymous verb *omnumi* signifies to make an oath, to declare or promise with an oath. See, e.g., Mark 6 : 23, in contrast to 5 : 7 (*horkizō*). See OATH and SWEAR.

For the A.V. ADMINISTER and ADMINISTRATION see MINISTER and MINISTRATION, SERVE and SERVICE.

For the A.V. ADMIRATION and ADMIRE see WONDER and MARVEL.

ADMONITION, ADMONISH
A. Noun.

NOUTHESIA (νουθεσία), lit., a putting in mind (*nous*, mind, *tithēmi*, to put), is used in 1 Cor. 10 : 11, of the purpose of the Scriptures ; in Eph. 6 : 4, of that which is ministered by the Lord : and in Tit. 3 : 10, of that which is to be administered for the correction of one who creates trouble in the church. *Nouthesia* is " the training by word," whether of encouragement, or, if necessary, by reproof or remonstrance. In contrast to this, the synonymous word *paideia* stresses training by act, though both words are used in each respect.¶

B. Verbs.

1. NOUTHETEŌ (νουθετέω), cp. the noun above, means to put in mind, admonish, Acts 20 : 31 (A.V., " warn ") ; Rom. 15 : 14 ; 1 Cor. 4 : 14

(A.V., " warn ") ; Col. 1 : 28 (A.V., " warning ") ; Col. 3 : 16 ; 1 Thess.
5 : 12, 14 (A.V., " warn ") ; 2 Thess. 3 : 15.

It is used, (a) of instruction, (b) of warning. It is thus distinguished
from *paideuō*, to correct by discipline, to train by act, Heb. 12 : 6 ;
cp. Eph. 6 : 4.

" The difference between ' admonish ' and ' teach ' seems to be that,
whereas the former has mainly in view the things that are wrong and call
for warning, the latter has to do chiefly with the impartation of positive
truth, cp. Col. 3 : 16 ; they were to let the word of Christ dwell richly in
them, so that they might be able (1) to teach and admonish one another,
and (2) to abound in the praises of God.

" Admonition differs from remonstrance, in that the former is warning
based on instruction ; the latter may be little more than expostulation.
For example, though Eli remonstrated with his sons, 1 Sam. 2 : 24, he
failed to admonish them, 3 : 13, LXX. Pastors and teachers in the
churches are thus themselves admonished, i.e., instructed and warned, by
the Scriptures, 1 Cor. 10 : 11, so to minister the Word of God to the saints,
that, naming the Name of the Lord, they shall depart from unrighteousness, 2 Tim. 2 : 19."* See WARN.¶

2. PARAINEŌ (παραινέω), to admonish by way of exhorting or
advising, is found in Acts 27 : 9 (" Paul admonished them ") and ver. 22
(" and now I exhort you "). See EXHORT.¶

3. CHRĒMATIZŌ (χρηματίζω), primarily, to transact business, then,
to give advice to enquirers (especially of official pronouncements of
magistrates), or a response to those consulting an oracle, came to signify
the giving of a Divine admonition or instruction or warning, in a general
way ; " admonished " in Heb. 8 : 5, A.V. (R.V., " warned "). Elsewhere
it is translated by the verb to warn.

The word is derived from *chrēma*, an affair, business. Names were
given to men from the nature of their business (see the same word in Acts
11 : 26 ; Rom. 7 : 3) ; hence the idea of dealing with a person and receiving
instruction. In the case of oracular responses, the word is derived from
chrēsmos, an oracle. See CALL, REVEAL, SPEAK, WARN.

ADO

THORUBEŌ (θορυβέω), to make an uproar, to throw into confusion,
or to wail tumultuously, is rendered " make . . . ado," in Mark 5 : 39 ;
elsewhere in Matt. 9 : 23 ; Acts 17 : 5 ; 20 : 10. See NOISE, TROUBLE,
UPROAR.¶

Note : For the corresponding noun, *thorubos*, see TUMULT, UPROAR.

ADOPTION

HUIOTHESIA (υἱοθεσία), from *huios*, a son, and *thesis*, a placing,

---

* From Notes on Thessalonians by Hogg and Vine, pp. 179, 180.

akin to *tithēmi*, to place, signifies the place and condition of a son given to one to whom it does not naturally belong. The word is used by the Apostle Paul only.

In Rom. 8 : 15, believers are said to have received " the Spirit of adoption," that is, the Holy Spirit who, given as the Firstfruits of all that is to be theirs, produces in them the realisation of sonship and the attitude belonging to sons. In Gal. 4 : 5 they are said to receive " the adoption of sons," i.e., sonship bestowed in distinction from a relationship consequent merely upon birth ; here two contrasts are presented, (1) between the sonship of the believer and the unoriginated Sonship of Christ, (2) between the freedom enjoyed by the believer and bondage, whether of Gentile natural condition, or of Israel under the Law. In Eph. 1 : 5 they are said to have been foreordained unto " adoption as sons " through Jesus Christ, R.V. : the A.V., " adoption of children " is a mistranslation and misleading. God does not adopt believers as children ; they are begotten as such by His Holy Spirit through faith. Adoption is a term involving the dignity of the relationship of believers as sons ; it is not a putting into the family by spiritual birth, but a putting into the position of sons. In Rom. 8 : 23 the adoption of the believer is set forth as still future, as it there includes the redemption of the body, when the living will be changed and those who have fallen asleep will be raised. In Rom. 9 : 4 adoption is spoken of as belonging to Israel, in accordance with the statement in Ex. 4 : 12, " Israel is My Son." Cp. Hos. 11 : 1. Israel was brought into a special relation with God, a collective relationship, not enjoyed by other nations, Deut. 14 : 1 ; Jer. 31 : 9, etc.¶

ADORN, ADORNING
A. Verb.

KOSMEŌ (κοσμέω), primarily to arrange, to put in order (Eng., cosmetic), is used of furnishing a room, Matt. 12 : 44 ; Luke 11 : 25, and of trimming lamps, Matt. 25 : 7. Hence, to adorn, to ornament, as of garnishing tombs, Matt. 23 : 29 ; buildings, Luke 21 : 5 ; Rev. 21 : 19 ; one's person, 1 Tim. 2 : 9 ; 1 Pet. 3 : 5 ; Rev. 21 : 2 ; metaphorically, of adorning a doctrine, Tit. 2 : 10. See GARNISH, TRIM.¶

B. Noun.

KOSMOS (κόσμος), a harmonious arrangement or order, then, adornment, decoration, hence came to denote the world, or the universe, as that which is Divinely arranged. The meaning " adorning " is found in 1 Pet. 3 : 3. Elsewhere it signifies the world. Cp. *kosmios*, decent, modest, 1 Tim. 2 : 9 ; 3 : 2. See WORLD.

ADULTERER (-ESS), ADULTEROUS, ADULTERY
A. Nouns.

1. MOICHOS (μοιχός) denotes one who has unlawful intercourse

with the spouse of another, Luke 18 : 11 ; 1 Cor. 6 : 9 ; Heb. 13 : 4. As to Jas. 4 : 4, see below.¶

2. MOICHALIS (μοιχαλίς), an adulteress, is used (a) in the natural sense, 2 Pet. 2 : 14 ; Rom. 7 : 3 ; (b) in the spiritual sense, Jas. 4 : 4 ; here the R.V. rightly omits the word " adulterers." It was added by a copyist. As in Israel the breach of their relationship with God through their idolatry, was described as adultery or harlotry (e.g., Ezek. 16 : 15, etc. ; 23 : 43), so believers who cultivate friendship with the world, thus breaking their spiritual union with Christ, are spiritual adulteresses, having been spiritually united to Him as wife to husband, Rom. 7 : 4. It is used adjectivally to describe the Jewish people in transferring their affections from God, Matt. 12 : 39 ; 16 : 4 ; Mark 8 : 38. In 2 Pet. 2 : 14, the lit. translation is " full of an adulteress " (R.V. marg.).¶

3. MOICHEIA (μοιχεία), adultery, is found in Matt. 15 : 19 ; Mark 7 : 21 ; John 8 : 3 (A.V. only).¶

B. Verbs.

1. MOICHAŌ (μοιχάω), used in the Middle Voice in the N.T, is said of men in Matt. 5 : 32 ; 19 : 9 ; Mark 10 : 11 ; of women in Mark 10 : 12.¶

2. MOICHEUŌ (μοιχεύω) is used in Matt. 5 : 27, 28, 32 (in ver. 32 some texts have No. 1) ; 19 : 18 ; Mark 10 : 19 ; Luke 16 : 18 ; 18 : 20 ; John 8 : 4 ; Rom. 2 : 22 ; 13 : 9 ; Jas. 2 : 11 ; in Rev. 2 : 22, metaphorically, of those who are by a Jezebel's solicitations drawn away to idolatry.¶

ADVANCE

PROKOPTŌ (προκόπτω), lit., to strike forward, cut forward a way, i.e., to make progress, is translated " advanced " in Luke 2 : 52, R.V., of the Lord Jesus (A.V., " increased ") ; in Gal. 1 : 14 " advanced," of Paul's former progress in the Jews' religion (A.V., " profited ") ; in Rom. 13 : 12, " is far spent," of the advanced state of the " night " of the world's spiritual darkness ; in 2 Tim. 2 : 16, " will proceed further," of profane babblings ; in 3 : 9 " shall proceed no further," of the limit Divinely to be put to the doings of evil men ; in ver. 13, of the progress of evil men and impostors, " shall wax," lit., ' shall advance to the worse.' See INCREASE, PROCEED, PROFIT, SPENT, WAX.¶

Note : The corresponding noun *prokopē* is found in Phil. 1 : 12 and 25, " progress " (A.V., " furtherance ") ; 1 Tim. 4 : 15, " progress " (A.V., " profiting," an inadequate meaning).¶

ADVANTAGE
A. Nouns.

1. PERISSOS (περισσός), primarily, what is above and over, superadded, hence came to denote what is superior and advantageous, Rom. 3 : 1, in a comparison between Jew and Gentile ; only here with this meaning. See ABUNDANT, C, No. 1.

2. OPHELOS (ὄφελος), akin to *ophellō*, to increase, comes from a root signifying to increase ; hence, advantage, profit ; it is rendered as a verb in its three occurrences, 1 Cor. 15 : 32 (A.V., " advantageth ; " R.V., " doth it profit ") ; Jas. 2 : 14, 16, lit., ' What (is) the profit ? ' See PROFIT.¶ In the Sept., Job 15 : 3.¶

3. ŌPHELEIA (ὠφέλεια), an alternative form to No. 2, akin to C, No. 1, is found in Rom. 3 : 1, " profit," and Jude 16, " advantage." (i.e., they shew respect of persons for the sake of what they may gain from them). See PROFIT.¶

Note : Ō*phelimos*, profitable, is used only in the Pastoral Epistles, 1 Tim. 4 : 8 ; 2 Tim. 3 : 16 ; Tit. 3 : 8. See PROFIT.¶

B. Verbs.

1. ŌPHELEŌ (ὠφελέω) signifies to be useful, do good, profit, Rom. 2 : 25 ; with a negative, to be of no use, to effect nothing, Matt. 27 : 24 ; John 6 : 63, " profiteth ; " 12 : 19, " prevail ; " in Luke 9 : 25, A.V., " (what is a man) advantaged ? " R.V., " profited." See BETTERED (to be), PREVAIL, PROFIT.

2. PLEONEKTEŌ (πλεονεκτέω), lit., to seek to get more (*pleon*, more, *echō*, to have) ; hence to get an advantage of, to take advantage of. In 2 Cor. 7 : 2 the A.V. has "defrauded," the R.V., " took advantage of ; " in 1 Thess. 4 : 6, A.V., " defraud," R.V., " wrong." In the other three places the R.V. consistently translates it by the verb to take advantage of, 2 Cor. 2 : 11, of Satan's effort to gain an advantage over the church, through their neglect to restore the backslider ; in 2 Cor. 12 : 17, 18, A.V., " make a gain of." See DEFRAUD, GAIN, WRONG.¶

Note : Cp. *pleonektēs*, a covetous person, *pleonexia*, covetousness.

ADVENTURE

DIDŌMI (δίδωμι), to give, is once used of giving oneself to go into a place, to adventure into, Acts 19 : 31, of Paul's thought of going into the midst of the mob in the theatre at Ephesus. See BESTOW, COMMIT, DELIVER, GIVE.

ADVERSARY

A. Noun.

ANTIDIKOS (ἀντίδικος), firstly, an opponent in a lawsuit, Matt. 5 : 25 (twice) ; Luke 12 : 58 ; 18 : 3, is also used to denote an adversary or an enemy, without reference to legal affairs, and this is perhaps its meaning in 1 Pet. 5 : 8, where it is used of the Devil. Some would regard the word as there used in a legal sense, since the Devil accuses men before God.¶

B. Verb.

ANTIKEIMAI (ἀντικείμαι) is, lit., to lie opposite to, to be set over against. In addition to its legal sense it signifies to withstand ; the present participle of the verb with the article, which is equivalent to a noun, signifies an adversary, e.g., Luke 13 : 17 ; 21 : 15 ; 1 Cor. 16 : 9 ;

Phil. 1 : 28 ; 1 Tim. 5 : 14. This construction is used of the Man of Sin, in 2 Thess. 2 : 4, and is translated " He that opposeth," where, adopting the noun form, we might render by ' the opponent and self-exalter against . . .' In Gal. 5 : 17 it is use of the antagonism between the Holy Spirit and the flesh in the believer ; in 1 Tim. 1 : 10, of anything, in addition to persons, that is opposed to the doctrine of Christ. In these two places the word is rendered " contrary to."¶ In the Sept. it is used of Satan, Zech. 3 : 1, and of men, Job 13 : 24 ; Isa. 66 : 6. See CONTRARY, OPPOSE.¶

C. Adjective.

HUPENANTIOS (ὑπεναντίος), contrary, opposed, is a strengthened form of *enantios* (*en*, in, and *antios*, set against). The intensive force is due to the preposition *hupo*. It is translated " contrary to, " in Col. 2 : 14, of ordinances ; in Heb. 10 : 27, " adversaries." In each place a more violent form of opposition is suggested than in the case of *enantios*. See CONTRARY.¶

For ADVERSITY, in Heb. 13 : 3, where the verb *kakoucheomai* is translated in the A.V., " suffer adversity," see SUFFER, (*b*), No. 6.

ADVICE, ADVISE

1. GNŌMĒ (γνώμη), connected with *ginōskō*, to know, perceive, firstly means the faculty of knowledge, reason ; then, that which is thought or known, one's mind. Under this heading there are various meanings : (1) a view, judgment, opinion, 1 Cor. 1 : 10 ; Philm. 14 ; Rev. 17 : 13, 17 ; (2) an opinion as to what ought to be done, either (*a*) by oneself, and so a resolve, or purpose, Acts 20 : 3 ; or (*b*) by others, and so, judgment. advice, 1 Cor. 7 : 25, 40 ; 2 Cor. 8 : 10. See AGREE, JUDGMENT, MIND, PURPOSE, WILL.¶

2. BOULĒ (βουλή), from a root meaning a will, hence a counsel, a piece of advice, is to be distinguished from *gnōmē* ; *boulē* is the result of determination, *gnōmē* is the result of knowledge. *Boulē* is everywhere rendered by " counsel " in the R.V. except in Acts 27 : 12, " advised," lit., ' gave counsel.' In Acts 13 : 36 the A.V. wrongly has " by the will of God fell on sleep ; " the R.V., " after he had served the counsel of God, fell on sleep." The word is used of the counsel of God, in Luke 7 : 30 ; Acts 2 : 23 ; 4 : 28 ; 13 : 36 ; 20 : 27 ; Eph. 1 : 11 ; Heb. 6 : 17 ; in other passages, of the counsel of men, Luke 23 : 51 ; Acts 27 : 12, 42 ; 1 Cor. 4 : 5. See COUNSEL, WILL.¶

For ADVOCATE see COMFORTER.

AFAR

1. MAKRAN (μακράν), from *makros*, far, Matt. 8 : 30 (A.V., " a good way ; " R.V., " afar "), a long way off, is used with *eis*, unto, in Acts 2 : 39,

" afar off." With the article, in Eph. 2 : 13, 17, it signifies " the (ones) far off." See FAR and WAY.

2. MAKROTHEN (μακρόθεν), also from *makros*, signifies afar off, from far, Matt. 26 : 58 ; 27 : 55, etc. It is used with *apo*, from, in Mark 5 : 6 ; 14 : 54 ; 15 : 40, etc. ; outside the Synoptists, three times, Rev. 18 : 10, 15, 17.

3. PORROTHEN (πόρρωθεν), afar off, from *porrō*, at a distance, a great way off, is found in Luke 17 : 12 and Heb. 11 : 13.¶

Note : In 2 Pet. 1 : 9, *muōpazō*, to be shortsighted, is translated " cannot see afar off " (A.V.) ; R.V., " seeing only what is near."

AFFAIR (-S)

PRAGMATIA, or PRAGMATEIA (πραγματία), from *pragma*, a deed, denotes a business, occupation, the prosecution of any affair ; in the plural, pursuits, affairs (of life), 2 Tim. 2 : 4.¶

Notes : (1) *Ta kata*, lit., the (things), with, or respecting a (person), is translated " affairs " in Eph. 6 : 21 and Col. 4 : 7, R.V.

(2) *Ta peri*, lit., the (things) concerning (a person), is translated " affairs " in the A.V. of Eph. 6 : 22 and Phil. 1 : 27 (R.V., " state," in each place).

AFFECT

KAK(Ō (κακόω), from *kakos*, evil, to treat badly, to hurt, also means to make evil affected, to embitter, Acts 14 : 2. See EVIL, HARM, HURT.

Note : Zēloō, akin to *zeō*, to boil (Eng., zeal), means (*a*) to be jealous, Acts 7 : 9 ; 17 : 5 ; to envy, 1 Cor. 13 : 4 ; to covet, Jas. 4 : 2 ; in a good sense (" jealous over "), in 2 Cor. 11 : 2 ; (*b*) to desire earnestly, 1 Cor. 12 : 31 ; 14 : 1, 39 ; to take a warm interest in, to seek zealously, Gal. 4 : 17, 18, A.V., " zealously affect," " to be zealously affected." The R.V. corrects this to " zealously seek," etc. See COVET, DESIRE, ENVY, JEALOUS, ZEALOUS.¶

AFFECTION (-S), AFFECTED
A. Nouns.

1. PATHOS (πάθος), from *paschō*, to suffer, primarily denotes whatever one suffers or experiences in any way ; hence, an affection of the mind, a passionate desire. Used by the Greeks of either good or bad desires, it is always used in the N.T. of the latter, Rom. 1 : 26 (A.V., " affections," R.V., " passions ") ; Col. 3 : 5 (A.V., " inordinate affection," R.V., " passion ") ; 1 Thess. 4 : 5 (A.V., " lust," R.V., " passion "). See LUST.¶

2. SPLANCHNA (σπλάγχνα), lit., the bowels, which were regarded by the Greeks as the seat of the more violent passions, by the Hebrews as the seat of the tender affections ; hence the word denotes " tender

mercies " and is rendered " affections " in 2 Cor. 6 : 12 (A.V., " bowels ") ;
" inward affection," 2 Cor. 7 : 15. See BOWELS, COMPASSION, HEART,
MERCY. Cp. *epithumia*, desire.

3. PATHĒMA (πάθημα), akin to No. 1, translated " affections " in
Gal. 5 : 24, A.V., is corrected to " passions " in the R.V. See AFFLICTION,
B, No. 3.

B. Adjectives.

1. ASTORGOS (ἄστοργος) signifies without natural affection (*a*,
negative, and *storgē*, love of kindred, especially of parents for children
and children for parents ; a fanciful etymology associates with this the
" stork "), Rom. 1 : 31 ; 2 Tim. 3 : 3.¶

2. PHILOSTORGOS (φιλόστοργος), tenderly loving (from *philos*,
friendly, *storgē*, see No. 1), is used in Rom. 12 : 10, R.V., " tenderly
affectioned " (A.V., " kindly affectioned ").¶

Notes : (1) *Phroneō*, to think, to set the mind on, implying moral
interest and reflexion, is translated " set your affection on " in Col. 3 : 2,
A.V. (R.V., " set your mind on "). See CAREFUL, MIND, REGARD,
SAVOUR, THINK, UNDERSTAND.

(2) For *homeiromai* (or *himeiromai*), to be affectionately desirous of,
1 Thess. 2 : 8, see DESIRE.¶

AFFIRM

1. DIABEBAIOOMAI (διαβεβαιόομαι), *dia*, intensive, and *bebaioō*,
to confirm, make sure, denotes to assert strongly, " affirm confidently,"
1 Tim. 1 : 7 ; Tit. 3 : 8 (A.V., " affirm constantly ").¶

2. DIISCHURIZOMAI (διισχυρίζομαι), as in No. 1, and *ischurizomai*,
to corroborate (*ischuros* " strong ; " see ABILITY, A, No. 2 and C, No. 2,
Note), primarily signifies to lean upon, then, to affirm stoutly, assert
vehemently, Luke 22 : 59 ; Acts 12 : 15.¶

3. PHASKŌ (φάσκω), a frequentative form of the verb *phēmi* (No. 4),
denotes to allege, to affirm by way of alleging or professing, Acts 24 : 9
(R.V., " affirming," A.V., " saying ") ; 25 : 19 ; Rom. 1 : 22, " professing."
Some mss. have it in Rev. 2 : 2, instead of the verb *legō*, to say. See
PROFESS, SAY.¶

4. PHĒMI (φημί), to say (primarily by way of enlightening, explaining),
is rendered " affirm " in Rom. 3 : 8. See SAY.

AFFLICT (-ED), AFFLICTION
A. Verbs.

1. KAKOŌ (κακόω) is translated " afflict," in Acts 12 : 1, R.V.
(A.V., " vex "). See AFFECT.

2. KAKOUCHEŌ (κακουχέω), from *kakos*, evil, and *echō*, to have,
signifies, in the Passive Voice, to suffer ill, to be maltreated, tormented,
Heb. 11 : 37 (A.V., " tormented," R.V., " afflicted ") ; 13 : 3, A.V.,

"suffer adversity," R.V., "evil entreated." See ENTREAT, TORMENT.¶ In the Sept., 1 Kings, 2 : 26 ; 11 : 39.¶

Note : Sunkakoucheō (*sun*, with, and No. 1), to be evil entreated with, is used in Heb. 11 : 25.¶

3. KAKOPATHEŌ (κακοπαθέω), from *kakos*, evil, *pathos*, suffering, signifies to suffer hardship. So the R.V. in 2 Tim. 2 : 9 ; and 4 : 5 ; in Jas. 5 : 13, "suffer" (A.V., "afflicted"). See ENDURE, SUFFER.¶

Note : For *sunkakopatheō*, 2 Tim. 1 : 8, see HARDSHIP.

4. THLIBŌ (θλίβω), to suffer affliction, to be troubled, has reference to sufferings due to the pressure of circumstances, or the antagonism of persons, 1 Thess. 3 : 4 ; 2 Thess. 1 : 6, 7 ; "straitened," in Matt. 7 : 14 (R.V.) ; "throng," Mark 3 : 9 ; "afflicted," 2 Cor. 1 : 6 ; 7 : 5 (R.V.) ; 1 Tim. 5 : 10 ; Heb. 11 : 37 ; "pressed," 2 Cor. 4 : 8. Both the verb and the noun (see B, No. 4), when used of the present experience of believers, refer almost invariably to that which comes upon them from without. See NARROW, PRESS, STRAITENED, THRONG, TRIBULATION, TROUBLE.¶

5. TALAIPŌREŌ (ταλαιπωρέω), to be afflicted, is used in Jas. 4 : 9, in the Middle Voice ('afflict yourselves'). It is derived from *tlaō*, to bear, undergo, and *pōros*, a hard substance, a callus, which metaphorically came to signify that which is miserable.¶

Note : Talaipōria (akin to No. 5) denotes misery, hardship, Rom. 3 : 16 ; Jas. 5 : 1.¶ The corresponding adjective is *talaipōros*, "wretched," Rom. 7 : 24 ; Rev. 3 : 17.¶

B. Nouns.

1. KAKOPATHEIA (κακοπάθεια), from *kakos*, evil, and *paschō*, to suffer, is rendered "suffering" in Jas. 5 : 10, R.V. (A.V., "suffering affliction").¶ In Sept., Mal. 1 : 13.¶

2. KAKŌSIS (κάκωσις), affliction, ill treatment, is used in Acts 7 : 34.¶

3. PATHĒMA (πάθημα), from *pathos*, suffering, signifies affliction. The word is frequent in Paul's Epistles and is found three times in Hebrews, four in 1 Peter ; it is used (*a*) of afflictions, Rom. 8 : 18 etc. ; of Christ's sufferings, 1 Pet. 1 : 11 ; 5 : 1 ; Heb. 2 : 9 ; of those as shared by believers, 2 Cor. 1 : 5 ; Phil. 3 : 10 ; 1 Pet. 4 : 13 ; 5 : 1 ; (*b*) of an evil emotion, passion, Rom. 7 : 5 ; Gal. 5 : 24. The connection between the two meanings is that the emotions, whether good or evil, were regarded as consequent upon external influences exerted on the mind (cp. the two meanings of the English "passion"). It is more concrete than No. 1, and expresses in sens (*b*) the uncontrolled nature of evil desires, in contrast to *epithumia*, the general and comprehensive term, lit., what you set your heart upon (Trench, Syn. § lxxxvii). Its concrete character is seen in Heb. 2 : 9. See AFFECTION, MOTION, PASSION, SUFFERING.

Note : The corresponding verbal form *pathētos*, used in Acts 26 : 23 of the sufferings of Christ, signifies destined to suffer.¶

4. THLIPSIS (θλίψις) primarily means a pressing, pressure (see A,

No. 4), anything which burdens the spirit. In two passages in Paul's Epistles it is used of future retribution, in the way of affliction, Rom. 2 : 9 ; 2 Thess. 1 : 6. In Matt. 24 : 9, the A.V. renders it as a verb, " to be afflicted," (R.V., " unto tribulation.") It is coupled with *stenochōria,* anguish, in Rom. 2 : 9 ; 8 : 35 ; with *anankē,* distress, 1 Thess. 3 : 7 ; with *diōgmos,* persecution, Matt. 13 : 21 ; Mark 4 : 17 ; 2 Thess. 1 : 4. It is used of the calamities of war, Matt. 24 : 21, 29 ; Mark 13 : 19, 24 ; of want, 2 Cor. 8 : 13, lit., ' distress for you ; ' Phil. 4 : 14 (cp. 1 : 16) ; Jas. 1 : 27 ; of the distress of woman in child-birth, John 16 : 21 ; of persecution, Acts 11 : 19 ; 14 : 22 ; 20 : 23 ; 1 Thess. 3 : 3, 7 ; Heb. 10 : 33 ; Rev. 2 : 10 ; 7 : 14 ; of the afflictions of Christ, from which (His vicarious sufferings apart) his followers must not shrink, whether sufferings of body or mind, Col. 1 : 24 ; of sufferings in general, 1 Cor. 7 : 28 ; 1 Thess. 1 : 6 etc. See ANGUISH, BURDENED, DISTRESS, PERSECUTION, TRIBULATION, TROUBLE.

AFFRIGHTED

A. Adjective.

EMPHOBOS (ἔμφοβος), lit., in fear (*en*, in, *phobos*, fear), means " affrighted," Luke 24 : 5, R.V. (A.V., " afraid ") ; 24 : 37 ; Acts 10 : 4, R.V. (A.V., " afraid ") ; Rev. 11 : 13. The R.V. omits it in Acts 22 : 9. See TREMBLE.

B. Verbs.

1. PTURŌ (πτύρω), to frighten, scare, is used in the Passive Voice in Phil. 1 : 28, " be affrighted," R.V., " be terrified," A.V. See TERRIFY.¶

2. EKTHAMBEŌ (ἐκθαμβέω), to throw into terror, is used in the Passive sense, to be amazed, " affrighted," Mark 16 : 5, 6, A.V. (R.V., " amazed ") ; Mark 9 : 15, " were greatly amazed ; " 14 : 33, " to be greatly amazed " (R.V.), " to be sore amazed " (A.V.). See AMAZE, B, No. 4.¶

For AFOOT see FOOT, B, No. 2

AFORE, AFOREHAND

The Greek words with these meanings consist of prefixes to verbs, signifying to come, prepare, promise, write afore, etc. See under these words.

AFOREPROMISED

PROEPANGELLOMAI (προεπαγγέλλομαι), to promise before (*pro*, before, *epangellomai*, to promise), is translated by the one word " aforepromised," in the R.V. of 2 Cor. 9 : 5 ; in Rom. 1 : 2, " promised afore."¶

AFORETIME

1. POTE (ποτέ) signifies once, at some time, John 9 : 13 (cp. *proteron*, in ver. 8) ; Eph. 2 : 2, 11 ; Col. 3 : 7 ; Tit. 3 : 3 ; Philm. 11 ; 1 Pet. 3 : 5, 20. In all these the R.V. translates it "aforetime." The A.V. varies it with "in time past," "some time," "sometimes," "in the old time."

2. PROTERON (πρότερον), the comparative of *pro*, before, aforetime, as being definitely antecedent to something else, is more emphatic than *pote* in this respect. See, e.g., John 6 : 62 ; 7 : 50 ; 9 : 8 ; 2 Cor. 1 : 13 ; Gal. 4 : 13 ; 1 Tim. 1 : 13 ; Heb. 4 : 6 ; 7 : 27 ; 10 : 32 ; 1 Pet. 1 : 14. See BEFORE, FIRST, FORMER.¶

For AFRAID see AFFRIGHTED, A, FEAR, A, No. 2, B, No. 3, D, SORE

For AFRESH see under CROSS, CRUCIFY, B

AFTER, AFTERWARD (-S)

The following are adverbs only. For prepositions and conjunctions see Note † p. 9.

1. EKEITHEN (ἐκεῖθεν), thence, is once used to signify "afterwards," in the sense of "then," from that time, Acts 13 : 21. See THENCE.

2 HEXĒS (ἑξῆς) denotes "after" with the significance of a succession of events, an event following next in order after another, Luke 7 : 11 ; 9 : 37 ; Acts 21 : 1 ; 25 : 17 ; 27 : 18.¶

3. KATHEXĒS (καθεξῆς), a strengthened form of No. 2, denotes "afterward," or "in order" (*kata*, according to, and No. 2), Luke 1 : 3 ; 8 : 1 ; Acts 3 : 24 ; 11 : 4 ; 18 : 23.¶

4. METEPEITA (μετέπειτα), afterwards, without necessarily indicating an order of events, as in Nos. 1 and 2, is found in Heb. 12 : 17.¶

5. HUSTERON (ὕστερον), afterwards, with the suggestion of at length, is found in Matt. 4 : 2 ; 21 : 29, 32, 37 (A.V., "last of all") ; 22 : 27 ; 25 : 11 ; 26 : 60 (A.V., "at the last") ; Mark 16 : 14 ; Luke 4 : 2 ; 20 : 32 (A.V., "last") ; John 13 : 36 ; Heb. 12 : 11. See LAST.¶

Note : Eita and *epeita*, then, afterwards, or thereupon, are translated "afterward" or "afterwards" in the A.V. of Mark 4 : 17 (*eita*) and Gal. 1 : 21 ; 1 Cor. 15 : 23, 46 (*epeita*) ; always "then" in the R.V. See THEN.

AGAIN

1. DIS (δίς), the ordinary numeral adverb signifying twice, is rendered "again" in Phil. 4 : 16, "ye sent once and again unto my need," and in 1 Thess. 2 : 18, where Paul states that he would have come to the Thessalonians "once and again," that is, twice at least he had attempted to do so. See TWICE.

2. PALIN (πάλιν), the regular word for "again," is used chiefly in two senses, (*a*) with reference to repeated action ; (*b*) rhetorically, in

the sense of " moreover " or " further," indicating a statement to be added in the course of an argument, e.g., Matt. 5 : 33 ; or with the meaning ' on the other hand,' ' in turn,' Luke 6 : 43 ; 1 Cor. 12 : 21 ; 2 Cor. 10 : 7 ; 1 John 2 : 8. In the first chapter of Hebrews, ver. 5, *palin* simply introduces an additional quotation ; in ver. 6 this is not so. There the R.V. rightly puts the word " again " in connection with " He bringeth in the firstborn into the world," " When He again bringeth etc." That is to say, *palin* is here set in contrast to the time when God *first* brought His Son into the world. This statement, then, refers to the future Second Advent of Christ. The word is used far more frequently in the Gospel of John than in any other book in the New Testament.

Note : Other words are rendered " again " in the A.V., which the R.V. corrects, namely, *deuteros* and *anōthen*. *Deuteros* signifies " a second time," John 9 : 24 ; Acts 11 : 9. *Anōthen* signifies from above, or anew. See the R.V. of John 3 : 3, 7, and the A.V. and R.V. of ver. 31. Nicodemus was not puzzled about birth from Heaven ; what perplexed him was that a person must be born a second time. This the context makes clear. This is really the meaning in Gal. 4 : 9, where it is associated with *palin*, " over again." The idea is " anew," for, though the bondage would be the same in essence and effect, it would be new in not being in bondage to idols but to the Law. See also Matt. 27 : 51 ; Mark 15 : 38 ; John 19 : 23, " from the top." *Anōthen* may mean " from the first," in Luke 1 : 3 and Acts 26 : 5. For the meaning " from above," see Jas. 1 : 17 ; 3 : 15, 17.¶

AGAINST : see Note, † p. 9.

AGE
A. Nouns.

1. AIŌN (αἰών), an age, era (to be connected with *aei*, ever, rather than with *aō*, to breathe), signifies a period of indefinite duration, or time viewed in relation to what takes place in the period.

The force attaching to the word is not so much that of the actual length of a period, but that of a period marked by spiritual or moral characteristics. This is illustrated in the use of the adjective [see Note (1) below] in the phrase " life eternal," in John 17 : 3, in respect of the increasing knowledge of God.

The phrases containing this word should not be rendered literally, but consistently with its sense of indefinite duration. Thus *eis ton aiōna* does not mean " unto the age " but " for ever " (see, e.g., Heb. 5 : 6). The Greeks contrasted that which came to an end with that which was expressed by this phrase, which shows that they conceived of it as expressing interminable duration.

The word occurs most frequently in the Gospel of John, the Hebrews and Revelation. It is sometimes wrongly rendered " world." See COURSE, ETERNAL, WORLD. It is a characteristic word of John's Gospel.

Notes : (1) *Aiōnios*, the adjective corresponding, denoting eternal, is set in contrast with *proskairos*, lit., ' for a season,' 2 Cor. 4 : 18. It is used of that which in nature is endless, as, e.g., of God, Rom. 16 : 26, His power, 1 Tim. 6 : 16, His glory, 1 Pet. 5 : 10, the Holy Spirit, Heb. 9 : 14, redemption, Heb. 9 : 12, salvation, 5 : 9, life in Christ, John 3 : 16, the resurrection body, 2 Cor. 5 : 1, the future rule of Christ, 2 Pet. 1 : 11, which is declared to be without end, Luke 1 : 33, of sin that never has forgiveness, Mark 3 : 29, the judgment of God, Heb. 6 : 2, and of fire, one of its instruments, Matt. 18 : 8 ; 25 : 41 ; Jude 7. See ETERNAL, EVER-LASTING.

(2) In Rev. 15 : 3, the R.V. has " King of the ages," according to the texts which have *aiōnōn ;* the A.V. has " of saints " (*hagiōn*, in inferior mss.). There is good ms. evidence for *ethnōn*, " nations," (A.V., marg.), probably a quotation from Jer. 10 : 7.

2. GENEA (γενεά), connected with *ginomai*, to become, primarily signifies a begetting, or birth ; then that which has been begotten, a family ; or successive members of a genealogy, Matt. 1 : 17, or of a race of people, possessed of similar characteristics, pursuits, etc., (of a bad character) Matt. 17 : 17 ; Mark 9 : 19 ; Luke 9 : 41 ; 16 : 8 ; Acts 2 : 40 ; or of the whole multitude of men living at the same time, Matt. 24 : 34 ; Mark 13 : 30 ; Luke 1 : 48 ; 21 : 32 ; Phil. 2 : 15, and especially of those of the Jewish race living at the same period, Matt. 11 : 16, etc. Trans-ferred from people to the time in which they lived, the word came to mean an age, i.e., a period ordinarily occupied by each successive generation, say, of thirty or forty years, Acts 14 : 16 ; 15 : 21 ; Eph. 3 : 5 ; Col. 1 : 26 ; see also, e.g., Gen. 15 : 16. In Eph. 3 : 21 *genea* is combined with *aiōn* in a remarkable phrase in a doxology : " Unto Him be the glory in the church and in Christ Jesus, unto all generations for ever and ever (wrongly in A.V. ' all ages, world without end ')." The word *genea* is to be distinguished from *aiōn*, as not denoting a period of unlimited duration. See GENERATION, NATION, TIME.

3. HĒLIKIA (ἡλικία), primarily an age, as a certain length of life, came to mean (*a*) a particular time of life, as when a person is said to be " of age," John 9 : 21, 23, or beyond a certain stage of life, Heb. 11 : 11 ; (*b*) elsewhere only of stature, e.g., Matt. 6 : 27 ; Luke 2 : 52 ; 12 : 25 ; 19 : 3 ; Eph. 4 : 13. Some regard Matt. 6 : 27 and Luke 12 : 25 as coming under (*a*). It is to be distinguished from *aiōn* and *genea*, since it has to do simply with matters relating to an individual, either his time of life or his height. See STATURE.¶

4. HĒMERA (ἡμέρα), a day, is rendered " age " in Luke 2 : 36, " of a great age " (lit., ' advanced in many days '). In Luke 3 : 23 there is no word in the original corresponding to age. The phrase is simply " about thirty years." See DAY, JUDGMENT, TIME, YEAR.

B. Adjectives.

1. HUPERAKMOS (ὑπέρακμος) in 1 Cor. 7 : 36 is rendered " past the

flower of her age ; " more lit., ' beyond the bloom or flower (*acme*) of life.'¶

2. TELEIOS (τέλειος), complete, perfect, from *telos*, an end, is translated " of full age " in Heb. 5 : 14, A.V. (R.V., " fullgrown man ").

Note : In Mark 5 : 42, R.V., " old," A.V., " of the age of," is, lit., ' of twelve years.' For " of great age," Luke 2 : 36, see STRICKEN. For " of mine own age," Gal. 1 : 14, R.V., see EQUAL, B, No. 2.

AGED
A. Nouns.

1. PRESBUTES (πρεσβύτης), an elderly man, is a longer form of *presbus*, the comparative degree of which is *presbuteros*, a senior, elder, both of which, as also the verb *presbeuō*, to be elder, to be an ambassador, are derived from *proeisbainō*, to be far advanced. The noun is found in Luke 1 : 18, " an old man ; " Tit. 2 : 2, " aged men," and Philm. 9, where the R.V. marg., " Paul an ambassador," is to be accepted, the original almost certainly being *presbeutēs* (not *presbutēs*), an ambassador. So he describes himself in Eph. 6 : 20. As Lightfoot points out, he is hardly likely to have made his age a ground of appeal to Philemon, who, if he was the father of Archippus, cannot have been much younger than Paul himself. See OLD.

2. PRESBUTIS (πρεσβῦτις), the feminine of No. 1, an aged woman, is found in Tit. 2 : 3.¶

B. Verb.

GĒRASKŌ (γηράσκω), from *gēras*, old age, signifies to grow old, John 21 : 18 (" when thou shalt be old ") and Heb. 8 : 13 (R.V., " that which . . . waxeth aged," A.V., " old "). See OLD.¶

For AGO see LONG, A, No. 5, and in combination with other words.

AGONY

AGŌNIA (ἀγωνία), Eng., agony, was used among the Greeks as an alternative to *agōn*, a place of assembly ; then for the contests or games which took place there, and then to denote intense emotion. It was more frequently used eventually in this last respect, to denote severe emotional strain and anguish. So in Luke 22 : 44, of the Lord's agony in Gethsemane.¶

AGREE, AGREEMENT
A. Verbs.

1. SUMPHŌNEŌ (συμφωνέω), lit., to sound together (*sun*, together, *phōnē*, a sound), i.e., to be in accord, primarily of musical instruments, is used in the N.T. of the agreement (*a*) of persons concerning a matter, Matt. 18 : 19 ; 20 : 2, 13 ; Acts 5 : 9 ; (*b*) of the writers of Scripture, Acts 15 : 15 ; (*c*) of things that are said to be congruous in their nature, Luke 5 : 36.¶

Note : Cp. *sumphōnēsis*, concord, 2 Cor. 6 : 15,¶, and *sumphōnia*, music, Luke 15 : 25.¶

2. SUNTITHĒMI (συντίθημι), lit., to put together (*sun*, with, *tithēmi*, to put), in the Middle Voice, means to make an agreement, or to assent to ; translated " covenanted " in Luke 22 : 5, " agreed " in John 9 : 22, and Acts 23 : 20 ; " assented " in Acts 24 : 9.¶

Note : For the synonym *sunkatatithēmi*, a strengthened form of No. 2, see CONSENT, No. 4.

3 EUNOEŌ (εὐνοέω), lit., to be well-minded, well-disposed (*eu*, well, *nous*, the mind), is found in Matt. 5 : 25, " agree with,"¶

4. PEITHŌ (πείθω), to persuade, is rendered " agreed " in Acts 5 : 40, where the meaning is " they yielded to him."   See ASSURE, BELIEVE, CONFIDENT, FRIEND, OBEY, PERSUADE, TRUST, YIELD.

B. Nouns.

1. GNŌMĒ (γνώμη), mind, will, is used with *poieō*, to make, in the sense of to agree, Rev. 17 : 17 (twice), lit., ' to do His mind, and to make one mind ; ' R.V., " to come to one mind," A.V., " to agree." See ADVICE, JUDGMENT, MIND, PURPOSE, WILL.

2. SUNKATATHESIS (συνκατάθεσις), akin to A, No. 3, occurs in 2 Cor. 6 : 16.¶

C. Adjectives.

1. ASUMPHŌNOS (ἀσύμφωνος), inharmonious (*a*, negative, *sumphōnos*, harmonious), is used in Acts 28 : 25, " they agreed not."¶

2. ISOS (ἴσος), equal, is used with the verb to be, signifying to agree, Mark 14 : 56, 59, lit., ' their thought was not equal one with the other.' See EQUAL, LIKE, MUCH.

Note : *Sumphōnos*, harmonious, agreeing, is used only with the preposition *ek* in the phrase *ek sumphōnou*, by consent, lit., out of agreement, 1 Cor. 7 : 5. In Mark 14 : 70 some texts have the verb *homoiazō*, " agreeth," A.V.

For AGROUND see RUN, No. 11

AH !

1. OUA (οὐά), an interjection of derision and insult, is translated Ha ! in Mark 15 : 29, R.V.¶

2. EA (ἔα), an interjection of surprise, fear and anger, was the ejaculation of the man with the spirit of an unclean demon, Luke 4 : 34, R.V. ; the A.V. renders it " Let us alone " (see R.V. marg.).¶

AIM

PHILOTIMEOMAI (φιλοτιμέομαι), lit., to be fond of honour (*phileō*, to love, *timē*, honour), and so, actuated by this motive, to strive to bring something to pass ; hence, to be ambitious, to make it one's aim, Rom.

15 : 20, of Paul's aim in Gospel pioneering, R.V. (A.V., "strive");
2 Cor. 5 : 9, of the aim of believers " to be well-pleasing " unto the Lord,
R.V. (A.V., " labour ") ; in 1 Thess. 4 : 11, of the aim of believers to be
quiet, do their own business and work with their own hands ; both Versions
translate it " study."   Some would render it, ' strive restlessly ; ' perhaps ' strive earnestly ' is nearer the mark, but ' make it one's aim ' is
a good translation in all three places.   See Labour, Strive, Study.¶

AIR

1. AĒR (ἀήρ), (Eng., air), signifies the atmosphere, certainly in five of
the seven occurrences, Acts 22 : 23 ; 1 Cor. 9 : 26 ; 14 : 9 ; Rev. 9 : 2 ;
16 : 17, and almost certainly in the other two, Eph. 2 : 2 and
1 Thess. 4 : 17.¶

2. OURANOS (οὐρανός) denotes the heaven.   The R.V. always renders
it " heaven."   The A.V. translates it " air " in Matt. 8 : 20.   In the
phrase " the fowls (or birds) of the heaven " the A.V. always has " air ; "
" sky " in Matt. 16 : 2, 3 ; Luke 12 : 56 ; in all other instances " heaven."
The word is probably derived from a root meaning to cover or encompass.
See Heaven, Sky.

For ALABASTER see CRUSE

For ALAS ! see WOE

ALBEIT

HINA (ἵνα), a conjunction, meaning " that," and so rendered in
Philm. 19, R.V., for A.V., " albeit."

ALIEN

ALLOTRIOS (ἀλλότριος), primarily, belonging to another (the opposite
to idios, one's own), hence came to mean foreign, strange, not of one's
own family, alien, an enemy ; " aliens " in Heb. 11 : 34, elsewhere
" strange," etc.   See Man's, Note (1), Strange, Stranger.

ALIENATE

APALLOTRIOŌ (ἀπαλλοτριόω) consists of apo, from, and the above ;
it signifies to be rendered an alien, to be alienated.   In Eph. 2 : 12 the
R.V. corrects to the verbal form " alienated," for the noun " aliens ; "
elsewhere in Eph. 4 : 18 and Col. 1 : 21 ; the condition of the unbeliever
is presented in a threefold state of alienation, (a) from the commonwealth
of Israel, (b) from the life of God, (c) from God Himself.¶   The word is
used of Israelites in the Sept. of Ezek. 14 : 5 (" estranged ") and of the
wicked in general, Psa. 58 : 3.

ALIKE

Note : In Rom. 14 : 5, this word is in italics. This addition is not needed in the translation.

For ALIVE see LIFE, C, LIVE, No. 6

ALL

A. Adjectives.

1. PAS (πᾶς) radically means "all." Used without the article it means "every," every kind or variety. So the R.V. marg. in Eph. 2 : 21, "every building," and the text in 3 : 15, "every family," and the R.V. marg. of Acts 2 : 36, "every house ; " or it may signify the highest degree, the maximum of what is referred to, as, "with all boldness" Acts 4 : 29. Before proper names of countries, cities and nations, and before collective terms, like "Israel," it signifies either "all" or "the whole," e.g., Matt. 2 : 3 ; Acts 2 : 36. Used with the article, it means the whole of one object. In the plural it signifies the totality of the persons or things referred to. Used without a noun it virtually becomes a pronoun, meaning "everyone" or "anyone." In the plural with a noun it means "all." The neuter singular denotes "everything" or "anything what- soever." One form of the neuter plural (*panta*) signifies wholly, together, in all ways, in all things, Acts 20 : 35 ; 1 Cor. 9 : 25. The neuter plural without the article signifies all things severally, e.g., John 1 : 3 ; 1 Cor. 2 : 10 ; preceded by the article it denotes all things, as constituting a whole, e.g., Rom. 11 : 36 ; 1 Cor. 8 : 6 ; Eph. 3 : 9. See EVERY, *Note* (1), WHOLE.

2. HAPAS (ἅπας), a strengthened form of *pas*, signifies quite all, the whole, and, in the plural, all, all things. Preceded by an article and followed by a noun it means the whole of. In 1 Tim. 1 : 16 the significance is ' the whole of His longsuffering,' or ' the fulness of His longsuffering.' See EVERY, WHOLE.

3. HOLOS (ὅλος), the whole, all, is most frequently used with the article followed by a noun, e.g., Matt. 4 : 23. It is used with the article alone, in John 7 : 23, "every whit ; " Acts 11 : 26 ; 21 : 31 ; 28 : 30 ; Tit. 1 : 11 ; Luke 5 : 5, in the best texts. See ALTOGETHER.

Note : The adjective *holoklēros*, lit., whole-lot, entire, stresses the separate parts which constitute the whole, no part being incomplete. See ENTIRE.

B. Adverbs.

1. HOLŌS (ὅλως) signifies "at all," Matt. 5 : 34 ; 1 Cor. 15 : 29 ; "actually," 1 Cor. 5 : 1, R.V. (A.V., wrongly, "commonly ") ; "alto- gether," 1 Cor. 6 : 7 (A.V., "utterly ").¶

Notes : (1) *Holotelēs*, from A, No. 3, and *telos*, complete, signifies wholly, through and through, 1 Thess. 5 : 23, lit., ' whole complete ' ; there, not an increasing degree of sanctification is intended, but the sanctification of the believer in every part of his being.¶

(2) The synonym *katholou*, a strengthened form of *holou* signifies " at all," Acts 4 : 18.¶

2. PANTŌS (πάντως), when used without a negative, signifies wholly, entirely, by all means, Acts 18 : 21 (A.V.) ; 1 Cor. 9 : 22 ; altogether, 1 Cor. 9 : 10 ; no doubt, doubtless, Luke 4 : 23, R.V. (A.V., " surely ") ; Acts 28 : 4. In 21 : 22 it is translated " certainly," R.V., for A.V., " needs " (lit., ' by all means '). With a negative it signifies in no wise, Rom. 3 : 9 ; 1 Cor. 5 : 10 ; 16 : 12 (" at all "). See ALTOGETHER, DOUBT (No), MEANS, SURELY, WISE.¶

C. Pronoun.

HOSA (ὅσα), the neuter plural of *hosos*, as much as, chiefly used in the plural, is sometimes rendered " all that," e.g., Acts 4 : 23 ; 14 : 27. It really means " whatsoever things." See Luke 9 : 10, R.V., " what things."

ALLEGE

PARATITHĒMI (παρατίθημι), to place beside or to set before (*para*, beside, *tithēmi*, to put), while often used in its literal sense of material things, as well as in its more common significance, to commit, entrust, twice means to set before one in teaching, as in putting forth a parable, Matt. 13 : 24, 31, R.V. Once it is used of setting subjects before one's hearers by way of argument and proof, of Paul, in " opening and alleging " facts concerning Christ, Acts 17 : 3. See COMMEND, COMMIT, PUT, SET.

Note : Legō is rendered " put forth " in the A.V. of Luke 14 : 7 ; but *legō* signifies to speak ; hence the R.V., " spake." The A.V. seems to be an imitation of *paratithēmi* in Matt. 13 : 24, 31. See SAY.

ALLEGORY

ALLĒGOREŌ (ἀλληγορέω), translated in Gal. 4 : 24 " contain an allegory " (A.V., " are an allegory "), formed from *allos*, other, and *agoreuō*, to speak in a place of assembly (*agora*, the market-place), came to signify to speak, not according to the primary sense of the word, but so that the facts stated are applied to illustrate principles. The allegorical meaning does not do away with the literal meaning of the narrative. There may be more than one allegorical meaning though, of course, only one literal meaning. Scripture histories represent or embody spiritual principles, and these are ascertained, not by the play of the imagination, but by the rightful application of the doctrines of Scripture.¶

For ALLELUIA (which has been robbed of its initial aspirate) see HALLELUJAH.

For ALTERED see OTHER, No. 2

ALLOW

1. DOKIMAZŎ (δοκιμάζω), to prove with a view to approving, is twice translated by the verb to allow in the A.V. ; the R.V. corrects to " approveth " in Rom. 14 : 22, and " have been approved," 1 Thess. 2 : 4, of being qualified to be entrusted with the Gospel ; in Rom. 1 : 28, with the negative, the R.V. has " refused," for A.V., " did not like." See APPROVE.

2. GINŌSKŌ (γινώσκω), to know, is rendered " allow " in Rom. 7 : 15 (A.V.) ; the R.V. has " that which I do I know not ; " i.e., ' I do not recognize, as a thing for which I am responsible.' See AWARE, CAN, FEEL, KNOW, PERCEIVE, RESOLVE, SPEAK, SURE, UNDERSTAND.

3. SUNEUDOKEŌ (συνευδοκέω), to consent or fully approve (sun, with, eu, well, dokeō, to think), is translated " allow " in Luke 11 : 48 ; " was consenting " in Acts 8 : 1 ; 22 : 20. See CONSENT.

4. PROSDECHOMAI (προσδέχομαι), mistranslated " allow " in Acts 24 : 15, A.V., means to wait for, in contrast to rejection, there said of entertaining a hope ; hence the R.V., " look for." See ACCEPT, A, No. 3.

For ALLURE see BEGUILE, No. 4, ENTICE

ALMIGHTY

PANTOKRATŌR (παντοκράτωρ), almighty, or ruler of all (pas, all, krateō, to hold, or to have strength), is used of God only, and is found, in the Epistles, only in 2 Cor. 6 : 18, where the title is suggestive in connection with the context ; elsewhere only in the Apocalypse, nine times. In one place, 19 : 6, the A.V. has " omnipotent," R.V., " (the Lord our God,) the Almighty."¶ The word is introduced in the Sept. as a translation of " Lord (or God) of hosts," e.g., Jer. 5 : 14 and Amos 4 : 13.

ALMOST
A. Adverb.

SCHEDON (σχεδόν) is used either (a) of locality, Acts 19 : 26, or (b) of degree, Acts 13 : 44 ; Heb. 9 : 22.¶
B. Verb.

MELLŌ (μέλλω), to be about to do anything, or to delay, is used in connection with a following verb in the sense of " almost," in Acts 21 : 27, lit., ' And when the seven days were about to be completed.' In Acts 26 : 28 the A.V., " Almost 'thou persuadest me to be a Christian " obscures the sense ; the R.V. rightly has " with but little persuasion ; " lit., ' in a little.' See ABOUT, B.

ALMS, ALMSDEEDS

ELEĒMOSUNĒ (ἐλεημοσύνη), connected with eleēmōn, merciful, signifies (a) mercy, pity, particularly in giving alms, Matt. 6 : 1 (see below), 2, 3, 4 ; Acts 10 : 2 ; 24 : 17 ; (b) the benefaction itself, the alms (the effect for the cause), Luke 11 : 41 ; 12 : 33 ; Acts 3 : 2, 3, 10 ; 9 : 36, " alms-deeds " ; 10 : 2, 4, 31.¶

Note : In Matt. 6 : 1, the R.V., translating *dikaiosunē*, according to the most authentic texts, has " righteousness," for A.V., " alms."

ALOES

ALOĒ (*ἀλόη*), an aromatic tree, the soft, bitter wood of which was used by Orientals for the purposes of fumigation and embalming, John 19 : 39 (see also Num. 24 : 6 ; Psa. 45 : 8 ; Prov. 7 : 17).¶ In the Sept., S. of Sol. 4 : 14.¶

ALONE (LET ALONE)
A. Adjective.

MONOS (*μόνος*) denotes single, alone, solitary, Matt. 4 : 4 etc. See ONLY, SELF.

B. Adverbs.

1. MONON (*μόνον*), the neuter of A., meaning only, exclusively, e.g., Rom. 4 : 23 ; Acts 19 : 26, is translated " alone " in the A.V. of John 17 : 20 ; R.V., " only." See ONLY.

2. KATA MONAS (*κατὰ μόνας*) signifies apart, in private, alone, Mark 4 : 10 ; Luke 9 : 18. Some texts have the phrase as one word.¶

C. Verb.

APHIĒMI (*ἀφίημι*) signifies to send away, set free ; also to let alone, Matt. 15 : 14 ; Mark 14 : 6 ; Luke 13 : 8 ; John 11 : 48 ; 12 : 7 (R.V., " suffer her ") ; in Acts 5 : 38 some texts have *easate* from *eaō*, to permit. See CRY, FORGIVE, FORSAKE, LAY, *Note* (2), LEAVE, LET, OMIT, PUT, No. 16, *Note*, REMIT, SEND, SUFFER, YIELD.

Notes : (1) The phrase *kath' heautēn* means " by (or in) itself," Jas. 2 : 17, R.V., for A.V., " being alone " (see A.V., margin).

(2) The phrase *kat' idian*, Mark 4 : 34, signifies in private, " privately," R.V. (A.V., " when they were alone ").

(3) For " let us alone " see AH !

For ALONG see the R.V. of Acts 17 : 23 and 27 : 13.

For ALOUD see CRY, B, No. 2

ALREADY

ĒDĒ (*ἤδη*) is always used of time in the N.T. and means now, at (or by) this time, sometimes in the sense of " already," i.e. without mentioning or insisting upon anything further, e.g., 1 Tim. 5 : 15. In 1 Cor. 4 : 8 and 1 John 2 : 8 the R.V. corrects the A.V. " now," and, in 2 Tim. 4 : 6, the A.V. " now ready to be," by the rendering " already."

See also John 9 : 27 (A.V., " already," R.V., " even now ") and 1 Cor. 6 : 7 (A.V., " now," R.V., " already ").

Notes : (1) *Phthanō*, to anticipate, be beforehand with, signifies to attain already, in Phil. 3 : 16. See ATTAIN, COME, PRECEDE.

(2) *Proamartanō*, to sin before, or heretofore, is translated " have sinned already " in 2 Cor. 12 : 21, A.V. ; both Versions have " heretofore " in 13 : 2.

ALSO

1. KAI (*καί*) has three chief meanings, " and," " also," " even." When *kai* means " also " it precedes the word which it stresses. In English the order should be reversed. In John 9 : 40, e.g., the R.V. rightly has " are we also blind ? " instead of " are we blind also ? " In Acts 2 : 26 the R.V. has " moreover My flesh also," instead of " moreover also . . ." See EVEN.

2. ETI (*ἔτι*), " yet " or " further," is used (*a*) of time, (*b*) of degree, and in this sense is once translated " also," Luke 14 : 26, " his own life also." Here the meaning probably is ' and, further, even his own life ' (the force of the *kai* being " even "). No other particles mean " also." See EVEN, FURTHER, LONGER, MORE, MOREOVER, STILL, THENCEFORTH, YET.

Note : The particle *te* means " both " or " and."

ALTAR

1. THUSIASTĒRION (*θυσιαστήριον*), probably the neuter of the adjective *thusiastērios*, is derived from *thusiazō*, to sacrifice. Accordingly it denotes an altar for the sacrifice of victims, though it was also used for the altar of incense, e.g., Luke 1 : 11. In the N.T. this word is reserved for the altar of the true God, Matt. 5 : 23, 24 ; 23 : 18–20, 35 ; Luke 11 : 51 ; 1 Cor. 9 : 13 ; 10 : 18, in contrast to *bōmos*, No. 2, below. In the Sept. *thusiastērion* is mostly, but not entirely, used for the Divinely appointed altar ; it is used for idol altars, e.g., in Judg. 2 : 2 ; 6 : 25 ; 2 Kings 16 : 10.

2. BŌMOS (*βωμός*), properly, an elevated place, always denotes either a pagan altar or an altar reared without Divine appointment. In the N.T. the only place where this is found is Acts 17 : 23, as this is the only mention of such. Three times in the Sept., but only in the Apocrypha, *bōmos* is used for the Divine altar. In Josh. 22 the Sept. translators have carefully observed the distinction, using *bōmos* for the altar which the two and a half tribes erected, verses 10, 11, 16, 19, 23, 26, 34, no Divine injunction being given for this ; in verses 19, 28, 29, where the altar ordained of God is mentioned, *thusiastērion* is used.¶

For ALTERED see OTHER, No. 2

ALTHOUGH: see Note †, p. 9

ALTOGETHER
A. Adjective.

HOLOS (ὅλος), whole, is rendered "altogether" in John 9 : 34. It is sometimes subjoined to an adjective or a verb, as in this case, to show that the idea conveyed by the adjective or verb belongs to the whole person or thing referred to. So here, lit., 'thou wast altogether (i.e., completely) born in sins.' Cp. Matt. 13 : 33, R.V.; Luke 11 : 36; 13 : 21; John 13 : 10, R.V. (rendered "every whit"). See ALL, and EVERY WHIT.

B. Adverbs.

1. PANTOS (πάντως), from pas, "all," is translated in various ways. The rendering "altogether" is found only in 1 Cor. 5 : 10 (where the R.V. margin gives the alternative meaning, "not at all meaning the fornicators of this world") and 9 : 10 (marg., "doubtless"). The other renderings are, in Luke 4 : 23, "doubtless" (A.V., "surely"); in Acts 18 : 21, "by all means," (A.V., only); so in 1 Cor. 9 : 22, both R.V. and A.V.; in Acts 21 : 22, "certainly" (A.V., "needs," which does not give an accurate meaning); in Acts 28 : 4, "no doubt;" in Rom. 3 : 9, "in no wise" (lit., 'not at all'), so in 1 Cor. 16 : 12. In Acts 26 : 29 the A.V. has given a misleading rendering in the phrase "both almost and altogether;" there is no Greek word here which means "altogether;" the R.V. corrects to "whether with little or with much." See ALL.¶

2. HOLOS denotes altogether or actually, or assuredly. See ACTUALLY, and ALL, B, No. 1.

ALWAY, ALWAYS

1. AEI (ἀεί) has two meanings: (a) perpetually, incessantly, Acts 7 : 51; 2 Cor. 4 : 11; 6 : 10; Tit. 1 : 12; Heb. 3 : 10; (b) invariably, at any and every time, of successive occurrences, when some thing is to be repeated, according to the circumstances, 1 Pet. 3 : 15; 2 Pet. 1 : 12. See EVER.¶

2. HEKASTOTE (ἑκάστοτε), from hekastos, each, is used in 2 Pet. 1 : 15, R.V., "at every time" (A.V., "always"). See TIME.¶

3. DIAPANTOS (διαπαντός) is, lit., 'through all,' i.e., 'through all time,' (dia, through, pas, all). In the best texts the words are separated. The phrase, which is used of the time throughout which a thing is done, is sometimes rendered "continually," sometimes "always;" "always" or "alway" in Mk. 5 : 5; Acts 10 : 2; 24 : 16; Rom. 11 : 10; "continually" in Luke 24 : 53; Heb. 9 : 6; 13 : 15, the idea being that of a continuous practice carried on without being abandoned. See CONTINUALLY.¶

4 and 5. PANTE (πάντη) and PANTOTE (πάντοτε) are derived from pas, all. The former is found in Acts 24 : 3.¶ The latter is the usual word for "always." See EVER, EVERMORE.

Note: Two phrases, rendered "always" or "alway" in the A.V., are *en panti kairō* (lit., ' in every season '), Luke 21 : 36, R.V., " at every season," Eph. 6 : 18, R.V., " at all seasons," and *pasas tas hēmeras*, (lit., ' all the days '), Matt. 28 : 20, A.V. and R.V., " alway."

AMAZE, AMAZEMENT
A. Nouns.

1. EKSTASIS (ἔκστασις) is, lit., ' a standing out (*ek*, out of, *stasis*, a standing).' Eng. " ecstasy " is a transliteration. It is translated " amazement " in Acts 3 : 10. It was said of any displacement, and hence, especially, with reference to the mind, of that alteration of the normal coñdition by which the person is thrown into a state of surprise or fear, or both ; or again, in which a person is so transported out of his natural state that he falls into a trance, Acts 10 : 10 ; 11 : 5 ; 22 : 17. As to the other meaning, the R.V. has " amazement " in Mark 5 : 42 and Luke 5 : 26, but " astonishment " in Mark 16 : 8. See TRANCE.¶

2. THAMBOS (θάμβος), amazement, wonder, is probably connected with a root signifying to render immovable ; it is frequently associated with terror as well as astonishment, as with the verb (No. 3, below) in Acts 9 : 6. It occurs in Luke 4 : 36 ; 5 : 9 ; Acts 3 : 10. See WONDER.¶

Note : Ptoēsis signifies " terror," not " amazement," 1 Pet. 3 : 6, R.V.¶

B. Verbs.

1. EXISTĒMI (ἐξίστημι), akin to A, No. 1, lit. means to stand out from. Like the noun, this is used with two distinct meanings : (*a*) in the sense of amazement, the word should be invariably rendered " amazed," as in the R.V., e.g., in the case of Simon Magus (for A.V., " bewitched "), Acts 8 : 9 and 11. It is used, in the Passive Voice, of Simon himself in the 13th ver., R.V., " he was amazed," for A.V., " wondered." " Amaze " is preferable to " astonish " throughout ; (*b*) in Mark 3 : 21 and 2 Cor. 5 : 13 it is used with its other meaning of being beside oneself. See BESIDE ONESELF (to be), BEWITCH, WONDER.

2. EKPLĒSSŌ (ἐκπλήσσω), from *ek*, out of, *plēssō*, to strike, lit., to strike out, signifies to be exceedingly struck in mind, to be astonished (*ek*, intensive). The English " astonish " should be used for this verb, and " amaze " for *existēmi*, as in the R.V. ; see Matt. 19 : 25 ; Luke 2 : 48 ; 9 : 43.

3. THAMBEŌ (θαμβέω), akin to A, Nò. 2, is used in Mark 1 : 27 ; 10 : 24, 32 (and Acts 9 : 6, A.V.)'. The R.V. has " amazed " in each place ; A.V., " astonished," in Mark 10 : 24.¶

4. EKTHAMBEŌ (ἐκθαμβέω), an intensive form of No. 3, is found in Mark's Gospel only ; in 9 : 15, " were greatly amazed ; " in 14 : 33, A.V., " were sore amazed ; " in 16 : 5, R.V., " were amazed," A.V., " were affrighted ; " in ver. 6, R.V., " be not amazed," A.V., " be not affrighted." See AFFRIGHTED.¶

C. Adjective.

EKTHAMBOS (ἔκθαμβος), a strengthened form of A, No. 2, is found in

Acts 3 : 11. The intensive force of the word is brought out by the rendering " greatly wondering." See WONDER.¶

AMBASSADOR, AMBASSAGE
A. Verb.

PRESBEUŌ (πρεσβεύω) denotes (a) to be elder or eldest, prior in birth or age ; (b) to be an ambassador, 2 Cor. 5 : 20, and Eph. 6 : 20 ; for Philm. 9 see under AGED. There is a suggestion that to be an ambassador for Christ involves the experience suggested by the word " elder." Elder men were chosen as ambassadors.

B. Noun.

PRESBEIA (πρεσβεία), primarily, age, eldership, rank, hence, an embassy or ambassage, is used in Luke 14 : 32 ; in 19 : 14, R.V., " ambassage," for A.V., " message."¶

AMEN

AMĒN (ἀμήν) is transliterated from Hebrew into both Greek and English. " Its meanings may be seen in such passages as Deut. 7 : 9, ' the faithful (the Amen) God,' Isa. 49 : 7, ' Jehovah that is faithful,' 65 : 16, ' the God of truth,' marg., ' the God of Amen.' And if God is faithful His testimonies and precepts are ' sure (amen),' Psa. 19 : 7 ; 111 : 7, as are also His warnings, Hos. 5 : 9, and promises, Isa. 33 : 16 ; 55 : 3. ' Amen ' is used of men also, e.g., Prov. 25 : 13.

" There are cases where the people used it to express their assent to a law and their willingness to submit to the penalty attached to the breach of it, Deut. 27 : 15, cp. Neh. 5 : 13. It is also used to express acquiescence in another's prayer, 1 Kings 1 : 36, where it is defined as ' (let) God say so too,' or in another's thanksgiving, 1 Chron. 16 : 36, whether by an individual, Jer. 11 : 5, or by the congregation, Psa. 106 : 48.

" Thus ' Amen ' said by God = ' it is and shall be so,' and by men, ' so let it be.'

" Once in the N.T. ' Amen ' is a title of Christ, Rev. 3 : 14, because through Him the purposes of God are established, 2 Cor. 1 : 20.

" The early Christian churches followed the example of Israel in associating themselves audibly with the prayers and thanksgivings offered on their behalf, 1 Cor. 14 : 16, where the article ' the ' points to a common practice. Moreover this custom conforms to the pattern of things in the Heavens, see Rev. 5 : 14, etc.

" The individual also said ' Amen ' to express his ' let it be so ' in response to the Divine ' thus it shall be,' Rev. 22 : 20. Frequently the speaker adds ' Amen ' to his own prayers and doxologies, as is the case at Eph. 3 : 21, e.g.

" The Lord Jesus often used ' Amen,' translated ' verily,' to introduce new revelations of the mind of God. In John's Gospel it is always repeated, ' Amen, Amen,' but not elsewhere. Luke does not use it at all, but where Matthew, 16 : 28, and Mark, 9 : 1, have 'Amen,' Luke has 'of a truth ; ' thus by varying the translation of what the Lord said, Luke throws light on His meaning."* See VERILY.

AMEND

ECHŌ KOMPSOTERON, lit., to have more finely, i.e., to be better, is used in John 4 : 52, " to amend." The latter word in the phrase is the comparative of *kompsos*, elegant, nice, fine. Cp. Eng., " he's doing nicely."¶

AMETHYST

AMETHUSTOS (ἀμέθυστος), primarily meaning " not drunken " (*a*, negative, and *methu*, wine), became used as a noun, being regarded as possessing a remedial virtue against drunkenness. Pliny, however, says that the reason for its name lay in the fact that in colour it nearly approached that of wine, but did not actually do so, Rev. 21 : 20.¶

For AMIDST see MIDST

AMISS
A. Adjective.

ATOPOS (ἄτοπος), lit., out of place (*a*, negative, *topos*, a place), hence denotes unbecoming, not befitting. It is used four times in the N.T., and is rendered " amiss " three times in the R.V. ; in the malefactor's testimony of Christ, Luke 23 : 41 ; in Festus's words concerning Paul, Acts 25 : 5, " if there is anything amiss in the man " (A.V., " wickedness ") ; in Acts 28 : 6, of the expected effect of the viper's attack upon Paul (A.V., " harm ") ; in 2 Thess. 3 : 2, of men capable of outrageous conduct, " unreasonable." See HARM, UNREASONABLE.

B. Adverb.

KAKŌS (κακῶς), akin to *kakos*, evil, is translated " amiss " in Jas. 4 : 3 ; elsewhere in various ways. See EVIL, GRIEVOUS, MISERABLE, SORE.

AMONG : See Note †, p. 9

For ANATHEMA see under CURSE

ANCHOR

ANKURA (ἄγκυρα), Eng., anchor, was so called because of its curved form (*ankos*, a curve), Acts 27 : 29, 30, 40 ; Heb. 6 : 19. In Acts 27 : 13 the verb *airō*, to lift, signifies to lift anchor (the noun being understood), R.V., " they weighed anchor " (A.V., " loosing thence ").¶

---

* From Notes on Galatians by Hogg and Vine, pp. 26, 27.

ANEW

ANŌTHEN (ἄνωθεν), lit., 'from above,' in the phrase rendered " anew " in the R.V. (A.V., " again ") of John 3 : 3, 7. See AGAIN.

Note : In Phil. 3 : 21 " fashion anew " translates the verb *metaschēmatizō*, which signifies to change the form of.

ANGEL

ANGELOS (ἄγγελος), a messenger (from *angellō*, to deliver a message), sent whether by God or by man or by Satan, " is also used of a guardian or representative in Rev. 1 : 20, cp. Matt. 18 : 10 ; Acts 12 : 15 (where it is better understood as = ' ghost '), but most frequently of an order of created beings, superior to man, Heb. 2 : 7 ; Psa. 8 : 5, belonging to Heaven, Matt. 24 : 36 ; Mark 12 : 25, and to God, Luke 12 : 8, and engaged in His service, Psa. 103 : 20. Angels are spirits, Heb. 1 : 14, i.e., they have not material bodies as men have ; they are either human in form, or can assume the human form when necessary, cp. Luke 24 : 4, with ver. 23, Acts 10 : 3 with ver. 30.

" They are called ' holy ' in Mark 8 : 38, and ' elect,' 1 Tim. 5 : 21, in contrast with some of their original number, Matt. 25 : 41, who ' sinned,' 2 Pet. 2 : 4, ' left their proper habitation,' Jude 6, *oikētērion*, a word which occurs again, in the N.T., only in 2 Cor. 5 : 2. Angels are always spoken of in the masculine gender, the feminine form of the word does not occur."*

Note : Isangelos, " equal to the angels," occurs in Luke 20 : 36.¶

ANGER, ANGRY (to be)
A. Noun.

ORGĒ (ὀργή), originally any natural impulse, or desire, or disposition, came to signify anger, as the strongest of all passions. It is used of the wrath of man, Eph. 4 : 31 ; Col. 3 : 8 ; 1 Tim. 2 : 8 ; Jas. 1 : 19, 20 ; the displeasure of human governments, Rom. 13 : 4, 5 ; the sufferings of the Jews at the hands of the Gentiles, Luke 21 : 23 ; the terrors of the Law, Rom. 4 : 15 ; the anger of the Lord Jesus, Mark 3 : 5 ; God's anger with Israel in the wilderness, in a quotation from the O.T., Heb. 3 : 11 ; 4 : 3 ; God's present anger with the Jews nationally, Rom. 9 : 22 ; 1 Thess. 2 : 16 ; His present anger with those who disobey the Lord Jesus in His Gospel, John 3 : 36 ; God's purposes in judgment, Matt. 3 : 7 ; Luke 3 : 7 ; Rom. 1 : 18 ; 2 : 5, 8 ; 3 : 5 ; 5 : 9 ; 12 : 19 ; Eph. 2 : 3 ; 5 : 6 ; Col. 3 : 6 ; 1 Thess. 1 : 10 ; 5 : 9. See INDIGNATION, VENGEANCE, WRATH.¶

Notes : (1) *Thumos*, wrath (not translated " anger "), is to be distinguished from *orgē*, in this respect, that *thumos* indicates a more agitated condition of the feelings, an outburst of wrath from inward indignation, while *orgē* suggests a more settled or abiding condition of mind, frequently with a view to taking revenge. *Orgē* is less sudden in its rise than *thumos*,

---

* From Notes on Thessalonians by Hogg and Vine, p. 229.

but more lasting in its nature. *Thumos* expresses more the inward feeling, *orgē* the more active emotion. *Thumos* may issue in revenge, though it does not necessarily include it. It is characteristic that it quickly blazes up and quickly subsides, though that is not necessarily implied in each case.

(2) *Parorgismos*, a strengthened form of *orgē*, and used in Eph. 4 : 26, R.V. margin, " provocation," points especially to that which provokes the wrath, and suggests a less continued state than No. (1). " The first keenness of the sense of provocation must not be cherished, though righteous resentment may remain " (Westcott). The preceding verb, *orgizō*, in this verse implies a just occasion for the feeling. This is confirmed by the fact that it is a quotation from Psa. 4 : 4 (Sept.), where the Hebrew word signifies to quiver with strong emotion.

Thumos is found eighteen times in the N.T., ten of which are in the Apocalypse, in seven of which the reference is to the wrath of God ; so in Rom. 2 : 8, R.V., " wrath (*thumos*) and indignation " (*orgē*) ; the order in the A.V. is inaccurate. Everywhere else the word *thumos* is used in a bad sense. In Gal. 5 : 20, it follows the word jealousies, which when smouldering in the heart break out in wrath. *Thumos* and *orgē* are coupled in two places in the Apocalypse, 16 : 19, " the fierceness (*thumos*) of His wrath " (*orgē*) ; and 19 : 15, " the fierceness of the wrath of Almighty God." See WROTH (be).

(3) *Aganaktēsis* originally signified physical pain or irritation (probably from *agan*, very much, and *achomai*, to grieve), hence, annoyance, vexation, and is used in 2 Cor. 7 : 11, " indignation."¶

B. Verbs.

1. ORGIZŌ (ὀργίζω), to provoke, to arouse to anger, is used in the Middle Voice in the eight places where it is found, and signifies to be angry, wroth. It is said of individuals, in Matt. 5 : 22 ; 18 : 34 ; 22 : 7 ; Luke 14 : 21 ; 15 : 28, and Eph. 4 : 26 (where a possible meaning is " be ye angry with yourselves ") ; of nations, Rev. 11 : 18 ; of Satan as the Dragon, 12 : 17. See WRATH.¶

2. PARORGIZŌ (παροργίζω) is to arouse to wrath, provoke (*para*, used intensively, and No. 1) ; Rom. 10 : 19, " will I anger ; " Eph. 6 : 4, " provoke to wrath." See PROVOKE.¶

3. CHOLAŌ (χολάω), connected with *cholē*, gall, bile, which became used metaphorically to signify bitter anger, means to be enraged, John 7 : 23, " wroth," R.V., in the Lord's remonstrance with the Jews on account of their indignation at His having made a man whole on the Sabbath Day.¶

Notes : (1) *Thumomacheō* (from *thumos*, wrath, *machomai*, to fight) originally denoted to fight with great animosity, and hence came to mean to be very angry, to be exasperated, Acts 12 : 20, of the anger of Herod, " was highly displeased."¶

(2) *Thumoō*, the corresponding verb, signifies to provoke to anger,

but in the Passive Voice to be wroth, as in Matt. 2 : 16, of the wrath of Herod, " was exceeding wroth."¶

(3) *Aganakteō*, see A, Note (3), is rendered in various ways in the seven places where it is used ; " moved with indignation," Matt. 20 : 24 and 21 : 15, R.V. (A.V., " sore displeased ") ; " had indignation," Matt. 26 : 8 ; Mark 14 : 4. In Mark 10 : 14 the R.V. has " was moved with indignation " (A.V., " was much displeased "), said of the Lord Jesus. The same renderings are given in ver. 41. In Luke 13 : 14 (A.V., " with indignation "), the R.V. rightly puts " being moved with indignation." These words more particularly point to the cause of the vexation. See DISPLEASE, INDIGNATION.¶

(4) In Col. 3 : 21 *erethizō* signifies to provoke. The R.V. correctly omits " to anger."

C. Adjective.

ORGILOS (ὀργίλος), angry, prone to anger, irascible (see B, Nos. 1, 2), is rendered " soon angry " in Tit. 1 : 7.¶

ANGUISH
A. Nouns.

1. THLIPSIS (θλῖψις) ; see AFFLICTION (No. 4).

2. STENOCHŌRIA (στενοχωρία), lit., narrowness of place (*stenos*, narrow, *chōra*, a place), metaphorically came to mean the distress arising from that condition, anguish. It is used in the plural, of various forms of distress, 2 Cor. 6 : 4 and 12 : 10, and of anguish or distress in general, Rom. 2 : 9 ; 8 : 35, R.V., " anguish " for A.V., " distress." The opposite state, of being in a large place, and so metaphorically in a state of joy, is represented by the word *platusmos* in certain Psalms as, e.g., Psa. 118 : 5 ; see also 2 Sam. 22 : 20. See DISTRESS.¶

3. SUNOCHĒ (συνοχή), lit., a holding together, or compressing (*sun*, together, *echō*, to hold), was used of the narrowing of a way. It is found only in its metaphorical sense, of straits, distress, anguish, Luke 21 : 25, " distress of nations," and 2 Cor. 2 : 4, " anguish of heart." See DISTRESS.¶

Note : *Ananké* is associated with *thlipsis*, and signifies a condition of necessity arising from some form of compulsion. It is therefore used not only of necessity but of distress, Luke 21 : 23 ; 1 Thess. 3 : 7, and in the plural in 2 Cor. 6 : 4 ; 12 : 10.

B. Verbs.

1. STENOCHŌREŌ (στενοχωρέω), akin to A, No. 2, lit., to crowd into a narrow space, or, in the Passive Voice to be pressed for room, hence, metaphorically, to be straitened, 2 Cor. 4 : 8 and 6 : 12 (twice), is found in its literal sense in two places in the Sept., in Josh. 17 : 15 and Isa. 49 : 19, and in two places in its metaphorical sense, in Judg. 16 : 16, where Delilah is said to have pressed Samson sore with her words continually, and to have " straitened him," and in Isa. 28 : 20. See DISTRESS, STRAITENED.¶

2. SUNECHŌ (συνέχω), akin to A, No. 3, lit., to hold together, is used physically of being held, or thronged, Luke 8 : 45 ; 19 : 43 ; 22 : 63 ; of being taken with a malady, Matt. 4 : 24 ; Luke 4 : 38 ; Acts 28 : 8 ; with fear, Luke 8 : 37 ; of being straitened or pressed in spirit, with desire, Luke 12 : 50 ; Acts 18 : 5 ; Phil. 1 : 23 ; with the love of Christ, 2 Cor. 5 : 14.   In one place it is used of the stopping of their ears by those who killed Stephen.   See CONSTRAIN, HOLD, KEEP, PRESS, SICK (lie), STOP, STRAIT (be in a), STRAITENED, TAKE, THRONG.

3. ODUNAŌ (ὀδυνάω), in the Middle and Passive Voices, signifies to suffer pain, be in anguish, be greatly distressed (akin to odunē, pain, distress) ; it is rendered " sorrowing " in Luke 2 : 48; in 16 : 24, 25, R.V., " in anguish," for A.V., " tormented ; " in Acts 20 : 38, " sorrowing." See SORROW, TORMENT.¶

For ANIMALS (2 Pet. 2 : 12, R.V.), see NATURAL.

ANISE
ANĒTHON (ἄνηθον), dill, anise, was used for food and for pickling, Matt. 23 : 23.¶

ANKLE-BONES
SPHURON (σφυρόν) or SPHUDRON (σφυδρόν) denotes the ankle, or ankle-bone (from sphura, a hammer, owing to a resemblance in the shape), Acts 3 : 7.¶

ANNOUNCE
ANANGELLŌ (ἀναγγέλλω), to declare, announce (ana, up, angellō, to report), is used especially of heavenly messages, and is translated " announced " in the R.V. of 1 Pet. 1 : 12, for A.V., " reported," and in 1 John 1 : 5, R.V., " announce," for A.V., " declare." See DECLARE, REHEARSE, REPORT, SHOW, SPEAK, TELL.

ANOINT, ANOINTING
A. Verbs.
1. ALEIPHŌ (ἀλείφω) is a general term used for an anointing of any kind, whether of physical refreshment after washing, e.g., in the Sept. of Ruth 3 : 3 ; 2 Sam. 12 : 20 ; Dan. 10 : 3 ; Micah 6 : 15 ; in the N.T., Matt. 6 : 17 ; Luke 7 : 38, 46 ; John 11 : 2 ; 12 : 3 ; or of the sick, Mark 6 : 13 ; Jas. 5 : 14 ; or a dead body, Mark 16 : 1.   The material used was either oil, or ointment, as in Luke 7 : 38, 46.¶   In the Sept. it is also used of anointing a pillar, Gen. 31 : 13, or captives, 2 Chron. 28 : 15, or of daubing a wall with mortar, Ezek. 13 : 10, 11, 12, 14, 15 ; and, in the sacred sense, of anointing priests, in Ex. 40 : 15 (twice), and Numb. 3 : 3.

2. CHRIŌ (χρίω) is more limited in its use than No. 1 ; it is confined to sacred and symbolical anointings ; of Christ as the Anointed of God, Luke 4 : 18 ; Acts 4 : 27 ; 10 : 38, and Heb. 1 : 9, where it is used meta-

phorically in connection with " the oil of gladness." The title Christ signifies " The Anointed One." The word (*Christos*) is rendered " (His) Anointed " in Acts 4 : 26, R.V. Once it is said of believers, 2 Cor. 1 : 21. *Chrio* is very frequent in the Sept., and is used of kings, 1 Sam. 10 : 1, and priests, Ex. 28 : 41, and prophets, 1 Kings 19 : 16. Among the Greeks it was used in other senses than the ceremonial, but in the Scriptures it is not found in connection with secular matters.¶

Note : The distinction referred to by Trench (Syn. § xxxviii), that *aleiphō* is the mundane and profane, *chriō*, the sacred and religious word, is not borne out by evidence. In a papyrus document *chrisis* is used of " a lotion for a sick horse " (Moulton and Milligan, Vocab. of Greek Test).

3. ENCHRIŌ (ἐγχρίω), primarily, to rub in, hence, to besmear, to anoint, is used metaphorically in the command to the church in Laodicea to anoint their eyes with eyesalve, Rev. 3 : 18.¶ In the Sept., Jer. 4 : 30, it is used of the anointing of the eyes with a view to beautifying them.

4. EPICHRIŌ (ἐπιχρίω), primarily, to rub on (*epi*, upon), is used of the blind man whose eyes Christ anointed, and indicates the manner in which the anointing was done, John 9 : 6, 11.¶

5. MURIZŌ (μυρίζω) is used of anointing the body for burial, in Mark 14 : 8.¶

B. Noun.

CHRISMA (χρίσμα), the corresponding noun to No. 2, above, signifies an unguent, or an anointing. It was prepared from oil and aromatic herbs. It is used only metaphorically in the N.T. ; by metonymy, of the Holy Spirit, 1 John 2 : 20, 27, twice. The R.V. translates it " anointing " in all three places, instead of the A.V. " unction " and " anointing."

That believers have " an anointing from the Holy One " indicates that this anointing renders them holy, separating them to God. The passage teaches that the gift of the Holy Spirit is the all-efficient means of enabling believers to possess a knowledge of the truth. In the Sept., it is used of the oil for anointing the high priest, e.g., Ex. 29 : 7, lit., ' Thou shalt take of the oil of the anointing.' In Ex. 30 : 25, etc., it is spoken of as " a holy anointing oil." In Dan. 9 : 26 *chrisma* stands for the anointed one, " Christ," the noun standing by metonymy for the Person Himself, as for the Holy Spirit in 1 John 2. See UNCTION.¶

Notes : (1) *Aleimma*, akin to A, No. 1 (not in the N.T.), occurs three times in the Sept., Ex. 30 : 31, of the anointing of the priests ; Isa. 61 : 3, metaphorically, of the oil of joy ; Dan. 10 : 3, of physical refreshment.

(2) *Muron*, a word akin to A, No. 5, denotes ointment. The distinction between this and *elaion*, oil, is observable in Christ's reproof of the Pharisee who, while desiring Him to eat with him, failed in the ordinary marks of courtesy ; " My head with oil (*elaion*) thou didst not anoint, but she hath anointed My feet with ointment " (*muron*), Luke 7 : 46.

ANON

Note : This is the A.V. rendering of *euthus*, in Matt. 13 : 20 and Mark 1 : 30, R.V., "straightway."

ANOTHER

ALLOS (ἄλλος) and HETEROS (ἕτερος) have a difference in meaning, which despite a tendency to be lost, is to be observed in numerous passages. *Allos* expresses a numerical difference and denotes another of the same sort ; *heteros* expresses a qualitative difference and denotes another of a different sort. Christ promised to send "another Comforter" (*allos*, another like Himself, not *heteros*), John 14 : 16. Paul says "I see a different (A.V., 'another') law," *heteros*, a law different from that of the spirit of life (not *allos*, a law of the same sort), Rom. 7 : 23. After Joseph's death "another king arose," *heteros*, one of quite a different character, Acts 7 : 18. Paul speaks of "a different gospel (*heteros*), which is not another" (*allos*, another like the one he preached), Gal. 1 : 6, 7. See *heteros* (not *allos*) in Matt. 11 : 3, and Acts 27 : 1 ; in Luke 23 : 32 *heteroi* is used of the two malefactors crucified with Christ. The two words are only apparently interchanged in 1 Cor. 1 : 16 and 6 : 1 ; 12 : 8–10 ; 14 : 17 and 19, e.g., the difference being present, though not so readily discernible.

They are not interchangeable in 1 Cor. 15 : 39–41 ; here *heteros* is used to distinguish the heavenly glory from the earthly, for these differ in genus, and *allos* to distinguish the flesh of men, birds, and fishes, which in each case is flesh differing not in genus but in species. *Allos* is used again to distinguish between the glories of the heavenly bodies, for these also differ not in kind but in degree only. For *allos*, see MORE, OTHER, etc. For *heteros*, see OTHER, STRANGE.

Note : The distinction comes out in the compounds of *heteros*, viz., *heteroglōssos*, "strange tongues," 1 Cor. 14 : 21 ; ¶ ; *heterodidaskaleō*, "to teach a different doctrine," 1 Tim. 1 : 3 ; 6 : 3 ; ¶ ; *heterozugō*, "to be unequally yoked" (i.e., with those of a different character), 2 Cor. 6 : 14.¶

ANSWER
A. Nouns.

1. APOKRISIS (ἀπόκρισις), lit., a separation or distinction, is the regular word for "answer," Luke 2 : 47 ; 20 : 26 ; John 1 : 22 and 19 : 9.¶

2. APOKRIMA (ἀπόκριμα), akin to No. 1, denotes a judicial "sentence," 2 Cor. 1 : 9, A.V., and R.V., margin, or an "answer" (R.V., text), an answer of God to the Apostle's appeal, giving him strong confidence. In an ancient inscription it is used of an official decision. In a papyrus document it is used of a reply to a deputation. See SENTENCE.¶

3. CHRĒMATISMOS (χρηματισμός), a Divine response, an oracle, is used in Rom. 11 : 4, of the answer given by God to Elijah's complaint against Israel.¶ See the verb under CALL.

4. APOLOGIA (ἀπολογία), a verbal defence, a speech in defence, is sometimes translated "answer," in the A.V., Acts 25 : 16; 1 Cor. 9 : 3; 2 Tim. 4 : 16, all which the R.V. corrects to "defence." See Acts 22 : 1; Phil. 1 : 7, 16; 2 Cor. 7 : 11, "clearing." Once it signifies an "answer," 1 Pet. 3 : 15. Cp. B, No. 4. See CLEARING, DEFENCE.¶

Note : Eperōtēma, 1 Pet. 3 : 21, is not, as in the A.V., an "answer." It was used by the Greeks in a legal sense, as a demand or appeal. Baptism is therefore the ground of an appeal by a good conscience against wrong doing.¶

B. Verbs.

1. APOKRINOMAI (ἀποκρίνομαι), akin to A, No. 1, above, signifies either to give an answer to a question (its more frequent use) or to begin to speak, but always where something has preceded, either statement or act to which the remarks refer, e.g., Matt. 11 : 25; Luke 14 : 3; John 2 : 18. The R.V. translates by "answered," e.g., Matt. 28 : 5; Mark 12 : 35; Luke 3 : 16, where some have suggested 'began to say' or 'uttered solemnly,' whereas the speaker is replying to the unuttered thought or feeling of those addressed by him.

2. ANTAPOKRINOMAI (ἀνταποκρίνομαι), anti, against, and No. 1, a strengthened form, to answer by contradiction, to reply against, is found in Luke 14 : 6 and Rom. 9 : 20.¶

3. HUPOLAMBANŌ (ὑπολαμβάνω) signifies (a) to take or bear up from beneath, Acts 1 : 9; (b) to receive, 3 John 8; (c) to suppose, Luke 7 : 43; Acts 2 : 15; (d) to catch up (in speech), to answer, Luke 10 : 3c; in sense (d) it indicates that a person follows what another has said, either by controverting or supplementing it. See RECEIVE, SUPPOSE.¶

4. APOLOGEOMAI (ἀπολογέομαι), cp. A, No. 4, lit., to talk oneself off from (apo, from, legō, to speak), to answer by way of making a defence for oneself (besides its meaning to excuse, Rom. 2 : 15; 2 Cor. 12 : 19), is translated "answer" in Luke 12 : 11; 21 : 14; in Acts 19 : 33, A.V. and R.V. both have "made defence;" in Acts 24 : 10; 25 : 8; 26 : 1, 2, the R.V. has the verb to make a defence, for the A.V., to answer, and in 26 : 24 for the A.V., "spake for himself." See DEFENCE, EXCUSE, SPEAK.¶

5. ANTILEGŌ (ἀντιλέγω), to speak against, is rendered "answering again" in the A.V. of Tit. 2 : 9 (R.V., "gainsaying"). See CONTRADICT, DENY, GAINSAY, SPEAK.

6. SUSTOICHEŌ (συστοιχέω), lit., to be in the same line or row with (sun, with, stoichos, a row), is translated "answereth to" in Gal. 4 : 25.¶

Note : Cp. *stoicheō*, to walk (in line), 5 : 25; 6 : 16. For *hupakouō*, rendered to answer in Acts 12 : 13, R.V., see HEARKEN, No. 1, *Note*.

ANTICHRIST

ANTICHRISTOS (ἀντίχριστος) can mean either against Christ or instead of Christ, or perhaps, combining the two, "one who, assuming the guise of Christ, opposes Christ " (Westcott). The word is found only in John's Epistles, (a) of the many antichrists who are forerunners of the Antichrist himself, 1 John 2 : 18, 22 ; 2 John 7 ; (b) of the evil power which already operates anticipatively of the Antichrist, 1 John 4 : 3.¶

What the Apostle says of him so closely resembles what he says of the first beast in Rev. 13, and what the Apostle Paul says of the Man of Sin in 2 Thess. 2, that the same person seems to be in view in all these passages, rather than the second beast in Rev. 13, the false prophet ; for the latter supports the former in all his Antichristian assumptions.

Note : The term *pseudochristos*, a false Christ, is to be distinguished from the above ; it is found in Matt. 24 : 24 and Mark 13 : 22. The false Christ does not deny the existence of Christ, he trades upon the expectation of His appearance, affirming that he is the Christ. The Antichrist denies the existence of the true God (Trench, Syn. §, xxx).¶

For ANXIETY and ANXIOUS see CARE, A, No. 1, B, No. 1

ANY : see Note †, p. 9

ANYTHING

Note : See the R.V. of Mark 15 : 5 ; John 16 : 23 ; 1 Tim. 6 : 7 ; in Luke 24 : 41, the R.V. suitably has " anything to eat," for, A.V., " any meat."

APART

1. CHŌRIS (χωρίς) is used both as an adverb and as a preposition. As an adverb it signifies separately, by itself, John 20 : 7, of the napkin which had been around the Lord's head in the tomb ; as a preposition (its more frequent use), apart from, without, separate from. It is rendered " apart from " in the R.V. of John 15 : 5 ; Rom. 3 : 21, 28 ; 4 : 6 ; 2 Cor. 12 : 3 ; Heb. 9 : 22, 28 ; 11 : 40 ; Jas. 2 : 18, 20, 26. See BESIDE, WITHOUT.

Note : The opposite of *chōris* is *sun*, with. A synonymous preposition, *aneu*, denotes without, Matt. 10 : 29 ; 1 Pet. 3 : 1 and 4 : 9.¶

2. KAT' IDIAN (κατ' ἰδίαν), lit., according to one's own, i.e., privately, alone, is translated " apart " in Matt. 14 : 13, 23 ; 17 : 1, 19 ; 20 : 17 ; Mark 6 : 31, 32 (A.V., " privately ") ; 9 : 2.

3. KATA MONAS (κατὰ μόνας) : see ALONE.

APIECE

ANA (ἀνά), used with numerals or measures of quantity with a distributive force, is translated " apiece " in Luke 9 : 3, " two coats apiece," A.V. ; in John 2 : 6, " two or three firkins apiece." In Matt. 20 : 9, 10, " every man a penny," is a free rendering for " a penny apiece ; " in

Luke 9 : 14, the R.V. adds "each" to translate the *ana*; in 10 : 1, *ana duo* is "two by two." See Rev. 4 : 8, "each." See EACH, EVERY.

APOSTLE, APOSTLESHIP

1. APOSTOLOS (ἀπόστολος) is, lit., one sent forth (*apo*, from, *stellō*, to send). "The word is used of the Lord Jesus to describe His relation to God, Heb. 3 : 1; see John 17 : 3. The twelve disciples chosen by the Lord for special training were so called, Luke 6 : 13; 9 : 10. Paul, though he had seen the Lord Jesus, 1 Cor. 9 : 1; 15 : 8, had not 'companied with' the Twelve 'all the time' of His earthly ministry, and hence was not eligible for a place among them, according to Peter's description of the necessary qualifications, Acts 1 : 22. Paul was commissioned directly, by the Lord Himself, after His Ascension, to carry the Gospel to the Gentiles.

"The word has also a wider reference. In Acts 14 : 4, 14, it is used of Barnabas as well as of Paul; in Rom. 16 : 7 of Andronicus and Junias. In 2 Cor. 8 : 23 (R.V., margin) two unnamed brethren are called 'apostles of the churches;' in Phil. 2 : 25 (R.V., margin) Epaphroditus is referred to as 'your apostle.' It is used in 1 Thess. 2 : 6 of Paul, Silas and Timothy, to define their relation to Christ."*

2. APOSTOLĒ (ἀποστολή), a sending, a mission, signifies an apostleship, Acts 1 : 25; Rom. 1 : 5; 1 Cor. 9 : 2; Gal. 2 : 8.¶

Note : Pseudapostoloi, "false apostles," occurs in 2 Cor. 11 : 13.¶

APPAREL, APPARELLED

1. ESTHĒS (ἐσθής) and ESTHĒSIS (ἔσθησις), connected with *hennumi*, to clothe mean clothing, raiment, usually suggesting the ornate, the goodly. The former is found in Luke 23 : 11, R.V., "apparel" (A.V., "robe"); 24 : 4 (A.V., "garments"); Acts 10 : 30 (A.V., "clothing"); 12 : 21; Jas. 2 : 2 (R.V., "clothing," twice; A.V., "apparel" and "raiment"); 2 : 3 ("clothing"). *Esthēsis* is used in Acts 1 : 10, "apparel." See CLOTHING.¶

2. HIMATION (ἱμάτιον), a diminutive of *heima*, a robe, was used especially of an outer cloak or mantle, and in general of raiment, "apparel" in 1 Pet. 3 : 3. The word is not in the original in·the next verse, but is supplied in English to complete the sentence. See CLOTHING, No. 2, GARMENT, RAIMENT, ROBE.

3. HIMATISMOS (ἱματισμός), a collective word, is translated "apparelled" in Luke 7 : 25, and preceded by *en*, "in," lit., 'in apparel.' See CLOTHING, No. 4, RAIMENT, VESTURE.

4. KATASTOLĒ (καταστολή), connected with *katastellō*, to send or let down, to lower (*kata*, down, *stellō*, to send), was primarily a garment let down; hence, dress, attire, in general (cp. *stolē*, a loose outer garment worn by kings and persons of rank,—Eng., stole); 1 Tim. 2 : 9, "apparel." See CLOTHING.¶

---

* From Notes on Thessalonians by Hogg and Vine, pp. 59, 60.

APPARITION

PHANTASMA (φάντασμα), a phantasm or phantom (from *phainō*, to appear), is translated " apparition " in the R.V. of Matt. 14 : 26 and Mark 6 : 49 (A.V., " spirit ").¶ In the Sept., Job 20 : 8 ; Is. 28 : 7.¶

APPEAL

EPIKALEŌ (ἐπικαλέω), to call upon, has the meaning appeal in the Middle Voice, which carries with it the suggestion of a special interest on the part of the doer of an action in that in which he is engaged. Stephen died " calling upon the Lord," Acts 7 : 59. In the more strictly legal sense the word is used only of Paul's appeal to Cæsar, Acts 25 : 11, 12, 21, 25 ; 26 : 32 ; 28 : 19. See CALL (upon), SURNAME. See also *eperotēma*, under ANSWER.

APPEAR, APPEARING
A. Verbs.

1. PHAINŌ (φαίνω) signifies, in the Active Voice, to shine ; in the Passive, to be brought forth into light, to become evident, to appear. In Rom. 7 : 13, concerning sin, the R.V. has " might be shewn to be," for A.V., " appear."

It is used of the appearance of Christ to the disciples, Mark 16 : 9 ; of His future appearing in glory as the Son of Man, spoken of as a sign to the world, Matt. 24 : 30 ; there the gen tive is subjective, the sign being the appearing of Christ Himself ; of Christ as the light, John 1 : 5 ; of John the Baptist, 5 : 35 ; of the appearing of an angel of the Lord, either visibly, Matt. 1 : 20, or in a dream, 2 : 13 ; of a star, 2 : 7 ; of men who make an outward show, Matt. 6 : 5 ; 6 : 18 (see the R.V.) ; 23 : 27, 28 ; 2 Cor. 13 : 7 ; of tares, Matt. 13 : 26 ; of a vapour, Jas. 4 : 14 ; of things physical in general, Heb. 11 : 3 ; used impersonally in Matt. 9 : 33, " it was never so seen ; " also of what appears to the mind, and so in the sense of to think, Mark 14 : 64, or to seem, Luke 24 : 11 (R.V., " appeared "). See SEE, SEEM, SHINE, THINK.

2. EPIPHAINŌ (ἐπιφαίνω), a strengthened form of No. 1 but differing in meaning, *epi* signifying upon, is used in the Active Voice with the meaning to give light, Luke 1 : 79 ; in the Passive Voice, to appear, become visible. It is said of heavenly bodies, e.g., the stars, Acts 27 : 20 (R.V., " shone ") ; metaphorically, of things spiritual, the grace of God, Tit. 2 : 11 ; the kindness and the love of God, 3 : 4. See LIGHT.¶ Cp. *epiphaneia*, B, No. 2.

3. ANAPHAINŌ (ἀναφαίνω), *ana*, forth, or up, perhaps originally a nautical term, to come up into view, hence, in general, to appear suddenly, is used in the Passive Voice, in Luke 19 : 11, of the Kingdom of God ; Active Voice, in Acts 21 : 3, to come in sight of, R.V. ; " having sighted " would be a suitable rendering (A.V., " having discovered ").¶

4. PHANEROŌ (φανερόω), akin to No. 1, signifies, in the Active

Voice, to manifest; in the Passive Voice, to be manifested; so, regularly, in the R.V., instead of to appear. See 2 Cor. 7 : 12 ; Col. 3 : 4 ; Heb. 9 : 26 ; 1 Pet 5 : 4 ; 1 John 2 : 28 ; 3 : 2 ; Rev. 3 : 18. To be manifested, in the Scriptural sense of the word, is more than to appear. A person may appear in a false guise or without a disclosure of what he truly is ; to be manifested is to be revealed in one's true character ; this is especially the meaning of *phaneroō*, see, e.g., John 3 : 21 ; 1 Cor. 4 : 5 ; 2 Cor. 5 : 10, 11 ; Eph. 5 : 13.

5 EMPHANIZŌ (ἐμφανίζω), from *en*, in, intensive, and *phainō*, to shine, is used, either of physical manifestation, Matt. 27 : 53 ; Heb. 9 : 24 ; cp. John 14 : 22, or, metaphorically, of the manifestation of Christ by the Holy Spirit in the spiritual experience of believers who abide in His love, John 14 : 21. It has another, secondary meaning, to make known, signify, inform. This is confined to the Acts, where it is used five times, 23 : 15, 22 ; 24 : 1 ; 25 : 2, 15. There is perhaps a combination of the two meanings in Heb. 11 : 14, i.e., to declare by oral testimony and to manifest by the witness of the life. See INFORM, MANIFEST, SHEW, SIGNIFY.¶

6. OPTOMAI (ὄπτομαι), to see (from *ōps*, the eye ; cp. Eng. optical, etc.), in the Passive sense, to be seen, to appear, is used (*a*) objectively, with reference to the person or thing seen, e.g., 1 Cor. 15 : 5, 6, 7, 8, R.V. "appeared," for A.V., "was seen ; " (*b*) subjectively, with reference to an inward impression or a spiritual experience, John 3 : 36, or a mental occupation, Acts 18 : 15, "look to it ; " cp. Matt. 27 : 4, 24, "see (thou) to it," "see (ye) to it," throwing responsibility on others. *Optomai* is to be found in dictionaries under the word *horaō*, to see ; it supplies some forms that are lacking in that verb.

These last three words, *emphanizo*, *phaneroō* and *optomai* are used with reference to the appearances of Christ in the closing verses of Heb. 9 ; *emphanizō* in ver. 24, of His presence before the face of God for us ; *phaneroō* in ver. 26, of His past manifestation for " the sacrifice of Himself ; " *optomai* in ver. 28, of His future appearance for His saints.

7. OPTANŌ (ὀπτάνω), in the Middle Voice signifies to allow oneself to be seen. It is rendered " appearing " in Acts 1 : 3, R.V., for A.V., " being seen," of the Lord's appearances after His resurrection ; the Middle Voice expresses the Personal interest the Lord took in this.¶

Note : In Acts 22 : 30 *sunerchomai* (in its aorist form), to come together, is translated " appear," A.V. ; R.V., " come together."

B. Nouns.

1. APOKALUPSIS (ἀποκάλυψις), lit., an uncovering, unveiling (*apo*, from, *kaluptō*, to hide, cover), denotes a revelation, or appearing (Eng., apocalypse). It is translated " the appearing " in 1 Pet. 1 : 7, A.V. (R.V., " revelation "). See COMING, MANIFESTATION, REVELATION.

2. EPIPHANEIA (ἐπιφάνεια), Eng., epiphany, lit., ' a shining forth was used of the appearance of a god to men, and of an enemy to an army

in the field, etc. In the N.T. it occurs of (*a*) the advent of the Saviour when the Word became flesh, 2 Tim. 1 : 10 ; (*b*) the coming of the Lord Jesus into the air to the meeting with His saints, 1 Tim. 6 : 14; 2 Tim. 4 : 1, 8 ; (*c*) the shining forth of the glory of the Lord Jesus " as the lightning cometh forth from the east, and is seen even unto the west," Matt. 24 : 27, immediately consequent on the unveiling, *apokalupsis*, of His *Parousia* in the air with His saints, 2 Thess. 2 : 8 ; Tit. 2 : 13.¶*

Notes : (1) *Phanerōsis*, akin to A, No. 4, a manifestation, is used in 1 Cor. 12 : 7 and 2 Cor. 4 : 2.¶

(2) For *phaneros*, wrongly translated " may appear," in 1 Tim. 4 : 15, A.V. (R.V., " may be manifest," not mere appearance), see MANIFEST.

(3) *Emphanēs*, akin to A, No. 5, manifest, is used in Acts 10 : 40 and Rom. 10 : 20. See MANIFEST, OPENLY.¶

(4) For *adēlos*, " which appear not," Luke 11 : 44, see UNCERTAIN.

APPEARANCE
A. Nouns.

1. EIDOS (εἶδος), properly that which strikes the eye, that which is exposed to view, signifies the external appearance, form, or shape, and in this sense is used of the Holy Spirit in taking bodily form, as a dove, Luke 3 : 22 ; of Christ, 9 : 29, " the fashion of His countenance." Christ used it, negatively, of God the Father, when He said " Ye have neither heard His voice at any time, nor seen His form," John 5 : 37. Thus it is used with reference to each Person of the Trinity. Probably the same meaning attaches to the word in the Apostle's statement, " We walk by faith, not by sight (*eidos*)," 2 Cor. 5 : 7, where *eidos* can scarcely mean the act of beholding, but the visible appearance of things which are set in contrast to that which directs faith. The believer is guided, then, not only by what he beholds but by what he knows to be true though it is invisible.

It has a somewhat different significance in 1 Thess. 5 : 22, in the exhortation " Abstain from every form of evil," i.e., every sort or kind of evil (not " appearance," A.V.). This meaning was common in the papyri, the Greek writings of the closing centuries, B.C., and the New Testament era. See FASHION, SHAPE, SIGHT.¶ Cp. No. 4.

2. PROSŌPON (πρόσωπον), *pros*, towards, ὄψ, an eye, lit. the part round the eye, the face, in a secondary sense the look, the countenance, as being the index of the inward thoughts and feelings (cp. 1 Pet. 3 : 12, there used of the face of the Lord), came to signify the presentation of the whole person (translated " person," e.g., in Matt. 22 : 16). Cp. the expression in O.T. passages, as Gen. 19 : 21 (A.V. marg., " thy face "), where it is said by God of Lot, and 33 : 10, where it is said by Jacob of Esau ; see also Deut. 10 : 17 (" persons "), Lev. 19 : 15 (" person "). It also signifies the presence of a person, Acts 3 : 13 ; 1 Thess. 2 : 17 ; or the

---

* From Notes on Thessalonians by Hogg and Vine, p. 263.

presence of a company, Acts 5 : 41. In this sense it is sometimes rendered "appearance," 2 Cor. 5 : 12. In 2 Cor. 10 : 7, A.V., "appearance," the R.V. corrects to "face." See COUNTENANCE, FACE, FASHION, PERSON, PRESENCE.

3. OPSIS (ὄψις), from ὄps, the eye, connected with horaō, to see (cp. No. 2), primarily denotes seeing, sight ; hence, the face, the countenance, John 11 : 44 ("face") ; Rev. 1 : 16 ("countenance") ; the outward "appearance," the look, John 7 : 24, only here, of the outward aspect of a person. See COUNTENANCE, FACE.

4. EIDEA (εἰδέα), an aspect, appearance, is used in Matt. 28 : 3, R.V., "appearance ; " A.V., "countenance."¶

B. Verb.

PHANTAZŌ (φαντάζω), to make visible, is used in its participial form (Middle Voice), with the neuter article, as equivalent to a noun, and is translated "appearance," R.V., for A.V., "sight," Heb. 12 : 21.¶

APPEASE

KATASTELLŌ (καταστέλλω), to quiet (lit., to send down, kata, down, stellō, to send), in the Passive Voice, to be quiet, or to be quieted, is used in Acts 19 : 35 and 36, in the former verse in the Active Voice, A.V., "appeased ; " R.V., "quieted ; " in the latter, the Passive, "to be quiet " (lit., ' to be quieted '). See QUIET.¶

APPOINT, APPOINTED

1. HISTĒMI (ἵστημι), to make to stand, means to appoint, in Acts 17 : 31, of the day in which God will judge the world by Christ. In Acts 1 : 23, with reference to Joseph and Barnabas, the R.V. has " put forward ; " for these were not both appointed in the accepted sense of the term, but simply singled out, in order that it might be made known which of them the Lord had chosen. See ABIDE, No. 10.

2. KATHISTĒMI (καθίστημι), a strengthened form of No. 1, usually signifies to appoint a person to a position. In this sense the verb is often translated to make or to set, in appointing a person to a place of authority, e.g., a servant over a household, Matt. 24 : 45, 47 ; 25 : 21, 23 ; Luke 12 : 42, 44 ; a judge, Luke 12 : 14 ; Acts 7 : 27, 35 ; a governor, Acts 7 : 10 ; man by God over the work of His hands, Heb. 2 : 7. It is rendered "appoint," with reference to the so-called seven deacons in Acts 6 : 3. The R.V. translates it by "appoint " in Tit. 1 : 5, instead of "ordain," of the elders whom Titus was to appoint in every city in Crete. Not a formal ecclesiastical ordination is in view, but the appointment, for the recognition of the churches, of those who had already been raised up and qualified by the Holy Spirit, and had given evidence of this in their life and service (see No. 11). It is used of the priests of old, Heb. 5 : 1 ; 7 : 28 ; 8 : 3 (R.V., "appointed"). See CONDUCT, MAKE, ORDAIN, SET.

3. TITHĒMI (τίθημι), to put, is used of appointment to any form of service. Christ used it of His followers, John 15 : 16 (R.V., " appointed " for A.V., " ordained "). " I set you " would be more in keeping with the metaphor of grafting. The verb is used by Paul of his service in the ministry of the Gospel, 1 Tim. 1 : 12 (R.V., " appointing " for " putting ") ; 2 : 7 (R.V., " appointed " for " ordained ") ; and 2 Tim. 1 : 11 (R.V., " appointing " for " putting ") ; of the overseers, or bishops, in the local church at Ephesus, as those appointed by the Holy Ghost, to tend the church of God, Acts 20 : 28 (" hath made ") ; of the Son of God, as appointed Heir of all things, Heb. 1 : 2. It is also used of appointment to punishment, as of the unfaithful servant, Matt. 24 : 51 ; Luke 12 : 46 ; of unbelieving Israel, 1 Pet. 2 : 8. Cp. 2 Pet. 2 : 6. See Bow, Commit, Conceive, Lay, Make, Ordain, Purpose, Put, Set, Sink.

Note : Akin to *tithemi* is the latter part of the noun *prothesmia*, Gal. 4 : 2, of a term or period appointed.¶

4. DIATITHĒMI (διατίθημι), a strengthened form of No. 3 (*dia*, through, intensive), is used in the Middle Voice only. The Lord used it of His disciples with reference to the Kingdom which is to be theirs hereafter, and of Himself in the same respect, as that which has been appointed for Him by His Father, Luke 22 : 29. For its use in connection with a covenant, see Make and Testator.

5. TASSŌ (τάσσω), to place in order, arrange, signifies to appoint, e.g., of the place where Christ had appointed a meeting with His disciples after His resurrection, Matt. 28 : 16 ; of positions of military and civil authority over others, whether appointed by men, Luke 7 : 8, or by God, Rom. 13 : 1, " ordained." It is said of those who, having believed the Gospel, " were ordained to eternal life," Acts 13 : 48. The house of Stephanas at Corinth had " set themselves " to the ministry of the saints (A.V., " addicted "), 1 Cor. 16 : 15. Other instances of the arranging of special details occur in Acts 15 : 2 ; 22 : 10 ; 28 : 23. See Determine, Ordain, Set.¶

6. DIATASSŌ (διατάσσω), a strengthened form of No. 5 (*dia*, through, intensive), frequently denotes to arrange, appoint, prescribe, e.g., of what was appointed for tax collectors to collect, Luke 3 : 13 ; of the tabernacle, as appointed by God for Moses to make, Acts 7 : 44 ; of the arrangements appointed by Paul with regard to himself and his travelling companions, Acts 20 : 13 ; of what the Apostle " ordained " in all the churches in regard to marital conditions, 1 Cor. 7 : 17 ; of what the Lord " ordained " in regard to the support of those who proclaimed the Gospel, 1 Cor. 9 : 14 ; of the Law as Divinely " ordained," or administered, through angels, by Moses, Gal. 3 : 19.

In Tit. 1 : 5, A.V., " had appointed thee," the sense is rather that of commanding, R.V., " gave thee charge." See Command, No. 1, Ordain, Order.

7. SUNTASSŌ (συντάσσω), *sun*, with, and No. 5, lit., to arrange

together with, hence to appoint, prescribe, is used twice, in Matt. 26 : 19 of what the Lord appointed for His disciples, and in 27 : 10, in a quotation concerning the price of the potter's field.¶

8. PROTASSŌ (προτάσσω), *pro*, before, and No. 5, to appoint before, is used in Acts 17 : 26 (R.V., " appointed "), of the seasons arranged by God for nations, and the bounds of their habitation.¶

9. KEIMAI (κεῖμαι), to lie, is used in 1 Thess. 3 : 3 of the appointment of affliction for faithful believers. It is rendered " set " in Luke 2 : 34 and Phil. 1 : 16, R.V., where the sense is the same. The verb is a perfect tense, used for the perfect Passive of *tithēmi*, to place, ' I have been placed,' i.e., ' I lie.' See LAY, LIE, MADE (be), SET.

10. APOKEIMAI (ἀποκεῖμαι), *apo*, from, and No. 9, signifies to be laid, reserved, Luke 19 : 20 ; Col. 1 : 5 ; 2 Tim. 4 : 8 ; " appointed," in Heb. 9 : 27, where it is said of death and the judgment following (R.V., marg., " laid up "). See LAY.¶

11. CHEIROTONEŌ (χειροτονέω), primarily used of voting in the Athenian legislative assembly and meaning to stretch forth the hands (*cheir*, the hand, *teinō*, to stretch), is not to be taken in its literal sense ; it could not be so taken in its compound *procheirotoneō*, to choose before, since it is said of God, Acts 10 : 41. *Cheirotoneō* is said of the appointment of elders by apostolic missionaries in the various churches which they revisited, Acts 14 : 23, R.V., " had appointed," i.e., by the recognition of those who had been manifesting themselves as gifted of God to discharge the functions of elders (see No. 2). It is also said of those who were appointed (not by voting, but with general approbation) by the churches in Greece to accompany the Apostle in conveying their gifts to the poor saints in Judæa, 2 Cor. 8 : 19. See CHOOSE, ORDAIN.¶

12. PROCHEIRIZŌ (προχειρίζω), from *procheiros*, at hand, signifies (*a*) to deliver up, appoint, Acts 3 : 20 (R.V., " appointed ") ; (*b*) in the Middle Voice, to take into one's hand, to determine, appoint beforehand, translated " appointed " in Acts 22 : 14, R.V. (for A.V., " hath chosen "), and " to appoint " in 26 : 16 (for A.V., " to make ").¶

13. HORIZŌ (ὁρίζω) (Eng., horizon), lit., to mark by a limit, hence, to determine, ordain, is used of Christ as ordained of God to be a Judge of the living and the dead, Acts 17 : 31 ; of His being ' marked out ' as the Son of God, Rom. 1 : 4 ; of Divinely appointed seasons, Acts 17 : 26, " having determined." See DEFINE.

14. ANADEIKNUMI (ἀναδείκνυμι), lit., to show up, to show clearly, also signifies to appoint to a position or a service ; it is used in this sense of the 70 disciples, Luke 10 : 1 ; for the meaning " show," see Acts 1 : 24.¶

15. POIEŌ (ποιέω), to do, to make, is rendered " appointed " in Heb. 3 : 2, of Christ. For Mark 3 : 14, R.V., see ORDAIN, *Note* (2).

Note : *Epithanatios*, " appointed to death," doomed to it by condemnation, 1 Cor. 4 : 9, A.V., is corrected to " doomed to death " in the R.V. (*epi*, for, *thanatos*, death).

For APPORTIONED (R.V. in 2 Cor. 10 : 13) see DISTRIBUTE

APPREHEND

1. KATALAMBANŌ (καταλαμβάνω) properly signifies to lay hold of; then, to lay hold of so as to possess as one's own, to appropriate. Hence it has the same twofold meaning as the Eng. " apprehend ; " (a), to seize upon, take possession of, (1) with a beneficial effect, as of laying hold of the righteousness which is of faith, Rom. 9 : 30 (not there a matter of attainment, as in the Eng. Versions, but of appropriation) ; of the obtaining of a prize, 1 Cor. 9 : 24 (R.V., " attain ") ; of the Apostle's desire to apprehend, or lay hold of, that for which he was apprehended by Christ, Phil. 3 : 12, 13 ; (2) with a detrimental effect, e.g., of demon power, Mark 9 : 18 ; of human action in seizing upon a person, John 8 : 3, 4 ; metaphorically, with the added idea of overtaking, of spiritual darkness in coming upon people, John 12 : 35 ; of the day of the Lord, in suddenly coming upon unbelievers as a thief, 1 Thess. 5 : 4 ; (b), to lay hold of with the mind, to understand, perceive, e.g., metaphorically, of darkness with regard to light, John 1 : 5, though possibly here the sense is that of (a) as in 12 : 35 ; of mental perception, Acts 4 : 13 ; 10 : 34 ; 25 : 25 ; Eph. 3 : 18. See ATTAIN, No. 2, COME, *Note* (8), FIND, OBTAIN, OVERTAKE, PERCEIVE, TAKE.¶

Note : Cp. *epilambanō*, to take hold of, always in the Middle Voice in the N.T. See HOLD.

2. PIAZŌ (πιάζω), to lay hold of, with the suggestion of firm pressure or force, is used in the Gospels only in John, six times of efforts to seize Christ. and is always rendered " take " in the R.V., 7 : 30, 32, 44 ; 8 : 20 ; 10 : 39 ; 11 : 57. The A.V. has " laid hands on " in 8 : 20. In Acts 12 : 4 and 2 Cor. 11 : 32 (A.V.), it is translated respectively " apprehended " and " apprehend " (R.V., " had taken," and " take "). In Rev. 19 : 20 it is used of the seizure of the Beast and the False Prophet. In John 21 : 3, 10 it is used of catching fish. Elsewhere in Acts 3 : 7. See CATCH, LAY HANDS ON, TAKE.¶ In the Sept., S. of Sol. 2 : 15.¶

APPROACH

A. Verb.

ENGIZŌ (ἐγγίζω), to draw near, to approach, from *engus*, near, is used (a) of place and position, literally and physically, Matt. 21 : 1 ; Mark 11 : 1 ; Luke 12 : 33 ; 15 : 25 ; figuratively, of drawing near to God, Matt. 15 : 8 ; Heb. 7 : 19 ; Jas. 4 : 8 ; (b) of time, with reference to things that are imminent, as the Kingdom of Heaven, Matt. 3 : 2 ; 4 : 17 ; 10 : 7 ; the Kingdom of God, Mark 1 : 15 ; Luke 10 : 9, 11 ; the time of fruit, Matt. 21 : 34 ; the desolation of Jerusalem, Luke 21 : 8 ; redemption, 21 : 28 ; the fulfilment of a promise, Acts 7 : 17 ; the Day of Christ in contrast to the present night of the world's spiritual darkness, Rom.

13 : 12 ; Heb. 10 : 25 ; the coming of the Lord, Jas. 5 : 8 ; the end of all things, 1 Pet. 4 : 7.   It is also said of one who was drawing near to death, Phil. 2 : 30. See COME, *Note* (16), DRAW, *B*, No. 1, HAND (at), NIGH.

B. Adjective.

APROSITOS (ἀπρόσιτος), unapproachable, inaccessible (*a*, negative, and an adjective formed from *proseimi*, to go to), is used, in 1 Tim. 6 : 16, of the light in which God dwells (A.V., " which no man can approach unto ; " R.V., " unapproachable ").¶

APPROVE, APPROVED
A. Verbs.

1. DOKIMAZŌ (δοκιμάζω), primarily, of metals (e.g., the Sept. of Prov. 8 : 10 ; 17 : 3), signifies to prove, e.g., 1 John 4 : 1, more frequently to prove with a view to approval, e.g., Rom. 1 : 28, A.V., " they did not like to retain God in their knowledge ; " R.V., " they refused ; " marg., " did not approve," the true meaning.   Their refusal was not the outcome of ignorance ; they had the power to make a deliberate choice ; they wilfully disapproved of having God in their knowledge.

In the next chapter, the Apostle speaks of the Jew as " approving things that are excellent," 2 : 18.   The Jew knew God's will, and mentally approved of the things in which God had instructed him out of the Law.

In Rom. 14 : 22, he is said to be happy who " judgeth not himself in that which he approveth ; " that is to say, in that which he approves of after having put the matter to the test.   The A.V. " alloweth " has not now this meaning.

As to the gifts from the church at Corinth for poor saints in Judæa, those who were " approved " by the church to travel with the offering would be men whose trustworthiness and stability had been proved, 1 Cor. 16 : 3 (the R.V. margin seems right, " whomsoever ye shall approve, them will I send with letters ") ; cp. 2 Cor. 8 : 22.

In Phil. 1 : 10 the Apostle prays that the saints may " approve the things that are excellent " or ' things that differ,' i.e., approve after distinguishing and discerning.

In 1 Thess. 2 : 4, the Apostle and his fellow-missionaries were " approved of God to be entrusted with the Gospel " (not " allowed," A.V.).   Not permission to preach, but Divine approval after Divine testing is intended. See ALLOW, DISCERN, EXAMINE, LIKE, PROVE, REFUSE, TRY.

Note : Cp. *dokimē*, proof, experience ; see also B.

2. SUNISTĒMI (συνίστημι), lit., to set together (*sun*, with, *histēmi*, to stand), hence signifies to set one person or thing with another by way of presenting and commending. This meaning is confined to Romans and 2 Corinthians. The saints at Corinth had ' approved themselves in everything to be pure,' in the matter referred to, 2 Cor. 7 : 11.   The word often denotes to commend, so as to meet with approval, Rom. 3 : 5 ;

5 : 8 ; 16 : 1 ; 2 Cor. 4 : 2 ; 6 : 4 (R.V.) ; 10 : 18 ; 12 : 11, etc. See COMMEND, COMPACTED, CONSIST (No. 2), STAND.

3. APODEIKNUMI (ἀποδείκνυμι), lit., to point out, to exhibit (apo, forth, deiknumi, to show), is used once in the sense of proving by demonstration, and so bringing about an approval. The Lord Jesus was " a Man approved of God by mighty works and wonders and signs," Acts 2 : 22. See PROVE, SET, No. 17, SHEW.

B. Adjective.

DOKIMOS (δόκιμος), akin to dechomai, to receive, always signifies " approved ; " so the R.V. everywhere, e.g., in Jas. 1 : 12 for A.V., " when he is tried." The word is used of coins and metals in the Sept. ; in Gen. 23 : 16, " four hundred didrachms of silver approved with merchants ; " in Zech. 11 : 13, in regard to the 30 pieces of silver, " Cast them into a furnace and I will see if it is good (approved) metal."

APRON

SIMIKINTHION (σιμικίνθιον), a thing girded round half the body (Latin, semicinctium), was a narrow apron, or linen covering, worn by workmen and servants, Acts 19 : 12.¶

For APT see TEACH, B

ARCHANGEL

ARCHANGELOS (ἀρχάγγελος) " is not found in the O.T., and in the N.T. only in 1 Thess. 4 : 16 and Jude 9, where it is used of Michael, who in Daniel is called ' one of the chief princes,' and ' the great prince ' (Sept., ' the great angel '), 10 : 13, 21 ; 12 : 1. Cp. also Rev. 12 : 7. . . . Whether there are other beings of this exalted rank in the heavenly hosts, Scripture does not say, though the description ' one of the chief princes ' suggests that this may be the case ; cp. also Rom. 8 : 38 ; Eph. 1 : 21 ; Col. 1 : 16, where the word translated ' principalities ' is archē, the prefix in archangel."* In 1 Thess. 4 : 16 the meaning seems to be that the voice of the Lord Jesus will be of the character of an archangelic shout.¶

For ARIGHT (R.V. of 2 Tim. 2 : 15) see HANDLE, No. 5

ARISE, AROSE, AROUSE, RAISE, RISE, ROUSE

1. ANISTĒMI (ἀνίστημι), to stand up or to make to stand up, according as its use is intransitive or transitive (ana, up, histēmi, to stand), is used (a) of a physical change of position, e.g., of rising from sleep, Mark 1 : 35 ; from a meeting in a synagogue, Luke 4 : 29 ; of the illegal rising of the high priest in the tribunal in Matt. 26 : 62 ; of an invalid rising from his couch, Luke 5 : 25 ; the rising up of a disciple from his

---

* From Notes on Thessalonians by Hogg and Vine, p. 142.

vocation to follow Christ, Luke 5 : 28 ; cp. John 11 : 31 ; rising up from prayer, Luke 22 : 45 ; of a whole company, Acts 26 : 30 ; 1 Cor. 10 : 7 ; (b) metaphorically, of rising up antagonistically against persons, e.g., of officials against people, Acts 5 : 17 ; of a seditious leader, 5 : 36 ; of the rising up of Satan, Mark 3 : 26 ; of false teachers, Acts 20 : 30 ; (c) of rising to a position of pre-eminence or power ; e.g., of Christ as a Prophet, Acts 3 : 22 ; 7 : 37 ; as God's servant in the midst of the nation of Israel, Acts 3 : 26 ; as the Son of God in the midst of the nation, 13 : 33 (not here of Resurrection, but with reference to the Incarnation : the A.V. " again " has nothing corresponding to it in the original, it was added as a misinterpretation : the mention of His Resurrection is in the next verse, in which it is stressed by way of contrast and by the addition, " from the dead ") ; as a Priest, Heb. 7 : 11, 15 ; as King over the nations, Rom. 15 : 12 ; (d) of a spiritual awakening from lethargy, Eph. 5 : 14 ; (e) of resurrection from the dead : (1) of the Resurrection of Christ, Matt. 17 : 9 ; 20 : 19 ; Mark 8 : 31 ; 9 : 9, 10, 31 ; 10 : 34 ; Luke 18 : 33 ; 24 : 7, 46 ; John 20 : 9 ; Acts 2 : 24, 32 ; 10 : 41 ; 13 : 34 ; 17 : 3, 31 ; 1 Thess. 4 : 14 ; (2) of believers, John 6 : 39, 40, 44, 54 ; 11 : 24 ; 1 Thess. 4 : 16 ; of unbelievers, Matt. 12 : 41. See LIFT, RAISE (up), STAND.

2. EXANISTĒMI (ἐξανίστημι), a strengthened form of No. 1 (ex, i.e., ek, intensive), signifies to raise up, Mark 12 : 19 ; Luke 20 : 28 ; intransitively, to rise up, Acts 15 : 5.¶

3. EGEIRŌ (ἐγείρω) is frequently used in the N.T. in the sense of raising (Active Voice), or rising (Middle and Passive Voices) : (a) from sitting, lying, sickness, e.g., Matt. 2 : 14 ; 9 : 5, 7, 19 ; Jas. 5 : 15 ; Rev. 11 : 1 ; (b) of causing to appear, or, in the Passive, appearing, or raising up so as to occupy a place in the midst of people, Matt. 3 : 9 ; 11 : 11 ; Mark 13 : 22 ; Acts 13 : 22. It is thus said of Christ in Acts 13 : 23 ; cp. No. 1, (c) ; (c) of rousing, stirring up, or rising against, Matt. 24 : 7 ; Mark 13 : 8 ; (d) of raising buildings, John 2 : 19, 20 ; (e) of raising or rising from the dead ; (1) of Christ, Matt. 16 : 21 ; and frequently elsewhere (but not in Phil., 2 Thess., 1 Tim., Tit., Jas., 2 Pet., Epp. of John and Jude) ; (2) of Christ's raising the dead, Matt. 11 : 5 ; Mark 5 : 41 ; Luke 7 : 14 ; John 12 : 1, 9, 17 ; (3) of the act of the disciples, Matt. 10 : 8 ; (4) of the resurrection of believers, Matt. 27 : 52 ; John 5 : 21 ; 1 Cor. 15 : 15, 16, 29, 32, 35, 42, 43, 44, 52 ; 2 Cor. 1 : 9 ; 4 : 14 ; of unbelievers, Matt. 12 : 42 (cp. ver. 41, No. 1).

Egeirō stands in contrast to anistēmi (when used with reference to resurrection) in this respect, that egeirō is frequently used both in the transitive sense of raising up and the intransitive of rising, whereas anistēmi is comparatively infrequent in the transitive use. See AWAKE.

4. DIEGEIRŌ (διεγείρω), a strengthened form of No. 3 (dia, through, intensive), signifies to rouse, to awaken from sleep. The Active Voice is not used intransitively. In Matt. 1 : 24, R.V., " Joseph arose from his sleep," the Passive Participle is, lit., ' being aroused.' In Mark

4 : 39 (A.V., " he arose," R.V., " he awoke "), the lit. rendering is ' he being awakened.' In John 6 : 18 the imperfect tense of the Passive Voice is used, and the rendering should be, ' the sea was being aroused.' See AWAKE, No. 2.

5. GINOMAI (γίνομαι), to become, to take place, is sometimes suitably translated " arise ; " e.g., Matt. 8 : 24 ; Mark 4 : 37, "there arose a great tempest." So of the arising of persecution, Matt. 13 : 21 ; Mark 4 : 17 ; this might be translated ' taketh place ;' of a tumult, Matt. 27 : 24, R.V., " arising,'" for A.V., " made ; " of a flood, Luke 6 : 48 ; a famine, 15 : 14 ; a questioning, John 3 : 25 ; a murmuring, Acts 6 : 1 ; a tribulation, 11 : 19 (R.V.) ; a stir in the city, 19 : 23 ; a dissension, 23 : 7 ; a great clamour, ver. 9. See BECOME.

6. ANABAINŌ (ἀναβαίνω), to go up, to ascend, is once rendered " arise " in the R.V., Luke 24 : 38, of reasonings in the heart ; in Rev. 13 : 1, R.V., " coming up," for A.V., " rise up," with reference to the beast ; in 17 : 8, A.V., " ascend," for R.V., " to come up ; " in 19 : 3, R.V., " goeth up," for A.V., " rose up." See CLIMB UP, COME, ENTER, GO, GROW, RISE, SPRING.

7. SUNEPHISTĒMI (συνεφίστημι), to rise up together (sun, together, epi, up, histēmi, to stand), is used in Acts 16 : 22, of the rising up of a multitude against Paul and Silas.¶

8. EISERCHOMAI (εἰσέρχομαι), lit., to go in (eis, in, erchomai, to go), to enter, is once rendered "arose," metaphorically, with reference to a reasoning among the disciples which of them should be the greatest, Luke 9 : 46. See COME, ENTER, GO.

9. ANATELLŌ (ἀνατέλλω), to arise, is used especially of things in the natural creation, e.g., the rising of the sun, moon and stars ; metaphorically, of light, in Matt. 4 : 16, " did spring up ; " of the sun, Matt. 5 : 45 ; 13 : 6 (R.V.) ; Mark 4 : 6 ; James 1 : 11 ; in Mark 16 : 2 the R.V. has " when the sun was risen," keeping to the verb form, for the A.V., " at the rising of ; " of a cloud, Luke 12 : 54 ; of the day-star, 2 Pet. 1 : 19 ; in Heb. 7 : 14 metaphorically, of the Incarnation of Christ : " Our Lord hath sprung out of Judah," more lit., ' Our Lord hath arisen out of Judah,' as of the rising of the light of the sun. See RISE, SPRING, UP.¶

Notes : (1) A corresponding noun, anatolē, signifies the east, i.e., the place of the sunrising.

(2) In Acts 27 : 14, the verb ballō, to beat (intransitive), is translated " arose " in the A.V. ; R.V., " beat."

ARK

KIBŌTOS (κιβωτός), a wooden box, a chest, is used of (a) Noah's vessel, Matt. 24 : 38 ; Luke 17 : 27 ; Heb. 11 : 7 ; 1 Pet. 3 : 20 ; (b) the ark of the Covenant in the Tabernacle, Heb. 9 : 4 ; (c) the ark seen in vision in the Heavenly Temple, Rev. 11 : 19.¶

ARM (physical)

1. ANKALĒ (ἀγκάλη), used in the plural, in Luke 2 : 28, originally denoted the curve, or the inner angle, of the arm. The word is derived from a term signifying to bend, to curve ; the Eng. " angle " is connected.¶

Note : Enankalizomai (en, in, and a verb akin to No. 1), to take into the arms, to embrace, is used in Mark 9 : 36 and 10 : 16, of the tenderness of Christ towards little children.¶

2. BRACHIŌN (βραχίων), the shorter part of the arm, from the shoulder to the elbow, is used metaphorically to denote strength, power, and always in the N.T. of the power of God, Luke 1 : 51 ; John 12 : 38 ; Acts 13 : 17 ; frequently so in the O.T., especially in Deuteronomy, the Psalms and Isaiah ; see, e.g., Deut. 4 : 34 ; 5 : 15 ; Psa. 44 : 3 ; 71 : 18, where " strength " is, lit., ' arm ; ' 77 : 15 ; Isa. 26 : 11, where " hand " is, lit., ' arm ; ' 30 : 30 ; 40 : 10, 11, etc.¶

ARMS (weapons), ARMOUR, TO ARM
A. Nouns.

1. HOPLON (ὅπλον), originally any tool or implement for preparing a thing, became used in the plural for weapons of warfare. Once in the N.T. it is used of actual weapons, John 18 : 3 ; elsewhere, metaphorically, of (a) the members of the body as instruments of unrighteousness and as instruments of righteousness, Rom. 6 : 13 ; (b) the armour of light, Rom. 13 : 12 ; the armour of righteousness, 2 Cor. 6 : 7 ; the weapons of the Christian's warfare, 2 Cor. 10 : 4.¶

2. PANOPLIA (πανοπλία), Eng., panoply, lit., all armour, full armour, (*pas,* all, *hoplon,* a weapon), is used (a) of literal armour, Luke 11 : 22 ; (b) of the spiritual helps supplied by God for overcoming the temptations of the Devil, Eph. 6 : 11, 13. Among the Greeks the *panoplia* was the complete equipment used by heavily armed infantry.¶

B. Verbs.

1. HOPLIZŌ (ὁπλίζω), to arm oneself, is used in 1 Pet. 4 : 1, in an exhortation to arm ourselves with the same mind as that of Christ in regard to His sufferings.¶

2. KATHOPLIZŌ (καθοπλίζω) is an intensive form, to furnish fully with arms, *kata,* down, intensive, *hoplon,* a weapon, Luke 11 : 21, lit., ' a strong man fully armed.'¶ In the Sept., Jer. 46 : 9.¶

ARMY

1. STRATEUMA (στράτευμα) denotes (a) an army of any size, large or small, Matt. 22 : 7 ; Rev. 9 : 16 ; 19 : 14, 19 (twice) ; (b) a company of soldiers, such as Herod's bodyguard, Luke 23 : 11 (R.V., " soldiers "), or the soldiers of a garrison, Acts 23 : 10, 27 (R.V., " the soldiers," for A.V., " an army "). See SOLDIER, WAR.¶

2. STRATOPEDON (στρατόπεδον), from *stratos,* a military host, *pedon,* a plain, strictly denotes an army encamped, a camp ; in Luke

21 : 20, of the soldiers which were to be encamped about Jerusalem in fulfilment of the Lord's prophecy concerning the destruction of the city ; the phrase might be translated ' by camps ' (or encampments).¶

3. PAREMBOLĒ (παρεμβολή), lit., a casting in among, an insertion (*para*, among, *ballō*, to throw), in the Macedonian dialect, was a military term.   In the N.T. it denotes the distribution of troops in army formation, " armies," Heb. 11 : 34 ; a camp, as of the Israelites, Ex. 19 : 17 ; 29 : 14 ; 32 : 17 ; hence, in Heb. 13 : 11, 13, of Jerusalem, since the city was to the Jews what the camp in the wilderness had been to the Israelites ; in Rev. 20 : 9, the armies or camp of the saints, at the close of the Millennium.

It also denoted a castle or barracks, Acts 21 : 34, 37 ; 22 : 24 ; 23 : 10, 16, 32.¶

AROUND : see Note †, p. 9.

For ARRAY, see CLOTHE, No. 6, PUT

ARRIVE

1. KATANTAŌ (καταντάω), to come to, arrive at, is used (*a*) literally, of locality, Acts 16 : 1, " came to ; " so 18 : 19, 24 ; 20 : 15 (" came ") ; 21 : 7 ; 25 : 13 ; 27 : 12 (A.V., " attain to," R.V., " reach ") ; 28 : 13 ; (*b*) metaphorically, of attainment, Acts 26 : 7, " attain ; " so Eph. 4 : 13 ; Phil. 3 : 11.   In 1 Cor. 10 : 11 (" upon whom the ends of the ages are come," R.V.), the metaphor is apparently that of an inheritance as coming down or descending to an heir, the " ends " (*telē*) being the spiritual revenues (cp. Matt. 17 : 25, revenues derived from taxes, and Rom. 13 : 7, where the singular, *telos*, " custom," is used) ; the inheritance metaphor is again seen in 1 Cor. 14 : 36, of the coming (or descending) of the word of God to the Corinthians.   See ATTAIN.

2. KATAPLEŌ (καταπλέω) denotes to sail down (*kata*, down, *pleō*, to sail), i.e., from the high sea to the shore, Luke 8 : 26.¶

3. PARAGINOMAI (παραγίνομαι), lit., to become near, hence, to come on the scene, Matt. 3 : 1, of John the Baptist, is translated, " arrive " in the R.V. of 1 Cor. 16 : 3, for A.V., " come."   See COME, GO, PRESENT.

4. PARABALLŌ (παραβάλλω), *para*, alongside, *ballō*, to throw, signifies, nautically, " touched at ; " so the R.V. of Acts 20 : 15 (A.V., " arrived ") ; or, perhaps, to strike across, from one place to another.   In Mark 4 : 30, some mss. have this verb (A.V., " compare ") ; the most authentic have *tithēmi*, to set forth (with the word " parable ").   See COMPARE.

5. PHTHANŌ (φθάνω), to anticipate, reach to, is translated " did arrive at," Rom. 9 : 31, R.V., of Israel's failure to attain to the Law (A.V., " hath attained to ").   See ATTAIN, COME, PRECEDE.

ART, ARTS

1. TECHNĒ (τέχνη), an art, handicraft, trade, is used in Acts 17 : 29, of the plastic art ; in Acts 18 : 3, of a trade or craft (A.V., " occupation,"

R.V., " trade ") ; in Rev. 18 : 22, " craft " (cp. *technitēs*, a craftsman, Eng., technical). See CRAFT, OCCUPATION, TRADE.¶

2. PERIERGOS (περίεργος), lit., a work about (*peri*, about, *ergon*, a work), hence, ' busy about trifles,' is used, in the plural, of things superfluous, " curious (or magical) arts," Acts 19 : 19 ; in 1 Tim. 5 : 13, " busybodies." See BUSYBODY.¶

AS (and connected phrases) : see Note †, p. 9.

For ASCEND see ARISE, No. 6

ASHAMED (to be), SHAME
A. Verbs.

1. AISCHUNŌ (αἰσχύνω), from *aischos*, shame, always used in the Passive Voice, signifies (*a*) to have a feeling of fear or shame which prevents a person from doing a thing, e.g., Luke 16 : 3 ; (*b*) the feeling of shame arising from something that has been done, e.g., 2 Cor. 10 : 8 ; Phil. 1 : 20 ; 1 John 2 : 28, of the possibility of being ashamed before the Lord Jesus at His Judgment Seat in His Parousia with His saints ; in 1 Pet. 4 : 16, of being ashamed of suffering as a Christian.¶

2. EPAISCHUNOMAI (ἐπαισχύνομαι), a strengthened form of No. 1 (*epi*, upon, intensive), is used only in the sense (*b*) in the preceding paragraph. It is said of being ashamed of persons, Mark 8 : 38 ; Luke 9 : 26 ; the Gospel, Rom. 1 : 16 ; former evil doing, Rom. 6 : 21 ; " the testimony of our Lord," 2 Tim. 1 : 8 ; suffering for the Gospel, ver. 12 ; rendering assistance and comfort to one who is suffering for the Gospel's sake, ver. 16. It is used in Heb., of Christ in calling those who are sanctified His brethren, 2 : 11, and of God in His not being ashamed to be called the God of believers, 11 : 16.¶ In the Sept., in Job 34 : 19 ;. Ps. 119 : 6 ; Is. 1 : 29.¶

3. KATAISCHUNŌ (καταισχύνω), another strengthened form (*kata*, down, intensive), is used (*a*) in the Active Voice, to put to shame, e.g., Rom. 5 : 5 ; 1 Cor. 1 : 27 (A.V., " confound ") ; 11 : 4, 5 (" dishonoureth "), and ver. 22 ; (*b*) in the Passive Voice, Rom. 9 : 33 ; 10 : 11 ; 2 Cor. 7 : 14 ; 1 Pet. 2 : 6 ; 3 : 16. See CONFOUND, DISHONOUR, SHAME.

4. ENTREPŌ (ἐντρέπω), to put to shame, in the Passive Voice, to be ashamed, lit. means to turn in (*en*, in, *trepō*, to turn), that is, to turn one upon himself and so produce a feeling of shame, a wholesome shame which involves a change of conduct, 1 Cor. 4 : 14 ; 2 Thess. 3 : 14 ; Titus 2 : 8, the only places where it has this meaning. See also REGARD, REVERENCE.

B. Nouns.

1. AISCHUNĒ (αἰσχύνη), shame, akin to A, No. 1, signifies (*a*) subjectively, the confusion of one who is ashamed of anything, a sense of shame, Luke 14 : 9 ; those things which shame conceals, 2 Cor. 4 : 2 ;

(*b*) objectively, ignominy, that which is visited on a person by the wicked, Heb. 12 : 2 ; that which should arise from guilt, Phil. 3 : 19 ; (*c*) concretely, a thing to be ashamed of, Rev. 3 : 18 ; Jude 13, where the word is in the plural, lit., ' basenesses,' ' disgraces.' See DISHONESTY.¶

2. ENTROPĒ (ἐντροπή), akin to A, No. 4, lit., a turning in upon oneself, producing a recoil from what is unseemly or vile, is used in 1 Cor. 6 : 5 ; 15 : 34. It is associated with *aischunē* in the Psalms, in the Sept., e.g., 35 : 26, where it follows *aischunē*, " let them be clothed with shame (*aischunē*) and confusion (*entropē*) ; " 44 : 15, " all the day my shame is before me and the confusion of my face has covered me ; " 69 : 19, " Thou knowest my reproach and my shame and my confusion ; " so in 71 : 13. In 109 : 29 the words are in the opposite order.¶

Note : Aidōs, used in 1 Tim. 2 : 9, denotes modesty, shamefastness (the right spelling for the A.V., " shamefacedness "). In comparison with *aischunē*, *aidōs* is " the nobler word, and implies the nobler motive : in it is involved an innate moral repugnance to the doing of the dishonourable act, which moral repugnance scarcely or not at all exists in *aischunē* " (Trench, Syn. § xix). See SHAMEFASTNESS.¶

C. Adjectives.

1. AISCHROS (αἰσχρός), base (akin to No. 1), is used in 1 Cor. 11 : 6 ; 14 : 35 ; Eph. 5 : 12. See FILTHY, B, No. 1. ¶Cp. *aischrotēs*, filthiness, Eph. 5 : 4.¶

2. ANEPAISCHUNTOS (ἀνεπαίσχυντος), an intensive adjective (*a*, negative, *n* euphonic, *epi*, upon, intensive, *aischunē*, shame), not ashamed, having no cause for shame, is used in 2 Tim. 2 : 15.¶

ASHES
A. Noun.

SPODOS (σποδός), ashes, is found three times, twice in association with sackcloth, Matt. 11 : 21 and Luke 10 : 13, as tokens of grief (cp. Esth. 4 : 1, 3 ; Isa. 58 : 5 ; 61 : 3 ; Jer. 6 : 26 ; Jonah 3 : 6) ; of the ashes resulting from animal sacrifices, Heb. 9 : 13 ; in the O.T., metaphorically, of one who describes himself as dust and ashes, Gen. 18 : 27, etc.¶

B. Verb.

TEPHROŌ (τεφρόω), to turn to ashes, is found in 2 Pet. 2 : 6, with reference to the destruction of Sodom and Gomorrah.¶

Notes : (1) *Tephra*, frequently used of the ashes of a funeral pile, is not found in the N.T.

(2) The Hebrew verb, rendered " accept " in Psa. 20 : 3, " accept thy burnt sacrifice," signifies to turn to ashes (i.e., by sending fire from heaven). See also Ex. 27 : 3, and Num. 4 : 13, " shall take away the ashes."

For ASHORE (Acts 27 : 29), see CAST, A, No. 3

For ASIDE see LAY, No. 8, TAKE, No. 3, TURN, Nos. 3, 17, *Note* (1)

ASK
A. Verbs.

1. AITEŌ (αἰτέω), to ask, is to be distinguished from No. 2. *Aiteō* more frequently suggests the attitude of a suppliant, the petition of one who is lesser in position than he to whom the petition is made ; e.g., in the case of men in asking something from God, Matt. 7 : 7 ; a child from a parent, Matt. 7 : 9, 10 ; a subject from a king, Acts 12 : 20 ; priests and people from Pilate, Luke 23 : 23 (R.V., " asking " for A.V., " requiring ") ; a beggar from a passer by, Acts 3 : 2. With reference to petitioning God, this verb is found in Paul's Epistles in Eph. 3 : 20 and Col. 1 : 9 ; in James four times, 1 : 5, 6 ; 4 : 2, 3 ; in 1 John, five times, 3 : 22 ; 5 : 14, 15 (twice), 16. See BEG, CALL FOR, CRAVE, DESIRE, REQUIRE.

2. ERŌTAŌ (ἐρωτάω) more frequently suggests that the petitioner is on a footing of equality or familiarity with the person whom he requests. It is used of a king in making request from another king, Luke 14 : 32 ; of the Pharisee who " desired " Christ that He would eat with him, an indication of the inferior conception he had of Christ, Luke 7 : 36 ; cp. 11 : 37 ; John 9 : 15 ; 18 : 19.

In this respect it is significant that the Lord Jesus never used *aiteō* in the matter of making request to the Father. " The consciousness of His equal dignity, of His potent and prevailing intercession, speaks out in this, that as often as He asks, or declares that He will ask anything of the Father, it is always *erōtaō*, an asking, that is, upon equal terms, John 14 : 16 ; 16 : 26 ; 17 : 9, 15, 20, never *aiteō*, that He uses. Martha, on the contrary, plainly reveals her poor unworthy conception of His person, that . . . she ascribes that *aiteō* to Him which He never ascribes to Himself, John 11 : 22 " (Trench, Syn. § xl).

In passages where both words are used, the distinction should be noticed, even if it cannot be adequately represented in English. In John 16 : 23, " in that day ye shall ask Me nothing," the verb is *erōtaō*, whereas in the latter part of the verse, in the sentence, " If ye shall ask anything of the Father," the verb is *aiteō*. The distinction is brought out in the R.V. margin, which renders the former clause " Ye shall ask Me no question," and this meaning is confirmed by the fact that the disciples had been desirous of asking Him a question (*erōtaō*, ver. 19). If the Holy Spirit had been given, the time for asking questions from the Lord would have ceased. In John 14 : 14, where, not a question, but a request is made by the disciples, *aiteō* is used.

Both verbs are found in 1 John 5 : 16 : in the sentence " he shall ask, and God will give him life for them that sin not unto death," the verb is *aiteō*, but with regard to the sin unto death, in the sentence " not concerning this do I say that he shall make request," the verb is *erōtaō*.

Later, the tendency was for *erotaō* to approximate to *aiteō*. See BESEECH, DESIRE, INTREAT, PRAY, REQUEST.

Note : In Matt. 19 : 17, the R.V., following the most authentic mss., has " Why askest (*erotaō*) thou Me concerning that which is good ? "

3. EPERŌTAŌ (ἐπερωτάω), a strengthened form of No. 2 (*epi*, in addition), is frequently used in the Synoptic Gospels, but only twice in the Gospel of John, 18 : 7, 21. In Rom. 10 : 20 it is rendered " asked of " (A.V., " asked after "). The more intensive character of the asking may be observed in Luke 2 : 46 ; 3 : 14 ; 6 : 9 ; 17 : 20 ; 20 : 21, 27, 40 ; 22 : 64 ; 23 : 3, 6, 9. In Matt. 16 : 1, it virtually signifies to demand (its meaning in later Greek). See DEMAND, DESIRE, QUESTION.

Note : For the corresponding noun *eperōtēma*, see ANSWER.

4. PUNTHANOMAI (πυνθάνομαι), to ask by way of enquiry, not by way of making a request for something, is found in the Gospels and the Acts, five times in the former, seven in the latter ; in Matt. 2 : 4, A.V., " demanded," R.V., " enquired," so Acts 21 : 33. See DEMAND, INQUIRE, UNDERSTAND.

5. EXETAZŌ (ἐξετάζω), to search out (*ek*, out, intensive, *etazō*, to examine), is translated " ask," in John 21 : 12, A.V. (R.V., " inquire ") ; in Matt. 2 : 8, A.V., " search ; " R.V., " search out," expressing the intensive force of the verb, so Matt. 10 : 11 (A.V., " inquire "). See INQUIRE, SEARCH.¶

6. LEGŌ (λέγω), to say, occasionally signifies to ask, as of an enquiry, the reason being that *legō* is used for every variety of speaking, e.g., Acts 25 : 20, " I asked whether he would come to Jerusalem." See BID, BOAST, CALL, DESCRIBE, GIVE, NAME, PUT, *Note* (2), SAY, SPEAK, TELL, UTTER.

7. ANAKRINŌ (ἀνακρίνω), to judge, sometimes has the meaning to ask a question ; e.g., 1 Cor. 10 : 25, 27. See DISCERN, EXAMINE, JUDGE, SEARCH.

Notes : (1) For *apaiteō*, Luke 6 : 30, see REQUIRE, No. 3. (2) In Luke 22 : 31, R.V., *exaiteomai* is rendered " hath asked to have."¶

B. Noun.

AITĒMA (αἴτημα), akin to No. 1, lit., that which has been asked for, is used in Luke 23 : 24, R.V., " what they asked for " (A.V., " required ") ; Phil. 4 : 6, " requests ; " 1 John 5 : 15, " petitions." See PETITION, REQUEST, REQUIRE.¶

ASLEEP, SLEEP
A. Verbs.

1. KATHEUDŌ (καθεύδω); to go to sleep, is chiefly used of natural sleep, and is found most frequently in the Gospels, especially Matthew and Luke. With reference to death it is found in the Lord's remark concerning Jairus' daughter, Matt. 9 : 24 ; Mark 5 : 39 ; Luke 8 : 52. In the Epistles of Paul it is used as follows : (*a*) of natural sleep, e.g., 1 Thess. 5 : 7 ; (*b*) of carnal indifference to spiritual things on the part of believers, Eph. 5 : 14 ; 1 Thess. 5 : 6, 10 (as in Mark 13 : 36), a condition of insensibility to Divine things involving conformity to the world (cp. *hupnos* below).

2. KOIMAOMAI (κοιμάομαι) is used of natural sleep, Matt. 28 : 13 ; Luke 22 : 45 ; John 11 : 12 ; Acts 12 : 6 ; of the death of the body, but only of such as are Christ's ; yet never of Christ Himself, though He is " the firstfruits of them that have fallen asleep," 1 Cor. 15 : 20; of saints who departed before Christ came, Matt. 27 : 52 ; Acts 13 : 36 ; of Lazarus, while Christ was yet upon the earth, John 11 : 11 ; of believers since the Ascension, 1 Thess. 4 : 13, 14, 15, and Acts 7 : 60 ; 1 Cor. 7 : 39 ; 11 : 30 ; 15 : 6, 18, 51 ; 2 Pet. 3 : 4.¶

Note : " This metaphorical use of the word sleep is appropriate, because of the similarity in appearance between a sleeping body and a dead body ; restfulness and peace normally characterise both. The object of the metaphor is to suggest that, as the sleeper does not cease to exist while his body sleeps, so the dead person continues to exist despite his absence from the region in which those who remain can communicate with him, and that, as sleep is known to be temporary, so the death of the body will be found to be. . . .

" That the body alone is in view in this metaphor is evident, (*a*) from the derivation of the word *koimaomai*, from *keimai*, to lie down (cp. *anastasis*, resurrection, from *ana*, ' up,' and *histēmi*, to cause to stand) ; cp. Is. 14 : 8, where for ' laid down,' the Sept. has ' fallen asleep ; ' (*b*) from the fact that in the N.T. the word resurrection is used of the body alone ; (*c*) from Dan. 12 : 2, where the physically dead are described as ' them that sleep (Sept. *katheudō*, as at 1 Thess. 5 : 6) in the dust of the earth,' language inapplicable to the spiritual part of man ; moreover, when the body returns whence it came, Gen. 3 : 19, the spirit returns to God who gave it, Eccles. 12 : 7.

" When the physical frame of the Christian (the earthly house of our tabernacle, 2 Cor. 5 : 1) is dissolved and returns to the dust, the spiritual part of his highly complex being, the seat of personality, departs to be with Christ, Phil. 1 : 23. And since that state in which the believer, absent from the body, is at home with the Lord, 2 Cor. 5 : 6–9, is described as ' very far better ' than the present state of joy in communion with God and of happy activity in His service, everywhere reflected in Paul's writings, it is evident the word ' sleep,' where applied to the departed Christians, is not intended to convey the idea that the spirit is unconscious. . . .

" The early Christians adopted the word *koimētērion* (which was used by the Greeks of a rest-house for strangers) for the place of interment of the bodies of their departed ; thence the English word ' cemetery,' ' the sleeping place,' is derived."*

3. EXUPNIZO (ἐξυπνίζω), to awake (*ek*, out, *hupnos*, sleep), to awake out of sleep, is used in John 11 : 11.¶ In the Sept., Judg. 16 : 14, 20; 1 Kings 3 : 15 ; Job. 14 : 12.¶

4. APHUPNOŌ (ἀφυπνόω), to fall asleep (*apo*, away), is used of natural

---

* From Notes on Thessalonians by Hogg and Vine, p. 172.

sleep, Luke 8 : 23, of the Lord's falling asleep in the boat on the lake of Galilee.¶

B. Adjective.

EXUPNOS (ἔξυπνος), Acts 16 : 27, signifies " out of sleep."¶

C. Noun.

HUPNOS (ὕπνος) is never used of death. In five places in the N.T. it is used of physical sleep ; in Rom. 13 : 11, metaphorically, of a slumbering state of soul, i.e., of spiritual conformity to the world, out of which believers are warned to awake.

ASP

ASPIS (ἀσπίς), a small and very venomous serpent, the bite of which is fatal, unless the part affected is at once cut away, in Rom. 3 : 13 is said, metaphorically, of the conversation of the ungodly.¶

ASS

1. ONOS (ὄνος) is the usual word. *Onarion*, the diminutive of *onos*, a young ass, or ass's colt, is used in John 12 : 14, together with *onos*.¶

2. HUPOZUGION (ὑποζύγιον), lit., under a yoke (*hupo*, under, *zugos*, a yoke), is used as an alternative description of the same animal, in Matt. 21 : 5, where both words are found together, " Behold, thy king cometh unto thee, meek and riding upon an ass (*onos*), and upon a colt the foal of an ass (*hupozugion*)." It was upon the colt that the Lord sat, John 12 : 14. In 2 Pet. 2 : 16, it is used of Balaam's ass.¶

ASSASSIN

SIKARIOS (σικάριος) is a Latin word (*sicarius*, from *sica*, a dagger) denoting one who carries a dagger or short sword under his clothing, an assassin, Acts 21 : 38, R.V. Here it is used as a proper name (see the R.V.) of the Sicarii, Assassins, the fanatical Jewish faction which arose in Judæa after Felix had rid the country of the robbers referred to by Josephus (Ant., XX). They mingled with the crowds at Festivals and stabbed their political opponents unobserved (A.V., " murderers ").¶

ASSAULT

A. Verb.

EPHISTĒMI (ἐφίστημι), lit., to stand over (*epi*, over, *histēmi*, to stand), signifies to assault ; said in Acts 17 : 5, of those who attacked the house of Jason. For its usual meanings see COME (in, to, upon), HAND (at), INSTANT, PRESENT, STAND.

B. Noun.

HORMĒ (ὁρμή), rendered " assault " in Acts 14 : 5, A.V. ; R.V., " onset," corresponds to *hormaō*, to rush. See IMPULSE, ONSET.¶

For ASSAY see TRY, No. 2

ASSEMBLE

1. SUNAGŌ (συνάγω), to assemble (sun, together, agō, to bring), is used of the gathering together of people or things ; in Luke 12 : 17, 18, " bestow," with reference to the act of gathering one's goods ; so in Luke 15 : 13, suggesting that the Prodigal, having gathered all his goods together, sold them off ; in John 6 : 12, of gathering up fragments ; in John 18 : 2, " resorted," with reference to the assembling of Christ with His disciples in the garden of Gethsemane, there in the Passive Voice (unsuitable, however, in an English translation). In Acts 11 : 26, the R.V. has " were gathered together (with the church)," for A.V., " assembled themselves " (possibly ' they were hospitably entertained by '). The verb is not found in the most authentic mss. in Rev. 13 : 10. See BESTOW, GATHER, LEAD, TAKE, No. 29.

Note : Episunagō, to gather together, is found only in the Synoptic Gospels ; twice of the gathering together of people, Mark 1 : 33 ; Luke 12 : 1 ; twice of the desire of the Lord to gather together the inhabitants of Jerusalem, Matt. 23 : 37 ; Luke 13 : 34 ; twice of His future act in gathering together His elect through the instrumentality of the angels, Matt. 24 : 31 ; Mark 13 : 27. See GATHER.¶

2. SUNALIZŌ (συναλίζω), to gather together, to assemble, with the suggestion of a crowded meeting (sun, with, halizō, to crowd, or mass : the corresponding adjective is halēs, thronged), is used in Acts 1 : 4. The meaning to eat with, suggested by some, as if the word were derived from hals, " salt," is not to be accepted.¶

3. SUNERCHOMAI (συνέρχομαι), to come together (sun, together, erchomai, to come), is once rendered " assemble," Mark 14 : 53, A.V. It is frequently used of " coming together," especially of the gathering of a local church, 1 Cor. 11 : 17, 18, 20, 33, 34 ; 14 : 23, 26 ; it is rendered " resorted " in Acts 16 : 13, A.V., where the R.V. adheres to the lit. rendering, " came together." See ACCOMPANY.

Notes : (1) In Acts 15 : 25, *ginomai*, to become, is translated " having come to (one accord)," correcting the A.V., " being assembled with (one accord)."

(2) *Sunagōgē*, akin to A, No. 1, is, lit., a place where people assemble. In Acts 13 : 43 the R.V. suitably has " synagogue," for the A.V. " congregation," the building standing by metonymy for the people therein (cp. Matt. 10 : 17, etc.). In Jas. 2 : 2 (A.V., " assembly ") the word is " synagogue " (R.V.). See SYNAGOGUE.

(3) *Episunagōgē*, akin to No. 1, *Note*, an assembling together, is used in 2 Thess. 2 : 1, of the Rapture of the saints into the air to meet the Lord, " our gathering together ; " in Heb. 10 : 25, of the gatherings of believers on earth during the present period. See GATHERING.

ASSEMBLY

1. EKKLESIA (ἐκκλησία), from ek, out of, and klēsis, a calling (kaleō,

to call), was used among the Greeks of a body of citizens gathered to discuss the affairs of State, Acts 19 : 39. In the Sept. it is used to designate the gathering of Israel, summoned for any definite purpose, or a gathering regarded as representative of the whole nation.   In Acts 7 : 38 it is used of Israel ; in 19 : 32, 41, of a riotous mob.   It has two applications to companies of Christians, (a) to the whole company of the redeemed throughout the present era, the company of which Christ said, " I will build My Church," Matt. 16 : 18, and which is further described as " the Church which is His Body," Eph. 1 : 22 ; 5 : 23, (b) in the singular number (e.g., Matt. 18 : 17, R.V. marg., " congregation "), to a company consisting of professed believers, e.g., Acts 20 : 28 ; 1 Cor. 1 : 2 ; Gal. 1 : 13 ; 1 Thess. 1 : 1 ; 2 Thess. 1 : 1 ; 1 Tim. 3 : 5, and in the plural, with reference to churches in a district.

There is a apparent exception in the R.V. of Acts 9 : 31, where, while the A.V. has " churches," the singular seems to point to a district ; but the reference is clearly to the church as it was in Jerusalem, from which it had just been scattered, 8 : 1.   Again, in Rom. 16 : 23, that Gaius was the host of " the whole church," simply suggests that the assembly in Corinth had been accustomed to meet in his house, where also Paul was entertained.   See CHURCH.

2. PANĒGURIS (πανήγυρις), from pan, all, and agora, any kind of assembly, denoted, among the Greeks, an assembly of the people in contrast to the Council of National Leaders, or a gathering of the people in honour of a god, or for some public festival, such as the Olympic games. The word is used in Heb. 12 : 23, coupled with the word Church, as applied to all believers who form the Body of Christ.¶

3. PLĒTHOS (πλῆθος), a multitude, the whole number, is translated " assembly " in Acts 23 : 7, R.V.   See BUNDLE, COMPANY, MULTITUDE.

Note : For sunagōgē, see ASSEMBLE, Note (2).

For ASSENT see AGREE, No. 2

For ASSIST see HELP, B, Note

ASSURANCE, ASSURE, ASSUREDLY
A. Nouns.

1. PISTIS (πίστις), faith, has the secondary meaning of an assurance or guarantee, e.g., Acts 17 : 31 ; by raising Christ from the dead, God has given " assurance " that the world will be judged by Him (the A.V. margin, " offered faith " does not express the meaning).   Cp. 1 Tim. 5 : 12, where " faith " means " pledge."   See BELIEF, FAITH, FIDELITY.

2. PLĒROPHORIA (πληροφορία), a fulness, abundance, also means full assurance, entire confidence ; lit., a ' full-carrying ' (plēros, full, pherō, to carry).   Some explain it as full fruitfulness (cp. R.V., " fulness " in Heb. 6 : 11).   In 1 Thess. 1 : 5 it describes the willingness and freedom

of spirit enjoyed by those who brought the Gospel to Thessalonica ; in Col. 2 : 2, the freedom of mind and confidence resulting from an understanding in Christ ; in Heb. 6 : 11 (A.V., " full assurance," R.V., " fulness "), the engrossing effect of the expectation of the fulfilment of God's promises ; in Heb. 10 : 22, the character of the faith by which we are to draw near to God. See FULNESS.¶

3. HUPOSTASIS (ὑπόστασις), lit., a standing under, support (hupo, under, histēmi, to stand), hence, an " assurance," is so rendered in Heb. 11 : 1, R.V., for A.V., " substance." It here may signify a title-deed, as giving a guarantee, or reality. See CONFIDENCE, PERSON, SUBSTANCE.

Note : In Acts 16 : 10, for the A.V. (of sumbibazomai), " assuredly gathering," see CONCLUDE.

B. Verbs.

1. PISTOŌ (πιστόω), to trust or give assurance to (cp. A, No. 1), has a secondary meaning, in the Passive Voice, to be assured of, 2 Tim. 3 : 14.¶

2. PLĒROPHOREŌ (πληροφορέω), akin to A, No. 2, to bring in full measure, to fulfil, also signifies to be fully assured, Rom. 4 : 21, R.V., of Abraham's faith. In 14 : 5 it is said of the apprehension of the will of God. So in Col. 4 : 12 in the best mss. In these three places it is used subjectively, with reference to an effect upon the mind. For its other and objective use, referring to things external, see FULFIL ; see also BELIEVE, KNOW, PERSUADE, PROOF.¶ In the Sept., Eccl. 8 : 11.¶

3. PEITHŌ (πείθω), to persuade, is rendered " assure " in 1 John 3 : 19 (marg., " persuade "), where the meaning is that of confidence toward God consequent upon loving in deed and in truth. See BELIEVE, CONFIDENCE, FRIEND, OBEY, PERSUADE, TRUST, YIELD.

C. Adverb.

ASPHALŌS (ἀσφαλῶς) means (a) safely, Mark 14 : 44 ; Acts 16 : 23 ; (b) assuredly, Acts 2 : 36 ; the knowledge there enjoined involves freedom from fear of contradiction, with an intimation of the impossibility of escape from the effects. See SAFELY.

For ASTONISH and ASTONISHMENT see AMAZE and AMAZEMENT

For ASTRAY see ERR

For ASUNDER see BREAK, BURST, CUT, PART, PUT, REND and SAW

AT: see Note †, p. 9

For ATHIRST see THIRST

ATONEMENT

KATALLAGĒ (καταλλαγή), translated " atonement " in the A.V.

of Rom. 5 : 11, signifies, not "atonement," but "reconciliation," as in the R.V. See also Rom. 11 : 15 ; 2 Cor. 5 : 18, 19.¶ So with the corresponding verb *katallassō*, see under RECONCILE. "Atonement" (the explanation of this English word as being at-one-ment is entirely fanciful) is frequently found in the O.T. See, for instance, Leviticus, chapters 16 and 17. The corresponding N.T. words are *hilasmos*, propitiation, 1 Jno. 2 : 2 ; 4 : 10, and *hilastērion*, Rom. 3 : 25 ; Heb. 9 : 5, "mercy-seat," the covering of the ark of the Covenant. These describe the means (in and through the Person and work of the Lord Jesus Christ, in His death on the Cross by the shedding of His blood in His vicarious sacrifice for sin) by which God shows mercy to sinners. See PROPITIATION.

ATTAIN

1. KATANTAŌ (καταντάω), a strengthened form of *antaō*, to come opposite to, signifies to reach, to arrive at. It is used in its local significance several times in the Acts, e.g., 27 : 12, R.V., " could reach."

In its metaphorical sense of attaining to something it is used in three places : Acts 26 : 7, of the fulfilment of the promise of God made to the ancestors of Israel, to which promise the twelve tribes " hope to attain " (R.V.) ; in Eph. 4 : 13, of attaining to the unity of the faith and of the knowledge of the Son of God ; in Phil. 3 : 11, of the paramount aims of the Apostle's life, " if by any means," he says, " I might attain unto the resurrection from the dead," not the physical resurrection, which is assured to all believers hereafter, but to the present life of identification with Christ in His Resurrection. For the metaphorical sense in 1 Cor. 10 : 11 and 14 : 36, see ARRIVE, A, No. 1. See also COME, No. 28.

2. KATALAMBANŌ (καταλαμβάνω), to seize, to apprehend, whether physically or mentally, is rendered " attain " in the sense of making something one's own, appropriating a thing, Rom. 9 : 30, said of the Gentiles, who through the Gospel have attained to, or laid hold of, the righteousness which is of faith, in contrast to the present condition of Israel ; in 1 Cor. 9 : 24, of securing a prize, R.V., " attain," for A.V., " obtain." See APPREHEND.

3. PHTHANŌ (φθάνω), to anticipate, also means to reach, attain to a thing ; negatively of Israel (see ARRIVE, No. 5). The only other passage where it has this significance is Phil. 3 : 16, " we have attained." See COME, PREVENT.

4. TUNCHANŌ (τυγχάνω), to reach, meet with, signifies to attain to, in Luke 20 : 35, R.V. (for A.V., " obtain "). See CHANCE, ENJOY, OBTAIN.

Notes : (1) *Parakoloutheō*, rendered " attained " in 1 Tim. 4 : 6, A.V. (R.V., " hast followed "), does not signify attainment, but following fully. It is an intensive form of *akoloutheō*, to follow. So in 2 Tim. 3 : 10, R.V., " didst follow " (A.V., " fully known ") ; ' follow fully ' would be suitable. In Mark 16 : 17 it is translated " follow ; " in Luke 1 : 3, ' having traced " (R.V.). See FOLLOW, KNOW, *Notes* (1), UNDERSTAND.¶

(2) *Lambanō*, incorrectly translated "attained" in the A.V. of Phil. 3 : 12, means "obtained" (R.V.).

ATTEND, ATTENDANCE, ATTENDANT
A. Verbs.

1. PROSECHŌ (προσέχω), to take heed, give heed, is said of the priests who "gave attendance at the altar," Heb. 7 : 13. It suggests devotion of thought and effort to a thing. In 1 Tim. 4 : 13 (in the exhortation regarding the public reading of the Scriptures), the R.V. translates it "give heed," for the A.V., "give attendance." In Acts 16 : 14, "to give heed" (for A.V., "attended"). See BEWARE, GIVE, No. 17, REGARD.

2. PROSKARTEREŌ (προσκαρτερέω), to be stedfast, a strengthened form of *kartereō* (*pros*, towards, intensive, *karteros*, strong), denotes to continue stedfastly in a thing and give unremitting care to it, e.g., Rom. 13 : 6, of rulers in the discharge of their functions. See CONTINUE, WAIT. In the Sept., Numb. 13 : 21.¶

B. Adjective.

EUPAREDROS (εὐπάρεδρος), lit., sitting well beside (*eu*, well, *para*, beside, *hedra*, a seat), i.e., sitting constantly by, and so applying oneself diligently to, anything, is used in 1 Cor. 7 : 35, with *pros*, upon, "that ye may attend upon." Some mss. have *euprosedron*.¶

C. Noun.

HUPERETES (ὑπηρέτης), lit., an under-rower ; hence, a servant, is rendered "attendant" in Luke 4 : 20 and Acts 13 : 5, R.V. See MINISTER, OFFICER, SERVANT.

For ATTENTIVE, in the A.V. of Luke 19 : 48, see HANG, No. 2

For AUDIENCE see HEARING, A, No. 1, B, No. 1

AUGHT
AUGHT : See † page 9 (footnote). It is wrongly spelt "ought" in the A.V. in some places, e.g., in John 4 : 33, "ought to eat" (there is no word in the original there for "aught ").

AUSTERE
AUSTEROS (αὐστηρός), akin to *auō*, to dry up (Eng., austere), primarily denotes stringent to the taste, like new wine not matured by age, unripe fruit, etc. ; hence, harsh, severe, Luke 19 : 21, 22.¶
Note : Synonymous with *austeros*, but to be distinguished from it, is *sklēros* (from *skellō*, to be dry). It was applied to that which lacks moisture, and so is rough and disagreeable to the touch, and hence came to denote harsh, stern, hard. It is used by Matthew to describe the un-profitable servant's remark concerning his master, in the parable corres-ponding to that in Luke 19 (see *austeros*, above). *Austeros* is derived from

a word having to do with the taste, *sklēros*, with the touch. *Austēros* is not necessarily a term of reproach, whereas *sklēros* is always so, and indicates a harsh, even inhuman, character. *Austēros* is "rather the exaggeration of a virtue pushed too far, than an absolute vice" (Trench, Syn. § xiv). *Sklēros* is used of the character of a man, Matt. 25 : 24 ; of a saying, John 6 : 60 ; of the difficulty and pain of kicking against the ox-goads, Acts 9 : 5 ; 26 : 14 ; of rough winds, Jas. 3 : 4 and of harsh speeches, Jude 15. See FIERCE, HARD.¶ Cp. *sklērotēs*, hardness, *sklērunō*, to harden, *sklērokardia*, hardness of heart, and *sklērotrachēlos*, stiff-necked.

AUTHOR

1. AITIOS (αἴτιος), an adjective (cp. *aitia*, a cause), denotes that which causes something. This and No. 2 are both translated "author" in Hebrews. *Aitios*, in Heb. 5 : 9, describes Christ as the "Author of eternal salvation unto all them that obey Him," signifying that Christ, exalted and glorified as our High Priest, on the ground of His finished work on earth, has become the Personal mediating cause (R.V., margin) of eternal salvation. It is difficult to find an adequate English equivalent to express the meaning here. Christ is not the merely formal cause of our salvation. He is the concrete and active cause of it. He has not merely caused or effected it, He is, as His Name, "Jesus," implies, our salvation itself, Luke 2 : 30 ; 3 : 6.

2. ARCHĒGOS (ἀρχηγός), translated "Prince" in Acts 3 : 15 (marg., "Author") and 5 : 31, but "Author" in Heb. 2 : 10, R.V., "Captain," R.V. marg., and A.V., and "Author" in 12 : 2, primarily signifies one who takes a lead in, or provides the first occasion of, anything. In the Sept. it is used of the chief of a tribe or family, Num. 13 : 2 (R.V., prince) ; of the "heads" of the children of Israel, ver. 3 ; a captain of the whole people, 14 : 4 ; in Micah 1 : 13, of Lachish as the leader of the sin of the daughter of Sion : there, as in Heb. 2 : 10, the word suggests a combination of the meaning of leader with that of the source from whence a thing proceeds. That Christ is the Prince of life signifies, as Chrysostom says, that "the life He had was not from another ; the Prince or Author of life must be He who has life from Himself." But the word does not necessarily combine the idea of the source or originating cause with that of leader. In Heb. 12 : 2 where Christ is called the "Author and Perfecter of faith," He is represented as the One who takes precedence in faith and is thus the perfect Exemplar of it. The pronoun "our" does not correspond to anything in the original, and may well be omitted. Christ in the days of His flesh trod undeviatingly the path of faith, and as the Perfecter has brought it to a perfect end in His own Person. Thus He is the leader of all others who tread that path. See PRINCE.¶

Note : In 1 Cor. 14 : 33, the A.V., "the author," represents no word in the original ; R.V. "a God of."

AUTHORITY
A. Nouns.

1. EXOUSIA (ἐξουσία) denotes authority (from the impersonal verb *exesti*, " it is lawful "). From the meaning of leave or permission, or liberty of doing as one pleases, it passed to that of the ability or strength with which one is endued, then to that of the power of authority, the right to exercise power, e.g., Matt. 9 : 6 ; 21 : 23 ; 2 Cor. 10 : 8 ; or the power of rule or government, the power of one whose will and commands must be obeyed by others, e.g., Matt. 28 : 18 ; John 17 : 2 ; Jude 25 ; Rev. 12 : 10 ; 17 : 13 ; more specifically of apostolic authority, 2 Cor. 10 : 8 ; 13 : 10 ; the power of judicial decision, John 19 : 10 ; of managing domestic affairs, Mark 13 : 34. By metonymy, or name-change (the substitution of a suggestive word for the name of the thing meant), it stands for that which is subject to authority or rule, Luke 4 : 6 (R.V. " authority," for the A.V. " power ") ; or, as with the English " authority," one who possesses authority, a ruler, magistrate, Rom. 13 : 1-3 ; Luke 12 : 11 ; Tit. 3 : 1 ; or a spiritual potentate, e.g., Eph. 3 : 10 ; 6 : 12 ; Col. 1 : 16 ; 2 : 10, 15 ; 1 Pet. 3 : 22. The R.V. usually translates it " authority."

In 1 Cor. 11 : 10 it is used of the veil with which a woman is required to cover herself in an assembly or church, as a sign of the Lord's authority over the Church. See JURISDICTION, LIBERTY, POWER, RIGHT, STRENGTH.

2. EPITAGĒ (ἐπιταγή), an injunction (from *epi*, upon, *tassō*, to order), is once rendered " authority," Tit. 2 : 15 (R.V., marg., " commandment "). See COMMANDMENT.

Note : The corresponding verb is *epitassō*, to command. See COMMAND.

3. HUPEROCHĒ (ὑπεροχή), primarily, a projection, eminence, as a mountain peak, hence, metaphorically, pre-eminence, superiority, excellency, is once rendered " authority," 1 Tim. 2 : 2, A.V. (marg., " eminent place "), R.V., " high place," of the position of magistrates ; in 1 Cor. 2 : 1, " excellency " (of speech). Cp. *huperechō*, to surpass. See EXCELLENCY.¶

4. DUNASTĒS (δυνάστης), akin to *dunamis*, power, Eng., dynasty, signifies a potentate, a high officer ; in Acts 8 : 27, of a high officer, it is rendered " of great authority ; " in Luke 1 : 52, R.V., " princes," (A.V., " the mighty ") ; in 1 Tim. 6 : 15 it is said of God (" Potentate "). See MIGHTY, POTENTATE. ¶

B. Verbs.

1. EXOUSIAZŌ (ἐξουσιάζω), akin to A, No. 1, signifies to exercise power, Luke 22 : 25 ; 1 Cor. 6 : 12 ; 7 : 4 (twice). See POWER.¶

2. KATEXOUSIAZŌ (κατεξουσιάζω), *kata*, down, intensive, and No. 1, to exercise authority upon, is used in Matt. 20 : 25, and Mark 10 : 42.¶

3. AUTHENTEŌ (αὐθεντέω), from *autos*, self, and a lost noun *hentēs*,

probably signifying working (Eng., authentic), to exercise authority on one's own account, to domineer over, is used in 1 Tim. 2 : 12, A.V., " to usurp authority," R.V., " to have dominion." In the earlier usage of the word it signified one who with his own hand killed either others or himself. Later it came to denote one who acts on his own authority ; hence, to exercise authority, dominion. See DOMINION, *Note*.¶

AUTUMN

PHTHINOPŌRINOS (φθινοπωρινός), an adjective signifying autumnal (from *phthinopōron*, late autumn, from *phthinō*, to waste away, or wane, and *opōra*, autumn), is used in Jude 12, where unfruitful and worthless men are figuratively described as trees such as they are at the close of autumn, fruitless and leafless (A.V., " trees whose fruit withereth ").¶

AVAIL

ISCHUŌ (ἰσχύω) signifies (*a*) to be strong in body, to be robust, in sound health, Matt. 9 : 12 ; Mark 2 : 17 ; (*b*) to have power, as of the Gospel, Acts 19 : 20 ; to prevail against, said of spiritual enemies, Rev. 12 : 8 ; of an evil spirit against exorcists, Acts 19 : 16 ; (*c*) to be of force, to be effective, capable of producing results, Matt. 5 : 13 (" it is good for nothing ; " lit., ' it availeth nothing ') ; Gal. 5 : 6 ; in Heb. 9 : 17 it apparently has the meaning to be valid (R.V., " for doth it ever avail . . .? ", for A.V., " it is of no strength "). It is translated " avail " with reference to prayer, in Jas. 5 : 16 ; cp. the strengthened form *exischuō* in Eph. 3 : 18. See ABLE, CAN, GOOD, MAY, PREVAIL, STRENGTH, WHOLE, WORK.

AVENGE, AVENGER
A. Verb.

EKDIKEŌ (ἐκδικέω), *ek*, from, *dikē*, justice, i.e., that which proceeds from justice, means (*a*) to vindicate a person's right, (*b*) to avenge a thing. With the meaning (*a*), it is used in the parable of the unjust judge, Luke 18 : 3, 5, of the vindication of the rights of the widow ; with the meaning (*b*) it is used in Rev. 6 : 10 and 19 : 2, of the act of God in avenging the blood of the saints ; in 2 Cor. 10 : 6, of the Apostle's readiness to use his apostolic authority in punishing disobedience on the part of his readers ; here the R.V. substitutes " avenge " for the A.V., " revenge ; " in Rom. 12 : 19 of avenging oneself, against which the believer is warned.¶

Note : In Rev. 18 : 20, the A.V. mistranslates *krinō* and *krima* " hath avenged you ; " R.V., " hath judged your judgement."

B. Nouns.

1. EKDIKOS (ἔκδικος), primarily, without law, then, one who exacts a penalty from a person, an avenger, a punisher, is used in Rom. 13 : 4 of a civil authority in the discharge of his function of executing wrath on the evildoer (A.V., wrongly, " revenger ") ; in 1 Thess. 4 : 6, of God as the Avenger of the one who wrongs his brother, here particularly in the matter of adultery.¶

2. EKDIKĒSIS (ἐκδίκησις), vengeance, is used with the verb *poieō*, to make, i.e., to avenge, in Luke 18 : 7, 8 ; Acts 7 : 24 ; twice it is used in statements that " vengeance " belongs to God, Rom. 12 : 19 ; Heb. 10 : 30. In 2 Thess. 1 : 8 it is said of the act of Divine justice which will be meted out to those who know not God and obey not the Gospel, when the Lord comes in flaming fire at His Second Advent. In the Divine exercise of judgment there is no element of vindictiveness, nothing by way of taking revenge. In Luke 21 : 22, it is used of the days of vengeance upon the Jewish people ; in 1 Pet. 2 : 14, of civil governors as those who are sent of God " for vengeance on evildoers " (A.V. " punishment ") ; in 2 Cor. 7 : 11, of the self-avenging of believers, in their godly sorrow for wrong doing, R.V., " avenging," for A.V., " revenge." See PUNISHMENT, VENGEANCE.¶

AVOID

1. EKKLINŌ (ἐκκλίνω), to turn away from, to turn aside, lit., to bend out of (*ek*, out, *klinō*, to bend), is used in Rom. 3 : 12, of the sinful condition of mankind, A.V., " gone out of the way," R.V., " turned aside ; " in Rom. 16 : 17, of turning away from those who cause offences and occasions of stumbling (A.V., " avoid ") ; in 1 Pet. 3 : 11 of turning away from evil (A.V., " eschew "). See ESCHEW, WAY.¶

2. EKTREPŌ (ἐκτρέπω), lit., to turn or twist out, is used in the Passive Voice in Heb. 12 : 13, " that which is lame be not turned out of the way " (or rather, ' put out of joint ') ; in the sense of the Middle Voice (though Passive in form) of turning aside, or turning away from, 2 Tim. 4 : 4 (A.V., " shall be turned unto fables," R.V., " shall turn aside ") ; in 1 Tim. 1 : 6, of those who, having swerved from the faith, have turned aside unto vain talking ; in 5 : 15, of those who have turned aside after Satan ; in 6 : 20, R.V., of " turning away from (A.V., " avoiding ") profane babblings and oppositions of the knowledge which is falsely so called." See TURN. In the Sept., Amos 5 : 8.¶

3. PARAITEOMAI (παραιτέομαι), lit., to ask aside (*para*, aside, *aiteō*, to ask), signifies (*a*) to beg of (or from) another, Mark 15 : 6, in the most authentic mss. ; (*b*) to deprecate, (1) to entreat (that) not, Heb. 12 : 19 ; (2) to refuse, decline, avoid, 1 Tim. 4 : 7 ; 5 : 11 ; 2 Tim. 2 : 23 ; Tit. 3 : 10 (see No. 4 for ver. 9) ; Heb. 12 : 25 ; (*c*) to beg off, ask to be excused, Luke 14 : 18, 19 (some would put Heb. 12 : 25 here). See EXCUSE, INTREAT, REFUSE, REJECT.¶

4. PERIISTĒMI (περιίστημι), in the Active Voice, means to stand around (*peri*, around, *histēmi*, to stand), John 11 : 42 ; Acts 25 : 7 ; in the Middle Voice, to turn oneself about, for the purpose of avoiding something, to avoid, shun, said of profane babblings, 2 Tim. 2 : 16 ; of foolish questions, genealogies, strife, etc., Tit. 3 : 9 (A.V., " avoid "). See SHUN, STAND.¶

5. STELLŌ (στέλλω), to place, sometimes signifies, in the Middle

Voice, to take care against a thing, to avoid, 2 Cor. 8 : 20 ; in 2 Thess. 3 : 6, of withdrawing from a person. See WITHDRAW.¶

For AWAIT (A.V. of Acts 9 : 24 ; 20 : 3, 19 ; 23 : 30) see PLOT

AWAKE

1. EGEIRŌ (ἐγείρω) is used, (a) in the Active Voice, of arousing a person from sleep ; in Matt. 8 : 25 of the act of the disciples in awaking the Lord ; in Acts 12 : 7, of the awaking of Peter R.V., " awake him " ; (b) in the Passive Voice, with a Middle significance, of the virgins, in arousing themselves from their slumber, Matt. 25 : 7 ; in Rom. 13 : 11, and Eph. 5 : 14, metaphorically, of awaking from a state of moral sloth. See ARISE, LIFT, RAISE, REAR, RISE, STAND, TAKE.

2. DIEGEIRŌ (διεγείρω) is used of awaking from natural sleep, Matt. 1 : 24 ; Mark 4 : 38 ; of the act of the disciples in awaking the Lord, Luke 8 : 24 (cp. egeirō, in Matt. 8 : 25) ; metaphorically, of arousing the mind, 2 Pet. 1 : 13 ; 3 : 1. See ARISE, RAISE, STIR UP.

3. EKNĒPHŌ (ἐκνήφω), primarily, to return to one's sense from drunkenness, to become sober, is so used in the Sept., e.g., Gen. 9 : 24 ; metaphorically, in Joel 1 : 5 ; Hab. 2 : 7 ; lit., in 2 : 19, of the words of an idolater to an image ; in the N.T. in 1 Cor. 15 : 34, " Awake up righteously and sin not " (R.V.), suggesting a return to soberness of mind from the stupor consequent upon the influence of evil doctrine.¶

4. EXUPNIZŌ (ἐξυπνίζω), from ek, out of, and hupnos, sleep, to rouse a person out of sleep, is used metaphorically, in John 11 : 11.¶

5. DIAGRĒGOREŌ (διαγρηγορέω), dia, intensive, grēgoreō, to watch, is used in Luke 9 : 32, R.V., " were fully awake." A.V. " were awake."¶

For AWARE see KNOW, A, No. 1, end of 1st par.

AWAY

Note : This word is to be taken in connection with various verbs. The verb airō, to seize, to lift up, take away, is translated " away with," in Luke 23 : 18 ; John 19 : 15 ; Acts 21 : 36 ; 22 : 22, implying a forcible removal for the purpose of putting to death. See BEAR, No. 9.

AWE

DEOS (δέος), awe, is so rendered in Heb. 12 : 28, R.V. ; the previous word " reverence " represents the inferior reading aidōs (see SHAME-FASTNESS).

AXE

AXINĒ (ἀξίνη), an axe, akin to agnumi, to break, is found in Matt. 3 : 10, and Luke 3 : 9.¶

B

BABBLER, BABBLINGS

1. SPERMOLOGOS (σπερμολόγος), a babbler, is used in Acts 17 : 18. Primarily an adjective, it came to be used as a noun signifying a crow, or some other bird, picking up seeds (*sperma*, a seed, *legō*, to collect). Then it seems to have been used of a man accustomed to hang about the streets and markets, picking up scraps which fall from loads; hence a parasite, who lives at the expense of others, a hanger on.

Metaphorically it became used of a man who picks up scraps of information and retails them secondhand, a plagiarist, or of those who make a show, in unscientific style, of knowledge obtained from misunderstanding lectures. Prof. Ramsay points out that there does not seem to be any instance of the classical use of the word as a babbler or a mere talker. He finds in the word a piece of Athenian slang, applied to one who was outside any literary circle, an ignorant plagiarist. Other suggestions have been made, but without satisfactory evidence.¶

2. KENOPHONIA (κενοφωνία), babbling (from *kenos*, empty, and *phonē*, a sound), signifies empty discussion, discussion on useless subjects, 1 Tim. 6 : 20 and 2 Tim. 2 : 16.¶

BABE

1. BREPHOS (βρέφος) denotes (*a*) an unborn child, as in Luke 1 : 41, 44; (*b*) a newborn child, or an infant still older, Luke 2 : 12, 16; 18 : 15; Acts 7 : 19; 2 Tim. 3 : 15; 1 Pet. 2 : 2. See CHILD, INFANT.¶

2. NĒPIOS (νήπιος), lit., 'without the power of speech,' denotes a little child, the literal meaning having been lost in the general use of the word. It is used (*a*) of infants, Matt. 21 : 16; (*b*) metaphorically, of the unsophisticated in mind and trustful in disposition, Matt. 11 : 25 and Luke 10 : 21, where it stands in contrast to the wise; of those who are possessed merely of natural knowledge, Rom. 2 : 20; of those who are carnal, and have not grown, as they should have done, in spiritual understanding and power, the spiritually immature, 1 Cor. 3 : 1, those who are so to speak partakers of milk, and "without experience of the word of righteousness," Heb. 5 : 13; of the Jews, who, while the Law was in force, were in a state corresponding to that of childhood, or minority, just as the word "infant" is used of a minor, in English law, Gal. 4 : 3, "children;" of believers in an immature condition, impressionable and

liable to be imposed upon instead of being in a state of spiritual maturity, Eph. 4 : 14, " children." Immaturity is always associated with this word. See CHILD, No. 7 ¶

Note : The corresponding verb, *nēpiazō*, is found in 1 Cor. 14 : 20, where believers are exhorted to be as " babes " (R.V.) in malice, unable to think or speak maliciously.¶

BACK (Noun)

NŌTOS (νῶτος), the back, is derived from a root *nō*—, signifying to bend, curve. It is used in Rom. 11 : 10.¶

BACK (Adverb), BACKSIDE, BACKWARD

1. OPISŌ (ὀπίσω), connected with *hepomai*, to follow, is used adverbially, of place, with the meaning " back," " backward," in the phrase *eis ta opisō*, lit., unto the things behind, in Mark 13 : 16 ; Luke 9 : 62 ; 17 : 31 ; John 6 : 66 ; 18 : 6 ; 20 : 14. Cp. Phil. 3 : 13, " the things which are behind." See BEHIND.

2. OPISTHEN (ὄπισθεν), of place, behind, after, is rendered " backside " in Rev. 5 : 1, A.V. (R.V., " back "). See BEHIND.

BACKBITER, BACKBITING

KATALALOS (κατάλαλος), a backbiter, and KATALALIA (καταλαλία), backbiting, are formed from *kata*, against, and *laleō*, to speak. *Katalalos* is used in Rom. 1 : 30.¶ *Katalalia* is translated " evil speaking " in 1 Pet. 2 : 1, " backbiting " in 2 Cor. 12 : 20.¶

Note : The corresponding verb *katalaleō* the R.V. translates " speak against," in its five occurrences, Jas. 4 : 11 (three times) ; 1 Pet. 2 : 12, and 3 : 16 ; A.V., " speak evil," in all the passages except 1 Pet. 2 : 12.¶

For BADE see BID

BAD

1. KAKOS (κακός) indicates the lack in a person or thing of those qualities which should be possessed ; it means bad in character (*a*) morally, by way of thinking, feeling or acting, e.g., Mark 7 : 21, " thoughts ; " 1 Cor. 15 : 33, " company ; " Col. 3 : 5, " desire ; " 1 Tim. 6 : 10, " all kinds of evil ; " 1 Pet. 3 : 9, " evil for evil ; " (*b*) in the sense of what is injurious or baneful, e.g., the tongue as " a restless evil," Jas. 3 : 8 ; " evil beasts," Tit. 1 : 12 ; " harm," Acts 16 : 28 ; once it is translated " bad," 2 Cor. 5 : 10. It is the opposite of *agathos*, good. See EVIL, HARM, ILL, NOISOME, WICKED.

2. PONĒROS (πονηρός), connected with *ponos*, labour, expresses especially the active form of evil, and is practically the same in meaning as (*b*), under No. 1. It is used, e.g., of thoughts, Matt. 15 : 19 (cp. *kakos*, in Mark 7 : 21) ; of speech, Matt. 5 : 11 (cp. *kakos*, in 1 Pet. 3 : 10) ; of

acts, 2 Tim. 4 : 18. Where *kakos* and *ponēros* are put together, *kakos* is always put first and signifies bad in character, base, *ponēros*, bad in effect, malignant : see 1 Cor. 5 : 8, and Rev. 16 : 2. *Kakos* has a wider meaning, *ponēros* a stronger meaning. *Ponēros* alone is used of Satan and might well be translated ' the malignant one,' e.g., Matt. 5 : 37 and five times in 1 John (2 : 13, 14 ; 3 : 12 ; 5 : 18, 19, R.V.) ; of demons, e.g., Luke 7 : 21. Once it is translated " bad," Matt. 22 : 10. See EVIL, GRIEVOUS, HARM, LEWD, MALICIOUS, WICKED.

3. SAPROS (σαπρός), corrupt, rotten (akin to *sēpō*, to rot), primarily, of vegetable and animal substances, expresses what is of poor quality, unfit for use, putrid. It is said of a tree and its fruit, Matt. 7 : 17, 18 ; 12 : 33 ; Luke 6 : 43 ; of certain fish, Matt. 13 : 48 (here translated " bad ") ; of defiling speech, Eph. 4 : 29. See CORRUPT.¶

BAG

1. GLŌSSOKOMON (γλωσσόκομον), from *glōssa*, a tongue, and *komeō*, to tend, was, firstly, a case in which to keep the mouthpiece of wind instruments ; secondly, a small box for any purpose, but especially a casket or purse, to keep money in. It is used of the bag which Judas carried, John 12 : 6 ; 13 : 29 ; in the Sept. of 2 Chron. 24 : 8, 10, used of the box appointed by King Joash for offerings for the repair of the Temple.¶

2. BALLANTION (βαλλάντιον), from *ballō*, to cast, a money-box or purse, is found in Luke's Gospel, four times, 10 : 4 ; 12 : 33 (A.V., " bag ") ; 22 : 35, 36. See PURSE.¶

Note : Zōnē, a girdle or belt, also served as a purse for money, Matt. 10 : 9 ; Mark 6 : 8. See GIRDLE.

BAGGAGE

EPISKEUAZŌ (ἐπισκευάζω), to furnish with things necessary ; in the Middle Voice, to furnish for oneself ; it was used of equipping baggage animals for a journey ; in Acts 21 : 15, R.V., it is translated " we took up our baggage " (A.V., " we took up our carriages "). The form is the 1st aorist participle, and lit. means ' having made ready (the things that were necessary for the journey).'¶

Note : Some mss. have the verb *aposkeuazō*, which has the same meaning.

BALANCE

ZUGOS (ζυγός), a yoke, also has the meaning of a pair of scales, Rev. 6 : 5. So the Sept. of Lev. 19 : 36 ; Isa. 40, 12. See YOKE.¶

BAND

1. SPEIRA (σπεῖρα), primarily anything round, and so whatever might be wrapped round a thing, a twisted rope, came to mean a body

of men at arms, and was the equivalent of the Roman *manipulus*. It was also used for a larger body of men, a cohort, about 600 infantry, commanded by a tribune. It is confined to its military sense. See, e.g., Matt. 27 : 27, and corresponding passages.

2. DESMOS (δεσμός), a band, fetter, anything for tying (from *deō*, to bind, fasten with chains etc.), is sometimes translated " band," sometimes " bond ; " " bands," in Luke 8 : 29 ; Acts 16 : 26 ; 22 : 30, A.V. only. In the case of the deaf man who had an impediment in his speech, whom the Lord took aside, Mark 7 : 35, the A.V. says " the string of his tongue was loosed ; " the R.V., more literally, " the bond of his tongue." See BOND, CHAIN, STRING.

3. SUNDESMOS (σύνδεσμος), an intensive form of No. 2, denoting that which binds firmly together, is used metaphorically of the joints and bands of the mystic Body of Christ, Col. 2 : 19 ; otherwise in the following phrases, " the bond of iniquity," Acts 8 : 23 ; " the bond of peace," Eph. 4 : 3 ; " the bond of perfectness," Col. 3 : 14. See BOND.¶

4. ZEUKTĒRIA (ζευκτηρία), a bond (connected with *zugos*, a yoke), is found once, of the rudder band of a ship, Acts 27 : 40.¶

BANDED

POIEŌ SUSTROPHĒN (ποιέω συστροφήν), Acts 23 : 12, of the Jews who " banded together " with the intention of killing Paul, consists of the verb *poieō*, to make, and the noun *sustrophē*, primarily a twisting up together, a binding together ; then, a secret combination, a conspiracy. Accordingly it might be translated ' made a conspiracy.' The noun is used elsewhere in 19 : 40. See CONCOURSE.¶

BANK, BANKERS

1. TRAPEZA (τράπεζα), primarily a table, denotes (*a*) an eating-table, e.g., Matt. 15 : 27 ; (*b*) food etc. placed on a table, Acts 6 : 2 ; 16 : 34 ; (*c*) a feast, a banquet, 1 Cor. 10 : 21 ; (*d*) the table or stand of a money-changer, where he exchanged money for a fee, or dealt with loans and deposits, Matt. 21 : 12 ; Mark 11 : 15 ; Luke 19 : 23 ; John 2 : 15. See MEAT, TABLE.

2. TRAPEZITĒS (τραπεζίτης), a money-changer, broker, banker ; translated " bankers " in Matt. 25 : 27, R.V. (A.V., " exchangers ").¶

Note : For *charax*, Luke 19 : 43, see TRENCH.

For BANQUETING see CAROUSINGS

BAPTISM, BAPTIST, BAPTIZE
A. Nouns.

1. BAPTISMA (βάπτισμα), baptism, consisting of the processes of immersion, submersion and emergence (from *baptō*, to dip), is used

(a) of John's baptism, (b) of Christian baptism, see B. below ; (c) of the overwhelming afflictions and judgments to which the Lord voluntarily submitted on the Cross, e.g., Luke 12 : 50 ; (d) of the sufferings His followers would experience, not of a vicarious character, but in fellowship with the sufferings of their Master. Some mss. have the word in Matt. 20 : 22, 23 ; it is used in Mark 10 : 38, 39, with this meaning.

2. BAPTISMOS (βαπτισμός), as distinct from *baptisma* (the ordinance), is used of the ceremonial washing of articles, Mark 7 : 4, 8, in some texts ; Heb. 9 : 10 ; once in a general sense, Heb. 6 : 2.¶ See WASHING.

3. BAPTISTĒS (βαπτιστής), a baptist, is used only of John the Baptist, and only in the Synoptists, 14 times.

B. Verb.

BAPTIZŌ (βαπτίζω), to baptize, primarily a frequentative form of *baptō*, to dip, was used among the Greeks to signify the dyeing of a garment, or the drawing of water by dipping a vessel into another, etc. Plutarchus uses it of the drawing of wine by dipping the cup into the bowl (*Alexis*, 67) and Plato, metaphorically, of being overwhelmed with questions (*Euthydemus*, 277 D).

It is used in the N.T. in Luke 11 : 38 of washing oneself (as in 2 Kings 5 : 14, " dipped himself," Sept.) ; see also Isa. 21 : 4, lit., ' lawlessness overwhelms me.' In the early chapters of the four Gospels and in Acts 1 : 5 ; 11 : 16 ; 19 : 4, it is used of the rite performed by John the Baptist who called upon the people to repent that they might receive remission of sins. Those who obeyed came " confessing their sins," thus acknowledging their unfitness to be in the Messiah's coming Kingdom. Distinct from this is the baptism enjoined by Christ, Matt. 28 : 19, a baptism to be undergone by believers, thus witnessing to their identification with Him in death, burial and resurrection, e.g., Acts 19 : 5 ; Rom. 6 : 3, 4 ; 1 Cor. 1 : 13–17 ; 12 : 13 ; Gal. 3 : 27 ; Col. 2 : 12. The phrase in Matt. 28 : 19, " baptizing them into the Name " (R.V. ; cp. Acts 8 : 16, R.V.), would indicate that the baptized person was closely bound to, or became the property of, the one into whose Name he was baptized.

In Acts 22 : 16 it is used in the Middle Voice, in the command given to Saul of Tarsus, " arise and be baptized," the significance of the Middle Voice form being ' get thyself baptized.' The experience of those who were in the ark at the time of the Flood was a figure or type of the facts of spiritual death, burial and resurrection, Christian baptism being an *antitupon*, " a corresponding type," a " like figure," 1 Pet. 3 : 21. Likewise the nation of Israel was figuratively baptized when made to pass through the Red Sea under the cloud, 1 Cor. 10 : 2. The verb is used metaphorically also in two distinct senses : firstly, of baptism by the Holy Spirit, which took place on the day of Pentecost ; secondly, of the calamity which would come upon the nation of the Jews, a baptism of the fire of Divine judgment for rejection of the will and word of God, Matt. 3 : 11 ; Luke 3 : 16.

BARBARIAN, BARBAROUS

BARBAROS (βάρβαρος) properly meant one whose speech is rude, or harsh ; the word is onomatopœic, indicating in the sound the uncouth character represented by the repeated syllable " bar-bar." Hence it signified one who speaks a strange or foreign language. See 1 Cor. 14 : 11. It then came to denote any foreigner ignorant of the Greek language and culture. After the Persian war it acquired the sense of rudeness and brutality. In Acts 28 : 2, 4, it is used unreproachfully of the inhabitants of Malta, who were of Phœnician origin. So in Rom. 1 : 14, where it stands in distinction from Greeks, and in implied contrast to both Greeks and Jews. Cp. the contrasts in Col. 3 : 11, where all such distinctions are shown to be null and void in Christ. " Berber " stood similarly in the language of the Egyptians for all non-Egyptian peoples.¶

BARE (Adjective)

GUMNOS (γυμνός), naked, is once translated " bare," 1 Cor. 15 : 37, where, used of grain, the meaning is made clearer by translating the phrase by " a bare grain," R.V. See NAKED.

For BARE (Verb) see BEAR

BARLEY
A. Noun.

KRITHĒ (κριθή), barley, is used in the plural in Rev. 6 : 6.¶
B. Adjective.

KRITHINOS (κρίθινος) signifies made of barley, John 6 : 9, 13.¶

BARN

APOTHĒKĒ (ἀποθήκη), lit., a place where anything is stored (Eng., apothecary), hence denoted a garner, granary, barn, Matt. 3 : 12 ; 6 : 26 ; 13 : 30 ; Luke 3 : 17 ; 12 : 18, 24. See also under GARNER.¶

Note : For *tameion,* a storehouse, store-chamber, more especially an inner chamber or secret room, Matt. 6 : 6 ; 24 : 26 ; Luke 12 : 3, 24, see CHAMBER.¶

BARREN

1. STEIROS (στεῖρος), from a root *ster*— meaning hard, firm (hence Eng., sterile), signifies barren, not bearing children, and is used with the natural significance three times in the Gospel of Luke, 1 : 7, 36 ; 23 : 29 ; and with a spiritual significance in Gal. 4 : 27, in a quotation from Is. 54 : 1. The circumstances of Sarah and Hagar, which Isaiah no doubt had in mind, are applied by the Apostle to the contrast between the works of the Law and the promise by grace.¶

2. ARGOS (ἀργός), denoting idle, barren, yielding no return, because of inactivity, is found in the best mss. in Jas. 2 : 20 (R.V., " barren ") ;

it is rendered " barren " in 2 Pet. 1 : 8, A.V., (R.V., " idle "). In Matt. 12 : 36, the " idle word " means the word that is thoughtless or profitless. See IDLE, SLOW ; cp. *katargeō*, under ABOLISH.

BASE, BASER

1. AGENĒS (ἀγενής), of low birth (*a*, negative, *genos*, family, race), hence denoted that which is of no reputation, of no account, 1 Cor. 1 : 28, " the base things of the world," i.e., those which are of no account or fame in the world's esteem. That the neuter plural of the adjective bears reference to persons is clear from verse 26.¶

2. TAPEINOS (ταπεινός), primarily that which is low, and does not rise far from the ground, as in the Sept. of Ezek. 17 : 24, hence, metaphorically, signifies lowly, of no degree. So the R.V. in 2 Cor. 10 : 1. Cp. Luke 1 : 52 and Jas. 1 : 9, " of low degree." Cp. *tapeinophrosunē*, lowliness of mind, and *tapeinoō*, to humble. See CAST, *Note* (7), HUMBLE, LOW, LOWLY.

3. AGORAIOS (ἀγοραῖος), translated in the A.V. of Acts 17 : 5 " of the baser sort," R.V., " of the rabble," signifies, lit., relating to the market place ; hence, frequenting markets, and so sauntering about idly. It is also used of affairs usually transacted in the market-place, and hence of judicial assemblies, Acts 19 : 38, R.V., " courts " (A.V., " law ") ; the margin in both R.V. and A.V. has " court days are kept." See COURT.¶

BASKET, BASKETFUL

1. KOPHINOS (κόφινος) was a wicker basket, originally containing a certain measure of capacity, Matt. 14 : 20 ; 16 : 9 ; Mark 6 : 43 (R.V., " basketfuls ") ; 8 : 19 ; Luke 9 : 17 ; 13 : 8 in some mss. ; John 6 : 13.¶

2. SPURIS (σπυρίς), or *sphuris*, signifies something round, twisted or folded together (connected with *speira*, anything rolled into a circle ; Eng., sphere) ; hence a reed basket, plaited, a capacious kind of hamper, sometimes large enough to hold a man, Matt. 15 : 37 ; 16 : 10 ; Mark 8 : 8, 20 (R.V., " basketfuls ") ; Acts 9 : 25.¶

3. SARGANĒ (σαργάνη) denotes (*a*) a braided rope or band, (*b*) a large basket made of ropes, or a wicker basket made of entwined twigs, 2 Cor. 11 : 33. That the basket in which Paul was let down from a window in Damascus is spoken of by Luke as a *spuris*, and by Paul himself as a *sarganē*, is quite consistent, the two terms being used for the same article.¶

BASON

NIPTĒR (νιπτήρ), the vessel into which the Lord poured water to wash the disciples' feet, was a large ewer, John 13 : 5. The word is connected with the verb *niptō*, to wash.¶

BASTARD

NOTHOS (νόθος) denotes an illegitimate child, one born out of lawful wedlock, Heb. 12 : 8.¶

BATHED

LOUŌ (λούω) signifies to bathe or to wash. In John 13 : 10 the R.V. " bathed " is necessary to distinguish the act from the washing of feet. See WASH.

BATTLE

POLEMOS (πόλεμος), a war, is incorrectly rendered " battle " in the A.V. of 1 Cor. 14 : 8 ; Rev. 9 : 7, 9 ; 16 : 14 ; 20 : 8 ; R.V., invariably, " war."

BAY

KOLPOS (κόλπος), translated " bay " in the R.V. of Acts 27 : 39, is wider than a " creek " (A.V.). Eng., gulf, is connected. See BOSOM.

For BE see BEING

BEACH

AIGIALOS (αἰγιαλός), translated " shore " in the A.V. in each place where it is used, Matt. 13 : 2, 48 ; John 21 : 4 ; Acts 21 : 5 ; 27 : 39, 40, is always in the R.V. translated " beach." It is derived from a root signifying to press, drive ; *aigis* denotes a wind-storm.¶

BEAM

DOKOS (δοκός), a beam, is perhaps etymologically connected with the root *dek—*, seen in the word *dechomai*, to receive, beams being received at their ends into walls or pieces of timber. The Lord used it metaphorically, in contrast to a mote, of a great fault, or vice, Matt. 7 : 3, 4, 5 ; Luke 6 : 41, 42.¶

BEAR (*in the sense of carrying, supporting*)
For the verb to bear in the sense of begetting, see BEGET.

1. BASTAZŌ (βαστάζω) signifies to support as a burden. It is used with the meaning (*a*) to take up, as in picking up anything, stones, John 10 : 31 ; (*b*) to carry something, Matt. 3 : 11 ; Mark 14 : 13 ; Luke 7 : 14 ; 22 : 10 ; Acts 3 : 2 ; 21 : 35 ; Rev. 17 : 7 ; to carry on one's person, Luke 10 : 4 ; Gal. 6 : 17 ; in one's body, Luke 11 : 27 ; to bear a name in testimony, Acts 9 : 15 ; metaphorically, of a root bearing branches, Rom. 11 : 18 ; (*c*) to bear a burden, whether physically, as of the Cross, John 19 : 17, or metaphorically in respect of sufferings endured in the cause of Christ, Luke 14 : 27 ; Rev. 2 : 3 ; it is said of physical endurance, Matt. 20 : 12 ; of sufferings borne on behalf of others, Matt. 8 : 17 ;

Rom. 15 : 1 ; Gal. 6 : 2 ; of spiritual truths not able to be borne, John 16 : 12 ; of the refusal to endure evil men, Rev. 2 : 2 ; of religious regulations imposed on others, Acts 15 : 10 ; of the burden of the sentence of God to be executed in due time, Gal. 5 : 10 ; of the effect at the Judgment Seat of Christ, to be borne by the believer for failure in the matter of discharging the obligations of discipleship, Gal. 6 : 5 ; (d) to bear by way of carrying off, John 12 : 6 ; 20 : 15. See CARRY, TAKE.¶

2. PHERŌ (φέρω), to bring or bear, is translated in the R.V. by the latter verb in Luke 23 : 26 ; John 2 : 8 (twice) ; 12 : 24 ; 15 : 2 (twice) ; Heb. 13 : 13. See BRING, No. 1 and words there.

3. ANAPHERŌ (ἀναφέρω), No. 2, with ana, up, is used of leading persons up to a higher place, and, in this respect, of the Lord's Ascension, Luke 24 : 51. It is used twice of the Lord's propitiatory sacrifice, in His bearing sins on the Cross, Heb. 9 : 28 and 1 Pet. 2 : 24 ; the A.V. margin, " to the tree," is to be rejected. The A.V. text, " on," and the R.V. " upon " express the phrase rightly. See BRING, CARRY, LEAD, OFFER.

4. EKPHERŌ (ἐκφέρω), No. 2, with ek, out, is used, literally, of carrying something forth, or out, e.g., a garment, Luke 15 : 22 ; sick folk, Acts 5 : 15 ; a corpse, Acts 5 : 6, 9, 10 ; of the impossibility of carrying anything out from this world at death, 1 Tim. 6 : 7. The most authentic mss. have this word in Mark 8 : 23, of the blind man, whom the Lord brought out of the village (R.V.). It is also used of the earth, in bringing forth produce, Heb. 6 : 8. See BRING, CARRY.¶

5. PERIPHERŌ (περιφέρω), No. 2, with peri, about, signifies to carry about, or bear about, and is used literally, of carrying the sick, Mark 6 : 55, or of physical sufferings endured in fellowship with Christ, 2 Cor. 4 : 10 ; metaphorically, of being carried about by different evil doctrines, Eph. 4 : 14 ; Heb. 13 : 9 ; Jude 12. See CARRY.

6. HUPOPHERŌ (ὑποφέρω), lit., to bear up under, is best rendered by " endure," as 1 Cor. 10 : 13, R.V., of enduring temptations ; of enduring persecutions, 2 Tim. 3 : 11 ; grief, 1 Pet. 2 : 19. See ENDURE.¶

7. PHOREŌ (φορέω), a frequentative form of pherō, is to be distinguished from it as denoting, not a simple act of bearing, but a continuous or habitual condition, e.g., of the civil authority in bearing the sword as symbolic of execution, Rom. 13 : 4 ; of a natural state of bodily existence in this life, spoken of as " the image of the earthy," and the spiritual body of the believer hereafter, " the image of the heavenly," 1 Cor. 15 : 49, the word " image " denoting the actual form and not a mere similitude. See WEAR.

8. TROPOPHOREŌ (τροποφορέω), from tropos, a manner, and phoreō, to endure, is found in Acts 13 : 18, where some ancient authorities have the verb trophophoreō, " He bare them as a nursing father," (from trophos, a feeder, a nurse, and phoreō to carry).¶

9. AIRŌ (αἴρω) signifies (a) to raise up, to lift, to take upon oneself and carry what has been raised, physically (its most frequent use), or as

applied to the mind, to suspend, to keep in suspense, as in John 10 : 24, lit., ' How long doth thou suspend our souls ? ; ' (b) to take away what is attached to anything, to remove, as of Christ, in taking (or bearing, marg.) away the sin of the world, John 1 : 29 ; Christ " was manifested to take away sins," 1 John 3 : 5, where, not the nature of the Atonement is in view, but its effect in the believer's life. See CARRY, DOUBT, No. 6, LIFT, LOOSE, PUT, No. 17, REMOVE, SUSPENSE, TAKE.

10. POIEŌ (ποιέω), to do, sometimes means to produce, bear, Luke 8 : 8 ; 13 : 9 ; Jas. 3 : 12 (A.V., " bear," R.V., " yield ") ; Rev. 22 : 2. See COMMIT, DO.

11. STEGŌ (στέγω), primarily to protect, or preserve by covering, hence means to keep off something which threatens, to bear up against, to hold out against, and so to endure, bear, forbear, 1 Cor. 9 : 12. The idea of supporting what is placed upon a thing is prominent in 1 Thess. 3 : 1, 5 (" forbear "), and 1 Cor. 13 : 7. See FORBEAR and SUFFER.¶

12. ANECHOMAI (ἀνέχομαι) signifies to hold up against a thing and so to bear with (ana, up, and echomai, the Middle Voice of echō, to have, to hold), e.g., Matt. 17 : 7 ; 1 Cor. 4 : 12 ; 2 Cor. 11 : 1, 4, 19, 20 ; Heb. 13 : 22, etc. See ENDURE, FORBEAR, SUFFER.

13. METRIOPATHEŌ (μετριοπαθέω), to treat with mildness, or moderation, to bear gently with (metrios, moderate, and paschō, to suffer), is used in Heb. 5 : 2 (R.V. and A.V. marg.). The idea is that of not being unduly disturbed by the faults and ignorance of others ; or rather perhaps of feeling in some measure, in contrast to the full feeling with expressed in the verb sumpatheō in 4 : 15, with reference to Christ as the High Priest. See COMPASSION, No. 5.¶

14. MAKROTHUMEŌ (μακροθυμέω), to be long-tempered (makros, long, thumos, temper), is translated " is longsuffering over " in Luke 18 : 7, R.V. (A.V., " bear long with "). See PATIENT, SUFFER.

Notes : (1) For " bear (or give) witness," see WITNESS.

(2) For " bear up into," in Acts 27 : 15, see FACE.

(3) In 1 Cor. 10 : 13 the adjective anthrōpinos, human (from anthrōpos, man) is translated " is common to man," A.V. (R.V., " man can bear ").

(4) For karpophoreō, to bear fruit, e.g., Mark 4 : 20, (karpos, fruit, and No. 7), A.V., " bring forth," see FRUIT.

(5) In Acts 20 : 9, R.V., katapherō is rendered " borne down." See GIVE. No. 12.

BEAR (animal)

ARK(T)OS (ἄρκος), a bear, occurs in Rev. 13 : 2.¶

BEAST

1. ZŌON (ζῶον) primarily denotes a living being (zōē, life). The Eng., " animal," is the equivalent, stressing the fact of life as the characteristic feature. In Heb. 13 : 11 the A.V. and the R.V. translate it " beasts "

("animals" would be quite suitable). In 2 Pet. 2 : 12 and Jude 10, the A.V. has "beasts," the R.V. "creatures." In the Apocalypse, where the word is found some 20 times, and always of those beings which stand before the Throne of God, who give glory and honour and thanks to Him, 4 : 6, and act in perfect harmony with His counsels, 5 : 14 ; 6 : 1–7, e.g., the word "beasts" is most unsuitable ; the R.V., "living creatures," should always be used ; it gives to zōon its appropriate significance. See CREATURE.

2. THĒRION (θηρίον), to be distinguished from zōon, almost invariably denotes a wild beast. In Acts 28 : 4, "venomous beast" is used of the viper which fastened on Paul's hand. Zōon stresses the vital element, thērion the bestial. The idea of a beast of prey is not always present. Once, in Heb. 12 : 20, it is used of the animals in the camp of Israel, such, e.g., as were appointed for sacrifice. But in the Sept. thērion is never used of sacrificial animals ; the word ktēnos (see below) is reserved for these.

Thērion, in the sense of wild beast, is used in the Apocalypse for the two Antichristian potentates who are destined to control the affairs of the nations with Satanic power in the closing period of the present era, 11 : 7 ; 13 : 1–18 ; 14 : 9, 11 ; 15 : 2 ; 16 : 2, 10, 13 ; 17 : 3–17 ; 19 : 19, 20 ; 20 : 4, 10.

3. KTĒNOS (κτῆνος) primarily denotes property (the connected verb ktaomai means to possess) ; then, property in flocks and herds. In Scripture it signifies, (a) a beast of burden, Luke 10 : 34 ; Acts 23 : 24, (b) beasts of any sort, apart from those signified by thērion (see above), 1 Cor. 15 : 39 ; Rev. 18 : 13, (c) animals for slaughter ; this meaning is not found in the N.T., but is very frequent in the Sept.¶

4. TETRAPOUS (τετράπους), a four-footed beast (tetra, four, and pous, a foot) is found in Acts 10 : 12 ; 11 : 6 ; Rom. 1 : 23.¶

5. SPHAGION (σφάγιον), from sphazō, to slay, denotes a victim, slaughtered for sacrifice, a slain beast, Acts 7 : 42, in a quotation from Amos 5 : 25.¶

BEAT

1. DERŌ (δέρω), from a root der—, skin (derma, a skin, cp. Eng., dermatology), primarily to flay, then to beat, thrash or smite, is used of the treatment of the servants of the owner of the vineyard by the husband-men, in the parable in Matt. 21 : 35 ; Mark 12 : 3, 5 ; Luke 20 : 10, 11 ; of the treatment of Christ, Luke 22 : 63, R.V., "beat," for A.V., "smote ;" John 18 : 23 ; of the followers of Christ, in the synagogues, Mark 13 : 9 ; Acts 22 : 19 ; of the punishment of unfaithful servants, Luke 12 : 47, 48 ; of the beating of apostles by the High Priest and the Council of the Sanhedrin, Acts 5 : 40 ; by magistrates, 16 : 37. The significance of flogging does not always attach to the word ; it is used of the infliction of a single blow, John 18 : 23 ; 2 Cor. 11 : 20, and of beating the air,

1 Cor. 9 : 26.   The usual meaning is that of thrashing or cudgelling, and when used of a blow it indicates one of great violence.   See SMITE.¶

2. TUPTŌ (τύπτω), from a root *tup*—, meaning a blow, (*tupos*, a figure or print : Eng., type) denotes to smite, strike, or beat, usually not with the idea of giving a thrashing as with *derō*.   It frequently signifies a blow of violence, and, when used in a continuous tense, indicates a series of blows. In Matt. 27 : 30 the imperfect tense signifies that the soldiers kept on striking Christ on the head.   So Mark 15 : 19.   The most authentic mss. omit it in Luke 22 : 64.   In that verse the word *paiō*, to smite, is used of the treatment given to Christ (*derō* in the preceding verse).   The imperfect tense of the verb is again used in Acts 18 : 17, of the beating given to Sosthenes.   Cp. Acts 21 : 32, which has the present participle.   It is used in the metaphorical sense of wounding, in 1 Cor. 8 : 12.   See SMITE, STRIKE, WOUND.

3. RHABDIZŌ (ῥαβδίζω), to beat with a rod, or stick, to cudgel, is the verbal form of *rhabdos*, a rod, or staff, Acts 16 : 22 ; 2 Cor. 11 : 25.¶

4. BALLŌ (βάλλω), to throw or cast, is once rendered " beat," Acts 27 : 14 R.V., of the tempestuous wind that beat down upon the ship. So the A.V. margin.   See CAST.

5. EPIBALLŌ (ἐπιβάλλω), No. 4, with *epi*, upon, to cast upon, or lay hands upon, signifies to beat into, in Mark 4 : 37, of the action of the waves.   See CAST, No. 7, FALL, No. 11, LAY, PUT, No. 8, STRETCH, THINK, No. 15.

6. PROSKOPTŌ (προσκόπτω), to stumble, to strike against (*pros*, to or against, *koptō*, to strike), is once used of a storm beating upon a house, Matt. 7 : 27.   See DASH, STUMBLE, and cp. *proskomma* and *proskopē*, a stumbling-block, offence.

7. PROSPIPTŌ (προσπίπτω), to fall upon (*pros*, to, *piptō*, to fall), is translated " beat " in Matt. 7 : 25 ; elsewhere, to fall down at or before. See FALL.

PROSRĒGNUMI (προσρήγνυμι), to break upon, is translated "beat vehemently upon," or against (*pros*, upon, *rhēgnumi; to break), in Luke 6:48, 49, of the violent action of a flood (R.V., "brake") ¶

Note: In Luke 10:30, the phrase lit. rendered 'inflicting blows,' is translated "wounded" (A.V.), R.V., correctly, "beat."

BEAUTIFUL

1. HŌRAIOS (ὡραῖος) describes that which is seasonable, produced at the right time, as of the prime of life, or the time when anything is at its loveliest and best (from *hōra*, a season, a period fixed by natural laws and revolutions, and so the best season of the year).   It is used of the outward appearance of whited sepulchres in contrast to the corruption within, Matt. 23:27; of the Jerusalem gate caled "Beautiful," Acts 3:2, 10; of the feet of those that bring glad tidings, Rom. 10:15.¶

In the Sept. it is very frequent, and especially in Genesis and the

Song of Solomon. In Genesis it is said of all the trees in the garden of Eden, 2 : 9, especially of the tree of the knowledge of good and evil, 3 : 6 ; of the countenances of Rebekah, 26 : 7, Rachel, 29 : 17 and Joseph, 39 : 6. It is used five times in the Song of Solomon, 1 : 16 ; 2 : 14 ; 4 : 3 and 6 : 3, 5.

2. ASTEIOS (ἀστεῖος), connected with *astu*, a city, was used primarily of that which befitted the town, town-bred (corresponding Eng. words are " polite," " polished," connected with *polis*, a town ; cp. " urbane," from Lat., *urbs*, a city). Among Greek writers it is set in contrast to *agroikos*, rustic, and *aischros*, base, and was used, e.g., of clothing. It is found in the N.T. only of Moses, Acts 7 : 20, " (exceeding) fair," lit., ' fair (to God),' and Heb. 11 : 23, " goodly " (A.V., " proper "). See FAIR, GOODLY, *Note*, PROPER.¶

Notes : (1) In the Sept. it is far less frequent than *hōraios*. It is said of Moses in Ex. 2 : 2 ; negatively, of Balaam's procedure in the sight of God, Num. 22 : 32 ; of Eglon in Judg. 3 : 17.

(2) *Asteios* belongs to the realm of art, *hōraios*, to that of nature. *Asteios* is used of that which is beautiful because it is elegant ; *hōraios* describes that which is beautiful because it is, in its season, of natural excellence.

(3) *Kalos*, good, describes that which is beautiful as being well proportioned in all its parts, or intrinsically excellent. See BETTER, FAIR, GOOD, etc.

For BECAME see BECOME

BECAUSE : see Note † p. 9

BECKON

1. NEUŌ (νεύω), lit., to give a nod, to signify by a nod, is used in John 13 : 24, of Peter's beckoning to John to ask the Lord of whom He had been speaking ; in Acts 24 : 10, of the intimation given by Felix to Paul to speak.¶

2. DIANEUŌ (διανεύω), to express one's meaning by a sign (No. 1, with *dia*, through, used intensively), is said of the act of Zacharias, Luke 1 : 22 (R.V., " continued making signs," for A.V., " beckoned "). In Sept., Psa. 35 : 19, " wink."¶

3. KATANEUŌ (κατανεύω), No. 1, with *kata*, down, intensive, is used of the fishermen-partners in Luke 5 : 7, " beckoned."¶

4. KATASEIŌ (κατασείω), lit., to shake down (*kata*, down, *seiō*, to shake), of shaking the hand, or waving, expresses a little more vigorously the act of beckoning, Acts 12 : 17 ; 13 : 16 ; 19 : 33 ; 21 : 40. *Neuō* and its compounds have primary reference to a movement of the head ; *kataseiō*, to that of the hand.¶

BECOME (to be fitting)
A. Verb.

PREPŌ (πρέπω) means to be conspicuous among a number, to be eminent, distinguished by a thing, hence, to be becoming, seemly, fit. The adornment of good works " becometh women professing godliness," 1 Tim. 2 : 10. Those who minister the truth are to speak " the things which befit the sound doctrine," Tit. 2 : 1. Christ, as a High Priest " became us," Heb. 7 : 26. In the impersonal sense, it signifies it is fitting, it becometh, Matt. 3 : 15 ; 1 Cor. 11 : 13 ; Eph. 5 : 3 ; Heb. 2 : 10. See BEFIT, COMELY.¶

B. Adjective.

HIEROPREPĒS (ἱεροπρεπής), from *hieros*, sacred, with the adjectival form of *prepō*, denotes suited to a sacred character, that which is befitting in persons, actions or things consecrated to God, Tit. 2 : 3, R.V., " reverent," A.V., " as becometh holiness," (marg., " holy women "). Trench (Syn. §xcii) distinguishes this word from *kosmios*, modest, and *semnos*, grave, honourable.¶

Notes : (1) The A.V. translates the adverb *axiōs*, " as becometh," in Rom. 16 : 2 ; Phil. 1 : 27 (R.V. corrects to " worthily " and " worthy ").

(2) *Ginomai*, to become, is mentioned under various other headings.

(3) For " become of no effect," Gal. 5 : 4, A.V., R.V., " severed from," see ABOLISH.

BED

1. KLINĒ (κλίνη), akin to *klinō*, to lean (Eng., recline, incline etc.), a bed, e.g., Mark 7 : 30, also denotes a couch for reclining at meals, Mark 4 : 21, or a couch for carrying the sick, Matt. 9 : 2, 6. The metaphorical phrase ' to cast into a bed,' Rev. 2 : 22, signifies to afflict with disease (or possibly, to lay on a bier). In Mark 7 : 4 the A.V. curiously translates the word " tables " (marg., " beds "), R.V., marg. only, " couches." See COUCH.

2. KLINARION (κλινάριον), a diminutive of No. 1, a small bed, is used in Acts 5 : 15. Some mss. have *klinōn*. See also No. 4. See COUCH.¶

3. KOITĒ (κοίτη), primarily a place for lying down (connected with *keimai*, to lie), denotes a bed, Luke 11 : 7; the marriage bed, Heb. 13 : 4; in Rom. 13 : 13, it is used of sexual intercourse. By metonymy, the cause standing for the effect, it denotes conception, Rom. 9 : 10.¶

4. KRABBATOS (κράββατος), a Macedonian word (Lat. *grabatus*), is a somewhat mean bed, pallet, or mattress for the poor, Mark 2 : 4, 9, 11, 12 ; 6 : 55 ; John 5 : 8–11 ; Acts 5 : 15 ; 9 : 33. See also No. 2. See COUCH.¶

Note : The verb *strōnnuō* or *strōnnumi*, to spread, signifies, in Acts 9 : 34, to make a bed ; elsewhere it has its usual meaning. See FURNISH, SPREAD.

BEFALL

1. GINOMAI (γίνομαι), to become, is rendered " befell " in Mark 5 : 16 ; " hath befallen " in Rom. 11 : 25, R.V., for A.V., " is happened to ; " so the R.V. in 2 Cor. 1 : 8 ; 2 Tim. 3 : 11.

2. SUMBAINŌ (συμβαίνω), lit., to walk, or go together (sun, with, bainō, to go), is used of things which happen at the same time ; hence, to come to pass, " befall," Acts 20 : 19. In 21 : 35, it is translated " so it was." See HAPPEN.

3. SUNANTAŌ (συναντάω), to meet with (sun, with, antaō, to meet), is used much in the same way as sumbainō, of events which come to pass ; " befall," Acts 20 : 22. See MEET.

Note : The phrase in Matt. 8 : 33, " what was befallen to them that were possessed with demons," is, lit., ' the things of the demonized.'

BEFIT, BEFITTING

1. PREPŌ (πρέπω) is translated " befit " in Tit. 2 : 1, R.V. (A.V., " become "). See BECOME.

2. ANĒKŌ (ἀνήκω), primarily, to have arrived at, reached to, pertained to, came to denote what is due to a person, one's duty, what is befitting. It is used ethically in the N.T. ; Eph. 5 : 4, R.V., " are (not) befitting," for A.V., " are (not) convenient " ; Col. 3 : 18, concerning the duty of wives towards husbands, R.V., " as is fitting," for A.V., " as it is fit." In Philm. 8, the participle is used with the article, signifying " that which is befitting," R.V. (A.V., " that which is convenient "). See CONVENIENT. For synonymous words see BECOME.¶

BEFORE, BEFORETIME

A. Adverbs.

1. PRŌTON (πρῶτον), the neuter of the adjective prōtos (the superlative degree of pro, before), signifies first, or at the first, (a) in order of time, e.g., Luke 10 : 5 ; John 18 : 13 ; 1 Cor. 15 : 46 ; 1 Thess. 4 : 16 ; 1 Tim. 3 : 10 ; (b) in enumerating various particulars, e.g., Rom. 3 : 2 ; 1 Cor. 11 : 18 ; 12 : 28 ; Heb. 7 : 2 ; Jas. 3 : 17. It is translated " before " in John 15 : 18. See CHIEFLY, FIRST.

2. PROTERON (πρότερον), the neuter of proteros, the comparative degree of pro, is always used of time, and signifies aforetime, " before," e.g., John 6 : 62 ; 9 : 8 ; 2 Cor. 1 : 15 ; Heb. 7 : 27 ; in Gal. 4 : 13, " the first time " (R.V.), lit., ' the former time,' i.e., the former of two previous visits ; in Heb. 10 : 32 it is placed between the article and the noun, " the former days ; " so in 1 Pet. 1 : 14, " the former lusts," i.e., the lusts formerly indulged. See FIRST, FORMER.

3. PRIN (πρίν), before, formerly (etymologically akin to pro, before), has the force of a conjunction, e.g., Matt. 1 : 18 ; 26 : 34, 75 ; John 14 : 29 ; Acts 7 : 2.

4. EMPROSTHEN (ἔμπροσθεν) is used of place or position only; adverbially, signifying in front, Luke 19 : 28 ; Phil. 3 : 13 ; Rev. 4 : 6 ; as a preposition, e.g., Matt. 5 : 24 ; John 10 : 4 ; with the meaning ' in the sight of a person,' e.g., Matt. 5 : 16 ; 6 : 1 ; 17 : 2 ; Luke 19 : 27 ; John 12 : 37 ; 1 Thess. 2 : 19, R.V., " before ; " A.V., " in the presence of ; " Rev. 19 : 10, R.V., " before," especially in phrases signifying in the sight of God, as God wills, Matt. 11 : 26 ; 18 : 14 (lit., ' a thing willed before your Father,' R.V., marg.) ; Luke 10 : 21 ; in the sense of priority of rank or position or dignity, John 1 : 15, 30 (in some texts, ver. 27) ; in an antagonistic sense, " against," Matt. 23 : 13 (R.V., marg., " before ").

5. ENANTION (ἐναντίον), from en, in, and anti, over against, the neuter of the adjective enantios, and virtually an adverb, is also used as a preposition signifying in the presence of, in the sight of, Luke 20 : 26 ; Acts 7 : 10 : 8 : 32 ; in the judgment of, Luke 24 : 19.¶

6. ENANTI (ἔναντι), an adverb, used as a preposition, has meanings like those of No. 5, " before," Luke 1 : 8 ; in the judgment of, Acts 8 : 21. Some texts have the word in Acts 7 : 10.¶

7. APENANTI (ἀπέναντι), apo, from, with No. 6, denotes (a) opposite, Matt. 27 : 61 ; (b) in the sight of, before, Matt. 27 : 24 ; Acts 3 : 16 ; Rom. 3 : 18 ; (c) against, Acts 17 : 7. See CONTRARY, PRESENCE.¶

8. KATENANTI (κατέναντι), kata, down, with No. 6, lit., down over against, is used (a) of locality, e.g., Mark 11 : 2 ; 13 : 3 ; Luke 19 : 30 ; (b) as ' in the sight of,' Rom. 4 : 17 ; in most mss. in 2 Cor. 2 : 17 ; 12 : 19.

9. ENŌPION (ἐνώπιον), from en, in, and ōps, the eye, is the neuter of the adjective enōpios, and is used prepositionally, (a) of place, that which is before or opposite a person, towards which he turns his eyes, e.g. Luke 1 : 19 ; Acts 4 : 10 ; 6 : 6 ; Rev. 1 : 4 ; 4 : 10 ; 7 : 15 ; (b) in metaphorical phrases after verbs of motion, Luke 1 : 17 ; 12 : 9 ; Acts 9 : 15, etc. ; signifying in the mind or soul of persons, Luke 12 : 6 ; Acts 10 : 31 ; Rev. 16 : 19 ; (c) in one's sight or hearing, Luke 24 : 43 ; John 20 : 30 ; 1 Tim. 6 : 12 ; metaphorically, Rom. 14 : 22 ; especially in Gal. 1 : 20 ; 1 Tim. 5 : 21 ; 6 : 13 ; 2 Tim. 2 : 14 ; 4 : 1 ; before, as having a person present to the mind, Acts 2 : 25 ; Jas. 4 : 10 ; in the judgment of a person, Luke 16 : 15 ; 24 : 11, R.V., " in their sight," for A.V., " to ; " Acts 4 : 19 ; Rom. 3 : 20 ; 12 : 17 ; 2 Cor. 8 : 21 ; 1 Tim. 2 : 3 ; in the approving sight of God, Luke 1 : 75 ; Acts 7 : 46 ; 10 : 33 ; 2 Cor. 4 : 2 ; 7 : 12. See PRESENCE, SIGHT OF (in the).

10. KATENŌPION (κατενώπιον), kata, against, with No. 9, signifies right over against, opposite ; (a) of place, Jude 24 ; (b) before God as Judge, Eph. 1 : 4 ; Col. 1 : 22. See No. 8 (b).¶

B. Verb.

PROUPARCHŌ (προυπάρχω), to exist before, or be beforehand, is found in Luke 23 : 12, and Acts 8 : 9, " beforetime."¶ In the Sept., Job 42 : 18.¶

BEG, BEGGAR, BEGGARLY
A. Verb.

1. EPAITEŌ (ἐπαιτέω), a strengthened form of *aiteō*, is used in Luke 16 : 3.¶

2. PROSAITEŌ (προσαιτέω), lit., to ask besides (*pros*, towards. used intensively, and *aiteō*), to ask earnestly, to importune, continue asking, is said of the blind beggar in John 9 : 8. In Mark 10 : 46 and Luke 18 : 35 certain mss. have this verb ; the most authentic have *prosaitēs*, a beggar, a word used in John 9 : 8, as well as the verb (see the R.V.).¶

Note : " Begged " in Matt. 27 : 58 and Luke 23 : 52, R.V., " asked for," translates the verb *aiteō* ; see ASK.

B. Adjective.

PTŌCHOS (πτωχός), an adjective describing one who crouches and cowers, is used as a noun, a beggar (from *ptōssō*, to cower down or hide oneself for fear), Luke 14 : 13, 21 (" poor ") ; 16 : 20, 22 ; as an adjective, " beggarly " in Gal. 4 : 9, i.e., poverty-stricken, powerless to enrich, metaphorically descriptive of the religion of the Jews.

While *prosaitēs* is descriptive of a beggar, and stresses his begging, *ptōchos* stresses his poverty-stricken condition. See POOR.

For BEGAN see BEGIN

BEGET, BEAR (of begetting), BORN
A. Verbs.

1. GENNAŌ (γεννάω), to beget, in the Passive Voice, to be born, is chiefly used of men begetting children, Matt. 1 : 2–16 ; more rarely of women begetting children, Luke 1 : 13, 57, " brought forth " (for " delivered," in this ver., see No. 4) ; 23 : 29 ; John 16 : 21, " is delivered of," and of the child, " is born " (for " is in travail " see No. 4). In Gal. 4 : 24, it is used allegorically, to contrast Jews under bondage to the Law, and spiritual Israel, A.V., " gendereth," R.V., " bearing children," to contrast the natural birth of Ishmael and the supernatural birth of Isaac. In Matt. 1 : 20 it is used of conception, " that which is conceived in her." It is used of the act of God in the Birth of Christ, Acts 13 : 33 ; Heb. 1 : 5 ; 5 : 5, quoted from Psalm 2 : 7, none of which indicate that Christ became the Son of God at His Birth.

It is used metaphorically (*a*) in the writings of the Apostle John, of the gracious act of God in conferring upon those who believe the nature and disposition of " children," imparting to them spiritual life, John 3 : 3, 5, 7 ; 1 John 2 : 29 ; 3 : 9 ; 4 : 7 ; 5 : 1, 4, 18 ; (*b*) of one who by means of preaching the Gospel becomes the human instrument in the impartation of spiritual life, 1 Cor. 4 : 15 ; Philm. 10 ; (*c*) in 2 Pet. 2 : 12, with reference to the evil men whom the Apostle is describing, the R.V. rightly has " born mere animals " (A.V., " natural brute beasts ") ; (*d*) in the sense of gendering strife, 2 Tim. 2 : 23. See A, No. 3, BRING, CONCEIVE, DELIVER, GENDER, SPRING.

2. ANAGENNAŌ (ἀναγεννάω), *ana*, again, or from above, with No. 1, is found in 1 Pet. 1 : 3, 23.¶

Note : In John 3 : 3, 5, 7, the adverb *anōthen*, anew, or from above, accompanies the simple verb *gennaō*. See ABOVE.

3. APOKUEŌ (ἀποκυέω), to give birth to, to bring forth (from *kueō*, to be pregnant), is used metaphorically of spiritual birth by means of the Word of God, Jas. 1 : 18, and of death as the offspring of sin (ver. 15 ; so in the best texts). See BRING, A, No. 30.¶

4. TIKTŌ (τίκτω), to bring forth, Luke 1 : 57 ; John 16 : 21 ; Heb. 11 : 11 ; Rev. 12 : 2, 4, or, to be born, said of the Child, Matt. 2 : 2 ; Luke 2 : 11, is used metaphorically in Jas. 1 : 15, of lust as bringing forth sin. See *apokueō*, above, used in the same verse. See BRING, DELIVER, TRAVAIL (be in).

B. Nouns.

1. GENOS (γένος), a generation, kind, stock, is used in the dative case, with the article, to signify "by race," in Acts 18 : 2 and 24, R.V., for the A.V., "born." See COUNTRYMEN, DIVERSITY, GENERATION, KIND, KINDRED, NATION, OFFSPRING, STOCK.

2. EKTRŌMA (ἔκτρωμα) denotes an abortion, an untimely birth ; from *ektitrōskō*, to miscarry. In 1 Cor. 15 : 8 the Apostle likens himself to " one born out of due time ; " i.e., in point of time, inferior to the rest of the Apostles, as an immature birth comes short of a mature one.¶

C. Adjectives.

1. GENNĒTOS (γεννητός), born (related to *gennaō*, verb No. 1), is used in Matt. 11 : 11 and Luke 7 : 28 in the phrase "born of women," a periphrasis for " men," and suggestive of frailty.¶

2. ARTIGENNĒTOS (ἀρτιγέννητος), newborn (*arti*, newly, recently, and No. 1), is used in 1 Pet. 2 : 2.¶

Notes : (1) For *prōtotokos* see FIRSTBORN.

(2) For *monogenēs*, see ONLY BEGOTTEN.

For BEGGAR see BEG

BEGIN, BEGINNING, BEGINNER
A. Verbs.

1. ARCHOMAI (ἄρχομαι) denotes to begin. In Luke 3 : 23 the present participle is used in a condensed expression, lit., ' And Jesus Himself was beginning about thirty years.' Some verb is to be supplied in English. The R.V. has " when He began to teach, was about thirty years of age." The meaning seems to be that He was about thirty years when He began His public career (cp. Acts 1 : 1). The A.V. has " began to be about thirty years of age." In Acts 11 : 4 the R.V. suitably has " began,

and expounded," instead of " from the beginning." See B, No. 1, below, and REIGN, RULE.

2. ENARCHOMAI (ἐνάρχομαι), lit., to begin in (en, in, with No. 1), is used in Gal. 3 : 3 (" having begun in the Spirit "), to refer to the time of conversion ; similarly in Phil. 1 : 6, " He which began a good work in you." The en may be taken in its literal sense in these places.¶

3. PROENARCHOMAI (προενάρχομαι), lit., to begin in before (pro, with No. 2), is used in 2 Cor. 8 : 6, " he had made a beginning before ; " and in ver. 10, " were the first to make a beginning " (R.V.).¶

4. MELLŌ (μέλλω), to be about to, is rendered " begin " in the A.V. of Rev. 10 : 7 ; R.V. suitably, " when he is about to sound." See COME, INTEND, MEAN, MIND, READY, SHALL, SHOULD, TARRY, WILL, WOULD.

Note : For " began to wax " in 1 Tim. 5 : 11, see WANTON, B, No. 2.

B. Noun.

ARCHĒ (ἀρχή) means a beginning. The root arch— primarily indicated what was of worth. Hence the verb archō meant ' to be first,' and archōn denoted a ruler. So also arose the idea of a beginning, the origin, the active cause, whether a person or thing, e.g., Col. 1 : 18.

In Heb. 2 : 3 the phrase " having at the first been spoken " is, lit., ' having received a beginning to be spoken.' In 2 Thess. 2 : 13 (" God chose you from the beginning "), there is a well supported alternative reading, " chose you as first-fruits " (i.e., aparchēn, instead of ap' archēs). In Heb. 6 : 1, where the word is rendered " first principles," the original has ' let us leave the word of the beginning of Christ,' i.e., the doctrine of the elementary principles relating to Christ.

In John 8 : 25, Christ's reply to the question " Who art Thou ?," " Even that which I have spoken unto you from the beginning," does not mean that He had told them before ; He declares that He is consistently the unchanging expression of His own teaching and testimony from the first, the immutable embodiment of His doctrine. See CORNER, FIRST, MAGISTRATE, POWER, PRINCIPALITY, RULE.

Note : In the following passages the A.V. faulty translations, " since the world began " etc. are rightly rendered in the R.V. by " before times eternal " and similar phrases, Rom. 16 : 25 ; Eph. 3 : 9 ; 2 Tim. 1 : 9 ; Tit. 1 : 2. The alteration has not been made, however, in Luke 1 : 70 ; John 9 : 32 ; Acts 3 : 21 ; 15 : 18.

C. Adverb.

PRŌTON (πρῶτον), the neuter of prōtos (the superlative degree of proteros), first, at the first, is rendered " at the beginning " in John 2 : 10, A.V., R.V., " setteth on first." See BEFORE.

For BEGOTTEN see BEGET

BEGUILE

1. APATAŌ (ἀπατάω), to deceive, is rendered " beguiled " in the R.V. of 1 Tim. 2 : 14. See No. 2.

2. EXAPATAŌ (ἐξαπατάω), a strengthened form of No. 1, is rendered " beguile," 2 Cor. 11 : 3 ; the more adequate rendering would be ' as the serpent thoroughly beguiled Eve.' So in 1 Tim. 2 : 14, in the best mss., this stronger form is used of Satan's deception of Eve, lit., ' thoroughly beguiled ; ' the simpler verb, No. 1, is used of Adam. In each of these passages the strengthened form is used. So of the influence of sin, Rom. 7 : 11 (R.V., " beguile ") ; of self-deception, 1 Cor. 3 : 18 (R.V., " deceive ") ; of evil men, who cause divisions, Rom. 16 : 18 (R.V., " beguile ") ; of deceitful teachers, 2 Thess. 2 : 3 (R.V., " beguile "). See DECEIVE.¶ In the Sept., Ex. 8 : 29.¶

3. PARALOGIZOMAI (παραλογίζομαι), lit. and primarily, to reckon wrong, hence means to reason falsely (para, from, amiss, logizomai, to reason) or to deceive by false reasoning ; translated " delude " in Col. 2 : 4, R.V. (A.V., " beguile ") and Jas. 1 : 22 (A.V., " deceive "). See DECEIVE, DELUDE.¶

4. DELEAZŌ (δελεάζω) originally meant to catch by a bait (from delear, a bait) ; hence to beguile, entice by blandishments : in Jas. 1 : 14, " entice ; " in 2 Pet. 2 : 14, A.V., " beguile ; " in ver. 18, A.V., " allure ; " R.V., " entice " in both. See ENTICE.¶

Note : In Col. 2 : 18, the verb katabrabeuō, to give judgment against, condemn, is translated " beguile . . . of your reward," A.V. ; R.V., " rob . . . of your prize." The verb was used of an umpire's decision against a racer ; hence the translations (or paraphrases) in the Eng. Versions. See ROB.

BEHALF

1. MEROS (μέρος), a part, is translated " behalf " in the A.V. of 2 Cor. 9 : 3 (R.V., " respect ") and 1 Pet. 4 : 16 ; here the most authentic texts have onoma, a name ; hence R.V., " in this name." See COAST, CRAFT, PART, PIECE, PORTION, RESPECT, SORT.

2. HUPER (ὑπέρ), on behalf of, is to be distinguished from anti, instead of. See Note †, p. 9.

BEHAVE, BEHAVIOUR

A. Verbs.

1. ANASTREPHŌ (ἀναστρέφω), to turn back, return (ana, back, strephō, to turn), hence, to move about in a place, to sojourn, and, in the Middle and Passive Voices, to conduct oneself, indicating one's manner of life and character, is accordingly rendered " behave " in 1 Tim. 3 : 15, lit., ' how it is necessary to behave,' not referring merely to Timothy himself, but to all the members of the local church (see the whole Epistle) ; in Eph. 2 : 3, A.V., " we had our conversation," R.V., " we lived ; " in 2 Cor. 1 : 12 " behaved ourselves," for A.V. " have had our conversation." See ABIDE, etc.

2. GINOMAI (γίνομαι), to become, is rendered " behave " in 1 Thess. 2 : 10 ; lit., ' we became among you ' (cp. 1 : 5).

3. ATAKTEŌ (ἀτακτέω), lit., to be disorderly (a, negative, and *taxis*, order), to lead a disorderly life, is rendered " behave disorderly " in 2 Thess. 3 : 7.¶ Cp. *ataktos*, disorderly, unruly, and *ataktōs*, disorderly.

4. ASCHĒMONEŌ (ἀσχημονέω), to be unseemly (a, negative, and *schēma*, a form), is used in 1 Cor. 7 : 36, " behave (himself) unseemly," i.e., so as to run the risk of bringing the virgin daughter into danger or disgrace, and in 13 : 5, " doth (not) behave itself unseemly."¶

B. Nouns.

1. ANASTROPHĒ (ἀναστροφή), lit., a turning back (cp. No. 1, above), is translated " manner of life," " living," etc. in the R.V., for A.V., " conversation," Gal. 1 : 13 ; Eph. 4 : 22 ; 1 Tim. 4 : 12 ; Heb. 13 : 7 ; Jas. 3 : 13 ; 1 Pet. 1 : 15, 18 ; 2 : 12 (" behaviour ") ; 3 : 1, 2, 16 (ditto) ; 2 Pet. 2 : 7 ; 3 : 11. See CONVERSATION, LIFE.¶

2. KATASTĒMA (κατάστημα), akin to *kathistēmi* (see APPOINT, No. 2), denotes a condition, or constitution of anything, or deportment, Tit. 2 : 3, " demeanour," R.V., for A.V., " behaviour." See DEMEANOUR.¶

C. Adjective.

KOSMIOS (κόσμιος), orderly, modest, is translated " orderly " in 1 Tim. 3 : 2, R.V., for A.V., " of good behaviour." Both have " modest " in 1 Tim. 2 : 9. Cp. *kosmeō*, to adorn, *kosmos*, adornment.¶

BEHEAD

1. APOKEPHALIZŌ (ἀποκεφαλίζω), apo, from, off, *kephalē*, a head, is found in Matt. 14 : 10 ; Mark 6 : 16, 27 ; Luke 9 : 9.¶

2. PELEKIZŌ (πελεκίζω) denotes, to cut with an axe (from *pelekus*, an axe), Rev. 20 : 4.¶

BEHIND, COME BEHIND
A. Adverbs.

1. OPISTHEN (ὄπισθεν), behind, is used only of place, e.g., Matt. 9 : 20 ; Mark 5 : 27 ; Luke 8 : 44 ; Rev. 4 : 6 ; as a preposition, Matt. 15 : 23 (" after "), and Luke 23 : 26 ; in Rev. 5 : 1, R.V., " on the back ; " A.V., " backside." See BACK.¶

2. OPISŌ (ὀπίσω), after (see BACK, adverb).

B. Verbs.

1. HUSTEREŌ (ὑστερέω), to come late, be behind, is translated " come behind," in 1 Cor. 1 : 7 ; " to be behind," 2 Cor. 11 : 5 and 12 : 11. See COME, No. 39, DESTITUTE, FAIL, LACK, NEED, B, *Note*, WANT, WORSE.

2. HUPOMENŌ (ὑπομένω), to abide, endure, is once rendered " tarry behind," Luke 2 : 43. See ABIDE.

Note : In 1 Thess. 3 : 1, the R.V. " left behind " adequately expresses the verb *kataleipō*.

C. Noun.

HUSTEREMA (ὑστέρημα), akin to B.1, denotes that which is lacking, 1 Cor. 16 : 17 ; Phil. 2 : 30 ; Col. 1 : 24 (A.V., " that which is behind of the afflictions of Christ "), R.V., " that which is lacking ; " 1 Thess. 3 : 10. For the other meaning, " want," see LACK, PENURY, WANT.

BEHOLD, BEHELD

1. HORAŌ (ὁράω), with its aorist form *eidon*, to see (in a few places the A.V. uses the verb to behold), is said (*a*) of bodily vision, e.g., Mark 6 : 38 ; John 1 : 18, 46 ; (*b*) of mental perception, e.g., Rom. 15 : 21 ; Col. 2 : 18 ; (*c*) of taking heed, e.g., Matt. 8 : 4 ; 1 Thess. 5 : 15 ; (*d*) of experience, as of death, Luke 2 : 26 ; Heb. 11 : 5 ; life, John 3 : 36 ; corruption, Acts 2 : 27 ; (*e*) of caring for, Matt. 27 : 4 ; Acts 18 : 15 (here the form *opsomai* is used). See APPEAR, HEED, LOOK, PERCEIVE, SEE, SHEW.

2. BLEPŌ (βλέπω) is also used of (*a*) bodily and (*b*) mental vision, (*a*) to perceive, e.g., Matt. 13 : 13 ; (*b*) to take heed, e.g., Mark 13 : 23, 33 ; it indicates greater vividness than *horaō*, expressing a more intent, earnest contemplation ; in Luke 6 : 41, of beholding the mote in a brother's eye ; Luke 24 : 12, of beholding the linen clothes in the empty tomb ; Acts 1 : 9, of the gaze of the disciples when the Lord ascended. The greater earnestness is sometimes brought out by the rendering " regardest," Matt. 22 : 16. See BEWARE, HEED, LIE, LOOK, PERCEIVE, REGARD, SEE, SIGHT.

3. EMBLEPŌ (ἐμβλέπω), from *en*, in (intensive), and No. 2, (not to be rendered literally), expresses earnest looking, e.g., in the Lord's command to behold the birds of the heaven, with the object of learning lessons of faith from them, Matt. 6 : 26. See also 19 : 26 ; Mark 8 : 25 ; 10 : 21, 27 ; 14 : 67 ; Luke 20 : 17 ; 22 : 61 ; John 1 : 36 ; of the Lord's looking upon Peter, John 1 : 42 ; Acts 1 : 11 ; 22 : 11. See GAZE, LOOK, SEE.¶

4. IDE and IDOU (ἴδε and ἰδού) are Imperative Moods, Active and Middle Voices, respectively, of *eidon*, to see, calling attention to what may be seen or heard or mentally apprehended in any way. These are regularly rendered " behold." See especially the Gospels, Acts and the Apocalypse. See LO, SEE.

5. EPIDE (ἔπιδε), a strengthened form of No. 4 (with *epi*, upon, prefixed), is used in Acts 4 : 29 of the entreaty made to the Lord to behold the threatenings of persecutors.¶

6. THEŌREŌ (θεωρέω), from *theōros*, a spectator, is used of one who looks at a thing with interest and for a purpose, usually indicating the careful observation of details ; this marks the distinction from No. 2 ; see, e.g., Mark 15 : 47 ; Luke 10 : 18 ; 23 : 35 ; John 20 : 6 (R.V., " beholdeth," for A.V., " seeth ; ") ; so in verses 12 and 14 ; " consider," in Heb. 7 : 4. It is used of experience, in the sense of partaking of, in John 8 : 51 ; 17 : 24. See CONSIDER, LOOK, PERCEIVE, SEE. Cp. *theōria*, sight, Luke 23 : 48, only.

7. ANATHEŌREŌ (ἀναθεωρέω), *ana*, up (intensive), and No. 6, to view with interest, consider contemplatively, is translated " beheld," in Acts 17 : 23, R.V., " observed ; " " considering " in Heb. 13 : 7. See Consider.¶

8. THEAOMAI (θεάομαι), to behold, view attentively, contemplate, had, in earlier Greek usage, the sense of a wondering regard. This idea was gradually lost. It signifies a more earnest contemplation than the ordinary verbs for to see, " a careful and deliberate vision which interprets . . . its object," and is more frequently rendered " behold " in the R.V. than the A.V. Both translate it by " behold " in Luke 23 : 55 (of the sepulchre) ; " we beheld," in John 1 : 14, of the glory of the Son of God ; " beheld," R.V., in John 1 : 32 ; Acts 1 : 11 ; 1 John 1 : 1 (more than merely seeing) ; 4 : 12, 14. See Look, See.

9. EPOPTEUŌ (ἐποπτεύω), from *epi*, upon, and a form of *horaō*, to see, is used of witnessing as a spectator, or overseer, 1 Pet. 2 : 12 ; 3 : 2.¶

Note : The corresponding noun *epoptēs*, an eye-witness, found in 2 Pet. 1 : 16, was used by the Greeks of those who had attained to the highest grade of certain mysteries, and the word is perhaps purposely used here of those who were at the transfiguration of Christ. See Eye-witness.¶

10. ATENIZŌ (ἀτενίζω) from *atenēs*, strained, intent, denotes to gaze upon, " beholding earnestly," or " stedfastly " in Acts 14 : 9 ; 23 : 1. See Fasten, Look, Set, B, *Note* (5).

11. KATANOEŌ (κατανοέω), a strengthened form of *noeō*, to perceive, (*kata*, intensive), denotes the action of the mind in apprehending certain facts about a thing ; hence, to consider ; " behold," Acts 7 : 31, 32 ; Jas. 1 : 23, 24. See Consider, Discover, Perceive.

12. KATOPTRIZŌ (κατοπτρίζω), from *katoptron*, a mirror (*kata*, down, *ōps*, an eye or sight), in the Active Voice, signifies to make to reflect, to mirror ; in the Middle Voice, to reflect as a mirror ; so the R.V. in 2 Cor. 3 : 18, for A.V., " beholding as in a glass." The whole context in the 3rd chapter and the first part of the 4th bears out the R.V.¶

Note : For *epeidon* (from *ephoraō*), Acts 4 : 29, see Look, No. 9. For *prooraō*, Acts 2 : 25, R.V., " behold," see Foresee.

BEHOVE

1. OPHEILŌ (ὀφείλω), to owe, is once rendered " behove," Heb. 2 : 17 ; it indicates a necessity, owing to the nature of the matter under consideration ; in this instance, the fulfilment of the justice and love of God, voluntarily exhibited in what Christ accomplished, that He might be a merciful and faithful High Priest. See Bound, Debt, Due, Duty, Guilty, Indebted, Must, Need, Ought, Owe.

2. DEI (δεῖ), " it is necessary," is rendered " behoved," in Luke 24 : 46 ; R.V., (that the Christ) " should " (suffer). *Dei* expresses a logical necessity, *opheilō*, a moral obligation ; cp. *chrē*, Jas. 3 : 10, " ought,"

which expresses a need resulting from the fitness of things (Trench, § cvii). See MEET, MUST, NEED, OUGHT.

BEING

When not part of another verb (usually the participle), or part of a phrase, this word translates one of the following :—

(a) the present participle of *eimi*, to be, the verb of ordinary existence ;

(b) the participle of *ginomai*, to become, signifying origin or result ;

(c) the present participle of *huparchō*, to exist, which always involves a pre-existent state, prior to the fact referred to, and a continuance of the state after the fact. Thus in Phil. 2 : 6, the phrase " who being (*huparchōn*) in the form of God," implies His pre-existent Deity, previous to His Birth, and His continued Deity afterwards.

In Acts 17 : 28 the phrase " we have our being " represents the present tense of the verb to be, " we are."

BELIAL

BELIAL (βελίαλ, or βελίαρ) is a word frequently used in the Old Testament, with various meanings, especially in the books of Samuel, where it is found nine times. See also Deut. 13 : 13 ; Judg. 19 : 22 ; 20 : 13 ; 1 Kings 21 : 10, 13 ; 2 Chron. 13 : 7. Its original meaning was either worthlessness or hopeless ruin (see the R.V., margin). It also had the meanings of extreme wickedness and destruction, the latter indicating the destiny of the former. In the period between the O.T. and the N.T. it came to be a proper name for Satan. There may be an indication of this in Nahum 1 : 15, where the word translated " the wicked one " is Belial.

The oldest form of the word is Beliar, possibly from a phrase signifying " Lord of the forest," or perhaps simply a corruption of the form Belial, due to harsh Syriac pronunciation. In the N.T., in 2 Cor. 6 : 15, it is set in contrast to Christ, and represents a personification of the system of impure worship connected especially with the cult of Aphrodite.¶

BELIEF, BELIEVE, BELIEVERS
A. Verbs.

1. PISTEUŌ (πιστεύω), to believe, also to be persuaded of, and hence, to place confidence in, to trust, signifies, in this sense of the word, reliance upon, not mere credence. It is most frequent in the writings of the Apostle John, especially the Gospel. He does not use the noun (see below). For the Lord's first use of the verb, see 1 : 50. Of the writers of the Gospels, Matthew uses the verb ten times, Mark ten, Luke nine, John ninety-nine. In Acts 5 : 14 the present participle of the verb is translated " believers." See COMMIT, INTRUST, TRUST.

2. PEITHŌ (πείθω), to persuade, in the Middle and Passive Voices

signifies to suffer oneself to be persuaded, e.g., Luke 16 : 31 ; Heb. 13 : 18 ; it is sometimes translated " believe " in the R.V., but not in Acts 17 : 4, R.V., " were persuaded," and 27 : 11, " gave (more) heed ; " in Acts 28 : 24, " believed." See AGREE, ASSURE, OBEY, PERSUADE, TRUST, YIELD.

Note : For *apisteō*, the negative of No. 1, and *apeitheō*, the negative of No. 2, see DISBELIEVE, DISOBEDIENT.

B. Noun.

PISTIS (πίστις), faith, is translated " belief " in Rom. 10 : 17 ; 2 Thess. 2 : 13. Its chief significance is a conviction respecting God and His Word and the believer's relationship to Him. See ASSURANCE, FAITH, FIDELITY.

Note : In 1 Cor. 9 : 5 the word translated " believer " (R.V.), is *adelphē*, a sister, so 7 : 15 ; Rom. 16 : 1 ; Jas. 2 : 15, used, in the spiritual sense, of one connected by the tie of the Christian faith.

C. Adjective.

PISTOS (πιστός), (a) in the Active sense means believing, trusting ; (b) in the Passive sense, trusty, faithful, trustworthy. It is translated " believer " in 2 Cor. 6 : 15 ; " them that believe " in 1 Tim. 4 : 12, R.V. (A.V., " believers ") ; in 1 Tim. 5 : 16, " if any woman that believeth," lit., ' if any believing woman.' So in 6 : 2, " believing masters." In 1 Pet. 1 : 21 the R.V., following the most authentic mss., gives the noun form, " are believers in God " (A.V., " do believe in God "). In John 20 : 27 it is translated " believing." It is best understood with significance (a), above, e.g., in Gal. 3 : 9 ; Acts 16 : 1 ; 2 Cor. 6 : 15 ; Tit. 1 : 6 ; it has significance (b), e.g., in 1 Thess. 5 : 24 ; 2 Thess. 3 : 3 (see Notes on Thess. p. 211, and Gal. p. 126, by Hogg and Vine). See FAITHFUL, SURE.

Notes : (1) The corresponding negative verb is *apisteō*, 2 Tim. 2 : 13, A.V., " believe not " R.V., " are faithless," in contrast to the statement " He abideth faithful."

(2) The negative noun *apistia*, " unbelief," is used twice in Matthew (13 : 58 ; 17 : 20), three times in Mark (6 : 6 ; 9 : 24 ; 16 : 14), four times in Romans (3 : 3 ; 4 : 20 ; 11 : 20, 23) ; elsewhere in 1 Tim. 1 : 13 and Heb. 3 : 12, 19.¶

(3) The adjective *apistos* is translated " unbelievers " in 1 Cor. 6 : 6, and 2 Cor. 6 : 14 ; in ver. 15, R.V., " unbeliever " (A.V., " infidel ") ; so in 1 Tim. 5 : 8 ; " unbelieving " in 1 Cor. 7 : 12, 13, 14, 15 ; 14 : 22, 23, 24 ; 2 Cor. 4 : 4 ; Tit. 1 : 15 ; Rev. 21 : 8 ; " that believe not " in 1 Cor. 10 : 27. In the Gospels it is translated " faithless " in Matt. 17 : 17 ; Mark 9 : 19 ; Luke 9 : 41 ; John 20 : 27, but in Luke 12 : 46, R.V., " unfaithful," A.V., " unbelievers." Once it is translated " incredible," Acts 26 : 8. See FAITHLESS, INCREDIBLE, UNBELIEVER.¶

(4) *Plērophoreō*, in Luke 1 : 1 (A.V., " are most surely believed," lit., have had full course), the R.V. renders " have been fulfilled." See FULFIL, KNOW, PERSUADE, PROOF.

BELLY

1. KOILIA (κοιλία), from koilos, hollow (Lat., coelum, heaven, is connected), denotes the entire physical cavity, but most frequently was used to denote the womb. In John 7 : 38 it stands metaphorically for the innermost part of man, the soul, the heart. See WOMB.

2. GASTĒR (γαστήρ), (cp. Eng., gastritis), is used much as No. 1, but in Tit. 1 : 12, by synecdoche (a figure of speech in which the part is put for the whole, or vice versa), it is used to denote " gluttons," R.V., for A.V., " bellies." See GLUTTON, WOMB.

BELONG

Note : This word represents (a) a phrase consisting of *eimi*, to be, with or without a preposition and a noun, and usually best rendered, as in the R.V., by the verb to be, Mark 9 : 41, lit., ' ye are of Christ ; ' Luke 23 : 7 and Heb. 5 : 14 ; cp. Rom. 12 : 19, " belongeth unto Me," R.V. ; (b) a phrase consisting of the neuter plural of the definite article, either with the preposition *pros*, unto, as in Luke 19 : 42, where the phrase " the things which belong unto peace " (R.V.) is, lit., ' the (things) unto peace,' or with the genitive case of the noun, as in 1 Cor. 7 : 32, A.V., " the things that belong to the Lord," R.V., suitably, " the things of the Lord ; " (c) a distinct verb, e.g., *metechō*, to partake of, share in, Heb. 7 : 13 R.V., " belongeth to (another tribe)," A.V., " pertaineth to."

BELOVED
A. Adjective.

AGAPĒTOS (ἀγαπητός), from *agapaō*, to love, is used of Christ as loved by God, e.g., Matt. 3:17; of believers (ditto), e.g., Rom. 1:7; of believers, one of another, 1 Cor. 4:14; often, as a form of address, e.g., 1 Cor. 10:14. Whenever the A.V. has "dearly beloved," the R.V. has "beloved;" so, "well beloved" in 3 John 1; in 1 John 2:7, A.V., "brethren" (*adelphos*), the R.V. has "beloved," according to the mss. which have *agapētos*. See DEAR.

B. Verb.

AGAPAŌ (ἀγαπάω), in its perfect participle Passive form, is translated "beloved" in Rom. 9:25; Eph. 1:6; Col. 3:12; 1 Thess. 1:4; 2 Thess. 2:13. In Jude 1 the best texts have this verb (R.V.) ; the A.V., "sanctified" follows those which have *hagiazō*. See LOVE.

Note: In Luke 9:35, the R.V., translating from the most authentic mss., has "My chosen" (*eklegō*), for A.V., "beloved" (*agapētos*) ; so in Philm. 2, "sister" (*adelphē*).

BENEATH

KATŌ (κάτω) signifies (a) down, downwards, Matt. 4 : 6 ; Luke 4 : 9 ; John 8 : 6, 8 ; Acts 20 : 9 ; (b) below, beneath, of place, Mark 14 : 66 ; the realms that lie below in contrast to heaven, John 8 : 23 ; the earth, as contrasted with the heavens, Acts 2 : 19 ; with *heōs*, unto, Matt. 27 : 51 ; Mark 15 : 38. The comparative degree, *katōterō*, under, is used in Matt. 2 : 16. See BOTTOM, UNDER.¶

BENEFIT, BENEFACTOR

1. EUERGESIA (εὐεργεσία), lit., ' good work (*eu*, well, *ergon*, work),' is found in Acts 4 : 9, " good deed," and 1 Tim. 6 : 2, " benefit."¶

2. EUERGETĒS (εὐεργέτης), a benefactor, expresses the agent, Luke 22 : 25.¶

Note : Cp. *euergeteō*, to do good.

3. CHARIS (χάρις), grace, is once rendered " benefit," 2 Cor. 1 : 15 ; it stresses the character of the benefit, as the effect of the gracious disposition of the benefactor. See ACCEPTABLE, FAVOUR, GRACE, LIBERALITY, PLEASURE, THANK.

4. AGATHON (ἀγαθόν), the neuter of *agathos*, used as a noun in Philm. 14, is translated " benefit," A.V. ; R.V., " goodness." See GOOD.

BENEVOLENCE

EUNOIA (εὔνοια), good will (*eu*, well, *nous*, the mind), is rendered " benevolence " in 1 Cor. 7 : 3, A.V. The R.V., following the texts which have *opheilēn* (" due "), has " her due," a more comprehensive expression ; in Eph. 6 : 7, " good will."¶

BEREAVED, BEREFT

1. APORPHANIZOMAI (ἀπορφανίζομαι), lit., to be rendered an orphan (*apo*, from, with the thought of separation, and *orphanos*, an orphan), is used metaphorically in 1 Thess. 2 : 17 (A.V., " taken from ; " R.V., " bereaved "), in the sense of being bereft of the company of the saints through being compelled to leave them (cp. the similes in 7 and 11). The word has a wider meaning than that of being an orphan.¶

Note : The corresponding adjective, *orphanos*, is translated " desolate " in John 14 : 18 (A.V., " comfortless ") ; " fatherless " in Jas. 1 : 27 ; see DESOLATE, FATHERLESS.¶

2. APOSTEREŌ, to rob, defraud, deprive, is used in 1 Tim. 6 : 5, in the Passive Voice, of being deprived or " bereft " (of the truth), with reference to false teachers (A.V., " destitute "). See DEFRAUD, DESTITUTE, FRAUD.

BERYL

BĒRULLOS (βήρυλλος), beryl, is a precious stone of a sea-green colour, Rev. 21 : 20 (cp. Ex. 28 : 20).¶

BESEECH

1. PARAKALEŌ (παρακαλέω), the most frequent word with this meaning, lit. denotes to call to one's side, hence, to call to one's aid. It

is used for every kind of calling to a person which is meant to produce a particular effect, hence, with various meanings, such as comfort, exhort, desire, call for, in addition to its significance to beseech, which has a stronger force than *aiteō* (see ASK). See, e.g., the R.V. " besought " in Mark 5 : 18 ; Acts 8 : 31 ; 19 : 31 ; 1 Cor. 16 : 12. See CALL, No. 6, Note (2), COMFORT, DESIRE, EXHORT, INTREAT, PRAY.

2. ERŌTAŌ (ἐρωτάω), often translated by the verb to beseech, in the Gospels, is elsewhere rendered " beseech " in 1 Thess. 4 : 1 ; 5 : 12 ; 2 Thess. 2 : 1 ; 2 John 5. See under ASK, No. 2.

3. DEOMAI (δέομαι), to desire, to long for, usually representing the word " need," is sometimes translated " beseech," e.g., Luke 5 : 12 ; Acts 21 : 39 ; 2 Cor. 10 : 2 ; Gal. 4 : 12. It is used of prayer to God, in Matt. 9 : 38 ; Luke 10 : 2 ; 21 : 36 ; 22 : 32 ; Acts 4 : 31 ; 8 : 22, 24 ; 10 : 2 ; Rom. 1 : 10 ; 1 Thess. 3 : 10. See PRAY, REQUEST.

Note : *Proskuneō* is wrongly rendered " besought " in the A.V. marg. of Matt. 18 : 26. The word signifies " to worship."

BESET

EUPERISTATOS (εὐπερίστατος), used in Heb. 12 : 1, and translated " which doth so easily beset," lit. signifies ' standing well (i.e., easily) around ' (*eu*, well, *peri*, around, *statos*, standing, i.e., easily encompassing). It describes sin as having advantage in favour of its prevailing.¶

BESIDE, BESIDES

1. CHŌRIS (χωρίς), separately, apart from, besides, is translated " beside " in Matt. 14 : 21 ; 15 : 38 ; 2 Cor. 11 : 28. See APART, SEPARATE, WITHOUT.

2. LOIPON (λοιπόν) is rendered " besides " in 1 Cor. 1 : 16. See FINALLY.

Notes : (1) *Pareiserchomai*, in Rom. 5 : 20, signifies to come in beside, i.e., of the Law, as coming in addition to sin committed previously apart from law, the prefix *par–* (i.e., *para*) denoting " beside " (the A.V., " entered " is inadequate) ; in Gal. 2 : 4 (" came in privily "). See COME.¶

(2) In Philm. 19, *prosopheilō* signifies to owe in addition (*pros*, besides, and *opheilō*, to owe) : " thou owest (to me even thine own self) besides."¶

(3) In 2 Pet. 1 : 5, the phrase, wrongly translated in the A.V., " beside this," means " for this very cause " (R.V.).

BESIDE ONESELF (to be)

1. EXISTĒMI (ἐξίστημι), primarily and lit. means to put out of position, displace ; hence, (*a*) to amaze, Luke 24 : 22 (for A.V., " make . . . astonished ") ; Acts 8 : 9, 11 (A.V., " bewitched ") ; or to be amazed, astounded, Matt. 12 : 23 ; Mark 6 : 51 ; (*b*) to be out of one's mind, to be beside oneself, Mark 3 : 21 ; 2 Cor. 5 : 13, in the latter of which it is contrasted with *sōphroneō*, to be of a sound mind, sober. See AMAZE.

2. MAINOMAI (μαίνομαι), to be mad, to rave, is said of one who so

speaks that he appears to be out of his mind, Acts 26 : 24, translated " thou art beside thyself," A.V. ; R.V., " thou art mad." In ver. 25 ; John 10 : 20 ; Acts 12 : 15 ; 1 Cor. 14 : 23, both Versions use the verb to be mad. See MAD.¶

Note : For *paraphroneō*, 2 Cor. 11 : 23, R.V., see FOOL, B, No. 2.

BEST

1. PRŌTOS (πρῶτος) is one of two words translated " best " in the A.V., but the only one so rendered in the R.V. In Luke 15 : 22 " the best (robe) " is, lit., ' the first (robe),' i.e., chief, principal, first in rank or quality. See BEFORE, BEGINNING, CHIEF, FIRST, FORMER.

2. MEIZŌN (μείζων), greater, is translated " best " in 1 Cor. 12 : 31, " the best gifts," greater, not in quality, but in importance and value. It is the comparative degree of *megas*, great ; the superlative, *megistos*, is used only in 2 Pet. 1 : 4. See ELDER, GREATER and MORE.

BESTOW

1. DIDŌMI (δίδωμι), to give, is rendered " bestow " in 1 John 3 : 1, the implied idea being that of giving freely. The A.V. has it in 2 Cor. 8 : 1 ; the R.V. adheres to the lit. rendering, " the grace of God which hath been given in the churches of Macedonia." See ADVENTURE and especially GIVE.

2. SUNAGŌ (συνάγω), to bring together (*sun*, together, *agō*, to bring), is used in the sense of bestowing, or stowing, by the rich man who laid up his goods for himself, Luke 12 : 17, 18. See ASSEMBLE, COME, GATHER, LEAD, RESORT, TAKE.

3. KOPIAŌ (κοπιάω), (*a*) to grow tired with toil, Matt. 11 : 28 ; John 4 : 6 ; Rev. 2 : 3, also means (*b*) to bestow labour, work with toil, Rom. 16 : 6 ; Gal. 4 : 11 ; in John 4 : 38, A.V., " bestowed (no) labour," R.V., " have (not) laboured," and, in the same verse, A.V. and R.V., " laboured." See LABOUR, TOIL, WEARY.

4. PSŌMIZŌ (ψωμίζω), primarily to feed by putting little bits into the mouths of infants or animals, came to denote simply to give out food, to feed, and is rendered by the phrase " bestow . . . to feed " in 1 Cor. 13 : 3 ; " feed," Rom. 12 : 20 ; there the person to be fed is mentioned : in 1 Cor. 13 : 3 the material to be given is specified, and the rendering " bestow . . . to feed " is necessary. See FEED.¶

5. PERITITHĒMI (περιτίθημι), to put around or on (*peri*, around, *tithēmi*, to put), is translated in 1 Cor. 12 : 23 (metaphorically) " bestow " (marg., " put on "). See PUT, SET, No. 5.

6. CHARIZOMAI (χαρίζομαι), to show favour, grant, bestow, is rendered " bestowed " in Luke 7 : 21, R.V., for A.V., " gave." Here and in Gal. 3 : 18, the verb might be translated " graciously conferred." See DELIVER, FORGIVE, GIVE, GRANT.

Note : For " freely bestowed " see ACCEPT, A, *Note.*

BETRAY, BETRAYER
A. Verb.

PARADIDŌMI (παραδίδωμι), to betray (*para*, up, *didōmi*, to give), lit., to give over, is used either (*a*) in the sense of delivering a person or thing to be kept by another, to commend, e.g., Acts 28 : 16 ; (*b*) to deliver to prison or judgment, e.g., Matt. 4 : 12 ; 1 Tim. 1 : 20 ; (*c*) to deliver over treacherously by way of betrayal, Matt. 17 : 22 (R.V., " delivered ") ; 26 : 16 ; John 6 : 64 etc. ; (*d*) to hand on, deliver, e.g., 1 Cor. 11 : 23 : (*e*) to allow of something being done, said of the ripening of fruit, Mark 4 : 29, R.V., " is ripe " (marg., " alloweth "). See BRING, p. 153, *Note* (4), CAST, COMMIT, DELIVER, GIVE, HAZARD, PUT (in prison), RECOMMEND.

B. Noun.

PRODOTĒS (προδότης), a betrayer (akin to A), is translated " betrayers " in Acts 7 : 52 ; " traitor," " traitors," in Luke 6 : 16 and 2 Tim. 3 : 4. See TRAITOR.¶

BETROTH

MNĒSTEUŌ (μνηστεύω), in the Active Voice, signifies to woo a woman and ask for her in marriage ; in the N.T., only in the Passive Voice, to be promised in marriage, to be betrothed, Matt. 1 : 18 ; Luke 1 : 27 ; 2 : 5, R.V., " betrothed," (A.V., " espoused "). See ESPOUSED.¶

BETTER

1. KREISSŌN (κρείσσων), from *kratos*, strong (which denotes power in activity and effect), serves as the comparative degree of *agathos*, good (good or fair, intrinsically). *Kreissōn* is especially characteristic of the Epistle to the Hebrews, where it is used 12 times ; it indicates what is (*a*) advantageous or useful, 1 Cor. 7 : 9, 38 ; 11 : 17 ; Heb. 11 : 40 ; 12 : 24 ; 2 Pet. 2 : 21 ; Phil. 1 : 23, where it is coupled with *mallon*, more, and *pollō*, much, by far, " very far better " (R.V.) ; (*b*) excellent, Heb. 1 : 4 ; 6 : 9 ; 7 : 7, 19, 22 ; 8 : 6 ; 9 : 23 ; 10 : 34 ; 11 : 16, 35.¶

2. KALON . . . MALLON (καλὸν . . . μᾶλλον), the neuter of *kalos*, with *mallon*, more, is used in Mark 9 : 42, " it were better (lit., much better) for him if a great millstone were hanged about his neck." In verses 43, 45, 47, *kalos* is used alone (R.V., " good," for A.V., " better ").

Note : In Luke 5 : 39 the most authentic texts have *chrēstos*, good, instead of the comparative, *chrēstoteros*, better.

BETTER (be)

1. DIAPHERŌ (διαφέρω), used (*a*) transitively, means to carry through or about (*dia*, through, *pherō*, to carry), Mark 11 : 16 (" carry . . . through ") ; Acts 13 : 49 ; 27 : 27 (" driven to and fro ") ; (*b*) intransitively, (1) to differ, Rom. 2 : 18 ; Gal. 2 : 6 ; Phil. 1 : 10 ; (2) to excel, be better, e.g., Matt. 6 : 26 ; 10 : 31 (" of more value ") ; 12 : 12 ; Luke

12 : 7, 24 ; 1 Cor. 15 : 41 ; Gal. 4 : 1 ; some would put Rom. 2 : 18 and Phil. 1 : 10 here (see marg.). See CARRY, DIFFER, DRIVE, EXCELLENT, MATTER (make), PUBLISH.¶

2. PERISSEUŌ (περισσεύω), to be over or above (a number), to be more than enough, to be pre-eminent, superior, Matt. 5 : 20, is translated " are we the better," in 1 Cor. 8 : 8 (cp. 15 : 58 ; Rom. 15 : 13 ; 2 Cor. 3 : 9 ; 8 : 7 ; Phil. 1 : 9 ; Col. 2 : 7 ; 1 Thess. 4 : 1, 10). See ABOUND.

3. LUSITELEŌ (λυσιτελέω) signifies to indemnify, pay expenses, pay taxes (from luō, to loose, telos, toll, custom) ; hence, to be useful, advantageous, to be better, Luke 17 : 2.¶

4. HUPERECHŌ (ὑπερέχω) lit. means to hold or have above (huper, above, echō, to hold) ; hence, metaphorically, to be superior to, to be better than, Phil. 2 : 3 ; 1 Pet. 2 : 13, " supreme," in reference to kings ; in Rom. 13 : 1, " higher;" Phil. 3 : 8, " excellency," more strictly ' the surpassing thing, (namely, the knowledge of Christ) ' ; in 4 : 7 " passeth." See EXCELLENCY, HIGHER, PASS, SUPREME.¶

Notes : (1) In Rom. 3 : 9 the R.V. rightly translates *proechō* (which there is used in the Passive Voice, not the Middle) " are we in worse case than . . . ? ," i.e., ' are we surpassed ? ' ' are we at a disadvantage ? ' The question is, are the Jews, so far from being better off than the Gentiles, in such a position that their very privileges bring them into a greater disadvantage or condemnation than the Gentiles ? The A.V. " are we better " does not convey the meaning.

(2) *Sumpherō*, in Matt. 18 : 6, A.V., is translated " it were better for him," R.V., " profitable." See Matt. 5 : 29, 30 etc. See BRING, EXPEDIENT, GOOD, D, *Note* (2), PROFITABLE.

BETTERED (to be)

ŌPHELEŌ (ὠφελέω) in the Active Voice signifies to help, to succour, to be of service ; in the Passive to receive help, to derive profit or advantage ; in Mark 5 : 26, " was (nothing) bettered," of the woman who had an issue of blood. See under ADVANTAGE, C, No. 1, and cp. A, Nos. 2, 3 and B.

BETWEEN

In addition to the prepositions *en* and *pros* (see Note † p. 9), the following have this meaning :

1. ANA MESON (ἀνὰ μέσον), lit., up to the middle of, i.e., among, or in the midst of, hence, between, is used in 1 Cor. 6 : 5, of those in the church able to decide between brother and brother, instead of their going to law with one another in the world's courts.

2. METAXU (μεταξύ), in the midst, or between (from *meta*, and *xun*, i.e., *sun*, with), is used as a preposition, (a) of mutual relation, Matt. 18 : 15 ; Acts 15 : 9 ; Rom. 2 : 15, R.V., " one with another," lit., ' between one another,' for A.V., " the meanwhile ; " (b) of place, Matt.

23 : 35 ; Luke 11 : 51 ; 16 : 26 ; Acts 12 : 6 ; (c) of time, " meanwhile," John 4 : 31. In Acts 13 : 42, the A.V. marg. has " in the week between," the literal rendering. See WHILE.¶

Note : The phrase *ek meta* (*ek*, out of, *meta*, with) is translated " between . . . and " in the A.V. of John 3 : 25 (R.V., " on the part of . . . with ").

BEWAIL

1. KLAIŌ (κλαίω), to wail, whether with tears or any external expression of grief, is regularly translated " weep " in the R.V. ; once in the A.V. it is rendered " bewail," Rev. 18 : 9. See WEEP.

Note : The associated noun is *klauthmos*, weeping. Cp. *dakruō*, to weep, John 11 : 35.¶

2. KOPTŌ (κόπτω), primarily, to beat, smite ; then, to cut off, Matt. 21 : 8 ; Mark 11 : 8, is used in the Middle Voice, of beating oneself, beating the breast, as a token of grief ; hence, to bewail, Matt. 11 : 17 (R.V., " mourn," for A.V., " lament ") ; 24 : 30, " mourn ; " Rev. 1 : 7 (R.V., " mourn ; " A.V., " wail ") ; in Luke 8 : 52 ; 23 : 27 " bewail ; " in Rev. 18 : 9, " wail " (for A.V., " lament "). See CUT, MOURN.¶ Cp. *kopetos*, lamentation, Acts 8 : 2.¶

3. PENTHEŌ (πενθέω) denotes to lament, mourn, especially for the dead ; in 2 Cor. 12 : 21, R.V., " mourn " (A.V., " bewail "). See also Rev. 18 : 11, 15, 19. Cp. *penthos*, mourning. See MOURN.

Notes : (1) *Thrēneō*, to sing a dirge, to lament, is rendered " wail " in Matt. 11 : 17, R.V. ; " mourned " in Luke 7 : 32 ; to lament in Luke 23 : 27 and John 16 : 20.¶ *Thrēnos*, lamentation, occurs in Matt. 2 : 18.¶

(2) *Odurmos* from *oduromai*, to wail (a verb not found in the N.T.), denotes " mourning," Matt. 2 : 18 and 2 Cor. 7 : 7.¶

(3) Cp. *lupeomai*, to grieve, and see Trench, Syn. § lxv.

BEWARE

1. BLEPŌ (βλέπω), to see, is applied to mental vision, and is sometimes used by way of warning to take heed against an object, Mark 8 : 15 ; 12 : 38 ; Acts 13 : 40 ; Phil. 3 : 2 (three times) ; in Col. 2 : 8, R.V., " take heed," marg., " see whether." See BEHOLD.

2. PROSECHŌ (προσέχω), lit., to hold to (*pros*, to, *echō*, to have, to hold), hence, to turn one's mind or attention to a thing by being on one's guard against it, is translated " beware " in Matt. 7 : 15 ; 10 : 17 ; 16 : 6, 11, 12 ; Luke 12 : 1 ; 20 : 46. See ATTEND, HEED, REGARD.

3. PHULASSŌ (φυλάσσω), to guard, watch, keep, is used, in the Middle Voice, of being on one's guard against (the Middle V. stressing personal interest in the action), Luke 12 : 15, " beware of," R.V., " keep yourselves from," as in Acts 21 : 25 ; in 2 Tim. 4 : 15, " be thou ware ; " in 2 Pet. 3 : 17, " beware." See GUARD, KEEP, OBSERVE, SAVE.

BEWITCH

1. BASKAINŌ (βασκαίνω), primarily, to slander, to prate about anyone ; then to bring evil on a person by feigned praise, or mislead by an evil eye, and so to charm, bewitch (Eng., fascinate is connected), is used figuratively in Gal. 3 : 1, of leading into evil doctrine.¶

2. EXISTEMI (ἐξίστημι) is rendered "bewitch" in Acts 8 : 9, 11, A.V., concerning Simon the sorcerer ; it does not mean to bewitch, as in the case of the preceding verb, but to confuse, amaze (R.V.). See AMAZE, B. No. 1.

BEWRAY

Note : The word "bewrayeth", Matt. 26 : 73, is a translation of *poieō*, to make, with *dēlos*, manifest, evident ; lit., 'maketh thee manifest.'

BEYOND

In addition to the preposition *huper*, over, rendered "beyond" in 2 Cor. 8 : 3, the following adverbs have this meaning :

1. EPEKEINA (ἐπέκεινα), *epi*, upon, and *ekeina*, those, the word "parts" being understood, is used in Acts 7 : 43.¶

2. PERAN (πέραν), on the other side, across, is used with the definite article, signifying the regions beyond, the opposite shore, Matt. 8 : 18 etc. With verbs of going it denotes direction towards and beyond a place, e.g., John 10 : 40. It frequently indicates "beyond," of locality, without a verb of direction, Matt. 16 : 5 ; Mark 10 : 1, R.V. ; John 1 : 28 ; 3 : 26. See FARTHER, SIDE.

Note : In 2 Cor. 10 : 14, the verb *huperekteinō,* to stretch overmuch, is so rendered in the R.V., for A.V., ". . . beyond our measure."¶ In 2 Cor. 10 : 16 the adverb *huperekeina*, beyond, is used as a preposition.

BID, BIDDEN, BADE, BID AGAIN

1. KALEŌ (καλέω), to call, often means to bid, in the sense of invite, e.g., Matt. 22 : 3, 4, 8, 9 ; Luke 14 : 7, 8, 9, 10, 13, R.V. ; Rev. 19 : 9, R.V. See CALL, NAME, SURNAME.

2. KELEUŌ (κελεύω), to command, is translated "bid" in Matt. 14 : 28, only. See COMMAND, No. 5. Compare the synonym *entellō*, to command.

3. EIPON (εἶπον), used as the aorist tense of *legō*, to speak, to say, sometimes has the meaning of commanding, or bidding, and is translated "bid," or "bade," e.g., in Matt. 16 : 12 ; 23 : 3 ; Luke 10 : 40 ; 9 : 54, A.V., "command," R.V., "bid ;" Acts 11 : 12 ; "bidding," Acts 22 : 24, R.V. See SAY, SPEAK.

4. ANTIKALEŌ (ἀντικαλέω), to bid again, invite in turn, is found in Luke 14 : 12.¶

Notes : (1) *Legō*, to say, is translated "bid" and "biddeth" in the A.V. of 2 John 10, 11 ; R.V., " give (him no greeting)," " giveth (him greeting "). See GREETING.

(2) In Matt. 1 : 24, *prostassō*, to command, is translated " had bidden," A.V. ; R.V., " commanded." See COMMAND.

BID FAREWELL

1. APOTASSŌ (ἀποτάσσω) is used in the Middle Voice to signify to bid adieu to a person. It primarily means to set apart, separate (*apo*, from, *tassō*, to set, arrange) ; then, to take leave of, to bid farewell to, Mark 6 : 46 (R.V.) ; Luke 9 : 61 ; to give parting instructions to, Acts 18 : 18, 21 ; 2 Cor. 2 : 13 ; to forsake, renounce, Luke 14 : 33. See FORSAKE, RENOUNCE, SEND, *Note* (2) at end.¶

2. APASPAZOMAI (ἀπασπάζομαι), to bid farewell (*apo*, from, *aspazomai*, to greet), is used in Acts 21 : 6, A.V., " had taken our leave of ; " R.V., " bade . . . farewell."¶

BIER

SOROS (σορός) originally denoted a receptacle for containing the bones of the dead, a cinerary urn ; then a coffin, Gen. 50 : 26 ; Job. 21 : 32 ; then, the funeral couch or bier on which the Jews bore their dead to burial, Luke 7 : 14.¶

BILL

1. BIBLION (βιβλίον), primarily a small book, a scroll, or any sheet on which something has been written ; hence, in connection with *apostasion*, divorce, signifies a bill of divorcement, Matt. 19 : 7 (A.V., " writing ") ; Mark 10 : 4. See BOOK, SCROLL, WRITING.

2. GRAMMA (γράμμα), from *graphō*, to write (Eng., graph, graphic etc.), in Luke 16 : 6, A.V., is translated " bill." It lit. signifies that which is drawn, a picture ; hence, a written document ; hence, a bill, or bond, or note of hand, showing the amount of indebtedness. In the passage referred to the word is in the plural, indicating perhaps, but not necessarily, various bills. The bonds mentioned in Rabbinical writings, were formal, signed by witnesses and the Sanhedrin of three, or informal, when only the debtor signed. The latter were usually written on wax, and easily altered. See LEARNING, LETTER, SCRIPTURE, WRITING.

For BILLOWS, Luke 21; 25, R.V., see WAVE

BIND, BINDING (see also BOUND)

1. DEŌ (δέω), to bind, is used (*a*) literally, of any sort of binding, e.g., Acts 22 : 5 ; 24 : 27, (*b*) figuratively, of the Word of God, as not being bound, 2 Tim. 2 : 9, i.e., its ministry, course and efficacy were not hindered by the bonds and imprisonment suffered by the Apostle. A woman who was bent together, had been " bound " by Satan through the work of a

demon, Luke 13 : 16. Paul speaks of himself, in Acts 20 : 22, as being
" bound in the spirit," i.e. compelled by his convictions, under the
constraining power of the Spirit of God, to go to Jerusalem. A wife is
said to be " bound " to her husband, Rom. 7 : 2 ; 1 Cor. 7 : 39 ; and the
husband to the wife, 1 Cor. 7 : 27. The Lord's words to the Apostle
Peter in Matt. 16 : 19, as to binding, and to all the disciples in 18 : 18,
signify, in the former case, that the Apostle, by his ministry of the Word of
Life, would keep unbelievers outside the kingdom of God, and admit those
who believed. So with regard to 18 : 18, including the exercise of disciplinary measures in the sphere of the local church ; the application of the
Rabbinical sense of forbidding is questionable. See BOND, KNIT, Note.
TIE.

2. PERIDEŌ (περιδέω), peri, around, with No. 1, to bind around, is
used in John 11 : 44 of the napkin around the face of Lazarus.¶ Cp.
Job 12 : 18, Sept.

3. HUPODEŌ (ὑποδέω), hupō, under, with No. 1, to bind underneath,
is used of binding of sandals, Acts 12 : 8 ; rendered " shod " in Mark 6 : 9
and Eph. 6 : 15. See SHOD.¶

4. KATADEŌ (καταδέω), kata, down, with No. 1, to bind or tie down,
or bind up, is used in Luke 10 : 34 of the act of the good Samaritan.¶

5. SUNDEŌ (συνδέω), sun, together, and No. 1, to bind together,
implying association, is used in Heb. 13 : 3 of those bound together in
confinement.¶

6. DESMEUŌ or DESMEŌ (δεσμεύω) signifies to put in fetters or any
kind of bond, Luke 8 : 29 ; Acts 22 : 4, or to bind a burden upon a person,
Matt. 23 : 4. The verb is connected with No. 1.¶

Notes : (1) Cp. desmos, a band, bond, fetter, e.g., Luke 13 : 16, and
desmios, " bound," Acts 25 : 14, A.V. (R.V., " a prisoner ") ; in Heb.
13 : 3, " them that are in bonds." See BOND, CHAIN, PRISONER, STRING.

(2) Sundesmos (see No. 5, above), that which binds together, is
translated " bands," in Col. 2 : 19. See BONDS.

7. PROTEINŌ (προτείνω), lit., to stretch forth (pro, forth, teinō, to
stretch), is used in Acts 22 : 25, A.V., " they bound ; " R.V., " they had
tied (him) up," in reference to the preparations made for scourging, probably, to stretch the body forward, to make it tense for severer punishment. See TIE.¶

BIRD (Fowl)

1. ORNEON (ὄρνεον) is probably connected with a word signifying
to perceive, to hear ; Rev. 18 : 2 ; 19 : 17, 21. See FOWL. Cp. ornis,
a hen.¶

2. PETEINON (πετεινόν) signifies that which is able to fly, winged.
It is connected with ptenon signifying " feathered, winged," which is
used in 1 Cor. 15 : 39. Cp. petomai and petaomai, to fly. In the Gospels
the R.V. always translates it " birds," e.g., Matt. 6 : 26 ; but " fowls "

in Acts 10 : 12 ; 11 : 6.   The A.V. unsuitably has " fowls," in the Gospels, except Matt. 8 : 20 ; 13 : 32 ; Luke 9 : 58.

BIRTH

1. GENNĒSIS (γέννησις), a birth, begetting, producing (related to *gennaō*, to beget), is used in Matt. 1 : 18 and Luke 1 : 14.   Some mss. have *genesis*, lineage, birth (from *ginomai*, to become).¶

2. GENETĒ (γενετή), a being born, or the hour of birth (related to *genea*, race, generation), is connected with *ginomai*, to become, to be born, and is used in John 9 : 1.¶

Notes (1) For *genesis* and *gennēma* see FRUIT, GENERATION, NATURE.

(2) In Gal. 4 : 19, *ōdinō*, to have birth pangs, is rendered " travail in birth," A.V. ; R.V., " am in travail."   See Rev. 12 : 2.

BIRTHDAY

GENESIA (γενέσια), a neuter plural (akin to *genesis*, lineage, from *ginomai*), primarily denoted the festivities of a birthday, a birthday feast, though among the Greeks it was also used of a festival in commemoration of a deceased friend.   It is found in Matt. 14 : 6 and Mark 6 : 21.   Some have regarded it as the day of the king's accession, but this meaning is not confirmed in Greek writings.¶

BIRTHRIGHT

PRŌTOTOKIA (πρωτοτόκια), a birthright (from *prōtos*, first, *tiktō*, to beget), is found in Heb. 12 : 16, with reference to Esau (cp. *prōtotokos*, firstborn).   The birthright involved pre-eminence and authority, Gen. 27 : 29 ; 49 : 3.   Another right was that of the double portion, Deut. 21 : 17 ; 1 Chron. 5 : 1, 2.   Connected with the birthright was the progenitorship of the Messiah.   Esau transferred his birthright to Jacob for a paltry mess of pottage, profanely despising this last spiritual privilege, Gen. 25 and 27.   In the history of the nation God occasionally set aside the birthright, to show that the objects of His choice depended not on the will of the flesh, but on His own authority.   Thus Isaac was preferred to Ishmael, Jacob to Esau, Joseph to Reuben, David to his elder brethren, Solomon to Adonijah.   See FIRSTBORN.¶

BISHOP (Overseer)

1. EPISKOPOS (ἐπίσκοπος), lit., an overseer (*epi*, over, *skopeō*, to look or watch), whence Eng. " bishop," which has precisely the same meaning, is found in Acts 20 : 28 ; Phil. 1 : 1 ; 1 Tim. 3 : 2 ; Tit. 1 : 7 ; 1 Pet. 2 : 25.   See OVERSEER.¶

Note : *Presbuteros*, an elder, is another term for the same person as bishop or overseer.   See Acts 20 : 17 with verse 28.   The term " elder " indicates the mature spiritual experience and understanding of those so described ; the term " bishop," or " overseer," indicates the character of the work undertaken. According to the Divine will and appointment, as in the N.T., there were to be bishops in every local church, Acts 14 : 23 ; 20 : 17 ; Phil. 1 : 1 ; Tit. 1 : 5 ; Jas. 5 : 14. Where the singular is used, the passage is describing what a bishop should be, 1 Tim. 3 : 2 ; Tit. 1 : 7. Christ Himself is spoken of as " the . . . Bishop of our souls," 1 Pet. 2 : 25. See ELDER.

2. EPISKOPĒ (ἐπισκοπή), besides its meaning, visitation, e.g., 1 Pet. 2 : 12 (cp. the Sept. of Ex. 3 : 16 ; Is. 10 : 3 ; Jer. 10 : 15), is rendered " office," in Acts 1 : 20, R.V. (A.V., " bishoprick ") ; in 1 Tim. 3 : 1," the office of a bishop," lit., ' (if any one seeketh) overseership,' there is no word representing office.

Note : The corresponding verb is *episkopeō*, which, in reference to the work of an overseer, is found in 1 Pet. 5 : 2, R.V., " exercising the oversight," for A.V. " taking the oversight." See OVERSIGHT.

For BIT see BRIDLE

BITE

DAKNŌ (δάκνω), to bite, in Gal. 5 : 15, " if ye bite and devour one another," is used metaphorically of wounding the soul, or rending with reproaches.¶

BITTER, BITTERLY, BITTERNESS
A. Adjective.

PIKROS (πικρός), from a root *pik—*, meaning to cut, to prick, hence, lit., pointed, sharp, keen, pungent to the sense of taste, smell, etc., is found in Jas. 3 : 11, 14. In ver. 11 it has its natural sense, with reference to water ; in ver. 14 it is used metaphorically of jealousy, R.V.¶

B. Verb.

PIKRAINŌ (πικραίνω), related to A, signifies, in the Active Voice, to be bitter, Col. 3 : 19, or to embitter, irritate, or to make bitter, Rev. 10 : 9 ; the Passive Voice, to be made bitter, is used in Rev. 8 : 11 ; 10 : 10.¶

C. Noun.

PIKRIA (πικρία) denotes bitterness. It is used in Acts 8 : 23, metaphorically, of a condition of extreme wickedness, " gall of bitterness " or " bitter gall ; " in Rom. 3 : 14, of evil speaking ; in Eph. 4 : 31, of bitter hatred ; in Heb. 12 : 15, in the same sense, metaphorically, of a root of bitterness, producing bitter fruit.¶

D. Adverb.

PIKRŌS (πικρῶς), bitterly, is used of the poignant grief of Peter's weeping for his denial of Christ, Matt. 26 : 75 ; Luke 22 : 62.¶

Note : In the Sept., *pikris* (not in the N.T.), a bitter herb, is used in Ex. 12 : 8 ; Num. 9 : 11.¶

BLACK, BLACKNESS
A. Adjective.

MELAS (μέλας), black, Matt. 5 : 36 ; Rev. 6 : 5, 12, is derived from a root *mal*—, meaning to be dirty ; hence Latin, *malus*, bad.   See INK.

B. Nouns.

1. GNOPHOS (γνόφος), Heb. 12 : 18, blackness, gloom, seems to have been associated with the idea of a tempest.   It is related to *skotos*, darkness, in that passage, and in the Sept. of Ex. 10 : 22 ; Deut. 4 : 11 ; Zeph. 1 : 15.¶

2. ZOPHOS (ζόφος), akin to No. 1, especially the gloom of the regions of the lost, is used four times ; 2 Pet. 2 : 4, " darkness " (R.V.) ; 2 : 17, R.V., " blackness," for A.V., " mist ; " Jude 6, " darkness ; " ver. 13, " blackness," suggesting a kind of emanation.   See DARKNESS, MIST.¶

For BLADE see GRASS

BLAME, BLAMELESS
A. Verb.

MŌMAOMAI (μωμάομαι), to find fault with, to blame, or calumniate, is used in 2 Cor. 6 : 3, of the ministry of the Gospel ; in 8 : 20, of the ministration of financial help.¶

Notes : (1) Cp. the synonymous verb, *memphomai*, to find fault, Mark 7 : 2 ; Rom. 9 : 19 ; Heb. 8 : 8.   See FAULT.¶

(2) In Gal. 2 : 11, *kataginōskō* is rightly rendered " stood condemned," R.V., for A.V., " was to be blamed."   See CONDEMN.

B. Adjectives.

1. AMŌMOS (ἄμωμος) : See BLEMISH, B.

2. AMŌMĒTOS (ἀμώμητος), translated in Phil. 2 : 15 " without blemish " (A.V., " without rebuke "), is rendered " blameless " in 2 Pet. 3 : 14 (A.V. and R.V.).¶

3. AMEMPTOS (ἄμεμπτος), related to *memphomai* (A., Note), is translated " unblameable " in 1 Thess. 3 : 13 ; " blameless," in Luke 1 : 6 ; Phil. 2 : 15 ; 3 : 6 ; " faultless " in Heb. 8 : 7.   See FAULTLESS, UNBLAMEABLE.¶

" If *amōmos* is the unblemished,' *amemptos* is the ' unblamed.' . . . Christ was *amōmos* in that there was in Him no spot or blemish, and He could say, ' Which of you convinceth (convicteth) Me of sin ? ' but in strictness of speech He was not *amemptos* (unblamed), nor is this epithet ever given to Him in the N.T., seeing that He endured the contradiction of sinners against Himself, who slandered His footsteps and laid to His charge ' things that He knew not ' (i.e., of which He was guiltless)." Trench, Syn. §103.

4. ANAITIOS (ἀναίτιος), guiltless (*a*, negative, *n*, euphonic, and *aitia*, a charge), is translated, " blameless " in the A.V. of Matt. 12 : 5,

" guiltless " in 12 : 7. The R.V. has " guiltless " in both places ¶ In the Sept., in Deut. 19 : 10, 13, and 21 : 8, 9.¶ See GUILTLESS.

5. ANEPILĒPTOS (ἀνεπίληπτος), lit., that cannot be laid hold of, hence, not open to censure, irreproachable (from *a*, negative, *n*, euphonic, and *epilambanō*, to lay hold of), is used in 1 Tim. 3 : 2 ; 5 : 7 ; 6 : 14 (in all three places the R.V. has " without reproach ; " in the first two, A.V., " blameless," in the last, " unrebukeable ; " an alternative rendering would be ' irreprehensible '). See REPROACH, UNREBUKEABLE.¶

6. ANENKLĒTOS (ἀνέγκλητος) signifies that which cannot be called to account (from *a*, negative, *n*, euphonic, and *enkaleō*, to call in), i.e., with nothing laid to one's charge (as the result of public investigation) , in 1 Cor. 1 : 8, R.V., " unreproveable," A.V., " blameless ; " in Col. 1 : 22, A.V. and R.V., " unreproveable ; " in 1 Tim. 3 : 10 and Tit. 1 : 6, 7, A.V. and R.V., " blameless." It implies not merely acquittal, but the absence of even a charge or accusation against a person. This is to be the case with elders.¶

C. Adverb.

AMEMPTŌS (ἀμέμπτως), in 1 Thess. 2 : 10, " unblameably ; " in 5 : 23, " without blame," A.V., " blameless," is said of believers at the Judgment-Seat of Christ in His Parousia (His presence after His coming), as the outcome of present witness and stedfastness. See B, No. 3, above.¶

BLASPHEME, BLASPHEMY, BLASPHEMER, BLASPHEMOUS
A. Noun.

BLASPHĒMIA (βλασφημία), either from *blax*, sluggish, stupid, or, probably, from *blaptō*, to injure, and *phēmē*, speech, Eng. " blasphemy," is so translated thirteen times in the R.V., but " railing " in Matt. 15 . 19 ; Mark 7 : 22 ; Eph. 4 : 31 ; Col. 3 : 8 ; 1 Tim. 6 : 4 ; Jude 9. The word " blasphemy " is practically confined to speech defamatory of the Divine Majesty. See Note, below. See EVIL SPEAKING, RAILING.

B. Verb.

BLASPHĒMEŌ (βλασφημέω), to blaspheme, rail at or revile, is used (*a*) in a general way, of any contumelious speech, reviling, calumniating, railing at etc., as of those who railed at Christ, e.g., Matt. 27 : 39 ; Mark 15 : 29 ; Luke 22 : 65 (R.V., " reviling ") ; 23 : 39 ; (*b*) of those who speak contemptuously of God or of sacred things, e.g., Matt. 9 : 3 ; Mark 3 : 28 ; Rom. 2 : 24 ; 1 Tim. 1 : 20 ; 6 : 1 ; Rev. 13 : 6 ; 16 : 9, 11, 21 ; " hath spoken blasphemy," Matt. 26 : 65 ; " rail at," 2 Pet. 2 : 10 ; Jude 8, 10 ; " railing," 2 Pet. 2 : 12 ; " slanderously reported," Rom. 3 : 8 ; " be evil spoken of," Rom. 14 : 16 ; 1 Cor. 10 : 30 ; 2 Pet. 2 : 2 ; " speak evil of," Tit. 3 : 2 ; 1 Pet. 4 : 4 ; " being defamed," 1 Cor. 4 : 13. The verb (in the present participial form) is translated " blasphemers " in Acts 19 : 37 ; in Mark 2 : 7, " blasphemeth," R.V., for A.V., " speaketh blasphemies."

There is no noun in the original representing the English " blasphemer."

This is expressed either by the verb, or by the adjective *blasphemos*. See DEFAME, RAIL, REPORT, REVILE.

C. Adjective.

BLASPHĒMOS (βλάσφημος), abusive, speaking evil, is translated " blasphemous," in Acts 6 : 11, 13; "a blasphemer," 1 Tim. 1 : 13; " railers," 2 Tim. 3 : 2, R.V. ; " railing," 2 Pet. 2 : 11. See RAIL.¶

Note : As to Christ's teaching concerning blasphemy against the Holy Spirit, e.g., Matt. 12 : 32, that anyone, with the evidence of the Lord's power before His eyes, should declare it to be Satanic, exhibited a condition of heart beyond Divine illumination and therefore hopeless. Divine forgiveness would be inconsistent with the moral nature of God. As to the Son of Man, in his state of humiliation, there might be misunderstanding, but not so with the Holy Spirit's power demonstrated.

BLAZE ABROAD

DIAPHĒMIZŌ (διαφημίζω), to spread abroad (*dia*, throughout, *phēmizō*, to speak), is so translated in the R.V. in Matt. 9 : 31 ; 28 : 15 (A.V., " commonly reported ") ; Mark 1 : 45 (A.V., " blaze abroad ").¶

BLEMISH
A. Noun.

MŌMOS (μῶμος), akin to *mōmaomai* (see BLAME, A), signifies (*a*) a blemish (Sept. only) ; (*b*) a shame, a moral disgrace, metaphorical of the licentious, 2 Pet. 2 : 13.¶

B. Adjective.

AMŌMOS (ἄμωμος), without blemish, is always so rendered in the R.V., Eph. 1 : 4 ; 5 : 27 ; Phil. 2 : 15 ; Col. 1 : 22 ; Heb. 9 : 14 ; 1 Pet. 1 : 19 ; Jude 24 ; Rev. 14 : 5. This meaning is to be preferred to the various A.V. renderings, " without blame," Eph. 1 : 4, " unblameable," Col. 1 : 22, " faultless," Jude 24, " without fault," Rev. 14 : 5. The most authentic mss. have *amōmos*," without blemish," in Phil. 2 : 15, for *amōmētos*, " without rebuke."¶ In the Sept., in reference to sacrifices, especially in Lev. and Num., the Psalms and Ezek., of blamelessness in character and conduct. See BLAME, FAULT.

BLESS, BLESSED, BLESSEDNESS, BLESSING
A. Verbs.

1. EULOGEŌ (εὐλογέω), lit., to speak well of (*eu*, well, *logos*, a word), signifies, (*a*) to praise, to celebrate with praises, of that which is addressed to God, acknowledging His goodness, with desire for His glory, Luke 1 : 64 ; 2 : 28 ; 24 : 51, 53 ; Jas. 3 : 9 ; (*b*) to invoke blessings upon a person, e.g., Luke 6 : 28 ; Rom. 12 : 14. The present participle Passive, blessed, praised, is especially used of Christ in Matt. 21 : 9 ; 23 : 39, and the parallel passages ; also in John 12 : 13 ; (*c*) to consecrate a thing with solemn prayers, to ask God's blessing on a thing, e.g., Luke 9 : 16 ; 1 Cor.

10 : 16 ; (d) to cause to prosper, to make happy, to bestow blessings on, said of God, e.g., in Acts 3 : 26 ; Gal. 3 : 9 ; Eph. 1 : 3. Cp. the synonym *aineō*, to praise. See PRAISE.

2. ENEULOGEOMAI (ἐνευλογέομαι), to bless, is used in the Passive Voice, Acts 3 : 25, and Gal. 3 : 8. The prefix *en* apparently indicates the person on whom the blessing is conferred.¶

3. MAKARIZŌ (μακαρίζω), from a root *mak*—, meaning large, lengthy, found also in *makros*, long, *mēkos*, length, hence denotes to pronounce happy, blessed, Luke 1 : 48 and Jas. 5 : 11. See HAPPY.¶

B. Adjectives.

1. EULOGĒTOS (εὐλογητός), akin to A, 1, means blessed, praised ; it is applied only to God, Mark 14 : 61 ; Luke 1 : 68 ; Rom. 1 : 25 ; 9 : 5 ; 2 Cor. 1 : 3 ; 11 : 31 ; Eph. 1 : 3 ; 1 Pet. 1 : 3.¶ In the Sept. it is also applied to man, e.g., in Gen. 24 : 31 ; 26 : 29 ; Deut. 7 : 14 ; Judg. 17 : 2 ; Ruth 2 : 20 ; 1 Sam. 15 : 13.

2. MAKARIOS (μακάριος), akin to A, No. 3, is used in the beatitudes in Matt. 5 and Luke 6, is especially frequent in the Gospel of Luke, and is found seven times in Revelation, 1 : 3 ; 14 : 13 ; 16 : 15 ; 19 : 9 ; 20 : 6 ; 22 : 7, 14. It is said of God twice, 1 Tim. 1 : 11 ; 6 : 15. In the beatitudes the Lord indicates not only the characters that are blessed, but the nature of that which is the highest good.

C. Nouns.

1. EULOGIA (εὐλογία), akin to A, 1, lit., good speaking, praise, is used of (a) God and Christ, Rev. 5 : 12, 13 ; 7 : 12 ; (b) the invocation of blessings, benediction, Heb. 12 : 17 ; Jas. 3 : 10 ; (c) the giving of thanks, 1 Cor. 10 : 16 ; (d) a blessing, a benefit bestowed, Rom. 15 : 29 ; Gal. 3 : 14 ; Eph. 1 : 3 ; Heb. 6 : 7 ; of a monetary gift sent to needy believers, 2 Cor. 9 : 5, 6 ; (e) in a bad sense, of fair speech, Rom. 16 : 18, R.V., where it is joined with *chrēstologia*, smooth speech, the latter relating to the substance, *eulogia* to the expression. See BOUNTY.¶

2. MAKARISMOS (μακαρισμός), akin to A, 3, blessedness, indicates an ascription of blessing rather than a state ; hence in Rom. 4 : 6, where the A.V. renders it as a noun, " (describeth) the blessedness ; " the R.V. rightly puts " (pronounceth) blessing." So ver. 9. In Gal. 4 : 15 the A.V. has " blessedness," R.V., " gratulation." The Galatian believers had counted themselves happy when they heard and received the Gospel. Had they lost that opinion ? See GRATULATION.¶

Note : In Acts 13 : 34, *hosia*, lit., 'holy things,' is translated " mercies " (A.V.), " blessings " (R.V.).

For BLEW see BLOW

BLIND, BLINDNESS
A. Verbs.

1. TUPHLOŌ (τυφλόω), to blind (from a root *tuph*—, to burn, smoke ;

cp. *tuphos*, smoke), is used metaphorically, of the dulling of the intellect,
John 12 : 40 ; 2 Cor. 4 : 4 ; 1 John 2 : 11.¶

2. PŎROŌ (πωρόω) signifies to harden (from *pŏros*, a thick skin, a
hardening) ; rendered " blinded," A.V., in Rom. 11 : 7 and 2 Cor. 3 : 14
(R.V., " hardened ") ; cp. 4 : 4. See HARDEN.

B. Adjective.

TUPHLOS (τυφλός), blind, is used both physically and metaphorically,
chiefly in the Gospels ; elsewhere four times ; physically, Acts 13 : 11 ;
metaphorically, Rom. 2 : 19 ; 2 Pet. 1 : 9 ; Rev. 3 : 17. The word is
frequently used as a noun, signifying a blind man.

C. Noun.

PŎRŌSIS (πώρωσις), akin to A. No. 2, primarily means a covering with
a callus, a " hardening," Rom. 11 : 25 and Eph. 4 : 18, R.V., for A.V.,
" blindness ; " Mark 3 : 5, R.V., for A.V., " hardness." It is metaphorical
of a dulled spiritual perception. See HARDNESS.¶

Note : In John 9 : 8, the most authentic mss. have *prosaitēs*, a beggar,
R.V., instead of *tuphlos*, blind.

BLINDFOLD

PERIKALUPTŌ (περικαλύπτω) signifies to blindfold (*peri*, around,
kaluptō, to hide), Luke 22 : 64. See COVER, OVERLAY.

BLOOD
A. Nouns.

1. HAIMA (αἷμα), (hence Eng., prefix *hæm*—), besides its natural
meaning, stands, (*a*) in conjunction with *sarx*, flesh, " flesh and blood,"
Matt. 16 : 17 ; 1 Cor. 15 : 50 ; Gal. 1 : 16 ; the original has the opposite
order, blood and flesh, in Eph. 6 : 12 and Heb. 2 : 14 ; this phrase signifies,
by *synecdoche*, man, human beings. It stresses the limitations of
humanity ; the two are essential elements in man's physical being ; " the
life of the flesh is in the blood," Lev. 17 : 11 ; (*b*) for human generation,
John 1 : 13 ; (*c*) for blood shed by violence, e.g., Matt. 23 : 35 ; Rev.
17 : 6 ; (*d*) for the blood of sacrificial victims, e.g., Heb. 9 : 7 ; of the blood
of Christ, which betokens His death by the shedding of His blood in
expiatory sacrifice ; to drink His blood is to appropriate the saving
effects of His expiatory death, John 6 : 53. As " the life of the flesh
is in the blood," Lev. 17 : 11, and was forfeited by sin, life eternal can
be imparted only by the expiation made, in the giving up of the life by
the sinless Saviour.

2. HAIMATEKCHUSIA (αἱματεκχυσία) denotes shedding of blood,
Heb. 9 : 22 (*haima*, blood, *ekchunō*, to pour out, shed).¶

B. Verb.

HAIMORRHOEŌ (αἱμορροέω), from *haima*, blood, *rheō*, to flow
(Eng., hæmorrhage), signifies to suffer from a flow of blood, Matt. 9 : 20.¶

Notes : (1) In Mark 5 : 25 and Luke 8 : 43, different constructions are used, the translations respectively being " having a flowing of blood " and " being in (i.e., with) a flowing of blood."

(2) In Acts 17 : 26 (R.V., " of one ; " A.V., " of one blood "), the most authentic mss. do not contain the noun *haima*, blood. So with the phrase " through His blood," in Col. 1 : 14.

(3) For " bloody flux " in Acts 28 : 8, A.V., see DYSENTERY (R.V.).

BLOT OUT

EXALEIPHŌ (ἐξαλείφω), from *ek*, out, used intensively, and *aleiphō*, to wipe, signifies to wash, or to smear completely. Hence, metaphorically, in the sense of removal, to wipe away, wipe off, obliterate ; Acts 3 : 19, of sins ; Col. 2 : 14, of writing ; Rev. 3 : 5, of a name in a book ; Rev. 7 : 17 ; 21 : 4, of tears.¶

BLOW (Noun)

RHAPISMA (ῥάπισμα), (*a*) a blow with a rod or staff, (*b*) a blow with the hand, a slap or cuff, is found in three places, of the maltreatment of Christ by the officials or attendants of the high priest, Mark 14 : 65, R.V., " received (according to the most authentic mss.) Him with blows of their hands," (A.V., " did strike Him with the palms of their hands ") ; that they received, or took, Him would indicate their rough handling of Him ; John 18 : 22 and 19 : 3 ; in all three places the R.V. marg. gives the meaning (*a*), as to the use of a rod.¶

So with the corresponding verb *rhapizō*, in Matt. 26 : 67. The soldiers subsequently beat Him with a reed, 27 : 30, where *tuptō*, to beat, is used ; *rhapizō* occurs elsewhere in Matt. 5 : 39. See SMITE.¶

BLOW (Verb)

1. PNEŌ (πνέω) signifies (*a*) to blow, e.g., Matt. 7 : 25 ; John 3 : 8 ; in Acts 27 : 40 the present participle is used as a noun, lit., ' to the blowing ' (i.e., to the wind) ; (*b*) to breathe. See BREATHE.

2. HUPOPNEŌ (ὑποπνέω), *hupo*, under (indicating repression), and No. 1, denotes to blow softly, Acts 27 : 13.¶

Note : In Acts 28 : 13, *epiginomai*, to come on, is used of the springing up of a wind, A.V., " blew ; " R.V., " sprang up."

BOARD

SANIS (σανίς) denotes a plank, or board, Acts 27 : 44.¶

BOAST, BOASTER, BOASTFUL
A. Verbs.

1. KAUCHAOMAI (καυχάομαι), and its related words *katakauchaomai*, to glory or boast and the nouns *kauchēsis* and *kauchēma*, translated " boast," and " boasting," in the A.V., are always translated " glory,"

and " glorying " in the R.V., e.g., 2 Cor. 10 : 15 ; 11 : 10, 17 ; Eph. 2 : 9. See GLORY.

2. MEGALAUCHEŌ (μεγαλαυχέω), from *megala*, great things, and *aucheō*, to lift up the neck, hence, to boast, is found in some texts of Jas. 3 : 5. The most authentic mss. have the two words separated. It indicates any kind of haughty speech which stirs up strife or provokes others.¶

Note : In Acts 5 : 36, the verb *legō*, to say, is rendered " boasting " in the A.V. ; " giving out " (R.V.).

B. Nouns.

1. ALAZŌN (ἀλαζών), a boaster, Rom. 1 : 30 and 2 Tim. 3 : 2, A.V., " boasters," R.V., " boastful," primarily signifies a wanderer about the country (from *alē*, wandering), a vagabond ; hence, an impostor.¶

2. ALAZONEIA (ἀλαζονεία), the practice of an *alazōn*, denotes quackery ; hence, arrogant display, or boastings, Jas. 4 : 16, R.V., " vauntings ; " in 1 John 2 : 16, R.V., " vainglory ; " A.V., " pride." See PRIDE, VAUNT.¶

Note : In 2 Cor. 9 : 4, *hupostasis*, a support, substance, means " confidence " (R.V.) ; A.V., " confident boasting."

BOAT

1. PLOIARION (πλοιάριον), a skiff or small boat, is a diminutive of *ploion* (No. 2), Mark 3 : 9 ; 4 : 36 ; John 6 : 22 (but No. 2 in the 2nd part of the verse), 23 (here some texts have No. 2), 24 ; 21 : 8.¶

2. PLOION (πλοῖον), A.V., " ship," is preferably translated " boat " (R.V.) in the Gospels, where it is of frequent use ; it is found 18 times in Acts, where, as in Jas. 3 : 4 ; Rev. 8 : 9 ; 18 : 19, it signifies a ship. See SHIP.

3. SKAPHĒ (σκάφη) is, lit., anything dug or scooped out (from *skaptō*, to dig), as a trough, a tub, and hence a light boat, or skiff, a boat belonging to a larger vessel, Acts 27 : 16, 30, 32.¶

BODY, BODILY
A. Nouns.

1. SŌMA (σῶμα) is the body as a whole, the instrument of life, whether of man living, e.g., Matt. 6 : 22, or dead, Matt. 27 : 52 ; or in resurrection, 1 Cor. 15 : 44 ; or of beasts, Heb. 13 : 11 ; of grain, 1 Cor. 15 : 37, 38 ; of the heavenly hosts, 1 Cor. 15 : 40. In Rev. 18 : 13 it is translated " slaves." In its figurative uses the essential idea is preserved.

Sometimes the word stands, by *synecdoche*, for the complete man, Matt. 5 : 29 ; 6 : 22 ; Rom. 12 : 1 ; Jas. 3 : 6 ; Rev. 18 : 13. Sometimes the person is identified with his or her body, Acts 9 : 37 ; 13 : 36, and this is so even of the Lord Jesus, John 19 : 40 with 42. The body is not the man, for he himself can exist apart from his body, 2 Cor. 12 : 2, 3. The body is an essential part of the man and therefore the redeemed are not perfected till the resurrection, Heb. 11 : 40 ; no man in his final state will be without his body, John 5 : 28, 29 ; Rev. 20 : 13.

The word is also used for physical nature, as distinct from *pneuma*, the spiritual nature, e.g., 1 Cor. 5 : 3, and from *psuchē*, the soul, e.g., 1 Thess. 5 : 23. "*Sōma*, body, and *pneuma*, spirit, may be separated; *pneuma* and *psuchē*, soul, can only be distinguished " (Cremer).

It is also used metaphorically, of the mystic Body of Christ, with reference to the whole Church, e.g., Eph. 1 : 23 ; Col. 1 : 18, 22, 24 ; also of a local church, 1 Cor. 12 : 27.

2. CHRŌS (χρώς) signifies the surface of a body, especially of the human body, Acts 19 : 12, with reference to the handkerchiefs carried from Paul's body to the sick.¶

3. PTŌMA (πτῶμα) denotes, lit., a fall (akin to *piptō*, to fall) ; hence, that which is fallen, a corpse, Matt. 14 : 12 ; 24 : 28, " carcase ; " Mark 6 : 29 ; 15 : 45, " corpse ; " Rev. 11 : 8, 9, " dead bodies " (Gk., " carcase," but plural in the 2nd part of ver. 9). See CARCASE, CORPSE.¶

B. Adjectives.

1. SUSSŌMOS (σύσσωμος), *sun*, with, and A, No. 1., means united in the same body, Eph. 3 : 6, of the Church.¶

2. SŌMATIKOS (σωματικός), bodily, is used in Luke 3 : 22, of the Holy Spirit in taking a bodily shape ; in 1 Tim. 4 : 8 of bodily exercise.¶

C. Adverb.

SŌMATIKŌS (σωματικῶς), bodily, corporeally, is used in Col. 2 : 9.¶

BOISTEROUS

Note : The A.V. " boisterous " in Matt. 14 : 30 is a rendering of the word *ischuros*, " strong " (see margin) ; it is not in the most authentic mss.

BOLD, BOLDNESS, BOLDLY
A. Verbs.

1. THARREŌ (θαρρέω), a later form of *tharseō* (see CHEER, COMFORT), is connected with *therō*, to be warm (warmth of temperament being associated with confidence) ; hence, to be confident, bold, courageous ; R.V., invariably, to be of good courage ; 2 Cor. 5 : 6, 8 (A.V., to be confident) ; 7 : 16 (A.V., to have confidence) ; 10 : 1, 2 (A.V., to be bold) ; Heb. 13 : 6, A.V., " boldly ; " R.V., " with good courage " (lit., ' being courageous '). See COURAGE.

2. PARRHĒSIAZOMAI (παρρησιάζομαι), to speak boldly, or freely, primarily had reference to speech (see B, below), but acquired the meaning of being bold, or waxing bold, 1 Thess. 2 : 2 ; in Acts 13 : 46, R.V., " spake out boldly " (the aorist participle here signifies ' waxing bold ') ; Acts 9 : 27, 29, " preached boldly " (see also 18 : 26 ; 19 : 8) ; in 26 : 26, " speak freely." See FREELY.

3. TOLMAŌ (τολμάω) signifies to dare to do, or to bear, something

terrible or difficult ; hence, to be bold, to bear oneself boldly, deal boldly ; it is translated " be bold " in 2 Cor. 10 : 2, as contrasted with *tharreō* in verse 1, and the first line of verse 2, " shew courage " (see No. 1, above) ; in 10 : 12, R.V., " are not bold to," for A.V., " dare not make ourselves of." *Tharreō* denotes confidence in one's own powers, and has reference to character ; *tolmaō* denotes boldness in undertaking and has reference to manifestation (Thayer). See COURAGE, DARE.

4. APOTOLMAŌ (ἀποτολμάω), *apo* (intensive), with No. 3, means to be very bold, to speak out boldly, and is used in Rom. 10 : 20.¶

B. Noun.

PARRHĒSIA (παρρησία), from *pas*, all, *rhēsis*, speech (see A, No. 2), denotes (*a*), primarily, freedom of speech, unreservedness of utterance, Acts 4 : 29, 31 ; 2 Cor. 3 : 12 ; 7 : 4 ; Philm. 8 ; or to speak without ambiguity, plainly, John 10 : 24 ; or without figures of speech, John 16 : 25 ; (*b*) the absence of fear in speaking boldly ; hence, confidence, cheerful courage, boldness, without any connection necessarily with speech ; the R.V. has " boldness " in the following ; Acts 4 : 13 ; Eph. 3 : 12 ; 1 Tim. 3 : 13 ; Heb. 3 : 6 ; 4 : 16 ; 10 : 19, 35 ; 1 John 2 : 28 ; 3 : 21 ; 4 : 17 ; 5 : 14 ; (*c*) the deportment by which one becomes conspicuous, John 7 : 4 ; 11 : 54, acts openly, or secures publicity, Col. 2 : 15. See CONFIDENCE, OPENLY, PLAINNESS.

C. Adverb.

TOLMĒROTERŌS (τολμηροτέρως), the comparative degree of *tolmērōs*, means the more boldly, Rom. 15 : 15 ; in some texts, *tolmēroteron*. Cp. A, No. 3.¶ Cp. *tolmētēs*, presumptuous ; R.V., " daring," 2 Pet. 2 : 10.¶

BOND

1. DESMOS (δεσμός), from *deō*, to bind (see BAND), is usually found in the plural, either masculine or neuter ; (*a*) it stands thus for the actual bonds which bind a prisoner, as in Luke 8 : 29 ; Acts 16 : 26 ; 20 : 23 (the only three places where the neuter plural is used) ; 22 : 30 ; (*b*) the masculine plural stands frequently in a figurative sense for a condition of imprisonment, Phil. 1 : 7, 13, i.e., ' so that my captivity became manifest as appointed for the cause of Christ ' ; verses 14, 16 ; Col. 4 : 18 ; 2 Tim. 2 : 9 ; Philm. 10, 13 ; Heb. 10 : 34.

In Mark 7 : 35 " the bond (A.V., string) " stands metaphorically for the infirmity which caused an impediment in his speech. So in Luke 13 : 16, of the infirmity of the woman who was bowed together. See BAND, CHAIN, STRING.

2. DESMIOS (δέσμιος), a binding, denotes " a prisoner," e.g., Acts 25 : 14, R.V., for the A.V., " in bonds ; " Heb. 13 : 3, " them that are in bonds." Paul speaks of himself as a prisoner of Christ, Eph. 3 : 1 ; 2 Tim. 1 : 8 ; Philm. 1, 9 ; " in the Lord," Eph. 4 : 1. See PRISONER.

3. SUNDESMOS (σύνδεσμος), that which binds together (*sun*, with, and No. 1), is said of " the bond of iniquity," Acts 8 : 23 ; " the bond of

peace," Eph. 4 : 3 ; " the bond of perfectness," Col. 3 : 14 (figurative of the ligaments of the body) ; elsewhere, Col. 2 : 19, " bands," figuratively of the bands which unite the Church, the Body of Christ. See BAND.¶

4. HALUSIS (ἅλυσις) denotes a chain ; so the R.V. in Eph. 6 : 20, for A.V., " bonds." See CHAIN.

5. GRAMMA (γράμμα), in Luke 16 : 6, R.V., means a bill or note of hand. See BILL, No. 2.

6. CHEIROGRAPHOS (χειρόγραφος), a handwriting, is rendered " bond " in Col. 2 : 14, R.V.

BONDAGE
A. Noun.

DOULEIA (δουλεία), akin to *deō*, to bind, primarily the condition of being a slave, came to denote any kind of bondage, as, e.g., of the condition of creation, Rom. 8 : 21 ; of that fallen condition of man himself which makes him dread God, ver. 15, and fear death, Heb. 2 : 15 ; of the condition imposed by the Mosaic Law, Gal. 4 : 24. See SERVE.

B. Verbs.

1. DOULEUŌ (δουλεύω), to serve as a slave, to be a slave, to be in bondage, is frequently used without any association of slavery, e.g., Acts 20 : 19 ; Rom. 6 : 6 ; 7 : 6 ; 12 : 11 ; Gal. 5 : 13. See SERVE.

2. DOULOŌ (δουλόω), different from No. 1, in being transitive instead of intransitive, signifies to make a slave of, to bring into bondage, Acts 7 : 6 ; 1 Cor. 9 : 19, R.V. ; in the Passive Voice, to be brought under bondage, 2 Pet. 2 : 19 ; to be held in bondage, Gal. 4 : 3 (lit., ' were reduced to bondage ') ; Tit. 2 : 3, of being enslaved to wine ; Rom. 6 : 18, of service to righteousness (lit., ' were made bondservants '). As with the purchased slave there were no limitations either in the kind or the time of service, so the life of the believer is to be lived in continuous obedience to God. See ENSLAVED, GIVE, SERVANT.

3. DOULAGŌGEŌ (δουλαγωγέω), to bring into bondage (from A, above, and *agō*, to bring), is used in 1 Cor. 9 : 27, concerning the body, R.V., " bondage," for A.V., " subjection."¶

4. KATADOULOŌ (καταδουλόω), to bring into bondage, occurs in 2 Cor. 11 : 20 ; Gal. 2 : 4.¶

BONDMAN, BONDMAID

DOULOS (δοῦλος), from *deō*, to bind, a slave, originally the lowest term in the scale of servitude, came also to mean one who gives himself up to the will of another, e.g., 1 Cor. 7 : 23 ; Rom. 6 : 17, 20, and became the most common and general word for " servant," as in Matt. 8 : 9, without any idea of bondage. In calling himself, however, a ' bondslave of Jesus Christ,' e.g., Rom. 1 : 1, the Apostle Paul intimates (1) that he had been formerly a bondslave of Satan, and (2) that, having been bought by Christ, he was now a willing slave, bound to his new Master. See SERVANT.

The feminine, *doulē*, signifies a handmaid, Luke 1 : 38, 48 ; Acts 2 : 18.¶

PAIDISKĒ (παιδίσκη), a young girl, maiden, also denoted a young female slave, bondwoman, or handmaid. For the A.V., " bondmaid " or " bondwoman," in Gal. 4 : 22, 23, 30, 31, the R.V. has " handmaid." See DAMSEL, HANDMAID, MAID.

For BONDSERVANT see SERVANT

BONE

OSTEON (ὀστέον), probably from a word signifying strength, or firmness, sometimes denotes hard substances other than bones, e.g., the stone or kernel of fruit. In the N.T. it always denotes bones, Matt. 23 : 27 ; Luke 24 : 39 ; John 19 : 36 ; Heb. 11 : 22.¶

Note : As to Eph. 5 : 30, R.V., " We are members of His body " (in contrast to the A.V.), " the words that follow in the common text are an unintelligent gloss, in which unsuccessful endeavour is made to give greater distinctness to the Apostle's statement " (Westcott).

BOOK

1. BIBLOS (βίβλος), Eng. " Bible," was the inner part, or rather the cellular substance, of the stem of the papyrus (Eng. " paper "). It came to denote the paper made from this bark in Egypt, and then a written book, roll, or volume. It is used in referring to books of Scripture, the book, or scroll, of Matthew's Gospel, Matt. 1 : 1 ; the Pentateuch, as the book of Moses, Mark 12 : 26 ; Isaiah, as " the book of the words of Isaiah," Luke 3 : 4 ; the Psalms, Luke 20 : 42 and Acts 1 : 20 ; " the prophets," Acts 7 : 42 ; to " the Book of Life," Phil. 4 : 3 ; Rev. 3 : 5 ; 20 : 15. Once only it is used of secular writings, Acts 19 : 19.¶

2. BIBLION (βιβλίον), a diminutive of No. 1, had in Hellenistic Greek almost lost its diminutive force and was ousting *biblos* in ordinary use ; it denotes a scroll or a small book. It is used in Luke 4 : 17, 20, of the book of Isaiah ; in John 20 : 30, of the Gospel of John ; in Gal. 3 : 10 and Heb. 10 : 7, of the whole of the O.T. ; in Heb. 9 : 19, of the book of Exodus ; in Rev. 1 : 11 ; 22 : 7, 9, 10, 18 (twice), 19, of the Apocalypse ; in John 21 : 25 and 2 Tim. 4 : 13, of books in general ; in Rev. 13 : 8 ; 17 : 8 ; 20 : 12 ; 21 : 27, of the Book of Life (see Note, below) ; in Rev. 20 : 12, of other books to be opened in the Day of Judgment, containing, it would seem, the record of human deeds. In Rev. 5 : 1–9 the Book represents the revelation of God's purposes and counsels concerning the world. So with the " little book " in Rev. 10 : 8. In 6 : 14 it is used of a scroll, the rolling up of which illustrates the removal of the heaven.

In Matt. 19 : 7 and Mark 10 : 4 the word is used of a bill of divorcement. See BILL.¶

Note : In Rev. 22 : 19, the most authentic mss. have *xulon*, tree (of life), instead of " *biblion*."

3. BIBLARIDION (βιβλαρίδιον), another diminutive of No. 1, is always rendered " little book," in Rev. 10 : 2, 9, 10. Some texts have it also in verse 8, instead of *biblion* (but see beginning of No. 2).¶

BOON

DŌRĒMA (δώρημα), translated " boon " in Jas. 1 : 17, R.V., is thus distinguished, as the thing given, from the preceding word in the verse, *dosis*, the act of giving (A.V., " gift " in each case) ; elsewhere in Rom. 5 : 16. It is to be distinguished also from *dōron*, the usual word for a gift. See GIFT.¶

BORDER

1. KRASPEDON (κράσπεδον) was primarily the extremity or prominent part of a thing, an edge ; hence the fringe of a garment, or a little fringe, hanging down from the edge of the mantle or cloak. The Jews had these attached to their mantles to remind them of the Law, according to Num. 15 : 38, 39 ; Deut. 22 : 12 ; Zech. 8 : 23.¶. This is the meaning in Matt. 23 : 5. In Matt. 9 : 20 ; 14 : 36 ; Mark 6 : 56 ; Luke 8 : 44, it is used of the border of Christ's garment (A.V. " hem," in the first two places). See HEM.¶

2. HORION (ὅριον), the border of a country or district (cp. Eng., horizon), is always used in the plural. The A.V. has " coasts," but " borders " in Matt. 4 : 13 ; the R.V. always " borders," Matt. 2 : 16 ; 4 : 13 ; 8 : 34 ; 15 : 22, 39 ; 19 : 1 ; Mark 5 : 17 ; 7 : 31 (twice) ; 10 : 1 ; Acts 13 : 50. In some of these it signifies territory. See COAST.¶

3. METHORION (μεθόριον), *meta*, with, and No. 2, similar in meaning, is found, in some mss., in Mark 7 : 24.¶ Cp. *horothesia*, under BOUND.

For BORN see BEGET

For BORNE see BEAR

BORROW

DANEIZŌ (δανείζω), in the Active Voice, signifies to lend money, as in Luke 6 : 34, 35 ; in the Middle Voice, to have money lent to one-self, to borrow, Matt. 5 : 42.¶ Cp. *dan(e)ion*, a debt, Matt. 18 : 27,¶ and *dan(e)istēs*, a creditor, Luke 7 : 41.¶ See LEND.

BOSOM

KOLPOS (κόλπος) signifies (*a*) the front of the body between the arms ; hence, to recline in the bosom was said of one who so reclined at table that his head covered, as it were, the bosom of the one next to him, John 13 : 23. Hence, figuratively, it is used of a place of blessedness with another, as with Abraham in Paradise, Luke 16 : 22, 23 (plural in ver. 23), from the custom of reclining at table in the bosom, a place of honour ;

of the Lord's eternal and essential relation with the Father, in all its blessedness and affection as intimated in the phrase, " The Only-begotten Son, which is in the bosom of the Father " (John 1 : 18) ; (b) of the bosom of a garment, the hollow formed by the upper forepart of a loose garment, bound by a girdle and used for carrying or keeping things ; thus figuratively of repaying one liberally, Luke 6 : 38 ; cp. Isa. 65 : 6; Jer. 39 : 18 ; (c) of an inlet of the sea, because of its shape, like a bosom, Acts 27 : 39.   See Bay, Creek.¶

BOTH : see Note †, p. 9.

For BOTTLE see SKIN

BOTTOM, BOTTOMLESS
A. Adverb.
KATŌ (κάτω) ; for this see Beneath.
B. Adjective.
ABUSSOS (ἄβυσσος), bottomless (from a, intensive, and bussos, a depth; akin to bathus, deep ; Eng., bath), is used as a noun denoting the abyss (A.V., " bottomless pit ").   It describes an immeasurable depth, the underworld, the lower regions, the abyss of Sheol.   In Rom. 10 : 7, quoted from Deut. 30 : 13, the abyss (the abode of the lost dead) is substituted for the sea (the change in the quotation is due to the facts of the Death and Resurrection of Christ); the A.V. has "deep" here and in Luke 8 : 31 ; the reference is to the lower regions as the abode of demons, out of which they can be let loose, Rev. 11 : 7 ; 17 : 8 ; it is found seven times in the Apocalypse, 9 : 1, 2, 11 ; 11 : 7 ; 17 : 8 ; 20 : 1, 3 ; in 9 : 1, 2 the R.V. has " the pit of the abyss."   See Deep.¶

For BOUGHT see BUY

BOUND (Noun)
HOROTHESIA (ὁροθεσία), the fixing of a boundary, rather than the boundary itself (from horos, a boundary, and tithēmi, to place), is used in Acts 17 : 26, " bounds."¶

BOUND (to be)
(a) of obligation :
OPHEILŌ (ὀφείλω), to owe, whether of a debt or any obligation, is translated " we are bound," in 2 Thess. 1 : 3 and 2 : 13 (the Apostle expressing his obligation to give thanks for his readers).   See Behove.
Note : Dei, it is necessary (for which see Must), expresses, not the obligation (as does opheilō) but the certainty or inevitableness of what is bound to happen, e.g., John 3 : 15, " must be lifted up " (i.e., inevitably), and Acts 4 : 12, " wherein we must be saved " (i.e., there is a certainty of salvation).

(b) of binding :

PERIKEIMAI (περίκειμαι), lit., to lie around (*peri*, around, *keimai*, to lie), to be compassed, is used of binding fetters around a person, Acts 28 : 20 ; in Mark 9 : 42, and Luke 17 : 2, to hang about a person's neck ; in Heb. 5 : 2, to compass about, metaphorically of infirmities ; in 12 : 1, of those who have witness borne to their faith. See COMPASS, HANG.¶

Note : For " bound " in Acts 22 : 5 ; 24 : 27, see BIND, No. 1 ; for Acts 22 : 25, A.V., see BIND, No. 7 ; for Luke 8 : 29, see BIND, No. 6.

BOUNTY, BOUNTIFULLY

1. EULOGIA (εὐλογία), a blessing, has the meaning of bounty in 2 Cor. 9 : 5, of the offering sent by the church at Corinth to their needy brethren in Judæa.

Note : In the next verse the adverb " bountifully " is a translation of the phrase *ep' eulogiais*, lit., 'with blessings' (R.V. marg.), that is, that blessings may accrue. See BLESSING.

2. HAPLOTĒS (ἁπλότης), from *haplous*, simple, single, is translated " bountifulness " in 2 Cor. 9 : 11, A.V. ; R.V., " liberality " (marg., " singleness ") ; cp. 8 : 2 ; 9 : 13 ; from sincerity of mind springs " liberality." The thought of sincerity is present in Rom. 12 : 8 ; 2 Cor. 11 : 3 ; Eph. 6 : 5 ; Col. 3 : 22. See LIBERAL, SIMPLICITY, SINGLENESS.¶

3. CHARIS (χάρις), grace, is rendered, " bounty " in 1 Cor. 16 : 3, R.V., (A.V., " liberality "), by metonymy for a material gift. See BENEFIT, No. 3.

4. HADROTĒS (ἁδρότης), lit., fatness (from *hadros*, thick, well-grown), is used of a monetary gift, in 2 Cor. 8 : 20, A.V., " abundance," R.V., " bounty."¶

BOW, BOWED (Verb)

1. KAMPTŌ (κάμπτω), to bend, is used especially of bending the knees in religious veneration, Rom. 11 : 4 ; 14 : 11 ; Eph. 3 : 14 ; Phil. 2 : 10.¶

2. SUNKAMPTŌ (συγκάμπτω) signifies to bend completely together, to bend down by compulsory force, Rom. 11 : 10.¶

3. SUNKUPTŌ (συγκύπτω), to bow together (*sun*, together with, *kuptō*, to bow), is said, in Luke 13 : 11, of the woman crippled with a physical infirmity.¶

4. KLINŌ (κλίνω), to incline, to bow down, is used of the women who in their fright bowed their faces to the earth at the Lord's empty tomb, Luke 24 : 5 ; of the act of the Lord on the Cross immediately before giving up His Spirit. What is indicated in the statement " He bowed His head," is not the helpless dropping of the head after death, but the deliberate putting of His head into a position of rest, John 19 : 30. The

verb is deeply significant here.   The Lord reversed the natural order.   The same verb is used in His statement in Matt. 8 : 20 and Luke 9 : 58, " the Son of Man hath not where to lay His head."   It is used, too, of the decline of day, Luke 9 : 12 ;   24 : 29 ;   of turning enemies to flight, Heb. 11 : 34. See LAY, SPENT, No. 7, TURN, WEAR.¶

5. TITHĒMI (τίθημι), to put, or place, is said of the soldiers who mockingly bowed their knees to Christ, Mark 15 : 19.   See APPOINT.

Note : For *gonupeteō*, to bow the knee, Matt. 27 : 29, see KNEEL.

BOW (Noun)
TOXON (τόξον), a bow, is used in Rev. 6 : 2.   Cp. Hab. 3 : 8, 9.   The instrument is frequently mentioned in the Sept., especially in the Psalms.¶

BOWELS
SPLANCHNON (σπλάγχνον), always in the plural, properly denotes the physical organs of the intestines, and is once used in this respect, Acts 1 : 18 (for the use by Greeks and Hebrews, see AFFECTION, No. 2). The R.V. substitutes the following for the word " bowels : " " affections," 2 Cor. 6 : 12 ; " affection," 2 Cor. 7 : 15 ; " tender mercies," Phil. 1 : 8 ; 2 : 1 ; " a heart (of compassion)," Col. 3 : 12 ; " heart," Philm. 12, 20 ; " hearts," Philm. 7 ; " compassion," 1 John 3 : 17.   The word is rendered " tender " in the A.V. and R.V. of Luke 1 : 78, in connection with the word " mercy."   See AFFECTION, No. 2, COMPASSION, A, No. 2 and B, No. 2.¶

BOWL
PHIALĒ (φιάλη), Eng., phial, denotes a bowl ; so the R.V., for A.V., " vial," in Rev. 5 : 8 ; 15 : 7 ; 16 : 1, 2, 3, 4, 8, 10, 12, 17 ; 17 : 1 ; 21 : 9 ; the word is suggestive of rapidity in the emptying of the contents.   While the seals (ch. 6) give a general view of the events of the last " week " or " hebdomad," in the vision given to Daniel, Dan. 9 : 23–27, the " trumpets " refer to the judgments which, in a more or less extended period, are destined to fall especially, though not only, upon apostate Christendom and apostate Jews.   The emptying of the bowls betokens the final series of judgments in which this exercise of the wrath of God is " finished " (Rev. 15 : 1, R.V.).   These are introduced by the 7th trumpet.   See Rev. 11 : 15 and the successive order in ver. 18, " the nations were wroth, and Thy wrath came . . . ; " see also 6 : 17 ; 14 : 19, 20 ; 19 : 11–21.¶

BOX
ALABASTRON (ἀλάβαστρον), an alabaster vessel, is translated, in the A.V. of Matt. 26 : 7 ; Mark 14 : 3 ; Luke 7 : 37, " box," R.V., " cruse." The breaking refers to the seal, not to the box or cruse.   See CRUSE.¶

BOY

PAIS (παῖς) denotes a boy (in contrast to *paidion*, a diminutive of *pais*, and to *teknon*, a child). With reference to Christ, instead of the A.V. " child," the R.V. suitably translates otherwise as follows : Luke 2 : 43, " the boy Jesus ; " Acts 4 : 27, 30, " Thy Holy Servant, Jesus." So in the case of others, Matt. 17 : 18 and Luke 9 : 42 (" boy "). See CHILD, MAID, MANSERVANT, SERVANT, SON, YOUNG MAN.

BRAIDED (A.V., BROIDED)

PLEGMA (πλέγμα) signifies what is woven (from *plekō*, to weave, plait), whether a net or basket (Josephus uses it of the ark of bulrushes in which the infant Moses was laid), or of a web, plait, braid. It is used in 1 Tim. 2 : 9, of " braided hair," which the Vulgate signifies as ringlets, curls.¶

Notes : (1) Cp. *emplokē*, 1 Pet. 3 : 3, " plaiting," i.e., intertwining the hair in ornament.¶

(2) " Broided " is to be distinguished from " broidered," which means to adorn with needlework (not to plait).

For BRAMBLE BUSH see BUSH

For BRAKE see BREAK

BRANCH

1. KLADOS (κλάδος), from *klaō*, to break (cp. *klasma*, a broken piece), properly a young tender shoot, broken off for grafting, is used for any kind of branch, Matt. 13 : 32 ; 21 : 8 ; 24 : 32 ; Mark 4 : 32 ; 13 : 28 ; Luke 13 : 19 ; the descendants of Israel, Rom. 11 : 16–19, 21.¶

2. KLĒMA (κλῆμα), akin to *klaō*, to break, denotes a tender, flexible branch, especially the shoot of a vine, a vine sprout, John 15 : 2, 4, 5, 6.¶

3. STOIBAS or STIBAS (στοιβάς), from *steibō*, to tread on, primarily denoted a layer of leaves, reeds, twigs or straw, serving for a bed ; then a branch full of leaves, soft foliage, which might be used in making a bed, or for treading upon, Mark 11 : 8.¶

4. BAION (βαῖον), of Egyptian origin, frequent in the papyri writings, denotes a branch of the palm tree, John 12 : 13.¶

Note : Matthew, Mark and John each use a different word for ' branch ' in narrating Christ's entry into Jerusalem.

BRANDED

KAUSTĒRIAZO (καυστηριάζω), to burn in with a branding iron (cp. Eng., caustic), is found, in the best mss., in 1 Tim. 4 : 2, R.V. " branded." Others have *kautēriazō* (from *kautērion*, a branding-iron, Eng., cauterize), to mark by branding, an act not quite so severe as that indicated by the former. The reference is to apostates whose consciences are branded with the effects of their sin. See SEARED.¶

Note : In the R.V. of Gal. 6 : 17, " branded " does not represent a word in the original ; it serves to bring out the force of the Apostle's metaphor of bearing in his body the *stigmata*, the marks, of the Lord Jesus. The reference is not to the branding of slaves, soldiers and criminals, but rather to the religious devotee, who branded himself with the mark of the god whom he specially worshipped. So Paul describes the physical marks due to the lictor's rods at Philippi and to the stones at Lystra, marks which, while not self-inflicted, betokened his devotion to Christ and his rejoicing therein.

BRASS, BRAZEN

1. CHALKOS (χαλκός), primarily, copper, became used for metals in general, later was applied to bronze, a mixture of copper and tin, then, by metonymy, to any article made of these metals, e.g., money, Matt. 10 : 9 ; Mark 6 : 8 ; 12 : 41, or a sounding instrument, 1 Cor. 13 : 1, figurative of a person destitute of love. See Rev. 18 : 12. See MONEY.¶

2. CHALKEOS (χάλκεος), made of brass or bronze, is used of idols, Rev. 9 : 20.¶

3. CHALKION (χαλκίον) is used in Mark 7 : 4 of brazen vessels.¶

4. CHALKOLIBANON (χαλκολίβανον) is used of white or shining copper or bronze, and describes the feet of the Lord, in Rev. 1 : 15 and 2 : 18.¶

5. CHALKEUS (χαλκεύς) denotes a coppersmith, 2 Tim. 4 : 14.¶

BRAWLER

1. PAROINOS (πάροινος), an adjective, lit., tarrying at wine (*para*, at, *oinos*, wine), " given to wine," 1 Tim. 3 : 3 and Tit. 1 : 7, A.V., probably has the secondary sense, of the effects of wine-bibbing, viz., abusive brawling. Hence R.V., " brawler." See WINE.¶

2. AMACHOS (ἄμαχος), an adjective, lit., not fighting (*a*, negative, *machē*, a fight), came to denote, metaphorically, not contentious, 1 Tim. 3 : 3, and Tit. 3 : 2, R.V., for A.V., " not a brawler," " not brawlers." See CONTENTIOUS.¶

BREAD (Loaf)

1. ARTOS (ἄρτος), bread (perhaps derived from *arō*, to fit together, or from a root *ar*—, the earth), signifies (*a*) a small loaf or cake, composed of flour and water, and baked, in shape either oblong or round, and about as thick as the thumb ; these were not cut, but broken and were consecrated to the Lord every Sabbath and called the shewbread (loaves of presentation), Matt. 12 : 4 ; when the shewbread was reinstituted by Nehemiah (Neh. 10 : 32) a poll-tax of ⅓ shekel was laid on the Jews, Matt. 17 : 24 ; (*b*) the loaf at the Lord's Supper, e.g., Matt. 26 : 26 (" Jesus took a loaf," R.V., marg.) ; the breaking of bread became the name for this institution, Acts 2 : 42 ; 20 : 7 ; 1 Cor. 10 : 16 ; 11 : 23 ; (*c*) bread of

any kind, Matt. 16 : 11 ; (d) metaphorically, of Christ as the Bread of God, and of Life, John 6 : 33, 35 ; (e) food in general, the necessities for the sustenance of life, Matt. 6 : 11 ; 2 Cor. 9 : 10, etc.

2. AZUMOS (ἄζυμος) denotes unleavened bread, i.e., without any process of fermentation ; hence, metaphorically, of a holy, spiritual condition, 1 Cor 5 : 7, and of sincerity and truth (ver. 8). With the article it signifies the feast of unleavened bread, Matt. 26 : 17 ; Mark 14 : 1, 12 ; Luke 22 : 1, 7 ; Acts 12 : 3 ; 20 : 6.¶

For BREADTH see BROAD

BREAK, BREAKER, BREAKING, BRAKE
A. Verbs.

1. KLAŎ or KLAZŎ (κλάω), to break, to break off pieces, is used of breaking bread, (a) of the Lord's act in providing for people, Matt. 14 : 19 ; 15 : 36 ; Mark 8 : 6, 19 ; (b) of the breaking of bread in the Lord's Supper, Matt. 26 : 26 ; Mark 14 : 22 ; Luke 22 : 19 ; Acts 20 : 7 ; 1 Cor. 10 : 16 ; 11 : 24 ; (c) of an ordinary meal, Acts 2 : 46 ; 20 : 11 ; 27 : 35 ; (d) of the Lord's act in giving evidence of His resurrection, Luke 24 : 30.¶

2. EKKLAŎ (ἐκκλάω), ek, off, and No. 1, to break off, is used meta-phorically of branches, Rom. 11 : 17, 19, 20.¶

3. KATAKLAŎ (κατακλάω), kata, down, and No. 1, is used in Mark 6 : 41 and Luke 9 : 16, of Christ's breaking loaves for the multitudes.¶

4. LUŎ (λύω), to loosen, especially by way of deliverance, sometimes has the meaning of breaking, destructively, e.g., of breaking command-ments, not only infringing them, but loosing the force of them, rendering them not binding, Matt. 5 : 19 ; John 5 : 18 ; of breaking the Law of Moses, John 7 : 23 ; Scripture, John 10 : 35 ; of the breaking up of a ship, Acts 27 : 41 ; of the breaking down of the middle wall of partition, Eph. 2 : 14 ; of the marriage tie, 1 Cor. 7 : 27. See DESTROY, DISSOLVE, LOOSE, MELT, PUT, Note (5), UNLOOSE.

5. SUNTRIBŎ (συντρίβω), lit., to rub together, and so to shatter, shiver, break in pieces by crushing, is said of the bruising of a reed, Matt. 12 : 20 (No. 9 is used in the next clause) ; the breaking of fetters in pieces, Mark 5 : 4 ; the breaking of an alabaster cruse, Mark 14 : 3 ; an earthenware vessel, Rev. 2 : 27 ; of the physical bruising of a person possessed by a demon, Luke 9 : 39 ; concerning Christ, " a bone of Him shall not be broken," John 19 : 36 ; metaphorically of the crushed condition of a " broken-hearted " person, Luke 4 : 18 (A.V. only) ; of the eventual crushing of Satan, Rom. 16 : 20. See BRUISE.¶ This verb is frequent in the Sept. in the Passive Voice, e.g., Ps. 51 : 17 ; Is. 57 : 15, of a contrite heart, perhaps a figure of stones made smooth by being rubbed together in streams. Cp. suntrimma, destruction.

6. RHĒGNUMI (ῥήγνυμι), to tear, rend, as of garments etc., is trans-lated " break " in the A.V. of Matt. 9 : 17, of wine-skins (R.V., " burst ") ;

as in Mark 2 : 22 and Luke 5 : 37 ; " break forth " in Gal. 4 : 27. See
BURST, REND, TEAR.

7. DIARRHĒGNUMI (διαρρήγνυμι), *dia*, through (intensive), and No.
6, to burst asunder, to rend, cleave, is said of the rending of garments,
Matt. 26 : 65 ; Mark 14 : 63 ; Acts 14 : 14 ; of the breaking of a net,
Luke 5 : 6 ; of fetters, 8 : 29. See REND.¶

8. PROSRHĒGNUMI (προσρήγνυμι) : see BEAT, No. 8.

9. KATAGNUMI (κατάγνυμι), *kata*, down (intensive), and No. 6,
is used of the breaking of a bruised reed, Matt. 12 : 20, and of the breaking
of the legs of those who were crucified, John 19 : 31, 32, 33.¶

10. SUNTHLAŌ (συνθλάω), *sun*, together (intensive), and *thlaō*, to
break or crush, to break in pieces, to shatter, is used in Matt. 21 : 44 and
Luke 20 : 18 of the physical effect of falling on a stone.¶

11. SUNTHRUPTŌ (συνθρύπτω), *sun*, and *thruptō*, to crush, to break
small, weaken, is used metaphorically of breaking one's heart, Acts 21 : 13.¶

12. SCHIZŌ (σχίζω), to split, to rend open, is said of the veil of the
temple, Matt. 27 : 51 ; the rending of rocks, Matt. 27 : 51 ; the rending
of the heavens, Mark 1 : 10 ; a garment, Luke 5 : 36 ; John 19 : 24 ; a
net, John 21 : 11 ; in the Passive Voice, metaphorically, of being divided
into factions, Acts 14 : 4 ; 23 : 7. See DIVIDE, *Note*, OPEN, REND,
RENT.

Note : Cp. *schisma* (Eng., schism), said of the rent in a garment,
Matt. 9 : 16. See DIVISION, RENT, SCHISM.

13. DIORUSSŌ (διορύσσω), lit., to dig through (*dia*, through, *orussō*,
to dig), is used of the act of thieves in breaking into a house, Matt. 6 : 19,
20 ; 24 : 43 ; Luke 12 : 39.¶

14. EXORUSSŌ (ἐξορύσσω), lit., to dig out (cp. No. 13), is used of the
breaking up of part of a roof, Mark 2 : 4, and, in a vivid expression, of
plucking out the eyes, Gal. 4 : 15. See PLUCK.¶

Note : For *aristaō*, to break one's fast, see DINE.

B. Nouns.

1. KLASIS (κλάσις), a breaking (akin to A, No. 1), is used in Luke
24 : 35 and Acts 2 : 42, of the breaking of bread.¶

2. KLASMA (κλάσμα), a broken piece, fragment, is always used of
remnants of food, Matt. 14 : 20 ; 15 : 37 and corresponding passages.
See PIECE.

3. PARABASIS (παράβασις), a transgression (*para*, across, *bainō*, to
go), is translated " breaking " in Rom. 2 : 23, A.V. ; R.V., " transgression ; " A.V. and R.V. ditto in 4 : 15 ; 5 : 14 ; Gal. 3 : 19 ; 1 Tim. 2 :
14 ; Heb. 2 : 2 ; 9 : 15. See TRANSGRESSION.

4. PARABATĒS (παραβάτης), a transgressor (cp. No. 3), is translated
" breaker," Rom. 2 : 25, A.V. ; R.V., " transgressor." In ver. 27 the
A.V. turns it into a verb, " dost transgress." See Gal. 2 : 18 ; Jas. 2 : 9,
11.¶

BREAST

1. STĒTHOS (στῆθος), connected with *histēmi*, to stand, i.e., that which stands out, is used of mourners in smiting the breast, Luke 18 : 13 ; 23 : 48 ; of John in reclining on the breast of Christ, John 13 : 25 ; 21 : 20 ; of the breasts of the angels in Rev. 15 : 6.¶

2. MASTOS (μαστός), used in the plural, " paps," Luke 11 : 27 ; 23 : 29 ; Rev. 1 : 13, A.V., is preferably rendered " breasts," in the R.V.¶

BREASTPLATE

THŌRAX (θώραξ), primarily, the breast, denotes a breastplate or corselet, consisting of two parts and protecting the body on both sides, from the neck to the middle. It is used metaphorically of righteousness, Eph. 6 : 14 ; of faith and love, 1 Thess. 5 : 8, with perhaps a suggestion of the two parts, front and back, which formed the coat of mail (an alternative term for the word in the N.T. sense) ; elsewhere in Rev. 9 : 9, 17.¶

BREATH, BREATHE
A. Nouns.

1. PNOĒ (πνοή), akin to *pneō*, to blow, lit., a blowing, signifies (a) breath, the breath of life, Acts 17 : 25 ; (b) wind, Acts 2 : 2. See WIND.¶

2. PNEUMA (πνεῦμα), spirit, also denotes breath, Rev. 11 : 11 and 13 : 15, R.V. In 2 Thess. 2 : 8, the A.V. has " spirit " for R.V., " breath." See GHOST, LIFE, SPIRIT, WIND.

B. Verbs.

1. EMPNEŌ (ἐμπνέω), lit., to breathe in, or on, is used in Acts 9 : 1, indicating that threatening and slaughter were, so to speak, the elements from which Saul drew and expelled his breath.¶

2. EMPHUSAŌ (ἐμφυσάω), to breathe upon, is used of the symbolic act of the Lord Jesus in breathing upon His Apostles the communication of the Holy Spirit, John 20 : 22.¶

BRIDE, BRIDE-CHAMBER, BRIDEGROOM

BRIDE, BRIDECHAMBER, BRIDEGROOM

NUMPHĒ (νύμφη), Eng. nymph, a bride, or young wife, John 3 : 29 ; Rev. 18 : 23 ; 21 : 2, 9 ; 22 : 17, is probably connected with the Latin *nubō*, to veil ; the bride was often adorned with embroidery and jewels (see Rev. 21 : 2), and was led veiled from her home to the bridegroom. Hence the secondary meaning of daughter-in-law, Matt. 10 : 35 ; Luke 12 : 53. See DAUGHTER-IN-LAW.¶ For the relationship between Christ and a local church, under this figure, see 2 Cor. 11 : 2 ; regarding the whole Church, Eph. 5 : 23–32 ; Rev. 22 : 17.

NUMPHIOS (νυμφίος), a bridegroom, occurs fourteen times in the

Gospels, and in Rev. 18 : 23. " The friend of the bridegroom," John 3 : 29, is distinct from " the sons of the bride-chamber " who were numerous. When John the Baptist speaks of " the friend of the Bridegroom," he uses language according to the customs of the Jews.

NUMPHŌN (νυμφών) signifies (a) the room or dining hall in which the marriage ceremonies were held, Matt. 22 : 10 ; some mss. have gamos, a wedding, here ; (b) the chamber containing the bridal bed, " the sons of the bride-chamber " being the friends of the bridegroom, who had the charge of providing what was necessary for the nuptials, Matt. 9 : 15 ; Mark 2 : 19 ; Luke 5 : 34.¶

BRIDLE
A. Noun.

CHALINOS (χαλινός), a bridle, is used in Jas. 3 : 3 (A.V., " bits "), and Rev. 14 : 20. " The primitive bridle was simply a loop on the halter-cord passed round the lower jaw of the horse. Hence in Ps. 32 : 9 the meaning is bridle and halter " (Hastings, Bib. Dic.).¶

B. Verb.

CHALINAGŌGEŌ (χαλιναγωγέω), from chalinos and agō, to lead, signifies to lead by a bridle, to bridle, to hold in check, restrain ; it is used metaphorically of the tongue and of the body in Jas. 1 : 26 and 3 : 2.¶

BRIEFLY

DI' OLIGŌN (δι' ὀλίγων) lit. means ' by few.' In 1 Pet. 5 : 12 it signifies by means of few words, " briefly." The R.V. of Rom. 13 : 9 omits " briefly," the meaning being " it is summed up."¶

For BRIER see THISTLE

BRIGHT, BRIGHTNESS
A. Adjectives.

1. PHŌTEINOS (φωτεινός), bright (from phōs, light), is said of a cloud, Matt. 17 : 5 ; metaphorically of the body, Matt. 6 : 22, " full of light ; " Luke 11 : 34, 36. See LIGHT.¶

2. LAMPROS (λαμπρός), shining, brilliant, bright, is used of the clothing of an angel, Acts 10 : 30 and Rev. 15 : 6 ; symbolically, of the clothing of the saints in glory, Rev. 19 : 8, R.V., in the best texts (A.V., " white ") ; of Christ as the Morning Star, 22 : 16 ; of the water of life, 22 : 1, A.V., " clear." See CLEAR, GAY, GOODLY, GORGEOUS, WHITE. *Note :* Cp. lamprōs, sumptuously, Luke 16 : 19.¶

B. Nouns.

1. LAMPROTĒS (λαμπρότης), brightness, akin to A, No. 2, above, is found in Acts 26 : 13.¶

2. APAUGASMA (ἀπαύγασμα), a shining forth (apo, from, augē, bright-

ness), of a light coming from a luminous body, is said of Christ in Heb. 1 : 3, A.V., " brightness," R.V., " effulgence," i.e., shining forth (a more probable meaning than reflected brightness).¶

Note : Epiphaneia (ἐπιφάνεια), lit., shining forth or upon, is rendered " brightness " in the A.V. of 2 Thess. 2 : 8 ; R.V., " manifestation." See APPEARING.

BRIM

ANŌ (ἄνω), above, on high, in a higher place, in John 2 : 7 is used to denote the brim of a waterpot, lit., up to above, i.e., up to the higher parts, i.e., the brim. See ABOVE, HIGH, UP.

BRIMSTONE

1. THEION (θεῖον) originally denoted fire from heaven. It is connected with sulphur. Places touched by lightning were called *theia*, and, as lightning leaves a sulphurous smell, and sulphur was used in pagan purifications, it received the name of *theion*, Luke 17 : 29 ; Rev. 9 : 17, 18 ; 14 : 10 ; 19 : 20 ; 20 : 10 ; 21 : 8.¶

2. THEIŌDĒS (θειώδης), akin to No. 1, signifies brimstone-like, or consisting of brimstone, Rev. 9 : 17.¶

BRING, BRINGING, BROUGHT
A. Verbs.

1. PHERŌ (φέρω), to bear, or carry, is used also of bearing or bringing forth fruit, Mark 4 : 8 ; John 15 : 5, etc. To bring is the most frequent meaning. See BEAR, CARRY, DRIVE, ENDURE, GO, LEAD, MOVE, REACH, RUSHING, UPHOLD.

Compounds of No. 1, translated by the verb to bring, are as follows :

2. ANAPHERŌ (ἀναφέρω) denotes to bring up, Matt. 17 : 1. See BEAR, No. 3.

3. APOPHERŌ (ἀποφέρω), to carry forth, is rendered " bring," in the A.V. of 1 Cor. 16 : 3 ; Acts 19 : 12 (R.V., " carried away ") ; some mss. have *epipherō* here. See CARRY.

4. EISPHERŌ (εἰσφέρω), denotes to bring to, Acts 17 : 20 ; to bring into, Luke 5 : 18, 19 ; 1 Tim. 6 : 7 ; Heb. 13 : 11. See LEAD, No. 11.

5. EKPHERŌ (ἐκφέρω), to bring forth. See BEAR, No. 4.

6. EPIPHERŌ (ἐπιφέρω), signifies (a) to bring upon, or to bring against, Jude 9 ; (b) to impose, inflict, visit upon, Rom. 3 : 5. Some mss. have it in Acts 25 : 18 (for No. 1) ; some in Phil. 1 : 16 (R.V., ver. 17, " raise up," translating *egeirō*).¶

7. PROPHERŌ (προφέρω) denotes to bring forth, Luke 6 : 45, twice.¶

8. PROSPHERŌ (προσφέρω) means (a) to bring (in addition), Matt. 25 : 20 ; to bring unto, Matt. 5 : 23 (R.V., " art offering ") ; Mark 10 : 13 ; (b) to offer, Matt. 5 : 24. See DEAL WITH, DO, OFFER, PRESENT, PUT.

9. SUMPHERŌ (συμφέρω), to bring together, has this meaning in Acts 19 : 19. See BETTER (be), EXPEDIENT, GOOD, PROFIT.

10. AGO (ἄγω), to lead, to lead along, to bring, has the meaning to bring (besides its occurrences in the Gospels and Acts) in 1 Thess. 4 : 14, 2 Tim. 4 : 11, and Heb. 2 : 10. See CARRY, GO, KEEP, LEAD.

Compounds of this verb are :

11. ANAGŌ (ἀνάγω), to lead or bring up to, Luke 2 : 22 ; Acts 9 : 39 etc. ; to bring forth, Acts 12 : 4 ; to bring again, Heb. 13 : 20 ; to bring up again, Rom. 10 : 7. See DEPART, LAUNCH, LEAD, LOOSE, OFFER, TAKE UP, SAIL.

12. APAGŌ (ἀπάγω), to lead away, bring forth, bring unto, Acts 23 : 17. See CARRY, DEATH, LEAD, TAKE.

13. EISAGŌ (εἰσάγω), to bring in, into, Luke 2 : 27 etc. See LEAD.

14. EXAGŌ (ἐξάγω), to lead out, bring forth, Acts 5 : 19 ; 7 : 36, 40 etc. See FETCH, LEAD.

15. EPAGŌ (ἐπάγω), to bring upon, Acts 5 : 28 ; 2 Pet. 2 : 1, 5.¶

16. KATAGŌ (κατάγω), to bring down, Acts 9 : 30 ; 22 : 30 ; 23 : 15, 20 ; Rom. 10 : 6 ; to bring forth, Acts 23 : 28 ; of boats, to bring to land, Luke 5 : 11. See LAND, TOUCH.

17. PAREISAGŌ (παρεισάγω), to bring in privily (lit., to bring in beside), to introduce secretly, 2 Pet. 2 : 1.¶

18. PROAGŌ (προάγω), to bring or lead forth, e.g., Acts 12 : 6 ; 16 : 30 ; 25 : 26. See GO, No. 10.

19. PROSAGŌ (προσάγω), to bring to, or unto, Acts 16 : 20 ; 1 Pet. 3 : 18. For Acts 27 : 27 see DRAW, (B), No. 3.¶

Other verbs are :

20. KOMIZŌ (κομίζω), usually, to receive, to bring in, Luke 7 : 37. See RECEIVE.

21. PARECHŌ (παρέχω), usually, to offer, furnish, supply (lit., to have near), to bring, in the sense of supplying, Acts 16 : 16 ; 19 : 24. See DO, GIVE, KEEP, MINISTER, OFFER, SHEW, TROUBLE.

22. APOSTREPHŌ (ἀποστρέφω), to turn, or put, back, is translated " brought back " in Matt. 27 : 3. See PERVERT, PUT, TURN.

23. KATABIBAZŌ (καταβιβάζω), in the Active Voice, to cause to go down, is used in the Passive in the sense of being brought down, Luke 10 : 15 (A.V., " thrust down ") ; " go down " in Matt. 11 : 23 (marg., " be brought down ").¶

24. SUMBIBAZŌ (συμβιβάζω), rendered " brought " in Acts 19 : 33.

25. PROPEMPŌ (προπέμπω), to send forth, to bring on one's way, Acts 15 : 3 ; 20 : 38, R.V. ; 21 : 5 ; Rom. 15 : 24 ; 1 Cor. 16 : 6, 11 ; 2 Cor. 1 : 16 ; Tit. 3 : 13 ; 3 John 6. See ACCOMPANY, CONDUCT.¶

26. BLASTANŌ (βλαστάνω), to bud, spring up, translated " brought forth " (i.e., caused to produce), in Jas. 5 : 18. See BUD, SPRING.

27. POIEŌ (ποιέω), to make, to do, used of the bringing forth of fruit, Matt. 3 : 8, 10 ; 7 : 17, 18. See DO.

28. EKBALLŌ (ἐκβάλλω), to cast out, used of bringing forth good and evil things from the heart, Matt. 12 : 35. See CAST, No. 5.

29. TIKTŌ (τίκτω), to beget, " bring forth," Matt. 1 : 21, 23, 25 ; Jas. 1 : 15 (first part of verse, according to the best mss.) ; Rev. 12 : 5 (R.V., " was delivered of "). See BEGET, BORN, DELIVER.

30. APOKUEŌ (ἀποκύεω), to bear young, " bringeth forth " in Jas. 1 : 15 (end of verse) and " brought forth," ver. 18 (A.V., " begat "). See BEGET.¶

31. GENNAŌ (γεννάω), to beget, translated " brought forth " in Luke 1 : 57. See BEGET, A, No. 1.

32. EUPHOREŌ (εὐφορέω), to bear well, be productive, " brought forth plentifully ", Luke 12 : 16.¶ Cp. karpophoreō, Mark 4 : 20, R.V. " bear ; " so, Col. 1 : 6.

33. TREPHŌ (τρέφω), to rear, bring up, Luke 4 : 16. See FEED, NOURISH.

34. ANATREPHŌ (ἀνατρέφω), to nourish, Acts 7 : 20, 21; " brought up," Acts 22 : 3.¶

35. EKTREPHŌ (ἐκτρέφω), to nourish, Eph. 5 : 29 ; " bring up," 6 : 4, A.V. ; R.V., " nurture." See NURTURE.¶

36. APANGELLŌ (ἀπαγγέλλω), to announce, is translated " bring word " in Matt. 2 : 8, R.V. (the A.V. unnecessarily adds " again ") ; 28 : 8. See DECLARE, REPORT, SHEW, TELL.

B. Noun.

EPEISAGŌGĒ (ἐπεισαγωγή), lit., ' a bringing in besides,' is translated " a bringing in thereupon " in Heb. 7 : 19.¶

Notes: (1) In Mark 4 : 21, erchomai, to come, is translated "is brought," lit., ' (does a lamp) come.'

(2) In Mark 13 : 9, the verb translated " be brought," A.V., is histēmi, to stand (R.V.) ; in Acts 27 : 24, paristēmi, to stand before (A.V., " be brought before ").

(3) In Acts 5 : 36, ginomai, to become, is rendered " came (to nought)," R.V., for A.V., " were brought." So in 1 Cor. 15 : 54, " come to pass," for " shall be brought to pass."

(4) In Mark 4 : 29, paradidōmi is rendered " is ripe," R.V. and A.V. marg., for A.V., " brought forth."

(5) In Matt. 1 : 11, 12, 17, metoikesia signifies a removal, or carrying away (not " they were brought," ver. 12, A.V.).

(6) In Acts 13 : 1, suntrophos denotes a foster-brother, R.V. (A.V., marg.).¶

(7) In 1 Cor. 4 : 17, for " bring you into remembrance " (R.V., " put . . . "), see REMEMBRANCE.

(8) In Luke 1 : 19, for R.V., " bring you good tidings," and Acts 13 : 32, and Rom. 10 : 15 (end), see PREACH.

(9) In 1 Cor. 1 : 19, atheteō, to reject (R.V.), is rendered " bring to nothing " (A.V.). See DESPISE, Note (1).

(10) For *katargeō*, " bring to nought," R.V., " destroy," 1 Cor. 6 : 13 etc., see ABOLISH, DESTROY.

(11) For *eipon* in Matt. 2 : 13, A.V., " bring . . . word," see TELL.

(12) See also DESOLATION, No. 1, PERFECTION, B.

(13) For " bring into bondage " see BONDAGE, B.

(14) In Matt. 16 : 8 some mss. have *lambanō* (A.V., " ye have brought ").

BROAD, BREADTH
A. Adjective.

EURUCHŌROS (εὐρύχωρος), from *eurus*, broad, and *chōra*, a place, signifies, lit., (with) a broad place, i.e., broad, spacious, Matt. 7 : 13.¶

B. Verb.

PLATUNŌ (πλατύνω), connected with *plak*, a flat, broad surface, signifies to make broad; said of phylacteries, Matt. 23 : 5; used figuratively in 2 Cor. 6 : 11, 13, " to be enlarged," in the ethical sense, of the heart.¶

C. Noun.

PLATOS (πλάτος) denotes breadth, Eph. 3 : 18 ; Rev. 20 : 9 ; 21 : 16 (twice).¶

For BROIDED see BRAIDED

For BROKENHEARTED, see BREAK, A, No. 5.

BROILED

OPTOS (ὀπτός), broiled (from *optaō*, to cook, roast), is said of food prepared by fire, Luke 24 : 42.¶

For BROKEN see BREAK

BROOD

NOSSIA (νοσσιά), primarily, a nest, denotes a brood, Luke 13 : 34. Some texts have *nossion* in the plural, as Matt. 23 : 37, " chicken."¶

BROOK

CHEIMARRHOS (χείμαρρος), lit., winter-flowing (from *cheima*, winter, and *rheō*, to flow), a stream which runs only in winter or when swollen with rains, a brook, John 18 : 1.¶

BROTHER, BRETHREN, BROTHERHOOD, BROTHERLY

ADELPHOS (ἀδελφός) denotes a brother, or near kinsman ; in the plural, a community based on identity of origin or life. It is used of :—

(1) male children of the same parents, Matt. 1 : 2 ; 14 : 3 ; (2) male descendants of the same parents, Acts 7 : 23, 26 ; Heb. 7 : 5 ; (3) male children of the same mother, Matt. 13 : 55 ; 1 Cor. 9 : 5 ; Gal. 1 : 19 ; (4) people of the same nationality, Acts 3 : 17, 22 ; Rom. 9 : 3. With

" men " (*anēr*, male), prefixed, it is used in addresses only, Acts 2 : 29, 37, etc. ; (5) any man, a neighbour, Luke 10 : 29; Matt. 5 : 22; 7 : 3; (6) persons united by a common interest, Matt. 5 : 47 ; (7) persons united by a common calling, Rev. 22 : 9 ; (8) mankind, Matt. 25 : 40 ; Heb. 2 : 17; (9) the disciples, and so, by implication, all believers, Matt. 28 : 10 ; John 20 : 17 ; (10) believers, apart from sex, Matt. 23 : 8 ; Acts 1 : 15 ; Rom. 1 : 13 ; 1 Thess. 1 : 4 ; Rev. 19 : 10 (the word " sisters " is used of believers, only in 1 Tim. 5 : 2) ; (11) believers, with *anēr*, male, prefixed, and with " or sister " added, 1 Cor. 7 : 14 (R.V.), 15 ; Jas. 2 : 15, male as distinct from female, Acts 1 : 16 ; 15 : 7, 13, but not 6 : 3.*

Notes : (1) Associated words are *adelphotēs*, primarily, a brotherly relation, and so, the community possessed of this relation, a brotherhood, 1 Pet. 2 : 17 (see 5 : 9, marg.)¶ ; *philadelphos*, (*phileō*, to love, and *adelphos*), fond of one's brethren, 1 Pet. 3 : 8 ; " loving as brethren," R.V.¶ ; *philadelphia*, " brotherly love," Rom. 12 : 10 ; 1 Thess, 4 : 9 ; Heb. 13 : 1 ; " love of the brethren," 1 Pet. 1 : 22 and 2 Pet. 1 : 7, R.V.¶ ; *pseudadelphos*, " false brethren," 2 Cor. 11 : 26 ; Gal. 2 : 4.¶

(2) In Luke 6 : 16 and Acts 1 : 13, the R.V. has " son," for A.V., " brother."

(3) In Acts 13 : 1, for *suntrophos*, see BRING, B, Note (6).

For BROUGHT see BRING

BROW

OPHRUS (ὀφρύς), an eyebrow, stands for the brow of a hill, Luke 4 : 29, from the resemblance to an eyebrow, i.e., a ridge with an overhanging bank.¶

BRUISE

1. SUNTRIBŌ (συντρίβω) : see BREAK, A, No. 5.

2. THRAUŌ (θραύω), to smite through, shatter, is used in Luke 4 : 18, " them that are bruised," i.e., broken by calamity.¶

BRUTE

ALOGOS (ἄλογος), translated " brute " in the A.V. of 2 Pet. 2 : 12 and Jude 10, signifies " without reason," R.V., though, as J. Hastings points out, " brute beasts " is not at all unsuitable, as " brute " is from Latin *brutus*, which means dull, irrational ; in Acts 25 : 27 it is rendered " unreasonable."¶

BUD

BLASTANŌ (βλαστάνω), to bud, is said of Aaron's rod, Heb. 9 : 14 ; " spring up," Matt. 13 : 26, and Mark 4 : 27; elsewhere, in Jas. 5 : 18. See BRING, No. 26, SPRING, No. 6.¶

---

* From Notes on Thessalonians by Hogg and Vine, p. 32.

BUFFET

1. KOLAPHIZŌ (κολαφίζω) signifies to strike with clenched hands, to buffet with the fist (kolaphos, a fist), Matt. 26 : 67 ; Mark 14 : 65 ; 1 Cor. 4 : 11 ; 2 Cor. 12 : 7 ; 1 Pet. 2 : 20.¶

2. HUPŌPIAZŌ (ὑπωπιάζω), lit., to strike under the eye (from hupōpion, the part of the face below the eye ; hupo, under, ōps, an eye), hence, to beat the face black and blue (to give a black eye), is used metaphorically, and translated " buffet " in 1 Cor. 9 : 27 (A.V., " keep under "), of Paul's suppressive treatment of his body, in order to keep himself spiritually fit (R.V. marg., " bruise ") ; so R.V. marg. in Luke 18 : 5, of the persistent widow, text, " wear out " (A.V., " weary "). See KEEP, WEAR, WEARY.¶

BUILD, BUILDER, BUILDING
A. Verbs.

1. OIKODOMEŌ (οἰκοδομέω), lit., to build a house (oikos, a house, domeō, to build), hence, to build anything, e.g., Matt. 7 : 24 ; Luke 4 : 29 ; 6 : 48, R.V., " well builded " (last clause of verse) ; John 2 : 20 ; is frequently used figuratively, e.g., Acts 20 : 32 (some mss. have No. 3 here) ; Gal. 2 : 18 ; especially of edifying, Acts 9 : 31 ; Rom. 15 : 20 ; 1 Cor. 10 : 23 ; 14 : 4 ; 1 Thess. 5 : 11 (R.V.). In 1 Cor. 8 : 10 it is translated " emboldened " (marg., " builded up "). The participle with the article (equivalent to a noun) is rendered " builder," Matt. 21 : 42 ; Acts 4 : 11 ; 1 Pet. 2 : 7. See EDIFY, EMBOLDEN.

2. ANOIKODOMEŌ (ἀνοικοδομέω) signifies to build again (ana, again), Acts 15 : 16.¶

3. EPOIKODOMEŌ (ἐποικοδομέω) signifies to build upon (epi, upon), 1 Cor. 3 : 10, 12, 14 : Eph. 2 : 20 ; Jude 20 ; or up, Acts 20 : 32 ; Col. 2 : 7.¶

4. SUNOIKODOMEŌ (συνοικοδομέω), to build together (sun, with), is used in Eph. 2 : 22, metaphorically, of the Church, as a spiritual dwelling-place for God.¶

5. KATASKEUAZŌ (κατασκευάζω), to prepare, establish, furnish, is rendered " builded " and " built " in Heb. 3 : 3, 4. See MAKE, ORDAIN, PREPARE.

B. Nouns.

1. OIKODOMĒ (οἰκοδομή), a building, or edification (see A, No. 1), is used (a) literally, e.g., Matt. 24 : 1; Mark 13 : 1, 2 ; (b) figuratively, e.g., Rom. 14 : 19 (lit., ' the things of building up ') ; 15 : 2 ; of a local church as a spiritual building, 1 Cor. 3 : 9, or the whole Church, the Body of Christ, Eph. 2 : 21. It expresses the strengthening effect of teaching, 1 Cor. 14 : 3, 5, 12, 26 ; 2 Cor. 10 : 8 ; 12 : 19 ; 13 : 10, or other ministry, Eph. 4 : 12, 16, 29 (the idea conveyed is progress resulting from patient effort). It is also used of the believer's resurrection body, 2 Cor. 5 : 1. See EDIFICATION, EDIFY.¶

2. ENDŌMĒSIS (ἐνδώμησις), a thing built, structure (*en*, in, *dōmaō*, to build), is used of the wall of the heavenly city, Rev. 21 : 18 (some suggest that the word means a fabric ; others, a roofing or coping ; these interpretations are questionable ; the probable significance is a building).¶

3. KTISIS (κτίσις), a creation, is so translated in the R.V. of Heb. 9 : 11 (A.V. " building,"). See CREATION, B, No. 1, CREATURE, ORDINANCE.

4. TECHNITĒS (τεχνίτης), an artificer, one who does a thing by rules of art, is rendered " builder " in Heb. 11 : 10, marg., " architect," which gives the necessary contrast between this and the next noun in the verse. See CRAFTSMAN, No. 2.

For BULL see OX

BUNDLE

1. DESMĒ (δέσμη), from *deō*, to bind (similarly, Eng. " bundle " is akin to " bind "), is used in Matt. 13 : 30.¶

2. PLĒTHOS (πλῆθος), a great number (akin to *pleō*, to fill), is the word for the bundle of sticks which Paul put on the fire, Acts 28 : 3. See COMPANY, MULTITUDE.

BURDEN, BURDENED, BURDENSOME
A. Nouns.

1. BAROS (βάρος) denotes a weight, anything pressing on one physically, Matt. 20 : 12, or that makes a demand on one's resources, whether material, 1 Thess. 2 : 6 (to be burdensome), or spiritual, Gal. 6 : 2 ; Rev. 2 : 24, or religious, Acts 15 : 28. In one place it metaphorically describes the future state of believers as " an eternal weight of glory," 2 Cor. 4 : 17. See WEIGHT.¶

2. PHORTION (φορτίον), lit., something carried (from *pherō*, to bear), is always used metaphorically (except in Acts 27 : 10, of the lading of a ship) ; of that which, though " light," is involved in discipleship of Christ, Matt. 11 : 30 ; of tasks imposed by the Scribes, Pharisees and lawyers, Matt. 23 : 4 ; Luke 11 : 46 ; of that which will be the result, at the Judgment-Seat of Christ, of each believer's work, Gal. 6 : 5.¶

Note : The difference between *phortion* and *baros* is, that *phortion* is simply something to be borne, without reference to its weight, but *baros* always suggests what is heavy or burdensome. Thus Christ speaks of His burden (*phortion*) as " light ; " here *baros* would be inappropriate ; but the burden of a transgressor is *baros*, " heavy." Contrast *baros* in Gal. 6 : 2, with *phortion* in ver. 5.

3. GOMOS (γόμος), from a root *gem-*, signifying full, or heavy, seen in *gemō*, to be full, *gemizō*, to fill, Lat. *gemo*, to groan, denotes the lading of freight of a ship, Acts 21 : 3, or merchandise conveyed in a ship, and so merchandise in general, Rev. 18 : 11, 12. See MERCHANDISE.¶

B. Verbs.

1. BAREŌ (βαρέω), akin to A, No. 1, is used of the effect of drowsiness, " were heavy," Matt. 26 : 43 ; Mark 14 : 40 ; Luke 9 : 32 ; of the effects of gluttony, Luke 21 : 34 (" overcharged ") ; of the believer's present physical state in the body, 2 Cor. 5 : 4 ; of persecution, 2 Cor. 1 : 8 ; of a charge upon material resources, 1 Tim. 5 : 16 (R.V.). See CHARGE, HEAVY, PRESS.¶

2. EPIBAREŌ (ἐπιβαρέω), epi, upon (intensive), to burden heavily, is said of material resources, 1 Thess. 2 : 9 (R.V.) ; 2 Thess. 3 : 8, R.V., " burden," A.V., " be chargeable to ; " of the effect of spiritual admonition and discipline, 2 Cor. 2 : 5, R.V., " press heavily," A.V., " overcharge." See CHARGEABLE, PRESS.¶

3. KATABAREŌ (καταβαρέω), to weigh down (kata, down), overload, is used of material charges, in 2 Cor. 12 : 16.¶

4. KATANARKAŌ (καταναρκάω), to be a burden, to be burdensome, primarily signifies to be numbed or torpid, to grow stiff (narkē is the torpedo or cramp fish, which benumbs anyone who touches it) ; hence to be idle to the detriment of another person (like a useless limb), 2 Cor. 11 : 9 ; 12 : 13, 14. See CHARGEABLE.¶

Note : For thlipsis, distress, affliction, " burdened " (A.V. of 2 Cor. 8 : 13), see AFFLICTION, B. No. 4.

C. Adjective.

ABARĒS (ἀβαρής), without weight (a, negative, and baros, see A, No. 1), is used in 2 Cor. 11 : 9, lit. ' I kept myself burdensomeless.'¶

BURIAL, BURY, BURYING

A. Nouns.

1. ENTAPHIASMOS (ἐνταφιασμός), lit., an entombing (from en, in, taphos, a tomb), " burying," occurs in Mark 14 : 8 ; John 12 : 7. Cp. B.1.¶

2. TAPHĒ (ταφή), a burial (cp. No. 1, and Eng., epitaph), is found in Matt. 27 : 7, with eis, unto, lit. ' with a view to a burial (place) for strangers.'¶

B. Verbs.

1. ENTAPHIAZŌ (ἐνταφιάζω), see A, No. 1, to prepare a body for burial, is used of any provision for this purpose, Matt. 26 : 12 ; John 19 : 40.¶

2. THAPTŌ (θάπτω) occurs in Matt. 8: 21, 22, and parallels in Luke ; Matt. 14 : 12 ; Luke 16 : 22 ; Acts 2 : 29 ; 5 : 6, 9, 10 ; of Christ's burial, 1 Cor. 15 : 4.¶

3. SUNTHAPTŌ (συνθάπτω), akin to A. 2, to bury with, or together (sun), is used in the metaphorical sense only, of the believer's identification with Christ in His burial, as set forth in baptism, Rom. 6 : 4 ; Col. 2 : 12.¶

BURN, BURNING
A. Verbs.

1. KAIŌ (καίω), to set fire to, to light; in the Passive Voice, to be lighted, to burn, Matt. 5 : 15; John 15 : 6; Heb. 12 : 18; Rev. 4 : 5; 8 : 8, 10; 19 : 20; 21 : 8; 1 Cor. 13 : 3, is used metaphorically of the heart, Luke 24 : 32; of spiritual light, Luke 12 : 35; John 5 : 35. See LIGHT.¶

2. KATAKAIŌ (κατακαίω), from *kata*, down (intensive), and No. 1, signifies to burn up, burn utterly, as of chaff, Matt. 3 : 12; Luke 3 : 17; tares, Matt. 13 : 30, 40; the earth and its works, 2 Pet. 3 : 10; trees and grass, Rev. 8 : 7. This form should be noted in Acts 19 : 19; 1 Cor. 3 : 15; Heb. 13 : 11; Rev. 17 : 16. In each place the full rendering ' burn utterly ' might be used, as in Rev. 18 : 8.¶

3. EKKAIŌ (ἐκκαίω), from *ek*, out (intensive), and No. 1, lit., to burn out, in the Passive Voice, to be kindled, burn up, is used of the lustful passions of men, Rom. 1 : 27.¶

4. PUROOMAI (πυρόομαι), from *pur*, fire, to glow with heat, is said of the feet of the Lord, in the vision in Rev. 1 : 15; it is translated " fiery " in Eph. 6 : 16 (of the darts of the evil one); used metaphorically of the emotions, in 1 Cor. 7 : 9; 2 Cor. 11 : 29; elsewhere literally, of the heavens, 2 Pet. 3 : 12; of gold, Rev. 3 : 18 (R.V., " refined "). See FIERY, FIRE, TRY.¶

5. EMPIPRĒMI (ἐμπίπρημι), or EMPRĒTHŌ, to burn up, occurs in Matt. 2 : 7.¶

B. Nouns.

1. KAUSIS (καῦσις), akin to A, No. 1 (Eng., caustic), is found in Heb. 6 : 8, lit., ' whose end is unto burning.'¶ Cp. BRANDED.

2. KAUSŌN (καύσων) is rendered " burning heat " in Jas. 1 : 11, A.V. (R.V., " scorching "). See HEAT.

3. PURŌSIS (πύρωσις), akin to A. No. 4, is used literally in Rev. 18 : 9, 18; metaphorically in 1 Pet. 4 : 12, " fiery trial." See TRIAL.¶

BURNISHED

CHALKOLIBANON (χαλκολίβανον) : see BRASS.

BURNT (offering)

HOLOKAUTŌMA (ὁλοκαύτωμα) denotes a whole burnt offering (*holos*, whole, *kautos*, for *kaustos*, a verbal adjective from *kaiō*, to burn), i.e., a victim, the whole of which is burned, as in Ex. 30 : 20; Lev. 5 : 12; 23 : 8, 25, 27. It is used in Mark 12 : 33, by the scribe who questioned the Lord as to the first commandment in the Law, and in Heb. 10 : 6, 8, R.V., " whole burnt offerings." See OFFERING.¶

BURST (asunder)

1. RHĒGNUMI (ῥήγνυμι); see BREAK, A. No. 6.

2. LAKEŌ or LASKŌ (λάσκω), primarily, to crack, or crash, denotes to burst asunder with a crack, crack open (always of making a noise), is used in Acts 1 : 18.¶

For BURY see BURIAL

BUSH

BATOS (βάτος) denotes a bramble bush, as in Luke 6 : 44. In Mark 12 : 26 and Luke 20 : 37 the phrase " in the place concerning the Bush " signifies in that part of the book of Exodus concerning it. See also Acts 7 : 30, 35.¶

BUSHEL

MODIOS (μόδιος) was a dry measure containing about a peck, Matt. 5 : 15 ; Mark 4 : 21 ; Luke 11 : 33.¶

BUSINESS
A. Nouns.

1. CHREIA (χρεία), translated " business " in Acts 6 : 3, of the distribution of funds, signifies a necessity, a need, and is used in this place concerning duty or business. See LACK, NECESSITY, NEED, USE, WANT.

2. ERGASIA (ἐργασία) denotes a business, Acts 19 : 24, 25, R.V., A.V., " gain " and " craft " (from *ergon*, work). See DILIGENCE.

B. Adjective.

IDIOS (ἴδιος) expresses what is one's own (hence, Eng. " idiot," in a changed sense, lit., a person with his own opinions) ; the neuter plural with the article (*ta idia*) signifies one's own things. In 1 Thess. 4 : 11, the noun is not expressed in the original but is supplied in the English Versions by " business," " your own business." For the same phrase, otherwise expressed, see John 1 : 11, " His own (things) ; " 16 : 32 and 19 : 27, " his own (home) ; " Acts 21 : 6, " home." In Luke 2 : 49, the phrase " in My Father's house " (R.V.), " about My Father's business " (A.V.), is, lit., ' in the (things, the neuter plural of the article) of my Father.' See ACQUAINTANCE, COMPANY, No. 8, DUE, HOME, OWN, PRIVATE, PROPER, SEVERAL.

Notes : (1) In the A.V. of Rom. 16 : 2 *pragma* is translated " business," R.V., " matter." See MATTER, THING, WORK.

(2) In Rom. 12 : 11 *spoudē*, translated " business " (A.V.), signifies " diligence " (R.V.). See DILIGENCE.

BUSYBODY
A. Verb.

PERIERGAZOMAI (περιεργάζομαι), lit., to be working round about, instead of at one's own business (*peri*, around, *ergon*, work), signifies to take more pains than enough about a thing, to waste one's labour, to be meddling with, or bustling about, other people's matters. This is found in 2 Thess. 3 : 11, where, following the verb *ergazomai*, to work, it forms a paronomasia. This may be produced in a free rendering : ' some who are not busied in their own business, but are overbusied in that of others.'¶

B. Adjective.

PERIERGOS (περίεργος), akin to A, denoting taken up with trifles, is used of magic arts in Acts 19 : 19 ; " busybodies " in 1 Tim. 5 : 13, i.e., meddling in other persons' affairs. See CURIOUS.¶

C. Noun.

ALLOTRIOEPISKOPOS (ἀλλοτριοεπίσκοπος), from *allotrios*, belonging to another person, and *episkopos*, an overseer, translated " busybody " in the A.V. of 1 Pet. 4 : 15, " meddler," R.V., was a legal term for a charge brought against Christians as being hostile to civilized society, their purpose being to make Gentiles conform to Christian standards. Some explain it as a pryer into others' affairs. See MEDDLER.¶

BUY, BOUGHT

1. AGORAZŌ (ἀγοράζω), primarily, to frequent the market-place, the *agora*, hence to do business there, to buy or sell, is used lit., e.g., in Matt. 14 : 15. Figuratively Christ is spoken of as having bought His redeemed, making them His property at the price of His blood (i.e., His death through the shedding of His blood in expiation for their sins), 1 Cor. 6 : 20 ; 7 : 23 ; 2 Pet. 2 : 1 ; see also Rev. 5 : 9 ; 14 : 3, 4 (not as A.V., " redeemed "). *Agorazō* does not mean to redeem. See REDEEM.

2. ŌNEOMAI (ὠνέομαι), to buy, in contradistinction to selling, is used in Acts 7 : 16, of the purchase by Abraham of a burying place.¶

Note : In Jas. 4 : 13 (A.V.) the verb *emporeuomai* (Eng., emporium) is rendered " buy and sell." Its meaning is to trade, traffic, R.V. It primarily denotes to travel, to go on a journey, then, to do so for traffic purposes ; hence to trade ; in 2 Pet. 2 : 3, " make merchandise of." See MERCHANDISE.¶

BY. See Note †, p. 9.

Note : The phrase " by and by " in the A.V. is in several places misleading. The three words *exautēs*, Mark 6 : 25, *euthus*, Matt. 13 : 21, and *eutheōs*, Luke 17 : 7 ; 21 : 9, mean " straightway," " immediately." See under these words.

C

CAGE

PHULAKĒ (φυλακή), from *phulassō*, to guard, denotes (a) a watching, keeping watch, Luke 2 : 8 ; (b) persons keeping watch, a guard, Acts 12 : 10 ; (c) a period during which watch is kept, e.g., Matt. 24 : 43 ; (d) a prison, a hold. In Rev. 18 : 2, A.V., Babylon is described figuratively, first as a " hold " and then as a " cage " of every unclean and hateful bird (R.V., " hold " in both clauses ; marg., " prison "). The word is almost invariably translated " prison." See HOLD, IMPRISONMENT, PRISON, WARD, WATCH.

CALF

MOSCHOS (μόσχος) primarily denotes anything young, whether plants or the offspring of men or animals, the idea being that which is tender and delicate ; hence a calf, young bull, heifer, Luke 15 : 23, 27, 30 ; Heb. 9 : 12, 19 ; Rev. 4 : 7.¶

MOSCHOPOIEŌ (μοσχοποιέω) signifies to make a calf (*moschos*, and *poieō*, to make), Acts 7 : 41.¶

CALL, CALLED, CALLING
A. Verbs.

1. KALEŌ (καλέω), derived from the root *kal*—, whence Eng. " call " and " clamour " (see B. and C., below), is used (a) with a personal object, to call anyone, invite, summon, e.g., Matt. 20 : 8 ; 25 : 14 ; it is used particularly of the Divine call to partake of the blessings of redemption, e.g., Rom. 8 : 30 ; 1 Cor. 1 : 9 ; 1 Thess. 2 : 12 ; Heb. 9 : 15 ; cp. B. and C., below ; (b) of nomenclature or vocation, to call by a name, to name ; in the Passive Voice, to be called by a name, to bear a name. Thus it suggests either vocation or destination ; the context determines which, e.g., Rom. 9 : 25, 26 ; " surname," in Acts 15 : 37, A.V., is incorrect (R.V., " was called "). See BID, NAME.

2. EISKALEŌ (εἰσκαλέω), lit., to call in, hence, to invite (*eis*, in, and No. 1), is found in Acts 10 : 23.¶

3. EPIKALEŌ (ἐπικαλέω), *epi*, upon, and No. 1., denotes (a) to surname ; (b) to be called by a person's name ; hence it is used of being declared to be dedicated to a person, as to the Lord, Acts 15 : 17 (from Amos 9 : 12) ; Jas. 2 : 7 ; (c) to call a person by a name by charging him with an offence, as the Pharisees charged Christ with doing His works

by the help of Beelzebub, Matt. 10 : 25 (the most authentic reading has *epikaleō*, for *kaleō*) ; (*d*) to call upon, invoke ; in the Middle Voice, to call upon for oneself (i.e., on one's behalf), Acts 7 : 59, or to call upon a person as a witness, 2 Cor. 1 : 23, or to appeal to an authority, Acts 25 : 11, etc. ; (*e*) to call upon by way of adoration, making use of the Name of the Lord, Acts 2 : 21 ; Rom. 10 : 12, 13, 14 ; 2 Tim. 2 : 22. See APPEAL, SURNAME.

4. METAKALEŌ (μετακαλέω), *meta*, implying change, and No. 1, to call from one place to another, to summon (cp. the Sept. of Hos. 11 : 1), is used in the Middle Voice only, to call for oneself, to send for, call hither, Acts 7 : 14 ; 10 : 32 ; 20 : 17 ; 24 : 25.¶

5. PROSKALEŌ (προσκαλέω), *pros*, to, and No. 1, signifies (*a*) to call to oneself, to bid to come ; it is used only in the Middle Voice, e.g., Matt. 10 : 1 ; Acts 5 : 40 ; Jas. 5 : 14 ; (*b*) God's call to Gentiles through the Gospel, Acts 2 : 39 ; (*c*) the Divine call in entrusting men with the preaching of the Gospel, Acts 13 : 2 ; 16 : 10.¶

6. SUNKALEŌ (συγκαλέω) signifies to call together, Mark 15 : 16 ; Luke 9 : 1 ; 15 : 6, 9 ; 23 : 13 ; Acts 5 : 21 ; 10 : 24 ; 28 : 17.¶

Notes : (1) *Enkaleō*, Acts 19 : 40, A.V., " called in question," signifies to accuse, as always in the R.V. See ACCUSE, IMPLEAD.

(2) *Parakaleō*, to beseech, intreat, is rendered " have called for " in Acts 28 : 20, A.V. ; R.V., " did intreat " (marg., " call for "). It is used only here with this meaning. See BESEECH.

7. AITEŌ (αἰτέω), to ask, is translated " called for " in Acts 16 : 29 (" he called for lights "). See ASK, A. No. 1.

Note : For the R.V. of Matt. 19 : 17 (A.V., " callest "), see ASK (A, No. 2, *Note*).

8. PHŌNEŌ (φωνέω), to sound (Eng., 'phone), is used of the crowing of a cock, e.g., Matt. 26 : 34 ; John 13 : 38 ; of calling out with a clear or loud voice, to cry out, e.g., Mark 1 : 26 (some mss. have *krazō* here) ; Acts 16 : 28 ; of calling to come to oneself, e.g., Matt. 20 : 32 ; Luke 19 : 15 ; of calling forth, as of Christ's call to Lazarus to come forth from the tomb, John 12 : 17 ; of inviting, e.g., Luke 14 : 12 ; of calling by name, with the implication of the pleasure taken in the possession of those called, e.g., John 10 : 3 ; 13 : 13. See CROW, CRY.

9. LEGŌ (λέγω), to speak, is used of all kinds of oral communication, e.g., to call, to call by name, to surname, Matt. 1 : 16 ; 26 : 36 ; John 4 : 5 ; 11 : 54 ; 15 : 15 ; Rev. 2 : 2, R.V., " call themselves," etc. See ASK.

10. EPILEGŌ (ἐπιλέγω), *epi*, upon, and No. 9, signifies to call in addition, i.e., by another name besides that already intimated, John 5 : 2 ; for its other meaning in Acts 15 : 40, see CHOOSE.¶

11. CHRĒMATIZO (χρηματίζω) occasionally means to be called or named, Acts 11 : 26 (of the name " Christians ") and Rom. 7 : 3, the only places where it has this meaning. Its primary significance, to have

business dealings with, led to this. They "were (publicly) called" Christians, because this was their chief business. See ADMONISH, REVEAL, SPEAK, WARN.

12. EIPON (εἶπον), to say, speak, means to call by a certain appellation, John 10 : 35. See BID, No. 3.

13. KRINŌ (κρίνω), to judge, is translated to call in question, in Acts 23 : 6 ; 24 : 21.

Notes : (1) For *onoma*, a name, translated " called," A.V., in Luke 24 : 13, Acts 10 : 1, *onomazō*, to name, translated " called," A.V., 1 Cor. 5 : 11, and *eponomazō*, to surname, translated " art called," Rom. 2 : 17, see NAME and SURNAME.

(2) *Legō*, to say, is rendered " calleth " in 1 Cor. 12 : 3, A.V., which the R.V. corrects to " saith ; " what is meant is not calling Christ " Anathema," but making use of the phrase " Anathema Jesus," i.e., ' Jesus is accursed.'

(3) *Prosagoreuō*, Heb. 5 : 10, means " to be named." See NAME.¶

(4) *Metapempō*, rendered " call for," in Acts 10 : 5, A.V., and 11 : 13, signifies to fetch, R.V. See FETCH, SEND, No. 9.

(5) *Sunathroizō*, to assemble, is translated " he called together," in the A.V. of Acts 19 : 25 ; R.V., " he gathered together."

(6) *Lambanō*, to take or receive, is found with the noun *hupomnēsis*, remembrance, in 2 Tim. 1 : 5 ; R.V., " having been reminded " (lit., ' having received remembrance '), for A.V., " when I call to remembrance."

(7) In Acts 10 : 15 and 11 : 9, *koinoō*, to make common (R.V.) is translated " call common " in the A.V.

(8) For *prosphōneō*, to call unto, see SPEAK, No. 12.

B. Noun.

KLĒSIS (κλῆσις), a calling (akin to A, No. 1), is always used in the N.T. of that calling the origin, nature and destiny of which are heavenly (the idea of invitation being implied) ; it is used especially of God's invitation to man to accept the benefits of salvation, Rom. 11 : 29 ; 1 Cor. 1 : 26 ; 7 : 20 (said there of the condition in which the calling finds one) ; Eph. 1 : 18, " His calling ; " Phil. 3 : 14, the " high calling ; " 2 Thess. 1 : 11 and 2 Pet. 1 : 10, " your calling ; " 2 Tim. 1 : 9, a " holy calling ; " Heb. 3 : 1, a " heavenly calling ; " Eph. 4 : 1, " the calling wherewith ye were called ; " 4 : 4, " in one hope of your calling." See VOCATION.¶

C. Adjective.

KLĒTOS (κλητός), called, invited, is used, (*a*) of the call of the Gospel, Matt. 20 : 16 ; 22 : 14, not there an effectual call, as in the Epistles, Rom. 1 : 1, 6, 7 ; 8 : 28 ; 1 Cor. 1 : 2, 24 ; Jude 1 ; Rev. 17 : 14 ; in Rom. 1 : 7 and 1 Cor. 1 : 2 the meaning is ' saints by calling ; ' (*b*) of an appointment to apostleship, Rom. 1 : 1 ; 1 Cor. 1 : 1.¶

CALM

GALĒNĒ (γαλήνη) primarily signifies calmness, cheerfulness (from a root *gal—*, from which *gelaō*, to smile, is also derived ; hence the calm of the sea, the smiling ocean being a favourite metaphor of the poets), Matt. 8 : 26 ; Mark 4 : 39 ; Luke 8 : 24.¶

CALVARY

KRANION (κρανίον), *kara*, a head (Eng., cranium), a diminutive of *kranon*, denotes a skull (Latin *calvaria*), Matt. 27 : 33 ; Mark 15 : 22 ; Luke 23 : 33 ; John 19 : 17. The corresponding Aramaic word is Golgotha (Heb. *gulgōleth* ; see Judg. 9 : 53 ; 2 Kings 9 : 35).¶

For CAME see COME

CAMEL

KAMĒLOS (κάμηλος), from a Hebrew word signifying a bearer, carrier, is used in proverbs to indicate (*a*) something almost or altogether impossible, Matt. 19 : 24, and parallel passages, (*b*) the acts of a person who is careful not to sin in trivial details, but pays no heed to more important matters, Matt. 23 : 24.

For CAMP see ARMY

CAN (CANST, COULD, CANNOT)

1. DUNAMAI (δύναμαι) ; see ABILITY, B, No. 1.

2. ISCHUŌ (ἰσχύω) is translated " I can do " in Phil. 4 : 13 ; see ABLE, B, No. 4.

3. ECHŌ (ἔχω), to have, is translated " could " in Mark 14 : 8, lit., ' she hath done what she had ; ' in Luke 14 : 14, for the A.V., " cannot," the R.V. has " they have not wherewith ; " in Acts 4 : 14, " could say nothing against " is, lit., ' had nothing to say against ; ' in Heb. 6 : 13, " he could swear " is, lit., ' He had (by none greater) to swear.' See ABLE, HAVE.

4. GINŌSKŌ (γινώσκω), to know, is so rendered in the R.V. of Matt. 16 : 3, " ye know how to," for A.V., " ye can " (*dunamai* is used in the next sentence). This verb represents knowledge as the effect of experience. In Acts 21 : 37, for " canst thou speak Greek ? " the R.V. has " dost . . ." See ALLOW, KNOW.

5. OIDA (οἶδα), to know by perception, is the word in Pilate's remark " make it as sure as ye can " (marg. " sure, as ye know "), Matt. 27 : 65. The phrases " cannot tell," " canst not tell," etc., are in the R.V. rendered " know not " etc., Matt. 21 : 27 ; Mark 11 : 33 ; Luke 20 : 7 ; John 3 : 8 ; 8 : 14 ; 16 : 18 ; 2 Cor. 12 : 2, 3. See KNOW.

6. ESTI (ἐστί), meaning " it is," is translated " we cannot," in Heb. 9 : 5, lit., ' it is not possible (now to speak) ; ' so in 1 Cor. 11 : 20 ; see margin.

7. ENDECHOMAI (ἐνδέχομαι), to accept, admit, allow of, is used impersonally in Luke 13 : 33, " it can (not) be," i.e., it is not admissible.¶

For CANDLE and CANDLESTICK see LAMP and LAMPSTAND

For CANKER see GANGRENE and RUST

CAPTAIN

1. CHILIARCHOS (χιλίαρχος), denoting a commander of 1000 soldiers (from *chilios*, a thousand, and *archō*, to rule), was the Greek word for the Persian vizier, and for the Roman military tribune, the commander of a Roman cohort, e.g., John 18 : 12 ; Acts 21 : 31-33, 37. One such commander was constantly in charge of the Roman garrison in Jerusalem. The word became used also for any military commander, e.g., a captain or chief captain, Mark 6 : 21 ; Rev. 6 : 15 ; 19 : 18.

2. STRATĒGOS (στρατηγός), originally the commander of an army (from *stratos*, an army, and *agō*, to lead), came to denote a civil commander, a governor (Latin, *duumvir*), the highest magistrate, or any civil officer in chief command, Acts 16 : 20, 22, 35, 36, 38 ; also the chief captain of the Temple, himself a Levite, having command of the Levites who kept guard in and around the Temple, Luke 22 : 4, 52 ; Acts 4 : 1 ; 5 : 24, 26. Cp. Jer. 20 : 1.¶

3. ARCHĒGOS (ἀρχηγός) : see AUTHOR (No. 2).

Note : In Acts 28 : 16 some mss. have the word *stratopedarchēs* (lit., camp-commander), which some take to denote a prætorian prefect, or commander of the prætorian cohorts, the Emperor's bodyguard, " the captain of the prætorian guard." There were two prætorian prefects, to whose custody prisoners sent bound to the Emperor were consigned. But the word probably means the commander of a detached corps connected with the commissariat and the general custody of prisoners.

CAPTIVE, CAPTIVITY
A. Nouns.

1. AICHMALŌTOS (αἰχμάλωτος), lit., one taken by the spear (from *aichmē*, a spear, and *halōtos*, a verbal adjective, from *halōnai*, to be captured), hence denotes a captive, Luke 4:18.¶

2. AICHMALŌSIA (αἰχμαλωσία), captivity, the abstract noun in contrast to No. 1, the concrete, is found in Rev. 13:10 and Eph. 4:8, where "He led captivity captive" (marg., "a multitude of captives") seems to be an illusion to the triumphal procession by which a victory was celebrated, the captives taken forming part of the procession. See Judg. 5:12. The quotation is from Psa. 68:18, and probably is a forceful expression for Christ's victory, through His Death, over the hostile powers of darkness. An alternative suggestion is that at His Ascension Christ transferred the redeemed Old Testament saints from Sheol to His own presence in glory.¶

B. Verbs.

1. AICHMALŌTEUŌ (αἰχμαλωτεύω) signifies (*a*) to be a prisoner of

war, (b) to make a prisoner of war. The latter meaning is the only one used in the N.T., Eph. 4 : 8.¶

2. AICHMALŌTIZŌ (αἰχμαλωτίζω), practically synonymous with No. 1, denotes either to lead away captive, Luke 21 : 24, or to subjugate, to bring under control, said of the effect of the Law in one's members in bringing the person into captivity under the law of sin, Rom. 7 : 23 ; or of subjugating the thoughts to the obedience of Christ, 2 Cor. 10 : 5 ; or of those who took captive " silly women laden with sins," 2 Tim. 3 : 6.¶

3. ZŌGREŌ (ζωγρέω) lit. signifies to take men alive (from zōos, alive, and agreuō, to hunt or catch), Luke 5 : 10 (marg. " take alive "), there of the effects of the work of the Gospel ; in 2 Tim. 2 : 26 it is said of the power of Satan to lead men astray. The verse should read ' and that they may recover themselves out of the snare of the Devil (having been taken captive by him), unto the will of God.' This is the probable meaning rather than to take alive or for life. See CATCH.¶

CARCASE

1. KŌLON (κῶλον) primarily denotes a member of a body, especially the external and prominent members, particularly the feet, and so, a dead body (see, e.g., the Sept., in Lev. 26 : 30 ; Num. 14 : 29, 32 ; Is. 66 : 24, etc.). The word is used in Heb. 3 : 17, from Num. 14 : 29, 32.¶

2. PTŌMA (πτῶμα) : see BODY, No. 3.

CARE (noun and verb), CAREFUL, CAREFULLY, CAREFULNESS

A. Nouns.

1. MERIMNA (μέριμνα), probably connected with merizō, to draw in different directions, distract, hence signifies that which causes this, a care, especially an anxious care, Matt. 13 : 22 ; Mark 4 : 19 ; Luke 8 : 14 ; 21 : 34 ; 2 Cor. 11 : 28 (R.V., " anxiety for ") ; 1 Pet. 5 : 7 (R.V., " anxiety "). See ANXIETY.¶

Note : The negative adjective amerimnos (a, negative) signifies free from care, Matt. 28 : 14, R.V., " we will . . . rid you of care," A.V., " we will . . . secure you " (" secure " lit. means ' free from care ') ; 1 Cor. 7 : 32, A.V., " without carefulness."¶

2. SPOUDĒ (σπουδή), primarily haste, zeal, diligence, hence means earnest care, carefulness, 2 Cor. 7 : 11, 12 ; 8 : 16 (R.V., " earnest care," in each place). Merimna conveys the thought of anxiety, spoudē, of watchful interest and earnestness. See BUSINESS, DILIGENCE (A, No. 2), EARNESTNESS, FORWARDNESS, HASTE.

B. Verbs.

1. MERIMNAŌ (μεριμνάω), akin to A, No. 1, signifies to be anxious about, to have a distracting care, e.g., Matt. 6 : 25, 28, R.V., " be anxious," for A.V., " take thought ; " 10 : 19 ; Luke 10 : 41 (R.V., " anxious," for A.V., " careful ") ; 12 : 11 (R.V., " anxious ") ; to be careful for, 1 Cor.

7 : 32, 33, 34 ; to have a care for, 1 Cor. 12 : 25 ; to care for, Phil. 2 : 20 ; " be anxious," Phil. 4 : 6, R.V. See THOUGHT (to take).

2. MELEI (μέλει), the third person sing. of melō, used impersonally, signifies that something is an object of care, especially the care of forethought and interest, rather than anxiety, Matt. 22 : 16 ; Mark 4 : 38 ; 12 : 14 ; Luke 10 : 40 ; John 10 : 13 ; 12 : 6 ; Acts 18 : 17 ; 1 Cor. 9 : 9 (R.V., " Is it for the oxen that God careth ? " The A.V. seriously misses the point. God does care for oxen, but there was a Divinely designed significance in the O.T. passage, relating to the service of preachers of the Gospel) ; 7 : 21 ; 1 Pet. 5 : 7.¶

3. EPIMELEOMAI (ἐπιμελέομαι) signifies to take care of, involving forethought and provision (epi indicating the direction of the mind toward the object cared for), Luke 10 : 34, 35, of the Good Samaritan's care for the wounded man, and in 1 Tim. 3 : 5, of a bishop's (or overseer's) care of a church—a significant association of ideas.¶

4. PHRONTIZŌ (φροντίζω), to think, consider, be thoughtful (from phrēn, the mind), is translated " be careful " in Tit. 3 : 8.¶

5. PHRONEŌ (φρονέω), translated " be careful," in Phil. 4 : 10, A.V. [R.V., " (ye did) take thought "], has a much wider range of meaning than No. 5, and denotes to be minded, in whatever way. See AFFECTION, B, Note (1), MIND, REGARD, SAVOUR, THINK, UNDERSTAND.

Note : Episkopeō, to oversee, is rendered " looking carefully," in Heb. 12 : 15, R.V. See OVERSIGHT.¶

C. Adverbs.

1. AKRIBŌS (ἀκριβῶς), carefully ; see ACCURATELY.

Note : For akribesteron, more carefully, see EXACTLY.

2. SPOUDAIOTERŌS, the comparative adverb corresponding to A, No. 2, signifies " the more diligently," Phil. 2 : 28, R.V. (A.V., " carefully ").¶ The adverb spoudaiōs denotes " diligently," 2 Tim. 1 : 17 (some mss. have the comparative here) ; Tit. 3 : 13 ; or " earnestly," Luke 7 : 4 (A.V., " instantly "). See also spoudaios and its comparative, in 2 Cor. 8 : 17, 22, R.V., " earnest," " more earnest."¶

CARNAL, CARNALLY

1. SARKIKOS (σαρκικός), from sarx, flesh, signifies (a) having the nature of flesh. i.e., sensual, controlled by animal appetites, governed by human nature, instead of by the Spirit of God, 1 Cor. 3 : 3 (for ver. 1, see below ; some mss. have it in ver. 4) ; having its seat in the animal nature, or excited by it, 1 Pet. 2 : 11, " fleshly ; " or as the equivalent of " human," with the added idea of weakness, figuratively of the weapons of spiritual warfare, " of the flesh " (A.V., " carnal "), 2 Cor. 10 : 4 ; or with the idea of unspirituality, of human wisdom, " fleshly," 2 Cor. 1 : 12 ; (b) pertaining to the flesh (i.e., the body), Rom. 15 : 27 ; 1 Cor. 9 : 11.¶

2. SARKINOS (σάρκινος), (a) consisting of flesh, 2 Cor. 3 : 3, " tables

that are hearts of flesh" (A.V., "fleshy tables of the heart"); (b) pertaining to the natural, transient life of the body, Heb. 7 : 16, " a carnal commandment ; " (c) given up to the flesh, i.e., with almost the same significance as *sarkikos*, above, Rom. 7 : 14, " I am carnal sold under sin ; " 1 Cor. 3 : 1 (some texts have *sarkikos*, in both these places, and in those in (a) and (b), but textual evidence is against it). It is difficult to discriminate between *sarkikos* and *sarkinos* in some passages. In regard to 1 Pet. 2 : 11, Trench (Syn §§ lxxi, lxxii) says that *sarkikos* describes the lusts which have their source in man's corrupt and fallen nature, and the man is *sarkikos* who allows to the flesh a place which does not belong to it of right ; in 1 Cor. 3 : 1 *sarkinos* is an accusation far less grave than *sarkikos* would have been. The Corinthian saints were making no progress, but they were not anti-spiritual in respect of the particular point with which the Apostle was there dealing. In vv. 3, 4, they are charged with being *sarkikos*. See FLESHLY, FLESHY.¶

CAROUSINGS

POTOS (πότος), lit., a drinking, signifies not simply a banquet but a drinking bout, a carousal, 1 Pet. 4 : 3 (R.V., " carousings," A.V., " banquetings ").¶ Synonymous is *kraipalē*, " surfeiting," Luke 21 : 34.¶

CARPENTER

TEKTŌN (τέκτων) denotes any craftsman, but especially a worker in wood, a carpenter, Matt. 13 : 55 ; Mark 6 : 3.¶

For CARRIAGE see BAGGAGE

CARRY

1. SUNKOMIZŌ (συγκομίζω), to carry together, to help in carrying (*sun*, with, *komizō*, to carry), is used in Acts 8 : 2, R.V., " buried," for A.V., " carried to his burial." The verb has also the meaning of recovering or getting back a body.¶

2. EKKOMIZŌ (ἐκκομίζω), to carry out, is found in Luke 7 : 12.¶

3. PHERŌ (φέρω), to bear, to bring, is translated " carry " only in John 21 : 18. See Note below.

4. DIAPHERŌ (διαφέρω) has the meaning " to carry through " in Mark 11 : 16. See BETTER, DIFFER, DRIVE, EXCELLENT, MATTER, PUBLISH, VALUE.

5. METATITHĒMI (μετατίθημι), to place among, put in another place (*meta*, implying change, and *tithēmi*, to put), has this latter meaning in Acts 7 : 16, " carried over." See CHANGE, REMOVE, TRANSLATE, TURN.

6. APAGŌ (ἀπάγω), to lead away (*apo*, from, *agō*, to lead), is rendered " carried " in 1 Cor. 12 : 2, A.V. (R.V., " were led "). See BRING.

7. SUNAPAGŌ (συναπάγω), to carry away with (*sun*, with, and No. 6), is used in a bad sense, in Gal. 2 : 13 and 2 Pet. 3 : 17, " being carried

away with " (R.V.) ; in a good sense in Rom. 12 : 16 ; the R.V. marg. " be carried away with " is preferable to the text " condescend " (R.V., and A.V.), and to the A.V. marg., " be contented (with mean things)." A suitable rendering would be ' be led along with.'¶

Notes : (1) For *pherō*, to carry, or bring, *apopherō*, to carry away, *peripherō*, to carry about, *ekpherō*, to carry forth, *anapherō*, to carry up, *airō*, to lift and carry away, to take away, *bastazō*, to support, carry about, *agō*, to lead or carry, *apagō*, to carry away, see BEAR and BRING.

(2) For *elaunō*, rendered " carry " in 2 Pet. 2 : 17, see DRIVE.

CARRYING AWAY
A. Noun.

METOIKESIA (μετοικεσία), a change of abode, or a carrying away by force (*meta*, implying change, *oikia*, a dwelling), is used only of the carrying away to Babylon, Matt. 1 : 11, 12, 17.¶
B. Verb.

METOIKIZŌ (μετοικίζω), akin to A, is used of the removal of Abraham into Canaan, Acts 7 : 4, and of the carrying into Babylon, 7 : 43.¶

CASE

1. AITIA (αἰτία) : see under ACCUSATION, A, No. 1.

2. ECHŌ (ἔχω), to have, is idiomatically used in the sense of being in a case or condition, as with the infirm man at the pool of Bethesda, John 5 : 6, lit., ' that he had already much time (in that case).'

Note : In Acts 25 : 14 the phrase in the original is ' the things concerning Paul,' A.V., " cause " (as if translating *aitia*) ; R.V., " Festus laid Paul's case before the king."

3. PROECHŌ (προέχω), lit., to have before, in the Middle Voice, Rom. 3 : 9, is rightly translated " are we in worse case ? " (R.V.), as is borne out by the context. See BETTER (be), Note (1).¶

4. The preposition *en*, followed by the dative of the pronoun, lit., ' in me,' is translated in the R.V.," in my case," in 1 Cor. 9 : 15 ; " unto me," in 1 Cor. 14 : 11 (marg. " in my case"). Similarly, in the plural, in 1 John 4 : 16, R.V. " in us " (marg., " in our case ") ; A.V., incorrectly, " to us."

Note : In Matt. 5 : 20 the strong double negative *ou mē* is translated " in no case " (A.V.) : R.V., " in no wise."

CAST
A. Verbs.

1. BALLŌ (βάλλω), to throw, hurl, in contrast to striking, is frequent in the four Gospels and Revelation ; elsewhere it is used only in Acts. In Matt. 5 : 30 some mss. have this verb (A.V., " should be cast ") ; the most authentic have *aperchomai*, to go away, R.V., " go." See ARISE, BEAT, DUNG, LAY, POUR, PUT, SEND, STRIKE, THROW, THRUST.

2. RHIPTŌ (ῥίπτω) denotes to throw with a sudden motion, to jerk, cast forth ; " cast down," Matt. 15 : 30 and 27 : 5 ; "thrown down," Luke 4 : 35 ; " thrown," 17 : 2 (A.V., " cast ") ; [rhipteō in Acts 22 : 23 (A.V., " cast off "), of the casting off of clothes (in the next sentence ballō, No. 1, is used of casting dust into the air)] ; in 27 : 19 " cast out," of the tackling of a ship ; in ver. 29 " let go " (A.V., " cast "), of anchors ; in Matt. 9 : 36, " scattered," said of sheep. See THROW, SCATTER.¶

3. EKPIPTŌ (ἐκπίπτω), lit., to fall out, is translated " be cast ashore," in Acts 27 : 29, R.V., A.V., " have fallen upon ". See EFFECT, FAIL, FALL, NOUGHT.

A number of compound verbs consisting of ballō or rhiptō, with prepositions prefixed, denote to cast, with a corresponding English preposition. Compounds of ballō are :

4. APOBALLŌ (ἀποβάλλω), to throw off from, to lay aside, to cast away, Mark 10 : 50 ; Heb. 10 : 35.¶

Note : Apobolē, " casting away " (akin to No. 4), is used of Israel in Rom. 11 : 15 ; elsewhere, Acts 27 : 22, " loss " (of life).¶

5. EKBALLŌ (ἐκβάλλω), to cast out of, from, forth, is very frequent in the Gospels and Acts ; elsewhere, in Gal. 4 : 30 ; 3 John 10 ; in Jas. 2 : 25, " sent out ; " in Rev. 11 : 2, " leave out " (marg., " cast without "). See BRING, No. 28, DRIVE, EXPEL, LEAVE, PLUCK, PULL, PUT, SEND, TAKE, THRUST.

6. EMBALLŌ (ἐμβάλλω), to cast into, is used in Luke 12 : 5.¶

7. EPIBALLŌ (ἐπιβάλλω), to cast on, or upon, is used in this sense in Mark 11 : 7 and 1 Cor. 7 : 35. See BEAT (No. 5), FALL, No. 11, LAY, PUT, No. 8, STRETCH.

8. KATABALLŌ (καταβάλλω) signifies to cast down, 2 Cor. 4 : 9, A.V., " cast down," R.V., " smitten down ; " Heb. 6 : 1, " laying " See LAY.¶ Some mss. have this verb in Rev. 12 : 10 (for ballō).

9. AMPHIBALLŌ (ἀμφιβάλλω), to cast around, occurs Mark 1 : 16.¶

10. PERIBALLŌ (περιβάλλω), to cast about, or around, is used in 23 of its 24 occurrences, of putting on garments, clothing, etc. ; it is translated " cast about " in Mark 14 : 51 ; Acts 12 : 8 ; in Luke 19 : 43, used of casting up a bank or palisade against a city (see R.V. and marg.), A.V., " shall cast a trench about thee." See CLOTHE, No. 6, PUT.

Compounds of rhiptō are :

11. APORIPTŌ (ἀπορίπτω), to cast off, Acts 27 : 43, of shipwrecked people in throwing themselves into the water.¶

12. EPIRIPTŌ (ἐπιρίπτω), to cast upon, (a) lit., of casting garments on a colt, Luke 19 : 35 ; (b) figuratively, of casting care upon God, 1 Pet. 5 : 7.¶

Other verbs are :

13. APŌTHEŌ (ἀπωθέω), to thrust away (apo, away, ōtheō, to thrust), in the N.T. used in the Middle Voice, signifying to thrust from oneself,

to cast off, by way of rejection, Acts 7 : 27, 39 ; 13 : 46 ; Rom. 11 : 1, 2 ; 1 Tim. 1 : 19. See PUT and THRUST.¶

14. KATHAIREŌ (καθαιρέω), *kata*, down, *haireō*, to take, to cast down, demolish, in 2 Cor. 10 : 5, of strongholds and imaginations. See DESTROY, PULL, PUT, TAKE.

Note : The corresponding noun *kathairesis*, a casting down, is so rendered in 2 Cor. 10 : 4 (A.V., " pulling down ") and 13 : 10 (A.V., " destruction ").

15. DIALOGIZOMAI (διαλογίζομαι), to reason (*dia*, through, *logizomai*, to reason), is translated " cast in (her) mind," Luke 1 : 29. See DISPUTE, MUSING, REASON, THINK.

16. APOTITHĒMI (ἀποτίθημι), to put off, lay aside, denotes, in the Middle Voice, to put off from oneself, cast off, used figuratively of works of darkness, Rom. 13 : 12, " let us cast off," (aorist tense, denoting a definite act). See LAY, No. 8, PUT, No. 5.

17. EKTITHĒMI (ἐκτίθημι), to expose, cast out (*ek*, out, *tithēmi*, to put), is said of a new-born child in Acts 7 : 21. In ver. 19 " cast out " translates the phrase *poieō*, to make, with *ekthetos*, exposed, a verbal form of *ektithēmi*. See EXPOUND.

18. PERIAIREŌ (περιαιρέω), to take away, is used in Acts 27 : 40, as a nautical term, R.V., " casting off," A.V., " taken up." See TAKE.

Notes : (1) For *zēmioō*, " cast away," Luke 9 : 25, see FORFEIT. (2) For *katakrēmnizō*, Luke 4 : 29 (A.V., " cast down headlong "), see THROW.¶ (3) For *oneidizō*, Matt. 27 : 44 (A.V., " cast in one's teeth "), see REPROACH. (4) For *paradidōmi*, Matt. 4 : 12 (A.V., " cast into prison "), see DELIVER. (5) For *atheteō*, 1 Tim. 5 : 12 (A.V., " cast off "), see REJECT. (6) For *ekteinō*, Acts 27 : 30 (A.V., " cast out "), see LAY No. 13. (7) For *tapeinos*, 2 Cor. 7 : 6 (A.V., " cast down "), see LOWLY

B. Noun.

BOLE (βολή) denotes a throw (akin to *ballō*, to throw), and is used in Luke 22 : 21 in the phrase " a stone's cast," of the distance from which the Lord was parted from the disciples in the garden of Gethsemane.¶

Note : In Jas. 1 : 17, *aposkiasma* (from *aposkiazō*, to cast a shadow), is rendered " shadow that is cast," R.V.¶

C. Adjective.

ADOKIMOS (ἀδόκιμος) signifies not standing the test, rejected, (*a*, negative, and *dokimos*, tested, approved) ; it is said of things, e.g., the land, Heb. 6 : 8, " rejected," and of persons, Rom. 1 : 28, " reprobate ; " 1 Cor. 9 : 27, A.V., " castaway," R.V. " rejected " (i.e., disapproved, and so rejected from present testimony, with loss of future reward) ; 2 Cor. 13 : 5, 6, 7, " reprobate " (sing. in R.V. in each verse), i.e., that will not stand the test ; 2 Tim. 3 : 8, " reprobate (concerning the faith)," Tit. 1 : 16, " reprobate." See REJECT, REPROBATE.¶

For CASTLE see ARMY (No. 3)

CATCH

1. HARPAZŌ (ἁρπάζω), to snatch or catch away, is said of the act of the Spirit of the Lord in regard to Philip in Acts 8 : 39 ; of Paul in being caught up to Paradise, 2 Cor. 12 : 2, 4 ; of the Rapture of the saints at the return of the Lord, 1 Thess. 4 : 17 ; of the rapture of the man child in the vision of Rev. 12 : 5. This verb conveys the idea of force suddenly exercised, as in Matt. 11 : 12, " take (it) by force ; " 12 : 29, " spoil " (some mss. have *diarpazō* here) ; in 13 : 19, R.V., " snatcheth ; " for forceful seizure, see also John 6 : 15 ; 10 : 12, 28, 29 ; Acts 23 : 10 ; in Jude 23, R.V., " snatching ". See PLUCK, PULL, SNATCH, TAKE (by force).¶

2. LAMBANŌ (λαμβάνω), to receive, is once used of catching by fraud, circumventing, 2 Cor. 12 : 16. In Matt. 21 : 39 and Mark 12 : 3, R.V. " took," for A.V. " caught." See ACCEPT, No. 4.

3. AGREUŌ (ἀγρεύω), to take by hunting (from *agra*, a hunt, a catch), is used metaphorically, of the Pharisees and Herodians in seeking to catch Christ in His talk, Mark 12 : 13.¶

4. THĒREUŌ (θηρεύω), to hunt or catch wild beasts (*thērion*, a wild beast), is used by Luke of the same event as in No. 3, Luke 11 : 54.¶

5. ZŌGREŌ (ζωγρέω), to take alive : see CAPTIVE, B, No. 3.

6. PIAZŌ (πιάζω), to capture : see APPREHEND, No. 2.

7. SUNARPAZŌ (συναρπάζω), *sun*, used intensively, and No. 1, to snatch, to seize, to keep a firm grip of, is used only by Luke, and translated " caught " in the A.V. of Luke 8 : 29, of demon-possession ; in Acts 6 : 12, of the act of the elders and scribes in seizing Stephen, R.V., more suitably, " seized." So in Acts 19 : 29. In 27 : 15, it is used of the effects of wind upon a ship. See SEIZE.¶

8. SULLAMBANŌ (συλλαμβάνω), *sun*, and No. 2, to seize, is used, similarly to No. 7, in Acts 26 : 21, of the act of the Jews in seizing Paul in the temple. See CONCEIVE, HELP, SEIZE, TAKE.

9. EPILAMBANŌ (ἐπιλαμβάνω), to lay hold (*epi*, intensive, and No. 2), is translated " caught " in Acts 16 : 19, A.V. ; R.V., " laid hold." See HOLD, TAKE.

CATTLE

1. THREMMA (θρέμμα), whatever is fed or nourished (from *trephō*, to nourish, nurture, feed), is found in John 4 : 12.¶

2. KTĒNOS (κτῆνος), cattle as property : see BEAST, No. 3.

Note : The verb *poimainō*, to act as a shepherd (*poimēn*), to keep sheep, is translated " keeping sheep " in Luke 17 : 7, R.V., for A.V., " feeding cattle."

CAUSE (Noun and Verb)
A. Nouns.

1. AITIA (αἰτία), a cause : see ACCUSATION, A, No. 1.

2. AITION (αἴτιον), a fault (synonymous with No. 1, but more limited in scope), is translated " cause (of death) " in Luke 23 : 22 ; " cause " in Acts 19 : 40 (of a riot); " fault " in Luke 23 : 4, 14. See FAULT.¶

3. LOGOS (λόγος), a word spoken for any purpose, denotes, in one place, a cause or reason assigned, Matt. 5 : 32.

The following phrases are rendered by an English phrase containing the word " cause " (see WHEREFORE) :

" For this cause "

1. ANTI TOUTOU (ἀντὶ τούτου), lit., instead of this, i.e., for this cause, signifying the principle or motive, Eph. 5 : 31.

2. DIA TOUTO (διὰ τοῦτο), lit., on account of this, for this cause, signifying the ground or reason, e.g., R.V. in Mark 12 : 24 ; John 1 : 31 ; 5 : 16, 18 ; 6 : 65 ; 7 : 22 ; 8 : 47 ; 12 : 18, 27, 39 ; Rom. 1 : 26 ; 4 : 16 ; 13 : 6 ; 1 Cor. 4 : 17 ; 11 : 10, 30 ; Eph. 1 : 15 ; Col. 1 : 9 ; 1 Thess. 2 : 13 ; 3 : 5, 7 ; 2 Thess. 2 : 11 ; 1 Tim. 1 : 16 ; Heb. 9 : 15 ; 1 John 3 : 1.

3. HENEKEN TOUTOU (ἕνεκεν τούτου), lit., for the sake of this, therefore, as a reason for, Matt. 19 : 5 ; Mark 10 : 7 ; heneka toutōn, ' for the sake of these things,' Acts 26 : 21 ; and heneken tou, for the cause of the (one) etc., 2 Cor. 7 : 12 (twice).

4. CHARIN TOUTOU, or TOUTOU CHARIN (τούτου χάριν), for this cause, not simply as a reason, as in the preceding phrase, but in favour of, Eph. 3 : 1, 14 ; Tit. 1 : 5.

" For this very cause "

AUTO TOUTO (αὐτὸ τοῦτο), lit., (as to) this very thing, 2 Pet. 1 : 5.

Notes : (1) This phrase often represents one containing aitia (see above).

(2) In John 18 : 37, eis touto, unto this, denotes " unto this end," R.V. (A.V., " for this cause ").

(3) For the phrase " for which cause " (dio), Rom. 15 : 22 ; 2 Cor. 4 : 16, see WHEREFORE, Note (2) (R.V.).

(4) In Phil. 2 : 18, to auto, is rendered " for the same cause," A.V. ; R.V., " in the same manner."

" without a cause "

DŌREAN (δωρεάν), lit., as a gift, gratis, (connected with dōron, a gift), is rendered " without a cause," John 15 : 25 ; " for nought," 2 Cor. 11 : 7 ; Gal. 2 : 21 ; 2 Thess. 3 : 8 ; " freely," Matt. 10 : 8 ; Rom. 3 : 24 ; Rev. 21 : 6 ; 22 : 17.¶

Notes : (1) Eikē, " in vain," " without a cause," Matt. 5 : 22 (A.V.), is absent from the most authentic mss.

(2) For " cause," in Acts 25 : 14, A.V., see CASE.

(3) In 2 Cor. 5 : 13 (R.V., " unto you "), the A.V. has " for your cause."

B. Verbs.

1. POIEŌ (ποιέω), to do, is translated by the verb to cause in John 11 : 37 ; Acts 15 : 3 ; Rom. 16 : 17 ; Col. 4 : 16 ; Rev. 13 : 15, 16. See Do.

2. DIDŌMI (δίδωμι), to give, is translated " cause " in 1 Cor. 9 : 12, R.V., for A.V., " (lest we) should."

Notes : (1) In Matt. 5 : 32 the R.V. translates *poieō* " maketh (her an adulteress) : " in Rev. 13 : 12, R.V., " maketh," for A.V., " causeth."

(2) In 2 Cor. 9 : 11, *katergazomai*, to work, is translated " causeth " in the A.V. ; R.V., " worketh."

(3) In 2 Cor. 2 : 14, *thriambeuō* is rendered " causeth us to triumph," A.V. ; R.V., " leadeth us in triumph," the metaphor being taken from the circumstances of the procession of a Roman " triumph."

CAVE

1. OPĒ (ὀπή), perhaps from ōps, sight, denotes a hole, an opening, such as a fissure in a rock, Heb. 11 : 38. In Jas. 3 : 11, the R.V. has " opening," of the orifice of a fountain (A.V., " place "). See PLACE.¶

2. SPĒLAION (σπήλαιον), a grotto, cavern, den (Lat., *spelunca*), " cave," John 11 : 38, is said of the grave of Lazarus ; in the R.V. in Heb. 11 : 38 and Rev. 6 : 15 (A.V., " dens ") ; in the Lord's rebuke concerning the defilement of the Temple, Matt. 21 : 13 ; Mark 11 : 17 ; Luke 19 : 46, " den " is used.¶

CEASE
A. Verbs.

1. PAUŌ (παύω), to stop, to make an end, is used chiefly in the Middle Voice in the N.T., signifying to come to an end, to take one's rest, a willing cessation (in contrast to the Passive Voice which denotes a forced cessation), Luke 5 : 4, of a discourse ; 8 : 24, of a storm ; 11 : 1, of Christ's prayer ; Acts 5 : 42, of teaching and preaching ; 6 : 13, of speaking against ; 13 : 10, of evil doing ; 20 : 1, of an uproar ; 20 : 31, of admonition ; 21 : 32, of a scourging ; 1 Cor. 13 : 8, of tongues ; Eph. 1 : 16, of giving thanks ; Col. 1 : 9, of prayer ; Heb. 10 : 2, of sacrifices ; 1 Pet. 4 : 1, of ceasing from sin. It is used in the Active Voice in 1 Pet. 3 : 10, ' let him cause his tongue to cease from evil.' See LEAVE, REFRAIN.¶

2. DIALEIPŌ (διαλείπω), lit., to leave between, i.e., to leave an interval, whether of space or time (*dia*, between, *leipō*, to leave) ; hence, to intermit, desist, cease, in Luke 7 : 45 is used of the kissing of the Lord's feet.¶

3. HĒSUCHAZŌ (ἡσυχάζω), to be quiet, still, at rest, is said of Paul's friends in Cæsarea, in ceasing to persuade him not to go to Jerusalem, Acts 21 : 14 ; it is used of silence (save in Luke 23 : 56 and 1 Thess. 4 : 11) in Luke 14 : 4 and Acts 11 : 18. See PEACE (hold one's), QUIET, REST.¶

4. KOPAZŌ (κοπάζω), to cease through being spent with toil, to cease raging (from *kopos*, labour, toil, *kopiaō*, to labour), is said of the wind only, Matt. 14 : 32 ; Mark 4 : 39 ; 6 : 51.¶

5. APHIĔMI (ἀφίημι), to let go, is translated " let us cease to " in

Heb. 6 : 1, R.V. (marg., " leave ") for A.V., " leaving." See FORGIVE, LEAVE.

6. KATAPAUŌ (καταπαύω), to rest (kata, down, intensive, and No. 1), is so translated in Heb. 4 : 10, for the A.V. " hath ceased." See REST, RESTRAIN.

Notes : (1) *Katargeō*, to render inactive, to bring to naught, to do away, is so rendered in Gal. 5 : 11, R.V., for the A.V. " ceased." See ABOLISH.

(2) *Akatapaustos*, incessant, not to be set at rest (from *a*, negative, *kata*, down, *pauō*, to cease), is used in 2 Pet. 2 : 14, of those who " cannot cease " from sin, i.e., who cannot be restrained from sinning.¶

B. Adjective.

ADIALEIPTOS (ἀδιάλειπτος), unceasing (from *a*, negative, *dia*, through, *leipō*, to leave), is used of incessant heart pain, Rom. 9 : 2, A.V., " continual," R.V., " unceasing," and in 2 Tim. 1 : 3, of remembrance in prayer ; the meaning in each place is not that of unbroken continuity, but without the omission of any occasion. Cp. A, No. 2. See CONTINUAL.¶

C. Adverb.

ADIALEIPTŌS (ἀδιαλείπτως), unceasingly, without ceasing, is used with the same significance as the adjective, not of what is not interrupted, but of that which is constantly recurring ; in Rom. 1 : 9 and 1 Thess. 5 : 17, of prayer ; in 1 Thess. 1 : 3, of the remembrance of the work, labour and patience of saints ; in 1 Thess. 2 : 13, of thanksgiving.¶

Note : *Ektenēs*, lit., stretched out, signifies earnest, fervent ; Acts 12 : 5, R.V., for A.V., " without ceasing." See 1 Pet. 4 : 8, " fervent."¶

For CELESTIAL see HEAVEN, HEAVENLY, B, No. 2

CELL

OIKĒMA (οἴκημα), lit., a habitation (akin to *oikeō*, to dwell), is euphemistically put for a prison, in Acts 12 : 7, R.V., " cell." See PRISON.¶

CELLAR

KRUPTĒ (κρυπτή),—Eng., crypt -a covered way or vault (akin to *kruptos*, hidden, secret), is used in Luke 11 : 33, of lighting a lamp and putting it " in a cellar," R.V. See PLACE, *Note* (8).¶

CENSER

1. THUMIATĒRION (θυμιατήριον), a vessel ior burning incense (2 Chron. 26 : 19 ; Ezek. 8 : 11), is found in Heb. 9 : 4.¶

2. LIBANŌTOS (λιβανωτός) denotes frankincense, the gum of the *libanos*, the frankincense tree ; in a secondary sense, a vessel in which to burn incense, Rev. 8 : 3, 5.¶

Note : No. 1 derives its significance from the act of burning (*thumiaō*) ; No. 2 from that which was burned in the vessel.

CENTURION

1. HEKATONTARCHOS (ἑκατόνταρχος), a centurion, denotes a military officer commanding from 50 to 100 men, according to the size of the legion of which it was a part (hekaton, a hundred, archō, to rule), e.g., Matt. 8 : 5, 8.

2. HEKATONTARCHĒS (ἑκατοντάρχης) has the same meaning as No. 1, e.g., Acts 10 : 1, 22. The Sept. has this word frequently, to denote captains of hundreds.

3. KENTURION (κεντυρίων) is a Greek transliteration of the Latin centurio, signifying practically the same as No. 1, Mark 15 : 39, 44, 45. There were ten centurions to a cohort when the numbers were complete. There were several at Jerusalem under the chief captain mentioned in Acts 21 : 31.¶

CERTAIN, CERTAINTY, CERTAINLY, CERTIFY
A. Noun.

ASPHALEIA (ἀσφάλεια), primarily, not liable to fall, stedfast, firm, hence denoting safety, Acts 5 : 23, and 1 Thess. 5 : 3, has the further meaning, "certainty," Luke 1 : 4. See SAFETY.¶

B. Adjective.

ASPHALĒS (ἀσφαλής), safe, is translated "certainty," Acts 21 : 34 ; 22 : 30 ; "certain," Acts 25 : 26 ; "safe," Phil. 3 : 1 ; "sure," Heb. 6 : 19. See SAFE, SURE.¶

Notes : (1) Dēlos, evident, visible, is translated "certain" in 1 Tim. 6 : 7, A.V. The most authentic mss. omit it.

(2) The rendering "certain," is frequently changed in the R.V., or omitted, e.g., Luke 5 : 12 ; 8 : 22 ; Acts 23 : 17 ; Heb. 2 : 6 ; 4 : 4.

(3) The indefinite pronoun tis signifies anyone, some one, a certain one ; the neuter, ti, a certain thing, e.g., Matt. 20 : 20 ; Mark 14 : 51.

(4) In the A.V. of Gal. 1 : 11, gnōrizō is rendered "certify," R.V., "to make known."

(5) For "a certain island," Acts 27 : 16, see the R.V., "small island."

(6) In 1 Cor. 4 : 11, the verb astateō, to be unsettled, to lead a homeless life, is rendered "we . . . have no certain dwelling place." The unsettlement conveyed by the word has suggested the meaning "we are vagabonds" or "we lead a vagabond life," a probable significance.¶

C. Adverbs.

1. ONTŌS (ὄντως), really, actually, verily (from eimi, to be), is translated "certainly" in Luke 23 : 47. See CLEAN, INDEED, TRUTH, VERILY.

2. PANTŌS (πάντως) : see ALTOGETHER, B.

CHAFF

ACHURON (ἄχυρον), chaff, the stalk of the grain from which the kernels have been beaten out, or the straw broken up by a threshing machine, is found in Matt. 3 : 12 and Luke 3 : 17.¶

CHAIN

HALUSIS (ἅλυσις) denotes a chain or bond for binding the body, or any part of it (the hands or feet). Some derive the word from *a*, negative, and *luō*, to loose, i.e., not to be loosed ; others from a root connected with a word signifying to restrain. It is used in Mark 5 : 3, 4 ; Luke 8 : 29 ; Acts 12 : 6, 7 ; 21 : 33 ; 28 : 20 ; Eph. 6 : 20 ; 2 Tim. 1 : 16 ; Rev. 20 : 1. See BOND.¶

Notes : (1) Some ancient authorities have *seira*, a cord, rope, band, chain, in 2 Pet. 2 : 4, instead of *seiros*, a cavern, R.V., " pits."

(2) In Jude 6 the R.V. renders *desmos* by " bonds " (for the A.V. " chains "). See BOND.¶

CHALCEDONY

CHALKĒDŌN (χαλκηδών), the name of a gem, including several varieties, one of which resembles a cornelian, is " supposed to denote a green silicate of copper found in the mines near Chalcedon " (*Swete, on the Apocalypse*), Rev. 21 : 19.¶

CHAMBER (Store-chamber)

1. TAMEION (ταμεῖον) denotes, firstly, a store-chamber, then, any private room, secret chamber, Matt. 6 : 6 ; R.V., " inner chamber " (A.V., " closet ") ; 24 : 26, " inner (A.V., secret) chambers ; " Luke 12 : 3, R.V., ditto, for A.V., " closets ; " it is used in Luke 12 : 24 (" store-chamber ") of birds.¶

2. HUPERŌON (ὑπερῷον), the neuter of *huperōos*, " above," denotes an upper room, upper chamber (*huper*, above), Acts 1 : 13 ; 9 : 37, 39 ; 20 : 8. See ROOM.¶

CHAMBERING

KOITĒ (κοίτη), primarily a place in which to lie down, hence, a bed, especially the marriage bed, denotes, in Rom. 13 : 13, illicit intercourse. See BED, CONCEIVE.

CHAMBERLAIN

HO EPI TOU KOITŌNOS, lit., the (one) over the bedchamber (*epi*, over, *koitōn*, a bedchamber), denotes a chamberlain, an officer who had various duties in the houses of kings and nobles. The importance of the position is indicated by the fact that the people of Tyre and Sidon sought the favour of Herod Agrippa through the mediation of Blastus, Acts 12 : 20.

Note : In Rom. 16 : 23, *oikonomos*, a person who manages the domestic affairs of a family, in general, a manager, a steward, is translated " chamberlain " in the A.V., which the R.V. corrects to " treasurer."

CHANCE

1. SUNKURIA (συγκυρία), lit., a meeting together with, a coincidence of circumstances, a happening, is translated " chance " in Luke 10 : 31. But concurrence of events is what the word signifies, rather than chance.¶

Note : Some texts have *tucha* here (from *tunchanō*, to happen).

2. EI TUCHOI (εἰ τύχοι), lit., ' if it may happen ' (*ei*, if, *tunchanō*, to happen), signifies " it may chance," 1 Cor. 15 : 37.¶

CHANGE (Noun and Verb)

A. Noun.

METATHESIS (μετάθεσις), a transposition, or a transference from one place to another (from *meta*, implying change, and *tithēmi*, to put), has the meaning of change in Heb. 7 : 12, in connection with the necessity of a change of the Law (or, as margin, law), if the priesthood is changed (see B, No. 3). It is rendered " translation " in 11 : 5, " removing " in 12 : 27. See REMOVING, TRANSLATION.¶

B. Verbs.

1. ALLASSŌ (ἀλλάσσω), to make other than it is (from *allos*, another), to transform, change, is used (*a*) of the effect of the Gospel upon the precepts of the Law, Acts 6 : 14 ; (*b*) of the effect, on the body of a believer, of Christ's Return, 1 Cor. 15 : 51, 52 ; (*c*) of the final renewal of the material creation, Heb. 1 : 12 ; (*d*) of a change in the Apostle's mode of speaking (or dealing), Gal. 4 : 20. In Rom. 1 : 23 it has its other meaning, to exchange.¶

2. METALLASSŌ (μεταλλάσσω), from *meta*, implying change, and No. 1, to change one thing for another, or into another, Rom. 1 : 25, 26, is translated " exchange " in ver. 25. See EXCHANGE.¶

3. METATITHĒMI (μετατίθημι), to place differently, to change, (akin to A, above), is said of priesthood, Heb. 7 : 12. See CARRY, No. 5.

4. METABALLŌ (μεταβάλλω), *meta*, as in No. 2, and *ballō*, to throw, signifies to turn quickly, or, in the Middle Voice, to change one's mind, and is found in Acts 28 : 6.¶

Notes : (1) In Phil. 3 : 21, for the A.V. rendering of *metaschēmatizō*, " change," the R.V. has " fashion anew ; " in 2 Cor. 3 : 18 *metamorphoō* is rendered " change," in the A.V. (R.V., " transform ").

(2) For *metanoia*, a change of mind, see REPENTANCE.

CHANGER (Money-changer)

1. KOLLUBISTĒS (κολλυβιστής), from *kollubos* (lit., clipped), a small coin or rate of change (*koloboō* signifies to cut off, to clip, shorten, Matt. 24 : 22), denotes a money-changer, lit., money-clipper, Matt. 21 : 12 ; Mark 11 : 15 ; John 2 : 15.¶

2. KERMATISTĒS (κερματιστής), from *kermatizō* (not found in the N.T.), to cut into small pieces, to make small change (*kerma* signifies a small coin, John 2 : 15 ; akin to *keirō*, to cut short). In the court of the

Gentiles, in the Temple precincts, were the seats of those who sold selected and approved animals for sacrifice, and other things. The magnitude of this traffic had introduced the bankers' or brokers' business, John 2 : 14.¶

CHARGE (Nouns, Adjective and Verbs), CHARGEABLE
A. Nouns.
(a) With the meaning of an accusation.

1. AITIA (αἰτία), a cause, accusation, is rendered "charges" in Acts 25 : 27 (A.V., "crimes"); cp. ver. 18. See ACCUSATION, CAUSE.

2. AITIŌMA (αἰτίωμα), in some texts aitiama, denotes a charge, Acts 25 : 7. See ACCUSATION, A, No. 2.

3. ENKLĒMA (ἔγκλημα) : see ACCUSATION, A, No. 3.

(b) With the meaning of something committed or bestowed.

4. KLĒROS (κλῆρος), a lot, allotment, heritage (whence Eng. "clergy"), is translated in 1 Pet. 5 : 3, R.V., "the charge allotted to you;" here the word is in the plural, lit., 'charges.' See INHERITANCE, LOT, PART.

5. OPSŌNION (ὀψώνιον), from opson, meat, and ōneomai, to buy, primarily signified whatever is brought to be eaten with bread, provisions, supplies for an army, soldier's pay, "charges," 1 Cor. 9 : 7, of the service of a soldier. It is rendered "wages" in Luke 3 : 14; Rom. 6 : 23; 2 Cor. 11 : 8. See WAGES.¶

6. PARANGELIA (παραγγελία), a proclamation, a command or commandment, is strictly used of commands received from a superior and transmitted to others. It is rendered "charge" in Acts. 16 : 24; 1 Thess. 4 : 2, R.V. (where the word is in the plural); 1 Tim. 1 : 5 (R.V.) and ver. 18. In Acts 5 : 28 the lit. meaning is 'Did we not charge you with a charge?' See also COMMANDMENT, STRAITLY. Cp. C, No. 8, below.¶

B. Adjective.

ADAPANOS (ἀδάπανος), lit., 'without expense' (a, negative, and dapanē, expense, cost), is used in 1 Cor. 9 : 18, "without charge" (of service in the Gospel).¶

C. Verbs.

1. DIAMARTUROMAI (διαμαρτύρομαι), a strengthened form of marturomai (dia, through, intensive), is used in the Middle Voice; primarily it signifies to testify through and through, bear a solemn witness; hence, to charge earnestly, 1 Tim. 5 : 21; 2 Tim. 2 : 14; 4 : 1. See TESTIFY, WITNESS.

2. DIASTELLOMAI (διαστέλλομαι), lit., to draw asunder (dia, asunder, steliō, to draw), signifies to admonish, order, charge, Matt. 16 : 20; Mark 5 : 43; 7 : 36 (twice); 8 : 15; 9 : 9. In Acts 15 : 24 it is translated "gave commandment;" in Heb. 12 : 20, A.V., "commanded," R.V., "enjoined." See COMMAND, Note (2).¶

3. DIATASSŌ (διατάσσω) : see APPOINT, No. 6.

4. EMBRIMAOMAI (ἐμβριμάομαι), from *en*, in, intensive, and *brimē*, strength, primarily signifies to snort with anger, as of horses. Used of men it signifies to fret, to be painfully moved ; then, to express indignation against ; hence, to rebuke sternly, to charge strictly, Matt. 9 : 30 ; Mark 1 : 43 ; it is rendered " murmured against " in Mark 14 : 5 ; " groaned " in John 11 : 33 ; " groaning " in ver. 38. See GROAN, MURMUR.¶

5. ENKALEŌ (ἐγκαλέω) : see ACCUSE, B, No. 2.

6. ENTELLOMAI (ἐντέλλομαι), to order, command, enjoin (from *en*, in, used intensively, and *teleō*, to fulfil), is translated by the verb to give charge, Matt. 4 : 6 ; 17 : 9 (A.V.) ; Luke 4 : 10. See COMMAND, ENJOIN.

7. EPITIMAŌ (ἐπιτιμάω) signifies (*a*) to put honour upon (*epi*, upon, *timē*, honour) ; (*b*) to adjudge, to find fault with, rebuke ; hence to charge, or rather, to charge strictly (*epi*, intensive), e.g., Matt. 12 : 16 ; Mark 3 : 12, " charged much ; " Mark 8 : 30 ; in 10 : 48, R.V., " rebuked." See REBUKE.

8. PARANGELLŌ (παραγγέλλω), lit., to announce beside (*para*, beside, *angellō*, to announce), to hand on an announcement from one to another, usually denotes to command, to charge, Luke 5 : 14 ; 8 : 56 ; 1 Cor. 7 : 10 (A.V., " command "), " give charge," R.V. ; 11 : 17, " in giving you this charge," R.V. ; 1 Tim. 1 : 3 ; 6 : 13, R.V., and 6 : 17. It is rendered by the verb to charge in the R.V. of Acts 1 : 4 ; 4 : 18 ; 5 : 28 ; 15 : 5 ; 1 Thess. 4 : 11. See Acts 5 : 28 under A, No. 6. See COMMAND, DECLARE.

9. PROAITIAOMAI (προαιτιάομαι), to accuse beforehand, to have already brought a charge (*pro*, before, *aitia*, an accusation), is used in Rom. 3 : 9, " we before laid to the charge."¶

10. TĒREŌ (τηρέω), to keep, to guard, is translated " to be kept in charge," in Acts 24 : 23 ; 25 : 4, R.V. (A.V., " kept "). See HOLD, KEEP, OBSERVE, PRESERVE, WATCH.

Notes : (1) *Martureō*, to testify, translated " charged " in 1 Thess. 2 : 11, A.V., is found there in the most authentic mss. and translated " testifying " in the R.V. (2) *Enorkizō*, to adjure (*en*, in, used intensively, *horkos*, an oath), is translated " I adjure," in 1 Thess. 5 : 27, R.V., for A.V., " I charge." Some mss. have *horkizō* here. (3) The following are translated by the verb to charge or to be chargeable in the A.V., but differently in the R.V., and will be found under the word BURDEN : *bareō*, B, No. 1 ; *epibareō*, B, No. 2 ; *katanarkaō*, B, No. 5. (4) *Epitassō*, to command, is so translated in Mark 9 : 25, R.V., for the A.V., " charge." (5) *Dapanaō*, to be at the expense of anything (cp. B, above), is translated " be at charges," in Acts 21 : 24. See CONSUME, SPEND. (6) In 2 Tim. 4 : 16, *logizomai* is rendered " laid to (their) charge," A.V. ; R.V., " . . . account." (7) In Acts 8 : 27, the R.V. translates the verb *eimi*, to be, with *epi*, over, " was over," A.V., " had the charge of." (8) In Acts 7 : 60 *histēmi*, to cause to stand, is rendered " lay . . . to the charge."

CHARGER

PINAX (πίναξ), primarily a board or plank, came to denote various articles of wood ; hence, a wooden trencher, charger, Matt. 14 : 8, 11 ; Mark 6 : 25, 28 ; Luke 11 : 39. See PLATTER.¶

CHARIOT

1. HARMA (ἅρμα), akin to *arariskō*, to join, denotes a war chariot with two wheels, Acts 8 : 28, 29, 38 ; Rev. 9 : 9.¶

2. RHEDĒ (ῥέδη), a waggon with four wheels, was chiefly used for travelling purposes, Rev. 18 : 13.¶

For CHARITY see LOVE

CHASTE

HAGNOS (ἁγνός) signifies (a) pure from every fault, immaculate, 2 Cor. 7 : 11 (A.V., " clear ") ; Phil. 4 : 8 ; 1 Tim. 5 : 22 ; Jas. 3 : 17 ; 1 John 3 : 3 (in all which the R.V. rendering is " pure "), and 1 Pet. 3 : 2, " chaste ; " (b) pure from carnality, modest, 2 Cor. 11 : 2, R.V., " pure ; " Tit. 2 : 5, " chaste." See CLEAR, HOLY, PURE.¶

Note : Cp. *hagios*, holy, as being free from admixture of evil ; *hosios*, holy, as being free from defilement ; *eilikrinēs*, pure, as being tested, lit., judged by the sunlight ; *katharos*, pure, as being cleansed.

CHASTEN, CHASTENING, CHASTISE, CHASTISEMENT

A. Verb.

PAIDEUŌ (παιδεύω) primarily denotes to train children, suggesting the broad idea of education (*pais*, a child), Acts 7 : 22 ; 22 : 3 ; see also Tit. 2 : 12, " instructing " (R.V.), here of a training gracious and firm ; grace, which brings salvation, employs means to give us full possession of it ; hence, to chastise, this being part of the training, whether (a) by correcting with words, reproving, and admonishing, 1 Tim. 1 : 20 (R.V., " be taught ") ; 2 Tim. 2 : 25, or (b) by chastening by the infliction of evils and calamities, 1 Cor. 11 : 32 ; 2 Cor. 6 : 9 ; Heb. 12 : 6, 7, 10 ; Rev. 3 : 19. The verb also has the meaning to chastise with blows, to scourge, said of the command of a judge, Luke 23 : 16, 22. See CORRECTION, B, INSTRUCT, LEARN, TEACH, and cp. CHILD (Nos. 4 to 6).¶

B. Noun.

PAIDEIA (παιδεία) denotes the training of a child, including instruction ; hence, discipline, correction, " chastening," Eph. 6 : 4, R.V. (A.V., " nurture "), suggesting the Christian discipline that regulates character; so in Heb. 12 : 5, 7, 8 (in ver. 8, A.V., " chastisement," the R.V. corrects to " chastening ") ; in 2 Tim. 3 : 16, " instruction." See INSTRUCTION, NURTURE.¶

CHEEK

SIAGŌN (σιαγών) primarily denotes the jaw, the jaw-bone ; hence "cheek," Matt. 5 : 39 ; Luke 6 : 29.¶

CHEER, CHEERFUL, CHEERFULLY, CHEERFULNESS
A. Verbs.

1. EUTHUMEŌ (εὐθυμέω) signifies, in the Active Voice, to put in good spirits, to make cheerful (*eu*, well, *thumos*, mind or passion) ; or, intransitively, to be cheerful, Acts 27 : 22, 25 ; Jas. 5 : 13 (R.V., "cheerful," for A.V., "merry"). See MERRY.¶

2. THARSEŌ (θαρσέω), to be of good courage, of good cheer (*tharsos*, courage, confidence), is used only in the Imperative Mood, in the N.T. ; "be of good cheer," Matt. 9 : 2, 22 ; 14 : 27 ; Mark 6 : 50 ; 10 : 49 ; Luke 8 : 48 ; John 16 : 33 ; Acts 23 : 11. See BOLD, A, No. 1, COMFORT, COURAGE.¶

B. Adjectives.

1. EUTHUMOS (εὔθυμος) means of good cheer (see A, No. 1), Acts 27 : 36.¶

2. HILAROS (ἱλαρός), from *hileōs*, propitious, signifies that readiness of mind, that joyousness, which is prompt to do anything ; hence, cheerful (Eng., hilarious), 2 Cor. 9 : 7, " God loveth a cheerful (hilarious) giver."¶

Note : In the Sept. the verb *hilarunō* translates a Hebrew word meaning " to cause to shine," in Ps. 104 : 15.¶

C. Adverb.

EUTHUMŌS (εὐθύμως), cheerfully (see A, No. 1), is found in the most authentic mss., in Acts 24 : 10, instead of the comparative degree, *euthumoteron*.¶

D. Noun.

HILAROTĒS (ἱλαρότης), cheerfulness (akin to B, No. 2), is used in Rom. 12 : 8, in connection with shewing mercy.¶

CHERISH

THALPŌ (θάλπω) primarily means to heat, to soften by heat ; then, to keep warm, as of birds covering their young with their feathers, Deut. 22 : 6, Sept. ; metaphorically, to cherish with tender love, to foster with tender care, in Eph. 5 : 29 of Christ and the Church ; in 1 Thess. 2 : 7 of the care of the saints at Thessalonica by the Apostle and his associates, as of a nurse for her children.¶

CHERUBIM

CHEROUBIM (χερουβίμ) are regarded by some as the ideal representatives of redeemed animate creation. In the Tabernacle and Temple they were represented by the two golden figures of two-winged living-creatures. They were all of one piece with the golden lid of the Ark of the Covenant in the Holy of Holies, signifying that the prospect of redeemed and glorified creatures was bound up with the sacrifice of Christ.

This in itself would indicate that they represent redeemed human beings in union with Christ, a union seen, figuratively, proceeding out of the Mercy Seat. Their faces were towards this Mercy Seat, suggesting a consciousness of the means whereby union with Christ has been produced.

The first reference to the cherubim is in Gen. 3 : 24, which should read '. . . at the East of the Garden of Eden He caused to dwell in a tabernacle the cherubim, and the flaming sword which turned itself to keep the way of the Tree of Life.' This was not simply to keep fallen human beings out ; the presence of the cherubim suggests that redeemed men, restored to God on God's conditions, would have access to the Tree of Life. (See Rev. 22 : 14).

Certain other references in the O.T. give clear indication that angelic beings are upon occasion in view, e.g., Psalm 18 : 10 ; Ezek. 28 : 4. So with the Vision of the Cherubim in Ezek. 10 : 1–20 ; 11 : 22. In the N.T. the word is found in Heb. 9 : 5, where the reference is to the Ark in the Tabernacle, and the thought is suggested of those who minister to the manifestation of the glory of God.

We may perhaps conclude, therefore, that, inasmuch as in the past and in the present angelic beings have functioned and do function administratively in the service of God, and that redeemed man in the future is to act administratively in fellowship with Him, the Cherubim in Scripture represent one or other of these two groups of created beings according to what is set forth in the various passages relating to them. ¶

For CHICKEN see BROOD

CHIEF, CHIEFEST, CHIEFLY
A. Adjective.

PRŌTOS (πρῶτος) denotes the first, whether in time or place. It is translated " chief " in Mark 6 : 21, R.V., of men of Galilee ; in Acts 13 : 50, of men in a city ; in 28 : 7, of the chief man in the island of Melita ; in 17 : 4, of chief women in a city ; in 28 : 17, of Jews ; in 1 Tim. 1 : 15, 16, of a sinner. In the following, where the A.V. has " chief," or " chiefest," the R.V. renderings are different : Matt. 20 : 27 and Mark 10 : 44, " first ; " Luke 19 : 47 and Acts 25 : 2, " principal men ; " Acts 16 : 12, said of Philippi, " the first (city) of the district," R.V., for incorrect A.V., " the chief city of that part of Macedonia." Amphipolis was the chief city of that part. *Prōtos* here must mean the first in the direction in which the Apostle came. See BEGINNING, BEFORE, BEST, FIRST, FORMER.

B. Nouns.

1. KEPHALAION (κεφάλαιον), akin to the adjective *kephalaios*,

belonging to the head, and *kephalē*, the head, denotes the chief point or principal thing in a subject, Heb. 8 : 1, " the chief point is this " (A.V., " the sum ") ; elsewhere in Acts 22 : 28 (of principal, as to money), " (a great) sum." See SUM.¶

Certain compound nouns involving the significance of chief, are as follows :

2. ARCHIEREUS (ἀρχιερεύς), a chief priest, high priest (*archē*, first, *hiereus*, a priest), is frequent in the Gospels, Acts and Hebrews, but there only in the N.T. It is used of Christ, e.g., in Heb. 2 : 17 ; 3 : 1 ; of chief priests, including ex-high-priests and members of their families, e.g., Matt. 2 : 4 ; Mark 8 : 31.

3. ARCHIPOIMĒN (ἀρχιποίμην), a chief shepherd (*archē*, chief, *poimēn*, a shepherd), is said of Christ only, 1 Pet. 5 : 4. Modern Greeks use it of tribal chiefs.¶

4. ARCHITELŌNĒS (ἀρχιτελώνης) denotes a chief tax-collector, or publican, Luke 19 : 2.¶

5. AKROGŌNIAIOS (ἀκρογωνιαῖος) denotes a chief corner-stone (from *akros*, highest, extreme, *gōnia*, a corner, angle), Eph. 2 : 20 and 1 Pet. 2 : 6.¶ In the Sept., Is. 28 : 16.¶

6. PRŌTOKATHEDRIA (πρωτοκαθεδρία), a sitting in the first or chief seat (*prōtos*, first, *kathedra*, a seat), is found in Matt. 23 : 6 ; Mark 12 : 39 ; Luke 11 : 43 ; 20 : 46.¶

7. PRŌTOKLISIA (πρωτοκλισία), the first reclining place, the chief place at table (from *prōtos*, and *klisia*, a company reclining at a meal ; cp. *klinō*, to incline), is found in Matt. 23 : 6 ; Mark 12 : 39 (as with No. 6) ; Luke 14 : 7, 8 ; 20 : 46.¶

8. CHILIARCHOS (χιλίαρχος) denotes a chief captain : see CAPTAIN, No. 1.

9. ASIARCHĒS ('Ασιαρχής), an Asiarch, was one of certain officers elected by various cities in the province of Asia, whose function consisted in celebrating, partly at their own expense, the public games and festivals ; in Acts 19 : 31, R.V., the word is translated " chief officers of Asia " (A.V., " chief of Asia ").

It seems probable, according to Prof. Ramsay, that they were " the high priests of the temples of the Imperial worship in various cities of Asia ; " further, that " the Council of the Asiarchs sat at stated periods in the great cities alternately . . . and were probably assembled at Ephesus for such a purpose when they sent advice to St. Paul to consult his safety." A festival would have brought great crowds to the city.¶

10. ARCHŌN (ἄρχων), a ruler, is rendered " chief " in the A.V. of Luke 14 : 1 (R.V., " ruler ") ; " chief rulers," in John 12 : 42, R.V., " rulers (of the people)," i.e., of members of the Sanhedrin ; " chief," in Luke 11 : 15 (R.V., " prince "), in reference to Beelzebub, the prince of demons. See MAGISTRATE, PRINCE, RULER.

11. ARCHISUNAGŌGOS (ἀρχισυνάγωγος), a ruler of a synagogue,

translated " chief ruler of the synagogue," in Acts 18 : 8, 17, A.V., was the administrative officer supervising the worship.

C. Verb.

HĒGEOMAI (ἡγέομαι), to lead the way, to preside, rule, be the chief, is used of the ambition to be chief among the disciples of Christ, Luke 22 : 26 ; of Paul as the chief speaker in Gospel testimony at Lystra, Acts 14 : 12 ; of Judas and Silas, as chief (or rather, ' leading ') men among the brethren at Jerusalem, Acts 15 : 22. See ACCOUNT, COUNT, ESTEEM, GOVERNOR, JUDGE, SUPPOSE, THINK.

D. Adverbs.

1. HUPERLIAN (ὑπερλίαν), chiefest (huper, over, lian, exceedingly, pre-eminently, very much), is used in 2 Cor. 11 : 5 ; 12 : 11, of Paul's place among the Apostles.¶

2. MALISTA (μάλιστα), the superlative of mala, very, very much, is rendered " chiefly " in 2 Pet. 2 : 10 and in the A.V. of Phil. 4 : 22 (R.V., " especially "). See ESPECIALLY, MOST.

Note : In Rom. 3 : 2, R.V., the adverb prōton is translated " first of all " (A.V., " chiefly ").

CHILD, CHILDREN, CHILD-BEARING, CHILDISH, CHILDLESS

1. TEKNON (τέκνον), a child (akin to tiktō, to beget, bear), is used in both the natural and the figurative senses. In contrast to huios, son (see below), it gives prominence to the fact of birth, whereas huios stresses the dignity and character of the relationship. Figuratively, teknon is used of children of (a) God, John 1 : 12 ; (b) light, Eph. 5 : 8 ; (c) obedience, I Pet. 1 : 14 ; (d) a promise, Rom. 9 : 8 ; Gal. 4 : 28 ; (e) the Devil, I John 3 : 10 ; (f) wrath, Eph. 2 : 3 ; (g) cursing, 2 Pet. 2 : 14 ; (h) spiritual relationship, 2 Tim. 2 : 1 ; Philm. 10. See DAUGHTER, SON.

2. TEKNION (τεκνίον), a little child, a diminutive of No. 1, is used only figuratively in the N.T., and always in the plural. It is found frequently in I John, see 2 : 1, 12, 28 ; 3 : 7, 18 ; 4 : 4 ; 5 : 21 ; elsewhere, once in John's Gospel, 13 : 33, once in Paul's Epistles, Gal. 4 : 19. It is a term of affection by a teacher to his disciples under circumstances requiring a tender appeal, e.g., of Christ to the Twelve just before His death ; the Apostle John used it in warning believers against spiritual dangers ; Paul, because of the deadly errors of Judaism assailing the Galatian churches. Cp. his use of teknon in Gal. 4 : 28.¶

3. HUIOS (υἱός), a son, is always so translated in the R.V., except in the phrase " children of Israel," e.g., Matt. 27 : 9 ; and with reference to a foal, Matt. 21 : 5. The A.V. does not discriminate between teknon and huios. In the 1st Ep. of John, the Apostle reserves the word for the Son of God. See teknia, " little children " (above), and tekna, " children," in John 1 : 12 ; 11 : 52. See paidion (below). For the other use of huios, indicating the quality of that with which it is connected, see SON.

4. PAIS (παῖς) signifies (a) a child in relation to descent, (b) a boy or

girl in relation to age, (c) a servant, attendant, maid, in relation to condition. As an instance of (a) see Matt. 21 : 15, " children," and Acts 20 : 12 (R.V., " lad "). In regard to (b) the R.V. has " boy " in Matt. 17 : 18 and Luke 9 : 42. In Luke 2 : 43 it is used of the Lord Jesus. In regard to (c), see Matt. 8 : 6, 8, 13, etc. As to (a) note Matt. 2 : 16, R.V., " male children." See MAID, MANSERVANT, SERVANT, SON, YOUNG MAN.

5. PAIDION (παιδίον), a diminutive of *pais*, signifies a little or young child ; it is used of an infant just born, John 16 : 21 ; of a male child recently born, e.g., Matt. 2 : 8 ; Heb. 11 : 23 ; of a more advanced child, Mark 9 : 24 ; of a son, John 4 : 49 ; of a girl, Mark 5 : 39, 40, 41 ; in the plural, of children, e.g., Matt. 14 : 21. It is used metaphorically of believers who are deficient in spiritual understanding, 1 Cor. 14 : 20, and in affectionate and familiar address by the Lord to His disciples, almost like the Eng., " lads," John 21 : 5 ; by the Apostle John to the youngest believers in the family of God, 1 John 2 : 13, 18 ; there it is to be distinguished from *teknia*, which term he uses in addressing all his readers (vv. 1, 12, 28 : see *teknia*, above). See DAMSEL.

Note : The adverb *paidiothen*, " from (or of) a child," is found in Mark 9 : 21.¶

6. PAIDARION (παιδάριον), another diminutive of *pais*, is used of boys and girls, in Matt. 11 : 16 (the best texts have *paidiois* here), and a lad, John 6 : 9 ; the tendency in colloquial Greek was to lose the diminutive character of the word.¶

7. NĒPIOS (νήπιος), lit., not-speaking (from *nē*, a negative, and *epos*, a word is rendered " childish " in 1 Cor. 13 : 11 : see BABE.

8. MONOGENĒS (μονογενής), lit., only-begotten, is translated " only child " in Luke 9 : 38. See ONLY, ONLY-BEGOTTEN.

9. TEKNOGONIA (τεκνογονία), *teknon* and a root *gen*—, whence *gennaō*, to beget, denotes bearing children, implying the duties of motherhood, 1 Tim. 2 : 15.¶

B. Verbs.

1. NĒPIAZŌ (νηπιάζω), to be a babe, is used in 1 Cor. 14 : 20, " (in malice) be ye babes " (akin to No 7, above).¶

2. TEKNOTROPHEŌ (τεκνοτροφέω), to rear young, *teknon*, and *trephō*, to rear, signifies to bring up children, 1 Tim. 5 : 10.¶

3. TEKNOGONEŌ (τεκνογονέω), to bear children (*teknon*, and *gennaō*, to beget), see No. 9 above, is found in 1 Tim. 5 : 14.¶

C. Adjectives.

1. ENKUOS (ἔγκυος) denotes " great with child " (*en*, in, and *kuō*, to conceive), Luke 2 : 5.¶

2. PHILOTEKNOS (φιλότεκνος), from *phileō*, to love, and *teknon*, signifies loving one's children, Tit. 2 : 4.¶

3. ATEKNOS (ἄτεκνος), from *a*, negative, and *teknon*, signifies " childless," Luke 20 : 28, 29, 30.¶

Notes : (1) For *brephos*, a new born babe, always rendered " babe "

or " babes " in the R.V. (A.V., " young children ", Acts 7 : 19 ; " child,"
2 Tim. 3 : 15), see under BABE.

(2) *Huiothesia*, " adoption of children," in the A.V. of Eph. 1 : 5, is
corrected to " adoption as sons " in the R.V. See on ADOPTION.

CHOKE

1. PNIGŌ (πνίγω) is used, in the Passive Voice, of perishing by
drowning, Mark 5 : 13 ; in the Active, to seize a person's throat, to throttle,
Matt. 18 : 28. See THROAT.¶

2. APOPNIGŌ (ἀποπνίγω), a strengthened form of No. 1 (*apo*, from,
intensive ; cp. Eng., to choke off), is used metaphorically, of thorns
crowding out seed sown and preventing its growth, Matt. 13 : 7 ; Luke
8 : 7. It is Luke's word for suffocation by drowning, Luke 8 : 33 (cp.
Mark 5 : 13, above).¶

3. SUMPNIGŌ (συμπνίγω) gives the suggestion of choking together
(*sun*, with), i.e., by crowding, Matt. 13 : 22 ; Mark 4 : 7, 19 ; Luke 8 : 14.
It is used in Luke 8 : 42, of the crowd that thronged the Lord, almost,
so to speak, to suffocation.¶

CHOICE, CHOOSE, CHOSEN
A. Verbs.

1. EKLEGŌ (ἐκλέγω), to pick out, select, means, in the Middle Voice,
to choose for oneself, not necessarily implying the rejection of what is
not chosen, but choosing with the subsidiary ideas of kindness or favour
or love, Mark 13 : 20 ; Luke 6 · 13 ; 9 : 35 (R.V.) ; 10 · 42 ; 14 : 7 ;
John 6 : 70 ; 13 : 18 ; 15 : 16, 19 ; Acts 1 : 2, 24 ; 6 · 5 ; 13 : 17 ; 15 : 22,
25 ; in 15 : 7 it is rendered " made choice ; " 1 Cor. 1 : 27, 28 ; Eph. 1 : 4 ;
Jas. 2 : 5.¶

2. EPILEGŌ (ἐπιλέγω), in the Middle Voice, signifies to choose,
either in addition or in succession to another. It has this meaning in
Acts 15 : 40, of Paul's choice of Silas. For its other meaning, to call or
name, John 5 : 2, see CALL.¶

3. HAIREŌ (αἱρέω), to take, is used in the Middle Voice only, in the
sense of taking for oneself, choosing, 2 Thess. 2 : 13, of a choice made by
God (as in Deut. 7 : 6, 7 ; 26 : 18, Sept.) ; in Phil. 1 : 22 and Heb. 11 : 25,
of human choice. Its special significance is to select rather by the act of
taking, than by shewing preference or favour.¶

4. HAIRETIZŌ (αἱρετίζω), akin to the verbal adjective *hairetos*,
that which may be taken (see No. 3), signifies to take, with the implication
that what is taken is eligible or suitable ; hence, to choose, by reason of
this suitability, Matt. 12 : 18, of God's delight in Christ as His " chosen."¶
It is frequent in the Sept., e.g., Gen. 30 : 20 ; Num. 14 : 8 ; Psa. 25 : 12 ;
119 : 30, 173 ; 132 : 13, 14 ; Hos. 4 : 18 ; Hag. 2 : 23 (" he hath chosen the
Canaanites ") ; Zech. 1 : 17 ; 2 : 12 ; Mal. 3 : 17.

5. CHEIROTONEŌ (χειροτονέω) : see APPOINT, No. 11.

6. PROCHEIROTONEŌ (προχειροτονέω) signifies to choose before, Acts 10 : 41, where it is used of a choice made before by God.¶

Notes : (1) For *procheirizō* see APPOINT, No. 12.

(2) *Stratologeō*, in 2 Tim. 2 : 4 (A.V., " chosen to be a soldier "), signifies to enrol as a soldier (R.V.). See SOLDIER.

B. Adjective.

EKLEKTOS (ἐκλεκτός), akin to A, No. 1, signifies chosen out, select, e.g., Matt. 22 : 14 ; Luke 23 : 35 ; Rom 16 : 13 (perhaps in the sense of eminent) ; Rev. 17 : 14. In 1 Pet. 2 : 4, 9, the R.V. translates it " elect." See ELECT.

C. Noun.

EKLOGĒ (ἐκλογή), akin to A, No. 1 and B, a picking out, choosing (Eng., eclogue), is translated " chosen " in Acts 9 : 15, lit., ' he is a vessel of choice unto Me.' In the six other places where this word is found it is translated " election." See ELECTION.

CHRIST

CHRISTOS (χριστός), anointed, translates, in the Sept., the word Messiah, a term applied to the priests who were anointed with the holy oil, particularly the High Priest, e.g., Lev. 4 : 3, 5, 16. The prophets are called *hoi christoi Theou,* " the anointed of God," Psa. 105 : 15. A king of Israel was described upon occasion as *christos tou Kuriou,* " the anointed of the Lord," 1 Sam. 2 : 10, 35 ; 2 Sam. 1 : 14 ; Ps. 2 : 2 ; 18 : 50 ; Hab. 3 : 13 ; the term is used even of Cyrus, Is. 45 : 1.

The title *ho Christos,* " the Christ," is not used of Christ in the Sept. Version of the Inspired Books of the O.T. In the N.T. the word is frequently used with the article, of the Lord Jesus, as an appellative rather than a title, e.g., Matt. 2 : 4 ; Acts 2 : 31 ; without the article, Luke 2 : 11 ; 23 : 2 ; John 1 : 41. Three times the title was expressly accepted by the Lord Himself, Matt. 16 : 17 ; Mark 14 : 61, 62 ; John 4 : 26.

It is added as an appellative to the proper name " Jesus," e.g., John 17 : 3, the only time when the Lord so spoke of Himself ; Acts 9 : 34 ; 1 Cor. 3 : 11 ; 1 John 5 : 6. It is distinctly a proper name in many passages, whether with the article, e.g., Matt. 1 : 17 ; 11 : 2 ; Rom. 7 : 4 ; 9 : 5 ; 15 : 19 ; 1 Cor. 1 : 6, or without the article, Mark 9 : 41 ; Rom. 6 : 4 ; 8 : 9, 17 ; 1 Cor. 1 : 12 ; Gal. 2 : 16. The single title *Christos* is sometimes used without the article to signify the One who by His Holy Spirit and power indwells believers and moulds their character in conformity to His likeness, Rom. 8 : 10 ; Gal. 2 : 20 ; 4 : 19 ; Eph. 3 : 17. As to the use or absence of the article, the title with the article specifies the Lord Jesus as " the Christ ; " the title without the article stresses His character and His relationship with believers. Again, speaking generally, when the title is the subject of a sentence it has the article ; when it forms part of the predicate the article is absent. See also JESUS.

FALSE CHRISTS

PSEUDOCHRISTOS (ψευδόχριστος) denotes one who falsely lays claim to the Name and office of the Messiah, Matt. 24 : 24 ; Mark 13 : 22.¶ See Note under ANTICHRIST.

CHRISTIAN

CHRISTIANOS (χριστιανός), Christian, a word formed after the Roman style, signifying an adherent of Jesus, was first applied to such by the Gentiles and is found in Acts 11 : 26 ; 26 : 28 ; 1 Pet. 4 : 16.

Though the word rendered " were called " in Acts 11 : 26 (see under CALL) might be used of a name adopted by oneself or given by others, the Christians do not seem to have adopted it for themselves in the times of the Apostles. In 1 Pet. 4 : 16, the Apostle is speaking from the point of view of the persecutor ; cp. " as a thief," " as a murderer." Nor is it likely that the appellation was given by Jews. As applied by Gentiles there was no doubt an implication of scorn, as in Agrippa's statement in Acts 26 : 28. Tacitus, writing near the end of the first century, says, " The vulgar call them Christians. The author or origin of this denomination, Christus, had, in the reign of Tiberius, been executed by the Procurator, Pontius Pilate " (Annals xv. 44). From the second century onward the term was accepted by believers as a title of honour.¶

CHRYSOLITE

CHRUSOLITHOS (χρυσόλιθος), lit., a gold stone (chrusos, gold, lithos, a stone), is the name of a precious stone of a gold colour, now called a topaz, Rev. 21 : 20 (see also Ex. 28 : 20 and Ezek. 28 : 13).¶

CHRYSOPRASUS

CHRUSOPRASOS (χρυσόπρασος), from chrusos, gold, and prasos, a leek), is a precious stone like a leek in colour, a translucent, golden green. Pliny reckons it among the beryls. The word occurs in Rev. 21 : 20.¶

For CHURCH see ASSEMBLY and CONGREGATION

CINNAMON

KINNAMOMON (κιννάμωμον) is derived from an Arabic word signifying to emit a smell ; the substance was an ingredient in the holy oil for anointing, Ex. 30 : 23. See also Prov. 7 : 17 and S. of S. 4 : 14. In the N.T. it is found in Rev. 18 : 13. The cinnamon of the present day is the inner bark of an aromatic tree called *canella zeylanica*.¶

CIRCUIT

PERIERCHOMAI (περιέρχομαι), to go about (peri, about, erchomai, to go), is said of navigating a ship under difficulty owing to contrary winds, Acts 28 : 13, R.V., " we made a circuit," for A.V., " we fetched a compass." See COMPASS, STROLLING, WANDER.

CIRCUMCISION, UNCIRCUMCISION, CIRCUMCISE
A. Nouns.

1. PERITOME (περιτομή), lit., a cutting round, circumcision (the verb is *peritemnō*), was a rite enjoined by God upon Abraham and his male descendants and dependents, as a sign of the covenant made with him, Gen. 17 ; Acts 7 : 8 ; Rom. 4 : 11. Hence Israelites termed Gentiles " the uncircumcised," Judg. 15 : 18 ; 2 Sam. 1 : 20. So in the N.T., but without the suggestion of contempt, e.g., Rom. 2 : 26 ; Eph. 2 : 11.

The rite had a moral significance, Ex. 6 : 12, 30, where it is metaphorically applied to the lips ; so to the ear, Jer. 6 : 10, and the heart, Deut. 30 : 6 ; Jer. 4 : 4. Cp. Jer. 9 : 25, 26. It refers to the state of circumcision, in Rom. 2 : 25–28 ; 3 : 1 ; 4 : 10 ; 1 Cor. 7 : 19 ; Gal. 5 : 6 ; 6 : 15 ; Col. 3 : 11.

" In the economy of grace no account is taken of any ordinance performed on the flesh ; the old racial distinction is ignored in the preaching of the Gospel, and faith is the sole condition upon which the favour of God in salvation is to be obtained, Rom. 10 : 11–13; 1 Cor. 7 : 19. See also Rom. 4 : 9–12."*

Upon the preaching of the Gospel to, and the conversion of, Gentiles, a sect of Jewish believers arose who argued that the Gospel, without the fulfilment of circumcision, would make void the Law and make salvation impossible, Acts 15 : 1. Hence this party was known as " the circumcision," Acts 10 : 45 ; 11 : 2 ; Gal. 2 : 12 ; Col. 4 : 11 ; Tit. 1 : 10 (the term being used by metonymy, the abstract being put for the concrete, as with the application of the word to Jews generally, Rom. 3 : 30 ; 4 : 9, 12 ; 15 : 8 ; Gal. 2 : 7–9 ; Eph. 2 : 11). It is used metaphorically and spiritually of believers with reference to the act, Col. 2 : 11 and Rom. 2 : 29 ; to the condition, Phil. 3 : 3.

The Apostle Paul's defence of the truth, and his contention against this propaganda, form the main subject of the Galatian Epistle. Cp. *katatomē*, " concision," Phil. 3 : 2. See CONCISION.

2. AKROBUSTIA (ἀκροβυστια), uncircumcision, is used (a) of the physical state, in contrast to the act of circumcision, Acts 11 : 3 (lit., ' having uncircumcision ') ; Rom. 2 : 25, 26 ; 4 : 10, 11 (" though they be in uncircumcision," R.V.), 12 ; 1 Cor. 7 : 18, 19 ; Gal. 5 : 6 ; 6 : 15 ; Col. 3 : 11 ; (b) by metonymy, for Gentiles, e.g., Rom. 2 : 26, 27 ; 3 : 30 ; 4 : 9 ; Gal. 2 : 7 ; Eph. 2 : 11 ; (d) in a metaphorical or transferred sense, of the moral condition in which the corrupt desires of the flesh still operate, Col. 2 : 13.¶

Note : In Rom. 4 : 11, the phrase " though they be in uncircum-

---

* From Notes on Galatians by Hogg and Vine, p. 69.

cision" translates the Greek phrase *di' akrobustias*, lit., 'through uncircumcision;' here *dia* has the local sense of proceeding from and passing out.

B. Adjective.

APERITMĒTOS (ἀπερίτμητος), uncircumcised (*a*, negative, *peri*, around, *temnō*, to cut), is used in Acts 7 : 51, metaphorically, of "heart and ears."¶

C. Verbs.

1. PERITEMNŌ (περιτέμνω), to circumcise, is used (*a*) lit., e.g., Luke 1 : 59; 2 : 21; of receiving circumcision, Gal. 5 : 2, 3; 6 : 13, R.V.; (*b*) metaphorically, of spiritual circumcision, Col. 2 : 11.

2. EPISPAOMAI (ἐπισπάομαι), lit., to draw over, to become uncircumcised, as if to efface Judaism, appears in 1 Cor. 7 : 18.¶

For CIRCUMSPECTLY see ACCURATELY

CITIZEN, CITIZENSHIP

1. POLITĒS (πολίτης), a member of a city or state, or the inhabitant of a country or district, Luke 15 : 15, is used elsewhere in Luke 19 : 14; Acts 21 : 39, and, in the most authentic mss., in Heb. 8 : 11 (where some texts have *plēsion*, a neighbour). Apart from Heb. 8 : 11, the word occurs only in the writings of Luke (himself a Greek).¶

2. SUMPOLITĒS (συμπολίτης), *sun*, with, and No. 1, denotes a fellow-citizen, i.e., possessing the same citizenship, Eph. 2 : 19, used metaphorically in a spiritual sense.¶

3. POLITEIA (πολιτεία) signifies (*a*) the relation in which a citizen stands to the state, the condition of a citizen, citizenship, Acts 22 : 28, "with a great sum obtained I this citizenship" (A.V., "freedom"). While Paul's citizenship of Tarsus was not of advantage outside that city, yet his Roman citizenship availed throughout the Roman Empire and, besides private rights, included (1) exemption from all degrading punishments; (2) a right of appeal to the Emperor after a sentence; (3) a right to be sent to Rome for trial before the Emperor if charged with a capital offence. Paul's father might have obtained citizenship (1) by manumission; (2) as a reward of merit; (3) by purchase; the contrast implied in Acts 22 : 28 is perhaps against the last mentioned; (*b*) a civil polity, the condition of a state, a commonwealth, said of Israel, Eph. 2 : 12. See COMMONWEALTH.¶

4. POLITEUMA (πολίτευμα) signifies the condition, or life, of a citizen, citizenship; it is said of the heavenly status of believers, Phil. 3 : 20, "our citizenship (A.V., "conversation") is in Heaven." The R.V. marg. gives the alternative meaning, "commonwealth," i.e., community. See COMMONWEALTH, FREEDOM.¶

Note : *Politeuō*, Phil. 1 : 27, signifies to be a *politēs* (see No. 1), and is used in the Middle Voice, signifying, metaphorically, conduct characteristic of heavenly citizenship, R.V., " let your manner of life (A.V., " conversation ") be worthy (marg., ' behave as citizens worthily ') of the Gospel of Christ."   In Acts 23 : 1 it is translated " I have lived."   See CONVERSATION, LIVE.¶

CITY

POLIS (πόλις), primarily a town enclosed with a wall (perhaps from a root plē—, signifying fulness, whence also the Latin pleo, to fill, Eng., polite, polish, politic etc.), is used also of the heavenly Jerusalem, the abode and community of the redeemed, Heb. 11 : 10, 16 ; 12 : 22 ; 13 : 14. In the Apocalypse it signifies the visible capital of the Heavenly Kingdom, as destined to descend to earth in a coming age, e.g., Rev. 3 : 12 ; 21 : 2, 14, 19.   By metonymy the word stands for the inhabitants, as in the English use, e.g., Matt. 8 : 34 ; 12 : 25 ; 21 : 10 ; Mark 1 : 33 ; Acts 13 : 44.

Note : In Acts 16 : 13, the most authentic mss. have pulē, gate, R.V., " without the gate."

CLAMOUR

KRAUGĒ (κραυγή), an onomatopœic word, imitating the raven's cry, akin to krazō and kraugazō, to cry, denotes an outcry, " clamour," Acts 23 : 9, R.V. ; Eph. 4 : 31, where it signifies the tumult of controversy. See CRY.

CLANGING

ALALAZŌ (ἀλαλάζω), an onomatopœic word, from the battle-cry, *alala*, is used of raising the shout of battle, Josh. 6 : 20 ; hence, to make a loud cry or shout, e.g., Psa. 47 : 1 ; to wail, Jer. 29 : 2 ; in the N.T., in Mark 5 : 38, of wailing mourners ; in 1 Cor. 13 : 1, of the " clanging " of cymbals (A.V., " tinkling ").¶

CLAY

PĒLOS (πηλός), clay, especially such as was used by a mason or potter, is used of moist clay, in John 9 : 6, 11, 14, 15, in connection with Christ's healing the blind man ; in Rom. 9 : 21, of potter's clay, as to the potter's right over it as an illustration of the prerogatives of God in His dealings with men.¶

CLEAN, CLEANNESS, CLEANSE, CLEANSING
A. Adjective.

KATHAROS (καθαρός), free from impure admixture, without blemish, spotless, is used (a) physically, e.g., Matt. 23 : 26 ; 27 : 59 ; John 13 : 10 (where the Lord, speaking figuratively, teaches that one who has been entirely cleansed, needs not radical renewal, but only to be cleansed from every sin into which he may fall) ; 15 : 3 ; Heb. 10 : 22 ;

Rev. 15 : 6 ; 19 : 8, 14 ; 21 : 18, 21 ; (b) in a Levitical sense, Rom. 14 : 20 ; Tit. 1 : 15, " pure ; " (c) ethically, with the significance free from corrupt desire, from guilt, Matt. 5 : 8 ; John 13 : 10, 11 ; Acts 20 : 26 ; 1 Tim. 1 : 5 ; 3 : 9 ; 2 Tim. 1 : 3 ; 2 : 22 ; Tit. 1 : 15 ; Jas. 1 : 27 ; blameless, innocent (a rare meaning for this word), Acts 18 : 6 ; (d) in a combined Levitical and ethical sense ceremonially, Luke 11 : 41, " all things are clean unto you." See CLEAR, C, Note (2), PURE.¶

B. Verbs.

1. KATHARIZŌ (καθαρίζω), akin to A, signifies (1) to make clean, to cleanse (a) from physical stains and dirt, as in the case of utensils, Matt. 23 : 25 (figuratively in verse 26) ; from disease, as of leprosy, Matt. 8 : 2 ; (b) in a moral sense, from the defilement of sin, Acts 15 : 9 ; 2 Cor. 7 : 1 ; Heb. 9 : 14 ; Jas. 4 : 8, " cleanse " from the guilt of sin, Eph. 5 : 26 ; 1 John 1 : 7 ; (2) to pronounce clean in a Levitical sense, Mark 7 : 19, R.V. ; Acts 10 : 15 ; 11 : 9 ; to consecrate by cleansings, Heb. 9 : 22, 23 ; 10 : 2. See PURGE, PURIFY.

2. DIAKATHARIZŌ (διακαθαρίζω), to cleanse thoroughly, is used in Matt. 3 : 12, R.V.¶

Note : For *kathairō*, John 15 : 2, R.V., see PURGE, No. 1. For *diakathairō*, Luke 3 : 17, R.V., see PURGE, No. 3.

C. Nouns.

1. KATHARISMOS (καθαρισμός), akin to A, denotes cleansing, (a) both the action and its results, in the Levitical sense, Mark 1 : 44 ; Luke 2 : 22, " purification ; " 5 : 14, " cleansing ; " John 2 : 6 ; 3 : 25, " purifying ; " (b) in the moral sense, from sins, Heb. 1 : 3 ; 2 Pet. 1 : 9, R.V., " cleansing." See PURGE, PURIFICATION, PURIFYING.¶

2. KATHAROTĒS (καθαρότης), akin to B, cleanness, purity, is used in the Levitical sense in Heb. 9 : 13, R.V., " cleanness." See PURIFY.¶

Note : In 2 Pet. 2 : 18, some inferior mss. have *ontōs*, " certainly " (A.V., " clean "), for *oligōs*, " scarcely " (R.V., " just ").

CLEAR, CLEARING, CLEARLY
A. Verb.

KRUSTALLIZŌ (κρυσταλλίζω), to shine like crystal, to be of crystalline brightness, or transparency, is found in Rev. 21 : 11, " clear as crystal." The verb may, however, have a transitive force, signifying to crystallize or cause to become like crystal. In that case it would speak of Christ (since He is the " Lightgiver," see the preceding part of the verse), as the One who causes the saints to shine in His own likeness.¶

B. Adjective.

LAMPROS (λαμπρός) is said of crystal, Rev. 22 : 1, A.V., " clear," R.V., " bright." See BRIGHT, GAY, GOODLY, GORGEOUS, WHITE.

Note : The corresponding adverb *lamprōs* signifies " sumptuously."

C. Adverb.

TĒLAUGŌS (τηλαυγῶς), from *tēle*, afar, and *augē*, radiance, signifies conspicuously, or clearly, Mark 8 : 25, of the sight imparted by Christ to one who had been blind.¶ Some mss. have *dēlaugōs*, clearly (*dēlos*, clear).

Notes : (1) In 2 Cor. 7 : 11, A.V., *hagnos* is rendered " clear." See PURE. (2) In Rev. 21 : 18, *katharos*, (" pure," R.V.) is rendered " clear," in the A.V. See CLEAN. (3) *Apologia* (Eng., apology), a defence against an accusation, signifies, in 2 Cor. 7 : 11, a clearing of oneself. (4) For *diablepō*, to see clearly, Matt. 7 : 5 ; Luke 6 : 42, and *kathoraō*, ditto, Rom. 1 : 20, see SEE.

CLEAVE, CLAVE

1. KOLLAŌ (κολλάω), to join fast together, to glue, cement, is primarily said of metals and other materials (from *kolla*, glue). In the N.T. it is used only in the Passive Voice, with reflexive force, in the sense of cleaving unto, as of cleaving to one's wife, Matt. 19 : 5 ; some mss. have the intensive Verb No. 2, here ; 1 Cor. 6 : 16, 17, " joined." In the corresponding passage in Mark 10 : 7, the most authentic mss. omit the sentence. In Luke 10 : 11 it is used of the cleaving of dust to the feet ; in Acts 5 : 13 ; 8 : 29 ; 9 : 26 ; 10 : 28 ; 17 : 34, in the sense of becoming associated with a person so as to company with him, or be on his side, said, in the last passage, of those in Athens who believed : in Rom. 12 : 9, ethically, of cleaving to that which is good. For its use in Rev. 18 : 5 see REACH (R.V.,marg. " clave together "). See COMPANY, JOIN.¶

2. PROSKOLLAŌ (προσκολλάω), in the Passive Voice, used reflexively, to cleave unto, is found in Eph. 5 : 31 (A.V. " joined to ").

3. PROSMENŌ (προσμένω), lit., to abide with (*pros.* toward or with, and *menō*, to abide), is used of cleaving unto the Lord, Acts 11 : 23. See ABIDE.

CLEMENCY

EPIEIKEIA (ἐπιείκεια), mildness, gentleness, kindness (what Matthew Arnold has called " sweet reasonableness "), is translated " clemency " in Acts 24 : 4 ; elsewhere, in 2 Cor. 10 : 1, of the gentleness of Christ. See GENTLENESS.¶ Cp. *epieikēs* (see FORBEARANCE).

For CLERK, see under TOWNCLERK

CLIMB UP

ANABAINŌ (ἀναβαίνω), to ascend, is used of climbing up, in Luke 19 : 4 and John 10 : 1. See ARISE.

CLOKE (Pretence)

1. EPIKALUMMA (ἐπικάλυμμα) is a covering, a means of hiding (*epi*, upon, *kaluptō*, to cover) ; hence, a pretext, a cloke, for wickedness,

1 Pet. 2 : 16.¶ In the Sept. it is used in Ex. 26 : 14 ; 39 : 21," coverings ; " 2 Sam. 17 : 19 ; Job 19 : 29, " deceit." ¶

2. PROPHASIS (πρόφασις), either from *pro*, before, and *phainō*, to cause to appear, shine, or, more probably, from *pro*, and *phēmi*, to say, is rendered " cloke " (of covetousness) in 1 Thess. 2 : 5 ; " excuse " in John 15 : 22 (A.V. " cloke ") ; " pretence " in Matt. 23 : 14 ; Mark 12 : 40 ; Luke 20 : 47 (A.V. " shew ") ; Phil. 1 : 18 ; " colour " in Acts 27 : 30. It signifies the assuming of something so as to disguise one's real motives. See PRETENCE, SHEW.¶

CLOKE (Garment)

For the various words for garments, see CLOTHING.

CLOSE (Verb)

1. KAMMUŌ (καμμύω), derived by syncope (i.e., shortening and assimilation of *t* to *m*) from *katamuō*, i.e., *kata*, down, and *muō*, from a root *mu*—, pronounced by closing the lips, denotes to close down ; hence, to shut the eyes, Matt. 13 : 15 and Acts 28 : 27, in each place of the obstinacy of Jews in their opposition to the Gospel.¶

2. PTUSSŌ (πτύσσω), to fold, double up, is used of a scroll of parchment, Luke 4 : 20.¶ Cp. *anaptussō*, to open up, ver. 17.¶

Notes : (1) For " close-sealed," Rev. 5 : 1, see SEAL.

(2) In Luke 9 : 36, *sigaō*, to be silent, is translated " they kept it close," A.V. (R.V., " they held their peace ").

CLOSE (Adverb)

ASSON (ἆσσον), the comparative degree of *anchi*, near, is found in Acts 27 : 13, of sailing close by a place.¶

For the word CLOSET see CHAMBER

CLOTH

RHAKOS (ῥάκος) denotes a ragged garment, or a piece of cloth torn off, a rag ; hence, a piece of undressed cloth, Matt. 9 : 16 ; Mark 2 : 21. *Note :* For other words, *othonion*, *sindon*, see LINEN, Nos. 1 and 3.¶

CLOTHE

1. AMPHIENNUMI (ἀμφιέννυμι), to put clothes round (*amphi*, around, *hennumi*, to clothe), to invest, signifies, in the Middle Voice, to put clothing on oneself, e.g., Matt. 6 : 30 ; 11 : 8 ; Luke 7 : 25 ; 12 : 28.¶

2. ENDUŌ (ἐνδύω), Eng., endue), signifies to enter into, get into, as into clothes, to put on, e.g., Mark 1 : 6 ; Luke 8 : 27 (in the best mss.) ; 24 : 49 (A.V., " endued ") ; 2 Cor. 5 : 3 ; Rev. 1 : 13 ; 19 : 14. See ARRAY, ENDUE, PUT ON.

3. ENDIDUSKŌ (ἐνδιδύσκω) has the same meaning as No. 2 ; the termination, —skō suggests the beginning or progress of the action. The verb is used in the Middle Voice in Luke 16 : 19 (of a rich man). Some mss. have it in 8 : 27, for No. 2 (of a demoniac). In Mark 15 : 17 the best texts have this verb (some have No. 2). See WEAR.¶

4. EPENDUŌ (ἐπενδύω), a strengthened form of No. 2, used in the Middle Voice, to cause to be put on over, to be clothed upon, is found in 2 Cor. 5 : 2, 4, of the future spiritual body of the redeemed.¶

5. HIMATIZŌ (ἱματίζω) means to put on raiment (see himation, below), Mark 5 : 15 ; Luke 8 : 35.¶

6. PERIBALLŌ, to cast around or about, to put on, array, or, in the Middle and Passive Voices, to clothe oneself, e.g., Matt. 25 : 36, 38, 43, is most frequent in the Apocalypse, where it is found some 12 times (see peribolaion, below). See CAST, No. 10, PUT, No. 9).

Note : The verb enkomboomai, to gird oneself with a thing, in 1 Pet. 5 : 5, is rendered in the A.V., " be clothed with."

CLOTHING, CLOTHS, CLOTHES, CLOKE, COAT

1. PHELONĒS, or phailonēs (φαιλόνης), probably by metathesis from phainolēs (Latin paenula), a mantle, denotes a travelling cloak for protection against stormy weather, 2 Tim. 4 : 13. Some, however, regard it as a Cretan word for chitōn, a tunic. It certainly was not an ecclesiastical vestment. The Syriac renders it a case for writings (some regard it as a book-cover), an explanation noted by Chrysostom, but improbable. It may have been " a light mantle like a cashmere dust-cloak, in which the books and parchments were wrapped " (Mackie in Hastings' Dic. of the Bible).¶

2. HIMATION (ἱμάτιον), an outer garment, a mantle, thrown over the chitōn. In the plural, clothes (the cloak and the tunic), e.g., Matt. 17 : 2 ; 26 : 65 ; 27 : 31, 35. See APPAREL, No. 2.

3. CHITŌN (χιτών) denotes the inner vest or under garment, and is to be distinguished, as such, from the himation. The distinction is made, for instance, in the Lord's command in Matt. 5 : 40 : " If any man would go to law with thee, and take away thy coat (chitōn), let him have thy cloke (himation) also." The order is reversed in Luke 6 : 29, and the difference lies in this, that in Matt. 5 : 40 the Lord is referring to a legal process, so the claimant is supposed to claim the inner garment, the less costly. The defendant is to be willing to let him have the more valuable one too. In the passage in Luke an act of violence is in view, and there is no mention of going to law. So the outer garment is the first one which would be seized.

When the soldiers had crucified Jesus they took His garments (himation, in the plural), His outer garments, and the coat, the chitōn, the inner garment, which was without seam, woven from the top throughout,

John 19 : 23. The outer garments were easily divisible among the four soldiers, but they could not divide the *chitōn* without splitting it, so they cast lots for it.

Dorcas was accustomed to make coats (*chitōn*) and garments (*himation*), Acts 9 : 39, that is, the close fitting under garments and the long, flowing outer robes.

A person was said to be " naked " (*gumnos*), whether he was without clothing, or had thrown off his outer garment, e.g., his *ependutēs*, (No. 6, below), and was clad in a light undergarment, as was the case with Peter, in John 21 : 7. The High Priest, in rending his clothes after the reply the Lord gave him in answer to his challenge, rent his under garments (*chitōn*), the more forcibly to express his assumed horror and indignation, Mark 14 : 63. In Jude 23, " the garment spotted by the flesh " is the *chitōn*, the metaphor of the under garment being appropriate ; for it would be that which was brought into touch with the pollution of the flesh.

4. HIMATISMOS (ἱματισμός), in form a collective word, denoting vesture, garments, is used generally of costly or stately raiment, the apparel of kings, of officials, etc. See Luke 7 : 25, where " gorgeously apparelled " is, lit., ' in gorgeous vesture.' See also Acts 20 : 33 and 1 Tim. 2 : 9, " costly raiment." This is the word used of the Lord's white and dazzling raiment on the Mount of Transfiguration, Luke 9 : 29. It is also used of His *chitōn*, His under-garment (see note above), for which the soldiers cast lots, John 19 : 23, 24, " vesture ; " in Matt. 27 : 35 it is also translated " vesture." See APPAREL, RAIMENT, VESTURE.¶

5. ENDUMA (ἔνδυμα), akin to *enduō* (see CLOTHE, No. 2), denotes anything put on, a garment of any kind. It was used of the clothing of ancient prophets, in token of their contempt of earthly splendour, 1 Kings 19 : 13 ; 2 Kings 1 : 8, R.V. ; Zech. 13 : 4. In the N.T. it is similarly used of John the Baptist's raiment, Matt. 3 : 4 ; of raiment in general, Matt. 6 : 25, 28 ; Luke 12 : 23 ; metaphorically, of sheep's clothing, Matt. 7 : 15 ; of a wedding garment, 22 : 11, 12 ; of the raiment of the angel at the tomb of the Lord after His resurrection, 28 : 3. See GARMENT, RAIMENT.¶

6. EPENDUTĒS (ἐπενδύτης) denotes an upper garment (*epi*, upon, *enduō*, to clothe). The word is found in John 21 : 7, where it apparently denotes a kind of linen frock, which fishermen wore when at their work. See No. 3.¶

7. ESTHĒS (ἐσθής), " clothing," Acts 10 : 30 ; see APPAREL, No. 1.

8. STOLĒ (στολή), (Eng., stole), denotes any stately robe, a long garment reaching to the feet or with a train behind. It is used of the long clothing in which the scribes walked, making themselves conspicuous in the eyes of men, Mark 12 : 38 ; Luke 20 : 46 ; of the robe worn by the young man in the Lord's tomb, Mark 16 : 5 ; of the best or, rather, the chief robe, which was brought out for the returned prodigal, Luke 15 : 22 ; five times in the Apocalypse, as to glorified saints, 6 : 11 ; 7 : 9, 13, 14 ;

22 : 14.¶ In the Sept. it is used of the holy garments of the priests, e.g., Ex. 28 : 2 ; 29 : 21 ; 31 : 10.

Notes : (1) *Peribolaion*, from *periballō*, to throw around, lit., that which is thrown around, was a wrap or mantle. It is used in 1 Cor. 11 : 15, of the hair of a woman which is given to her as a veil ; in Heb. 1 : 12, of the earth and the heavens, which the Lord will roll up " as a mantle," R.V., for A.V., " vesture." The other word in that verse rendered " garment," R.V., is *himation*.¶

(2) *Endusis*, is " a putting on (of apparel)," 1 Pet. 3 : 3. Cp. No. 5.¶

(3) *Esthēsis*. See APPAREL, No. 1.

(4) The *chlamus* was a short cloak or robe, worn over the *chitōn* (No. 3), by emperors, kings, magistrates, military officers, etc. It is used of the scarlet robe with which Christ was arrayed in mockery by the soldiers in Pilate's Judgment Hall, Matt. 27 : 28, 31.

What was known as purple was a somewhat indefinite colour. There is nothing contradictory about its being described by Mark and John as " purple," though Matthew speaks of it as " scarlet." The soldiers put it on the Lord in mockery of His Kingship.¶

(5) The *podērēs* was another sort of outer garment, reaching to the feet (from *pous*, the foot, and *arō*, to fasten). It was one of the garments of the high priests, a robe (Hebrew, *chetoneth*), mentioned after the ephod in Ex. 28 : 4, etc. It is used in Ezek. 9 : 2, where instead of " linen " the Sept. reads " a long robe ; " and in Zech. 3 : 4, " clothe ye him with a long robe ; " in the N.T. in Rev. 1 : 13, of the long garment in which the Lord is seen in vision amongst the seven golden lampstands. There, *podērēs* is described as " a garment down to the feet," indicative of His High Priestly character and acts.¶

(6) For *katastolē*, see APPAREL, No. 4.

CLOUD

1. NEPHOS (νέφος) denotes a cloudy, shapeless mass covering the heavens. Hence, metaphorically, of a dense multitude, a throng, Heb. 12 : 1.¶

2. NEPHELĒ (νεφέλη), a definitely shaped cloud, or masses of clouds possessing definite form, is used, besides the physical element, (a) of the cloud on the mount of transfiguration, Matt. 17 : 5 ; (b) of the cloud which covered Israel in the Red Sea, 1 Cor. 10 : 1, 2 ; (c), of clouds seen in the Apocalyptic visions, Rev. 1 : 7 ; 10 : 1 ; 11 : 12 ; 14 : 14, 15, 16 ; (d), metaphorically in 2 Pet. 2 : 17, of the evil workers there mentioned ; but R.V., " and mists " (*homichlē*), according to the most authentic mss.

In 1 Thess. 4 : 17, the clouds referred to in connection with the Rapture of the saints are probably the natural ones, as also in the case of those in connection with Christ's Second Advent to the earth. See Matt. 24 : 30 ; 26 : 64, and parallel passages. So at the Ascension, Acts 1 : 9.

CLOVEN

DIAMERIZŌ (διαμερίζω), to part asunder (*dia*, asunder, *meros*, a part), is translated " cloven " in the A.V. of Acts 2 : 3, R.V., " parting asunder." See DIVIDE, PART.

CLUSTER

BOTRUS (βότρυς), a cluster, or bunch, bunch of grapes, is found in Rev. 14 : 18.¶

Note : Cp. *staphulē*, a bunch of grapes, the ripe cluster, stressing the grapes themselves, Matt. 7 : 16 ; Luke 6 : 44 ; Rev. 14 : 18.¶

COALS

1. ANTHRAX (ἄνθραξ), a burning coal (cp. Eng., *anthracite*), is used in the plural in Rom. 12 : 20, metaphorically in a proverbial expression, " thou shalt heap coals of fire on his head " (from Prov. 25 : 22), signifying retribution by kindness, i.e., that, by conferring a favour on your enemy, you recall the wrong he has done to you, so that he repents, with pain of heart.¶

2. ANTHRAKIA (ἀνθρακία), akin to No. 1, is a heap of burning coals, or a charcoal fire, John 18 : 18 ; 21 : 9.¶

COAST, COASTING
A. Noun.

HORION (ὅριον), a bound, boundary, limit, frontier (akin to *horizō*, to bound, limit), is rendered " coasts " ten times in the A.V., but " borders " in Matt. 4 : 13, and is always translated " borders " in the R.V. See BORDER.

B. Adjective.

PARALIOS (παράλιος), by the sea (*para*, by, *hals*, salt), hence denotes a sea coast, Luke 6 : 17.¶ In the Sept., Gen. 49 : 13 ; Deut. 1 : 7 ; 33 : 19; Josh. 9 : 1 ; 11 : 3 (twice) ; Job 6 : 3 ; Is. 9 : 1.

C. Verb.

PARALEGŌ (παραλέγω) is used, in the Middle Voice, as a nautical term, to sail past, Acts 27 : 8, " coasting along ; " ver. 13, " sailed by."¶

Notes : (1) *Methorion* (*meta*, with, and A), in Mark 7 : 24, is translated " borders." (2) The phrase " upon the sea coast," Matt. 4 : 13, A.V., translates *parathalassios* (*para*, by, *thalassa*, the sea), R.V. " by the sea."¶ (3) *Meros*, a part, is translated " coasts " in Matt. 15 : 21 ; 16 : 13, A.V. (R.V., " parts,") ; " country," R.V., in Acts 19 : 1, A.V. " coasts ; " this refers to the high land in the interior of Asia Minor. See BEHALF, CRAFT, PART, PARTICULAR, PIECE, PORTION, RESPECT, SOMEWHAT, SORT. (4) *Chōra*, a country, rendered " coasts " in Acts 26 : 20, A.V., is corrected in the R.V. to " country." See COUNTRY, FIELD, GROUND, LAND, REGION. (5) In Acts 27 : 2 the phrase in the R.V., " on the coast of," translates the preposition *kata*, along, and the complete clause, "unto the places on the coast of Asia," R.V., is curiously condensed in the A.V. to "by the coasts of Asia."

For COAT (*ependeutēs*) see CLOKE, CLOTHING

COCK, COCK-CROWING

1. ALEKTŌR (ἀλέκτωρ), a cock, perhaps connected with a Hebrew phrase for the on-coming of the light, is found in the passages concerning Peter's denial of the Lord, Matt. 26 : 34, 74, 75 ; Mark 14 : 30, 68, 72 ; Luke 22 : 34, 60, 61 ; John 13 : 38 ; 18 : 27.¶

2. ALEKTOROPHŌNIA (ἀλεκτοροφωνία) denotes cock-crowing (*alektōr*, and *phōnē*, a sound), Mark 13 : 35. There were two cock-crowings, one after midnight, the other before dawn. In these watches the Jews followed the Roman method of dividing the night. The first cock-crowing was at the third watch of the night. That is the one mentioned in Mark 13 : 35. Mark mentions both ; see 14 : 30. The latter, the second, is that referred to in the other Gospels and is mentioned especially as " the cock-crowing."¶

COLD
A. Noun.

PSUCHOS (ψύχος), coldness, cold, appears in John 18 : 18 ; Acts 28 : 2 ; 2 Cor. 11 : 27.¶

B. Adjective.

PSUCHROS (ψυχρός), cool, fresh, cold, chilly (fuller in expression than *psuchos*), is used in the natural sense in Matt. 10 : 42, " cold water ; " metaphorically in Rev. 3 : 15, 16.¶

C. Verb.

PSUCHŌ (ψύχω), to breathe, blow, cool by blowing, Passive Voice, grow cool, is used metaphorically in Matt. 24 : 12, in the sense of waning zeal or love.¶

COLLECTION

LOGIA (λογία), akin to *legō*, to collect, is used in 1 Cor. 16 : 1, 2 ; in the latter verse, A.V. " gatherings," R.V., " collections," as in ver. 1. See GATHERING.¶

COLONY

KOLŌNIA (κολωνία) transliterates the Latin *colonia*. Roman colonies belonged to three periods and classes, (*a*) those of the earlier republic before 100 B.C., which were simply centres of Roman influence in conquered territory ; (*b*) agrarian colonies, planted as places for the overflowing population of Rome ; (*c*) military colonies during the time of the Civil wars and the Empire, for the settlement of disbanded soldiers. This third class was established by the *imperator*, who appointed a legate to exercise his authority. To this class Philippi belonged as mentioned in Acts 16 : 12, R.V., " a Roman colony." They were watch-towers of the Roman State and formed on the model of Rome itself. The full organization of Philippi as such was the work of Augustus, who, after the battle of Actium, 31 B.C., gave his soldiers lands in Italy and transferred most of the inhabitants there to other quarters including Philippi. These communities possessed the right of Roman freedom, and of holding the soil under Roman law, as well as exemption from poll-tax and tribute. Most Roman colonies were established on the coast.¶

For the word COLOUR (Acts 27 : 30) see CLOKE

COLT

PŌLOS (πῶλος), a foal, whether colt or filly, had the general significance of a young creature ; in Matt. 21 : 2, and parallel passages, an ass's colt.

COME, CAME (see also COMING)

1. ERCHOMAI (ἔρχομαι), the most frequent verb, denoting either to come, or to go, signifies the act, in contrast with *hēkō* (see No. 22, below), which stresses the arrival, as, e.g., ' I am come and am here,' John 8 : 42 and Heb. 10 : 9. See BRING, B, *Note* (1), FALL, GO, GROW, LIGHT, PASS, RESORT.

Compounds of this with prepositions are as follows (2 to 11) :

2. EISERCHOMAI (εἰσέρχομαι), to come into, or to go into (*eis*, into), e.g., Luke 17 : 7. See ENTER.

3. EXERCHOMAI (ἐξέρχομαι), to come out, or go out or forth (*ek*, out), e.g., Matt. 2 : 6. See DEPART, ESCAPE, GET, (*b*), No. 3, GO, *Note* (1), PROCEED, SPREAD.

4. EPANERCHOMAI (ἐπανέρχομαι), to come back again, return (*epi*, on, *ana*, again), Luke 10 : 35 ; 19 : 15.¶

5. DIERCHOMAI (διέρχομαι), to come or go through (*dia*, through), e.g., Acts 9 : 38. See DEPART, GO, PASS, PIERCE, TRAVEL, WALK.

6. EPERCHOMAI (ἐπέρχομαι), to come or go upon (*epi*, upon), e.g., Luke 1 : 35 ; in Luke 21 : 26, used of coming events, suggesting their certainty ; in Eph. 2 : 7, said of the on-coming of the ages ; in Acts 14 : 19, of Jews coming to (lit., upon) a place.

7. KATERCHOMAI (κατέρχομαι), to come down (*kata*, down), e.g., Luke 9 : 37. See DEPART, DESCEND, GO, *Note* (1), LAND.

8. PAREISERCHOMAI (παρεισέρχομαι), lit., to come in (*eis*) beside or from the side (*para*) so as to be present with, is used (*a*) in the literal sense, of the coming in of the Law in addition to sin, Rom. 5 : 20 ; (*b*) in Gal. 2 : 4, of false brethren, suggesting their coming in by stealth. See ENTER.¶

9. PARERCHOMAI (παρέρχομαι), (*para*, by or away), signifies (*a*) to

come or go forth, or arrive, e.g., Luke 12 : 37 ; 17 : 7 (last part) ; Acts 24 : 7 ; (b) to pass by, e.g., Luke 18 : 37 ; (c) to neglect, e.g., Luke 11 : 42. See Go, Pass, Transgress.

10. PROSERCHOMAI (προσέρχομαι) denotes to come or go near to (pros, near to), e.g., Matt. 4 : 3 ; Heb. 10 : 1, A.V., " comers," R.V., " them that draw nigh." See Consent, Draw, Go, Note (1).

11. SUNERCHOMAI (συνέρχομαι), to come together (sun with), e.g., John 18 : 20, is often translated by the verb to assemble ; see the R.V. of 1 Cor. 11 : 20 ; 14 : 23. See Accompany, Assemble, Company, Go with, Resort.

Note : Aperchomai, to come away or from, is differently translated in the R.V. ; see, e.g., Mark 3 : 13 where it signifies that they went from the company or place where they were to Him ; it usually denotes to go away.

12. GINOMAI (γίνομαι) to become, signifies a change of condition, state or place, e.g., Mark 4 : 35. In Acts 27 : 33, the verb is used with mellō, to be about to, to signify the coming on of day.

13. PARAGINOMAI (παραγίνομαι), para, near or by, denotes to arrive, to be present, e.g., Matt. 2 : 1. See Go, Present.

14. SUMPARAGINOMAI (συμπαραγίνομαι), (sun, with, para, near), to come together, is used in Luke 23 : 48 ; 2 Tim. 4 : 16, lit., ' stood at my side with me.' See Stand.¶

Note : For " come by " in Acts 27 : 16, A.V., the R.V. suitably has " secure."

Compounds of the verb bainō, to go, are as follows (15 to 21) :

15. ANABAINŌ (ἀναβαίνω), to come upon, to arrive in a place (ana, up or upon), is translated " come into " in Acts 25 : 1. See Arise, Ascend, Enter, Go, Climb, Grow, Rise, Spring.

16. EPIBAINŌ (ἐπιβαίνω), to come to or into, or go upon, is rendered, in Acts 20 : 18, R.V., " set foot in." See Enter, Go, Take, Note (16).

17. EKBAINŌ (ἐκβαίνω), to come or go out, appears in the best mss. in Heb. 11 : 15 ; A.V., " came out," R.V., " went out."¶

18. DIABAINŌ (διαβαίνω), to pass through, is translated " come over " in Acts 16 : 9 ; " pass " in Luke 16 : 26 ; " pass through " in Heb. 11 : 29. See Pass.¶

19. KATABAINŌ (καταβαίνω) signifies to come down, e.g., Matt. 8 : 1. See Descend, Fall, Get, Go, Step (down).

20. SUNANABAINŌ (συναναβαίνω), to come up with (sun, with, ana, up), is used in Mark 15 : 41 ; Acts 13 : 31.¶

21. EMBAINŌ (ἐμβαίνω), to go into, is rendered, in Mark 5 : 18, A.V., " was come into," R.V., " was entering." See Enter, Get, Go, Step.

Note : Apobainō, to go away, is rendered, in the A.V. of John 21 : 9, " were come to ; " R.V., " got out upon."

22. HĒKŌ (ἥκω) means (a) to come, to be present (see above, on No. 1); (b) to come upon, of time and events, Matt. 24 : 14 ; John 2 : 4 ; 2 Pet.

3 : 10 ; Rev. 18 : 8 ; (c) metaphorically, to come upon one, of calamitous times, and evils, Matt. 23 : 36 ; Luke 19 : 43.

23. APHIKNEOMAI (ἀφικνέομαι), to arrive at a place, is used in Rom. 16 : 19, " come abroad " (of the obedience of the saints).¶

24. CHOREO (χωρέω), lit., to make room (chōra, a place) for another, and so to have place, receive, is rendered " come " (followed by " to repentance ") in 2 Pet. 3 : 9 ; the meaning strictly is ' have room (i.e., space of time) for repentance.' See CONTAIN, GO, PLACE, ROOM, RECEIVE.

25. EIMI (εἰμί), to be, is, in the Infinitive Mood, rendered " come," in John 1 : 46 and in the future Indicative "will come," in 2 Tim. 4 : 3.

26. ENISTEMI (ἐνίστημι), lit., to stand in, or set in (en, in, histēmi, to stand), hence to be present or to be imminent, is rendered " shall come " in 2 Tim. 3 : 1 ; it here expresses permanence, ' shall settle in (upon you).' See AT HAND, PRESENT.

27. EPHISTEMI (ἐφίστημι) signifies to stand by or over (epi, upon), Luke 2 : 9, R.V. ; Acts 12 : 7 ; " before," Acts 11 : 11 ; to come upon, Luke 20 : 1 (here with the idea of suddenness) ; Acts 4 : 1 ; 6 : 12 ; 23 : 27 ; 1 Thess. 5 : 3 ; " coming up," of the arrival of Anna at the Temple, Luke 2 : 38 ; " came up to (Him)," of Martha, Luke 10 : 40 ; " is come," 2 Tim. 4 : 6 (probably with the same idea as in Luke 20 : 1). The R.V. is significant in all these places. See ASSAULT, AT HAND, PRESENT, STAND.

28. KATANTAO (καταντάω) denotes (a) to come to, or over against, a place, arrive, Acts 16 : 1 ; 18 : 19, 24 ; 20 : 15 (in 21 : 7 and 25 : 13, R.V., " arrived ; " in 27 : 12 ," reach," for A.V., " attain to) ; 28 : 13 ; (b) of things or events, to arrive at a certain time, or come upon certain persons in the period of their lifetime, 1 Cor. 10 : 11 ; or to come to persons so that they partake of, as of the Gospel, 1 Cor. 14 : 36. For the remaining instances, Acts 26 : 7 ; Eph. 4 : 13 ; Phil. 3 : 11, see ATTAIN.¶

29. MELLO (μέλλω), to be about (to do something), often implying the necessity and therefore the certainty of what is to take place, is frequently rendered " to come," e.g., Matt. 3 : 7 ; 11 : 14 ; Eph. 1 : 21 ; 1 Tim. 4 : 8 ; 6 : 19 ; Heb. 2 : 5. See ALMOST, BEGIN, MEAN, MIND, SHALL, TARRY, WILL.

30. PARISTEMI (παρίστημι), to stand by or near, to be at hand (para, near), is translated " is come," of the arrival of harvest, Mark 4 : 29. See BRING, COMMEND, GIVE, PRESENT, PROVE, PROVIDE, SHEW, STAND, YIELD.

31. PHERO (φέρω), to bear, carry, is rendered " came," in the sense of being borne from a place, in 2 Pet. 1 : 17, 18, 21. See BEAR, CARRY.

32. PHTHANO (φθάνω) denotes to anticipate, to come sooner than expected, 1 Thess. 2 : 16, " is come upon," of Divine wrath ; cp. Rom. 9 : 31, " did not arrive at ; " or to come in a different manner from what

was expected, Matt. 12 : 28, " come upon ; " Luke 11 : 20, of the Kingdom of God ; so of coming to a place, 2 Cor. 10 : 14. See ATTAIN, PRECEDE, PREVENT.¶

Two of the compounds of the verb poreuomai, to go, proceed, are translated " come," with a preposition or adverb :

33. EKPOREUŌ (ἐκπορεύω), in the Middle Voice, to come forth (*ek*, out of), Mark 7 : 15, 20 ; John 5 : 29. See DEPART, GO, ISSUE, PROCEED.

34. PROSPOREUOMAI (προσπορεύομαι), in Mark 10 : 35, is translated " come near unto."¶

Notes : (1) No. 33 is rendered " proceed " in the R.V. of Mark 7 : 15, 20, 23 (A.V., " come "). (2) For *epiporeuomai*, in Luke 8 : 4, see RESORT.¶

35. PROSENGIZŌ (προσεγγίζω) denotes to come near (*pros*, to, *engizō*, to be near, to approach), Mark 2 : 4, used of those who tried to bring a palsied man to Christ.¶

36. SUMPLĒROŌ (συμπληρόω), to fill completely (*sun*, with, intensive), is used, in the Passive Voice, of time to be fulfilled or completed, Luke 9 : 51, " the days were well-nigh come ; " Acts 2 : 1, " the day . . . was now come " (A.V. " was fully come "). In Luke 8 : 23, it is used in the Active Voice, of the filling of a boat in a storm. See FILL.¶

37. SUNTUNCHANŌ (συντυγχάνω), to meet with (*sun*, with, and *tunchanō*, to reach), is rendered " to come at " in Luke 8 : 19, (of the efforts of Christ's mother and brethren to get at Him through a crowd).¶

38. KUKLOŌ (κυκλόω), to compass (Eng., cycle), is translated " came round about," in John 10 : 24. See COMPASS, ROUND, STAND.

39. HUSTEREŌ (ὑστερέω), to be behind, is translated " to have come short," in Heb. 4 : 1. See BEHIND, B, No. 1.

Notes : (1) *Deuro*, hither, here, is used (sometimes with verbs of motion) in the singular number, in calling a person to come, Matt. 19 : 21 ; Mark 10 : 21 ; Luke 18 : 22 ; John 11 : 43 ; Acts 7 : 3, 34 ; Rev. 17 : 1 ; 21 : 9. For its other meaning, " hitherto," Rom. 1 : 13, see HITHERTO.¶ It has a plural, *deute*, frequent in the Gospels ; elsewhere in Rev. 19 : 17. *In the following the R.V. has a different rendering :* (2) In Mark 14 : 8, *prolambanō*, to anticipate, to be beforehand, A.V., ' hath come aforehand to anoint My body," R.V., " hath anointed My body aforehand." (3) In Acts 7 : 45, *diadechomai*, to succeed one, to take the place of, A.V., " who came after," R.V., " in their turn."¶ (4) In Luke 8 : 55, *epistrephō*, to return to, A.V., " came again," R.V., " returned." (5) In Acts 24 : 27, *lambanō*, with *diadochos*, a successor, A.V., " came into the room of," R.V., " was succeeded by." (6) In Mark 9 : 23, for *episuntrechō*, to come running together, see under RUN.¶ (7) In Acts 5 : 38, *kataluō*, to destroy, A.V., " will come to nought," R.V., " will be overthrown." (8) In John 12 : 35, *katalambanō*, to seize, A.V., " come upon," R.V., " overtake." (9) In 2 Cor. 11 : 28, *epistasis* (in some mss. *episustasis*), lit., a standing

together upon, hence, a pressing upon, as of cares, A.V., " cometh upon,"
R.V., " presseth upon." (10) In Acts 19 : 27, *erchomai*, with *eis apelegmon*,
R.V., " come into disrepute," A.V., " be set at nought." (11) For *pareimi*,
John 7 : 6, see PRESENT, No. 1. (12) *Sunagō*, to gather together, is always
so rendered in R.V., e.g., Matt. 27 : 62 ; Mark 7 : 1 ; Luke 22 : 66 ; Acts
13 : 44 ; 15 : 6 ; 20 : 7. See GATHER, No. 1. (13) For come to nought
see NOUGHT. (14) For *eisporeuomai* see ENTER, No. 4. (15) For " was
come again," Acts 22 : 17, A.V., see RETURN, No. 4. (16) For *engizō*, to
come near, see APPROACH, NIGH.

For COME BEHIND, see BEHIND

COMELINESS, COMELY
A. Noun.

EUSCHĒMOSUNĒ (εὐσχημοσύνη), elegance of figure, gracefulness,
comeliness (*eu*, well, *schēma*, a form), is found in this sense in 1 Cor. 12 : 23.
B. Adjective.

EUSCHĒMŌN (εὐσχήμων), akin to A, elegant in figure, well formed,
graceful, is used in 1 Cor. 12 : 24, of parts of the body (see above) ; in
1 Cor. 7 : 35, R.V., " (that which is) seemly," A.V., " comely ; " " honourable," Mark 15 : 43 ; Acts 13 : 50 ; 17 : 12. See HONOURABLE.¶
Note : In 1 Cor. 11 : 13, *prepō*, to be becoming, is rendered in the
A.V., " is it comely ? " R.V., " is it seemly ? " See BECOME, SEEMLY.

COMFORT, COMFORTER, COMFORTLESS
A. Nouns.

1. PARAKLĒSIS (παράκλησις), means a calling to one's side (*para*,
beside, *kaleō*, to call) ; hence, either an exhortation, or consolation,
comfort, e.g., Luke 2 : 25 (here " looking for the consolation of Israel "
is equivalent to waiting for the coming of the Messiah) ; 6 : 24 ; Acts
9 : 31 ; Rom. 15 : 4, 5 ; 1 Cor. 14 : 3, " exhortation ; " 2 Cor. 1 : 3, 4, 5,
6, 7 ; 7 : 4, 7, 13 ; 2 Thess. 2 : 16 ; Philm. 7. In 2 Thess. 2 : 16 it
combines encouragement with alleviation of grief. The R.V. changes
" consolation " into " comfort," except in Luke 2 : 25 ; 6 : 24 ; Acts
15 : 31 ; in Heb. 6 : 18, " encouragement ; " in Acts 4 : 36, " exhortation."
R.V. (A.V., " consolation "). See CONSOLATION, ENCOURAGEMENT, EX-
HORTATION, INTREATY.

2. PARAMUTHIA (παραμυθία), primarily a speaking closely to anyone
(*para*, near, *muthos*, speech), hence denotes consolation, comfort, with a
greater degree of tenderness than No. 1, 1 Cor. 14 : 3.¶

3. PARAMUTHION (παραμύθιον) has the same meaning as No. 2,
the difference being that *paramuthia* stresses the process or progress of the
act, *paramuthion* the instrument as used by the agent, Phil. 2 : 1.¶

4. PARĒGORIA (παρηγορία), primarily an addressing, address, hence

denotes a soothing, solace, Col. 4 : 11.¶ A verbal form of the word signifies medicines which allay irritation (Eng., paregoric).

5. PARAKLĒTOS (παράκλητος), lit., called to one's side, i.e., to one's aid, is primarily a verbal adjective, and suggests the capability or adaptability for giving aid. It was used in a court of justice to denote a legal assistant, counsel for the defence, an advocate ; then, generally, one who pleads another's cause, an intercessor, advocate, as in 1 John 2 : 1, of the Lord Jesus.   In the widest sense, it signifies a succourer, comforter. Christ was this to His disciples, by the implication of His word " another (*allos*, another of the same sort, not *heteros*, different) Comforter," when speaking of the Holy Spirit, John 14 : 16.   In 14 : 26 ; 15 : 26 ; 16 : 7 He calls Him " the Comforter.¶ '"" Comforter " or " Consoler " corresponds to the name " *Menahem*," given by the Hebrews to the Messiah.

B. Verbs.

1. PARAKALEŌ (παρακαλέω) has the same variety of meanings as Noun, No. 1, above, e.g., Matt. 2 : 18 ; 1 Thess. 3 : 2, 7 ; 4 : 18.   In 2 Cor. 13 : 11, it signifies to be comforted (so the R.V.).   See BESEECH.

2. SUMPARAKALEŌ (συμπαρακαλέω), *sun*, with, and No. 1, signifies to comfort together, Rom. 1 : 12.¶

3. PARAMUTHEOMAI (παραμυθέομαι), akin to Noun No. 2, to soothe, console, encourage, is translated, in John 11 : 31, " comforted ; " in ver. 19, R.V., " console."   In 1 Thess. 2 : 11 and 5 : 14, R.V., " encourage," as the sense there is that of stimulating to the earnest discharge of duties.   See CONSOLE, ENCOURAGE.¶

4. EUPSUCHEŌ (εὐψυχέω) signifies to be of good comfort (*eu*, well, *psuchē*, the soul), Phil. 2 : 19.¶

Notes : (1) For the verb *tharseō*, " be of good comfort," see CHEER, No. 2.

(2) *Orphanos* is rendered " comfortless " in John 14 : 18, A.V. ; R.V., " desolate."   See DESOLATE, FATHERLESS.

COMING (Noun)

1. EISODOS (εἴσοδος), an entrance (*eis*, in, *hodos*, a way), an entering in, is once translated " coming," Acts 13 : 24, of the coming of Christ into the nation of Israel.   For its meaning " entrance " see 1 Thess. 1 : 9 ; 2 : 1 ; Heb. 10 : 19 ; 2 Pet. 1 : 11.   See ENTER, ENTRANCE.¶

2. ELEUSIS (ἔλευσις), a coming (from *erchomai*, to come), is found in Acts 7 : 52.¶

3. PAROUSIA (παρουσία), lit., a presence, *para*, with, and *ousia*, being (from *eimi*, to be), denotes both an arrival and a consequent presence with. For instance, in a papyrus letter a lady speaks of the necessity of her *parousia* in a place in order to attend to matters relating to her property there. Paul speaks of his *parousia* in Philippi, Phil. 2 : 12 (in contrast to his *apousia*, his absence ; see ABSENCE).   Other words denote the arrival (see *eisodos* and *eleusis*, above). *Parousia* is used to describe the

presence of Christ with His disciples on the Mount of Transfiguration, 2 Pet. 1 : 16. When used of the return of Christ, at the Rapture of the Church, it signifies, not merely His momentary coming for His saints, but His presence with them from that moment until His revelation and manifestation to the world. In some passages the word gives prominence to the beginning of that period, the course of the period being implied, 1 Cor. 15 : 23 ; 1 Thess. 4 : 15 ; 5 : 23 ; 2 Thess. 2 : 1 ; Jas. 5 : 7, 8 ; 2 Pet. 3 : 4. In some, the course is prominent, Matt. 24 : 3, 37 ; 1 Thess. 3 : 13 ; 1 John 2 : 28 ; in others the conclusion of the period, Matt. 24 : 27 ; 2 Thess. 2 : 8.

The word is also used of the Lawless One, the Man of Sin, his access to power and his doings in the world during his *parousia*, 2 Thess. 2 : 9. In addition to Phil. 2 : 12 (above), it is used in the same way of the Apostle, or his companions, in 1 Cor. 16 : 17 ; 2 Cor. 7 : 6, 7 ; 10 : 10 ; Phil. 1 : 26 ; of the Day of God, 2 Pet. 3 : 12. See PRESENCE.

Note : The word *apokalupsis*, rendered " coming " in 1 Cor. 1 : 7, A.V., denotes a " revelation " (R.V.). For a fuller treatment of *Parousia*, see *Notes on Thessalonians*, by Hogg and Vine, pp. 87, 88.

COMMAND (Verbs)

1. DIATASSŌ (διατάσσω) signifies to set in order, appoint, command, Matt. 11 : 1 ; Luke 8 : 55 ; 17 : 9, 10 ; Acts 18 : 2 ; 23 : 31 ; " gave order," 1 Cor. 16 : 1, R.V. So in Acts 24 : 23, where it is in the Middle Voice. See APPOINT, No. 6.

2. EPŌ (ἔπω) denotes to speak (connected with *eipon*, to say) ; hence, among various renderings, to bid, command, Matt. 4 : 3 ; M ;k 5 : 43 ; 8 : 7 ; Luke 4 : 3 ; 19 : 15. See BID.

Note : In 2 Cor. 4 : 6, the R.V. rightly has " said," followed by the quotation " Light shall shine out of darkness."

3. ENTELLŌ (ἐντέλλω) signifies to enjoin upon, to charge with ; it is used in the Middle Voice in the sense of commanding, Matt. 19 : 7 ; 28 : 20 ; Mark 10 : 3 ; 13 : 34 ; John 8 : 5 ; 15 : 14, 17 ; Acts 13 : 47 ; Heb. 9 : 20 ; 11 : 22, " gave commandment." See CHARGE, ENJOIN.

4. EPITASSŌ (ἐπιτάσσω) signifies to appoint over, put in charge (*epi*, over, *tassō*, to appoint) ; then, to put upon one as a duty, to enjoin, Mark 1 : 27 ; 6 : 27, 39 ; 9 : 25 ; Luke 4 : 36 ; 8 : 25, 31 ; 14 : 22 ; Acts 23 : 2 ; Philm. 8. See CHARGE, ENJOIN.¶

5. KELEUŌ (κελεύω), to urge, incite, order, suggests a stronger injunction than No. 6, Matt. 14 : 9, 19 ; 15 : 35 ; 18 : 25 ; 27 : 58, 64 ; Luke 18 : 40 ; Acts 4 : 15 (frequently in Acts, not subsequently in the N.T.). See BID.

6. PARANGELLŌ (παραγγέλλω), to announce beside (*para*, beside, *angellō*, to announce), to pass on an announcement, hence denotes to give the word, order, give a charge, command, e.g., Mark 6 : 8 ; Luke

8 : 29 ; 9 : 21 ; Acts 5 : 28 ; 2 Thess. 3 : 4, 6, 10, 12. See CHARGE, B, No. 8.

7. PROSTASSŌ (προστάσσω) denotes to arrange or set in order towards (pros, towards, tassō, to arrange) ; hence to prescribe, give command, Matt. 1 : 24 ; 8 : 4 ; Mark 1 : 44 ; Luke 5 : 14 ; Acts 10 : 33, 48. For Matt. 21 : 6 see Note (3) below. See BID.¶

Notes : (1) In Rev. 9 : 4, *rheō*, to speak, is translated " said " in the R.V. (A.V., " commanded "). (2) in Heb. 12 : 20 *diastellomai*, to charge, enjoin (so in the R.V.), is rendered " commanded " in the A.V. (3) in Matt. 21 : 6, the R.V., translating *suntassō*, as in the best mss., has " appointed," A.V., " commanded."

COMMANDMENT

1. DIATAGMA (διάταγμα) signifies that which is imposed by decree or law, Heb. 11 : 23. It stresses the concrete character of the commandment more than *epitagē* (No. 4). Cp. COMMAND, No. 1. For the verb in ver. 22 see No. 3 under COMMAND.¶

2. ENTOLĒ (ἐντολή), akin to No. 3, above, denotes, in general, an injunction, charge, precept, commandment. It is the most frequent term, and is used of moral and religious precepts, e.g., Matt. 5 : 19 ; it is frequent in the Gospels, especially that of John, and in his Epistles. See also, e.g., Acts 17 : 15 ; Rom. 7 : 8–13 ; 13 : 9 ; 1 Cor. 7 : 19 ; Eph. 2 : 15 ; Col. 4 : 10. See PRECEPT.

3. ENTALMA (ἔνταλμα), akin to No. 2, marks more especially the thing commanded, a commission ; in Matt. 15 : 9 ; Mark 7 : 7 ; Col. 2 : 22, R.V., " precepts," A.V., " commandments." See PRECEPT.¶

4. EPITAGĒ (ἐπιταγή), akin to No. 4, above, stresses the authoritativeness of the command ; it is used in Rom. 16 : 26 ; 1 Cor. 7 : 6, 25 ; 2 Cor. 8 : 8 ; 1 Tim. 1 : 1 ; Tit. 1 : 3 ; 2 : 15. See AUTHORITY.¶

Notes : (1) For *parangelia* (cp. *parangellō*, above), a proclamation, see CHARGE. (2) In Rev. 22 : 14 the R.V., " wash their robes " (for A.V., " do His commandments ") follows the most authentic mss.

COMMEND, COMMENDATION
A. Verbs.

1. EPAINEŌ (ἐπαινέω), to praise, is an intensive form of *aineō*, Luke 16 : 8. It is elsewhere translated by the verb to praise, in the R.V., Rom. 15 : 11 ; 1 Cor. 11 : 2, 17, 22. See LAUD, PRAISE.¶

2. PARADIDŌMI (παραδίδωμι), lit., to give or deliver over (para, over, didōmi, to give), is said of commending, or committing, servants of God to Him (A.V., " recommend "), Acts 14 : 26 ; 15 : 40. See BETRAY, BRING, B, *Note* (4), CAST, COMMIT, DELIVER, GIVE, HAZARD, PUT (in prison), RECOMMEND.

3. PARATITHĒMI (παρατίθημι), lit., to put near (para, near), in the

Middle Voice, denotes to place with someone, entrust, commit. In the sense of commending, it is said (a) of the Lord Jesus in commending His spirit into the Father's hands, Luke 23 : 46 ; (b) of commending disciples to God, Acts 14 : 23 ; (c) of commending elders to God, Acts 20 : 32. See ALLEGE, COMMIT, PUT, No. 3, SET, No. 4. Cp. No. 2.

4. PARISTĒMI (παρίστημι), lit., to place near, set before, (para, near, histēmi, to set), is used of self-commendation, 1 Cor. 8 : 8. See ASSIST, BRING, COME, GIVE, PRESENT, PROVE, PROVIDE, SHEW, STAND, YIELD.

5. SUNISTĒMI (συνίστημι), or SUNISTANŌ (συνιστάνω), lit., to place together, denotes to introduce one person to another, represent as worthy, e.g., Rom. 3 : 5 ; 5 : 8 ; 16 : 1 ; 2 Cor. 4 : 2 ; 6 : 4 ; 10 : 18 ; 12 : 11. In 2 Cor. 3 : 1 ; 5 : 12 and 10 : 12, the verb sunistanō is used. See APPROVE, CONSIST, MAKE, STAND.

B. Adjective.

SUSTATIKOS (συστατικός), akin to A, No. 5, lit., placing together, hence, commendatory, is used of letters of commendation, 2 Cor. 3 : 1, lit., 'commendatory letters.'¶

COMMIT, COMMISSION
A. Verbs.
(I) In the sense of doing or practising.

1. ERGAZOMAI (ἐργάζομαι), to work, is translated by the verb to commit (of committing sin), in Jas. 2 : 9. This is a stronger expression than poieō, to do, or prassō, to practise (Nos. 2 and 3). See DO, LABOUR, MINISTER, TRADE, WORK.

2. POIEŌ (ποιέω), to do, cause etc., sometimes signifies to commit, of any act, as of murder, Mark 15 : 7 ; sin, John 8 : 34 ; 2 Cor. 11 : 7 ; Jas. 5 : 15. See DO.

Note : In 1 John 3 : 4, 8, 9, the A.V. wrongly has " commit " (an impossible meaning in ver. 8) ; the R.V. rightly has " doeth," i.e., of a continuous habit, equivalent to prassō, to practise. The committal of an act is not in view in that passage.

3. PRASSŌ (πράσσω), to do, work, practise, is said of continuous action, or action not yet completed, Acts 25 : 11, 25 ; it is rendered " practise " in the R.V., for the incorrect A.V. " commit," in Rom. 1 : 32 ; 2 : 2. See DO, EXACT, KEEP, REQUIRE, USE.

(II) In the sense of delivering or entrusting something to a person.

1. PARADIDŌMI (παραδίδωμι), to give over, is often rendered by the verb to commit, e.g., to prison, Acts 8 : 3 ; to the grace of God, Acts 14 : 26 ; to God, 1 Pet. 2 : 23 ; by God to pits of darkness, 2 Pet. 2 : 4. See COMMEND, No. 2.

2. PISTEUŌ (πιστεύω) signifies to entrust, commit to, Luke 16 : 11 ; 1 Tim. 1 : 11, " committed to (my) trust." See BELIEVE.

3. TITHĒMI (τίθημι), to put, place, signifies, in the Middle Voice,

to put for oneself, assign, place in, 2 Cor. 5 : 19, " having committed
(unto us)."

4. PARATITHĒMI (παρατίθημι), see COMMEND, No. 3, signifies to
entrust, commit to one's charge, e.g., in Luke 12 : 48 ; 1 Tim. 1 : 18 ;
2 Tim. 2 : 2 ; 1 Pet. 4 : 19 (A.V., " commit the keeping ").

Notes : (1) *Didōmi*, to give, is rendered " committed " in the A.V.
of John 5 : 22 (R.V., " given "). (2) For *porneuō* (to commit fornication)
see FORNICATION. (3) In Rom. 2 : 22, *hierosuleō*, to rob temples, is so
rendered in the R.V., for A.V., " commit sacrilege." (4) In Acts 27 : 40,
eaō, to let, leave, is rendered in the R.V., " left (the anchors) in ",
for A.V., " committed themselves to."

B. Nouns.

1. PARATHĒKĒ (παραθήκη), a putting with, a deposit (*para*, with,
tithēmi, to put), and its longer form, *parakatathēkē*, are found, the former
in 2 Tim. 1 : 12, " that which He hath committed unto me," R.V., marg.,
lit., ' my deposit ' (perhaps, ' my deposit with Him '), the latter in 1 Tim.
6 : 20, where " guard that which is committed unto thee " is, lit., ' guard
the deposit,' and 2 Tim. 1 : 14, " that good thing which was committed unto thee," i.e., the good deposit ; R.V., marg., " the good
deposit."¶

2. EPITROPĒ (ἐπιτροπή) denotes a turning over (to another), a
referring of a thing to another (*epi*, over, *trepō*, to turn), and so a
committal of full powers, a commission, Acts 26 : 12.¶

COMMODIOUS (not)

ANEUTHETOS (ἀνεύθετος), not commodious, lit., ' not-well-placed '
(from *a*, not, *n*, euphonic, *eu*, well, *thetos*, from *tithēmi*, to put, place), is
found in Acts 27 : 12, where it is said of the haven at the place called
Fair Havens.¶

COMMON, COMMONLY
A. Adjective.

KOINOS (κοινός) denotes (*a*) common, belonging to several (Lat.,
communis), said of things had in common, Acts 2 : 44 ; 4 : 32 ; of faith,
Tit. 1 : 4 ; of salvation, Jude 3 ; it stands in contrast to *idios*, one's own ;
(*b*) ordinary, belonging to the generality, as distinct from what is peculiar
to the few ; hence the application to religious practices of Gentiles in
contrast with those of Jews ; or of the ordinary people in contrast with
those of the Pharisees ; hence the meaning unhallowed, profane, Leviti-
cally unclean (Lat., *profanus*), said of hands, Mark 7 : 2 (A.V., " defiled,")
R.V. marg., " common ; " of animals, ceremonially unclean, Acts 10 : 14 ;
11 : 8 ; of a man, 10 : 28 ; of meats, Rom. 14 : 14, " unclean ; " of the
blood of the covenant, as viewed by an apostate, Heb. 10 : 29, " unholy "
(R.V., marg., " common ") ; of everything unfit for the holy city, Rev.

21 : 27, R.V., " unclean " (marg., " common "). Some mss. have the verb here. See DEFILED, UNCLEAN, UNHOLY.¶

B. Verb.

KOINOŌ (κοινόω), to make, or count, common, has this meaning in Acts 10 : 15 ; 11 : 9. See DEFILE, POLLUTE, UNCLEAN.

Notes : (1) *Polus*, used of number, signifies many, numerous ; used of space, it signifies wide, far reaching ; hence, with the article it is said of a multitude as being numerous ; it is translated " common " (people) in Mark 12 : 37 (see the R.V., marg.). It does not, however, mean the ordinary folk, but the many folk. See ABUNDANT, GREAT, LONG, MANY, MUCH, PLENTY.

(2) *Ochlos* denotes a crowd, a great multitude ; with the article it is translated " the common people," in John 12 : 9, 12 (R.V., marg.). See COMPANY, CROWD, MULTITUDE, NUMBER, PEOPLE, PRESS.

(3) *Tunchanō*, to happen, is used as an adjective in Acts 28 : 2, of the kindness shown by the people of Melita to the shipwrecked company ; A.V., " (no) little ; " R.V., " (no) common ; " the idea suggested by the verb is that which might happen anywhere or at all times ; hence, little, ordinary, or casual. See CHANCE, ENJOY, OBTAIN.

(4) In Matt. 27 : 27, what the A.V. describes as " the common hall," is the prætorium, R.V., " palace," the official residence of the Governor of a Province (marg., " prætorium ").

(5) In Acts 5 : 18, *dēmosios* (A.V., " common," with reference to the prison) signifies " public," belonging to the people, *dēmos*, (R.V., " public ").

(6) In 1 Cor. 5 : 1, *holōs*, altogether (A.V., " commonly ") means " actually " (R.V.).

(7) In Matt. 28 : 15, *diaphēmizō*, to spread abroad (as in the R.V.), is rendered in the A.V., " is commonly reported." See SPREAD, *Note* (5).

COMMONWEALTH

1. POLITEIA (πολιτεία) : see CITIZENSHIP, No. 3.
2. POLITEUMA (πολίτευμα) : see CITIZENSHIP, No. 4.

For COMMOTION see CONFUSION, TUMULT

COMMUNE

1. DIALALEŌ (διαλαλέω) signifies to speak with anyone (*dia*, by turns, *laleō*, to speak), Luke 6 : 11 ; in 1 : 65, to talk over, to noise abroad. The idea that *laleō* and its compounds bear no reference to the word spoken or the sentiment, is unfounded. See NOISE.¶

2. HOMILEŌ (ὁμιλέω), from *homos*, together, signifies to be in company, to associate with any one ; hence, to have intercourse with,

Luke 24 : 14 (R.V., " communed ; " A.V., " talked "), 15 ; Acts 24 : 26 ; in 20 : 11, " talked with." See TALK.¶

3. SULLALEŌ (συλλαλέω), to talk together, is translated " communed " in Luke 22 : 4, of the conspiracy of Judas with the chief priests. See CONFER, SPEAK, TALK.

Note : *Laleō* and its compounds, and the noun *lalia*, speech, have a more dignified meaning in the Hellenistic Greek than to chatter, its frequent meaning in earlier times.

COMMUNICATE, COMMUNICATION
A. Verbs.

1. KOINŌNEŌ (κοινωνέω) is used in two senses, (*a*) to have a share in, Rom. 15 : 27 ; 1 Tim. 5 : 22 ; Heb. 2 : 14 ; 1 Pet. 4 : 13 ; 2 John 11 ; (*b*) to give a share to, go shares with, Rom. 12 : 13, R.V., " communicating," for A.V., " distributing ; " Gal. 6 : 6, " communicate ; " Phil. 4 : 15, A.V., " did communicate," R.V., " had fellowship with." See DISTRIBUTE, FELLOWSHIP, PARTAKE.¶

2. SUNKOINŌNEŌ (συγκοινωνέω), to share together with (*sun* and No. 1), is translated " communicated with " in Phil. 4 : 14 ; " have fellowship with," Eph. 5 : 11 ; " be . . . partakers of," Rev. 18 : 4 (R.V., " have fellowship "). The thought is that of sharing with others what one has, in order to meet their needs. See FELLOWSHIP, B, No. 2, PARTAKE, B, No. 2.¶

Note : *Anatithēmi*, to set forth, is rendered " laid before " in Gal. 2 : 2, R.V., for A.V., " communicated unto ; " in Acts 25 : 14, R.V., " laid before," for A.V., " declared."¶

B. Nouns.

1. KOINŌNIA (κοινωνία), akin to A (which see), is translated in Heb. 13 : 16 " to communicate," lit., ' be not forgetful of good deed and of fellowship ; ' " fellowship " (A.V., " communication ") in Philm. 6, R.V. See COMMUNION.

2. LOGOS (λόγος), a word, that which is spoken (*legō*, to speak), is used in the plural with reference to a conversation ; " communication," Luke 24 : 17. Elsewhere with this significance the R.V. renders it " speech," Matt. 5 : 37 ; Eph. 4 : 29. See ACCOUNT.

Note : In Col. 3 : 8, where the A.V. translates *aischrologia* by " filthy communication," the R.V. renders it " shameful speaking " (*aischros*, base, *legō*, to speak).

C. Adjective.

KOINŌNIKOS (κοινωνικός), akin to A, No. 1 and B, No. 1, means apt, or ready, to communicate, 1 Tim. 6 : 18.¶

Note : *Homilia*, a company, association, or intercourse with (see COMMUNE, No. 2), is translated " company " in 1 Cor. 15 : 33, R.V. (A.V., " communications ") ; the word is in the plural, " evil companies," i.e., associations. See COMPANY, No. 6.¶

COMMUNION
A. Noun.

KOINŌNIA (κοινωνία), a having in common (koinos), partnership, fellowship (see COMMUNICATE), denotes (a) the share which one has in anything, a participation, fellowship recognized and enjoyed ; thus it is used of the common experiences and interests of Christian men, Acts 2 : 42 ; Gal. 2 : 9 ; of participation in the knowledge of the Son of God, 1 Cor. 1 : 9 ; of sharing in the realization of the effects of the Blood (i.e., the Death) of Christ and the Body of Christ, as set forth by the emblems in the Lord's Supper, 1 Cor. 10 : 16 ; of participation in what is derived from the Holy Spirit, 2 Cor. 13 : 14 (R.V., " communion ") ; Phil. 2 : 1 ; of participation in the sufferings of Christ, Phil. 3 : 10 ; of sharing in the resurrection life possessed in Christ, and so of fellowship with the Father and the Son, 1 John 1 : 3, 6, 7 ; negatively, of the impossibility of communion between light and darkness, 2 Cor. 6 : 14 ; (b) fellowship manifested in acts, the practical effects of fellowship with God, wrought by the Holy Spirit in the lives of believers as the outcome of faith, Philm. 6, and finding expression in joint ministration to the needy, Rom. 15 : 26 ; 2 Cor. 8 : 4 ; 9 : 13 ; Heb. 13 : 16, and in the furtherance of the Gospel by gifts, Phil. 1 : 5.   See COMMUNICATION, CONTRIBUTION, DISTRIBUTION, FELLOWSHIP.¶

B. Adjective.

KOINŌNOS (κοινωνός), having in common, is rendered " have communion with (the altar), "—the altar standing by metonymy for that which is associated with it—in 1 Cor. 10 : 18, R.V. (for A.V., " are partakers of "), and in ver. 20, for A.V., " have fellowship with (demons)." See COMPANION.

COMPACTED

1. SUNISTĒMI (συνίστημι), and transitively sunistaō, to stand together (sun, with, histēmi, to stand), is rendered " compacted," in 2 Pet. 3 : 5, of the earth as formerly arranged by God in relation to the waters.   See APPROVE, COMMEND, CONSIST, MAKF STAND.

2. SUMBIBAZŌ (συμβιβάζω), to unite, to knit, is translated " compacted " in the A.V. of Eph. 4 : 16 (R.V., " knit together "), concerning the Church as the Body of Christ.   See CONCLUDE, GATHER, INSTRUCT, KNIT, PROVE.

COMPANION

1. SUNEKDĒMOS (συνέκδημος), a fellow-traveller (sun, with, ek, from, dēmos, people ; i.e., away from one's people), is used in Acts 19 : 29, of Paul's companions in travel ; in 2 Cor. 8 : 19, " travel with ; " a closer rendering would be ' (as) our fellow-traveller.'   See TRAVEL.¶

2. KOINŌNOS (κοινωνός) is rendered " companions " in the A.V. of Heb. 10 : 33 (R.V. " partakers "). So sunkoinōnos in Rev. 1 : 9, A.V., " companion ; " R.V , " partaker with you." See B, above, PARTAKER, PARTNER. Cp. COMMUNICATE.

3. SUNERGOS (συνεργός), a fellow-worker (sun, with, ergon, work), is translated in Phil. 2 : 25 " companion in labour," A.V. (R.V., " fellow-worker "). See HELPER, LABOURER, WORKER.

COMPANY (Noun and Verb)
A. Nouns and Phrases.

1. OCHLOS (ὄχλος), a throng of people, an irregular crowd, most usually a disorganised throng ; in Acts 6 : 7, however, it is said of a company of the priests who believed ; the word here indicates that they had not combined to bring this about. The R.V. usually translates this word " company " or " multitude." Cp. B, Note 3. See COMMON, CROWD, MULTITUDE, and Trench, Syn. §xcviii.

2. SUNODIA (συνοδία), lit., a way or journey together (sun, with, hodos, a way), denotes, by metonymy, a company of travellers ; in Luke 2 : 44, of the company from which Christ was missed by Joseph and Mary. (Eng., synod).¶

3. SUMPOSION (συμπόσιον), lit. denotes a drinking together (sun, with, pinō, to drink), a drinking-party ; hence, by metonymy, any table party or any company arranged as a party. In Mark 6 : 39 the noun is repeated, in the plural, by way of an adverbial and distributive phrase, sumposia sumposia, lit., ' companies-companies ' (i.e., by companies).¶

4. KLISIA (κλισία), akin to klinō, to recline, primarily means a place for lying down in, and hence a reclining company, for the same purpose as No. 3. It is found in the plural in Luke 9 : 14, corresponding to Mark's word sumposia (No. 3, above), signifying companies reclining at a meal.¶

5. PLĒTHOS (πλῆθος), lit., a fulness, hence denotes a multitude, a large or full company, Luke 23 : 1 ; " a multitude," ver. 27 (A.V., " a great company "). See BUNDLE, MULTITUDE.

6. HOMILIA (ὁμιλία), an association of people, those who are of the same company (homos, same), is used in 1 Cor. 15 : 33, A.V., " (evil) communications ; " R.V., " (evil) company."¶

7. HOMILOS (ὅμιλος), akin to No. 6, a throng or crowd, is found, in some mss., in Rev. 18 : 17, " all the company in ships," A.V. Homilos denotes the concrete ; homilia is chiefly an abstract noun.¶

8. IDIOS (ἴδιος) one's own, is used in the plural with the article in Acts 4 : 23, to signify " their own (company)." See BUSINESS, B.

Notes : (1) The preposition ex (i.e., ek), of, with the first personal pronoun in the genitive plural (hēmōn, us), signifies " of our company," lit., ' of us,' in Luke 24 : 22 ; so ex autōn, in Acts 15 : 22, " men out of their company," lit., ' men out of them.' (2) The phrase in Acts 13 : 13, hoi peri Paulon, lit., ' the (ones) about Paul,' signifies " Paul and his company." (3) Murias, a noun connected with the adjective murios (numberless, infinite), signifies a myriad (whence the English word), and is used hyperbolically, of vast numbers, e.g., Heb. 12 : 22, A.V., an innumerable company ; R.V., " innumerable hosts." (Contrast *murioi*, 10,000, Matt. 18 : 24). (4) In Acts 21 : 8, the phrase translated " that were of Paul's company " is absent from the best texts.

B. Verbs.

1. SUNANAMIGNUMI (συναναμίγνυμι), lit., to mix up with (*sun*, with, *ana*, up, *mignumi*, to mix, mingle), signifies to have, or keep, company with, 1 Cor. 5 : 9, 11 ; 2 Thess. 3 : 14.¶

2. SUNERCHOMAI (συνέρχομαι), to come, or go, with, is rendered " have companied " in Acts 1 : 21. See COME, No. 11.

Notes : (1) *Aphorizō*, to separate, is translated " separate (you) from (their) company," in Luke 6 : 22, the latter part being added in italics to supply the meaning of excommunication. See DIVIDE.

(2) *Kollaō*, to join, is rendered " keep company," in Acts 10 : 28, A.V. ; R.V., " join himself." See CLEAVE, JOIN.

(3) *Ochlopoieō*, lit., to make a crowd (*ochlos*, a crowd, *poieō*, to make), is translated " gathered a company," in Acts 17 : 5, A.V. ; the R.V. corrects this to " gathering a crowd." See CROWD.¶

COMPARE, COMPARISON

1. SUNKRINŌ (συγκρίνω) denotes (*a*) to join fitly, to combine, 1 Cor. 2 : 13, either in the sense of combining spiritual things with spiritual, adapting the discourse to the subject, under the guidance of the Holy Spirit, or communicating spiritual things by spiritual things or words, or in the sense of interpreting spiritual things to spiritual men, R.V. and A.V., " comparing " (cp. the Sept. use, of interpreting dreams, etc. Gen. 40 : 8, 16, 22 ; 41 : 12, 15 ; Dan. 5 : 12) ; (*b*) to place together ; hence, judge or discriminate by comparison, compare, with or among, 2 Cor. 10 : 12 (thrice).¶

2. PARABALLŌ (παραβάλλω), to place side by side, to set forth, and the noun *parabolē* (Eng., parable), occur in Mark 4 : 30, R.V., " In what parable shall we set it forth ? ", A.V., " with what comparison shall we compare it ? " See ARRIVE.

Note : The preposition *pros*, towards, is sometimes used of mental direction, in the way of estimation, or comparison, as in the phrase " (worthy) to be compared," or ' (worthy) in comparison with,' Rom. 8 : 18.

COMPASS

1. KUKLEUŌ (κυκλεύω) denotes to encircle, surround, and is found in the best texts in John 10 : 24, " came round about," and Rev. 20 : 9, of a camp surrounded by foes ; some mss. have No. 2 in each place.¶

2. KUKLOŌ (κυκλόω), (cp. Eng., cycle), signifies to move in a circle, to compass about, as of a city encompassed by armies, Luke 21 : 20 ; Heb. 11 : 30 ; in Acts 14 : 20, " stood round about." See COME, No. 38, STAND.¶

3. PERIKUKLOŌ (περικυκλόω), *peri*, about, with No. 2, is used in Luke 19 : 43, " shall compass . . . round."¶

4. PERIAGŌ (περιάγω), to lead about, 1 Cor. 9 : 5, or, intransitively, to go about, to go up and down, is so used in Matt. 4 : 23 ; 9 : 35 ; Mark 6 : 6 ; Acts 13 : 11 ; to compass regions, Matt. 23 : 15. See GO, LEAD.¶

5. PERIKEIMAI (περίκειμαι), to be encompassed : see BOUND (*b*), HANG.

6. PERIERCHOMAI (περιέρχομαι), lit., to go, or come, about (*peri*, about, *erchomai*, to come), is translated in Acts 28 : 13, A.V., " fetched a compass." See CIRCUIT.

COMPASSION, COMPASSIONATE

A. Verbs.

1. OIKTEIRŌ (οἰκτείρω), to have pity, a feeling of distress through the ills of others, is used of God's compassion, Rom. 9 : 15.¶

2. SPLANCHNIZOMAI (σπλαγχνίζομαι), to be moved as to one's inwards (*splanchna*), to be moved with compassion, to yearn with compassion, is frequently recorded of Christ towards the multitude and towards individual sufferers, Matt. 9 : 36 ; 14 : 14 ; 15 : 32 ; 18 : 27 ; 20 : 34 ; Mark 1 : 41 ; 6 : 34 ; 8 : 2 ; 9 : 22 (of the appeal of a father for a demon-possessed son) ; Luke 7 : 13 ; 10 : 33 ; of the father in the parable of the prodigal son, 15 : 20. (Moulton and Milligan consider the verb to have been coined in the Jewish Dispersion).¶

3. SUMPATHEŌ (συμπαθέω), to suffer with another (*sun*, with, *paschō*, to suffer), to be affected similarly (Eng., sympathy), to have compassion upon, Heb. 10 : 34, of compassionating those in prison, is translated " be touched with " in Heb. 4 : 15, of Christ as the High Priest. See TOUCH.¶

4. ELEEŌ (ἐλεέω), to have mercy (*eleos*, mercy), to show kindness, by beneficence, or assistance, is translated " have compassion " in Matt. 18 : 33 (A.V.) ; Mark 5 : 19 and Jude 22. See MERCY.

5. METRIOPATHEŌ (μετριοπαθέω) is rendered " have compassion," in Heb. 5 : 2, A.V. See BEAR, No. 13.¶

B. Nouns.

1. OIKTIRMOS (οἰκτιρμός), akin to A, No. 1, is used with *splanchna* (see below), the viscera, the inward parts, as the seat of emotion, the " heart," Phil. 2 : 1 ; Col. 3 : 12, " a heart of compassion " (A.V., " bowels of mercies "). In Heb. 10 : 28 it is used with *chōris*, " without," (lit., ' without compassions '). It is translated " mercies " in Rom. 12 : 1 and 2 Cor. 1 : 3. See MERCY.¶

2. SPLANCHNON (σπλάγχνον), always used in the plural, is suitably rendered " compassion " in the R.V. of Col. 3 : 12 and 1 John 3 : 17 ; " compassions " in Phil. 2 : 1. Cp. A, No. 2. See BOWELS.

C. Adjective.

SUMPATHĒS (συμπαθής) denotes suffering with, "compassionate," 1 Pet. 3 : 8, R.V. (A.V., "having compassion"). See A, No. 3.¶

COMPEL

1. ANANKAZŌ (ἀναγκάζω) denotes to put constraint upon (from anankē, necessity), to constrain, whether by threat, entreaty, force or persuasion; Christ "constrained" the disciples to get into a boat, Matt. 14 : 22; Mark 6 : 45; the servants of the man who made a great supper were to constrain people to come in, Luke 14 : 23 (R.V., "constrain"); Saul of Tarsus "strove" to make saints blaspheme, Acts 26 : 11, R.V. (A.V., "compelled"); Titus, though a Greek, was not "compelled" to be circumcised, Gal. 2 : 3, as Galatian converts were, 6 : 12, R.V.; Peter was "compelling" Gentiles to live as Jews, Gal. 2 : 14; Paul was "constrained" to appeal to Cæsar, Acts 28 : 19, and was "compelled" by the church at Corinth to become foolish in speaking of himself, 2 Cor. 12 : 11. See CONSTRAIN.¶

2. ANGAREUŌ (ἀγγαρεύω), to despatch as an angaros (a Persian courier kept at regular stages with power of impressing men into service), and hence, in general, to impress into service, is used of compelling a person to go a mile, Matt. 5 : 41; of the impressing of Simon to bear Christ's Cross, Matt. 27 : 32; Mark 15 : 21.¶

COMPLAINER, COMPLAINT

1. MEMPSIMOIROS (μεμψίμοιρος) denotes one who complains, lit., complaining of one's lot (memphomai, to blame; moira, a fate, lot); hence, discontented, querulous, repining; it is rendered "complainers" in Jude 16.¶

2. MOMPHĒ (μομφή) denotes blame (akin to memphomai, see No. 1), an occasion of complaint, Col. 3 : 13 (A.V., "quarrel"). See QUARREL.¶

3. AITIŌMA (αἰτίωμα), a charge, is translated "complaints" in Acts 25 : 7, A.V. See CHARGE.¶

COMPLETE, COMPLETION, COMPLETELY
A. Verbs.

1. EPITELEŌ (ἐπιτελέω), to complete: see ACCOMPLISH, No. 4.

2. EXARTIZŌ (ἐξαρτίζω), to fit out (ek, out, intensive, artos, a joint; or from artios, perfect, lit., exactly right), is said of the equipment of the man of God, 2 Tim. 3 : 17, "furnished completely" (A.V., "throughly furnished"); elsewhere in Acts 21 : 5, "accomplished." Cp. B. See FURNISH.¶

3. SUNTELEŌ (συντελέω), to end together, bring quite to an end (sun, together, intensive, telos, an end), is said (a) of the completion of a period of days, Luke 4 : 2; Acts 21 : 27; (b) of completing something; some mss. have it in Matt. 7 : 28, of the Lord, in ending His discourse

(the best mss. have *teleō* to finish) ; of God, in finishing a work, Rom. 9 : 28, in making a new covenant, Heb. 8 : 8, marg., "accomplish ;" of the fulfilment of things foretold, Mark 13 : 4 ; of the Devil's temptation of the Lord, Luke 4 : 13. See END, FINISH, FULFIL, MAKE.¶

4. PLĒROŌ (πληρόω), to fill (in the Passive Voice, to be made full), is translated "complete" in the A.V. of Col. 2 : 10 (R.V., "made full ;" cp. v. 9). See ACCOMPLISH.

5. PLEROPHOREŌ (πληροφορέω), to be fully assured, is translated "complete" in Col. 4 : 12. See ASSURED, B, No. 2.

B. Adjective.

ARTIOS (ἄρτιος), fitted, complete (from *artos*, a limb, joint), is used in 2 Tim. 3 : 17, R.V., "complete," A.V., "perfect." See PERFECT.¶

C. Noun.

APARTISMOS (ἀπαρτισμός) is rendered "complete" in Luke 14 : 28, R.V.¶

For COMPREHEND see APPREHEND, John 1 : 5, A.V., and SUM UP

CONCEAL

PARAKALUPTŌ (παρακαλύπτω), to conceal thoroughly (*para*, beside, intensive, *kaluptō*, to hide), is found in Luke 9 : 45, of concealing from the disciples the fact of the delivering up of Christ.

CONCEITS

1. EN HEAUTOIS (ἐν ἑαυτοῖς), lit., 'in yourselves,' is used with *phronimos*, "wise," in Rom. 11 : 25, "(wise) in your own conceits (i.e., opinions)."

2. PAR' HEAUTOIS (παρ' ἑαυτοῖς), (*para*, with, in the estimation of), in Rom. 12 : 16 has the same rendering as No. 1.

CONCEIVE

1. GENNAŌ (γεννάω), to conceive, beget : see BEGET, A, No. 1.

2. SULLAMBANŌ (συλλαμβάνω), lit., to take together (*sun*, with, *lambanō*, to take or receive), is used (*a*) of a woman, to conceive, Luke 1 : 24, 31, 36 ; in the Passive Voice. Luke 2 : 21 ; (*b*) metaphorically, of the impulse of lust in the human heart, enticing to sin, Jas. 1 : 15. For its other meanings see CATCH, No. 8.

3. TITHĒMI (τίθημι), to put, set, is used in Acts 5 : 4, of the sin of Ananias, in conceiving a lie in his heart.

Notes : (1) The phrase *echō*, to have, with *koitē*, a lying down, a bed, especially the marriage bed, denotes to conceive, Rom. 9 : 10.¶

(2) The phrase *eis katabolēn*, lit., for a casting down, or in, is used of conception in Heb. 11 : 11.¶

CONCERN (-ETH)

1. The neuter plural of the article ('the things'), with the genitive case of a noun, is used in 2 Cor. 11 : 30 of Paul's infirmity, "the things that concern my infirmity," lit., 'the (things) of my infirmity.'

2. The neuter singular of the article, with the preposition *peri*, concerning, is used by the Lord in Luke 22 : 37, "that which concerneth," lit., 'the (thing) concerning (Me).' The same construction is found in Luke 24 : 27 ; Acts 19 : 8 ; 28 : 31.

CONCERNING : see Note †, p. 9.

CONCISION

KATATOMĒ (κατατομή), lit., a cutting off (*kata*, down, *temnō*, to cut), a mutilation, is a term found in Phil. 3 : 2, there used by the Apostle, by a paranomasia, contemptuously, for the Jewish circumcision with its Judaistic influence, in contrast to the true spiritual circumcision.¶

CONCLUDE

SUMBIBAZŌ (συμβιβάζω), lit., to make to come together, is translated "concluding" in Acts 16 : 10, R.V., for the A.V., "assuredly gathering." See COMPACTED, INSTRUCT, KNIT, PROVE.

Notes : (1) For *krinō*, to judge, give judgment, rendered "concluded" in the A.V. of Acts 21 : 25, R.V., "giving judgment," see JUDGMENT.

(2) For *logizomai*, to reckon, translated "conclude" in Rom. 3 : 28, A.V., R.V., "reckon," see RECKON.

(3) For *sunkleiō*, to shut up with, translated "concluded" in Rom. 11 : 32 ; Gal. 3 : 22, A.V., R.V., "shut up," see INCLOSE, SHUT.

CONCORD

SUMPHŌNĒSIS (συμφώνησις), lit., a sounding together (*sun*, with, *phōnē*, a sound ; Eng., symphony), is found in 2 Cor. 6 : 15, in the rhetorical question "what concord hath Christ with Belial?" See AGREE, A, No. 1.¶

CONCOURSE

SUNTROPHĒ (συντροφή), a turning together (*sun*, with, *trepō*, to turn), signifies (*a*) that which is rolled together ; hence (*b*) a dense mass of people, concourse, Acts 19 : 40.¶ See BANDED.

For CONCUPISCENCE (A.V. of Rom. 7 : 8 ; Col. 3 : 5 ; 1 Thess. 4 : 5), see COVET, DESIRE, LUST.

CONDEMN, CONDEMNATION
A. Verbs.

1. KATAGINŌSKŌ (καταγινώσκω), to know something against (*kata*,

against, *ginōskō*, to know by experience), hence, to think ill of, to condemn, is said, in Gal. 2 : 11, of Peter's conduct (R.V., " stood condemned "), he being self-condemned as the result of an exercised and enlightened conscience, and condemned in the sight of others ; so of self-condemnation due to an exercise of heart, 1 John 3 : 20, 21.   See BLAME.¶

2. KATADIKAZŌ (*καταδικάζω*) signifies to exercise right or law against anyone ; hence, to pronounce judgment, to condemn (*kata*, down, or against, *dikē*, justice), Matt. 12 : 7, 37 ;   Luke 6 : 37 ;   Jas. 5 : 6.¶

3. KRINŌ (*κρίνω*), to distinguish, choose, give an opinion upon, judge, sometimes denotes to condemn, e.g., Acts 13 : 27 ;   Rom. 2 : 27 ; Jas. 5 : 9 (in the best mss.).   Cp. No. 1, below.   See CALL (No. 13), CONCLUDE, DECREE, DETERMINE, ESTEEM, JUDGE, LAW (go to), ORDAIN, SUE, THINK.

4. KATAKRINŌ (*κατακρίνω*), a strengthened form of No. 3, signifies to give judgment against, pass sentence upon ; hence, to condemn, implying (*a*) the fact of a crime, e.g., Rom. 2 : 1 ;   14 : 23 ;   2 Pet. 2 : 6 ; some mss. have it in Jas. 5 : 9 ;   (*b*) the imputation of a crime, as in the condemnation of Christ by the Jews, Matt. 20 : 18 ;   Mark 14 : 64.   It is used metaphorically of condemning by a good example, Matt. 12 : 41, 42 ;   Luke 11 : 31, 32 ;   Heb. 11 : 7.

In Rom. 8 : 3, God's condemnation of sin is set forth in that Christ, His own Son, sent by Him to partake of human nature (sin apart) and to become an offering for sin, died under the judgment due to our sin.

B. Nouns.

1. KRIMA (*κρίμα*) denotes (*a*) the sentence pronounced, a verdict, a condemnation, the decision resulting from an investigation, e.g., Mark 12 : 40 ;   Luke 23 : 40 ;   1 Tim. 3 : 6 ;   Jude 4 ;   (*b*) the process of judgment leading to a decision, 1 Pet. 4 : 17 (" judgment "), where *krisis* (see No. 3, below) might be expected.   In Luke 24 : 20, " to be condemned " translates the phrase *eis krima*, " unto condemnation " (i.e., unto the pronouncement of the sentence of condemnation).   For the rendering " judgment," see, e.g., Rom. 11 : 33 ;   1 Cor. 11 : 34 ;   Gal. 5 : 10 ;   Jas. 3 : 1. In these (*a*) the process leading to a decision and (*b*) the pronouncement of the decision, the verdict, are to be distinguished.   In 1 Cor. 6 : 7 the word means a matter for judgment, a lawsuit.   See JUDGMENT.

2. KATAKRIMA (*κατάκριμα*), cp. No. 4, above, is the sentence pronounced, the condemnation with a suggestion of the punishment following ; it is found in Rom. 5 : 16, 18 ;   8 : 1.¶

3. KRISIS (*κρίσις*) (*a*) denotes the process of investigation, the act of distinguishing and separating (as distinct from *krima*, see No. 1 above) ; hence a judging, a passing of judgment upon a person or thing ;   it has a variety of meanings, such as judicial authority, John 5 : 22, 27 ;   justice, Acts 8 : 33 ;   Jas. 2 : 13 ;   a tribunal, Matt. 5 : 21, 22 ;   a trial, John 5 : 24 ; 2 Pet. 2 : 4 ;   a judgment, 2 Pet. 2 : 11 ;   Jude 9 ;   by metonymy, the

standard of judgment, just dealing, Matt. 12 : 18, 20 ; 23 : 23 ; Luke 11 : 42 ; Divine judgment executed, 2 Thess. 1 : 5 ; Rev. 16 : 7 ; (b) sometimes it has the meaning " condemnation," and is virtually equivalent to *krima* (a) ; see Matt. 23 : 33 ; John 3 : 19 ; Jas. 5 : 12, *hupo krisin*, " under judgment." See Accusation, A (Note), Damnation, Judgment.

Note : In John 9 : 39, " For judgment (*krima*) came I into this world," the meaning would appear to be, ' for being judged ' (as a touchstone for proving men's thoughts and characters), in contrast to 5 : 22, ' hath given all judging (*krisis*) to the Son ; ' in Luke 24 : 20, " delivered Him up to be condemned to death," the latter phrase is, lit., ' to a verdict (*krima*) of death ' (which they themselves could not carry out) ; in Mark 12 : 40, " these shall receive greater condemnation " (*krima*), the phrase signifies a heavier verdict (against themselves).

4. KATAKRISIS (κατάκρισις), a strengthened form of No. 3, denotes a judgment against, condemnation, with the suggestion of the process leading to it, as of " the ministration of condemnation," 2 Cor. 3 : 9 ; in 7 : 3, " to condemn," more lit., ' with a view to condemnation.'¶

C. Adjectives.

1. AUTOKATAKRITOS (αὐτοκατάκριτος), self-condemned (*auto*, self, *katakrinō*, to condemn), i.e., on account of doing himself what he condemns in others, is used in Tit. 3 : 11.¶

2. AKATAGNŌSTOS (ἀκατάγνωστος), akin to A, No. 1, with negative prefix, *a*, " not to be condemned," is said of sound speech, in Tit. 2 : 8.¶

CONDESCEND

SUNAPAGŌ (συναπάγω) : see Carry, No. 7.

CONDITIONS

Note : This translates the phrase *ta pros* in Luke 14 : 32, lit., ' the (things) towards,' i.e., the things relating to, or conditions of, (peace).

CONDUCT
A. Noun.

AGŌGĒ (ἀγωγή), from *agō*, to lead, properly denotes a teaching ; then, figuratively, a training, discipline, and so, the life led, a way or course of life, conduct, 2 Tim. 3 : 10, R.V., " conduct ; " A.V., " manner of life." See Life.¶

B. Verbs.

1. KATHISTĒMI (καθίστημι), lit., to stand down or set down (*kata*, down, *histēmi*, to stand), has, among its various meanings, the significance of bringing to a certain place, conducting, Acts 17 : 15 (so the Sept. in Josh. 6 : 23 ; 1 Sam. 5 : 3 ; 2 Chron. 28 : 15). See Appoint.

2. PROPEMPŌ (προπέμπω) signifies to set forward, conduct : see Accompany, No. 4.

CONFER, CONFERENCE

1. PROSANATITHĒMI (προσανατίθημι), lit., to put before (pros, towards, ana, up, and tithēmi, to put), i.e., to lay a matter before others so as to obtain counsel or instruction, is used of Paul's refraining from consulting human beings, Gal. 1 : 16 (translated " imparted " in 2 : 6 ; A.V., " added . . . in conference "). Cp. the shorter form anatithēmi, in 2 : 2, " laid before," the less intensive word being used there simply to signify the imparting of information, rather than conferring with others to seek advice. See ADD, IMPART.¶

2. SULLALEŌ (συλλαλέω), to speak together with (sun, with, laleō, to speak), is translated " conferred " in Acts 25 : 12 ; elsewhere of talking with Matt. 17 : 3 ; Mark 9 : 4 ; Luke 4 : 36 ; 9 : 30 ; " communed " in Luke 22 : 4. See COMMUNE, SPEAK, TALK.¶

3. SUMBALLŌ (συμβάλλω), lit., to throw together (sun, with, ballō, to throw), is used of conversation, to discourse or consult together, confer, Acts 4 : 15. See ENCOUNTER, HELP, MEET WITH, PONDER.

Note : For the A.V., " conference " in Gal. 2 : 6, see No. 1, above.

CONFESS, CONFESSION
A. Verbs.

1. HOMOLOGEŌ (ὁμολογέω), lit., to speak the same thing (homos, same, legō, to speak), to assent, accord, agree with, denotes, either (a) to confess, declare, admit, John 1 : 20 ; e.g., Acts 24 : 14 ; Heb. 11 : 13 ; (b) to confess by way of admitting oneself guilty of what one is accused of, the result of inward conviction, 1 John 1 : 9 ; (c) to declare openly by way of speaking out freely, such confession being the effect of deep conviction of facts, Matt. 7 : 23 ; 10 : 32 (twice) and Luke 12 : 8 (see next par.) ; John 9 : 22 ; 12 : 42 ; Acts 23 : 8 ; Rom. 10 : 9, 10 (" confession is made ") ; 1 Tim. 6 : 12 (R.V.) ; Tit. 1 : 16 ; 1 John 2 : 23 ; 4 : 2,15; 2 John 7 (in John's Epp. it is the necessary antithesis to Gnostic doceticism) ; Rev. 3 : 5, in the best mss. (some have No. 2 here) ; (d) to confess by way of celebrating with praise, Heb. 13 : 15 ; (e) to promise, Matt. 14 : 7.

In Matt. 10 : 32 and Luke 12 : 8 the construction of this verb with en, in, followed by the dative case of the personal pronoun, has a special significance, namely, to confess in a person's name, the nature of the confession being determined by the context, the suggestion being to make a public confession. Thus the statement, " every one . . . who shall confess Me (lit., in Me, i.e., in My case) before men, him (lit., in him, i.e., in his case) will I also confess before My Father . . .," conveys the thought of confessing allegiance to Christ as one's Master and Lord, and, on the other hand, of acknowledgment, on His part, of the faithful one as being His worshipper and servant, His loyal follower ; this is appropriate to the original idea in homologeō of being identified in thought or language. See PROFESS, PROMISE, THANK.¶

2. EXOMOLOGEŌ (ἐξομολογέω), *ek*, out, intensive, and No. 1, and accordingly stronger than No. 1, to confess forth, i.e., freely, openly, is used (*a*) of a public acknowledgment or confession of sins, Matt. 3 : 6 ; Mark 1 : 5 ; Acts 19 : 18 ; Jas. 5 : 16 ; (*b*) to profess or acknowledge openly, Matt. 11 : 25 (translated " thank," but indicating the fuller idea) ; Phil. 2 : 11 (some mss. have it in Rev. 3 : 5 : see No. 1) ; (*c*) to confess by way of celebrating, giving praise, Rom. 14 : 11 ; 15 : 9.   In Luke 10 : 21, it is translated " I thank," the true meaning being ' I gladly acknowledge.' In Luke 22 : 6 it signifies to consent (R.V.), for A.V., " promised."   See CONSENT, PROMISE, THANK.¶

B. Noun.

HOMOLOGIA (ὁμολογία), akin to A, No. 1, denotes confession, by acknowledgment of the truth, 2 Cor. 9 : 13 ; 1 Tim. 6 : 12, 13 ; Heb. 3 : 1 ; 4 : 14 ; 10 : 23 (A.V., incorrectly, " profession," except in 1 Tim. 6 : 13).¶

Note : For the adverb *homologoumenōs*, confessedly, see CONTROVERSY.

CONFIDENCE (Noun, or Verb with " have "), CONFIDENT (-LY)

A. Nouns.

1. PEPOITHĒSIS (πεποίθησις), akin to *peithō*, B, No. 1 below, denotes persuasion, assurance, confidence, 2 Cor. 1 : 15 ;   3 : 4, A.V., " trust ; " 8 : 22 ;   10 : 2 ;   Eph. 3 : 12 ;   Phil. 3 : 4.   See TRUST.¶

2. HUPOSTASIS (ὑπόστασις), lit., a standing under (*hupo*, under, *stasis*, a standing), that which stands, or is set, under, a foundation, beginning ;   hence, the quality of confidence which leads one to stand under, endure, or undertake anything, 2 Cor. 9 : 4 ;   11 : 17 ;   Heb. 3 : 14. Twice in Heb. it signifies substance, 1 : 3 (A.V., " Person ") and 11 : 1. See SUBSTANCE.¶

3. PARRHĒSIA (παῤῥησία), often rendered " confidence " in the A.V., is in all such instances rendered " boldness " in the R.V., Acts 28 : 31 ;   Heb. 3 : 6 ;   1 John 2 : 28 ;   3 : 21 ;   5 : 14.   See BOLDNESS, OPENLY, PLAINNESS.

B. Verbs.

1. PEITHŌ (πείθω), to persuade, or, intransitively, to have confidence, to be confident (cp. A, No. 1), has this meaning in the following, Rom. 2 : 19 ;   2 Cor. 2 : 3 ;   Gal. 5 : 10 ;   Phil. 1 : 6, 14 (R.V., " being confident," for A.V., " waxing confident "), 25 ;   3 : 3, 4 ;   2 Thess. 3 : 4 ;   Philm. 21. See AGREE, ASSURE, BELIEVE, OBEY, PERSUADE, TRUST, YIELD.

2. THARREŌ (θαρρέω), to be of good courage, is so translated in the R.V. of 2 Cor. 5 : 6 ;   7 : 16 (A.V., to have confidence, or be confident). See COURAGE.

Note : The adverb " confidently " is combined with the verb " affirm " to represent the verbs *diischurizomai*, Luke 22 : 59 and Acts 12 : 15, R.V. (A.V., " constantly affirmed "),¶, and *diabebaioomai*, 1 Tim. 1 : 7, A.V., " affirm," and Tit. 3 : 8, A.V., " affirm constantly."   See AFFIRM.¶

CONFIRM, CONFIRMATION
A. Verbs.

1. BEBAIOŌ (βεβαιόω), to make firm, establish, make secure (the connected adjective *bebaios* signifies stable, fast, firm), is used of confirming a word, Mark 16 : 20 ; promises, Rom. 15 : 8 ; the testimony of Christ, 1 Cor. 1 : 6 ; the saints by the Lord Jesus Christ, 1 Cor. 1 : 8 ; the saints by God, 2 Cor. 1 : 21 (" stablisheth ") ; in faith, Col. 2 : 7 ; the salvation spoken through the Lord and confirmed by the Apostles, Heb. 2 : 3 ; the heart by grace, Heb. 13 : 9 (" stablished ").¶

2. EPISTĒRIZŌ (ἐπιστηρίζω), to make to lean upon, strengthen (*epi*, upon, *stērix*, a prop, support), is used of confirming souls, Acts 14 : 22 ; brethren, 15 : 32 ; churches, 15 : 41 ; disciples, 18 : 23, in some mss. (" stablishing," R.V., " strengthening," A.V.) ; the most authentic mss. have *stērizō* in 18 : 23.   See STRENGTHEN.¶

3. KUROŌ (κυρόω), to make valid, ratify, impart authority or influence (from *kuros*, might, *kurios*, mighty, a head, as supreme in authority), is used of spiritual love, 2 Cor. 2 : 8 ; a human covenant, Gal. 3 : 15.¶.   In the Sept., see Gen. 23 : 20, e.g.

4. PROKUROŌ (προκυρόω), *pro*, before, and No. 3, to confirm or ratify before, is said of the Divine confirmation of a promise given originally to Abraham, Gen. 12, and confirmed by the vision of the furnace and torch, Gen. 15, by the birth of Isaac, Gen. 21, and by the oath of God, Gen. 22, all before the giving of the Law, Gal. 3 : 17.¶

5. MESITEUŌ (μεσιτεύω), to act as a mediator, to interpose, is rendered " confirmed," in the A.V. of Heb. 6 : 17 (marg., and R.V., " interposed "). See INTERPOSED.¶

B. Noun.

BEBAIŌSIS (βεβαίωσις), akin to A, No. 1, is used in two senses (*a*) of firmness, establishment, said of the confirmation of the Gospel, Phil. 1 : 7 ; (*b*) of authoritative validity imparted, said of the settlement of a dispute by an oath to produce confidence, Heb. 6 : 16.   The word is found frequently in the Papyri of the settlement of a business transaction.¶

CONFLICT (Noun)

1. AGŌN (ἀγών), from *agō*, to lead, signifies (*a*) a place of assembly, especially the place where the Greeks assembled for the Olympic and Pythian games ; (*b*) a contest of athletes, metaphorically, 1 Tim. 6 : 12 ; 2 Tim. 4 : 7, " fight ; " Heb. 12 : 1, " race ; " hence, (*c*) the inward conflict of the soul ; inward conflict is often the result, or the accompaniment, of outward conflict, Phil. 1 : 30 ; 1 Thess. 2 : 2, implying a contest against spiritual foes, as well as human adversaries ; so Col. 2 : 1, " conflict," A.V. ; R.V., " (how greatly) I strive," lit., ' how great a conflict I have.'   See CONTENTION, FIGHT, RACE.¶.   Cp. *agōnizomai* (Eng., agonize), 1 Cor. 9 : 25 etc.

2. ATHLĒSIS (ἄθλησις) denotes a combat, contest of athletes ; hence,

a struggle, fight, Heb. 10 : 32, with reference to affliction.   See FIGHT.¶
Cp. *athleō*, to strive, 2 Tim. 2 : 5 (twice).¶

CONFORMED, CONFORMABLE
A. Verb.

SUMMORPHIZŌ (συμμορφίζω), to make of like form with another person or thing, to render like (*sun*, with, *morphē*, a form), is found in Phil. 3 : 10 (in the Passive Participle of the verb), " becoming conformed " (or ' growing into conformity ') to the death of Christ, indicating the practical apprehension of the death of the carnal self, and fulfilling his share of the sufferings following upon the sufferings of Christ.   Some texts have the alternative verb *summorphoō*, which has practically the same meaning.

B. Adjectives.

1. SUMMORPHOS (σύμμορφος), akin to A, signifies having the same form as another, conformed to ;   (*a*) of the conformity of children of God " to the image of His Son," Rom. 8 : 29;   (*b*), of their future physical conformity to His body of glory, Phil. 3 : 21.   See FASHION.¶

2. SUSCHĒMATIZŌ (συσχηματίζω), to fashion or shape one thing like another, is translated " conformed " in Rom. 12 : 2, A.V. ;   R.V., " fashioned ; " " fashioning " in 1 Pet. 1 : 14.   This verb has more especial reference to that which is transitory, changeable, unstable ; *summorphizō*, to that which is essential in character and thus complete or durable, not merely a form or outline.   *Suschēmatizō* could not be used of inward transformation.   See FASHION (*schēma*) and FORM (*morphē*).¶

CONFOUND, CONFUSE, CONFUSION
A. Nouns.

1. AKATASTASIA (ἀκαταστασία), instability, (*a*, negative, *kata*, down, *stasis*, a standing), denotes a state of disorder, disturbance, confusion, tumult, 1 Cor. 14 : 33 ;   Jas. 3 : 16, revolution or anarchy ;   translated " tumults " in Luke 21 : 9 (A.V., " commotions ") ;   2 Cor. 6 : 5 ;   12 : 20.   See TUMULT.¶

2. SUNCHUSIS (σύγχυσις), a pouring or mixing together (*sun*, with, *cheō*, to pour) ;   hence a disturbance, confusion, a tumultuous disorder, as of riotous persons, is found in Acts 19 : 29.¶

B. Verbs.

1. SUNCHEŌ (συγχέω), or SUNCHUNNŌ or SUNCHUNŌ (the verb form of A. 2), lit., to pour together, commingle, hence (said of persons), means to trouble or confuse, to stir up, Acts 19 : 32 (said of the mind) ; to be in confusion, 21 : 31, R.V. (A.V., " was in an uproar ") ;   21 : 27, " stirred up ; " Acts 2 : 6 ;   9 : 22, " confounded."   See STIR, UPROAR.¶

2. KATAISCHUNŌ (καταισχύνω), to put to shame, is translated " confound " in 1 Cor. 1 : 27, and 1 Pet. 2 : 6, A.V. (R.V., " put to shame "). See ASHAMED, DISHONOUR, SHAME.

CONFUTE

DIAKATELENCHOMAI (διακατελέγχομαι), to confute powerfully, is an intensive form of *elenchō*, to convict (*dia*, through, *kata*, down, both intensive), Acts 18 : 28, implying that he met the opposing arguments in turn (*dia*), and brought them down to the ground (*kata*). It carries also the thought that he brought home moral blame to them.

CONGREGATION

1. EKKLĒSIA (ἐκκλησία) is translated " congregation " in Heb. 2 : 12, R.V., instead of the usual rendering " church." See ASSEMBLY.

2. SUNAGŌGĒ (συναγωγή) is translated " congregation " in Acts 13 : 43, A.V. (R.V., " synagogue "). See SYNAGOGUE.

CONQUER, CONQUEROR

1. NIKAŌ (νικάω), to overcome (its usual meaning), is translated " conquering " and " to conquer " in Rev. 6 : 2. See OVERCOME, PREVAIL, VICTORY.

2. HUPERNIKAŌ (ὑπερνικάω), to be more than conqueror (*huper*, over, and No. 1), to gain a surpassing victory, is found in Rom. 8 : 37, lit., ' we are hyper-conquerors,' i.e., we are pre-eminently victorious.¶

CONSCIENCE

SUNEIDĒSIS (συνείδησις), lit., a knowing with (*sun*, with, *oida*, to know), i.e., a co-knowledge (with oneself), the witness borne to one's conduct by conscience, that faculty by which we apprehend the will of God, as that which is designed to govern our lives ; hence (*a*) the sense of guiltiness before God; Heb. 10 : 2 ; (*b*) that process of thought which distinguishes what it considers morally good or bad, commending the good, condemning the bad, and so prompting to do the former, and avoid the latter ; Rom. 2 : 15 (bearing witness with God's Law) ; 9 : 1 ; 2 Cor. 1 : 12 ; acting in a certain way because conscience requires it, Rom. 13 : 5 ; so as not to cause scruples of conscience in another, 1 Cor. 10 : 28, 29 ; not calling a thing in question unnecessarily, as if conscience demanded it, 1 Cor. 10 : 25, 27 ; ' commending oneself to every man's conscience,' 2 Cor. 4 : 2 ; cp. 5 : 11. There may be a conscience not strong enough to distinguish clearly between the lawful and the unlawful, 1 Cor. 8 : 7, 10, 12 (some regard consciousness as the meaning here). The phrase " conscience toward God," in 1 Pet. 2 : 19, signifies a conscience (or perhaps here, a consciousness) so controlled by the apprehension of God's presence, that the person realizes that griefs are to be borne in accordance with His will. Heb. 9 : 9 teaches that sacrifices under the Law could not so perfect a person that he could regard himself as free from guilt.

For various descriptions of conscience see Acts 23 : 1 ; 24 : 16 ;

1 Cor. 8 : 7 ; 1 Tim. 1 : 5, 19 ; 3 : 9 ; 4 : 2 ; 2 Tim. 1 : 3 ; Tit. 1 : 15 ; Heb. 9 : 14 ; 10 : 22 ; 13 : 18 ; 1 Pet. 3 : 16, 21.¶

CONSECRATE

Note : In Heb. 7 : 28 the verb *teleioō* is translated " perfected " in the R.V., for A.V., " consecrated ; " so in 9 : 18 and 10 : 20, *enkainizō*, R.V., " dedicated." See DEDICATE, PERFECT.

CONSENT
A. Verbs.

1. EXOMOLOGEŌ (ἐξομολογέω), to agree openly, to acknowledge outwardly, or fully (*ex*, for *ek*, out, intensive), is translated " consented " in the R.V. of Luke 22 : 6 (A.V., " promised "). See CONFESS, THANK.

2. EPINEUŌ (ἐπινεύω), lit. signifies to nod to (*epi*, upon or to, *neuō*, to nod) ; hence, to nod assent, to express approval, consent, Acts 18 : 20.

3. PROSERCHOMAI (προσέρχομαι), to come to, signifies to consent, implying a coming to agreement with, in 1 Tim. 6 : 3. See COME, No. 10.

4. SUNKATATITHĒMI (συγκατατίθημι), lit., to put or lay down together with (*sun*, with, *kata*, down, *tithēmi*, to put), was used of depositing one's vote in an urn ; hence, to vote for, agree with, consent to. It is said negatively of Joseph of Arimathæa, who had not " consented " to the counsel and deed of the Jews, Luke 23 : 51 (Middle Voice).¶

5. SUMPHĒMI (συμφήμι), lit., to speak with (*sun*, with, *phēmi*, to speak), hence, to express agreement with, is used of consenting to the Law, agreeing that it is good, Rom. 7 : 16.¶

6. SUNEUDOKEŌ (συνευδοκέω), lit., to think well with (*sun*, with, *eu*, well, *dokeō*, to think), to take pleasure with others in anything, to approve of, to assent, is used in Luke 11 : 48, of consenting to the evil deeds of predecessors (A.V., " allow ") ; in Rom. 1 : 32, of consenting in doing evil ; in Acts 8 : 1 ; 22 : 20, of consenting to the death of another. All these are cases of consenting to evil things. In 1 Cor. 7 : 12, 13, it is used of an unbelieving wife's consent to dwell with her converted husband, and of an unbelieving husband's consent to dwell with a believing wife (A.V., " be pleased ; " R.V., " be content "). See ALLOW, CONTENT, PLEASE.¶

B. Phrases.

1. APO MIAS, lit., ' from one,' is found in Luke 14 : 18, some word like " consent " being implied ; e.g., " with one consent."¶

2. EK SUMPHŌNOU, lit., ' from (or by) agreement ' (*sun*, with, *phōnē*, a sound), i.e., by consent, is found in 1 Cor. 7 : 5. Cp. AGREE.¶

CONSIDER

1. EIDON (εἶδον), used as the aorist tense of *horaō*, to see, is translated " to consider " in Acts 15 : 6, of the gathering of the Apostles and elders regarding the question of circumcision in relation to the Gospel.

2. SUNEIDON (συνεῖδον), *sun*, with, and No. 1, used as the aorist tense of *sunoraō*, to see with one view, to be aware, conscious, as the result of mental perception, is translated "considered" in Acts 12 : 12, of Peter's consideration of the circumstances of his deliverance from See KNOW, PRIVY.

3. KATAMANTHANŎ (καταμανθάνω), lit., to learn thoroughly (*kata*, down, intensive, *manthanō*, to learn), hence, to note accurately, consider well, is used in the Lord's exhortation to consider the lilies, Matt. 6 : 28.¶

4. NOEŌ (νοέω), to perceive with the mind (*nous*), think about, ponder, is translated "consider," only in Paul's exhortation to Timothy in 2 Tim. 2 : 7. See PERCEIVE, THINK, UNDERSTAND.

5. KATANOEŌ (κατανοέω), to perceive clearly (*kata*, intensive, and No. 4), to understand fully, consider closely, is used of not considering thoroughly the beam in one's own eye, Matt. 7 : 3 and Luke 6 : 41 (A.V., "perceivest"); of carefully considering the ravens, Luke 12 : 24; the lilies, ver. 27; of Peter's full consideration of his vision, Acts 11 : 6; of Abraham's careful consideration of his own body, and Sarah's womb, as dead, and yet accepting by faith God's promise, Rom. 4 : 19 (R.V.); of considering fully the Apostle and High Priest of our confession, Heb. 3 : 1; of thoughtfully considering one another to provoke unto love and good works, Heb. 10 : 24. It is translated by the verbs behold, Acts 7 : 31, 32; Jas. 1 : 23, 24; perceive, Luke 20 : 23; discover, Acts 27 : 39. See BEHOLD, DISCOVER, PERCEIVE.¶

6. LOGIZOMAI (λογίζομαι) signifies to take account of, 2 Cor. 10 : 7 (R.V., "consider," A.V., "think"), the only place where the R.V. translates it "consider." See ACCOUNT.

7. THEŌREŌ (θεωρέω) : see BEHOLD, No. 6.

8. ANATHEŌREŌ (ἀναθεωρέω), to consider carefully : see BEHOLD, No. 7.

9. ANALOGIZOMAI (ἀναλογίζομαι), to consider, occurs in Heb. 12:3.¶

Notes : (1) *Skopeō*, to look, is translated "looking to" in Gal. 6 : 1, R.V. (A.V., "considering"). See HEED, LOOK, MARK. (2) *Suniēmi*, to understand, is translated "considered" in Mark 6 : 52 (A.V.), R.V., "understood." (3) In John 11 : 50 (A.V., *dialogizomai*) the best texts have No. 6.

CONSIST

1. EIMI (εἰμί), to be, is rendered "consist" (lit., 'is') in Luke 12 : 15.

2. SUNISTĒMI (συνίστημι), *sun*, with, *histēmi*, to stand, denotes, in its intransitive sense, to stand with or fall together, to be constituted, to be compact ; it is said of the universe as upheld by the Lord, Col. 1 : 17, lit., 'by Him all things stand together,' i.e., "consist" (the Latin *consisto*, to stand together, is the exact equivalent of *sunistēmi*). See APPROVE, COMMEND, MAKE, STAND.

CONSOLATION, CONSOLE
A. Nouns.

1. PARAKLĒSIS (παράκλησις) is translated " consolation," in both A.V. and R.V., in Luke 2 : 25 ; 6 : 24 ; Acts 15 : 31 ; in 1 Cor. 14 : 3, A.V., " exhortation," R.V., " comfort ; " in the following the A.V. has " consolation," the R.V., " comfort," Rom. 15 : 5 ; 2 Cor. 1 : 6, 7 ; 7 : 7 ; Phil. 2 : 1 ; 2 Thess. 2 : 16 ; Philm. 7 ; in Acts 4 : 36, R.V., " exhortation ; " in Heb. 6 : 18, R.V., " encouragement." See COMFORT.

2. PARAMUTHIA (παραμυθία), a comfort, consolation : see COMFORT, A, No. 2.

3. PARAMUTHION (παραμύθιον), an encouragement, " consolation ," Phil. 2 : 1, R.V., in the phrase " consolation of love." See COMFORT, A, No. 3.

B. Verb.

PARAMUTHEOMAI (παραμυθέομαι), to speak soothingly to, is translated " console," John 11 : 19, R.V. ; in ver. 31 " were comforting ; " in 1 Thess. 2 : 11 and 5 : 14, A.V., " comforted " and " comfort," R.V., " encouraged " and " encourage."

CONSORT (with)

PROSKLĒROŌ (προσκληρόω), lit., to assign by lot (pros, to, klēros, a lot), to allot, is found in Acts 17 : 4, " consorted with," imparting to the Passive Voice (the form of the verb there) a Middle Voice significance, i.e., ' they joined themselves to,' or ' threw in their lot with.' The Passive Voice significance can be retained by translating (in the stricter sense of the word), " they were allotted " (i.e., by God) to Paul and Silas, as followers or disciples.¶

CONSPIRACY

SUNŌMOSIA (συνωμοσία) denotes, lit., a swearing together (sun, with, omnumi, to swear), a being leagued by oath, and so a conspiracy, Acts 23 : 13.¶

For CONSTANTLY see AFFIRM

CONSTRAIN, CONSTRAINT
A. Verbs.

1. ANANKAZŌ (ἀναγκάζω) : see COMPEL, No. 1.

2. PARABIAZOMAI (παραβιάζομαι) primarily denotes to employ force contrary to nature and right, to compel by using force (para, alongside, intensive, biazō, to force), and is used only of constraining by intreaty, as the two going to Emmaus did to Christ, Luke 24:29; as Lydia did to Paul and his companions, Acts 16:15.¶

3. SUNECHŌ (συνέχω), to hold together, confine, secure, to hold fast (echō, to have or hold), to constrain, is said (a) of the effect of the word of the Lord upon Paul, Acts 18:5 (A.V., "was pressed in spirit," R.V.,

" was constrained by the word ") ; of the effect of the love of Christ, 2 Cor. 5 : 14 ; (b) of being taken with a disease, Matt. 4 : 24 ; Luke 4 : 38 ; Acts 28 : 8 ; with fear, Luke 8 : 37 ; (c) of thronging or holding in a person, Luke 8 : 45 ; being straitened, Luke 12 : 50 ; being in a strait betwixt two, Phil. 1 : 23 ; keeping a city in on every side, Luke 19 : 43 ; keeping a tight hold on a person, as the men who seized the Lord Jesus did, after bringing Him into the High Priest's house, Luke 22 : 63 ; (d) of stopping the ears in refusal to listen, Acts 7 : 57. Luke uses the word nine times out of its twelve occurrences in the N.T. See HOLD, KEEP, No. (1), PRESS, SICK (lie), STOP, STRAIT (be in a), TAKEN (be), THRONG.¶

Note : The verb *echō*, to have, with *anankē*, a necessity, is translated " I was constrained," in Jude 3, R.V. (A.V., " it was needful ").

B. Adverb.

ANANKASTŌS (ἀναγκαστῶς), akin to A, No. 1, by force, unwillingly, by constraint, is used in 1 Pet. 5 : 2.¶

CONSULT, CONSULTATION
A. Verbs.

1. BOULEUŌ (βουλεύω), used in the Middle Voice, means (a) to consult, Luke 14 : 31 ; (b) to resolve, John 12 : 10, A.V., " consulted ; " R.V., " took counsel." See COUNSEL.

2. SUMBOULEUŌ (συμβουλεύω), to take counsel together, is translated " consulted together," in Matt. 26 : 4, A.V. (R.V., " took counsel.") See COUNSEL.

B. Noun.

SUMBOULION (συμβούλιον), a word of the Græco-Roman period (akin to A, No. 2), counsel, advice, is translated " consultation " in Mark 15 : 1 (with *poieō*, to make), to hold a consultation ; elsewhere " counsel " in the R.V., except in Acts 25 : 12, where, by metonymy, it means a " council." See COUNCIL.

CONSUME

1. ANALISKŌ (ἀναλίσκω), to use up, spend up, especially in a bad sense, to destroy, is said of the destruction of persons, (a) literally, Luke 9:54 and the R.V. marg. of 2 Thess. 2:8 (text, "shall slay") ; (b) meta-phorically, Gal. 5:15 "(that) ye be not consumed (one of another)."¶

2. KATANALISKŌ (καταναλίσκω), to consume utterly, wholly (*kata*, intensive), is said, in Heb. 12:29, of God as "a consuming fire."¶

3. APHANIZŌ (ἀφανίζω), lit., to cause to disappear, put out of sight, came to mean to do away with (*a*, negative, *phainō*, to cause to appear), said of the destructive work of moth and rust, Matt. 6:19, 20 (R.V., "consume," A.V., "corrupt"). See CORRUPT, DISFIGURE, PERISH, VANISH.

Note: Dapanaō, to expend, be at an expense, is translated "consume" in the A.V. of James 4:3 (R.V., "spend"). See SPEND.

CONTAIN

1. CHŌREŌ (χωρέω) signifies (a), lit., to give space, make room (chōra, a place) ; hence, transitively, to have space or room for a thing, to contain, said of the waterpots as containing a certain quantity, John 2 : 6 ; of a space large enough to hold a number of people, Mark 2 : 2 ; of the world as not possible of containing certain books, John 21 : 25 ; (b) to go, Matt. 15 : 17 ; to have place, John 8 : 37 ; to come, 2 Pet. 3 : 9 ; (c) metaphorically, of receiving with the mind, Matt. 19 : 11, 12 ; or into the heart, 2 Cor. 7 : 2. See COME (No. 24), GO, PLACE, RECEIVE, ROOM.¶

2. PERIECHŌ (περιέχω), lit., to have round (peri, around, echō, to have), means to encompass, enclose, contain, as a writing contains details, 1 Pet. 2 : 6. Some mss. have it in Acts 23 : 25, lit., ' having this form ' (the most authentic have echō, to have). For the secondary meaning, amazed (A.V., " astonished "), Luke 5 : 9 (lit., amazement encompassed, i.e., seized, him).¶

Notes : (1) The verb *allēgoreō* in Gal. 4 : 24, R.V., is translated " contain an allegory " (A.V., " are an allegory "), i.e., they apply the facts of the narrative to illustrate principles. (2) In Eph. 2 : 15 " the law of commandments contained in ordinances " is, lit., the law of commandments in ordinances. (3) In Rom. 2 : 14, the R.V., translating literally, has " the things of the Law ; " the A.V. inserts the words " contained in." (4) In 1 Cor. 7 : 9, for the A.V., " if they cannot contain," see CONTINENCY.

For CONTEMPTIBLE, see ACCOUNT, No. 6

CONTEND (-ING)

1. ATHLEŌ (ἀθλέω), to engage in a contest (cp. Eng., athlete), to contend in public games, is used in 2 Tim. 2 : 5, R.V., " contend in the games," for the A.V., " strive for the masteries." See STRIVE.¶

Note : In 1 Cor. 9 : 25, the verb *agōnizomai*, to strive, is used in the same connection, R.V., " striveth in the games." Cp. No. 3.

2. DIAKRINŌ (διακρίνω), lit., to separate throughout or wholly (dia, asunder, krinō, to judge, from a root kri, meaning separation), then, to distinguish, decide, signifies, in the Middle Voice, to separate oneself from, or to contend with, as did the circumcisionists with Peter, Acts 11 : 2 ; as did Michael with Satan, Jude 9. See R.V. marg. of ver. 22, where the thought may be that of differing in opinion. See DIFFER, DISCERN, DOUBT, JUDGE, PARTIAL, STAGGER, WAVER.

3. EPAGŌNIZOMAI (ἐπαγωνίζομαι) signifies to contend about a thing, as a combatant (epi, upon or about, intensive, agōn, a contest), to contend earnestly, Jude 3. The word " earnestly " is added to convey the intensive force of the preposition.¶

CONTENT (to be), CONTENTMENT
A. Verb.

1. ARKEŌ (ἀρκέω) primarily signifies to be sufficient, to be possessed of sufficient strength, to be strong, to be enough for a thing ; hence, to defend, ward off ; in the Middle Voice, to be satisfied, contented with, Luke 3 : 14, with wages ; 1 Tim. 6 : 8, with food and raiment ; Heb. 13 : 5, with " such things as ye have ; " negatively of Diotrephes, in 3 John 10, " not content therewith." See ENOUGH, SUFFICE, SUFFICIENT.

2. SUNEUDOKEŌ (συνευδοκέω), in 1 Cor. 7 : 12, 13, R.V., signifies to be content : see CONSENT, No. 6.

B. Adjectives.

1. AUTARKĒS (αὐτάρκης), as found in the papyri writings, means sufficient in oneself (autos, self, arkeō, see A), self-sufficient, adequate, needing no assistance ; hence, content, Phil. 4 : 11.¶

2. HIKANOS (ἱκανός), sufficient, used with poieō, to do, in Mark 15 : 15, is translated " to content (the multitude)," i.e., to do sufficient to satisfy them. See ABLE.

C. Noun.

AUTARKEIA (αὐτάρκεια), contentment, satisfaction with what one has, is found in 1 Tim. 6 : 6. For its other meaning " sufficiency," in 2 Cor. 9 : 8, see SUFFICIENCY.¶

CONTENTION, CONTENTIOUS
A. Nouns.

1. ERIS (ἔρις), strife, quarrel, especially rivalry, contention, wrangling, as in the church in Corinth, 1 Cor. 1 : 11, is translated " contentions " in Tit. 3 : 9, A.V. See DEBATE, STRIFE, VARIANCE.

2. PAROXUSMOS (παροξυσμός), Eng., paroxysm, lit., a sharpening, hence a sharpening of the feeling, or action (para, beside, intensive, oxus, sharp), denotes an incitement, a sharp contention, Acts 15 : 39, the effect of irritation ; elsewhere in Heb. 10 : 24, " provoke," unto love. See PROVOKE.¶

3. PHILONEIKIA (φιλονεικία), lit., love of strife (phileō, to love, neikos, strife), signifies eagerness to contend ; hence, a contention, said of the disciples, Luke 22 : 24. Cp. B, 2.¶

B. Adjectives.

1. AMACHOS (ἄμαχος), lit., not fighting (a, negative, machē, a fight, combat, quarrel), primarily signifying invincible, came to mean not contentious, 1 Tim. 3 : 3, R.V. ; Tit. 3 : 2 (A.V., " not a brawler," " no brawlers ").¶

2. PHILONEIKOS (φιλόνεικος), akin to A, No. 3, is used in 1 Cor. 11 : 16.¶ In the Sept., Ezek. 3 : 7, " stubborn."¶

Notes : (1) Eritheia, " contention," A.V., in Phil. 1 : 17, is translated " faction," in the R.V. The phrase hoi ex eritheias, Rom. 2 : 8, lit., ' those

of strife,' is rendered " contentious," in the A.V. ; R.V., " factious."
See FACTIOUS, STRIFE.

(2) For *agōn*, a contest, " contention," 1 Thess. 2 : 2, A.V. ;
" conflict," R.V., see CONFLICT.

CONTINENCY

ENKRATEUOMAI (ἐγκρατεύομαι), *en*, in, *kratos*, power, strength,
lit., to have power over oneself, is rendered " (if) they have (not)
continency " (i.e., are lacking in self-control), in 1 Cor. 7 : 9, R.V. ; A.V.,
" can (not) contain ; " in 9 : 25, " is temperate." See TEMPERATE.¶

CONTINUAL, CONTINUALLY (see also CONTINUE)
A. Adverbial Phrases.

1. EIS TELOS (εἰς τέλος), lit., ' unto (the) end,' signifies " continual,"
in Luke 18 : 5, of the importunate widow's applications to the unrighteous
judge ; see also Matt. 10 : 22 ; 24 : 13 ; Mark 13 : 13 ; John 13 : 1 ;
1 Thess. 2 : 16. Cp. *heōs telous*, lit., ' until the end,' 1 Cor. 1 : 8 ; 2 Cor.
1 : 13 ; ¶ *mechri telous*, ditto, Heb. 3 : 6, 14 ; ¶ *achri telous*, Heb.
6 : 11 ; Rev. 2 : 26.¶

2. DIA PANTOS (διὰ παντός) is used of a period throughout or during
which anything is done ; it is said of the disciples' continuance in the
Temple after the Ascension of Christ, Luke 24 : 53 ; of the regular entrance
of the priests into the first tabernacle, Heb. 9 : 6, R.V. (A.V. " always ") ;
of the constant sacrifice of praise enjoined upon believers, Heb. 13 : 15.
See also Matt. 18 : 10 ; Mark 5 : 5 ; Acts 10 : 2 ; 24 : 16 ; Rom. 11 : 10 ;
2 Thess. 3 : 16, " at all times." See ALWAYS, No. 3, and Note under
No. 3 below).¶

3. EIS TO DIĒNEKES (εἰς τὸ διηνεκές), lit., unto the carried-through
(*dia*, through, *enenka*, to carry), i.e., unto (the) unbroken continuance, is
used of the continuous Priesthood of Christ, Heb. 7 : 3, and of the continual
offering of sacrifices under the Law, Heb. 10 : 1. It is translated " for
ever," in Heb. 10 : 12, of the everlasting session of Christ at the right
hand of God ; and in 10 : 14, of the everlasting effects of His sacrifice
upon " them that are sanctified," See EVER.¶

Note : No. 2 indicates that a certain thing is done frequently throughout a period ; No. 3 stresses the unbroken continuity of what is mentioned.
B. Adjective.

ADIALEIPTOS (ἀδιάλειπτος), continual, unceasing : see CEASE, B.

CONTINUE, CONTINUANCE

1. GINOMAI (γίνομαι) signifies (*a*) to begin to be (suggesting origin) ;
(*b*) to become (suggesting entrance on a new state) ; (*c*) to come to pass
(suggesting effect) ; hence with the meaning (*c*) it is translated
" continued " in Acts 19 : 10. See ARISE.

2. DIATELEŎ (διατελέω), to bring through to an end (*dia*, through,

telos, an end), to finish fully or, when used of time, continue right through, is said of continuing fasting up to the time mentioned, Acts 27 : 33.¶

3. MENŌ (μένω) : see ABIDE.

Compounds of menō with this meaning, are as follows :

4. DIAMENŌ (διαμένω), to continue throughout, i.e., without interruption (No. 3 with *dia*, through), is said of the dumbness of Zacharias, Luke 1 : 22, A.V., " remained ; " of the continuance of the disciples with Christ, Luke 22 : 28 ; of the permanency of the truth of the Gospel with churches, Gal. 2 : 5 ; of the unchanged course of things, 2 Pet. 3 : 4 ; of the eternal permanency of Christ, Heb. 1 : 11. See REMAIN.¶

5. EMMENŌ (ἐμμένω), to remain in (*en*, in), is used of abiding in a house, Acts 28 : 30 (in the best mss.) ; of continuing in the faith, Acts 14 : 22 ; in the Law, Gal. 3 : 10 ; in God's Covenant, Heb. 8 : 9.¶

6. EPIMENŌ (ἐπιμένω), lit., to remain on, i.e., in addition to (*epi*, upon, and No. 3), to continue long, still to abide, is used of continuing to ask, John 8 : 7 ; to knock, Acts 12 : 16 ; in the grace of God, 13 : 43 ; in sin, Rom. 6 : 1 ; in God's goodness, 11 : 22 ; in unbelief, 11 : 23 (A.V., " abide ") ; in the flesh, Phil. 1 : 24 ; in the faith, Col. 1 : 23 ; in doctrine, 1 Tim. 4 : 16 ; elsewhere of abiding in a place. See ABIDE, TARRY.

7. PARAMENŌ (παραμένω), to remain by or near (*para*, beside, and No. 3), hence, to continue or persevere in anything, is used of the inability of Levitical priests to continue, Heb. 7 : 23 ; of persevering in the law of liberty, Jas. 1 : 25 ; it is translated " abide " in Phil. 1 : 25 (2nd clause, in the best mss.), R.V. [see Note (1)], and in 1 Cor. 16 : 6. See ABIDE.¶

8. PROSMENŌ (προσμένω), to remain with (*pros*, with, and No. 3), to continue with a person, is said of the people with Christ, Matt. 15 : 32 ; Mark 8 : 2 (A.V., " been with ") ; of continuing in supplications and prayers, 1 Tim. 5 : 5. See ABIDE, CLEAVE (unto), TARRY.

9. PROSKARTEREŌ (προσκαρτερέω), lit., to be strong towards (*pros*, towards, used intensively, and *kartereō*, to be strong), to endure in, or persevere in, to be continually stedfast with a person or thing, is used of continuing in prayer with others, Acts 1 : 14 ; Rom. 12 : 12 ; Col. 4 : 2 ; in the Apostles' teaching, Acts 2 : 42 ; in the Temple, 2 : 46 (" continuing stedfastly," R.V.), the adverb representing the intensive preposition ; in prayer and the ministry, 6 : 4 (R.V., " will continue stedfastly ") ; of Simon Magus with Philip, 8 : 13. In Mark 3 : 9 and Acts 10 : 7, it signifies to wait on ; in Rom. 13 : 6, to attend continually upon. See ATTEND, INSTANT, WAIT.¶

10. DIANUKTEREUŌ (διανυκτερεύω), to pass the night through (*dia*, through, *nux*, a night), to continue all night, is found in Luke 6 : 12, of the Lord in spending all night in prayer.¶

Notes : (1) The following are translated by the verb to continue, in the A.V., in the places mentioned : *diatribō*, to tarry, (according to inferior mss.) John 11 : 54 ; Acts 15 : 35 (R.V., " tarried ") ; *histēmi*, to stand, Acts 26 : 22 (R.V., " stand ") : *kathizō*, to sit down, Acts 18 : 11

(R.V., "dwelt"): *parateinō*, to extend, stretch, Acts 20 : 7 (R.V., "prolonged"); *paramenō*, to abide together with, Phil. 1 : 25, R.V., "abide with;" the A.V., "continue," translating *sumparamenō* (in some mss.), marks the difference from the preceding *menō*. See ABIDE, No. 4.

(2) In Rom. 2 : 7, for A.V., "patient continuance," the R.V. has "patience" (lit., 'according to patience').

(3) In Rev. 13 : 5 *poieō*, to do, is rendered "to continue."

CONTRADICT, CONTRADICTION
A. Verb.

ANTILEGŌ (ἀντιλέγω), lit., to speak against (*anti*, against, *legō*, to speak), is translated "contradict" in Acts 13 : 45. See ANSWER, GAINSAY, SPEAK (against).

B. Noun.

ANTILOGIA (ἀντιλογία), akin to A, is translated "contradiction" in the A.V. of Heb. 7 : 7 ; 12 : 3, "dispute," and "gainsaying." See DISPUTE, GAINSAY, STRIFE.

CONTRARIWISE.

T'OUNANTION (τοὐναντίον), for *to enantion*, the contrary, on the contrary or contrariwise, is used in 2 Cor. 2 : 7 ; Gal. 2 : 7 ; 1 Pet. 3 : 9.¶

CONTRARY
A. Verb.

ANTIKEIMAI (ἀντίκειμαι), to be contrary (*anti*, against, *keimai*, to lie), Gal. 5 : 17 ; 1 Tim. 1 : 10. See ADVERSARY.

B. Prepositions.

1. PARA (παρά), beside, has the meaning "contrary to" in Acts 18 : 13 ; Rom. 11 : 24 ; 16 : 17 ; "other than" in Gal. 1 : 8.

2. APENANTI (ἀπέναντι), lit., from over against, opposite to (*apo*, from, *enantios*, against), is translated "contrary to" in Acts 17 : 7 ; "before" in Matt. 27 : 24 ; Rom. 3 : 18 ; "over against," in Matt. 27 : 61 ; "in the presence of," in Acts 3 : 16.¶

Note : The most authentic mss. have *katenanti*, "over against," in Matt. 21 : 2.

C. Adjectives.

1. ENANTIOS (ἐναντίος), over against (*en*, in, *antios*, against), is used primarily of place, Mark 15 : 39 ; of an opposing wind, Matt. 14 : 24 ; Mark 6 : 48 ; Acts 27 : 4 ; metaphorically, opposed as an adversary, antagonistic, Acts 26 : 9 ; 1 Thess. 2 : 15 ; Tit. 2 : 8 ; Acts 28 : 17, "against."¶

2. HUPENANTIOS (ὑπεναντίος), *hupo*, under, and No. 1, opposite to, is used of that which is contrary to persons, Col. 2 : 14, and as a noun, "adversaries," Heb. 10 : 27. See ADVERSARY.¶

CONTRIBUTION

KOINŌNIA (κοινωνία) is twice rendered "contribution," Rom. 15 : 26, and 2 Cor. 9 : 13, R.V., (A.V., "distribution"). See COMMUNION.

CONTROVERSY (without)

HOMOLOGOUMENŌS (ὁμολογουμένως), confessedly, by common consent, akin to *homologeō*, to confess (*homos*, same, *legō*, to speak), is rendered in 1 Tim. 3 : 16 "without controversy ; " some translate it "confessedly." See CONFESS, A, No. 1, and B.¶

CONVENIENT, CONVENIENTLY
A. Adjective.

EUKAIROS (εὔκαιρος), lit., well-timed (*eu*, well, *kairos*, a time, season), hence signifies timely, opportune, convenient ; it is said of a certain day, Mark 6 : 21 ; elsewhere, Heb. 4 : 16, "in time of need." See NEED.¶ Cp. *eukairia*, opportunity, Matt. 26 : 16 ; Luke 22 : 6 ;¶ *eukaireō*, to have opportunity, Mark 6 : 31 ; Acts 17 : 21 ("they spent their time," marg. "had leisure for nothing else "); 1 Cor. 16 : 12. See OPPORTUNITY, NEED, C, *Note*.¶

B. Adverb.

EUKAIRŌS (εὐκαίρως), conveniently, Mark 14 : 11, is used elsewhere in 2 Tim. 4 : 2, "in season."¶ See SEASON, C.

C. Verbs.

1. ANĒKŌ (ἀνήκω) is rendered "befitting" in Eph. 5 : 4, for A.V., "convenient ; " so in Philm. 8. See BEFIT.

2. KATHĒKŌ (καθήκω), to be fitting, is so translated in Rom. 1 : 28, R.V. ; A.V., "(not) convenient ; " in Acts 22 : 22, "it is (not) fit." See FIT.¶

CONVERSATION

This word is not used in the R.V., as it does not now express the meaning of the words so translated in the A.V. These are as follows :

A. Nouns.

1. ANASTROPHĒ (ἀναστροφή) : see BEHAVIOUR, B. No. 1.

2. TROPOS (τρόπος), a turning, a manner, is translated simply "be ye," R.V. in Heb. 13 : 5, instead of "let your conversation be." See MANNER, MEANS, WAY.

3. POLITEUMA (πολίτευμα) : see CITIZENSHIP, No. 4

B. Verbs.

1. ANASTREPHŌ (ἀναστρέφω) : see BEHAVE, A, No. 1.

2. POLITEUŌ (πολιτεύω) : see CITIZENSHIP, No. 4, Note.

CONVERT, CONVERSION
A. Verbs.

1. STREPHŌ (στρέφω), to turn, is translated "be converted" in Matt. 18 : 3, A.V. See TURN.

2. EPISTREPHŌ (ἐπιστρέφω), to turn about, turn towards (epi, towards and No. 1), is used transitively, and so rendered " convert " (of causing a person to turn) in Jas. 5 : 19, 20.   Elsewhere, where the A.V. translates this verb, either in the Middle Voice and intransitive use, or the Passive, the R.V. adheres to the Middle Voice significance, and translates by "turn again," Matt. 13 : 15;   Mark 4 : 12;   Luke 22 : 32; Acts 3 : 19; 28 : 27.   See COME (again), Note (4), GO (again), RETURN, TURN.

B. Noun.

EPISTROPHĒ (ἐπιστροφή), akin to A, No. 2, a turning about, or round, conversion, is found in Acts 15 : 3.   The word implies a turning from and a turning to ; corresponding to these are repentance and faith ; cp. " turned to God from idols " (1 Thess. 1 : 9).   Divine grace is the efficient cause, human agency the responding effect.¶

CONVEY

EKNEUŌ (ἐκνεύω), primarily, to bend to one side, to turn aside ; then to take oneself away, withdraw, is found in John 5 : 13, of Christ's conveying Himself away from one place to another.   Some have regarded the verb as having the same meaning as ekneō, to escape, as from peril, slip away secretly ; but the Lord did not leave the place where He had healed the paralytic in order to escape danger, but to avoid the applause of the throng.¶

CONVICT (including the A.V., " convince ")

1. ELENCHŌ (ἐλέγχω) signifies (a) to convict, confute, refute, usually with the suggestion of putting the convicted person to shame ; see Matt. 18 : 15, where more than telling the offender his fault is in view ; it is used of convicting of sin, John 8 : 46; 16 : 8; gainsayers in regard to the faith, Tit. 1 : 9; transgressors of the Law, Jas. 2 : 9; some texts have the verb in John 8 : 9; (b) to reprove, 1 Cor. 14 : 24, R.V. (for A.V., " convince "), for the unbeliever is there viewed as being reproved for, or convicted of, his sinful state ; so in Luke 3 : 19; it is used of reproving works, John 3 : 20; Eph. 5 : 11, 13 ; 1 Tim. 5 : 20; 2 Tim. 4 : 2; Tit. 1 : 13; 2 : 15; all these speak of reproof by word of mouth.   In Heb. 12 : 5 and Rev. 3 : 19, the word is used of reproving by action.   See FAULT, REBUKE, REPROVE.¶

2. EXELENCHŌ (ἐξελέγχω), an intensive form of No. 1, to convict thoroughly, is used of the Lord's future conviction of the ungodly, Jude 15.¶

Note : For diakatelenchō, to confute powerfully in disputation, Acts 18 : 28 (A.V., " convinced "), see CONFUTE.¶

COOL

KATAPSUCHŌ (καταψύχω), Luke 16 : 24, denotes to cool off, make cool (kata, down, psuchō, to cool).¶   In the Sept., Gen. 18 : 4.¶

For COPPERSMITH see under BRASS

COPY

HUPODEIGMA (ὑπόδειγμα), from *hupŏ*, under, *deiknumi*, to show, properly denotes what is shown below or privately ; it is translated "example," Heb. 8 : 5, A.V. (R.V., "copy "). It signifies (*a*) a sign suggestive of anything, the delineation or representation of a thing, and so, a figure, copy; in Heb. 9 : 23 the R.V. has "copies," for the A.V., "patterns ; " (*b*) an example for imitation, John 13 : 15 ; Jas. 5 : 10 ; for warning, Heb. 4 : 11 ; 2 Pet. 2 : 6 (A.V. "ensample "). See EXAMPLE, PATTERN.¶

Note : Cp. *hupogrammos* (*hupo*, under, *graphō*, to write), an under-writing, a writing copy, an example, is used in 1 Pet. 2 : 21.

CORBAN

KORBAN (κορβᾶν) signifies (*a*) an offering, and was a Hebrew term for any sacrifice, whether by the shedding of blood or otherwise; (*b*) a gift offered to God, Mark 7 : 11.¶ Jews were much addicted to rash vows ; a saying of the Rabbis was, " It is hard for the parents, but the law is clear, vows must be kept." The Sept. translates the word by *dōron*, a gift. See *korbanas*, under TREASURY, Matt. 27 : 6.¶

CORD

SCHOINION (σχοινίον), a cord or rope, a diminutive of *schoinos*, a rush, bulrush, meant a cord made of rushes ; it denotes (*a*) a small cord, John 2 : 15 (plural), (*b*) a rope, Acts 27 : 32. See ROPE.¶

CORN, CORNFIELD

1. SITOS (σῖτος), wheat, corn ; in the plural, grain, is translated " corn " in Mark 4 : 28 ; " wheat," Matt. 3 : 12 ; 13 : 25, 29, 30 ; Luke 3 : 17 ; 12 : 18 (some mss. have *genēmata*, " fruits," here) ; 16 : 7 ; 22 : 31 ; John 12 : 24 ; Acts 27 : 38 ; 1 Cor. 15 : 37 ; Rev. 6 : 6 ; 18 : 13. See WHEAT.¶

2. SITION (σίτιον), corn, grain, a diminutive of No. 1, is found in Acts 7 : 12.¶

3. SPORIMOS (σπόριμος), lit., sown, or fit for sowing (*speirō* to sow, scatter seed), denotes, in the plural, sown fields, fields of grain, corn-fields, Matt. 12 : 1, R.V. ; Mark 2 : 23 ; Luke 6 : 1 (cp. *spora*, 1 Pet. 1 : 23,¶ and *sporos*, seed).¶

4. STACHUS (στάχυς) means an ear of grain, Matt. 12 : 1 ; Mark 2 : 23 ; 4 : 28 ; Luke 6 : 1. Cp. the name *Stachys* in Rom. 16 : 9.¶

Notes : (1) *Aloaō*, to thresh, from *alōn*, a threshing-floor, is translated " treadeth out (the) corn," in 1 Cor. 9 : 9, 10 and 1 Tim. 5 : 18. Cp. THRESH, TREAD.¶

(2) *Kokkos*, a grain (its regular meaning), is translated " corn " in the A.V. of John 12 : 24 (R.V., " grain "). See GRAIN.

CORNER, CORNERSTONE

1. GŌNIA (γωνία), an angle (Eng., *coign*), signifies (a) an external angle, as of the corner of a street, Matt. 6 : 5 ; or of a building, 21 : 42 ; Mark 12 : 10 ; Luke 20 : 17 ; Acts 4 : 11 ; 1 Pet. 2 : 7, the corner stone or head-stone of the corner (see below) ; or the four extreme limits of the earth, Rev. 7 : 1 ; 20 : 8 ; (b) an internal corner, a secret place, Acts 26 : 26. See QUARTER.¶

2. ARCHĒ (ἀρχή), a beginning (its usual meaning), first in time, order, or place, is used to denote the extremities or corners of a sheet, Acts 10 : 11 ; 11 : 5. See BEGINNING.

Note : For the adjective *akrogōniaios* (from *akros*, extreme, highest, and No. 1), a chief corner stone, see CHIEF. They were laid so as to give strength to the two walls with which they were connected. So Christ unites Jew and Gentile, Eph. 2 : 20 ; again, as one may carelessly stumble over the corner stone, when turning the corner, so Christ proved a stumbling stone to Jews, 1 Pet. 2 : 6.

CORPSE

PTŌMA (πτῶμα) : see BODY, No. 3.

CORRECT, CORRECTION, CORRECTOR, CORRECTING
A. Nouns.

1. DIORTHŌMA (διόρθωμα) signifies a reform, amendment, correction, lit., a making straight (*dia*, through, *orthoō*, to make straight). In Acts 24 : 2, lit., ' reformations come about (or take place, lit., ' become '),' the R.V. has " evils are corrected," A.V., " worthy deeds are done ; " there is no word for " worthy " or for " deeds " in the original. Some texts have *katorthōma*, which has the same meaning.¶ See *diorthōsis*, " reformation," Heb. 9 : 10.¶

2. EPANORTHŌSIS (ἐπανόρθωσις), lit., a restoration to an upright or right state (*epi*, to, *ana*, up, or again, and *orthoō*, see No. 1), hence, " correction," is used of the Scripture in 2 Tim. 3 : 16, referring to improvement of life and character.¶

3. PAIDEUTĒS (παιδευτής) has two meanings, corresponding to the two meanings of the verb *paideuō* (see below) from which it is derived, (a) a teacher, preceptor, corrector, Rom. 2 : 20 (A.V., " instructor "), (b) a chastiser, Heb. 12 : 9, rendered " to chasten " (A.V., " which corrected ; " lit., ' chastisers '). See INSTRUCTOR.¶

B. Verb.

PAIDEUŌ (παιδεύω), to train up a child (*pais*), is rendered " correcting " in 2 Tim. 2 : 25, R.V., A.V., " instructing." See CHASTEN.

CORRUPT, verb and adjective.
CORRUPTION, CORRUPTIBLE, INCORRUPTION,
INCORRUPTIBLE

A. Verbs.

1. KAPĒLEUŌ (καπηλεύω) primarily signifies to be a retailer, to peddle, to hucksterize (from *kapēlos*, an inn-keeper, a petty retailer, especially of wine, a huckster, pedlar, in contrast to *emporos*, a merchant) ; hence, to get base gain by dealing in anything, and so, more generally, to do anything for sordid personal advantage. It is found in 2 Cor. 2 : 17, with reference to the ministry of the Gospel. The significance can be best ascertained by comparison and contrast with the verb *doloō* (δολόω) in 4 : 2 (likewise there only in the N.T.), to handle deceitfully. The meanings are not identical. While both involve the deceitful dealing of adulterating the word of truth, *kapēleuō* has the broader significance of doing so in order to make dishonest gain. Those to whom the Apostle refers in 2 : 17 are such as make merchandise of souls through covetousness (cp. Tit. 1 : 11 ; 2 Pet. 2 : 3, 14, 15 ; Jude 11, 16 ; Ezek. 13 : 19) ; accordingly " hucksterizing " would be the most appropriate rendering in this passage, while " handling deceitfully " is the right meaning in 4 : 2. See Trench, Syn. § lxii.¶ In Is. 1 : 22, the Sept. has " thy wine-merchants " (*kapēloi*, hucksterizers).¶

2. PHTHEIRŌ (φθείρω) signifies to destroy by means of corrupting, and so bringing into a worse state ; (*a*) with this significance it is used of the effect of evil company upon the manners of believers, and so of the effect of association with those who deny the truth and hold false doctrine, 1 Cor. 15 : 33 (this was a saying of the pagan poet Menander, which became a well known proverb) ; in 2 Cor. 7 : 2, of the effects of dishonourable dealing by bringing people to want (a charge made against the Apostle) ; in 11 : 3, of the effects upon the minds (or thoughts) of believers by corrupting them " from the simplicity and the purity that is toward Christ ; " in Eph. 4 : 22, intransitively, of the old nature in waxing corrupt, " morally decaying, on the way to final ruin " (Moule), " after the lusts of deceit ; " in Rev. 19 : 2, metaphorically, of the Babylonish harlot, in corrupting the inhabitants of the earth by her false religion.

(*b*) With the significance of destroying, it is used of marring a local church by leading it away from that condition of holiness of life and purity of doctrine in which it should abide, 1 Cor. 3 : 17 (A.V., " defile "), and of God's retributive destruction of the offender who is guilty of this sin (id.) ; of the effects of the work of false and abominable teachers upon themselves, 2 Pet. 2 : 12 (some texts have *kataphtheirō* ; A.V., " shall utterly perish "), and Jude 10 (A.V., " corrupt themselves." R.V., marg., " are corrupted "). See DEFILE AND DESTROY.¶

3. DIAPHTHEIRŌ (διαφθείρω), *dia*, through, intensive, and No. 2, to corrupt utterly, through and through, is said of men " corrupted in mind," whose wranglings result from the doctrines of false teachers,

1 Tim. 6 : 5 (the A.V. wrongly renders it as an adjective, " corrupt "). It is translated " destroyeth " instead of " corrupteth," in the R.V. of Luke 12 : 33, of the work of a moth ; in Rev. 8 : 9, of the effect of Divine judgments hereafter upon navigation ; in 11 : 18, of the Divine retribution of destruction upon those who have destroyed the earth ; in 2 Cor. 4 : 16 it is translated " is decaying," said of the human body. See DESTROY, PERISH.¶

4. KATAPHTHEIRŌ (καταφθείρω), kata, down, intensive, and No. 2, is said of men who are reprobate concerning the faith, " corrupted in mind " (A.V., " corrupt "), 2 Tim. 3 : 8. For 2 Pet. 2 : 12, R.V., " shall be destroyed," see No. 2.¶

5. SĒPŌ (σήπω) signifies to make corrupt, to destroy ; in the Passive Voice with Middle sense, to become corrupt or rotten, to perish, said of riches, Jas. 5 : 2, of the gold and silver of the luxurious rich who have ground down their labourers. The verb is derived from a root signifying to rot off, drop to pieces.¶

6. APHANIZŌ (ἀφανίζω) : see CONSUME, No. 3.

B. Nouns.

1. PHTHORA (φθορά), connected with phtheirō, No. 2, above, signifies a bringing or being brought into an inferior or worse condition, a destruction or corruption. It is used (a) physically, (1), of the condition of creation, as under bondage, Rom. 8 : 21 ; (2) of the effect of the withdrawal of life, and so of the condition of the human body in burial, 1 Cor. 15 : 42 ; (3) by metonymy, of anything which is liable to corruption, 1 Cor. 15 : 50 ; (4) of the physical effects of merely gratifying the natural desires and ministering to one's own needs or lusts, Gal. 6 : 8, to the flesh in contrast to the Spirit, " corruption " being antithetic to " eternal life ; " (5) of that which is naturally short-lived and transient, Col. 2 : 22, " perish ; " (b) of the death and decay of beasts, 2 Pet. 2 : 12, R.V., " destroyed " (first part of verse ; lit., ' unto . . . destruction ') ; (c) ethically, with a moral significance, (1) of the effect of lusts, 2 Pet. 1 : 4 ; (2) of the effect upon themselves of the work of false and immoral teachers, 2 Pet. 2 : 12, R.V., " destroying ; " A.V., " corruption," and verse 19. See DESTROY, PERISH.¶

Note : There is nothing in any of these words suggesting or involving annihilation.

2. DIAPHTHORA (διαφθορά), an intensified form of No. 1, utter or thorough corruption, referring in the N.T. to physical decomposition and decay, is used six times, five of which refer, negatively, to the body of God's " Holy One," after His death, which body, by reason of His absolute holiness, could not see corruption, Acts 2 : 27, 31 ; 13 : 34, 35, 37 ; once it is used of a human body, that of David, which, by contrast, saw corruption, Acts 13 : 36.¶

3. APHTHARSIA (ἀφθαρσία), incorruption, a, negative, with A, No. 2, is used (a) of the resurrection body, 1 Cor. 15 : 42, 50, 53, 54 ;

(*b*) of a condition associated with glory and honour and life, including perhaps a moral significance, Rom. 2 : 7 ; 2 Tim. 1 : 10 ; this is wrongly translated " immortality " in the A.V. ; (*c*) of love to Christ, that which is sincere and undiminishing, Eph. 6 : 24 (translated " uncorruptness "). See IMMORTALITY, SINCERITY.¶

Note : For Tit. 2 : 7 (where some texts have *aphtharsia*), see No. 4.

4. APHTHORIA (ἀφθορία), similar to No. 3, uncorruptness, free from (moral) taint, is said of doctrine, Tit. 2 : 7 (some texts have *adiaphthoria*, the negative form of No. 2, above).¶

C. Adjectives.

1. PHTHARTOS (φθαρτός), corruptible, akin to A, No. 2, is used (*a*) of man as being mortal, liable to decay (in contrast to God), Rom. 1 : 23 ; (*b*) of man's body as death-doomed, 1 Cor. 15 : 53, 54 ; (*c*) of a crown of reward at the Greek games, 1 Cor. 9 : 25 ; (*d*) of silver and gold, as specimens of corruptible things, 1 Pet. 1 : 18 ; (*e*) of natural seed, 1 Pet. 1 : 23.¶

2. APHTHARTOS (ἄφθαρτος), not liable to corruption or decay, incorruptible (*a*, negative, and A, No. 2), is used of (*a*) God, Rom. 1 : 23 ; 1 Tim 1 : 17 (A.V., " immortal ") ; (*b*) the raised dead, 1 Cor. 15 : 52 ; (*c*) rewards given to the saints hereafter, metaphorically described as a " crown," 1 Cor. 9 : 25 ; (*d*) the eternal inheritance of the saints, 1 Pet. 1 : 4 ; (*e*) the Word of God, as incorruptible seed, 1 Pet. 1 : 23 ; (*f*) a meek and quiet spirit, metaphorically spoken of as incorruptible apparel, 1 Pet. 3 : 4.   See IMMORTAL.¶

3. SAPROS (σαπρός), corrupt, akin to *sēpō*, A, No. 5 ; see BAD, No. 3.

Note : (1) Trench, Syn. § lxviii, contrasts this with *amarantos*, and *amarantinos*, unwithering, not fading away, 1 Pet. 1 : 4 ; 5 : 4.   These are, however, distinct terms (see FADE) and are not strictly synonymous, though used in the same description of the heavenly inheritance.

COST, COSTLINESS, COSTLY
A. Nouns.

1. DAPANĒ (δαπάνη), expense, cost (from *daptō*, to tear ; from a root *dap*— meaning to divide), is found in Luke 14 : 28, in the Lord's illustration of counting the cost of becoming His disciple.   Cp. *dapanaō*, to spend, and its compounds, under CHARGE, SPEND.¶

2. TIMIOTĒS (τιμιότης), costliness (from *timios*, valued at great price, precious ; see No. 3, below), is connected with *timē*, honour, price, and used in Rev. 18 : 19, in reference to Babylon.¶

B. Adjectives.

1. TIMIOS (τίμιος), akin to A, No. 2, is translated " costly " in 1 Cor. 3 : 12, of costly stones, in a metaphorical sense (A.V., " precious "). Cp. Rev. 17 : 4 ; 18 : 12, 16 ; 21 : 19.   See DEAR, HONOURABLE, PRECIOUS, REPUTATION.

2. POLUTELĒS (πολυτελής), primarily, the very end or limit (from

polus, much, *telos*, revenue), with reference to price, of highest cost, very expensive, is said of spikenard, Mark 14 : 3 ; raiment, 1 Tim. 2 : 9 ; metaphorically, of a meek and quiet spirit, 1 Pet. 3 : 4, " of great price ; " cp. No. 1 and A, No. 2, above. See PRECIOUS, PRICE.¶

3. POLUTIMOS (πολύτιμος), lit., of great value (see A, No. 2 and B, No. 1), is used of a pearl, Matt. 13 : 46 ; of spikenard, John 12 : 3 (R.V., " very precious," A.V. " very costly "). See PRICE.¶ The comparative *polutimo(v.l.iō)teros*, " much more precious," is used in 1 Pet. 1 : 7.¶

COUCH

1. KLINIDION (κλινίδιον), a small bed, a diminutive form of *klinē*, a bed (from *klinō*, to incline, recline), is used in Luke 5 : 19, 24 of the bed (*klinē*, in ver. 18) on which the palsied man was brought. See BED.¶

2. KRABBATOS (κράββατος) : see BED, No. 4.

COULD

1. ECHŌ (ἔχω), to have, is rendered " could " in Mark 14 : 8, " she hath done what she could," lit., ' she hath done what she had.' See HAVE.

2. ISCHUŌ (ἰσχύω), to have strength, is translated in Mark 14 : 37 " couldest thou not." See ABLE.

Notes : (1) *Emblepō* in Acts 22 : 11, lit., ' I was not seeing,' is translated " I could not see." See BEHOLD.

(2) See CAN, when not used as part of another verb.

COUNCIL, COUNCILLOR

1. SUMBOULION (συμβούλιον), a uniting in counsel (*sun*, together, *boulē*, counsel, advice), denotes (a) counsel which is given, taken and acted upon, e.g., Matt. 12 : 14, R.V., " took counsel," for A.V., " held a council ; " 22 : 15 ; hence (b) a council, an assembly of counsellors or persons in consultation, Acts 25 : 12, of the council with which Festus conferred concerning Paul. The governors and procurators of provinces had a board of advisers or assessors, with whom they took counsel, before pronouncing judgment. See CONSULTATION.

2. SUNEDRION (συνέδριον), properly, a settling together (*sun*, together, *hedra*, a seat), hence, (a) any assembly or session of persons deliberating or adjusting, as in the Sept. of Psa. 26 : 4 (lit., ' with a council of vanity ') ; Prov. 22 : 10 ; Jer. 15 : 17, etc. ; in the N.T., e.g., Matt. 10 : 17 ; Mark 13 : 9 ; John 11 : 47, in particular, it denoted (b) the Sanhedrin, the Great Council at Jerusalem, consisting of 71 members, namely, prominent members of the families of the high priest, elders and scribes. The Jews trace the origin of this to Num. 11 : 16. The more important causes came up before this tribunal. The Roman rulers of Judæa permitted the Sanhedrin to try such cases, and even to pronounce sentence of death, with the condition that such a sentence should be valid only if confirmed by the Roman Procurator. In John 11 : 47, it is used

of a meeting of the Sanhedrin ; in Acts 4 : 15, of the place of meeting.

3. BOULEUTĒS (βουλευτής) : Joseph of Arimathaea is described as " a councillor of honourable estate," Mark 15 : 43, R.V. ; cp. Luke 23 : 50 (not as A.V., " counsellor ").¶

COUNSEL. For COUNSELLOR see above.

A. Nouns.

1. BOULĒ (βουλή) : see under ADVICE.

2. SUMBOULOS (σύμβουλος), a councillor with, occurs in Rom. 11 : 34.¶

B. Verbs.

1. BOULEUŌ (βουλεύω), to take counsel, to resolve, is used in the Middle Voice in the N.T., " took counsel " in Acts 5 : 33, A.V. (R.V. translates *boulomai*) ; both in 27 : 39 ; in Luke 14 : 31, R.V. " take " counsel " (A.V., " consulteth ") ; in John 11 : 53, A.V. and R.V. (so the best mss.) ; 12 : 10, R.V., " took counsel," for A.V., " consulted ; " in 2 Cor. 1 : 17 (twice), " purpose." See CONSULT, MINDED, PURPOSE.¶

2. SUMBOULEUŌ (συμβουλεύω), in the Active Voice, to advise, to counsel, John 18 : 14, " gave counsel ; " in Rev. 3 : 18, " I counsel ; " in the Middle Voice, to take counsel, consult, Matt. 26 : 4, R.V., " took counsel together," for A.V., " consulted ; " Acts 9 : 23, " took counsel " (R.V. adds " together ") ; in some mss. John 11 : 53. See CONSULT.¶

COUNT

1. ECHŌ (ἔχω), to have, to hold ; then, to hold in the mind, to regard, to count, has this significance in Matt. 14 : 5, " they counted Him as a prophet ; " Philm. 17, " If then thou countest me a partner ; " Mark 11 : 32, A.V., (R.V., " hold ") ; Acts 20 : 24, A.V. See ABLE.

2. HĒGEOMAI (ἡγέομαι), primarily, to lead the way ; hence, to lead before the mind, account, is found with this meaning in Phil. 2 : 3, R.V. (A.V., " esteem ") ; 2 : 6, R.V. (A.V., " thought ") ; 2 : 25 (A.V., " supposed ") ; Phil. 3 : 7, 8 ; 2 Thess. 3 : 15 ; 1 Tim. 1 : 12 ; 6 : 1 ; Heb. 10 : 29 ; Jas. 1 : 2 ; Heb. 11 : 11 (A.V., " judged ") ; 2 Pet. 2 : 13 ; 3 : 9. See ACCOUNT.

3. LOGIZOMAI (λογίζομαι), to reckon, is rendered " count " in 2 Cor. 10 : 2, R.V. (A.V., " think ") ; " counted " in the A.V. of Rom. 2 : 26 ; 4 : 3, 5 ; 9 : 8 (R.V., " reckoned ").

4. PSĒPHIZŌ (ψηφίζω), akin to *psēphos*, a stone, used in voting, occurs in Luke 14 : 28 ; Rev. 13 : 18.¶

5. SUMPSĒPHIZŌ (συμψηφίζω), to count up, occurs in Acts 19 : 19.¶

Note : In Jas. 5 : 11, *makarizō*, to pronounce blessed, is rendered " count . . . happy," A.V. (R.V., " call . . . "). For *kataxioō* see ACCOUNT, No. 5. For " descent is counted " see GENEALOGY.

COUNTENANCE

1. OPSIS (ὄψις) : only Rev. 1 : 16 has " countenance." See APPEARANCE.

2. PROSŌPON (πρόσωπον) is translated " countenance " in Luke 9 : 29 ; Acts 2 : 28, and in the A.V. of 2 Cor. 3 : 7 (R.V., " face "). See APPEARANCE.

3. EIDEA (εἰδέα), akin to *eidon*, to see : see APPEARANCE.

Notes : (1) In Acts 13 : 24 *prosōpon* is translated " before " (lit., ' before the presence of His coming ').

(2) *Skuthrōpos*, " of a sad countenance " (*skuthros*, gloomy, sad, *ōps*, an eye), is used in Matt. 6 : 16 and Luke 24 : 17, " sad."

(3) *Stugnazō*, to be or become hateful, gloomy, in aspect, is translated " his countenance fell," Mark 10 : 22, R.V. (A.V., " he was sad "). It is used of the heaven or sky in Matt. 16 : 3, " lowring." See LOWRING.¶

COUNTRY
A. Nouns.

1. AGROS (ἀγρός) denotes a field, especially a cultivated field ; hence, the country in contrast to the town (Eng., agrarian, agriculture), e.g., Mark 5 : 14 ; 6 : 36 ; 15 : 21 ; 16 : 12 ; Luke 8 : 34 ; 9 : 12 (plural, lit., ' fields ') ; 23 : 26 ; a piece of ground, e.g., Mark 10 : 29 ; Acts 4 : 37. See FARM.

2. PATRIS (πατρίς) primarily signifies one's fatherland, native country, of one's own town, Matt. 13 : 54, 57 ; Mark 6 : 1, 4 ; Luke 4 : 23, 24 ; John 4 : 44 ; Heb. 11 : 14.¶

3. CHŌRA (χώρα) properly denotes the space lying between two limits or places ; accordingly it has a variety of meanings : " country," Matt. 2 : 12 ; 8 : 28 ; Mark 1 : 5, R.V. (A.V., " land ") ; 5 : 1, 10 ; Luke 2 : 8 ; 8 : 26 ; 15 : 13, 14, R.V. (A.V., " land "), 15 ; 19 : 12 ; 21 : 21 ; Acts 10 : 39, R.V. (A.V., " land ") ; 12 : 20 ; 26 : 20, R.V. (A.V., " coasts ") ; 27 : 27 ; in Mark 6 : 55 (in the best mss.) and Acts 18 : 23, R.V., " region." See COAST, FIELD, GROUND, LAND, REGION.

4. PERICHŌROS (περίχωρος), *peri*, around, and No. 3, signifies " country round about," Luke 8 : 37 ; " country about," Luke 3 : 3, A.V. (R.V., " region round about ") ; in Matt. 14 : 35 and Luke 4 : 37, A.V., " country round about " (R.V., " region round about ") ; Matt. 3 : 5 ; Mark 1 : 28 ; Luke 4 : 14 ; 7 : 17 ; Acts 14 : 6. See REGION.¶

5. MEROS (μέρος), a part, is rendered " country " in Acts 19 : 1, R.V.

Note : Some inferior mss. have No. 4 in Mark 6 : 55, for No. 3.

B. Adjectives.

1. ANŌTERIKOS (ἀνωτερικός), upper, is used in the plural in Acts 19 : 1, to denote upper regions, with A.V., "coast," R.V., " country," i.e., the high central plateau, in contrast to the roundabout way by the river through the valley. See COAST.¶

2. OREINOS (ὀρεινός), hilly (from *oros*, a hill, mountain), is translated " hill country " in Luke 1 : 39, 65.¶

C. Verb.

APODĒMEŌ (ἀποδημέω) signifies to go or travel into a far country, lit., ' to be away from one's people ' (*apo*, from, *dēmos*, a people), Matt. 21 : 33 ; 25 : 14 ; in ver. 15 the verb is translated in the R.V., " went on his journey " (A.V., " took his journey ") ; Mark 12 : 1 ; Luke 20 : 9, " went into another country," R.V. In Luke 15 : 13 both Versions translate by " took his journey " ("into a far country " being separately expressed) ; see JOURNEY.¶

Cp. *apodēmos*, lit., away from one's own people, gone abroad, Mark 13 : 34.¶

Notes : (1) *Gē*, earth, land, is translated "country " in the A.V. of Matt. 9 : 31 and Acts 7 : 3 ; R.V., "land." See LAND.

(2) *Genos*, a race, is mistranslated "country " in the A.V. of Acts 4 : 36 (R.V., "by race "). See below.

COUNTRYMEN

1. GENOS (γένος) properly denotes an offspring ; then, a family ; then, a race, nation ; otherwise, a kind or species ; it is translated "countrymen," in 2 Cor. 11 : 26, in Paul's reference to his fellow-nationals ; so in Gal. 1 : 14, R.V., for A.V., "nation." See BEGET.

2. SUMPHULETĒS (συμφυλέτης), lit., a fellow-tribesman (*sun*, with, *phulē*, a tribe, race, nation, people), hence, one who is of the same people, a fellow-countryman, is found in 1 Thess. 2 : 14.¶

COUPLED

Note : The word "coupled " is inserted in italics in 1 Pet. 3 : 2, the more adequately to express the original, which is, lit., ' your chaste behaviour in fear.'

COURAGE

A. Noun.

THARSOS (θάρσος), akin to *tharseō*, to be of good cheer, is found in Acts 28 : 15.¶

B. Verb.

THARREŌ (θαρρέω) is translated by some form of the verb to be of good courage, in the R.V. in five of the six places where it is used : 2 Cor. 5 : 6, "being of good courage " (A.V., "we are . . . confident ") ; 5 : 8, "we are of good courage " (A.V., "we are confident ") ; 7 : 16, "I am of good courage " (A.V., "I have confidence ") ; 10 : 1, "I am of good courage " (A.V., "I am bold ") ; 10 : 2, "show courage " (A.V., "be bold ") ; Heb. 13 : 6, "with good courage," lit., ' being of good courage ' (A.V., "boldly "). See BOLD, CONFIDENCE.¶

Note : Tharreō is a later form of *tharseō*. Cp. *tolmaō*, to be bold.

COURSE

A. Nouns.

1. AIŌN (αἰών), **an age** (see AGE), is sometimes wrongly spoken of as

a " dispensation," which does not mean a period of time, but a mode of dealing. It is translated " course " in Eph. 2 : 2, " the course of this world," i.e., the cycle or present round of things. See AGE, ETERNAL, EVER, WORLD.

2. DROMOS (δρόμος), properly, a running, a race (from *edramon*, to run), hence, metaphorically, denotes a career, course of occupation, or of life, viewed in a special aspect, Acts 13 : 25 ; 20 : 24 ; 2 Tim. 4 : 7.¶

3. EPHĒMERIA (ἐφημερία), primarily, daily service, as, e.g., in the Sept. of 2 Chron. 13 : 11 (from *epi*, upon, or by, *hēmera*, a day, Eng., ephemeral), hence denoted a class, or course, into which the priests were divided for the daily service in the Temple, each class serving for seven days (see 1 Chron. 9 : 25). In the N.T. it is used in Luke 1 : 5, 8.¶

Note : Cp. *ephēmeros*, " daily (food)," Jas. 2 : 15.¶

4. TROCHOS (τροχός), a wheel, is translated " wheel " in Jas. 3 : 6, R.V., with metaphorical reference to the round of human activity (A.V., " course "), as a glowing axle would set on fire the whole wooden wheel.¶

B. Verb.

CHŌREŌ (χωρέω), to make room for, to go forward, is rendered " hath not free course," in John 8 : 37, R.V. (A.V., " hath no place "). See COME, No. 24.

Notes : (1) Connected with *dromos*, A, No. 2, is *euthudromeō*, to make (or run) a straight course (*euthus*, straight), Acts 16 : 11 and 21 : 1.¶ (2) In 2 Thess. 3 : 1, *trechō*, to run (R.V.), is translated " have free course " (A.V.).¶ (3) In 1 Cor. 14 : 27, *ana meros*, " by turn," " in turn " (R.V.), is rendered " by course " (A.V.). (4) For *ploos*, a sailing or voyage, " course," Acts 21 : 7, A.V. (R.V., " voyage "), see VOYAGE.

COURT

1. AGORAIOS (ἀγοραῖος) is an adjective, signifying pertaining to the *agora*, any place of public meeting, and especially where trials were held, Acts 19 : 38 ; the R.V. translates the sentence " the courts are open ; " a more literal rendering is ' court days are kept.' In Acts 17 : 5 it is translated in the R.V., " rabble ; " A.V., " baser sort," lit., frequenters of the markets. See BASER.¶

2. AULĒ (αὐλή), primarily, an uncovered space around a house, enclosed by a wall, where the stables were, hence was used to describe (a) the courtyard of a house ; in the O.T. it is used of the courts of the Tabernacle and Temple ; in this sense it is found in the N.T. in Rev. 11 : 2 ; (b) the courts in the dwellings of well-to-do folk, which usually had two, one exterior, between the door and the street (called the *proaulion*, or porch, Mark 14 : 68.¶), the other, interior, surrounded by the buildings of the dwellings, as in Matt. 26 : 69 (in contrast to the room where the judges were sitting); Mark 14 : 66 ; Luke 22 : 55 ; A.V., " hall ; " R.V. " court " gives the proper significance, Matt. 26 : 3, 58 ; Mark 14 : 54 ; 15 : 16 (R.V., " Prætorium ") ; Luke 11 : 21 ; John 18 : 15. It is here

to be distinguished from the Prætorium, translated " palace."   See HALL, PALACE.   For the other meaning " sheepfold," John 10 : 1, 16, see FOLD.¶

3. BASILEION (βασίλειον), an adjective meaning " royal," signifies, in the neuter plural, a royal palace, translated " kings' courts " in Luke 7 : 25 ; in the singular, 1 Pet. 2 : 9, " royal."   See ROYAL.¶

COURTEOUS, COURTEOUSLY
A. Adjective.

TAPEINOPHRŌN (ταπεινόφρων), lowly-minded, is used in 1 Pet. 3 : 8, " be courteous," A.V. (R.V., " humble-minded ").¶

B. Adverbs.

1. PHILOPHRONŌS (φιλοφρόνως), lit., friendly, or, more fully, ' with friendly thoughtfulness ' (philos, friend, phrēn, the mind), is found in Acts 28 : 7, of the hospitality showed by Publius to Paul and his fellow-shipwrecked travellers.¶

Note : Some mss. have the corresponding adjective philophrōn, " courteous," in 1 Pet. 3 : 8 ; the most authentic mss. have tapeinophrōn, " humble-minded."

2. PHILANTHRŌPŌS (φιλανθρώπως) is translated " courteously " in Acts 27 : 3, A.V. ;   R.V., " kindly " (Eng., philanthropically).   See KINDLY.¶

COUSIN

1. ANEPSIOS (ἀνεψιός), in Col. 4 : 10 denotes a cousin rather than a nephew (A.V., " sister's son ").   " Cousin " is its meaning in various periods of Greek writers.¶   In this sense it is used in the Sept., in Numb. 36 : 11.¶   In later writings it denotes a nephew ; hence the A.V. rendering. As Lightfoot says, there is no reason to suppose that the Apostle would have used it in any other than its proper sense.   We are to understand, therefore, that Mark was the cousin of Barnabas.   See SISTER.

2. SUNGENIS (συγγενίς) in Luke 1 : 36 (so in the most authentic mss.) and sungenēs in ver. 58 (plural), A.V., " cousin " and " cousins," respectively signify " kinswoman " and " kinsfolk," (R.V.) ;   so the R.V. and A.V. in 2 : 44 and 21 : 16.   The word lit. signifies ' born with,' i.e., of the same stock, or descent ; hence kinsman, kindred.   See KIN, KINSFOLK, KINSWOMAN.

COVENANT (Noun and Verb)
A. Noun.

DIATHĒKĒ (διαθήκη) primarily signifies a disposition of property by will or otherwise.   In its use in the Sept., it is the rendering of a Hebrew word meaning a covenant or agreement (from a verb signifying to cut or divide, in allusion to a sacrificial custom in connection with covenant-making, e.g., Gen. 15 : 10, " divided " Jer. 34 : 18, 19).   In contradistinction to the English word " covenant " (lit., a coming together), which signifies a mutual undertaking between two parties or more, each binding himself to fulfil obligations, it does not in itself contain the idea of joint obligation, it mostly signifies an obligation undertaken by a single person. For instance, in Gal. 3 : 17 it is used as an alternative to a " promise " (vv. 16, 17 and 18). God enjoined upon Abraham the rite of circumcision, but His promise to Abraham, here called a covenant, was not conditional upon the observance of circumcision, though a penalty attached to its non-observance.

" The N.T. uses of the word may be analysed as follows : (a) a promise or undertaking, human or divine, Gal. 3 : 15 ; (b) a promise or undertaking on the part of God, Luke 1 : 72 ; Acts 3 : 25 ; Rom. 9 : 4 ; 11 : 27 ; Gal. 3 : 17 ; Eph. 2 : 12 ; Heb. 7 : 22 ; 8 : 6, 8, 10 ; 10 : 16 ; (c) an agreement, a mutual undertaking, between God and Israel, see Deut. 29 and 30 (described as a ' commandment,' Heb. 7 : 18, cp. ver. 22) ; Heb. 8 : 9 ; 9 : 20 ; (d) by metonymy, the token of the covenant, or promise, made to Abraham, Acts 7 : 8 ; (e) by metonymy, the record of the covenant, 2 Cor. 3 : 14 ; Heb. 9 : 4 ; cp. Rev. 11 : 19 ; (f) the basis, established by the death of Christ, on which the salvation of men is secured, Matt. 26 : 28 ; Mark 14 : 24 ; Luke 22 : 20 ; 1 Cor. 11 : 25 ; 2 Cor. 3 : 6 ; Heb. 10 : 29 ; 12 : 24 ; 13 : 20.

" This covenant is called the ' new,' Heb. 9 : 15, the ' second,' 8 : 7, the ' better,' 7 : 22. In Heb. 9 : 16, 17, the translation is much disputed. There does not seem to be any sufficient reason for departing in these verses from the word used everywhere else. The English word ' Testament ' is taken from the titles prefixed to the Latin Versions."*¶ See TESTAMENT.

B. Verb.

SUNTITHĒMI (συντίθημι), lit., to put together, is used only in the Middle Voice in the N.T., and, means to determine, agree, John 9 : 22 and Acts 23 : 20 ; to assent, Acts 24 : 9 ; to covenant, Luke 22 : 5. See AGREE, ASSENT.¶

Note : In Matt. 26 : 15 the A.V. translates *histēmi*, to place (in the balances), i.e., to weigh, " they covenanted with ; " R.V., " they weighed unto."

COVENANT-BREAKERS

ASUNTHETOS (ἀσύνθετος), from *suntithēmi* (see above), with the negative prefix *a*, hence signifies " not covenant-keeping," i.e., refusing to abide by covenants made, covenant-breaking, faithless, Rom. 1 : 31.¶ In the Sept. it is found in Jer. 3 : 8–11.¶ Cp. the corresponding verb, *asuntithēmi*, in the Sept. of Ps. 73 : 15, to deal treacherously (R.V.), and the noun *asunthesia*, transgression, or covenant-breaking, e.g., Ezra 9 : 2, 4 ; 10 : 6.

Note : Trench, Syn. § lii, notes the distinction between *asunthetos* and *aspondos*, " implacable," the latter, in 2 Tim. 3 : 3 only, being derived

---

* From Notes on Galatians by Hogg and Vine, p. 144.

from *spondē*, a sacrificial libation, which accompanied treaty-making ; hence, with the negative prefix *a*, " without a treaty or covenant," thus denoting a person who cannot be persuaded to enter into a covenant. He points out that *asunthetos* presumes a state of peace interrupted by the unrighteous, *aspondos* a state of war, which the implacable refuse to terminate equitably. The words are clearly not synonymous.

COVER, COVERING
A. Verbs.

1. KALUPTŌ (καλύπτω) signifies to cover, Matt. 8 : 24 ; 10 : 26 ; Luke 8 : 16 ; 23 : 30 ; Jas. 5 : 20 (R.V.) ; 1 Pet. 4 : 8 ; to veil, in 2 Cor. 4 : 3 (R.V. ; A.V., " hid "). See HIDE.¶

Note : Cp. the corresponding noun *kalumma*, a veil, 2 Cor. 3 : 13, 14, 15, 16. See VEIL.¶

2. EPIKALUPTŌ (ἐπικαλύπτω), to cover up or over (*epi*, over), is used in Rom. 4 : 7, lit., ' whose sins are covered over.'¶ Cp. *epikalumma*, a cloke, 1 Pet. 2 : 16.¶

3. PERIKALUPTŌ (περικαλύπτω), to cover around (*peri*, around), e.g., the face, and so, to blindfold, is translated " cover " in Mark 14 : 65, " blindfold " in Luke 22 : 64. In Heb. 9 : 4, it signifies to overlay. See BLINDFOLD, OVERLAY.¶

4. SUNKALUPTŌ (συγκαλύπτω), lit., to cover together ; the *sun-*, however, is intensive, and the verb signifies to cover wholly, to cover up, Luke 12 : 2.¶

5. KATAKALUPTŌ (κατακαλύπτω), to cover up (*kata*, intensive), in the Middle Voice, to cover oneself, is used in 1 Cor. 11 : 6, 7 (R.V., " veiled ").¶

Note : In 1 Cor. 11 : 4, " having his head covered " is, lit., ' having (something) down the head.'

B. Nouns.

1. PERIBOLAION (περιβόλαιον) lit. denotes something thrown around (*peri*, around, *ballō*, to throw) ; hence, a veil, covering, 1 Cor. 11 : 15 (marg.), or a mantle around the body, a vesture, Heb. 1 : 12. See CLOTHING, Note (1), VESTURE.¶

2. SKEPASMA (σκέπασμα), a covering (*skepazō*, to cover), strictly, a roofing, then, any kind of shelter or covering, is used in the plural in 1 Tim. 6 : 8 (A.V., " raiment ; " R.V., " covering ").¶

COVET, COVETOUS, COVETOUSNESS
A. Verbs.

1. EPITHUMEŌ (ἐπιθυμέω), to fix the desire upon (*epi*, upon, used intensively, *thumos*, passion), whether things good or bad ; hence, to long for, lust after, covet, is used with the meaning to covet evilly in Acts 20 : 33, of coveting money and apparel ; so in Rom. 7 : 7 ; 13 : 9. See DESIRE, FAIN, LUST.

2. ZĒLOŌ (ζηλόω) is rendered " covet earnestly," in 1 Cor. 12 : 31, A.V.; R.V., " desire earnestly," as in 14 : 39 (A.V., " covet "). See AFFECT, DESIRE, ENVY, JEALOUS, ZEALOUS.

3. OREGŌ (ὀρέγω), to stretch after, is rendered " covet after " in 1 Tim. 6 : 10, A.V.; R.V., " reaching after." See DESIRE, REACH.

B. Nouns.

1. EPITHUMĒTĒS (ἐπιθυμητής), a luster after (akin to A, No. 1), is translated in 1 Cor. 10 : 6, in verbal form, " should not lust after." See LUST.¶

2. EPITHUMIA (ἐπιθυμία) denotes " coveting," Rom. 7 : 7, 8, R.V.; A.V., " lust " and " concupiscence ; " the commandment here referred to convicted him of sinfulness in his desires for unlawful objects besides that of gain. See DESIRE, LUST.

3. PLEONEXIA (πλεονεξία), covetousness, lit., a desire to have more (pleon, more, echō, to have), always in a bad sense, is used in a general way in Mark 7 : 22 (plural, lit., ' covetings,' i.e., various ways in which covetousness shows itself) ; Rom. 1 : 29 ; Eph. 5 : 3 ; 1 Thess. 2 : 5. Elsewhere it is used, (a) of material possessions, Luke 12 : 15 ; 2 Pet. 2 : 3 ; 2 Cor. 9 : 5 (R.V., " extortion "), lit., ' as (a matter of) extortion,' i.e., a gift which betrays the giver's unwillingness to bestow what is due ; (b) of sensuality, Eph. 4 : 19, " greediness ; " Col. 3 : 5 (where it is called idolatry) ; 2 Pet. 2 : 14 (A.V., " covetous practices "). See EXTORTION.¶

Note : Cp. the corresponding verb pleonekteō, to gain, take advantage of, wrong. See ADVANTAGE, DEFRAUD, GAIN, B, Note (2), WRONG

C. Adjectives.

1. PLEONEKTĒS (πλεονέκτης), lit., (eager) to have more (see B, No. 3), i.e., to have what belongs to others ; hence, greedy of gain, covetous, 1 Cor. 5 : 10, 11 ; 6 : 10 ; Eph. 5 : 5 (" covetous man ").¶

2. PHILARGUROS (φιλάργυρος), lit., money-loving, is rendered " covetous " in the A.V. of Luke 16 : 14 and 2 Tim. 3 : 2 ; R.V., " lovers of money," the wider and due significance.¶

3. APHILARGUROS (ἀφιλάργυρος), No. 2, with negative prefix, is translated " without covetousness " in Heb. 13 : 5, A.V.; R.V., " free from the love of money." In 1 Tim. 3 : 3, the A.V. has " not covetous," the R.V., " no lover of money."

Note : Trench, Syn. § 24, points out the main distinction between pleonexia and philarguria as being that between covetousness and avarice, the former having a much wider and deeper sense, being " the genus of which philarguria is the species." The covetous man is often cruel as well as grasping, while the avaricious man is simply miserly and stinting.

CRAFT, CRAFTSMAN

1. TECHNĒ (τέχνη), craft, Rev. 18 : 22 : see ART.

2. TECHNITĒS (τεχνίτης), akin to No. 1, an artificer, artisan, craftsman, is translated " craftsman " in Acts 19 : 24, 38 and Rev. 18 : 22.

It is found elsewhere in Heb. 11 : 10, " builder ; " but this is practically
the same as " maker " (*demiourgos*, the next noun in the verse ; see
No. 5, Note). Trench, Syn. § cv, suggests that *technitēs* brings out the
artistic side of creation, viewing God as " moulding and fashioning . . .
the materials which He called into existence." This agrees with the usage
of the word in the Sept. See BUILDER.¶

3. ERGASIA (ἐργασία) : see DILIGENCE.

4. HOMOTECHNOS (ὁμότεχνος), one of the same trade (from *homos*,
same, and *technē*, see No. 1), is used in Acts 18 : 3 (R.V., " trade ").¶
Cp. *architektōn*, " master-builder," 1 Cor. 3 : 10.¶

5. MEROS (μέρος), a part, portion, is translated " craft " in Acts
19 : 27, A.V.; " trade," R.V. (cp. *ergasia* in ver. 25). See BEHALF,
COAST, PART, PIECE, PORTION, RESPECT, SORT.

Note : *Dēmiourgos*, a maker, properly signifies one who works for the
people, or whose work stands forth to the public gaze (*dēmos*, people,
ergon, work), but this idea has been lost in the use of the word, which
came to signify a maker, Heb. 11 : 10. This has reference to the structure,
No. 2 to the design. Cp. *ktistēs*, a creator.¶

CRAFTINESS, CRAFTY
A. Noun.

PANOURGIA (πανουργία), lit., ' all-working,' i.e., doing everything
(*pan*, all, *ergon*, work), hence, unscrupulous conduct, craftiness, is always
used in a bad sense in the N.T.. Luke 20 : 23 ; 1 Cor. 3 : 19 ; 2 Cor. 4 : 2 ;
11 : 3 ; Eph. 4 : 14, A.V., " cunning craftiness." See SUBTILTY.¶ In
the Sept. it is used in a good sense, Prov. 1 : 4 ; 8 : 5 ; indifferently in
Numb. 24 : 22 and Josh. 9 : 4.¶

B. Adjective.

PANOURGOS (πανοῦργος), cunning, crafty, is found in 2 Cor. 12 : 16,
where the Apostle is really quoting an accusation made against him by
his detractors.¶ In the Sept. it is used in a good sense in Prov. 13 : 1 ;
28 : 2.¶

C. Noun.

DOLOS (δόλος), primarily, a bait, hence, fraud, guile, deceit, is rendered
" craft " in the A.V. of Mark 14 : 1 (R.V. " subtilty "). See DECEIT,
GUILE, SUBTILTY.

CRAVE

Note : The word " crave," found in the A.V. of Mark 15 : 43, translates
the verb *aiteō*, to ask (R.V., " asked for "). See ASK.

CREATE, CREATION, CREATOR, CREATURE
A. Verb.

KTIZŌ (κτίζω), used among the Greeks to mean the founding of a
place, a city or colony, signifies, in Scripture, to create, always of the

act of God, whether (*a*) in the natural creation, Mark 13 : 19 ; Rom. 1 : 25 (where the title " The Creator " translates the article with the aorist participle of the verb) ; 1 Cor. 11 : 9 ; Eph. 3 : 9 ; Col. 1 : 16 ; 1 Tim. 4 : 3 ; Rev. 4 : 11 ; 10 : 6, or (*b*) in the spiritual creation, Eph. 2 : 10, 15 ; 4 : 24 ; Col. 3 : 10. See MAKE.¶

B. Nouns.

1. KTISIS (κτίσις), primarily the act of creating, or the creative act in process, has this meaning in Rom. 1 : 20 and Gal. 6 : 15. Like the English word " creation," it also signifies the product of the creative act, the creature, as in Mark 16 : 15, R.V. ; Rom. 1 : 25 ; 8 : 19 ; Col. 1 : 15 etc. ; in Heb. 9 : 11, A.V., " building." In Mark 16 : 15 and Col. 1 : 23 its significance has special reference to mankind in general. As to its use in Gal. 6 : 15 and 2 Cor. 5 : 17, in the former, apparently, " the reference is to the creative act of God, whereby a man is introduced into the blessing of salvation, in contrast to circumcision done by human hands, which the Judaizers claimed was necessary to that end. In 2 Cor. 5 : 17 the reference is to what the believer is in Christ ; in consequence of the creative act he has become a new creature."*

Ktisis is once used of human actions, 1 Pet. 2 : 13, " ordinance " (marg., " creation "). See BUILDING, ORDINANCE.

2. KTISMA (κτίσμα) has the concrete sense, the created thing, the creature, the product of the creative act, 1 Tim. 4 : 4 ; Jas. 1 : 18 ; Rev. 5 : 13 ; 8 : 9.¶

3. KTISTĒS (κτίστης), among the Greeks, the founder of a city etc., denotes in Scripture the Creator, 1 Pet. 4 : 19 (cp. Rom. 1 : 20, under B, No. 1, above).¶

Note : It is a significant confirmation of Rom. 1 : 20, 21, that in all non-Christian Greek literature these words are never used by Greeks to convey the idea of a Creator or of a creative act by any of their gods. The words are confined by them to the acts of human beings.

4. ZŌON (ζῶον), a living creature : see BEAST.

For CREDITOR see LEND, LENDER

For CREEK see BAY

CREEP, CREEPING, CREPT
A. Verbs.

1. ENDUNŌ (ἐνδύνω), properly, to envelop in (*en*, in, *dunō*, to enter), to put on, as of a garment, has the secondary and intransitive significance of creeping into, insinuating oneself into, and is found with this meaning in 2 Tim. 3 : 6. Cp. *enduō*, to clothe.¶

2. PAREISDUNŌ (παρεισδύνω), to enter in by the side (*para*, beside,

---

* From Notes on Galatians by Hogg and Vine, p. 339.

eis, in), to insinuate oneself into, by stealth, to creep in stealthily, is used in Jude 4.¶

B. Noun.

HERPETON (ἑρπετόν) signifies a creeping thing (*herpō*, to creep; Eng., " serpent " is from the same root), Jas. 3 : 7 (R.V., " creeping things," for A.V., " serpents," which form only one of this genus) ; it is set in contrast to quadrupeds and birds, Acts 10 : 12 ; 11 : 6 ; Rom. 1 : 23. See SERPENT.¶

For CRIME see CHARGE

For CRIPPLE see HALT

CROOKED

SKOLIOS (σκολιός), curved, crooked, was especially used (*a*) of a way, Luke 3 : 5, with spiritual import (see Prov. 28 : 18, Sept.) ; it is set in contrast to *orthos* and *euthus*, straight ; (*b*) metaphorically, of what is morally crooked, perverse, froward, of people belonging to a particular generation, Acts 2 : 40 (A.V., " untoward ") ; Phil. 2 : 15 ; of tyrannical or unjust masters, 1 Pet. 2 : 18, " froward ; " in this sense it is set in contrast to *agathos*, good.¶

CROSS, CRUCIFY
A. Noun.

STAUROS (σταυρός) denotes, primarily, an upright pale or stake. On such malefactors were nailed for execution. Both the noun and the verb *stauroō*, to fasten to a stake or pale, are originally to be distinguished from the ecclesiastical form of a two beamed cross. The shape of the latter had its origin in ancient Chaldea, and was used as the symbol of the god Tammuz (being in the shape of the mystic Tau, the initial of his name) in that country and in adjacent lands, including Egypt. By the middle of the 3rd cent. A.D. the churches had either departed from, or had travestied, certain doctrines of the Christian faith. In order to increase the prestige of the apostate ecclesiastical system pagans were received into the churches apart from regeneration by faith, and were permitted largely to retain their pagan signs and symbols. Hence the Tau or T, in its most frequent form, with the cross-piece lowered, was adopted to stand for the cross of Christ.

As for the Chi, or X, which Constantine declared he had seen in a vision leading him to champion the Christian faith, that letter was the initial of the word " Christ " and had nothing to do with " the Cross " (for *xulon*, a timber beam, a tree, as used for the *stauros*, see under TREE).

The method of execution was borrowed by the Greeks and Romans from the Phoenicians. The *stauros* denotes (*a*) the cross, or stake itself, e.g., Matt. 27 : 32 ; (*b*) the crucifixion suffered, e.g., 1 Cor. 1 : 17, 18, where " the word of the cross," R.V., stands for the Gospel ; Gal. 5 : 11, where crucifixion is metaphorically used of the renunciation of the world, that characterizes the true Christian life ; 6 : 12, 14 ; Eph. 2 : 16 ; Phil. 3 : 18.

The judicial custom by which the condemned person carried his stake to the place of execution, was applied by the Lord to those sufferings by which His faithful followers were to express their fellowship with Him, e.g., Matt. 10 : 38.

B. Verbs.

1. STAUROŌ (σταυρόω) signifies (a) the act of crucifixion, e.g., Matt. 20 : 19 ; (b) metaphorically, the putting off of the flesh with its passions and lusts, a condition fulfilled in the case of those who are " of Christ Jesus," Gal. 5 : 24, R.V. ; so of the relationship between the believer and the world, 6 : 14.

2. SUSTAUROŌ (συσταυρόω), to crucify with (su-, for, sun, with), is used (a) of actual crucifixion in company with another, Matt. 27 : 44 ; Mark 15 : 32 ; John 19 : 32 ; (b) metaphorically, of spiritual identification with Christ in His death, Rom. 6 : 6, and Gal. 2 : 20.¶

3. ANASTAUROŌ (ἀνασταυρόω) (ana, again) is used in Heb. 6 : 6 of Hebrew apostates, who as merely nominal Christians, in turning back to Judaism, were thereby virtually guilty of crucifying Christ again.¶

4. PROSPĒGNUMI (προσπήγνυμι), to fix or fasten to anything (pros, to, pēgnumi, to fix), is used of the crucifixion of Christ, Acts 2 : 23.¶

CROSS (Verb)

DIAPERAŌ (διαπεράω), to pass over, to cross over (dia, through, peraō, to pass : akin to this are peran, across, peras, a boundary, Latin, porta, a gate, Eng., portal, port, etc.), is translated by the verb to cross in the R.V., but differently in the A.V. ; in Matt. 9 : 1 ; Mark 5 : 21 ; 6 : 53 (A.V., " passed ") ; Matt. 14 : 34 (A.V., " were gone ") ; Luke 16 : 26 (A.V., " neither can they pass ") ; Acts 21 : 2 (A.V., " sailing "). See Go, Pass, Sail.¶ In the Sept., Deut. 30 : 13 ; Is. 23 : 2.¶

For the verb CROW (CREW) see CALL, A, No. 8

CROWD
A. Noun.

OCHLOS (ὄχλος), a confused throng, is usually translated " multitude." The R.V. translates it " crowd " (A.V., " press " in some) in Matt. 9 : 23, 25 ; Mark 2 : 4 ; 3 : 9 ; 5 : 27, 30 ; Luke 8 : 19 ; 19 : 3 ; Acts 21 : 34, 35 ; 24 : 12, 18. See Company, Multitude, Number, People.

B. Verb.

OCHLOPOIEŌ (ὀχλοποιέω), to make a crowd (A, with poieō, to make), is translated " gathered a crowd " in Acts 17 : 5, R.V. (A.V., " company ").

CROWN (Noun and Verb)
A. Nouns.

1. STEPHANOS (στέφανος), primarily, that which surrounds, as a wall or crowd (from stephō, to encircle), denotes (a) the victor's crown, the symbol of triumph in the games or some such contest ; hence, by metonymy, a reward or prize ; (b) a token of public honour for distinguished service, military prowess etc., or of nuptial joy, or festal gladness, especially at the parousia of kings. It was woven as a garland of oak, ivy, parsley, myrtle or olive, or in imitation of these in gold. In some passages the reference to the games is clear, 1 Cor. 9 : 25 ; 2 Tim. 4 : 8 (" crown of righteousness ") ; it may be so in 1 Pet. 5 : 4, where the fadeless character of " the crown of glory " is set in contrast to the garlands of earth. In other passages it stands as an emblem of life, joy, reward and glory, Phil. 4 : 1 ; 1 Thess. 2 : 19 ; Jas. 1 : 12 (" crown of life ") ; Rev. 2 : 10 (ditto) ; 3 : 11 ; 4 : 4, 10 : of triumph, 6 : 2 ; 9 : 7 ; 12 : 1 ; 14 : 14.

It is used of the crown of thorns which the soldiers plaited and put on Christ's head, Matt. 27 : 29 ; Mark 15 : 17 ; John 19 : 2, 5. At first sight this might be taken as an alternative for diadēma, a kingly crown (see below), but considering the blasphemous character of that masquerade, and the materials used, obviously diadēma would be quite unfitting and the only alternative was stephanos (see Trench § xxxii).¶

2. DIADĒMA (διάδημα) is never used as stephanos is ; it is always the symbol of kingly or imperial dignity, and is translated " diadem " instead of " crown " in the R.V., of the claims of the Dragon, Rev. 12 : 3 ; 13 : 1 ; 19 : 12. See DIADEM.¶

B. Verb.

STEPHANOŌ (στεφανόω), to crown, conforms in meaning to stephanos ; it is used of the reward of victory in the games, in 2 Tim. 2 : 5 ; of the glory and honour bestowed by God upon man in regard to his position in creation, Heb. 2 : 7 ; of the glory and honour bestowed upon the Lord Jesus in His exaltation, ver. 9.¶

For CRUCIFY see CROSS

CRUMB

PSICHION (ψιχίον), a small morsel, a diminutive of psix, a bit, or crumb ; of bread or meat, it is used in Matt. 15 : 27 and Mark 7 : 28 ; some mss. have it in Luke 16 : 21.¶

CRUSE

ALABASTRON (ἀλάβαστρον) was a vessel for holding ointment or perfume ; it derived its name from the alabaster stone, of which it was usually made. " Cruse," R.V., is a more suitable rendering than " box ; " Matt. 26 : 7 ; Mark 14 : 3 ; Luke 7 : 37.¶

CRUSH

APOTHLIBŌ (ἀποθλίβω), a strengthened form of *thlibō*, to throng (*apo*, intensive), is used in Luke 8 : 45, R.V., " crush," for A.V., " press," of the multitude who were pressing around Christ (cp. the preceding word *sunechō*, to press).¶ In the Sept., Numb. 22 : 25.¶

CRY (Noun and Verb), CRYING
A. Nouns.

1. KRAUGĒ (κραυγή), an onomatopœic word, is used in Matt. 25 : 6 ; Luke 1 : 42 (some mss. have *phōnē*) ; Acts 23 : 9, R.V., " clamour ; " Eph. 4 : 31, " clamour ; " Heb. 5 : 7 ; Rev. 21 : 4, " crying." Some mss. have it in Rev. 14 : 18 (the most authentic have *phōnē*). See CLAMOUR.¶

2. BOĒ (βοή), especially a cry for help, an onomatopœic word (cp. Eng., boo), connected with *boaō* (see B, No. 1), is found in Jas. 5 : 4.¶

B. Verbs.

1. BOAŌ (βοάω), akin to A, No. 2, signifies (*a*) to raise a cry, whether of joy, Gal. 4 : 27, or vexation, Acts 8 : 7 ; (*b*) to speak with a strong voice, Matt. 3 : 3 ; Mark 1 : 3 ; 15 : 34 ; Luke 3 : 4 ; 9 : 38 (some mss. have *anaboaō* here : see No. 2) ; John 1 : 23 ; Acts 17 : 6 ; 25 : 24 (some mss. have *epiboaō*, No. 3, here) ; (*c*) to cry out for help, Luke 18 : 7, 38.¶ For Acts 21 : 34, see No. 8.

2. ANABOAŌ (ἀναβοάω), *ana*, up, intensive, and No. 1, to lift up the voice, cry out, is said of Christ at the moment of His Death, a testimony to His supernatural power in giving up His life, Matt. 27 : 46 ; in some mss. in Mark 15 : 8, of the shouting of a multitude ; in some mss. in Luke 9 : 38, of the crying out of a man in a company (see No. 1).¶

3. EPIBOAŌ (ἐπιβοάω), *epi*, upon, intensive, and No. 1, to cry out, exclaim vehemently, is used in some mss. in Acts 25 : 24 (see No. 1.¶)

4. KRAZŌ (κράζω), akin to A, No. 1, to cry out, an onomatopœic word, used especially of the cry of the raven ; then, of any inarticulate cries, from fear, pain etc. ; of the cry of a Canaanitish woman, Matt. 15 : 22 (so the best mss., instead of *kraugazō*) ; of the shouts of the children in the Temple, Matt. 21 : 15 ; of the people who shouted for Christ to be crucified, 27 : 23 ; Mark 15 : 13, 14 ; of the cry of Christ on the Cross at the close of His sufferings, Matt. 27 : 50 ; Mark 15 : 39 (see No. 2, above).

In John's Gospel it is used three times, out of the six, of Christ's utterances, 7 : 28, 37 ; 12 : 44. In the Acts it is not used of cries of distress, but chiefly of the shouts of opponents ; in the Apocalypse, chiefly of the utterances of heavenly beings concerning earthly matters ; in Rom. 8 : 15 and Gal. 4 : 6, of the appeal of believers to God the Father ; in Rom. 9 : 27, of a prophecy concerning Israel ; in Jas. 5 : 4, metaphorically, of hire kept back by fraud.

Note : A recent translator renders this verb in Matt. 27 : 50 " uttered a scream," an utterly deplorable mistranslation, and a misrepresentation of the nature of the Lord's cry.

5. ANAKRAZŌ (ἀνακράζω), *ana*, up, intensive, and No. 4, signifies to cry out loudly, Mark 1 : 23 ; 6 : 49 ; Luke 4 : 33 ; 8 : 28 ; 23 : 18.¶

6. KRAUGAZŌ (κραυγάζω), a stronger form of No. 4, to make a clamour or outcry (A, No. 1), is used in Matt. 12 : 19, in a prophecy from Isaiah of Christ ; in Luke 4 : 41 (in the best mss., instead of *krazō*) ; John 11 : 43 ; 12 : 13 (in the best mss.) ; 18 : 40 ; 19 : 6, 12, 15 ; Acts 22 : 23.¶

7. PHŌNEŌ (φωνέω), to utter a loud sound or cry, whether of animals, e.g., Matt. 26 : 34 ; or persons, Luke 8 : 8 ; 16 : 24 ; this is the word which Luke uses to describe the cry of the Lord at the close of His sufferings on the Cross, Luke 23 : 46 (see under *anaboaō* and *krazō*, above) ; also, e.g., Acts 16 : 28 ; Rev. 14 : 18. See CALL, A, No. 8, CROW.

8. EPIPHŌNEŌ (ἐπιφωνέω), No. 7, with *epi*, upon, or against, signifies to shout, either against, Luke 23 : 21 ; Acts 21 : 34 (in the best mss., No. 1) ; 22 : 24, or in acclamation, Acts 12 : 22. See SHOUT.¶

Note : For *aphiēmi*, Mark 15 : 37, see UTTER.

Comparing the various verbs, *kaleō*, denotes to call out for any purpose, *boaō*, to cry out as an expression of feeling, *krazō*, to cry out loudly. *Kaleō* suggests intelligence, *boaō*, sensibilities, *krazō*, instincts.

CRYSTAL
A. Noun.

KRUSTALLOS (κρύσταλλος), from *kruos*, ice, and hence properly anything congealed and transparent, denotes crystal, a kind of precious stone, Rev. 4 : 6 ; 22 : 1. Rock-crystal is pure quartz ; it crystallizes in hexagonal prisms, each with a pyramidical apex.¶

B. Verb.

KRUSTALLIZŌ (κρυσταλλίζω), to be of crystalline brightness and transparency, to shine like crystal, is found in Rev. 21 : 11, where it is said of Christ as the " Light-giver " (*phōstēr*) of the Heavenly City (not *phōs*, light, R.V. and A.V.). Possibly there the verb has a transitive force, to transform into crystal splendour, as of the effect of Christ upon His saints.¶

CUBIT

PĒCHUS (πῆχυς) denotes the fore-arm, i.e., the part between the hand and the elbow-joint ; hence, a measure of length, not from the wrist to the elbow, but from the tip of the middle finger to the elbow joint, i.e., about a foot and a half, or a little less than two feet, Matt. 6 : 27 ; Luke 12 : 25 ; John 21 : 8 ; Rev. 21 : 17.¶

CUMBER

1. KATARGEŌ (καταργέω), lit., to reduce to idleness or inactivity (*kata*, down, and *argos*, idle), is once rendered " cumber," Luke 13 : 7. See ABOLISH.

2. PERISPAŌ (περισπάω), lit., to draw around (peri), draw away, distract, is used in the Passive Voice in the sense of being over-occupied about a thing, to be cumbered, Luke 10 : 40.¶

CUMMIN

KUMINON (κύμινον) is an umbelliferous plant with aromatic seeds, used as a condiment, Matt. 23 : 23.

For the A.V. CUNNING see CRAFTINESS. For CUNNINGLY see DEVISED

CUP

POTĒRION (ποτήριον), a diminutive of potēr, denotes, primarily, a drinking vessel ; hence, a cup (a) literal, as, e.g., in Matt. 10 : 42. The cup of blessing, 1 Cor. 10 : 16, is so named from the third (the fourth according to Edersheim) cup in the Jewish Passover Feast, over which thanks and praise were given to God. This connection is not to be rejected on the ground that the church at Corinth was unfamiliar with Jewish customs. That the contrary was the case, see 5 : 7 ; (b) figurative, of one's lot or experience, joyous or sorrowful (frequent in the Psalms ; cp. Ps. 116 : 18, "cup of salvation ") ; in the N.T. it is used most frequently of the sufferings of Christ, Matt. 20 : 22, 23 ; 26 : 39 ; Mark 10 : 38, 39 ; 14 : 36 ; Luke 22 : 42 ; John 18 : 11 ; also of the evil deeds of Babylon, Rev. 17 : 4 ; 18 : 6 ; of Divine punishments to be inflicted, Rev. 14 : 10 ; 16 : 19. Cp. Ps. 11 : 6 ; 75 : 8 ; Is. 51 : 17 ; Jer. 25 : 15 ; Ezek. 23 : 32–34 ; Zech. 12 : 2.

CURE (Noun and Verb)
A. Noun.

IASIS (ἴασις), a healing, a cure (akin to iaomai, to heal, and iatros, a physician), is used in the plural in Luke 13 : 32 ; in Acts 4 : 22, " healing ; " in 4 : 30 with the preposition eis, unto, lit., ' unto healing,' translated " heal." See HEALING.¶

B. Verb.

THERAPEUŌ (θεραπεύω), Eng., therapeutics, etc., denotes (a) primarily, to serve (cp. therapeia and therapōn), Acts 17 : 25 (A.V., " worshipped ") ; then, (b) to heal, restore to health, to cure ; it is usually translated " to heal," but " cure " in Matt. 17 : 16, 18 ; Luke 7 : 21 ; 9 : 1 ; John 5 : 10, Acts 28 : 9, R.V. See HEAL, WORSHIP.

CURIOUS

Note : For the adjective periergos, busy about trifles, see BUSYBODY : it is used of magic arts in Acts 19 : 19 (lit., ' things that are around work,' and thus superfluous), i.e., the arts of those who pry into forbidden things, with the aid of evil spirits. See also 1 Tim. 5 : 13, where the meaning is " inquisitive," prying into other people's affairs.¶

CURSE, CURSING (Noun and Verb), CURSED, ACCURSED

A. Nouns.

1. ARA (ἀρά), in its most usual meaning, a malediction, cursing (its other meaning is "a prayer"), is used in Rom. 3 : 14 (often in the Sept.).¶

2. KATARA (κατάρα), kata, down, intensive, and No. 1, denotes an execration, imprecation, curse, uttered out of malevolence, Jas. 3 : 10 ; 2 Pet. 2 : 14 ; or pronounced by God in His righteous judgment, as upon a land doomed to barrenness, Heb. 6 : 8 ; upon those who seek for justification by obedience, in part or completely, to the Law, Gal. 3 : 10, 13 ; in this 13th verse it is used concretely of Christ, as having " become a curse " for us, i.e., by voluntarily undergoing on the Cross the appointed penalty of the curse. He thus was identified, on our behalf, with the doom of sin. Here, not the verb in the Sept. of Deut. 21 : 23 is used (see B, No. 3), but the concrete noun.¶

3. ANATHEMA (ἀνάθεμα), transliterated from the Greek, is frequently used in the Sept., where it translates the Heb. *cherem*, a thing devoted to God, whether (a) for His service, as the sacrifices, Lev. 27 : 28 (cp. *anathēma*, a votive offering, gift), or (b) for its destruction, as an idol, Deut. 7 : 26, or a city, Josh. 6 : 17.   Later it acquired the more general meaning of the disfavour of Jehovah, e.g., Zech. 14 : 11.   This is the meaning in the N.T.   It is used of (a) the sentence pronounced, Acts 23 : 14 (lit., ' cursed themselves with a curse ; ' see *anathematizō* below) ; (b) of the object on which the curse is laid, " accursed ; " in the following, the R.V. keeps to the word " anathema," Rom. 9 : 3 ; 1 Cor. 12 : 3 ; 16 : 22 ; Gal. 1 : 8, 9, all of which the A.V. renders by " accursed " except 1 Cor. 16 : 22, where it has " Anathema."   In Gal. 1 : 8, 9, the Apostle declares in the strongest manner that the Gospel he preached was the one and only way of salvation, and that to preach another was to nullify the Death of Christ.¶

4. KATATHEMA (κατάθεμα), or, as in some mss., the longer form *katanathema*, is stronger than No. 3 (*kata*, intensive), and denotes, by metonymy, an accursed thing (the object cursed being put for the curse pronounced), Rev. 22 : 3.¶

B. Verbs.

1. ANATHEMATIZŌ (ἀναθεματίζω), akin to No. 3, signifies to declare anathema, i.e., devoted to destruction, accursed, to curse, Mark 14 : 71, or to bind by a curse, Acts 23 : 12, 14, 21.¶

2. KATANATHEMATIZŌ (καταναθεματίζω), a strengthened form of No. 1, denotes to utter curses against, Matt. 26 : 74 ; cp. Mark's word concerning the same occasion (No. 1).¶

3. KATARAOMAI (καταράομαι), akin to A, No. 2, primarily signifies to pray against, to wish evil against a person or thing ; hence to curse, Matt. 25 : 41 ; Mark 11 : 21 ; Luke 6 : 28 ; Rom. 12 : 14 ; Jas. 3 : 9. Some mss. have it in Matt. 5 : 44.¶

4. KAKOLOGEŌ (κακολογέω), to speak evil (kakos, evil, legō, to speak), is translated by the verb to curse in Matt. 15 : 4, and Mark 7 : 10, to speak evil of father and mother, not necessarily to curse, is what the Lord intended (R.V.). A.V. and R.V. have the verb to speak evil in Mark 9 : 39 and Acts 19 : 9. See EVIL.

C. Adjectives.

1. EPIKATARATOS (ἐπικατάρατος), cursed, accursed (epi, upon, and A, No. 2), is used in Gal. 3 : 10, 13.¶

2. EPARATOS (ἐπάρατος), accursed, is found, in the best mss., in John 7 : 49, R.V., " accursed," instead of No. 1.

For CUSHION see PILLOW

CUSTOM (Usage), ACCUSTOM (Verb)
A. Nouns.

1. ETHOS (ἔθος) denotes (a) a custom, usage, prescribed by law, Acts 6 : 14 ; 15 : 1 ; 25 : 16 ; a rite or ceremony, Luke 2 : 42 ; (b) a custom, habit, manner, Luke 22 : 39 ; John 19 : 40 ; Heb. 10 : 25 (A.V., " manner "). See MANNER, WONT.

2. SUNĒTHEIA (συνήθεια), sun, with, ethos (see No. 1), denotes (a) an intercourse, intimacy, a meaning not found in the N.T. ; (b) a custom, customary usage, John 18 : 39 ; 1 Cor. 11 : 16 ; or force of habit, 1 Cor. 8 : 7, R.V., " being used to " (some mss. here have suneidēsis, conscience ; whence A.V., " with conscience of ").¶

B. Verbs.

1. ETHIZŌ (ἐθίζω), akin to A, No. 1, signifies to accustom, or in the Passive Voice, to be accustomed. In the participial form it is equivalent to a noun, " custom," Luke 2 : 27.¶

2. ETHŌ (ἔθω), to be accustomed, as in the case of No. 1, is used in the Passive participle as a noun, signifying a custom, Luke 4 : 16 ; Acts 17 : 2 (A.V., " manner ; " R.V., " custom ") ; in Matt. 17 : 15 and Mark 10 : 1, " was wont." See MANNER, WONT.¶

CUSTOM (Toll)

1. TELOS (τέλος), an end, termination, whether of time or purpose, denotes, in its secondary significance, what is paid for public ends, a toll, tax, custom, Matt. 17 : 25 (R.V., " toll ") ; Rom. 13 : 7 (R.V. and A.V., " custom "). In Palestine the Herods of Galilee and Peræa received the custom ; in Judæa it was paid to the Procurator for the Roman Government. See END, FINALLY, UTTERMOST.

2. TELŌNION (τελώνιον) denotes a custom-house, for the collection of the taxes, Matt. 9 : 9 ; Mark 2 : 14 ; Luke 5 : 27 (R.V., " place of toll ").

CUT

1. KOPTŌ (κόπτω) denotes to cut by a blow, e.g., branches, Matt. 21 : 8 ; Mark 11 : 8. See BEWAIL, LAMENT, MOURN, WAIL.

2. APOKOPTŌ (ἀποκόπτω), to cut off, or cut away (apo, from, and No. 1), is used (a) literally, of members of the body, Mark 9 : 43, 45 ; John 18 : 10, 26 ; of ropes, Acts 27 : 32 ; (b) metaphorically, in the Middle Voice, of cutting off oneself, to excommunicate, Gal. 5 : 12, of the Judaizing teachers, with a reference, no doubt, to circumcision.¶

3. EKKOPTŌ (ἐκκόπτω), lit., to cut or strike out (ek, out or off, and No. 1), to cut down, is used (a) literally, Matt. 5 : 30 (in 3 : 10 and 7 : 19 and Luke 3 : 9, " hewn down ") ; 18 : 8 ; Luke 13 : 7, 9 ; (b) metaphorically, of cutting off from spiritual blessing, Rom. 11 : 22, 24 ; of depriving persons of an occasion for something, 2 Cor. 11 : 12. See HEW.¶

Note : In 1 Pet. 3 : 7 the best mss. have enkoptō, to hinder ; some have ekkoptō.

4. KATAKOPTŌ (κατακόπτω), lit., to cut down, cut in pieces (kata, down, intensive), Mark 5 : 5, of the demoniac.¶

5. DIAPRIŌ (διαπρίω) signifies to saw asunder (dia, asunder, priō, to saw), to divide by a saw (as in 1 Chron. 20 : 3, Sept.), hence, metaphorically, to be sawn through mentally, to be rent with vexation, to be cut to the heart, is used in Acts 5 : 33 ; 7 : 54.¶

6. DICHOTOMEŌ (διχοτομέω), lit., to cut into two parts (dicha, apart, temnō, to cut, tomē, a cutting), Matt. 24 : 51, to cut asunder, is used in Luke 12 : 46. Some take the reference to be to the mode of punishment by which criminals and captives were cut in two ; others, on account of the fact that in these passages the delinquent is still surviving after the treatment, take the verb to denote to cut up by scourging, to scourge severely, the word being used figuratively.

As to Matt. 24 : 51, it has been remarked that the cutting asunder was an appropriate punishment for one who had lived a double life. In both passages the latter part of the sentence applies to retribution beyond this life.¶ In the Sept. the verb is used in Ex. 29 : 17 of the dividing of the ram as a whole burnt offering at the consecration of the priests.¶ The corresponding noun is found in Gen. 15 : 11, 17 ; Ex. 29 : 17 ; Lev. 1 : 8 ; Ezek. 24 : 4.¶

7. SUNTEMNŌ (συντέμνω), lit., to cut together (sun, with, temnō, to cut ; the simple verb temnō is not found in the N.T.), signifies to contract by cutting, to cut short ; thus, to bring to an end or accomplish speedily ; it is said of a prophecy or decree, Rom. 9 : 28 (twice), from the Sept. of Is. 10 : 23. See SHORT.¶

8. APHAIREŌ (ἀφαιρέω), to take away, remove, is translated " cut off " in Mark 14 : 47, A.V., and Luke 22 : 50, and " smote off " in Matt. 26 : 51 ; R.V., " struck off " in each place. See SMITE, TAKE.

CYMBAL

KUMBALON (κύμβαλον), a cymbal, was so called from its shape (akin to kumbos, a hollow basin, kumbē, a cup), and was made of bronze, two being struck together, 1 Cor. 13 : 1.¶

D

DAILY (Adjective)

1. EPIOUSIOS (ἐπιούσιος) is found in Matt. 6 : 11 and Luke 11 : 3. Some would derive the word from *epi*, upon, and *eimi*, to be, as if to signify " (bread) present," i.e., sufficient bread, but this formation is questionable. The same objection applies to the conjecture, that it is derived from *epi*, and *ousia*, and signifies " (bread) for sustenance." The more probable derivation is from *epi*, and *eimi*, to go, (bread) for going on, i.e., for the morrow and after, or (bread) coming (for us). See the R.V. marg. This suits the added *sēmeron*, " to-day," i.e., the prayer is to be for bread that suffices for this day and next, so that the mind may conform to Christ's warning against anxiety for the morrow. Confirmation of this derivation is also to be found in the word *epiousę̄*, in the phrase " the next day," Acts 7 : 26 ; 16 : 11.¶

2. EPHĒMEROS (ἐφήμερος) signifies "for the day" (*epi*, upon, or for, *hēmera*, a day, Eng., ephemeral), Jas. 2 : 15.¶

3. KATHĒMERINOS (καθημερινός) means, lit., according to (*kata*) the day (*hēmera*), day by day, daily, Acts 6 : 1.¶

Notes : The following phrases contain the word *hēmera*, day, and are translated " daily " or otherwise : (*a*) *kath' hēmeran*, lit., according to, or for, (the) day, or throughout the day, " day by day," e.g., Luke 11 : 3 ; Acts 3 : 2 ; 16 : 5 ; 1 Cor. 15 : 31 ; Heb. 7 : 27 ; (*b*) *hēmera kai hēmera*, lit., day and day, " day by day," 2 Cor. 4 : 16 ; (*c*) *hēmeran ex hēmeras*, lit., day from day, " from day to day," 2 Pet. 2 : 8 ; (*d*) *sēmeron*, " this day," or " to-day," used outside the Synoptists and the Acts, in 2 Cor. 3 : 14, 15, eight times in Hebrews, and in Jas. 4 : 13 ; (*e*) *tēs sēmeron hēmeras*, " (unto) this very day," Rom. 11 : 8 (R.V.) ; (*f*) *tas hēmeras*, Luke 21 : 37, R.V., " every day," for A.V., " in the daytime ; " (*g*) *pasan hēmeran*, Acts 5 : 42, R.V., " every day ; " preceded by *kata* in Acts 17 : 17, R.V., " every day ; " (*h*) *kath' hekastēn hēmeran*, lit., ' according to each day,' Heb. 3 : 13, " day by day," R.V.

DAINTY

LIPAROS (λιπαρός) properly signifies oily, or anointed with oil (from *lipos*, grease, connected with *aleiphō*, to anoint) ; it is said of things which

pertain to delicate and sumptuous living ; hence, " dainty," Rev. 18 : 14.¶
In the Sept., Judg. 3 : 29 ; Neh. 9 : 35 ; Is. 30 : 23.¶

For DAMAGE see LOSS

For DAMNABLE, DAMNATION and DAMNED, see CONDEM-NATION, DESTRUCTION, JUDGE, JUDGMENT

DAMSEL

1. KORASION (κοράσιον), a diminutive of korē, a girl, denotes a little girl (properly a colloquial word, often used disparagingly, but not so in later writers) ; in the N.T. it is used only in familiar conversation, Matt. 9 : 24, 25 (A.V., " maid ") ; 14 : 11 ; Mark 5 : 41, 42 ; 6 : 22, 28.¶

2. PAIDION (παιδιον), a diminutive of pais, denotes a young child (male or female) in the A.V. of Mark 5 : 39, 40, 41 (1st line) ; the R.V. corrects " damsel " to " child," so as to distinguish between the narrative of facts, and the homely address to the little girl herself, in which, and in the following sentence, korasion is used. (See No. 1). See CHILD.

3. PAIDISKĒ (παιδίσκη) denotes a young girl, or a female slave ; " damsel," A.V., in John 18 : 17 ; Acts 12 : 13 ; 16 : 16 ; R.V. " maid " in each case. See BONDMAID, BONDWOMAN, MAID, MAIDEN.

DANCE

ORCHEŌ (ὀρχέω), cp. Eng., orchestra, probably originally signified to lift up, as of the feet ; hence, to leap with regularity of motion. It is always used in the Middle Voice, Matt. 11 : 17 ; 14 : 6 ; Mark 6 : 22 ; Luke 7 : 32. The performance by the daughter of Herodias is the only clear instance of artistic dancing, a form introduced from Greek customs.¶

DANCING

CHOROS (χορός), Eng., chorus, primarily denoted an enclosure for dancing ; hence, a company of dancers and singers. The supposition that the word is connected with orcheō by metathesis (i.e., change of place, of the letters ch and o) seems to be without foundation. The word is used in Luke 15 : 25.¶

DANGER, DANGEROUS
A. Verb.

KINDUNEUŌ (κινδυνεύω) properly signifies to run a risk, face danger, but is used in the N.T. in the sense of being in danger, jeopardy, Acts 19 : 27, 40. It is translated " were in jeopardy " in Luke 8 : 23, and " stand we in jeopardy," 1 Cor. 15 : 30.¶

Note : Kindunos, akin to A, peril, danger, is always rendered " peril," Rom. 8 : 35 and 2 Cor. 11 : 26 (eight times).¶

B. Adjectives.

1. ENOCHOS (ἔνοχος), lit., held in, contained in (*en*, in, *echō*, to have, hold), hence, bound under obligation to, liable to, subject to, is used in the sense of being in danger of the penal effect of a misdeed, i.e., in a forensic sense, signifying the connection of a person with (*a*) his crime, " guilty of an eternal sin," Mark 3 : 29, R.V. ; (*b*) the trial or tribunal, as a result of which sentence is passed, Matt. 5 : 21, 22, " the judgment," " the council ; " *enochos* here has the obsolete sense of control (J. Hastings) ; (*c*) the penalty itself, 5 : 22, " the hell of fire," and, with the translation " worthy " (A.V., " guilty "), of the punishment determined to be inflicted on Christ, Matt. 26 : 66 and Mark 14 : 64, " death ; " (*d*) the person or thing against whom or which the offence is committed, 1 Cor. 11 : 27, " guilty," the crime being against " the body and blood of the Lord ; " Jas. 2 : 10, " guilty " of an offence against all the Law, because of a breach of one commandment.

Apart from the forensic sense, this adjective is used of the thing by which one is bound, " subject to " (bondage), in Heb. 2 : 15. See GUILTY, SUBJECT, WORTHY.¶

2. EPISPHALES (ἐπισφαλής), lit., prone to fall (*epi*, upon, i.e., near upon, *sphallō*, to fall), hence, insecure, dangerous, is used in Acts 27 : 9.¶

DARE, DARING, DURST
A. Verb.

TOLMAŌ (τολμάω) signifies to dare, (*a*) in the sense of not dreading or shunning through fear, Matt. 22 : 46 ; Mark 12 : 34 ; Mark 15 : 43, " boldly," lit., ' having dared, went in ; ' Luke 20 : 40 ; John 21 : 12 ; Acts 5 : 13 ; 7 : 32 ; Rom. 15 : 18 ; 2 Cor. 10 : 2, R.V., " shew courage," (A.V., " be bold ") ; 10 : 12, R.V., " are (not) bold ; " 11 : 21 ; Phil. 1 : 14, " are bold ; " Jude 9 ; (*b*) in the sense of bearing, enduring, bringing oneself to do a thing, Rom. 5 : 7 ; 1 Cor. 6 : 1.¶ Cp. *apotolmaō*, to be very bold, Rom. 10 : 20.¶ See BOLD.

B. Adjective.

TOLMETES (τολμητής), akin to A, daring, is used in 2 Pet. 2 : 10, R.V., " daring " (A.V., " presumptuous "), shameless and irreverent daring.¶

DARK, DARKEN, DARKLY, DARKNESS
A. Adjectives.

1. SKOTEINOS (σκοτεινός), full of darkness, or covered with darkness, is translated " dark " in Luke 11 : 36 ; " full of darkness," in Matt. 6 : 23 and Luke 11 : 34, where the physical condition is figurative of the moral. The group of *skot*-words is derived from a root *ska*—, meaning to cover. The same root is to be found in *skēnē*, a tent.¶

Note : Contrast *phōteinos*, full of light, e.g., Matt. 6 : 22.

2. AUCHMEROS (αὐχμηρός), from *auchmos*, drought produced by

excessive heat, hence signifies dry, murky, dark, 2 Pet. 1 : 19 (R.V. marg., " squalid "). No. 1 signifies darkness produced by covering ; No. 2, darkness produced by being squalid or murky.¶

B. Nouns.

1. SKOTIA (σκοτία) is used (a) of physical darkness, " dark," John 6 : 17, lit., ' darkness had come on,' and 20 : 1, lit., ' darkness still being ; ' (b) of secrecy, in general, whether what is done therein is good or evil, Matt. 10 : 27 ; Luke 12 : 3 ; (c) of spiritual or moral darkness, emblematic of sin, as a condition of moral or spiritual depravity, Matt. 4 : 16 ; John 1 : 5 ; 8 : 12 ; 12 : 35, 46 ; 1 John 1 : 5 ; 2 : 8, 9, 11.¶

2. SKOTOS (σκότος), an older form than No. 1, grammatically masculine, is found in some mss. in Heb. 12 : 18.¶

3. SKOTOS (σκότος), a neuter noun, frequent in the Sept., is used in the N.T. as the equivalent of No. 1 ; (a) of physical darkness, Matt. 27 : 45 ; 2 Cor. 4 : 6 ; (b) of intellectual darkness, Rom. 2 : 19 (cp. C, No. 1) ; (c) of blindness, Acts 13 : 11 ; (d) by metonymy, of the place of punishment, e.g., Matt. 8 : 12 ; 2 Pet. 2 : 17 ; Jude 13 ; (e) metaphorically, of moral and spiritual darkness, e.g., Matt. 6 : 23 ; Luke 1 : 79 ; 11 : 35 ; John 3 : 19 ; Acts 26 : 18 ; 2 Cor. 6 : 14 ; Eph. 6 : 12 ; Col. 1 : 13 ; 1 Thess. 5 : 4, 5 ; 1 Pet. 2 : 9 ; 1 John 1 : 6 ; (f) by metonymy, of those who are in moral or spiritual darkness, Eph. 5 : 8 ; (g) of evil works, Rom. 13 : 12 ; Eph. 5 : 11 ; (h) of the evil powers that dominate the world, Luke 22 : 53 ; (i) of secrecy [as in No. 1, (b)]. While skotos is used more than twice as many times as skotia in the N.T., the Apostle John uses skotos only once, 1 John 1 : 6, but skotia 15 times out of the 18.

" With the exception of the significance of secrecy [No. 1, (b) and No. 3 (i)], darkness is always used in a bad sense. Moreover the different forms of darkness are so closely allied, being either cause and effect, or else con-current effects of the same cause, that they cannot always be distinguished ; 1 John 1 : 5 ; 2 : 8, e.g., are passages in which both spiritual and moral darkness are intended."*

4. ZOPHOS (ζόφος) denotes the gloom of the nether world ; hence, thick darkness, darkness that may be felt ; it is rendered " darkness " in Heb. 12 : 18 ; 2 Pet. 2 : 4 and Jude 6 ; in 2 Pet. 2 : 17, R.V., " black-ness," A.V., " mists ; " in Jude 13, R.V. and A.V., " blackness." See BLACKNESS, B, Nos. 1 and 2, MIST.¶

C. Verbs.

1. SKOTIZŌ (σκοτίζω), to deprive of light, to make dark, is used in the N.T. in the Passive Voice only, (a) of the heavenly bodies, Matt. 24 : 29 ; Mark 13 : 24 ; Rev. 8 : 12 ; (b) metaphorically, of the mind, Rom. 1 : 21 ; 11 : 10 ; (some mss. have it in Luke 23 : 45).¶

2. SKOTOŌ (σκοτόω), to darken, is used (a) of the heavenly bodies, Rev. 9 : 2 ; 16 : 10 ; (b) metaphorically, of the mind, Eph. 4 : 18.¶

---

* From Notes on Thessalonians by Hogg and Vine, pp. 157, 158.

Note : The phrase *en ainigmati*, lit., ' in an enigma,' is rendered " darkly " in 1 Cor. 13 : 12. *Ainigma* is akin to the verb *ainissomai*, to hint obscurely. The allusion is to Numb. 12 : 8 (Sept.), " not in (*dia*, by means of) dark speeches " (lit., enigmas) ; God's communications to Moses were not such as in the case of dreams, etc. After the same analogy, what we see and know now is seen " darkly " compared with the direct vision in the presence of God hereafter. The riddles of seeming obscurity in life will all be made clear.

DART

BELOS (βέλος), akin to *ballō*, to throw, denotes a missile, an arrow, javelin, dart, etc., Eph. 6 : 16 (see FIERY).¶ Cp. *bolē*, a stone's throw or cast, Luke 22 : 41,¶ ; *bolizō*, to sound (to fathom the depth of water), Acts 27 : 28.¶

Note : The noun *bolis*, a dart, is found in some texts in Heb. 12 : 20 (see A.V.).¶

DASH

1. PROSKOPTŌ (προσκόπτω) denotes to beat upon or against, to strike against, dash against (*pros*, to or against, *koptō*, to strike, beat) ; hence, of the foot, to stumble, " dash " (A.V. and R.V.), Matt. 4 : 6 ; Luke 4 : 11. See BEAT, STUMBLE.

2. RHĒGNUMI (ῥήγνυμι), to tear, rend, break, is used of the action of a demon upon a human victim, Mark 9 : 18, " dasheth . . . down," R.V. ; (A.V., marg. ; A.V., text, " teareth ") ; Luke 9 : 42, R.V., " dashed . . . down " (A.V., " threw . . . down "). See BREAK, No. 6.

3. EDAPHIZŌ (ἐδαφίζω), to beat level with the earth, e.g., as a threshing floor (cp. *edaphos*, the ground), Luke 19 : 44 ; R.V., " shall dash (thee) to the ground ; " (A.V., " shall lay (thee) even with the ground "). See GROUND.¶

DAUGHTER, DAUGHTER-IN-LAW

1. THUGATĒR (θυγάτηρ), a daughter, (etymologically, Eng., daughter is connected), is used of (*a*) the natural relationship (frequent in the Gospels) ; (*b*) spiritual relationship to God, 2 Cor. 6 : 18, in the sense of the practical realization of acceptance with, and the approval of, God (cp. Isa. 43 : 6), the only place in the N.T. where it applies to spiritual relationship ; (*c*) the inhabitants of a city or region, Matt. 21 : 5 ; John 12 : 15 (" of Zion ") ; cp. Is. 37 : 22 ; Zeph. 3 : 14 (Sept.) ; (*d*) the women who followed Christ to Calvary, Luke 23 : 28 ; (*e*) women of Aaron's posterity, Luke 1 : 5 ; (*f*) a female descendant of Abraham, Luke 13 : 16.

2. THUGATRION (θυγάτριον), a diminutive of No. 1, denotes a little daughter, Mark 5 : 23 ; 7 : 25.¶

3. PARTHENOS (παρθένος), a maiden, virgin, e.g., Matt. 1 : 23,

signifies a virgin-daughter in 1 Cor. 7 : 36, 37, 38 (R.V.) ; in Rev. 14 : 4, it is used of chaste persons. See VIRGIN.

4. NUMPHĒ (νύμφη), Eng., nymph, denotes a bride, John 3 : 29 ; also a daughter-in-law, Matt. 10 : 35 ; Luke 12 : 53. See BRIDE.

Note : In 1 Pet. 3 : 6, *teknon*, a child, is translated " daughters " (A.V.), " children " (R.V.).

DAWN
A. Verbs.

1. AUGAZŌ (αὐγάζω), to shine, is used metaphorically of the light of dawn, in 2 Cor. 4 : 4 (some texts have *kataugazō*). Cp. *augē*, brightness or break of day, Acts 20 : 11. The word formerly meant to see clearly, and it is possible that this meaning was continued in general usage.¶

2. DIAUGAZŌ (διαυγάζω) signifies to shine through (*dia*, through, *augē*, brightness) ; it describes the breaking of daylight upon the darkness of night, metaphorically in 2 Pet. 1 : 19, of the shining of spiritual light into the heart. A probable reference is to the Day to be ushered in at the Second Coming of Christ : ' until the Day gleam through the present darkness, and the Light-bringer dawn in your hearts.'¶

Note : Cp. *diaugēs*, translucent, transparent, Rev. 21 : 21 (some texts have *diaphanēs*, " transparent ").¶

3. EPIPHŌSKŌ (ἐπιφώσκω), to grow light (*epi*, upon, *phōs*, light), in the sense of shining upon, is used in Matt. 28 : 1 ; in Luke 23 : 54, " drew on " (of the Sabbath-day) ; R.V., marg., " began to dawn." See DRAW.¶

B. Noun.

ORTHROS (ὄρθρος), daybreak, denotes " at early dawn," Luke 24 : 1 (R.V.), " early in the morning " (A.V.), and John 8 : 2 (A.V. and R.V.) ; in Acts 5 : 21, R.V., " about daybreak," for A.V., " early in the morning."¶

Note : Cp. *orthrios*, " early," in some texts in Luke 24 : 22 ;¶ *orthrinos*, a later form of *orthros*, in some mss. in Rev. 22 : 16 ;¶ *orthrizō*, to do anything early in the morning, in Luke 21 : 38.¶

DAY
A. Nouns.

1. HĒMERA (ἡμέρα), a day, is used of (*a*) the period of natural light, Gen. 1 : 5 ; Prov. 4 : 18 ; Mark 4 : 35 ; (*b*) the same, but figuratively, for a period of opportunity for service, John 9 : 4 ; Rom. 13 : 13 ; (*c*) one period of alternate light and darkness, Gen. 1 : 5 ; Mark 1 : 13 ; (*d*) a period of undefined length marked by certain characteristics, such as " the day of small things," Zech. 4 : 10 ; of perplexity and distress, Isa. 17 : 11 ; Obad. 12–14 ; of prosperity and of adversity, Ecc. 7 : 14 ; of trial or testing, Psa. 95 : 8 ; of salvation, Isa. 49 : 8 ; 2 Cor. 6 : 2 ; cp. Luke 19 : 42 ; of evil, Eph. 6 : 13 ; of wrath and revelation of the judg-

ments of God, Rom. 2 : 5 ; (e) an appointed time, Ecc. 8 : 6 ; Eph. 4 : 30 ;
(f) a notable defeat in battle, etc. Isa. 9 : 4 ; Psa. 137 : 7 ; Ezek. 30 : 9 ;
Hos. 1 : 11 ; (g) by metonymy = 'when,' 'at the time when ;' (1), of
the past, Gen. 2 : 4 ; Numb. 3 : 13 ; Deut. 4 : 10, (2), of the future, Gen.
2 : 17 ; Ruth 4 : 5 ; Matt. 24 : 50 ; Luke 1 : 20 ; (h) a judgment or doom,
Job. 18 : 20.* (i) of a time of life, Luke 1 : 17, 18 (" years ").

As the day throws light upon things that have been in darkness, the
word is often associated with the passing of judgment upon circumstances.
In 1 Cor. 4 : 3, "man's day," A.V., "man's judgement," R.V., denotes
mere human judgment upon matters (" man's " translates the adjective
anthrōpinos, human), a judgment exercised in the present period of
human rebellion against " God ; " probably therefore " the Lord's Day,"
Rev. 1 : 10, or ' the Day of the Lord ' (where an adjective, *kuriakos*, is
similarly used), is the Day of His manifested judgment on the world.

The phrases " the day of Christ, " Phil. 1 : 10 ; 2 : 16 ; " the day of Jesus
Christ," 1 : 6 ; " the day of the Lord Jesus," 1 Cor. 5 : 5 ; 2 Cor. 1 : 14 ;
" the day of our Lord Jesus Christ," 1 Cor. 1 : 8, denote the time of the
Parousia of Christ with His saints, subsequent to the Rapture, 1 Thess. 4 : 16,
17.   In 2 Pet. 1 : 19 this is spoken of simply as " the day," (see DAY-STAR).

From these the phrase " the day of the Lord " is to be distinguished ;
in the O.T. it had reference to a time of the victorious interposition by
God for the overthrow of the foes of Israel, e.g., Is. 2 : 12 ; Amos 5 : 18 ;
if Israel transgressed in the pride of their hearts, the Day of the Lord would
be a time of darkness and judgment.   For their foes, however, there
would come ' a great and terrible day of the Lord,' Joel 2 : 31 ; Mal. 4 : 5.
That period, still future, will see the complete overthrow of Gentile
power and the establishment of Messiah's Kingdom, Isa. 13 : 9–11 ;
34 : 8 ; Dan. 2 : 34, 44 ; Obad. 15 ; cp. Isa. 61 : 2 ; John 8 : 56.

In the N.T. " the day of the Lord " is mentioned in 1 Thess. 5 : 2 and
2 Thess. 2 : 2, R.V., where the Apostle's warning is that the church at
Thessalonica should not be deceived by thinking that " the Day of the
Lord is now present."   This period will not begin till the circumstances
mentioned in verses 3 and 4 take place.

For the eventual development of the Divine purposes in relation to
the human race see 2 Pet. 3 : 12, " the Day of God."

2. AUGĒ (αὐγή), brightness, bright, shining, as of the sun ; hence,
the beginning of daylight, is translated " break of day " in Acts 20 : 11.¶

B. Adverb.

ENNUCHA (ἔννυχα), the neuter plural of *ennuchos*, used adverbially,
lit., in night (*en*, in, *nux*, night, with *lian*, " very "), signifies very early,
yet in the night, " a great while before day," Mark 1 : 35.¶

Notes : (1) For phrases, see DAILY.   (2) In Mark 6 : 35, the clause
" the day was far spent " is, lit., ' a much hour (i.e., a late hour) having

---

* From Notes on Thessalonians by Hogg and Vine. pp. 150, 151.

become,' or, perhaps, ' many an hour having become,' i.e. many hours having passed.   In the end of the ver., R.V., " day," for A.V., " time." (3) In Mark 2 : 26, A.V., " in the days of," there is no word for " days "in the original ; R.V. (from best mss.), " when ; " in Acts 11 : 28, " in the days of ".   (4) In John 21 : 4, the adjective *prōios*, at early morn, is translated " day " (R.V., for A.V., " the morning ") ;   see Matt. 27 : 1.¶   (5) In 2 Thess. 2 : 3, " that day shall not come " (A.V.) translates nothing in the original ; it is inserted to supply the sense (see the R.V.) ; cp. Luke 7 : 11 (R.V., " soon afterwards ") ;   1 Cor. 4 : 13 (R.V., " even until now ").

(6) For " day following " see MORROW.

For DAYBREAK (R.V., in Acts 5 : 21), see DAWN, B

DAYSPRING

ANATOLĒ (ἀνατολή), lit., a rising up (cp. *anatellō*, to cause to rise), is used of the rising of the sun and stars ; it chiefly means the east, as in Matt. 2 : 1, etc. ;   rendered " dayspring " in Luke 1 : 78.   Its other meaning, " a shoot," is found in the Sept. in Jer. 23 : 5 ; Zech. 6 : 12. See also the margin of Luke 1 : 78, " branch." See EAST.

DAY-STAR

PHŌSPHOROS (φωσφόρος), Eng., phosphorus, lit., light-bearing (*phōs*, light, *phērō*, to bear), is used of the morning star, as the light-bringer, 2 Pet. 1 : 19, where it indicates the arising of the light of Christ as the Personal fulfilment, in the hearts of believers, of the prophetic Scriptures concerning His Coming to receive them to Himself.¶

DAZZLING

1. ASTRAPTŌ (ἀστράπτω), to flash forth, lighten, is said of lightning, Luke 17 : 24, and of the apparel of the two men by the Lord's sepulchre, 24 : 4, A.V., " shining." See LIGHTEN, SHINE.¶

2. EXASTRAPTŌ (ἐξαστράπτω), a strengthened form of No. 1 (*ek*, out of), signifies to flash like lightning, gleam, be radiant, in Luke 9 : 29 of the Lord's raiment at His transfiguration, R.V., " dazzling ; " A.V., " glistering."¶   In the Sept., Ezek. 1 : 4, 7 ; Nahum 3 : 3.¶

DEACON

DIAKONOS (διάκονος), whence Eng. deacon, primarily denotes a servant, whether as doing servile work, or as an attendant rendering free service, without particular reference to its character. The word is probably connected with the verb *diōkō*, to hasten after, pursue (perhaps originally said of a runner).   " It occurs in the N.T. of domestic servants, John 2 : 5, 9 ; the civil ruler, Rom. 13 : 4 ; Christ, Rom. 15 : 8 ; Gal. 2 : 17 ; the followers of Christ in relation to their Lord, John 12 : 26 ; Eph. 6 : 21 ; Col. 1 : 7 ; 4 : 7 ; the followers of Christ in relation to one another,

Matt. 20 : 26 ; 23 : 11 ; Mark 9 : 35 ; 10 : 43 ; the servants of Christ in the work of preaching and teaching, 1 Cor. 3 : 5 ; 2 Cor. 3 : 6 ; 6 : 4 ; 11 : 23 ; Eph. 3 : 7 ; Col. 1 : 23, 25 ; 1 Thess. 3 : 2 ; 1 Tim. 4 : 6 ; those who serve in the churches, Rom. 16 : 1 (used of a woman here only in N.T.) ; Phil. 1 : 1 ; 1 Tim. 3 : 8, 12 ; false apostles, servants of Satan, 2 Cor. 11 : 15. Once *diakonos* is used where, apparently, angels are intended, Matt. 22 : 13 ; in ver. 3, where men are intended, *doulos* is used."*

Diakonos is, generally speaking, to be distinguished from *doulos*, a bondservant, slave ; *diakonos* views a servant in relationship to his work ; *doulos* views him in relationship to his master. See, e.g., Matt. 22 : 2–14 ; those who bring in the guests (vv. 3, 4, 6, 8, 10) are *douloi ;* those who carry out the king's sentence (v. 13) are *diakonoi.*¶

Note : As to synonymous terms, *leitourgos* denotes one who performs public duties ; *misthios* and *misthōtos*, a hired servant ; *oiketēs*, a household servant ; *hupēretēs*, a subordinate official waiting on his superior (originally an under-rower in a war-galley) ; *therapōn*, one whose service is that of freedom and dignity. See MINISTER, SERVANT.

The so-called Seven Deacons in Acts 6 are not there mentioned by that name, though the kind of service in which they were engaged was of the character of that committed to such.

DEAD

A. Noun and Adjective.

NEKROS (νεκρός) is used of (a) the death of the body, cp. Jas. 2 : 26, its most frequent sense : (b) the actual spiritual condition of unsaved men, Matt. 8 : 22 ; John 5 : 25 ; Eph. 2 : 1, 5 ; 5 : 14 ; Phil. 3 : 11 ; Col. 2 : 13 ; cp. Luke 15 : 24 : (c) the ideal spiritual condition of believers in regard to sin, Rom. 6 : 11 : (d) a church in declension, inasmuch as in that state it is inactive and barren, Rev. 3 : 1 : (e) sin, which apart from law cannot produce a sense of guilt, Rom. 7 : 8 : (f) the body of the believer in contrast to his spirit, Rom. 8 : 10 : (g) the works of the Law, inasmuch as, however good in themselves, Rom. 7 : 13, they cannot produce life, Heb. 6 : 1 ; 9 : 14 : (h) the faith that does not produce works, Jas. 2 : 17, 26 ; cp. ver. 20.†

B. Verbs.

1. NEKROŌ (νεκρόω), to put to death, is used in the Active Voice in the sense of destroying the strength of, depriving of power, with reference to the evil desires which work in the body, Col. 3 : 5. In the Passive Voice it is used of Abraham's body as being " as good as dead," Rom. 4 : 19 with Heb. 11 : 12.¶

2. THANATOŌ (θανατόω), to put to death : see DEATH, C. No. 1.

---

* From Notes on Thessalonians by Hogg and Vine, p. 91.
† From Notes on Thessalonians by Hogg and Vine, p. 143.

DEADLY

1. THANATĒPHOROS (θανατηφόρος), lit., death-bearing, deadly (*thanatos*, death, *pherō*, to bear), is used in Jas. 3 : 8.¶ In the Sept., Numb. 18 : 22 ; Job 33 : 23.¶

2. THANASIMOS (θανάσιμος), from *thanatos* (see No. 1), belonging to death, or partaking of the nature of death, is used in Mark 16 : 18.¶

HALF DEAD

HĒMITHANĒS (ἡμιθανής), from *hēmi*, half, and *thnēskō*, to die, is used in Luke 10 : 30.¶

DEADNESS

NEKRŌSIS (νέκρωσις), a putting to death (cp. DEAD, A and B), is rendered " dying " in 2 Cor. 4 : 10 ; " deadness " in Rom. 4 : 19, i.e., the state of being virtually dead.¶

DEAF

KŌPHOS (κωφός), akin to *koptō*, to beat, and *kopiaō*, to be tired (from a root *kop*—, to cut), signifies blunted, dull, as of a weapon ; hence, blunted in tongue, dumb, Matt. 9 : 32 etc. ; in hearing, deaf, Matt. 11 : 5 ; Mark 7 : 32, 37 ; 9 : 25 ; Luke 7 : 22. See DUMB.

For a GREAT DEAL see GREAT

DEAL

MERIZŌ (μερίζω) signifies to divide into parts (*meros*, a portion, part) ; hence, to distribute, divide out, deal out to, translated " hath dealt " in Rom. 12 : 3. See DIFFERENCE, DISTRIBUTE, DIVIDE.

DEAL WITH, HAVE DEALINGS WITH

1. POIEŌ (ποιέω), to do, used to describe almost any act, whether complete or repeated, like the Eng. " do," is translated to deal with, in Luke 2 : 48. In Luke 1 : 25, A.V., " hath dealt with (me)," the R.V., adhering to the ordinary meaning, translates by " hath done unto (me) ".

2. PROSPHERŌ (προσφέρω), to bring or bear to (*pros*, to, *pherō*, to bear), signifies, in the Middle Voice, to bear oneself towards any one, to deal with anyone in a certain manner, Heb. 12 : 7, " God dealeth with you." See BRING, OFFER, PRESENT.

3. SUNCHRAOMAI (συγχράομαι), lit., to use with (*sun*, with, *chraomai*, to use), to have in joint use, and hence to have dealings with, is said, in John 4 : 9, of Jews and Samaritans.¶

Notes : (1) In Acts 25 : 24, *entunchanō*, to fall in with, meet and talk with, and hence to make suit to a person by way of pleading with him, is translated " have dealt with " in the A.V. ; correctly in the R.V., " have made suit to," of the Jews in appealing to Festus against Paul.   See INTERCESSION.

(2) *Katasophizomai*, to circumvent by fraud, conquer by subtle devices (*kata*, down, intensive, and *sophizō*, to devise cleverly or cunningly; cp. Eng., sophist, sophistry), is translated " dealt subtilly," in Acts 7 : 19, of Pharaoh's dealings with the Israelites.¶   This is the word in the Sept. of Ex. 1 : 10.   See SUBTILLY.¶

(3) In 1 Thess. 2 : 11 the italicised phrase " we dealt with " (R.V.), has no corresponding word in the original, but is inserted in order to bring out the participial forms of the verbs " exhorting," " encouraging," " testifying," as showing the constant practice of the apostles at Thessalonica.   The incompleteness of the sentence in the original illustrates the informal homeliness of the Epistle.

(4) In 2 Cor. 13 : 10, the verb *chraomai*, to use, is rendered, in the R.V., " deal (sharply)," A.V., " use (sharpness)."

DEAR

1. TIMIOS (τίμιος), from *timē*, honour, price, signifies (*a*), primarily, accounted as of great price, precious, costly, 1 Cor. 3 : 12 ; Rev. 17 : 4 ; 18 : 12, 16 ; 21 : 19, and in the superlative degree, 18 : 12 ; 21 : 11 ; the comparative degree is found in 1 Pet. 1 : 7 (*polutimoteros*, in the most authentic mss., " much more precious ") ; (*b*) in the metaphorical sense, held in honour, esteemed, very dear, Acts 5 : 34, " had in honour," R.V. (A.V., " had in reputation ") ; so in Heb. 13 : 4, R.V., " let marriage be had in honour ; " A.V., " is honourable ; " Acts 20 : 24, " dear," negatively of Paul's estimate of his life ; Jas. 5 : 7, " precious " (of fruit) ; 1 Pet. 1 : 19, " precious " (of the blood of Christ) ; 2 Pet. 1 : 4 (of God's promises).   See COSTLY, HONOURABLE, REPUTATION, PRECIOUS.¶   Cp. *timiōtes*, preciousness, Rev. 18 : 19.¶

2. ENTIMOS (ἔντιμος), held in honour (*timē*, see above), precious, dear, is found in Luke 7 : 2, of the centurion's servant ; 14 : 8, " more honourable ; " Phil. 2 : 29, " honour " (A.V., " reputation "), of devoted servants of Christ ; in 1 Pet. 2 : 4, 6, " precious," of stones, metaphorically. See HONOURABLE, REPUTATION, PRECIOUS.¶

3. AGAPĒTOS (ἀγαπητός), from *agapē*, love, signifies beloved ; it is rendered " very dear " in 1 Thess. 2 : 8 (A.V., " dear "), of the affection of Paul and his fellow-workers for the saints at Thessalonica ; in Eph. 5 : 1 and Col. 1 : 7, A.V., " dear ; " R.V., " beloved."   See BELOVED.

Note :   In Col. 1 : 13, *agapē* is translated " dear " in the A.V. ; the R.V., adhering to the noun, has " the Son of His love."

For DEARLY see BELOVED

For DEARTH see FAMINE

DEATH, DEATH-STROKE
(*See also DIE*)
A. Nouns.

1. THANATOS (θάνατος), death, is used in Scripture of :

(*a*) the separation of the soul (the spiritual part of man) from the body (the material part), the latter ceasing to function and turning to dust, e.g., John 11 : 13 ; Heb. 2 : 15 ; 5 : 7 ; 7 : 23. In Heb. 9 : 15, the A.V., " by means of death " is inadequate ; the R.V., " a death having taken place " is in keeping with the subject. In Rev. 13 : 3, 12, the R.V., " death-stroke " (A.V., " deadly wound ") is, lit., the stroke of death :

(*b*) the separation of man from God ; Adam died on the day he disobeyed God, Gen. 2 : 17, and hence all mankind are born in the same spiritual condition, Rom. 5 : 12, 14, 17, 21, from which, however, those who believe in Christ are delivered, John 5 : 24 ; 1 John 3 : 14. Death is the opposite of life ; it never denotes non-existence. As spiritual life is " conscious existence in communion with God," so spiritual death is " conscious existence in separation from God."

" Death, in whichever of the above-mentioned senses it is used, is always, in Scripture, viewed as the penal consequence of sin, and since sinners alone are subject to death, Rom. 5 : 12, it was as the Bearer of sin that the Lord Jesus submitted thereto on the Cross, 1 Pet. 2 : 24. And while the physical death of the Lord Jesus was of the essence of His sacrifice, it was not the whole. The darkness symbolised, and His cry expressed, the fact that He was left alone in the Universe, He was ' forsaken ; ' cp. Matt. 27 : 45, 46."*

2. ANAIRESIS (ἀναίρεσις), another word for death, lit. signifies a taking up or off (*ana*, up, *airō*, to take), as of the taking of a life, or putting to death ; it is found in Acts 8 : 1, of the murder of Stephen. Some mss. have it in 22 : 20. See *anaireō*, under KILL.¶ In the Sept., Numb. 11 : 15 ; Judg. 15 : 17, " the lifting of the jawbone."¶

3. TELEUTĒ (τελευτή), an end, limit (cp. *telos*, see END), hence, the end of life, death, is used of the death of Herod, Matt. 2 : 15.¶

B. Adjective.

EPITHANATIOS (ἐπιθανάτιος), doomed to death (*epi*, upon, *thanatos*, A, No. 1), is said of the apostles, in 1 Cor. 4 : 9.¶

C. Verbs.

1. THANATOŌ (θανατόω), to put to death (akin to A, No. 1), in Matt. 10 : 21 ; Mark 13 : 12 ; Luke 21 : 16, is translated " shall . . . cause (them) to be put to death," lit., ' shall put (them) to death ' (R.V. marg.). It is used of the Death of Christ in Matt. 26 : 59 ; 27 : 1 ; Mark 14 : 55 and 1 Pet. 3 : 18. In Rom. 7 : 4 (Passive Voice) it is translated " ye . . . were made dead," R.V. (for A.V., " are become "), with reference to the change from bondage to the Law to union with Christ ;

---

* From Notes on Thessalonians by Hogg and Vine, p. 134.

in 8 : 13, " mortify " (marg., " make to die "), of the act of the believer in regard to the deeds of the body ; in 8 : 36, " are killed ; " so in 2 Cor. 6 : 9. See KILL, MORTIFY.¶

2. ANAIREŌ (ἀναιρέω), lit., to take or lift up or away (see A, No. 2), hence, to put to death, is usually translated to kill or slay ; in two places " put to death," Luke 23 : 32 ; Acts 26 : 10. It is used 17 times, with this meaning, in Acts. See KILL, SLAY, TAKE.

3. APAGŌ (ἀπάγω), lit., to lead away (apo, away, agō, to lead), is used especially in a judicial sense, to put to death, e.g., Acts 12 : 19. See BRING, CARRY, LEAD, TAKE.

4. APOKTEINŌ (ἀποκτείνω), to kill, is so translated in the R.V., for the A.V., " put to death," in Mark 14 : 1 ; Luke 18 : 33 ; in John 11 : 53 ; 12 : 10 and 18 : 31, R.V., " put to death." See KILL, SLAY.

Note : The phrase *eschatōs echō*, lit., to have extremely, i.e., to be in extremity, *in extremis*, at the last (gasp), to be at the point of death, is used in Mark 5 : 23.¶

For the A.V., DEBATE (Rom. 1 : 29 and 2 Cor. 12 : 20), see STRIFE.

DEBT

1. OPHEILĒ (ὀφειλή), that which is owed (see Note, below), is translated " debt " in Matt. 18 : 32 ; in the plural, " dues," Rom. 13 : 7 ; " (her) due," 1 Cor. 7 : 3, of conjugal duty : some texts here have *opheilomenēn (eunoian)* " due (benevolence)," A.V. ; the context confirms the R.V. See DUE.¶

2. OPHEILĒMA (ὀφείλημα), a longer form of No. 1, expressing a debt more concretely, is used (a) literally, of that which is legally due, Rom. 4 : 4 ; (b) metaphorically, of sin as a debt, because it demands expiation, and thus payment by way of punishment, Matt. 6 : 12.¶

3. DANEION (δάνειον), a loan (akin to *danos*, a gift), is translated " debt " in Matt. 18 : 27 (R.V., marg., " loan "), of the ten thousand talents debtor.¶ Cp. *daneizō*, to lend, and *daneistēs*, a money-lender, a creditor.

Note : In Matt. 18 : 30, *opheilō*, to owe, is translated " debt " in the A.V. (R.V., " that which was due."). See DUE.

DEBTOR

1. OPHEILETĒS (ὀφειλέτης), one who owes anything to another, primarily in regard to money ; in Matt. 18 : 24, " who owed " (lit., ' one was brought, a debtor to him of ten thousand talents '). The slave could own property, and so become a debtor to his master, who might seize him for payment.

It is used metaphorically,

(a) of a person who is under an obligation, Rom. 1 : 14, of Paul, in the matter of preaching the Gospel ; in Rom. 8 : 12, of believers, to mortify the deeds of the body ; in Rom. 15 : 27, of Gentile believers, to assist afflicted Jewish believers ; in Gal. 5 : 3, of those who would be justified by circumcision, to do the whole Law : (b) of those who have not yet made amends to those whom they have injured, Matt. 6 : 12, " our debtors ; " of some whose disaster was liable to be regarded as a due punishment, Luke 13 : 4 (R.V., " offenders ; " A.V., " sinners ; " marg., " debtors ").¶

2. CHREŌPHEILETĒS (χρεωφειλέτης), lit., a debt-ower (chreōs, a loan, a debt, and No. 1), is found in Luke 7 : 41, of the two debtors mentioned in the Lord's parable addressed to Simon the Pharisee, and in 16 : 5, of the debtors in the parable of the unrighteous steward. This parable indicates a system of credit in the matter of agriculture.¶ In the Sept., Job 31 : 37, " having taken nothing from the debtor ; " Prov. 29 : 13, " when the creditor and the debtor meet together."¶ The word is more expressive than No. 1.

Note : In Matt. 23 : 16 opheilō, to owe (see DEBT), is translated " he is a debtor." The R.V. marg., keeping the verbal form, has " bound by his oath " (A.V., marg., " bound "). In the 18th verse the A.V., " he is guilty," means that he is under obligation to make amends for his misdeeds.

DECAY

1. PALAIOŌ (παλαιόω), to make old (palaios), is translated in Heb. 8 : 13, firstly, " hath made . . . old," secondly (Passive Voice), R.V. " is becoming old " (A.V., " decayeth ") ; " wax old," Luke 12 : 33 and Heb. 1 : 11. See OLD.¶

2. DIAPHTHEIRŌ (διαφθείρω), to destroy utterly, as used in 2 Cor. 4 : 16 (here in the Passive Voice, lit., ' is being destroyed '), is rendered " is decaying " (R.V., for A.V., " perish "). See CORRUPT, DESTROY.

DECEASE
A. Noun.

EXODOS (ἔξοδος), Eng., exodus, lit. signifies a way out (ex, out, hodos, a way) ; hence, a departure, especially from life, a decease ; in Luke 9 : 31, of the Lord's Death, " which He was about to accomplish ; " in 2 Pet. 1 : 15, of Peter's death (marg., " departure " in each case) ; " departure " in Heb. 11 : 22, R.V. See DEPARTURE.¶

B. Verb.

TELEUTAŌ (τελευτάω), lit., to end, is used intransitively and translated " deceased " in Matt. 22 : 25. See DEATH, A, No. 3, DIE.

DECEIT, DECEITFUL, DECEITFULLY, DECEITFULNESS, DECEIVE, DECEIVABLENESS
A. Nouns.

1. APATĒ (ἀπάτη), deceit or deceitfulness (akin to apataō, to cheat,

deceive, beguile), that which gives a false impression, whether by appearance, statement or influence, is said of riches, Matt. 13 : 22 ; Mark 4 : 19 ; of sin, Heb. 3 : 13. The phrase in Eph. 4 : 22, " deceitful lusts," A.V., " lusts of deceit," R.V., signifies lusts excited by deceit, of which deceit is the source of strength, not lusts deceitful in themselves. In 2 Thess. 2 : 10, " all deceit of unrighteousness," R.V., signifies all manner of unscrupulous words and deeds designed to deceive (see Rev. 13 : 13-15). In Col. 2 : 8, " vain deceit " suggests that deceit is void of anything profitable.¶

Note : In 2 Pet. 2 : 13, the most authentic texts have " revelling in their love-feasts," R.V. (*agapais*), for A.V., " deceivings " (*apatais*).

2. DOLOS (δόλος), primarily a bait, snare ; hence, craft, deceit, guile, is translated " deceit " in Mark 7 : 22 ; Rom. 1 : 29. See CRAFT, GUILE, SUBTILTY.

Notes : (1) *Planē*, rendered " deceit " in 1 Thess. 2 : 3, A.V., signifies wandering (cp. Eng., " planet "), hence, " error " (R.V.), i.e., a wandering from the right path ; in Eph. 4 : 14, " wiles of error," A.V., " to deceive." See DELUDE, ERROR.

(2) For *dolioō*, to use deceit, see C, No. 4.

B. Adjective.

DOLIOS (δόλιος), deceitful, is used in 2 Cor. 11 : 13, of false apostles as " deceitful workers ; " cp. A, No. 2 and Note (2).¶

C. Verbs.

1. APATAŌ (ἀπατάω), to beguile, deceive (see A, No. 1), is used (*a*) of those who deceive " with empty words," belittling the true character of the sins mentioned, Eph. 5 : 6 ; (*b*) of the fact that Adam was " not beguiled," 1 Tim. 2 : 14, R.V. (cp. what is said of Eve ; see No. 2 below) ; (*c*) of the self-deceit of him who thinks himself religious, but bridles not his tongue, Jas. 1 : 26.¶

2. EXAPATAŌ (ἐξαπατάω), ek (ex), intensive, and No. 1, signifies to beguile thoroughly, to deceive wholly, 1 Tim. 2 : 14, R.V. See BEGUILE.

3. PHRENAPATAŌ (φρεναπατάω), lit., to deceive in one's mind (*phrēn*, the mind, and No. 1), " to deceive by fancies " (Lightfoot), is used in Gal. 6 : 3, with reference to self-conceit, which is self-deceit, a sin against common sense. Cp. Jas. 1 : 26 (above).¶

Note : Cp. *phrenapatēs*, No. 2, under DECEIVER.

4. DOLIOŌ (δολιόω), to lure, as by a bait (see A, No. 2), is translated " have used deceit " in Rom. 3 : 13.¶

5. DOLOŌ (δολόω), a short form of No. 4, primarily signifies to ensnare ; hence, to corrupt, especially by mingling the truths of the Word of God with false doctrines or notions, and so handling it deceitfully, 2 Cor. 4 : 2.¶ Cp. *kapēleuō*, to corrupt by way of hucksterizing, 2 : 17.¶ For the difference between the words see CORRUPT, A, No. 1.

6. PLANAŌ (πλανάω), akin to *planē*, A, Note (1) (Eng., planet), in the Passive form sometimes means to go astray, wander, Matt. 18 : 12 ;

1 Pet. 2 : 25 ; Heb. 11 : 38 ; frequently Active, to deceive, by leading into error, to seduce, e.g., Matt. 24 : 4, 5, 11, 24 ; John 7 : 12, " leadeth astray," R.V. (cp. 1 John 3 : 7). In Rev. 12 : 9 the present participle is used with the definite article, as a title of the Devil, " the Deceiver," lit., ' the deceiving one.' Often it has the sense of deceiving oneself, e.g., 1 Cor. 6 : 9 ; 15 : 33 ; Gal. 6 : 7 ; Jas. 1 : 16, " be not deceived," R.V., " do not err," A.V. See ERR, LEAD (astray), SEDUCE, WANDER, WAY (be out of the).

7. PARALOGIZOMAI (παραλογίζομαι) ; see BEGUILE, No. 3.

DECEIVER

1. PLANOS (πλάνος) is, properly, an adjective, signifying wandering, or leading astray, seducing, 1 Tim. 4 : 1, " seducing (spirits) ; " used as a noun, it denotes an impostor of the vagabond type, and so any kind of deceiver or corrupter, Matt. 27 : 63 ; 2 Cor. 6 : 8 ; 2 John 7 (twice), in the last of which the accompanying definite article necessitates the translation " the deceiver," R.V. See SEDUCE.¶

2. PHRENAPATĒS (φρεναπάτης), akin to C, No. 3, under DECEIVE, lit., a mind-deceiver, is used in Tit. 1 : 10.¶

Note : For " the deceiver," in Rev. 12 : 9, see DECEIVE, C, No. 6.

DECENTLY

EUSCHĒMONŌS (εὐσχημόνως) denotes gracefully, becomingly, in a seemly manner (*eu*, well, *schēma*, a form, figure) ; " honestly," in Rom. 13 : 13 (marg., " decently "), in contrast to the shamefulness of Gentile social life ; in 1 Thess. 4 : 12, the contrast is to idleness and its concomitant evils and the resulting bad testimony to unbelievers ; in 1 Cor. 14 : 40, " decently," where the contrast is to disorder in oral testimony in the churches. See HONESTLY.¶

Note : Cp. *euschēmosunē*, comeliness, 1 Cor. 12 : 23.¶, and *euschēmōn*, comely, honourable. See COMELY.

DECIDE, DECISION
A. Verb.

DIAKRINŌ (διακρίνω) primarily signifies to make a distinction, hence, to decide, especially judicially, to decide a dispute, to give judgment, 1 Cor. 6 : 5, A.V., " judge ; " R.V., " decide," where church members are warned against procuring decisions by litigation in the world's law courts. See CONTEND.

B. Nouns.

1. DIAGNŌSIS (διάγνωσις), transliterated in English, primarily denotes a discrimination (*dia*, apart, *ginōskō*, to know), hence, a judicial decision, which is its meaning in Acts 25 : 21, R.V., " for the decision of the Emperor " (A.V., " hearing ").¶

Note : Cp. *diaginōskō*, to distinguish, Acts 23 : 15, to judge (A.V.,

" enquire "), or " determine," 24 : 22, R.V. (A.V., " know the uttermost of ").¶

2. DIAKRISIS (διάκρισις), a distinguishing, and so a decision (see A), signifies " discerning " in 1 Cor. 12 : 10 ; Heb. 5 : 14, lit., ' unto a discerning of good and evil ' (translated " to discern ") ; in Rom. 14 : 1, " not to (doubtful) disputations " is more literally rendered in the margin " not for decisions (of doubts)." See DISCERN. Cp. JUDGE.¶ In the Sept., Job. 37 : 16.¶

_____

DECK (Verb)

CHRUSOŌ (χρυσόω), lit., to gild with gold (chrusos, gold), is used in Rev. 17 : 4 ; 18 : 16.¶

_____

DECLARE, DECLARATION
A. Verbs.

1. ANANGELLŌ (ἀναγγέλλω) signifies to announce, report, bring back tidings (ana, back, angellō, to announce). Possibly the ana carries the significance of upward, i.e., heavenly, as characteristic of the nature of the tidings. In the following, either the A.V. or the R.V. translates the word by the verb to declare ; in John 4 : 25, R.V., " declare," A.V., " tell ; " in 16 : 13, 14, 15, R.V., " declare," A.V., " shew ; " in Acts 15 : 4, R.V., " rehearsed," A.V., " declared ; " in 19 : 18, R.V., " declaring," A.V., " shewed " (a reference, perhaps, to the destruction of their idols, in consequence of their new faith) ; in 20 : 20, R.V., " declaring," A.V., " have shewed ; " in 1 John 1 : 5, R.V., " announce," A.V., " declare." See REHEARSE, REPORT, SHEW, SPEAK, TELL.

2. APANGELLŌ (ἀπαγγέλλω) signifies to announce or report from a person or place (apo, from) ; hence, to declare, publish ; it is rendered " declare " in Luke 8 : 47 ; Heb. 2 : 12 ; 1 John 1 : 3. It is very frequent in the Gospels and Acts ; elsewhere, other than the last two places mentioned, only in 1 Thess. 1 : 9 and 1 John 1 : 2. See BRING, A, No. 36.

3. DIANGELLŌ (διαγγέλλω), lit., to announce through, hence, to declare fully, or far and wide (dia, through), is translated " declaring " in Acts 21 : 26, R.V. (A.V., " to signify ") ; in Luke 9 : 60, R.V., " publish abroad " (for A.V. " preach "), giving the verb its fuller significance ; so in Rom. 9 : 17, for A.V., " declared." See PREACH, SIGNIFY.¶

4. KATANGELLŌ (καταγγέλλω), lit., to report down (kata, intensive), is ordinarily translated to preach ; " declare " in Acts 17 : 23, A.V. (R.V., " set forth ") ; in 1 Cor. 2 : 1, R.V., " proclaiming," for A.V., " declaring." It is nowhere translated by " declare " in the R.V. See PREACH, SHEW, SPEAK, TEACH.

5. PARANGELLŌ (παραγγέλλω) : see CHARGE, B, No. 8.

6. DIĒGEOMAI (διηγέομαι), to conduct a narration through to the end (dia, through, intensive, hegēomai, to lead), hence denotes to recount, to relate in full, Mark 5 : 16 ; Luke 8 : 39 ; 9 : 10 ; Acts 8 : 33 ; 9 : 27 ; 12 : 17 ; in Mark 9 : 9 and Heb. 11 : 32, " tell." See SHEW, TELL.¶

7. EKDIĒGEOMAI (ἐκδιηγέομαι), properly, to narrate in full, came to denote, to tell, declare ; it is used in Acts 13 : 41 ; 15 : 3.¶

8. EXĒGEOMAI (ἐξηγέομαι), lit., to lead out, signifies to make known, rehearse, declare, Luke 24 : 35 (A.V., " told ; " R.V., rehearsed "); Acts 10 : 8 ; 15 : 12, 14 ; 21 : 19. In John 1 : 18, in the sentence " He hath declared Him," the other meaning of the verb is in view, to unfold in teaching, to declare by making known. See TELL.¶

9. HORIZŌ (ὁρίζω), to mark off by boundaries, signifies to determine, usually of time ; in Rom. 1 : 4, Christ is said to have been marked out as the Son of God, by the fact of His resurrection ; " declared " (R.V., marg., " determined "). See DEFINE.

10. DĒLOŌ (δηλόω), to make plain, is rendered to declare in 1 Cor. 1 : 11, A.V. ; 3 : 13 ; Col. 1 : 8. See SIGNIFY.

11. PHRAZŌ (φράζω), to declare, occurs in Matt. 15 : 15 and (in some texts) in 13 : 36 (as A.V.).

Note : For *gnōrizō*, to make known, rendered to declare in John 17 : 26 ; 1 Cor. 15 : 1 and Col. 4 : 7, see KNOW, A, No. 8. For *emphanizō*, to declare plainly, Heb. 11 : 14, A.V., see MANIFEST, B, No. 2. For *phaneroō*, see MANIFEST, B, No. 1. For *anatithēmi*, Acts 25 : 14, A.V., see COMMUNICATE. For " declare glad tidings " see TIDINGS.

B. Noun.

ENDEIXIS (ἔνδειξις), a showing, pointing out (*en*, in, *deiknumi*, to show), is said of the showing forth of God's righteousness, in Rom. 3 : 25, 26, A.V., " to declare ; " R.V., " to shew," and " (for) the shewing." In 2 Cor. 8 : 24, " proof ; " Phil. 1 : 28, " an evident token." See SHEW, TOKEN.¶

Notes : (1) In Luke 1 : 1, *diēgēsis* is a " narrative " (R.V.), not a " declaration " (A.V.).

(2) In 2 Cor. 8 : 19, " declaration " does not represent any word in the original.

DECREASE (Verb)

ELATTOŌ (ἐλαττόω) signifies to make less or inferior, in quality, position or dignity ; " madest . . . lower " and " hast made . . . lower," in Heb. 2 : 7, 9. In John 3 : 30, it is used in the Middle Voice, in John the Baptist's " I must decrease," indicating the special interest he had in his own decrease, i.e., in authority and popularity. See LOWER.¶

DECREE (Noun and Verb)

DOGMA (δόγμα), transliterated in English, primarily denoted an opinion or judgment (from *dokeō*, to be of opinion), hence, an opinion expressed with authority, a doctrine, ordinance, decree ; " decree," Luke 2 : 1 ; Acts 16 : 4 ; 17 : 7 ; in the sense of ordinances, Eph. 2 : 15 ; Col. 2 : 14. See ORDINANCE.¶

Note : *Krinō*, to determine, is translated " hath decreed " in 1 Cor. 7 : 37, A.V. ; R.V., " hath determined."

DEDICATE, DEDICATION
A. Verb.

ENKAINIZŌ (ἐγκαινίζω) primarily means to make new, to renew (*en*, in, *kainos*, new), as in the Sept. of 2 Chron. 15 : 8 ; then, to initiate or dedicate, Heb. 9 : 18, with reference to the first Covenant, as not dedicated without blood ; in 10 : 20, of Christ's dedication of the new and living way (A.V., " consecrated ; " R.V., " dedicated "). See CON-SECRATE.¶ In the Sept. it has this meaning in Deut. 20 : 5 ; 2 Chron. 7 : 5 ; Isa. 16 : 11 ; 41 : 1 ; 45 : 16, " keep a feast (to Me)."

B. Noun.

ENKAINIA (ἐγκαίνια), akin to A, frequent in the Sept., in the sense of dedication, became used particularly for the annual eight days' feast beginning on the 25th of Chisleu (mid. of Dec.), instituted by Judas Maccabæus, 164, B.C., to commemorate the cleansing of the Temple from the pollutions of Antiochus Epiphanes ; hence it was called the Feast of the Dedication, John 10 : 22. This Feast could be celebrated anywhere. The lighting of lamps was a prominent feature ; hence the description " Feast of Lights." Westcott suggests that John 9 : 5 refers to this.¶

DEED, DEEDS

1. ERGON (ἔργον) denotes a work (Eng., " work " is etymologically akin), deed, act. When used in the sense of a deed or act, the idea of working is stressed, e.g., Rom. 15 : 18 ; it frequently occurs in an ethical sense of human actions, good or bad, e.g., Matt. 23 : 3 ; 26 : 10 ; John 3 : 20, 21 ; Rom. 2 : 7, 15 ; 1 Thess. 1 : 3 ; 2 Thess. 1 : 11, etc. ; sometimes in a less concrete sense, e.g., Tit. 1 : 16 ; Jas. 1 : 25 (R.V., " that worketh," lit., ' of work '). See LABOUR, WORK.

2. PRAXIS (πρᾶξις) denotes a doing, transaction, a deed the action of which is looked upon as incomplete and in progress (cp. *prassō*, to practise) ; in Matt. 16 : 27, R.V., " deeds," for A.V., " works ; " in Luke 23 : 51, " deed " ; in ver. 41, the verb is used [see Note (2) below] ; Acts 19 : 18 ; Rom. 8 : 13 ; Col. 3 : 9. In Rom. 12 : 4 it denotes an action, business, or function, translated " office." See OFFICE, WORK.¶

Note : Contrast *pragma*, that which has been done, an accomplished act, e.g., Jas. 3 : 16, R.V., " deed," A.V., " work."

3. POIĒSIS (ποίησις), a doing (akin to *poieō*, to do), is translated " deed " in Jas. 1 : 25, A.V. (R.V., " doing ").¶

Note : Cp. *poiēma*, a work done, Rom. 1 : 20 ; Eph. 2 : 10.¶

4. EUERGESIA (εὐεργεσία) : see BENEFIT, No. 1.

Notes : (1) *Katergazomai*, to work out, bring about something, to perpetrate a deed, is used with the neuter demonstrative pronoun *touto*, this, in 1 Cor. 5 : 3, " hath (so) done this deed," A.V. ; R.V., " hath (so) wrought this thing."

(2) *Prassō* (see No. 2), is used in Luke 23 : 41, with the neuter plural

of the relative pronoun, " of our deeds ; " lit., ' (the things) which we practised.'

(3) In 2 Cor. 12 : 12 the phrase " mighty deeds " (R.V., " mighty works ") translates *dunameis*, " powers " (marg.). See WORK.

(4) In Acts 24 : 2, *diorthōma*, a straightening, with *ginomai*, to become, is translated in the A.V., " very worthy deeds are done," R.V., " evils are corrected ; " more lit., ' reforms take place.'¶ For the variant reading *katorthōma* see CORRECTION, No. 1.

DEEM

HUPONOEŌ (ὑπονοέω), to suppose, conjecture, surmise, is translated " deemed " in Acts 27 : 27, A.V. (R.V., " surmised "); in 13 : 25, " think ye " (A.V.) ; R.V., " suppose ye ; " in 25 : 18, " supposed." See SUPPOSE, THINK.¶

DEEP (Noun and Adjective), DEEPNESS, DEEPLY, DEPTH
A. Nouns.

1. BATHOS (βάθος) is used (a) naturally, in Matt. 13 : 5, " deepness ; " Mark 4 : 5, A.V., " depth," R.V., " deepness ; " Luke 5 : 4, of deep water ; Rom. 8 : 39 (contrasted with *hupsōma*, height) ; (b) metaphorically, in Rom. 11 : 33, of God's wisdom and knowledge ; in 1 Cor. 2 : 10, of God's counsels ; in Eph. 3 : 18, of the dimensions of the sphere of the activities of God's counsels, and of the love of Christ which occupies that sphere ; in 2 Cor. 8 : 2, of deep poverty ; some mss. have it in Rev. 2 : 24.¶

2. BUTHOS (βυθός), a depth, is used in the N.T. only in the natural sense, of the sea, 2 Cor. 11 : 25.¶

Notes : (1) Cp. *buthizō*, to sink (intransitive), Middle Voice, Luke 5 : 7 ; (transitive) to drown, 1 Tim. 6 : 9.¶

(2) *Abussos*, Eng., abyss, is translated " the deep " in Luke 8 : 31 and Rom. 10 : 7, A.V. See ABYSS, BOTTOM.

B. Adjective and Adverb.

BATHUS (βαθύς), akin to A, No. 1, deep, is said in John 4 : 11, of a well ; in Acts 20 : 9, of sleep ; in Rev. 2 : 24 the plural is used, of the deep things, the evil designs and workings, of Satan.

Notes : (1) In Luke 24 : 1, some mss. have *batheos*, the genitive case, with *orthros*, dawn ; the most authentic mss. have *batheōs*, deeply, i.e., very early.

(2) In Mark 8 : 12, " He sighed deeply " represents *anastenazō*, to fetch a deep-drawn sigh (*ana*, up, *stenazō*, to sigh or groan). See SIGH.¶

C. Verb.

BATHUNŌ (βαθύνω), to deepen, make deep, is used in Luke 6 : 48 (A.V., " digged deep "). The original has two separate verbs, *skaptō*, to dig, and *bathunō* ; the R.V. therefore has " digged and went deep."¶

DEFAME

DUSPHĒMEŌ (δυσφημέω), lit., to speak injuriously (from *dus*—, an inseparable prefix signifying opposition, injury etc., and *phēmi*, to speak), is translated " defamed," 1 Cor. 4 : 13.   Some mss. have *blasphēmeō*. See BLASPHEME.¶

DEFECT

HĒTTĒMA (ἥττημα), primarily a lessening, a decrease, diminution, denotes a loss.   It is used of the loss sustained by the Jewish nation in that they had rejected God's testimonies and His Son and the Gospel, Rom. 11 : 12, the reference being not only to national diminution but to spiritual loss ;   R.V., " loss," for A.V., " diminishing."   Here the contrasting word is *plērōma*, fulness.   In 1 Cor. 6 : 7 the reference is to the spiritual loss sustained by the church at Corinth because of their discord and their litigious ways in appealing to the world's judges.   Here the R.V. has " defect " (marg. " loss "), for A.V., " fault."   The preceding adverb " altogether " shows the comprehensiveness of the defect ;   the loss affected the whole church, and was " an utter detriment."

In the Sept. of Isa. 31 : 8 the word signifies the loss of a defeat, with reference to the overthrow of the Assyrians ;   lit. ' his young men shall be for loss ' (i.e., " tributary ").   See DIMINISHING, FAULT, LOSS.¶

Note :   Cp. *hēttaō*, to make inferior, used in the Passive Voice, to be overcome (of spiritual defeat, 2 Pet. 2 : 20), and the adjective *hēttōn* or *hēssōn*, less, worse.

DEFENCE
A. Noun.

APOLOGIA (ἀπολογία), a speech made in defence.   See ANSWER.

B. Verb.

APOLOGEOMAI (ἀπολογέομαι) :   see ANSWER, B, No. 4.

DEFEND

AMUNŌ (ἀμύνω), to ward off, is used in the Middle Voice in Acts 7 : 24, of the assistance given by Moses to his fellow-Israelite against an Egyptian (translated " defended ").   The Middle Voice indicates the special personal interest Moses had in the act.¶

DEFER

ANABALLŌ (ἀναβάλλω), lit., to throw up (*ana*, up, *ballō*, to throw), hence to postpone, is used in the Middle Voice in Acts 24 : 22, in the forensic sense of deferring the hearing of a case.¶

Note :   Cp. *anabolē*, a putting off, delay, Acts 25 : 17.¶

DEFILE, DEFILEMENT
A. Verbs.

1. KOINOŌ (κοινόω) denotes (*a*) to make common ;   hence, in a

ceremonial sense, to render unholy, unclean, to defile, Matt. 15 : 11, 18, 20 ;
Mark 7 : 15, 18, 20, 23 ; Acts 21 : 28 (R.V., " defiled ; " A.V., " polluted ") ;
Heb. 9 : 13 (R.V., " them that have been defiled," A.V., " the unclean ") ;
(b) to count unclean, Acts 10 : 15 ; 11 : 9. In Rev. 21 : 27, some mss.
have this verb, " defileth ; " the most authentic have the adjective,
koinos, " unclean." See CALL, COMMON.¶

2. MIAINŌ (μιαίνω), primarily, to stain, to tinge or dye with another
colour, as in the staining of a glass, hence, to pollute, contaminate, soil,
defile, is used (a) of ceremonial defilement, John 18 : 28 ; so in the Sept.,
in Lev. 22 : 5, 8 ; Num. 19 : 13, 20 etc. ; (b) of moral defilement, Tit.
1 : 15 (twice) ; Heb. 12 : 15 ; of moral and physical defilement, Jude 8.
See B, Nos. 1 and 2.¶

3. MOLUNŌ (μολύνω) properly denotes to besmear, as with mud or
filth, to befoul. It is used in the figurative sense, of a conscience defiled
by sin, 1 Cor. 8 : 7 ; of believers who have kept themselves (their
" garments ") from defilement, Rev. 3 : 4, and of those who have not
soiled themselves by adultery or fornication, Rev. 14 : 4.¶

Note : The difference between *miainō* and *molunō* is that the latter is
not used in a ritual or ceremonial sense, as *miainō* is (Trench, Syn. xxxi).

4. SPILOŌ (σπιλόω), to make a stain or spot, and so to defile, is used
in Jas. 3 : 6 of the defiling effects of an evil use of the tongue ; in Jude 23,
" spotted," with reference to moral defilement. See SPOT.¶

Note : (1) Cp. *spilos*, a spot, a moral blemish, Eph. 5 : 27 ; 2 Pet.
2 : 13 ;¶ *aspilos*, without spot, spotless, 1 Tim. 6 : 14 ; Jas. 1 : 27 ; 1 Pet.
1 : 19 ; 2 Pet. 3 : 14 ; ¶ *spilas*, Jude 12, " hidden rocks," R.V. (A.V.
" spots," a late meaning, equivalent to *spilos*).¶

5. PHTHEIRŌ (φθείρω) : see CORRUPT, A, No. 2.

B. Nouns.

1. MIASMA (μίασμα), whence the Eng. word, denotes defilement
(akin to A, No. 2), and is found in 2 Pet. 2 : 20, A.V., " pollutions," R.V.,
" defilements," the vices of the ungodly which contaminate a person in
his intercourse with the world.¶

2. MIASMOS (μιασμός), also akin to A, No. 2, primarily denotes the
act of defiling, the process, in contrast to the defiling thing (No. 1). It
is found in 2 Pet. 2 : 10 (A.V., " uncleanness," R.V., " defilement.")¶

3. MOLUSMOS (μολυσμός), akin to A, No. 3, denotes defilement, in
the sense of an action by which anything is defiled, 2 Cor. 7 : 1.¶ Cp. the
synonymous word *spilos*, A, No. 4, Note.

C. Adjective.

KOINOS (κοινός), akin to A, No. 1, common, and, from the idea of
coming into contact with everything, " defiled," is used in the ceremonial
sense in Mark 7 : 2 ; in ver. 5, R.V., " defiled," for A.V., " unwashen "
(the verb is used in 7 : 15). See COMMON, UNCLEAN.

DEFINE

HORIZŌ (ὁρίζω), Eng., horizon, primarily means to mark out the boundaries of a place (as in the Sept. of Numb. 34 : 6 ; Josh. 13 : 27) ; hence to determine, appoint. In Heb. 4 : 7, where the reference is to the time of God's invitation to enter into His rest, in contrast to Israel's failure to do so, the word may mean either the appointing of the day (i.e., the period), or the defining of the day, i.e., marking its limits. So the R.V. (A.V., " limiteth "). See DECLARE, DETERMINE, LIMIT, ORDAIN.

DEFRAUD

1. APOSTEREŌ (ἀποστερέω) signifies to rob, despoil, defraud, Mark 10 : 19 ; 1 Cor. 6 : 8 ; 7 : 5 (of that which is due to the condition of natural relationship of husband and wife) ; in the Middle Voice, to allow one-self to be defrauded, 1 Cor. 6 : 7 ; in the Passive Voice, " bereft," 1 Tim. 6 : 5, R.V., with reference to the truth, with the suggestion of being retributively robbed of the truth, through the corrupt condition of the mind. Some mss. have this verb in Jas. 5 : 4 for aphustereō, to keep back by fraud. See BEREFT, DESTITUTE, FRAUD.¶ In the Sept., Ex. 21 : 10 ; in some mss., Deut. 24 : 14.¶

2. PLEONEKTEŌ (πλεονεκτέω), translated " defraud " in 1 Thess. 4 : 6, A.V. (R.V. " wrong "), the reference being to the latter part of the Tenth Commandment. See ADVANTAGE, C, No. 2.

DEGREE

BATHMOS (βαθμός) denotes a step, primarily of a threshold or stair, and is akin to bainō, to go ; figuratively, a standing, a stage in a career, position, degree, 1 Tim. 3 : 13, of faithful deacons.¶

Note : Tapeinos, low, humble, whether in condition or mind, is translated " of low degree " in Luke 1 : 52 and Jas. 1 : 9.¶

DELAY
A. Verbs.

1. OKNEŌ (ὀκνέω), akin to oknos, a shrinking, to be loath or slow to do a thing, to hesitate, delay, is used in Acts 9 : 38.¶ In the Sept. in Numb. 22 : 16, " do not delay " ; Judg. 18 : 9.¶

2. CHRONIZŌ (χρονίζω), from chronos, time, lit. means to while away time, i.e., by way of lingering, tarrying, delaying ; " delayeth," Matt. 24 : 48 ; Luke 12 : 45 ; " tarried," Matt. 25 : 5 ; " tarried so long," Luke 1 : 21 ; " will (not) tarry," Heb. 10 : 37. See TARRY.¶

B. Noun.

ANABOLĒ (ἀναβολή) lit. signifies that which is thrown up (ana, up, ballō, to throw) ; hence a delay, Acts 25 : 17. See DEFER.¶

Note : In Rev. 10 : 6, chronos is translated " delay " in R.V. marg., and is to be taken as the true meaning.

DELICACIES

Note : For *strēnos*, rendered "delicacies" in Rev. 18 : 3, A.V., denoting "wantonness" (R.V.), i.e., arrogant luxury, see WANTON.¶ Cp. the verb *strēniaō*, below, under DELICATELY.

DELICATELY (live)
A. Verbs.

TRUPHAŌ (τρυφάω), from *thruptō*, to enervate, signifies to lead a voluptuous life, to give oneself up to pleasure, Jas. 5 : 5, R.V., " ye have lived delicately ; " A.V., " ye have lived in pleasure."¶

Notes : (1) Cp. *spatalaō*, from *spatalē*, wantonness, to live riotously, used with A in Jas. 5 : 5, " ye have lived in pleasure " (R.V., " have taken your . . . ") ; cp. 1 Tim. 5 : 6, of carnal women in the church, A.V., " liveth in pleasure," R.V., "giveth herself to pleasure." See PLEASURE.¶

(2) Cp. also *strēniaō*, to run riot, translated " lived deliciously," in Rev. 18 : 7, 9, A.V. (R.V., " waxed wanton " and " lived wantonly "). Cp. DELICACIES (above). See WANTON.¶ Cp. the intensive form *kata-strēniaō*, to wax utterly wanton, 1 Tim. 5 : 11.¶

(3) *Spatalaō* " might properly be laid to the charge of the prodigal, scattering his substance in riotous living, Luke 15 : 13 ; . . . *truphaō* to the charge of the rich man, faring sumptuously every day, Luke 16 : 19 ; *strēniaō* to Jeshurun, when, waxing fat, he kicked, Deut. 32 : 15 " (Trench, Syn. § liv).

B. Noun.

TRUPHĒ (τρυφή), akin to A, is used with *en*, in the phrase *en truphē*, luxuriously, " delicately," Luke 7 : 25, and denotes effeminacy, softness ; " to revel " in 2 Pet. 2 : 13 (A.V., " riot "), lit., 'counting revelling in the day time a pleasure.' See REVEL, RIOT.¶

Note : *Entruphaō*, to revel luxuriously, is used in 2 Pet. 2 : 13, R.V., " revelling " (A.V., " sporting themselves ").¶

For DELICIOUSLY, Rev. 18 : 7, 9, A.V., see Note (1) above.

DELIGHT IN

SUNĒDOMAI (συνήδομαι), lit., to rejoice with (anyone), to delight in (a thing) with (others), signifies to delight with oneself inwardly in a thing, in Rom. 7 : 22.¶

Note : Cp. *hēdonē*, desire, pleasure.

DELIVER, DELIVERANCE, DELIVERER
A. Verbs.

1. DIDŌMI (δίδωμι), to give, is translated " delivered " in Luke 7 : 15 ; R.V., " gave ; " so 19 : 13. See GIVE.

2. ANADIDŌMI (ἀναδίδωμι), *ana*, up, and No. 1, to deliver over, give up, is used of delivering the letter mentioned in Acts 23 : 33.¶

Note : For the different verb in Acts 15 : 30, see No. 4.

3. APODIDŌMI (ἀποδίδωμι), *apo*, from, and No. 1, lit., to give away, hence, to give back or up, is used in Pilate's command for the Lord's body to be given up, Matt. 27 : 58 ; in the sense of giving back, of the Lord's act in giving a healed boy back to his father, Luke 9 : 42. See GIVE, PAY, PAYMENT, PERFORM, RECOMPENSE, RENDER, REPAY, REQUITE, RESTORE, REWARD, SELL, YIELD.

4. EPIDIDŌMI (ἐπιδίδωμι), lit., to give upon or in addition, as from oneself to another, hence, to deliver over, is used of the delivering of the roll of Isaiah to Christ in the synagogue, Luke 4 : 17 ; of the delivering of the epistle from the elders at Jerusalem to the church at Antioch, Acts 15 : 30. See DRIVE (let), GIVE, OFFER.

5. PARADIDŌMI (παραδίδωμι), to deliver over, in Rom. 6 : 17, R.V. " that form of teaching whereunto ye were delivered," the figure being that of a mould which gives its shape to what is cast in it (not as the A.V.). In Rom. 8 : 32 it is used of God in delivering His Son to expiatory Death ; so 4 : 25 ; see Mark 9 : 31 ; of Christ in delivering Himself up, Gal. 2 : 20 ; Eph. 5 : 2, 25. See BETRAY, A. In Mark 1 : 14, R.V., it is used of delivering John the Baptist to prison. See PUT, No. 12.

6. APALLASSŌ (ἀπαλλάσσω), lit., to change from (*apo*, from, *allassō*, to change), to free from, release, is translated " might deliver " in Heb. 2 : 15 ; in Luke 12 : 58, it is used in a legal sense of being quit of a person, i.e., the opponent being appeased and withdrawing his suit. For its other meaning, to depart, in Acts 19 : 12, see DEPART.¶

7. ELEUTHEROŌ (ἐλευθερόω), to set free, is translated " deliver " in Rom. 8 : 21. In six other places it is translated " make free," John 8 : 32, 36 ; Rom. 6 : 18, 22 ; 8 : 2 ; Gal. 5 : 1, R.V., " set free." See FREE.¶

8. EXAIREŌ (ἐξαιρέω), lit., to take out, denotes, in the Middle Voice, to take out for oneself, hence, to deliver, to rescue, the person who does so having a special interest in the result of his act. Thus it is used, in Gal. 1 : 4, of the act of God in delivering believers " out of this present evil world," the Middle Voice indicating His pleasure in the issue of their deliverance. It signifies to deliver by rescuing from danger, in Acts 12 : 11 ; 23 : 27 ; 26 : 17 ; from bondage, Acts 7 : 10, 34. For its other meaning, to pluck out of, Matt. 5 : 29 ; 18 : 9, see PLUCK.¶

9. KATARGEŌ (καταργέω) : see ABOLISH.

10. RHUOMAI (ῥύομαι), to rescue from, to preserve from, and so, to deliver, the word by which it is regularly translated, is largely synonymous with *sōzō*, to save, though the idea of rescue from is predominant in *rhuomai* (see Matt. 27 : 43), that of preservation from, in *sōzō*. In Rom. 11 : 26 the present participle is used with the article, as a noun, " the Deliverer." This is the construction in 1 Thess. 1 : 10, where Christ is similarly spoken of. Here the A.V. wrongly has " which delivered " (the tense is not past) ; R.V., " which delivereth ; " the translation might well be (as in Rom. 11 : 26), ' our Deliverer,' that is, from the retributive

calamities with which God will visit men at the end of the present age. From that wrath believers are to be delivered. The verb is used with *apo*, away from, in Matt. 6 : 13 ; Luke 11 : 4 (in some mss.) ; so also in 11 : 4 ; Rom. 15 : 31 ; 2 Thess. 3 : 2 ; 2 Tim. 4 : 18 ; and with *ek*, from, out of, in Luke 1 : 74 ; Rom. 7 : 24 ; 2 Cor. 1 : 10 ; Col. 1 : 13, from bondage ; in 2 Pet. 2 : 9, from temptation ; in 2 Tim. 3 : 11, from persecution ; but *ek* is used of ills impending, in 2 Cor. 1 : 10 ; in 2 Tim. 4 : 17, *ek* indicates that the danger was more imminent than in ver. 18, where *apo* is used. Accordingly the meaning ' out of the midst of ' cannot be pressed in 1 Thess. 1 : 10.¶

11. CHARIZOMAI (χαρίζομαι), to gratify, to do what is pleasing to anyone, is translated " deliver " in the A.V. of Acts 25 : 11, 16 ; R.V., " give up " (marg., " grant by favour," i.e., to give over to the Jews so as to gratify their wishes). See FORGIVE, GIVE, GRANT.

Note : For *gennaō* and *tiktō*, to bear, to be delivered (said of women at childbirth), see BEGET.

B. Nouns.

1. APOLUTRŌSIS (ἀπολύτρωσις) denotes redemption (*apo*, from, *lutron*, a price of release). In Heb. 11 : 35 it is translated " deliverance ; " usually the release is effected by the payment of a ransom, or the required price, the *lutron* (ransom). See REDEMPTION.

2. APHESIS (ἄφεσις) denotes a release, from bondage, imprisonment etc. (the corresponding verb is *aphiēmi*, to send away, let go) ; in Luke 4 : 18 it is used of liberation from captivity (A.V., " deliverance," R.V., " release "). See FORGIVENESS, REMISSION.

3. LUTRŌTĒS (λυτρωτής), a redeemer, one who releases (see No. 1), is translated " deliverer " in Acts 7 : 35 (R.V. marg., " redeemer ").¶

Note : See also DELIVER, A, No. 10.

C. Verbal Adjective.

EKDOTOS (ἔκδοτος), lit., given up (*ek*, out of, *didōmi*, to give), delivered up (to enemies, or to the power or will of someone), is used of Christ in Acts 2 : 23.¶

DELUDE, DELUSION
A. Verb.
PARALOGIZOMAI (παραλογίζομαι) : see BEGUILE.
B. Noun.
PLANĒ (πλάνη), lit., a wandering, whereby those who are led astray roam hither and thither, is always used in the N.T., of mental straying, wrong opinion, error in morals or religion. In 2 Thess. 2 : 11, A.V., it is translated " delusion," R.V., " error." See DECEIT, ERROR.

DEMAND
Note : For DEMAND (Matt. 2 : 4 and Acts 21 : 33), see INQUIRE ; for its use in Luke 3 : 14 and 17 : 20, see under ASK.

DEMEANOUR

KATASTĒMA (κατάστημα) : see BEHAVIOUR, B, No. 2.

DEMON, DEMONIAC
A. Nouns.

1. DAIMŌN (δαίμων), a demon, signified, among pagan Greeks, an inferior deity, whether good or bad. In the N.T. it denotes an evil spirit. It is used in Matt. 8 : 31, mistranslated " devils."

Some would derive the word from a root *da*—, meaning to distribute. More probably it is from a similar root *da*—, meaning to know, and hence means a knowing one.¶

2. DAIMONION (δαιμόνιον), not a diminutive of *daimōn*, No. 1, but the neuter of the adjective *daimonios*, pertaining to a demon, is also mistranslated " devil," " devils." In Acts 17 : 18, it denotes an inferior pagan deity. Demons are the spiritual agents acting in all idolatry. The idol itself is nothing, but every idol has a demon associated with it who induces idolatry, with its worship and sacrifices, 1 Cor. 10 : 20, 21 ; Rev. 9 : 20 ; cp. Deut. 32 : 17 ; Isa. 13 : 21 ; 34 : 14 ; 65 : 3, 11. They disseminate errors among men, and seek to seduce believers, 1 Tim. 4 : 1. As seducing spirits they deceive men into the supposition that through mediums (those who have " familiar spirits," Lev. 20 : 6, 27, e.g.) they can converse with deceased human beings. Hence the destructive deception of Spiritism, forbidden in Scripture, Lev. 19 : 31 ; Deut. 18 : 11 ; Isa. 8 : 19. Demons tremble before God, Jas. 2 : 19 ; they recognized Christ as Lord and as their future Judge, Matt. 8 : 29 ; Luke 4 : 41. Christ cast them out of human beings by His own power. His disciples did so in His Name, and by exercising faith, e.g., Matt. 17 : 20.

Acting under Satan (cp. Rev. 16 : 13, 14), demons are permitted to afflict with bodily disease, Luke 13 : 16. Being unclean they tempt human beings with unclean thoughts, Matt. 10 : 1 ; Mark 5 : 2 ; 7 : 25 ; Luke 8 : 27–29 ; Rev. 16 : 13 ; 18 : 2, e.g. They differ in degrees of wickedness, Matt. 12 : 45. They will instigate the rulers of the nations at the end of this age to make war against God and His Christ, Rev. 16 : 14. See DEVIL.

B. Verb.

DAIMONIZOMAI (δαιμονίζομαι) signifies to be possessed of a demon, to act under the control of a demon. Those who were thus afflicted expressed the mind and consciousness of the demon or demons indwelling them, e.g., Luke 8 : 28. The verb is found chiefly in Matt. and Mark ; Matt. 4 : 24 ; 8 : 16, 28, 33 ; 9 : 32 ; 12 : 22 ; 15 : 22 ; Mark 1 : 32 ; 5 : 15, 16, 18 ; elsewhere in Luke 8 : 36 and John 10 : 21, " him that hath a devil (demon)."¶

C. Adjective.

DAIMONIŌDĒS (δαιμονιώδης) signifies proceeding from, or resembling, a demon, " demoniacal ; " see marg. of Jas. 3 : 15, R.V. (text, " devilish ").¶

DEMONSTRATION

APODEIXIS (ἀπόδειξις), lit., a pointing out (apo, forth, deiknumi, to show), a showing or demonstrating by argument, is found in 1 Cor. 2 : 4, where the Apostle speaks of a proof, a showing forth or display, by the operation of the Spirit of God in him, as affecting the hearts and lives of his hearers, in contrast to the attempted methods of proof by rhetorical arts and philosophic arguments.¶

DEN

SPĒLAION (σπήλαιον) : see CAVE.

DENY

1. ARNEOMAI (ἀρνέομαι) signifies (a) to say . . . not, to contradict, e.g., Mark 14 : 70 ; John 1 : 20 ; 18 : 25, 27 ; 1 John 2 : 22 ; (b) to deny by way of disowning a person, as, e.g., the Lord Jesus as Master, e.g., Matt. 10 : 33 ; Luke 12 : 9 ; John 13 : 38 (in the best mss.) ; 2 Tim. 2 : 12 ; or, on the other hand, of Christ Himself, denying that a person is His follower, Matt. 10 : 33 ; 2 Tim. 2 : 12 ; or to deny the Father and the Son, by apostatizing and by disseminating pernicious teachings, to deny Jesus Christ as Master and Lord by immorality under a cloak of religion, 2 Pet. 2 : 1 ; Jude 4 ; (c) to deny oneself, either in a good sense, by disregarding one's own interests, Luke 9 : 23, or in a bad sense, to prove false to oneself, to act quite unlike oneself, 2 Tim. 2 : 13 ; (d) to abrogate, forsake, or renounce a thing, whether evil, Tit. 2 : 12, or good, 1 Tim. 5 : 8 ; 2 Tim. 3 : 5 ; Rev. 2 : 13 ; 3 : 8 ; (e) not to accept, to reject something offered, Acts 3 : 14 ; 7 : 35, " refused ; " Heb. 11 : 24, " refused." See REFUSE.

2. APARNEOMAI (ἀπαρνέομαι), a strengthened form of No. 1, with apo, from, prefixed (Lat., abnego), means (a) to deny utterly, to abjure, to affirm that one has no connection with a person, as in Peter's denial of Christ, Matt. 26 : 34, 35, 75 ; Mark 14 : 30, 31, 72 ; Luke 22 : 34, 61 (some mss. have it in John 13 : 38). This stronger form is used in the Lord's statements foretelling Peter's denial, and in Peter's assurance of fidelity ; the simple verb (No. 1) is used in all the records of his actual denial. The strengthened form is the verb used in the Lord's warning as to being " denied " in the presence of the angels, Luke 12 : 9 ; in the preceding clause, " he that denieth Me," the simple verb arneomai is used ; the rendering therefore should be ' he that denieth Me in the presence of men, shall be utterly denied in the presence of the angels of God ; ' (b) to deny oneself as a follower of Christ, Matt. 16 : 24 ; Mark 8 : 34 ; Luke 9 : 23.¶

3. ANTILEGŌ (ἀντιλέγω) means to speak against, contradict.

In Luke 20 : 27, the R.V., " they which say that there is no resurrection," follows the texts which have the simple verb *lego ;* for the A.V., which translates the verb *antilego*, " which deny that there is any resurrection." See ANSWER, CONTRADICT, GAINSAY, SPEAK, No. 6.

DEPART

(a) Compounds of agō.

1. ANAGŌ (ἀνάγω), lit., to lead up (*ana*, up, *agō*, to lead), is used, in the Middle Voice, as a nautical term, signifying to set sail, put to sea ; " to depart," Acts 27 : 12, A.V. (R.V., " put to sea ") ; 28 : 10 (R.V., " sailed ") ; ver. 11 (R.V., " set sail "). Cp. *epanagō*, in Luke 5 : 3, to put out. See BRING, No. 11.

2. PARAGŌ (παράγω), used intransitively, means to pass by (*para*, by, beside), and is so translated everywhere in the Gospels, except in the A.V. of Matt. 9 : 27, " departed ; " R.V., " passed by." Outside the Gospels it is used in its other meaning, to pass away, 1 Cor. 7 : 31 ; 1 John 2 : 8 (R.V.), 17. See PASS.

3. HUPAGŌ (ὑπάγω), to go, translated " depart " in Jas. 2 : 16, A.V., primarily and lit. meant to lead under (*hupo*, under) ; in its later use, it implied a going, without noise or notice, or by stealth. In this passage the idea is perhaps that of a polite dismissal, ' Go your ways.' See GET, GO.

(b) Compounds of erchomai.

4. APERCHOMAI (ἀπέρχομαι), lit., to come or go away (*apo*), hence, to set off, depart, e.g., Matt. 8 : 18, is frequent in the Gospels and Acts ; Rev. 18 : 14, R.V., " are gone." See COME, No. 11 (Note), GO, PASS.

5. DIERCHOMAI (διέρχομαι), to come or go through, to pass through to a place, is translated " departed " in Acts 13 : 14, A.V. ; R.V., " passing through ; " elsewhere it is usually translated " pass through " or " go through." See COME, No. 5.

6. EXERCHOMAI (ἐξέρχομαι) denotes to come out, or go out of, to go forth. It is frequently translated by the verb to depart, e.g., Matt. 9 : 31 ; in Luke 4 : 42, for the A.V., " He departed and went (No. 8)," the R.V. has " He came out and went ; " in 9 : 6 the A.V. and R.V. agree. See COME, No. 3.

7. KATERCHOMAI (κατέρχομαι), to come down (its usual meaning), is translated " departed " in Acts 13 : 4, A.V. (R.V., " went down "). See COME, No. 7.

(c) Poreuō and a compound.

8. POREUŌ (πορεύω), akin to *poros*, a passage, in the Middle Voice signifies to go on one's way, to depart from one place to another. In some places, where the A.V. has the verb to depart, the R.V. translates by to go one's way, e.g., Matt. 2 : 9, " went their way ; " 11 : 7 ; 24 : 1, " was going on His way." In the following the R.V. has the verb to go, for the A.V. depart, Luke 4 : 42 (latter part of verse) ; 13 : 31 ; John 16 : 7 ;

2 Tim. 4 : 10.   In Luke 21 : 8, " go (after)," is said of disciples or partisans.
In some places both A.V. and R.V. translate by the verb to depart, e.g.,
Matt. 19 : 15 ;   25 : 41 ;   Acts 5 : 41 ;   Acts 22 : 21.   This verb is to be
distinguished from others signifying to go.   It is best rendered, as often
as possible, to go on one's way.   See Go, Journey, Walk.

9.   EKPOREUŌ (ἐκπορεύω), ek, from, in the Middle and Passive, to
proceed from or forth, more expressive of a definite course than simply
to go forth, is translated " go forth," in Mark 6 : 11 ;   "'went out " in
Matt. 20 : 29, R.V. (A.V., " departed ") ;   both have " depart " in Acts
25 : 4.   It is frequently translated by the verb to proceed, and is often
best so rendered, e.g., in Rev. 9 : 17, 18, R.V., for A.V., " issued."   See
Come, No. 33.

(d) Compounds of chōreō.

10.   ANACHŌREŌ (ἀναχωρέω), to go back, recede, retire (ana, back
or up, chōreō, to make room for, betake oneself, chōros, a place), is
translated " departed " in Matt. 2 : 12, 13, 14 ;   4 : 12 (R.V., " withdrew ") ;   so in 14 : 13 and 15 : 21, but " departed " in 27 : 5 ;   " withdrew"
in John 6 : 15.   In Matt. 2 : 22 the R.V. has " withdrew," which is
preferable to the A.V., " turned aside."   The most suitable translation
wherever possible, is by the verb to withdraw.   See Place, B, No. 1, Go,
No. 15, Turn, *Note* (1), Withdraw.

11.   APOCHŌREŌ (ἀποχωρέω), to depart from (apo), is so translated
in Matt. 7 : 23 ;   Luke 9 : 39 ;   Acts 13 : 13 (both A.V. and R.V.).   Some
mss. have it in Luke 20 : 20.¶

12.   EKCHŌREŌ (ἐκχωρέω) signifies to depart out (ek), to leave a
place, Luke 21 : 21.¶

(e) Chōrizō and compounds.

13.   CHŌRIZŌ (χωρίζω), to put apart, separate, means, in the Middle
Voice, to separate oneself, to depart from, Acts 1 : 4 ;   18 : 1, 2 ;   in
marital affairs, 1 Cor. 7 : 10, 11, 15 ;   " departed " (R.V. corrects to " was
parted "), Phlm. 15.   The verb is also used in Matt. 19 : 6 ;   Mark 10 : 9 ;
Rom. 8 : 35, 39 ;   Heb. 7 : 26.   See Put, No. 14, Separate.¶

14.   APOCHŌRIZŌ (ἀποχωρίζω) signifies to separate off (apo) ;   in
the Middle Voice, to depart from, Acts 15 : 39, A.V., " departed asunder ; "
R.V., " parted asunder ; "   Rev. 6 : 14, R.V., " was removed."   See
Part, Remove.¶

15.   DIACHŌRIZŌ (διαχωρίζω), lit., to separate throughout (dia),
i.e., completely, in the Middle Voice, to separate oneself definitely from,
is used in Luke 9 : 33, R.V., " were parting from."¶

(f) Various other verbs.

16.   ANALUŌ (ἀναλύω), lit., to unloose, undo (ana, up, or again),
signifies to depart, in the sense of departing from life, Phil. 1 : 23, a
metaphor drawn from loosing moorings preparatory to setting sail, or,
according to some, from breaking up an encampment, or from the

unyoking of baggage animals. See DEPARTING, No. 1. In Luke 12 : 36, it has its other meaning, to return. See RETURN.¶

17. APOLUŌ (ἀπολύω), to loose from (apo), in the Middle Voice, signifies to depart, Luke 2 : 29 ; Acts 23 : 22, R.V., " let go ; " 28 : 25. See DISMISS.

18. EXEIMI (ἔξειμι), to go out (ex, out, eimi, to go), is rendered " went out " in Acts 13 : 42 ; in 27 : 43, " got," of mariners getting to shore ; in 17 : 15, " departed ; " in 20 : 7, " to depart." See GET, GO.¶

19. METAIRŌ (μεταίρω), to make a distinction, to remove, to lift away (in its transitive sense), is used intransitively in the N.T., signifying to depart, and is said of Christ, in Matt. 13 : 53 ; 19 : 1. It could be well translated " removed."¶

20. APHISTĒMI (ἀφίστημι), in the Active Voice, used transitively, signifies to cause to depart, to cause to revolt, Acts 5 : 37 ; used intransitively, to stand off, or aloof, or to depart from anyone, Luke 4 : 13 ; 13 : 27 ; Acts 5 : 38 (" refrain from ") ; 12 : 10 ; 15 : 38 ; 19 : 9 ; 22 : 29 ; 2 Cor. 12 : 8 ; metaphorically, to fall away, 2 Tim. 2 : 19 ; in the Middle Voice, to withdraw or absent oneself from, Luke 2 : 37 ; to apostatize, Luke 8 : 13 ; 1 Tim. 4 : 1 ; Heb. 3 : 12, R.V., " falling away." See DRAW (away), FALL, No. 14, REFRAIN, WITHDRAW.¶

21. APALLASSŌ (ἀπαλλάσσω), lit., to change from (apo, from, allassō, to change), is used once of departing, said of the removal of diseases, Acts 19 : 12. In Heb. 2 : 15 it signifies to deliver, release. In Luke 12 : 58, it is used in a legal sense, to be quit of. See DELIVER.¶

22. METABAINŌ (μεταβαίνω) is rendered to depart in Matt. 8 : 34 ; 11 : 1 ; 12 : 9 ; 15 : 29 ; John 7 : 3 ; 13 : 1 ; Acts 18 : 7.

DEPARTING, DEPARTURE

1. ANALUSIS (ἀνάλυσις), an unloosing (as of things woven), a dissolving into separate parts (Eng., analysis), is once used of departure from life, 2 Tim. 4 : 6, where the metaphor is either nautical, from loosing from moorings (thus used in Greek poetry), or military, from breaking up an encampment ;   cp. kataluō in 2 Cor. 5 : 1 (cp. DEPART, No. 16).¶

2. APHIXIS (ἄφιξις), most frequently an arrival (akin to aphikneomai, see COME), also signifies a departure (apo, from, hikneomai, to come : etymologically, to come far enough, reach ; cp. hikanos, sufficient), the departure being regarded in relation to the end in view. Thus Paul speaks of his " departing," Acts 20 : 29.¶

3. EXODOS (ἔξοδος) : see DECEASE.

DEPOSE

KATHAIREŌ (καθαιρέω) lit. signifies to take down (kata, down, haireō, to take), the technical term for removing a body after crucifixion, e.g., Mark 15 : 36 ; hence, to pull down, demolish ; in Acts 19 : 27, according to the most authentic mss., the translation is (as the R.V.) " that she

(Diana) should even be deposed from her magnificence " (possibly, in the partitive sense of the genitive, ' destroyed from, or diminished in, somewhat of her magnificence '). See Cast, Destroy, Pull, Put, Take (down).

For DEPOSIT see COMMIT, B, No. 1

DEPTH

1. BATHOS (βάθος) : see Deep.

2. PELAGOS (πέλαγος), the sea, Acts 27 : 5, denotes also " the depth " (of the sea), Matt. 18 : 6. The word is most probably connected with a form of *plēssō*, to strike, and *plēgē*, a blow, suggestive of the tossing of the waves. Some would connect it with *plax*, a level board, but this is improbable, and less applicable to the general usage of the word, which commonly denotes the sea in its restless character. See Sea.¶

For DEPUTY see PROCONSUL

DERIDE

Note : For *ekmuktērizō*, lit., to turn up the nose at, to deride out and out, Luke 16 : 14 ; 23 : 35, see Scoff.¶

DESCEND

1. KATABAINŌ (καταβαίνω), to go down (*kata*, down, *bainō*, to go), used for various kinds of motion on the ground (e.g., going, walking, stepping), is usually translated to descend. The R.V. uses the verb to come down, for A.V., descend, in Mark 15 : 32 ; Acts 24 : 1 ; Rev. 21 : 10. See Come, No. 19.

2. KATERCHOMAI (κατέρχομαι), to come or go down, is translated " descendeth," in Jas. 3 : 15, A.V. ; R.V., " cometh down." See Come, No. 7.

DESCENT

KATABASIS (κατάβασις) denotes a going down, akin to No. 1 under Descend, a way down, Luke 19:37.¶

Note: For descent" (A.V. in Heb. 7:3, 6), see Genealogy (the R.V. rendering).

DESCRIBE

1. GRAPHŌ (γράφω), to write, is rendered "describeth" in Rom. 10:5, A.V., "For Moses describeth the righteousness which is of the Law . . . ;" this the R.V. corrects to "For Moses writeth that the man that doeth the righteousness which is of the Law . . ." See Write.

2. LEGŌ   to say, is rendered "describeth" in Rom. 4:6, A.V., "David describeth the blessedness . . . ;" this the R.V. corrects to,

" David pronounceth blessing upon . . ."   This might be regarded as the meaning, if David is considered as the human agent acting for God as the real pronouncer of blessing.   Otherwise the verb *lego* is to be taken in its ordinary sense of telling or relating ;   especially as the blessedness (*makarismos*) is not an act, but a state of felicity resulting from God's act of justification.

DESERT (Noun and Adjective)
A. Noun.

EREMIA (ἐρημία), primarily a solitude, an uninhabited place, in contrast to a town or village, is translated " deserts " in Heb. 11 : 38 ; " the wilderness " in Matt. 15 : 33, A.V., " a desert place," R.V. ;   so in Mark 8 : 4 ;   " wilderness " in 2 Cor. 11 : 26.   It does not always denote a barren region, void of vegetation ;   it is often used of a place uncultivated, but fit for pasturage.   See WILDERNESS.¶

B. Adjective.

EREMOS (ἔρημος), used as a noun, has the same meaning as *eremia* ; in Luke 5 : 16 and 8 : 29, R.V., " deserts," for A.V., " wilderness ; " in Matt. 24 : 26 and John 6 : 31, R.V., " wilderness," for A.V., " desert." As an adjective, it denotes (*a*), with reference to persons, " deserted," desolate, deprived of the friends and kindred, e.g., of a woman deserted by a husband, Gal. 4 : 27 ; (*b*) so of a city, as Jerusalem, Matt. 23 : 38 ; or uninhabited places, " desert," e.g., Matt. 14 : 13, 15 ; Acts 8 : 26 ; in Mark 1 : 35, R.V., " desert," for A.V., " solitary." See DESOLATE, WILDERNESS.

DESIRE (Noun and Verb), DESIROUS
A. Nouns.

1. EPITHUMIA (ἐπιθυμία), a desire, craving, longing, mostly of evil desires, frequently translated " lust," is used in the following, of good desires :   of the Lord's wish concerning the last Passover, Luke 22 : 15 ; of Paul's desire to be with Christ, Phil. 1 : 23 ; of his desire to see the saints at Thessalonica again, 1 Thess. 2 : 17.

With regard to evil desires, in Col. 3 : 5 the R.V. has " desire," for the A.V., " concupiscence ; " in 1 Thess 4 : 5, R.V., " lust," for A.V., " concupiscence ; " there the preceding word *pathos* is translated " passion," R.V., for A.V., " lust " (see AFFECTION) ;   also in Col. 3 : 5 *pathos* and *epithumia* are associated, R.V., " passion," for A.V., " inordinate affection."   *Epithumia* is combined with *pathema*, in Gal. 5 : 24 ; for the A.V., " affections and lusts," the R.V. has " passions, and the lusts thereof." *Epithumia* is the more comprehensive term, including all manner of lusts and desires ;   *pathema* denotes suffering ;   in the passage in Gal. (l.c.) the sufferings are those produced by yielding to the flesh ;   *pathos* points more to the evil state from which lusts spring.   Cp. *orexis*, lust, Rom. 1 : 27.   See CONCUPISCENCE, LUST, and Trench, Syn. lxxxvii.

2. EUDOKIA (εὐδοκία), lit., good pleasure (*eu*, well, *dokeō*, to seem), implies a gracious purpose, a good object being in view, with the idea of a resolve, shewing the willingness with which the resolve is made.   It is often translated " good pleasure," e.g., Eph. 1 : 5, 9 ; Phil. 2 : 13 ; in Phil. 1 : 15, " good will ; " in Rom. 10 : 1, " desire," (marg., " good pleasure ") ; in 2 Thess. 1 : 11, R.V., " desire," A.V. and R.V., marg., " good pleasure."

It is used of God in Matt. 11 : 26 (" well pleasing," R.V., for A.V., " seemed good ") ; Luke 2 : 14, R.V., " men in whom He is well pleased," lit., ' men of good pleasure ' (the construction is objective) ; 10 : 21 ; Eph. 1 : 5, 9 ; Phil. 2 : 13. See PLEASURE, SEEM, WILL.¶

3. EPIPOTHĒSIS (ἐπιπόθησις), an earnest desire, a longing for (*epi*, upon, intensive, *potheo*, to desire), is found in 2 Cor. 7 : 7, 11, A.V., " earnest desire," and " vehement desire ; " R.V., " longing " in both places. See LONGING.¶

4. EPIPOTHIA (ἐπιποθία), with the same meaning as No. 3, is used in Rom. 15 : 23, R.V., " longing," A.V., " great desire."¶ Cp. *epipothetos*, Phil. 4 : 1, " longed for "¶, and *epipotheō*, to long for [see B, Note (4)]. See LONGING.

5. THELĒMA (θέλημα) denotes a will, that which is willed (akin to B, No. 6). It is rendered " desires," in Eph. 2 : 3. See PLEASURE, WILL.

Note : In 1 Pet. 4 : 3, R.V., *boulēma* is rendered " desire." See WILL.

B. Verbs.

1. AXIOŌ (ἀξιόω), to deem worthy, is translated " desire " in Acts 28 : 22, where a suitable rendering would be ' We think it meet (or good) to hear of thee ; ' so in 15 : 38. See THINK.

2. EPITHUMEŌ (ἐπιθυμέω), to desire earnestly (as with A, No. 1), stresses the inward impulse rather than the object desired. It is translated to desire in Luke 16 : 21 ; 17 : 22 ; 22 : 15 ; 1 Tim. 3 : 1 ; Heb. 6 : 11 ; 1 Pet. 1 : 12 ; Rev. 9 : 6. See COVET.

3. ERŌTAŌ (ἐρωτάω), in Luke 7 : 36 is translated " desired ; " in 14 : 32, R.V., " asketh," for A.V., " desireth ; " so in John 12 : 21 ; Acts 16 : 39 ; 18 : 20 ; 23 : 20 ; in ver. 18 " asked," for A.V., " prayed." See ASK.

4. HOMEIROMAI, or HIMEIROMAI (ὁμείρομαι), to have a strong affection for, a yearning after, is found in 1 Thess. 2 : 8, " being affectionately desirous of you." It is probably derived from a root indicating remembrance.¶

5. OREGŌ (ὀρέγω), to reach or stretch out, is used only in the Middle Voice, signifying the mental effort of stretching oneself out for a thing, of longing after it, with stress upon the object desired (cp. No. 2) ; it is translated " desire " in Heb. 11 : 16 ; in 1 Tim. 3 : 1, R.V., " seeketh," for A.V., " desireth ; " in 1 Tim. 6 : 10, R.V., " reached after," for A.V., " coveted after." In Heb. 11 : 16, a suitable rendering would be ' reach after.' See COVET, SEEK.¶ Cp. *orexis*, lust, Rom. 1 : 27.¶

6. THELŌ(θέλω), to will, to wish, implying volition and purpose, frequently a determination, is most usually rendered to will. It is translated to desire in the R.V. of the following : Matt. 9 : 13 ; 12 : 7 ; Mark 6 : 19 ; Luke 10 : 29 ; 14 : 28 ; 23 : 20 ; Acts 24 : 27 ; 25 : 9 ; Gal. 4 : 17 ; 1 Tim. 5 : 11 ; Heb. 12 : 17 ; 13 : 18. See DISPOSED, FORWARD, INTEND, LIST, LOVE, MEAN, PLEASED, RATHER, VOLUNTARY, WILL.

7. BOULOMAI (βούλομαι), to wish, to will deliberately, expresses more strongly than *thelō* (No. 6) the deliberate exercise of the will ; it is translated to desire in the R.V. of the following : Acts 22 : 30 ; 23 : 38 ; 27 : 43 ; 28 : 18 ; 1 Tim. 2 : 8 ; 5 : 14 ; 6 : 9 and Jude 5. See DISPOSED, INTEND, LIST, MINDED, WILLING, WISH, WOULD.

8. ZĒLOŌ (ζηλόω), to have a zeal for, to be zealous towards, whether in a good or evil sense, the former in 1 Cor. 14 : 1, concerning spiritual gifts R.V., " desire earnestly," A.V., " desire ; " in an evil sense, in Jas. 4 : 2, R.V., " covet," for A.V., " desire to have."

9. AITEŌ (αἰτέω), to ask, is rendered to desire in A.V., e.g., in Matt. 20 : 20 ; Luke 23 : 25 [R.V., always ' to ask (for) '].

10. SPEUDŌ (σπεύδω) is translated " earnestly desiring " in 2 Pet. 3 : 12, R.V. See HASTE.

Note : The following are translated by the verb to desire in the A.V. (1) *Eperōtaō*, No. 3, with *epi*, intensive, to ask, interrogate, inquire of, consult, or to demand of a person ; in Matt. 16 : 1, R.V., " asked." See ASK. (2) *Zēteō*, to seek ; in Matt. 12 : 46, 47, R.V., " seeking ; " in Luke 9 : 9, R.V., " sought." See ENDEAVOUR, GO, *Note* (2), (*a*), INQUIRE, REQUIRE, SEEK. (3) *Epizēteō*, to seek earnestly (No. 2, with *epi*, intensive), in Acts 13 : 7, R.V., " sought ; " in Phil. 4 : 17, R.V., " seek for " (twice). See INQUIRE, SEEK. (4) *Epipotheō*, to long after, to lust ; in 2 Cor. 5 : 2, R.V., " longing ; " in 1 Thess. 3 : 6 and 2 Tim. 1 : 4, R.V., " longing ; " in 1 Pet. 2 : 2, R.V., " long for." See A, Nos. 3, 4. See LONG, LUST. (5) *Exaiteomai*, intensive of No. 9, occurs in Luke 22 : 31.¶ (6) For *parakaleō*, see BESEECH, EXHORT, INTREAT. (7) For " desirous of vain glory," see VAINGLORY.

DESOLATE (Verb and Adjective), DESOLATION

A. Verbs.

1. ERĒMOŌ (ἐρημόω) signifies to make desolate, lay waste. From the primary sense of making quiet comes that of making lonely. It is used only in the Passive Voice in the N.T. ; in Rev. 17 : 16, " shall make desolate " is, lit., ' shall make her desolated ; ' in 18 : 17, 19, " is made desolate ; " in Matt. 12 : 25 and Luke 11 : 17, " is brought to desolation." See NOUGHT (come to).¶ Cp. DESERT.

2. MONOŌ (μονόω), to leave alone (akin to *monos*, alone), is used in 1 Tim. 5 : 5, in the Passive Voice, but translated " desolate," lit., ' was made desolate ' or ' left desolate.'¶

B. Adjectives.

1. EREMOS (ἔρημος) is translated "desolate" in the Lord's words against Jerusalem, Matt. 23 : 38 ; some mss. have it in Luke 13 : 35 ; in reference to the habitation of Judas, Acts 1 : 20, and to Sarah, from whom, being barren, her husband had turned, Gal. 4 : 27. See DESERT.

2. ORPHANOS (ὀρφανός) (Eng., orphan ; Lat., orbus), signifies bereft of parents or of a father. In Jas. 1 : 27 it is translated "fatherless." It was also used in the general sense of being friendless or desolate. In John 14 : 18 the Lord uses it of the relationship between Himself and His disciples, He having been their Guide, Teacher and Protector ; R.V., "desolate," A.V., "comfortless." Some mss. have the word in Mark 12 : 40. See FATHERLESS.¶

C. Noun.

EREMOSIS (ἐρήμωσις), akin to A, No. 1, denotes desolation, (a) in the sense of making desolate, e.g., in the phrase "the abomination of desolation," Matt. 24 : 15 ; Mark 13 : 14 ; the genitive is objective, ' the abomination that makes desolate ; ' (b) with stress upon the effect of the process, Luke 21 : 20, with reference to the desolation of Jerusalem.¶

DESPAIR

1. EXAPOREO (ἐξαπορέω) is used in the N.T. in the Passive Voice, with Middle sense, to be utterly without a way (ek, out of, intensive, a, negative, poros, a way through ; cp. poreuō, to go through ; Eng., ' ferry ' is connected), to be quite at a loss, without resource, in despair. It is used in 2 Cor. 1 : 8, with reference to life ; in 4 : 8, in the sentence "perplexed, yet not unto (A.V. ' in ') despair," the word "perplexed" translates the verb aporeō, and the phrase "unto despair" translates the intensive form exaporeō, a play on the words.¶ In the Sept., Ps. 88 : 15, where the translation is "having been lifted up, I was brought low and into despair."¶

2. APELPIZO (ἀπελπίζω), lit., to hope away (apo, away from, elpizō, to hope), i.e., to give up in despair, to despair, is used in Luke 6 : 35, R.V., "nothing despairing," i.e., without anxiety as to the result, or not despairing of the recompense from God ; this is probably the true meaning ; A.V., "hoping for nothing again." The marg., "of no man," is to be rejected.¶

DESPISE, DESPISER
A. Verbs.

1. EXOUTHENEO (ἐξουθενέω), to make of no account (ex, out, oudeis, nobody, alternatively written, outheis), to regard as nothing, to despise utterly, to treat with contempt. This is usually translated to set at nought, Luke 18 : 9, R.V., A.V., "despised." So in Rom. 14 : 3. Both have "set at nought" in Luke 23 : 11 ; Acts 4 : 11 ; Rom. 14 : 10. Both have "despise" in 1 Cor. 16 : 11 ; Gal. 4 : 14, and 1 Thess. 5 : 20 ;

in 2 Cor. 10 : 10, R.V., " of no account," for A.V., " contemptible ; " in 1 Cor. 1 : 28, A.V. and R.V., " despised." For the important rendering in 1 Cor. 6 : 4, R.V., see ACCOUNT.¶

Note : In Mark 9 : 12 some mss. have this verb ; the most authentic have the alternative spelling *exoudeneō,* " set at nought."

2. KATAPHRONEŌ (καταφρονέω), lit., to think down upon or against anyone (*kata,* down, *phrēn,* the mind), hence signifies to think slightly of, to despise, Matt. 6 : 24 ; 18 : 10 ; Luke 16 : 13 ; Rom. 2 : 4 ; 1 Cor. 11 : 22 ; 1 Tim. 4 : 12 ; 6 : 2 ; Heb. 12 : 2 ; 2 Pet. 2 : 10.¶

3. PERIPHRONEŌ (περιφρονέω) lit. denotes to think round a thing, to turn over in the mind ; hence, to have thoughts beyond, to despise, Tit. 2 : 15.¶

Notes : The following verbs, translated to despise etc. in the A.V., are given suitable meanings in the R.V. :

(1) *Atheteō,* lit., to displace, to set aside, R.V., to reject, Luke 10 : 16 ; 1 Thess. 4 : 8 ; in 1 Tim. 5 : 12, " rejected," for A.V., " cast off ; " in Heb. 10 : 28, " hath set at nought ; " so Jude 8. See DISANNUL, REJECT, VOID, No. 2. (2) *Atimazō,* to dishonour (*a,* negative, *timē,* honour) ; in Jas. 2 : 6, R.V., " have dishonoured." See DISHONOUR, ENTREAT, SHAME, C, No. 1, SHAMEFULLY. (3) *Oligōreō,* to care little for, regard lightly (*oligos,* little) ; in Heb. 12 : 5, R.V., " regard lightly." See REGARD.¶ (4) The phrase *logizomai eis ouden* signifies to reckon as nothing ; in the Passive Voice, to be counted as nothing ; in Acts 19 : 27, R.V., " be made of no account."

B. Adjective.

ATIMOS (ἄτιμος), without honour, see Note (2), above, is translated as a verb in 1 Cor. 4 : 10, A.V., " are despised ; " R.V., " have dishonour," lit., ' (we are) without honour ; ' " without honour " in Matt. 13 : 57 ; Mark 6 : 4. The comparative degree *atimoteros,* " less honourable," is used in 1 Cor. 12 : 23.¶

Note : *Aphilagathos,* not loving the good (*a,* negative, *phileō,* to love, *agathos,* good), is used in 2 Tim. 3 : 3, A.V., " despisers of those that are good," R.V., " no lovers of good."See LOVER.¶

C. Noun.

KATAPHRONĒTĒS (καταφρονητής), lit., one who thinks down against, hence, a despiser (see A, No. 2), is found in Acts 13 : 41.¶ In the Sept., Hab. 1 : 5 ; 2 : 5 and Zeph. 3 : 4.¶

DESPITE, DESPITEFUL, DESPITEFULLY (use)

1. ENUBRIZŌ (ἐνυβρίζω), to treat insultingly, with contumely (*en,* intensive, *hubrizō,* to insult ; some connect it with *huper,* above, over, Lat. *super,* which suggests the insulting disdain of one who considers himself superior), is translated " hath done despite " in Heb. 10 : 29.¶

Notes : (1) *Hubrizō,* to insult, act with insolence, is translated " to use despitefully " in Acts 14 : 5, A.V. ; R.V., " to entreat . . . shamefully." See (ENTREAT) SHAMEFULLY, (ENTREAT) SPITEFULLY, REPROACH, B, No. 2.

(2) The noun *hubristēs*, a violent man, is translated " despiteful " in Rom. 1 : 30, A.V. ; R.V., " insolent ; " in 1 Tim. 1 : 13, " injurious."¶

2. EPĒREAZŌ (ἐπηρεάζω), for which see ACCUSE, B, No. 3, is found in some mss. in Matt. 5 : 44, and translated " despitefully use," A.V. (the R.V. follows the mss. which omit the sentence). In the corresponding passage in Luke 6 : 28, the A.V. and R.V. have " despitefully use ; " in 1 Pet. 3 : 16, A.V., " falsely accuse," R.V., " revile." See ACCUSE, REVILE.¶

DESTITUTE (be, etc.)

1. APOSTEREŌ (ἀποστερέω) : see DEFRAUD.

2. HUSTEREŌ (ὑστερέω), primarily, to be behind, to be last, hence, to lack, fail of, come short of, is translated " being destitute " in Heb. 11 : 37. See BEHIND, B, No. 1.

3. LEIPŌ (λείπω) signifies to leave, forsake ; in the Passive Voice, to be left, forsaken, destitute ; in Jas. 2 : 15, A.V., " destitute," R.V., " be in lack." See LACK, WANT.

DESTROY, DESTROYER, DESTRUCTION, DESTRUCTIVE
A. Verbs.

1. APOLLUMI (ἀπόλλυμι), a strengthened form of *ollumi*, signifies to destroy utterly ; in Middle Voice, to perish. The idea is not extinction but ruin, loss, not of being, but of well-being. This is clear from its use, as, e.g., of the marring of wine skins, Luke 5 : 37 ; of lost sheep, i.e., lost to the shepherd, metaphorical of spiritual destitution, Luke 15 : 4, 6, etc. ; the lost son, 15 : 24 ; of the perishing of food, John 6 : 27 ; of gold, 1 Pet. 1 : 7. So of persons, Matt. 2 : 13, " destroy ; " 8 : 25, " perish ; " 22 : 7 ; 27 : 20; of the loss of well-being in the case of the unsaved hereafter, Matt. 10 : 28 ; Luke 13 : 3, 5 ; John 3 : 16 (ver. 15 in some mss.) ; 10 : 28 ; 17 : 12 ; Rom. 2 : 12 ; 1 Cor. 15 : 18 ; 2 Cor. 2 : 15, " are perishing ; " 4 : 3 ; 2 Thess. 2 : 10 ; Jas. 4 : 12 ; 2 Pet. 3 : 9. Cp. B, II, No. 1. See DIE, LOSE, MARRED, PERISH.

2. KATARGEŌ (καταργέω) : see ABOLISH.

3. KATHAIREŌ (καθαιρέω), to cast down, pull down by force, etc., is translated to destroy in Acts 13 : 19. In Acts 19 : 27, A.V., " should be destroyed," the R.V. suitably has " should be deposed." See CAST, No. 13, PULL, PUT, TAKE.

4. LUŌ (λύω), to loose, dissolve, sever, break, demolish, is translated " destroy," in 1 John 3 : 8, of the works of the Devil. See BREAK, A, No. 4.

5. KATALUŌ (καταλύω), *kata*, down, intensive, and No. 4, to destroy utterly, to overthrow completely, is rendered " destroy," in Matt. 5 ; 17,

twice, of the Law; Matt. 24 : 2 ; 26 : 61 ; 27 : 40 ; Mark 13 : 2 ; 14 : 58 ; 15 : 29 ; Luke 21 : 6, of the Temple ; in Acts 6 : 14, of Jerusalem ; in Gal. 2 : 18, of the Law as a means of justification ; in Rom. 14 : 20 (A.V., " destroy," R.V., " overthrow "), of the marring of a person's spiritual well-being (in ver. 15 *apollumi*, No. 1, is used in the same sense) ; in Acts 5 : 38 and 39 (R.V., " overthrow ") of the failure of purposes ; in 2 Cor. 5 : 1, of the death of the body (" dissolved "). See DISSOLVE, NOUGHT (come to), OVERTHROW, THROW.

For its other meaning, to lodge, see Luke 9 : 12 and 19 : 7. See GUEST, LODGE.¶

6. OLOTHREUŌ (ὀλοθρεύω), to destroy, especially in the sense of slaying, is found in Heb. 11 : 28, where the R.V. translates the present participle with the article by the noun " destroyer."¶ See B, below. The verb occurs frequently in the Sept., e.g., Ex. 12 : 23 ; Josh. 3 : 10 ; 7 : 25 ; Jer. 2 : 30 ; 5 : 6 ; 22 : 7.

7. EXOLOTHREUŌ (ἐξολοθρεύω), *ek*, out of (intensive), and No. 6, to destroy utterly, to slay wholly, is found in Acts 3 : 23, R.V., " utterly destroyed," referring to the destruction of one who would refuse to hearken to the voice of God through Christ.¶ This verb is far more abundantly used in the Sept. than No. 6 ; it occurs 35 times in Deut. ; 34 in Josh. ; 68 in the Psalms.

8. PHTHEIRŌ (φθείρω) : see CORRUPT, A, No. 2.

9. DIAPHTHEIRŌ (διαφθείρω) ; see CORRUPT, A, No. 3.

Note : *Portheō*, to ruin by laying waste, to make havock of, is translated " destroyed " in Acts 9 : 21, of the attacks upon the church in Jerusalem by Saul of Tarsus ; " wasted," in Gal. 1 : 13, with reference to the same ; " destroyed " in Gal. 1 : 23, where " the faith " is put by metonymy (one thing being put for another associated with it), for those who held the faith. In each of these places the R.V. consistently translates by " made havock of." See HAVOCK, WASTE.¶

B. Nouns.

(I) (*Personal : DESTROYER*)

OLOTHREUTĒS (ὀλοθρευτής), akin to A, No. 6, a destroyer, is found in 1 Cor. 10 : 10.¶

Note : For the construction in Heb. 11 : 28, " the destroyer," see A, No. 6. Cp. *apolluōn*, in Rev. 9 : 11, the present participle of *apollumi*, A, No. 1, used as a proper noun.¶

(II) (*Abstract : DESTRUCTION*)

1. APŌLEIA (ἀπώλεια), akin to A, No. 1, and likewise indicating loss of well-being, not of being, is used (*a*) of things, signifying their waste, or ruin ; of ointment, Matt. 26 : 8 ; Mark 14 : 4 ; of money, Acts 8 : 20 (" perish ") ; (*b*) of persons, signifying their spiritual and eternal perdition, Matt. 7 : 13 ; John 17 : 12 ; 2 Thess. 2 : 3, where " son of perdition " signifies the proper destiny of the person mentioned ; metaphorically of men persistent in evil, Rom. 9 : 22, where " fitted " is in the Middle Voice,

indicating that the vessels of wrath fitted themselves for destruction ; of the adversaries of the Lord's people, Phil. 1 : 28 (" perdition ") ; of professing Christians, really enemies of the Cross of Christ, Phil. 3 : 19 (R.V., " perdition ") ; of those who are subjects of foolish and hurtful lusts, 1 Tim. 6 : 9 (for the preceding word " destruction " see No. 3, below) ; of professing Hebrew adherents who shrink back into unbelief, Heb. 10 : 39 ; of false teachers, 2 Pet. 2 : 1, 3 ; of ungodly men, 3 : 7 ; of those who wrest the Scriptures, 3 : 16 ; of the Beast, the final head of the revived Roman Empire, Rev. 17 : 8, 11 ; (c) of impersonal subjects, as heresies, 2 Pet. 2 : 1, where " destructive heresies " (R.V. ; A.V., " damnable ") is, lit., ' heresies of destruction ' (marg., " sects of perdition ") ; in ver. 2 the most authentic mss. have *aselgeiais*, " lascivious," instead of *apōleiais*. See PERDITION, PERNICIOUS, WASTE.¶

2. KATHAIRESIS (καθαίρεσις), akin to A, No. 3, a taking down, a pulling down, is used three times in 2 Cor.," casting down " in the R.V. in each place ; in 10 : 4 (A.V., " pulling down ") ; in 10 : 8 and 13 : 10 (A.V., " destruction "). See PULL.¶

3. OLETHROS (ὄλεθρος), ruin, destruction, akin to A, No. 6, always translated " destruction," is used in 1 Cor. 5 : 5, of the effect upon the physical condition of an erring believer for the purpose of his spiritual profit ; in 1 Thess. 5 : 3 and 2 Thess. 1 : 9, of the effect of the Divine judgments upon men at the ushering in of the Day of the Lord and the revelation of the Lord Jesus ; in 1 Tim. 6 : 9, of the consequences of the indulgence of the flesh, referring to physical ruin and possibly that of the whole being, the following word *apōleia* (see No. 1) stressing the final, eternal and irrevocable character of the ruin.¶

4. PHTHORA (φθορά), akin to A, No. 8, denotes the destruction that comes with corruption. In 2 Pet. 2 : 12 it is used twice ; for the A.V., " made to be taken and destroyed . . . shall utterly perish (*phtheirō*) in their own corruption," the R.V. has " to be taken and destroyed (lit., unto capture and destruction, *phthora*) . . . shall in their destroying (*phthora*) surely be destroyed," taking the noun in the last clause in the sense of their act of destroying others. See CORRUPT, CORRUPTION.

5. SUNTRIMMA (σύντριμμα), a breaking in pieces, shattering (the corresponding verb is *suntribō ;* see under BREAK, BRUISE), hence, ruin, destruction, is compounded of *sun*, together, and *trimma*, a rubbing or wearing away. The latter, and *tribō*, to beat, are derived from a root, signifying to rub, wear away ; hence Eng., tribulation and trouble. It is used, metaphorically, of destruction, in Rom. 3 : 16 (from Isa. 59 : 7), which, in a passage setting forth the sinful state of mankind in general, suggests the wearing process of the effects of cruelty.¶ The word is frequent in the Sept., especially in Isaiah and Jeremiah.

DETERMINE, DETERMINATE

1. KRINŌ (κρίνω), primarily, to separate, hence, to be of opinion,

approve, esteem, Rom. 14 : 5, also to determine, resolve, decree, is used in this sense in Acts 3 : 13 ; 20 : 16 ; 25 : 25 ; 27 : 1 ; 1 Cor. 2 : 2 ; 2 Cor. 2 : 1 ; Tit. 3 : 12. See CONDEMN, JUDGE, JUDGMENT, LAW, B, No. 2.

2. HORIZŌ (ὁρίζω) denotes to bound, to set a boundary (Eng., horizon) ; hence, to mark out definitely, determine ; it is translated to determine in Luke 22 : 22, of the fore-ordained pathway of Christ ; Acts 11 : 29, of a determination to send relief ; 17 : 26, where it is used of fixing the bounds of seasons. In Acts 2 : 23 the verb is translated " determinate," with reference to counsel. Here the verbal form might have been adhered to by the translation ' determined ; ' that is to say, in the sense of ' settled.'

In Rom. 1 : 4 it is translated " declared," where the meaning is that Christ was marked out as the Son of God by His resurrection and that of others (see under DECLARE). In Acts 10 : 42 and 17 : 31 it has its other meaning of ordain, that is, to appoint by determined counsel. In Heb. 4 : 7, it is translated " limiteth," but preferably in the R.V., " defineth," with reference to a certain period ; here again it approaches its primary meaning of marking out the bounds of. See DECLARE, No. 9, LIMIT, ORDAIN.¶

3. PROORIZŌ (προορίζω), pro, beforehand, and No. 2, denotes to mark out beforehand, to determine before, foreordain ; in Acts 4 : 28, A.V., " determined before," R.V., " foreordained ; " so the R.V. in 1 Cor. 2 : 7, A.V., " ordained ; " in Rom. 8 : 29, 30 and Eph. 1 : 5, 11, A.V., " predestinate," R.V., " foreordain." See ORDAIN, Note (1), PREDESTINATE.¶

4. EPILUŌ (ἐπιλύω), lit., to loosen upon, denotes to solve, expound, Mark 4 : 34 ; to settle, as of a controversy, Acts 19 : 39, A.V., " it shall be determined," R.V., " it shall be settled." See EXPOUND, SETTLE.¶

5. DIAGINŌSKŌ (διαγινώσκω), besides its meaning to ascertain exactly, Acts 23 : 15, was an Athenian law term signifying to determine, so used in 24 : 22, R.V., " determine ; " A.V., " know the uttermost of."¶

6. TASSŌ (τάσσω) : see APPOINT, No. 5.

Note : Boulomai, to be minded, to purpose, is translated " determined " in Acts 15 : 37 ; R.V., " was minded." See MINDED, No. 2.

DEVICE

1. ENTHUMĒSIS (ἐνθύμησις), a cogitation, an inward reasoning (generally, evil surmising or supposition), is formed from en, in, and thumos, strong feeling, passion (cp. thumoō, in the Middle Voice, to be wroth, furious) ; Eng., fume is akin ; the root, thu, signifies to rush, rage. The word is translated " device " in Acts 17 : 29, of man's production of images ; elsewhere, " thoughts," Matt. 9 : 4 ; 12 : 25 ; Heb. 4 : 12, where the accompanying word ennoia denotes inward intentions. See THOUGHT.¶

2. NOĒMA (νόημα) denotes thought, that which is thought out (cp. *noeō*, to understand) ; hence, a purpose, device ; translated " devices " in 2 Cor. 2 : 11 ; " minds " in 2 Cor. 3 : 14 ; 4 : 4 ; 11 : 3 ; in 2 Cor. 10 : 5, " thought ; " in Phil. 4 : 7, A.V., " minds," R.V., " thoughts." See MIND, THOUGHT.¶

DEVIL, DEVILISH

DIABOLOS (διάβολος), an accuser, a slanderer (from *diaballō*, to accuse, to malign), is one of the names of Satan.   From it the English word " Devil " is derived, and should be applied only to Satan, as a proper name.   *Daimōn*, a demon, is frequently, but wrongly, translated " devil ; " it should always be translated " demon," as in the R.V. margin. There is one Devil, there are many demons.   Being the malignant enemy of God and man, he accuses man to God, Job 1 : 6–11 ; 2 : 1–5 ; Rev. 12 : 9, 10, and God to man, Gen. 3.   He afflicts men with physical sufferings, Acts 10 : 38.   Being himself sinful, 1 John 3 : 8, he instigated man to sin, Gen. 3, and tempts man to do evil, Eph. 4 : 27 ; 6 : 11, encouraging him thereto by deception, Eph. 2 : 2.   Death having been brought into the world by sin, the Devil had the power of death, but Christ through His own Death, has triumphed over him, and will bring him to nought, Heb. 2 : 14 ; his power over death is intimated in his struggle with Michael over the body of Moses, Jude 9.   Judas, who gave himself over to the Devil, was so identified with him, that the Lord described him as such, John 6 : 70 (see 13 : 2).   As the Devil raised himself in pride against God and fell under condemnation, so believers are warned against similar sin, 1 Tim. 3 : 6 ; for them he lays snares, ver. 7, seeking to devour them as a roaring lion, 1 Pet. 5 : 8 ; those who fall into his snare may be recovered therefrom unto the will of God, 2 Tim. 2 : 26, " having been taken captive by him (i.e., by the Devil) ; " " by the Lord's servant " is an alternative, which some regard as confirmed by the use of *zōgreō* (to catch alive) in Luke 5 : 10 ; but the general use is that of taking captive in the usual way.   If believers resist he will flee from them, Jas. 4 : 7.   His fury and malignity will be especially exercised at the end of the present age, Rev. 12 : 12.   His doom is the lake of fire, Matt. 25 : 41 ; Rev. 20 : 10. The noun is applied to slanderers, false accusers, 1 Tim. 3 : 11 ; 2 Tim. 3 : 3 ; Tit. 2 : 3.

Note : For " devilish," Jas. 3 : 17, see DEMON, C.

DEVISED (cunningly)

SOPHIZŌ (σοφίζω), from *sophos*, wise (connected etymologically with *sophēs*, tasty), in the Active Voice signifies to make wise, 2 Tim. 3 : 15 (so in the Sept. of Ps. 19 : 7, e.g., " making babes wise ; " in 119 : 98, " Thou hast made me wiser than mine enemies "). In the Middle Voice it means (*a*) to become wise ; it is not used thus in the N.T., but is so found in the Sept., e.g., in Eccles. 2 : 15, 19 ; 7 : 17 ; (*b*) to play the sophist, to devise cleverly ; it is used with this meaning in the Passive Voice in 2 Pet. 1 : 16, " cunningly devised fables." See WISE.¶

Note : Cp. *katasophizomai*, to deal subtilly. See DEAL WITH, *Note* (2).

DEVOTION

Note : For this word, in Acts 17 : 23, A.V., which translates *sebasma*, " devotions," marg., " gods that ye worship," R.V., " objects of your worship," in 2 Thess. 2 : 4, " that is worshipped," see WORSHIP.¶ Cp. Acts 14 : 15, where, in translating *mataia*, the A.V. has " vanities," the abstract for the concrete (R.V., " vain things ").

DEVOUR

1. ESTHIŌ (ἐσθίω) is a strengthened form of an old verb *edō*, from the root *ed*—, whence Lat., *edo*, Eng., eat. The form *ephagon*, used as the 2nd Aorist Tense of this verb, is from the root *phag*—, to eat up. It is translated " devour " in Heb. 10 : 27 ; elsewhere, by the verb to eat. See EAT.

2. KATESTHIŌ and KATAPHAGŌ (κατεσθίω and καταφάγω), *kata*, down, intensive, and No. 1, signifies (*a*) to consume by eating, to devour, said of birds, Matt. 13 : 4 ; Mark 4 : 4 ; Luke 8 : 5 ; of the Dragon, Rev. 12 : 4 ; of a prophet, eating up a book, suggestive of spiritually eating and digesting its contents, Rev. 10 : 9 (cp. Ezek. 2 : 8 ; 3 : 1-3 ; Jer. 15 : 16) ; (*b*) metaphorically, to squander, to waste, Luke 15 : 30 ; to consume one's physical powers by emotion, John 2 : 17 ; to devour by forcible appropriation, as of widows' property, Matt. 23 : 14 (A.V. only) ; Mark 12 : 40 ; to demand maintenance, as false apostles did to the church at Corinth, 2 Cor. 11 : 20 ; to exploit or prey on one another, Gal. 5 : 15, where " bite . . . devour . . . consume " form a climax, the first two describing a process, the last the act of swallowing down ; to destroy by fire, Rev. 11 : 5 ; 20 : 9. See EAT.¶

3. KATAPINŌ (καταπίνω), from *kata*, down, intensive, *pinō*, to drink, in 1 Pet. 5 : 8 is translated " devour," of Satan's activities against believers. The meaning to swallow is found in Matt. 23 : 24 ; 1 Cor. 15 : 54 ; 2 Cor. 2 : 7 ; 5 : 4 ; Heb. 11 : 29, R.V. (for A.V., " drowned ") ; Rev. 12 : 16. See SWALLOW.¶

DEVOUT

1. EULABĒS (εὐλαβής), lit., taking hold well (*eu*, well, *lambanō*, to take hold), primarily, cautious, signifies in the N.T., careful as to the realization of the presence and claims of God, reverencing God, pious, devout ; in Luke 2 : 25 it is said of Simeon ; in Acts 2 : 5, of certain Jews ; in 8 : 2, of those who bore Stephen's body to burial ; of Ananias, 22 : 12 (see No. 2). " In that mingled fear and love which, combined, constitute the piety of man toward God, the Old Testament placed its emphasis on the fear, the New places it on the love (though there was

love in the fear of God's saints then, as there must be fear in their love now)," Trench, Syn., § xlviii.¶

Note : Cp. the noun *eulabeia*, reverence, and the verb *eulabeomai*, to reverence.

2. EUSEBĒS (εὐσεβής), from *eu*, well, *sebomai*, to reverence, the root *seb*– signifying sacred awe, describes reverence exhibited especially in actions, reverence or awe well directed. Among the Greeks it was used, e.g., of practical piety towards parents. In the N.T. it is used of a pious attitude towards God, Acts 10 : 2, 7 ; (in some mss. in 22 : 12) ; " godly," in 2 Pet. 2 : 9. See GODLY.¶ In the Sept., Prov. 12 : 12 ; Is. 24 : 16 ; 26 : 7 ; 32 : 8 ; Mic. 7 : 2.¶

Notes : (1) While *eulabēs* especially suggests the piety which characterizes the inner being, the soul, in its attitude towards God, *eusebēs* directs us rather to the energy which, directed by holy awe of God, finds expression in devoted activity.¶

(2) Cp. *theosebeia*, and *theosebēs*, which, by their very formation (*theos*, God, and *sebomai*), express reverence towards God. See Trench (§ xlviii).

3. SEBOMAI (σέβομαι), to feel awe, whether before God or man, to worship, is translated " devout," in Acts 13 : 43, R.V. (A.V., " religious ") ; 13 : 50 ; 17 : 4, 17. See WORSHIP.

DIADEM

DIADĒMA (διάδημα) is derived from *diadeō*, to bind round. It was the kingly ornament for the head, and especially the blue band marked with white, used to bind on the turban or tiara of Persian kings. It was adopted by Alexander the Great and his successors. Among the Greeks and Romans it was the distinctive badge of royalty. Diocletian was the first Roman Emperor to wear it constantly. The word is found in Rev. 12 : 3 ; 13 : 1 ; 19 : 12, in which passages it symbolises the rule respectively of the Dragon, the Beast, and Christ.¶ In the Sept., Esth. 1 : 11 ; 2 : 17 ; in some mss. in 6 : 8 and 8 : 15 ; also in Is. 62 : 3.¶ For the distinction between this and *stephanos*, see CROWN.

DIE, DEAD (to be, become), DYING

1. THNĒSKŌ (θνήσκω), to die (in the perf. tense, to be dead), in the N.T. is always used of physical death, except in 1 Tim. 5 : 6, where it is metaphorically used of the loss of spiritual life. The noun *thanatos*, and the verb *thanatoō* (below) are connected. The root of this group of words probably had the significance of the breathing out of the last breath. Cp. words under DEATH.

2. APOTHNĒSKŌ (ἀποθνήσκω), lit., to die off or out, is used (*a*) of the separation of the soul from the body, i.e., the natural death of human beings, e.g., Matt. 9 : 24 ; Rom. 7 : 2 ; by reason of descent from Adam, 1 Cor. 15 : 22 ; or of violent death, whether of men or animals ; with

regard to the latter it is once translated " perished," Matt. 8 : 32 ; of vegetation, Jude 12 ; of seeds, John 12 : 24 ; 1 Cor. 15 : 36; it is used of death as a punishment in Israel under the Law, in Heb. 10 : 28 ; (b) of the separation of man from God ; all who are descended from Adam not only die physically, owing to sin, see (a) above, but are naturally in the state of separation from God, 2 Cor. 5 : 14. From this believers are freed both now and eternally, John 6 : 50 ; 11 : 26, through the Death of Christ, Rom. 5 : 8, e.g. ; unbelievers, who die physically as such, remain in eternal separation from God, John 8 : 24. Believers have spiritually died to the Law as a means of life, Gal. 2 : 19 ; Col. 2 : 20 ; to sin, Rom. 6 : 2, and in general to all spiritual association with the world and with that which pertained to their unregenerate state, Col. 3 : 3, because of their identification with the Death of Christ, Rom. 6 : 8 (see No. 3, below). As life never means mere existence, so death, the opposite of life, never means non-existence. See PERISH.

3. SUNAPOTHNĒSKŌ (συναποθνήσκω), to die with, to die together, is used of association in physical death, Mark 14 : 31 ; in 2 Cor. 7 : 3, the Apostle declares that his love to the saints makes separation impossible, whether in life or in death. It is used once of association spiritually with Christ in His death, 2 Tim. 2 : 11. See No. 2 (b).¶

4. TELEUTAŌ (τελευτάω), to end (from *telos*, an end), hence, to end one's life, is used (a) of the death of the body, Matt. 2 : 19 ; 9 : 18 ; 15 : 4, where " die the death " means " surely die," R.V., marg., lit., ' let him end by death ; ' Mark 7 : 10 ; Matt. 22 : 25, " deceased ; " Luke 7 : 2 ; John 11 : 39, some mss. have verb No. 1 here ; Acts 2 : 29 ; 7 : 15 ; Heb. 11 : 22 (R.V., " his end was nigh ") ; (b) of the gnawings of conscience in self reproach, under the symbol of a worm, Mark 9 : 48 (vv. 44 and 46, A.V.). See DECEASE.¶

5. KOIMAŌ (κοιμάω), in the Middle and Passive Voices, its only use in the N.T., signifies to fall asleep. It is connected etymologically with *keimai*, to lie down, the root *ki*— signifying to lie. Hence it is used metaphorically of death, Matt. 27 : 52, etc. It is translated " be dead " in 1 Cor. 7 : 39. See ASLEEP.

6. APOGINOMAI (ἀπογίνομαι), lit., to be away from (*apo*, from, *ginomai*, to be, become ; *apo* here signifies separation), is used in 1 Pet. 2 : 24 of the believer's attitude towards sin as the result of Christ's having borne our sins in His body on the Tree ; R.V., " having died unto sins," the aorist or momentary tense, expressing an event in the past.¶

Note : Apollumi, to destroy, is found in the Middle Voice in some mss. in John 18 : 14, and translated " die." The most authentic mss. have *apothnēskō* (No. 2, above).

DIFFER, DIFFERING, DIFFERENT, DIFFERENCE
A. Verbs.

1. DIAPHERŌ (διαφέρω), lit., to bear through, carry different ways,

hence, to be different from, is said of the stars, 1 Cor. 15 : 41 ; of a child under age in comparison with a servant, Gal. 4 : 1 ; in Phil. 1 : 10, marg., " things that differ," for " things that are excellent." See BETTER (be)

2. MERIZŌ (μερίζω) denotes to divide (from *meros*, a part : the root *mer*— indicates distribution, or measuring out, and is seen in *meris*, a district). In 1 Cor. 7 : 34 the perfect tense of the Passive Voice is translated " there is a difference." Some take the verb with what precedes, with reference to the married brother, and translate " he has been divided." See DEAL, DISTRIBUTE, DIVIDE, GIVE, PART.

3. DIAKRINŌ (διακρίνω), lit., to separate throughout, to make a distinction, Acts 15 : 9, R.V., is translated to make to differ, in 1 Cor. 4 : 7. In Jude 22, where the Middle Voice is used, the A.V. has " making a difference ; " the R.V., adopting the alternative reading, the accusative case, has " who are in doubt," a meaning found in Matt. 21 : 21 ; Mark 11 : 23 ; Acts 10 : 20 ; Rom. 14 : 23 ; Jas. 1 : 6 ; 2 : 4. See CONTEND.

B. Nouns.

1. DIAIRESIS (διαίρεσις) lit. signifies to take asunder, from *dia*, apart, and *haireō*, to take (Eng., diæresis, i.e., distinguishing two successive vowels as separate sounds) ; it is rendered in the A.V., " diversities " in 1 Cor. 12 : 4 and 6 ; " differences " in ver. 5 ; R.V., " diversities," in each place.¶

2. DIASTOLĒ (διαστολή) signifies a setting asunder (*dia*, asunder, *stellō*, to set, place, arrange), hence, a distinction ; in Rom. 3 : 22 and 10 : 12, A.V., " difference ; " R.V., " distinction ; " in 1 Cor. 14 : 7 it is used of the distinction in musical sounds.¶

C. Adjectives.

1. DIAPHOROS (διάφορος), akin to A, No. 1, signifies varying in kind, different, diverse. It is used of spiritual gifts, Rom. 12 : 6 ; of ceremonial washings, Heb. 9 : 10 (" divers "). See DIVERS, and for its other meaning, in Heb. 1 : 4 ; 8 : 6, see EXCELLENT.¶

2. HETEROS (ἕτερος), R.V., " different," for A.V., " another," in Rom. 7 : 23 ; 2 Cor. 11 : 4 ; Gal. 1 : 6 ; cp. 1 Tim. 1 : 3 ; 6 : 3. See ANOTHER.

DIFFICULTY

MOLIS (μόλις) signifies with difficulty, hardly (from *molos*, toil). In Luke 9 : 39, it is rendered " hardly," of the difficulty in the departure of a demon. In Acts 27 : 7, 8, 16, where the A.V. has three different renderings, " scarce," " hardly," and " much work," respectively, the R.V. has " with difficulty " in each place. For its other meanings, scarce, scarcely, see Acts 14 : 18 ; Rom. 5 : 7 ; 1 Pet. 4 : 18. See HARDLY, No. 3.¶

DIG, DIG DOWN

1. ORUSSŌ (ὀρύσσω), to dig, dig up soil, dig a pit, is said of a place

for a winepress, Matt. 21 : 33 ; Mark 12 : 1 ; of digging a pit for hiding something, Matt. 25 : 18.¶

Notes : (1) *Diorussō*, lit., to dig through (*dia*, through), is translated to break through (or up) in Matt. 6 : 19, 20 ; 24 : 43 ; Luke 12 : 39. See BREAK.¶

(2) *Exorussō*, lit., to dig out, is translated to break up in Mark 2 : 4 ; to pluck out (the eyes) in Gal. 4 : 15. See BREAK, PLUCK.¶

2. SKAPTŌ (σκάπτω), primarily, to dig, by way of hollowing out, hence, denotes to dig. The root *skap* is seen in *skapanē*, a spade, *skapetos*, a ditch, *skaphē*, a boat, and in Eng., scoop, skiff, and ship (i.e., something hollowed out). The verb is found in Luke 6 : 48 ; 13 : 8 ; 16 : 3.¶

3. KATASKAPTŌ (κατασκάπτω), to dig down (*kata*, down, and No. 2), is found in Rom. 11 : 3, of altars, and in some mss. in Acts 15 : 16, " ruins," lit., ' the things dug down.' Here the best texts have *katastrephō*, to overthrow, overturn.¶

DIGNITY, DIGNITIES

DOXA (δόξα) primarily denotes an opinion, estimation, repute ; in the N.T., always good opinion, praise, honour, glory, an appearance commanding respect, magnificence, excellence, manifestation of glory ; hence, of angelic powers, in respect of their state as commanding recognition, " dignities," 2 Pet. 2 : 10 ; Jude 8. See GLORY, HONOUR, PRAISE, WORSHIP.

DILIGENCE, DILIGENT, DILIGENTLY
A. Nouns.

1. ERGASIA (ἐργασία), (*a*) lit., a working (akin to *ergon*, work), is indicative of a process, in contrast to the concrete, *ergon*, e.g., Eph. 4 : 19, lit., ' unto a working ' (R.V. marg., ' to make a trade of ') ; contrast *ergon* in ver. 12 ; (*b*) " business," Acts 19 : 25, R.V. (for A.V., " craft ") ; or gain got by work, Acts 16 : 16, 19 ; 19 : 24 ; (*c*) endeavour, pains, " diligence," Luke 12 : 58. See CRAFT, GAIN, WORK.¶

2. SPOUDĒ (σπουδή), earnestness, zeal, or sometimes the haste accompanying this, Mark 6 : 25 ; Luke 1 : 39, is translated " diligence " in Rom. 12 : 8 ; in ver. 11, A.V., " business " (R.V., " diligence ") ; in 2 Cor. 8 : 7, A.V., " diligence," R.V., " earnestness ; " both have " diligence " in Heb. 6 : 11 ; 2 Pet. 1 : 5 ; Jude 3 ; in 2 Cor. 7 : 11, 12, R.V., " earnest care," A.V., " carefulness," and " care." See CARE.¶

B. Verbs.

1. SPOUDAZŌ (σπουδάζω) has meanings corresponding to A, No. 2 ; it signifies to hasten to do a thing, to exert oneself, endeavour, give diligence ; in Gal. 2 : 10, of remembering the poor, A.V., " was forward," R.V., " was zealous ; " in Eph. 4 : 3, of keeping the unity of the Spirit, A.V. " endeavouring," R.V., " giving diligence ; " in 1 Thess. 2 : 17, of going to see friends, " endeavoured ; " in 2 Tim. 4 : 9 ; 4 : 21, " do thy diligence ; " in the following the R.V. uses the verb to give diligence :

2 Tim. 2 : 15, A.V., " study ; " Tit. 3 : 12, A.V., " be diligent ; " Heb. 4 : 11, of keeping continuous Sabbath rest, A.V., " let us labour ; " in 2 Pet. 1 : 10, of making our calling and election sure ; in 2 Pet. 1 : 15, of enabling believers to call Scripture truth to remembrance, A.V., " endeavour ; " in 2 Pet. 3 : 14, of being found in peace without fault and blameless, when the Lord comes, A.V., " be diligent." See ENDEAVOUR, FORWARD, LABOUR, STUDY, ZEALOUS.¶

2. MELETAŎ (μελετάω), signifies to care for, attend carefully (from *meletē*, care) ; in 1 Tim. 4 : 15, A.V., " meditate," R.V., " be diligent in ; " in Acts 4 : 25, " imagine " (marg., " meditate ") ; in Mark 13 : 11, the most authentic mss. have *promerimnaō*. See IMAGINE, MEDITATE.¶

C. Adjectives.

1. SPOUDAIOS (σπουδαῖος), akin to A, No. 2 and B, No. 1, primarily signifies in haste ; hence, diligent, earnest, zealous, 2 Cor. 8 : 22, A.V., " diligent," R.V., " earnest." See EARNEST, FORWARD.¶ In the Sept., Ezek. 41 : 25, " stout (planks)."¶

2. SPOUDAIOTEROS (σπουδαιότερος), the comparative degree of No. 1, 2 Cor. 8 : 22, A.V., " more diligent," R.V., " more earnest ; " in ver. 17, A.V., " more forward," R.V., " very earnest." See EARNEST ; cp. FORWARD.¶

D. Adverbs.

1. EPIMELŌS (ἐπιμελῶς), from *epi*, intensive, and an adverbial form of the impersonal verb *melei*, it is a care (cp. B, No. 2), signifies carefully, diligently, Luke 15 : 8.¶

2. PUGMĒ (πυγμῇ), the dative case of *pugmē*, a fist, lit. means ' with the fist ' (one hand being rubbed with the clenched fist of the other), a metaphorical expression for thoroughly, in contrast to what is superficial ; Mark 7 : 3, R.V. and A.V. marg., " diligently " (A.V., text, " oft "). It also signified boxing (not in the N.T.) ; cp. *puktēs* and *pugmachos*, a boxer (Lat., *pugnus* and *pugno* ; Eng., pugilist).¶ In the Sept., Ex. 21 : 18 ; Is. 58 : 4.¶

3. SPOUDAIŌS (σπουδαίως), speedily, earnestly, diligently (cp. the corresponding noun, verb and adjective above), is translated " earnestly " in the R.V. of Luke 7 : 4 (A.V., " instantly ") ; " diligently " in Tit. 3 : 13. See INSTANTLY.

4. SPOUDAIOTERŌS (σπουδαιοτέρως), the comparative degree of No. 3, " more diligently," is used in Phil. 2 : 28, R.V., " the more diligently " (A.V., " the more carefully "). See CAREFULLY.¶

Notes : (1) Some mss. have the neuter of the comparative adjective *spoudaioteron* in 2 Tim. 1 : 17. The most authentic texts have the adverb, No. 4.

(2) *Akribōs* (ἀκριβῶς) means accurately, exactly. The A.V. translates it " diligently " in Matt. 2 : 8 and Acts 18 : 25 ; " perfectly " in 1 Thess. 5 : 2 (cp. Luke 1 : 3). See ACCURATELY, CAREFUL, CIRCUMSPECTLY, PERFECTLY.

DIMINISHING

HÊTTÊMA (ἥττημα) : see DEFECT.

DINE, DINNER
A. Verb.

ARISTAÖ (ἀριστάω), primarily, to breakfast (see B), was later used also with the meaning to dine, e.g., Luke 11 : 37 ; in John 21 : 12, 15, R.V., " break your fast," and " had broken their fast," for A.V., " dine ; " obviously there it was the first meal in the day.¶ In the Sept., Gen. 43 : 25 ; 1 Sam. 14 : 24 ; 1 Chron. 13 : 7.¶

B. Noun.

ARISTON (ἄριστον), primarily, the first food, taken early in the morning before work ; the meal in the Pharisee's house, in Luke 11 : 37, was a breakfast or early meal (see R.V., marg.) ; the dinner was called *deipnon*. Later the breakfast was called *akratisma* (not in N.T.), and dinner, *ariston*, as in Matt. 22 : 4 ; Luke 11 : 38 ; 14 : 12.¶

DIP, DIPPED, DIPPETH

1. BAPTÖ (βάπτω), to immerse, dip (derived from a root signifying deep), also signified to dye, which is suggested in Rev. 19 : 13, of the Lord's garment " dipped (i.e., dyed) in blood " (R.V., " sprinkled " translates the verb *rhantizō* : see SPRINKLED. It is elsewhere translated to dip, Luke 16 : 24 ; John 13 : 26. Cp. the longer form *baptizō* (primarily a frequentative form). See BAPTIZE.¶

2. EMBAPTÖ (ἐμβάπτω), *en*, in, and No. 1, to dip into, is used of the act of Judas in dipping his hand with that of Christ in the dish, Matt. 26 : 23 ; Mark 14 : 20.¶

DIRECT

KATEUTHUNÖ (κατευθύνω), to make straight (*kata*, down, intensive, *euthus*, straight, *euthunō*, to straighten), is translated " guide " in Luke 1 : 79, of the Lord's guidance of the feet of His people ; " direct," in 1 Thess. 3 : 11, of His directing the way of His servants ; in 2 Thess. 3 : 5, of His directing the hearts of His saints into the love of God. See GUIDE.¶

DISALLOW

APODOKIMAZÖ (ἀποδοκιμάζω), to reject as the result of disapproval (*apo*, away from, *dokimazō*, to approve), is always translated to reject, except in the A.V. of 1 Pet. 2 : 4 and 7. See REJECT.

DISANNUL, DISANNULLING
A. Verbs.

1. ATHETEÖ (ἀθετέω) signifies to put as of no value (*a*, negative, *theton*, what is placed, from *tithēmi*, to put, place) ; hence, (*a*) to act

towards anything as though it were annulled ; e.g., to deprive a law of its force by opinions or acts contrary to it, Gal. 3 : 15, A.V., " disannulleth," R.V., " maketh void ; " (b) to thwart the efficacy of anything, to nullify, to frustrate it, Luke 7 : 30, " rejected ; " 1 Cor. 1 : 19, " will I reject ; " to make void, Gal. 2 : 21 ; to set at nought, Jude 8, R.V. (A.V., " despised ") ; the parallel passage, in 2 Pet. 2 : 10, has *kataphroneō*. In Mark 6 : 26, the thought is that of breaking faith with. See DESPISE, A, Note (1).

2. AKUROŌ (ἀκυρόω), to deprive of authority (*a*, negative, *kuros*, force, authority; cp. *kurios*, a lord, *kuroō*, to strengthen), hence, to make of none effect, Matt. 15 : 6; Mark 7 : 13, with reference to the commandment or word of God, R.V., to make void, is translated " disannul " in Gal. 3 : 17, of the inability of the Law to deprive of force God's covenant with Abraham. This verb stresses the effect of the act, while No. 1 stresses the attitude of the rejector. See VOID.¶

B. Noun.

ATHETĒSIS (ἀθέτησις), akin to A, No. 1, a setting aside, abolition, is translated " disannulling " in Heb. 7 : 18, with reference to a command-ment ; in 9 : 26 " to put away," with reference to sin, lit., ' for a putting away.' See PUTTING, *Note*.¶

DISBELIEVE

APISTEŌ (ἀπιστέω), to be unbelieving (*a*, negative, *pistis*, faith ; cp. *apistos*, unbelieving), is translated " believed not," etc. in the A.V. (except in 1 Pet. 2 : 7, " be disobedient ") ; " disbelieve " (or " dis-believed ") in the R.V., in Mark 16 : 11, 16 ; Luke 24 : 11, 41 ; Acts 28 : 24 ; " disbelieve " is the best rendering, implying that the unbeliever has had a full opportunity of believing and has rejected it ; some mss. have *apeitheō*, to be disobedient,in 1 Pet. 2 : 7 ; Rom. 3 : 3, R.V., " were without faith ; " 2 Tim. 2 : 13, R.V., " are faithless." Cp. DISOBEDIENT, C. See BELIEVE.¶

DISCERN, DISCERNER, DISCERNMENT
A. Verbs.

1. ANAKRINŌ (ἀνακρίνω), to distinguish, or separate out so as to investigate (*krinō*) by looking throughout (*ana*, intensive) objects or particulars, hence signifies to examine, scrutinize, question, to hold a preliminary judicial examination preceding the trial proper (this first examination, implying more to follow, is often present in the non-legal uses of the word), e.g., Luke 23 : 14 ; figuratively, in 1 Cor. 4 : 3 ; it is said of searching the Scriptures in Acts 17 : 11 ; of discerning or deter-mining the excellence or defects of a person or thing, e.g., 1 Cor. 2 : 14, A.V., " discerned ;" R.V., " judged ; " in 1 Cor. 10 : 27, " asking (no) question " (i.e., not raising the question as to whether the meat is the residue from an idolatrous sacrifice). Except in Luke 23 : 14, this word is found only in Acts and 1 Cor. See EXAMINE, JUDGE.

2. DIAKRINŌ (διακρίνω) signifies to separate, discriminate ; then, to learn by discriminating, to determine, decide. It is translated " discern " in Matt. 16 : 3, of discriminating between the varying conditions of the sky (see *dokimazō*, No. 3, below, in Luke 12 : 56), and in 1 Cor. 11 : 29, with reference to partaking of the bread and the cup of the Lord's Supper unworthily, by not discerning or discriminating what they represent ; in ver. 31, the R.V. has " discerned," for the A.V., " would judge," of trying oneself, discerning one's condition, and so judging any evil before the Lord ; in 14 : 29, regarding oral testimony in a gathering of believers, it is used of discerning what is of the Holy Spirit, R.V., " discern " (A.V., " judge "). See CONTEND, DECIDE, DIFFER, etc.

3. DOKIMAZŌ (δοκιμάζω) signifies to test, prove, scrutinize, so as to decide. It is translated " discern " in the A.V. of Luke 12 : 56 ; R.V., " interpret " (marg., " prove "). See APPROVE.

B. Noun.

DIAKRISIS (διάκρισις), cp. A, No. 2, a distinguishing, a clear discrimination, discerning, judging, is translated " discernings " in 1 Cor. 12 : 10, of discerning spirits, judging by evidence whether they are evil or of God. In Heb. 5 : 14 the phrase consisting of *pros*, with this noun, lit., ' towards a discerning,' is translated " to discern," said of those who are capable of discriminating between good and evil. In Rom. 14 : 1 the word has its other sense of decision or judgment, and the phrase " doubtful disputations " is, lit., ' judgments of reasonings ' (marg., " not for decisions of doubts," i.e., not to act as a judge of the weak brother's scruples). See DECISION, B, No. 2.¶

Note : For " discernment," Phil. 1 : 19, see JUDGMENT, *Note* (4).

C. Adjective.

KRITIKOS (κριτικός) signifies that which relates to judging (*krinō*, to judge), fit for, or skilled in, judging (Eng., critical), found in Heb. 4 : 12, of the Word of God as " quick to discern the thoughts and intents of the heart," (lit., ' critical of etc.'), i.e., discriminating and passing judgment on the thoughts and feelings.¶

DISCHARGED

KATARGEŌ (καταργέω) means to reduce to inactivity. " Discharged " is the R.V. translation of the word in Rom. 7 : 2 and 6 (A.V., " is loosed," and " are delivered "). In ver. 2 the meaning is that the death of a woman's first husband makes void her status as a wife in the eyes of the Law ; she is therefore discharged from the prohibition against re-marrying ; the prohibition is rendered ineffective in her case. So, in ver. 6, with the believer in relation to the Law, he has been made dead to the Law as a means of justification and life. It is not the Law that has died (A.V.), but the believer (see the R.V.), who has been discharged, through being put to death, as to the old nature, in identification with the Death of Christ, that he might have life in Christ. See ABOLISH.

DISCIPLE
A. Nouns.

1. MATHĒTĒS (μαθητής), lit., a learner (from *manthanō*, to learn, from a root *math*—, indicating thought accompanied by endeavour), in contrast to *didaskalos*, a teacher ; hence it denotes one who follows one's teaching, as the disciples of John, Matt. 9 : 14 ; of the Pharisees, Matt. 22 : 16 ; of Moses, John 9 : 28 ; it is used of the disciples of Jesus (*a*) in a wide sense, of Jews who became His adherents, John 6 : 66 ; Luke 6 : 17, some being secretly so, John 19 : 38 ; (*b*) especially of the twelve Apostles, Matt. 10 : 1 ; Luke 22 : 11, e.g. ; (*c*) of all who manifest that they are His disciples by abiding in His Word, John 8 : 31 ; cp. 13 : 35 ; 15 : 8 ; (*d*) in the Acts, of those who believed upon Him and confessed Him, 6 : 1, 2, 7 ; 14 : 20, 22, 28 ; 15 : 10 ; 19 : 1 etc.

A disciple was not only a pupil, but an adherent ; hence they are spoken of as imitators of their teacher ; cp. John 8 : 31 ; 15 : 8.

2. MATHĒTRIA (μαθήτρια), a female disciple, is said of Tabitha, Acts. 9 : 36.¶

3. SUMMATHĒTĒS (συμμαθητής) means a fellow-disciple (*sun*, with, and No. 1), John 11 : 16.¶

Note : In Acts 1 : 15, the R.V. translates the mss. which have *adelphōn*, " brethren ; " in 20 : 7, R.V., " we," for A.V., " disciples."

B. Verb.

MATHĒTEUŌ (μαθητεύω) is used in the Active Voice, intransitively, in some mss., in Matt. 27 : 57, in the sense of being the disciple of a person ; here, however, the best mss. have the Passive Voice, lit., ' had been made a disciple,' as in Matt. 13 : 52, R.V., " who hath been made a disciple." It is used in this transitive sense in the Active Voice in 28 : 19 and Acts 14 : 21.¶

DISCIPLINE

SŌPHRONISMOS (σωφρονισμός), from *sōphrōn*, lit., saving the mind, from *saos*, contracted to *sōs*, safe (cp. *sōzō*, to save), *phrēn*, the mind, primarily, an admonishing or calling to soundness of mind, or to self-control, is used in 2 Tim. 1 : 7, A.V., " a sound mind ; " R.V., " discipline." Cp. *sōphroneō* (to be of sound mind), *sōphronizō* (to admonish), *sōphronōs* (soberly), and *sōphrōn*, of sound mind. See MIND.¶ Cp. CHASTISEMENT.

DISCOURAGE (-D)

ATHUMEŌ (ἀθυμέω), to be disheartened, dispirited, discouraged (*a*, negative, *thumos*, spirit, courage, from the root *thu*, found in *thuō*, to rush, denoting feeling, passion ; hence Eng., fume), is found in Col. 3 : 21.¶

DISCOURSE

DIALEGOMAI (διαλέγομαι) primarily denotes to ponder, resolve in one's mind (*dia*, through, *legō*, to say) ; then, to converse, dispute, discuss, discourse with; most frequently, to reason or dispute with. In Heb. 12 : 5 the R.V., "reasoneth with" is to be preferred to the A.V., "speaketh unto." The A.V. translates it "preached," in Acts 20 : 7 and 9; this the R.V. corrects to "discoursed," lit., 'dialogued,' i.e., not by way of a sermon, but by a discourse of a more conversational character. See DISPUTE, PREACH, REASON, SPEAK. In the Sept., Ex. 6 : 27; Judg. 8 : 1; Is. 63 : 1.

DISCOVER

Two verbs are translated by the verb to discover, in the A.V. The R.V. translates differently in each case.

1. ANAPHAINŌ (ἀναφαίνω) : see APPEAR, A, No. 3.

2. KATANOEŌ (κατανοέω), to perceive distinctly, discern clearly, descry, is translated "discovered" in Acts 27 : 39, A.V., of finding a bay with a creek (R.V., "perceived"). See BEHOLD.

DISCREET, DISCREETLY
A. Adjective.

SŌPHRŌN (σώφρων), of sound mind, self-controlled (for the derivation, see DISCIPLINE), is translated "sober-minded," in its four occurrences in the R.V., 1 Tim. 3 : 2 (A.V., "sober"); Tit. 1 : 8 (A.V., ditto); 2 : 2 (A.V., "temperate"); 2 : 5 (A.V., "discreet"). See SOBER, TEMPERATE.¶

B. Adverb.

NOUNECHŌS (νουνεχῶς), lit., mind-possessing (nous, mind, understanding, echō, to have), hence denotes discreetly, sensibly, prudently. Mark 12 : 34.¶

DISEASE, DISEASED (BE)
A. Nouns.

1. ASTHENEIA (ἀσθένεια), lit., lacking strength (a, negative, sthenos, strength), weakness, infirmity, is translated "diseases" in Matt. 8 : 17, R.V., for A.V., "sicknesses," and in Acts 28 : 9. Its usual rendering is "infirmity" or "infirmities;" "sickness," in John 11 : 4. Cp. B, No. 1. See INFIRMITY, SICKNESS, WEAKNESS.

2. MALAKIA (μαλακία) primarily denotes softness (cp. malakos, soft, Matt. 11 : 8 etc.); hence, debility, disease. It is found in Matthew only, 4 : 23; 9 : 35; 10 : 1.¶ It is frequent in the Sept., e.g., Gen. 42 : 4; 44 : 29; Deut. 7 : 15; 28 : 61; Is. 38 : 9; 53 : 3.

3. NOSOS (νόσος), akin to Lat. nocere, to injure (Eng., nosology), is the regular word for disease, sickness, Matt. 4 : 23; 8 : 17; 9 : 35; 10 : 1, R.V., "disease," A.V., "sickness;" in Matt. 4 : 24; Mark 1 : 34; Luke 4 : 40; 6 : 17; 9 : 1; Acts 19 : 12, A.V. and R.V. render it "diseases." In Luke 7 : 21, A.V. has "infirmities." The most authentic mss. omit the word in Mark 3 : 15. See SICKNESS.¶

4. NOSĒMA (νόσημα), an alternative form of No. 3, is found in some mss. in John 5 : 4.¶ Cp. *noseō*, to dote about, have a diseased craving for, 1 Tim. 6 : 4.¶

B. Verbs.

1. ASTHENEŌ (ἀσθενέω), akin to A, No. 1, to lack strength, to be weak, sick, is translated "were diseased" in John 6 : 2, A.V. (R.V., "were sick"). See IMPOTENT, SICK, WEAK.

2. ECHŌ KAKŌS (ἔχω κακῶς), lit., to have badly, i.e., to be ill or in an evil case, is used in Matt. 14 : 35 (A.V., "were diseased," R.V., "were sick") ; so in Mark 1 : 32 ; Luke 7 : 2. See SICK.¶

DISFIGURE

APHANIZŌ (ἀφανίζω) primarily means to cause to disappear, hence (*a*) to make unsightly, to disfigure, as of the face, Matt. 6 : 16 ; (*b*) to cause to vanish away, consume, Matt. 6 : 19, 20 ; (*c*) in the Passive Voice, to perish, Acts 13 : 41, or to vanish away, Jas. 4 : 14. See CONSUME.¶

DISH

TRUBLION (τρύβλιον) denotes a bowl, somewhat deep, Matt. 26 : 23 ; Mark 14 : 20 ; among the Greeks it was a measure in medical prescriptions.¶

DISHONESTY

AISCHUNĒ (αἰσχύνη), shame, so the R.V. in 2 Cor. 4 : 2 (for A.V., "dishonesty"), is elsewhere rendered "shame," Luke 14 : 9 ; Phil. 3 : 19 ; Heb. 12 : 2 ; Jude 13 ; Rev. 3 : 18. See SHAME.¶

DISHONOUR
A. Noun.

ATIMIA (ἀτιμία), from *a*, negative, *timē*, honour, denotes dishonour, ignominy, disgrace, in Rom. 1 : 26, "vile passions" (R.V.), lit., 'passions of dishonour ;' in Rom. 9 : 21, "dishonour," of vessels designed for meaner household purposes (in contrast to *timē*, honour, as in 2 Tim. 2 : 20) ; in 1 Cor. 11 : 14, said of long hair, if worn by men, R.V., "dishonour," for A.V., "shame," in contrast to *doxa*, glory, ver. 15 ; so in 1 Cor. 15 : 43, of the "sowing" of the natural body, and in 2 Cor. 6 : 8, of the Apostle Paul's ministry. In 2 Cor. 11 : 21 he uses it in self-disparagement, A.V., "reproach," R.V., "disparagement." See DISPARAGEMENT, REPROACH, SHAME, VILE.¶

B. Adjective.

ATIMOS (ἄτιμος), akin to A : see DESPISE, B.

C. Verbs.

1. ATIMAZŌ (ἀτιμάζω) akin to A, signifies to dishonour, treat shamefully, insult, whether in word, John 8 : 49, or deed, Mark 12 : 4 ; Luke 20 : 11, R.V., "handled (him) shamefully," (A.V. "entreated . . .

shamefully ") ; Rom. 1 : 24 ; 2 : 23, " dishonourest ; " Jas. 2 : 6, R.V.,
" ye have dishonoured (the poor)," (A.V., " despised ") ; in the Passive
Voice, to suffer dishonour, Acts 5 : 41 (A.V., " suffer shame "). See
DESPISE, A, Note (2).¶

Note : Atimaō is found in some mss. in Mark 12 : 4.

2. KATAISCHUNŌ (καταισχύνω) : see ASHAMED, No. 3.

DISMISS (-ED)

APOLUŌ (ἀπολύω), lit., to loose from (*apo*, from, *luō*, to loose), is
translated " dismiss " in Acts 15 : 30, 33, R.V. (A.V., " let go ") and
19 : 41. See DEPART, DIVORCE, FORGIVE, GO, LIBERTY, LOOSE, PUT,
No. 16, RELEASE, SEND.

DISOBEDIENCE, DISOBEDIENT
A. Nouns.

1. APEITHEIA (ἀπείθεια), lit., the condition of being unpersuadable
(*a*, negative, *peithō*, to persuade), denotes obstinacy, obstinate rejection
of the will of God ; hence, " disobedience ; " Eph. 2 : 2 ; 5 : 6 ; Col. 3 : 6,
and in the R.V. of Rom. 11 : 30, 32 and Heb. 4 : 6, 11 (for A.V.,
" unbelief "), speaking of Israel, past and present. See UNBELIEF.¶

2. PARAKOĒ (παρακοή), primarily, hearing amiss (*para*, aside,
akouō, to hear), hence signifies a refusal to hear ; hence, an act of
disobedience, Rom. 5 : 19 ; 2 Cor. 10 : 6 ; Heb. 2 : 2. It is broadly to
be distinguished from No. 1, as an act from a condition, though *parakoē*
itself is the effect, in transgression, of the condition of failing or refusing
to hear. Carelessness in attitude is the precursor of actual disobedience.
In the O.T. disobedience is frequently described as a refusing to hear,
e.g., Jer. 11 : 10 ; 35 : 17 ; cp. Acts 7 : 57. See Trench, Syn. § lxvi.¶

B. Adjective.

APEITHĒS (ἀπειθής), akin to A, No. 1, signifies unwilling to be
persuaded, spurning belief, disobedient, Luke 1 : 17 ; Acts 26 : 19 ;
Rom. 1 : 30 ; 2 Tim. 3 : 2 ; Tit. 1 : 16 ; 3 : 3.¶

Note : In 1 Tim. 1 : 9 *anupotaktos*, insubordinate, unsubjected (*a*,
negative, *n*, euphonic, *hupo*, under, *tassō*, to order), is translated
" disobedient " in the A.V. ; the R.V. has " unruly," as in Tit. 1 : 6, 10 ;
in Heb. 2 : 8, " not subject " (R.V.), " not put under " (A.V.). See
PUT, UNRULY.¶

C. Verb.

APEITHEŌ (ἀπειθέω), akin to A, No. 1, and B, to refuse to be
persuaded, to refuse belief, to be disobedient, is translated " disobedient,"
or by the verb to be disobedient, in the R.V. of Acts 14 : 2 (A.V.,
" unbelieving "), and 19 : 9 (A.V., " believed not ") ; it is absent from
the most authentic mss. in Acts 17 : 5 ; in John 3 : 36 " obeyeth not,"
R.V. (A.V., " believeth not ") ; in Rom. 2 : 8 " obey not ; " in 10 : 21,
" disobedient ; " in 11 : 30, 31, " were disobedient " (A.V., " have not

believed ") ; so in 15 : 31 ; Heb. 3 : 18 ; 11 : 31 ; in 1 Pet. 2 : 8,
" disobedient ; " so in 3 : 20 ; in 3 : 1 and 4 : 17, " obey not." In 2 : 7
the best mss. have *apisteō*, to disbelieve. See OBEY, B, No. 4, UN-
BELIEVING.¶

DISORDERLY
A. Adjective.

ATAKTOS (ἄτακτος) signifies not keeping order (*a*, negative, *tassō*,
to put in order, arrange) ; it was especially a military term, denoting
not keeping rank, insubordinate ; it is used in 1 Thess. 5 : 14, describing
certain church members who manifested an insubordinate spirit, whether
by excitability or officiousness or idleness. See UNRULY.¶

B. Adverb.

ATAKTŌS (ἀτακτῶς) signifies disorderly, with slackness (like soldiers
not keeping rank), 2 Thess. 3 : 6 ; in ver. 11 it is said of those in the
church who refused to work, and became busybodies (cp. 1 Tim. 5 : 13).¶

C. Verb.

ATAKTEŌ (ἀτακτέω) signifies to be out of rank, out of one's place,
undisciplined, to behave disorderly : in the military sense, to break rank ;
negatively in 2 Thess. 3 : 7, of the example set by the Apostle and his
fellow-missionaries, in working for their bread while they were at
Thessalonica so as not to burden the saints. See BEHAVE.¶

DISPARAGEMENT
For this R.V. translation of *atimia* in 2 Cor. 11 : 21, see DISHONOUR, A.

DISPENSATION
OIKONOMIA (οἰκονομία) primarily signifies the management of a
household or of household affairs (*oikos*, a house, *nomos*, a law) ; then the
management or administration of the property of others, and so a
stewardship, Luke 16 : 2, 3, 4 ; elsewhere only in the Epistles of Paul,
who applies it (*a*) to the responsibility entrusted to him of preaching the
Gospel, 1 Cor. 9 : 17 (R.V., " stewardship," A.V., " dispensation ") ;
(*b*) to the stewardship committed to him " to fulfil the Word of God,"
the fulfilment being the unfolding of the completion of the Divinely
arranged and imparted cycle of truths which are consummated in the
truth relating to the Church as the Body of Christ, Col. 1 : 25 (R.V. and
A.V., " dispensation ") ; so in Eph. 3 : 2, of the grace of God given him
as a stewardship (" dispensation ") in regard to the same " mystery " ;
(*c*) in Eph. 1 : 10 and 3 : 9, it is used of the arrangement or administration
by God, by which in " the fulness of the times " (or seasons) God will
sum up all things in the heavens and on earth in Christ. In Eph. 3 : 9
some mss. have *koinōnia*, " fellowship," for *oikonomia*, " dispensation."
In 1 Tim. 1 : 4 *oikonomia* may mean either a stewardship in the sense of
(*a*) above, or a dispensation in the sense of (*c*). The reading *oikodomia*,

" edifying," in some mss., is not to be accepted. See Stewardship.¶

Note : A dispensation is not a period or epoch (a common, but erroneous, use of the word), but a mode of dealing, an arrangement or administration of affairs. Cp. *oikonomos*, a steward, and *oikonomeō*, to be a steward.

DISPERSE, DISPERSION
A. Verbs.

1. DIALUŌ (διαλύω), to dissolve, is used in Acts 5 : 36 of the breaking up and dispersion of a company of men, R.V., " dispersed," A.V., " scattered." See Scatter.¶

2. SKORPIZŌ (σκορπίζω), to scatter (probably from a root, *skarp-*, signifying to cut asunder, akin to *skorpios*, a scorpion), is used in Matt. 12 : 30 ; Luke 11 : 23 ; John 10 : 12 ; 16 : 32 ; in the R.V. of 2 Cor. 9 : 9, " scattered abroad " (A.V., " he hath dispersed abroad "), of one who liberally dispenses benefits. See Scatter.¶

3. DIASKORPIZŌ (διασκορπίζω), *dia*, through, and No. 2, signifies to scatter abroad, in Matt. 26 : 31 ; Mark 14 : 27, metaphorically of sheep ; in Luke 1 : 51, of the proud ; in John 11 : 52, of the scattering of the children of God ; in Acts 5 : 37, of the followers of Judas of Galilee (A.V., " were dispersed ") ; cp. No. 1, re ver. 36 ; of scattering grain by winnowing, Matt. 25 : 24, 26 ; in Luke 15 : 13 and 16 : 1, it signifies to waste. See Scatter, Strawed, Waste.¶

4. DIASPEIRŌ (διασπείρω), to scatter abroad (*dia*, through, *speirō*, to sow), is used in Acts 8 : 1, 4 ; 11 : 19.¶
B. Noun.

DIASPORA (διασπορά), akin to A, No. 4, a scattering, a dispersion, was used of the Jews who from time to time had been scattered among the Gentiles, John 7 : 35 ; later with reference to Jews, so scattered, who had professed, or actually embraced, the Christian faith, " the Dispersion," Jas. 1 : 1, R.V. ; especially of believers who were converts from Judaism and scattered throughout certain districts, " sojourners of the Dispersion," 1 Pet. 1 : 1, R.V.¶ In the Sept., of Israelites, scattered and exiled, e.g., Deut. 28 : 25 ; 30 : 4 ; Neh. 1 : 9.

DISPLEASED

1. AGANAKTEŌ (ἀγανακτέω), from *agan*, much, and *achomai*, to grieve, primarily meant to feel a violent irritation, physically ; it was used, too, of the fermenting of wine ; hence, metaphorically, to show signs of grief, to be displeased, to be grieved, vexed ; it is translated " sore displeased " in Matt. 21 : 15, A.V. ; " much displeased," in Mark 10 : 14, 41 ; the R.V. always renders it to be moved with, or to have, indignation, as the A.V. elsewhere, Matt. 20 : 24 ; 26 : 8 ; Mark 14 : 4 ; Luke 13 : 14. See Indignation.¶

2. PROSOCHTHIZŌ (προσοχθίζω), to be wroth or displeased with

(*pros*, toward, or with, *ochtheō*, to be sorely vexed), is used in Heb. 3 : 10, 17 (A.V., " grieved ; " R.V., " displeased "). " Grieved " does not adequately express the righteous anger of God intimated in the passage. See GRIEVE.¶

3. THUMOMACHEŌ (θυμομαχέω), lit., to fight with great animosity (*thumos*, passior, *machomai*, to fight), hence, to be very angry, to be highly displeased, is said of Herod's displeasure with the Tyrians and Sidonians, Acts 12 : 20.¶

DISPOSED (to be)

1. BOULOMAI (βούλομαι), to wish, to purpose, to will deliberately, indicating a predisposition acting through the deliberate will, is trans- lated " was disposed " in Acts 18 : 27, A.V. (R.V., " was minded "). It expresses more strongly than *thelō* (No. 2) the deliberate exercise of the will. See DESIRE, B, No. 7.

2. THELŌ (θέλω) means to will ; it signifies more especially the natural impulse or volition, and indicates a less formal or deliberate purpose than No. 1. It is translated " are disposed " in 1 Cor. 10 : 27. See DESIRE, B, No. 6.

DISPOSITION

DIATAGĒ (διαταγή), an ordinance, e.g., Rom. 13 : 2 (cp. *diatassō*, to appoint, ordain), is rendered " disposition " in Acts 7 : 53 ; R.V., " as it (the law) was ordained by angels " (marg., " as the ordinance of angels ; " lit., ' unto ordinances of angels '). Angels are mentioned in connection with the giving of the Law of Moses in Deut. 33 : 2. In Gal. 3 : 19 and Heb. 2 : 2 the purpose of the reference to them is to show the superiority of the Gospel to the Law. In Acts 7 : 53 Stephen mentions the angels to stress the majesty of the Law. See ORDAIN, ORDINANCE.¶

DISPUTATION

1. ZĒTĒSIS (ζήτησις) denotes, firstly, a seeking (*zēteō*, to seek), then, a debate, dispute, questioning, Acts 15 : 2, 7 (some texts have *suzētēsis*, reasoning, in both verses), R.V., " questioning," for A.V., " disputation " and " disputing ; " for John 3 : 25 ; Acts 25 : 20 ; 1 Tim. 1 : 4 ; 6 : 4 ; 2 Tim. 2 : 23 ; Tit. 3 : 9, see QUESTION, QUESTIONING.¶

2. DIALOGISMOS (διαλογισμός) is translated " disputations " in Rom. 14 : 1. See below.

DISPUTE, DISPUTER, DISPUTING
A. Nouns.

1. DIALOGISMOS (διαλογισμός) denotes, primarily, an inward reasoning, an opinion (*dia*, through, suggesting separation, *logismos*, a reasoning), e.g., Luke 2 : 35 ; 5 : 22 ; 6 : 8 ; then, a deliberating, ques- tioning, Luke 24 : 38 ; (more strongly) a disputing, Phil. 2 : 14 ; 1 Tim. 2 : 8 (A.V., " doubtings ") ; in Rom. 14 : 1, " disputations ; " marg., " (not

for decisions) of doubts " (lit., ' not unto discussions of doubts,' which is perhaps a suitable rendering). Cp. *dialogizomai*, to reason. See DOUBTING, IMAGINATION, REASONING, THOUGHT.

2. LOGOMACHIA (λογομαχία) denotes a dispute about words (*logos*, a word, *machē*, a fight), or about trivial things, 1 Tim. 6 : 4, R.V., " disputes," A.V., " strifes." See STRIFE.¶

3. DIAPARATRIBĒ (διαπαρατριβή) denotes a constant or incessant wrangling (*dia*, through, *para*, beside, *tribō*, to wear out, suggesting the attrition or wearing effect of contention), 1 Tim. 6 : 5, R.V., " wranglings," A.V., " perverse disputings." Some mss. have the word *paradiatribē*, in the opposite order of the prefixed prepositions. See WRANGLING.¶

4. ANTILOGIA (ἀντιλογία) denotes a gainsaying, contradiction (*anti*, against, *legō*, to speak), Heb. 6 : 16 (A.V., " strife," R.V., " dispute,") ; 7 : 7, a gainsaying (R.V., " dispute ; " A.V., " contradiction ") ; 12 : 3 (R.V., " gainsaying ; " A.V., " contradiction ") ; Jude 11 (" gainsaying "). See CONTRADICTION, B.¶

5. SUZĒTĒTĒS (συζητητής), from *sun*, with, *zēteō*, to seek, denotes a disputer, 1 Cor. 1 : 20, where the reference is especially to a learned disputant, a sophist.¶

B. Verbs.

1. DIALEGOMAI (διαλέγομαι), akin to A, No. 1, primarily signifies to think different things with oneself, to ponder ; then, with other persons, to converse, argue, dispute ; it is translated to dispute in Mark 9 : 34 (for ver. 33 see No. 2), the R.V. and A.V. " had disputed " is somewhat unsuitable here, for the delinquency was not that they had wrangled, but that they had reasoned upon the subject at all ; in Acts 17 : 17, A.V. (R.V., " reasoned," as in the A.V. of 18 : 4, 19) ; in 19 : 8, 9 (R.V., " reasoning ") ; in 24 : 12, " disputing ; " in Jude 9, " disputed." See DISCOURSE.

2. DIALOGIZOMAI (διαλογίζομαι), akin to A, No. 1, to bring together different reasons, to reckon them up, to reason, discuss, in Mark 9 : 33 is translated " ye disputed among yourselves," A.V. ; R.V., " were reasoning." See CAST, No. 15, REASON.

3. SUZĒTEŌ (συζητέω), akin to A, No. 5, lit., to seek or examine together, signifies to discuss, but is translated to dispute in Acts 6 : 9, and 9 : 29 ; elsewhere only in Mark and Luke. See INQUIRE, QUESTION, REASON.

DISREPUTE

APELEGMOS (ἀπελεγμός), from *apo*, from, and *elenchō*, to refute, denotes censure, repudiation (of something shown to be worthless), hence, contempt, " disrepute," Acts 19 : 27, R.V., " (come into) disrepute," for A.V., " (to be) set at nought." It is akin to *apelenchō*, to convict, refute (not in the N.T.), *elenchō*, to convict, *elenxis*, rebuke, and *elegmos*, reproof. See NOUGHT.¶

For DISSEMBLE see DISSIMULATION

DISSENSION

STASIS (στάσις), akin to *histēmi*, to stand, denotes (*a*) a standing, stability, Heb. 9 : 8, " (while as the first tabernacle) is yet standing ; " (*b*) an insurrection, uproar, Mark 15 : 7 ; Luke 23 : 19, 25 ; Acts 19 : 40 ; 24 : 5 ; (*c*) a dissension, Acts 15 : 2 ; 23 : 7, 10. See INSURRECTION, SEDITION, STANDING, UPROAR.¶

DISSIMULATION, DISSEMBLE
A. Noun.

HUPOKRISIS (ὑπόκρισις), primarily, a reply, came to mean the acting of a stage-player, because such answered one another in dialogue ; hence the meaning dissembling or pretence. It is translated " dissimulation " in Gal. 2 : 13 (see B). See HYPOCRISY.

B. Verb.

SUNUPOKRINOMAI (συνυποκρίνομαι), *sun*, with, *hupokrinomai*, akin to A, to join in acting the hypocrite, in pretending to act from one motive, whereas another motive really inspires the act. So in Gal. 2 : 13, Peter with other believing Jews, in separating from believing Gentiles at Antioch, pretended that the motive was loyalty to the Law of Moses, whereas really it was fear of the Judaizers.¶

C. Adjective.

ANUPOKRITOS (ἀνυπόκριτος), from *a*, negative, *n*, euphonic, and an adjectival form corresponding to A, signifies unfeigned ; it is said of love, 2 Cor. 6 : 6 ; 1 Pet. 1 : 22 ; Rom. 12 : 9, A.V., " without dissimulation," R.V., " without hypocrisy ; " of faith, 1 Tim. 1 : 5 ; 2 Tim. 1 : 5, " unfeigned ; " of the wisdom that is from above, Jas. 3 : 17, " without hypocrisy." See HYPOCRISY.¶

DISSOLVE

1. LUŌ (λύω), to loose, is used of the future demolition of the elements or heavenly bodies, 2 Pet. 3 : 10, 11, 12 ; in ver. 10, A.V., " shall melt," R.V., " shall be dissolved ; " in verses 11, 12, A.V. and R.V., " dissolved." See BREAK.

2. KATALUŌ (καταλύω) : see DESTROY, A, No. 5.

For DISTINCTION (*diastolē*) see DIFFERENCE

DISTRACTION (without)

APERISPASTŌS (ἀπερισπάστως), from *a*, negative, *perispaō*, to draw around, draw away, distract (for which see CUMBER), is found in 1 Cor. 7 : 35.¶

DISTRESS, DISTRESSED
A. Nouns.

1. ANANKĒ (ἀνάγκη) denotes (a) a necessity, imposed whether by external circumstances, e.g., Luke 23 : 17, or inward pressure, e.g., 1 Cor. 9 : 16 ; (b) straits, distress, Luke 21 : 23 (in ver. 25, " distress " translates No. 3) ; 1 Cor. 7 : 26 ; 1 Thess. 3 : 7 ; the last two refer to the lack of material things. See NECESSARY, NECESSITY, NEEDS.

2. STENOCHŌRIA (στενοχωρία) : see ANGUISH.

3. SUNOCHĒ (συνοχή) : see ANGUISH.

4. THLIPSIS (θλίψις) : see AFFLICTION, B, No. 5.

B. Verbs.

1. BASANIZŌ (βασανίζω), properly signifies to test by rubbing on the touchstone (basanos, a touchstone), then, to question by applying torture ; hence to vex, torment ; in the Passive Voice, to be harassed, distressed ; it is said of men struggling in a boat against wind and waves, Matt. 14 : 24, R.V., " distressed " (A.V., " tossed ") ; Mark 6 : 48, R.V., " distressed " (A.V., " toiling "). See PAIN, TOIL, TORMENT, VEX.

2. SKULLŌ (σκύλλω) primarily signifies to skin, to flay ; then to rend, mangle ; hence, to vex, trouble, annoy ; it is found in the most authentic mss. in Matt. 9 : 36, R.V., " distressed " (of the multitudes who applied to the Lord for healing) ; A.V., " fainted," translating the alternative reading, ekluō, lit., to loosen out. It is also used in Mark 5 : 35 ; Luke 7 : 6 ; 8 : 49. See TROUBLE.¶

3. STENOCHŌREŌ (στενοχωρέω) : see ANGUISH.

4. KATAPONEŌ (καταπονέω), primarily, to tire down with toil, exhaust with labour (kata, down, ponos, labour), hence signifies to afflict, oppress ; in the Passive Voice, to be oppressed, much distressed ; it is translated " oppressed " in Acts 7 : 24, and " sore distressed " in 2 Pet. 2 : 7, R.V., (A.V., " vexed "). See OPPRESS, VEX.¶

DISTRIBUTE, DISTRIBUTION
A. Verbs.

1. DIADIDŌMI (διαδίδωμι), lit., to give through, (dia, through, didōmi, to give), as from one to another, to deal out, is said of distributing to the poor, Luke 18 : 22 ; Acts 4 : 35, " distribution was made," or to a company of people, John 6 : 11. It is translated " divideth " in Luke 11 : 22. In Rev. 17 : 13 the most authentic mss. have the verb didōmi, to give, instead of the longer form.¶

2. MERIZŌ (μερίζω) is translated " hath distributed " in 1 Cor. 7 : 17, and in the A.V. of 2 Cor. 10 : 13, where, however, this rendering is unsuitable, as it is not a case of distributing among a number, but apportioning a measure to the Apostle and his co-workers ; hence the R.V., " apportioned." See DIFFER, A, No. 2.

Note : Koinōneō, to share in common with, is translated " distributing " in Rom. 12 : 13, A.V. The verb does not mean to distribute ; hence

R.V., " communicating." Similarly *koinōnia*, fellowship, communion, is translated " distribution " in 2 Cor. 9 : 13, A.V. ; R.V., " contribution."

B. Adjective.

EUMETADOTOS (εὐμετάδοτος), ready to impart (*eu*, well, *meta*, with, *didōmi*, to give : see A, No. 1), is used in 1 Tim. 6 : 18, "ready to distribute."¶

DISTRICT

MERIS (μερίς) denotes a part (akin to *merizō*, DISTRIBUTE, A., No. 2), Luke 10 : 42 ; Acts 8 : 21 ; 2 Cor. 6 : 15 ; Col. 1 : 12 (lit., ' unto the part,' or share, of the inheritance). In Acts 16 : 12 the R.V. translates it " district," with reference to Macedonia. See PART.¶

DITCH

BOTHUNOS (βόθυνος), any kind of deep hole or pit (probably connected with *bathos*, deep), is translated " ditch " in the A.V. of Matt. 15 : 14 and Luke 6 : 39, R.V., " pit " in each place, as in both Versions of Matt. 12 : 11. See PIT.¶

DIVERS
A. Adjectives.

1. DIAPHOROS (διάφορος) is rendered " divers " in Heb. 9 : 10. See DIFFER, C.

2. POIKILOS (ποικίλος) denotes parti-coloured, variegated (*poikillō* means to make gay : the root of the first syllable is *pik*—, found in Eng., picture), hence " divers," Matt. 4 : 24 ; Mark 1 : 34 ; Luke 4 : 40 ; 2 Tim. 3 : 6 ; Tit. 3 : 3 ; Heb. 2 : 4 (R.V., " manifold ") ; 13 : 9 ; Jas. 1 : 2 (R.V., " manifold ") ; in 1 Pet. 1 : 6 and 4 : 10, " manifold," both A.V. and R.V. See MANIFOLD.¶

Notes : (1) Cp. *polupoikilos*, Eph. 3 : 10, " manifold " (lit., ' much varied ').

(2) The pronoun *tines*, " some " (the plural of *tis*, someone), is translated " divers " in the A.V. of Mark 8 : 3 and Acts 19 : 9 ; R.V., " some."

(3) In 1 Cor. 12 : 28, *genos*, in the plural, is rendered " divers kinds." See DIVERSITIES.

B. Adverb.

POLUTROPOS (πολυτρόπως) means in many ways (*polus*, much, *tropos*, a manner, way ; Eng., trope), " in divers manners," Heb. 1 : 1.¶

Note : The phrase *kata topous*, lit., throughout places (*kata*, down, or throughout, in a distributive sense, *topos*, a place), is translated " in divers places," in Matt. 24 : 7 ; Mark 13 : 8 and Luke 21 : 11.

DIVERSITY, DIVERSITIES

DIAIRESIS (διαίρεσις) : See DIFFER, B, No. 1.

Note : Genos, a kind, class, sort (Eng., genus), is translated " diversities " in the A.V. of 1 Cor. 12 : 28 (marg., " kinds ") ; R.V., " divers kinds."

DIVIDE, DIVIDER, DIVIDING
A. Verbs.

1. APHORIZŌ (ἀφορίζω), lit., to mark off by boundaries or limits (*apo*, from, *horizō*, to determine, mark out), denotes to separate ; " divideth," Matt. 25 : 32, A.V. ; R.V., " separateth," as in the preceding part of the verse. See SEPARATE, SEVER.

2. DIAIREŌ (διαιρέω), lit., to take asunder (see DIFFER, B, No. 1), to divide into parts, to distribute, is found in Luke 15 : 12 and 1 Cor. 12 : 11.¶

3. DIADIDŌMI (διαδίδωμι) : see DISTRIBUTE, A, No. 1.

4. DIAKRINŌ (διακρίνω), to separate, discriminate, hence, to be at variance with oneself, to be divided in one's mind, is rendered " divided " in Jas. 2 : 4, R.V. ; A.V., " partial." See DISCERN.

5. GINOMAI (γίνομαι), to become, is translated " was divided " in Rev. 16 : 19 (of " the great city "), lit., ' became into three parts.'

6. MERIZŌ (μερίζω), akin to *meros*, a part, to part, divide into, in the Middle Voice means to divide anything with another, to share with. The usual meaning is to divide, Matt. 12 : 25, 26 ; Mark 3 : 24, 25, 26 ; 6 : 41 ; Luke 12 : 13 (Middle Voice) ; Rom. 12 : 3, " hath dealt ; " 1 Cor. 1 : 13 ; Heb. 7 : 2, R.V. (A.V., " gave a part "). Elsewhere with other meanings, 1 Cor. 7 : 17, 34 ; 2 Cor. 10 : 13. See DEAL, DIFFER, A, No. 2, DISTRIBUTE, A, No. 2, GIVE.¶

7. DIAMERIZŌ (διαμερίζω), *dia*, through, and No. 6, to divide through, i.e., completely, to divide up, is translated to divide in Luke 11 : 17, 18 ; 12 : 52, 53 ; 22 : 17 ; " parted " in Matt. 27 : 35 ; Mark 15 : 24 ; Luke 23 : 34 ; John 19 : 24 ; Acts 2 : 45 ; in Acts 2 : 3, A.V., " cloven," R.V., " parting asunder." See CLOVEN.¶

8. ORTHOTOMEŌ (ὀρθοτομέω), lit., to cut straight (*orthos*, straight, *temnō*, to cut), is found in 2 Tim. 2 : 15, A.V., " rightly dividing," R.V., " handling aright " (the word of truth) ; the meaning passed from the idea of cutting or dividing, to the more general sense of rightly dealing with a thing. What is intended here is not dividing Scripture from Scripture, but teaching Scripture accurately.¶ In the Sept., of directing one's paths, Prov. 3 : 6 and 11 : 5 (" righteousness traces out blameless paths ").¶

Note : In Acts 13 : 19, the A.V., " He divided their land . . . by lot," represents the verb *kataklērodoteō*, from *kata*, suggesting distribution, *klēros*, a lot, *didōmi*, to give. The most authentic mss. have *kataklēronomeō*, to distribute, as an inheritance, from *klēronomia*, an inheritance ; hence R.V., " He gave them their land for an inheritance."¶ For *schizō*, Acts 14 : 4 ; 23 : 7, see BREAK, No. 12.

B. Nouns.

1. MERISTĒS (μεριστής), a divider, is found in Luke 12 : 14.¶

2. MERISMOS (μερισμός), akin to No. 1, primarily denotes a division, partition (*meros*, a part) ; hence, (*a*) a distribution, Heb. 2 : 4, " gifts "

(marg. of R.V., " distributions ") ; (b) a dividing or separation, Heb. 4 : 12, " dividing " (A.V., " dividing asunder "). Some take this in the Active sense, " as far as the cleaving asunder or separation of soul and spirit ; " others in the Passive sense, " as far as the division (i.e., the dividing line) between soul and spirit," i.e., where one differs from the other. The former seems more in keeping with the meaning of the word. See GIFT.¶

DIVINATION

PUTHŌN (πύθων), Eng., python, in Greek mythology was the name of the Pythian serpent or dragon, dwelling in Pytho, at the foot of mount Parnassus, guarding the oracle of Delphi, and slain by Apollo. Thence the name was transferred to Apollo himself. Later the word was applied to diviners or soothsayers, regarded as inspired by Apollo. Since demons are the agents inspiring idolatry, 1 Cor. 10 : 20, the young woman in Acts 16 : 16 was possessed by a demon instigating the cult of Apollo, and thus had " a spirit of divination."¶

DIVINE
A. Adjective.

THEIOS (θεῖος), divine (from theos, God), is used of the power of God, 2 Pet. 1 : 3, and of His nature, ver. 4, in each place, as that which proceeds from Himself. In Acts 17 : 29 it is used as a noun with the definite article, to denote " the Godhead," the Deity (i.e., the one true God). This word, instead of theos, was purposely used by the Apostle in speaking to Greeks on Mars Hill, as in accordance with Greek usage. Cp. DIVINITY.¶ In the Sept., Ex. 31 : 3 ; 35 : 31 ; Job 27 : 3 ; 33 : 4 ; Prov. 2 : 17.¶
B. Noun.

LATREIA (λατρεία), akin to latreuō, to serve, primarily, any service for hire, denotes in Scripture the service of God according to the requirements of the Levitical Law, Rom. 9 : 4 ; Heb. 9 : 1, 6, " Divine service." It is used in the more general sense of service to God, in John 16 : 2 ; Rom. 12 : 1. See SERVICE.¶

DIVINITY

THEIOTĒS (θειότης), divinity, the R.V. rendering in Rom. 1 : 20 (A.V., " Godhead "), is derived from theios (see DIVINE, A), and is to be distinguished from theotēs, in Col. 2 : 9, " Godhead." In Rom. 1 : 20 the Apostle " is declaring how much of God may be known from the revelation of Himself which He has made in nature, from those vestiges of Himself which men may everywhere trace in the world around them. Yet it is not the personal God whom any man may learn to know by these aids ; He can be known only by the revelation of Himself in His Son ; . . . But in the second passage (Col. 2 : 9), Paul is declaring that in the Son there dwells all the fulness of absolute Godhead ; they were no mere rays of Divine glory which gilded Him, lighting up His Person for a season and with a splendour not His own ; but He was, and is, absolute and perfect God ; and the Apostle uses *theotēs* to express this essential and personal Godhead of the Son " (Trench, Syn. § ii). *Theotēs* indicates the Divine essence of Godhood, the Personality of God ; *theiotēs*, the attributes of God, His Divine nature and properties. See GODHEAD.¶

DIVISION

1. DIAMERISMOS (διαμερισμός), primarily, a parting, distribution, denotes a discussion, dissension, division or discord, breaking up as of family ties (*dia*, asunder, *meros*, a part), it is found in Luke 12 : 51, where it is contrasted with *eirēnē*, peace. Cp. DIVIDE, A, No. 7.

2. DICHOSTASIA (διχοστασία), lit., a standing apart (*dichē*, asunder, apart, *stasis*, a standing ; the root *di*— indicating division, is found in many words in various languages), is used in Rom. 16 : 17, where believers are enjoined to mark those who cause division and to turn away from them ; and in Gal. 5 : 20, R.V. (A.V., " seditions "), where divisions are spoken of as " works of the flesh." Some mss. have this noun in 1 Cor. 3 : 3.¶

3. SCHISMA (σχίσμα), Eng., schism, denotes a cleft, a rent, Matt. 9 : 16 ; Mark 2 : 21 ; then, metaphorically, a division, dissension, John 7 : 43 ; 9 : 16 ; 10 : 19 ; 1 Cor. 1 : 10 ; 11 : 18 ; in 1 Cor. 12 : 25 it is translated " schism " (marg., " division "). The root is *skid*—, seen in the corresponding verb *schizō*, to cleave (Lat. *scindo*). See SCHISM. Cp. *hairesis*, a sect.¶

DIVORCE, DIVORCEMENT
A. Verb.

APOLUŌ (ἀπολύω), to let loose from, let go free (*apo*, from, *luō*, to loose), is translated " is divorced " in the A.V. of Matt. 5 : 32 (R.V., " is put away ") ; it is further used of divorce in Matt. 1 : 19 ; 19 : 3, 7–9 ; Mark 10 : 2, 4, 11 ; Luke 16 : 18. The Lord also used it of the case of a wife putting away her husband, Mark 10 : 12, a usage among Greeks and Romans, not among Jews. See DISMISS.

B. Noun.

APOSTASION (ἀποστάσιον), primarily, a defection, lit., a standing off (*apo*, from, *stasis*, a standing ; cp. *aphistēmi*, to cause to withdraw), denotes, in the N.T., a writing or bill of divorcement, Matt. 5 : 31 ; 19 : 7 ; Mark 10 : 4.¶ In Sept., Deut. 24 : 3 ; Isa. 50 : 1 ; Jer. 3 : 8.¶

DO, DONE

In English the verb to do serves the purpose of a large number of verbs, and has a large variety of meanings. It therefore translates a considerable number of Greek verbs. These, with their specific meanings, are as follows :

1. POIEŌ (ποιέω) signifies (a) to make, (b) to do, i.e., to adopt a way of expressing by act the thoughts and feelings. It stands for a number of such acts, chiefly to make, produce, create, cause, e.g., Matt. 17 : 4. See ABIDE, APPOINT, BEAR, BRING, CAUSE, COMMIT, CONTINUE, DEAL, EXECUTE, EXERCISE, FULFIL, GAIN, GIVE, HOLD, KEEP, MAKE, MEAN, OBSERVE, ORDAIN, PERFORM, PROVIDE, PURPOSE, PUT, SHEW, SHOOT FORTH, SPEND, TAKE, TARRY, WORK, YIELD.

2. PRASSŌ (πράσσω) signifies to practise, though this is not always to be pressed. The Apostle John, in his Epistles, uses the continuous tenses of *poieō*, to indicate a practice, the habit of doing something, e.g., 1 John 3 : 4 (the A.V., " committeth " and " commit " in 1 John 3 : 8 and 9, e.g., is wrong ; " doeth," R.V., in the sense of practising, is the meaning). He uses *prassō* twice in the Gospel, 3 : 20 and 5 : 29. The Apostle Paul uses *prassō* in the sense of practising, and the R.V. so renders the word in Rom. 1 : 32 ; 2 : 2, instead of A.V., " commit," though, strangely enough, the R.V. translates it " committed," instead of " practised," in 2 Cor. 12 : 21.

Generally speaking, in Paul's Epistles *poieō* denotes an action complete in itself, while *prassō* denotes a habit. The difference is seen in Rom. 1 : 32, R.V. Again, *poieō* stresses the accomplishment, e.g., " perform," in Rom. 4 : 21 ; *prassō* stresses the process leading to the accomplishment, e.g., " doer," in 2 : 25. In Rom. 2 : 3 he who does, *poieō*, the things mentioned, is warned against judging those who practise them, *prassō*.

The distinction in John 3 : 20, 21 is noticeable : " Every one that doeth (*prassō*, practiseth) ill . . . he that doeth (*poieō*) the truth." While we cannot draw the regular distinction, that *prassō* speaks of doing evil things, and *poieō* of doing good things, yet very often " where the words assume an ethical tinge, there is a tendency to use the verbs with this distinction " (Trench, Syn., § xcvi). See COMMIT, EXACT, KEEP, REQUIRE, USE.

3. GINOMAI (γίνομαι), to become, is sometimes translated " do " or " done," e.g., Luke 4 : 23, " done (at Capernaum)," followed by *poieō* in the next clause. In Matt. 21 : 42 and Mark 12 : 11, this verb is translated, in the A.V., " (the Lord's) doing ; " R.V., " this was from the Lord." See BECOME.

4. ERGAZOMAI (ἐργάζομαι) denotes to work (*ergon*, work). In Gal. 6 : 10 the R.V. renders it " let us work," for A.V., " let us do ; " in 3 John 5, " thou doest." See COMMIT, LABOUR, MINISTER, TRADE, WORK.

5. KATERGAZOMAI (κατεργάζομαι), *kata* (intensive), is a more emphatic verb than No. 4. In Rom. 2 : 9 the R.V. has " worketh " for A.V., " doeth." In Rom. 7 : 15, 17, both translate it " I do " (R.V. marg., " work ") ; so in ver. 20, " I that do." In 1 Cor. 5 : 3 the R.V. has " wrought," for A.V., " done." In Eph. 6 : 13 both render it " having done (all) ; " more suitably, ' having wrought (all) ; ' the A.V. marg.

" having overcome " does not give the correct meaning. See CAUSE, B,
Note (2), PERFORM, WORK, WROUGHT.

6. ISCHUŌ (ἰσχύω) signifies to be strong, to prevail. It is translated
" I can do," in Phil. 4 : 13. See ABLE, etc.

7. PARECHŌ (παρέχω) lit. means to hold near (*para*, beside, and
echō, to have), i.e., to present, offer, supply. It is translated " do for " in
Luke 7 : 4. See BRING, No. 21.

Notes: (1) In Phil. 2 : 13 *energeō*, to work, is translated " to do," A.V.;
R.V., " to work." (2) In Luke 13 : 32 *apoteleō*, to complete, perform, is
translated " I . . . do," A.V.; R.V., " I perform " (some mss. have
epiteleō here). (3) In Acts 15 : 36, *echō*, to have, to hold, sometimes used
to express the condition in which a person is, how he is faring, is translated
" (how) they do," A.V.; R.V., " how they fare." It is often used of a
physical condition, e.g., Matt. 4 : 24 (see SICK). (4) In Acts 25 : 9
katatithēmi, to deposit, or lay up, for future use, to lay up favour for oneself with a person, is translated " to do (the Jews a pleasure)," A.V.;
R.V., " to gain (favour with the Jews)." (5) In John 16 : 2 *prospherō*,
to bring near, offer, present, is translated " doeth (service)," A.V.;
R.V., " offereth (service)." (6) In Heb. 4 : 13 the phrase *hēmin ho logos*,
rendered " (with whom) we have to do," is, lit., ' (with whom is) the
account to us.' (7) In 1 Cor. 13 : 10, *katargeō*, to render inactive, abolish,
so is translated " shall be done away ; " 2 Cor, 3 : 7, A.V., " was to be
done away," R.V., " was passing away ; " ver. 11. See ABOLISH, DE-
STROY. (8) For " done aforetime," Rom. 3 : 25, R.V., see PAST. For
" did," 2 Tim. 4 : 14, A.V., see SHEW, No. 3. For " do good " see GOOD.

For DOING see DEED, No. 3, DO, No. 3

DOCTOR

1. DIDASKALOS (διδάσκαλος), a teacher (from *didaskō*, to teach),
cp. *didaskalia*, teaching, doctrine, instruction, is translated " doctors,"
with reference to the teachers of the Jewish religion, Luke 2 : 46. Cp.
paideutēs, a teacher. See MASTER, TEACHER.

2. NOMODIDASKALOS (νομοδιδάσκαλος), a teacher of the Law
(*nomos*, a law, and No. 1), with reference to the teachers of the Mosaic
Law, is used in the same sense as No. 1, Luke 5 : 17 ; Acts 5 : 34 ; also
of those who went about among Christians, professing to be instructors
of the Law, 1 Tim. 1 : 7. See TEACHER.¶ See under LAW.

DOCTRINE

1. DIDACHĒ (διδαχή), akin to No. 1, under DOCTOR, denotes teaching,
either (*a*) that which is taught, e.g., Matt. 7 : 28, A.V., " doctrine," R.V.,
" teaching ; " Tit. 1 : 9, R.V.; Rev. 2 : 14, 15, 24, or (*b*) the act of
teaching, instruction, e.g., Mark 4 : 2, A.V., " doctrine," R.V.,

" teaching ; " the R.V. has " the doctrine " in Rom. 16 : 17. See Note (1) below.

2. DIDASKALIA (διδασκαλία) denotes, as No. 1 (from which, however, it is to be distinguished), (a) that which is taught, doctrine, Matt. 15 : 9 ; Mark 7 : 7 ; Eph. 4 : 14 ; Col. 2 : 22 ; 1 Tim. 1 : 10 ; 4 : 1, 6 ; 6 : 1, 3 ; 2 Tim. 4 : 3 ; Tit. 1 : 9 (" doctrine," in last part of verse : see also No. 1) ; 2 : 1, 10 ; (b) teaching, instruction, Rom. 12 : 7, " teaching ; " 15 : 4, " learning ; " 1 Tim. 4 : 13, A.V., " doctrine," R.V., " teaching ; " ver. 16, A.V., " the doctrine," R.V., (correctly) " thy teaching ; " 5 : 17, A.V., " doctrine," R.V. " teaching ; " 2 Tim. 3 : 10, 16 (ditto) ; Tit. 2 : 7, " thy doctrine." Cp. No. 1, under DOCTOR. See LEARNING.¶

Notes : (1) Whereas *didachē* is used only twice in the Pastoral Epistles, 2 Tim. 4 : 2, and Tit. 1 : 9, *didaskalia* occurs fifteen times. Both are used in the active and passive senses (i.e., the act of teaching and what is taught), the passive is predominant in *didachē*, the active in *didaskalia ;* the former stresses the authority, the latter the act (Cremer). Apart from the Apostle Paul, other writers make use of *didachē* only, save in Matt. 15 : 9 and Mark 7 : 7 (*didaskalia*).

(2) In Heb. 6 : 1, *logos*, a word, is translated " doctrine," A.V. ; the R.V. margin gives the lit. rendering, " the word (of the beginning of Christ)," and, in the text, " the (first) principles (of Christ)."

DOER

POIĒTĒS (ποιητής), akin to *poieō*, see Do, No. 1, signifies a doer, Rom. 2 : 13 ; Jas. 1 : 22, 23, 25 ; 4 : 11. Its meaning " poet " is found in Acts 17 : 28.¶

Notes : (1) For *prassō*, rendered " doer " in Rom. 2 : 25, see Do, No. 2.

(2) In 2 Tim. 2 : 9, *kakourgos* is rendered " evil doer " (R.V., " malefactor ").

DOG

1. KUŌN (κύων) is used in two senses, (a) natural, Matt. 7 : 6 ; Luke 16 : 21 ; 2 Pet. 2 : 22, (b) metaphorical, Phil. 3 : 2 ; Rev. 22 : 15, of those whose moral impurity will exclude them from the New Jerusalem. The Jews used the term of Gentiles, under the idea of ceremonial impurity. Among the Greeks it was an epithet of impudence. Lat., *canis*, and Eng., hound are etymologically akin to it.¶

2. KUNARION (κυνάριον), a diminutive of No. 1, a little dog, a puppy, is used in Matt. 15 : 26, 27 ; Mark 7 : 27, 28.¶

DOMINION (have . . . over)
A. Nouns.

1. KRATOS (κράτος), force, strength, might, more especially manifested power, is derived from a root *kra*—, to perfect, to complete : " creator " is probably connected. It also signifies dominion, and is so

rendered frequently in doxologies, 1 Pet. 4 : 11 ; 5 : 11 ; Jude 25 ; Rev. 1 : 6 ; 5 : 13 (R.V.) ; in 1 Tim. 6 : 16, and Heb. 2 : 14 it is translated " power." See MIGHT, POWER, STRENGTH.

Note : Synonymous words are *bia*, force, often oppressive, *dunamis*, power, especially inherent power ; *energeia*, power especially in exercise, operative power ; *exousia*, primarily liberty of action, then authority either delegated or arbitrary ; *ischus*, strength, especially physical, power as an endowment.

2. KURIOTĒS (κυριότης) denotes lordship (*kurios*, a lord), power, dominion, whether angelic or human, Eph. 1 : 21 ; Col. 1 : 16 ; 2 Pet. 2 : 10 (R.V., for A.V., " government ") ; Jude 8. In Eph. and Col. it indicates a grade in the angelic orders, in which it stands second.¶

B. Verbs.

1. KURIEUŌ (κυριεύω), to be lord over, rule over, have dominion over (akin to A, No. 2), is used of (*a*) Divine authority over men, Rom. 14 : 9, " might be Lord ; " (*b*) human authority over men, Luke 22 : 25, " lordship," 1 Tim. 6 : 15, " lords " (R.V., marg., " them that rule as lords ") ; (*c*) the permanent immunity of Christ from the dominion of death, Rom. 6 : 9 ; (*d*) the deliverance of the believer from the dominion of sin, Rom. 6 : 14 ; (*e*) the dominion of law over men, Rom. 7 : 1 ; (*f*) the dominion of a person over the faith of other believers, 2 Cor. 1 : 24 (R.V., " lordship "). See LORD.¶

2. KATAKURIEUŌ (κατακυριεύω), *kata*, down (intensive), and No. 1, to exercise, or gain, dominion over, to lord it over, is used of (*a*) the lordship of Gentile rulers, Matt. 20 : 25, A.V., " exercise dominion," R.V., " lord it ; " Mark 10 : 42, A.V., " exercise lordship," R.V., " lord it ; " (*b*) the power of demons over men, Acts 19 : 16, A.V., " overcame," R.V., " mastered ; " (*c*) of the evil of elders in lording it over the saints under their spiritual care, 1 Pet. 5 : 3. See LORDSHIP, OVERCOME.

Note : For *authenteō*, to have dominion, 1 Tim, 2 : 12, R.V., see AUTHORITY, No. 3.

DOOMED

For R.V. in 1 Cor. 4 : 9, see APPOINT (Note at end), DEATH, B.

DOOR

THURA (θύρα), a door, gate (Eng., door is connected), is used (*a*) literally, e.g., Matt. 6 : 6 ; 27 : 60 ; (*b*) metaphorically, of Christ, John 10 : 7, 9 ; of faith, by acceptance of the Gospel, Acts 14 : 27 ; of openings for preaching and teaching the Word of God, 1 Cor. 16 : 9 ; 2 Cor. 2 : 12 ; Col. 4 : 3 ; Rev. 3 : 8 ; of entrance into the Kingdom of God, Matt. 25 : 10 ; Luke 13 : 24, 25 ; of Christ's entrance into a repentant believer's heart, Rev. 3 : 20 ; of the nearness of Christ's Second Advent, Matt. 24 : 33 ; Mark 13 : 29 ; cp. Jas. 5 : 9 ; of access to behold visions relative to the purposes of God, Rev. 4 : 1.

Note : For the phrase " that kept the door," *thurōros,* John 18 : 16, 17 (" porter " in Mark 13 : 34 ; John 10 : 3), see PORTER.¶

DOTE

NOSEŌ (*voσéω*) signifies to be ill, to be ailing, whether in body or mind ; hence, to be taken with such a morbid interest in a thing as is tantamount to a disease, to dote, 1 Tim. 6 : 4 (marg., " sick "). The primary meaning of dote is to be foolish (cp. Jer. 50 : 36), the evident meaning of *noseō,* in this respect, is to be unsound.¶

DOUBLE
A. Adjective.

DIPLOUS (*διπλοῦς*) denotes twofold, double, 1 Tim. 5 : 17 ; Rev. 18 : 6 (twice).¶ The comparative degree *diploteron* (neuter) is used adverbially in Matt. 23 : 15, " twofold more."¶
B. Verb.

DIPLOŌ (*διπλόω*) signifies to double, to repay or render twofold, Rev. 18 : 6.¶

DOUBLE-MINDED

DIPSUCHOS (*δίψυχος*) lit. means two-souled (*dis,* twice, *psuchē,* a soul), hence, double-minded, Jas. 1 : 8 ; 4 : 8.¶

DOUBLE-TONGUED

DILOGOS (*δίλογος*) primarily means saying the same thing twice, or given to repetition (*dis,* twice, *logos,* a word, or speech) ; hence, saying a thing to one person and giving a different view of it to another, double-tongued, 1 Tim. 3 : 8.¶

DOUBT (be in, make to), DOUBTFUL, DOUBTING
A. Verbs.

1. APOREŌ (*ἀπορέω*), always used in the Middle Voice, lit. means to be without a way (*a,* negative, *poros,* a way, transit), to be without resources, embarrassed, in doubt, perplexity, at a loss, as was Herod regarding John the Baptist, Mark 6 : 20 (R.V., following the most authentic mss., " was much perplexed ") ; as the disciples were, regarding the Lord's betrayal, John 13 : 22, " doubting ; " and regarding the absence of His body from the tomb, Luke 24 : 4, " were perplexed ; " as was Festus, about the nature of the accusations brought against Paul, Acts 25 : 20, A.V. " doubted," R.V., " being perplexed ; " as Paul was, in his experiences of trial, 2 Cor. 4 : 8, " perplexed," and, as to the attitude of the believers of the churches in Galatia towards Judaistic errors, Gal. 4 : 20, A.V., " I stand in doubt," R.V., " I am perplexed." Perplexity is the main idea. See PERPLEX.¶ Cp. the noun *aporia,* " distress," Luke 21 : 25.¶

2. DIAPOREŌ (διαπορέω), *dia*, asunder (intensive), and No. 1, signi-
fies to be thoroughly perplexed, with a perplexity amounting to despair,
Acts 2 : 12 ; 5 : 24 and 10 : 17, A.V., " were in doubt," " doubted,"
R.V., " were (was) perplexed." See also Luke 9 : 7 (some mss. have it in
Luke 24 : 4, where the most authentic have No. 1).   See PERPLEX.¶

3. DIAKRINŌ (διακρίνω) : see CONTEND and DIFFER, A, No. 2 ;
in Acts 11 : 12, A.V., " nothing doubting," R.V., " making no distinction ; " in Jude 22, R.V., " who are in doubt " (A.V., " making a
difference," R.V., marg., " while they dispute ") ; in Jas. 1 : 6, A.V.,
" wavereth," R.V., " doubteth." This verb suggests, not so much
weakness of faith, as lack of it (contrast, Nos. 4 and 5).

4. DISTAZŌ (διστάζω), to stand in two ways (*dis*, double, *stasis*, a
standing), implying uncertainty which way to take, is used in Matt.
14 : 31 and 28 : 17 ; said of believers whose faith is small. Cp. No. 5.¶

5. METEŌRIZŌ (μετεωρίζω), from *meteōros* (Eng., meteor), signifying
in mid air, raised on high, was primarily used of putting a ship out to sea,
or of raising fortifications, or of the rising of the wind. In the Sept.,
it is used, e.g., in Micah 4 : 1, of the exaltation of the Lord's house ; in
Ezek. 10 : 16, of the lifting up of the wings of the cherubim ; in Obad. 4,
of the mounting up of the eagle ; in the N.T. metaphorically, of being
anxious, through a distracted state of mind, of wavering between hope
and fear, Luke 12 : 29, " neither be ye of doubtful mind " (A.V., marg.,
" live not in careful suspense "), addressed to those who have little faith.
Cp. No. 4.   The interpretation " do not exalt yourselves " is not in keeping
with the context.¶

6. PSUCHĒN AIRŌ (ψυχὴν αἴρω), lit., to raise the breath, or to lift
the soul, signifies to hold in suspense, R.V. of John 10 : 24 (A.V., " make
us to doubt "), suggestive of " an objective suspense due to lack of light "
(Warfield), through a failure of their expectations, rather than, subjectively,
through unbelief.   The meaning may thus be, ' How long dost Thou raise
our expectations without satisfying them ? '

B. Noun.

DIALOGISMOS (διαλογισμός) expresses reasoning or questioning
hesitation, 1 Tim. 2 : 8. See DISPUTE, A, No. 1.

Note : For A.V., " doubtful " in Rom. 14 : 1 see DECISION, B, No. 2.

DOUBT (No), DOUBTLESS

PANTŌS (πάντως) : see ALTOGETHER, B.

Notes : (1) In 2 Cor. 12 : 1 the best texts have no word representing
" doubtless." (2) In Luke 11 : 20, the particle *ara*, A.V., " no doubt,"
means " then " (R.V.). (3) In 1 Cor. 9 : 10 the conjunction *gar*, A.V.,
" no doubt," here means " assuredly," or " yea " (R.V.). (4) In Phil.
3 : 8, the opening phrase means " yea, verily," as R.V. (5) In 1 Cor. 9 : 2,
the R.V., " at least," gives the right sense (not " doubtless,"

DOVE, TURTLE-DOVE

1. PERISTERA (περιστερά) denotes a dove or pigeon, Matt. 3 : 16 ; 10 : 16 (indicating its proverbial harmlessness) ; 21 : 12 ; Mark 1 : 10 ; 11 : 15 ; Luke 2 : 24 (" pigeons ") ; 3 : 22 ; John 1 : 32 ; 2 : 14, 16.¶

2. TRUGŌN (τρυγών) denotes a turtle-dove (from *truzō*, to murmur, to coo), Luke 2 : 24.¶

DOWN : see Note †, p. 9

DRAG

1. SURŌ (σύρω), to draw, drag, haul, is used of a net, John 21 : 8 ; of violently dragging persons along, Acts 8 : 3, " haling ; " 14 : 19, R.V., " dragged," A.V., " drew ; " 17 : 6 (ditto) ; Rev. 12 : 4, A.V., " drew," R.V., " draweth." See DRAW, HALE.¶

Note : Cp. the strengthened form *katasurō*, to hale, used in Luke 12 : 58.¶

2. HELKUŌ (or HELKŌ) (ἑλκύω or ἕλκω), to draw, differs from *surō*, as drawing does from violent dragging. It is used of drawing a net, John 21 : 6, 11 (cp. No. 1, in ver. 8) ; Trench remarks, " At vv. 6 and 11 *helkō* (or *helkuō*) is used ; for there a *drawing* of the net to a certain point is intended ; by the disciples to themselves in the ship, by Peter to himself upon the shore. But at ver. 8 *helkō* gives place to *surō :* for nothing is there intended but the *dragging* of the net, which had been fastened to the ship, after it through the water " (Syn., § xxi).

This less violent significance, usually present in *helkō*, but always absent from *surō*, is seen in the metaphorical use of *helkō*, to signify drawing by inward power, by Divine impulse, John 6 : 44 ; 12 : 32. So in the Sept., e.g., S. of S., 1 : 4, and Jer. 31 : 3, " with lovingkindness have I drawn thee." It is used of a more vigorous action, in John 18 : 10, of drawing a sword ; in Acts 16 : 19 ; 21 : 30, of forcibly drawing men to or from a place ; so in Jas. 2 : 6, A.V., " draw," R.V., " drag." See DRAW.¶

DRAGON

DRAKŌN (δράκων) denoted a mythical monster, a dragon ; also a large serpent, so called because of its keen power of sight (from a root *derk—*, signifying to see). Twelve times in the Apocalypse it is used of the Devil, 12 : 3, 4, 7, 9, 13, 16, 17 ; 13 : 2, 4, 11 ; 16 : 13 ; 20 : 2.¶

For DRANK see DRINK

DRAUGHT

1. AGRA (ἄγρα), a hunting, catching (from *agō*, to lead), is used only in connection with fishing. In Luke 5 : 4 it signifies the act of catching fish ; in ver. 9 it stands for the catch itself.¶

2. APHEDRŌN (ἀφεδρών), a latrine, a sink, drain, is found in Matt. 15 : 17 and Mark 7 : 19.¶

For DRAVE and DROVE see DRIVE

DRAW (Away, Back, Nigh, On, Out, Up)

(A) *In the sense of dragging, pulling, or attracting :*

1. ANABIBAZŌ (ἀναβιβάζω), a causal form of *anabainō*, to go up, denotes, lit., to make go up, cause to ascend (*ana*, up, *bibazō*, to cause to mount), hence, to draw a boat up on land, Matt. 13 : 48.¶

2. HELKŌ (ἕλκω) is translated to draw in the A.V., of Acts 21 : 30 and Jas. 2 : 6 ; see DRAG, No. 2.

3. SURŌ (σύρω) : see DRAG, No. 1.

4. SPAŌ (σπάω), to draw or pull, is used, in the Middle Voice, of drawing a sword from its sheath, Mark 14 : 47 ; Acts 16 : 27.¶

5. ANASPAŌ (ἀνασπάω), *ana*, up, and No. 4, to draw up, is used of drawing up an animal out of a pit, Luke 14 : 5 (R.V., " draw up ; " A.V., " pull out "), and of the drawing up of the sheet into heaven, in the vision in Acts 11 : 10.¶

6. APOSPAŌ (ἀποσπάω), *apo*, from, and No. 4, to draw away, lit., to wrench away from, is used of a sword, Matt. 26 : 51 ; of drawing away disciples into error, Acts 20 : 30 ; of Christ's withdrawal from the disciples, in Gethsemane, Luke 22 : 41, A.V., " was withdrawn," R.V., " was parted " (or ' was reft away from them ') ; of parting from a company, Acts 21 : 1 (A.V., " were gotten," R.V., " were parted "). See GET, PART.¶

7. ANTLEŌ (ἀντλέω) signified, primarily, to draw out a ship's bilge-water, to bale or pump out (from *antlos*, bilge-water), hence, to draw water in any way (*ana*, up, and a root, *tel*—, to lift, bear), John 2 : 8, 9 ; 4 : 7, 15.¶

Note : In John 4 : 11, " to draw with " translates the corresponding noun *antlēma*, a bucket for drawing water by a rope.¶

8. EXELKŌ (ἐξέλκω), *ek*, out of, and No. 2, to draw away, or lure forth, is used metaphorically in Jas. 1 : 14, of being drawn away by lust. As in hunting or fishing the game is lured from its haunt, so man's lust allures him from the safety of his self-restraint.¶

9. ANATASSOMAI (ἀνατάσσομαι), to arrange in order, is used in Luke 1 : 1 ; R.V., " to draw up " (some interpret the word to mean to bring together from memory assisted by the Holy Spirit).¶

(B) *In the sense of approaching or withdrawing :*

1. ENGIZŌ (ἐγγίζω), to come near, draw nigh (akin to *engus*, near), is translated by the verb draw near or nigh, in the R.V., Luke 12 : 33, A.V., " approacheth ; " Heb. 10 : 25, A.V., " approaching ; " Luke 18 : 35 ; 19 : 29, 37 ; Acts 22 : 6, A.V., " was come nigh ; " Luke 7 : 12, " came nigh ; " Acts 9 : 3, " came near " See APPROACH.

2. PROSERCHOMAI (προσέρχομαι) is translated " draw near " in

Heb. 4 : 16 ; 7 : 25, R.V., and 10 : 22, A.V. and R.V. ; in Acts 7 : 31, ' drew near." See COME, GO.

3. PROSAGŌ (προσάγω), used transitively, to bring to ; intransitively, to draw near, is so rendered in Acts 27 : 27. See BRING.

4. HUPOSTELLŌ (ὑποστέλλω), to draw back, withdraw, perhaps a metaphor from lowering a sail and so slackening the course, and hence of being remiss in holding the truth ; in the Active Voice, rendered " drew back " in Gal. 2 : 12, R.V. (A.V., " withdrew ") ; in the Middle, in Heb. 10 : 38, " shrink back " R.V. (A.V., " draw back ") ; the prefix *hupo*, underneath, is here suggestive of stealth. In verse 39 the corresponding noun, *hupostolē*, is translated " of them that shrink back," R.V. ; A.V., " draw back " (lit., ' of shrinking back '). In Acts 20 : 20, 27, " shrank," R.V. See KEEP, *Note* (6), SHRINK, SHUN, WITHDRAW.¶

5. APHISTĒMI (ἀφίστημι) : see DEPART, A, No. 20.

6. GINOMAI (γίνομαι), to become, begin to be, is translated " drawing nigh," in John 6 : 19. See BECOME.

7. EPIPHŌSKŌ (ἐπιφώσκω), to dawn (lit., to make to shine upon), is said of the approach of the Sabbath, Luke 23 : 54 (marg., " began to dawn ") ; cp. Matt. 28 : 1.¶ See DAWN, A, No. 3.

Notes : (1) In Mark 6 : 53, *prosormizō*, to bring a ship (or boat) to anchor, cast anchor, land at a place (*pros*, to, *hormizō*, to moor, bring to anchorage), is translated " moored to the shore," in the R.V., for A.V., " drew."¶

(2) In Acts 19 : 33, where the most authentic mss. have *sumbibazō*, the R.V. translates it " brought " (marg., " instructed "), A.V., " draw out." Some mss. have *probibazō*, to bring or drag forward. See BRING, No. 24.

DREAM (noun and verb), DREAMER
A. Nouns.

1. ONAR (ὄναρ) is a vision in sleep, in distinction from a waking vision, Matt. 1 : 20 ; 2 : 12, 13, 19, 22 ; 27 : 19.¶

2. ENUPNION (ἐνύπνιον), is, lit., what appears in sleep (*en*, in, *hupnos*, sleep), an ordinary dream, Acts 2 : 17. For synonymous nouns see VISION.¶

B. Verb.

ENUPNIAZŌ (ἐνυπνιάζω), akin to A, No. 2, is used in Acts 2 : 17, in the Passive Voice, in a phrase (according to the most authentic mss.) which means ' shall be given up to dream by dreams,' translated " shall dream dreams ; " metaphorically in Jude 8, of being given over to sensuous " dreamings," R.V., A.V., " dreamers," and so defiling the flesh.¶

DRESSED
Note : This is the A.V. translation of the Passive of *geōrgeō*, Heb. 6 : 7, to till the ground, to practise as a farmer ; R.V., " is tilled." See TILL.¶

DRESSER

Note: For *ampelourgos*, "dresser," Luke 13 : 7, A.V. (R.V., "vine-dresser "), see VINEDRESSER.

---

for DRIED see DRY, B

DRIFT

PARARHEŌ (παραρέω), lit., to flow past, glide by (*para*, by, *rheō*, to flow), is used in Heb. 2 : 1, where the significance is to find oneself flowing or passing by, without giving due heed to a thing, here " the things that were heard," or perhaps the salvation of which they spoke ; hence the R.V., " lest haply we drift away from them," for A.V., " let them slip." The A.V. marg. " run out as leaking vessels," does not give the meaning.¶ In the Sept., Prov. 3 : 21 ; Isa. 44 : 4.¶

DRINK (-ETH, -ER, -ING), DRANK
A. Nouns.

1. POMA (πόμα), akin to B, No. 1, denotes the thing drunk (from a root *po*—, found in the Eng., potion ; it is connected with the root *pi*— ; see B, No. 3), 1 Cor. 10 : 4 ; Heb. 9 : 10.¶

2. POSIS (πόσις), akin to B, No. 1, suggests the act of drinking, John 6 : 55 (where it is practically equivalent to No. 1) ; Rom. 14 : 17, " drinking," R.V. ; Col. 2 : 16.¶

3. SIKERA (σίκερα) is a strong, intoxicating drink, made from any sweet ingredients, whether grain, vegetables, or the juice of fruits, or a decoction of honey ; " strong drink," Luke 1 : 15.¶ In the Sept., Lev. 10 : 9 ; Num. 6 : 3 ; 28 : 7 ; Deut 14 : 26 ; 29 : 6 ; Isa 5 : 11, 22 ; 24 : 9 ; 28 : 7 ; 29 : 9.

B. Verbs.

1. PINŌ (πίνω), to drink, is used chiefly in the Gospels and in 1 Cor., whether literally (most frequently), or figuratively, (*a*) of drinking of the Blood of Christ, in the sense of receiving eternal life, through His Death, John 6 : 53, 54, 56 ; (*b*) of receiving spiritually that which refreshes, strengthens and nourishes the soul, John 7 : 37 ; (*c*) of deriving spiritual life from Christ, John 4 : 14, as Israel did typically, 1 Cor. 10 : 4 ; (*d*) of sharing in the sufferings of Christ humanly inflicted, Matt. 20 : 22, 23 ; Mark 10 : 38, 39 ; (*e*) of participating in the abominations imparted by the corrupt religious and commercial systems emanating from Babylon, Rev. 18 : 3 ; (*f*) of receiving Divine judgment, through partaking unworthily of the Lord's Supper, 1 Cor. 11 : 29 ; (*g*) of experiencing the wrath of God, Rev. 14 : 10 ; 16 : 6 ; (*h*) of the earth's receiving the benefits of rain, Heb. 6 : 7.

2. METHUŌ (μεθύω), from *methu*, wine, to be drunk, is used in John 2 : 10 in the Passive Voice, and is translated in the P.V., " have drunk freely ; " A.V., " have well drunk." See DRUNK.

3. POTIZŌ (ποτιζω), to give to drink, to make to drink, is used (a) in the material sense, in Matt. 10 : 42 ; 25 : 35, 37, 42 (here of ministering to those who belong to Christ and thus doing so virtually to Him) ; 27 : 48 ; Mark 9 : 41 ; 15 : 36 ; Luke 13 : 15 (" to watering ") ; Rom. 12 : 20 ; 1 Cor. 3 : 7, 8 ; (b) figuratively, with reference to teaching of an elementary character, 1 Cor. 3 : 2, " I fed (you with milk) ; " of spiritual watering by teaching the word of God, 3 : 6 ; of being provided and satisfied by the power and blessing of the Spirit of God, 1 Cor. 12 : 13 ; of the effect upon the nations of partaking of the abominable mixture, provided by Babylon, of paganism with details of the Christian faith, Rev. 14 : 8. See FEED, WATER.¶

4. SUMPINŌ (συμπίνω), to drink together (sun, with, and B, No. 1), is found in Acts 10 : 41.¶

5. HUDROPOTEŌ (ὑδροποτέω), to drink water (hudōr, water, poteō, to drink), is found in 1 Tim. 5 : 23, R.V., " be (no longer) a drinker of water."¶

DRIVE, DRIVEN, DRAVE, DROVE

1. EKBALLŌ (ἐκβάλλω) denotes, lit., to cast forth, with the suggestion of force (ek, out, ballō, to cast) ; hence to drive out or forth. It is translated " driveth " in Mark 1 : 12, R.V., " driveth forth." In John 2 : 15 for the A.V., " drove," the R.V. has " cast," the more usual translation. See CAST, No. 5.

2. EKDIŌKŌ (ἐκδιώκω), to chase away, drive out (ek, out, diōkō, to pursue), is used in 1 Thess. 2 : 15, R.V., " drave out," A.V., " have persecuted." Some mss. have this verb for diōkō, in Luke 11 : 49.¶

3. ELAUNŌ (ἐλαύνω) signifies to drive, impel, urge on. It is used of rowing, Mark 6 : 48 and John 6 : 19 ; of the act of a demon upon a man, Luke 8 : 29 ; of the power of winds upon ships, Jas. 3 : 4 ; and of storms upon mists, 2 Pet. 2 : 17, A.V., " carried," R.V., " driven." See also CARRY, Note (2), Row.

4. APELAUNŌ (ἀπελαύνω), apo, from, and No. 3, to drive from, is used in Acts 18 : 16.¶

5. EXŌTHEŌ (ἐξωθέω), to thrust out (ek, out, ōtheō, to push, thrust), is translated " thrust " in Acts 7 : 45, R.V. (A.V., " drave ") ; in 27 : 39, of driving a storm-tossed ship ashore (R.V., " drive," A.V., " thrust "). Cp. No. 6. See THRUST.¶

6. PHERŌ (φέρω), to bear, is translated " driven " in Acts 27 : 15, 17, of being borne in a storm-tossed ship. See BEAR, etc.

7. DIAPHERŌ (διαφέρω), lit., to bear through (dia, through, and No. 6), in Acts 27 : 27 signifies to be borne hither and thither (R.V., " were driven to and fro ; " A.V., " up and down "). See BETTER (be), No. 1.

8. ANEMIZŌ (ἀνεμίζω), to drive by the wind (anemos, wind), is used in Jas. 1 : 6.¶

Note : For " let . . . drive," Acts 27 : 15, see GIVE, No. 3.

DROP (Noun)

THROMBOS (θρόμβος), a large, thick drop of clotted blood (etymologically akin to *trephō*, to curdle), is used in Luke 22 : 44, in the plural, in the narrative of the Lord's agony in Gethsemane.¶

DROPSY

HUDRŌPIKOS (ὑδρωπικός), dropsical, suffering from dropsy (*hudrops*, dropsy), is found in Luke 14 : 2, the only instance recorded of the healing of this disease by the Lord.¶

DROWN

1. BUTHIZŌ (βυθίζω), to plunge into the deep, to sink (*buthos*, bottom, the deep, the sea), akin to *bathos*, depth, and *abussos*, bottomless, and Eng., bath, is used in Luke 5 : 7 of the sinking of a boat ; metaphorically in 1 Tim. 6 : 9, of the effect of foolish and hurtful lusts, which " drown men in destruction and perdition." See SINK.¶

2. KATAPINŌ (καταπίνω), lit., to drink down (*pinō*, to drink, prefixed by *kata*, down), signifies to swallow up (R.V., in Heb. 11 : 29, for A.V., " were drowned "). It is elsewhere translated by the verb to swallow, or swallow up, except in 1 Pet. 5 : 8, " devour." See DEVOUR, No. 3, SWALLOW.

3. KATAPONTIZŌ (καταποντίζω), to throw into the sea (*kata*, down, *pontos*, the open sea), in the Passive Voice, to be sunk in, to be drowned, is translated " were drowned," in Matt. 18 : 6, A.V. (R.V., " should be sunk ") ; elsewhere in 14 : 30, " (beginning) to sink." See SINK.¶

DRUNK, (-EN, be), DRUNKARD, DRUNKENNESS

A. Verbs.

1. METHUŌ (μεθύω) signifies to be drunk with wine (from *methu*, mulled wine ; hence Eng., mead, honey-wine ; originally it denoted simply a pleasant drink). For John 2 : 10 see under DRINK. The verb is used of being intoxicated in Matt. 24 : 49 ; Acts 2 : 15 ; 1 Cor. 11 : 21 ; 1 Thess. 5 : 7*b* ; metaphorically, of the effect upon men of partaking of the abominations of the Babylonish system, Rev. 17 : 2 ; of being in a state of mental intoxication, through the shedding of men's blood profusely, ver. 6.¶

2. METHUSKŌ (μεθύσκω) signifies to make drunk, or to grow drunk (an inceptive verb, marking the process of the state expressed in No. 1), to become intoxicated, Luke 12 : 45 ; Eph. 5 : 18 ; 1 Thess. 5 : 7*a*.¶

B. Adjective.

METHUSOS (μέθυσος), drunken (cp. No. 2), is used as noun, in the singular, in 1 Cor. 5 : 11, and in the plural, in 6 : 10, " drunkard," " drunkards."¶

C. Noun.

METHĒ (μέθη), strong drink (akin to *methu*, wine, see under A. 1, above), denotes drunkenness, habitual intoxication, Luke 21 : 34 ; Rom. 13 : 13 ; Gal. 5 : 21.¶

DRY
A. Adjectives.

1. XĒROS (ξηρός) is used (a) naturally, of dry land, Heb. 11 : 29 ; or of land in general, Matt. 23 : 15, "land ; " or of physical infirmity, "withered," Matt. 12 : 10 ; Mark 3 : 3 ; Luke 6 : 6, 8 ; John 5 : 3 ; (b) figuratively, in Luke 23 : 31, with reference to the spiritual barrenness of the Jews, in contrast to the character of the Lord. Cp. Ps. 1 : 3 ; Isa. 56 : 3 ; Ezek. 17 : 24 ; 20 : 47. See LAND, WITHERED.¶

2. ANUDROS (ἄνυδρος), waterless (a, negative, n, euphonic, hudōr, water), is rendered "dry" in Matt. 12 : 43, A.V., and Luke 11 : 24 (R.V., "waterless") ; "without water" in 2 Pet. 2 : 17 and Jude 12. See WATER.¶

B. Verb.

XĒRAINŌ (ξηραίνω), akin to A. 1, to dry, dry up, make dry, wither, is translated "dried" (of physical infirmity), in Mark 5 : 29 ; of a tree, in the A.V. of Mark 11 : 20 (R.V., "withered away") ; of water, in Rev. 16 : 12. It is translated "ripe" (R.V., "over-ripe") in Rev. 14 : 15, of a harvest (used figuratively of the gathered nations against Jerusalem at the end of this age) ; "pineth away," in Mark 9 : 18. See OVER-RIPE, PINE AWAY, RIPE, WITHER.

DUE
A. Adjective.

IDIOS (ἴδιος), one's own, is applied to kairos, a season, in Gal. 6 : 9, "in due season," i.e., in the season Divinely appointed for the reaping. So in 1 Tim. 2 : 6, "the testimony to be borne in its own (A.V., ' due ') times (seasons) ; " 6 : 15, "in its own (idios) times (seasons) ; " similarly in Tit. 1 : 3. See BUSINESS, B.

Note : For axios, "the due reward," see REWARD, Note (1).

B. Verbs.

1. OPHEILŌ (ὀφείλω) signifies to owe, to be indebted, especially financially, Matt. 18 : 30, R.V., "that which was due ; " 18 : 34, "all that was due." See BEHOVE, BOUND (to be).

2. DEI (δεῖ), an impersonal verb signifying "it is necessary," is translated "was due" in Rom. 1 : 27, R.V. (A.V., "was meet"). See BEHOVE.

C. Noun.

OPHEILĒ (ὀφειλή), akin to B, No. 1, is rendered "dues" in Rom. 13 : 7. In 1 Cor. 7 : 3, R.V., it is translated "her due" (the A.V. "due benevolence" follows another reading)..

Notes : (1) In the phrases "in due season" in Matt. 24 : 45 ; Luke 12 : 42 ; Rom. 5 : 6 (lit., ' according to time '), and "in due time,"

1 Pet. 5 : 6, there is no word representing " due " in the original, and the phrases are, lit., " in season," " in time."

(2) For the phrase "born out of due time," in 1 Cor. 15 : 8, see BEGET, B, No. 2.

DULL
A. Adjective.

NŌTHROS (νωθρός), slow, sluggish, indolent, dull (the etymology is uncertain), is translated " dull " in Heb. 5 : 11 (in connection with *akoē*, hearing ; lit., 'in hearings ') ; " sluggish," in 6 : 12. See SLOTH-FUL, SLUGGISH.¶ In the Sept., Prov. 22 : 29.¶ Cp. *nōthrokardios*, " slow of heart " (*kardia*, the heart), Prov. 12 : 8.¶

Note : In Luke 24 : 25 " slow (of heart) " translates the synonymous word *bradus*. Of these Trench says (Syn. § civ), " *Bradus* differs from the words with which it is here brought into comparison, in that no moral fault or blame is necessarily involved in it ; so far indeed is it from this, that of the three occasions on which it is used in the N.T. two are in honour ; for to be ' slow ' to evil things, to rash speaking, or to anger (Jas. 1 : 19, twice), is a grace, and not the contrary. . . . There is a deeper, more inborn sluggishness implied in *nōthros*, and this bound up as it were in the very life, more than in either of the other words of this group." Trench compares and contrasts *argos*, idle, but this word is not strictly synonymous with the other two.¶

B. Adverb.

BAREŌS (βαρέως), heavily, with difficulty (*barus*, heavy), is used with *akouō*, to hear, in Matt. 13 : 15 , and Acts 28 : 27 (from Isa. 6 : 10), lit., to hear heavily, to be dull of hearing.¶ In the Sept., Gen. 31 : 35 (lit., ' bear it not heavily ') ; Isa. 6 : 10.¶

DUMB
A. Adjectives.

1. ALALOS (ἄλαλος), lit., speechless (*a*, negative, and *laleō*, to speak), is found in Mark 7 : 37 ; 9 : 17, 25.¶ In the Sept., Ps. 38 : 13.¶

2. APHŌNOS (ἄφωνος), lit., voiceless, or soundless (*a*, negative, and *phōnē*, a sound), has reference to voice, Acts 8 : 32 ; 1 Cor. 12 : 2 ; 2 Pet. 2 : 16, while *alalos* has reference to words. In 1 Cor. 14 : 10 it is used metaphorically of the significance of voices or sounds, " without signifi-cation."¶ In the Sept. Isa. 53 : 7.¶

3. KŌPHOS (κωφός) denotes blunted or dulled ; see DEAF.

B. Verb.

SIŌPAŌ (σιωπάω), from *siōpē*, silence, to be silent, is used of Zacharias' dumbness, Luke 1 : 20. See PEACE (hold one's).

DUNG

1. SKUBALON (σκύβαλον) denotes refuse, whether (*a*) excrement, that

which is cast out from the body, or (b) the leavings of a feast, that which is thrown away from the table. Some have derived it from *kusibalon* (with *metathesis* of k and s), "thrown to dogs;" others connect it with a root meaning "shred." Judaizers counted Gentile Christians as dogs, while they themselves were seated at God's banquet. The Apostle, reversing the image, counts the Judaistic ordinances as refuse upon which their advocates feed, Phil. 3 : 8.¶

2. KOPRION (κόπριον), manure, Luke 13 : 8, used in the plural with *ballō*, to throw, is translated by the verb to dung. Some mss. have the accusative case of the noun *kopria*, a dunghill. See below.¶

DUNGHILL

KOPRIA (κοπρία), a dunghill, is found in Luke 14 : 35.¶

For DURE see under WHILE, *Note* 1

DURING : see Note †, p. 9.

For DURST see DARE

DUST
A. Nouns.

1. CHOUS, or CHOOS (χοῦς or χόος), from *cheō*, to pour, primarily, earth dug out, an earth heap, then, loose earth or dust, is used in Mark 6 : 11 and Rev. 18 : 19.¶

2. KONIORTOS (κονιορτός), raised or flying dust (*konia*, dust, *ornumi*, to stir up), is found in Matt. 10 : 14 ; Luke 9 : 5 ; 10 : 11 ; Acts 13 : 51 ; 22 : 23.¶

B. Verb.

LIKMAŌ (λικμάω), primarily, to winnow (from *likmos*, a winnowing-fan), hence, to scatter as chaff or dust, is used in Matt. 21 : 44 and Luke 20 : 18, R.V., "scatter as dust," A.V., "grind to powder." There are indications in the papyri writings that the word came to denote to ruin, to destroy.¶

DUTY

OPHEILŌ (ὀφείλω), to owe, to be indebted, is translated "it was our duty," in Luke 17 : 10, lit., 'we owe (ought) to do ;' so in Rom. 15 : 27, A.V., "their duty is :" R.V., "they owe it." See BEHOVE, BOUND.

DWELL, DWELLERS, DWELLING (place)
A. Verbs.

1. OIKEŌ (οἰκέω), to dwell (from *oikos*, a house), to inhabit as one's abode, is derived from the Sanskrit, *vic*, a dwelling place (the Eng. termination —wick is connected). It is used (a) of God as dwelling in

light, 1 Tim. 6 : 16 ; (b) of the indwelling of the Spirit of God in the believer, Rom. 8 : 9, 11, or in a church, 1 Cor. 3 : 16 ; (c) of the indwelling of sin, Rom. 7 : 20 ; (d) of the absence of any good thing in the flesh of the believer, Rom. 7 : 18 ; (e) of the dwelling together of those who are married, 1 Cor. 7 : 12, 13.¶

2. KATOIKEŌ (κατοικέω), kata, down, and No. 1, the most frequent verb with this meaning, properly signifies to settle down in a dwelling, to dwell fixedly in a place. Besides its literal sense, it is used of (a) the indwelling of the totality of the attributes and powers of the Godhead in Christ, Col. 1 : 19 ; 2 : 9 ; (b) the indwelling of Christ in the hearts of believers (' may make a home in your hearts '), Eph. 3 : 17 ; (c) the dwelling of Satan in a locality, Rev. 2 : 13 ; (d) the future indwelling of righteousness in the new heavens and earth, 2 Pet. 3 : 13. It is translated " dwellers " in Acts 1 : 19 ; 2 : 9 ; " inhabitants " in Rev. 17 : 2, A.V. (R.V., " they that dwell "), " inhabiters " in Rev. 8 : 13 and 12 : 12, A.V. (R.V., " them that dwell ").

Cp. the nouns katoikēsis (below), katoikia, habitation, Acts 17 : 26¶ ; katoikētērion, a habitation, Eph. 2 : 22 ; Rev. 18 : 2.¶ Contrast paroikeō, to sojourn, the latter being temporary, the former permanent. See HABITATION, INHABITANT.

3. KATOIKIZŌ (κατοικίζω), to cause to dwell, is said of the act of God concerning the Holy Spirit in Jas. 4 : 5, R.V. (some mss. have No. 2).¶

4. ENOIKEŌ (ἐνοικέω), lit., to dwell in (en, in, and No. 1), is used, with a spiritual significance only, of (a) the indwelling of God in believers, 2 Cor. 6 : 16 ; (b) the indwelling of the Holy Spirit, Rom. 8 : 11 ; 2 Tim. 1 : 14 ; (c) the indwelling of the word of Christ, Col. 3 : 16 ; (d) the indwelling of faith, 2 Tim. 1 : 5 ; (e) the indwelling of sin in the believer, Rom. 7 : 17.¶

5. PERIOIKEŌ (περιοικέω), peri, around, and No. 1, to dwell around, be a neighbour, is used in Luke 1 : 65.¶ Cp. perioikos, a neighbour, Luke 1 : 58.¶

6. SUNOIKEŌ (συνοικέω), sun, with, and No. 1, to dwell with, is used in 1 Pet. 3 : 7.¶

7. ENKATOIKEŌ (ἐγκατοικέω), en, in, and No. 2, to dwell among, is used in 2 Pet. 2 : 8.¶

8. MENŌ (μένω), to abide, remain, is translated to dwell, in the A.V. of John 1 : 38, 39 ; 6 : 56 ; 14 : 10, 17 ; Acts 28 : 16. The R.V. adheres throughout to the verb to abide. See ABIDE.

9. SKĒNOŌ (σκηνόω), to pitch a tent (skēnē), to tabernacle, is translated " dwelt," in John 1 : 14, A.V., R.V. marg., " tabernacled ; " in Rev. 7 : 15, A.V., " shall dwell," R.V., " shall spread (His) tabernacle ; " in Rev. 12 : 12 ; 13 : 6 ; 21 : 3, " dwell." See TABERNACLE.

10. KATASKĒNOŌ (κατασκηνόω), to pitch one's tent (kata, down, skēnē, a tent), is translated " lodge " in Matt. 13 : 32 ; Mark 4 : 32 ; Luke 13 : 19 ; in Acts 2 : 26, R.V., " dwell," A.V., " rest."¶

11. EMBATEUŌ (ἐμβατεύω), primarily, to step in, or on (from *embainō*, to enter), hence (*a*) to frequent, dwell in, is used metaphorically in Col. 2 : 18, R.V., " dwelling in " (marg., " taking his stand upon ") ; (*b*) with reference to the same passage, alternatively, to invade, to enter on ; perhaps used in this passage as a technical term of the mystery religions, denoting the entrance of the initiated into the new life (A.V., " intruding into "). A suggested alternative reading involves the rendering " treading on air," i.e., indulging in vain speculations, but evidences in the papyri writings make the emendation unnecessary.¶

12. KATHĒMAI (κάθημαι), to sit down, is translated " dwell," in Luke 21 : 35. See SET, SIT.

13. KATHIZŌ (καθίζω), to sit down, denotes to dwell, in Acts 18 : 11 (R.V., " dwelt," for A.V., " continued ").

14. ASTATEŌ (ἀστατέω), to wander about (*a*, negative, *histēmi*, to stand), to have no fixed dwelling-place, is used in 1 Cor. 4 : 11.¶ Cp. *akatastatos*, unstable, Jas. 1 : 8 ; 3 : 8.¶ ; *akatastasia*, revolution, confusion, e.g., 1 Cor. 14 : 33.

B. Nouns.

1. PAROIKIA (παροικία) denotes a sojourning, Acts 13 : 17, lit., ' in the sojourning,' translated " when they sojourned," R.V. (A.V., " dwelt as strangers ") ; in 1 Pet. 1 : 17, " sojourning."¶

2. KATOIKĒSIS (κατοίκησις), akin to A, No. 2, a dwelling, a habitation, is used in Mark 5 : 3.¶

Note : Cp. *oikia*, and *oikos*, a house, *oikēma*, a prison, *katoikia*, a habitation (see A, No. 2).

3. MISTHŌMA (μίσθωμα), primarily, a price, a hire (akin to *misthos*, wages, hire, and *misthoō*, to let out for hire), is used in Acts 28 : 30 to denote a hired dwelling.¶

For DYING see DEADNESS

DYSENTERY

DUSENTERION (δυσεντέριον), whence Eng., dysentery, is so translated in Acts 28 : 8, R.V., for A.V. " bloody flux " (*enteron* denotes an intestine).¶

E

EACH, EACH MAN, EACH ONE

1. HEKASTOS (ἕκαστος), each or every, is used of any number separately, either (a) as an adjective qualifying a noun, e.g., Luke 6 : 44 ; John 19 : 23 ; Heb. 3 : 13, where " day by day," is, lit., ' according to each day ; ' or, more emphatically with *heis*, one, in Matt. 26 : 22 ; Luke 4 : 40 ; 16 : 5 ; Acts 2 : 3, 6 ; 20 : 31 ; I Cor. 12 : 18 ; Eph. 4 : 7, 16, R.V., " each (several)," for A.V., " every ; " Col. 4 : 6 ; I Thess. 2 : 11 ; 2 Thess. I : 3 ; (b) as a distributive pronoun, e.g., Acts 4 : 35 ; Rom. 2 : 6 ; Gal. 6 : 4 ; in Phil. 2 : 4, it is used in the plural ; some mss. have it thus in Rev. 6 : 11. The repetition in Heb. 8 : 11 is noticeable, " every man " (i.e., everyone). Prefixed by the preposition *ana*, apiece (a colloquialism), it is used, with stress on the individuality, in Rev. 21 : 21, of the gates of the heavenly city, " each one of the several," R.V. ; in Eph. 5 : 33, preceded by *kath' hena*, ' by one,' it signifies " each (one) his own."

2. The phrase *hen kath' hen*, lit., ' one by one,' is used in Rev. 4 : 8, " each one of them."

EACH OTHER

ALLĒLŌN (ἀλλήλων), a reciprocal pronoun, preceded by the preposition *meta*, with, signifies " with each other," Luke 23 : 12, R.V., for A.V., " together." Similarly in 24 : 14 *pros allēlous*, where *pros* suggests greater intimacy. See ONE ANOTHER.

EAGLE

AETOS (ἀετός), an eagle (also a vulture), is perhaps connected with *aēmi*, to blow, as of the wind, on account of its windlike flight. In Matt. 24 : 28 and Luke 17 : 37 the vultures are probably intended. The meaning seems to be that, as these birds of prey gather where the carcase is, so the judgments of God will descend upon the corrupt state of humanity. The figure of the eagle is used in Ezek. 17 to represent the great powers of Egypt and Babylon, as being employed to punish corrupt and faithless Israel. Cp. Job 39 : 30 ; Prov. 30 : 17. The eagle is mentioned elsewhere in the N.T. in Rev. 4 : 7 ; 8 : 13 (R.V.) ; 12 : 14. There are eight species in Palestine.¶

In the following pages † indicates that the word referred to (preposition, conjunction, or particle) is not dealt with in this volume.

¶ indicates that all the N.T. occurrences of the Greek word under consideration are mentioned under the heading or sub-heading.

EAR (of the body)

1. OUS (οὖς), Latin *auris*, is used (*a*) of the physical organ, e.g., Luke 4 : 21 ; Acts 7 : 57 ; in Acts 11 : 22, in the plural with *akouō*, to hear, lit., ' was heard into the ears of someone,' i.e., came to the knowledge of ; similarly, in the singular, Matt. 10 : 27, in familiar private conversation ; in Jas. 5 : 4 the phrase is used with *eiserchomai*, to enter into ; in Luke 1 : 44, with *ginomai*, to become, to come ; in Luke 12 : 3, with *lalein*, to speak and *pros*, to ; (*b*) metaphorically, of the faculty of perceiving with the mind, understanding and knowing, Matt. 13 : 16 ; frequently with *akouō*, to hear, e.g., Matt. 11 : 15 ; 13 : 9, 43 ; Rev. 2 and 3, at the close of each of the messages to the churches ; in Matt. 13 : 15 and Acts 28 : 27, with *bareōs*, heavily, of being slow to understand and obey ; with a negative in Mark 8 : 18 ; Rom. 11 : 8 ; in Luke 9 : 44 the lit. meaning is ' put those words into your ears,' i.e., take them into your mind and keep them there ; in Acts 7 : 51 it is used with *aperitmētos*, uncircumcised. As seeing is metaphorically associated with conviction, so hearing is with obedience (*hupakoē*, lit., hearing under ; the Eng., " obedience " is etymologically ' hearing over against,' i.e., with response in the hearer).

2. ŌTION (ὠτίον), a diminutive of No. 1, but without the diminutive force, it being a common tendency in everyday speech to apply a diminutive form to most parts of the body, is used in Matt. 26 : 51 ; Mark 14 : 47 (in some mss.) ; Luke 22 : 51 ; John 18 : 10 (in some mss.) and ver. 26, all with reference to the ear of Malchus.¶

Note : The most authentic mss. have the alternative diminutive *ōtarion*, in Mark 14 : 47 and John 18 : 10.¶

3. AKOĒ (ἀκοή), hearing, akin to *akouō*, to hear, denotes (*a*) the sense of hearing, e.g., 1 Cor. 12 : 17 ; 2 Pet. 2 : 8 ; (*b*) that which is heard, a report, e.g., Matt. 4 : 24 ; (*c*) the physical organ, Mark 7 : 35, standing for the sense of hearing ; so in Luke 7 : 1, R.V., for A.V., " audience ; " Acts 17 : 20 ; 2 Tim. 4 : 3, 4 (in ver. 3, lit., ' being tickled as to the ears ') ; (*d*) a message or teaching, John 12 : 38 ; Rom. 10 : 16, 17 ; Gal. 3 : 2, 5 ; 1 Thess. 2 : 13 ; Heb. 4 : 2, R.V., " (the word) of hearing," for A.V., " (the word) preached." See FAME, HEARING, PREACH, REPORT, RUMOUR.

Note : In Matt. 28 : 14, the verb *akouō* is used with the preposition *epi*, upon or before (or *hupo*, by, in some mss.), lit., ' if this come to a hearing before the governor.'

EAR (of corn)

STACHUS (στάχυς) is found in Matt. 12 : 1 ; Mark 2 : 23 ; 4 : 28 (" ear," twice) ; Luke 6 : 1. The first part of the word is derived from the root *sta—* found in parts of the verb *histēmi*, to cause to stand. It is used as a proper name in Rom. 16 : 9.¶

EARLY
A. Noun.

ORTHROS (ὄρθρος) denotes daybreak, dawn (cp. Lat. *orior*, to rise). Used with the adverb *batheōs*, deeply, in Luke 24 : 1, it means " at early dawn " (R.V.). In John 8 : 2 it is used in the genitive case, *orthrou*, at dawn, i.e., " early in the morning." In Acts 5 : 21, it is used with the article and preceded by the preposition *hupo*, under, or about, lit., ' about the dawn,' " about daybreak," R.V. (for A.V., " early in the morning.").¶

B. Adjectives.

1. ORTHRINOS (ὀρθρινός) early, akin to A., is a later form of *orthrios*. It is found, in the most authentic mss., in Luke 24 : 22, of the women at the sepulchre, lit., ' early ones ' (some texts have the form *orthrios*, at daybreak).¶

2. PRŌIMOS (πρώϊμος) or *proimos*, a longer and later form of *proios*, pertaining to the morning, is formed from *prō*, before (cp. *prōtos*, first), and used in Jas. 5 : 7, of the early rain.¶

C. Adverb.

PRŌI (πρωΐ), early in the day, at morn, is derived from *prō*, before (see B, No. 2, above). In Mark 16 : 2, A.V., it is translated " early in the morning ; " in Mark 16 : 9 and John 18 : 28 ; 20 : 1, " early ; " in Matt. 16 : 3 ; 20 : 1 ; 21 : 18 ; Mark 1 : 35 ; 11 : 20 ; 13 : 35 ; 15 : 1, " in the morning ; " in Acts 28 : 23. " (from) morning." See MORNING.¶

Note : In Matt. 20 : 1, *hama*, at once, is rendered " early."

EARNEST (Noun)

ARRABŌN (ἀρραβών), originally, earnest-money deposited by the purchaser and forfeited if the purchase was not completed, was probably a Phœnician word, introduced into Greece. In general usage it came to denote a pledge or earnest of any sort ; in the N.T. it is used only of that which is assured by God to believers ; it is said of the Holy Spirit as the Divine pledge of all their future blessedness, 2 Cor. 1 : 22 ; 5 : 5 ; in Eph. 1 : 14, particularly of their eternal inheritance.¶ In the Sept., Gen. 38 : 17, 18, 20.¶ In modern Greek *arrabōna* is an engagement ring.

EARNEST, EARNESTNESS, EARNESTLY
A. Noun.

SPOUDE (σπουδή), akin to *speudō*, to hasten, denotes haste, Mark 6 : 25 ; Luke 1 : 39 ; hence, " earnestness," 2 Cor. 8 : 7, R.V., for A.V., " diligence," and ver. 8, for A.V., " forwardness ; " in 7 : 12, " earnest care," for A.V., " care ; " in 8 : 16, " earnest care." See BUSINESS, CARE, CAREFULNESS, DILIGENCE, FORWARDNESS, HASTE.

B. Adjective.

SPOUDAIOS (σπουδαῖος), akin to A, denotes active, diligent, earnest,

2 Cor. 8 : 22, R.V., " earnest," for A.V., " diligent ; " in the latter part of the verse the comparative degree, *spoudaioteros*, is used, R.V., " more earnest," for A.V., " more diligent ; " in ver. 17, R.V., in the superlative sense, " very earnest," for A.V., " more forward." See DILIGENT, FORWARD.¶

C. Adverbs.

1. EKTENŌS (ἐκτενῶς), earnestly (*ek*, out, *teinō*, to stretch ; Eng., tension, etc.), is used in Acts 12 : 5, " earnestly," R.V., for A.V., " without ceasing " (some mss. have the adjective *ektenēs*, earnest) ; in 1 Pet. 1 : 22, " fervently." The idea suggested is that of not relaxing in effort, or acting in a right spirit. See FERVENTLY.¶

2. EKTENESTERON (ἐκτενέστερον), the comparative degree of No. 1, used as an adverb in this neuter form, denotes more earnestly, fervently, Luke 22 : 44.¶

3. SPOUDAIŌS (σπουδαίως), akin to B, signifies with haste, or with zeal, earnestly, Luke 7 : 4, R.V., " earnestly," for A.V., " instantly ; " in 2 Tim. 1 : 17, R.V., and Tit. 3 : 13, " diligently ; "¶ in Phil. 2 : 28, the comparative *spoudaioteros*, R.V., " the more diligently," A.V., " the more carefully." See CAREFULLY, DILIGENTLY, INSTANTLY.¶

D. Adverbial Phrase.

EN EKTENEIA (ἐν ἐκτενείᾳ), lit., ' in earnestness,' cp. C, No. 1, is translated " earnestly " in Acts 26 : 7, R.V., for A.V., " instantly." See INSTANTLY.¶

Notes : (1) For the phrase " earnest expectation," Rom. 8 : 19 and Phil. 1 : 20, see EXPECTATION. (2) In 1 Cor. 12 : 31 ; 14 : 1, 39, *zēloō*, to be zealous about, is translated " desire earnestly." See DESIRE. (3) In 2 Pet. 3 : 12, *speudō* is translated " earnestly desiring," for A.V., " hasting unto." See HASTEN. (4) In Jude 3, *epagōnizō*, to contend earnestly, is so translated.¶ (5) In Jas. 5 : 17 the dative case of the noun *proseuchē* is translated " earnestly " (A.V.), in connection with the corresponding verb, lit., ' he prayed with prayer ' (R.V., " fervently "), implying persevering continuance in prayer with fervour. Cp., e.g., Ps. 40 : 1, lit., ' in waiting I waited.' See FERVENT. (6) *Atenizō*, akin to C, No. 1, to fix the eyes upon, gaze upon, is translated " earnestly looked " in Luke 22 : 56, A.V. (R.V., " looking stedfastly ") ; in Acts 3 : 12, A.V., " look ye earnestly," R.V., " fasten ye your eyes on ; " in Acts 23 : 1, A.V., " earnestly beholding," R.V., " looking stedfastly on." (7) In Heb. 2 : 1, *prosechō*, to give heed, is used with the adverb *perissoterōs*, more abundantly, to signify " to give the more earnest heed ; " lit., ' to give heed more exceedingly.' For the verb see ATTEND, GIVE, No. 16, HEED, REGARD.

EARTH

1. GĒ (γῆ) denotes (*a*) earth as arable land, e.g., Matt. 13 : 5, 8, 23 ; in 1 Cor. 15 : 47 it is said of the earthly material of which " the first man "

was made, suggestive of frailty ; (b) the earth as a whole, the world, in contrast, whether to the heavens, e.g., Matt. 5 : 18, 35, or to Heaven, the abode of God, e.g., Matt. 6 : 19, where the context suggests the earth as a place characterized by mutability and weakness ; in Col. 3 : 2 the same contrast is presented by the word " above ; " in John 3 : 31 (R.V., " of the earth," for A.V., " earthly ") it describes one whose origin and nature are earthly and whose speech is characterized thereby, in contrast with Christ as the One from Heaven ; in Col. 3 : 5 the physical members are said to be " upon the earth," as a sphere where, as potential instruments of moral evils, they are, by metonymy, spoken of as the evils themselves ; (c) the inhabited earth, e.g., Luke 21 : 35 ; Acts 1 : 8 ; 8 : 33 ; 10 : 12 ; 11 : 6 ; 17 : 26 ; 22 : 22 ; Heb. 11 : 13 ; Rev. 13 : 8. In the following the phrase " on the earth " signifies ' among men,' Luke 12 : 49 ; 18 : 8 ; John 17 : 4 ; (d) a country, territory, e.g., Luke 4 : 25 ; John 3 : 22 ; (e) the ground, e.g., Matt. 10 : 29 ; Mark 4 : 26, R.V., " (upon the) earth," for A.V., " (into the) ground ; " (f) land, e.g., Mark 4 : 1 ; John 21 : 8, 9, 11. Cp. Eng. words beginning with ge—, e.g., geodetic, geodesy, geology, geometry, geography. See COUNTRY, GROUND, LAND, WORLD.

2. OIKOUMENE (οἰκουμένη), the present participle, Passive Voice, of oikeō, to dwell, inhabit, denotes the inhabited earth. It is translated " world " in every place where it has this significance, save in Luke 21 : 26, A.V., where it is translated " earth." See WORLD.

Note : For *epigeios*, translated " on earth " in Phil. 2 : 10, *ostrakinos*, " of earth," 2 Tim. 2 : 20, and *katachthonios*, " under the earth," Phil. 2 : 10,¶ see EARTHEN.

EARTHEN, EARTHLY, EARTHY

1. OSTRAKINOS (ὀστράκινος) signifies made of earthenware or clay (from *ostrakon*, baked clay, potsherd, shell ; akin to *osteon*, a bone), 2 Tim. 2 : 20, " of earth ; " 2 Cor. 4 : 7, " earthen."¶

2. EPIGEIOS (ἐπίγειος), on earth (*epi*, on, *gē*, the earth), is rendered " earthly " in John 3 : 12 ; 2 Cor. 5 : 1 ; Phil 3 : 19 ; Jas. 3 : 15 ; in Phil. 2 : 10, " on earth," R.V. ; " terrestrial " in 1 Cor. 15 : 40 (twice). See TERRESTRIAL.¶

3. CHOÏKOS (χοϊκός) denotes " earthy," made of earth, from *chous*, soil, earth thrown down or heaped up, 1 Cor. 15 : 47, 48, 49.¶

4. KATACHTHONIOS (καταχθόνιος), under the earth, subterranean (*kata*, down, *chthōn*, the ground, from a root signifying that which is deep), is used in Phil. 2 : 10.¶

EARTHQUAKE

SEISMOS (σεισμός), a shaking, a shock, from *seiō*, to move to and fro, to shake, chiefly with the idea of concussion (Eng., seismic, seismology, seismometry), is used (a) of a tempest in the sea, Matt. 8 : 24 ; (b) of earthquakes, Matt. 24 : 7 ; 27 : 54 ; 28 : 2 ; Mark 13 : 8 ; Luke 21 : 11 ;

Acts 16 : 26 ; Rev. 6 : 12 ; 8 : 5 ; 11 : 13 (twice), 19 ; 16 : 18 (twice).
See TEMPEST.¶

EASE, EASED
A. Verb.

ANAPAUŌ (ἀναπαύω) signifies to cause or permit one to cease from
any labour or movement so as to recover strength.   It implies previous
toil and care.   Its chief significance is that of taking, or causing to take,
rest ; it is used in the Middle Voice in Luke 12 : 19, " take (thine) ease,"
indicative of unnecessary, self-indulgent relaxation.   In the papyri it is
used technically, as an agricultural term.   Cp. *anapausis*, rest.   See
REFRESH, REST.

B. Noun.

ANESIS (ἄνεσις) denotes a letting loose, relaxation, easing, it is
connected with *aniēmi*, to loosen, relax (*ana*, back, and *hiēmi*, to send).
It signifies rest, not from toil, but from endurance and suffering.   Thus
it is said (*a*) of a less vigorous condition in imprisonment, Acts 24 : 23,
" indulgence," A.V., " liberty ; "   (*b*) relief from anxiety, 2 Cor. 2 : 13 ;
7 : 5, " relief " (A.V., " rest ") ; (*c*) relief from persecutions, 2 Thess. 1 : 7,
" rest ; "   (*d*) of relief from the sufferings of poverty, 2 Cor. 8 : 13, " be
eased," lit., ' (that there should be) easing for others (trouble to you).'
Cp. the synonymous word *anapausis*, cessation or rest (akin to A).   See
INDULGENCE, LIBERTY, RELIEF, REST.¶   In the Sept., 2 Chron. 23 : 15.¶

For EASILY see EASY

EAST

ANATOLE (ἀνατολή), primarily a rising, as of the sun and stars,
corresponds to *anatellō*, to make to rise, or, intransitively, to arise, which
is also used of the sunlight, as well as of other objects in nature.   In
Luke 1 : 78 it is used metaphorically of Christ as " the Dayspring," the
One through Whom light came into the world, shining immediately into
Israel, to dispel the darkness which was upon all nations.   Cp. Mal. 4 : 2.
Elsewhere it denotes the east, as the quarter of the sun's rising, Matt. 2 : 1,
2, 9 ; 8 : 11 ; 24 : 27 ; Luke 13 : 29 ; Rev. 7 : 2 ; 16 : 12 ; 21 : 13.   The
east in general stands for that side of things upon which the rising of
the sun gives light.   In the heavenly city itself, Rev. 21 : 13, the reference
to the east gate points to the outgoing of the influence of the city eastward.
See DAYSPRING.¶

EASTER

PASCHA (πάσχα), mistranslated " Easter " in Acts 12 : 4, A.V., denotes
the Passover (R.V.).   The phrase " after the Passover " signifies after the
whole festival was at an end.   The term Easter is not of Christian origin.
It is another form of *Astarte*, one of the titles of the Chaldean goddess.

the queen of heaven. The festival of Pasch held by Christians in post-apostolic times was a continuation of the Jewish feast, but was not instituted by Christ, nor was it connected with Lent. From this Pasch the Pagan festival of Easter was quite distinct and was introduced into the apostate Western religion, as part of the attempt to adapt Pagan festivals to Christianity. See Passover.

EASY, EASIER, EASILY

1. CHRĒSTOS (χρηστός) primarily signifies fit for use, able to be used (akin to *chraomai*, to use), hence, good, virtuous, mild, pleasant (in contrast to what is hard, harsh, sharp, bitter). It is said (*a*) of the character of God as kind, gracious, Luke 6 : 35 ; 1 Pet. 2 : 3 ; good, Rom. 2 : 4, where the neuter of the adjective is used as a noun, " the goodness " (cp. the corresponding noun *chrēstotēs*, " goodness," in the same verse) ; of the yoke of Christ, Matt. 11 : 30, " easy " (a suitable rendering would be ' kindly ') ; (*c*) of believers, Eph. 4 : 32 ; (*d*) of things, as wine, Luke 5 : 39, R.V., " good," for A.V., " better " (cp. Jer. 24 : 3, 5, of figs) ; (*e*) ethically, of manners, 1 Cor. 15 : 33. See Good, Gracious, Kind.¶

2. EUKOPŌTEROS (εὐκοπώτερος), the comparative degree of *eukopos*, easy, with easy labour (*eu*, well, *kopos*, labour), hence, of that which is easier to do, is found in the Synoptists only, Matt. 9 : 5 ; 19 : 24 ; Mark 2 : 9 ; 10 : 25 ; Luke 5 : 23 ; 16 : 17 ; 18 : 25.¶

Notes : (1) The adverb " easily " is included in the translation of *euperistatos* in Heb. 12 :1, " easily beset," lit., ' the easily besetting sin,' probably a figure from a garment, ' easily surrounding,' and therefore easily entangling. See Beset. (2) In 1 Cor. 13 : 5, A.V., " is not easily provoked," there is no word in the original representing " easily ; " R.V., " is not provoked." (3) For " easy to be entreated " see Intreat. For " easy to be understood " see Understand.

EAT, EAT WITH, EATING
A. Verbs.

1. ESTHIŌ (ἐσθίω) signifies to eat (as distinct from *pinō*, to drink) ; it is a lengthened form from *edō* (Lat., *edō* ; cp. Eng., edible) ; in Heb. 10 : 27, metaphorically, " devour ; " it is said of the ordinary use of food and drink, 1 Cor. 9 : 7 ; 11 : 22 ; of partaking of food at table, e.g., Mark 2 : 16 ; of revelling, Matt. 24 : 49 ; Luke 12 : 45. Cp. the strengthened form *katesthiō*, and the verb *sunesthiō*, below. See Devour.

2. PHAGŌ (φάγω), to eat, devour, consume, is obsolete in the present and other tenses, but supplies certain tenses which are wanting in No. 1, above. In Luke 8 : 55 the A.V. has " (to give her) meat," the R.V. " (that something be given her) to eat." The idea that this verb combines both eating and drinking, while No. 1 differentiates the one from the other, is not borne out in the N.T. The word is very frequent in the Gospels and is used eleven times in 1 Cor. See also No. 3. See Meat.

3. TRŌGŌ (τρώγω), primarily, to gnaw, to chew, stresses the slow process ; it is used metaphorically of the habit of spiritually feeding upon Christ, John 6 : 54, 56, 57, 58 (the aorists here do not indicate a definite act, but view a series of acts seen in perspective) ; of the constant custom of eating in certain company, John 13 : 18 ; of a practice unduly engrossing the world, Matt. 24 : 38.

In John 6, the change in the Lord's use from the verb *esthiō* (*phagō*) to the stronger verb *trōgō*, is noticeable. The more persistent the unbelief of His hearers, the more difficult His language and statements became. In vv. 49 to 53 the verb *phagō* is used ; in 54, 58, *trōgō* (in ver. 58 it is put into immediate contrast with *phagō*). The use of *trōgō* in Matt. 24 : 38 and John 13 : 18 is a witness against pressing into the meaning of the word the sense of munching or gnawing ; it had largely lost this sense in its common usage.¶

4. GEUŌ (γεύω), primarily, to cause to taste, to give one a taste of, is used in the Middle Voice and denotes (*a*) to taste, its usual meaning ; (*b*) to take food, to eat, Acts 10 : 10 ; 20 : 11 ; 23 : 14 ; the meaning to taste must not be pressed in these passages, the verb having acquired the more general meaning. As to whether Acts 20 : 11 refers to the Lord's Supper or to an ordinary meal, the addition of the words " and eaten " is perhaps a sufficient indication that the latter is referred to here, whereas ver. 7, where the single phrase " to break bread " is used, refers to the Lord's Supper. A parallel instance is found in Acts 2 : 43, 46. In the former verse the phrase " the breaking of bread," unaccompanied by any word about taking food, clearly stands for the Lord's Supper ; whereas in ver. 46 the phrase " breaking bread at home " is immediately explained by " they did take their food," indicating their ordinary meals. See TASTE.

5. BIBRŌSKŌ (βιβρώσκω), to eat, is derived from a root, *bor*—, to devour (likewise seen in the noun *brōma*, food, meat ; cp. Eng., car-nivorous, voracious, from Lat. *vorax*). This verb is found in John 6 : 13. The difference between this and *phagō*, No. 2, above, may be seen perhaps in the fact that whereas in the Lord's question to Philip in ver. 5, *phagō* intimates nothing about a full supply, the verb *bibrōskō*, in ver. 13, indicates that the people had been provided with a big meal, of which they had partaken eagerly.¶

6. KATAPHAGŌ (καταφάγω) signifies to eat up (*kata*, used intensively, and No. 2), John 2 : 17 ; Rev. 10 : 9, 10 ; elsewhere it is translated " devour," as also is *katesthiō* (see No. 1). See DEVOUR.

7. KORENNUMI (κορέννυμι), to satiate, to satisfy, as with food, is used in the Middle Voice in Acts 27 : 38, " had eaten enough ; " in 1 Cor. 4 : 8, " ye are filled." See FILL.¶

8. SUNESTHIŌ (συνεσθίω), to eat with (*sun*, with, and No. 1), is found in Luke 15 : 2 ; Acts 10 : 41 ; 11 : 3 ; 1 Cor. 5 : 11 ; Gal. 2 : 12.¶

9. NOMĒN ECHŌ (νομὴν ἔχω) is a phrase consisting of the noun *nomē*, denoting (*a*) pasturage, (*b*) growth, increase, and *echō*, to have. In John 10 : 9 the phrase signifies to find pasture (*a*). In 2 Tim. 2 : 17, with the meaning (*b*), the phrase is, lit., 'will have growth,' translated "will eat," i.e., 'will spread like a gangrene.' It is used in Greek writings, other than the N.T., of the spread of a fire, and of ulcers. See PASTURE.¶

Note : The verb *metalambanō*, to take a part or share of anything with others, to partake of, share, is translated "did eat," in Acts 2 : 46, corrected in the R.V. to "did take ; " a still more suitable rendering would be ' shared,' the sharing of food being suggested ; cp. *metadidōmi*, to share, e.g., Luke 3 : 11.

B. Nouns.

1. BRŌSIS (βρῶσις), akin to A, No. 5, denotes (*a*) the act of eating, e.g., Rom. 14 : 17 ; said of rust, Matt. 6 : 19, 20 ; or, more usually, (*b*) that which is eaten, food (like *brōma*, food), meat, John 4 : 32 ; 6 : 27, 55 ; Col. 2 : 16 ; Heb. 12 : 16 ("morsel of meat ") ; "food," 2 Cor. 9 : 10 ; "eating," 1 Cor. 8 : 4. See FOOD, MEAT, RUST.¶

2. PROSPHAGION (προσφάγιον), primarily a dainty or relish (especially cooked fish), to be eaten with bread (*pros*, to, and A, No. 2), then, fish in general, is used in John 21 : 5, "Have ye aught to eat ? " (A.V., "have ye any meat ? "). Moulton remarks that the evidences of the papyri are to the effect that *prosphagion*, "is not so broad a word as ' something to eat.' The apostles had left even loaves behind them once, Mark 8 : 14 ; they might well have left the ' relish ' on this occasion. It would normally be fish ; cp. Mark 6 : 38 " (Gram. of N.T. Greek, Vol. 1, p. 170).¶

C. Adjective.

BRŌSIMOS (βρώσιμος), akin to A, No. 5, and B., signifying eatable, is found in Luke 24 : 41, R.V., appropriately, "to eat," for the A.V., "meat."¶ In the Sept., Lev. 19 : 23 ; Neh. 9 : 25 ; Ezek. 47 : 12.¶

EDGE, EDGED
A. Noun.

STOMA (στόμα), the mouth (cp. Eng., stomach, from *stomachos*, 1 Tim. 5 : 23), has a secondary and figurative meaning in reference to the edge of a sharp instrument, as of a sword, Luke 21 : 24 ; Heb. 11 : 34 (cp. the Sept., e.g., Gen. 34 : 26 ; Jud. 18 : 27). See FACE, MOUTH.

B. Adjective.

DISTOMOS (δίστομος), lit., double-mouthed (*dis*, twice, and A.), two-edged, is used of a sword with two edges, Heb. 4 : 12 ; Rev. 1 : 16 ; 2 : 12.¶ In the Sept., Judg. 3 : 16 ; Psa. 149 : 6 ; Prov. 5 : 4.¶

EDIFICATION, EDIFY, EDIFYING
A. Noun.

OIKODOMĒ (οἰκοδομή) denotes (*a*) the act of building (*oikos*, a home, and *demō*, to build) ; this is used only figuratively in the N.T., in the sense of edification, the promotion of spiritual growth (lit., the things of building up), Rom. 14 : 19 ; 15 : 2 ; 1 Cor. 14 : 3, 5, 12, 26, e.g. ; (b) a building, edifice, whether material, Matt. 24 : 1, e.g., or figurative, of the future body of the believer, 2 Cor. 5 : 1, or of a local church, 1 Cor. 3 : 9, or the whole Church, " the body of Christ," Eph. 2 : 21. See BUILDING.

B. Verb.

OIKODOMEŌ (οἰκοδομέω), lit., to build a house (see above), (a) usually signifies to build, whether literally, or figuratively ; the present participle, lit., ' the (ones) building,' is used as a noun, " the builders," in Matt. 21 : 42 ; Mark 12 : 10 ; Luke 20 : 17 ; Acts 4 : 11 (in some mss. ; the most authentic have the noun *oikodomos*) ; 1 Pet. 2 : 7 ; (b) is used metaphorically, in the sense of edifying, promoting the spiritual growth and development of character of believers, by teaching or by example, suggesting such spiritual progress as the result of patient labour. It is said (1) of the effect of this upon local churches, Acts 9 : 31 ; 1 Cor. 14 : 4 ; (2) of the individual action of believers towards each other, 1 Cor. 8 : 1 ; 10 : 23 ; 14 : 17 ; 1 Thess. 5 : 11 ; (3) of an individual in regard to himself, 1 Cor. 14 : 4. In 1 Cor. 8 : 10, where it is translated " emboldened," the Apostle uses it with pathetic irony, of the action of a brother in " building up " his brother who had a weak conscience, causing him to compromise his scruples ; ' strengthened,' or ' confirmed,' would be suitable renderings. See BUILD, EMBOLDEN.

EFFECT (of none)

1. AKUROŌ (ἀκυρόω) signifies to render void, deprive of force and authority (from *a*, negative, and *kuros*, might, authority ; *kurios*, a lord, is from the same root), the opposite to *kuroō*, to confirm (see CONFIRM). It is used of making void the Word of God, Matt. 15 : 6 ; Mark 7 : 13 (A.V., " making of none effect "), and of the promise of God to Abraham as not being deprived of authority by the Law 430 years after, Gal. 3 : 17, " disannul." *Kuroō* is used in verse 15. See DISANNUL, VOID.¶

2. KATARGEŌ (καταργέω), to reduce to inactivity, to render useless, is translated to make of none effect, in Rom. 3 : 3, 31 ; 4 : 14 ; Gal. 3 : 17 (cp. *akuroō*, No. 1, in the same verse), and in the A.V. of Gal. 5 : 4, R.V., " ye are severed " (from Christ). For the meaning and use of the word see ABOLISH and DESTROY.

3. KENOŌ (κενόω), to make empty, to empty, is translated " should be made of none effect " in 1 Cor. 1 : 17, A.V. (R.V. " made void ") ; it is used (a) of the Cross of Christ, there ; (b) of Christ, in emptying Himself, Phil. 2 : 7 ; (c) of faith, Rom. 4 : 14 ; (d) of the Apostle Paul's glorying in the Gospel ministry, 1 Cor. 9 : 15 ; (e) of his glorying on behalf of the church at Corinth, 2 Cor. 9 : 3. See EMPTY, VAIN, VOID.¶

Note : In Rom. 9 : 6 the verb *ekpiptō*, lit., to fall out of, as of a ship falling out of its course (cp. the same word in Acts 27 : 17, " were driven "), is translated " hath taken none effect," A.V. (R.V., " hath come to nought "). See NOUGHT.

EFFECTUAL
A. Adjective.

ENERGĒS (ἐνεργής) denotes active, powerful in action (en, in, ergon, work ; Eng. " energy ;" the word " work " is derived from the same root). It is translated "effectual" in 1 Cor. 16:9, of the door opened for the Gospel in Ephesus, and made effectual in the results of entering it ; and in Philm. 6, of the fellowship of Philemon's faith " in the knowledge of every good thing " (R.V.). In Heb. 4 : 12 it describes the Word of God as " active," R.V. (A.V., " powerful "), i.e., full of power to achieve results. See ACTIVE, POWERFUL.¶

B. Verb.

ENERGEŌ (ἐνεργέω), to put forth power, be operative, to work (its usual meaning), is rendered by the verb to work effectually, or to be effectual, in the A.V. of 2 Cor. 1 : 6 ; Gal. 2 : 8 and 1 Thess. 2 : 13 ; in each case the R.V. translates it by the simple verb to work (past tense, " wrought "). In Jas. 5 : 16 the R.V. omits the superfluous word " effectual," and translates the sentence " the supplication of a righteous man availeth much in its working," the verb being in the present participial form. Here the meaning may be ' in its inworking,' i.e., in the effect produced in the praying man, bringing him into line with the will of God, as in the case of Elijah. For a fuller treatment of the word see WORK. See also DO, MIGHTY, SHEW, Note (11).

Note : The noun energeia, working, is translated " effectual working," in the A.V. of Eph. 3 : 7, and 4 : 16.

EFFEMINATE

MALAKOS (μαλακός), soft, soft to the touch (Lat., mollis, Eng., mollify, emollient, etc., are from the same root), is used (a) of raiment, Matt. 11 : 8 (twice) ; Luke 7 : 25 ; (b) metaphorically, in a bad sense, 1 Cor. 6 : 9, " effeminate," not simply of a male who practises forms of lewdness, but persons in general, who are guilty of addiction to sins of the flesh, voluptuous.¶

EFFULGENCE

APAUGASMA (ἀπαύγασμα), radiance, effulgence, is used of light shining from a luminous body (apo, from, and augē, brightness). The word is found in Heb. 1 : 3, where it is used of the Son of God as " being the effulgence of His glory." The word " effulgence " exactly corresponds (in its Latin form) to apaugasma. The glory of God expresses all that He is in His nature and His actings and their manifestation. The Son, being one with the Father in Godhood, is in Himself, and ever was, the shining forth of the glory, manifesting in Himself all that God is and does, all, for instance, that is involved in His being " the very image of His substance," and in His creative acts, His sustaining power, and in His making purification of sins, with all that pertains thereto and issues from it. ¶

EGG

ŌON (ᾠόν) denotes an egg (Lat., *ovum*), Luke 11 : 12.¶

EIGHT, EIGHTEEN, EIGHTH

OKTŌ (ὀκτώ), eight (Lat., *octo, octavus ;* cp. Eng., octagon, octave, octavo, October, etc.), is used in Luke 2 : 21 ; 9 : 28 ; John 20 : 26 ; Acts 9 : 33 ; 25 : 6 ; 1 Pet. 3 : 20 ; in composition with other numerals, *oktō kai deka*, lit., eight and ten, eighteen, Luke 13 : 4, 11, 16 ; *triakonta kai oktō*, thirty and eight, John 5 : 5.¶

OGDOOS (ὄγδοος), eighth (connected with the preceding), is used in Luke 1 : 59 ; Acts 7 : 8 ; 2 Pet. 2 : 5 ; Rev. 17 : 11 ; 21 : 20.¶

OKTAĒMEROS (ὀκταήμερος), an adjective, signifying an eighth-day person or thing, eight days old (*oktō*, and *hēmera*, a day), is used in Phil. 3 : 5. This, and similar numerical adjectives not found in the N.T., indicate duration rather than intervals. The Apostle shows by his being an ' eighth-day ' person as to circumcision, that his parents were neither Ishmaelites (circumcised in their thirteenth year) nor other Gentiles, converted to Judaism (circumcised on becoming Jews).¶

EITHER

Ē (ἤ) is a disjunctive particle. One of its uses is to distinguish things which exclude each other, or one of which can take the place of another. It is translated " either " in Matt. 6 : 24 ; 12 : 33 ; Luke 16 : 13 ; Acts 17 : 21 ; 1 Cor. 14 : 6. The R.V. rightly omits it in Luke 6 : 42, and translates it by " or " in Luke 15 : 8 ; Phil. 3 : 12 and Jas. 3 : 12.

Note : The adverb *enteuthen*, denoting " hence," is repeated in the phrase rendered " on either side," (lit., ' hence and hence ') in John 19 : 18. The R.V. of Rev. 22 : 2 translates it " on this side," distinguishing it from *ekeithen*, " on that side ; " the A.V., following another reading for the latter adverb, has " on either side." See HENCE.

ELDER, ELDEST
A. Adjectives.

1. PRESBUTEROS (πρεσβύτερος), an adjective, the comparative degree of *presbus*, an old man, an elder, is used (*a*) of age, whether of the elder of two persons, Luke 15 : 25, or more, John 8 : 9, " the eldest ; " or of a person advanced in life, a senior, Acts 2 : 17 ; in Heb. 11 : 2, the " elders " are the forefathers in Israel ; so in Matt. 15 : 2 ; Mark 7 : 3, 5 ; the feminine of the adjective is used of elder women in the churches, 1 Tim.

5 : 2, not in respect of position but in seniority of age ; (*b*) of rank or positions of responsibility, (1) among Gentiles, as in the Sept. of Gen. 50 : 7 ; Num. 22 : 7 ; (2) in the Jewish nation, firstly, those who were the heads or leaders of the tribes and families, as of the seventy who assisted Moses, Num. 11 : 16 ; Deut. 27 : 1, and those assembled by Solomon ; secondly, members of the Sanhedrin, consisting of the chief priests, elders and scribes, learned in Jewish Law, e.g., Matt. 16 : 21 ; 26 : 47 ; thirdly, those who managed public affairs in the various cities, Luke 7 : 3 ; (3) in the Christian churches, those who, being raised up and qualified by the work of the Holy Spirit, were appointed to have the spiritual care of, and to exercise oversight over, the churches. To these the term bishops, *episkopoi*, or overseers, is applied (see Acts 20, ver. 17 with ver. 28, and Tit. 1 : 5 and 7), the latter term indicating the nature of their work, *presbuteroi* their maturity of spiritual experience. The Divine arrangement seen throughout the N.T. was for a plurality of these to be appointed in each church, Acts 14 : 23 ; 20 : 17 ; Phil. 1 : 1 ; 1 Tim. 5 : 17 ; Tit. 1 : 5. The duty of elders is described by the verb *episkopeō*. They were appointed according as they had given evidence of fulfilling the Divine qualifications, Tit. 1 : 6 to 9 ; cp. 1 Tim. 3 : 1-7 and 1 Pet. 5 : 2 ; (4) the twenty-four elders enthroned in Heaven around the throne of God, Rev. 4 : 4, 10 ; 5 : 5-14 ; 7 : 11, 13 ; 11 : 16 ; 14 : 3 ; 19 : 4. The number twenty-four is representative of earthly conditions. The word " elder " is nowhere applied to angels. See OLD.

2. SUMPRESBUTEROS (συμπρεσβύτερος), a fellow-elder (*sun*, with), is used in 1 Pet. 5 : 1.¶

3. MEIZŌN (μείζων), greater, the comparative degree of *megas*, great, is used of age, and translated " elder " in Rom. 9 : 12, with reference to Esau and Jacob. See GREATER, GREATEST, MORE.

B. Noun.

PRESBUTERION (πρεσβυτέριον), an assembly of aged men, denotes (*a*) the Council or Senate among the Jews, Luke 22 : 66 ; Acts 22 : 5 ; (*b*) the elders or bishops in a local church, 1 Tim. 4 : 14, " the presbytery." For their functions see A, No. 1, (3).

ELECT, ELECTED, ELECTION
A. Adjectives.

1. EKLEKTOS (ἐκλεκτός) lit. signifies picked out, chosen (*ek*, from, *legō*, to gather, pick out), and is used of (*a*) Christ, the chosen of God, as the Messiah, Luke 23 : 35 (for the verb in 9 : 35 see Note below), and metaphorically as a " living Stone," " a chief corner Stone," 1 Pet. 2 : 4, 6 ; some mss. have it in John 1 : 34, instead of *huios*, Son ; (*b*) angels, 1 Tim. 5 : 21, as chosen to be of especially high rank in administrative association with God, or as His messengers to human beings, doubtless in contrast to fallen angels (see 2 Pet. 2 : 4 and Jude 6) ; (*c*) believers (Jews or Gentiles), Matt. 24 : 22, 24, 31 ; Mark 13 : 20, 22, 27 ; Luke 18 : 7 ;

Rom. 8 : 33 ; Col. 3 : 12 ; 2 Tim. 2 : 10 ; Tit. 1 : 1 ; 1 Pet. 1 : 1 ; 2 : 9 (as a spiritual race) ; Matt. 20 : 16 ; 22 : 14 and Rev. 17 : 14, " chosen ; " individual believers are so mentioned in Rom. 16 : 13 ; 2 John 1, 13.¶

Believers were chosen " before the foundation of the world " (cp. " before times eternal," 2 Tim. 1 : 9), in Christ, Eph. 1 : 4, to adoption, Eph. 1 : 5 ; good works, 2 : 10 ; conformity to Christ, Rom. 8 : 29 ; salvation from the delusions of the Antichrist and the doom of the deluded, 2 Thess. 2 : 13 ; eternal glory, Rom. 9 : 23.

The source of their election is God's grace, not human will, Eph. 1 : 4, 5 ; Rom. 9 : 11 ; 11 : 5. They are given by God the Father to Christ as the fruit of His Death, all being foreknown and foreseen by God, John 17 : 6 and Rom. 8 : 29. While Christ's Death was sufficient for all men, and is effective in the case of the elect, yet men are treated as responsible, being capable of the will and power to choose. For the rendering ' being chosen as firstfruits,' an alternative reading in 2 Thess. 2 : 13, see FIRSTFRUITS. See CHOICE, B.

2. SUNEKLEKTOS (συνεκλεκτός) means " elect together with," 1 Pet. 5 : 13.¶

B. Noun.

EKLOGĒ (ἐκλογή) denotes a picking out, selection (Eng., eclogue), then, that which is chosen ; in Acts 9 : 15, said of the choice of God of Saul of Tarsus, the phrase is, lit., ' a vessel of choice.' It is used four times in Romans ; in 9 : 11, of Esau and Jacob, where the phrase " the purpose . . . according to election " is virtually equivalent to ' the electing purpose ; ' in 11 : 5, the " remnant according to the election of grace " refers to believing Jews, saved from among the unbelieving nation ; so in ver. 7 ; in ver. 28, " the election " may mean either the act of choosing or the chosen ones ; the context, speaking of the fathers, points to the former, the choice of the nation according to the covenant of promise. In 1 Thess. 1 : 4, " your election " refers not to the church collectively, but to the individuals constituting it ; the Apostle's assurance of their election gives the reason for his thanksgiving. Believers are to give ' the more diligence to make their calling and election sure,' by the exercise of the qualities and graces which make them fruitful in the knowledge of God, 2 Pet. 1 : 10.¶ For the corresponding verb eklegomai, see CHOOSE.

ELEMENTS

STOICHEION (στοιχεῖον), used in the plural, primarily signifies any first things from which others in a series, or a composite whole, take their rise ; the word denotes an element, first principle (from stoichos, a row, rank, series ; cp. the verb stoicheō, to walk or march in rank ; see WALK) ; it was used of the letters of the alphabet, as elements of speech. In the N.T. it is used of (a) the substance of the material world, 2 Pet. 3 : 10, 12 ; (b) the delusive speculations of Gentile cults and of Jewish theories, treated as elementary principles, " the rudiments of the world," Col. 2 : 8, spoken of as " philosophy and vain deceit ; " these were presented as superior to faith in Christ ; at Colossæ the worship of angels, mentioned in ver. 18, is explicable by the supposition, held by both Jews and Gentiles in that district, that the constellations were either themselves animated heavenly beings, or were governed by them ; (c) the rudimentary principles of religion, Jewish or Gentile, also described as " the rudiments of the world," Col. 2 : 20, and as " weak and beggarly rudiments," Gal. 4 : 3, 9, R.V., constituting a yoke of bondage ; (d) the elementary principles (the A.B.C.) of the O.T., as a revelation from God, Heb. 5 : 12, R.V., " rudiments," lit., ' the rudiments of the beginning of the oracles of God,' such as are taught to spiritual babes. See PRINCIPLES, RUDIMENTS.¶

ELEVEN, ELEVENTH
HENDEKA (ἕνδεκα), lit., one ten (Lat., *undecim*), is used only of the eleven Apostles remaining after the death of Judas Iscariot, Matt. 28 : 16 ; Mark 16 : 14 ; Luke 24 : 9, 33 ; Acts 1 : 26 ; 2 : 14.¶
HENDEKATOS (ἑνδέκατος), an adjective derived from the above, is found in Matt. 20 : 6, 9 ; Rev. 21 : 20.¶

ELOQUENT
LOGIOS (λόγιος), an adjective, from *logos*, a word, primarily meant learned, a man skilled in literature and the arts. In the A.V. of Acts 18 : 24, it is translated " eloquent," said of Apollos ; the R.V. is almost certainly right in translating it " learned." It was much more frequently used among the Greeks of one who was erudite than of one who was skilled in words. He had stores of learning and could use it convincingly.¶

ELSE
EPEI (ἐπεί), a conjunction, when used of cause, meaning " since," " otherwise," " for then," " because ; " in an ellipsis, " else," as in 1 Cor. 7 : 14, where the ellipsis would be ' if the unbelieving husband were not sanctified in the wife, your children would be unclean ; ' cp. Rom. 11 : 6, 22 ; 1 Cor. 5 : 10 ; Heb. 9 : 26. Sometimes it introduces a question, as in Rom. 3 : 6 ; 1 Cor. 14 : 16 ; 15 : 29 ; Heb. 10 : 2. It is translated " else " in 1 Cor. 14 : 16 and in the R.V. in Heb. 9 : 26 and 10 : 2, for A.V., " for then."

ELSEWHERE
ALLACHOU (ἀλλαχοῦ), connected with *allos*, another, is used in Mark 1 : 38 (R.V. only).¶

For EMBARK (R.V., in Acts 27 : 2) see ABOARD

EMBOLDEN

OIKODOMEŌ (οἰκοδομέω) is rendered " embolden " in 1 Cor. 8 : 10, in reference to blameworthy actions (see marg.), the delinquent being built up, so to speak, to do what is contrary to his conscience. See BUILD, EDIFICATION.

EMBRACE

1. ASPAZOMAI (ἀσπάζομαι) lit. signifies to draw to oneself ; hence, to greet, salute, welcome, the ordinary meaning, e.g., in Rom. 16, where it is used 21 times. It also signifies to bid farewell, e.g., Acts 20 : 1 , R.V., " took leave of " (A.V., " embraced "). A salutation or farewell was generally made by embracing and kissing (see Luke 10 : 4, which indicates the possibility of delay on the journey by frequent salutation). In Heb. 11 : 13 it is said of those who greeted the promises from afar, R.V., " greeted," for A.V., " embraced." Cp. *aspasmos*, a salutation. See GREET, LEAVE (take), SALUTE.

Note : In Acts 21 : 6 the most authentic texts have *apaspazomai* (*apo*, and No. 1), to bid farewell.

2. SUMPERILAMBANŌ (συμπεριλαμβάνω), lit., to take around with; (*sun*, with, *peri*, around, *lambanō*, to take), to embrace, is used in Acts 20 : 10, in connection with Paul's recovery of Eutychus.¶ In the Sept., Ezra 5 : 3, " to enclose."¶

EMPEROR

SEBASTOS (σεβαστός), august, reverent, the masculine gender of an adjective (from *sebas*, reverential awe), became used as the title of the Roman Emperor, Acts 25 : 21, 25, R.V., for A.V., " Augustus ; " then, taking its name from the Emperor, it became a title of honour applied to certain legions or cohorts or battalions, marked for their valour, Acts 27 : 1.¶ Cp. *sebazomai*, to worship, Rom. 1 : 25 ;¶ *sebasma*, an object of worship, Acts 17 : 23 ; 2 Thess. 2 : 4.¶

EMERALD

A. Noun.

SMARAGDOS (σμάραγδος) is a transparent stone of a light green colour, occupying the first place in the second row on the high priest's breastplate, Ex. 28 : 18. Tyre imported it from Syria, Ezek. 27 : 16. It is one of the foundations of the Heavenly Jerusalem, Rev. 21 : 19. The name was applied to other stones of a similar character, such as the carbuncle.¶

B. Adjective.

SMARAGDINOS (σμαράγδινος), emerald in character, descriptive of the rainbow round about the Throne in Rev. 4 : 3, is used in the papyri to denote emerald green.¶

EMPTY

A. Verbs.

1. KENOŌ (κενόω), to empty, is so translated in Phil. 2 : 7, R.V., for A.V., " made . . . of no reputation." The clauses which follow the verb are exegetical of its meaning, especially the phrases " the form of a servant," and " the likeness of men." Christ did not empty Himself of Godhood. He did not cease to be what He essentially and eternally was. The A.V., while not an exact translation, goes far to express the act of the Lord (see GIFFORD on the Incarnation). For other occurrences of the word see Rom. 4 : 14 ; 1 Cor. 1 : 17 ; 9 : 15 ; 2 Cor. 9 : 3.¶ In the Sept., Jer. 14 : 2 ; 15 : 9.¶

2. SCHOLAZŌ (σχολάζω), from scholē, leisure, that for which leisure is employed, such as a lecture (hence, the place where lectures are given ; Eng., school), is used of persons, to have time for anything and so to be occupied in, 1 Cor. 7 : 5 ; of things, to be unoccupied, empty, Matt. 12 : 44 (some mss. have it in Luke 11 : 25). See GIVE (oneself to).¶

B. Adjective.

KENOS (κενός) expresses the hollowness of anything, the absence of that which otherwise might be possessed. It is used (a) literally, Mark 12 : 3 ; Luke 1 : 53 ; 20 : 10, 11 ; (b) metaphorically, of imaginations, Acts 4 : 25 ; of words which convey erroneous teachings, Eph. 5 : 6 ; of deceit, Col. 2 : 8 ; of a person whose professed faith is not accompanied by works, Jas. 2 : 20 ; negatively, concerning the grace of God, 1 Cor. 15 : 10 ; of refusal to receive it, 2 Cor. 6 : 1 ; of faith, 1 Cor. 15 : 14 ; of preaching (id.) ; and other forms of Christian activity and labour, 1 Cor. 15 : 58 ; Gal. 2 : 2 ; Phil. 2 : 16 ; 1 Thess. 2 : 1 ; 3 : 5.¶ The synonymous word mataios, vain, signifies void of result, it marks the aimlessness of anything. The vain (kenos) man in Jas. 2 : 20 is one who is empty of Divinely imparted wisdom ; in 1 : 26 the vain (mataios) religion is one that produces nothing profitable. Kenos stresses the absence of quality, mataios, the absence of useful aim or effect. Cp. the corresponding adverb kenōs, " in vain," in Jas. 4 : 5,¶ the noun kenodoxia, vainglory, Phil. 2 : 3,¶ the adjective kenodoxos, vainglorious, Gal. 5 : 26,¶ and the noun kenophōnia, vain, or empty, babblings, 1 Tim. 6 : 20 ; 2 Tim. 2 : 16.¶

For EMULATION, A.V. (Rom. 11 : 14 ; Gal. 5 : 20) see JEALOUSY

ENABLE

ENDUNAMOŌ (ἐνδυναμόω), to render strong (en, in, dunamis, power), is translated " enabled " in 1 Tim. 1 : 12, more lit., ' in-strengthened,' ' inwardly strengthened,' suggesting strength in soul and purpose (cp. Phil. 4 : 13). See STRENGTH, STRONG. (In the Sept., Judg. 6 : 34 ; 1 Chron. 12 : 18 ; Psa. 52 : 7.¶)

ENACT

NOMOTHETEŌ (νομοθετέω), to ordain by law, to enact (nomos, a law, tithēmi, to put), is used in the Passive Voice, and rendered " enacted " in Heb. 8 : 6, R.V., for A.V., " established ; " in 7 : 11, used intransitively, it is rendered " received the Law." See ESTABLISH, LAW.¶

For ENCLOSE see INCLOSE

ENCOUNTER

SUMBALLŌ (συμβάλλω), lit., to throw together (sun, with, ballō, to throw), is used of encountering in war, Luke 14 : 31, R.V., " to encounter . . . (in war)," for A.V., " to make war against ; " of meeting in order to discuss, in Acts 17 : 18, " encountered," of the philosophers in Athens and the Apostle. See CONFER, HELP, MAKE, MEET, PONDER.

ENCOURAGE, ENCOURAGEMENT
A. Verbs.

1. PROTREPŌ (προτρέπω), to urge forward, persuade, is used in Acts 18 : 27 in the Middle Voice, R.V., " encouraged," indicating their particular interest in giving Apollos the encouragement mentioned ; the A.V., " exhorting," wrongly connects the verb.¶

2. PARAMUTHEOMAI (παραμυθέομαι), from para, with, and muthos, counsel, advice, is translated " encouraging " in 1 Thess. 2 : 11, R.V., and " encourage " in 5 : 14, R.V., there signifying to stimulate to the discharge of the ordinary duties of life. In John 11 : 19, 31, it means to comfort. See COMFORT.¶

Cp. the nouns paramuthia, 1 Cor. 14 : 3, ¶ and paramuthion, Phil 2 : 1, comfort.¶

B. Noun.

PARAKLĒSIS (παράκλησις), a calling to one's aid (para, by the side, kaleō, to call), then, an exhortation, encouragement, is translated " encouragement " in Heb. 6 : 18, R.V., for A.V., " consolation ; " it is akin to parakaleō, to beseech or exhort, encourage, comfort, and paraklētos, a paraclete or advocate. See COMFORT, CONSOLATION, EXHORTATION, INTREATY.

END, ENDING
A. Nouns.

1. TELOS (τέλος) signifies (a) the limit, either at which a person or thing ceases to be what he or it was up to that point, or at which previous activities were ceased, 2 Cor. 3 : 13 ; 1 Pet. 4 : 7 ; (b) the final issue or result of a state or process, e.g., Luke 1 : 33 ; in Rom. 10 : 4, Christ is described as " the end of the Law unto righteousness to everyone that believeth ; " this is best explained by Gal. 3 : 23–26 ; cp. Jas. 5 : 11 ; the following more especially point to the issue or fate of a thing, Matt.

26 : 58 ; Rom. 6 : 21 ; 2 Cor. 11 : 15 ; Phil. 3 : 19 ; Heb. 6 : 8 ; 1 Pet. 1 : 9 ; (c) a fulfilment, Luke 22 : 37, A.V. " (have) an end ; " (d) the utmost degree of an act, as of the love of Christ towards His disciples, John 13 : 1 ; (e) the aim or purpose of a thing, 1 Tim. 1 : 5 ; (f) the last in a succession or series Rev. 1 : 8 (A.V., only, " ending ") ; 21 : 6 ; 22 : 13. See CONTINUAL, CUSTOM (Toll), FINALLY, UTTERMOST.

Note : The following phrases contain *telos* (the word itself coming under one or other of the above) : *eis telos,* " unto the end," e.g., Matt. 10 : 22 ; 24 : 13 ; Luke 18 : 5, " continual ; " John 13 : 1 (see above) ; 2 Cor. : 13, " on the end " (R.V.) ; *heōs telous,* " unto the end," 1 Cor. 1 : 8 ; 2 Cor. 1 : 13 ;¶ *achri telous,* " even to the end " (a stronger expression than the preceding), Heb. 6 : 11 ; Rev. 2 : 26 (where ' even ' might well have been added) ;¶ *mechri telous,* with much the same meaning as *achri telous,* Heb. 3 : 6, 14.¶ See other expressions in the Notes after C.

2. SUNTELEIA (συντέλεια) signifies a bringing to completion together (*sun* with, *teleō,* to complete, akin to No. 1), marking the completion or consummation of the various parts of a scheme. In Matt. 13 : 39, 40, 49 ; 24 : 3 ; 28 : 20, the rendering " the end of the world " (A.V. and R.V., text) is misleading ; the R.V. marg., " the consummation of the age," is correct. The word does not denote a termination, but the heading up of events to the appointed climax. *Aiōn* is not the world, but a period or epoch or era in which events take place. In Heb. 9 : 26, the word translated " world " (A.V.) is in the plural, and the phrase is ' the consummation of the ages.' It was at the heading up of all the various epochs appointed by Divine counsels that Christ was manifested (i.e., in His Incarnation) " to put away sin by the sacrifice of Himself."¶

3. PERAS (πέρας), a limit, boundary (from *pera,* beyond), is used (a) of space, chiefly in the plural, Matt. 12 : 42, R.V., " ends," for A.V., " uttermost parts ; " so Luke 11 : 31 (A.V., " utmost ") ; Rom. 10 : 18 (A.V. and R.V., " ends ") ; (b) of the termination of something occurring in a period, Heb. 6 : 16, R.V., " final," for A.V., " an end," said of strife. See UTTERMOST.¶

4. EKBASIS (ἔκβασις) denotes a way out (*ek,* out, *bainō,* to go), 1 Cor. 10 : 13, " way of escape ; " or an issue, Heb. 13 : 7 (A.V., " end," R.V., " issue "). See ISSUE.¶

B. Verbs.

1. TELEŌ (τελέω), to complete, finish, bring to an end, is translated " had made an end," in Matt. 11 : 1. See ACCOMPLISH.

2. SUNTELEŌ (συντελέω), cp. A, No. 2, signifies (a) to bring to an end, finish completely (*sun,* together, imparting a perfective significance to *teleō*), Matt. 7 : 28 (in some mss.) ; Luke 4 : 2, 13 ; Acts 21 : 27, R.V., " completed ; " (b) to bring to fulfilment, Mark 13 : 4 ; Rom. 9 : 28 ; (c) to effect, make, Heb. 8 : 8. See FINISH, FULFIL, MAKE.¶

3. PLĒROŌ (πληρόω), (a) to fill, (b) to fulfil, complete, end, is trans-

lated " had ended " in Luke 7 : 1 ; " were ended " (Passive) in Acts 19 : 21. See ACCOMPLISH.

Note : In John 13 : 2, the verb *ginomai*, there signifying to be in progress, and used in the present participle, is translated " during supper " (R.V.). A less authentic reading, is *genomenou*, " being ended " (A.V.).

C. Adjective.

ESCHATOS (ἔσχατος), last, utmost, extreme, is used as a noun (*a*) of time, rendered " end " in Heb. 1 : 2, R.V., " at the end of these days," i.e., at the end of the period under the Law, for A.V., " in these last days ; " so in 1 Pet. 1 : 20, " at the end of the times." In 2 Pet. 2 : 20, the plural, *ta eschata*, lit., ' the last things,' is rendered " the latter end," A.V., (R.V., " the last state ") ; the same phrase is used in Matt. 12 : 45 ; Luke 11 : 26 ; (*b*) of place, Acts 13 : 47, A.V., " ends (of the earth)," R.V., " uttermost part." See LAST, LOWEST, UTTERMOST.

Notes : (1) In Matt. 28 : 1, *opse*, late (in the evening), is rendered " in the end (of)," A.V., R.V., " late (on)." (2) In 1 Pet. 1 : 13, *teleiōs*, " perfectly," R.V., is rendered " to the end," in A.V. (3) The phrase *eis touto*, lit., ' unto this,' signifies " to this end," John 18 : 37, R.V. (twice ; A.V., " for this cause," in the second clause) ; so Mark 1 : 38 ; Acts 26 : 16 ; Rom. 14 : 9 ; 2 Cor. 2 : 9 ; 1 Tim. 4 : 10 (A.V., " therefore "); 1 Pet. 4 : 6 ; 1 John 3 : 8 (A.V., " for this purpose "). (4) *Eis*, unto, followed by the article and the infinitive mood of a verb, signifies " to the end that . . , " marking the aim of an action, Acts 7 : 19 ; Rom. 1 : 11 ; 4 : 16, 18 ; Eph. 1 : 12 ; 1 Thess. 3 : 13 ; 2 Thess. 1 : 5 ; 2 : 2, 6 ; 1 Pet. 3 : 7. In Luke 18 : 1, *pros*, to, has the same construction and meaning. (5) The conjunction *hina*, in order that, is sometimes rendered " to the end that," Eph. 3 : 17 ; 2 Thess. 3 : 14 ; Tit. 3 : 8. (6) In Matt. 24 : 31, the prepositions *apo*, from, and *heōs*, unto, are used with the plural of *akros*, highest, extreme, signifying " from one end . . . to the other," lit., ' from extremities . . . to extremities.'

ENDEAVOUR

1. SPOUDAZO (σπουδάζω), to make haste, to be zealous, and hence, to be diligent, is rendered " endeavouring " in Eph. 4 : 3, A.V. ; R.V., " giving diligence." In 2 Pet. 1 : 15, A.V., " endeavour," R.V., " give diligence." Both have " endeavoured " in 1 Thess. 2 : 17. See DILIGENCE.

2. ZĒTEŌ (ζητέω), to seek after, is translated " endeavour " in Acts 16 : 10, A.V., R.V., " sought." See ABOUT (to be), DESIRE, INQUIRE, SEEK.

ENDLESS

1. AKATALUTOS (ἀκατάλυτος) denotes indissoluble (from *a*, negative, *kata*, down, *luō*, to loose), Heb. 7 : 16, " endless ; " see the R.V., marg.,

i.e., a life which makes its Possessor the holder of His priestly office for evermore.¶

2. APERANTOS (ἀπέραντος), from *a*, negative and *perainō*, to complete, finish, signifies interminable, endless ; it is said of genealogies, I Tim. I : 4.¶ In the Sept., Job 36 : 26.¶

ENDUE

ENDUŌ (ἐνδύω), in the Middle Voice, to put on oneself, be clothed with, is used metaphorically of power, Luke 24 : 49, R.V., " clothed." See CLOTHE.

Note : In Jas. 3 : 13 the adjective *epistēmōn*, knowing, skilled, is translated " endued with knowledge," A.V., R.V., " understanding."¶

ENDURE, ENDURING
A. Verbs.

1. MENŌ (μένω), to abide, is rendered to endure in the A.V. of John 6 : 27 and I Pet. I : 25 (R.V., " abideth ") ; Heb. 10 : 34, A.V., " enduring (substance)," R.V., " abiding." See ABIDE.

2. HUPOMENŌ (ὑπομένω), a strengthened form of No. 1, denotes to abide under, to bear up courageously (under suffering), Matt. 10 : 22 ; 24 : 13 ; Mark 13 : 13 ; Rom. 12 : 12, translated " patient ; " I Cor. 13 : 7 ; 2 Tim. 2 : 10, 12 (A.V., " suffer ") ; Heb. 10 : 32 ; 12 : 2, 3, 7 ; Jas. I : 12 ; 5 : II ; I Pet. 2 : 20, " ye shall take it patiently." It has its other significance, to tarry, wait for, await, in Luke 2 : 43 ; Acts 17 : 14 (in some mss., Rom. 8 : 24).¶ Cp. B. See ABIDE, PATIENT, SUFFER, TARRY. Cp. *makrothumeō*, to be longsuffering (see No. 7).

3. PHERŌ (φέρω), to bear, is translated " endured " in Rom. 9 : 22 and Heb. 12 : 20. See BEAR.

4. HUPOPHERŌ (ὑποφέρω), a strengthened form of No. 3, to bear or carry, by being under, is said metaphorically of enduring temptation, I Cor. 10 : 13, A.V., " bear ; " persecutions, 2 Tim. 3 : 11 ; griefs, I Pet. 2 : 19. See BEAR.¶

5. ANECHŌ (ἀνέχω), to hold up (*ana*, up, *echō*, to hold or have), always in the Middle Voice in the N.T., is rendered " endure " in 2 Thess. I : 4, of persecutions and tribulations ; in 2 Tim. 4 : 3, of sound doctrine. See BEAR.

6. KARTEREŌ (καρτερέω), to be stedfast, patient, is used in Heb. II : 27, " endured," of Moses in relation to Egypt.¶ In the Sept., Job 2 : 9 ; Isa. 42 : 14.¶

7. MAKROTHUMEŌ (μακροθυμέω), to be long-tempered (*makros*, long, *thumos*, mind), is rendered " patiently endured " in Heb. 6 : 15, said of Abraham. See B. below. See BEAR, LONGSUFFERING, PATIENCE, SUFFER.

Note : In 2 Tim. 2 : 9, *kakopatheō*, to suffer evil (*kakos*, evil, *paschō*, to suffer), is translated " endure hardness," A.V. ; R.V., " suffer hardship ; " so in 4 : 5, A.V., " endure afflictions ; " elsewhere in Jas. 5 : 13.¶ In 2 Tim. 2 : 3 the most authentic mss. have *sunkakopatheō*, to suffer hardship with, as in 1 : 8.¶ See HARDSHIP, SUFFER.

B. Noun.

HUPOMONĒ (ὑπομονή), patience, lit., a remaining under (akin to A, No. 2), is translated " patient enduring " in 2 Cor. 1 : 6, R.V., for A.V., "enduring." Cp. *makrothumia*, longsuffering (akin to A, No. 7). See PATIENCE.

ENEMY

ECHTHROS (ἐχθρός), an adjective, primarily denoting hated or hateful (akin to *echthos*, hate ; perhaps associated with *ektos*, outside), hence, in the Active sense, denotes hating, hostile ; it is used as a noun signifying an enemy, adversary, and is said (*a*) of the Devil, Matt. 13 : 39 ; Luke 10 : 19 ; (*b*) of death, 1 Cor. 15 : 26 ; (*c*) of the professing believer who would be a friend of the world, thus making Himself an enemy of God, Jas. 4 : 4 ; (*d*) of men who are opposed to Christ, Matt. 13 : 25, 28 ; 22 : 44 ; Mark 12 : 36 ; Luke 19 : 27 ; 20 : 43 ; Acts 2 : 35 ; Rom. 11 : 28 ; Phil. 3 : 18 ; Heb. 1 : 13 ; 10 : 13 ; or to His servants, Rev. 11 : 5, 12 ; to the nation of Israel, Luke 1 : 71, 74 ; 19 : 43 ; (*e*) of one who is opposed to righteousness, Acts 13 : 10 ; (*f*) of Israel in its alienation from God, Rom. 11 : 28 ; (*g*) of the unregenerate in their attitude toward God, Rom. 5 : 10 ; Col. 1 : 21 ; (*h*) of believers in their former state, 2 Thess. 3 : 15 ; (*i*) of foes, Matt. 5 : 43, 44 ; 10 : 36 ; Luke 6 : 27, 35 ; Rom. 12 : 20 ; 1 Cor. 15 : 25 ; of the Apostle Paul because he told converts " the truth," Gal. 4 : 16. See FOE. Cp. *echthra*, enmity.¶

ENGRAFTED

Note : This is the A.V. rendering of *emphutos*, Jas. 1 : 21, an adjective derived from *emphuō*, to implant ; the R.V. has " implanted."¶ The metaphor is that of a seed rooting itself in the heart ; cp. Matt. 13 : 21 ; 15 : 13 ; 1 Cor. 3 : 6, and the kindred word *sumphutos*, Rom. 6 : 5, " planted together " (*sun*, with).¶ The A.V. " engrafted " would translate the word *emphuteuton* (from *emphuteuō*, to graft), which is not found in the N.T. ; it uses *enkentrizō* in Rom. 11. Cp. *ekphuō*, to cause to grow out, put forth (leaves), Matt. 24 : 32 ; Mark 13 : 28.

ENGRAVE

ENTUPOŌ (ἐντυπόω), to imprint, engrave (*en*, in, *tupos*, a mark, impression, form, type), is used of the engraving of the Law on the two stones, or tablets, 2 Cor. 3 : 7.¶ In the Sept., Ex. 36 : 39 (some texts have *ektupoō*).¶ See also GRAVEN.

ENJOIN

1. ENTELLOMAI (ἐντέλλομαι) is translated "hath enjoined" in the A.V. of Heb. 9 : 20. See COMMAND (R.V.).

2. EPITASSŌ (ἐπιτάσσω), lit., to set or arrange over, to charge, command, is rendered "enjoin" in Philm. 8. See COMMAND. Cp. *keleuō*, to order.

ENJOY

A. Verb.

TUNCHANŌ (τυγχάνω), used transitively, denotes to hit upon, meet with ; then, to reach, get, obtain ; it is translated "enjoy" (i.e., obtain to our satisfaction) in Acts 24 : 2. See CHANCE, COMMON, *Note* (3), OBTAIN.

B. Noun.

APOLAUSIS (ἀπόλαυσις), enjoyment (from *apolauō*, to take hold of, enjoy a thing), suggests the advantage or pleasure to be obtained from a thing (from a root, *lab*— seen in *lambanō*, to obtain) ; it is used with the preposition *eis*, in 1 Tim. 6 : 17, lit., ' unto enjoyment,' rendered "to enjoy ; " with *echō*, to have, in Heb. 11 : 25, lit., ' to have pleasure (of sin),' translated "to enjoy the pleasures."¶ See PLEASURE.

ENLARGE

1. MEGALUNŌ (μεγαλύνω) denotes to make great (from *megas*, great), Matt. 23 : 5, " enlarge ; " 2 Cor. 10 : 15, A.V., " enlarged," R.V., " magnified ; " elsewhere in the A.V. it is rendered by the verb to magnify, except in Luke 1 : 58, A.V., " had shewed great (mercy)," R.V., " had magnified (His mercy) ; see Luke 1 : 46 ; Acts 5 : 13 ; 10 : 46 ; 19 : 17 ; Phil. 1 : 20. See MAGNIFY.¶

2. PLATUNŌ (πλατύνω), to make broad, from *platus*, broad, is translated " enlarged " in 2 Cor. 6 : 11, 13 (metaphorically), " make broad," Matt. 23 : 5 (literally). From the primary sense of freedom comes that of the joy that results from it. See BROAD.¶ Cp. *platos*, breadth, and *plateia*, a street.

ENLIGHTEN

PHŌTIZŌ (φωτίζω), from *phōs*, light, (a), used intransitively, signifies to give light, shine, Rev. 22 : 5 ; (b), used transitively, to enlighten, illumine, is rendered " enlighten " in Eph. 1 : 18, metaphorically of spiritual enlightenment ; so John 1 : 9, i.e., " lighting every man " (by reason of His coming) ; Eph. 3 : 9, " to make (all men) see " (R.V. marg., " to bring to light ") ; Heb. 6 : 4, " were enlightened ; " 10 : 32, R.V., " enlightened," A.V., " illuminated." See ILLUMINATED, LIGHT. Cp. *phōtismos*, light, and *phōteinos*, full of light.

ENMITY

ECHTHRA (ἔχθρα), from the adjective *echthros* (see ENEMY) is rendered "enmity" in Luke 23 : 12; Rom. 8 : 7; Eph. 2 : 15, 16; Jas. 4 : 4; "enmities," Gal. 5 : 20, R.V., for A.V., "hatred." It is the opposite of *agapē*, love.¶

ENOUGH
A. Adjectives.

1. ARKETOS (ἀρκετός), sufficient, akin to *arkeō* (see B, No. 1), is rendered "enough" in Matt. 10 : 25; "sufficient" in Matt. 6 : 34; "suffice" in 1 Pet. 4 : 3, lit., "(is) sufficient." See SUFFICE, SUFFICIENT.¶

2. HIKANOS (ἱκανός), sufficient, competent, fit (akin to *hikanō* and *hikō*, to reach, attain and *hikanoō*, to make sufficient), is translated "enough" in Luke 22 : 38, of the Lord's reply to Peter concerning the swords. See ABLE.

Note : In Luke 15 : 17 the verb *perisseuō*, to have abundance, is translated "have enough and to spare." In Acts 27 : 38 the verb *korennumi*, to satisfy, is translated "had eaten enough."

B. Verbs.

1. ARKEŌ (ἀρκέω), to ward off; hence, to aid, assist; then, to be strong enough, i.e., to suffice, to be enough (cp. A, No. 1), is translated "be enough" in Matt. 25 : 9. See CONTENT.

2. APECHŌ (ἀπέχω), lit., to hold off from, to have off or out (*apō*, from, *echō*, to have), i.e., to have in full, to have received, is used impersonally in Mark 14 : 41, "it is enough," in the Lord's words to His slumbering disciples in Gethsemane. It is difficult, however, to find examples of this meaning in Greek usage of the word, and *apechō* may here refer, in its commercial significance, to Judas (who is mentioned immediately afterwards), with the meaning 'he hath received' (his payment); cp. the same use in Matt. 6 : 2, 5, 16 (see Deissmann, *Light from the Ancient East*, pp. 110 ff.). See ABSTAIN, HAVE, RECEIVE.

For ENQUIRE see INQUIRE

ENRICH

PLOUTIZŌ (πλουτίζω), to make rich (from *ploutos*, wealth, riches), is used metaphorically, of spiritual riches, in 1 Cor. 1 : 5, "ye were enriched;" 2 Cor. 6 : 10, "making rich;" 2 Cor. 9 : 11, "being enriched." See RICH.¶

ENROL, ENROLMENT
A. Verb.

APOGRAPHŌ (ἀπογράφω) primarily signifies to write out, to copy; then, to enrol, to inscribe, as in a register. It is used of a census, Luke 2 : 1, R.V., "be enrolled," for A.V., "be taxed;" in the Middle Voice, vv. 3, 5, to enrol oneself, A.V., "be taxed." Confirmation that this census (not taxation) was taken in the dominions of the Roman Empire is given by the historians Tacitus and Suetonius. Augustus himself drew up a sort of Roman Doomsday Book, a Rationarium, afterwards epitomized into a Breviarium, to include the allied kingdoms, appointing twenty commissioners to draw up the lists. In Heb. 12 : 23 the members of the Church of the firstborn are said to be " enrolled," R.V.¶

Note : For R.V., I Tim. 5 : 9, *katalegō*, see TAKE, *Note* (18) ; for R.V., 2 Tim. 2 : 4, *stratologeō*, see SOLDIER, B, *Note* (2).

B. Noun.

APOGRAPHĒ (ἀπογραφή) primarily denotes a written copy, or, as a law term, a deposition ; then, a register, census, enrolment, Luke 2 : 2 ; Acts 5 : 37, R.V., for A.V.," taxing." Luke's accuracy has been vindicated, as against the supposed inconsistency that as Quirinius was Governor of Syria in A.D. 6, ten years after the birth of Christ, the census, as " the first " (R.V.), could not have taken place. At the time mentioned by Luke, Cilicia, of which Quirinius was Governor, was separated from Cyprus and joined to Syria. His later direct governorship of Syria itself accounts for the specific inclusion of, and reference to, his earlier connection with that Province. Justin Martyr, a native of Palestine, writing in the Middle of the 2nd century, asserts thrice that Quirinius was present in Syria at the time mentioned by Luke (see Apol., I : 34, 46 ; Trypho 78). Noticeable, too, are the care and accuracy taken by Luke in his historical details, I : 3, R.V.

As to charges made against Luke's accuracy, Moulton and Milligan say as follows :—" The deduction so long made . . . about the census apparently survives the demonstration that the blunder lay only in our lack of information : the microbe is not yet completely expelled. Possibly the salutary process may be completed by our latest inscriptional evidence that Quirinius was a legate in Syria for census purposes in 8–6 B.C."¶

ENSAMPLE

1. TUPOS (τύπος) primarily denoted a blow (from a root *tup*—, seen also in *tuptō*, to strike), hence, (*a*) an impression, the mark of a blow, John 20 : 25 ; (*b*) the impress of a seal, the stamp made by a die, a figure, image, Acts 7 : 43 ; (*c*) a form or mould, Rom. 6 : 17 (see R.V.) ; (*d*) the sense or substance of a letter, Acts 23 : 25 ; (*e*) an ensample, pattern, Acts 7 : 44 ; Heb. 8 : 5, " pattern ; " in an ethical sense, I Cor. 10 : 6 ; Phil. 3 : 17 ; I Thess. I : 7 ; 2 Thess. 3 : 9 ; I Tim. 4 : 12, R.V., " ensample ; " Tit. 2 : 7, R.V., " ensample," for A.V., " pattern ; " I Pet. 5 : 3 ; in a doctrinal sense, a type, Rom. 5 : 14. See EXAMPLE, FASHION, FIGURE, FORM, MANNER, PATTERN, PRINT.¶

2. HUPOTUPŌSIS (ὑποτύπωσις), an outline, sketch, akin to *hupotupoō*, to delineate, is used metaphorically to denote a pattern, an ensample, I Tim. I : 16, R.V., " ensample," for A.V., " pattern ; " 2 Tim. I : 13, R.V., " pattern," for A.V., " form." See FORM, PATTERN.¶

3. HUPODEIGMA (ὑπόδειγμα), lit., that which is shown (from *hupo*, under, and *deiknumi*, to show), hence, (*a*) a figure, copy, Heb. 8 : 5, R.V., " copy," for A.V., " example ; " 9 : 23 ; (*b*) an example, whether for imitation, John 13 : 15 ; Jas. 5 : 10, or for warning, Heb. 4 : 11 ; 2 Pet. 2 : 6, R.V., " example." See EXAMPLE, PATTERN.¶

ENSLAVED

DOULOŌ (δουλόω), to make a slave of, is rendered "enslaved" (to much wine) in Tit. 2 : 3, R.V., for A.V., " given to." See BONDAGE.

ENSNARE

PAGIDEUŌ (παγιδεύω), to entrap, lay snares for (from *pagis*, anything which fixes or grips, hence, a snare), is used in Matt. 22 : 15, of the efforts of the Pharisees to entrap the Lord in His speech, A.V., " entangle." See ENTANGLE.¶

For ENSUE see PURSUE

ENTANGLE

1. PAGIDEUŌ : see ENSNARE.

2. EMPLEKŌ (ἐμπλέκω), to weave in (*en*, in, *plekō*, to weave), hence, metaphorically, to be involved, entangled in, is used in the Passive Voice in 2 Tim. 2 : 4, " entangleth himself ; " 2 Pet. 2 : 20, " are entangled."¶ In the Sept., Prov. 28 : 18.¶

3. ENECHŌ (ἐνέχω), to hold in, is said (*a*) of being entangled in a yoke of bondage, such as Judaism, Gal. 5 : 1. Some mss. have the word in 2 Thess. 1 : 4, the most authentic have *anechō*, to endure ; (*b*) with the meaning to set oneself against, be urgent against, said of the plotting of Herodias against John the Baptist, Mark 6 : 19, R.V., " set herself against," A.V., " had a quarrel against ; " of the effort of the Scribes and Pharisees to provoke the Lord to say something which would provide them with a ground of accusation against Him, Luke 11 : 53, R.V., " to press upon," marg., " to set themselves vehemently against," A.V., " to urge."¶

ENTER, ENTERING, ENTRANCE

A. Verbs.

1. EISERCHOMAI (εἰσέρχομαι), to come into (*eis*, in, *erchomai*, to come), is frequently rendered " entered " in the R.V. for A.V., " went into," e.g., Matt. 9 : 25 ; 21 : 12 ; or " go in," e.g., Matt. 7 : 13 ; Luke 8 : 51 ; " go," Luke 18 : 25 ; " was coming in," Acts 10 : 25. See COME, No. 2, Go (Notes).

2. SUNEISERCHOMAI (συνεισέρχομαι), to enter together, is used in John 6 : 22 (in the best mss. ; see No. 6) and 18 : 15.¶

3. PAREISERCHOMAI (παρεισέρχομαι), (a) to come in beside (para, beside, and No. 1), is rendered " entered " in Rom. 5 : 20, A.V., for R.V., " came in beside," the meaning being that the Law entered in addition to sin ; (b) to enter secretly, by stealth, Gal. 2 : 4, " came in privily," to accomplish the purposes of the circumcision party. See COME, No. 8.¶ Cp. pareisduō (or —dunō), Jude 4, " crept in privily."¶

4. EISPOREUOMAI (εἰσπορεύομαι), to go into, found only in the Synoptists and Acts, is translated to enter, in the R.V. of Mark 1 : 21 ; 6 : 56 ; 11 : 2 ; Luke 8 : 16 ; 11 : 33 (A.V., " come in ") ; 19 : 30 (A.V., " at your entering ") ; 22 : 10 ; in the following the R.V. has the verb to go, for the A.V., to enter, Matt. 15 : 17 ; Mark 5 : 40 ; 7 : 15, 18, 19 ; in Acts 28 : 30, " went," A.V., " came ; " in 9 : 28, R.V., " going," A.V,, " coming ; " in the following both A.V. and R.V. have the verb to enter, Mark 4 : 19 ; Luke 18 : 24 (in the best mss.) ; Acts 3 : 2 ; 8 : 3. See Go, No. 5.¶

5. ANABAINŌ (ἀναβαίνω), to go up (ana, up, bainō, to go), is translated " entered " in 1 Cor. 2 : 9, metaphorically, of coming into the mind. In John 21 : 3, the best mss. have No. 6. See ARISE, No. 6.

6. EMBAINŌ (ἐμβαίνω), to go in (en, in), is used only in the Gospels, of entering a boat, Matt. 8 : 23 ; 9 : 1 ; 13 : 2 ; 14 : 22, 32 ; 15 : 39 ; Mark 4 : 1 ; 5 : 18 ; 6 : 45 ; 8 : 10, 13 ; Luke 5 : 3 ; 8 : 22, 37 ; John 6 : 17, (in some mss., in ver. 22), 24, R.V., " got into the boats," for A.V., " took shipping ; " 21 : 3 (some mss. have No. 5 here) ; Acts 21 : 6 (in the best mss.) ; of stepping into water, John 5 : 4 (R.V. omits the verb). See COME, No. 21, GET, No. 5, GO, Note (2), m, STEP, TAKE, Note (3).¶

7. EPIBAINŌ (ἐπιβαίνω), to go upon (epi, upon), is used of going on board ship, Acts 21 : 2 ; 27 : 2, A.V., " entering into," R.V., " embarking in." See ABOARD, COME, No. 16, SIT, Note.

8. EISEIMI (εἴσειμι), to go into (eis, into, eimi, to go), Acts 3 : 3 ; 21 : 18, 26, A.V., " entered ; " Heb. 9 : 6, R.V., " go in," for A.V., " went into." See GO, No. 12.¶

Notes : (1) Erchomai, to come, is never translated to enter, in the R.V. ; in the A.V., Mark 1 : 29 ; Acts 18 : 7. (2) In 2 John 7, the most authentic mss. have the verb exerchomai, " gone forth," R.V., for A.V. (No. 1), " entered." (3) In Luke 16 : 16, biazō, to force, to enter in violently, is so rendered in the R.V., for A.V., " presseth."

B. Noun.

EISODOS (εἴσοδος), lit., a way in (eis, in, hodos, a way), an entrance, is used (a) of the coming of Christ into the midst of the Jewish nation, Acts 13 : 24, R.V. marg., " entering in ; " (b) of entrance upon Gospel work in a locality, 1 Thess. 1 : 9 ; 2 : 1 ; (c) of the present access of believers into God's presence, Heb. 10 : 19, lit., ' for entrance into ; ' (d) of their entrance into Christ's eternal Kingdom, 2 Pet. 1 : 11. See COMING.¶

ENTERTAIN

XENIZŌ (ξενίζω) signifies (a) to receive as a guest (xenos, a guest), rendered "entertained" in Acts 28 : 7, R.V., for A.V., "lodged ; " in Heb. 13 : 2, "have entertained ; " (b) to be astonished by the strangeness of a thing, Acts 17 : 20 ; 1 Pet. 4 : 4, 12. See LODGE, STRANGE (think).

Note : In Heb. 13 : 2 (first part), *philoxenia*, lit., love of strangers (*phileō*, to love, and *xenos*, a stranger or guest), is translated to show love to, R.V., for A.V., "entertain." See HOSPITALITY.

ENTICE, ENTICING
A. Verb.

DELEAZŌ (δελεάζω), primarily, to lure by a bait (from *delear*, a bait), is used metaphorically in Jas. 1 : 14, of the enticement of lust ; in 2 Pet. 2 : 14, of seducers, R.V., "enticing," for A.V., "beguiling ; " in ver. 18, R.V., "entice (in)," for A.V., "allure (through)."¶

B. Adjective.

PEITHOS (πειθός), apt to persuade (from *peithō*, to persuade), is used in 1 Cor. 2 : 4, A.V., "enticing," R.V., "persuasive."¶

Note : In Col. 2 : 4, *pithanologia*, persuasive speech (from *pithanos*, persuasive, plausible, akin to the above, and *logos*, speech), is rendered "enticing" in the A.V. (R.V., "persuasiveness of.") It signifies the employment of plausible arguments, in contrast to demonstration.¶ Cp. *eulogia*, "fair speech," Rom. 16 : 18, i.e., ' nice style.'¶

ENTIRE

HOLOKLĒROS (ὁλόκληρος), complete, sound in every part (*holos*, whole, *klēros*, a lot, i.e., with all that has fallen by lot), is used ethically in 1 Thess. 5 : 23, indicating that every grace present in Christ should be manifested in the believer ; so Jas. 1 : 4.¶ In the Sept. the word is used, e.g., of a full week, Lev. 23 : 15 ; of altar stones unhewn, Deut. 27 : 6 and Josh. 8 : 31 ; of a full-grown vine tree, useless for work, Ezek. 15 : 5 ; of the sound condition of a sheep, Zech. 11 : 16.

The corresponding noun *holoklēria* is used in Acts 3 : 16, "perfect soundness."¶ The synonymous word *teleios*, used also in Jas. 1 : 4, "perfect," indicates the development of every grace into maturity.

The Heb. *shalom*, peace, is derived from a root meaning "wholeness." See, e.g., Is. 42 : 19, marg., "made perfect," for text, "at peace ; " cp. 26 : 3. Cp. also Col. 1 : 28 with 2 Pet. 3 : 14.

For ENTREAT, to request, see INTREAT ;
for ENTREATY see INTREATY

ENTREAT (to deal with, to treat)
Note : The distinction between this and the preceding word is main-

tained in the R.V., which confines the initial " e " to the sense of dealing with, or uses the Verb to treat.

CHRAOMAI (χράομαι) denotes (a) to use (of things) ; (b) to use well or ill, to treat, deal with (of persons) ; " treated (kindly)," Acts 27 : 3, R.V., A.V., " (courteously) entreated." The remaining ten instances come under (a). See USE.

Note : In Luke 20 : 11, *atimazō*, to dishonour (a, negative, *timē*, honour), is translated " entreated shamefully," A.V. (R.V., " handled shamefully "). For *kakoucheō*, Heb. 11 : 37, R.V., and *sunkakoucheomai*, Heb. 11 : 25, R.V., see SUFFER, Nos. 6 and 7.

ENVY, ENVYING
A. Noun.

PHTHONOS (φθόνος), envy, is the feeling of displeasure produced by witnessing or hearing of the advantage or prosperity of others ; this evil sense always attaches to this word, Matt. 27 : 18 ; Mark 15 : 10 ; Rom. 1 : 29 ; Gal. 5 : 21 ; Phil. 1 : 15 ; 1 Tim. 6 : 4 ; Tit. 3 : 3 ; 1 Pet. 2 : 1 ; so in Jas. 4 : 5, where the question is rhetorical and strongly remonstrative, signifying that the Spirit (or spirit) which God made to dwell in us was certainly not so bestowed that we should be guilty of envy.¶

Note : *Zēlos*, zeal or jealousy, translated " envy " in the A.V., in Acts 13 : 45 ; Rom. 13 : 13 ; 1 Cor. 3 : 3 ; 2 Cor. 12 : 20 ; Jas. 3 : 14, 16, is to be distinguished from *phthonos*, and, apart from the meanings " zeal " and " indignation," is always translated " jealousy " in the R.V. The distinction lies in this, that envy desires to deprive another of what he has, jealousy desires to have the same or the same sort of thing for itself. See FERVENT, INDIGNATION, JEALOUSY, ZEAL.

B. Verbs.

1. PHTHONEŌ (φθονέω), to envy (akin to A.), is used in Gal. 5 : 26.¶

2. ZĒLOŌ (ζηλόω) denotes to be zealous, moved with jealousy, Acts 7 : 9 and 17 : 5, R.V., " moved with jealousy " (A.V., " moved with envy ") ; both have " envieth " in 1 Cor. 13 : 4. See the Note under A. See AFFECT, COVET, DESIRE, JEALOUS, ZEALOUS.

EPHPHATHA

Note : *Ephphatha* is an Aramaic word signifying to open, used in the Imperative Mood, " be opened," Mark 7 : 34 ; while the application in this case was to the ears, the tongue was remedially affected.

EPILEPTIC

SELĒNIAZŌ (σεληνιάζω), lit., to be moon struck (from *selēnē*, the moon), is used in the Passive Voice with Active significance, R.V., " epileptic," for A.V., " lunatick," Matt. 4 : 24 ; 17 : 15 ; the corresponding English word is lunatic. Epilepsy was supposed to be influenced by the moon.¶

EPISTLE

EPISTOLĒ (ἐπιστολή), primarily a message (from *epistellō*, to send to), hence, a letter, an epistle, is used in the singular, e.g., Acts 15 : 30 ; in the plural, e.g., Acts 9 : 2 ; 2 Cor. 10 : 10. " Epistle is a less common word for a letter. A letter affords a writer more freedom, both in subject and expression, than does a formal treatise. A letter is usually occasional, that is, it is written in consequence of some circumstance which requires to be dealt with promptly. The style of a letter depends largely on the occasion that calls it forth."* " A broad line is to be drawn between the letter and the epistle. The one is essentially a spontaneous product dominated throughout by the image of the reader, his sympathies and interests, instinct also with the writer's own soul : it is virtually one half of an imaginary dialogue, the suppressed responses of the other party shaping the course of what is actually written . . .; the other has a general aim, addressing all and sundry whom it may concern : it is like a public speech and looks towards publication " (J. V. Bartlet, in *Hastings' Bib. Dic.*).

In 2 Pet. 3 : 16 the Apostle includes the Epistles of Paul as part of the God-breathed Scriptures.

EQUAL, EQUALITY
A. Adjective.

ISOS (ἴσος), the same in size, number, quality, etc., is translated " equal " in John 5 : 18 ; Phil. 2 : 6 ; in the latter the word is in the neuter plural, lit., ' equalities ; ' " in the R.V. the words are translated ' on an equality with God,' instead of ' equal with God,' as in the A.V. The change is of great importance to the right interpretation of the whole passage. The rendering ' equal with God,' is evidently derived from the Latin Version. . . . It was apparently due at first to the fact that the Latin language had no adequate mode of representing the exact form and meaning of the Greek. The neuter plural denotes the various modes or states in which it was possible for the nature of Deity to exist and manifest itself as Divine."†

Note : Cp. *isotimos*, equally precious, 2 Pet. 1 : 1 ;¶ *isopsuchos* of equal soul, like-minded, Phil. 2 : 20 ;¶ also Eng. words beginning with the prefix *iso*—.

B. Nouns.

1. ISOTĒS (ἰσότης), equality (akin to A.), is translated " equality " in 2 Cor. 8 : 14, twice ; in Col. 4 : 1, with the article, " that which is . . . equal," (lit., ' the equality,' as marg.), i.e., equity, fairness, what is equitable.¶ In the Sept., Job 36 : 29 ; Zech. 4 : 7.¶

2. SUNĒLIKIŌTĒS (συνηλικιώτης) denotes one of the same age, an equal in age (*sun*, with, *hēlikia*, an age), a contemporary, Gal. 1 : 14,

---

* From Notes on Thessalonians by Hogg and Vine, p. 5.
† Gifford, The Incarnation, p. 20.

R.V., " of mine own age," for A.V. " mine equals," the reference being to the Apostle's good standing among his fellow-students in the Rabbinical Schools ; cp. Acts 22 : 3.¶

ERE : see Note † p. 9.

ERR

1. PLANAŌ (πλανάω), in the Active Voice, signifies to cause to wander, lead astray, deceive (planē, a wandering ; cp. Eng., planet) ; in the Passive Voice, to be led astray, to err. It is translated " err," in Matt. 22 : 29 ; Mark 12 : 24, 27 ; Heb. 3 : 10 ; Jas. 1 : 16 (A.V., " do not err," R.V., " be not deceived ") ; 5 : 19. See DECEIVE, SEDUCE, WANDER, WAY, *Note* (5).

2. APOPLANAŌ (ἀποπλανάω), to cause to wander away from, to lead astray from (apō, from, and No. 1), is used metaphorically of leading into error, Mark 13 : 22, A.V., " seduce," R.V., " lead astray ; " 1 Tim. 6 : 10, in the Passive Voice, A.V., " have erred," R.V., " have been led astray." See SEDUCE.¶

3. ASTOCHEŌ (ἀστοχέω), to miss the mark, fail (a, negative, *stochos*, a mark), is used only in the Pastoral Epistles, 1 Tim. 1 : 6, " having swerved ; " 6 : 21 and 2 Tim. 2 : 18, " have erred." See SWERVE.¶

ERROR

1. PLANĒ (πλάνη), akin to *planaō* (see ERR, No. 1), " a wandering, a forsaking of the right path, see Jas. 5 : 20, whether in doctrine, 2 Pet. 3 : 17 ; 1 John 4 : 6, or in morals, Rom. 1 : 27 ; 2 Pet. 2 : 18 ; Jude 11, though, in Scripture, doctrine and morals are never divided by any sharp line. See also Matt. 27 : 64, where it is equivalent to ' fraud.' "*

Errors in doctrine are not infrequently the effect of relaxed morality, and vice versa.

In Eph. 4 : 14 the R.V. has " wiles of error," for A.V., " they lie in wait to deceive ; " in 1 Thess. 2 : 3, R.V., " error," for A.V., " deceit ; " in 2 Thess. 2 : 11, R.V., " a working of error," for A.V., " strong delusion." See DECEIT.¶ Cp. *planētēs*, a wandering, Jude 13,¶ and the adjective *planos*, leading astray, deceiving, a deceiver.

2. AGNOĒMA (ἀγνόημα), a sin of ignorance (cp. *agnoia*, ignorance, and *agnoeō*, to be ignorant), is used in the plural in Heb. 9 : 7.¶

ESCAPE
A. Verbs.

1. PHEUGŌ (φεύγω), to flee (Lat., *fuga*, flight, etc. ; cp. Eng., fugitive, subterfuge), is rendered " escape " in Matt. 23 : 33 ; Heb. 11 : 34. See FLEE.

---

* From Notes on Thessalonians by Hogg and Vine, p. 53.

2. APOPHEUGŌ (ἀποφεύγω), to flee away from (*apo*, from, and No. 1), is used in 2 Pet. 1 : 4 ; 2 : 18, 20.¶

3. DIAPHEUGŌ (διαφεύγω), lit., to flee through, is used of the escaping of prisoners from a ship, Acts 27 : 42. For the word in verse 44 see No. 5.¶

4. EKPHEUGŌ (ἐκφεύγω), to flee out of a place (*ek*, out of, and No. 1), is said of the escape of prisoners, Acts 16 : 27 ; of Sceva's sons, fleeing from the demoniac, 19 : 16 ; of Paul's escape from Damascus, 2 Cor. 11 : 33 ; elsewhere with reference to the judgments of God, Luke 21 : 36 ; Rom. 2 : 3 ; Heb. 2 : 3 ; 12 : 25 ; 1 Thess. 5 : 3. See FLEE.¶

5. DIASŌZŌ (διασώζω), in the Active Voice, to bring safely through a danger (*dia*, through, intensive, *sōzō*, to save), to make completely whole, to heal, Luke 7 : 3 ; to bring safe, Acts 23 : 24 ; to save, 27 : 43 ; in the Passive Voice, Matt. 14 : 36, " were made whole ; " 1 Pet. 3 : 20 ; It is also used in the Passive Voice, signifying to escape, said of ship-wrecked mariners, Acts 27 : 44 ; 28 : 1, 4. See HEAL, SAFE, SAVE.¶

Note : Exerchomai, to come or go out of a place, is rendered " He escaped," in John 10 : 39, A.V., an unsuitable translation, both in meaning and in regard to the circumstances of the Lord's departure from His would-be captors. The R.V. " went forth " is both accurate and appropriate to the dignity of the Lord's actions.

B. Noun.

EKBASIS (ἔκβασις), a way out (*ek*, out, *bainō*, to go), denotes (*a*) an escape, 1 Cor. 10 : 13, used with the definite article and translated " the way of escape," as afforded by God in case of temptation ; (*b*) an issue or result, Heb. 13 : 7. See END, ISSUE.¶ Cp. *ekbainō*, to go out, Heb. 11 : 15 (some mss. have *exerchomai*).¶

ESCHEW

EKKLINŌ (ἐκκλίνω), to turn aside (*ek*, from, *klinō*, to turn, bend), is used metaphorically (*a*) of leaving the right path, Rom. 3 : 12, R.V., " turned aside," for A.V., " gone out of the way ; " (*b*) of turning away from division-makers, and errorists, 16 : 17, R.V., " turn away from ; " (*c*) of turning away from evil, 1 Pet. 3 : 11, R.V., " turn away from," A.V., " eschew." See AVOID, TURN.¶ In the Sept. the verb is frequently used of declining or swerving from God's ways, e.g., Job 23 : 11 ; Psa. 44 : 18 ; 119 : 51, 157.

ESPECIALLY

MALISTA (μάλιστα), most, most of all, above all, is the superlative of *mala*, very much ; translated " especially " in Acts 26 : 3 ; Gal. 6 : 10 ; 1 Tim. 5 : 17 ; 2 Tim. 4 : 13 ; Phil. 4 : 22, R.V. (for A.V., " chiefly ") ; " specially," Acts 25 : 26 ; 1 Tim. 4 : 10 ; 5 : 8 ; Tit. 1 : 10 ; Philm. 16 ; in Acts 20 : 38, " most of all." See CHIEFLY, MOST.

ESPOUSED

1. HARMOZŌ (ἁρμόζω), to fit, join (from *harmos*, a joint, joining; the root *ar*—, signifying to fit, is in evidence in various languages; cp. *arthron*, a joint, *arithmos*, a number, etc.), is used in the Middle Voice, of marrying or giving in marriage; in 2 Cor. 11 : 2 it is rendered "espoused," metaphorically of the relationship established between Christ and the local church, through the Apostle's instrumentality. The thought may be that of fitting or joining to one Husband, the Middle Voice expressing the Apostle's interest or desire in doing so.¶

2. MNĒSTEUŌ (μνηστεύω), to woo and win, to espouse or promise in marriage, is used in the Passive Voice in Matt. 1 : 18; Luke 1 : 27; 2 : 5, all with reference to the Virgin Mary, R.V., "betrothed," for A.V., "espoused," in each case. See BETROTH.¶

ESTABLISH

1. STĒRIZŌ (στηρίζω), to fix, make fast, to set (from *stērix*, a prop), is used of establishing or stablishing (i.e., the confirmation) of persons; the Apostle Peter was called by the Lord to establish his brethren, Luke 22 : 32, translated "strengthen;" Paul desired to visit Rome that the saints might be "established," Rom. 1 : 11; cp. Acts 8 : 23; so with Timothy at Thessalonica, 1 Thess. 3 : 2; the confirmation of the saints is the work of God, Rom. 16 : 25, "to stablish (you);" 1 Thess. 3 : 13, "stablish (your hearts);" 2 Thess. 2 : 17, "stablish them (in every good work and word);" 1 Pet. 5 : 10, "stablish;" the means used to effect the confirmation is the ministry of the Word of God, 2 Pet. 1 : 12, "are established (in the truth which is with you);" James exhorts Christians to "stablish" their hearts, Jas. 5 : 8; cp. Rev. 3 : 2, R.V.

The character of this confirmation may be learned from its use in Luke 9 : 51, "stedfastly set;" 16 : 26, "fixed," and in the Sept. in Ex. 17 : 12, "stayed up" (also from its strengthened form *epistērizō*, to confirm, in Acts 14 : 22; 15 : 32, 41; in some mss. to strengthen, in 18 : 23; see CONFIRM ¶). Neither the laying on of hands nor the impartation of the Holy Spirit is mentioned in the N.T. in connection with either of these words, or with the synonymous verb *bebaioō* (see 1 Cor. 1 : 8; 2 Cor. 1 : 21, etc.). See FIX, SET, STRENGTHEN.¶

2. STEREOŌ (στερεόω), to make firm, or solid (akin to *stereos*, hard, firm, solid; cp. Eng., stereotype), is used only in Acts, (a) physically, 3 : 7, "received strength;" 3 : 16, "hath made strong;" (b) metaphorically, of establishment in the faith, 16 : 5, R.V., "strengthened," for A.V., "established."¶

3. HISTĒMI (ἵστημι), to cause to stand, is translated "establish" in Rom. 3 : 31; 10 : 3; Heb. 10 : 9. See ABIDE, APPOINT, STAND, etc.

4. BEBAIOŌ (βεβαιόω), to confirm, is rendered "stablish," 2 Cor.

I : 21 ; "stablished," Col. 2 : 7 ; "be established," Heb. 13 : 9 : see
CONFIRM.

5. NOMOTHETEŌ (νομοθετέω) : see ENACT.

ESTATE, STATE

1. EUSCHĒMŌN (εὐσχήμων), signifying elegant, graceful, comely
(*eu*, well, *schēma*, figure, fashion), is used (*a*) in a moral sense, seemly,
becoming, I Cor. 7 : 35 ; (*b*) in a physical sense, comely, I Cor. 12 : 24 ;
(*c*) with reference to social degree, influential, a meaning developed in
later Greek, and rendered of " honourable estate " in the R.V. of Mark
15 : 43 ; Acts 13 : 50 ; 17 : 12 (for A.V., " honourable "). See COMELY,
HONOURABLE.¶

2. TAPEINŌSIS (ταπείνωσις) denotes abasement, humiliation, low
estate (from *tapeinos*, lowly), Luke I : 48, " low estate ; " Acts 8 : 33,
" humiliation ; " Phil. 3 : 21, R.V., " of humiliation," for A.V., " vile ;"
Jas. I : 10, " is made low," lit., ' in his low estate.' See HUMILIATION,
LOW, VILE.¶

3. HUPSOS (ὕψος), signifying height, is rendered " (in his) high
estate," Jas. I : 9, R.V., for A.V., " in that he is exalted ; " " on high,"
Luke I : 78 ; 24 : 49 ; Eph. 4 : 8 ; " height," Eph. 3 : 18 ; Rev. 21 : 16.
See EXALT HEIGHT, HIGH.¶

Notes : (1) In Acts 22 : 5, *presbuterion*, presbytery, a body of elders,
is translated " estate of the elders," lit., ' the presbytery,' i.e., the
Sanhedrin.   (2) In Col. 4 : 7 the plural of the definite article with the
preposition *kata*, and the singular personal pronoun with *panta*, all, is
rendered " all my state," A.V., R.V., " all my affairs ; " in ver. 8 the
preposition *peri*, with the personal pronoun, lit., ' the things concerning
us,' is translated " our estate," i.e., ' how we fare ; ' so in Phil. 2 : 19, 20,
" your state," i.e., ' your condition.'   (3) In Mark 6 : 21 *prōtos*, lit., first,
is rendered " chief estates," A.V., R.V., " the chief men," i.e., the men
to whom belongs the dignity.   (4) In Rom. 12 : 16 *tapeinos*, in the plural
with the article, lit., the lowly, is translated " men of low estate," A.V.,
R.V., " things that are lowly."   (5) In Jude 6 *archē*, " principality," R.V.,
A.V. has " first estate,"   (6) For " last state " see LAST, p. 311, ll. 4–6.

ESTEEM

1. HĒGEOMAI (ἡγέομαι) signifies to lead ; then, to lead before the
mind, to suppose, consider, esteem ; translated " esteem " in Phil. 2 : 3,
A.V., R.V., " counting ; " in I Thess. 5 : 13, " esteem ; " in Heb. 11 : 26,
A.V., " esteeming," R.V., " accounting."

2. KRINŌ (κρίνω) signifies to separate, choose ; then, to approve,
esteem ; translated " esteemeth " in Rom. 14 : 5 (twice), said of days ;
here the word " alike " (A.V.) is rightly omitted in the R.V., the meaning
being that every day is especially regarded as sacred.   See DETERMINE.

3. LOGIZOMAI (λογίζομαι), to reckon, is translated " esteemeth " in Rom. 14 : 14 (R.V., " accounteth "). See ACCOUNT.

Notes : (1) In 1 Cor. 6 : 4, A.V., *exoutheneō*, to set at nought, is rendered " are least esteemed ; " the meaning is that judges in the world's tribunals have no place (are not of account) in the church. See ACCOUNT. (2) In the A.V. marg. of 1 Pet. 2 : 17, *timaō*, to honour, is rendered " esteem." (3) For " highly esteemed," Luke 16 : 15, A.V., see EXALT, B.

ETERNAL

1. AIŌN (αἰών), an age, is translated " eternal " in Eph. 3 : 11, lit., ' (purpose) of the ages ' (marg.), and 1 Tim. 1 : 17, lit. ' (king) of the ages ' (marg.). See AGE.

2. AIŌNIOS (αἰώνιος) " describes duration, either undefined but not endless, as in Rom. 16 : 25 ; 2 Tim. 1 : 9 ; Tit. 1 : 2 ; or undefined because endless as in Rom. 16 : 26, and the other sixty-six places in the N.T.

" The predominant meaning of *aiōnios*, that in which it is used everywhere in the N.T., save the places noted above, may be seen in 2 Cor. 4 : 18, where it is set in contrast with *proskairos*, lit., ' for a season,' and in Philm. 15, where only in the N.T. it is used without a noun. Moreover it is used of persons and things which are in their nature endless, as, e.g., of God, Rom. 16 : 26 ; of His power, 1 Tim. 6 : 16, and of His glory, 1 Pet. 5 : 10 ; of the Holy Spirit, Heb. 9 : 14 ; of the redemption effected by Christ, Heb. 9 : 12, and of the consequent salvation of men, 5 : 9, as well as of His future rule, 2 Pet. 1 : 11, which is elsewhere declared to be without end, Luke 1 : 33 ; of the life received by those who believe in Christ, John 3 : 16, concerning whom He said, ' they shall never perish,' 10 : 28, and of the resurrection body, 2 Cor. 5 : 1, elsewhere said to be ' immortal,' 1 Cor. 15 : 53, in which that life will be finally realized, Matt. 25 : 46 ; Tit. 1 : 2.

" *Aiōnios* is also used of the sin that ' hath never forgiveness,' Mark 3 : 29, and of the judgment of God, from which there is no appeal, Heb. 6 : 2, and of the fire, which is one of its instruments, Matt. 18 : 8 ; 25 : 41 ; Jude 7, and which is elsewhere said to be ' unquenchable,' Mark 9 : 43.

" The use of *aiōnios* here shows that the punishment referred to in 2 Thess. 1 : 9, is not temporary, but final, and, accordingly, the phraseology shows that its purpose is not remedial but retributive."*

3. AÏDIOS (ἀΐδιος) ; see EVERLASTING.

EUNUCH
A. Noun.

EUNOUCHOS (εὐνοῦχος) denotes (a) an emasculated man, a eunuch, Matt. 19 : 12 ; (b) in the 3rd instance in that verse, one naturally incapaci-

---

* From Notes on Thessalonians by Hogg and Vine, pp. 232, 233.

tated for, or voluntarily abstaining from, wedlock ; (c) one such, in a position of high authority in a court, a chamberlain, Acts 8 : 27–39.¶

B. Verb.

EUNOUCHIZŌ (εὐνουχίζω), to make a eunuch (from A.), is used in Matt. 19 : 12, as under (b) in A. ; and in the Passive Voice, "were made eunuchs," probably an allusion by the Lord to the fact that there were eunuchs in the courts of the Herods, as would be well known to His hearers.¶

EVANGELIST

EUANGELISTĒS (εὐαγγελιστής), lit., a messenger of good (eu, well, angelos, a messenger), denotes a preacher of the Gospel, Acts 21 : 8 ; Eph. 4 : 11, which makes clear the distinctiveness of the function in the churches ; 2 Tim. 4 : 5.¶ Cp. euangelizō, to proclaim glad tidings, and euangelion, good news, gospel. Missionaries are evangelists, as being essentially preachers of the Gospel.

EVEN (Noun), EVENING, EVENTIDE
A. Nouns.

1. HESPERA (ἑσπέρα), properly, the feminine of the adjective hesperos, of, or at, evening, western (Lat., vesper, Eng., vespers), is used as a noun in Luke 24 : 29 ; Acts 4 : 3, "eventide ; " 28 : 23. Some mss. have the word in 20 : 15, 'in the evening (we touched),' instead of hetera, "next (day)."

2. OPSIA (ὀψία), the feminine of the adjective opsios, late, used as a noun, denoting evening, with hora, understood (see No. 1), is found seven times in Matthew, five in Mark, two in John, and in these places only in the N.T. (some mss. have it in Mark 11 : 11, see B.). The word really signifies the late evening, the latter of the two evenings as reckoned by the Jews, the first from 3 p.m. to sunset, the latter after sunset ; this is the usual meaning. It is used, however, of both, e.g., Mark 1 : 32 (cp. opsimos, latter, said of rain, Jas. 5 : 7).

B. Adverb.

OPSE (ὀψέ), long after, late, late in the day, at evening (in contrast to prōi, early, e.g., Matt. 20 : 1), is used practically as a noun in Mark 11 : 11, lit., 'the hour being at eventide ;' 11 : 19 ; 13 : 35 ; in Matt. 28 : 1 it is rendered "late on," R.V., for A.V., "in the end of." Here, however, the meaning seems to be "after," a sense in which the word was used by late Greek writers. See Late.¶ In the Sept., Gen. 24 : 11 ; Ex. 30 : 8 ; Jer. 2 : 23 ; Isa. 5 : 11.¶

Note : In Luke 12 : 38 some mss. have the adjective hesperinos, of the evening (see A, No. 1), lit., 'in the evening watch.'

EVEN (Adjective)

Notes : (1) In Luke 19 : 44 (A.V., "shall lay thee even with the ground "), there is no word representing " even ; " the verb edaphizō signifies to beat level (like a threshing floor) ; hence, to dash to the ground. See DASH.¶

(2) In Heb. 12 : 13 the adjective *orthos*, straight, is rendered " even " in the A.V., marg.

EVEN (Adverb, etc.), EVEN AS, EVEN SO

1. KAI (καί), a conjunction, is usually a mere connective, meaning " and ; " it frequently, however, has an ascensive or climactic use, signifying " even," the thing that is added being out of the ordinary, and producing a climax.   The determination of this meaning depends on the context.   Examples are Matt. 5 : 46, 47 ;   Mark 1 : 27 ;   Luke 6 : 33 (R.V.) ;   10 : 17 ; John 12 : 42 ; Gal. 2 : 13, 17, where " also " should be " even ; " Eph. 5 : 12.   Examples where the R.V. corrects the A.V. " and " or " also," by substituting " even," are Luke 7 : 49 ; Acts 17 : 28 ; Heb. 11 : 11 ; in 1 John 4 : 3 the R.V. rightly omits " even."

When followed by " if " or " though," *kai* often signifies " even," e.g., Matt. 26 : 35 ; John 8 : 14.   So sometimes when preceded by " if," e.g., 1 Cor. 7 : 11, where " but and if " should be " but even if."

The epexegetic or explanatory use of *kai* followed by a noun in apposition, and meaning " namely," or " even " is comparatively rare. Winer's cautionary word needs heeding, that " this meaning has been introduced into too many passages " (Gram. of the N.T., p. 546.).   Some think it has this sense in John 3 : 5, " water, even the Spirit," and Gal. 6 : 16, " even the Israel of God."

2. DE (δέ), usually signifying " but," is sometimes used for emphasis, signifying " even," e.g., Rom. 3 : 22 ; 9 : 30, " even the righteousness ; " Phil. 2 : 8 (R.V., " yea ").   This is to be distinguished from No. 1.

3. ETI (ἔτι), an adverb, as yet, still, is rendered " even " in Luke 1 : 15.

4. HŌS (ὥς), " as," in comparative sentences, is sometimes translated " even as," Matt. 15 : 28 ; Mark 4 : 36 ; Eph. 5 : 33 ; 1 Pet. 3 : 6 (A.V. only) ; Jude 7.

5. HOUTŌS (οὕτως), or *houtō*, so, thus, is frequently rendered " even so," e.g., Matt. 7 : 17 ; 12 : 45 ; 18 : 14 ; 23 : 28 ; " so " in 1 Cor. 11 : 12 and 1 Thess. 2 : 4, R.V.

6. KATHŌS (καθώς), according as (*kata*, according to, and No. 4), is frequently translated " even as," e.g., Mark 11 : 6 ; Luke 1 : 2 ; 1 Thess. 5 : 11.

7. HŌSPER (ὥσπερ), No. 4, strengthened by *per*, is translated " even as " in Matt. 20 : 28.

8. KATHAPER (καθάπερ), just as, even as, is rendered " even as " in Rom. 4 : 6 ; 9 : 13 ; 10 : 15 ; 12 : 4 (R.V.) ; 2 Cor. 3 : 18 ; 1 Thess. 3 : 6, 12 ; 4 : 5 ; Heb. 4 : 2 ; " according as," Rom. 11 : 8 ; elsewhere simply " as."

9. NAI (ναί), a particle of strong affirmation, yea, verily, even so, is

rendered " even so " in the A.V., " yea " in the R.V., in Matt. 11 : 26 ; Luke 10 : 21 ; Rev. 16 : 7 ; both A.V. and R.V. have it in Rev. 1 : 7 ; the most authentic mss. omit it in 22 : 20. See SURELY, TRUTH, VERILY, YEA, YES.

10. HOMŌS (ὅμως), yet, nevertheless, is translated " even " in 1 Cor. 14 : 7 (A.V., " and even ") ; elsewhere John 12 : 42, " nevertheless ; " Gal. 3 : 15, " yet " (i.e., ' nevertheless,' an example of hyperbaton, by which a word is placed out of its true position).¶

Notes : (1) In Rom. 1 : 26, there is no word representing " even " in the original. The A.V. seems to have put it for the particle *te*, which simply annexes the statement to the preceding and does not require translation. (2) In 1 Thess. 2 : 18 the A.V. renders the particle *men* by " even ; " if translated, it signifies " indeed." (3) In 1 Cor. 12 : 2, *hōs* (see No. 4, above), followed by the particle *an*, means " howsoever " (R.V., for A.V., " even as "). (4) In Matt. 23 : 37, " even as " translates the phrase *hon tropon*, lit., ' (in) what manner.' (5) In 1 Tim. 3 : 11, *hōsautōs*, a strengthened form of No. 4, likewise, in like manner, is rendered " even so," A.V. (R.V., " in like manner "). (6) *Kagō*, for *kai egō*, means either " even I " or " even so I " or " I also." In John 10 : 15, the R.V. has " and I " for the A.V., " even so . . . I ; " in 17 : 18 and 20 : 21, A.V. and R.V., " even so I ; " in the following, *kagō* is preceded by *hōs*, or *kathōs*, " even as I," 1 Cor. 7 : 8 ; 10 : 33 ; " even as I also," 11 : 1 ; " as I also," Rev. 2 : 27. (7) In Luke 12 : 7 the R.V. renders *kai* by " very " (for A.V., " even the very "). (8) In John 6 : 57 *kakeinos* (for *kai ekeinos*, " also he "), is translated " he also," R.V., for A.V., " even he." (9) In Eph. 1 : 10 there is no word in the original for " even." The R.V. expresses the stress on the pronoun by " in Him, I say."

EVER, FOR EVER, EVERMORE
A. Adverbs.

1. PANTOTE (πάντοτε), at all times, always (akin to *pas*, all), is translated " ever " in Luke 15 : 31 ; John 18 : 20 ; 1 Thess. 4 : 17 ; 5 : 15 ; 2 Tim. 3 : 7 ; Heb. 7 : 25 ; " evermore " in John 6 : 34 ; in 1 Thess. 5 : 16, R.V., " alway," for A.V., " evermore." It there means ' on all occasions,' as, e.g., in 1 Thess. 1 : 2 ; 3 : 6 ; 5 : 15 ; 2 Thess. 1 : 3, 11 ; 2 : 13. See ALWAYS.

2. AEI (ἀεί), ever, is used (*a*) of continuous time, signifying unceasingly, perpetually, Acts 7 : 51 ; 2 Cor. 4 : 11 ; 6 : 10 ; Tit. 1 : 12 ; Heb. 3 : 10 ; (*b*) of successive occurrences, signifying ' on every occasion,' 1 Pet. 3 : 15 ; 2 Pet. 1 : 12. Some texts have the word in Mark 15 : 8. See ALWAYS.¶

Note : The adjective *diēnekēs*, unbroken, continuous, is used in a phrase with *eis*, unto, and the article, signifying perpetually, for ever, Heb. 7 : 3 ; 10 : 1, 12, 14.¶

B. Phrases.

The following phrases are formed in connection with *aiōn*, an age : they are idiomatic expressions betokening undefined periods and are not to be translated literally : (*a*) *eis aiōna*, lit., ' unto an age,' Jude 13, " for ever ; " (*b*) *eis ton aiōna*, lit., ' unto the age,' " for ever " (or, with a negative, " never "), Matt. 21 : 19 ; Mark 3 : 29 ; 11 : 14 ; Luke 1 : 55 ; John 4 : 14 ; 6 : 51, 58 ; 8 : 35 (twice), 51, 52 ; 10 : 28 ; 11 : 26 ; 12 : 34 ; 13 : 8 ; 14 : 16 ; 1 Cor. 8 : 13 ; 2 Cor. 9 : 9 ; Heb. 5 : 6 ; 6 : 20 ; 7 : 17, 21, 24, 28 ; 1 Pet. 1 : 25 ; 1 John 2 : 17 ; 2 John 2 ; (*c*) *eis tous aiōnas*, lit., ' unto the ages,' " for ever," Matt. 6 : 13 (A.V. only) ; Luke 1 : 33 ; Rom. 1 : 25 ; 9 : 5 ; 11 : 36 ; 16 : 27 (some mss. have the next phrase here) ; 2 Cor. 11 : 31 ; Heb. 13 : 8 ; (*d*) *eis tous aiōnas tōn aiōnōn*, lit. ' unto the ages of the ages,' " for ever and ever," or " for evermore," Gal. 1 : 5 ; Phil. 4 : 20 ; 1 Tim. 1 : 17 ; 2 Tim. 4 : 18 ; Heb. 13 : 21 ; 1 Pet. 4 : 11 ; 5 : 11 [(*c*) in some mss.] ; Rev. 1 : 6 [(*c*) in some mss.] ; 1 : 18, " for evermore ; " 4 : 9, 10 ; 5 : 13 ; 7 : 12 ; 10 : 6 ; 11 : 15 ; 15 : 7 ; 19 : 3 ; 20 : 10 ; 22 : 5 ; (*e*) *eis aiōnas aiōnōn*, lit., ' unto ages of ages,' " for ever and ever," Rev. 14 : 11 ; (*f*) *eis ton aiōna tou aiōnos*, lit., ' unto the age of the age,' " for ever and ever," Heb. 1 : 8 ; (*g*) *tou aiōnos tōn aiōnōn*, lit., ' of the age of the ages,' " for ever and ever," Eph. 3 : 21 ; (*h*) *eis pantas tous aiōnas*, lit., ' unto all the ages,' Jude 25 (" for evermore," R.V. ; " ever," A.V.) ; (*i*) *eis hēmeran aiōnos*, lit., ' unto a day of an age,' " for ever," 2 Pet. 3 : 18.

EVERLASTING

1. AIŌNIOS (αἰώνιος) : see ETERNAL.

2. AIDIOS (ἀΐδιος) denotes everlasting (from *aei*, ever), Rom. 1 : 20, R.V., " everlasting," for A.V., " eternal ; " Jude 6, A.V. and R.V., " everlasting." *Aiōnios*, should always be translated " eternal " and *aidios*, " everlasting." " While *aiōnios* . . . negatives the end either of a space of time or of unmeasured time, and is used chiefly where something future is spoken of, *aidios* excludes interruption and lays stress upon permanence and unchangeableness " (Cremer).¶

EVERY, EVERYONE (MAN), EVERYTHING

1. PAS (πᾶς) signifies (1) with nouns without the article, (*a*) every one of the class denoted by the noun connected with *pas*, e.g., Matt. 3 : 10, " every tree ; " Mark 9 : 49, " every sacrifice ; " see also John 2 : 10 ; Acts 2 : 43 ; Rom. 2 : 9 ; Eph. 1 : 21 ; 3 : 15 ; 2 Thess. 2 : 4 ; 2 Tim. 3 : 16, R.V. ; (*b*) any and every, of every kind, " all manner of," e.g., Matt. 4 : 23 ; " especially with nouns denoting virtues or vices, emotions, condition, indicating every mode in which a quality manifests itself ; or any object to which the idea conveyed by the noun belongs " (Grimm-Thayer). This is often translated " all," e.g., Acts 27 : 20 ; Rom. 15 : 14 ; 2 Cor. 10 : 6 ; Eph. 4 : 19, 31 ; Col. 4 : 12, " all the will of God," i.e.,

everything God wills ; (2) without a noun, every one, everything, every man (i.e., person), e.g., Luke 16 : 16 ; or with a negative, not everyone, e.g., Mark 9 : 49 ; with a participle and the article, equivalent to a relative clause, everyone who, e.g., 1 Cor. 9 : 25 ; Gal. 3 : 10, 13 ; 1 John 2 : 29 ; 3 : 3, 4, 6, 10, 15, rendered " whosoever." So in the neuter, 1 John 2 : 16 ; 5 : 4, often rendered " whatsoever ; " governed by the preposition *en*, in, without a noun following, it signifies in every matter, or condition, Phil. 4 : 6 ; 1 Thess. 5 : 18 ; in every way or particular, 2 Cor. 4 : 8, translated " on every side ; " so 2 Cor. 7 : 5 ; " in everything," Eph. 5 : 24 ; Phil. 4 : 12, lit., ' in everything and (perhaps " even ") in all things.' See THOROUGHLY, WHOLE.

2. HAPAS (ἅπας), a strengthened form of No. 1, signifies all, the whole, altogether ; it is translated " every one " in Acts 5 : 16, where it occurs in the plural. In Mark 8 : 25, the A.V.," every man " translates the text with the masculine plural ; the best mss. have the neuter plural, R.V., " all things." See ALL, WHOLE.

3. HEKASTOS (ἕκαστος) : see EACH, No. 1. It is used with *heis*, one, in Acts 2 : 6, " every man," and in Eph. 4 : 16, " each several (part)," for A.V., " every (part)." In Rev. 22 : 2 the most authentic mss. omit the numeral in the phrase " every month." It is preceded by *kath hena* (*kata*, according to, *hena*, one), a strengthened phrase, in Eph. 5 : 33, A.V., " everyone . . . in particular," R.V., " severally, each one." The same kind of phrase with *ana*, each, before the numeral, is used in Rev. 21 : 21, R.V.," each one of the several (gates)," for A.V., " every several (gate)." See EACH, PARTICULAR, SEVERAL.

Notes : (1) The preposition *kata*, down, is sometimes found governing a noun, in the sense of " every," e.g., Luke 2 : 41, " every year ; " 16 : 19, " every day ; " Heb. 9 : 25, " every year " (R.V., " year by year ") ; so 10 : 3. This construction sometimes signifies " in every . . .," e.g., Acts 14 : 23, " in every church ; " 15 : 21, " in every city ; " so 20 : 23 ; Tit. 1 : 5 ; Acts 22 : 19, " in every synagogue " (plural) ; Acts 8 : 3 " (into) every house." In Luke 8 : 1 the phrase means " throughout every city," as in the A.V. ; in ver. 4 " of every city," R.V. In Acts 5 : 42 the R.V. renders *kat' oikon* " at home," for A.V., " in every house ; " in 2 : 46, for A.V., " from house to house " (marg., " at home "). In Acts 15 : 21 (last part) the adjective *pas* (all) is placed between the preposition and the noun for the sake of emphasis. In Acts 26 : 11, *kata*, followed by the plural of *pas* and the article before the noun, is rendered " in all the synagogues," R.V., for A.V., " in every synagogue." The presence of the article confirms the R.V. See SEVERALLY.

(2) In Matt. 20 : 9, 10, the preposition *ana*, upward (used distributively), governing the noun *dēnarion*, is translated " every man (a penny)." There is no word for " every man," and an appropriate rendering would be ' a penny apiece ; ' cp. Luke 9 : 14, " fifty each," R.V. ; 10 : 1, " two

and two ; " John 2 : 6, " two or three . . . apiece ; " Rev. 4 : 8,
" each . . . six wings."

(3) The pronoun *tis*, anyone, is rendered " any " in Acts 2 : 45, R.V.,
for the incorrect A.V., " every." In Mark 15 : 24, the interrogative form
is rendered " what each (should take) " (A.V., " every man "), lit., ' who
(should take) what.'

___

EVERYWHERE, EVERY QUARTER, EVERY SIDE

1. PANTACHĒ (πανταχῇ), everywhere, is used in Acts 21 : 28.¶

2. PANTACHOU (πανταχοῦ), a variation of No. 1, is translated
" everywhere " in Mark 1 : 28, R.V., of the report throughout Galilee
concerning Christ ; in Mark 16 : 20, of preaching ; Luke 9 : 6, of healing ;
Acts 17 : 30, of a Divine command for repentance ; 28 : 22, of disparagement of Christians ; 1 Cor. 4 : 17, of apostolic teaching ; in Acts 24 : 3,
it is rendered " in all places."¶ In the Sept., Isa. 42 : 22.¶ See PLACE.

3. PANTOTHEN (παντόθεν) or *pantachothen*, from all sides, is
translated " from every quarter," Mark 1 : 45 ; in Luke 19 : 43, " on
every side ; " in Heb. 9 : 4, " round about."¶

Notes : (1) In Phil. 4 : 12, the phrase *en panti*, A.V., " everywhere,"
is corrected to " in everything," in the R.V. ; in 2 Cor. 4 : 8, " on every
side."

(2) In 1 Tim. 2 : 8, *en panti topō*, " in every place," R.V., is translated
" everywhere " in the A.V.

___

EVERY WHIT

HOLOS (ὅλος), all, whole, complete, is rendered " every whit " in
John 7 : 23 ; 13 : 10. See ALL.

___

For EVIDENCE (Heb. 11 : 1) see REPROOF, A

___

EVIDENT, EVIDENTLY
A. Adjectives.

1. DĒLOS (δῆλος), properly signifying visible, clear to the mind,
evident, is translated " evident " in Gal. 3 : 11 and 1 Cor. 15 : 27, R.V.
(A.V., " manifest ") ; " bewrayeth," Matt. 26 : 73 ; " certain," 1 Tim.
6 : 7, A.V. Cp. *dēloō*, to declare, signify. See BEWRAY, CERTAIN,
MANIFEST.¶

2. KATADĒLOS (κατάδηλος), a strengthened form of No. 1, quite
manifest, evident, is used in Heb. 7 : 15 (A.V., " more evident ").¶ For
the preceding verse see No. 3.

3. PRODĒLOS (πρόδηλος), manifest beforehand (*pro*, before, and
No. 1), is used in Heb. 7 : 14 in the sense of ' clearly evident.' So in
1 Tim. 5 : 24, 25, R.V., " evident," for A.V., " open beforehand," and
" manifest beforehand." The *pro* is somewhat intensive.¶

Note : *Phaneros*, visible, manifest (akin to *phainomai*, to appear), is synonymous with the above, but is not translated "evident" in the N.T. For "evident token" see TOKEN.

B. Adverb.

PHANERŌS (φανερῶς), manifestly (see note above), is rendered "openly" in Mark 1 : 45 ; "publicly" in John 7 : 10, R.V. (opposite to "in secret ") ; in Acts 10 : 3, R.V., "openly," for A.V., "evidently." See OPENLY, PUBLICLY.¶

Note : For the A.V. "evidently" in Gal. 3 : 1, see OPENLY.

EVIL, EVIL-DOER
A. Adjectives.

1. KAKOS (κακός) stands for whatever is evil in character, base, in distinction (wherever the distinction is observable) from *ponēros* (see No. 2), which indicates what is evil in influence and effect, malignant. *Kakos* is the wider term and often covers the meaning of *ponēros*. *Kakos* is antithetic to *kalos*, fair, advisable, good in character, and to *agathos*, beneficial, useful, good in act ; hence it denotes what is useless, incapable, bad ; *ponēros* is essentially antithetic to *chrēstos*, kind, gracious, serviceable ; hence it denotes what is destructive, injurious, evil. As evidence that *ponēros* and *kakos* have much in common, though still not interchangeable, each is used of thoughts, cp. Matt. 15 : 19 with Mark 7 : 21 ; of speech, Matt. 5 : 11 with 1 Pet. 3 : 10 ; of actions, 2 Tim. 4 : 18 with 1 Thess. 5 : 15 ; of man, Matt. 18 : 32 with 24 : 48.

The use of *kakos* may be broadly divided as follows : (*a*) of what is morally or ethically evil, whether of persons, e.g., Matt. 21 : 41 ; 24 : 48 ; Phil. 3 : 2 ; Rev. 2 : 2, or qualities, emotions, passions, deeds, e.g., Mark 7 : 21 ; John 18 : 23, 30 ; Rom. 1 : 30 ; 3 : 8 ; 7 : 19, 21 ; 13 : 4 ; 14 : 20 ; 16 : 19 ; 1 Cor. 13 : 5 ; 2 Cor. 13 : 7 ; 1 Thess. 5 : 15 ; 1 Tim. 6 : 10 ; 2 Tim. 4 : 14 ; 1 Pet. 3 : 9, 12 ; (*b*) of what is injurious, destructive, baneful, pernicious, e.g., Luke 16 : 25 ; Acts 16 : 28 ; 28 : 5 ; Tit. 1 : 12 ; Jas. 3 : 8 ; Rev. 16 : 2, where *kakos* and *ponēros* come in that order, "noisome and grievous." See B, No. 3. For compounds of *kakos*, see below.

2. PONĒROS (πονηρός), akin to *ponos*, labour, toil, denotes evil that causes labour, pain, sorrow, malignant evil (see No. 1) ; it is used (*a*) with the meaning bad, worthless, in the physical sense, Matt. 7 : 17, 18 ; in the moral or ethical sense, evil, wicked ; of persons, e.g., Matt. 7 : 11 ; Luke 6 : 45 ; Acts 17 : 5 ; 2 Thess. 3 : 2 ; 2 Tim. 3 : 13 ; of evil spirits, e.g., Matt. 12 : 45 ; Luke 7 : 21 ; Acts 19 : 12, 13, 15, 16 ; of a generation, Matt. 12 : 39, 45 ; 16 : 4 ; Luke 11 : 29 ; of things, e.g., Matt. 5 : 11 ; 6 : 23 ; 20 : 15 ; Mark 7 : 22 ; Luke 11 : 34 ; John 3 : 19 ; 7 : 7 ; Acts 18 : 14 ; Gal. 1 : 4 ; Col. 1 : 21 ; 1 Tim. 6 : 4 ; 2 Tim. 4 : 18 ; Heb. 3 : 12 ; 10 : 22 ; Jas. 2 : 4 ; 4 : 16 ; 1 John 3 : 12 ; 2 John 11 ; 3 John 10 ; (*b*) with the meaning toilsome, painful, Eph. 5 : 16 ; 6 : 13 ; Rev. 16 : 2. Cp. *ponēria*, iniquity, wickedness. For its use as a noun see B, No. 2.

3. PHAULOS (φαῦλος) primarily denotes slight, trivial, blown about by every wind ; then, mean, common, bad, in the sense of being worthless, paltry or contemptible, belonging to a low order of things ; in John 5 : 29, those who have practised evil things, R.V., " ill " (phaula), are set in contrast to those who have done good things (agatha) ; the same contrast is presented in Rom. 9 : 11 and 2 Cor. 5 : 10, in each of which the most authentic mss. have phaulos for kakos ; he who practises evil things (R.V., " ill ") hates the light, John 3 : 20 ; jealousy and strife are accompanied by " every vile deed," Jas. 3 : 16. It is used as a noun in Tit. 2 : 8 (see B, No. 4). See BAD, ILL, VILE.¶

B. Nouns.

1. KAKIA (κακία), primarily, badness in quality (akin to A, No. 1), denotes (a) wickedness, depravity, malignity, e.g., Acts 8 : 22, " wickedness ;" Rom. 1 : 29, " maliciousness ; " in Jas. 1 : 21, A.V., " naughtiness ; " (b) the evil of trouble, affliction, Matt. 6 : 34, only, and here alone translated " evil." See MALICE, MALICIOUSNESS, NAUGHTINESS, WICKEDNESS.

2. PONĒROS (πονηρός), the adjective (A, No. 2), is used as a noun, (a) of Satan as the evil one, Matt. 5 : 37 ; 6 : 13 ; 13 : 19, 38 ; Luke 11 : 4 (in some texts) ; John 17 : 15 ; Eph. 6 : 16 ; 2 Thess. 3 : 3 ; 1 John 2 : 13, 14 ; 3 : 12 ; 5 : 18, 19 ; (b) of human beings, Matt. 5 : 45 ; (probably ver. 39) ; 13 : 49 ; 22 : 10 ; Luke 6 : 35 ; 1 Cor. 5 : 13 ; (c) neuter, " evil (things)," Matt. 9 : 4 ; 12 : 35 ; Mark 7 : 23 ; Luke 3 : 19 ; " that which is evil," Luke 6 : 45 ; Rom. 12 : 9 ; Acts 28 : 21, " harm."

3. KAKON (κακόν), the neuter of A, No. 1, is used with the article, as a noun, e.g., Acts 23 : 9 ; Rom. 7 : 21 ; Heb. 5 : 14 ; in the plural, " evil things," e.g., 1 Cor. 10 : 6 ; 1 Tim. 6 : 10, " all kinds of evil," R.V.

4. PHAULON (φαῦλον), the neuter of A, No. 3, is used as a noun in Tit. 2 : 8.

5. KAKOPOIOS (κακοποιός), properly the masculine gender of the adjective, denotes an evil-doer (kakon, evil, poieō, to do), 1 Pet. 2 : 12, 14 ; 4 : 15 ; in some mss. in 3 : 16 and John 18 : 30 (so the A.V.).¶ For a synonymous word see Note (1). Cp. the verb below. In the Sept., Prov. 12 : 4 ; 24 : 19. See MALEFACTOR.¶

Notes : (1) Kakourgos, an evil-worker (kakon, evil, ergon, a work), is translated " evil-doer " in 2 Tim. 2 : 9, A.V. (R.V., " malefactor "). Cp. Luke 23 : 32, 33, 39.¶

(2) Adikēma, an injustice (a, negative, dikaios, just), is translated " evil-doing," in Acts 24 : 20, A.V., R.V., " wrong-doing." See INIQUITY, WRONG.

C. Verbs.

1. KAKOŌ (κακόω), to ill-treat (akin to A, No. 1), is rendered to entreat evil in Acts 7 : 6, 19 ; " made (them) evil affected," 14 : 2. See AFFECT, AFFLICT, HARM, HURT, VEX.

2. KAKOPOIEŌ (κακοποιέω) signifies to do evil (cp. B, No. 5), Mark 3 : 4 (R.V., " to do harm ") ; so, Luke 6 : 9 ; in 3 John 11, " doeth evil ; " in 1 Pet. 3 : 17, "evil doing." See HARM.¶

Note : Cp. *kakologeō*, to speak evil (see CURSE, SPEAK) ; *kakopatheō*, to endure evil (see ENDURE, SUFFER) ; *kakopatheia*, suffering affliction (see SUFFER) ; *kakoucheō*, to suffer adversity (see SUFFER).

D. Adverb.

KAKŌS (κακῶς), badly, evilly, akin to A, No. 1, is used in the physical sense, to be sick, e.g., Matt. 4 : 24 ; Mark 1 : 32, 34 ; Luke 5 : 31 (see DISEASE). In Matt. 21 : 41 this adverb is used with the adjective, " He will miserably destroy those miserable men," more lit., ' He will evilly destroy those men (evil as they are),' with stress on the adjective ; (b) in the moral sense, to speak evilly, John 18 : 23 ; Acts 23 : 5 ; to ask evilly, Jas. 4 : 3. See AMISS, GRIEVOUSLY, SICK, SORE.

EVIL SPEAKING

1. BLASPHĒMIA (βλασφημία) is translated " evil speaking " in Eph. 4 : 31, A.V. (R.V., " railing "). See BLASPHEMY.

2. KATALALIA (καταλαλία), "evil speaking," 1 Pet. 2 : 1 : see BACK-BITING.

EXACT (Verb)

1. PRASSŌ (πράσσω), to do, to practise, also has the meaning of transacting, or managing in the matter of payment, to exact, to get money from a person, Luke 3 : 13 (R.V., " extort "). Cp. the English idiom ' to do a person.' This verb is rendered " required," in 19 : 23.

2. SUKOPHANTEŌ (συκοφαντέω), to accuse falsely, Luke 3 : 14, has its other meaning, to exact wrongfully, in 19 : 8. See ACCUSE.¶

EXACT, EXACTLY

AKRIBESTERON (ἀκριβέστερον), the comparative degree of *akribōs*, accurately, carefully, is used in Acts 18 : 26, A.V., " more perfectly," R.V., " more carefully ; " 23 : 15, A.V., " more perfectly," R.V., " more exactly ; " so ver. 20 ; 24 : 22, A.V., " more perfect," R.V., " more exact " (lit., ' knowing more exactly'). See CAREFULLY, PERFECTLY.¶

Cp. *akribeia*, precision, exactness, Acts 22 : 3,¶ and *akriboō*, to learn carefully, to enquire with exactness, Matt. 2 : 7, 16.¶

EXALT, EXALTED

A. Verbs.

1. HUPSOŌ (ὑψόω), to lift up (akin to *hupsos*, height), is used (a) literally of the lifting up of Christ in His crucifixion, John 3 : 14 ; 8 : 28 ; 12 : 32, 34 ; illustratively, of the serpent of brass, John 3 : 14 ;

(b) figuratively, of spiritual privileges bestowed on a city, Matt. 11 : 23 ; Luke 10 : 15 ; of raising to dignity and happiness, Luke 1 : 52 ; Acts 13 : 17 ; of haughty self-exaltation, and, contrastingly, of being raised to honour, as a result of self-humbling, Matt. 23 : 12 ; Luke 14 : 11 ; 18 : 14 ; of spiritual uplifting and revival, Jas. 4 : 10 ; 1 Pet. 5 : 6 ; of bringing into the blessings of salvation through the Gospel, 2 Cor. 11 : 7 ; (c) with a combination of the literal and metaphorical, of the exaltation of Christ by God the Father, Acts 2 : 33 ; 5 : 31. See LIFT.¶

2. HUPERUPSOŌ (ὑπερυψόω), to exalt highly (huper, over, and No. 1), is used of Christ, as in No. 1, (c), in Phil. 2 : 9.¶

3. EPAIRŌ (ἐπαίρω), to lift up (epi, up, airō, to raise), is said (a) literally, of a sail, Acts 27 : 40 ; hands, Luke 24 : 50 ; 1 Tim. 2 : 8 ; heads, Luke 21 : 28 ; eyes, Matt. 17 : 8, etc. ; (b) metaphorically, of exalting oneself, being lifted up with pride, 2 Cor. 10 : 5 ; 11 : 20. See LIFT.

4. HUPERAIRŌ (ὑπεραίρω), to raise over (huper, above, and airō, see No. 3), is used in the Middle Voice, of exalting oneself exceedingly, 2 Cor. 12 : 7 ; 2 Thess. 2 : 4.¶

B. Adjective.

HUPSĒLOS (ὑψηλός), high, lofty, is used metaphorically in Luke 16 : 15, as a noun with the article, R.V., " that which is exalted," A.V., " that which is highly esteemed." See ESTEEM, HIGH.

Note : For Jas. 1 : 9, R.V., " in his high estate," see ESTATE, No. 3.

EXAMINATION, EXAMINE
A. Noun.

ANAKRISIS (ἀνάκρισις), from *ana*, up or through, and *krinō*, to distinguish, was a legal term among the Greeks, denoting the preliminary investigation for gathering evidence for the information of the judges, Acts 25 : 26.¶

B. Verbs.

1. ANAKRINŌ (ἀνακρίνω), to examine, investigate, is used (a) of searching or enquiry, Acts 17 : 11 ; 1 Cor. 9 : 3 ; 10 : 25, 27 ; (b) of reaching a result of the enquiry, judging, 1 Cor. 2 : 14, 15 ; 4 : 3, 4 ; 14 : 24 ; (c) forensically, of examining by torture, Luke 23 : 14 ; Acts 4 : 9 ; 12 : 19 ; 24 : 8 ; 28 : 18. See ASK, DISCERN, JUDGE, SEARCH.¶

2. ANETAZŌ (ἀνετάζω), to examine judicially (ana, up, etazō, to test), is used in Acts 22 : 24, 29.¶ Cp. the synonymous verb *exetazō*, to search or enquire carefully, Matt. 2 : 8 ; 10 : 11 ; John 21 : 12.¶

3. DOKIMAZŌ (δοκιμάζω), to prove, test, approve, is rendered " examine " in 1 Cor. 11 : 28, A.V. (R.V., " prove "). See APPROVE.

4. PEIRAZŌ (πειράζω), to tempt, try, is rendered " examine " in 2 Cor. 13 : 5, A.V. (R.V., " try "). See GO, PROVE, TEMPT, TRY.

EXAMPLE
A. Nouns.

1. DEIGMA (δεῖγμα), primarily a thing shown, a specimen (akin to *deiknumi*, to show), denotes an example given as a warning, Jude 7.¶ *Note :* The corresponding word in 2 Pet. 2 : 6 is No. 2.

2. HUPODEIGMA (ὑπόδειγμα) : see ENSAMPLE, No. 3.

3. TUPOS (τύπος) : see ENSAMPLE, No. 1.

4. HUPOGRAMMOS (ὑπογραμμός), lit., an under-writing (from *hupographō*, to write under, to trace letters for copying by scholars) ; hence, a writing-copy, an example, 1 Pet. 2 : 21, said of what Christ left for believers, by His sufferings (not expiatory, but exemplary), that they might "follow His steps."

B. Verbs.

1. DEIGMATIZŌ (δειγματίζω), to make a show of, to expose (akin to A, No. 1), is translated "to make a public example," in Matt. 1 : 19 (some mss. have the strengthened form *paradeigmatizō* here ; "put . . . to an open shame," Heb. 6 : 6,¶) ; in Col. 2 : 15, "made a show of."¶

2. HUPODEIKNUMI (ὑποδείκνυμι), primarily, to show secretly (*hupo*, under, *deiknumi*, to show), to show by tracing out (akin to A, No. 2) ; hence, to teach, to show by example, Acts 20 : 35, R.V., " I gave you an example," for A.V., " I shewed you." Elsewhere, to warn, Matt. 3 : 7 ; Luke 3 : 7 ; 12 : 5, R.V., for A.V., " forewarn ; " to show, Luke 6 : 47 ; Acts 9 : 16. See FOREWARN, SHEW, WARN.¶

EXCEED, EXCEEDING, EXCEEDINGLY
A. Verbs.

1. HUPERBALLŌ (ὑπερβάλλω), to throw over or beyond (*huper*, over, *ballō*, to throw), is translated "exceeding" in 2 Cor. 9 : 14 ; Eph. 1 : 19 ; 2 : 7 ; "excelleth" (R.V., "surpasseth") in 2 Cor. 3 : 10 ; "passeth" in Eph. 3 : 19 (" surpasseth " might be the meaning here). See EXCEL, SURPASS.¶ Cp. *huperbolē*, under EXCEL, B, No. 1.

2. PERISSEUŌ (περισσεύω), to be over and above, over a certain number or measure, to abound, exceed, is translated "exceed" in Matt. 5 : 20 ; 2 Cor. 3 : 9. See ABUNDANCE, B, No. 1.

B. Adverbs and Adverbial Phrases.

1. LIAN (λίαν), very, exceedingly, is translated "exceeding" in Matt. 2 : 16 (for ver. 10, see No. 2) ; 4 : 8 ; 8 : 28 ; Mark 9 : 3 ; Luke 23 : 8. See GREATLY (GREAT), SORE, VERY.

2. SPHODRA (σφόδρα), properly the neuter plural of *sphodros*, excessive, violent (from a root indicating restlessness), signifies very, very much, exceedingly, Matt. 2 : 10 ; 17 : 6, " sore ; " 17 : 23 ; 18 : 31, R.V., " exceeding," for A.V., " very ; " 19 : 25 ; 26 : 22 ; 27 : 54, R.V., " exceedingly " for A.V., " greatly ; " Mark 16 : 4, " very ; " Luke 18 : 23 (ditto) ; Acts 6 : 7, R.V., " exceedingly," for A.V., " greatly ; " Rev. 16 : 21. See GREATLY, SORE, VERY.¶

3. SPHODRŌS (σφοδρῶς), exceedingly (see No. 2), is used in Acts 27 : 18.¶

4. PERISSŌS (περισσῶς) is used in Matt. 27 : 23, R.V., " exceedingly," for A.V., " the more ; " Mark 10 : 26, R.V., " exceedingly," for A.V., " out of measure ; " in Acts 26 : 11, " exceedingly." In Mark 15 : 14, the most authentic mss. have this word (R.V., " exceedingly ") for No. 5 (A.V., " the more exceedingly "). See MORE.¶

5. PERISSOTERŌS (περισσοτέρως), the comparative degree of No. 4, abundantly, exceedingly (akin to A, No. 2), Gal. 1 : 14, " more exceedingly ; " 1 Thess. 2 : 17, R.V., " the more exceedingly," for A.V., " the more abundantly ; " see ABUNDANCE, D, No. 2.

6. HUPEREKPERISSOU (ὑπερεκπερισσοῦ) denotes superabundantly (huper, over, ek, from, perissos, abundant) ; in 1 Thess. 3 : 10, " exceedingly ; " Eph. 3 : 20, " exceeding abundantly."¶ Another form, huperekperissōs (huper, and ek and No. 4), is used in 1 Thess. 5 : 13 (in the best mss.), " exceeding highly."¶ Cp. the verb huperperisseuō, to abound more exceedingly, Rom. 5 : 21 ; in 2 Cor. 7 : 4, " I overflow (with joy)," R.V., for A.V., " I am exceeding (joyful). See ABUNDANT, D, No. 2.

Notes : (1) In Acts 7 : 20, the phrase " exceeding fair " (asteios) is, lit., ' fair to God ' (see marg.). (2) In Matt. 26 : 7, barutimos (barus, weighty, *timē* value), is rendered " exceeding precious," R.V., for A.V., " very precious." (3) In Mark 4 : 41, " they feared exceedingly " is, lit., ' they feared a great fear.' See FEAR. (4) For other combinations of the adverb, see GLAD, GREAT, JOYFUL, SORROWFUL, SORRY.

EXCEL, EXCELLENCY, EXCELLENT
A. Verbs.

1. HUPERBALLŌ (ὑπερβάλλω), lit., to throw over : see EXCEED, No. 1.

2. PERISSEUŌ (περισσεύω), to be over and above, is rendered " abound in 1 Cor. 14 : 12, R.V., for A.V., " excel." See ABUNDANCE, B, No. 1, and EXCEED, A, No. 2.

3. HUPERECHŌ (ὑπερέχω), lit., to have over (huper, over, echō, to have), is translated " excellency " in Phil. 3 : 8, ' the surpassingness ' (Moule) ; the phrase could be translated ' the surpassing thing, which consists in the knowledge of Christ Jesus,' and this is the probable meaning. This verb is used three times in Philippians, here and in 2 : 3 ; 4 : 7. See also Rom. 13 : 1 ; 1 Pet. 2 : 13. See BETTER, No. 4.¶

4. DIAPHERŌ (διαφέρω), to differ, is used in the neuter plural of the present participle with the article, in Phil. 1 : 10, " the things that are excellent " (marg., " the things that differ "), lit., ' the excellent things.' See DIFFER.

B. Nouns.

1. HUPERBOLĒ (ὑπερβολή), lit., a throwing beyond, hence, a surpassing, an excellence, is translated " excellency " in 2 Cor. 4 : 7, A.V. ;

R.V., " exceeding greatness." It always betokens pre-eminence. It is used with *kata*, according to, in the phrase *kath' huperbolēn*, signifying beyond measure, exceedingly, Rom. 7 : 13, " exceeding sinful ; " in 2 Cor. 1 : 8, R.V., " exceedingly," for A.V., " out of measure ; " in Gal. 1 : 13, " beyond measure ; " in 1 Cor. 12 : 31, " more excellent." In 2 Cor. 4 : 17, there is an expanded phrase *kath' huperbolēn eis huperbolēn*, lit., ' according to a surpassing unto a surpassing,' R.V., " more and more exceedingly," which corrects the A.V., " a far more exceeding ; " the phrase refers to " worketh," showing the surpassing degree of its operation, and not to the noun " weight " (nor does it qualify " eternal "). In 2 Cor. 12 : 7, the R.V. has " exceeding greatness," the A.V., " abundance." See ABUNDANCE.¶

2. HUPEROCHĒ (ὑπεροχή), akin to A, No. 3, strictly speaking, the act of overhanging (*huper*, and *echō*, to hold) or the thing which overhangs, hence, superiority, pre-eminence, is translated " excellency (of speech) " in 1 Cor. 2 : 1 ; elsewhere, in 1 Tim. 2 : 2, R.V., " high place," for A.V., " authority." See AUTHORITY, PLACE.¶

Note : In 1 Pet. 2 : 9 R.V. renders *aretē* (virtue) " excellencies."

C. Adjectives.

1. MEGALOPREPĒS (μεγαλοπρεπής) signifies magnificent, majestic, that which is becoming to a great man (from *megas*, great, and *prepō*, to be fitting or becoming), in 2 Pet. 1 : 17, " excellent."¶

2. DIAPHORŌTEROS (διαφορώτερος), comparative degree of *diaphoros*, excellent, akin to A, No. 4, is used twice, in Heb. 1 : 4, " more excellent (name)," and 8 : 6, " more excellent (ministry)."¶ For the positive degree see Rom. 12 : 6 ; Heb. 9 : 10. See under DIFFER.¶

3. PLEIŌN (πλείων), more, greater, the comparative degree of *polus*, much, is translated " more excellent " in Heb. 11 : 4, of Abel's sacrifice ; *pleiōn* is used sometimes of that which is superior by reason of inward worth, cp. 3 : 3, " more (honour) ; " in Matt. 6 : 25, of the life in comparison with meat.

4. KRATISTOS (κράτιστος), mightiest, noblest, best, the superlative degree of *kratus*, strong (cp. *kratos*, strength), is used as a title of honour and respect, " most excellent," Luke 1 : 3 (Theophilus was quite possibly a man of high rank) ; Acts 23 : 26 ; 24 : 3 and 26 : 25, R.V., for A.V., " most noble."¶

Note : The phrase *kath' huperbolēn* (for which see B, No. 1) is translated " more excellent " in 1 Cor. 12 : 31.

EXCEPT, EXCEPTED

Note : For the negative conjunctions *ean mē* and *ei mē*, see † p. 9.

1. EKTOS (ἐκτός), an adverb, lit., outside, is used with *ei mē*, as an extended conjunction signifying " except ; " so in 1 Cor. 14 : 5 ; in 15 : 2, R.V., for A.V., " unless ; " in 1 Tim. 5 : 19, R.V., for A.V., " but."

It has the force of a preposition in the sense of (a) outside of, in 1 Cor. 6 : 18, "without ; " in 2 Cor. 12 : 2, "out of ; " (b) besides, except, in Acts 26 : 22, R.V., "but," for A.V., "other than ; " in 1 Cor. 15 : 27 "excepted." For its use as a noun see Matt. 23 : 26, "(the) outside." See OTHER, OUT OF, OUTSIDE, UNLESS, WITHOUT.¶

2. PAREKTOS (παρεκτός), a strengthened form of No. 1 (para, beside), is used (a) as an adverb, signifying "without," 2 Cor. 11 : 28 ; lit., ' the things without,' i.e., the things happening without ; (b) as a preposition signifying "except ; " in Matt. 5 : 32, "saving ; " in Acts 26 : 29, "except."¶

Note : In Matt. 19 : 9, the A.V. and R.V., translating the mss. which have the negative mē, followed by epi, render it "except for." The authorities mentioned in the R.V. marg. have parektos, followed by logou, i.e., ' saving for the cause of.'

3. PLĒN (πλήν), an adverb, most frequently signifying yet, howbeit, or only, sometimes has the meaning "except (that)," "save (that)," Acts 20 : 23 ; Phil. 1 : 18, R.V., "only that," for A.V., "notwithstanding." It is also used as a preposition, signifying except, save, Mark 12 : 32, "but ; " John 8 : 10, "but " (A.V. only) ; Acts 8 : 1, "except ; " Acts 15 : 28, "than ; " 27 : 22, "but (only)."

EXCESS

1. AKRASIA (ἀκρασία) lit. denotes want of strength (a, negative, kratos, strength), hence, want of self-control, incontinence, Matt. 23 : 25, "excess ; " 1 Cor. 7 : 5, "incontinency."¶ Cp. akratēs, powerless, incontinent, 2 Tim. 3 : 3, R.V., "without self-control."¶

2. ANACHUSIS (ἀνάχυσις), lit., a pouring out, overflowing (akin to anacheō, to pour out), is used metaphorically in 1 Pet. 4 : 4, "excess," said of the riotous conduct described in ver. 3.¶

Notes : (1) Asōtia denotes prodigality, profligacy, riot (from a, negative, and sōzō, to save) ; it is translated "riot " in Eph. 5 : 18, R.V., for A.V., "excess ; " in Tit. 1 : 6 and 1 Pet. 4 : 4, "riot " in A.V. and R.V. See RIOT.¶ Cp. the adverb asōtōs, wastefully, "in riotous living," Luke 15 : 13.¶ A synonymous noun is aselgeia, lasciviousness, out-rageous conduct, wanton violence.

(2) In 1 Pet. 4 : 3, oinophlugia, drunkenness, debauchery (oinos, wine, phluō, to bubble up, overflow), is rendered "excess of wine," A.V. (R.V., "winebibbings ") ¶

EXCHANGE
A. Noun.

ANTALLAGMA (ἀντάλλαγμα), the price received as an equivalent of, or in exchange for, an article, an exchange (anti, instead of, allassō, to change, akin to allos, another), hence denotes the price at which the exchange is effected, Matt. 16 : 26 ; Mark 8 : 37.¶ Connected with this is the conception of atonement, as in the word *lutron*, a ransom. Cp. *allagma* in the Sept., e.g., in Isa. 43 : 3.

B. Verb.

METALLASSŌ (μεταλλάσσω) denotes (*a*) to exchange, *meta*, with, implying change, and *allassō* (see A.), Rom. 1 : 25, of exchanging the truth for a lie, R.V., for A.V., " changed ; " (*b*) to change, ver. 26, a different meaning from that in the preceding verse. See CHANGE.¶ In the Sept., Esth. 2 : 7, 20.¶

Note : In Luke 24 : 17, " what communications are these that ye have one with another ? " the verb *antiballō*, to throw in turn, to exchange, is used of conversation, lit., ' what words are these that ye exchange one with another ? '

For EXCHANGERS see BANKERS

EXCLUDE

EKKLEIŌ (ἐκκλείω), to shut out (*ek*, from, *kleiō*, to shut), is said of glorying in works as a means of justification, Rom. 3 : 27 ; of Gentiles, who by Judaism would be excluded from salvation and Christian fellow-ship, Gal. 4 : 17.¶

EXCUSE
A. Noun.

PROPHASIS (πρόφασις), a pretence, pretext (from *pro*, before, and *phēmi*, to say), is translated " excuse " in John 15 : 22, R.V., for A.V., " cloke ; " " cloke in 1 Thess. 2 : 5, A.V. and R.V. See CLOKE, PRETENCE, SHOW (Noun).

B. Adjective (*negative*).

ANAPOLOGĒTOS (ἀναπολόγητος), without excuse, inexcusable (*a*, negative, *n*, euphonic, and *apologeomai*, see C, No. 1, below), is used, Rom. 1 : 20, " without excuse," of those who reject the revelation of God in creation ; 2 : 1, R.V., for A.V., " inexcusable," of the Jew who judges the Gentile.¶

C. Verbs.

1. APOLOGEOMAI (ἀπολογέομαι), lit., to speak oneself off, hence to plead for oneself, and so, in general, (*a*) to defend, as before a tribunal ; in Rom. 2 : 15, R.V., " excusing them," means one excusing others (not themselves) ; the preceding phrase " one with another " signifies one person with another, not one thought with another ; it may be para-phrased, ' their thoughts with one another, condemning or else excusing one another ; ' conscience provides a moral standard by which men judge one another ; (*b*) to excuse oneself, 2 Cor. 12 : 19 ; cp. B. See ANSWER.

2. PARAITEOMAI (παραιτέομαι) is used in the sense of begging off, asking to be excused or making an excuse, in Luke 14 : 18 (twice) and

ver. 19. In the first part of ver. 18 the verb is used in the Middle Voice, " to make excuse " (acting in imagined self-interest) ; in the latter part and in ver. 19 it is in the Passive Voice, " have me excused."

EXECUTE

1. POIEŌ (ποιέω), to do, to make, is thrice rendered " execute," of the Lord's authority and acts in executing judgment, (a) of His authority as the One to whom judgment is committed, John 5 : 27 ; (b) of the judgment which He will mete out to all transgressors at His Second Advent, Jude 15 ; (c) of the carrying out of His word (not " work," as in the A.V.) in the earth, especially regarding the nation of Israel, the mass being rejected, the remnant saved, Rom. 9 : 28. That He will " execute His word finishing and cutting it short," is expressive of the summary and decisive character of His action. See Do.

2. HIERATEUŌ (ἱερατεύω), to be a priest, to officiate as such, is translated " executed the priest's office," in Luke 1 : 8.¶ It occurs frequently in the Sept., and in Inscriptions. Cp. hierateuma, priesthood, 1 Pet. 2 : 5, 9,¶ hierateia, a priest's office, Luke 1 : 9 ; Heb. 7 : 5,¶ hiereus, a priest, and hieros, sacred.

For **EXECUTIONER**, Mark 6 : 27, see GUARD, A, No. 2

EXERCISE
A. Verbs.

1. GUMNAZŌ (γυμνάζω) primarily signifies to exercise naked (from gumnos, naked) ; then, generally, to exercise, to train the body or mind (Eng., gymnastic), 1 Tim. 4 : 7, with a view to godliness ; Heb. 5 : 14, of the senses, so as to discern good and evil ; 12 : 11, of the effect of chastening, the spiritual exercise producing the fruit of righteousness ; 2 Pet. 2 : 14, of certain evil teachers with hearts " exercised in covetousness," R.V.¶

2. ASKEŌ (ἀσκέω) signifies to form by art, to adorn, to work up raw material with skill ; hence, in general, to take pains, endeavour, exercise by training or discipline, with a view to a conscience void of offence, Acts 24 : 16.¶

3. POIEŌ (ποιέω), to do, is translated " exerciseth " in Rev. 13 : 12, said of the authority of the second " Beast." Cp. EXECUTE. See Do.

Notes : The following verbs contain in translation the word " exercise " but belong to other headings : *exousiazō*, to exercise authority over, Luke 22 : 25 (*exousia*, authority) ; in the first part of this verse, the verb *kurieuō*, to be lord, is translated " exercise lordship," A.V. (R.V., " have lordship ") ; *katexousiazō*, a strengthened form of the preceding (*kata*, down, intensive), Matt. 20 : 25 ; Mark 10 : 42, " exercise authority " (in the first part of these verses the synonymous verb *katakurieuō*, is rendered "lord it," R.V., for A.V., "exercise dominion," and "exercise lordship," respectively) ; *episkopeō*, to look over or upon (*epi*, over, *skopeō*, to look), to care for, 1 Pet. 5 : 2 (absent in some mss.), R.V., "exercising the oversight," for A.V. "taking etc."

B. Noun.

GUMNASIA (γυμνασία) primarily denotes gymnastic exercise (akin to A, No. 1), 1 Tim. 4 : 8, where the immediate reference is probably not to mere physical training for games but to discipline of the body such as that to which the Apostle refers in 1 Cor. 9 : 27, though there may be an allusion to the practices of asceticism.

EXHORT, EXHORTATION
A. Verbs.

1. PARAKALEŌ (παρακαλέω), primarily, to call to a person (*para*, to the side, *kaleō*, to call), denotes (*a*) to call on, entreat ; see BESEECH ; (*b*) to admonish, exhort, to urge one to pursue some course of conduct (always prospective, looking to the future, in contrast to the meaning to comfort, which is retrospective, having to do with trial experienced), translated "exhort" in the R.V. of Phil. 4 : 2 ; 1 Thess. 4 : 10 ; Heb. 13 : 19, 22, for A.V., "beseech ; " in 1 Tim. 5 : 1, for A.V., "intreat ; " in 1 Thess. 5 : 11, for A.V., "comfort ; " "exhorted" in 2 Cor. 8 : 6 and 12 : 18, for A.V., "desired ; " in 1 Tim. 1 : 3, for A.V., "besought." See BESEECH.

2. PARAINEŌ (παραινέω), primarily, to speak of near (*para*, near, and *aineō*, to tell of, speak of, then, to recommend), hence, to advise, exhort, warn, is used in Acts 27 : 9, "admonished," and ver. 22, "I exhort." See ADMONISH.¶

3. PROTREPŌ (προτρέπω), lit., to turn forward, propel (*pro*, before, *trepō*, to turn) ; hence, to impel morally, to urge forward, encourage, is used in Acts 18 : 27, R.V., "encouraged him" (Apollos), with reference to his going into Achaia ; A.V., "exhorting the disciples ; " while the encouragement was given to Apollos, a letter was written to the disciples in Achaia to receive him.¶

B. Noun.

PARAKLĒSIS (παράκλησις), akin to A, No. 1, primarily a calling to one's side, and so to one's aid, hence denotes (*a*) an appeal, "entreaty," 2 Cor. 8 : 4 ; (*b*) encouragement, exhortation, e.g., Rom. 12 : 8 ; in Acts 4 : 36, R.V., "exhortation," for A.V., "consolation ; " (*c*) consolation and comfort, e.g., Rom. 15 : 4. See COMFORT. Cp. *paraklētos*, an advocate, comforter.

EXIST
HUPARCHŌ (ὑπάρχω), primarily, to make a beginning (*hupo*, under, *archē*, a beginning), denotes to be, to be in existence, involving an existence

or condition both previous to the circumstances mentioned and continuing after it. This is important in Phil. 2 : 6, concerning the Deity of Christ. The phrase " being (existing) in the form (*morphē*, the essential and specific form and character) of God," carries with it the two facts of the antecedent Godhood of Christ, previous to His Incarnation, and the continuance of His Godhood at and after the event of His Birth (see Gifford, on the Incarnation, pp. 11, sqq.). It is translated " exist " in 1 Cor. 11 : 18, R.V., for A.V., " there be." Cp. Luke 16 : 14 ; 23 : 50 ; Acts 2 : 30 ; 3 : 2 ; 17 : 24 ; 22 : 3 etc. See BEING, GOODS, LIVE, POSSESS, SUBSTANCE.

EXORCIST

EXORKISTĒS (*ἐξορκιστής*) denotes (*a*) one who administers an oath ; (*b*) an exorcist (akin to *exorkizō*, to adjure, from *orkos*, an oath), one who employs a formula of conjuration for the expulsion of demons, Acts 19 :13. The practice of exorcism was carried on by strolling Jews, who used their power in the recitation of particular names.¶

EXPECT, EXPECTATION
A. Verbs.

1. EKDECHOMAI (*ἐκδέχομαι*), lit. and primarily, to take or receive from (*ek*, from, *dechomai*, to receive), hence denotes to await, expect, the only sense of the word in the N.T. ; it suggests a reaching out in readiness to receive something ; " expecting," Heb. 10 : 13 ; " expect," 1 Cor. 16 : 11, R.V. (A.V., " look for ") ; to wait for, John 5 : 3 (A.V. only) ; Acts 17 : 16 ; 1 Cor. 11 : 33, R.V. (A.V., " tarry for ") ; Jas. 5 : 7 ; to wait, 1 Pet. 3 : 20 in some mss. ; " looked for," Heb. 11 : 10. Cp. B, No. 1. See LOOK, TARRY, WAIT.¶

2. PROSDOKAŌ (*προσδοκάω*), to watch toward, to look for, expect (*pros*, toward, *dokeō*, to think : *dokaō* does not exist), is translated " expecting " in Matt. 24 : 50 and Luke 12 : 46, R.V. (A.V., " looketh for ") ; Luke 3 : 15, " were in expectation ; " Acts 3 : 5, " expecting " (A.V. and R.V.) ; 28 : 6 (twice), " expected that," R.V. (A.V., " looked when ") and " when they were long in expectation " (A.V., " after they had looked a great while "). See LOOK, TARRY, WAIT.

B. Nouns.

1. APOKARADOKIA (*ἀποκαραδοκία*), primarily a watching with outstretched head (*apo*, from, *kara*, the head, and *dokeō*, to look, to watch), signifies strained expectancy, eager longing, the stretching forth of the head indicating an expectation of something from a certain place, Rom. 8 : 19 and Phil. 1 : 20. The prefix *apo* suggests " abstraction and absorption " (Lightfoot), i.e., abstraction from anything else that might engage the attention, and absorption in the object expected " till the fulfilment is realized " (Alford). The intensive character of the noun, in comparison

with No. 2 (below), is clear from the contexts ; in Rom. 8 : 19 it is said figuratively of the creation as waiting for the revealing of the sons of God (" waiting " translates the verb *apekdechomai*, a strengthened form of A, No. 1 ; see WAIT FOR).   In Phil. 1 : 20 the Apostle states it as his " earnest expectation " and hope, that, instead of being put to shame, Christ shall be magnified in his body, " whether by life, or by death," suggesting absorption in the Person of Christ, abstraction from aught that hinders.¶

2. PROSDOKIA (προσδοκία), a watching for, expectation (akin to A, No. 2, which see), is used in the N.T. only of the expectation of evil, Luke 21 : 26, R.V., " expectation," A.V., " looking for," regarding impending calamities ; Acts 12 : 11, " the expectation," of the execution of Peter.¶

3. EKDOCHĒ (ἐκδοχή), primarily a receiving from, hence, expectation (akin to A, No. 1), is used in Heb. 10 : 27 (R.V., " expectation ; " A.V., " looking for "), of judgment.¶

EXPEDIENT

SUMPHERŌ (συμφέρω) signifies (*a*), transitively, lit., to bring together, (*sun*, with, *pherō*, to bring), Acts 19 : 19 ; (*b*) intransitively, to be an advantage, profitable, expedient (not merely ' convenient ') ; it is used mostly impersonally, " it is (it was) expedient ; " so in Matt. 19 : 10, R.V. (negatively), A.V., " it is (not) good ; " John 11 : 50 ; 16 : 7 ; 18 : 14 ; 1 Cor. 6 : 12 ; 10 : 23 ; 2 Cor. 8 : 10 ; 12 : 1 ; " it is profitable," Matt. 5 : 29, 30 ; 18 : 6, R.V. ; " was profitable," Acts 20 : 20 ; " to profit withal," 1 Cor. 12 : 7 ; in Heb. 12 : 10, used in the neuter of the present participle with the article as a noun, " for (our) profit."   See PROFIT.¶ Cp. the adjective *sumphoros* (or *sumpheron*), profitable, used with the article as a noun, 1 Cor. 7 : 35 ; 10 : 33.¶

For EXPELLED, Acts 13 : 50, A.V., see CAST, No. 5

EXPERIENCE (without), EXPERIMENT

1. APEIROS (ἄπειρος), without experience (*a*, negative, *peira*, a trial, experiment), is used in Heb. 5 : 13, R.V., " without experience," A.V., " unskilful," with reference to " the word of righteousness."¶   In the Sept., Numb. 14 : 23, of youths ; Jer. 2 : 6, of a land, " untried ; " Zech. 11 : 15, of a shepherd.¶

2. DOKIMĒ (δοκιμή) means (*a*) the process of proving ; it is rendered " experiment " in 2 Cor. 9 : 13, A.V., R.V., " the proving (of you) ; " in 8 : 2, A.V., " trial," R.V., " proof ; " (*b*) the effect of proving, approval, approvedness, R.V., " probation," Rom. 5 : 4 (twice), for A.V., " experience ; " A.V. and R.V., " proof " in 2 Cor. 2 : 9 ; 13 : 3 and Phil. 2 : 22. See EXPERIENCE, PROOF.¶ Cp. *dokimos*, approved, *dokimazō*, to prove, approve ; see APPROVE.

EXPERT

GNŌSTĒS (γνώστης), one who knows (akin to ginōskō, to know), denotes an expert, a connoisseur, Acts 26 : 3.¶ Cp. gnōstos, known.

EXPIRE

Note : In Acts 7 : 30, the A.V. " were expired " translates the verb *plēroō*, to fulfil (R.V.). See FULFIL. In Rev. 20 : 7, the A.V. " are expired " translates the verb *teleō*, to finish (R.V.). See FINISH.

EXPLAIN

DIASAPHEŌ (διασαφέω), to make clear, explain fully (*dia*, through, intensive, and *saphēs*, clear), is translated " explain " in Matt. 13 : 36 R.V. (A.V., " declare ") translates *pirazō* ; in 18 : 31, told," of the account of the unforgiving debtor's doings, given by his fellow-servants. The preferable rendering would be ' they made clear ' or ' they explained,' suggesting a detailed explanation of the circumstances.¶

EXPOUND

1. EKTITHĒMI (ἐκτίθημι), to set out, expose (*ek*, out, *tithēmi*, to place), is used (*a*) literally, Acts 7 : 21 ; (*b*) metaphorically, in the Middle Voice, to set forth, expound, of circumstances, Acts 11 : 4 ; of the way of God, 18 : 26 ; of the Kingdom of God, 28 : 23.¶

2. EPILUŌ (ἐπιλύω), primarily, to loose, release, a strengthened form of *luō*, to loose, signifies to solve, explain, expound, Mark 4 : 34, " expounded ; " in Acts 19 : 39, of settling a controversy, R.V., " it shall be settled," for A.V., " it shall be determined." See DETERMINE.¶ Cp. *epilusis*, an interpretation, 2 Pet. 1 : 20.¶

3. DIERMĒNEUŌ (διερμηνεύω), to interpret fully (*dia*, through, intensive, *hermēneuō*, to interpret ; Eng., hermeneutics), is translated " He expounded " in Luke 24 : 27, A.V., R.V., " interpreted ; " in Acts 9 : 36, " by interpretation," lit., ' being interpreted ; ' see also 1 Cor. 12 : 30 ; 14 : 5, 13. 27. See INTERPRET.¶

For EXPRESS, Heb. 1:3, A.V., see IMAGE, No. 2

EXPRESSLY

RHĒTŌS (ῥητῶς), meaning ' in stated terms ' (from *rhētos*, stated, specified ; from *rheō*, or *erō*, to say ; cp. *rhēma*, a word), is used in 1 Tim. 4 : 1, " expressly."¶

EXTORT, EXTORTION, EXTORTIONER
A. Verb.

PRASSŌ (πράσσω), to practise, has the special meaning " extort " in Luke 3 : 13, R.V. (A.V., " exact "). In Luke 19 : 23 it is translated

" required ; " it may be that the master, in addressing the slothful servant, uses the word ' extort ' or ' exact ' (as in 3 : 13), in accordance with the character attributed to him by the servant.

B. Nouns.

1. HARPAGĒ (ἁρπαγή) denotes pillage, plundering, robbery, extortion [akin to *harpazō*, to seize, carry off by force, and *harpagmos*, a thing seized, or the act of seizing ; from the root *arp* (sic), seen in Eng., rapacious ; an associated noun, with the same spelling, denoted a rake, or hook for drawing up a bucket] ; it is translated " extortion " in Matt. 23 : 25 ; Luke 11 : 39, R.V., A.V., " ravening ; " Heb. 10 : 34, " spoiling." See RAVENING, SPOILING.¶ Cp. C. below.

2. PLEONEXIA (πλεονεξία), covetousness, desire for advantage, is rendered " extortion " in 2 Cor. 9 : 5, R.V. (A.V. and R.V. marg., " covetousness "). See COVET.

C. Adjective.

HARPAX (ἅρπαξ), rapacious (akin to No. 1), is translated as a noun, " extortioners," in Luke 18 : 11 ; 1 Cor. 5 : 10, 11 ; 6 : 10 ; in Matt. 7 : 15 " ravening " (of wolves).¶ In the Sept., Gen. 49 : 27.¶

EYE

1. OPHTHALMOS (ὀφθαλμός), akin to *opsis*, sight, probably from a root signifying penetration, sharpness (Curtius, Gk. Etym.) (cp. Eng., ophthalmia, etc.), is used (*a*) of the physical organ, e.g., Matt. 5 : 38 ; of restoring sight, e.g., Matt. 20 : 33 ; of God's power of vision, Heb. 4 : 13 ; 1 Pet. 3 : 12 ; of Christ in vision, Rev. 1 : 14 ; 2 : 18 ; 19 : 12 ; of the Holy Spirit in the unity of Godhood with Christ, Rev. 5 : 6 ; (*b*) metaphorically, of ethical qualities, evil, Matt. 6 : 23 ; Mark 7 : 22 (by metonymy, for envy) ; singleness of motive, Matt. 6 : 22 ; Luke 11 : 34 ; as the instrument of evil desire, " the principal avenue of temptation," 1 John 2 : 16 ; of adultery, 2 Pet. 2 : 14 ; (*c*) metaphorically, of mental vision, Matt. 13 : 15 ; John 12 : 40 ; Rom. 11 : 8 ; Gal. 3 : 1, where the metaphor of the " evil eye " is altered to a different sense from that of bewitching (the posting up or placarding of an eye was used as a charm, to prevent mischief) ; by Gospel-preaching Christ had been, so to speak, placarded before their eyes ; the question may be paraphrased, ' What evil teachers have been malignly fascinating you ? ; ' Eph. 1 : 18, of the " eyes of the heart," as a means of knowledge.

2. OMMA (ὅμμα), sight, is used in the plural in Matt. 20 : 34 (No. 1 is used in ver. 33) ; Mark 8 : 23 (No. 1 is used in ver. 25). The word is more poetical in usage than No. 1, and the writers may have changed the word with a view to distinguishing the simple desire of the blind man from the tender act of the Lord Himself.¶

3. TRUMALIA (τρυμαλιά) is used of the eye of a needle, Mark 10 : 25 (from *trumē*, a hole, *truō*, to wear away).¶ Cp. *trēma*, a hole, perforation,

Matt. 19 : 24 (some texts have *trupēma*, a hole, from *trupaō*, to bore a hole) and Luke 18 : 25, as in the most authentic mss. (some texts have *trumalia* here).¶

EYE (with one)

MONOPHTHALMOS (μονόφθαλμος), one-eyed, deprived of one eye (*monos*, only, and No. 1, above), is used in the Lord's warning in Matt. 18 : 9 ; Mark 9 : 47.¶

EYE-SALVE

KOLLOURION (κολλούριον), primarily a diminutive of *kollura*, and denoting a coarse bread roll (as in the Sept. of 1 Kings 12 : after ver. 24, lines 30, 32, 39 ; Eng. Version, 14 : 3 ¶), hence an eye-salve, shaped like a roll, Rev. 3 : 18, of the true knowledge of one's condition and of the claims of Christ. The word is doubtless an allusion to the Phrygian powder used by oculists in the famous medical school at Laodicea (Ramsay, *Cities and Bishoprics of Phrygia*, Vol. I, p. 52).

EYE-SERVICE

OPHTHALMODOULIA (ὀφθαλμοδουλία) denotes service performed only under the master's eye (*ophthalmos*, an eye, *doulos*, a slave), diligently performed when he is looking, but neglected in his absence, Eph. 6 : 6 and Col. 3 : 22.¶

EYE-WITNESS

1. AUTOPTĒS (αὐτόπτης) signifies seeing with one's own eyes (*autos*, self, and a form, *optanō*, to see), Luke 1 : 2.¶

2. EPOPTĒS (ἐπόπτης), primarily an overseer (*epi*, over), then, a spectator, an eye-witness of anything, is used in 2 Pet. 1 : 16 of those who were present at the Transfiguration of Christ. Among the Greeks the word was used of those who had attained to the third grade, the highest, of the Eleusinian mysteries, a religious cult at Eleusis, with its worship, rites, festival and pilgrimages ; this brotherhood was open to all Greeks.¶ In the Sept., Esth. 5 : 1, where it is used of God as the Overseer and Preserver of all things.¶ Cp. *epopteuō*, to behold, 1 Pet. 2 : 12 and 3 : 2.¶

F

FABLE

MUTHOS (μῦθος) primarily signifies speech, conversation. The first syllable comes from a root *mu—*, signifying to close, keep secret, be dumb ; whence, *muō*, to close (eyes, mouth) and *mustērion*, a secret, a mystery ; hence, a story, narrative, fable, fiction (Eng., myth). The word is used of Gnostic errors and of Jewish and profane fables and genealogies, in 1 Tim. 1 : 4 ; 4 : 7 ; 2 Tim. 4 : 4 ; Tit. 1 : 14 ; of fiction, in 2 Pet. 1 : 16.¶

Muthos is to be contrasted with *alētheia*, truth, and with *logos*, a story, a narrative purporting to set forth facts, e.g., Matt. 28 : 15, a " saying " (i.e., an account, story, in which actually there is a falsification of facts) ; Luke 5 : 15, R.V., " report."

FACE

1. PROSŌPON (πρόσωπον) denotes the countenance, lit., the part towards the eyes (from *pros*, towards, *ōps*, the eye), and is used (*a*) of the face, Matt. 6 : 16, 17 ; 2 Cor. 3 : 7, 2nd part (A.V., " countenance ") ; in 2 Cor. 10 : 7, in the R.V., " things that are before your face " (A.V., " outward appearance "), the phrase is figurative of superficial judgment ; (*b*) of the look, i.e., the face, which by its various movements affords an index of inward thoughts and feelings, e.g., Luke 9 : 51, 53 ; 1 Pet. 3 : 12 ; (*c*) the presence of a person, the face being the noblest part, e.g., Acts 3 : 13, R.V., " before the face of," A.V., " in the presence of ;" 5 : 41, " presence ;" 2 Cor. 2 : 10, " person ;" 1 Thess. 2 : 17 (first part), " presence ;" 2 Thess. 1 : 9, R.V., " face," A.V., " presence ;" Rev. 12 : 14, " face ; " (*d*) the person himself, e.g., Gal. 1 : 22 ; 1 Thess. 2 : 17 (second part) ; (*e*) the appearance one presents by his wealth or poverty, his position or state, Matt. 22 : 16 ; Mark 12 : 14 ; Gal. 2 : 6 ; Jude 16 ; (*f*) the outward appearance of inanimate things, Matt. 16 : 3 ; Luke 12 : 56 ; 21 : 35 ; Acts 17 : 26.

To spit in a person's face was an expression of the utmost scorn and aversion, e.g., Matt. 26 : 67 (cp. 27 : 30 ; Mark 10 : 34 ; Luke 18 : 32). See APPEARANCE.

2. OPSIS (ὄψις) is primarily the act of seeing ; then, (*a*) the face ; of the body of Lazarus, John 11 : 44 ; of the countenance of Christ in a vision, Rev. 1 : 16 ; (*b*) the outward appearance of a person or thing, John 7 : 24. See APPEARANCE.¶

Note : The phrase " face to face " translates two phrases in Greek : (1) *kata prosōpon* (*kata,* over against, and No. 1), Acts 25 : 16 ; (2) *stoma pros stoma,* lit., ' mouth to mouth ' (*stoma,* a mouth), 2 John 12 ; 3 John 14. See MOUTH. (3) For *antophthalmeō,* Acts 27 : 15, R.V. has ' to face.'

FACTION, FACTIOUS

ERITHIA (or —*eia*) (ἐριθία) denotes ambition, self-seeking, rivalry, self-will being an underlying idea in the word ; hence it denotes party-making.　It is derived, not from *eris,* strife, but from *erithos,* a hireling ; hence the meaning of seeking to win followers, " factions," so rendered in the R.V. of 2 Cor. 12 : 20, A.V., " strifes ; " not improbably the meaning here is rivalries, or base ambitions (all the other words in the list express abstract ideas rather than factions) ; Gal. 5 : 20 (ditto) ; Phil. 1 : 17 (R.V. ; A.V., ver. 16, " contention ") ; 2 : 3 (A.V., " strife ") ; Jas. 3 : 14, 16 (ditto) ; in Rom. 2 : 8 it is translated as an adjective, " factious " (A.V., " contentious ").　The order strife, jealousy, wrath, faction, is the same in 2 Cor. 12 : 20 and Gal. 5 : 20.　Faction is the fruit of jealousy.¶ Cp. the synonymous adjective *hairetikos,* Tit. 3 : 10, causing division (marg., " factious "), not necessarily " heretical," in the sense of holding false doctrine.¶

FADE (away)
A. Verb.

MARAINŌ (μαραίνω) was used (*a*) to signify to quench a fire, and in the Passive Voice, of the dying out of a fire ; hence (*b*) in various relations, in the Active Voice, to quench, waste, wear out ; in the Passive, to waste away, Jas. 1 : 11, of the fading away of a rich man, as illustrated by the flower of the field.¶　In the Sept., Job 15 : 30 ; 24 : 24.¶

B. Adjectives (negative).

1. AMARANTOS (ἀμάραντος), unfading (*a,* negative, and A., above), whence the " amaranth," an unfading flower, a symbol of perpetuity (see *Paradise Lost,* iii. 353), is used in 1 Pet. 1 : 4 of the believer's inheritance, " that fadeth not away."　It is found in various writings in the language of the *Koinē,* e.g., on a gladiator's tomb ; and as a proper name (Moulton and Milligan, Vocab.).¶

2. AMARANTINOS (ἀμαράντινος) primarily signifies composed of amaranth (see No. 1) ; hence, unfading, 1 Pet. 5 : 4, of the crown of glory promised to faithful elders.¶　Cp. *rhodinos,* made of roses (*rhodon,* a rose).

FAIL
A. Verbs.

1. EKLEIPŌ (ἐκλείπω), to leave out (*ek,* out, *leipō,* to leave), used intransitively, means to leave off, cease, fail ; it is said of the cessation of earthly life, Luke 16 : 9 ; of faith, 22 : 32 ; of the light of the sun, 23 : 45 (in the best mss.) ; of the years of Christ, Heb. 1 : 12.¶

2. EPILEIPŌ (ἐπιλείπω), not to suffice for a purpose (*epi*, over), is said of insufficient time, in Heb. 11 : 32.¶

3. PIPTŌ (πίπτω), to fall, is used of the Law of God in its smallest detail, in the sense of losing its authority or ceasing to have force, Luke 16 : 17. In 1 Cor. 13 : 8 it is used of love (some mss. have *ekpiptō*, to fall off). See FALL.

Notes : (1) In 1 Cor. 13 : 8, *katargeō*, to reduce to inactivity (see ABOLISH), in the Passive Voice, to be reduced to this condition, to be done away, is translated " shall fail," A.V. This, however, misses the distinction between what has been previously said of love and what is here said of prophecies (see No. 3) ; the R.V. has " shall be done away ; " so also as regards knowledge (same verse). (2) In Heb. 12 : 15, *hustereō*, to come behind, fall short, miss, is rendered " fail " in the A.V., R.V., " falleth short." (3) In Luke 21 : 26, *apopsuchō*, lit., to breathe out life, hence, to faint, is translated " hearts failing," in the A.V., R.V., " fainting." See FAINT.¶

B. Adjective.

ANEKLEIPTOS (ἀνέκλειπτος), unfailing (*a*, negative, and A, No. 1), is rendered " that faileth not," in Luke 12 : 33.¶ In a Greek document dated A.D. 42, some contractors undertake to provide unfailing heat for a bath during the current year (Moulton and Milligan, Vocab.).¶

FAIN

1. BOULOMAI (βούλομαι), to will deliberately, wish, desire, be minded, implying the deliberate exercise of volition (contrast No. 3), is translated " would fain " in Philm. 13 (in the best mss.). See DISPOSED.

2. EPITHUMEŌ (ἐπιθυμέω), to set one's heart upon, desire, is translated " would fain " in Luke 15 : 16, of the prodigal son. See DESIRE.

3. THELŌ (θέλω), to wish, to design to do anything, expresses the impulse of the will rather than the intention (see No. 1) ; the R.V. translates it " would fain " in Luke 13 : 31, of Herod's desire to kill Christ, A.V., " will (kill) ; " in 1 Thess. 2 : 18, of the desire of the missionaries to return to the church in Thessalonica. See DISPOSED.

Note : In Acts 26 : 28, in Agrippa's statement to Paul, the R.V. rendering is " with but little persuasion thou wouldest fain make me a Christian." The lit. rendering is ' with (or in) little (labour or time) thou art persuading me so as to make (me) a Christian.' There is no verb for " wouldest " in the original, but it brings out the sense.

FAINT

1. EKLUŌ (ἐκλύω) denotes (*a*) to loose, release (*ek*, out, *luō*, to loose) ; (*b*) to unloose, as a bow-string, to relax, and so, to enfeeble, and is used in the Passive Voice with the significance to be faint, grow weary, (1) of the body, Matt. 15 : 32 ; (some mss. have it in 9 : 36) ; Mark 8 : 3 ;

(2) of the soul, Gal. 6 : 9 (last clause), in discharging responsibilities in obedience to the Lord ; in Heb. 12 : 3, of becoming weary in the strife against sin ; in ver. 5, under the chastening hand of God.¶ It expresses the opposite of *anazōnnumi*, to gird up, 1 Pet. 1 : 13.¶

2. ENKAKEŌ or EKKAKEŌ (ἐνκακέω), to lack courage, lose heart, be fainthearted (*en*, in, *kakos*, base), is said of prayer, Luke 18 : 1 ; of Gospel ministry, 2 Cor. 4 : 1, 16 ; of the effect of tribulation, Eph. 3 : 13 ; as to well doing, 2 Thess. 3 : 13, " be not weary " (A.V. marg., " faint not "). Some mss. have this word in Gal. 6 : 9 (No. 1).¶

3. KAMNŌ (κάμνω) primarily signified to work ; then, as the effect of continued labour, to be weary ; it is used in Heb. 12 : 3, of becoming weary (see also No. 1), R.V., " wax not weary ; " in Jas. 5 : 15, of sickness ; some mss. have it in Rev. 2 : 3, A.V., " hast (not) fainted," R.V., " grown weary." See SICK, WEARY.¶

Note : For *apopsuchō*, Luke 21 : 26, R.V., see FAIL, *Note* (3).¶

FAINTHEARTED

OLIGOPSUCHOS (ὀλιγόψυχος), lit., small-souled (*oligos*, small, *psuchē*, the soul), denotes despondent ; then, " fainthearted," 1 Thess. 5 : 14, R.V., for the incorrect A.V., " feeble-minded." ¶ In the Sept., similarly, in a good sense, Isa. 57 : 15, ' who giveth endurance to the fainthearted,' for R.V. " to revive the spirit of the humble ; " in a bad sense, Prov. 18 : 14, ' who can endure a fainthearted man ? '

FAIR

1. ASTEIOS (ἀστεῖος), lit., of the city (from *astu*, a city ; like Lat. *urbanus*, from *urbs*, a city ; Eng., urbane ; similarly, polite, from *polis*, a town), hence, fair, elegant (used in the papyri writings of clothing), is said of the external form of a child, Acts 7 : 20, of Moses " (exceeding) fair," lit., ' fair to God ; ' Heb. 11 : 23 (R.V., " goodly," A.V., " proper "). See BEAUTIFUL, GOODLY, *Note*.¶

2. EUDIA (εὐδία) denotes fair weather, Matt. 16 : 2, from *eudios*, calm ; from *eu*, good, and *dios*, divine, among the pagan Grceks, akin to the name for the god Zeus, or Jupiter. Some would derive *Dios* and the Latin *deus* (god) and *dies* (day) from a root meaning bright. Cp. the Latin *sub divo*, ' under a bright, open sky.'¶

3. KALOS (καλός), beautiful, fair, in appearance, is used as part of the proper name, Fair Havens, Acts 27 : 8. See BETTER, GOOD.

Notes : (1) In Rom. 16 : 18 *eulogia*, which generally signifies blessing, is used in its more literal sense, " fair speech," i.e., a fine style of utterance, giving the appearance of reasonableness.

(2) In Gal. 6 : 12 the verb *euprosōpeō*, to look well, lit., to be fair of face (*eu*, well, and *prosōpon*, a face), signifies to make a fair or plausible show, used there metaphorically of making a display of religious zeal.¶

FAITH

PISTIS (πίστις), primarily, firm persuasion, a conviction based upon hearing (akin to *peithō*, to persuade), is used in the N.T. always of faith in God or Christ, or things spiritual.

The word is used of (*a*) trust, e.g., Rom. 3 : 25 [see Note (4) below] ; 1 Cor. 2 : 5 ; 15 : 14, 17 ; 2 Cor. 1 : 24 ; Gal. 3 : 23 [see Note (5) below] ; Phil. 1 : 25 ; 2 : 17 ; 1 Thess. 3 : 2 ; 2 Thess. 1 : 3 ; 3 : 2 ; (*b*) trustworthiness, e.g., Matt. 23 : 23 ; Rom. 3 : 3, R.V., " the faithfulness of God ; " Gal. 5 : 22 (R.V., " faithfulness ") ; Tit. 2 : 10, " fidelity ; " (*c*) by metonymy, what is believed, the contents of belief, the faith, Acts 6 : 7 ; 14 : 22 ; Gal. 1 : 23 ; 3 : 25 [contrast 3 : 23, under (*a*)] ; 6 : 10 ; Phil. 1 : 27 ; 1 Thess. 3 : 10 ; Jude 3, 20 (and perhaps 2 Thess. 3 : 2) ; (*d*) a ground for faith, an assurance, Acts 17 : 31 (not as in A.V., marg., " offered faith ") ; (*e*) a pledge of fidelity, plighted faith, 1 Tim. 5 : 12.

The main elements in faith in its relation to the invisible God, as distinct from faith in man, are especially brought out in the use of this noun and the corresponding verb, *pisteuō* ; they are (1) a firm conviction, producing a full acknowledgement of God's revelation or truth, e.g., 2 Thess. 2 : 11, 12 ; (2) a personal surrender to Him, John 1 : 12 ; (3) a conduct inspired by such surrender, 2 Cor. 5 : 7. Prominence is given to one or other of these elements according to the context. All this stands in contrast to belief in its purely natural exercise, which consists of an opinion held in good faith without necessary reference to its proof. The object of Abraham's faith was not God's promise (that was the occasion of its exercise) ; his faith rested on God Himself, Rom. 4 : 17, 20, 21. See Assurance, Belief, Faithfulness, Fidelity.

Notes : (1) In Heb. 10 : 23, *elpis*, hope, is mistranslated " faith " in the A.V. (R.V., " hope "). (2) In Acts 6 : 8 the most authentic mss. have *charis*, grace, R.V., for *pistis*, faith. (3) In Rom. 3 : 3, R.V., *apistia*, is rendered " want of faith," for A.V., " unbelief " (so translated elsewhere). See Unbelief. The verb *apisteō* in that verse is rendered " were without faith," R.V., for A.V., " did not believe." (4) In Rom. 3 : 25, the A.V. wrongly links " faith " with " in His blood," as if faith is reposed in the blood (i.e., the Death) of Christ ; the *en* is instrumental ; faith rests in the living Person ; hence the R.V. rightly puts a comma after " through faith," and renders the next phrase " by His blood," which is to be connected with " a propitiation." Christ became a propitiation through His blood (i.e., His death in expiatory sacrifice for sin). (5) In Gal. 3 : 23, though the article stands before " faith " in the original, faith is here to be taken as under (*a*) above, and as in ver. 22, and not as under (*c*), the faith ; the article is simply that of renewed mention. (6) For the difference between the teaching of Paul and that of James, on faith and works, see Notes on Galatians, by Hogg and Vine, pp. 117–119.

FAITH (of little)

OLIGOPISTOS (ὀλιγόπιστος), lit., little of faith (oligos, little, pistis, faith), is used only by the Lord, and as a tender rebuke, for anxiety, Matt. 6 : 30 and Luke 12 : 28 ; for fear, Matt. 8 : 26 ; 14 : 31 ; 16 : 8.¶

FAITHFUL, FAITHFULLY, FAITHLESS

1. PISTOS (πιστός), a verbal adjective, akin to peithō (see FAITH), is used in two senses, (a) Passive, faithful, to be trusted, reliable, said of God, e.g., 1 Cor. 1 : 9 ; 10 : 13 ; 2 Cor. 1 : 18 (A.V., " true ") ; 2 Tim. 2 : 13 ; Heb. 10 : 23 ; 11 : 11 ; 1 Pet. 4 : 19 ; 1 John 1 : 9 ; of Christ, e.g., 2 Thess. 3 : 3 ; Heb. 2 : 17 ; 3 : 2 ; Rev. 1 : 5 ; 3 : 14 ; 19 : 11 ; of the words of God, e.g., Acts 13 : 34, " sure ; " 1 Tim. 1 : 15 ; 3 : 1 (A.V., " true ") ; 4 : 9 ; 2 Tim. 2 : 11 ; Tit. 1 : 9 ; 3 : 8 ; Rev. 21 : 5 ; 22 : 6 ; of servants of the Lord, Matt. 24 : 45 ; 25 : 21, 23 ; Acts 16 : 15 ; 1 Cor. 4 : 2, 17 ; 7 : 25 ; Eph. 6 : 21 ; Col. 1 : 7 ; 4 : 7, 9 ; 1 Tim. 1 : 12 ; 3 : 11 ; 2 Tim. 2 : 2 ; Heb. 3 : 5 ; 1 Pet. 5 : 12 ; 3 John 5 ; Rev. 2 : 13 ; 17 : 14 ; of believers, Eph. 1 : 1 ; Col. 1 : 2 ; (b) Active, signifying believing, trusting, relying, e.g., Acts 16 : 1 (feminine) ; 2 Cor. 6 : 15 ; Gal. 3 : 9 seems best taken in this respect, as the context lays stress upon Abraham's faith in God, rather than upon his faithfulness. In John 20 : 27 the context requires the Active sense, as the Lord is reproaching Thomas for his want of faith. See No. 2.

With regard to believers, they are spoken of sometimes in the Active sense, sometimes in the Passive, i.e., sometimes as believers, sometimes as faithful. See Lightfoot on Galatians, p. 155.

Note : In 3 John 5 the R.V. has " thou doest a faithful work," for A.V., " thou doest faithfully." The lit. rendering is ' thou doest (poieō) a faithful thing, whatsoever thou workest (ergazō).' That would not do as a translation. To do a faithful work is to do what is worthy of a faithful man. The A.V. gives a meaning but is not exact as a translation. Westcott suggests ' thou makest sure (piston) whatsoever thou workest ' (i.e., it will not lose its reward). The change between poieō, to do, and ergazō, to work, must be maintained. Cp. Matt. 26 : 10 (ergazō and ergon).

2. APISTOS (ἄπιστος) is used with meanings somewhat parallel to No. 1 ; (a) untrustworthy (a, negative, and No. 1), not worthy of confidence or belief, is said of things " incredible," Acts 26 : 8 ; (b) unbelieving, distrustful, used as a noun, " unbeliever," Luke 12 : 46 ; 1 Tim. 5 : 8 (R.V., for A.V., " infidel ") ; in Tit. 1 : 15 and Rev. 21 : 8, " unbelieving ; " " faithless " in Matt. 17 : 17 ; Mark 9 : 19 ; Luke 9 : 41 ; John 20 : 27. The word is most frequent in 1 and 2 Corinthians. See BELIEVE, INCREDIBLE, INFIDEL, UNBELIEVER, UNFAITHFUL. (In the Sept., Prov. 17 : 6 ; 28 : 25 ; Is. 17 : 10.¶).

FAITHFULNESS

Note : This is not found in the A.V. The R.V. corrects the A.V. " faith " to " faithfulness " in Rom. 3 : 3 ; Gal. 5 : 22. See FAITH.

FALL, FALLEN, FALLING, FELL

A. Nouns.

1. PTŌSIS (πτῶσις), a fall (akin to B, No. 1), is used (a) literally, of the overthrow of a building, Matt. 7 : 27 ; (b) metaphorically, Luke 2 : 34, of the spiritual fall of those in Israel who would reject Christ ; the word " again " in the A.V. of the next clause is misleading ; the " rising up " (R.V.) refers to those who would acknowledge and receive Him, a distinct class from those to whom the " fall " applies. The fall would be irretrievable, cp. (a) ; such a lapse as Peter's is not in view.¶

2. PARAPTŌMA (παράπτωμα), primarily a false step, a blunder (*para*, aside, *piptō*, to fall), then a lapse from uprightness, a sin, a moral trespass, misdeed, is translated " fall " in Rom. 11 : 11, 12, of the sin and downfall of Israel in their refusal to acknowledge God's claims and His Christ ; by reason of this the offer of salvation was made to Gentiles ; cp. *ptaiō*, to stumble, in ver. 11. See FAULT, OFFENCE, SIN, TRESPASS.

3. APOSTASIA (ἀποστασία), a defection, revolt, apostasy, is used in the N.T. of religious apostasy ; in Acts 21 : 21, it is translated " to forsake," lit., ' thou teachest apostasy from Moses.' In 2 Thess. 2 : 3 " the falling away " signifies apostasy from the faith. In papyri documents it is used politically of rebels.¶ *Note :* For " mighty fall," Rev. 18 : 21, R.V., see VIOLENCE.

B. Verbs.

1. PIPTŌ (πίπτω), to fall, is used (a) of descent, to fall down from, e.g., Matt. 10 : 29 ; 13 : 4 ; (b) of a lot, Acts 1 : 26 ; (c) of falling under judgment, Jas. 5 : 12 (cp. Rev. 18 : 2, R.V.) ; (d) of persons in the act of prostration, to prostrate oneself, e.g., Matt. 17 : 6 ; John 18 : 6 ; Rev. 1 : 17 ; in homage and worship, e.g., Matt. 2 : 11 ; Mark 5 : 22 ; Rev. 5 : 14 ; 19 : 4 ; (e) of things, falling into ruin, or failing, e.g., Matt. 7 : 25 ; Luke 16 : 17, R.V., " fall," for A.V., " fail ; " Heb. 11 : 30 ; (f) of falling in judgment upon persons, as of the sun's heat, Rev. 7 : 16, R.V., " strike," A.V., " light ; " of a mist and darkness, Acts 13 : 11 (some mss. have *epipiptō*) ; (g) of persons, in falling morally or spiritually, Rom. 14 : 4 ; 1 Cor. 10 : 8, 12 ; Rev. 2 : 5 (some mss. have No. 3 here). See FAIL, LIGHT (upon), STRIKE.

2. APOPIPTO (ἀποπίπτω), to fall from (*apo*, from), is used in Acts 9 : 18, of the scales which fell from the eyes of Saul of Tarsus.¶

3. EKPIPTŌ (ἐκπίπτω), to fall out of (*ek*, out, and No. 1), " is used in the N.T., literally, of flowers that wither in the course of nature, Jas. 1 : 11 ; 1 Pet. 1 : 24 ; of a ship not under control, Acts 27 : 17, 26, 29, 32 ; of shackles loosed from a prisoner's wrist, 12 : 7 ; figuratively, of the Word of God (the expression of His purpose), which cannot fall away from the end to which it is set, Rom. 9 : 6 ; of the believer who is warned

lest he fall away from the course in which he has been confirmed by the Word of God, 2 Pet. 3 : 17."* So of those who seek to be justified by law, Gal. 5 : 4, " ye are fallen away from grace." Some mss. have this verb in Mark 13 : 25, for No. 1 ; so in Rev. 2 : 5. See CAST, EFFECT.¶

4. EMPIPTŌ (ἐμπίπτω), to fall into, or among (en, in, and No. 1), is used (a) literally, Matt. 12 : 11 ; Luke 6 : 39 (some mss. have No. 1 here) ; 10 : 36 ; some mss. have it in 14 : 5 ; (b) metaphorically, into condemnation, 1 Tim. 3 : 6 ; reproach, 3 : 7 ; temptation and snare, 6 : 9 ; the hands of God in judgment, Heb. 10 : 31.¶

5. EPIPIPTŌ (ἐπιπίπτω), to fall upon (epi, upon, and No. 1), is used (a) literally, Mark 3 : 10, " pressed upon ; " Acts 20 : 10, 37 ; (b) metaphorically, of fear, Luke 1 : 12 ; Acts 19 : 17 ; Rev. 11 : 11 (No. 1, in some mss.) ; reproaches, Rom. 15 : 3 ; of the Holy Spirit, Acts 8 : 16 ; 10 : 44 ; 11 : 15.

Note : Some mss. have this verb in John 13 : 25 ; Acts 10 : 10 ; 13 : 11. See PRESS.¶

6. KATAPIPTŌ (καταπίπτω), to fall down (kata, down, and No. 1), is used in Luke 8 : 6 (in the best mss.) ; Acts 26 : 14 ; 28 : 6.¶

7. PARAPIPTŌ (παραπίπτω), akin to A, No. 2, properly, to fall in one's way (para, by), signifies to fall away (from adherence to the realities and facts of the faith), Heb. 6 : 6.¶

8. PERIPIPTŌ (περιπίπτω), to fall around (peri, around), hence signifies to fall in with, or among, to light upon, come across, Luke 10 : 30, " among (robbers) ; " Acts 27 : 41, A.V., " falling into," R.V., " lighting upon," a part of a shore ; Jas. 1 : 2, into temptation (i.e., trials). See LIGHT (to l. upon).¶ In the Sept., Ruth 2 : 3 ; 2 Sam. 1 : 6 ; Prov. 11 : 5.¶

9. PROSPIPTŌ (προσπίπτω), to fall towards anything (pros, towards), to strike against, is said of " wind," Matt. 7 : 25 ; it also signifies to fall down at one's feet, fall prostrate before, Mark 3 : 11 ; 5 : 33 ; 7 : 25 ; Luke 5 : 8 ; 8 : 28, 47 ; Acts 16 : 29.¶

10. HUSTEREŌ (ὑστερέω), to come late, to be last, behind, inferior, is translated " falleth short " in Heb. 12 : 15, R.V., for A.V., " fail," and " fall short " in Rom. 3 : 23, for A.V., " come short," which, in view of the preceding " have," is ambiguous, and might be taken as a past tense. See BEHIND.

11. EPIBALLŌ (ἐπιβάλλω), to cast upon (epi, on, ballō, to throw), also signifies to fall to one's share, Luke 15 : 12, " that falleth." The phrase is frequently found in the papyri documents as a technical formula. See CAST, A, No. 7.

12. ERCHOMAI (ἔρχομαι), to come, is translated " have fallen out," in Phil. 1 : 12, of the issue of circumstances. See COME.

13. GINOMAI (γίνομαι), to become, is translated " falling " (headlong) in Acts 1 : 18. See Note (1) below. See BECOME.

---

* From Notes on Galatians by Hogg and Vine, p. 242.

14. APHISTĒMI (ἀφίστημι), when used intransitively, signifies to stand off (apo, from, histēmi, to stand), to withdraw from ; hence, to fall away, to apostatize, 1 Tim. 4 : 1, R.V., " shall fall away," for A.V., " shall depart ; " Heb. 3 : 12, R.V., " falling away." See DEPART, No. 20.

15. PARABAINŌ (παραβαίνω), to transgress, fall (para, away, across, bainō, to go), is translated " fell away " in Acts 1 : 25, R.V., for A.V., " by transgression fell." See TRANSGRESS.

16. KATABAINŌ (καταβαίνω) denotes to come (or fall) down, Luke 22 : 44 ; in Rev. 16 : 21, " cometh down," R.V. See COME, DESCEND.

Notes : (1) In Rev. 16 : 2, ginomai, to become, is translated " it became," R.V., for A.V., " there fell." (2) In 2 Pet. 1 : 10, ptaiō, to stumble, is translated " stumble," R.V., for A.V., " fall." (3) In Rom. 14 : 13, skandalon, a snare, a means of doing wrong, is rendered " an occasion of falling," R.V., for A.V. " an occasion to fall." (4) Koimaō, in the Middle Voice, signifies to fall asleep, Matt. 27 : 52, R.V., " had fallen asleep," for A.V., " slept." See ASLEEP. (5) In Acts 27 : 34, apollumi, to perish, is translated " shall . . . perish," R.V., for A.V., " shall . . . fall." (6) In Jude 24 the adjective aptaistos, without stumbling, sure footed (a, negative, and ptaiō, to stumble), is translated " from stumbling," R.V., for A.V., " from falling." (7) In Acts 1 : 18 the phrase prēnēs, headlong, with the aorist participle of ginomai, to become, " falling headlong." lit., ' having become headlong,' is used of the suicide of Judas Iscariot. Some would render the word (it is a medical term) " swollen," (as connected with a form of the verb pimprēmi, to burn), indicating the condition of the body of certain suicides. (8) In Acts 20 : 9, A.V., katapherō, to bear down, is translated " being fallen into " (R.V., " borne down "), and then " he sunk down " (R.V., ditto), the first of gradual oppression, the second (the aorist tense) of momentary effect. (9) In Acts 19 : 35 diopetēs, from dios, heaven, piptō, to fall, i.e., fallen from the sky, is rendered " image which fell down from Jupiter " (R.V. marg., " heaven ").

FALSE, FALSEHOOD, FALSELY
A. Adjectives.

1. PSEUDĒS (ψευδής), is used of false witnesses, Acts 6 : 13 ; false apostles, Rev. 2 : 2, R.V., " false," A.V., " liars ; " Rev. 21 : 8, " liars."¶

Note : For compound words with this adjective, see APOSTLE, BRETHREN, CHRIST, PROPHET, WITNESS.

2. PSEUDŌNUMOS (ψευδώνυμος), under a false name (No. 1, and onoma, a name.; Eng., pseudonym), is said of the knowledge professed by the propagandists of various heretical cults, 1 Tim. 6 : 20.¶

B. Noun.

PSEUDOS (ψεῦδος), a falsehood (akin to A, No. 1), is so translated in Eph. 4 : 25, R.V. (A.V., " lying ") ; in 2 Thess. 2 : 9, " lying wonders " is lit. ' wonders of falsehood,' i.e., wonders calculated to deceive ; it is elsewhere rendered "lie," John 8 : 44 ; Rom. 1 : 25 ; 2 Thess. 2 : 11 ; 1 John 2 : 21, 27 ; Rev. 14 : 5, R.V. ; 21 : 27 ; 22 : 15. See GUILE, LIE.¶

C. Verb.

PSEUDŌ (ψεύδω), to deceive by lies, is used in the Middle Voice, translated "to say . . . falsely," in Matt. 5 : 11 ; it is elsewhere rendered to lie, Acts 5 : 3, 4 ; Rom. 9 : 1 ; 2 Cor. 11 : 31 ; Gal. 1 : 20 ; Col. 3 : 9 ; 1 Tim. 2 : 7. See LIE.

FAME
A. Noun.

PHĒMĒ (φήμη) originally denoted a Divine voice, an oracle ; hence, a saying or report (akin to phēmi, to say, from a root meaning to shine, to be clear ; hence, Lat., fama, Eng., fame), is rendered "fame" in Matt. 9 : 26 and Luke 4 : 14.¶

Notes : (1) In Luke 5 : 15, R.V., *logos,* a word, report, account, is translated "report," for A.V., "fame." See REPORT. (2) *Akoē,* a hearing, is translated "report" in the R.V. of Matt. 4 : 24 ; 14 : 1 ; Mark 1 : 28, for A.V., "fame." See EAR, No. 3, HEARING. (3) *Ēchos,* a noise, report, sound, is translated "rumour," in the R.V. of Luke 4 : 37, for A.V., "fame ;" "sound" in Acts 2 : 2 ; Heb. 12 : 19. See RUMOUR, SOUND.¶

B. Verb.

DIAPHĒMIZŌ (διαφημίζω) signifies to spread abroad a matter, Matt. 28 : 15, R.V. ; Mark 1 : 45, R.V. (from *dia,* throughout, and *phēmi,* to say) ; hence, to spread abroad one's fame, Matt. 9 : 31. All the passages under this heading relate to the testimony concerning Christ in the days of His flesh.¶

FAMILY

1. OIKOS (οἶκος) signifies (a) a dwelling, a house (akin to *oikeō,* to dwell) ; (b) a household, family, translated "family" in 1 Tim. 5 : 4, R.V., for A.V., "at home." See HOME, HOUSE, HOUSEHOLD, TEMPLE.

2. PATRIA (πατριά), primarily an ancestry, lineage, signifies in the N.T. a family or tribe (in the Sept. it is used of related people, in a sense wider than No. 1, but narrower than *phulē,* a tribe, e.g., Ex. 12 : 3 ; Numb. 32 : 28) ; it is used of the family of David, Luke 2 : 4, R.V., for A.V., "lineage ;" in the wider sense of nationalities, races, Acts 3 : 25, R.V., "families," for A.V., "kindreds ;" in Eph. 3 : 15, R.V., "every family," for A.V., "the whole family," the reference being to all those who are spiritually related to God the Father, He being the Author of their spiritual relationship to Him as His children, they being united to one another in family fellowship (*patria* is akin to *patēr,* a father) ; Luther's translation, "all who bear the name of children," is advocated by Cremer, p. 474. The phrase, however, is lit., 'every family.'¶ See KINDRED.¶

FAMINE

LIMOS (λιμός) is translated " hunger " in Luke 15 : 17 ; 2 Cor. 11 : 27 ;
elsewhere it signifies a famine, and is so translated in each place in the
R.V. ; the A.V. has the word " dearth " in Acts 7 : 11 and 11 : 28, and
" hunger " in Rev. 6 : 8 ; the R.V. " famine " is preferable there ; see
Matt. 24 : 7 ; Mark 13 : 8 ; Luke 4 : 25 ; 15 : 14 ; 21 : 11 ; Rom. 8 : 35 ;
Rev. 18 : 8. See HUNGER.¶

FAN

PTUON (πτύον) denotes a winnowing shovel or fan, with which
grain is thrown up against the wind, in order to separate the chaff,
Matt. 3 : 12 ; Luke 3 : 17.¶

FAR
A. Adjective.

MAKROS (μακρός) is used (a) of space and time, long, said of prayers
(in some mss., Matt. 23 : 14), Mark 12 : 40 ; Luke 20 : 47 ; (b) of distance,
far, far distant, Luke 15 : 13 ; 19 : 12. See LONG.¶

B. Adverbs.

1. MAKRAN (μακράν), properly a feminine form of the adjective
above, denotes a long way, far, (a) literally, Matt. 8 : 30, R.V., " afar off."
Luke 7 : 6 ; 15 : 20, R.V., " afar off ; " John 21 : 8 ; Acts 17 : 27 ; 22 : 21 ;
(b) metaphorically, " far (from the kingdom of God)," Mark 12 : 34 ; in
spiritual darkness, Acts 2 : 39 ; Eph. 2 : 13, 17. See AFAR.¶

2. MAKROTHEN (μακρόθεν), from far (akin to No. 1), Mark 8 : 3 :
see AFAR.

3. PORRŌ (πόρρω) is used (a) literally, Luke 14 : 32, " a great way
off ; " the comparative degree porrōteron, " further," is used in 24 : 28 ;
(b) metaphorically, of the heart in separation from God, Matt. 15 : 8 ;
Mark 7 : 6. See FURTHER, WAY.¶ Cp. porrōthen, afar off ; see AFAR.

Notes : (1) In Matt. 16 : 22, Peter's word to the Lord " be it far from
Thee " translates the phrase *hileōs soi,* lit., ' (God be) propitious to Thee,'
R.V., marg., " God have mercy on Thee." Some would translate it
" God avert this from Thee ! " Others render it " God forbid ! " Luther's
translation is ' spare Thyself.' Lightfoot suggests ' Nay, verily ! ' or
' Away with the thought ! ' It was the vehement and impulsive utterance
of Peter's horrified state of mind. *Hileōs* signifies propitious, " merciful,"
Heb. 8 : 12. See MERCY, C.¶ (2) In Luke 22 : 51, " thus far " translates
the phrase *heōs toutou,* lit., ' unto this.' (3) In Gal. 6 : 14 the R.V. " far
be it " translates the phrase *mē genoito,* lit., ' let it not be,' elsewhere
translated idiomatically " God forbid," e.g., Luke 20 : 16. See FORBID.
(4) In Heb. 7 : 15 the A.V. " far more " translates *perissoteron,* R.V.,
" more abundantly ; " see ABUNDANT. (5) In the following the verb
apodēmeō, to go abroad, is rendered, in the A.V., to go into a far country,
R.V.. to go into another country, Matt. 21 : 33 ; 25 : 14 ; Mark 12 : 1 ;

in Matt. 25 : 15, R.V., " he went on his journey " (A.V., " took etc."). In Luke 15 : 13 the A.V. and R.V. have " took (his) journey into a far country ;" in Luke 20 : 9, R.V., " another country," for A.V., " a far country."¶ The adjective *apodēmos* in Mark 13 : 34 is rendered in the A.V., " taking a far journey," R.V., " sojourning in another country." See JOURNEY.¶ (6) In 2 Cor. 4 : 17 the phrase *kath' huperbolēn* is translated " more and more," R.V., for A.V., " a far more." (7) In the following, *heōs*, used as a preposition, is translated " as far as " in the R.V., for different words in the A.V. ; Acts 17 : 14, in the best mss., instead of *hōs*, which the A.V. renders " as it were ; " 17 : 15, " unto ; " 23 : 23, " to." Both Versions have " as far as " in 11 : 19, 22 ; in Luke 24 : 50, the R.V. has " until they were over against," for A.V., " as far as to." (8) In Rev. 14 : 20, the preposition *apo*, from, is translated " as far as " in the R.V., for A.V., " by the space of."

FARE, FAREWELL

1. EUPHRAINŌ (εὐφραίνω), in the Active Voice, signifies to cheer, gladden, 2 Cor. 2 : 2 ; in the Passive, to rejoice, make merry ; translated " faring sumptuously " in Luke 16 : 19, especially of food (R.V., marg., " living in mirth and splendour"). See GLAD, MERRY, REJOICE.

2. RHŌNNUMI (ῥώννυμι), to strengthen, to be strong, is used in the Imperative Mood as a formula at the end of letters, signifying " Farewell," Acts 15 : 29 ; some mss. have it in 23 ; 30 (the R.V. omits it, as do most Versions).¶

3. ECHŌ (ἔχω), to have, is used idiomatically in Acts 15 : 36, R.V., " (how) they fare," A.V., " how they do."

4. CHAIRŌ (χαίρω), to joy, rejoice, be glad, is used in the Imperative Mood in salutations, (a) on meeting, " Hail," e.g., Matt. 26 : 49 ; or with *legō*, to say, to give a greeting, 2 John 11 ; in letters, " greeting," e.g., Acts 15 : 23 ; (b) at parting, the underlying thought being joy, 2 Cor. 13 : 11 (R.V., marg., " rejoice ") ; (c) on other occasions, see the R.V. marg. in Phil. 3 : 1 ; 4 : 4. See GLAD, GREETING, No. 2, HAIL, JOY, JOYFULLY.

Note : As " farewell " is inadequate to express *chairō*, which always conveys the thought of joy or cheer. (b) properly comes under (c).

5. APOTASSŌ (ἀποτάσσω) primarily denotes to set apart ; then, in the Middle Voice, (a) to take leave of, bid farewell to, Mark 6 : 46, " had taken leave of ; " cp. Acts 18 : 18, 21 ; 2 Cor. 2 : 13 (in these three verses, the verb may signify to give final instructions to) ; Luke 9 : 61, " to bid farewell ; " (b) to forsake, Luke 14 : 33. In the papyri, besides saying goodbye, the stronger meaning is found of getting rid of a person (Moulton and Milligan). See FORSAKE, LEAVE (take), RENOUNCE, SEND (away).¶

Note : For *aspazomai*, to bid farewell, see LEAVE (c), No. 2.

FARM

AGROS (ἀγρός) denotes (a) a field (cp. Eng., agriculture), e.g., Matt. 6 : 28 ; (b) the country, e.g., Mark 15 : 21, or, in the plural, country places, farms, Mark 5 : 14 ; 6 : 36, 56 ; Luke 8 : 34 ; 9 : 12 ; (c) a piece of ground, e.g., Mark 10 : 29 ; Acts 4 : 37 ; a farm, Matt. 22 : 5. See COUNTRY, FIELD, GROUND, LAND.

Note : For the synonymous word *chōra,* a country, land, see COUNTRY. Moulton and Milligan point out that *agros* is frequent in the Sept., and in the Synoptic Gospels, but that Luke uses *chōra* especially, and that possibly *agros* was a favourite word with translators from Hebrew and Aramaic.

For FARTHER SIDE, Mark 10 : 1, see BEYOND, No. 2

FARTHING

1. ASSARION (ἀσσάριον), a diminutive of the Latin *as,* was one-tenth of a drachma, or one-sixteenth of a Roman *denarius,* i.e., about three farthings, Matt. 10 : 29 ; Luke 12 : 6.¶

2. KODRANTĒS (κοδράντης) was the Latin *quadrans,* the fourth part of an *as* (see No. 1), about two thirds of a farthing, Matt. 5 : 26 ; Mark 12 : 42.¶

FASHION
A. Nouns.

1. EIDOS (εἶδος), that which is seen, an appearance, is translated " fashion " in Luke 9 : 29, of the Lord's countenance at the Transfiguration. See APPEARANCE, and Note under IMAGE, No. 1.

2. PROSŌPON (πρόσωπον), the face, countenance, is translated " fashion " in Jas. 1 : 11, of the flower of grass. See COUNTENANCE. Cp. ver. 24, " what manner of man," which translates *hopoios,* of what sort.

3. SCHĒMA (σχῆμα), a figure, fashion (akin to *echō,* to have), is translated " fashion " in 1 Cor. 7 : 31, of the world, signifying that which comprises the manner of life, actions, etc. of humanity in general ; in Phil. 2 : 8 it is used of the Lord in His being found " in fashion " as a man, and signifies what He was in the eyes of men, " the entire outwardly perceptible mode and shape of His existence, just as the preceding words *morphē,* form, and *homoiōma,* likeness, describe what He was in Himself as Man " (Gifford on the Incarnation, p. 44). " Men saw in Christ a human form, bearing, language, action, mode of life . . . in general the state and relations of a human being, so that in the entire mode of His appearance He made Himself known and was recognized as a man " (Meyer).

4. TUPOS (τύπος), a type, figure, example, is translated " fashion " in the A.V. of Acts 7 : 44, R.V., " figure," said of the Tabernacle. See ENSAMPLE.

B. Adverb.

HOUTŌS (οὕτως), thus, so, in this way, is rendered " on this fashion " in Mark 2 : 12. See EVEN, No. 5, LIKEWISE, MANNER, SO, THUS,WHAT.

C. Verbs.

1. METASCHĒMATIZŌ (μετασχηματίζω), to change in fashion or appearance (meta, after, here implying change, schēma, see A, No. 3), is rendered " shall fashion anew " in Phil. 3 : 21, R.V. ; A.V., " shall change," of the bodies of believers as changed or raised at the Lord's Return ; in 2 Cor. 11 : 13, 14, 15, the R.V. uses the verb to fashion oneself, for A.V., to transform, of Satan and his human ministers, false apostles ; in 1 Cor. 4 : 6 it is used by way of a rhetorical device, with the significance of transferring by a figure. See CHANGE, TRANSFORM.¶

2. SUSCHĒMATIZŌ (συσχηματίζω), to give the same figure or appearance as, to conform to (sun, with, schēma, cp. No. 1), used in the Passive Voice, signifies to fashion oneself, to be fashioned, Rom. 12 : 2, R.V., " be not fashioned according to," for A.V., " be not conformed to ; " 1 Pet. 1 : 14, " (not) fashioning yourselves." See CONFORMED.¶

Note : In Rom. 12 : 2 being outwardly conformed to the things of this age is contrasted with being transformed (or transfigured) inwardly by the renewal of the thoughts through the Holy Spirit's power. A similar distinction holds good in Phil. 3 : 21 ; the Lord will " fashion anew," or change outwardly, the body of our humiliation, and conform it in its nature (summorphos) to the body of His glory.

D. Adjective.

SUMMORPHOS (σύμμορφος), having like form with (sun, with, morphē, form), is used in Rom. 8 : 29 and Phil. 3 : 21 (A.V., " fashioned," R.V., " conformed "). See CONFORM.¶

FAST, FASTING
A. Nouns.

1. NĒSTEIA (νηστεία), a fasting, fast (from nē, a negative prefix, and esthiō, to eat), is used (a) of voluntary abstinence from food, Luke 2 : 37 ; Acts 14 : 23 (some mss. have it in Matt. 17 : 21 and Mark 9 : 29) ; fasting had become a common practice among Jews, and was continued among Christians ; in Acts 27 : 9, " the Fast " refers to the Day of Atonement, Lev. 16 : 29 ; that time of the year would be one of dangerous sailing ; (b) of involuntary abstinence (perhaps voluntary is included), consequent upon trying circumstances, 2 Cor. 6 : 5 ; 11 : 27.¶

2. NĒSTIS (νῆστις), not eating (see No. 1), fasting, is used of lack of food, Matt. 15 : 32 ; Mark 8 : 3.¶

Note : Asitia, Acts 27 : 21, means " without food " (not through lack of supplies), i.e., abstinence from food. See ABSTINENCE, and cp. C, below.

B. Verb.

NĒSTEUŌ (νηστεύω), to fast, to abstain from eating (akin to A, Nos.

1 and 2), is used of voluntary fasting, Matt. 4 : 2 ; 6 : 16, 17, 18 ; 9 : 14, 15 ; Mark 2 : 18, 19, 20 ; Luke 5 : 33, 34, 35 ; 18 : 12 ; Acts 13 : 2, 3. Some of these passages show that teachers to whom scholars or disciples were attached, gave them special instructions as to fasting. Christ taught the need of purity and simplicity of motive.

The answers of Christ to the questions of the disciples of John and of the Pharisees reveal His whole purpose and method. No doubt He and His followers observed such a Fast as that on the Day of Atonement, but He imposed no frequent fasts in addition. What He taught was suitable to the change of character and purpose which He designed for His disciples. His claim to be the Bridegroom, Matt. 9 : 15, and the reference there to the absence of fasting, virtually involved a claim to be the Messiah (cp. Zech. 8 : 19).¶ Some mss. have the verb in Acts 10 : 30.

C. Adjective.

ASITOS (ἄσιτος), without food (a, negative, sitos, corn, food), is used in Acts 27 : 33, " fasting." Cp. asitia, Note under A, No. 2.¶

FAST (to make)

ASPHALIZŌ (ἀσφαλίζω), to make secure, safe, firm (akin to asphalēs, safe), (a, negative, and sphallō, to trip up), is translated " make . . . fast," in Acts 16 : 24, of prisoners' feet in the stocks. In Matt. 27 : 64, 65, 66, it is rendered ' to make sure.' See SURE.¶

Note : For HOLD (fast) and STAND (fast), see HOLD and STAND, NO. 7

FASTEN

1. ATENIZŌ (ἀτενίζω), from atenēs, strained, intent, and teinō, to stretch, strain (from a root ten—, seen in Eng., tension, tense etc.), signifies to look fixedly, gaze, fasten one's eyes upon, and is found twelve times in the writings of Luke (ten in the Acts), out of its fourteen occurrences. It always has a strongly intensive meaning, and is translated to fasten the eyes upon in the A.V. and R.V. in Luke 4 : 20 ; Acts 3 : 4 ; 11 : 6 ; so in the R.V., where the A.V. has different renderings, in Acts 6 : 15 (for A.V., " looking stedfastly ") ; 10 : 4 (" looked ") ; 13 : 9 (" set his eyes ") ; 14 : 9 (" stedfastly beholding "). In Acts 7 : 55, both have " looked up stedfastly." In the following the R.V. also varies the translation, Luke 22 : 56 ; Acts 1 : 10 ; 3 : 12 ; 23 : 1 ; 2 Cor. 3 : 7, 13. See BEHOLD, LOOK.¶

2. KATHAPTŌ (καθάπτω), to fasten on, lay hold of, attack, is used of the serpent which fastened on Paul's hand, Acts 28 : 3.¶

FATHER
A. Noun.

PATĒR (πατήρ), from a root signifying a nourisher, protector, up-holder (Lat., pater, Eng., father, are akin), is used (a) of the nearest ancestor, e.g., Matt. 2 : 22 ; (b) of a more remote ancestor, the progenitor of the people, a forefather, e.g., Matt. 3 : 9 ; 23 : 30 ; 1 Cor. 10 : 1 ;

the patriarchs, 2 Pet. 3 : 4 ; (c) one advanced in the knowledge of Christ, I John 2 : 13 ; (d) metaphorically, of the originator of a family or company of persons animated by the same spirit as himself, as of Abraham, Rom. 4 : 11, 12, 16, 17, 18, or of Satan, John 8 : 38, 41, 44 ; (e) of one who, as a preacher of the Gospel and a teacher, stands in a father's place, caring for his spiritual children, I Cor. 4 : 15 (not the same as a mere title of honour, which the Lord prohibited, Matt. 23 : 9) ; (f) of the members of the Sanhedrin, as of those who exercised religious authority over others, Acts 7 : 2 ; 22 : 1 ; (g) of God in relation to those who have been born anew (John I : 12, 13), and so are believers, Eph. 2 : 18 ; 4 : 6 (cp. 2 Cor. 6 : 18), and imitators of their Father, Matt. 5 : 45, 48 ; 6 : 1, 4, 6, 8, 9, etc. Christ never associated Himself with them by using the personal pronoun " our ; " He always used the singular, " My Father," His relationship being unoriginated and essential, whereas theirs is by grace and regeneration, e.g., Matt. 11 : 27 ; 25 : 34 ; John 20 : 17 ; Rev. 2 : 27 ; 3 : 5, 21 ; so the Apostles spoke of God as the Father of the Lord Jesus Christ, e.g., Rom. 15 : 6 ; 2 Cor. 1 : 3 ; 11 : 31 ; Eph. 1 : 3 ; Heb. 1 : 5 ; I Pet. 1 : 3 ; Rev. 1 : 6 ; (h) of God, as the Father of lights, i.e., the Source or Giver of whatsoever provides illumination, physical and spiritual, Jas. 1 : 17 ; of mercies, 2 Cor. 1 : 3 ; of glory, Eph. 1 : 17 ; (i) of God, as Creator, Heb. 12 : 9 (cp. Zech. 12 : 1).

Note : Whereas the everlasting power and Divinity of God are manifest in creation, His Fatherhood in spiritual relationship through faith is the subject of N.T. revelation, and waited for the presence on earth of the Son, Matt. 11 : 27 ; John 17 : 25. The spiritual relationship is not universal, John 8 : 42, 44 (cp. John 1 : 12 and Gal. 3 : 26).

B. Adjectives.

1. PATRŌOS (πατρῷος) signifies of one's fathers, or received from one's fathers (akin to A), Acts 22 : 3 ; 24 : 14 ; 28 : 17.¶ In the Sept., Prov. 27 : 10.¶

2. PATRIKOS (πατρικός), from one's fathers, or ancestors, is said of that which is handed down from one's forefathers, Gal. 1 : 14.¶

3. APATŌR (ἀπάτωρ), without father (a, negative, and *patēr*), signifies, in Heb. 7 : 3, with no recorded genealogy.¶

4. PATROPARADOTOS (πατροπαράδοτος), handed down from one's fathers (*patēr*, and *paradidomi*, to hand down), is used in I Pet. 1 : 18.¶

FATHER-IN-LAW

PENTHEROS (πενθερός), a wife's father (from a root signifying a bond, union), is found in John 18 : 13.¶

FATHERLESS

ORPHANOS (ὀρφανός), properly, an orphan, is rendered " fatherless " in Jas. 1 : 27 ; " desolate " in John 14 : 18, for A.V., " comfortless." See COMFORTLESS.¶

FATHOM

ORGUIA (ὀργυιά), akin to *oregō*, to stretch, is the length of the outstretched arms, about six feet, Acts 27 : 28 (twice).¶

FATLING, FATTED

1. SITISTOS (σιτιστός), fattened, lit., ' fed with grain ' (from *siteuō*, to feed, to fatten), is used as a neuter plural noun, " fatlings," in Matt. 22 : 4.¶ Cp. *asitos*, under FASTING.

2. SITEUTOS (σιτευτός), fed (with grain), denotes " fatted," Luke 15 : 23, 27, 30.¶

FATNESS

PIOTĒS (πιότης), from *piōn*, fat, from a root, *pi—*, signifying swelling, is used metaphorically in Rom. 11 : 17. The Gentile believer had become a sharer in the spiritual life and blessing bestowed by Divine covenant upon Abraham and his descendants as set forth under the figure of " the root of (not ' and ') the fatness of the olive tree."¶

FAULT, FAULTLESS
A. Noun.

AITION (αἴτιον), properly the neuter of *aitios*, causative of, responsible for, is used as a noun, a crime, a legal ground for punishment, translated " fault " in Luke 23 : 4, 14 ; in ver. 22, " cause." See AUTHOR, CAUSE.

Notes : (1) For *aitia*, rendered " fault " in John 18 : 38 : 19 : 4, 6, A.V. (like *aition*, denoting a ground for punishment), see ACCUSATION, CAUSE, CHARGE. (2) For *hēttēma*, a loss, translated " fault " in 1 Cor. 6 : 7, A.V., see DEFECT (R.V.). (3) For *paraptōma*, a false step, a trespass, translated " fault " in Gal. 6 : 1, A.V., and " faults " in Jas. 5 : 16, A.V., see SIN, A, No. 2, *Note* (1), TRESPASS.

B. Adjective.

AMEMPTOS (ἄμεμπτος), without blame, is rendered " faultless," in Heb. 8 : 7. See BLAMELESS.

Note : For *amōmos*, without blemish, rendered " faultless," i.e., without any shortcoming, in Jude 24, and " without fault " in Rev. 14 : 5, A.V., see BLEMISH.

C. Verbs.

1. MEMPHOMAI (μέμφομαι), to blame, is translated " to find fault " in Rom. 9 : 19 and Heb. 8 : 8. Some mss. have the verb in Mark 7 : 2. See BLAME.

2. ELENCHŌ (ἐλέγχω), to convict, reprove, rebuke, is translated " shew (him) his fault " in Matt. 18 : 15. See CONVICT.

Note : In 1 Pet. 2 : 20, A.V., the verb *hamartanō*, to sin (strictly, to miss the mark) is rendered " for your faults." The R.V. corrects to " when ye sin (and are buffeted for it)."

FAVOUR, FAVOURED
A. Noun.

CHARIS (χάρις) denotes (a) objectively, grace in a person, graciousness, (b) subjectively, (1) grace on the part of a giver, favour, kindness, (2) a sense of favour received, thanks. It is rendered " favour " in Luke 1 : 30 ; 2 : 52 ; Acts 2 : 47 ; 7 : 10, 46 ; 24 : 27 and 25 : 9, R.V. (for A.V., " pleasure ") ; 25 : 3 ; see more fully under GRACE.

B. Verb.

CHARITOŌ (χαριτόω), akin to A., to endow with *charis*, primarily signified to make graceful or gracious, and came to denote, in Hellenistic Greek, to cause to find favour, Luke 1 : 28, " highly favoured " (marg., " endued with grace ") ; in Eph. 1 : 6, it is translated " made . . . accepted," A.V., " freely bestowed," R.V. (lit., ' graced ') ; it does not here mean to endue with grace. Grace implies more than favour ; grace is a free gift, favour may be deserved or gained.¶

FEAR, FEARFUL, FEARFULNESS
A. Nouns.

1. PHOBOS (φόβος) first had the meaning of flight, that which is caused by being scared ; then, that which may cause flight, (a) fear, dread, terror, always with this significance in the four Gospels ; also e.g., in Acts 2 : 43 ; ·19 : 17 ; 1 Cor. 2 : 3 ; 1 Tim. 5 : 20 (lit., ' may have fear ') ; Heb. 2 : 15 ; 1 John 4 : 18 ; Rev. 11 : 11 ; 18 : 10, 15 ; by metonymy, that which causes fear, Rom. 13 : 3 ; 1 Pet. 3 : 14, R.V., " (their) fear," A.V. " (their) terror," an adaptation of the Sept. of Isa. 8 : 12, " fear not their fear ; " hence some take it to mean, as there, ' what they fear,' but in view of Matt. 10 : 28, e.g., it seems best to understand it as that which is caused by the intimidation of adversaries ; (b) reverential fear, (1) of God, as a controlling motive of the life, in matters spiritual and moral, not a mere fear of His power and righteous retribution, but a wholesome dread of displeasing Him, a fear which banishes the terror that shrinks from His presence, Rom. 8 : 15, and which influences the disposition and attitude of one whose circumstances are guided by trust in God, through the indwelling Spirit of God, Acts 9 : 31 ; Rom. 3 : 18 ; 2 Cor. 7 : 1 ; Eph. 5 : 21 (R.V., " the fear of Christ ") ; Phil. 2 : 12 ; 1 Pet. 1 : 17 (a comprehensive phrase : the reverential fear of God will inspire a constant carefulness in dealing with others in His fear) ; 3 : 2, 15 ; the association of " fear and trembling," as, e.g., in Phil. 2 : 12, has in the Sept. a much sterner import, e.g., Gen. 9 : 2 ; Ex. 15 : 16 ; Deut. 2 : 25 ; 11 : 25 ; Ps. 55 : 5 ; Is. 19 : 16 ; (2) of superiors, e.g., Rom. 13 : 7 ; 1 Pet. 2 : 18. See TERROR.

2. DEILIA (δειλία), fearfulness (from *deos*, fright), is rightly rendered " fearfulness " in 2 Tim. 1 : 7, R.V. (for A.V., " fear "). That spirit is not given us of God. The word denotes cowardice and timidity and is

never used in a good sense, as No. 1 is.¶   Cp. *deilos*, B, No. 2, below, and *deiliaō*, to be fearful (A.V., " afraid "), John 14 : 27.¶

3. EULABEIA (εὐλάβεια) signifies, firstly, caution ; then, reverence, godly fear, Heb. 5 : 7 ; 12 : 28, in best mss., " reverence " ; in general, apprehension, but especially holy fear, "that mingled fear and love which, combined, constitute the piety of man toward God ; the O.T. places its emphasis on the fear, the N.T. . . . on the love, though there was love in the fear of God's saints then, as there must be fear in their love now" (Trench, Syn. § xlviii).¶ In the Sept., Josh. 22 : 24 ; Prov. 28 : 14.¶

Note : In Luke 21 : 11, *phobētron* (akin to No. 1) denotes a terror, R.V., " terrors," for A.V., " fearful sights," i.e., ' objects or instruments of terror.'¶

B. Adjectives.

1. PHOBEROS (φοβερός), fearful (akin to A, No. 1), is used only in the Active sense in the N.T., i.e., causing fear, terrible, Heb. 10 : 27, 31 ; 12 : 21, R.V., " fearful," for A.V., " terrible."¶

2. DEILOS (δειλός), cowardly (see A, No. 2), timid, is used in Matt. 8 : 26 ; Mark 4 : 40 ; Rev. 21 : 8 (here " the fearful " are first in the list of the transgressors).¶

3. EKPHOBOS (ἔκφοβος) signifies frightened outright (*ek*, out, intensive, and A, No. 1), Heb. 12 : 21 (with *eimi*, I am), " I exceedingly fear " (see No. 4) ; Mark 9 : 6, " sore afraid."¶

4. ENTROMOS (ἔντρομος), trembling with fear (*en*, in, intensive, and *tremō*, to tremble, quake ; Eng., tremor, etc.), is used with *ginomai*, to become, in Acts 7 : 32, " trembled ; " 16 : 29, R.V., " trembling for fear ; " with *eimi*, to be, in Heb. 12 : 21, " quake " (some mss. have *ektromos* here). See QUAKE, TREMBLE.¶ The distinction between No. 3 and No. 4, as in Heb. 12 : 21, would seem to be that *ekphobos* stresses the intensity of the fear, *entromos* the inward effect, ' I inwardly tremble (or quake).'

C. Adverb.

APHOBŌS (ἀφόβως) denotes " without fear " (*a*, negative, and A, No. 1), and is said of serving the Lord, Luke 1 : 74 ; of being among the Lord's people as His servant, 1 Cor. 16 : 10 ; of ministering the Word of God, Phil. 1 : 14 ; of the evil of false spiritual shepherds, Jude 12.¶ In the Sept., Prov. 1 : 33.¶

D. Verbs.

1. PHOBEŌ (φοβέω), in earlier Greek, to put to flight (see A, No. 1), in the N.T. is always in the Passive Voice, with the meanings either (*a*) to fear, be afraid, its most frequent use, e.g., Acts 23 : 10, according to the best mss. (see No. 2) ; or (*b*) to show reverential fear [see A, No. 1, (*b*)], (1) of men, Mark 6 : 20 ; Eph. 5 : 33, R.V., " fear," for A.V., " reverence ; " (2) of God, e.g., Acts 10 : 2, 22 ; 13 : 16, 26 ; Col. 3 : 22 (R.V., " the Lord ") ; 1 Pet. 2 : 17 ; Rev. 14 : 7 ; 15 : 4 ; 19 : 5 ; (*a*) and

(b) are combined in Luke 12 : 4, 5, where Christ warns His followers not to be afraid of men, but to fear God. See MARVEL, B, No. 1, *Note.*

2. EULABEOMAI (εὐλαβέομαι), to be cautious, to beware (see A, No. 3), signifies to act with the reverence produced by holy fear, Heb. 11 : 7, " moved with godly fear."

Notes : (1) In Acts 23 : 10 some mss. have this verb with the meaning (a) under No. 1.

(2) In Luke 3 : 14, *diaseiō,* to shake violently, to intimidate, to extort by violence, blackmail, is rendered " put no man in fear " in A.V. marg. See VIOLENCE.

FEAST
A. Nouns.

1. HEORTĒ (ἑορτή), a feast or festival, is used (a) especially of those of the Jews, and particularly of the Passover ; the word is found mostly in John's Gospel (seventeen times) ; apart from the Gospels it is used in this way only in Acts 18 : 21 ; (b) in a more general way, in Col. 2 : 16, A.V., " holy day," R.V., " a feast day."

2. DEIPNON (δεῖπνον) denotes (a) the chief meal of the day, dinner or supper, taken at or towards evening ; in the plural " feasts," Matt. 23 : 6 ; Mark 6 : 21 ; 12 : 39 ; Luke 20 : 46 ; otherwise translated " supper," Luke 14 : 12, 16, 17, 24 ; John 12 : 2 ; 13 : 2, 4 ; 21 : 20 ; 1 Cor. 11 : 21 (of a social meal) ; (b) the Lord's Supper, 1 Cor. 11 : 20 ; (c) the supper or feast which will celebrate the marriage of Christ with His spiritual Bride, at the inauguration of His Kingdom, Rev. 19 : 9 ; (d) figuratively, of that to which the birds of prey will be summoned after the overthrow of the enemies of the Lord at the termination of the war of Armageddon, 19 : 17 (cp. Ezek. 39 : 4, 17–20). See SUPPER.¶

3. DOCHĒ (δοχή), a reception feast, a banquet (from *dechomai,* to receive), Luke 5 : 29 ; 14 : 13 (not the same as No. 2 ; see ver. 12).¶

4. GAMOS (γάμος), a wedding, especially a wedding feast (akin to *gameō,* to marry) ; it is used in the plural in the following passages (the R.V. rightly has " marriage feast " for the A.V., " marriage," or " wedding "), Matt. 22 : 2, 3, 4, 9 (in verses 11, 12, it is used in the singular, in connection with the wedding garment) ; 25 : 10 ; Luke 12 : 36 ; 14 : 8 ; in the following it signifies a wedding itself, John 2 : 1, 2 ; Heb. 13 : 4 ; and figuratively in Rev. 19 : 7, of the marriage of the Lamb ; in ver. 9 it is used in connection with the supper, the wedding supper (or what in English is termed breakfast), not the wedding itself, as in ver. 7.

5. AGAPĒ (ἀγάπη), love, is used in the plural in Jude 12, signifying " love feasts," R.V. (A.V., " feasts of charity ") ; in the corresponding passage, 2 Pet. 2 : 13, the most authentic mss. have the word *apatē,* in the plural, " deceivings."

Notes : (1) In 1 Cor. 10 : 27 the verb *kaleō,* to call, in the sense of inviting to one's house, is translated " biddeth you (to a feast) ; " in the most authentic texts there is no separate phrase representing "to a feast," as in some mss., *eis deipnon* (No. 2). (2) In Mark 14 : 2 and John 2 : 23 the A.V. translates *heortē* (see No. 1) by "feast day" (R.V., "feast"). (3) For the Feast of the Dedication, John 10 : 22, see DEDICATION.

B. Verbs.

1. HEORTAZŌ (ἑορτάζω), to keep festival (akin to A, No. 1) is translated "let us keep the feast," in 1 Cor. 5 : 8. This is not the Lord's Supper, nor the Passover, but has reference to the continuous life of the believer as a festival or holy-day (see A.V., margin), in freedom from "the leaven of malice and wickedness, but with the unleavened bread of sincerity and truth."¶

2. SUNEUŌCHEŌ (συνευωχέω), to entertain sumptuously with, is used in the Passive Voice, denoting to feast sumptuously with (*sun*, together, and *euōchia*, good cheer), to revel with, translated "feast with" in 2 Pet. 2 : 13 and Jude 12.¶

FEEBLE

ASTHENĒS (ἀσθενής), without strength (*a*, negative, and *sthenos*, strength), is translated feeble in 1 Cor. 12 : 22, of members of the body. See IMPOTENT, SICK, STRENGTH, B, *Note* (5), WEAK.

Notes : (1) In Heb. 12 : 12 *paraluō*, to weaken, enfeeble, in the Passive Voice, to be enfeebled, as by a paralytic stroke, is translated "feeble" in the A.V. (R.V., "palsied"). (2) For "feeble-minded" in 1 Thess. 5 : 14, A.V., see FAINTHEARTED.

FEED, FED

1. BOSKŌ (βόσκω), to feed, is primarily used of a herdsman (from *boō*, to nourish, the special function being to provide food ; the root is *bo*, found in *botēr*, a herdsman or herd, and *botanē*, fodder, pasture) ; its uses are (*a*) literal, Matt. 8 : 30 ; in ver. 33, the R.V. corrects the A.V., "they that kept," to "they that fed," as in Mark. 5 : 14 (A.V. and R.V.) and Luke 8 : 34 ; in Mark 5 : 11 and Luke 8 : 32, "feeding ;" Luke 15 : 15 ; (*b*) metaphorical, of spiritual ministry, John 21 : 15, 17 (see note on No. 2). See KEEP.¶

2. POIMAINŌ (ποιμαίνω), to act as a shepherd (from *poimēn*, a shepherd), is used (*a*) literally, Luke 17 : 7, R.V., "keeping sheep," for A.V., "feeding cattle ;" 1 Cor. 9 : 7 ; (*b*) metaphorically, to tend, to shepherd ; said of Christ, Matt. 2 : 6, R.V., "shall be Shepherd of" (for A.V., "shall rule") ; of those who act as spiritual shepherds under Him, John 21 : 16, R.V., "tend" (for A.V. "feed") ; so 1 Pet. 5 : 2 ; Acts 20 : 28, "to feed" ('to tend' would have been a consistent rendering ; a shepherd does not only feed his flock) ; of base shepherds, Jude 12. See RULE.

Note : In John 21 : 15, 16, 17, the Lord, addressing Peter, first uses No. 1, *boskō* (ver. 15), then No. 2, *poimainō* (ver. 16), and then returns to *boskō* (ver. 17). These are not simply interchangeable (nor are other variations in His remarks) ; a study of the above notes will show this. Nor, again, is there a progression of ideas. The lesson to be learnt, as Trench points out (Syn. § xxv), is that, in the spiritual care of God's children, the feeding of the flock from the Word of God is the constant and regular necessity ; it is to have the foremost place. The tending (which includes this) consists of other acts, of discipline, authority, restoration, material assistance of individuals, but they are incidental in comparison with the feeding.

3. TREPHŌ (τρέφω) signifies (a) to make to grow, bring up, rear, Luke 4 : 16, " brought up ; " (b) to nourish, feed, Matt. 6 : 26 ; 25 : 37 ; Luke 12 : 24 ; Acts 12 : 20 ; Rev. 12 : 6, 14 ; of a mother, to give suck, Luke 23 : 29 (some mss. here have *thēlazō*, to suckle) ; to fatten, as of fattening animals, Jas. 5 : 5, " ye have nourished (your hearts)." See Bring, A, No. 33.¶

4. CHORTAZŌ (χορτάζω), to feed, to fatten, is used (a) primarily of animals, Rev. 19 : 21 ; (b) of persons, to fill or satisfy with food. It is usually translated by the verb " to fill," but is once rendered " to be fed," in Luke 16 : 21, of Lazarus, in his desire for the crumbs (he could be well supplied with them) that fell from the rich man's table, a fact which throws light upon the utter waste that went on at the table of the latter. The crumbs that fell would provide no small meal. See Fill, Satisfy.

5. PSŌMIZŌ (ψωμίζω) primarily denotes to feed with morsels, as nurses do children ; then, to dole out or supply with food, Rom. 12 : 20 ; 1 Cor. 13 : 3.¶ Cp. *psōmion*, a fragment, morsel, John 13 : 26, 27, 30 (" sop ").¶

6. POTIZŌ (ποτίζω), to give to drink, is translated " I fed (you with milk) " in 1 Cor. 3 : 2. See Drink, Water.

FEEL, FEELING, FELT

1. GINŌSKŌ (γινώσκω), to know, perceive, is translated " she felt (in her body)," of the woman with the issue of blood, Mark 5 : 29, i.e., she became aware of the fact. See Know.

2. PHRONEŌ (φρονέω), to think, to be minded, is translated " I felt " in the R.V. of 1 Cor. 13 : 11 (for A.V., " I understood "). See Careful.

3. PSĒLAPHAŌ (ψηλαφάω), to feel or grope about (from *psaō*, to touch), expressing the motion of the hands over a surface, so as to feel it, is used (a) metaphorically, of seeking after God, Acts 17 : 27 ; (b) literally, of physical handling or touching, Luke 24 : 39 with 1 John 1 : 1 ; Heb. 12 : 18. See Handle, Touch.¶

4. SUMPATHEŌ (συμπαθέω), to have a fellow-feeling for or with, is rendered " touched with the feeling of " in Heb. 4 : 15 ; " have compassion " in 10 : 34. See Compassion.¶

5. APALGEŌ (ἀπαλγέω) signifies to cease to feel pain for (*apo*, from,

algeō, to feel pain ; cp. Eng., neuralgia) ; hence, to be callous, " past feeling," insensible to honour and shame, Eph. 4 : 19.¶

Note : In Acts 28 : 5 *paschō*, to suffer, is rendered " felt (no harm)," R.V., " took," lit., ' suffered no ill (effect).'

For FEET see FOOT

FEIGN, FEIGNED
A. Verb.

HUPOKRINOMAI (ὑποκρίνομαι) primarily denotes to answer ; then, to answer on the stage, play a part, and so, metaphorically, to feign, pretend, Luke 20 : 20.¶ Cp. *hupokritēs*, a hypocrite, and *hupokrisis*, hypocrisy.

B. Adjective.

PLASTOS (πλαστός) primarily denotes formed, moulded (from *plassō*, to mould ; Eng., plastic) ; then, metaphorically, made up, fabricated, feigned, 2 Pet. 2 : 3.¶ Cp. *plasma*, that which is moulded, Rom. 9 : 20.¶

For FELL see FALL

FELLOW

1. ANĒR (ἀνήρ) denotes a man, in relation to his sex or age ; in Acts 17 : 5 (plural) it is rendered " fellows," as more appropriate to the accompanying description of them. See HUSBAND, MAN, SIR.

2. HETAIROS (ἑταῖρος), a companion, comrade, is translated " fellows " in Matt. 11 : 16 [where, however, the most authentic mss. have *heterois*, " (the) others "]. The word is used only by Matthew and is translated " friend " in 20 : 13 ; 22 : 12 ; 26 : 50. See FRIEND.¶

3. METOCHOS (μέτοχος), properly an adjective, signifying sharing in, partaking of, is translated " partners " in Luke 5 : 7 ; " partakers " in Heb. 3 : 1, 14 ; 6 : 4 ; 12 : 8 ; " fellows " in Heb. 1 : 9, of those who share in a heavenly calling, or have held, or will hold, a regal position in relation to the earthly, Messianic Kingdom. (Cp. *summetochos*, " fellow-partakers," in Eph. 3 : 6, R.V.). See PARTAKER, PARTNER.

Notes : (1) In Acts 24 : 5 *loimos*, a plague, a pest, is rendered " a pestilent fellow." This is a sample of the strongest use of the epithet " fellow." (2) *Toioutos*, an adjective, " such a one," is often used as a noun, e.g., Acts 22 : 22, where it is translated " such a fellow." (3) *Houtos*, this, is translated " this fellow " in the A.V. of Luke 23 : 2 (R.V., " this man "). So in John 9 : 29. Both Versions have " this man," e.g., in Mark 2 : 7 ; John 6 : 52, in the same contemptuous sense. (4) For the word in combination with various nouns see CITIZEN, DISCIPLE, ELDER, HEIR, HELPER, LABOURER, MEMBER, PARTNER, PRISONER, SERVANT, SOLDIER, WORK, WORKER.

FELLOWSHIP
A. Nouns.

1. KOINŌNIA (κοινωνία), (a) communion, fellowship, sharing in common (from koinos, common), is translated "communion" in 1 Cor. 10 : 16 ; Philm. 6, R.V., "fellowship," for A.V., "communication ; " it is most frequently translated "fellowship ; " (b) that which is the outcome of fellowship, a contribution, e.g., Rom. 15 : 26 ; 2 Cor. 8 : 4. See COMMUNION, CONTRIBUTION, etc.

Note : In Eph. 3 : 9, some mss. have koinōnia, instead of oikonomia, dispensation, R.V.

2. METOCHĒ (μετοχή), partnership (akin to No. 3, under FELLOW), is translated "fellowship" in 2 Cor. 6 : 14.¶ In the Sept., Ps. 122 : 3, "Jerusalem is built as a city whose fellowship is complete."¶ The word seems to have a more restricted sense than koinōnia. Cp. the verb form in Heb. 2 : 14.

3. KOINŌNOS (κοινωνός) denotes a partaker or partner (akin to No. 1) ; in 1 Cor. 10 : 20 it is used with ginomai, to become, " that ye should have communion with," R.V. (A.V., " fellowship with "). See COMPANION, PARTAKER, PARTNER.

B. Verbs.

1. KOINŌNEŌ (κοινωνέω), to have fellowship, is so translated in Phil. 4 : 15, R.V., for A.V., "did communicate." See COMMUNICATE.

2. SUNKOINŌNEŌ (συγκοινωνέω), to have fellowship with or in (sun, with, and No. 1), is used in Eph. 5 : 11 ; Phil. 4 : 14, R.V., " ye had fellowship," for A.V., " ye did communicate ; " Rev. 18 : 4, R.V., " have (no) fellowship with," for A.V., " be (not) partakers of." See COMMUNICATE, PARTAKER.¶

For FELT see FEEL

FEMALE

THĒLUS (θῆλυς), an adjective (from thēlē, a breast), is used in the form thēlu (grammatically neuter) as a noun, " female," in Matt. 19 : 4 ; Mark 10 : 6 ; Gal. 3 : 28 ; in the feminine form thēleia, in Rom. 1 : 26, " women ; " ver. 27 " woman." See WOMAN.¶

FERVENT, FERVENTLY
A. Adjective.

EKTENĒS (ἐκτενής) denotes strained, stretched (ek, out, teinō, to stretch) ; hence, metaphorically, " fervent," 1 Pet. 4 : 8. Some mss. have it in Acts 12 : 5, for the adverb (see B).¶ Cp. ekteneia (with en), intently, strenuously, in Acts 26 : 7, A.V., " instantly," R.V., " earnestly." Cp. EARNEST.

B. Adverb.

EKTENŌS (ἐκτενῶς), fervently (akin to A.), is said of love, in 1 Pet.

1 : 22 ; of prayer, in some mss., Acts 12 : 5 (see under A.) ; for the comparative degree in Luke 22 : 44, see EARNESTLY.¶

C. Verb.

ZEŌ (ζέω), to be hot, to boil (Eng. " zeal " is akin), is metaphorically used of fervency of spirit, Acts 18 : 25 ; Rom. 12 : 11.¶

Notes : (1) In Col. 4 : 12, the verb *agōnizomai*, to strive, is translated " labouring fervently," A.V. (R.V., " striving "). (2) In 2 Cor. 7 : 7, the noun *zēlos*, zeal (akin to C.), is translated " fervent mind," A.V. (R.V., " zeal "). (3) In Jas. 5 : 17, " he prayed fervently " (A.V., " earnestly ") translates the noun *proseuchē*, followed by the corresponding verb, lit., ' he prayed with prayer.' In ver. 16 *deēsis*, supplication, is so translated in the R.V., for the A.V., " effectual fervent prayer." There is nothing in the original corresponding to the word " effectual." The phrase, including the verb *energeomai*, to work in, is, lit., ' the inworking supplication,' suggesting a supplication consistent with inward conformity to the mind of God. (4) For "fervent heat " see HEAT, B.

FETCH

METAPEMPŌ (μεταπέμπω), to send after or for (*meta*, after, *pempō*, to send), in the Middle Voice, is translated " fetch " in the R.V. of Acts 10 : 5 and 11 : 13. See CALL.

Notes : (1) In Acts 16 : 37, the R.V. gives to *exagō*, to bring out, the adequate meaning " let them . . . bring us out," for the A.V., " let them fetch us out." " Fetch " is not sufficiently dignified for the just demand made. (2) For Acts 28 : 13, A.V., " fetched a compass," see CIRCUIT.

FETTER

PEDĒ (πέδη), a fetter (akin to *peza*, the instep, and *pous*, a foot ; cp. Eng. prefix *ped*—), occurs in Mark 5 : 4 and Luke 8 : 29. Cp. FOOT,¶

FEVER (to be sick of)
A. Noun.

PURETOS (πυρετός), feverish heat (from *pur*, fire), hence, a fever, occurs in Matt. 8 : 15 ; Mark 1 : 31 ; John 4 : 52 ; Acts 28 : 8 ; in Luke 4 : 38, with *megas*, great, a high fever ; ver. 39. Luke, as a physician, uses the medical distinction by which the ancients classified fevers into great and little.¶ In the Sept., Deut. 28 : 22.¶

B. Verb.

PURESSŌ (πυρέσσω) signifies to be ill of a fever (akin to A.), Matt. 8 : 14 ; Mark 1 : 30.¶

FEW
A. Adjectives.

1. OLIGOS (ὀλίγος), used of number, quantity, and size, denotes few, little, small, slight, e.g., Matt. 7 : 14 ; 9 : 37 ; 15 : 34 ; 20 : 16 ; neuter

plural, "a few things," Matt. 25 : 21, 23 ; Rev. 2 : 14 (20 in some mss.) ; in Eph. 3 : 3, the phrase *en oligō*, in brief, is translated "in a few words."

2. BRACHUS (βραχύς) denotes (*a*) short, in regard to time, e.g., Heb. 2 : 7 ; or distance, Acts 27 : 28 ; (*b*) few, in regard to quantity, Heb. 13 : 22, in the phrase *dia bracheōn*, lit., ' by means of few,' i.e., "in few words." See LITTLE.

Note : In Luke 10 : 42, in the Lord's words to Martha, many ancient authorities provide the rendering, ' but there is need of few things (neuter plural) or one.'

B. Adverb.

SUNTOMŌS (συντόμως), concisely, briefly, cut short (from *suntemnō*, to cut in pieces, *sun*, used intensively, *temnō*, to cut), occurs in the speech of Tertullus, Acts 24 : 4.¶

FICKLENESS

ELAPHRIA (ἐλαφρία) denotes lightness, levity, "fickleness," 2 Cor. 1 : 17, R.V. (for A.V., "lightness").¶ The corresponding adjective is *elaphros*, light, Matt. 11 : 30 ; 2 Cor. 4 : 17.¶

FIDELITY

PISTIS (πίστις), faith, faithfulness, is translated "fidelity" in Tit. 2 : 10. See FAITH (*b*).

FIELD, CORNFIELD

1. AGROS (ἀγρός), a cultivated field, or fields in the aggregate, e.g., Matt. 6 : 28 ; Mark 11 : 8 (some mss. here have *dendrōn*, trees) ; Luke 15 : 15. See FARM.

2. CHŌRA (χώρα), (*a*) a space, place, then, (*b*) land, country, region, is translated "fields" in John 4 : 35 ; Jas. 5 : 4. See COUNTRY.

3. CHŌRION (χωρίον), a diminutive of No. 2, denotes (*a*) a place, region, (*b*) a piece of land, property, rendered "field" in Acts 1 : 18, 19. See LAND, PARCEL, PLACE, POSSESSION.

4. SPORIMOS (σπόριμος) signifies fit for sowing (from *speirō*, to sow), and denotes a cornfield, Matt. 12 : 1 ; Mark 2 : 23 ; Luke 6 : 1.¶ In the Sept., Gen. 1 : 29 ; Lev. 11 : 37.¶

FIERCE, FIERCENESS
A. Adjectives.

1. ANĒMEROS (ἀνήμερος) signifies ' not tame,' savage (from *a*, negative, and *hēmeros*, gentle), 2 Tim. 3 : 3. Epictetus describes those who forget God as their Creator, as resembling lions, ' wild, savage and fierce (*anēmeroi*) ' (Moulton and Milligan, Greek Test. Vocab.).¶

2. CHALEPOS (χαλεπός), hard, (*a*) hard to do or deal with, difficult, fierce, is said of the Gadarene demoniacs, Matt. 8 : 28 ; (*b*) hard to bear,

painful, grievous, said of the last times, 2 Tim. 3 : 1, R.V., " grievous," for A.V., " perilous." See GRIEVOUS.¶

Notes : (1) In Jas. 3 : 4, *sklēros*, hard, rough, violent, is said of winds, R.V., " rough," for A.V., " fierce." (2) In Luke 23 : 5, the verb *epischuō*, to make or grow stronger (from *epi*, over, intensive, and *ischus*, strength), is used metaphorically, " they were the more urgent," R.V., for A.V., " the more fierce."¶

B. Nouns.

1. THUMOS (θυμός), hot anger, wrath, is rendered " fierceness " in Rev. 16 : 19 ; 19 : 15, of the wrath of God. See ANGER (A, Notes), INDIGNATION, WRATH.

2. ZĒLOS (ζῆλος), zeal, jealousy, is rendered " fierceness " in Heb. 10 : 27, R.V. (of fire).

FIERY

PUROŌ (πυρόω), to set on fire, burn up (from *pur*, fire), always used in the Passive Voice in the N.T., is translated " fiery " in Eph. 6 : 16, metaphorically of the darts of the evil one ; ' fire-tipped ' would perhaps bring out the verbal force of the word. The most ancient mss. have the article repeated, lit., ' the darts of the evil one, the fiery (darts),' marking them as particularly destructive. Some mss. omit the repeated article. In ancient times, darts were often covered with burning material. See BURN, FIRE, TRY, *Note* (1).

Notes : (1) For Heb. 10 : 27, R.V., see FIRE (cp. FIERCE, B, No. 2). (2) For *purōsis*, a fiery trial, 1 Pet. 4 : 12, (lit., a burning, as in Rev. 18 : 9, 18), a refining, or trial by fire, see TRIAL.

FIFTEEN, FIFTEENTH

DEKAPENTE (δεκαπέντε), lit., ten-five, occurs in John 11 : 18 ; Acts 27 : 28 ; Gal. 1 : 18.¶

Notes : (1) In Acts 7 : 14, " threescore and fifteen " translates a different numeral, lit., ' seventy-five.' This refers to all Joseph's kindred whom he sent for. There is no discrepancy between this and Gen. 46 : 26. The Sept. translations give the number as 75 in Gen. 46 : 27 and in Ex. 1 : 5, and this Stephen follows, being a Grecian Jew. (2) The corresponding ordinal numeral *pentekaidekatos*, fifteenth (lit., five and tenth) is found in Luke 3 : 1, where Luke dates the reign of Tiberias from the period of his joint rule with Augustus.

FIFTH

PEMPTOS (πέμπτος), akin to *pente*, five, is found only in the Apocalypse, 6 : 9 ; 9 : 1 ; 16 : 10 ; 21 : 20.¶

FIFTY

PENTĒKONTA (πεντήκοντα) is found in Luke 7 : 41 ; 16 : 6 ; John 8 : 57 ; 21 : 11 ; Acts 13 : 20 ; in Mark 6 : 40 with *kata* (in the most authentic mss.), according to, " by fifties ; " in Luke 9 : 14, with *ana*, up, used distributively, " fifty each," R.V. (Luke adds *hōsei*, " about ").¶

FIG

1. SUKON (σῦκον) denotes the ripe fruit of a *sukē*, a fig-tree (see below ; cp. No. 2), Matt. 7 : 16 ; Mark 11 : 13 ; Luke 6 : 44 ; Jas. 3 : 12.¶

2. OLUNTHOS (ὄλυνθος) denotes an unripe fig, which grows in winter and usually falls off in the Spring, Rev. 6 : 13.¶ In the Sept., S. of Sol., 2 : 13.¶

FIG-TREE

SUKĒ, or SUKEA (συκῆ), a fig tree, is found in Matt. 21 : 19, 20, 21 ; 24 : 32 ; Mark 11 : 13, 20, 21 ; 13 : 28 ; Luke 13 : 6, 7 ; 21 : 29 ; John 1 : 48, 50 ; Jas. 3 : 12 ; Rev. 6 : 13 (see *sukon*, above).¶

Note : A fig tree with leaves must have young fruits already, or it will be barren for the season. The first figs ripen in late May or early June. The tree in Mark 11 : 13 should have had fruit, unripe indeed, but existing. In some lands fig-trees bear the early fruit under the leaves and the later fruit above the leaves. In that case the leaves were a sign that there should have been fruit, unseen from a distance, underneath the leaves. The condemnation of this fig-tree lay in the absence of any sign of fruit.

FIGHT
A. Nouns.

1. AGŌN (ἀγών), akin to *agō*, to lead, primarily a gathering, then, a place of assembly, and hence, a contest, conflict, is translated " fight " in 1 Tim. 6 : 12 ; 2 Tim. 4 : 7. See CONFLICT.

2. ATHLĒSIS (ἄθλησις) is translated " fight " in Heb. 10 : 32, A.V. See CONFLICT.¶

Note : In Heb. 11 : 34, *polemos*, war, is translated " fight," A.V. (R.V., " war ") ; it is misrendered " battle " in the A.V. of 1 Cor. 14 : 8 ; Rev. 9 : 7, 9 ; 16 : 14 ; 20 : 8.

B. Verbs.

1. AGŌNIZOMAI (ἀγωνίζομαι), from A, No. 1, denotes (*a*) to contend in the public games, 1 Cor. 9 : 25 (" striveth in the games," R.V.) ; (*b*) to fight, engage in conflict, John 18 : 36 ; (*c*) metaphorically, to contend perseveringly against opposition and temptation, 1 Tim. 6 : 12 ; 2 Tim. 4 : 7 (cp. A, No. 1 ; in regard to the meaning there, the evidence of *Koinē* inscriptions is against the idea of games-contests) ; to strive as in a contest for a prize, straining every nerve to attain to the object, Luke 13 : 24 ; to put forth every effort, involving toil, Col. 1 : 29 ; 1 Tim. 4 : 10 (some mss. have *oneidizomai* here, to suffer reproach) ; to wrestle earnestly in prayer, Col. 4 : 12 (cp. *sunagōnizomai*, Rom. 15 : 30). See LABOUR, STRIVE.¶

FIG 425 FIG

2. PUKTEUŌ (πυκτεύω), to box (from *puktēs*, a pugilist), one of the events in the Olympic games, is translated "fight" in 1 Cor. 9 : 26.¶

3. MACHOMAI (μάχομαι), to fight, is so rendered in Jas. 4 : 2 (cp. "fightings," ver. 1, see below), and translated "strive" in 2 Tim. 2 : 24 ; "strove" in John 6 : 52 ; Acts 7 : 26. See STRIVE.¶

4. THĒRIOMACHEŌ (θηριομαχέω) signifies to fight with wild beasts (*thērion*, a beast, and No. 3), 1 Cor. 15 : 32. Some think that the Apostle was condemned to fight with wild beasts ; if so, he would scarcely have omitted it from 2 Cor. 11 : 23–end. Moreover, he would have lost his status as a Roman citizen. Probably he uses the word figuratively of contending with ferocious men. Ignatius so uses it in his Ep. to the Romans.¶

Notes : (1) In Rev. 2 : 16 and 12 : 7, A.V., *polemeō*, to war, is translated "to fight," R.V., "will make war," "*going forth* to war," and "warred." (2) In Acts 23 : 9 some mss. have the verb *theomacheō*, to fight against God. Cp. the corresponding adjective, below, under FIGHTING.

FIGHTING

A. Noun.

MACHĒ (μάχη), a fight, strife (akin to B, No. 3, under FIGHT), is always used in the plural in the N.T., and translated "fightings" in 2 Cor. 7 : 5 ; Jas. 4 : 1 ; and Tit. 3 : 9, R.V. (for A.V., "strivings") ; "strifes" in 2 Tim. 2 : 23. See STRIFE.¶

B. Adjective.

THEOMACHOS (θεομάχος), fighting against God (*theos*, God, and A, occurs in Acts 5 : 39 (A.V., "to fight"), lit., 'God-fighters.'¶

FIGURE

1. TUPOS (τύπος), a type, figure, pattern, is translated "figures" (i.e., representations of gods) in Acts 7 : 43 ; in the R.V. of ver. 44 (for A.V., "fashion") and in Rom. 5 : 14, of Adam as a "figure" of Christ. See ENSAMPLE.

2. ANTITUPOS (ἀντίτυπος), an adjective, used as a noun, denotes, lit., a striking back ; metaphorically, resisting, adverse ; then, in a Passive sense, struck back ; in the N.T. metaphorically, 'corresponding to,' (a) a copy of an archetype (*anti*, corresponding to, and No. 1), i.e., the event or person or circumstance corresponding to the type, Heb. 9 : 24, R.V., "like in pattern" (A.V., "the figure of"), of the Tabernacle, which, with its structure and appurtenances, was a pattern of that "holy place," "Heaven itself," "the true," into which Christ entered, "to appear before the face of God for us." The earthly Tabernacle anticipatively represented what is now made good in Christ ; it was a "figure" or "parable" (9 : 9), "for the time now present," R.V., i.e., pointing to the present time, not "then present," A.V. (see below) ;

(b) a corresponding type, 1 Pet. 3 : 21, said of baptism ; the circumstances of the flood, the ark and its occupants, formed a type, and baptism forms ' a corresponding type ' (not an antitype), each setting forth the spiritual realities of the death, burial, and resurrection of believers in their identification with Christ. It is not a case of type and antitype, but of two types, that in Genesis, the type, and baptism, the corresponding type.¶

3. PARABOLE (παραβολή), a casting or placing side by side (para, beside, ballō, to throw) with a view to comparison or resemblance, a parable, is translated " figure " in the A.V. of Heb. 9 : 9 (R.V., " a parable for the time now present ") and 11 : 19, where the return of Isaac was (parabolically, in the lit. sense of the term) figurative of resurrection (R.V., " parable "). See No. 2 (a). See PARABLE

Notes : (1) The synonymous noun *hupotupōsis*, an example, pattern, 1 Tim. 1 : 16 ; 2 Tim. 1 : 13, denotes simply a delineation or outline.¶ (2) For *metaschēmatizō*, rendered " I have in a figure transferred " in 1 Cor. 4 : 6, where the fact stated is designed to change its application, i.e., from Paul and Apollos to circumstances in Corinth, see FASHION.

FILL, FILL UP
A. Verbs.

1. PLĒROŌ (πληρόω) denotes (I) to make full, to fill to the full ; in the Passive Voice, to be filled, made full ; it is used (1) of things : a net, Matt. 13 : 48 ; a building, John 12 : 3 ; Acts 2 : 2 ; a city, Acts 5 : 28 ; needs, Phil. 4 : 19, A.V., " supply," R.V., " fulfil ; " metaphorically, of valleys, Luke 3 : 5 ; figuratively, of a measure of iniquity, Matt. 23 : 32 ; (2) of persons : (a) of the members of the Church, the Body of Christ, as filled by Him, Eph. 1 : 23 (' all things in all the members ') ; 4 : 10 ; in 3 : 19, of their being filled ' into ' (eis), R.V., " unto," A.V., " with " (all the fulness of God) ; of their being " made full " in Him, Col. 2 : 10 (R.V., for A.V., " complete ") ; (b) of Christ Himself : with wisdom, in the days of His flesh, Luke 2 : 40 ; with joy, in His return to the Father, Acts 2 : 28 ; (c) of believers : with the Spirit, Eph. 5 : 18 ; with joy, Acts 13 : 52 ; 2 Tim. 1 : 4 ; with joy and peace, Rom. 15 : 13 ; [from these are to be distinguished those passages which speak of joy as being fulfilled or completed, which come under FULFIL, John 3 : 29 ; 15 : 11 (R.V.) ; 16 : 24 (R.V.) ; Phil. 2 : 2 ; 1 John 1 : 4 (R.V.) ; 2 John 12 (R.V.)] ; with knowledge, Rom. 15 : 14 ; with comfort, 2 Cor. 7 : 4 ; with the fruits of righteousness, Phil. 1 : 11 (Gk. ' fruit ') ; with the knowledge of God's will, Col. 1 : 9 ; with abundance through material supplies by fellow-believers, Phil. 4 : 18 ; (d) of the hearts of believers as the seat of emotion and volition, John 16 : 6 (sorrow) ; Acts 5 : 3 (deceitfulness) ; (e) of the unregenerate who refuse recognition of God, Rom. 1 : 29 ; (II) to accomplish, complete, fulfil. See ACCOMPLISH, FULFIL.

2. ANAPLĒROŌ (ἀναπληρόω), to fill up adequately, completely (ana,

up, and No. 1), is twice translated by the verbs to fill, to fill up, in 1 Cor. 14 : 16, R.V. (for A.V., " occupieth "), of a believer as a member of an assembly, who fills the position or condition (not one who fills it by assuming it) of being unable to understand the language of him who had the gift of tongues ; in 1 Thess. 2 : 16, " to fill up their sins," of the Jews who persisted in their course of antagonism and unbelief. See FULFIL.

3. ANTANAPLĒROŌ (ἀνταναπληρόω), to fill up in turn (or on one's part ; *anti*, corresponding to, and No. 2), is used in Col. 1 : 24, of the Apostle's responsive devotion to Christ in filling up, or undertaking on his part a full share of, the sufferings which follow after the sufferings of Christ, and are experienced by the members of His Body, the Church. " The point of the Apostle's boast is that Christ, the sinless Master, should have left something for Paul, the unworthy servant, to suffer " (Lightfoot, on Col., p. 165).¶

4. SUMPLĒROŌ (συμπληρόω), to fill completely (*sun*, with, and No. 1), is used in the Passive Voice (*a*) of a boat filling with water, and, by metonymy, of the occupants themselves, Luke 8 : 23 (R.V., " were filling ") ; (*b*) of fulfilling, with regard to time, " when the days were well-nigh come," R.V., for A.V., " when the time was come " (R.V., marg., " were being fulfilled "), Luke 9 : 51 ; Acts 2 : 1, see R.V., marg. See COME.¶ In the Sept. Jer. 25 : 12.¶

5. PIMPLĒMI (πίμπλημι) and PLĒTHŌ (πλήθω), lengthened forms of *pleō*, to fill (*plēthō* supplies certain tenses of *pimplēmi*), is used (1) of things ; boats, with fish, Luke 5 : 7 ; a sponge, with vinegar, Matt. 27 : 48 (some mss. have this verb in John 19 : 29) ; a city, with confusion, Acts 19 : 29 ; a wedding, with guests, Matt. 22 : 10 ; (2) of persons (only in Luke's writings) : (*a*) with the Holy Spirit, Luke 1 : 15, 41, 67 ; Acts 2 : 4 ; 4 : 8, 31 ; 9 : 17 ; 13 : 9 ; (*b*) with emotions : wrath, Luke 4 : 28 ; fear, 5 : 26 ; madness, 6 : 11 ; wonder, amazement, Acts 3 : 10 ; jealousy, 5 : 17, R.V., for A.V., " indignation," and 13 : 45 (A.V., " envy "). For its other significance, to complete, see ACCOMPLISH.

6. EMPIPLĒMI (ἐμπίπλημι) or EMPLĒTHŌ (as in No. 5), to fill full, to satisfy, is used (*a*) of filling the hungry, Luke 1 : 53 ; John 6 : 12 ; of the abundance of the rich, Luke 6 : 25 ; (*b*) metaphorically, of a company of friends, Rom. 15 : 24, R.V., " satisfied," for A.V., " filled."¶

7. EMPIPLAŌ (ἐμπιπλάω), an alternative form of No. 6, is found in Acts 14 : 17, " filling (your hearts)," of God's provision for mankind.¶

8. CHORTAZŌ (χορτάζω), to fill or satisfy with food, e.g., Matt. 15 : 33 ; Phil. 4 : 12, is used metaphorically in Matt. 5 : 6 ; Luke 6 : 21. See FEED.

9. GEMIZŌ (γεμίζω), to fill or load full, is used of a boat, Mark 4 : 37 (R.V., " was filling ") ; a sponge, Mark 15 : 36 (cp. No. 5, Matt. 27 : 48) ; a house, Luke 14 : 23 ; the belly, Luke 15 : 16 ; waterpots, John 2 : 7 ;

baskets, 6 : 13 ; bowls, with fire, Rev. 8 : 5 ; the Temple, with smoke, 15 : 8.¶ Cp. *gemō*, to be full. See FULL.

10. KORENNUMI (κορέννυμι), to satisfy (akin to *koros*, a surfeit), is used metaphorically of spiritual things, in 1 Cor. 4 : 8, R.V., " ye are filled ; " in Acts 27 : 38, " had eaten enough," lit., ' having being satisfied with food ' See EAT, ENOUGH.¶

11. MESTOŌ (μεστόω), to fill full, from *mestos*, full, is used of being filled with wine, Acts 2 : 13, R.V., " are filled with."¶

B. Noun.

PLĒRŌMA (πλήρωμα), fulness, has two meanings, (*a*) in the active sense, that which fills up, a piece of undressed cloth on an old garment, Matt. 9 : 16 ; Mark 2 : 21, lit., ' the filling ' (R.V., " that which should fill it up "), i.e., the patch, which is probably the significance ; (*b*) that which has been completed, the fulness, e.g., Mark 8 : 20. See FULNESS.

Notes : (1) In Rev. 18 : 6, A.V., *kerannumi*, to mix, is incorrectly rendered to fill full (R.V., to mingle). (2) In Rev. 15 : 1, A.V., *teleō*, to finish, complete, is incorrectly rendered " filled up " (R.V., " finished ") ; the contents of the seven bowls are not the sum total of the Divine judgments ; they form the termination of them ; there are many which precede (see previous chapters), which are likewise comprised under " the wrath of God," to be executed at the closing period of the present age, e.g., 6 : 17 ; 11 : 18 ; 14 : 10, 19.

FILTH

1. PERIKATHARMA (περικάθαρμα) denotes offscouring, refuse (lit., cleanings, i.e., that which is thrown away in cleansing ; from *perikathairō*, to purify all around, i.e., completely, as in the Sept. of Deut. 18 : 10 ; Josh. 5 : 4.¶) It is once used in the Sept. (Prov. 21 : 18) as the price of expiation ; among the Greeks the term was applied to victims sacrificed to make expiation ; they also used it of criminals kept at the public expense, to be thrown into the sea, or otherwise killed, at the outbreak of a pestilence, etc. It is used in 1 Cor. 4 : 13 much in this sense (not of sacrificial victims), " the filth of the world," representing " the most abject and despicable men " (Grimm-Thayer), the scum or rubbish of humanity.¶

2. RHUPOS (ῥύπος) denotes dirt, filth, 1 Pet. 3 : 21.¶ Cp. *rhuparia*, filthiness (see A, No. 2, below) ; *rhuparos*, vile, Jas. 2 : 2 ; Rev. 22 : 11, in the best mss. (see B, No. 3, below) ;¶ *rhupoō*, to make filthy, Rev. 22 : 11 ;¶ *rhupainō* (see D. below).

FILTHINESS, FILTHY (to make)

A. Nouns.

1. AISCHROTĒS (αἰσχρότης), baseness (from *aischos*, shame, disgrace), is used in Eph. 5 : 4, of obscenity, all that is contrary to purity.¶

2. RHUPARIA (ῥυπαρία) denotes dirt, filth (cp. No. 2, under FILTH), and is used metaphorically of moral defilement in Jas. 1 : 21.¶

3. MOLUSMOS (μολυσμός), a soiling, defilement, is used in 2 Cor. 7 : 1. See DEFILEMENT.¶

4. ASELGEIA (ἀσέλγεια), wantonness, licentiousness, lasciviousness, is translated "filthy (conversation)," in 2 Pet. 2 : 7, A.V.; R.V., "lascivious (life)." See LASCIVIOUSNESS, WANTONNESS.

Notes : (1) Broadly speaking, *aischrotēs* signifies whatever is disgraceful; *rhuparia*, that which is characterized by moral impurity; *molusmos*, that which is defiling by soiling the clean ; *aselgeia*, that which is an insolent disregard of decency. (2) In Col. 3 : 8 *aischrologia*, which denotes any kind of base utterance, the utterance of an uncontrolled tongue, is rendered "filthy communication" in the A.V.; but this is only part of what is included in the more comprehensive R.V. rendering, "shameful speaking." In the papyri writings the word is used of abuse. In general it seems to have been associated more frequently with foul or filthy, rather than abusive, speaking (Moulton and Milligan).¶

B. Adjectives.

1. AISCHROS (αἰσχρός), base, shameful (akin to A, No. 1), is used of base gain, "filthy (lucre)," Tit. 1 : 11, and translated "shame" in 1 Cor. 11 : 6, with reference to a woman with shorn hair ; in 14 : 35, of oral utterances of women in a church gathering (R.V., "shameful") ; in Eph. 5 : 12, of mentioning the base and bestial practices of those who live lascivious lives. See SHAME.¶

2. AISCHROKERDĒS (αἰσχροκερδής), greedy of base gain (No. 1, and *kerdos*, gain), is used in 1 Tim. 3 : 8 and Tit. 1 : 7, "greedy of filthy lucre ;" some mss. have it also in 1 Tim. 3 : 3.¶

3. RHUPAROS (ῥυπαρός), akin to A, No. 2 (see also FILTH, No. 2), dirty, is said of shabby clothing, Jas. 2 : 2 : metaphorically, of moral defilement, Rev. 22 : 11 (in the best mss.).¶

Note : For *akathartos* see UNCLEAN, No. 1.

C. Adverb.

AISCHROKERDŌS (αἰσχροκερδῶς), eagerness for base gain (akin to B, No. 2), is used in 1 Pet. 5 : 2, "for filthy lucre."¶

D. Verb.

RHUPAINŌ (ῥυπαίνω), to make filthy, defile (from A, No. 2), is used in the Passive Voice, in an ethical sense, in Rev. 22 : 11 (cp. B, No. 3, in the same verse), "let him be made filthy," R.V. The tense (the aorist) marks the decisiveness of that which is decreed. Some texts have *rhupareuomai*, here, with the same meaning ; some have *rhupoō*, in the Middle Voice, to make oneself filthy.¶

FINAL, FINALLY
A. Nouns.

1. PERAS (πέρας), a limit, end, is translated "final" in Heb. 6 : 16,

R.V., " an oath is final for confirmation " (the A.V. connects the clauses differently). See END.

2. TELOS (τέλος), an end, most frequently of the termination of something, is used with the article adverbially, meaning " finally " or ' as to the end,' i.e., as to the last detail, 1 Pet. 3 : 8. See END.

B. Adverb.

LOIPON (λοιπόν) is the neuter of the adjective *loipos*, remaining (which is used in its different genders as a noun, ' the rest '), and is used either with the article or without, to signify " finally," lit., ' for the rest.' The Apostle Paul uses it frequently in the concluding portion of his Epistles, introducing practical exhortations, not necessarily implying that the letter is drawing to a close, but marking a transition in the subject-matter, as in Phil. 3 : 1, where the actual conclusion is for the time postponed and the farewell injunctions are resumed in 4 : 8. See also 1 Thess. 4 : 1 (A.V., " furthermore ") ; 2 Thess. 3 : 1.

FIND, FOUND

1. HEURISKŌ (εὑρίσκω) denotes (a) to find, either with previous search, e.g., Matt. 7 : 7, 8, or without, e.g., Matt. 27 : 32 ; in the Passive Voice, of Enoch's disappearance, Heb. 11 : 5 ; of mountains, Rev. 16 : 20 ; of Babylon and its occupants, 18 : 21, 22 ; (b) metaphorically, to find out by enquiry, or to learn, discover, e.g., Luke 19 : 48 ; John 18 : 38 ; 19 : 4, 6 ; Acts 4 : 21 ; 13 : 28 ; Rom. 7 : 10 ; Gal. 2 : 17, which indicates " the surprise of the Jew " who learned for the first time that before God he had no moral superiority over the Gentiles whom he superciliously dubbed " sinners," while he esteemed himself to be ' righteous ; ' 1 Pet. 1 : 7 ; Rev. 5 : 4 ; (c) in the Middle Voice, to find for oneself, gain, procure, obtain, e.g., Matt. 10 : 39 ; 11 : 29, " ye shall find (rest) ; " Luke 1 : 30 ; Acts 7 : 46 ; 2 Tim. 1 : 18. See GET, OBTAIN.

2. ANEURISKŌ (ἀνευρίσκω), to find out (by search), discover (*ana*, up, and No. 1), implying diligent searching, is used in Luke 2 : 16, of the shepherds in searching for and finding Mary and Joseph and the Child ; in Acts 21 : 4, of Paul and his companions, in searching for and finding " the disciples " at Tyre (in ver. 2, No. 1, is used).¶

3. LAMBANŌ (λαμβάνω), to take, receive, is translated " finding (occasion) " in Rom. 7 : 11, R.V. (A.V., " taking "). See ACCEPT.

4. KATALAMBANŌ (καταλαμβάνω), to lay hold of, said of mental action, to comprehend by laying hold of or finding facts, is translated " I found," of Festus regarding charges made against Paul, Acts 25 : 25. See APPREHEND.

Notes : (1) For *sunanapauomai*, to be refreshed in spirit, in Rom. 15 : 32, R.V., " find rest with," see FIND, REFRESH. (2) In Rom. 7 : 18, there is no word in the original for " find." Hence the R.V. has " is not." (3) In Rom. 11 : 33, *anexichniastos*, untraceable, is rendered " past finding out," A.V., R.V., " past tracing out " (*ichniazō*, to track out) ; in Eph. 3 : 8, " unsearchable." See TRACE, UNSEARCHABLE.¶

For FINE see BRASS, No. 4, FLOUR, GOODLY, Note, LINEN

FINGER

DAKTULOS (δάκτυλος), Matt. 23 : 4 ; Mark 7 : 33 ; Luke 11 : 46 ; 16 : 24 ; John 8 : 6 ; 20 : 25, 27, is used metaphorically in Luke 11 : 20, for the power of God, the effects of which are made visible to men (cp. Matt. 12 : 28, " by the Spirit of God ; " cp. also Ex. 8 : 19).¶

FINISH

1. TELEŌ (τελέω), to bring to an end (*telos*, an end), in the Passive Voice, to be finished, is translated by the verb to finish in Matt. 13 : 53 ; 19 : 1 ; 26 : 1 ; John 19 : 28, where the R.V. " are . . . finished " brings out the force of the perfect tense (the same word as in ver. 30, " It is finished "), which is missed in the A.V. ; as Stier says, " the word was in His heart before He uttered it ; " 2 Tim. 4 : 7 ; Rev. 10 : 7 ; 11 : 7 ; 20 : 3, R.V., " should be finished " (A.V., " fulfilled "), 5, 7, R.V., " finished " (A.V., " expired "). In Rev. 15 : 1 the verb is rightly translated " is finished," R.V., see FILL, Note (2). In 15 : 8 the R.V., " should be finished " corrects the A.V., " were fulfilled." See ACCOMPLISH.

2. TELEIOŌ (τελειόω), akin to the adjective *teleios*, complete, perfect, and to No. 1, denotes to bring to an end in the sense of completing or perfecting, and is translated by the verb to finish in John 4 : 34 ; 5 : 36 ; 17 : 4 ; Acts 20 : 24. See CONSECRATE, FULFIL, PERFECT.

3. EKTELEŌ (ἐκτελέω), lit., to finish out, i.e., completely (*ek*, out, intensive, and No. 1), is used in Luke 14 : 29, 30.¶

4. EPITELEŌ (ἐπιτελέω), to bring through to an end, is rendered " finish " in 2 Cor. 8 : 6, A.V. (R.V., " complete "). See ACCOMPLISH.

5. SUNTELEŌ (συντελέω), to bring to fulfilment, to effect, is translated " finishing " (A.V., " will finish ") in Rom. 9 : 28. See COMPLETE.

6. DIANUŌ (διανύω) is translated " had finished," in Acts 21 : 7, of the voyage from Tyre to Ptolemais. As this is so short a journey, and this verb is intensive in meaning, some have suggested the rendering ' but we having (thereby) completed our voyage (i.e., from Macedonia, 20 : 6), came from Tyre to Ptolemais.' In late Greek writers, however, the verb is used with the meaning to continue, and this is the probable sense here.¶

7. GINOMAI (γίνομαι), to become, to come into existence, is translated " were finished " in Heb. 4 : 3, i.e., were brought to their predestined end.

Notes : (1) In Luke 14 : 28, *apartismos* denotes a completion, and the phrase is, lit., ' unto a completion.' The A.V. has " to finish " (R.V., " to complete "). See COMPLETE.¶ (2) In Jas. 1 : 15, *apoteleō*, to perfect, to bring to maturity, to become " fullgrown," R.V. (A.V., " is finished "), is said of the full development of sin. (3) In Heb. 12 : 2, the R.V. suitably translates *teleiōtēs* " perfecter," for A.V., " finisher."

FIRE
A. Nouns.

1. PUR (πῦρ) (akin to which are No. 2, *pura*, and *puretos*, a fever, Eng., fire, etc.) is used (besides its ordinary natural significance) :

(*a*) of the holiness of God, which consumes all that is inconsistent therewith, Heb. 10 : 27 ; 12 : 29 ; cp. Rev. 1 : 14 ; 2 : 18 ; 10 : 1 ; 15 : 2 ; 19 : 12 ; similarly of the holy angels as His ministers, Heb. 1 : 7 ; in Rev. 3 : 18 it is symbolic of that which tries the faith of saints, producing what will glorify the Lord :

(*b*) of the Divine judgment, testing the deeds of believers, at the Judgment-Seat of Christ, 1 Cor. 3 : 13 and 15 :

(*c*) of the fire of Divine judgment upon the rejectors of Christ, Matt. 3 : 11 (where a distinction is to be made between the baptism of the Holy Spirit at Pentecost and the fire of Divine retribution ; Acts 2 : 3 could not refer to baptism); Luke 3 : 16 :

(*d*) of the judgments of God at the close of the present age previous to the establishment of the Kingdom of Christ in the world, 2 Thess. 1 : 8 ; Rev. 18 : 8 :

(*e*) of the fire of Hell, to be endured by the ungodly hereafter, Matt. 5 : 22 ; 13 : 42, 50 ; 18 : 8, 9 ; 25 : 41 ; Mark 9 : 43, 48 ; Luke 3 : 17 :

(*f*) of human hostility both to the Jews and to Christ's followers, Luke 12 : 49 :

(*g*) as illustrative of retributive judgment upon the luxurious and tyrannical rich, Jas. 5 : 3 :

(*h*) of the future overthrow of the Babylonish religious system at the hands of the Beast and the nations under him, Rev. 17 : 16 :

(*i*) of turning the heart of an enemy to repentance by repaying his unkindness by kindness, Rom. 12 : 20 :

(*j*) of the tongue, as governed by a fiery disposition and as exercising a destructive influence over others, Jas. 3 : 6 :

(*k*) as symbolic of the danger of destruction, Jude 23.

Note : See also under FLAME.

2. PURA (πυρά), from No. 1, denotes a heap of fuel collected to be set on fire (hence Eng., pyre), Acts 28 : 2, 3.¶

Note : In Mark 14 : 54, the italicised phrase " of the fire " is added in the Eng. Versions to indicate the light as coming from the fire.

B. Adjective.

PURINOS (πύρινος), " fiery " (akin to A, No. 1), is translated " of fire " in Rev. 9 : 17.¶ In the Sept., Ezek. 28 : 14, 16.¶

C. Verbs.

1. PUROŌ (πυρόω) is translated " being on fire " (Middle Voice) in 2 Pet. 3 : 12. See FIERY.

2. PHLOGIZŌ (φλογίζω), to set on fire, burn up, is used figuratively, in both Active and Passive Voices, in Jas. 3 : 6, of the tongue, firstly, of its disastrous effects upon the whole round of the circumstances of life ; secondly, of Satanic agency in using the tongue for this purpose.¶

FIRKIN

METRĒTĒS (μετρητής) is a liquid measure (akin to *metreō*, to measure), equivalent to one and a half Roman *amphoræ*, or about nine gallons, John 2 : 6.¶

FIRM

1. BEBAIOS (βέβαιος), firm, stedfast, secure (from *bainō*, to go), is translated " firm " in Heb. 3 : 6, of the maintenance of the boldness of the believer's hope, and in 3 : 14, R.V., of " the beginning of our confidence " (A.V., " stedfast "). See STEDFAST, SURE.

2. STEREOS (στερεός), solid, hard, stiff, is translated " firm " in 2 Tim. 2 : 19, R.V., " the firm (foundation of God)," A.V., " (standeth) sure ; " *stereos* is not part of the predicate ; " solid (food) " in Heb. 5 : 12, 14, R.V. ; " stedfast " in 1 Pet. 5 : 9. See SOLID, STEDFAST, STRONG.¶

Note : Cp. *stereoō*, to make strong, establish, Acts 3 : 7, 16 ; 16 : 5, and *stereōma*, stedfastness, Col. 2 : 5.¶

FIRST
A. Adjective.

PRŌTOS (πρῶτος), the superlative degree of *pro*, before, is used (I) of time or place, (*a*) as a noun, e.g., Luke 14 : 18 ; Rev. 1 : 17 ; opposite to ' the last,' in the neuter plural, Matt. 12 : 45 ; Luke 11 : 26 ; 2 Pet. 2 : 20 ; in the neuter singular, opposite to ' the second,' Heb. 10 : 9 ; in 1 Cor. 15 : 3, *en prōtois*, lit., ' in the first (things, or matters) ' denotes " first of all ; " (*b*) as an adjective, e.g., Mark 16 : 9, used with " day " understood, lit., ' the first (day) of (i.e., after) the Sabbath,' in which phrase the " of " is objective, not including the Sabbath, but following it (cp. B, No. 3) ; in John 20 : 4, 8 ; Rom. 10 : 19, e.g., equivalent to an English adverb ; in John 1 : 15, lit., ' first of me,' i.e., " before me " (of superiority) ; (II) of rank or dignity, see CHIEF. Cp. B, Nos. 3 and 4.
B. Adverbs.

1. PROTERON (πρότερον), the comparative degree of *pro* (see No. 1), former, before, denotes " first " in Heb. 7 : 27 ; in 4 : 6, R.V., " before " (A.V., " first "), speaking of Israel as having heard God's good tidings previously to the ministry of the Gospel ; in Gal. 4 : 13, " I preached . . . unto you the first time " means on the former of his two previous visits.

2. ANŌTHEN (ἄνωθεν), from above, is rendered " from the first " in Luke 1 : 3, R.V. ; it may mean ' from their beginning, or source.'

3. PRŌTŌS (πρώτως), firstly, is used in Acts 11 : 26, " first " (some mss. have No. 4 here).¶

4. PRŌTON (πρῶτον), the neuter of the adjective *prōtos*, is used as an adverb, signifying first, firstly, e.g., of time, Matt. 8 : 21 ; of order, Rom. 3 : 2 (A.V., " chiefly ") ; in John 7 : 51, R.V., " except it first hear from himself " (the A.V., " before it hear him," follows the mss. which have No. 1).

C. Numeral.

MIA (μία), a grammatically feminine form of *heis*, one, is translated " first " in certain occurrences of the phrase " on the first day of the week," e.g., Luke 24 : 1 ; 1 Cor. 16 : 2 ; cp. A. and see DAY ; also in Tit. 3 : 10, of a first admonition to a heretical man. See ONE.

D. Noun.

ARCHĒ (ἀρχή), a beginning, is translated " first " in Heb. 5 : 12, " of the first (principles of the oracles of God)," lit., ' (the principles) of the beginning (of the oracles of God) ; ' in 6 : 1 " the first (principles) of Christ," lit., ' (the account) of the beginning of Christ,' i.e., the elementary teaching concerning Christ. In Acts 26 : 4, where the word is preceded by *apo*, from, the A.V. has " at the first," the R.V., " from the beginning."

Notes : (1) In Jude 6 *archē* has the meaning " principality," as in the R.V. and the A.V. margin.

(2) In 2 Cor. 8 : 12 *prokeimai*, to be present, lit., to lie beforehand (*pro*, before, *keimai*, to lie), R.V. renders " (if the readiness) is there," for A.V., " if there be first (a willing mind)." See SET, A, No. 23.

FIRST-BEGOTTEN, FIRSTBORN

PRŌTOTOKOS (πρωτότοκος), firstborn (from *prōtos*, first, and *tiktō*, to beget), is used of Christ as born of the Virgin Mary, Luke 2 : 7 ; further, in His relationship to the Father, expressing His priority to, and preeminence over, creation, not in the sense of being the first to be born. It is used occasionally of superiority of position in the O.T. ; see Ex. 4 : 22 ; Deut. 21 : 16, 17, the prohibition being against the evil of assigning the privileged position of the firstborn to one born subsequently to the first child.

The five passages in the N.T. relating to Christ may be set forth chronologically thus : (a) Col. 1 : 15, where His eternal relationship with the Father is in view, and the clause means both that He was the Firstborn before all creation and that He Himself produced creation (the genitive case being objective, as ver. 16 makes clear) ; (b) Col. 1 : 18 and Rev. 1 : 5, in reference to His resurrection ; (c) Rom. 8 : 29, His position in relationship to the Church ; (d) Heb. 1 : 6, R.V., His Second Advent (the R.V. " when He again bringeth in," puts " again " in the right place, the contrast to His First Advent, at His Birth, being implied) ; cp. Psa. 89 : 27. The word is used in the plural, in Heb. 11 : 28, of the firstborn sons in the families of the Egyptians, and in 12 : 23, of the members of the Church.¶

Note : With (a) cp. John 1 : 30, " He was before me," lit., ' He was first (*prōtos*) of me,' i.e., ' in regard to me,' expressing all that is involved in His pre-existence and priority.

FIRSTFRUIT(S)

APARCHĒ (ἀπαρχή) denotes, primarily, an offering of firstfruits (akin to *aparchomai*, to make a beginning ; in sacrifices, to offer firstfruits). " Though the English word is plural in each of its occurrences save Rom. 11 : 16, the Greek word is always singular. Two Hebrew words are thus translated, one meaning the chief or principal part, e.g., Num. 18 : 12 ; Prov. 3 : 9 ; the other, the earliest ripe of the crop or of the tree, e.g., Ex. 23 : 16 ; Neh. 10 : 35 ; they are found together, e.g., in Ex. 23 : 19, " the first of the firstfruits."

" The term is applied in things spiritual, (*a*) to the presence of the Holy Spirit with the believer as the firstfruits of the full harvest of the Cross, Rom. 8 : 23 ; (*b*) to Christ Himself in resurrection in relation to all believers who have fallen asleep, 1 Cor. 15 : 20, 23 ; (*c*) to the earliest believers in a country in relation to those of their countrymen subsequently converted, Rom. 16 : 5 ; 1 Cor. 16 : 15 ; (*d*) to the believers of this age in relation to the whole of the redeemed, 2 Thess. 2 : 13 (see Note below) and Jas. 1 : 18. Cp. Rev. 14 : 4."¶*

Notes : (1) In Jas. 1 : 15 the qualifying phrase, " a kind of," may suggest a certain falling short, on the part of those mentioned, of what they might be. (2) In 2 Thess. 2 : 13, instead of *ap' archēs*, " from the beginning," there is an alternative reading, well supported, viz., *aparchēn*, ' (God chose you) as firstfruits.'

FISH

1. ICHTHUS (ἰχθύς) denotes a fish, Matt. 7 : 10 ; Mark 6 : 38, etc. ; apart from the Gospels, only in 1 Cor. 15 : 39.

2. ICHTHUDION (ἰχθύδιον) is a diminutive of No. 1, a little fish, Matt. 15 : 34 ; Mark 8 : 7.¶

3. OPSARION (ὀψάριον) is a diminutive of *opson*, cooked meat, or a relish, a dainty dish, especially of fish ; it denotes a little fish, John 6 : 9, 11 ; 21 : 9, 10, 13.¶

FISH (Verb), FISHER, FISHERMAN
A. Noun.

HALIEUS (ἁλιεύς), a fisherman, fisher (from *hals*, the sea), occurs in Matt. 4 : 18, 19 ; Mark 1 : 16, 17 ; Luke 5 : 2.¶
B. Verb.

HALIEUŌ (ἁλιεύω), to fish (akin to A.), occurs in John 21 : 3.¶ In the Sept., Jer. 16 : 16.¶

---

* From Notes on Thessalonians by Hogg and Vine, p. 271.

FIT (Adjective and Verb), FITLY, FITTING
A. Adjectives.

1. EUTHETOS (εὔθετος), ready for use, fit, well adapted, lit., well placed (*eu*, well, *tithēmi*, to place), is used (*a*) of persons, Luke 9 : 62, negatively, of one who is not fit for the Kingdom of God ; (*b*) of things, Luke 14 : 35, of salt that has lost its savour ; rendered " meet " in Heb. 6 : 7, of herbs. See MEET.¶

2. ARESTOS (ἀρεστός), pleasing (akin to *areskō*, to please), is translated " (it is not) fit," R.V. (A.V., " reason "), in Acts 6 : 2. See PLEASE, REASON.

B. Verbs.

1. ANĒKŌ (ἀνήκω), properly, to have come up to (*ana*, up, and *hēkō*, to arrive), is translated " is fitting," in Col. 3 : 18, R.V. See BEFITTING.

2. KATHĒKŌ (καθήκω), to come or reach down to (*kata*, down), hence, to befit, be proper, is translated " is (not fit)," in Acts 22 : 22 ; in Rom. 1 : 28, R.V., " fitting " (A.V., " convenient "). See CONVENIENT.¶

3. KATARTIZŌ (καταρτίζω), to make fit, to equip, prepare (*kata*, down, *artos*, a joint), is rendered " fitted " in Rom. 9 : 22, of vessels of wrath ; here the Middle Voice signifies that those referred to fitted themselves for destruction (as illustrated in the case of Pharaoh, the self-hardening of whose heart is accurately presented in the R.V. in the first part of the series of incidents in the Exodus narrative, which records Pharaoh's doings ; only after repeated and persistent obstinacy on his part is it recorded that God hardened his heart.) See FRAME, JOIN, PERFECT, PREPARE, RESTORE.

4. SUNARMOLOGEŌ (συναρμολογέω), to fit or frame together (*sun*, with, *harmos*, a joint, in building, and *legō*, to choose), is used metaphorically of the various parts of the Church as a building, Eph. 2 : 21, " fitly framed together ; " also of the members of the Church as the Body of Christ, 4 : 16, R.V., " fitly framed . . . together."¶

FIVE, FIVE TIMES

PENTE (πέντε) is derived by some from words suggesting the fingers of a hand, or a fist. The word is frequent in the Gospels. *Pentakis*, five times, is found in 2 Cor. 11 : 24 ;¶ *pentakosioi*, five hundred, in Luke 7 : 41 ; 1 Cor. 15 : 6 ;¶ *pentakischilioi*, five thousand (*chilios*, a thousand), in Matt. 14 : 21 ; 16 : 9 and corresponding passages. See FIFTEENTH, FIFTH, FIFTY.

FIX

STĒRIZŌ (στηρίζω), to set forth, make fast, fix, is translated " fixed " in Luke 16 : 26, of the great gulf separating Hades or Sheol from the region called " Abraham's bosom." See ESTABLISH.

FLAME, FLAMING

PHLOX (φλόξ), akin to Lat. *fulgeō*, to shine, is used apart from *pur*, fire, in Luke 16 : 24 ; with *pur*, it signifies a fiery flame, lit., a flame of fire, Acts 7 : 30 ; 2 Thess. 1 : 8, where the fire is to be understood as the instrument of Divine judgment ; Heb. 1 : 7, where the meaning probably is that God makes His angels as active and powerful as a flame of fire ; in Rev. 1 : 14 ; 2 : 18 ; 19 : 12, of the eyes of the Lord Jesus as emblematic of penetrating judgment, searching out evil.¶

FLATTERY (-ING)

KOLAKIA (or -EIA) (κολακία), akin to *kolakeuō*, to flatter, is used in 1 Thess. 2 : 5 of " words of flattery " (R.V.), adopted as " a cloke of covetousness," i.e., words which flattery uses, not simply as an effort to give pleasure, but with motives of self-interest.¶

FLAX

LINON (λίνον) primarily denotes flax (Eng., linen) ; then, that which is made of it, a wick of a lamp, Matt. 12 : 20 ; several ancient mss. have the word in Rev. 15 : 6 (A.V. only, " linen "). See LINEN.¶

FLEE, FLED

1. PHEUGŌ (φεύγω), to flee from or away (Lat., *fugio* ; Eng., fugitive, etc.), besides its literal significance, is used metaphorically, (a) transitively, of fleeing fornication, 1 Cor. 6 : 18 ; idolatry, 10 : 14 ; evil doctrine, questionings, disputes of words, envy, strife, railings, evil surmisings, wranglings, and the love of money, 1 Tim. 6 : 11 ; youthful lusts, 2 Tim. 2 : 22 ; (b) intransitively, of the flight of physical matter, Rev. 16 : 20 ; 20 : 11 ; of death, 9 : 6. See ESCAPE.

2. EKPHEUGŌ (ἐκφεύγω), to flee away, escape (*ek*, from, and No. 1), is translated " fled " in Acts 16 : 27 (A.V. only) ; 19 : 16. In Heb. 12 : 25 the best mss. have this verb instead of No. 1. See ESCAPE.

3. KATAPHEUGŌ (καταφεύγω), to flee for refuge (*kata*, used intensively, and No. 1), is used (a) literally in Acts 14 : 6 ; (b) metaphorically in Heb. 6 : 18, of fleeing for refuge to lay hold upon hope.¶

Note : For *apopheugō* and *diapheugō*, see ESCAPE.

FLESH

1. SARX (σάρξ) has a wider range of meaning in the N.T. than in the O.T. Its uses in the N.T. may be analysed as follows :

" (a) the substance of the body, whether of beasts or of men, 1 Cor. 15 : 39; (b) the human body, 2 Cor. 10 : 3a ; Gal. 2 : 20 ; Phil. 1 : 22 ; (c) by synecdoche, of mankind, in the totality of all that is essential to manhood, i.e., spirit, soul, and body, Matt. 24 : 22 ; John 1 : 13 ; Rom. 3 : 20 ; (d) by synecdoche, of the holy humanity of the Lord Jesus, in the totality

of all that is essential to manhood, i.e., spirit, soul, and body, John 1 : 14 ;
1 Tim. 3 : 16 ; 1 John 4 : 2 ; 2 John 7 ; in Heb. 5 : 7, ' the days of His
flesh,' i.e., His past life on earth in distinction from His present life in
resurrection ; (e) by synecdoche, for the complete person, John 6 : 51-57 ;
2 Cor. 7 : 5 ; Jas. 5 : 3 ; (f) the weaker element in human nature,
Matt. 26 : 41 ; Rom. 6 : 19 ; 8 : 3a ; (g) the unregenerate state of men,
Rom. 7 : 5 ; 8 : 8, 9 ; (h) the seat of sin in man (but this is not the same
thing as in the body), 2 Pet. 2 : 18 ; 1 John 2 : 16 ; (i) the lower and
temporary element in the Christian, Gal. 3 : 3 ; 6 : 8, and in religious
ordinances, Heb. 9 : 10 ; (j) the natural attainments of men, 1 Cor. 1 : 26 ;
2 Cor. 10 : 2, 3b ; (k) circumstances, 1 Cor. 7 : 28 ; the externals of life,
2 Cor. 7 : 1 ; Eph. 6 : 5 ; Heb. 9 : 13 ; (l) by metonymy, the outward
and seeming, as contrasted with the spirit, the inward and real, John 6 : 63 ;
2 Cor. 5 : 16 ; (m) natural relationship, consanguine, 1 Cor. 10 : 18 ;
Gal. 4 : 23, or marital, Matt. 19 : 5."*

In Matt. 26 : 41 ; Rom. 8 : 4, 13 ; 1 Cor. 5 : 5 ; Gal. 6 : 8 (not the
Holy Spirit, here), flesh is contrasted with spirit ; in Rom. 2 : 28, 29,
with heart and spirit ; in Rom. 7 : 25, with the mind ; cp. Col. 2 : 1, 5.
It is coupled with the mind in Eph. 2 : 3, and with the spirit in 2 Cor. 7 : 1.

Note : In Col. 2 : 18 the noun *sarx* is used in the phrase " (by his)
fleshly mind," lit., ' by the mind of his flesh' [see (h) above], whereas the
mind ought to be dominated by the Spirit.

2. KREAS (κρέας) denotes flesh in the sense of meat. It is used in
the plural in Rom. 14 : 21 ; 1 Cor. 8 : 13.¶

FLESHLY, FLESHY

1. SARKIKOS (σαρκικός), akin to No. 1, under FLESH, signifies
(a) associated with or pertaining to, the flesh, carnal, Rom. 15 : 27 ;
1 Cor. 9 : 11 ; (b) of the nature of the flesh, sensual, translated " fleshly "
in 2 Cor. 1 : 12, of wisdom ; in 1 Pet. 2 : 11, of lusts ; in 2 Cor. 10 : 4,
negatively, of the weapons of the Christian's warfare, R.V., " of the flesh "
(A.V., " carnal "). See CARNAL.

2. SARKINOS (σάρκινος) denotes 'of the flesh,' fleshly (the termination—*inos* signifying the substance or material of a thing) ; in 2 Cor.
3:3, R.V., "(tables that are hearts) of flesh," A.V., "fleshly (tables),"
etc. See CARNAL.

Note: The adjectives "fleshly," "carnal" are contrasted with
spiritual qualities in Rom. 7:14; 1 Cor. 3:1, 3, 4; 2 Cor. 1:12;
Col. 2:18 (lit., 'mind of flesh'). Speaking broadly, the carnal denotes
the sinful element in man's nature, by reason of descent from Adam; the
spiritual is that which comes by the regenerating operation of the Holy
Spirit.

---

* From Notes on Galatians by Hogg and Vine, pp. 111, 112.

FLIGHT
A. Noun.

PHUGĒ (φυγή), akin to *pheugō* (see FLEE), is found in Matt. 24 : 20. Some inferior mss. have it in Mark 13 : 18.¶

B. Verb.

KLINŌ (κλίνω), to make to bend, is translated " turned to flight " in Heb. 11 : 34. See Bow.

FLOCK

1. POIMNĒ (ποίμνη), akin to *poimēn*, a shepherd, denotes a flock (properly, of sheep), Matt. 26 : 31 ; Luke 2 : 8 ; 1 Cor. 9 : 7 ; metaphorically, of Christ's followers, John 10 : 16, R.V., for the erroneous A.V., " fold." What characterizes Christ's sheep is listening to His voice, and the flock must be one as He is one.¶

2. POIMNION (ποίμνιον), possibly a diminutive of No. 1, is used in the N.T. only metaphorically, of a group of Christ's disciples, Luke 12 : 32 ; of local churches cared for by elders, Acts 20 : 28, 29 ; 1 Pet. 5 : 2, 3.¶

FLOOD
A. Nouns.

1. KATAKLUSMOS (κατακλυσμός), a deluge (Eng., cataclysm), akin to *katakluzō*, to inundate, 2 Pet. 3 : 6, is used of the flood in Noah's time, Matt. 24 : 38, 39 ; Luke 17 : 27 ; 2 Pet. 2 : 5.¶

2. PLĒMMURA (πλήμμυρα), akin to *plēthō* and *pimplēmi*, to fill, a flood of sea or river, the latter in Luke 6 : 48.¶ In the Sept., Job 40 : 18 (ver. 23 in the E.V.).¶

3. POTAMOS (ποταμός), a river, stream, torrent, is translated " flood " in Matt. 7 : 25, 27 ; in Rev. 12 : 15, 16, A.V., " flood," R.V., " river." See RIVER, WATER.

B. Adjective.

POTAMOPHORĒTOS (ποταμοφόρητος) signifies carried away by a stream or river (A, No. 3, and *pherō*, to carry), Rev. 12 : 15, R.V., " carried away by the stream " (A.V., " of the flood ").¶

For FLOOR see THRESHING-FLOOR

FLOUR

SEMIDALIS (σεμίδαλις) denotes the finest wheaten flour, Rev. 18 : 13.¶

For FLOURISH in Phil. 4 : 10, see REVIVE

FLOW

RHEŌ (ῥέω), to flow, is used figuratively in John 7 : 38 of the Holy Spirit, acting in and through the believer.¶

FLOWER
A. Noun.

ANTHOS (ἄνθος), a blossom, flower (used in certain names of flowers), occurs in Jas. 1 : 10, 11 ; 1 Pet. 1 : 24 (twice).¶

B. Adjective.

HUPERAKMOS (ὑπέρακμος), past the bloom of youth (from *huper*, beyond, and *akmē*, the highest point of anything, the full bloom of a flower : Eng., acme), is used in 1 Cor. 7 : 36, " past the flower of her age ; " Lightfoot prefers the rendering " of full age."

For FLUX see DYSENTERY

FLUTE-PLAYERS

AULĒTĒS (αὐλητής), a flute-player (from *auleō*, to play the flute), occurs in Matt. 9 : 23 (A.V., " minstrel "), and Rev. 18 : 22 (A.V., " pipers "). In the papyri writings of the time the word is chiefly associated with religious matters (Moulton and Milligan, Vocab.). Cp. MINSTREL.¶

FLY

PETOMAI (πέτομαι), to fly (the root of which is seen in *pteron* and *pterux*, a wing, *ptilon*, a feather, etc.), is confined to the Apocalypse, 4 : 7 ; 8 : 13 ; 12 : 14 ; 14 : 6 ; 19 : 17. Some mss. have the verb *petaomai*, a frequentative form.¶

FOAL

HUIOS (υἱός), a son, primarily signifying the relation of offspring to parent, is used of the foal of an ass in Matt. 21 : 5. See SON.

FOAM
A. Verbs.

1. APHRIZŌ (ἀφρίζω) denotes to foam at the mouth (akin to *aphros*, foam ; see B.), Mark 9 : 18, 20.¶

2. EPAPHRIZŌ (ἐπαφρίζω), to foam out, or up (*epi*, up, and No. 1), is used metaphorically in Jude 13, of the impious libertines, who had crept in among the saints, and foamed out their own shame with swelling words. The metaphor is drawn from the refuse borne on the crest of waves and cast up on the beach.¶

B. Noun.

APHROS (ἀφρός), foam, occurs in Luke 9 : 39, where it is used with the preposition *meta*, with, lit., ' (teareth him) with (accompanied by) foam.'¶

FOE

ECHTHROS (ἐχθρός), an adjective signifying hated, hateful, or hostile, is used also as a noun denoting an enemy, translated " foes " in Matt. 10 : 36 and the A.V. of Acts 2 : 35. See ENEMY.

FOLD

AULĒ (αὐλή) first signifies an open courtyard before a house ; then, an enclosure in the open, a sheepfold, John 10 : 1, 16. In the papyri " the word is extremely common, denoting the court attached to a house " (Moulton and Milligan, Vocab.). The sheepfold was usually surrounded by a stone wall, Numb. 32 : 16, preferably near a well, Ex. 2 : 16 ; Psa. 23 : 2, and often protected by a tower, 2 Chron. 26 : 10 ; Mic. 4 : 8. See COURT, HALL, PALACE.

Note : For the erroneous A.V. rendering, " fold," of *poimnē*, a flock, in John 10 : 16, see FLOCK.

For FOLD UP see ROLL, A, No. 4

For FOLK see IMPOTENT, B, SICK, B, No. 2

FOLLOW, FOLLOW AFTER

1. AKOLOUTHEŌ (ἀκολουθέω), to be an *akolouthos*, a follower, or companion (from the prefix *a*, here expressing union, likeness, and *keleuthos*, a way ; hence, one going in the same way), is used (*a*) frequently in the literal sense, e.g., Matt. 4 : 25 ; (*b*) metaphorically, of discipleship, e.g., Mark 8 : 34 ; 9 : 38 ; 10 : 21. It is used 77 times in the Gospels, of following Christ, and only once otherwise, Mark 14 : 13.

2. EXAKOLOUTHEŌ (ἐξακολουθέω), to follow up, or out to the end (*ek*, out, used intensively, and No. 1), is used metaphorically, and only by the Apostle Peter in his Second Epistle : in 1 : 16, of cunningly devised fables ; 2 : 2, of lascivious doings ; 2 : 15, of the way of Balaam.¶ In the Sept., Job 31 : 9 ; Is. 56 : 11 ; Jer. 2 : 2 ; Amos 2 : 4.¶

3. EPAKOLOUTHEŌ (ἐπακολουθέω), to follow after, close upon (*epi*, upon, and No. 1). is used of signs following the preaching of the Gospel. Mark 16 : 20 ; of following good works, 1 Tim 5 : 10 ; of sins following after those who are guilty of them, 5 : 24 ; of following the steps of Christ, 1 Pet. 2 : 21.¶

4. KATAKOLOUTHEŌ (κατακολουθέω), to follow behind or intently after (*kata*, after, used intensively, and No. 1), is used of the women on their way to Christ's tomb, Luke 23 : 55 ; of the demon-possessed maid in Philippi in following the missionaries, Acts 16 : 17.¶

5. PARAKOLOUTHEŌ (παρακολουθέω) lit. signifying to follow close up, or side by side, hence, to accompany, to conform to (*para*, beside, and No. 1), is used of signs accompanying " them that believe," Mark 16 : 17 ; of tracing the course of facts, Luke 1 : 3, R.V. ; of following the good doctrine, 1 Tim. 4 : 6, R.V. (A.V., " attained ") ; similarly of

following teaching so as to practise it, 2 Tim. 3 : 10, R.V., " didst follow "
(A.V., " hast fully known "). See ATTAIN, KNOW, TRACE, UNDERSTAND.¶

6. SUNAKOLOUTHEŌ (συνακολουθέω), to follow along with, to
accompany a leader (*sun*, with, and No. 1), is given its true rendering in
the R.V. of Mark 5 : 37, " He suffered no man to follow with Him ; " in
14 : 51, of the young man who " followed with " Christ (inferior mss.
have No. 1 here) ; Luke 23 : 49, of the women who " followed with "
Christ from Galilee.¶

7. DIŌKŌ (διώκω) denotes (*a*) to drive away, Matt. 23 : 34 ; (*b*) to
pursue without hostility, to follow, follow after, said of righteousness,
Rom. 9 : 30 ; the Law, 9 : 31 ; 12 : 13, hospitality (" given to ") lit.,
' pursuing ' (as one would a calling) ; the things which make for peace,
14 : 19 ; love, 1 Cor. 14 : 1 ; that which is good, 1 Thess. 5 : 15 ; righteousness, godliness, faith, love, patience, meekness, 1 Tim. 6 : 11 ; righteousness, faith, love, peace, 2 Tim. 2 : 22 ; peace and sanctification, Heb. 12 : 14 ;
peace, 1 Pet. 3 : 11 ; (*c*) to follow on (used intransitively), Phil. 3 : 12, 14,
R.V., " I press on ; " ' follow after,' is an inadequate meaning. See
GIVE, PERSECUTE, PRESS, PURSUE.

8. KATADIŌKŌ (καταδιώκω), to follow up or closely, with the
determination to find (*kata*, down, intensive, giving the idea of a hard,
persistent search, and No. 7), Mark 1 : 36, " followed after (Him)," is said
of the disciples in going to find the Lord who had gone into a desert place
to pray.¶ The verb is found, e.g., in 1 Sam. 30 : 22 ; Psa. 23 : 6, and
with hostile intent in Gen. 31 : 36.

9. GINOMAI (γίνομαι), to become, to come into existence, is used in
Rev. 8 : 17 ; 11 : 15, 19, in the sense of taking place after, translated
" there followed." See BECOME.

10. EPEIMI (ἔπειμι), to come upon, or, of time, to come on or after
(*epi*, upon, and *eimi*, to go), is used in the present participle as an adjective,
in reference to a day, in Acts 7 : 26 ; 16 : 11 ; 20 : 15 ; 21 : 18 ; a night,
23 : 11, R.V., " following," in each place (A.V., " next ").¶

Notes : (1) In Luke 13 : 33, the present participle, Middle Voice, of
the verb *echō*, to have, to be next, is used with the article, the word
hēmera, a day, being understood, signifying " the day following." (2) In
John 1 : 43 and 6 : 22 the adverb *epaurion* with the article, " on the
morrow," is translated " the day following " in the A.V. See MORROW.
(3) In Acts 21 : 1 the adverb *hexēs*, in order, next, is translated " the
day following " (A.V.). (4) *Mimeomai*, to imitate, be an imitator, is so
translated always in the R.V., where the A.V. uses the verb to follow ;
it is always used in a good sense, 2 Thess. 3 : 7, 9 ; Heb. 13 : 7 ; 3 John 11.
So with the nouns *mimētēs*, an imitator, and *summimētēs*, an imitator
together. See IMITATE, IMITATOR. (5) In Matt. 4 : 19, *deute*, come
hither, with *opisō*, after, is translated " come ye after," R.V. (A.V.,
" follow "). (6) In Matt. 27 : 62, R.V., the phrase *eimi meta*, to be after,

is translated " (which) is (the day) after " (A.V., " that followed ").
(7) In 1 Pet. 1 : 11, the phrase *meta tauta*, lit., ' after these things,' is translated " that should follow," said of glories after the sufferings of Christ.
(8) In Luke 22 : 49, the phrase *to esomenon*, lit. ' the (thing) about to be '
(from *eimi*, to be), is translated " what would follow."   (9) In Acts 3 : 24,
the adverb *kathexēs*, successively, in order, is translated " (them) that
followed after," i.e., those who succeeded (him), lit., ' the (ones) successively (to him).' Cp. Note (3) above. See AFTERWARD.

FOLLY

ANOIA (ἄνοια) lit. signifies ' without understanding ' (*a*, negative,
nous, mind) ; hence, folly, or, rather, senselessness, 2 Tim. 3 : 9 ; in Luke
6 : 11 it denotes violent or mad rage, " madness." See MADNESS.¶
Cp. *anoētos*, foolish.

Note : For *aphrosunē*, rendered " folly " in 2 Cor. 11 : 1, A.V., see
FOOLISHNESS (R.V.).

FOOD

1. TROPHĒ (τροφή) denotes nourishment, food (akin to *trephō*, to
rear, nourish, feed) ; it is used literally, in the Gospels, Acts and Jas.
2 : 15 ; metaphorically, in Heb. 5 : 12, 14, R.V., " (solid) food," A.V.,
" (strong) meat," i.e., deeper subjects of the faith than that of elementary
instruction. The word is always rendered " food " in the R.V., where
the A.V. has " meat ; " e.g., Matt. 3 : 4 ; 6 : 25 ; 10 : 10 ; 24 : 45 ;
Luke 12 : 23 ; John 4 : 8 ; Acts 2 : 46, " did take their food," R.V. (A.V.,
" did eat their meat ") ; 9 : 19, " took food ; " 27 : 33, 34, 36. The A.V.
also has " food " in Acts 14 : 17 and Jas. 2 : 15.¶

2. DIATROPHĒ (διατροφή), sustenance, food, a strengthened form of
No. 1 (*dia*, through, suggesting a sufficient supply), is used in 1 Tim. 6 : 8.¶

3. BRŌSIS (βρῶσις), eating, the act of eating (akin to *bibrōskō*, to
eat) is translated " food " in 2 Cor. 9 : 10. See EATING, MEAT, RUST.

4. SITOMETRION (σιτομέτριον), a measured " portion of food "(*sitos*,
corn, *metreō*, to measure), is used in Luke 12 : 42, R.V.¶

5. BRŌMA (βρῶμα), akin to No. 3, frequently translated " meat,"
and always so in the A.V. except in Matt. 14 : 15, " victuals," is rendered
" food " in the R.V. in Matt. 14 : 15 ; Luke 3 : 11 ; 9 : 13.

Note : For *asitia*, without food, see ABSTINENCE.

FOOL, FOOLISH, FOOLISHLY, FOOLISHNESS
A. Adjectives.

1. APHRŌN (ἄφρων) signifies ' without reason ' (*a*, negative, *phrēn*,
the mind), " want of mental sanity and sobriety, a reckless and inconsiderate habit of mind " (Hort), or " the lack of commonsense perception
of the reality of things natural and spiritual . . . or the imprudent
ordering of one's life in regard to salvation " (G. Vos, in Hastings' Bible

Dic.) ; it is mostly translated " foolish " or " foolish ones " in the R.V. ; Luke 11 : 40 ; 12 : 20 ; Rom. 2 : 20 ; 1 Cor. 15 : 36 ; 2 Cor. 11 : 16 (twice), 19 (contrasted with *phronimos*, prudent) ; 12 : 6, 11 ; Eph. 5 : 17 ; 1 Pet. 2 : 15.¶

2. ANOĒTOS (ἀνόητος) signifies not understanding (*a*, negative, *noeō*, to perceive, understand), not applying *nous*, the mind, Luke 24 : 25 ; in Rom. 1 : 14 and Gal. 3 : 1, 3 it signifies senseless, an unworthy lack of understanding ; sometimes it carries a moral reproach (in contrast with *sōphrōn*, sober-minded, self-controlled) and describes one who does not govern his lusts, Tit. 3 : 3 ; in 1 Tim. 6 : 9 it is associated with evil desires, lusts. See UNWISE.¶

3. MŌROS (μωρός) primarily denotes dull, sluggish (from a root *muh*, to be silly) ; hence, stupid, foolish ; it is used (*a*) of persons, Matt. 5 : 22, " Thou fool ; " here the word means morally worthless, a scoundrel, a more serious reproach than " Raca ; " the latter scorns a man's mind and calls him stupid ; *mōros* scorns his heart and character ; hence the Lord's more severe condemnation; in 7 : 26, " a foolish man ; " 23 : 17, 19, " fools ; " 25 : 2, 3, 8, " foolish ; " in 1 Cor. 3 : 18, " a fool ; " the Apostle Paul uses it of himself and his fellow-workers, in 4 : 10, " fools " (i.e., in the eyes of opponents) ; (*b*) of things, 2 Tim. 2 : 23, " foolish and ignorant questionings ; " so Tit. 3 : 9 ; in 1 Cor. 1 : 25, " the foolishness of God," not *mōria*, foolishness as a personal quality (see C, No. 1), but adjectively, that which is considered by the ignorant as a foolish policy or mode of dealing, lit., ' the foolish (thing) ; ' so in ver. 27, " the foolish (things) of the world."¶

4. ASUNETOS (ἀσύνετος) denotes without discernment, or understanding (*a*, negative, *suniēmi*, to understand) ; hence " senseless," as in the R.V. of Rom. 1 : 21 (A.V., " foolish "), of the heart ; in 10 : 19, A.V., " foolish," R.V., " void of understanding." See UNDERSTANDING.

Note : For " fools," Eph. 5 : 15, see UNWISE, No. 3.

B. Verbs.

1. MŌRAINŌ (μωραίνω) is used (*a*) in the causal sense, to make foolish, 1 Cor. 1 : 20 ; (*b*) in the passive sense, to become foolish, Rom. 1 : 22 ; in Matt. 5 : 13 and Luke 14 : 34 it is said of salt that has lost its flavour, becoming tasteless. See SAVOUR.¶

2. PARAPHRONEŌ (παραφρονέω), to be beside oneself (from *para*, contrary to, and *phrēn*, the mind), to be deranged, 2 Cor. 11 : 23, R.V., " as one beside himself," for A.V., " as a fool."¶

C. Nouns.

1. MŌRIA (μωρία) denotes foolishness (akin to A, No. 3 and B, No. 1), and is used in 1 Cor. 1 : 18, 21, 23 ; 2 : 14 ; 3 : 19.¶

2. APHROSUNĒ (ἀφροσύνη), senselessness, is translated " foolishness " in Mark 7 : 22 ; 2 Cor. 11 : 1, 17, 21, " foolishness," R.V. (A.V., " folly " and " foolishly "). See FOLLY.¶

Note : *Mōrologia* denotes foolish talking, Eph. 5 : 4. See TALKING.¶

FOOT, FEET
A. Nouns.

1. POUS (πούς), besides its literal meaning, is used, by metonymy, of a person in motion, Luke 1 : 79 ; Acts 5 : 9 ; Rom. 3 : 15 ; 10 : 15 ; Heb. 12 : 13. It is used in phrases expressing subjection, 1 Cor. 15 : 27, R.V. ; of the humility and receptivity of discipleship, Luke 10 : 39 ; Acts 22 : 3 ; of obeisance and worship, e.g., Matt. 28 : 9 ; of scornful rejection, Matt. 10 : 14 ; Acts 13 : 51. Washing the feet of another betokened the humility of the service and the comfort of the guest, and was a feature of hospitality, Luke 7 : 38 ; John 13 : 5 ; 1 Tim. 5 : 10 (here figuratively).

Note : In Acts 7 : 5 *bēma*, a step, is used with *podos*, the genitive case of *pous*, lit., ' the step of a foot,' i.e., a foot breadth, what the foot can stand on, " (not so much as) to set his foot on."

2. BASIS (βάσις), lit., a step (*akin to bainō*, to go), hence denotes that with which one steps, a foot, and is used in the plural in Acts 3 : 7.¶

B. Adjectives.

1. PODĒRĒS (ποδήρης) signifies reaching to the feet, from *pous*, and *arō*, to fit (akin to A, No. 1), and is said of a garment, Rev. 1 : 13.¶ In the Sept. it is used of the high priest's garment, e.g., Ex. 28 : 4.

2. PEZOS (πεζός), an adjective, " on foot," is used in one of its forms as an adverb in Matt. 14 : 13, and Mark 6 : 33, in each place signifying ' by land,' in contrast to ' by sea.'¶

Cp. *pezeuō*, to go on foot, Acts 20 : 13, R.V., " to go by land " (marg., " on foot ").

Notes : (1) In Acts 20 : 18, the R.V. " set foot in " expresses more literally the verb *epibainō* (lit., to go upon) than the A.V. " came into." So again in 21 : 4 (some mss. have *anabainō* here). (2) In Luke 8 : 5, *katapateō*, to tread down (*kata*, down, *pateō*, to tread, trample), is translated " was trodden under foot," R.V. (A.V., " was trodden down ").

FOOTSTOOL

HUPOPODION (ὑποπόδιον), from *hupo*, under, and *pous*, a foot, is used (a) literally in Jas. 2 : 3, (b) metaphorically, of the earth as God's footstool, Matt. 5 : 35 ; of the foes of the Lord, Matt. 22 : 44 (in some mss.) ; Mark 12 : 36, " underneath " (in some mss.) ; Luke 20 : 43 ; Acts 2 : 35 ; 7 : 49 ; Heb. 1 : 13 ; 10 : 13. The R.V., adhering to the literal rendering, translates the phrase " the footstool of My (Thy, His) feet," for the A.V., " My (etc.) footstool," but in Matt. 22 : 44, " (till I put Thine enemies) underneath thy feet."¶

FOR and FORASMUCH : see Note †, p. 9

For FORBADE see FORBID

FORBEAR, FORBEARANCE

A. Verbs.

1. ANECHŌ (ἀνέχω), to hold up (*ana*, up, *echō*, to have or hold), is used in the Middle Voice in the N.T., signifying to bear with, endure ; it is rendered " forbearing (one another) " in Eph. 4 : 2 and Col. 3 : 13. See BEAR. Cp. B, No. 1, below.

2. ANIĒMI (ἀνίημι), lit., to send up or back (*ana*, up, *hiēmi*, to send), hence, to relax, loosen, or, metaphorically, to desist from, is translated " forbearing " (threatening) in Eph. 6 : 9 (' giving up your threatening,' T. K. Abbott). SEE LEAVE, LOOSE.

3. PHEIDOMAI (φείδομαι), to spare (its usual meaning), to refrain from doing something, is rendered " I forbear " in 2 Cor. 12 : 6. See SPARE.

4. STEGŌ (στέγω) properly denotes to protect by covering ; then, to conceal ; then, by covering, to bear up under ; it is translated " forbear " in 1 Thess. 3 : 1, 5. See BEAR.

Note : In 1 Cor. 9 : 6, the verb *ergazomai*, to work, is used in the present infinitive, with a negative, and translated " to forbear working " (lit., ' not working ').

B. Noun.

ANOCHĒ (ἀνοχή), a holding back (akin to A, No. 1), denotes forbearance, a delay of punishment, Rom. 2 : 4 ; 3 : 25, in both places of God's forbearance with men ; in the latter passage His forbearance is the ground, not of His forgiveness, but of His prætermission of sins, His withholding punishment. In 2 : 4 it represents a suspense of wrath which must eventually be exercised unless the sinner accepts God's conditions ; in 3 : 25 it is connected with the passing over of sins in times past, previous to the atoning work of Christ.¶

Note : Cp. the noun *epieikeia*, Acts 24 : 4, " clemency ; " 2 Cor. 10 : 1, " gentleness." Synonymous with this are *makrothumia*, longsuffering, and *hupomonē*, patience (see Col. 1 : 11). *Anochē* and *makrothumia* are used together in Rom 2 : 4. See also Eph. 4 : 2 (where A, No. 1, is used in this combination). Trench (Syn.) and Abbott-Smith (Lex.) state that *hupomonē* expresses patience with regard to adverse things, *makrothumia* patience with regard to antagonistic persons. It must be observed, however, that in Heb. 6 : 15 the verb *makrothumeō* is used of Abraham's patience under the pressure of trying circumstances (cp. also Jas. 5 : 7, 8). *Makrothumia* and *hupomonē* are often found together, e.g., 2 Cor. 6 : 4 and 6 ; 2 Tim. 3 : 10.

" Longsuffering is that quality of self-restraint in the face of provocation which does not hastily retaliate or promptly punish ; it is the opposite of anger and is associated with mercy, and is used of God, Ex. 34 : 6, Sept. ; Rom. 2 : 4 ; 1 Pet. 3 : 20. Patience is the quality that does not surrender to circumstances or succumb under trial ; it is the opposite of despondency and is associated with hope, in 1 Thess. 1 : 3 ; it is not used of God."*

C. Adjectives.

1. ANEXIKAKOS (ἀνεξίκακος) denotes patiently forbearing evil, lit., ' patient of wrong,' (from *anechō*, A, No. 1 and *kakos*, evil), enduring ; it is rendered " forbearing " in 2 Tim. 2 : 24.¶

2. EPIEIKĒS (ἐπιεικής), an adjective (from *epi*, used intensively, and *eikos*, reasonable), is used as a noun with the article in Phil. 4 : 5, and translated " forbearance " in the R.V. ; A.V., " moderation," R.V., marg., " gentleness," ' sweet reasonableness ' (Matthew Arnold). See GENTLE.

FORBID, FORBADE
A. Verb.

KŌLUŌ (κωλύω), to hinder, restrain, withhold, forbid (akin to *kolos*, docked, lopped, clipped), is most usually translated to forbid, often an inferior rendering to that of hindering or restraining, e.g., 1 Thess. 2 : 16 ; Luke 23 : 2 ; 2 Pet. 2 : 16, where the R.V. has " stayed ; " in Acts 10 : 47 " forbid." In Luke 6 : 29, the R.V. has " withhold not (thy coat also)." See HINDER, KEEP, *Note* (7), STAY, SUFFER, A, *Note* (3), WITHHOLD, WITHSTAND, No. 1.

Notes : (1) The strengthened form *diakōluō* (*dia*, through, used intensively) is used in Matt. 3 : 14, where, for the A.V., " forbad " the R.V. has " would have hindered him " [" forbad " is unsuitable with reference to the natural and persistent (*dia*) effort to prevent Christ from being baptized.]¶

(2) The phrase *mē genoito*, lit., ' let it not be ' (*mē*, negative, and *ginomai*, to become), is idiomatically translated " God forbid " in Luke 20 : 16 ; Rom. 3 : 4, 6, 31 ; 6 : 2, 15 ; 7 : 7, 13 ; 9 : 14 ; 11 : 1, 11 ; 1 Cor. 6 : 15 ; Gal. 2 : 17 ; 3 : 21, and in the A.V. of 6 : 14 ; here the R.V. has " far be it from me (to glory)," which the American R.V. uses in the O.T. In Paul's Epistles it is almost entirely used to express the Apostle's repudiation of an inference which he apprehends may be drawn from his argument.

B. Adverb.

AKŌLUTŌS (ἀκωλύτως), without hindrance (*a*, negative, and A, No. 1), is translated " none forbidding him," in Acts 28 : 31. From the 2nd century A.D. onwards the word is found constantly in legal documents (Moulton and Milligan, Vocab., who draw attention to the triumphant note on which the word brings the Acts to a close).¶

FORCE
A. Adjective.

BEBAIOS (βέβαιος), firm, secure, is translated " of force " (present

---

* From Notes on Thessalonians by Hogg and Vine, pp. 183, 184.

usage would translate it ' in force ') in Heb. 9 : 17, of a testament, or covenant, in relation to a death.   See FIRM.

B. Verb.

1. HARPAZŌ (ἁρπάζω), to snatch away, carry off by force, is used in the next sentence in Matt. 11 : 12, to that referred to under No. 1, " men of violence (A.V. ' the violent ') take it by force," the meaning being, as determined by the preceding clause, that those who are possessed of eagerness and zeal, instead of yielding to the opposition of religious foes, such as the Scribes and Pharisees, press their way into the Kingdom, so as to possess themselves of it.   It is elsewhere similarly rendered in John 6 : 15, of those who attempted to seize the Lord, and in Acts 23 : 10, of the chief captain's command to the soldiers to rescue Paul.   See CATCH, PLUCK, PULL.   Cp. *diarpazō*, to plunder, e.g., Matt. 12 : 29, and *sunarpazō*, to seize and carry away, e.g., Acts 6 : 12, and *harpax*, rapacious, ravening, e.g., Matt. 7 : 15.

Notes : (1) *Biazō*, to force (from *bia*, force), is used in the Passive Voice in Matt. 11 : 12, of the Kingdom of Heaven as ' suffering violence ; ' so in Luke 16 : 16, " entereth violently into it," here in the Middle Voice, expressive of the special interest which the doer of the act has in what he is doing.   This meaning is abundantly confirmed by the similar use in the papyri.   Moulton and Milligan (Vocab.) remark that Luke's statement can be naturally rendered ' everyone is entering it violently.' See VIOLENCE.

(2) In Matt. 11 : 12, the corresponding noun, *biastēs*, violence, is rendered " men of violence," R.V. (see No. 2).   See VIOLENCE.

FOREFATHER

1. PROGONOS (πρόγονος), an adjective, primarily denoting born before (*pro*, before, and *ginomai*, to become), is used as a noun in the plural, 2 Tim. 1 : 3, " forefathers " (in 1 Tim. 5 : 4, " parents ").   See PARENTS.¶

2. PROPATŌR (προπάτωρ), a forefather (*pro*, before, *patēr*, a father), is used of Abraham in Rom. 4 : 1.¶

FOREGOING

PROAGŌ (προάγω), when used intransitively, signifies either to lead the way, or to go before, precede ; in Heb. 7 : 18, it is used of the commandment of the Law (ver. 16), as preceding the bringing in of " a better hope " (R.V., " foregoing ").   See BRING, GO.

FOREHEAD

METŌPON (μέτωπον), from *meta*, with, and *ōps*, an eye, occurs only in the Apocalypse, 7 : 3 ; 9 : 4 ; 13 : 16 ; 14 : 1, 9 ; 17 : 5 ; 20 : 4 ; 22 : 4.¶

FOREIGN, FOREIGNER

EXŌ (ἔξω), an adverb, signifying outside, without, is used in Acts 26 : 11, R.V., " foreign," for A.V. " strange," of cities beyond the limits of Palestine, lit., ' unto (the) cities without,' including Damascus. See FORTH, OUTWARD, STRANGE, WITHOUT.

Note : In Eph. 2 : 19, *paroikos*, lit., dwelling near (*para*, near, *oikos*, a dwelling), denotes an alien, a sojourner, in contrast to fellow-citizens, R.V., " sojourners " (A.V., " foreigners "); in 1 Pet. 2 : 11, A.V., " strangers ; " see also Acts 7 : 6, 29. See SOJOURNER, STRANGER. Cp. *allotrios*, e.g., Acts 7 : 6 ; Heb. 11 : 9, 34 ; *allophulos*, Acts 10 : 28 ;¶. *xenos*, Matt. 25 : 35, 38, 43 ; 27 : 7 ; Acts 17 : 21, etc.

FOREKNOW, FOREKNOWLEDGE
A. Verb.

PROGINŌSKŌ (προγινώσκω), to know before (*pro*, before, *ginoskō*, to know), is used (*a*) of Divine knowledge, concerning (1) Christ, 1 Pet. 1 : 20, R.V., " foreknown " (A.V., " foreordained "); (2) Israel as God's earthly people, Rom. 11 : 2 ; (3) believers, Rom. 8 : 29 ; the foreknowledge of God is the basis of His foreordaining counsels ; (*b*) of human knowledge, (1) of persons, Acts 26 : 5 ; (2) of facts, 2 Pet. 3 : 17.¶

B. Noun.

PROGNŌSIS (πρόγνωσις), a foreknowledge (akin to A.), is used only of Divine foreknowledge, Acts 2 : 23 ; 1 Pet. 1 : 2.¶ Foreknowledge is one aspect of omniscience ; it is implied in God's warnings, promises and predictions. See Acts 15 : 18. God's foreknowledge involves His electing grace, but this does not preclude human will. He foreknows the exercise of faith which brings salvation. The Apostle Paul stresses especially the actual purposes of God rather than the ground of the purposes, see, e.g., Gal. 1 : 16 ; Eph. 1 : 5, 11. The Divine counsels will ever be unthwartable. Cp. FORESHEW.

For FOREORDAIN see DETERMINE, No, 3, FOREKNOW, A

For FOREPART see FORESHIP

FORERUNNER

PRODROMOS (πρόδρομος), an adjective signifying running forward, going in advance, is used as a noun, of those who were sent before to take observations, acting as scouts, especially in military matters ; or of one sent before a king to see that the way was prepared, Isa. 40 : 3 ; (cp. Luke 9 : 52 ; and, of John the Baptist, Matt. 11 : 10, etc). In the N.T. it is said of Christ in Heb. 6 : 20, as going in advance of His followers who are to be where He is, when He comes to receive them to Himself.¶ In the Sept., Numb. 13 : 21, " forerunners (of the grape) ; " Is. 28 : 4, " an early (fig)."¶

FORESAIL

ARTEMŌN (ἀρτέμων), from *artaō*, to fasten to, is rendered " mainsail " in Acts 27 : 40, A.V. ; R.V., " foresail." As to the particular kind of sail there mentioned, Sir William Ramsay, quoting from Juvenal con- cerning the entrance of a disabled ship into harbour by means of a prow-sail, indicates that the *artemōn* would be a sail set on the bow.¶

FORESEE, FORESEEN

1. PROORAŌ (προοράω), with the aorist form *proeidon* (used to supply tenses lacking in *prooraō*), to see before (*pro*, before, *horaō*, to see), is used with reference (*a*) to the past, of seeing a person before, Acts 21 : 29 ; (*b*) to the future, in the sense of foreseeing a person or thing, Acts 2 : 25, with reference to Christ and the Father, R.V., " beheld " (here the Middle Voice is used).¶

2. PROEIDON (προεῖδον), an aorist tense form without a present, to foresee, is used of David, as foreseeing Christ, in Acts 2 : 31, R.V., " fore- seeing " (A.V., " seeing before ") ; in Gal. 3 : 8, it is said of the Scripture, personified, personal activity being attributed to it by reason of its Divine source (cp. ver. 22). " What saith the Scripture ? " was a common formula among the Rabbis.¶ In the Sept., Gen. 37 : 18 ; Ps. 16 : 8 (*prooraō*) ; 139 : 3.¶

3. PROBLEPŌ (προβλέπω), from *pro*, before, and *blepō*, to see, per- ceive, is translated " having provided " in Heb. 11 : 40 (Middle Voice), marg., " foreseen," which is the lit. meaning of the verb, as with Eng. ' provide.'¶ In the Sept., Psa. 37 : 13.¶

FORESHEW

PROKATANGELLŌ (προκαταγγέλλω), to announce beforehand (*pro*, before, *katangellō*, to proclaim), is translated " foreshewed " in Acts 3 : 18, R.V. (A.V., " before had shewed ") ; in 7 : 52, A.V. and R.V., " shewed before."¶

FORESHIP

PRŌRA (πρῶρα) denotes the forward part of a ship, the prow, Acts 27 : 30 ; in ver. 41 (A.V., " forepart ") in contrast to *prumna*, the stern.¶

FORETELL

PROLEGŌ (προλέγω), with the aorist form *proeipon*, and a perfect form *proeirēka* (from *proereō*), signifies (1) to declare openly or plainly, or to say or tell beforehand (*pro*, before, *legō*, to say), translated in 2 Cor. 13 : 2 (in the first sentence), R.V., " I have said beforehand," A.V., " I told . . . before ; " in the next sentence, A.V., " I foretell," R.V., " I do say beforehand " (marg., " plainly ") ; not prophecy is here in view, but a warning given before and repeated (see under FOREWARN) ; (2) to speak before, of prophecy, as foretelling the future, Mark 13 : 23,

A.V., " have foretold," R.V., " have told . . . beforehand ; " Acts 1 : 16 (of the prophecy concerning Judas) ; Rom. 9 : 29 ; 2 Pet. 3 : 2 ; Jude 17 ; some inferior mss. have it in Heb. 10 : 15.   See FOREWARN, SPEAK, TELL.

Note : In Acts 3 : 24 some mss. have *prokatangellō* (see FORESHEW) ; the most authentic have *katangellō*, R.V., " told."

FOREWARN

PROLEGŌ (προλέγω), with verbal forms as mentioned above, is translated " I forewarn " and " I did forewarn," in the R.V. of Gal. 5 : 21, A.V., " I tell (you) before " and " I have told (you) in time past ; " here, however, as in 2 Cor. 13 : 2 and 1 Thess. 3 : 4 (see below), the R.V. marg., " plainly " is to be preferred to " beforehand " or " before " (see under FORETELL) ; the meaning in Gal. 5 : 21 is not so much that Paul prophesied the result of the practice of the evils mentioned, but that he had told them before of the consequence and was now repeating his warning, as leaving no possible room for doubt or misunderstanding ; in 1 Thess. 3 : 4, the subject told before was the affliction consequent upon the preaching of the Gospel ; in 1 Thess. 4 : 6, " we forewarned," the warning was as to the consequences of whatsoever violates chastity.

Note : In Luke 12 : 5 the verb *hupodeiknumi*, to shew, teach, make known, is translated " will warn " in the R.V. (A.V., " forewarn "). See EXAMPLE (B, No. 2), SHEW, WARN.

FORFEIT

ZĒMIOŌ (ζημιόω), in the Active Voice, signifies to damage ; in the Passive, to suffer loss, forfeit, Matt. 16 : 26 and Mark 8 : 36, of the " life," R.V. ; A.V., and R.V. marg., " soul ;" in each place the R.V. has " forfeit," for A.V., " lose ; " Luke 9 : 25, " his own self " (R.V., " forfeit," A.V., " be cast away ; " here the preceding word " lose " translates *apollumi*, to destroy). What is in view here is the act of forfeiting what is of the greatest value, not the casting away by Divine judgment, though that is involved, but losing or penalising one's own self, with spiritual and eternal loss.   The word is also used in 1 Cor. 3 : 15 ; 2 Cor. 7 : 9 ; Phil. 3 : 8. See CAST, LOSE, LOSS (suffer).¶

FORGET, FORGETFUL
A. Verbs.

1. LANTHANŌ (λανθάνω), to escape notice, is translated " they (wilfully) forget " in 2 Pet. 3 : 5, R.V., lit., ' this escapes them (i.e., their notice, wilfully on their part),' A.V., " they willingly are ignorant of ; " in ver. 8, R.V., " forget not," lit., ' let not this one thing escape you ' (your notice), A.V., " be not ignorant of." See HIDE, IGNORANT, UNAWARES.

2. EPILANTHANOMAI (ἐπιλανθάνομαι), to forget, or neglect (*epi*, upon, used intensively, and No. 1),is said (*a*) negatively of God, indicating

His remembrance of sparrows, Luke 12 : 6, and of the work and labour of love of His saints, Heb. 6 : 10 ; (b) of the disciples regarding taking bread, Matt. 16 : 5 ; Mark 8 : 14 ; (c) of Paul regarding " the things which are behind," Phil. 3 : 13 ; (d) of believers, as to shewing love to strangers, Heb. 13 : 2, R.V., and as to doing good and communicating, ver. 16 ; (d) of a person who, after looking at himself in a mirror, forgets what kind of person he is, Jas. 1 : 24.¶

3. EKLANTHANOMAI (ἐκλανθάνομαι), to forget utterly (ek, out, intensive), is used in the Middle Voice in Heb. 12 : 5, of forgetting an exhortation.¶

B. Nouns.

1. LĒTHĒ (λήθη), forgetfulness (from lēthō, to forget, an old form of lanthanō, see A, No. 1 ; cp. Eng. lethal, lethargy, and the mythical river Lethe, which was supposed to cause forgetfulness of the past to those who drank of it), is used with lambanō, to take, in 2 Pet. 1 : 9, " having forgotten," lit., ' having taken forgetfulness ' (cp. 2 Tim. 1 : 5, lit., ' having taken reminder '), a periphrastic expression for a single verb.¶

2. EPILĒSMONĒ (ἐπιλησμονή), forgetfulness (akin to A, No. 2), is used in Jas. 1 : 25, " a forgetful hearer," R.V., " a hearer that forgetteth," lit., ' a hearer of forgetfulness,' i.e., a hearer characterized by forgetfulness.¶

FORGIVE, FORGAVE, FORGIVENESS
A. Verbs.

1. APHIĒMI (ἀφίημι), primarily, to send forth, send away (apo, from, hiēmi, to send), denotes, besides its other meanings, to remit or forgive (a) debts, Matt. 6 : 12 ; 18 : 27, 32, these being completely cancelled ; (b) sins, e.g., Matt. 9 : 2, 5, 6 ; 12 : 31, 32 ; Acts 8 : 22 (" the thought of thine heart ") ; Rom. 4 : 7 ; Jas. 5 : 15 ; 1 John 1 : 9 ; 2 : 12. In this latter respect the verb, like its corresponding noun (below), firstly signifies the remission of the punishment due to sinful conduct, the deliverance of the sinner from the penalty Divinely, and therefore righteously, imposed ; secondly, it involves the complete removal of the cause of offence ; such remission is based upon the vicarious and pro-pitiatory sacrifice of Christ. In the O.T. atoning sacrifice and forgiveness are often associated, e.g., Lev. 4 : 20, 26. The verb is used in the N.T. with reference to trespasses (paraptōma), e.g., Matt. 6 : 14, 15 ; sins (hamartia), e.g., Luke 5 : 20 ; debts (see above) (opheilēma), Matt. 6 : 12 ; (opheilē), 18 : 32 ; (daneion), 18 : 27 ; the thought (dianoia) of the heart, Acts 8 : 22. Cp. kaluptō, to cover, 1 Pet. 4 : 8 ; Jas. 5 : 20 ; and epikaluptō, to cover over, Rom. 4 : 7, representing the Hebrew words for atonement.

Human forgiveness is to be strictly analogous to Divine forgiveness, e.g., Matt. 6 : 12. If certain conditions are fulfilled, there is no limitation to Christ's law of forgiveness, Matt. 18 : 21, 22. The conditions are repentance and confession, Matt. 18 : 15-17 ; Luke 17 : 3.

As to limits to the possibility of Divine forgiveness, see Matt. 12 : 32, 2nd part (see BLASPHEMY) and 1 John 5 : 16 (see DEATH).   See FORSAKE, LAY, *Note* (2) at end, LEAVE, LET, OMIT, PUT, No. 16, *Note*, REMIT, SEND, *Note* (1), SUFFER, YIELD.

2. CHARIZOMAI (χαρίζομαι), to bestow a favour unconditionally, is used of the act of forgiveness, whether Divine, Eph. 4 : 32 ; Col. 2 : 13 ; 3 : 13 ;   or human, Luke 7 : 42, 43 (debt) ; 2 Cor. 2 : 7, 10 ; 12 : 13 ; Eph. 4 : 32 (1st mention).   Paul uses this word frequently, but No. 1 only, in Rom. 4 : 7, in this sense of the word.   See DELIVER.

Note : Apoluō, to let loose from (*apo*, from, *luō*, to loose), to release, is translated " forgive," " ye shall be forgiven," Luke 6 : 37, A.V. (R.V., " release," " ye shall be released "), the reference being to setting a person free as a quasi-judicial act.   The verb does not mean to forgive. See DISMISS, RELEASE.

B. Noun.

APHESIS (ἄφεσις) denotes a dismissal, release (akin to A, No. 1) ; it is used of the remission of sins, and translated " forgiveness " in Mark 3 : 29 ; Eph. 1 : 7 ; Col. 1 : 14, and in the A.V. of Acts 5 : 31 ; 13 : 38 ; 26 : 18, in each of which the R.V. has " remission."   Eleven times it is followed by " of sins," and once by " of trespasses."   It is never used of the remission of sins in the Sept., but is especially connected with the year of Jubilee (Lev. 25 : 10, etc.).   Cp. the R.V. of Luke 4 : 18, " release " (A.V., " liberty ").   For the significance in connection with remission of sins and the propitiatory sacrifice of Christ, see A, No. 1.   See DELIVERANCE, LIBERTY, RELEASE, REMISSION.   Cp. the different word *paresis*, a passing over, a remission, of sins committed under the old Covenant, Rom. 3 : 25.   The R.V. should be used here.   This passing over, or by, was neither forgetting nor forgiving ; it was rather a suspension of the just penalty ; cp. Acts 17 : 30, " the times of ignorance God overlooked," R.V. ;   see also, e.g., Ps. 78 : 38.

FORM (Noun)

1. MORPHĒ (μορφή) denotes the special or characteristic form or feature of a person or thing ; it is used with particular significance in the N.T., only of Christ, in Phil. 2 : 6, 7, in the phrases " being in the form of God," and " taking the form of a servant."   An excellent definition of the word is that of Gifford :   " *morphē* is therefore properly the nature or essence, not in the abstract, but as actually subsisting in the individual, and retained as long as the individual itself exists. . . . Thus in the passage before us *morphē Theou* is the Divine nature actually and inseparably subsisting in the Person of Christ. . . . For the interpretation of ' the form of God ' it is sufficient to say that (1) it includes the whole nature and essence of Deity, and is inseparable from them, since they could have no actual existence without it ;   and (2) that it does not include in itself anything ' accidental ' or separable, such as particular

modes of manifestation, or conditions of glory and majesty, which may at one time be attached to the ' form,' at another separated from it. . . .

The true meaning of *morphē* in the expression ' form of God ' is confirmed by its recurrence in the corresponding phrase, ' form of a servant.' It is universally admitted that the two phrases are directly antithetical, and that ' form ' must therefore have the same sense in both."*

The definition above mentioned applies to its use in Mark 16 : 12, as to the particular ways in which the Lord manifested Himself.¶

Note : For the synonymous word *schēma*, see FASHION. For the verb *morphoō*, see FORMED, No. 1, below.

2. MORPHŌSIS (μόρφωσις), a form or outline, denotes, in the N.T., an image or impress, an outward semblance, Rom. 2 : 20, of knowledge of the truth ; 2 Tim. 3 : 5, of godliness. It is thus to be distinguished from *morphē* (No. 1) ; it is used in almost the same sense as *schēma*, fashion (which see), but is not so purely the outward form as *schēma* is.¶

3. TUPOS (τύπος), the representation or pattern of anything (for which see ENSAMPLE), is rendered " form " in Rom. 6 : 17, " that form (or mould) of teaching whereunto ye were delivered," R.V. The metaphor is that of a cast or frame into which molten material is poured so as to take its shape. The Gospel is the mould ; those who are obedient to its teachings become conformed to Christ, whom it presents. In Acts 23 : 25, it is used of a letter, R.V., " form " (A.V., " manner "), with reference to the nature of the contents.

4. EIDOS (εἶδος), lit., that which is seen (*eidon*, to see), an appearance or external form, is rendered " form " in the R.V. of Luke 3 : 22, of the Holy Spirit's appearance at the baptism of Christ ; in John 5 : 37, in the Lord's testimony concerning the Father ; in Luke 9 : 29 it is said of Christ Himself ; it is translated " sight " in 2 Cor. 5 : 7, the Christian being guided by what he knows to be true, though unseen ; in 1 Thess. 5 : 22 Christians are exhorted to abstain from " every form of evil," R.V. (the A.V., " appearance " is inadequate), i.e., from every kind of evil. See FASHION, SHAPE, SIGHT.¶

5. HUPOTUPŌSIS (ὑποτύπωσις), an outline, sketch (akin to *hupotupoō*, to delineate, *hupo*, under, and No. 3), is used metaphorically to denote a pattern, example, " form," in 2 Tim. 1 : 13, " of sound words " (R.V., " pattern ") ; in 1 Tim. 1 : 16, " pattern " and " ensample." See ENSAMPLE.¶

FORMED
A. Verbs.

1. MORPHOŌ (μορφόω), like the noun (A, No. 1), refers, not to the external and transient, but to the inward and real ; it is used in Gal. 4 : 19, expressing the necessity of a change in character and conduct to correspond

---

* From Gifford, " The Incarnation," pp. 16, 19, 39.

with inward spiritual condition, so that there may be moral conformity to Christ.¶

Cp. *metamorphoō*, to transform, transfigure, *summorphizō* and *suschematizō*, to conform to.

2. PLASSŌ (πλάσσω), to mould, to shape, was used of the artist who wrought in clay or wax (Eng., plastic, plasticity), and occurs in Rom. 9 : 20 ; 1 Tim. 2 : 13.¶

B. Noun.

PLASMA (πλάσμα) denotes anything moulded or shaped into a form (akin to A, No. 2), Rom. 9 : 20, " the thing formed."¶ Cp. the adjective *plastos*, made up, fabricated, feigned, 2 Pet. 2 : 3.¶

FORMER

1. PRŌTOS (πρῶτος), first, is translated " former " in Acts 1 : 1, of Luke's first treatise ; in Rev. 21 : 4, R.V., " first " (A.V., " former "). See BEFORE, FIRST.

2. PROTEROS (πρότερος), before, former, is translated " former " in Eph. 4 : 22 ; Heb. 10 : 32 ; 1 Pet. 1 : 14. See BEFORE.

FORNICATION, FORNICATOR
A. Nouns.

1. PORNEIA (πορνεία) is used (*a*) of illicit sexual intercourse, in John 8 : 41 ; Acts 15 : 20, 29 ; 21 : 25 ; 1 Cor. 5 : 1 ; 6 : 13, 18 ; 2 Cor. 12 : 21 ; Gal. 5 : 19 ; Eph. 5 : 3 ; Col. 3 : 5 ; 1 Thess. 4 : 3 ; Rev. 2 : 21 ; 9 : 21 ; in the plural in 1 Cor. 7 : 2 ; in Matt. 5 : 32 and 19 : 9 it stands for, or includes, adultery ; it is distinguished from it in 15 : 19 and Mark 7 : 21 ; (*b*) metaphorically, of the association of pagan idolatry with doctrines of, and professed adherence to, the Christian faith, Rev. 14 : 8 ; 17 : 2, 4 ; 18 : 3 ; 19 : 2 ; some suggest this as the sense in 2 : 21.¶

2. PORNOS (πόρνος) denotes a man who indulges in fornication, a fornicator, 1 Cor. 5 : 9, 10, 11 ; 6 : 9 ; Eph. 5 : 5, R.V. ; 1 Tim. 1 : 10, R.V. ; Heb. 12 : 16 ; 13 : 4, R.V. ; Rev. 21 : 8 and 22 : 15, R.V. (A.V., " whoremonger ").¶

B. Verbs.

1. PORNEUŌ (πορνεύω), to commit fornication, is used (*a*) literally, Mark 10 : 19 ; 1 Cor. 6 : 18 ; 10 : 8 ; Rev. 2 : 14, 20, see (*a*) and (*b*) above ; (*b*) metaphorically, Rev. 17 : 2 ; 18 : 3, 9.¶

2. EKPORNEUŌ (ἐκπορνεύω), a strengthened form of No. 1, (*ek*, used intensively), to give oneself up to fornication, implying excessive indulgence, Jude 7.¶

FORSAKE
A. Verbs.

1. KATALEIPŌ (καταλείπω), a strengthened form of *leipō*, to leave, signifies (*a*) to leave, to leave behind, e.g., Matt. 4 : 13 ; (*b*) to leave

remaining, reserve, e.g., Luke 10 : 40 ; (c) to forsake, in the sense of abandoning, translated to forsake in the R.V. of Luke 5 : 28 and Acts 6 : 2 ; in Heb. 11 : 27 and 2 Pet. 2 : 15, A.V. and R.V. In this sense it is translated to leave, in Mark 10 : 7 ; 14 : 52 ; Luke 15 : 4 ; Eph. 5 : 31. See LEAVE, RESERVE.

2. ENKATALEIPŌ (ἐγκαταλείπω), from en, in, and No. 1, denotes (a) to leave behind, among, leave surviving, Rom. 9 : 29 ; (b) to forsake, abandon, leave in straits, or helpless, said by, or of, Christ, Matt. 27 : 46 ; Mark 15 : 34 ; Acts 2 : 27, 31 (No. 1 in some mss.) ; of men, 2 Cor. 4 : 9 ; 2 Tim. 4 : 10, 16 ; by God, Heb. 13 : 5 ; of things, by Christians (negatively), Heb. 10 : 25. See LEAVE.¶

3. APHIĒMI (ἀφίημι) sometimes has the significance of forsaking, Mark 1 : 18 ; 14 : 50 (R.V., " left ") ; so Luke 5 : 11. See FORGIVE.

4. APOTASSŌ (ἀποτάσσω), primarily, to set apart (apo, off, from, tassō, to arrange), is used in the Middle Voice, meaning (a) to take leave of, e.g., Mark 6 : 46, (b) to renounce, forsake, Luke 14 : 33, A.V., " forsaketh," R.V., " renounceth " (" all that he hath "). See BID FAREWELL, RENOUNCE, SEND, Note (2) at end, TAKE, Note (14).

B. Noun.

APOSTASIA (ἀποστασία), an apostasy, defection, revolt, always in N.T. of religious defection, is translated " to forsake " in Acts 21 : 21, lit., ' (thou teachest) apostasy (from Moses) ; ' in 2 Thess. 2 : 3, " falling away." See FALL.¶

FORSOMUCH : see † p. 9

FORSWEAR

EPIORKEŌ (ἐπιορκέω) signifies to swear falsely, to undo one's swearing, forswear oneself (epi, against, orkos, an oath), Matt. 5 : 33.¶ Cp. epiorkos, a perjured person, a perjurer, 1 Tim. 1 : 10, " false swearers."¶

FORTH

EXŌ (ἔξω), outside, without (from, ek, out of, from), frequently signifies " forth," especially after verbs of motion, e.g., John 11 : 43 ; 19 : 4, 13. See OUTWARD, STRANGE, WITHOUT.

Notes : (1) For the word " forth " in combination with various verbs, see, e.g., BREAK, BRING, COME, PUT. (2) In Matt. 26 : 16, the R.V. omits " forth," as the phrase apo tote, ' from then,' simply means " from that time ; " in the similar phrase " from that day forth," Matt. 22 : 46 ; John 11 : 53, there is no word in the original representing " forth." (3) In John 2 : 11 the R.V. rightly omits " forth."

FORTHWITH

1. EXAUTĒS (ἐξαυτῆς), at once (from, ek, out of, and autēs, the genitive case of autos, self or very, agreeing with " hour " understood,

i.e., ' from that very hour '), is translated " forthwith " in the R.V. in Mark 6 : 25 (A.V., " by and by ") ; Acts 10 : 33 (A.V., " immediately ") ; 11 : 11 (ditto) ; 21 : 32 (ditto) ; 23 : 30 (A.V., " straightway ") ; Phil. 2 : 23 (A.V., " presently "). The word is frequent in the period of the *koinē* Greek (see Preface). See IMMEDIATELY, PRESENTLY, STRAIGHT-WAY.¶

2. EUTHEŌS (εὐθέως), at once, straightway (from the adjective, *euthus*, straight), is translated " forthwith," in the A.V. of Matt. 13 : 5 ; 26 : 49 ; (it occurs in some mss. in Mark 5 : 13 ; the R.V. omits it) ; Acts 12 : 10 ; 21 : 30 (R.V., " straightway," in each place). See IM-MEDIATELY, SHORTLY, STRAIGHTWAY.

3. EUTHUS (εὐθύς), an alternative adverb to No. 2, is translated " forthwith " in the A.V. of Mark 1 : 29 ; 1 : 43 (in the best mss.), and John 19 : 34 (R.V., " straightway "). See ANON, IMMEDIATELY, STRAIGHT-WAY.¶

Note : Parachrēma, a synonymous word denoting instantly, on the spot, is not translated " forthwith " in A.V. or R.V. See IMMEDIATELY.

FORTY

TESSARAKONTA (τεσσαράκοντα) is used in circumstances in Scripture which indicate the number as suggesting probation, separation or judg-ment, e.g., Matt. 4 : 2 ; Acts 1 : 3 ; Heb. 3 : 9, 17.

Note : Tessarakontaetēs, forty years (*etos*, a year), is found in Acts 7 : 23 ; 13 : 18.¶

FORWARD (be), FORWARDNESS

Notes : (1) The verb *thelō*, to will, wish, is translated " to be forward," in the A.V. of 2 Cor. 8 : 10, which the R.V. corrects to " to will." (2) In Gal. 2 : 10, *spoudazō*, to be zealous, is so rendered in the R.V. (A.V., " I was forward "). (3) In 2 Cor. 8 : 17, the corresponding adjective *spoudaios*, earnest, is so rendered in the R.V. (A.V., " forward "). So in ver. 8, the noun *spoudē*, earnestness, is thus rendered in the R.V. (A.V., " for-wardness "). (4) In 9 : 2, R.V., the noun *prothumia*, " readiness " (*pro*, before, *thumos*, impulse), is so rendered (A.V., " forwardness of mind "). (5) For the combination of this word with verbs see GO, PUT, SET, STRETCH.

FOSTER-BROTHER

SUNTROPHOS (σύντροφος) primarily denotes one nourished or brought up with another (*sun*, with, *trephō*, to rear) ; it is rendered " foster-brother " in Acts 13 : 1, R.V. It has, however, been found in Hellenistic usage as a court term, signifying an intimate friend of a king (Deissmann), and this would seem to be the meaning regarding Manaen and Herod the Tetrarch.

FOUL

AKATHARTOS (ἀκάθαρτος) denotes unclean, impure (*a*, negative, and *kathairō*, to purify), (*a*) ceremonially, e.g., Acts 10 : 14, 28 ; (*b*) morally, always, in the Gospels, of unclean spirits ; it is translated " foul " in the A.V. of Mark 9 : 25 and Rev. 18 : 2, but always " unclean " in the R.V. Since the word primarily had a ceremonial significance, the moral significance is less prominent as applied to a spirit, than when *poneros*, wicked, is so applied. Cp. *akatharsia*, uncleanness. See UNCLEAN.

Note : In Rev. 17 : 4 the best mss. have this word in the plural, R.V., " the unclean things " (*akathartēs*, filthiness, in some mss.).

FOUNDATION (to lay), FOUNDED
A. Nouns.

1. THEMELIOS, or THEMELION (θεμέλιος) is properly an adjective denoting belonging to a foundation (connected with *tithēmi*, to place). It is used (1) as a noun, with *lithos*, a stone, understood, in Luke 6 : 48, 49 ; 14 : 29 ; Heb. 11 : 10 ; Rev. 21 : 14, 19 ; (2) as a neuter noun in Acts 16 : 26, and metaphorically, (*a*) of the ministry of the gospel and the doctrines of the faith, Rom. 15 : 20 ; 1 Cor. 3 : 10, 11, 12 ; Eph. 2 : 20, where the " of " is not subjective (i.e., consisting of the apostles and prophets), but objective, (i.e., laid by the apostles, etc.) ; so in 2 Tim. 2 : 19, where " the foundation of God " is ' the foundation laid by God,'— not the Church (which is not a foundation), but Christ Himself, upon whom the saints are built ; Heb. 6 : 1 ; (*b*) of good works, 1 Tim. 6 : 19.¶

2. KATABOLĒ (καταβολή), lit., a casting down, is used (*a*) of conceiving seed, Heb. 11 : 11 ; (*b*) of a foundation, as that which is laid down, or in the sense of founding ; metaphorically, of the foundation of the world ; in this respect two phrases are used, (1) " from the foundation of the world," Matt. 25 : 34 (in the most authentic mss. in 13 : 35 there is no phrase representing " of the world ") ; Luke 11 : 50 ; Heb. 4 : 3 ; 9 : 26 ; Rev. 13 : 8 ; 17 : 8 ; (2) " before the foundation of the world," John 17 : 24 ; Eph. 1 : 4 ; 1 Pet. 1 : 20. The latter phrase looks back to the past eternity.¶

B. Verb.

THEMELIOŌ (θεμελιόω), to lay a foundation, to found (akin to A, No. 1), is used (*a*) literally, Matt. 7 : 25 ; Luke 6 : 48 ; Heb. 1 : 10 ; (*b*) metaphorically, Eph. 3 : 17, " grounded (in love) ; " Col. 1 : 23 (ditto, " in the faith ") ; 1 Pet. 5 : 10, A.V., " settle." See GROUND, SETTLE.¶

FOUNTAIN

PĒGĒ (πηγή), a spring or fountain, is used of (*a*) an artificial well, fed by a spring, John 4 : 6 ; (*b*) metaphorically (in contrast to such a well), the indwelling Spirit of God, 4 : 14 ; (*c*) springs, metaphorically in 2 Pet. 2 : 17, R.V., for A.V., " wells ; " (*d*) natural fountains or springs, Jas. 3 : 11, 12 ; Rev. 8 : 10 ; 14 : 7 ; 16 : 4 ; (*e*) metaphorically, eternal life

and the future blessings accruing from it, Rev. 7 : 17 ; 21 : 6 ; (*f*) a
flow of blood, Mark 5 : 29.¶

FOUR (-TH), FOURTEEN (-TH), FOUR HUNDRED

TESSARES (τέσσαρες), four, is not found in the N.T. outside the
Gospels, the Acts and Apocalypse ; in the last it is very frequent.
Tetartos, fourth, is found in Matt. 14 : 25 ; Mark 6 : 48 and seven times
in the Apocalypse ; also in Acts 10 : 30, " four days ago," lit., ' from
a fourth day.' *Dekatessares*, fourteen (lit., ten-four), is found in Matt.
1 : 17 ; 2 Cor. 12 : 2 ; Gal. 2 : 1 ;¶ *tessareskaidekatos*, fourteenth (lit.,
four-and-tenth), Acts 27 : 27, 33 ;¶ *tetrakosia*, four hundred, Acts 5 : 36 ;
7 : 6 ; 13 : 20 ; Gal. 3 : 17.¶ In Acts 7 : 6 the 400 years refers to Abraham's
descendants and to the sojourning and the bondage. This agrees with
Gen. 15 : 13. In Ex. 12 : 40 the 430 years dates from the call of Abraham
himself. Likewise the giving of the Law was 430 years from the promise
in Gen. 12 : 3, which agrees with Gal. 3 : 17. In John 11 : 39 *tetartaios*,
lit., ' a fourth day (one),' is rendered " four days."

FOURFOLD

TETRAPLOOS (τετραπλόος), an adjective, is found in Luke 19 : 8.¶

FOURFOOTED

TETRAPOUS (τετράπους), from *tetra*, four (used in compound words),
and *pous*, a foot, is used of beasts, Acts 10 : 12 ; 11 : 6 ; Rom. 1 : 23.¶

FOURSCORE

OGDOĒKONTA (ὀγδοήκοντα), from *ogdoos*, eighth, is found in Luke
2 : 37 ; 16 : 7.¶

FOURSQUARE

TETRAGŌNOS (τετράγωνος), four-cornered (from *tetra*, see above,
and *gōnia*, a corner, or angle), is found in Rev. 21 : 16.¶

For FOWL see BIRD

FOX

ALŌPĒX (ἀλώπηξ) is found in Matt. 8 : 20 ; Luke 9 : 58 ; metaphorically, of Herod, in Luke 13 : 32.¶

For FRAGMENTS see PIECE, No. 4

FRAME (Verb)

1. KATARTIZŌ (καταρτίζω), to fit, to render complete, is translated
" have been framed " in Heb. 11 : 3, of the worlds or ages. See FIT.

2. SUNARMOLOGEŌ (συναρμολογέω), to fit or frame together (*sun*,
with, *harmos*, a joint, *legō*, to choose), is used metaphorically of the Church

as a spiritual temple, the parts being " fitly framed together," Eph. 2 : 21 ; as a body, 4 : 16, R.V., " fitly framed," (for A.V., " fitly joined ").¶

FRANKINCENSE

LIBANOS (λίβανος), from a Semitic verb signifying to be white, is a vegetable resin, bitter and glittering, obtained by incisions in the bark of the *arbor thuris*, the incense tree, and especially imported through Arabia ; it was used for fumigation at sacrifices, Ex. 30 : 7 etc., or for perfume, S. of Sol., 3 : 6. The Indian variety is called *looban*. It was among the offerings brought by the wise men, Matt. 2 : 11. In Rev. 18 : 13 it is listed among the commodities of Babylon. The " incense " of Rev. 8 : 3 should be " frankincense." Cp. INCENSE.¶

FRANKLY

Note : In Luke 7 : 42, the verb *charizomai*, to forgive (as a matter of grace), is rendered " frankly forgave," so as to bring out the force of the grace in the action. Older versions had " forgave," and to this the R.V. returns.

FRAUD

APHUSTEREŌ (ἀφυστερέω), to keep back, deprive (*apo*, from, *hustereō*, to be lacking), is used in Jas. 5 : 4, " is kept back by fraud " (some mss. have *apostereō*, to defraud). The word is found in a papyrus writing of A.D. 42, of a bath insufficiently warmed (Moulton and Milligan, Vocab.). The Law required the prompt payment of the labourer, Deut. 24 : 15.¶

FREE, FREEDOM, FREELY, FREEMAN, FREEDMAN, FREEWOMAN

A. Adjective.

ELEÚTHEROS (ἐλεύθερος), primarily of freedom to go wherever one likes, is used (*a*) of freedom from restraint and obligation in general, Matt. 17 : 26 ; Rom. 7 : 3 ; 1 Cor. 7 : 39, R.V., " free," of the second marriage of a woman ; 9 : 1, 19 ; 1 Pet. 2 : 16 ; from the Law, Gal. 4 : 26 ; from sin, John 8 : 36 ; with regard to righteousness, Rom. 6 : 20 (i.e., righteousness laid no sort of bond upon them, they had no relation to it) ; (*b*) in a civil sense, free from bondage or slavery, John 8 : 33 ; 1 Cor. 7 : 21, 22, 2nd part (for ver. 22, 1st part, see C, No. 2) ; 12 : 13 ; Gal. 3 : 28 ; Eph. 6 : 8 ; Rev. 13 : 16 ; 19 : 18 ; as a noun, " freeman," Col. 3 : 11, R.V. ; Rev. 6 : 15 ; " freewoman," Gal. 4 : 22, 23, 30, and ver. 31. R.V.¶

Notes : (1) In Matt. 15 : 6 and Mark 7 : 11, the words " he shall be free," A.V., have nothing to represent them in the Greek. (2) In Heb. 13 : 5, R.V., " be ye free from the love of money," is an abbreviated rendering of the adjective *aphilarguros* (not loving money) with the noun *tropos*, turn (of mind) ; hence the marg., " let your turn of mind be free etc.," for A.V., " let your conversation be without covetousness."

B. Verb.

ELEUTHEROŌ (ἐλευθερόω), to make free (akin to A.), is used of deliverance from (a) sin, John 8 : 32, 36 ; Rom. 6 : 18, 22 ; (b) the Law, Rom. 8 : 2 ; Gal. 5 : 1 (see, however under C.) ; (c) the bondage of corruption, Rom. 8 : 21. See DELIVER.¶

Note : In Rom. 6 : 7, the verb *dikaioō*, translated " is freed," signifies to justify, as in the R.V., " is justified," i.e., in the legal sense ; death annuls all obligations. The death penalty which Christ endured holds good for the believer, through his identification with Christ in His death ; having been crucified as to his unregenerate nature, and justified from sin, he walks in newness of life in Christ.

C. Nouns.

1. ELEUTHERIA (ἐλευθερία), liberty (akin to A. and B.), is rendered " freedom " in Gal. 5 : 1, " with freedom did Christ set us free." The combination of the noun with the verb stresses the completeness of the act, the aorist (or point) tense indicating both its momentary and comprehensive character ; it was done once for all. The R.V. margin " for freedom " gives perhaps the preferable meaning, i.e., ' not to bring us into another form of bondage did Christ liberate us from that in which we were born, but in order to make us free from bondage.'

The word is twice rendered " freedom " in the R.V. of Gal. 5 : 13 (A.V., " liberty "). The phraseology is that of manumission from slavery, which among the Greeks was effected by a legal fiction, according to which the manumitted slave was purchased by a god ; as the slave could not provide the money, the master paid it into the temple Treasury in the presence of the slave, a document being drawn up containing the words " for freedom." No one could enslave him again, as he was the property of the god. Hence the word *apeleutheros*, No. 2. The word is also translated " freedom " in 1 Pet. 2 : 16, R.V. In 2 Cor. 3 : 17 the word denotes freedom of access to the presence of God. See LIBERTY.

2. APELEUTHEROS (ἀπελεύθερος), a freed man (*apo*, from, and A.), is used in 1 Cor. 7 : 22, " the Lord's freedman." See the illustration above under No. 1. Here the fuller word brings out the spiritual emancipation in contrast to the natural freedman.

Note : (1) In Acts 22 : 28, the word *politeia*, rendered " freedom " (A.V.), denotes citizenship, as in the R.V. (see CITIZENSHIP) ; in the next sentence the Greek is, lit., ' But I was even born ; ' the necessary word to be supplied is " Roman," from the previous verse ; hence the R.V., " But I am a Roman born." (2) For " free gift " (*charisma*), Rom. 5 : 15, 16 ; 6 : 23, see GIFT.

D. Adverb.

DŌREAN (δωρεάν), from *dōrea*, a gift, is used as an adverb in the sense " freely," in Matt. 10 : 8 ; Rom. 3 : 24 ; 2 Cor. 11 : 7 (R.V., " for nought ") ; Rev. 21 : 6 ; 22 : 17. Here the prominent thought is the grace of the Giver. See CAUSE.

Notes : (1) In Acts 26 : 26 *parrhēsiazomai*, to be bold in speech, is translated, to speak freely. (2) In Acts 2 : 29 the noun *parrhēsia* with the preposition *meta*, with, is rendered " freely," lit., ' with free-spokenness.' (3) For *charizomai*, to give freely, Rom. 8 : 32 ; 1 Cor. 2 : 12, see GIVE. (4) In 2 Thess. 3 : 1, A.V., the verb *trechō*, to run, is rendered " may have free course ; " this the R.V. corrects to " may run." (5) For *charitoō*, to bestow freely, Eph. 1 : 6, see ACCEPT, *Note*. (6) For " have drunk freely," John 2 : 10, R.V., see DRINK, B, No. 2.

FREIGHT

EKBOLĒ (ἐκβολή), lit., a throwing out (from *ekballō*, to throw out), denotes a jettison, a throwing out of cargo, Acts 27 : 18, lit., ' they made a throwing out,' R.V., " they began to throw the freight overboard," A.V., " they lightened the ship."¶   In the Sept., Ex. 11 : 1 ; Jonah 1 : 5.¶

For FREQUENT, 2 Cor. 11 : 23, see ABUNDANT, D

FRESH

NEOS (νέος), new (in respect of time, as distinct from *kainos*, new, in respect of quality), is translated " fresh " in the R.V. of Matt. 9 : 17 ; Mark 2 : 22 ; Luke 5 : 38, with reference to wineskins. See NEW.

Note : *Glukus*, sweet, is used in Jas. 3 : 11, 12 (in this verse, A.V., " fresh," R.V., " sweet," as in both elsewhere) ; Rev. 10 : 9, 10. See SWEET.¶

FRIEND (make one's)
A. Nouns.

1. PHILOS (φίλος), primarily an adjective, denoting loved, dear, or friendly, became used as a noun, (*a*) masculine, Matt. 11 : 19 ; fourteen times in Luke (once feminine, 15 : 9) ; six in John ; three in Acts ; two in James, 2 : 23, " the friend of God ; " 4 : 4, " a friend of the world ; " 3 John 14 (twice) ; (*b*) feminine, Luke 15 : 9, " her friends."

2. HETAIROS (ἑταῖρος), a comrade, companion, partner, is used as a term of kindly address in Matt. 20 : 13 ; 22 : 12 ; 26 : 50. This, as expressing comradeship, is to be distinguished from No. 1, which is a term of endearment. Some mss. have the word in Matt. 11 : 16 ; the best have *heterois*, others, A.V. and R.V., " fellows." See FELLOW.

Notes : (1) The phrase *hoi para autou*, in Mark 3 : 21, " his friends," lit. means ' the (ones) beside Him,' i.e., those belonging to him. (2) In Mark 5 : 19, " thy friends " represents the phrase *hoi soi*, lit., ' the (ones) to thee,' i.e., ' thine own.'

B. Verb.

PEITHŌ (πείθω), to persuade, influence, is rendered " having made

. . . their friend " in Acts 12 : 20, of the folks of Tyre and Sidon in winning the good will of Blastus, Herod's chamberlain, possibly with bribes. See ASSURE, B, No. 3.

FRIENDSHIP

PHILIA (φιλία), akin to *philos*, a friend (see above), is rendered in Jas. 4 : 4, " the friendship (of the world)." It involves " the idea of loving as well as being loved " (Mayor) ; cp. the verb in John 15 : 19.¶

FRO and FROM ; see † p. 9.

FROG

BATRACHOS (βάτραχος) is mentioned in Rev. 16 : 13. Quacks were represented as frogs and were associated metaphorically with serpents.¶

For FROWARD see CROOKED

FRUIT (bear), FRUITFUL, UNFRUITFUL
A. Nouns.

1. KARPOS (καρπός), fruit, is used (I) of the fruit of trees, fields, the earth, that which is produced by the inherent energy of a living organism, e.g., Matt. 7 : 17 ; Jas. 5 : 7, 18 ; plural, e.g., in Luke 12 : 17 [for the next verse, see Note (1) below] and 2 Tim. 2 : 6 ; of the human body, Luke 1 : 42 ; Acts 2 : 30 ; (II) metaphorically, (a) of works or deeds, fruit being the visible expression of power working inwardly and invisibly, the character of the fruit being evidence of the character of the power producing it, Matt. 7 : 16. As the visible expressions of hidden lusts are the works of the flesh, so the invisible power of the Holy Spirit in those who are brought into living union with Christ (John 15 : 2-8, 16) produces " the fruit of the Spirit," Gal. 5 : 22, the singular form suggesting the unity of the character of the Lord as reproduced in them, namely, " love, joy, peace, longsuffering, kindness, goodness, faithfulness, meekness, temperance," all in contrast with the confused and often mutually antagonistic " works of the flesh." So in Phil. 1 : 11, marg., " fruit of righteousness." In Heb. 12 : 11, the fruit of righteousness is described as " peaceable fruit," the outward effect of Divine chastening ; " the fruit of righteousness is sown in peace," Jas. 3 : 18, i.e., the seed contains the fruit ; those who make peace, produce a harvest of righteousness ; in Eph. 5 : 9, " the fruit of the light " (R.V., and see context) is seen in " goodness and righteousness and truth," as the expression of the union of the Christian with God (Father, Son and Holy Spirit) ; for God is good, Mark 10 : 18, the Son is " the righteous One," Acts 7 : 52, the Spirit is " the Spirit of truth," John 16 : 13 ; (b) of advantage, profit, consisting

(1) of converts as the result of evangelistic ministry, John 4 : 36 ; Rom. 1 : 13 ; Phil. 1 : 22 ; (2) of sanctification, through deliverance from a life of sin and through service to God, Rom. 6 : 22, in contrast to (3) the absence of anything regarded as advantageous as the result of former sins, ver. 21 ; (4) of the reward for ministration to servants of God, Phil. 4 : 17 ; (5) of the effect of making confession to God's Name by the sacrifice of praise, Heb. 13 : 15.

2. GENĒMA (γένημα), from *ginomai*, to come into being, denotes fruit (a) as the produce of the earth, e.g., the vine ; in the following the best mss. have this noun, Matt. 26 : 29 ; Mark 14 : 25 ; Luke 22 : 18 ; [12 : 18 in some mss. ; see Note (1)] ; (b) metaphorically, as " the fruits of . . . righteousness " (i.e., of material ministrations to the needy), 2 Cor. 9 : 10.¶

Notes : (1) In Luke 12 : 18 some mss. have *gennēmata*, a mistake for *genēmata* ; the best have *sitos*, corn. (2) *Genēma* is to be distinguished from *gennēma*, offspring (from *gennaō*, to beget), Matt. 3 : 7 ; 12 : 34 ; 23 : 33 ; Luke 3 : 7.¶

3. OPŌRA (ὀπώρα) primarily denotes late summer or early autumn, i.e., late July, all August and early September. Since that is the time of fruit-bearing, the word was used, by metonymy, for the fruits themselves, Rev. 18 : 14.¶

Note : Cp. *phthinopōrinos*, autumnal, in Jude 12, " autumn trees," bearing no fruit when fruit should be expected.¶

B. Adjectives.

1. KARPOPHOROS (καρποφόρος) denotes fruitful (A, No. 1, and *pherō*, to bear), Acts 14 : 17.¶ Cp. C. below.

2. AKARPOS (ἄκαρπος), unfruitful (a, negative, and A, No. 1), is used figuratively (a) of " the word of the Kingdom," rendered unfruitful in the case of those influenced by the cares of the world and the deceitfulness of riches, Matt. 13 : 22 ; Mark 4 : 19 ; (b) of the understanding of one praying with a " tongue," which effected no profit to the church without an interpretation of it, 1 Cor. 14 : 14 ; (c) of the works of darkness, Eph. 5 : 11 ; (d) of believers who fail " to maintain good works," indicating the earning of one's living so as to do good works to others, Tit. 3 : 14 ; of the effects of failing to supply in one's faith the qualities of virtue, knowledge, temperance, patience, godliness, love of the brethren, and love, 2 Pet. 1 : 8. In Jude 12 it is rendered " without fruit," of ungodly men, who oppose the Gospel while pretending to uphold it, depicted as " autumn trees " (see Note under A, No. 3).¶ In the Sept., Jer. 2 : 6.¶

C. Verb.

KARPOPHOREŌ (καρποφορέω), to bear or bring forth fruit (see B, No. 1), is used (a) in the natural sense, of the fruit of the earth, Mark 4 : 28 ; (b) metaphorically, of conduct, or that which takes effect in conduct, Matt. 13 : 23 ; Mark 4 : 20 ; Luke 8 : 15 ; Rom. 7 : 4, 5 (the latter, of evil fruit, borne " unto death," of activities resulting from a state of alienation from God) ; Col. 1 : 6, in the Middle Voice ; Col. 1: 10.¶

Note : For " bring forth fruit to perfection," Luke 8 : 14, see PER-
FECTION, B.

For FRUSTRATE, Gal. 2 : 21, see VOID

FULFIL, FULFILLING, FULFILMENT
A. Verbs.

1. PLĒROŌ (πληρόω) signifies (1) to fill (see FILL) ; (2) to fulfil,
complete, (*a*) of time, e.g., Mark 1 : 15 ; Luke 21 : 24 ; John 7 : 8 (A.V.,
" full come ") ; Acts 7 : 23, R.V., " he was well-nigh forty years old "
(A.V., " was full " etc.), lit., ' the time of forty years was fulfilled to him ; '
ver. 30, A.V., " were expired ; " 9 : 23 ; 24 : 27 (A.V.," after two years ; "
R.V., " when two years were fulfilled ") ; (*b*) of number, Rev. 6 : 11 ;
(*c*) of good pleasure, 2 Thess. 1 : 11 ; (*d*) of joy, Phil. 2 : 2 ; in the Passive
Voice, ' to be fulfilled,' John 3 : 29 and 17 : 13 ; in the following the verb
is rendered " fulfilled " in the R.V., for the A.V., " full," John 15 : 11 ;
16 : 24 ; 1 John 1 : 4 ; 2 John 12 ; (*e*) of obedience, 2 Cor. 10 : 6 ; (*f*) of
works, Rev. 3 : 2 ; (*g*) of the future Passover, Luke 22 : 16 ; (*h*) of
sayings, prophecies, etc., e.g., Matt. 1 : 22 (twelve times in Matt., two in
Mark, four in Luke, eight in John, two in Acts) ; Jas. 2 : 23 ; in Col.
1 : 25 the word signifies to preach fully, to complete the ministry of the
Gospel appointed. See FILL.

2. ANAPLĒROŌ (ἀναπληρόω), to fill up, fill completely (*ana*, up,
up to, and No. 1), is used (*a*) of Isaiah's prophecy of Israel's rejection of
God, fulfilled in the rejection of His Son, Matt. 13 : 14 ; (*b*) of the status of a
person in a church, R.V., " filleth the place," for A.V., " occupieth the
room," 1 Cor. 14 : 16 ; (*c*) of an adequate supply of service, 1 Cor. 16 : 17,
" supplied ; " Phil. 2 : 30, " to supply ; " (*d*) of sins, 1 Thess. 2 : 16 ;
(*e*) of the law of Christ, Gal. 6 : 2. See FILL, OCCUPY, SUPPLY.¶

3. TELEŌ (τελέω), to end (akin to *telos*, an end), signifies, among its
various meanings, to give effect to, and is translated " fulfil," of the Law,
intentionally, Jas. 2 : 8, or unconsciously, Rom. 2 : 27 ; of the prophetic
Scriptures concerning the Death of Christ, Acts 13 : 29 ; prohibitively,
of the lust of the flesh, Gal. 5 : 16. See ACCOMPLISH, FINISH.

Notes : (1) In regard to this word in Rev. 15 : 1 and 8, the R.V.,
" finished," corrects the A.V., " filled up," and " fulfilled," as the judgments there indicated finish the whole series of those consisting of the
wrath of God ; so in 20 : 3, of the thousand years of the Millennium (cp.
vv. 5, 7). (2) In 17 : 17, the R.V. has " should be accomplished," for
A.V., " shall be fulfilled."· (3) In Luke 22 : 37 the A.V. has " be accomplished " (R.V., " be fulfilled ").

4. SUNTELEŌ (συντελέω), to complete, is translated " fulfilled " in
the A.V. of Mark 13 : 4 (R.V., " accomplished "). See COMPLETE.

5. TELEIOŌ (τελειόω), to bring to an end, fulfil, is rendered to fulfil, of days. Luke 2 : 43 : of the Scripture, John 19 : 28 See FINISH.

6. PLĒROPHOREŌ (πληροφορέω), to bring in full measure, from *plēroō* (see No. 1), and *phoreō*, to bring ; hence, to fulfil, of circumstances relating to Christ, Luke 1 : 1, R.V., " have been fulfilled " (A.V. " are most surely believed ") ; of evangelical ministry, 2 Tim. 4 : 5, " fulfil " (A.V., " make full proof ") ; so in ver. 17, R.V., " fully proclaimed " (A.V., " fully known "). See ASSURE, PERSUADE.

7. EKPLĒROŌ (ἐκπληρόω), a strengthened form of No. 1, occurs in Acts 13 : 33.¶

Notes : (1) *Poieō*, to do, is so rendered in the R.V., for A.V. " fulfil," in Acts 13 : 22 ; Eph. 2 : 3 ; Rev. 17 : 17 [for the end of this verse see Note (2) under *teleō*, above]. (2) *Ginomai*, to become, to take place, is rendered " fulfilled " in the A.V. of Matt. 5 : 18 ; 24 : 34 ; Luke 21 : 32, R.V., " accomplished," in each place.

B. Nouns.

1. PLĒRŌMA (πλήρωμα) stands for the result of the action expressed in *pleroō*, to fill. It is used to signify (*a*) that which has been completed, the complement, fulness, e.g., John 1 : 16 ; Eph. 1 : 23 ; some suggest that the " fulness " here points to the Body as the filled receptacle of the power of Christ (words terminating in —*ma* are frequently concrete in character ; cp. *dikaiōma* in Rom. 5 : 18, act of righteousness) ; in Mark 8 : 20 the rendering " basketfuls " (R.V.) represents the plural of this word, lit., ' the fulnesses of (how many baskets) ; ' (*b*) that which fills up, Matt. 9 : 16 ; Mark 2 : 21 (see FILL) ; (*c*) a filling up, fulfilment, Rom. 13 : 10, of the fulfilling of the Law. See FULNESS (below).

2. TELEIŌSIS (τελείωσις), a fulfilment, is so rendered in Luke 1 : 45, R.V. (A.V., " performance "). See PERFECTION.

FULL
A. Adjectives.

1. PLĒRĒS (πλήρης) denotes full, (*a*) in the sense of being filled, materially, Matt. 14 : 20 ; 15 : 37 ; Mark 8 : 19 (said of baskets full of bread crumbs) ; of leprosy, Luke 5 : 12 ; spiritually, of the Holy Spirit, Luke 4 : 1 ; Acts 6 : 3 ; 7 : 55 ; 11 : 24 ; grace and truth, John 1 : 14 ; faith, Acts 6 : 5 ; grace and power, 6 : 8 ; of the effects of spiritual life and qualities, seen in good works, Acts 9 : 36 ; in an evil sense, of guile and villany, Acts 13 : 10 ; wrath, 19 : 28 ; (*b*) in the sense of being complete, " full corn in the ear," Mark 4 : 28 ; of a reward hereafter, 2 John 8.¶ .

2. MESTOS (μεστός), probably akin to a root signifying to measure, hence conveys the sense of having full measure, (*a*) of material things, a vessel, John 19 : 29 ; a net, 21 : 11 ; (*b*) metaphorically, of thoughts and feelings, exercised (1) in evil things, hypocrisy, Matt. 23 : 28 ; envy,

murder, strife, deceit, malignity, Rom. 1 : 29 ; the utterances of the tongue, Jas. 3 : 8 ; adultery, 2 Pet. 2 : 14 ; (2) in virtues, goodness, Rom. 15 : 14 ; mercy, etc., Jas. 3 : 17.¶

B. Verb.

GEMŌ (γέμω), to be full, to be heavily laden with, was primarily used of a ship; it is chiefiy used in the N.T. of evil contents, such as extortion and excess, Matt. 23 : 25 ; dead men's bones, ver. 27 ; extortion and wickedness, Luke 11 : 39 ; cursing, Rom. 3 : 14 ; blasphemy, Rev. 17 : 3 ; abominations, ver. 4 ; of Divine judgments, 15 : 17 ; 21 : 9 ; (R.V., " laden," A.V., " full ") ; of good things, 4 : 6, 8 ; 5 : 8.¶

Notes : (1) *Gemizō* (see FILL, A, No. 9) is always rendered to fill in R.V. (2) For Acts 2 : 13, A.V., see FILL, No. 11. (3) For " fullgrown," Heb. 5 : 14, R.V., see AGE, No. 2 ; for Jas. 1 : 15, R.V., see FINISH, *Note* (2).

FULLER

GNAPHEUS (γναφεύς), akin to *knaptō*, to card wool, denotes a cloth-carder, or dresser (*gnaphos*, the prickly teasel-cloth ; hence, a carding comb) ; it is used of the raiment of the Lord in Mark 9 : 3.¶

FULLGROWN: see AGE, B, No. 2, FINISH, *Note* (2)

FULLY: see ASSURED, COME, KNOW, PERSUADE, PREACH, RIPE

FULNESS

PLERŌMA (πλήρωμα) denotes fulness, that of which a thing is full ; it is thus used of the grace and truth manifested in Christ, John 1 : 16 ; of all His virtues and excellencies, Eph. 4 : 13 ; "the blessing of Christ," Rom. 15 : 29, R.V. (not as A.V.) ; the conversion and restoration of Israel, Rom. 11 : 12 ; the completion of the number of Gentiles who receive blessing through the Gospel, ver. 25 ; the complete products of the earth, 1 Cor. 10 : 26 ; the end of an appointed period, Gal 4 : 4 ; Eph. 1 : 10 ; God, in the completeness of His Being, Eph. 3 : 19 ; Col. 1 : 19 ; 2 : 9 ; the Church as the complement of Christ, Eph. 1 : 23. In Mark 6 : 43, " basketfuls," R.V., is, lit., ' fulnesses of baskets.' For Matt 9 : 16 ; Mark 2 : 21 see FILL, (B) ; for 8 : 20 see FULFIL, B.

Note : For *plērophoria*, " fulness," Heb. 6 : 11, R.V., see ASSURANCE.

FURLONG

STADION (στάδιον) denotes (*a*) a stadium, i.e., a measure of length, 600 Greek feet, or one-eighth of a Roman mile, Matt. 14 : 24 (in the best mss.) ; Luke 24 : 13 ; John 6 : 19 ; 11 : 18 ; Rev. 14 : 20 ; 21 : 16 ; (*b*) a race course, the length of the Olympic course, 1 Cor. 9 : 24.¶

FURNACE

KAMINOS (κάμινος), an oven, furnace, kiln (whence Lat. *caminus*,

Eng., chimney), used for smelting, or for burning earthenware, occurs in Matt. 13 : 42, 50 ; Rev. 1 : 15 ; 9 : 2.¶

FURNISH

1. STRŌNNUMI (στρώννυμι), or *strōnnuō*, to spread, is used of furnishing a room, Mark 14 : 15 ; Luke 22 : 12 ; of making a bed, Acts 9 : 34 ; in Matt. 21 : 8 ; Mark 11 : 8, " spread " (A.V., " strawed," twice). See SPREAD.¶

2. EXARTIZŌ (ἐξαρτίζω), to fit out, to prepare perfectly, to complete for a special purpose (*ex*, out, used intensively, and *artios*, joined, *artos*, a joint), is used of accomplishing days, Acts 21 : 5, i.e., of terminating a space of time ; of being " completely furnished," by means of the Scriptures, for spiritual service, 2 Tim. 3 : 17. See ACCOMPLISH.

3. PLĒTHŌ (πλήθω), Matt. 21 : 10, " furnished " R.V., " filled." See FILL, No. 5.

FURTHER

1. ETI (ἔτι), yet, still, further, is used (*a*) of time, most usually translated " yet," e.g., Matt. 12 : 46 ; or negatively, " any more," " no more," e.g., Heb. 8 : 12 ; (*b*) of degree, translated " further," or " any further," Matt. 26 : 65 ; Mark 5 : 35 ; 14 : 63 ; Luke 22 : 71 ; Heb. 7 : 11 ; in Acts 21 : 28, R.V., " moreover " (A.V., " further "). See LONGER, MORE, MOREOVER, STILL, THENCEFORTH, YET.

2. PORRŌTERON (πορρώτερον), the comparative degree of *porrō*, far off, signifies " further," Luke 24 : 28. See FAR.

Note : In Acts 27 : 28, *brachu*, a little, is rendered " a little further," A.V. (R.V., " after a little space ").

FURTHERANCE

Notes : (1) In Phil. 1 : 12, 25, A.V., *prokopē*, a striking forward (*pro*, forward, *koptō*, to cut), is translated " furtherance ; " " progress " in R.V., as in 1 Tim. 4 : 15. Originally the word was used of a pioneer cutting his way through brushwood. See PROGRESS.¶ (2) In Phil. 1 : 5 the R.V. " (for your fellowship) in furtherance of the Gospel," and in 2 : 22, " in furtherance of the Gospel," are, lit., ' unto the Gospel.'

FURTHERMORE

EITA (εἶτα), which is chiefly used of time or enumerations, signifying ' then ' or ' next,' is once used in argument, signifying ' furthermore,' Heb. 12 : 9. See AFTERWARD, THEN.

Note : In 1 Thess. 4 : 1 the A.V. " furthermore " translates the phrase *to loipon*, lit., ' for the rest,' R.V., " finally." See FINALLY.

G

GAIN (Noun and verb)
A. Nouns.

1. ERGASIA (ἐργασία) signifies (a) work, working, performance (from *ergon*, work), Eph. 4 : 19 ; in Luke 12 : 58, "diligence ; " (b) business or gain got by work, Acts 16 : 16, 19 ; in 19 : 24, 25, the R.V. adheres to the meaning "business" (A.V., "gain" and "craft"). See CRAFT, DILIGENCE.¶

2. PORISMOS (πορισμός) primarily denotes a providing (akin to *porizō*, to procure), then, a means of gain, 1 Tim. 6 : 5 (R.V., "a way of gain ") ; 6 : 6.¶

3. KERDOS (κέρδος), gain (akin to *kerdainō*, see below), occurs in Phil. 1 : 21 ; 3 : 7 ; Tit. 1 : 11. See LUCRE.¶

B. Verbs.

1. KERDAINŌ (κερδαίνω), akin to A, No. 3, signifies (I), literally, (a) to gain something, Matt. 16 : 26 ; 25 : 16 (in the best mss.), 17, 20, 22 ; Mark 8 : 36 ; Luke 9 : 25 ; (b) to get gain, make a profit, Jas. 4 : 13 ; (II), metaphorically, (a) to win persons, said (1) of gaining an offending brother who by being told privately of his offence, and by accepting the representations, is won from alienation and from the consequences of his fault, Matt. 18 : 15 ; (2) of winning souls into the Kingdom of God by the Gospel, 1 Cor. 9 : 19, 20 (twice), 21, 22, or by godly conduct, 1 Pet. 3 : 1 (R.V., "gained ") ; (3) of so practically appropriating Christ to oneself that He becomes the dominating power in and over one's whole being and circumstances, Phil. 3 : 8 (R.V., "gain ") ; (b) to gain things, said of getting injury and loss, Acts 27 : 21, R.V. "gotten." See GET.¶

2. DIAPRAGMATEUOMAI (διαπραγματεύομαι) signifies to gain by trading, Luke 19 : 15 (from *dia*, through, used intensively, and *pragmateuomai*, to busy oneself, to be engaged in business).¶

3. PERIPOIEŌ (περιποιέω), to save for oneself, gain, is in the Middle Voice in the best mss. in Luke 17 : 33, R.V., "gain." See PURCHASE.

Notes : (1) In Luke 19 : 16, A.V., *prosergazomai*, to work out in addition, or to earn in addition, is translated "gained " (R.V., "made ") ; in ver. 18 the verb *poieō*, to make, is translated in the same way, the English verb "make " standing both for earning and for producing. (2) In 2 Cor. 12 : 17, 18, *pleonekteō*, to claim unduly, to overreach, is translated "make a gain of," A.V. (R.V., "take advantage of "). (3) For *ergazomai*, Rev. 18 : 17, R.V., see TRADE. (4) In Acts 25 : 9, R.V., *katatithēmi*, Middle Voice, to lay up for oneself, is rendered "to gain."

GAINSAY, GAINSAYER, GAINSAYING
A. Verbs.

1. ANTILEGŌ (ἀντιλέγω), to contradict, oppose, lit., say against, is translated "gainsaying" in Rom. 10 : 21 and Tit. 2 : 9, R.V. (A.V., "answering again"), of servants in regard to masters ; in Tit. 1 : 9 "gainsayers." Moulton and Milligan (Vocab.) illustrate from the papyri "the strong sense of antilegō in Rom. 10 : 21, 'contradict,' 'oppose'." See ANSWER, CONTRADICT.

2. ANTEIPON (ἀντεῖπον), which serves as an aorist tense of No. 1, is rendered "gainsay" in Luke 21 : 15 ; "say against" in Acts 4 : 14. See SAY.¶

B. Noun.

ANTILOGIA (ἀντιλογία), akin to A, No. 1, is rendered "gainsaying," in Heb. 12 : 3, R.V., and Jude 11. Opposition in act seems to be implied in these two places ; though this sense has been questioned by some, it is confirmed by instances from the papyri (Moulton and Milligan, Vocab.). See CONTRADICTION, DISPUTE, STRIFE.

C. Adjective.

ANANTIRRHĒTOS (ἀναντίρρητος), lit., not to be spoken against (a, negative, n, euphonic, anti, against, rhētos, spoken), is rendered "cannot be gainsaid" in Acts 19 : 36, R.V.¶

D. Adverb.

ANANTIRRHĒTŌS (ἀναντιρρήτως), corresponding to C, is translated "without gainsaying" in Acts 10 : 29 ; it might be rendered 'unquestioningly.'¶

GALL

CHOLĒ (χολή), a word probably connected with chloē, yellow, denotes gall, (a) literal, Matt. 27 : 34 (cp. Ps. 69 : 21) ; some regard the word here as referring to myrrh, on account of Mark 15 : 23 ; (b) metaphorical, Acts 8 : 23, where "gall of bitterness" stands for extreme wickedness, productive of evil fruit.¶ In the O.T. it is used (a) of a plant characterized by bitterness (probably wormwood), Deut. 29 : 18 ; Hos. 10 : 4 ; Amos 6 : 12 ; (b) as the translation of the word mererah, bitterness, Job. 13 : 26, e.g. ; (c) as the translation of rôsh, venom ; in Deut. 32 : 32 "(grapes) of gall." In Job 20 : 25, the gall bladder is referred to (the receptacle of bile). The ancients supposed that the poison of serpents lay in the gall (see Job 20 : 14).

GAMES, see CONTEND

GANGRENE

GANGRAINA (γάγγραινα), an eating sore, spreading corruption and producing mortification, is used, in 2 Tim. 2 : 17, of errorists in the church, who, pretending to give true spiritual food, produce spiritual gangrene (A.V., "canker," R.V., "gangrene").¶

GARDEN

KĒPOS (κῆπος), a garden, occurs in Luke 13 : 19, in one of the Lord's parables ; in John 18 : 1, 26, of the garden of Gethsemane ; in 19 : 41, of the garden near the place of the Lord's crucifixion.¶

GARDENER

KĒPOUROS (κηπουρός), lit., a garden-keeper (from kēpos, see above, and ouros, a watcher), occurs in John 20 : 15.¶

GARLAND

STEMMA (στέμμα) denotes a wreath (from stephō, to put around, enwreath), as used in sacrifices, Acts 14 : 13.¶

GARMENT

Note : For himation, the usual word for "garment," see CLOTHING, where see also esthēsis (translated "garments" in the A.V. of Luke 24 : 4, R.V., "apparel"), enduma, chitōn, and stolē (R.V., "robe" in Mark 16 : 5). The fact of the wedding garment, enduma in Matt. 22, vv. 11, 12, indicates that persons of high rank showed their magnificence by providing the guests with festal garments. See APPAREL.

GARNER

APOTHĒKĒ (ἀποθήκη), a storehouse, granary (from apo, away, and tithēmi, to put), is translated "garner" in Matt. 3 : 12 and Luke 3 : 17. See BARN.

GARNISH

KOSMEŌ (κοσμέω) is translated by the verb to garnish in Matt. 12 : 44 ; 23 : 29 ; Luke 11 : 25 ; and in the A.V. of Rev. 21 : 19. See ADORN.

For GARRISON see GUARD, B, No. 3

GATE

1. PULĒ (πύλη) is used (a) literally, for a larger sort of gate, in the wall either of a city or palace or temple, Luke 7 : 12, of Nain (burying places were outside the gates of cities) ; Acts 3 : 10 ; 9 : 24 ; 12 : 10 ; Heb. 13 : 12 ; (b) metaphorically, of the gates at the entrances of the ways leading to life and to destruction, Matt. 7 : 13, 14 ; some mss. have pulē, for thura, a door, in Luke 13 : 24 (see the R.V.) ; of the gates of Hades, Matt. 16 : 18, than which nothing was regarded as stronger. The importance and strength of gates made them viewed as synonymous with power. By metonymy, the gates stood for those who held government and administered justice there.¶

2. PULŌN (πυλών), akin to No. 1, primarily signifies a porch or

vestibule, e.g., Matt. 26 : 71 ; Luke 16 : 20 ; Acts 10 : 17 ; 12 : 13, 14 ; then, the gateway or gate tower of a walled town, Acts 14 : 13 ; Rev. 21 : 12, 13, 15, 21, 25 ; 22 : 14.¶

Notes : (1) In Acts 3 : 2 *thura* denotes, not a gate, but a door, R.V. See Door. (2) *Probatikos*, signifying of, or belonging to, sheep, denotes a sheep gate in John 5 : 2, R.V., and A.V. marg. (3) The conjectural emendation which suggests the idea of " floods " for " gates " in Matt. 16 : 18 is not sufficiently substantiated to be accepted.

GATHER, GATHERING
A. Verbs.

1. SUNAGŌ (συνάγω), to gather or bring together, is said of (*a*) persons, e.g., Matt. 2 : 4 ; (*b*) things, e.g., Matt. 13 : 30 ; in Luke 15 : 13 the idea is that of gathering his goods together for sale, i.e., ' having sold off all.' See Assemble, Bestow, Come, Resort.

2. EPISUNAGŌ (ἐπισυνάγω), to gather together, suggesting stress upon the place at which the gathering is made (*epi*, to), is said of a hen and her chickens, Matt. 23 : 37 ; and so of the Lord's would-be protecting care of the people of Jerusalem, *id.*, and Luke 13 : 34 ; of the gathering together of the elect, Matt. 24 : 31 ; Mark 13 : 27 ; of the gathering together of a crowd, Mark 1 : 33 ; Luke 12 : 1.¶

3. SULLEGŌ (συλλέγω), to collect, gather up or out (*sun*, with *legō*, to pick out), is said of gathering grapes and figs, Matt. 7 : 16 ; Luke 6 : 44 (cp. No. 5) ; tares, Matt. 13 : 28, 29, 30, 40 ; good fish, 13 : 48 ; " all things that cause stumbling, and them that do iniquity," 13 : 41.¶

4. SUSTREPHŌ (συστρέφω) signifies (*a*) to twist together or roll into a mass (*sun*, together, *strephō*, to turn), said of the bundle of sticks gathered by Paul, Acts 28 : 3 ; (*b*) to assemble or gather together (possibly, to journey about together), of persons, Matt. 17 : 22 (in the best mss.), R.V., marg.¶

5. TRUGAŌ (τρυγάω) signifies to gather in, of harvest, vintage, ripe fruits (*trugē* denotes fruit, etc., gathered in autumn), Luke 6 : 44, of grapes (last part of ver. ; for the previous clause, as to figs, see No. 3) ; metaphorically, of the clusters of " the vine of the earth," Rev. 14 : 18 ; of that from which they are gathered, ver. 19.¶

6. ATHROIZŌ (ἀθροίζω) denotes to assemble, gather together, Luke 24 : 33 (according to the best mss.) ; the word is akin to *athroos*, assembled in crowds (not found in the N.T.).¶

7. SUNATHROIZŌ (συναθροίζω), *sun*, together, and No. 6, signifies (*a*) to gather together, Acts 19 : 25, R.V. (A.V., " called together ") ; in the Passive Voice, 12 : 12.¶

8. EPATHROIZŌ (ἐπαθροίζω), to assemble besides (*epi*), said of multitudes, Luke 11 : 29, is rendered " were gathering together " (Middle Voice), R.V. (A.V., " were gathered thick together ").¶

Notes : (1) In Eph. 1 : 10, A.V., the verb *anakephalaioō*, to sum up,

head up, is rendered " might gather together in one " (R.V., " sum up ").
(2) In Luke 8 : 4, A.V. (*suneimi*, to come together) as " were gathered
together " (see R.V.). (4) For " assuredly gathering " see CONCLUDE.

B. Noun.

EPISUNAGŌGĒ (ἐπισυναγωγή), a gathering together, is used in
2 Thess. 2 : 1, of the ' rapture ' of the saints ; for Heb. 10 : 25, see
ASSEMBLE.

Note : For *logia*, 1 Cor. 16 : 2, A.V., see COLLECTION.

For GAY see GOODLY, A, *Note.*

For GAZE see BEHOLD, No. 3.

GAZINGSTOCK

THEATRIZŌ (θεατρίζω) signifies to make a spectacle (from *theatron*,
a theatre, spectacle, show) ; it is used in the Passive Voice in Heb.
10 : 33, " being made a gazingstock."¶

GEAR

SKEUOS (σκεῦος), an implement, vessel, utensil, is used of the tackling
or gear of a ship, Acts 27 : 17, R.V. (A.V., " sail ").

For GENDER see BEGET, No. 1

GENEALOGY
A. Noun.

GENEALOGIA (γενεαλογία) is used in 1 Tim. 1 : 4 and Tit. 3 : 9,
with reference to such genealogies as are found in Philo, Josephus and
the book of Jubilees, by which Jews traced their descent from the
patriarchs and their families, and perhaps also to Gnostic genealogies and
orders of æons and spirits. Amongst the Greeks, as well as other nations,
mythological stories gathered round the birth and genealogy of their
heroes. Probably Jewish genealogical tales crept into Christian communities. Hence the warnings to Timothy and Titus.¶

B. Verb.

GENEALOGEŌ (γενεαλογέω), to reckon or trace a genealogy (from
genea, a race, and *legō*, to choose, pick out), is used, in the Passive Voice,
of Melchizedek in Heb. 7 : 6, R.V., " whose genealogy (A.V., ' descent ')
is not counted."¶

C. Adjective *(negative).*

AGENEALOGĒTOS (ἀγενεαλόγητος), denoting without recorded
pedigree (*a*, negative, and an adjectival form from B.), is rendered
" without genealogy " in Heb. 7 : 3. The narrative in Gen. 14 is so
framed in facts and omissions as to foreshadow the Person of Christ.¶

For GENERAL (Assembly) see ASSEMBLY, No. 2

GENERATION

1. GENEA (γενεά) : see AGE, No. 2.

2. GENESIS (γένεσις) denotes an origin, a lineage, or birth, translated " generation " in Matt. 1 : 1. See NATURAL, NATURE.

Notes : (1) For *gennēma,* translated " generation " in the A.V. of Matt. 3 : 7 ; 12 : 34 ; 23 : 33 ; Luke 3 : 7, see OFFSPRING¶ (2) For *genos,* translated " generation " in 1 Pet. 2 : 9, A.V., see KIND.

GENTILES
A. Nouns.

1. ETHNOS (ἔθνος), whence Eng., " heathen," denotes, firstly, a multitude or company ; then, a multitude of people of the same nature or genus, a nation, people ; it is used in the singular, of the Jews, e.g., Luke 7 : 5 ; 23 : 2 ; John 11 : 48, 50–52 ; in the plural, of nations (Heb., *goiim*) other than Israel, e.g., Matt. 4 : 15 ; Rom. 3 : 29 ; 11 : 11 ; 15 : 10 ; Gal. 2 : 8 ; occasionally it is used of Gentile converts in distinction from Jews, e.g., Rom. 11 : 13 ; 16 : 4 ; Gal. 2 : 12, 14 ; Eph. 3 : 1.

2. HELLĒN (ἕλλην) originally denoted the early descendants of Thessalian Hellas ; then, Greeks as opposed to barbarians, Rom. 1 : 14. It became applied to such Gentiles as spoke the Greek language, e.g., Gal. 2 : 3 ; 3 : 28. Since that was the common medium of intercourse in the Roman Empire, Greek and Gentile became more or less interchangeable terms. For this term the R.V. always adheres to the word " Greeks," e.g., John 7 : 35 ; Rom. 2 : 9, 10 ; 3 : 9 ; 1 Cor. 10 : 32, where the local church is distinguished from Jews and Gentiles ; 12 : 13.

B. Adjective.

ETHNIKOS (ἐθνικός) is used as noun, and translated " Gentiles " in the R.V. of Matt. 5 : 47 ; 6 : 7 ; " the Gentile " in 18 : 17 (A.V., " an heathen man ") ; " the Gentiles " in 3 John 7, A.V. and R.V.¶

C. Adverb.

ETHNIKŌS (ἐθνικῶς), in Gentile fashion, in the manner of Gentiles, is used in Gal. 2 : 14, " as do the Gentiles," R.V.¶

Notes : (1) For the synonymous word *laos,* a people, see PEOPLE. (2) When, under the new order of things introduced by the Gospel the mystery of the Church was made known, the word *ethnos* was often used in contrast to the local church, 1 Cor. 5 : 1 ; 10 : 20 ; 12 : 2 ; 1 Thess. 4 : 5 ; 1 Pet. 2 : 12.

GENTLE, GENTLENESS, GENTLY
A. Adjectives.

1. EPIEIKĒS (ἐπιεικής), from *epi,* unto, and *eikos,* likely, denotes seemly, fitting ; hence, equitable, fair, moderate, forbearing, not insisting on the letter of the law ; it expresses that considerateness that

looks " humanely and reasonably at the facts of a case " ; it is rendered
" gentle " in 1 Tim. 3 : 3, R.V. (A.V., " patient "), in contrast to con-
tentiousness ; in Tit. 3 : 2, " gentle," in association with meekness ; in
Jas. 3 : 17, as a quality of the wisdom from above ; in 1 Pet. 2 : 18, in
association with the good ; for the R.V. rendering " forbearance " in
Phil. 4 : 5, R.V., see FORBEARANCE. Cp. B. See PATIENT.¶ In the Sept.,
Esth. 8 : 13 ; Ps. 86 : 5.¶

2. ĒPIOS (ἤπιος), mild, gentle, was frequently used by Greek writers
as characterizing a nurse with trying children or a teacher with refractory
scholars, or of parents toward their children. In 1 Thess. 2 : 7, the
Apostle uses it of the conduct of himself and his fellow-missionaries
towards the converts at Thessalonica (cp. 2 Cor. 11 : 13, 20) ; in 2 Tim.
2 : 24, of the conduct requisite for a servant of the Lord.¶

B. Noun.

EPIEIKEIA (ἐπιείκεια), or epieikia, denotes fairness, moderation,
gentleness, " sweet reasonableness " (Matthew Arnold) ; it is said of Christ,
2 Cor. 10 : 1, where it is coupled with praütēs, " meekness " ; for its
meaning in Acts 24 : 4, see CLEMENCY.¶. Trench (Syn. § xlviii) considers
that the ideas of equity and justice, which are essential to the meaning,
do not adequately express it in English. In contrast with praütēs
(meekness), which is more especially a temperament or habit of mind,
epieikeia expresses an active dealing with others.

Notes : (1) For *chrēstotēs*, kindness, goodness of heart, rendered
" gentleness " in Gal. 5 : 22, A.V., see KINDNESS. The corresponding
adjective *chrēstos* is translated " good," " kind," " easy," " gracious."

(2) For *metriopatheō*, to bear gently with, Heb. 5 : 2, see BEAR, No. 13.

GET, GOT, GOTTEN

(a) *In the sense of acquiring :*

1. HEURISKŌ (εὑρίσκω), to find, is translated " get " in Luke
9 : 12, of victuals. See FIND.

2. KTAOMAI (κτάομαι), to acquire, procure for oneself, gain, is
rendered " get " in the R.V. of Matt. 10 : 9 and A.V. marg. (A.V., text,
" provide ") ; in Luke 18 : 12 (for A.V., " possess "). See OBTAIN,
POSSESS, PROVIDE, PURCHASE.

3. KERDAINŌ (κερδαίνω), to gain, is rendered " have gotten "
in Acts 27 : 21, R.V. (of injury and loss) ; the word is there used metaphorically, however, of avoiding, or saving oneself from. For the meaning,
to get gain, Jas. 4 : 13, see GAIN.

Notes : (1) For *pleonekteō*, to get an advantage of (A.V., in 2 Cor.
2 : 11 ; R.V., " an advantage may be gained over,"), see ADVANTAGE.
(2) In Rev. 15 : 2, A.V., *nikaō*, to conquer, prevail over, is translated
" had gotten the victory " (R.V., " come victorious "). (3) In Rev.
3 : 17, R.V., *plouteō*, to become rich, is rendered " I have gotten riches."

(b) In the sense of going :

1. EXEIMI (ἔξειμι), to go or come out, is used in Acts 27 : 43 of getting to land. See DEPART, GO, No. 23.

2. HUPAGŌ (ὑπάγω), to go away, withdraw, is rendered " get," " get . . . hence," in Matt. 4 : 10 ; 16 : 23 ; Mark 8 : 33 ; some mss. have it in Luke 4 : 8. See DEPART, GO, No. 8.

3. EXERCHOMAI (ἐξέρχομαι), to come or go out, is translated " get . . . out " in Luke 13 : 31 ; Acts 7 : 3 ; 22 : 18. See COME, No. 3, GO (Notes).

4. KATABAINŌ (καταβαίνω), to descend, is translated " get . . . down," in Acts 10 : 20. See COME, No. 19.

5. EMBAINŌ (ἐμβαίνω), to enter, is translated " they got into " in John 6 : 24 (of boats), R.V. [A.V., " took (shipping)."]. See COME, No. 21.

6. APOBAINŌ (ἀποβαίνω), to go from, is translated " they got out " in John 21 : 9, R.V. (A.V., " were come to "). See COME, 21 (Note).

Note : In Acts 21 : 1, A.V., *apospaō*, to withdraw or part from, is rendered " we had gotten (from)," R.V., " had parted (from)." After the scene described at the end of ch. 20, it may well have the force of being reft away (or tearing themselves away) from them. Cp. the same verb in Luke 22 : 41 (' He was reft away from them '). See DRAW, PART, WITHDRAW.

For GHOST see SPIRIT

GHOST (give up the)

1. EKPNEŌ (ἐκπνέω), lit., to breathe out (*ek*, out, *pneō*, to breathe), to expire, is used in the N.T., without an object, " soul " or " life " being understood, Mark 15 : 37, 39, and Luke 23 : 46, of the Death of Christ. In Matt. 27 : 50 and John 19 : 30, where different verbs are used, the act is expressed in a way which stresses it as of His own volition : in the former, " Jesus . . . yielded up His spirit (*pneuma*) ; in the latter, " He gave up His spirit."¶

2. EKPSUCHŌ (ἐκψύχω), to expire, lit., to breathe out the soul (or life), to give up the ghost (*ek*, out, *psuchē*, the soul), is used in Acts 5 : 5, 10 ; 12 : 23.¶

GIFT, GIVING

1. DŌRON (δῶρον), akin to *didōmi*, to give, is used (*a*) of gifts presented as an expression of honour, Matt. 2 : 11 ; (*b*) of gifts for the support of the temple and the needs of the poor, Matt. 15 : 5 ; Mark 7 : 11 ; Luke 21 : 1, 4 ; (*c*) of gifts offered to God, Matt. 5 : 23, 24 ; 8 : 4 ; 23 : 18, 19 ; Heb. 5 : 1 ; 8 : 3, 4 ; 9 : 9 ; 11 : 4 ; (*d*) of salvation by grace, as the gift of God, Eph. 2 : 8 ; (*e*) of presents for mutual celebration of an occasion, Rev. 11 : 10. See OFFERING.¶

2. DŌREA (δωρεά) denotes a free gift, stressing its gratuitous

character ; it is always used in the N.T. of a spiritual or supernatural gift, John 4 : 10 ; Acts 8 : 20 ; 11 : 17 ; Rom. 5 : 15 ; 2 Cor. 9 : 15 ; Eph. 3 : 7 ; Heb. 6 : 4 ; in Eph. 4 : 7, " according to the measure of the gift of Christ," the gift is that given by Christ ; in Acts 2 : 28, " the gift of the Holy Ghost," the clause is epexegetical, the gift being the Holy Ghost Himself ; cp. 10 : 45 ; 11 : 17, and the phrase, " the gift of righteousness," Rom. 5 : 17.¶

Note : For *dōrean*, a form of this noun, used adverbially, see FREELY.

3. DŌRĒMA (δώρημα) : see BOON.

4. DOMA (δόμα) lends greater stress to the concrete character of the gift, than to its beneficent nature, Matt. 7 : 11 ; Luke 11 : 13 ; Eph. 4 : 8 ; Phil. 4 : 17.¶

5. DOSIS (δόσις) denotes, properly, the act of giving, Phil. 4 : 15, euphemistically referring to gifts as a matter of debt and credit accounts ; then, objectively, a gift, Jas. 1 : 17 (1st mention ; see BOON).¶

6. CHARISMA (χάρισμα), a gift of grace, a gift involving grace (*charis*) on the part of God as the Donor, is used (*a*) of His free bestowments upon sinners, Rom. 5 : 15, 16 ; 6 : 23 ; 11 : 29 ; (*b*) of His endowments upon believers by the operation of the Holy Spirit in the churches, Rom. 12 : 6 ; 1 Cor. 1 : 7 ; 12 : 4, 9, 28, 30, 31 ; 1 Tim. 4 : 14 ; 2 Tim. 1 : 6 ; 1 Pet. 4 : 10 ; (*c*) of that which is imparted through human instruction, Rom. 1 : 11 ; (*d*) of the natural gift of continence, consequent upon the grace of God as Creator, 1 Cor. 7 : 7 ; (*e*) of gracious deliverances granted in answer to the prayers of fellow-believers, 2 Cor. 1 : 11.¶

Note : In the A.V. of 2 Cor. 8 : 4 *charis*, grace, is translated " gift." The R.V., " in regard of this grace," adheres to the true meaning, as in ver. 6.

7. MERISMOS (μερισμός), a dividing (from *meros*, a part), is translated " gifts " in Heb. 2 : 4, " gifts of the Holy Ghost " (marg., " distributions ") ; in 4 : 12, " dividing ". See DIVIDING.¶

Note : In the A.V. of Luke 21 : 5 *anathēma*, a votive offering, is translated " gifts " (R.V., " offerings ").¶

GIRD, GIRDED, GIRT (about, up)

1. ZŌNNUMI (ζώννυμι), or ZŌNNUŌ, to gird, in the Middle Voice, to gird oneself, is used of the long garments worn in the east, John 21 : 18 : Acts 12 : 8 (*perizōnnumi* in some mss.).¶

2. ANAZŌNNUMI (ἀναζώννυμι), to gird up (*ana*, up, and No. 1), is used metaphorically of the loins of the mind, 1 Pet. 1 : 13 ; cp. Luke 12 : 35 (see No. 4). The figure is taken from the circumstances of the Israelites as they ate the passover in readiness for their journey, Ex. 12 : 11; the Christian is to have his mental powers alert in expectation of Christ's Coming. The verb is in the Middle Voice, indicating the special interest the believer is to take in so doing.¶

3. DIAZŌNNUMI (διαζώννυμι), to gird round, i.e., firmly (*dia*, throughout, used intensively), is used of the Lord's act in girding Himself with a towel, John 13 : 4, 5, and of Peter's girding himself with his coat, 21 : 7.¶

4. PERIZŌNNUMI (περιζώννυμι), to gird around or about, is used (*a*) literally, of girding oneself for service, Luke 12 : 37 ; 17 : 8 ; for rapidity of movement, Acts 12 : 8 ; (*b*) figuratively, of the condition for service on the part of the followers of Christ, Luke 12 : 35 ; Eph. 6 : 14 ; (*c*) emblematically, of Christ's Priesthood, Rev. 1 : 13, indicative of majesty of attitude and action, the Middle Voice suggesting the particular interest taken by Christ in girding Himself thus ; so of the action of the angels mentioned in 15 : 6.¶

GIRDLE

ZŌNĒ (ζώνη), Eng., zone, denotes a belt or girdle, Matt. 3 : 4 ; Mark 1 : 6 ; Acts 21 : 11 ; Rev. 1 : 13 ; 15 : 6 ; it was often hollow, and hence served as a purse, Matt. 10 : 9 ; Mark 6 : 8.¶

GIVE

1. DIDŌMI (δίδωμι), to give, is used with various meanings according to the context ; it is said, e.g., of seed yielding fruit, Mark 4 : 7, 8 ; of giving (i.e., exercising) diligence, Luke 12 : 58 ; of giving lots, Acts 1 : 26, R.V. (A.V., " gave forth ") ; of rendering vengeance, 2 Thess. 1 : 8 ; of striking or smiting Christ, John 18 : 22 (lit., ' gave a blow ') and 19 : 3 (lit., ' they gave Him blows ') ; of putting a ring on the hand, Luke 15 : 22 ; of Paul's adventuring himself into a place, Acts 19 : 31.   (In Rev. 17 : 13 some mss. have *diadidōmi*, to divide). See ADVENTURE, BESTOW, No. 1, COMMIT, *Note* (1), DELIVER, GRANT, MAKE, MINISTER, OFFER, PUT, SET, SHEW, SUFFER, TAKE, UTTER, YIELD.

Note : In the following the R.V. gives the correct rendering : Acts 7 : 25, " was giving them deliverance " (A.V., " would deliver them ") ; Acts 10 : 40, " gave Him to be made manifest " (A.V., " shewed Him openly ") ; Rev. 13 : 14, 15, " it was given him " (A.V., " he had power ").

2. APODIDŌMI (ἀποδίδωμι) signifies to give up or back, to restore, return, render what is due, to pay, give an account (*apo*, back, and No. 1), e.g., of an account. Matt. 5 : 26 ; 12 : 36 ; Luke 16 : 2 ; Acts. 19 : 40 ; Heb. 13 : 17 ; 1 Pet. 4 : 5 ; of wages, etc., e.g., Matt. 18 : 25-34 ; 20 : 8 ; of conjugal duty, 1 Cor. 7 : 3 ; of a witness, Acts 4 : 33 ; frequently of recompensing or rewarding, 1 Tim. 5 : 4 ; 2 Tim. 4 : 8, 14 ; 1 Pet. 3 : 9 ; Rev. 18 : 6 ; 22 : 12.   In the Middle Voice it is used of giving up what is one's own ; hence, to sell, Acts 5 : 8 ; 7 : 9 ; Heb. 12 : 16.   See DELIVER.

3. EPIDIDŌMI (ἐπιδίδωμι) signifies (*a*) to give by handing, to hand (*epi*, over), e.g., Matt. 7 : 9, 10 ; Luke 4 : 17 ; 24 : 30, here of the Lord's act in handing the broken loaf to the two at Emmaus, an act which was the means of the revelation of Himself as the crucified and risen Lord ; the simple verb, No. 1, is used of His handing the bread at the institution

of the Lord's Supper, Matt. 26 : 26 ; Mark 14 : 22 ; Luke 22 : 19 ; this meaning of the verb *epididōmi* is found also in Acts 15 : 30, " they delivered ; " (*b*) to give in, give way, Acts 27 : 15, R.V., " we gave way to it." See DELIVER.

4. METADIDŌMI (μεταδίδωμι), to give a share of, impart (*meta*, with), as distinct from giving. The Apostle Paul speaks of sharing some spiritual gift with Christians at Rome, Rom. 1 : 11, " that I may impart," and exhorts those who minister in things temporal, to do so as sharing, and that generously, 12 : 8, " he that giveth ; " so in Eph. 4 : 28 ; Luke 3 : 11 ; in 1 Thess. 2 : 8 he speaks of himself and his fellow-missionaries as having been well pleased to impart to the converts both God's Gospel and their own souls (i.e., so sharing those with them as to spend themselves and spend out their lives for them). See IMPART.¶

5. PARADIDŌMI (παραδίδωμι), to give or hand over, is said of giving up the ghost, John 19 : 30 ; of giving persons up to evil, Acts 7 : 42 ; Rom. 1 : 24, 26 ; of giving one's body to be burned, 1 Cor. 13 : 3 ; of Christ's giving Himself up to death, Gal. 2 : 20 ; Eph. 5 : 2, 25. See BETRAY, COMMIT, DELIVER.

6. PRODIDŌMI (προδίδωμι), to give before, or first (*pro*, before), is found in Rom. 11 : 35.¶

7. CHARIZOMAI (χαρίζομαι) primarily denotes to show favour or kindness, as in Gal. 3 : 18, R.V., " hath granted " (A.V., " gave ") ; then, to give freely, bestow graciously ; in this sense it is used almost entirely of that which is given by God, Acts 27 : 24, " God hath granted thee all them that sail with thee " (R.V.) ; in Rom. 8 : 32, " shall . . . freely give ; " 1 Cor. 2 : 12, " are freely given ; " Phil. 1 : 29, " it hath been granted " (said of believing on Christ and suffering for Him) ; 2 : 9, " hath given " (said of the Name of Jesus as given by God) ; Philm. 22, " I shall be granted unto you " (R.V.). In Luke 7 : 21, it is said in regard to the blind, upon whom Christ " bestowed " sight (R.V.). The only exceptions, in this sense of the word, as to Divinely imparted gifts, are Acts 3 : 14, of the granting of Barabbas by Pilate to the Jews, and Acts 25 : 11, 16, of the giving up of a prisoner to his accusers or to execution. See DELIVER, FORGIVE, GRANT.

8. PARECHŌ (παρέχω), in the Active Voice, signifies to afford, furnish, provide, supply (lit., to hold out or towards ; *para*, near, *echō*, to hold) ; it is translated " hath given " in Acts 17 : 31 ; " giveth " in 1 Tim. 6 : 17 (in the sense of affording) ; in Col. 4 : 1, R.V., " render " (A.V., " give "). See BRING, DO, KEEP, MINISTER, OFFER, RENDER, SHEW, TROUBLE.

9. DŌREŌ (δωρέω), akin to No. 1, and used in the Middle Voice, to bestow, make a gift of, is translated in the R.V. by the verb to grant, instead of the A.V., to give, Mark 15 : 45 ; 2 Pet. 1 : 3, 4. See GRANT.¶

10. APONEMŌ (ἀπονέμω), to assign, apportion (*apo*, away, *nemō*, to distribute), is rendered " giving " in 1 Pet. 3 : 7, of giving honour

to the wife. In the papyri writings it is said of a prefect who gives to all their dues.¶ In the Sept., Deut. 4 : 19.¶

11. POIEŌ (ποιέω), to do, is used in Jude 3 of giving diligence (the Middle Voice indicating Jude's especial interest in his task).

12. KATAPHERŌ (καταφέρω), to bring down or against (kata, down), said of an accusation in Acts 25 : 7 (in the best mss.), and of being " borne down " with sleep, 20 : 9, R.V., is used of casting a ballot or giving a vote in 26 : 10. See FALL, Note (8), SINK.¶

13. PROSTITHĒMI (προστίθημι), lit., to put in addition (pros, to, tithēmi, to put), to give more, is translated " shall more be given," in Mark 4 : 24 (Passive Voice). See ADD.

14. SCHOLAZŌ (σχολάζω), to be at leisure, hence, to have time or opportunity for, to be occupied in, is said of ' giving oneself ' to prayer, 1 Cor. 7 : 5 ; of an " empty " house, ' lying vacant,' Matt. 12 : 44.¶

15. LEGŌ (λέγω), to say, is rendered " giving out," of the self-advertisement of Simon Magus, Acts 8 : 9. See SAY.

16. PROSECHŌ (προσέχω), to turn one's mind to, attend to, is used of giving oneself up to, 1 Tim. 3 : 8 (to wine) ; of giving heed to, Acts 8 : 6, 10, 11 (R.V.) ; 16 : 14 (R.V.) ; 1 Tim. 1 : 4 ; 4 : 1, 13 (R.V.) ; Tit. 1 : 14 ; Heb. 2 : 1. See ATTEND.

17. DIŌKŌ (διώκω), to pursue, is translated " given to " in Rom. 12 : 13, lit., ' pursuing hospitality.' See FOLLOW.

Notes : (1) In John 10 : 11, R.V., tithēmi, to put, lay down etc., is rendered " layeth down," for the A.V., " giveth." (2) For pareispherō, to add, rendered " giving " in 2 Pet. 1 : 5, A.V., see ADD. (3) For martureō, to bear witness, A.V., " gave (record) " in 1 John 5 : 10, R.V., " hath borne (witness)," see WITNESS. (4) For chorēgeō, to supply, minister, rendered " giveth " (R.V., " supplieth ") in 1 Pet. 4 : 11, see MINISTER. (5) For merizō, to divide into parts, rendered " gave a part " (R.V., " divided ") in Heb. 7 : 2, see DIVIDE. (6) For paristēmi, to place by, rendered " give " in Matt. 26 : 53, A.V. (R.V., " send "), see SEND. (7) For douloō, in the Passive Voice, to be enslaved, rendered " given to " in Tit. 2 : 3, A.V., see ENSLAVE. (8) In 1 Tim. 4 : 15, the Imperative Mood of eimi, to be, with en, in, lit., ' be in,' is translated " give thyself wholly to." (9) In Luke 10 : 7, the phrase, lit., ' the (things) by them,' is rendered " such things as they give." (10) For epikrinō, see SENTENCE. (11) For proskartereō, to give oneself continually, Acts 6 : 4, see CONTINUE. (12) See CHARGE, COMMANDMENT, DRINK, HOSPITALITY, LAW, LIGHT, MARRIAGE, PLACE, PLEASURE, SUCK, THANKS.

GIVER

DOTĒS (δότης), akin to didōmi, to give, is used in 2 Cor. 9 : 7 of him who gives cheerfully (hilariously) and is thereby loved of God.¶

GLAD (be, make), GLADLY
A. Verbs.

1. CHAIRŌ (χαίρω) is the usual word for rejoicing, being glad; it is rendered by the verb to be glad in Mark 14 : 11 ; Luke 15 : 32 ; 22 : 5 ; 23 : 8 ; John 8 : 56 ; 11 : 15 ; 20 : 20 ; Acts 11 : 23 ; 13 : 48 ; in the following the R.V. has ' to rejoice ' for A.V., ' to be glad,' Rom. 16 : 19 ; 1 Cor. 16 : 17 ; 2 Cor. 13 : 9 ; 1 Pet. 4 : 13 ; Rev. 19 : 7. See FAREWELL, No. 4, GREETING, HAIL, JOY, REJOICE.

2. AGALLIAŌ (ἀγαλλιάω), to exult, rejoice greatly, is chiefly used in the Middle Voice (Active in Luke 1 : 47 ; some mss. have the Passive in John 5 : 35, ' to be made glad '). In the O.T., it is found abundantly in the Psalms, from 2 : 11 onward to 149 : 2, 5 (Sept.). It conveys the idea of jubilant exultation, spiritual gladness, Matt. 5 : 12, " be exceeding glad," the Lord's command to His disciples ; Luke 1 : 47, in Mary's song ; 10 : 21, of Christ's exultation (" rejoiced ") ; cp. Acts 2 : 26, " (My tongue) was glad," A.V. (R.V., " rejoiced ") ; John 8 : 56, of Abraham ; Acts 16 : 34, R.V., " rejoiced greatly " (of the Philippian jailor) ; 1 Pet. 1 : 6, 8 ; 4 : 13 (" with exceeding joy "), of believers in general ; in Rev. 19 : 7, R.V., " be exceeding glad " (A.V., " rejoice "). See REJOICE.¶

3. EUPHRAINŌ (εὐφραίνω), to cheer, gladden, is rendered " maketh . . . glad " in 2 Cor. 2 : 2. See FARE, MERRY, REJOICE.

B. Adverbs.

1. HĒDEŌS (ἡδέως), gladly (from hēdus, sweet), is used in Mark 6 : 20 ; 12 : 37 ; 2 Cor. 11 : 19.¶

2. HĒDISTA (ἥδιστα), the superlative degree of No. 1, most gladly, most delightedly, with great relish, is rendered " most gladly " in 2 Cor. 12 : 9, and in ver. 15 (R.V. ; A.V., " very gladly ").¶

3. ASMENŌS (ἀσμένως), with delight, delightedly, gladly, is found in Acts 21 : 17. It is absent from the best texts in 2 : 41 (see the R.V.).¶

GLADNESS

1. CHARA (χαρά), joy, delight (akin to A, No. 1 above), is rendered " gladness " in the A.V. of Mark 4 : 16 ; Acts 12 : 14 and Phil. 2 : 29 (R.V. " joy ", as elsewhere in both Versions). See JOY.

2. AGALLIASIS (ἀγαλλίασις), exultation, exuberant joy (akin to A, No. 2), is translated " gladness " in Luke 1 : 14 ; Acts 2 : 6 ; Heb. 1 : 9 ; " joy " in Luke 1 : 44 ; " exceeding joy " in Jude 24. It indicates a more exultant joy than No. 1. In the Sept. this word is found chiefly in the Psalms, where it denotes joy in God's redemptive work, e.g., 30 : 5 ; 42 : 4 ; 45 : 7, 15. See JOY.

3. EUPHROSUNĒ (εὐφροσύνη), good cheer, joy, mirth, gladness of heart (akin to A, No. 3), from eu, well, and phrēn, the mind, is rendered " gladness " in Acts 2 : 28, R.V. (A.V., " joy ") and 14 : 17. See JOY.¶

GLASS, GLASSY
A. Nouns.

1. HUALOS (ὕαλος) primarily denoted anything transparent, e.g., a transparent stone or gem, hence, a lens of crystal, a glass, Rev. 21 : 18, 21.¶

2. ESOPTRON (ἔσοπτρον), a mirror, is rendered "glass" in the A.V. of 1 Cor. 13 : 12 and Jas. 1 : 23. See MIRROR.¶

Note : For the corresponding verb *katoptrizō* in 2 Cor. 3 : 18 (Middle Voice), see BEHOLD, No. 12.

B. Adjective.

HUALINOS (ὑάλινος) signifies glassy, made of glass (akin to A, No. 1), Rev. 4 : 6 ; 15 : 2 (twice), R.V., "glassy."¶

For GLISTERING see DAZZLING and SHINE, No. 4

GLORIFY

1. DOXAZŌ (δοξάζω) primarily denotes "to suppose" (from *doxa*, an opinion) ; in the N.T. (*a*) to magnify, extol, praise (see DOXA below), especially of glorifying God, i.e., ascribing honour to Him, acknowledging Him as to His being, attributes and acts, i.e., His glory (see GLORY), e.g., Matt. 5 : 16 ; 9 : 8 ; 15 : 31 ; Rom. 15 : 6, 9 ; Gal. 1 : 24 ; 1 Pet. 4 : 16 ; the word of the Lord, Acts 13 : 48 ; the Name of the Lord, Rev. 15 : 4 ; also of glorifying oneself, John 8 : 54 ; Rev. 18 : 7 ;. (*b*) to do honour to, to make glorious, e.g., Rom. 8 : 30 ; 2 Cor. 3 : 10 ; 1 Pet. 1 : 8, "full of glory," Passive Voice (lit., ' glorified ') ; said of Christ, e.g., John 7 : 39 ; 8 : 54, R.V., "glorifieth," for A.V., "honour" and "honoureth" (which would translate *timaō*, to honour) ; of the Father, e.g., John 13 : 31, 32 ; 21 : 19 ; 1 Pet. 4 : 11 ; of glorifying one's ministry, Rom. 11 : 13, R.V., "glorify" (A.V., "magnify") ; of a member of the body, 1 Cor. 12 : 26, "be honoured" (R.V. marg., "be glorified").

"As the glory of God is the revelation and manifestation of all that He has and is . . . , it is said of a Self-revelation in which God manifests all the goodness that is His, John 12 : 28. So far as it is Christ through whom this is made manifest, He is said to glorify the Father, John 17 : 1, 4 ; or the Father is glorified in Him, 13 : 31 ; 14 : 13 ; and Christ's meaning is analogous when He says to His disciples, ' Herein is My Father glorified, that ye bear much fruit ; and so shall ye be My disciples,' John 15 : 8. When *doxazō* is predicated of Christ . . . , it means simply that His innate glory is brought to light, is made manifest ; cp. 11 : 4. So 7 : 39 ; 12 : 16, 23 ; 13 : 31 ; 17 : 1, 5. It is an act of God the Father in Him. . . . As the revelation of the Holy Spirit is connected with the glorification of Christ, Christ says regarding Him, ' He shall glorify Me,' 16 : 14 " (Cremer).

2. ENDOXAZŌ (ἐνδοξάζω), No. 1 prefixed by *en*, "in," signifies, in

the Passive Voice, to be glorified, i.e., to exhibit one's glory ; it is said of God, regarding His saints in the future, 2 Thess. 1 : 10, and of the Name of the Lord Jesus as glorified in them in the present, ver. 12.¶

3. SUNDOXAZŌ (συνδοξάζω), to glorify together (*sun*, with), is used in Rom. 8 : 17.¶

GLORY, GLORIOUS
A. Nouns.

1. DOXA (δόξα), glory (from *dokeō*, to seem), primarily signifies an opinion, estimate, and hence, the honour resulting from a good opinion. It is used (I) (*a*) of the nature and acts of God in self-manifestation, i.e., what He essentially is and does, as exhibited in whatever way he reveals Himself in these respects, and particularly in the Person of Christ, in whom essentially His glory has ever shone forth and ever will do, John 17 : 5, 24 ; Heb. 1 : 3 ; it was exhibited in the character and acts of Christ in the days of His flesh, John 1 : 14 ; John 2 : 11 ; at Cana both His grace and His power were manifested, and these constituted His glory ; so also in the resurrection of Lazarus, 11 : 4, 40 ; the glory of God was exhibited in the resurrection of Christ, Rom. 6 : 4, and in His ascension and exaltation, 1 Pet. 1 : 21, likewise on the Mount of Transfiguration, 2 Pet. 1 : 17. In Rom. 1 : 23 His " everlasting power and Divinity " are spoken of as His glory, i.e., His attributes and power as revealed through creation ; in Rom. 3 : 23 the word denotes the manifested perfection of His character, especially His righteousness, of which all men fall short ; in Col. 1 : 11 " the might of His glory " signifies the might which is characteristic of His glory ; in Eph. 1 : 6, 12, 14, " the praise of the glory of His grace " and " the praise of His glory " signify the due acknowledgement of the exhibition of His attributes and ways ; in Eph. 1 : 17, " the Father of glory " describes Him as the source from whom all Divine splendour and perfection proceed in their manifestation, and to whom they belong ; (*b*) of the character and ways of God as exhibited through Christ to and through believers, 2 Cor. 3 : 18 and 4 : 6 ; (*c*) of the state of blessedness into which believers are to enter hereafter through being brought into the likeness of Christ, e.g., Rom. 8 : 18, 21 ; Phil. 3 : 21 (R.V., " the body of His glory ") ; 1 Pet. 5 : 1, 10 ; Rev. 21 : 11 ; (*d*) brightness or splendour, (1) supernatural, emanating from God (as in the Shekinah glory, in the pillar of cloud and in the Holy of Holies, e.g., Ex. 16 : 10 ; 25 : 22), Luke 2 : 9 ; Acts 22 : 11 ; Rom. 9 : 4 ; 2 Cor. 3 : 7 ; Jas. 2 : 1 ; in Tit. 2 : 13 it is used of Christ's return, " the appearing of the glory of our great God and Saviour Jesus Christ " (R.V.) ; cp. Phil. 3 : 21, above ; (2) natural, as of the heavenly bodies, 1 Cor. 15 : 40, 41 ; (II) of good reputation, praise, honour, Luke 14 : 10 (R.V., " glory," for A.V., " worship ") ; John 5 : 41 (R.V., " glory," for A.V., " honour ") ; 7 : 18 ; 8 : 50 ; 12 : 43 (R.V., " glory," for A.V., " praise ") ; 2 Cor. 6 : 8 (R.V., " glory," for A.V. " honour ") ; Phil. 3 : 19 ; Heb. 3 : 3 ; in 1 Cor.

11 : 7, of man as representing the authority of God, and of woman as rendering conspicuous the authority of man ; in 1 Thess. 2 : 6, " glory " probably stands, by metonymy, for material gifts, an honorarium, since in human estimation glory is usually ·expressed in things material.

The word is used in ascriptions of praise to God, e.g., Luke 17 : 18 ; John 9 : 24, R.V., " glory " (A.V., " praise ") ; Acts 12 : 23 ; as in doxologies (lit., glory-words), e.g., Luke 2 : 14 ; Rom. 11 : 36 ; 16 : 27 ; Gal. 1 : 5 ; Rev. 1 : 6. See DIGNITY, HONOUR, PRAISE, WORSHIP.

2. KLEOS (κλέος), good report, fame, renown, is used in 1 Pet. 2 : 20.¶ The word is derived from a root signifying hearing ; hence, the meaning ' reputation.'

Note : In 2 Cor. 3 : 11 the phrase *dia doxēs*, through (i.e., by means of) glory, is rendered " with glory " in the R.V. (A.V., " glorious ") ; in the same verse *en doxē*, " in glory " (R.V.), i.e., accompanied by glory, is rendered " glorious " in the A.V. The first is said of the ministration of the Law, the second of that of the Gospel.

B. Adjective.

ENDOXOS (ἔνδοξος) signifies (*a*) held in honour (*en*, in, *doxa*, honour), of high repute, 1 Cor. 4 : 10, R.V., " have glory " (A.V., " are honourable ") ; (*b*) splendid, glorious, said of apparel, Luke 7 : 25, " gorgeously ; " of the works of Christ, 13 : 17 ; of the Church, Eph. 5 : 27. See GORGEOUSLY, HONOURABLE.¶

GLORY (to boast), GLORYING
A. Verbs.

1. KAUCHAOMAI (καυχάομαι), to boast or glory, is always translated in the R.V. by the verb to glory, where the A.V. uses the verb to boast (see, e.g., Rom. 2 : 17, 23 ; 2 Cor. 7 : 14 ; 9 : 2 ; 10 : 8, 13, 15, 16) ; it is used (*a*) of vainglorying, e.g., 1 Cor. 1 : 29 ; 3 : 21 ; 4 : 7 ; 2 Cor. 5 : 12 ; 11 : 12, 18 ; Eph. 2 : 9 ; (*b*) of valid glorying, e.g., Rom. 5 : 2, " rejoice ; " 5 : 3, 11 (R.V., " rejoice ") ; 1 Cor. 1 : 31 ; 2 Cor. 9 : 2 ; 10 : 8 ; 12 : 9 ; Gal. 6 : 14 ; Phil. 3 : 3 and Jas. 1 : 9, R.V., " glory " (A.V., " rejoice "). See BOAST, JOY, REJOICE.

2. KATAKAUCHAOMAI (κατακαυχάομαι), a strengthened form of No. 1 (*kata*, intensive), signifies to boast against, exult over, Rom. 11 : 18, R.V., " glory " (A.V., " boast ") ; Jas. 2 : 13, R.V., " glorieth " (A.V., " rejoiceth ") ; 3 : 14, " glory (not)." See BOAST, REJOICE.¶

3. ENKAUCHAOMAI (ἐνκαυχάομαι), *en*, in, and No. 1, to glory in, is found, in the most authentic mss., in 2 Thess. 1 : 4.¶

Note : Cp. *perpereuomai*, to vaunt oneself, to be *perperos*, vainglorious, 1 Cor. 13 : 4.¶

B. Nouns.

1. KAUCHĒMA (καύχημα), akin to A, No. 1, denotes (*a*) that in which one glories, a matter or ground of glorying, Rom. 4 : 2 and Phil. 2 : 16, R.V., " whereof to glory " (for Rom. 3 : 27, see No. 2) ; in the following

the meaning is likewise a ground of glorying : 1 Cor. 5 : 6 ; 9 : 15, " glorying," 16, " to glory of ; " 2 Cor. 1 : 14, R.V. ; 9 : 3, R.V. ; Gal. 6 : 4, R.V. (A.V., " rejoicing ") ; Phil. 1 : 26 (ditto) ; Heb. 3 : 6 (ditto). In 2 Cor. 5 : 12 and 9 : 3 the word denotes the boast itself, yet as distinct from the act (see No. 2).¶

2. KAUCHĒSIS (καύχησις) denotes the act of boasting, Rom. 3 : 27 ; 15 : 17, R.V., " (my) glorying " (A.V., " whereof I may glory ") ; 1 Cor. 15 : 31, R.V., " glorying ; " 2 Cor. 1 : 12 (ditto) ; 7 : 4, 14 (A.V., " boasting ") ; 8 : 24 ; 11 : 10, and 17 (ditto) ; 1 Thess. 2 : 19 (A.V., " rejoicing ") ; Jas. 4 : 16 (ditto). The distinction between this and No. 1 is to be observed in 2 Cor. 8 : 24, speaking of the Apostle's act of glorying in the liberality of the Corinthians, while in 9 : 3 he exhorts them not to rob him of the ground of his glorying (No. 1). Some take the word in 2 Cor. 1 : 12 (see above) as identical with No. 1, a boast, but there seems to be no reason for regarding it as different from its usual sense, No. 2.¶

Note : Cp. *alazoneia* (or -*ia*), vainglory, ostentatious (or arrogant) display, Jas. 4 : 16 and 1 John 2 : 16,¶ and *alazōn*, a boaster, Rom. 1 : 30 and 2 Tim. 3 : 2.¶

GLUTTON

GASTĒR (γαστήρ) denotes a belly ; it is used in Tit. 1 : 12, with the adjective *argos*, idle, metaphorically, to signify a glutton, R.V., " (idle) gluttons " [A.V. " (slow) bellies "] ; elsewhere, Luke 1 : 31. See WOMB.¶

GLUTTONOUS

PHAGOS (φάγος), akin to *phagō*, to eat, a form used for the aorist or past tense of *esthiō*, denotes a glutton, Matt. 11 : 19 ; Luke 7 : 34.¶

GNASH, GNASHING
A. Verbs.

1. BRUCHŌ (βρύχω), primarily, to bite or eat greedily (akin to *brukō*, to chew), denotes to grind or gnash with the teeth, Acts 7 : 54.¶
2. TRIZŌ (τρίζω), primarily used of the sounds of animals, to chirp, cry, squeak, came to signify to grind or gnash with the teeth, Mark 9 : 18.¶
B. Noun.

BRUGMOS (βρυγμός), akin to A, No. 1, denotes " gnashing " (" of teeth " being added), Matt. 8 : 12 ; 13 : 42, 50 ; 22 : 13 ; 24 : 51 ; 25 : 30 ; Luke 13 : 28.¶

GNAT

KŌNŌPS (κώνωψ) denotes the wine-gnat or midge, which breeds in fermenting or evaporating wine, Matt. 23 : 24, where the A.V., " strain at " is corrected to " strain out," in the R.V.¶

GNAW

MASAOMAI or MASSAOMAI (μασάομαι) denotes to bite or chew, Rev. 16 : 10.¶ In the Sept., Job. 30 : 4.¶

GO (WENT), GO ONWARD, etc.

1. POREUOMAI (πορεύομαι), to go on one's way, to proceed from one place to another (from *poros*, a passage, a ford, Eng., pore), is always used in the Middle Voice in the N.T. and the Sept., and is the most frequent verb signifying to go ; it is more distinctly used to indicate procedure or course than the verb *eimi*, to go (not found in the N.T.). It is often rendered " go thy (your) way," in Oriental usage the customary dismissal, marking the close of a case in court. Hence, in ordinary parlance, marking the end of a conversation, etc., e.g., Luke 7 : 22 ; 17 : 19 ; John 4 : 50 ; Acts 9 : 15 ; 24 : 25 ; cp. Dan. 12 : 9 ; in Rom. 15 : 24 (1st part), R.V., " go " (A.V., " take my journey ") ; in Acts 9 : 3 and 26 : 13, " journeyed " (A.V. and R.V.). See DEPART, JOURNEY, WALK.

2. PARAPOREUOMAI (παραπορεύομαι) denotes to go past, to pass by (*para*, by, and No. 1), Mark 2 : 23, A.V., " went (through)," R.V., " was going (through) ; " some mss. have No. 4 here. See PASS.

3. PROPOREUOMAI (προπορεύομαι), to go before (*pro*, and No. 1), is used in Luke 1 : 76 and Acts 7 : 40.¶

4. DIAPOREUOMAI (διαπορεύομαι), to go through (*dia*, through, and No. 1), to pass across, is translated to go through, in Luke 6 : 1 ; 13 : 22, " went on His way through," R.V. ; Acts 16 : 4 ; " going by " in Luke 18 : 36, R.V. (A.V., " pass by ") ; " in my journey " in Rom. 15 : 24 (2nd part). For Mark 2 : 23 see No. 2. See JOURNEY.

5. EISPOREUOMAI (εἰσπορεύομαι), to go in, enter, is never rendered by the verb to come in, in the R.V. See, e.g., Luke 11 : 33, " enter ; " Acts 9 : 28, " going in ; " 28 : 30, " went in." See ENTER.

6. SUMPOREUOMAI (συμπορεύομαι), to go together with (*sun*, with), is used in Mark 10 : 1, R.V., " come together " (A.V., " resort ") ; Luke 7 : 11 ; 14 : 25 ; 24 : 15. See RESORT.¶

7. AGŌ (ἄγω), to bring, lead, is used intransitively, signifying " let us go " (as if to say, ' let us be leading on,' with the point of departure especially in view), Matt. 26 : 46 ; Mark 1 : 38 ; 14 : 42 ; John 11 : 7, 15, 16 ; 14 : 31. See BRING.

8. HUPAGŌ (ὑπάγω), to go away or to go slowly away, to depart, withdraw oneself, often with the idea of going without noise or notice (*hupo*, under, and No. 7), is very frequent in the Gospels ; elsewhere it is used in Jas. 2 : 16 ; 1 John 2 : 11 ; Rev. 10 : 8 ; 13 : 10 ; 14 : 4 ; 16 : 1 ; 17 : 8, 11. It is frequently rendered " go your (thy) way," See DEPART.

9. PERIAGŌ (περιάγω), to lead about (*peri*, about, and No. 7), as in 1 Cor. 9 : 5, is used intransitively with the meaning to go about ; " went about," Matt. 4 : 23 ; 9 : 35 ; Mark 6 : 6 ; Acts 13 : 11 ; in Matt. 23 : 15, " ye compass." See COMPASS, LEAD.¶

10. PROAGŌ (προάγω), to lead forth, used intransitively signifies to go before, usually of locality, e.g., Matt. 2 : 9 ; figuratively, in 1 Tim. 1 : 18, "went before" (R.V., marg., "led the way to "), of the exercise of the gifts of prophecy which pointed to Timothy as one chosen by God for the service to be committed to him ; in 5 : 24, of sins " going before unto judgment." In 2 John 9, where the best mss. have this verb (instead of parabainō, to transgress, A.V.), the R.V. renders it " goeth onward " (marg., " taketh the lead "), of not abiding in the doctrine of Christ. Cp. Mal. 4 : 4. See BRING.

11. APEIMI (ἄπειμι), to go away, is found in Acts 17 : 10.¶

12. EISEIMI (εἴσειμι), to go into, enter, is used in Acts 3 : 3 ; 21 : 18, 26 ; Heb. 9 : 6, R.V., " go in " (A.V., " went . . . into "). See ENTER.¶

13. METABAINŌ (μεταβαίνω), to go or pass over from one place to another, is translated " go " in Luke 10 : 7. See DEPART.

14. APERCHOMAI (ἀπέρχομαι), to go away (apo, from), is chiefly used in the Gospels ; it signifies to go aside in Acts 4 : 15. See DEPART.

15. ANACHŌREŌ (ἀναχωρέω) signifies to withdraw, often in the sense of avoiding danger, e.g., Acts 23 : 19, R.V., " going aside " (A.V., " went . . . aside "). See DEPART.

16. HUPOCHŌREŌ (ὑποχωρέω), to go back, retire (hupo, under, suggesting privacy), Luke 5 : 16 ; 9 : 10, A.V., " went aside " (R.V., " withdrew apart "). See WITHDRAW.¶

17. PROERCHOMAI (προέρχομαι), to go before, precede, go forward or farther (pro, before), is used of (a) place, e.g., Matt. 26 : 39 ; Acts 12 : 10, " passed on through ; " (b) time, Luke 1 : 17 ; Acts 20 : 5, 13 ; 2 Cor. 9 : 5. See OUTGO, PASS.

18. EPIDUŌ (ἐπιδύω) signifies to go down, and is said of the sun in Eph. 4 : 26 ; i.e., put wrath away before sunset (see ANGER, A, Note (2). In the Sept., Deut. 24 : 15 ; Josh. 8 : 29 ; Jer. 15 : 9.¶

19. SUNKATABAINŌ (συνκαταβαίνω), to go down with, is used in Acts 25 : 5.¶ In the Sept., Psa. 49 : 17.¶

20. PROBAINŌ (προβαίνω), to go on, forwards, advance, is used of locality, Matt. 4 : 21 ; Mark 1 : 19 ; for the metaphorical use with reference to age, Luke 1 : 7, 18 ; 2 : 36, see AGE, STRICKEN.¶

21. APOBAINŌ (ἀποβαίνω), to go away or from, is translated " had gone out," in Luke 5 : 2, i.e., disembarked. See COME, 21, Note, TURN.

22. PROSANABAINŌ (προσαναβαίνω), to go up higher (pros, towards), is used of moving to a couch of greater honour at a feast, Luke 14 : 10.¶

23. EXEIMI (ἔξειμι), to go out, is so rendered in Acts 13 : 42. See DEPART, GET.

24. SBENNUMI (σβέννυμι), to quench, is used in the Passive Voice, of the going out of the light of a torch or lamp, Matt. 25 : 8, " are going out " (R.V.). See QUENCH.

25. TELEŌ (τελέω), to finish, is rendered to go through or over in Matt. 10 : 23, of going through the cities of Israel (A.V., marg., " end," or " finish "). See END, FINISH.

26. DIODEUŌ (διοδεύω), to travel throughout or along (dia, through, hodos, a way), is used in Luke 8 : 1, of going throughout (A.V.) or about through (R.V.) cities and villages ; of passing through towns, Acts 17 : 1. See PASS.

27. APODĒMEŌ (ἀποδημέω), to be abroad, is translated "going into another country," in Matt. 25 : 14 (A.V., " travelling etc."). See JOURNEY.

28. ANERCHOMAI (ἀνέρχομαι), to go up (ana), occurs in John 6 : 3 ; Gal. 1 : 17, 18.¶

29. PERIERCHOMAI (περιέρχομαι), to go around, or about, is translated "going about" in 1 Tim. 5 : 13, R.V. (A.V., " wandering about ") ; "went about" in Heb. 11 : 37, R.V. (A.V., " wandered about "). See CIRCUIT.

30. EPICHEIREŌ (ἐπιχειρέω), lit., to put the hand to (epi, to, cheir, the hand), to take in hand, undertake, occurs in Luke 1 : 1, " have taken in hand ; " in Acts 9 : 29, " they went about ; " in 19 : 13, " took upon them." See TAKE.¶

Notes : (1) The following verbs signify both to come and to go, with prefixed prepositions accordingly, and are mentioned under the word COME : erchomai (No. 1) ; eiserchomai (No. 2) ; exerchomai (No. 3) ; dierchomai (No. 5) ; katerchomai (No. 7) ; Luke 17 : 7, parerchomai (No. 9) ; proserchomai, " go near," Acts 8 : 29 (No. 10) ; sunerchomai, " went with," Acts 9 : 39 ; 15 : 38 ; 21 : 16 (No. 11) ; anabainō, (No. 15) ; katabainō (No. 19) ; paraginomai, Acts 23 : 16, A.V., " went," R.V. " entered " (No. 13) ; ekporeuō (No. 33) ; chōreō, Matt. 15 : 17, A.V., " goeth," R.V.," passeth " (No. 24) ; anabainō, Luke 19 : 28, R.V.," going up " ; ekbainō (No. 17).

(2) In the following, the verbs mentioned, translated in the A.V. by some form of the verb to go, are rendered in the R.V. more precisely in accordance with their true meaning : (a) zēteō, to seek, so the R.V. in John 7 : 19, 20 ; Acts 21 : 31 ; Rom. 10 : 3 (A.V., to go about) ; (b) peirazō, to make an attempt, Acts 24 : 6, R.V., " assayed " (A.V., " have gone about ") ; (c) peiraō, to attempt, Acts 26 : 21, R.V., " assayed " A.V., " went about ") ; (d) epistrephō, to return, Acts 15 : 16, R.V., " let us return " (A.V., " let us go again ") ; (e) huperbainō, to overstep, 1 Thess. 4 : 6, R.V., " transgress " (A.V., " go beyond ") ; (f) diistēmi, to set apart, make an interval, Acts 27 : 28, R.V., " (after) a space " (A.V., " had gone further ") ; (g) suneiserchomai, to go in with, John 6 : 22 and 18 : 15, R.V., " entered (in) with " (A.V., " went . . . with ") ; (h) pherō, in the Middle Voice, lit., to bear oneself along, Heb. 6 · 1, R.V., " let us press on " (A.V., " let us go on ") ; (i) ekklinō, to bend or turn away, Rom. 3 : 12, R.V., " have turned aside " (A.V., " have gone out of

the way ") ; (*j*) *diaperaō*, to pass through, or across, Matt. 14 : 34, R.V., " had crossed over " (A.V., " were gone over ") ; (*k*) *strateuomai*, to serve in war, 1 Cor. 9 : 7, R.V., " (what) soldier . . . serveth " (A.V., " goeth a warfare ") ; (*l*) *hodoiporeō*, to be on a journey, Acts 10 : 9, R.V., " as they were on their journey " (A.V., " as they went etc.") ; (*m*) *embainō*, to enter, Matt. 13 : 2 and Luke 8 : 22, R.V., " entered " (A.V., " went into ") ; in ver. 37 (A.V., " went up into ") ; (*n*) *apoluō*, to set free, Luke 23 : 22 and John 19 : 12, R.V., " release " (A.V., " let . . . go ") ; Acts 15 : 33, R.V., " dismissed " (A.V., ditto) ; Acts 28 : 18, R.V., " set at liberty " (A.V., ditto) ; (*o*) *epibainō*, to go upon, Acts 21 : 4, R.V., " set foot " (A.V., " go ") ; some mss. have *anabainō* ; (*p*) *apangellō*, to announce, Acts 12 : 17, R.V., " tell " (A.V., " go shew ") ; (*q*) *aperchomai*, to go away, Matt. 5 : 30, R.V., " go " (A.V., " be cast ") ; some mss. have *ballō*, to cast ; (*r*) *peripateō*, to walk, Mark 12 : 38, R.V., " walk " (A.V. " go ") ; (*s*) *For* " gone by," Acts 14 : 16, R.V., see PASS, No. 17.

GOAD

KENTRON (κέντρον), from *kenteō*, to prick, denotes (*a*) a sting, Rev. 9 : 10 ; metaphorically, of sin as the sting of death, 1 Cor. 15 : 55, 56 ; (*b*) a goad, Acts 26 : 14, R.V., " goad " (marg., " goads "), for A.V., " pricks " (in some mss. also in 9 : 5), said of the promptings and misgivings which Saul of Tarsus had resisted before conversion.¶

GOAL

SKOPOS (σκοπός), primarily, a watcher (from *skopeō*, to look at ; Eng., scope), denotes a mark on which to fix the eye, and is used metaphorically of an aim or object in Phil. 3 : 14, R.V., " goal " (A.V., " mark "), See MARK.

GOAT

1. ERIPHOS (ἔριφος) denotes a kid or goat, Matt. 25 : 32 (R.V., marg., " kids ") ; Luke 15 : 29, " a kid ; " some mss. have No. 2 here, indicating a sneer on the part of the elder son, that his father had·never given him even a tiny kid.¶

2. ERIPHION (ἐρίφιον), a diminutive of No. 1, is used in Matt. 25 : 33. In ver. 32 *eriphos* is purely figurative ; in ver 33, where the application is made, though metaphorically, the change to the diminutive is suggestive of the contempt which those so described bring upon themselves by their refusal to assist the needy.¶

3. TRAGOS (τράγος) denotes a he-goat, Heb. 9 : 12, 13, 19 ; 10 : 4, the male prefiguring the strength by which Christ laid down His own life in expiatory sacrifice.

GOATSKIN

Note : The adjective *aigeios* signifies belonging to a goat (from *aix*, a goat) ; it is used with *derma*, a skin, in Heb. 11 : 37.

GOD

THEOS (θέος), (A) in the polytheism of the Greeks, denoted a god or deity, e.g., Acts 14 : 11 ; 19 : 26 ; 28 : 6 ; 1 Cor. 8 : 5 ; Gal. 4 : 8.

(B) (*a*) Hence the word was appropriated by Jews and retained by Christians to denote the one true God. In the Sept. *theos* translates (with few exceptions) the Hebrew words Elohim and Jehovah, the former indicating His power and pre-eminence, the latter His unoriginated, immutable, eternal and self-sustained existence.

In the N.T., these and all the other Divine attributes are predicated of Him. To Him are ascribed, e.g., His unity, or monism, e.g., Mark 12 : 29 ; 1 Tim. 2 : 5 ; self-existence, John 5 : 26 ; immutability, Jas. 1 : 17 ; eternity, Rom. 1 : 20 ; universality, Matt. 10 : 29 ; Acts 17 : 26–28 ; almighty power, Matt. 19 : 26 ; infinite knowledge, Acts 2 : 23 ; 15 : 18 ; Rom. 11 : 33 ; creative power, Rom. 11 : 36 ; 1 Cor. 8 : 6 ; Eph. 3 : 9 ; Rev. 4 : 11 ; 10 : 6 ; absolute holiness, 1 Pet. 1 : 15 ; 1 John 1 : 5 ; righteousness, John 17 : 25 ; faithfulness, 1 Cor. 1 : 9 ; 10 : 13 ; 1 Thess. 5 : 24 ; 2 Thess. 3 : 3 ; 1 John 1 : 9 ; love, 1 John 4 : 8, 16 ; mercy, Rom. 9 : 15, 18 ; truthfulness, Tit. 1 : 2 ; Heb. 6 : 18. See GOOD, No. 1 (*b*).

(*b*) The Divine attributes are likewise indicated or definitely predicated of Christ, e.g., Matt. 20 : 18–19 ; John 1 : 1–3 ; 1 : 18, R.V., marg. ; 5 : 22–29 ; 8 : 58 ; 14 : 6 ; 17 : 22–24 ; 20 : 28 ; Rom. 1 : 4 ; 9 : 5 ; Phil. 3 : 21 ; Col. 1 : 15 ; 2 : 3 ; Tit. 2 : 13, R.V. ; Heb. 1 : 3 ; 13 : 8 ; 1 John 5 : 20 ; Rev. 22 : 12, 13.

(*c*) Also of the Holy Spirit, e.g., Matt. 28 : 19 ; Luke 1 : 35 ; John 14 : 16 ; 15 : 26 ; 16 : 7–14 ; Rom. 8 : 9, 26 ; 1 Cor. 12 : 11 ; 2 Cor. 13 : 14.

(*d*) *Theos* is used (1) with the definite article, (2) without (i.e., as an anarthrous noun). "The English may or may not have need of the article in translation. But that point cuts no figure in the Greek idiom. Thus in Acts 27 : 23 (' the God whose I am,' R.V.) the article points out the special God whose Paul is, and is to be preserved in English. In the very next verse (*ho theos*) we in English do not need the article" (A. T. Robertson, Gram. of Greek, N.T., p. 758).

As to this latter it is usual to employ the article with a proper name, when mentioned a second time. There are, of course, exceptions to this, as when the absence of the article serves to lay stress upon, or give precision to, the character or nature of what is expressed in the noun. A notable instance of this is in John 1 : 1, " and the Word was God ; " here a double stress is on *theos*, by the absence of the article and by the emphatic position. To translate it literally, ' a god was the Word,' is entirely misleading. Moreover, that " the Word " is the subject of the sentence, exemplifies the rule that the subject is to be determined by its having the article when the predicate is anarthrous (without the article). In Rom. 7 : 22, in the phrase " the law of God," both nouns have the article ; in ver. 25, neither has the article. This is in accordance with a general rule that if two nouns are united by the genitive case (the " of " case), either both have the article, or both are without. Here, in the first instance, both nouns, " God " and " the law " are definite, whereas in ver. 25 the word " God " is not simply titular, the absence of the article stresses His character as Lawgiver.

Where two or more epithets are applied to the same person or thing, one article usually serves for both (the exceptions being when a second article lays stress upon different aspects of the same person or subject, e.g., Rev. 1 : 17). In Tit. 2 : 13 the R.V. correctly has " our great God and Saviour Jesus Christ." Moulton (Prol., p. 84) shows, from papyri writings of the early Christian era, that among Greek-speaking Christians this was " a current formula " as applied to Christ. So in 2 Pet. 1 : 1 (cp. 1 : 11 ; 3 : 18).

In the following titles God is described by certain of His attributes ; the God of glory, Acts 7 : 2 ; of peace, Rom. 15 : 33 ; 16 : 20 ; Phil. 4 : 9 ; 1 Thess. 5 : 23 ; Heb. 13 : 20 ; of love and peace, 2 Cor. 13 : 11 ; of patience and comfort, Rom. 15 : 5 ; of all comfort, 2 Cor. 1 : 3 ; of hope, Rom. 15 : 13 ; of all grace, 1 Pet. 5 : 10. These describe Him, not as in distinction from other persons, but as the Source of all these blessings ; hence the employment of the definite article. In such phrases as ' the God of a person,' e.g., Matt. 22 : 32, the expression marks the relationship in which the person stands to God and God to him.

(e) In the following the nominative case is used for the vocative, and always with the article ; Mark 15 : 34 ; Luke 18 : 11, 13 ; John 20 : 28 ; (Acts 4 : 24 in some mss.) ; Heb. 1 : 8 ; 10 : 7.

(f) The phrase " the things of God " (translated literally or otherwise) stands for (1) His interests, Matt. 16 : 23 ; Mark 8 : 33 ; (2) His counsels, 1 Cor. 2 : 11 ; (3) things which are due to Him, Matt. 22 : 21 ; Mark 12 : 17 ; Luke 20 : 25. The phrase " things pertaining to God," Rom. 15 : 17 ; Heb. 2 : 17 ; 5 : 1, describes, in the Heb. passages, the sacrificial service of the priest ; in the Rom. passage the Gospel ministry as an offering to God.

(C) The word is used of Divinely appointed judges in Israel, as representing God in His authority, John 10 : 34, quoted from Psa. 82 : 6, which indicates that God Himself sits in judgment on those whom He has appointed. The application of the term to the Devil, 2 Cor. 4 : 4, and the belly, Phil. 3 : 19, virtually places these instances under (A).

For GOD-SPEED see GREETING

GOD (without)

ATHEOS (ἄθεος), cp. Eng., atheist, primarily signifies godless (a, negative), i.e., destitute of God ; in Eph. 2 : 12 the phrase indicates, not only that the Gentiles were void of any true recognition of God, and hence became morally godless (Rom. 1 : 19–32), but that, being given up by God, they were excluded from communion with God and from the privileges granted to Israel (see the context and cp. Gal. 4 : 8). As to pagan ideas, the popular cry against the early Christians was " away with the atheists " (see the account of the martyrdom of Polycarp, in Eusebius, Eccles. Hist. iv. 15, 19).¶

GODDESS

THEA (θεά) is found in Acts 19 : 27 (in some mss. in vv. 35, 37).¶

For GODHEAD see DIVINE, DIVINITY

GODLINESS, GODLY

A. Nouns.

1. EUSEBEIA (εὐσέβεια), from *eu*, well, and *sebomai*, to be devout, denotes that piety which, characterized by a Godward attitude, does that which is well-pleasing to Him. This and the corresponding verb and adverb (see below) are frequent in the Pastoral Epistles, but do not occur in previous Epistles of Paul. The Apostle Peter has the noun four times in his 2nd Epistle, 1 : 3, 6, 7 ; 3 : 11. Elsewhere it occurs in Acts 3 : 12 ; 1 Tim. 2 : 2 ; 3 : 16 ; 4 : 7, 8 ; 6 : 3, 5, 6, 11 ; 2 Tim. 3 : 5 ; Tit. 1 : 1. In 1 Tim. 6 : 3 " the doctrine which is according to godliness " signifies that which is consistent with godliness, in contrast to false teachings ; in Tit. 1 : 1, " the truth which is according to godliness " is that which is productive of godliness ; in 1 Tim. 3 : 16, " the mystery of godliness " is godliness as embodied in, and communicated through, the truths of the faith concerning Christ ; in 2 Pet. 3 : 11, the word is in the plural, signifying acts of godliness.¶

2. THEOSEBEIA (θεοσέβεια) denotes the fear or reverence of God, from *theos*, god, and *sebomai* (see No. 1), 1 Tim. 2 : 10.¶ Cp. the adjective *theosebēs*, God-fearing, John 9 : 31.¶ In the Sept., Gen. 20 : 11 and Job 28 : 28.¶

Note : For *eulabeia*, godly fear, Heb. 5 : 7 ; 12 : 28, see FEAR, A, No. 3 ; for *eulabeomai*, to reverence, Heb. 11 : 7 (" for His godly fear "), see FEAR, D, No. 2 ; for the verb *eusebeō*, to show piety, 1 Tim. 5 : 4 ; to worship, Acts 17 : 23, see PIETY and WORSHIP.¶

B. Adjective.

EUSEBĒS (εὐσεβής), akin to A, No. 1, denotes pious, devout, godly, indicating reverence manifested in actions ; it is rendered " godly " in 2 Pet. 2 : 9. See DEVOUT.

C. Adverb.

EUSEBŌS (εὐσεβῶς) denotes piously, godly ; it is used with the verb to live (of manner of life) in 2 Tim. 3 : 12 ; Tit. 2 : 12.¶

Notes : (1) In the following the word " godly " translates the genitive case of the noun *theos*, lit., ' of God,' 2 Cor. 1 : 12, A.V., " godly (sincerity)," R.V., " (sincerity) of God ; " 2 Cor. 11 : 2, " a godly jealousy," lit., ' a jealousy of God ' (R.V., marg.) ; 1 Tim. 1 : 4, R.V., " a dispensation of God " (*oikonomia*, in the best mss.), A.V., " godly edifying " (*oikodomē*, lit., ' an edifying of, i.e., by, God '). (2) In 2 Cor. 7 : 10, " godly (sorrow)," and in vv. 9 and 11, " after a godly sort," are in all three places, lit., ' according to God.' (3) In 3 John 6, where the A.V. translates the adverb *axiōs*, with the noun *theos*, " after a godly sort," the R.V. rightly substitutes " worthily of God."

GODWARD

Note : This translates the phrase *pros ton theon*, lit., ' toward God,' in 2 Cor. 3 : 4, and 1 Thess. 1 : 8.

GOLD, GOLDEN
A. Nouns.

1. CHRUSOS (χρυσός) is used (*a*) of coin, Matt. 10 : 9 ; Jas. 5 : 3 ; (*b*) of ornaments, Matt. 23 : 16, 17 ; Jas. 5 : 3 (perhaps both coin and ornaments) ; Rev. 18 : 12 ; some mss. have it instead of No. 2 in 1 Cor. 3 : 12 ; (*c*) of images, Acts 17 : 29 ; (*d*) of the metal in general, Matt. 2 : 11 ; Rev. 9 : 7 (some mss. have it in Rev. 18 : 16).¶

2. CHRUSION (χρυσίον), a diminutive of No. 1, is used (*a*) of coin, primarily smaller than those in No. 1 (*a*), Acts 3 : 6 ; 20 : 33 ; 1 Pet. 1 : 18 ; (*b*) of ornaments, 1 Pet. 3 : 3, and the following (in which some mss. have No. 1), 1 Tim. 2 : 9 ; Rev. 17 : 4 ; 18 : 16 ; (*c*) of the metal in general, Heb. 9 : 4 ; 1 Pet. 1 : 7 ; Rev. 21 : 18, 21 ; metaphorically, (*d*) of sound doctrine and its effects, 1 Cor. 3 : 12 ; (*e*) of righteousness of life and conduct, Rev. 3 : 18.¶

B. Adjective.

CHRUSEOS (χρυσέος) denotes golden, i.e., made of, or overlaid with, gold, 2 Tim. 2 : 20 ; Heb. 9 : 4, and fifteen times in the Apocalypse.

GOLD RING

CHRUSODAKTULIOS (χρυσοδακτύλιος), an adjective denoting ' with a gold ring ' (*daktulos*, a finger), occurs in Jas. 2 : 2.¶

GOOD, GOODLY, GOODNESS
A. Adjectives.

1. AGATHOS (ἀγαθός) describes that which, being good in its character or constitution, is beneficial in its effect ; it is used (*a*) of things physical, e.g., a tree, Matt. 7 : 17 ; ground, Luke 8 : 8 ; (*b*) in a moral sense, frequently of persons and things. God is essentially, absolutely and consummately good, Matt. 19 : 17 ; Mark 10 : 18 ; Luke 18 : 19. To certain persons the word is applied in Matt. 20 : 15 ; 25 : 21, 23 ; Luke 19 : 17 ; 23 : 50 ; John 7 : 12 ; Acts 11 : 24 ; Tit. 2 : 5 ; in a general application, Matt. 5 : 45 ; 12 : 35 ; Luke 6 : 45 ; Rom. 5 : 7 ; 1 Pet. 2 : 18.

The neuter of the adjective with the definite article signifies that which is good, lit., ' the good,' as being morally honourable, pleasing to God, and therefore beneficial. Christians are to prove it, Rom. 12 : 2 ; to cleave to it, 12 : 9 ; to do it, 13 : 3 ; Gal. 6 : 10 ; 1 Pet. 3 : 11 (here, and here only, the article is absent) ; John 5 : 29 (here, the neuter plural is used, ' the good things ') ; to work it, Rom. 2 : 10 ; Eph. 4 : 28 ; 6 : 8 ; to follow after it, 1 Thess. 5 : 15 ; to be zealous of it, 1 Pet. 3 : 13 ; to imitate it, 3 John 11 ; to overcome evil with it, Rom. 12 : 21. Governmental authorities are ministers of good, i.e., that which is salutary, suited to the course of human affairs, Rom. 13 : 4. In Philm. 14, " thy goodness," R.V. (lit., ' thy good '), means ' thy benefit.' As to Matt. 19 : 17, " why askest thou Me concerning that which is good ? " the R.V. follows the most ancient mss.

The neuter plural is also used of material goods, riches, etc., Luke 1 : 53 ; 12 : 18, 19 ; 16 : 25 ; Gal. 6 : 6 (of temporal supplies) ; in Rom. 10 : 15 ; Heb. 9 : 11 ; 10 : 1, the good things are the benefits provided through the sacrifice of Christ, in regard both to those conferred through the Gospel and to those of the coming Messianic Kingdom. See further under No. 2. See BENEFIT, GOODS.

2. KALOS (καλός) denotes that which is intrinsically good, and so, goodly, fair, beautiful, as (a) of that which is well adapted to its circumstances or ends, e.g., fruit, Matt. 3 : 10 ; a tree, 12 : 33 ; ground, 13 : 8, 23 ; fish, 13 : 48 ; the Law, Rom. 7 : 16 ; 1 Tim. 1 : 8 ; every creature of God, 1 Tim. 4 : 4 ; a faithful minister of Christ and the doctrine he teaches, 4 : 6 ; (b) of that which is ethically good, right, noble, honourable, e.g., Gal. 4 : 18 ; 1 Tim. 5 : 10, 25 ; 6 : 18 ; Tit. 2 : 7, 14 ; 3 : 8, 14. The word does not occur in the Apocalypse, nor indeed after 1 Peter.

Christians are to " take thought for things honourable " (kalos), 2 Cor. 8 : 21, R.V. ; to do that which is honourable, 13 : 7 ; not to be weary in well doing, Gal. 6 : 9 ; to hold fast "that which is good," 1 Thess. 5 : 21 ; to be zealous of good works, Tit. 2 : 14 ; to maintain them, 3 : 8 ; to provoke to them, Heb. 10 : 24 ; to bear testimony by them, 1 Pet. 2 : 12.

Kalos and *agathos* occur together in Luke 8 : 15, an " honest " (*kalos*) heart, i.e., the attitude of which is right towards God ; a " good " (*agathos*) heart, i.e., one that, instead of working ill to a neighbour, acts beneficially towards him. In Rom. 7 : 18, " in me . . . dwelleth no good thing " (*agathos*) signifies that in him is nothing capable of doing good, and hence he lacks the power " to do that which is good " (*kalos*). In 1 Thess. 5 : 15, " follow after that which is good " (*agathos*), the good is that which is beneficial ; in ver. 21, " hold fast that which is good (*kalos*)," the good describes the intrinsic value of the teaching. See BETTER, FAIR, HONEST, MEET, WORTHY.

3. CHRĒSTOS (χρηστός), said of things, that which is pleasant, said of persons, kindly, gracious, is rendered " good " in 1 Cor. 15 : 33 ; " goodness " in Rom. 2 : 4. See EASY.

Note : Lampros denotes gay, bright, " goodly " in Jas. 2 : 2, A.V.,
(R.V., " fine ") ; in 2 : 3, A.V., " gay ; " in Rev. 18 : 14 (R.V., " sumptuous "). See GORGEOUS, SUMPTUOUS. For *asteios*, " goodly," Heb.
11 : 23, R.V., see BEAUTIFUL. For *hikanos*, Acts 18 : 18, A.V., " a good
while " see WHILE. *Note* (16).

B. Nouns.

1. CHRĒSTOTĒS (χρηστότης), akin to A, No. 3, denotes goodness
(*a*) in the sense of what is upright, righteous, Rom. 3 : 12 (translated
" good ") ; (*b*) in the sense of kindness of heart or act, said of God, Rom.
2 : 4 ; 11 : 22 (thrice) ; Eph. 2 : 7 (" kindness ") ; Tit. 3 : 4 (" kindness ") ;
said of believers and rendered " kindness," 2 Cor. 6 : 6 ; Col. 3 : 12 ;
Gal. 5 : 22 (R.V. ; A.V., " gentleness "). It signifies " not merely
goodness as a quality, rather it is goodness in action, goodness expressing
itself in deeds ; yet not goodness expressing itself in indignation against
sin, for it is contrasted with severity in Rom. 11 : 22, but in grace and
tenderness and compassion."* See GENTLENESS, KINDNESS.¶

2. AGATHŌSUNĒ (ἀγαθωσύνη), goodness, signifies that moral
quality which is described by the adjective *agathos* (see A, No. 1). It
is used, in the N.T., of regenerate persons, R^m. 15 : 14 ; Gal. 5 : 22 ;
Eph. 5 : 9 ; 2 Thess. 1 : 11 ; in the last, the phrase " every desire of
goodness " (R.V. ; the addition of " His " in the A.V. is an interpolation ;
there is no pronoun in the original) may be either subjective, i.e., desire
characterised by goodness, good desire, or objective, i.e., desire after
goodness, to be and do good.¶

Trench, following Jerome, distinguishes between *chrēstotēs* and
agathōsunē in that the former describes the kindlier aspects of goodness,
the latter includes also the sterner qualities by which doing good to others
is not necessarily by gentle means. He illustrates the latter by the act of
Christ in cleansing the temple, Matt. 21 : 12, 13, and in denouncing the
Scribes and Pharisees, 23 : 13–29 ; but *chrēstotēs* by His dealings with the
penitent woman, Luke 7 : 37–50. Lightfoot regards *chrēstotēs* as a kindly
disposition towards others ; *agathōsunē* as a kindly activity on their behalf.

J. A. Robertson (on Eph. 5 : 9) remarks that *agathōsunē* is " the
kindlier, as *dikaiosunē* (righteousness) the sterner, element in the ideal
character."

3. EUPOIIA (εὐποιία), beneficence, doing good (*eu*, well, *poieō*, to do),
is translated as a verb in Heb. 13 : 16, " to do good."¶

C. Adverbs.

1. KALŌS (καλῶς), well, finely, is used in some mss. in Matt. 5 : 44,
with *poieō*, to do, and translated " do good." In Jas. 2 : 3 it is rendered
" in a good place " (A.V. marg., " well " or " seemly "). See WELL.

2. EU (εὖ), well, used with *poieō*, is translated " do . . . good " in
Mark 14 : 7. See WELL.

---

* From Notes on Galatians, by Hogg and Vine, p. 292.

D. Verbs (to do, or be, good).

1. AGATHOPOIEŌ (ἀγαθοποιέω), from A, No. 1, and *poieō*, to do, is used (*a*) in a general way, to do well, 1 Pet. 2 : 15, 20 ; 3 : 6, 17 ; 3 John 11 ; (*b*) with pointed reference to the benefit of another, Luke 6 : 9, 33, 35 ; in Mark 3 : 4 the parts of the word are separated in some mss. Some mss. have it in Acts 14 : 17, for No. 2.¶ Cp. the noun *agathopoiia*, well-doing, 1 Pet. 4 : 19, and the adjective *agathopoios*, doing well, 1 Pet. 2 : 14.

2. AGATHOURGEŌ (ἀγαθουργέω), for *agathoergeō*, to do good (from A, No. 1, and *ergon*, a work), is used in Acts 14 : 17 (in the best mss. ; see No. 1), where it is said of God's beneficence towards man, and 1 Tim. 6 : 18, where it is enjoined upon the rich.¶

3. EUERGETEŌ (εὐεργετέω), to bestow a benefit, to do good (*eu*, well, and a verbal form akin to *ergon*), is used in Acts 10 : 38.¶

Notes : (1) The verb *ischuo*, to be strong (*ischus*, strength), to have efficacy, force or value, is said of salt in Matt. 5 : 13, negatively, " it is good for nothing." (2) In Matt. 19 : 10, A.V., *sumpherō*, to be profitable, expedient (*sun*, together, *pherō*, to bring), is rendered with a negative " it is not good " (R.V., " it is not expedient "). (3) In Mark 14 : 7, the two words *eu*, well, and *poieō*, to do, are in some mss. treated as one verb *eupoieō*, to do good.

GOODMAN

OIKODESPOTĒS (οἰκοδεσπότης) denotes the master of a house (*oikos*, a house, *despotēs*, a master), a householder. It occurs only in the Synoptists, and there 12 times. It is rendered " goodman " in Luke 22 : 11, where " of the house " is put separately ; in Matt. 20 : 11, where the A.V. has " the goodman of the house " for the one word, the R.V. renders it by " householder," as in ver. 1 ; in 24 : 43, " master ; " so in Luke 12 : 39 ; in Mark 14 : 14, both have " the goodman of the house." See HOUSEHOLDER, MASTER.

GOODS

1. For the neuter plural of *agathos*, used as a noun, " goods," see Luke 12 : 18, 19, where alone this word is so rendered.

2. HUPARXIS (ὕπαρξις), primarily, subsistence, then, substance, property, goods (akin to *huparchō*, to exist, be, belong to), is translated " goods " in Acts 2 : 45 ; " possession," R.V. (A.V., " substance ") in Heb. 10 : 34.¶

3. BIOS (βίος), which denotes (*a*) life, lifetime, (*b*) livelihood, living, means of living, is translated " goods " in 1 John 3 : 17, R.V. (A.V., " good "). See LIFE, No. 2.

4. SKEUOS (σκεῦος), a vessel, denotes " goods " in Matt. 12 : 29 ; Mark 3 : 27 ; Luke 17 : 31, R.V. (A.V., " stuff "). See VESSEL.

Notes : (1) The neuter plural of the present participle of *huparchō*, is used as a noun denoting goods, in Matt. 24 : 47, A.V. " his goods,"

R.V., " that he hath ; " " goods " in Matt. 25 : 14 ; Luke 11 : 21 ; 16 : 1 ;
19 : 8 ; 1 Cor. 13 : 3 ; in Heb. 10 : 34 (1st part). (2) In Luke 6 : 30
" thy goods " translates the neuter plural of the possessive pronoun with
the article, lit., ' thy things,' or possessions. (3) In Rev. 3 : 17, the A.V.
" I am . . . increased with goods " translates the perfect tense of the
verb *plouteō*, to be rich; R.V., " I have gotten riches." (4) See SUBSTANCE.

GORGEOUS, GORGEOUSLY

LAMPROS (λαμπρός), bright, splendid, is rendered " gorgeous " in
Luke 23 : 11, of the apparel in which Herod and his soldiers arrayed
Christ. See BRIGHT.

Note : For the A.V., " gorgeously apparelled " in Luke 7 : 25, see
GLORIOUS, B.

GOSPEL (Noun and Verb : to preach)
A. Noun.

EUANGELION (εὐαγγέλιον) originally denoted a reward for good
tidings ; later, the idea of reward dropped, and the word stood for the good
news itself. The Eng. word gospel, i.e. good message, is the equivalent
of *euangelion* (Eng., evangel). In the N.T. it denotes the good tidings of
the Kingdom of God and of salvation through Christ, to be received by
faith, on the basis of His expiatory death, His burial, resurrection, and
ascension, e.g., Acts 15 : 7 ; 20 : 24 ; 1 Pet. 4 : 17. Apart from those
references and those in the Gospels of Matthew and Mark, and Rev. 14 : 6,
the noun is confined to Paul's Epistles. The Apostle uses it of two
associated yet distinct things, (*a*) of the basic facts of the death, burial
and resurrection of Christ, e.g., 1 Cor. 15 : 1–3 ; (*b*) of the interpretation
of these facts, e.g., Rom. 2 : 16 ; Gal. 1 : 7, 11 ; 2 : 2 ; in (*a*) the Gospel
is viewed historically, in (*b*) doctrinally, with reference to the interpretation
of the facts, as is sometimes indicated by the context.

The following phrases describe the subjects or nature or purport of the
message ; it is the gospel of God, Mark 1 : 14 ; Rom. 1 : 1 ; 15 : 16 ;
2 Cor. 11 : 7 ; 1 Thess. 2 : 2, 9 ; 1 Pet. 4 : 17 ; God, concerning His Son,
Rom. 1 : 1–3 ; His Son, Rom. 1 : 9 ; Jesus Christ, the Son of God, Mark
1 : 1 ; our Lord Jesus, 2 Thess. 1 : 8 ; Christ, Rom. 15 : 19, etc. ; the glory
of Christ, 2 Cor. 4 : 4 ; the grace of God, Acts 20 : 24 ; the glory of the
blessed God, 1 Tim. 1 : 11 ; your salvation, Eph. 1 : 13 ; peace, Eph. 6 : 15.
Cp. also " the gospel of the Kingdom," Matt. 4 : 23 ; 9 : 35 ; 24 : 14 ;
" an eternal gospel," Rev. 14 : 6.

In Gal. 2 : 14, " the truth of the gospel " denotes, not the true gospel,
but the true teaching of it, in contrast to perversions of it.

The following expressions are used in connection with the Gospel :
(*a*) with regard to its testimony ; (1) *kērussō*, to preach it as a herald, e.g.,
Matt. 4 : 23 ; Gal. 2 : 2 (see PREACH) ; (2) *laleō*, to speak, 1 Thess. 2 : 2 ;
(3) *diamarturomai*, to testify (thoroughly), Acts 20 : 24 ; (4) *euangelizō*,

to preach, e.g., 1 Cor. 15 : 1 ; 2 Cor. 11 : 7 ; Gal. 1 : 11 (see B, No. 1 below) ; (5) *katangellō*, to proclaim, 1 Cor. 9 : 14 ; (6) *douleuō eis*, to serve unto (" in furtherance of "), Phil. 2 : 22 ; (7) *sunathleō en*, to labour with in, Phil. 4 : 3 ; (8) *hierourgeō*, to minister, Rom. 15 : 16 ; (8) *plēroō*, to preach fully, Rom. 15 : 19 ; (10) *sunkakopatheō*, to suffer hardship with, 2 Tim. 1 : 8 ; (*b*) with regard to its reception or otherwise : (1) *dechomai*, to receive, 2 Cor. 11 : 4 ; *hupakouō*, to hearken to, or obey, Rom. 10 : 16 ; 2 Thess. 1 : 8 ; *pisteuō en*, to believe in, Mark 1 : 15 ; *metastrephō*, to pervert, Gal. 1 : 7.

Note : In connection with (*a*), the Apostle's statement in 1 Cor. 9 : 23 is noticeable, " I do all things for the Gospel's sake, that I may be a joint partaker thereof," R.V., for the incorrect A.V., " that I might be partaker thereof with you."

B. Verbs.

1. EUANGELIZŌ (*εὐαγγελίζω*), to bring or announce glad tidings (Eng., evangelize), is used (*a*) in the Active Voice in Rev. 10 : 7 (" declared ") and 14 : 6 (" to proclaim," R.V., A.V., " to preach ") ; (*b*) in the Passive Voice, of matters to be proclaimed as glad tidings, Luke 16 : 16 ; Gal. 1 : 11 ; 1 Pet. 1 : 25 ; of persons to whom the proclamation is made, Matt. 11 : 5 ; Luke 7 : 22 ; Heb. 4 : 2, 6 ; 1 Pet. 4 : 6 ; (*c*) in the Middle Voice, especially of the message of salvation, with a personal object, either of the Person preached, e.g., Acts 5 : 42 ; 11 : 20 ; Gal. 1 : 16, or, with a preposition, of the persons evangelized, e.g., Acts 13 : 32, " declare glad tidings ; " Rom. 1 : 15 ; Gal. 1 : 8 ; with an impersonal object, e.g., " the word," Acts 8 : 4 ; " good tidings," 8 : 12 ; " the word of the Lord," 15 : 35 ; " the gospel," 1 Cor. 15 : 1 ; 2 Cor. 11 : 7 ; " the faith," Gal. 1 : 23 ; " peace," Eph. 2 : 17 ; " the unsearchable riches of Christ," 3 : 8. See PREACH, SHEW, TIDINGS.

2. PROEUANGELIZOMAI (*προευαγγελίζομαι*), to announce glad tidings beforehand, is used in Gal. 3 : 8.¶

Note : For other verbs see above.

For GOT and GOTTEN see GET

GOVERNMENT

KUBERNĒSIS (*κυβέρνησις*), from *kubernaō*, to guide (whence Eng., govern), denotes (*a*) steering, pilotage ; (*b*) metaphorically, governments or governings, said of those who act as guides in a local church, 1 Cor. 12 : 28.¶ Cp. *kubernētēs*, a pilot, Acts 27 : 11 ; Rev. 18 : 17.¶

Note : For *kuriotēs*, lordship, dominion, rendered " government " in 2 Pet. 2 : 10, A.V., see DOMINION.

GOVERNOR
A. Nouns.

1. HĒGEMŌN (*ἡγεμών*) is a term used (*a*) for rulers generally, Mark

13 : 9; 1 Pet. 2 : 14; translated "princes" (i.e., leaders) in Matt. 2 : 6; (b) for the Roman Procurators, referring, in the Gospels to Pontius Pilate, e.g., Matt. 27 : 2 ; Luke 20 : 20 (so designated by Tacitus, Annals, xv. 44) ; to Felix, Acts 23 : 26. Technically the Procurator was a financial official under a proconsul or propraetor, for collecting the Imperial revenues, but entrusted also with magisterial powers for decisions of questions relative to the revenues. In certain provinces, of which Judæa was one (the Procurator of which was dependent on the Legate of Syria), he was the general administrator and supreme judge, with sole power of life and death. Such a governor was a person of high social standing. Felix, however, was an ex-slave, a freedman, and his appointment to Judæa could not but be regarded by the Jews as an insult to the nation. The headquarters of the governor of Judæa was Cæsarea, which was made a garrison town. See PRINCE, RULER. For *anthupatos*, a proconsul, see PROCONSUL.

2. ETHNARCHĒS (ἐθνάρχης), an ethnarch, lit. a ruler of a nation (*ethnos*, a people, *archē*, rule), is translated " governor " in 2 Cor. 11 : 32 ; it describes normally the ruler of a nation possessed of separate laws and customs among those of a different race. Eventually it denoted a ruler of a Province, superior to a tetrarch, but inferior to a king (e.g., Aretas).¶

3. OIKONOMOS (οἰκονόμος), lit., one who rules a house (*oikos*, a house, *nomos*, a law), Gal. 4 : 2, denotes a superior servant responsible for the family housekeeping, the direction of other servants, and the care of the children under age. See CHAMBERLAIN, STEWARD.

4. ARCHITRIKLINOS (ἀρχιτρίκλινος), from *archē*, rule, and *triklinos*, a room with three couches, denotes the ruler of a feast, John 2 : 8, R.V. (A.V., " the governor of the feast "), a man appointed to see that the table and couches were duly placed and the courses arranged, and to taste the food and wine.¶

B. Verbs.

1. HĒGEOMAI (ἡγέομαι), akin to A, No. 1, is used in the present participle to denote a governor, lit., ' (one) governing,' Matt. 2 : 6; Acts 7 : 10.

2. HĒGEMONEUŌ (ἡγεμονεύω), to be a *hēgemōn*, to lead the way, came to signify to be a governor of a Province ; it is used of Quirinius, governor of Syria, Luke 2 : 2, R.V. (for the circumstances see under ENROLMENT) ; of Pontius Pilate, governor of Judæa, 3 : 1.¶ In the first clause of this verse the noun *hēgemonia*, a rule or sovereignty, is translated " reign ; " Eng., hegemony.¶

Note. In Jas. 3 : 4, the verb *euthunō*, to make or guide straight, is used in the present participle, as a noun, denoting the " steersman " (R.V.) or pilot of a vessel, A.V., " governor."

GRACE

1. CHARIS (χάρις) has various uses, (a) objective, that which bestows

or occasions pleasure, delight, or causes favourable regard ; it is applied, e.g., to beauty, or gracefulness of person, Luke 2 : 40 ; act, 2 Cor. 8 : 6, or speech, Luke 4 : 22, R.V., " words of grace " (A.V., " gracious words ") ; Col. 4 : 6 ; (b) subjective, (1) on the part of the bestower, the friendly disposition from which the kindly act proceeds, graciousness, loving-kindness, goodwill generally, e.g., Acts 7 : 10 ; especially with reference to the Divine favour or grace, e.g., Acts 14 : 26 ; in this respect there is stress on its freeness and universality, its spontaneous character, as in the case of God's redemptive mercy, and the pleasure or joy He designs for the recipient ; thus it is set in contrast with debt, Rom. 4 : 4, 16, with works, 11 : 6, and with law, John 1 : 17 ; see also, e.g., Rom. 6 : 14, 15 ; Gal. 5 : 4 ; (2) on the part of the receiver, a sense of the favour bestowed, a feeling of gratitude, e.g., Rom. 6 : 17 (" thanks ") ; in this respect it sometimes signifies to be thankful, e.g., Luke 17 : 9 (" doth he thank the servant ? " lit., ' hath he thanks to ') ; 1 Tim. 1 : 12 ; (c) in another objective sense, the effect of grace, the spiritual state of those who have experienced its exercise, whether (1) a state of grace, e.g., Rom. 5 : 2 ; 1 Pet. 5 : 12 ; 2 Pet. 3 : 18, or (2) a proof thereof in practical effects, deeds of grace, e.g., 1 Cor. 16 : 3, R.V., " bounty " (A.V., " liberality ") ; 2 Cor. 8 : 6, 19 (in 2 Cor. 9 : 8 it means the sum of earthly blessings) ; the power and equipment for ministry, e.g., Rom. 1 : 5 ; 12 : 6 ; 15 : 15 ; 1 Cor. 3 : 10 ; Gal. 2 : 9 ; Eph. 3 : 2, 7.

To be in favour with is to find grace with, e.g., Acts 2 : 47 ; hence it appears in this sense at the beginning and the end of several Epistles, where the writer desires grace from God for the readers, e.g., Rom. 1 : 7 ; 1 Cor. 1 : 3 ; in this respect it is connected with the imperative mood of the word *chairō*, to rejoice, a mode of greeting among Greeks, e.g., Acts 15 : 23 ; Jas. 1 : 1 (marg.) ; 2 John 10, 11, R.V., " greeting " (A.V., " God speed ").

The fact that grace is received both from God the Father, 2 Cor. 1 : 12, and from Christ, Gal. 1 : 6 ; Rom. 5 : 15 (where both are mentioned), is a testimony to the Deity of Christ.   See also 2 Thess. 1 : 12, where the phrase " according to the grace of our God and the Lord Jesus Christ " is to be taken with each of the preceding clauses, " in you," " and ye in Him."

In Jas. 4 : 6, " But He giveth more grace " (Greek, ' a greater grace,' R.V., marg.), the statement is to be taken in connection with the preceding verse, which contains two remonstrating, rhetorical questions, " Think ye that the Scripture speaketh in vain ? " and " Doth the Spirit (the Holy Spirit) which He made to dwell in us long unto envying ? " (see the R.V.). The implied answer to each is ' it cannot be so.'   Accordingly, if those who are acting so flagrantly, as if it were so, will listen to the Scripture instead of letting it speak in vain, and will act so that the Holy Spirit may have His way within, God will give even ' a greater grace,' namely, all that follows from humbleness and from turning away from the world. See BENEFIT, BOUNTY, LIBERALITY, THANK.

Note : The corresponding verb *charitoō*, to endue with Divine favour or grace, is used in Luke 1 : 28, " highly favoured " (marg., " endued with grace ") and Eph. 1 : 6, A.V., " hath made . . . accepted ; " R.V., " freely bestowed " (marg., " endued.").¶

2. EUPREPEIA (εὐπρέπεια), comeliness, goodly appearance, is said of the outward appearance of the flower of the grass, Jas. 1 : 11.¶

GRACIOUS

CHRĒSTOS (χρηστός) is rendered " gracious " in 1 Pet. 2 : 3, as an attribute of the Lord. See EASY, GOOD, KIND.

Note : *Euphēmos*, fair-sounding (*eu*, well, *phēmē*, a saying, or report), " of good report," Phil. 4 : 8, is rendered " gracious " in the R.V. marg.

GRAFF, GRAFT (R.V.)

ENKENTRIZŌ (ἐνκεντρίζω) denotes to graft in (*en*, in, *kentrizō*, to graft), to insert a slip of a cultivated tree into a wild one. In Rom. 11 : 17, 19, 23, 24, however, the metaphor is used " contrary to nature " (ver. 24), of grafting a wild olive branch (the Gentile) into the good olive tree (the Jews) ; that unbelieving Jews (branches of the good tree) were broken off that Gentiles might be grafted in, afforded no occasion for glorying on the part of the latter. Jew and Gentile alike must enjoy the Divine blessings by faith alone. So Jews who abide not in unbelief shall, as " the natural branches, be grafted into their own olive tree."¶

GRAIN

KOKKOS (κόκκος) denotes a grain, Matt. 13 : 31 ; 17 : 20 ; Mark 4 : 31 ; Luke 13 : 19 ; 17 : 6 ; John 12 : 24 (A.V., " corn ") ; 1 Cor. 15 : 37 (where the R.V. has " a . . . grain," to distinguish it from grain in general). See CORN.¶

GRANDCHILDREN

EKGONOS (ἔκγονος), an adjective, denoting born of (*ek*, from, *ginomai*, to become or be born), was used as a noun, signifying a child ; in the plural, descendants, " grand-children," 1 Tim. 5 : 4, R.V. (A.V., " nephews ").¶

GRANDMOTHER

MAMMĒ (μάμμη), an onomatopœic word, was primarily a child's name for its mother ; later it denoted a grandmother, 2 Tim. 1 : 5.¶

GRANT

1. DIDŌMI (δίδωμι), to give, is rendered " grant " in Mark 10 : 37 ; Luke 1 : 74 ; Acts 4 : 29 ; 11 : 18 ; 14 : 3. See GIVE.

2. DŌREŌ (δωρέω), to present, bestow (akin to No. 1), is rendered "granted" in Mark 15 : 45, R.V. (A.V., "gave"); in 2 Pet. 1 : 3, 4, "hath granted," "He hath granted," R.V. (A.V., "hath given" and "are given"); in each place Middle Voice. See GIVE.¶

3. CHARIZOMAI (χαρίζομαι) primarily signifies to show favour or kindness (akin to *charis*, see GRACE), Gal. 3 : 18, R.V., "hath granted" (A.V., "gave"; it signifies more than to give); then, to give freely, bestow, rendered to grant in Acts 3 : 14; 27 : 24, R.V. (A.V., "given"); Phil. 1 : 29, R.V.; Philm. 22, R.V. See DELIVER.

GRAPE

STAPHULĒ (σταφυλή) denotes a bunch of grapes, or a grape, Matt. 7 : 16; Luke 6 : 44; Rev. 14 : 18. It is to be distinguished from *omphax*, an unripe grape (not in N.T.), e.g., in the Sept. of Job 15 : 33, and from *botrus*, a cluster, used together with *staphulē* in Rev. 14 : 18.¶

GRASS

CHORTOS (χόρτος) primarily denoted a feeding enclosure (whence Latin *hortus*, a garden; Eng., yard, and garden); then, food, especially grass for feeding cattle; it is translated "grass" in Matt. 6 : 30; 14 : 19; Mark 6 : 39 (where "the green grass" is the first evidence of early spring); Luke 12 : 28; John 6 : 10; Jas. 1 : 10, 11; 1 Pet. 1 : 24; Rev. 8 : 7; 9 : 4; "blade" in Matt. 13 : 26; Mark 4 : 28; "hay" in 1 Cor. 3 : 12, used figuratively. In Palestine or Syria there are 90 genera and 243 species of grass.¶

GRATULATION

MAKARISMOS (μακαρισμός) denotes a declaration of blessedness, a felicitation; it is translated "gratulation" in Gal. 4:15, R.V. (A.V., "blessedness"); the Galatian converts had counted themselves happy when they heard and received the Gospel from Paul; he asks them rhetorically what had become of that spirit which had animated them; the word is rendered "blessing" in Rom. 4:6, 9. See BLESSING, C, No. 2.¶

GRAVE (Noun)

1. MNĒMEION (μνημεῖον) primarily denotes a memorial (akin to *mnaomai*, to remember), then, a monument (the significance of the word rendered "tombs," A.V., "sepulchres," in Luke 11:47), anything done to preserve the memory of things and persons; it usually denotes a tomb, and is translated either 'tomb" or "sepulchre" or "grave." Apart from the Gospels, it is found only in Acts 13:29. Among the Hebrews it was generally a cavern, closed by a door or stone, often decorated. Cp. Matt. 23:29. See TOMB.

2. MNÊMA (μνῆμα), akin to No. 1, like which it signified a memorial or record of a thing or a dead person, then a sepulchral monument, and hence a tomb ; it is rendered " graves " in the A.V. of Rev. 11 : 9 (R.V., " a tomb ") ; " tomb " or " tombs," Mark 5 : 3, 5 (some mss. have No. 1, as in 15 : 46, A.V., " sepulchre ") and 16 : 2 (A.V., " sepulchre ") ; Luke 8 : 27 ; Acts 2 : 29 and 7 : 16 (A.V., " sepulchre "). See TOMB.

Note : In 1 Cor. 15 : 55, where some texts have " Hades," A.V., " grave," the most authentic have *thanatos*, death.

GRAVE (Adjective)

SEMNOS (σεμνός) first denoted reverend, august, venerable (akin to *sebomai*, to reverence) ; then, serious, grave, whether of persons, 1 Tim. 3 : 8, 11 (deacons and their wives) ; Tit. 2 : 2 (aged men) ; or things, Phil. 4 : 8, R.V., " honourable " (marg., " reverend "), A.V., " honest." Trench (Syn.,§ xcii) points out that " grave " and " gravity " fail to cover the full meaning of their original ; " the word we want is one in which the sense of gravity and dignity is combined." Cremer describes it as denoting what inspires reverence and awe, and says that *semnos* and *hosios*, holy, consecrated, are only secondary designations of the conception of holiness. " The word points to seriousness of purpose and to self-respect in conduct " (Moule).¶ Cp. *semnotēs*, gravity (see below).

GRAVE-CLOTHES

KEIRIA (κειρία) denotes, firstly, a band either for a bed girth, or bed sheets themselves (Sept. of Prov. 7 : 16.¶) ; then, the swathings wrapped round a corpse ; it is used in the plural in John 11 : 44.¶

GRAVEN

CHARAGMA (χάραγμα), from *charassō*, to engrave (akin to *charaktēr*, an impress, R.V., marg., of Heb. 1 : 3), denotes (*a*) a mark or stamp, e.g., Rev. 13 : 16, 17 ; 14 : 9, 11 ; 16 : 2 ; 19 : 20 ; 20 : 4 ; 15 : 2 in some mss. ; (*b*) a thing graven, Acts 17 : 29.¶

GRAVITY

SEMNOTĒS (σεμνότης) denotes venerableness, dignity ; it is a necessary characteristic of the life and conduct of Christians, 1 Tim. 2 : 2, R.V., " gravity " (A.V., " honesty "), a qualification of a bishop or overseer in a church, in regard to his children, 1 Tim. 3 : 4 ; a necessary characteristic of the teaching imparted by a servant of God, Tit. 2 : 7.¶ Cp. the adjective *semnos*, under GRAVE.

GREAT

1. MEGAS (μέγας) is used (*a*) of external form, size, measure, e.g., of a stone, Matt. 27 : 60 ; fish, John 21 : 11 ; (*b*) of degree and intensity, e.g., of fear, Mark 4 : 41 ; wind, John 6 : 18 ; Rev. 6 : 13, R.V., " great "

(A.V., " mighty ") ; of a circumstance, I Cor. 9 : 11 ; 2 Cor. 11 : 15 ; in Rev. 5 : 2, 12, the R.V. has " great " (A.V., " loud "), of a voice ; (c) of rank, whether of persons, e.g., God, Tit. 2 : 13 ; Christ as a " great Priest," Heb. 10 : 21, R.V. ; Diana, Acts 19 : 27 ; Simon Magus, Acts 8 : 9 " (some) great one ; " in the plural, " great ones," Matt. 20 : 25 ; Mark 10 : 42, those who hold positions of authority in Gentile nations ; or of things, e.g., a mystery, Eph. 5 : 32. Some mss. have it in Acts 8 : 8, of joy (see No. 2). See also Note (2) below. See GREATEST, HIGH, LOUD, MIGHTY, STRONG.

2. POLUS (πολύς), much, many, great, is used of number, e.g., Luke 5 : 6 ; Acts 11 : 21 ; degree, e.g., of harvest, Matt. 9 : 37 [See Note (8)] ; mercy, I Pet. 1 : 3, R.V., " great " (A.V., " abundant ") ; glory, Matt. 24 : 30 ; joy, Philm. 7, R.V., " much " (A.V., " great ") ; peace, Acts 24 : 2. The best mss. have it in Acts 8 : 8 (R.V., " much "), of joy. See ABUNDANT, COMMON, Note (1), LONG, MANY, MUCH, OFT, SORE, STRAITLY.

3. HIKANOS (ἱκανός), lit., reaching to (from hikanō, to reach), denotes sufficient, competent, fit, and is sometimes rendered " great," e.g., of number (of people), Mark 10 : 46 ; of degree (of light), Acts 22 : 6. See ABLE, ENOUGH, GOOD, LARGE, LONG, MANY, MEET, MUCH, SECURITY, SUFFICIENT, WORTHY.

4. HĒLIKOS (ἡλίκος) primarily denotes as big as, as old as (akin to hēlikia, an age) ; then, as an indirect interrogation, what, what size, how great, how small (the context determines the meaning), said of a spiritual conflict, Col. 2 : 1, A.V., " what great (conflict) I have ; " R.V., " how greatly (I strive) ; " of much wood as kindled by a little fire, Jas. 3 : 5 (twice in the best mss.), " how much (wood is kindled by) how small (a fire)," R.V., said metaphorically of the use of the tongue. Some mss. have No. 4 in Gal 6 : 11 ; the most authentic have No. 5.¶

5. PĒLIKOS (πηλίκος), primarily a direct interrogative, how large ? how great ? is used in exclamations, indicating magnitude, like No. 4 (No. 6 indicates quantity), in Gal. 6 : 11, of letter characters (see No. 4, Note) ; in Heb. 7 : 4, metaphorically, of the distinguished character of Melchizedek.¶

6. POSOS (πόσος), an adjective of number, magnitude, degree etc., is rendered " how great " in Matt. 6 : 23. See MANY, MUCH.

7. HOSOS (ὅσος), how much, how many, is used in the neuter plural to signify how great things, Mark 5 : 19, 20 ; Luke 8 : 39 (twice) ; Acts 9 : 16, A.V. (R.V., " how many things ") ; in Rev. 21 : 16 (in the best mss.), " as great as," R.V. (A.V., " as large as," said of length). See ALL, MANY, No. 5, WHATSOEVER.

8. TOSOUTOS (τοσοῦτος), so great, so many, so much, of quantity, size, etc., is rendered " so great," in Matt. 8 : 10, and Luke 7 : 9, of faith ; Matt. 15 : 33, of a multitude ; Heb. 12 : 1, of a cloud of witnesses ; Rev. 18 : 17, of riches. See LARGE, LONG, MANY, MUCH.

9. TĒLIKOUTOS (τηλικοῦτος), so great, is used in the N.T. of things only, a death, 2 Cor. 1 : 10 ; salvation, Heb. 2 : 3 ; ships, Jas. 3 : 4 ; an earthquake, Rev. 16 : 18, A.V., " so mighty," corrected in the R.V. to " so great." See MIGHTY.¶

Notes : (1) In Mark 7 : 36, " so much the more a great deal " translates a phrase lit. signifying ' more abundantly ; ' in 10 : 48, " the more a great deal " translates a phrase lit. signifying ' more by much.'   (2) For the noun *megistan*, in the plural, rendered " Lords " in the A.V. of Mark 6 : 21, see LORD ; in Rev. 6 : 15 and 18 . 23, see PRINCE.   (3) In Luke 1 : 58, the verb *megalunō*, to magnify, make great (akin to No. 1), is rendered " had magnified (His mercy)," R.V. [A.V., " had shewed great (mercy) "].   (4) In Luke 10 : 13, the adverb *palai*, of old, long ago, is so rendered in the R.V. (A.V., " a great while ago ").   (5) In 2 Pet. 1 : 4, *megistos*, the superlative of *megas* (No. 1), said of the promises of God, is rendered " exceeding great."¶ (6) In Matt. 21 : 8, *pleistos*, the superlative of *polus* (No. 2), said of a multitude, is rendered " very great " in the A.V. (R.V., " the most part ").   (7) In Rev. 21 : 10, the most authentic mss. omit " that great " [R.V., " the holy (city) "].   (8) In Luke 10 : 2, the R.V. renders *polus* by " plenteous " (A.V., " great ").   (9) In Mark 1 : 35, the adverb *lian*, exceedingly (see GREATLY), is rendered " a great while." See DAY, B.   (10) In Luke 1 : 49 some texts have *megaleia*, " great things ; " the best have No. 1.

GREATER

1. MEIZŌN (μείζων) is the comparative degree of *megas* (see GREAT, No. 1), e.g., Matt. 11 : 11 ; in Matt. 13 : 32, the R.V. rightly has " greater than " (A.V., " the greatest among ") ;   23 : 17 ; in Luke 22 : 26, R.V., " the greater (among you) " (A.V., " greatest ") ; in Jas. 3 : 1, R.V., " the heavier (marg., greater) judgment " (A.V., " the greater con-demnation ") ;   it is used in the neuter plural in John 1 : 50, " greater things ; " in 14 : 12, " greater works " (lit.,   greater things ') ;   in 1 Cor. 12 : 31, R.V., " the greater," A.V., " the best ".   See GREATEST, No. 2.

Note : In Matt. 20 : 31, the neuter of *meizōn*, used as an adverb, is translated " the more." See MORE.

2. MEIZOTEROS (μειζότερος), a double comparative of *megas* (cp. No. 1, above), is used in 3 John 4, of joy.¶

3. PLEIŌN (πλείων), the comparative of *polus* (see GREAT, No. 2), is used (*a*) as an adjective, greater, more, e.g., Acts 15 : 28 ; (*b*) as a noun, e.g., Matt. 12 : 41, " a greater (than Jonah) ; " ver. 42, " a greater (than Solomon) ; " in these instances the neuter *pleion*, ' something greater,' is " a fixed or stereotyped form " of the word ; in 1 Cor. 15 : 6, " the greater part " (masculine plural) ; (*c*) as an adverb, e.g., Matt. 5 : 20, lit., ' (except your righteousness abound) more greatly (than of scribes

and Pharisees) ; ' so 26 : 53, " more " ; Luke 9 : 13. See ABOVE, LONGER, MANY, MORE, MOST, YET.

4. PERISSOTEROS (περισσότερος), the comparative of *perissos*, over and above, abundant, signifies more abundant, greater, e.g., of condemnation, Mark 12 : 40 ; Luke 20 : 47. See ABUNDANT, C, No. 2.

GREATEST

1. MEGAS (μέγας), for which see GREAT, No. 1, is translated " the greatest," in Acts 8 : 10 and Heb. 8 : 11. The whole phrase, lit., ' from small to great,' is equivalent to the Eng. idiom " one and all." It is used in the Sept., e.g., in 1 Sam. 5 : 9 (' God smote the people of Gath from the least to the greatest,' " both small and great ") So 1 Sam. 30 : 19 ; 2 Chron. 34 : 30, etc. See GREAT.

2. MEIZON (μείζων), the comparative of No. 1, is sometimes translated " greatest ; " besides the two cases given under GREATER, No. 1, where the R.V. corrects the A.V., " greatest " to " greater " (Matt. 13 : 32 and Luke 22 : 26), the R.V. itself has " greatest " for this comparative in the following, and relegates " greater " to the margin, Matt. 18 : 1, 4 ; 23 : 11 ; Mark 9 : 34 ; Luke 9 : 46 ; 22 : 24. See GREATER, MORE.

GREATLY

1. LIAN (λίαν), very, exceedingly, is rendered " greatly " in Matt. 27 : 14, of wonder ; 2 Tim. 4 : 15, of opposition ; 2 John 4 and 3 John 3, of joy. See EXCEEDING, SORE, VERY.

2. POLUS (πολύς) is used in the neuter singular (*polu*) or the plural (*polla*), as an adverb ; in the sing., e.g., Mark 12 : 27 ; in the plur., e.g., Mark 1 : 45, " much ; " 5 : 23, " greatly " (R.V., " much ') ; ver. 38, A.V. and R.V., " greatly ; " 1 Cor. 16 : 12 (R.V., " much "). See LONG, MUCH.

Note : In Acts 28 : 6, A.V., *polu* is rendered " a great while " (R.V., " long ").

3. MEGALOS (μεγάλως), from *megas* (GREAT, No. 1), is used of rejoicing, Phil. 4 : 10. ¶

4. CHARA (χαρά), joy, is used in the dative case adverbially with the verb *chairō*, to rejoice, in John 3 : 29, " rejoiceth greatly," lit., ' rejoiceth with joy.'

Notes : (1) For *sphodra*, R.V., " exceedingly," in Matt. 27 : 54 and Acts 6 : 7, see EXCEED, B, No. 2. (2) In the following the R.V. omits " greatly," as the verbs are adequately translated without, Phil. 1 : 8 ; 1 Thess. 3 : 6 ; 2 Tim. 1 : 4. In the following the R.V. adds " greatly " to express the fuller force of the verb, Luke 1 : 29 ; Acts 16 : 34 ; 1 Pet. 1 : 8. (3) In 1 Pet. 1 : 6, " ye greatly rejoice," the adverb is not separately expressed, but is incorporated in the rendering of the verb *agalliaō*, to rejoice much, to exult.

GREATNESS

1. MEGETHOS (μέγεθος), akin to *megas* (see GREAT, No. 1), is said of the power of God, in Eph. 1 : 19.¶

2. HUPERBOLE (ὑπερβολή) denotes "exceeding greatness," 2 Cor. 4 : 7 ; 12 : 7. see EXCEL, B, No. 1.

For GREEDILY see RUN, No. 9

For GREEDINESS see COVETOUSNESS, B, No. 3

For GREEDY see LUCRE

GREEN

1. CHLOROS (χλωρός), akin to *chloe*, tender foliage (cp. the name Chloe, 1 Cor. 1 : 11, and Eng., chlorine), denotes (*a*) pale green, the colour of young grass, Mark 6 : 39 ; Rev. 8 : 7 ; 9 : 4, "green thing ; " hence, (*b*) pale, Rev. 6 : 8, the colour of the horse whose rider's name is Death. See PALE.¶

2. HUGROS (ὑγρός) denotes wet, moist (the opposite of *xēros*, dry) ; said of wood, sappy, "green," Luke 23 : 31, i.e., if they thus by the fire of their wrath treated Christ, the guiltless, holy, the fruitful, what would be the fate of the perpetrators, who were like the dry wood, exposed to the fire of Divine wrath.¶

GREET, GREETING
A. Verbs.

1. ASPAZOMAI (ἀσπάζομαι) signifies to greet, welcome, or salute. In the A.V. it is chiefly rendered by either of the verbs to greet or to salute. "There is little doubt that the Revisers have done wisely in giving ' salute ' . . . in the passages where A.V. has ' greet.' For the cursory reader is sure to imagine a difference of Greek and of meaning when he finds, e.g., in Phil. 4 : 21, ' Salute every saint in Christ Jesus. The brethren which are with me greet you,' or in 3 John 14, ' Our friends salute thee. Greet the friends by name ' " (Hastings, Bible Dic.). In Acts 25 : 13 the meaning virtually is ' to pay his respects to.'

In two passages the renderings vary otherwise ; in Acts 20 : 1, of bidding farewell, A.V., " embraced them," R.V., " took leave of them," or, as Ramsay translates it, ' bade them farewell ' ; in Heb. 11 : 13, of welcoming promises, A.V., " embraced," R.V., " greeted."

The verb is used as a technical term for conveying greetings at the close of a letter, often by an amanuensis, e.g., Rom. 16 : 22, the only instance of the use of the first person in this respect in the N.T. ; see also 1 Cor. 16 : 19, 20 ; 2 Cor. 13 : 13 ; Phil. 4 : 22 ; Col. 4 : 10-15 ; 1 Thess. 5 : 26 ; 2 Tim. 4 : 21 ; Tit. 3 : 15 ; Philm. 23 ; Heb. 13 : 24 ; 1 Pet. 5 : 13, 14 ; 2 John 13. This special use is largely illustrated in the papyri, one example of this showing how keenly the absence of the greeting was felt. The papyri also illustrate the use of the addition " by name," when several persons are included in the greeting, as in 3 John 14 (Moulton and Milligan, Vocab). See EMBRACE, LEAVE, SALUTE.

2. CHAIRŌ (χαίρω), to rejoice, is thrice used as a formula of salutation in Acts 15 : 23, A.V., " send greeting," R.V., " greeting ; " so 23 : 26 ; Jas. 1 : 1. In 2 John 10, 11, the R.V substitutes the phrase (to give) greeting, for the A.V. (to bid) God speed. See FAREWELL, GLAD, HAIL, JOY, REJOICE.

B. Noun.

ASPASMOS (ἀσπασμός), a salutation, is always so rendered in the R.V. ; A.V., " greetings " in Matt. 23 : 7 ; Luke 11 : 43 ; 20 : 46 ; it is used (a) orally in those instances and in Mark 12 : 38 ; Luke 1 : 29, 41, 44 ; (b) in written salutations, 1 Cor. 16 : 21 (cp. A, No. 1, in ver. 20) ; Col. 4 : 18 ; 2 Thess. 3 : 17.¶

GRIEF, GRIEVE
A. Noun.

LUPĒ (λύπη) signifies pain, of body or mind ; it is used in the plural in 1 Pet. 2 : 19 only, R.V., " griefs " (A.V., " grief ") ; here, however, it stands, by metonymy, for ' things that cause sorrow,' grievances ; hence Tyndale's rendering, " grief," for Wycliffe's " sorews ; " everywhere else it is rendered " sorrow," except in Heb. 12 : 11, where it is translated " grievous " (lit., ' of grief '). See HEAVINESS, SORROW.

B. Verbs.

1. LUPEŌ (λυπέω), akin to A, denotes (a), in the Active Voice, to cause pain, or grief, to distress, grieve, e.g., 2 Cor. 2 : 2 (twice, Active and Passive Voices) ; ver. 5 (twice), R.V., " hath caused sorrow " (A.V., " have caused grief," and " grieved ") ; 7 : 8, " made (you) sorry " ; Eph. 4 : 30, of grieving the Holy Spirit of God (as indwelling the believer) ; (b) in the Passive Voice, to be grieved, to be made sorry, to be sorry, sorrowful, e.g., Matt. 14 : 9, R.V., " (the king) was grieved " (A.V., " was sorry ") ; Mark 10 : 22, R.V., " (went away) sorrowful " (A.V., " grieved ") ; John 21 : 17, " (Peter) was grieved ; " Rom. 14 : 15, " (if . . . thy brother) is grieved ; " 2 Cor. 2 : 4, " (not that) ye should be made sorry," R.V., A.V., " ye should be grieved." See HEAVINESS, SORROW, SORROWFUL, SORRY.

2. SUNLUPEŌ (συνλυπέω), or sullupeō, is used in the Passive Voice in Mark 3 : 5, to be grieved or afflicted together with a person, said of Christ's grief at the hardness of heart of those who criticised His healing on the Sabbath Day ; it here seems to suggest the sympathetic nature of His grief because of their self-injury. Some suggest that the sun indicates the mingling of grief with His anger.¶

3. STENAZŌ (στενάζω), to groan (of an inward, unexpressed feeling of sorrow), is translated " with grief " in Heb. 13 : 17 (marg. " groaning ").

It is rendered "sighed" in Mark 7 : 34 ; "groan," in Rom. 8 : 23 ;
2 Cor. 5 : 2, 4 ; "murmur," in Jas. 5 : 9, R.V. (A.V., "grudge"). See
GROAN, MURMUR, SIGH.¶

Notes : (1) *Diaponeō*, to work out with labour, in the Passive Voice,
to be sore troubled, is rendered "being grieved" in Acts 4 : 2 and 16 : 18,
A.V. (R.V., "sore troubled"). See TROUBLE.¶ In some mss., Mark
14 : 4. (2) *Prosochthizō*, to be angry with, is rendered "was grieved"
in Heb. 3 : 10, 17, A.V. (R.V., "was displeased"). See DISPLEASE.¶

GRIEVOUS, GRIEVOUSLY
A. Adjectives.

1. BARUS (βαρύς) denotes heavy, burdensome ; it is always used
metaphorically in the N.T., and is translated "heavy" in Matt. 23 : 4,
of Pharisaical ordinances ; in the comparative degree "weightier,"
23 : 23, of details of the Law of God ; "grievous," metaphorically of
wolves, in Acts 20 : 29 ; of charges, 25 : 7 ; negatively of God's commandments, 1 John 5 : 3 (causing a burden on him who fulfils them) ; in 2 Cor.
10 : 10, "weighty," of Paul's letters. See HEAVY, WEIGHTY.¶

2. PONĒROS (πονηρός), painful, bad, is translated "grievous" in
Rev. 16 : 2, of a sore inflicted retributively. See BAD.

3. DUSBASTAKTOS (δυσβάστακτος), hard to be borne (from *dus*,
an inseparable prefix, like Eng. mis-, and un-, indicating difficulty,
injuriousness, opposition, etc., and *bastazō*, to bear), is used in Luke
11 : 46 and, in some mss., in Matt. 23 : 4, "grievous to be borne ;" in
the latter the R.V. marg. has "many ancient authorities omit."¶

4. CHALEPOS (χαλεπός), hard, signifies (*a*) hard to deal with, Matt.
8 : 28 (see FIERCE) ; (*b*) hard to bear, grievous, 2 Tim. 3 : 1, R.V.,
"grievous" (A.V., "perilous"), said of a characteristic of the last days
of this age. See FIERCE.¶

Notes : (1) For the noun *lupē*, "grievous," in Heb. 12 : 11, see GRIEF.
(2) In Phil. 3 : 1, the adjective *oknēros*, shrinking, or causing shrinking,
hence, tedious (akin to *okneō*, to shrink), is rendered "irksome" in the
R.V. (A.V., "grievous") ; the Apostle intimates that, not finding his
message tedious, he has no hesitation in giving it. In Matt. 25 : 26 and
Rom. 12 : 11, "slothful."¶

B. Adverbs.

1. DEINŌS (δεινῶς), akin to *deos*, fear, signifies (*a*) terribly, Matt.
8 : 6, "grievously (tormented) ;" (*b*) vehemently, Luke 11 : 53. See
VEHEMENTLY.¶

2. KAKŌS (κακῶς), badly, ill, is translated "grievously (vexed),"
in Matt. 15 : 22. See AMISS, EVIL, MISERABLY, SORE.

Notes : (1) In Mark 9 : 20 and Luke 9 : 42, the R.V. renders the verb
susparassō "tare (him) grievously," the adverb bringing out the intensive
force of the prefix *su*—(i.e., *sun*) ; the meaning may be 'threw violently
to the ground.' (2) In Matt. 17 : 15, the idiomatic phrase, consisting of

No. 2 (above) with *echō*, to have, (lit., ' hath badly '), is rendered " suffereth grievously," R.V. (A.V., " is . . . sore vexed ").

GRIND

1. ALĒTHŌ (ἀλήθω) signifies to grind at the mill, Matt. 24 : 41 ; Luke 17 : 35.¶ The Sept. has both the earlier form *aleō*, Is. 47 : 2,¶, and the later one *alēthō*, used in the *Koinē* period, Numb. 11 : 8 ; Judg. 16 : 21 ; Eccles. 12 : 3, 4.¶

2. TRIZO (τρίζω), primarily of animal sounds, to chirp, cry, etc., is used of grinding the teeth, Mark 9 : 18, R.V. " grindeth " (A.V., " gnasheth with "). See GNASH.¶

Note : In Matt. 21 : 44 and Luke 20 : 18, *likmaō*, to winnow, as of grain, by throwing it up against the wind, to scatter the chaff and straw, hence has the meaning to scatter, as chaff or dust, and is translated " will scatter . . . as dust," R.V. (A.V., " will grind . . . to powder "). In the Sept. it is used of being scattered by the wind or of sifting (cp. Amos 9 : 9). The use of the verb in the papyri writings suggests the meaning, to ruin, destroy (Deissmann).¶

GROAN, GROANING
A. Verbs.

1. EMBRIMAOMAI (ἐμβριμάομαι), from *en*, in, and *brimē*, strength, is rendered " groaned " in John 11 : 33 (preferable to the R.V. marg., " He had indignation ") ; so in ver. 38. The Lord was deeply moved doubtless with the combination of circumstances, present and in the immediate future. Indignation does not here seem to express His feelings. See CHARGE.

2. STENAZŌ (στενάζω) : see GRIEVE, B, No. 3.

3. SUSTENAZŌ (συστενάζω), to groan together (*sun*, with, and No. 2), is used of the creation in Rom. 8 : 22. In ver. 23, No. 2 is used.¶.

B. Noun.

STENAGMOS (στεναγμός), akin to A, No. 2, is used in Acts 7 : 34, in a quotation from Ex. 3 : 7, but not from the Sept., which there has *kraugē*, a cry ; the word is used, however, in Ex. 2 : 24 ; in Rom. 8 : 26, in the plural, of the intercessory groanings of the Holy Spirit.¶

GROSS (to wax)

PACHUNŌ (παχύνω), from *pachus*, thick, signifies to thicken, fatten ; in the Passive Voice, to grow fat ; metaphorically said of the heart, to wax gross or dull, Matt. 13 : 15 ; Acts 28 : 27.¶

GROUND, GROUNDED
A. Nouns.

1. GĒ (γῆ), the earth, land, etc., often denotes the ground, e.g., Matt. 10 : 29 ; Mark 8 : 6. See EARTH.

2. EDAPHOS (ἔδαφος), a bottom, base, is used of the ground in Acts 22 : 7, suggestive of that which is level and hard.¶   Cp. B, No. 1, below.

3. CHŌRA (χώρα), land, country, is used of property, ground, in Luke 12 : 16, " the ground (of a certain rich man)." See COUNTRY.

4. CHŌRION (χωρίον), a diminutive of No. 3, a piece of land, a place, estate, is translated " parcel of ground " in John 4 : 5. See FIELD.

5. HEDRAIŌMA (ἑδραίωμα), a support, bulwark, stay (from *hedraios*, stedfast, firm ; from *hedra*, a seat), is translated " ground " in 1 Tim. 3 : 15 (said of a local church) ; the R.V. marg., " stay " is preferable.¶

Notes : (1) In Mark 4 : 16 the R.V. rightly has " rocky places " (*petrōdēs*) for A.V., " stony ground." (2) In Acts 27 : 29, for the A.V., " rocks " the R.V. has " rocky ground," lit., ' rough places,' i.e., a rocky shore. (3) In Luke 14 : 18, *agros*, a field, is translated " a piece of ground," A.V., R.V., " a field." See FIELD.

B. Verbs.

1. EDAPHIZŌ (ἐδαφίζω), akin to A, No. 2 : see DASH.

2. THEMELIOŌ (θεμελιόω) signifies to lay the foundation of, to found (akin to *themelios*, a foundation ; from *tithēmi*, to put), and is rendered " grounded " in Eph. 3 : 17, said of the condition of believers with reference to the love of Christ ; in Col. 1 : 23, of their continuance in the faith. See FOUND.

C. Adverb.

CHAMAI (χαμαί) (akin to Lat., *humi*, on the ground, and *homo*, man), signifies " on the ground," John 9 : 6, of the act of Christ in spitting on the ground before anointing the eyes of a blind man ; in 18 : 6, " to the ground," of the fall of the rabble that had come to seize Christ in Gethsemane.¶

GROW

1. AUXANŌ (αὐξάνω), to grow or increase, of the growth of that which lives, naturally or spiritually, is used (*a*) transitively, signifying to make to increase, said of giving the increase, 1 Cor. 3 : 6, 7 ; 2 Cor. 9 : 10, the effect of the work of God, according to the analogy of His operations in nature ; to grow, become greater, e.g. of plants and fruit, Matt. 6 : 28 ; used in the Passive Voice in 13 : 32 and Mark 4 : 8, " increase ; " in the Active in Luke 12 : 27 ; 13 : 19 ; of the body, Luke 1 : 80 ; 2 : 40 ; of Christ, John 3 : 30, " increase ; " of the work of the Gospel of God, Acts 6 : 7, " increased ; " 12 : 24 ; 19 : 20 ; of people, Acts 7 : 17 ; of faith, 2 Cor. 10 : 15 (Passive Voice), R.V., " groweth " (A.V., " is increased ") ; of believers individually, Eph. 4 : 15 ; Col. 1 : 6, R.V., 10 (Passive Voice), " increasing ; " 1 Pet. 2 : 2 ; 2 Pet. 3 : 18 ; of the Church, Col. 2 : 19 ; of churches, Eph. 2 : 21. See INCREASE.¶

Note : Cp. *auxēsis*, increase, Eph. 4 : 16 ; Col. 2 : 19.¶

2. GINOMAI (γίνομαι), to become or come to be, is translated " grow "

in Acts 5 : 24, of the development of apostolic work. See ARISE, No. 5.

Notes : (1) In Matt. 21 : 19, for A.V., " let (no fruit) grow," the R.V., more strictly, has " let there be (no fruit)." (2) In Heb. 11 : 24, *ginomai* is used with *megas*, great, of Moses, lit., ' had become great,' R.V., " had grown up " (A.V., " had come to years ").

3. ERCHOMAI (ἔρχομαι), to come or go, is translated " grew (worse)," in Mark 5 : 26. See COME, No. 1.

4. ANABAINŌ (ἀναβαίνω), to ascend, when used of plants, signifies to grow up, Mark 4 : 7, 32 ; in 4 : 8, of seed, " growing up," R.V., A.V., " that sprang up," (for the next word, " increasing," see No. 1). See ARISE, No. 6.

5. MĒKUNOMAI (μηκύνομαι), to grow long, lengthen, extend (from *mēkos*, length), is used of the growth of plants, in Mark 4 : 27.¶

Note : Three different words are used in Mark 4 of the growth of plants or seed, Nos. 1, 4, 5.

6. HUPERAUXANŌ (ὑπεραυξάνω), to increase beyond measure (*huper*, over, and No. 1), is used of faith and love, in their living and practical effects, 2 Thess. 1 : 3. Lightfoot compares this verb and the next in the verse (*pleonazō*, to abound) in that the former implies " an internal, organic growth, as of a tree," the latter " a diffusive or expansive character, as of a flood irrigating the land."¶

7. SUNAUXANŌ (συναυξάνω), to grow together, is in Matt. 13 : 30.¶

8. PHUŌ (φύω), to produce, is rendered " grew " (Passive V.) in Luke 8 : 6. See SPRING.

9. SUMPHUŌ (συμφύω) is used in Luke 8 : 7, R.V., " grow with."¶

For GRUDGE (Jas. 5 : 9), GRIEVE, B, No. 3, GRUDGING (1 Pet. 4 : 9) see MURMUR

GRUDGINGLY

Note : In 2 Cor. 9 : 7, the phrase *ek lupēs*, lit., ' out of sorrow ' (*ek*, out of, or from, *lupē*, sorrow, grief), is translated " grudgingly " (R.V. marg., " of sorrow ") ; the grudging regret is set in contrast to cheerfulness enjoined in giving, as is the reluctance expressed in " of necessity.'

GUARD (Noun and Verb)
A. Nouns.

1. KOUSTŌDIA (κουστωδία), a guard, (Latin, *custodia* ; Eng., custodian), is used of the soldiers who guarded Christ's sepulchre, Matt. 27 : 65, 66 and 28 : 11, and is translated " (ye have) a guard," " the guard (being with them)," and " (some of) the guard," R.V., A.V., " . . . a watch," " (setting a) watch," and ". . . the watch." This was the Temple Guard, stationed under a Roman officer in the Tower of Antonia, and having charge of the high priestly vestments. Hence the significance of Pilate's words " Ye have a guard." See WATCH.¶

2. SPEKOULATŌR (σπεκουλάτωρ), Latin, *speculator*, primarily denotes a lookout officer, or scout, but, under the Emperors, a member of the bodyguard ; these were employed as messengers, watchers and executioners ; ten such officers were attached to each legion ; such a guard was employed by Herod Antipas, Mark 6 : 27, R.V., " a soldier of his guard " (A.V., " executioner ").¶

3. PHULAX (φύλαξ), a guard, keeper (akin to *phulassō*, to guard, keep), is translated " keepers " in Acts 5 : 23 ; in 12 : 6, 19, R.V., " guards " (A.V., " keepers "). See KEEPER.¶

Notes : (1) In Acts 28 : 16, some mss. have the sentence containing the word *stratopedarchēs*, a captain of the guard. See CAPTAIN. (2) In Phil. 1 : 13, the noun *praitōrion*, the " Prætorian Guard," is so rendered in the R.V. (A.V., " palace ").

B. Verbs.

1. PHULASSŌ (φυλάσσω), to guard, watch, keep (akin to A, No. 3), is rendered by the verb to guard in the R.V. (A.V., to keep) of Luke 11 : 21 ; John 17 : 12 ; Acts 12 : 4 ; 28 : 16 ; 2 Thess. 3 : 3 ; 1 Tim. 6 : 20 ; 2 Tim. 1 : 12, 14 ; 1 John 5 : 21 ; Jude 24. In Luke 8 : 29, " was kept under guard," R.V. (A.V., " kept "). See BEWARE, KEEP, OBSERVE, PRESERVE, SAVE, WARE OF, WATCH.

2. DIAPHULASSŌ (διαφυλάσσω), a strengthened form of No. 1 (*dia*, through, used intensively), to guard carefully, defend, is found in Luke 4 : 10 (from the Sept. of Psa. 91 : 11), R.V., " to guard " (A.V., " to keep ").¶

3. PHROUREŌ (φρουρέω), a military term, to keep by guarding, to keep under guard, as with a garrison (*phrouros*, a guard, or garrison), is used, (a) of blocking up every way of escape, as in a siege ; (b) of providing protection against the enemy, as a garrison does ; see 2 Cor. 11 . 32, " guarded," A.V., " kept," i.e., kept the city, " with a garrison." It is used of the security of the Christian until the end, 1 Pet. 1 : 5, R.V., " are guarded," and of the sense of that security that is his when he puts all his matters into the hand of God, Phil. 4 : 7, R.V., " shall guard." In these passages the idea is not merely that of protection, but of inward garrisoning as by the Holy Spirit ; in Gal. 3 : 23 (" were kept in ward "), it means rather a benevolent custody and watchful guardianship in view of worldwide idolatry (cp. Is. 5 : 2). See KEEP.¶

GUARDIAN

EPITROPOS (ἐπίτροπος), lit., one to whose care something is committed (*epi*, upon, *trepō*, to turn or direct), is rendered " guardians " in Gal. 4 : 2, R.V., A.V., " tutors " (in Matt. 20 : 8 and Luke 8 : 3, " steward ").¶

" The corresponding verb, *epitrepō*, is translated ' permit,' ' give leave,' ' suffer ; ' see 1 Cor. 14 : 34 ; 16 : 7 ; 1 Tim. 2 : 12, e.g., . . . An allied noun, *epitropē*, is translated ' commission ' in Acts 26 : 12 (¶) and refers to delegated authority over persons. This usage of cognate words suggests that the *epitropos* was a superior servant responsible for the persons composing the household, whether children or slaves."*

GUEST

ANAKEIMAI (ἀνάκειμαι), to recline at table, frequently rendered to sit at meat, is used in its present participial form (lit., ' reclining ones ') as a noun denoting " guests," in Matt. 22 : 10, 11. See LEAN, LIE, SIT.

Note : For *kataluō*, to unloose, rendered to be a guest in Luke 19 : 7, A.V., (R.V., to lodge), see LODGE.

GUEST-CHAMBER

KATALUMA (κατάλυμα), akin to *kataluō* (see Note above), signifies (a) an inn, lodging-place, Luke 2 : 7 ; (b) a guest-room, Mark 14 : 14 ; Luke 22 : 11. The word lit. signifies a loosening down (*kata*, down, *luō*, to loose), used of the place where travellers and their beasts untied their packages, girdles and sandals. " In the East, no figure is more invested with chivalry than the guest. In his own right he cannot cross the threshold, but when once he is invited in, all do him honour and unite in rendering service ; cp. Gen. 18 : 19 ; Judg. 19 : 9, 15." These two passages in the N.T. " concern a room in a private house, which the owner readily placed at the disposal of Jesus and His disciples for the celebration of the Passover . . . At the festivals of Passover, Pentecost and Tabernacles the people were commanded to repair to Jerusalem ; and it was a boast of the Rabbis that, notwithstanding the enormous crowds, no man could truthfully say to his fellow, ' I have not found a fire where to roast my paschal lamb in Jerusalem,' or ' I have not found a bed in Jerusalem to lie in,' or ' My lodging is too strait in Jerusalem ' " (Hastings, Bib. Dic., GUEST-CHAMBER and INN). See INN.¶

GUIDE (Noun and Verb)
A. Noun.

HODĒGOS (ὁδηγός), a leader on the way (*hodos*, a way, *hēgeomai*, to lead), a guide, is used (a) literally, in Acts 1 : 16 ; (b) figuratively, Matt. 15 : 14, R.V., " guides " (A.V., ' leaders ") ; Matt. 23 : 16, 24, " guides ; " Rom. 2 : 19, " a guide." Cp. B, No. 1.¶

B. Verbs.

1. HODĒGEŌ (ὁδηγέω), to lead the way (akin to A), is used (a) literally, R.V., " guide " (A.V., " lead "), of guiding the blind, in Matt. 15 : 14 ; Luke 6 : 39 ; of guiding unto fountains of waters of life, Rev. 7 : 17 ; (b) figuratively, in John 16 : 13, of guidance into the truth by the Holy Spirit ; in Acts 8 : 31, of the interpretation of Scripture. See LEAD.¶

---

* From Notes on Galatians, by Hogg and Vine, p. 180.

2. KATEUTHUNŌ (κατευθύνω), to make straight, is said of guiding the feet into the way of peace, Luke 1 : 79. See DIRECT.

Notes : (1) In 1 Tim. 5 : 14, the R.V. rightly translates the verb *oikodespoteō* by " rule the household " (A.V., " guide the house "), the meaning being that of the management and direction of household affairs. See RULE.¶ (2) *Hēgeomai*, to lead, in Heb. 13 : 7, 24, is rendered " that had the rule over " and " that have etc.," more lit., ' them that were (are) your leaders,' or guides.

GUILE

DOLOS (δόλος), a bait, snare, deceit, is rendered " guile " in John 1 : 47, negatively of Nathanael ; Acts 13 : 10, R.V., A.V., " subtlety " (of Bar-Jesus) ; 2 Cor. 12 : 16, in a charge made against Paul by his detractors, of catching the Corinthian converts by guile (the Apostle is apparently quoting the language of his critics) ; 1 Thess. 2 : 3, negatively, of the teaching of the Apostle and his fellow-missionaries ; 1 Pet. 2 : 1, of that from which Christians are to be free ; 2 : 22, of the guileless speech of Christ (cp. GUILELESS, No. 2) ; 3 : 10, of the necessity that the speech of Christians should be guileless. See also Matt. 26 : 4 ; Mark 7 : 22 ; 14 : 1. See CRAFT, DECEIT, SUBTILTY.¶

Note : In Rev. 14 : 5, some mss. have *dolos* ; the most authentic have *pseudos*, a " lie."

GUILELESS (WITHOUT GUILE)

1. ADOLOS (ἄδολος), without guile (*a*, negative, and *dolos*, see GUILE), pure, unadulterated, is used metaphorically of the teaching of the Word of God, 1 Pet. 2 : 2, R.V. It is used in the papyri writings of seed, corn, wheat, oil, wine, etc.¶

2. AKAKOS (ἄκακος), lit., without evil (*a*, negative, *kakos*, evil), signifies simple, guileless, Rom. 16 : 18, " simple," of believers (perhaps = unsuspecting, or, rather, innocent, free from admixture of evil) ; in Heb. 7 : 26, R.V., " guileless " (A.V., " harmless "), the character of Christ (more lit., ' free from evil ').¶ Cp. Sept., Job 2 : 3 ; 8 : 20 ; Prov. 1 : 4 ; 14 : 15. See HARMLESS.

GUILTLESS

ANAITIOS (ἀναίτιος), innocent, guiltless (*a*, negative, *n*, euphonic, *aitia*, a charge of crime), is translated " blameless " in Matt. 12 : 5, A.V., " guiltless " in ver. 7 ; R.V., " guiltless " in each place. See BLAMELESS.¶

GUILTY (Adjective)

ENOCHOS (ἔνοχος), lit., held in, bound by, liable to a charge or action at law : see DANGER.

Notes : (1) In Rom. 3 : 19, A.V., *hupodikos*, brought to trial, lit.,

' under judgment ' (*hupo*, under, *dikē*, justice), is incorrectly rendered " guilty ; " R.V., " under the judgement of." See JUDGMENT. (2) In Matt. 23 : 18, *opheilō*, to owe, to be indebted, to fail in duty, be a delinquent, is misrendered " guilty " in the A.V. ; R.V., " a debtor."

GULF

CHASMA (χάσμα), akin to *chaskō*, to yawn (Eng., chasm), is found in Luke 16 : 26.¶ In the Sept., 2 Sam. 18 : 17, two words are used with reference to Absalom's body, *bothunos* which signifies a great pit, and *chasma*, a yawning abyss, or precipice, with a deep pit at the bottom, into which the body was cast.¶

GUSH OUT

EKCHUNŌ, or EKCHUNNŌ (ἐκχύνω), a Hellenistic form of *ekcheō*, to pour forth, is translated " gushed out " in Acts 1 : 18, of the bowels of Judas Iscariot. See POUR, RUN, SHED, SPILL.

H

For HA (Mark 15 : 29, R.V.) see AH

HABITATION

1. OIKĒTĒRION (οἰκητήριον), a habitation (from oikētēr, an inhabitant, and oikos, a dwelling), is used in Jude 6, of the heavenly region appointed by God as the dwelling place of angels ; in 2 Cor. 5 : 2, R.V., "habitation," A.V., "house," figuratively of the spiritual bodies of believers when raised or changed at the return of the Lord.   See HOUSE.¶

2. KATOIKĒTĒRION (κατοικητήριον), (kata, down, used intensively, and No. 1), implying more permanency than No. 1, is used in Eph. 2 : 22 of the Church as the dwelling-place of the Holy Spirit ; in Rev. 18 : 2 of Babylon, figuratively, as the dwelling-place of demons.¶

3. KATOIKIA (κατοικία), a settlement, colony, dwelling (kata, and oikos, see above), is used in Acts 17 : 26, of the localities Divinely appointed as the dwelling-places of the nations.¶

4. EPAULIS (ἔπαυλις), a farm, a dwelling (epi, upon, aulis, a place in which to pass the night, a country-house, cottage or cabin, a fold), is used in Acts 1 : 20 of the habitation of Judas.¶

5. SKĒNĒ (σκηνή), akin to skēnoō, to dwell in a tent or tabernacle, is rendered "habitations" in Luke 16 : 9, A.V. (R.V., "tabernacles"), of the eternal dwelling-places of the redeemed.   See TABERNACLE.

6. SKĒNŌMA (σκήνωμα), a booth, or tent pitched (akin to No. 5), is used of the Temple as God's dwelling, as that which David desired to build, Acts 7 : 46 (R.V., "habitation," A.V., "tabernacle") ; metaphorically of the body as a temporary tabernacle, 2 Pet. 1 : 13, 14.¶   See TABERNACLE.

HADES

HADĒS (ᾅδης), the region of departed spirits of the lost (but including the blessed dead in periods preceding the Ascension of Christ).   It has been thought by some that the word etymologically meant the unseen (from a, negative, and eidō, to see), but this derivation is questionable ; a more probable derivation is from hadō, signifying all-receiving.   It corresponds to "Sheol" in the O.T.   In the A.V. of the O.T. and N.T., it has been unhappily rendered "Hell," e.g., Psa. 16 : 10 ; or "the grave," e.g., Gen. 37 : 35 ; or "the pit," Num. 16 : 30, 33 ; in the N.T. the Revisers have always used the rendering "Hades ;" in the O.T.

they have not been uniform in the translation, e.g., in Isa. 14 : 15, " hell " (marg., " Sheol ") ; usually they have " Sheol " in the text and " the grave " in the margin. It never denotes the grave, nor is it the permanent region of the lost ; in point of time it is, for such, intermediate between decease and the doom of Gehenna. For the condition, see Luke 16 : 23-31.

The word is used four times in the Gospels, and always by the Lord, Matt. 11 : 23 ; 16 : 18 ; Luke 10 : 15 ; 16 : 23 ; it is used with reference to the soul of Christ, Acts 2 : 27, 31 ; Christ declares that He has the keys of it, Rev. 1 : 18 ; in Rev. 6 : 8 it is personified, with the signification of the temporary destiny of the doomed ; it is to give up those who are therein, 20 : 13, and is to be cast into the lake of fire, ver. 14.¶

Note : In 1 Cor. 15 : 55 the most authentic mss. have *thanatos*, death, in the 2nd part of the verse, instead of *Hades*, which the A.V. wrongly renders " grave " (" hell," in the marg.).

HAIL (Noun)

CHALAZA (χάλαζα), akin to *chalaō*, to let loose, let fall, is always used as an instrument of Divine judgment, and is found in the N.T. in Rev. 8 : 7 ; 11 : 19 ; 16 : 21.¶

HAIL (Verb)

CHAIRŌ (χαίρω), to rejoice, is used in the imperative mood, (a) as a salutation, only in the Gospels ; in this respect it is rendered simply " hail," in mockery of Christ, Matt. 26 : 49 ; 27 : 29 ; Mark 15 : 18 ; John 19 : 3 ; (b) as a greeting, by the angel Gabriel to Mary, Luke 1 : 28, and, in the plural, by the Lord to the disciples after His resurrection, Matt. 28 : 9.

HAIR
A. Nouns.

1. THRIX (θρίξ) denotes the hair, whether of beast, as of the camel's hair which formed the raiment of John the Baptist, Matt. 3 : 4 ; Mark 1 : 6 ; or of man. Regarding the latter (a) it is used to signify the minutest detail, as that which illustrates the exceeding care and protection bestowed by God upon His children, Matt. 10 : 30 ; Luke 12 : 7 ; 21 : 18 ; Acts 27 : 34 ; (b) as the Jews swore by the hair, the Lord used the natural inability to make one hair white or black, as one of the reasons for abstinence from oaths, Matt. 5 : 36 ; (c) while long hair is a glory to a woman (see B), and to wear it loose or dishevelled is a dishonour, yet the woman who wiped Christ's feet with her hair (in place of the towel which Simon the Pharisee omitted to provide), despised the shame in her penitent devotion to the Lord (slaves were accustomed to wipe their masters' feet), Luke 7 : 38, 44 (R.V., " hair ") ; see also John 11 : 2 ; 12 : 3 ; (d) the dazzling whiteness of the head and hair of the Son of Man

in the vision of Rev. 1 (ver. 14) is suggestive of the holiness and wisdom of " the Ancient of Days ; " (e) the long hair of the spirit-beings described as locusts in Rev. 9 : 8 is perhaps indicative of their subjection to their Satanic master (cp. 1 Cor. 11 : 10, R.V.) ; (f) Christian women are exhorted to refrain from adorning their hair for outward show, 1 Pet. 3 : 3.¶

Note : Goat's hair was used in tent-making, as, e.g., in the case of Paul's occupation, Acts 18 : 3 ; the haircloth of Cilicia, his native province was noted, being known in commerce as *cilicium.*

2. KOMĒ (κόμη) is used only of human hair, but not in the N.T. of the ornamental. The word is found in 1 Cor. 11 : 15, where the context shows that the " covering " provided in the long hair of the woman is as a veil, a sign of subjection to authority, as indicated in the headships spoken of in vers. 1–10.¶

B. Verb.

KOMAŌ (κομάω) signifies to let the hair grow long, to wear long hair, a glory to a woman, a dishonour to a man (as taught by nature), 1 Cor. 11 : 14, 15.¶

C. Adjective.

TRICHINOS (τρίχινος), akin to A, No. 1, signifies hairy, made of hair, Rev. 6 : 12, lit., ' hairy sackcloth.' Cp. SACKCLOTH.¶

HALE (Verb)

1. SURŌ (σύρω) to drag, haul, is rendered " haling " in Acts 8 : 3, of taking to trial or punishment. See DRAG.

2. KATASURŌ (κατασύρω), an intensive form of No. 1, lit., to pull down (*kata*), hence, to drag away, is used in Luke 12 : 58, of haling a person before a judge.¶

HALF

HĒMISUS (ἥμισυς), an adjective, is used (a) as such in the neuter plural, in Luke 19 : 8, lit., ' the halves (of my goods) ; ' (b) as a noun, in the neuter sing., " the half," Mark 6 : 23 ; " half (a time)," Rev. 12 : 14 ; " a half," 11 : 9, 11, R.V.¶

For HALF-SHEKEL see SHEKEL

HALL

1. AULĒ (αὐλή), a court, most frequently the place where a governor dispensed justice, is rendered " hall " in Mark 15 : 16 and Luke 22 . 55, A.V. (R.V., " court "). See COURT, FOLD, PALACE.

2. PRAITŌRION (πραιτώριον) is translated " common hall " in Matt. 27 : 27, A.V. (R.V., " palace ") ; " Prætorium " in Mark 15 : 16 ; " hall of judgment " or " judgment hall " in John 18 : 28, 33 ; 19 : 9 ; Acts 23 : 35 (R.V., " palace," in each place) ; " prætorian guard," Phil. 1 : 13 (A.V., " palace "). See PALACE.¶

HALLELUJAH

HALLĒLOUIA ('Αλληλουιά) signifies " Praise ye Jah." It occurs as a short doxology in the Psalms, usually at the beginning, e.g., 111, 112, or the end, e.g., 104, 105, or both, e.g., 106, 135 (where it is also used in ver. 3), 146-150. In the N.T. it is found in Rev. 19 : 1, 3, 4, 6, as the key-note in the song of the great multitude in Heaven. Alleluia, without the initial H, is a misspelling.¶

HALLOW

HAGIAZŌ (ἁγιάζω), to make holy (from *hagios*, holy), signifies (*a*) to set apart for God, to sanctify, to make a person or thing the opposite of *koinos*, common ; it is translated " Hallowed," with reference to the Name of God the Father in the Lord's Prayer, Matt. 6 : 9 ; Luke 11 : 2. See SANCTIFY.

HALT

CHŌLOS (χωλός), lame, is translated " halt " in Matt. 18 : 8 ; Mark 9 : 45 ; John 5 : 3 ; in Acts 14 : 8, " cripple ; " in Luke 14 : 21, A.V., " halt," R.V., " lame ; " elsewhere, " lame," Matt. 11 : 5 ; 15 : 30, 31 ; 21 : 14 ; Luke 7 : 22 ; 14 : 13 ; Acts 3 : 2 ; 8 : 7 ; Heb. 12 : 13 ; some mss. have it in Acts 3 : 11 (A.V., " the lame man "), R.V., " he," translating *autou*, as in the best texts.¶

Note : For *kullos*, Matt. 18 : 8, R.V., " halt," see MAIMED, No. 2.

HAND

CHEIR (χείρ), the hand (cp. Eng., chiropody), is used, besides its ordinary significance, (*a*) in the idiomatic phrases, by the hand of, at the hand of, etc., to signify by the agency of, Acts 5 : 12 ; 7 : 35 ; 17 : 25 ; 14 : 3 ; Gal. 3 : 19 (cp. Lev. 26 : 46) ; Rev. 19 : 2 ; (*b*) metaphorically, for the power of God, e.g., Luke 1 : 66 ; 23 : 46 ; John 10 : 28, 29 ; Acts 11 : 21 ; 13 : 11 ; Heb. 1 : 10 ; 2 : 7 ; 10 : 31 ; (*c*) by metonymy, for power, e.g., Matt. 17 : 22 ; Luke 24 : 7 ; John 10 : 39 ; Acts 12 : 11.

AT HAND
A. Adverb.

ENGUS (ἐγγύς), near, nigh, frequently rendered " at hand," is used (*a*) of place, e.g., of the Lord's sepulchre, John 19 : 42, " nigh at hand ; " (*b*) of time, e.g., Matt. 26 : 18 ; Luke 21 : 30, 31, R.V., " nigh," A.V., " nigh at hand ; " in Phil. 4 : 5, " the Lord is at hand," it is possible to regard the meaning as that either of (*a*) or (*b*) ; the following reasons may point to (*b*) : (1) the subject of the preceding context has been the return of Christ, 3 : 20, 21 ; (2) the phrase is a translation of the Aramaic Maran-atha, 1 Cor. 16 : 22, a Christian watchword, and the use of the title " the Lord " is appropriate ; (3) the similar use of the adverb in Rev. 1 : 3 and 22 : 10 ; (4) the similar use of the corresponding verb (see B) in Rom.

13 : 12 ; Heb. 10 : 25, " drawing nigh," R.V. ; Jas. 5 : 8 ; cp. 1 Pet. 4 : 7.
See NEAR, NIGH, READY.

B. Verb.

ENGIZŌ (ἐγγίζω) : See APPROACH, A.

Notes : (1) In 2 Thess. 2 : 2, A.V., the verb *enistēmi,* to be present
(*en,* in, *histēmi,* to cause to stand), is wrongly translated " is at hand ; "
the R.V. correctly renders it, " is (now) present ; " the Apostle is counter-
acting the error of the supposition that " the Day of the Lord " (R.V.), a
period of Divine and retributive judgments upon the world, had already
begun.

(2) In 2 Tim. 4 : 6, A.V., the verb *ephistēmi,* to stand by, to come to
or upon (*epi,* upon, *histēmi,* to make to stand), is rendered " is at hand,"
of the Apostle's departure from this life ; the R.V. " is come " represents
the vivid force of the statement, expressing suddenness or imminence.

HAND˙ (lead by the)
A. Adjective.

CHEIRAGŌGOS (χειραγωγός), lit., a hand-leader (*cheir,* the hand,
agō, to lead), is used as a noun (plural) in Acts 13 : 11, " some to lead him
by the hand."¶

B. Verb.

CHEIRAGŌGEŌ (χειραγωγέω), to lead by the hand, is used in
Acts 9 : 8 ; 22 : 11.¶

HANDED DOWN

PATROPARADOTOS (πατροπαράδοτος), an adjective, denoting handed
down from one's fathers, is used in 1 Pet. 1 : 18, R.V., for A.V., " *received
by tradition from your fathers* " (from *patēr,* a father, and *paradidōmi,* to
hand down).¶

HAND (with one's own)

AUTOCHEIR (αὐτόχειρ), a noun (*autos,* self, *cheir,* the hand), is used
in the plural in Acts 27 : 19, " with their own hands."¶

HAND (take in)

EPICHEIREŌ (ἐπιχειρέω), to put the hand to (*epi,* to, *cheir,* the hand),
is rendered " have taken in hand " in Luke 1 : 1. See TAKE.

For LAY HANDS ON (*krateō* in Matt. 18 : 28 ; 21 : 46 ; *piazō* in
John 8 : 20), see HOLD and APPREHEND.

HANDS (made by, not made with)

1. CHEIROPOIĒTOS (χειροποίητος), made by hand, of human
handiwork (*cheir,* and *poieō,* to make), is said of the temple in Jerusalem,
Mark 14 : 58 ; temples in general, Acts 7 : 48 (R.V., " houses ") ; 17 : 24 ;

negatively, of the heavenly and spiritual tabernacle, Heb. 9 : 11 ; of the holy place in the earthly tabernacle, ver. 24 ; of circumcision, Eph. 2 : 11.¶ In the Sept., of idols, Lev. 26 : 1, 30 ; Isa. 2 : 18 ; 10 : 11 ; 16 : 12 ; 19 : 1 ; 21 : 9 ; 31 : 7 ; 46 : 6.¶

2. ACHEIROPOIĒTOS (ἀχειροποίητος), not made by hands (a, negative, and No. 1), is said of an earthly temple, Mark 14 : 58 ; of the resurrection body of believers, metaphorically as a house, 2 Cor. 5 : 1 ; metaphorically, of spiritual circumcision, Col. 2 : 11.¶ This word is not found in the Sept.

HANDKERCHIEF

SOUDARION (σουδάριον), a Latin word, *sudarium* (from *sudor*, sweat), denotes (a) a cloth for wiping the face, etc., Luke 19 : 20 ; Acts 19 : 12 ; (b) a head-covering for the dead, John 11 : 44 ; 20 : 7. See NAPKIN.¶

HANDLE

1. PSĒLAPHAŌ (ψηλαφάω), to feel, touch, handle, is rendered by the latter verb in Luke 24 : 39, in the Lord's invitation to the disciples to accept the evidence of His resurrection in His being bodily in their midst ; in 1 John 1 : 1, in the Apostle's testimony (against the Gnostic error that Christ had been merely a phantom) that he and his fellow-apostles had handled Him. See FEEL.

2. THINGANŌ (θιγγάνω) signifies (a) to touch, to handle (though to handle is rather stronger than the actual significance compared with No 1). In Col. 2 : 21 the R.V. renders it " touch," and the first verb (*haptō*, to lay hold of) " handle," i.e., ' handle not, nor taste, nor touch ; ' " touch " is the appropriate rendering ; in Heb. 12 : 20 it is said of a beast's touching Mount Sinai ; (b) to touch by way of injuring, Heb. 11 : 28. See TOUCH.¶ In the Sept., Ex. 19 : 12.¶

Note : The shortened form found in the passages mentioned is an aorist (or point) tense of the verb.

3. DOLOŌ (δολόω), to corrupt, is used in 2 Cor. 4 : 2, " handling (the Word of God) deceitfully," in the sense of using guile (*dolos*) ; the meaning approximates to that of adulterating (cp. *kapēleuō*, in 2 : 17).¶

4. ATIMAZŌ (ἀτιμάζω), to dishonour, insult, is rendered " handled shamefully " in Mark 12 : 4. Some mss. have the alternative verb *atimaō*. See DESPISE, DISHONOUR.

5. ORTHOTOMEŌ (ὀρθοτομέω), to cut straight, as in road-making (*orthos*, straight, *temnō*, to cut), is used metaphorically in 2 Tim. 2 : 15, of ' handling aright (the word of truth),' R.V. (A.V., " rightly dividing "). The stress is on *orthos* ; the Word of God is to be handled strictly along the lines of its teaching.   If the metaphor is taken from ploughing, cutting a straight furrow, the word would express a careful cultivation, the Word of God viewed as ground designed to give the best results from its ministry and in the life. See DIVIDE.¶

In the Sept., in Prov. 3 : 6 and 11 : 5, the knowledge of God's wisdom and the just dealing of the upright are enjoined as producing a straight walk in the life.¶

For HANDMAID and HANDMAIDEN see under BONDMAN

For HANDWRITING see BOND

HANG

1. KREMANNUMI (κρεμάννυμι) is used (*a*) transitively in Acts 5 : 30 ; 10 : 39 ; in the Passive Voice, in Matt. 18 : 6, of a millstone about a neck, and in Luke 23 : 39, of the malefactors ; (*b*) intransitively, in the Middle Voice, in Matt. 22 : 40, of the dependence of " the Law and the prophets " (i.e., that which they enjoin) upon the one great principle of love to God and one's neighbour (as a door hangs on a hinge, or as articles hang on a nail) ; in Acts 28 : 4, of the serpent hanging from Paul's hand ; in Gal. 3 : 13 the word is used in a quotation from the Sept. of Deut. 21 : 23.¶

2. EKKREMANNUMI (ἐκκρεμάννυμι), to hang from, or upon (*ek*, and No. 1), is used in the Middle Voice (*ekkremamai*) metaphorically in Luke 19 : 48, R.V., " (the people all) hung upon (Him, listening)," A.V., " were very attentive."¶ In the Sept., Gen. 44 : 30.¶

3. PARIĒMI (παρίημι) signifies (*a*) to disregard, leave alone, leave undone, Luke 11 : 42 (some mss. have *aphiēmi*, here) ; (*b*) to relax, loosen, and, in the Passive Voice, to be relaxed, exhausted, said of hands that hang down in weakness, Heb. 12 : 12.¶

4. PERIKEIMAI (περίκειμαι) signifies to lie round (*peri*, around, *keimai*, to lie) ; then, to be hanged round, said of " a great millstone " (lit., ' a millstone turned by an ass '), Mark 9 : 42, R.V., and marg., to be hung round the neck of him who causes one of Christ's " little ones " to stumble ; in Luke 17 : 2, " a millstone." See BOUND (to be).

5. APANCHŌ (ἀπάγχω) signifies to strangle ; in the Middle Voice, to hang oneself, Matt. 27 : 5.¶ In the Sept. it is said of Ahithophel (2 Sam. 17 : 23).¶

HAPLY (if, lest)

1. EI ARA (εἰ ἄρα) denotes if therefore, if accordingly (i.e., if in these circumstances), e.g., Mark 11 : 13, of Christ and the fig tree (not ' if perchance,' but marking a correspondence in point of fact).

2. EI ARAGE (εἰ ἄραγε) denotes if in consequence, e.g., Acts 17 : 27, " if haply " they might feel after God, in consequence of seeking Him.

3. MĒ POTE (μή ποτε), lit., lest ever, " lest haply," e.g., Luke 14 : 29, of laying a foundation, with the possibility of being unable to finish the building ; Acts 5 : 39, of the possibility of being found fighting against God ; Heb. 3 : 12, R.V., " lest haply," of the possibility of having an evil heart of unbelief. The R.V. usually has " lest haply " (A.V. " lest at

any time "), e.g., Matt. 4 : 6 ; 5 : 25 ; 13 : 15 ; Mark 4 : 12 ; Luke 4 : 11 ; 21 : 34 ; Heb. 2 : 1 ; in Matt. 25 : 9, the R.V. has " peradventure ; " in 2 Tim. 2 : 25, A.V. and R.V., have " if peradventure ; " in John 7 : 26 the R.V. has " Can it be that," for the word " Do " in the A.V.

4. MĒ PŌS (μή πως) denotes lest in any way, by any means, e.g., 2 Cor. 9 : 4, A.V., " lest haply," R.V., " lest by any means."

5. MĒ POU (μή που) denotes lest somehow ; the R.V. has " lest haply " in Acts 27 : 29 (some mss. have No. 4, here).

HAPPEN

1. SUMBAINŌ (συμβαίνω), lit., to go or come together (sun, with, bainō, to go), signifies to happen together, of things or events, Mark 10 : 32 ; Luke 24 : 14 ; Acts 3 : 10 ; 1 Cor. 10 : 11 ; 1 Pet. 4 : 12 ; 2 Pet. 2 : 22 ; " befell " in Acts 20 : 19 ; in Acts 21 : 35, " so it was." See BEFALL.¶

Notes : (1) In Phil. 1 : 12, the phrase *ta kat'* (i.e., *kata*) *eme*, lit., ' the things relating to me,' is rendered " the things *which happened* unto me." (2) In Luke 24 : 35, the phrase " the things *that happened* in the way," R.V. (A.V., " what things were done in the way "), is, lit., ' the things in the way.'

HAPPY, HAPPIER
A. Adjective.

MAKARIOS (μακάριος), blessed, happy, is rendered " happy " in the R.V., in two places only, as in the A.V., Acts 26 : 2 and Rom. 14 : 22 (where " blessed " would have done) ; also the comparative " happier " in 1 Cor. 7 : 40. Elsewhere the R.V. uses " blessed " for A.V. " happy," e.g., John 13 : 17 ; 1 Pet. 3 : 14 ; 4 : 14. See BLESSED.

B. Verb.

MAKARIZŌ (μακαρίζω), to call blessed, Luke 1 : 48, is rendered " we count . . . happy " in Jas. 5 : 11. See BLESSED.¶

HARD, HARDEN, HARDENING, HARDNESS
A. Adjectives.

1. SKLĒROS (σκληρός), from *skellō*, to dry, signifies trying, exacting : see AUSTERE.

2. DUSKOLOS (δύσκολος) primarily means hard to satisfy with food (*dus*, a prefix like Eng., *un*— or *mis*—, indicating difficulty, opposition, injuriousness, etc., the opposite of, *eu*, well, and *kolon*, food) ; hence, difficult, Mark 10 : 24, of the difficulty, for those who trust in riches, to enter into the Kingdom of God.¶

B. Nouns.

1. SKLĒROTĒS (σκληρότης), akin to A, No. 1, is rendered " hardness " in Rom 2 : 5.¶

2. PŌRŌSIS (πώρωσις) denotes a hardening, a covering with a *pōros*, a kind of stone, indicating a process (from *pōroō*, C, No. 1), and is used

metaphorically of dulled spiritual perception, Mark 3 : 5, R.V., " at the hardening of their hearts ; " Rom. 11 : 25, R.V., " a hardening " (A.V., " blindness "), said of the state of Israel ; Eph. 4 : 18, R.V., " hardening," of the heart of Gentiles. See BLINDNESS.¶

Note : See also under HARDSHIP and HEART (hardness of).

C. Verbs.

1. PŌROŌ (πωρόω), to make hard, callous, to petrify (akin to B, No. 2), is used metaphorically, of the heart, Mark 6 : 52 ; 8 : 17 ; John 12 : 40 ; of the mind (or thoughts), 2 Cor. 3 : 14, of those in Israel who refused the revealed will and ways of God in the Gospel, as also in Rom. 11 : 7, R.V., " hardened " (A.V., " blinded "), in both places. See BLINDNESS.¶

2. SKLĒRUNŌ (σκληρύνω), to make dry or hard (akin to A, No. 1 and B, No. 1), is used in Acts 19 : 9 ; in Rom. 9 : 18, illustrated by the case of Pharaoh, who first persistently hardened his heart (see the R.V. marg. of Ex. 7 : 13, 22 ; 8 : 19 ; text of ver. 32 and 9 : 7), all producing the retributive hardening by God, after His much long-suffering, 9 : 12, etc. ; in Heb. 3 : 8, 13, 15 ; 4 : 7, warnings against the hardening of the heart.¶

HARDLY

1. DUSKOLŌS (δυσκόλως), the adverbial form of HARD, A, No. 2, is used in Matt. 19 : 23 ; Mark 10 : 23 ; Luke 18 : 24 of the danger of riches.¶

2. MOGIS (μόγις), with labour, pain, trouble (akin to *mogos*, toil), is found in some mss. in Luke 9 : 39, instead of No. 3.¶

3. MOLIS (μόλις), with difficulty, scarcely, hardly (akin to *molos*, toil), is used as an alternative for No. 2, and occurs in the most authentic mss. in Luke 9 : 39 ; it is rendered " hardly " in Acts 27 : 8, A.V. See DIFFICULTY.

HARDSHIP (to suffer)

1. KAKOPATHEŌ (κακοπαθέω), to suffer evil, is translated " suffer hardship " in three places in the R.V., 2 Tim. 2 : 3 (in some mss. ; see No. 2), A.V., " endure hardness ; " 2 : 9, A.V., " suffer trouble ; " 4 : 5, A.V., " endure affliction ; " in Jas. 5 : 13, R.V., " suffering " (A.V., " afflicted "). See AFFLICT, ENDURE, SUFFER.¶ In the Sept., Jonah 4 : 10.¶

2. SUNKAKOPATHEŌ (συγκακοπαθέω), to suffer hardship with, is so rendered in 2 Tim. 1 : 8, R.V., A.V., " be thou partaker of the afflictions " (of the Gospel), and, in the best mss., in 2 : 3, " suffer hardship with me." See AFFLICTION, No. 3, *Note*.¶

HARLOT

PORNĒ (πόρνη), a prostitute, harlot (from *pernēmi*, to sell), is used (*a*) literally, in Matt. 21 : 31, 32, of those who were the objects of the mercy shown by Christ ; in Luke 15 : 30, of the life of the prodigal ; in

1 Cor. 6 : 15, 16, in a warning to the Corinthian church against the prevailing licentiousness which had made Corinth a byword ; in Heb. 11 : 31 and Jas. 2 : 25, of Rahab ; (b) metaphorically, of mystic Babylon, Rev. 17 : 1, 5 (A.V., " harlots "), 15, 16 ; 19 : 2, R.V., for A.V., " whore."¶

HARM

A. Nouns.

1. KAKOS (κακός), evil, is rendered " harm " in Acts 16 : 28 ; 28 : 5. See EVIL.

2. PONĒROS (πονηρός), evil, generally of a more malignant sort than No. 1, is translated " harm " in Acts 28 : 21.   See EVIL.

3. ATOPOS (ἄτοπος) : see AMISS.

4. HUBRIS (ὕβρις) primarily denotes wantonness, insolence ; then, an act of wanton violence, an outrage, injury, 2 Cor. 12 : 10, R.V., " injuries," A.V., " reproaches " (more than reproach is conveyed by the term) ; metaphorically of a loss by sea, Acts 27 : 10, R.V., " injury," A.V., " hurt," and ver. 21, R.V., " injury," A.V., " harm."   See HURT, INJURY, REPROACH.¶

B. Verb.

1. KAKOŌ (κακόω), to do evil to a person (akin to A, No. 1), is rendered " harm " in 1 Pet. 3 : 13, and in the R.V. of Acts 18 : 10 (A.V., " hurt "). See AFFECT, EVIL.

2. KAKOPOIEŌ (κακοποιέω), to do harm (A, No. 1, and poieō, to do), is so rendered in the R.V. of Mark 3 : 4 and Luke 6 : 9 (A.V., " to do evil "), with reference to the moral character of what is done ; in 1 Pet. 3 : 17, " evil doing ; " 3 John 11, " doeth evil."¶

HARMLESS

1. AKERAIOS (ἀκέραιος), lit., unmixed, with absence of foreign mixture (from a, negative, and kerannumi, to mix), pure, is used metaphorically in the N.T. of what is guileless, sincere, Matt. 10 : 16, " harmless " (marg., " simple "), i.e., with the simplicity of a single eye, discerning what is evil, and choosing only what glorifies God ; Rom. 16 : 19, " simple (unto that which is evil)," A.V. marg., " harmless ; " Phil. 2 : 15, " harmless," A.V. marg., " sincere."   The Greeks used it of wine unmixed with water, of unalloyed metal ; in the papyri writings it is used of a loan the interest of which is guaranteed (Moulton and Milligan, Vocab.).   Trench compares it and synonymous words as follows : " as the akakos (see No. 2, below) has no harmfulness in him, and the adolos no guile, so the akeraios no foreign mixture, and the haplous no folds " (Syn., § lvi).   Haplous is said of the single eye, Matt. 6 : 22 ; Luke 11 : 34.¶

2. AKAKOS (ἄκακος), the negative of kakos (see HARM, A, No. 1), void of evil, is rendered " harmless " in Heb. 7 : 26 (R.V., " guileless "), of the character of Christ as a High Priest ; in Rom. 16 : 18, R.V., " innocent," A.V., " simple."¶

HARP
A. Noun.

KITHARA (κιθάρα), whence Eng., guitar, denotes a lyre or harp; it is described by Josephus as an instrument of ten strings, played by a plectrum (a smaller instrument was played by the hand); it is mentioned in I Cor. 14:7; Rev. 5:8; 14:2; 15:2.¶

B. Verb.

KITHARIZO (κιθαρίζω) signifies to play on the harp, I Cor. 14:7; Rev. 14:2.¶ In the Sept., Isa. 23:16.¶

HARPER

KITHARŌDOS (κιθαρωδός) denotes one who plays and sings to the lyre (from *kithara*, a lyre, and *aoidos*, a singer), Rev. 14:2; 18:22.¶

HARVEST

THERISMOS (θερισμός), akin to *therizō*, to reap, is used (a) of the act of harvesting, John 4:35; (b) the time of harvest, figuratively, Matt. 13:30, 39; Mark 4:29; (c) the crop, figuratively, Matt. 9:37, 38; Luke 10:2; Rev. 14:15. The beginning of harvest varied according to natural conditions, but took place on the average about the middle of April in the eastern lowlands of Palestine, in the latter part of the month in the coast plains and a little later in high districts. Barley harvest usually came first and then wheat. Harvesting lasted about seven weeks, and was the occasion of festivities.¶

HASTE, WITH HASTE, HASTILY
A. Noun.

SPOUDE (σπουδή) denotes (a) haste, speed, accompanied by " with," Mark 6:25; Luke 1:39; (b) zeal, diligence, earnestness: see BUSINESS, CARE, CAREFULNESS, DILIGENCE, FORWARDNESS.

B. Verb.

SPEUDŌ (σπεύδω) denotes (a) intransitively, to hasten, Luke 2:16, " with haste," lit., ' (they came) hastening; ' Luke 19:5, 6; Acts 20:16; 22:18; (b) transitively, to desire earnestly, 2 Pet. 3:12, R.V., " earnestly desiring " (marg., " hastening "), A.V., " hasting " (the day of God), i.e., in our practical fellowship with God as those who are appointed by Him as instruments through prayer and service for the accomplishment of His purposes, purposes which will be unthwartably fulfilled both in time and manner of accomplishment. In this way the earnest desire will find its fulfilment.¶

C. Adverb.

TACHEŌS (ταχέως), quickly, is used in a warning to lay hands " hastily " on no man (with a suggestion of rashness), I Tim. 5:22, R.V. (A.V., " suddenly "); in John 11:31, R.V., " (she rose up) quickly " (A.V., " hastily "). See QUICKLY, SHORTLY, SUDDENLY.

HATE, HATEFUL, HATER, HATRED
A. Verb.

MISEŌ (μισέω), to hate, is used especially (a) of malicious and un-justifiable feelings towards others, whether towards the innocent or by mutual animosity, e.g., Matt. 10 : 22 ; 24 : 10 ; Luke 6 : 22, 27 ; 19 : 14 ; John 3 : 20, of hating the light (metaphorically) ; 7 : 7 ; 15 : 18, 19, 23–25 ; Tit. 3 : 3 ; 1 John 2 : 9, 11 ; 3 : 13, 15 ; 4 : 20 ; Rev. 18 : 2, where " hateful " translates the perfect participle Passive Voice of the verb, lit., ' hated,' or ' having been hated ; ' (b) of a right feeling of aversion from what is evil ; said of wrong doing, Rom. 7 : 15 ; iniquity, Heb. 1 : 9 ; " the garment (figurative) spotted by the flesh," Jude 23 ; " the works of the Nicolaitans," Rev. 2 : 6 (and ver. 15, in some mss. ; see the A.V.) ; (c) of relative preference for one thing over another, by way of expressing either aversion from, or disregard for, the claims of one person or thing relatively to those of another, Matt. 6 : 24, and Luke 16 : 13, as to the impossibility of serving two " masters ; " Luke 14 : 26, as to the claims of parents relatively to those of Christ ; John 12 : 25, of disregard for one's life relatively to the claims of Christ ; Eph. 5 : 29, negatively, of one's flesh, i.e. of one's own, and therefore a man's wife as one with him.

Note : In 1 John 3 : 15, he who hates his brother is called a murderer ; for the sin lies in the inward disposition, of which the act is only the outward expression.

B. Adjective.

STUGĒTOS (στυγητός), hateful (from *stugeō*, to hate, not found in the N.T.), is used in Tit. 3 : 3.¶

C. Nouns.

1. ECHTHRA (ἔχθρα), hatred : see ENMITY.

2. THEOSTUGĒS (θεοστυγής), from *theos*, God, and *stugeō* (see B), is used in Rom. 1 : 30, A.V., and R.V. marg., " haters of God," R.V., " hateful to God ; " the former rendering is appropriate to what is expressed by the next words, " insolent," " haughty," but the R.V. text seems to give the true meaning. Lightfoot quotes from the Epistle of Clement of Rome, in confirmation of this, " those who practise these things are hateful to God."¶

HAUGHTY

HUPERĒPHANOS (ὑπερήφανος), showing oneself above others (*huper*, over, *phainomai*, to appear), though often denoting pre-eminent, is always used in the N.T. in the evil sense of arrogant, disdainful, haughty ; it is rendered " haughty " in Rom. 1 : 30 and 2 Tim. 3 : 2, R.V., A.V., " proud," but " proud " in both Versions in Luke 1 : 51 ; Jas. 4 : 6, and 1 Pet. 5 : 5 ; in the last two it is set in opposition to *tapeinos*, humble, lowly. Cp. the noun *huperēphania*, Mark 7 : 22, pride.¶

HAVE

(*Note :* The following are distinct from the word when it is auxiliary to the tenses of other verbs.)

1. ECHŌ (ἔχω), the usual verb for to have, is used with the following meanings : (*a*) to hold, in the hand, etc., e.g., Rev. 1 : 16 ; 5 : 8 ; (*b*) to hold fast, keep, Luke 19 : 20 ; metaphorically, of the mind and conduct, e.g., Mark 16 : 8 ; John 14 : 21 ; Rom. 1 : 28 ; 1 Tim. 3 : 9 ; 2 Tim. 1 : 13 ; (*c*) to hold on, cling to, be next to, e.g., of accompaniment, Heb. 6 : 9. "things that accompany (salvation)," lit., ' the things holding themselves of salvation ' (R.V., marg., " are near to ") ; of place, Mark 1 : 38, " next (towns)," lit., ' towns holding nigh ; ' of time, e.g., Luke 13 : 33, " (the day) following," lit., ' the holding (day) ; ' Acts 13 : 44 ; 20 : 15 ; 21 : 26 ; (*d*) to hold, to count, consider, regard, e.g., Matt. 14 : 5 ; 21 : 46 ; Mark 11 : 32 ; Luke 14 : 18 ; Philm. 17 ; (*e*) to involve, Heb. 10 : 35 ; Jas. 1 : 4 ; 1 John 4 : 18 ; (*f*) to wear, of clothing, arms, etc., e.g., Matt. 3 : 4 ; 22 : 12 ; John 18 : 10 ; (*g*) to be (with child), of a woman, Mark 13 : 17 ; Rom. 9 : 10 (lit., ' having conception ') ; (*h*) to possess, the most frequent use, e.g., Matt. 8 : 20 ; 19 : 22 ; Acts 9 : 14 ; 1 Thess. 3 : 6 ; (*i*) of complaints, disputes, Matt. 5 : 23 ; Mark 11 : 25 ; Acts 24 : 19 ; Rev. 2 : 4, 20 ; (*j*) of ability, power, e.g., Luke 12 : 4 ; Acts 4 : 14 (lit., ' had nothing to say ') ; (*k*) of necessity, e.g., Luke 12 : 50 ; Acts 23 : 17-19 ; (*l*) to be in a certain condition, as, of readiness, Acts 21 : 13 (lit., ' I have readily ') ; of illness, Matt. 4 : 24, " all that were sick " (lit., ' that had themselves sickly ') ; Mark 5 : 23, " lieth (lit., ' hath herself ') at the point of death ; " Mark 16 : 18, " they shall recover " (lit., ' shall have themselves well ') ; John 4 : 52, " he began to amend " (lit., ' he had himself better ') ; of evil works, 1 Tim. 5 : 25, " they that are otherwise," (lit., ' the things having otherwise ') ; to be so, e.g., Acts 7 : 1, " are these things so ? " (lit., ' have these things thus ? ') ; of time, Acts 24 : 25, " for this time " (lit., ' the thing having now ').

2. APECHŌ (ἀπέχω) denotes to have in full, to have received (*apo*, from, and No. 1), Matt. 6 : 2, 5, 16, R.V., " have received," for A.V., " have ; " Luke 6 : 24, A.V. and R.V., " have received," but Phil. 4 : 18, " I have ; " Philm. 15, " (that) thou shouldest have (him) " (A.V., " receive "). Deissmann, in *Light from the Ancient East*, and Moulton and Milligan (Vocab. of Gk. Test.) show that the verb was constantly used " as a technical expression in drawing up a receipt. Consequently in the Sermon on the Mount we are led to understand ' they have received their reward ' as ' they have signed the receipt of their reward : their right to receive their reward is realised, precisely as if they had already given a receipt for it.' "

Is there not a hint of this in Paul's word to Philemon concerning receiving Onesimus (ver. 17) ? Philemon would give the Apostle a receipt for his payment in sending him. This is in keeping with the metaphorical terms of finance in vv. 18, 19. See ABSTAIN.

3. GINOMAI (γίνομαι), to begin to be, come to pass, happen, is rendered " have " in Matt. 18 : 12 ; " had " in Acts 15 : 2 ; " shall have " in 1 Cor. 4 : 5, lit., ' praise shall be,' or come to pass. See BECOME.

4. METALAMBANŌ (μεταλαμβάνω), to have, or get a share of, is rendered " I have (a convenient season)," in Acts 24 : 25. See EAT, PARTAKE, RECEIVE, TAKE.

5. HUPARCHŌ (ὑπάρχω), to be in existence, to be ready, at hand, is translated by the verb to have in Acts 3 : 6, lit., ' silver and gold is not to me ' (in the next clause, " such as I have," echō is used) ; 4 : 37, " having (land)," lit., ' (land) being (to him) ; ' Matt. 19 : 21, " that (thou) hast," lit., ' (things that) are (thine),' i.e., ' thy belongings ; ' similarly Luke 12 : 33, 44 ; 14 : 33. See BEING.

6. ANTIBALLŌ (ἀντιβάλλω), lit., to throw in turn, exchange (anti, corresponding to, ballō, to throw), hence, metaphorically, to exchange thoughts, is used in Luke 24 : 27, " ye have," i.e., ' ye exchange.'¶

7. EIMI (εἰμί), to be, is often used in its various forms with some case of the personal pronoun, to signify to be to, or of, a person, e.g., Matt. 19 : 27, " (what then) shall we have," lit., ' what then shall be to us ? ; ' Acts 21 : 23, " we have four men," lit., ' there are to us, etc.'

8. ENDUŌ (ἐνδύω), to put on, is rendered " having on " in Eph. 6 : 14. See CLOTHE.

Notes : (1) In John 5 : 4 (in those mss. which contain the passage), *katechō*, to hold fast, is used in the Passive Voice, in the phrase " whatsoever disease he had," lit., ' (by whatsoever disease) he was held.' (2) In Mark 12 : 22, in some mss., *lambanō*, to take or receive, is translated " had," in the statement " the seven had her ; " in Acts 25 : 16, R.V., " have had " (A.V., " have ") ; in Heb. 11 : 36, " had." (3) In Matt. 27 : 19, " Have thou nothing to do with that righteous man " translates what is lit. ' nothing to thee and that righteous man,' the verb being omitted. Similarly with the phrase, " What have I to do with thee ? " lit., ' what (is) to me and thee ? ' Mark 5 : 7 ; Luke 8 : 28 ; John 2 : 4, where Westcott translates it ' What is there to Me and to thee ? ; ' Ellicott, ' What is that to Me and to thee," i.e., ' What is My concern and thine in the matter ? ' There is certainly nothing disparaging in the question. On the contrary, it answers what must have been the thought in Mary's heart, and suggests that while there is no obligation either on Him or her, yet the need is a case for rendering help. For the construction with the plural pronoun see Matt. 8 : 29 ; Mark 1 : 24 ; Luke 4 : 34. (4) In Heb. 4 : 13, " with whom we have to do " is, lit., ' with whom (is) the account (*logos*) to us.' (5) In Heb. 13 : 5, " such things as ye have " is, lit., ' the (things) present ' (6) In Mark 5 : 26, " all that she had " is, lit., ' all the (things) with her.' (7) For Luke 15 : 31, A.V., " all that I have," lit., ' all my (things),' see R.V. (8) For *eneimi*, Luke 11 : 41, " ye have," see WITHIN, *Note* (h).

HAVEN

LIMĒN (λιμήν) is mentioned in Acts 27 : 8, " Fair Havens," and ver. 12 ; for the first of these see FAIR. The first mention in the Bible is in Gen. 49 : 13 (see R.V. marg.).¶

HAVOCK

1. PORTHEŌ (πορθέω), to destroy, ravage, lay waste, is used of the persecution inflicted by Saul of Tarsus on the church in Jerusalem, Acts 9 : 21, and Gal. 1 : 23, R.V., " made havock," for A.V., " destroyed ; " Gal. 1 : 13, ditto, for A.V., " wasted." See DESTROY, Note.¶

2. LUMAINOMAI (λυμαίνομαι), to maltreat, outrage (lumē, an outrage), is translated " made havock " in Acts 8 : 3, A.V. (R.V., " laid waste.")¶

For HAY see GRASS

HAZARD

1. PARADIDŌMI (παραδίδωμι), to give over, deliver, signifies to risk, to hazard, in Acts 15 : 26, of Barnabas and Paul, who hazarded their lives for the Name of the Lord Jesus. See BETRAY.

2. PARABOLEUOMAI (παραβολεύομαι), lit., to throw aside (para, aside, ballō, to throw), hence, to expose oneself to danger, to hazard one's life, is said of Epaphroditus in Phil. 2 : 30, R.V., " hazarding." Some mss. have parabouleuomai here, to consult amiss, A.V., " not regarding."¶

HE

Note : This pronoun is generally part of the translation of a verb. Frequently it translates the article before nouns, adjectives, numerals, adverbs, prepositional phrases and the participial form of verbs. Apart from these it translates one of the following :

1. AUTOS (αὐτός), he himself and no other, emphatic, e.g., Matt. 1 : 21, where the R.V. brings out the emphasis by the rendering " it is He ; " 3 : 11 (last clause), where the repeated " He " brings out the emphasis ; in some cases it can be marked only by a circumlocution which would not constitute a translation, e.g., 8 : 24 ; this use is very frequent, especially in the Gospels, the Epistles of John and the Apocalypse ; see also, e.g., Eph. 2 : 14 ; 4 : 11 ; 5 : 23, 27. See SAME, SELF, THIS, VERY.

2. HOUTOS (οὗτος), this, this person here, is always emphatic ; it is used with this meaning, sometimes to refer to what precedes, e.g., Matt. 5 : 19, " he (shall be called great) ; " John 6 : 46, " he (hath seen) ; " often rendered " this," e.g., Rom. 9 : 9, or " this man," e.g., Matt. 27 : 58, R.V. ; Jas. 1 : 25 ; " the same," e.g., Luke 9 : 48. See THAT, THIS, THESE.

3. EKEINOS (ἐκεῖνος) denotes that one, that person (in contrast to No. 2) ; its use marks special distinction, favourable or unfavourable ; this form of emphasis should always be noted ; e.g., John 2 : 21 " (But)

He (spake) ; " 5 : 19, " (what things soever) He (doeth) ; " 7 : 11 ; 2 Cor. 10 : 18, lit., ' for not he that commendeth himself, he (*ekeinos*) is approved ;' 2 Tim. 2 : 13, " He (in contrast to " we ") abideth faithful ; " 1 John 3 : 3, " (even as) He (is pure) ; " ver. 5, " He (was manifested) ; " ver. 7, " He (is righteous) ; " ver. 16, " He laid down ; " 4 : 17, " (as) He (is)." See OTHER, THAT, THIS.

Note : The indefinite pronoun *tis*, anyone, any man, is rendered " he " in Acts 4 : 35, A.V. (R.V., rightly, " any one ") ; in Heb. 10 : 28, R.V., " a man."

HE HIMSELF

1. AUTOS (αὐτός) : see No. 1, above.

2. HEAUTON (ἑαυτόν), oneself, himself, a reflexive of No. 1, is rendered " he himself " in Luke 23 : 2 and Acts 25 : 4.

HE THAT

1. HOS (ὅς), the relative pronoun who, is sometimes rendered " he that," e.g., Matt. 10 : 38 ; with the particle *an*, expressing possibility, uncertainty or a condition, signifying whosoever, Mark 3 : 29, A.V. (R.V., " whosoever ") ; 4 : 25 and 9 : 40 (with *an*, in the best mss.). See WHAT-SOEVER, WHICH, WHO, WHOSOEVER.

2. HOSGE (ὅσγε), who even (No. 1, and the particle *ge*), indicates a greater in regard to a less, Rom. 8 : 32, " He that (spared not)."

Notes : (1) In Rev. 13 : 10, *ei tis*, if anyone, is rendered " if any man " in the R.V., for A.V., " he that."

(2) In Matt. 23 : 12, *hostis*, No. 1, combined with the indefinite pronoun *tis* (see preceding note), is properly rendered " whosoever," R.V., for A.V., " he that."

HEAD

KEPHALĒ (κεφαλή), besides its natural significance, is used (*a*) figuratively in Rom. 12 : 20, of heaping coals of fire on a head (see COALS) ; in Acts 18 : 6, " Your blood be upon your own heads," i.e., ' your blood-guiltiness rest upon your own persons,' a mode of expression frequent in the O.T., and perhaps here directly connected with Ezek. 3 : 18, 20 ; 33 : 6, 8 ; see also Lev. 20 : 16 ; 2 Sam. 1 : 16 ; 1 Kings 2 : 37 ; (*b*) metaphorically, of the authority or direction of God in relation to Christ, of Christ in relation to believing men, of the husband in relation to the wife, 1 Cor. 11 : 3 ; of Christ in relation to the Church, Eph. 1 : 22 ; 4 : 15 ; 5 : 23 ; Col. 1 : 18 ; 2 : 19 ; of Christ in relation to principalities and powers, Col. 2 : 10. As to 1 Cor. 11 : 10, taken in connection with the context, the word " authority " probably stands, by metonymy, for a sign of authority (R.V.), the angels being witnesses of the pre-eminent relationship as established by God in the creation of man as just mentioned, with the spiritual significance regarding the position of Christ in relation

to the Church ; cp. Eph. 3 : 10 ; it is used of Christ as the foundation of
the spiritual building set forth by the Temple, with its " corner stone,"
Matt. 21 : 42 ; symbolically also of the Imperial rulers of the Roman
power, as seen in the Apocalyptic visions, Rev. 13 : 1, 3 ; 17 : 3, 7, 9.

HEAD (to wound in the)

KEPHALIOŌ, or KEPHALAIOŌ (κεφαλιόω), from *kephalion*, a
diminutive of *kephalē*, usually meant to sum up, to bring under heads ;
in Mark 12 : 4 it is used for wounding on the head, the only place where
it has this meaning.¶

HEADLONG (to cast, to fall)

1. KATAKRĒMNIZO (κατακρημνίζω) signifies to throw over a
precipice (*kata*, down, *krēmnos*, a steep bank, etc.), said of the purpose
of the people of Nazareth to destroy Christ, Luke 4 : 29.¶

2. PRĒNĒS (πρηνής), an adjective denoting headlong, prone, is used
with the verb *ginomai*, to become, in Acts 1 : 18, of the death of Judas,
" falling headlong ; " various suggestions have been made as to the
actual details ; some ascribe to the word the meaning " swelling up."¶

HEADSTRONG (R.V.), HEADY (A.V.)

PROPETĒS (προπετής) lit. means falling forwards (from *pro*, forwards,
and *piptō*, to fall) ; it is used metaphorically to signify precipitate, rash,
reckless, and is said (*a*) of persons, 2 Tim. 3 : 4 ; " headstrong " is the
appropriate rendering ; (*b*) of things, Acts 19 : 36, R.V., " (nothing) rash "
(A.V., " rashly ").¶

HEAL, HEALING
A. Verbs.

1. THERAPEUŌ (θεραπεύω) primarily signifies to serve as a *therapōn*,
an attendant ; then, to care for the sick, to treat, cure, heal (Eng., therapeutics). It is chiefly used in Matthew and Luke, once in John (5 : 10),
and, after the Acts, only Rev. 13 : 3 and 12. See CURE.

2. IAOMAI (ἰάομαι), to heal, is used (*a*) of physical treatment 22 times ;
in Matt. 15 : 28, A.V., " made whole," R.V., " healed ; " so in Acts
9 : 34 ; (*b*) figuratively, of spiritual healing, Matt. 13 : 15 ; John 12 : 40 ;
Acts 28 : 27 ; Heb. 12 : 13 ; 1 Pet. 2 : 24 ; possibly, Jas. 5 : 16 includes
both (*a*) and (*b*) ; some mss. have the word, with sense (*b*), in Luke 4 : 18.
Apart from this last, Luke, the physician, uses the word fifteen times.
See WHOLE.

3. SŌZŌ (σώζω), to save, is translated by the verb to heal in the A.V.
of Mark 5 : 23 and Luke 8 : 36 (R.V., to make whole ; so A.V. frequently) ;
the idea is that of saving from disease and its effects. See SAVE.

4. DIASŌZŌ (διασώζω), to save thoroughly (*dia*, through, and No. 3),
is translated " heal " in Luke 7 : 3, A.V. (R.V., " save "). See ESCAPE.

B. Nouns.

1. THERAPEIA (θεραπεία), akin to A, No. 1, primarily denotes care, attention, Luke 12 : 42 (see HOUSEHOLD) ; then, medical service, healing (Eng., therapy), Luke 9 : 11 ; Rev. 22 : 2, of the effects of the leaves of the tree of life, perhaps here with the meaning " health."¶

2. IAMA (ἴαμα), akin to A, No. 2, formerly signified a means of healing ; in the N.T., a healing (the result of the act), used in the plural, in 1 Cor. 12 : 9, 28, 30, R.V., " healings ; " of Divinely imparted gifts in the churches in Apostolic times.¶

3. IASIS (ἴασις), akin to A, No. 2, stresses the process as reaching completion, Luke 13 : 32, " cures," of the acts of Christ in the days of His flesh ; Acts 4 : 22, 30, " to heal," lit. ' unto healing.'¶

HEALTH (to be in)

HUGIAINŌ (ὑγιαίνω) denotes to be healthy, sound, in good health (Eng., hygiene), rendered " mayest be in health," in 3 John 2 ; rendered " safe and sound " in Luke 15 : 27. See SAFE, D, No. 2, SOUND, WHOLE, B, No. 1.

Note : In Acts 27 : 34, *sōtēria*, salvation, safety, is translated " health " in the A.V. ; the R.V., gives the right meaning, " safety."

HEAP (to)

1. SŌREUŌ (σωρεύω), to heap one thing on another, is said of heaping coals of fire on the head, Rom. 12 : 20 (for the meaning see COALS) ; in 2 Tim. 3 : 6 it is used metaphorically of women " laden " (or overwhelmed) with sins. See LADEN.¶ In the Sept., Prov. 25 : 22.¶

2. EPISŌREUŌ (ἐπισωρεύω), to heap upon or together (*epi*, upon, and No. 1), is used metaphorically in 2 Tim. 4 : 3 of appropriating a number of teachers to suit the liking of those who do so. The reference may be to those who, like the Athenians, run about to hear and follow those who proclaim new ideas of their own invention.¶

HEAR, HEARING
A. Verbs.

1. AKOUŌ (ἀκούω), the usual word denoting to hear, is used (*a*) intransitively, e.g., Matt. 11 : 15 ; Mark 4 : 23 ; (*b*) transitively when the object is expressed, sometimes in the accusative case, sometimes in the genitive. Thus in Acts 9 : 7, " hearing the voice," the noun " voice " is in the partitive genitive case [i.e., hearing (something) of], whereas in 22 : 9, " they heard not the voice," the construction is with the accusative. This removes the idea of any contradiction. The former indicates a hearing of the sound, the latter indicates the meaning or message of the voice (this they did not hear). " The former denotes the sensational perception, the latter (the accusative case) the thing perceived " (Cremer). In John 5 : 25, 28, the genitive case is used, indicating a " sensational

perception " that the Lord's voice is sounding ; in 3 : 8, of hearing the wind, the accusative is used, stressing " the thing perceived."

That God hears prayer signifies that He answers prayer, e.g., John 9 : 31 ; 1 John 5 : 14, 15. Sometimes the verb is used with *para* (from beside), e.g., John 1 : 40, " one of the two which heard John speak," lit., ' heard from beside John,' suggesting that he stood beside him ; in John 8 : 26, 40, indicating the intimate fellowship of the Son with the Father ; the same construction is used in Acts 10 : 22 and 2 Tim. 2 : 2, in the latter case, of the intimacy between Paul and Timothy. See HEARKEN.

2. EISAKOUŌ (εἰσακούω), to listen to (*eis*, to, and No. 1), has two meanings, (*a*) to hear and to obey, 1 Cor. 14 : 21, " they will not hear ; " (*b*) to hear so as to answer, of God's answer to prayer, Matt. 6 : 7 ; Luke 1 : 13 ; Acts 10 : 31 ; Heb. 5 : 7.¶

3. DIAKOUŌ (διακούω), to hear through, hear fully (*dia*, through, and No. 1), is used technically, of hearing judicially, in Acts 23 : 35, of Felix in regard to the charges against Paul.¶ In the Sept., Deut. 1 : 16 ; Job 9 : 33.¶

4. EPAKOUŌ (ἐπακούω), to listen to, hear with favour, at or upon an occasion (*epi*, upon, and No. 1), is used in 2 Cor. 6 : 2 (R.V., " hearken ").¶

5. EPAKROAOMAI (ἐπακροάομαι), to listen attentively to (*epi*, used intensively, and a verb akin to No. 1), is used in Acts 16 : 25, " (the prisoners) were listening to (them)," R.V., expressive of rapt attention.¶

6. PROAKOUŌ (προακούω) signifies to hear before (*pro*), Col. 1 : 5, where Lightfoot suggests that the preposition contrasts what they heard before, the true Gospel, with the false gospel of their recent teachers.¶

7. PARAKOUŌ (παρακούω) primarily signifies to overhear, hear amiss or imperfectly (*para*, beside, amiss, and No. 1) ; then (in the N.T.) to hear without taking heed, to neglect to hear, Matt. 18 : 17 (twice) ; in Mark 5 : 36 the best mss. have this verb, which the R.V. renders " not heeding " (marg., " overhearing ") ; some mss. have No. 1, A.V., " hearing." It seems obvious that the Lord paid no attention to those from the ruler's house and their message that his daughter was dead.¶ Cp. the noun *parakoē*, disobedience.

B. Nouns.

1. AKOĒ (ἀκοή), akin to A, No. 1, denotes (*a*) the sense of hearing, 1 Cor. 12 : 17 ; 2 Pet. 2 : 8 ; a combination of verb and noun is used in phrases which have been termed Hebraic as they express somewhat literally an O.T. phraseology, e.g., " By hearing ye shall hear," Matt. 13 : 14 ; Acts 28 : 26, R.V., a mode of expression conveying emphasis ; (*b*) the organ of hearing, Mark 7 : 35, " ears ; " Luke 7 : 1, R.V., " ears," for A.V., " audience ; " Acts 17 : 20 ; 2 Tim. 4 : 3, 4 ; Heb. 5 : 11, " dull of hearing," lit., ' dull as to ears ; ' (*c*) a thing heard, a message or teaching,

John 12 : 38, " report ; " Rom. 10 : 16 ; 1 Thess. 2 : 13, " the word of the message," lit. ' the word of hearing' (A.V., "which ye heard"); Heb. 4 : 2, " the word of hearing," R.V., for A.V., " the word preached ; " in a somewhat similar sense, a rumour, report, Matt. 4 : 24 ; 14 : 1 ; Mark 1 : 28, A.V., " fame," R.V., " report ; " Matt. 24 : 6 ; Mark 13 : 7, " rumours (of wars) ; " (d) the receiving of a message, Rom. 10 : 17, something more than the mere sense of hearing [see (a)] ; so with the phrase " the hearing of faith," Gal. 3 : 2, 5, which it seems better to understand so than under (c). See EAR, FAME, PREACH, REPORT, RUMOUR.¶

Notes : (1) For *diagnōsis* (investigation, followed by decision), rendered " hearing " in Acts 25 : 21, A.V., see DECISION. (2) For the phrase to be dull of hearing, lit., ' to hear heavily,' Matt. 13 : 15 ; Acts 28 : 27, see DULL. (3) For *akroatērion*, a place of hearing, Acts 25 : 23, see PLACE.¶

HEARER

AKROATĒS (ἀκροατής), from *akroaomai*, to listen, is used in Rom. 2 : 13, " of a law ; " Jas. 1 : 22, 23, " of the word ; " ver. 25, " a (forgetful) hearer."¶

Note : In Eph. 4 : 29 and 2 Tim. 2 : 14, the verb *akouō*, to hear, is rendered " hearers " in the A.V. (R.V., " them that hear ").

HEARKEN

1. AKOUŌ (ἀκούω), to hear, is rendered " hearken " in the A.V. and R.V., in Mark 4 : 3 ; Acts 4 : 19 ; 7 : 2 ; 15 : 13 ; Jas. 2 : 5 ; in the R.V. only, in Acts 3 : 22, 23 ; 13 : 16 (A.V., " give audience ") ; 15 : 12, " hearkened " (A.V. " gave audience "). See HEAR, No. 1.

Note : In Acts 12 : 13, *hupakouō*, lit., to hearken, with the idea of stillness, or attention (*hupo*, under, *akouō*, to hear), signifies to answer a knock at a door, R.V., " to answer " (A.V., " to hearken "). See OBEY.

2. EPAKOUŌ (ἐπακούω) denotes to hearken to, 2 Cor. 6 : 2, R.V. (see HEAR, A, No. 4).¶

3. ENŌTIZOMAI (ἐνωτίζομαι), to give ear to, to hearken (from *en*, in, and *ous*, an ear), is used in Acts 2 : 14, in Peter's address to the men of Israel.¶

4. PEITHARCHEŌ (πειθαρχέω), to obey one in authority, be obedient (*peithomai*, to be persuaded, *archē*, rule), is translated to hearken unto in Acts 27 : 21, in Paul's reminder to the shipwrecked mariners that they should have given heed to his counsel. See OBEY.

HEART, HEARTILY

KARDIA (καρδία), the heart (Eng., cardiac, etc.), the chief organ of physical life (" for the life of the flesh is in the blood," Lev. 17 : 11), occupies the most important place in the human system. By an easy transition the word came to stand for man's entire mental and moral activity, both the rational and the emotional elements. In other words, the heart is used figuratively for the hidden springs of the personal life. " The Bible describes human depravity as in the ' heart,' because sin is a principle which has its seat in the centre of man's inward life, and then ' defiles ' the whole circuit of his action, Matt. 15 : 19, 20. On the other hand, Scripture regards the heart as the sphere of Divine influence, Rom. 2 : 15 ; Acts 15 : 9. . . . The heart, as lying deep within, contains ' the hidden man,' 1 Pet. 3 : 4, the real man. It represents the true character but conceals it " (J. Laidlaw, in Hastings' Bible Dic.).

As to its usage in the N.T. it denotes (*a*) the seat of physical life, Acts 14 : 17 ; Jas. 5 : 5 ; (*b*) the seat of moral nature and spiritual life, the seat of grief, John 14 : 1 ; Rom. 9 : 2 ; 2 Cor. 2 : 4 ; joy, John 16 : 22 ; Eph. 5 : 19 ; the desires, Matt. 5 : 28 ; 2 Pet. 2 : 14 ; the affections, Luke 24 : 32 ; Acts 21 : 13 ; the perceptions, John 12 : 40 ; Eph. 4 : 18 ; the thoughts, Matt. 9 : 4 ; Heb. 4 : 12 ; the understanding, Matt. 13 : 15 ; Rom. 1 : 21 ; the reasoning powers, Mark 2 : 6 ; Luke 24 : 38 ; the imagination, Luke 1 : 51 ; conscience, Acts 2 : 37 ; 1 John 3 : 20 ; the intentions, Heb. 4 : 12, cp. 1 Pet. 4 : 1 ; purpose, Acts 11 : 23 ; 2 Cor. 9 : 7 ; the will, Rom. 6 : 17 ; Col. 3 : 15 ; faith, Mark 11 : 23 ; Rom. 10 : 10 ; Heb. 3 : 12.

The heart, in its moral significance in the O.T., includes the emotions, the reason and the will.

2. PSUCHĒ (ψυχή), the soul, or life, is rendered " heart " in Eph. 6 : 6 (marg., " soul "), " doing the will of God from the heart." In Col. 3 : 23, a form of the word *psuchē* preceded by *ek*, from, lit., ' from (the) soul,' is rendered " heartily."

Notes : (1) The R.V., " heart " is substituted for A.V., " bowels," in Col. 3 : 12 ; Philm. 7, 12, 20. (2) In 2 Cor. 3 : 3, the R.V. has " tables that are hearts of flesh," for A.V., " fleshy tables of the heart." (3) In Eph. 1 : 18, the best mss. have *kardia*, " (the eyes of your) heart ; " some have *dianoia*, " understanding " (A.V.). (4) In Heb. 8 : 10 and 10 : 16, the A.V. has " in their hearts " and " into their hearts ; " R.V., " on their heart." (5) In Luke 21 : 26, where there is no word for " hearts " in the original, the R.V. has " men fainting (for fear)." (6) In 2 Cor. 7 : 2, the verb *chōreō*, to make room for, " receive " (A.V.), is translated, or rather, interpreted, " open your hearts," R.V., marg., " make room for (us)."

HEART (hardness of)

SKLĒROKARDIA (σκληροκαρδία), hardness of heart (*sklēros*, hard, and *kardia*), is used in Matt. 19 : 8 ; Mark 10 : 5 ; 16 : 14.¶ In the Sept., Deut. 10 : 16 ; Jer. 4 : 4.¶

HEART (knowing the)

KARDIOGNŌSTĒS (καρδιογνώστης), a knower of hearts (*kardia* and *ginōskō*, to know), is used in Acts 1 : 24 ; 15 : 8.¶

HEAT
A. Nouns.

1. KAUSŌN (καύσων) denotes a burning heat (from *kaiō*, to burn; cp. Eng., caustic, cauterize), Matt. 20 : 12 ; Luke 12 : 55 (A.V., " heat "), R.V., in each place, " scorching heat " (marg., " hot wind ") ; in Jas. 1 : 11, " a burning heat," A.V., R.V., " the scorching wind," like the Sirocco. Cp. Amos 4 : 9, where the Sept. has *purōsis*, burning (*pur*, fire). See BURNING.

2. KAUMA (καῦμα), heat (akin to No. 1), signifies the result of burning, or the heat produced, Rev. 7 : 16 ; 16 : 9 ;¶ cp. *kaumatizō*, to scorch, *kausis*, burning, *kautēriazomai*, to brand, sear.

3. THERMĒ (θέρμη) denotes warmth, heat, Acts 28 : 3 (Eng., thermal, etc.).¶

B. Verb.

KAUSOŌ (καυσόω) was used as a medical term, of a fever ; in the N.T., to burn with great heat (akin to A, No. 1), said of the future destruction of the natural elements, 2 Pet. 3 : 10, 12, " with fervent heat," Passive Voice, lit., ' being burned.'¶

For HEATHEN see GENTILES

HEAVEN, HEAVENLY (-IES)
A. Nouns.

1. OURANOS (οὐρανός), probably akin to *ornumi*, to lift, to heave, is used in the N.T. (*a*) of the aërial heavens, e.g., Matt. 6 : 26 ; 8 : 20 ; Acts 10 : 12 ; 11 : 6 (R.V., " heaven," in each place, A.V., " air ") ; Jas. 5 : 18 ; (*b*) the sidereal, e.g., Matt. 24 : 29, 35 ; Mark 13 : 25, 31 ; Heb. 11 : 12, R.V., " heaven," A.V., " sky ; " Rev. 6 : 14 ; 20 : 11 ; they, (*a*) and (*b*), were created by the Son of God, Heb. 1 : 10, as also by God the Father, Rev. 10 : 6 ; (*c*) the eternal dwelling place of God, Matt. 5 : 16 ; 12 : 50 ; Rev. 3 : 12 ; 11 : 13 ; 16 : 11 ; 20 : 9. From thence the Son of God descended to become Incarnate, John 3 : 13, 31 ; 6 : 38, 42. In His ascension Christ " passed through the heavens," Heb. 4 : 14, R.V. ; He " ascended far above all the heavens," Eph. 4 : 10, and was " made higher than the heavens," Heb. 7 : 26 ; He " sat down on the right hand of the throne of the Majesty in the heavens," Heb. 8 : 1 ; He is " on the right hand of God," having gone into Heaven, 1 Pet. 3 : 22. Since His Ascension it is the scene of His present life and activity, e.g., Rom. 8 : 34 ; Heb. 9 : 24. From thence the Holy Spirit descended at Pentecost, 1 Pet. 1 : 12. It is the abode of the angels, e.g., Matt. 18 : 10 ; 22 : 30 ; cp. Rev. 3 : 5. Thither Paul was " caught up," whether in the body or out of the body, he knew not, 2 Cor. 12 : 2. It is to be the eternal dwelling-place of the saints in resurrection glory, 2 Cor. 5 : 1. From thence Christ will descend to the air to receive His saints at the Rapture, 1 Thess. 4 : 16 ; Phil. 3 : 20, 21, and will subsequently come with His saints and with His

holy angels at His Second Advent, Matt. 24 : 30 ; 2 Thess. 1 : 7. In the present life heaven is the region of the spiritual citizenship of believers, Phil. 3 : 20. The present heavens, with the earth, are to pass away, 2 Pet. 3 : 10, " being on fire," ver. 12 (see ver. 7) ; Rev. 20 : 11, and new heavens and earth are to be created, 2 Pet. 3 : 13 ; Rev. 21 : 1, with Is. 65 : 17, e.g.

In Luke 15 : 18, 21, heaven is used, by metonymy, for God. See AIR.

Notes : (1) For the phrase in Luke 11 : 13, see Note on B, No. 2. (2) In Luke 11 : 2, the A.V., " as in heaven," translates a phrase found in some mss.

2. MESOURANĒMA (μεσουράνημα) denotes mid-heaven, or the midst of the heavens (*mesos*, middle, and No. 1), Rev. 8 : 13 ; 14 : 6 ; 19 : 17.¶

B. Adjectives.

1. OURANIOS (οὐράνιος), signifying of heaven, heavenly, corresponding to A, No. 1, is used (*a*) as an appellation of God the Father, Matt. 6 : 14, 26, 32, " your heavenly Father ; " 15 : 13, " My heavenly Father ; " (*b*) as descriptive of the holy angels, Luke 2 : 13 ; (*c*) of the vision seen by Paul, Acts 26 : 19.¶

2. EPOURANIOS (ἐπουράνιος), heavenly, what pertains to, or is in, heaven (*epi*, in the sense of ' pertaining to,' not here, ' above '), has meanings corresponding to some of the meanings of *ouranos*, A, No. 1. It is used (*a*) of God the Father, Matt. 18 : 35 ; (*b*) of the place where Christ " sitteth at the right hand of God " (i.e., in a position of Divine authority), Eph. 1 : 20; and of the present position of believers in relationship to Christ, 2 : 6; where they possess ' every spiritual blessing,' 1 : 3 ; (*c*) of Christ as " the Second Man," and all those who are related to Him spiritually, 1 Cor. 15 : 48 ; (*d*) of those whose sphere of activity or existence is above, or in contrast to that of earth, of " principalities and powers," Eph. 3 : 10 ; of " spiritual hosts of wickedness," 6 : 12, R.V., " in heavenly places," for A.V., " in high places ; " (*e*) of the Holy Spirit, Heb. 6 : 4 ; (*f*) of " heavenly things," as the subjects of the teaching of Christ, John 3 : 12, and as consisting of the spiritual and heavenly Sanctuary and " true tabernacle " and all that appertains thereto in relation to Christ and His sacrifice as antitypical of the earthly tabernacle and sacrifices under the Law, Heb. 8 : 5 ; 9 : 23 ; (*g*) of the " calling " of believers, Heb. 3 : 1 ; (*h*) of Heaven as the abode of the saints, " a better country " than that of earth, Heb. 11 : 16, and of the spiritual Jerusalem, 12 : 22 ; (*i*) of the Kingdom of Christ in its future manifestation, 2 Tim. 4 : 18 ; (*j*) of all beings and things, animate and inanimate, that are " above the earth," Phil. 2 : 10 ; (*k*) of the resurrection and glorified bodies of believers, 1 Cor. 15 : 49 ; (*l*) of the heavenly orbs, 1 Cor. 15 : 40 (" celestial," twice, and so rendered here only).¶

Note : In connection with (*a*), the word " heavenly," used of God the Father in Luke 11 : 13, represents the phrase *ex ouranou*, ' from heaven.'

C. Adverb.

OURANOTHEN (οὐρανόθεν), formed from A, No. 1, and denoting 'from heaven,' is used of (a) the aërial heaven, Acts 14 : 17 ; (b) heaven, as the uncreated sphere of God's abode, 26 : 13.¶

HEAVY, HEAVINESS
A. Nouns.

1. LUPĒ (λύπη), grief, sorrow, is rendered " heaviness " in the A.V. of Rom. 9 : 2 ; 2 Cor. 2 : 1 (R.V., " sorrow," in both places). See GRIEF, SORROW.

2. KATĒPHEIA (κατήφεια) probably denotes a downcast look, expressive of sorrow ; hence, dejection, heaviness ; it is used in Jas. 4 : 9.¶

B. Verbs.

1. ADĒMONEŌ (ἀδημονέω), to be troubled, much distressed, is used of the Lord's sorrow in Gethsemane, Matt. 26 : 37 ; Mark 14 : 33, A.V., " to be very heavy," R.V., " to be sore troubled ; " of Epaphroditus, because the saints at Philippi had received news of his sickness, Phil. 2 : 26, A.V., " was full of heaviness," R.V., " was sore troubled." See TROUBLE, B, No. 12.¶

2. LUPEŌ (λυπέω), to distress, grieve (akin to A, No. 1), is rendered " are in heaviness " in 1 Pet. 1 : 6, A.V. (R.V., " have been put to grief ") ; here, as frequently, it is in the Passive Voice. See GRIEF, SORROWFUL.

3. BAREŌ (βαρέω), always in the Passive Voice in the N.T., is rendered " were heavy " in Matt. 26 : 43 ; Mark 14 : 40 ; Luke 9 : 32. See BURDEN.

Note : For " heavy laden," Matt. 11 : 28, see LADE, No. 3.

C. Adjective.

BARUS (βαρύς), heavy (akin to B, No. 3), is so rendered in Matt. 23 : 4. See GRIEVOUS.

HEDGE

PHRAGMOS (φραγμός) denotes any sort of fence, hedge, palings or wall (akin to *phrassō*, to fence in, stop). It is used (a) in its literal sense, in Matt. 21 : 33, lit. ' (he put) a hedge (around) ; ' Mark 12 : 1 ; Luke 14 : 23 ; (b) metaphorically, of the " partition " which separated Gentile from Jew, which was broken down by Christ through the efficacy of His expiatory sacrifice, Eph. 2 : 14.¶

HEED (to give, to take)

1. BLEPŌ (βλέπω), to look, see, usually implying more especially an intent, earnest contemplation, is rendered " take heed " in Matt. 24 : 4 ; Mark 4 : 24 ; 13 : 5, 9, 23, 33 ; Luke 8 : 18 ; 21 : 8 ; 1 Cor. 3 : 10 ; 8 : 9 ; 10 : 12 ; Gal. 5 : 15 ; Col. 2 : 8 (A.V., " beware ") ; 4 : 17 ; Heb. 3 : 12. See BEHOLD, BEWARE, LIE, LOOK, PERCEIVE, REGARD, SEE.

2. HORAŌ (ὁράω), to see, usually expressing the sense of vision, is

rendered " take heed " in Matt. 16 : 6 ; 18 : 10, A.V. (R.V., " see ") ;
Mark 8 : 15 ; Luke 12 : 15 ; Acts 22 : 26 (A.V. only). See BEHOLD, SEE.

3. PROSECHŌ (προσέχω), lit., to hold to, signifies to turn to, turn
one's attention to ; hence, to give heed ; it is rendered " take heed " in
Matt. 6 : 1 ; Luke 17 : 3 ; 21 : 34 ; Acts 5 : 35 ; 20 : 28 ; 2 Pet. 1 : 19 ;
to give heed to, in Acts 8 : 6, 10 ; in ver. 11 (A.V., " had regard to ") ;
16 : 14 (A.V., " attended unto ") ; 1 Tim. 1 : 4 ; 4 : 1, 13 (A.V., " give
attendance to ") ; Tit. 1 : 14 ; Heb. 2 : 1, lit., ' to give heed more
earnestly.' See ATTEND, BEWARE, GIVE, REGARD.

4. EPECHŌ (ἐπέχω), lit., to hold upon, then, to direct towards, to
give attention to, is rendered " gave heed," in Acts 3 : 5 ; " take heed,"
in 1 Tim. 4 : 16. See HOLD (forth), MARK, STAY.

Notes : (1) In Luke 11 : 35, A.V., *skopeō*, to look, is translated " take
heed (that)," R.V., " look (whether)." (2) Nos. 2 and 3 are used together
in Matt. 16 : 6 ; Nos. 2 and 1, in that order, in Mark 8 : 15 ; but in Luke
12 : 15 the R.V. rightly follows No. 2 by " keep yourselves from "
(*phulassō*, to guard). (3) For the R.V. of Mark 5 : 36, " not heeding,"
see under HEAR, No. 7. (4) In Rom. 11 : 21 the A.V. adds " take heed,"
because of a variant reading which introduces the clause by a conjunctive
phrase signifying " lest."

HEEL

PTERNA (πτέρνα) is found in John 13 : 18, where the Lord quotes
from Ps. 41 : 9 ; the metaphor is that of tripping up an antagonist in
wrestling.¶ Cp. the verb in Gen. 27 : 36 ; Jer. 9 : 4 ; Hos. 12 : 3.

HEIFER

DAMALIS (δάμαλις), etymologically one of fit age to be tamed to the
yoke (*damaō*, to tame), occurs in Heb. 9 : 13, with reference to the " red
heifer " of Numb. 19.¶

HEIGHT

1. HUPSOS (ὕψος), a summit, top, is translated " height " in Eph.
3 : 18, where it may refer either to " the love of Christ " or to " the fulness
of God ; " the two are really inseparable, for they who are filled into the
fulness of God thereby enter appreciatively into the love of Christ, which
' surpasseth knowledge ; ' in Rev. 21 : 16, of the measurement of the
Heavenly Jerusalem. See ESTATE, HIGH.

2. HUPSŌMA (ὕψωμα), more concrete than No. 1, is used (*a*) of a
height, as a mountain or anything definitely termed a height, Rom. 8 : 39
(metaphorically) ; (*b*) of a high thing lifted up as a barrier or in antagonistic
exaltation, 2 Cor. 10 : 5. See HIGH.¶ Cp. *hupsoō*, to exalt.

HEIR
A. Noun.

1. KLĒRONOMOS (κληρονόμος) lit. denotes one who obtains a lot or

portion (*klēros*, a lot, *nemomai*, to possess), especially of an inheritance. The N.T. usage may be analysed as under : " (a) the person to whom property is to pass on the death of the owner, Matt. 21 : 38 ; Mark 12 : 7 ; Luke 20 : 14 ; Gal. 4 : 1 ; (b) one to whom something has been assigned by God, on possession of which, however, he has not yet entered, as Abraham, Rom. 4 : 13, 14 ; Heb. 6 : 17 ; Christ, Heb. 1 : 2 ; the poor saints, Jas. 2 : 5 ; (c) believers, inasmuch as they share in the new order of things to be ushered in at the return of Christ, Rom. 8 : 17 ; Gal. 3 : 29 ; 4 : 7 ; Tit. 3 : 7 ; (d) one who receives something other than by merit, as Noah, Heb. 11 : 7."*¶

In the Sept., Judg. 18 : 7 ; 2 Sam. 14 : 7 ; Jer. 8 : 10 ; Mic. 1 : 15.¶

2. SUNKLĒRONOMOS (συγκληρονόμος), a joint-heir, co-inheritor (*sun*, with, and No. 1), " is used of Isaac and Jacob as participants with Abraham in the promises of God, Heb. 11 : 9 ; of husband and wife who are also united in Christ, 1 Pet. 3 : 7 ; of Gentiles who believe, as participants in the gospel with Jews who believe, Eph. 3 : 6 ; and of all believers as prospective participants with Christ in His glory, as recompense for their participation in His sufferings, Rom. 8 : 17."*¶

B. Verb.

KLĒRONOMEŌ (κληρονομέω), to be an heir to, to inherit (see A, No. 1), is rendered " shall (not) inherit with " in Gal. 4 : 30, R.V., A.V., " shall (not) be heir with ; " in Heb. 1 : 14, R.V., " shall inherit," A.V., " shall be heirs of." See INHERIT. Cp. *klēroomai*, to be taken as an inheritance, *klēronomia*, an inheritance, *klēros*, a lot, an inheritance.

HELL

1. GEENNA (γέεννα) represents the Hebrew Gê-Hinnom (the valley of Tophet) and a corresponding Aramaic word ; it is found twelve times in the N.T.,eleven of which are in the Synoptists, in every instance as uttered by the Lord Himself. He who says to his brother, Thou fool (see under FOOL), will be in danger of " the hell of fire," Matt. 5 : 22 ; it is better to pluck out (a metaphorical description of irrevocable law) an eye that causes its possessor to stumble, than that his " whole body be cast into hell," ver. 29 ; similarly with the hand, ver. 30 ; in Matt. 18 : 8, 9, the admonitions are repeated, with an additional mention of the foot ; here, too, the warning concerns the person himself (for which obviously the " body " stands in chapt. 5) ; in ver. 8, " the eternal fire " is mentioned as the doom, the character of the region standing for the region itself, the two being combined in the phrase " the hell of fire," ver. 9. To the passage in Matt. 18, that in Mark 9 : 43-47, is parallel ; here to the word " hell " are applied the extended descriptions " the unquenchable fire " and " where their worm dieth not and the fire is not quenched."

---

* From Notes on Galatians, by Hogg and Vine, pp. 177, 178.
* ditto, p. 178.

That God, "after He hath killed, hath power to cast into hell," is assigned as a reason why He should be feared with the fear that keeps from evil doing, Luke 12 : 5 ; the parallel passage to this in Matt. 10 : 28 declares, not the casting in, but the doom which follows, namely, the destruction (not the loss of being, but of well-being) of " both soul and body."

In Matt. 23 the Lord denounces the Scribes and Pharisees, who in proselytizing a person "make him two-fold more a son of hell" than themselves (ver. 15), the phrase here being expressive of moral characteristics, and declares the impossibility of their escaping " the judgment of hell," ver. 33.   In Jas. 3 : 6 hell is described as the source of the evil done by misuse of the tongue ; here the word stands for the powers of darkness, whose characteristics and destiny are those of hell.¶

For terms descriptive of hell, see e.g., Matt. 13 : 42 ; 25 : 46 ; Phil. 3 : 19 ; 2 Thess. 1 : 9 ; Heb. 10 : 39 ; 2 Pet. 2 : 17 ; Jude 13 ; Rev. 2 : 11 ; 19 : 20 ; 20 : 6, 10, 14 ; 21 : 8.

Notes : (1) For the rendering " hell " as a translation of Hades, corresponding to Sheol, wrongly rendered " the grave " and " hell," see HADES.   (2) The verb *tartaroō*, translated " cast down to hell " in 2 Pet. 2 : 4, signifies to consign to Tartarus, which is neither Sheol nor Hades nor Hell, but the place where those angels whose special sin is referred to in that passage are confined " to be reserved unto judgment ; " the region is described as " pits of darkness," RV.¶

For HELM (Jas. 3 : 4) see RUDDER

HELMET

PERIKEPHALAIA (περικεφαλαία), from *peri*, around, and *kephalē*, a head, is used figuratively in Eph. 6 : 17, with reference to salvation, and 1 Thess. 5 : 8, where it is described as " the hope of salvation."   The head is not to be regarded here as standing for the seat of the intellect ; the word is not so used elsewhere in Scripture.   In Eph. 6 : 17 salvation is a present experience of the Lord's deliverance of believers as those who are engaged in spiritual conflict ; in 1 Thess. 5 : 8, the hope is that of the Lord's Return, which encourages the believer to resist the spirit of the age in which he lives.¶

HELP, HOLPEN
A. Nouns.

1. ANTILĒPSIS or ANTILĒMPSIS (ἀντίληψις) properly signifies a laying hold of, an exchange (*anti*, in exchange, or, in its local sense, in front, and *lambanō*, to take, lay hold of, so as to support) ; then, a help (akin to B, No. 1) ; it is mentioned in 1 Cor. 12 : 28, as one of the ministrations in the local church, by way of rendering assistance, perhaps especially of help ministered to the weak and needy.   So Theophylact defines the

injunction in 1 Thess. 5 : 14, "support the weak ; " cp. Acts 20 : 35 ; not official functionaries are in view in the term " helps," but rather the functioning of those who, like the household of Stephanas, devote themselves to minister to the saints. Hort defines the ministration as " anything that would be done for poor or weak or outcast brethren."¶

2. BOĒTHEIA (βοήθεια), from boē, a shout, and theō, to run, denotes help, succour, Heb. 4 : 16, lit., ' (grace) unto (timely) help ; ' in Acts 27 : 17, where the plural is used, the term is nautical, ' frapping.'¶

3. EPIKOURIA (ἐπικουρία) strictly denotes such aid as is rendered by an epikouros, an ally, an auxiliary ; Paul uses it in his testimony to Agrippa, " having therefore obtained the help that is from God," Acts 26 : 22, R.V.¶

B. Verbs.

1. ANTILAMBANŌ (ἀντιλαμβάνω), lit., to take instead of, or in turn (akin to A, No. 1), is used in the Middle Voice, and rendered " He hath holpen " in Luke 1 : 54 ; " to help," R.V., " to support," A.V., in Acts 20 : 35 ; its other meaning, to partake of, is used of partaking of things, 1 Tim. 6 : 2, " that partake of," for A.V., " partakers of." See PARTAKE, SUPPORT.¶

2. SULLAMBANŌ (συλλαμβάνω), to assist, take part with (sun, with, and lambanō), is used, in the Middle Voice, of rendering help in what others are doing, Luke 5 : 7, of bringing in a catch of fish ; in Phil. 4 : 3, in an appeal to Synzygus (" yokefellow ") to help Euōdia and Syntychē (ver. 2). See CATCH, CONCEIVE.

3. SUNANTILAMBANŌ (συναντιλαμβάνω) signifies to take hold with at the side for assistance (sun, with, and No. 1) ; hence, to take a share in, help in bearing, to help in general. It is used, in the Middle Voice, in Martha's request to the Lord to bid her sister help her, Luke 10 : 40 ; and of the ministry of the Holy Spirit in helping our infirmities, Rom. 8 : 26.¶ In the Sept., Ex. 18 : 22 ; Num. 11 : 17 ; Ps. 89 : 21.

4. BOĒTHEŌ (βοηθέω), to come to the aid of anyone, to succour (akin to A, No. 2), is used in Matt. 15 : 25 ; Mark 9 : 22, 24 ; Acts 16 : 9 ; 21 : 28 ; 2 Cor. 6 : 2, " did I succour ; " Heb. 2 : 18, " to succour ; " Rev. 12 : 16.¶

5. SUMBALLŌ (συμβάλλω), lit., to throw together (sun, with, ballō, to throw), is used in the Middle Voice in Acts 18 : 27, of helping or benefiting believers by discussion or ministry of the Word of God. See CONFER, ENCOUNTER, MAKE (war), MEET, PONDER.

6. SUNUPOURGEŌ (συνυπουργέω) denotes to help together, join in helping, to serve with anyone as an underworker (sun, with, hupourgeō, to serve ; hupo, under, ergon, work) ; it is used in 2 Cor. 1 : 11.¶

7. SUNERGEŌ (συνεργέω), to help in work, to co-operate, be a co-worker, is rendered " that helpeth with " in 1 Cor. 16 : 16. See WORK.

Note : Paristēmi, to place beside (para, by, histēmi, to cause to stand), to stand by, be at hand, is used of standing up for help, in Rom. 16 : 2, "that ye assist," and 2 Tim. 4 : 17, "stood with." See BRING, COME, COMMEND, GIVE, PRESENT, PROVE, PROVIDE, SHEW, STAND, YIELD.

HELPER, FELLOW-HELPER

1. BOËTHOS (βοηθός), an adjective, akin to A, No. 2, and B, No. 4, under HELP, signifying helping, is used as a noun in Heb. 13 : 6, of God as the Helper of His saints.¶

2. SUNERGOS (συνεργός), an adjective, akin to B, No. 7, under HELP, a fellow-worker, is translated "helper" in the A.V. of Rom. 16 : 3, 9, R.V., "fellow-worker;" in 2 Cor. 1 : 24, A.V. and R.V., "helpers;" in 2 Cor. 8 : 23, A.V., "fellow-helper," R.V., "fellow-worker;" so the plural in 3 John 8: See COMPANION, LABOURER, etc.

For HEM see BORDER

HEN

ORNIS (ὄρνις), a bird, is used, in the N.T., only of a hen, Matt. 23 : 37 ; Luke 13 : 34.¶

HENCE

1. ENTHEN (ἔνθεν) is found in the best mss. in Matt. 17 : 20 ; Luke 16 : 26.¶

2. ENTEUTHEN (ἐντεῦθεν), akin to No. 1, is used (a) of place, "hence," or "from hence," Luke 4 : 9 ; 13 : 31 ; John 2 : 16 ; 7 : 3 ; 14 : 31 ; 18 : 36 ; in John 19 : 18, "on either side (one)," lit., 'hence and hence;' in Rev. 22 : 2, it is contrasted with ekeithen, thence, R.V., "on this side . . . on that" (A.V., "on either side"), lit. 'hence . . . . thence;' (b) causal, Jas. 4 : 1, "(come they not) hence," i.e., 'owing to.'¶

Notes : (1) For *makran*, "far hence," in Acts 22 : 21, see FAR. (2) In Acts 1 : 5, the phrase "not many days hence" is, lit., 'not after (*meta*) many days.'

HENCEFORTH (from, and negatives), HENCEFORWARD.

Notes : (1) Positively, "henceforth" stands for the following : (a) *ap' arti* (i.e., *apo arti*), lit., 'from now,' e.g., Matt. 26 : 64 ; Luke 22 : 69; John 13 : 19, R.V., and A.V. marg., "from henceforth"; Rev. 14 : 13 (where *aparti* is found as one word in the best mss.) ; (b) *to loipon*, lit., (for) the remaining (time), Heb. 10 : 13 ; *tou loipou*, Gal. 6 : 17 ; (c) *apo tou nun*, lit., 'from the now,' e.g., Luke 1 : 48 ; 5 : 10 ; 12 : 52 ; Acts 18 : 6 ; 2 Cor. 5 : 16 (1st part) ; (2) negatively, "henceforth . . . not" (or "no more") translates one or other of the negative adverbs *ouketi* and *mēketi*, no longer, e.g., Acts 4 : 17, A.V., and R.V., "henceforth (to no man) ;" in the following the R.V. has "no longer" for the A.V., "henceforth" (with a negative), John 15 : 15 ; Rom. 6 : 6 ; 2 Cor. 5 : 15 ;

Eph. 4 : 17 ; in 2 Cor. 5 : 16 (last part), R.V., " no more ; " in Matt. 21 : 19 and Mark 11 : 14, " no (fruit . . .) henceforward ; " A.V. in the latter, " hereafter." See HEREAFTER.

For HER and HERSELF see the forms under HE

HERB

1. LACHANON (λάχανον) denotes a garden herb, a vegetable (from *lachainō*, to dig), in contrast to wild plants, Matt. 13 : 32 ; Mark 4 : 32 ; Luke 11 : 42 ; Rom. 14 : 2.¶

2. BOTANĒ (βοτάνη) denotes grass, fodder, herbs (from *boskō*, to feed : Eng., botany), Heb. 6 : 7.¶

HERD

AGELĒ (ἀγέλη), from *agō*, to lead, is used, in the N.T., only of swine, Matt. 8 : 30, 31, 32 ; Mark 5 : 11, 13 ; Luke 8 : 32, 33.¶

HERE

1. HŌDE (ὧδε), an adverb signifying (*a*) here (of place), e.g., Matt. 12 : 6 ; Mark 9 : 1 ; used with the neuter plural of the article, Col. 4 : 9, " (all) things (that are done) here," lit., ' (all) the (things) here ; ' in Matt. 24 : 23, *hōde* is used in both parts, hence the R.V., " Lo, here (is the Christ, or) Here ; " in Mark 13 : 21 *hōde* is followed by *ekei*, " there." The word is used metaphorically in the sense of in this circumstance, or connection, in 1 Cor. 4 : 2 ; Rev. 13 : 10, 18 ; 14 : 12 ; 17 : 9. See HITHER.

2. ENTHADE (ἐνθάδε) has the same meanings as No. 1 ; " here " in Luke 24 : 41 ; Acts 16 : 28 ; 25 : 24. See HITHER (John 4 : 15, 16 ; Acts 25 : 17).¶

3. AUTOU (αὐτοῦ), the genitive case of *autos*, self, signifies ' just here ' in Matt. 26 : 36. See THERE, No. 5.

HERE (to be, be present)

PAREIMI (πάρειμι), to be by or beside or here (*para*, by, and *eimi*, to be), is rendered " to have been here " in Acts 24 : 19. See COME, PRESENT.

Note : For *sumpareimi*, to be here present, see PRESENT.

HEREAFTER

Notes : (1) This adverb translates the phrase *meta tauta*, lit., ' after these things,' John 13 : 7 ; Rev. 1 : 19, and frequently in the Apocalypse, see 4 : 1 (twice) ; 7 : 9 ; 9 : 12 ; 15 : 5 ; 18 : 1 ; 19 : 1 ; 20 : 3. (2) For Matt. 26 : 64 and Luke 22 : 69 (A.V., " hereafter ") see HENCEFORTH ; for Mark 11 : 14 see HENCEFORWARD. (3) In John 14 : 30, *ouk eti* is rendered " no more " in the R.V. (A.V., " Hereafter . . . not "). (4) In 1 Tim. 1 : 16, " hereafter " translates the verb *mellō*, to be about to.

HEREBY

Notes : (1) This translates the phrase *en toutǭ*, lit., ' in this,' 1 Cor. 4 : 4 ; 1 John 2 : 3, 5 ; 3 : 16, 19, 24 ; 4 : 2, 13 ; 5 : 2 (R.V., " hereby," A.V., " by this "). (2) In 1 John 4 : 6, A.V., *ek toutou*, lit., ' out of this,' i.e., in consequence of this, is rendered " hereby " (R.V., " by this ").¶

HEREIN

Note : This translates the phrase *en toutǭ*, ' in this,' in John 4 : 37 ; 9 : 30 ; 15 : 8 ; Acts 24 : 16 ; 2 Cor. 8 : 10 ; 1 John 4 : 9 (A.V., " in this "), 10, 17.¶

HEREOF

Notes : (1) This translates the word *hautē*, this, the feminine of *houtos*, this, in Matt. 9 : 26, lit., ' this (fame),' A.V., and R.V. marg. (2) In Heb. 5 : 3, A.V., *dia tautēn*, lit., ' by reason of (*dia*) this ' (i.e., this infirmity), is rendered " hereof ; " the best texts have *autēn*, R.V., " thereof."

HERESY

HAIRESIS (*αἵρεσις*) denotes (*a*) a choosing, choice (from *haireomai*, to choose) ; then, that which is chosen, and hence, an opinion, especially a self-willed opinion, which is substituted for submission to the power of truth, and leads to division and the formation of sects, Gal. 5 : 20 (marg., " parties ") ; such erroneous opinions are frequently the outcome of personal preference or the prospect of advantage ; see 2 Pet. 2 : 1, where " destructive " (R.V.) signifies leading to ruin ; some assign even this to (*b*) ; in the papyri the prevalent meaning is " choice " (Moulton and Milligan, Vocab.) ; (*b*) a sect ; this secondary meaning, resulting from (*a*), is the dominating significance in the N.T., Acts 5 : 17 ; 15 : 5 ; 24 : 5, 14 ; 26 : 5 ; 28 : 22 ; " heresies " in 1 Cor. 11 : 19 (see marg.). See SECT.¶

HERETICAL

HAIRETIKOS (*αἱρετικός*), akin to the above, primarily denotes capable of choosing (*haireomai*) ; hence, causing division by a party spirit, factious, Tit. 3 : 10, R.V., " heretical ".¶

For HERETOFORE see SIN, C, No. 2

HEREUNTO

Note : This translates the phrase *eis touto*, lit., ' unto this,' in 1 Pet. 2 : 21.

For *HEREWITH* see TRADE, A, No. 2

HERITAGE

KLĒROŌ (*κληρόω*), primarily, to cast lots or to choose by lot, then, to assign a portion, is used in the Passive Voice in Eph. 1 : 11, " we were made a heritage," R.V. (A.V., " we have obtained an inheritance "). The R.V. is in agreement with such O.T. passages as Deut. 4 : 20, " a people of inheritance ; " 9 : 29 ; 32 : 9 ; Psa. 16 : 6. The meaning ' were chosen by lot,' as in the Vulgate, and in 1 Sam. 14 : 41, indicating the freedom of election without human will (so Chrysostom and Augustine), is not suited to this passage.¶

HEW, HEW DOWN, HEWN
A. Verbs.

1. EKKOPTŌ (ἐκκόπτω), to cut out or down (*ek*, out of, *koptō*, to cut), is rendered to hew down, of trees, Matt. 3 : 10 ; 7 : 19 (a similar testimony by John the Baptist and Christ) ; Luke 3 : 9. See CUT, HINDER.

2. LATOMEŌ (λατομέω) signifies to hew out stones (from *latomos*, a stone-cutter ; *las*, a stone, *temnō*, to cut), and is used of the sepulchre which Joseph of Arimathæa had hewn out of a rock for himself, where the body of the Lord was buried, Matt. 27 : 60 ; Mark 15 : 46.¶

B. Adjective.

LAXEUTOS (λαξευτός) denotes hewn in stone (*las*, a stone, *xeō*, to scrape ; cp. A, No. 2), is used of Christ's tomb, in Luke 23 : 53.¶

HIDE, HID, HIDDEN
A. Verbs.

1. KRUPTŌ (κρύπτω), to cover, conceal, keep secret (Eng., crypt, cryptic, etc.), is used (*a*) in its physical significance, e.g., Matt. 5 : 14 ; 13 : 44 ; 25 : 18 (some mss. have No. 2) ; (*b*) metaphorically, e.g., Matt. 11 : 25 (some mss. have No. 2 here) ; 13 : 35, R.V., " (things) hidden ; " A.V., " (things) which have been kept secret ; " Luke 18 : 34 ; 19 : 42 ; John 19 : 38, " secretly." See SECRET.

2. APOKRUPTŌ (ἀποκρύπτω), to conceal from, to keep secret (*apo*, from, and No. 1), is used metaphorically, in Luke 10 : 21, of truths hidden from the wise and prudent and revealed to babes ; 1 Cor. 2 : 7, of God's wisdom ; Eph. 3 : 9, of the mystery of the unsearchable riches of Christ, revealed through the gospel ; Col. 1 : 26, of the mystery associated with the preceding.¶

3. ENKRUPTŌ (ἐγκρύπτω), to hide in anything (*en*, in, and No. 1), is used in Matt. 13 : 33, of leaven hidden in meal.¶

4. PERIKRUPTŌ (περικρύπτω) signifies to hide by placing something around, to conceal entirely, to keep hidden (*peri*, around, used intensively, and No. 1), Luke 1 : 24.¶

5. KALUPTŌ (καλύπτω) signifies to cover, conceal, so that no trace of it can be seen (hence somewhat distinct from No. 1) ; it is not translated to hide in the R.V. ; in 2 Cor. 4 : 3 it is rendered " veiled," suitably continuing the subject of 3 : 13-18 ; in Jas. 5 : 20, " shall hide," A.V. (R.V., " shall cover "). See COVER.

6. PARAKALUPTŌ (παρακαλύπτω), lit., to cover with a veil, A.V., " hid," in Luke 9 : 45, ' it was veiled from them ; ' see CONCEAL.¶

7. LANTHANŌ (λανθάνω), to escape notice, to be hidden from, is rendered " (could not) be hid " in Mark 7 : 24, of Christ ; " was (not) hid," Luke 8 : 47, of the woman with the issue of blood ; " is hidden," Acts 26 : 26, of the facts concerning Christ ; the sentence might be rendered ' none of these things has escaped the king's notice.' See FORGET, UNAWARES.

B. Adjectives.

1. KRUPTOS (κρυπτός), akin to A, No. 1, hidden, secret, is translated " hid " in Matt. 10 : 26 ; Mark 4 : 22 ; Luke 8 : 17, R.V., for A.V., " secret ; " 12 : 2 (last part) ; in 1 Cor. 4 : 5, " hidden (things of darkness) ; " 2 Cor. 4 : 2, " hidden (things of shame) ; " 1 Pet. 3 : 4, " hidden (man of the heart)." See INWARDLY, SECRET.

2. APOKRUPHOS (ἀπόκρυφος), hidden away from (corresponding to A, No. 2 ; cp. Eng., apocryphal), is translated, " made (A.V., kept) secret," in Mark 4 : 22 ; in Luke 8 : 17, R.V., " secret," for A.V., " hid ; " in Col. 2 : 3, R.V., " hidden," A.V., " hid." See SECRET.¶

HIGH (from on, most), HIGHLY
A. Adjectives.

1. HUPSĒLOS (ὑψηλός), high, lofty, is used (a) naturally, of mountains, Matt. 4 : 8 ; 17 : 1 ; Mark 9 : 2 ; Rev. 21 : 10 ; of a wall, Rev. 21 : 12 ; (b) figuratively, of the arm of God, Acts 13 : 17 ; of heaven, " on high," plural, lit., ' in high (places),' Heb. 1 : 3 ; (c) metaphorically, Luke 16 : 15, R.V., " exalted " (A.V., " highly esteemed ") ; Rom. 11 : 20, in the best texts, " high-minded " [lit., ' mind (not) high things '] ; 12 : 16.¶

2. HUPSISTOS (ὕψιστος), most high, is a superlative degree, the positive not being in use ; it is used of God in Luke 1 : 32, 35, 76 ; 6 : 35, in each of which the R.V. has " the most High," for A.V., " the highest ; " A.V. and R.V. in Mark 5 : 7 ; Luke 8 : 28 ; Acts 7 : 48 ; 16 : 17 ; Heb. 7 : 1. See HIGHEST (below).

3. MEGAS (μέγας), great, is translated " high " in John 19 : 31, of the Sabbath Day at the Passover season ; here the meaning is virtually equivalent to ' holy.' See GREAT.

Note : In Heb. 10 : 21, the R.V. rightly has " a great (priest)," A.V., " high." For " high places," Eph. 6 : 12, A.V., see HEAVENLY, B, No. 2.

B. Nouns.

1. HUPSOS (ὕψος), height, is used with *ex* (ek) from, in the phrase " on high," Luke 1 : 78 ; 24 : 49 ; with *eis*, in or into, Eph. 4 : 8. See ESTATE, HEIGHT, NO. 1.

2. HUPSŌMA (ὕψωμα), high thing, 2 Cor. 10 : 5 ; in Rom. 8 : 39, " height." See HEIGHT, No. 2.¶

C. Adverb.

ANŌ (ἄνω), above, upward, is used in Phil. 3 : 14, of the "high calling of God in Christ Jesus," the prize of which is set before believers as their goal, lit., ' calling upward ' (R.V., marg.), a preferable rendering to ' heavenly calling.' See ABOVE.

HIGHER

A. Adverb.

1. ANŌTERON (ἀνώτερον), the neuter of anōteros, higher, the comparative of anō (see C, under HIGH), is used as an adverb of place in Luke 14 : 10 ; for the meaning "above," in Heb. 10 : 8, see ABOVE.¶

B. Verb.

HUPERECHŌ (ὑπερέχω), lit., to hold over anything, as being superior, is used metaphorically in Rom. 13 : 1, of rulers, as the "higher" powers ; cp. 1 Pet. 2 : 13, "supreme." See BETTER, EXCELLENCY, PASS, SUPREME.

HIGHEST

HUPSISTOS (ὕψιστος) is used in the plural in the phrase "in the highest," i.e., in the highest regions, the abode of God, Matt. 21 : 9 ; Mark 11 : 10 ; Luke omits the article, Luke 2 : 14 ; 19 : 38 ; for its use as a title of God, see HIGH, A, No. 2.

For HIGHLY see DISPLEASE, EXALT, EXCEEDING, FAVOUR, THINK

HIGH-MINDED

1. TUPHOŌ (τυφόω) properly means to wrap in smoke (from tuphos, smoke ; metaphorically, for conceit) ; it is used in the Passive Voice, metaphorically in 1 Tim. 3 : 6, " puffed up," R.V. (A.V., " lifted up with pride ") ; so 6 : 4, A.V., " proud," and 2 Tim. 3 : 4, A.V., " high-minded." See PROUD, PUFF (up).¶ Cp. tuphomai, to smoke, Matt. 12 : 20,¶ and tuphōnikos, tempestuous (with anemos, wind, understood), Acts 27 : 14.¶

2. HUPSĒLOPHRONEŌ (ὑψηλοφρονέω), to be highminded, is used in 1 Tim. 6 : 17.¶

HIGHWAY, HIGHWAYSIDE

HODOS (ὁδός), a way, path, road, is rendered "highways" in Matt. 22 : 10 ; Luke 14 : 23 ; in Mark 10 : 46, R.V., " way side," A.V., " highway side ; " in Matt. 22 : 9, the word is used with diexodoi (ways out through), and the phrase is rightly rendered in the R.V., " the partings of the highways " (i.e., the crossroads), A.V., " the highways." See WAY.

HILL

1. OROS (ὄρος), a hill or mountain, is translated "hill" in Matt. 5 : 14 ; Luke 4 : 29 ; "mountain" in Luke 9 : 37, R.V., A.V., "hill" (of the mount of transfiguration) as in ver. 28. See MOUNTAIN.

2. OREINOS (ὀρεινός), an adjective meaning mountainous, hilly, is used in the feminine, oreinē, as a noun, and rendered "hill country" in Luke 1 : 39, 65. See COUNTRY.¶

3. BOUNOS (βουνός), a mound, heap, height, is translated "hill" in Luke 3 : 5 ; "hills" in 23 : 30.¶

Note : In Acts 17 : 22, A.V., *pagos* is translated "hill." "The Areopagus," R.V., stands for the Council (not hill) held near by.

For HIM and HIMSELF see HE

HINDER, HINDRANCE
A. Verbs.

1. ENKOPTŌ (ἐγκόπτω), lit., to cut into (*en*, in, *koptō*, to cut), was used of impeding persons by breaking up the road, or by placing an obstacle sharply in the path ; hence, metaphorically, of detaining a person unnecessarily, Acts 24 : 4 ; of hindrances in the way of reaching others, Rom. 15 : 22 ; or returning to them, 1 Thess. 2 : 18 ; of hindering progress in the Christian life, Gal. 5 : 7 (*anakoptō* in some mss.), where the significance virtually is 'who broke up the road along which you were travelling so well ? ' ; of hindrances to the prayers of husband and wife, through low standards of marital conduct, 1 Pet. 3 : 7 (*ekkoptō*, to cut out, repulse, in some mss.).¶

2. KŌLUŌ (κωλύω), to hinder, forbid, restrain, is translated to hinder in Luke 11 : 52 ; Acts 8 : 36 ; Rom. 1 : 13, R.V. (A.V., "was let") ; Heb. 7 : 23, R.V. (A.V., "were not suffered"). See FORBID.

3. DIAKŌLUŌ (διακωλύω), a strengthened form of No. 2, to hinder thoroughly, is used in Matt. 3 : 14, of John the Baptist's endeavour to hinder Christ from being baptized, A.V., "forbad," R.V., "would have hindered," lit., 'was hindering.'¶

B. Noun.

ENKOPĒ (ἐγκοπή), a hindrance, lit., a cutting in, akin to A, No. 1, with corresponding significance, is used in 1 Cor. 9 : 12, with *didōmi*, to give, R.V., "(that) we may cause (no) hindrance," A.V., "(lest) we should hinder."¶

For HINDER (part) see STERN

HIRE, HIRED
A. Noun.

MISTHOS (μισθός) denotes (*a*) wages, hire, Matt. 20 : 8 ; Luke 10 : 7 ; Jas. 5 : 4 ; in 1 Tim. 5 : 18 ; 2 Pet. 2 : 13 ; Jude 11, R.V., "hire" (A.V.,

" reward ") ; in 2 Pet. 2 : 15, R.V., " hire " (A.V., " wages "). See
REWARD.

B. Verb.

MISTHOŌ (μισθόω), to let out for hire, is used in the Middle Voice,
signifying to hire, to engage the services of anyone by contract, Matt.
20 : 1, 7.¶

Note : In ver. 9 there is no word for " hired " in the original.

HIRED HOUSE

MISTHŌMA (μίσθωμα), akin to A and B, above, primarily denotes a
hire, as in the Sept. of Deut. 23 : 18 ; Prov. 19 : 13 ; Ezek. 16 : 31, 34, 41,
etc. ; in the N.T., it is used of a hired dwelling, Acts 28 : 30.¶

HIRED SERVANT, HIRELING

1. MISTHŌTOS (μισθωτός), an adjective denoting hired, is used as a
noun, signifying one who is hired, " hired servants," Mark 1 : 20 ; " hireling," John 10 : 12, 13 ; here, it expresses, not only one who has no
real interest in his duty (that may or may not be present in its use in
Mark 1 : 20, and in *misthios*, No. 2), but one who is unfaithful in the
discharge of it ; that sense attaches always to the word rendered " hireling."¶

2. MISTHIOS (μίσθιος), an adjective, akin to No. 1, and similarly
signifying a hired servant, is used in Luke 15 : 17, 19 (in some texts,
ver. 21).¶

HIS, HIS OWN

Note : These translate (*a*) forms of pronouns under HE, No. 1 (a frequent use : in 1 Pet. 2 : 24, " His own self ") ; the form *autou*, " his,"
becomes emphatic when placed between the article and the noun, e.g.,
1 Thess. 2 : 19 ; Tit. 3 : 5 ; Heb. 2 : 4 ; also under HE, No. 3 (in which
" his " is emphasized), e.g., John 5 : 47 ; 9 : 28 ; 1 Cor. 10 : 28 ; 2 Cor.
8 : 9 ; 2 Tim. 2 : 26 ; Tit. 3 : 7 ; 2 Pet. 1 : 16 ; (*b*) *heautou*, of himself,
his own ; the R.V. rightly puts " his own," for the A.V., " his," in Luke
11 : 21 ; 14 : 26 ; Rom. 4 : 19 ; 5 : 8, " His own (love) ; " 1 Cor. 7 : 37 ;
Gal. 6 : 8 ; Eph. 5 : 28, 33 ; 1 Thess. 2 : 11, 12 ; 4 : 4 ; in Rev. 10 : 7
the change has not been made ; it should read ' his own servants ; '
(*c*) *idios*, one's own, " his own," in the R.V., in Matt. 22 : 5 ; John 5 : 18 ;
2 Pet. 2 : 16 ; in Matt. 25 : 15, it is rendered " his several ; " in John
19 : 27, " his own home," lit., ' his own things ; ' in 1 Tim. 6 : 15, R.V.,
" its own (times)," referring to the future appearing of Christ ; in Heb.
4 : 10 (end of verse), both A.V. and R.V. have " his," where it should
be ' his own ; ' so in Acts 24 : 23, for A.V. and R.V., " his ; " in 1 Cor.
7 : 7, R.V., " his own," A.V., " his proper ; " (*d*) in Acts 17 : 28, the
genitive case of the definite article, " His (offspring)," lit., ' of the ' (i.e.,
the one referred to, namely, God).

HITHER

1. HŌDE (ὧδε), primarily an adverb of manner, then, of place, (a) of motion or direction towards a place, e.g., Matt. 8 : 29 ; Mark 11 : 3 ; Luke 9 : 41 ; John 6 : 25 ; (b) of position ; see HERE, PLACE.

2. ENTHADE (ἐνθάδε) has the same meaning as No. 1 ; " hither," John 4 : 15, 16 ; Acts 17 : 6 ; 25 : 17. See HERE.

Note : For *deuro*, " come hither," see COME, and HITHERTO, *Note* (2).

HITHERTO

Notes : (1) The phrase *heōs arti*, until now, is rendered " hitherto " in John 16 : 24, A.V., and R.V. ; in 5 : 17, R.V., " even until now," which more definitely expresses the meaning than the A.V., " hitherto ; " the rest of the Father and the Son having been broken by man's sin, they were engaged in the accomplishment of their counsels of grace with a view to redemption. (2) The phrase *achri tou deuro*, lit., ' until the hither,' or ' the present,' is used of time in Rom. 1 : 13, " hitherto." (3) In 1 Cor. 3 : 2, A.V., *oupō*, not yet, is translated " hitherto . . . not," R.V., " not yet."

HOISE UP, HOIST UP

1. AIRŌ (αἴρω), to raise, is used of hoisting up a skiff, or little boat, before undergirding the ship, Acts 27 : 17, R.V., " had hoisted up," for A.V., " had taken up." See AWAY, TAKE.

2. EPAIRŌ (ἐπαίρω), to raise up (*epi*, up, and No. 1), is used of hoisting up the foresail of a vessel, Acts 27 : 40, R.V., " hoisting up." See EXALT, LIFT.

HOLD (Noun)

1. TĒRĒSIS (τήρησις), translated " hold " in Acts 4 : 3, A.V., " prison " in 5 : 18 (R.V., " ward "), signifies (a) a watching, guarding ; hence, imprisonment, ward (from *tēreō*, to watch, keep) ; the R.V., has " ward " in both places ; (b) a keeping, as of commandments, 1 Cor. 7 : 19. See KEEPING, WARD.¶

2. PHULAKĒ (φυλακή), a guarding or guard (akin to *phulassō*, to guard or watch), also denotes a prison, a hold, Rev. 18 : 2 (twice), R.V., " hold " in both places, A.V., " cage," in the second (R.V., marg., " prison," in both). See CAGE, IMPRISONMENT, PRISON.

HOLD (down, fast, forth, on, to, up), HELD, HOLDEN, (take) HOLD

1. ECHŌ (ἔχω), to have or hold, is used of mental conception, to consider, account, e.g., Matt. 21 : 26 ; of stedfast adherence to faith, or the faith, e.g., 1 Tim. 1 : 19 ; 3 : 9 ; 2 Tim. 1 : 13. See HAVE.

2. KATECHŌ (κατέχω), to hold firmly, hold fast (*kata*, down, and No. 1), is rendered " hold fast " in 1 Cor. 11 : 2, R.V. (A.V., " keep ") ; 1 Thess. 5 : 21 ; Heb. 3 : 6, 14 (R.V.) ; 10 : 23 ; " hold down," Rom.

1 : 18, R.V., of unrighteous men who restrain the spread of truth by their unrighteousness, or, as R.V. marg., " who hold the truth in (or with) unrighteousness," contradicting their profession by their conduct (cp. 2 : 15, R.V.) ; in Rom. 7 : 6, R.V., " holden," A.V., " held," of the Law as that which had held in bondage those who through faith in Christ were made dead to it as a means of life. See KEEP, MAKE (toward), POSSESS, RESTRAIN, RETAIN, SEIZE, STAY, TAKE.

3. ANTECHŌ (ἀντέχω), anti, against, or to, and No. 1, signifies in the Middle Voice, (a) to hold firmly to, cleave to, of holding or cleaving to a person, Matt. 6 : 24 ; Luke 16 : 13 ; of holding to the faithful word, Tit. 1 : 9, R.V., A.V., " holding fast ; " (b) to support, 1 Thess. 5 : 14 (the weak). See SUPPORT.¶

4. SUNECHŌ (συνέχω), sun, with, intensive, and No. 1, is used of holding a prisoner, in Luke 22 : 63. See CONSTRAIN, KEEP, PRESS, STOP, STRAIT, STRAITENED, TAKE.

5. EPECHŌ (ἐπέχω) is used in Phil. 2 : 16, of holding forth the word of life (epi, forth, and No. 1). See (give) HEED, (take) HEED, MARK, STAY.

6. KRATEŌ (κρατέω), to be strong, mighty, to prevail, (1) is most frequently rendered to lay or take hold on (a) literally, e.g., Matt. 12 : 11 ; 14 : 3 ; 18 : 28 and 21 : 46, R.V. (A.V., " laid hands on ") ; 22 : 6, R.V. (A.V., " took ") ; 26 : 55, A.V. (R.V., " took ") ; 28 : 9, R.V., " took hold of " (A.V., " held by ") ; Mark 3 : 21 ; 6 : 17 ; 12 : 12 ; 14 : 51 ; Acts 24 : 6, R.V. (A.V., " took ") ; Rev. 20 : 2 ; (b) metaphorically, of laying hold of the hope of the Lord's return, Heb. 6 : 18 ; (2) also signifies to hold or hold fast, i.e., firmly, (a), literally, Matt. 26 : 48, A.V. (R.V., " take ") ; Acts 3 : 11 ; Rev. 2 : 1 ; (b) metaphorically, of holding fast a tradition or teaching, in an evil sense, Mark 7 : 3, 4, 8 ; Rev. 2 : 14, 15 ; in a good sense, 2 Thess. 2 : 15 ; Rev. 2 : 25 ; 3 : 11 ; of holding Christ, i.e., practically apprehending Him, as the Head of His Church, Col. 2 : 19 ; a confession, Heb. 4 : 14 ; the Name of Christ, i.e., abiding by all that His Name implies, Rev. 2 : 13 ; of restraint, Luke 24 : 16, " (their eyes) were holden ; " of the winds, Rev. 7 : 1 ; of the impossibility of Christ's being holden of death, Acts 2 : 24. See KEEP, RETAIN (of sins), TAKE.

7. EPILAMBANŌ (ἐπιλαμβάνω), to lay hold of, to take hold of (epi, upon, lambanō, to take), with a special purpose, always in the Middle Voice, is so translated in Luke 20 : 20, 26, of taking hold of Christ's words ; in 23 : 26 and Acts 21 : 33, R.V., of laying hold of persons ; in 1 Tim. 6 : 12, 19, of laying hold on eternal life, i.e., practically appropriating all the benefits, privileges and responsibilities involved in the possession of it ; in Heb. 2 : 16, R.V. " He taketh hold " (A.V., " took on "), perhaps to be viewed in connection with " deliver " (v. 15) and " succour " (v. 18). See APPREHEND, CATCH, TAKE.

8. TĒREŌ (τηρέω), akin to A, No. 1, under HOLD (Noun), to watch

over, keep, give heed to, observe, is rendered " hold fast " in Rev. 3 : 3,
A.V. (R.V., " keep "). See KEEP, OBSERVE, RESERVE, WATCH.

9. EIMI (εἰμί), to be, is used in the imperfect tense, with the preposition, *sun*, with, in the idiomatic phrase " held with," in Acts 14 : 4, lit.,
' were with.'

Notes : (1) In Rom. 14 : 4, *histēmi*, to cause to stand, in the Passive
Voice, to be made to stand, is used in both forms, the latter in the first
part, R.V., " he shall be made to stand " (A.V., " he shall be holden
up "), the Active Voice in the second part, A.V., and R.V., " to make
stand." (2) In Matt. 12 : 14, R.V., *lambanō*, to take, is translated "took
(counsel)," A.V., " held (a council)." (3) In Mark 15 : 1, some mss. have
the verb *poieō*, to make, rendered " held (a consultation) ; " the most
authentic have *hetoimazō*, to prepare, also translated " held."

HOLE

1. PHŌLEOS (φωλεός), a lair, burrow, den or hole, is used of foxes
in Matt. 8 : 20 and Luke 9 : 58.¶

2. OPĒ (ὀπή) is translated " holes " in Heb. 11 : 38, R.V., A.V.
" caves." See CAVE, OPENING.

HOLINESS, HOLY, HOLILY
A. Nouns.

1. HAGIASMOS (ἁγιασμός), translated "holiness" in the A.V.
of Rom. 6 : 19, 22 ; 1 Thess. 4 : 7 ; 1 Tim. 2 : 15 ; Heb. 12 : 14, is always
rendered " sanctification " in the R.V. It signifies (*a*) separation to God,
1 Cor. 1 : 30 ; 2 Thess. 2 : 13 ; 1 Pet. 1 : 2 ; (*b*) the resultant state, the
conduct befitting those so separated, 1 Thess. 4 : 3, 4, 7, and the four
other places mentioned above. Sanctification is thus the state predetermined by God for believers, into which in grace He calls them, and in
which they begin their Christian course and so pursue it. Hence they are
called " saints " (*hagioi*). See SANCTIFICATION.¶

Note : The corresponding verb *hagiazō* denotes to set apart to God.
See HALLOW, SANCTIFY.

2. HAGIŌSUNĒ (ἁγιωσύνη) denotes the manifestation of the quality
of holiness in personal conduct ; (*a*) it is used in Rom. 1 : 4, of the absolute
holiness of Christ in the days of His flesh, which distinguished Him from
all merely human beings ; this (which is indicated in the phrase " the spirit
of holiness ") and (in vindication of it) His resurrection from the dead,
marked Him out as (He was " declared to be ") the Son of God ;
(*b*) believers are to be " perfecting holiness in the fear of God," 2 Cor. 7 : 1,
i.e., bringing holiness to its predestined end, whereby (*c*) they may be
found " unblameable in holiness " in the Parousia of Christ, 1 Thess.
3 : 13.¶

" In each place character is in view, perfect in the case of the Lord
Jesus, growing toward perfection in the case of the Christian. Here the

exercise of love is declared to be the means God uses to develop likeness to Christ in His children. The sentence may be paraphrased thus :— ' The Lord enable you more and more to spend your lives in the interests of others, in order that He may so establish you in Christian character now, that you may be vindicated from every charge that might possibly be brought against you at the Judgment-seat of Christ ; ' cp. I John 4 : 16, 17.''*

3. HAGIOTĒS (ἁγιότης), sanctity, the abstract quality of holiness, is used (a) of God, Heb. 12 : 10 ; (b) of the manifestation of it in the conduct of the Apostle Paul and his fellow-labourers, 2 Cor. 1 : 12 (in the best mss., for haplotēs).¶

4. HOSIOTĒS (ὁσιότης) is to be distinguished from No. 3, as denoting that quality of holiness which is manifested in those who have regard equally to grace and truth ; it involves a right relation to God ; it is used in Luke 1 : 75 and Eph. 4 : 24, and in each place is associated with righteousness.¶

Notes : (1) In Acts 3 : 12, the A.V. translates eusebeia, by " holiness," R.V., " godliness," as everywhere, the true meaning of the word. See GODLINESS. (2) In Tit. 2 : 3, A.V., hieroprepēs, which denotes suited to a sacred character, reverent, is rendered " as becometh holiness," R.V., " reverent." See REVERENT.¶

B. Adjectives.

1. HAGIOS (ἅγιος), akin to A, Nos. 1 and 2, which are from the same root as hagnos (found in hazō, to venerate), fundamentally signifies separated (among the Greeks, dedicated to the gods), and hence, in Scripture in its moral and spiritual significance, separated from sin and therefore consecrated to God, sacred.

(a) It is predicated of God (as the absolutely Holy One, in His purity, majesty and glory) : of the Father, e.g., Luke 1 : 49 ; John 17 : 11 ; 1 Pet. 1 : 15, 16 ; Rev. 4 : 8 ; 6 : 10 ; of the Son, e.g., Luke 1 : 35 ; Acts 3 : 14 ; 4 : 27, 30 ; 1 John 2 : 20 ; of the Spirit, e.g., Matt. 1 : 18 and frequently in all the Gospels, Acts, Romans, 1 and 2 Cor., Eph., 1 Thess. ; also in 2 Tim. 1 : 14 ; Tit. 3 : 5 ; 1 Pet. 1 : 12 ; 2 Pet. 1 : 21 ; Jude 20.

(b) It is used of men and things (see below) in so far as they are devoted to God. Indeed the quality, as attributed to God, is often presented in a way which involves Divine demands upon the conduct of believers. These are called hagioi, saints, i.e., ' sanctified ' or ' holy ones.'

This sainthood is not an attainment, it is a state into which God in grace calls men ; yet believers are called to sanctify themselves (consistently with their calling, 2 Tim. 1 : 9), cleansing themselves from all defilement, forsaking sin, living a holy manner of life, 1 Pet. 1 : 15 ; 2 Pet. 3 : 11, and experiencing fellowship with God in His holiness. The saints are thus figuratively spoken of as " a holy temple," 1 Cor. 3 : 17 (a local

---

* From Notes on Thessalonians by Hogg and Vine, pp. 108, 115.

church) ; Eph. 2 : 21 (the whole Church), cp. 5 : 27 ; " a holy priesthood,"
1 Pet. 2 : 5 ; " a holy nation," 2 : 9.

" It is evident that *hagios* and its kindred words . . . express something more and higher than *hieros*, sacred, outwardly associated with
God ; . . . something more than *semnos*, worthy, honourable ; something more than *hagnos*, pure, free from defilement. *Hagios* is . . .
more comprehensive. . . . It is characteristically godlikeness " (G. B.
Stevens, in Hastings' Bib. Dic.).

The adjective is also used of the outer part of the Tabernacle, Heb.
9 : 2 (R.V., " the Holy place ") ; of the inner sanctuary, 9 : 3, R.V.,
" the Holy of Holies ; " 9 : 24, " a holy place," R.V. ; ver. 25 (plural),
of the Presence of God in Heaven, where there are not two compartments
as in the Tabernacle, all being " the holy place;" 9 : 8, 12 (neuter plural) ;
10 : 19, " the holy place," R.V. (A.V., " the holiest," neut. plural), see
SANCTUARY ; of the city of Jerusalem, Rev. 11 : 2 ; its temple, Acts 6 : 13 ;
of the faith, Jude 20 ; of the greetings of saints, 1 Cor. 16 : 20 ; of angels,
e.g., Mark 8 : 38 ; of apostles and prophets, Eph. 3 : 5 ; of the future
heavenly Jerusalem, Rev. 21 : 2, 10 ; 22 : 19.

2. HOSIOS (ὅσιος), akin to A, No. 4, signifies religiously right, holy,
as opposed to what is unrighteous or polluted. It is commonly associated
with righteousness (see A, No. 4). It is used " of God, Rev. 15 : 4 ; 16 : 5 ;
and of the body of the Lord Jesus, Acts 2 : 27 ; 13 : 35, citations from
Ps. 16 : 10, Sept. ; Heb. 7 : 26 ; and of certain promises made to David,
which could be fulfilled only in the resurrection of the Lord Jesus, Acts
13 : 34. In 1 Tim. 2 : 8 and Tit. 1 : 8, it is used of the character of
Christians. . . . In the Sept., *hosios* frequently represents the Hebrew
word *chasid*, which varies in meaning between ' holy ' and ' gracious,'
or ' merciful ; ' cp. Ps. 16 : 10 with 145 : 17."*

Notes : (1) For Acts 13 : 34, see the R.V. and the A.V. marg. ; the
R.V. in Rev. 16 : 5, " Thou Holy One," translates the most authentic
mss. (A.V. " and shalt be "). (2) For *hieros* (see No. 1), subserving a
sacred purpose, translated " holy " in 2 Tim. 3 : 15, A.V. (of the Scriptures), see SACRED.

C. Adverb.

HOSIŌS (ὁσίως), akin to A, No. 4, and B No. 2, " holily," i.e., pure
from evil conduct, and observant of God's will, is used in 1 Thess. 2 : 10,
of the conduct of the Apostle and his fellow-missionaries.¶

D. Verb.

HAGIAZŌ (ἁγιάζω), to hallow, sanctify, in the Passive Voice, to be
made holy, be sanctified, is translated " let him be made holy " in Rev.
22 : 11, the aorist or point tense expressing the definiteness and completeness of the Divine act ; elsewhere it is rendered by the verb to
sanctify. See HALLOW, SANCTIFY.

---

* From Notes on Thessalonians by Hogg and Vine, p. 64.

For HOLY GHOST see under SPIRIT and HOLY, B, No. 1 (a)

HOLYDAY

HEORTĒ (ἑορτή) denotes a feast, festival; it is translated "a holyday" in the A.V. of Col. 2:16; R.V., "a feast day." See FEAST.

HOME, AT HOME (to be; workers)

A. Noun and Phrases.

1. OIKOS (οἶκος), a house, dwelling, is used (a) with the preposition *eis*, unto, with the meaning 'to home,' lit., to a house, in Mark 8:3, R.V., "to (their) home," A.V., "to (their own) houses;" so 8:26, "to (his) home;" Luke 15:6, "home," lit., 'into the house;' (b) with the preposition *en*, in, 1 Cor. 11:34, "(let him eat) at home;" 14:35, "(let them ask . . .) at home;" (c) with the preposition *kata*, down, Acts 2:46, "(breaking bread) at home," R.V. (A.V., "from house to house"); so in 5:42 (A.V., "in every house").

Notes: (1) In Mark 3:19, the A.V. and R.V. marg., have "home," for the text "to a house;" the latter seems the more probable. See HOUSE. (2) In 1 Tim. 5:4, the phrase *ton idion oikon*, is rendered "at home," of the necessity that children should show piety there; R.V., "towards their own family," the house being put by metonymy for the family.

2. The neuter plural of *idios*, one's own, with the article, preceded by *eis*, unto, lit., 'unto one's own (things),' is translated "home" in Acts 21:6; in John 19:27, "unto his own home" ("home" being italicised).

Note: In John 16:32, this phrase is rendered "to his own" (of the predicted scattering of the disciples), A.V. marg., "his own home;" cp. John 1:11, "His own things," R.V., marg. (i.e., 'His possessions'). For *oikia* in Matt. 8:6, A.V., "at home," see HOUSE.

3. In Luke 24:12 the reflexive pronoun *hauton* (in some mss. *heauton*), preceded by *pros*, to, is rendered "to his home," R.V. (lit., 'to himself'), of the departure of Peter from the Lord's tomb; in John 20:10, the same construction is used, in the plural, of Peter and John on the same occasion, and rendered "unto their own home."

B. Adjective.

OIKOURGOS (οἰκουργός), working at home (*oikos*, and a root of *ergon*, work), is used in Tit. 2:5, "workers at home," R.V., in the injunction given to elder women regarding the training of the young women. Some mss. have *oikouros*, watching or keeping the home (*oikos*, and *ouros*, a keeper), A.V., "keepers at home."¶

C. Verb.

ENDĒMEŌ (ἐνδημέω), lit., to be among one's people (*en*, in, *dēmos*, people; *endēmos*, one who is in his own place or land), is used metaphorically of the life on earth of believers, 2 Cor. 5:6, "at home (in the body);" in ver. 8 of the life in Heaven of the spirits of believers, after their decease,

ver... absent ..., the Lord)," R.V. (A.V., " present "); in ver. 9, " at
absent ..., the Lord); in ... resent") refers again to the life on earth. In each
Lord); in ... resent") refers again to be away from home, to be
so in ver. 9, ...rasted with *ekdēmeō*, to be away from home (from the
Lord " after death are absent," i.e., away from home of the body);
ness of the spirit, ...bsent " (i.e., away from the home with the
... implication in being " at home with the
... against the doctrine of the unconscious-
... the natural body.¶

HONEST, HONESTY

A.

1. KALOS (καλός), good, admi...y, meaning of what is fair, right, honour... esteem; it is translated " honest " [cp...oming, has also the ethical
honour)], which has the same double meaning ...uch conduct as deserves
namely, regarded with honour, honourable, and *honest* (from *honos*,
coming; in Luke 8 : 15 (A.V., and R.V.), " an honest "... in the A.V.,
heart; " Rom. 12 : 17; 2 Cor. 8 : 21 and 13 : 7, R.V., ...ing honour, be-
(A.V., " honest "), of things which are regarded with esteem ... good (*agathos*)
2 : 12, of behaviour, R.V., " seemly," A.V., " honest " (i.e., be...ming).
See GOOD.

Note : In Tit. 3 : 14, the R.V. and A.V. margins give what is probably
the accurate meaning, " (to profess) honest occupations " (A.V., " trades ");
in the texts " (to maintain) good works."

2. SEMNOS (σεμνός), august, venerable, is rendered "honest" in
Phil. 4 : 8, A.V. (marg., " venerable "), R.V., " honourable " (marg.,
" reverent "). Matthew Arnold suggests ' nobly serious.' See GRAVE.

Note : In Acts 6 : 3, " men of honest (R.V., good) report " translates
the Passive Voice of *martureō*, lit., ' having had witness borne.'

B. Adverbs.

1. KALŌS (καλῶς), corresponding to A, No. 1, is used in Heb. 13 : 18,
" honestly," i.e., honourably. See PLACE, C, *Note* (4), WELL.

2. EUSCHĒMONŌS (εὐσχημόνως), becomingly, decently, is rendered
" honestly " in Rom. 13 : 13, where it is set in contrast with the confusion
of Gentile social life, and in 1 Thess. 4 : 12, of the manner of life of
believers as a witness to " them that are without; " in 1 Cor. 14 : 40,
" decently," in contrast with confusion in the churches. See DECENTLY.¶

C. Noun.

SEMNOTĒS (σεμνότης) denotes gravity, dignified seriousness; it is
rendered " honesty " in the A.V. of 1 Tim. 2 : 2, R.V., " gravity." See
GRAVITY.

HONEY

MELI (μέλι) occurs with the adjective *agrios*, wild, in Matt. 3 : 4;
Mark 1 : 6; in Rev. 10 : 9, 10, as an example of sweetness.¶ As honey

is liable to ferment, it was precluded from offer... ...s regarded
The liquid honey mentioned in Psa. 19 : 10 a... to Ahijah by
as the best ; a cruse of it was part of the ...
Jeroboam's wife, 1 Kings 14 : 3.

bees from *melissa*, a bee,

MELISSIOS (μελίσσιος), signify...

HONEY ...n Luke 24 : 42. ¶

is found, with *kerion*, a comb, in ...i and Verb)

HONO...ouns.

...valuing, hence, objectively, (*a*) a price

1. TIMĒ (τιμή), prir... 27 : 6, 9 ; Acts 4 : 34 ; 5 : 2, 3 ; 7 : 16,
paid or received, e.g. ...n ") ; 19 : 19 ; 1 Cor. 6 : 20 ; 7 : 23 ; (*b*) of the
R.V., " price " (A.V...nto believers, 1 Pet. 2 : 7, R.V., i.e., the honour
preciousness of ...ue of Christ as appropriated by believers, who are
and inestimabl...stones, to Him the Corner-Stone ; (*c*) in the sense of
joined, as livi... ordinances, valueless against the indulgence of the
value, of ...man flesh, o...perhaps of no value in attempts at asceticism, Col. 2 : 23 (see
extended note under INDULGENCE, No. 2) ; (*d*) honour, esteem, (1) used
in ascriptions of worship to God, 1 Tim. 1 : 17 ; 6 : 16 ; Rev. 4 : 9, 11 ;
5 : 13 ; 7 : 12 ; to Christ, 5 : 12, 13 ; (2) bestowed upon Christ by the
Father, Heb. 2 : 9 ; 2 Pet. 1 : 17 ; (3) bestowed upon man, Heb. 2 : 7 ;
(4) bestowed upon Aaronic priests, Heb. 5 : 4 ; (5) to be the reward hereafter of " the proof of faith " on the part of tried saints, 1 Pet. 1 : 7, R.V. ;
(6) used of the believer who as a vessel is " meet for the Master's use,"
2 Tim. 2 : 21 ; (7) to be the reward of patience in well-doing, Rom. 2 : 7,
and of working good (a perfect life to which man cannot attain, so as to be
justified before God thereby), 2 : 10 ; (8) to be given to all to whom it is
due, Rom. 13 : 7 (see 1 Pet. 2 : 17, under B, No. 1) ; (9) as an advantage
to be given by believers one to another instead of claiming it for self,
Rom. 12 : 10 ; (10) to be given to elders that rule well (" double honour "),
1 Tim. 5 : 17 (here the meaning may be an honorarium) ; (11) to be given
by servants to their master, 1 Tim. 6 : 1 ; (12) to be given to wives by
husbands, 1 Pet. 3 : 7 ; (13) said of the husband's use of the wife, in
contrast to the exercise of the passion of lust, 1 Thess. 4 : 4 (some regard
the " vessel " here as the believer's body) ; (14) of that bestowed upon
parts of the body, 1 Cor. 12 : 23, 24 ; (15) of that which belongs to the
builder of a house in contrast to the house itself, Heb. 3 : 3 ; (16) of that
which is not enjoyed by a prophet in his own country, John 4 : 44 ; (17) of
that bestowed by the inhabitants of Melita upon Paul and his fellow-
passengers, in gratitude for his benefits of healing, Acts 28 : 10 ; (18) of
the festive honour to be possessed by nations, and brought into the
Holy City, the Heavenly Jerusalem, Rev. 21 : 26 (in some mss., ver. 24) ;
(19) of honour bestowed upon things inanimate, a potters' vessel, Rom.

9 : 21 ; 2 Tim. 2 : 20. See PRECIOUSNESS, PRICE, SUM, VALUE.¶

Note : For *entimos*, ' in honour,' see HONOURABLE, No. 2.

2. DOXA (δοξά), glory, is translated " honour " in the A.V. of John 5 : 41, 44 (twice) ; 8 : 54 ; 2 Cor. 6 : 8, and Rev. 19 : 7 ; the R.V. keeps to the word " glory," as the A.V. everywhere else. See GLORY.

B. Verbs.

1. TIMAŌ (τιμάω), to honour (akin to A, No. 1), is used of (*a*) valuing Christ at a price, Matt. 27 : 9, cp. A, No. 1, (*a*) ; (*b*) honouring a person : (1) the honour done by Christ to the Father, John 8 : 49 ; (2) honour bestowed by the Father upon him who serves Christ, John 12 : 26 ; (3) the duty of all to honour the Son equally with the Father, 5 : 23 ; (4) the duty of children to honour their parents, Matt. 15 : 4 ; 19 : 19 ; Mark 7 : 10 ; 10 : 19 ; Luke 18 : 20 ; Eph. 6 : 2 ; (5) the duty of Christians to honour the king, and all men, 1 Pet. 2 : 17 ; (6) the respect and material assistance to be given to widows " that are widows indeed," 1 Tim. 5 : 3 ; (7) the honour done to Paul and his companions by the inhabitants of Melita, Acts 28 : 10 ; (8) mere lip profession of honour to God, Matt. 15 : 8 ; Mark 7 : 6.¶

2. DOXAZŌ (δοξάζω), to glorify (from *doxa*, A, No. 2), is rendered " honour " and " honoureth " in the A.V. of John 8 : 54 ; in 1 Cor. 12 : 26, however, in reference to the members of the body, both A.V. and R.V. have " honoured " (R.V. marg., " glorified "). Everywhere else it is translated by some form of the verb to glorify, have glory, or be made glorious, except in Rom. 11 : 13, " magnify," A.V. See GLORIFY.

HONOURABLE, WITHOUT HONOUR

1. ENDOXOS (ἔνδοξος) denotes (*a*) held in honour (*en*, in, *doxa*, honour ; cp. HONOUR, A, No. 2), of high repute, 1 Cor. 4 : 10, A.V. " (are) honourable," R.V., " (have) glory," in contrast to *atimos*, without honour (see No. 6 below). See GLORIOUS, GORGEOUSLY.

2. ENTIMOS (ἔντιμος), lit., in honour (*en*, in, *timē*, honour : see HONOUR, A, No. 1), is used of the centurion's servant in Luke 7 : 2, " dear " (R.V. marg., " precious . . . or honourable ") ; of self-sacrificing servants of the Lord, said of Epaphroditus, Phil. 2 : 29, R.V. " (hold such) in honour " (A.V., " in reputation ; " marg., " honour such ") ; of Christ, as a precious stone, 1 Pet. 2 : 4, 6 (R.V. marg., " honourable "). Cp. *timios* in 1 : 7, 19 ; see No. 4.¶

The comparative degree, *entimoteros*, is used (in the best mss.) of degrees of honour attached to persons invited to a feast, a marriage feast, Luke 14 : 8, " a more honourable man." See PRECIOUS.¶

3. EUSCHĒMŌN (εὐσχήμων) signifies elegant, comely, of honourable position, A.V., " honourable," R.V., " of honourable estate," Mark 15 : 43 ; Acts 13 : 50 ; 17 : 12 ; for other renderings in 1 Cor. 7 : 35 and 12 : 24 see COMELY, B.

4. TIMIOS (τίμιος), precious, valuable, honourable (akin to timē, honour; see No. 2), is used of marriage in Heb. 13 : 4, A.V , as a statement, " (marriage) is honourable (in all)," R.V., as an exhortation, " let (marriage) be had in honour (among all)." See DEAR, PRECIOUS, REPU-TATION.

5. KALOS (καλός), good, fair, is translated " honourable " in Rom. 12 : 17 ; 2 Cor. 8 : 21 ; 13 : 7, R.V. (A.V., " honest). See GOOD, HONEST.

6. ATIMOS (ἄτιμος), without honour (a, negative, or privative, timē, honour), despised, is translated " without honour " in Matt. 13 : 57 : Mark 6 : 4 ; " dishonour " in 1 Cor. 4 : 10, R.V. (A.V., " despised "). See DESPISE.¶

The comparative degree atimoteros is used in the best mss. in 1 Cor. 12 : 23, " less honourable."¶

Note : For *semnos*, honourable, Phil. 4 : 8, R.V., see GRAVE.

HOOK

ANKISTRON (ἄγκιστρον), a fish-hook (from *ankos*, a bend ; Lat. *angulus ;* Eng., anchor and angle are akin), is used in Matt. 17 : 27.¶ In the Sept., 2 Kings 19 : 28 ; Job 40 : 20 ; Is. 19 : 8 ; Ezek. 32 : 3 ; Hab. 1 : 15.¶

HOPE (Noun and Verb), HOPE (for)

A. Noun.

ELPIS (ἐλπίς), in the N.T., favourable and confident expectation (contrast the Sept. in Isa. 28 : 19, " an evil hope "). It has to do with the unseen and the future, Rom. 8 : 24, 25. Hope describes (a) the happy anticipation of good (the most frequent significance), e.g., Tit. 1 : 2 ; 1 Pet. 1 : 21 ; (b) the ground upon which hope is based, Acts 16 : 19 ; Col. 1 : 27, " Christ in you the hope of glory ; " (c) the object upon which the hope is fixed, e.g., 1 Tim. 1 : 1.

Various phrases are used with the word hope, in Paul's Epistles and speeches : (1) Acts 23 : 6, " the hope and resurrection of the dead ; " this has been regarded as a hendiadys (one by means of two), i.e., the hope of the resurrection ; but the *kai*, " and," is epexegetic, defining the hope, namely, the resurrection ; (2) Acts 26 : 6, 7, " the hope of the promise (i.e., the fulfilment of the promise) made unto the fathers ; " (3) Gal. 5 : 5, " the hope of righteousness ; " i.e., the believer's complete conformity to God's will, at the Coming of Christ ; (4) Col. 1 : 23, " the hope of the Gospel," i.e., the hope of the fulfilment of all the promises presented in the Gospel ; cp. 1 : 5 ; (5) Rom. 5 : 2, " (the) hope of the glory of God," i.e., as in Tit. 2 : 13, " the blessed hope and appearing of the glory of our great God and Saviour Jesus Christ ; " cp. Col. 1 : 27 ; (6) 1 Thess. 5 : 8, " the hope of salvation," i.e., of the Rapture of believers, to take place at the opening of the Parousia of Christ ; (7) Eph. 1 : 18, "the hope of His (God's) calling," i.e., the prospect before those who respond to His call in the Gospel ; (8) Eph. 4 : 4, "the hope of your calling," the same as (7), but regarded from the point of view of the called ; (9) Tit. 1 : 2, and 3 : 7, "the hope of eternal life," i.e., the full manifestation and realization of that life which is already the believer's possession ; (10) Acts 28 : 20, "the hope of Israel," i.e., the expectation of the coming of the Messiah. See Notes on Galatians by Hogg and Vine, pp. 248, 249.

In Eph. 1 : 18 ; 2 : 12 and 4 : 4, the hope is objective. The objective and subjective use of the word need to be distinguished ; in Rom. 15 : 4, e.g., the use is subjective.

In the N.T. three adjectives are descriptive of hope : "good," 2 Thess. 2 : 16 ; "blessed," Tit. 2 : 13 ; "living," 1 Pet. 1 : 3. To these may be added Heb. 7 : 19, "a better hope," i.e., additional to the commandment, which became disannulled (v. 18), a hope centred in a new Priesthood.

In Rom. 15 : 13 God is spoken of as "the God of hope," i.e., He is the Author, not the Subject, of it. Hope is a factor in salvation, Rom. 8 : 24 ; it finds its expression in endurance under trial, which is the effect of waiting for the Coming of Christ, 1 Thess. 1 : 3 ; it is "an anchor of the soul," staying it amidst the storms of this life, Heb. 6 : 18, 19 ; it is a purifying power, "every one that hath this hope set on Him (Christ) purifieth himself, even as He is pure," 1 John 3 : 3, R.V. (the Apostle John's one mention of hope).

The phrase "fulness of hope," Heb. 6 : 11, R.V., expresses the completeness of its activity in the soul ; cp. "fulness of faith," 10 : 22, and "of understanding," Col. 2 : 2 (R.V., marg.).

B. Verbs.

1. ELPIZŌ (ἐλπίζω), to hope, is not infrequently translated in the A.V., by the verb to trust ; the R.V. adheres to some form of the verb to hope, e.g., John 5 : 45, "Moses, on whom ye have set your hope ;" 2 Cor. 1 : 10, "on whom we have set our hope ;" so in 1 Tim. 4 : 10 ; 5 : 5 ; 6 : 17 ; see also, e.g., Matt. 12 : 21 ; Luke 24 : 21 ; Rom. 15 : 12, 24.

The verb is followed by three prepositions : (1) *eis*, rendered " on " in John 5 : 45 (as above) ; the meaning is really " in " as in 1 Pet. 3 : 5, "who hoped in God ;" the hope is thus said to be directed to, and to centre in, a Person ; (2) *epi*, "on," Rom. 15 : 12, "On Him shall the Gentiles hope," R.V. ; so 1 Tim. 4 : 10 ; 5 : 5 (in the best mss.) ; 6 : 17, R.V. ; this expresses the ground upon which hope rests ; (3) *en*, "in," 1 Cor. 15 : 19, "we have hoped in Christ," R.V., more lit., ' we are (men) that have hoped in Christ,' the preposition expresses that Christ is not simply the ground upon whom, but the sphere and element in whom, the hope is placed. The form of the verb (the perfect participle with the verb to be, lit., ' are having hoped ') stresses the character of those who

hope, more than the action ; hope characterizes them, showing what sort
of persons they are. See TRUST.

2. PROELPIZŌ (προελπίζω), to hope before (pro, before, and No. 1),
is found in Eph. 1 : 12.¶

3. APELPIZŌ (ἀπελπίζω), lit., to hope from (apo, and No. 1) : see
DESPAIR.

HORN

KERAS (κέρας), a horn, is used in the plural, as the symbol of strength,
(a) in the Apocalyptic visions ; (1) on the head of the Lamb as symbolic
of Christ, Rev. 5 : 6 ; (2) on the heads of beasts as symbolic of national
potentates, Rev. 12 : 3 ; 13 : 1, 11 ; 17 : 3, 7, 12, 16 (cp. Dan. 7 : 8 ; 8 : 9 ;
Zech. 1 : 18, etc.) ; (3) at the corners of the golden altar, Rev. 9 : 13
(cp. Ex. 30 : 2 ; the horns were of one piece with the altar, as in the case
of the brazen altar, 27 : 2, and were emblematic of the efficacy of the
ministry connected with it) ; (b) metaphorically, in the singular, " a horn
of salvation," Luke 1 : 69 (a frequent metaphor in the O.T., e.g., Psa.
18 : 2 ; cp. 1 Sam. 2 : 10 ; Lam. 2 : 3).¶

HORSE

HIPPOS (ἵππος), apart from the fifteen occurrences in the Apocalypse,
occurs only in Jas. 3 : 3 ; in the Apocalypse horses are seen in visions
in 6 : 2, 4, 5, 8 ; 9 : 7, 9, 17 (twice) ; 14 : 20 ; 19 : 11, 14, 19, 21 ; otherwise in 18 : 13 ; 19 : 18.¶

HORSEMEN

1. HIPPEUS (ἱππεύς), a horseman, is used in the plural in Acts 23 : 23,
32.¶

2. HIPPIKOS (ἱππικός), an adjective signifying ' of a horse ' or ' of
horsemen,' equestrian, is used as a noun denoting cavalry, in Rev. 9 : 16,
" horsemen," numbering " twice ten thousand times ten thousand,"
R.V.¶

HOSANNA

HŌSANNA (ὡσαννά), in the Hebrew, means " save, we pray." The
word seems to have become an utterance of praise rather than of prayer,
though originally, probably, a cry for help. The people's cry at the
Lord's triumphal entry into Jerusalem (Matt. 21 : 9, 15 ; Mark 11 : 9, 10 ;
John 12 : 13) was taken from Psa. 118, which was recited at the Feast of
Tabernacles (see FEAST) in the great Hallel (Psalms 113 to 118) in responses
with the priest, accompanied by the waving of palm and willow branches.
" The last day of the feast " was called " the great Hosanna ; " the boughs
also were called hosannas.¶

HOSPITALITY
A. Noun.

PHILOXENIA (φιλοξενία), love of strangers (*philos*, loving, *xenos*, a stranger), is used in Rom. 12 : 13 ; Heb. 13 : 2, lit. ' (be not forgetful of) hospitality.'   See ENTERTAIN, Note.¶

B. Adjective.

PHILOXENOS (φιλόξενος), hospitable, occurs in 1 Tim. 3 : 2; Tit. 1 : 8; 1 Pet. 4 : 9.¶

Note : For *xenodocheō*, 1 Tim. 5 : 10, see STRANGER, B.¶

HOST (of guests)

1. XENOS (ξένος), in addition to the meaning stranger, mentioned above under A, denotes one or other of the parties bound by ties of hospitality, (*a*) the guest (not in the N.T.), (*b*) the host, Rom. 16 : 23.¶

2. PANDOCHEUS (πανδοχεύς), lit., one who receives all (*pas*, all, *dechomai*, to receive), denotes an innkeeper, host, Luke 10 : 35.¶

HOST (of angels, etc.)

STRATIA (στρατιά), an army, is used of angels, Luke 2 : 13 ; of stars, Acts 7 : 42 ; some mss. have it instead of *strateia*, in 2 Cor. 10 : 4 (" warfare ").¶ Cp. *strateuma*, an army.

HOT

ZESTOS (ζεστός), boiling hot (from *zeō*, to boil, be hot, fervent ; Eng., zest), is used, metaphorically, in Rev. 3 : 15, 16.¶

HOUR

HŌRA (ὥρα), whence Lat., *hora*, Eng., hour, primarily denoted any time or period, expecially a season.   In the N.T. it is used to denote (*a*) a part of the day, especially a twelfth part of day or night, an hour, e.g., Matt. 8 : 13 ; Acts 10 : 3, 9 ; 23 : 23 ; Rev. 9 : 15 ; in 1 Cor. 15 : 30, " every hour " stands for ' all the time ; ' in some passages it expresses duration, e.g., Matt. 20 : 12 ; 26 : 40 ; Luke 22 : 59 ; inexactly, in such phrases as " for a season," John 5 : 35 ; 2 Cor. 7 : 8 ; " for an hour," Gal. 2 : 5 ; " for a short season," 1 Thess. 2 : 17, R.V. (A.V., " for a short time," lit., ' for the time of an hour ') ; (*b*) a period more or less extended, e.g., 1 John 2 : 18, " it is the last hour," R.V. ; (*c*) a definite point of time, e.g., Matt. 26 : 45, " the hour is at hand ; " Luke 1 : 10 ; 10 : 21 ; 14 : 17, lit., ' at the hour of supper ; ' Acts 16 : 18 ; 22 : 13 ; Rev. 3 : 3 ; 11 : 13 ; 14 : 7 ; a point of time when an appointed action is to begin, Rev. 14 : 15 ; in Rom. 13 : 11, " it is high time," lit., ' it is already an hour,' indicating that a point of time has come later than would have been the case had responsibility been realised.   In 1 Cor. 4 : 11, it indicates a point of time previous to which certain circumstances have existed.

Notes : (1) In 1 Cor. 8 : 7, A.V., " unto this hour," the phrase in the

original is simply, " until now," as R.V.   (2) In Rev. 8 : 1, *hēmiōron*,
half an hour (*hēmi*, half, and *hōra*), is used with *hōs*, " about," of a period
of silence in Heaven after the opening of the 7th seal, a period corresponding to the time customarily spent in silent worship in the Temple
during the burning of incense.¶

HOUSE
A. Nouns.

1. OIKOS (*oîkos*) denotes (*a*) a house, a dwelling, e.g., Matt. 9 : 6, 7 ;
11 : 8 ; it is used of the Tabernacle, as the House of God, Matt. 12 : 4,
and the Temple similarly, e.g., Matt. 21 : 13 ;   Luke 11 : 51, A.V.,
" temple," R.V., " sanctuary ; "   John 2 : 16, 17 ; called by the Lord
" your house " in Matt. 23 : 38 and Luke 13 : 35 (some take this as the
city of Jerusalem) ; metaphorically of Israel as God's house, Heb. 3 : 2, 5,
where " his house " is not Moses', but God's ; of believers, similarly,
ver. 6, where Christ is spoken of as " over God's House " (the word " own "
is rightly omitted in the R.V.) ; Heb. 10 : 21 ; 1 Pet. 2 : 5 ; 4 : 17 ; of the
body, Matt. 12 : 44 ; Luke 11 : 24 ; (*b*) by metonymy, of the members
of a household or family, e.g., Luke 10 : 5 ; Acts 7 : 10 ; 11 : 14 ; 1 Tim.
3 : 4, 5, 12 ; 2 Tim. 1 : 16 ; 4 : 19, R.V. (A.V., " household ") ; Tit. 1 : 11
(plural) ; of a local church, 1 Tim. 3 : 15 ; of the descendants of Jacob
(Israel) and David, e.g., Matt. 10 : 6 ; Luke 1 : 27, 33 ; Acts 2 : 36 ; 7 : 42.
See HOME, A, No. 1, *Note* (1), HOUSEHOLD.

2. OIKIA (*oikía*) is akin to No. 1, and used much in the same way ;
in Attic law *oikos* denoted the whole estate, *oikia* stood for the dwelling
only ; this distinction was largely lost in later Greek.   In the N.T. it
denotes (*a*) a house, a dwelling, e.g., Matt. 2 : 11 ; 5 : 15 ; 7 : 24–27 ;
2 Tim. 2 : 20 ; 2 John 10 ; it is not used of the Tabernacle or the Temple,
as in the case of No. 1 ; (*b*) metaphorically, the heavenly abode, spoken
of by the Lord as " My Father's house," John 14 : 2, the eternal dwelling
place of believers ; the body as the dwelling place of the soul, 2 Cor. 5 : 1 ;
similarly the resurrection body of believers (*id.*) ; property, e.g., Mark
12 : 40 ; by metonymy, the inhabitants of a house, a household, e.g.,
Matt. 12 : 25 ; John 4 : 53 ; 1 Cor. 16 : 15.   See HOUSEHOLD.

B. Adverb.

PANOIKEI (*πανοικεί*) denotes ' with all the house,' Acts 16 : 34,
i.e., the household.¶

Notes : (1) In 2 Cor. 5 : 2, *oikētērion*, a habitation (see R.V.) is translated " house " in the A.V., of the resurrection body (cp. *oikia* in the
preceding verse ; see above). (2) In 1 Tim. 5 : 13, " from house to house " is,
lit., ' the houses.' (3) For " in every house," Acts 5 : 42 (cp. 2 : 46), see HOME.
(4) For " them which are of the house," 1 Cor. 1 : 11, A.V., see HOUSEHOLD.

For GOODMAN of the HOUSE see HOUSEHOLDER

For MASTER of the HOUSE see HOUSEHOLDER

HOUSEHOLD

A. Nouns.

1. OIKOS (οἶκος) is translated "household" in Acts 16 : 15 ; 1 Cor. 1 : 16 ; in the A.V. of 2 Tim. 4 : 19 (R.V., "house"). See HOUSE, No. 1.

2. OIKIA (οἰκία) is translated "household" in Phil. 4 : 22. See HOUSE, No. 2.

3. OIKETEIA (οἰκετεία) denotes a household of servants, Matt. 24 : 45 (some mss. have No. 4 here).¶

4. THERAPEIA (θεραπεία), service, care, attention, is also used in the collective sense of a household, in Luke 12 : 42 (see No. 3). See HEALING.

Notes : (1) In Rom. 16 : 10, 11, the phrase "those of the household" translates a curtailed phrase in the original, lit., ' the (persons) of (*ek*, consisting of) the (members of the household of).' (2) In 1 Cor. 1 : 11, " they which are of the household (A.V., house) of Chloe " is, lit., ' the . . . of Chloe,' the Eng. translation being necessary to express the idiom.

B. Adjectives.

1. OIKEIOS (οἰκεῖος), akin to A, No. 1, primarily signifies of, or belonging to, a house, hence, of persons, one's household, or kindred, as in 1 Tim. 5 : 8, R.V., "household," A.V. "house," marg., "kindred ; " in Eph. 2 : 19, "the household of God" denotes the company of the redeemed ; in Gal. 6 : 10, it is called " the household of the faith," R.V. In these two cases *oikeios* is used in the same sense as those mentioned under *oikos* (A, No. 1).¶

2. OIKIAKOS (οἰκιακός), from A, No. 2, denotes belonging to one's household, one's own ; it is used in Matt. 10 : 25, 36.¶

HOUSEHOLDER

A. Noun.

OIKODESPOTĒS (οἰκοδεσπότης), a master of a house (*oikos*, a house, *despotēs*, a master), is rendered "master of the house " in Matt. 10 : 25 ; Luke 13 : 25, and 14 : 21, where the context shows that the authority of the householder is stressed ; in Matt. 24 : 43 and Luke 12 : 39, the R.V. " master of the house " (A.V., " goodman of the house ", does not give the exact meaning) ; " householder " is the rendering in both Versions in Matt. 13 : 27, 52 ; 20 : 1 ; 21 : 33 ; so the R.V. in 20 : 11 (for A.V., " goodman of the house ") ; both have " goodman of the house " in Mark 14 : 14 ; in Luke 22 : 11, " goodman." See GOODMAN.¶

B. Verb.

OIKODESPOTEŌ (οἰκοδεσποτέω), corresponding to A, to rule a house, is used in 1 Tim. 5 : 14, R.V., " rule the household " (A.V., " guide the house ").¶

HOUSEHOLD-SERVANT

OIKETĒS (οἰκέτης), a house-servant, is translated "household-servants" in Acts 10 : 7 ; elsewhere, "servant" or "servants," Luke 16 : 13 ; Rom. 14 : 4 ; 1 Pet. 2 : 18. See SERVANT.¶

HOUSETOP

DŌMA (δῶμα), akin to demō, to build, denotes a housetop. The housetop was flat, and guarded by a low parapet wall (see Deut. 22 : 8). It was much frequented and used for various purposes, e.g., for proclamations, Matt. 10 : 27 ; Luke 12 : 3 ; for prayer, Acts 10 : 9. The house was often built round a court, across the top of which cords were fixed from the parapet walls for supporting a covering from the heat. The housetop could be reached by stairs outside the building ; the paralytic in Luke 5 : 19 could be let down into the court or area by rolling back the covering. External flight from the housetop in time of danger is enjoined in Matt. 24 : 17 ; Mark 13 : 15 ; Luke 17 : 31.¶

HOW and HOWBEIT, see † p. 9.

For HOW GREAT see GREAT, Nos. 4, 5, 6

HOWL

OLOLUZŌ (ὀλολύζω), an onomatopœic verb (expressing its significance in its sound), to cry aloud (the Sept. uses it to translate the Heb. yālal, e.g., Is. 13 : 6 ; 15 : 3 ; Jer. 4 : 8 ; Ezek. 21 : 12 ; Lat., ululare, and Eng., howl are akin), was primarily used of crying aloud to the gods ; it is found in Jas. 5 : 1 in an exhortation to the godless rich.¶

HUMBLE (Adjective and Verb)
A. Adjectives.

1. TAPEINOS (ταπεινός) primarily signifies low-lying. It is used always in a good sense in the N.T., metaphorically, to denote (a) of low degree, brought low, Luke 1 : 52 ; Rom. 12 : 16, A.V., "(men) of low estate," R.V., "(things that are) lowly" (i.e., of low degree) ; 2 Cor. 7 : 6, A.V., "cast down," R.V., "lowly ; " the preceding context shows that this occurrence belongs to (a) ; Jas. 1 : 9, "of low degree ; " (b) humble in spirit, Matt. 11 : 29 ; 2 Cor. 10 : 1, R.V., "lowly," A.V. "base ; " Jas. 4 : 6 ; 1 Pet. 5 : 5. See BASE, CAST, Note (7), DEGREE (Note), LOWLY.¶

2. TAPEINOPHRŌN (ταπεινόφρων), "humble-minded" (phrēn, the mind), 1 Pet. 3 : 8 ; see COURTEOUS.¶

B. Verb.

TAPEINOŌ (ταπεινόω), akin to A, signifies to make low, (a) literally, of mountains and hills, Luke 3 : 5 (Passive Voice) ; (b) metaphorically, in the Active Voice, Matt. 18 : 4 ; 23 : 12 (2nd part) ; Luke 14 : 11 (2nd part) ; 18 : 14 (2nd part) ; 2 Cor. 11 : 7 ("abasing ") ; 12 : 21 ; Phil. 2 : 8 ; in the Passive Voice, Matt. 23 : 12 (1st part), R.V., "shall be humbled," A.V., "shall be abased ; " Luke 14 : 11 (ditto) ; 18 : 14 (ditto) ; Phil. 4 : 12, "to be abased ; " in the Passive, with Middle Voice sense, Jas. 4 : 10, "humble yourselves ; " 1 Pet. 5 : 6 (ditto). See ABASE, Low (to bring).¶

HUMBLENESS OF MIND, HUMILITY

TAPEINOPHROSUNĒ (ταπεινοφροσύνη), lowliness of mind (*tapeinos*, see A, above, under HUMBLE, and *phrēn*, the mind), is rendered "humility of mind" in Acts 20 : 19, A.V. (R.V., "lowliness of mind ") ; in Eph. 4 : 2, "lowliness ; " in Phil. 2 : 3, "lowliness of mind ; " in Col. 2 : 18, 23, of a false humility ; in Col. 3 : 12, A.V., "humbleness of mind," R.V., "humility ; " 1 Pet. 5 : 5, "humility." See LOWLINESS.¶

HUMILIATION

TAPEINŌSIS (ταπείνωσις), akin to *tapeinos* (see above), is rendered "low estate" in Luke 1 : 48 ; "humiliation," Acts 8 : 33 ; Phil. 3 : 21, R.V. "(the body of our) humiliation," A.V., "(our) vile (body) ; " Jas. 1 : 10, where "in that he is made low," is, lit., 'in his humiliation.' See ESTATE, LOW.¶

HUNDRED, HUNDREDFOLD

1. HEKATON (ἑκατόν), an indeclinable numeral, denotes a hundred, e.g., Matt. 18 : 12, 28 ; it also signifies a hundredfold, Matt. 13 : 8, 23, and the R.V. in the corresponding passage, Mark 4 : 8, 20 (for A.V., "hundred "), signifying the complete productiveness of sown seed. In the passage in Mark the phrase is, lit., 'in thirty and in sixty and in a hundred.' In Mark 6 : 40 it is used with the preposition *kata*, in the phrase "by hundreds." It is followed by other numerals in John 21 : 11 ; Acts 1 : 15 ; Rev. 7 : 4 ; 14 : 1, 3 ; 21 : 17.

2. HEKATONTAPLASIŌN (ἑκατονταπλασίων), an adjective, denotes a hundredfold, Mark 10 : 30 ; Luke 8 : 8 ; the best mss. have it in Matt. 19 : 29 for *pollaplasiōn*, many times more. See the R.V. margin.¶

For multiples of a hundred, see under the numerals TWO, THREE, etc. For "a hundred years," see YEARS.

HUNGER (Noun and Verb), HUNGERED, HUNGRY
A. Noun.

LIMOS (λιμός) has the meanings famine and hunger ; hunger in Luke 15 : 17 ; 2 Cor. 11 : 27 ; in Rev. 6 : 8, R.V. "famine " (A.V., "hunger "). See FAMINE.

B. Verb.

PEINAŌ (πεινάω), to hunger, be hungry, hungered, is used (*a*) literally, e.g., Matt. 4 : 2 ; 12 : 1 ; 21 : 18 ; Rom. 12 : 20 ; 1 Cor. 11 : 21, 34 ; Phil. 4 : 12 ; Rev. 7 : 16 ; Christ identifies Himself with His saints in speaking of Himself as suffering in their sufferings in this and other respects, Matt. 25 : 35, 42 ; (b) metaphorically, Matt. 5 : 6 ; Luke 6 : 21, 25 ; John 6 : 35.

C. Adjective.

PROSPEINOS (πρόσπεινος) signifies hungry (pros, intensive, peina, hunger), Acts 10 : 10, A.V., " very hungry," R.V., " hungry."¶

HURT (Noun and Verb), HURTFUL
A. Noun.

HUBRIS (ὔβρις) is rendered " hurt " in Acts 27 : 10, A.V. only. See HARM.

B. Verbs.

1. ADIKEŌ (ἀδικέω) signifies, intransitively, to do wrong, do hurt, act unjustly (a, negative, and dikē, justice), transitively, to wrong, hurt or injure a person. It is translated to hurt in the following : (a), intransitively, Rev. 9 : 19 ; (b) transitively, Luke 10 : 19 ; Rev. 2 : 11 (Passive) ; 6 : 6 ; 7 : 2, 3 ; 9 : 4, 10 ; 11 : 5. See INJURE, OFFENDER, UNJUST, UNRIGHTEOUSNESS, WRONG, WRONG-DOER.

2. BLAPTŌ (βλάπτω) signifies to injure, mar, do damage to, Mark 16 : 18, " shall (in no wise) hurt (them)" ; Luke 4 : 35, " having done (him no) hurt," R.V. Adikeō stresses the unrighteousness of the act, blaptō stresses the injury done.¶

3. KAKOŌ (κακόω), to do evil to anyone : see HARM.

C. Adjective.

BLABEROS (βλαβερός), akin to B, No. 2, signifies hurtful, 1 Tim. 6 : 9, said of lusts.¶ In the Sept., Prov. 10 : 26.¶

HUSBAND
A. Noun.

ANĒR (ἀνήρ) denotes, in general, a man, an adult male (in contrast to anthrōpos, which generically denotes a human being, male or female) ; it is used of man in various relations, the context deciding the meaning ; it signifies a husband, e.g., Matt. 1 : 16, 19 ; Mark 10 : 12 ; Luke 2 : 36 ; 16 : 18 ; John 4 : 16, 17, 18 ; Rom. 7 : 23. See MAN.

B. Adjectives.

1. PHILANDROS (φίλανδρος), primarily, loving man, signifies ' loving a husband,' Tit. 2 : 4, in instruction to young wives to love their husbands, lit., ' (to be) lovers of their husbands.'¶ The word occurs frequently in epitaphs.

2. HUPANDROS (ὔπανδρος), lit., ' under (i.e. subject to) a man,' married, and therefore, according to Roman law under the legal authority of the husband, occurs in Rom. 7 : 2, " that hath a husband."¶

HUSBANDMAN

GEŌRGOS (γεωργός), from gē, land, ground, and ergō (or erdō), to do (Eng., George), denotes (a) a husbandman, a tiller of the ground, 2 Tim. 2 : 6 ; Jas. 5 : 7 ; (b) a vine-dresser, Matt. 21 : 33-35, 38, 40, 41 ; Mark 12 : 1, 2, 7, 9 ; Luke 20 : 9, 10, 14, 16 ; John 15 : 1, where Christ speaks of the Father as the Husbandman, Himself as the Vine, His disciples as the branches, the object being to bear much fruit, life in Christ producing the fruit of the Spirit, i.e., character and ways in conformity to Christ.¶

HUSBANDRY

GEŌRGION (γεώργιον), akin to the above, denotes tillage, cultivation, husbandry, 1 Cor. 3 : 9, where the local church is described under this metaphor (A.V., marg., " tillage," R.V., marg., " tilled land "), suggestive of the diligent toil of the Apostle and his fellow-missionaries, both in the ministry of the gospel, and the care of the church at Corinth ; suggestive, too, of the effects in spiritual fruitfulness.¶ Cp. geōrgeomai, to till the ground, Heb. 6 : 7.¶

HUSKS

KERATION (κεράτιον), a little horn (a diminutive of keras, a horn ; see HORN), is used in the plural in Luke 15 : 16, of carob-pods, given to swine, and translated " husks."¶

HYMN (Noun and Verb)

A. Noun.

HUMNOS (ὕμνος) denotes a song of praise addressed to God (Eng., hymn), Eph. 5 : 19 ; Col. 3 : 16, in each of which the punctuation should probably be changed ; in the former " speaking to one another " goes with the end of ver. 18, and should be followed by a semi-colon ; similarly in Col. 3 : 16, the first part of the verse should end with the words " admonishing one another," where a semi-colon should be placed.¶

Note : The *psalmos* denoted that which had a musical accompaniment ; the ōdē (Eng., ode) was the generic term for a song ; hence the accompanying adjective " spiritual."

B. Verb.

HUMNEŌ (ὑμνέω), akin to A, is used (a) transitively, Matt. 26 : 30 ; Mark 14 : 26, where the hymn was that part of the Hallel consisting of Psalms 113-118 ; (b) intransitively, where the verb itself is rendered to sing praises or praise, Acts 16 : 25 ; Heb. 2 : 12. The Psalms are called, in general, " hymns," by Philo ; Josephus calls them " songs and hymns."¶

HYPOCRISY

HUPOKRISIS (ὑπόκρισις) primarily denotes a reply, an answer (akin to *hupokrinomai*, to answer) ; then, play-acting, as the actors spoke in dialogue ; hence, pretence, hypocrisy ; it is translated " hypocrisy " in Matt. 23 : 28 ; Mark 12 : 15 ; Luke 12 : 1 ; 1 Tim. 4 : 2 ; the plural in 1 Pet. 2 : 1. For Gal. 2 : 13 and *anupokritos*, " without hypocrisy," in Jas. 3 : 17, see DISSIMULATION.¶

HYPOCRITE

HUPOKRITĒS (ὑποκριτής), corresponding to the above, primarily denotes one who answers ; then, a stage-actor ; it was a custom for Greek and Roman actors to speak in large masks with mechanical devices for augmenting the force of the voice ; hence the word became used metaphorically of a dissembler, a hypocrite. It is found only in the Synoptists, and always used by the Lord, fifteen times in Matthew ; elsewhere, Mark 7 : 6 ; Luke 6 : 42 ; 11 : 44 (in some mss.) ; 12 : 56 ; 13 : 15.

HYSSOP

HUSSŌPOS (ὕσσωπος), a bunch of which was used in ritual sprinklings, is found in Heb. 9 : 19 ; in John 19 : 29 the reference is apparently to a branch or rod of hyssop, upon which a sponge was put and offered to the Lord on the Cross. The suggestion has been made that the word in the original may have been *hussos*, a javelin ; there seems to be no valid reason for the supposition.¶

I

I

EGŌ (ἐγώ) is the nominative case of the first personal pronoun. The pronoun, " I," however, generally forms a part of the verb itself in Greek ; thus *luō* itself means " I loose," the pronoun being incorporated in the verb form. Where the pronoun *ego* is added to the verb, it is almost invariably, if not entirely, emphatic. The emphasis may not be so apparent in some instances, as e.g., Matt. 10 : 16, but even here it may be taken that something more of stress is present than if the pronoun were omitted. By far the greater number of instances are found in the Gospel of John, and there in the utterances of the Lord concerning Himself, e.g., 4 : 14, 26, 32, 38 ; 5 : 34, 36, 43, 45 ; 6 : 35, 40, 41, 48, 51 (twice), 63, 70 ; instances in the Epistles are Rom. 7 : 9, 14, 17, 20 (twice), 24, 25 ; there are more in that chapter than in any other outside the Gospel of John.

In other cases of the pronoun than the nominative, the pronoun is usually more necessary to the meaning, apart from any stress.

For *k'agō* (i.e., *kai egō*), see EVEN, *Note* (6).

IDLE

ARGOS (ἀργός) denotes inactive, idle, unfruitful, barren (*a*, negative, and *ergon*, work ; cp. the verb *katargeō*, to reduce to inactivity : see ABOLISH) ; it is used (*a*) literally, Matt. 20 : 3, 6 ; 1 Tim. 5 : 13 (twice) ; Tit. 1 : 12, R.V., " idle (gluttons) ; " 2 Pet. 1 : 8, R.V., " idle," A.V., " barren ; " (*b*) metaphorically in the sense of ineffective, worthless, as of a word, Matt. 12 : 36 ; of faith unaccompanied by works, Jas. 2 : 20 (some mss. have *nekra*, dead).¶

For IDLE TALES (Luke 24 : 11, R.V., " idle talk ") see TALK

IDOL

EIDŌLON (εἴδωλον), primarily a phantom or likeness (from *eidos*, an appearance, lit., that which is seen), or an idea, fancy, denotes in the N.T. (*a*) an idol, an image to represent a false god, Acts 7 : 41 ; 1 Cor. 12 : 2 ; Rev. 9 : 20 ; (*b*) the false god worshipped in an image, Acts 15 : 20 ; Rom. 2 : 22 ; 1 Cor. 8 : 4, 7 ; 10 : 19 ; 2 Cor. 6 : 16 ; 1 Thess. 1 : 9 ; 1 John 5 : 21.¶

" The corresponding Heb. word denotes ' vanity,' Jer. 14 : 22 ; 18 : 15 ; ' thing of nought,' Lev. 19 : 4, marg., cp. Eph. 4 : 17. Hence what

represented a deity to the Gentiles, was to Paul a 'vain thing,' Acts 14 :
15 ; 'nothing in the world,' 1 Cor. 8 : 4 ; 10 : 19.   Jeremiah calls the idol a
' scarecrow ' (' pillar in a garden,' 10 : 5, marg.), and Isaiah, 44 : 9-20, etc.,
and Habakkuk, 2 : 18, 19 and the Psalmist, 115 : 4-8, etc., are all equally
scathing.   It is important to notice, however, that in each case the people
of God are addressed.   When he speaks to idolaters, Paul, knowing that
no man is won by ridicule, adopts a different line, Acts 14 : 15-18 ; 17 : 16,
21-31."*

IDOLS (full of)

KATEIDŌLOS (κατείδωλος), an adjective denoting " full of idols "
(kata, throughout, and eidōlon), is said of Athens in Acts 17 : 16, R.V.,
and A.V., marg. (A.V., " wholly given to idolatry ").¶

IDOLS (offered to, sacrificed to)

1. EIDŌLOTHUTOS (εἰδωλόθυτος) is an adjective signifying sacrificed
to idols (eidōlon, as above, and thuō, to sacrifice), Acts 15 : 29 ; 21 : 25 ;
1 Cor. 8 : 1, 4, 7, 10 ; 10 : 19 (in all these the R.V. substitutes " sacrificed "
for the A.V.) ;   Rev. 2 : 14, 20 (in these the R.V. and A.V. both have
" sacrificed ").   Some inferior mss. have this adjective in 1 Cor. 10 : 28 ;
see No. 2.   The flesh of the victims, after sacrifice, was eaten or sold.¶
2. HIEROTHUTOS (ἱερόθυτος), " offered in sacrifice " (hieros, sacred,
and thuō, to sacrifice), is found in the best mss. in 1 Cor. 10 : 28 (see No. 1).¶

IDOL'S TEMPLE

EIDŌLION (or eidōleion) (εἰδώλιον), an idol's temple, is mentioned in
1 Cor. 8 : 10 ;   feasting in the temple usually followed the sacrifice.¶

IDOLATER

EIDŌLOLATRĒS (εἰδωλολάτρης), an idolater (from eidōlon, and
latris, a hireling), is found in 1 Cor. 5 : 10, 11 ; 6 : 9 ; 10 : 7 ; the warning
is to believers against turning away from God to idolatry, whether
" openly or secretly, consciously or unconsciously " (Cremer) ;   Eph.
5 : 5 ;   Rev. 21 : 8 ;   22 : 15.¶

IDOLATRY

EIDŌLOLATRIA (or -EIA) (εἰδωλολατρία), whence Eng., idolatry,
(from eidōlon, and latreia, service), is found in 1 Cor. 10 : 14 ;   Gal. 5 : 20 ;
Col. 3 : 5 ;   and, in the plural, in 1 Pet. 4 : 3.¶
Heathen sacrifices were sacrificed to demons, 1 Cor. 10 : 19 ;   there was
a dire reality in the cup and table of demons and in the involved communion with demons.   In Rom. 1 : 22-25, idolatry, the sin of the mind
against God (Eph. 2 : 3), and immorality, sins of the flesh, are associated,

---

* From Notes on Thessalonians, pp. 44, 45, by Hogg and Vine.

and are traced to lack of the acknowledgment of God and of gratitude to Him. An idolater is a slave to the depraved ideas his idols represent, Gal. 4 : 8, 9 ; and thereby, to divers lusts, Tit. 3 : 3 (see Notes on Thess. by Hogg and Vine, p. 44).

For IDOLATRY (wholly given to) see IDOLS (full of)

IF : See † p. 9.

IGNORANCE, IGNORANT, IGNORANTLY
A. Nouns.

1. AGNOIA (ἄγνοια), lit., want of knowledge or perception (akin to *agnoeō*, to be ignorant), denotes ignorance on the part of the Jews regarding Christ, Acts 3 : 17 ; of Gentiles in regard to God, 17 : 30 ; Eph. 4 : 18 (here including the idea of wilful blindness : see Rom. 1 : 28, not the ignorance which mitigates guilt) ; 1 Pet. 1 : 14, of the former unregenerate condition of those who became believers (R.V., " in *the time of* your ignorance ").¶

2. AGNŌSIA (ἀγνωσία) denotes ignorance as directly opposed to *gnōsis*, which signifies knowledge as a result of observation and experience (*a*, negative, *ginōskō*, to know ; cp. Eng., agnostic) ; 1 Cor. 15 : 34 (" no knowledge ") ; 1 Pet. 2 : 15. In both these passages reprehensible ignorance is suggested. See KNOWLEDGE.¶

3. AGNOĒMA (ἀγνόημα), a sin of ignorance, occurs in Heb. 9 : 7, " errors " (R.V. marg., " ignorances ").¶ For the corresponding verb in Heb. 5 : 2 see B, No. 1. What is especially in view in these passages is unwitting error. For Israel a sacrifice was appointed, greater in proportion to the culpability of the guilty, greater, for instance, for a priest or ruler than for a private person. Sins of ignorance, being sins, must be expiated. A believer guilty of a sin of ignorance needs the efficacy of the expiatory sacrifice of Christ, and finds " grace to help." Yet, as the conscience of the believer receives enlightenment, what formerly may have been done in ignorance becomes a sin against the light and demands a special confession, to receive forgiveness, 1 John 1 : 8, 9.¶

4. IDIŌTĒS (ἰδιώτης), primarily a private person in contrast to a State official, hence, a person without professional knowledge, unskilled, uneducated, unlearned, is translated " unlearned " in 1 Cor. 14 : 16, 23, 24, of those who have no knowledge of the facts relating to the testimony borne in and by a local church ; " rude " in 2 Cor. 11 : 6, of the Apostle's mode of speech in the estimation of the Corinthians ; " ignorant men," in Acts 4 : 13, of the speech of the Apostle Peter and John in the estimation of the rulers, elders and scribes in Jerusalem.

While *agrammatoi* (" unlearned ") may refer to their being unacquainted with Rabbinical learning, *idiōtai* would signify ' laymen,' in contrast with the religious officials. See RUDE, UNLEARNED.¶

B. Verbs.

1. AGNOEŌ (ἀγνοέω), signifies (a) to be ignorant, not to know, either intransitively, 1 Cor. 14 : 38 (in the 2nd occurrence in this verse, the R.V. text translates the Active Voice, the margin the Passive) ; 1 Tim. 1 : 13, lit., ' being ignorant (I did it) ; ' Heb. 5 : 2, " ignorant ; " or transitively, 2 Pet. 2 : 12, A.V., " understand not," R.V., " are ignorant (of) ; " Acts 13 : 27, " knew (Him) not ; " 17 : 23, R.V., " (what ye worship) in ignorance," for A.V., "(whom ye) ignorantly (worship)," lit., '(what) not knowing (ye worship) ; ' also rendered by the verb to be ignorant that, or to be ignorant of, Rom. 1 : 13 ; 10 : 3 ; 11 : 25 ; 1 Cor. 10 : 1 ; 12 : 1 ; 2 Cor. 1 : 8 ; 2 : 11 ; 1 Thess 4 : 13 ; to know not, Rom. 2 : 4 ; 6 : 3 ; 7 : 1 ; to be unknown (Passive Voice), 2 Cor. 6 : 9 ; Gal. 1 : 22 ; (b) not to understand, Mark 9 : 32 ; Luke 9 : 45. See KNOW, UNDERSTAND.¶

2. LANTHANŌ (λανθάνω) ; for 2 Pet. 3 : 5, 8, A.V., see FORGET.

Note : For adjectives see UNLEARNED.

ILL

KAKOS (κακός), bad, is used in the neuter as a noun in Rom. 13 : 10, and translated " ill." See BAD.

Note : For *phaulos*, John 5 : 29, R.V., see EVIL, A, No. 3.

For ILLUMINATED (Heb. 10 : 32) see ENLIGHTEN

IMAGE

1. EIKŌN (εἰκών) denotes an image ; the word involves the two ideas of representation and manifestation. " The idea of perfection does not lie in the word itself, but must be sought from the context " (Lightfoot) ; the following instances clearly show any distinction between the imperfect and the perfect likeness.

The word is used (1) of an image or a coin (not a mere likeness), Matt. 22 : 20 ; Mark 12 : 16 ; Luke 20 : 24 ; so of a statue or similar represent tion (more than a resemblance), Rom. 1 : 23 ; Rev. 13 : 14, 15 (thrice) ; 14 : 9, 11 ; 15 : 2 ; 16 : 2 ; 19 : 20 ; 20 : 4 ; of the descendants of Adam as bearing his image, 1 Cor. 15 : 49, each a representation derived from the prototype ; (2) of subjects relative to things spiritual, Heb. 10 : 1, negatively of the Law as having " a shadow of the good things to come, not the very image of the things," i.e., not the essential and substantial form of them ; the contrast has been likened to the difference between a statue and the shadow cast by it ; (3) of the relations between God the Father, Christ, and man, (a) of man as he was created as being a visible representation of God, 1 Cor. 11 : 7, a being corresponding to the Original ; the condition of man as a fallen creature has not entirely effaced the image ; he is still suitable to bear responsibility, he still has Godlike qualities, such as love of goodness and beauty, none of which are found in a mere animal ; in the Fall man ceased to be a perfect vehicle for the representation of God ; God's grace in Christ will yet accomplish more than what Adam lost ; (*b*) of regenerate persons, in being moral representations of what God is, Col. 3 : 10 ; cp. Eph. 4 : 24 ; (c) of believers, in their glorified state, not merely as resembling Christ but representing Him, Rom. 8 : 29 ; 1 Cor. 15 : 49 ; here the perfection is the work of Divine grace ; believers are yet to represent, not something like Him, but what He is in Himself, both in His spiritual body and in His moral character ; (*d*) of Christ in relation to God, 2 Cor. 4 : 4, " the image of God," i.e., essentially and absolutely the perfect expression and representation of the Archetype, God the Father ; in Col. 1 : 15, " the image of the invisible God " gives the additional thought suggested by the word " invisible," that Christ is the visible representation and manifestation of God to created beings ; the likeness expressed in this manifestation is involved in the essential relations in the Godhead, and is therefore unique and perfect ; " he that hath seen Me hath seen the Father," John 14 : 9. " The epithet ' invisible ' . . . must not be confined to the apprehension of the bodily senses, but will include the cognisance of the inward eye also " (Lightfoot).¶

As to synonymous words, *homoiōma*, likeness, stresses the resemblance to an archetype, though the resemblance may not be derived, whereas *eikōn* is a derived likeness (see LIKENESS) ; *eidos*, a shape, form, is an appearance, " not necessarily based on reality " (see FORM) ; *skia*, is " a shadowed resemblance " (see SHADOW) ; *morphē* is " the form, as indicative of the inner being " (Abbott-Smith) ; see FORM. For *charaktēr*, see No. 2.

2. CHARAKTĒR (χαρακτήρ) denotes, firstly, a tool for graving (from *charassō*, to cut into, to engross ; cp. Eng., character, characteristic) ; then, a stamp or impress, as on a coin or a seal, in which case the seal or die which makes an impression bears the image produced by it, and, *vice versa*, all the features of the image correspond respectively with those of the instrument producing it. In the N.T. it is used metaphorically in Heb. 1 : 3, of the Son of God as " the very image (marg., ' the impress ') of His substance," R.V. The phrase expresses the fact that the Son " is both personally distinct from, and yet literally equal to, Him of whose essence He is the adequate imprint " (Liddon). The Son of God is not merely his image (His *charaktēr*), He is the image or impress of His substance, or essence. It is the fact of complete similarity which this word stresses in comparison with those mentioned at the end of No. 1.¶ In the Sept., Lev. 13 : 28, ' the mark (of the inflammation).'¶

" In John 1 : 1–3, Col. 1 : 15–17, and Heb. 1 : 2, 3, the special function of creating and upholding the universe is ascribed to Christ under His titles of Word, Image, and Son, respectively. The kind of Creatorship so predicated of Him is not that of a mere instrument or artificer in the formation of the world, but that of One ' by whom, in whom, and for whom ' all things are made, and through whom they subsist. This implies the assertion of His true and absolute Godhood " (Laidlaw, in Hastings' Bib. Dic.).

Note : The similar word *charagma*, a mark (see GRAVEN and MARK), has the narrower meaning of the thing impressed, without denoting the special characteristic of that which produces it, e.g., Rev. 13 : 16, 17. In Acts 17 : 29 the meaning is not " graven (*charagma*) by art," but 'an engraved work of art.'

IMAGINATION

1. LOGISMOS (λογισμός), a reasoning, a thought (akin to *logizomai*, to count, reckon), is translated " thoughts " in Rom. 2 : 15, suggestive of evil intent, not of mere reasonings ; " imaginations " in 2 Cor. 10 : 5 (R.V., marg., " reasonings," in each place). The word suggests the contemplation of actions as a result of the verdict of conscience. See THOUGHT.¶

2. DIALOGISMOS (διαλογισμός), dia, and No. 1, is rendered " imaginations " in Rom. 1 : 21, carrying with it the idea of evil purposes, R.V., " reasonings "; it is most frequently translated " thoughts." See DISPUTE.

3. DIANOIA (διάνοια), strictly, a thinking over, denotes the faculty of thinking ; then, of knowing ; hence, the understanding, and in general, the mind, and so, the faculty of moral reflection ; it is rendered " imagination " in Luke 1 : 51, " the imagination of their heart " signifying their thoughts and ideas. See MIND, UNDERSTANDING.

IMAGINE

MELETAŌ (μελετάω) signifies to care for (*meletē*, care) ; then, to attend to, " be diligent in," 1 Tim. 4 : 15, R.V., i.e., to practise as the result of devising or planning ; thirdly, to ponder, " imagine," Acts 4 : 25, R.V., marg., " meditate." Some inferior mss. have it in Mark 13 : 11. See DILIGENT, MEDITATE.¶

IMITATE, IMITATOR
A. Verb.

MIMEOMAI (μιμέομαι), a mimic, an actor (Eng., mime, etc.), is always translated to imitate in the R.V., for A.V., to follow, (*a*) of imitating the conduct of missionaries, 2 Thess. 3 : 7, 9; the faith of spiritual guides, Heb. 13 : 7 ; (*b*) that which is good, 3 John 11. The verb is always used in exhortations, and always in the continuous tense, suggesting a constant habit or practice. See FOLLOW.

B. Nouns.

1 MIMĒTĒS (μιμητής), akin to A, an imitator, so the R.V. for A.V., " follower," is always used in a good sense in the N.T. In 1 Cor. 4 : 16 ; 11 : 1 ; Eph. 5 : 1 ; Heb. 6 : 12, it is used in exhortations, accompanied

by the verb *ginomai*, to be, become, and in the continuous tense (see A) except in Heb. 6 : 12, where the aorist or momentary tense indicates a decisive act with permanent results ; in 1 Thess. 1 : 6 ; 2 : 14, the accompanying verb is in the aorist tense, referring to the definite act of conversion in the past. These instances, coupled with the continuous tenses referred to, teach that what we became at conversion we must diligently continue to be thereafter. See FOLLOW, *Note* (4).¶

2. SUMMIMĒTĒS (συμμιμητής) denotes a fellow-imitator (*sun*, with, and No. 1), Phil. 3 : 17, R.V., " imitators together " (A.V., " followers together "). See FOLLOW, *Note* (4).¶

IMMEDIATELY

1. PARACHRĒMA (παραχρῆμα), lit., with the matter (or business) itself (*para*, with, *chrēma*, a business, or event), and so, immediately, Matt. 21 : 19 (A.V., " presently "), 20 ; Luke 1 : 64 ; 4 : 39 ; 5 : 25 ; 8 : 44, 47, 55 ; 13 : 13 ; 18 : 43 ; 19 : 11 ; 22 : 60 ; Acts 3 : 7 ; 5 : 10 ; 12 : 23 ; 13 : 11 ; 16 : 26, 33 ; it is thus used by Luke only, save for the two instances in Matthew. See FORTHWITH. It is also rendered " presently," " soon," " straightway."¶

2. EUTHUS (εὐθύς) : see FORTHWITH.

3. EUTHEŌS (εὐθέως) : ditto.

4. EXAUTĒS (ἐξαυτῆς) : ditto.

IMMORTAL, IMMORTALITY

ATHANASIA (ἀθανασία), lit., deathlessness (*a*, negative, *thanatos*, death), is rendered " immortality " in 1 Cor. 15 : 53, 54, of the glorified body of the believer ; 1 Tim. 6 : 16, of the nature of God. Moulton and Milligan (Vocab.) show that in early times the word had the wide connotation of freedom from death ; they also quote Ramsay (*Luke the Physician*, p. 273), with reference to the use of the word in sepulchral epitaphs. In a papyrus writing of the sixth century, " a petitioner says that he will send up ' unceasing (*athanatous*) ' hymns to the Lord Christ for the life of the man with whom he is pleading." In the N.T., however, *athanasia* expresses more than deathlessness, it suggests the quality of the life enjoyed, as is clear from 2 Cor. 5 : 4 ; for the believer what is mortal is to be " swallowed up of life."¶

Note : The adjective *aphthartos*, translated " immortal " in 1 Tim. 1 : 17, A.V., does not bear that significance, it means ' incorruptible.' So with the noun *aphtharsia*, incorruption, translated " immortality," in the A.V. of Rom. 2 : 7 and 2 Tim. 1 : 10. See CORRUPT, B, No. 3, and C, No. 2.

IMMUTABLE, IMMUTABILITY

AMETATHETOS (ἀμετάθετος), an adjective signifying immutable (*a*, negative, *metatithēmi*, to change), Heb. 6 : 18, where the " two immutable things " are the promise and the oath. In ver. 17 the word is

used in the neuter with the article, as a noun, denoting " the immutability," with reference to God's counsel. Examples from the papyri
show that the word was used as a technical term in connection with wills,
" The connotation adds considerably to the force of Heb. 6 : 17 (and foll.) "
(Moulton and Milligan).¶

IMPART

1. PROSANATITHĒMI (προσανατίθημι) is used in the Middle Voice
in the N.T., in Gal. 1 : 16, " conferred," or ' had recourse to,' and 2 : 6,
R.V., " imparted." See CONFER.¶

2. METADIDŌMI (μεταδίδωμι) : see GIVE, No. 4.

IMPEDIMENT

MOGILALOS (μογιλάλος) denotes speaking with difficulty (mogis,
hardly, laleō, to talk), stammering, Mark 7 : 32 ; some mss. have mog-
gilalos, thick-voiced (from moggos, with a hoarse, hollow voice).¶ In the
Sept., Isa. 35 : 6 " (the tongue) of stammerers."¶

IMPENITENT

AMETANOĒTOS (ἀμετανόητος), lit., without change of mind (a,
negative, metanoeō, to change one's mind, meta, signifying change, nous,
the mind), is used in Rom. 2 : 5, " impenitent " (or ' unrepentant ').¶
Moulton and Milligan show from the papyri writings that the word is
also used " in a passive sense, ' not affected by change of mind,' like
ametamelētos in Rom. 11 : 29," " without repentance."

IMPLACABLE

ASPONDOS (ἄσπονδος) lit. denotes without a libation (a, negative,
spondē, a libation), i.e., without a truce, as a libation accompanied the
making of treaties and compacts ; then, one who cannot be persuaded to
enter into a covenant, " implacable," 2 Tim. 3 : 3 (A.V., " truce-breakers ").
Some mss. have this word in Rom. 1 : 31.¶

Note : Trench (Syn., § lii) contrasts aspondos with asunthetos ; see
Note under COVENANT-BREAKERS. Aspondos may signify untrue to one's
promise, asunthetos not abiding by one's covenant, treacherous.

For IMPLEAD see ACCUSE, B, No. 2

IMPLANTED

EMPHUTOS (ἔμφυτος), implanted, or rooted (from emphuō, to
implant), is used in Jas. 1 : 21, R.V., " implanted," for A.V., " engrafted,"
of the word of God, " as the ' rooted word,' i.e., a word whose property
it is to root itself like a seed in the heart. " The A.V. seems to identify
it with emphuteuton, which however would be out of place here, since the
word is sown, not grafted, in the heart " (Mayor).¶

IMPORTUNITY

ANAIDIA (or ANAIDEIA) (ἀναιδία) denotes shamelessness, importunity (a, negative, n, euphonic, and aidōs, shame, modesty), and is used in the Lord's illustration concerning the need of earnestness and perseverance in prayer, Luke 11 : 8. If shameless persistence can obtain a boon from a neighbour, then certainly earnest prayer will receive our Father's answer.¶

IMPOSED

EPIKEIMAI (ἐπίκειμαι) denotes to be placed on, to lie on, (a) literally, as of the stone on the sepulchre of Lazarus, John 11 : 38 ; of the fish on the fire of coals, 21 : 9 ; (b) figuratively, of a tempest (to press upon), Acts 27 : 20 ; of a necessity laid upon the Apostle Paul, 1 Cor. 9 : 16 ; of the pressure of the multitude upon Christ to hear Him, Luke 5 : 1, " pressed upon ; " of the insistence of the chief priests, rulers and people that Christ should be crucified, Luke 23 : 23, " were instant ; " of carnal ordinances " imposed " under the Law until a time of reformation, brought in through the High-Priesthood of Christ, Heb. 9 : 10. See INSTANT, LIE, PRESS.¶

IMPOSSIBLE
A. Adjectives.

1. ADUNATOS (ἀδύνατος), from a, negative, and dunatos, able, strong, is used (a) of persons, Acts 14 : 8, " impotent ; " figuratively, Rom. 15 : 1, " weak ; " (b) of things, " impossible," Matt. 19 : 26 ; Mark 10 : 27 ; Luke 18 : 27 ; Heb. 6 : 4, 18 ; 10 : 4 ; 11 : 6 ; in Rom. 8 : 3, " for what the Law could not do," is, more lit., ' the inability of the law ; ' the meaning may be either ' the weakness of the Law,' or ' that which was impossible for the Law ; ' the latter is perhaps preferable ; literalism is ruled out here, but the sense is that the Law could neither justify nor impart life.¶

2. ANENDEKTOS (ἀνένδεκτος) signifies inadmissible (a, negative, n, euphonic, and endechomai, to admit, allow), Luke 17 : 1, of occasions of stumbling, where the meaning is ' it cannot be but that they will come.'¶
B. Verb.

ADUNATEŌ (ἀδυνατέω) signifies to be impossible (corresponding to A, No. 1), unable ; in the N.T. it is used only of things, Matt. 17 : 20, " (nothing) shall be impossible (unto you) ; " Luke 1 : 37, A.V. " (with God nothing) shall be impossible ; " R.V., " (no word from God—a different construction in the best mss.) shall be void of power ; " rhēma may mean either " word " or " thing " (i.e., fact).¶ In the Sept. the verb is always used of things and signifies either to be impossible or to be impotent, e.g., Gen. 18 : 14 ; Lev. 25 : 35, " he fail ; " Deut. 17 : 8 ; Job 4 : 4, " feeble ; " 42 : 2 ; Dan. 4 : 6 ; Zech. 8 : 6.

IMPOSTORS

GOĒS (γόης) primarily denotes a wailer (goaō, to wail) ; hence, from the howl in which spells were chanted, a wizard, sorcerer, enchanter, and hence, a juggler, cheat, impostor, rendered " impostors " in 2 Tim. 3 : 13, R.V. (A.V., " seducers ") ; possibly the false teachers referred to practised magical arts ; cp. ver. 8.¶

IMPOTENT
A. Adjectives.

1. ADUNATOS (ἀδύνατος) : see IMPOSSIBLE, A, No. 1.
2. ASTHENĒS (ἀσθενής), without strength (a, negative, sthenos, strength), is translated " impotent " in Acts 4 : 9. See FEEBLE, SICK, WEAK.

B. Verb.

ASTHENEŌ (ἀσθενέω), to be without strength (akin to A, No. 2), is translated " impotent folk " in John 5 : 3, A.V. ; cp. ver. 7 (the present participle, lit., ' being impotent '). See DISEASED, SICK, WEAK.

IMPRISON, IMPRISONMENT
A. Verb.

PHULAKIZŌ (φυλακίζω), to imprison, akin to phulax, a guard, a keeper, and phulassō, to guard, and B, below, is used in Acts 22 : 19.¶

B. Noun.

PHULAKĒ (φυλακή), besides its other meanings, denotes imprisonment, in 2 Cor. 6 : 5 (plural) and Heb. 11 : 36. See CAGE.

IMPULSE

HORMĒ (ὁρμή) denotes (a) an impulse or violent motion, as of the steersman of a vessel, Jas. 3 : 4, R.V., " impulse " (A.V. omits) ; (b) an assault, onset, Acts 14 : 5. See ASSAULT.¶

IMPUTE

1. LOGIZOMAI (λογίζομαι), to reckon, take into account, or, metaphorically, to put down to a person's account, is never rendered in the R.V. by the verb to impute. In the following, where the A.V. has that rendering, the R.V. uses the verb to reckon, which is far more suitable ; Rom. 4 : 6, 8, 11, 22, 23, 24 ; 2 Cor. 5 : 19 ; Jas. 2 : 23. See ACCOUNT, and especially, in the above respect, RECKON.

2. ELLOGAŌ, or -EŌ (ἐλλογάω) (the -ao termination is the one found in the Koinē, the language covering the N.T. period), denotes to charge to one's account, to lay to one's charge, and is translated " imputed " in Rom. 5 : 13, of sin as not being " imputed when there is no law." This principle is there applied to the fact that between Adam's transgression and the giving of the Law at Sinai, sin, though it was in the world, did not partake of the character of transgression ; for there was no law.

The law of conscience existed, but that is not in view in the passage, which deals with the fact of external commandments given by God.   In Philm. 18 the verb is rendered " put (that) to (mine) account." See ACCOUNT.¶

IN : See † p. 9.

INASMUCH AS

1. KATHO (καθό), lit., according to what (kata, according to, and ho, the neuter of the relative pronoun), is translated " inasmuch as " in 1 Pet. 4 : 13, A.V. (R.V., " insomuch as ") ; in Rom. 8 : 26, " as (we ought) ; " in 2 Cor. 8 : 12, R.V., " according as " (A.V., " according to that ").   See INSOMUCH.¶

2. EPH'HOSON (ἐφ'ὅσον), lit., upon how much (epi, upon, hosos, how much), is translated " inasmuch as " in Matt. 25 : 40, 45 ; Rom. 11 : 13.¶

3. KATHOTI (καθότι) : see·ACCORDING AS, No. 1.

4. KATH' HOSON (καθ' ὅσον), kata, according to, and hosos, how much, is translated " inasmuch as " in Heb. 3 : 3, A.V. (R.V., " by so much as ") ; 7 : 20 ; 9 : 27, R.V. (A.V., " as ").

Note : In Phil. 1 : 7, the phrase " inasmuch as " translates the present participle of the verb eimi, to be, lit., ' (ye) being (all partakers).'

INCENSE (burn)
A. Noun.

THUMIAMA (θυμίαμα) denotes fragrant stuff for burning, incense (from thuō, to offer in sacrifice), Luke 1 : 10, 11 ; in the plural, Rev. 5 : 8 and 18 : 13, R.V. (A.V., " odours ") ; 8 : 3, 4, signifying frankincense here. In connection with the Tabernacle, the incense was to be prepared from stacte, onycha, and galbanum, with pure frankincense, an equal weight of each ; imitation for private use was forbidden, Ex. 30 : 34–38. See ODOUR.¶ Cp. thumiatērion, a censer, Heb. 9 : 4, and libanos, frank-incense, Rev. 18 : 13 ; see FRANKINCENSE.¶

B. Verb.

THUMIAŌ (θυμιάω), to burn incense (see A), is found in Luke 1 : 9.¶

INCLOSE

SUNKLEIŌ (συγκλείω), to shut together, shut in on all sides (sun, with, kleiō, to shut), is used of a catch of fish, Luke 5 : 6 ; metaphorically in Rom. 11 : 32, of God's dealings with Jew and Gentile, in that He has " shut up (A.V., concluded) all unto disobedience, that He might have mercy upon all."   There is no intimation in this of universal salvation. The meaning, from the context, is that God has ordered that all should be convicted of disobedience without escape by human merit, that He might display His mercy, and has offered the Gospel without national distinction, and that when Israel is restored, He will, in the resulting Millennium, show

His mercy to all nations. The word " all " with reference to Israel, is to be viewed in the light of ver. 26, and, in reference to the Gentiles, in the light of verses 12–25 ; in Gal. 3 : 22, 23 (" the Scripture hath shut up all things under sin "), the Apostle shows that, by the impossibility of being justified by keeping the Law, all, Jew and Gentile, are under sin, so that righteousness might be reckoned to all who believe. See CONCLUDE, SHUT.¶

INCONTINENCY, INCONTINENT
A. Noun.

AKRASIA (ἀκρασία) denotes want of power (a, negative, kratos, power) ; hence, want of self-control, incontinency, 1 Cor. 7 : 5 ; in Matt. 23 : 25, " excess." See EXCESS.¶

B. Adjective.

AKRATĒS (ἀκρατής) denotes powerless, impotent ; in a moral sense, unrestrained, " without self-control," 2 Tim. 3 : 3, R.V. (A.V., " incontinent "). See SELF-CONTROL.¶

For INCORRUPTIBLE and INCORRUPTION, see under CORRUPT

For the noun INCREASE, see GROW, No. 1, Note

INCREASE (Verb)

1. AUXANŌ (αὐξάνω) : see GROW, No. 1.

2. PERISSEUŌ (περισσεύω), to be over and above, to abound, is translated " increased " in Acts 16 : 5, of churches ; " increase " in the A.V. of 1 Thess. 4 : 10 (R.V., " abound "). See ABOUND, under ABUNDANCE, B, No. 1.

3. PLEONAZO (πλεονάζω), to make to abound, is translated " make (you) to increase " in 1 Thess. 3 : 12, with No. 2. See ABUNDANCE, B, No. 3.

4. PROKOPTŌ (προκόπτω) is translated by the verb to increase in Luke 2 : 52 and in the A.V. of 2 Tim. 2 : 16 (R.V., " will proceed further "). See ADVANCE, PROCEED.

5. PROSTITHĒMI (προστίθημι), to put to, add to, is translated " increase " in Luke 17 : 5. See ADD, No. 2.

Note : For " increased in strength " see STRENGTH.

INCREDIBLE

APISTOS (ἄπιστος) is once rendered " incredible," Acts 26 : 8, of the doctrine of resurrection ; elsewhere it is used of persons, with the meaning unbelieving. See BELIEF, C, *Note* (3).

INDEBTED (to be)

OPHEILŌ (ὀφείλω), to owe, to be a debtor, is translated " is indebted " in Luke 11 : 4. Luke does not draw a parallel between our forgiving and God's ; he speaks of God's forgiving sins, of our forgiving debts, moral debts, probably not excluding material debts.   Matthew speaks of our sins as *opheilēmata*, debts, and uses parallel terms.   Ellicott and others suggest that Luke used a term more adapted to the minds of Gentile readers. The inspired language provides us with both, as intended by the Lord.

INDEED

1. MEN (μέν), a conjunctive particle (originally a form of *mēn*, verily, truly, found in Heb. 6 : 14.¶), usually related to an adversative conjunction or particle, like *de*, in the following clause, which is placed in opposition to it.   Frequently it is untranslateable ; sometimes it is rendered " indeed," e.g., Matt. 3 : 11 ;   13 : 32 ;   17 : 11, R.V. (A.V., " truly ") ; 20 : 23 ;   26 : 41 ;   (some mss. have it in Mark 1 : 8) ;   Mark 9 : 12, R.V. (A.V., " verily ").

2. ALĒTHĒS (ἀληθής), true, is rendered " indeed " in John 6 : 55 (twice), see R.V. marg. ;   some mss. have No. 3 here.

3. ALĒTHŌS (ἀληθῶς), truly (from No. 2), is translated " indeed " in John 1 : 47 ;   4 : 42 ;   8 : 31.

4. ONTŌS (ὄντως), an adverb from *ōn*, the present participle of *eimi*, to be, denotes really, actually ;   it is translated " indeed " in Mark 11 : 32 (R.V., " verily ") ;   Luke 24 : 34 ;   John 8 : 36 ;   1 Cor. 14 : 25, R.V. (A.V., " of a truth ") ;   1 Tim. 5 : 3, 5, 16 ; 6 : 19, R.V., where some mss. have *aiōnios*, " eternal " (A.V.) ;   in Gal. 3 : 21, " verily."

5. KAI GAR (καὶ γάρ) signifies ' and in fact,' ' for also ' (*kai*, and, or even, or also ;   *gar*, for ;   *gar*, always comes after the first word in the sentence) ;   it is translated " For indeed " in the R.V. of Acts 19 : 40 ; 2 Cor. 5 : 4 ;   1 Thess. 4 : 10 (A.V., " And indeed ") ;   A.V. and R.V. in Phil. 2 : 27.   This phrase has a confirmatory sense, rather than a modifying effect, e.g., Matt. 15 : 27, R.V., " for even," instead of the A.V. " yet ; "   the woman confirms that her own position as a Gentile ' dog ' brings privilege, ' for indeed the dogs, etc.'

6. OUDE GAR (οὐδὲ γάρ), for neither, is rendered " neither indeed " in Rom. 8 : 7.

7. ALLA KAI (ἀλλὰ καί), but even, or but also, is rendered " nay indeed " in 2 Cor. 11 : 1, R.V. (A.V., " and indeed ; " R.V. marg., " but indeed ").

8. KAI (καί), preceded by the particle *ge*, ' at least,' ' ever,' is rendered " indeed " in Gal. 3 : 4, R.V. (A.V., " yet "). *Kai* alone is rendered " indeed " in Phil. 4 : 10, R.V. (A.V., " also ").

9. EI MĒTI (εἰ μήτι), if not indeed, is rendered " unless indeed " in 2 Cor. 13 : 5, R.V. (A.V., " except ").

INDIGNATION
A. Noun.

AGANAKTĒSIS (ἀγανάκτησις) is rendered " indignation " in 2 Cor. 7 : 11.   See ANGER, A, Note (3).¶

Notes : (1) *Orgē*, wrath, is translated " indignation " in Rev. 14 : 10, A.V. ; R.V., " anger." See ANGER, A, No. 1. (2) For *thumos*, see ANGER, A, Notes (1) and (2). (3) In Acts 5 : 17, the A.V. translates *zēlos* by " indignation " (R.V. " jealousy ") ; in Heb. 10 : 27, A.V., " indignation " (R.V., " fierceness ; " marg., " jealousy "). See JEALOUSY.

B. Verb.

AGANAKTEŌ (ἀγανακτέω), to be indignant, to be moved with indignation (from *agan*, much, *achomai*, to grieve), is translated " were moved with indignation " of the ten disciples against James and John, Matt. 20 : 24 ; in Mark 10 : 41, R.V. (A.V., " they began to be much displeased ") ; in Matt. 21 : 15, of the chief priests and scribes, against Christ and the children, R.V., " they were moved with indignation " (A.V., " they were sore displeased ") ; in 26 : 8, of the disciples against the woman who anointed Christ's feet, " they had indignation ; " so Mark 14 : 4 ; in Mark 10 : 14, of Christ, against the disciples, for rebuking the children, " He was moved with indignation," R.V. (A.V., " he was much displeased ") ; in Luke 13 : 14, of the ruler of the synagogue against Christ for healing on the Sabbath, " being moved with indignation," R.V., A.V., " (answered) with indignation." See ANGER, B, Note (3).¶

INDULGENCE

1. ANESIS (ἄνεσις), a loosening, relaxation of strain (akin to *aniēmi*, to relax, loosen), is translated " indulgence " in Acts 24 : 23, R.V. (A.V., " liberty "), in the command of Felix to the centurion, to moderate restrictions upon Paul. The papyri and inscriptions illustrate the use of the word as denoting relief (Moulton and Milligan, Vocab.) In the N.T. it always carries the thought of relief from tribulation or persecution ; so 2 Thess. 1 : 7, " rest " ; in 2 Cor. 2 : 13 and 7 : 5 it is rendered " relief," R.V. (A.V., " rest ") ; in 8 : 13, " eased." Josephus speaks of the rest or relief (*anesis*) from ploughing and tillage, given to the land in the year of Jubilee. See EASE, LIBERTY, RELIEF, REST.¶

2. PLĒSMONĒ (πλησμονή), a filling up, satiety (akin to *pimplēmi*, to fill), is translated " indulgence (of the flesh) " in Col. 2 : 23, R.V. (A.V., " satisfying "). Lightfoot translates the passage " yet not really of any value to remedy indulgence of the flesh." A possible meaning is, ' of no value in attempts at asceticism.' Some regard it as indicating that the ascetic treatment of the body is not of any honour to the satisfaction of the flesh (the reasonable demands of the body) : this interpretation is unlikely. The following paraphrase well presents the contrast between the asceticism which " practically treats the body as an enemy, and the Pauline view which treats it as a potential instrument of a righteous life : " ordinances, ' which in fact have a specious look of wisdom (where there is no true wisdom), by the employment of self-chosen acts of religion and humility (and) by treating the body with brutality instead of treating it

with due respect, with a view to meeting and providing against over-indulgence of the flesh' (Parry, in the Camb. Greek Test.).¶

For INEXCUSABLE see EXCUSE

For INFALLIBLE see PROOF

For INFANT see BABE

INFERIOR

HĒTTAOMAI, or HĒSSAOMAI (ἡττάομαι), to be less or inferior, is used in the Passive Voice, and translated "ye were made inferior," in 2 Cor. 12 : 13, R.V., for A.V., " ye were inferior," i.e., were treated with less consideration than other churches, through his independence in not receiving gifts from them. In 2 Pet. 2 : 19, 20 it signifies to be over-come, in the sense of being subdued and enslaved. See OVERCOME.¶ Cp. hēssōn, less, 2 Cor. 12 : 15; in 1 Cor. 11 : 17, "worse;"¶ hēttēma, a loss, a spiritual defect, Rom. 11 : 12; 1 Cor. 6 : 7.¶ Also elattoō, to decrease, make lower, John 3 : 30; Heb. 2 : 7, 9.¶

For INFIDEL (R.V., UNBELIEVER), see BELIEF, C. Note (3)

INFIRMITY

1. ASTHENEIA (ἀσθένεια), lit., want of strength (a, negative, sthenos, strength), weakness, indicating inability to produce results, is most frequently translated "infirmity," or "infirmities;" in Rom. 8 : 26, the R.V. has "infirmity" (A.V., "infirmities"); in 2 Cor. 12 : 5, 9, 10, "weaknesses" and in 11 : 30, "weakness" (A.V., "infirmities"); in Luke 13 : 11 the phrase "a spirit of infirmity" attributes her curvature directly to Satanic agency. The connected phraseology is indicative of trained medical knowledge on the part of the writer.

2. ASTHENĒMA (ἀσθένημα), akin to No. 1, is found in the plural in Rom. 15 : 1, "infirmities," i.e., those scruples which arise through weak-ness of faith. The strong must support the infirmities of the weak (adunatos) by submitting to self-restraint.¶

Note : In Luke 7 : 21, A.V., nosos, a disease, is translated "infirmities" (R.V., "diseases").

INFLICTED

Note : This is inserted in 2 Cor. 2 : 6 to complete the sentence; there is no corresponding word in the original, which lit. reads 'this punish-ment, the (one) by the majority.'

INFORM

1. EMPHANIZŌ (ἐμφανίζω), to manifest, exhibit, in the Middle and

Passive Voices, to appear, also signifies to declare, make known, and is translated " informed " in Acts 24 : 1 ; 25 : 2, 15. For all the occurrences of the word see APPEAR, A, No. 5.

2. KATĒCHEŌ (κατηχέω) primarily denotes to resound (kata, down, ēchos, a sound) ; then, to sound down the ears, to teach by word of mouth, instruct, inform (Eng., catechize, catechumen) ; it is rendered, in the Passive Voice, by the verb to inform, in Acts 21 : 21, 24. Here it is used of the large numbers of Jewish believers at Jerusalem whose zeal for the Law had been stirred by information of accusations made against the Apostle Paul, as to certain anti-Mosaic teaching he was supposed to have given the Jews. See INSTRUCT, TEACH.

For INHABITANTS, INHABITERS, see DWELL, A, No. 2

INHERIT, INHERITANCE
A. Verbs.

1. KLĒRONOMEŌ (κληρονομέω) strictly means to receive by lot (klēros, a lot, nemomai, to possess) ; then, in a more general sense, to possess oneself of, to receive as one's own, to obtain. The following list shows how in the N.T. the idea of inheriting broadens out to include all spiritual good provided through and in Christ, and particularly all that is contained in the hope grounded on the promises of God.

The verb is used of the following objects :

" (a) birthright, that into the possession of which one enters in virtue of sonship, not because of a price paid or of a task accomplished, Gal. 4 : 30 ; Heb. 1 : 4 ; 12 : 17 :

(b) that which is received as a gift, in contrast with that which is received as the reward of law-keeping, Heb. 1 : 14 ; 6 : 12 (' through,' i.e., ' through experiences that called for the exercise of faith and patience,' but not ' on the ground of the exercise of faith and patience.') :

(c) that which is received on condition of obedience to certain precepts, 1 Pet. 3 : 9, and of faithfulness to God amidst opposition Rev. 21 : 7 :

(d) the reward of that condition of soul which forbears retaliation and self-vindication, and expresses itself in gentleness of behaviour . . ., Matt. 5 : 5. The phrase " inherit the earth," or " land," occurs several times in O.T. See especially Psa. 37 : 11, 22 :

(e) the reward (in the coming age, Mark 10 : 30) of the acknowledgment of the paramountcy of the claims of Christ, Matt. 19 : 29. In the three accounts given of this incident, see Mark 10 : 17–31, Luke 18 : 18–30, the words of the question put to the Lord are, in Matthew, ' that I may have,' in Mark and Luke, ' that I may inherit.' In the report of the Lord's word to Peter in reply to his subsequent question, Matthew has ' inherit eternal life,' while Mark and Luke have ' receive eternal life.' It seems to follow that the meaning of the word ' inherit ' is here ruled by the words ' receive ' and ' have,' with which it is interchanged in each of the three Gospels, i.e., the less common word ' inherit ' is to be regarded as equivalent to the more common words ' receive ' and ' have.' Cp. Luke 10 : 25 :

(*f*) the reward of those who have shown kindness to the ' brethren ' of the Lord in their distress, Matt. 25 : 34 :

(*g*) the Kingdom of God, which the morally corrupt cannot inherit, 1 Cor. 6 : 9, 10, the inheritance of which is likewise impossible to the present physical constitution of man, 1 Cor. 15 : 50 :

(*h*) incorruption, impossible of inheritance by corruption, 1 Cor. 15 : 50."*

See HEIR.¶

Note : In regard to (*e*), the word clearly signifies entrance into eternal life without any previous title ; it will not bear the implication that a child of God may be divested of his inheritance by the loss of his right of succession.

2. KLĒROŌ (κληρόω) is used in the Passive Voice in Eph. 1 : 11, A.V., " we have obtained an inheritance ; " R.V., " we were made a heritage." See HERITAGE.¶

B. Nouns.

1 KLĒRONOMIA (κληρονομία), a lot (see A), properly an inherited property, an inheritance. " It is always rendered inheritance in N.T., but only in a few cases in the Gospels has it the meaning ordinarily attached to that word in English, i.e., that into possession of which the heir enters only on the death of an ancestor. The N.T. usage may be set out as follows: (*a*) that property in real estate which in ordinary course passes from father to son on the death of the former, Matt. 21 : 38 ; Mark 12 : 7 ; Luke 12 : 13 ; 20 : 14 ; (*b*) a portion of an estate made the substance of a gift, Acts 7 . 5 ; Gal. 3 : 18, which also is to be included under (*c*) ; (*c*) the prospective condition and possessions of the believer in the new order of things to be ushered in at the return of Christ, Acts 20 : 32 ; Eph. 1 : 14 ; 5 : 5 ; Col. 3 : 24 ; Heb. 9 : 15 ; 1 Pet. 1 : 4 ; (*d*) what the believer will be to God in that age, Eph. 1 : 18."†

Note : In Gal. 3 : 18, " if the inheritance is of the Law," the word " inheritance " stands for ' the title to the inheritance.'

2. KLĒROS (κλῆρος), (whence Eng., clergy), denotes (*a*) a lot, given or cast (the latter as a means of obtaining Divine direction), Matt. 27 : 35 ; Mark 15 : 24 ; Luke 23 : 24 ; John 19 : 24 ; Acts 1 : 26 ; (*b*) a person's share in anything, Acts 1 : 17, R.V., " portion " (A.V., " part ") ; 8 : 21, " lot ; " (*c*) a charge (lit., ' charges ') " allotted," to elders, 1 Pet. 5 : 3, R.V. [A.V., " (God's) heritage "] ; the figure is from portions of lands allotted to be cultivated ; (*d*) an inheritance, as in No. 1 (*c*) ; Acts 26 : 18 ; Col. 1 : 12. See CHARGE, A, No. 4, LOT(S), PART, PORTION.¶

---

* From Notes on Galatians, by Hogg and Vine, pp. 286–289.
† From Notes on Galatians, by Hogg and Vine, pp. 146, 147.

INIQUITY

1. ANOMIA (ἀνομία), lit., lawlessness (*a*, negative, *nomos*, law), is used in a way which indicates the meaning as being lawlessness or wickedness. Its usual rendering in the N.T. is " iniquity," which lit. means unrighteousness. It occurs very frequently in the Sept., especially in the Psalms, where it is found about 70 times. It is used (*a*) of iniquity in general, Matt. 7 : 23 ; 13 : 41 ; 23 : 28 ; 24 : 12 ; Rom. 6 : 19 (twice) ; 2 Cor. 6 : 14, R.V., " iniquity " (A.V., " unrighteousness ") ; 2 Thess. 2 : 3, in some mss. ; the A.V. and R.V. follow those which have *hamartia*, " (man of) sin ; " 2 : 7, R.V., " lawlessness " (A.V., " iniquity ") ; Tit. 2 : 14 ; Heb. 1 : 9 ; 1 John 3 : 4 (twice), R.V., " (doeth) . . . lawlessness " and " lawlessness " (A.V., " transgresseth the law " and " transgression of the law ") ; (*b*) in the plural, of acts or manifestations of lawlessness, Rom. 4 : 7 ; Heb. 10 : 17 (some inferior mss. have it in 8 : 12, for the word *hamartia*). See LAWLESSNESS, TRANSGRESSION, UNRIGHTEOUSNESS.¶

Note : In the phrase " man of sin," 2 Thess. 2 : 3, the word suggests the idea of contempt of Divine law, since the Antichrist will deny the existence of God.

2. ADIKIA (ἀδικία) denotes unrighteousness, lit., ' unrightness ' (*a*, negative, *dikē*, right), a condition of not being right, whether with God, according to the standard of His holiness and righteousness, or with man, according to the standard of what man knows to be right by his conscience. In Luke 16 : 8 and 18 : 6, the phrases lit. are, ' the steward of unrighteousness ' and ' the judge of injustice,' the subjective genitive describing their character ; in 18 : 6 the meaning is ' injustice ' and so perhaps in Rom. 9 : 14. The word is usually translated " unrighteousness," but is rendered " iniquity " in Luke 13 : 27 ; Acts 1 : 18 ; 8 : 23 ; 1 Cor. 13 : 6, A.V. (R.V., " unrighteousness ") ; so in 2 Tim. 2 : 19 ; Jas. 3 : 6.

3. ADIKEMA (ἀδίκημα) denotes a wrong, injury, misdeed (akin to No. 2 ; from *adikeō*, to do wrong), the concrete act, in contrast to the general meaning of No. 2, and translated " a matter of wrong," in Acts 18 : 14 ; " wrong-doing," 24 : 20 (A.V., " evil-doing ") ; " iniquities," Rev. 18 : 5. See EVIL, WRONG.¶

4. PONERIA (πονηρία), akin to *poneō*, to toil (cp. *poneros*, bad, worthless ; see BAD), denotes wickedness, and is so translated in Matt. 22 : 18 ; Mark 7 : 22 (plural) ; Luke 11 : 39 ; Rom. 1 : 29 ; 1 Cor. 5 : 8 ; Eph. 6 : 12 ; in Acts 3 : 26, " iniquities." See WICKEDNESS.¶ Cp. *kakia*, evil.

5. PARANOMIA (παρανομία), law-breaking (*para*, against, *nomos*, law), denotes transgression, so rendered in 2 Pet. 2 : 16, for A.V., " iniquity."¶

INJURE, INJURIOUS, INJURY
A. Verb.

ADIKEO (ἀδικέω), akin to Nos. 2 and 3, under INIQUITY, is usually translated either to hurt, or by some form of the verb to do wrong. In the A.V. of Gal. 4 : 12, it is rendered " ye have (not) injured me," which the R.V. corrects, both in tense and meaning, to " ye did (me no) wrong." See HURT.

B. Adjective.

HUBRISTĒS (ὑβριστής), a violent, insolent man (akin to C), is translated " insolent " in Rom. 1 : 30, R.V., for A.V., " despiteful ; " in 1 Tim. 1 : 13, " injurious." See DESPITEFUL, INSOLENT.¶

C. Noun.

HUBRIS (ὕβρις) : see HARM, A, No. 4.

INK

MELAN (μέλαν), the neuter of the adjective *melas*, black (see Matt. 5 : 36 ; Rev. 6 : 5, 12), denotes ink, 2 Cor. 3 : 3 ; 2 John 12 ; 3 John 13.¶

INN

1. KATALUMA (κατάλυμα) : see GUEST-CHAMBER.

2. PANDOCHEION (πανδοχεῖον), lit., a place where all are received (*pas*, all, *dechomai*, to receive), denotes a house for the reception of strangers, a *caravanserai*, translated " inn," in Luke 10 : 34, in the parable of the Good Samaritan. Cattle and beasts of burden could be sheltered there, and this word must thereby be distinguished from No. 1.¶ Cp. *pandocheus* in the next verse, " (the) host."¶

INNER

1. ESŌ (ἔσω), an adverb connected with *eis*, into, is translated " inner " in the A.V. of Eph. 3 : 16 (R.V., " inward ") ; after verbs of motion, it denotes ' into,' Mark 15 : 16 ; after verbs of rest, " within." See WITHIN.

2. ESŌTEROS (ἐσώτερος), the comparative degree of No. 1, denotes " inner," Acts 16 : 24 (of a prison) ; Heb. 6 : 19, with the article, and practically as a noun, " that which is within (the veil)," lit., ' the inner (of the veil).'¶ Cp. Eng., esoteric.

Note : For " inner chamber(s) " see CHAMBER, No. 1.

INNOCENT

1. ATHŌOS (ἀθῶος) primarily denotes unpunished (*a*, negative, *thōē*, a penalty) ; then, innocent, Matt. 27 : 4, " innocent blood," i.e., the blood of an innocent person, the word " blood " being used both by synecdoche (a part standing for the whole), and by metonymy (one thing standing for another), i.e., for death by execution (some mss. have *dikaion*, righteous) ; ver. 24, where Pilate speaks of himself as " innocent."¶

2. AKAKOS (ἄκακος), lit., not bad (*a*, negative, *kakos*, bad), denotes guileless, innocent, Rom. 16 : 18, R.V., " innocent " (A.V., " simple ") ; " harmless " in Heb. 7 : 26. See HARMLESS.¶

INNUMERABLE

1. ANARITHMĒTOS (ἀναρίθμητος), *a*, negative, *n*, euphonic, *arithmeō*, to number, is used in Heb. 11 : 12.¶

2. MURIAS (μυριάς) denotes either ten thousand, or, indefinitely, a myriad, a numberless host, in the plural, Acts 19 : 19 ; lit. ' five ten-thousands,' Rev. 5 : 11 ; 9 : 16 ; in the following, used of vast numbers, Luke 12 : 1, A.V., " an innumerable multitude," R.V., " the many thousands " (R.V. marg., " the myriads ") ; Acts 21 : 20, " thousands ; " Heb. 12 : 22, " innumerable hosts ; " Jude 14, " ten thousands " (R.V., marg., in each place, " myriads "). See COMPANY, THOUSANDS.¶ Cp. the adjective *murios*, ten thousand, Matt. 18 : 24 ; 1 Cor. 4 : 15 ; 14 : 19.¶

For INORDINATE see AFFECTION, No. 1

INQUIRE, INQUIRY (make)
A. Verbs.

1. PUNTHANOMAI (πυνθάνομαι), to inquire, is translated " inquired " in Matt. 2 : 4, and Acts 21 : 33, R.V. (A.V., " demanded ") ; in Luke 15 : 26 ; 18 : 36 and Acts 4 : 7 (A.V., " asked ") ; " inquired " (A.V., " enquired ") in John 4 : 52 ; " inquire " (A.V., " enquire ") in Acts 23 : 20 ; in Acts 23 : 34 it denotes to learn by enquiry, A.V., and R.V., " when (he) understood ; " elsewhere it is rendered by the verb to ask, Acts 10 : 18, 29 ; 23 : 19. See ASK, UNDERSTAND.¶

2. ZĒTEŌ (ζητέω), to seek, is rendered " inquire " in John 16 : 19 ; " inquire . . . for " in Acts 9 : 11. See ABOUT, B, Note, DESIRE, ENDEAVOUR, GO, *Note* (2), *a*, REQUIRE, SEEK.

3. DIERŌTAŌ (διερωτάω), to find by inquiry, to inquire through to the end (*dia*, intensive, *erōtaō*, to ask), is used in Acts 10 : 17.¶

4. EXETAZŌ (ἐξετάζω), to examine, seek out, inquire thoroughly, is translated " enquire " in Matt. 10 : 11, A.V. (R.V., " search out ") ; in John 21 : 12, " durst) inquire," R.V. [A.V., " (durst) ask "] ; in Matt. 2 : 8, R.V., " search out " (A.V., " search "). See ASK, SEARCH.¶

Notes : (1) *Epizēteō*, to seek after or for (*epi*, after, *zēteō*, to seek), is rendered " enquire " in Acts 19 : 39, A.V. (R.V., " seek "). (2) *Sunzēteō*, to search or examine together, is rendered " to enquire " in Luke 22 : 23, A.V. (R.V., " to question "). (3) *Ekzēteō*, to seek out, search after, is rendered " have inquired " in 1 Pet. 1 : 10, A.V. (R.V., " sought "). (4) *Diaginōskō*, to ascertain exactly, or to determine, is rendered " enquire " in Acts 23 : 15, A.V. (R.V., " judge "). (5) *Akriboō*, to learn by diligent or exact inquiry, is rendered " enquired diligently " and " had diligently enquired " respectively, in Matt. 2 : 7, 16, A.V. (R.V., " learned carefully," and " had carefully learned "). (6) In 2 Cor. 8 : 23, the words " any inquire " are inserted to complete the meaning, lit., ' whether about Titus.'

B. Noun.

ZĒTĒSIS (ζήτησις) primarily denotes a search; then, an inquiry, a questioning, debate; it forms part of a phrase translated by the verb to inquire, in Acts 25 : 20, R.V., " how to inquire," lit. ' (being perplexed as to) the inquiry.' See QUESTION.

INSCRIPTION

ˊEPIGRAPHŌ (ἐπιγράφω), to write upon, inscribe (epi, upon, graphō, to write), is usually rendered by the verb to write upon, over, or in, Mark 15 : 26; Heb. 8 : 10; 10 : 16; Rev. 21 : 12; it is translated by a noun phrase in Acts 17 : 23, " (with this) inscription," lit., ' (on which) had been inscribed.'¶ Cp. the noun epigraphē, a superscription.

INSIDE

1. ENTOS (ἐντός), an adverb denoting within, or among, is once used with the article, as a noun, of " the inside (of the cup and of the platter)," Matt. 23 : 26, R.V. (A.V., " that which is within etc."); elsewhere, Luke 17 : 21. See WITHIN.¶

2. ESŌTHEN (ἔσωθεν), an adverb denoting from within, or within, is used with the article, as a noun, of the inner being, the secret intents of the heart, which, the Lord declared, God made, as well as the visible physical frame, Luke 11 : 40. In ver. 39, it is rendered " inward part." See INWARD, WITHIN.

INSOLENT

HUBRISTĒS (ὑβριστής), violent, injurious, insolent, is rendered " insolent " in Rom. 1 : 30, R.V. (A.V., " despiteful "). See DESPITEFUL, INJURIOUS.

INSOMUCH THAT, or AS

1. HŌSTE (ὥστε), a consecutive particle, is used with the meaning " insomuch that," or " so that," or " that," to express the effect or result of anything, e.g., Matt. 8 : 24; 13 : 54; 15 : 31; 27 : 14; Acts 1 : 19 (A.V., " insomuch as "); 5 : 15; 19 : 12 (A.V., " so that "); 2 Cor. 1 : 8; Gal. 2 : 13. See WHEREFORE.

2. EIS TO (εἰς τό), lit., unto the, followed by the infinitive mood, is sometimes used of result, and is rendered " insomuch that " in 2 Cor. 8 : 6.

3. KATHO (καθό) is translated " insomuch as " in 1 Pet. 4 : 13, R.V. (A.V., " inasmuch as "). See INASMUCH.

INSPIRATION OF GOD, INSPIRED OF GOD

THEOPNEUSTOS (θεόπνευστος), inspired by God (Theos, God, pneō, to breathe), is used in 2 Tim. 3 : 16, of the Scriptures as distinct from non-inspired writings. Wycliffe, Tyndale, Coverdale and the Great Bible have the rendering " inspired of God."¶

INSTANT, BE INSTANT, INSTANTLY
A. Verbs.

1. EPIKEIMAI (ἐπίκειμαι), to lie or press upon, is rendered "they were instant" in Luke 23 : 23 (Amer. R.V., "they were urgent"). See IMPOSE.

2. EPHISTĒMI (ἐφίστημι), to set upon or by, is used in the N.T. intransitively, either in the Middle Voice, or in certain tenses of the Active, signifying to stand by, be present, be at hand, come on or upon, and is translated "be instant" in 2 Tim. 4 : 2. See ASSAULT, COME, etc.

Note : For *proskartereō*, in Rom. 12 : 12, A.V., rendered "continuing instant," R.V., "stedfastly," see CONTINUE, No. 9.

B. Noun.

Note : The word *hōra*, an hour, is translated "instant" in Luke 2 : 38, A.V. ; the R.V. renders it "hour." See HOUR.

C. Adverb.

SPOUDAIŌS (σπουδαίως), earnestly, diligently, is rendered "instantly" in Luke 7 : 4, A.V. (R.V., "earnestly"). See EARNEST.

Note : For the phrase *en ekteneią*, rendered "instantly" in Acts 26 : 7, A.V., see EARNEST, D.

INSTRUCT, INSTRUCTION, INSTRUCTOR
A. Verbs.

1. KATĒCHEŌ (κατηχέω), to teach orally, inform, instruct, is translated by the verb to instruct in Luke 1 : 4 ; Acts 18 : 25 (R.V. marg., "taught by word of mouth") ; Rom. 2 : 18 ; 1 Cor. 14 : 19, R.V. (A.V., "teach"). See INFORM, TEACH.

2. PAIDEUŌ (παιδεύω), to train children, teach, is rendered "was instructed," in Acts 7 : 22, R.V. (A.V., "learned") ; "instructing" in 2 Tim. 2 : 25, A.V. (R.V., "correcting") ; Tit. 2 : 12, R.V., "instructing" (A.V., "teaching"). The verb is used of the family discipline, as in Heb. 12 : 6, 7, 10 ; cp. 1 Cor. 11 : 32 ; 2 Cor. 6 : 9 ; Rev. 3 : 19. In 1 Tim. 1 : 20 (Passive Voice) it is translated "might be taught," R.V. (A.V., "may learn"), but, "however the passage is to be understood, it is clear that not the impartation of knowledge but severe discipline is intended. In Luke 23 : 16, 22, Pilate, since he had declared the Lord guiltless of the charge brought against Him, and hence could not punish Him, weakly offered, as a concession to the Jews, to ' chastise, *paideuō*, Him, and let Him go.' "*

This sense of *paideuō* is confirmed by Heb. 12 : 6, where it is joined (in a quotation from the Sept. of Prov. 3 : 12) with to lash or scourge. Cp. the scene in the *Pilgrim's Progress* where a shining one with a whip of small cords " chastised sore " the pilgrims foolishly caught in the net of the flatterer and said to them, " As many as I love I rebuke and chasten " (*paideuō*). See CORRECT, TEACH.¶

---

* From Notes on Galatians, by Hogg and Vine, p. 165.

3. MATHĒTEUŌ (μαθητεύω), used transitively, to make a disciple, is translated " which is instructed " in Matt. 13 : 52, A.V. (R.V., " who hath been made a disciple "). See DISCIPLE.

4. MUEŌ (μυέω), to initiate into the mysteries, is used in the Passive Voice, in Phil. 4 : 12, A.V., " I am instructed," R.V., " have I learned the secret." See LEARN.¶

5. PROBIBAZŌ (προβιβάζω), to lead forward, lead on (the causal of *probainō*, to go forward ; *pro*, forward, *bibazō*, to lift up), is used in the Passive Voice in Matt. 14 : 8, and translated, A.V., " being before instructed," R.V., " being put forward." Some mss. have it in Acts 19 : 33, instead of No. 6.¶

6. SUMBIBAZŌ (συμβιβάζω), to join, knit, unite (*sun*, with), then, to compare, and so, to prove, hence, to teach, instruct, is so rendered in I Cor. 2 : 16 ; it is found in the best mss. in Acts 19 : 33 (R.V. marg., " instructed "). See COMPACTED, CONCLUDE, KNIT TOGETHER, PROVE.

B. Nouns.
(INSTRUCTION)

PAIDEIA (παιδεία), training, instruction, is translated " instruction " in 2 Tim. 3 : 16. See CHASTEN.

(INSTRUCTOR)

1. PAIDAGŌGOS (παιδαγωγός), a guide, or guardian or trainer of boys, lit., a child-leader (*pais*, a boy, or child, *agō*, to lead), a tutor, is translated " instructors " in I Cor. 4 : 15, A.V. (R.V., " tutors ") ; here the thought is that of pastors rather than teachers ; in Gal. 3 : 24, 25, A.V., " schoolmaster " (R.V., " tutor,"), but here the idea of instruction is absent. " In this and allied words the idea is that of training, discipline, not of impartation of knowledge. The *paidagōgos* was not the instructor of the child ; he exercised a general supervision over him and was responsible for his moral and physical well-being. Thus understood, *paidagōgos* is appropriately used with ' kept in ward ' and ' shut up,' whereas to understand it as equivalent to ' teacher ' introduces an idea entirely foreign to the passage, and throws the Apostle's argument into confusion."*¶ Cp. *epitropos*, a steward, guardian, tutor.

2. PAIDEUTĒS (παιδευτής), akin to A, No. 2, denotes (*a*) an instructor, a teacher, Rom. 2 : 20, A.V., " an instructor " (R.V., " a corrector ") ; (*b*) one who disciplines, corrects, chastens, Heb. 12 : 9, R.V., " to chasten " [A.V., " which corrected " (lit., ' correctors ')]. In (*a*) the discipline of the school is in view ; in (*b*) that of the family. See CORRECTOR.¶. Cp. *epitropos*, a steward, guardian, tutor.

INSTRUMENTS

HOPLON (ὅπλον), a tool, instrument, weapon, is used metaphorically in Rom. 6 : 13 of the members of the body as " instruments " (marg.,

---

* From Notes on Galatians, by Hogg and Vine, pp. 163, 164.

" weapons "), negatively, of unrighteousness, positively, of righteousness. The metaphor is probably military (cp. ver. 23, " wages," i.e., soldiers' pay) ; Moule renders it ' implements ; ' ' weapons ' seems to be the meaning. See ARMOUR, WEAPONS.

INSURRECTION
A. Nouns.

1. STASIS (στάσις), akin to *histēmi*, to make to stand, denotes (*a*) primarily, a standing or place, Heb. 9 : 8 ; (*b*) an insurrection, sedition, translated " insurrection " in Mark 15 : 7 ; " insurrections " in Acts 24 : 5, R.V. (A.V., " sedition ") ; in Luke 23 : 19, 25 (A.V. " sedition ") · " riot," Acts 19 : 40, R.V. (A.V., " uproar ") ; (*c*) a dissension, Acts 15 : 2 ; in Acts 23 : 7, 10, " dissension." See DISSENSION.¶

2. STASIASTĒS (στασιαστής) denotes a rebel, revolutionist, one who stirs up sedition (from *stasiazō*, to stir up sedition), Mark 15 : 7, " had made insurrection." Some mss. have *sustasiastēs*, a fellow-rioter, a fellow-mover of sedition, A.V., " had made insurrection with (him)."¶

B. Verb.

KATEPHISTĒMI (κατεφίστημι) signifies to rise up against (lit., to cause to stand forth against, *kata*, against, *epi*, forth, *histēmi*, to cause to stand), Acts 18 : 12, A.V., " made insurrection " (R.V., " rose up against.")¶

INTEND

1. BOULOMAI (βούλομαι), to will, wish, desire, purpose (expressing a fixed resolve, the deliberate exercise of volition), is translated " intend " in Acts 5 : 28, and " intending " in 12 : 4. See DESIRE.

2. THELŌ (θέλω), to will, be willing, desire (less strong, and more frequent than No. 1), is translated " intending " in Luke 14 : 28, A.V. (R.V., " desiring "). See DESIRE.

3. MELLŌ (μέλλω), to be about to do a thing, indicating simply the formation of a design, is translated " intend " in Acts 5 : 35, A.V. (R.V., " are about ") ; " intending," in Acts 20 : 7, R.V. (A.V., " ready ") ; 20 : 13 (1st part) ; in the 2nd part of the ver., R.V., " intending " (A.V., " minding ").

INTENT

1. ENNOIA (ἔννοια), primarily a thinking, idea, consideration, denotes purpose, intention, design (*en*, in, *nous*, mind) ; it is rendered " intents " in Heb. 4 : 12 ; " mind," in 1 Pet. 4 : 1 (R.V., marg., " thought "). See MIND.¶ Cp. *Enthumēsis*, thought (see DEVICE).

2. LOGOS (λόγος), a word, account, etc., sometimes denotes a reason, cause, intent, e.g., Matt. 5 : 32, " cause ; " it is rendered " intent " in Acts 10 : 29. See CAUSE.

Notes : (1) The phrase *eis touto*, lit., ' unto this,' i.e., for this purpose, is rendered " for this (A.V., ' that ') intent " in Acts 9 : 21, R.V.

(2) The phrase *eis to*, ' unto the,' followed by a verb in the infinitive mood, is translated " to the intent " in 1 Cor. 10 : 6.   (3) The phrase *pros ti*, lit., ' in reference to what,' is rendered " for what intent " in John 13 : 28. (4) In John 11 : 15 the conjunction *hina*, to the end that, is translated " to the intent," and in Eph. 3 : 10, " to the intent that."

INTERCESSIONS
A. Noun.

ENTEUXIS (ἔντευξις) primarily denotes a lighting upon, meeting with (akin to B) ; then, a conversation ; hence, a petition, a meaning frequent in the papyri ; it is a technical term for approaching a king, and so for approaching God in intercession ; it is rendered " prayer " in 1 Tim. 4 : 5 ; in the plural in 2 : 1 (i.e., seeking the presence and hearing of God on behalf of others).¶   For the synonymous words, *proseuchē, deēsis*, see PRAYER.

B. Verbs.

1. ENTUNCHANŌ (ἐντυγχάνω), primarily to fall in with, meet with in order to converse ; then, to make petition, especially to make intercession, plead with a person, either for or against others ; (a) against, Acts 25 : 24, " made suit to (me)," R.V. [A.V., " have dealt with (me) "], i.e., against Paul ; in Rom. 11 : 2, of Elijah in ' pleading ' with God, R.V. (A.V., " maketh intercession to "), against Israel ; (b) " for," in Rom. 8 : 27, of the intercessory work of the Holy Spirit for the saints ; ver. 34, of the similar intercessory work of Christ ; so Heb. 7 : 25. See DEAL WITH, PLEAD, SUIT.¶

2. HUPERENTUNCHANŌ (ὑπερεντυγχάνω), to make a petition or intercede on behalf of another (*huper*, on behalf of, and No. 1), is used in Rom. 8 : 26 of the work of the Holy Spirit in making intercession (see No. 1, ver. 27).¶

INTEREST

TOKOS (τόκος), primarily a bringing forth, birth (from *tiktō*, to beget), then, an offspring, is used metaphorically of the produce of money lent out, interest, usury, Matt. 25 : 27 ; Luke 19 : 23. See USURY.¶

INTERPOSED

MESITEUŌ (μεσιτεύω), to mediate, give surety (akin to *mesitēs*, a mediator), is translated " interposed " in Heb. 6 : 17, R.V. See CONFIRM, No. 5.¶

INTERPRET, INTERPRETATION, INTERPRETER
A. Verbs.

1. HERMĒNEUŌ (ἑρμηνεύω), (cp. *Hermēs*, the Greek name of the pagan god Mercury, who was regarded as the messenger of the gods), denotes to explain, interpret (Eng., hermeneutics), and is used of explaining the meaning of words in a different language, John 1 : 38 (in some mss.),

see No. 3 ; 9 : 7 (" Siloam," interpreted as " sent ") ; Heb. 7 : 2 (Melchizedec, " by interpretation," lit., ' being interpreted,' King of righteousness).¶

2. DIERMĒNEUŌ (διερμηνεύω), a strengthened form of No. 1 (dia, through, used intensively), signifies to interpret fully, to explain. In Luke 24 : 27, it is used of Christ in interpreting to the two on the way to Emmaus " in all the Scriptures the things concerning Himself," R.V., " interpreted " (A.V., " expounded ") ; in Acts 9 : 36, it is rendered " is by interpretation," lit., ' being interpreted ' (of Tabitha, as meaning Dorcas) ; in 1 Cor. 12 : 30 and 14 : 5, 13, 27, it is used with reference to the temporary gift of tongues in the churches ; this gift was inferior in character to that of prophesying, unless he who spoke in a " tongue " interpreted his words, 14 : 5 ; he was, indeed, to pray that he might interpret, ver. 13 ; only two, or at the most three, were to use the gift in a gathering, and that " in turn " (R.V.) ; one was to interpret ; in the absence of an interpreter, the gift was not to be exercised, ver. 27. See Expound.¶

3. METHERMĒNEUŌ (μεθερμηνεύω), to change or translate from one language to another (meta, implying change, and No. 1), to interpret, is always used in the Passive Voice in the N.T., " being interpreted," of interpreting the names, Immanuel, Matt. 1 : 23 ; Golgotha, Mark 15 : 22 ; Barnabas, Acts 4 : 36 ; in Acts 13 : 8, of Elymas, the verb is rendered " is . . . by interpretation," lit., ' is interpreted ; ' it is used of interpreting or translating sentences in Mark 5 : 41 ; 15 : 34 ; in the best mss., John 1 : 38 (Rabbi, interpreted as " Master ") ; ver. 41 (Messiah, interpreted as " Christ ") ; see No. 1.¶

B. Nouns.
(Interpretation)

1. HERMĒNEIA (or -ia) (ἑρμηνία), akin to A, No. 1, is used in 1 Cor. 12 : 10 ; 14 : 26 (see A, No. 2).¶

2. EPILUSIS (ἐπίλυσις), from epiluō, to loose, solve, explain, denotes a solution, explanation, lit., a release (epi, up, luō, to loose), 2 Pet. 1 : 20, " (of private) interpretation ; " i.e., the writers of Scripture did not put their own construction upon the ' God-breathed ' words they wrote.¶
Note : For "hard of interpretation," Heb. 5 : 11, R.V., see Utter, Note (1).

(Interpreter)

DIERMĒNEUTĒS (διερμηνευτής), lit., a thorough interpreter (cp. A, No. 2), is used in 1 Cor. 14 : 28 (some mss. have hermēneutēs).¶

INTERROGATION

EPERŌTĒMA (ἐπερώτημα), primarily a question or enquiry, denotes a demand or appeal ; it is found in 1 Pet. 3 : 21, R.V., " interrogation " (A.V., " answer "). See Answer, Note. Some take the word to indicate that baptism affords a good conscience, an appeal against the accuser.¶

INTO : see † p. 9.

INTREAT, INTREATY
A. Verbs.

1. ERŌTAŌ (ἐρωτάω), to ask, beseech, is rendered " intreat," e.g., in Phil. 4 : 3, A.V. (R.V., " beseech "). See ASK.

2. PARAKALEŌ (παρακαλέω), to beseech, comfort, exhort, is rendered by the verb to intreat in Luke 8 : 31, R.V., " intreated " (A.V., " besought ") ; 15 : 28 ; Acts 9 : 38, R.V., " intreating " (A.V., " desiring ") ; 28 : 20, R.V. (A.V., " called for ") ; 1 Cor. 4 : 13 ; 2 Cor. 9 : 5, R.V. (A.V., " exhort ") ; 10 : 1, R.V. (A.V., " beseech ") ; 1 Tim. 5 : 1, A.V. (R.V., " exhort "). See BESEECH.

3. PARAITEOMAI (παραιτέομαι), to ask to be excused, to beg, etc., is rendered " intreated " in Heb. 12 : 19. See AVOID.

B. Adjective.

EUPEITHĒS (εὐπειθής), ready to obey (eu, well, peithomai, to obey, to be persuaded), compliant, is translated " easy to be intreated " in Jas. 3 : 17, said of the wisdom that is from above.¶

C. Noun.

PARAKLĒSIS (παράκλησις), an appeal, a comfort, exhortation, etc., is translated " intreaty " in 2 Cor. 8 : 4.

For INTRUDE (Col. 2 : 18) see DWELL, A, No. 11

INTRUST

PISTEUŌ (πιστεύω), to believe, also means to entrust, and in the Active Voice is translated to commit, in Luke 16 : 11 ; John 2 : 24 ; in the Passive Voice, to be intrusted with, Rom. 3 : 2, R.V., " they were intrusted with " (A.V., " unto them were committed "), of Israel and the oracles of God ; 1 Cor. 9 : 17, R.V., " I have . . . intrusted to me " (A.V., " is committed unto me "), of Paul and the stewardship of the Gospel ; so Gal. 2 : 7 ; Tit. 1 : 3 ; in 1 Thess. 2 : 4, where he associates with himself his fellow-missionaries, R.V., " to be intrusted with " (A.V., " to be put in trust with "). See BELIEVE, COMMIT.

INVENTORS

EPHEURETĒS (ἐφευρετής), an inventor, contriver (akin to epheuriskō, to find out ; epi, on, used intensively, heuriskō, to find), occurs in the plural in Rom. 1 : 30.¶

INVISIBLE

AORATOS (ἀόρατος), lit., unseen (a, negative, horaō, to see), is translated " invisible " in Rom. 1 : 20, of the power and Divinity of God ; of God Himself, Col. 1 : 15 ; 1 Tim. 1 : 17 ; Heb. 11 : 27 ; of things unseen, Col. 1 : 16.¶ In the Sept., Gen. 1 : 2 ; Is. 45 : 3, " unseen (treasures)."¶

INWARD (man, part), INWARDLY

1. ESŌ (ἔσω), within, inward, is used adjectivally in Rom. 7 : 22, " (the) inward (man) ; " 2 Cor. 4 : 16, with " man " expressed in the preceding clause, but not repeated in the original, " (our) inward (man) " (some mss. have esōthen, from within) ; Eph. 3 : 16, R.V., " (the) inward (man) " (A.V., " inner "). See INNER, WITHIN.

2. ESŌTHEN (ἔσωθεν) is used in Luke 11 : 39, as a noun with the article, " part " being understood, " (your) inward part ; " in Matt. 7 : 15 it has its normal use as an adverb, " inwardly." See WITHIN.

Note : In Rom. 2 : 29 the phrase *en tō kruptō*, lit., in (the) secret, or hidden (' part ' being understood) is rendered " inwardly," said of a spiritual Jew, in contrast to the one who is merely naturally circumcised and so is one outwardly. See HIDE, SECRET.

IRKSOME

OKNĒROS (ὀκνηρός), shrinking, timid (from *okneō*, to shrink, delay), is used negatively in Phil. 3 : 1, R.V., " irksome " (A.V., " grievous "), i.e., ' I do not hesitate ' ; in Matt. 25 : 26, and Rom. 12 : 11, " slothful." See GRIEVOUS, SLOTHFUL.¶

IRON
A. Noun.

SIDĒROS (σίδηρος), iron, occurs in Rev. 18 : 12.¶
B. Adjective.

SIDĒREOS (σιδήρεος), of iron, occurs in Acts 12 : 10, of an iron gate ; " of iron," Rev. 2 : 27 ; 9 : 9 ; 12 : 5 ; 19 : 15.¶

ISLAND, ISLE

1. NĒSOS (νῆσος), an island, occurs in Acts 13 : 6 ; 27 : 26 ; 28 : 1, 7, 9, 11 ; Rev. 1 : 9 ; 6 : 14 ; 16 : 20.¶

2. NĒSION (νησίον), a diminutive of No. 1, a small island, occurs in Acts 27 : 16, Cauda, R.V.¶

ISSUE
A. Nouns.

1. EKBASIS (ἔκβασις), a way out, " way of escape," 1 Cor. 10 : 13 (*ek*, out, *bainō*, to go), is rendered " issue " in Heb. 13 : 7, R.V., for A.V., " end," regarding the manner of life of deceased spiritual guides. See END.¶

2. RHUSIS (ῥύσις), a flowing (akin to *rheō*, to flow), an issue, is used in Mark 5 : 25 ; Luke 8 : 43, 44.¶

Note : In Matt. 22 : 25, A.V., *sperma*, seed, is translated " issue " (R.V., " seed ").

B. Verb.

EKPOREUŌ (ἐκπορεύω), to cause to go forth (*ek*, out, *poreuō*, to cause to go), is used in the Middle Voice in Rev. 9 : 17, 18, of the coming forth of fire, smoke and brimstone from the mouths of the symbolic horses in a vision, A.V., " issued " (the R.V. renders it by the verb to proceed). See COME, DEPART, GO, PROCEED.

IT

Note : The pronouns used are the same, in their neuter forms, as Nos. 1, 2, 3 under HE.

ITCHING

KNĒTHŌ (κνήθω), to scratch, tickle, is used in the Passive Voice, metaphorically, of an eagerness to hear, in 2 Tim. 4 : 3, lit., ' itched (as to the hearing),' of those who, not enduring sound doctrine, heap to themselves teachers.¶

ITSELF

Note : The pronouns used are the same in their neuter forms, as those under HIMSELF.

IVORY

ELEPHANTINOS (ἐλεφάντινος), an adjective from *elephas* (whence Eng., elephant), signifies ' of ivory,' Rev. 18 : 12.¶

J

JACINTH
A. Noun.

HUAKINTHOS (ὑάκινθος) primarily denoted a hyacinth, probably the dark blue iris ; then, a precious stone, most likely the sapphire, Rev. 21 : 20.¶

B. Adjective.

HUAKINTHINOS (ὑακίνθινος) signifies hyacinthine, perhaps primarily having the colour of the hyacinth. Some regard its colour as that of the martagon lily, a dusky red. According to Swete, the word in Rev. 9 : 17 is " doubtless meant to describe the blue smoke of a sulphurous flame."¶

JAILOR

DESMOPHULAX (δεσμοφύλαξ), a prison-keeper, gaoler (desmos, a band, phulax, a guard, keeper), occurs in Acts 16 : 23, 27, 36.¶

For JANGLING (1 Tim. 1 : 6, A.V.) see TALKING (vain)

JASPER

IASPIS (ἴασπις), a Phœnician word (cp. Heb. yāsh'pheh, e.g., Ex. 28 : 20 ; 39 : 16), seems to have denoted a translucent stone of various colours, especially that of fire, Rev. 4 : 3 ; 21 : 11, 18, 19. The sardius and the jasper, of similar colour, were the first and last stones on the breastplate of the High Priest, Ex. 28 : 17, 20.¶

JEALOUS, JEALOUSY
A. Noun.

ZĒLOS (ζῆλος), zeal, jealousy, is rendered " jealousy " in the R.V. (A.V., " envying ") in Rom. 13 : 13 ; 1 Cor. 3 : 3 ; Jas. 3 : 14, 16 ; in 2 Cor. 12 : 20 (A.V., " envyings ") ; in Gal. 5 : 20, R.V. " jealousies " (A.V., " emulations ") ; in Acts 5 : 17 (A.V., " indignation ") ; in 13 : 45 (A.V., " envy ") ; in 2 Cor. 11 : 2 it is used in the phrase " with a godly jealousy," lit., ' with a jealousy of God ' (R.V., marg.). See ENVY.

B. Verbs.

1. ZĒLOŌ (ζηλόω), akin to A, to be jealous, to burn with jealousy (otherwise, to seek or desire eagerly), is rendered " moved with jealousy," in Acts 7 : 9 and 17 : 5, R.V. (A.V., " moved with envy ") ; in 1 Cor. 13 : 4, " envieth (not)," A.V. and R.V. ; in Jas. 4 : 2, R.V. marg., " are jealous " (text " covet ; " A.V., " desire to have "). See AFFECT, Note, DESIRE.

2. PARAZĒLOŌ (παραζηλόω), to provoke to jealousy (*para*, beside, used intensively, and No. 1), is found in Rom. 10 : 19 and 11 : 11, of God's dealings with Israel through his merciful dealings with Gentiles ; in 11 : 14, R.V., " I may provoke to jealousy " (A.V., " . . . emulation "), of the Apostle's evangelical ministry to Gentiles with a view to stirring his fellow-nationals to a sense of their need and responsibilities regarding the Gospel ; in 1 Cor. 10 : 22, of the provocation of God on the part of believers who compromise their Divine relationship by partaking of the table of demons ; in Gal 5 : 20, of the works of the flesh.¶

For JEOPARDY see DANGER

JESTING

EUTRAPELIA (εὐτραπελία) properly denotes wit, facetiousness, versatility (lit., easily turning, from *eu*, well, *trepō*, to turn). It was used in the literal sense to describe the quick movements of apes and persons. Pericles speaks of the Athenians of his day (430 B.C.) as distinguished by a happy and gracious ' flexibility.' In the next century Aristotle uses it of ' versatility ' in the give and take of social intercourse, quick repartee. In the sixth century, B.C., the poet Pindar speaks of one Jason as never using a word of ' vain lightness,' a meaning approaching to its latest use. Its meaning certainly deteriorated, and it came to denote coarse jesting, ribaldry, as in Eph. 5 : 4, where it follows *mōrologia*, foolish talking.¶

JESUS

IĒSOUS ('Ιησοῦs) is a transliteration of the Heb. " Joshua," meaning ' Jehovah is salvation,' i.e., ' is the Saviour,' " a common name among the Jews, e.g., Ex. 17 : 9 ; Luke 3 : 29 (R.V.) ; Col. 4 : 11. It was given to the Son of God in Incarnation as His personal name, in obedience to the command of an angel to Joseph, the husband of His Mother, Mary, shortly before He was born, Matt. 1 : 21. By it He is spoken of throughout the Gospel narratives generally, but not without exception, as in Mark 16 : 19, 20 ; Luke 7 : 13, and a dozen other places in that Gospel, and a few in John.

" ' Jesus Christ' occurs only in Matt. 1 : 1, 18 ; 16 : 21, marg. ; Mark 1 : 1 ; John 1 : 17 ; 17 : 3. In Acts the name ' Jesus ' is found frequently. ' Lord Jesus ' is the normal usage, as in Acts 8 : 16 ; 19 : 5, 17 ; see also the reports of the words of Stephen, 7 : 59, of Ananias, 9 : 17, and of Paul, 16 : 31 ; though both Peter, 10 : 36, and Paul, 16 : 18, also used ' Jesus Christ.'

" In the Epp. of James, Peter, John and Jude, the personal name is not once found alone, but in Rev. eight times (R.V.), 1 : 9 ; 12 : 17 ; 14 : 12 ; 17 : 6 ; 19 : 10 (twice) ; 20 : 4 ; 22 : 16.

" In the Epp. of Paul ' Jesus ' appears alone just thirteen times, and in the Hebrews eight times ; in the latter the title ' Lord ' is added once only, at 13 : 20. In the Epp. of James, Peter, John, and Jude, men who had companied with the Lord in the days of His flesh, ' Jesus Christ ' is the invariable order (in the R.V.) of the Name and Title, for this was the order of their experience ; as ' Jesus ' they knew Him first, that He was Messiah they learnt finally in His resurrection. But Paul came to know Him first in the glory of heaven, Acts 9 : 1–6, and his experience being thus the reverse of theirs, the reverse order, ' Christ Jesus,' is of frequent occurrence in his letters, but, with the exception of Acts 24 : 24, does not occur elsewhere in the R.V.

" In Paul's letters the order is always in harmony with the context. Thus ' Christ Jesus ' describes the Exalted One who emptied Himself, Phil. 2 : 5, and testifies to His pre-existence ; ' Jesus Christ ' describes the despised and rejected One Who was afterwards glorified, Phil. 2 : 11, and testifies to His resurrection. ' Christ Jesus ' suggests His grace, ' Jesus Christ ' suggests His glory."*

JEW(-S) (live as do the), JEWESS, JEWISH, JEWRY, JEWS' RELIGION

A. Adjectives.

1. IOUDAIOS ('Ιουδαῖος) is used (a) adjectivally, with the lit. meaning, ' Jewish,' sometimes with the addition of *anēr*, a man, Acts 10 : 28 ; 22 : 3 ; in 21 : 39 with *anthrōpos*, in some mss. (a man in the generic sense) ; the best mss. omit the phrase here ; in 13 : 6, lit., ' a Jewish false-prophet ; ' in John 3 : 22, with the word *chōra*, land or country, signifying ' Judæan,' lit., ' Judæan country ; ' used by metonymy for the people of the country ; (b) as a noun, a Jew, Jews, e.g., Matt. 2 : 2 ; Mark 7 : 3. The name ' Jew ' is primarily " tribal " (from ' Judah '). It is first found in 2 Kings 16 : 6, as distinct from Israel, of the Northern Kingdom. After the Captivity it was chiefly used to distinguish the race from Gentiles, e.g., John 2 : 6 ; Acts 14 : 1 ; Gal. 2 : 15, where it denotes Christians of Jewish race ; it distinguishes Jews from Samaritans, in John 4 : 9 ; from proselytes, in Acts 2 : 10. The word is most frequent in John's Gospel and the Acts ; in the former " it especially denotes the typical representatives of Jewish thought contrasted with believers in Christ . . . or with other Jews of less pronounced opinions, e.g., John 3 : 25 ; 5 : 10 ; 7 : 13 ; 9 : 22 " (Lukyn Williams, in Hastings' Bib. Dic.) ; such representatives were found, generally, in opposition to Christ ; in the Acts they are chiefly those who opposed the apostles and the Gospel. In Rom. 2 : 28, 29 the word is used of ideal Jews, i.e., Jews in spiritual reality, believers, whether Jews or Gentiles by natural birth. The feminine, " Jewess," is found in Acts 16 : 1 ; 24 : 24.

It also denotes Judæa, e.g., Matt. 2 : 1 ; Luke 1 : 5 ; John 4 : 3, the word ' country ' being understood [cp. (a) above]. In Luke 23 : 5 and

---

* From Notes on Thessalonians, by Hogg and Vine, pp. 26, 29.

John 7 : 1, where the A.V. has " Jewry," the R.V. translates it as usual, " Judæa."

2. IOUDAIKOS ('Ιουδαϊκός) denotes " Jewish," Tit. 1 : 14.¶

B. Noun.

IOUDAISMOS ('Ιουδαϊσμός), Judaism, denotes " the Jews' religion," Gal. 1 : 13, 14, and stands, not for their religious beliefs, but for their religious practices, not as instituted by God, but as developed and extended from these by the traditions of the Pharisees and scribes. In the Apocrypha it denotes comprehensively " the Government, laws, institutions and religion of the Jews."¶

C. Verb.

IOUDAIZO ('Ιουδαΐζω), lit., to Judaize, i.e., to conform to Jewish religious practices and manners, is translated " to live as do the Jews," in Gal. 2 : 14.¶

D. Adverb.

IOUDAIKOS ('Ιουδαϊκῶς), in Jewish fashion, is translated " as do the Jews," in Gal. 2 : 14.¶

JEWELS

CHRUSION (χρυσίον), gold, is used of ornaments in 1 Pet. 3 : 3, R.V., " jewels." See GOLD, No. 2.

JOIN

1. KOLLAO (κολλάω), primarily, to glue or cement together, then, generally, to unite, to join firmly, is used in the Passive Voice signifying to join oneself to, to be joined to, Luke 15 : 15 ; Acts 5 : 13 ; 8 : 29 ; 9 : 26 ; 10 : 28, R.V. (A.V., " to keep company with ") ; 1 Cor. 6 : 16, 17 ; elsewhere, to cleave to, Luke 10 : 11 ; Acts 17 : 34 ; Rom. 12 : 9. See CLEAVE.¶

2. PROSKOLLAO (προσκολλάω), to stick to, a strengthened form of No. 1, with pros, to, intensive, is used in the Passive Voice, reflexively, in a metaphorical sense, with the meanings (a) to join oneself to, in Acts 5 : 36 ; (b) to cleave to, of the husband with regard to the wife, Matt. 19 : 5 ; Mark 10 : 7 ; in Eph. 5 : 31, R.V., " shall cleave to " (A.V., " shall be joined to "). See CLEAVE.¶

3. SU(N)ZEUGNUMI (συνζεύγνυμι), to yoke together (sun, with, zugos, a yoke), is used metaphorically of union in wedlock, in Matt. 19 : 6 ; Mark 10 : 9.¶

4. SUNOMOREO (συνομορέω), to border on, is used of a house as being contiguous with a synagogue, in Acts 18 : 7, " joined hard to."¶

Notes : (1) In 1 Cor. 1 : 10, katartizo, to render complete, to perfect (kata, down, intensive, and artios, complete, jointed), to restore, is translated " be perfectly joined together," A.V. (R.V., " be perfected together ") ; see FIT. (2) In Eph. 4 : 16, sunarmologeo, to fit or frame together, is translated " fitly joined together," A.V. (R.V., " fitly framed . . . together ") ; cp. 2 : 21.¶

JOINT

1. HARMOS (ἁρμός), a joining, joint (akin to *harmozō*, to fit, join), is found in Heb. 4 : 12, figuratively (with the word " marrow ") of the inward moral and spiritual being of man, as just previously expressed literally in the phrase " soul and spirit."¶

2. HAPHĒ (ἁφή), a ligature, joint (akin to *haptō*, to fit, to fasten), occurs in Eph. 4 : 16 and Col. 2 : 19.¶

For JOINT-HEIR see HEIR

JOT

IŌTA (ἰῶτα), from the Heb. *yod*, the smallest Hebrew letter, is mentioned by the Lord in Matt. 5 : 18 (together with *keraia*, a little horn, a tittle, the point or extremity which distinguishes certain Hebrew letters from others), to express the fact that not a single item of the Law will pass away or remain unfulfilled.¶

JOURNEY (Noun and Verb), JOURNEYINGS
A. Nouns.

1. HODOS (ὁδός), a way, path, road, used of a traveller's way, a journey, is rendered " journey " in Matt. 10 : 13 ; Mark 6 : 8 ; Luke 2 : 44, " a day's journey " (probably to Beeroth, six miles north of Jerusalem) ; 9 : 3 ; 11 : 6 ; Acts 1 : 12, " a Sabbath day's journey," i.e., the journey which a Jew was allowed to take on the Sabbath, viz., about 2,000 yards or cubits (estimates vary). The regulation was not a Mosaic enactment, but a Rabbinical tradition, based upon an exposition of Ex. 16 : 29, and a comparison of the width of the suburb of a Levitical city as enjoined in Num. 35 : 4, 5, and the distance between the Ark and the people at the crossing of the Jordan, Josh. 3 : 4. In regard to Acts 1 : 12, there is no discrepancy between this and Luke 24 : 50, where the R.V. rightly translates by " over against Bethany," which does not fix the exact spot of the Ascension. See HIGHWAY, WAY.

2. HODOIPORIA (ὁδοιπορία), a way-faring, journeying (No. 1, and *poros*, a way, a passage), is used of the Lord's journey to Samaria, John 4 : 6, and of Paul's " journeyings," 2 Cor. 11 : 26. Cp. B, No. 3.

Note : In Luke 13 : 22 the noun *poreia*, a journey, a going (cp. *poros*, No. 2, above), is used with the verb *poieō*, to make, with the meaning ' to journey,' lit., ' making (for Himself, Middle Voice) a way ', " journeying." In Jas. 1 : 11, " ways." See WAY.¶

B. Verbs.

1. POREUOMAI (πορεύομαι) is used in the Middle Voice in the N.T., signifying to go, proceed, go on one's way ; it is translated by the verb to journey in Acts 9 : 3 ; 22 : 6, " as I made (my) journey ; " 26 : 13 ; Rom. 15 : 24 (1st part), A.V., " I take my journey," R.V., " I go " (for the 2nd part, " in my journey," see No. 2). See GO, No. 1.

2. DIAPOREUŌ (διαπορεύω), to carry over, used in the Passive Voice with the meaning to pass by, to journey through, is translated " in my journey," in Rom. 15 : 24, lit., ' journeying through ; ' in Luke 18 : 36, R.V., " going by " (A.V. " pass by "). See Go, No. 4.

3. HODOIPOREŌ (ὁδοιπορέω), to travel, journey (akin to A, No. 2), is found in Acts 10 : 9.¶

4. HODEUŌ (ὁδεύω), to be on the way, journey (from *hodos*, a way), the simplest form of the verbs denoting to journey, is used in the parable of the Good Samaritan, Luke 10 : 33.¶

5. SUNODEUŌ (συνοδεύω), *sun*, with, and No. 4, to journey with, occurs in Acts 9 : 7.¶ In the Sept., Zech. 8 : 21.¶

6. EUODOŌ (εὐοδόω), to help on one's way (*eu*, well, and *hodos*), is used in the Passive Voice with the meaning ' to have a prosperous journey ; ' so the A.V. of Rom. 1 : 10 ; the R.V., " I may be prospered " rightly expresses the metaphorical use which the verb acquired, without reference to a journey ; see 1 Cor. 16 : 2 ; 3 John 2.¶

7. PROPEMPŌ (προπέμπω), to send before or forth (*pro*, before, *pempō*, to send), also means to set forward on a journey, to escort ; in 1 Cor. 16 : 6, " may set (me) forward on my journey," R.V. [A.V., " may bring (me) etc."] ; so Tit. 3 : 13, and 3 John 6. See ACCOMPANY, CONDUCT, WAY.

8. APODĒMEŌ (ἀποδημέω) denotes to go on a journey to another country, go abroad, Matt. 21 : 33 ; 25 : 14, 15 ; Mark 12 : 1 ; Luke 15 :13 ; 20 : 9. See COUNTRY.¶

Note : For the adjective *apodēmos*, Mark 13 : 34, A.V., " taking a far journey," R.V., " sojourning in another country," see COUNTRY.

JOY (Noun and Verb), JOYFULNESS, JOYFULLY, JOYOUS
A. Nouns.

1. CHARA (χαρά), joy, delight (akin to *chairō*, to rejoice), is found frequently in Matthew and Luke, and especially in John, once in Mark (4 : 16, R.V., " joy," A.V., " gladness ") ; it is absent from 1 Cor. (though the verb is used three times), but is frequent in 2 Cor., where the noun is used five times (for 7 : 4, R.V., see Note below), and the verb eight times, suggestive of the Apostle's relief in comparison with the circumstances of the 1st Epistle ; in Col. 1 : 11, A.V., " joyfulness," R.V., " joy." The word is sometimes used, by metonymy, of the occasion or cause of joy, Luke 2 : 10 (lit., ' I announce to you a great joy ') ; in 2 Cor. 1 : 15, in some mss., for *charis*, " benefit " ; Phil. 4 : 1, where the readers are called the Apostle's joy ; so 1 Thess. 2 : 19, 20 ; Heb. 12 : 2, of the object of Christ's joy ; Jas. 1 : 2, where it is connected with falling into trials ; perhaps also in Matt. 25 : 21, 23, where some regard it as signifying, concretely, the circumstances attending co-operation in the authority of the Lord. See also the Note following No. 3.

Note : In Heb. 12 : 11, " joyous " represents the phrase *meta*, with, followed by *chara*, lit., ' with joy.' So in 10 : 34, "joyfully ; " in 2 Cor. 7 : 4 the noun is used with the Middle Voice of *huperperisseuō*, to abound more exceedingly, and translated " (I overflow) with joy," R.V. (A.V., " I am exceeding joyful ").

2. AGALLIASIS (ἀγαλλίασις), exultation, exuberant joy. Cp. B, No. 3, below. See GLADNESS.

3. EUPHROSUNĒ (εὐφροσύνη) is rendered " joy " in the A.V. of Acts 2 : 28, R.V., " gladness," as in 14 : 17. See GLADNESS.¶

Note : Joy is associated with life, e.g., 1 Thess. 3 : 8, 9. Experiences of sorrow prepare for, and enlarge, the capacity for joy, e.g., John 16 : 20 ; Rom. 5 : 3, 4 ; 2 Cor. 7 : 4 ; 8 : 2 ; Heb. 10 : 34 ; Jas. 1 : 2. Persecution for Christ's sake enhances joy, e.g., Matt. 5 : 11, 12 ; Acts 5 : 41. Other sources of joy are faith, Rom. 15 : 13 ; Phil. 1 : 25 ; hope, Rom. 5 : 2 (*kauchaomai*, see B, No. 2) ; 12 : 12 (*chairō*, see B, No. 1) ; the joy of others, 12 : 15, which is distinctive of Christian sympathy. Cp. 1 Thess. 3 : 9. In the O.T. and the N.T. God Himself is the ground and object of the believer's joy, e.g., Ps. 35 : 9 ; 43 : 4 ; Is. 61 : 10 ; Luke 1 : 47 ; Rom. 5 : 11 ; Phil. 3 : 1 ; 4 : 4.

B. Verbs.

1. CHAIRŌ (χαίρω), to rejoice, be glad, is translated " joyfully " in Luke 19 : 6, lit., ' rejoicing ; ' " we joyed," 2 Cor. 7 : 13 ; " I joy," Phil. 2 : 17 ; " do ye joy," 2 : 18 ; " joying," Col. 2 : 5 ; " we joy," 1 Thess. 3 : 9. It is contrasted with weeping and sorrow, e.g., in John 16 : 20, 22 ; Rom. 12 : 15 ; 1 Cor. 7 : 30 (cp. Ps. 30 : 5). See FAREWELL, GLAD, GREETING, HAIL, REJOICE.

2. KAUCHAOMAI (καυχάομαι), to boast, glory, exult, is rendered " we joy," in Rom. 5 : 11, A.V. (R.V., " we rejoice "). It would have been an advantage to translate this word distinctively by the verbs to glory or to exult.

3. AGALLIAŌ (ἀγαλλιάω), to exult, rejoice greatly, is translated " with exceeding joy " in 1 Pet. 4 : 13 (Middle Voice), lit., ' (ye rejoice, *chairō*) exulting.' Cp. A, No. 2. See GLAD, REJOICE.

4. ONINĒMI (ὀνίνημι), to benefit, profit, in the Middle Voice, to have profit, derive benefit, is translated " let me have joy " in Philm. 20 (R.V. marg., " help ") ; the Apostle is doubtless continuing his credit and debit metaphors and using the verb in the sense of ' profit.'¶

JUDGE (Noun and Verb)
A. Nouns.

1. KRITĒS (κριτής), a judge (from *krino*, see B, No. 1), is used (*a*) of God, Heb. 12 : 23, where the order in the original is ' to a Judge who is God of all ; ' this is really the significance ; it suggests that He who is the Judge of His people is at the same time their God ; that is the order in 10 : 30 ; the word is also used of God in Jas. 4 : 12, R.V. ; (*b*) of Christ,

Acts 10 : 42 ; 2 Tim. 4 : 8 ; Jas. 5 : 9 ; (c) of a ruler in Israel in the times of the Judges, Acts 13 : 20 ; (d) of a Roman procurator, Acts 24 : 10 ; (e) of those whose conduct provides a standard of judging, Matt. 12 : 27 ; Luke 11 : 19 ; (f) in the forensic sense, of one who tries and decides a case, Matt. 5 : 25 (twice) ; Luke 12 : 14 (some mss. have No. 2 here) ; 12 : 58 (twice) ; 18 : 2 ; 18 : 6 (lit., 'the judge of unrighteousness,' expressing subjectively his character) ; Acts 18 : 15 ; (g) of one who passes, or arrogates to himself, judgment on anything, Jas. 2 : 4 (see the R.V.) ; 4 : 11.

2. DIKASTĒS (δικαστής) denotes a judge (from dikē, right, a judicial hearing, justice ; akin to dikazō, to judge), Acts 7 : 27, 35 ; some mss. have it in Luke 12 : 14 (see No. 1) ; while dikastēs is a forensic term, kritēs "gives prominence to the mental process" (Thayer). At Athens the dikastēs acted as a juryman, the kritēs being the presiding judge.¶

B. Verbs.

1. KRINŌ (κρίνω) primarily denotes to separate, select, choose ; hence, to determine, and so to judge, pronounce judgment. "The uses of this verb in the N.T. may be analysed as follows : (a) to assume the office of a judge, Matt. 7 : 1 ; John 3 : 17 ; (b) to undergo process of trial, John 3 : 18 ; 16 : 11 ; 18 : 31 ; Jas. 2 : 12 ; (c) to give sentence, Acts 15 : 19 ; 16 : 4 ; 21 : 25 ; (d) to condemn, John 12 : 48 ; Acts 13 : 27 ; Rom. 2 : 27 ; (e) to execute judgment upon, 2 Thess. 2 : 12 ; Acts 7 : 7 ; (f) to be involved in a lawsuit, whether as plaintiff, Matt. 5 : 40 ; 1 Cor. 6 : 1 ; or as defendant, Acts 23 : 6 ; (g) to administer affairs, to govern, Matt. 19 : 28 ; cp. Judg. 3 : 10 ; (h) to form an opinion, Luke 7 : 43 ; John 7 : 24 ; Acts 4 : 19 ; Rom. 14 : 5 ; (i) to make a resolve, Acts 3 : 13 ; 20 : 16 ; 1 Cor. 2 : 2 "*

See CALL, No. 13, CONCLUDE, CONDEMN, DECREE, DETERMINE, ESTEEM, LAW (go to), ORDAIN, SENTENCE, THINK.

Note : In Acts 21 : 25, the R.V. has "giving judgement" (A.V., "concluded") ; see JUDGMENT, Note (5).

2. ANAKRINŌ (ἀνακρίνω), to examine, investigate, question (ana, up, and No. 1), is rendered "judged" in 1 Cor. 2 : 14, R.V. (A.V., "are . . . discerned ;" R.V. marg., "examined"), said of the things of the Spirit of God ; in ver. 15, "judgeth" (R.V. marg., "examineth"), said of the exercise of a discerning judgment of all things as to their true value, by one who is spiritual ; in the same verse, "is judged (of no man)," R.V. marg., "examined", i.e., the merely natural mind cannot estimate the motives of the spiritual ; in 4 : 3, "I should be judged," i.e., as to examining and passing sentence on the fulfilment or non-fulfilment of the Apostle's stewardship ; so in the same verse, "I judge (not mine own self)," and in ver. 4 "(he that) judgeth (me is the Lord) ;" in 14 : 24, "he is judged (of all)," i.e., the light of the heart-searching testimony of the

---

* From Notes on Thessalonians by Hogg and Vine, p. 267.

assembly probes the conscience of the unregenerate, sifting him judicially. See Ask, No. 7, Discern, A, No. 1.

3. DIAKRINŌ (διακρίνω) denotes to separate throughout (dia, and No. 1), discriminate, discern, and hence, to decide, to judge (also to contend, to hesitate, to doubt) ; it is rendered " to judge " in 1 Cor. 6 : 5, in the sense of arbitrating ; in 11 : 31 (1st part), the R.V. has " (if we) discerned (ourselves)," A.V. " (if we would) judge " (krinō, No. 1, is used in the 2nd part) ; so in 14 : 29, R.V., " discern " (A.V., " judge "). See Decide, A, Discern, A. No. 2.

Notes : (1) In 1 Cor. 6 : 2 (last clause) " to judge " represents the noun *kritērion*, which denotes a tribunal, a law court, and the meaning thus is ' are ye unworthy of sitting upon tribunals of least importance ? ' (see R.V. marg.), i.e., to judge matters of smallest importance. Some would render it ' cases,' but there is no clear instance elsewhere of this meaning. See Judgment-seat. (2) In Heb. 11 : 11, the verb *hēgeomai*, to consider, think, account, is rendered " she judged (Him faithful)," A.V. (R.V., " she counted "). See Count, No. 2.

JUDGMENT

1. KRISIS (κρίσις) primarily denotes a separating, then, a decision, judgment, most frequently in a forensic sense, and especially of Divine judgment. For the variety of its meanings, with references, see Condemnation, B, No. 3.

Notes : (1) The Holy Spirit, the Lord said, would convict the world of (peri, in respect of), i.e., of the actuality of, God's judgment, John 16 : 8, 11. Cp. 2 Thess. 1 : 5. (2) In Rom. 2 : 5 the word *dikaiokrisia*, " righteous judgment," combines the adjective *dikaios*, righteous, with *krisis*, the two words which are used separately in 2 Thess. 1 : 5.¶

2. KRIMA (κρίμα) denotes the result of the action signified by the verb *krinō*, to judge ; for its general significance see Condemnation, B, No. 1 : it is used (a) of a decision passed on the faults of others, Matt. 7 : 2 ; (b) of judgment by man upon Christ, Luke 24 : 20 ; (c) of God's judgment upon men, e.g., Rom. 2 : 2, 3 ; 3 : 8 ; 5 : 16 ; 11 : 33 ; 13 : 2 ; 1 Cor. 11 : 29 ; Gal. 5 : 10 ; Heb. 6 : 2 ; Jas. 3 : 1 ; through Christ, e.g., John 9 : 39 ; (d) of the right of judgment, Rev. 20 : 4 ; (e) of a law-suit, 1 Cor. 6 : 7.

3. HĒMERA (ἡμέρα), a day, is translated " judgment " in 1 Cor. 4 : 3, where " man's judgment " (lit., ' man's day,' marg.) is used of the present period in which man's mere judgment is exercised, a period of human rebellion against God. The adjective *anthrōpinos*, human, belonging to man (anthrōpos), is doubtless set in contrast here to *kuriakos*, belonging to the Lord (kurios, a lord), which is used in the phrase " the Day of the Lord," in Rev. 1 : 10, " The Lord's Day," a period of Divine judgments. See Day.

4. GNŌMĒ (γνώμη), primarily a means of knowing (akin to ginōskō, to know), came to denote a mind, understanding; hence (a) a purpose, Acts 20 : 3, lit., ' (it was his) purpose ; ' (b) a royal purpose, a decree, Rev. 17 : 17, R.V., " mind " (A.V., " will "); (c) judgment, opinion, I Cor. I : 10, " (in the same) judgment ; " Rev. 17 : 13, " mind ; " (d) counsel, advice, I Cor. 7 : 25, " (I give my) judgment ; " 7 : 40, " (after my) judgment ; " Philm. 14, " mind." See MIND, PURPOSE, WILL.¶

Notes : (1) In I Cor. 6 : 4, A.V., *kritērion*, a tribunal, is rendered " judgments " (R.V., " to judge," marg., " tribunals "). See JUDGE, B, No. 3, Note (1). (2) In Rom. I : 32, A.V., *dikaiōma*, an ordinance, righteous act, is translated " judgment " (R.V. " ordinance "); in Rev. 15 : 4, " judgments " (R.V., " righteous acts "). (3) In Acts 25 : 15, A.V., *katadikē*, a sentence, condemnation, is translated " judgment " (R.V., " sentence "). Some mss. have *dikē*. See SENTENCE. (4) In Phil. I : 9, A.V., *aisthēsis*, perception, discernment, is translated " judgment " (R.V., " discernment "). (5) In Acts 21 : 25, in the record of the decree from the Apostles and elders at Jerusalem to the churches of the Gentiles, the verb *krinō* (see JUDGE, B, No. 1), is translated " giving judgement," R.V. (A.V., " concluded ").

B. Adjective.

HUPODIKOS (ὑπόδικος). brought to trial, answerable to (*hupo*, under, *dikē*, justice), Rom. 3 : 19, is translated " under the judgement," R.V. (A.V., " guilty ").¶

For HALL OF JUDGMENT, JUDGMENT HALL, see HALL

JUDGMENT-SEAT

I. BĒMA (βῆμα), primarily, a step, a pace (akin to *bainō*, to go), as in Acts 7 : 5, translated " to set (his foot) on," lit., ' foot-room,' was used to denote a raised place or platform, reached by steps, originally that at Athens in the Pnyx Hill, where was the place of assembly ; from the platform orations were made. The word became used for a tribune, two of which were provided in the law-courts of Greece, one for the accuser and one for the defendant ; it was applied to the tribunal of a Roman magistrate or ruler, Matt. 27 : 19 ; John 19 : 13 ; Acts 12 : 21, translated " throne ; " 18 : 12, 16, 17 ; 25 : 6, 10, 17.

In two passages the word is used of the Divine tribunal before which all believers are hereafter to stand. In Rom. 14 : 10 it is called " The judgement-seat of God," R.V. (A.V., " of Christ "), according to the most authentic mss. The same tribunal is called " the judgment-seat of Christ," 2 Cor. 5 : 10, to whom the Father has given all judgment, John 5 : 22, 27. At this *bēma* believers are to be made manifest, that each may ' receive the things done in (or through) the body,' according to what he has done, ' whether it be good or bad.' There they will receive rewards for their faithfulness to the Lord. For all that has been contrary in their lives to His will they will suffer loss, 1 Cor. 3 : 15.   This judgment-seat is to be distinguished from the pre-millennial, earthly Throne of Christ, Matt. 25 : 31, and the post-millennial " Great White Throne," Rev. 20 : 11, at which only " the dead " will appear.   The judgment-seat of Christ will be a tribunal held ' in His Parousia,' i.e., His presence with His saints after His return to receive them to Himself.¶

2. KRITĒRION (κριτήριον) primarily a means of judging (akin to *krinō*, to judge : Eng., criterion), then, a tribunal, law-court, or lawsuit, 1 Cor. 6 : 2 (last clause), for which see JUDGE, B, No. 3, Note (1) ; 6 : 4, for which see JUDGMENT, Note (1) at end ; Jas. 2 : 6.¶

JURISDICTION

EXOUSIA (ἐξουσία), power, authority, is used, by metonymy, to denote jurisdiction, in Luke 23 : 7.   For the different meanings of the word and other instances of its use by metonymy, see AUTHORITY, A, No. 1.

JUST, JUSTLY
A. Adjectives.

1. DIKAIOS (δίκαιος) was first used of persons observant of *dikē*, custom, rule, right, especially in the fulfilment of duties towards gods and men, and of things that were in accordance with right.   The Eng. word " righteous " was formerly spelt ' rightwise ', i.e., (in a) straight way. In the N.T. it denotes righteous, a state of being right, or right conduct, judged whether by the Divine standard, or according to human standards, of what is right.   Said of God, it designates the perfect agreement between His nature and His acts (in which He is the standard for all men).   See RIGHTEOUSNESS.   It is used (1) in the broad sense, of persons : (*a*) of God, e.g., John 17 : 25 ; Rom. 3 : 26 ; 1 John 1 : 9 ; 2 : 29 ; 3 : 7 ; (*b*) of Christ, e.g., Acts 3 : 14 ; 7 : 52 ; 22 : 14 ; 2 Tim. 4 : 8 ; 1 Pet. 3 : 18 ; 1 John 2 : 1 ; (*c*) of men, Matt. 1 : 19 ; Luke 1 : 6 ; Rom. 1 : 17 ; 2 : 13 ; 5 : 7.   (2) of things ;   blood (metaphorical), Matt. 23 : 35 ;   Christ's judgment, John 5 : 30 ;   any circumstance, fact or deed, Matt. 20 : 4 (v. 7, in some mss.)) ; Luke 12 : 57 ; Acts 4 : 19 ; Eph. 6 : 1 ; Phil. 1 : 7 ; 4 : 8 ; Col. 4 : 1 ; 2 Thess. 1 : 6 ; " the commandment " (the Law), Rom. 7 : 12 ; works, 1 John 3 : 12 ; the ways of God, Rev. 15 : 3.   See RIGHTEOUS.

2. ENDIKOS (ἔνδικος), just, righteous (*en*, in, *dikē*, right), is said of the condemnation of those who say " Let us do evil, that good may come," Rom. 3 : 8 ; of the recompense of reward of transgressions under the Law, Heb. 2 : 2.¶

Note : As to the distinction between No. 1 and No. 2, " *dikaios* characterizes the subject so far as he or it is (so to speak) one with *dikē*, right ;   *endikos*, so far as he occupies a due relation to *dikē* ;   . . . in Rom. 3 : 8 *endikos* presupposes that which has been decided righteously, which leads to the just sentence " (Cremer).

B. Adverb.

DIKAIŌS (δικαίως), justly, righteously, in accordance with what is right, is said (a) of God's judgment, 1 Pet. 2 : 23 ; (b) of men, Luke 23 : 41, " justly ; " 1 Cor. 15 : 34, R.V., " righteously " (A.V., " to righteousness ") ; 1 Thess. 2 : 10, R.V., " righteously ; " Tit. 2 : 12.¶

JUSTICE

DIKĒ (δίκη), primarily custom, usage, came to denote what is right ; then, a judicial hearing ; hence, the execution of a sentence, " punishment," 2 Thess. 1 : 9, R.V. ; Jude 7, " punishment," R.V. (A.V., " vengeance "). In Acts 28 : 4 (A.V., " vengeance ") it is personified and denotes the goddess Justice or Nemesis (Lat., *Justitia*), who the Melita folk supposed was about to inflict the punishment of death upon Paul by means of the viper. See PUNISHMENT, VENGEANCE.¶

JUSTIFICATION, JUSTIFIER, JUSTIFY
A. Nouns.

1. DIKAIŌSIS (δικαίωσις) denotes the act of pronouncing righteous, justification, acquittal ; its precise meaning is determined by that of the verb *dikaioō*, to justify (see B) ; it is used twice in the Ep. to the Romans, and there alone in the N.T., signifying the establishment of a person as just by acquittal from guilt. In Rom. 4 : 25 the phrase " for our justification," is, lit., ' because of our justification ' (parallel to the preceding clause " for our trespasses," i.e., because of trespasses committed), and means, not with a view to our justification, but because all that was necessary on God's part for our justification had been effected in the Death of Christ. On this account He was raised from the dead. The propitiation being perfect and complete, His resurrection was the confirmatory counterpart. In 5 : 18, " justification of life " means ' justification which results in life ' (cp. ver. 21). That God justifies the believing sinner on the ground of Christ's Death, involves His free gift of life. On the distinction between *dikaiōsis* and *dikaiōma*, see below.¶ In the Sept., Lev. 24 : 22.¶

2. DIKAIŌMA (δικαίωμα) has three distinct meanings, and seems best described comprehensively as " a concrete expression of righteousness ; " it is a declaration that a person or thing is righteous, and hence, broadly speaking, it represents the expression and effect of *dikaiōsis* (No. 1). It signifies (a) an ordinance, Luke 1 : 6 ; Rom. 1 : 32, R.V., " ordinance," i.e., what God has declared to be right, referring to His decree of retribution (A.V., " judgment ") ; Rom. 2 : 26, R.V., " ordinances of the Law " (i.e., righteous requirements enjoined by the Law) ; so 8 : 4, " ordinance of the Law," i.e., collectively, the precepts of the Law, all that it demands as right ; in Heb. 9 : 1, 10, ordinances connected with the Tabernacle ritual; (b) a sentence of acquittal, by which God acquits men of their guilt, on the conditions (1) of His grace in Christ, through His expiatory sacrifice, (2) the acceptance of Christ by faith, Rom. 5 : 16 ; (c) a righteous act,

Rom. 5 : 18, " (through one) act of righteousness," R.V., not the act of justification, nor the righteous character of Christ (as suggested by the A.V. : *dikaiōma* does not signify character, as does *dikaiosunē*, righteousness), but the Death of Christ, as an act accomplished consistently with God's character and counsels ; this is clear as being in antithesis to the " one trespass " in the preceding statement.   Some take the word here as meaning a decree of righteousness, as in ver. 16 ; the Death of Christ could indeed be regarded as fulfilling such a decree, but as the Apostle's argument proceeds, the word, as is frequently the case, passes from one shade of meaning to another, and here stands not for a decree, but an act ; so in Rev. 15 : 4, R.V., " righteous acts " (A.V., " judgments "), and 19 : 8, " righteous acts (of the saints) " (A.V., " righteousness ").¶

Note :   For *dikaiosunē*, always translated " righteousness," see RIGHTEOUSNESS.

B. Verb.

DIKAIOŌ (δικαιόω) primarily, to deem to be right, signifies, in the N.T., (*a*) to show to be right or righteous ; in the Passive Voice, to be justified, Matt. 11 : 19 ; Luke 7 : 35 ; Rom. 3 : 4 ; 1 Tim. 3 : 16 ; (*b*) to declare to be righteous, to pronounce righteous, (1) by man, concerning God, Luke 7 : 29 (see Rom. 3 : 4, above) ; concerning himself, Luke 10 : 29 ; 16 : 15 ; (2) by God concerning men, who are declared to be righteous before Him on certain conditions laid down by Him.

Ideally the complete fulfilment of the Law of God would provide a basis of justification in His sight, Rom. 2 : 13.   But no such case has occurred in mere human experience, and therefore no one can be justified on this ground, Rom. 3 : 9–20 ; Gal. 2 : 16 ; 3 : 10, 11 ; 5 : 4.   From this negative presentation in Rom. 3, the Apostle proceeds to show that, consistently with God's own righteous character, and with a view to its manifestation, He is, through Christ, as " a propitiation . . . by (*en*, instrumental) His blood," 3 : 25, R.V., " the Justifier of him that hath faith in Jesus " (ver. 26), justification being the legal and formal acquittal from guilt by God as Judge, the pronouncement of the sinner as righteous, who believes on the Lord Jesus Christ.   In ver. 24, " being justified " is in the present continuous tense, indicating the constant process of justification in the succession of those who believe and are justified.   In 5 : 1, " being justified " is in the aorist, or point, tense, indicating the definite time at which each person, upon the exercise of faith, was justified.   In 8 : 1, justification is presented as " no condemnation."   That justification is in view here is confirmed by the preceding chapters and by verse 34. In 3 : 26, the word rendered " Justifier " is the present participle of the verb, lit., ' justifying ; '   similarly in 8 : 33 (where the article is used), " God that justifieth," is, more lit., ' God is the (One) justifying,' with stress upon the word " God."

Justification is primarily and gratuitously by faith, subsequently and evidentially by works. In regard to justification by works, the so-called contradiction between James and the Apostle Paul is only apparent. There is harmony in the different views of the subject. Paul has in mind Abraham's attitude toward God, his acceptance of God's word. This was a matter known only to God. The Romans Epistle is occupied with the effect of this Godward attitude, not upon Abraham's character or actions, but upon the contrast between faith and the lack of it, namely, unbelief, cp. Rom. 11 : 20. James (2 : 21–26) is occupied with the contrast between faith that is real and faith that is false, a faith barren and dead, which is not faith at all.

Again, the two writers have before them different epochs in Abraham's life—Paul, the event recorded in Gen. 15, James, that in Gen. 22. Contrast the words ' believed ' in Gen. 15 : 6 and ' obeyed ' in 22 : 18.

Further, the two writers use the words ' faith ' and ' works ' in somewhat different senses. With Paul, faith is acceptance of God's word ; with James, it is acceptance of the truth of certain statements about God, (ver. 19), which may fail to affect one's conduct. Faith, as dealt with by Paul, results in acceptance with God., i.e., justification, and is bound to manifest itself. If not, as James says ' Can that faith save him ? ' (ver. 14). With Paul, works are dead works ; with James they are life works. The works of which Paul speaks could be quite independent of faith : those referred to by James can be wrought only where faith is real, and they will attest its reality.

So with righteousness, or justification : Paul is occupied with a right relationship with God, James, with right conduct. Paul testifies that the ungodly can be justified by faith, James that only the right-doer is justified. See also under RIGHTEOUS, RIGHTEOUSNESS.

K

KEEP, KEEPING (Noun)
A. Verbs.

1. TĒREŌ (τηρέω) denotes (a) to watch over, preserve, keep, watch, e.g., Acts 12 : 5, 6 ; 16 : 23 ; in 25 : 21, R.V. (1st part), " kept " (A.V., " reserved ") ; the present participle is translated " keepers " in Matt. 28 : 4, lit. ' the keeping (ones) ; ' it is used of the keeping power of God the Father and Christ, exercised over His people, John 17 : 11, 12, 15 ; 1 Thess. 5 : 23, " preserved ; " 1 John 5 : 18, where " He that was begotten of God," R.V., is said of Christ as the Keeper (" keepeth him," R.V., for A.V., " keepeth himself ") ; Jude 1, R.V., " kept for Jesus Christ " (A.V., " preserved in Jesus Christ ") ; Rev. 3 : 10 ; of their inheritance, 1 Pet. 1 : 4 (" reserved ") ; of judicial reservation by God in view of future doom, 2 Pet. 2 : 4, 9, 17 ; 3 : 7 ; Jude 6, 13 ; of keeping the faith, 2 Tim. 4 : 7 ; the unity of the Spirit, Eph. 4 : 3 ; oneself, 2 Cor. 11 : 9 ; 1 Tim. 5 : 22 ; Jas. 1 : 27 ; figuratively, one's garments, Rev. 16 : 15 ; (b) to observe, to give heed to, as of keeping commandments, etc., e.g., Matt. 19 : 17 ; John 14 : 15 ; 15 : 10 ; 17 : 6 ; Jas. 2 : 10 ; 1 John 2 : 3, 4, 5 ; 3 : 22, 24 ; 5 : 2 (in some mss.), 3 ; Rev. 1 : 3 ; 2 : 26 ; 3 : 8, 10 ; 12 : 17 ; 14 : 12 ; 22 : 7, 9. See RESERVE.

2. DIATĒREŌ (διατηρέω), to keep carefully (dia, intensive, and No. 1), is said of " the Mother of Jesus," in keeping His sayings in her heart, Luke 2 : 51, and of the command of the Apostles and elders in Jerusalem to Gentile converts in the churches to keep themselves from the evils mentioned in Acts 15 : 29.¶

3. SUNTĒREŌ (συντηρέω) denotes to preserve, keep safe, keep close (sun, together with, used intensively, and No. 1), in Luke 2 : 19, as in ver. 51 (see No. 2, above), of the Mother of Jesus in regard to the words of the shepherds ; in Mark 6 : 20 it is used of Herod's preservation of John the Baptist from Herodias, R.V., " kept (him) safe," A.V., " observed (him) " (marg., " kept ") ; in Matt. 9 : 17 (in some mss., Luke 5 : 38), of the preservation of wine-skins. See OBSERVE, PRESERVE.¶

4. PHULASSŌ (φυλάσσω) denotes (a) to guard, watch, keep watch, e.g., Luke 2 : 8 ; in the Passive Voice, 8 : 29 ; (b) to keep by way of pro- tection, e.g., Luke 11 : 21 ; John 12 : 25 ; 17 : 12 (2nd part ; No. 1 in 1st part and in ver. 11) ; (c) metaphorically, to keep a law, precept, etc., e.g., Matt. 19 : 20 and Luke 18 : 21, " have observed ; " Luke 11 : 28 ; John 12 : 47 (in the best mss.) ; Acts 7 : 53 ; 16 : 4 ; 21 : 24 ; Rom. 2 : 26 ; Gal. 6 : 13 ; 1 Tim. 5 : 21 (" observe ") ; in the Middle Voice, Mark 10 : 20 (" have observed ") ; (d) in the Middle Voice, to keep oneself

from, Acts 21 : 25 ; elsewhere translated by the verb to beware. See BEWARE, No. 3, GUARD, B, No. 1.

5. DIAPHULASSŌ (διαφυλάσσω), an intensive form of No. 4, to guard thoroughly ; see GUARD.

6. PHROUREŌ (φρουρέω), to keep with a military guard, e.g., Gal. 3 : 23, R.V., " kept in ward ; " see GUARD, B, No. 3.

7. POIEŌ (ποιέω), to do, make, signifies to keep, in Matt. 26 : 18, in the Lord's statement, " I will keep the passover ; " so in Acts 18 : 21, in some mss. ; in John 7 : 19, where the A.V. has " keepeth (the law)," the R.V. adheres to the usual meaning " doeth."

8. ECHŌ (ἔχω), to have, to hold, is rendered " I kept " in Luke 19 : 20, R.V. (A.V., " I have kept "), of keeping a pound laid up in a napkin. See HAVE.

9. KRATEŌ (κρατέω), to be strong, get possession of, hold fast, is used in Mark 9 : 10, " (and) they kept (the saying)," i.e., they held fast to the Lord's command to refrain from telling what they had seen in the mount of Transfiguration. See HOLD.

10. NOSPHIZŌ (νοσφίζω), to set apart, remove, signifies, in the Middle Voice, to set apart for oneself, to purloin, and is rendered " purloining " in Tit. 2 : 10 ; " kept back " (and " keep ") in Acts 5 : 2, 3, of the act of Ananias and his wife in retaining part of the price of the land.¶

11. SUNECHŌ (συνέχω), to hold together, is translated " shall . . . keep (thee) in," in Luke 19 : 43. See also Note (8), below. See CONSTRAIN.

Notes : (1) In Acts 22 : 2, A.V., *parechō*, to afford, give, cause, is rendered " kept (the more silence)," R.V., " were (the more quiet)." (2) In Matt. 14 : 6 some mss. have the verb *agō*, to lead, hold (of a feast), of keeping Herod's birthday ; the most authentic have *ginomai*, to become, take place ; hence the R.V., " when Herod's birthday came." The verb *agō* is used in Acts 19 : 38 of keeping certain occasions, as of the holding of law courts, R.V. " (the courts) are open," A.V. marg., " court days are kept ; " Moulton and Milligan illustrate from the papyri the use of the adjective *agoraios*, in the plural with *hēmerai*, days, understood, in regard to certain market days ; certain court days are what are indicated here. The conjecture that the meaning is ' courts are now being held ' (*sunodoi* being understood as meetings of the court instead of ' days ') is scarcely so appropriate to the circumstances. (3) In Matt. 8 : 33, *boskō*, to feed (swine etc.), is translated " (they that) fed," R.V. for A.V. " (they that) kept." (4) In Acts 9 : 33, *katakeimai*, to lie down, is used with *epi*, upon, with the meaning to keep one's bed (see LIE, No. 2). (5) In Rom. 2 : 25, *prassō*, to do (continuously), to practise, is rendered " be a doer of," R.V. (A.V., " keep "). (6) In Acts 20 : 20, *hupostellō*, to shrink, draw back from, is translated " I shrank (not) " (Middle Voice), R.V., A.V., " I kept back (nothing)." (7) In Acts 27 : 43, *kōluō*, to hinder, is translated " stayed (them from)," R.V., A.V., " kept (them from)." (8) In Luke 8 : 15 and 1 Cor. 11 : 2, *katechō*, to hold fast (a strengthened form of *echō*, No. 8), is translated " hold fast," R.V., A.V., " keep ; " in 15 : 2, R.V., " hold fast," A.V., " keep in memory." (9) For keep secret, see SECRET. (10) For keep under, see BUFFET. (11) *Paratithēmi* is rendered " commit the keeping " in 1 Pet. 4 : 19, A.V.. (12) For " keep the feast " see FEAST, B, No. 2

B. Noun.

TĒRĒSIS (τήρησις), akin to A, No. 1, denotes (a) a watching, and hence, imprisonment, prison, Acts 4 : 3 and 5 : 18, " ward," R.V. (A.V., " hold " and " prison ") ; (b) " keeping," 1 Cor. 7 : 19. See HOLD, PRISON.¶

KEEPER

PHULAX (φύλαξ), akin to A, No. 4, above, a guard : see GUARD.
Note : For *tēreō*, in Matt. 28 : 4, see A, No. 1, above.

KEY

KLEIS (κλείς), a key, is used metaphorically (a) of " the keys of the kingdom of heaven," which the Lord committed to Peter, Matt. 16 : 19, by which he would open the door of faith, as he did to Jews at Pentecost, and to Gentiles in the person of Cornelius, acting as one commissioned by Christ, through the power of the Holy Spirit ; he had precedence over his fellow-disciples, not in authority, but in the matter of time, on the ground of his confession of Christ (ver. 16) ; equal authority was committed to them (18 : 18) ; (b) of " the key of knowledge," Luke 11 : 52, i.e., knowledge of the revealed will of God, by which men entered into the life that pleases God ; this the religious leaders of the Jews had presumptuously ' taken away,' so that they neither entered in themselves, nor permitted their hearers to do so ; (c) of " the keys of death and of Hades," Rev. 1 : 18, R.V. (see HADES), indicative of the authority of the Lord over the bodies and souls of men ; (d) of " the key of David," Rev. 3 : 7, a reference to Is. 22 : 22, speaking of the deposition of Shebna and the investiture of Eliakim, in terms evidently Messianic, the metaphor being that of the right of entrance upon administrative authority ; the mention of David is symbolic of complete sovereignty ; (e) of " the key of the pit of the abyss," Rev. 9 : 1 ; here the symbolism is that of competent authority ; the pit represents a shaft or deep entrance into the region (see ABYSS), from whence issued smoke, symbolic of blinding delusion ; (f) of " the key of the abyss," Rev. 20 : 1 ; this is to be distinguished from (e) : the symbolism is that of the complete supremacy of God over the region of the lost, in which, by angelic agency, Satan is destined to be confined for a thousand years.¶

KICK

LAKTIZŌ (λακτίζω), to kick (from *lax*, an adverb signifying ' with the foot '), is used in Acts 26 : 14 (some mss. have it in 9 : 5).

For KID see GOAT

KILL

1. APOKTEINŌ (ἀποκτείνω), to kill, is used (a) physically, e.g., Matt. 10 : 28 ; 14 : 5, " put . . . to death," similarly rendered in John 18 : 31 ; often of Christ's Death ; in Rev. 2 : 13, R.V., " was killed " (A.V., " was slain ") ; 9 : 15, R.V., " kill " (A.V., " slay ") ; 11 : 13, R.V., " were killed " (A.V., " were slain ") ; so in 19 : 21 ; (b) metaphorically, Rom. 7 : 11, of the power of sin, which is personified, as " finding occasion, through the commandment," and inflicting deception and spiritual death, i.e., separation from God, realized through the presentation of the command-ment to conscience, breaking in upon the fancied state of freedom ; the argument shows the power of the Law, not to deliver from sin, but to enhance its sinfulness ; in 2 Cor. 3 : 6, " the letter killeth," signifies not the literal meaning of Scripture as contrasted with the spiritual, but the power of the Law to bring home the knowledge of guilt and its punishment ; in Eph. 2 : 16 " having slain the enmity " describes the work of Christ through His death in annulling the enmity, " the Law " (ver. 15), between Jew and Gentile, reconciling regenerate Jew and Gentile to God in spiritual unity " in one body." See DEATH, C, No. 4, SLAY.

2. ANAIREŌ (ἀναιρέω) denotes (a) to take up (ana, up, haireō, to take), said of Pharaoh's daughter, in taking up Moses, Acts 7 : 21 ; (b) to take away in the sense of removing, Heb. 10 : 9, of the legal appointment of sacrifices, to bring in the will of God in the sacrificial offering of the Death of Christ ; (c) to kill, used physically only (not metaphorically as in No. 1), e.g., Luke 22 : 2 ; in 2 Thess. 2 : 8, instead of the future tense of this verb, some texts (followed by R.V. marg.) read the future of analiskō, to consume. See DEATH, C, No. 2, SLAY.

3. THUŌ (θύω) primarily denotes to offer firstfruits to a god ; then (a) to sacrifice by slaying a victim, Acts 14 : 13, 18, to do sacrifice ; 1 Cor. 10 : 20, to sacrifice ; 1 Cor. 5 : 7, " hath been sacrificed," of the Death of Christ as our Passover ; (b) to slay, kill, Matt. 22 : 4 ; Mark 14 : 12 ; Luke 15 : 23, 27, 30 ; 22 : 7 ; John 10 : 10 ; Acts 10 : 13 ; 11 : 7.¶

4. PHONEUŌ (φονεύω), to murder, akin to phoneus, a murderer, is always rendered by the verb to kill (except in Matt. 19 : 18, A.V., " do . . . murder," and in Matt. 23 : 35, A.V. and R.V., " ye slew ") ; Matt. 5 : 21 (twice) ; 23 : 31 ; Mark 10 : 19 ; Luke 18 : 20 ; Rom. 13 : 9 ; Jas. 2 : 11 (twice) ; 4 : 2 ; 5 : 6.¶

5. THANATOŌ (θανατόω), to put to death (from thanatos, death), is translated " are killed " in Rom. 8 : 36 ; " killed " in 2 Cor. 6 : 9. See DEATH, C, No. 1.

6. DIACHEIRIZŌ (διαχειρίζω), primarily, to have in hand, manage (cheir, the hand), is used in the Middle Voice, in the sense of laying hands on with a view to kill, or of actually killing, Acts 5 : 30, " ye slew ;" 26 : 21, " to kill." See SLAY.¶

7. SPHAZŌ, or SPHATTŌ (σφάζω), to slay, to slaughter, especially victims for sacrifice, is most frequently translated by the verb to slay; so the R.V. in Rev. 6 : 4 (A.V., " should kill "); in 13 : 3, R.V., " smitten unto death " (A.V., " wounded "). See SLAY, WOUND. Cp. *katasphazō*, to kill off, Luke 19 : 27 ;¶ *sphagē*, slaughter, e.g., Acts 8 : 32, and *sphagion*, a victim for slaughter, Acts 7 : 42.¶

KIN, KINSFOLK, KINSMAN, KINSWOMAN
A. Adjective.

SUNGENĒS (συγγενής), primarily denoting congenital, natural, innate (*sun*, with, *genos*, a family, race, offspring), then, ' akin to,' is used as a noun, denoting (*a*) of family relationship, kin, a kinsman, kinsfolk(s), Luke 1 : 58, R.V., " kinsfolk " (A.V., " cousins "); 14 : 12; 21 : 16; John 18 : 26; Acts 10 : 24; (*b*) of tribal or racial kinship, fellow-nationals, Rom. 9 : 3; 16 : 7, 11, 21.¶

B. Nouns.

1. SUNGENIS (συγγενίς), a late feminine form of A (some mss. have *sungenēs*), denotes a kinswoman, Luke 1 : 36, R.V., " kinswoman " (A.V., " cousin "). Cp. *sungeneia* (see KINDRED).¶

2. SUNGENEUS (συγγενεύς), an alternative form of A, is used in Mark 6 : 4, " kin," and Luke 2 : 44, " kinsfolk."¶

KIND (Noun)

1. GENOS (γένος), akin to *ginomai*, to become, denotes (*a*) a family, Acts 4 : 6, " kindred; " 7 : 13, R.V., " race " (A.V., " kindred "); 13 : 26, " stock "; (*b*) an offspring, Acts 17 : 28; Rev. 22 : 16; (*c*) a nation, a race, Mark 7 : 26, R.V., " race " (A.V., " nation "); Acts 4 : 36, R.V. " (a man of Cyprus) by race," A.V., " of the country (of Cyprus); " *genos* does not mean a country, the word here signifies parentage (Jews had settled in Cyprus from, or even before, the reign of Alexander the Great); 7 : 19, R.V., " race " (A.V., " kindred "); 18 : 2, 24, R.V., " by race " (A.V., " born "); 2 Cor. 11 : 26, " countrymen; " Gal. 1 : 14, R.V., " countrymen " (A.V., " nation "); Phil. 3 : 5, " stock; " 1 Pet. 2 : 9, R.V., " race " (A.V., " generation "); (*d*) a kind, sort, class, Matt. 13 : 47, " kind; " in some mss. in 17 : 21, A.V., " kind; " Mark 9 : 29, " kind; " 1 Cor. 12 : 10, 28, " kinds " (A.V., " diversities "); 14 : 10 (ditto).¶ See BEGET, B.

2. PHUSIS (φύσις) among its various meanings denotes the nature, the natural constitution or power of a person or thing, and is translated " kind " in Jas. 3 : 7 (twice), " kind " (of beasts etc.), and " (man)kind," lit., ' human kind.' See NATURE, NATURAL.

Notes : (1) The indefinite pronoun *tis*, some, a certain, one, is used adjectively with the noun *aparchē*, firstfruits, in Jas. 1 : 18, " a kind of." (2) In 1 Cor. 15 : 37, R.V., " some other kind " (A.V., " some other grain ") translates a phrase which, lit. rendered, is ' some (one) of the rest (*loipos*).'

(3) In 2 Cor. 6 : 13, " (for a recompense) in like kind," R.V. (A.V., " in the same "), is, lit., ' (as to) the same (recompense).'

KIND (Adjective), KIND (be), KINDLY, KINDNESS
A. Adjectives.

1. CHRĒSTOS (χρηστός), serviceable, good, pleasant (of things), good, gracious, kind (of persons), is translated " kind " in Luke 6 : 35, of God ; in Eph. 4 : 32, enjoined upon believers. See BETTER, EASY, GOOD, GOODNESS, GRACIOUS.

2. AGATHOS (ἀγαθός), good, is translated " kind " in Tit. 2 : 5, R.V. See GOOD.

B. Verb.
CHRĒSTEUOMAI (χρηστεύομαι), akin to A, No. 1, to be kind, is said of love, 1 Cor. 13 : 4.¶

C. Nouns.

1. CHRĒSTOTĒS (χρηστότης), akin to A, No. 1, and B, used of goodness of heart, kindness, is translated " kindness " in 2 Cor. 6 : 6 ; Gal. 5 : 22, R.V. (A.V., " gentleness ") ; Eph. 2 : 7 ; Col. 3 : 12 ; Tit. 3 : 4. See GOODNESS.

2. PHILANTHRŌPIA (φιλανθρωπία), from philos, loving, anthrōpos, man (Eng., philanthropy), denotes kindness, and is so translated in Acts 28 : 2, of that which was shown by the inhabitants of Melita to the shipwrecked voyagers ; in Tit. 3 : 4, of the kindness of God, translated " (His) love toward man." See LOVE.¶

D. Adverb.
PHILANTHRŌPŌS (φιλανθρώπως), akin to C, No. 2, humanely, kindly, is translated " kindly " in Acts 27 : 3 (A.V., " courteously "). See COURTEOUSLY.¶

KINDLE

1. HAPTŌ (ἅπτω), properly, to fasten to, is used in Acts 28 : 2 (in the most authentic mss., some mss. have No. 3), of kindling a fire. See No. 2.

Note : Haptō is used of lighting a lamp, in Luke 8 : 16 ; 11 : 33 ; 15 : 8. For the Middle Voice see TOUCH.

2. PERIAPTŌ (περιάπτω), properly, to tie about, attach (peri, around, and No. 1), is used of lighting a fire in the midst of a court in Luke 22 : 55 (some mss. have No. 1).¶

3. ANAPTŌ (ἀνάπτω), to light up (ana, up, and No. 1), is used (a) literally, in Jas. 3 : 5, " kindleth ; " (b) metaphorically, in the Passive Voice, in Luke 12 : 49, of the kindling of the fire of hostility ; see FIRE, A (f). For Acts 28 : 2, see No. 1, above.¶

KINDRED

1. SUNGENEIA (συγγένεια) primarily denotes kinship ; then, kinsfolk, kindred (cp. sungenēs, a kinsman ; see KIN), Luke 1 : 61 ; Acts. 7 : 3, 14.¶

2. GENOS (γένος) ; see KIND (Noun), No. 1.

Notes : (1) *Phulē*, a tribe, rendered " kindreds " in the A.V. of Rev. 1 : 7 ; 7 : 9 ; 11 : 9 ; 13 : 7, " kindred " in 5 : 9 ; 14 : 6, and elsewhere, " tribe," " tribes," is always translated by the latter in the R.V. See TRIBE. (2) For *patria*, rendered " kindreds " in Acts 3 : 25, A.V., see FAMILY.

KING
A. Noun.

BASILEUS (βασιλεύς), a king (cp. Eng., Basil), e.g., Matt. 1 : 6, is used of the Roman Emperor in 1 Pet. 2 : 13, 17 (a command of general application) ; this reference to the Emperor is illustrated frequently in the *koinē* (for which see Preface to Vol. I) ; of Herod the Tetrarch (used by courtesy), Matt. 14 : 9 ; of Christ, as the King of the Jews, e.g., Matt. 2 : 2 ; 27 : 11, 29, 37 ; as the King of Israel, Mark 15 : 32 ; John 1 : 49 ; 12 : 13 ; as King of kings, Rev. 17 : 14 ; 19 : 16 ; as " the King " in judging nations and men at the establishment of the Millennial Kingdom, Matt. 25 : 34, 40 ; of God, " the great King," Matt. 5 : 35 ; " the King eternal, incorruptible, invisible," 1 Tim. 1 : 17 ; " King of kings," 1 Tim. 6 : 15, see Note (2) below ; " King of the ages," Rev. 15 : 3, R.V. (A.V., " saints "). Christ's Kingship was predicted in the O.T., e.g., Psa. 2 : 6, and in the N.T., e.g., Luke 1 : 32, 33 ; He came as such, e.g., Matt. 2 : 2 ; John 18 : 37 ; was rejected and died as such, Luke 19 : 14 ; Matt. 27 : 37 ; is now a King Priest, after the order of Melchizedek, Heb. 5 : 6 ; 7 : 1, 17 ; and will reign for ever and ever, Rev. 11 : 15.

Notes : (1) In Rev. 1 : 6 and 5 : 10, the most authentic mss. have the word *basileia*, kingdom, instead of the plural of *basileus*, A.V., " kings ; " R.V., " a kingdom (to be priests)," and " a kingdom (and priests)." The kingdom was conditionally offered by God to Israel, that they should be to Him " a kingdom of priests," Ex. 19 : 6, the entire nation fulfilling priestly worship and service. Their failure to fulfil His covenant resulted in the selection of the Aaronic priesthood. The bringing in of the new and better covenant of grace has constituted all believers a spiritual Kingdom, a holy and royal priesthood, 1 Pet. 2 : 5, 9. (2) In 1 Tim. 6 : 15, the word " kings " translates the present participle of the verb *basileuō*, to be king, to have kingship, lit., ' of (those) who are kings.' See REIGN. (3) Deissmann has shown that the title " king of kings " was " in very early eastern history a decoration of great monarchs and also a divine title " (*Light from the Ancient East*, pp. 367, f.). Moulton and Milligan illustrate the use of the title among the Persians, from documents discovered in Media.

B. Adjectives.

1. BASILEIOS (βασίλειος), denoting royal, as in 1 Pet. 2 : 9, is used in the plural, of the courts or palaces of kings, Luke 7 : 25, " kings' courts ; " a possible meaning is ' among royal courtiers or persons.'¶

2. BASILIKOS (βασιλικός), royal, belonging to a king, is used in Acts 12 : 20 with ' country ' understood, " their country was fed from the king's," lit., ' the royal (country).' See NOBLEMAN, ROYAL.

KINGDOM

BASILEIA (βασιλεία) is primarily an abstract noun, denoting sovereignty, royal power, dominion, e.g., Rev. 17 : 18, translated " (which) reigneth," lit., ' hath a kingdom ' (R.V. marg.) ; then, by metonymy, a concrete noun, denoting the territory or people over whom a king rules, e.g., Matt. 4 : 8 ; Mark 3 : 24. It is used especially of the Kingdom of God and of Christ.

" The Kingdom of God is (a) the sphere of God's rule, Ps. 22 : 28 ; 145 : 13 ; Dan. 4 : 25 ; Luke 1 : 52 ; Rom. 13 : 1, 2. Since, however, this earth is the scene of universal rebellion against God, e.g., Luke 4 : 5, 6 ; 1 John 5 : 19 ; Rev. 11 : 15-18, the Kingdom of God is (b) the sphere in which, at any given time, His rule is acknowledged. God has not relinquished His sovereignty in the face of rebellion, demoniac and human, but has declared His purpose to establish it, Dan. 2 : 44 ; 7 : 14 ; 1 Cor. 15 : 24, 25. Meantime, seeking willing obedience, He gave His law to a nation and appointed kings to administer His Kingdom over it, 1 Chron. 28 : 5. Israel, however, though declaring still a nominal allegiance shared in the common rebellion, Isa. 1 : 2-4, and, after they had rejected the Son of God, John 1 : 11 (cp. Matt. 21 : 33-43), were " cast away," Rom. 11 : 15, 20, 25. Henceforth God calls upon men everywhere, without distinction of race or nationality, to submit voluntarily to His rule. Thus the Kingdom is said to be ' in mystery ' now, Mark 4 : 11, that is, it does not come within the range of the natural powers of observation, Luke 17 : 20, but is spiritually discerned, John 3 : 3 (cp. 1 Cor. 2 : 14). When, hereafter, God asserts His rule universally, then the Kingdom will be in glory, that is, it will be manifest to all ; cp. Matt. 25 : 31-34 ; Phil. 2 : 9-11 ; 2 Tim. 4 : 1, 18.

" Thus, speaking generally, references to the Kingdom fall into two classes, the first, in which it is viewed as present and involving suffering for those who enter it, 2 Thess. 1 : 5 ; the second, in which it is viewed as future and is associated with reward, Matt. 25 : 34, and glory, 13 : 43. See also Acts 14 : 22.

" The fundamental principle of the Kingdom is declared in the words of the Lord spoken in the midst of a company of Pharisees, " the Kingdom of God is in the midst of you," Luke 17 : 21, marg., that is, where the King is, there is the Kingdom. Thus at the present time and so far as this earth is concerned, where the King is and where His rule is acknowledged, is, first, in the heart of the individual believer, Acts 4 : 19 ; Eph. 3 : 17 ; 1 Pet. 3 : 15 ; and then in the churches of God, 1 Cor. 12 : 3, 5, 11 ; 14 : 37 ; cp. Col. 1 : 27, where for " in " read ' among.'

"Now, the King and His rule being refused, those who enter the Kingdom of God are brought into conflict with all who disown its allegiance, as well as with the desire for ease, and the dislike of suffering and unpopularity, natural to all. On the other hand, subjects of the Kingdom are the objects of the care of God, Matt. 6 : 33, and of the rejected King, Heb. 13 : 5.

"Entrance into the Kingdom of God is by the new birth, Matt. 18 : 3 ; John 3 : 5, for nothing that a man may be by nature, or can attain to by any form of self-culture, avails in the spiritual realm. And as the new nature, received in the new birth, is made evident by obedience, it is further said that only such as do the will of God shall enter into His Kingdom, Matt. 7 : 21, where, however, the context shows that the reference is to the future, as in 2 Pet. 1 : 10, 11. Cp. also 1 Cor. 6 : 9, 10 ; Gal. 5 : 21 ; Eph. 5 : 5.

"The expression 'Kingdom of God' occurs four times in Matthew, 'Kingdom of the Heavens' usually taking its place. The latter (cp. Dan. 4 : 26) does not occur elsewhere in N.T., but see 2 Tim. 4 : 18, "His heavenly Kingdom." . . . This Kingdom is identical with the Kingdom of the Father (cp. Matt. 26 : 29 with Mark 14 : 25), and with the Kingdom of the Son (cp. Luke 22 : 30). Thus there is but one Kingdom, variously described : of the Son of Man, Matt. 13 : 41 ; of Jesus, Rev. 1 : 9 ; of Christ Jesus, 2 Tim. 4 : 1 ; " of Christ and God," Eph. 5 : 5 ; " of our Lord, and of His Christ," Rev. 11 : 15 ; " of our God, and the authority of His Christ," 12 : 10 ; " of the Son of His love," Col. 1 : 13.

"Concerning the future, the Lord taught His disciples to pray, " Thy Kingdom come," Matt. 6 : 10, where the verb is in the point tense, precluding the notion of gradual progress and development, and implying a sudden catastrophe as declared in 2 Thess. 2 : 8.

"Concerning the present, that a man is of the Kingdom of God is not shown in the punctilious observance of ordinances, which are external and material, but in the deeper matters of the heart, which are spiritual and essential, viz., ' righteousness, and peace, and joy in the Holy Spirit,' Rom. 14 : 17."*

"With regard to the expressions ' the Kingdom of God ' and the ' Kingdom of the Heavens,' while they are often used interchangeably, it does not follow that in every case they mean exactly the same and are quite identical.

" The Apostle Paul often speaks of the Kingdom of God, not dispensationally but morally, e.g., in Rom. 14 : 17 ; 1 Cor. 4 : 20, but never so of the Kingdom of Heaven. ' God ' is not the equivalent of ' the heavens.' He is everywhere and above all dispensations, whereas ' the heavens ' are distinguished from the earth, until the Kingdom comes in judgment

---

* From Notes on Thessalonians by Hogg and Vine, pp. 68–70.

and power and glory (Rev. 11 : 15, R.V.) when rule in heaven and on earth will be one.

"While, then, the sphere of the Kingdom of God and the Kingdom of Heaven are at times identical, yet the one term cannot be used indiscriminately for the other. In the 'Kingdom of Heaven' (32 times in Matt.), heaven is in antithesis to earth, and the phrase is limited to the Kingdom in its earthly aspect for the time being, and is used only dispensationally and in connection with Israel. In the 'Kingdom of God', in its broader aspect, God is in antithesis to 'man' or 'the world,' and the term signifies the entire sphere of God's rule and action in relation to the world. It has a moral and spiritual force and is a general term for the Kingdom at any time. The Kingdom of Heaven is always the Kingdom of God, but the Kingdom of God is not limited to the Kingdom of Heaven, until in their final form, they become identical; e.g., Rev. 11 : 15, R.V.; John 3 : 5; Rev. 12 : 10." (*An Extract*).

For KINSFOLK and KINSMAN see KIN

KISS (Noun and Verb)
A. Noun.

PHILĒMA (φίλημα), a kiss (akin to B), Luke 7 : 45; 22 : 48, was a token of Christian brotherhood, whether by way of welcome or farewell, "a holy kiss," Rom. 16 : 16; 1 Cor. 16 : 20; 2 Cor. 13 : 12; 1 Thess. 5 : 26, "holy" (*hagios*), as free from anything inconsistent with their calling as saints (*hagioi*); "a kiss of love," 1 Pet. 5 : 14. There was to be an absence of formality and hypocrisy, a freedom from prejudice arising from social distinctions, from discrimination against the poor, from partiality towards the well-to-do. In the churches masters and servants would thus salute one another without any attitude of condescension on the one part or disrespect on the other. The kiss took place thus between persons of the same sex. In the "Apostolic Constitutions," a writing compiled in the 4th century, A.D., there is a reference to the custom whereby men sat on one side of the room where a meeting was held, and women on the other side of the room (as is frequently the case still in parts of Europe and Asia), and the men are bidden to salute the men, and the women the women, with "the kiss of the Lord."¶

B. Verbs.

1. PHILEŌ (φιλέω), to love, signifies to kiss, in Matt. 26 : 48; Mark 14 : 44; Luke 22 : 47.

2. KATAPHILEŌ (καταφιλέω) denotes to kiss fervently (*kata*, intensive, and No. 1); the stronger force of this verb has been called in question, but the change from *phileō* to *kataphileō* in Matt. 26 : 49 and Mark 14 : 45 can scarcely be without significance, and the act of the traitor was almost certainly more demonstrative than the simple kiss of salu-

tation.   So with the kiss of genuine devotion, Luke 7 : 38, 45 ; 15 : 20 ;
Acts 20 : 37, in each of which this verb is used.¶

KNEE

GONU (γόνυ). a knee (Latin, *genu*), is used (*a*) metaphorically in
Heb. 12 : 12, where the duty enjoined is that of " courageous self-recovery
in God's strength ; " (*b*) literally, of the attitude of a suppliant, Luke
5 : 8 ; Eph. 3 : 14 ; of veneration, Rom. 11 : 4 ; 14 : 11 ; Phil. 2 : 10 ;
in mockery, Mark 15 : 19.   See KNEEL.

KNEEL

1. GONUPETEŌ (γονυπετέω) denotes to bow the knees, kneel, from
gonu (see above) and *piptō*, to fall prostrate, the act of one imploring
aid, Matt. 17 : 14 ; Mark 1 : 40 ; of one expressing reverence and honour,
Mark 10 : 17 ; in mockery, Matt. 27 : 29.¶

2. A phrase consisting of *tithēmi*, to put, with *gonata*, the plural of
gonu, the knee (see above), signifies to kneel, and is always used of an
attitude of prayer, Luke 22 : 41 (lit., ' placing the knees ') ; Acts 7 : 60 ;
9 : 40 ; 20 : 36 ; 21 : 5.¶

KNIT TOGETHER

SUMBIBAZŌ (συμβιβάζω) signifies to cause to coalesce, to join or knit
together, Eph. 4 : 16, R.V., " knit together " (A.V., " compacted)" ;
Col. 2 : 2, where some would assign the alternative meaning, to instruct,
as, e.g., in 1 Cor. 2 : 16 ; in Col. 2 : 19, " knit together," it is said of the
Church, as the Body of which Christ is the Head.   See COMPACTED.

Note : In Acts 10 : 11 some mss. have the verb *deō*, to bind, translated
" knit," of the four corners of the sheet in Peter's vision.   The R.V.
" let down " translates the verb *kathiēmi*, found in the best texts.

KNOCK

KROUŌ (κρούω), to strike, knock, is used in the N.T. of knocking
at a door, (*a*) literally, Luke 12 : 36 ; Acts 12 : 13, 16 ; (*b*) figuratively,
Matt. 7 : 7, 8 ; Luke 11 : 9, 10 (of importunity in dealing with God) ;
13 : 25 ; Rev. 3 : 20.¶

KNOW, KNOWN, KNOWLEDGE, UNKNOWN
A. Verbs.

1. GINŌSKŌ (γινώσκω) signifies to be taking in knowledge, to come
to know, recognize, understand, or to understand completely, e.g.,
Mark 13 : 28, 29 ; John 13 : 12 ; 15 : 18 ; 21 : 17 ; 2 Cor. 8 : 9 ; Heb.
10 : 34 ; 1 John 2 : 5 ; 4 : 2, 6 (twice), 7, 13 ; 5 : 2, 20 ; in its past tenses
it frequently means to know in the sense of realising, the aorist or point
tense usually indicating definiteness, Matt. 13 : 11 ; Mark 7 : 24 ; John
7 : 26 ; in 10 : 38 " that ye may know (aorist tense) and understand, (present tense) ; " 19 : 4 ; Acts 1 : 7 ; 17 : 19 ; Rom. 1 : 21 ; 1 Cor. 2 : 11 (2nd

part), 14; 2 Cor. 2:4; Eph. 3:19; 6:22; Phil. 2:19; 3:10; 1 Thess. 3:5; 2 Tim. 2:19; Jas. 2:20; 1 John 2:13 (twice), 14; 3:6; 4:8; 2 John 1; Rev. 2:24; 3:3, 9. In the Passive Voice, it often signifies to become known, e.g., Matt. 10:26; Phil. 4:5. In the sense of complete and absolute understanding on God's part, it is used, e.g., in Luke 16:15; John 10:15 (of the Son as well as the Father); 1 Cor. 3:20. In Luke 12:46, A.V., it is rendered " he is . . . aware."

In the N.T. *ginōskō* frequently indicates a relation between the person knowing and the object known; in this respect, what is known is of value or importance to the one who knows, and hence the establishment of the relationship, e.g., especially of God's knowledge, 1 Cor. 8:3, " if any man love God, the same is known of Him; " Gal. 4:9, " to be known of God; " here the knowing suggests approval and bears the meaning ' to be approved ; ' so in 2 Tim. 2:19; cp. John 10:14, 27; Gen. 18:19; Nahum 1:7; the relationship implied may involve remedial chastisement, Amos 3:2. The same idea of appreciation as well as knowledge underlies several statements concerning the knowledge of God and His truth on the part of believers, e.g., John 8:32; 14:20, 31; 17:3; Gal. 4:9 (1st part); 1 John 2:3, 13, 14; 4:6, 8, 16; 5:20; such knowledge is obtained, not by mere intellectual activity, but by operation of the Holy Spirit consequent upon acceptance of Christ. Nor is such knowledge marked by finality; see, e.g., 2 Pet. 3:18; Hos. 6:3, R.V.

The verb is also used to convey the thought of connection or union, as between man and woman, Matt. 1:25; Luke 1:34.

2. OIDA (οἶδα), from the same root as *eidon*, to see, is a perfect tense with a present meaning, signifying, primarily, to have seen or perceived; hence, to know, to have knowledge of, whether absolutely, as in Divine knowledge, e.g., Matt. 6:8, 32; John 6:6, 64; 8:14; 11:42; 13:11; 18:4; 2 Cor. 11:31; 2 Pet. 2:9; Rev. 2:2, 9, 13, 19; 3:1, 8, 15; or in the case of human knowledge, to know from observation, e.g., 1 Thess. 1:4, 5; 2:1; 2 Thess. 3:7.

The differences between *ginōskō* (No. 1) and *oida* demand consideration : (a) *ginōskō*, frequently suggests inception or progress in knowledge, while *oida* suggests fulness of knowledge, e.g., John 8:55, " ye have not known Him " (*ginōskō*), i.e., begun to know, " but I know Him " (*oida*), i.e., ' know Him perfectly ; ' 13:7, " What I do thou knowest not now," i.e. Peter did not yet perceive (*oida*) its significance, " but thou shalt understand," i.e., ' get to know (*ginōskō*), hereafter ; ' 14:7, " If ye had known Me " (*ginōskō*), i.e., ' had definitely come to know Me,' " ye would have known My Father also " (*oida*), i.e., ' would have had perception of : ' " from henceforth ye know Him " (*ginōskō*), i.e., having unconsciously been coming to the Father, as the One who was in Him, they would now consciously be in the constant and progressive experience of knowing Him; in Mark 4:13, " Know ye not (*oida*) this parable ? and how shall ye know (*ginōskō*) all the parables ? " (R.V.), i.e., ' Do ye not understand this parable ? How shall ye come to perceive all . . . ' the intimation being that the first parable is a leading and testing one ; (*b*) while *ginōskō* frequently implies an active relation between the one who knows and the person or thing known (see No. 1, above), *oida* expresses the fact that the object has simply come within the scope of the knower's perception ; thus in Matt. 7 : 23 " I never knew you " (*ginōskō*) suggests ' I have never been in approving connection with you,' whereas in 25 : 12, " I know you not " (*oida*) suggests ' you stand in no relation to Me.'

3. EPIGINŌSKŌ (*ἐπιγινώσκω*) denotes (*a*) to observe, fully perceive, notice attentively, discern, recognize (*epi*, upon, and No. 1) ; it suggests generally a directive, a more special, recognition of the object known than does No. 1 ; it also may suggest advanced knowledge or special appreciation ; thus, in Rom. 1 : 32, " knowing the ordinance of God " (*epiginōskō*) means ' knowing full well,' whereas in verse 21 " knowing God " (*ginōskō*) simply suggests that they could not avoid the perception. Sometimes *epiginōskō* implies a special participation in the object known, and gives greater weight to what is stated ; thus in John 8 : 32, " ye shall know the truth," *ginōskō* is used, whereas in 1 Tim. 4 : 3, " them that believe and know the truth," *epiginōskō* lays stress on participation in the truth. Cp. the stronger statement in Col. 1 : 6 (*epiginōskō*) with that in 2 Cor. 8 : 9 (*ginōskō*), and the two verbs in 1 Cor. 13 : 12, " now I know in part (*ginōskō*) ; but then shall I know (*piginōskō*) even as also I have been known (*epiginōskō*)," a knowledge " which perfectly unites the subject with the object ; " (*b*) to discover, ascertain, determine, e.g., Luke 7 : 37 ; 23 : 7 ; Acts 9 : 30 ; 19 : 34 ; 22 : 29 ; 28 : 1 ; in 24 : 11 the best mss. have this verb instead of No. 1 ; hence the R.V., " take knowledge." J. Armitage Robinson (on Ephesians) points out that *epignōsis* is " knowledge directed towards a particular object, perceiving, discerning," whereas *gnōsis* is knowledge in the abstract. See ACKNOWLEDGE.

4. PROGINŌSKŌ (*προγινώσκω*), to know beforehand, is used (*a*) of the Divine foreknowledge concerning believers, Rom. 8 : 29 ; Israel, 11 : 2 ; Christ as the Lamb of God, 1 Pet. 1 : 20, R.V., " foreknown " (A.V., " foreordained ") ; (*b*) of human previous knowledge, of a person, Acts 26 : 5, R.V., " having knowledge of " (A.V., " which knew ") ; of facts, 2 Pet. 3 : 17. See FOREKNOW.¶

5. EPISTAMAI (*ἐπίσταμαι*), to know, know of, understand (probably an old Middle Voice form of *ephistēmi*, to set over), is used in Mark 14 : 68, " understand," which follows *oida* " I (neither) know ; " most frequently in the Acts, 10 : 28 ; 15 : 7 ; 18 : 25 ; 19 : 15, 25 ; 20 : 18 ; 22 : 19 ; 24 : 10 ; 26 : 26 ; elsewhere, 1 Tim. 6 : 4 ; Heb. 11 : 8 ; Jas. 4 : 14 ; Jude 10. See UNDERSTAND.¶

6. SUNOIDA (σύνοιδα), *sun*, with,and No. 2, a perfect tense with a present meaning, denotes (*a*) to share the knowledge of, be privy to, Acts 5 : 2 ; (*b*) to be conscious of, especially of guilty consciousness, 1 Cor. 4 : 4, " I know nothing against (A.V., by) myself." The verb is connected with *suneidon*, found in Acts 12 : 12 ; 14 : 6 (in the best texts). See CONSIDER, PRIVY, WARE.¶

7. AGNOEŌ (ἀγνοέω), not to know, to be ignorant : see IGNORANT.

8. GNŌRIZŌ (γνωρίζω) signifies (*a*) to come to know, discover, know, Phil. 1 : 22, " I wot (not)," i.e., ' I know not,' ' I have not come to know ' (the R.V., marg. renders it, as under (*b*), " I do not make known ") ; (*b*) to make known, whether (I) communicating things before unknown, Luke 2 : 15, 17 ; in the latter some mss. have the verb *diagnōrizō* (hence the A.V., " made known abroad) ; " John 15 : 15, " I have made known ; " 17 : 26 ; Acts 2 : 28 ; 7 : 13 (1st part), see Note (3) below ; Rom. 9 : 22, 23 ; 16 : 26 (Passive Voice) ; 2 Cor. 8 : 1, " we make known (to you)," R.V., A.V., " we do (you) to wit ; " Eph. 1 : 9 ; 3 : 3, 5, 10 (all three in the Passive Voice) ; 6 : 19, 21 ; Col. 1 : 27 ; 4 : 7, 9, " shall make known " (A.V., " shall declare ") ; 2 Pet. 1 : 16 ; or (II) reasserting things already known, 1 Cor. 12 : 3, " I give (you) to understand " (the Apostle reaffirms what they knew) ; 15 : 1, of the Gospel ; Gal. 1 : 11 (he reminds them of what they well knew, the ground of his claim to Apostleship) ; Phil. 4 : 6 (Passive Voice), of requests to God. See CERTIFY, DECLARE (Note), UNDERSTAND, WIT, WOT.¶

Notes : (1) In 2 Tim. 3 : 10, A.V., *parakoloutheō*, to follow closely, follow as a standard of conduct, is translated " hast fully known " (R.V., " didst follow "). See FOLLOW. (2) In 2 Tim. 4 : 17, A.V., *plērophoreō*, to fulfil, accomplish, is translated " might be fully known " (R.V., " might be fully proclaimed "). See FULFIL. (3) In Acts 7 : 13, some mss. have the verb *anagnōrizō*, to make oneself known, " was made known," instead of No. 8 (which see).¶ (4) In Acts 7 : 13 (2nd part) the A.V., " was made known " translates the phrase *phaneros ginomai*, to become manifest (R.V., " became manifest "). See MANIFEST. (5) For *diagnōrizō*, to make known, in Luke 2 : 17, see No. 8. (6) For *diaginōskō*, in Acts 24 : 22, " I will know the uttermost of," see DETERMINE, No. 5.

B. Adjectives.

1. GNŌSTOS (γνωστός), a later form of *gnōtos* (from No. 1), most frequently denotes " known ; " it is used ten times in the Acts, always with that meaning (save in 4 : 16, where it means " notable ") ; twice in the Gospel of John, 18 : 15, 16 ; in Luke 2 : 44 and 23 : 49 it denotes " acquaintance ; " elsewhere only in Rom. 1 : 19, " (that which) may be known (of God)," lit., ' the knowable of God,' referring to the physical universe, in the creation of which God has made Himself knowable, that is, by the exercise of man's natural faculties, without such supernatural revelations as those given to Israel. See ACQUAINTANCE.

2. PHANEROS (φανερός), visible, manifest, is translated "known" in Matt. 12 : 16 and Mark 3 : 12. See APPEAR, MANIFEST, OPENLY, OUTWARDLY.

3. EPISTĒMŌN (ἐπιστήμων), akin to A, No. 5, knowing, skilled, is used in Jas. 3 : 13, A.V., "endued with knowledge" (R.V. "understanding ").¶

4. AGNŌSTOS (ἄγνωστος), the negative of No. 1, "unknown," is found in Acts 17 : 23.¶

C. Nouns.

1. GNŌSIS (γνῶσις), primarily a seeking to know, an enquiry, investigation (akin to A, No. 1), denotes, in the N.T., knowledge, especially of spiritual truth ; it is used (a) absolutely, in Luke 11 : 52 ; Rom. 2 : 20 ; 15 : 14 ; 1 Cor. 1 : 5 ; 8 : 1 (twice), 7, 10, 11 ; 13 : 2, 8 ; 14 : 6 ; 2 Cor. 6 : 6 ; 8 : 7 ; 11 : 6 ; Eph. 3 : 19 ; Col. 2 : 3 ; 1 Pet. 3 : 7 ; 2 Pet. 1 : 5, 6 ; (b) with an object : in respect of (1) God, 2 Cor. 2 : 14 ; 10 : 5 ; (2) the glory of God, 2 Cor. 4 : 6 ; (3) Christ Jesus, Phil. 3 : 8 ; 2 Pet. 3 : 18 ; (4) salvation, Luke 1 : 77 ; (c) subjectively, of God's knowledge, Rom. 11 : 33 ; the word of knowledge, 1 Cor. 12 : 8 ; knowledge falsely so called, 1 Tim. 6 : 20.¶

2. EPIGNŌSIS (ἐπίγνωσις), akin to A, No. 3, denotes exact or full knowledge, discernment, recognition, and is a strengthened form of No. 1, expressing a fuller or a full knowledge, a greater participation by the knower in the object known, thus more powerfully influencing him. It is not found in the Gospels and Acts. Paul uses it 15 times (16 if Heb. 10 : 26 is included) out of the 20 occurrences ; Peter 4 times, all in his 2nd Epistle. Contrast Rom. 1 : 28 (epignōsis) with the simple verb in ver. 21. " In all the four Epistles of the first Roman captivity it is an element in the Apostle's opening prayer for his correspondents' well-being, Phil. 1 : 9 ; Eph. 1 : 17 ; Col. 1 : 9 ; Philm. 6 " (Lightfoot).

It is used with reference to God in Rom. 1 : 28 ; 10 : 2 ; Eph. 1 : 17 ; Col. 1 : 10 ; 2 Pet. 1 : 3 ; God and Christ, 2 Pet. 1 : 2 ; Christ, Eph. 4 : 13 ; 2 Pet. 1 : 8 ; 2 : 20 ; the will of the Lord, Col. 1 : 9 ; every good thing, Philm. 6, R.V. (A.V., " acknowledging ") ; the truth, 1 Tim. 2 : 4 ; 2 Tim. 2 : 25, R.V. ; 3 : 7 ; Tit. 1 : 1, R.V. ; the mystery of God, Col. 2 : 2, R.V., " (that they) may know " (A.V., " to the acknowledgment of "), lit., 'into a full knowledge.' It is used without the mention of an object in Phil. 1 : 9 ; Col. 3 : 10, R.V., " (renewed) unto knowledge." See ACKNOWLEDGE.¶

3. AGNŌSIA (ἀγνωσία), the negative of No. 1, ignorance, is rendered " no knowledge " in 1 Cor. 15 : 34, R.V. (A.V., " not the knowledge ") ; in 1 Pet. 2 : 15, " ignorance." See IGNORANCE.¶

Note : In Eph. 3 : 4, A.V., *sunesis*, understanding, is translated knowledge ;' R.V., " understanding." For *kardiognōstēs* see p. 207.

L

LABOUR (Noun and Verb)
A. Nouns.

1. KOPOS (κόπος) primarily denotes a striking, beating (akin to *koptō*, to strike, cut) ; then, toil resulting in weariness, laborious toil, trouble ; it is translated " labour " or " labours " in John 4 : 38 ; 1 Cor. 3 : 8 ; 15 : 58 ; 2 Cor. 6 : 5 ; 10 : 15 ; 11 : 23, 27, R.V., " labour " (A.V., " weariness ") ; 1 Thess. 1 : 3 ; 2 : 9 ; 3 : 5 ; 2 Thess. 3 : 8 ; (in some mss., Heb. 6 : 10) ; Rev. 2 : 2 (R.V. " toil ") ; 14 : 13. In the following the noun is used as the object of the verb *parechō*, to afford, give, cause, the phrase being rendered to trouble, lit., to cause toil or trouble, to embarrass a person by giving occasion for anxiety, as some disciples did to the woman with the ointment, perturbing her spirit by their criticisms, Matt. 26 : 10 ; Mark 14 : 6 ; or by distracting attention or disturbing a person's rest, as the importunate friend did, Luke 11 : 7 ; 18 : 5 ; in Gal. 6 : 17, " let no man trouble me," the Apostle refuses, in the form of a peremptory prohibition, to allow himself to be distracted further by the Judaizers, through their proclamation of a false gospel and by their malicious attacks upon himself.¶

2. PONOS (πόνος) denotes (*a*) labours, toil, Col. 4 : 13, in the best mss. (some have *zēlos*, zeal, A.V.) ; (*b*) the consequence of toil, viz., distress, suffering, pain, Rev. 16 : 10, 11 ; 21 : 4. See PAIN.¶

Notes : (1) In Phil. 1 : 22, A.V., *ergon*, work, is translated " labour " (R.V., " work ") ; work refers to what is done, and may be easy and pleasant ; *kopos* suggests the doing, and the pains taken therein. (2) A synonymous word is *mochthos*, toil, hardship, distress, 2 Cor. 11 : 27 ; 1 Thess. 2 : 9 ; 2 Thess. 3 : 8.¶

B. Verbs.

1. KOPIAŌ (κοπιάω), akin to A, No. 1, has the two different meanings (*a*) growing weary, (*b*) toiling ; it is sometimes translated to bestow labour (see under BESTOW, No. 3). It is translated by the verb to labour in Matt. 11 : 28 ; John 4 : 38 (2nd part) ; Acts 20 : 35 ; Rom. 16 : 12 (twice) ; 1 Cor. 15 : 10 ; 16 : 16 ; Eph. 4 : 28 ; Phil. 2 : 16 ; Col. 1 : 29 ; 1 Thess. 5 : 12 ; 1 Tim. 4 : 10 ; 5 : 17 ; 2 Tim. 2 : 6 ; Rev. 2 : 3 ; 1 Cor. 4 : 12, R.V., " toil " (A.V., " labour "). See TOIL.

2. CHEIMAZŌ (χειμάζω), from *cheima*, winter-cold, primarily, to expose to winter cold, signifies to drive with a storm ; in the Passive Voice, to be driven with storm, to be tempest-tossed, Acts 27 : 18, R.V., " as (we) laboured with the storm " (A.V., " being . . . tossed with a tempest ").¶

3. SUNATHLEŌ (συναθλέω), to contend along with a person (sun, with, athleō, to contend), is said in Phil. 4 : 3 of two women who " laboured with " the Apostle in the Gospel ; in 1 : 27, R.V., " striving (for)," marg., " with," A.V., " striving together (for)."   See STRIVE.¶

Notes : (1) In John 6 : 27 and 1 Thess. 2 : 9, A.V., *ergazomai*, to work, is translated respectively " labour " and " labouring " (R.V., " working "). It is used of manual work here and in 4 : 11 and Eph. 4 : 28 ; of work for Christ in general, in 1 Cor. 16 : 10.   See COMMIT.   (2) In Heb. 4 : 11, A.V., *spoudazō*, to be diligent, is translated " let us labour " (R.V., " let us give diligence ").   (3) In Col. 4 : 12, A.V., *agōnizomai*, to strive, wrestle, is translated " labouring fervently " (R.V., and A.V., marg., " striving "). (4) In 2 Cor. 5 : 9, A.V., *philotimeomai*, to seek after honour, and hence, to be ambitious, is translated " we labour," marg., " endeavour " (R.V., " we make it our aim," marg., " are ambitious ") ; cp. Rom. 15 : 20 ; 1 Thess. 4 : 11, R.V., marg.¶

LABOURER, FELLOW-LABOURER

ERGATĒS (ἐργάτης), akin to *ergazomai*, to work, and *ergon*, work, denotes (*a*) a field-labourer, a husbandman, Matt. 9 : 37, 38 ; 20 : 1, 2, 8 ; Luke 10 : 2 (twice) ; Jas. 5 : 4 ; (*b*) a workman, labourer, in a general sense, Matt. 10 : 10 ; Luke 10 : 7 ; Acts 19 : 25 ; 1 Tim. 5 : 18 ; it is used (*c*) of false apostles and evil teachers, 2 Cor. 11 : 13 ; Phil. 3 : 2 ; (*d*) of a servant of Christ, 2 Tim. 2 : 15 ; (*e*) of evildoers, Luke 13 : 27.¶

Note : In the A.V. of Philm. 1 and 24, *sunergos*, a fellow-worker, is translated " fellow-labourer," R.V., " fellow-worker " ; in Phil. 4 : 3, the plural, R.V., " fellow-workers ; " in Phil. 2 : 25, A.V., " companion in labour," R.V., " fellow-worker ;" in 1 Cor. 3 : 9, A.V., " labourers together (with God)," R.V., " God's fellow-workers," i.e., fellow-workers belonging to and serving God ; in 3 John 8, A.V., " fellow-helpers " (to the truth), R.V., " fellow-workers (with the truth)," i.e., acting together with the truth as an operating power ; in 1 Thess. 3 : 2, some ancient authorities have the clause " fellow-worker (with God)," R.V., marg. ; it is absent from the most authentic mss.   See HELPER.

LACK, LACKING
A. Noun.

HUSTERĒMA (ὑστέρημα) denotes (*a*) that which is lacking, deficiency, shortcoming (akin to *hustereō*, to be behind, in want), 1 Cor. 16 : 17 ; Phil. 2 : 30 ; Col. 1 : 24, R.V., " that which is lacking " [A.V., " that which is behind " (of the afflictions of Christ)], where the reference is not to the vicarious sufferings of Christ, but to those which He endured previously, and those which must be endured by His faithful servants ; 1 Thess. 3 : 10, where " that which is lacking " means that which Paul had not been able to impart to them, owing to the interruption of his spiritual instruction among them ; (*b*) need, want, poverty, Luke 21 : 4,

R.V., " want " (A.V., " penury ") ; 2 Cor. 8 : 14 (twice), " want ; " 9 : 12, " wants " (A.V., " want ") ; 11 : 9, R.V., " (the measure of my) want " [A.V., " that which was lacking (to me) "]. See BEHIND, PENURY, WANT.¶

Note : In 1 Thess. 4 : 12, A.V., *chreia*, need, is translated " lack " (R.V., " need "). See NEED.

B. Adjective.

ENDEĒS (ἐνδεής), from *endeō*, to lack, signifies needy, in want, translated " that lacked " in Acts 4 : 34.¶

C. Verbs.

1. HUSTEREŌ (ὑστερέω), akin to A, to come or be behind, is used in the sense of lacking certain things, Matt. 19 : 20 ; Mark 10 : 21 (" one thing ; " cp. No. 3 in Luke 18 : 22) ; Luke 22 : 35 ; in the sense of being inferior, 1 Cor. 12 : 24 (Middle Voice). Elsewhere it is translated in various ways ; see BEHIND, B, No. 1, COME, No. 39, DESTITUTE, FAIL, *Note* (2), NEED, WANT, WORSE.

2. ELATTONEŌ (ἐλαττονέω), to be less (from *elattōn*, less), is translated " had no lack," 2 Cor. 8 : 15 (quoted from the Sept. of Ex. 16 : 18), the circumstance of the gathering of the manna being applied to the equalising nature of cause and effect in the matter of supplying the wants of the needy.¶

3. LEIPŌ (λείπω), to leave, denotes (*a*) transitively, in the Passive Voice, to be left behind, to lack, Jas. 1 : 4, " ye may be lacking in (nothing)," R.V. (A.V., " wanting ") ; ver. 5, " lacketh " (A.V., " lack ") ; 2 : 15, R.V., " be . . . in lack " (A.V., " be . . . destitute ") ; (*b*) intransitively, Active Voice, Luke 18 : 22, " (one thing thou) lackest," is, lit., ' (one thing) is lacking (to thee) ; ' Tit. 1 : 5, " (the things) that were wanting ; " 3 : 13, " (that nothing) be wanting." See DESTITUTE, WANTING.¶

Note : In 2 Pet. 1 : 9, " he that lacketh " translates a phrase the lit. rendering of which is ' (he to whom these things) are not present ' (*pareimi*, to be present).

For LAD, in John 6 : 9, see CHILD, A, No. 6

LADE, LADEN

1. SŌREUŌ (σωρεύω) signifies (*a*) to heap on (from *sōros*, a heap, not in the N.T. ; in the Sept., e.g., Josh. 7 : 26 ; 8 : 29 ; 2 Sam. 18 : 17 ; 2 Chron. 31 : 6–9), Rom. 12 : 20, of coals of fire ; 2 Tim. 3 : 6, said of silly women (' womanlings ') laden with sins. See HEAP.¶ In the Sept., Prov. 25 : 22.¶

2. GEMŌ (γέμω), to be full, is translated " laden " in Rev. 21 : 9, R.V. See FULL.

3. PHORTIZŌ (φορτίζω), to load (akin to *pherō*, to bear), is used in the Active Voice in Luke 11 : 46, " ye lade ; " in the Passive Voice,

metaphorically, in Matt. 11 : 28, " heavy laden." See BURDEN.¶ In the Sept., Ezek. 16 : 33.¶

Note : In Acts 28 : 10, A.V., *epitithēmi*, to put on (*epi*, on, *tithēmi*, to put), is translated " they laded (us) with," R.V., " they put on (board)."

LADING

PHORTION (φορτίον), a burden, load (a diminutive of *phortos*, a load, from *pherō*, to bear), is used of the cargo of a ship, Acts 27 : 10, " lading," (some mss. have *phortos*). See BURDEN, A, No. 2.

LADY

KURIA (κυρία) is the person addressed in 2 John 1 and 5. Not improbably it is a proper name (Eng., Cyria), in spite of the fact that the full form of address in ver. 1 is not quite in accord, in the original, with those in ver. 13 and in 3 John 1. The suggestion that the Church is addressed is most unlikely. Possibly the person is one who had a special relation with the local church.¶

For LAID see LAY

LAKE

LIMNĒ (λίμνη), a lake, is used (*a*) in the Gospels, only by Luke, of the Sea of Galilee, Luke 5 : 2 ; 8 : 22, 23, 33, called Gennesaret in 5 : 1 (Matthew and Mark use *thalassa*, a sea) ; (*b*) of the lake of fire, Rev. 19 : 20 ; 20 : 10, 14, 15 ; 21 : 8.¶

LAMA

LAMA (λαμά) is the Hebrew word for " Why ? " (the variant *lema* is the Aramaic form), Matt. 27 : 46 ; Mark 15 : 34.¶

LAMB

1. ARĒN (ἀρήν), a noun the nominative case of which is found only in early times, occurs in Luke 10 : 3. In normal usage it was replaced by *arnion* (No. 2), of which it is the equivalent.¶

2. ARNION (ἀρνίον) is a diminutive in form, but the diminutive force is not to be pressed (see Note under No. 3). The general tendency in the vernacular was to use nouns in -*ion* freely, apart from their diminutive significance. It is used only by the Apostle John, (*a*) in the plural, in the Lord's command to Peter, John 21 : 15, with symbolic reference to young converts ; (*b*) elsewhere, in the singular, in the Apocalypse, some 28 times, of Christ as the Lamb of God, the symbolism having reference to His character and His vicarious Sacrifice, as the basis both of redemption and of Divine vengeance. He is seen in the position of sovereign glory and honour, e.g., 7 : 17, which He shares equally with the Father, 22 : 1, 3, the centre of angelic beings and of the redeemed and the object of their

veneration, e.g. 5 : 6, 8, 12, 13 ; 15 : 3, the Leader and Shepherd of His saints, e.g., 7 : 17 ; 14 : 4, the Head of His spiritual Bride, e.g., 21 : 9, the luminary of the heavenly and eternal city, 21 : 23, the One to whom all judgment is committed, e.g., 6 : 1, 16 ; 13 : 8, the Conqueror of the foes of God and His people, 17 : 14 ; the song that celebrates the triumph of those who ' gain the victory over the Beast,' is the song of Moses . . . and the song of the Lamb, 15 : 3.   His sacrifice, the efficacy of which avails for those who accept the salvation thereby provided, forms the ground of the execution of Divine wrath for the rejector, and the defier of God, 14 : 10 ; (c) in the description of the second " Beast," Rev. 13 : 11, seen in the vision " like a lamb," suggestive of his acting in the capacity of a false Messiah, a travesty of the true.   For the use in the Sept. see Note under No. 3.

3. AMNOS (ἀμνός), a lamb, is used figuratively of Christ, in John 1 : 29, 36, with the article, pointing Him out as the expected One, the One to be well known as the Personal fulfilment and embodiment of all that had been indicated in the O.T., the One by whose sacrifice deliverance from Divine judgment was to be obtained ; in Acts 8 : 32 (from the Sept. of Is. 53 : 7) and 1 Pet. 1 : 19, the absence of the article stresses the nature and character of His sacrifice as set forth in the symbolism.   The reference in each case is to the lamb of God's providing, Gen. 22 : 8, and the Paschal lamb of God's appointment for sacrifice in Israel, e.g., Ex. 12 : 5, 14, 27 (cp. 1 Cor. 5 : 7).¶

Note : The contrast between *arnion* and *amnos* does not lie in the diminutive character of the former as compared with the latter. As has been pointed out under No. 2, *arnion* lost its diminutive force.   The contrast lies in the manner in which Christ is presented in the two respects. The use of *amnos* points directly to the fact, the nature and character of His sacrifice ;   *arnion* (only in the Apocalypse) presents Him, on the ground, indeed, of His Sacrifice, but in His acquired majesty, dignity, honour, authority and power.

In the Sept. *arnion* is used in Ps. 114 : 4, 6 ; in Jer. 11 : 19, with the adjective *akakos*, innocent ; in Jer. 27 : 45, " lambs."   There is nothing in these passages to suggest a contrast between a lamb in the general sense of the term and the diminutive ; the contrast is between lambs and sheep.   Elsewhere in the Sept. *amnos* is in general used some 100 times in connection with lambs for sacrifice.

For LAME see HALT

For LAMENT and LAMENTATION see BEWAIL

LAMP

1. LAMPAS (λαμπάς) denotes a torch (akin to *lampō*, to shine), frequently fed, like a lamp, with oil from a little vessel used for the purpose

(the *angeion* of Matt. 25 : 4) ; they held little oil and would frequently need replenishing. Rutherford (*The New Phrynichus*) points out that it became used as the equivalent of *luchnos* (No. 2), as in the parable of the Ten Virgins, Matt. 25 : 1, 3, 4, 7, 8 ; John 18 : 3, " torches ; " Acts 20 : 8, " lights ; " Rev. 4 : 5 ; 8 : 10 (R.V., " torch," A.V., " lamp "). See Note below.¶ Cp. *phanos*, a torch, John 18 : 3 (translated " lanterns ").¶

2. LUCHNOS (λύχνος), frequently mistranslated " candle," is a portable lamp usually set on a stand (see LAMPSTAND) ; the word is used (*a*) literally, Matt. 5 : 15 ; Mark 4 : 21 ; Luke 8 : 16 ; 11 : 33, 36 ; 15 : 8 ; Rev. 18 : 23 ; 22 : 5 ; (*b*) metaphorically, of Christ as the Lamb, Rev. 21 : 23, R.V., " lamp " (A.V., " light ") ; of John the Baptist, John 5 : 35, R.V., " the lamp " (A.V., " a . . . light ") ; of the eye, Matt. 6 : 22, and Luke 11 : 34, R.V., " lamp ; " of spiritual readiness, Luke 12 : 35, R.V., " lamps ; " of " the word of prophecy," 2 Pet. 1 : 19, R.V., " lamp." See LIGHT.¶

" In rendering *luchnos* and *lampas* our Translators have scarcely made the most of the words at their command. Had they rendered *lampas* by ' torch ' not once only (John 18 : 3), but always, this would have left ' lamp,' now wrongly appropriated by *lampas*, disengaged. Altogether dismissing ' candle,' they might then have rendered *luchnos* by ' lamp ' wherever it occurs. At present there are so many occasions where ' candle ' would manifestly be inappropriate, and where, therefore, they are obliged to fall back on ' light,' that the distinction between *phōs* and *luchnos* nearly, if not quite, disappears in our Version. The advantages of such a re-distribution of the words would be many. In the first place, it would be more accurate. *Luchnos* is not a ' candle ' (' candela,' from ' candeo,' the white wax light, and then any kind of taper), but a hand-lamp, fed with oil. Neither is *lampas* a ' lamp,' but a ' torch ' " (Trench Syn., § xlvi).

Note : There is no mention of a candle in the original either in the O.T. or in the N.T. The figure of that which feeds upon its own substance to provide its light would be utterly inappropriate. A lamp is supplied by oil, which in its symbolism is figurative of the Holy Spirit.

LAMPSTAND

LUCHNIA (λυχνία) is mistranslated " candlestick " in every occurrence in the A.V. and in certain places in the R.V. ; the R.V. has " stand " in Matt. 5 : 15 ; Mark 4 : 21 ; Luke 8 : 16 ; 11 : 33 ; " candlestick " in Heb. 9 : 2 ; Rev. 1 : 12, 13, 20 (twice) ; 2 : 1, 5 ; 11 : 4 ; the R.V. marg., gives " lampstands " in the passages in Rev., but not in Heb. 9 : 2.¶

LAND

A. Nouns.

1. GE (γῆ), in one of its usages, denotes (*a*) land as distinct from sea or other water, e.g., Mark 4 : 1 ; 6 : 47 ; Luke 5 : 3 ; John 6 : 21 ; (*b*) land

as subject to cultivation, e.g., Luke 14 : 35 (see GROUND) ; (c) land as describing a country or region, e.g., Matt. 2 : 20, 21 ; 4 : 15 ; Luke 4 : 25 ; in 23 : 44, R.V., " (the whole) land," A.V., " (all the) earth ; " Acts 7 : 29 ; Heb. 11 : 9, R.V., " a land (not his own)," A.V. " a (strange) country ; " Jude 5. In Acts 7 : 11 the A.V. follows a reading of the noun with the definite article which necessitates the insertion of " land." See EARTH.

2. CHŌRA (χώρα) is used with the meaning land, (a) of a country, region, e.g., Mark 1 : 5 ; Luke 15 : 14 ; sometimes translated " region," e.g., Matt. 4 : 16 ; Luke 3 : 1 ; Acts 8 : 1 ; 13 : 49 ; 16 : 6 ; (b) of property, Luke 12 : 16, " ground." See COUNTRY, A, No. 3.

3. CHŌRION (χωρίον), a diminutive of No. 2, in form, but not in meaning, is translated " land " in the sense of property, in Acts 4 : 34 ; 5 : 3, 8 ; 28 : 7, R.V., " lands " (A.V., " possessions "). See FIELD, GROUND, A, No. 4, PLACE, POSSESSION.

4. AGROS (ἀγρός), a field, or piece of ground, or the country as distinct from the town, is translated " lands " in Matt. 19 : 29 ; Mark 10 : 29, 30 ; Acts 4 : 37 (cp. No. 3 in ver. 34). See COUNTRY, A, No. 1, FARM, FIELD, GROUND.

B. Adjective.

XĒROS (ξηρός), dry, " dry land," Matt. 23 : 15 (gē, land, being understood) ; Heb. 11 : 29 : see DRY.

Note : In Luke 4 : 26, the R.V., " in the land (of) " and A.V., " a city (of)," represent no word in the original, but give the sense of the phrase.

C. Verb.

KATERCHOMAI (κατέρχομαι), to come down, or go down, descend, is used of coming to port by ship, in Acts 18 : 22, " landed ; " 21 : 3 (ditto) ; 27 : 5, " came to." See COME, No. 7, GO, Note (1).

Notes : (1) In Acts 28 : 12, R.V., *katagō*, to bring down, used as a nautical term in the Passive Voice, is translated " touching " (A.V., " landing "). (2) In Acts 21 : 3, some mss. have the verb *katagō*, with reference to Cyprus. (3) In Acts 20 : 13, *pezeuō*, to travel by land or on foot (*pezos*, on foot ; *pous*, a foot), is translated " to go by land," R.V., A.V., " to go afoot," and R.V. marg., " to go on foot."¶

LANE

RHUMĒ (ῥύμη) in earlier Greek meant the force or rush or swing of a moving body ; in later times, a narrow road, lane or street ; it is translated " lanes " in Luke 14 : 21 ; " streets " in Matt. 6 : 2 ; " street " in Acts 9 : 11 ; 12 : 10. See STREET.¶ In the Sept., Is. 15 : 3.¶

LANGUAGE

DIALEKTOS (διάλεκτος), primarily a conversation, discourse (akin to *dialegomai*, to discourse or discuss), came to denote the language or dialect of a country or district ; in the A.V. and R.V. of Acts 2 : 6 it is translated " language ; " in the following the R.V. retains " language," for A.V.,

"tongue," Acts 1 : 19 ; 2 : 8 ; 21 : 40 ; 22 : 2 ; 26 : 14.   See TONGUE.¶
In the Sept., Esth. 9 : 26.¶

LANTERN

PHANOS (φανός) denotes either a torch or a lantern (from *phainō*, to
cause to shine, to give light), John 18 : 3, where it is distinguished from
lampas (see LAMP, No. 1) ; it was " a link or torch consisting of strips of
resinous wood tied together " (Rutherford).   " Torch " would seem to
be the meaning.¶

LARGE

1. MEGAS (μέγας), great, large, of physical magnitude, is translated
" large " in Mark 14 : 15 and Luke 22 : 12, of the upper room.   See GREAT,
No. 1.

2. HIKANOS (ἱκανός), of persons, denotes sufficient, competent, fit ;
of things, sufficient, enough, much, many (so of time) ; it is translated
" large " in Matt. 28 : 12, of money.   See ABLE, C, No. 2.

3. PĒLIKOS (πηλίκος), how large, is used of letters of the alphabet,
characters in writing, Gal. 6 : 11, " with how large (letters) ; " it is said
of personal greatness in Heb. 7 : 4.   See GREAT, No. 5.¶

LASCIVIOUS, LASCIVIOUSNESS

ASELGEIA (ἀσέλγεια) denotes excess, licentiousness, absence of
restraint, indecency, wantonness ; " lasciviousness " in Mark 7 : 22, one
of the evils that proceed from the heart ; in 2 Cor. 12 : 21, one of the evils
of which some in the church at Corinth had been guilty ; in Gal. 5 : 19,
classed among the works of the flesh ; in Eph. 4 : 19, among the sins of
the unregenerate who are " past feeling ; " so in 1 Pet. 4 : 3 ; in Jude 4,
of that into which the grace of God had been turned by ungodly men ; it
is translated " wantonness " in Rom. 13 : 13, one of the sins against which
believers are warned ; in 2 Pet. 2 : 2, according to the best mss.,
" lascivious (doings)," R.V. (the A.V. " pernicious ways " follows those
texts which have *apōleiais*) ; in ver. 7, R.V., " lascivious (life)," A.V.,
" filthy (conversation)," of the people of Sodom and Gomorrah ; in 2 : 18,
R.V., " lasciviousness " (A.V., " wantonness "), practised by the same
persons as mentioned in Jude.   The prominent idea is shameless conduct.
Some have derived the word from *a*, negative, and *selgē*, a city in Pisidia.
Others, with similar improbability, trace it to *a*, negative, and *selgō*, or
thelgō, to charm.   See WANTONNESS.¶

LAST
A. Adjective.

ESCHATOS (ἔσχατος), last, utmost, extreme, is used (*a*) of place, e.g.,
Luke 14 : 9, 10, " lowest ; " Acts 1 : 8 and 13 : 47, " uttermost part ; "
(*b*) of rank, e.g., Mark 9 : 35 ; (*c*) of time, relating either to persons or

things, e.g., Matt. 5 : 26, " the last (farthing)," (A.V., " uttermost ") ;
Matt. 20 : 8, 12, 14 ; Mark 12 : 6, 22 ; 1 Cor. 4 : apostles as last in the
programme of a spectacular display ; 1 Cor. 15 the last Adam ;"
Rev. 2 : 19 ; of the last state of persons, Matt. 12 neuter plural, lit.,
' the last (things) ; ' so Luke 11 : 26 ; 2 Pet. 2 : 20, the last state "
(A.V., " the latter end ") ; of Christ as the Eternal Rev. 1 : 17 (in
some mss. ver. 11) ; 2 : 8 ; 22 : 13 ; in eschatological ses as follows :
(a) " the last day," a comprehensive term including b e time of the
resurrection of the redeemed, John 6 : 39, 40, 44, 54 and 24, and the
ulterior time of the judgment of the unregenerate, at t reat White
Throne, John 12 : 48 ; (b) " the last days," Acts 2 : 17, a od relative
to the supernatural manifestation of the Holy Spirit at Pent st and the
resumption of the Divine interpositions in the affairs of the rld at the
end of the present age, before " the great and notable Day of he Lord,"
which will usher in the Messianic Kingdom ; (c) in 2 Tim. 3 : 1, " the last
days " refers to the close of the present age of world conditions ; (d) in
Jas. 5 : 3, the phrase " in the last days " (R.V.) refers both to the period
preceding the Roman overthrow of the city and the land in A.D. 70, and
to the closing part of the age in consummating acts of Gentile persecution
including " the time of Jacob's trouble " (cp. verses 7, 8) ; (e) in 1 Pet.
1 : 5, " the last time " refers to the time of the Lord's Second Advent ;
(f) in 1 John 2 : 18, " the last hour " (R.V.) and, in Jude 18, " the last
time " signify the present age previous to the Second Advent.

Notes : (1) In Heb. 1 : 2, R.V., " at the end of these days " (A.V., " in
these last days "), the reference is to the close of the period of the testimony
of the prophets under the Law, terminating with the presence of Christ
and His redemptive sacrifice and its effects, the perfect tense " hath
spoken " indicating the continued effects of the message embodied in the
risen Christ ; so in 1 Pet. 1 : 20, R.V., " at the end of the times " (A.V.,
" in these last times ").

B. Adverb.

HUSTERON (ὕστερον), the neuter of the adjective *husteros*, is used as
an adverb signifying ' afterwards,' ' later,' see AFTER, No. 5. Cp. the
adjective, under LATER.

Note : In Phil. 4 : 10 the particle *pote*, sometime, used after *ēdē*, now,
already, to signify " now at length," is so rendered in the R.V., A.V.,
" (now) at the last."

LATCHET

HIMAS (ἱμάς) denotes a thong, strap, whether for binding prisoners,
Acts 22 : 25, " (the) thongs " (for scourging ; see BIND, No. 7), or for
fastening sandals, Mark 1 : 7 ; Luke 3 : 16 ; John 1 : 27. " Among the
Orientals everything connected with the feet and shoes is defiled and
debasing, and the stooping to unfasten the dusty latchet is the most
insignificant in such service " (Mackie, in Hastings' Bib. Dic.).¶

LATE

OPSE (ὀψέ) an adverb of time, besides its meaning at evening or at eventide, denotes late in, or on, Matt. 28 : 1, R.V., "late on (the Sabbath day) " (A.V., "in the end of ") ; it came also to denote ' late after,' which seems to be the meaning here. See EVENING.

Note : In John 11 : 8, A.V., *nun,* now, is translated " of late " (R.V., " but now ").

LATELY

PROSPHATŌS (προσφάτως) denotes recently, lately, from the adjective *prosphatos,* new, fresh, recent ; primarily, newly slain, Heb. 10 : 20 (*phatos,* slain), is also found in Acts 18 : 2.¶ In the Sept., Deut. 24 : 5 ; Ezek. 11 : 3.¶

LATER

HUSTEROS (ὕστερος) denotes later or latter and is used in 1 Tim. 4 : 1, R.V., " in later (times)," A.V., " in (the) latter (times)." Several mss. have it in Matt. 21 : 31, ' the former,' for *prōtos,* " the first."¶

LATIN

RHŌMAISTI (ῥωμαϊστί), an adverb, " in Latin," occurs in John 19 : 20, lit., ' in Roman.'¶

Note : In Luke 23 : 38, some mss. have the adjective *Rhōmaikos,* ' of Latin,' agreeing with " letters."

LATTER

OPSIMOS (ὄψιμος), akin to *opse* and *opsios* (see LATE), denotes late, or latter, and is used of " the latter rain " in Jas. 5 : 7 (the most authentic mss. omit *huetos,* rain ; some have *karpos,* fruit) ; this rain falls in March and April, just before the harvest, in contrast to the early rain, in October.¶ In the Sept., Deut. 11 : 14 ; Prov. 16 : 15 ; Jer. 5 : 24 ; Hos. 6 : 3 ; Joel 2 : 23 ; Zech. 10 : 1.¶

Note : For " latter " (*husteros*) in the A.V. of 1 Tim. 4 : 1 see LATER, and for 2 Pet. 2 : 20 see LAST.

For LAUD (Rom. 15 : 11, A.V.) see PRAISE, B, No. 1

LAUGH, LAUGH TO SCORN

1. GELAŌ (γελάω), to laugh, is found in Luke 6 : 21, 25. This signifies loud laughter in contrast to demonstrative weeping.¶

2. KATAGELAŌ (καταγελάω) denotes to laugh scornfully at, more emphatic than No. 1 (*kata,* down, used intensively, and No. 1), and signifies derisive laughter, Matt. 9 : 24 ; Mark 5 : 40 ; Luke 8 : 53.¶ Cp. *ekmuktērizō,* to deride.

Note : The laughter of incredulity, as in Gen. 17 : 17 and 18 : 12, is not mentioned in the N.T.

LAUGHTER

GELŌS (γέλως) denotes laughter, Jas. 4 : 9.¶ This corresponds to the kind of laughter mentioned above (see LAUGH, No. 1).

LAUNCH

1. ANAGŌ (ἀνάγω), to bring up (ana, up, agō, to lead), is used in the Middle Voice as a nautical term signifying to put to sea ; it is translated " launch forth " in Luke 8 : 22 ; " set sail " in Acts 13 : 13, R.V. (A.V., " loosed ") ; similarly in 16 : 11 ; in 18 : 21, for A.V., " sailed ; " similarly in 20 : 3, 13 ; in 21 : 1, R.V., " set sail," (A.V., " launched "), and in ver. 2, for A.V., " set forth ; " in 27 : 2 and 4 the R.V. has the verb to put to sea, for A.V. to launch; in ver. 12 for A.V., " depart ;" in ver. 21, R.V., " set sail " (A.V., " loosed ") ; in 28 : 10, 11, " sailed " and " set sail " (A.V., " departed "). See BRING, DEPART, LEAD, LOOSE, OFFER, PUT, SAIL, SET.

2. EPANAGŌ (ἐπανάγω), to lead up upon (epi, upon, and No. 1), is used as a nautical term with ploion, a ship, understood, denoting to put out to sea, translated in Luke 5 : 3, " put out," R.V. (A.V., " thrust out ") ; in ver. 4, for A.V., " launch." For the non-nautical significance to return, see Matt. 21 : 18. See PUT, RETURN, THRUST.¶ In the Sept., Zech. 4 : 12, " that communicate with (the golden oil vessels)."

LAW
A. Nouns.

1. NOMOS (νόμος), akin to nemō, to divide out, distribute, primarily meant that which is assigned ; hence, usage, custom, and then, law, law as prescribed by custom, or by statute ; the word ēthos, custom, was retained for unwritten law, while nomos became the established name for law as decreed by a state and set up as the standard for the administration of justice.

In the N.T. it is used (a) of law in general, e.g., Rom. 2 : 12, 13, " a law " (R.V.), expressing a general principle relating to law ; ver. 14, last part ; 3 : 27, " By what manner of law ? " i.e., ' by what sort of principle (has the glorying been excluded) ? '; 4 : 15 (last part) ; 5 : 13, referring to the period between Adam's trespass and the giving of the Law ; 7 : 1 (1st part, R.V. marg., " law ") ; against those graces which constitute the fruit of the Spirit " there is no law," Gal. 5 : 23 ; " the ostensible aim of the law is to restrain the evil tendencies natural to man in his fallen estate ; yet in experience law finds itself not merely ineffective, it actually provokes those tendencies to greater activity. The intention of the gift of the Spirit is to constrain the believer to a life in which the natural tendencies shall have no place, and to produce in him their direct contraries. Law, therefore, has nothing to say against the fruit of the Spirit ; hence the believer is not only not under law, ver. 18, the law finds no scope in his life, inasmuch as, and in so far as, he is led by the Spirit ; "*

---

* From Notes on Galatians by Hogg and Vine, p. 298.

(*b*) of a force or influence impelling to action, Rom. 7 : 21, 23 (1st part), " a different law," R.V. ; (*c*) of the Mosaic Law, the Law of Sinai, (1) with the definite article, e.g., Matt. 5 : 18 ; John 1 : 17 ; Rom. 2 : 15, 18, 20, 26, 27 ; 3 : 19 ; 4 : 15 ; 7 : 4, 7, 14, 16, 22 ; 8 : 3, 4, 7 ; Gal. 3 : 10, 12, 19, 21, 24 ; 5 : 3 ; Eph. 2 : 15 ; Phil. 3 : 6 ; 1 Tim. 1 : 8 ; Heb. 7 : 19 ; Jas. 2 : 9 ; (2) without the article, thus stressing the Mosaic Law in its quality as law, e.g., Rom. 2 : 14 (1st part) ; 5 : 20 ; 7 : 9, where the stress on the quality lies in this, that " the commandment which was unto (i.e., which he thought would be a means of) life," he found to be " unto (i.e., to have the effect of revealing his actual state of) death ; " 10 : 4 ; 1 Cor. 9 : 20 ; Gal. 2 : 16, 19, 21 ; 3 : 2, 5, 10 (1st part), 11, 18, 23 ; 4 : 4, 5, 21 (1st part) ; 5 : 4, 18 ; 6 : 13 ; Phil. 3 : 5, 9 ; Heb. 7 : 16 ; 9 : 19 ; Jas. 2 : 11 ; 4 : 11 ; (in regard to the statement in Gal. 2 : 16, that " a man is not justified by the works of the Law," the absence of the article before *nomos* indicates the assertion of a principle, ' by obedience to law,' but evidently the Mosaic law is in view. Here the Apostle is maintaining that submission to circumcision entails the obligation to do the whole Law. Circumcision belongs to the ceremonial part of the Law, but, while the Mosaic Law is actually divisible into the ceremonial and the moral, no such distinction is made or even assumed in Scripture. The statement maintains the freedom of the believer from the law of Moses in its totality as a means of justification) ;

(*d*) by metonymy, of the books which contain the law, (1) of the Pentateuch, e.g., Matt. 5 : 17 ; 12 : 5 ; Luke 16 : 16 ; 24 : 44 ; John 1 : 45 ; Rom. 3 : 21 ; Gal. 3 : 10 ; (2) of the Psalms, John 10 : 34 ; 15 : 25 ; of the Psalms, Isaiah, Ezekiel and Daniel, 12 : 34 ; the Psalms and Isaiah, Rom. 3 : 19 (with vv. 10–18) ; Isaiah, 1 Cor. 14 : 21 ; from all this it may be inferred that " the law " in the most comprehensive sense was an alternative title to " The Scriptures."

The following phrases specify laws of various kinds ; (*a*) " the law of Christ," Gal. 6 : 2, i.e., either given by Him (as in the Sermon on the Mount and in John 13 : 14, 15 ; 15 : 4), or the law or principle by which Christ Himself lived (Matt. 20 : 28 ; John 13 : 1) ; these are not actual alternatives, for the law imposed by Christ was always that by which He Himself lived in the " days of His flesh." He confirmed the Law as being of Divine authority (cp. Matt. 5 : 18) ; yet He presented a higher standard of life than perfunctory obedience to the current legal rendering of the Law, a standard which, without annulling the Law, He embodied in His own character and life (see, e.g., Matt. 5 : 21–48 ; this breach with legalism is especially seen in regard to the ritual or ceremonial part of the Law in its wide scope) ; He showed Himself superior to all human interpretations of it ; (*b*) " a law of faith," Rom. 3 : 27, i.e., a principle which demands only faith on man's part ; (*c*) " the law of my mind," Rom. 7 : 23, that principle which governs the new nature in virtue of the new birth ; (*d*) " the law of sin," Rom. 7 : 23, the principle by which sin exerts its influence and power despite the desire to do what is right ; " of sin and death," 8 : 2, death being the effect ; (e) " the law of liberty," Jas. 1 : 25 ; 2 : 12, a term comprehensive of all the Scriptures, not a law of compulsion enforced from without, but meeting with ready obedience through the desire and delight of the renewed being who is subject to it ; into it he looks, and in its teaching he delights ; he is " under law (*ennomos*, ' in law,' implying union and subjection) to Christ," 1 Cor. 9 : 21 ; cp., e.g., Ps. 119 : 32, 45, 97 ; 2 Cor. 3 : 17 ; (f) " the royal law," Jas. 2 : 8, i.e., the law of love, royal in the majesty of its power, the law upon which all others hang, Matt. 22 : 34-40 ; Rom. 13 : 8 ; Gal. 5 : 14 ; (g) " the law of the Spirit of life," Rom. 8 : 2, i.e., the animating principle by which the Holy Spirit acts as the Imparter of life (cp. John 6 : 63) ; (h) " a law of righteousness," Rom. 9 : 31, i.e., a general principle presenting righteousness as the object and outcome of keeping a law, particularly the Law of Moses (cp. Gal. 3 : 21) ; (i) " the law of a carnal commandment," Heb. 7 : 16, i.e., the law respecting the Aaronic priesthood, which appointed men conditioned by the circumstances and limitations of the flesh. In the Epistle to the Hebrews the Law is treated of especially in regard to the contrast between the Priesthood of Christ and that established under the Law of Moses, and in regard to access to God and to worship. In these respects the Law " made nothing perfect," 7 : 19. There was " a disannulling of a fore-going commandment . . . and a bringing in of a better hope." This is established under the " new Covenant," a covenant instituted on the basis of " better promises," 8 : 6.

Notes : (1) In Gal. 5 : 3, the statement that to receive circumcision constitutes a man a debtor to do " the whole Law," views the Law as made up of separate commands, each essential to the whole, and predicates the unity of the Law; in ver. 14, the statement that " the whole law " is fulfilled in the one commandment concerning love, views the separate commandments as combined to make a complete law. (2) In Rom. 8 : 3, " what the law could not do," is lit., ' the inability (*adunaton*, the neuter of the adjective *adunatos*, unable, used as a noun) of the Law ; ' this may mean either ' the weakness of the Law ' or ' that which was impossible for the Law ; ' the latter is preferable ; the significance is the same in effect ; the Law could neither give freedom from condemnation nor impart life. (3) For the difference between the teaching of Paul and that of James in regard to the Law, see under JUSTIFICATION. (4) For Acts 19 : 38, A.V., " the law is open " (R.V., " courts " etc.) see COURT, No. 1. (5) For *nomodidaskaloi*, " doctors of the law," Luke 5 : 17, singular in Acts 5 : 34, " teachers of the law," 1 Tim. 1 : 7, see DOCTOR.

2. NOMOTHESIA (νομοθεσία) denotes legislation, lawgiving (No. 1, and *tithēmi*, to place, to put), Rom. 9 : 4, " (the) giving of the law." Cp. B, No. 1.¶

B. Verbs.

1. NOMOTHETEŌ (νομοθετέω), (a) used intransitively, signifies to make laws (cp. A, No. 2, above) ; in the Passive Voice, to be furnished with laws, Heb. 7 : 11, " received the law," lit., ' was furnished with (the) law ; ' (b) used transitively, it signifies to ordain by law, to enact ; in the Passive Voice, Heb. 8 : 6. See ENACT.¶

2. KRINŌ (κρίνω), to esteem, judge, etc., signifies to go to law, and is so used in the Middle Voice in Matt. 5 : 40, R.V., " go to law " (A.V., " sue . . . at the law ") ; 1 Cor. 6 : 1, 6. See ESTEEM.

Note : In 1 Cor. 6 : 7, the A.V., " go to law," is a rendering of the phrase *echō krimata*, to have lawsuits, as in the R.V.

3. PARANOMEŌ (παρανομέω), to transgress law (*para*, contrary to, and *nomos*), is used in the present participle in Acts 23 : 3, and translated " contrary to the law," lit., ' transgressing the law.'¶

C. Adjectives.

1. NOMIKOS (νομικός) denotes relating to law ; in Tit. 3 : 9 it is translated " about the law," describing " fightings " (A.V., " strivings ") ; see LAWYER.

2. ENNOMOS (ἔννομος), (a) lawful, legal, lit., in law (*en*, in, and *nomos*), or, strictly, what is within the range of law, is translated " lawful " in Acts 19 : 39, A.V. (R.V., " regular "), of the legal tribunals in Ephesus ; (b) " under law " (R.V.), in relation to Christ, 1 Cor. 9 : 21, where it is contrasted with *anomos* (see No. 3 below) ; the word as used by the Apostle suggests not merely the condition of being under law, but the intimacy of a relation established in the loyalty of a will devoted to his Master. See LAWFUL.

3. ANOMOS (ἄνομος) signifies " without law " (*a*, negative) and has this meaning in 1 Cor. 9 : 21 (four times). See LAWLESS, TRANSGRESSOR, UNLAWFUL, WICKED.

D. Adverb.

ANOMŌS (ἀνόμως), without law (the adverbial form of C, No. 3), is used in Rom. 2 : 12 (twice), where " (have sinned) without law " means in the absence of some specifically revealed law, like the law of Sinai ; " (shall perish) without law " predicates that the absence of such a law will not prevent their doom ; the law of conscience is not in view here. The succeeding phrase " under law " is lit., ' in law,' not the same as the adjective *ennomos* (C, No. 2), but two distinct words.¶

LAWFUL, LAWFULLY
A. Verb.

EXESTI (ἔξεστι), an impersonal verb, signifying it is permitted, it is lawful (or interrogatively, is it lawful ?), occurs most frequently in the Synoptic Gospels and the Acts ; elsewhere in John 5 : 10 ; 18 : 31 ; 1 Cor. 6 : 12 ; 10 : 23 ; 2 Cor. 12 : 4 ; in Acts 2 : 29, it is rendered " let me (speak)," lit., ' it being permitted ; ' in the A.V. of 8 : 37, " thou mayest," lit., ' it is permitted ; ' 16 : 21 ; in 21 : 37, " may I," lit., ' is it permitted ? ' See LET, MAY.

Note : For *ennomos*, see C, No. 2, (under LAW).

B. Adverb.

NOMIMŌS (νομίμως), lawfully, is used in 1 Tim. 1 : 8, " the Law is good, if a man use it lawfully," i.e., agreeably to its design ; the meaning here is that, while no one can be justified or obtain eternal life through its instrumentality, the believer is to have it in his heart and to fulfil its requirements ; walking " not after the flesh but after the spirit," Rom. 8 : 4, he will " use it lawfully." In 2 Tim. 2 : 5 it is used of contending in the games and adhering to the rules.¶

LAWGIVER

NOMOTHETĒS (νομοθέτης), a lawgiver (see LAW, A, No. 2, and B, No. 1), occurs in Jas. 4 : 12, of God, as the sole Lawgiver ; therefore, to criticize the Law is to presume to take His place, with the presumption of enacting a better law.¶

LAWLESS, LAWLESSNESS
A. Adjective.

ANOMOS (ἄνομος), without law, also denotes lawless, and is so rendered in the R.V. of Acts 2 : 23, " lawless (men)," marg., " (men) without the law," A.V., " wicked (hands) ; " 2 Thess. 2 : 8, " the lawless one " (A.V., " that wicked "), of the man of sin (ver. 4) ; in 2 Pet. 2 : 8, of deeds (A.V., " unlawful "), where the thought is not simply that of doing what is unlawful, but of flagrant defiance of the known will of God. See LAW, C, No. 3.

B. Noun.

ANOMIA (ἀνομία), lawlessness, akin to A, is most frequently translated " iniquity ; " in 2 Thess. 2 : 7, R.V., " lawlessness " (A.V., " iniquity ") ; " the mystery of lawlessness " is not recognized by the world, for it does not consist merely in confusion and disorder (see A) ; the display of lawlessness by the lawless one (ver. 8) will be the effect of the attempt by the powers of darkness to overthrow the Divine government. In 1 John 3 : 4, the R.V. adheres to the real meaning of the word, " every one that doeth sin (a practice, not the committal of an act) doeth also lawlessness : and sin is lawlessness." This definition of sin sets forth its essential character as the rejection of the law, or will, of God and the substitution of the will of self. See INIQUITY and synonymous words.

LAWYER

NOMIKOS (νομικός), an adjective, learned in the law (see Tit. 3 : 9, under LAW, C, No. 1), is used as a noun, a lawyer, Matt. 22 : 35 ; Luke 7 : 30 ; 10 : 25 ; 11 : 45, 46, 52 (ver. 53 in some mss.) ; 14 : 3 ; Tit. 3 : 13, where Zenas is so named. As there is no evidence that he was one skilled in Roman jurisprudence, the term may be regarded in the usual N.T. sense as applying to one skilled in the Mosaic Law.¶

The usual name for a scribe is *grammateus*, a man of letters; for a doctor of the law, *nomodidaskalos* (see DOCTOR). " A comparison of Luke 5 : 17 with ver. 21 and Mark 2 : 6 and Matt. 9 : 3 shows that the three terms were used synonymously, and did not denote three distinct classes. The scribes were originally simply men of letters, students of Scripture, and the name first given to them contains in itself no reference to the law ; in course of time, however, they devoted themselves mainly, though by no means exclusively, to the study of the law. They became jurists rather than theologians, and received names which of themselves called attention to that fact. Some would doubtless devote themselves more to one branch of activity than to another; but a ' lawyer ' might also be a ' doctor,' and the case of Gamaliel shows that a ' doctor ' might also be a member of the Sanhedrin, Acts 5 : 34 " (Eaton, in Hastings' Bib. Dic.).

LAY

1. TITHĒMI (τίθημι), to put, place, set, frequently signifies to lay, and is used of (*a*) laying a corpse in a tomb, Matt. 27 : 60 ; Mark 6 : 29 ; 15 : 47 ; 16 : 6 ; Luke 23 : 53, 55 ; John 11 : 34 ; 19 : 41, 42 ; 20 : 2, 13, 15 ; Acts 7 : 16 ; 13 : 29 ; Rev. 11 : 9, R.V., " to be laid " (A.V., " to be put ") ; in an upper chamber, Acts 9 : 37 ; (*b*) laying the sick in a place, Mark 6 : 56 ; Luke 5 : 18 ; Acts 3 : 2 ; 5 : 15 ; (*c*) laying money at the Apostles' feet, Acts 4 : 35, 37 ; 5 : 2 ; (*d*) Christ's laying His hands upon children, Mark 10 : 16, R.V., " laying " (A.V., " put ") ; upon John, Rev. 1 : 17 (in the best mss.) ; (*e*) laying down one's life, (1) of Christ, John 10 : 11, R.V., " layeth down " (A.V., " giveth ") ; vers. 17, 18 (twice) ; 1 John 3 : 16 ; (2) of Peter for Christ's sake, John 13 : 37, 38 ; (3) of Christ's followers, on behalf of others, 1 John 3 : 16 ; (4) of anyone, for his friends, John 15 : 13 ; (*f*) laying up sayings in one's heart, Luke 1 : 66 (Middle Voice, in the sense of ' for themselves ') ; in 9 : 44, of letting Christ's words " sink " (Middle Voice, in the sense of ' for oneself ; ' A.V., " sink down ") into the ears ; (*g*) laying a foundation (1) literally, Luke 6 : 48 ; 14 : 29 ; (2) metaphorically, of Christ in relation to an assembly, 1 Cor. 3 : 10, 11 ; (*h*) God in laying Christ as a " stone of stumbling " for Israel, Rom. 9 : 33 ; (*i*) Christ's laying aside His garments, John 13 : 4 ; (*j*) Christians, in laying money in store for the help of the needy, 1 Cor. 16 : 2 (lit., ' let him put ') ; (*k*) depositing money, Luke 19 : 21, 22. See APPOINT.

2. KATATITHĒMI (κατατίθημι), to lay down (*kata*), is used in Mark 15 : 46 of the act of Joseph of Arimathæa in laying Christ's body in the tomb (some mss. have No. 1 here). See DO, Note (4), SHEW.

3. BALLŌ (βάλλω), to cast, throw, place, put, is used in the Passive Voice signifying to be laid, e.g., Mark 7 : 30 ; Luke 16 : 20 ; for Matt. 8 : 14, R.V., " lying " (A.V., " laid ") and 9 : 2, see LIE, No. (3). See CAST.

4. EPIBALLŌ (ἐπιβάλλω), to lay upon, is used of seizing men, to imprison them, Acts 4 : 3. See CAST.

5. KATABALLŌ (καταβάλλω), to cast down (kata), is used metaphorically in Heb. 6 : 1, in the Middle Voice, negatively, of laying a foundation of certain doctrines. See CAST.

6. KLINŌ (κλίνω), to make to bend, to bow, or to make to lean, to rest, is used in Matt. 8 : 20 and Luke 9 : 58, in the Lord's statement, " the Son of man hath not where to lay His head ; " it is significant that this verb is used in John 19 : 30 of the Lord's act at the moment of His Death in placing His head into a position of rest, not a helpless drooping of the head as in all other cases of crucifixion. He reversed the natural order, by first reclining His head (indicative of His submission to His Father's will), and then ' giving up His spirit.' The rest He found not on earth in contrast to His creatures the foxes and birds, He found in this consummating act on the Cross. See BOW.

7. ANAKLINŌ (ἀνακλίνω), to lay down, make to recline (in the Passive Voice, to lie back, recline), is used in Luke 2 : 7, of the act of the Virgin Mary in laying her Child in a manger. See SIT.

8. APOTITHĒMI (ἀποτίθημι), to put off from oneself (apo, from, and No. 1), always in the Middle Voice in the N.T., is used metaphorically in Heb. 12 : 1, " laying aside (every weight) ; " in Jas. 1 : 21, A.V., " lay apart," R.V., " putting away ; " in Acts 7 : 58 of laying down garments, after taking them off, for the purpose of stoning Stephen. See CAST, PUT.

9. HUPOTITHĒMI (ὑποτίθημι), to place under, lay down (hupo, under, and No. 1), is used metaphorically in Rom. 16 : 4, of risking one's life, " laid down " (their own necks). In the Middle Voice in 1 Tim. 4 : 6 it is used of putting persons in mind, R.V., (A.V., " in remembrance "). See REMEMBRANCE.¶

10. EPITITHĒMI (ἐπιτίθημι), to add to, lay upon, etc., is used of laying hands on the sick, for healing, Matt. 9 : 18 ; 19 : 13, R.V., " lay " (A.V., " put ") ; 19 : 15 ; Mark 5 : 23 ; 6 : 5 ; 7 : 32 ; 8 : 23, R.V., " laid " (A.V., " put ") ; so in ver. 25 ; 16 : 18 ; Luke 4 : 40 ; 13 : 13 ; Acts 6 : 6 ; 8 : 17, 19 ; 9 : 12 and 17, R.V., " laying " (A.V., " putting ") ; 13 : 3 ; 19 : 6 ; 28 : 8 ; in some mss. in Rev. 1 : 17, see No. 1, (d) ; of laying hands on a person by way of public recognition, 1 Tim. 5 : 22 ; of a shepherd's laying a sheep on his shoulders, Luke 15 : 5 ; of laying the Cross on Christ's shoulders, Luke 23 : 26 ; of laying on stripes, Acts 16 : 23 ; wood on a fire, 28 : 3 ; metaphorically, of laying burden's on men's shoulders, Matt. 23 : 4 ; similarly of giving injunctions, Acts 15 : 28 (cp. " put . . . upon " in ver. 10). See LADE, PUT, SET, SURNAME, WOUND.

11. ANATITHĒMI (ἀνατίθημι), to put up or before (ana), is used in the Middle Voice of laying a case before an authority, Acts 25 : 14, R.V., " laid before," for A.V., " declared unto ; " of setting forth a matter for

consideration, Gal. 2 : 2, R.V., " laid before (them the gospel)," for A.V., " communicated unto." See COMMUNICATE, DECLARE.¶

12. PROSTITHĒMI (προστίθημι), to put to, add, is used in the Passive Voice in Acts 13 : 36, " was laid " (unto his fathers), of the burial of David. See ADD, No. 2.

13. EKTEINŌ (ἐκτείνω), to stretch out or forth, especially of the hand, is used of laying out anchors from a vessel, in Acts 27 : 30, R.V., " lay out " (A.V., " cast . . . out "). See CAST, Notes, STRETCH.

14. KEIMAI (κεῖμαι), to be laid, to lie, is used as the Passive Voice of tithēmi, to put, and is translated by some part of the verb to be laid in Matt. 3 : 10 and Luke 3 : 9, of an axe ; Luke 12 : 19, of goods ; John 21 : 9, where the verb has been omitted from the translation, after the words " a fire of coals " (for epikeimai, of the fish, see No. 15) ; 1 Cor. 3 : 11, of Christ, as a foundation. See APPOINT, LIE, MADE (be), SET.

Notes : (1) In Luke 23 : 53, the R.V. has " had lain " (intransitive : see LIE), for A.V., " was laid." (2) In Luke 24 : 12, some mss. have the verb, with reference to the linen cloths (the clause is absent in the best mss.) ; the translation should be " lying," not as A.V., " laid." (3) In John 11 : 41, the verb is not found in the best mss.

15. EPIKEIMAI (ἐπίκειμαι), to be placed, to lie on (epi, upon, and No. 14), is translated by the verb to be laid upon, in John 21 : 9, of a fish ; in 1 Cor. 9 : 16, of necessity. See IMPOSED, INSTANT, LIE, PRESS.

16. APOKEIMAI (ἀπόκειμαι), to be laid away, or up, is used of money in a napkin, Luke 19 : 20 ; metaphorically, of a hope, Col. 1 : 5 ; the crown of righteousness, 2 Tim. 4 : 8. In Heb. 9 : 27, said of physical death, it is translated " it is appointed " (R.V. marg., " laid up "). See APPOINT.¶

17. THĒSAURIZŌ (θησαυρίζω), to lay up, store up (akin to thēsauros, a treasury, a storehouse, a treasure), is used of laying up treasures, on earth, Matt. 6 : 19 ; in Heaven, ver. 20 ; in the last days, Jas. 5 : 3, R.V., " ye have laid up your treasure " (A.V., " ye have heaped treasure together ") ; in Luke 12 : 21, " that layeth up treasure (for himself) ; " in 1 Cor. 16 : 2, of money for needy ones (here the present participle is translated " in store," lit. ' treasuring.' or ' storing,' the ' laying by ' translating the preceding verb tithēmi, see No. 1) ; in 2 Cor. 12 : 14, negatively, of children for parents ; metaphorically, of laying up wrath, Rom. 2 : 5, " treasurest up." In 2 Pet. 3 : 7 the Passive Voice is used of the heavens and earth as " stored up " for fire, R.V. (marg., " stored " with fire), A.V., " kept in store." See STORE, TREASURE.¶

18. TRACHĒLIZŌ (τραχηλίζω), to seize and twist the neck (from trachēlos, the throat), was used of wrestlers, in the sense of taking by the throat. The word is found in Heb. 4 : 13, " laid open," R.V. (A.V., " opened "). The literal sense of the word seems to be ' with the head thrown back and the throat exposed.' Various suggestions have been made as to the precise significance of the word in this passage. Some

have considered that the metaphor is from the manner of treating victims about to be sacrificed. Little help, however, can be derived from these considerations. The context serves to explain the meaning and the R.V. rendering is satisfactory.¶

Notes : (1) In Acts 25 : 7, A.V., *pherō,* to bear, bring, is rendered "laid . . . (complaints)," R.V., "bringing . . . (charges)." (2) In Mark 7 : 8, A.V., *aphiēmi,* to leave, is translated "laying aside" (R.V., "ye leave"). (3) For *epilambanō,* to lay hold, see HOLD, No. 7.

For LAY WAIT see LIE IN WAIT

For LAYING (Acts 9 : 24) see PLOT

LAY WASTE

LUMAINOMAI (λυμαίνομαι), to maltreat, to outrage (from *lumē,* a brutal outrage), is translated "laid waste" (the church), in Acts 8 : 3, R.V. (A.V., "made havock of").¶

LAYING ON

EPITHESIS (ἐπίθεσις), a laying on (*epi,* on, *tithēmi,* to put), is used in the N.T. (*a*) of the laying on of hands by the Apostles, accompanied by the impartation of the Holy Spirit in outward demonstration, in the cases of those in Samaria who had believed, Acts 8 : 18 ; such supernatural manifestations were signs especially intended to give witness to Jews as to the facts of Christ and the faith ; they were thus temporary ; there is no record of their continuance after the time and circumstances narrated in Acts 19 (in ver. 6 of which the corresponding verb *epitithēmi* is used ; see below), nor was the gift delegated by the Apostles to others (see LAY, Nos. 1 and 10) ; (*b*) of the similar act by the elders of a church on occasions when a member of a church was set apart for a particular work, having given evidence of qualifications necessary for it, as in the case of Timothy, 1 Tim. 4 : 14 ; of the impartation of a spiritual gift through the laying on of the hands of the Apostle Paul, 2 Tim. 1 : 6, R.V., "laying" (A.V., "putting") ; cp. the verb *epitithēmi* in Acts 6 : 6, on the appointment of the Seven, and in the case of Barnabas and Saul, 13 : 3 ; also in 19 : 6 ; (*c*) in Heb. 6 : 2, the doctrine of the laying on of hands refers to the act enjoined upon an Israelite in connection, e.g., with the peace offerings, Lev. 3 : 2, 8, 13 ; 4 : 29, 33 ; upon the priests in connection with the sin offering, 4 : 4 ; 16 : 21 ; upon the elders, 4 : 15 ; upon a ruler, 4 : 24.¶

The principle underlying the act was that of identification on the part of him who did it with the animal or person upon whom the hands were laid. In the Sept., 2 Chron. 25 : 27 ; Ezek. 23 : 11.¶

Note : For the laying of Christ's hands on the sick, see LAY, No. 10.

LEAD, LED

1. AGŌ (ἄγω), to bear, bring, carry, lead, is translated by the verb to

lead, e.g., in Mark 13 : 11 ; Luke 4 : 1 ; 4 : 9, R.V. ; 4 : 29 ; 22 : 54 ; 23 : 1, A.V. only ; 23 : 32 ; John 18 : 28 (present tense, R.V.) ; Acts 8 : 32 ; metaphorically in Rom. 2 : 4, of the goodness of God ; 8 : 14 and Gal. 5 : 18, of the Spirit of God ; 1 Cor. 12 : 2, of the powers of darkness instigating to idolatry ; 2 Tim. 3 : 6, of divers lusts (in some mss., *aichmalōteuō*). In Luke 24 : 21 *agō* is used of the passing (or spending) of a day, and translated " it is (now the third day) ; " here the verb is probably to be taken impersonally, according to idiomatic usage, in the sense 'there is passing the third day.' See BRING, No. 10, KEEP, Note (2).

2. ANAGŌ (*ἀνάγω*), to lead up (*ana*, up), is used of Christ in being led up by the Spirit into the wilderness, Matt. 4 : 1 ; Luke 4 : 5 (A.V., " taking up ") ; by the elders of the people into their council, Luke 22 : 66, " led away." See BRING, No. 11.

3. APAGŌ (*ἀπάγω*), to lead away (*apo*, away), is used of a way leading to destruction, Matt. 7 : 13 ; to life, ver. 14 ; of those who led Christ away from Gethsemane, Mark 14 : 44 ; in some mss., John 18 : 13, to Annas (the best mss. have No. 1 here) ; to Caiaphas, Matt. 26 : 57 ; Mark 14 : 53 ; to Pilate, Matt. 27 : 2 ; to the Prætorium, Mark 15 : 16 ; to crucifixion, Matt. 27 : 31 ; Luke 23 : 26 ; in some mss. John 19 : 16 ; of leading an animal away to watering, Luke 13 : 15 ; of being led away to idolatry, 1 Cor. 12 : 2, R.V., " led away " (A.V., " carried away "). Some mss. have it in Acts 24 : 7 (A.V., " took away "). It is translated " bring " in 23 : 17. In 12 : 19 it signifies to put to death. See BRING, No. 12, DEATH, C, No. 3.¶

4. PERIAGŌ (*περιάγω*), used transitively, denotes to lead about, 1 Cor. 9 : 5. For the intransitive use, see GO, No. 9.

5. PHERŌ (*φέρω*), to bear, carry, is used metaphorically of a gate, as leading to a city, Acts 12 : 10. See BRING, No. 1.

6. HODĒGEŌ (*ὁδηγέω*), to lead the way : see GUIDE, B, No. 1.

7. EISAGŌ (*εἰσάγω*), to bring into, is translated " to be led into " in Acts 21 : 37, A.V. (R.V., " to be brought into "). See BRING, A, No. 13.

8. SUNAPAGŌ (*συναπάγω*), always in the Passive Voice, to be carried or led away with, is translated " being led away with " in 2 Pet. 3 : 17, A.V. (R.V., " being carried away with "). See CARRY.

9. EXAGŌ (*ἐξάγω*), to lead out, is rendered by the verb to lead, out or forth, in Mark 15 : 20 (in some mss. in 8 : 23, the best have *ekpherō*, to bring out) ; Luke 24 : 50 ; John 10 : 3 ; Acts 7 : 36, 40 (A.V. " brought "), and 13 : 17, R.V. ; Acts 21 : 38 ; Heb. 8 : 9. See BRING, No. 14.

10. ANAPHERŌ (*ἀναφέρω*), to carry or lead up, is translated " leadeth . . . up " in the A.V. of Mark 9 : 2 (R.V. " bringeth . . . up "). See BRING, No. 2.

11. EISPHERŌ (*εἰσφερω*), to bring in, or into, is translated " lead (us not) into," in Matt. 6 : 13 and Luke 11 : 4 (R.V., " bring . . . into "), of temptation. See BRING, No. 4.

12. PLANAŌ (πλανα.
is translated "lead . . . a3
and Mark 13 : 5, 6 (A.V., "c ̣ ̣ay (akin to *planē*, a wandering),
13. APOPLANAŌ (ἀποπλαὶ ̣horically, in Matt. 24 : 4, 5, 11
from, and No. 12), is used metà
13 : 22, R.V., "lead astray" (A. ̣ ̣e to go astray (*apo*, away
1 Tim. 6 : 10 (A.V., " erred ").¶ f leading into error, Mark
Notes : (1) In Rev. 13 : 10, some msse ") ; Passive Voice in
translated "leadeth (into captivity)," A.\
" is for "). (2) For the verb *diagō*, to lead ̣ago, to bring together,
No. 7. (3) For *thriambeuō*, to "lead in triun ̣V. marg. (R.V. text,
see. TRIUMPH. (4) See also HAND (lead by the). ̣im. 2 : 2, see LIVE,
Cor. 2 : 14, R.V.,

For LEADERS (Matt. 15 : 14) see GU⸲

LEAF

PHULLON (φύλλον), a leaf (originally *phulion*, Lat., *foliun* ̣ Eng.,
folio, foliaceous, foliage, foliate, folious, etc.), is found in Matt. 21 ̣19 ;
24 : 32 ; Mark 11 : 13 (twice) ; 13 : 28 ; Rev. 22 : 2.¶

LEAN

1. ANAKEIMAI (ἀνάκειμαι), to be laid up, to lie, is used of reclining
at table, and translated "leaning (on Jesus' bosom) " in the A.V. of
John 13 : 23, R.V., " reclining " (for ver. 25 see No. 2). In ver. 28, it is
translated "at the table," lit., ' of (those) reclining.' See GUEST, RECLINE,
SIT, TABLE (at the).

2. ANAPIPTŌ (ἀναπίπτω), lit., to fall back (*ana*, back, *piptō*, to fall),
is used of reclining at a repast and translated " leaning back, (as he was, on
Jesus' breast) " in John 13 : 25, R.V. (the A.V. follows the mss. which have
epipiptō, and renders it ' lying ') ; in 21 : 20, " leaned back," the Apostle's
reminder of the same event in his experience. See SIT.

LEAP

1. HALLOMAI (ἄλλομαι), to leap (akin to *halma*, a leap), is used
(a) metaphorically, of the springing up of water, John 4 : 14 ; (b) literally,
of the leaping of healed cripples, Acts 3 : 8 (2nd part) ; 14 : 10.¶

2. SKIRTAŌ (σκιρτάω), to leap, is found in Luke 1 : 41, 44, and
6 : 23, there translated " leap for joy ; " in 1 : 44 the words " for joy "
are expressed separately.¶

3. EXALLOMAI (ἐξάλλομαι), to leap up (lit., out, *ek*, and No. 1), is
said in Acts 3 : 8 (1st part) of the cripple healed by Peter (cp. No. 1,
above).¶

4. EPHALLOMAI (ἐφάλλομαι), to leap upon (*epi*, upon, and No. 1),
is said of the demoniac in Acts 19 : 16.¶

...ED (be)

(a) to learn (akin to *mathētēs*, a

1. MANTHANŌ (μανθ...), ...LEAge, or be increased in knowledge, disciple), to increase ...observation, e.g., Matt. 9 : 13 ; 11 : 29 ; frequently to learn by on5 ; Rom. 16 : 17 ; 1 Cor. 4 : 6 ; 14 : 35 ; 24 : 32 ; Mark 13 : 28 ; erv. 14 : 3 ; said of learning Christ, Eph. Phil. 4 : 9 ; 2 Tim. ... of Christ, but Christ Himself, a process not 4 : 20, not simply th... ...e Person but of so applying the knowledge as merely of getting t... ...he rest of the Gentiles ; (b) to ascertain, Acts to walk differentl... ...(A.V., " understood ") ; Gal. 3 : 2, " This only 23 : 27, R.V., " ja," perhaps with a tinge of irony in the enquiry, the would I learn f...uld settle the question of the validity of the new answer to whi...ey were receiving ; (c) to learn by use and practice, to Judaistic go... of, be accustomed to, e.g., Phil. 4 : 11 ; 1 Tim. 5 : 4, 13 ; acquire the...eb. 5 : 8. See UNDERSTAND. Tit. 3 : 14...

2. GI...SKŌ (γινώσκω), to know by observation and experience, is translat...d to learn, in the R.V. of Mark 15 : 45 ; John 12 : 9. See ALL...

3. AKRIBOŌ (ἀκριβόω), to learn carefully, is so translated in Matt. 2 : 7, 16, R.V. (A.V., " diligently enquired ").¶

4. MUEŌ (μυέω), to initiate into mysteries, is translated " I have learned the secret " (Passive Voice, perfect tense) in Phil. 4 : 12, R.V. (A.V., " I am instructed "). See INSTRUCT.¶

Note : *Paideuō*, to teach, instruct, train, is translated " instructed " in Acts 7 : 22, R.V. (A.V., " learned ") ; in 1 Tim. 1 : 20, " (that) they might be taught," A.V., " (that) they may learn."

LEARNING (Noun)

1. GRAMMA (γράμμα), a letter, is used in the plural in Acts 26 : 24, with the meaning " learning," " (thy much) learning (doth turn thee to madness)," R.V., possibly an allusion to the Jewish Scriptures, to which the Apostle had been appealing ; in John 7 : 15, " (How knoweth this Man) letters " (A.V. marg., " learning "), the succeeding phrase " not having learned " is illustrated in the papyri, where it indicates inability to write. See BILL.

2. DIDASKALIA (διδασκαλία), teaching, instruction (akin to *didaskō*, to teach), is translated " learning " in Rom. 15 : 4. See DOCTRINE.

LEAST

1. ELACHISTOS (ἐλάχιστος), least, is a superlative degree formed from the word *elachus*, little, the place of which was taken by *mikros* (the comparative degree being *elassōn*, less) ; it is used of (a) size, Jas. 3 : 4 ; (b) amount ; of the management of affairs, Luke 16 : 10 (twice) ; 19 : 17, " very little ; " (c) importance, 1 Cor. 6 : 2, " smallest (matters) ; " (d) authority : of commandments, Matt. 5 : 19 ; (e) estimation, as to

persons, Matt. 5 : 19 (2nd part) ; 25 : 40, 45 ; 1 Cor. 15 : 9 ; as to a town, Matt. 2 : 6 ; as to activities or operations, Luke 12 : 26 ; 1 Cor. 4 : 3, " a very small thing."¶

2. ELACHISTOTEROS (ἐλαχιστότερος), a comparative degree formed from No. 1, is used in Eph. 3 : 8, " less than the least."¶

3. MIKROS (μικρός), small, little, is translated " the least " in Acts 8 : 10 and Heb. 8 : 11, with reference to rank or influence. See LITTLE, A, No. 1.

4. MIKROTEROS (μικρότερος), the comparative of No. 3, is used of (a) size, Matt. 13 : 32, A.V., " the least," R.V., " less ; " Mark 4 : 31 [cp. No. 1 (a)] ; (b) estimation, Matt. 11 : 11 and Luke 7 : 28, A.V., " least," R.V., " but little," marg., " lesser " (in the Kingdom of Heaven), those in the Kingdom itself being less than John the Baptist [cp. No. 1 (e)] ; Luke 9 : 48. See LESS.¶

Notes : (1) In 1 Cor. 6 : 4, A.V., *exoutheneō*, in the Passive Voice, to be of no account, is translated " is least esteemed " (R.V., " are of no account ") ; see ACCOUNT. (2) In Luke 19 : 42, the adverbial phrase *kai ge*, " at least," is found in some mss. ; the R.V. follows those in which it is absent. (3) In 1 Cor. 9 : 2, A.V., the phrase *alla ge* is rendered " doubtless ; " R.V., " at least." (4) In Acts 5 : 15, the phrase *k'an* (for *kai ean*, even if) denotes " at the least."

LEATHERN

DERMATINOS (δερμάτινος) denotes of skin, leathern (from *derma*, skin, hide of beasts, akin to *derō*, to flay ; whence Eng., derm, dermal, dermatology) ; it is translated " leathern " in Matt. 3 : 4, of John the Baptist's girdle ; in Mark 1 : 6, R.V. (A.V., " of a skin "). See SKIN.¶

LEAVE, LEFT

(a) *In the sense of leaving, abandoning, forsaking.*

1. APHIĒMI (ἀφίημι), *apo*, from, and *hiēmi*, to send, has three chief meanings, (a) to send forth, let go, forgive ; (b) to let, suffer, permit ; (c) to leave, leave alone, forsake, neglect. It is translated by the verb to leave (c), in Matt. 4 : 11 ; 4 : 20, 22, and parallel passages ; 5 : 24 ; 8 : 15, and parallel passages ; 8 : 22, R.V., " leave (the dead)," A.V., " let," and the parallel passage ; 13 : 36, R.V., " left (the multitude)," A.V., " sent . . . away ; " 18 : 12 ; 19 : 27, and parallel passages, R.V., " we have left " (A.V., " we have forsaken ") ; so ver. 29 ; 22 : 22, 25 ; 23 : 23, R.V., " have left undone " (A.V., " have omitted," in the 1st part, " leave undone " in the second) ; 23 : 38, and the parallel passage ; 24 : 2, 40, 41, and parallel passages ; 26 : 56, R.V., " left ; " Mark 1 : 18, " left ; " 1 : 31 ; 7 : 8, R.V., " ye leave ; " 8 : 13 ; 10 : 28, 29 ; 12 : 12, 19–22 ; 13 : 34 ; Luke 10 : 30 ; 11 : 42 (in some mss.) ; Luke 12 : 39, R.V. " have left," A.V. " have suffered " (No. 9 in Matt. 24 : 43) ; John 4 : 3, 28, 52 ; 8 : 29 ; 10 : 12 ; 14 : 18, 27 ; 16 : 28, 32 ; Rom. 1 : 27 ; 1 Cor. 7 : 11, R.V.,

" leave " (A.V., " put away ") ; 7 : 13 (A.V. and R.V.) ; Heb. 2 : 8 ; 6 : 1 ; Rev. 2 : 4.   See FORGIVE.

2. ANIĒMI (ἀνίημι), ana, back and hiēmi, to send, denotes to let go, loosen, forbear ; it is translated " I will (never) leave (thee) " in Heb. 13 : 5.   See FORBEAR.

3. KATALEIPŌ (καταλείπω), to leave behind (kata, down, leipō, to leave), is everywhere rendered by the verb to leave except in the following : the A.V. of Rom. 11 : 4, " I have reserved " (R.V., " I have left ") ; Heb. 11 : 27, " he forsook ; " 2 Pet. 2 : 15, A.V., " have forsaken," R.V., " forsaking."   See FORSAKE, RESERVE.

4. APOLEIPŌ (ἀπολείπω), to leave behind (apo, from), is used (a) in the Active Voice, of leaving behind a cloak, 2 Tim. 4 : 13 ; a person, 2 Tim. 4 : 20 ; of abandoning a principality (by angels), Jude 6, R.V. ; (b) in the Passive Voice, to be reserved, to remain, Heb. 4 : 6, 9 ; 10 : 26. See REMAIN, No. 3.¶   In the papyri it is used as a technical term in wills (Moulton and Milligan, Vocab.).

5. ENKATALEIPŌ (ἐγκαταλείπω), lit., to leave behind in (en, in, and No. 3), signifies (a) to leave behind, Rom. 9 : 29, " a seed ; " (b) to abandon, forsake, translated by the verb to leave in Acts 2 : 27, 31 (in some mss., No. 3) of the soul of Christ ; in the following, by the verb to forsake, Matt. 27 : 46 ; Mark 15 : 34 ; 2 Cor. 4 : 9 ; 2 Tim. 4 : 10, 16 ; Heb. 10 : 25 ; 13 : 5 (see No. 2 in the same ver.).   See FORSAKE.¶

6. HUPOLEIPŌ (ὑπολείπω), to leave remaining; lit., to leave under (hupo), is used in the Passive Voice in Rom. 11 : 3, of a survivor.¶

7. PERILEIPŌ (περιλείπω), to leave over, is used in the Passive Voice in 1 Thess. 4 : 15, 17, R.V., " that are left " (A.V., " that remain "), lit., ' left over,' i.e., the living believers at the Lord's return.   See REMAIN.¶

8. PAUŌ (παύω), to make to cease, is used in the Middle Voice, sig-nifying to cease, leave off, and is translated " had left " in Luke 5 : 4 ; " left " in Acts 21 : 32 ; elsewhere, to cease.   See CEASE.

9. EAŌ (ἐάω) signifies (a) to let, permit, suffer, e.g., Matt. 24 : 43 ; (b) to leave, Acts 23 : 32, of leaving horsemen ; 27 : 40, of leaving anchors in the sea, R.V. [A.V., " committed (themselves) "].   See COMMIT, SUFFER.

10. HUPOLIMPANŌ (ὑπολιμπάνω), limpanō being a late form for leipō, to leave, is used in 1 Pet. 2 : 21, " leaving (us an example)."¶

11. PERISSEUŌ (περισσεύω), to be over and above (the number), hence, to be or remain over, is translated " was left," in Matt. 15 : 37, A.V. (R.V., " remained over," as in 14 : 20 ; Luke 9 : 17 ; John 6 : 12 and ver. 13, where the A.V. adds " and above "), of the broken fragments after the feeding of the multitudes.   See ABOUND.

Note : The corresponding noun, perisseuma, that which is over and above, is used in the plural in Mark 8 : 8, R.V., " (of broken pieces) that remained over," A.V., " (of the broken meat) that was left," lit., ' of fragments of broken pieces.'   See REMAIN.

12. EKBALLŌ (ἐκβάλλω), to cast out (ek, from, ballō, to cast), to drive out, is used in the sense of rejecting or leaving out, in Rev. 11 : 2, as to the measuring of the court of the Temple (marg., " cast without "). See CAST, No. 5.

(b) *In the sense of giving leave.*

EPITREPŌ (ἐπιτρέπω) lit. denotes to turn to (epi, upon, to, trepō, to turn), and so (a) to commit, entrust (not in N.T.) ; (b) to permit, give leave, send, of Christ's permission to the unclean spirits to enter the swine, Mark 5 : 13 ; in Luke 8 : 32, R.V., " give . . . leave," " gave . . . leave " (A.V., " suffer " and " suffered ") ; in John 19 : 38, of Pilate's permission to Joseph to take away the body of the Lord ; in Acts 21 : 39, of Paul's request to the chief captain to permit him to address the people, R.V., " give . . . leave " (for A.V., " suffer ") ; in 21 : 40, " he had given him leave " (A.V., " . . . licence "). See LET, LIBERTY, LICENCE, PERMIT, SUFFER.

(c) *In the sense of taking leave of, bidding farewell to.*

1. APOTASSŌ (ἀποτάσσω), used in the Middle Voice in the N.T., lit. signifies to arrange oneself off (apo, from, tassō, to arrange) ; hence, to take leave of, Mark 6 : 46, R.V., " had taken leave of " (A.V., " had sent . . . away ") ; Acts 18 : 18 ; 18 : 21, R.V., " taking his leave of " (A.V., " bade . . . farewell ") ; 2 Cor. 2 : 13 ; in Luke 9 : 61, " to bid farewell ; " in Luke 14 : 33 it has its other meaning " renouncing " (A.V., " forsaking "). See FAREWELL, FORSAKE, RENOUNCE.¶

2. APASPAZOMAI (ἀπασπάζομαι), to embrace, salute, take leave of (apo, from, aspazomai, to salute), is used in Acts 21 : 6, A.V., " when we had taken our leave " (R.V., " bade . . . farewell "). Some mss. have the simple verb aspazomai.¶

LEAVEN (Noun and Verb)
A. Noun.

ZUMĒ (ζύμη), leaven, sour dough, in a high state of fermentation, was used in general in making bread. It required time to fulfil the process. Hence, when food was required at short notice, unleavened cakes were used, e.g., Gen. 18 : 6 ; 19 : 3 ; Ex. 12 : 8. The Israelites were forbidden to use leaven for seven days at the time of Passover, that they might be reminded that the Lord brought them out of Egypt " in haste," Deut. 16 : 3, with Ex. 12 : 11 ; the unleavened bread, insipid in taste, reminding them, too, of their afflictions, and of the need of self-judgment, is called " the bread of affliction." Leaven was forbidden in all offerings to the Lord by fire, Lev. 2 : 11 ; 6 : 17. Being bred of corruption and spreading through the mass of that in which it is mixed, and therefore symbolizing the pervasive character of evil, leaven was utterly inconsistent in offerings which typified the propitiatory sacrifice of Christ.

In the O.T. leaven is not used in a metaphorical sense. In the N.T. it is used (a) metaphorically (1) of corrupt doctrine, Matt. 13 : 33 and

Luke 13 : 21, of error as mixed with the truth (there is no valid reason for regarding the symbol here differently from its application elsewhere in the N.T.) ; Matt. 16 : 6, 11 ; Mark 8 : 15 (1st part) ; Luke 12 : 1 ; that the Kingdom of heaven is likened to leaven, does not mean that the Kingdom is leaven. The same statement, as made in other parables, shows that it is the whole parable which constitutes the similitude of the Kingdom ; the history of Christendom confirms the fact that the pure meal of the doctrine of Christ has been adulterated with error ; (2) of corrupt practices, Mark 8 : 15 (2nd part), the reference to the Herodians being especially applied to their irreligion ; 1 Cor. 5 : 7, 8 ; (b) literally, in Matt. 16 : 12, and in the general statements in 1 Cor. 5 : 6 and Gal. 5 : 9, where the implied applications are to corrupt practice and corrupt doctrine respectively.¶

B. Verb.

ZUMOŌ (ζυμόω) signifies to leaven, to act as leaven, Passive Voice in Matt. 13 : 33 and Luke 13 : 21 ; Active Voice in 1 Cor. 5 : 6 and Gal. 5 : 9.¶

For LED see LEAD

LEE

Note : This forms part of the R.V. rendering of two verbs, (1) *hupopleō*, to sail under (i.e., under the lee of), from *hupo*, under, *pleō*, to sail, Acts 27 : 4, 7 (A.V., " sailed under ") ;¶ (2) *hupotrechō*, to run in under (in navigation), to run under the lee of (*hupo*, and a form *hupodramōn*, used as an aorist participle of the verb), Acts 27 : 16, R.V., " running under the lee of " (A.V., " running under "). See RUN, SAIL.¶

For LEFT (Verb) see LEAVE

LEFT (Adjective)

1. ARISTEROS (ἀριστερός), is used (a) of the left hand, in Matt. 6 : 3, the word " hand " being understood ; in connection with the armour of righteousness, in 2 Cor. 6 : 7, " (on the right hand and) on the left," lit., ' (of the weapons . . . the right and) the left ; ' (b) in the phrase " on the left," formed by *ex* (for *ek*), from, and the genitive plural of this adjective, Mark 10 : 37 (some mss. have No. 2 here) ; Luke 23 : 33.¶

2. EUŌNUMOS (εὐώνυμος), lit., of good name, or omen (*eu*, well, *onoma*, a name), a word adopted to avoid the ill-omen attaching to the left (omens from the left being unlucky, but a good name being desired for them, cp. *aristeros*, lit., ' better of two,' euphemistic for the ill-omened *laios* and *skaios* ; cp., too, the Eng., sinister, from the Latin word meaning ' left '), is used euphemistically for No. 1, either (a) simply as an adjective in Rev. 10 : 2, of the left foot ; in Acts 21 : 3, " on the

left " (lit., ' left ') ; or (*b*) with the preposition *ex* (for *ek*), signifying on the left hand, Matt. 20 : 21, 23 ; 25 : 33, 41 ; 27 : 38 ; Mark 10 : 40 (for ver. 37, in some mss., see No. 1) ; 15 : 27.¶

LEG

SKELOS (σκέλος), the leg from the hip downwards, is used only of the breaking of the legs of the crucified malefactors, to hasten their death, John 19 : 31–33 (a customary act, not carried out in the case of Christ, in fulfilment of Ex. 12 : 46 ; Numb. 9 : 12). The practice was known as *skelokopia* (from *koptō*, to strike), or, in Latin, *crurifragium* (from *crus*, a leg, and *frango*, to break).¶

LEGION

LEGIŌN (λεγιών), otherwise spelt *legeōn*, a legion, occurs in Matt. 26 : 53, of angels ; in Mark 5 : 9, 15, and Luke 8 : 30, of demons. Among the Romans a legion was primarily a chosen (*lego*, to choose) body of soldiers divided into ten cohorts, and numbering from 4,200 to 6,000 men (Gk. *speira*, see BAND). In the time of our Lord it formed a complete army of infantry and cavalry, of upwards of 5,000 men. The legions were not brought into Judæa till the outbreak of the Jewish war (A.D. 66), as they were previously employed in the frontier Provinces of the Empire. Accordingly in its N.T. use the word has its other and more general significance of a large number.¶

LEISURE (to have)

EUKAIREŌ (εὐκαιρέω), to have leisure or opportunity (*eu*, well, *kairos*, a time or season), is translated " they had . . . leisure " in Mark 6 : 31 ; in Acts 17 : 21, " spent their time " (R.V., marg., " had leisure for ") ; in 1 Cor. 16 : 12," he shall have opportunity," R.V. (A.V., " . . . convenient time "). See CONVENIENT, OPPORTUNITY, SPEND.¶ This verb differs from *scholazō*, to have leisure ; it stresses the opportunity of doing something, whereas *scholazō* stresses the leisure for engaging in it, e.g., 1 Cor. 7 : 5, " (that) ye may give yourselves to."

LEND, LENDER
A. Verbs.

1. DANEIZŌ (δανείζω) is translated to lend in Luke 6 : 34, 35 : see BORROW.

2. KICHRĒMI (κίχρημι), or CHRAŌ (χράω), to lend, is used in the aorist (or ' point ') tense, Active Voice, in Luke 11 : 5, in the request, " lend me three loaves." The radical sense of the verb is to furnish what is needful (akin to *chreia*, which means both use and need, and to *chrē*, it is needful). Hence it is distinct from No. 1, the basic idea of which is to lend on security or return.¶

B. Noun.

DANISTĒS or DANEISTĒS (δανειστής) denotes a money-lender (akin to A, No. 1), translated " lender " in Luke 7 : 41,R.V. (A.V., " creditor ").¶ In the Sept., 2 Kings 4 : 1 ; Ps. 109 : 11 ; Prov. 29 : 13.¶

LENGTH

MĒKOS (μῆκος), length, from the same root as makros, long (see FAR, LONG), occurs in Eph. 3 : 18 and Rev. 21 : 16 (twice).¶

LENGTH (at)

POTE (ποτέ) is translated " at length " in Rom. 1 : 10, where the whole phrase " if by any means now at length " suggests not only ardent desire but the existence of difficulties for a considerable time. See AFORETIME.

LEOPARD

PARDALIS (πάρδαλις) denotes a leopard or a panther, an animal characterized by swiftness of movement and sudden spring, in Dan. 7 : 6 symbolic of the activities of Alexander the Great, and the formation of the Grecian Kingdom, the third seen in the vision there recorded. In Rev. 13 : 2 the imperial power, described there also as a " beast," is seen to concentrate in himself the characteristics of those mentioned in Dan. 7.¶

LEPER

LEPROS (λεπρός), an adjective, primarily used of psoriasis, characterized by an eruption of rough, scaly patches ; later, leprous, but chiefly used as a noun, a leper, Matt. 8 : 2 ; 10 : 8 ; 11 : 5 ; Mark 1 : 40 ; Luke 4 : 27 ; 7 : 22 ; 17 : 12 ; especially of Simon, mentioned in Matt. 26 : 6 ; Mark 14 : 3.¶

LEPROSY

LEPRA (λέπρα), akin to lepros (above), is mentioned in Matt. 8 : 3 ; Mark 1 : 42 ; Luke 5 : 12, 13.¶ In the removal of other maladies the verb to heal (iaomai) is used, but in the removal of leprosy, the verb to cleanse (katharizō), save in the statement concerning the Samaritan, Luke 17 : 15, " when he saw that he was healed." Matt. 10 : 8 and Luke 4 : 27 indicate that the disease was common in the nation. Only twelve cases are recorded in the N.T., but these are especially selected. For the Lord's commands to the leper mentioned in Matthew 8 and to the ten in Luke 17, see Lev. 14 : 2–32.

LESS

1. ELASSŌN (ἐλάσσων) serves as a comparative degree of mikros, little (see LEAST), and denotes ' less ' in (a) quality, as of wine, John 2 : 10, " worse ; " (b) age, Rom. 9 : 12, " younger ; " 1 Tim. 5 : 9, " under "

neuter, adverbially) ; (c) rank, Heb. 7 : 7. See UNDER, WORSE, YOUNG.¶

2. MIKROTEROS (μικρότερος), the comparative of *mikros*, is translated "less" in Matt. 13 : 32, R.V. (A.V., "least"), and Mark 4 : 31. See LEAST.

3. HĒSSŌN (ἥσσων), inferior, is used in the neuter adverbially in 2 Cor. 12 : 15, "the less." See WORSE.

LEST

1. MĒ (μή), a negative particle, often used as a conjunction, is frequently translated "lest," e.g., Mark 13 : 36 (in ver. 5, R.V., "that no," for A.V., "lest") ; Acts 13 : 40 ; 23 : 10.

2. HINA MĒ (ἵνα μή), in order that not, is rendered "lest," e.g., in Matt. 17 : 27 ; in some instances the R.V. renders the phrase "that . . . not," e.g., Luke 8 : 12, or "that . . . no," 1 Cor. 9 : 12 (A.V., "lest").

3. MĒPOTE or MĒ POTE (μήποτε) denotes lest ever, lest perhaps, lest at any time, e.g., Matt. 4 : 6 ; "lest haply," Matt. 7 : 6, R.V. (A.V., "lest"), and in 13 : 15 (A.V., "lest at any time") ; in 25 : 9, R.V., "peradventure" (A.V., "lest"). The R.V. does not translate this simply by "lest," as in the A.V. ; see further, e.g., in Matt. 27 : 64 ; Mark 14 : 2 ; Luke 12 : 58 ; the addition of *pote* requires the fuller rendering.

Note : In Luke 14 : 29, the conjunctive phrase *hina mēpote*, "lest haply," is used.

4. MĒPŌS, or MĒ PŌS (μήπως), used as a conjunction, denotes lest somehow, lest haply, lest by any means, e.g., 2 Cor. 2 : 7, R.V., "lest by any means" (A.V., "lest perhaps") ; so 12 : 20 (twice) and Gal. 4 : 11 (A.V., "lest") ; in 1 Thess. 3 : 5 (A.V., "lest by some means").

5. MĒPOU, or MĒ POU (μήπου), lest perhaps, is used in Acts 27 : 29, R.V., "lest haply" (A.V., "lest").

Note : In 2 Cor. 4 : 4, A.V., the phrase *eis* (unto) *to* (the) *mē* (not), i.e., 'in order that . . . not,' is rendered "lest (the light) . . . should ; " R.V., "that (the light) . . . should not."

LET (alone, go)

1. APHIĒMI (ἀφίημι), for the meanings of which see LEAVE, No. 1, frequently denotes to let, suffer, permit, e.g., Matt. 5:40 (translated "let . . . have") ; 7:4; 13:30; 15:14; 27:49 and Mark 15:36, R.V., "let be," probably short for 'let us see' (Moulton and Milligan, Vocab.) ; Mark 7:27; 11:6 ("let . . . go") ; 14:6 ("let . . . alone") ; so Luke 13:8; John 11:48; in Acts 5:38 (where some mss. have *eaō*, to permit, let, suffer) ; in John 11:44 and 18:8 ("let") ; 1 Cor. 7:11, 12, R.V., "let . . . leave," A.V., "let . . . put away;" 7:13 ("let .. leave").

2. EPITREPŌ (ἐπιτρέπω), for the meanings of which see LEAVE (b), is translated "let (me)" in Luke 9:61, A.V., R.V., "suffer (me)."

3. APOLUŌ (ἀπολύω) signifies to set free, release, loose (*apo*, from,

luō, to loose), e.g., Luke 13 : 12 ; John 19 : 10 ; forgive, Luke 6 : 37 ; to release, dismiss, send away, translated to let go, e.g., in Luke 14 : 4 ; in some mss. 22 : 68 ; in Luke 23 : 22, John 19 : 12 and Acts 3 : 13, A.V., " let . . . go " (R.V., " release ") ; in Acts 4 : 21, " they let . . . go ; " in ver. 23 (Passive Voice), " being let go ; " 5 : 40 ; in 15 : 33, A.V., " let go " (R.V., " dismissed ") ; 16 : 35, 36 ; 17 : 9 ; in 23 : 22, R.V., " let . . . go " (A.V., " let . . . depart ") ; in 28 : 18, A.V., " let . . . go " (R.V., " set . . . at liberty "). See DISMISS.

4. EAŌ (*ἐάω*), to let, occurs in Acts 27 : 32. See SUFFER.

Note : In Acts 2 : 29, the impersonal verb *exesti*, it is permitted, it is lawful, is rendered " let me," A.V. (R.V. and A.V., marg., " I may ").

For LET (A.V. in Rom. 1 : 13 and 2 Thess. 2 : 7) see HINDER and RESTRAIN

LET DOWN

1. KATHIĒMI (*καθίημι*), to send, or let down (*kata*, down, *hiēmi*, to send), is translated to let down, with reference to (*a*) the paralytic in Luke 5 : 19 ; (*b*) Saul of Tarsus, Acts 9 : 25 ; (*c*) the great sheet in Peter's vision, 10 : 11 and 11 : 5.¶

2. CHALAŌ (*χαλάω*), to slacken, loosen, let loose, denotes in the N.T., to let down, to lower ; it is used with reference to (*a*) the paralytic, in Mark 2 : 4, cp. No. 1 (*a*) ; (*b*) Saul of Tarsus, Acts 9 : 25, " lowering " [see also No. 1 (*b*)] ; 2 Cor. 11 : 33, " was I let down " (Passive Voice) ; (*c*) nets, Luke 5 : 4, 5 (in the latter, R.V., " nets ;" A.V., " net ") ; (*d*) the gear of a ship, Acts 27 : 17, R.V., " they lowered (the gear)," A.V., " they strake (sail) ; " (*e*) a ship's boat, ver. 30, R.V., " lowered " (A.V., " let down "). See LOWER, STRIKE.¶

LET OUT

EKDIDŌMI (*ἐκδίδωμι*), primarily, to give out, give up, surrender (*ek*, out, from, *didōmi*, to give), denotes to let out for hire; in the N.T. it is used, in the Middle Voice, with the meaning to let out to one's advantage, in the parable of the husbandman and his vineyard, Matt. 21:33, 41; Mark 12:1; Luke 20:9, A.V., "let . . . forth;" R.V., "let . . . out."¶

LETTER

1. GRAMMA (*γράμμα*) primarily denotes that which is traced or drawn, a picture; then, that which is written, (*a*) a character, letter of the alphabet, 2 Cor. 3:7; "written," lit., '(in) letters'; Gal. 6:11; here the reference is not to the length of the Epistle (Paul never uses *gramma*, either in the singular or the plural. of his Epistles; of these he uses *epistolē*, No. 2), but to the size of the characters written by his own hand (probably from this verse to the end, as the use of the past tense, "I have written,"

is, according to Greek idiom, the equivalent of our 'I am writing'). Moreover, the word for " letters " is here in the dative case, *grammasin,* ' with (how large) letters ; ' (*b*) a writing, a written document, a bond (A.V., " bill ") Luke 16 : 6, 7 ; (*c*) a letter, by way of correspondence, Acts 28 : 21 ; (*d*) the Scriptures of the O.T., 2 Tim. 3 : 15 ; (*e*) learning, John 7 : 15, " letters ; " Acts 26 : 24, " (much) learning " (lit., ' many letters ') ; in the papyri an illiterate person is often spoken of as one who does not know letters, "which never means anything else than inability to write " (Moulton and Milligan) ; (*f*) " the letter," the written commandments of the Word of God, in contrast to the inward operation of the Holy Spirit under the New Covenant, Rom. 2 : 27, 29 ; 7 : 6 ; 2 Cor. 3 : 6 ; (*g*) the books of Moses, John 5 : 47.¶

2. EPISTOLE (ἐπιστολή) : see EPISTLE.

For LEVEL see PLACE, *Note* (4)

For LEWD and LEWDNESS see VILE and VILLANY

LIAR
A. Nouns.
PSEUSTES (ψεύστης), a liar, occurs in John 8 : 44, 55 ; Rom. 3 : 4 ; 1 Tim. 1 : 10 ; Tit. 1 : 12 ; 1 John 1 : 10 ; 2 : 4, 22 ; 4 : 20 ; 5 : 10.¶
B. Adjective.
PSEUDES (ψευδής), lying, false (Eng., pseudo-), rendered " false " in Acts 6 : 13 and in the R.V. of Rev. 2 : 2 (A.V., " liars "), is used as a noun, " liars," in Rev. 21 : 8. See FALSE.¶

Note : Many compound nouns are formed by the prefix *pseudo-* : see, e.g., APOSTLES, BRETHREN, CHRISTS, PROPHETS, TEACHERS, WITNESS.

LIBERAL, LIBERALITY, LIBERALLY
A. Noun.
1. HAPLOTES (ἁπλότης) denotes (*a*) simplicity, sincerity, unaffectedness (from *haplous*, single, simple, in contrast to *diplous*, double), Rom. 12 : 8, " simplicity ; " 2 Cor. 11 : 3 (in some mss. in 1 : 12) ; Eph. 6 : 5 and Col. 3 : 22, " singleness ; " (*b*) simplicity as manifested in generous giving, " liberality," 2 Cor. 8 : 2 ; 9 : 11 (A.V., " bountifulness," R.V. marg., " singleness ") ; 9 : 13 (A.V., " liberal "). See BOUNTY, No. 2.¶

2. CHARIS (χάρις) is rendered " liberality " in 1 Cor. 16 : 3, A.V. See BOUNTY, No. 3.

B. Adverb.
HAPLOS (ἁπλῶς), liberally, with singleness of heart, is used in Jas. 1 : 5 of God as the gracious and liberal Giver. The word may be taken either (*a*) in a logical sense, signifying unconditionally, simply, or (*b*) in a moral sense, generously ; for the double meaning compare A, No. 1.¶ On this passage Hort writes as follows : " Later writers comprehend under the

one word the whole magnanimous and honourable type of character in which singleness of mind is the central feature."

LIBERTY
A. Nouns.

1. ANESIS (ἄνεσις), a loosening, relaxation, is translated " liberty " in Acts 24 : 23, A.V. See INDULGENCE.

2. APHESIS (ἄφεσις), dismissal, release, forgiveness, is rendered " liberty " in the A.V. of Luke 4 : 18, R.V., " release." See FORGIVENESS.

3. ELEUTHERIA (ἐλευθερία) : see FREEDOM.

4. EXOUSIA (ἐξουσία), authority, right, is rendered "liberty " in 1 Cor. 8 : 9 (marg., " power "), " this liberty of yours," or ' this right which you assert.' See UTHORITY.

B. Adjective.

ELEUTHEROS (ἐλεύθερος) is rendered " at liberty " in 1 Cor. 7 : 39, A.V. (R.V. " free "). See FREE.

C. Verbs.

1. APOLUŌ (ἀπολύω), for the meanings of which see LET, No. 3, is translated "to set at liberty " in Acts 26 : 32 and Heb. 13 : 23. See DISMISS.

2. APOSTELLŌ (ἀποστέλλω), to send away, is translated " to set at liberty " in Luke 4 : 18. See SEND.

Note : In Acts 27 : 3, A.V., *epitrepō* is rendered " gave . . . liberty " (R.V. " gave . . . leave "). See LEAVE (*b*).

For LICENCE (in Acts 21 : 40 and 25 : 16, A.V.) see LEAVE (*b*) and OPPORTUNITY, A, No. 3

LICK

EPILEICHŌ (ἐπιλείχω), to lick over (*epi*, over, *leichō*, to lick), is said of the dogs in Luke 16 : 21. Some mss. have *apoleichō*, to lick off.¶

LIE (falsehood : Noun and Verb)
A. Nouns.

1. PSEUDOS (ψεῦδος), a falsehood, lie (see also under LIAR), is translated " lie " in John 8 : 44 (lit., ' the lie ') ; Rom. 1 : 25, where it stands by metonymy for an idol, as, e.g., in Isa. 44 : 20 ; Jer. 10 : 14 ; 13 : 25 ; Amos 2 : 4 (plural) ; 2 Thess. 2 : 11, with special reference to the lie of ver. 4, that man is God (cp. Gen. 3 : 5) ; 1 John 2 : 21, 27 ; Rev. 21 : 27 ; 22 : 15 ; in Eph. 4 : 25, A.V. " lying," R.V., " falsehood," the practice ; in Rev. 14 : 5, R.V., " lie " (some mss. have *dolos*, " guile," A.V.) ; 2 Thess. 2 : 9, where " lying wonders " is, lit., ' wonders of falsehood,' i.e., wonders calculated to deceive (cp. Rev. 13 : 13–15), the purpose being to deceive people into the acknowledgement of the spurious claim to deity on the part of the Man of Sin.¶

Note : In Rom. 1 : 25 the lie or idol is the outcome of pagan religion ;

in 1 John 2 : 21, 22 the lie is the denial that Jesus is the Christ ; in 2 Thess. 2 : 11 the lie is the claim of the Man of Sin.

2. PSEUSMA (ψεῦσμα), a falsehood, or an acted lie, Rom. 3 : 7, where " my lie " is not idolatry, but either the universal false attitude of man toward God or that with which his detractors charged the Apostle ; the former seems to be the meaning.¶

B. Adjectives.

1. PSEUDOLOGOS (ψευδολόγος) denotes speaking falsely (pseudēs, false, logos, a word) in 1 Tim. 4 : 2, where the adjective is translated " that speak lies," R.V. (A.V., " speaking lies ") and is applied to " demons," the actual utterances being by their human agents.¶

2. APSEUDĒS (ἀψευδής) denotes free from falsehood (a, negative, pseudēs, false), truthful, Tit. 1 : 2, of God, " who cannot lie."¶

C. Verb.

PSEUDŌ (ψεύδω), to deceive by lies (always in the Middle Voice in the N.T.), is used (a) absolutely, in Matt. 5 : 11, " falsely," lit., ' lying ' (A.V., marg.) ; Rom. 9 : 1 ; 2 Cor. 11 : 31 ; Gal. 1 : 20 ; Col. 3 : 9 (where the verb is followed by the preposition eis, to) ; 1 Tim. 2 : 7 ; Heb. 6 : 18 ; Jas. 3 : 14 (where it is followed by the preposition kata, against) ; 1 John 1 : 6 ; Rev. 3 : 9 ; (b) transitively, with a direct object (without a preposition following), Acts 5 : 3 (with the accusative case), " to lie to (the Holy Ghost)," R.V. marg., " deceive ; " ver. 4 (with the dative case) " thou hast (not) lied (unto men, but unto God)."¶

LIE (to lie down, on, upon)

1. KEIMAI (κεῖμαι), to be laid, to lie, used as the Passive Voice of tithēmi, to lay (see LAY, No. 14), is said (a) of the Child Jesus, Luke 2 : 12, 16 ; (b) of the dead body of the Lord, Matt. 28 : 6 ; John 20 : 12 ; in Luke 23 : 53, " had . . . lain," R.V., A.V., " was laid " [see LAY, No. 14, Note (1)], in the tomb as hitherto empty ; (c) of the linen cloths, John 20 : 5, 6, 7 ; (d) figuratively of a veil as lying upon the hearts of the Jews, 2 Cor. 3 : 15, R.V., " lieth " (A.V., " is ") ; (e) metaphorically, of the world as lying in the evil one, 1 John 5 : 19, R.V. ; (f) of the Heavenly City, Rev. 21 : 16. For other instances in which the rendering is in the Passive Voice, see LAY, No. 14. See APPOINT.

2. KATAKEIMAI (κατάκειμαι), to lie down (kata, down, and No. 1), is used of the sick, Mark 1 : 30 ; 2 : 4 ; Luke 5 : 25 ; John 5 : 3, 6 ; Acts 28 : 8 ; in Acts 9 : 33 it is rendered " had kept (his bed)," lit., ' lying (on a bed).' See SIT.

3. BALLŌ (βάλλω), to throw, cast, is used in the Passive Voice, with reference to the sick, with the meaning to be laid, to lie, in Matt. 8 : 6, " (my servant) lieth (in the house)," lit., ' is laid ; ' 8 : 14, " lying," R.V. (A.V., " laid ") ; 9 : 2, " lying (on a bed)." See CAST.

4. EPIKEIMAI (ἐπίκειμαι), to lie upon, be laid upon, is translated with this meaning, intransitively in John 11 : 38 and Acts 27 : 20 ; tran-

sitively, in the Passive Voice, in John 21 : 9 and 1 Cor. 9 : 16. See IMPOSED.

Notes : (1) In Mark 5 : 40, some mss. have the verb *anakeimai*, to be laid up, translated " was lying," A.V. In the most authentic the word is absent. (2) In Acts 27 : 12, A.V., *blepō*, to look, is rendered " lieth," of the situation of the haven Phœnix (A.V., Phenice); R.V., "looketh." (3) In John 11 : 17, A.V., the verb *echō*, to have, to hold, used with *en*, in, signifying to be in a certain condition, is translated " had *lain* " (R.V., " had been "). (4) In John 13 : 25, *anapiptō*, lit., to fall back (some mss. have *epipiptō*, lit., to fall upon, hence the A.V., " lying "), is used of John's position at the table, R.V., "leaning back (. . . on Jesus' breast)."

LIE IN WAIT
A. Verb.

ENEDREUŌ (ἐνεδρεύω), to lie in wait for, to lay wait for (from *en*, in, and *hedra*, a seat, cp. B), occurs in Luke 11 : 54, " laying wait for ; " Acts 23 : 21, " there lie in wait for."¶

Note : In Acts 23 : 30, the word *epiboulē*, a plot, necessitates the R.V. " (that there would be) a plot." For Eph. 4 : 14, A.V., see WILES.

B. Noun.

ENEDRA or ENEDRON (ἐνέδρα), akin to A, a lying in wait, an ambush, occurs in Acts 23 : 16 (where some mss. have the form *enedron*) ; 25 : 3, " laying wait," lit., ' making an ambush.'¶ In the Sept., Josh. 8 : 7, 9 ; Ps. 10 : 8.¶

LIFE, LIVING, LIFETIME, LIFE-GIVING
A. Nouns.

1. ZŌĒ (ζωή) (Eng., zoo, zoology) is used in the N.T. " of life as a principle, life in the absolute sense, life as God has it, that which the Father has in Himself, and which He gave to the Incarnate Son to have in Himself, John 5 : 26, and which the Son manifested in the world, 1 John 1 : 2. From this life man has become alienated in consequence of the Fall, Eph. 4 : 18, and of this life men become partakers through faith in the Lord Jesus Christ, John 3 : 15, who becomes its Author to all such as trust in Him, Acts 3 : 15, and who is therefore said to be ' the life ' of the believer, Col. 3 : 4, for the life that He gives He maintains, John 6 : 35, 63. Eternal life is the present actual possession of the believer because of his relationship with Christ, John 5 : 24 ; 1 John 3 : 14, and that it will one day extend its domain to the sphere of the body is assured by the Resurrection of Christ, 2 Cor. 5 : 4 ; 2 Tim. 1 : 10. This life is not merely a principle of power and mobility, however, for it has moral associations which are inseparable from it, as of holiness and righteousness. Death and sin, life and holiness, are frequently contrasted in the Scriptures.

" ZŌĒ is also used of that which is the common possession of all animals and men by nature, Acts 17 : 25 ; 1 John 5 : 16, and of the present sojourn of man upon the earth with reference to its duration, Luke 16 : 25 ;

1 Cor. 15 : 19 ; 1 Tim. 4 : 8 ; 1 Pet. 3 : 10. ' This life ' is a term equivalent to ' the gospel,' ' the faith,' ' Christianity,' Acts 5 : 20."*

Death came through sin, Rom. 5 : 12, which is rebellion against God. Sin thus involved the forfeiting of the life. " The life of the flesh is in the blood," Lev. 17 : 11. Therefore the impartation of life to the sinner must be by a death caused by the shedding of that element which is the life of the flesh. " It is the blood that maketh atonement by reason of the life " (*id.*, R.V.). The separation from God caused by the forfeiting of the life could be removed only by a sacrifice in which the victim and the offerer became identified. This which was appointed in the typical offerings in Israel received its full accomplishment in the voluntary sacrifice of Christ. The shedding of the blood in the language of Scripture involves the taking or the giving of the life. Since Christ had no sins of his own to die for, His death was voluntary and vicarious, John 10 : 15 with Isa. 53 : 5, 10, 12 ; 2 Cor. 5 : 21. In His sacrifice He endured the Divine judgment due to man's sin. By this means the believer becomes identified with Him in His deathless life, through His resurrection, and enjoys conscious and eternal fellowship with God.

2. BIOS (βίος) (cp. Eng. words beginning with *bio-*), is used in three respects (*a*) of the period or duration of life, e.g., in the A.V. of 1 Pet. 4 : 3, " the time past of our life " (the R.V. follows the mss. which omit " of our life ") ; Luke 8 : 14 ; 2 Tim. 2 : 4 ; (*b*) of the manner of life, life in regard to its moral conduct, 1 Tim. 2 : 2 ; 1 John 2 : 16 ; (*c*) of the means of life, livelihood, maintenance, living, Mark 12 : 44 ; Luke 8 : 43 ; 15 : 12, 30 ; 21 : 4 ; 1 John 3 : 17, " goods," R.V. (A.V., " good "). See GOODS.¶

Note : " While *zōē* is life intensive . . . *bios* is life extensive. . . . In *bios*, used as manner of life, there is an ethical sense often inhering which, in classical Greek at least, *zōē* does not possess." In Scripture *zōē* is " the nobler word, expressing as it continually does, all of highest and best which the saints possess in God " (Trench, Syn. §xxvii).

3. PSUCHĒ (ψυχή), besides its meanings, heart, mind, soul, denotes life in two chief respects, (*a*) breath of life, the natural life, e.g., Matt. 2 : 20 ; 6 : 25 ; Mark 10 : 45 ; Luke 12 : 22 ; Acts 20 : 10 ; Rev. 8 : 9 ; 12 : 11 (cp. Lev. 17 : 11 ; Esth. 8 : 11) ; (*b*) the seat of personality, e.g., Luke 9 : 24, explained in ver. 25 as " own self." See list under SOUL. See also HEART, MIND.

Notes : (1) " Speaking generally, *psuchē*, is the individual life, the living being, whereas *zōē*, is the life of that being, cp. Ps. 66 : 9, ' God . . . which holdeth our soul (*psuchē*) in life (*zōē*),' and John 10 : 10, ' I came that they may have life (*zōē*),' with ver. 11, ' The Good Shepherd layeth down His life (*psuchē*) for the sheep.' "† (2) In Rev. 13 : 15, A.V., *pneuma*, breath, is translated " life " (R.V., " breath "). (3) In 2 Cor. 1 : 8,

---

* From Notes on Galatians by Hogg and Vine, pp. 324, 325.
† From Notes on Thessalonians by Hogg and Vine, p. 325.

" we despaired even of life," the verb *zaō*, to live, is used in the Infinitive Mood, as a noun, and translated "life " (lit., ' living '). In Heb. 2 : 15 the Infinitive Mood of the same verb is translated "lifetime."

4. BIŌSIS (βίωσις), from *bioō*, to spend one's life, to live, denotes a manner of life, Acts 26 : 4.¶

5. AGŌGĒ (ἀγωγή), a manner of life, 2 Tim. 3 : 10 ; see CONDUCT.

6. ANASTROPHĒ (ἀναστροφή), behaviour, conduct, is translated " manner of life " (A.V. " conversation ") in the R.V. of Gal. 1 : 13 ; 1 Tim. 4 : 12 ; 1 Pet. 1 : 18 ; 3 : 16 ; "living," in 1 Pet. 1 : 15. See BEHAVIOUR.

B. Adjectives.

1. BIŌTIKOS (βιωτικός), pertaining to life (*bios*), is translated " of this life," in Luke 21 : 34, with reference to cares ; in 1 Cor. 6 : 3," (things) that pertain to this life," and ver. 4, " (things) pertaining to this life," i.e., matters of this world, concerning which Christians at Corinth were engaged in public lawsuits one with another ; such matters were to be regarded as relatively unimportant in view of the great tribunals to come under the jurisdiction of saints hereafter. Moulton and Milligan (Vocab.) illustrate the word from phrases in the papyri, e.g., " business (documents) ;" "business concerning my livelihood ; " " (stories) of ordinary life."¶

2. APSUCHOS (ἄψυχος) denotes lifeless, inanimate (*a*, negative, and *psuchē*, see A, No. 3), " without life," 1 Cor. 14 : 7.¶

C. Verb.

ZŌOPOIEŌ (ζωοποιέω), to make alive, cause to live, quicken (from *zōē*, life, and *poieō*, to make), is used as follows :

" (*a*) of God as the Bestower of every kind of life in the universe, 1 Tim. 6 : 13 (*zōogoneō*, to preserve alive, is the alternative reading adopted by most editors ; see LIVE, No. 6), and, particularly, of resurrection life, John 5 : 21 ; Rom. 4 : 17 ; (*b*) of Christ, who also is the Bestower of resurrection life, John 5 : 21 (2nd part) ; 1 Cor. 15 : 45 ; cp. ver. 22 ; (*c*) of the resurrection of Christ in " the body of His glory," 1 Pet. 3 : 18 ; (*d*) of the power of reproduction inherent in seed, which presents a certain analogy with resurrection, 1 Cor. 15 : 36 ; (*e*) of the ' changing,' or ' fashioning anew,' of the bodies of the living, which corresponds with, and takes place at the same time as, the resurrection of the dead in Christ, Rom. 8 : 11 ; (*f*) of the impartation of spiritual life, and the communication of spiritual sustenance generally, John 6 : 63 ; 2 Cor. 3 : 6 ; Gal. 3 : 21."¶* See QUICKEN, and cp. *sunzōopoieō*, to quicken together with, Eph. 2 : 5 and Col. 2 : 13.¶

Notes : (1) For the verb *diagō*, to lead a life, see LIVE, No. 7. (2) For *politeuō*, in Phil. 1 : 27, R.V., "let your manner of life be," see LIVE, No. 8.

---

* From Notes on Galatians by Hogg and Vine, pp. 154, 155.

LIFT

1. EGEIRŌ (ἐγείρω), to awaken, raise up, is used in Matt. 12 : 11, of lifting a sheep out of a pit. In the following the R.V. has "raised" for A.V., "lifted : " Mark 1 : 31 ; 9 : 27 ; Acts 3 : 7. See ARISE, AWAKE, RAISE.

2. AIRŌ (αἴρω) signifies (a) to raise, take up, lift, draw up, (b) to bear, carry, (c) to take or carry away. It is used of lifting up the voice, Luke 17 : 13 ; Acts 4 : 24 ; eyes, John 11 : 41 ; hand, Rev. 10 : 5. See AWAY, BEAR, CARRY, DOUBT, A, No. 6, LOOSE, PUT, No. 17, REMOVE, TAKE.

3. EPAIRŌ (ἐπαίρω), to lift up, raise (epi, upon, and No. 2), is used of lifting up the eyes, Matt. 17 : 8 ; Luke 6 : 20 ; 16 : 23 ; 18 : 13 ; John 4 : 35 ; 6 : 5 ; 17 : 1 ; the head, Luke 21 : 28 ; the hands, Luke 24 : 50 ; 1 Tim. 2 : 8 ; the voice, Luke 11 : 27 ; Acts 2 : 14 ; 14 : 11 ; 22 : 22 ; a foresail, Acts 27 : 40 ("hoisting," R.V.) ; metaphorically, of the heel, John 13 : 18, as of one lifting up the foot before kicking ; the expression indicates contempt and violence ; in the Passive Voice, Acts 1 : 9, of Christ's Ascension, "was taken up ; " 2 Cor. 10 : 5, "is exalted" (with pride) ; 11 : 20, "exalteth himself." See EXALT, HOIST, TAKE.¶

4. HUPSOŌ (ὑψόω), to lift or raise up (akin to hupsos, height), is rendered by the verb to lift up in John 3 : 14, of the brazen serpent ; of Christ in crucifixion (id.), and 8 : 28 ; 12 : 32, 34 ; metaphorically, to exalt, lift up, e.g., Jas. 4 : 10, A.V., "shall lift . . . up," R.V., "shall exalt." See EXALT.

5. ANISTĒMI (ἀνίστημι), to raise up (ana, up, histēmi, to cause to stand), is translated "lifted (her) up," in Acts 9 : 41, A.V. ; R.V., "raised (her) up." See ARISE, RAISE.

6. ANORTHOŌ (ἀνορθόω), to set upright (ana, up, orthos, straight), is used of lifting up "hands that hang down," Heb. 12 : 12 ; of setting up a building, restoring ruins, Acts 15 : 16 (cp., e.g., 2 Sam. 7 : 13, 16 ; 1 Chron. 17 : 12 ; Jer. 10 : 12 ; often so used in the papyri) ; of the healing of the woman with a spirit of infirmity, Luke 13 : 13, "was made straight" (for ver. 11, see No. 7). See SET, STRAIGHT.¶

7. ANAKUPTŌ (ἀνακύπτω), to lift oneself up, is used (a) of the body, Luke 13 : 11 ; John 8 : 7, 10 ; (b) metaphorically, of the mind, to look up, to be elated, Luke 21 : 28 (followed by No. 3, "lift up") ; an instance is found in the papyri in which a person speaks of the impossibility of ever looking up again in a certain place, for very shame (Moulton and Milligan, Vocab.).¶ In the Sept., Job 10 : 15.¶

LIGHT, Noun, and Verb (bring to, give), LIGHTEN
A. Nouns.

1. PHŌS (φῶς), akin to phaō, to give light (from roots pha— and phan—, expressing light as seen by the eye, and, metaphorically, as

reaching the mind, whence *phainō*, to make to appear, *phaneros*, evident, etc.) ; cp. Eng., phosphorus (lit., light-bearing). " Primarily light is a luminous emanation, probably of force, from certain bodies, which enables the eye to discern form and colour. Light requires an organ adapted for its reception (Matt. 6 : 22). Where the eye is absent, or where it has become impaired from any cause, light is useless. Man, naturally, is incapable of receiving spiritual light inasmuch as he lacks the capacity for spiritual things, 1 Cor. 2 : 14. Hence believers are called ' sons of light,' Luke 16 : 8, not merely because they have received a revelation from God, but because in the New Birth they have received the spiritual capacity for it.

" Apart from natural phenomena, light is used in Scripture of (a) the glory of God's dwelling-place, 1 Tim. 6 : 16 ; (b) the nature of God, 1 John 1 : 5 ; (c) the impartiality of God, Jas. 1 : 17 ; (d) the favour of God, Ps. 4 : 6 ; of the King, Prov. 16 : 15 ; of an influential man, Job 29 : 24 ; (e) God, as the illuminator of His people, Isa. 60 : 19, 20 ; (f) the Lord Jesus as the illuminator of men, John 1 : 4, 5, 9 ; 3 : 19 ; 8 : 12 ; 9 : 5 ; 12 : 35, 36, 46 ; Acts 13 : 47 ; (g) the illuminating power of the Scriptures, Ps. 119 : 105 ; and of the judgments and commandments of God, Isa. 51 : 4 ; Prov. 6 : 23, cp. Ps. 43 : 3 ; (h) the guidance of God, Job 29 : 3 ; Ps. 112 : 4 ; Isa. 58 : 10 ; and, ironically, of the guidance of man, Rom. 2 : 19 ; (i) salvation, 1 Pet. 2 : 9 ; (j) righteousness, Rom. 13 : 12 ; 2 Cor. 11 : 14, 15 ; 1 John 2 : 9, 10 ; (k) witness for God, Matt. 5 : 14, 16 ; John 5 : 35 ; (l) prosperity and general well-being, Esth. 8 : 16 ; Job 18 : 18 ; Isa. 58 : 8–10."*

2. PHŌSTĒR (φωστήρ) denotes a luminary, light, or light-giver ; it is used figuratively of believers, as shining in the spiritual darkness of the world, Phil. 2 : 15 ; in Rev. 21 : 11 it is used of Christ as the Light reflected in and shining through the Heavenly City (cp. ver. 23).¶ In the Sept., Gen. 1 : 14, 16.¶

3. PHŌTISMOS (φωτισμός), an illumination, light, is used metaphorically in 2 Cor. 4 : 4, of the light of the Gospel, and in ver. 6, of the knowledge of the glory of God.¶ In the Sept., Job 3 : 9 ; Psa. 27 : 1 ; 44 : 3 ; 78 : 14 ; 90 : 8 ; 139 : 11.¶

4. PHENGOS (φέγγος), brightness, lustre, is used of the light of the moon, Matt. 24 : 29 ; Mark 13 : 24 ; of a lamp, Luke 11 : 33 (some mss. have *phōs*, here).¶

5. LUCHNOS (λύχνος), a hand-lamp : see Lamp.

6. LAMPAS (λαμπάς), a torch : see Lamp.

B. Verbs.

1. PHŌTIZŌ (φωτίζω), used (a) intransitively, signifies to shine, give light, Rev. 22 : 5 ; (b) transitively, (1) to illumine, to light, enlighten,

---

* From Notes on Thessalonians by Hogg and Vine, pp. 159, 160.

to be lightened, Luke 11 : 36 ; Rev. 21 : 23 ; in the Passive Voice, Rev. 18 : 1 ; metaphorically, of spiritual enlightenment, John 1 : 9 ; Eph. 1 : 18 ; 3 : 9, " to make . . . see ; " Heb. 6 : 4 ; 10 : 32, " ye were enlightened," R.V. (A.V., " . . . illuminated ") ; (2) to bring to light, 1 Cor. 4 : 5 (of God's act in the future) ; 2 Tim. 1 : 10 (of God's act in the past). See ENLIGHTEN, ILLUMINATE.¶

2. EPIPHAUSKŌ (ἐπιφαύσκω), or possibly *epiphauō*, to shine forth, is rendered " shall give . . . light," in Eph. 5 : 14, A.V. (R.V., " shall shine upon "), of the glory of Christ, illumining the believer who fulfils the conditions, so that being guided by His light he reflects His character. See SHINE.¶ Cp. *epiphōskō*, to dawn (really a variant form of *epiphauskō*).

3. LAMPŌ (λάμπω), to give the light of a torch, is rendered " giveth light " in Matt. 5 : 15, A.V. (R.V., " shineth "). See SHINE.

4. EPIPHAINŌ (ἐπιφαίνω), transitively, to show forth (*epi*, upon, *phainō*, to cause to shine), is used intransitively and metaphorically in Luke 1 : 79, and rendered " to give light," A.V. (R.V., " to shine upon "). See APPEAR, SHINE.

5. HAPTŌ (ἅπτω), to kindle a fire and so give light : see KINDLE, No. 1, Note.

6. KAIŌ (καίω), to burn, is translated " do (men) light " in Matt. 5 : 15. See BURN.

7. ASTRAPTŌ (ἀστράπτω), to flash forth, lighten as lightning (akin to *astrapē*, lightning), occurs in Luke 17 : 24 ; 24 : 4 (A.V. " shining ; " R.V., " dazzling "). See DAZZLING.

Note : In Luke 2 : 32, A.V., the noun *apokalupsis*, an unveiling, revelation, preceded by *eis*, unto, with a view to, is rendered " to lighten " (R.V., " for revelation ; " marg., " (the) unveiling "). See REVELATION.

C. Adjective.

PHŌTEINOS (φωτεινός), from *phōs* (A, No. 1), bright, is rendered " full of light " in Matt. 6 : 22 ; Luke 11 : 34, 36 (twice), figuratively, of the single-mindedness of the eye, which acts as the lamp of the body ; in Matt. 17 : 5, " bright," of a cloud. See BRIGHT.¶

LIGHT (to light upon)

Notes : (1) In Matt. 3 : 16, A.V., *erchomai*, to come, is translated " lighting ; " R.V., " coming." (2) In Rev. 7 : 16, A.V., *piptō*, to fall, is translated " shall . . . light " (R.V., " shall . . . strike "). See STRIKE. (3) For Acts 27 : 41, R.V., see FALL, B, No. 8.

LIGHT, LIGHTEN (as to weight)
A. Adjective.

ELAPHROS (ἐλαφρός), light in weight, easy to bear, is used of the burden imparted by Christ, Matt. 11 : 30 ; of affliction, 2 Cor. 4 : 17.¶

B. Verb.

KOUPHIZŌ (κουφίζω), to make light, lighten (the adjective *kouphos*, not in N.T., denotes slight, light, empty), is used of lightening the ship, in Acts 27 : 38.

Note : For the phrase in ver. 18, A.V., " they lightened the ship," see FREIGHT.

C. Noun.

ELAPHRIA (ἐλαφρία), lightness, 2 Cor. 1 : 17, A.V. : see FICKLENESS.

LIGHT OF (make), LIGHTLY

AMELEŌ (ἀμελέω) denotes (*a*) to be careless, not to care (*a*, negative, and *melei*, an impersonal verb, signifying it is a care : see CARE), Matt. 22 : 5, " they made light of (it)," lit., ' making light of (it),' aorist participle, indicating the definiteness of their decision. See NEGLECT, NEGLIGENT, REGARD.

Note : In Mark 9 : 39, A.V., the adverb *tachu*, quickly, is translated " lightly " (R.V., " quickly "). See QUICKLY.

LIGHTNING

ASTRAPĒ (ἀστραπή) denotes (*a*) lightning (akin to LIGHT, B, No. 7), Matt. 24 : 27 ; 28 : 3 ; Luke 10 : 18 ; 17 : 24 ; in the plural, Rev. 4 : 5 ; 8 : 5 ; 11 : 19 ; 16 : 18 ; (*b*) " bright shining," or shining brightness, Luke 11 : 36. See SHINING.¶

LIKE, LIKE (as to, unto), (be) LIKE, (make) LIKE, LIKE (things), LIKEN

A. Adjectives.

1. HOMOIOS (ὅμοιος), like, resembling, such as, the same as, is used (*a*) of appearance or form, John 9 : 9 ; Rev. 1 : 13, 15 ; 2 : 18 ; 4 : 3 (twice), 6, 7 ; 9 : 7 (twice), 10, 19 ; 11 : 1 ; 13 : 2, 11 ; 14 : 14 ; (*b*) of ability, condition, nature, Matt. 22 : 39 ; Acts 17 : 29 ; Gal. 5 : 21, " such like," lit., ' and the (things) similar to these ; ' 1 John 3 : 2 ; Rev. 13 : 4 ; 18 : 18 ; 21 : 11, 18 ; (*c*) of comparison in parables, Matt. 13 : 31, 33, 44, 45, 47 ; 20 : 1 ; Luke 13 : 18, 19, 21 ; (*d*) of action, thought, etc., Matt. 11 : 16 ; 13 : 52 ; Luke 6 : 47, 48, 49 ; 7 : 31, 32 ; 12 : 36 ; John 8 : 55 ; Jude 7.¶

2. ISOS (ἴσος), equal (the same in size, quality, etc.), is translated " like," of the gift of the Spirit, Acts 11 : 17. See EQUAL, MUCH (AS).

3. PAROMOIOS (παρόμοιος), much like (*para*, beside, and No. 1), is used in Mark 7 : 13, in the neuter plural, " (many such) like things."¶

B. Verbs.

1. HOMOIOŌ (ὁμοιόω), to make like (akin to A, No. 1), is used (*a*) especially in the parables, with the significance of comparing, likening, or, in the Passive Voice, ' being likened,' Matt. 7 : 24, 26 ; 11 : 16 ; 13 : 24 ; 18 : 23 ; 22 : 2 (R.V., " likened ") ; 25 : 1 ; Mark 4 : 30 ; Luke 7 : 31 ;

13 : 18, R.V., " liken " (A.V., " resemble ") ; ver. 20 ; in several of these instances the point of resemblance is not a specific detail, but the whole circumstances of the parable ; (b) of making like, or, in the Passive Voice, of being made or becoming like, Matt. 6 : 8 ; Acts 14 : 11, " in the likeness of (men)," lit., ' being made like ' (aorist participle, Passive) ; Rom. 9 : 29 ; Heb. 2 : 17, of Christ in being " made like " unto His brethren, i.e., in partaking of human nature, apart from sin (cp. ver. 14).¶

2. EOIKA (ἔοικα), a perfect tense with a present meaning (from an obsolete present, eikō), denotes to be like, to resemble, Jas. 1 : 6, 23.¶ In the Sept., Job 6 : 3, 25.¶

3. PAROMOIAZŌ (παρομοιάζω), to be like (from para, by, and a verbal form from homoios, A, No. 1), is used in Matt. 23 : 27 (perhaps with intensive force), in the Lord's comparison of the scribes and Pharisees to whitened sepulchres.¶

4. APHOMOIOŌ (ἀφομοιόω), to make like (apo, from, and No. 1), is used in Heb. 7 : 3, of Melchizedek as " made like " the Son of God, i.e., in the facts related and withheld in the Genesis record.¶

Note : For the A.V. of Rom. 1 : 23, " made like," see LIKENESS, No. 1.

C. Adverbs.

1. HŌS (ὡς), used as a relative adverb of manner, means as, like as, etc. and is translated " like," e.g., in Matt. 6 : 29 ; Mark 4 : 31 ; Luke 12 : 27 ; in Acts 3 : 22 and 7 : 37 (see R.V., marg.) ; in 8 : 32 (2nd part), R.V., " as " (A.V., " like ") ; Rev. 2 : 18, R.V. (the rendering should have been " as " here) ; 18 : 21, R.V., " as it were " (A.V., " like ") ; 21 : 11, 2nd part (ditto).

2. HŌSPER (ὥσπερ), just as, is rendered " like as " in Rom. 6 : 4.

Notes : (1) In Heb. 4 : 15, the phrase kath'homoiotēta (kata, according to, homoiotēs, a likeness, i.e., ' after the similitude '), is rendered " like as," in the statement that Christ has been tempted in all points " like as we are, yet without sin ; " this may mean either ' according to the likeness of our temptations,' or ' in accordance with His likeness to us.' (2) In the following the most authentic mss. have hōs, as, for hōsei, like, in the A.V. ; Mark 1 : 10 ; Luke 3 : 22 ; John 1 : 32 ; Rev. 1 : 14. (3) In John 7 : 46, A.V., the combination of the adverb houtōs, thus, with hōs, as, is translated " like," R.V. " (never man) so (spake)." (4) For " in like manner " see MANNER. (5) In 1 Thess. 2 : 14, A.V., ta auta, the same (things), is translated " like (things)," R.V., " the same (things)."

For (DID NOT) LIKE, Rom. 1 : 28, A.V., see REFUSE, No. 3

LIKEMINDED

1. ISOPSUCHOS (ἰσόψυχος), lit., of equal soul (isos, equal, psuchē, the soul), is rendered " like-minded " in Phil. 2 : 20.¶ In the Sept., Psa. 55 : 13.¶

2. HOMOPHRŌN (ὁμόφρων), (homos, the same, phrēn, the mind), occurs in 1 Pet. 3 : 8, R.V., " likeminded " (A.V., " of one mind ").

Note: In Rom. 15 : 5 ; Phil. 2 : 2, *phroneō to auto*, to think the same thing, is translated, A.V., " be likeminded " (R.V., " be of the same mind ").

LIKENESS, LIKENESS OF (in the)

1. HOMOIŌMA (ὁμοίωμα) denotes that which is made like something, a resemblance, (a) in the concrete sense, Rev. 9 : 7, " shapes " (R.V., marg., " likenesses ") ; (b) in the abstract sense, Rom. 1 : 23, R.V., " (for) the likeness (of an image) ; " the A.V. translates it as a verb, " (into an image) made like to ; " the association here of the two words *homoiōma* and *eikōn* (see IMAGE) serves to enhance the contrast between the idol and " the glory of the incorruptible God," and is expressive of contempt ; in 5 : 14, " (the) likeness of Adam's transgression " (A.V., " similitude ") ; in 6 : 5, " (the) likeness (of His death) ; in 8 : 3, " (the) likeness (of sinful flesh) ; in Phil. 2 : 7, " the likeness of men." " The expression ' likeness of men ' does not of itself imply, still less does it exclude or diminish, the reality of the nature which Christ assumed. That . . . is declared in the words ' form of a servant.' ' Paul justly says *in the likeness of men*, because, in fact, Christ, although certainly perfect Man (Rom. 5 : 15 ; 1 Cor. 15 : 21 ; 1 Tim. 2 : 5), was, by reason of the Divine nature present in Him, not simply and merely man . . . but the Incarnate Son of God ' " (Gifford, quoting Meyer). See SHAPE.¶ Ch. LIKE, B, (b).

2. HOMOIŌSIS (ὁμοίωσις), a making like, is translated " likeness " in Jas. 3 : 9, R.V. (A.V., " similitude ").¶

3. HOMOIOTĒS (ὁμοιότης) is translated " likeness " in Heb. 7 : 15, R.V. (A.V., " similitude ").

4. ANTITUPON (ἀντίτυπον) is rendered " after a true likeness," in 1 Pet. 3 : 21, R.V. (marg., " in the antitype "). See FIGURE, No. 2.

LIKEWISE

1. HOMOIŌS (ὁμοίως), in like manner (from the adjective *homoios*, see LIKE, A, No. 1), is rendered " likewise " in the A.V. of Matt. 22 : 26 ; 27 : 41, Luke 10 : 32 ; 16 : 25 ; John 5 : 19 ; Jas. 2 : 25 ; 1 Pet. 3 : 1, 7 ; Jude 8 ; Rev. 8 : 12 (in all these the R.V. has " in like manner ") ; in the following, A.V. and R.V. have " likewise ; " Matt. 26 : 35 ; Luke 5 : 33 ; 6 : 31 ; 10 : 37 ; 17 : 28, 31 ; 22 : 36 ; John 6 : 11 ; 21 : 13 ; Rom. 1 : 27 ; 1 Pet. 5 : 5.¶ See MANNER, So.

2. HŌSAUTŌS (ὡσαύτως), a strengthened form of *hōs*, as, denotes in like manner, just so, likewise ; it is sometimes translated " likewise," e.g., Matt. 20 : 5 ; 21 : 30.

3. KAI (καί), and, even, is translated " likewise " in the A.V. and R.V. of Matt. 20 : 10 (last *kai* in the verse), more lit., ' even they ; ' elsewhere the R.V. has " also," for the A.V., " likewise," Matt. 18 : 35 ;

24 : 33 ; Luke 3 : 14 ; 17 : 10 ; 19 : 19 ; 21 : 31 ; Acts 3 : 24 ; 1 Cor. 14 : 9 ; Col. 4 : 16 ; 1 Pet. 4 : 1 ; in Matt. 21 : 24, the A.V. has " in like wise " (R.V., " likewise ").

4. PARAPLĒSIŌS (παραπλησίως), from *para*, beside, and the adjective *plēsios*, near (akin to the adverb *pelas*, near, hard by), is used in Heb. 2 : 14, A.V., " likewise " (R.V., " in like manner "), expressing the true humanity of Christ in partaking of flesh and blood.¶

Notes : (1) In Matt. 17 : 12 and Rom. 6 : 11, A.V., the adverb *houtōs*, thus, so, is translated " likewise " (R.V., " so ") ; in Luke 15 : 7 and 10, A.V., " likewise," R.V., " even so ; " in Luke 14 : 33, A.V., followed by *oun*, therefore, it is rendered " so likewise " (R.V., " so therefore ").

LILY

KRINON (κρίνον) occurs in Matt. 6 : 28 and Luke 12 : 27 ; in the former the Lord speaks of " the lilies of the field ; " the lily referred to was a flower of rich colour, probably including the Gladiolus and Iris species. The former " grow among the grain, often overtopping it and illuminating the broad fields with their various shades of pinkish purple to deep violet purple and blue. . . . Anyone who has stood among the wheat fields of Galilee . . . will see at once the appropriateness of our Saviour's allusion. They all have a reedy stem, which, when dry, would make such fuel as is used in the ovens. The beautiful Irises . . . have gorgeous flowers, and would suit our Saviour's comparison even better than the above. But they are plants of pasture grounds and swamps, and seldom found in grain fields. If, however, we understand by ' lilies of the field ' simply wild lilies, these would also be included in the expression. Our Saviour's comparison would then be like a ' composite photograph,' a reference to all the splendid colours and beautiful shapes of the numerous wild plants comprehended under the name ' lily ' " (G. E. Post, in Hastings' Bib. Dic.).

For LIMIT, in Heb. 4 : 7, A.V., see DEFINE

For LINE see PROVINCE, No. 2

For LINEAGE in Luke 2 : 4, A.V., see FAMILY

LINEN, LINEN CLOTH, FINE LINEN

1. SINDŌN (σινδών) was a fine linen cloth, an article of domestic manufacture (Prov. 31 : 24) used (*a*) as a garment or wrap, the " linen cloth " of Mark 14 : 51, 52 ; (*b*) as shrouds or winding sheets, Matt. 27 : 59 ; Mark 15 : 46, R.V., " linen cloth," for A.V., " linen ; " Luke 23 : 53 (ditto).¶ In the Sept., Judg. 14 : 12, " (thirty) sheets ; " Prov. 31 : 24 (see above).¶ The Mishna (the Great Collection of legal decisions by the

ancient Rabbis) records that the material was sometimes used for curtains.

2. LINON (λίνον) denotes (a) flax, Matt. 12 : 20 ; (b) linen, in Rev. 15 : 6, A.V. ; the best texts have *lithos*, " stone," R.V. See FLAX.

3. OTHONION (ὀθόνιον), a piece of fine linen, is used in the plural, of the strips of cloth with which the body of the Lord was bound, after being wrapped in the *sindōn*, Luke 24 : 12 ; John 19 : 40 ; 20 : 5, 6, 7.¶ In the Sept., Judg. 14 : 13, " changes of raiment ; " Hos. 2 : 5, 9.¶ The word is a diminutive of *othonē*, a sheet (see SHEET).

4. BUSSOS (βύσσος), fine linen, made from a special species of flax, a word of Aramæan origin, used especially for the Syrian *byssus* (Arab. *bûs* is still used for native linen). Cp. Heb. *bûs*, in all O.T. passages quoted here, except Ezek. 27 : 7 ; Syriac *bûsâ* in Luke 16 : 19. It is the material mentioned in 1 Chron. 4 : 21, wrought by the house of Ashbea ; 15 : 27, *bussinos*, No. 5 (David's robe) ; 2 Chron. 3 : 14, *bussos* (the veil of the Temple) ; 5 : 12, *bussinos* (the clothing of the Levite singers) ; Esth. 1 : 6 (the cords of the hangings in the king's garden) ; 8 : 15 (Mordecai's dress) ; Ezek. 27 : 7 (*bussos*, in Syrian trade with Tyre). In the N.T., Luke 16 : 19, the clothing of the " rich man."¶

5. BUSSINOS (βύσσινος), an adjective formed from No. 4, denoting made of fine linen. This is used of the clothing of the mystic Babylon, Rev. 18 : 12, 16, and of the suitable attire of the Lamb's wife, 19 : 8, 14, figuratively describing " the righteous acts of the saints." The presumption of Babylon is conspicuous in that she arrays herself in that which alone befits the Bride of Christ.¶ For examples of the use in the Sept. see No. 4.

LINGER

ARGEŌ (ἀργέω), to be idle, to linger (akin to *argos*, idle : see *katargeō*, under ABOLISH), is used negatively regarding the judgment of the persons mentioned in 2 Pet. 2 : 3.¶ In the Sept., Ezra 4 : 24 ; Eccles. 12 : 3.¶

LION

LEŌN (λέων) occurs in 2 Tim. 4 : 17, probably figurative of the imminent peril of death, the figure being represented by the whole phrase, not by the word " lion " alone ; some suppose the reference to be to the lions of the amphitheatre ; the Greek commentators regarded the lion as Nero ; others understand it to be Satan. The language not improbably recalls that of Psa. 22 : 21 and Dan. 6 : 20. The word is used metaphorically, too, in Rev. 5 : 5, where Christ is called " the Lion of the tribe of Judah." Elsewhere it has the literal meaning, Heb. 11 : 33 ; 1 Pet. 5 : 8 ; Rev. 4 : 7 ; 9 : 8, 17 ; 10 : 3 ; 13 : 2.¶ Taking the O.T. and N.T. occurrences the allusions are to the three great features of the lion, (1) its majesty and strength, indicative of royalty, e.g., Prov. 30 : 30, (2) its courage, e.g., Prov. 28 : 1, (3) its cruelty, e.g., Psa. 22 : 13.

LIP

CHEILOS (χεῖλος) is used (a) of the organ of speech, Matt. 15 : 8 and Mark 7 : 6, where honouring with the lips, besides meaning empty words, may have reference to a Jewish custom of putting to the mouth the tassel of the tallith (the woollen scarf wound round the head and neck during prayer), as a sign of acceptance of the Law from the heart ; Rom. 3 : 13 ; 1 Cor. 14 : 21 (from Isa. 28 : 11, 12, speaking of the Assyrian foe as God's message to disobedient Israel) ; Heb. 13 : 15 ; 1 Pet. 3 : 10 ; (b) meta-phorically, of the brink or edge of things, as of the sea shore, Heb. 11 : 12, lit., ' the shore (of the sea) '.¶

LIST (Verb)

1. THELŌ (θέλω), to will, wish, is translated by the verb to list in Matt. 17 : 12 ; Mark 9 : 13 ; John 3 : 8. See DESIRE, B, No. 6.

2. BOULOMAI (βούλομαι), to will, be minded, is translated " listeth " in Jas. 3 : 4 (R.V., " willeth "). See DESIRE, B, No. 7.

LITTLE

A. Adjectives.

1. MIKROS (μικρός), little, small (the opposite of *megas*, great), is used (a) of persons, with regard to (1) station, or age, in the singular, Mark 15 : 40, of James " the less " (R.V. marg., " little "), possibly referring to age ; Luke 19 : 3 ; in the plural, little ones, Matt. 18 : 6, 10, 14 ; Mark 9 : 42 ; (2) rank or influence, e.g., Matt. 10 : 42 (see context) ; Acts 8 : 10 ; 26 : 22, " small," as in Rev. 11 : 18 ; 13 : 16 ; 19 : 5, 18 ; 20 : 12 ; (b) of things, with regard to (1) size, e.g., Jas. 3 : 5 (some mss. have No. 2 here) ; (2) quantity, Luke 12 : 32 ; 1 Cor. 5 : 6 ; Gal. 5 : 9 ; Rev. 3 : 8 ; (3) time, John 7 : 33 ; 12 : 35 ; Rev. 6 : 11 ; 20 : 3. See B, No. 1. See LEAST, SMALL.

2. OLIGOS (ὀλίγος), little, few (the opposite of *polus*, much), is translated " short " in Rev. 12 : 12 ; in the neut. sing., e.g., 2 Cor. 8 : 15. For Jas. 3 : 5, see No. 1. See FEW, SHORT, SMALL.

3. BRACHUS (βραχύς), short, is used to some extent adverbially of (a) time, with the preposition *meta*, after, Luke 22 : 58, " (after) a little while ; " in Acts 5 : 34, without a preposition, R.V., " a little while " (A.V., " a little space ") ; in Heb. 2 : 7, 9, " a little " (A.V. marg. in ver. 7, and R.V. marg., in both, " a little while "), where the writer transfers to time what the Sept. in Psa. 8 : 5 says of rank ; (b) of quantity, John 6 : 7 ; in Heb. 13 : 22, preceded by the preposition *dia*, by means of, and with *logōn*, words (genitive plural) understood, " (in) few words ; " (c) of distance, Acts 27 : 28, R.V., " a little space " (A.V., " a little further "). See FEW, FURTHER, SPACE.¶

4. ELACHISTOS (ἐλάχιστος), which serves as the superlative of No. 1, is translated " a very little " in Luke 19 : 17. See LEAST.

Note : For *mikroteros*, " but little," see LEAST, No. 4.

B. Adverbs.

1. MIKRON (μικρόν), the neuter of A, No. 1, is used adverbially (a) of distance, Matt. 26 : 39 ; Mark 14 : 35 ; (b) of quantity, 2 Cor. 11 : 1, 16 ; (c) of time, Matt. 26 : 73, "a while ; " Mark 14 : 70 ; John 13 : 33, "a little while ; " 14 : 19 ; 16 : 16–9 ; Heb. 10 : 37, with the repeated *hoson,* "how very," lit., 'a little while, how little, how little ! ' See WHILE.¶

2. OLIGON (ὀλίγον), the neuter of A, No. 2, is used adverbially of (a) time, Mark 6 : 31, "a while ; " 1 Pet. 1 : 6, R.V., "a little while (A.V., "a season ") ; 5 : 10, R.V., "a little while " (A.V., "a while ") ; Rev. 17 : 10, R.V., "a little while " (A.V., "a short space ")) ; (b) space, Mark 1 : 19 ; Luke 5 : 3 ; (c) extent, with the preposition *pros,* for, in 1 Tim. 4 : 8, R.V., "(for) a little " (A.V., and R.V. marg., "little "), where, while the phrase might refer to duration (as A.V. marg.), yet the antithesis "for all things " clearly indicates extent, i.e., 'physical training is profitable towards few objects in life.' See BRIEFLY, FEW, SEASON, C, *Note.*

3. METRIŌS (μετρίως), moderately, occurs in Acts 20 : 12, "a little."¶

For (NO) LITTLE see COMMON, B, *Note* (3)

LIVE

1. ZAŌ (ζάω), to live, be alive, is used in the N.T. of " (a) God, Matt. 16 : 16 ; John 6 : 57 ; Rom. 14 : 11 ; (b) the Son in Incarnation, John 6 : 57 ; (c) the Son in Resurrection, John 14 : 19 ; Acts 1 : 3 ; Rom. 6 : 10 ; 2 Cor. 13 : 4 ; Heb. 7 : 8 ; (d) spiritual life, John 6 : 57 ; Rom. 1 : 17 ; 8 : 13b ; Gal. 2 : 19, 20 ; Heb. 12 : 9 ; (e) the present state of departed saints, Luke 20 : 38 ; 1 Pet. 4 : 6 ; (f) the hope of resurrection, 1 Pet. 1 : 3 ; (g) the resurrection of believers, 1 Thess. 5 : 10 ; John 5 : 25 ; Rev. 20 : 4, and of unbelievers, ver. 5, cp. ver. 13 ; (h) the way of access to God through the Lord Jesus Christ, Heb. 10 : 20 ; (i) the manifestation of Divine power in support of Divine authority, 2 Cor. 13 : 4b ; cp. 12 : 10, and 1 Cor. 5 : 5 ; (j) bread, figurative of the Lord Jesus, John 6 : 51 ; (k) a stone, figurative of the Lord Jesus, 1 Pet. 2 : 4 ; (l) water, figurative of the Holy Spirit, John 4 : 10 ; 7 : 38 ; (m) a sacrifice, figurative of the believer, Rom. 12 : 1 ; (n) stones, figurative of the believer, 1 Pet. 2 : 5 ; (o) the oracles, *logion,* Acts 7 : 38, and word, *logos,* Heb. 4 : 12 ; 1 Pet. 1 : 23, of God ; (p) the physical life of men, 1 Thess. 4 : 15 ; Matt. 27 : 63 ; Acts 25 : 24 ; Rom. 14 : 9 ; Phil. 1 : 21 (in the infinitive mood used as a noun, with the article, 'living '), 22 ; 1 Pet. 4 : 5 ; (q) the maintenance of physical life, Matt. 4 : 4 ; 1 Cor. 9 : 14 ; (r) the duration of physical life, Heb. 2 : 15 ; (s) the enjoyment of physical life, 1 Thess. 3 : 8 ; (t) the recovery of physical life from the power of disease, Mark 5 : 23 ; John 4 : 50 ; (u) the recovery of physical life from the power of death, Matt. 9 : 18 ; Acts 9 : 41 ; Rev. 20 : 5 ; (v) the course, conduct, and character of men, (1) good, Acts 26 : 5 ; 2 Tim. 3 : 12 ; Tit. 2 : 12 ; (2) evil, Luke

15 : 13 ; Rom. 6 : 2 ; 8 : 13*a* ; 2 Cor. 5 : 15*b* ; Col. 3 : 7 ; (3) undefined, Rom. 7 : 9 ; 14 : 7 ; Gal. 2 : 14 ; (*w*) restoration after alienation, Luke 15 : 32.

"*Note :* In 1 Thess. 5 : 10, to live means to experience that change, 1 Cor. 15 : 51, which is to be the portion of all in Christ who will be alive upon the earth at the Parousia of the Lord Jesus, cp. John 11 : 25, and which corresponds to the resurrection of those who had previously died in Christ, 1 Cor. 15 : 52–54.

" 2. SUNZAŌ (συνζάω), to live together with (*sun*, with, and *zaō*, to live), may be included with *zaō* in the above analysis as follows : (*g*) Rom. 6 : 8 ; 2 Tim. 2 : 11 ; (*s*), 2 Cor. 7 : 3.¶

" 3. ANAZAŌ (ἀναζάω) *ana*, again, and *zaō*, denotes ' to live again,' ' to revive,' Luke 15 : 24 ; cp. (*w*) in list above, and Rom. 7 : 9, to manifest activity again."¶*

Note: *Zaō* is translated " quick " (i.e., " living ") in Acts 10 : 42 ; 2 Tim. 4 : 1 ; 1 Pet. 4 : 5 ; in Heb. 4 : 12, A.V. (R.V., " living ").

4. BIOŌ (βιόω), to spend life, to pass one's life, is used in 1 Pet. 4 : 2.¶

5. ANASTREPHŌ (ἀναστρέφω), used metaphorically, in the Middle Voice, to conduct oneself, behave, live, is translated to live, in Heb. 13 : 18 (" honestly ") ; in 2 Pet. 2 : 18 (" in error "). See ABIDE, BEHAVE, etc.

6. ZŌOGONEŌ (ζωογονέω) denotes to preserve alive (from *zōos*, alive, and *ginomai*, to come to be, become, be made) ; in Luke 17 : 33, " shall preserve (it)," i.e., his life, R.V. marg., " save (it) alive ; " cp. the parallels *sōzō*, to save, in Matt. 16 : 25, and *phulassō*, to keep, in John 12 : 25 ; in Acts 7 : 19, " live," negatively of the efforts of Pharaoh to destroy the babes in Israel ; in 1 Tim. 6 : 13, according to the best mss. (some have *zōopoieō*, to cause to live), " quickeneth " (R.V., marg., " preserveth . . . alive," the preferable rendering). See PRESERVE, QUICKEN.¶

7. DIAGŌ (διάγω) is used of time in the sense of passing a life, 1 Tim. 2 : 2, " (that) we may lead (a tranquil and quiet, R.V.) life ; " Tit. 3 : 3, " living (in malice and envy)."¶

8. POLITEUŌ (πολιτεύω), to be a citizen (*politēs*), to live as a citizen, is used metaphorically of conduct as in accordance with the characteristics of the heavenly community ; in Acts 23 : 1, " I have lived ; " in Phil. 1 : 27, " let your manner of life (A.V., conversation) be." See CITIZENSHIP, No. 4, *Note.*¶

9. HUPARCHŌ (ὑπάρχω), to be in existence, to be, is translated " live (delicately) " in Luke 7 : 25. See BEING.

Note : In 1 Cor. 9 : 13, A.V., *esthiō*, to eat, is translated " live of." In Tim. 5 : 6 the A.V. renders *spatalaō* " liveth in pleasure."

LIVE LONG

MAKROCHRONIOS (μακροχρόνιος), an adjective denoting of long

duration, long-lived (*makros*, long, *chronos*, time), is used in Eph. 6 : 3, " (that thou mayest) live long," lit., ' (that thou mayest be) long-lived.'¶ In the Sept., Ex. 20 : 12 ; Deut. 4 : 40 ; 5 : 16 ; 17 : 20.¶

LIVELY

Note : This is the A.V. translation of the present participle of the verb *zaō*, to live, in three passages, in each of which the R.V. has " living," Acts 7 : 38 ; 1 Pet. 1 : 3 ; 2 : 5.

For LIVING see BEHAVIOUR, B, No. 1, LIFE, Nos. 2, 6, and LIVE, No. 3, *Note*

For LIVING CREATURES see BEAST

L

LO !

1. IDE (ἴδε), an aorist or point tense, marking a definite point of time, of the imperative mood of *eidon*, to see (taken as part of *horaō*, to see), is used as an interjection, addressed either to one or many persons, e.g., Matt. 25 : 20, 22, 25 ; John 1 : 29, 36, 47 ; Gal. 5 : 2, the only occurrence outside Matthew, Mark and John. See BEHOLD, SEE.

2. IDOU (ἰδού), a similar tense of No. 1, but in the Middle Voice, e.g., Matt. 1 : 20, 23 ; very frequent in the Synoptists and Acts and the Apocalypse.

For LOAF see BREAD

LOCUST

AKRIS (ἀκρίς) occurs in Matt. 3 : 4 and Mark 1 : 6, of the animals themselves, as forming part of the diet of John the Baptist ; they are used as food ; the Arabs stew them with butter, after removing the head, legs and wings. In Rev. 9 : 3, 7, they appear as monsters representing Satanic agencies, let loose by Divine judgments inflicted upon men for five months, the time of the natural life of the locust. For the character of the judgment see the whole passage.¶

LODGE, LODGING
A. Verbs.

1. AULIZOMAI (αὐλίζομαι), properly, to lodge in a courtyard (*aulē*, see COURT, No. 2), then, to lodge in the open, denotes, in the N.T., to pass the night, to lodge anywhere, Matt. 21 : 17 ; Luke 21 : 37, R.V., " lodged " (A.V., " abode ").¶ See the metaphorical use in the Sept. and the Heb. of Psa. 30 : 5, ' (weeping) may come in to lodge (at even),' i.e., as a passing stranger. See ABIDE.

2. KATASKĒNOŌ (κατασκηνόω), to pitch one's tent (*kata*, down, *skēnē*, a tent), is rendered to lodge, of birds, in Matt. 13 : 32 ; Mark 4 : 32 ; Luke 13 : 19.   In Acts 2 : 26, it is used of the body of the Lord in the tomb, as dwelling in hope, R.V., " shall dwell " (marg., " tabernacle "), A.V., " shall rest."   See DWELL, REST.¶ Cp. *kataskēnōsis*, a roosting place.

3. KATALUŌ (καταλύω), in one of its meanings, signifies to unloose (*kata*, down, *luō*, to loose), unyoke, as of horses, etc., hence intransitively,

---

In the following pages † indicates that the word referred to (preposition, conjunction, or particle) is not dealt with in this volume.

¶ indicates that all the N.T. occurrences of the Greek word under consideration are mentioned under the heading or sub-heading.

to take up one's quarters, to lodge, Luke 9 : 12 ; 19 : 7, R.V., " to lodge "
(A.V., " to be a guest "). See COME, Note (7) (come to nought), DESTROY,
DISSOLVE, OVERTHROW, THROW. Cp. *kataluma*, a guest chamber, inn.

4. XENIZŌ (ξενίζω), to receive as a guest (*xenos*, a guest, stranger),
to entertain, lodge, is used in the Active Voice in Acts 10 : 23 ; 28 : 7, R.V.,
" entertained " (A.V., " lodged ") ; Heb. 13 : 2, " have entertained ; "
in the Passive Voice, Acts 10 : 6 (lit., ' he is entertained '), 18, 32 ;
21 : 16. Its other meaning, to think strange, is found in 1 Pet. 4 : 4, 12.
See ENTERTAIN, STRANGE.

B. Noun.

XENIA (ξενία), akin to A, No. 4, denotes (*a*) hospitality, entertainment, Philm. 22 ; (*b*) by metonymy, a place of entertainment, a lodging-
place, Acts 28 : 23 (some put Philm. 22 under this section).¶

For LOFT, Acts 20 : 9, see STORY

LOINS

OSPHUS (ὀσφύς) is used (*a*) in the natural sense in Matt. 3 : 4 ;
Mark 1 : 6 ; (*b*) as the seat of generative power, Heb. 7 : 5, 10 ; metaphorically in Acts 2 : 30 ; (*c*) metaphorically, (1) of girding the loins in
readiness for active service for the Lord, Luke 12 : 35 ; (2) the same, with
truth, Eph. 6 : 14, i.e., bracing up oneself so as to maintain perfect
sincerity and reality as the counteractive in Christian character against
hypocrisy and falsehood ; (3) of girding the loins of the mind, 1 Pet. 1 : 13,
R.V., " girding," suggestive of the alertness necessary for sobriety and for
setting one's hope perfectly on " the grace to be brought . . . at the
revelation of Jesus Christ " (the present participle, " girding," is
introductory to the rest of the verse).¶

LONG (Adjective and Adverb)

A. Adjectives.

1. MAKROS (μακρός) is used of long prayers (Matt. 23 : 14, in some
mss.), Mark 12 : 40 ; Luke 20 : 47. It denotes " far " in Luke 15 : 13 ;
19 : 12. See FAR.¶

2. HIKANOS (ἱκανός), sufficient, much, long, is used with *chronos*,
time, in Luke 8 : 27 ; in 20 : 9 and 23 : 8 (A.V., " season ") the plural is
used, lit., ' long times ; ' Acts 8 : 11 ; 14 : 3. See ABLE (ABILITY), C,
No. 2, MANY, MUCH.

3. POLUS (πολύς), much, is used with *chronos*, time, in Matt. 25 : 19 ;
John 5 : 6 ; in Acts 27 : 21, with *asitia*, A.V., " long abstinence," R.V.,
" long without food." See COMMON, Note (1).

4. TOSOUTOS (τοσοῦτος), so long, is used with *chronos* in John 14 : 9
and Heb. 4 : 7.

5. POSOS (πόσος), how much, is used with *chronos*, in Mark 9 : 21,
" how long time," R.V. (A.V., " how long ago ").

6. HOSOS (ὅσος), how much, so much, is used after the preposition

epi (*eph'*), and as an adjective qualifying *chronos*, signifying " for so long time," in Rom. 7 : 1 ; 1 Cor. 7 : 39 ; Gal. 4 : 1 ; see also B, No. 4.

Notes : (1) In Acts 14 : 28, A.V., the adjective *oligos*, little, with the negative *ou*, not, and qualifying *chronos*, is rendered " long time ; " R.V., " no little (time)." (2) For the comparative adjective, *pleiōn*, see Longer, B.

B. Adverbs.

1. POLUS (πολύς), in one or other of its neuter forms, singular or plural, is used (*a*) of degree, greatly, much, many, e.g., Mark 1 : 45 ; (*b*) of time, e.g., Acts 27 : 14. Cp. A, No. 3. See Great, Much, Oft, Sore, Straitly, While.

2. EPH' HIKANON (ἐφ' ἱκανόν), lit., ' unto much (time),' is rendered " a long while " in Acts 20 : 11. Cp. A, No. 2.

3. HEŌS POTE (ἕως πότε), lit., ' until when ? ' signifies " how long ? " Matt. 17 : 17 (twice) ; Mark 9 : 19 (twice) ; Luke 9 : 41 ; John 10 : 24 ; Rev. 6 : 10.

4. EPH' HOSON (ἐφ' ὅσον) signifies so long as, as long as (*epi*, upon, *hosos*, how much), Matt. 9 : 15 ; Mark 2 : 19 ; 2 Pet. 1 : 13. See Inasmuch, No. 2.

Notes : (1) For the adverb Longer, see below. (2) In 2 Pet. 2 : 3, A.V., the adverb *ekpalai*, " from of old," R.V. (*ek*, from, *palai*, of old, formerly), is translated " of a long time."

LONG (Verb), LONG (after, for), LONGING
A. Verb.

EPIPOTHEŌ (ἐπιποθέω), to long for greatly (a strengthened form of *potheō*, to long for, not found in the N.T.), is translated " I long," in Rom. 1 : 11 ; in 2 Cor. 5 : 2, R.V., " longing " (A.V., " earnestly desiring ") ; in 1 Thess. 3 : 6 and 2 Tim. 1 : 4, R.V., " longing " (A.V., " desiring greatly ") ; to long after, in 2 Cor. 9 : 14 ; Phil. 1 : 8 ; 2 : 26 ; to long for, in 1 Pet. 2 : 2, R.V. (A.V., " desire ") ; Jas. 4 : 5, R.V., " long." See Desire.¶

B. Adjective.

EPIPOTHĒTOS (ἐπιπόθητος), akin to A, and an intensive form of *pothētos*, desired, greatly desired, " longed for," is used in Phil. 4 : 1.¶

C. Nouns.

1. EPIPOTHIA (ἐπιποθία), a longing (akin to A and B), is found in Rom. 15 : 23, R.V., " longing " (A.V., " great desire "). See Desire.¶

2. EPIPOTHĒSIS (ἐπιπόθησις), a longing (perhaps stressing the process more than No. 1), is found in 2 Cor. 7 : 7, R.V., " longing " (A.V., " earnest desire ") ; 7 : 11, R.V., " longing " (A.V., " vehement desire ").¶

LONGER
A. Adverbs.

1. ETI (ἔτι), yet, as yet, still, is translated " longer " in Luke 16 : 2

(with separate negative) ; "any longer" in Rom. 6 : 2. See ALSO, EVEN, FURTHER, MORE, MOREOVER, STILL, THENCEFORTH, YET.

2. OUKETI (οὐκέτι), no more, no longer (ou, not, k, euphonic, and No. 1), is rendered "no longer" in the R.V. of Mark 7 : 12 (A.V., "no more ") ; John 15 : 15, R.V. (A.V., "henceforth not ") ; Rom. 14 : 15, R.V. (A.V., "now . . . not ") ; Gal. 2 : 20, R.V. (A.V., "yet not ") ; Gal. 3 : 25 ; 4 : 7 (A.V., "no more ") ; Philm. 16 (A.V., "not now "). See HENCEFORTH, MORE, NOW, YET.

3. MĒKETI (μηκέτι) also means no more, no longer, but generally suggests what is a matter of thought or supposition, whereas No. 1 refers to what is a matter of fact. It is rendered "any longer" in Acts 25 : 24 ; "no longer," in Mark 2 : 2, R.V., "no longer (room)," A.V., "no (room) ; " 2 Cor. 5 : 15, R.V. (A.V., "not henceforth ") ; Eph. 4 : 14, R.V. (A.V., "no more ") ; 4 : 17, R.V. (A.V., "henceforth . . . not ") ; 1 Thess. 3 : 1, 5 ; 1 Tim. 5 : 23 ; 1 Pet. 4 : 2. See (negatively) HENCEFORTH, HENCEFORWARD, HEREAFTER, NO MORE.

4. PLEION (πλεῖον), the neuter of pleiōn, more, the comparative degree of polu, much, is rendered "longer" in Acts 20 : 9, R.V. (A.V., "long ").

B. Adjective.

PLEIŌN (πλείων), more, (cp. A, No. 4), is used with chronos, time, in Acts 18 : 20, "a longer time," R.V. (A.V., "longer ").

LONGSUFFERING (Noun and Verb)

A. Noun.

MAKROTHUMIA (μακροθυμία), forbearance, patience, longsuffering (makros, long, thumos, temper), is usually rendered "longsuffering," Rom. 2 : 4 ; 9 : 22 ; 2 Cor. 6 : 6 ; Gal. 5 : 22 ; Eph. 4 : 2 ; Col. 1 : 11 ; 3 : 12 ; 1 Tim. 1 : 16 ; 2 Tim. 3 : 10 ; 4 : 2 ; 1 Pet. 3 : 20 ; 2 Pet. 3 : 15 ; "patience " in Heb. 6 : 12 and Jas. 5 : 10. See PATIENCE, and Note under FORBEAR.¶

B. Verb.

MAKROTHUMEŌ (μακροθυμέω), akin to A, to be patient, long-suffering, to bear with, lit., to be long-tempered, is rendered by the verb to be longsuffering in Luke 18 : 7, R.V. (A.V., "bear long ") ; in 1 Thess. 5 : 14, R.V. (A.V., "be patient ") ; so in Jas. 5 : 7, 8 ; in 2 Pet. 3 : 9, A.V. and R.V., "is longsuffering." See BEAR, No. 14, ENDURE, PATIENT, SUFFER.

Note : "Longsuffering is that quality of self-restraint in the face of provocation which does not hastily retaliate or promptly punish ; it is the opposite of anger, and is associated with mercy, and is used of God, Ex. 34 : 6 (Sept.) ; Rom. 2 : 4 ; 1 Pet. 3 : 20. Patience is the quality that does not surrender to circumstances or succumb under trial ; it is the opposite of despondency and is associated with hope, 1 Thess. 1 : 3 ; it is not used of God."*

---

* From Notes on Thessalonians by Hogg and Vine, pp. 183, 184.

LOOK
A. Verbs.

1. BLEPŌ (βλέπω), primarily, to have sight, to see, then, observe, discern, perceive, frequently implying special contemplation (cp. No. 4), is rendered by the verb to look in Luke 9 : 62, " looking (back) ; " John 13 : 22 " (the disciples) looked (one on another) " ; Acts 1 : 9, R.V., " were looking " (A.V., " beheld ") ; 3 : 4, " look (on us) ; " 27 : 12, R.V., looking," A.V., " that lieth (towards)," of the haven Phenix ; Eph. 5 : 15, R.V., " look (therefore carefully how ye walk)," A.V., " see (that ye walk circumspectly) ; " Rev. 11 : 9 and 18 : 9, R.V., " look upon " (A.V., " shall see "). See BEHOLD.

2. ANABLEPŌ (ἀναβλέπω), denotes (a) to look up (ana, up, and No. 1), e.g., Matt. 14 : 19 ; Mark 8 : 24 (in some mss. ver. 25) ; (b) to recover sight, e.g., Matt. 11 : 5 ; 20 : 34, R.V., " received their sight ; " John 9 : 11. See SIGHT. Cp. anablepsis, recovering of sight, Luke 4 : 18.

3. PERIBLEPŌ (περιβλέπω), to look about, or round about, on (peri, around, and No. 1), is used in the Middle Voice, Mark 3 : 5, 34 ; 5 : 32 ; 9 : 8 ; 10 : 23 ; 11 : 11 ; Luke 6 : 10.¶

4. APOBLEPŌ (ἀποβλέπω) signifies to look away from (apo) all else at one object ; hence, to look stedfastly, Heb. 11 : 26, R.V., " he looked " (A.V., " he had respect ").¶ Cp. No. 8.

5. EMBLEPŌ (ἐμβλέπω), to look at (en, in, and No. 1), is translated to look upon in Mark 10 : 27 ; 14 : 67 ; Luke 22 : 61 ; John 1 : 36. This verb implies a close, penetrating look, as distinguished from Nos. 6 and 9. See BEHOLD, No. 3, GAZE, SEE, No. 6.

6. EPIBLEPŌ (ἐπιβλέπω), to look upon (epi, upon), is used in the N.T. of favourable regard, Luke 1 : 48, R.V., " he hath looked upon " (A.V., " hath regarded "), of the low estate of the Virgin Mary ; in 9 : 38, in a request to the Lord to look upon an afflicted son ; in Jas. 2 : 3, R.V., " ye have regard " (A.V., " . . . respect "), of having a partial regard for the well-to-do. See REGARD, RESPECT.¶

7. EIDON (εἶδον), used as the aorist tense of horaō, to see, in various senses, is translated to look, in the A.V. of John 7 : 52, R.V., " see ; " Rev. 4 : 1 (R.V., " I saw ") ; so in 6 : 8 ; 14 : 1, 14 (as in A.V. of ver. 6), and 15 : 5. See BEHOLD, CONSIDER, HEED, No. 2, PERCEIVE, SEE, SHEW.

8. APHORAŌ (ἀφοράω), to look away from one thing so as to see another (apo, from, and No. 7), to concentrate the gaze upon, occurs in Phil. 2 : 23, " I shall see ; " Heb. 12 : 2, " looking."¶

9. EPEIDON (ἐπεῖδον) denotes to look upon (epi, upon), (a) favourably, Luke 1 : 25 ; (b) unfavourably, in Acts 4 : 29.¶

10. PARAKUPTŌ (παρακύπτω), lit. and primarily, to stoop sideways (para, aside, kuptō, to bend forward), denotes to stoop to look into, Luke 24 : 12, " stooping and looking in " (A.V., " stooping down ") ; John 20 : 5, 11 ; metaphorically in Jas. 1 : 25, of looking into the perfect

law of liberty ; in 1 Pet. 1 : 12 of things which the angels desire " to look " into.¶

11. ANAKUPTŌ (ἀνακύπτω), to lift oneself up (ana, up), is translated " look up " in Luke 21 : 28, of being elated in joyous expectation (followed by epairō, to lift up). See LIFT.

12. SKOPEŌ (σκοπέω), to look at, consider (Eng., scope), implying mental consideration, is rendered "while we look . . . at " in 2 Cor. 4 : 18 ; " looking to " (A.V., " on ") in Phil. 2 : 4. See HEED, MARK.

13. EPISKOPEŌ (ἐπισκοπέω), lit., to look upon (epi, and No. 12), is rendered " looking carefully " in Heb. 12 : 15, R.V. (A.V., " looking diligently "), epi being probably intensive here ; in 1 Pet. 5 : 2, to exercise the oversight, to visit, care for. See OVERSIGHT.¶

14. EPISKEPTOMAI (ἐπισκέπτομαι), a later form of No. 13, to visit, has the meaning of seeking out, and is rendered " look ye out " in Acts 6 : 3. See VISIT.

15. ATENIZŌ (ἀτενίζω), to look fixedly, gaze, is translated " looking stedfastly " in Luke 22 : 56, R.V. (A.V., " . . . earnestly ") ; in Acts 1 : 10, " looking stedfastly ; " in 3 : 12, A.V., " look . . . earnestly " (R.V., " fasten ye your eyes," as in 3 : 4 and 11 : 6) ; so in the R.V. of 6 : 15 ; 10 : 4 ; 13 : 9 ; 14 : 9 ; in 7 : 55, " looked up stedfastly ; " in 23 : 1, " looking stedfastly on " (A.V., " earnestly beholding ") ; in 2 Cor. 3 : 7, R.V., " look stedfastly " (A.V., " stedfastly behold ") ; in 3 : 13, R.V., ditto (A.V., " stedfastly look "). In Luke 4 : 20, " were fastened " (ophthalmoi, eyes, being used separately). See BEHOLD, No. 10.¶

16. THEAOMAI (θεάομαι), to behold (of careful contemplation), is translated " look " in John 4 : 35, of looking on the fields ; in 1 John 1 : 1, A.V. (R.V., " we beheld "), of the Apostles' personal experiences of Christ in the days of His flesh, and the facts of His Godhood and Manhood. See BEHOLD, No. 8.

17. THEŌREŌ (θεωρέω), to look at, gaze at, behold, is translated " looking on " in Mark 15 : 40, A.V. (R.V., " beholding "). See BEHOLD, No. 6.

B. Noun.

HORASIS (ὅρασις), akin to A, No. 7, denotes (a) a vision (so the associated noun horama, e.g., Acts 7 : 31 ; horasis signifies especially the act of seeing, horama that which is seen), Acts 2 : 17 ; Rev. 9 : 17 ; (b) an appearance, Rev. 4 : 3, translated " to look upon " (twice in the R.V. ; in the second instance the A.V. has " in sight ").¶

LOOK (for), LOOKING (after, for)
A. Verbs.

1. PROSDOKAŌ (προσδοκάω), to await, expect (pros, to or towards, dokeō, to think, be of opinion), is translated to look for, e.g., in Matt. 11 : 3 ; 2 Pet. 3 : 12, 13, 14 ; the R.V. renders it by the verb to expect, to be in

expectation, in some instances, as does the A.V. in Luke 3 : 15 ; Acts 3 : 5. See EXPECT.

2. PROSDECHOMAI (προσδέχομαι), to receive favourably, also means to expect, and is rendered to look for, e.g., in Luke 2 : 38 ; 23 : 51 ; Acts 24 : 15, R.V. (A.V., " allow ") ; Tit. 2 : 13 ; Jude 21. See ACCEPT, A, No. 3, ALLOW, No. 4.

3. EKDECHOMAI (ἐκδέχομαι), primarily to receive from another, hence, to expect, to await, is translated " he looked for " in Heb. 11 : 10 ; in 1 Cor. 16 : 11, A.V., " I look for " (R.V., " I expect "). See EXPECT, No. 1.

Notes : (1) In Phil. 3 : 20 and Heb. 9 : 28, A.V., *apekdechomai* (the verb in the preceding No. extended by *apo*, from), to await or expect eagerly, is translated " look for " (R.V., " wait for ; " so A.V. everywhere else). See WAIT. (2) In Acts 28 : 6, A.V., *prosdokaō*, to expect, is translated " they looked " (R.V., " they expected "), and " they had looked " (R.V., " they were long in expectation ").

B. Nouns.

1. PROSDOKIA (προσδοκία); akin to A, No. 1, is translated " a looking after " in Luke 21 : 26, A.V. (R.V., " expectation," as in Acts 12 : 11, A.V. and R.V.). See EXPECTATION.¶

2. EKDOCHĒ (ἐκδοχή), akin to A, No. 3, is translated " looking for " in Heb. 10 : 27, A.V. See EXPECTATION.¶

LOOK (to)

1. BLEPŌ (βλέπω), to look (see LOOK, No. 1), has the meaning of taking heed, looking to oneself, in 2 John 8. See HEED.

2. HORAŌ (ὁράω), to see (see LOOK, No. 7), has the meaning of seeing to or caring for a thing in Matt. 27 : 4, " see (thou to it) ; " in Acts 18 : 15, " look to it (yourselves) ; " the future (sing. *opsei*, plural, *opsesthe*), is used for the tense which is wanting in *horaō*, and stands for the imperative.

LOOSE

A. Verbs.

1. LUŌ (λύω) denotes (a) to loose, unbind, release, (1) of things, e.g., in Acts 7 : 33, R.V., " loose (the shoes)," A.V., " put off ; " Mark 1 : 7 ; (2) of animals, e.g., Matt. 21 : 2 ; (3) of persons, e.g., John 11 : 44 ; Acts 22 : 30 ; (4) of Satan, Rev. 20 : 3, 7, and angels, Rev. 9 : 14, 15 ; (5) metaphorically, of one diseased, Luke 13 : 16 ; of the marriage tie, 1 Cor. 7 : 27 ; of release from sins, Rev. 1 : 5 (in the most authentic mss.) ; (b) to loosen, break up, dismiss, dissolve, destroy ; in this sense it is translated to loose in Acts 2 : 24, of the pains of death ; in Rev. 5 : 2, of the seals of a roll. See BREAK, DESTROY, DISSOLVE, MELT, PUT (off), UNLOOSE.

2. APOLUŌ (ἀπολύω), *apo*, from, and No. 1, denotes (a) to set free, release, translated " loosed " in Luke 13 : 12, of deliverance from an

infirmity; in Matt. 18 : 27, A.V., "loosed" (R.V., "released"), of a debtor; (b) to let go, dismiss, e.g., Matt. 14 : 15, 22. See DEPART, DISMISS, DIVORCE, FORGIVE, LET (go), LIBERTY, PUT (away), RELEASE, SEND (away).

3. ANIĒMI (ἀνίημι), to send back (ana, back, hiēmi, to send), to leave, forbear, is translated to loose, in Acts 16 : 26, of the loosening of bonds; 27 : 40, rudder-bands. Elsewhere, Eph. 6 : 9; Heb. 13 : 5. See FORBEAR, LEAVE.¶

4. ANAGŌ (ἀνάγω): see LAUNCH.

Notes: (1) In Acts 27 : 13, A.V., *airō*, to lift, is translated "loosing (thence)" (R.V., "they weighed anchor"). (2) For *katargeō*, translated "she is loosed" in Rom. 7 : 2, A.V. (R.V. "discharged"), see ABOLISH.

B. Noun.

LUSIS (λύσις), a loosening (akin to A, No. 1), 1 Cor. 7 : 27, of divorce, is translated "to be loosed," lit., 'loosing.' In the second part of the verse the verb *luō* is used.¶ In the Sept., Eccles. 8 : 1, with the meaning "interpretation."¶

LORD, LORDSHIP
A. Nouns.

1. KURIOS (κύριος), properly an adjective, signifying having power (*kuros*) or authority, is used as a noun, variously translated in the N.T., "'Lord,' 'master,' 'Master,' 'owner,' 'Sir,' a title of wide significance, occurring in each book of the N.T. save Tit. and the Epp. of John. It is used (a) of an owner, as in Luke 19 : 33, cp. Matt. 20 : 8; Acts 16 : 16; Gal. 4 : 1; or of one who has the disposal of anything, as the Sabbath, Matt. 12 : 8; (b) of a master, i.e., one to whom service is due on any ground, Matt. 6 : 24; 24 : 50; Eph. 6 : 5; (c) of an Emperor or King, Acts 25 : 26; Rev. 17 : 14; (d) of idols, ironically, 1 Cor. 8 : 5, cp. Isa. 26 : 13; (e) as a title of respect addressed to a father, Matt. 21 : 30, a husband, 1 Pet. 3 : 6, a master, Matt. 13 : 27; Luke 13 : 8, a ruler, Matt. 27 : 63, an angel, Acts 10 : 4; Rev. 7 : 14; (f) as a title of courtesy addressed to a stranger, John 12 : 21; 20 : 15; Acts 16 : 30; from the outset of His ministry this was a common form of address to the Lord Jesus, alike by the people, Matt. 8 : 2; John 4 : 11, and by His disciples, Matt. 8 : 25; Luke 5 : 8; John 6 : 68; (g) *kurios* is the Sept. and N.T. representative of Heb. Jehovah ('LORD' in Eng. versions), see Matt. 4 : 7; Jas. 5 : 11, e.g., of *adon*, Lord, Matt. 22 : 44, and of *Adonay*, Lord, 1 : 22; it also occurs for *Elohim*, God, 1 Pet. 1 : 25.

"Thus the usage of the word in the N.T. follows two main lines: one—a—f, customary and general, the other, g, peculiar to the Jews, and drawn from the Greek translation of the O.T.

"Christ Himself assumed the title, Matt. 7 : 21, 22; 9 : 38; 22 : 41-45; Mark 5 : 19 (cp. Ps. 66 : 16; the parallel passage, Luke 8 : 39, has 'God'); Luke 19 : 31; John 13 : 13, apparently intending it in the higher senses of its current use, and at the same time suggesting its O.T. associations.

"His purpose did not become clear to the disciples until after His resurrection, and the revelation of His Deity consequent thereon. Thomas, when he realised the significance of the presence of a mortal wound in the body of a living man, immediately joined with it the absolute title of Deity, saying, ' My Lord and my God,' John 20 : 28. Thereafter, except in Acts 10 : 4 and Rev. 7 : 14, there is no record that *kurios* was ever again used by believers in addressing any save God and the Lord Jesus ; cp. Acts 2 : 47 with 4 : 29, 30.

"How soon and how completely the lower meaning had been super- seded is seen in Peter's declaration in his first sermon after the resurrection, ' God hath made Him—Lord,' Acts 2 : 36, and that in the house of Cornelius, ' He is Lord of all,' 10 : 36 ; cp. Deut. 10 : 14 ; Matt. 11 : 25 ; Acts 17 : 24. In his writings the implications of his early teaching are confirmed and developed. Thus Ps. 34 : 8, ' O taste and see that Jehovah is good,' is applied to the Lord Jesus, 1 Pet. 2 : 3, and ' Jehovah of Hosts, Him shall ye sanctify,' Isa. 8 : 13, becomes ' sanctify in your hearts Christ as Lord,' 3 : 15.

"So also James who uses *kurios* alike of God, 1 : 7 (cp. v. 5) ; 3 : 9 ; 4 : 15 ; 5 : 4, 10, 11, and of the Lord Jesus, 1 : 1 (where the possibility that *kai* is intended epexegetically, i.e.=even, cp. 1 Thess. 3 : 11, should not be overlooked) ; 2 : 1 (lit., ' our Lord Jesus Christ of glory,' cp. Ps. 24 : 7 ; 29 : 3 ; Acts 7 : 2 ; 1 Cor. 2 : 8) ; 5 : 7, 8, while the language of 4 : 10 ; 5 : 15, is equally applicable to either.

"Jude, v. 4, speaks of ' our only—Lord, Jesus Christ,' and immediately, v. 5, uses ' Lord ' of God (see the remarkable marg. here), as he does later, vv. 9, 14.

"Paul ordinarily uses *kurios* of the Lord Jesus, 1 Cor. 1 : 3, e.g., but also on occasion, of God, in quotations from the O.T., 1 Cor. 3 : 20, e.g., and in his own words, 1 Cor. 3 : 5, cp. v. 10. It is equally appropriate to either in 1 Cor. 7 : 25 ; 2 Cor. 3 : 16 ; 8 : 21 ; 1 Thess. 4 : 6, and if 1 Cor. 11 : 32 is to be interpreted by 10 : 21, 22, the Lord Jesus is intended, but if by Heb. 12 : 5–9, then *kurios* here also=God. 1 Tim. 6 : 15, 16 is probably to be understood of the Lord Jesus, cp. Rev. 17 : 14.

"Though John does not use ' Lord ' in his Epp., and though, like the other Evangelists, he ordinarily uses the personal Name in his narrative, yet he occasionally speaks of Him as ' the Lord,' John 4 : 1 ; 6 : 23 ; 11 : 2 ; 20 : 20 ; 21 : 12.

"The full significance of this association of Jesus with God under the one appellation, ' Lord,' is seen when it is remembered that these men belonged to the only monotheistic race in the world. To associate with the Creator one known to be a creature, however exalted, though possible to Pagan philosophers, was quite impossible to a Jew.

"It is not recorded that in the days of His flesh any of His disciples either addressed the Lord, or spoke of Him, by His personal Name. Where

Paul has occasion to refer to the facts of the gospel history he speaks of what the Lord Jesus said, Acts 20 : 35, and did, 1 Cor. 11 : 23, and suffered, 1 Thess. 2 : 15 ; 5 : 9, 10. It is our Lord Jesus who is coming, 1 Thess. 2 : 19, etc. In prayer also the title is given, 3 : 11 ; Eph. 1 : 3 ; the sinner is invited to believe on the Lord Jesus, Acts 16 : 31 ; 20 : 21, and the saint to look to the Lord Jesus for deliverance, Rom. 7 : 24, 25, and in the few exceptional cases in which the personal Name stands alone a reason is always discernible in the immediate context.

" The title ' Lord,' as given to the Saviour, in its full significance rests upon the resurrection, Acts 2 : 36 ; Rom. 10 : 9 ; 14 : 9, and is realised only in the Holy Spirit, 1 Cor. 12 : 3."*

2. DESPOTĒS (δεσπότης), a master, lord, one who possesses supreme authority, is used in personal address to God in Luke 2 : 29 ; Acts 4 : 24 ; Rev. 6 : 10 ; with reference to Christ, 2 Pet. 2 : 1 ; Jude 4 ; elsewhere it is translated " master," " masters," 1 Tim. 6 : 1, 2 ; 2 Tim. 2 : 21 (of Christ) ; Tit. 2 : 9 ; 1 Pet. 2 : 18. See MASTER.¶

Note : For *rabboni*, rendered " Lord " in the A.V of Mark 10 : 51, see RABBONI.

3. MEGISTAN (μεγιστάν), akin to *megistos*, greatest, the superlative degree of *megas*, great, denotes chief men, nobles ; it is rendered " lords " in Mark 6 : 21, of nobles in Herod's entourage ; " princes " in Rev. 6 : 15 and 18 : 23, R.V. (A.V., " great men ").¶

B. Verbs.

1. KURIEUŌ (κυριεύω) denotes to be lord of, to exercise lordship over, Luke 22 : 25 ; Rom. 6 : 9, 14 ; 7 : 1 ; 14 : 9 ; 2 Cor. 1 : 24 ; 1 Tim. 6 : 15 ; see DOMINION, B, No. 1.¶

2. KATAKURIEUŌ (κατακυριεύω), a strengthened form of No. 1, is rendered " lording it " in 1 Pet. 5 : 3, R.V. : see DOMINION, B, No. 2.

C. Adjective.

KURIAKOS (κυριακός), from *kurios* (A, No. 1), signifies pertaining to a lord or master ; ' lordly ' is not a legitimate rendering for its use in the N.T., where it is used only of Christ ; in 1 Cor. 11 : 20, of the Lord's Supper, or the Supper of the Lord (see FEAST) ; in Rev. 1 : 10, of the Day of the Lord (see DAY, No. 1).¶

LOSE, (Suffer) LOSS, LOST

1. APOLLUMI (ἀπόλλυμι) signifies (I) In the Active Voice, (*a*) to destroy, destroy utterly, kill, e.g., Matt. 10 : 28 ; Mark 1 : 24 ; 9 : 22 ; (*b*) to lose utterly, e.g., Matt. 10 : 42, of losing a reward ; Luke 15 : 4 (1st part), of losing a sheep ; Luke 9 : 25, of losing oneself (of the loss of well-being hereafter) ; metaphorically, John 6 : 39, of failing to save ; 18 : 9, of Christ's not losing His own ; (II) in the Middle Voice, (*a*) to perish, of things, e.g., John 6 : 12 " (that nothing) be lost " ; of persons, e.g., Matt. 8 : 25, " we perish ; " of the loss of eternal life, usually (always in the R.V.)

---

* From Notes on Thessalonians by Hogg and Vine, p. 25.

translated to perish, John 3 : 16 ; 17 : 12, A.V., " is lost," R.V., " perished ; " 2 Cor. 4 : 3, " are perishing," A.V., " are lost " (see PERISH) ; (b) to be lost, e.g., Luke 15 : 4 (2nd part), " which is lost ; " metaphorically, from the relation between shepherd and flock, of spiritual destitution and alienation from God, Matt. 10 : 6, " (the) lost (sheep) " of the house of Israel ; Luke 19 : 10 (the perfect tense translated " lost " is here intransitive). See DESTROY.

2. ZĒMIOŌ (ζημιόω), to damage (akin to zēmia, damage, e.g., Acts 27 : 10, 21), is used in the N.T., in the Passive Voice, signifying to suffer loss, forfeit, lose, Matt. 16 : 26 ; Mark 8 : 36, of losing one's soul or life ; Luke 9 : 25, R.V., " forfeit (his own self)," A.V., " be cast away " (for the preceding verb see No. 1) ; 1 Cor. 3 : 15, " he shall suffer loss," i.e., at the Judgment-Seat of Christ (see ver. 13 with 2 Cor. 5 : 10) ; 2 Cor. 7 : 9, " (that) ye might suffer loss," R.V. (A.V., " might receive damage ") ; though the Apostle did regret the necessity of making them sorry by his letter, he rejoiced that they were made sorry after a godly sort, and that they thus suffered no spiritual loss, which they would have done had their sorrow been otherwise than after a godly manner ; in Phil. 3 : 8, " I suffered the loss (of all things)," R.V., i.e., of all things which he formerly counted gain (especially those in verses 5 and 6, to which the article before " all things " points). See CAST, FORFEIT.¶

LOSS

1. ZĒMIA (ζημία), akin to No. 2, above, is used in Acts 27 : 10, R.V., " loss " (A.V., " damage ") ; ver. 21, A.V. and R.V., " loss," of ship and cargo ; in Phil. 3 : 7, 8 of the Apostle's estimate of the things which he formerly valued, and of all things on account of " the excellency of the knowledge of Christ Jesus."¶

2. APOBOLĒ (ἀποβολή), lit., casting away (apo, away, ballō, to cast), is translated " loss " in Acts 27 : 22 ; in Rom. 11 : 15, " casting away," of the temporary exclusion of the nation of Israel from its position of Divine favour, involving the reconciling of the world (i.e., the provision made through the gospel, which brings the world within the scope of reconciliation).¶

3. HĒTTĒMA (ἥττημα) denotes a defect, loss, Rom. 11 : 12, R.V., " loss," A.V., " diminishing " (for the meaning of which in regard to Israel see No. 2) ; 1 Cor. 6 : 7, R.V., " defect " (A.V., " fault "). See DEFECT.

Note : For " suffer loss " see LOSE, No. 2.

LOT, LOTS

A. Noun.

KLĒROS (κλῆρος) denotes (a) an object used in casting or drawing lots, which consisted of bits, or small tablets, of wood or stone (the probable derivation is from klaō, to break) ; these were sometimes inscribed with the names of persons, and were put into a receptacle or a garment (a lap, Prov. 16 : 33), from which they were cast, after being shaken together ; he whose lot first fell out was the one chosen. The method was employed in a variety of circumstances, e.g., of dividing or assigning property, Matt. 27 : 35 ; Mark 15 : 24 ; Luke 23 : 34 ; John 19 : 24 (cp., e.g., Numb. 26 : 55) ; of appointing to office, Acts 1 : 26 (cp., e.g., 1 Sam. 10 : 20) ; for other occurrences in the O.T., see, e.g., Josh. 7 : 14 (the earliest instance in Scripture) ; Lev. 16 : 7–10 ; Esth. 3 : 7 ; 9 : 24 ; (b) what is obtained by lot, an allotted portion, e.g., of the ministry allotted to the Apostles, Acts 1 : 17, R.V., " portion," marg., " lot " (A.V., " part ") ; in some mss. ver. 25, A.V., " part " (the R.V. follows those which have topos, " place ") ; Acts 8 : 21 ; it is also used like klēronomia, an inheritance, in Acts 26 : 18, of what God has in grace assigned to the sanctified ; so Col. 1 : 12 ; in 1 Pet. 5 : 3 it is used of those the spiritual care of, and charge over, whom is assigned to elders, R.V., " the charge allotted to you " (plural, lit., ' the charges '), A.V., " (God's) heritage." From klēros the word " clergy " is derived (a transposition in the application of the term). See CHARGE, No. 4.¶

B. Verb.

LANCHANŌ (λαγχάνω) denotes (a) to draw lots, John 19 : 24 ; (b) to obtain by lot, to obtain, Luke 1 : 9, " his lot was," lit., ' he received by lot,' i.e., by Divine appointment ; Acts 1 : 17, of the portion allotted by the Lord to His Apostles in their ministry (cp. A, above) ; 2 Pet. 1 : 1, " that have obtained (a like precious faith)," i.e., by its being allotted to them, not by acquiring it for themselves, but by Divine grace (an act independent of human control, as in the casting of lots). See OBTAIN.¶

Note : For divide by lot see DIVIDE.

LOUD

MEGAS (μέγας), great, is used, besides other meanings, of intensity, as, e.g., of the force of a voice, e.g., Matt. 27 : 46, 50 ; in the following the R.V. has " great " for the A.V., " loud," Rev. 5 : 2, 12 ; 6 : 10 ; 7 : 2, 10 ; 8 : 13 ; 10 : 3 ; 12 : 10 ; 14 : 7, 9, 15, 18. See GREAT.

LOVE (Noun and Verb)
A. Verbs.

1. AGAPAŌ (ἀγαπάω) and the corresponding noun agapē (B, No. 1 below) present " the characteristic word of Christianity, and since the Spirit of revelation has used it to express ideas previously unknown, enquiry into its use, whether in Greek literature or in the Septuagint, throws but little light upon its distinctive meaning in the N.T. Cp., however, Lev. 19 : 18 ; Deut. 6 : 5.

" *Agapē* and *agapaō* are used in the N.T. (a) to describe the attitude of God toward His Son, John 17 : 26 ; the human race, generally, John 3 : 16 ; Rom 5 : 8 ; and to such as believe on the Lord Jesus Christ, particularly, John 14 : 21 ; (b) to convey His will to His children concerning their attitude one toward another, John 13 : 34, and toward all men, 1 Thess. 3 : 12 ; 1 Cor. 16 : 14 ; 2 Pet. 1 : 7 ; (c) to express the essential nature of God, 1 John 4 : 8.

" Love can be known only from the actions it prompts. God's love is seen in the gift of His Son, 1 John 4 : 9, 10. But obviously this is not the love of complacency, or affection, that is, it was not drawn out by any excellency in its objects, Rom. 5 : 8. It was an exercise of the Divine will in deliberate choice, made without assignable cause save that which lies in the nature of God Himself, cp. Deut. 7 : 7, 8.

" Love had its perfect expression among men in the Lord Jesus Christ, 2 Cor. 5 : 14 ; Eph. 2 : 4 ; 3 : 19 ; 5 : 2 ; Christian love is the fruit of His Spirit in the Christian, Gal. 5 : 22.

" Christian love has God for its primary object, and expresses itself first of all in implicit obedience to His commandments, John 14 : 15, 21, 23 ; 15 : 10 ; 1 John 2 : 5 ; 5 : 3 ; 2 John 6. Self-will, that is, self-pleasing, is the negation of love to God.

" Christian love, whether exercised toward the brethren, or toward men generally, is not an impulse from the feelings, it does not always run with the natural inclinations, nor does it spend itself only upon those for whom some affinity is discovered. Love seeks the welfare of all, Rom. 15 : 2, and works no ill to any, 13 : 8–10 ; love seeks opportunity to do good to ' all men, and especially toward them that are of the household of the faith,' Gal. 6 : 10. See further 1 Cor. 13 and Col. 3 : 12–14."*

In respect of agapaō as used of God, it expresses the deep and constant love and interest of a perfect Being towards entirely unworthy objects, producing and fostering a reverential love in them towards the Giver, and a practical love towards those who are partakers of the same, and a desire to help others to seek the Giver. See BELOVED.

2. PHILEŌ (φιλέω) is to be distinguished from agapaō in this, that phileō more nearly represents tender affection. The two words are used for the love of the Father for the Son, John 3 : 35 (No. 1), and 5 : 20 (No. 2) ; for the believer, 14 : 21 (No. 1) and 16 : 27 (No. 2) ; both, of Christ's love for a certain disciple, 13 : 23 (No. 1), and 20 : 2 (No. 2). Yet the distinction between the two verbs remains, and they are never used indiscriminately in the same passage ; if each is used with reference to the same objects, as just mentioned, each word retains its distinctive and essential character.

Phileō is never used in a command to men to love God ; it is, however, used as a warning in 1 Cor. 16 : 22 ; agapaō is used instead, e.g., Matt. 22 : 37 ; Luke 10 : 27 ; Rom. 8 : 28 ; 1 Cor. 8 : 3 ; 1 Pet. 1 : 8 ; 1 John 4 : 21. The distinction between the two verbs finds a conspicuous instance in the narrative of John 21 : 15–17. The context itself indicates that

---

* From Notes on Thessalonians by Hogg and Vine, p. 105.

agapaō in the first two questions suggests the love that values and esteems (cp. Rev. 12 : 11). It is an unselfish love, ready to serve. The use of *phileō* in Peter's answers and the Lord's third question, conveys the thought of cherishing the Object above all else, of manifesting an affection characterised by constancy, from the motive of the highest veneration. See also Trench, Syn., §xii.

Again, to love (*phileō*) life, from an undue desire to preserve it, forgetful of the real object of living, meets with the Lord's reproof, John 12 : 25. On the contrary, to love life (*agapaō*) as used in 1 Pet. 3 : 10, is to consult the true interests of living. Here the word *phileō* would be quite inappropriate.

Note : In Mark 12 : 38, A.V., *thelō*, to wish, is translated " love " (R.V., " desire ").

B. Nouns.

1. AGAPĒ (ἀγάπη), the significance of which has been pointed out in connection with A, No. 1, is always rendered " love " in the R.V. where the A.V. has " charity," a rendering nowhere used in the R.V. ; in Rom. 14 : 15, where the A.V. has " charitably," the R.V., adhering to the translation of the noun, has " in love."

Note : In the two statements in 1 John 4 : 8 and 16, " God is love," both are used to enjoin the exercise of love on the part of believers. While the former introduces a declaration of the mode in which God's love has been manifested (vv. 9, 10), the second introduces a statement of the identification of believers with God in character, and the issue at the Judgment-Seat hereafter (ver. 17), an identification represented ideally in the sentence " as He is, so are we in this world."

2. PHILANTHRŌPIA (φιλανθρωπία) denotes, lit., love for man (*phileō* and *anthrōpos*, man) ; hence, kindness, Acts 28 : 2 ; in Tit. 3 : 4, " (His) love toward man."¶ Cp. the adverb *philanthrōpōs*, humanely, kindly, Acts 27 : 3.¶ See KINDNESS.

Note : For *philarguria*, love of money, 1 Tim. 6 : 10, see MONEY (love of). For *philadelphia*, see BROTHER, Note (1).

LOVE-FEASTS

AGAPĒ (ἀγάπη) is used in the plural in Jude 12, and in some mss. in 2 Pet. 2 : 13 ; R.V. marg., " many ancient authorities read ' deceivings,' " (*apatais*) ; so the A.V. These love-feasts arose from the common meals of the early churches (cp. 1 Cor. 11 : 21). They may have had this origin in the private meals of Jewish households, with the addition of the observance of the Lord's Supper. There were, however, similar common meals among the pagan religious brotherhoods. The evil dealt with at Corinth (l.c.) became enhanced by the presence of immoral persons, who degraded the feasts into wanton banquets, as mentioned in 2 Pet. and Jude. In later times the *agapē* became detached from the Lord's Supper.

LOVELY

PROSPHILĒS (προσφιλής), pleasing, agreeable, lovely (pros, toward, phileō, to love), occurs in Phil. 4 : 8.¶ In the Sept., Esth. 5 : 1 (3rd sentence).¶

LOVER

This is combined with other words, forming compound adjectives as follows :

1. PHILOTHEOS (φιλόθεος), a lover of God, 2 Tim. 3 : 4.¶

2. PHILOXENOS (φιλόξενος), loving strangers (xenia, hospitality), translated " a lover of hospitality " in Tit. 1 : 8, A.V. (R.V., " given to h.") ; elsewhere, in 1 Tim. 3 : 2 ; 1 Pet. 4 : 9. See HOSPITALITY.¶

3. PHILAGATHOS (φιλάγαθος), loving that which is good (agathos), Tit. 1 : 8, " a lover of good," R.V.¶

Note : The negative aphilagathos is found in 2 Tim. 3 : 3, " no lovers of good."¶

4. PHILARGUROS (φιλάργυρος), loving money (arguros, silver), translated " lovers of money " in Luke 16 : 14 ; 2 Tim. 3 : 2, R.V. (A.V., " covetous "). See COVETOUS.¶

5. PHILAUTOS (φίλαυτος), loving oneself, 2 Tim. 3 : 2, " R.V.¶

6. PHILĒDONOS (φιλήδονος), loving pleasure (hēdonē, pleasure), 2 Tim. 3 : 4, " lovers of pleasure."¶

Note : For loving warmly, Rom. 12 : 10, see AFFECTION, B, No. 2.¶

For aphilarguros, no lover of money, 1 Tim. 3 : 3, R.V., and Heb. 13 : 5, R.V., see COVETOUS.¶

LOW (to bring, to make), LOW (estate, degree)
A. Verb.

TAPEINOŌ (ταπεινόω), to bring low, to humble, is translated " shall be brought low " in Luke 3 : 5. See HUMBLE.

B. Adjective.

TAPEINOS (ταπεινός) denotes of low degree or estate, Rom. 12 : 16, " things that are lowly," R.V. (A.V., " men of low estate "). See BASE, DEGREE, ESTATE, HUMBLE, LOWLY.

C. Noun.

TAPEINŌSIS (ταπείνωσις), abasement, humiliation, low estate, is translated " low estate " in Luke 1 : 48 ; in Jas. 1 : 10, " that he is made low," lit., ' in his abasement.' See HUMILIATION.

LOWER (Adjective, and Verb, to make), LOWEST
A. Adjectives.

1. KATŌTEROS (κατώτερος), the comparative degree of katō, beneath, is used in Eph. 4 : 9, of Christ's descent into " the lower parts of the earth ; " two of the various interpretations of this phrase are (1) that the earth is in view in contrast to heaven, (2) that the region is that of Hades,

the Sheol of the O.T. Inasmuch as the passage is describing the effects not merely of the Incarnation but of the Death and Resurrection of Christ, the second interpretation is to be accepted; cp., e.g., Ps. 16 : 10 ; 63 : 9 ; where the Sept. has the superlative ; 139 : 15 ; Acts 2 : 31. Moreover, as Westcott says, it is most unlikely that the phrase would be used to describe the earth. The word *merē* (plural of *meros*), " parts," would have no force in such a meaning.¶

2. ESCHATOS (ἔσχατος), last, utmost, lowest, is rendered " lowest " in Luke 14 : 9, 10, of the lowest place at a meal. See LAST.

B. Verb.

ELATTOŌ (ἐλαττόω) denotes to make less (*elattōn*, less), and is used in the Active Voice in Heb. 2 : 7, " Thou madest (Him) . . . lower," and in the Passive in ver. 9, " was made . . . lower," and John 3 : 30, " (I must) decrease," (lit., ' be made less ').¶

For LOWER (Verb, to let down) see LET DOWN, No. 2 (*d*)

LOWLINESS, LOWLY
A. Noun.

TAPEINOPHROSUNĒ (ταπεινοφροσύνη), lowliness of mind, humbleness, is translated " lowliness " or " lowliness of mind " in Acts 20 : 19, R.V.; Eph. 4 : 2 ; Phil. 2 : 3. See HUMBLENESS OF MIND.

B. Adjective.

TAPEINOS (ταπεινός), low, lowly : see HUMBLE and LOW, B.

LOWRING (to be)

STUGNAZŌ (στυγνάζω), to have a gloomy, sombre appearance (akin to *stugnos*, sombre, gloomy, from a root *stug*—, to hate ; cp. *stugētos*, hateful, Tit. 3 : 3), is said of the human countenance, Mark 10 : 22, R.V., " his countenance fell " (A.V., " he was sad ") ; of the sky, Matt. 16 : 3, " lowring." See COUNTENANCE, Note (3).¶ In the Sept., Ezek. 27 : 35 ; 28 : 19 ; 32 : 10.¶

LUCRE (filthy)
A. Noun.

KERDOS (κέρδος), gain (cp. *kerdainō*, to gain, get gain), is translated " gain " in Phil. 1 : 21 and 3 : 7 ; " lucre " in Tit. 1 : 11 (preceded by *aischros*, filthy). See GAIN.¶

B. Adjective.

AISCHROKERDĒS (αἰσχροκερδής) denotes greedy of base gains (*aischros*, and A, as above), 1 Tim. 3 : 8, " greedy of filthy lucre ; " so the R.V. in Tit. 1 : 7, A.V., " given to) filthy lucre." In some mss. 1 Tim. 3 : 3.¶

AISCHROKERDŌS (αἰσχροκερδῶς) denotes ' from eagerness for base gain,' 1 Pet. 5 : 2, " for filthy lucre."¶

LUKEWARM

CHLIAROS (χλιαρός), tepid, warm (akin to *chliō*, to become warm, not found in the N.T. or Sept.), is used metaphorically in Rev. 3 : 16, of the state of the Laodicean church, which afforded no refreshment to the Lord, such as is ministered naturally by either cold or hot water.¶

LUMP

PHURAMA (φύραμα) denotes that which is mixed or kneaded (*phuraō*, to mix) ; hence, a lump, either of dough, Rom. 11 : 16 (cp. Numb. 15 : 21) ; 1 Cor. 5 : 6, 7 ; Gal. 5 : 9 (see under LEAVEN) ; of potter's clay, Rom. 9 : 21.¶

For LUNATIC see EPILEPTIC

LUST (Noun and Verb)

A. Nouns.

1. EPITHUMIA (ἐπιθυμία) denotes strong desire of any kind, the various kinds being frequently specified by some adjective (see below). The word is used of a good desire in Luke 22 : 15 ; Phil. 1 : 23, and 1 Thess. 2 : 17 only. Everywhere else it has a bad sense. In Rom. 6 : 12 the injunction against letting sin reign in our mortal body to obey the lust thereof, refers to those evil desires which are ready to express themselves in bodily activity. They are equally the lusts of the flesh, Rom. 13 : 14 ; Gal. 5 : 16, 24 ; Eph. 2 : 3 ; 2 Pet. 2 : 18 ; 1 John 2 : 16, a phrase which describes the emotions of the soul, the natural tendency towards things evil. Such lusts are not necessarily base and immoral, they may be refined in character, but are evil if inconsistent with the will of God.

Other descriptions besides those already mentioned are :—" of the mind," Eph. 2 : 3 ; " evil (desire)," Col. 3 : 5 ; " the passion of," 1 Thess. 4 : 5, R.V. ; " foolish and hurtful," 1 Tim. 6 : 9 ; " youthful," 2 Tim. 2 : 22 ; " divers," 2 Tim. 3 : 6 and Tit. 3 : 3 ; " their own," 2 Tim. 4 : 3 ; 2 Pet. 3 : 3 ; Jude 16 ; " worldly," Tit. 2 : 12 ; " his own," Jas. 1 : 14 ; " your former," 1 Pet. 1 : 14, R.V. ; " fleshly," 2 : 11 ; " of men," 4 : 2 ; " of defilement," 2 Pet. 2 : 10 ; " of the eyes," 1 John 2 : 16 ; of the world (" thereof "), ver. 17 ; " their own ungodly," Jude 18. In Rev. 18 : 14 " (the fruits) which thy soul lusted after " is, lit., ' of thy soul's lust.' See DESIRE, A, No. 1 (where associated words are noted).

2. OREXIS (ὄρεξις), lit., a reaching or stretching after (akin to *oregomai*, to stretch oneself out, reach after), a general term for every kind of desire, is used in Rom. 1 : 27, " lust."¶

3. HĒDONĒ (ἡδονή), pleasure, is translated " lusts," in the A.V. of Jas. 4 : 1, 3 (R.V., " pleasures "). See PLEASURE.

Note : In 1 Thess. 4 : 5, A.V., *pathos*, passion (R.V., " passion "), is translated " lust," which is the better rendering of the next word *epithumia*, rendered " concupiscence." *Pathos* is described by Trench as " the diseased condition out of which *epithumia* springs." In 1 Cor. 12 6 : *epithumētēs*, a luster after, is rendered to lust.

B. Verb.

EPITHUMEŌ (ἐπιθυμέω), akin to A, No. 1, has the same twofold meaning as the noun, namely (*a*) to desire, used of the Holy Spirit against the flesh, Gal. 5 : 17 (see below) ; of the Lord Jesus, Luke 22 : 15, " I have desired ; " of the holy angels, 1 Pet. 1 : 12 ; of good men, for good things, Matt. 13 : 17 ; 1 Tim. 3 : 1 ; Heb. 6 : 11 ; of men, for things without moral quality, Luke 15 : 16 ; 16 : 21 ; 17 : 22 ; Rev. 9 : 6 ; (*b*) of evil desires, in respect of which it is translated to lust in Matt. 5 : 28 ; 1 Cor. 10 : 6 ; Gal. 5 : 17 (1st part ; see below) ; Jas. 4 : 2 ; to covet, Acts 20 : 23 ; Rom. 7 : 7 ; 13 : 9. See COVET, DESIRE, B, No. 2.¶

Notes : (1) in Gal. 5 : 17, in the statement, " the flesh lusteth against the Spirit, and the Spirit against the flesh," the Holy Spirit is intended, as in the preceding verse. To walk by the Spirit involves the opposition here referred to. The verb " lusteth " is not repeated in the second part of the statement, but must in some way be supplied. Since in modern English the word " lust " is used exclusively in a bad sense, it is unsuitable as a translation of *epithumeō*, where the word is used in a good sense. As the rendering " desire " is used of the Lord Jesus (as mentioned above), it may be best so understood here in respect of the Holy Spirit.

(2) In James 4 : 5 the R.V. translates correctly in giving two questions, each of a rhetorical character, asked by way of remonstrance. The first draws attention to the fact that it is impossible for the Scripture to speak in vain ; the second to the impossibility that the Holy Spirit, whom God has caused to dwell in the believer, should " long (unto envying)," *epipotheō* (A.V., " lust "). Here again, not the human spirit is in view, but the Spirit of God ; cp. 1 Cor. 6 : 19. See LONG.

For LYING (falsehood) see LIE, and for LYING (in wait) see LIE IN WAIT.

M

MAD, MADNESS
A. Verbs.

1. MAINOMAI (μαίνομαι), to rage, be mad, is translated by the verb to be mad in John 10 : 20 ; Acts 12 : 15 ; 26 : 24, 25 ; 1 Cor. 14 : 23 ; see BESIDE ONESELF, No. 2.

2. EMMAINOMAI (ἐμμαίνομαι), an intensive form of No. 1, prefixed by *en*, in, implying fierce rage, to be furious against ; it is rendered " being exceedingly mad " in Acts 26 : 11 (cp. 9 : 1).¶

B. Nouns.

1. MANIA (μανία), akin to A, and transliterated into English, denotes frenzy, madness, Acts 26 : 24 " (thy much learning doth turn thee to) madness," R.V. ; A.V., " (doth make thee) mad."¶

2. ANOIA (ἄνοια), lit., without understanding (*a*, negative, *nous*, mind, understanding), denotes folly, 2 Tim. 3 : 9, and this finding its expression in violent rage, Luke 6 : 11. See FOLLY.¶

3. PARAPHRONIA (παραφρονία), madness (from *para*, contrary to, and *phrēn*, the mind), is used in 2 Pet. 2 : 16.¶ Cp. *paraphroneō*, 2 Cor. 11 : 23, ' I speak like one distraught.'¶

MADE (be)
A. Verbs.

1. GINOMAI (γίνομαι), to become, is sometimes translated by the Passive Voice of the verb to make, e.g., Matt. 9 : 16 ; John 1 : 3 (three times), 10 ; 8 : 33 ; Rom. 11 : 9 ; 1 Cor. 1 : 30 ; 3 : 13 ; 4 : 9, 13 ; Eph. 2 : 13 ; 3 : 7 ; Phil. 2 : 7 (but R.V. marg., " becoming ") ; Col. 1 : 23, 25 ; Heb. 5 : 5 ; 6 : 4 ; 7 : 12, 16, 21, 26 ; 11 : 3 ; Jas. 3 : 9 ; 1 Pet. 2 : 7. In many places the R.V. translates otherwise, and chiefly by the verb to become, e.g., Matt. 25 : 6, " there is ; " 27 : 24, " was arising ; " John 1 : 14, " became ; " John 2 : 9, " become ; " Rom. 1 : 3, " born ; " 2 : 25, " is become ; " 10 : 20, " became ; " Gal. 3 : 13, " having become ; " 4 : 4, " born " (twice) ; Heb. 3 : 14, " are become ; " 7 : 22, " hath . . . become."

2. KEIMAI (κεῖμαι), to lie, is sometimes used as the Passive Voice of *tithēmi*, to put ; it is translated " is (not) made " in 1 Tim. 1 : 9, of the Law, where a suitable rendering would be ' is (not) enacted.'

Notes : (1) In 2 Pet. 2 : 12, A.V., the verb *gennaō*, to beget, in the

Passive Voice, to be born, is translated " made " (R.V., " born "). (2) In Luke 3 : 5, A.V. (3rd statement), the future tense of *eimi*, to be, is translated " shall be made " (R.V., " shall become ") ; in the next sentence there is nothing in the original representing " *shall be* made ". (3) In Acts 16 : 13, A.V., the infinitive mood of *eimi*, to be, is translated " to be made " (of prayer), R.V., " there was (a place of prayer)." (4) For the translation of words in which the Eng. " made " forms a part of another verb, see under those words, e.g., CONFESSION, KNOWN, LIKE, LOW, PAYMENT, RICH, SUBJECT.

B. Noun.

POIĒMA (ποίημα), whence Eng., poem, denotes that which is made (from *poieō*, to do, make), Rom. 1 : 20, " the things that are made ; " Eph. 2 : 10, " (His) workmanship."¶

MAGISTRATE

1. STRATĒGOS (στρατηγός), besides its application to the captain of the Temple (see CAPTAIN), denotes a magistrate or governor, Acts 16 : 20, 22, 35, 36, 38. These were, in Latin terminology, the *duumviri* or *prætores*, so called in towns which were Roman colonies. They were attended by lictors or " serjeants," who executed their orders. In the circumstances of Acts 16 they exceeded their powers, in giving orders for Roman " citizens " to be scourged ; hence they became suppliants. See CAPTAIN.

2. ARCHŌN (ἄρχων), a ruler, denotes, in Luke 12 : 58, a local authority, a magistrate, acting in the capacity of one who received complaints, and possessing higher authority than the judge, to whom the magistrate remits the case. See CHIEF, PRINCE, RULER.

Notes : (1) In Luke 12 : 11, A.V., *archē*, a beginning, rule, principality, is translated " magistrates ; " the word, however, denotes rulers in general : hence the R.V., " rulers." (2) For the A.V. of Tit. 3 : 1, " to obey magistrates," see OBEY, B, No. 3.

MAGNIFICENCE

MEGALEIOTĒS (μεγαλειότης) denotes splendour, magnificence (from *megaleios*, magnificent, " mighty," Acts 2 : 11, *megas*, great), translated " magnificence " in Acts 19 : 27, of the splendour of the goddess Diana. In Luke 9 : 43, R.V. (A.V., " mighty power ") ; in 2 Pet. 1 : 16, " majesty." In the papyri writings it is frequent as a ceremonial title.¶

MAGNIFY

MEGALUNŌ (μεγαλύνω), to make great (*megas*), is translated to magnify in Luke 1 : 46 ; in ver. 58, R.V., " had magnified (His mercy)," A.V., " had shewed great (mercy) ; " Acts 5 : 13 ; 10 : 46 ; 19 : 17 ; 2 Cor. 10 : 15, R.V. (A.V., " we shall be enlarged "), i.e., by their faith in its practical effect he will be so assisted as to enlarge the scope of his Gospel ministry and carry its message to regions beyond them ; in Phil. 1 : 20, of the magnifying of Christ by him in his body, i.e., in all his activities and ways. In Matt. 23 : 5, it signifies to enlarge. See ENLARGE.¶

Note : In Rom. 11 : 13, A.V., the verb *doxazō*, to glorify, is translated " I magnify (my office)," R.V., " I glorify (my ministry)." See GLORIFY.

MAID, MAIDEN, MAIDSERVANT

1. PAIS (παῖς), a child, denotes a maid or maiden in Luke 8 : 51 and 54, R.V., " maiden " in both places. See CHILD, MANSERVANT, SERVANT, SON, YOUNG MAN.

2. PAIDISKĒ (παιδίσκη), a diminutive of No. 1, is translated " maid ", " maids," in the A.V. and R.V. in Mark 14 : 66, 69 ; Luke 22 : 56 ; in the R.V. (A.V., " damsel "), in Matt. 26 : 69 ; John 18 : 17 ; Acts 12 : 13 ; 16 : 16 ; in Luke 12 : 45, " maidservants " (A.V. " maidens ") ; in Gal. 4 : 22, 23, 30, 31, R.V., " handmaid " (A.V., " bondmaid " or " bond- woman "). See BONDMAID, DAMSEL.¶

3. KORASION (κοράσιον), a colloquial, familiar term, is translated " maid " in Matt. 9 : 24, 25, A.V. (R.V., " damsel "). See DAMSEL, No. 1.

MAIMED

1. ANAPĒROS, or ANAPEIROS (ἀνάπηρος), crippled, maimed (from *ana*, up, and *pēros*, disabled in a limb), is found in Luke 14 : 13, 21.¶

2. KULLOS (κυλλός) denotes crooked, crippled (akin to *kuliō*, to roll) : in Matt. 15 : 30, 31, translated " maimed " ; so in 18 : 8, A.V. (R.V., " halt ") and Mark 9 : 43 (A.V. and R.V.). See HALT.¶

For MAINSAIL see FORESAIL

MAINTAIN

PROISTĒMI (προΐστημι), to preside, rule, also means to maintain, Tit. 3 : 8 and 14, " to maintain (good works)," R.V. marg., " profess honest occupations " (A.V., marg. . . . " trades "). The usage of the phrase *kala erga* (good works) in the Pastoral Epistles is decisive for the rendering " good works," here. See OVER (to be), RULE.

MAJESTY

1. MEGALEIOTĒS (μεγαλειότης) : see MAGNIFICENCE.

2. MEGALŌSUNĒ (μεγαλωσύνη), from *megas*, great, denotes greatness, majesty ; it is used of God the Father, signifying His greatness and dignity, in Heb. 1 : 3, " the Majesty (on high)," and 8 : 1, " the Majesty (in the Heavens) ; " and in an ascription of praise acknowledging the attributes of God in Jude 25.¶

MAKE

1. POIEŌ (ποιέω), to do, to make, is used in the latter sense (a) of constructing or producing anything, of the creative acts of God, e.g.,

Matt. 19 : 4 (2nd part) ; Acts 17 : 24 ; of the acts of human beings, e.g.,
Matt. 17 : 4 ; Acts 9 : 39 ; (b) with nouns denoting a state or condition,
to be the author of, to cause, e.g., peace, Eph. 2 : 15 ; Jas. 3 : 18 ;
stumblingblocks, Rom. 16 : 17 ; (c) with nouns involving the idea of action
(or of something accomplished by action), so as to express the idea of the
verb more forcibly (the Middle Voice is commonly used in this respect,
suggesting the action as being of special interest to the doer) ; for the
Active Voice see, e.g., Mark 2 : 23, of making one's way, where the idea is
not that the disciples made a path through the standing corn, but simply
that they went, the phrase being equivalent to going, " (they began) as
they went (to pluck the ears) ; " other instances of the Active are Rev.
13 : 13, 14 ; 16 : 14 ; 19 : 20 ; for the Middle Voice (the ' dynamic ' or
' subjective ' Middle), see, e.g., John 14 : 23, " will make Our abode ; "
in Acts 20 : 24, " none of these things move me," lit., ' I make account of
none of these things ;' 25 : 17, " I made no delay," R.V. ; Rom. 15 : 26 ;
Eph. 4 : 16 ; Heb. 1 : 2 ; 2 Pet. 1 : 10 ; (d) to make ready or prepare,
e.g., a dinner, Luke 14 : 12 ; a supper, John 12 : 2 ; (e) to acquire, provide
a thing for oneself, Matt. 25 : 16 ; Luke 19 : 18 ; (f) to render or make
one or oneself anything, or cause a person or thing to become something,
e.g., Matt. 4 : 19 ; 12 : 16, " make (Him known) ; " John 5 : 11, 15, to
make whole ; 16 : 2, lit., ' they shall make (you put out of the synagogue) ;'
Eph. 2 : 14 ; Heb. 1 : 7 ; to change one thing into another, Matt. 21 : 13 ;
John 2 : 16 ; 4 : 46 ; 1 Cor. 6 : 15 ; (g) to constitute one anything, e.g.,
Acts 2 : 36 ; (h) to declare one or oneself anything, John 5 : 18, " making
(Himself equal with God) ; " 8 : 53 ; 10 : 33 ; 19 : 7, 12 ; 1 John 1 : 10 ;
5 : 10 ; (i) to make one do a thing, e.g., Luke 5 : 34 ; John 6 : 10 ; Rev.
3 : 9. See Do, No. 1, and other renderings there.

2. TITHEMI (τίθημι), to put, is used in the same way as No. 1 (f),
Matt. 22 : 44 ; Mark 12 : 36 ; Luke 20 : 43 ; Acts 2 : 35 ; 1 Cor. 9 : 18
(of making the Gospel without charge) ; Heb. 1 : 13 ; 10 : 13 ; 2 Pet.
2 : 6 ; as No. 1 (g), Acts 20 : 28 ; Rom. 4 : 17. See Appoint, No. 3.

3. DIATITHĒMI (διατίθημι), to covenant, is rendered " I will make "
(the noun diathēkē, a covenant, being expressed additionally), in the
Middle Voice, in Acts 3 : 25 ; Heb. 8 : 10 and 10 : 16, lit., ' I will covenant '
(see R.V., marg.). See Appoint, No. 4.

4. KATHISTĒMI (καθίστημι), to set down, set in order, appoint, is
used in the same way as No. 1 (g) in Acts 7 : 10, 27, 35 ; Heb. 7 : 28, A.V.
(R.V., " appointeth ") ; as No. 1 (f) in Rom. 5 : 19 (twice). See
Appoint, No. 2.

5. SUNISTĒMI (συνίστημι), to commend, prove, establish, is used in
Gal. 2 : 18, much as in No. 1 (g), " I make myself (a transgressor),"
i.e., ' I constitute (or prove) myself etc.' See Approve, No. 2.

6. DIDŌMI (δίδωμι), to give, is used in 2 Thess. 3 : 9 in much the same
sense as No. 1 (g), " to make (ourselves an ensample) ; " in Rev. 3 : 9

(1st part), R.V., " I will give," the sense is virtually the same as *poieō* in the 2nd part of the verse, see No. 1 (*i*).   See GIVE.

7. EPITELEŌ (ἐπιτελέω), to complete, is translated " to make " in Heb. 8 : 5 (1st part), R.V. marg., " complete " [in the 2nd part No. 1 is used in sense (*a*)].   See ACCOMPLISH.

8. SUNTELEŌ (συντελέω), to end, fulfil, is translated " I will make " in Heb. 8 : 8 :, said of the new covenant.   See END.

9. EIMI (εἰμί), to be, is translated " make " in Mark 12 : 42, lit., 'which is (a farthing).'

10. PROSPOIEŌ (προσποιέω), primarily, to claim, is used in the Middle Voice with the meaning to make as if, in Luke 24 : 28, of the Lord's action regarding the two on the way to Emmaus.¶   In the Sept., 1 Sam. 21 : 13 ; Job 19 : 14.¶

11. KATECHŌ (κατέχω), to hold fast (*kata*, down, intensive, *echō*, to hold), is used of making for a place, in Acts 27 : 40, R.V., " they made for " (A.V., " they made toward ").   See HOLD.

12. PROKATARTIZŌ (προκαταρτίζω), to render fit (fitted ; *artos*, a joint) beforehand, is used in 2 Cor. 9 : 5, " to make up beforehand."¶

Notes : (1) In Heb. 9 : 2, A.V., *kataskeuazō*, to prepare, is translated " made " (R.V., " prepared ").   (2) In Eph. 2 : 15, A.V., *ktizō*, to create, is translated " make " (R.V., " create ").   (3) In Acts 26 : 16, A.V., *procheirizō*, to determine, choose, is translated " make " (R.V., " appoint ").   (4) In Gal. 3 : 16, A.V., *erō*, to speak, is translated " were . . . made " (R.V., " were . . . spoken ").   (5) In Luke 14 : 31, A.V., *sumballō*, to meet with, in hostile sense, is rendered in combination with the phrase *eis polemon*, in war, " to make war ; " R.V., " to encounter (in war)."   (6) In Rom. 14 : 19 " the things which make for peace " is, lit., ' the things of peace.'   (7) In Acts 22 : 1 the verb " I make " represents no word in the original, lit., ' hear now my defence unto you.' (8) The Eng. verb to make forms with many other verbs a rendering of single Greek verbs which are given under the respective headings.   (9) For " made," Luke 19 : 16, R.V., see GAIN, *Note* (1).

MAKER

DĒMIOURGOS (δημιουργός), lit., one who works for the people (from *dēmos*, people, *ergon*, work ; an ancient inscription speaks of the magistrates of Tarsus as *dēmiourgoi* : the word was formerly used thus regarding several towns in Greece ; it is also found used of an artist), came to denote, in general usage, a builder or maker, and is used of God as the Maker of the Heavenly City, Heb. 11 : 10.   In that passage the first word of the two, *technitēs*, denotes an architect, designer, the second, *dēmiourgos*, is the actual Framer ; the city is the archetype of the earthly one which God chose for His earthly people.¶   Cp. *ktistēs*, creator.

For TENT-MAKER see Vol. IV, p. 118

MALE

ARSĒN or ARRĒN (ἄρσην) is translated " men " in Rom. 1 : 27 (three times) ; " man child " in Rev. 12 : 5 (ver. 13 in some mss.) ; " male " in Matt. 19 : 4 ; Mark 10 : 6 ; Luke 2 : 23 ; Gal. 3 : 28, " (there can be no) male (and female)," R.V., i.e., sex-distinction does not obtain in Christ ; sex is no barrier either to salvation or the development of Christian graces. See MAN.¶

MALEFACTOR

1. KAKOURGOS (κακοῦργος), an adjective, lit., evil-working (kakos, evil, ergon, work), is used as a noun, translated " malefactor(-s) " in Luke 23 : 32, 33, 39, and in the R.V. in 2 Tim. 2 : 9 (A.V., " evil doer "). See EVIL, B, Note (1).   In the Sept., Prov. 21 : 15.¶

2. KAKOPOIOS (κακοποιός), an adjective, lit., doing evil, is used in 1 Pet. 2 : 12, 14 ; 3 : 16 (in some mss.) ; 4 : 15.   See EVIL, B, No. 5.¶

MALICE, MALICIOUSNESS, MALICIOUS

KAKIA (κακία), badness in quality (the opposite of aretē, excellence), " the vicious character generally " (Lightfoot), is translated " malice " in 1 Cor. 5 : 8 ; 14 : 20 ; Eph. 4 : 31 ; Col. 3 : 8 ; Tit. 3 : 3 ; 1 Pet. 2 : 1, A.V. (R.V., " wickedness " ;   marg., " malice ") ;   " maliciousness " in Rom. 1 : 29 ; in 1 Pet. 2 : 16, A.V. (R.V., " wickedness ;" marg., " malice "). Elsewhere, Matt. 6 : 34 ; Acts 8 : 22 ; Jas. 1 : 21 (R.V. marg., " malice "). See EVIL, B, No. 1.¶

Note : In 2 John 10, A.V., ponēros, evil, wicked (see EVIL, A, No. 2), is translated " malicious " (R.V., " wicked ").

MALIGNITY

KAKOĒTHEIA (κακοήθεια), lit., bad manner or character (kakos, bad, ēthos, manner), hence, an evil disposition that tends to put the worst construction on everything, malice, malevolence, craftiness, occurs in Rom. 1 : 29, as the accompaniment of dolos, guile.¶

MAMMON

MAMŌNAS (μαμωνᾶς), a common Aramaic word for riches, akin to a Hebrew word signifying to be firm, stedfast (whence Amen), hence, that which is to be trusted ; Gesenius regards it as derived from a Heb. word signifying " treasure " (Gen. 43 : 23) ; it is personified in Matt. 6 : 24 ; Luke 16 : 9, 11, 13.¶

MAN (see also MEN)

1. ANTHRŌPOS (ἄνθρωπος) is used (a) generally, of a human being, male or female, without reference to sex or nationality, e.g., Matt. 4 : 4 ; 12 : 35 ; John 2 : 25 ; (b) in distinction from God, e.g., Matt. 19 : 6 ;

John 10 : 33 ; Gal. 1 : 11 ; Col. 3 : 23 ; (c) in distinction from animals etc., e.g., Luke 5 : 10 ; (d) sometimes, in the plural, of men and women, people, e.g., Matt. 5 : 13, 16 ; in Mark 11 : 2 and 1 Tim. 6 : 16, lit., ' no one of men ; ' (e) in some instances with a suggestion of human frailty and imperfection, e.g., 1 Cor. 2 : 5 ; Acts 14 : 15 (2nd part) ; (f) in the phrase translated " after man," " after the manner of men," " as a man " (A.V.), lit. ' according to (kata) man,' is used only by the Apostle Paul, of " (1) the practices of fallen humanity, 1 Cor. 3 : 3 ; (2) anything of human origin, Gal. 1 : 11 ; (3) the laws that govern the administration of justice among men, Rom. 3 : 5 ; (4) the standard generally accepted among men, Gal. 3 : 15 ; (5) an illustration not drawn from Scripture, 1 Cor. 9 : 8 ; (6) probably=' to use a figurative expression ' (see A.V., marg.), i.e., to speak evil of men with whom he had contended at Ephesus as ' beasts ' (cp. 1 Cor. 4 : 6), 1 Cor. 15 : 32 ; Lightfoot prefers ' from worldly motives ; ' but the other interpretation, No. (4), seems to make better sense. See also Rom. 6 : 19, where, however, the Greek is slightly different, anthrōpinos, ' pertaining to mankind ; ' " the meaning is as Nos. (5) and (6).*

(g) in the phrase " the inward man," the regenerate person's spiritual nature personified, the inner self of the believer, Rom. 7 : 22, as approving of the Law of God ; in Eph. 3 : 16, as the sphere of the renewing power of the Holy Spirit ; in 2 Cor. 4 : 16 (where anthrōpos is not repeated), in contrast to " the outward man," the physical frame, the man as cognizable by the senses ; the " inward " man is identical with " the hidden man of the heart," 1 Pet. 3 : 4.

(h) in the expressions " the old man," " the new man," which are confined to Paul's Epistles, the former standing for the unregenerate nature personified as the former self of a believer, which, having been crucified with Christ, Rom. 6 : 6, is to be apprehended practically as such, and to be " put off," Eph. 4 : 22 ; Col. 3 : 9, being the source and seat of sin ; the latter, " the new man," standing for the new nature personified as the believer's regenerate self, a nature " created in righteousness and holiness of truth," Eph. 4 : 24, and having been " put on " at regeneration, Col. 3 : 10 ; being " renewed after the image of Him that created him," it is to be " put on " in practical apprehension of these facts.

(i) often joined with another noun, e.g., Matt. 11 : 19, lit., ' a man, a glutton ; ' 13 : 52, lit., ' a man, a householder ; ' 18 : 23, " a certain king," lit., ' a man, a king.'

(j) as equivalent simply to ' a person,' or ' one,' whether man or woman, e.g., Acts 19 : 16 ; Rom. 3 : 28 ; Gal. 2 : 16 ; Jas. 1 : 19 ; 2 : 24 ; 3 : 8 (like the pronoun tis, someone ; tis is rendered " man " in Matt. 8 : 28) ; or, again (as tis sometimes signifies), " a man," e.g., Matt. 17 : 14 ; Luke 13 : 19.

---

* From Notes on Galatians by Hogg and Vine, p. 139.

(*k*) definitely, with the article, of some particular person, Matt. 12 : 13 ; Mark 3 : 3, 5 ; or with the demonstrative pronoun and the article, e.g., Matt. 12 : 45 ; Luke 14 : 30. For the phrase " the Son of man " see Son of Man. For " the man of sin," 2 Thess. 2 : 3, see Iniquity, No. 1

(*l*) in the phrase " the man of God," 2 Tim. 3 : 17, not used as an official designation, nor denoting a special class of believers, it specifies what every believer should be, namely, a person whose life and conduct represent the mind of God and fulfil His will ; so in 1 Tim. 6 : 11, " O man of God." Some regard this in the O.T. sense as of a prophet acting in a distinctive character, possessed of Divine authority ; but the context is of such a general character as to confirm the more extended designation here.

Notes : (1) In Gal. 3 : 28, the R.V. adds the italicised word " man " (" ye all are one *man* in Christ Jesus "), in accordance with Eph. 2 : 15, which speaks of Jew and Gentile as becoming " one new man " in Christ. The figure is closely analogous to that of " the body." In these two passages " one " is masculine, i.e., ' one person ;' in John 10 : 30 ; 11 : 52 ; 17 : 21, 22, 23, " one " is neuter, ' one thing,' as in 1 Cor. 3 : 8 ; 11 : 5. The first two, in Gal. 3 and Eph. 2, express vital union, present and eternal ; in John 17 the union is moral, a process in course of accomplishment. (2) For *philanthrōpia*, Tit. 3 : 4, " (His) love toward man," see Kind, C, No. 2.

(3) In Rev. 9 : 20, the R.V. translates the genitive plural of *anthrōpos* with the article, " mankind " (A.V., " the men ") ; it might have been rendered ' (the rest) of men.'

2. ANĒR (ἀνήρ) is never used of the female sex ; it stands (*a*) in distinction from a woman, Acts 8 : 12 ; 1 Tim. 2 : 12 ; as a husband, Matt. 1 : 16 ; John 4 : 16 ; Rom. 7 : 2 ; Tit. 1 : 6 ; (*b*) as distinct from a boy or infant, 1 Cor. 13 : 11 ; metaphorically in Eph. 4 : 13 ; (*c*) in conjunction with an adjective or noun, e.g., Luke 5 : 8, lit., ' a man, a sinner ;' 24 : 19, lit., ' a man, a prophet ;' often in terms of address, e.g., Acts 1 : 16 ; 13 : 15, 26 ; 15 : 7, 13, lit., ' men, brethren ;' with gentilic or local names (virtually a title of honour), e.g., Acts 2 : 14 ; 22 : 3, lit., ' Judæan men,' ' a Judæan man ;' 3 : 12 ; 5 : 35, lit., ' Israelite men ;' 17 : 22, ' Athenian men ;' 19 : 35, lit., ' Ephesian men ;' in Acts 14 : 15 it is used in addressing a company of men, without any descriptive term. In this verse, however, the distinction between *anēr* and *anthrōpos* (2nd part) is noticeable ; the use of the latter comes under No. 1 (*e*) ; (*d*) in general, a man, a male person (used like the pronoun *tis*, No. 3), " a man " (i.e., a certain man), e.g., Luke 8 : 41 ; in the plural, Acts 6 : 11.

3. TIS (τις), some one, a certain one, is rendered " a man," a certain man, e.g., in Matt. 22 : 24 ; Mark 8 : 4, A.V. (R.V., " one ") ; 12 : 19 ; John 3 : 3, 5 ; 6 : 50 ; 14 : 23 ; 15 : 6, 13 ; Acts 13 : 41, A.V. (R.V., ' one ') ;

1 Cor. 4 : 2 ; 1 Tim. 1 : 8 ; 2 Tim. 2 : 5, 21 ; Jas. 2 : 14, 18 ; 1 Pet. 2 : 19 ; 1 John 4 : 20.

4. ARRĒN and ARSĒN (ἄρσην) : see MALE.

5. TELEIOS (τέλειος), perfect, is translated " men " in 1 Cor. 14 : 20, R.V. marg., " of full age," A.V. marg., " perfect, or, of a ripe age." See PERFECT.

Note : In many cases the word " man " is combined with an adjective to translate one word in the original. These will be found under various other headings.

For MAN-CHILD see MALE

MAN'S, OF MAN, MANKIND (see also MEN)

ANTHRŌPINOS (ἀνθρώπινος), human, belonging to man (from *anthrōpos*, see MAN, No. 1), is used (a) of man's wisdom, in 1 Cor. 2 : 13 (some mss. have it in ver. 4, where indeed it is implied ; see, however, the R.V.) ; (b) of " man's judgement," 1 Cor. 4 : 3 (marg., " day : " see DAY) ; (c) of " mankind," Jas. 3 : 7, lit., " the human nature," R.V. marg. (A.V. marg., " nature of man ") ; (d) of human ordinance, 1 Pet. 2 : 13 ; Moulton and Milligan show from the papyri how strongly anti-thetic to the Divine the use of the word is in this respect ; (e) of tempta-tion, 1 Cor. 10 : 13, R.V., " such as man can bear " (A.V., " such as is common to man "), i.e., such as must and does come to men ; (f) of men's hands, Acts 17 : 25 ; (g) in the phrase " after the manner of men," Rom. 6 : 19.¶

Notes : (1) In Luke 16 : 12, A.V., *allotrios*, belonging to another (*allos*, another), here used as a pronoun, is translated " another man's " (R.V., " another's ") ; so, as an adjective, in Rom. 14 : 4 ; 15 : 20 ; 2 Cor. 10 : 15, 16 (in this last the R.V. omits " man "). (2) In Acts 27 : 22 there is no word representing " *man's* ; " the R.V. has " of life." (3) In Rom. 5 : 17, the R.V. rightly has " the trespass of the one," for A.V., " one man's offence."

MANGER

PHATNĒ (φάτνη), a manger, Luke 2 : 7, 12, 16, also denotes a stall, 13 : 15.¶ So in the Sept., the word denoted not only a manger but, by metonymy, the stall or " crib " (Prov. 14 : 4) containing the manger.

MANIFEST (Adjective and Verb)
A. Adjectives.

1. EMPHANĒS (ἐμφανής), manifest (akin to *emphainō*, to show in, to exhibit ; *en*, in, *phainō*, to cause to shine), is used (a) literally in Acts 10 : 40, R.V. " (gave Him to be made) manifest ; " (b) metaphorically in Rom. 10 : 20, " (I was made) manifest ". See OPENLY.¶ Cp. B, No. 2.

2. PHANEROS (φανερός), open to sight, visible, manifest (the root

phan—, signifying shining, exists also in No. 1), is translated " manifest " in Luke 8 : 17; Acts 4 : 16; 7 : 13, R.V. (A.V., "known "); Rom. 1 : 19; 1 Cor. 3 : 13; 11 : 19; 14 : 25; Gal. 5 : 19; Phil. 1 : 13; 1 Tim. 4 : 15 (A.V., "appear "); 1 John 3 : 10. See Appear, B, Note (2), Know, B, No. 2, Openly, Outwardly.

3. APHANĒS (ἀφανής) denotes unseen, hidden, Heb. 4 : 13, "not manifest " (*a*, negative, and *phainō*).¶ In the Sept., Neh. 4 : 8; Job 24 : 20.¶

Notes : (1) In 1 Cor. 15 : 27, A.V. *dēlos*, evident, is translated "manifest " (R.V., "evident "). (2) So with *ekdēlos*, 2 Tim. 3 : 9, an intensive form of *dēlos*, signifying quite evident.¶ (3) In 1 Tim. 5 : 25, A.V., *prodēlos*, evident beforehand, clearly evident, is translated "manifest beforehand " (R.V., "evident "); see Evident. (4) For "manifest token," see Token.

B. Verbs.

1. PHANEROŌ (φανερόω), to make visible, clear, manifest, known (akin to A, No. 2), is used especially in the writings of the Apostles John and Paul), occurring 9 times in the Gospel, 9 times in 1 John, 2 in Rev.; in the Pauline Epistles (including Heb.) 24 times; in the other Gospels, only in Mark, 3 times; elsewhere in 1 Pet. 1 : 20; 5 : 4.

The true meaning is to uncover, lay bare, reveal. The following are variations in the rendering, which should be noted : Mark 16 : 12, 14 (R.V., "was manifested," A.V., "appeared "); John 21 : 1 (R.V., "manifested," A.V., "shewed ; " cp. ver. 14); Rom. 1 : 19 (R.V., "manifested," A.V., "hath shewed "); 2 Cor. 3 : 3 (R.V., "being made manifest," A.V., "are manifestly declared "); 2 Cor. 5 : 10; 7 : 12 and Rev. 3 : 18 (R.V., "be made manifest," A.V., "appear "); 2 Cor. 11 : 6 (R.V., "we have made it manifest," A.V., "we have been throughly made manifest "); Col. 1 : 26 (R.V., "hath it been manifested," A.V., "is made manifest "); 3 : 4 (R.V., "be manifested," A.V., "appear ; " so 1 Pet. 5 : 4); 1 Tim. 3 : 16 (R.V., "was manifested," A.V., "was manifest "); 2 Tim. 1 : 10 (R.V., "hath . . . been manifested," A.V., "is . . . made manifest ; " cp. Rom. 16 : 26; 2 Cor. 4 : 10, 11; 1 Pet. 1 : 20); Heb. 9 : 26 (R.V., "hath He been manifested," A.V., "hath He appeared "); 1 John 2 : 28; 3 : 2 (R.V., "is . . . made manifest," A.V., "doth appear "). See Appear, A, No. 4.

2. EMPHANIZŌ (ἐμφανίζω), akin to A, No. 1, is translated to manifest, make manifest, in John 14 : 21, 22; Heb. 11 : 14, R.V.; see Appear, A, No. 5.

Note : For the adverb *phanerōs*, manifestly, see Evidently, Openly.

MANIFESTATION

PHANERŌSIS (φανέρωσις), a manifestation (akin to *phaneros* and *phaneroō* ; see Manifest), occurs in 1 Cor. 12 : 7 and 2 Cor. 4 : 2.¶

Note : In Rom. 8 : 19, A.V., *apokalupsis*, an uncovering, laying bare, revealing, revelation, is translated " manifestation " (R.V., " revealing "). See REVELATION.

MANIFOLD

1. POIKILOS (ποικίλος), varied, is translated "manifold" in 1 Pet. 1 : 6 ; 4 : 10 and in Jas. 1 : 2, R.V. (A.V., " divers "). See DIVERS, A, No. 2.

2. POLUPOIKILOS (πολυποίκιλος), much varied (polus, much, and No. 1), is said of the wisdom of God, in Eph. 3 : 10.¶

3. POLLAPLASIŌN (πολλαπλασίων), many times more (from polus, much), occurs in Luke 18 : 30, " manifold more," and in many ancient authorities in Matt. 19 : 29 (R.V., marg. ; some editions in text) ; A.V. and R.V. text, " a hundredfold," translating hekatontaplasiona.¶

For MANKIND see MAN, No. 1, Note (3), MAN'S (c), ABUSERS

MANNA

MANNA (μάννα), the supernaturally provided food for Israel during their wilderness journey (for details see Ex. 16 and Numb. 11). The Hebrew equivalent is given in Ex. 16 : 15, R.V. marg., " man hu." The translations are, R.V., " what is it ? " ; A.V. and R.V. marg., " it is manna." It is described in Ps. 78 : 24, 25 as " the corn of heaven " and " the bread of the mighty," R.V. text and A.V. marg. (" angels' food," A.V. text), and in 1 Cor. 10 : 3, as " spiritual meat." The vessel appointed to contain it as a perpetual memorial, was of gold, Heb. 9 : 4, with Ex. 16 : 33. The Lord speaks of it as being typical of Himself, the true Bread from Heaven, imparting eternal life and sustenance to those who by faith partake spiritually of Him, John 6 : 31–35. The " hidden manna " is promised as one of the rewards of the overcomer, Rev. 2 : 17 ; it is thus suggestive of the moral excellence of Christ in His life on earth, hid from the eyes of men, by whom He was " despised and rejected ; " the path of the overcomer is a reflex of His life.

None of the natural substances called manna is to be identified with that which God provided for Israel.¶

MANNER
A. Nouns.

1. ETHOS (ἔθος), a habit, custom (akin to the verb ethō, to be accustomed), is always translated " custom " in the R.V. (" manner " in the A.V. of John 19 : 40 ; Acts 15 : 1 ; 25 : 16 ; Heb. 10 : 25). See CUSTOM, No. 1.

2. ĒTHOS (ἦθος), primarily a haunt, abode, then, a custom, manner, occurs in the plural in 1 Cor. 15 : 33, i.e., ethical conduct, morals.¶

3. TROPOS (τρόπος), a turning, fashion, manner, character, way of life, is translated " manner " in Acts 1 : 11, with reference to the Lord's

Ascension and Return ; in Jude 7, of the similarity of the evil of those mentioned in vv. 6 and 7. See CONVERSATION, MEANS, WAY.

Note : In Acts 15 : 11, the phrase *kath' hon tropon,* ' according to what manner,' is translated " in like manner as," R.V. (A.V., " even as ").

4. TUPOS (τύπος), a mark or impress, is translated " manner " in Acts 23 : 25. See FORM, No. 3.

5. AKRIBEIA (ἀκρίβεια), exactness, precision (akin to *akribēs,* exact, careful ; see *akriboō,* to enquire carefully, and *akribōs,* carefully), occurs in Acts 22 : 3, R.V., " strict manner " (A.V., " perfect manner ").¶

Notes : (1) The verb *ethō,* to be accustomed, has a perfect tense *eiōtha,* with a present meaning, the neuter of the participle of which, *eiōthos,* used with the article, signifies " custom," Luke 4 : 16. In Acts 17 : 2 the A.V. translates it " manner " (R.V., " custom "). See CUSTOM, WONT. (2) For *agōgē,* in 2 Tim. 3 : 10, A.V., " manner of life " (R.V., " conduct "), see CONDUCT. (3) For *anastrophē,* " manner of life," see LIFE, A, No. 6 ; cp. LIVE, No. 5. *Agōge* suggests conduct according to one's leading ; *anastrophē,* conduct as one goes about and mingles with others.

B. Adjectives and Pronouns.

1. POTAPOS (ποταπός), primarily, from what country, then, of what sort, is rendered " what manner of man," Matt. 8 : 27 : so 2 Pet. 3 : 11 ; Mark 13 : 1 (twice) ; Luke 1 : 29 ; 7 : 39 ; 1 John 3 : 1.¶

2. POIOS (ποῖος), of what sort, is translated " by what manner of (death) " in John 21 : 19, R.V., (A.V., " by what ") ; in Acts 7 : 49, " what manner of (house) ; " Rom. 3 : 27, " what manner of law ; " 1 Cor. 15 : 35, " what manner of body."

3. HOIOS (οἷος), a relative pronoun, signifying what sort of or manner of, is translated by the latter phrase in 1 Thess. 1 : 5 ; some mss. have it in Luke 9 : 55, as in A.V. ; the R.V. follows those in which it is absent.

4. HOPOIOS (ὁποῖος) is rendered " what manner of " in 1 Thess. 1 : 9 ; Jas. 1:24. See SORT, A.

C. Adverbs.

1. POLUTROPOS (πολυτρόπως), lit., ' much turning ' (*polus,* much, *tropos,* a turning), ' in many ways (or manners),' is rendered " in divers manners " in Heb. 1 : 1.¶

2. HOUTOS or HOUTO (οὕτως), thus, in this way, is rendered " after this manner " in Matt. 6 : 9 ; 1 Pet. 3 : 5 ; Rev. 11 : 5. See SO, THUS.

3. HŌSAUTOS (ὡσαύτως), a strengthened form of *hōs,* thus, signifies just so, likewise, in like manner e.g., 1 Tim. 2 : 9 ; in the following the R.V. has " in like manner," for A.V., " likewise ; " Mark 14 : 31 ; Luke 22 : 20 ; Rom. 8 : 26 ; 1 Tim. 3 : 8 ; 5 : 25 ; in Luke 20 : 31 the R.V. has " likewise," A.V., " in like manner." See LIKEWISE.

4. HOMOIOS (ὁμοίως), akin to the adjective *homoios,* like, signifies in like manner, equally ; in the following the R.V. has " in like manner " for A.V., " likewise ; " Matt. 27 : 41 ; Mark 4 : 16 ; 15 : 31 ; Luke 10 : 32 ; 13 : 3 ; 16 : 25 ; John 5 : 19 ; (Heb. 9 : 21 ;) Jas. 2 : 25 ; 1 Pet. 3 : 1, 7 ;

Rev. 8 : 12 ; in Rev. 2 : 15 the A.V. " which thing I hate " translates a variant reading (*ho misō*). See LIKEWISE, SO.

5. PŌS (πῶς), how, is translated " after what manner " in Acts 20 : 18. See MEANS.

Note : For *paraplēsiōs*, Heb. 2 : 14, R.V., see LIKEWISE, No. 4.

D. Preposition.

KATA (κατά), according to, is translated " after the manner " in John 2 : 6, i.e., ' in accordance with ; ' in Rom. 3 : 5 ; 1 Cor. 3 : 3 ; 9 : 8, R.V., " after the manner of " (A.V., " as ").

E. Verb.

TROPOPHOREŌ (τροποφορέω), to bear another's manners, is translated " suffered He (their) manners " in Acts 13 : 18. For this and the alternative reading see BEAR, No. 8.¶

Notes : (1) In the following the phrase *kata tauta*, or *kata ta auta*, lit., ' according to the same things,' is translated " in (the) like (R.V., same) manner," Luke 6 : 23 ; ver. 26, R.V. (A.V., " so ") ; 17 : 30, R.V., " after the same manner " (A.V., " even thus "). (2) In Phil. 2 : 18 the phrase *to . . . auto*, lit., ' the same (thing),' used adverbially, is translated " in the same manner," R.V. (A.V., " for the same cause "). (3) In Mark 13 : 29, A.V., *kai*, also (so R.V.), is translated " in like manner." (4) In Acts 15 : 23 some mss. have the demonstrative pronoun *tode* used adverbially and rendered " after this manner " (A.V.). The R.V., adhering to the mss. in which it is absent, inserts the word " *thus* " in italics. (5) In Acts 25 : 20 a phrase lit. rendered ' (as to) the enquiry concerning these things ' (or according to some mss. ' this person,' whether " Jesus " or " Paul," ver. 19), is translated " of such manner of questions," A.V. (R.V., " how to inquire concerning these things "). (6) In Luke 1 : 66, A.V., *ara*, " then " (so R.V.), is rendered freely " (what) manner." (7) In Luke 24 : 17, A.V., the pronoun *tis*, who, what, in the plural (R.V., " what ") is translated " what manner of ; " similarly, in the singular in Mark 4 : 41 ; Luke 8 : 25 (R.V., " who ") ; John 7 : 36. (8) In Gal. 2 : 14, A.V., the adverb *ethnikōs*, in Gentile fashion (*ethnos*, a nation : in the plural, Gentiles or nations), is translated " after the manner of Gentiles " (R.V., " as do . : "). (9) In Matt. 12 : 31 ; Luke 11 : 42 ; Rev. 18 : 12, A.V., *pas*, " every " (so R.V.), is translated " all manner."

MANSERVANT

PAIS (παῖς), a child, boy, youth, also means a servant, attendant ; in Luke 12 : 45 it is used in the plural " menservants," in contrast to *paidiskē*, a maidservant. See CHILD, No. 4.

MANSIONS

MONĒ (μονή), primarily a staying, abiding (akin to *menō*, to abide), denotes an abode (Eng., manor, manse, etc.), translated " mansions " in John 14 : 2 ; " abode " in ver. 23. There is nothing in the word to indicate separate compartments in Heaven; neither does it suggest temporary resting-places on the road.¶

MANSLAYERS

ANDROPHONOS (ἀνδροφόνος), from *anēr*, a man, and *phoneus*, a murderer, occurs in the plural in 1 Tim. 1 : 9.¶

MANTLE

PERIBOLAION (περιβόλαιον), lit., that which is thrown around, is translated "mantle" in Heb. 1 : 12, R.V. (A.V., "vesture.") See COVERING, VEIL.

MANY

1. POLUS (πολύς), much, many, great, is used especially of number when its significance is "many," e.g., Matt. 8 : 30; 9 : 10; 13 : 17; so the R.V. of Matt. 12 : 15, where some mss. follow the word by *ochloi*, multitudes; 1 Cor. 12 : 12; Rev. 1 : 15; it is more frequently used as a noun, "many (persons)," e.g., Matt. 3 : 7; 7 : 22; 22 : 14; with the article, "the many," e.g., Matt. 24 : 12, R.V.; Mark 9 : 26, R.V., "the more part" (A.V. "many"); Rom. 5 : 15, 19 (twice), R.V.; 12 : 5; 1 Cor. 10 : 17; ver. 33, R.V.; so 2 Cor. 2 : 17; in 1 Cor. 11 : 30, R.V., "not a few." In Luke 12 : 47 it is translated "many stripes," the noun being understood. See GREAT, MUCH.

Notes: (1) In Luke 23 : 8 some mss. have *polla*, "many things," though it is absent from the most authentic; see the R.V. (2) In Mark 6 : 20 the R.V., following the mss. which have *aporeō*, to be perplexed, translates *polla* by "much;" some mss. have *poieō*, to do; hence A.V., "did many things." (3) In Gal. 4 : 27 the plural of *polus*, with *mallon*, more, is translated "more" in the R.V. (A.V., "many more"), lit., 'many are the children of the desolate more than of her that etc.,' the phrase implying that both should have many children, but the desolate more than the other. (4) In John 7 : 40 there is no word in the original representing "*some*" or "*many*."

2. PLEIŌN (πλείων), more, greater, the comparative of No. 1, is translated "many" in Acts 2 : 40; 13 : 31; 21 : 10; 24 : 17; 25 : 14; 27 : 20; 28 : 23 (A.V.; R.V., "in great number"); with the article, "most," R.V. (or rather, 'the more part'), Acts 19 : 32; 1 Cor. 10 : 5, and Phil. 1 : 14 (for A.V., "many," an important change); in 2 Cor. 2 : 6, R.V., "the many" (marg., "the more"); so 4 : 15; in 9 : 2, "very many" (marg., "the more part"); in Heb. 7 : 23, R.V., "many in number" (A.V., "many"). See GREATER, MORE.

3. HIKANOS (ἱκανός), sufficient, when used of number sometimes signifies many, suggesting a sufficient number, (a) with nouns, Luke 8 : 32; 23 : 9; Acts 9 : 23, 43; 20 : 8; 27 : 7; (b) absolutely, some noun being

understood, e.g., Acts 12 : 12 ; 14 : 21 ; 19 : 19 ; 1 Cor. 11 : 30. See ABLE, C, No. 2.

4. HOSOS (ὅσος), how much, how many, how great, as much as, as many as, is translated " as many as," e.g., in Matt. 14 : 36 ; Mark 3 : 10 ; Luke 9 : 5, R.V. (A.V., " whosoever ") ; Acts 2 : 39 ; in 9 : 16, R.V., " how many things " (A.V., " how great things ") ; in Rom. 6 : 3 the R.V. renders it by " all we who " (A.V., " so many of us as "), a necessary alteration, not singling out some believers from others, as if some were not baptized, but implying what was recognized as true of all (see Acts 18 : 8) ; in 2 Cor. 1 : 20, R.V., " how many soever be " (A.V., " all "). See ALL, C.

5. POSOS (πόσος), how much, how great, how many, has the last meaning in Matt. 15 : 34 ; 16 : 9, 10 ; 27 : 13 (" how many things ") ; Mark 6 : 38 ; 8 : 5, 19, 20 ; 15 : 4 (" how many things ") ; Luke 15 : 17 ; Acts 21 : 20. See GREAT.

6. TOSOUTOS (τοσοῦτος), so great, so much, so many, (a) qualifying a noun, is rendered " these many (years) " in Luke 15 : 29 ; " so many," John 12 : 37 ; 1 Cor. 14 : 10 ; (b) without a noun, John 6 : 9 ; 21 : 11 ; Gal. 3 : 4, " so many things." See GREAT.

Note : In John 17 : 2, A.V., the neuter of *pas*, all, followed by the neuter of the relative pronoun ' what,' and then by the plural of the personal pronoun, is translated " to as many as " (R.V., " whatsoever . . . to them ").

MARAN-ATHA

MARAN-ATHA (μαρὰν ἀθά), an expression used in 1 Cor. 16 : 22, is the Greek spelling for two Aramaic words, formerly supposed by some to be an imprecatory utterance or " a curse reinforced by a prayer," an idea contrary to the intimations conveyed by its use in early Christian documents, e.g., " The Teaching of the Apostles," a document of the beginning of the 2nd cent., and in the " Apostolic Constitutions " (vii. 26), where it is used as follows : " Gather us all together into Thy Kingdom which Thou hast prepared. Maranatha, Hosanna to the Son of David ; blessed is He that cometh etc."

The first part, ending in ' n,' signifies ' Lord ;' as to the second part, the " Fathers " regarded it as a past tense, " has come." Modern expositors take it as equivalent to a present, " cometh," or future, " will come." Certain Aramaic scholars regard the last part as consisting of ' tha,' and regard the phrase as an ejaculation, ' Our Lord, come,' or ' O Lord, come.' The character of the context, however, indicates that the Apostle is making a statement rather than expressing a desire or uttering a prayer.

As to the reason why it was used, most probably it was a current ejaculation among early Christians, as embodying the consummation of their desires.

" At first the title *Marana* or *Maran*, used in speaking to and of

Christ was no more than the respectful designation of the Teacher on the part of the disciples." After His resurrection they used the title of or to Him as applied to God, " but it must here be remembered that the Aramaic-speaking Jews did not, save exceptionally, designate God as ' Lord ; ' so that in the ' Hebraist ' section of the Jewish Christians the expression ' our Lord ' (*Marana*) was used in reference to Christ only " (Dalman, *The Words of Jesus*).¶

MARBLE

MARMAROS (μάρμαρος) primarily denoted any glistering stone (from *maraino*, to glisten) ; hence, marble, Rev. 18 : 12.¶

MARINERS

NAUTĒS (ναύτης), a seaman, mariner, sailor (from *naus*, a ship, Eng., nautical), is translated " sailors " in Acts 27 : 27, 30, R.V. (A.V., " shipmen ") ; in Rev. 18 : 17, R.V., " mariners " (A.V., " sailors ").¶

MARK (Noun)

1. CHARAGMA (χάραγμα) denotes a stamp, impress, translated " mark " in Rev. 13 : 16, 17, etc. See GRAVEN.

2. STIGMA (στίγμα) denotes a tattooed mark or a mark burnt in, a brand (akin to *stizo*, to prick), translated " marks " in Gal. 6 : 17.¶ " It is probable that the Apostle refers to the physical sufferings he had endured since he began to proclaim Jesus as Messiah and Lord [e.g., at Lystra and Philippi]. It is probable, too, that this reference to his scars was intended to set off the insistence of the Judaizers upon a body-mark which cost them nothing. Over against the circumcision they demanded as a proof of obedience to the law he set the indelible tokens, sustained in his own body, of his loyalty to the Lord Jesus. As to the origin of the figure, it was indeed customary for a master to brand his slaves, but this language does not suggest that the Apostle had been branded by His Master. Soldiers and criminals also were branded on occasion ; but to neither of these is the case of Paul as here described analogous. The religious devotee branded himself with the peculiar mark of the god whose cult he affected ; so was Paul branded with the marks of his devotion to the Lord Jesus. It is true such markings were forbidden by the law, Lev. 19 : 28, but then Paul had not inflicted these on himself.

" The marks of Jesus cannot be taken to be the marks which the Lord bears in His body in consequence of the Crucifixion ; they were different in character."*

3. SKOPOS (σκοπός), primarily a watcher, watchman (as in the Sept., e.g., Ezek. 3 : 17), then, a mark on which to fix the eye (akin to *skopeo*, to look at), is used metaphorically in Phil. 3 : 14, of an aim or object, R.V., " goal." See GOAL.¶

---

* From Notes on Galatians by Hogg and Vine, p. 344.

MARK (Verb)

1. EPECHŌ (ἐπέχω), lit., to hold upon (*epi*, upon, *echō*, to hold), signifies (like *parechō*) to hold out, Phil. 2 : 16, of the word of life ; then, to hold one's mind towards, to observe, translated "marked" in Luke 14 : 7, of the Lord's observance of those who chose the chief seats. See HEED, HOLD, STAY.

2. SKOPEŌ (σκοπέω), to look at, behold, watch, contemplate, (akin to *skopos*, a mark, see Noun above), is used metaphorically of looking to, and translated "mark" in Rom. 16 : 17, of a warning against those who cause divisions, and in Phil. 3 : 17, of observing those who walked after the example of the Apostle and his fellow-workers, so as to follow their ways. See HEED, Note (1), LOOK.

MARKET, MARKET-PLACE

AGORA (ἀγορά), primarily an assembly, or, in general, an open space in a town (akin to *ageirō*, to bring together), became applied, according to papyri evidences, to a variety of things, e.g., a judicial assembly, a market, or even supplies, provisions (Moulton and Milligan, Vocab.). In the N.T. it denotes a place of assembly, a public-place or forum, a market-place. A variety of circumstances, connected with it as a public gathering-place, is mentioned, e.g., business dealings such as the hiring of labourers, Matt. 20 : 3; the buying and selling of goods, Mark 7 : 4 (involving risk of pollution) ; the games of children, Matt. 11 : 16 ; Luke 7 : 32 ; exchange of greetings, Matt. 23 : 7 ; Mark 12 : 38 ; Luke 11 : 43 ; 20 : 46 ; the holding of trials, Acts 16 : 19 ; public discussions, Acts 17 : 17. Mark 6 : 56 records the bringing of the sick there. The word always carries with it the idea of publicity, in contrast to private circumstances.

The R.V. always translates it "market-place" or in the plural. The A.V. sometimes changes the rendering to "markets" and translates it "streets" in Mark 6 : 56. See STREET.¶

MARRED

Note : In Mark 2 : 22, *apollumi*, to destroy, perish, is found in the most authentic mss. as applying both to the wine and the wine skins, R.V., "perisheth ; " the A.V. follows the mss. which tell of the wine being "spilled" (*ekcheō*, to pour out), and the skins (A.V., "bottles") being "marred." See DESTROY, No. 1.

MARRIAGE (give in), MARRY
A. Noun.

GAMOS (γάμος), a marriage, wedding, or wedding feast, is used to denote (*a*) the ceremony and its proceedings, including the marriage feast, John 2 : 1, 2 ; of the marriage ceremony only, figuratively, Rev. 19 : 7, as distinct from the marriage feast (ver. 9) ; (*b*) the marriage feast, R.V.

in Matt. 22 : 2, 3, 4, 9 ; in ver. 8, 10, "wedding ; " in 25 : 10, R.V., "marriage feast ; " so Luke 12 : 36 ; 14 : 8 ; in Matt. 22 : 11, 12, the "wedding garment " is, lit., 'a garment of a wedding.' In Rev. 19, where, under the figure of a marriage, the union of Christ, as the Lamb of God, with His Heavenly Bride is so described, the marriage itself takes place in Heaven during the Parousia, ver. 7 (the aorist or point tense indicating an accomplished fact ; the Bride is called " His wife ") ; the marriage feast or supper is to take place on earth, after the Second Advent, ver. 9. That Christ is spoken of as the Lamb points to His atoning sacrifice as the ground upon which the spiritual union takes place. The background of the phraseology lies in the O.T. description of the relation of God to Israel, e.g., Is. 54 : 4, ff. ; Ezek. 16 : 7, ff. ; Hos. 2 : 19 ; (c) marriage in general, including the married state, which is to be " had in honour," Heb. 13 : 4, R.V. ¶

Note : Among the Jews the marriage-supper took place in the husband's house and was the great social event in the family life. Large hospitality, and resentment at the refusal of an invitation, are indicated in Matt. 22 : 1–14. The marriage in Cana exhibits the way in which a marriage feast was conducted in humbler homes. Special honour attached to the male friends of the bridegroom, " the sons of the bride-chamber," Matt. 9 : 15, R.V. (see BRIDE-CHAMBER). At the close the parents conducted the bride to the nuptial chamber (cp. Judg. 15 : 1).

B. Verbs.

1. GAMEŌ (γαμέω), to marry (akin to A), is used (a) of the man, Matt. 5 : 32 ; 19 : 9, 10 ; 22 : 25 (R.V. ; A.V., " married a wife ") ; ver. 30 ; 24 : 38 ; Mark 6 : 17 ; 10 : 11 ; 12 : 25 ; Luke 14 : 20 ; 16 : 18 ; 17 : 27, R.V., " married " (A.V., " married wives ") ; 20 : 34, 35 ; 1 Cor. 7 : 28 (1st part) ; ver. 33 ; (b) of the woman, in the Active Voice, Mark 10 : 12 ; 1 Cor. 7 : 28 (last part) ; ver. 34 ; 1 Tim. 5 : 11, 14 ; in the Passive Voice, 1 Cor. 7 : 39 ; (c) of both sexes, 1 Cor. 7 : 9, 10, 36 ; 1 Tim. 4 : 3.¶

2. GAMIZŌ (γαμίζω), to give in marriage, is used in the Passive Voice in Matt. 22 : 30 (2nd clause), some mss. have No. 5 here ; Mark 12 : 25 (No. 3 in some mss.) ; Luke 17 : 27 (No. 5 in some mss.) ; 20 : 35 (last word), Passive (Nos. 3 and 4 in some mss.) ; in the Active Voice Matt. 24 : 38 (Nos. 3 and 5 in some mss.) ; further, of giving a daughter in marriage, 1 Cor. 7 : 38 (twice), R.V. (No. 5 in some mss.), which, on the whole, may be taken as the meaning. In this part of the Epistle, the Apostle was answering a number of questions on matters about which the church at Corinth had written to him, and in this particular matter the formal transition from marriage in general to the subject of giving a daughter in marriage, is simple. Eastern customs naturally would involve the inclusion of the latter in the enquiry and the reply.¶

3. GAMISKŌ (γαμίσκω), an alternative for No. 2, Luke 20 : 34 (some mss. have No. 4) ; in some mss. in Mark 12 : 25; Luke 20 : 35.¶

4. EKGAMISKŌ (ἐκγαμίσκω), to give out in marriage (ek, out, and No. 3) : see Nos. 2 and 3.

5. EKGAMIZŌ (ἐκγαμίζω), an alternative for No. 4 : see Nos. 2 and 3.¶

6. EPIGAMBREUŌ (ἐπιγαμβρεύω), to take to wife after (epi, upon, gambros, a connection by marriage), signifies to marry (of a deceased husband's next of kin, Matt. 22 : 24).¶ Cp. Gen. 38 : 8.

Note : In Rom. 7 : 3 (twice) and ver. 4, A.V., *ginomai*, to become (here, to become another man's), is translated " be married " (R.V., " be joined ").

MARROW

MUELOS (μυελός), marrow, occurs in Heb. 4 : 12, where, by a natural metaphor, the phraseology changes from the material to the spiritual.¶

For MARTYR see WITNESS

MARVEL (Noun and Verb), MARVELLOUS
A. Noun.

THAUMA (θαῦμα), a wonder (akin to *theaomai*, to gaze in wonder), is found in the most authentic mss. in 2 Cor. 11 : 14 (some mss. have the adjective *thaumastos :* see C, below), " (no) marvel ; " in Rev. 17 : 6, R.V., " wonder " (A.V., " admiration "), said of John's astonishment at the vision of the woman described as Babylon the Great.¶ In the Sept., Job 17 : 8 ; 18 : 20 ; in some mss., 20 : 8 and 21 : 5.¶ Cp. *teras*, a wonder ; *sēmeion*, a sign ; *thambos*, wonder ; *ekstasis*, amazement.

B. Verbs.

1. THAUMAZŌ (θαυμάζω) signifies to wonder at, marvel (akin to A) ; the following are R.V. differences from the A.V. : Luke 2 : 33, " were marvelling " for " marvelled ; " Luke 8 : 25 and 11 : 14, " marvelled " for " wondered ; " 9 : 43, " were marvelling " for " wondered ; " 2 Thess. 1 : 10, " marvelled at " for " admired " (of the Person of Christ at the time of the shining forth of His Parousia, at the Second Advent). See WONDER.

Note : In Matt. 9 : 8, A.V. translates this verb ; R.V., *phobeō*, " were afraid."

2. EKTHAUMAZŌ (ἐκθαυμάζω), a strengthened form of No. 1 (*ek*, intensive), is found in the best mss. in Mark 12 : 17, R.V., " wondered greatly " (some mss. have No. 1).¶

C. Adjective.

THAUMASTOS (θαυμαστός), marvellous (akin to A and B), is said (a) of the Lord's doing in making the rejected Stone the Head of the corner, Matt. 21 : 42 ; Mark 12 : 11 ; (b) of the erstwhile blind man's astonishment that the Pharisees knew not from whence Christ had come, and yet He had given him sight, John 9 : 30, R.V., " the marvel," A.V., " a marvellous thing ; " (c) of the spiritual light into which believers are brought, 1 Pet. 2 : 9 ; (d) of the vision of the seven angels having the seven last plagues, Rev. 15 : 1 ; (e) of the works of God, 15 : 3.¶

MASTER (Noun and Verb)
A. Nouns.

1. DIDASKALOS (διδάσκαλος), a teacher (from *didaskō*, to teach), is frequently rendered " Master " in the four Gospels, as a title of address to Christ, e.g., Matt. 8 : 19 ; Mark 4 : 38 (there are more instances in Luke than in the other Gospels) ; John 1 : 38, where it interprets " Rabbi ; " 20 : 16, where it interprets " Rabboni." It is used by Christ of Himself in Matt. 23 : 8 (see No. 6) and John 13 : 13, 14 ; by others concerning Him, Matt. 17 : 24 ; 26 : 18 ; Mark 5 : 35 ; 14 : 14 ; Luke 8 : 49 ; 22 : 11 ; John 11 : 28. In John 3 : 10, the Lord uses it in addressing Nicodemus, R.V., " the teacher " (A.V., " a master "), where the article does not specify a particular teacher, but designates the member of a class ; for the class see Luke 2 : 46, " the doctors " (R.V., marg., " teachers "). It is used of the relation of a disciple to his master, in Matt. 10 : 24, 25 ; Luke 6 : 40. It is not translated " masters " in the rest of the N.T., save in the A.V. of Jas. 3 : 1 " (be not many) masters," where obviously the R.V. " teachers " is the meaning. See TEACHER.

2. KURIOS (κύριος), a lord, one who exercises power, is translated " masters " in Matt. 6 : 24 ; 15 : 27 ; Mark 13 : 35 ; Luke 16 : 13 ; Acts 16 : 16, 19 ; Rom. 14 : 4, A.V. (R.V., " lord ") ; Eph. 6 : 5, 9 (twice), the 2nd time of Christ ; so in Col. 3 : 22 ; 4 : 1. See LORD.

3. DESPOTĒS (δεσπότης), one who has " absolute ownership and uncontrolled power," is translated " masters " in 1 Tim. 6 : 1, 2 ; Tit. 2 : 9 ; 1 Pet. 2 : 18 ; of Christ, 2 Tim. 2 : 21 ; 2 Pet. 2 : 1, R.V. (for A.V., " Lord ") ; in Jude 4, R.V., it is applied to Christ " (our only) Master (and Lord, Jesus Christ)," A.V. " (the only) Lord (God) ; " in Rev. 6 : 10, R.V., in an address to God, " O Master " (A.V., " O Lord "). It is rendered " Lord " in Luke 2 : 29 and Acts 4 : 24. See LORD.¶

Note : For " master of the house," see GOODMAN.

4. RABBEI (ῥαββεί) was an Aramaic word signifying " my master," a title of respectful address to Jewish teachers.

" The Aramaic word *rabbei*, transliterated into Greek, is explicitly recognized as the common form of address to Christ, Matt. 26 : 25 (cp., however, ver. 22, *kurios*) ; 26 : 49 ; Mark 9 : 5, but Matt. 17 : 4, *kurios* " (Dalman, *The Words of Jesus*).

In the following the R.V. has " Rabbi " for A.V. " Master ; " Matt. 26 : 25, 49 ; Mark 9 : 5 ; 11 : 21 ; 14 : 45 ; John 4 : 31 ; 9 : 2 ; 11 : 8. In other passages the A.V. has " Rabbi," Matt. 23 : 7, 8 ; John 1 : 38, 49 ; 3 : 2, 26 ; 6 : 25.¶

Note : The form *Rabbounei* (*Rabboni*), in Mark 10 : 51, is retained in the R.V. (for A.V., " Lord ") ; in John 20 : 16, in both A.V. and R.V. This title is said to be Galilean ; hence it would be natural in the lips of a woman of Magdala. It does not differ materially from Rabbi.¶

5. EPISTATĒS (ἐπιστάτης) denotes a chief, a commander, overseer, master. It is used by the disciples in addressing the Lord, in recognition

of His authority rather than His instruction (Nos. 1 and 6) ; it occurs only in Luke: 5 : 5; 8 : 24, 45; 9 : 33, 49; 17 : 13.¶ In the Sept., 2 Kings 25 : 19 ; 2 Chron. 31 : 12 ; Jer. 36 : 26 ; 52 : 25.¶

Note : " The form *epistata* . . . alongside of the commoner *didaskale* is . . . a Greek synonym for the latter, and both are to be traced back to the Aramaic *rabbei*." Christ forbade His disciples to allow themselves to be called *rabbi*, " on the ground that He alone was their Master, Matt. 23 : 8. In reference to Himself the designation was expressive of the real relation between them. The form of address ' Good Master ' He, however, refused to allow, Mark 10 : 17, 18 . . . in the mouth of the speaker it was mere insolent flattery . . . the Lord was unwilling that anyone should thoughtlessly deal with such an epithet ; and here, as always, the honour due to the Father was the first consideration with Him. . . . The primitive community never ventured to call Jesus ' Our Teacher ' after He had been exalted to the Throne of God. The title *rabbi*, expressing the relation of the disciple to the teacher, vanished from use ; and there remained only the designation *maran*, the servant's appropriate acknowledgement of his Lord " (Dalman).

6. KATHĒGĒTĒS (καθηγητής), properly a guide (akin to *kathēgeomai*, to go before, guide ; *kata*, down, *hēgeomai*, to guide), denotes a master, a teacher, Matt. 23 : 10 (twice) ; some mss. have it in ver. 8, where the most authentic have No. 1.¶

7. KUBERNĒTĒS (κυβερνήτης), the pilot or steersman of a ship, or, metaphorically, a guide or governor (akin to *kubernaō*, to guide : Eng., govern is connected ; cp. *kubernēsis*, a steering, pilotage, 1 Cor. 12 : 28, " governments "), is translated " master " in Acts 27 : 11 ; " shipmaster " in Rev. 18 : 17.¶ In the Sept., Prov. 23 : 34 ; Ezek. 27 : 8, 27, 28.¶

B. Verb.

KATAKURIEUŌ (κατακυριεύω), to exercise lordship (*kata*, down upon, *kurios*, a lord), is translated " mastered " in Acts 19 : 16, R.V., of the action of the evil spirit on the sons of Sceva (A.V., " overcame "). In translating the word *amphoterōn* by its primary meaning, " both," the R.V. describes the incident as referring to two only. It has been shown, however, that in the period of the *Koinē* (see Foreword to Vol. I) *amphoteroi*, " both," was no longer restricted to two persons. Ramsay ascribes the abruptness of the word here to the vivid narrative of an eye witness. See DOMINION, LORD, LORDSHIP.

MASTERBUILDER

ARCHITEKTŌN (ἀρχιτέκτων), from *archē*, rule, beginning, and *tektōn*, an artificer (whence Eng., architect), a principal artificer, is used figuratively by the Apostle in 1 Cor. 3 : 10, of his work in laying the foundation of the local church in Corinth, inasmuch as the inception of the spiritual work there devolved upon him. The examples from the papyri and from inscriptions, as illustrated by Moulton and Milligan, show that the word had a wider application than our " architect," and confirm the rendering " masterbuilder " in this passage, which is of course borne out by the context.¶

MATTER, MATTERS

1. LOGOS (λόγος), a word, speech, discourse, account, hence also that which is spoken of, a matter, affair, thing, is translated " matter " in Mark 1 : 45 ; Acts 8 : 21 ; 15 : 6 ; 19 : 38 ; in the R.V. of Phil. 4 : 15, " in the matter of " (A.V., " concerning "). See ACCOUNT.

2. PRAGMA (πρᾶγμα), akin to *prassō*, to do, denotes (*a*) that which has been done, a deed, translated " matters " in Luke 1 : 1, R.V. (A.V., " things ") ; " matter " in 2 Cor. 7 : 11 ; (*b*) that which is being done, an affair, translated " matter " in Rom. 16 : 2, R.V. (A.V., " business ") ; 1 Cor. 6 : 1, in a forensic sense, a law-suit (frequently found with this meaning in the papyri) ; 1 Thess. 4 : 6, " in the matter," i.e., the matter under consideration, which, as the preceding words show, is here the sin of adultery. See BUSINESS, B, Note (1), THING.

3. ENKLĒMA (ἔγκλημα), an accusation, charge, Acts 25 : 16, R.V., " matter laid against him ; " elsewhere, Acts 23 : 29, " charge ; " see ACCUSATION, A, No. 3.¶

Notes : (1) In Gal. 2 : 6, the statement " it maketh no matter " translates the verb *diapherō*, to bear asunder, make a difference, with *ouden*, nothing, used adverbially, i.e., ' it makes no difference (to me) ; ' his commission from the Lord relieved him of responsibility to the authority of the Apostles. (2) In 1 Cor. 9 : 11, R.V., the neuter of the adjective *megas*, great, is translated " a great matter " (A.V., " a great thing "). (3) In Jas. 3 : 5, A.V., *hulē*, a wood, forest, is translated " a matter " (R.V., and A.V. marg., " wood "). In older English the word " matter " actually meant " wood " (like its Latin original, *materia*). (4) In Acts 17 : 32, the A.V. adds " *matter* " to the pronoun " this," R.V., " (concerning) this." (5) In 2 Cor. 8 : 19, R.V., the phrase, lit., ' in this grace ' is translated " in *the matter of* (A.V., with) this grace." (6) In 2 Cor. 8 : 20, R.V., the phrase, lit., ' in this bounty ' is translated " in *the matter of* this bounty " (A.V., " in this abundance "). (7) In 2 Cor. 9 : 5, the phrase, lit., ' as a bounty ' is amplified to " as a matter of bounty." (8) For 1 Pet. 4 : 15 see BUSYBODY. See also OTHER, THIS, THESE, WEIGHTIER, WRONG.

MAY, MAYEST, MIGHT

1. DUNAMAI (δύναμαι), to be able, have power, whether by personal ability, permission, or opportunity, is sometimes rendered " may " or " might," e.g., Matt. 26 : 9 ; Mark 14 : 5 ; Acts 17 : 19 ; 1 Thess. 2 : 6. In the following the R.V. substitutes " can," " canst," " couldst," for the A.V., e.g., Matt. 26 : 42 ; Mark 4 : 32 ; 14 : 7 ; Luke 16 : 2 ; Acts 24 : 11 ; 25 : 11 ; 27 : 12 ; 1 Cor. 7 : 21 ; 14 : 31 (here the alteration is especially

important, as not permission for all to prophesy, but ability to do so, is
the meaning) ; Eph. 3 : 4. In the following the R.V. substitutes the verb
to be able, Acts 19 : 40 ; 24 : 8 ; Rev. 13 : 17. See ABLE, B, No. 1.

2. EXESTI (ἔξεστι), it is permitted, lawful (eimi, to be, prefixed by
ek, from), is rendered " (I) may " in Acts 2 : 29, R.V. [A.V., " let (me) "] ;
in Acts 21 : 37, " may (I)," lit., ' is it permitted (me to speak) ? ' Some
mss. have it in 8 : 37, " thou mayest " (A.V.). See LAWFUL.

3. ISŌS (ἴσως), equally (from the adjective isos, equal), is translated
" it may be " in Luke 20 : 13 (i.e., ' perhaps ').¶

4. TUNCHANŌ (τυγχάνω), to meet with, reach, obtain, denotes,
intransitively, to happen, chance, befall ; used impersonally with the
conjunction ei, if, it signifies ' it may be,' ' perhaps,' e.g., 1 Cor. 14 : 10 ;
15 : 37, " it may chance ; " 16 : 6.

Notes : (1) In Matt. 8 : 28, A.V., ischuō, to have strength, be strong,
be well able, is translated " might " (R.V., " could "). (2) " May,"
" might," sometimes translate the prepositional phrase eis, unto, with the
definite article, followed by the infinitive mood of some verb, expressing
purpose, e.g., Acts 3 : 19, " may be blotted out," lit., ' unto the blotting
out of ; ' Rom. 3 : 26, " that he might be," lit., ' unto his being ; ' so
8 : 29 ; 2 Cor. 1 : 4, " that we may be able," lit., ' unto our being able ; '
Eph. 1 : 18, " that ye may know," lit., ' unto your knowing ; ' Acts
7 : 19 ; Rom. 1 : 11 ; 4 : 16 ; 12 : 2 ; 15 : 13 ; Phil. 1 : 10 ; 1 Thess.
3 : 10, 13 ; 2 Thess. 1 : 5 ; 2 : 6, 10 ; Heb. 12 : 10. In Luke 20 : 20 the
best mss. have hōste, " so as to," R.V., as, e.g., in 1 Pet. 1 : 21. Sometimes
the article with the infinitive mood without a preceding preposition,
expresses result, e.g., Luke 21 : 22 ; Acts 26 : 18 (twice), " that they may
turn," R.V. ; cp. Rom. 6 : 6 ; 11 : 10 ; 1 Cor. 10 : 13 ; Phil. 3 : 10, " that
I may know ; " Jas. 5 : 17.

(3) The phrases " may be," " might be," are frequently the rendering
of the verb to be, in the subjunctive or optative moods, preceded by a
conjunction introducing a condition, or expressing a wish or purpose,
e.g., Matt. 6 : 4 ; John 14 : 3 ; 17 : 11. Sometimes the phrase translates
simply the infinitive mood of the verb eimi, to be, e.g., Luke 8 : 38, lit.,
' to be (with Him) ; ' so the R.V. in 2 Cor. 5 : 9; in 2 Cor. 9 : 5, " that
(the same) might be," lit., ' (the same) to be.'

(4) In Heb. 7 : 9 the phrase hōs (' so ') epos (' a word ') eipein (' to say '),
i.e., lit., ' so to say a word ' is an idiom, translated in the R.V., " so to
say " (A.V., " if I may so say ") ; the Eng. equivalent is ' one might
almost say.'

ME

Notes : (1) The pronoun, whether alone or with some English preposition,
e.g., of, to, for, in, translates one or other of the oblique cases of ego, ' I.'
(2) In Philm. 13 the reflexive pronoun emauton, myself, is translated " me,"
governed by the preposition pros, with, lit., ' with myself.' (3) In Tit.

1 : 3, for the A.V., "is committed unto me," the R.V. has "I was intrusted." (4) In Phil. 2 : 23, "how it will go with me," is, lit., 'the (things) concerning me.' (5) The phrase *en emoi*, 'in me,' is used (*a*) instrumentally (*en*, instrumental, by or through), e.g., 2 Cor. 13 : 3 ; (*b*) subjectively, 'within me,' e.g., Gal. 2 : 20 ; (*c*) objectively, 'in my case,' e.g., 1 Cor. 9 : 15 ; 14 : 11 ; Gal. 1 : 16, 24 ; 1 Tim. 1 : 16. (6) In Luke 22 : 19 the possessive pronoun *emos*, my, is rendered "of Me," lit., '(into) My (remembrance).'

MEAL

ALEURON (ἄλευρον), meal (akin to *aleuō*, to grind, and therefore, lit., 'what is ground'), occurs in Matt. 13 : 33 ; Luke 13 : 21.¶

MEAN (Adjective)

ASĒMOS (ἄσημος), lit., without mark (*a*, negative, *sēma*, a mark), i.e., undistinguished, obscure, was applied by the Apostle Paul negatively, to his native city, Tarsus, Acts 21 : 39.¶ Moulton and Milligan (Vocab.) have a note as follows : " This word occurs perpetually in the papyri to denote a man who is 'not distinguished' from his neighbours by the convenient scars on eyebrow or arm or right shin, which identify so many individuals in formal documents." Deissmann suggests that the word may have been the technical term for "uncircumcised," among the Greek Egyptians. In another papyrus document a pair of silver bracelets are described as of "unstamped" (*asēmos*) silver.

MEAN (Verb)

1. EIMI (εἰμί), to be, in certain of its forms, has an explicative force, signifying to denote, to import, e.g., Matt. 9 : 13 ; 12 : 7, " (what this) meaneth," lit. '(what this) is ;' Luke 18 : 36, "meant" (lit., 'might be'); Acts 10 : 17, "might mean," R.V. (lit., 'might be'); in Luke 15 : 26 the R.V. keeps to the verb to be, "(what these things) might be " (A.V., "meant "). In Acts 2 : 12 the verb to be is preceded by *thelō*, to will, and the phrase is translated " (what) meaneth (this)," lit., '(what) does (this) will to be ? ' in 17 : 20, lit., '(what do these things) will to be ? '

2. LEGŌ (λέγω), to say, sometimes has the significance of meaning something ; so the R.V. in 1 Cor. 1 : 12 ; A.V., " (this) I say."

Notes : (1) In Acts 27 : 2, A.V., *mellō*, to be about to, is translated " meaning " (R.V., " was about to "), with reference to the ship (according to the best mss.). (2) In Acts 21 : 13, A.V., *poieō*, to do, is translated " (what) mean ye (to weep) ; " R.V., " (what) do ye, (weeping)." (3) The abbreviated original in 2 Cor. 8 : 13 is rendered by the italicised additions, A.V., " *I mean* (not)," R.V., " *I say* (not) *this*." Cp. the R.V. italics in Mark 6 : 2.

MEANING

DUNAMIS (δύναμις), power, force, is used of the significance or force of what is spoken, 1 Cor. 14 : 11. See MIGHT, POWER.

MEANS (by all, by any, etc.)

1. PANTŌS (πάντως), an adverb from *pas*, all, denoting wholly, altogether, entirely, is used in 1 Cor. 9 : 22, " by all means." When the Apostle says, " I am become all things to all men, that I may by all means save some," he is simply speaking of his accommodating himself to various human conditions consistently with fidelity to the truth, with no unscriptural compliance with men, but in the exercise of self denial ; " by all means " refers to the preceding context from ver. 18, and stresses his desire to be used in the salvation of some. It is found in Acts 21 : 22, R.V., " certainly." Some mss. have the word in this sense in Acts 18 : 21 (A.V.). See ALTOGETHER, B, No. 1.

2. PŌS (πως), at all, somehow, in any way, is used after the conjunction (a) *ei*, if, meaning ' if by any means,' e.g., Acts 27 : 12 ; Rom. 1 : 10 ; 11 : 14 ; Phil. 3 : 11 ; (b) *mē*, lest, ' lest by any means,' e.g., 1 Cor. 8 : 9 ; 9 : 27 ; 2 Cor. 2 : 7, R.V. (A.V., " perhaps ") ; 9 : 4, R.V. (A.V., " haply ") ; 11 : 3 ; 12 : 20, R.V. ; Gal. 2 : 2 ; 4 : 11, R.V. (A.V., " lest ") ; 1 Thess. 3 : 5 (A.V., " lest by some means ").

3. EK (ἐκ), out of, from, by, suggesting the source from which something is done, is sometimes rendered " by means of," e.g., Luke 16 : 9, R.V., " by means of (the mammon of unrighteousness) ; " A.V., " of ; " 2 Cor. 1 : 11, " by (the) means of (many)."

4. DIA (διά), by, by means of, when followed by the genitive case, is instrumental, e.g., 2 Pet. 3 : 6, R.V., " by which means " (A.V., " whereby ").

5. PŌS (πῶς), an interrogative adverb (different from No. 2), how, in what way, Luke 8 : 36, A.V., " by what means," R.V., " how ; " so John 9 : 21 ; cp. Note (4) below.

Notes : (1) In Luke 5 : 18 the A.V. adds the word " *means* " in italics. (2) The word *tropos*, a manner, way, is sometimes used in a prepositional phrase, e.g., 2 Thess. 2 : 3, A.V., " by any means," R.V., " in any wise," lit., ' in any manner ; ' 3 : 16, A.V., " by all means," R.V., " in all ways," lit., ' in every manner.' (3) The double negative *ou mē*, i.e., ' no not,' ' not at all,' is translated " by no means," Matt. 5 : 26 ; in Luke 10 : 19, " by any means," A.V. (R.V., " in any wise ") ; Luke 12 : 59, R.V., " by no means " (A.V., " not "). (4) In Acts 4 : 9, the phrase *en*, in or by, with *tini* (from *tis*, who), lit., " in whom " (R.V., marg.), is translated " by what means." (5) In Heb. 9 : 15, R.V., the verb *ginomai*, to come to be, become, take place, used in its 2nd aorist participle, is rightly translated " (a death) having taken place ; " A.V., " by means of (death)." (6) In Rev. 13 : 14, R.V., *dia*, followed by the accusative case, is rightly translated

" by reason of," i.e., ' on account of ' (A.V., wrongly, " by *the means of* ").

For MEANWHILE see WHILE

MEASURE (Noun and Verb)
A. Nouns.

1. METRON (μέτρον) denotes (I) that which is used for measuring, a measure, (*a*) of a vessel, figuratively, Matt. 23 : 32 ; Luke 6 : 38 (twice) ; in John 3 : 34, with the preposition *ek*, " (He giveth not the Spirit) by measure," R.V. (which is a necessary correction ; the italicized words " *unto him*," A.V., detract from the meaning). Not only had Christ the Holy Spirit without measure, but God so gives the Spirit through Him to others. It is the Ascended Christ who gives the Spirit to those who receive His testimony and set their seal to this, that God is true. The Holy Spirit is imparted neither by degrees, nor in portions, as if He were merely an influence, He is bestowed Personally upon each believer, at the time of the new birth ; (*b*) of a graduated rod or rule for measuring, figuratively, Matt. 7 : 2 ; Mark 4 : 24 ; literally, Rev. 21 : 15 (in the best mss. ; see the R.V.) ; ver. 17 ; (II) that which is measured, a determined extent, a portion measured off, Rom. 12 : 3 ; 2 Cor. 10 : 13 (twice) ; Eph. 4 : 7, " (according to the) measure (of the gift of Christ) ; " the gift of grace is measured and given according to the will of Christ ; whatever the endowment, His is the bestowment and the adjustment ; ver. 13, " the measure (of the stature of the fulness of Christ)," the standard of spiritual stature being the fulness which is essentially Christ's ; ver. 16, " (according to the working in due) measure (of each several part)," i.e., according to the effectual working of the ministration rendered in due measure by every part.¶

2. MEROS (μέρος), a part, portion, is used with the preposition *apo*, from, with the meaning " in some measure," Rom. 15 : 15, R.V. (A.V., " . . . sort"). See COAST, PART.

3. SATON (σάτον) is a Hebrew dry measure (Heb., *seah*), about a peck and a half, Matt. 13 : 33 ; Luke 13 : 21 ; " three measures " would be the quantity for a baking (cp. Gen. 18 : 6 ; Judg. 6 : 19 ; 1 Sam. 1 : 24 ; the " ephah " of the last two passages was equal to three *sata*).¶

4. KOROS (κόρος) denotes a *cor*, the largest Hebrew dry measure (ten *ephahs*), containing about 11 bushels, Luke 16 : 7 ; the hundred measures amounted to a very considerable quantity.¶

5. BATOS (βάτος) denotes a *bath*, a Jewish liquid measure (the equivalent of an *ephah*), containing between 8 and 9 gallons, Luke 16 : 6.¶

6. CHOINIX (χοῖνιξ), a dry measure of rather less than a quart, about " as much as would support a person of moderate appetite for a day," occurs in Rev. 6 : 6 (twice). Usually eight *chœnixes* could be bought for a *denarius* (about 9½d.) ; this passage predicts circumstances in which

the *denarius* is the price of one *chœnix*.¶ In the Sept., Ezek. 45 : 10, 11, where it represents the Heb. *ephah* and *bath*.¶

Notes : (1) In 2 Cor. 10 : 14, A.V., *huperekteinō*, to stretch out overmuch, is translated " we stretch (not ourselves) beyond measure," (R.V., " . . . overmuch) ". (2) In 2 Cor. 11 : 9, R.V., *prosanaplēroō*, to fill up by adding to, to supply fully, is translated " supplied the measure " (A.V., " supplied "). See SUPPLY. (3) For the phrases in the A.V., " beyond measure," Gal. 1 : 13 ; " out of measure," 2 Cor. 1 : 8, see ABUNDANCE, A, No. 4, EXCEL, B. (4) In Mark 6 : 51, some mss. have the phrase *ek perissou*, " beyond measure " (A.V.). (5) For the phrase " be exalted above measure," 2 Cor. 12 : 7, A.V., see EXALT, A, No. 4.

B. Adverbs.

1. HUPERBALLONTŌS (ὑπερβαλλόντως), beyond measure (*huper*, over, beyond, *ballō*, to throw ; for the verb *huperballō*, see EXCEEDING), is rendered " above measure " in 2 Cor. 11 : 23.¶

2. PERISSŌS (περισσῶς), Mark 10 : 26 ; see EXCEED, B, No. 4.

3. HUPERPERISSŌS (ὑπερπερισσῶς), Mark 7 : 37 : see ABUNDANCE D, No. 3.¶

C. Adjective.

AMETROS (ἄμετρος), without measure (*a*, negative, and A, No. 1), is used in the neuter plural in an adverbial phrase in 2 Cor. 10 : 13, 15, *eis ta ametra*, lit., ' unto the (things) without measure,' R.V., " (we will not glory) beyond our measure ; " A.V.,"(we will not boast) of things without measure," referring to the sphere Divinely appointed for the Apostle as to his Gospel ministry ; this had reached to Corinth, and by the increase of the faith of the church there, would extend to regions beyond. His opponents had no scruples about intruding into the spheres of other men's work.¶

D. Verbs.

1. METREŌ (μετρέω), to measure (akin to A, No. 1), is used (*a*) of space, number, value, etc., Rev. 11 : 1, 2 ; 21 : 15, 16, 17 ; metaphorically, 2 Cor. 10 : 12 ; (*b*) in the sense of measuring out, giving by measure, Matt. 7 : 2, " ye mete " (some mss. have No. 2) ; Mark 4 : 24 ; in some mss. in Luke 6 : 38 (see No. 2).¶

2. ANTIMETREŌ (ἀντιμετρέω), to measure in return (*anti*, back, in return and No. 1), is used in the Passive Voice, and found in some mss. in Matt. 7 : 2 (the most authentic have No. 1) ; in Luke 6 : 38 the most authentic have this verb.¶ It is not found in the Sept.

MEAT

1. BRŌMA (βρῶμα), food (akin to *bibrōskō*, to eat, John 6 : 13¶), solid food in contrast to milk, is translated " food " in Matt. 14 : 15, R.V. (A.V., " victuals ") ; " meats," Mark 7 : 19 ; 1 Cor. 6 : 13 (twice) ; 1 Tim. 4 : 3 ; Heb. 9 : 10 ; 13 : 9 ; " meat," John 4 : 34 ; Rom. 14 : 15

(twice), 20 ; 1 Cor. 3 : 2 ; 8 : 8, 13 ; 10 : 3 ; "food," R.V., for A.V., "meat," Luke 3 : 11 ; 9 : 13.¶

2. BRŌSIS (βρῶσις), akin to No. 1, denotes (a) the act of eating, 1 Cor. 8 : 4 (see EAT) ; (b) food, translated "meat" in John 4 : 32 (for ver. 34, see No. 1) ; 6 : 27 (twice, the second time metaphorically, of spiritual food) ; 6 : 55, R.V., marg., "(true) meat ;" Rom. 14 : 17, A.V., "meat," R.V., "eating ;" Col. 2 : 16 ; in Heb. 12 : 16, R.V., "mess of meat," A.V., "morsel of meat ;" in 2 Cor. 9 : 10, "food ;" in Matt. 6 : 19, 20, "rust." See EAT, EATING, B.¶

3. BRŌSIMOS (βρώσιμος), eatable, Luke 24 : 41, A.V., "any meat" (R.V., "anything to eat"). See EAT, C.¶

4. TROPHĒ (τροφή), nourishment, food, is translated "meat" in the A.V. (R.V. "food") except in two instances. See FOOD, No. 1.

5. PHAGŌ (φάγω), to eat, is used as a noun, in the infinitive mood, and translated "meat" in Matt. 25 : 35, 42 (lit., ' to eat ') ; in Luke 8 : 55 the R.V. translates it literally, "to eat" (A.V., "meat"). See EAT, No. 2.

6. TRAPEZA (τράπεζα), a table (Eng., trapeze), is used, by metonymy, of the food on the table, in Acts 16 : 34 (R.V., marg., "a table"), and translated "meat ;" cp. "table" in Rom. 11 : 9 ; 1 Cor. 10 : 21. See TABLE.

Notes : (1) For *prosphagion,* John 21 : 5, A.V., "any meat," see EAT, B, No. 2. (2) In Luke 12 : 42, *sitometrion* denotes a measured portion of food (*sitos,* food, *metrios,* within measure). (3) In Matt. 15 : 37 and Mark 8 : 8, the A.V. translates the plural of *klasma,* a broken piece (from *klaō,* to break), "broken meat" (R.V., "broken pieces"). (4) In John 12 : 2, R.V., *anakeimai,* to recline at table, is translated "sat at meat" (A.V., "sat at the table") ; in Mark 6 : 26, R.V., according to the best mss., "sat at meat," some have *sunanakeimai* (A.V., "sat with him") ; in Mark 6 : 22, R.V., *sunanakeimai,* to recline at table together, is translated "that sat at meat with him." (5) In Acts 15 : 29, A.V., the neuter plural of *eidōlothutos,* sacrificed to idols, is translated "meats offered to idols" (R.V., "things . . . ," as elsewhere in the A.V.). See IDOLS (offered to.) (6) For *kataklinō,* to sit down to (recline at) meat, see SIT, No. 7.

MEDIATOR

MESITĒS (μεσίτης), lit., a go-between (from *mesos,* middle, and *eimi,* to go), is used in two ways in the N.T., (a) one who mediates between two parties with a view to producing peace, as in 1 Tim. 2 : 5, though more than mere mediatorship is in view, for the salvation of men necessitated that the Mediator should Himself possess the nature and attributes of Him towards whom He acts, and should likewise participate in the nature of those for whom He acts (sin apart) ; only by being possessed both of Deity and humanity could He comprehend the claims of the one and the needs of the other ; further, the claims and the needs could be met only by One who, Himself being proved sinless, would offer Himself an expiatory sacrifice on behalf of men ; (b) one who acts as a guarantee so as to secure something which otherwise would not be obtained. Thus in Heb. 8 : 6 ; 9 : 15 ; 12 : 24 Christ is the Surety of " the better covenant," " the new covenant," guaranteeing its terms for His people.

In Gal. 3 : 19 Moses is spoken of as a mediator, and the statement is made that " a mediator is not a mediator of one," ver. 20, that is, of one party. Here the contrast is between the promise given to Abraham and the giving of the Law. The Law was a covenant enacted between God and the Jewish people, requiring fulfilment by both parties. But with the promise to Abraham, all the obligations were assumed by God, which is implied in the statement, " but God is one."¶ In the Sept., Job 9 : 33, " daysman."¶

MEDITATE

1. MELETAŌ (μελετάω), primarily, to care for (akin to *meletē*, care ; cp. *melei*, it is a care), denotes (a) to attend to, practise, 1 Tim. 4 : 15, R.V., " be diligent in " (A.V., " meditate upon ") ; to practise is the prevalent sense of the word, and the context is not against this significance in the R.V. rendering ; some mss. have it in Mark 13 : 11 ; (b) to ponder, imagine, Acts 4 : 25. See IMAGINE.¶

2. PROMELETAŌ (προμελετάω), to premeditate, is used in Luke 21 : 14.¶

Note : In the corresponding passage in Mark 13 : 11, the most authentic mss. have the verb *promerimnaō*, to be anxious beforehand (R.V.) ; see No. 1.

For MEDDLER see BUSYBODY

MEEK, MEEKNESS
A. Adjective.

PRAÜS or PRAOS (πραΰς) denotes gentle, mild, meek ; for its significance see the corresponding noun, below, B. Christ uses it of His own disposition, Matt. 11 : 29 ; He gives it in the third of His Beatitudes, 5 : 5 ; it is said of Him as the King Messiah, 21 : 5, from Zech. 9 : 9 ; it is an adornment of the Christian profession, 1 Pet. 3 : 4.¶ Cp. *ēpios*, gentle, of a soothing disposition, 1 Thess. 2 : 7 ; 2 Tim. 2 : 24.¶

B. Nouns.

1. PRAUTĒS, or PRAOTĒS, an earlier form, (πραΰτης) denotes meekness. In its use in Scripture, in which it has a fuller, deeper significance than in non-scriptural Greek writings, it consists not in a person's " outward behaviour only ; nor yet in his relations to his fellow-men ; as little in his mere natural disposition. Rather it is an inwrought grace of the soul ; and the exercises of it are first and chiefly towards God. It is that temper of spirit in which we accept His dealings with us as good, and therefore without disputing or resisting ; it is closely linked with the word

tapeinophrosunē [humility], and follows directly upon it, Eph. 4 : 2 ; Col. 3 : 12 ; cp. the adjectives in the Sept. of Zeph. 3 : 12, " meek and lowly ; " . . . it is only the humble heart which is also the meek, and which, as such, does not fight against God and more or less struggle and contend with Him. This meekness, however, being first of all a meekness before God, is also such in the face of men, even of evil men, out of a sense that these, with the insults and injuries which they may inflict, are permitted and employed by Him for the chastening and purifying of His elect " (Trench, Syn. § xlii). In Gal. 5 : 23 it is associated with *enkrateia*, self-control.

The meaning of *praütēs* " is not readily expressed in English, for the terms meekness, mildness, commonly used, suggest weakness and pusillanimity to a greater or less extent, whereas *praütēs* does nothing of the kind. Nevertheless, it is difficult to find a rendering less open to objection than ' meekness ; ' ' gentleness ' has been suggested, but as *praütēs* describes a condition of mind and heart, and as ' gentleness ' is appropriate rather to actions, this word is no better than that used in both English Versions. It must be clearly understood, therefore, that the meekness manifested by the Lord and commended to the believer is the fruit of power. The common assumption is that when a man is meek it is because he cannot help himself ; but the Lord was ' meek ' because he had the infinite resources of God at His command. Described negatively, meekness is the opposite to self-assertiveness and self-interest ; it is equanimity of spirit that is neither elated nor cast down, simply because it is not occupied with self at all.

" In 2 Cor. 10 : 1 the Apostle appeals to the ' meekness . . . of Christ.' Christians are charged to show ' all meekness toward all men,' Tit. 3 : 2, for meekness becomes ' God's elect,' Col. 3 : 12. To this virtue the ' man of God ' is urged ; he is to ' follow after meekness ' for his own sake, 1 Tim. 6 : 11 (the best texts have No. 2 here, however), and in his service, and more especially in his dealings with the ' ignorant and erring,' he is to exhibit ' a spirit of meekness,' 1 Cor. 4 : 21, and Gal. 6 : 1 ; even ' they that oppose themselves ' are to be corrected in meekness, 2 Tim. 2 : 25. James exhorts his ' beloved brethren ' to ' receive with meekness the implanted word,' 1 : 21. Peter enjoins ' meekness ' in setting forth the grounds of the Christian hope, 3 : 15."*¶

2. PRAÜPATHIA (πραϋπαθία), a meek disposition, meekness (*praus*, meek, *paschō*, to suffer), is found in the best texts in 1 Tim. 6 : 11.¶

MEET (Adjective and Verb)
A. Adjectives.

1. AXIOS (ἄξιος) has the meaning of being of weight, value, worth ; also befitting, becoming, right on the ground of fitness, e.g., Matt. 3 : 8,

---

* From Notes on Galatians by Hogg and Vine, pp. 294, 295.

A.V., " meet " (R.V., " worthy ") ; so Acts 26 : 20 ; Luke 3 : 8 (" worthy") ;
23 : 41 (" due reward "). See REWARD, WORTHY.

2. HIKANOS (ἱκανός), sufficient, competent, fit, is translated " meet "
in 1 Cor. 15 : 9. See ENOUGH, SUFFICIENT.

3. KALOS (καλός), good, is translated " meet " in Matt. 15 : 26 and
Mark 7 : 27. See GOOD.

4. EUTHETOS (εὔθετος), well-placed, is translated " meet " in
Heb. 6 : 7 : see FIT.

Note : In Phil. 1 : 7 and 2 Pet. 1 : 13, A.V., *dikaios*, just, is translated
" meet " (R.V., " right "). For " meet . . . for use," 2 Tim. 2 : 21, see
USE, *Note*.

B. Verbs.

1. DEI (δεῖ), an impersonal verb, it is necessary, one must, is translated
" it was meet," in Luke 15 : 32 ; in Rom. 1 : 27, A.V., " was meet " (R.V.,
" was due "). See DUE, B, No. 2.

2. HIKANOŌ (ἱκανόω), to render fit, meet, to make sufficient, is
translated " hath made . . . meet " in Col. 1 : 12 ; in 2 Cor. 3 : 6, R.V.,
" made . . . sufficient " (A.V., " hath made . . . able "). See ABLE.¶

MEET (Verb), MEET WITH, MET
A. Verbs.

1. APANTAŌ (ἀπαντάω), to go to meet, to meet (*apo*, from, *antaō*,
to meet with, come face to face with), is used in Mark 14 : 13 and Luke
17 : 12. Some mss. have this verb for No. 3 in Matt. 28 : 9 ; Mark 5 : 2 ;
Luke 14 : 31 ; John 4 : 51 ; Acts 16 : 16.¶

2. SUNANTAŌ (συναντάω), to meet with, lit., to meet together with
(*sun*, with, and *antaō*, see No. 1), is used in Luke 9 : 37 (in ver. 18, in some
mss.) ; 22 : 10 ; Acts 10 : 25 ; Heb. 7 : 1, 10 ; metaphorically in Acts
20 : 22 (" shall befall "). See BEFALL.¶

3. HUPANTAŌ (ὑπαντάω), to go to meet, to meet, has the same
meaning as No. 1, and is used in Matt. 8 : 28 ; Luke 8 : 27 ; John 11 : 20,
30, and, in the most authentic mss., in Matt. 28 : 9 ; Mark 5 : 2 ; Luke
14 : 31 (of meeting in battle) ; John 4 : 51 ; 12 : 18 and Acts 16 : 16 (see
No. 1).¶

4. PARATUNCHANŌ (παρατυγχάνω), to happen to be near or present,
to chance to be by (*para*, beside, near, *tunchanō*, to happen), occurs in
Acts 17 : 17, " met with (him)."¶

5. SUMBALLŌ (συμβάλλω), to confer, to fall in with, meet with, is
translated " met " in Acts 20 : 14, R.V. (A.V., " met with "), of the
Apostle Paul's meeting his companions at Assos. See CONFER, No. 3.

B. Nouns.

1. HUPANTĒSIS (ὑπάντησις), a going to meet (akin to A, No. 3),
preceded by the preposition *eis*, unto, lit., ' unto a meeting,' translated
" to meet," is found in John 12 : 13, and in the most authentic mss. in
Matt. 8 : 34 (see No. 3) and 25 : 1 (see No. 2).¶

2. APANTĒSIS (ἀπάντησις), a meeting (akin to A, No. 1), occurs in

Matt. 25 : 6 (in some mss. in ver. 1, and in 27 : 32, in some mss.) ; Acts 28 : 15 ; 1 Thess. 4 : 17. It is used in the papyri of a newly arriving magistrate. " It seems that the special idea of the word was the official welcome of a newly arrived dignitary " (Moulton, Greek Test. Gram. Vol. I, p. 14).¶

3. SUNANTĒSIS (συνάντησις), a coming to meet with (akin to A, No. 2), is found in some mss. in Matt. 8 : 34, of the coming out of all the people of a city to meet the Lord (see No. 1).¶

MELODY (Verb)

PSALLŌ (ψάλλω), primarily to twitch, twang, then, to play a stringed instrument with the fingers, and hence, in the Sept., to sing with a harp, sing psalms, denotes, in the N.T., to sing a hymn, sing praise ; in Eph. 5 : 19, " making melody " (for the preceding word adō, see SING). Elsewhere it is rendered " sing," Rom. 15 : 9 ; 1 Cor. 14 : 15 ; in Jas. 5 : 13, R.V., " let him sing praise " (A.V., " let him sing psalms "). See SING.¶

MELT

TĒKŌ (τήκω), to melt, melt down, is used in the Passive Voice in 2 Pet. 3 : 12, " shall melt " (lit., ' shall be melted '), of the elements (Eng., ' thaw ' is etymologically connected).¶

Note : In verse 10, the A.V. " shall melt " represents the verb luō, to loosen, dissolve (R.V., " shall be dissolved," Passive Voice) ; so in vv. 11, 12.

MEMBER

MELOS (μέλος), a limb of the body, is used (a) literally, Matt. 5 : 29, 30 ; Rom. 6 : 13 (twice), 19 (twice) ; 7 : 5, 23 (twice) ; 12 : 4 (twice) ; 1 Cor. 12 : 12 (twice), 14, 18–20, 22, 25, 26 (twice) ; Jas. 3 : 5, 6 ; 4 : 1 ; in Col. 3 : 5, " mortify therefore your members which are upon the earth ; " since our bodies and their members belong to the earth, and are the instruments of sin, they are referred to as such (cp. Matt. 5 : 29, 30 ; Rom. 7 : 5, 23, mentioned above) ; the putting to death is not physical, but ethical ; as the physical members have distinct individualities, so those evils, of which the physical members are agents, are by analogy regarded as examples of the way in which the members work if not put to death ; this is not precisely the same as " the old man," ver. 9, i.e., the old nature, though there is a connection ; (b) metaphorically, of believers as members of Christ, 1 Cor. 6 : 15 (1st part) ; of one another, Rom. 12 : 5 (as with the natural illustration, so with the spiritual analogy, there is not only vital unity, and harmony in operation, but diversity, all being essential to effectivity ; the unity is not due to external organization but to common and vital union in Christ) ; there is stress in ver. 5 upon " many " and " in Christ " and " members ; " 1 Cor. 12 : 27 (of the members of a local church as a body) ; Eph. 4 : 25 (of the members of the whole Church as the mystical body of Christ) ; in 1 Cor. 6 : 15 (2nd part), of one who practises fornication.¶

MEMORIAL

MNĒMOSUNON (μνημόσυνον) denotes a memorial, that which keeps alive the memory of someone or something (from *mnēmōn*, mindful), Matt. 26 : 13 ; Mark 14 : 9 ; Acts 10 : 4.¶

For MEMORY (keep in) see KEEP, Note (8)

MEN

Notes : (1) For this plural see the nouns under MAN. (2) For *anthrōpinos*, e.g., Rom. 6 : 19, " after the manner of men," see MAN'S. No. 1. (3) For the phrase *kat' anthrōpon*, " after the manner of men," see MAN, No. 1(*f*). (4) The phrase " quit you like men," 1 Cor. 16 : 13, translates the verb *andrizō*, in the Middle Voice, to play the man (a verb illustrated in the papyri). (5) See also ALL, GOOD, GREAT, LOW (estate), THESE, (of) WAR.

MEN-PLEASERS

ANTHRŌPARESKOS (ἀνθρωπάρεσκος), an adjective signifying study-ing to please men (*anthrōpos*, man, *areskō*, to please), designates, " not simply one who is pleasing to men . . . , but one who endeavours to please men and not God " (Cremer). It is used in Eph. 6 : 6 and Col. 3 : 22.¶ In the Sept., Psa. 53 : 5.¶

MENSERVANTS

PAIS (παῖς), for the meanings of which see CHILD, No. 4, is translated " menservants " in Luke 12 : 45.

MEN-STEALERS

ANDRAPODISTĒS (ἀνδραποδιστής), a slave-dealer, kidnapper, from *andrapodon*, a slave captured in war, a word found in the plural in the papyri, e.g., in a catalogue of property and in combination with *tetrapoda*, four-footed things (*andrapodon, anēr*, a man, *pous*, a foot) ; *andrapodon* " was never an ordinary word for slave ; it was too brutally obvious a reminder of the principle which made quadruped and human chattels differ only in the number of their legs " (Moulton and Milligan, Vocab.). The verb *andrapodizō* supplied the noun " with the like odious meaning," which appears in 1 Tim. 1 : 10.¶

MEND

KATARTIZŌ (καταρτίζω), from *kata,* down, intensive and *artios,* fit, has three meanings, (*a*) to mend, repair, Matt. 4 : 21; Mark 1 : 19, of nets; (*b*) to complete, furnish completely, equip, prepare, Luke 6 : 40; Rom. 9 : 22; Heb. 11 : 3 and in the Middle Voice, Matt. 21 : 16; Heb.

10 : 5 ; (c) ethically, to prepare, perfect, Gal. 6 : 1 ; 1 Thess. 3 : 10 ; 1 Pet. 5 : 10 ; Heb. 13 : 21 ; and in the Passive Voice, 1 Cor. 1 : 10 ; 2 Cor. 13 : 11. See FIT, FRAME, JOIN, PERFECT, PREPARE, RESTORE.¶

MENTION (Noun and Verb)
A. Noun.

MNEIA (μνεία), remembrance, mention (akin to *mimnēskō*, to remind, remember), is always used in connection with prayer, and translated " mention " in Rom. 1 : 9 ; Eph. 1 : 16 ; 1 Thess. 1 : 2 ; Philm. 4, in each of which it is preceded by the verb to make ; " remembrance " in Phil. 1 : 3 ; 1 Thess. 3 : 6 ; 2 Tim. 1 : 3. Some mss. have it in Rom. 12 : 13, instead of *chreiais*, necessities. See REMEMBRANCE.¶ Cp. *mnēmē*, memory, remembrance, 2 Pet. 1 : 15.¶

B. Verb.

MNĒMONEUŌ (μνημονεύω), which most usually means to call to mind, remember, signifies to make mention of, in Heb. 11 : 22. See REMEMBER.

MERCHANDISE (Noun, and Verb, to make)
A. Nouns.

1. EMPORIA (ἐμπορία) denotes commerce, business, trade [akin to No. 2, and to *emporos*, one on a journey (*en*, in, *poros*, a journey), a merchant], occurs in Matt. 22 : 5.¶

2. EMPORION (ἐμπόριον) denotes a trading-place, exchange (Eng., emporium), John 2 : 16, " (a house) of merchandise."¶

3. GOMOS (γόμος) is translated " merchandise " in Rev. 18 : 11, 12 : see BURDEN, A, No. 3.

B. Verb.

EMPOREUOMAI (ἐμπορεύομαι) primarily signifies to travel, especially for business ; then, to traffic, trade, Jas. 4 : 13 ; then, to make a gain of, make merchandise of, 2 Pet. 2 : 3.¶

MERCHANT

EMPOROS (ἔμπορος) denotes a person on a journey (*poros*, a journey), a passenger on shipboard ; then, a merchant, Matt. 13 : 45 ; Rev. 18 : 3, 11, 15, 23.¶

MERCIFUL (Adjective, and Verb, to be), MERCY (Noun, and Verb, to have, etc.)
A. Nouns.

1. ELEOS (ἔλεος) " is the outward manifestation of pity ; it assumes need on the part of him who receives it, and resources adequate to meet the need on the part of him who shows it. It is used (a) of God, who is rich in mercy, Eph. 2 : 4, and who has provided salvation for all men, Tit. 3 : 5, for Jews, Luke 1 : 72, and Gentiles, Rom. 15 : 9. He is merciful to those who fear him, Luke 1 : 50, for they also are compassed with

infirmity, and He alone can succour them. Hence they are to pray boldly for mercy, Heb. 4 : 16, and if for themselves, it is seemly that they should ask for mercy for one another, Gal. 6 : 16 ; 1 Tim. 1 : 2. When God brings His salvation to its issue at the Coming of Christ, His people will obtain His mercy, 2 Tim. 1 : 16 ; Jude 21 ; (b) of men ; for since God is merciful to them, He would have them show mercy to one another, Matt. 9 : 13 ; 12 : 7 ; 23 : 23 ; Luke 10 : 37 ; Jas. 2 : 13.

" Wherever the words mercy and peace are found together they occur in that order, except in Gal. 6 : 16. Mercy is the act of God, peace is the resulting experience in the heart of man. Grace describes God's attitude toward the law-breaker and the rebel ; mercy is His attitude toward those who are in distress."*

" In the order of the manifestation of God's purposes of salvation grace must go before mercy . . . only the forgiven may be blessed. . . . From this it follows that in each of the apostolic salutations where these words occur, grace precedes mercy, 1 Tim. 1 : 2 ; 2 Tim. 1 : 2 ; Tit. 1 : 4 (in some mss.) ; 2 John 3 " (Trench, Syn. § xlvii).

2. OIKTIRMOS (οἰκτιρμός), pity, compassion for the ills of others, is used (a) of God, Who is " the Father of mercies," 2 Cor. 1 : 3 ; His mercies are the ground upon which believers are to present their bodies a living sacrifice, holy, acceptable to God, as their reasonable service, Rom. 12 : 1 ; under the Law he who set it at nought died without compassion, Heb. 10 : 28 ; (b) of men ; believers are to feel and exhibit compassions one toward another, Phil. 2 : 1, R.V. " compassions," and Col. 3 : 12, R.V. " (a heart) of compassion ; " in these two places the word is preceded by No. 3, rendered " tender mercies " in the former, and " a heart " in the latter, R.V.¶

3. SPLANCHNON (σπλάγχνον), affections, the heart, always in the plural in the N.T., has reference to feelings of kindness, goodwill, pity, Phil. 2 : 1, R.V., " tender mercies ; " see AFFECTION, No. 2, and BOWELS.

Note : In Acts 13 : 34 the phrase, lit., ' the holy things, the faithful things (of David) ' is translated, " the holy and sure *blessings*," R.V. ; the A.V., following the mss. in which the words " holy and " are absent, has " the sure mercies," but notices the full phrase in the margin.

B. Verbs.

1. ELEEŌ (ἐλεέω), akin to A, No. 1, signifies, in general, to feel sympathy with the misery of another, and especially sympathy manifested in act, (a) in the Active Voice, to have pity or mercy on, to shew mercy to, e.g., Matt. 9 : 27 ; 15 : 22 ; 17 : 15 ; 18 : 33 ; 20 : 30, 31 (three times in Mark, four in Luke) ; Rom. 9 : 15, 16, 18 ; 11 : 32 ; 12 : 8 ; Phil. 2 : 27 ; Jude 22, 23 ; (b) in the Passive Voice, to have pity or mercy shown one, to obtain mercy, Matt. 5 : 7 ; Rom. 11 : 30, 31 ; 1 Cor. 7 : 25 ; 2 Cor. 4 : 1 ; 1 Tim. 1 : 13, 16 ; 1 Pet. 2 : 10.

---

* From Notes on Galatians by Hogg and Vine, pp. 340, 341.

2. OIKTEIRŌ (οἰκτείρω), akin to A, No. 2, to have pity on (from *oiktos*, pity: *oi*, an exclamation,=oh !), occurs in Rom. 9 : 15 (twice), where it follows No. 1 (twice) ; the point established there and in Ex. 33 : 19, from the Sept. of which it is quoted, is that the mercy and compassion shown by God are determined by nothing external to His attributes. Speaking generally *oikteirō* is a stronger term than *eleeō*.¶

3. HILASKOMAI (ἱλάσκομαι) in profane Greek meant to conciliate, appease, propitiate, cause the gods to be reconciled ; their goodwill was not regarded as their natural condition, but as something to be earned. The heathen believed their gods to be naturally alienated in feeling from man. In the N.T. the word never means to conciliate God ; it signifies (a) to be propitious, merciful, Luke 18 : 13, in the prayer of the publican ; (b) to expiate, make propitiation for, Heb. 2 : 17, " make propitiation."

That God is not of Himself already alienated from man, see John 3 : 16. His attitude toward the sinner does not need to be changed by his efforts. With regard to his sin, an expiation is necessary, consistently with God's holiness and for His righteousness' sake, and that expiation His grace and love have provided in the atoning Sacrifice of His Son ; man, himself a sinner, justly exposed to God's wrath (John 3 : 36), could never find an expiation. As Lightfoot says, " when the N.T. writers speak at length on the subject of Divine wrath, the hostility is represented, not as on the part of God, but of men." Through that which God has accomplished in Christ, by His death, man, on becoming regenerate, escapes the merited wrath of God. The making of this expiation [(b) above], with its effect in the mercy of God (a) is what is expressed in *hilaskomai*.¶ The Sept. uses the compound verb *exilaskomai*, e.g., Gen. 32 : 20 ; Ex. 30 : 10, 15, 16 ; 32 : 30, and frequently in Lev. and Numb. See PROPITIATION.

C. Adjectives.

1. ELEĒMŌN (ἐλεήμων), merciful, akin to A, No. 1, not simply possessed of pity but actively compassionate, is used of Christ as a High Priest, Heb. 2:17, and of those who are like God, Matt. 5:7 (cp. Luke 6:35, 36, where the R.V., "sons" is to be read, as representing characteristics resembling those of their Father).¶

2. OIKTIRMŌN (ὀικτίρμων), pitiful, compassionate for the ills of others, a stronger term than No. 1 (akin to A, No. 2), is used twice in Luke 6:36, "merciful" (of the character of God, to be expressed in His people) ; Jas. 5:11, R.V., "merciful," A.V., "of tender mercy."¶

3. HILEŌS (ἵλεως), propitious, merciful (akin to B, No. 3), was used in profane Greek just as in the case of the verb (which see). There is nothing of this in the use of the word in Scripture. The quality expressed by it there essentially appertains to God, though man is undeserving of it. It is used only of God, Heb. 8:12; in Matt. 16:22, "Be it far from Thee" (Peter's word to Christ) may have the meaning given in the R.V. marg., "(God) have mercy on Thee," lit., 'propitious to Thee' (A.V. marg., "Pity Thyself")¶ Cp. the Sept., 2 Sam. 20:20; 23:17.

4. ANELEOS or ANILEŌS (ἀνέλεος or ἀνίλεως), unmerciful, merciless (*a*, negative, *n*, euphonic, and A, No. 1, or C, No. 3), occurs in Jas. 2 : 13, said of judgment on him who shows no mercy.¶

MERCY-SEAT

HILASTĒRION (ἱλαστήριον), the lid or cover of the ark of the Covenant, signifies the Propitiatory, so called on account of the expiation made once a year on the great day of atonement, Heb. 9 : 5. For the formation see Ex. 25 : 17–21. The Heb. word is *kapporeth*, the cover, a meaning connected with the covering or removal of sin (Psa. 32 : 1) by means of expiatory sacrifice. This mercy-seat, together with the ark, is spoken of as the footstool of God, 1 Chron. 28 : 2 ; cp. Ps. 99 : 5 ; 132 : 7. The Lord promised to be present upon it and to commune with Moses " from above the mercy-seat, from between the two cherubim," Ex. 25 : 22 (see CHERUBIM). In the Sept. the word *epithēma*, which itself means a cover, is added to *hilastērion*; *epithēma* was simply a translation of *kapporeth*; accordingly, *hilastērion*, not having this meaning, and being essentially connected with propitiation, was added. Eventually *hilastērion* stood for both. In 1 Chron. 28 : 11 the Holy of Holies is called " the House of the Kapporeth " (see R.V., marg.).

Through His voluntary expiatory sacrifice in the shedding of His blood, under Divine judgment upon sin, and through His Resurrection, Christ has become the Mercy-Seat for His people. See Rom. 3 : 25, and see PROPITIATION, B, No. 1.¶

MERRY (to be, to make)

1. EUPHRAINŌ (εὐφραίνω), in the Active Voice, to cheer, make glad, 2 Cor. 2 : 2, is used everywhere else in the Passive Voice, signifying, to be happy, rejoice, make merry, and translated to be merry in Luke 12 : 19 ; 15 : 23, 24, 29, 32 ; in 16 : 19, " fared (sumptuously) ; " in Rev. 11 : 10, " make merry." See FARE, GLAD, REJOICE.

2. EUTHUMEŌ (εὐθυμέω), from *eu*, well, and *thumos*, the soul, as the principle of feeling, especially strong feeling, signifies to make cheerful ; it is used intransitively in the N.T., to be of good cheer, Acts 27 : 22, 25 ; in Jas. 5 : 13, R.V., " is (any) cheerful ? " (A.V., " . . . merry ? "). See CHEER.¶

MESS

BRŌSIS (βρῶσις), eating, food, is translated " mess of meat " in Heb. 12 : 16, R.V. (A.V., " morsel of meat "). See FOOD, MEAT, No. 2.

MESSAGE

1. ANGELIA (ἀγγελία), akin to *angellō*, to bring a message, proclaim, denotes a message, proclamation, news, 1 John 1 : 5 [some mss. have *epangelia* : see Note (1)] ; 1 John 3 : 11, where the word is more precisely

defined (by being followed by the conjunction " that," expressing the purpose that we should love one another) as being virtually equivalent to an order.¶

Notes : (1) *Epangelia* (*epi*, upon, and No. 1), a promise, is found in some mss. in 1 John 1 : 5, " message " (see No. 1). See PROMISE. (2) In Luke 19 : 14, A.V., *presbeia*, is translated " a message ; " R.V., " an ambassage," as in 14 : 32. See AMBASSAGE.¶

2. AKOĒ (ἀκοή), hearing, also denotes the thing heard, a message ; in 1 Thess. 2 : 13, it is associated with *logos*, a word, lit., ' the word of hearing ' (R.V. marg.), R.V., " the word of the message," A.V., " the word . . . which ye heard ; " so in Heb. 4 : 2, R.V., " the word of hearing " (A.V., " the word preached "). See HEARING.

3. KĒRUGMA (κήρυγμα), that which is proclaimed by a herald, a proclamation, preaching, is translated " the message " in Tit. 1 : 3, R.V. (A.V., " preaching "). See PREACHING.

MESSENGER

1. ANGELOS (ἄγγελος), a messenger, an angel, one sent, is translated " messenger," of John the Baptist, Matt. 11 : 10 ; Mark 1 : 2 ; Luke 7 : 27 ; in the plural, of John's messengers, 7 : 24 ; of those whom Christ sent before Him when on His journey to Jerusalem, 9 : 52 ; of Paul's " thorn in the flesh," " a messenger of Satan," 2 Cor. 12 : 7 ; of the spies as received by Rahab, Jas. 2 : 25. See ANGEL.

2. APOSTOLOS (ἀπόστολος), an apostle, is translated " messengers " in 2 Cor. 8 : 23 regarding Titus and " the other brethren," whom Paul describes to the Church at Corinth as " messengers of the churches," in respect of offerings from those in Macedonia for the needy in Judæa ; in Phil. 2 : 25, of Epaphroditus as the " messenger " of the church at Philippi to the Apostle in ministering to his need ; R.V. marg. in each case, " apostle." See APOSTLE.

For METE see MEASURE

For MID see MIDST

MIDDAY

Note : In Acts 26 : 13, " at midday " translates the adjective *mesos*, middle, and the noun *hēmera*, a day, in a combined adverbial phrase. See MIDST.

For MIDDLE see WALL

MIDNIGHT

MESONUKTION (μεσονύκτιον), an adjective denoting at, or of, midnight, is used as a noun in Mark 13 : 35 ; Luke 11 : 5 ; Acts 16 : 25 ; 20 : 7.¶

Note : In Matt. 25 : 6 "at midnight" translates the adjective *mesos*, and noun *nux*, night, in the combined adverbial phrase. In Acts 27 : 27 "about midnight" translates an adverbial phrase consisting of *kata*, towards, followed by *mesos*, middle and *nux*, night, with the article, lit., 'towards (the) middle of the night.' See MIDST.

MIDST
A. Adjective and Adverb.

MESOS (μέσος), an adjective denoting middle, in the middle or midst, is used in the following, in which the English requires a phrase, and the adjectival rendering must be avoided : Luke 22 : 55, "Peter sat in the midst of them," lit., 'a middle one of (them) ;' Luke 23 : 45, of the rending of the veil "in the midst ;" here the adjective idiomatically belongs to the verb "was rent," and is not to be taken literally, as if it meant 'the middle veil ;' John 1 : 26, "in the midst of you (standeth One)," R.V. (lit., 'a middle One '); Acts 1 : 18, where the necessity of avoiding the lit. rendering is obvious. Cp. the phrases "at midday," "at midnight" (see MIDDAY, MIDNIGHT, above).

Notes : (1) *Mesos* is used adverbially, in prepositional phrases, (a) *ana m.*, e.g., 1 Cor. 6 : 5, "between ;" Matt. 13 : 25, "among ;" Rev. 7 : 17, "in the midst ;" (b) *dia m.*, e.g., Luke 4 : 30 ; 17 : 11, "through the midst ;" (c) *en m.*, Luke 10 : 3, R.V., "in the midst," A.V., "among ;" so 22 : 27 ; 1 Thess. 2 : 7 ; with the article after *en*, e.g., Matt. 14 : 6, R.V., "in the midst," A.V., "before ;" (d) *eis m.*, Mark 14 : 60, "in the midst ;" with the article, e.g., Mark 3 : 3, "forth" (lit., 'into the midst') ; (e) *ek m.*, "out of the way," lit., 'out of the midst,' Col. 2 : 14 ; 2 Thess. 2 : 7, where, however, removal is not necessarily in view ; there is no accompanying verb signifying removal, as in each of the other occurrences of the phrase ; with the article, e.g., 1 Cor. 5 : 2 ; 2 Cor. 6 : 17 ; see WAY ; (f) *kata m.*, Acts 27 : 27, "about mid(night)."

(2) The neuter, *meson*, is used adverbially in Matt. 14 : 24, in some mss., "in the midst (of the waves) ;" in Phil. 2 : 15 in the best mss. (where some mss. have *en m.* . . .). (3) For Rev. 8 : 13, see HEAVEN, A, No. 2.

B. Verb.

MESOŌ (μεσόω), to be in the middle, is used of time in John 7 : 14, translated "when it was . . . the midst (of the feast)." lit., '(the feast) being in the middle.'¶

MIGHT (Noun), MIGHTY, MIGHTILY, MIGHTIER
A. Nouns.

1. DUNAMIS (δύναμις), power, (a) used relatively, denotes inherent ability, capability, ability to perform anything, e.g., Matt. 25 : 15,

" ability ; " Acts 3 : 12, " power " ; 2 Thess. 1 : 7, R.V., " (angels) of His power " (A.V., " mighty ") ; Heb. 11 : 11, R.V., " power " (A.V., " strength ") ; see ABILITY ; (b) used absolutely, denotes (1) power to work, to carry something into effect, e.g., Luke 24 : 49 ; (2) power in action, e.g., Rom. 1 : 16 ; 1 Cor. 1 : 18 ; it is translated " might " in the A.V. of Eph. 1 : 21 (R.V., " power ") ; so 3 : 16 ; Col. 1 : 11 (1st clause) ; 2 Pet. 2 : 11 ; in Rom. 15 : 19, A.V., this noun is rendered " mighty ; " R.V., " (in the) power of signs." The R.V. consistently avoids the rendering " might " for *dunamis;* the usual rendering is " power." Under this heading comes the rendering " mighty works," e.g., Matt. 7 : 22, R.V. (A.V., " wonderful works ") ; 11 : 20-23 ; singular number in Mark 6 : 5 ; in Matt. 14 : 2 and Mark 6 : 14 the R.V. has " powers ; " in 2 Cor. 12 : 12, R.V., " mighty works " (A.V., " mighty deeds "). See MIRACLE, especially POWER.

Note : *Dunamis*, power, is to be distinguished from *exousia*, the right to exercise power. See DOMINION, Note.

2. ISCHUS (ἰσχύς) denotes might, strength, power, (a) inherent and in action as used of God, Eph. 1 : 19, R.V., " (the strength, *kratos*, of His) might," A.V., " (His mighty) power," i.e., power (over external things) exercised by strength ; Eph. 6 : 10, " of His might ; " 2 Thess. 1 : 9, R.V., " (from the glory) of His might " (A.V. " power ") ; Rev. 5 : 12, R.V., " might " (A.V., " strength ") ; 7 : 12, " might ; " (b) as an endowment, said (1) of angels, 2 Pet. 2 : 11 ; here the order is No. 2 and No. 1, R.V., " might and power," which better expresses the distinction than the A.V., " power and might ; " in some mss. in Rev. 18 : 2 it is said of the voice of an angel [see E, (c)] ; the most authentic mss. have the adjective *ischuros,* " mighty ; " (2) of men, Mark 12 : 30, 33 ; Luke 10 : 27 (R.V. and A.V., " strength," in all three verses) ; 1 Pet. 4 : 11, R.V., " strength " (A.V., " ability : " this belongs rather to No. 1). Either ' strength ' or ' might ' expresses the true significance of *ischus.* See ABILITY, POWER, STRENGTH.¶

Notes : (1) In Luke 9 : 43, A.V., *megaleiotēs*, greatness, majesty, is translated " mighty power " (R.V., " majesty "). (2) Cp. *kratos* (see POWER).

B. Adjectives.

1. DUNATOS (δυνατός), powerful, mighty (akin to A, No. 1), is used, with that significance, (1) of God, Luke 1 : 49, " mighty ; " Rom. 9 : 22, " power " (here the neuter of the adjective is used with the article, as a noun, equivalent to *dunamis*) ; frequently with the meaning " able " (see ABLE, C, No. 1) ; (2) of Christ, regarded as a prophet, Luke 24 : 19 (" in deed and word ") ; (3) of men : Moses, Acts 7 : 22 (" in his words and works ") ; Apollos, 18 : 24, " in the Scriptures ; " of those possessed of natural power, 1 Cor. 1 : 26 ; of those possessed of spiritual power, 2 Cor. 10 : 4. For the shades of meaning in the translation " strong,"

see Rom. 15 : 1 ; 2 Cor. 12 : 10 ; 13 : 9. For Rev. 6 : 15, see No. 2, below ; see STRONG. See also POSSIBLE.

2. ISCHUROS (ἰσχυρός), strong, mighty (akin to A, No. 2, and with corresponding adjectival significance), is usually translated " strong ; " " mighty " in Luke 15 : 14 (of a famine) ; Rev. 19 : 6 (of thunders) ; 19 : 18 (of men) : in the following, where the A.V. has " mighty," the R.V. substitutes " strong," 1 Cor. 1 : 27 ; Rev. 6 : 15 (A.V., " mighty men ") ; 18 : 10, 21 ; Heb. 11 : 34, R.V., " (waxed) mighty " (A.V., " valiant "). See BOISTEROUS, POWERFUL, STRONG (where the word is analysed).

3. ISCHUROTEROS (ἰσχυρότερος), stronger, mightier, the comparative degree of No. 2, is translated " mightier " in Matt. 3 : 11 ; Mark 1 : 7 ; Luke 3 : 16 ; " stronger " in Luke 11 : 22 ; 1 Cor. 1 : 25 ; 10 : 22. See STRONG.¶

4. BIAIOS (βίαιος), violent (from bia, force, violence, strength, found in Acts 5 : 26 ; 21 : 35 ; 24 : 7 ; 27 : 41¶), occurs in Acts 2 : 2, of wind.¶

5. KRATAIOS (κραταιός), strong, mighty (akin to kratos, strength, relative and manifested power : see MIGHTILY, below), is found in 1 Pet. 5 : 6, of the " mighty " hand of God.¶

6. MEGALEIOS (μεγαλεῖος) is rendered " mighty " in Acts 2 : 11, R.V. See WONDERFUL, Note (2).

Notes : (1) In Luke 1 : 52, A.V., *dunastēs*, a potentate, prince, is translated " mighty " (R.V., " princes "). (2) In Rev. 6 : 13, A.V., *megas*, great, is translated " mighty " (R.V., " great "), of a wind. (3) In Rev. 16 : 18, A.V., *tēlikoutos*, so great (when said of things), is translated " so mighty " (R.V., " so great "), of an earthquake.

C. Verb.

DUNATEŌ (δυνατέω), to be powerful (akin to A, No. 1 and B, No. 1), is found in the most authentic mss. in Rom. 14 : 4 (some have *dunatos*, B, No. 1), R.V. " (the Lord) hath power," A.V., " (God) is able ; " similarly, as regard mss., in 2 Cor. 9 : 8, where the R.V. and A.V. have " (God) is able ; " in 2 Cor. 13 : 3, A.V., " is mighty," R.V., " is powerful " (according to the general significance of *dunamis*).¶

Note : In Gal. 2 : 8, A.V., *energeō*, to work, work in (*en*, in, *ergon*, work), is first translated " wrought effectually," then " was mighty in " (R.V., " wrought for," in both places ; the probable meaning is ' in me '). See EFFECTUAL, WORK.

D. Adverb.

EUTONŌS (εὐτόνως), vigorously, vehemently (*eu*, well, *teinō*, to stretch), is translated " mightily " in Acts 18 : 28, A.V., of the power of Apollos in ' confuting ' the Jews (R.V., " powerfully ") ; in Luke 23 : 10 it is rendered " vehemently." See POWERFUL, VEHEMENTLY.¶ In the Sept., Josh. 6 : 7, " (let them sound) loudly."¶

E. Phrases.

The following phrases signify " mightily : " (a) *en dunamei*, Col. 1 : 29, of the inward power of God's working, lit., " in power," as R.V. marg.

(*en*, in, and A, No. 1) ; (*b*) *kata kratos*, Acts 19 : 20, of the increase of the word of the Lord in a place, lit., ' according to might ; ' (*c*) in Rev. 18 : 2 some mss. have *en ischui*, lit., ' in strength ' (*en*, in, and A, No. 2), of the voice of an angel.

MILE

MILION (μίλιον), a Roman mile, a word of Latin origin (1680 yards), is used in Matt. 5 : 41.¶

MILK

GALA (γάλα) is used (*a*) literally, 1 Cor. 9 : 7 ; (*b*) metaphorically, of rudimentary spiritual teaching, 1 Cor. 3 : 2 ; Heb. 5 : 12, 13 ; 1 Pet. 2 : 2 ; here the meaning largely depends upon the significance of the word *logikos*, which the A.V. renders " of the word," R.V. " spiritual." While *logos* denotes a **word**, the adjective *logikos* is never used with the meaning assigned to it in the A.V., nor does the context in 1 : 23 compel this meaning. While it is true that the Word of God, like milk, nourishes the soul, and this is involved in the exhortation, the only other occurrence in the N.T. is Rom. 12 : 1, where it is translated " reasonable," i.e., rational, intelligent (service), in contrast to the offering of an irrational animal ; so here the nourishment may be understood as of that spiritually rational nature which, acting through the regenerate mind, develops spiritual growth. God's Word is not given so that it is impossible to understand it, or that it requires a special class of men to interpret it ; its character is such that the Holy Spirit who gave it can unfold its truths even to the young convert. Cp. 1 John 2 : 27.¶

MILL

MULŌN (μύλων) denotes a mill-house, where the millstone is, Matt. 24 : 41 ; some mss. have *mulos* (see next word).¶ In the Sept., Jer. 52 : 11, " grinding house " (lit., ' house of a mill ').¶

MILLSTONE
A. Noun.

MULOS (μύλος) denotes a hand-mill, consisting of two circular stones, one above the other, the lower being fixed. From the centre of the lower a wooden pin passes through a hole in the upper, into which the grain is thrown, escaping as flour between the stones and falling on a prepared material below them. The handle is inserted into the upper stone near the circumference. Small stones could be turned by one woman (mill-grinding was a work deemed fit only for women and slaves ; cp. Judg. 16 : 21) ; larger ones were turned by two (cp. Matt. 24 : 41, under MILL), or more.

Still larger ones were turned by an ass (*onikos*), Matt. 18 : 6, R.V., " a great millstone " (marg., " a millstone turned by an ass "), indicating the immediate and overwhelming drowning of one who causes one young believer to stumble ; Mark 9 : 42 (where some mss. have *lithos mulikos*, a stone of a mill, as in Luke 17 : 2) ; Rev. 18 : 22 (some mss. have it in ver. 21, see below).¶

B. Adjectives.

1. MULIKOS (μυλικός), ' of a mill,' occurs in Luke 17 : 2 (see above).¶

2. MULINOS (μύλινος), made of millstone, is used with *lithos*, a stone; and with the adjective *megas*, great, in the best mss. in Rev. 18 : 21 (some have the word *mulos*; see A).¶

MIND (Noun and Verb)
A. Nouns.

1. NOUS (νοῦς), mind, denotes, speaking generally, the seat of reflective consciousness, comprising the faculties of perception and understanding, and those of feeling, judging and determining.

Its use in the N.T. may be analysed as follows : it denotes (*a*) the faculty of knowing, the seat of the understanding, Luke 24 : 45 ; Rom. 1 : 28 ; 14 : 5 ; 1 Cor. 14 : 15, 19 ; Eph. 4 : 17 ; Phil. 4 : 7 ; Col. 2 : 18 ; 1 Tim. 6 : 5 ; 2 Tim. 3 : 8 ; Tit. 1 : 15 ; Rev. 13 : 18 ; 17 : 9 ; (*b*) counsels, purpose, Rom. 11 : 34 (of the mind of God) ; 12 : 2 ; 1 Cor. 1 : 10 ; 2 : 16, twice (1) of the thoughts and counsels of God, (2) of Christ, a testimony to His Godhood ; Eph. 4 : 23 ; (*c*) the new nature, which belongs to the believer by reason of the new birth, Rom. 7 : 23, 25, where it is contrasted with " the flesh," the principle of evil which dominates fallen man. Under (*b*) may come 2 Thess. 2 : 2, where it stands for the determination to be stedfast amidst afflictions, through the confident expectation of the day of rest and recompense mentioned in the first chapter.¶

2. DIANOIA (διάνοια), lit. a thinking through, or over, a meditation, reflecting, signifies (*a*) like No. 1, the faculty of knowing, understanding, or moral reflection, (1) with an evil significance, a consciousness characterized by a perverted moral impulse, Eph. 2 : 3 (plural) ; 4 : 18 ; (2) with a good significance, the faculty renewed by the Holy Spirit, Matt. 22 : 37 ; Mark 12 : 30 ; Luke 10 : 27 ; Heb. 8 : 10 ; 10 : 16 ; 1 Pet. 1 : 13 ; 1 John 5 : 20 ; (*b*) sentiment, disposition (not as a function but as a product) ; (1) in an evil sense, Luke 1 : 51, " imagination ; " Col. 1 : 21 ; (2) in a good sense, 2 Pet. 3 : 1.¶

3. ENNOIA (ἔννοια), an idea, notion, intent, is rendered " mind " in 1 Pet. 4 : 1 ; see INTENT.

4. NOĒMA (νόημα), thought, design, is rendered " minds " in 2 Cor. 3 : 14 ; 4 : 4 ; 11 : 3 ; Phil. 4 : 7 ; see DEVICE, No. 2.

5. GNŌMĒ (γνώμη), a purpose, judgment, opinion, is translated " mind " in Philm. 14 and Rev. 17 : 13. See JUDGMENT, No. 4.

6. PHRONĒMA (φρόνημα) denotes what one has in the mind, the thought (the content of the process expressed in *phroneō*, to have in mind, to think) ; or an object of thought ; in Rom. 8 : 6 (A.V., " to be carnally

minded " and " to be spiritually minded "), the R.V., adhering to the use of the noun, renders by " the mind of the flesh," in vv. 6 and 7, and " the mind of the spirit," in ver. 6.   In ver. 27 the word is used of the mind of the Holy Spirit.¶

Notes : (1) This word is to be distinguished from *phronēsis*, which denotes an understanding, leading to right action, prudence, Luke 1 : 17 ; Eph. 1 : 8.¶ (2) In three places, Acts 14 : 2 ; Phil. 1 : 27 ; Heb. 12 : 3, the A.V. translates *psuchē*, the soul, by " mind " (R.V., " soul ").

B. Verbs.

1. PHRONEŌ (φρονέω) signifies (a) to think, to be minded in a certain way : (b) to think of, be mindful of.   It implies moral interest or reflection, not mere unreasoning opinion.   Under (a) it is rendered by the verb to mind in the following : Rom. 8 : 5, " (they that are after the flesh) do mind (the things of the flesh) ; " 12 : 16, " be of (the same) mind," lit., ' minding the same,' and " set (not) your mind on," R.V., A.V., " mind (not) ; " 15 : 5, " to be of (the same) mind," R.V., (A.V., " to be like-minded ") ; so the R.V. in 2 Cor. 13 : 11, A.V., " be of (one) mind ; " Gal. 5 : 10, " ye will be (none otherwise) minded ; " Phil. 1 : 7, R.V., " to be (thus) minded," A.V., " to think (this) ; " 2 : 2, R.V., " be of (the same) mind," A.V., " be likeminded," and " being . . . of (one) mind," lit., ' minding (the one thing) ;' 2 : 5, R.V., " have (this) mind," A.V., " let (this) mind be," lit., ' mind this ;' 3 : 15, " let us . . . be (thus) minded," and " (if) . . . ye are (otherwise) minded " (some mss. have the verb in ver. 16) ; 3 : 19, " (who) mind (earthly things) ; " 4 : 2, " be of (the same) mind ; " Col. 3 : 2, R.V. and A.V. marg., " set your mind," lit., ' mind (the things above),' A.V., " set your affection." See CAREFUL, B,   6, REGARD, SAVOUR, THINK, UNDERSTAND.

2. ANAMIMNĒSKŌ (ἀναμιμνήσκω), to remind, call to remembrance (*ana*, up, *mimnēskō*, to remind), is translated " called to mind," in Mark 14 : 72 (Passive Voice). See REMEMBRANCE.

Note : The lengthened form *epanamimnēskō* is used in Rom. 15 : 15, A.V., " putting (you) in mind ; " R.V., " putting (you) again (*epi*) in remembrance."¶

3. HUPOMIMNĒSKŌ (ὑπομιμνήσκω), to cause one to remember, put one in mind (*hupo*, under), is translated " put (them) in mind " in Tit. 3 : 1. See REMEMBER, REMEMBRANCE.

4. HUPOTITHĒMI (ὑποτίθημι), lit., to place under (*hupo*, under, *tithēmi*, to place), to lay down (of risking the life, Rom. 16 : 4), also denotes to suggest, put into one's mind, 1 Tim. 4 : 6, R.V., " put . . . in mind " (A.V., " put . . . in remembrance "). See LAY.¶

5. SŌPHRONEŌ (σωφρονέω) signifies (a) to be of sound mind, or in one's right mind, sober-minded (*sōzō*, to save, *phrēn*, the mind), Mark 5 : 15 and Luke 8 : 35, " in his right mind ; " 2 Cor. 5 : 13, R.V., " we are of sober mind " (A.V., " we be sober ") ; (b) to be temperate, self-con-trolled, Tit. 2 : 6, to be sober-minded ; " 1 Pet. 4 : 7, R.V., " be ye . . .

of sound mind" (A.V., " be ye sober "). See also Rom. 12 : 3. See
SOBER.¶

Note : In Acts 20 : 13, A.V., *mellō*, to be about to, to intend, is translated " minding " (R.V., " intending "). See INTEND.

C. Adjective.

HOMOPHRŌN (ὁμόφρων), agreeing, of one mind (*homos*, same, *phrēn*,
the mind), is used in 1 Pet. 3 : 8.¶

Notes : (1) For the noun *sōphronismos*, in 2 Tim. 1 : 7, see
DISCIPLINE.¶ (2) In Rom. 15 : 6, A.V., the adverb *homothumadon*, of
one accord, is translated " with one mind " (R.V., " of one accord ").
See ACCORD. (3) See also CAST, CHANGE, DOUBTFUL, FERVENT, FOR-
WARDNESS, HUMBLENESS, HUMILITY, LOWLINESS, READINESS, READY,
WILLING.

MINDED

1. PHRONEŌ (φρονέω) : see MIND, B, No. 1.

2. BOULOMAI (βούλομαι), to wish, will, desire, purpose (akin to
boulē, counsel, purpose), is translated " was minded " in Matt. 1 : 19 ;
Acts 15 : 37, R.V. (A.V., " determined ") ; 18 : 27, R.V. (A.V., " was
disposed ") ; 19 : 30, R.V. (A.V., " would have ") ; 5 : 33, R.V., " were
minded " (A.V., " took counsel ") ; 18 : 15, R.V., " I am (not) minded
(to be)," A.V., " I will (be no) ; " Heb. 6 : 17, " being minded," R.V.
(A.V., " willing "), said of God. See COUNSEL.

3. BOULEUŌ (βουλεύω), to take counsel, is translated to be minded
in Acts 27 : 39 ; 2 Cor. 1 : 17, Middle Voice in each case. See COUNSEL,
B, No. 1.

Note : For the noun *phronēma* in Rom. 8 : 6, see MIND, A, No. 6.

MINDFUL OF (to be)

1. MIMNĒSKŌ (μιμνήσκω), the tenses of which are from the older
verb *mnaomai*, signifies to remind ; but in the Middle Voice, to remember,
to be mindful of, in the sense of caring for, e.g., Heb. 2 : 6, " Thou art
mindful ; " in 13 : 3, " remember ; " in 2 Tim. 1 : 4, R.V., " remembering "
(A.V., " being mindful of ") ; so in 2 Pet. 3 : 2. See REMEMBER.

2. MNĒMONEUŌ (μνημονεύω), to call to mind, remember, is rendered
" they had been mindful " in Heb. 11 : 15. See MENTION, B, REMEMBER.

For MINE, MINE OWN (self), see MY

MINGLE

1. MIGNUMI (μίγνυμι), to mix, mingle (from a root *mik* ; Eng., *mix*
is akin), is always in the N.T. translated to mingle, Matt. 27 : 34 ; Luke
13 : 1 ; Rev. 8 : 7 ; 15 : 2.¶

2. KERANNUMI (κεράννυμι), to mix, to mingle, chiefly of the diluting
of wine, implies " a mixing of two things, so that they are blended and

form a compound, as in wine and water, whereas *mignumi* (No. 1) implies a mixing without such composition, as in two sorts of grain " (Liddell and Scott, Lex.). It is used in Rev. 18 : 6 (twice) ; in 14 : 10, R.V., " prepared " (marg., " mingled ; " A.V., " poured out "), lit., ' mingled,' followed by *akratos*, unmixed, pure (*a*, negative, and *kratos*, an adjective, from this verb *kerannumi*), the two together forming an oxymoron, the combination in one phrase of two terms that are ordinarily contradictory.¶

Note : For the verb *smurnizō*, to mingle with myrrh, Mark 15 : 23, see MYRRH.¶

MINISTER (Noun and Verb)
A. Nouns.

1. DIAKONOS (διάκονος), a servant, attendant, minister, deacon, is translated " minister " in Mark 10 : 43 ; Rom. 13 : 4 (twice) ; 15 : 8 ; 1 Cor. 3 : 5 ; 2 Cor. 3 : 6 ; 6 : 4 ; 11 : 15 (twice) ; Gal. 2 : 17 ; Eph. 6 : 21 ; Col. 1 : 7, 23, 25 ; 4 : 7 ; 1 Thess. 3 : 2 ; 1 Tim. 4 : 6. See DEACON.

2. LEITOURGOS (λειτουργός) denoted among the Greeks, firstly, one who discharged a public office at his own expense, then, in general, a public servant, minister. In the N.T. it is used (*a*) of Christ, as a " Minister of the sanctuary " (in the Heavens), Heb. 8 : 2 ; (*b*) of angels, Heb. 1 : 7 (Psa. 104 : 4) ; (*c*) of the Apostle Paul, in his evangelical ministry, fulfilling it as a serving-priest, Rom. 15 : 16 ; that he used it figuratively and not in an ecclesiastical sense, is obvious from the context ; (*d*) of Epaphroditus, as ministering to Paul's needs on behalf of the church at Philippi, Phil. 2 : 25 ; here, representative service is in view ; (*e*) of earthly rulers, who though they do not all act consciously as servants of God, yet discharge functions which are the ordinance of God, Rom. 13 : 6.¶

3. HUPĒRETĒS (ὑπηρέτης), properly an under rower (*hupo*, under, *eretēs*, a rower), as distinguished from *nautēs*, a seaman (a meaning which lapsed from the word), hence came to denote any subordinate acting under another's direction ; in Luke 4 : 20, R.V., " attendant," A.V., " minister," it signifies the attendant at the Synagogue service ; in Acts 13 : 5, it is said of John Mark, R.V., " attendant," A.V., " minister ; " in Acts 26 : 16, " a minister," it is said of Paul as a servant of Christ in the Gospel ; so in 1 Cor. 4 : 1, where the Apostle associates others with himself, as Apollos and Cephas, as " ministers of Christ." See ATTEND, C, OFFICER.

Note : Other synonymous nouns are *doulos*, a bondservant ; *oiketēs*, a household servant ; *misthios*, a hired servant ; *misthōtos* (ditto) ; *pais*, a boy, a household servant. For all these see SERVANT. Speaking broadly, *diakonos* views a servant in relation to his work ; *doulos*, in relation to his master ; *hupēretēs*, in relation to his superior ; *leitourgos*, in relation to public service.

B. Verbs.

1. DIAKONEŌ (διακονέω), akin to A, No. 1, signifies to be a servant, attendant, to serve, wait upon, minister. In the following it is translated

to minister, except where to serve is mentioned : it is used (a) with a general significance, e.g., Matt. 4 : 11 ; 20 : 28 ; Mark 1 : 13 ; 10 : 45 ; John 12 : 26 (" serve," twice) ; Acts 19 : 22 ; Philm. 13 ; (b) of waiting at table, ministering to the guests, Matt..8 : 15 ; Luke 4 : 39 ; 8 : 3 ; 12 : 37 ; 17 : 8, " serve ; " 22 : 26, " serve," ver. 27, " serveth," twice ; the 2nd instance, concerning the Lord, may come under (a) ; so of women preparing food, etc., Mark 1 : 31 ; Luke 10 : 40, " serve ; " John 12 : 2, " served ; " (c) of relieving one's necessities, supplying the necessaries of life, Matt. 25 : 44 ; 27 : 55 ; Mark 15 : 41 ; Acts 6 : 2, " serve ; " Rom. 15 : 25 ; Heb. 6 : 10 ; more definitely in connection with such service in a local church, 1 Tim. 3 : 10, 13 [there is nothing in the original representing the word " office ; " R.V., " let them serve as deacons," " they that have served (well) as deacons "] ; (d) of attending, in a more general way, to anything that may serve another's interests, as of the work of an amanuensis, 2 Cor. 3 : 3 (metaphorical) : of the conveyance of material gifts for assisting the needy, 2 Cor. 8 : 19, 20, R.V., " is ministered " (A.V., " is administered ") ; of a variety of forms of service, 2 Tim. 1 : 18 ; of the testimony of the O.T. prophets, 1 Pet. 1 : 12 ; of the ministry of believers one to another in various ways, 1 Pet. 4 : 10, 11 (not here of discharging ecclesiastical functions).¶

Note : In Heb. 1 : 14, A.V. (2nd part), the phrase *eis diakonian* is translated " to minister," R.V., " to do service," lit., ' for service ; ' for the noun " ministering " in the 1st part, see MINISTERING, B.

2. LEITOURGEŌ (λειτουργέω), (akin to A, No. 2), in classical Greek, signified at Athens to supply public offices at one's own cost, to render public service to the State ; hence, generally, to do service, said, e.g., of service to the gods. In the N.T. (see Note below) it is used (a) of the prophets and teachers in the church at Antioch, who " ministered to the Lord," Acts 13 : 2 ; (b) of the duty of churches of the Gentiles to minister in " carnal things " to the poor Jewish saints at Jerusalem, in view of the fact that the former had " been made partakers " of the " spiritual things " of the latter, Rom. 15 : 27 ; (c) of the official service of priests and Levites under the Law, Heb. 10 : 11 (in the Sept., e.g., Ex. 29 : 30 ; Numb. 16 : 9).¶

Note : The synonymous verb *latreuō* (properly, to serve for hire), which is used in the Sept. of the service of both priests and people (e.g., Ex. 4 : 3 ; Deut. 10 : 12, and in the N.T., e.g., Heb. 8 : 5), and, in the N.T., of Christians in general, e.g., Rev. 22 : 3, is to be distinguished from *leitourgeō*, which has to do with the fulfilment of an office, the discharge of a function, something of a representative character (Eng., liturgy).

3. HUPĒRETEŌ (ὑπηρετέω), to do the service of a *hupēretēs* (see A, No. 3), properly, to serve as a rower on a ship, is used (a) of David, as serving the counsel of God in his own generation, Acts 13 : 36, R.V., expressive of the lowly character of his service for God ; (b) of Paul's toil in working with his hands, and his readiness to avoid any pose of ecclesias-

tical superiority, Acts 20 : 34 ; (c) of the service permitted to Paul's friends to render to him, 24 : 23.¶

4. HIEROURGEŌ (ἱερουργέω), to minister in priestly service (akin to *hierourgos*, a sacrificing priest, a word not found in the Sept. or N.T. : from *hieros*, sacred, and *ergon*, work), is used by Paul metaphorically of his ministry of the Gospel, Rom. 15 : 16 ; the offering connected with his priestly ministry is " the offering up of the Gentiles," i.e., the presentation by Gentile converts of themselves to God.¶ The Apostle uses words proper to the priestly and Levitical ritual, to explain metaphorically his own priestly service. Cp. *prosphora*, " offering up," and *leitourgos*, in the same verse.

5. PARECHŌ (παρέχω), to furnish, provide, supply, is translated " minister " in 1 Tim. 1 : 4, of the effect of " fables and endless genealogies." See BRING, A, No. 21.

6. ERGAZOMAI (ἐργάζομαι), to work, work out, perform, is translated " minister " in 1 Cor. 9 : 13 ; the verb is frequently used of business, or employment, and here the phrase means ' those employed in sacred things ' or ' those who are assiduous in priestly functions.' See COMMIT, A, No. 1.

Notes : (1) The verb *chorēgeō*, rendered " minister " in the A.V. of 2 Cor. 9 : 10, and the strengthened form *epichorēgeō*, rendered by the same verb in the A.V. of 2 Cor. 9 : 10 ; Gal. 3 : 5 ; Col. 2 : 19 ; 2 Pet. 1 : 11, in ver. 5, " add," are always translated to supply in the R.V. Both verbs suggest an abundant supply, and are used of material or of spiritual provision. See SUPPLY. (2) In Eph. 4 : 29, A.V., *didōmi*, to give, is translated " minister " (R.V., " give ").

MINISTERING, MINISTRATION, MINISTRY
A. Nouns.

1. DIAKONIA (διακονία), the office and work of a *diakonos* (see MINISTER, A, No. 1), service, ministry, is used (a) of domestic duties, Luke 10 : 40 ; (b) of religious and spiritual ministration, (1) of apostolic ministry, e.g., Acts 1 : 17, 25 ; 6 : 4 ; 12 : 25 ; 21 : 19 ; Rom. 11 : 13, R.V. (A.V., " office ") ; (2) of the service of believers, e.g., Acts 6 : 1 ; Rom. 12 : 7 ; 1 Cor. 12 : 5, R.V., " ministrations " (A.V., " administrations ") ; 1 Cor. 16 : 15 ; 2 Cor. 8 : 4 ; 9 : 1 ; 9 : 12, R.V., " ministration ; " ver. 13 ; Eph. 4 : 12, R.V., " ministering " (A.V., " the ministry," not in the sense of an ecclesiastical function) ; 2 Tim. 4 : 11, R.V., " (for) ministering ; " collectively of a local church, Acts 11 : 29, " relief " (R.V. marg., " for ministry ") ; Rev. 2 : 19, R.V., " ministry " (A.V., " service ") ; of Paul's service on behalf of poor saints, Rom. 15 : 31 ; (3) of the ministry of the Holy Spirit in the Gospel, 2 Cor. 3 : 8 ; (4) of the ministry of angels, Heb. 1 : 14, R.V., " to do service " (A.V., " to minister ") ; (5) of the work of the Gospel, in general, e.g., 2 Cor. 3 : 9, " of righteousness ; " 5 : 18, " of reconciliation ; " (6) of the general ministry of a servant of the Lord in preaching and teaching, Acts 20 : 24 ; 2 Cor. 4 : 1 ; 6 : 3 ; 11 : 8 ;

1 Tim. 1 : 12, R.V., " (to His) service ; " 2 Tim. 4 : 5 ; undefined in Col. 4 : 17 ; (7) of the Law, as a ministration of death, 2 Cor. 3 : 7 ; of condemnation, 3 : 9.¶

2. LEITOURGIA (λειτουργία), akin to *leitourgos* (see MINISTER, A, No. 2), to which the meanings of *leitourgia* correspond, is used in the N.T. of sacred ministrations, (*a*) priestly, Luke 1 : 23 ; Heb. 8 : 6 ; 9 : 21 ; (*b*) figuratively, of the practical faith of the members of the church at Philippi regarded as priestly sacrifice, upon which the Apostle's life-blood might be poured out as a libation, Phil. 2 : 17 ; (*c*) of the ministration of believers one to another, regarded as priestly service, 2 Cor. 9 : 12 ; Phil. 2 : 30. See SERVICE.¶

B. Adjective.

LEITOURGIKOS (λειτουργικός), of or pertaining to service, ministering, is used in Heb. 1 : 14, of angels as " ministering spirits " (for the word " do service " in the next clause, see A, No. 1).¶ In the Sept., Ex. 31 : 10 ; 39 : 13 ; Numb. 4 : 12, 26 ; 7 : 5 ; 2 Chron. 24 : 14.¶

MINSTREL

MOUSIKOS (μουσικός) is found in Rev. 18 : 22, R.V., " minstrels " (A.V., " musicians ") ; inasmuch as other instrumentalists are mentioned, some word like " minstrels " is necessary to make the distinction, hence the R.V. ; Bengel and others translate it ' singers.' Primarily the word denoted ' devoted to the Muses ' (the nine goddesses who presided over the principal departments of letters), and was used of anyone devoted to or skilled in arts and sciences, or ' learned.'¶

MINT

HEDUOSMON (ἡδύοσμον), an adjective denoting sweet-smelling (*hēdus*, sweet, *osmē*, a smell), is used as a neuter noun signifying mint, Matt. 23 : 23 ; Luke 11 : 42.¶

MIRACLE

1. DUNAMIS (δύναμις), power, inherent ability, is used of works of a supernatural origin and character, such as could not be produced by natural agents and means. It is translated " miracles " in the R.V. and A.V. in Acts 8 : 13 (where variant readings give the words in different order) ; 19 : 11 ; 1 Cor. 12 : 10, 28, 29 ; Gal. 3 : 5 ; A.V. only, in Acts 2 : 22 (R.V., " mighty works ") ; Heb. 2 : 4 (R.V., " powers "). In Gal. 3 : 5, the word may be taken in its widest sense, to include miracles both physical and moral. See MIGHT, A, No. 1, POWER, WORK.

2. SEMEION (σημεῖον), a sign, mark, token (akin to *sēmainō*, to give a sign ; *sēma*, a sign), is used of miracles and wonders as signs of Divine authority ; it is translated " miracles " in the R.V. and A.V. of Luke 23 : 8 ; Acts 4 : 16, 22 ; most usually it is given its more appropriate meaning " sign," " signs," e.g., Matt. 12 : 38, 39, and in every occurrence

in the Synoptists, except Luke 23 : 8 ; in the following passages in John's Gospel the R.V. substitutes " sign " or " signs " for the A.V., " miracle " or " miracles ; " 2 : 11, 23 ; 3 : 2 ; 4 : 54 ; 6 : 2, 14, 26 ; 7 : 31 ; 9 : 16 ; 10 : 41 ; 11 : 47 ; 12 : 18, 37 ; the A.V. also has " signs " elsewhere in this Gospel ; in Acts, R.V., " signs," A.V., " miracles," in 6 : 8 ; 8 : 6 ; 15 : 12 ; elsewhere only in Rev. 13 : 14 ; 16 : 14 ; 19 : 20. See SIGN, TOKEN, WONDER.

MIRE

BORBOROS ($\beta\acute{o}\rho\beta o\rho o\varsigma$), mud, filth, occurs in 2 Pet. 2 : 22.¶ In the Sept., Jer. 38 : 6 (twice), of the mire in the dungeon into which Jeremiah was cast.¶

MIRROR

ESOPTRON ($\check{\epsilon}\sigma o\pi\tau\rho o\nu$), rendered " glass " in the A.V., is used of any surface sufficiently smooth and regular to reflect rays of light uniformly, and thus produce images of objects which actually in front of it appear to the eye as if they were behind it. Mirrors in Biblical times were, it seems, metallic ; hence the R.V. adopts the more general term " mirror ; " in 1 Cor. 13 : 12, spiritual knowledge in this life is represented metaphorically as an image dimly perceived in a mirror ; in Jas. 1 : 23, the " law of liberty " is figuratively compared to a mirror ; the hearer who obeys not is like a person who, having looked into the mirror, forgets the reflected image after turning away ; he who obeys is like one who gazes into the mirror and retains in his soul the image of what he should be.¶

Note : For the verb *katoptrizō*, to reflect as a mirror (some regard it as meaning ' beholding in a mirror '), in 2 Cor. 3 : 18, see BEHOLD, No. 12.

For MISCHIEF, Acts 13 : 10, see VILLANY

MISERABLE, MISERABLY, MISERY
A. Adjectives.

1. ELEEINOS ($\grave{\epsilon}\lambda\epsilon\epsilon\iota\nu\acute{o}\varsigma$), pitiable, miserable (from *eleos*, mercy, pity ; see MERCY), is used in Rev. 3 : 17, in the Lord's description of the church at Laodicea ; here the idea is probably that of a combination of misery and pitiableness.¶

Note : For the comparative degree *eleeinoteros*, rendered " most pitiable " in 1 Cor. 15 : 19, R.V. (A.V., " most miserable "), see PITIABLE.

2. KAKOS ($\kappa a\kappa\acute{o}\varsigma$), bad, evil, is translated " miserable " in Matt. 21 : 41, R.V. (A.V., " wicked "). See BAD.

B. Adverb.

KAKŌS ($\kappa a\kappa\hat{\omega}\varsigma$), badly, ill, is translated " miserably " in Matt. 21 : 41 (see A, No. 2). Adhering to the meaning ' evil,' and giving the designed stress, the sentence may be rendered, ' evil (as they are) he will evilly destroy them.'

C. Noun.

TALAIPŌRIA (ταλαιπωρία), hardship, suffering, distress (akin to *talaipōros*, wretched, Rom. 7 : 24 ; Rev. 3 : 17,¶ and to *talaipōreō*, in the Middle Voice, to afflict oneself, in Jas. 4 : 9, " be afflicted "¶), is used as an abstract noun, " misery," in Rom. 3 : 16 ; as a concrete noun, " miseries," in Jas. 5 : 1.¶

MIST

1. ACHLUS (ἀχλύς), a mist, especially a dimness of the eyes, is used in Acts 13 : 11.   " In the single place of its N.T. use it attests the accuracy in the selection of words, and not least of medical words, which ' the beloved physician ' so often displays.   For him it expresses the mist of darkness . . . which fell on the sorcerer Elymas, being the outward and visible sign of the inward spiritual darkness which would be his portion for a while in punishment for his resistance to the truth " (Trench, Syn., § c).¶

2. HOMICHLĒ (ὁμίχλη), a mist (not so thick as *nephos* and *nephelē*, a cloud), occurs in 2 Pet. 2 : 17 (1st part), R.V., " mists ; " some mss. have *nephelai*, " clouds " (A.V.).¶

3. ZOPHOS (ζόφος) is rendered " mist " in the A.V. of 2 Pet. 2 : 17 (2nd part), R.V., " blackness ; " ' murkiness ' would be a suitable rendering.   For this and other synonymous terms see BLACKNESS, DARKNESS.

MITE

LEPTON (λεπτόν), the neuter of the adjective *leptos*, signifying, firstly, peeled, then, fine, thin, small, light, became used as a noun, denoting a small copper coin, often mentioned in the Mishna as proverbially the smallest Jewish coin.   It was valued at ½th of the Roman *as*, and the $\frac{1}{128}$th part of the *denarius* : its legal value was about one third of an English farthing ; Mark 12 : 42 lit. reads ' two *lepta*, which make a *kodrantēs* (a *quadrans*) ; ' in Luke 12 : 59 ' the last *lepton* ' corresponds in effect to Matt. 5 : 26, ' the uttermost *kodrantēs*,' " farthing ; " elsewhere Luke 21 : 2 ; see FARTHING.¶

MIXED (with)

Note : In Heb. 4 : 2, A.V., *sunkerannumi*, lit., to mix with (*sun*, with, *kerannumi*, see MINGLE, No. 2), is so translated ; R.V., " were (not) united (by faith) with " [A.V., " (not) being mixed . . . in], as said of persons ; in 1 Cor. 12 : 24 " hath tempered."   See TEMPER TOGETHER.¶

MIXTURE

MIGMA (μίγμα), a mixture (akin to *mignumi*, to mix, mingle : see MINGLE, No. 1), occurs in John 19 : 39 (some mss. have *heligma*, a roll).¶

Note : In Rev. 14 : 10, A.V., *akratos* (*a*, negative, and *kerannumi*, to

mingle) is translated " without mixture " (R.V., " unmixed ").¶ In the
Sept., Psa. 75 : 8 ; Jer. 32 : 1.¶

MOCK, MOCKER, MOCKING
A. Verbs.

1. EMPAIZŌ (ἐμπαίζω), a compound of *paizō*, to play like a child
(*pais*), to sport, jest, prefixed by *en*, in or at, is used only in the Synoptists,
and, in every instance, of the mockery of Christ, except in Matt. 2 : 16
(there in the sense of deluding, or deceiving, of Herod by the wise men)
and in Luke 14 : 29, of ridicule cast upon the one who after laying a
foundation of a tower is unable to finish it. The word is used (*a*) prophetically by the Lord, of His impending sufferings, Matt. 20 : 19 ;
Mark 10 : 34 ; Luke 18 : 32 ; (*b*) of the actual insults inflicted upon Him
by the men who had taken Him from Gethsemane, Luke 22 : 63 ; by
Herod and his soldiers, Luke 23 : 11 ; by the soldiers of the governor,
Matt. 27 : 29, 31 ; Mark 15 : 20 ; Luke 23 : 36 ; by the chief priests,
Matt. 27 : 41 ; Mark 15 : 31.¶

2. MUKTĒRIZŌ (μυκτηρίζω), from *muktēr*, the nose, hence, to turn
up the nose at, sneer at, treat with contempt, is used in the Passive Voice
in Gal. 6 : 7, where the statement " God is not mocked " does not mean
that men do not mock Him (see Prov. 1 : 30, where the Sept. has the same
verb) ; the Apostle vividly contrasts the essential difference between
God and man. It is impossible to impose upon Him who discerns the
thoughts and intents of the heart.¶

Note : Ekmuktērizō, a strengthened form of the above, to scoff at, is
used in Luke 16 : 14 and 23 : 35 (R.V., " scoffed at ; " A.V., " derided ").
See DERIDE, SCOFF.¶

3. CHLEUAZŌ (χλευάζω), to jest, mock, jeer at (from *chleuē*, a jest),
is said of the ridicule of some of the Athenian philosophers at the Apostle's
testimony concerning the resurrection of the dead, Acts 17 : 32.¶

4. DIACHLEUAZŌ (διαχλευάζω), an intensive form of No. 3, to scoff
at, whether by gesture or word, is said of those who jeered at the testimony
given on the day of Pentecost, Acts 2 : 13 (some mss. have No. 3).¶

B. Nouns.

1. EMPAIKTĒS (ἐμπαίκτης), a mocker (akin to A, No. 1), is used in
2 Pet. 3 : 3, R.V., " mockers " (A.V., " scoffers ") ; Jude 18, R.V. and
A.V., " mockers."¶ In the Sept., Is. 3 . 4.¶

2. EMPAIGMOS (ἐμπαιγμός), the act of the *empaiktēs*, a mocking, is
used in Heb. 11 : 36, " mockings."¶ In the Sept., Psa. 38 : 7 ; Ezek.
22 : 4.¶

3. EMPAIGMONĒ (ἐμπαιγμονή), an abstract noun, mockery, is used
in 2 Pet. 3 : 3 (some mss. omit it, as in A.V.) : (see also No. 1, above).¶

For MODERATION, Phil. 4 : 5, A.V., see FORBEARANCE, C, No. 2

MODEST

KOSMIOS (κόσμιος), orderly, well-arranged, decent, modest (akin to *kosmos*, in its primary sense as harmonious arrangement, adornment; cp. *kosmikos*, of the world, which is related to *kosmos* in its secondary sense as the world), is used in 1 Tim. 2 : 9 of the apparel with which Christian women are to adorn themselves; in 3 : 2 (R.V., " orderly; " A.V., " of good behaviour "), of one of the qualifications essential for a bishop or overseer. " The well-ordering is not of dress and demeanour only, but of the inner life, uttering indeed and expressing itself in the outward conversation " (Trench, Syn., §xcii).¶ In the Sept., Eccl. 12 : 9.¶

MOISTURE

IKMAS (ἰκμάς), moisture (probably from an Indo-European root *sik*— indicating wet), is used in Luke 8 : 6.¶ In the Sept., Job 26 : 14; Jer. 17 : 8.¶

MOMENT
A. Nouns.

1. ATOMOS (ἄτομος) lit. means indivisible (from *a*, negative, and *temnō*, to cut; Eng., atom); hence it denotes a moment, 1 Cor. 15 : 52.¶

2. STIGMĒ (στιγμή), a prick, a point (akin to *stizō*, to prick), is used metaphorically in Luke 4 : 5, of a moment, with *chronos*, " a moment (of time)."¶

Note : It is to be distinguished from *stigma*, a mark or brand, Gal. 6 : 17, which is, however, also connected with *stizō*.

B. Adverb.

PARAUTIKA (παραυτίκα), the equivalent of *parauta*, immediately (not in the N.T.), i.e., *para auta*, with *ta pragmata* understood, ' at the same circumstances,' is used adjectivally in 2 Cor. 4 : 17 and translated " which is but for a moment; " the meaning is not, however, simply that of brief duration, but that which is present with us now or immediate (*para*, beside, with), in contrast to the future glory; the clause is, lit., ' for the present lightness (i.e., light burden, the adjective *elaphron*, light, being used as a noun) of (our) affliction.'¶ This meaning is confirmed by its use in the Sept. of Psa. 70 : 3, ' (let them be turned back) immediately,' where the rendering could not be ' for a moment.'¶

MONEY

1. ARGURION (ἀργύριον), properly, a piece of silver, denotes (*a*) silver, e.g., Acts 3 : 6; (*b*) a silver coin, often in the plural, " pieces of silver," e.g., Matt. 26 : 15; so 28 : 12, where the meaning is ' many, (*hikanos*) pieces of silver '; (*c*) money; it has this meaning in Matt. 25 : 18, 27; 28 : 15; Mark 14 : 11; Luke 9 : 3; 19 : 15, 23; 22 : 5; Acts 8 : 20 (here the R.V. has " silver ").

Note : In Acts 7 : 16, for the A.V., " (a sum of) money," the R.V. has " (a price in) silver." See SILVER.

2. CHRĒMA (χρῆμα), lit., a thing that one uses (akin to *chraomai*, to use), hence, (*a*) wealth, riches, Mark 10 : 23, 24 ; Luke 18 : 24 ; (*b*) money, Acts 4 : 37, singular number, a sum of money ; plural in 8 : 18, 20 ; 24 : 26.¶ See RICHES.

3. CHALKOS (χαλκός), copper, is used, by metonymy, of copper coin, translated " money," in Mark 6 : 8 ; 12 : 41. See BRASS.

4. KERMA '(κέρμα), primarily a slice (akin to *keirō*, to cut short), hence, a small coin, change, is used in the plural in John 2 : 15, " the changers' money," probably considerable heaps of small coins.¶

5. NOMISMA (νόμισμα), primarily that which is established by custom (*nomos*, a custom, law), hence, the current coin of a state, currency, is found in Matt. 22 : 19, " (tribute) money."¶   In the Sept., Neh. 7 : 71.¶

Note : In Matt. 17 : 27, A.V., *statēr* (a coin, estimated at a little over three shillings, equivalent to four *drachmæ*, the temple-tax for two persons), is translated " piece of money " (R.V., " shekel "). See SHEKEL.¶

For MONEY-CHANGER, CHANGER OF MONEY, see CHANGER

MONEY (love of)

PHILARGURIA (φιλαργυρία), from *phileō*, to love, and *arguros*, silver, occurs in 1 Tim. 6 : 10 (cp. *philarguros*, covetous, avaricious). Trench contrasts this with *pleonexia*, covetousness. See under COVET, COVETOUSNESS.¶

MONTH, MONTHS

1. MĒN (μήν), connected with *mēnē*, the moon, akin to a Sanskrit root *mā*—, to measure (the Sanskrit *māsa* denotes both moon and month, cp., e.g., Lat. *mensis*, Eng., moon and month, the moon being in early times the measure of the month). The interval between the 17th day of the second month (Gen. 7 : 11) and the 17th day of the seventh month, is said to be 150 days (8 : 3, 4), i.e., five months of 30 days each ; hence the year would be 360 days (cp. Dan. 7 : 25 ; 9 : 27 ; 12 : 7 with Rev. 11 : 2, 3 ; 12 : 6, 14 ; 13 : 5 ; whence we conclude that 3½ years or 42 months=1260 days, i.e., one year=360 days) ; this was the length of the old Egyptian year ; later, five days were added to correspond to the solar year. The Hebrew year was as nearly solar as was compatible with its commencement, coinciding with the new moon, or first day of the month. This was a regular feast day, Numb. 10 : 10 ; 28 : 11–14 ; the Passover coincided with the full moon (the 14th of the month Abib : see PASSOVER).

Except in Gal. 4 : 10 ; Jas. 5 : 17 ; Rev. 9 : 5, 10, 15 ; 11 : 2 ; 13 : 5 ; 22 : 2, the word is found only in Luke's writings, Luke 1 : 24, 26, 36, 56 ; 4 : 25 ; Acts 7 : 20 ; 18 : 11 ; 19 : 8 ; 20 : 3 ; 28 : 11, examples of Luke's care as to accuracy of detail.¶

2. TRIMĒNOS (τρίμηνος), an adjective, denoting of three months (*tri*, for *treis*, three, and No. 1), is used as a noun, a space of three months,

in Heb. 11 : 23.¶

3. TETRAMĒNOS (τετράμηνος), an adjective, denoting of four months
(tetra, for tessares, four, and No. 1), is used as a noun in John 4 : 35 (where
chronos, time, may be understood).¶

MOON

1. SELĒNĒ (σελήνη), from selas, brightness (the Heb. words are
yarēach, wandering, and lebānāh, white), occurs in Matt. 24 : 29 ; Mark
13 : 24 ; Luke 21 : 25 ; Acts 2 : 20 ; 1 Cor. 15 : 41 ; Rev. 6 : 12 ; 8 : 12 ;
12 : 1 ; 21 : 23.   In Rev. 12 : 1, " the moon under her feet " is suggestive
of derived authority, just as her being clothed with the sun is suggestive
of supreme authority ; everything in the symbolism of the passage
centres in Israel.   In 6 : 12 the similar symbolism of the sun and moon is
suggestive of the supreme authority over the world, and of derived
authority, at the time of the execution of Divine judgments upon nations
at the close of the present age.¶

2. NEOMĒNIA (νεομηνία), or NOUMĒNIA, denoting a new moon
(neos, new, mēn, a month : see MONTH), is used in Col. 2 : 16, of a Jewish
festival.¶   Judaistic tradition added special features in the liturgy of the
synagogue in connection with the observance of the first day of the
month, the new moon time.

In the O.T. the R.V. has " new moon " for A.V., " month " in Numb.
29 : 6 ; 1 Sam. 20 : 27 ; Hos. 5 : 7.   For the connection with feast days
see Lev. 23 : 24 ; Numb. 10 : 10 ; 29 : 1 ; Psa. 81 : 3.

For MOOR see DRAW, B, *Note* (1)

MORE
A. Adverbs.

1. MALLON (μᾶλλον), the comparative degree of mala, very, very
much, is used (a) of increase, " more," with qualifying words, with pollǭ,
much, e.g., Mark 10 : 48, " the more (a great deal) ; " Rom. 5 : 15, 17,
" (much) more ; " Phil. 2 : 12 (ditto) ; with posǭ, how much, e.g., Luke
12 : 24 ; Rom. 11 : 12 ; with tosoutǭ, by so much, Heb. 10 : 25 ; (b) without
a qualifying word, by way of comparison, " the more," e.g., Luke 5 : 15,
" so much the more ; " John 5 : 18, " the more ; " Acts 5 : 14 (ditto) ;
Phil. 1 : 9 ; 1 Thess. 4 : 1, 10, " more and more ; " 2 Pet. 1 : 10, R.V.,
" the more " (A.V., " the rather ") ; in Acts 20 : 35, by a periphrasis, it
is translated " more (blessed) ; " in Gal. 4 : 27, " more (than)," lit., ' rather
(than) ; ' (c) with qualifying words, similarly to (a), e.g., Mark 7 : 36.
See RATHER.

2. ETI (ἔτι), yet, as yet, still, used of degree is translated " more "
in Matt. 18 : 16, " (one or two) more ; " Heb. 8 : 12 and 10 : 17, " (will I
remember no) more ; " 10 : 2, " (no) more (conscience) ; " 11 : 32, " (what
shall I) more (say) ? " Rev. 3 : 12, " (he shall go out thence no) more ; "

7 : 16, " (no) more " and " any more ; " 9 : 12, A.V., " more " (R.V., " hereafter ") ; 18 : 21–23, " (no) more," " any more " (5 times) ; 20 : 3, " (no) more ; " 21 : 1, 4 (twice) ; 22 : 3. See ALSO, No. 2.

3. OUKETI (οὐκέτι), ouk, not, and No. 2, combined in one word, is translated " no more," e.g., in Matt. 19 : 6 ; Luke 15 : 19, 21 ; Acts 20 : 25, 38 ; Eph. 2 : 19. See HENCEFORTH, HEREAFTER, LONGER, NOW, Note (2).

4. PERISSOTERON (περισσότερον), the neuter of the comparative degree of *perissos*, more abundant, is used as an adverb, " more," e.g., Luke 12 : 4 ; 2 Cor. 10 : 8, A.V. (R.V., " abundantly ") ; Heb. 7 : 15, R.V., " more abundantly " (A.V., " far more "). See ABUNDANTLY, C, No. 2.

Note : For the corresponding adverbs *perissōs* and *perissoterōs*, see ABUNDANTLY, EXCEEDINGLY.

5. MEIZON (μεῖζον), the neuter of *meizōn*, greater, the comparative degree of *megas*, great, is used as an adverb, and translated " the more " in Matt. 20 : 31. See GREATER.

6. HUPER (ὑπέρ), a preposition, over, above, etc., is used as an adverb in 2 Cor. 11 : 23, " (I) more."

7. HOSON (ὅσον), neuter of *hosos*, how much, is used adverbially in Mark 7 : 36 (1st part), " the more."

B. Adjectives (*some with adverbial uses*).

1. PLEIŌN (πλείων), the comparative degree of *polus*, much, is used (*a*) as an adjective, e.g., John 15 : 2 ; Acts 24 : 11, R.V., " (not) more (than) " (A.V., " yet but ") ; Heb. 3 : 3 ; (*b*) as a noun, or with a noun understood, e.g., Matt. 20 : 10 ; Mark 12 : 43 ; Acts 19 : 32 and 27 : 12, " the more part ; " 1 Cor. 9 : 19 ; (*c*) as an adverb, Matt. 5 : 20, " shall exceed," lit., ' (shall abound) more (than) ; ' 26 : 53 ; Luke 9 : 13. See ABOVE, No. 3, Note, GREATER.

2. PERISSOS (περισσός), more than sufficient, over and above, abundant (a popular substitute for No. 3), is translated " more," e.g., in Matt. 5 : 37. 47. In John 10 : 10 the neuter form is rendered " more abundantly," A.V., R.V., " abundantly " (marg., " abundance ").

3. PERISSOTEROS (περισσότερος), the comparative degree of No. 2, is translated " much more (than a prophet) " in Matt. 11 : 9, R.V. (A.V., " more ") ; in Luke 7 : 26 both R.V. and A.V. have " much more." See ABUNDANT, C.

Notes : (1) In Matt. 25 : 20 (2nd part), A.V., *allos*, " other " (so the R.V.), is translated " more." (2) In Jas. 4 : 6, A.V., the adjective *meizōn*, greater (see A, No. 5, above), is translated " more (grace) " (R.V. marg., " a greater grace "). See GRACE (at end). (3) Various uses of the word " more " occur in connection with other words, especially in the comparative degree. The phrase " more than " translates certain prepositions and particles : in Rom. 1 : 25, A.V., *para*, beside, compared with, is translated " more than " (R.V., " rather than ") : cp. Rom. 12 : 3 ; *huper*, over, above, " more than," in Matt. 10 : 37 (twice) ; in Philm. 21, A.V., " more than " (R.V., " beyond "). In Mark 14 : 5, A.V., *epanō*, above, is translated " more than " (R.V., " above "). In Luke 15 : 7 the particle *ē*, than, is necessarily rendered " more than ; " cp. Luke 17 : 2 and 1 Cor. 14 : 19, " rather than." In Mark 8 : 14, the conjunction *ei*, if, with the negative *mē*, lit., ' if not,' signifying ' except,' is translated " more than (one loaf)."

MOREOVER

1. ETI (ἔτι), yet, as yet, still, is translated " moreover " in Acts 2 : 26 ; in 21 : 28, R.V. (A.V., " further ") ; Heb. 11 : 36. See MORE, A, No. 2.

2. KAI (καί), and, is translated " moreover " in Acts 24 : 6 ; in the A.V., where the R.V. has " and," Acts 19 : 26.

3. DE (δέ), a particle signifying ' and ' or ' but,' is translated " moreover " in Matt. 18 : 15, A.V. (R.V., " and ") ; Acts 11 : 12 (R.V., " and ") ; Rom. 5 : 20, A.V. (R.V., " but ") ; 8 : 30 (" and ") ; 1 Cor. 15 : 1 (R.V., " now ") ; 2 Cor. 1 : 23 (R.V., " but ") ; 2 Pet. 1 : 15 (R.V., " yea ").

4. ALLA KAI (ἀλλὰ καί), but also, yea even, is translated " moreover " in Luke 24 : 22, R.V. (A.V., " yea, and ") ; in 16 : 21, A.V., " moreover " (R.V., " yea, even ").

5. DE KAI (δὲ καί), but also, is translated " moreover " in 1 Tim. 3 : 7.

6. KAI . . . DE (καὶ . . . δέ) is translated " moreover " in Heb. 9 : 21.

7. LOIPON (λοιπόν), the neuter of the adjective *loipos*, the rest, used adverbially, most usually rendered " finally," is translated " moreover " in 1 Cor. 4 : 2 (some mss. have *ho de loipon*, lit., ' but what is left,' A.V., " moreover," for *hōde loipon*, " here, moreover," as in the R.V.). See FINALLY.

Note : In 1 Cor. 10 : 1, A.V., *gar*, ' for,' is translated " moreover " (R.V., " for ") ; the R.V. is important here, as it introduces a reason for what has preceded in chap. 9, whereas " moreover " may indicate that a new subject is being introduced ; this incorrect rendering tends somewhat to dissociate the two passages, whereas *gar* connects them intimately.

MORNING (in the, early in the)
A. Adjectives.

1. PRŌIOS (πρώϊος), early, at early morn (from *pro*, before), is used as a noun in the feminine form *prōïa*, " morning " in Matt. 27 : 1 and John 21 : 4 (in some mss. in Matt. 21 : 18 and John 18 : 28, for B, No. 1, which see). Its adjectival force is retained by regarding it as qualifying the noun *hōra*, an hour, i.e., ' at an early hour.'¶

2. PRŌINOS (πρώϊνος), a later form of No. 1, qualifies *astēr*, star, in Rev. 2 : 28 and 22 : 16 (where some mss. have No. 3). That Christ will give to the overcomer " the morning star " indicates a special interest for

such in Himself, as He thus describes Himself in the later passage. For Israel He will appear as "the sun of righteousness; " as the morning Star which precedes He will appear for the Rapture of the Church. ¶

3. ORTHRINOS or ORTHRIOS (ὀρθρινός), pertaining to dawn or morning, in some mss. in Rev. 22 : 16 (see No. 2) ; see DAWN, B, Note.

B. Adverb.

PRŌÏ (πρωΐ), early, is translated "in the morning" in Matt. 16 : 3 ; 20 : 1 (with hama, "early"); 21 : 18 ; Mark 1 : 35 ; 11 : 20 ; 13 : 35 ; 15 : 1 ; "early" in Mark 16 : 2 (with lian, very ; A.V., "early in the morning"); 16 : 9 ; Matt. 21 : 18 and John 18 : 28 (in the best texts, for A, No. 1) ; 20 : 1 ; Acts 28 : 23 (with apo, from). ¶

C. Noun.

ORTHROS (ὄρθρος) denotes daybreak, dawn, Luke 24 : 1 ; John 8 : 2 ; Acts 5 : 21 ; see DAWN, B. ¶

D. Verb.

ORTHRIZŌ (ὀρθρίζω), to do anything early in the morning, is translated "came early in the morning," in Luke 21 : 38. ¶

MORROW

1. AURION (αὔριον), an adverb denoting to-morrow, is used (a) with this meaning in Matt. 6 : 30 ; Luke 12 : 28 ; 13 : 32, 33 ; Acts 23 : 15 (in some mss.), 20 ; 25 : 22 ; 1 Cor. 15 : 32 ; Jas. 4 : 13 ; (b) with the word hēmera, day, understood (occurring thus in the papyri), translated as a noun, "(the) morrow," Matt. 6 : 34 (twice) ; Luke 10 : 35 ; Acts 4 : 3 (A.V., "next day"); 4 : 5 ; Jas. 4 : 14. ¶

2. EPAURION (ἐπαύριον), epi, upon, and No. 1, is used as in (b) above ; the R.V. always translates it "on (the) morrow ; " in the following the A.V. has "(the) next day," Matt. 27 : 62 ; John 1 : 29, 35 ("the next day after"); 12 : 12 ; Acts 14 : 20 ; 21 : 8 ; 25 : 6 ; "(the) day following," John 1 : 43 ; 6 : 22 ; "the morrow after," Acts 10 : 24.

Note : In Acts 25 : 17, A.V., the adverb hexēs, next, successively, in order, is translated "on (the) morrow." See NEXT.

For MORSEL see MEAT, No. 2

MORTAL, MORTALITY

THNĒTOS (θνητός), subject or liable to death, mortal (akin to thnēskō, to die), occurs in Rom. 6 : 12, of the body, where it is called "mortal," not simply because it is liable to death, but because it is the organ in and through which death carries on its death-producing activities ; in 8 : 11, the stress is on the liability to death, and the quickening is not reinvigoration but the impartation of life at the time of the Rapture, as in 1 Cor. 15 : 53, 54 and 2 Cor. 5 : 4 (R.V., "what is mortal ; " A.V., "mortality ") ; in 2 Cor. 4 : 11, it is applied to the flesh, which stands, not simply for the body, but the body as that which consists of the element of decay, and is thereby death-doomed. Christ's followers are in this life delivered unto death, that His life may be manifested in that which naturally is the seat of decay and death. That which is subject to suffering is that in which the power of Him who suffered here is most manifested.¶

MORTIFY

1. THANATOŌ (θανατόω), to put to death (from *thanatos*, death, akin to *thnētos*, mortal, see above), is translated "mortify" in Rom. 8 : 13 (Amer. R.V., "put to death"); in 7 : 4, "ye were made dead" (Passive Voice), betokens the act of God on the believer, through the Death of Christ; here in 8 : 13 it is the act of the believer himself, as being responsible to answer to God's act, and to put to death "the deeds of the body." See DEATH, C, No. 1.

2. NEKROŌ (νεκρόω), to make dead (from *nekros*, see DEAD, A), is used figuratively in Col. 3 : 5 and translated "mortify" (Amer. R.V., "put to death"). See DEAD, B, No. 1.

MOST

1. PLEION (πλεῖον), the neuter of *pleiōn*, more, is used adverbially and translated "most" (of degree) in Luke 7 : 42 (without the article); in ver. 43 (with the article, 'the most'); 1 Cor. 10 : 5, R.V., "most" (A.V., "many"); Phil. 1 : 14 (ditto). See MORE.

2. PLEISTOS (πλεῖστος), the superlative degree of *polus*, is used (*a*) as an adjective in Matt. 11 : 20; 21 : 8, R.V., "(the) most part of" (A.V., "a very great"); (*b*) in the neuter, with the article, adverbially, "at the most," 1 Cor. 14 : 27; (*c*) as an elative (i.e., intensively) in Mark 4 : 1 (in the best mss.; some have *polus*), "a very great (multitude)."

3. MALISTA (μάλιστα), an adverb, the superlative of *mala*, very, is translated "most of all" in Acts 20 : 38. See ESPECIALLY.

Note : For combinations in the translation of other words, see BELIEVE, C, Note (4), EXCELLENT, GLADLY, HIGH, STRAITEST.

MOTE

KARPHOS (κάρφος), a small, dry stalk, a twig, a bit of dried stick (from *karphō*, to dry up), or a tiny straw or bit of wool, such as might fly into the eye, is used metaphorically of a minor fault, Matt. 7 : 3, 4, 5; Luke 6 : 41, 42 (twice), in contrast with *dokos*, a beam supporting the roof of a building (see BEAM).¶ In the Sept., Gen. 8 : 11.¶

MOTH

SĒS (σής) denotes a clothes moth, Matt. 6 : 19, 20; Luke 12 : 33.¶ In Job 4 : 19 "crushed before the moth" alludes apparently to the fact that woollen materials, riddled by the larvæ of moths, become so fragile that a touch demolishes them. In Job 27 : 18 "He buildeth his house as a moth" alludes to the frail covering which a larval moth constructs out of the material which it consumes. The rendering " spider " (marg.) seems an attempt to explain a difficulty.

MOTH-EATEN

SĒTOBRŌTOS (σητόβρωτος), from *sēs*, a moth, and *bibrōskō*, to eat, is used in Jas. 5 : 2.¶ In the Sept. Job 13 : 28.¶

MOTHER

1. MĒTĒR (μήτηρ) is used (*a*) of the natural relationship, e.g., Matt. 1 : 18 ; 2 Tim. 1 : 5 ; (*b*) figuratively, (1) of one who takes the place of a mother, Matt. 12 : 49, 50 ; Mark 3 : 34, 35 ; John 19 : 27 ; Rom. 16 : 13 ; 1 Tim. 5 : 2 ; (2) of the Heavenly and spiritual Jerusalem, Gal. 4 : 26, which is " free " (not bound by law imposed externally, as under the Law of Moses), " which is our mother " (R.V.), i.e., of Christians, the metropolis, mother-city, used allegorically, just as the capital of a country is " the seat of its government, the centre of its activities, and the place where the national characteristics are most fully expressed ; " (3) symbolically, of Babylon, Rev. 17 : 5, as the source from which has proceeded the religious harlotry of mingling pagan rites and doctrines with the Christian faith.

Note : In Mark 16 : 1 the article, followed by the genitive case of the name " James," the word " mother " being omitted, is an idiomatic mode of expressing the phrase " the mother of James."

2. MĒTROLŌAS, or MĒTRALŌAS (μητραλῴας) denotes a matricide (No. 1, and *aloiaō*, to smite) ; 1 Tim. 1 : 9, " murderers of mothers ; " it probably has, however, the broader meaning of " smiters " (R.V., marg.), as in instances elsewhere than the N.T.¶

3. AMĒTŌR (ἀμήτωρ), without a mother (*a*, negative, and No. 1), is used in Heb. 7 : 3, of the Genesis record of Melchizedek, certain details concerning him being purposely omitted, in order to conform the description to facts about Christ as the Son of God.   The word has been found in this sense in the writings of Euripides the dramatist and Herodotus the historian.   See also under FATHER.¶

MOTHER-IN-LAW

PENTHERA (πενθερά), the feminine of *pentheros* (a father-in-law), occurs in Matt. 8 : 14 ;   10 : 35 ;   Mark 1 : 30 ;   Luke 4 : 38 ;   12 : 53 (twice).¶

For MOTION, Rom. 7 : 5, A.V., see PASSION

MOUNT, MOUNTAIN

OROS (ὄρος) is used (*a*) without specification, e.g., Luke 3 : 5 (distinct from *bounos*, a hill, see HILL, No. 3) ; John 4 : 20 ; (*b*) of the mount of Transfiguration, Matt. 17 : 1, 9 ; Mark 9 : 2, 9 ; Luke 9 : 28, 37 (A.V.,

" hill ") ; 2 Pet. 1 : 18 ; (c) of Zion, Heb. 12 : 22 ; Rev. 14 : 1 ; (d) of Sinai, Acts 7 : 30, 38 ; Gal. 4 : 24, 25 ; Heb. 8 : 5 ; 12 : 20 ; (e) of the Mount of Olives, Matt. 21 : 1 ; 24 : 3 ; Mark 11 : 1 ; 13 : 3 ; Luke 19 : 29, 37 ; 22 : 39 ; John 8 : 1 ; Acts 1 : 12 ; (f) of the hill districts as distinct from the lowlands, especially of the hills above the Sea of Galilee, e.g., Matt. 5 : 1 ; 8 : 1 ; 18 : 12 ; Mark 5 : 5 ; (g) of the mountains on the east of Jordan and those in the land of Ammon and the region of Petra, etc., Matt. 24 : 16 ; Mark 13 : 14 ; Luke 21 : 21 ; (h) proverbially, of over-coming difficulties, or accomplishing great things, 1 Cor. 13 : 2 ; cp. Matt. 17 : 20 ; 21 : 21 ; Mark 11 : 23 ; (i) symbolically, of a series of the imperial potentates of the Roman Dominion, past and future, Rev. 17 : 9. See HILL.

MOURN, MOURNING
A. Verbs.

1. KOPTŌ (κόπτω), to cut or beat, used in the Middle Voice of beating the breast or head in mourning (cp. Luke 23 : 27), is translated " shall mourn " in Matt. 24 : 30. See BEWAIL, No. 2, CUT, WAIL.

2. PENTHEŌ (πενθέω), to mourn for, lament, is used (a) of mourning in general, Matt. 5 : 4 ; 9 : 15 ; Luke 6 : 25 ; (b) of sorrow for the death of a loved one, Mark 16 : 10 ; (c) of mourning for the overthrow of Babylon and the Babylonish system, Rev. 18 : 11, 15, R.V., " mourning " (A.V., " wailing ") ; ver. 19 (ditto) ; (c) of sorrow for sin or for condoning it, Jas. 4 : 9 ; 1 Cor. 5 : 2 ; (d) of grief for those in a local church who show no repentance for evil committed, 2 Cor. 12 : 21, R.V., " mourn " (A.V., " bewail "). See BEWAIL, No. 3.¶

3. THRĒNEŌ (θρηνέω), to lament, wail (akin to thrēnos, a lamentation, a dirge), is used (a) in a general sense, of the disciples during the absence of the Lord, John 16 : 20, " lament ; " (b) of those who sorrowed for the sufferings and the impending crucifixion of the Lord, Luke 23 : 27, " lamented ; " the preceding word is koptō (No. 1) ; (c) of mourning as for the dead, Matt. 11 : 17, R.V., " wailed " (A.V., " have mourned ") ; Luke 7 : 32 (ditto). See BEWAIL, Note (1).¶

Notes : (1) Trench points out that pentheō is often joined with klaiō, to weep, 2 Sam. 19 : 1 ; Mark 16 : 10 ; Jas. 4 : 9 ; Rev. 18 : 15, indicating that pentheō is used especially of external manifestation of grief (as with koptō and thrēneō), in contrast to lupeomai, which may be used of inward grief (Syn. §xlv) ; though in Classical Greek pentheō was used of grief without violent manifestations (Grimm-Thayer). (2) Among the well-to-do it was common to hire professional mourners (men and women), who accompanied the dead body to the grave with formal music and the singing of dirges. At the death of Jairus' daughter male flute-players were present, Matt. 9 : 23 (see, however, Jer. 9 : 17).

B. Nouns.

1. ODURMOS (ὀδυρμός), lamentation, mourning, is translated

"mourning" in Matt. 2 : 18 and 2 Cor. 7 : 7 : see BEWAIL, Note (2).¶

2. PENTHOS (πένθος), akin to A, No. 2, mourning, is used in Jas. 4 : 9; Rev. 18 : 7 (twice), R.V., "mourning" (A.V., "sorrow"); ver. 8, "mourning;" 21 : 4, R.V., "mourning" (A.V., "sorrow"). See SORROW.¶

MOUTH
A. Noun.

STOMA (στόμα), akin to *stomachos* (which originally meant a throat, gullet), is used (*a*) of the mouth of man, e.g., Matt. 15 : 11; of animals, e.g., Matt. 17 : 27; 2 Tim. 4 : 17 (figurative); Heb. 11 : 33; Jas. 3 : 3; Rev. 13 : 2 (2nd occurrence); (*b*) figuratively, of inanimate things, of the "edge" of a sword, Luke 21 : 24; Heb. 11 : 34; of the earth, Rev. 12 : 16; (*c*) figuratively, of the mouth, as the organ of speech, (1) of Christ's words, e.g., Matt. 13 : 35; Luke 11 : 54; Acts 8 : 32; 22 : 14; 1 Pet. 2 : 22; (2) of human, e.g., Matt. 18 : 16; 21 : 16; Luke 1 : 64; Rev. 14 : 5; as emanating from the heart, Matt. 12 : 34; Rom. 10 : 8, 9; of prophetic ministry through the Holy Spirit, Luke 1 : 70; Acts 1 : 16; 3 : 18; 4 : 25; of the destructive policy of two world potentates at the end of this age, Rev. 13 : 2, 5, 6; 16 : 13 (twice); of shameful speaking, Eph. 4 : 29 and Col. 3 : 8; (3) of the Devil speaking as a dragon or serpent, Rev. 12 : 15, 16; 16 : 13; (*d*) figuratively, in the phrase "face to face" (lit., 'mouth to mouth'), 2 John 12; 3 John 14; (*e*) metaphorically, of the utterances of the Lord, in judgment, 2 Thess. 2 : 8; Rev. 1 : 16; 2 : 16; 19 : 15, 21; of His judgment upon a local church for its lukewarmness, Rev. 3 : 16; (*f*) by metonymy, for speech, Matt. 18 : 16; Luke 19 : 22; 21 : 15; 2 Cor. 13 : 1.

Note : In Acts 15 : 27, *logos*, a word, is translated "word of mouth," R.V. (A.V., "mouth," marg., "word").

B. Verb.

EPISTOMIZO (ἐπιστομίζω), to bridle (*epi*, upon, and A), is used metaphorically of stopping the mouth, putting to silence, Tit. 1 : 11.¶ Cp. *phrassō*, to stop, close, said of stopping the mouths of men, in Rom. 3 : 19. See STOP.

MOVE, MOVED, MOVER, MOVING, UNMOVEABLE
A. Verbs.

1. KINEO (κινέω), to set in motion, move (hence, e.g., Eng. kinematics, kinetics, cinema), is used (*a*) of wagging the head, Matt. 27 : 39; Mark 15 : 29; (*b*) of the general activity of the human being, Acts 17 : 28; (*c*) of the moving of mountains, Rev. 6 : 14, in the sense of removing, as in Rev. 2 : 5, of removing a lampstand (there figuratively of causing a local church to be discontinued); (*d*) figuratively, of exciting, stirring up feelings and passions, Acts 21 : 30 (Passive Voice); 24 : 5, "a mover;"

(e) of moving burdens, Matt. 23 : 4. See REMOVE, WAG.¶ Cp. *sunkineo*, to stir up, Acts 6 : 12.¶

2. METAKINEŌ (μετακινέω), in the Active Voice, to move something away (not in the N.T. ; in the Sept., e.g., Deut. 19 : 14 ; Is. 54 : 10) ; in the Middle Voice, to remove oneself, shift, translated in the Passive in Col. 1 : 23, " be . . . not moved away (from the hope of the gospel)."¶

3. SEIŌ (σείω), to shake, move to and fro, usually of violent concussion (Eng., seismic, seismograph, seismology), is said (a) of the earth as destined to be shaken by God, Heb. 12 : 26 ; (b) of a local convulsion of the earth, at the Death of Christ, Matt. 27 : 51, " did quake ; " (c) of a fig tree, Rev. 6 : 13 ; (d) metaphorically, to stir up with fear or some other emotion, Matt. 21 : 10, of the people of a city ; 28 : 4, of the keepers or watchers, at the Lord's tomb, R.V., " did quake " (A.V., " did shake ").¶

4. SALEUŌ (σαλεύω), to shake, properly of the action of stormy wind, then, to render insecure, stir up, is rendered " I should (not) be moved " in Acts 2 : 25, in the sense of being cast down or shaken from a sense of security and happiness, said of Christ, in a quotation from Psa. 16 : 8. See SHAKE, STIR (up).

5. SAINŌ (σαίνω), properly, of dogs, to wag the tail, fawn ; hence, metaphorically of persons, to disturb, disquiet, 1 Thess. 3 : 3, Passive Voice, " (that no man) be moved (by these afflictions)." Some have suggested the primary meaning, to be wheedled, befooled, by pleasing utterances ; but Greek interpreters regard it as synonymous with No. 3, or with *tarassō*, to disturb, and this is confirmed by the contrast with " establish " in ver. 2, and " stand fast " in ver. 8. A variant reading gives the verb *siainesthai*, to be disheartened, unnerved.¶

6. PHERŌ (φέρω), to bear, carry, is rendered " being moved " in 2 Pet. 1 : 21, signifying that they were ' borne along,' or impelled, by the Holy Spirit's power, not acting according to their own wills, or simply expressing their own thoughts, but expressing the mind of God in words provided and ministered by Him.

Notes : (1) In Mark 15 : 11, A.V., *anaseiō*, to shake to and fro, stir up, is translated " moved " (R.V., " stirred up," as in Luke 23 : 5, A.V. and R.V.).¶ (2) In Acts 20 : 24 some mss. have a phrase translated " none of these things move me." The text for which there is most support gives the rendering " but I hold not my life of any account, as dear unto myself." Field suggests a reading, the translation of which is, ' neither make I account of anything, nor think my life dear unto myself.' (3) In 1 Cor. 15 : 34, for the more literal A.V., " I speak this to your shame," the R.V. has " I speak this to move you to shame." (4) For " moved with godly fear " see FEAR, D, No. 2. (5) See also COMPASSION, ENVY, FEAR, INDIGNATION.

B. Adjectives.

1. ASALEUTOS (ἀσάλευτος), unmoved, immoveable (from *a*, negative, and A, No. 4), is translated " unmoveable " in Acts 27 : 41 ; " which

cannot be moved " in Heb. 12 : 28, A.V. (R.V., " that cannot be shaken ").¶ In the Sept., Ex. 13 : 16 ; Deut. 6 : 8 ; 11 : 18.¶

2. AMETAKINĒTOS (ἀμετακίνητος), firm, immoveable (a, negative, and A, No. 2), is used in 1 Cor. 15 : 58.¶

C. Noun.

KINĒSIS (κίνησις), a moving (akin to A, No. 1), is found in John 5 : 3 (in many ancient authorities, R.V., marg.), of the moving of the water at the pool of Bethesda.¶

MOW

AMAŌ (ἀμάω), to mow, is translated " mowed " in Jas. 5 : 4, R.V. (A.V., " have reaped down "). " The cognate words seem to shew that the sense of cutting or mowing was original, and that of gathering-in secondary " (Liddell and Scott, Lex.).¶

MUCH

1. POLUS (πολύς) is used (a) as an adjective of degree, e.g., Matt. 13 : 5, " much (earth) ; " Acts 26 : 24, " much (learning) ; " in ver. 29, in the answer to Agrippa's " with but little persuasion," some texts have pollō (some megalō, ' with great '), R.V., " (whether with little or) with much ; " of number, e.g., Mark 5 : 24, R.V., " a great (multitude)," A.V., " much (people) ; " so Luke 7 : 11 ; John 12 : 12 ; Rev. 19 : 1, etc. ; (b) in the neuter singular form (polu), as a noun, e.g., Luke 16 : 10 (twice) ; in the plural (polla), e.g., Rom. 16 : 6, 12, " (laboured) much," lit., ' many things ; ' (c) adverbially, in the neuter singular, e.g., Acts 18 : 27 ; James 5 : 16 ; Matt. 26 : 9 (a genitive of price) ; in the plural, e.g., Mark 5 : 43, R.V., " much " (A.V., " straitly ") ; Mark 9 : 26, R.V., " much " (A.V., " sore ") ; John 14 : 30 ; and with the article, Acts 26 : 24 ; Rom. 15 : 22 ; 1 Cor. 16 : 19 ; Rev. 5 : 4. See GREAT.

2. HIKANOS (ἱκανός), enough, much, many, is translated " much," e.g., in Luke 7 : 12 (in some mss. Acts 5 : 37 ; see the R.V.) ; Acts 11 : 24, 26 ; 19 : 26 ; 27 : 9. See ABLE, ENOUGH, A, No. 2, GREAT, LARGE, MANY, MEET, SECURITY, SORE, SUFFICIENT, WORTHY.

Notes : (1) For " much more," " so much the more," see MORE. (2) In John 12 : 9, the R.V. has " the common people " for " much people." (3) In Acts 27 : 16, A.V., ischuō, to be able, with molis, scarcely, is translated " had much work " (R.V., " were able, with difficulty "). (4) in Luke 19 : 15, A.V., the pronoun ti, " what " (R.V.), is translated " how much." (5) The adjective tosoutos, so great, so much, is translated " so much (bread)," in Matt. 15 : 33, plural, R.V., " so many (loaves) ; " in the genitive case, of price, in Acts 5 : 8, " for so much ; " in the dative case, of degree, in Heb. 1 : 4, R.V., " by so much " (A.V., " so much ") ; so in Heb. 10 : 25 ; in Heb. 7 : 22 " by so much " translates the phrase kata tosouto ; in Rev. 18 : 7, " so much." (6) See DISPLEASED, EXHORTATION, PERPLEX, SPEAKING, WORK.

MUCH (AS)

Notes : (1) In Luke 6 : 34 the phrase *ta isa*, lit., ' the equivalent (things),' is translated " as much " (of lending, to receive back the equivalent). (2) In Rom. 1 : 15, the phrase *to kat' eme*, lit., ' the (thing) according to me,' signifies " as much as in me is ; " cp. the A.V. marg. in 1 Pet. 5 : 2 [lit., ' the (extent) in, or among, you ; ' the text takes the word ' flock ' as understood, the marg. regards the phrase as adverbially idiomatic] ; in Rom. 12 : 18 " as much as in you lieth " translates a similar phrase, lit., ' the (extent) out of you.'   (3) In Heb. 12 : 20, A.V., *kai ean* (contracted to *k'an*), " if even " (R.V.), is translated " and if so much as."   (4) The negatives *oude* and *mēde*, " not even " (R.V.) are translated " not so much as " in the A.V. in Mark 2 : 2 ; Luke 6 : 3 and 1 Cor. 5 : 1 ; in the following the R.V. and A.V. translate them " not so much as," Mark 3 : 20 (some mss. have *mēte*, with the same meaning) ; Acts 19 : 2 ; in Mark 6 : 31 " no (leisure) so much as."   (5) In Rom. 3 : 12, *heōs*, as far as, even unto, is translated " so much as " in the R.V. ; the A.V. supplies nothing actually corresponding to it.   (6) In John 6 : 11 *hosos* denotes " as much as."

MULTIPLY

1. PLĒTHUNŌ (πληθύνω), used (*a*) transitively, denotes to cause to increase, to multiply, 2 Cor. 9 : 10 ; Heb. 6 : 14 (twice) ; in the Passive Voice, to be multiplied, Matt. 24 : 12, R.V., " (iniquity) shall be multiplied " (A.V., " shall abound ") ; Acts 6 : 7 ; 7 : 17 ; 9 : 31 ; 12 : 24 ; 1 Pet. 1 : 2 ; 2 Pet. 1 : 2 ; Jude 2 ; (*b*) intransitively it denotes to be multiplying, Acts 6 : 1, R.V., " was multiplying " (A.V., " was multiplied "). See ABUNDANCE, B, No. 5.¶

2. PLEONAZŌ (πλεονάζω), used intransitively, to abound, is translated " being multiplied " in the R.V. cf 2 Cor. 4 : 15 (A.V., " abundant ") ; the Active Voice, aorist tense, here would be more accurately rendered ' having superabounded ' or ' superabounding ' or ' multiplying.' See ABUNDANCE, B, No. 3.

MULTITUDE

1. OCHLOS (ὄχλος) is used frequently in the four Gospels and the Acts ; elsewhere only in Rev. 7 : 9 ; 17 : 15 ; 19 : 1, 6 ; it denotes (*a*) a crowd or multitude of persons, a throng, e.g., Matt. 14 : 14, 15 ; 15 : 33 ; often in the plural, e.g., Matt. 4 : 25 ; 5 : 1 ; with *polus*, much or great, it signifies " a great multitude," e.g., Matt. 20 : 29, or " the common people," Mark 12 : 37, perhaps preferably ' the mass of the people.'   Field supports the meaning in the text, but either rendering is suitable.   The mass of the people was attracted to Him (for the statement " heard Him gladly " cp. what is said in Mark 6 : 20 of Herod Antipas concerning John the Baptist) ; in John 12 : 9, " the common people," R.V., stands in contrast with their leaders (ver. 10) ; Acts 24 : 12, R.V., " crowd ; " (*b*) the populace, an unorganised multitude, in contrast to *dēmos*. the people as a body politic, e.g., Matt. 14 : 5 ; 21 : 26 ; John 7 : 12 (2nd part) ;

(c) in a more general sense, a multitude or company, e.g., Luke 6 : 17, R.V., "a (great) multitude (of His disciples)," A.V., "the company ; " Acts 1 : 15, "a multitude (of persons)," R.V., A.V., "the number (of names) ; " Acts 24 : 18, R.V., "crowd" (A.V., "multitude "). See COMPANY, No. 1, NUMBER.

2. PLĒTHOS (πλῆθος), lit., a fulness, hence, a large company, a multitude, is used (a) of things : of fish, Luke 5 : 6 ; John 21 : 6 ; of sticks ("bundle"), Acts 28 : 3 ; of stars and of sand, Heb. 11 : 12 ; of sins, Jas. 5 : 20 ; 1 Pet. 4 : 8 ; (b) of persons, (1) a multitude : of people, e.g., Mark 3 : 7, 8 ; Luke 6 : 17 ; John 5 : 3 ; Acts 14 : 1 ; of angels, Luke 2 : 13 ; (2) with the article, the whole number, the multitude, the populace, e.g., Luke 1 : 10 ; 8 : 37 ; Acts 5 : 16 ; 19 : 9 ; 23 : 7 ; a particular company, e.g., of disciples, Luke 19 : 37 ; Acts 4 : 32 ; 6 : 2, 5 ; 15 : 30 ; of elders, priests, and scribes, 23 : 7 ; of the Apostles and the elders of the church in Jerusalem, Acts 15 : 12. See ASSEMBLY, No. 3, BUNDLE, No. 2, COMPANY, No. 5.

Note : In Luke 12 : 1, A.V., the phrase, lit., ' the myriads of the multitude ' is translated " an innumerable multitude of people " (where " people " translates No. 1, above), R.V., " the many thousands of the multitude" (where " multitude " translates No. 1).

MURDER

PHONOS (φόνος) is used (a) of a special act, Mark 15 : 7 ; Luke 23 : 19, 25 ; (b) in the plural, of murders in general, Matt. 15 : 19 ; Mark 7 : 21 (Gal. 5 : 21, in some inferior mss.) ; Rev. 9 : 21 ; in the singular, Rom. 1 : 29 ; (c) in the sense of slaughter, Heb. 11 : 37, " they were slain with the sword," lit., ' (they died by) slaughter (of the sword) ; ' in Acts 9 : 1, " slaughter." See SLAUGHTER.¶

Note : In Matt. 19 : 18, A.V., *phoneuō*, to kill (akin to *phoneus*, see below), is translated " thou shalt do (no) murder " (R.V., " thou shalt (not) kill "). See KILL, SLAY.

MURDERER

1. PHONEUS (φονεύς), akin to *phoneuō* and *phonos* (see above), is used (a) in a general sense, in the singular, 1 Pet. 4 : 15 ; in the plural, Rev. 21 : 8 ; 22 : 15 ; (b) of those guilty of particular acts, Matt. 22 : 7 ; Acts 3 : 14, lit. ' a man (*anēr*), a murderer ; ' 7 : 52 ; 28 : 4.¶

2. ANTHROPOKTONOS (ἀνθρωποκτόνος), an adjective, lit., ' man-slaying,' used as a noun, a manslayer, murderer (*anthrōpos*, a man, *kteinō*, to slay), is used of Satan, John 8 : 44 ; of one who hates his brother, and who, being a murderer, has not eternal life, 1 John 3 : 15 (twice).¶

3. PATROLOAS (or PATRAL-) (πατρολῴας), a murderer of one's father, occurs in 1 Tim. 1 : 9.¶

Note : For *sikarios*, in the plural, " murderers," in Acts 21 : 38, see ASSASSIN.¶ See MOTHER, No. 2.

MURMUR, MURMURING
A. Verbs.

1. GONGUZŌ (γογγύζω), to mutter, murmur, grumble, say anything in a low tone (Eng., gong), an onomatopœic word, representing the significance by the sound of the word, as in the word " murmur " itself, is used of the labourers in the parable of the householder, Matt. 20 : 11 ; of the scribes and Pharisees, against Christ, Luke 5 : 30 ; of the Jews, John 6 : 41, 43 ; of the disciples, 6 : 61 ; of the people, 7 : 32 (of debating secretly) ; of the Israelites, 1 Cor. 10 : 10 (twice), where it is also used in a warning to believers.¶ In the papyri it is used of the murmuring of a gang of workmen ; also in a remark interposed, while the Emperor (late 2nd cent. A.D.) was interviewing a rebel, that the Romans were then murmuring (Moulton and Milligan, Vocab.).

2. DIAGONGUZŌ (διαγογγύζω), lit., to murmur through (dia, i.e., through a whole crowd, or among themselves), is always used of indignant complaining, Luke 15 : 2 ; 19 : 7.¶

3. EMBRIMAOMAI (ἐμβριμάομαι) is rendered " murmured against " in Mark 14 : 5 ; it expresses indignant displeasure : see CHARGE, C, No. 4.

Note : For *stenazō*, Jas. 5 : 9, R.V., " murmur," see GRIEVE, No. 3.

B. Noun.

GONGUSMOS (γογγυσμός), a murmuring, muttering (akin to A, No. 1), is used (*a*) in the sense of secret debate among people, John 7 : 12 (as with the verb in ver. 32) ; (*b*) of displeasure or complaining (more privately than in public), said of Grecian Jewish converts against Hebrews, Acts 6 : 1 ; in general admonitions, Phil. 2 : 14 ; 1 Pet. 4 : 9, R.V., " murmuring " (A.V., " grudging ").¶

MURMURER

GONGUSTĒS (γογγυστής), a murmurer (akin to A, No. 1, and B, above), one who complains, is used in Jude 16, especially perhaps of utterances against God (see ver. 15).¶

For MUSING (*dialogizomai*, in Luke 3 : 15, A.V.) see REASON (Verb)

MUSIC

SUMPHŌNIA (συμφωνία), lit., a sounding together (Eng., symphony), occurs in Luke 15 : 25.¶ In the Sept., Dan. 3 : 5, 7, 10, 15, for Aramaic *sumpŏnyâ* (not in ver. 7), itself a loan word from the Greek ; translated " dulcimer " (R.V., marg., " bagpipe ").¶

For MUSICIAN, Rev. 18 : 22, A.V., see MINSTREL

MUST

1. DEI (δεῖ), an impersonal verb, signifying ' it is necessary ' or ' one must,' ' one ought,' is found most frequently in the Gospels, Acts and the

Apocalypse, and is used (*a*) of a necessity lying in the nature of the case, e.g., John 3 : 30 ; 2 Tim. 2 : 6 ; (*b*) of necessity brought about by circumstances, e.g., Matt. 26 : 35, R.V., " must," A.V., " should ; " John 4 : 4 ; Acts 27 : 21, " should ; " 2 Cor. 11 : 30 ; in the case of Christ, by reason of the Father's will, e.g., Luke 2 : 49 ; 19 : 5 ; (*c*) of necessity as to what is required that something may be brought about, e.g., Luke 12 : 12, " ought ; " John 3 : 7 ; Acts 9 : 6 ; 1 Cor. 11 : 19 ; Heb. 9 : 26 ; (*d*) of a necessity of law, duty, equity, e.g., Matt. 18 : 33, " shouldest ; " 23 : 23, " ought ; " Luke 15 : 32, " it was meet ; " Acts 15 : 5, " it is needful " (R.V.) ; Rom. 1 : 27, R.V., " was due," A.V., " was meet " (of a recompense due by the law of God) ; frequently requiring the rendering " ought," e.g., Rom. 8 : 26 ; 12 : 3 ; 1 Cor. 8 : 2 ; (*e*) of necessity arising from the determinate will and counsel of God, e.g., Matt. 17 : 10 ; 24 : 6 ; 26 : 54 ; 1 Cor. 15 : 53, especially regarding the salvation of men through the Death, Resurrection and Ascension of Christ, e.g., John 3 : 14 ; Acts 3 : 21 ; 4 : 12. See BEHOVE, No. 2 (where see the differences in the meanings of synonymous words), MEET, NEED, NEEDFUL, OUGHT, SHOULD.

2. OPHEILŌ (ὀφείλω), to owe, is rendered "must . . . needs" in 1 Cor. 5 : 10. See BEHOVE, No. 1.

Notes : (1) In Mark 14 : 49, A.V., the conjunction *hina* with the subjunctive mood, in order that, is represented by " must " (R.V., " that . . . might "). (2) In Heb. 13 : 17, A.V., the future participle of *apodidōmi*, to give, is translated " they that must give " (R.V., " they that shall give "). (3) In 2 Pet. 1 : 14, A.V., the verb to be, with *apothesis*, a putting off, is translated " I must put off," R.V., " (the) putting off . . . cometh," lit., ' is (swift).' (4) Sometimes the infinitive mood of a verb, with or without the article, is necessarily rendered by a phrase involving the word " must," e.g., 1 Pet. 4 : 17, A.V., " must (begin) ; " or " should," Heb. 4 : 6, R.V., " should " (A.V. " must "). (5) Sometimes the subjunctive mood of a verb, used as a deliberative, is rendered " must," etc., John 6 : 28, " (what) must (we do)," R.V. (A.V., " shall ").

MUSTARD

SINAPI (σίναπι), a word of Egyptian origin, is translated " mustard seed " in the N.T. " The conditions to be fulfilled by the mustard are that it should be a familiar plant, with a very small seed, Matt. 17 : 20 ; Luke 17 : 6, sown in the earth, growing larger than garden herbs, Matt. 13 : 31, having large branches, Mark 4 : 31, . . . attractive to birds, Luke 13 : 19 [R.V., ' (became) a tree ']. The cultivated mustard is *sinapis nigra.* The seed is well known for its minuteness. The mustards are annuals, reproduced with extraordinary rapidity . . . In fat soil they often attain a height of 10 or 12 feet, and have branches which attract passing birds " (A. E. Post, in Hastings' Bib. Dic.).¶

The correct R.V. translation in Matt. 13 : 32, " greater than the herbs," for the A.V., " greatest among herbs " (the mustard is not a herb), should be noted.

As the parable indicates, Christendom presents a sort of Christianity that has become conformed to the principles and ways of the world, and the world has favoured this debased Christianity. Contrast the testimony of the N.T., e.g., in John 17 : 14 ; Gal. 6 : 14 ; 1 Pet. 2 : 11 ; 1 John 3 : 1.

MUTUAL

Note : This is the A.V. rendering of the phrase *en allēlois* in Rom. 1 : 12, translated in the R.V., " each of us by the other's (faith)." See OTHER, No. 5.

MUZZLE

PHIMOŌ (φιμόω), to close the mouth with a muzzle (*phimos*), is used (*a*) of muzzling the ox when it treads out the corn, 1 Cor. 9 : 9, A.V., " muzzle the mouth of," R.V., " muzzle," and 1 Tim. 5 : 18, with the lesson that those upon whom spiritual labour is bestowed should not refrain from ministering to the material needs of those who labour on their behalf ; (*b*) metaphorically, of putting to silence, or subduing to stillness, Matt. 22 : 12, 34 ; Mark 1 : 25 ; 4 : 39 ; Luke 4 : 35 ; 1 Pet. 2 : 15. See PEACE (hold), SILENCE.¶

MY (MINE)

EMOS (ἐμός), a possessive adjective of the first person, often used as a possessive pronoun with greater emphasis than the oblique forms of *egō* (see below), a measure of stress which should always be observed ; it denotes (I) subjectively, (*a*) what I possess, e.g., John 4 : 34 ; 7 : 16 (1st part) ; 13 : 35 ; 1 Cor. 16 : 21 ; Gal. 6 : 11 ; Col. 4 : 18 (1st clause) ; as a pronoun, absolutely (i.e., not as an adjective), e.g., Matt. 20 : 15 ; 25 : 27 ; Luke 15 : 31, R.V., " (all that is) mine," A.V., " (all that) I have " ; John 16 : 14, 15 ; 17 : 10 ; (*b*) ' proceeding from me,' e.g. Mark 8 : 38 ; John 7 : 16 (2nd part) ; 8 : 37 (here the repetition of the article with the pronoun, after the article with the noun, lends special stress to the pronoun ; more lit., ' the word, that which is mine ') ; so in John 15 : 12. Such instances are to be distinguished from the less emphatic order where the pronoun comes between the article and the noun, as in John 7 : 16, already mentioned ; (*c*) in the phrase ' it is mine ' (i.e., ' it rests with me '), e.g., Matt. 20 : 23 ; Mark 10 : 40 ; (II) objectively, pertaining or relating to me : (*a*) ' appointed for me,' e.g., John 7 : 6, " My time " (with the repeated article and special stress just referred to) ; (*b*) equivalent to an objective genitive (' of me ') e.g., Luke 22 : 19, " (in remembrance) of Me " (lit., ' in My remembrance ') ; so 1 Cor. 11 : 24.

Notes : (1) This pronoun frequently translates oblique forms of the first personal pronoun *egō*, I, e.g., of me, to me. These instances are usually unemphatic, always less so than those under *emos* (above).

(2) For " my affairs " and " my state " see AFFAIR, Notes. (3) In Matt. 26 : 12, " for My burial " translates a phrase consisting of the preposition *pros* (towards) governing the article with the infinitive mood, aorist tense, of *entaphiazō*, to bury, followed by the personal pronoun " Me," as the object, where the infinitive is virtually a noun, lit., ' towards the burying (of) Me.' (4) In 1 Tim. 1 : 11, " was committed to my trust " is, lit., ' (with) which I was entrusted ' (*pisteuō*, to entrust).

MYRRH

A. Noun.

SMURNA (σμύρνα), whence the name Smyrna, a word of Semitic origin, Heb., *mōr*, from a root meaning bitter, is a gum resin from a shrubby tree, which grows in Yemen and neighbouring regions of Africa ; the fruit is smooth and somewhat larger than a pea. The colour of myrrh varies from pale reddish-yellow to reddish-brown or red. The taste is bitter, and the substance astringent, acting as an antiseptic and a stimulant. It was used as a perfume, Ps. 45 : 8, where the language is symbolic of the graces of the Messiah ; Prov. 7 : 17 ; S. of Sol. 1 : 13 ; 5 : 5 ; it was one of the ingredients of the " holy anointing oil " for the priests, Ex. 30 : 23 (R.V., " flowing myrrh ") ; it was used also for the purification of women, Esth. 2 : 12 ; for embalming, John 19 : 39 ; as an anodyne (see B) ; it was one of the gifts of the Magi, Matt. 2 : 11.¶

B. Verb.

SMURNIZŌ (σμυρνίζω) is used transitively in the N.T., with the meaning to mingle or drug with myrrh, Mark 15 : 23 ; the mixture was doubtless offered to deaden the pain (Matthew's word " gall " suggests that myrrh was not the only ingredient). Christ refused to partake of any such means of alleviation ; He would retain all His mental power for the complete fulfilment of the Father's will.¶

MYSELF

1. EMAUTOU (ἐμαυτοῦ), a reflexive pronoun, of the first person, lit., of myself, is used (*a*) frequently after various prepositions, e.g., *hupo*, under, Matt. 8 : 9 ; Luke 7 : 8 ; R.V., " under myself ; " *peri*, concerning, John 5 : 31 ; 8 : 14, 18 ; Acts 24 : 10 ; *apo*, from, John 5 : 30 ; 7 : 17, R.V., " from " (A.V., " of," which is ambiguous) ; so ver. 28 ; 8 : 28, 42 ; 10 : 18 ; 14 : 10 (R.V., " from ") ; *pros*, unto, John 12 : 32, R.V., " unto Myself ; " 14 : 3 ; Philm. 13, " with me ; " *eis*, to, 1 Cor. 4 : 6 ; *huper*, on behalf of, 2 Cor. 12 : 5 ; *ek* (*ex*), out of, or from, John 12 : 49, R.V., " from Myself ; " (*b*) as the direct object of a verb, Luke 7 : 7 ; John 8 : 54 ; 14 : 21 ; 17 : 19 ; Acts 26 : 2 ; 1 Cor. 4 : 3 ; 9 : 19 ; 2 Cor. 11 : 7, 9 ; Gal. 2 : 18 ; Phil. 3 : 13 ; (*c*) in other oblique cases of the pronoun, without a preposition, e.g., Acts 20 : 24, " unto " (or to) ; 26 : 9, " with " (or ' to ') ; Rom. 11 : 4, R.V., " for " (A.V., " to ") ; 1 Cor. 4 : 4, R.V.,

" against myself " (A.V., inaccurately, " by ") ; in all these instances the pronoun is in the dative case ; in I Cor. 10 : 33, " mine own " (the genitive case) ; in I Cor. 7 : 7, " I myself " (the accusative case).¶

2. AUTOS (αὐτός), self (a) with egō, I, " I myself," Luke 24 : 39 ; Acts 10 : 26 ; Rom. 7 : 25 ; 9 : 3 ; 2 Cor. 10 : 1 ; 12 : 13 ; (b) without the personal pronoun, Acts 24 : 16 (as the subject of a verb) ; in the nominative case, Acts 25 : 22 ; I Cor. 9 : 27 ; Phil. 2 : 24 ; in the genitive case, Rom. 16 : 2, R.V., " of mine own self."

MYSTERY

MUSTĒRION (μυστήριον), primarily that which is known to the mustēs, the initiated (from mueō, to initiate into the mysteries ; cp. Phil. 4 : 12, mueomai, " I have learned the secret," R.V.). In the N.T. it denotes, not the mysterious (as with the Eng. word), but that which, being outside the range of unassisted natural apprehension, can be made known only by Divine revelation, and is made known in a manner and at a time appointed by God, and to those only who are illumined by His Spirit. In the ordinary sense a mystery implies knowledge withheld ; its Scriptural significance is truth revealed.   Hence the terms especially associated with the subject are " made known," " manifested," " revealed," " preached," " understand," " dispensation."   The definition given above may be best illustrated by the following passage : " the mystery which hath been hid from all ages and generations : but now hath it been manifested to His saints " (Col. 1 : 26, R.V.).   " It is used of :

" (a) spiritual truth generally, as revealed in the gospel, I Cor. 13 : 2 ; 14 : 2 [cp. I Tim. 3 : 9].   Among the ancient Greeks ' the mysteries ' were religious rites and ceremonies practised by secret societies into which any one who so desired might be received.   Those who were initiated into these ' mysteries ' became possessors of certain knowledge, which was not imparted to the uninitiated, and were called ' the perfected,' cp. I Cor. 2 : 6-16 where the Apostle has these ' mysteries ' in mind and presents the gospel in contrast thereto ; here ' the perfected ' are, of course, the believers, who alone can perceive the things revealed ; (b) Christ, who is God Himself revealed under the conditions of human life, Col. 2 : 2 ; 4 : 3, and submitting even to death, I Cor. 2 : 1 [in some mss., for marturion, testimony], 7, but raised from among the dead, I Tim. 3 : 16, that the will of God to co-ordinate the universe in Him, and subject it to Him, might in due time be accomplished, Eph. 1 : 9 (cp. Rev. 10 : 7), as is declared in the gospel, Rom. 16 : 25 ; Eph. 6 : 19 ; (c) the Church, which is Christ's Body, i.e., the union of redeemed men with God in Christ, Eph. 5 : 32 [cp. Col. 1 : 27] ; (d) the rapture into the presence of Christ of those members of the Church which is His Body who shall be alive on the earth at His Parousia, I Cor. 15 : 51 ; (e) the operation of those hidden forces that either retard or accelerate the Kingdom of Heaven (i.e., of God), Matt. 13 : 11 ; Mark 4 : 11 ; (f) the cause of the present condition of

Israel, Rom. 11 : 25 ; (g) the spirit of disobedience to God, 2 Thess. 2 : 7 ;
Rev. 17 : 5, 7 ; cp. Eph. 2 : 2."*

To these may be added (h) the seven local churches, and their angels,
seen in symbolism, Rev. 1 : 20 ; (i) the ways of God in grace, Eph. 3 : 9.
The word is used in a comprehensive way in 1 Cor. 4 : 1.†

---

* From Notes on Thessalonians by Hogg and Vine, pp. 256, 257.
† See The Twelve Mysteries of Scripture by Vine.

N

NAIL (Noun and Verb)
A. Noun.

HĒLOS (ἧλος) occurs in the remarks of Thomas regarding the print of the nails used in Christ's crucifixion, John 20 : 25.¶

B. Verb.

PROSĒLOŌ (προσηλόω), to nail to (*pros*, to, and a verbal form of A), is used in Col. 2 : 14, in which the figure of a bond (ordinances of the Law) is first described as cancelled, and then removed ; the idea in the verb itself is not that of the cancellation, to which the taking out of the way was subsequent, but of nailing up the removed thing in triumph to the Cross. The Death of Christ not only rendered the Law useless as a means of salvation, but gave public demonstration that it was so.¶

NAKED (Adjective and Verb), NAKEDNESS
A. Adjective.

GUMNOS (γυμνός) signifies (a) unclothed, Mark 14 : 52 ; in ver. 51 it is used as a noun (" *his* " and " *body* " being italicised) ; (b) scantily or poorly clad, Matt. 25 : 36, 38, 43, 44 ; Acts 19 : 16 (with torn garments) ; Jas. 2 : 15 ; (c) clad in the undergarment only (the outer being laid aside), John 21 : 7 (see CLOTHING) ; (d) metaphorically, (1) of a bare seed, 1 Cor. 15 : 37 ; (2) of the soul without the body, 2 Cor. 5 : 3 ; (3) of things exposed to the all-seeing eye of God, Heb. 4 : 13 ; (4) of the carnal condition of a local church, Rev. 3 : 17 ; (5) of the similar state of an individual, 16 : 15 ; (b) of the desolation of religious Babylon, 17 : 16.¶

B. Verb.

GUMNITEUŌ (γυμνιτεύω), to be naked or scantily clad (akin to A), is used in 1 Cor. 4 : 11.   In the *Koinē* writings (see Preface to Vol. 1) it is used of being light-armed.¶

C. Noun.

GUMNOTĒS (γυμνότης), nakedness (akin to A), is used (a) of want of sufficient clothing, Rom. 8 : 35 ; 2 Cor. 11 : 27 ; (b) metaphorically, of the nakedness of the body, said of the condition of a local church, Rev. 3 : 18.¶

NAME
A. Noun.

ONOMA (ὄνομα) is used (I) in general of the name by which a person or thing is called, e.g., Mark 3 : 16, 17, " (He) surnamed," lit., ' (He added) the name ; ' 14 : 32, lit.,' (of which) the name (was) ; ' Luke 1 : 63 ; John 18 : 10 ; sometimes translated " named," e.g., Luke 1 : 5, " named (Zacharias)," lit., ' by name ; ' in the same verse, " named (Elizabeth)," lit., ' the name of her,' an elliptical phrase, with ' was ' understood ; Acts 8 : 9, R.V., " by name," 10 : 1 ; the name is put for the reality in Rev. 3 : 1 ; in Phil. 2 : 9, the Name represents ' the title and dignity ' of the Lord, as in Eph. 1 : 21 and Heb. 1 : 4 ;

(II) for all that a name implies, of authority, character, rank, majesty, power, excellence, etc., of everything that the name covers : (a) of the Name of God as expressing His attributes, etc., e.g., Matt. 6 : 9 ; Luke 1 : 49 ; John 12 : 28 ; 17 : 6, 26 ; Rom. 15 : 9 ; 1 Tim. 6 : 1 ; Heb. 13 : 15 ; Rev. 13 : 6 ; (b) of the Name of Christ, e.g., Matt. 10 : 22 ; 19 : 29 ; John 1 : 12 ; 2 : 23 ; 3 : 18 ; Acts 26 : 9 ; Rom. 1 : 5 ; Jas. 2 : 7 ; 1 John 3 : 23 ; 3 John 7 ; Rev. 2 : 13 ; 3 : 8 ; also the phrases rendered ' in the name ; ' these may be analysed as follows : (1) representing the authority of Christ, e.g., Matt. 18 : 5 (with *epi,* ' on the ground of My authority ') ; so Matt. 24 : 5 (falsely) and parallel passages ; as substantiated by the Father, John 14 : 26 ; 16 : 23 (last clause), R.V. ; (2) in the power of (with *èn,* in), e.g., Mark 16 : 17 ; Luke 10 : 17 ; Acts 3 : 6 ; 4 : 10 ; 16 : 18 ; Jas. 5 : 14 ; (3) in acknowledgement or confession of, e.g., Acts 4 : 12 ; 8 : 16 ; 9 : 27, 28 ; (4) in recognition of the authority of (sometimes combined with the thought of relying or resting on), Matt. 18 : 20 ; cp. 28 : 19 ; Acts 8 : 16 ; 9 : 2 (*eis,* into) ; John 14 : 13 ; 15 : 16 ; Eph. 5 : 20 ; Col. 3 : 17 ; (5) owing to the fact that one is called by Christ's Name or is identified with Him, e.g. 1 Pet. 4 : 14 (with *en,* in) ; with *heneken,* for the sake of, e.g., Matt. 19 : 29 ; with *dia,* on account of, Matt. 10 : 22 ; 24 : 9 ; Mark 13 : 13 ; Luke 21 : 17 ; John 15 : 21 ; 1 John 2 : 12 ; Rev. 2 : 3 (for 1 Pet. 4 : 16, see Note below) ;

(III) as standing, by metonymy, for persons, Acts 1 : 15 ; Rev. 3 : 4 ; 11 : 13 (R.V., " persons ").

Note : In Mark 9 : 41, the use of the phrase *en* with the dative case of *onoma* (as in the best mss.) suggests the idea of ' by reason of ' or ' on the ground of ' (i.e., ' because ye are My disciples ') ; 1 Pet. 4 : 16, R.V., " in this Name " (A.V., " on this behalf "), may be taken in the same way.

B. Verbs.

1. ONOMAZŌ (ὀνομάζω) denotes (a) to name, mention, or address by name, Acts 19 : 13, R.V., " to name " (A.V., " to call ") ; in the Passive Voice, Rom. 15 : 20 ; Eph. 1 : 21 ; 5 : 3 ; to make mention of the Name of the Lord in praise and worship, 2 Tim. 2 : 19 ; (b) to name, call, give a name to, Luke 6 : 13, 14 ; Passive Voice, 1 Cor. 5 : 11, R.V., " is named " (A.V., " is called ") ; Eph. 3 : 15 (some mss. have the verb in this sense in Mark 3 : 14 and 1 Cor. 5 : 1). See CALL, Note (1).¶

2. EPONOMAZŌ (ἐπονομάζω), to call by a name, surname (*epi,* on, and No. 1), is used in Rom. 2 : 17, Passive Voice, R.V., " bearest the name of " (A.V., " art called "). See CALL, Note (1).¶

3. PROSAGOREUŌ (προσαγορεύω) primarily denotes to address, greet, salute ; hence, to call by name, Heb. 5 : 10, R.V., " named (of God a High Priest) " (A.V., " called "), expressing the formal ascription of the title to Him whose it is ; " called " does not adequately express the significance. Some suggest the meaning ' addressed,' but this is doubtful. The reference is to Ps. 110 : 4, a prophecy confirmed at the Ascension.¶ In the Sept., Deut. 23 : 6.¶

4. KALEŌ (καλέω), to call, is translated " named " in Acts 7 : 58, R.V. (A.V., " whose name was "). See CALL, No. 1 (b).

Notes : (1) In Luke 19 : 2, A.V., *kaleō*, to call (with the dative case of *onoma*, ' by name '), is translated " named " (R.V., " called by name ") ; in Luke 2 : 21, A.V., the verb alone is rendered " named " (R.V., " called "). (2) In Matt. 9 : 9 and Mark 15 : 7, A.V., the verb *legō*, to speak, to call by name, is rendered " named " (R.V., " called "). See CALL, No. 9.

NAMELY

Notes : (1) In Rom. 13 : 9, the preposition *en*, in, with the article, lit., ' in the,' is translated " namely." (2) In 1 Cor. 7 : 26 the R.V., " *namely*," and A.V., " *I say*," do not translate anything in the original, but serve to reintroduce the phrase " that this is good."

NAPKIN

SOUDARION (σουδάριον), for which see HANDKERCHIEF, is translated " napkin " in Luke 19 : 20 ; John 11 : 44 ; 20 : 7. In Luke 19 : 20 the reference may be to a towel or any kind of linen cloth or even a sort of head-dress, any of which might be used for concealing money.

NARRATIVE

DIĒGĒSIS (διήγησις), translated " a declaration " in the A.V. of Luke 1 : 1, denotes a " narrative," R.V. (akin to *diēgeomai*, to set out in detail, recount, describe). See DECLARE, B, Note (1).¶ In the Sept., Judg. 7 : 15 ; Hab. 2 : 6.¶

NARROW
A. Adjective.

STENOS (στενός), from a root *sten-*, seen in *stenazō*, to groan, *stenagmos*, groaning (Eng., stenography, lit., narrow writing), is used figuratively in Matt. 7 : 13, 14, of the gate which provides the entrance to eternal life, narrow because it runs counter to natural inclinations, and " the way " is similarly characterized ; so in Luke 13 : 24 (where the more intensive word *agōnizomai*, " strive," is used) ; R.V., " narrow " (A.V., " strait ") in each place. Cp. *stenochōreō*, to be straitened, and *stenochōria*, narrowness, anguish, distress.¶

B. Verb.

THLIBŌ (θλίβω), to press, is translated " narrow " in Matt. 7 : 14,

A.V., lit., ' narrowed ' (R.V., " straitened ; " the verb is in the perfect participle, Passive Voice), i.e., hemmed in, like a mountain gorge ; the way is ' rendered narrow ' by the Divine conditions, which make it impossible for any to enter who think the entrance depends upon self-merit, or who still incline towards sin, or desire to continue in evil. See AFFLICT, No. 4.

NATION

1. ETHNOS (ἔθνος), originally a multitude, denotes (a) a nation or people, e.g., Matt. 24 : 7 ; Acts 10 : 35 ; the Jewish people, e.g., Luke 7 : 5 ; 23 : 2 ; John 11 : 48, 50–52 ; Acts 10 : 22 ; 24 : 2, 10, 17 ; in Matt. 21 : 43, the reference is to Israel in its restored condition ; (b) in the plural, the nations as distinct from Israel. See GENTILES.

2. GENOS (γένος), a race : see KIND (Noun).

3. ALLOPHULOS (ἀλλόφυλος), foreign, of another race (allos, another, phulon, a tribe), is used in Acts 10 : 28, " one of another nation."¶

Note : For Phil. 2 : 15, *genea* (A.V., " nation," R.V., " generation "), see AGE.

NATURAL, NATURALLY
A. Adjectives.

1. PHUSIKOS (φυσικός) originally signifying produced by nature, inborn, from *phusis*, nature (see below), cp. Eng., physical, physics, etc., denotes (a) according to nature, Rom. 1 : 26, 27 ; (b) governed by mere natural instincts, 2 Pet. 2 : 12, R.V., " (born) mere animals ", A.V. and R.V. marg., " natural (brute beasts)."¶

2. PSUCHIKOS (ψυχικός), belonging to the *psuchē*, soul (as the lower part of the immaterial in man), natural, physical, describes the man in Adam and what pertains to him (set in contrast to *pneumatikos*, spiritual), 1 Cor. 2 : 14 ; 15 : 44 (twice), 46 (in the latter used as a noun) ; Jas. 3 : 15, " sensual " (R.V. marg., " natural " or " animal "), here relating perhaps more especially to the mind, a wisdom in accordance with, or springing from, the corrupt desires and affections ; so in Jude 19.¶

B. Noun.

GENESIS (γένεσις), birth, is used in Jas. 1 : 23, of the " natural face," lit., ' the face of his birth,' " what God made him to be " (Hort). See GENERATION, NATURE, No. 2.

Note : In Rom. 11 : 21, 24 the preposition *kata*, according to, with the noun *phusis*, nature, is translated " natural," of branches, metaphorically describing members of the nation of Israel.

C. Adverb.

PHUSIKŌS (φυσικῶς), naturally, by nature (akin to A, No. 1), is used in Jude 10.¶

Note : In Phil. 2 : 20, A.V., *gnēsiōs*, sincerely, honourably, truly (from the adjective *gnēsios*, true, sincere, genuine; see, e.g., Phil. 4 : 3), is translated " naturally " (R.V., " truly ; " marg., " genuinely ").¶

NATURE

1. PHUSIS (φύσις), from *phuō*, to bring forth, produce, signifies (*a*) the nature (i.e., the natural powers or constitution) of a person or thing, Eph. 2 : 3 ; Jas. 3 : 7 (" kind ") ; 2 Pet. 1 : 4 ; (*b*) origin, birth, Rom. 2 : 27, one who by birth is a Gentile, uncircumcised, in contrast to one who, though circumcised, has become spiritually uncircumcised by his iniquity ; Gal. 2 : 15 ; (*c*) the regular law or order of nature, Rom. 1 : 26, against nature (*para*, against) ; 2 : 14, adverbially, " by nature " (for 11 : 21, 24, see NATURAL, Note) ; 1 Cor. 11 : 14 ; Gal. 4 : 8, " by nature (are no gods)," here " nature " is the emphatic word, and the phrase includes demons, men regarded as deified, and idols ; these are gods only in name (the negative, *mē*, denies not simply that they were gods, but the possibility that they could be).¶

2. GENESIS (γένεσις) is used in the phrase in Jas. 3 : 6, " the wheel of nature," R.V. (marg., " birth "). Some regard this as the course of birth or of creation, or the course of man's nature according to its original Divine purpose ; Mayor (on the Ep. of James) regards *trochos* here as a wheel, " which, catching fire from the glowing axle, is compared to the wide-spreading mischief done by the tongue," and shows that " the fully developed meaning " of *genesis* denotes " the incessant change of life . . . the sphere of this earthly life, meaning all that is contained in our life." The significance, then, would appear to be the whole round of human life and activity. Moulton and Milligan illustrate it in this sense from the papyri. See NATURAL, B.

For NAUGHTINESS, Jas. 1 : 21, A.V., see WICKEDNESS

NAY

1. OU (οὐ), no, not, expressing a negation absolutely, is rendered " nay," e.g., in Matt. 5 : 37 ; 13 : 29 ; John 7 : 12, A.V. (R.V., " not so ") ; Acts 16 : 37 ; 2 Cor. 1 : 17, 18, 19 ; Jas. 5 : 12.

2. OUCHI (οὐχί), a strengthened form of No. 1, is used, e.g., in Luke 12 : 51 ; 13 : 3, 5 ; 16 : 30 ; Rom. 3 : 27.

3. ALLA (ἀλλά), but, to mark contrast or opposition, is rendered " nay " in Rom. 3 : 31, R.V., " nay " (A.V., " yea ") ; in 7 : 7, R.V., " howbeit " (A.V., " nay ") ; 8 : 37 ; 1 Cor. 3 : 2, R.V. ; 6 : 8 ; 12 : 22 ; in Heb. 3 : 16, R.V., " nay " (A.V., " howbeit ").

4. MENOUNGE (μενοῦνγε), (i.e., *men oun ge*), nay rather, is rendered " nay but " in Rom. 9 : 20 (in Rom. 10 : 18 and Phil. 3 : 8, " yea verily," A.V., " yea doubtless "). See YEA.¶

NEAR (Adverb), NEAR (come, draw), NEARER
A. Adverbs.

1. ENGUS (ἐγγύς), near, nigh, is used (*a*) of place, e.g., Luke 19 : 11, " nigh ;" John 3 : 23 ; 11 : 54, " near ;" 6 : 19, 23, " nigh ;" meta-

phorically in Rom. 10 : 8 ; Eph. 2 : 13, 17, "nigh ; " (b) of time, e.g., Matt. 24 : 32, 33, "nigh ; " so Luke 21 : 30, 31 ; as a preposition, Heb. 6 : 8, "nigh unto (a curse)," and 8 : 13, "nigh unto (vanishing away)." See HAND (at), NIGH, READY.

2. ENGUTERON (ἐγγύτερον), the comparative degree of No. 1, and the neuter of the adjective *enguteros*, used adverbially, occurs in Rom. 13 : 11.¶

3. PLESION (πλησίον), near, close by, neighbouring (the neuter of the adjective *plēsios*, used as an adverb), occurs in John 4 : 5. See NEIGHBOUR.

B. Adjective.

ANANKAIOS (ἀναγκαῖος), necessary, is used, in a secondary sense, of persons connected by bonds of nature or friendship, with the meaning ' intimate,' in Acts 10 : 24, " (his) near (friends) ; " it is found in this sense in the papyri. See NECESSARY, NEEDFUL.

C. Verbs.

1. ENGIZO (ἐγγίζω), transitively, to bring near (not in N.T. ; in the Sept., e.g., Gen. 48 : 10 ; Is. 5 : 8) ; intransitively, to draw near, e.g., Matt. 21 : 34 ; Luke 18 : 40 ; 19 : 41, R.V., " draw nigh ; " see APPROACH, A.

2. PROSERCHOMAI (προσέρχομαι), to come to, go to, is translated " drew near " in Acts 7 : 31 and Heb. 10 : 22. See COME, No. 10.

3. PROSAGO (προσάγω) is used (a) transitively, to bring, Acts 16 : 20 ; 1 Pet. 3 : 18 ; (b) intransitively, to draw near, in the latter sense in Acts 27 : 27.¶

NECESSARY

1. ANANKAIOS (ἀναγκαῖος), necessary (from *ananke*, necessity ; see below), is so rendered in Acts 13 : 46 ; 1 Cor. 12 : 22 ; 2 Cor. 9 : 5 ; Phil. 2 : 25 ; Tit. 3 : 14 ; Heb. 8 : 3, R.V. (A.V., " of necessity ") ; for Acts 10 : 24, " near friends," see NEAR, B.¶

2. ANANKE (ἀνάγκη), a necessity (see No. 1), is rendered " (it was) necessary " in Heb. 9 : 23, lit., ' it was a necessity.' See DISTRESS, A, No. 1.

3. EPANANKES (ἐπανάγκης), an adjective akin to the preceding, with *epi*, used intensively, found only in the neuter form, is used as an adverb signifying ' of necessity ' and translated as an adjective in Acts 15 : 28, " necessary," lit., ' (things) of necessity.'¶

Note : For the A.V. of Acts 28 : 10 see NEED, A, No. 1.

NECESSITY (-TIES)

1. ANANKE (ἀνάγκη) signifies (a) a necessity, what must needs be (see NEEDS), translated " necessity " (in some mss. in Luke 23 : 17) in 1 Cor. 7 : 37 ; 9 : 16 ; 2 Cor. 9 : 7 (with *ek*, out of) ; Philm. 14 (with *kata*, according to) ; Heb. 7 : 12 ; 9 : 16 ; (b) distress, pain, translated

"necessities" in 2 Cor. 6 : 4 ; 12 : 10. See DISTRESS, No. 1, and the synonymous words there, and NEEDS, NEEDFUL (also CONSTRAIN, Note).

2. CHREIA (χρεία), a need, and almost always so translated, is used in the plural in Acts 20 : 34, "necessities ;" Rom. 12 : 13, R.V. (A.V., "necessity") ; in Phil. 4 : 16, A.V., "necessity," R.V., "need". See NEED, NEEDFUL.

NECK

TRACHĒLOS (τράχηλος) is used (a) literally, Matt. 18 : 6 ; Mark 9 : 42 ; Luke 17 : 2 ; of embracing, Luke 15 : 20 ; Acts 20 : 37 ; (b) metaphorically, in Acts 15 : 10, of putting a yoke upon ; Rom. 16 : 4, singular in the original,' (laid down their) neck,' indicating the figurative use of the term rather than the literal. Prisca and Aquila in some way had risked their lives for the Apostle (the phrase is found with this significance in the papyri).¶

NEED, NEEDS, NEEDFUL
A. Nouns.

1. CHREIA (χρεία) denotes a need, in such expressions as 'there is a need ;' or 'to have need of' something, e.g., Matt. 3 : 14 ; 6 : 8 ; 9 : 12, R.V., "(have no) need," A.V., "need (not)," the R.V. adheres to the noun form ; so in 14 : 16 ; Mark 14 : 63 ; Luke 5 : 31 ; 22 : 71 ; Eph. 4 : 28 ; 1 Thess. 4 : 9 ; in the following, however, both R.V. and A.V. use the verb form, to need (whereas the original has the verb *echō*, to have, with the noun *chreia* as the object, as in the instances just mentioned) : Luke 15 : 7 ; John 2 : 25 ; 13 : 10 ; 16 : 30 ; 1 Thess. 1 : 8 ; 1 John 2 : 27 ; Rev. 22 : 5 ; in all these the verb to have could well have been expressed in the translation.

In Luke 10 : 42 it is translated "needful," where the "one thing" is surely not one dish, or one person, but is to be explained according to Matt. 6 : 33 and 16 : 26. In Eph. 4 : 29, for the A.V., "(to) the use (of edifying)," the R.V. more accurately has "(for edifying) as the need may be," marg., "the building up of the need," i.e., 'to supply that which needed in each case ;' so Westcott, who adds "The need represents a gap in the life which the wise word ' builds up,' fills up solidly and surely." In Phil. 4 : 19 the R.V. has " every need of yours " (A.V., "all your need ") ; in 1 Thess. 4 : 12, R.V., "need" (A.V., "lack") ; in Acts 28 : 10, R.V., "(such things) as we needed " (A.V., "as were necessary "), lit., ' the things for the needs (plural).' See BUSINESS, A, No. 1, LACK, NECESSITY, USE, WANT.

2. ANANKĒ (ἀνάγκη), a necessity, need, is translated "it must needs be " in Matt. 18 : 7, with the verb 'to be' understood (according to the best mss.) ; in Luke 14 : 18, "I must needs " translates the verb *echō*, to have, with this noun as the object, lit., 'I have need ;' in Rom. 13 : 5 "(ye) must needs," lit., '(it is) necessary (to be subject).' See NECESSARY, No. 2, NECESSITY, No. 1. See also DISTRESS.

B. Verbs.

1. CHRĒZŌ (χρήζω), to need, to have need of (akin to *chrē*, it is necessary, fitting), is used in Matt. 6 : 32 ; Luke 11 : 8 ; 12 : 30 ; Rom. 16 : 2, R.V., " may have need " (A.V., " hath need ") ; 2 Cor. 3 : 1.¶

2. DEI (δεῖ), an impersonal verb, signifying ' it is necessary,' is rendered " must needs " in Mark 13 : 7 ; John 4 : 4 ; Acts 1 : 16, A.V. (R.V., " it was needful ") ; 17 : 3, A.V. (R.V., " it behoved ") ; (in some mss. in Acts 21 : 22) ; 2 Cor. 11 : 30 ; 12 : 1 ; in Acts 15 : 5, " it was needful."

3. DEON (δέον), the neuter of the present participle of No. 2, is used as a noun, signifying that which is needful, due, proper, in 1 Pet. 1 : 6, with the meaning ' need,' " (if) need (be)," with the verb to be understood. See OUGHT.

4. PROSDEOMAI (προσδέομαι), to want besides, to need in addition (*pros*, besides, *deomai*, to want), is used in Acts 17 : 25, " (as though) He needed (anything) ; " the literal sense of *pros* is not to be stressed.¶ In the Sept., Prov. 12 : 9, " lacking (bread)."¶

5. OPHEILŌ (ὀφείλω), to owe, be bound, obliged to do something, is translated " must ye needs," in 1 Cor. 5 : 10 ; in 7 : 36 it is used impersonally, signifying ' it is due,' and followed by the infinitive mood of *ginomai*, to become, to occur, come about, lit. ' it is due to become,' translated " (if) need (so) require." See BEHOVE, BOUND, DEBT, DUE, DUTY, GUILTY, INDEBTED, MUST, OUGHT, OWE.

Note : In Phil. 4 : 12, A.V., *hustereō*, to come short, fail, to be in want, is translated " to suffer need " (R.V., " to be in want "). See BEHIND.

C. Adjectives.

1. ANANKAIOTEROS (ἀναγκαιότερος), the comparative degree of *anankaios*, necessary, is translated " more needful " in Phil. 1 : 24. See NECESSARY, No. 1.

2. EPITĒDEIOS (ἐπιτήδειος), primarily, suitable, convenient, then, useful, necessary, is translated " needful " in Jas. 2 : 16, neuter plural, ' necessaries.' ¶ In the Sept., 1 Chron. 28 : 2, " suitable."¶

Note : In Heb. 4 : 16 *eukairos*, timely, seasonable, qualifying the noun *boētheia*, help, is translated " time of need," lit., ' for opportune help.' See CONVENIENT.

NEEDLE

1. RHAPHIS (ῥαφίς), from *rhaptō*, to sew, occurs in Matt. 19 : 24 ; Mark 10 : 25.¶

2. BELONĒ (βελόνη), akin to *belos*, a dart, denotes a sharp point, hence, a needle, Luke 18 : 25 (some mss. have No. 1).¶

Note : The idea of applying ' the needle's eye ' to small gates seems to be a modern one ; there is no ancient trace of it. The Lord's object in the statement is to express human impossibility and there is no need to endeavour to soften the difficulty by taking the needle to mean anything more than the ordinary instrument. Mackie points out (Hastings' Bib.

Dic.) that "an attempt is sometimes made to explain the words as a reference to the small door, a little over 2 feet square, in the large heavy gate of a walled city. This mars the figure without materially altering the meaning, and receives no justification from the language and traditions of Palestine."

NEGLECT, NEGLIGENT

1. AMELEŌ (ἀμελέω) denotes (a) to be careless, not to care (a, negative, melei, it is a care ; from melō, to care, to be a care), Matt. 22 : 5, " made light of ; " (b) to be careless of, neglect, 1 Tim. 4 : 14 ; Heb. 2 : 3 ; 8 : 9, " I regarded (them) not." See LIGHT OF (make), REGARD.¶ (In the Sept., Jer. 4 : 17 ; 38 : 32.¶)

2. PARATHEŌREŌ (παραθεωρέω), primarily, to examine side by side, compare (para, beside, theōreō, to look at), hence, to overlook, to neglect, is used in Acts 6 : 1, of the neglect of widows in the daily ministration in Jerusalem.¶

Note : In 2 Pet. 1 : 12, some mss. have No. 1, hence the A.V., " I will not be negligent ; " the R.V. follows those which have the future tense of mellō, to be ready. See READY. For " neglect to hear " see HEAR, No. 7.

For NEGLECTING (Col. 2 : 23) see SEVERITY

NEIGHBOUR

1. GEITŌN (γείτων), lit., one living in the same land, denotes a neighbour, always plural in the N.T., Luke 14 : 12 ; 15 : 6, 9 ; John 9 : 8.¶

2. PERIOIKOS (περίοικος), an adjective, lit., dwelling around (peri, around, oikos, a dwelling), is used as a noun in Luke 1 : 58, " neighbours."¶

3. PLĒSION (πλησίον), the neuter of the adjective plēsios (from pelas, near), is used as an adverb accompanied by the article, lit., ' the (one) near ; ' hence, one's neighbour ; see refs. below.

This and Nos. 1 and 2 have a wider range of meaning than that of the Eng. word neighbour. There were no farmhouses scattered over the agricultural areas of Palestine ; the populations, gathered in villages, went to and fro to their toil. Hence domestic life was touched at every point by a wide circle of neighbourhood. The terms for neighbour were therefore of a very comprehensive scope. This may be seen from the chief characteristics of the privileges and duties of neighbourhood as set forth in Scripture, (a) its helpfulness, e.g., Prov. 27 : 10 ; Luke 10 : 36 ; (b) its intimacy, e.g., Luke 15 : 6, 9 (see No. 1) ; Heb. 8 : 11 ; (c) its sincerity and sanctity, e.g., Ex. 22 : 7, 10 ; Prov. 3 : 29 ; 14 : 21 ; Rom. 13 : 10 ; 15 : 2 ; Eph. 4 : 25 ; Jas. 4 : 12. The N.T. quotes and expands the command in Lev. 19 : 18, to love one's neighbour as oneself ; see, e.g., Matt. 5 : 43 ; 19 : 19 ; 22 : 39 ; Mark 12 : 31, 33 ; Luke 10 : 27 ; Gal. 5 : 14 ; Jas. 2 : 8. See also Acts 7 : 27.

Note : In Rom. 13 : 8, for heteron, another, R.V. has " his neighbour."

NEIGHBOURHOOD

Note : This, in Acts 28 : 7, R.V., translates a phrase consisting of the dative plural of the article followed by *peri*, around, governed by the preposition *en*, in, " in the neighbourhood of (that place)," A.V., " in the (same quarters)," lit., ' in the (parts) around (that place).'

NEITHER. See † p. 9

For NEITHER AT ANY TIME, Luke 15 : 29, see NEVER

For NEPHEWS see GRANDCHILDREN

NEST

KATASKĒNŌSIS (κατασκήνωσις), properly an encamping, taking up one's quarters, then, a lodging, abode (*kata*, down over, *skēnē*, a tent), is used of birds' nests in Matt. 8 : 20 and Luke 9 : 58.¶ In the Sept., 1 Chron. 28 : 2, " the building ; " Ezek. 37 : 27, " (My) tabernacle."¶

The word *nossia*, signifying a brood, Luke 13 : 34, used in the Sept. to denote a nest, e.g., in Deut. 22 : 6 ; 32 : 11, signifies the actual receptacle built by birds in which to lay their eggs (having special reference to the prospective brood) ; but the word *kataskēnōsis*, used by the Lord, denotes a resting or roosting place. This lends force to His comparison. Not only was He without a home, He had not even a lodging-place (cp. *kataskēnoō*, to lodge, e.g., Matt. 13 : 32 ; Acts 2 : 26, R.V. marg., ' shall tabernacle ; ' see LODGE).

NET

1. AMPHIBLĒSTRON (ἀμφίβληστρον), lit., something thrown around (*amphi*, around, *ballō*, to throw), denotes a casting-net, a somewhat small net, cast over the shoulder, spreading out in a circle and made to sink by weights, Matt. 4 : 18 (in some mss. in Mark 1 : 16 : the best have the verb *amphiballō* alone).¶

2. DIKTUON (δίκτυον), a general term for a net (from an old verb *dikō*, to cast : akin to *diskos*, a quoit), occurs in Matt. 4 : 20, 21 ; Mark 1 : 18, 19 ; Luke 5 : 2, 4–6 ; John 21 : 6, 8, 11 (twice).¶ In the Sept. it was used for a net for catching birds, Prov. 1 : 17, in other ways, e.g., figuratively of a snare, Job. 18 : 8 ; Prov. 29 : 5.

3. SAGĒNĒ (σαγήνη) denotes a drag-net, a *seine ;* two modes were employed with this, either by its being let down into the water and drawn together in a narrowing circle, and then into the boat, or as a semicircle drawn to the shore, Matt. 13 : 47, where Nos. 1 and 2 would not have suited so well. The Greek historian Herodotus uses the corresponding verb *sagēneuō* of a device by which the Persians are said to have cleared a conquered island of its inhabitants.¶

NEVER

1. OUDEPOTE (οὐδέποτε), from *oude*, not even, and *pote*, at any time, is used in definite negative statements, e.g., Matt. 7 : 23 ; 1 Cor. 13 : 8 ; Heb. 10 : 1, 11, or questions, e.g., Matt. 21 : 16, 42 ; in Luke 15 : 29 (1st part), R.V., " never " (A.V., " neither . . . at any time ") ; A.V. and R.V., " never " (2nd part).

2. MĒDEPOTE (μηδέποτε), virtually the same as No. 1, the negative *mē*, however, conveying a less strong declarative negation, 2 Tim. 3 : 7.¶

3. OUDEPŌ (οὐδέπω), not yet, is translated " never (man) yet " in John 19 : 41 (" man " representing the idiomatically used negative pronoun *oudeis*, ' no one ') ; some mss. have it in Luke 23 : 53, instead of *oupō*, not yet.

Notes : (1) In Mark 14 : 21, A.V., the negative particle *ouk*, not, is translated " never " (R.V., " not ") ; the negative particle *mē*, not (which suggests non-existence when the existence was after all possible, or even probable, in contrast to *ou*, which implies non-existence absolutely), is translated " never " in John 7 : 15, A.V. and R.V. (2) The phrase *eis ton aiona*, for ever (not to be rendered literally, ' unto the age,' see ETERNAL), preceded by the double negative *ou mē*, denotes ' never,' John 4 : 14 ; 8 : 51, 52 ; 10 : 28 ; 11 : 26 ; 13 : 8 ; so, preceded by *ouk*, not, in Mark 3 : 29. (3) In 2 Pet. 1 : 10, " never " is the translation of *ou mē pote*, i.e., ' by no means ever ; ' so with the double negative followed by the extended word *pōpote*, i.e., ' by no means not even at any time,' John 6 : 35 (2nd part). (4) *Pōpote* follows *oudeis*, no one, in the dative case (' to no man ') in John 8 : 33, R.V., " never yet " (A.V., " never ") ; so in Luke 19 : 30, where *oudeis* is in the nominative case, R.V., " no man ever yet " (A.V., " yet never man ").

NEVERTHELESS : see † p. 9

NEW

1. KAINOS (καινός) denotes new, of that which is unaccustomed or unused, not new in time, recent, but new as to form or quality, of different nature from what is contrasted as old. " ' The new tongues,' *kainos*, of Mark 16 : 17 are the ' other tongues,' *heteros*, of Acts 2 : 4. These languages, however, were ' new ' and ' different,' not in the sense that they had never been heard before, or that they were new to the hearers, for it is plain from v. 8 that this is not the case ; they were new languages to the speakers, different from those in which they were accustomed to speak.

" The new things that the Gospel brings for present obedience and realization are : a new covenant, Matt. 26 : 28 in some texts ; a new commandment, John 13 : 34 ; a new creative act, Gal. 6 : 15 ; a new creation, 2 Cor. 5 : 17 ; a new man, i.e., a new character of manhood, spiritual and moral, after the pattern of Christ, Eph. 4 : 24 ; a new man, i.e., ' the Church which is His (Christ's) body,' Eph. 2 : 15.

" The new things that are to be received and enjoyed hereafter are : a new name, the believer's, Rev. 2 : 17 ; a new name, the Lord's, Rev. 3 : 12 ; a new song, Rev. 5 : 9 ; a new Heaven and a new Earth, Rev. 21 : 1 ; the new Jerusalem, Rev. 3 : 12 ; 21 : 2 ; ' And He that sitteth on the Throne said, Behold, I make all things new,' Rev. 21 : 5."*

Kainos is translated " fresh " in the R.V. of Matt. 9 : 17 ; Mark 2 : 22 (in the best texts) and Luke 5 : 38, of wineskins. Cp. *kainotēs*, newness (below).

2. NEOS (νέος) signifies new in respect of time, that which is recent ; it is used of the young, and so translated, especially the comparative degree " younger ; " accordingly what is *neos* may be a reproduction of the old in quality or character. *Neos* and *kainos* are sometimes used of the same thing, but there is a difference, as already indicated. Thus the " new man " in Eph. 2 : 15 (*kainos*) is new in differing in character ; so in 4 : 24 (see No. 1) ; but the " new man " in Col. 3 : 10 (*neos*) stresses the fact of the believer's new experience, recently begun, and still proceeding. " The old man in him . . . dates as far back as Adam ; a new man has been born, who therefore is fitly so called " [i.e., *neos*], Trench, Syn. §lx. The new Covenant in Heb. 12 : 24 is new (*neos*) compared with the Mosaic, nearly fifteen hundred years before ; it is new (*kainos*) compared with the Mosaic, which is old in character, ineffective, 8 : 8, 13 ; 9 : 15.

The new wine of Matt. 9 : 17 ; Mark 2 : 22 ; Luke 5 : 37–39, is *neos*, as being of recent production ; the new wine of the Kingdom, Matt. 26 : 29 ; Mark 14 : 25, is *kainos*, since it will be of a different character from that of this world. The rendering " new " (*neos*) is elsewhere used metaphorically in 1 Cor. 5 : 7, " a new lump." See YOUNG, YOUNGER.

3. PROSPHATOS (πρόσφατος), originally signifying freshly slain, acquired the general sense of new, as applied to flowers, oil, misfortune, etc. It is used in Heb. 10 : 20 of the " living way " which Christ " dedicated for us . . . through the veil . . . His flesh " (which stands for His expiatory death by the offering of His body, ver. 10).¶ In the Sept., Numb. 6 : 3 ; Deut. 32 : 17 ; Psa. 81 : 9 ; Eccl. 1 : 9.¶ Cp. the adverb *prosphatōs*, lately, recently, Acts 18 : 2.¶

Note : In Matt. 9 : 16 and Mark 2 : 21, A.V., *agnaphos* is translated " new " (R.V., " undressed "). Moulton and Milligan give an instance in the papyri of its use in respect of a " new white shirt." See UNDRESSED.¶

For NEWBORN, 1 Pet. 2 : 2, see BEGET, C, No. 2

NEWNESS

KAINOTĒS (καινότης), akin to *kainos*, is used in the phrases (a) " newness of life," Rom. 6 : 4, i.e., life of a new quality (see NEW, No. 1) ; the believer, being a new creation (2 Cor. 5 : 17), is to behave himself consistently with this in contrast to his former manner of life ; (b) newness

---

* From Notes on Galatians by Hogg and Vine, pp. 337, 338.

of the spirit, R.V., Rom. 7 : 6, said of the believer's manner of serving the Lord. While the phrase stands for the new life of the quickened spirit of the believer, it is impossible to dissociate this (in an objective sense) from the operation of the Holy Spirit, by whose power the service is rendered.¶

NEXT

1. HEXĒS (ἐξῆς), an adverb (akin to echō, to have) denoting ' in order,' successively, next, is used adjectivally, qualifying the noun " day " in Luke 9 : 37 ; Acts 21 : 1, R.V., " next " (A.V., " following ") ; 25 : 17, R.V., " next " (A.V., " on the morrow ") ; in 27 : 18, with hēmera, day, understood ; in Luke 7 : 11, in the best mss., with the word chronos, time, understood, " soon afterwards " (marg., " on the next day," according to some ancient authorities). See AFTER, FOLLOW, Note (3), MORROW.

2. METAXU (μεταξύ) signifies between, " next," in Acts 13 : 42. See BETWEEN, No. 2.

3. ECHŌ (ἔχω), to have, in the Middle Voice, sometimes signifies to be next to, said of towns, in Mark 1 : 38 ; of a day, Acts 21 : 26 ; in 20 : 15 (2nd part), hēmera, day, is unexpressed. See HAVE.

4. ERCHOMAI (ἔρχομαι), to come, is used in the present participle in Acts 13 : 44, " (the) next (sabbath)." See COME.

Note : In Acts 7 : 26, A.V., epeimi, to come on or after, used with hēmera, day, is translated " next " (R.V., " following ") ; so with hēmera, understood, Acts 16 : 11 ; 20 : 15 (1st part) ; in 21 : 18, R.V. and A.V., " following."

NEXT DAY

Notes : (1) For aurion, to-morrow, translated " next day " in Acts 4 : 3, and epaurion, on the morrow, Matt. 27 : 62 ; John 1 : 29, 35 ; 12 : 12 ; Acts 14 : 20 ; 25 : 6, see MORROW. (2) For echō, Acts 20 : 15, see NEXT, No. 3. (3) For epeimi, without the noun hēmera, " day," see NEXT (end of Note). (4) In Acts 20 : 15 (mid. of verse) heteros, other, signifies " next," with hēmera, understood. (5) In Acts 28 : 13 (end of ver.) the adjective deuteraios, second, is used in the masculine plural adverbially, signifying " the second (day)," R.V., A.V., " the next (day)."

NIGH
A. Adverbs.

1. ENGUS (ἐγγύς), nigh or near, is translated in both ways in Matt. 24 : 32, 33 and Mark 13 : 28, 29, A.V. (R.V., " nigh " in both) ; in Acts 1 : 12, with echon, present participle neuter of echō, to have, R.V., " nigh unto . . . off " (A.V., " from "). See NEAR, No. 1.

2. PARAPLĒSION (παραπλήσιον), the neuter of the adjective paraplēsios, para, beside, plēsios, near, nearly resembling, is translated " nigh unto," with reference to death, in Phil. 2 : 27.¶

B. Verb.

ENGIZŌ (ἐγγίζω) : see APPROACH.

C. Preposition.

PARA (παρά), beside, alongside of, is translated "nigh unto" in Matt. 15 : 29 ; in Mark 5 : 21, R.V., " by " (A.V., " nigh unto ").

Note : In Mark 5 : 11, A.V., *pros*, towards, on the side of, is translated "nigh unto (the mountain)," R.V., " on (the mountain) side ; " the swine were not simply near the mountain.

NIGHT (by, in the)

NUX (νύξ) is used (I) literally, (*a*) of the alternating natural period to that of the day, e.g., Matt. 4 : 2 ; 12 : 40 ; 2 Tim. 1 : 3 ; Rev. 4 : 8 ; (*b*) of the period of the absence of light, the time in which something takes place, e.g., Matt. 2 : 14 (27 : 64, in some mss.) ; Luke 2 : 8 ; John 3 : 2 (7 : 50, in some mss.) ; Acts 5 : 19 ; 9 : 25 ; (*c*) of point of time, e.g., Matt. 14 : 27 (in some mss.), 30 ; Luke 12 : 20 ; Acts 27 : 23 ; (*d*) of duration of time, e.g., Luke 2 : 37 ; 5 : 5 ; Acts 20 : 31 ; 26 : 7 (note the difference in the phrase in Mark 4 : 27) ; (II) metaphorically, (*a*) of the period of man's alienation from God, Rom. 13 : 12 ; 1 Thess. 5 : 5, lit., 'not of night,' where "of" means 'belonging to;' cp. "of the Way," Acts 9 : 2 ; "of shrinking back" and "of faith," Heb. 10 : 39, marg. ; (*b*) of death, as the time when work ceases, John 9 : 4.

NIGHT AND A DAY (A)

NUCHTHĒMEROS (νυχθήμερος), an adjective denoting lasting a night and a day (from *nux*, night, and *hēmera*, a day), is used in 2 Cor. 11 : 25, in the neuter gender, as a noun, the object of the verb *poieō*, to do, lit., ' I have done a night-and-a-day.'¶

NINE

ENNEA (ἐννέα) is found in Luke 17 : 17, and in connection with "ninety" (see below).¶

NINETY

ENENĒKONTA, or ENNĒN—(ἐνενήκοντα) is found in Matt. 18 : 12, 13 ; Luke 15 : 4, 7.¶

NINTH

ENATOS, or ENN—(ἔνατος) is found in reference (*a*) to the ninth hour (3 o'clock, p.m.) in Matt. 20 : 5 ; 27 : 45, 46 ; Mark 15 : 33, 34 ; Luke 23 : 44 ; Acts 3 : 1 ; 10 : 3, 30 ; (*b*) to the topaz as the ninth foundation of the city wall in the symbolic vision in Rev. 21 (ver. 20).¶

NO : see † p. 9.

NO LONGER, NO MORE

1. OUKETI (οὐκέτι), a negative adverb of time, signifies no longer, no more (ou, not, k, euphonic, eti longer), denying absolutely and directly, e.g., Matt. 19 : 6 ; John 4 : 42, " now . . . not ; " 6 : 66 ; Acts 20 : 25, 38 ; 2 Cor. 1 : 23, A.V., " not as yet ; " Eph. 2 : 19 ; with another negative, to strengthen the negation, e.g., Matt. 22 : 46 ; Mark 14 : 25 ; 15 : 5, R.V., " no more (anything)," A.V., " yet . . . no (thing) ; " Acts 8 : 39 ; Rev. 18 : 11, 14.

2. MĒKETI (μηκέτι), with the same meaning as No. 1, but generally expressing a prohibition, e.g., Matt. 21 : 19 ; John 5 : 14 ; Rom. 14 : 13 ; Eph. 4 : 28 ; 1 Tim. 5 : 23 ; 1 Pet. 4 : 2 ; indicating some condition expressed or implied, e.g., 1 Thess. 3 : 5 ; or non-existence, when the existence might have been possible under certain conditions, e.g., Mark 1 : 45 ; 2 : 2, R.V., " no longer " (A.V., " no "). See HENCEFORTH.

Notes : (1) The double negative *ou mē*, by no means, in no wise, followed by *eti*, longer, still, yet, is rendered " no more " in Heb. 8 : 12 ; 10 : 17 ; Rev. 3 : 12. (2) In John 15 : 4, A.V., *houtōs*, so, followed by *oude*, neither, is translated " no more " (R.V., " so neither ").

NO MAN, NO ONE, NEITHER ANY MAN

Note : *Oudeis* and *mēdeis*, no one, no man, are related to one another in much the same way as indicated above under *ouketi* and *mēketi*. Instances of *oudeis* are Matt. 6 : 24 ; 9 : 16 ; 24 : 36 (R.V., " no one ") ; John 1 : 18 ; 3 : 2, 13, 32 ; 14 : 6 and 16 : 22 (R.V., " no one ") ; 2 Cor. 7 : 2 (thrice) ; Heb. 12 : 14 ; 1 John 4 : 12 ; Rev. 2 : 17, R.V., " no one ; " so 5 : 3, 4 ; 19 : 12 ; in 3 : 7, 8 and 15 : 8 (R.V., " none ") ; in 7 : 9 and 14 : 3, " no man." In all these cases " man " stands for " person." The spelling *outheis* occurs occasionally in the mss. ; Westcott and Hort adopt it in 2 Cor. 11 : 8, in the genitive case *outhenos*.

Instances of *mēdeis* are Matt. 8 : 4 (almost all those in the Synoptists are cases of prohibition or admonition) ; Acts 9 : 7 ; Rom. 12 : 17 ; 1 Cor. 3 : 18, 21 ; Gal. 6 : 17 ; Eph. 5 : 6 ; Col. 2 : 18 ; 1 Thess. 3 : 3 ; 1 Tim. 4 : 12 ; Rev. 3 : 11, R.V., " no one."

Notes : (1) In some mss. the negative *mē* and the indefinite pronoun *tis*, some one, anyone, appear as one word, *mētis* (always separated in the best mss.), e.g., Matt. 8 : 28, " no man ; " so in 1 Cor. 16 : 11 ; 2 Cor. 11 : 16 ; 2 Thess. 2 : 3. The words are separated also in Matt. 24 : 4 ; 2 Cor. 8 : 20 (R.V., " any man," after " avoiding ") ; Rev. 13 : 17. These instances represent either impossibility or prohibition (see under No LONGER, No. 2) ; contrast *ouch* (i.e., *ou*) . . . *tis* in Heb. 5 : 4, " no man (taketh)," where a direct negative statement is made. (2) In 2 Cor. 11 : 10 the negative *ou*, " not," is translated " no man " (A.V. marg. " not ") ; in 1 Cor. 4 : 6, e.g., the negative *mē* is translated " no one ; " in Rom. 14 : 13, the negative *mē*, used in an admonition, is translated " no man."

NO WISE (in), ANYWISE (in)

1. OU MĒ (οὐ μή), a double negative, strongly expressing a negation, is translated "in no wise" in Matt. 5 : 18, 20, R.V. (A.V., "in no case"); 10 : 42; Luke 18 : 17; John 6 : 37; Acts 13 : 41; Rev. 21 : 27; in Matt. 13 : 14 (twice, R.V.; A.V., "not"); so in Mark 9 : 1; Luke 9 : 27; John 4 : 48; Acts 28 : 26 (twice); 1 Thess. 4 : 15; in Luke 10 : 19, R.V. "(nothing) . . . in any wise" (A.V., "by any means").

Note : In 2 Thess. 2 : 3, R.V., "(no man) . . . in any wise" (A.V., "by any means"), the double negative is *mē . . . mēdena.*

2. OUDAMŌS (οὐδαμῶς), akin to the adjective *oudamos*, not even one (not in the N.T.), denotes by no means, in no wise, Matt. 2 : 6.¶

3. OU PANTŌS (οὐ πάντως), lit., 'not altogether,' i.e., 'wholly not' (from *pas*, all), is rendered "in no wise" in Rom. 3 : 9.

Note : In Luke 13 : 11 the phrase *eis to panteles*, lit., unto the complete end (*pas*, all, *telos*, an end), i.e., completely, utterly, preceded by the negative *mē*, is translated "in no wise" ('who was utterly unable to lift herself up'). Cp. Heb. 7 : 25, where the same phrase is used without a negative, signifying "to the uttermost."

For ON THIS WISE see THUS (*b*)

NOBLE

1. EUGENĒS (εὐγενής), an adjective, lit., well born (*eu*, well, and *genos*, a family, race), (*a*) signifies noble, 1 Cor. 1 : 26; (*b*) is used with *anthrōpos*, a man, i.e., a nobleman, in Luke 19 : 12.¶ In the Sept., Job 1 : 3.¶

2. EUGENESTEROS (εὐγενέστερος), the comparative degree of No. 1, occurs in Acts 17 : 11, "more noble," i.e., more noble-minded.¶

3. KRATISTOS (κράτιστος) is translated "most noble" in the A.V. of Acts 24 : 3 and 26 : 25 (R.V., "most excellent"). See EXCELLENT.

NOBLEMAN

BASILIKOS (βασιλικός), an adjective, royal, belonging to a king (*basileus*), is used of the command, 'thou shalt love thy neighbour as thyself,' "the royal law," Jas. 2 : 8; this may mean a law which covers or governs other laws and therefore has a specially regal character (as Hort suggests), or because it is made by a King (a meaning which Deissmann assigns) with whom there is no respect of persons; it is used with the pronoun *tis*, a certain one, in John 4 : 46, 49, of a courtier, one in the service of a king, "a nobleman" (some mss. have the noun *basiliskos*, a petty king, in these two verses). It is used of a country in Acts 12 : 20, "the king's (country)," and of royal apparel in ver. 21. See KING, ROYAL.¶

Note : For *eugenēs* in Luke 19 : 12, see NOBLE, No. 1.

NOISE
A. Adverb.
RHOIZĒDON (ῥοιζηδόν), from *rhoizos*, the whistling of an arrow, signifies ' with rushing sound,' as of roaring flames, and is used in 2 Pet. 3 : 10, of the future passing away of the heavens.¶

B. Verbs.
1. AKOUŌ (ἀκούω), to hear, is translated " it was noised " in Mark 2 : 1 (Passive Voice), of the rapid spread of the information that Christ was " in the house " in Capernaum. See HEAR.

2. DIALALEŌ (διαλαλέω), lit., to speak through, is rendered " were noised abroad " in Luke 1 : 65. See COMMUNE.

Notes : (1) In Rev. 6 : 1, A.V., *phōnē*, a voice or sound, is translated " noise " (R.V., " voice ") ; it is used with *ginomai* in Acts 2 : 6, A.V., " (this) was noised abroad," R.V., " (this) sound was heard." (2) In Matt. 9 : 23, A.V., *thorubeō*, to make a tumult or uproar, in the Middle Voice, as in Mark 5 : 39 and Acts 20 : 10, is translated " making a noise " (R.V., " making a tumult "). See ADO, TROUBLE, TUMULT, UPROAR.

NOISOME
KAKOS (κακός), evil, is translated " noisome " in Rev. 16 : 2. See BAD.

For NONE see NO MAN

NOON
MESĒMBRIA (μεσημβρία), lit., middle-day (*mesos*, middle, and *hēmera*, a day), signifies (*a*) noon, Acts 22 : 6 ; (*b*) the south, Acts 8 : 26.¶

NOR : see † p. 9

NORTH
BORRAS (βορρᾶς), primarily Boreas, the North Wind, came to denote the north (cp. Borealis), Luke 13 : 29 ; Rev. 21 : 13.¶

NORTH EAST, NORTH WEST
CHŌROS (χῶρος), Lat., *corus*, the Latin name for the north-west wind, hence, the north-west, occurs in Acts 27 : 12, A.V., R.V., " (north-east and) south-east," as the N.W. wind blows towards the S.E.¶

Note : In the same ver., *lips*, the south-west (lit., Libyan) wind, hence, the south-west (so A.V.), is rendered " north-east " in R.V., as the S.W. wind blows towards the N.E. The difficulty is that Lutro (commonly identified with Phœnix) faces E., not W. But there is a harbour opposite Lutro which does look S.W. and N.W., bearing the name Phineka (R.V. marg. renders the whole phrase literally). This seems the best solution.

NOT : see † p. 9

NOTABLE, OF NOTE

1. GNŌSTOS (γνωστός), an adjective, signifying ' known ' (from ginōskō, to know), is used (a) as an adjective, most usually translated "known," whether of facts, e.g., Acts 1 : 19 ; 2 : 14 ; 4 : 10 ; or persons, John 18 : 15, 16 ; it denotes "notable" in Acts 4 : 16, of a miracle ; (b) as a noun, "acquaintance," Luke 2 : 44 and 23 : 49. See ACQUAINTANCE, KNOWN.

2. EPISĒMOS (ἐπίσημος) primarily meant bearing a mark, e.g., of money, ' stamped,' ' coined,' (from epi, upon, and sēma, a mark, a sign ; cp. sēmainō, to give a sign, signify, indicate, and sēmeioō, to note ; see below) ; it is used in the N.T., metaphorically, (a) in a good sense, Rom. 16 : 7, " of note," illustrious, said of Andronicus and Junias ; (b) in a bad sense, Matt. 27 : 16, " notable," of the prisoner Barabbas.¶ In the Sept., Gen. 30 : 42 ; Esth. 5 : 4 ; 8 : 13, toward the end of the verse, " a distinct (day) ".¶

3. EPIPHANĒS (ἐπιφανής), illustrious, renowned, notable (akin to epiphainō, to show forth, appear ; Eng., epiphany), is translated " notable " in Acts 2 : 20, of the great Day of the Lord. The appropriateness of this word (compared with Nos. 1 and 2) to that future occasion is obvious.¶

NOTE (Verb)

SĒMEIOŌ (σημειόω), from sēmeion, a sign, token, signifies to mark, to note, in the Middle Voice, to note for oneself, and is so used in 2 Thess. 3 : 14, in an injunction to take cautionary note of one who refuses obedience to the Apostle's word by the Epistle.¶ In the Sept. Ps. 5 : 6.¶

NOTHING

1. OUDEN (οὐδέν), the neuter of oudeis, no one, occurs, e.g., in Matt. 5 : 13 ; 10 : 26 ; 23 : 16 ; adverbially, e.g., in Matt. 27 : 24 ; 2 Cor. 12 : 11 (1st part), " in nothing ; " 1 Tim. 4 : 4 ; in the dative case, after en, " in," Phil. 1 : 20. Westcott and Hort adopt the spelling outhen in Luke 22 : 35 ; 23 : 14 ; Acts 15 : 9 ; 19 : 27 ; 26 : 26 ; 1 Cor. 13 : 2.

2. MĒDEN (μηδέν), the neuter of mēdeis, no one, is related to No. 1, in the same way as the masculine genders are ; so with the negatives ou and mē, not, in all their usage and connections (see under NO MAN). Thus it is found, not in direct negative statements, as with No. 1, but in warnings, prohibitions, etc., e.g., Matt. 27 : 19 ; Acts 19 : 36 ; in expressions conveying certain impossibilities, e.g., Acts 4 : 21 ; comparisons, e.g., 2 Cor. 6 : 10 ; intimating a supposition to the contrary, 1 Tim. 6 : 4 ; adverbially, e.g., 2 Cor. 11 : 5, " not a whit." Westcott and Hort adopt the spelling mēthen in Acts 27 : 33.

3. OU (οὐ), not, is translated " nothing " in Luke 8 : 17 ; 11 : 6 ; 1 Cor. 9 : 16 ; 2 Cor. 8 : 15 (in each case, an absolute and direct negative).

4. MĒ (μή), not, is translated " nothing " in John 6 : 39 in a clause

expressing purpose ; in the A.V. of Luke 7 : 42 (R.V., " not "), in a temporal clause.

5. OU . . . TI (οὐ . . . τί), followed by the subjunctive mood, " (have) nothing (to eat)," lit., ' (they have) not what (they should eat),' in Matt. 15 : 32 (in some mss. in Mark 6 : 36) ; Mark 8 : 2 ; the phrase conveys more stress than the simple negative (No. 3).

6. MĒ . . . TI (μὴ . . . τί), followed by the subjunctive mood, " (they had) nothing (to eat)," R.V., " (having) nothing (to eat)," A.V., lit., ' not (having) what (they should eat),' in Mark 8 : 1 ; the negative is *mē* here because it is attached to a participle, ' having ; ' whereas in No. 5 the negative *ou* is attached to the indicative mood, ' they have.'

7. MĒ TI (μή τι), lit., ' not anything,' not used in simple, direct negations (see under No Man), occurs in John 6 : 12 in a clause of purpose ; in 1 Cor. 4 : 5, in a prohibition.

8. OUDE TI (οὐδέ τι), not even anything, is found in 1 Tim. 6 : 7 (2nd part); it is a more forceful expression than the simple *ouden* in the 1st part of the verse, as if to say, ' it is a fact that we brought nothing into the world, and most certainly we can carry out not even the slightest thing, whatever we may have possessed.'

Notes : (1) For " nothing " in Luke 1 : 37, A.V. see WORD, No. 2 (R.V.). (2) In John 11 : 49 the double negative *ouk* (not) . . . *ouden* (nothing) is translated " nothing at all." (3) In Acts 11 : 8 *pan*, everything, with *oudepote*, not even ever, is rendered " nothing . . . ever," R.V., A.V., " nothing . . . at any time." (4) In 1 Cor. 1 : 19, A.V., *atheteō*, to set aside, make void, reject, is translated " I will bring to nothing " (R.V., " will I reject ").

For NOTICE BEFORE, 2 Cor. 9 : 5, A.V., see AFOREPROMISED

NOTWITHSTANDING

Note : This is the A.V. rendering of (1) *alla*, but, in Rev. 2 : 20 (R.V., " but ") ; (2) *plēn*, howbeit, yet, except that, in Luke 10 : 11, 20, and Phil. 1 : 18 (R.V., " only that ") ; in 4 : 14, A.V., " notwithstanding " (R.V., " howbeit ").

NOUGHT (for, bring to, come to, set at)
A. Pronoun.
OUDEN (οὐδέν), nothing (the neuter of *oudeis*, no one), is translated " nought " in Acts 5 : 36. See NOTHING.
B. Adverb.
DŌREAN (δωρεάν), freely, as a gift, is translated " for nought " in Gal. 2 : 21, R.V. (A.V., " in vain ") ; in 2 Thess. 3 : 8, in a denial by the Apostle that he lived on the hospitality of others at Thessalonica. See FREELY.

C. Verbs.

1. KATARGEŌ (καταργέω) is used in 1 Cor. 1 : 28, " (that) He might bring to nought ; " 1 Cor. 2 : 6 (Passive Voice in the original) ; 1 Cor. 6 : 13, R.V., " will bring to nought " (A.V. " will destroy ") ; so 2 Thess. 2 : 8 and Heb. 2 : 14. See ABOLISH.

2. EXOUTHENEŌ (ἐξουθενέω), to set at nought, treat with utter contempt, despise, is translated " set at nought " in Luke 18 : 9, R.V. (A.V., " despised ") ; in 23 : 11, " set (Him) at nought ; " " was set at nought " in Acts 4 : 11 ; in Rom. 14 : 3, R.V., " set at nought " (A.V., " despise ") ; ver. 10, " set at nought." See ACCOUNT, DESPISE.

3. EXOUDENEŌ or EXOUDENOŌ (ἐξουδενέω) has the same meaning as No. 2, and is virtually the same word (outhen being another form of ouden, nothing), i.e., to treat as nothing (ex, intensive), and is translated " be set at nought " in Mark 9 : 12.¶

4. EKPIPTŌ (ἐκπίπτω), to fall out, is used in Rom. 9 : 6 in the sense of falling from its place, failing, of the word of God, R.V., " hath come to nought " (A.V., " hath taken none effect "). See FALL.

5. ATHETEŌ (ἀθετέω), to set aside, reject, is translated " set at nought " in Heb. 10 : 28, R.V. (A.V., " despised ") ; so Jude 8. See NOTHING, Note (4).

Notes : (1) In Acts 5 : 38, A.V., *kataluō*, lit., to loosen down, hence, to overthrow, is translated " it will come to nought " (R.V., " it will be overthrown "). See DESTROY. (2) In Rev. 18 : 17, A.V., *erēmoō*, to make desolate, is translated " is come to nought " (R.V., " is made desolate "). See DESOLATE. (3) In Acts 19 : 27, A.V., the accusative case of *apelegmos*, confutation, disrepute, preceded by the verb *erchomai*, to come, and *eis*, unto or into, is translated " be set at nought " (R.V., " come into disrepute "). See DISREPUTE.¶

NOURISH, NOURISHMENT

1. TREPHŌ (τρέφω), to rear, feed, nourish, is translated by the verb to nourish in Jas. 5 : 5 (of luxurious living) ; Rev. 12 : 14 (of God's care for Israel against its enemies) ; so ver. 6, R.V. (A.V., " feed ") ; in Acts 12 : 20, R.V., " was fed " (A.V., " was nourished "). See FEED.

2. ANATREPHŌ (ἀνατρέφω), to nurse, bring up (ana, up, and No. 1), is translated " nourished " in Acts 7 : 20 (A.V., " nourished up ") ; in 21, " nourished," A.V. and R.V. See BRING.

3. EKTREPHŌ (ἐκτρέφω), ek, from, out of, and No. 1, primarily used of children, to nurture, rear, is translated " nurture " of the care of one's own flesh, Eph. 5 : 29, and in Eph. 6 : 4, R.V. (A.V., " bring . . . up "). See BRING.¶

4. ENTREPHŌ (ἐντρέφω), to train up, nurture, is used metaphorically, in the Passive Voice, in 1 Tim. 4 : 6, of being nourished in the faith.¶

For NOURISHMENT MINISTERED, Col. 2 : 19, see SUPPLY

NOVICE

NEOPHUTOS (νεόφυτος), an adjective, lit., newly-planted (from *neos*, new, and *phuō*, to bring forth, produce), denotes a new convert, neophyte, novice, 1 Tim. 3 : 6, of one who by inexperience is unfitted to act as a bishop or overseer in a church.¶ In the Sept., Job 14 : 9 ; Psa. 128 : 3 ; 144 : 12 ; Is. 5 : 7.¶

NOW

A. Adverbs.

1. NUN (νῦν) is used (*a*) of time, the immediate present, whether in contrast to the past, e.g., John 4 : 18 ; Acts 7 : 52, or to the future, e.g., John 12 : 27 ; Rom. 11 : 31 ; sometimes with the article, singular or plural, e.g., Acts 4 : 29 ; 5 : 38 ; (*b*) of logical sequence, often partaking also of the character of (*a*), now therefore, now however, as it is, e.g., Luke 11 : 39 ; John 8 : 40 ; 9 : 41 ; 15 : 22, 24 ; 1 Cor. 5 : 11, R.V. marg., " as it is."

Note : Under (*a*) comes the phrase in 2 Cor. 8 : 14, with *kairos*, a time, all governed by *en*, in, or at, A.V., " now at this time " (R.V., " at this present time ").

2. NUNI (νυνί), a strengthened form of No. 1, is used (*a*) of time, e.g., Acts 22 : 1 (in the best mss.) ; 24 : 13 ; Rom. 6 : 22 ; 15 : 23, 25 ; (*b*) with logical import, e.g., Rom. 7 : 17 ; 1 Cor. 13 : 13, which some regard as temporal (*a*) ; but if this is the significance, " the clause means, ' but faith, hope, love, are our abiding possession now in this present life.' The objection to this rendering is that the whole course of thought has been to contrast the things which last only for the present time with the things which survive. And the main contrast so far has been between love and the special [then] present activity of prophecy, tongues, knowledge. There is something of disappointment, and even of bathos, in putting as a climax to these contrasts the statement that in this present state faith, hope, love abide ; that is no more than can be said of [the then existing] prophecies, tongues and knowledge. If there is to be a true climax the ' abiding ' must cover the future as well as the present state. And that involves as a consequence that *nuni* must be taken in its logical meaning, i.e., ' as things are,' ' taking all into account ' . . . This logical sense of *nuni* . . . is enforced by the dominant note of the whole passage " (R. St. John Parry, in the Camb. Greek Test.).

It is certain that love will continue eternally ; and hope will not cease at the Parousia of Christ, for hope will ever look forward to the accomplishment of God's eternal purposes, a hope characterised by absolute assurance ; and where hope is in exercise faith is its concomitant. Faith will not be lost in sight.

3. ĒDĒ (ἤδη) denotes already, now already, " the subjective present, with a suggested reference to some other time, or to some expectation "

(Thayer), e.g., Matt. 3 : 10 ; 14 : 24 ; Luke 11 : 7 ; John 6 : 17 ; Rom. 1 : 10 ; 4 : 19 ; 13 : 11 ; Phil. 4 : 10.

4. ARTI (ἄρτι), expressing coincidence, and denoting strictly present time, signifies ' just now,' this moment, in contrast (a) to the past, e.g., Matt. 11 : 12 ; John 2 : 10 ; 9 : 19, 25 ; 13 : 33 ; Gal 1 : 9, 10 ; (b) to the future, e.g., John 13 : 37 ; 16 : 12, 31 ; 1 Cor. 13 : 12 (cp. No. 2 in ver. 13) ; 2 Thess. 2 : 7 ; 1 Pet. 1 : 6, 8 : (c) sometimes without necessary reference to either, e.g., Matt. 3 : 15 ; 9 : 18 ; 26 : 53 ; Gal. 4 : 20 ; Rev. 12 : 10.

5. APARTI (ἀπάρτι), sometimes written separately, ap'arti, i.e., apo, from, and No. 4, denotes ' from now,' henceforth, John 13 : 19 ; 14 : 7 ; Rev. 14 : 13. See HENCEFORTH.¶

6. LOIPON (λοιπόν), the neuter of loipos, the rest, from now, is used adverbially with the article and translated " now " in Mark 14 : 41.

B. Conjunctions and Particles.

1. OUN (οὖν), therefore, so then, is sometimes used in continuing a narrative, e.g., Acts 1 : 18 ; 1 Cor. 9 : 25 ; or resuming it after a digression, usually rendered " therefore," e.g., Acts 11 : 19 ; 25 : 1, R.V. (A.V., " now "). In the following it is absent from the best mss., Mark 12 : 20 ; Luke 10 : 36 ; John 16 : 19 ; 18 : 24 ; 19 : 29.

Note : In 2 Cor. 5 : 20 *oun* is simply " therefore," as in R.V. (A.V., " now then ").

2. DE (δέ), but, and, now, often implying an antithesis, is rendered " now " in John 19 : 23 ; 1 Cor. 10 : 11 ; 15 : 50 ; Gal. 1 : 20 ; Eph. 4 : 9 ; in Acts 27 : 9 (1st part), R.V., " and " (A.V., " now ") ; in Gal. 4 : 1, R.V., " but " (A.V. " now ").

3. DĒ (δή), a consecutive particle, giving stress to the word or words to which it is attached, sometimes with hardly any exact Eng. equivalent, is translated " now " in Luke 2 : 15, in the words of the shepherds ; in Acts 15 : 36, R.V. (A.V., " and "). Some mss. have it in 2 Cor. 12 : 1 ; see R.V. marg.

Notes : (1) In 1 Cor. 4 : 7, A.V., B, No. 2, followed by *kai*, and, is translated " now " (R.V., " but "). (2) In Rom. 14 : 15 and Philm. 16, A.V., *ouketi*, no longer, is translated " now . . . not " and " not now " (R.V., " no longer ") ; cp. John 4 : 42 and 21 : 6, " now . . . not." (3) The particle *ara*, then, expressing a more informal inference than *oun* (B, No. 1 above), is often in Paul's Epistles coupled with *oun*, the phrase meaning " so then," as A.V. and R.V. in Rom. 7 : 3, 25 ; 9 : 16 ; 14 : 12 ; in R.V. only (A.V., " therefore "), Rom. 5 : 18 ; 8 : 12 ; 9 : 18 ; 14 : 19 ; Gal. 6 : 10 ; 1 Thess. 5 : 6 ; 2 Thess. 2 : 15. In Eph. 2 : 19 the A.V. renders it " now therefore." (4) In 1 Tim. 1 : 4, the R.V. " *so do I now* " (A.V., " *so do* ") is added to complete the sentence. (5) In Heb. 9 : 9, R.V., the perfect participle of *enistēmi*, to be present, is translated " (the time) *now* present " (A.V., " then present," which misses the meaning). See COME, (AT) HAND, PRESENT.

NUMBER
A. Nouns.

1. ARITHMOS (ἀριθμός), number, a number (Eng., arithmetic, etc.), occurs in Luke 22 : 3 ; John 6 : 10 ; Rom. 9 : 27 ; elsewhere five times in Acts, ten times in the Apocalypse.

2. OCHLOS (ὄχλος), a multitude, is translated " number " in Luke 6 : 17, R.V. (A.V., " multitude ") ; in Mark 10 : 46 and Acts 1 : 15 the renderings are reversed. See COMMON, COMPANY, CROWD, MULTITUDE, PEOPLE.

B. Verbs.

1. ARITHMEŌ (ἀριθμέω), akin to A, is found in Matt. 10 : 30 ; Luke 12 : 7 ; Rev. 7 : 9.¶

2. KATARITHMEŌ (καταριθμέω), to number or count among (kata, and No. 1), is used in Acts 1 : 17.¶

3. ENKRINŌ (ἐγκρίνω), to reckon among (en, in, krinō, to judge or reckon), is translated " to number . . . (ourselves) with " in 2 Cor. 10 : 12 (R.V. marg., " to judge ourselves among or . . . with "), of the Apostle's dissociation of himself and his fellow-missionaries from those who commended themselves.¶

4. SUNKATAPSEPHIZŌ (συγκαταψηφίζω), to vote or reckon (one) a place among (sun, with or among, kata, down, and psēphizō, to count or vote, originally with pebbles, psēphos, a pebble), is used of the numbering of Matthias with the eleven Apostles, Acts 1 : 26.¶

Notes : (1) Some mss. have verse 28 in Mark 15 (A.V.), where *logizomai*, to reckon, is translated " He was numbered." (2) For *katalegō* 1 Tim. 5 : 9 (A.V., " let . . . be taken into the number "), see TAKE, *Note* (18). (3) In Mark 5 : 13 see the italicised words in R.V. (4) In Heb. 7 : 23, R.V., the adjective *pleiōn*, more, many, is translated " many in number " (A.V., " many ") ; in Acts 28 : 23, R.V., " a great number " (A.V., " many ").

NURSE

TROPHOS (τροφός), translated " nurse " in 1 Thess. 2 : 7, there denotes a nursing mother, as is clear from the statement " cherisheth her own children ; " this is also confirmed by the word *ēpios*, gentle (in the same verse), which was commonly used of the kindness of parents towards children. Cp. *trephō*, to bring up (see NOURISH).

For NURTURE (Eph. 6 : 4) see CHASTENING

O

OATH

1. HORKOS (ὅρκος) is primarily equivalent to *herkos*, a fence, an enclosure, that which restrains a person ; hence, an oath. The Lord's command in Matt. 5 : 33 was a condemnation of the minute and arbitrary restrictions imposed by the scribes and Pharisees in the matter of adjurations, by which God's Name was profaned. The injunction is repeated in Jas. 5 : 12. The language of the Apostle Paul, e.g., in Gal. 1 : 20 and 1 Thess. 5 : 27 was not inconsistent with Christ's prohibition, read in the light of its context. Contrast the oaths mentioned in Matt. 14 : 7, 9 ; 26 : 72 ; Mark 6 : 26.

Heb. 6 : 16 refers to the confirmation of a compact among men, guaranteeing the discharge of liabilities ; in their disputes " the oath is final for confirmation." This is referred to in order to illustrate the greater subject of God's oath to Abraham, confirming His promise ; cp. Luke 1 : 73 ; Acts 2 : 30.¶ Cp. the verbs *horkizō*, and *exorkizō*, under ADJURE.

2. HORKŌMOSIA (ὁρκωμοσία) denotes an affirmation on oath (from No. 1 and *omnumi*, to swear). This is used in Heb. 7 : 20, 21 (twice), 28, of the establishment of the Priesthood of Christ, the Son of God, appointed a Priest after the order of Melchizedek, and " perfected for evermore."¶ In the Sept., Ezek. 17 : 18, 19.¶

Note : For *anathematizo* in Acts 23 : 21, A.V., " have bound (themselves) with an oath," see CURSE.

OBEDIENCE, OBEDIENT, OBEY
A. Nouns.

1. HUPAKOĒ (ὑπακοή), obedience (*hupo*, under, *akouō*, to hear), is used (*a*) in general, Rom. 6 : 16 (1st part), R.V., " (unto) obedience," A.V., " (to) obey ; " here obedience is not personified, as in the next part of the verse, " servants . . . of obedience " [see (*c*)], but is simply shown to be the effect of the presentation mentioned ; (*b*) of the fulfilment of apostolic counsels, 2 Cor. 7 : 15 ; 10 : 6 ; Philm. 21 ; (*c*) of the fulfilment of God's claims or commands, Rom. 1 · 5 and 16 : 26, " obedience of faith," which grammatically might be objective, to the faith (marg.), or subjective, as in the text. Since faith is one of the main subjects of the Epistle, and is the initial act of obedience in the new life, as well as an essential characteristic thereof, the text rendering is to be preferred ; Rom. 6 : 16

(2nd part); 15 : 18, R.V. " (for) the obedience," A.V., " (to make) obedient ; " 16 : 19 ; 1 Pet. 1 : 2, 14, R.V., " (children of) obedience," i.e., characterized by obedience, A.V., " obedient (children) ; " ver. 22, R.V., " obedience (to the truth)," A.V., " obeying (the truth) ; " (d) of obedience to Christ (objective), 2 Cor. 10 : 5 ; (e) of Christ's obedience, Rom. 5 : 19 (referring to His death ; cp. Phil. 2 : 8) ; Heb. 5 : 8, which refers to His delighted experience in constant obedience to the Father's will (not to be understood in the sense that He learned to obey).¶

2. HUPOTAGĒ (ὑποταγή), subjection (hupo, under, tassō, to order), is translated " obedience " in 2 Cor. 9 : 13, R.V. (A.V., " subjection "). See SUBJECTION.

B. Verbs.

1. HUPAKOUŌ (ὑπακούω), to listen, attend (as in Acts 12 : 13), and so, to submit, to obey, is used of obedience (a) to God, Heb. 5 : 9 ; 11 : 8 ; (b) to Christ, by natural elements, Matt. 8 : 27 ; Mark 1 : 27 ; 4 : 41 ; Luke 8 : 25 ; (c) to disciples of Christ, Luke 17 : 6 ; (d) to the faith, Acts 6 : 7 ; the Gospel, Rom. 10 : 16 ; 2 Thess. 1 : 8 ; Christian doctrine, Rom. 6 : 17 (as to a form or mould of teaching) ; (e) to apostolic injunctions, Phil. 2 : 12 ; 2 Thess. 3 : 14 ; (f) to Abraham by Sarah, 1 Pet. 3 : 6 ; (g) to parents by children, Eph. 6 : 1 ; Col. 3 : 20 ; (h) to masters by servants, Eph. 6 : 5 ; Col. 3 : 22 ; (i) to sin, Rom. 6 : 12 ; (j) in general, Rom. 6 : 16.¶

2. PEITHŌ (πείθω), to persuade, to win over, in the Passive and Middle Voices, to be persuaded, to listen to, to obey, is so used with this meaning, in the Middle Voice, e.g., in Acts 5 : 36, 37 (in ver. 40, Passive Voice, " they agreed ") ; Rom. 2 : 8 ; Gal. 5 : 7 ; Heb. 13 : 17 ; Jas. 3 : 3. The obedience suggested is not by submission to authority, but result.ng from persuasion.

" Peithō and pisteuō, ' to trust,' are closely related etymologically ; the difference in meaning is that the former implies the obedience that is produced by the latter, cp. Heb. 3 : 18, 19, where the disobedience of the Israelites is said to be the evidence of their unbelief. Faith is of the heart, invisible to men ; obedience is of the conduct and may be observed. When a man obeys God he gives the only possible evidence that in his heart he believes God. Of course it is persuasion of the truth that results in faith (we believe because we are persuaded that the thing is true, a thing does not become true because it is believed), but peithō, in N.T. suggests an actual and outward result of the inward persuasion and consequent faith."* See ASSURANCE, B, No. 3.

3. PEITHARCHEŌ (πειθαρχέω), to obey one in authority (No. 2, and archē, rule), is translated " obey " in Acts 5 : 29, 32 ; " to be obedient," Tit. 3 : 1, R.V. (A.V., " to obey magistrates ") ; in Acts 27 : 21, " hearkened." See HEARKEN.¶

---

* From Notes on Thessalonians by Hogg and Vine, pp. 254, 255.

4. APEITHEŌ (ἀπειθέω), to disobey, be disobedient (*a*, negative, and No. 2), is translated " obey not " in Rom. 2 : 8 ; 1 Pet. 3 : 1 ; 4 : 17. See DISOBEDIENT.

Note : In 1 Cor. 14 : 34, A.V., *hupotassō*, to be in subjection (R.V.), is translated "to be under obedience ; " so Tit. 2 : 5, R.V., " being in subjection " (A.V., " obedient ") ; and ver. 9, R.V. (A.V., " to be obedient "). See SUBJECTION.

C. Adjective.

HUPĒKOOS (ὑπήκοος), obedient (akin to A, No. 1), giving ear, subject, occurs in Acts 7 : 39, R.V., " (would not be) obedient," A.V., " (would not) obey ; " 2 Cor. 2 : 9 ; Phil. 2 : 8, where the R.V. " *even* " is useful as making clear that the obedience was not to death but to the Father.¶

For the verb OBJECT, Acts 24 : 19, see ACCUSATION, B, No. 4

For OBJECTS, R.V., in Acts 17 : 23, see WORSHIP

OBSERVATION, OBSERVE
A. Noun.

PARATĒRĒSIS (παρατήρησις), attentive watching (akin to *paratēreō*, to observe), is used in Luke 17 : 20, of the manner in which the Kingdom of God (i.e., the operation of the spiritual Kingdom in the hearts of men) does not come, " in such a manner that it can be watched with the eyes " (Grimm-Thayer), or, as A.V. marg., " with outward show."¶

B. Verbs.

1. ANATHEŌREŌ (ἀναθεωρέω), to observe carefully, consider well (*ana*, up, intensive, and *theōreō*, to behold), is used in Acts 17 : 23, R.V., " observed " (of Paul's notice of the objects of Athenian worship), and Heb. 13 : 7, " considering." See BEHOLD.¶

2. TĒREŌ (τηρέω) : see KEEP, No. 1.

3. SUNTĒREŌ (συντηρέω) : see KEEP, No. 3.

4. PARATĒREŌ (παρατηρέω), to watch closely, observe narrowly (*para*, used intensively, and No. 2), is translated " ye observe " in Gal. 4 : 10, where the Middle Voice suggests that their religious observance of days etc. was not from disinterested motives, but with a view to their own advantage. See WATCH. Cp. *phroneō* (to think), " regardeth " in Rom. 14 : 6, where the subject is connected with the above, though the motive differs.

5. PHULASSŌ (φυλάσσω) : see KEEP, No. 4.

6. POIEŌ (ποιέω), to do, is translated " to observe " in Acts 16 : 21. See DO.

OBTAIN, OBTAINING
A. Verbs.

1. TUNCHANŌ (τυγχάνω), to meet with, light upon, also signifies to obtain, attain to, reach, get (with regard to things), translated to obtain

in Acts 26 : 22, of " the help that is from God ; " 2 Tim. 2 : 10, of " the salvation which is in Christ Jesus with eternal glory ; " Heb. 8 : 6, of the ministry obtained by Christ ; 11 : 35, of " a better resurrection." See CHANCE.

2. EPITUNCHANŌ (ἐπιτυγχάνω), primarily, to light upon (epi, upon, and No. 1), denotes to obtain, Rom. 11 : 7 (twice) ; Heb. 6 : 15 ; 11 : 33 ; Jas. 4 : 2.¶

3. LANCHANŌ (λαγχάνω), to obtain by lot, is translated " that have obtained " in 2 Pet. 1 : 1 ; in Acts 1 : 17, A.V., " had obtained " (R.V., " received "), with klēros, a lot or portion. See LOTS.

4. KTAOMAI (κτάομαι), to procure for oneself, get, gain, acquire, is translated " obtained " in Acts 1 : 18, R.V. (A.V., " purchased ") ; 8 : 20, R.V. (A.V., " may be purchased ") ; 22 : 28. See POSSESS, PROVIDE, PURCHASE.

5. KRATEŌ (κρατέω), to be strong, also means to get possession of, obtain, e.g., in Acts 27 : 13, " they had obtained (their purpose)." See HOLD.

6. LAMBANŌ (λαμβάνω), to take, to receive, is translated by the verb to obtain in 1 Cor. 9 : 25 ; Phil. 3 : 12, R.V.," (not that) I have (already) obtained " (contrast katantaō, to attain, ver. 11) ; Moule translates it ' not that I have already received,' i.e., the prize ; the verb does not signify to attain ; Heb. 4 : 16, A.V., " obtain." See ACCEPT, No. 4.

7. HEURISKŌ (εὑρίσκω) denotes to find ; in the Middle Voice, to find for oneself, to procure, get, obtain, with the suggestion of accomplishing the end which had been in view ; so in Heb. 9 : 12, " having obtained (eternal redemption)."

Notes : (1) In 1 Cor. 9 : 24, A.V., katalambanō, a strengthened form of No. 6 (kata, used intensively), is translated " obtain " (R.V., " attain "). (2) In Heb. 11 : 2, 4, 39, A.V., martureō, to bear witness, and in the Passive Voice, to have witness borne to one, is translated to obtain a good report, or to obtain witness (R.V., " had witness borne "). See WITNESS. (3) For the A.V. of Heb. 1 : 4, " He hath by inheritance obtained " (R.V., " He hath inherited "), and of Eph. 1 : 11, see INHERIT. (4) For the phrase to obtain mercy, the Passive Voice of eleeō in Matt. 5 : 7 ; Rom. 11 : 30, 31 ; 1 Cor. 7 : 25 ; 2 Cor. 4 : 1 (R.V.) ; 1 Tim. 1 : 13, 16 ; 1 Pet. 2 : 10 (twice), see MERCY.

B. Noun.

PERIPOIĒSIS (περιποίησις), lit., a making around (peri, around, poieō, to do or make), denotes (a) the act of obtaining anything, as of salvation in its completeness, 1 Thess. 5 : 9 ; 2 Thess. 2 : 14 ; (b) a thing acquired, an acquisition, possession, Eph. 1 : 14, R.V., " (God's own) possession " [some would put this under (a)] ; so 1 Pet. 2 : 9, R.V., A.V., " a peculiar (people) ; " cp. Is. 43 : 21 ; (c) preservation ; this may be the meaning in Heb. 10 : 39, " saving " (R.V. marg., " gaining ") ; cp. the

corresponding verb in Luke 17 : 33 (in the best texts), " preserve."¶
In the Sept. the noun has the meaning (b) in Hag. 2 : 10 and Mal. 3 : 17,
(c) in 2 Chron. 14 : 13.¶

OCCASION

APHORMĒ (ἀφορμή), properly a starting point, was used to denote a
base of operations in war.   In the N.T. it occurs as follows : " (a) the Law
provided sin with a base of operations for its attack upon the soul, Rom.
7 : 8, 11 ; (b) the irreproachable conduct of the Apostle provided
his friends with a base of operations against his detractors, 2 Cor.
5 : 12 ; (c) by refusing temporal support at Corinth he deprived these
detractors of their base of operations against him, 2 Cor. 11 : 12 ; (d)
Christian freedom is not to provide a base of operations for the flesh,
Gal. 5 : 13 ; (e) unguarded behaviour on the part of young widows (and
the same is true of all believers) would provide Satan with a base of
operations against the faith, 1 Tim. 5 : 14."*¶
   The word is found frequently in the papyri with meanings which
illustrate those in the N.T.   In the Sept., Prov. 9 : 9 ; Ezek. 5 : 7.¶
   Notes : (1) For the R.V. renderings " occasion (or ' occasions ') of
stumbling," " occasion of falling," see FALLING, B, Note (3), OFFENCE.
(2) In 2 Cor. 8 : 8, A.V., the phrase " by occasion of " translates the
preposition *dia*, through, by means of (R.V., " through ").

For OCCUPATION, Acts 18 : 3, A.V., see TRADE
   Notes : The phrase " of like occupation " in Acts 19 : 25 translates
the phrase *peri* (about) *ta* (the) *toiauta* (such things), i.e., lit., ' (occupied)
about such things.'

OCCUPY

PERIPATEŌ (περιπατέω), to walk, is sometimes used of the state in
which one is living, or of that to which a person is given, e.g., Heb. 13 : 9,
" (meats, wherein they that) occupied themselves," R.V. (marg.,
" walked ; " A.V., " have been occupied "), i.e., exercising themselves
about different kinds of food, regarding some as lawful, others as unlawful
(referring especially to matters of the ceremonial details of the law).
   Notes : (1) For " occupy," in the A.V. of Luke 19 : 13, see TRADE.
(2) For " occupieth," in the A.V. of 1 Cor. 14 : 16, see FILL, No. 2.

ODOUR

OSMĒ (ὀσμή), a smell, an odour (akin to *ozō*, to smell), is translated
" odour " in John 12 : 3 ; it is used metaphorically in Eph. 5 : 2, R.V.,
" an odour (of a sweet smell)," A.V., " (a sweet smelling) savour," of the
effects Godward of the Sacrifice of Christ ; in Phil. 4 : 18 of the effect of

---

* From Notes on Galatians by Hogg and Vine, p. 269.

sacrifice, on the part of those in the church at Philippi, who sent material assistance to the Apostle in his imprisonment. The word is translated " savour " in 2 Cor. 2 : 14, 16 (twice).¶

Note : For *thumiama,* incense, translated " odours " in the A.V. of Rev. 5 : 8 (R.V., " incense "), see INCENSE. For *amōmon* (quoted in R.V. marg. in the Latinized form *amomum*) in Rev. 18 : 13, see SPICE.

OF

Note : (1) In addition to the rendering of a number of prepositions, " of " translates the genitive case of nouns, with various shades of meaning. Of these the subjective and objective are mentioned here, which need careful distinction. Thus the phrase " the love of God," e.g., in 1 John 2 : 5 and 3 : 16, is subjective, signifying " God's love ; " in 1 John 5 : 3, it is objective, signifying our love to God. Again, " the witness of God," e.g., 1 John 5 : 9, is subjective, signifying the witness which God Himself has given ; in Rev. 1 : 2, 9, and 19 : 10, e.g., " the testimony of Jesus " is objective, signifying the testimony borne to Him. In the A.V. " the faith of " is sometimes ambiguous ; with reference to Christ it is objective, i.e., faith in Him, not His own faith, in the following passages in which the R.V., " in " gives the correct meaning ; Rom. 3 : 22 ; Gal. 2 : 16 (twice), 20, R.V., " I live in faith, the faith which is in the Son of God ; " 3 : 22 ; Eph. 3 : 12 ; Phil. 3 : 9 (cp. Col. 2 : 12, " faith in the working of God "). In Eph. 2 : 20, " the foundation of the apostles and prophets " is subjective, i.e., the foundation laid by the apostles and prophets (" other foundation can no man lay than . . . Jesus Christ," 1 Cor. 3 : 11). (2) In the A.V. of John 16 : 13, " He shall not speak of Himself, " the preposition is *apo,* " from," as in the R.V. ; the Spirit of God often speaks of Himself in Scripture, the Lord's assurance was that the Holy Spirit would not be the Source of His utterances. So with regard to Christ's utterances, John 7 : 17, R.V., " I speak from (*apo*) Myself : " and 14 : 10. (3) In John 6 : 46 ; 15 : 15 ; 17 : 7 ; Acts 17 : 9, the R.V., " from " is to be observed, as rightly translating *para* (A.V., " of "). (4) The following are instances in which " of " translates *ek,* or *ex,* out of, from, Matt. 21 : 25 (R.V., " from ") ; 1 Cor. 1 : 30 ; 15 : 6 ; 2 Cor. 5 : 1 (R.V., " from ") ; Jas. 4 : 1. (5) In the following, *peri,* concerning, is so translated in the R.V. (for A.V., " of "), e.g., Acts 5 : 24 ; 1 Cor. 1 : 11 ; 1 John 1 : 1 (the R.V. is important) ; cp. John 16 : 8. (6) *Epi,* over, is so translated in Matt. 18 : 13, R.V. ; " concerning " in Acts 4 : 9. (7) *Huper,* on behalf of, is so rendered in 2 Cor. 7 : 4, R.V. (A.V., " of ") ; (8) For *hupo,* by, see the R.V. of Matt. 1 : 22 ; 2 : 16 ; 11 : 27 ; Luke 9 : 7 ; Acts 15 : 4 ; 1 Cor. 14 : 24 ; 2 Cor. 8 : 19 ; Phil. 3 : 12. (9) For other prepositions, etc., see † p. 9.

OFF : see † p. 9

OFFENCE
A. Nouns.

1. SKANDALON (σκάνδαλον) originally was " the name of the part of a trap to which the bait is attached, hence, the trap or snare itself, as in Rom. 11 : 9, R.V., ' stumblingblock,' quoted from Psa. 69 : 22, and in Rev. 2 : 14, for Balaam's device was rather a trap for Israel than a stumblingblock to them, and in Matt. 16 : 23, for in Peter's words the Lord perceived a snare laid for Him by Satan.

" In N.T. *skandalon* is always used metaphorically, and ordinarily of anything that arouses prejudice, or becomes a hindrance to others, or causes them to fall by the way. Sometimes the hindrance is in itself good, and those stumbled by it are the wicked."*

Thus it is used (a) of Christ in Rom. 9 : 33, " (a rock) of offence ; " so 1 Pet. 2 : 8 ; 1 Cor. 1 : 23 (A.V. and R.V., " stumblingblock "), and of His Cross, Gal. 5 : 11 (R.V., ditto) ; of the " table " provided by God for Israel, Rom. 11 : 9 (see above) ; (b) of that which is evil, e.g., Matt. 13 : 41, R.V., " things that cause stumbling " (A.V., " things that offend "), lit., ' all stumblingblocks ; ' 18 : 7, R.V., " occasions of stumbling " and " occasion ; " Luke 17 : 1 (ditto) ; Rom. 14 : 13, R.V., " an occasion of falling " (A.V., " an occasion to fall "), said of such a use of Christian liberty as proves a hindrance to another ; 16 : 17, R.V., " occasions of stumbling," said of the teaching of things contrary to sound doctrine ; 1 John 2 : 10, " occasion of stumbling," of the absence of this in the case of one who loves his brother and thereby abides in the light. Love, then, is the best safeguard against the woes pronounced by the Lord upon those who cause others to stumble. See FALL, B, *Note* (3).¶ Cp. the Sept. in Hos. 4 : 17, " Ephraim partaking with idols hath laid stumblingblocks in his own path."

2. PROSKOMMA (πρόσκομμα), an obstacle against which one may dash his foot (akin to *proskoptō*, to stumble or cause to stumble ; *pros*, to or against, *koptō*, to strike), is translated " offence " in Rom. 14 : 20, in ver. 13, " a stumblingblock," of the spiritual hindrance to another by a selfish use of liberty (cp. No. 1 in the same verse) ; so in 1 Cor. 8 : 9. It is used of Christ, in Rom. 9 : 32, 33, R.V., " (a stone) of stumbling," and 1 Pet. 2 : 8, where the A.V. also has this rendering.¶ Cp. the Sept. in Ex. 23 : 33, " these (the gods of the Canaanites) will be an offence (stumblingblock) unto thee."

3. PROSKOPĒ (προσκοπή), like No. 2, and formed from the same combination, occurs in 2 Cor. 6 : 3, R.V., " occasion of stumbling " (A.V., " offence "), something which leads others into error or sin.¶ Cp. the Sept. in Prov. 16 : 18, " a haughty spirit (becomes) a stumblingblock " (i.e., to oneself).

Notes : (1) In the A.V. of Rom. 4 : 25 ; 5 : 15 (twice), 16, 17, 18, 20,

---

* From Notes on Galatians by Hogg and Vine, p. 262.

paraptōma, a trespass, is translated " offence." See TRESPASS. (2) In 2 Cor. 11 : 7, A.V., *hamartia*, a sin, is translated " an offence." See SIN.

B. Adjective.

APROSKOPOS (ἀπρόσκοπος), akin to A, No. 3, with *a*, negative, prefixed, is used (*a*) in the Active sense, not causing to stumble, in 1 Cor. 10 : 32, metaphorically of refraining from doing anything to lead astray either Jews or Greeks or the church of God (i.e., the local church), R.V., " no occasion of stumbling " (A.V., " none offence ") ; (*b*) in the Passive sense, blameless, without stumbling, Acts 24 : 16, " (a conscience) void of offence ; " Phil. 1 : 10, " void of (A.V., without) offence." The adjective is found occasionally in the papyri writings.¶

OFFEND

SKANDALIZŌ (σκανδαλίζω), from *skandalon* (OFFENCE, No. 1), signifies to put a snare or stumblingblock in the way, always metaphorically in the N.T., in the same ways as the noun, which see. It is used 14 times in Matthew, 8 in Mark, twice in Luke, twice in John ; elsewhere in 1 Cor. 8 : 13 (twice) and 2 Cor. 11 : 29. It is absent in the most authentic mss. in Rom. 14 : 21. The R.V. renders it by the verb to stumble, or cause to stumble, in every place save the following, where it uses the verb to offend, Matt. 13 : 57 ; 15 : 12 ; 26 : 31, 33 ; Mark 6 : 3 ; 14 : 27, 29.

Notes : (1) In Jas. 2 : 10 ; 3 : 2 (twice), A.V., *ptaiō*, to stumble, is translated " offend ; " see FALL, STUMBLE. (2) In Acts 25 : 8, A.V., *hamartanō*, to sin, is translated " have I offended ; " see SIN.

OFFENDER

OPHEILETĒS (ὀφειλέτης), a debtor, is translated " offenders " in Luke 13 : 4, R.V. (R.V. and A.V. marg., " debtors ; " A.V., " sinners "). See DEBTOR.

Note : In Acts 25 : 11, A.V., *adikeō*, to do wrong, is translated " be an offender " (R.V., " am a wrong-doer ").

OFFER, OFFERING
A. Verbs.

1. PROSPHERŌ (προσφέρω), primarily, to bring to (*pros*, to, *pherō*, to bring), also denotes to offer, (*a*) of the sacrifice of Christ Himself, Heb. 8 : 3 ; of Christ in virtue of his High Priesthood (R.V., " this *high priest* ; " A. V., " this man ") ; 9 : 14, 25 (negative), 28 ; 10 : 12 ; (*b*) of offerings under, or according to, the Law, e.g., Matt. 8 : 4 ; Mark 1 : 44 ; Acts 7 : 42 ; 21 : 26 ; Heb. 5 : 1, 3 ; 8 : 3 ; 9 : 7, 9 ; 10 : 1, 2, 8, 11 ; (*c*) of offerings previous to the Law, Heb. 11 : 4, 17 (of Isaac by Abraham) ; (*d*) of gifts offered to Christ, Matt. 2 : 11, R.V., " offered " (A.V., " presented unto ") ; (*e*) of prayers offered by Christ, Heb. 5 : 7 ; (*f*) of the vinegar offered to Him in mockery by the soldiers at the Cross, Luke 23 : 36 ; (*g*) of the slaughter of disciples by persecutors, who think they

are ' offering ' service to God, John 16 : 2, R.V. (A.V., " doeth ") ; (h) of money offered by Simon the sorcerer, Acts 8 : 18. See BRING, A, No. 8, DEAL WITH, No. 2.

2. ANAPHERŌ (ἀναφέρω), primarily, to lead or carry up (ana), also denotes to offer, (a) of Christ's sacrifice, Heb. 7 : 27 ; (b) of sacrifices under the Law, Heb. 7 : 27 ; (c) of such previous to the Law, Jas. 2 : 21 (of Isaac by Abraham) ; (d) of praise, Heb. 13 : 15 ; (e) of spiritual sacrifices in general, 1 Pet. 2 : 5. See BEAR, No. 3, BRING, A, No. 2.

3. DIDŌMI (δίδωμι), to give, is translated " to offer " in Luke 2 : 24 ; in Rev. 8 : 3, A.V., " offer " (R.V., " add ; " marg., " give "). See GIVE.

4. PARECHŌ (παρέχω), to furnish, offer, present, supply, is used in Luke 6 : 29, of offering the other cheek to be smitten after receiving a similar insult ; for the A.V. marg., in Acts 17 : 31, see ASSURANCE, A, No. 1. See BRING, A, No. 21.

5. SPENDŌ (σπένδω), to pour out as a drink offering, make a libation, is used figuratively in the Passive Voice in Phil. 2 : 17, " offered " (R.V. marg., " poured out as a drink offering ; " A.V. marg., " poured forth "). In 2 Tim. 4 : 6, " I am already being offered," R.V. (marg., " poured out as a drink-offering "), the Apostle is referring to his approaching death, upon the sacrifice of his ministry.¶ This use of the word is exemplified in the papyri writings.

Notes : (1) In Luke 11 : 12, A.V, *epididōmi*, to give (*epi*, over, in the sense of instead of, and No. 3), is translated " will he offer " (R.V., and A.V. marg., " will he give "). (2) In Acts 7 : 41, A.V., *anagō*, to lead up or bring up, is rendered " offered " (R.V., " brought "). (3) In Acts 15 : 29 ; 21 : 25 and 1 Cor. 8 : 1, 4, 10 ; 10 : 19, A.V., *eidōlothutos*, sacrificed to idols, is translated " offered to idols " (*thuō* denotes to sacrifice). See SACRIFICE.

B. Nouns.

1. PROSPHORA (προσφορά), lit., a bringing to (akin to A, No. 1), hence an offering, in the N.T. a sacrificial offering, (a) of Christ's sacrifice, Eph. 5 : 2 ; Heb. 10 : 10 (of His body) ; 10 : 14 ; negatively, of there being no repetition, 10 : 18 ; (b) of offerings under, or according to, the Law, Acts 21 : 26 ; Heb. 10 : 5, 8 ; (c) of gifts in kind conveyed to needy Jews, Acts 24 : 17 ; (d) of the presentation of believers themselves (saved from among the Gentiles) to God, Rom. 15 : 16.¶

2. HOLOKAUTŌMA (ὁλοκαύτωμα), a burnt offering : see BURNT.

3. ANATHĒMA (ἀνάθημα) denotes a gift set up in a temple, a votive offering (ana, up, tithēmi, to place), Luke 21 : 5, R.V. " offerings " (A.V., " gifts ").¶ Cp. *anathema* (see CURSE).

Notes : (1) In Luke 21 : 4, A.V., the plural of *dōron*, a gift, is translated " offerings " (R.V., " gifts "). (2) In Rom. 8 : 3 and Heb. 13 : 11, the R.V., " *as an offering* " is added to complete the sacrificial meaning of *peri*.

OFFICE

A. Nouns.

1. PRAXIS (πρᾶξις), a doing, deed (akin to *prassō*, to do or practise), also denotes an acting or function, translated "office" in Rom. 12 : 4. See DEED.

2. HIERATEIA (ἱερατεία), or *hieratia*, denotes a priest's office, Luke 1 : 9; Heb. 7 : 5, R.V., "priest's office" (A.V., "office of the priesthood").¶

B. Verb.

HIERATEUŌ (ἱερατεύω), to officiate as a priest (akin to A, No. 2), is translated "he executed the priest's office" in Luke 1 : 8. The word is frequent in Inscriptions.¶

Notes : (1) In Rom. 11 : 13, A.V., *diakonia*, a ministry, is translated "office" (R.V., "ministry"). (2) In Acts 1 : 20, R.V., *episkopē*, an overseership, is translated "office" (marg., "overseership;" A.V., "bishoprick"). (3) In 1 Tim. 3 : 1, the word "office," in the phrase "the office of a bishop," has nothing to represent it in the original; the R.V. marg. gives "overseer" for "bishop," and the phrase lit. is 'overseership;' so in vv. 10, 13, where the A.V. has "use (and 'used') the office of a deacon," the R.V. rightly omits "office," and translates the verb *diakoneō*, to serve, "let them serve as deacons" and "(they that) have served (well) as deacons."

OFFICER

1. HUPĒRETĒS (ὑπηρέτης), for the original of which see MINISTER, A, No. 3, is translated "officer," with the following applications, (a) to a magistrate's attendant, Matt. 5 : 25; (b) to officers of the Synagogue, or officers or bailiffs of the Sanhedrin, Matt. 26 : 58; Mark 14 : 54, 65; John 7 : 32, 45, 46; 18 : 3, 12, 18, 22; 19 : 6; Acts 5 : 22, 26. See MINISTER, SERVANT.

2. PRAKTŌR (πράκτωρ), lit., one who does, or accomplishes (akin to *prassō*, to do), was used in Athens of one who exacts payment, a collector (the word is frequently used in the papyri of a public accountant); hence, in general, a court officer, an attendant in a court of justice (so Deissmann); the word is used in Luke 12 : 58 (twice).¶ In the Sept., Isa. 3 : 12.¶

OFFSCOURING

PERIPSĒMA (περίψημα), that which is wiped off (akin to *peripsaō*, to wipe off all round; *peri*, around, *psaō*, to wipe), hence, offscouring, is used metaphorically in 1 Cor. 4 : 13. This and the synonymous word *perikatharma*, refuse, rubbish, "were used especially of condemned criminals of the lowest classes, who were sacrificed as expiatory offerings . . . because of their degraded life" (Lightfoot).¶

OFFSPRING

1. GENNĒMA (γέννημα), akin to *gennaō*, to beget, denotes the off-spring of men and animals, Matt. 3 : 7 ; 12 : 34 ; 23 : 33 ; Luke 3 : 7. R.V., " offspring " (A.V., " generation "). See FRUIT.¶

2. GENOS (γένος), a race, family (akin to *ginomai*, to become), denotes an offspring, Acts 17 : 28, 29 ; Rev. 22 : 16. See GENERATION, KIND.

OFT, OFTEN, OFTENER, OFTENTIMES, OFT-TIMES
A. Adverbs.

1. POLLAKIS (πολλάκις), akin to *polus*, much, many, is variously translated, e.g., " oft-times," Matt. 17 : 15 (A.V., " oft," 2nd part) ; " many times," 2 Cor. 8 : 22, R.V. (A.V., " oftentimes ") ; " oft," 2 Cor. 11 : 23 ; " often " (ver. 26).

2. POLLA (πολλά), the neuter plural of *polus*, is translated " oft " in Matt. 9 : 14 ; some ancient authorities omit it here (see R.V. marg.) ; in Rom. 15 : 22, with the article, R.V., " these many times " (A.V., " much ").

3. POSAKIS (ποσάκις), an interrogative numeral adverb, how many times, how oft (or often) ? occurs in Matt. 18 : 21 ; 23 : 37 ; Luke 13 : 34.¶

4. HOSAKIS (ὁσάκις), a relative adverb, as often (or oft) as, 1 Cor. 11 : 25, 26 ; Rev. 11 : 6.¶

5. PUKNA (πυκνά), the neuter plural of *puknos* (see B), used adverbially, is translated " often " in Luke 5 : 33.

6. PUKNOTERON (πυκνότερον), the neuter singular of the comparative degree of *puknos* (cp. No. 5, and see B), very often, or so much the oftener, Acts 24 : 26, " the oftener."¶

Notes : (1) In Luke 8 : 29, the phrase *pollois chronois*, lit., ' many times,' is translated " oftentimes " (R.V. marg., " of a long time "). (2) For the rendering " oft " in Mark 7 : 3, see DILIGENTLY, D, No. 2.

B. Adjective.

PUKNOS (πυκνός) primarily signifies close, compact, solid ; hence, frequent, often, 1 Tim. 5 : 23. Cp. A, Nos. 5 and 6.

OIL

ELAION (ἔλαιον), olive-oil, is mentioned over 200 times in the Bible. Different kinds were known in Palestine. The " pure," R.V. (A.V., " beaten "), mentioned in Ex. 27 : 20 ; 29 : 40 ; Lev. 24 : 2 ; Numb. 28 : 5 (now known as virgin oil), extracted by pressure, without heat, is called " golden " in Zech. 4 : 12. There were also inferior kinds. In the N.T. the uses mentioned were (a) for lamps, in which the oil is a symbol of the Holy Spirit, Matt. 25 : 3, 4, 8 ; (b) as a medicinal agent, for healing, Luke 10 : 34 ; (c) for anointing at feasts, Luke 7 : 46 ; (d) on festive occasions, Heb. 1 : 9, where the reference is probably to the consecration of kings ; (e) as an accompaniment of miraculous power, Mark 6 : 13, or of the prayer of faith, Jas. 5 : 14. For its general use in commerce, see Luke 16 : 6 ; Rev. 6 : 6 ; 18 : 13.¶

OINTMENT

MURON (μύρον), a word derived by the ancients from *murō*, to flow, or from *murra*, myrrh-oil (it is probably of foreign origin ; see MYRRH). The ointment is mentioned in the N.T. in connection with the anointing of the Lord on the occasions recorded in Matt. 26 : 7, 9, 12 ; Mark 14 : 3, 4 ; Luke 7 : 37, 38, 46; John 11 : 2 ; 12 : 3 (twice), 5. The alabaster cruse mentioned in the passages in Matthew, Mark and Luke was the best of its kind, and the spikenard was one of the costliest of perfumes. Ointments were used in preparing a body for burial, Luke 23 : 56 (" ointments "). Of the act of the woman mentioned in Matt. 26 : 6–13, the Lord said, " she did it to prepare Me for burial ; " her devotion led her to antedate the customary ritual after death, by showing both her affection and her understanding of what was impending. For the use of the various kinds of ointments as articles of commerce, see Rev. 18 : 13.¶

OLD
A. Adjectives.

1. ARCHAIOS (ἀρχαῖος), original, ancient (from *archē*, a beginning : Eng., archaic, archæology, etc.), is used (*a*) of persons belonging to a former age," (to) them of old time," Matt. 5 : 21, 33, R.V. ; in some mss. ver. 27 ; the R.V. rendering is right ; not ancient teachers are in view ; what was said to them of old time was " to be both recognized in its significance and estimated in its temporary limitations, Christ intending His words to be regarded not as an abrogation, but a deepening and fulfilling " (Cremer) ; of prophets, Luke 9 : 8, 19 ; (*b*) of time long gone by, Acts 15 : 21 ; (*c*) of days gone by in a person's experience, Acts 15 : 7, " a good while ago," lit., ' from old (days),' i.e., from the first days onward in the sense of originality, not age ; (*d*) of Mnason, " an early disciple," Acts 21 : 16, R.V., not referring to age, but to his being one of the first who had accepted the Gospel from the beginning of its proclamation ; (*e*) of things which are old in relation to the new, earlier things in contrast to things present, 2 Cor. 5 : 17, i.e., of what characterized and conditioned the time previous to conversion in a believer's experience, R.V., " they are become new," i.e., they have taken on a new complexion and are viewed in an entirely different way ; (*f*) of the world (i.e., the inhabitants of the world) just previous to the Flood, 2 Pet. 2 : 5 ; (*g*) of the Devil, as " that old serpent," Rev. 12 : 9 ; 20 : 2, old, not in age, but as characterized for a long period by the evils indicated.¶

Note : For the difference between this and No. 2, see below.

2. PALAIOS (παλαιός), akin to C, No. 1 (Eng., palæology, etc.), of what is of long duration, old in years, etc., a garment, wine (in contrast to *neos* ; see NEW), Matt. 9 : 16, 17 ; Mark 2 : 21, 22 (twice) ; Luke 5 : 36, 37,

39 (twice) ; of the treasures of Divine truth, Matt. 13 : 52 (compared with *kainos :* see NEW) ; of what belongs to the past, e.g., the believer's former self before his conversion, his " old man," old because it has been superseded by that which is new, Rom. 6 : 6 ; Eph. 4 : 22 (in contrast to *kainos*) ; Col. 3 : 9 (in contrast to *neos*) ; of the covenant in connection with the Law, 2 Cor. 3 : 14 ; of leaven, metaphorical of moral evil, 1 Cor. 5 : 7, 8 (in contrast to *neos*) ; of that which was given long ago and remains in force, an old commandment, 1 John 2 : 7 (twice), that which was familiar and well known in contrast to that which is fresh (*kainos*).¶

Note : Palaios denotes old, " without the reference to beginning and origin contained in *archaios* " (Abbott-Smith), a distinction observed in the papyri (Moulton and Milligan). While sometimes any difference seems almost indistinguishable, yet " it is evident that wherever an emphasis is desired to be laid on the reaching back to a beginning, whatever that beginning may be, *archaios* will be preferred (e.g., of Satan, Rev. 12 : 9 ; 20 : 2, see No. 1). That which . . . is old in the sense of more or less worn out . . . is always *palaios* " (Trench).

3. PRESBUTEROS (πρεσβύτερος), older, elder, is used in the plural, as a noun, in Acts 2 : 17, " old men." See ELDER.

B. Nouns.

1. GERON (γέρων) denotes an old man (from the same root comes Eng., grey), John 3 : 4.¶

2. PRESBUTES (πρεσβύτης), " an old man," Luke 1 : 18, is translated " aged " in Tit. 2 : 2 ; Philm. 9 (for this, however, see the R.V. marg. See AGED.

3. GERAS (γῆρας), old age, occurs in Luke 1 : 36.¶

Note : Augustine (quoted by Trench, §cvii, 2) speaks of the distinction observed among Greeks, that *presbutes* conveys the suggestion of gravity.

C. Adverbs.

1. PALAI (πάλαι) denotes long ago, of old, Heb. 1 : 1, R.V., " of old time " (A.V., " in time past ") ; in Jude 4, " of old ; " it is used as an adjective in 2 Pet. 1 : 9, " (his) old (sins)," lit., ' his sins of old.' See WHILE.

2. EKPALAI (ἔκπαλαι), from of old, for a long time (*ek*, from, and No. 1), occurs in 2 Pet. 2 : 3, R.V., " from of old " (A.V., " of a long time ") ; 3 : 5. See LONG, B, *Note* (2).

Note : In 1 Pet. 3 : 5, A.V., the particle *pote*, once, formerly, ever, sometime, is translated " in the old time " (R.V., " aforetime ") ; in 2 Pet. 1 : 21, " in old time " (R.V., " ever "), A.V. marg., " at any time."

D. Verbs.

1. PALAIOO (παλαιόω), akin to A, No. 2, denotes, in the Active Voice, to make or declare old, Heb. 8 : 13 (1st part) ; in the Passive Voice, to become old, of things worn out by time and use, Luke 12 : 33 ; Heb. 1 : 11, " shall wax old," lit., ' shall be made old,' i.e., worn out ; in 8 : 13 (2nd part), R.V., " is becoming old " (A.V. " decayeth ") ; here and in the

1st part of the verse, the verb may have the meaning to abrogate ; for the next verb in the verse, see No. 2.¶

2. GĒRASKŌ (γηράσκω), from gēras, old age (akin to B, No. 1), to grow old, is translated " thou shalt be old," in John 21 : 18 ; " waxeth aged," Heb. 8 : 13, R.V. (A.V., " waxeth old ").¶

Notes : (1) In John 8 : 57, *echō*, to have, is used with " fifty years " as the object, signifying, " Thou art (not yet fifty years) old," lit., ' Thou hast not yet fifty years.' (2) In Mark 5 : 42, R.V., the verb *eimi*, to be, with the phrase ' of twelve years ' is translated " was . . . old " (A.V., ' was *of the age* of ').

OLDNESS

PALAIOTĒS (παλαιότης), from *palaios* (see A, No. 2, above), occurs in Rom. 7 : 6, of " the letter," i.e., the law, with its rules of conduct, mere outward conformity to which has yielded place in the believer's service to a response to the inward operation of the Holy Spirit. The word is contrasted with *kainotēs*, newness.¶

OLD WIVES'

GRAŌDĒS (γραώδης), an adjective, signifying old-womanish (from *graus*, an old woman), is said of fables, in 1 Tim. 4 : 7.¶

OLIVES (OLIVE BERRIES), OLIVE TREE

1. ELAIA (ἐλαία) denotes (a) an olive tree, Rom. 11 : 17, 24 ; Rev. 11 : 4 (plural) ; the Mount of Olives was so called from the numerous olive-trees there, and indicates the importance attached to such ; the Mount is mentioned in the N.T. in connection only with the Lord's life on earth, Matt. 21 : 1 ; 24 : 3 ; 26 : 30 ; Mark 11 : 1 ; 13 : 3 ; 14 : 26 ; Luke 19 : 37 ; 22 : 39 ; John 8 : 1 ; (b) an olive, Jas. 3 : 12, R.V. (A.V., " olive berries ").¶

2. ELAIŌN (ἐλαιών), an olive-grove or olive-garden, the ending —ōn, as in this class of noun, here indicates " a place set with trees of the kind designated by the primitive " (Thayer) ; hence it is applied to the Mount of Olives, Luke 19 : 29 ; 21 : 37 ; Acts 1 : 12 (" Olivet ") : in the first two of these and in Mark 11 : 1, some mss. have the form of the noun as in No. 1.¶

3. KALLIELAIOS (καλλιέλαιος), the garden olive (from *kallos*, beauty, and No. 1), occurs in Rom. 11 : 24, " a good olive tree."¶

4. AGRIELAIOS (ἀγριέλαιος), an adjective (from *agrios*, growing in the fields, wild, and No. 1), denoting ' of the wild olive,' is used as a noun in Rom. 11 : 17, 24, " a wild olive tree " (R.V., in the latter verse).¶

For OMITTED (Matt. 23 : 23, A.V.) see LEAVE (undone), No. 1

For OMNIPOTENT (Rev. 19 : 6) see ALMIGHTY

ON : see †, p. 9

ONCE (at ; for all)

1. HAPAX (ἅπαξ) denotes (a) once, one time, 2 Cor. 11 : 25 ; Heb. 9 : 7, 26, 27 ; 12 : 26, 27 ; in the phrase " once and again," lit., ' once and twice,' Phil. 4 : 16 ; 1 Thess. 2 : 18 ; (b) once for all, of what is of perpetual validity, not requiring repetition, Heb. 6 : 4 ; 9 : 28 ; 10 : 2 ; 1 Pet. 3 : 18 ; Jude 3, R.V., " once for all " (A.V., " once ") ; ver. 5 (ditto) ; in some mss. 1 Pet. 3 : 20 (so the A.V.).¶

2. EPHAPAX (ἐφάπαξ), a strengthened form of No. 1 (epi, upon), signifies (a) once for all, Rom. 6 : 10 ; Heb. 7 : 27, R.V. (A.V., " once ") ; 9 : 12 (ditto) ; 10 : 10 ; (b) at once, 1 Cor. 15 : 6.¶

3. POTE (ποτέ) denotes once upon a time, formerly, sometime, e.g., Rom. 7 : 9 ; Gal. 1 : 23, 1st part, R.V., " once " (A.V., " in times past ") ; 2nd part, A.V. and R.V., " once ; " Gal. 2 : 6, R.V. marg., " what they once were " (to be preferred to the text, " whatsoever they were "), the reference probably being to the association of the twelve Apostles with the Lord during His ministry on earth ; upon this their partisans based their claim for the exclusive authority of these Apostles, which Paul vigorously repudiated ; in Eph. 5 : 8, R.V., " once " (A.V., " sometimes "). See AFORETIME, LAST, LENGTH (at), TIME (past).

Note : In Luke 23 : 18, A.V., *pamplēthei*, denoting with the whole multitude (*pas*, all, *plēthos*, a multitude), is rendered " all at once," R.V., " all together ").¶

ONE
A. Numeral.

HEIS (εἷς), the first cardinal numeral, masculine (feminine and neuter nominative forms are *mia* and *hen*, respectively), is used to signify (1) (a) one in contrast to many, e.g., Matt. 25 : 15 ; Rom. 5 : 18, R.V., " (through) one (trespass)," i.e., Adam's transgression, in contrast to the " one act of righteousness," i.e., the Death of Christ (not as A.V., " the offence of one," and " the righteousness of one ") ; (b) metaphorically, union and concord, e.g., John 10 : 30 ; 11 : 52 ; 17 : 11, 21, 22 ; Rom. 12 : 4, 5 ; Phil. 1 : 27 ; (2) emphatically, (a) a single (one), to the exclusion of others, e.g., Matt. 21 : 24 ; Rom. 3 : 10 ; 1 Cor. 9 : 24 ; 1 Tim. 2 : 5 (twice) ; (b) one, alone, e.g., Mark 2 : 7, R.V. (A.V., " only ") ; 10 : 18 ; Luke 18 : 19 ; (c) one and the same, e.g., Rom. 3 : 30, R.V., " God is one," i.e., there is not one God for the Jew and one for the Gentile ; cp. Gal. 3 : 20, which means that in a promise there is no other party ; 1 Cor. 3 : 8 ; 11 : 5 ; 12 : 11 ; 1 John 5 : 8 (lit., ' and the three are into one,' i.e., united in one and the same witness) ; (3) a certain one, in the same sense as the indefinite pronoun *tis* (see B, No. 1), e.g., Matt. 8 : 19, R.V., " a (scribe)," marg., " one (scribe)," A.V., " a certain (scribe) ; " 19 : 16, " one ; " in Rev. 8 : 13, R.V. marg., " one (eagle) ; " *heis tis* are used together in Luke 22 : 50 ;

John 11 : 49 ; this occurs frequently in the papyri (Moulton, Prol., p. 96) ; (4) distributively, with *hekastos*, each, i.e., every one, e.g., Luke 4 : 40 ; Acts 2 : 6, " every man " (lit., ' every one ') ; in the sense of ' one . . . and one,' e.g., John 20 : 12 ; or one . . . followed by *allos* or *heteros*, the other, e.g., Matt. 6 : 24 ; or by a second *heis*, e.g., Matt. 24 : 40, R.V., " one ; " John 20 : 12 ; in Rom. 12 : 5 *heis* is preceded by *kata* (*kath'*) in the sense of " severally (members) one (of another)," R.V. (A.V., " every one . . . one ") ; cp. Mark 14 : 19 ; in 1 Thess. 5 : 11 the phrase in the 2nd part, " each other," R.V. (A.V., " one another "), is, lit., ' one the one ; ' (5) as an ordinal number, equivalent to *prōtos*, first, in the phrase " the first day of the week," lit. and idiomatically, ' one of sabbaths,' signifying ' the first day after the sabbath,' e.g., Matt. 28 : 1 ; Mark 16 : 2 ; Acts 20 : 7 ; 1 Cor. 16 : 2.   Moulton remarks on the tendency for certain cardinal numerals to replace ordinals (Prol., p. 96).

B. Pronouns.

1. TIS (τις), an indefinite pronoun signifying a certain one, some one, any one, one (the neuter form *ti* denotes a certain thing), is used (*a*) like a noun, e.g., Acts 5 : 25 ; 19 : 32 ; 21 : 34 ; 1 Cor. 3 : 4 ; or with the meaning ' someone,' e.g., Acts 8 : 31, R.V., " some one " (A.V., " some man ") ; Rom. 5 : 7 ; (*b*) as an adjective ; see CERTAIN, Note (3), SOME.

2. HOS (ὅς), as a relative pronoun, signifies " who ; " as a demonstrative pronoun, " this," or " the one " in contrast with " the other," or " another," e.g., Rom. 14 : 2, A.V. (R.V., " one man ") ; 1 Cor. 12 : 8.

Notes : (1) The R.V. often substitutes " one " for " man," e.g., Matt. 17 : 8 (*oudeis*, no one) ; 1 Cor. 3 : 21 (i.e., ' no person ') ; 1 Cor. 15 : 35 ; 1 Thess. 5 : 15 ; 2 Tim. 4 : 16 ; 1 John 2 : 27 ; 3 : 3.   (2) The pronoun *houtos* is sometimes translated " this one," e.g., Luke 7 : 8.   (3) In 1 Pet. 3 : 8, A.V., *homophrōn*, " likeminded " (R.V.), is translated " of one mind " (lit., ' of the same mind ').   (4) In Acts 7 : 26, " at one," is, lit., ' unto peace ' (see PEACE).   (5) For " every one " in Acts 5 : 16 see EVERY, No. 2.   (6) In Mark 9 : 26 *nekros*, dead, is translated " one dead."   (7) In Acts 2 : 1 " in one place " translates *epi to auto*, lit., ' to the same,' which may mean ' for the same (purpose) ; ' in 1 Cor. 11 : 20 and 14 : 23, the R.V. translates it " together."   (8) In Mark 1 : 7, A.V., the article *ho*, the, is rendered " one " (R.V., " he that ").   (9) In Mark 7 : 14, A.V., the plural of *pas*, " all " (so R.V.), is translated " every one ; " in Matt. 5 : 28, A.V., *pas*, with the article, is translated " whosoever " (R.V. " every one who "). (10) In Acts 1 : 24, A.V., " whether " is, lit., and as the R.V., " the one whom."   (11) In 2 Thess. 2 : 7, the article is rendered " one that," R.V. (A.V., " he who ").

See also ACCORD, CONSENT, B, No. 1, END, C, Note (6), EYE (with one), GREAT, HOLY, LITTLE, MIND, NATION, WICKED.

ONE ANOTHER or ONE . . . ANOTHER, ONE . . . THE OTHER

Notes : (1) This translates a number of words and phrases, (*a*) *allēlōn*, a reciprocal pronoun in the genitive plural, signifying of, or from, one another (akin to *allos*, another), e.g., Matt. 25 : 32 ; John 13 : 22 ; Acts 15 : 39 ; 19 : 38 ; 1 Cor. 7 : 5 ; Gal. 5 : 17 ; the accusative *allēlous* denotes " one another," e.g., Acts 7 : 26, lit., ' why do ye wrong one another ? ' ; 2 Thess. 1 : 3, R.V. ; in Eph. 4 : 32 and Col. 3 : 13, e.g., R.V., " each other ; " in 1 Thess. 5 : 15, " one (toward) another," R.V. ; the dative *allēlois* denotes " one to another," e.g., Luke 7 : 32 ; (*b*) different forms of the plural of *heautou*, of himself, used as a reciprocal pronoun, e.g., Eph. 5 : 19, R.V., " one to another " (A.V., and R.V. marg., " to your-selves ") ; see also Note (5) ; (*c*) *allos pros allon*, " one to another," Acts 2 : 12 ; (*d*) *allos . . . heteros*, 1 Cor. 12 : 8 (for the difference between *allos* and *heteros*, see ANOTHER) ; (*e*) *hos men . . . hos de* (in various forms of the pronoun), lit., ' this indeed . . . but that,' e.g., Luke 23 : 33 ; Rom. 9 : 21 ; 14 : 5 ; 1 Cor. 11 : 21 ; 2 Cor. 2 : 16 ; Phil. 1 : 16, 17 ; (*f*) *heteros . . . heteros*, one . . . another, 1 Cor. 15 : 40. (2) In Matt. 24 : 2 ; Mark 13 : 2 ; Luke 19 : 44, and 21 : 6, " one (stone upon) another " is, lit., ' stone upon stone.' (3) In Heb. 10 : 25, " *one another* " is necessarily added in English to complete the sense of *parakaleō*, to exhort. (4) In 1 Pet. 3 : 8, A.V., " one of another " represents nothing in the original (the R.V., " compassionate " sufficiently translates the adjective *sum-pathēs*: see COMPASSION, C.). (5) In Mark 9 : 10, A.V., *pros heautous*, " among yourselves " (R.V.), is translated " one with another." (6) In 1 Tim. 5 : 21, A.V., the accusative case of *prosklisis*, partiality, preceded by *kata*, according to, is translated " preferring one before another " (R.V., " prejudice ; " marg., " preference," lit., ' according to partiality ').

ONLY
A. Adjectives.

1. MONOS (μόνος), alone, solitary, is translated " only," e.g., in Matt. 4 : 10 ; 12 : 4 ; 17 : 8 ; 1 Cor. 9 : 6 ; 14 : 36 ; Phil. 4 : 15 ; Col. 4 : 11 ; 2 John 1 ; it is used as an attribute of God in John 5 : 44 ; 17 : 3 ; Rom. 16 : 27 ; 1 Tim. 1 : 17 ; 1 Tim. 6 : 15, 16 ; Jude 4, 25 ; Rev. 15 : 4. See ALONE, A.

2. MONOGENĒS (μονογενής), only begotten (No. 1 and *genos*, offspring), has the meaning " only," of human offspring, in Luke 7 : 12 ; 8 : 42 ; 9 : 38 ; the term is one of endearment, as well as of singleness. For Heb. 11 : 17 see ONLY BEGOTTEN.

B. Adverbs.

1. MONON (μόνον), the neuter of A, No. 1, only, exclusively, is translated " only," e.g., in Matt. 5 : 47 ; 8 : 8 ; John 5 : 18 ; 11 : 52 ; 12 : 9 ; 13 : 9 ; frequently in Acts, Romans and Galatians. See ALONE, B, No. 1.

2. PLĒN (πλήν), howbeit, except that, is translated " only that " in the R.V. of Phil. 1 : 18 (A.V., " notwithstanding ") ; " only " in 3 : 16 (A.V., " nevertheless ").

Notes : (1) In Mark 2 : 7, A.V., *heis*, " one " (so R.V.), is translated " only ; " in Jas. 4 : 12, R.V., " one only " (A.V., " one "). (2) For " only that " in Acts 21 : 25, A.V., see the R.V. (3) The conjunction *ei*, if, with the negative *mē*, not, is translated " but only " in Luke 4 : 26, R.V. (A.V., " save ") ; 4 : 27 (A.V., " saving ") ; " only " in 1 Cor. 7 : 17 (A.V., " but ") ; in some mss. in Acts 21 : 25 (A.V. " save only ").

ONLY BEGOTTEN

MONOGENĒS (μονογενής) is used five times, all in the writings of the Apostle John, of Christ as the Son of God ; it is translated " only begotten " in Heb. 11 : 17 of the relationship of Isaac to Abraham.

With reference to Christ, the phrase " the only begotten from the Father," John 1 : 14, R.V. (see also the marg.), indicates that as the Son of God He was the sole representative of the Being and character of the One who sent Him. In the original the definite article is omitted both before " only begotten " and before " Father," and its absence in each case serves to lay stress upon the characteristics referred to in the terms used. The Apostle's object is to demonstrate what sort of glory it was that he and his fellow-Apostles had seen. That he is not merely making a comparison with earthly relationships is indicated by *para*, " from." The glory was that of a unique relationship and the word " begotten " does not imply a beginning of His Sonship. It suggests relationship indeed, but must be distinguished from generation as applied to man.

We can only rightly understand the term " the only begotten " when used of the Son, in the sense of unoriginated relationship. " The begetting is not an event of time, however remote, but a fact irrespective of time. The Christ did not *become*, but necessarily and eternally *is* the Son. He, a Person, possesses every attribute of pure Godhood. This necessitates eternity, absolute being ; in this respect He is not ' after ' the Father " (Moule). The expression also suggests the thought of the deepest affection, as in the case of the O.T. word *yachid*, variously rendered, " only one," Gen. 22 : 2, 12 ; " only son," Jer. 6 : 26 ; Amos 8 : 10 ; Zech. 12 : 10 ; " only beloved," Prov. 4 : 3, and " darling," Psa. 22 : 20 ; 35 : 17.

In John 1 : 18 the clause " The Only Begotten Son, which is in the bosom of the Father," expresses both His eternal union with the Father in the Godhead and the ineffable intimacy and love between them, the Son sharing all the Father's counsels and enjoying all His affections. Another reading is *monogenēs Theos*, ' God only-begotten.' In John 3 : 16 the statement, " God so loved the world that He gave His Only Begotten Son," must not be taken to mean that Christ became the Only Begotten Son by Incarnation. The value and the greatness of the gift lay in the Sonship of Him who was given. His Sonship was not the effect of His being given. In John 3 : 18 the phrase " the Name of the Only Begotten Son of God " lays stress upon the full revelation of God's character and will, His love and grace, as conveyed in the Name of One who, being in a unique relationship to Him, was provided by Him as the Object of faith. In 1 John 4 : 9 the statement " God hath sent His Only Begotten Son into the world " does not mean that God sent out into the world one who at His birth in Bethlehem had become His Son. Cp. the parallel statement, " God sent forth the Spirit of His Son," Gal. 4 : 6, R.V., which could not mean that God sent forth One who became His Spirit when He sent Him.¶

For ONSET, Acts 14 : 5, R.V., see ASSAULT and IMPULSE

For ONWARD, 2 John 9, R.V., see GO, No. 10

OPEN, OPENING (for OPENLY, see below)
A. Verbs.

1. ANOIGŌ (ἀνοίγω) is used (1) transitively, (a) literally, of a door or gate, e.g., Acts 5 : 19 ; graves, Matt. 27 : 52 ; a sepulchre, Rom. 3 : 13 ; a book, e.g., Luke 4 : 17 (some mss. have No. 4) ; Rev. 5 : 2–5 ; 10 : 8 ; the seals of a roll, e.g., Rev. 5 : 9 ; 6 : 1 ; the eyes, Acts 9 : 40 ; the mouth of a fish, Matt. 17 : 27 ; " the pit of the abyss," Rev. 9 : 2, R.V. ; heaven and the heavens, Matt. 3 : 16 ; Luke 3 : 21 ; Acts 10 : 11 (for 7 : 56, see No. 2) ; Rev. 19 : 11 ; " the temple of the tabernacle of the testimony in heaven," Rev. 15 : 5 ; by metonymy, for that which contained treasures, Matt. 2 : 11 ; (b) metaphorically, e.g., Matt. 7 : 7, 8 ; 25 : 11 ; Rev. 3 : 7 ; Hebraistically, to open the mouth, of beginning to speak, e.g., Matt. 5 : 2 ; 13 : 35 ; Acts 8 : 32, 35 ; 10 : 34 ; 18 : 14 ; Rev. 13 : 6 (cp., e.g., Numb. 22 : 28 ; Job. 3 : 1 ; Isa. 50 : 5) ; and of recovering speech, Luke 1 : 64 ; of the earth opening, Rev. 12 : 16 ; of the opening of the eyes, Acts 26 : 18 ; the ears, Mark 7 : 35 (in the best mss. ; some have No. 2) ; (2) intransitively (perfect tense, active, in the Greek), (a) literally, of the heaven, John 1 : 51, R.V., " opened ; " (b) metaphorically, of speaking freely, 2 Cor. 6 : 11.

2. DIANOIGŌ (διανοίγω), to open up completely (dia, through, intensive, and No. 1), is used (a) literally, Luke 2 : 23 ; Acts 7 : 56, in the best mss. ; (b) metaphorically, of the eyes, Mark 7 : 34 ; Luke 24 : 31 ; of the Scriptures, ver. 32 and Acts 17 : 3 ; of the mind, Luke 24 : 45, R.V. (A.V., " understanding ") ; of the heart, Acts 16 : 14.¶

3. AGŌ (ἄγω), to lead, or to keep or spend a day, is so used in Acts 19 : 38 : see KEEP, Note (2).

4. ANAPTUSSŌ (ἀναπτύσσω), to unroll (ana, back, ptussō, to roll), is found in some mss. in Luke 4 : 17 (of the roll of Isaiah), and translated " He had opened " (A.V.) ; see No. 1.¶

Notes : (1) For Heb. 4 : 13, " laid open," R.V. (A.V., " opened ") see LAY, No. 18. (2) In 2 Cor. 3 : 18, A.V., *anakaluptō*, to unveil, is translated " open " (R.V., " unveiled," which consistently continues the metaphor of the veil upon the heart of Israel). (3) In Mark 1 : 10, A.V., *schizō*, to rend or split, is translated " opened," of the heavens, R.V., " rent asunder," A.V. marg., " cloven, or, rent." (4) For *prodēlos*, in 1 Tim. 5 : 24, A.V., " open beforehand," see EVIDENT, A, No. 3. (5) For " be opened " see EPHPHATHA. (6) For " open (your hearts)," 2 Cor. 7 : 2, R.V., see RECEIVE, No. 18.

B. Nouns.

1. ANOIXIS (ἄνοιξις), an opening (akin to A, No. 1), is used in Eph. 6 : 19, metaphorically of the opening of the mouth as in A, No. 1 (2), (*b*).¶

2. OPE (ὀπή), an opening, a hole, is used in Jas. 3 : 11, of the orifice of a fountain : see CAVE, HOLE, PLACE.

OPENLY

1. PARRHĒSIA (παρρησία), freedom of speech, boldness, is used adverbially in the dative case and translated " openly " in Mark 8 : 32, of a saying of Christ ; in John 7 : 13, of a public statement ; in 11 : 54, of Christ's public appearance ; in 7 : 26 and 18 : 20, of His public testimony ; preceded by the preposition *en*, in, John 7 : 4, lit., ' in boldness' (cp. ver. 10, R.V., " publicly "). See BOLD, B.

2. PHANERŌS (φανερῶς), manifestly, openly : see EVIDENT, B.

Notes : (1) In Gal. 3 : 1, " openly set forth " translates the verb *prographō*, lit., ' to write before,' as of the O.T., Rom. 15 : 4 (cp. Jude 4), and of a previous letter, Eph. 3 : 3. In Gal. 3 : 1, however, " it is probably used in another sense, unexampled in the Scriptures but not uncommon in the language of the day,=' proclaimed,' ' placarded,' as a magistrate proclaimed the fact that an execution had been carried out, placarding his proclamation in a public place. The Apostle carries on his metaphor of the ' evil eye ; ' as a preventive of such mischief it was common to post up charms on the walls of houses, a glance at which was supposed to counteract any evil influence to which a person may have been subjected. ' Notwithstanding,' he says, in effect, ' that the fact that Christ had been crucified was placarded before your very eyes in our preaching, you have allowed yourselves to be . . . fascinated by the enemies of the Cross of Christ, when you had only to look at Him to escape their malignant influence ; ' cp. the interesting and instructive parallel in Num. 21 : 9."* (2) In some mss. in Matt. 6 : 4, 6, 18, the phrase *en tō phanerō*, lit., ' in the manifest,' is found (A.V., " openly ") ; see the R.V. (3) For *emphanēs*, rendered " openly " in Acts 10 : 40, A.V., see MANIFEST. (4) In Acts 16 : 37, A.V., the dative case of the adjective *dēmosios*, belonging to the people (*dēmos*, a people), " public " (so R.V.), used adverbially, is translated " openly ; " in 18 : 28 and 20 : 20, " publicly." For the adjective itself, " public," see Acts 5 : 18. See PUBLIC.¶

For OPERATION see WORKING

---

* From Notes on Galatians by Hogg and Vine, pp. 106, 107.

OPPORTUNITY (lack)
A. Nouns.

1. KAIROS (καιρός), primarily, a due measure, is used of a fixed and definite period, a time, season, and is translated " opportunity " in Gal. 6 : 10 and Heb. 11 : 15. See SEASON, TIME, WHILE.

2. EUKAIRIA (εὐκαιρία), a fitting time, opportunity (eu, well, and No. 1), occurs in Matt. 26 : 16 and Luke 22 : 6.¶ Cp. eukairos, seasonable ; see CONVENIENT.

3. TOPOS (τόπος), a place, is translated " opportunity " in Acts 25 : 16, R.V. (A.V., " licence "). See PLACE, ROOM.

B. Verbs.

1. EUKAIREŌ (εὐκαιρέω), to have time or leisure (akin to A, No. 2), is translated " he shall have opportunity " in 1 Cor. 16 : 12, R.V. (A.V., " convenient time "). See LEISURE.

2. AKAIREOMAI (ἀκαιρέομαι), to have no opportunity (a, negative, and kairos, season), occurs in Phil. 4 : 10.¶

OPPOSE

1. ANTIKEIMAI (ἀντίκειμαι) : see ADVERSARY, B.

2. ANTITASSŌ (ἀντιτάσσω) is used in the Middle Voice in the sense of setting oneself against (anti, against, tassō, to order, set), opposing oneself to, Acts 18 : 6 ; elsewhere rendered by the verb to resist, Rom. 13 : 2 ; Jas. 4 : 6 ; 5 : 6 ; 1 Pet. 5 : 5. See RESIST.¶

3. ANTIDIATITHĒMI (ἀντιδιατίθημι) signifies to place oneself in opposition, oppose (anti, against, dia, through, intensive, tithēmi, to place), 2 Tim. 2 : 25. The A.V. and R.V. translate this as a Middle Voice, " them (A.V., those) that oppose themselves." Field (Notes on the Trans. of the N.T.) points out that in the only other known instance of the verb it is Passive. The sense is practically the same if it is rendered ' those who are opposed.'¶

OPPOSITIONS

ANTITHESIS (ἀντίθεσις), a contrary position (anti, against, tithēmi, to place ; Eng., antithesis), occurs in 1 Tim. 6 : 20.¶

OPPRESS

1. KATADUNASTEUŌ (καταδυναστεύω), to exercise power over (kata, down, dunastēs, a potentate : dunamai, to have power), to oppress, is used, in the Passive Voice, in Acts 10 : 38 ; in the Active, in Jas. 2 : 6.¶

2. KATAPONEŌ (καταπονέω) : see DISTRESS, B, No. 4.

OR : see † p. 9

ORACLE

LOGION (λόγιον), a diminutive of logos, a word, narrative, statement, denotes a Divine response or utterance, an oracle ; it is used of (a) the contents of the Mosaic Law, Acts 7 : 38 ; (b) all the written utterances of God through O.T. writers, Rom. 3 : 2 ; (c) the substance of Christian doctrine, Heb. 5 : 12 ; (d) the utterances of God through Christian teachers, 1 Pet. 4 : 11.¶

Note : Divine oracles were given by means of the breastplate of the High Priest, in connection with the service of the Tabernacle, and the Sept. uses the associated word *logeion* in Ex. 28 : 15, to describe the breastplate.

ORATION

DĒMĒGOREŌ (δημηγορέω), from *dēmos*, the people and *agoreuō*, to speak in the public assembly, to deliver an oration, occurs in Acts 12 : 21.¶

ORATOR

RHĒTŌR (ῥήτωρ), from an obsolete present tense, *rheō*, to say (cp. Eng., rhetoric), denotes a public speaker, an orator, Acts 24 : 1, of Tertullus. Such a person, distinct from the professional lawyer, was hired, as a professional speaker, to make a skilful presentation of a case in court. His training was not legal but rhetorical.¶

ORDAIN

1. TITHĒMI (τίθημι), to put : see APPOINT, No. 3.

2. KATHISTĒMI (καθίστημι), from *kata*, down, or over against, and *histēmi*, to cause to stand, to set, is translated to ordain in the A.V. of Tit. 1 : 5 ; Heb. 5 : 1 ; 8 : 3. See APPOINT, No. 2.

3. TASSŌ (τάσσω) is translated to ordain, in Acts 13 : 48 and Rom. 13 : 1. See APPOINT, No. 5.

4. DIATASSŌ (διατάσσω) is translated to ordain in 1 Cor. 7 : 17 ; 9 : 14 ; Gal. 3 : 19, the last in the sense of ' administered.' Cp. *diatagē*, under DISPOSITION. See APPOINT, No. 6.

5. HORIZŌ (ὁρίζω) is twice used of Christ as Divinely " ordained " to be the Judge of men, Acts 10 : 42 ; 17 : 31. See DETERMINE, No. 2.

6. KRINŌ (κρίνω), to divide, separate, decide, judge, is translated " ordained " in Acts 16 : 4, of the decrees by the Apostles and elders in Jerusalem. See JUDGE.

Notes : (1) In 1 Cor. 2 : 7, A.V., *proorizō*, to foreordain (see R.V.) is translated " ordained." See DETERMINE, No. 3. (2) In Mark 3 : 14, A.V., *poieō*, to make, is translated " ordained " (R.V., " appointed "). (3) In Heb. 9 : 6, A.V., *kataskeuazō*, to prepare (so R.V.), is translated " were . . . ordained." See PREPARE. (4) In Acts 14 : 23, A.V., *cheirotoneō*, to appoint (R.V.), is translated " they had ordained." See APPOINT, No. 11. (5) In Eph. 2 : 10, A.V., *proetoimazō*, to prepare before, is translated " hath before ordained " (R.V., " afore prepared ") ; see PREPARE. (6) In Jude 4, A.V., *prographō*, lit., to write before, is translated " were before . . . ordained " (R.V., " were . . . set forth "). See SET (forth).   (7) In Acts 1 : 22, A.V., *ginomai*, to become, is translated " be ordained " (R.V., " become ").   (8) In Rom. 7 : 10, A.V., " *ordained* " represents no word in the original (see R.V.).

ORDER (Noun and Verb)
A. Nouns.

1. TAXIS (τάξις), an arranging, arrangement, order (akin to *tassō*, to arrange, draw up in order), is used in Luke 1 : 8 of the fixed succession of the course of the priests ; of due order, in contrast to confusion, in the gatherings of a local church, 1 Cor. 14 : 40 ; of the general condition of such, Col. 2 : 5 (some give it a military significance here) ; of the Divinely appointed character or nature of a priesthood, of Melchizedek, as fore-shadowing that of Christ, Heb. 5 : 6, 10 ; 6 : 20 ; 7 : 11 (where also the character of the Aaronic priesthood is set in contrast) ; 7 : 17 (in some mss., ver. 21).¶

2. TAGMA (τάγμα), a more concrete form of No. 1, signifying that which has been arranged in order, was especially a military term, denoting a company ; it is used metaphorically in 1 Cor. 15 : 23 of the various classes of those who have part in the first resurrection.¶

B. Verbs.

1. ANATASSOMAI (ἀνατάσσομαι), to arrange in order (*ana*, up, and the Middle Voice of *tassō*, to arrange), is used in Luke 1 : 1, A.V., " to set forth in order " (R.V., " to draw up ") ; the probable meaning is to bring together and so arrange details in order.¶

2. DIATASSŌ (διατάσσω), to appoint, arrange, charge, give orders to, is used, in the Middle Voice, in Acts 24 : 23, " gave order " (R.V.) ; 1 Cor. 11 : 34, " will I set in order ; " in the Active Voice, in 1 Cor. 16 : 1, " I gave order " (R.V.).   See COMMAND, No. 1.

3. EPIDIORTHOŌ (ἐπιδιορθόω), to set in order (*epi*, upon, *dia*, through, intensive, and *orthos*, straight), is used in Tit. 1 : 5, in the sense of setting right again what was defective, a commission to Titus, not to add to what the Apostle himself had done, but to restore what had fallen into disorder since the Apostle had laboured in Crete ; this is suggested by the *epi*.¶

C. Adverb.

KATHEXĒS (καθεξῆς) is translated " in order " in Luke 1 : 3 ; Acts 11 : 4, R.V. (A.V., " by order ") ; Acts 18 : 23.   See AFTERWARD, No. 3.

Note : In 2 Cor. 11 : 32, R.V., the phrase " in order to " (as with the A.V., " desirous to ") represents nothing in the original : the infinitive mood of the verb *piazō* expresses the purpose, viz., " to take."

ORDERLY

KOSMIOS (κόσμιος), an adjective signifying decent, modest, orderly (akin to *kosmos*, order, adornment), is translated " modest " in 1 Tim.

2 : 9; "orderly" in 3 : 2, R.V. (A.V., "of good behaviour"). See
MODEST.¶

Note : For *stoicheō*, in Acts 21 : 24, "thou walkest orderly," see WALK.

ORDINANCE
A. Nouns.

1. DIKAIŌMA (δικαίωμα) : see JUSTIFICATION, No. 2.

2. DIATAGĒ (διαταγή) is translated "ordinances," in Rom. 13 : 2.
See DISPOSITION.

3. DOGMA (δόγμα) is translated "ordinances" in Eph. 2 : 15 and
Col. 2 : 14. See DECREE.

4. KTISIS (κτίσις), a creation, creature, is translated "ordinance"
in 1 Pet. 2 : 13. See CREATE, B, No. 1.

Note : In 1 Cor. 11 : 2, A.V., *paradosis*, a tradition (marg., and R.V.,
" traditions "), is translated "ordinances." See TRADITION.
B. Verb.

DOGMATIZŌ (δογματίζω), akin to A, No. 3, to decree, signifies, in the
Middle Voice, to subject oneself to an ordinance, Col. 2 : 20.¶ In the
Sept., Esth. 3 : 9 ; in some texts, Dan. 2 : 13, 15.¶

OTHER

1. ALLOS (ἄλλος) indicates numeral distinction of objects of similar
character, and is used (*a*) absolutely, e.g., Matt. 20 : 3 (plural) ; (*b*) attached
to a noun, e.g., Matt. 21 : 36 ; (*c*) with the article, e.g. Matt. 5 : 39 ; 1 Cor.
14 : 29 (plural, R.V.) ; in Matt. 13 : 5 ; Luke 9 : 19 ; John 9 : 9, e.g.,
R.V., "others" (A.V., " some ") ; in Matt. 25 : 20, R.V., "other" (A.V.,
" beside them . . . more "). See ANOTHER, MORE, B, Note (1), SOME.

2. HETEROS (ἕτερος) indicates either numerical distinction, e.g.,
Luke 4 : 43 ; 5 : 7 ; or generic distinction, different in character, etc.,
e.g., Luke 9 : 29, " (the fashion of His countenance) was altered," lit.,
' became other ; ' 23 : 32, " two others, (malefactors)," R.V., where the
plural serves to make the necessary distinction between them and Christ ;
Acts 2 : 4 ; 19 : 39 (" other matters ") ; 1 Cor. 14 : 21, A.V., " other "
(R.V., " strange ") ; 2 Cor. 11 : 4 (2nd and 3rd parts, R.V., " different ; "
in the 1st clause, *allos*, " another "). For the distinction between this and
No. 1, see under ANOTHER.

3. LOIPOS (λοιπός) signifies remaining, the rest. It is translated
" other," or " others," e.g., in Matt. 25 : 11 ; Mark 4 : 19 ; Luke 18 : 9 ;
24 : 10 (in ver. 9, " the rest ") ; but in Luke 8 : 10 ; Acts 28 : 9 ; Rom.
1 : 13 ; 1 Cor. 9 : 5 ; Eph. 2 : 3 ; 1 Thess. 4 : 13 ; 5 : 6 ; 1 Tim. 5 : 20,
e.g., the R.V. renders this word " the rest " (A.V., " other " or " others ") ;
in Eph. 4 : 17, some mss. have *loipa*, neuter plural, A.V., " other
(Gentiles) ; " see the R.V. See REMNANT, REST (the).

4. ALLOTRIOS (ἀλλότριος), belonging to another, not one's own, is
translated " other men's " in 2 Cor. 10 : 15 ; 1 Tim. 5 : 22 ; in Heb.

9 : 25, R.V., " not his own " (A.V., " of others "). See ALIEN, MAN'S, Note (1), STRANGE, STRANGER.

5. ALLĒLŌN (ἀλλήλων), in Rom. 1 : 12, used in the dative case, is translated in the R.V. " (each of us by the) other's " (A.V., " mutual ") ; the accusative is translated " other " in Phil. 2 : 3. See MUTUAL and ONE ANOTHER.

6. HEIS (εἷς), one, is sometimes translated " other " when expressing the second of a pair, e.g., Matt. 24 : 40, A.V. (R.V., " one "). See ONE, A (4).

7. EKEINOS (ἐκεῖνος), signifying that one, implying remoteness as compared with *houtos*, this, is translated " the other," e.g., in Matt. 23 : 23 ; Luke 11 : 42 ; 18 : 14.

Notes : (1) In Acts 26 : 22, A.V., *ouden ektos*, lit., ' nothing besides ' is translated " none other things " (R.V., " nothing but "). (2) The plural of the definite article is translated " others " in Acts 17 : 32 ; in Jude 23, A.V., " others " (R.V., " some "). (3) In Luke 24 : 1, the plural of *tis*, a certain one, is found in some mss., and translated " certain others " in the A.V.

For OTHER SIDE and OTHER WAY see SIDE and WAY

OTHERWISE

1. ALLOS (ἄλλος) is used, in its neuter form, *allo*, in Gal. 5 : 10, lit., ' another thing,' with the meaning " otherwise." See OTHER, No. 1.

2. ALLŌS (ἄλλως), the adverb corresponding to No. 1, is translated " otherwise " in 1 Tim. 5 : 25 ; the contrast is not with works that are not good (No. 3 would signify that), but with good works which are not evident.¶

3. HETERŌS (ἑτέρως) is used in Phil. 3 : 15, " otherwise (minded)," i.e. differently minded.¶ Contrast No. 2, and for the corresponding difference between the adjectives *allos* and *heteros*, see ANOTHER.

4. EPEI (ἐπεί), when used of time, means since or when ; used of cause, it means since, because ; used elliptically it means otherwise or else ; " otherwise " in Rom. 11 : 6 (the 2nd part of the ver. is absent from the most authentic mss.) ; ver. 22 ; in Heb. 9 : 17, A.V., " otherwise (it is of no strength at all)," R.V., " for (doth it ever avail ?)." See ELSE.

Note : The phrase *ei*, if, *de*, but, *mēge*, not indeed, i.e., ' but if not indeed,' is translated " otherwise " in the A.V. of Matt. 6 : 1 ; Luke 5 : 36 (R.V., " else," in each place) ; in 2 Cor. 11 : 16, A.V., " if otherwise " (R.V., " but if ye do "). See also TEACH.

For the pronoun OUGHT (A.V.) see AUGHT

OUGHT (Verb)

1. DEI (δεῖ) denotes ' it is necessary,' one must ; in Luke 24 : 26,

A.V., " ought " (R.V., " behoved it ") ; the neuter of the present participle, used as a noun, is translated " things which they ought (not) " in 1 Tim. 5 : 13 ; in Acts 19 : 36, " ye ought " (see NEED). See MUST, No. 1.

2. OPHEILŌ (ὀφείλω), to owe, is translated " ought," with various personal pronouns, in John 13 : 14 ; 19 : 7 ; Acts 17 : 29 ; Rom. 15 : 1 ; Heb. 5 : 3, A.V. (R.V., " he is bound ") ; 5 : 12 ; 1 John 3 : 16 ; 4 : 11 ; 3 John 8 ; with other subjects in 1 Cor. 11 : 7, 10 ; 2 Cor. 12 : 14 ; Eph. 5 : 28 ; 1 John 2 : 6. See BEHOVE, OWE, etc.

3. CHRĒ (χρή), an impersonal verb (akin to *chraomai*, to use), occurs in Jas. 3 : 10, " (these things) ought (not so to be)," lit., ' it is not befitting, these things so to be.'¶

OUR, OURS

Notes : (1) This usually translates *hēmōn*, the genitive of *hēmeis*, " we," lit., ' of us,' e.g., Matt. 6 : 9, 11, 12. It is translated " ours," e.g., in Mark 12 : 7 ; Luke 20 : 14 ; 1 Cor. 1 : 2 ; 2 Cor. 1 : 14. (2) In 1 John 4 : 17, the phrase *meta hēmōn*, rendered " our (love) " in the A.V., is accurately translated in the R.V. " (herein is love made perfect) with us," i.e., Divine love in Christ finds its expression in our manifestation of it to others. (3) In Luke 17 : 5, " increase our faith " is, lit., ' add faith to us.' (4) In Luke 24 : 22, " of our company " is, lit., ' from among us.' (5) *Hēmeteros*, a possessive pronoun, more emphatic than *hēmeis*, is used in Luke 16 : 12, in the best mss. (some have *humeteros*, ' your own ') ; Acts 2 : 11 ; 24 : 6, in some mss. ; 26 : 5 ; 2 Tim. 4 : 15 ; Tit. 3 : 14, " ours ; " 1 John 1 : 3 ; 2 : 2, " ours." (6) In Luke 23 : 41, " of our deeds," is, lit., ' of what things we practised.' (7) In 1 Cor. 9 : 10, " for our sake," R.V. (twice), is, lit., ' on account of us.'

OUR OWN

1. HEAUTŌN (ἑαυτῶν) is sometimes used as a reflexive pronoun of the 1st person plural, signifying our own selves, translated " our own " in 1 Thess. 2 : 8, lit., ' (the souls) of ourselves.'

2. IDIOS (ἴδιος), one's own, signifies " our own " in Acts 3 : 12 ; 1 Cor. 4 : 12 ; in Acts 2 : 8, with *hēmōn*, forming a strong possessive, lit., ' each in his own language of us.'

OURSELVES

Notes : (1) This translates (a) *autoi*, the plural of *autos*, self, used emphatically either alone, e.g., John 4 : 42 ; Rom. 8 : 23 (1st part) ; 2 Cor. 1 : 4 (last part) ; 1 : 9, R.V., " we ourselves " (1st part) ; or joined with the plural pronouns, e.g., *hēmeis*, we, Rom. 8 : 23 (2nd part) ; (b) the plural *hemeis* alone, e.g., Tit. 3 : 3 ; in 2 Cor. 4 : 7, R.V., *ex hēmōn*, is translated " from ourselves " (A.V., " of us ") ; (c) *heautōn*, governed by the preposition *apo*, from, e.g., 2 Cor. 3 : 5 (1st part), lit., ' from ourselves ' ("of ourselves," in the text) ; (*d*) *heautois*, the dative case of (*c*), e.g., Rom. 15 : 1 ; governed by *en*, in, 2 Cor. 1 : 9 (1st part) ; by *epi*, on (2nd part). (*e*) *heautous*, the accusative case, e.g., Acts 23 : 14 ; 2 Cor. 3 : 1 ; 4 : 2, 5. (2) In Acts 6 : 4, A.V., *proskartereō*, to continue stedfastly (R.V.), is translated "give ourselves continually." (3) In 2 Cor. 10 : 12, A.V., *enkrinō*, to number (R.V.), is translated "to make ourselves of the number."

OUT, OUT OF

Notes : (1) The preposition *ek* (or *ex*), which frequently signifies "out of" or "from the midst of," has a variety of meanings, among which is "from," as virtually equivalent to *apo*, away from, e.g., 2 Cor. 1 : 10, "who delivered us out of so great a death, and will deliver ; " since death was not actually experienced, but was impending, *ek* here does not signify "out of the midst of." In Acts 12 : 7 it is used in the statement "his chains fell off from his hands." In Matt. 17 : 9 it is used of descending from a mountain, not 'out of ; ' "we are not to suppose that they had been in a cave" (Dr. A. T. Robertson, *Gram. of the Greek N.T.*). In 1 Thess. 1 : 10, "even Jesus, which delivereth us from the wrath to come," R.V., the question whether *ek* here means ' out of the midst of ' or ' away from,' is to be determined by some statement of Scripture where the subject is specifically mentioned ; this is provided, e.g., in 5 : 9, the context of which makes clear that believers are to be delivered from (not ' out of ') the Divine wrath to be executed on the nations at the end of the present age. (2) For the phrase *ek mesou*, "out of the way," see MIDST, Note (1), (*e*). (3) In Luke 8 : 4, A.V., the phrase *kata polin* is translated "out of every city" (R.V., "of every city," to be taken in connection with "they"). (4) *Ektos*, outside of, is translated "out of" in 2 Cor. 12 : 2 ; in 12 : 3 the best mss. have *chōris*, "apart from," R.V. (A.V., *ektos*, "out of"). (4) For other prepositions, and adverbs, see † p. 9.

OUTER

EXŌTEROS (ἐξώτερος), the comparative degree of *exō*, without, is used of the outer darkness, Matt. 8 : 12 ; 22 : 13 ; 25 : 30.¶

OUTGO

PROERCHOMAI (προέρχομαι), to go forward, go in advance, outgo, is used of time in Mark 6 : 33, "outwent," of the people who in their eagerness reached a spot earlier than Christ and His disciples. See Go, No. 17.

OUTRUN

PROTRECHŌ (προτρέχω), primarily, to run forward (*pro*, forward or before, *trechō*, to run), is used with *tachion*, more quickly, in John 20 : 4, "outran," R.V. (A.V., "did outrun"), lit., ' ran forward more quickly ; '

in Luke 19 : 4, " he ran on before," R.V. (A.V., " ran before "). See RUN.¶ In the Sept., 1 Sam. 8 : 11 ; in some texts, Job 41 : 13, " destruction runneth before him," in the Eng. Versions, ver. 22.¶

OUTSIDE

1. EXŌTHEN (ἔξωθεν), an adverb formed from exō, without, properly signifies ' from without,' Mark 7 : 18 (in ver. 15 it is used as a preposition) ; with the article it is equivalent to a noun, " the outside," Matt. 23 : 25 (for ver. 27, see OUTWARD, No. 2) ; Luke 11 : 39 ; in ver. 40, R.V., " the outside " (A.V., " that which is without "). See OUTWARD, OUTWARDLY, WITHOUT.

2. EKTOS (ἐκτός) is once used with the article, " the outside," Matt. 23 : 26. See EXCEPT, No. 1.

OUTWARD, OUTWARDLY

1. EXŌ (ἔξω), without, is used metaphorically of the physical frame, " the outward man," 2 Cor. 4 : 16. See WITHOUT.

2. EXŌTHEN (ἔξωθεν) is translated " outward " in Matt. 23 : 27 (R.V., " outwardly ") ; it is used with the article, adjectivally, in 1 Pet. 3 : 3, of outward adorning. See OUTSIDE, No. 1.

Notes : (1) The phrase *en tō phanerō*, lit., ' in the open ' (manifest), is rendered " outwardly " in Rom. 2 : 28. (2) For " with outward shew," A.V., marg., Luke 17 : 20, see OBSERVATION. (3) For the A.V., of 2 Cor. 10 : 7, " outward appearance," see FACE, No. 1.

OVEN

KLIBANOS (κλίβανος) is mentioned in Matt. 6 : 30 and Luke 12 : 28. The form of oven commonly in use in the east indicates the kind in use as mentioned in Scripture. A hole is sunk in the ground about 3 feet deep and somewhat less in diameter. The walls are plastered with cement. A fire is kindled inside, the fuel being grass, or dry twigs, which heat the oven rapidly and blacken it with smoke and soot (see Lam. 5 : 10). When sufficiently heated the surface is wiped, and the dough is moulded into broad thin loaves, placed one at a time on the wall of the oven to fit its concave inner circle. The baking takes a few seconds. Such ovens are usually outside the house, and often the same oven serves for several families (Lev. 26 : 26). An oven of this sort is doubtless referred to in Ex. 8 : 3 (see Hastings, Bib. Dic.).¶

OVER, OVER AGAINST : see Note † p. 9

OVER (to be, to have)

1. PROISTĒMI (προίστημι), lit., ' to stand before,' hence to lead, to direct, attend to, is translated ' rule,' with reference to the family, in 1 Tim. 3 : 4, 5, 12 ; with reference to the church, in Rom. 12 : 8 ; 1 Thess.

5 : 12, " are over ; " 1 Tim. 5 : 17. In Tit. 3 : 8, 14, it signifies to maintain. See MAINTAIN.¶

2. PLEONAZŌ (πλεονάζω), used intransitively, signifies to abound, to superabound ; in 2 Cor. 8 : 15 it is used with the negative *ou*, " had nothing over," lit., ' had not more ' (*pleon*, the comparative degree of *polus*, much).

For OVERBOARD, Acts 27 : 18, R.V., see FREIGHT, and, in 27 : 43, R.V., see CAST, No. 11.

OVERCHARGE

1. BAREŌ (βαρέω), or *barunō*, is rendered " overcharged " in Luke 21 : 34. See BURDEN, B, No. 1.

2. EPIBAREŌ (ἐπιβαρέω) is rendered " overcharge " in 2 Cor. 2 : 5, A.V. See BURDEN, B, No. 2, and PRESS.

OVERCOME

1. NIKAŌ (νικάω) is used (*a*) of God, Rom. 3 : 4 (a law term), R.V., " mightest prevail ; " (*b*) of Christ, John 16 : 33 ; Rev. 3 : 21 ; 5 : 5 ; 17 : 14 ; (*c*) of His followers, Rom. 12 : 21 (2nd part) ; 1 John 2 : 13, 14 ; 4 : 4 ; 5 : 4, 5 ; Rev. 2 : 7, 11, 17, 26 ; 3 : 5, 12, 21 ; 12 : 11 ; 15 : 2 ; 21 : 7 ; (*d*) of faith, 1 John 5 : 4 ; (*e*) of evil (Passive Voice), Rom. 12 : 21 ; (*f*) of predicted human potentates, Rev. 6 : 2 ; 11 : 7 ; 13 : 7.¶

2. HĒTTAOMAI (ἡττάομαι), to be made inferior, be enslaved, is rendered " is (are) overcome," in 2 Pet. 2 : 19, 20. See INFERIOR.

3. KATAKURIEUŌ (κατακυριεύω) is translated " overcome " in Acts 19 : 16 ; see MASTER, B.

OVERFLOW, OVERFLOWING
A. Verbs.

1. HUPERPERISSEUŌ (ὑπερπερισσεύω), to abound more exceedingly, Rom. 5 : 20, is used in the Middle Voice in 2 Cor. 7 : 4, R.V., " I overflow (with joy)," A.V., " I am exceeding (joyful)." See ABUNDANCE, B, No. 2.

2. KATAKLUZŌ (κατακλύζω), to inundate, deluge (*kata*, down, *kluzō*, to wash or dash over, said, e.g., of the sea), is used in the Passive Voice in 2 Pet. 3 : 6, of the Flood.¶

B. Noun.

PERISSEIA (περισσεία) is translated " overflowing " in Jas. 1 : 21, R.V. See ABUNDANCE, A, No. 2.

OVERLAY

PERIKALUPTŌ (περικαλύπτω) denotes to cover around, cover up, or over ; it is translated " overlaid " in Heb. 9 : 4. See BLINDFOLD, COVER.

OVERLOOK

HUPEREIDON (ὑπερεῖδον), to overlook (an aorist form), is used in Acts 17 : 30, R.V. (A.V., " winked at "), i.e., God bore with them without interposing by way of punishment, though the debasing tendencies of idolatry necessarily developed themselves.¶

OVERMUCH

PERISSOTEROS (περισσότερος), the comparative degree of *perissos*, abundant, is translated " overmuch " in 2 Cor. 2 : 7. See ABUNDANCE, C, No. 2.

Notes : (1) In 2 Cor. 10 : 14, R.V., the verb *huperekteinō*, to stretch out over, is translated " we stretch (not ourselves) overmuch " (A.V., . . . beyond *our measure* "). See STRETCH.¶ (2) In 2 Cor. 12 : 7 (twice), R.V., *huperairō*, in the Middle Voice, to uplift oneself, is translated " I should (not) be exalted overmuch," A.V., " . . . above measure." See EXALT.

OVER-RIPE

XĒRAINŌ (ξηραίνω) denotes to dry up, wither, translated in Rev. 14 : 15, " over-ripe," R.V. (A.V., " ripe "), said figuratively of the harvest of the earth, symbolizing the condition of the world, political, especially connected with Israel (Joel 3 : 9, 14), and religious, comprehensive of the whole scene of Christendom (Matt. 13 : 38). See DRY.

For OVERSEER see BISHOP

OVERSHADOW

1. EPISKIAZŌ (ἐπισκιάζω), to throw a shadow upon (*epi*, over, *skia*, a shadow), to overshadow, is used (*a*) of the bright cloud at the Transfiguration, Matt. 17 : 5 ; Mark 9 : 7 ; Luke 9 : 34 ; (*b*) metaphorically of the power of " the Most High " upon the Virgin Mary, Luke 1 : 35 ; (*c*) of the Apostle Peter's shadow upon the sick, Acts 5 : 15.¶

2. KATASKIAZŌ (κατασκιάζω), lit., to shadow down, is used of the " overshadowing " (R.V.) of the cherubim of glory above the mercy-seat, Heb. 9 : 5 (A.V., " shadowing ").¶

OVERSIGHT (exercise, take)

EPISKOPEŌ (ἐπισκοπέω), lit., to look upon (*epi*, upon, *skopeō*, to look at, contemplate), is found in 1 Pet. 5 : 2 (some ancient authorities omit it), " exercising the oversight," R.V. (A.V., " taking . . .") ; " exercising " is the right rendering ; the word does not imply the entrance upon such responsibility, but the fulfilment of it. It is not a matter of assuming a position, but of the discharge of the duties. The word is found elsewhere in Heb. 12 : 15, " looking carefully," R.V. See LOOK.¶ Cp. *episkopē* in 1 Tim. 3 : 1 (see BISHOP, No. 2).

OVERTAKE

1. KATALAMBANŌ (καταλαμβάνω), to lay hold of, has the significance of overtaking, metaphorically, in John 12 : 35 (R.V., " overtake," A.V., " come upon ") and 1 Thess. 5 : 4. See APPREHEND, No. 1.

2. PROLAMBANŌ (προλαμβάνω), to anticipate (pro, before, lambanō, to take), is used of the act of Mary, in Mark 14 : 8 [see COME, Note (2)] ; of forestalling the less favoured at a social meal, 1 Cor. 11 : 21 ; of being overtaken in any trespass, Gal. 6 : 1, where the meaning is not that of detecting a person in the act, but of his being caught by the trespass, through his being off his guard (see 5 : 21 and contrast the premeditated practice of evil in 5 : 26). The modern Greek Version is ' even if a man, through lack of circumspection, should fall into any sin.' See TAKE.¶

OVERTHROW (Noun and Verb)

A. Noun.

KATASTROPHĒ (καταστροφή), lit., a turning down (kata, down, strophē, a turning ; Eng., catastrophe), is used (a) literally, 2 Pet. 2 : 6 ; (b) metaphorically, 2 Tim. 2 : 14, " subverting," i.e., the overthrowing of faith.¶ Cp. kathairesis, a pulling down, 2 Cor. 10 : 4, 8 ; 13 : 10.¶

B. Verbs.

1. KATASTREPHŌ (καταστρέφω), akin to A, lit. and primarily, to turn down or turn over, as, e.g., the soil, denotes to overturn, overthrow, Matt. 21 : 12 ; Mark 11 : 15 ; in Acts 15 : 16, Passive Voice, " ruins," lit., ' the overthrown (things) of it ' (some mss. have kataskaptō, to dig down). See RUIN.¶

2. ANASTREPHŌ (ἀναστρέφω) is found in some mss. in John 2 : 15 (see No. 3). See ABIDE, No. 8.

3. ANATREPŌ (ἀνατρέπω), lit., to turn up or over (ana, up, trepō, to turn), to upset, is used (a) literally, in the most authentic mss., in John 2 : 15 (see No. 2) ; (b) metaphorically, in 2 Tim. 2 : 18, " overthrow (the faith of some) ; " in Tit. 1 : 11, R.V., " overthrow (whole houses)," A.V., " subvert . . . ," i.e., households. Moulton and Milligan (Vocab.) give an apt illustration from a 2nd cent. papyrus, of the complete upsetting of a family by the riotous conduct of a member.¶

4. KATALUŌ (καταλύω), lit., to loosen down, signifies to overthrow in Acts 5 : 38, R.V., " it will be overthrown " (A.V., " it will come to nought "); Rom. 14 : 20, R.V., " overthrow " (A.V., " destroy "). See DESTROY.

5. KATASTRŌNNUMI (καταστρώννυμι), primarily, to strew or spread over (kata, down, strōnnumi, or strōnnuō, to spread), then, to overthrow, has this meaning in 1 Cor. 10 : 5, " they were overthrown."¶ In the Sept., Numb. 14 : 16 ; Job 12 : 23.¶

OWE

A. Verbs.

1. OPHEILŌ (ὀφείλω), to owe, to be a debtor (in the Passive Voice,

to be owed, to be due), is translated by the verb to owe in Matt. 18 : 28 (twice) ; Luke 7 : 41 ; 16 : 5, 7 ; Rom. 13 : 8 ; in 15 : 27, R.V., " they (Gentile converts) owe it " (A.V., " it is their duty ") ; Philm. 18. See BEHOVE, DEBT, DUE, DUTY, GUILTY, INDEBTED, MUST, NEED, OUGHT.

2. PROSOPHEILŌ (προσοφείλω), to owe besides (pros, in addition, and No. 1), is used in Philm. 19, " thou owest (to me even thine own self) besides," i.e., ' thou owest me already as much as Onesimus' debt, and in addition even thyself' (not ' thou owest me much more ').

B. Noun.
OPHEILETĒS (ὀφειλέτης), a debtor (akin to A, No. 1), is translated " which owed " in Matt. 18 : 24, lit., ' a debtor (of ten thousand talents).' See DEBTOR.

OWN (Adjective)
Notes : (1) Gnēsios, primarily, lawfully begotten, and hence ' true,' ' genuine,' is translated " own " in the A.V. of 1 Tim. 1 : 2 and Tit. 1 : 4 (R.V., " true "). See SINCERITY, TRUE. (2) In Acts 5 : 4, " was it not thine own ? " is, lit., ' did it not remain (menō) to thee ? ' (3) In Jude 6 (1st part), A.V., heautōn, of themselves, " their own " (R.V.), is rendered " their ; " in the 2nd part, R.V., idios, one's own, is translated " their proper " (A.V., " their own "). (4) In Gal. 1 : 14, R.V., sunēlikiōtēs, is rendered " of mine own age " (A.V., " my equals ; " marg., " equals in years ").¶ (5) For " its own " in 1 Tim. 2 : 6, R.V., see DUE, A. (6) For association with other words see ACCORD, BUSINESS, COMPANY, CONCEITS, COUNTRY.

OWNER
1. KURIOS (κύριος), one having power (kuros) or authority, a lord, master, signifies an owner in Luke 19 : 33. See LORD, MASTER, SIR.

2. NAUKLĒROS (ναύκληρος), a ship owner (naus, a ship, klēros, a lot), a shipmaster, occurs in Acts 27 : 11, " (the) owner of the ship."¶

OWNETH
Note : In Acts 21 : 11, " that owneth this girdle," is lit., ' whose is (esti) this girdle.'

OX
1. BOUS (βοῦς) denotes an ox or a cow, Luke 13 : 15 ; 14 : 5, 19 ; John 2 : 14, 15 ; 1 Cor. 9 : 9 (twice) ; 1 Tim. 5 : 18.¶

2. TAUROS (ταῦρος), Latin taurus, is translated " oxen " in Matt. 22 : 4 and Acts 14 : 13 ; " bulls " in Heb. 9 : 13 and 10 : 4.¶

P

PAIN (Noun and Verb)
A. Nouns.

1. PONOS (πόνος) is translated "pain" in Rev. 16 : 10 ; 21 : 4 ; "pains" in 16 : 11. See LABOUR.

2. ŌDIN (ὠδίν), a birth pang, travail-pain, is rendered "travail," metaphorically, in Matt. 24 : 8 and Mark 13 : 8, R.V. (A.V., "sorrows") ; by way of comparison, in 1 Thess. 5 : 3 ; translated "pains (of death)," Acts 2 : 24 (R.V., "pangs"). See SORROW, TRAVAIL.¶ Cp. ōdinō, to travail in birth.

B. Verb.

BASANIZŌ (βασανίζω) primarily signifies to rub on the touchstone, to put to the test (from basanos, a touchstone, a dark stone used in testing metals) ; hence, to examine by torture, and, in general, to distress ; in Rev. 12 : 2, "in pain," R.V. (A.V., "pained"), in connection with parturition. See TORMENT. (In the Sept., 1 Sam. 5 : 3.¶).

Note : For Rom. 8 : 22, "travaileth in pain together," see TRAVAIL.

For PAINFULNESS (2 Cor. 11 : 27, A.V.) see TRAVAIL

PAIR

ZEUGOS (ζεῦγος), a yoke (akin to *zeugnumi*, to yoke), is used (*a*) of beasts, Luke 14 : 19 ; (*b*) of a pair of anything ; in Luke 2 : 24, of turtle-doves. See YOKE.¶

Note : In Rev. 6 : 5, A.V., *zugos*, a yoke (akin to *zeugos*), is translated "a pair of balances" (R.V., "a balance"). See BALANCE, YOKE.

PALACE

1. AULĒ (αὐλή), a court, dwelling, palace : see COURT.

2. PRAITŌRION (πραιτώριον) signified originally a general's (prætor's) tent. Then it was applied to the council of army officers ; then to the official residence of the Governor of a Province ; finally, to the imperial bodyguard. In the A.V. the word appears only once, Mark 15 : 16, "the hall, called Prætorium" (R.V., "within the court which is the Prætorium," marg., "palace") ; in the Greek of the N.T. it also occurs in Matt. 27 : 27, A.V., "the common hall," marg., "the governor's house ;" R.V., 'palace," see marg. ; John 18 : 28 (twice), A.V., "the hall of judgment ;"

and "judgment hall," marg., "Pilate's house," R.V., "palace;" 18 : 33 and 19 : 9, A.V., "judgment hall," R.V., "palace," see marg.; so in Acts 23 : 35; in Phil. 1 : 13, A.V., "in all the palace," marg., "Cæsar's court," R.V., "throughout the whole prætorian guard," marg., "in the whole Prætorium."

"In the Gospels the term denotes the official residence in Jerusalem of the Roman governor, and the various translations of it in our versions arose from a desire either to indicate the special purpose for which that residence was used on the occasion in question, or to explain what particular building was intended. But whatever building the governor occupied was the Prætorium. It is most probable that in Jerusalem he resided in the well-known palace of Herod. . . . Pilate's residence has been identified with the castle of Antonia, which was occupied by the regular garrison. The probability is that it was the same as Herod's palace. Herod's palace in Cæsarea was used as the Prætorium there, and the expression in Acts 23 : 35, marg.,' Herod's prætorium,' is abbreviated from ' the .prætorium of Herod's palace.' " (Hastings' Bib. Dic.).

In Phil. 1 : 13, marg., " the whole Prætorium " has been variously explained. It has been spoken of as ' the palace;' in connection with 4 : 22, where allusion is made to believers who belong to Cæsar's household. Others have understood it of the barracks of the prætorian guard, but Lightfoot shows that this use of the word cannot be established, neither can it be regarded as referring to the barracks of the palace guard. The phrase ' and to all the rest ' in 1 : 13 indicates that persons are meant. Mommsen, followed by Ramsay (*St. Paul the Traveller*, p. 357) regards it as improbable that the Apostle was committed to the prætorian guard and holds the view that Julius the centurion, who brought Paul to Rome, belonged to a corps drafted from legions in the provinces, whose duty it was to supervise the corn supply and perform police service, and that Julius probably delivered his prisoners to the Commander of his corps. Eventually Paul's case came before the prætorian council, which is the prætorium alluded to by the Apostle, and the phrase " to all the rest " refers to the audience of the trial.¶

Note : Some scholars, believing that this Epistle was written during an Ephesian imprisonment, take the Prætorium here to be the residence in Ephesus of the Proconsul of the Province of Asia, and "Cæsar's household" to be the local Imperial Civil Service (Deissmann etc.).

PALE

CHLŌROS (χλωρός), pale green, is translated " pale " (of a horse) in Rev. 6 : 8, symbolizing death. See GREEN.

PALM (of the hand)

Note : For *rhapizō*, to strike with a rod or with the palm of the hand, Matt. 26 : 67 (cp. 5 : 39), see SMITE.¶ For *rhapisma*, a blow, with *didōmi*, to give, translated " did strike (and, struck) . . . with the palm of his hand " (A.V., in Mark 14 : 65 ; John 18 : 22), see BLOW.

PALM (palm tree)

PHOINIX (φοῖνιξ) denotes the date palm ; it is used of palm trees in John 12 : 13, from which branches were taken ; of the branches themselves in Rev. 7 : 9.¶ The palm gave its name to Phœnicia and to Phœnix in Crete, Acts 27 : 12, R.V. Jericho was the city of palm trees, Deut. 34 : 3 ; Judg. 1 : 16 ; 3 : 13 ; 2 Chron. 28 : 15. They were plentiful there in the time of Christ.

PALSY (sick of)
A. Adjective.

PARALUTIKOS (παραλυτικός), paralytic, sick of the palsy, is found in Matt. 4 : 24 (R.V., " palsied ") ; 8 : 6 ; 9 : 2 (twice), 6 ; Mark 2 : 3, 4, 5, 9, 10 ; in some mss. Luke 5 : 24 (see B).¶

B. Verb.

PARALUŌ (παραλύω), lit., to loose from the side, hence, to set free, is used in the Passive Voice of being enfeebled by a paralytic stroke, palsied, Luke 5 : 18, R.V., " palsied " (A.V., " taken with a palsy ") ; 5 : 24 (ditto), in the best mss. ; Acts 8 : 7 (ditto) ; 9 : 33, R.V., " he was palsied " (A.V., " was sick of the palsy ") ; Heb. 12 : 12, R.V., " palsied (knees)," A.V., " feeble." See FEEBLE.¶

For PANGS, Acts 2 : 24, R.V., see PAIN

For PAPS see BREAST

PAPER

CHARTĒS (χάρτης), a sheet of paper made of strips of papyrus (whence Eng., " paper "), Eng., chart, charter, etc. ; the word is used in 2 John 12.¶ The papyrus reed grew in ancient times in great profusion in the Nile and was used as a material for writing. From Egypt its use spread to other countries and it was the universal material for writing in general in Greece and Italy during the most flourishing periods of their literature.

The pith of the stem of the plant was cut into thin strips, placed side by side to form a sheath. Another layer was laid upon this at right angles to it. The two layers were united by moisture and pressure and frequently with the addition of glue. The sheets, after being dried and polished, were ready for use. Normally, the writing is on that side of the papyrus on which the fibres lie horizontally, parallel to the length of the roll, but where the material was scarce the writer used the other side also (cp. Rev. 5 : 1). Papyrus continued to be used until the seventh cent., A.D., when the conquest of Egypt by the Arabs led to the disuse of the material for literary purposes and the use of vellum till the 12th century.

PARABLE

1. PARABOLĒ (παραβολή) lit. denotes a placing beside (akin to paraballō, to throw or lay beside, to compare). It signifies a placing of one thing beside another with a view to comparison (some consider that the thought of comparison is not necessarily contained in the word). In the N.T. it is found outside the Gospels, only in Heb. 9 : 9 and 11 : 19. It is generally used of a somewhat lengthy utterance or narrative drawn from nature or human circumstances, the object of which is to set forth a spiritual lesson, e.g., those in Matt. 13 and Synoptic parallels; sometimes it is used of a short saying or proverb, e.g., Matt. 15 : 15; Mark 3 : 23; 7 : 17; Luke 4 : 23; 5 : 36; 6 : 39. It is the lesson that is of value; the hearer must catch the analogy if he is to be instructed (this is true also of a proverb). Such a narrative or saying, dealing with earthly things with a spiritual meaning, is distinct from a fable, which attributes to things what does not belong to them in nature.

Christ's parables most frequently convey truths connected with the subject of the Kingdom of God. His withholding the meaning from His hearers as He did from the multitudes, Matt. 13 : 34, was a Divine judgment upon the unworthy.

Two dangers are to be avoided in seeking to interpret the parables in Scripture, that of ignoring the important features, and that of trying to make all the details mean something.

2. PAROIMIA (παροιμία) denotes a wayside saying (from paroimos, by the way), a byword, maxim, or problem, 2 Pet. 2 : 22. The word is sometimes spoken of as a parable, John 10 : 6, i.e., a figurative discourse (R.V. marg., " proverb "); see also 16 : 25, 29, where the word is rendered " proverbs " (marg. " parables ") and " proverb."¶

PARADISE

PARADEISOS (παράδεισος) is an Oriental word, first used by the historian Xenophon, denoting the parks of Persian kings and nobles. It is of Persian origin (Old Pers. pairidæza, akin to Gk. peri, around, and teichos, a wall) whence it passed into Greek. See the Sept., e.g., in Neh. 2 : 8; Eccl. 2 : 5; S. of Sol. 4 : 13. The Sept. translators used it of the garden of Eden, Gen. 2 : 8, and in other respects, e.g., Numb. 24 : 6; Is. 1 : 30; Jer. 29 : 5; Ezek. 31 : 8, 9.

In Luke 23 : 43, the promise of the Lord to the repentant robber was fulfilled the same day; Christ, at His death, having committed His spirit to the Father, went in spirit immediately into Heaven itself, the dwelling place of God (the Lord's mention of the place as Paradise must have been a great comfort to the malefactor; to the oriental mind it expressed the sum total of blessedness). Thither the Apostle Paul was caught up, 2 Cor. 12 : 4, spoken of as " the third heaven " (ver. 3 does not introduce a different vision), beyond the heavens of the natural creation (see Heb. 4 : 14, R.V., with reference to the Ascension). The same region is mentioned in Rev. 2 : 7, where the " tree of life," the figurative antitype of that in Eden, held out to the overcomer, is spoken of as being in " the Paradise of God " (R.V.), marg., " garden," as in Gen. 2 : 8.¶

For PARCEL see GROUND, No. 4

PARCHMENT

MEMBRANA (μεμβράνα) is a Latin word, properly an adjective, from *membrum*, a limb, but denoting skin, parchment. The Eng. word ' parchment ' is a form of *pergamena*, an adjective signifying ' of Pergamum,' the city in Asia Minor where parchment was either invented or brought into use. The word *membrana* is found in 2 Tim. 4 : 13, where Timothy is asked to bring to the Apostle " the books, especially the parchments." The writing material was prepared from the skin of the sheep or goat. The skins were first soaked in lime for the purpose of removing the hair, and then shaved, washed, dried, stretched and ground or smoothed with fine chalk or lime and pumice-stone. The finest kind is called vellum, and is made from the skins of calves or kids.¶

PARENTS

1. GONEUS (γονεύς), a begetter, a father (akin to *ginomai*, to come into being, become), is used in the plural in the N.T., Matt. 10 : 21 ; Mark 13 : 12 ; six times in Luke (in Luke 2 : 43, R.V., " His parents," A.V., " Joseph and His mother ") ; six in John ; elsewhere, Rom. 1 : 30 ; 2 Cor. 12 : 14 (twice) ; Eph. 6 : 1 ; Col. 3 : 20 ; 2 Tim. 3 : 2.¶

2. PROGONOS (πρόγονος), an adjective signifying born before (*pro*, before, and *ginomai*, see No. 1), is used as a noun, in the plural, (a) of ancestors, " forefathers," 2 Tim. 1 : 3 ; (b) of living parents, 1 Tim. 5 : 4. See FOREFATHER.¶

3. PATĒR (πατήρ), a father, is used in Heb. 11 : 23, in the plural, of both father and mother, the " parents " of Moses. See FATHER.

PART (Noun, a portion ; Verb, to give or divide, partake)
A. Nouns.

1. MEROS (μέρος) denotes (a) a part, portion, of the whole, e.g., John 13 : 8 ; Rev. 20 : 6 ; 22 : 19 ; hence, a lot or destiny, e.g., Rev. 21 : 8 ; in Matt. 24 : 51 and Luke 12 : 46, " portion ; " (b) a part as opposite to the whole, e.g., Luke 11 : 36 ; John 19 : 23 ; 21 : 6, " side ; " Acts 5 : 2 ; 23 : 6 ; Eph. 4 : 16 ; Rev. 16 : 19 ; a party, Acts 23 : 9 ; the divisions of a province, e.g., Matt. 2 : 22 ; Acts 2 : 10 ; the regions belonging to a city, e.g., Matt. 15 : 21, R.V., " parts " (A.V., " coasts ") ; 16 : 13 (ditto) ; Mark 8 : 10, A.V. and R.V., " parts ; " " the lower parts of the earth," Eph. 4 : 9 ; this phrase means the regions beneath the earth (see LOWER, A, No. 1) ; (c) a class, or category (with *en*, in, " in respect of "), Col. 2 : 16 ; " in this respect," 2 Cor. 3 : 10 ; 9 : 3, R.V. (A.V.,

" in this behalf "). See BEHALF, COAST, CRAFT, PIECE, PORTION, RESPECT.

2. MERIS (μερίς) denotes (a) a part or portion, Luke 10 : 42 ; Acts 8 : 21 ; 2 Cor. 6 : 15 (R.V., " portion ") ; in Col. 1 : 12, " partakers," lit., ' unto the part of ; ' (b) a district or division, Acts 16 : 12, R.V., " district " (A.V., " part "). See DISTRICT, PARTAKER.¶

3. KLIMA (κλίμα), primarily an incline, slope (Eng., clime, climate), is used of a region, Rom. 15 : 23, A.V., " parts " (R.V., " regions ") ; 2 Cor. 11 : 10, A.V. and R.V., " regions ; " Gal. 1 : 21 (ditto). See REGION.¶

4. ESCHATOS (ἔσχατος), an adjective signifying last, utmost, extreme, is often used as a noun ; in Acts 13 : 47, R.V., " uttermost part " (A.V., " ends "). See END, LAST, LOWEST, UTTERMOST.

5. TOPOS (τόπος), a place, is translated " parts " in Acts 16 : 3, R.V. (A.V., " quarters "). See PLACE, etc.

6. The plural of the article, followed first by the particle *men*, indeed, and then by *de*, but, is translated " part . . . and part " in Acts 14 : 4.

7. PERAS (πέρας), an end, boundary, is translated " utmost parts " in the A.V. of Matt. 12 : 42 and Luke 11 : 31. See END, A, No. 3.

Notes : (1) *Meros* is used with certain prepositions in adverbial phrases, (a) with *ana*, used distributively, 1 Cor. 14 : 27, " in turn," R.V., A.V., " by course " ; (b) with *kata*, according to, Heb. 9 : 5, R.V., " severally " (A.V., " particularly ") ; (c) with *apo*, from, " in part," Rom. 11 : 25 ; 2 Cor. 1 : 14 ; 2 : 5 (see also MEASURE) ; (d) with *ek*, from, 1 Cor. 13 : 9, 10, 12 ; in 1 Cor. 12 : 27, R.V., " severally," marg., " each in his part " (A.V., " in particular "). (2) In Mark 4 : 38 and Acts 27 : 41, A.V., *prumna*, a stern, is translated " hinder part " (R.V., " stern "). (3) In Acts 1 : 17, A.V., *klēros*, a lot, is translated " part " (R.V., " portion ; " marg., " lot "), of that portion allotted to Judas in the ministry of the Twelve. See INHERITANCE, LOT. (4) In Acts 1 : 25, where the best mss. have *topos*, a place, R.V., " (to take) the place (in this ministry)," some texts have *klēros*, which the A.V. translates " part." (5) In Mark 9 : 40, A.V., the preposition *huper*, on behalf of, is translated " on (our) part," R.V., " for (us)." (6) In 1 Pet. 4 : 14, A.V., " on (their) part," " on (your) part," represents the preposition *kata*, according to, followed by the personal pronouns ; the statements are not found in the most authentic mss. (7) In Acts 9 : 32, A.V., the phrase *dia pantōn*, lit., ' through all,' is rendered " throughout all *quarters* " (R.V., " throughout all **parts** "). (8) In 1 Cor. 12 : 23, the R.V. has " *parts* " for " *members* ; " A.V. and R.V. have " *parts* " in the end of the ver. ; see also ver. 24. (9) In 2 Cor. 10 : 16, the R.V. translates the neuter plural of the article " the parts " (A.V., " the *regions* "). (10) For " inward part " see INWARD.

B. Verbs.

1. MERIZŌ (μερίζω), to divide, to distribute (akin to A, No. 1), is translated " divided (A.V., gave) a . . . part " in Heb. 7 : 2, R.V. See DEAL.

2. METECHŌ (μετέχω), to partake of, share in, Heb. 2 : 14 : see PARTAKE.

3. PARAGINOMAI (παραγίνομαι), to be beside, support (*para*, beside, *ginomai*, to become), is rendered " took (my) part " in 2 Tim. 4 : 16 (A.V., " stood with ") ; some mss. have *sunparaginomai*. See COME, No. 13, GO, PRESENT (to be).

Notes : (1) In Rev. 6 : 8, *tetartos*, a fourth, is rendered " the fourth part." (2) See GREATER, HINDER, INWARD, MORE, TENTH, THIRD, UTMOST, UTTERMOST.

PART (Verb, to separate)

1. DIAMERIZŌ (διαμερίζω), to part among, to distribute, is translated by the verb to part (*a*) in the Middle Voice, with reference to the Lord's garments, Matt. 27 : 35, 1st part (in some mss., 2nd part) ; Mark 15 : 24 ; Luke 23 : 34 ; John 19 : 24 ; (*b*) in the Active Voice, of the proceeds of the sale of possessions and goods, Acts 2 : 45 ; (*c*) in the Passive Voice in Acts 2 : 3, of the " parting asunder " (R.V.) of tongues like fire (A.V., " cloven "). See CLOVEN, DIVIDE, No. 7.

2. DIISTĒMI (διΐστημι), to set apart, separate (*dia*, apart, *histēmi*, to cause to stand), is used in the Active Voice in Luke 24 : 51, R.V., " He parted (from them)," A.V., " was parted." See GO, SPACE.

3. APOSPAŌ (ἀποσπάω), to draw off or tear away, is used in the Passive Voice in Luke 22 : 41, R.V., " He was parted " (A.V., " was withdrawn "), lit. ' He was torn away,' indicating the reluctance with which Christ parted from the loving sympathy of the disciples. Moulton and Milligan suggest that the ordinary use of the verb does not encourage this stronger meaning, but since the simpler meaning is not found in the N.T., except in Acts 21 : 1, and since the idea of withdrawal is expressed in Matt. by *anachōreō*, Luke may have used *apospaō* here in the stronger sense. See DRAW, A, No. 6.

4. CHŌRIZŌ (χωρίζω), in Philm. 15, R.V., " parted : " see DEPART, No. 13.

5. APOCHŌRIZŌ (ἀποχωρίζω), to part from, Acts 15 : 39, R.V. : see DEPART, No. 14.

PARTAKE, PARTAKER
A. Nouns.

1. KOINŌNOS (κοινωνός), an adjective, signifying having in common (*koinos*, common), is used as a noun, denoting a companion, partner, partaker, translated " partakers " in Matt. 23 : 30 ; 1 Cor. 10 : 18, A.V. (see COMMUNION, B) ; 2 Cor. 1 : 7 ; Heb. 10 : 33, R.V. (see COMPANION, No. 2) ; 2 Pet. 1 : 4 ; " partaker " in 1 Pet. 5 : 1. See PARTNER.

2. SUNKOINŌNOS (συγκοινωνός) denotes partaking jointly with (*sun*, and No. 1), Rom. 11 : 17, R.V., " (didst become) partaker with them " (A.V., " partakest ") ; 1 Cor. 9 : 23, R.V., " a joint partaker,"

i.e., with the Gospel, as co-operating in its activity; the A.V. misplaces the "with" by attaching it to the superfluous italicised pronoun "*you*"; Phil. 1 : 7, "partakers with (me of grace)," R.V., and A.V. marg. ; not as A.V. text, "partakers (of my grace);" Rev. 1 : 9, "partaker with (you in the tribulation, etc.)," A.V., "companion." See COMPANION.¶

3. METOCHOS (μέτοχος): see FELLOW, No. 3, PARTNER.

4. SUMMETOCHOS (συμμέτοχος), partaking together with (*sun*, with, and No. 3), is used as a noun, a joint-partaker, Eph. 3 : 6, R.V., "fellow-partakers" (A.V., "partakers"); in 5 : 7, R.V. and A.V., "partakers."¶

Notes : (1) For *antilambanō*, to partake of, rendered "partakers" in 1 Tim. 6 : 2, A.V., see B, No. 4. (2) For the phrase "to be partakers," Col. 1 : 12, see PART, A, No. 2.

B. Verbs.

1. KOINŌNEŌ (κοινωνέω), to have a share of, to share with, take part in (akin to A, No. 1), is translated to be partaker of in 1 Tim. 5 : 22 ; Heb. 2 : 14 (1st part), A.V., "are partakers of," R.V., "are sharers in" (for the 2nd part see No. 3); 1 Pet. 4 : 13; 2 John 11, R.V., "partaketh in" (A.V., "is partaker of"); in the Passive Voice in Rom. 15 : 27. See COMMUNICATE, DISTRIBUTE.

2. SUNKOINŌNEŌ (συγκοινωνέω): see FELLOWSHIP, B, No. 2.

3. METECHŌ (μετέχω), to partake of, share in (*meta*, with, *echō*, to have), akin to A, No. 3, is translated "of partaking" in 1 Cor. 9 : 10, R.V. (A.V., "be partaker of"); "partake of" in 9 : 12, R.V. (A.V., "be partakers of"); so in 10 : 17, 21; in ver. 30 "partake"; in Heb. 2 : 14, the A.V. "took part of" is awkward; Christ "partook of" flesh and blood, R.V.; cp. No. 1 in this verse; in Heb. 5 : 13, metaphorically, of receiving elementary spiritual teaching, R.V., "partaketh of (milk)," A.V., "useth;" in Heb. 7 : 13, it is said of Christ (the antitype of Melchizedek) as 'belonging to' (so R.V.) or 'partaking of' (R.V. marg.) another tribe than that of Levi (A.V., "pertaineth to"). See PERTAIN, USE.¶ See PARTNER, Note.

4. ANTILAMBANŌ (ἀντιλαμβάνω), to take hold of, to lay hold of something before one, has the meaning to partake of in 1 Tim. 6 : 2, R.V., "partake of," marg., "lay hold of," A.V., "are . . . partakers of" (*anti*, in return for, *lambanō*, to take or receive); the benefit mentioned as partaken of by the masters would seem to be the improved quality of the service rendered; the benefit of redemption is not in view here. See HELP.

5. METALAMBANŌ (μεταλαμβάνω), to have, or get, a share of, is translated to be partaker (or partakers) of in 2 Tim. 2 : 6 and Heb. 12 : 10. See EAT, HAVE, RECEIVE, TAKE.

6. SUMMERIZŌ (συμμερίζω), primarily, to distribute in shares (*sun*, with, *meros*, a part), in the Middle Voice, to have a share in, is used in 1 Cor. 9 : 13, A.V., "are partakers with (the altar)," R.V., "have their

portion with," i.e., they feed with others on that which, having been sacrificed, has been placed upon an altar ; so the believer feeds upon Christ (who is the altar in Heb. 13 : 10).¶

PARTIAL, PARTIALITY
A. Verb.

DIAKRINŌ (διακρίνω), to separate, distinguish, discern, judge, decide (*dia*, asunder, *krinō*, to judge), also came to mean to be divided in one's mind, to hesitate, doubt, and had this significance in Hellenistic Greek (though not so found in the Sept.). For the A.V., " are ye (not) partial " in Jas. 2 : 4, see DIVIDE, No. 4. " ' This meaning seems to have had its beginning in near proximity to Christianity.' It arises very naturally out of the general sense of making distinctions " (Moulton and Milligan).

B. Noun.

PROSKLISIS (πρόσκλισις) denotes inclination (*pros*, towards, *klinō*, to lean) ; it is used with *kata* in 1 Tim. 5 : 21, lit., 'according to partiality.'¶

C. Adjective.

ADIAKRITOS (ἀδιάκριτος) primarily signifies not to be parted (*a*, negative, and an adjectival form akin to A), hence, without uncertainty, or indecision, Jas. 3 : 17, A.V., " without partiality " (marg. " wrangling "), R.V., " without variance " (marg., " Or, doubtfulness Or, partiality "). See VARIANCE.¶ In the Sept., Prov. 25 : 1.¶

For PARTICULAR and PARTICULARLY see EVERY, No. 3, SEVERALLY

Note : In Acts 21 : 19, for the A.V. " particularly " the R.V. has " one by one," translating the phrase. lit., ' according to each one.'

For PARTING see HIGHWAY

PARTITION

PHRAGMOS (φραγμός), primarily a fencing in (akin to *phrassō*, to fence in, stop, close), is used metaphorically in Eph. 2 : 14, of " the middle wall of partition ; " " the partition " is epexegetic of " the middle wall," i.e., ' the middle wall, namely, the partition ' between Jew and Gentile. J. A. Robinson suggests that Paul had in mind the barrier between the outer and inner courts of the Temple, notices fixed to which warned Gentiles not to proceed further on pain of death (see Josephus, *Antiq.* xv. 11. 5 ; *B. J.* v. 5. 2 ; vi. 2. 4 ; cp. Acts 21 : 29). See HEDGE.

PARTLY

Notes : (1) In the statement " I partly believe it," 1 Cor. 11 : 18, " partly " represents the phrase ' *meros* (part) *ti* (some),' used adverbially, i.e., ' in some part,' ' in some measure.' (2) In Heb. 10 : 33, " partly . . . partly " is a translation of the antithetic phrases ' *touto men*, this indeed,' and '*touto de*, but this,' i.e., ' on the one hand . . . and on the other hand.'

PARTNER

1. KOINŌNOS (κοινωνός), an adjective, signifying having in common (*koinos*), is used as a noun, " partners " in Luke 5 : 10, " partner " in 2 Cor. 8 : 23 ; Philm. 17 (in spiritual life and business). See COMMUNION, B, COMPANION, No. 2, PARTAKER.

2. METOCHOS (μέτοχος), an adjective, signifying having with, sharing, is used as a noun, " partners " in Luke 5 : 7. See FELLOW, PARTAKER.

Note : *Koinōnos* stresses the fact of having something in common, *metochos*, the fact of sharing ; the latter is less thorough in effect than the former.

PASS, COME TO PASS (see Notes below)

1. PARERCHOMAI (παρέρχομαι), from *para*, by, *erchomai*, to come or go, denotes (I), literally, to pass, pass by, (*a*) of persons, Matt. 8 : 28 ; Mark 6 : 48 ; Luke 18 : 37 ; Acts 16 : 8 ; (*b*) of things, Matt. 26 : 39, 42 ; of time, Matt. 14 : 15 ; Mark 14 : 35 ; Acts 27 : 9, A.V., " past " (R.V., " gone by ") ; 1 Pet. 4 : 3 ; (II), metaphorically, (*a*) to pass away, to perish, Matt. 5 : 18 ; 24 : 34, 35 ; Mark 13 : 30, 31 ; Luke 16 : 17 ; 21 : 32, 33 ; 2 Cor. 5 : 17 ; Jas. 1 : 10 ; 2 Pet. 3 : 10 ; (*b*) to pass by, disregard, neglect, pass over, Luke 11 : 42 ; 15 : 29, " transgressed." For the meaning to come forth or come, see Luke 12 : 37 ; 17 : 7, R.V. (Acts 24 : 7 in some mss.). See COME, No. 9.¶

2. DIERCHOMAI (διέρχομαι) denotes to pass through or over, (*a*) of persons, e.g., Matt. 12 : 43, R.V., " passeth (A.V., walketh) through ; " Mark 4 : 35, A.V., " pass (R.V., go) over ; " Luke 19 : 1, 4 ; Heb. 4 : 14, R.V., " passed through " (A.V. " into ") ; Christ passed through the created heavens to the Throne of God ; (*b*) of things, e.g., Matt. 19 : 24, " to go through ; " Luke 2 : 35, " shall pierce through " (metaphorically of a sword). See COME, No. 5.

3. APERCHOMAI (ἀπέρχομαι), to go away, is rendered to pass in Rev. 9 : 12 ; 11 : 14 ; " passed away " in Rev. 21 : 4. See DEPART, No. 4.

4. PROERCHOMAI (προέρχομαι), to go forward, is translated " passed on " in Acts 12 : 10. See GO.

5. ANTIPARERCHOMAI (ἀντιπαρέρχομαι) denotes to pass by opposite to (*anti*, over against, and No. 1), Luke 10 : 31, 32.¶

6. DIABAINŌ (διαβαίνω), to step across, cross over, is translated " to pass " in Luke 16 : 26 (of passing across the fixed gulf : for the A.V. in the 2nd part of the ver., see No. 13) ; in Heb. 11 : 29, " passed through." See COME, No. 18.

7. METABAINŌ (μεταβαίνω), to pass over from one place to another (*meta*, implying change), is translated " we have passed out of " (A.V.,

" from ") in 1 John 3 : 14, R.V., as to the change from death to life. See REMOVE, No. 1.

8. ANASTREPHŌ (ἀναστρέφω), lit., to turn back (ana, back, strephō, to turn), in the Middle Voice, to conduct oneself, behave, live, is translated " pass (the time) " in 1 Pet. 1 : 17. See ABIDE, No. 8.

9. PARAGŌ (παράγω), to pass by, pass away, in Matt. 9 : 9, R.V., " passed by " (A.V., " forth "), is used in the Middle Voice in 1 John 2 : 8, R.V., " is passing away " (A.V., " is past "), of the passing of spiritual darkness through the light of the Gospel, and in ver. 17 of the world. See DEPART, No. 2.

10. PARAPOREUOMAI (παραπορεύομαι), primarily, to go beside, accompany (para, beside, poreuomai, to proceed), denotes to go past, pass by, Matt. 27 : 39; Mark 9 : 30, " passed through " (some mss. have poreuomai); 11 : 20; 15 : 29; in Mark 2 : 23, " going . . . through." See GO.¶

11. DIAPOREUOMAI (διαπορεύομαι), to pass across, journey through, is used in the Middle Voice, translated " pass by " in Luke 18 : 36, A.V., R.V., " going by." See GO.

12. HUPERBALLŌ (ὑπερβάλλω), in Eph. 3 : 19, " passeth : " see EXCEED, A, No. 1.

13. HUPERECHŌ (ὑπερέχω), " passeth " in Phil. 4 : 7 : see BETTER (be), No. 4.

14. DIAPERAŌ (διαπεράω), to pass over, cross over (used in Luke 16 : 26, 2nd part : see No. 6) : see CROSS.

15. DIODEUŌ (διοδεύω), to travel through, or along (dia, through, hodos a way), is translated " they had passed through " in Acts 17 : 1, lit., ' having passed through ; ' in Luke 8 : 1, " He went about," R.V. (A.V., " throughout ").¶

16. CHŌREŌ (χωρέω), used intransitively, signifies to make room, retire, pass; in Matt. 15 : 17, R.V., " passeth (into the belly)," A.V., " goeth." See COME, No. 24.

17. KATARGEŌ (καταργέω) is translated " was passing away " in 2 Cor. 3 : 7 (A.V., " was to be done away "); " passeth away " in 3 : 11, R.V. (A.V., " is done away "). See ABOLISH.

18. PAROICHOMAI (παροίχομαι), to have passed by, to be gone by, is used in Acts 14 : 16, of past generations, A.V., " (in times) past," R.V., " (in the generations) gone by."¶

Notes : (1) Ginomai, to become, take place, is often translated to come to pass ; frequently in the Synoptic Gospels and Acts (note the R.V. of Luke 24 : 21) ; elsewhere in John 13 : 19 ; 14 : 22, R.V., " (what) is come to pass . . .? " A.V., " (how) is it . . .? " ; 14 : 29 (twice) ; 1 Thess. 3 : 4 ; Rev. 1 : 1. (2) In Acts 2 : 17, 21 ; 3 : 23 and Rom. 9 : 26, the A.V. translates the future of eimi, to be, " it shall come to pass " (R.V., " it shall be "). (3) In Acts 5 : 15, A.V., erchomai, to come, is translated " passing by " (R.V., " came by "). (4) For the A.V., " passing " in Acts

27 : 8, see COASTING, C.   (5) In Mark 6 : 35, A.V., " the time is far passed "
(R.V., " the day is . . far spent ") is, lit., ' the hour is much (*polus*).'   (6)
For *huperakmos* in 1 Cor. 7 : 36, R.V., " past the flower of her age," see
FLOWER.

PASSING OVER

PARESIS (πάρεσις), primarily a letting go, dismissal (akin to *pariēmi*,
to let alone, loosen), denotes a passing by or prætermission (of sin), a
suspension of judgment, or withholding of punishment, Rom. 3 : 25,
R.V., " passing over" (A.V., "remission"), with reference to sins committed previously to the propitiatory sacrifice of Christ, the passing by not
being a matter of Divine disregard but of forbearance.¶

PASSION
A. Nouns.

1. PATHĒMA (πάθημα), a suffering or a passive emotion, is translated
" passions " in Rom. 7 : 5, R.V., " (sinful) passions," A.V., " motions,'
and Gal. 5 : 24, R.V. ; see AFFECTION, A, No. 3, AFFLICT, B, No. 3.

2. PATHOS (πάθος) : see AFFECTION, A, No. 1.

B. Verb.

PASCHŌ (πάσχω), to suffer, is used as a noun, in the aorist infinitive
with the article, and translated " passion " in Acts 1 : 3, of the suffering of
Christ at Calvary.   See SUFFER.

C. Adjective.

HOMOIOPATHĒS (ὁμοιοπαθής), of like feelings or affections (*homoios*,
like, and A, No. 2 ; Eng., homœopathy), is rendered "of like passions "in
Acts 14 : 15 (R.V. marg., "nature ") ; in Jas. 5 : 17, R.V., ditto (A.V.,
" subject to like passions ").¶

PASSOVER

PASCHA (πάσχα), the Greek spelling of the Aramaic word for the
Passover, from the Hebrew *pāsach*, to pass over, to spare, a feast instituted
by God in commemoration of the deliverance of Israel from Egypt, and
anticipatory of the expiatory sacrifice of Christ.   The word signifies
(I) the Passover Feast, e.g., Matt. 26 : 2 ; John 2 : 13, 23 ; 6 : 4 ; 11 : 55 ;
12 : 1 ; 13 : 1 ; 18 : 39 ; 19 : 14 ; Acts 12 : 4 ; Heb. 11 : 28 ; (II) by
metonymy, (*a*) the Paschal Supper, Matt. 26 : 18, 19 ; Mark 14 : 16 ;
Luke 22 : 8, 13 ; (*b*) the Paschal lamb, e.g., Mark 14 : 12 (cp. Ex. 12 : 21) ;
Luke 22 : 7 ; (*c*) Christ Himself, 1 Cor. 5 : 7.

PAST
A. Verbs.

1. GINOMAI (γίνομαι), to become, come to pass, is translated " was
past " in Luke 9 : 36, A.V., and R.V. marg. (R.V., " came "), of the voice
of God the Father at the Transfiguration ; " is past," 2 Tim. 2 : 18.

2. DIAGINOMAI (διαγίνομαι), *dia*, through, a stronger form than No. 1, used of time, denotes to intervene, elapse, pass, Mark 16 : 1, " was past ; " Acts 25 : 13, R.V., " were passed ; " 27 : 9, " was spent."¶

3. PROGINOMAI (προγίνομαι), to happen before (*pro*, before, and No. 1), is used in Rom. 3 : 25, A.V., " that are past " (R.V., " done aforetime "), of sins committed in times previous to the atoning sacrifice of Christ (see PASSING OVER).¶

Note : For the past tense of the verb to pass, see PASS, e.g., Nos. 1 and 17.

B. Particle.

POTE (ποτέ), once, formerly, sometime, is translated " in time (or times) past," in Rom. 11 : 30 ; Gal. 1 : 13 ; ver. 23, A.V. (R.V., " once ") ; Eph. 2 : 2, 11 (R.V., " aforetime ") ; ver. 3 (R.V., " once ") ; Philm. 11 (R.V., " aforetime ") ; 1 Pet. 2 : 10.

PASTOR

POIMĒN (ποιμήν), a shepherd, one who tends herds or flocks (not merely one who feeds them), is used metaphorically of Christian " pastors," Eph. 4 : 11. Pastors guide as well as feed the flock ; cp. Acts 20 : 28, which, with ver. 17, indicates that this was the service committed to elders (overseers or bishops) ; so also in 1 Pet. 5 : 1, 2, " tend the flock . . . exercising the oversight," R.V. ; this involves tender care and vigilant superintendence. See SHEPHERD.

PASTURE

NOMĒ (νομή) denotes (*a*) pasture, pasturage, figuratively in John 10 : 9 ; (*b*) grazing, feeding, figuratively in 2 Tim. 2 : 17, of the doctrines of false teachers, lit., ' their word will have feeding as a gangrene.' See EAT.¶

PATH

1. TRIBOS (τρίβος), a beaten track (akin to *tribō*, to rub, wear down), a path, is used in Matt. 3 : 3 ; Mark 1 : 3 ; Luke 3 : 4.¶

2. TROCHIA (τροχία), the track of a wheel (*trochos*, a wheel ; *trechō*, to run), hence, a track, path, is used figuratively in Heb. 12 : 13.¶ In the Sept., Prov. 2 : 15 ; 4 : 11, 26, 27 ; 5 : 6, 21 ; in some texts, Ezek. 27 : 19.¶

PATIENCE, PATIENT, PATIENTLY
A. Nouns.

1. HUPOMONE (ὑπομονή), lit., an abiding under (*hupo*, under, *menō*, to abide), is almost invariably rendered " patience." " Patience, which grows only in trial, Jas. 1 : 3, may be passive, i.e.,= endurance, as, (*a*) in trials, generally, Luke 21 : 19 (which is to be understood by Matt. 24 : 13) ; cp. Rom. 12 : 12 ; Jas. 1 : 12 ; (*b*) in trials incident to service in the gospel, 2 Cor. 6 : 4 ; 12 : 12 ; 2 Tim. 3 : 10 ; (*c*) under chastisement,

which is trial viewed as coming from the hand of God our Father, Heb. 12 : 7 ; (d) under undeserved affliction, 1 Pet. 2 : 20 ; or active, i.e.= persistence, perseverance, as (e) in well doing, Rom. 2 : 7 (A.V., ' patient continuance ') ; (f) in fruit bearing, Luke 8 : 15 ; (g) in running the appointed race, Heb. 12 : 1.

"Patience perfects Christian character, Jas. 1 : 4, and fellowship in the patience of Christ is therefore the condition upon which believers are to be admitted to reign with Him, 2 Tim. 2 : 12 ; Rev. 1 : 9. For this patience believers are ' strengthened with all power,' Col. 1 : 11, ' through His Spirit in the inward man,' Eph. 3 : 16.

"In 2 Thess. 3 : 5, the phrase ' the patience of Christ,' R.V., is possible of three interpretations, (a) the patient waiting for Christ, so A.V. paraphrases the words, (b) that they might be patient in their sufferings as Christ was in His, see Heb. 12 : 2, (c) that since Christ is ' expecting till His enemies be made the footstool of His feet,' Heb. 10 : 13, so they might be patient also in their hopes of His triumph and their deliverance. While a too rigid exegesis is to be avoided, it may, perhaps, be permissible to paraphrase : ' the Lord teach and enable you to love as God loves, and to be patient as Christ is patient.' "*

In Rev. 3 : 10, " the word of My patience " is the word which tells of Christ's patience, and its effects in producing patience on the part of those who are His (see above on 2 Thess. 3 : 5).

2. MAKROTHUMIA (μακροθυμία), long-suffering (see B, No. 2), is rendered " patience " in Heb. 6 : 12 ; Jas. 5 : 10 ; see LONGSUFFERING.

B. Verbs.

1. HUPOMENŌ (ὑπομένω), akin to A, No. 1, (a) used intransitively, means to tarry behind, still abide, Luke 2 : 43 ; Acts 17 : 14 ; (b) transitively, to wait for, Rom. 8 : 24 (in some mss.), to bear patiently, endure, translated " patient " (present participle) in Rom. 12 : 12 ; " ye take it patiently," 1 Pet. 2 : 20 (twice). See also under A, No. 1.

2. MAKROTHUMEŌ (μακροθυμέω), akin to A, No. 2, to be long-tempered, is translated to have patience, or to be patient, in Matt. 18 : 26, 29 ; 1 Thess. 5 : 14, A.V. (R.V., " be longsuffering ") ; Jas. 5 : 7 (1st part, " be patient ; " 2nd part, R.V., " being patient," A.V., " hath long patience ") ; in Heb. 6 : 15, R.V., " having (A.V., after he had) patiently endured." See LONGSUFFERING.

C. Adjectives.

Notes : (1) For epieikēs, translated " patient " in 1 Tim. 3 : 3, A.V., see GENTLE. (2) For anexikakos, translated " patient " in 2 Tim. 2 : 24, A.V., see FORBEAR.¶

D. Adverb.

MAKROTHUMŌS (μακροθύμως), akin to A, No. 2, and B, No. 2, denotes " patiently," Acts 26 : 3.¶

---

* From Notes on Thessalonians by Hogg and Vine, pp. 222, 285.

PATRIARCH

PATRIARCHĒS (πατριάρχης), from *patria*, a family, and *archō*, to rule, is found in Acts 2 : 29 ; 7 : 8, 9 ; Heb. 7 : 4.¶ In the Sept., 1 Chron. 24 : 31 ; 27 : 22 ; 2 Chron. 19 : 8 ; 23 : 20 ; 26 : 12.¶

PATTERN

A. Nouns.

1. TUPOS (τύπος) is translated " pattern " in Tit. 2 : 7, A.V. ; Heb. 8 : 5 (A.V. and R.V.). See ENSAMPLE.

2. HUPOTUPŌSIS (ὑποτύπωσις) is translated " pattern " in 1 Tim. 1 : 16, A.V. ; 2 Tim. 1 : 13, R.V. See ENSAMPLE, FORM.¶

3. HUPODEIGMA (ὑπόδειγμα) is translated " patterns " in Heb. 9 : 23, A.V. See COPY.

B. Adjective.

ANTITUPOS (ἀντίτυπος) is translated " like in pattern " in Heb. 9 : 24, R.V. See FIGURE, No. 2.

PAVEMENT

LITHOSTRŌTOS (λιθόστρωτος), an adjective, denoting paved with stones (*lithos*, a stone, and *strōnnuō*, to spread), especially of tessellated work, is used as a noun in John 19 : 13, of a place near the Prætorium in Jerusalem, called Gabbatha, a Greek transliteration of an Aramaic word.¶ In the Sept., 2 Chron. 7 : 3 ; Esth. 1 : 6 ; S. of Sol. 3 : 10.¶

PAY (Verb), PAYMENT

1. APODIDŌMI (ἀποδίδωμι), to give back, to render what is due, to pay, used of various obligations in this respect, is translated to pay, to make payment, in Matt. 5 : 26 ; 18 : 25 (twice), 26, 28, 29, 30, 34 ; 20 : 8, R.V. (A.V., " give "). See DELIVER.

2. TELEŌ (τελέω), to bring to an end, complete, fulfil, has the meaning to pay in Matt. 17 : 24 and Rom. 13 : 6. See ACCOMPLISH.

Notes : (1) In Matt. 23 : 23, A.V., *apodekatoō*, to tithe, is translated " ye pay tithe " (R.V., " ye tithe "). (2) In Heb. 7 : 9, *dekatoō* (Passive Voice), to pay tithe, is translated " hath paid tithes," R.V. (perfect tense). See TITHE.

PEACE, PEACEABLE, PEACEABLY

A. Noun.

EIRĒNĒ (εἰρήνη) " occurs in each of the books of the N.T., save 1 John and save in Acts 7 : 26 [' (at) one again '] it is translated " peace " in the R.V. It describes (*a*) harmonious relationships between men, Matt. 10 : 34 ; Rom. 14 : 19 ; (*b*) between nations, Luke 14 : 32 ; Acts 12 : 20 ; Rev. 6 : 4 ; (*c*) friendliness, Acts 15 : 33 ; 1 Cor. 16 : 11 ; Heb. 11 : 31 ; (*d*) freedom from molestation, Luke 11 : 21 ; 19 : 42 ; Acts 9 : 31 (R.V., ' peace,' A.V., ' rest ') ; 16 : 36 ; (*e*) order, in the State,

Acts 24 : 2 (R.V., ' peace,' A.V., ' quietness ') ; in the churches, 1 Cor.
14 : 33 ; (f) the harmonised relationships between God and man,
accomplished through the gospel, Acts 10 : 36 ; Eph. 2 : 17 ; (g) the sense
of rest and contentment consequent thereon, Matt. 10 : 13 ; Mark 5 : 34 ;
Luke 1 : 79 ; 2 : 29 ; John 14 : 27 ; Rom. 1 : 7 ; 3 : 17 ; 8 : 6 ; in certain
passages this idea is not distinguishable from the last, Rom. 5 : 1."*

"The God of peace " is a title used in Rom. 15 : 33 ; 16 : 20 ; Phil. 4 : 9 ;
1 Thess. 5 : 23 ; Heb. 13 : 20 ; cp. 1 Cor. 14 : 33 ; 2 Cor. 13 : 11. The
corresponding Heb. word *shalom* primarily signifies wholeness : see its
use in Josh. 8 : 31, " unhewn ; " Ruth 2 : 12, " full ; " Neh. 6 : 15,
" finished ; " Is. 42 : 19, marg., " made perfect." Hence there is a close
connection between the title in 1 Thess. 5 : 23 and the word *holoklēros*,
" entire," in that verse. In the Sept. *shalom* is often rendered by *sōtēria*,
salvation, e.g., Gen. 26 : 31 ; 41 : 16 ; hence the " peace-offering " is
called the " salvation offering." Cp. Luke 7 : 50 ; 8 : 48. In 2 Thess.
3 : 16, the title " the Lord of peace " is best understood as referring to
the Lord Jesus. In Acts 7 : 26, " would have set them at one " is, lit.,
' was reconciling them (conative imperfect tense, expressing an earnest
effort) into peace.'

B. Verbs.

1. EIRĒNEUŌ (εἰρηνεύω), primarily, to bring to peace, reconcile,
denotes in the N.T., to keep peace or to be at peace : in Mark 9 : 50, R.V.,
the Lord bids the disciples " be at peace " with one another, gently
rebuking their ambitious desires ; in Rom. 12 : 18 (R.V.," be at peace,"
A.V.," live peaceably ") the limitation " if it be possible, as much as in
you lieth," seems due to the phrase " with all men," but is not intended
to excuse any evasion of the obligation imposed by the command ; in
2 Cor. 13 : 11 it is rendered " live in peace," a general exhortation to
believers ; in 1 Thess. 5 : 13, " be at peace (among yourselves)."¶

2. EIRĒNOPOIEŌ (εἰρηνοποιέω), to make peace (*eirēnē*, and *poieō*, to
make), is used in Col. 1 : 20.¶ In the Sept., Prov. 10 : 10.¶

C. Adjective.

EIRĒNIKOS (εἰρηνικός), akin to A, denotes peaceful. It is used
(a) of the fruit of righteousness, Heb. 12 : 11, " peaceable " (or ' peaceful ')
because it is produced in communion with God the Father, through His
chastening ; (b) of " the wisdom that is from above," Jas. 3 : 17.¶

Note : In 1 Tim. 2 : 2, A.V., *hēsuchios*, quiet, is translated " peaceable "
(R.V., " quiet ").

PEACE (hold one's)

1. SIGAŌ (σιγάω) signifies (a), used intransitively, to be silent (from
sigē, silence), translated to hold one's peace, in Luke 9 : 36 ; 18 : 39 ;
20 : 26 ; Acts 12 : 17 ; 15 : 13 (in ver. 12, " kept silence ; " similarly

rendered in 1 Cor. 14 : 28, 30, A.V., " hold his peace," 34) ; (b) used transitively, to keep secret ; in the Passive Voice, to be kept secret, Rom. 16 : 25, R.V., " hath been kept in silence." See SECRET, SILENCE.

2. SIŌPAŌ (σιωπάω), to be silent or still, to keep silence (from siōpē, silence), is translated to hold one's peace, in Matt. 20 : 31 ; 26 : 63 ; Mark 3 : 4 ; 9 : 34 ; 10 : 48 ; 14 : 61 ; Luke 19 : 40 ; Acts 18 : 9 ; in the Lord's command to the sea, in Mark 4 : 39, it is translated " peace " (for the next word " be still " see No. 4) ; in Luke 1 : 20, R.V., " thou shalt be silent " (A.V., " dumb "). See DUMB, B.¶

3. HĒSUCHAZŌ (ἡσυχάζω) signifies to be still ; it is used of holding one's peace, being silent, Luke 14 : 4 ; Acts 11 : 18 ; 21 : 14, " we ceased." See CEASE, A, No. 3, QUIET.

4. PHIMOŌ (φιμόω), to muzzle, is used metaphorically in the Passive Voice, in Mark 1 : 25 and Luke 4 : 35, " hold thy peace ; " in Mark 4 : 39, " be still." See MUZZLE.

PEACEMAKER
EIRĒNOPOIOS (εἰρηνοποιός), an adjective signifying peace-making (eirēnē, and poieō, to make), is used in Matt. 5 : 9, " peacemakers." Cp. PEACE, B, No. 2.¶

PEARL
MARGARITĒS (μαργαρίτης), a pearl (Eng., Margaret), occurs in Matt. 7 : 6 (proverbially and figuratively) ; 13 : 45, 46 ; 1 Tim. 2 : 9 ; Rev. 17 : 4 ; 18 : 12, 16 ; 21 : 21 (twice).¶

For PECULIAR see POSSESSION, B, No. 3, and C

PEN
KALAMOS (κάλαμος), a reed, reed-pipe, flute, staff, measuring rod, is used of a writing-reed or pen in 3 John 13. This was used on papyrus. Different instruments were used on different materials ; the kalamos may have been used also on leather. " Metal pens in the form of a reed or quill have been found in the so-called Grave of Aristotle at Eretria." See REED.

PENCE, PENNY, PENNYWORTH
DĒNARION (δηνάριον), a Roman coin, a denarius, a little less than the value of the Greek drachmē (see PIECE), now estimated as amounting to about 9½d. in the time of our Lord, occurs in the singular, e.g., Matt. 20 : 2 ; 22 : 19 ; Mark 12 : 15 ; Rev. 6 : 6 ; in the plural, e.g., Matt. 18 : 28 ; Mark 14 : 5 ; Luke 7 : 41 ; 10 : 35 ; John 12 : 5 ; " pennyworth " in Mark 6 : 37 and John 6 : 7, lit., ' (loaves of two hundred) pence.' Considering the actual value, " shilling " would have been a more accurate translation, as proposed by the American translators, retaining " penny " for the as, and " farthing " for the quadrans.

PENTECOST

PENTĒKOSTOS (πεντηκοστός), an adjective denoting fiftieth, is used as a noun, with " day " understood, i.e., the fiftieth day after the Passover, counting from the second day of the Feast, Acts 2 : 1 ; 20 : 16 ; 1 Cor. 16 : 8.¶ For the Divine instructions to Israel see Ex. 23 : 16 ; 34 : 22 ; Lev. 23 : 15–21 ; Num. 28 : 26–31 ; Deut. 16 : 9–11.

For PENURY (Luke 21 : 4, A.V., R.V., " want ") see LACK

PEOPLE

1. LAOS (λαός) is used of (a) the people at large, especially of people assembled, e.g., Matt. 27 : 25 ; Luke 1 : 21 ; 3 : 15 ; Acts 4 : 27 ; (b) a people of the same race and language, e.g., Rev. 5 : 9 ; in the plural, e.g., Luke 2 : 31 ; Rom. 15 : 11 ; Rev. 7 : 9 ; 11 : 9 ; especially of Israel, e.g., Matt. 2 : 6 ; 4 : 23 ; John 11 : 50 ; Acts 4 : 8 ; Heb. 2 : 17 ; in distinction from their rulers and priests, e.g., Matt. 26 : 5 ; Luke 20 : 19 ; Heb. 5 : 3 ; in distinction from Gentiles, e.g., Acts 26 : 17, 23 ; Rom. 15 : 10 ; (c) of Christians as the people of God, e.g., Acts 15 : 14 ; Tit. 2 : 14 ; Heb. 4 : 9 ; 1 Pet. 2 : 9.

2. OCHLOS (ὄχλος), a crowd, throng : see CROWD, MULTITUDE.

3. DĒMOS (δῆμος), the common people, the people generally (Eng., demagogue, democracy, etc.), especially the mass of the people assembled in a public place, Acts 12 : 22 ; 17 : 5 ; 19 : 30, 33.¶

4. ETHNOS (ἔθνος) denotes (a) a nation, e.g., Matt. 24 : 7 ; Acts 10 : 35 ; the Jewish people, e.g., Luke 7 : 5 ; Acts 10 : 22 ; 28 : 19 ; (b) in the plural, the rest of mankind in distinction from Israel or the Jews, e.g., Matt. 4 : 15 ; Acts 28 : 28 ; (c) the people of a city, Acts 8 : 9 ; (d) Gentile Christians, e.g., Rom. 10 : 19 ; 11 : 13 ; 15 : 27 ; Gal. 2 : 14. See GENTILES, NATION.

5. ANTHRŌPOS (ἄνθρωπος), man, without distinction of sex (cp. anēr, a male), is translated " people " in John 6 : 10, R.V. (A.V., " men ").

PERADVENTURE

A. Adverb.

TACHA (τάχα), primarily quickly (from tachus, quick), signifies " peradventure " in Rom. 5 : 7 ; in Philm. 15, " perhaps." See PERHAPS.¶

B. Conjunction.

MĒPOTE (μήποτε), often written as two words, usually signifies lest ever, lest haply, haply ; in indirect questions, ' if haply ' or ' whether haply,' e.g., Luke 3 : 15, R.V. ; in Matt. 25 : 9, R.V., " peradventure " (A.V., " lest ") ; " if peradventure," in 2 Tim. 2 : 25. See HAPLY.

PERCEIVE

1. GINŌSKŌ (γινώσκω), to know by experience and observation, is translated to perceive in Matt. 12 : 15, R.V. (A.V., " knew ") ; 16 : 8 ;

21 : 45 ; 22 : 18 ; 26 : 10, R.V., (A.V., " understood ") ; Mark 8 : 17 ; 12 : 12 and 15 : 10, R.V. (A.V., " knew ") ; so Luke 9 : 11 ; 18 : 34 ; in Luke 7 : 39, R.V. (A.V., " known ") ; 20 : 19 (cp. No. 7 in ver. 23) ; John 6 : 15 ; 8 : 27, R.V. (A.V., " understood ") ; 16 : 19, R.V. (A.V., " knew ") ; Acts 23 : 6 ; Gal. 2 : 9 ; in 1 John 3 : 16, A.V., " perceive " (R.V., " know," perfect tense, lit., ' we have perceived,' and therefore know). See KNOW.

2. EPIGINŌSKŌ (ἐπιγινώσκω), a strengthened form of No. 1, to gain a full knowledge of, to become fully acquainted with, is translated to perceive in Mark 5 : 30, R.V. (A.V., " knowing ") ; Luke 1 : 22 ; 5 : 22 ; Acts 19 : 34, R.V. (A.V., " knew "). See ACKNOWLEDGE, KNOW.

3. EIDON (εἶδον) (akin to oida, to know), an aorist form used to supply that tense of horaō, to see, is translated to perceive in Matt. 13 : 14 ; Mark 4 : 12 ; Acts 28 : 26 ; in Luke 9 : 47, A.V. (R.V., " saw ") ; in Acts 14 : 9, A.V., " perceiving " (R.V., " seeing "). See BEHOLD, No. 1.

4. THEŌREŌ (θεωρέω), to be a spectator of, look at, discern, is translated to perceive in John 4 : 19 (indicating the woman's earnest contemplation of the Lord) ; so Acts 17 : 22 ; in John 12 : 19, R.V., " behold " (A.V., " perceive ye "). See BEHOLD, No. 6.

5. AISTHANOMAI (αἰσθάνομαι), to perceive, to notice, understand, is used in Luke 9 : 45, R.V., " (that they should not) perceive," A.V., " (that) they perceived . . . (not)."¶

6. NOEŌ (νοέω), to perceive with the mind, to understand, is translated to perceive in Matt. 15 : 17, R.V. (A.V., " understand ") ; so 16 : 9, 11 ; John 12 : 40 ; Rom. 1 : 20 ; Eph. 3 : 4 ; in Mark 7 : 18 and 8 : 17, A.V. and R.V., " perceive." See CONSIDER, No. 4.

7. KATANOEŌ (κατανοέω), a strengthened form of No. 6, to take note of, consider carefully, is translated to perceive in Luke 6 : 41, A.V. (R.V., " considerest ") ; 20 : 23 ; Acts 27 : 39, R.V. (A.V., " discovered "). See BEHOLD, No. 11.

8. KATALAMBANŌ (καταλαμβάνω), to lay hold of, apprehend, comprehend, is translated to perceive in Acts 4 : 13 ; 10 : 34. See APPREHEND, No. 1.

Notes : (1) In Mark 12 : 28 the best mss. have oida, to know (so R.V.), for eidon, to see, perceive (A.V.). (2) In Acts 8 : 23, A.V., horaō, to see, is translated " I perceive " (R.V., " I see "). (3) In 2 Cor. 7 : 8, A.V., blepō, to look at, consider, see, is translated " I perceive " (R.V., " I see "). (4) In Acts 23 : 29, A.V., heuriskō, to find, is translated " perceived " (R.V., " found ").

For PERDITION see DESTRUCTION, No. 1

PERFECT (Adjective and Verb), PERFECTLY
A. Adjectives.

1. TELEIOS (τέλειος) signifies having reached its end (*telos*), finished,

complete, perfect. It is used (I) of persons, (a) primarily of physical development, then, with ethical import, fully grown, mature, I Cor. 2 : 6 ; 14 : 20 (" men ; " marg., " of full age ") ; Eph. 4 : 13 ; Phil. 3 : 15 ; Col. 1 : 28 ; 4 : 12 ; in Heb. 5 : 14, R.V., " fullgrown " (marg., " perfect "), A.V., " of full age " (marg., " perfect ") ; (b) complete, conveying the idea of goodness without necessary reference to maturity or what is expressed under (a), Matt. 5 : 48 ; 19 : 21 ; Jas. 1 : 4 (2nd part) ; 3 : 2. It is used thus of God in Matt. 5 : 48 ; (II) of things, complete, perfect, Rom. 12 : 2 ; 1 Cor. 13 : 10 (referring to the complete revelation of God's will and ways, whether in the completed Scriptures or in the hereafter) ; Jas. 1 : 4 (of the work of patience) ; ver. 25 ; 1 John 4 : 18.¶

2. TELEIOTEROS (τελειότερος), the comparative degree of No. 1, is used in Heb. 9 : 11, of the very presence of God.¶

3. ARTIOS (ἄρτιος) is translated " perfect " in 2 Tim. 3 : 17 : see COMPLETE, B.

B. Verbs.

1. TELEIOŌ (τελειόω), to bring to an end by completing or perfecting, is used (I) of accomplishing (see FINISH, FULFIL) ; (II) of bringing to completeness, (a) of persons : of Christ's assured completion of His earthly course, in the accomplishment of the Father's will, the successive stages culminating in His Death, Luke 13 : 32 ; Heb. 2 : 10, to make Him perfect, legally and officially, for all that He would be to His people on the ground of His sacrifice ; cp. 5 : 9 ; 7 : 28, R.V., " perfected " (A.V., " consecrated ") ; of His saints, John 17 : 23, R.V., " perfected " (A.V., " made perfect ") ; Phil. 3 : 12 ; Heb. 10 : 14 ; 11 : 40 (of resurrection glory) ; 12 : 23 (of the departed saints) ; 1 John 4 : 18 ; of former priests (negatively), Heb. 9 : 9 ; similarly of Israelites under the Aaronic priest-hood, 10 : 1 ; (b) of things, Heb. 7 : 19 (of the ineffectiveness of the Law) ; Jas. 2 : 22 (of faith made perfect by works) ; 1 John 2 : 5, of the love of God operating through him who keeps His word ; 4 : 12,of the love of God in the case of those who love one another ; 4 : 17, of the love of God as " made perfect with " (R.V.) those who abide in God, giving them to be possessed of the very character of God, by reason of which ' as He is, even so are they in this world.'

2. EPITELEŌ (ἐπιτελέω), to bring through to the end (epi, intensive, in the sense of ' fully,' and teleō, to complete), is used in the Middle Voice in Gal. 3 : 3, " are ye (now) perfected," continuous present tense, in-dicating a process, lit., ' are ye now perfecting yourselves ; ' in 2 Cor. 7 : 1, ." perfecting (holiness) ; " in Phil. 1 : 6, R.V., " will perfect (it)," A.V., " will perform." See ACCOMPLISH, No. 4.

3. KATARTIZŌ (καταρτίζω), to render fit, complete (artios), " is used of mending nets, Matt. 4 : 21 ; Mark 1 : 19, and is translated ' restore ' in Gal. 6 : 1. It does not necessarily imply, however, that that to which it is applied has been damaged, though it may do so, as in these passages ; it signifies, rather, right ordering and arrangement,

Heb. 11 : 3, ' framed ; ' it points out the path of progress, as in Matt. 21 : 16 ; Luke 6 : 40 ; cp. 2 Cor. 13 : 9 ; Eph. 4 : 12, where corresponding nouns occur. It indicates the close relationship between character and destiny, Rom. 9 : 22, ' fitted.' It expresses the pastor's desire for the flock, in prayer, Heb. 13 : 21, and in exhortation, 1 Cor. 1 : 10, R.V., ' perfected ' (A.V., ' perfectly joined ') ; 2 Cor. 13 : 11, as well as his conviction of God's purpose for them, 1 Pet. 5 : 10. It is used of the Incarnation of the Word in Heb. 10 : 5, ' prepare,' quoted from Ps. 40 : 6 (Sept.), where it is apparently intended to describe the unique creative act involved in the Virgin Birth, Luke 1 : 35. In 1 Thess. 3 : 10 it means to supply what is necessary, as the succeeding words show."* See FIT, B, No. 3.¶

Note : Cp. *exartizō*, rendered " furnished completely," in 2 Tim. 3 : 17, R.V. ; see ACCOMPLISH, No. 1.

C. Adverbs.

1. AKRIBŌS (ἀκριβῶς), accurately, is translated " perfectly " in 1 Thess. 5 : 2, where it suggests that Paul and his companions were careful ministers of the Word. See ACCURATELY, and see Note (2) below.

2. AKRIBESTERON (ἀκριβέστερον), the comparative degree of No. 1, Acts 18 : 26 ; 23 : 15 : see CAREFULLY, EXACTLY.

3. TELEIŌS (τελείως), perfectly, is so translated in 1 Pet. 1 : 13, R.V. (A.V., " to the end "), of setting one's hope on coming grace. See END.¶

Notes : (1) In Rev. 3 : 2, A.V., *plēroō*, to fulfil, is translated " perfect " (R.V., " fulfilled "). (2) For the adverb *akribōs* in Luke 1 : 3, A.V., see ACCURATELY ; in Acts 24 : 22, A.V., see EXACT. (3) For the noun *akribeia* in Acts 22 : 3, see MANNER.

PERFECTION, PERFECTING (noun), PERFECTNESS
A. Nouns.

1. KATARTISIS (κατάρτισις), a making fit, is used figuratively in an ethical sense in 2 Cor. 13 : 9, R.V., " perfecting " (A.V., " perfection "), implying a process leading to consummation (akin to *katartizō*, see PERFECT, B, No. 3).¶

2. KATARTISMOS (καταρτισμός) denotes, in much the same way as No. 1, a fitting or preparing fully, Eph. 4 : 12.¶

3. TELEIŌSIS (τελείωσις) denotes a fulfilment, completion, perfection, an end accomplished as the effect of a process, Heb. 7 : 11 ; in Luke 1 : 45, R.V., " fulfilment " (A.V., " performance ").¶

4. TELEIOTĒS (τελειότης) denotes much the same as No. 3, but stressing perhaps the actual accomplishment of the end in view, Col. 3 : 14, " perfectness ; " Heb. 6 : 1, " perfection."¶ In the Sept., Judg. 9 : 16, 19 ; Prov. 11 : 3 ; Jer. 2 : 2.¶

---

* From Notes on Thessalonians by Hogg and Vine, p. 101.

B. Verb.

TELESPHOREŌ (τελεσφορέω), to bring to a completion or an end in view (*telos*, an end, *pherō*, to bear), is said of plants, Luke 8 : 14.¶

PERFORM, PERFORMANCE

1. TELEŌ (τελέω), to finish, is translated " performed " in Luke 2 : 39, A.V. : see ACCOMPLISH, No. 3.

2. APOTELEŌ (ἀποτελέω), to bring to an end, accomplish, is translated " I perform " in Luke 13 : 32, R.V. (A.V., " I do ") ; some mss. have No. 3 ; in Jas. 1 : 15, it is used of sin, " fullgrown " R.V. (A.V., " finished "). See FINISH, Note 2.¶

3. EPITELEŌ (ἐπιτελέω), Rom. 15 : 28, A.V., " performed " (R.V., " accomplished ") ; 2 Cor. 8 : 11, A.V., " perform " (R.V., " complete ") ; Phil. 1 : 6, A.V., " perform " (R.V., " perfect ") : see ACCOMPLISH, No. 4.

4. POIEŌ (ποιέω), to do, is translated " to perform " in Rom. 4 : 21 ; in Luke 1 : 72, A.V. (R.V., " to shew "). See SHEW.

5. APODIDŌMI (ἀποδίδωμι), to give back, or in full, is translated " thou . . . shalt perform " in Matt. 5 : 33. See DELIVER. No. 3.

Notes : (1) In Rom. 7 : 18, A.V., *katergazomai*, to work, is translated " to perform " (R.V., " to do ; " marg., " work "). (2) In Luke 1 : 20, A.V., *ginomai*, to come to pass (R.V.), is translated " shall be performed." (3) For " performance " in Luke 1 : 45, see FULFILMENT.

PERHAPS

1. TACHA (τάχα) is translated " perhaps " in Philm. 15. See PERADVENTURE.

2. ARA (ἄρα), a particle, ' then,' sometimes marking a result about which some uncertainty is felt, is translated " perhaps " in Acts 8 : 22.

Note : In 2 Cor. 2 : 7, A.V., *pōs*, anyhow, " by any means " (R.V.), is translated " perhaps."

PERIL, see DANGER, Note : PERILOUS see GRIEVOUS

PERISH

1. APOLLUMI (ἀπόλλυμι), to destroy, signifies, in the Middle Voice, to perish, and is thus used (*a*) of things, e.g., Matt. 5 : 29, 30 ; Luke 5 : 37 ; Acts 27 : 34, R.V., " perish " (in some texts *piptō*, to fall, as A.V.) ; Heb. 1 : 11 ; 2 Pet. 3 : 6 ; Rev. 18 : 14 (2nd part), R.V., " perished " (in some texts *aperchomai*, to depart, as A.V.) ; (*b*) of persons, e.g., Matt. 8 : 25 ; John 3 : (15), 16 ; 10 : 28 ; 17 : 12, R.V., " perished " (A.V., " is lost ") ; Rom. 2 : 12 ; 1 Cor. 1 : 18, lit., ' the perishing,' where the perfective force of the verb implies the completion of the process of destruction (Moulton, *Proleg.*, p. 114) ; 8 : 11 ; 15 : 18 ; 2 Pet. 3 : 9 ; Jude 11. For the meaning of the word see DESTROY, No. 1.

2. SUNAPOLLUMI (συναπόλλυμι), in the Middle Voice, denotes to perish together (sun, with, and No. 1), Heb. 11 : 31.¶

3. APOTHNĒSKŌ (ἀποθνήσκω), to die; in Matt. 8 : 32 "perished." See DIE, No. 2.

4. APHANIZŌ (ἀφανίζω), to make unseen (a, negative, phainō, to cause to appear), in the Passive Voice, is translated "perish" in Acts 13 : 41 (R.V., marg., "vanish away"). See DISFIGURE.

5. DIAPHTHEIRŌ (διαφθείρω), to corrupt, is rendered "perish" in 2 Cor. 4 : 16, A.V. (R.V., "is decaying"). See CORRUPT, No. 3, DECAY.

Notes: (1) In Acts 8 : 20, "(thy money) perish" is a translation of a phrase, lit, 'be unto destruction,' apōleia ; see DESTRUCTION, B, (II), No. 1. (2) In Col. 2 : 22, "to perish" is a translation of the phrase eis pthoran, lit., 'unto corruption ;' see CORRUPT, B, No. 1. (3) For "shall utterly perish," in 2 Pet. 2 : 12, A.V., see CORRUPT, B, No. 1 (b).

For PERJURED PERSON see FORSWEAR

PERMISSION

SUNGNŌMĒ (συγγνώμη), lit., a joint opinion, mind or understanding (sun, with, gnōmē, an opinion), a fellow-feeling, hence, a concession, allowance, is translated "permission," in contrast to "commandment," in 1 Cor. 7 : 6.¶

PERMIT

EPITREPŌ (ἐπιτρέπω), lit., to turn to (epi, to, trepō, to turn), to entrust, signifies to permit, Acts 26 : 1 ; 1 Cor. 14 : 34 ; 1 Cor. 16 : 7 ; 1 Tim. 2 : 12, R.V. "permit" (A.V., "suffer") ; Heb. 6 : 3. See LEAVE.

For PERNICIOUS, 2 Pet. 2 : 2, A.V., see LASCIVIOUS

PERPLEX, PERPLEXITY
A. Verbs.

1. APOREŌ (ἀπορέω) is rendered "perplexed" in 2 Cor. 4 : 8, and in the most authentic mss. in Luke 24 : 4 ; see DOUBT, A, No. 1.

2. DIAPOREŌ (διαπορέω), "was much perplexed" in Luke 9 : 7 ; see DOUBT, A, No. 2.

B. Noun.

APORIA (ἀπορία), akin to A, No. 1, is translated "perplexity" in Luke 21 : 25 (lit., 'at a loss for a way,' a, negative, poros, a way, resource), of the distress of nations, finding no solution to their embarrassments ; papyri illustrations are in the sense of being at one's wit's end, at a loss how to proceed, without resources.¶

PERSECUTE, PERSECUTION
A. Verbs.

1. DIŌKŌ (διώκω) has the meanings (a) to put to flight, **drive** away,

(b) to pursue, whence the meaning to persecute, Matt. 5 : 10–12, 44 ; 10 : 23 ; 23 : 34 ; Luke 11 : 49 (No. 2 in some mss.) ; 21 : 12 ; John 5 : 16 ; 15 : 20 (twice) ; Acts 7 : 52 ; 9 : 4, 5, and similar passages ; Rom. 12 : 14 ; 1 Cor. 4 : 12 ; 15 : 9 ; 2 Cor. 4 : 9, A.V. (R.V., " pursued ") ; Gal. 1 : 13, 23 ; 4 : 29 ; Gal. 5 : 11, R.V., " am . . . persecuted " (A.V., " suffer persecution ") ; so 6 : 12 ; Phil. 3 : 6 ; 2 Tim. 3 : 12, " shall suffer persecution ; " Rev. 12 : 13. See FOLLOW, PURSUE.

2. EKDIŌKŌ (ἐκδιώκω), ek, out, and No. 1, is used in 1 Thess. 2 : 15, A.V., " persecuted " (R.V., " drave out "). See also No. 1. See DRIVE, No. 2.¶

B. Noun.

DIŌGMOS (διωγμός), akin to A, No. 1, occurs in Matt. 13 : 21 ; Mark 4 : 17 ; 10 : 30 ; Acts 8 : 1 ; 13 : 50 ; Rom. 8 : 35 ; 2 Cor. 12 : 10 ; 2 Thess. 1 : 4 ; 2 Tim. 3 : 11, twice (for ver. 12, see A, No. 1).¶ In the Sept., Prov. 11 : 19 ; Lam. 3 : 19.¶

Note : In Acts 11 : 19, A.V., *thlipsis*, " tribulation " (R.V.), is translated " persecution."

PERSECUTOR

DIŌKTĒS (διώκτης), akin to *diōkō* (see above), occurs in 1 Tim. 1 : 13.¶

PERSEVERANCE

PROSKARTERĒSIS (προσκαρτέρησις) occurs in Eph. 6 : 18. Cp. the verb (and the formation) under ATTEND, No. 2.¶

PERSON

1. PROSŌPON (πρόσωπον), for the meaning of which see APPEARANCE, No. 2, is translated " person " or " persons " in Matt. 22 : 16 ; Mark 12 : 14 ; Luke 20 : 21 ; 2 Cor. 1 : 11 ; 2 Cor. 2 : 10 ; Gal. 2 : 6 ; Jude 16, lit., ' (admiring, or shewing respect of, R.V.) persons.'

2. ANTHRŌPOS (ἄνθρωπος), a generic name for man, is translated " persons " in Rev. 11 : 13, R.V. (A.V., " men ").

Notes : (1) In Heb. 1 : 3, A.V., *hupostasis*, substance, is translated " person ; " see SUBSTANCE. (2) In Matt. 27 : 24, R.V., *toutou*, " of this . . . (man)," is translated " of this . . . person " (A.V.). (3) In Philm. 12, the pronoun *autos*, he, placed in a position of strong emphasis, is translated " in his own person," R.V., stressing the fact that in spite of the Apostle's inclination to retain Onesimus, he has sent him, as being, so to speak, ' his very heart,' instead of adopting some other method. (4) In 1 Cor. 5 : 13, A.V., the adjective *ponēros*, wicked, used as a noun, is translated " wicked person " (R.V., ". . . man "). (5) In 2 Pet. 2 : 5, A.V., *ogdoos*, " eighth," is translated " the (lit., an) eighth *person* " (R.V., " with seven others "). (6) Various adjectives are used with the word " persons," e.g., devout, perjured, profane.

PERSONS (respect of)
A. Nouns.

1. PROSŌPOLĒMPTĒS (προσωπολήμπτης) denotes a respecter of persons (prosōpon, a face or person, lambanō, to lay hold of), Acts 10 : 34.¶

2. PROSŌPOLĒMPSIA (in inferior texts without the letter m) (προσωπολημψία) denotes respect of persons, partiality (akin to No. 1), the fault of one who, when responsible to give judgment, has respect to the position, rank, popularity, or circumstances of men, instead of their intrinsic conditions, preferring the rich and powerful to those who are not so, Rom. 2 : 11 ; Eph. 6 : 9 ; Col. 3 : 25 ; Jas. 2 : 1.¶

B. Verb.

PROSŌPOLĒMPTEŌ (προσωπολημπτέω), to have respect of persons (see above), occurs in Jas. 2 : 9.¶

C. Adverb.

APROSŌPOLĒMPTŌS (ἀπροσωπολήμπτως), without respect of persons, impartially (a, negative), occurs in 1 Pet. 1 : 17.¶

PERSUADE

1. PEITHŌ (πείθω) in the Active Voice, signifies to apply persuasion, to prevail upon or win over, to persuade, bringing about a change of mind by the influence of reason or moral considerations, e.g., in Matt. 27 : 20 ; 28 : 14 ; Acts 13 : 43 ; 19 : 8 ; in the Passive Voice, to be persuaded, believe (see BELIEVE, No. 2, and OBEY), e.g., Luke 16 : 31 ; 20 : 6 ; Acts 17 : 4, R.V. (A.V., " believed ") ; 21 : 14 ; 26 : 26 ; Rom. 8 : 38 ; 14 : 14 ; 15 : 14 ; 2 Tim. 1 : 5, 12 ; Heb. 6 : 9 ; 11 : 13, in some mss. ; 13 : 18, R.V. (A.V., " trust "). See ASSURANCE, B, No. 3.

Note : For Acts 26 : 28, A.V., " thou persuadest," see FAIN, Note.

2. ANAPEITHŌ (ἀναπείθω), to persuade, induce, in an evil sense (ana, back, and No. 1), is used in Acts 18 : 13.¶ In the Sept., Jer. 29 : 8.¶

Note : For *plērophoreō*, rendered " being fully persuaded," in Rom. 4 : 21 and 14 : 5, A.V., see ASSURANCE, B, No. 2.

PERSUASIVE, PERSUASIVENESS
A. Adjective.

PEITHOS (πειθός), an adjective (akin to *peithō*), not found elsewhere, is translated " persuasive " in 1 Cor. 2 : 4, R.V. (A.V., " enticing ") ; see ENTICE, B.¶

B. Noun.

PITHANOLOGIA (πιθανολογία), persuasiveness of speech, is used in Col. 2 : 4, R.V. See ENTICE, B, Note.¶

PERSUASION

PEISMONĒ (πεισμονή), akin to *peithō*, is used in Gal. 5 : 8, where the meaning is ' this influence that has won you over, or that seems likely to do so ; ' the use of *peithō*, in the sense of to obey, in ver. 7, suggests a play upon words here.¶

PERTAIN TO

METECHŌ (μετέχω), Heb. 7 : 13, A.V. ; see BELONG, Note (*c*), PARTAKE, B, No. 3.

Notes : (1) In Rom. 15 : 17, the phrase *ta pros*, lit., ' the (things) towards ' is translated " things pertaining to," R.V. (A.V., " those things which pertain to ") ; in Heb. 2 : 17 and 5 : 1, R.V. and A.V., " things pertaining to." (2) In Acts 1 : 3, A.V., the phrase *ta peri*, " the (things) concerning " (R.V.), is translated " the things pertaining to." (3) In Rom. 9 : 4, the R.V. rightly translates the relative pronoun *hōn*, lit., ' of whom ' (from *hos*, who), by " whose is " (A.V., " to whom *pertaineth* "). (4) In Rom. 4 : 1, A.V., *kata*, " according to " (R.V.), is translated " as pertaining to." (5) For 1 Cor. 6 : 3, 4, see LIFE, B, No. 1.

PERVERSE, PERVERT

1. APOSTREPHŌ (ἀποστρέφω), to turn away (*apo*, from, *strephō*, to turn), is used metaphorically in the sense of perverting in Luke 23 : 14 (cp. No. 2 in ver. 2). See BRING, No. 22.

2. DIASTREPHŌ (διαστρέφω), to distort, twist (*dia*, through, and *strephō*), is translated to pervert in Luke 23 : 2 (cp. No. 1 in ver. 14) ; Acts 13 : 10 [in ver. 8, " to turn aside " (A.V., " away ")] ; in the perfect participle, Passive Voice, it is translated " perverse," lit., ' turned aside,' ' corrupted,' in Matt. 17 : 17 ; Luke 9 : 41 ; Acts 20 : 30 ; Phil. 2 : 15.¶

3. METASTREPHŌ (μεταστρέφω), to transform into something of an opposite character (*meta*, signifying a change, and *strephō*,) as the Judaizers sought to " pervert the gospel of Christ," Gal. 1 : 7 ; cp. " the sun shall be turned into darkness," Acts 2 : 20 ; laughter into mourning and joy to heaviness, Jas. 4 : 9. See TURN.¶

4. EKSTREPHŌ (ἐκστρέφω), to turn inside out (*ek*, out), to change entirely, is used metaphorically in Tit. 3 : 11, R.V., " is perverted " (A.V., " is subverted "). See SUBVERT.¶

Note : For " perverse disputings," 1 Tim. 6 : 5, A.V., see DISPUTE, A, No. 3.

PESTILENCE, PESTILENT FELLOW

LOIMOS (λοιμός), a pestilence, any deadly infectious malady, is used in the plural in Luke 21 : 11 (in some mss., Matt. 24 : 7) ; in Acts 24 : 5, metaphorically, " a pestilent fellow." See FELLOW.¶

PETITION

AITĒMA (αἴτημα), from *aiteō*, to ask, is rendered " petitions " in 1 John 5 : 15 : see ASK, B, and cp. the distinction between A, Nos. 1 and 2.¶ Cp. *deēsis* (see PRAYER).

PHARISEES

PHARISAIOS (φαρισαῖος), from an Aramaic word *peras* (found in Dan. 5 : 28), signifying to separate, owing to a different manner of life from that of the general public. The Pharisees and Sadducees appear as distinct parties in the latter half of the 2nd cent. B.C., though they represent tendencies traceable much earlier in Jewish history, tendencies which became pronounced after the return from Babylon (537 B.C.). The immediate progenitors of the two parties were, respectively, the Hasidæans and the Hellenizers ; the latter, the antedecents of the Sadducees, aimed at removing Judaism from its narrowness and sharing in the advantages of Greek life and culture. The Hasidæans, a transcription of the Hebrew *chasidim*, i.e., pious ones, were a society of men zealous for religion, who acted under the guidance of the scribes, in opposition to the godless Hellenizing party ; they scrupled to oppose the legitimate High Priest even when he was on the Greek side. Thus the Hellenizers were a political sect, while the Hasidæans, whose fundamental principle was complete separation from non-Jewish elements, were the strictly legal party among the Jews, and were ultimately the more popular and influential party. In their zeal for the Law they almost deified it and their attitude became merely external, formal, and mechanical. They laid stress, not upon the righteousness of an action, but upon its formal correctness. Consequently their opposition to Christ was inevitable ; His manner of life and teaching was essentially a condemnation of theirs ; hence His denunciation of them, e.g., Matt. 6 : 2, 5, 16 ; 15 : 7 and chapter 23.

While the Jews continued to be divided into these two parties, the spread of the testimony of the Gospel must have produced what in the public eye seemed to be a new sect, and in the extensive development which took place at Antioch, Acts 11 : 19–26, the name " Christians " seems to have become a popular term applied to the disciples as a sect, the primary cause, however, being their witness to Christ (see CALL, A, No. 11). The opposition of both Pharisees and Sadducees (still mutually antagonistic, Acts 23 : 6–10) against the new " sect " continued unabated during apostolic times.

PHILOSOPHER

PHILOSOPHOS (φιλόσοφος), lit., loving wisdom (*philos*, loving, *sophia*, wisdom), occurs in Acts 17 : 18.¶

PHILOSOPHY

PHILOSOPHIA (φιλοσοφία) denotes the love and pursuit of wisdom, hence, philosophy, the investigation of truth and nature ; in Col. 2 : 8, the so-called philosophy of false teachers. " Though essentially Greek as a name and as an idea, it had found its way into Jewish circles . . . Josephus speaks of the three Jewish sects as three ' philosophies ' . . .

It is worth observing that this word, which to the Greeks denoted the highest effort of the intellect, occurs here alone in Paul's writings . . . the Gospel had deposed the term as inadequate to the higher standard whether of knowledge or of practice, which it had introduced " (Lightfoot).¶

PHYLACTERY

PHULAKTĒRION (φυλακτήριον), primarily an outpost, or fortification (phulax, a guard), then, any kind of safeguard, became used especially to denote an amulet. In the N.T. it denotes a prayer-fillet, a phylactery, a small strip of parchment, with portions of the Law written on it ; it was fastened by a leathern strap either to the forehead or to the left arm over against the heart, to remind the wearer of the duty of keeping the commandments of God in the head and in the heart ; cp. Ex. 13 : 16 ; Deut. 6 : 8 ; 11 : 18. It was supposed to have potency as a charm against evils and demons. The Pharisees broadened their phylacteries to render conspicuous their superior eagerness to be mindful of God's Law, Matt. 23 : 5.¶

PHYSICIAN

IATROS (ἰατρός), akin to iaomai, to heal, a physician, occurs in Matt. 9 : 12 ; Mark 2 : 17 ; 5 : 26 ; Luke 4 : 23 ; 5 : 31 (in some mss., 8 : 43) ; Col. 4 : 14.¶

PIECE

1. EPIBLĒMA (ἐπίβλημα) primarily denotes that which is thrown over, a cover (epi, over, ballō, to throw) ; then, that which is put on, or sewed on, to cover a rent, a patch, Matt. 9 : 16 ; Mark 2 : 21 ; in the next sentence, R.V., " that which should fill " (A.V., " the new piece that filled "), there is no word representing " piece " (lit., ' the filling,' plērōma) ; see FILL, B ; Luke 5 : 36.¶

2. DRACHMĒ (δραχμή), a drachma, firstly, an Attic weight, as much as one can hold in the hand (connected with drassomai, to grasp with the hand, lay hold of, 1 Cor. 3 : 19), then, a coin, nearly equal to the Roman denarius (see PENNY), is translated " pieces of silver " in Luke 15 : 8, 1st part ; " piece," 2nd part and ver. 9.¶

3. MEROS (μέρος), a part, is translated " a piece (of a broiled fish) " in Luke 24 : 42. See BEHALF, PART.

4. KLASMA (κλάσμα), a broken piece (from klaō, to break), is used of the broken pieces from the feeding of the multitudes, R.V., " broken pieces," A.V., " fragments," Matt. 14 : 20 ; Mark 6 : 43 ; 8 : 19, 20 ; Luke 9 : 17 ; John 6 : 12, 13 ; in Matt. 15 : 37 and Mark 8 : 8, R.V., " broken pieces " (A.V., " broken meat ").¶

5. ARGURION (ἀργύριον), which frequently denotes " money," also represents a silver coin, of the value of a shekel or tetradrachmon (four

times the *drachmē*, see No. 2) ; it is used in the plural in Matt. 26 : 15 ; 27 : 3-9. In Acts 19 : 19, " fifty thousand pieces of silver," is, lit., ' fifty thousand of silver ' (probably drachmas). See MONEY, SILVER.

Notes : (1) In Acts 27 : 44, for A.V., " *broken pieces,*" the R.V. translates *epi* (on) *tinōn* (certain things) *tōn* (the, i.e., those namely) by " on *other* things ; " there is no word in the original representing " pieces." (2) For the phrase to break to (in) pieces, Matt. 21 : 44, R.V., and Mark 5 : 4, see BREAK, A, Nos. 10 and 5 respectively. (3) In Luke 14 : 18, A.V., *agros*, a field (R.V.), is translated " a piece of ground." (4) In Matt. 17 : 27, A.V., *statēr*, a shekel (R.V.), a *tetradrachmon* (see No. 5, above), is translated " a piece of money."

PIERCE

1. DIIKNEOMAI (διικνέομαι), to go through, penetrate (*dia*, through, *ikneomai*, to go), is used of the power of the Word of God, in Heb. 4 : 12, " piercing."¶ In the Sept., Ex. 26 : 28.¶

2. DIERCHOMAI (διέρχομαι), to go through, is translated " shall pierce through " in Luke 2 : 35. See COME, No. 5.

3. EKKENTEŌ (ἐκκεντέω), primarily, to prick out (*ek*, out, *kenteō*, to prick), signifies to pierce, John 19 : 37 ; Rev. 1 : 7.¶

4. NUSSŌ (νύσσω), to pierce or pierce through, often of inflicting severe or deadly wounds, is used of the piercing of the side of Christ, John 19 : 34 (in some mss., Matt. 27 : 49).¶

5. PERIPEIRŌ (περιπείρω), to put on a spit, hence, to pierce, is used metaphorically in 1 Tim. 6 : 10, of torturing one's soul with many sorrows, " have pierced (themselves) through."¶

PIETY (to shew)

EUSEBEŌ (εὐσεβέω), to reverence, to show piety towards any to whom dutiful regard is due (akin to *eusebēs*, pious, godly, devout), is used in 1 Tim. 5 : 4 of the obligation on the part of children and grandchildren (R.V.) to express in a practical way their dutifulness " towards their own family ; " in Acts 17 : 23 of worshipping God. See WORSHIP.¶

For PIGEON see DOVE, No. 1

PILGRIM

PAREPIDĒMOS (παρεπίδημος), an adjective signifying ' sojourning in a strange place, away from one's own people ' (*para*, from, expressing a contrary condition, and *epidēmeō*, to sojourn ; *dēmos*, a people), is used of O.T. saints, Heb. 11 : 13, " pilgrims " (coupled with *xenos*, a foreigner) ; of Christians, 1 Pet. 1 : 1, " sojourners (of the Dispersion)," R.V.; 2 : 11, " pilgrims " (coupled with *paroikos*, an alien, sojourner) ; the word is thus used metaphorically of those to whom Heaven is their own country, and who are sojourners on earth.¶

PILLAR

STULOS (στῦλος), a column supporting the weight of a building, is used (a) metaphorically, of those who bear responsibility in the churches, as of the elders in the church at Jerusalem, Gal. 2 : 9 ; of a local church as to its responsibility, in a collective capacity, to maintain the doctrines of the faith by teaching and practice, 1 Tim. 3 : 15 ; some would attach this and the next words to the statement in ver. 16 ; the connection in the Eng. Versions seems preferable ; (b) figuratively in Rev. 3 : 12, indicating a firm and permanent position in the spiritual, heavenly and eternal Temple of God ; (c) illustratively, of the feet of the angel in the vision in Rev. 10 : 1, seen as flames rising like columns of fire. indicative of holiness and consuming power, and thus reflecting the glory of Christ as depicted in 1 : 15 ; cp. Ezek. 1 : 7.¶

PILLOW

PROSKEPHALAION (προσκεφάλαιον) denotes a pillow, a cushion for the head (pros, to, kephalē, a head), Mark 4 : 38 (R.V., "cushion").¶ In the Sept., Ezek. 13 : 18.¶

PINE AWAY

XĒRAINŌ (ξηραίνω), to dry up, wither, is rendered " pineth away " in Mark 9 : 18. See DRY.

PINNACLE

PTERUGION (πτερύγιον) denotes (a) a little wing (diminutive of pterux, a wing) ; (b) anything like a wing, a turret, battlement, of the temple in Jerusalem, Matt. 4 : 5 and Luke 4 : 9 (of the hieron, the entire precincts, or parts of the main building, as distinct from the naos, the sanctuary). This " wing " has been regarded (1) as the apex of the sanctuary, (2) the top of Solomon's porch, (3) the top of the Royal Portico, which Josephus describes as of tremendous height (Antiq. xv. 11.5).¶ It is used in the Sept. of the fins of fishes, e.g., Lev. 11 : 9–12 ; of the part of a dress, hanging down in the form of a wing, Ruth 3 : 9 ; 1 Sam. 24 : 5.

PIPE (Noun and Verb)
A. Noun.

AULOS (αὐλός), a wind instrument, e.g., a flute (connected with aēmi, to blow), occurs in 1 Cor. 14 : 7.¶
B. Verb.

AULEŌ (αὐλέω), to play on an aulos, is used in Matt. 11 : 17 ; Luke 7 : 32 ; 1 Cor. 14 : 7 (2nd part).¶

For PIPERS, Rev. 18 : 22, A.V., see FLUTE-PLAYERS

PIT

1. PHREAR (φρέαρ), a well, dug for water (distinct from pēgē, a

fountain), denotes a pit in Rev. 9 : 1, 2, R.V., " the pit (of the abyss)," " the pit," i.e., the shaft leading down to the abyss, A.V., " (bottomless) pit ; " in Luke 14 : 5, R.V., " well " (A.V., " pit ") ; in John 4 : 11, 12, " well." See WELL.¶

2. BOTHUNOS (βόθυνος) is rendered " pit " in Matt. 12 : 11 : see DITCH.

3. ABUSSOS (ἄβυσσος) : see BOTTOMLESS, B.

4. HUPOLĒNION (ὑπολήνιον) denotes a vessel or trough beneath a winepress, to receive the juice, Mark 12 : 1, R.V., " a pit for the wine-press " (A.V., " a place for . . . the wine-fat ").¶

Note : For " pits," 2 Pet. 2 : 4, R.V., see CHAIN *Note* (1).

PITCH (Verb)

PĒGNUMI (πήγνυμι), to make fast, to fix (cp. *prospēgnumi*, Acts 2 : 23, of crucifixion), is used of pitching a tent ; in Heb. 8 : 2, of the " true tabernacle," the Heavenly and spiritual, which " the Lord pitched."¶

PITCHER

KERAMION (κεράμιον), an earthen vessel (*keramos*, potter's clay), a jar or jug, occurs in Mark 14 : 13 ; Luke 22 : 10.¶

PITIABLE (most)

ELEEINOTEROS (ἐλεεινότερος), the comparative degree of *eleeinos*, miserable, pitiable (*eleos*, pity), is used in 1 Cor. 15 : 19, " most pitiable " (R.V.), lit., ' more pitiable than all men.' See MISERABLE.¶

PITIFUL, PITY

1. POLUSPLANCHNOS (πολύσπλαγχνος) denotes very pitiful or full of pity (*polus*, much, *splanchnon*, the heart ; in the plural, the affections), occurs in Jas. 5 : 11, R.V., " full of pity."¶

2. EUSPLANCHNOS (εὔσπλαγχνος), compassionate, tenderhearted, lit., ' of good heartedness ' (*eu*, well, and *splanchnon*), is translated " pitiful " in 1 Pet. 3 : 8, A.V., R.V., " tenderhearted," as in Eph. 4 : 32.¶

PLACE (Noun, Verb, Adverb)

A. Nouns.

1. TOPOS (τόπος), Eng., topic, topography etc., is used of a region or locality, frequently in the Gospels and Acts ; in Luke 2 : 7 and 14 : 22, " room ; " of a place which a person or thing occupies, a couch at table, e.g., Luke 14 : 9, 10, R.V., " place " (A.V., " room ") ; of the destiny of Judas Iscariot, Acts 1 : 25 ; of the condition of the " unlearned " or non-gifted in a church gathering, 1 Cor. 14 : 16, R.V., " place ; " the sheath of a sword, Matt. 26 : 52 ; a place in a book, Luke 4 : 17 ; see also Rev. 2 : 5 ; 6 : 14 ; 12 : 8 ; metaphorically, of condition, occasion, opportunity Acts 25 : 16, R.V., " opportunity " (A.V., " licence ") ; Rom. 12 : 19 ; Eph. 4 : 27. See OPPORTUNITY, ROOM.

2. CHŌRION (χωρίον), a region (a diminutive of *chōra*, a land, country), is used of Gethsemane, Matt. 26 : 36; Mark 14 : 32. See FIELD.

3. HUPEROCHĒ (ὑπεροχή), "high place," 1 Tim. 2 : 2 : see AUTHORITY, No. 3.

4. PERIOCHĒ (περιοχή), primarily a circumference, compass (*peri*, around, *echō*, to have), hence denotes a portion circumscribed, that which is contained, and in reference to a writing or book, a portion or passage of its contents, Acts 8 : 32, " (the) place."¶

5. AKROATĒRION (ἀκροατήριον) denotes a place of audience (*akroaomai*, to listen), Acts 25 : 23, " place of hearing."¶

6. PRŌTOKLISIA (πρωτοκλισία) : see CHIEF, B, No. 7.

Notes : (1) For *opē*, a hole, Jas. 3 : 11, A.V., " place," see OPENING : see also CAVE. (2) For " place of toll," Matt. 9 : 9 ; Mark 2 : 14, see CUSTOM (TOLL), No. 2. (3) In Heb. 4 : 5 " in this place " is, lit., ' in this,' i.e., ' in this (passage).' (4) In Luke 6 : 17, R.V., *topos*, with *pedinos*, level, is translated " level place " (A.V., " plain "). (5) For *amphodon*, rendered " a place where two ways met," Mark 11 : 4 (R.V., " the open street "), see STREET.¶ (6) For *erēmia*, a desert place, see DESERT, A. (7) In 1 Cor. 11 : 20 and 14 : 23, A.V., the phrase *epi to auto*, lit., ' to the same,' is translated " into one place," R.V., " together ; " perhaps = ' in assembly.' (8) For " secret place," Luke 11 : 33, A.V., see CELLAR. (9) For " place of prayer," Acts 16 : 13, R.V., see PRAYER. (10) For Phil. 1 : 13 (A.V., " in all other places "), R.V., " to all the rest," see PALACE. (11) For " rocky places," Mark 4 : 16, see ROCKY.

B. Verbs.

1. ANACHŌREŌ (ἀναχωρέω), to withdraw (*ana*, back, *chōreō*, to make room, retire), is translated " give place " in Matt. 9 : 24. See DEPART, No. 10.

2. EIKŌ (εἴκω), to yield, give way, is rendered " gave place " in Gal. 2 : 5.¶

3. GINOMAI (γίνομαι), to become, take place, is translated " (a death) having taken place " in Heb. 9 : 15, R.V., A.V., " by means of (death)," referring, not to the circumstances of a testamentary disposition, but to the sacrifice of Christ as the basis of the new covenant.

Note : For *chōreō* in John 8 : 37, A.V., " hath . . . place," see COURSE, B.

C. Adverbs, etc.

1. HŌDE (ὧδε), here, hither, is translated " to (unto, R.V.) this place " in Luke 23 : 5. See HERE.

2. PANTACHOU (πανταχοῦ), everywhere, is translated " in all places " in Acts 24 : 3. See EVERYWHERE, No. 2.

Notes : (1) For " in divers places," Matt. 24 : 7, etc., see DIVERS, B, Note. (2) In the following the R.V. gives the correct meaning : in Mark 6 : 10, *ekeithen*, " thence " (A.V., " from that place ") ; in Heb.

2 : 6 and 4 : 4, *pou*, " somewhere " (A.V., " in a certain place ") ; in Matt. 12 : 6, *hōde*, " here " (A.V., " in this place ") ; in Mark 6 : 10, *hopou ean*, " wheresoever " (A.V., " in what place soever "). (3) The adjective *entopios*, " of that place," occurs in Acts 21 : 12.¶ (4) In Jas. 2 : 3 *kalōs*, well (A.V., marg.), is rendered " in a good place." See DWELLING, HEAVENLY, HOLY, MARKET, SKULL, STEEP, YONDER.

PLAGUE

1. MASTIX (μάστιξ), a whip, scourge, Acts 22 : 24, " by scourging ; " Heb. 11 : 36, " scourgings," is used metaphorically of disease or suffering, Mark 3 : 10 ; 5 : 29, 34 ; Luke 7 : 21. See SCOURGING.¶

2. PLĒGĒ (πληγή), a stripe, wound (akin to *plēssō*, to smite), is used metaphorically of a calamity, a plague, Rev. 9 : 20 ; 11 : 6 ; 15 : 1, 6, 8 ; 16 : 9, 21 (twice) ; 18 : 4, 8 ; 21 : 9 ; 22 : 18. See STRIPE, WOUND.

For PLAIN (Noun) see PLACE, A, Note (4)

PLAIN (Adverb), PLAINLY, PLAINNESS

1. ORTHŌS (ὀρθῶς), rightly (from *orthos*, straight), is translated " plain," in Mark 7 : 35, of restored speech. See RIGHTLY.

2. PARRHĒSIA (παρρησία), boldness, is used adverbially in its dative case and rendered " plainly " in John 10 : 24 ; 11 : 14 ; 16 : 25 ; 16 : 29 (with *en*, lit., ' in plainness'). See BOLD, B, where see also " plainness of speech," 2 Cor. 3 : 12, R.V.

PLAIT

PLEKŌ (πλέκω), to weave, twist, plait, is used of the crown of thorns inflicted on Christ, Matt. 27 : 29 ; Mark 15 : 17 ; John 19 : 2.¶

For PLAITING (of the hair) see BRAIDED, Note (1)

For PLANK see BOARD

PLANT (Noun, Verb, Adjective)

A. Noun.

PHUTEIA (φυτεία), firstly, a planting, then that which is planted, a plant (from *phuō*, to bring forth, spring up, grow, *phuton*, a plant), occurs in Matt. 15 : 13.¶ In the Sept., 2 Kings 19 : 29 ; Ezek. 17 : 7 ; Mic. 1 : 6.¶

B. Verb.

PHUTEUŌ (φυτεύω), to plant, is used (*a*) literally, Matt. 21 : 33 ; Mark 12 : 1 ; Luke 13 : 6 ; 17 : 6, 28 ; 20 : 9 ; 1 Cor. 9 : 7 ; (*b*) metaphorically, Matt. 15 : 13 ; 1 Cor. 3 : 6, 7, 8.¶

C. Adjective.

SUMPHUTOS (σύμφυτος), firstly, congenital, innate (from *sumphuō*, to make to grow together), then, planted or grown along with, united with, Rom. 6 : 5, A.V., " planted together," R.V., " united with *Him*," indicating the union of the believer with Christ in experiencing spiritually " the likeness of His death." See UNITED.¶ Cp. *emphutos*, Jas. 1 : 21, R.V., " implanted " (marg., " inborn "). See ENGRAFTED.

PLATTER

1. PAROPSIS (παροψίς), firstly, a side-dish of dainties (*para*, beside, *opson*, cooked) ; then, the dish itself, Matt. 23 : 25 ; ver. 26, in some mss.¶
2. PINAX (πίναξ) is translated platter in Luke 11 : 39 ; see CHARGER.

PLAY

PAIZŌ (παίζω), properly, to play as a child (*pais*), hence denotes to play as in dancing and making merry, 1 Cor. 10 : 7.¶ Cp. *empaizō*, to mock.

PLEAD

ENTUNCHANŌ (ἐντυγχάνω), to make petition, is used of the pleading of Elijah against Israel, Rom. 11 : 2, R.V., " pleadeth with " (A.V., " maketh intercession to "). See DEAL WITH, INTERCESSIONS.

PLEASE, PLEASING (Noun), WELL-PLEASING, PLEASURE
A. Verbs.

1. ARESKŌ (ἀρέσκω) signifies (*a*) to be pleasing to, be acceptable to, Matt. 14 : 6 ; Mark 6 : 22 ; Acts 6 : 5 ; Rom. 8 : 8 ; 15 : 2 ; 1 Cor. 7 : 32-34 ; Gal. 1 : 10 ; 1 Thess. 2 : 15 ; 4 : 1 (where the preceding *kai*, " and," is epexegetical, 'even,' explaining the 'walking,' i.e., Christian manner of life, as ' pleasing God ; ' in Gen. 5 : 22, where the Hebrew has " Enoch walked with God," the Sept. has " Enoch pleased God ; " cp. Mic. 6 : 8 ; Heb. 11 : 5) ; 2 Tim. 2 : 4 ; (*b*) to endeavour to please, and so, to render service, doing so evilly in one's own interests, Rom. 15 : 1, which Christ did not, ver. 3 ; or unselfishly, 1 Cor. 10 : 33 ; 1 Thess. 2 : 4. This sense of the word is illustrated by Moulton and Milligan (Vocab.) from numerous Inscriptions, especially describing " those who have proved themselves of use to the commonwealth."¶

2. EUARESTEŌ (εὐαρεστέω) signifies to be well-pleasing (*eu*, well, and a form akin to No. 1) ; in the Active Voice, Heb. 11 : 5, R.V., " he had been well-pleasing (unto God)," A.V., " he pleased ; " so ver. 6 ; in the Passive Voice, Heb. 13 : 16.¶

3. EUDOKEŌ (εὐδοκέω) signifies (*a*) to be well pleased, to think it good [*eu*, well, and *dokeō*, see Note (1) below], not merely an understanding of what is right and good as in *dokeō*, but stressing the willingness and freedom of an intention or resolve regarding what is good, e.g., Luke 12 : 32, " it is (your Father's) good pleasure ; " so Rom. 15 : 26, 27, R.V. ; 1 Cor. 1 : 21 ; Gal. 1 : 15 ; Col. 1 : 19 ; 1 Thess. 2 : 8, R.V., " we

were well pleased " (A.V., " we were willing ") ; this meaning is frequently found in the papyri in legal documents ; (*b*) to be well pleased with, or take pleasure in, e.g., Matt. 3 : 17 ; 12 : 18 ; 17 : 5 ; 1 Cor. 10 : 5 ; 2 Cor. 12 : 10 ; 2 Thess. 2 : 12 ; Heb. 10 : 6, 8, 38 ; 2 Pet. 1 : 17.

4. THELŌ (θέλω), to will, wish, desire, is translated " it pleased (Him) " in 1 Cor. 12 : 18 ; 15 : 38, R.V.   See DESIRE, B, No. 6.

5. SPATALAŌ (σπαταλάω), to live riotously, is translated " giveth herself to pleasure " in 1 Tim. 5 : 6, R.V. (A.V., " liveth in pleasure ") ; " taken your pleasure " in Jas. 5 : 5, A.V., " been wanton."¶

Notes : (1) In Acts 15 : 22, A.V., *dokeō*, to seem good to (R.V.), is translated " it pleased " (in some mss., ver. 34) ; in Heb. 12 : 10, A.V., " (after their own) pleasure," R.V.," (as) seemed good (to them)."   (2) For *suneudokeō*, rendered " have pleasure in " in Rom. 1 : 32, A.V., see CONSENT, No. 6.   (3) For *truphaō*, rendered " lived in pleasure " in Jas. 5 : 5, A.V., see DELICATELY.

B. Adjectives.

1. ARESTOS (ἀρεστός) denotes pleasing, agreeable, John 8 : 29, R.V., " (the things that are) pleasing," A.V., " (those things that) please ; " A.V. and R.V. in 1 John 3 : 22 ; in Acts 6 : 2, " fit " (R.V. marg., " pleasing ") ; 12 : 3, " it pleased," lit., ' it was pleasing.'   See FIT.¶

2. EUARESTOS (εὐάρεστος), *eu*, well, and No. 1, is translated " well-pleasing " in the R.V. except in Rom. 12 : 1, 2 (see marg., however). See ACCEPT, B, No. 4.

C. Noun.

ARESKEIA (or -*ia*) (ἀρεσκεία), a " pleasing," a giving pleasure, Col. 1 : 10, of the purpose Godward of a walk worthy of the Lord (cp. 1 Thess. 4 : 1).   It was used frequently in a bad sense in classical writers.   Moulton and Milligan illustrate from the papyri its use in a favourable sense, and Deissmann (*Bible Studies*) from an inscription.¶   In the Sept., Prov. 31 : 30.¶

PLEASURE
A. Nouns.

1. HĒDONĒ (ἡδονή), pleasure, is used of the gratification of the natural desire or sinful desires (akin to *hēdomai*, to be glad, and *hēdeōs*, gladly), Luke 8 : 14 ; Tit. 3 : 3 ; Jas. 4 : 1, 3, R.V., " pleasures " (A.V., " lusts ") ; in the singular, 2 Pet. 2 : 13.   See LUST.¶

2. EUDOKIA (εὐδοκία), good pleasure (akin to *eudokeō*, PLEASE, No. 3), Eph. 1 : 5, 9; Phil. 2 : 13; 2 Thess. 1 : 11.   See DESIRE, A. No. 2.

3. APOLAUSIS (ἀπόλαυσις), enjoyment, is used with *echō*, to have, and rendered " enjoy the pleasures " (lit., ' pleasure ') in Heb. 11 : 25. See ENJOY.

Notes : (1) In Rev. 4 : 11, A.V., *thelēma*, a will, is translated " (for Thy) pleasure," R.V., " (because of Thy) will."   (2) For *charis*, translated " pleasure " in the A.V. of Acts 24 : 27 and 25 : 9, see FAVOUR, A.

B. Adjective.

PHILĒDONOS (φιλήδονος), loving pleasure (philos, loving, and A, No. 1), occurs in 2 Tim. 3 : 4, R.V., "lovers of pleasure" (A.V., ". . . pleasures"). See LOVER.¶

Note : In 1 Tim. 5 : 6 the R.V. renders *spatalaō* " giveth herself to pleasure."

PLENTEOUS

POLUS (πολύς), much, is rendered " plenteous " in Matt. 9 : 37, of a harvest of souls, and Luke 10 : 2, R.V. (A.V., " great "). See GREAT.

PLENTIFULLY

Note : This translates the prefix *eu* (well) of the verb *euphoreō*, to produce well, in Luke 12 : 16, " brought forth plentifully."¶

PLOT

EPIBOULĒ (ἐπιβουλή), lit., a plan against (*epi*, against, *boulē*, a counsel, plan), is translated " plot " in the R.V. (A.V., " laying await " and " lying in wait ") in Acts 9 : 24 ; 20 : 3, 19 ; 23 : 30.¶

PLOUGH, PLOW
A. Noun.

AROTRON (ἄροτρον), from *aroō*, to plough, occurs in Luke 9 : 62.¶
B. Verb.

AROTRIAŌ (ἀροτριάω), akin to A, a later form of *aroō*, to plough, occurs in Luke 17 : 7 and 1 Cor. 9 : 10.¶

PLUCK (out)

1. TILLŌ (τίλλω) is used of plucking off ears of corn, Matt. 12 : 1 ; Mark 2 : 23 ; Luke 6 : 1.¶   In the Sept., Isa. 18 : 7.¶

2. HARPAZŌ (ἁρπάζω), to seize, snatch, is rendered " pluck " in John 10 : 28, 29, A.V., R.V., " snatch." For the meaning, see CATCH, No. 1.

3. EXAIREŌ (ἐξαιρέω), to take out (*ex* for *ek*, out, *haireō*, to take), is translated " pluck out," of the eye as the occasion of sin, in Matt. 5 : 29 ; 18 : 9, indicating that, with determination and promptitude, we are to strike at the root of unholy inclinations, ridding ourselves of whatever would stimulate them. Cp. Note (2) below. See DELIVER, No. 8.

4. EXORUSSŌ (ἐξορύσσω), to dig out or up, is rendered " ye would have plucked out (your eyes) " in Gal. 4 : 15, an indication of their feelings of gratitude to, and love for, the Apostle. The metaphor affords no real ground for the supposition of a reference to some weakness of his sight, and certainly not to the result of his temporary blindness at his conversion, the recovery from which must have been as complete as the infliction. There would be some reason for such an inference had the pronoun " ye " been stressed ; but the stress is on the word " eyes ; "

their devotion prompted a readiness to part with their most treasured possession on his behalf. For Mark 2 : 4 see BREAK, No. 14, DIG, No. 1, Note (2).¶ In the Sept., 1 Sam. 11 : 2 ; Prov. 29 : 22.¶

5. EKRIZOŌ (ἐκριζόω), to pluck up by the roots (ek, out, rhiza, a root), is so translated in Jude 12 (figuratively), and in the A.V. in Luke 17 : 6, R.V., " rooted up ; " " root up," Matt. 13 : 29 ; " shall be rooted up," 15 : 13. See ROOT.¶

Notes : (1) In Mark 5 : 4, A.V., *diaspaō*, to rend asunder (R.V.), is translated " plucked asunder," said of chains. (2) In Mark 9 : 47, A.V., *ekballō*, to cast out (R.V.), is translated " pluck . . . out." Cp. No. 3, above.

POET

POIĒTĒS (ποιητής), primarily a maker, later a doer (*poieō* to make, to do), was used, in classical Greek, of an author, especially a poet ; so Acts 17 : 28. See DOER.

POINT, POINTS
A. Phrases.

Notes : (1) In Heb. 4 : 15, " in all points " represents the phrase *kata* with the neuter plural of *pas*, all, lit., ' according to all (things).' (2) ' To be at the point of death ' is a translation (a) of the verb *mellō*, to be about, with *teleutaō*, to end one's life, die, Luke 7 : 2 ; see DIE, No. 4 ; (b) of *mellō* with *apothnēskō*, to die, John 4 : 47 ; (c) of the phrase mentioned under DEATH, C, Note. (3) In Jas. 2 : 10, *en heni* (the dative case of *heis*, one), lit., ' in one,' is rendered " in one *point*."

B. Noun.

KEPHALAION (κεφάλαιον), the neuter of the adjective *kephalaios*, of the head, is used as a noun, signifying (a) a sum, amount, of money, Acts 22 : 28 ; (b) a chief point, Heb. 8 : 1, not the summing up of the subject, as the A.V. suggests, for the subject was far from being finished in the Epistle ; on the contrary, in all that was being set forth by the writer " the chief point " consisted in the fact that believers have " a High Priest " of the character already described. See SUM.¶

C. Verb.

DĒLOŌ (δηλόω), to make plain (*dēlos*, evident), is translated " did point unto " in 1 Pet. 1 : 11, R.V. (A.V., " did signify "), of the operation of " the Spirit of Christ " in the prophets of the Old Testament in pointing on to the time and its characteristics, of the sufferings of Christ and subsequent glories. See SHEW, SIGNIFY.

POISON

IOS (ἰός) denotes something active as (a) rust, as acting on metals, affecting their nature, Jas. 5 : 3 ; (b) poison, as of asps, acting destructively on living tissues, figuratively of the evil use of the lips as the organs of speech, Rom. 3 : 13 ; so of the tongue, Jas. 3 : 8.¶

For POLLUTE see DEFILE, A, No. 1

POLLUTION

ALISGĒMA (ἀλίσγημα), akin to a late verb *alisgeō*, to pollute, denotes a pollution, contamination, Acts 15 : 20, " pollutions of idols," i.e., all the contaminating associations connected with idolatry including meats from sacrifices offered to idols.¶

Note : For *miasma*, A.V., " pollutions," in 2 Pet. 2 : 20, see DEFILE-MENT, B, No. 1.¶

POMP

PHANTASIA (φαντασία), as a philosophic term, denoted an imagination ; then, an appearance, like *phantasma*, an apparition ; later, a show, display, pomp (Eng., phantasy), Acts 25 : 23.¶ In the Sept., Hab. 2 : 18 ; 3 : 10 ; Zech. 10 : 1.¶

PONDER

SUMBALLŌ (συμβάλλω), to throw together, confer, etc., has the meaning to ponder, i.e., to put one thing with another in considering circumstances, in Luke 2 : 19. See CONFER.

POOL

KOLUMBĒTHRA (κολυμβήθρα) denotes a swimming pool (akin to *kolumbaō*, to swim, Acts 27 : 43), John 5 : 2 (ver. 4 in some mss.), 7 ; 9 : 7 (ver. 11 in some mss.).¶

POOR
A. Adjectives.

1. PTŌCHOS (πτωχός), for which see BEG, B, has the broad sense of " poor," (*a*) literally, e.g., Matt. 11 : 5 ; 26 : 9, 11 ; Luke 21 : 3 (with stress on the word, ' a conspicuously poor widow ') ; John 12 : 5, 6, 8 ; 13 : 29 ; Jas. 2 : 2, 3, 6 ; the poor are constantly the subjects of injunctions to assist them, Matt. 19 : 21 ; Mark 10 : 21 ; Luke 14 : 13, 21 ; 18 : 22 ; Rom. 15 : 26 ; Gal. 2 : 10 ; (*b*) metaphorically, Matt. 5 : 3 ; Luke 6 : 20 ; Rev. 3 : 17.

2. PENICHROS (πενιχρός), akin to B, needy, poor, is used of the widow in Luke 21 : 2 (cp. No. 1, of the same woman, in ver. 3) ; it is used frequently in the papyri.¶ In the Sept., Ex. 22 : 25 ; Prov. 28 : 15 ; 29 : 7.¶

B. Noun.

PENĒS (πένης), a labourer (akin to *penomai*, to work for one's daily bread), is translated " poor " in 2 Cor. 9 : 9.¶

C. Verb.

PTŌCHEUŌ (πτωχεύω), to be poor as a beggar (akin to A, No. 1), to be destitute, is said of Christ in 2 Cor. 8 : 9.¶

PORCH

1. STOA (στοά), a portico, is used (a) of the porches at the pool of Bethesda, John 5 : 2 ; (b) of the covered colonnade in the Temple, called Solomon's porch, ·John 10 : 23 ; Acts 3 : 11 ; 5 : 12, a portico on the eastern side of the temple ; this and the other porches existent in the time of Christ were almost certainly due to Herod's restoration. Cp. *Stoics* (Acts 17 : 18), ' philosophers of the porch.'¶

2. PULŌN (πυλών), akin to *pulē*, a gate (Eng., pylon), is used of a doorway, porch or vestibule of a house or palace, Matt. 26 : 71. In the parallel passage Mark 14 : 68, No. 3 is used, and *pulōn* doubtless stands in Matt. 26 for *proaulion*. See GATE, No. 2.

3. PROAULION (προαύλιον), the exterior court or vestibule, between the door and the street, in the houses of well-to-do folk, Mark 14 : 68, " porch " (R.V. marg., " forecourt ").¶

PORTER

THURŌROS (θυρωρός), a door-keeper (*thura*, a door, *ouros*, a guardian), is translated " porter " in Mark 13 : 34 ; John 10 : 3 ; it is used of a female in John 18 : 16, 17, translated " (her) that kept the door."¶ In the Sept., 2 Sam. 4 : 6 ; 2 Kings 7 : 11 ; Ezek. 44 : 11.¶

PORTION
A. Nouns.

1. MEROS (μέρος), a part, is translated " portion " in Matt. 24 : 51 ; Luke 12 : 46 ; 15 : 12. See PART.

2. KLĒROS (κλῆρος), a lot, is translated " portion " in Acts 1 : 17, R.V. See CHARGE, INHERITANCE, LOT.

3. MERIS (μερίς), a part, is translated " portion " in 2 Cor. 6 : 15, R.V. See PART.

Note : For " portion of food," Luke 12 : 42, R.V., see FOOD, No. 4.

B. Verb.

SUMMERIZŌ (συμμερίζω), to have a part with (akin to A, No. 3), is translated " have their portion with " in 1 Cor. 9 : 13, R.V. See PARTAKER.¶

C. Adverb.

POLUMERŌS (πολυμερῶς) signifies ' in many parts ' or portions (*polus*, many, and A, No. 1), Heb. 1 : 1, R.V. (A.V.,"at sundry times ").¶

POSSESS, POSSESSION
A. Verbs.

1. KATECHŌ (κατέχω), to hold fast, hold back, signifies to possess, in 1 Cor. 7 : 30 and 2 Cor. 6 : 10. See HOLD.

2. KTAOMAI (κτάομαι), to procure for oneself, acquire, obtain, hence, to possess (akin to B, No. 1), has this meaning in Luke 18 : 12 and 1 Thess. 4 : 4 ; in Luke 21 : 19, R.V., " ye shall win " (A.V., " possess ye "), where

the probable meaning is 'ye shall gain the mastery over your souls,' i.e., instead of giving way to adverse circumstances. See OBTAIN.

3. HUPARCHŌ (ὑπάρχω), to be in existence, and, in a secondary sense, to belong to, is used with this meaning in the neuter plural of the present participle with the article signifying one's possessions, " the things which he possesseth," Luke 12 : 15 ; Acts 4 : 32 ; in Heb. 10 : 34, R.V., " possessions " (A.V., " goods ") ; cp. B, No. 4. See GOODS.

4. DAIMONIZOMAI (δαιμονίζομαι), to be possessed of a demon or demons : see DEMON, B.

Note : In Acts 8 : 7 and 16 : 16, A.V., *echō*, have, is translated to be possessed of, in the sense of No. 4, above, R.V., " had " and " having."

B. Nouns.

1. KTĒMA (κτῆμα), akin to A, No. 2, denotes a possession, property, Matt. 19 : 22 ; Mark 10 : 22 ; Acts 2 : 45 ; 5 : 1.¶

2. KATASCHESIS (κατάσχεσις), primarily a holding back (akin to A, No. 1), then, a holding fast, denotes a possession, Acts 7 : 5, or taking possession, ver. 45, with the article, lit., ' in the (i.e., their) taking possession.'¶

3. PERIPOIĒSIS (περιποίησις), an obtaining, an acquisition, is translated " (*God's* own) possession " in Eph. 1 : 14, R.V., which may mean ' acquisition,' A.V., " purchased possession ; " 1 Pet. 2 : 9, R.V., " *God's* own possession ", A.V., " a peculiar (people)." See OBTAIN.

4. HUPARXIS (ὕπαρξις), primarily subsistence (akin to A, No. 3), later denoted substance, property, " possession " in Heb. 10 : 34, R.V. (A.V., " substance "). See GOODS, SUBSTANCE.

Note : In Acts 28 : 7, A.V., *chōria*, lands (R.V.), is translated " possessions."

C. Adjective.

PERIOUSIOS (περιούσιος), of one's own possession, one's own, qualifies the noun *laos*, people, in Tit. 2 : 14, A.V., " peculiar," see R.V.¶ In the Sept., Ex. 19 : 5 ; 23 . 22 ; Deut. 7 : 6 ; 14 : 2 ; 26 : 18.¶

POSSESSOR

KTĒTŌR (κτήτωρ), a possessor, an owner (akin to *ktaomai*, see POSSESS, No. 2), occurs in Acts 4 : 34.¶

POSSIBLE
A. Adjective.

DUNATOS (δυνατός), strong, mighty, powerful, able (to do), in its neuter form signifies " possible," Matt. 19 : 26 ; 24 : 24 ; 26 : 39 ; Mark 9 : 23 ; 10 : 27 ; 13 : 22 ; 14 : 35, 36 ; Luke 18 : 27 ; Acts 2 : 24 ; 20 : 16 (27 : 39, in some mss. ; *dunamai*, to be able, in the most authentic, R.V., " they could ") ; Rom. 12 : 18 ; Gal. 4 : 15. See ABLE.

B. Verb.

EIMI (εἰμί), to be, is used in the third person singular, impersonally, with the meaning " it is possible," negatively in 1 Cor. 11 : 20, R.V. (A.V., " it is not "), and Heb. 9 : 5, " we cannot," lit., ' it is not possible.'

Note: For Heb. 10 : 4, A.V., " it is not possible," see IMPOSSIBLE.

POT

1. XESTES (ξέστης) was a Sicilian corruption of the Latin liquid measure *sextarius*, about a pint ; in Mark 7 : 4 (ver. 8 also in some mss.) it denotes a pitcher, of wood or stone.¶

2. STAMNOS (στάμνος), primarily an earthen jar for racking off wine, hence, any kind of jar, occurs in Heb. 9 : 4.¶

For POTENTATE, used of God, 1 Tim. 6 : 15, see AUTHORITY, No. 4

POTTER
A. Noun.

KERAMEUS (κεραμεύς), a potter (from *kerannumi*, to mix, akin to *keramos*, potter's clay), is used (*a*) in connection with the " potter's field," Matt. 27 : 7, 10 ; (*b*) illustratively of the potter's right over the clay, Rom. 9 : 21, where the introductory " or " suggests the alternatives that either there must be a recognition of the absolute discretion and power of God, or a denial that the potter has power over the clay. There is no suggestion of the creation of sinful beings, or of the creation of any simply in order to punish them. What the passage sets forth is God's right to deal with sinful beings according to His own counsel.¶

B. Adjective.

KERAMIKOS (κεραμικός) denotes ' of (or made by) a potter ' (Eng., ceramic), earthen, Rev. 2 : 27.¶

POUND

1. LITRA (λίτρα) was a Sicilian coin, the equivalent of a Latin *libra* or *as* (whence the metric unit, litre) ; in the N.T. it is used as a measure of weight, a pound, John 12 : 3 ; 19 : 39.¶

2. MNA (μνᾶ), a Semitic word, both a weight and a sum of money, 100 shekels (cp. 1 Kings 10 : 17, *maneh*; Dan. 5 : 25, 26, *mene*), in Attic Greek 100 *drachmai*, in weight about 15 oz., in value near about £4 1s. 3d. (see PIECE), occurs in Luke 19 : 13, 16 (twice), 18 (twice), 20, 24 (twice), 25.¶

POUR

1. BALLO (βάλλω), to throw, is used of pouring liquids, Matt. 26 : 12, R.V., marg., " cast " (of ointment) ; John 13 : 5 (of water). See CAST, No. 1.

2. KATACHEO (καταχέω), to pour down upon (*kata*, down, *cheo*, to pour), is used in Matt. 26 : 7 (cp. No. 1 in ver. 12) and Mark 14 : 3, of ointment.¶

3. EKCHEŌ (ἐκχέω), to pour out (*ek*, out), is used (*a*) of Christ's act as to the changers' money, John 2 : 15 ; (*b*) of the Holy Spirit, Acts 2 : 17, 18, 33, R.V., "He hath poured forth" (A.V., " . . . shed forth ") ; Tit. 3 : 6, R.V., "poured out" (A.V., "shed ")) ; (*c*) of the emptying of the contents of the bowls (A.V., vials) of Divine wrath, Rev. 16 : 1–4, 8, 10, 12, 17 ; (*d*) of the shedding of the blood of saints by the foes of God, Rev. 16 : 6, R.V., "poured out" (A.V., "shed ")) ; some mss. have it in Acts 22 : 20. See RUN, SHED, SPILL.

4. EKCHUNŌ (ἐκχύνω) or *ekchunnō*, a Hellenistic form of No. 3, is used of the blood of Christ, Luke 22 : 20, R.V., "is poured out" (A.V., "is shed ")) ; of the Holy Spirit, Acts 10 : 45. See GUSH OUT, RUN, SHED, SPILL.

5. EPICHEŌ (ἐπιχέω), to pour upon (*epi*), is used in Luke 10 : 34, of the oil and wine used by the good Samaritan on the wounds of him who had fallen among robbers.¶

Note : For the A.V., "poured out" in Rev. 14 : 10 (R.V., "prepared"), see MINGLE, No. 2.

POVERTY

PTŌCHEIA (πτωχεία), destitution (akin to *ptōcheuō*, see POOR), is used of the poverty which Christ voluntarily experienced on our behalf, 2 Cor. 8 : 9 ; of the destitute condition of saints in Judæa, ver. 2 ; of the condition of the church in Smyrna, Rev. 2 : 9, where the word is used in a general sense. Cp. synonymous words under POOR.¶

For POWDER see GRIND

POWER (Noun, and Verb, to have, bring under)
A. Nouns.

1. DUNAMIS (δύναμις), for the different meanings of which see ABILITY, MIGHT, is sometimes used, by metonymy, of persons and things, e.g., (*a*) of God, Matt. 26 : 64 ; Mark 14 : 62 ; (*b*) of angels, e.g., perhaps in Eph. 1 : 21, R.V., "power," A.V., "might" (cp. Rom. 8 : 38 ; 1 Pet. 3 : 22) ; (*c*) of that which manifests God's power : Christ, 1 Cor. 1 : 24 ; the Gospel, Rom. 1 : 16 ; (*d*) of mighty works (R.V., marg., "power" or "powers"), e.g., Mark 6 : 5, "mighty work;" so 9 : 39, R.V. (A.V., "miracle ")) ; Acts 2 : 22 (ditto) ; 8 : 13, "miracles ;" 2 Cor. 12 : 12, R.V., "mighty works" (A.V., "mighty deeds ").

Note : For different meanings of synonymous terms, see Note under DOMINION, A, No. 1.

2. EXOUSIA (ἐξουσία) denotes freedom of action, right to act ; used of God, it is absolute, unrestricted, e.g., Luke 12 : 5 (R.V. marg., "authority ")) ; in Acts 1 : 7 'right of disposal' is what is indicated ; used of men, authority is delegated. Angelic beings are called "powers" in Eph. 3 : 10 (cp. 1 : 21) ; 6 : 12 ; Col. 1 : 16 ; 2 : 15 (cp. 2 : 10). See AUTHORITY, No. 1, see also PRINCIPALITY.

3. ISCHUS (ἰσχύς), ability, force, strength, is nowhere translated "power" in the R.V. (A.V. in 2 Thess. 1 : 9). See ABILITY, No. 2.

4. KRATOS (κράτος) is translated "power" in the R.V. and A.V. in 1 Tim. 6 : 16 ; Heb. 2 : 14 ; in Eph. 1 : 19 (last part) ; 6 : 10, A.V., "power" (R.V., "strength") : see DOMINION, A, No. 1, STRENGTH, A, No. 3.

5 DUNATON (δυνατόν), the neuter of the adjective *dunatos*, powerful (akin to No. 1), is used as a noun with the article in Rom. 9 : 22, " (to make His) power (known)." See ABLE.

6. ARCHĒ (ἀρχή), a beginning, rule, is translated "power" in Luke 20 : 20, A.V. (R.V., "rule"). See BEGINNING, B.

B. Verb.

EXOUSIAZŌ (ἐξουσιάζω), to exercise authority (akin to A, No. 2), is used (*a*) in the Active Voice, Luke 22 : 25, R.V., "have authority" (A.V., "exercise authority"), of the power of rulers ; 1 Cor. 7 : 4 (twice), of marital relations and conditions ; (*b*) in the Passive Voice, 1 Cor. 6 : 12, to be brought under the power of a thing ; here, this verb and the preceding one connected with it, *exesti*, present a paronomasia, which Lightfoot brings out as follows : ' All are within my power ; but I will not put myself under the power of any one of all things.' See AUTHORITY, B, No. 1.¶

Notes : (1) In Rev. 13 : 14, 15, A.V., *didōmi*, to give, is translated "(he) had power ;" R.V., "it was given (him)" and "it was given *unto him* ;" the A.V. misses the force of the permissive will of God in the actings of the Beast. (2) In Rom. 16 : 25, A.V., *dunamai*, to be able, is translated "that is of power" (R.V., "that is able"). See ABLE. (3) The subject of power in Scripture may be viewed under the following heads : (*a*) its original source, in the Persons in the Godhead ; (*b*) its exercise by God in creation, its preservation and its government ; (*c*) special manifestations of Divine power, past, present and future ; (*d*) power existent in created beings, other than man, and in inanimate nature ; (*e*) committed to man, and misused by him ; (*f*) committed to those who, on becoming believers, were empowered by the Spirit of God, are indwelt by Him, and will exercise it hereafter for God's glory.

POWERFUL, POWERFULLY
A. Adjectives.

1. ENERGĒS (ἐνεργής) : see ACTIVE.

2. ISCHUROS (ἰσχυρός), strong, mighty, akin to *ischus* (see POWER, A, No. 3), is translated "powerful" in 2 Cor. 10 : 10, A.V. (R.V., "strong"). See STRONG.

B. Adverb.

EUTONŌS (εὐτόνως) signifies vigorously, vehemently (*eu*, well, *teinō*, to stretch), Luke 23 : 10, "vehemently," of the accusation of the chief priests and scribes against Christ ; Acts 18 : 28, R.V., "powerfully"

(A.V., " mightily "), of Apollos in confuting Jews.¶ In the Sept.,
Josh. 6 : 8.¶

Note : For " is powerful," 2 Cor. 13 : 3, R.V., see MIGHTY, C.

For PRACTICES see COVETOUS, B, No. 3

PRACTISE

PRASSŌ (πράσσω) is translated by the verb to practise in the R.V.
in the following passages (the A.V. nowhere renders the verb thus) :
John 3 : 20 (marg.) ; 5 : 29 (marg.) ; Acts 19 : 19 ; Rom. 1 : 32 (twice) ;
2 : 1, 2, 3 ; 7 : 15, 19 ; Gal. 5 : 21. See Do, No. 2.

For PRÆTORIUM and PRÆTORIAN GUARD see PALACE

PRAISE
A. Nouns.

1. AINOS (αἶνος), primarily a tale, narration, came to denote praise ;
in the N.T. only of praise to God, Matt. 21 : 16 ; Luke 18 : 43.¶

2. EPAINOS (ἔπαι), a strengthened form of No. 1 (*epi*, upon),
denotes approbation, commendation, praise ; it is used (*a*) of those on
account of, and by reason of, whom as God's heritage, praise is to be
ascribed to God, in respect of His glory (the exhibition of His character
and operations), Eph. 1 : 12 ; in ver. 14, of the whole company, the
Church, viewed as " *God's* own possession " (R.V.) ; in ver. 6, with particular reference to the glory of His grace towards them ; in Phil. 1 : 11,
as the result of " the fruits of righteousness " manifested in them through
the power of Christ ; (*b*) of praise bestowed by God, upon the Jew
spiritually (Judah = praise), Rom. 2 : 29 ; bestowed upon believers
hereafter at the Judgment-Seat of Christ, 1 Cor. 4 : 5 (where the definite
article indicates that the praise will be exactly in accordance with each
person's actions) ; as the issue of present trials, " at the revelation of
Jesus Christ," 1 Pet. 1 : 7 ; (*c*) of whatsoever is praiseworthy, Phil. 4 : 8 ;
(*d*) of the approbation by churches of those who labour faithfully in the
ministry of the Gospel, 2 Cor. 8 : 18 ; (*e*) of the approbation of well-doers
by human rulers, Rom. 13 : 3 ; 1 Pet. 2 : 14.¶

3. AINESIS (αἴνεσις), praise (akin to No. 1), is found in Heb. 13 : 15,
where it is metaphorically represented as a sacrificial offering.¶

Notes : (1) In 1 Pet. 2 : 9, A.V., *aretē*, virtue, excellence, is translated
" praises " (R.V., " excellencies "). (2) In the following the A.V. translates *doxa*, glory, by " praise " (R.V., " glory ") ; John 9 : 24, where
" give glory to God " signifies ' confess thy sins ' (cp. Josh. 7 : 19, indicating the genuine confession of facts in one's life which gives glory to God) ;
12 : 43 (twice) ; 1 Pet. 4 : 11.

B. Verbs.

1. AINEŌ (αἰνέω), to speak in praise of, to praise (akin to A, No. 1),

is always used of praise to God, (a) by angels, Luke 2 : 13 ; (b) by men, Luke 2 : . ; 19 : 37 ; 24 : 53 ; Acts 2 : 20 47 ; 3 : 8, 9 ; Rom. 15 : 11 (No. 2 in some texts) ; Rev. 19 : 5.¶

2. EPAINEŌ (ἐπαινέω), akin to A, No. 2, is rendered " praise," 1 Cor. 11 : 2, 17, 22 : see COMMEND, No. 1.

3. HUMNEŌ (ὑμνέω) denotes (a) transitively, to sing, to laud, sing to the praise of (Eng., hymn), Acts 16 : 25, A.V., " sang praises " (R.V., " singing hymns ") ; Heb. 2 : 12, R.V., " will I sing (Thy) praise," A.V., " will I sing praise (unto Thee), " lit., ' I will hymn Thee ; ' (b) intransitively, to sing, Matt. 26 : 30 ; Mark 14 : 26, in both places of the singing of the paschal hymns (Psa. 113–118, and 136), called by Jews the Great Hallel.¶

4. PSALLŌ (ψάλλω), primarily, to twitch or twang (as a bowstring, etc.), then, to play (a stringed instrument with the fingers), in the Sept., to sing psalms, denotes, in the N.T., to sing a hymn, sing praise ; in Jas. 5 : 13, R.V., " sing praise " (A.V., " sing psalms "). See MELODY, SING.

5. EXOMOLOGEŌ (ἐξομολογέω) in Rom. 15 : 9, R.V., " will I give praise " (A.V., and R.V. marg., " I will confess ") : see CONFESS, A, No. 2 (c).

Note : In Luke 1 : 64, A.V., *eulogeō*, to bless, is translated " praised " (R.V., " blessing ").

PRATE

PHLUAREŌ (φλυαρέω) signifies to talk nonsense (from *phluō*, to babble ; cp. the adjective *phluaros*, babbling, garrulous, " tattlers," 1 Tim. 5 : 13), to raise false accusations, 3 John 10.¶

PRAY, PRAYER
A. Verbs.

1. EUCHOMAI (εὔχομαι), to pray (to God), is used with this meaning in 2 Cor. 13 : 7 ; ver. 9, R.V., " pray " (A.V., " wish ") ; Jas. 5 : 16 ; 3 John 2, R.V., " pray " (A.V., wish). Even when the R.V. and A.V. translate by " I would," Acts 26 : 29, or " wished for," Acts 27 : 29 (R.V., marg., " prayed "), or " could wish," Rom. 9 : 3 (R.V., marg., " could pray "), the indication is that prayer is involved.¶

2. PROSEUCHOMAI (προσεύχομαι), to pray, is always used of prayer to God, and is the most frequent word in this respect, especially in the Synoptists and Acts, once in Romans, 8 : 26 ; in Ephesians, 6 : 18 ; in Philippians, 1 : 9 ; in 1 Timothy, 2 : 8 ; in Hebrews, 13 : 18 ; in Jude, ver. 20. For the injunction in 1 Thess. 5 : 17, see CEASE, C.

3. ERŌTAŌ (ἐρωτάω), to ask, is translated by the verb to pray in Luke 14 : 18, 19 ; 16 : 27 ; John 4 : 31 ; 14 : 16 ; 16 : 26 ; 17 : 9, 15, 20 ; in Acts 23 : 18, R.V., " asked " (A.V. " prayed ") ; in 1 John 5 : 16, R.V., " should make request " (A.V. " shall pray "). See ASK, A, No. 2.

4. DEOMAI (δέομαι), to desire, in 2 Cor. 5 : 20 ; 8 : 4, R.V., " beseech " (A.V., " pray ") : see BESEECH, No. 3.

Notes : (1) *Parakaleō*, to call to one's aid, is rendered by the verb to pray in the A.V. in the following : Matt. 26 : 53 (R.V., " beseech ") ; so Mark 5 : 17, 18 ; Acts 16 : 9 ; in 24 : 4, R.V., " intreat ; " in 27 : 34, R.V., " beseech." See BESEECH, No. 1. (2) In 1 Thess. 5 : 23 and 2 Tim. 4 : 16, there is no word in the original for " I pray," see the R.V.

B. Nouns.

1. EUCHĒ (εὐχή), akin to A, No. 1, denotes a prayer, Jas. 5 : 15 ; a vow, Acts 18 : 18 and 21 : 23. See Vow.¶

2 PROSEUCHĒ (προσευχή), akin to A, No. 2, denotes (*a*) prayer (to God), the most frequent term, e.g., Matt. 21 : 22 ; Luke 6 : 12, where the phrase is not to be taken literally as if it meant, ' the prayer of God ' (subjective genitive), but objectively, " prayer to God." In Jas. 5 : 17, " He prayed fervently," R.V., is, lit., ' he prayed with prayer ' (a Hebraistic form) ; in the following the word is used with No. 3 : Eph. 6 : 18 ; Phil. 4 : 6 ; 1 Tim. 2 : 1 ; 5 : 5 ; (*b*) " a place of prayer," Acts 16 : 13, 16, a place outside the city wall, R.V.

3. DEĒSIS (δέησις), primarily a wanting, a need (akin to A, No. 4), then, an asking, entreaty, supplication, in the N.T. is always addressed to God and always rendered " supplication " or " supplications " in the R.V. ; in the A.V. " prayer," or " prayers," in Luke 1 : 13 ; 2 : 37 ; 5 : 33 ; Rom. 10 : 1 ; 2 Cor. 1 : 11 ; 9 : 14 ; Phil. 1 : 4 (in the 2nd part, " request ") ; 1 : 19 ; 2 Tim. 1 : 3 ; Heb. 5 : 7 ; Jas. 5 : 16 ; 1 Pet. 3 : 12.

4. ENTEUXIS (ἔντευξις) is translated " prayer " in 1 Tim. 4 : 5 ; see INTERCESSION.

Notes : (1) *Proseuchē* is used of prayer in general ; *deēsis* stresses the sense of need ; it is used sometimes of request from man to man. (2) In the papyri *enteuxis* is the regular word for a petition to a superior. For the synonymous word *aitēma* see PETITION ; for *hiketēria*, Heb. 5 : 7, see SUPPLICATION.

(3) " Prayer is properly addressed to God the Father, Matt. 6 : 6 ; John 16 : 23 ; Eph. 1 : 17 ; 3 : 14, and the Son, Acts 7 : 59 ; 2 Cor. 12 : 8 ; but in no instance in the N.T. is prayer addressed to the Holy Spirit distinctively, for whereas the Father is in Heaven, Matt. 6 : 9, and the Son is at His right hand, Rom. 8 : 34, the Holy Spirit is in and with the believers, John 14 : 16, 17.

" Prayer is to be offered in the Name of the Lord Jesus, John 14 : 13, that is, the prayer must accord with His character, and must be presented in the same spirit of dependence and submission that marked Him, Matt. 11 : 26 ; Luke 22 : 42.

" The Holy Spirit, being the sole interpreter of the needs of the human heart, makes His intercession therein ; and inasmuch as prayer is impossible to man apart from His help, Rom. 8 : 26, believers are exhorted to pray at all seasons in the Spirit, Eph. 6 : 18 ; cp. Jude 20, and Jas.

5 : 16, the last clause of which should probably be read ' the inwrought [i.e., by the Holy Spirit] supplication of a righteous man availeth much ' (or ' greatly prevails,' *ischuō*, as in Acts 19 : 16, 20).

" None the less on this account is the understanding to be engaged in prayer, 1 Cor. 14 : 15, and the will, Col. 4 : 12 ; Acts 12 : 5 (where ' earnestly ' is, lit., ' stretched out ') and so in Luke 22 : 44.

" Faith is essential to prayer, Matt. 21 : 22 ; Mark 11 : 24 ; Jas. 1 : 5–8, for faith is the recognition of, and the committal of ourselves and our matters to, the faithfulness of God.

" Where the Jews were numerous, as at Thessalonica, they had usually a Synagogue, Acts 17 : 1 ; where they were few, as at Philippi, they had merely a *proseuchē*, or ' place of prayer,' of much smaller dimensions, and commonly built by a river for the sake of the water necessary to the preliminary ablutions prescribed by Rabbinic tradition, Acts 16 : 13, 16."*

PREACH, PREACHING
A. Verbs.

1. EUANGELIZŌ (εὐαγγελίζω) is almost always used of the good news concerning the Son of God as proclaimed in the Gospel [exceptions are, e.g., Luke 1 : 19 ; 1 Thess. 3 : 6, in which the phrase " to bring (or shew) good (or glad) tidings " does not refer to the Gospel] ; Gal. 1 : 8 (2nd part). With reference to the Gospel the phrase to bring, or declare, good, or glad, tidings is used in Acts 13 : 32 ; Rom. 10 : 15 ; Heb. 4 : 2.

In Luke 4 : 18 the R.V. " to preach good tidings " gives the correct quotation from Isaiah, rather than the A.V. " to preach the Gospel." In the Sept. the verb is used of any message intended to cheer the hearers, e.g., 1 Sam. 31 : 9 ; 2 Sam. 1 : 20. See GOSPEL, B, No. 1.

2. KĒRUSSŌ (κηρύσσω) signifies (*a*) to be a herald, or, in general, to proclaim, e.g., Matt. 3 : 1 ; Mark 1 : 45, " publish ; " in Luke 4 : 18, R.V., " to proclaim," A.V., " to preach ; " so verse 19 ; Luke 12 : 3 ; Acts 10 : 37 ; Rom. 2 : 21 ; Rev. 5 : 2. In 1 Pet. 3 : 19 the probable reference is, not to glad tidings (which there is no real evidence that Noah preached, nor is there evidence that the spirits of antediluvian people are actually " in prison "), but to the act of Christ after His resurrection in proclaiming His victory to fallen angelic spirits ; (*b*) to preach the Gospel as a herald, e.g., Matt. 24 : 14 ; Mark 13 : 10, R.V., " be preached " (A.V., " be published ") ; 14 : 9 ; 16 : 15, 20 ; Luke 8 : 1 ; 9 : 2 ; 24 : 47 ; Acts 8 : 5 ; 19 : 13 ; 28 : 31 ; Rom. 10 : 14, present participle, lit., ' (one) preaching,' " a preacher ; " 10 : 15 (1st part) ; 1 Cor. 1 : 23 ; 15 : 11, 12 ; 2 Cor. 1 : 19 ; 4 : 5 ; 11 : 4 ; Gal. 2 : 2 ; Phil. 1 : 15 ; Col. 1 : 23 ; 1 Thess. 2 : 9 ; 1 Tim. 3 : 16 ; (*c*) to preach the word, 2 Tim. 4 : 2 (of the ministry of the Scriptures, with special reference to the Gospel). See PROCLAIM, PUBLISH.

---

* From Notes on Thessalonians by Hogg and Vine, pp. 189, 190.

3. PROEUANGELIZOMAI (προευαγγελίζομαι) : see GOSPEL, B, No. 2.

4. PROKĒRUSSŌ (προκηρύσσω), lit., to proclaim as a herald (*pro*, before, and No. 2), is used in Acts 13 : 24, " had first preached." Some mss. have the verb in Acts 3 : 20 ; for the best see APPOINT, No. 12.¶

5. PARRHĒSIAZOMAI (παρρησιάζομαι), to be bold in speech, is translated to preach boldly in Acts 9 : 27 (2nd part) ; in ver. 29, R.V. (A.V., " he spake boldly "). See BOLD, A, No. 2.

Notes : (1) For *diangellō*, translated " preach " in Luke 9 : 60, see DECLARE, A, No. 3. (2) *Katangellō*, to proclaim, is always so translated in the R.V. ; the A.V. renders it by to preach in Acts 4 : 2 ; 13 : 5, 38 ; 15 : 36 ; 17 : 3, 13 ; 1 Cor. 9 : 14 ; Col. 1 : 28. (3) *Laleō*, to speak, is translated " preached," Mark 2 : 2, A.V., " preached " (R.V., " spake ") ; in Acts 8 : 25, 1st part, A.V. (R.V., " spoken ") ; so in 13 : 42 and 14 : 25 ; " preaching " in Acts 11 : 19, A.V., but what is indicated here is not a formal preaching by the believers scattered from Jerusalem, but a general testimony to all with whom they came into contact ; in 16 : 6, R.V., " to speak " (A.V., " to preach "). (4) For *dialegomai*, in A.V. of Acts 20 : 7, 9, see DISCOURSE. (5) For A.V., " preached " in Heb. 4 : 2 (2nd part), see HEARING. (6) In Rom. 15 : 19 *plēroō*, to fulfil (R.V., marg.), is rendered " I have fully preached."

B. Nouns.

KĒRUGMA (κήρυγμα), a proclamation by a herald (akin to A, No. 2), denotes a message, a preaching (the substance of what is preached as distinct from the act of preaching), Matt. 12 : 41 ; Luke 11 : 32 ; Rom. 16 : 25 ; 1 Cor. 1 : 21 ; 2 : 4 ; 15 : 14 ; in 2 Tim. 4 : 17 and Tit. 1 : 3, R.V., " message," marg., " proclamation," A.V., " preaching." See MESSAGE.¶ In the Sept., 2 Chron. 30 : 5 ; Prov. 9 : 3 ; Jonah 3 : 2.¶

Note : In 1 Cor. 1 : 18, A.V., *logos*, a word, is translated " preaching," R.V., " the word (of the Cross)," i.e., not the act of preaching, but the substance of the testimony, all that God has made known concerning the subject. For Heb. 4 : 2, A.V., see HEAR, B, No. 1.

PREACHER

KĒRUX (κῆρυξ), a herald (akin to A, No. 2 and B, above), is used (*a*) of the preacher of the Gospel, 1 Tim. 2 : 7 ; 2 Tim. 1 : 11 ; (*b*) of Noah, as a preacher of righteousness, 2 Pet. 2 : 5.¶

Notes : (1) For " a preacher," in Rom. 10 : 14, where the verb *kērussō* is used, see PREACH, A, No. 2. (2) *Kērux* indicates the preacher as giving a proclamation ; *euangelistēs* points to his message as glad tidings ; *apostolos* suggests his relationship to Him by whom he is sent.

PRECEDE

PHTHANŌ (φθάνω), to anticipate, to come sooner, is translated " shall (in no wise) precede " in 1 Thess. 4 : 15, R.V. (A.V., " prevent "), i.e., ' shall in no wise obtain any advantage over ' (the verb does not convey the thought of a mere succession of one event after another) ; the Apostle, in reassuring the bereaved concerning their departed fellow-believers, declares that, as to any advantage, the dead in Christ will " rise first." See ATTAIN, No. 3, COME, No. 32.

PRECEPT

1. ENTOLĒ (ἐντολή), a commandment, is translated " precept " in Mark 10 : 5 (R.V., " commandment ") ; so Heb. 9 : 19. See COMMANDMENT, No. 2.

2. ENTALMA (ἔνταλμα) is always translated " precepts " in the R.V. ; see COMMANDMENT, No. 3.

PRECIOUS, PRECIOUSNESS

1. TIMIOS (τίμιος), translated " precious," e.g., in Jas. 5 : 7 ; 1 Pet. 1 : 19 ; 2 Pet. 1 : 4 ; in 1 Cor. 3 : 12, A.V. (R.V., " costly ") : see COSTLY, B, No. 1, DEAR, No. 1.

2. ENTIMOS (ἔντιμος), " precious," 1 Pet. 2 : 4, 6 : see DEAR, No. 2.

3. POLUTELĒS (πολυτελής), very expensive, translated " very precious " in Mark 14 : 3, A.V. (R.V., " very costly ") : see COSTLY, B, No. 2.

4. POLUTIMOS (πολύτιμος), of great value ; comparative degree in 1 Pet. 1 : 7 ; see COSTLY, B, No. 3, DEAR, No. 1 (for a less authentic reading).

5. BARUTIMOS (βαρύτιμος), of great value, exceeding precious (barus, weighty, timē, value), is used in Matt. 26 : 7.¶

6. ISOTIMOS (ἰσότιμος), of equal value, held in equal honour (isos, equal, and timē), is used in 2 Pet. 1 : 1, " a like precious (faith)," R.V. (marg., " an equally precious ").¶

Note : In 1 Pet. 2 : 7, A.V., the noun timē, is translated " precious " (R.V., " preciousness "). See HONOUR, No. 1.

PREDESTINATE

PROORIZŌ : see DETERMINE.
Note: This verb is to be distinguished from proginōskō, to foreknow; the latter has special reference to the persons foreknown by God; proorizō has special reference to that to which the subjects of His foreknowledge are predestinated. See FOREKNOW, A and B.

PRE-EMINENCE (to have the)

1. PRŌTEUŌ (πρωτεύω), to be first (prōtos), to be pre-eminent, is used of Christ in relation to the Church, Col. 1:18.¶

2. PHILOPRŌTEUŌ (φιλοπρωτεύω), lit., to love to be pre-eminent (philos, loving), to strive to be first, is said of Diotrephes, 3 John 9.¶

PREFER, PREFERRING

PROĒGEOMAI (προηγέομαι), to go before and lead, is used in Rom.

12 : 10, in the sense of taking the lead in showing deference one to another, " (in honour) preferring one another."¶

Notes : (1) In John 1 : 15, 30, A.V., *ginomai*, to become, is translated " is preferred " (R.V., " is become ") ; some mss. have it again in ver. 27. (2) For *prokrima*, 1 Tim. 5 : 21 (A.V., " preferring one before another "), see PREJUDICE.

PREJUDICE

PROKRIMA (πρόκριμα) denotes pre-judging (akin to *prokrinō*, to judge beforehand), 1 Tim. 5 : 21, R.V., " prejudice " (marg., " preference "), preferring one person, another being put aside, by unfavourable judgment due to partiality.¶

PREMEDITATE

Note : This is the A.V. rendering of *meletaō*, to care for, which occurs in some mss. in Mark 13 : 11, " (neither) do ye premeditate." It is absent from the best mss. See IMAGINE.

PREPARATION, PREPARE, PREPARED
A. Nouns.

1. HETOIMASIA (ἐτοιμασία) denotes (*a*) readiness, (*b*) preparation ; it is found in Eph. 6 : 15, of having the feet shod with the preparation of the Gospel of peace ; it also has the meaning of firm footing (foundation), as in the Sept. of Ps. 89 : 14 (R.V., " foundation ") ; if that is the meaning in Eph. 6 : 15, the Gospel itself is to be the firm footing of the believer, his walk being worthy of it and therefore a testimony in regard to it. See READY.¶

2. PARASKEUĒ (παρασκευή) denotes preparation, equipment. The day on which Christ died is called " the Preparation " in Mark 15 : 42 and John 19 : 31 ; in John 19 : 42 " the Jews' Preparation," R.V. ; in 19 : 14 it is described as " the Preparation of the Passover ; " in Luke 23 : 54, R.V., " the day of the Preparation (and the Sabbath drew on)." The same day is in view in Matt. 27 : 62, where the events recorded took place on " the day after the Preparation " (R.V.). The reference would be to the 6th day of the week. The title arose from the need of preparing food etc. for the Sabbath. Apparently it was first applied only to the afternoon of the 6th day ; later, to the whole day. In regard to the phraseology in John 19 : 14, many hold this to indicate the preparation for the paschal feast. It probably means ' the Preparation day,' and thus falls in line with the Synoptic Gospels. In modern Greek and ecclesiastical Latin, *Parasceve* = Friday.¶
B. Verbs.

1. HETOIMAZŌ (ἐτοιμάζω), to prepare, make ready, is used (I) absolutely, e.g., Mark 14 : 15 ; Luke 9 : 52 ; (II) with an object, e.g., (*a*) of those things which are ordained (1) by God, such as future positions of

authority, Matt. 20 : 23 ; the coming Kingdom, 25 : 34 ; salvation personified in Christ, Luke 2 : 31 ; future blessings, 1 Cor. 2 : 9 ; a city, Heb. 11 : 16 ; a place of refuge for the Jewish remnant, Rev. 12 : 6 ; Divine judgments on the world, Rev. 8 : 6 ; 9 : 7, 15 ; 16 : 12 ; eternal fire, for the Devil and his angels, Matt. 25 : 41 ; (2) by Christ : a place in Heaven for His followers, John 14 : 2, 3 ; (b) of human preparation for the Lord, e.g., Matt. 3 : 3 ; 26 : 17, 19 ; Luke 1 : 17 (" make ready "), 76 ; 3 : 4, A.V. (R.V., " make ye ready ") ; 9 : 52 (" to make ready ") ; 23 : 56 ; Rev. 19 : 7 ; 21 : 2 ; in 2 Tim. 2 : 21, of preparation of oneself for " every good work ; " (c) of human preparations for human objects, e.g., Luke 12 : 20, R.V., " thou hast prepared " (A.V., " provided ") ; Acts 23 : 23 ; Philm. 22.

2. KATARTIZŌ (καταρτίζω), to furnish completely, prepare, is translated " didst Thou prepare " in Heb. 10 : 5 (A.V., " hast Thou prepared "), of the body of the Lord Jesus. See FIT, B, No. 3.

3. KATASKEUAZŌ (κατασκευάζω), to prepare, make ready (kata, used intensively, skeuē, equipment), is so translated in Matt. 11 : 10 ; Mark 1 : 2 ; Luke 1 : 17 ; 7 : 27 ; Heb. 9 : 2, R.V. (A.V., " made ") ; 9 : 6, R.V. (A.V., " were . . . ordained ") ; 11 : 7 ; 1 Pet. 3 : 20. See BUILD, No. 5.

4. PARASKEUAZŌ (παρασκευάζω), to prepare, make ready (para, beside), is used of making ready a meal, Acts 10 : 10 : in the Middle Voice, of preparing oneself for war, 1 Cor. 14 : 8, R.V. ; in the Passive Voice, of preparing an offering for the needy, 2 Cor. 9 : 2, " hath been prepared," R.V. (A.V., " was ready ") ; ver. 3, " ye may be prepared," R.V. (A.V., " ye may be ready "). See READY.¶

5. PROETOIMAZŌ (προετοιμάζω), to prepare beforehand (pro, before, and No. 1), is used of good works which God " afore prepared," for fulfilment by believers, Eph. 2 : 10, R.V. (A.V., " hath before ordained," marg., " prepared ") ; of " vessels of mercy," as " afore prepared " by God " unto glory," Rom. 9 : 23. See ORDAIN.¶

Notes : (1) Etymologically, the difference between hetoimazō and paraskeuazō, is that the former is connected with what is real (etumos) or ready, the latter with skeuos, an article ready to hand, an implement, vessel. (2) In Mark 14 : 15, A.V., hetoimos, ready, is translated " prepared " (R.V., " ready '). It is absent in some mss. See READY.

For PRESBYTERY see ELDER, A and B

PRESENCE
A. Nouns.

1. PROSŌPON (πρόσωπον) : see FACE, No. 1 (also APPEARANCE, No. 2).

2. PAROUSIA (παρουσία) : see COMING (Noun), No. 3.

B. Adverbs and Prepositions.

1. EMPROSTHEN (ἔμπροσθεν) : see BEFORE, A, No. 4.

2. ENŌPION (ἐνώπιον) is translated " in the presence of " in Luke
1 : 19 ; 13 : 26 ; 14 : 10 ; 15 : 10 ; John 20 : 30 ; Rev. 14 ˙ 10 (twice) ;
in 1 Cor. 1 : 29, A.V., " in His presence " (R.V., " before God ") : see
BEFORE, A, No. 9.

3. KATENŌPION (κατενώπιον), kata, down, and No. 2, in the very
presence of, is translated " before the presence of " in Jude 24. See
BEFORE, A, No. 10.

4. APENANTI (ἀπέναντι), over against, opposite to, is translated
" in the presence of " in Acts 3 : 16. See BEFORE, A, No. 7.

PRESENT (to be)
A. Verbs.

1. PAREIMI (πάρειμι) signifies (a) to be by, at hand or present, of
persons, e.g., Luke 13 : 1 ; Acts 10 : 33 ; 24 : 19 ; 1 Cor. 5 : 3 ; 2 Cor.
10 : 2, 11 ; Gal. 4 : 18, 20 ; of things, John 7 : 6, of a particular season in
the Lord's life on earth, " is (not yet) come," or ' is not yet at hand ; '
Heb. 12 : 11, of chastening " (for the) present " (the neuter of the present
participle, used as a noun) ; in 13 : 5 " such things as ye have " is, lit.,
' the things that are present ; ' 2 Pet. 1 : 12, of the truth " (which) is
with (you) " (not as A.V., " the present truth," as if of special doctrines
applicable to a particular time) ; in ver. 9 " he that lacketh " is lit., ' to
whom are not present ; ' (b) to have arrived or come, Matt. 26 : 50, " thou
art come," R.V. ; John 11 : 28 ; Acts 10 : 21 ; Col. 1 : 6.

2. ENISTĒMI (ἐνίστημι), to set in, or, in the Middle Voice and perfect
tense of the Active V., to stand in, be present, is used of the present in
contrast with the past, Heb. 9 : 9, where the R.V. correctly has " (for
the time) now present " (for the incorrect A.V., " then pr.") ; in contrast
to the future, Rom. 8 : 38 ; 1 Cor. 3 : 22 ; Gal. 1 : 4, " present ; "
1 Cor. 7 : 26, where " the present distress " is set in contrast to both the
past and the future ; 2 Thess. 2 : 2, where the R.V., " is now present "
gives the correct meaning (A.V., incorrectly, " is at hand ") ; the saints
at Thessalonica, owing to their heavy afflictions, were possessed of the
idea that " the day of the Lord," R.V. (not as A.V., " the day of Christ "),
had begun ; this mistake the Apostle corrects ; 2 Tim. 3 : 1, " shall come."
See COME, No. 26.¶

3. EPHISTĒMI (ἐφίστημι), to set over, stand over, is translated
" present " in Acts 28 : 2. See ASSAULT, A, COME, No. 27.

4. PARAGINOMAI (παραγίνομαι), to be beside (para, by, ginomai, to
become), is translated " were present " in Acts 21 : 18. See COME, No. 13.

5. PARAKEIMAI (παράκειμαι), to lie beside (para, and keimai, to lie),
to be near, is translated " is present " in Rom. 7 : 18, 21.¶

6. SUMPAREIMI (συμπάρειμι), to be present with (sun, with, and
No. 1), is used in Acts 25 : 24.¶

B. Adverbs.

1. ARTI (ἄρτι), just, just now, this moment, is rendered " (this) present (hour) " in 1 Cor. 4 : 11 ; in 1 Cor. 15 : 6, R.V., " now " (A.V., " this present "). See Now.

2. NUN (νῦν), now, is translated " present," with reference to this age or period (" world "),in Rom. 8 : 18 ; 11 : 5 ; 2 Tim. 4 : 10 ; Tit. 2 : 12. See HENCEFORTH, NOW.

Notes : (1) *Endēmeō,* to be at home, is so rendered in 2 Cor. 5 : 6 (A.V. and R.V.) ; in vv. 8, 9, R.V., " at home " (A.V., " present "). See HOME. (2) In John 14 : 25, A.V., *menō,* to abide, is translated " being present " (R.V., " abiding "). (3) In Luke 5 : 17 the R.V. has " with Him," for A.V., italicised, " *present.*"

PRESENT (Verb)

1. PARISTĒMI (παρίστημι) denotes, when used transitively, to place beside (*para,* by, *histēmi,* to set), to present, e.g., Luke 2 : 22 ; Acts 1 : 3, " He shewed (Himself) ; " 9 : 41 ; 23 : 33 ; Rom. 6 : 13 (2nd part), R.V., " present," A.V., " yield ; " so 6 : 19 (twice) ; 12 : 1 ; 2 Cor. 4 : 14 ; 11 : 2 ; Eph. 5 : 27 ; Col. 1 : 22, 28 ; 2 Tim. 2 : 15, R.V. (A.V., " shew "). See SHEW.

2. PARISTANŌ (παριστάνω), a late present form of No. 1, is used in Rom. 6 : 13 (1st part) and ver. 16, R.V., " present " (A.V., " yield ").

Notes : (1) In Jude 24, A.V., *histēmi,* to cause to stand, to set, is trans-lated " to present " (R.V., " to set "). (2) In Matt. 2 : 11, A.V., *prospherō,* to offer, is translated " presented " (R.V., " offered ").

For PRESENTLY see FORTHWITH, No. 1, and IMMEDIATELY, No. 1

PRESERVE

1. TĒREŌ (τηρέω) is translated to preserve in 1 Thess. 5 : 23, where the verb is in the singular number, as the threefold subject, " spirit and soul and body," is regarded as the unit, constituting the person. The aorist or ' point ' tense regards the continuous preservation of the believer as a single, complete act, without reference to the time occupied in its accomplishment ; in Jude 1, A.V. (R.V., " kept "). See KEEP, No. 1.

2. SUNTĒREŌ (συντηρέω) : see KEEP, No. 3.

3. ZŌOGONEŌ (ζωογονέω), to preserve alive : see LIVE, No. 6.

4. PHULASSŌ (φυλάσσω), to guard, protect, preserve, is translated " preserved " in 2 Pet. 2 : 5, R.V. (A.V., " saved "). See GUARD.

Note : In 2 Tim. 4 : 18, A.V., *sōzō,* to save, is translated " will preserve " (R.V., " will save ").

For PRESS (Noun) see CROWD, A

PRESS (Verb)
A. Verbs.

1. THLIBŌ (θλίβω), to press, distress, trouble, is translated " pressed " in 2 Cor. 4 : 8, R.V. (A.V., " troubled "). See AFFLICT, No. 4.

2. APOTHLIBŌ (ἀποθλίβω), translated " press " in Luke 8 : 45 (end) : see CRUSH.

3. BIAZO (βιάζω), in the Middle Voice, to press violently or force one's way into, is translated " presseth " in Luke 16 : 16, A.V., R.V., " entereth violently," a meaning confirmed by the papyri. Moulton and Milligan also quote a passage from D. S. Sharp's *Epictetus and the N.T.*, speaking of " those who (try to) force their way in ; " the verb suggests forceful endeavour. See ENTER, Note (3), VIOLENCE, B, No. 2.

4. SUNECHŌ (συνέχω) : for the significance of this in Acts 18 : 5, " was constrained by the word," R.V., i.e., Paul felt the urge of the word of his testimony to the Jews in Corinth, see CONSTRAIN, No. 3. It is used with No. 1 in Luke 8 : 45, R.V., " press " (A.V., " throng ").

5. ENECHŌ (ἐνέχω), lit., to hold in, also signifies to set oneself against, be urgent against, as the scribes and Pharisees were regarding Christ, Luke 11 : 53, R.V., " to press upon," marg., " set themselves vehemently against " (A.V., " to urge "). See ENTANGLE, No. 3.

6. EPIKEIMAI (ἐπίκειμαι), to lie upon, press upon, is rendered " pressed upon " in Luke 5 : 1. See IMPOSED.

7. EPIPIPTŌ (ἐπιπίπτω), to fall upon, is rendered " pressed upon " in Mark 3 : 10. See FALL, B, No. 5.

8. BAREŌ (βαρέω), to weigh down, burden, is rendered " we were pressed " in 2 Cor. 1 : 8, A.V. (R.V., " we were weighed down "). See BURDEN, B, No. 1.

9. EPIBAREŌ (ἐπιβαρέω), 2 Cor. 2 : 5, R.V., " I press (not) too heavily " (A.V., " overcharge "). See BURDEN, B, No. 2, OVERCHARGE.

10. PIEZŌ (πιέζω), to press down together, is used in Luke 6 : 38, " pressed down," of the character of the measure given in return for giving.¶ In the Sept., Mic. 6 : 15.¶

11. DIŌKŌ (διώκω), to pursue, is used as a metaphor from the foot-race, in Phil. 3 : 12, 14, of speeding on earnestly, R.V., " I press on." See FOLLOW, No. 7.

12. PHERŌ (φέρω), to bear, carry, is used in the Passive Voice in Heb. 6 : 1, " let us . . . press on," R.V., lit., ' let us be borne on ' (A.V., " go on "). See Go, Note (2), (h).

B. Noun.

EPISTASIS (ἐπίστασις), primarily a stopping, halting (as of soldiers), then, an incursion, onset, rush, pressure (akin to *ephistēmi*, to set upon), is so used in 2 Cor. 11 : 28, " (that which) presseth upon (me)," A.V., " cometh upon," lit., ' (the daily) pressure (upon me) ; ' some have taken the word in its other meaning ' attention,' which perhaps is accounted for by the variant reading of the pronoun (*mou*, ' my ', instead of *moi*, ' to me,' ' upon me '), but that does not adequately describe the pressure or onset due to the constant call upon the Apostle for all kinds of help, advice, counsel, exhortation, decisions as to difficulties, disputes, etc. Cp. the other occurrence of the word in Acts 24 : 12, " stirring up," R.V. (A.V., " raising "), lit. ' making a stir ' (in some mss., *episustasis*). See COME, Notes at end (9).¶

For PRESUMPTUOUS see DARING, B

PRETENCE

PROPHASIS (πρόφασις) : see CLOKE (Pretence), No. 2

PREVAIL

1. ISCHUŌ (ἰσχύω), to be strong, powerful, is translated to prevail in Acts 19 : 16, 20 ; Rev. 12 : 8. See ABLE, B, No. 4.

2. KATISCHUŌ (κατισχύω), to be strong against (*kata*, against, and No. 1), is used in Matt. 16 : 18, negatively of the gates of Hades ; in Luke 21 : 36 (in the most authentic mss. ; some have *kataxioō*, to count worthy ; see A.V.), of prevailing to escape judgments at the close of this age ; in Luke 23 : 23, of the voices of the chief priests, rulers and people against Pilate regarding the crucifixion of Christ.¶

3. ŌPHELEŌ (ὠφελέω), to benefit, do good, profit, is translated " prevailed " in Matt. 27 : 24, R.V. (A.V., " could prevail "), of the conclusion formed by Pilate concerning the determination of the chief priests, elders and people. The meaning of the verb with the negative is better expressed by the phrase ' he would do no good ; ' so in John 12 : 19, " ye prevail (nothing)," lit., ' ye are doing no good.' See ADVANTAGE, BETTERED, PROFIT.

4. NIKAŌ (νικάω), to conquer, prevail, is used as a law term in Rom. 3 : 4, " (that) Thou . . . mightest prevail [A.V., ' overcome '] (when Thou comest into judgment) ; " that the righteousness of the judge's verdict compels an acknowledgement on the part of the accused, is inevitable where God is the Judge. God's promises to Israel provided no guarantee that an unrepentant Jew would escape doom. In Rev. 5 : 5, A.V., " hath prevailed " (R.V., " hath overcome "). See CONQUER, No. 1.

For PREVENT, 1 Thess. 4 : 15, A.V., see PRECEDE : Matt. 17 : 25, A.V., see SPEAK No. 11

PRICE
A. Noun.

TIMĒ (τιμή) denotes a valuing, hence, objectively, (*a*) price paid or received, Matt. 27 : 6, 9 ; Acts 4 : 34 (plural) ; 5 : 2, 3 ; 7 : 16, R.V., " price (in silver)," A.V., " sum (of money) ; " 19 : 19 (plural) ; 1 Cor.

6 : 20 ; 7 : 23 ; (b) value, honour, preciousness.   See HONOUR, PRECIOUS-
NESS.

B. Verb.

TIMAŌ (τιμάω), to fix the value, to price, is translated " was priced "
and " did price " in the R.V. of Matt. 27 : 9 (A.V., " was valued " and
" did value ").   See HONOUR.

C. Adjectives.

1. POLUTELĒS (πολυτελής), " of great price," 1 Pet. 3 : 4 : see COST,
B, No. 2.

2. POLUTIMOS (πολύτιμος), " of great price," Matt. 13 : 46 : see
COST, B, No. 3.

For PRICK (Noun) see GOAD

PRICK (Verb)

KATANUSSŌ (κατανύσσω), primarily, to strike or prick violently, to
stun, is used of strong emotion, in Acts 2 : 37 (Passive Voice), " they
were pricked (in their heart)."¶   Cp. katanuxis, stupor, torpor of mind,
Rom. 11 : 8.¶

PRIDE
A. Nouns.

1. ALAZONIA (or —EIA) (ἀλαζονία) is translated " pride " in 1 John
2 : 16, A.V.   See BOAST, B, No. 2, VAINGLORY.

2. HUPERĒPHANIA (ὑπερηφανία), pride, Mark 7 : 22 : see HAUGHTY.¶

B. Verb.

TUPHOŌ (τυφόω), " lifted up with pride," 1 Tim. 3 : 6, A.V. (R.V.,
" puffed up ").   See HIGH-MINDED.

PRIEST

1. HIEREUS (ἱερεύς), one who offers sacrifice and has the charge of
things pertaining thereto, is used (a) of a priest of the pagan god Zeus,
Acts 14 : 13 ; (b) of Jewish priests, e.g., Matt. 8 : 4 ; 12 : 4, 5 ;
Luke 1 : 5, where allusion is made to the 24 courses of priests appointed
for service in the Temple (cp. 1 Chron. 24 : 4ff.) ; John 1 : 19; Heb. 8 : 4 ;
(c) of believers, Rev. 1 : 6 ; 5 : 10 ; 20 : 6.   Israel was primarily designed
as a nation to be a kingdom of priests, offering service to God, e.g., Ex.
19 : 6 ; the Israelites having renounced their obligations, Ex. 20 : 19, the
Aaronic priesthood was selected for the purpose, till Christ came to fulfil
His ministry in offering up Himself ; since then the Jewish priesthood
has been abrogated, to be resumed nationally, on behalf of Gentiles, in the
Millennial Kingdom, Is. 61 : 6 ; 66 : 21.   Meanwhile all believers, from
Jews and Gentiles, are constituted " a kingdom of priests," Rev. 1 : 6
(see above), " a holy priesthood," 1 Pet. 2 : 5, and " royal," ver. 9.
The N.T. knows nothing of a sacerdotal class in contrast to the laity ; all

believers are commanded to offer the sacrifices mentioned in Rom. 12 : 1 ; Phil. 2 : 17 ; 4 : 18 ; Heb. 13 : 15, 16 ; 1 Pet. 2 : 5 ; (d) of Christ, Heb. 5 : 6 ; 7 : 11, 15, 17, 21 ; 8 : 4 (negatively) ; (e) of Melchizedek, as the foreshadower of Christ, Heb. 7 : 1, 3.

2. ARCHIEREUS (ἀρχιερεύς) designates (a) the high priests of the Levitical order, frequently called " chief priests " in the N.T., and including ex-high priests and members of high priestly families, e.g., Matt. 2 : 4 ; 16 : 21 ; 20 : 18 ; 21 : 15 ; in the singular, a " high priest," e.g., Abiathar, Mark 2 : 26 ; Annas and Caiaphas, Luke 3 : 2, where the R.V. rightly has " in the high-priesthood of A. and C." (cp. Acts 4 : 6). As to the combination of the two in this respect, Annas was the high priest from A.D. 7–14, and, by the time referred to, had been deposed for some years ; his son-in-law, Caiaphas, the fourth high priest since his deposition, was appointed about A.D. 24. That Annas was still called the high priest is explained by the facts (1) that by the Mosaic law the high-priesthood was held for life, Numb. 35 : 25 ; his deposition was the capricious act of the Roman procurator, but he would still be regarded legally and religiously as high priest by the Jews ; (2) that he probably still held the office of deputy-president of the Sanhedrin (cp. 2 Kings 25 : 18) ; (3) that he was a man whose age, wealth and family connections gave him a preponderant influence, by which he held the real sacerdotal power ; indeed at this time the high-priesthood was in the hands of a clique of some half dozen families ; the language of the writers of the Gospels is in accordance with this, in attributing the high-priesthood rather to a caste than a person ; (4) the high priests were at that period mere puppets of Roman authorities who deposed them at will, with the result that the title was used more loosely than in former days.

The Divine institution of the priesthood culminated in the high priest, it being his duty to represent the whole people, e.g., Lev. 4 : 15, 16 ; ch. 16. The characteristics of the Aaronic high priests are enumerated in Heb. 5 : 1–4 ; 8 : 3 ; 9 : 7, 25 ; in some mss., 10 : 11 (R.V., marg.) ; 13 : 11.

(b) Christ is set forth in this respect in the Ep. to the Hebrews, where He is spoken of as " a high priest," 4 : 15 ; 5 : 5, 10 ; 6 : 20 ; 7 : 26 ; 8 : 1, 3 (R.V.) ; 9 : 11 ; " a great high priest," 4 : 14 ; " a great priest," 10 : 21 ; " a merciful and faithful high priest," 2 : 17 ; " the Apostle and high priest of our confession," 3 : 1, R.V. ; " a high priest after the order of Melchizedek," 5 : 10. One of the great objects of this Epistle is to set forth the superiority of Christ's High Priesthood as being of an order different from and higher than the Aaronic, in that He is the Son of God (see especially 7 : 28), with a priesthood of the Melchizedek order. Seven outstanding features of His priesthood are stressed, (1) its character, 5 : 6, 10 ; (2) His commission, 5 : 4, 5 ; (3) His preparation, 2 : 17 ; 10 : 5 ; (4) His sacrifice, 8 : 3 ; 9 : 12, 14, 27, 28 ; 10 : 4–12 ; (5) His sanctuary, 4 : 14 ; 8 : 2 ; 9 : 11, 12, 24 ; 10 : 12, 19 ; (6) His ministry, 2 : 18 ; 4 : 15 ;

7 : 25 ; 8 : 6 ; 9 : 15, 24 ; (7) its effects, 2 : 15 ; 4 : 16 ; 6 : 19, 20 ; 7 : 16, 25 ; 9 : 14, 28 ; 10 : 14–17, 22, 39 ; 12 : 1 ; 13 : 13–17.

Note : In Acts 4 : 6 the adjective *hieratikos,* high priestly, is translated " of the high priest."

PRIESTHOOD, PRIEST'S OFFICE
A. Nouns.

1. HIERATEUMA (ἱεράτευμα) denotes a priesthood (akin to *hierateuō,* see below), a body of priests, consisting of all believers, the whole Church (not a special order from among them), called " a holy priesthood," 1 Pet. 2 : 5 ; " a royal priesthood," ver. 9 ; the former term is associated with offering spiritual sacrifices, the latter with the royal dignity of shewing forth the Lord's excellencies (R.V.)¶ In the Sept., Ex. 19 : 6 ; 23 : 22.¶

2. HIEROSUNE (ἱερωσύνη), a priesthood, signifies the office, quality, rank and ministry of a priest, Heb. 7 : 11, 12, 24, where the contrasts between the Levitical priesthood and that of Christ are set forth.¶   In the Sept., 1 Chron. 29 : 22.¶

3. HIERATEIA (ἱερατεία), a priesthood, denotes the priest's office, Luke 1 : 9 ; Heb. 7 . 5, R.V., " priest's office."¶
B. Verb.

HIERATEUŌ (ἱερατεύω) signifies to officiate as a priest, Luke 1 : 8, " he executed the priest's office."¶

PRINCE

1. ARCHĒGOS (ἀρχηγός), primarily an adjective signifying originating, beginning, is used as a noun, denoting a founder, author, prince or leader, Acts 3 : 15, " Prince " (marg., " Author ") ; 5 : 31 ; see AUTHOR, No. 2.

2. ARCHŌN (ἄρχων), the present participle of the verb *archō,* to rule, denotes a ruler, a prince.   It is used as follows (" p " denoting " prince," or " princes ; " " r," " ruler " or " rulers ") : (a) of Christ, as " the Ruler (A.V., Prince) of the kings of the earth," Rev. 1 : 5 ; (b) of rulers of nations, Matt. 20 : 25, R.V., " r," A.V., " p ; " Acts 4 : 26, " r ; " 7 : 27, " r ; " 7 : 35, " r " (twice) ; (c) of judges and magistrates, Acts 16 : 19, " r ; " Rom. 13 : 3, " r ; " (d) of members of the Sanhedrin, Luke 14 : 1, R.V., " r " (A.V., " chief ") ; 23 : 13, 35, " r ; " so 24 : 20 ; John 3 : 1 ; 7 : 26, 48 ; 12 : 42, R.V., " r " (A.V., " chief r.") ; " r " in Acts 3 : 17 ; 4 : 5, 8 ; 13 : 27 ; 14 : 5 ; (e) of rulers of synagogues, Matt. 9 : 18, 23, " r ; " so Luke 8 : 41 ; 18 : 18 ; (f) of the Devil, as " prince " of this world, John 12 : 31 ; 14 : 30 ; 16 : 11 ; of the power of the air, Eph. 2 : 2, " the air " being that sphere in which the inhabitants of the world live and which, through the rebellious and godless condition of humanity, constitutes the seat of his authority ; (g) of Beelzebub, the prince of the demons, Matt. 9 : 24 ; 12 : 24 ; Mark 3 : 22 ; Luke 11 : 15. See CHIEF, B, No. 10.¶

3. HĒGEMŌN (ἡγεμών), a leader, ruler, is translated "princes" (i.e., leaders) in Matt. 2 : 6 : see GOVERNOR, A, No. 1.

Note : For *megistan,* Rev. 6 : 15 ; 18 : 23, R.V., "princes," see LORD, No. 3.

PRINCIPAL

PRŌTOS (πρῶτος), first, is translated "principal men " in the R.V. of Luke 19 : 47 and Acts 25 : 2. See CHIEF, A.

Note : In Acts 25 : 23 the phrase *kat' exochēn,* lit., 'according to eminence,' is translated "principal (men) ; " *exochē,* primarily a projection (akin to *exechō,* to stand out), is used here metaphorically of eminence.¶ In the Sept., Job 39 : 28.¶

PRINCIPALITY

ARCHĒ (ἀρχή), beginning, government, rule, is used of supramundane beings who exercise rule, called " principalities ; " (a) of holy angels, Eph. 3 : 10, the Church in its formation being to them the great expression of "the manifold (or ' much-varied ') wisdom of God ; " Col. 1 : 16 ; (b) of evil angels, Rom. 8 : 38 ; Col. 2 : 15, some would put this under (a), but see SPOIL, B, No. 4 ; (a) and (b) are indicated in Col. 2 : 10. In Eph. 1 : 21, the R.V. renders it " rule " (A.V., " principality ") and in Tit. 3 : 1, " rulers " (A.V., " principalities "). In Jude 6, R.V., it signifies, not the first estate of fallen angels (as A.V.), but their authoritative power, " their own " indicating that which had been assigned to them by God, which they left, aspiring to prohibited conditions. See BEGIN, B.

PRINCIPLES

1. ARCHĒ (ἀρχή), beginning, is used in Heb. 6 : 1, in its relative significance, of the beginning of the thing spoken of ; here " the first principles of Christ," lit., ' the account (or word) of the beginning of Christ,' denotes the teaching relating to the elementary facts concerning Christ. See BEGIN, B.

2. STOICHEION (στοιχεῖον) is translated " principles " in Heb. 5 : 12. See ELEMENTS.

PRINT

TUPOS (τύπος), for which see ENSAMPLE, No. 1, is translated " print " in John 20 : 25 (twice), of the marks made by the nails in the hands of Christ.

PRISON, PRISON-HOUSE

1. DESMŌTĒRION (δεσμωτήριον), a place of bonds (from *desmos,* a bond, *deō,* to bind), a prison, occurs in Matt. 11 : 2 ; in Acts 5 : 21, 23 and 16 : 26, R.V., " prison-house " (A.V., " prison ").¶

2. PHULAKĒ (φυλακή), for the various meanings of which see CAGE, denotes a prison, e.g., Matt. 14 : 10 ; Mark 6 : 17 ; Acts 5 : 19 ; 2 Cor.

11 : 23 ; in 2 Cor. 6 : 5 and Heb. 11 : 36 it stands for the condition of imprisonment ; in Rev. 2 : 10 ; 18 : 2, " hold " (twice, R.V., marg., " prison ; " in the 2nd case, A.V., " cage ") ; 20 : 7.

3. TĒRĒSIS (τήρησις), a watching, keeping, then, a place of keeping, is translated " prison " in Acts 5 : 18, A.V. (R.V., " ward "). See KEEPING, B.

Notes : (1) For *oikēma* in Acts 12 : 7, A.V., " prison," see CELL. (2) In Matt. 4 : 12, A.V., *paradidōmi*, to betray, deliver up, is translated " was cast into prison " (R.V., " was delivered up ") ; see BETRAY. In Mark 1 : 14, A.V., " was put in prison," R.V., as in Matt. 4 : 12 ; see PUT, No. 12.

For PRISON-KEEPER see JAILOR

PRISONER

1. DESMIOS (δέσμιος), an adjective, primarily denotes binding, bound, then, as a noun, the person bound, a captive, prisoner (akin to *deō*, to bind), Matt. 27 : 15, 16 ; Mark 15 : 6 ; Acts 16 : 25, 27 ; 23 : 18 ; 25 : 14, R.V. (A.V., " in bonds "), 27 ; 28 : 16, 17 ; Eph. 3 : 1 ; 4 : 1 ; 2 Tim. 1 : 8 ; Philm. 1, 9 ; in Heb. 10 : 34 and 13 : 3, " in bonds." See BOND, No. 2.¶

Note : The prison at Jerusalem (Acts 5) was controlled by the priests and probably attached to the high priest's palace, or the temple. Paul was imprisoned at Jerusalem in the fort Antonia, Acts 23 : 10 ; at Cæsarea, in Herod's Prætorium, 23 : 35 ; probably his final imprisonment in Rome was in the Tullianum dungeon.

2. DESMŌTĒS (δεσμώτης), akin to No. 1, occurs in Acts 27 : 1, 42.¶

3. SUNAICHMALŌTOS (συναιχμάλωτος), a fellow-prisoner, primarily one of fellow-captives in war (from *aichmē*, a spear, and *haliskomai*, to be taken), is used by Paul of Andronicus and Junias, Rom. 16 : 7 ; of Epaphras, Philm. 23 ; of Aristarchus, Col. 4 : 10, on which Lightfoot remarks that probably his relations with the Apostle in Rome excited suspicion and led to a temporary confinement, or that he voluntarily shared his captivity by living with him.¶

PRIVATE, PRIVATELY
A. Adjective.

IDIOS (ἴδιος), one's own, is translated " private " in 2 Pet. 1 : 20 (see under INTERPRETATION). See BUSINESS, B.

B. Adverbial Phrase.

KAT' IDIAN (κατ' ἰδίαν) is translated " privately " in Matt. 24 : 3 ; Mark 4 : 34, R.V. (A.V., " when they were alone ") ; 6 : 32 (A.V. only) ; 7 : 33, R.V. ; 9 : 28 ; 13 : 3 ; Luke 10 : 23 ; Acts 23 : 19 ; Gal. 2 : 2. Contrast 2 : 14.

PRIVILY

LATHRA (λάθρα), secretly, covertly (from a root *lath*— indicating unnoticed, unknown, seen in *lanthanō*, to escape notice, *lēthē*, forgetfulness), is translated "privily" in Matt. 1 : 19; 2 : 7; Acts 16 : 37; "secretly" in John 11 : 28 (in some mss., Mark 5 : 33). See SECRETLY.¶

Note: In Gal. 2 : 4, *pareisaktos*, an adjective (akin to *pareisagō*, lit., to bring in beside, i.e., secretly, from *para*, by the side, *eis*, into, *agō*, to bring), is used, "privily brought in," R.V. (A.V., "unawares etc."), i.e., as spies or traitors. Strabo, a Greek historian contemporary with Paul, uses the word of enemies introduced secretly into a city by traitors within.¶ In the same verse the verb *pareiserchomai* (see COME, No. 8) is translated "came in privily," of the same Judaizers, brought in by the circumcision party to fulfil the design of establishing the ceremonial law, and thus to accomplish the overthrow of the faith; cp. in Jude 4 the verb *pareisduō* (or—*dunō*), to slip in secretly, steal in, R.V., "crept in privily" (A.V., ". . . unawares"). See CREEP, No. 2.

PRIVY

SUNOIDA (σύνοιδα) : see KNOW, No. 6

PRIZE

1. BRABEION (βραβεῖον), a prize bestowed in connection with the games (akin to *brabeus*, an umpire, and *brabeuō*, to decide, arbitrate, "rule," Col. 3 : 15), 1 Cor. 9 : 24, is used metaphorically of the reward to be obtained hereafter by the faithful believer, Phil. 3 : 14; the preposition *eis*, "unto," indicates the position of the goal. The prize is not "the high calling," but will be bestowed in virtue of, and relation to, it, the heavenly calling, Heb. 3 : 1, which belongs to all believers and directs their minds and aspirations heavenward; for the prize see especially 2 Tim. 4 : 7, 8.¶

2. HARPAGMOS (ἁρπαγμός), akin to *harpazō*, to seize, carry off by force, is found in Phil. 2 : 6, "(counted it not) a prize," R.V. (marg., "a thing to be grasped"), A.V., "(thought it not) robbery;" it may have two meanings, (*a*) in the Active sense, the act of seizing, robbery, a meaning in accordance with a rule connected with its formation; (*b*) in the Passive sense, a thing held as a prize. The subject is capably treated by Gifford in "*The Incarnation*," pp. 28, 36, from which the following is quoted :

"In order to express the meaning of the clause quite clearly, a slight alteration is required in the R.V., 'Counted it not a prize to be on an equality with God.' The form ' to be ' is ambiguous and easily lends itself to the erroneous notion that to be on equality with God was something to be acquired in the future. The rendering ' counted it not a prize that He was on an equality with God,' is quite as accurate and more free from ambiguity. . . . Assuming, as we now may, that the equality was something which Christ possessed prior to His Incarnation, and then for a time resigned, we have . . . to choose between two meanings of the word *harpagmos* : (1) with the active sense ' robbery ' or ' usurpation ' we get the following meaning : ' Who *because* He was subsisting in the essential form of God, did not regard it as any usurpation that He was on an equality of glory and majesty with God, *but yet* emptied Himself of that co-equal glory. . . . ' (2) The passive sense gives a different meaning to the passage : ' Who *though* He was subsisting in the essential form of God, *yet* did not regard His being on an equality of glory and majesty with God as a prize and a treasure to be held fast, *but* emptied himself thereof.''

After reviewing the arguments *pro* and *con* Gifford takes the latter to be the right meaning, as conveying the purpose of the passage '' to set forth Christ as the supreme example of humility and self-renunciation.''

Note : For *katabrabeuō* (*kata*, down, and *brabeuō*, see No. 1), translated '' rob (you) of your prize,'' Col. 2 : 18, see BEGUILE, Note.

For PROBATION, R.V. in Rom. 5 : 4, see EXPERIENCE, No. 2

PROCEED

1. EKPOREUOMAI (ἐκπορεύομαι), to go forth, is translated to proceed out of in Matt. 4 : 4 ; 15 : 11, R.V. ; 15 : 18 ; Mark 7 : 15, R.V. ; 7 : 20, R.V. ; 7 : 21 ; 7 : 23, R.V. ; Luke 4 : 22 ; John 15 : 26 ; Eph. 4 : 29 ; Rev. 1 : 16, R.V. ; 4 : 5 ; 9 : 17, 18, R.V. (A.V., '' issued '') ; 11 : 5 ; 19 : 15, R.V. ; 19 : 21, A.V. (R.V., '' came forth '') ; 22 : 1.   See COME, No. 33, GO, Note (1).

2. EXERCHOMAI (ἐξέρχομαι) is translated '' proceed '' in Matt. 15 : 19, A.V. (R.V., '' come forth '') ; John 8 : 42, R.V., '' came forth ; '' Jas. 3 : 10. The verb to proceed is not so suitable. See COME, No. 3.

3. PROKOPTŌ (προκόπτω), lit., to cut forward (a way), is translated '' will proceed '' in 2 Tim. 2 : 16, R.V. (A.V., '' will increase '') and '' shall proceed'' (both Versions) in 3 : 9.   See INCREASE.

4. PROSTITHĒMI (προστίθημι), to put to, to add, is translated '' proceeded '' in Acts 12 : 3 (a Hebraism). See ADD, No. 2.

PROCLAIM

1. KĒRUSSŌ (κηρύσσω) is translated to proclaim in the R.V., for A.V., to preach, in Matt. 10 : 27 ; Luke 4 : 19 ; Acts 8 : 5 ; 9 : 20. See PREACH, No. 2.

2. KATANGELLŌ (καταγγέλλω), to declare, proclaim, is translated to proclaim in the R.V., for A.V., to shew, in Acts 16 : 17 ; 26 : 23 ; 1 Cor. 11 : 26, where the verb makes clear that the partaking of the elements at the Lord's Supper is a proclamation (an evangel) of the Lord's Death ; in Rom. 1 : 8, for A.V., '' spoken of ; '' in 1 Cor. 2 : 1, for A.V., '' declaring.'' See also PREACH, Note (2), and DECLARE, A, No. 4.

3. PLĒROPHOREŌ (πληροφορέω), to bring in full measure (*plērēs*,

full, *pherō*, to bring), hence, to fulfil, accomplish, is translated "might be fully proclaimed," in 2 Tim. 4 : 17, R.V., with *kērugma*, marg., "proclamation" (A.V. " . . . known "). See ASSURE, B, No. 2, BELIEVE, C, Note (4), FULFIL, No. 6, KNOW, Note (2), PERSUADE, No. 2, Note, PROOF.

PROCONSUL

ANTHUPATOS (ἀνθύπατος), from *anti*, instead of, and *hupatos*, supreme, denotes a consul, one acting in place of a consul, a proconsul, the governor of a senatorial province (i.e., one which had no standing army). The proconsuls were of two classes, (*a*) ex-consuls, the rulers of the provinces of Asia and Africa, who were therefore proconsuls, (*b*) those who were ex-prætors or proconsuls of other senatorial provinces (a prætor being virtually the same as a consul). To the former belonged the proconsuls at Ephesus, Acts 19 : 38 (A.V., " deputies ") ; to the latter, Sergius Paulus in Cyprus, Acts 13 : 7, 8, 12, and Gallio at Corinth, 18 : 12. In the N.T. times Egypt was governed by a prefect. Provinces in which a standing army was kept were governed by an imperial legate (e.g., Quirinius in Syria, Luke 2 : 2) : see GOVERNOR, A, No. 1.¶

Note : *Anthupateō*, to be proconsul, is in some texts in Acts 18 : 12.

PROFANE (Adjective and Verb)
A. Adjective.

BEBĒLOS (βέβηλος), primarily, permitted to be trodden, accessible (from *bainō*, to go, whence *bēlos*, a threshold), hence, unhallowed, profane (opposite to *hieros*, sacred), is used of (*a*) persons, 1 Tim. 1 : 9 ; Heb. 12 : 16 ; (*b*) things, 1 Tim. 4 : 7 ; 6 : 20 ; 2 Tim. 2 : 16. " The natural antagonism between the profane and the holy or divine grew into a moral antagonism. . . . Accordingly *bebēlos* is that which lacks all relationship or affinity to God " (Cremer, who compares *koinos*, common, in the sense of ritual uncleanness).¶

B. Verb.

BEBĒLOŌ (βεβηλόω), primarily, to cross the threshold (akin to A, which see), hence, to profane, pollute, occurs in Matt. 12 : 5 and Acts 24 : 6 (the latter as in 21 : 28, 29 : cp. DEFILE, A, No. 1, PARTITION).¶

PROFESS, PROFESSION
A. Verbs.

1. EPANGELLŌ (ἐπαγγέλλω), to announce, proclaim, profess, is rendered to profess in 1 Tim. 2 : 10, of godliness, and 6 : 21, of " the knowledge . . . falsely so called." See PROMISE.

2. HOMOLOGEŌ (ὁμολογέω) is translated to profess in Matt. 7 : 23 and Tit. 1 : 16 ; in 1 Tim. 6 : 12, A.V. (R.V., " confess "). See CONFESS.

3. PHASKŌ (φάσκω), to affirm, assert : see AFFIRM, No. 3.

B. Noun.

HOMOLOGIA (ὁμολογία), akin to A, No. 2, confession, is translated " profession " and " professed " in the A.V. only. See CONFESS.

PROFIT (Noun and Verb), PROFITABLE, PROFITING

A. Nouns.

1. ŌPHELEIA (ὠφέλεια) primarily denotes assistance ; then, advantage, benefit, " profit," Rom. 3 : 1. See ADVANTAGE, No. 3.

2. OPHELOS (ὄφελος), " profit " in Jas. 2 : 14, 16 : see ADVANTAGE, No. 2.

3. SUMPHERON (συμφέρον), the neuter form of the present participle of *sumpherō* (see B, No. 1), is used as a noun with the article in Heb. 12 : 10, " (for our) profit ; " in some mss. in 1 Cor. 7 : 35 and 10 : 33 (see No. 4) ; in 1 Cor. 12 : 7, preceded by *pros*, with a view to, towards, translated " to profit withal," lit., ' towards the profiting.'¶

4. SUMPHOROS (σύμφορος), akin to No. 3, an adjective, signifying profitable, useful, expedient, is used as a noun, and found in the best texts, with the article, in 1 Cor. 7 : 35 (see No. 3) and 10 : 33 (1st part), the word being understood in the 2nd part.¶

5. PROKOPĒ (προκοπή), translated " profiting " in 1 Tim. 4 : 15, A.V. (R.V., " progress ") ; see FURTHERANCE.

B. Verbs.

1. SUMPHERŌ (συμφέρω), to be " profitable," Matt. 5 : 29, 30 ; Acts 20 : 20 : see EXPEDIENT.

2. ŌPHELEŌ (ὠφελέω), akin to A, No. 1, is translated ' to profit ' in Matt. 15 : 5 ; 16 : 26 ; Mark 7 : 11 ; 8 : 36 ; Luke 9 : 25, R.V. ; John 6 : 63 ; Rom. 2 : 25 ; 1 Cor. 13 : 3 ; 14 : 6 ; Gal. 5 : 2 ; Heb. 4 : 2 ; 13 : 9. See ADVANTAGE, BETTERED, PREVAIL.

3. PROKOPTŌ (προκόπτω) is translated " I profited " in Gal. 1 : 14, A.V. See ADVANCE.

C. Adjectives.

1. CHRĒSIMOS (χρήσιμος), useful (akin to *chraomai*, to use), is translated as a noun in 2 Tim. 2 : 14, " to (no) profit," lit., ' to (nothing) profitable.'¶

2. EUCHRĒSTOS (εὔχρηστος), useful, serviceable (*eu*, well, *chrēstos*, serviceable, akin to *chraomai*, see No. 1), is used in Philm. 11, " profitable," in contrast to *achrēstos*, " unprofitable " (*a*, negative), with a delightful play upon the name " Onesimus," signifying " profitable " (from *onēsis*, profit), a common name among slaves. Perhaps the prefix *eu* should have been brought out by some rendering like ' very profitable,' ' very serviceable,' the suggestion being that whereas the runaway slave had done great disservice to Philemon, now after his conversion, in devotedly serving the Apostle in his confinement, he had thereby already become particularly serviceable to Philemon himself, considering that the latter would have most willingly rendered service to Paul, had it been possible. Onesimus, who had belied his name, was now true to it on behalf of his erstwhile master, who also owed his conversion to the Apostle.

It is translated " meet for (the master's) use " in 2 Tim. 2 : 21 ;

" useful " in 4 : 11, R.V. (A.V., " profitable "). See USEFUL.¶ In the
Sept., Prov. 31 : 13.¶

3. ŌPHELIMOS (ὠφέλιμος), useful, profitable (akin to B, No. 2), is
translated " profitable " in 1 Tim. 4 : 8, both times in the R.V. (A.V.,
" profiteth " in the 1st part), of physical exercise, and of godliness ; in
2 Tim. 3 : 16 of the God-breathed Scriptures ; in Tit. 3 : 8, of maintaining
good works.¶

PROGRESS

PROKOPĒ (προκοπή) is translated " progress " in Phil. 1 : 12, 25
and 1 Tim. 4 : 15 : see FURTHERANCE.¶

PROLONG

PARATEINŌ (παρατείνω), to stretch out along (para, along, teinō, to
stretch), is translated " prolonged " in Acts 20 : 7, R.V., of Paul's discourse : see CONTINUE, Note (1).¶

PROMISE (Noun and Verb)
A. Nouns.

1. EPANGELIA (ἐπαγγελία), primarily a law term, denoting a
summons (epi, upon, angellō, to proclaim, announce), also meant an
undertaking to do or give something, a promise. Except in Acts 23 : 21
it is used only of the promises of God. It frequently stands for the thing
promised, and so signifies a gift graciously bestowed, not a pledge secured
by negotiation ; thus, in Gal. 3 : 14, " the promise of the Spirit " denotes
' the promised Spirit : ' cp. Luke 24 : 49 ; Acts 2 : 33 and Eph. 1 : 13 ;
so in Heb. 9 : 15, " the promise of the eternal inheritance " is ' the promised
eternal inheritance.' On the other hand, in Acts 1 : 4, " the promise of
the Father," is the promise made by the Father.

In Gal. 3 : 16, the plural " promises " is used because the one promise
to Abraham was variously repeated (Gen. 12 : 1–3 ; 13 : 14–17 ; 15 : 18 ;
17 : 1–14 ; 22 : 15–18), and because it contained the germ of all subsequent promises ; cp. Rom. 9 : 4 ; Heb. 6 : 12 ; 7 : 6 ; 8 : 6 ; 11 : 17.
Gal. 3 is occupied with showing that the promise was conditional upon
faith and not upon the fulfilment of the Law. The Law was later than,
and inferior to, the promise, and did not annul it, ver. 21 ; cp. 4 : 23, 28.
Again, in Eph. 2 : 12, " the covenants of the promise " does not indicate
different covenants, but a covenant often renewed, all centring in Christ
as the promised Messiah-Redeemer, and comprising the blessings to be
bestowed through Him.

In 2 Cor. 1 : 20 the plural is used of every promise made by God :
cp. Heb. 11 : 33 ; in 7 : 6, of special promises mentioned. For other
applications of the word, see, e.g., Eph. 6 : 2 ; 1 Tim. 4 : 8 ; 2 Tim. 1 : 1 ;
Heb. 4 : 1 ; 2 Pet. 3 : 4, 9 ; in 1 John 1 : 5 some mss. have this word,
instead of angelia, " message."

The occurrences of the word in relation to Christ and what centres in Him, may be arranged under the headings (1) the contents of the promise, e.g., Acts 26 : 6 ; Rom. 4 : 20 ; 1 John 2 : 25 ; (2) the heirs, e.g., Rom. 9 : 8 ; 15 : 8 ; Gal. 3 : 29 ; Heb. 11 : 9 ; (3) the conditions, e.g., Rom. 4 : 13, 14 ; Gal. 3 : 14–22 ; Heb. 10 : 36.

2. EPANGELMA (ἐπάγγελμα) denotes a promise made, 2 Pet. 1 : 4 ; 3 : 13.¶

B. Verbs.

1. EPANGELLŌ (ἐπαγγέλλω), to announce, proclaim, has in the N.T. the two meanings to profess and to promise, each used in the Middle Voice ; to promise (a) of promises of God, Acts 7 : 5 ; Rom. 4 : 21 ; in Gal. 3 : 19, Passive Voice ; Tit. 1 : 2 ; Heb. 6 : 13 ; 10 : 23 ; 11 : 11 ; 12 : 26 ; Jas. 1 : 12 ; 2 : 5 ; 1 John 2 : 25 ; (b) made by men, Mark 14 : 11 ; 2 Pet. 2 : 19. See PROFESS.

2. PROEPANGELLŌ (προεπαγγέλλω), in the Middle Voice, to promise before (pro, and No. 1), occurs in Rom. 1 : 2 ; 2 Cor. 9 : 5. See AFORE-PROMISED:¶

3. HOMOLOGEŌ (ὁμολογέω), to agree, confess, signifies to promise in Matt. 14 : 7. See CONFESS.

Note : For *exomologeō* in Luke 22 : 6, see CONSENT, No. 1.

PRONOUNCE

LEGŌ (λέγω), to say, declare, is rendered " pronounceth (blessing) " in Rom. 4 : 6, R.V., which necessarily repeats the verb in ver. 9 (it is absent from the original), for A.V., " *cometh* " (italicised). See ASK, A, No. 6, DESCRIBE, No. 2, SAY.

PROOF

1. DOKIMĒ (δοκιμή) : see EXPERIENCE, No. 2.

2. DOKIMION (δοκίμιον), a test, a proof, is rendered " proof " in Jas. 1 : 3, R.V. (A.V., " trying ") ; it is regarded by some as equivalent to *dokimeion*, a crucible, a test ; it is the neuter form of the adjective *dokimios*, used as a noun, which has been taken to denote the means by which a man is tested and proved (Mayor), in the same sense as *dokimē* (No. 1) in 2 Cor. 8 : 2 ; the same phrase is used in 1 Pet. 1 : 7, R.V., " the proof (of your faith)," A.V., " the trial;" where the meaning probably is ' that which is approved [i.e., as genuine] in your faith ; ' this interpretation, which was suggested by Hort, and may hold good for Jas. 1 : 3, has been confirmed from the papyri by Deissmann (*Bible Studies*, p. 259, ff). Moulton and Milligan (Vocab.) give additional instances.¶

3. ENDEIXIS (ἔνδειξις) : see DECLARE, B. Cp. the synonymous word *endeigma*, a token, 2 Thess. 1 : 5, which refers rather to the thing proved, while *endeixis* points to the act of proving.

4. TEKMĒRION (τεκμήριον), a sure sign, a positive proof (from *tekmar*, a mark, sign), occurs in Acts 1 : 3, R.V., " proofs " (A.V., " in-

fallible proofs ; " a proof does not require to be described as infallible, the adjective is superfluous).¶

Note : For the A.V. in 2 Tim. 4 : 5, " make full proof," R.V.," fulfil " (*plērophoreō*), see FULFIL.

PROPER

1. ASTEIOS (ἀστεῖος) is translated " proper " in Heb. 11 : 23, R.V., " goodly : " see BEAUTIFUL, No. 2.

2. IDIOS (ἴδιος), one's own, is found in some mss. in Acts 1 : 19, A.V., " proper ; " in 1 Cor. 7 : 7, R.V., " own " (A.V., " proper ") ; in Jude 6, R.V., " their proper (habitation)," A.V., " their own."

PROPHECY, PROPHESY, PROPHESYING
A. Noun.

PROPHĒTEIA (προφητεία) signifies the speaking forth of the mind and counsel of God (*pro*, forth, *phēmi*, to speak : see PROPHET) ; in the N.T. it is used (*a*) of the gift, e.g., Rom. 12 : 6 ; 1 Cor. 12 : 10 ; 13 : 2 ; (*b*) either of the exercise of the gift or of that which is prophesied, e.g., Matt. 13 : 14 ; 1 Cor. 13 : 8 ; 14 : 6, 22 and 1 Thess. 5 : 20, " prophesying (s) ; " 1 Tim. 1 : 18 ; 4 : 14 ; 2 Pet. 1 : 20, 21 ; Rev. 1 : 3 ; 11 : 6 ; 19 : 10 ; 22 : 7, 10, 18, 19.¶

" Though much of O.T. prophecy was purely predictive, see Micah 5 : 2, e.g., and cp. John 11 : 51, prophecy is not necessarily, nor even primarily, fore-telling. It is the declaration of that which cannot be known by natural means, Matt. 26 : 68, it is the forth-telling of the will of God, whether with reference to the past, the present, or the future, see Gen. 20 : 7 ; Deut. 18 : 18 ; Rev. 10 : 11 ; 11 : 3. . . .

" In such passages as 1 Cor. 12 : 28 ; Eph. 2 : 20, the ' prophets ' are placed after the ' Apostles,' since not the prophets of Israel are intended, but the ' gifts ' of the ascended Lord, Eph. 4 : 8, 11 ; cp. Acts 13 : 1 ; . . . . ; the purpose of their ministry was to edify, to comfort, and to encourage the believers, 1 Cor. 14 : 3, while its effect upon unbelievers was to show that the secrets of a man's heart are known to God, to convict of sin, and to constrain to worship, vv. 24, 25.

" With the completion of the canon of Scripture prophecy apparently passed away, 1 Cor. 13 : 8, 9. In his measure the teacher has taken the place of the prophet, cp. the significant change in 2 Pet. 2 : 1. The difference is that, whereas the message of the prophet was a direct revelation of the mind of God for the occasion, the message of the teacher is gathered from the completed revelation contained in the Scriptures."*

B. Adjective.
PROPHĒTIKOS (προφητικός), of or relating to prophecy, or proceeding

---

* From Notes on Thessalonians by Hogg and Vine, pp. 196, 197.

from a prophet, prophetic, is used of the O.T. Scriptures, Rom. 16 : 26, "of the prophets," lit., ' (by) prophetic (Scriptures) ; ' 2 Pet. 1 : 19, "the word of prophecy (*made* more sure) ", i.e., confirmed by the Person and work of Christ (A.V., "a more sure etc."), lit., ' the prophetic word.'¶

C. Verb.

PROPHĒTEUŌ (προφητεύω), to be a prophet, to prophesy, is used (*a*) with the primary meaning of telling forth the Divine counsels, e.g., Matt. 7 : 22 ; 26 : 68 ; 1 Cor. 11 : 4, 5 ; 13 : 9 ; 14 : 1, 3-5, 24, 31, 39 ; Rev. 11 : 3 ; (*b*) of foretelling the future, e.g., Matt. 15 : 7 ; John 11 : 51 ; 1 Pet. 1 : 10 ; Jude 14.

PROPHET

1. PROPHĒTĒS (προφήτης), one who speaks forth or openly (see PROPHECY, A), a proclaimer of a divine message, denoted among the Greeks an interpreter of the oracles of the gods.

In the Sept. it is the translation of the word *rôeh*, a seer; 1 Sam. 9 : 9, indicating that the prophet was one who had immediate intercourse with God. It also translates the word *nābhî*, meaning either one in whom the message from God springs forth or one to whom anything is secretly communicated. Hence, in general, the prophet was one upon whom the Spirit of God rested, Numb. 11 : 17–29, one, to whom and through whom God speaks, Numb. 12 : 2 ; Amos 3 : 7, 8. In the case of the O.T. prophets their messages were very largely the proclamation of the Divine purposes of salvation and glory to be accomplished in the future ; the prophesying of the N.T. prophets was both a preaching of the Divine counsels of grace already accomplished and the fore-telling of the purposes of God in the future.

In the N.T. the word is used (*a*) of the O.T. prophets, e.g., Matt. 5 : 12 ; Mark 6 : 15 ; Luke 4 : 27 ; John 8 : 52 ; Rom. 11 : 3 ; (*b*) of prophets in general, e.g., Matt. 10 : 41 ; 21 : 46 ; Mark 6 : 4 ; (*c*) of John the Baptist, Matt. 21 : 26 ; Luke 1 : 76 ; (*d*) of prophets in the churches, e.g., Acts 13 : 1 ; 15 : 32 ; 21 : 10 ; 1 Cor. 12 : 28, 29 ; 14 : 29, 32, 37 ; Eph. 2 : 20 ; 3 : 5 ; 4 : 11 ; (*e*) of Christ, as the afore-promised Prophet, e.g., John 1 : 21 ; 6 : 14 ; 7 : 40 ; Acts 3 : 22 ; 7 : 37, or, without the article, and, without reference to the Old Testament, Mark 6 : 15, Luke 7 : 16 ; in Luke 24 : 19 it is used with *anēr*, a man ; John 4 : 19 ; 9 : 17 ; (*f*) of two witnesses yet to be raised up for special purposes, Rev. 11 : 10, 18 ; (*g*) of the Cretan poet Epimenides, Tit. 1 : 12 ; (*h*) by metonymy, of the writings of prophets, e.g., Luke 24 : 27 ; Acts 8 : 28.

2. PSEUDOPROPHĒTĒS (ψευδοπροφήτης), a false prophet, is used of such (*a*) in O.T. times, Luke 6 : 26 ; 2 Pet. 2 : 1 ; (*b*) in the present period since Pentecost, Matt. 7 : 15 ; 24 : 11, 24 ; Mark 13 : 22 ; Acts 13 : 6 ; 1 John 4 : 1 ; (*c*) with reference to a false prophet destined to arise as the supporter of the " beast " at the close of this age, Rev. 16 : 13 ; 19 : 20 ; 20 : 10 (himself described as " another beast," 13 : 11).¶

PROPHETESS

PROPHĒTIS (προφῆτις), the feminine of *prophētēs* (see above), is used of Anna, Luke 2 : 36 ; of the self-assumed title of " the woman Jezebel " in Rev. 2 : 20.¶

PROPITIATION
A. Verb.

HILASKOMAI (ἱλάσκομαι) was used amongst the Greeks with the significance to make the gods propitious, to appease, propitiate, inasmuch as their good will was not conceived as their natural attitude, but something to be earned first. This use of the word is foreign to the Greek Bible, with respect to God, whether in the Sept. or in the N.T. It is never used of any act whereby man brings God into a favourable attitude or gracious disposition. It is God who is propitiated by the vindication of His holy and righteous character, whereby, through the provision He has made in the vicarious and expiatory sacrifice of Christ, He has so dealt with sin that He can shew mercy to the believing sinner in the removal of his guilt and the remission of his sins.

Thus in Luke 18 : 13 it signifies to be propitious or merciful to (with the person as the object of the verb), and in Heb. 2 : 17 to expiate, to make propitiation for (the object of the verb being sins) ; here the R.V.," to make propitiation " is an important correction of the A.V., " to make reconciliation." Through the propitiatory sacrifice of Christ, he who believes upon Him is by God's own act delivered from justly deserved wrath, and comes under the covenant of grace. Never is God said to be reconciled, a fact itself indicative that the enmity exists on man's part alone, and that it is man who needs to be reconciled to God, and not God to man. God is always the same and, since He is Himself immutable, His relative attitude does change towards those who change. He can act differently towards those who come to Him by faith, and solely on the ground of the propitiatory sacrifice of Christ, not because He has changed, but because He ever acts according to His unchanging righteousness.

The expiatory work of the Cross is therefore the means whereby the barrier which sin interposes between God and man is broken down. By the giving up of His sinless life sacrificially, Christ annuls the power of sin to separate between God and the believer.

In the O.T. the Hebrew verb *kaphar* is connected with *kopher*, a covering (see MERCY-SEAT), and is used in connection with the burnt offering, e.g., Lev. 1 : 4 ; 14 : 20 ; 16 : 24, the guilt offering, e.g., Lev. 5 : 16, 18, the sin offering, e.g., Lev. 4 : 20, 26, 31, 35, the sin offering and burnt offering together, e.g., Lev. 5 : 10 ; 9 : 7, the meal offering and peace offering, e.g., Ezek. 45 : 15, 17, as well as in other respects. It is used of the ram offered at the consecration of the high priest, Ex. 29 : 33, and of the blood which God gave upon the altar to make propitiation for the souls of the people, and that because " the life of the flesh is in the blood," Lev. 17 : 11, and " it is the blood that maketh atonement by reason of the life " (R.V.). Man has forfeited his life on account of sin and God has provided the one and only way whereby eternal life could be bestowed, namely, by the voluntary laying down of His life by His Son, under Divine retribution. Of this the former sacrifices appointed by God were foreshadowings.

B. Nouns.

1. HILASTĒRION (ἱλαστήριον), akin to A, is regarded as the neuter of an adjective signifying propitiatory. In the Sept. it is used adjectivally in connection with *epithēma*, a cover, in Ex. 25 : 17 and 37 : 6, of the lid of the ark (see MERCY-SEAT), but it is used as a noun (without *epithēma*), of locality, in Ex. 25 : 18, 19, 20, 21, 22 ; 31 : 7 ; 35 : 12 ; 37 : 7, 8, 9 ; Lev. 16 : 2, 13, 14, 15 ; Numb. 7 : 89, and this is its use in Heb. 9 : 5.

Elsewhere in the N.T. it occurs in Rom. 3 : 25, where it is used of Christ Himself ; the R.V. text and punctuation in this verse are important : " whom God set forth *to be* a propitiation, through faith, by His blood." The phrase " by His blood " is to be taken in immediate connection with " propitiation." Christ, through His expiatory death, is the Personal means by whom God shows the mercy of His justifying grace to the sinner who believes. His " blood " stands for the voluntary giving up of His life, by the shedding of His blood in expiatory sacrifice, under Divine judgment righteously due to us as sinners, faith being the sole condition on man's part.

Note : " By metonymy, ' blood ' is sometimes put for ' death,' inasmuch as, blood being essential to life, Lev. 17 : 11, when the blood is shed life is given up, that is, death takes place. The fundamental principle on which God deals with sinners is expressed in the words ' apart from shedding of blood,' i.e., unless a death takes place, ' there is no remission ' of sins, Heb. 9 : 22.

" But whereas the essential of the type lay in the fact that blood was shed, the essential of the antitype lies in this, that the blood shed was that of Christ. Hence, in connection with Jewish sacrifices, ' the blood ' is mentioned without reference to the victim from which it flowed, but in connection with the great antitypical sacrifice of the N.T. the words ' the blood ' never stand alone ; the One Who shed the blood is invariably specified, for it is the Person that gives value to the work ; the saving efficacy of the Death depends entirely upon the fact that He Who died was the Son of God."*

2. HILASMOS (ἱλασμός), akin to *hileōs* (merciful, propitious), signifies an expiation, a means whereby sin is covered and remitted. It is used in the N.T. of Christ Himself as " the propitiation," in 1 John 2 : 2 and 4 : 10, signifying that He Himself, through the expiatory sacrifice of His Death, is the Personal means by whom God shows mercy to the sinner who believes

---

* From Notes on Thessalonians by Hogg and Vine, p. 168.

on Christ as the One thus provided.   In the former passage He is described as " the propitiation for our sins ; and not for ours only, but also for the whole world."   The italicised addition in the A.V., " *the sins of*," gives a wrong interpretation.   What is indicated is that provision is made for the whole world, so that no one is, by Divine pre-determination, excluded from the scope of God's mercy ; the efficacy of the propitiation, however, is made actual for those who believe.   In 4 : 10, the fact that God " sent His Son to be the propitiation for our sins," is shown to be the great expression of God's love toward man, and the reason why Christians should love one another.¶   In the Sept., Lev. 25 : 9 ; Numb. 5 : 8 ; 1 Chron. 28 : 20 ; Ps. 130 : 4 ; Ezek. 44 : 27 ; Amos 8 : 14.¶

PROPORTION

ANALOGIA (ἀναλογία), Eng., analogy, signified in classical Greek " the right relation, the coincidence or agreement existing or demanded according to the standard of the several relations, not agreement as equality " (Cremer).   It is used in Rom. 12 : 6, where " let us prophesy according to the proportion of our faith," R.V., recalls ver. 3.   It is a warning against going beyond what God has given and faith receives. This meaning, rather than the other rendering, " according to the analogy of the faith," is in keeping with the context.   The word *analogia* is not to be rendered literally.   " Proportion " here represents its true meaning. The fact that there is a definite article before " faith " in the original does not necessarily afford an intimation that the faith, the body of Christian doctrine, is here in view.   The presence of the definite article is due to the fact that faith is an abstract noun.   The meaning " the faith" is not relevant to the context.¶

PROSELYTE

PROSĒLUTOS (προσήλυτος), akin to *proserchomai*, to come to, primarily signifies one who has arrived, a stranger ; in the N.T. it is used of converts to Judaism, or foreign converts to the Jewish religion, Matt. 23 : 15 ; Acts 2 : 10 ; 6 : 5 ; 13 : 43.¶   There seems to be no connexion necessarily with Palestine, for in Acts 2 : 10 and 13 : 43 it is used of those who lived abroad.   Cp. the Sept., e.g., in Ex. 22 : 21 ; 23 : 9 ; Deut. 10 : 19, of the " stranger " living among the children of Israel.

PROSPER

EUODOŌ (εὐοδόω), to help on one's way (*eu*, well, *hodos*, a way or journey), is used in the Passive Voice signifying to have a prosperous journey, Rom. 1 : 10 ; metaphorically, to prosper, be prospered, 1 Cor. 16 : 2, R.V., " (as) he may prosper," A.V., " (as God) hath prospered (him)," lit., ' in whatever he may be prospered,' i.e., in material things ; the continuous tense suggests the successive circumstances of varying prosperity as week follows week ; in 3 John 2, of the prosperity of physical and spiritual health.¶

PROTEST

Note : In 1 Cor. 15 : 31, " I protest by " is a rendering of *nē*, a particle of strong affirmation used in oaths.¶   In the Sept., Gen. 42 : 15, 16.¶

PROUD

HUPERĒPHANOS (ὑπερήφανος) signifies showing oneself above others, pre-eminent (*huper*, above, *phainomai*, to appear, be manifest) ; it is always used in Scripture in the bad sense of arrogant, disdainful, proud, Luke 1 : 51 ; Rom. 1 : 30 ; 2 Tim. 3 : 2 ; Jas. 4 : 6 ; 1 Pet. 5 : 5.¶

Note : For the A.V. renderings of the verb *tuphoō*, in 1 Tim. 3 : 6 ; 6 : 4 ; 2 Tim. 3 : 4, see HIGH-MINDED.

PROVE
A. Verbs.

1. DOKIMAZŌ (δοκιμάζω), to test, prove, with the expectation of approving, is translated to prove in Luke 14 : 19 ; Rom. 12 : 2 ; 1 Cor. 3 : 13, R.V. (A.V., " shall try ") ; 11 : 28, R.V. (A.V., " examine ") ; 2 Cor. 8 : 8, 22 ; 13 : 5 ; Gal. 6 : 4 ; Eph. 5 : 10 ; 1 Thess. 2 : 4 (2nd part), R.V. (A.V., " trieth ") ; 5 : 21 ; 1 Tim. 3 : 10 ; in some mss., Heb. 3 : 9 (the most authentic have the noun *dokimasia*, a proving¶) ; 1 Pet. 1 : 7, R.V. (A.V., " tried ") ; 1 John 4 : 1, R.V. (A.V., " try "). See APPROVE.

2. APODEIKNUMI (ἀποδείκνυμι), to show forth, signifies to prove in Acts 25 : 7. See APPROVE, No. 3.

3. PARISTĒMI (παρίστημι), to present, signifies to prove in Acts 24 : 13. See COMMEND, No. 4.

4. PEIRAZŌ (πειράζω), to try, either in the sense of attempting, e.g., Acts 16 : 7, or of testing, is rendered " to prove " in John 6 : 6. See EXAMINE, TEMPT.

5. SUMBIBAZŌ (συμβιβάζω), to join together, signifies to prove in Acts 9 : 22. See COMPACTED, No. 2.

6. SUNISTĒMI or SUNISTANŌ (συνίστημι), to commend, to prove, is translated " I prove (myself a transgressor) " in Gal. 2 : 18 (A.V., " I make "). See COMMEND.

B. Noun.

PEIRASMOS (πειρασμός), (*a*) a trying, testing, (*b*) a temptation, is used in sense (*a*) in 1 Pet. 4 : 12, with the preposition *pros*, towards or with a view to, R.V., " to prove " (A.V., " to try "), lit., ' for a testing.' See TEMPTATION.

Notes : (1) In Luke 10 : 36, R.V., *ginomai*, to become, come to be, is translated " proved (neighbour)," A.V., " was . . . ; " so in Heb. 2 : 2. (2) In Rom. 3 : 9, A.V., *proaitiaomai*, to accuse beforehand, is translated " we have before proved " (marg., " charged ") ; for the R.V., see CHARGE, C, No. 9.

For PROVERB see PARABLE, No. 2

PROVIDE, PROVIDENCE, PROVISION
A. Verbs.

1. HETOIMAZŌ (ἐτοιμάζω), to prepare, is translated " hast provided " in Luke 12 : 20, A.V. See PREPARE.

2. KTAOMAI (κτάομαι), to get, to gain, is rendered " provide " in Matt. 10 : 9. See OBTAIN, POSSESS.

3. PARISTĒMI (παρίστημι), to present, signifies to provide in Acts 23 : 24. See COMMEND, PROVE, No. 3.

4. PROBLEPŌ (προβλέπω), to foresee, is translated " having provided " in Heb. 11 : 40. See FORESEE.¶

5. PRONOEŌ (προνοέω), to take thought for, provide, is translated " provide . . . for " in 1 Tim. 5 : 8 ; in Rom. 12 : 17 and 2 Cor. 8 : 21, R.V., to take thought for (A.V., to provide).¶

Note : In Luke 12 : 33, A.V., *poieō*, to make (R.V.), is translated " provide."

B. Noun.

PRONOIA (πρόνοια), forethought (*pro*, before, *noeō*, to think), is translated " providence " in Acts 24 : 2 ; " provision " in Rom. 13 : 14.¶

PROVINCE

1. EPARCHEIA, or -IA (ἐπαρχεία) was a technical term for the administrative divisions of the Roman Empire. The original meaning was the district within which a magistrate, whether consul or prætor, exercised supreme authority. The word *provincia* acquired its later meaning when Sardinia and Sicily were added to the Roman territories, 227 B.C. On the establishment of the Empire the proconsular power over all provinces was vested in the Emperor. Two provinces, Asia and Africa, were consular, i.e., held by ex-consuls ; the rest were prætorian. Certain small provinces, e.g. Judæa and Cappadocia, were governed by procurators. They were usually districts recently added to the Empire and not thoroughly Romanized. Judæa was so governed in the intervals between the rule of native kings ; ultimately it was incorporated in the province of Syria. The province mentioned in Acts 23 : 34 and 25 : 1 was assigned to the jurisdiction of an *eparchos*, a prefect or governor (cp. GOVERNOR, PROCONSUL).¶ In the Sept., Esth. 4 : 11.¶

2. KANŌN (κανών) originally denoted a straight rod, used as a ruler or measuring instrument, or, in rare instances, the beam of a balance, the secondary notion being either (*a*) of keeping anything straight, as of a rod used in weaving, or (*b*) of testing straightness, as a carpenter's rule ; hence its metaphorical use to express what serves to measure or determine anything. By a common transition in the meaning of words, that which measures, was used for what was measured ; thus a certain space at Olympia was called a *kanōn*. So in music, a canon is a composition in which a given melody is the model for the formation of all the parts. In general the word thus came to serve for anything regulating the actions

of men, as a standard or principle. In Gal. 6 : 16, those who " walk by this rule (*kanōn*) " are those who make what is stated in vv. 14 and 15 their guiding line in the matter of salvation through faith in Christ alone, apart from works, whether following the principle themselves or teaching it to others. In 2 Cor. 10 : 13, 15, 16, it is translated " province," R.V. (A.V., " rule " and " line of things " ; marg., " line ; " R.V. marg., " limit " or " measuring rod.") Here it signifies the limits of the responsibility in gospel service as measured and appointed by God.¶

For PROVING (*elenchos*) see REPROOF, A

PROVOCATION, PROVOKE
A. Nouns.

1. PARAPIKRASMOS (παραπικρασμός), from *para*, amiss or from, used intensively, and *pikrainō*, to make bitter (*pikros*, sharp, bitter), provocation, occurs in Heb. 3 : 8, 15.¶ In the Sept., Psa. 95 : 8.¶

2. PAROXUSMOS (παροξυσμός) denotes a stimulation (Eng., paroxysm), (cp. B, No. 2) : in Heb. 10 : 24, " to provoke," lit., ' unto a stimulation (of love).' See CONTENTION, No. 2.

B. Verbs.

1. PARAPIKRAINŌ (παραπικραίνω), to embitter, provoke (akin to A, No. 1), occurs in Heb. 3 : 16.¶

2. PAROXUNŌ (παροξύνω), primarily, to sharpen (akin to A, No. 2), is used metaphorically, signifying to rouse to anger, to provoke, in the Passive Voice, in Acts 17 : 16, R.V., " was provoked " (A.V., " was stirred ") ; in 1 Cor. 13 : 5, R.V., " is not provoked " (the word " easily " in A.V., represents no word in the original). See STIR.¶

3. ERETHIZŌ (ἐρεθίζω), to excite, stir up, provoke, is used (*a*) in a good sense in 2 Cor. 9 : 2, A.V., " hath provoked," R.V., " hath stirred up ; " (*b*) in an evil sense in Col. 3 : 21, " provoke." See STIR.¶

4. PARORGIZŌ (παροργίζω), to provoke to wrath : see ANGER, B, No. 2.

5. PARAZĒLOŌ (παραζηλόω), to provoke to jealousy : see JEALOUSY.

6. APOSTOMATIZŌ (ἀποστοματίζω) in classical Greek meant to speak from memory, to dictate to a pupil (*apo*, from, *stoma*, a mouth) ; in later Greek, to catechize ; in Luke 11 : 53, " to provoke (Him) to speak."¶

7. PROKALEŌ (προκαλέω), to call forth, as to a contest, hence to stir up what is evil in another, occurs in the Middle Voice in Gal. 5 : 26.¶

PRUDENCE, PRUDENT
A. Nouns.

1. PHRONĒSIS (φρόνησις), akin to *phroneō*, to have understanding (*phrēn*, the mind), denotes practical wisdom, prudence in the management of affairs. It is translated " wisdom " in Luke 1 : 17 ; " prudence " in Eph. 1 : 8. See WISDOM.¶

2. SUNESIS (σύνεσις), understanding, is rendered "prudence" in 1 Cor. 1 : 19, R.V. (A.V., "understanding"); it suggests quickness of apprehension, the penetrating consideration which precedes action. Cp. B, in the same verse. See KNOWLEDGE, UNDERSTANDING.

B. Adjective.

SUNETOS (συνετός) signifies intelligent, sagacious, understanding (akin to suniēmi, to perceive), translated "prudent" in Matt. 11 : 25, A.V. (R.V., "understanding"); Luke 10 : 21 (ditto); Acts 13 : 7, R.V., " (a man) of understanding; " in 1 Cor. 1 : 19, " prudent," R.V. and A.V.¶ Cp. asunetos, "without understanding."

PSALM

PSALMOS (ψαλμός) primarily denoted a striking or twitching with the fingers (on musical strings); then, a sacred song, sung to musical accompaniment, a psalm. It is used (a) of the O.T. book of Psalms, Luke 20 : 42; 24 : 44; Acts 1 : 20; (b) of a particular psalm, Acts 13 : 33 (cp. ver. 35); (c) of psalms in general, 1 Cor. 14 : 26; Eph. 5 : 19; Col. 3 : 16.¶

Note: For *psallō*, rendered "let him sing psalms" in Jas. 5 · 13, see MELODY, SING.

PUBLIC, PUBLICLY
A. Adjective.

DĒMOSIOS (δημόσιος), belonging to the people (*dēmos*, the people), is translated "public" in Acts 5 : 18, R.V., "public (ward)", A.V., " common (prison)."

B. Adverbs.

PHANERŌS (φανερῶς): see OPENLY, No. 2.

Note: For a form of *dēmosios* used as an adverb, "publicly," see OPENLY, Note (4).

PUBLICAN

TELŌNĒS (τελώνης) primarily denoted a farmer of the tax (from *telos*, toll, custom, tax), then, as in the N.T., a subsequent subordinate of such, who collected taxes in some district, a tax-gatherer; such were naturally hated intensely by the people; they are classed with " sinners ", Matt. 9 : 10, 11; 11 : 9; Mark 2 : 15, 16; Luke 5 : 30; 7 : 34; 15 : 1; with harlots, Matt. 21 : 31, 32; with " the Gentile," Matt. 18 : 17; some mss. have it in Matt. 5 : 47, the best have *ethnikoi*, " Gentiles." See also Matt. 5 : 46; 10 : 3; Luke 3.: 12; 5 : 27, 29; 7 : 29; 18 : 10, 11, 13.¶

Note: For *architelōnēs*, a chief publican, see CHIEF, B, No. 4.

PUBLISH

1. KĒRUSSŌ (κηρύσσω), to be a herald, to proclaim, preach, is translated to publish in Mark 1 : 45; 5 : 20; 7 : 36; 13 : 10, A.V. (R.V., " preached "); Luke 8 : 39. See PREACH, PROCLAIM.

2. DIAPHERŌ (διαφέρω), to bear through, is translated " was published " in Acts 13 : 49, A.V. (R.V., " was spread abroad "). See BETTER (be), No. 1.

3. GINOMAI (γίνομαι), to become, come to be, is translated " was published " in Acts 10 : 37, lit., ' came to be.'

4. DIANGELLŌ (διαγγέλλω), to publish abroad, is so translated in Luke 9 : 60, R.V. (A.V., " preach "), and Rom. 9 : 17. See DECLARE, A, No. 3.

PUFF (up)

1. PHUSIOŌ (φυσιόω), to puff up, blow up, inflate (from *phusa*, bellows), is used metaphorically in the N.T., in the sense of being puffed up with pride, 1 Cor. 4 : 6, 18, 19 ; 5 : 2 ; 8 : 1 ; 13 : 4 ; Col. 2 : 18.¶

2. TUPHOŌ (τυφόω) is always rendered to puff up in the R.V. See HIGH-MINDED, PROUD.

PULL (down)

KATHAIREŌ (καθαιρέω), to take down, is translated ·" I will pull down " in Luke 12 : 18. See DESTROY, No. 3.

Notes : (1) In Jude 23, A.V., *harpazo*, to seize, snatch away, is rendered " pulling . . . out." See SNATCH. (2) In Acts 23 : 10, A.V., *diaspaō*, to rend or tear asunder, is translated " should have been pulled in pieces " (R.V., " should be torn in pieces "). (3) *Ekballō*, to cast out, is translated to pull out in Matt. 7 : 4 and Luke 6 : 42 (twice), A.V. (R.V., " cast out "). See CAST, No. 5. (4) For *anaspaō*, rendered " pull out " in Luke 14 : 5, A.V., see DRAW, No. 5. (5) For *kathairesis*, a casting down, 2 Cor. 10 : 4, see CAST, A, No. 14, Note.

PUNISH

1. KOLAZŌ (κολάζω) primarily denotes to curtail, prune, dock (from *kolos*, docked) ; then, to check, restrain, punish ; it is used in the Middle Voice in Acts 4 : 21 ; Passive Voice in 2 Pet. 2 : 9, A.V., to be punished (R.V., " under punishment," lit., ' being punished '), a futurative present tense.¶

2. TIMŌREŌ (τιμωρέω), primarily, to help, then, to avenge (from *timē*, value, honour, and *ouros*, a guardian), i.e., to help by redressing injuries, is used in the Active Voice in Acts 26 : 11, R.V., " punishing " (A.V., " I punished ") ; Passive V. in 22 : 5, lit., ' (that) they may be punished.' Cp. No. 5, below.¶

Note : For 2 Thess. 1 : 9, " shall suffer punishment," R.V., see JUSTICE. See SUFFER, *Note* (10).

PUNISHMENT

1. EKDIKĒSIS (ἐκδίκησις) : for 1 Pet. 2 : 14, A.V., " punishment " (R.V., " vengeance "), see AVENGE, B, No. 2.

2. EPITIMIA (ἐπιτιμία) in the N.T. denotes penalty, punishment, 2 Cor. 2 : 6.¶ Originally it signified the enjoyment of the rights and privileges of citizenship; then it became used of the estimate (timē) fixed by a judge on the infringement of such rights, and hence, in general, a penalty.

3. KOLASIS (κόλασις), akin to kolazō (PUNISH, No. 1), punishment, is used in Matt. 25 : 46, " (eternal) punishment," and 1 John 4 : 18, " (fear hath) punishment," R.V. (A.V., " torment "), which there describes a process, not merely an effect; this kind of fear is expelled by perfect love; where God's love is being perfected in us, it gives no room for the fear of meeting with His reprobation; the punishment referred to is the immediate consequence of the sense of sin, not a holy awe but a slavish fear, the negation of the enjoyment of love.¶

4. DIKĒ (δίκη), justice, or the execution of a sentence, is translated " punishment " in Jude 7, R.V. (A.V., " vengeance "). See JUSTICE.

5. TIMŌRIA (τιμωρία), primarily help (see PUNISH, No. 2), denotes vengeance, punishment, Heb. 10 : 29.¶

Note : The distinction, sometimes suggested, between No. 3 as being disciplinary, with special reference to the sufferer, and No. 5, as being penal, with reference to the satisfaction of him who inflicts it, cannot be maintained in the *Koinē* Greek of N.T. times.

PURCHASE

1. KTAOMAI (κτάομαι) : see OBTAIN, A, No. 4.

2. PERIPOIEŌ (περιποιέω) signifies to gain or get for oneself, purchase; Middle Voice in Acts 20 : 28 and 1 Tim. 3 : 13 (R.V., " gain "); see GAIN.

3. AGORAZŌ (ἀγοράζω) is rendered to purchase in the R.V. of Rev. 5 : 9; 14 : 3, 4. See BUY, No. 1.

Note : For *peripoiēsis,* " purchased possession," Eph. 1 : 14, see POSSESSION.

PURE, PURENESS, PURITY
A. Adjectives.

1. HAGNOS (ἁγνός), pure from defilement, not contaminated (from the same root as *hagios,* holy), is rendered " pure " in Phil. 4 : 8; 1 Tim. 5 : 22; Jas. 3 : 17; 1 John 3 : 3; see CHASTE.

2. KATHAROS (καθαρός), pure, as being cleansed, e.g., Matt. 5 : 8; 1 Tim. 1 : 5; 3 : 9; 2 Tim. 1 : 3; 2 : 22; Tit. 1 : 15; Heb. 10 : 22; Jas. 1 : 27; 1 Pet. 1 : 22; Rev. 15 : 6; 21 : 18; 22 : 1 (in some mss.). See CHASTE, Note, CLEAN, A.

Note : In 1 Pet. 1 : 22 the A.V., " with a pure heart," follows those mss. which have this adjective (R.V., " from the heart ").

3. EILIKRINĒS (εἰλικρινής) signifies unalloyed, pure; (a) it was used of unmixed substances; (b) in the N.T. it is used of moral and ethical purity, Phil. 1 : 10, " sincere ;" so the R.V. in 2 Pet. 3 : 1 (A.V., " pure ").

ne regard the etymological meaning as ' tested by the sunlight '
remer).¶ See CHASTE, Note, SINCERE.

Note : Wine mixed with water may be *hagnos*, not being contaminated ;
it is not *katharos*, when there is the admixture of any element even
though the latter is pure in itself.

B. Nouns.

1. HAGNOTĒS (ἁγνότης), the state of being *hagnos* (A, No. 1), occurs
in 2 Cor. 6 : 6, " pureness ; " 11 : 3, in the best mss., " (and the) purity,"
R.V.¶

2. HAGNEIA (ἁγνεία), synonymous with No. 1, " purity ", occurs
in 1 Tim. 4 : 12 ; 5 : 2, where it denotes the chastity which excludes all
impurity of spirit, manner, or act.¶

PURGE

1. KATHAIRŌ (καθαίρω), akin to *katharos* (see PURE, A, No. 2), to
cleanse, is used of pruning, John 15 : 2, A.V., " purgeth " (R.V.,
" cleanseth ").¶ In the Sept., 2 Sam. 4 : 6 ; Isa. 28 : 27 ; Jer. 38 : 28.¶

2. EKKATHAIRŌ (ἐκκαθαίρω), to cleanse out, cleanse thoroughly, is
said of purging out leaven, 1 Cor. 5 : 7 ; in 2 Tim. 2 : 21, of purging oneself
from those who utter " profane babblings," vv. 16–18.¶

3. DIAKATHAIRŌ (διακαθαίρω), to cleanse thoroughly, is translated
" will throughly purge " in Luke 3 : 17, A.V. (R.V., " thoroughly to
cleanse ; " less authentic mss. have No. 5).¶

4. KATHARIZŌ (καθαρίζω), to cleanse, make clean, is translated
" purging (all meats)," in Mark 7 : 19, A.V., R.V., " making (all meats)
clean ; " Heb. 9 : 14, A.V., " purge " (R.V., " cleanse ") ; so 9 : 22 (for
ver. 23, see PURIFY) and 10 : 2. See CLEAN, B, No. 1.

5. DIAKATHARIZŌ (διακαθαρίζω), to cleanse thoroughly, is translated " will throughly purge " in Matt. 3 . 12, A.V. See CLEAN, B, No. 2.
Cp. the synonymous verb No. 3.¶

Notes : (1) For Heb. 1 : 3, A.V., " had purged," see PURIFICATION.
(2) For the A.V. rendering of the noun *katharismos*, cleansing, " that he
was purged," see CLEAN, C, No. 1.

PURIFICATION, PURIFY, PURIFYING
A. Nouns.

1. KATHARISMOS (καθαρισμός) is rendered a cleansing (akin to
No. 4, above), Mark 1 : 44 ; Luke 5 : 14 ; in Heb. 1 : 3, R.V., " purification "

2. KATHAROTĒS (καθαρότης), cleansing, Heb. 9 : 13. See CLEAN,
C, No. 2.¶

3. HAGNISMOS (ἁγνισμός) denotes a ceremonial purification, Acts
21 : 26, for the circumstances of which with reference to the vow of a
Nazirite (R.V.), see Numb. 6 : 9–13.¶

B. Verbs.

1. HAGNIZŌ (ἁγνίζω), akin to *hagnos*, pure (see CHASTE), to purify, cleanse from defilement, is used of purifying (*a*) ceremonially, John 11 : 55 ; Acts 21 : 24, 26 (cp. No. 3 above) ; 24 : 18 ; (*b*) morally, the heart, Jas. 4 : 8 ; the soul, 1 Pet. 1 : 22 ; oneself, 1 John 3 : 3.¶

2. KATHARIZŌ (καθαρίζω), to cleanse, make free from admixture, is translated to purify in Acts 15 : 9, A.V. (R.V., " cleansing ") ; Tit. 2 : 14 ; Heb. 9 : 23, A.V. (R.V., " cleansed "). See CLEAN, B, No. 1.

PURLOIN

NOSPHIZŌ (νοσφίζω) is translated " purloining " in Tit. 2 : 10. See KEEP, A, No. 10.

PURPLE
A. Noun.

PORPHURA (πορφύρα) originally denoted the purple-fish, then, purple dye (extracted from certain shell fish) : hence, a purple garment, Mark 15 : 17, 20 ; Luke 16 : 19 ; Rev. 18 : 12.¶

B. Adjective.

PORPHUREOS (πορφύρεος), purple, a reddish purple, is used of the robe put in mockery on Christ, John 19 : 2, 5 ; in Rev. 17 : 4 (in the best texts ; some have No. 1) ; 18 : 16, as a noun (with *himation*, a garment, understood).¶

PURPLE (seller of)

PORPHUROPŌLIS (πορφυρόπωλις) denotes a seller of purple fabrics (from *porphura*, and *pōleō*, to sell), Acts 16 : 14.¶

PURPOSE (Noun and Verb)
A. Nouns.

1. BOULĒMA (βούλημα), a purpose or will (akin to *boulomai*, to will, wish, purpose), a deliberate intention, occurs in Acts 27 : 43, " purpose ; " Rom. 9 : 19, " will ; " 1 Pet. 4 : 3, in the best mss. (some have *thelēma*), A.V., " will," R.V., " desire." See WILL.¶

2. PROTHESIS (πρόθεσις), a setting forth (used of the " shewbread "), a purpose (akin to B, No. 3), is used (*a*) of the purposes of God, Rom. 8 : 28 ; 9 : 11 ; Eph. 1 : 11 ; 3 : 11 ; 2 Tim. 1 : 9 ; (*b*) of human purposes, as to things material, Acts 27 : 13 ; spiritual, Acts 11 : 23 ; 2 Tim. 3 : 10. See SHEWBREAD.

3. GNŌMĒ (γνώμη), an opinion, purpose, judgment, is used in the genitive case with *ginomai*, to come to be, in Acts 20 : 3, " he purposed," A.V. (R.V., " he determined "), lit., ' he came to be of purpose.'

Notes : The following phrases are translated with the word " purpose : " (*a*) *eis auto touto*, " for this same (or very) purpose," lit., ' unto this same (thing),' Rom. 9 : 17 ; Eph. 6 : 22 ; Col. 4 : 8 ; (*b*) *eis touto*, " for this purpose," Acts 26 : 16, A.V. (R.V., " to this end "), lit., ' unto this ; ' so

1 John 3 : 8 ; (c) *eis ti*, " to what purpose," Matt. 26 : 8, lit., ' unto what ; ' Mark 14 : 4, R.V., " to what purpose " (A.V., " why ").

B. Verbs.

1. BOULEUŌ (βουλεύω), to take counsel, resolve, always in the Middle Voice in the N.T., to take counsel with oneself, to determine with oneself, is translated " I purpose " in 2 Cor. 1 : 17 (twice). See COUNSEL, B, No. 1.

2. TITHĒMI (τίθημι), to put, place, is used in the Middle Voice in Acts 19 : 21, " purposed," in the sense of resolving.

3. PROTITHĒMI (προτίθημι), to set before, set forth (*pro*, before, and No. 2, akin to A, No. 2), is used in Rom. 3 : 25, " set forth," R.V. marg., " purposed," A.V. marg., " foreordained," Middle Voice, which lays stress upon the Personal interest which God had in so doing ; either meaning, to set forth or to purpose, would convey a Scriptural view, but the context bears out the former as being intended here ; in Rom. 1 : 13, " I purposed ; " Eph. 1 : 9, " He purposed (in Him)," R.V. See SET.¶

4. POIEŌ (ποιέω), to make, is translated " He purposed " in Eph. 3 : 11 (for the noun *prothesis*, in the same verse, see A, No. 2). See DO, No. 1.

5. PROAIREŌ (προαιρέω), to bring forth or forward, or, in the Middle Voice, to take by choice, prefer, purpose, is translated " He hath purposed " in 2 Cor. 9 : 7, R.V. (A.V., " he purposed ").¶

For PURSE see BAG, No. 2 and Note

PURSUE

DIŌKŌ (διώκω), to put to flight, pursue, persecute, is rendered to pursue in 2 Cor. 4 : 9, R.V. (A.V., " persecute "), and is used metaphorically of seeking eagerly after peace in 1 Pet. 3 : 11, R.V. (A.V., " ensue "). See FOLLOW.

PUT

1. TITHĒMI (τίθημι), to place, lay, set, put, is translated to put in Matt. 5 : 15 ; 12 : 18 ; in Matt. 22 : 44, R.V., " put (underneath Thy feet) ; " Mark 4 : 21 (1st part), in the 2nd part, R.V., " put " (in some texts, No. 4, A.V., " set ") ; 10 : 16, A.V. (R.V., " laying ") ; Luke 8 : 16 (1st part) ; 2nd part, R.V. (A.V., " setteth ") ; 11 : 33 ; John 19 : 19 ; Acts 1 : 7, A.V. (R.V., " set ") ; 4 : 3 ; 5 : 18, 25 ; 12 : 4 ; Rom. 14 : 13 ; 1 Cor. 15 : 25 ; 2 Cor. 3 : 13 ; 1 Tim. 1 : 12, A.V. (R.V., " appointing ") ; Rev. 11 : 9, A.V. (R.V., " laid "). See APPOINT, No. 3.

2. PERITITHĒMI (περιτίθημι), to put around or on (*peri*, around, and No. 1), is so used in Matt. 27 : 28 ; Mark 15 : 17, R.V., " put on " (A.V., " . . . about ") ; 15 : 36 ; John 19 : 29. See BESTOW, No. 5.

3. PARATITHĒMI (παρατίθημι), to set before (para, beside or before), is rendered to put forth (of a parable) in Matt. 13 : 24, 31, A.V. (R.V., " set before "). See SET.

4. EPITITHĒMI (ἐπιτίθημι), to put on, upon, is so rendered in Matt. 19 : 13, A.V. (R.V., " lay ") ; so Mark 7 : 32 ; 8 : 25 (some mss. have No. 1, here) ; Matt. 21 : 7 ; 27 : 29 ; John 9 : 15 ; 19 : 2 (1st part) ; Acts 9 : 12 (R.V., " laying . . . on ") ; 15 : 10. See ADD, No. 1.

5. APOTITHĒMI (ἀποτίθημι), always in the Middle Voice in the N.T., to put off (apo) from oneself, is rendered " to put away " in the R.V. in the following : Eph. 4 : 22 (A.V., " put off ") ; Col. 3 : 8 (A.V., ditto) ; Eph. 4 : 25 ; Jas. 1 : 21 (A.V., " laying apart ") ; 1 Pet. 2 : 1 (A.V., " laying aside "). See CAST, No. 16.

6. BALLŌ (βάλλω), to throw, cast, put, is translated to put, in Matt. 9 : 17 (twice) ; 25 : 27 ; 27 : 6 ; Mark 2 : 22 ; 7 : 33 ; Luke 5 : 37 ; John 5 : 7 ; 12 : 6 ; 13 : 2 (of putting into the heart by the Devil) ; 18 : 11 (of putting up a sword) ; 20 : 25 (R.V. twice, A.V., " put " and " thrust ") ; ver. 27, R.V. ; Jas. 3 : 3 ; Rev. 2 : 24 (R.V., " cast "). See CAST, No. 1.

Note : BLĒTEOS (a gerundive form from *ballō*), meaning ' (that which) one must put,' is found in Luke 5 : 38, and, in some mss., Mark 2 : 22.¶

7. EKBALLŌ (ἐκβάλλω), to cast out, is translated to put forth or out in Matt. 9 : 25 ; Mark 5 : 40 (Luke 8 : 54 in some mss.) ; John 10 : 4 ; Acts 9 : 40. See CAST, No. 5.

8. EPIBALLŌ (ἐπιβάλλω), to put to or unto, is so translated in Matt. 9 : 16 ; Luke 5 : 36 ; 9 : 62 ; in Acts 12 : 1, R.V., " put forth (his hands)," A.V., " stretched forth." See CAST, No. 7.

9. PERIBALLŌ (περιβάλλω), to put or throw around, is translated " put on " in John 19 : 2, A.V. (R.V., " arrayed . . . in "). See CAST, No. 10, CLOTHE, No. 6.

10. PROBALLŌ (προβάλλω), to put forward, is so used in Acts 19 : 33. See SHOOT FORTH.

11. DIDŌMI (δίδωμι), to give, is rendered to put in Luke 15 : 22, of the ring on the returned prodigal's finger ; 2 Cor. 8 : 16 and Rev. 17 : 17, of putting into the heart by God ; Heb. 8 : 10, of laws into the mind (A.V., marg., " give ") ; 10 : 16, of laws on (R.V. : A.V., " into ") the heart. See GIVE.

12. PARADIDŌMI (παραδίδωμι), to give or hand over, is rendered " put in prison " in Mark 1 : 14, A.V. (R.V., " delivered up "). See BETRAY.

13. POIEŌ (ποιέω), to do, make, is translated " to put " (with *exō*, " forth ") in Acts 5 : 34, lit., ' do (them) outside.'

14. CHŌRIZŌ (χωρίζω), to separate, divide (cp. *chōris*, apart, separate from), is translated to put asunder in Matt. 19 : 6 ; Mark 10 : 9, of putting away a wife.

15. EKPHUŌ (ἐκφύω), to cause to grow out, put forth (*ek*, out, *phuō*, to bring forth, produce, beget), is used of the leaves of a tree, Matt. 24 : 32 ; Mark 13 : 28, "putteth forth."¶

16. APOLUŌ (ἀπολύω), to set free, let go, is rendered to put away in reference to one who is betrothed, Matt. 1 : 19 ; a wife, 5 : 31, 32 (twice ; in 2nd part, R.V. ; A.V., "is divorced ") ; 19 : 3, 7, 8, 9 (twice) ; Mark 10 : 2, 4, 11, 12 ; Luke 16 : 18 (twice). See DISMISS.

Note : In 1 Cor. 7 : 11, 12, A.V., *aphiēmi*, to send away, is translated to put away (R.V., " leave "), of the act of the husband toward the wife ; in ver. 13, "leave," of the act of the wife toward the husband.

17. AIRŌ (αἴρω), to take up, remove, is rendered " put away," of bitterness, wrath, anger, clamour, railing and malice, Eph. 4 : 31 ; in 1 Cor. 5 : 2 of the Divine effects of church discipline. See BEAR, No. 9.

18. EXAIRŌ (ἐξαίρω), to put away from the midst of (*ek*, from, and No. 17), is used of church discipline, 1 Cor. 5 : 13.¶

19. KATARGEŌ (καταργέω) is rendered " I put away " in 1 Cor. 13 : 11 ; in 15 : 24, A.V., " shall have put down " (R.V., " abolished "). See ABOLISH.

20. KATHAIREŌ (καθαιρέω), to take down, put down, is rendered " He hath put down " in Luke 1 : 52. See CAST, A, No. 14.

21. APOSTELLŌ (ἀποστέλλω), to send forth (*apo*, from or forth, *stellō*, to send), is said of using the sickle, Mark 4 : 29, R.V., " he putteth forth," marg., " sendeth forth " (A.V., " putteth in "). See SEND, SET.

22. APEKDUŌ (ἀπεκδύω), to strip off clothes or arms, is used in the Middle Voice in the N.T., Col. 2 : 15, R.V., " having put off from Himself," (A.V., " having spoiled ") ; in 3 : 9, " ye have put off," of " the old man " (see MAN). See SPOIL.¶

23. METHISTĒMI or METHISTANŌ (μεθίστημι), to change, remove (*meta*, implying change, *histēmi*, to cause to stand), is used of putting a man out of his stewardship, Luke 16 : 4 (Passive Voice). See REMOVE, TRANSLATE, TURN (away).

24. ANAGŌ (ἀνάγω), to lead or bring up, is used nautically of ' putting out to sea,' Acts 27 : 2, 4, R.V. See LAUNCH.

25. EPANAGŌ (ἐπανάγω), to bring up or back, is used in the same sense as No. 24, in Luke 5 : 3, 4. See LAUNCH.

26. ENDUŌ (ἐνδύω), used in the Middle Voice, of putting on oneself, or on another, is translated to put on (*a*) literally, Matt. 6 : 25 ; 27 : 31 ; Mark 6 : 9 ; 15 : 20 ; Luke 12 : 22 ; 15 : 22 ; (*b*) metaphorically, of putting on the armour of light, Rom. 13 : 12 ; the Lord Jesus Christ, 13 : 14 ; Christ, Gal. 3 : 27 ; incorruption and immortality (said of the body of the believer), 1 Cor. 15 : 53, 54 ; the new man, Eph. 4 : 24 ; Col. 3 : 10 ; the whole armour of God, Eph. 6 : 11 ; the breastplate of

righteousness, 6 : 14, R.V. ; the breastplate of faith and love, 1 Thess. 5 : 8 ; various Christian qualities, Col. 3 : 12. See CLOTHE, No. 2.

27. EMBIBAZŌ (ἐμβιβάζω), to put in (en, in, bibazō, not found in the N.T.), is used of putting persons on board ship, Acts 27 : 6.¶ In the Sept., 2 Kings 9 : 28 ; Prov. 4 : 11.¶

28. PROBIBAZŌ (προβιβάζω), to put forward, hence, to induce, incite, is rendered " being put forward " in Matt. 14 : 8, R.V. (A.V., " being before instructed ").¶ In the Sept., Ex. 35 : 34 ; Deut. 6 : 7.¶

29. APOSTREPHŌ (ἀποστρέφω), to turn away, remove, return, is used of ' putting up again ' a sword into its sheath, Matt. 26 : 52. See BRING, A, No. 22.

Notes : (1) *Ekteinō*, to stretch forth (always so translated in the R.V., save in Acts 27 : 30, " lay out," of anchors), is rendered to put forth in the A.V. of Matt. 8 : 3 ; Mark 1 : 41 ; Luke 5 : 13. (2) In Luke 14 : 7, A.V., *legō*, to speak (see R.V.), is translated " He put forth." (3) In Acts 13 : 46, A.V., *apōtheō*, to thrust away (R.V.), is rendered " put . . . from ; " in 1 Tim. 1 : 19, A.V., " having put away " (R.V., " having thrust from "), Middle Voice in each ; so in Acts 7 : 27, A.V. and R.V., " thrust away." See CAST, No. 13, THRUST. (4) For " to put away " in Heb. 9 : 26, see PUTTING, *Note* (below). (5) In Acts 7 : 33, A.V., *luō*, to loose (R.V.), is translated " put off." See LOOSE. (6) For the A.V. of *hupotassō*, " put under " in 1 Cor. 15 : 27, 28 ; Eph. 1 : 22 ; Heb. 2 : 8, see SUBJECT, and for the connected negative adjective *anupotaktos*, rendered " not put under " in Heb. 2 : 8, A.V., see DISOBEDIENT, B, (Note). (7) In John 19 : 29, A.V., *prospherō*, to bring to, is translated " they put it to (His mouth)," R.V., " they brought it . . ." (8) For *anamimnēskō*, to put in remembrance, 1 Cor. 4 : 17, R.V., see REMEMBRANCE. (9) For *apokteinō*, to kill, rendered " put to death " in Mark 14 : 1, etc., see DEATH, C, No. 4. (10) For 1 Thess. 2 : 4, A.V., " to be put in trust," see INTRUST. (11) For the phrase " put . . . to . . . account " in Philm. 18, see ACCOUNT, A, No. 2. (12) In Acts 15 : 9, A.V., *diakrinō*, to make a distinction (R.V.), is translated " put (no) difference." (13) In Matt. 9 : 16, A.V., *plērōma*, the fulness or filling, is rendered " (that) which is put in to fill it up," R.V., " (that) which should fill it up." See FILL. (14) For *paradeigmatizō*, to put to an open shame, Heb. 6 : 6, see SHAME. (15) For *phimoō*, to put to silence, see SILENCE. (16) For " I will put My trust," Heb. 2 : 13, see TRUST.

PUTTING

1. ENDUSIS (ἔνδυσις), a putting on (akin to *enduō*, PUT, No. 26), is used of apparel, 1 Pet. 3 : 3.¶ In the Sept., Esth. 5 : 1 ; Job 41 : 4.¶

2. EPITHESIS (ἐπίθεσις), a putting on (akin to *epitithēmi*, PUT, No. 4), is used of the putting or laying on of hands ; in 2 Tim. 1 : 6, R.V., " laying " (A.V., " putting "). See LAYING ON.

3. APOTHESIS (ἀπόθεσις), a putting off or away (akin to *apotithēmi*, PUT, No. 5), is used metaphorically in 1 Pet. 3 : 21, of the " putting away " of the filth of the flesh ; in 2 Pet. 1 : 14, R.V., of " the putting off " of the body (as a tabernacle) at death (A.V., " I must put off ").¶

4. APEKDUSIS (ἀπέκδυσις), a putting off, stripping off (akin to *apekduō*, PUT, No. 22), is used in Col. 2 : 11, of " the body of the flesh " (R.V., an important rendering).¶

Note : For *athetēsis*, a putting away, translated " to put away " in Heb. 9 : 26, lit., ' (unto) a setting aside,' see DISANNUL, B.¶

Q

QUAKE

1. ENTROMOS (ἔντρομος), an adjective signifying trembling with fear (en, in, tremō, to tremble), is used with eimi, to be, in Heb. 12 : 21 (some mss. have ektromos, with the same meaning), " I quake," lit., ' I am trembling.' It is used with ginomai, to become, in Acts 7 : 32, " trembled," lit., ' became trembling,' and 16 : 29, R.V., " trembling for fear " (A.V., " came trembling "). See TREMBLE.¶

2. SEIŌ (σείω), " did quake," Matt. 27 : 51, and 28 : 4, R.V. (A.V., " did shake "). See MOVE, No. 3, SHAKE, TREMBLE.

For QUARREL see COMPLAINT, No. 2, and SET, No. 15, Mark 6 : 19, R.V.

QUARTER

PANTOTHEN (πάντοθεν), from all sides, is translated " from every quarter " in Mark 1 : 45. See EVERY SIDE, ROUND ABOUT.

Notes : (1) In Rev. 20 : 8, A.V., gōnia, an angle, corner, is rendered " quarter " (R.V., " corner "). (2) In Acts 16 : 3, A.V., topois, " parts " (R.V.) is translated " quarters." (3) In Acts 9 : 32 the phrase dia pantōn, lit., ' throughout all,' is rendered " throughout all parts," R.V. (meros, a part, being understood), A.V., " throughout all *quarters.*" (4) For " quarters " in Acts 28 : 7, A.V., see NEIGHBOURHOOD.

QUATERNION

TETRADION (τετράδιον), a group of four (*tetra*—, four), occurs in Acts 12 : 4. A quaternion was a set of four men occupied in the work of a guard, two soldiers being chained to the prisoner and two keeping watch ; alternatively one of the four watched while the other three slept. The night was divided into four watches of three hours each ; there would be one quaternion for each watch by day and by night.¶ Cp. the " guard " in Matt. 27 : 65 and 28 : 11.

QUEEN

BASILISSA (βασίλισσα), the feminine of basileus, a king, is used (a) of the Queen of Sheba, Matt. 12 : 42 ; Luke 11 : 31 ; of Candace, Acts 8 : 27 ; (b) metaphorically, of Babylon, Rev. 18 : 7.¶

QUENCH, UNQUENCHABLE
A. Verb.

SBENNUMI (σβέννυμι) is used (*a*) of quenching fire or things on fire, Matt. 12 : 20, quoted from Is. 42 : 3, figurative of the condition of the feeble ; Heb. 11 : 34 ; in the Passive Voice, Matt. 25 : 8, of torches (see LAMP), R.V., " are going out," lit., ' are being quenched ; ' of the retributive doom hereafter of sin unrepented of and unremitted in this life, Mark 9 : 48 (in some mss. in vv. 44, 46) ; (*b*) metaphorically, of quenching the fire-tipped darts of the evil one, Eph. 6 : 16 ; of quenching the Spirit, by hindering His operations in oral testimony in the church gatherings of believers, 1 Thess. 5 : 19. " The peace, order, and edification of the saints were evidence of the ministry of the Spirit among them, 1 Cor. 14 : 26, 32, 33, 40, but if, through ignorance of His ways, or through failure to recognise, or refusal to submit to, them, or through impatience with the ignorance or self-will of others, the Spirit were quenched, these happy results would be absent. For there was always the danger that the impulses of the flesh might usurp the place of the energy of the Spirit in the assembly, and the endeavour to restrain this evil by natural means would have the effect of hindering His ministry also. Apparently then, this injunction was intended to warn believers against the substitution of a mechanical order for the restraints of the Spirit."*¶ Cp. S. of Sol. 8 : 7.

B. Adjective.

ASBESTOS (ἄσβεστος), not quenched (*a*, negative, and A), is used of the doom of persons described figuratively as " chaff," Matt. 3 : 12 and Luke 3 : 17, " unquenchable ; " of the fire of Gehenna (see HELL), Mark 9 : 43, R.V., " unquenchable fire " (in some mss. ver. 45).¶ In the Sept., Job 20 : 26.¶

QUESTION (Noun and Verb), QUESTIONING
A. Nouns.

1. ZĒTĒSIS (ζήτησις), primarily a seeking, search (*zēteō*, to seek), for which see DISPUTATION, is used in John 3 : 25 ; Acts 25 : 20, R.V., " (being perplexed) how to inquire (concerning these things)," A.V. " (because I doubted of such manner) of questions," lit., ' being perplexed as to the enquiry (or discussion) concerning these things ; ' in 1 Tim. 1 : 4 (in some mss.) ; 6 : 4 ; 2 Tim. 2 : 23 ; Tit. 3 : 9. See INQUIRY.

2. ZĒTĒMA (ζήτημα), synonymous with No. 1, but, generally speaking, suggesting in a more concrete form the subject of an enquiry, occurs in Acts 15 : 2 ; 18 : 15 ; 23 : 29 ; 25 : 19 ; 26 : 3.¶

3. LOGOS (λόγος), a word, is translated " question " in Matt. 21 : 24 (A.V., " thing ") ; in Mark 11 : 29 (R.V., marg., " word ") and Luke 20 : 3, A.V., " one thing : " there is no word in the original for " one," hence the R.V., " a question."

---

* From Notes on Thessalonians, by Hogg and Vine, p. 196.

4. EKZĒTĒSIS (ἐκζήτησις), a questioning, is found in the best texts in 1 Tim. 1 : 4 (see R.V.) ; cp. No. 1.¶

Notes : (1) In Matt. 22 : 41, there is no word in the original for " question." (2) For *suzētēsis* or *sunzētēsis*, a questioning together (*sun*, with), see DISPUTATION. (3) In Acts 19 : 40, A.V., *enkaleō*, to bring a charge against, is translated " to be called in question " (R.V., " to be accused ").

B. Verbs.

1. SUZĒTEŌ (συζητέω) or SUNZĒTEŌ, to search together (cp. Note, above), to discuss, dispute, is translated to question (or q. with or together) in Mark 1 : 27 ; 8 : 11 ; 9 : 10, 14, 16 ; 12 : 28, R.V. (A.V., " reasoning together ") ; Luke 22 : 23, R.V. (A.V., " enquire ") ; 24 : 15, R.V. (A.V., " reasoned "). See DISPUTE, B, No. 3, INQUIRE, REASON.

2. EPERŌTAŌ (ἐπερωτάω), to ask, is translated " asked . . . a question," in Matt. 22 : 35, 41 ; in Luke 2 : 46, " asking . . . questions ; " " questioned " in Luke 23 : 9. See ASK, A, No. 3.

For QUICK, see DISCERN, C, LIVE, No. 3, Note

QUICKEN

1. ZŌOPOIEŌ (ζωοποιέω), to make alive : see LIFE, C.

2. ZŌOGONEŌ (ζωογονέω), to endue with life, produce alive, preserve alive : see LIVE, No. 6.

3. SUZŌOPOIEŌ (συζωοποιέω) or SUNZŌOPOIEŌ, to quicken together with, make alive with (*sun*, with and No. 1), is used in Eph. 2 : 5 ; Col. 2 : 13, of the spiritual life with Christ, imparted to believers at their conversion.¶

QUICKLY

1. TACHU (ταχύ), the neuter of *tachus*, swift, quick, signifies quickly, Matt. 5 : 25 ; 28 : 7, 8 ; Mark 9 : 39, R.V. (A.V., " lightly ") ; Luke 15 : 22 ; John 11 : 29 ; Rev. 2 : 16 (ver. 5 in some mss.) ; 3 : 11 ; 11 : 14 ; 22 : 7, 12, 20. See LIGHTLY.¶

2. TACHEION (τάχειον), the comparative degree of No. 1, is trans- lated " quickly " in John 13 : 27 ; " out(ran) " in 20 : 4, R.V., lit., ' (ran before) more quickly (than Peter) ; ' " shortly " in 1 Tim. 3 : 14 and Heb. 13 : 23 ; in 13 : 19, " (the) sooner." See SHORTLY.¶

3. TACHEŌS (ταχέως), akin to No. 1, is translated " quickly " in Luke 14 : 21 ; 16 : 6 ; John 11 : 31, R.V. ; " shortly " in 1 Cor. 4 : 19 ; Phil. 2 : 19, 24 ; 2 Tim 4 : 9 ; with a suggestion of rashness in the following, Gal. 1 : 6, R.V., " quickly " (A.V., " soon ") ; 2 Thess. 2 : 2 ; and 1 Tim. 5 : 22, " hastily," (A.V., " suddenly "). See HASTILY, C.¶

4. EN TACHEI (ἐν τάχει), lit., in, or with, swiftness, with speed (*en*, in, and the dative case of *tachos*, speed), is translated " quickly " in Acts 12 : 7 ; 22 : 18 ; " speedily " in Luke 18 : 8 ; " shortly " in Acts 25 : 4 ;

Rom. 16 : 20; 1 Tim. 3 : 14 in some texts; Rev. 1 : 1; 22 : 6. In the last two places, "with speed" is probably the meaning. See Shortly, Speedily.¶

QUICKSANDS

Note : This is the A.V. rendering in Acts 27 : 17 of *Surtis*, "Syrtis" (R.V.). The Syrtes, Major and Minor, lie on the North coast of Africa, between the headlands of Tunis and Barca. They have been regarded as dangerous to mariners from very early times, both from the character of the sands and from the cross currents of the adjoining waters. In the voyage described in this chapter the vessel had left the shelter of the island of Cauda and was drifting before the N.E. wind Euraquilo. The mariners might well fear that they would be driven on the Syrtes on the leeward of their course. The changing character of the tempest, however, drove them into the sea of Adria.¶

QUIET, QUIETNESS
A. Adjectives.

1. ĒREMOS (ἤρεμος), quiet, tranquil, occurs in 1 Tim. 2 : 2, R.V., "tranquil" (A.V., "quiet"); it indicates tranquillity arising from without.¶

2. HĒSUCHIOS (ἡσύχιος) has much the same meaning as No. 1, but indicates tranquillity arising from within, causing no disturbance to others. It is translated "quiet" in 1 Tim. 2 : 2, R.V. (A.V., "peaceable"); "quiet" in 1 Pet. 3 : 4, where it is associated with "meek," and is to characterize the spirit or disposition. See Peaceable.¶

B. Verbs.

1. HĒSUCHAZŌ (ἡσυχάζω), akin to A, No. 2, to be still, to live quietly: see Cease, A, No. 3.¶

2. KATASTELLŌ (καταστέλλω) denotes to quiet: see Appease.

C. Nouns.

1. EIRĒNĒ (εἰρήνη), peace, is translated "quietness" in Acts 24 : 2, A.V. (R.V., "peace"). See Peace (e).

2. HĒSUCHIA (ἡσυχία), akin to A, No. 2, and B. No. 1, denotes quietness, 2 Thess. 3 : 12; it is so translated in the R.V. of 1 Tim. 2 : 11, 12 (A.V., "silence"); in Acts 22 : 2, R.V., "(they were the more) quiet," A.V., "(they kept the more) silence," lit., ' they kept quietness the more.'¶

QUIT

1. APALLASSŌ (ἀπαλλάσσω), to free from, is used in the Passive Voice in Luke 12 : 58, R.V., "to be quit" (A.V., "to be delivered"). See Deliver, A, No. 6.

2. ANDRIZŌ (ἀνδρίζω) signifies to make a man of (*anēr*, a man); in the Middle Voice, in 1 Cor. 16 : 13, to play the man, "quit you like men."¶

R

RABBI

RABBEI or RABBI (ῥαββεί), from a word *rab*, primarily denoting " master " in contrast to a slave ; this with the added pronominal suffix signified " my master " and was a title of respect by which teachers were addressed. The suffix soon lost its specific force, and in the N.T. the word is used as courteous title of address. It is applied to Christ in Matt. 26 : 25, 49 ; Mark 9 : 5 ; 11 : 21 ; 14 : 45 ; John 1 : 38 (where it is interpreted as *didaskalos*, " master," marg., " teacher " (see also " Rabboni " in John 20 : 16) ; ver. 49 ; 3 : 2 ; 4 : 31 ; 6 : 25 ; 9 : 2 ; 11 : 8 ; to John the Baptist in John 3 : 26. In Matt. 23 : 7, 8 Christ forbids his disciples to covet or use it. In the latter verse it is again explained as *didaskalos*, " master " (some mss. have *kathēgētēs*, a guide).¶

RABBONI

RABBOUNEI or RABBŌNI (ῥαββουνεί), formed in a similar way to the above, was an Aramaic form of a title almost entirely applied to the president of the Sanhedrin, if such was a descendant of Hillel. It was even more respectful than Rabbi, and signified ' My great master ; ' in its use in the N.T. the pronominal force of the suffix is apparently retained (contrast Rabbi above) ; it is found in Mark 10 : 51 in the best texts, R.V., " Rabboni " (A.V., " Lord "), addressed to Christ by blind Bartimæus, and in John 20 : 16 by Mary Magdalene, where it is interpreted by *didaskalos*, " Master " (marg., " Teacher ").¶

For RABBLE see COURT, No. 1

RACA

RAKA (ῥακά) is an Aramaic word akin to the Heb. *rêq*, empty, the first *a* being due to a Galilæan change. In the A.V. of 1611 it was spelt *racha ;* in the edition of 1638, *raca*. It was a word of utter contempt, signifying empty, intellectually rather than morally, empty-headed, like Abimelech's hirelings, Judg. 9 : 4, and the " vain " man of Jas. 2 : 20. As condemned by Christ, Matt. 5 : 22, it was worse than being angry, inasmuch as an outrageous utterance is worse than a feeling unexpressed or somewhat controlled in expression ; it does not indicate such a loss of self-control as the word rendered " fool," a godless, moral reprobate.¶

For RACE (kindred) see KIND

RACE (contest)

1. AGŌN (ἀγών) is translated " race " in Heb. 12 : 1, one of the modes of athletic contest, this being the secondary meaning of the word. See CONFLICT.

2. STADION (στάδιον), a stadium, denotes a racecourse, 1 Cor. 9 : 24. The stadium (about 600 Greek feet or ⅛ of a Roman mile) was the length of the Olympic course. See FURLONG.

Note : No. 1 signifies the race itself ; No. 2 the course.

RAGE, RAGING
A. Verb.

PHRUASSŌ (φρυάσσω) was primarily used of the snorting, neighing and prancing of horses ; hence, metaphorically, of the haughtiness and insolence of men, Acts 4 : 25.¶ In the Sept., Psa. 2 : 1.¶

B. Noun.

KLUDŌN (κλύδων), a billow, surge (akin to *kluzō*, " to wash over," said of the sea ; cp. *kludōnizomai*, to be tossed by the waves, Eph. 4 : 14), is translated " raging " in Luke 8 : 24 ; in Jas. 1 : 6, R.V., " surge " (A.V., " wave ").¶

Note : In Jude 13, A.V., the adjective *agrios*, wild, is translated " raging " (R.V., " wild "). See WILD.

RAIL, RAILER, RAILING
A. Verb.

BLASPHĒMEŌ (βλασφημέω), to blaspheme, rail, revile (for the meanings of which see BLASPHEME), is translated to rail at, or on, in Matt. 27 : 39, R.V. (A.V., " reviled ") ; Mark 15 : 29 ; Luke 23 : 39 ; 2 Pet. 2 : 10, R.V. (A.V., " to speak evil of ") ; 2 : 12, R.V. (A.V., " speak evil of "). Cp. *loidoreō*, to revile (see REVILE), and B, No. 2 and C, No. 2.

B. Nouns.

1. BLASPHĒMIA (βλασφημία) is translated " railings " in Matt. 15 : 19, R.V. ; 1 Tim. 6 : 4, A.V. and R.V. ; " railing " in Mark 7 : 22, R.V. ; Col. 3 : 8, R.V. ; Jude 9, A.V. and R.V., lit., ' judgment of railing ; ' in Eph. 4 : 31, R.V. (A.V., " evil speaking "). See BLASPHEMY.

2. LOIDORIA (λοιδορία), abuse, railing, reviling, is rendered " reviling " in the R.V., 1 Pet. 3 : 9 (twice) ; in 1 Tim. 5 : 14, A.V. marg., " for their reviling." See REVILE, C.¶

C. Adjectives.

1. BLASPHĒMOS (βλάσφημος), akin to A, and B, No. 1 ; see BLASPHEME, C.

2. LOIDOROS (λοίδορος), an adjective denoting reviling, railing (akin to B, No. 2), is used as a noun, " a railer," 1 Cor. 5 : 11. See REVILE.

RAIMENT

Notes : (1) For *himation*, rendered " raiment " in Matt. 17 : 2, A.V. (R.V., " garments "), so Matt. 27 : 31 ; Mark 9 : 3 ; Luke 23 : 34 ; John 19 : 24 ; Acts 22 : 20 ; Rev. 3 : 5, 18 ; 4 : 4 ; A.V. and R.V., Acts 18 : 6, see CLOTHING, No. 2 and ROBE. *Himatismos* is rendered " raiment " in Luke 9 : 29 ; *enduma* in Matt. 3 : 4 ; 6 : 25, 28 ; 28 : 3 and Luke 12 : 23. For *esthēs*, translated " raiment " in Jas.2 : 2 (2nd part), A.V., see APPAREL. (2) For *skepasma*, a covering, rendered " raiment " in 1 Tim. 6 : 8, A.V., see COVER, B, No. 2.

RAIN (Noun and Verb)

A. Nouns.

1. HUETOS (ὑετός), from *huō*, to rain, is used especially, but not entirely, of showers, and is found in Acts 14 : 17 ; 28 : 2 ; Heb. 6 : 7 ; Jas. 5 : 7 (see EARLY AND LATTER) ; 5 : 18 ; Rev. 11 : 6 (see B).¶
2. BROCHĒ (βροχή), akin to B, below, lit., a wetting, hence, rain, is used in Matt. 7 : 25, 27.¶ In the Sept., Ps. 68 : 9 ; 105 : 32.¶ It is found in the papyri in connection with irrigation in Egypt (Deissmann, *Light from the Ancient East*).

B. Verb.

BRECHŌ (βρέχω), akin to A, No. 2, signifies (*a*) to wet, Luke 7 : 38, 44, R.V. (A.V., to wash) ; (*b*) to send rain, Matt. 5 : 45 ; to rain, Luke 17 : 29 (of fire and brimstone) ; Jas. 5 : 17, used impersonally (twice) ; Rev. 11 : 6, where *huetos* (A, No. 1) is used as the subject, lit., ' (that) rain rain (not).'¶

RAINBOW

IRIS (ἶρις), whence Eng., iris, the flower, describes the rainbow seen in the heavenly vision, " round about the throne, like an emerald to look upon," Rev. 4 : 3, emblematic of the fact that, in the exercise of God's absolute sovereignty and perfect counsels, He will remember His covenant concerning the earth (Gen. 9 : 9–17) ; in Rev. 10 : 1, " the rainbow," R.V., the definite article suggests a connection with the scene in 4 : 3 ; here it rests upon the head of an angel who declares that " there shall be delay no longer " (ver. 6, R.V. marg., the actual meaning) ; the mercy to be shown to the earth must be preceded by the execution of Divine judgments upon the nations who defy God and His Christ. Cp. Ezek. 1 : 28.¶

RAISE (up)

1. EGEIRŌ (ἐγείρω), for the various meanings of which see ARISE, No. 3, is used (*a*) of raising the dead, Active and Passive Voices, e.g. of the resurrection of Christ, Matt. 16 : 21 ; 17 : 23 ; 20 : 19, R.V. ; 26 : 32, R.V., " (after) I am raised up " (A.V., ". . . risen again ") ; Luke 9 : 22 ; 20 : 37 ; John 2 : 19 ; Acts 3 : 15 ; 4 : 10 [not 5 : 30, see (*c*) below] ; 10 : 40 [not 13 : 23 in the best texts, see (*c*) below] ; 13 : 30, 37 ; Rom. 4 : 24, 25 ;

6 : 4, 9 ; 7 : 4 ; 8 : 11 (twice) ; 8 : 34, R.V. ; 10 : 9 ; 1 Cor. 6 : 14 (1st part) ; 15 : 13, 14, R.V. ; 15 : 15 (twice), 16, 17 ; 15 : 20, R.V. ; 2 Cor. 4 : 14 ; Gal. 1 : 1 ; Eph. 1 : 20 ; Col. 2 : 12 ; 1 Thess. 1 : 10 ; 1 Pet. 1 : 21 ; in 2 Tim. 2 : 8, R.V., " risen " ; (b) of the resurrection of human beings, Matt. 10 : 8 ; 11 : 5 ; Matt. 27 : 52, R.V. (A.V., " arose ") ; Mark 12 : 26, R.V. ; Luke 7 : 22 ; John 5 : 21 ; 12 : 1, 9, 17 ; Acts 26 : 8 ; 1 Cor. 15 : 29 and 32, R.V. ; 15 : 35, 42, 43 (twice), 44, 52 ; 2 Cor. 1 : 9 ; 4 : 14 ; Heb. 11 : 19 ; (c) of raising up a person to occupy a place in the midst of a people, said of Christ, Acts 5 : 30 ; in 13 : 23, A.V. only (the best texts have agō, to bring, R.V., " hath . . . brought ") ; of David, Acts 13 : 22 (for ver. 33 see No. 2) ; (d) metaphorically, of a horn of salvation, Luke 1 : 69 ; (e) of children, from stones, by creative power, Luke 3 : 8 ; (f) of the Temple, as the Jews thought, John 2 : 20, R.V., " wilt Thou raise (it) up " (A.V., " rear ") ; (g) of lifting up a person, from physical infirmity, Mark 1 : 31, R.V., " raised . . . up " (A.V., " lifted ") ; so 9 : 27 ; Acts 3 : 7 ; 10 : 26, R.V. (A.V., " took ") ; Jas. 5 : 15, " shall raise . . . up ; " (h) metaphorically, of raising up affliction, Phil. 1 : 17, R.V. (in the best texts ; the A.V., ver. 16, following those which have epipherō, has " to add "). See AWAKE, No. 1.

2. ANISTĒMI (ἀνίστημι), for the various applications of which see ARISE, No. 1, is translated to raise or raise up, (a) of the resurrection of the dead by Christ, John 6 : 39, 40, 44, 54 ; (b) of the resurrection of Christ from the dead, Acts 2 : 24 (for ver. 30 see R.V., kathizō, to set, as in the best texts) ; 2 : 32 ; 13 : 34, see (c) below ; Acts 17 : 31 ; (c) of raising up a person to occupy a place in the midst of a nation, said of Christ, Acts 3 : 26 ; 7 : 37 ; 13 : 33, R.V., " raised up Jesus," not here by resurrection from the dead, as the superfluous " again " of the A.V. would suggest ; this is confirmed by the latter part of the verse, which explains the raising up as being by way of His Incarnation, and by the contrast in ver. 34, where stress is laid upon His being raised " from the dead," the same verb being used : (d) of raising up seed, Matt. 22 : 24 ; (e) of being raised from natural sleep, Matt. 1 : 24, A.V., " being raised " (R.V., " arose ") ; here some mss. have diegeirō, to arouse completely ; see ARISE, No. 4.

Note : For the contrast between No. 1 and No. 2 see ARISE, No. 3 (parag. 2).

3. EXEGEIRŌ (ἐξεγείρω), ek, out of, and No. 1, is used (a) of the resurrection of believers, 1 Cor. 6 : 14 [2nd part ; see No. 1 (a) for the 1st part] ; (b) of raising a person to public position, Rom. 9 : 17, " did I raise thee up," R.V., said of Pharaoh.¶

4. EXANISTĒMI (ἐξανίστημι), ek, out of, and No. 2, is used of raising up seed, Mark 12 : 19 ; Luke 20 : 28 ; elsewhere, Acts 15 : 5, to rise up. See RISE.¶

5. SUNEGEIRŌ (συνεγείρω), to raise together (sun, with, and No. 1), is used of the believer's spiritual resurrection with Christ, Eph. 2 : 6 ;

Passive Voice in Col. 2 : 12, R.V., " ye were . . . raised (with Him)," A.V., " ye are risen ; " so 3 : 1. See RISE.

Notes : (1) In Acts 13 : 50, A.V., *epegeirō*, to rouse up, excite, is translated " raised " (R.V., " stirred up," as in A.V. and R.V. in 14 : 2). (2) In Acts 24 : 12, *poieō*, to make, is used with *epistasis*, a collection of people, and translated " stirring up (a crowd)," R.V., lit., ' making a collection (of a crowd) ' ; some mss. have *episustasis*, a riotous throng, A.V., " raising up (the people)." (3) In Heb. 11 : 35, A.V., the noun *anastasis*, a resurrection, preceded by *ex* (i.e., *ek*), out of, or by, instrumental, is translated " raised to life again " (a paraphrase), R.V., " by a resurrection."

For RAN see RUN

RANKS

PRASIA (πρασιά), a garden-bed or plot (probably from *prason*, a leek), is used metaphorically in Mark 6 : 40 of ranks of persons arranged in orderly groups.¶

RANSOM

1. LUTRON (λύτρον), lit., a means of loosing (from *luō*, to loose), occurs frequently in the Sept., where it is always used to signify equivalence. Thus it is used of the ransom for a life, e.g., Ex. 21 : 30, of the redemption price of a slave, e.g., Lev. 19 : 20, of land, 25 : 24, of the price of a captive, Isa. 45 : 13. In the N.T. it occurs in Matt. 20 : 28 and Mark 10 : 45, where it is used of Christ's gift of Himself as " a ransom for many." Some interpreters have regarded the ransom price as being paid to Satan ; others, to an impersonal power such as death, or evil, or " that ultimate necessity which has made the whole course of things what it has been." Such ideas are largely conjectural, the result of an attempt to press the details of certain Old Testament illustrations beyond the actual statements of New Testament doctrines.

That Christ gave up His life in expiatory sacrifice under God's judgment upon sin and thus provided a ransom whereby those who receive Him on this ground obtain deliverance from the penalty due to sin, is what Scripture teaches. What the Lord states in the two passages mentioned involves this essential character of His death. In these passages the preposition is *anti*, which has a vicarious significance, indicating that the ransom holds good for those who, accepting it as such, no longer remain in death since Christ suffered death in their stead. The change of preposition in 1 Tim. 2 : 6, where the word *antilutron*, a substitutionary ransom, is used, is significant. There the preposition is *huper*, on behalf of, and the statement is made that He " gave Himself a ransom for all," indicating that the ransom was provisionally universal, while being of a vicarious character. Thus the three passages consistently show that while the provision was universal, for Christ died for all men, yet it is actual for those only who accept God's conditions, and who are described in the Gospel statements as "the many." The giving of His life was the giving of His entire Person, and while His death under Divine judgment was alone expiatory, it cannot be dissociated from the character of His life which, being sinless, gave virtue to His death and was a testimony to the fact that His death must be of a vicarious nature.¶

2. ANTILUTRON (ἀντίλυτρον), 1 Tim. 2 : 6. See under No. 1.¶

_____

For RASH, RASHLY see HEADSTRONG

_____

RATHER
A. Adverb.

MALLON (μᾶλλον), the comparative degree of *mala*, very, very much, is frequently translated " rather," e.g., Matt. 10 : 6, 28 ; 1 Cor. 14 : 1, 5 ; sometimes followed by " than," with a connecting particle, e.g., Matt. 18 : 13 (" more than ") ; or without, e.g., John 3 : 19 ; Acts 4 : 19, R.V. (A.V., " more ") ; in 1 Cor. 9 : 12, A.V., " rather " (R.V., " yet more ") ; 12 : 22, R.V., " rather " (A.V., " more ") ; 2 Cor. 3 : 9 (ditto) ; Philm. 16 (ditto) ; in 2 Pet. 1 : 10, A.V., " the rather " (R.V., " the more "). See MORE.

B. Verb.

THELŌ (θέλω), to will, wish, is translated " I had rather " in 1 Cor. 14 : 19. See DESIRE, B, No. 6.

C. Preposition.

PARA (παρά), beyond, in comparison with, is translated " rather than " in Rom. 1 : 25, R.V. (A.V., " more than ; " marg., " rather ").

D. Conjunction.

ALLA (ἀλλά), but, on the contrary, is translated " and rather " in Luke 17 : 8.

Notes : (1) In Heb. 13 : 19, A.V., *perissoterōs*, " the more exceedingly " (R.V.), is translated " the rather." (2) In Luke 11 : 41 and 12 : 31, A.V., *plēn*, an adverb signifying yet, howbeit, is translated " rather " (R.V., " howbeit "). (3) In Rom. 3 : 8, A.V., the negative particle *mē*, " not," is translated with " *rather* " in italics (R.V., " why not "). (4) In Luke 10 : 20, A.V., " rather rejoice," there is no word in the original for " rather " (see the R.V.).

_____

RAVEN

KORAX (κόραξ), a raven (perhaps onomatopœic, representing the sound), occurs in the plural in Luke 12 : 24. The Heb. *oreb* and the Arabic *ghurab* are from roots meaning ' to be black ; ' the Arabic root also has the idea of leaving home. Hence the evil omen attached to the bird. It is the first bird mentioned in the Bible, Gen. 8 : 7. Christ used the ravens to illustrate and enforce the lesson of God's provision and care.¶

RAVENING
A. Adjective.

HARPAX (ἅρπαξ), an adjective signifying rapacious, is translated "ravening" (of wolves) in Matt. 7 : 15 : see Extort, C.

B. Noun.

HARPAGĒ (ἁρπαγή) is translated "ravening" in Luke 11 : 39, A.V. : see Extort, B, No. 1.

REACH

1. AKOLOUTHEŌ (ἀκολουθέω), to follow, is translated "have reached," in Rev. 18 : 5, of the sins of Babylon. Some mss. have the verb kollaomai, to cleave together, R.V., marg. ; see Follow.

2. OREGŌ (ὀρέγω), to reach or stretch out, is rendered "reached after " in 1 Tim. 6 : 10, R.V. ; see Desire, B, No. 5.

3. PHERŌ (φέρω), to bear, carry, is used of reaching forth the hand in John 20 : 27 (twice). See Bear, No. 2.

4. EPHIKNEOMAI (ἐφικνέομαι), to come to, reach, is used in 2 Cor. 10 : 13, 14.¶

5. KATANTAŌ (καταντάω), to come to a place, is translated "reach " in Acts 27 : 12, R.V. (A.V., "attain to "). See Come, No. 28.

Note : In Phil. 3 : 13, A.V., epekteinō, in the Middle Voice, to stretch forward, is translated "reaching forth " (R.V., "stretching forward ").

READ, READING
A. Verb.

ANAGINŌSKŌ (ἀναγινώσκω), primarily, to know certainly, to know again, recognize (ana, again, ginōskō, to know), is used of reading written characters, e.g., Matt. 12 : 3, 5 ; 21 : 16 ; 24 : 15 ; of the private reading of Scripture, Acts 8 : 28, 30, 32 ; of the public reading of Scripture, Luke 4 : 16 ; Acts 13 : 27 ; 15 : 21 ; 2 Cor. 3 : 15 ; Col. 4 : 16 (thrice) ; 1 Thess. 5 : 27 ; Rev. 1 : 3. In 2 Cor. 1 : 13 there is a purposive play upon words ; firstly, " we write none other things unto you, than what ye read (anaginōskō) " signifies that there is no hidden or mysterious meaning in his Epistles ; whatever doubts may have arisen and been expressed in this respect, he means what he says ; then follows the similar verb epiginōskō, to acknowledge, " or even acknowledge, and I hope ye will acknowledge unto the end." The *paronomasia* can hardly be reproduced in English. Similarly, in 3 : 2 the verb ginōskō, to know, and anaginōskō, to read, are put in that order, and metaphorically applied to the church at Corinth as being an epistle, a message to the world, written by the Apostle and his fellow-missionaries, through their ministry of the gospel and the consequent change in the lives of the converts, an epistle " known and read of all men." For other instances of *paronomasia* see, e.g., Rom. 12 : 3, *phroneō, huperphroneō, sōphroneō ;* 1 Cor. 2 : 13, 14, *sunkrinō, anakrinō ;* 2 Thess. 3 : 11, *ergazomai,* and *periergazomai ;* 1 Cor.

7 : 31, *chraomai* and *katachraomai ;* 11 : 31, *diakrinō* and *krinō ;* 12 : 2, *agō* and *apagō ;* Phil. 3 : 2, 3, *katatomē* and *peritomē*.

B. Noun.

ANAGNŌSIS (ἀνάγνωσις) in non-Biblical Greek denoted recognition or a survey (the latter found in the papyri) ; then, reading ; in the N.T. the public reading of Scripture, Acts 13 : 15 ; 2 Cor. 3 : 14 ; 1 Tim. 4 : 13, where the context makes clear that the reference is to the care required in reading the Scriptures to a company, a duty ever requiring the exhortation " take heed." Later, readers in churches were called *anagnōstai*.¶ In the Sept., Neh. 8 : 8.¶

READINESS

1. PROTHUMIA (προθυμία), eagerness, willingness, readiness (*pro*, forward, *thumos*, mind, disposition, akin to *prothumos*, READY, A, No. 2), is translated " readiness of mind " in Acts 17 : 11, " readiness " in 2 Cor. 8 : 11 ; in ver. 12, R.V. (A.V., " a willing mind ") ; in ver. 19, R.V. " (our) readiness," A.V., " (your) ready mind ; " in 9 : 2, R.V., " readiness " (A.V., " forwardness of . . . mind ; " see FORWARDNESS, Note (4).¶

2. HETOIMOS (ἕτοιμος), an adjective (see READY, A, No. 1), is used with *echō*, to have, and *en*, in, idiomatically, as a noun, in 2 Cor. 10 : 6, R.V., " being in readiness " (A.V., " having in readiness "), of the Apostle's aim for the church to be obedient to Christ. Cp. READY, C.

READY
A. Adjectives.

1. HETOIMOS (ἕτοιμος), prepared, ready (akin to *hetoimasia*, preparation), is used (*a*) of persons, Matt. 24: 44 ; 25 : 10 ; Luke 12 : 40 ; 22 : 33 ; Acts 23 : 15, 21 (for 2 Cor. 10 : 6, see above) ; Tit. 3 : 1 ; 1 Pet. 3 : 15 ; (*b*) of things, Matt. 22 : 4 (2nd part), 8 ; Mark 14 : 15, R.V., " ready " (A.V., " prepared ") ; Luke 14 : 17 ; John 7 : 6 ; 2 Cor. 9 : 5 ; 10 : 16, R.V., " things ready " (A.V., " things made ready ") ; 1 Pet. 1 : 5. See PREPARE, No. 5, Note (2).¶

2. PROTHUMOS (πρόθυμος), predisposed, willing (akin to *prothumia*, see READINESS), is translated " ready " in Rom. 1 : 15, expressive of willingness, eagerness : in Mark 14 : 38, R.V., " willing " (A.V., " ready ") ; in Matt. 26 : 41, " willing." See WILLING.¶

B. Verbs.

1. MELLŌ (μέλλω), to be about to, is translated to be ready in 2 Pet. 1 : 12, R.V., where the future indicates that the Apostle will be prepared, as in the past and the present, to remind his readers of the truths they know (some mss. have *ouk amelēsō*, " I will not be negligent," A.V. ; cp., however, ver. 15. Field, in *Notes on the Translation of the N.T.*, suggests that the true reading is *melēsō*, the future of *melō*, to be a care, or an object of care) ; in Rev. 3 : 2, R.V., " were ready " (some texts have the present tense, as in the A.V.). Elsewhere, where the A.V. has the

rendering to be ready, the R.V. gives renderings in accordance with the usual significance as follows : Luke 7 : 2, " was . . . at the point of ; " Acts 20 : 7, " intending ; '" Rev. 12 : 4, " about (to)."

2. HETOIMAZŌ (ἑτοιμάζω), make ready : see PREPARE, B, No. 1.

3. PARASKEUAZŌ (παρασκευάζω), to prepare, make ready : see PREPARE, B, No. 4.

Note : On the difference between No. 2 and No. 3, see PREPARE, Note (1) under No. 5.

C. Adverb.

HETOIMŌS (ἑτοίμως) readily (akin to A, No. 1), is used with *echō*, to have, lit., ' to have readily,' i.e., to be in readiness, to be ready, Acts 21 : 13 ; 2 Cor. 12 : 14 ; 1 Pet. 4 : 5.¶

Notes : (1) In Heb. 8 : 13, A.V., *engus*, near, is translated " ready " (R.V., " nigh "). See NIGH. (2) For " ready to distribute," 1 Tim. 6 : 18, see DISTRIBUTE, B. (3) In 2 Tim. 4 : 6, A.V., *spendomai*, " I am being offered," R.V., with *ēdē*, " already," is translated " I am now ready to be offered." See OFFER. (4) In 1 Pet. 5 : 2 *prothumōs*, willingly, with alacrity, is rendered " of a ready mind."¶

REAP

THERIZŌ (θερίζω), to reap (akin to *theros*, summer, harvest), is used (*a*) literally, Matt. 6 : 26 ; 25 : 24, 26 ; Luke 12 : 24 ; 19 : 21, 22 ; Jas. 5 : 4 (2nd part), A.V., " have reaped " ; (*b*) figuratively or in proverbial expressions, John 4 : 36 (twice), 37, 38, with immediate reference to bringing Samaritans into the Kingdom of God, in regard to which the disciples would enjoy the fruits of what Christ Himself had been doing in Samaria ; the Lord's words are, however, of a general application in respect of such service ; in 1 Cor. 9 : 11, with reference to the right of the Apostle and his fellow-missionaries to receive material assistance from the church, a right which he forbore to exercise ; in 2 Cor. 9 : 6 (twice), with reference to rendering material help to the needy, either " sparingly " or " bountifully," the reaping being proportionate to the sowing ; in Gal. 6 : 7, 8 (twice), of reaping " corruption," with special reference, according to the context, to that which is naturally shortlived transient (though the statement applies to every form of sowing to the flesh), and of reaping eternal life (characteristics and moral qualities being in view), as a result of sowing " to the Spirit," the reference probably being to the new nature of the believer, which is, however, under the controlling power of the Holy Spirit, ver. 9, the reaping (the effect of well doing) being accomplished, to a limited extent, in this life, but in complete fulfilment at and beyond the Judgment-Seat of Christ ; diligence or laxity here will then produce proportionate results ; in Rev. 14 : 15 (twice), 16, figurative of the discriminating judgment Divinely to be fulfilled at the close of this age, when the wheat will be separated from the tares (see Matt. 13 : 30).¶

For REAP DOWN, Jas. 5 : 4, see MOW

REAPER

THERISTĒS (θεριστής), a reaper (akin to *therizō*, see above), is used of angels in Matt. 13 : 30, 39.¶

For REAR UP, John 2 : 20, see RAISE, No. 1 (f)

REASON (Noun)

LOGOS (λόγος), a word, etc., has also the significance of the inward thought itself, a reckoning, a regard, a reason, translated "reason" in Acts 18 : 14, in the phrase "reason would," *kata logon*, lit., 'according to reason (I would bear with you) ; ' in 1 Pet. 3 : 15, "a reason (concerning the hope that is in you)." See WORD.

Note : In Acts 6 : 2, A.V., the adjective *arestos*, pleasing, agreeable, is translated "reason" (R.V., "fit," marg., "pleasing"). See FIT, No. 2.

For the prepositions rendered BY REASON OF see †p. 9

REASON (Verb)

1. DIALOGIZOMAI (διαλογίζομαι), to bring together different reasons and reckon them up, to reason, is used in the N.T. (a) chiefly of thoughts and considerations which are more or less objectionable, e.g., of the disciples who reasoned together, through a mistaken view of Christ's teaching regarding leaven, Matt. 16 : 7, 8 and Mark 8 : 16, 17 ; of their reasoning as to who was the greatest among them, Mark 9 : 33, R.V., "were ye reasoning," A.V., "ye disputed" (for ver. 34, see DISPUTE) ; of the Scribes and Pharisees in criticising Christ's claim to forgive sins, Mark 2 : 6, 8 (twice) and Luke 5 : 21, 22 ; of the chief priests and elders in considering how to answer Christ's question regarding John's baptism, Matt. 21 : 25 ; Mark 11 : 31 (some mss. have *logizomai*, here, which is nowhere else rendered "to reason") ; of the wicked husbandmen, and their purpose to murder the heir and seize his inheritance, Luke 20 : 14 ; of the rich man who "reasoned" within himself, R.V. (A.V., "thought"), as to where to bestow his fruits, Luke 12 : 17 (some mss. have it in John 11 : 50, the best have *logizomai* ; see ACCOUNT, No. 4) ; (b) of considerations not objectionable, Luke 1 : 29, "cast in (her) mind ; " 3 : 15, R.V., and A.V., marg., "reasoned" (A.V., "mused"). See CAST, No. 15, DISPUTE, B, No. 2.¶

2. DIALEGOMAI (διαλέγομαι), to think different things with oneself, to ponder, then, to dispute with others, is translated to reason in Acts 17 : 2, A.V. and R.V. ; 17 : 17, R.V. ; 18 : 4, 19, A.V. and R.V. ; 19 : 8, 9, R.V. ; 24 : 25, A.V. and R.V. ; Heb. 12 : 5, R.V., "reasoneth (with you)," A.V., "speaketh (unto you)." See DISPUTE, B, No. 1.

3. SULLOGIZOMAI (συλλογίζομαι), to compute (*sun*, with, and *logizomai* ; cp. Eng., syllogism), also denotes to reason, and is so rendered in Luke 20 : 5.¶

4. SUZĒTEŌ (συζητέω), to seek or examine together (*sun*, with, *zēteō*, to seek), to discuss, is translated " reasoning " in Mark 12 : 28, A.V. (R.V., " questioning ") ; similarly in Luke 24 : 15. See DISPUTE, B, No. 3.

REASONABLE

LOGIKOS (λογικός), pertaining to the reasoning faculty, reasonable, rational, is used in Rom. 12 : 1, of the service (*latreia*) to be rendered by believers in presenting their bodies " a living sacrifice, holy, acceptable to God." The sacrifice is to be intelligent, in contrast to those offered by ritual and compulsion ; the presentation is to be in accordance with the spiritual intelligence of those who are new creatures in Christ and are mindful of " the mercies of God." For the significance of the word in 1 Pet. 2 : 2, see under MILK.¶

REASONING

DIALOGISMOS (διαλογισμός), a thought, reasoning, inward questioning [akin to *dialogizomai*, see REASON (Verb), No. 1], is translated " reasoning " or " reasonings " in Luke 5 : 22, R.V. (A.V., " thoughts ") ; 9 : 46 ; ver. 47, R.V. (A.V., " thoughts ") ; 24 : 38 (A.V., " thoughts ") ; Rom. 1 : 21 (A.V., " imaginations ") ; 1 Cor. 3 : 20 (A.V., " thoughts "). See DISPUTE, A, No. 1.

Note : In those mss. which contain Acts 28 : 29, occurs *suzētēsis*, a disputation, which is translated " reasoning " (A.V.).¶

REBUKE (Verb and Noun)
A. Verbs.

1. EPITIMAŌ (ἐπιτιμάω), primarily, to put honour upon, then, to adjudge, hence signifies to rebuke. Except for 2 Tim. 4 : 2 and Jude 9, it is confined in the N.T. to the Synoptic Gospels, where it is frequently used of the Lord's rebukes to (*a*) evil spirits, e.g., Matt. 17 : 18 ; Mark 1 : 25 ; 9 : 25 ; Luke 4 : 35, 41 ; 9 : 42 ; (*b*) winds, Matt. 8 : 26 ; Mark 4 : 39 ; Luke 8 : 24 ; (*c*) fever, Luke 4 : 39 ; (*d*) disciples, Mark 8 : 33 ; Luke 9 : 55 ; contrast Luke 19 : 39. For rebukes by others see Matt. 16 : 22 ; 19 : 13 ; 20 : 31 ; Mark 8 : 32 ; 10 : 13 ; 10 : 48, R.V., " rebuked " (A.V., " charged ") ; Luke 17 : 3 ; 18 : 15, 39 ; 23 : 40. See CHARGE, C, No. 7.

2. ELENCHŌ (ἐλέγχω), to convict, refute, reprove, is translated to rebuke in the A.V. of the following (the R.V. always has the verb to reprove) : 1 Tim. 5 : 20 ; Tit. 1 : 13 ; 2 : 15 ; Heb. 12 : 5 ; Rev. 3 : 19. See CONVICT, No. 1.

Note : While *epitimaō* signifies simply a rebuke which may be either undeserved, Matt. 16 : 22, or ineffectual, Luke 23 : 40, *elenchō* implies a rebuke which carries conviction.

3. EPIPLĒSSŌ (ἐπιπλήσσω), to strike at (*epi*, upon or at, *plēssō*, to

strike, smite), hence, to rebuke, is used in the injunction against rebuking an elder, 1 Tim. 5 : 1,¶

Note : In Phil. 2 : 15, the best texts have *amōmos*, without blemish (*a*, negative, *mōmos*, a blemish, a moral disgrace), R.V., " without blemish ; " some mss. have *amōmētos* (*a*, negative, and *mōmaomai*, to blame), A.V., " without rebuke." Contrast *amemptos* in the same verse, blameless on account of absence of inconsistency or ground of reproof, whereas *amōmos* indicates absence of stain or blemish. We may have blemish, with freedom from blame.

B. Noun.

ELENXIS (ἔλεγξις), akin to A, No. 2, denotes rebuke ; in 2 Pet. 2 : 16, it is used with *echō*, to have, and translated " he was rebuked," lit., ' he had rebuke.'¶ In the Sept., Job 21 : 4, " reproof ; " 23 : 2, " pleading."¶

For RECEIPT see CUSTOM (Toll), No. 2

RECEIVE, RECEIVING
A. Verbs.

1. LAMBANŌ (λαμβάνω) denotes either to take or to receive, (I) literally, (*a*) without an object, in contrast to asking, e.g., Matt. 7 : 8 ; Mark 11 : 24, R.V., " have received " (the original has no object) ; (*b*) in contrast to giving, e.g., Matt. 10 : 8 ; Acts 20 : 35 ; (*c*) with objects, whether things, e.g., Mark 10 : 30 ; Luke 18 : 30, in the best mss. (some have No. 4) ; John 13 : 30 ; Acts 9 : 19, R.V., " took " (A.V., " received ") ; 1 Cor. 9 : 25, R.V., " receive " (A.V., " obtain ") ; or persons, e.g., John 6 : 21 ; 13 : 20 ; 16 : 14, R.V., " take ; " 2 John 10 ; in Mark 14 : 65, R.V., " received (Him with blows of their hands) ; " this has been styled a vulgarism ; (II) metaphorically, of the word of God, Matt. 13 : 20 ; Mark 4 : 16 ; the sayings of Christ, John 12 : 48 ; the witness of Christ, John 3 : 11 ; a hundredfold in this life, and eternal life in the world to come, Mark 10 : 30 ; mercy, Heb. 4 : 16, R.V., " may receive " (A.V., " may obtain ") ; a person (*prosōpon*, see FACE), Luke 20 : 21, " acceptest," and Gal. 2 : 6, " accepteth," an expression used in the O.T. either in the sense of being gracious or kind to a person, e.g., Gen. 19 : 21 ; 32 : 20, or (negatively) in the sense of being impartial, e.g., Lev. 19 : 15 ; Deut. 10 : 17 ; this latter is the meaning in the two N.T. passages just mentioned. See ACCEPT, A, No. 4, TAKE, etc.

Lambanō and *prosōpon* are combined in the nouns *prosōpolēmpsia*, respect of persons, and *prosōpolēmptēs*, respecter of persons, and in the verb *prosōpolēmptō*, to have respect of persons : see PERSON.

2. PARALAMBANŌ (παραλαμβάνω), to receive from another (*para*, from beside), or to take, signifies to receive, e.g., in Mark 7 : 4 ; John 1 : 11 ; 14 : 3 ; 1 Cor. 11 : 23 ; 15 : 1, 3 ; Gal. 1 : 9, 12 ; Phil. 4 : 9 ; Col. 2 : 6 ; 4 : 17 ; 1 Thess. 2 : 13 (1st part) ; 4 : 1 ; 2 Thess. 3 : 6 ; Heb. 12 : 28. See TAKE.

3. ANALAMBANŌ (ἀναλαμβάνω), to take up (ana), to take to oneself, receive, is rendered to receive in Mark 16 : 19 ; Acts 1 : 2, 11, 22, R.V., " He was received up " (A.V., " taken ") ; 10 : 16 ; 1 Tim. 3 : 16. See TAKE.

4. APOLAMBANŌ (ἀπολαμβάνω) signifies to receive from another, (a) to receive as one's due (for Luke 18 : 30, see No. 1) ; Luke 23 : 41 ; Rom. 1 : 27 ; Col. 3 : 24 ; 2 John 8 ; (b) without the indication of what is due, Luke 16 : 25 ; Gal. 4 : 5 (in some mss. 3 John 8, for No. 7) ; (c) to receive back, Luke 6 : 34 (twice) ; 15 : 27. For its other meaning, to take apart, Mark 7 : 33, see TAKE.¶

5. PROSLAMBANŌ (προσλαμβάνω) denotes to take to oneself (pros, to) or to receive, always in the Middle Voice, signifying a special interest on the part of the receiver, suggesting a welcome, Acts 28 : 2 ; Rom. 14 : 1, 3 ; 15 : 7 ; Philm. 12 (in some mss. ; the best omit it) ; ver. 17. See TAKE.

6. METALAMBANŌ (μεταλαμβάνω), to have or get a share of, partake of (meta, with), is rendered " receiveth " in Heb. 6 : 7. See EAT, HAVE, PARTAKE, TAKE. In the Sept., Esth. 5 : 1.¶

7. HUPOLAMBANŌ (ὑπολαμβάνω), to take or bear up (hupo, under), to receive, is rendered " received " in Acts 1 : 9, of the cloud at the Ascension ; in 3 John 8, R.V., " welcome " (A.V., " receive "). See ANSWER, B, No. 3, SUPPOSE, WELCOME.

8. DECHOMAI (δέχομαι), to receive by deliberate and ready reception of what is offered, is used of (a) taking with the hand, taking hold, taking hold of or up, e.g., Luke 2 : 28, R.V., " he received (Him)," A.V., " took he (Him) up ; " 16 : 6, 7 ; 22 : 17 ; Eph. 6 : 17 ; (b) receiving, said of a place receiving a person, of Christ into the Heavens, Acts 3 : 21 ; or of persons in giving access to someone as a visitor, e.g., John 4 : 45 ; 2 Cor. 7 : 15 ; Gal. 4 : 14 ; Col. 4 : 10 ; by way of giving hospitality, etc., e.g., Matt. 10 : 14, 40 (four times), 41 (twice) ; 18 : 5 ; Mark 6 : 11 ; 9 : 37 ; Luke 9 : 5, 48, 53 ; 10 : 8, 10 ; 16 : 4 ; ver. 9, of reception, " into the eternal tabernacles," said of followers of Christ who have used " the mammon of unrighteousness " to render assistance to (" make . . . friends of ") others ; of Rahab's reception of the spies, Heb. 11 : 31 ; of the reception, by the Lord, of the spirit of a departing believer, Acts 7 : 59 ; of receiving a gift, 2 Cor. 8 : 4 (in some mss. ; R.V. follows those which omit it) ; of the favourable reception of testimony and teaching, etc., Luke 8 : 13 ; Acts 8 : 14 ; 11 : 1 ; 17 : 11 ; 1 Cor. 2 : 14 ; 2 Cor. 8 : 17 ; 1 Thess. 1 : 6 ; 2 : 13, where paralambanō (No. 2) is used in the 1st part, " ye received," dechomai in the 2nd part, " ye accepted," R.V. (A.V., " received "), the former refers to the ear, the latter, adding the idea of appropriation, to the heart ; Jas. 1 : 21 ; in 2 Thess. 2 : 10, " the love of the truth," i.e., love for the truth ; cp. Matt. 11 : 14, " if ye are willing to receive it," an elliptical construction frequent in Greek writings ; of receiving, by way of bearing with, enduring, 2 Cor. 11 : 16 ;

of receiving by way of getting, Acts 22 : 5 ; 28 : 21 ; of becoming partaker of benefits, Mark 10 : 15 ; Luke 18 : 17 ; Acts 7 : 38 ; 2 Cor. 6 : 1 ; 11 : 4 (last clause " did accept : " cp. *lambanō* in previous clauses) ; Phil. 4 : 18.¶

Note : There is a certain distinction between *lambanō* and *dechomai* (more pronounced in the earlier, classical use), in that in many instances *lambanō* suggests a self-prompted taking, whereas *dechomai* more frequently indicates "a welcoming or an appropriating reception" (Grimm-Thayer).

9. ANADECHOMAI (ἀναδέχομαι), to receive gladly, is used in Acts 28 : 7, of the reception by Publius of the shipwrecked company in Melita ; in Heb. 11 : 17, of Abraham's reception of God's promises, R.V., " gladly (*ana*, up, regarded as intensive) received." Moulton and Milligan point out the frequency of this verb in the papyri in the legal sense of taking the responsibility of something, becoming security for, under-taking, and say " The predominance of this meaning suggests its application in Heb. 11 : 17. The statement that Abraham had ' under-taken,' ' assumed the responsibility of,' the promises, would not perhaps be alien to the thought." The responsibility would surely be that of his faith in receiving the promises. In Classical Greek it had the meaning of receiving, and it is a little difficult to attach any other sense to the circumstances, save perhaps that Abraham's faith undertook to exercise the assurance of the fulfilment of the promises.¶

10. APODECHOMAI (ἀποδέχομαι), to welcome, to accept gladly (*apo*, from), to receive without reserve, is used (*a*) literally, Luke 8 : 40, R.V., " welcomed ; " 9 : 11 (in the best texts, some have No. 8) ; Acts 18 : 27 ; 21 : 17 ; 28 : 30 ; (*b*) metaphorically, Acts 2 : 41 ; 24 : 3, " we accept," in the sense of acknowledging, the term being used in a tone of respect. See ACCEPT, A No. 2.¶

11. EISDECHOMAI (εἰσδέχομαι), to receive into (*eis*), is used only in 2 Cor. 6 : 17, where the verb does not signify to accept, but to admit (as antithetic to "come ye out," and combining Isa. 52 : 11 with Zeph. 3 : 20).¶

12. EPIDECHOMAI (ἐπιδέχομαι), lit., to accept besides (*epi*, upon), to accept (found in the papyri, of accepting the terms of a lease), is used in the sense of accepting in 3 John 9 ; in ver. 10, in the sense of receiving with hospitality, in each verse said negatively concerning Diotrephes.¶

13. PARADECHOMAI (παραδέχομαι), to receive or admit with approval (*para*, beside), is used (*a*) of persons, Acts 15 : 4 (in some texts, No. 10) ; Heb. 12 : 6 ; (*b*) of things, Mark 4 : 20, A.V., " receive " (R.V., " accept ") ; Acts 16 : 21 ; 22 : 18 ; 1 Tim. 5 : 9.¶ In the Sept., Ex. 23 : 1 ; Prov. 3 : 12.¶

14. PROSDECHOMAI (προσδέχομαι), to receive to oneself, to receive favourably, also to look for, wait for, is used of receiving in Luke 15 : 2 ; Rom. 16 : 2 ; Phil. 2 : 29. See ACCEPT, A, No. 3, ALLOW, LOOK (for), TAKE, WAIT.

15. HUPODECHOMAI (ὑποδέχομαι) denotes to receive under one's

roof (*hupo*, under), receive as a guest, entertain hospitably, Luke 10 : 38 ; 19 : 6 ; Acts 17 : 7 ; Jas. 2 : 25.¶

16. KOMIZŌ (κομίζω) denotes to bear, carry, e.g., Luke 7 : 37 ; in the Middle Voice, to bear for oneself, hence (*a*) to receive, Heb. 10 : 36 ; 11 : 13 (in the best texts ; some have *lambanō*, No. 1), 39 ; 1 Pet. 1 : 9 ; 5 : 4 ; in some texts in 2 Pet. 2 : 13 (in the best mss. *adikeomai*, " suffering wrong," R.V.) ; (*b*) to receive back, recover, Matt. 25 : 27 ; Heb. 11 : 19 ; metaphorically, of requital, 2 Cor. 5 : 10 ; Col. 3 : 25, of ' receiving back again ' by the believer at the Judgment-Seat of Christ hereafter, for wrong done in this life ; Eph. 6 : 8, of receiving, on the same occasion, " whatsoever good thing each one doeth," R.V. ; see BRING, No. 20.¶

17. APECHŌ (ἀπέχω) denotes (*a*) transitively, to have in full, to have received ; so the R.V. in Matt. 6 : 2, 5, 16 (for A.V., " they have ") ; Luke 6 : 24, A.V., and R.V. ; in all these instances the present tense (to which the A.V. incorrectly adheres in the Matt. 6 verses) has a perfective force, consequent upon the combination with the prefix *apo* (from), not that it stands for the perfect tense, but that it views the action in its accomplished result ; so in Phil. 4 : 18, where the A.V. and R.V. translate it " I have ; " in Philm. 15, " (that) thou shouldest have (him for ever)," A.V., " shouldest receive ; " see HAVE, No. 2, and the reference to illustrations from the papyri of the use of the Verb in receipts ; (*b*) intransitively, to be away, distant, used with *porrō*, far, Matt. 15 : 8 ; Mark 7 : 6 ; with *makran*, far off, afar, Luke 7 : 6 ; 15 : 20 ; without an accompanying adverb, Luke 24 : 13, " which was from." See ABSTAIN, ENOUGH, HAVE.

18. CHŌREŌ (χωρέω), to give space, make room for (*chōra*, a place), is used metaphorically, of receiving with the mind, Matt. 19 : 11, 12 ; into the heart, 2 Cor. 7 : 2, R.V., " open your hearts," marg., " make room " (A.V., " receive "). See COME, No. 24, CONTAIN, No. 1, COURSE, B.

19. LANCHANŌ (λαγχάνω), to obtain by lot, is translated " received " in Acts 1 : 17, R.V. (A.V., " had obtained "). See LOT.

Notes : (1) In Mark 2 : 2, A.V., *chōreō* is translated " there was (no) room to receive " [R.V., " there was (no longer) room (for)]." (2) In Rev. 13 : 16, A.V., *didōmi* is translated " to receive " (marg., " to give them "), R.V., " (that) there be given (them)." (3) In 2 Cor. 7 : 9, A.V., *zēmioō*, to suffer loss (R.V.), is translated " ye might receive damage." (4) In Luke 7 : 22, R.V., *anablepō*, to recover sight, is translated " receive their sight " (A.V., " see "). (5) For " received (R.V., hath taken) tithes," Heb. 7 : 6, see TITHE. (6) For *eleeō*, in the Passive Voice, 2 Cor. 4 : 1, A.V., " having received mercy " (R.V., " obtained "), see MERCY. (7) For *patroparadotos*, in 1 Pet. 1 : 18, A.V., " *received* by tradition from your fathers," see HANDED DOWN. (8) In the A.V. of Matt. 13 : 19, 20, 22, 23, *speirō*, to sow seed, is translated " received seed ; " see SOW.

B. Nouns.

1. LĒPSIS or LĒMPSIS (λῆμψις), a receiving (akin to *lambanō*, A

No. 1), is used in Phil. 4 : 15.¶ In the Sept., Prov. 15 : 27, 29.¶

2. ANALĒ(M)PSIS (ἀνάλημψις), a taking up (ana, up, and No. 1), is used in Luke 9 : 51 with reference to Christ's Ascension ; " that He should be received up " is, lit., ' of the receiving up (of Him).' ¶ It has

3. METALĒ(M)PSIS (μετάλημψις), a participation, taking, receiving, is used in 1 Tim. 4 : 3, in connection with food, " to be received," lit., ' with a view to (eis) reception.'¶

4. PROSLĒ(M)PSIS (πρόσλημψις), pros, to, and No. 1, is used in Rom. 11 : 15, of the restoration of Israel.¶

RECKON, RECKONING

1. LOGIZOMAI (λογίζομαι) is properly used (a) of numerical calcu-lation, e.g., Luke 22 : 37 ; (b) metaphorically, by a reckoning of character-istics or reasons, to take into account, Rom. 2 : 26, " shall . . . be reckoned," R.V. (A.V., " counted "), of reckoning uncircumcision for circumcision by God's estimate in contrast to that of the Jew regarding his own condition (ver. 3) ; in 4 : 3, 5, 6, 9, 11, 22, 23, 24, of reckoning faith for righteousness, or reckoning righteousness to persons, in all of which the R.V. uses the verb to reckon instead of the A.V. to count or to impute ; in ver. 4 the subject is treated by way of contrast between grace and debt, which latter involves the reckoning of a reward for works ; what is owed as a debt cannot be reckoned as a favour, but the faith of Abraham and his spiritual children sets them outside the category of those who seek to be justified by self-effort, and, vice versa, the latter are excluded from the grace of righteousness bestowed on the sole condition of faith ; so in Gal. 3 : 6 (R.V., " was reckoned," A.V., " was accounted ") ; since Abraham, like all the natural descendants of Adam, was a sinner, he was destitute of righteousness in the sight of God ; if, then, his relationship with God was to be rectified (i.e., if he was to be justified before God), the rectification could not be brought about by works of merit on his part ; in Jas. 2 : 23, R.V., " reckoned," the subject is viewed from a different standpoint (see under JUSTIFICATION, B, last four paragraphs) ; for other instances of reckoning in this respect see Rom. 9 : 8, R.V., " are reckoned " (A.V., " are counted ") ; 2 Cor. 5 : 19, R.V., " (not) reckoning (trespasses)," A.V., " imputing ; " (c) to consider, calculate, translated to reckon in Rom. 6 : 11 ; 8 : 36 ; 2 Cor. 10 : 11, R.V., " let (such a one) reckon (this) ; " (d) to suppose, judge, deem, translated to reckon in Rom. 2 : 3, " reckonest thou (this)," R.V. (A.V., " thinkest ") ; 3 : 28 (A.V., " we conclude ") ; 8 : 18 ; 2 Cor. 11 : 5 (A.V., " I suppose ") ; see ACCOUNT, A, No. 4, CONSIDER, No. 6, COUNT, No. 3, SUPPOSE ; (e) to purpose, decide, 2 Cor. 10 : 2, R.V., " count " (A.V., " think ") ; see COUNT, No. 3.

2. LEGŌ (λέγω), to say, speak, also has the meaning to gather, reckon, account, used in this sense in Heb. 7 : 11, R.V., " be reckoned " (A.V., " be called "). See ASK, A, No. 6.

3. SUNAIRŌ (συναίρω), to take up together (sun, with, airō, to take),
is used with the noun logos, an account, signifying to settle accounts,
Matt. 18 : 23, R.V., " make a reckoning " (A.V., " take account ") ; ver.
24, A.V. and R.V., " to reckon " (logos being understood) ; 25 : 19, R.V.,
" maketh a reckoning " (A.V., " reckoneth "). This phrase occurs not
infrequently in the papyri in the sense of settling accounts (see Deissmann,
Light from the Ancient East, 118).¶   In the Sept. the verb occurs in its
literal sense in Ex. 23 : 5, " thou shalt help to raise " (lit., ' raise with ').¶

RECLINE

ANAKEIMAI (ἀνάκειμαι), lit., and in classical usage, to be laid up,
laid, denotes, in the N.T., to recline at table ; it is translated " reclining "
in John 13 : 23, R.V. (A.V., " leaning ") ; cp. anapiptō in ver. 25, R.V.,
" leaning back." See also ver. 12, marg. See LEAN, SIT, TABLE (at the)

For RECOMMEND, Acts 14 : 26 ; 15 : 40, A.V., see COMMEND, No. 2

RECOMPENCE, RECOMPENSE

A. Nouns.

1. ANTAPODOMA (ἀνταπόδομα), akin to antapodidōmi, to recompense
(see below), lit., a giving back in return (anti, in return, apo, back, didōmi,
to give), a requital, recompence, is used (a) in a favourable sense, Luke
14 : 12 ; (b) in an unfavourable sense, Rom. 11 : 9, indicating that the
present condition of the Jewish nation is the retributive effect of their
transgressions, on account of which that which was designed as a blessing
(" their table ") has become a means of judgment.¶

2. ANTAPODOSIS (ἀνταπόδοσις), derived, like No. 1, from
antapodidōmi, is rendered " recompense " in Col. 3 : 24, R.V. (A.V.,
" reward ").¶

3. ANTIMISTHIA (ἀντιμισθία), a reward, requital (anti, in return,
misthos, wages, hire), is used (a) in a good sense, 2 Cor. 6 : 13 ; (b) in a bad
sense, Rom. 1 : 27.¶

4. MISTHAPODOSIA (μισθαποδοσία), a payment of wages (from
misthos, see No. 3, and apodidōmi, B, No. 2), a recompence, is used
(a) of reward, Heb. 10 : 35 ; 11 : 26 ; (b) of punishment, Heb. 2 : 2.¶
Cp. misthapodotēs, a rewarder, Heb. 11 : 6.¶

B. Verbs.

1. ANTAPODIDŌMI (ἀνταποδίδωμι), akin to A, No. 1 and No. 2,
to give back as an equivalent, to requite, recompense (the anti expressing
the idea of a complete return), is translated " render " in 1 Thess. 3 : 9,
here only in the N.T. of thanksgiving to God (cp. the Sept. of Ps. 116 : 12) ;
elsewhere it is used of recompense, " whether between men (but in that
case only of good, not of evil, see No. 2 in 1 Thess. 5 : 15), Luke 14 : 14
a, cp. the corresponding noun in v. 12 ; or between God and evil-doers,
Rom. 12 : 19, R.V. (A.V., " repay ") ; Heb. 10 : 30, cp. the noun in Rom.

11 : 9; or between God and those who do well, Luke 14 : 14 *b*; Rom. 11 : 35, cp. the noun in Col. 3 : 24 ; in 2 Thess. 1 : 6 both reward and retribution are in view."*¶

2. APODIDŌMI (ἀποδίδωμι), to give up or back, restore, return, is translated " shall recompense " in the R.V. of Matt. 6 : 4, 6, 18 (A.V., " shall reward ") ; in Rom. 12 : 17, A.V., " recompense " (R.V., " render ") ; in 1 Thess. 5 : 15, " render." See DELIVER, GIVE, PAY, PERFORM, RENDER, REPAY, REQUITE, RESTORE, REWARD, SELL, YIELD.

RECONCILE, RECONCILIATION
A. Verbs.

1. KATALLASSŌ (καταλλάσσω) properly denotes to change, exchange (especially of money) ; hence, of persons, to change from enmity to friendship, to reconcile. With regard to the relationship between God and man, the use of this and connected words shows that primarily reconciliation is what God accomplishes, exercising His grace towards sinful man on the ground of the death of Christ in propitiatory sacrifice under the judgment due to sin, 2 Cor. 5 : 19, where both the verb and the noun are used (cp. No. 2, in Col. 1 : 21). By reason of this men in their sinful condition and alienation from God are invited to be reconciled to Him ; that is to say, to change their attitude, and accept the provision God has made, whereby their sins can be remitted and they themselves be justified in His sight in Christ.

Rom. 5 : 10 expresses this in another way : " For if, while we were enemies, we were reconciled to God through the death of His Son . . . ;" that we were " enemies " not only expresses man's hostile attitude to God but signifies that until this change of attitude takes place men are under condemnation, exposed to God's wrath. The death of His Son is the means of the removal of this, and thus we " receive the reconciliation," ver. 11, R.V. This stresses the attitude of God's favour toward us. The A.V. rendering " atonement " is incorrect. Atonement is the offering itself of Christ under Divine judgment upon sin. We do not receive atonement. What we do receive is the result, namely, " reconciliation."

The removal of God's wrath does not contravene His immutability. He always acts according to His unchanging righteousness and lovingkindness, and it is because He changes not that His relative attitude does change towards those who change. All His acts show that He is Light and Love. Anger, where there is no personal element, is a sign of moral health if, and if only, it is accompanied by grief. There can be truest love along with righteous indignation, Mark 3 : 5, but love and enmity cannot exist together. It is important to distinguish " wrath " and " hostility." The change in God's relative attitude toward those who

---

* From Notes on Thessalonians by Hogg and Vine, p. 226.

receive the reconciliation only proves His real unchangeableness. Not once is God said to be reconciled. The enmity is alone on our part. It was we who needed to be reconciled to God, not God to us, and it is propitiation, which His righteousness and mercy have provided, that makes the reconciliation possible to those who receive it.

When the writers of the N.T. speak upon the subject of the wrath of God, "the hostility is represented not as on the part of God, but of man. And this is the reason why the Apostle never uses *diallassō* [a word used only in Matt. 5 : 24, in the N.T.] in this connection, but always *katallassō*, because the former word denotes mutual concession after mutual hostility [frequently exemplified in the Sept.], an idea absent from *katallassō*" (Lightfoot, *Notes on the Epistles of Paul*, p. 288).

The subject finds its great unfolding in 2 Cor. 5 : 18-20, which states that God "reconciled us (believers) to Himself through Christ," and that "the ministry of reconciliation" consists in this, "that God was in Christ reconciling the world unto Himself." The insertion of a comma in the A.V. after the word "Christ" is misleading; the doctrine stated here is not that God was in Christ (the unity of the Godhead is not here in view), but that what God has done in the matter of reconciliation He has done in Christ, and this is based upon the fact that "Him who knew no sin He made to be sin on our behalf; that we might become the righteousness of God in Him." On this ground the command to men is "be ye reconciled to God."

The verb is used elsewhere in 1 Cor. 7 : 11, of a woman returning to her husband.¶

2. APOKATALLASSŌ (ἀποκαταλλάσσω), to reconcile completely (*apo*, from, and No. 1), a stronger form of No. 1, to change from one condition to another, so as to remove all enmity and leave no impediment to unity and peace, is used in Eph. 2 : 16, of the reconciliation of believing Jew and Gentile "in one body unto God through the Cross;" in Col. 1 : 21 not the union of Jew and Gentile is in view, but the change wrought in the individual believer from alienation and enmity, on account of evil works, to reconciliation with God; in ver. 20 the word is used of the Divine purpose to reconcile through Christ "all things unto Himself . . . whether things upon the earth, or things in the heavens," the basis of the change being the peace effected "through the blood of His Cross." It is the Divine purpose, on the ground of the work of Christ accomplished on the Cross, to bring the whole universe, except rebellious angels and unbelieving man, into full accord with the mind of God, Eph. 1 : 10. Things "under the earth," Phil. 2 : 10, are subdued, not reconciled.¶

3. DIALLASSŌ (διαλλάσσω), to effect an alteration, to exchange, and hence, to reconcile, in cases of mutual hostility yielding to mutual concession, and thus differing from No. 1 (under which see Lightfoot's remarks), is used in the Passive Voice in Matt. 5 : 24, which illustrates

the point. There is no such idea as " making it up " where God and man are concerned.¶

B. Noun.

KATALLAGĒ (καταλλαγή), akin to A, No. 1, primarily an exchange, denotes reconciliation, a change on the part of one party, induced by an action on the part of another ; in the N.T., the reconciliation of men to God by His grace' and love in Christ. The word is used in Rom. 5 : 11 and 11 : 15. The occasioning cause of the world-wide proclamation of reconciliation through the Gospel, was the casting away (partially and temporarily) of Israel. A new relationship Godward is offered to the Gentiles in the Gospel. The word also occurs in 2 Cor. 5 : 18, 19, where " the ministry of reconciliation " and " the word of reconciliation " are not the ministry of teaching the doctrine of expiation, but that of beseeching men to be reconciled to God on the ground of what God has wrought in Christ. See No. 1, above.¶

Note : In the O.T. in some passages the A.V. incorrectly has " reconciliation," the R.V. rightly changes the translation to " atonement," e.g., Lev. 8 : 15 ; Ezek. 45 : 20, R.V., " make atonement for " (A.V., " reconcile ").

For RECONCILIATION (MAKE), Heb. 2 : 17, A.V., see PROPITIATION

For RECORD (A.V.) see TESTIFY, No. 3, TESTIMONY, No. 2

RECOVER

1. SŌZŌ (σώζω), to save, is sometimes used of healing or restoration to health, the latter in John 11 : 12, R.V., " he will recover," marg., " be saved " (A.V., " he shall do well "). See HEAL, PRESERVE, SAVE, WHOLE.

2. ANANĒPHŌ (ἀνανήφω), to return to soberness, as from a state of delirium or drunkenness (*ana*, back, or again, *nēphō*, to be sober, to be wary), is used in 2 Tim. 2 : 26, " may recover themselves " (R.V. marg., " return to soberness," A.V. marg., " awake "), said of those who, opposing the truth through accepting perversions of it, fall into the snare of the Devil, becoming intoxicated with error ; for these recovery is possible only by " repentance unto the knowledge of the truth." For a translation of the verse see CAPTIVE, B, No. 3.¶

Notes : (1) For " recovering of sight," Luke 4 : 18, see SIGHT. (2) In Mark 16 : 18, the phrase *echō kalōs*, lit., ' to have well,' i.e., " to be well," is rendered " they shall recover."

RED
A. Adjectives.

1. PURRHOS (πυρρός) denotes fire-coloured (*pur*, fire), hence, fiery red, Rev. 6 : 4 ; 12 : 3, in the latter passage said of the Dragon, indicative of the cruelty of the Devil.¶

2. ERUTHROS (ἐρυθρός) den̄ ̄ ̄
root *rudh*— is seen, e.g., in the La ̄ ̄
It is applied to the Red Sea, Acts ̄ ̄ ̄
the name is uncertain ; it has been ̄ ̄ ̄
of the corals which cover the Red Sea ̄ due, ̄ etc.
of the mountains which border it, or to its shore ̄ ̄

B. Verb ̄

PURRHAZŌ (πυρράζω), to be fiery re ̄ ̄ A, No. 1), is ̄
the sky, Matt. 16 : 2, 3.¶ In the Sept., *pu̅*̄ ̄ Lev. 13 : 19, 42, 43, ̄
14 : 37.¶

REDEEM, REDEMPT ̄
A. Verbs.

1. EXAGORAZŌ (ἐξαγοράζω), a strengthen̄ ̄ ̄ *agorazō*, to
buy (see BUY, No. 1), denotes to buy out (*ex* for *ek*), especially ̄ purchasing
a slave with a view to his freedom. It is used *metaphorially* ̄ in Gal.
3 : 13 and 4 : 5, of the deliverance by Christ of Christian Jews from the
Law and its curse ; what is said of *lutron* (RANSOM, No. 1) is true of this
verb and of *agorazō*, as to the Death of Christ, that Scripture does not
say to whom the price was paid ; the various suggestions made are purely
speculative ; (*b*) in the Middle Voice, to buy up for oneself, Eph. 5 : 16
and Col. 4 : 5, of " buying up the opportunity " (R.V. marg. ; text,
" redeeming the time," where " time " is *karos*, a season, a time in which
something is seasonable), i.e., making the most of every opportunity,
turning each to the best advantage since none can be recalled if missed.¶

Note : In Rev. 5 : 9 ; 14 : 3, 4, A.V., *agorazō*, to purchase (R.V.) is
translated " redeemed." See PURCHASE.

2. LUTROŌ (λυτρόω), to release on receipt of ransom (akin to *lutron*,
a ransom), is used in the Middle Voice, signifying to release by paying a
ransom price, to redeem (*a*) in the natural sense of delivering, Luke 24 : 21,
of setting Israel free from the Roman yoke ; (*b*) in a spiritual sense, Tit.
2 : 14, of the work of Christ in redeeming men " from all iniquity "
(*anomia*, lawlessness, the bondage of self-will which rejects the will of
God) ; 1 Pet. 1 : 18 (Passive Voice), " ye were redeemed," from a vain
manner of life, i.e., from bondage to tradition. In both instances the
Death of Christ is stated as the means of redemption.¶

Note : While both No. 1 and No. 2 are translated to redeem, *exagorazō*
does not signify the actual redemption, but the price paid with a view to
it, *lutroō* signifies the actual deliverance, the setting at liberty.

B. Nouns.

1. LUTRŌSIS (λύτρωσις), a redemption (akin to A, No. 2), is used
(*a*) in the general sense of deliverance, of the nation of Israel, Luke 1 : 68,
R.V., " wrought redemption ; " 2 : 38 ; (*b*) of the redemptive work of
Christ, Heb. 9 : 12, bringing deliverance through His death, from the guilt

: 29, 48 ; Numb. 18 : 16 ;
Isa. 63 : 4.¶

sin.¶ In the Sngthened form of No. I, lit.,
Ps. 49 : 8 ; III som. It is used of (a) " deliver-
LUTRŌSIS (ἀπολύ 35, see DELIVER, B, No. I ; (b)
g, for (i.e., on payme t the Coming of Christ with His
rom physical torture er and great glory," Luke 21 : 28,
liverance of the peopl t the 'outshining of His Parousia,'
fied saints, " in a clou vent ; (c) forgiveness and justification,
redemption to be accom tion, deliverance from the guilt of sins,
Thess. 2 : 8, i.e., at His S ption that is in Christ Jesus ; " Eph. I : 7,
redemption as the result f our trespasses," R.V. ; so Col. I : 14,
Rom. 3 : 24, "through th indicating both the liberation from the
defined as "the forgive and the introduction into a life of liberty,
"the forgiveess of ou m. 6 : 4) ; Heb. 9 : 15, " for the redemption of
guilt and dom of si were under the first covenant," R.V., here
" newness clif " (R m. is equivalent to 'redemption from,' the genitive case
the transgr ions that the object from which the redemption is effected, not
"redempio 6" is equivalent uence of the transgressions, but from the transgressions
being used of the object from selves (d) the deliverance of the believer from the presence and
from the consequence of the and of his body from bondage to corruption, at the Coming
themselves (d) the deliverance in its inception) d the Lord Jesus, Rom. 8 : 23 ; I Cor. I : 30 ;
power of sin, and of his body rom : 14 ; 4 : 30.¶ See also PROPITIATION.
(the Parousia in its inception) d the Lord Jesus
Eph. I : 14 ; 4 : 30.¶ See also PROPITIATION.

For REDOUND, 2 Cor. 4 : 15 (R.V., " abound "), see ABUNDANCE,
B, No. I (c)

REED

KALAMOS (κάλαμος) denotes (a) the reed mentioned in Matt. 11 : 7 ;
12 : 20 ; Luke 7 : 24, the same as the Heb., qāneh (among the various reeds
in the O.T.), e.g., Isa. 42 : 3, from which Matt. 12 : 20 is quoted (cp. Job
40 : 21 ; Ezek. 29 : 6, a reed with jointed, hollow stalk) ; (b) a reed-staff,
staff, Matt. 27 : 29, 30, 48 ; Mark 15 : 19, 36 (cp. rhabdos, a rod ; in 2 Kings
18 : 21, rhabdos kalaminē) ; (c) a measuring reed or rod, Rev. 11 : 1 ;
21 : 15, 16 ; (d) a writing reed, a pen, 3 John 13 ; see PEN.¶

REFINED

PUROOMAI (πυρόομαι), to burn, is translated " refined," as of metals,
in Rev. I : 15 and 3 : 18, R.V. (A.V., " burned," and " tried "). See
BURN, No. 4.

For REFLECTING, 2 Cor. 3 : 18, R.V., see BEHOLD, No. 12

REFORMATION

DIORTHŌSIS (διόρθωσις), properly, a making straight (dia, through,

orthos, straight ; cp. *diorthōma* in Acts 24 : 2 ; see CORRECTION, No. 1),
denotes a " reformation " or reforming, Heb. 9 : 10 ; the word has the
meaning either (*a*) of a right arrangement, right ordering, or, more usually,
(*b*) of restoration, amendment, bringing right again ; what is here indicated
is a time when the imperfect, the inadequate, would be superseded by a
better order of things, and hence the meaning (*a*) seems to be the right
one ; it is thus to be distinguished from that of Acts 24 : 2, mentioned
above.¶ The word is used in the papyri in the other sense of the
rectification of things, whether by payments or manner of life.

REFRAIN

1. PAUŌ (παύω), to stop, is used in the Active Voice, in the sense
of making to cease, restraining in 1 Pet. 3 : 10, of causing the tongue to
refrain from evil ; elsewhere in the Middle Voice, see CEASE, No. 1.

2. APHISTĒMI (ἀφίστημι), to cause to depart, is used intransitively,
in the sense of departing from, refraining from, Acts 5 : 38. See DEPART,
No. 20.

REFRESH, REFRESHING
A. Verbs.

1. ANAPAUŌ (ἀναπαύω), to give intermission from labour, to give
rest, refresh (*ana*, back, *pauō*, to cause to cease), is translated to refresh
in 1 Cor. 16 : 18 ; 2 Cor. 7 : 13 ; Philm. 7, 20. See REST.

2. SUNANAPAUOMAI (συναναπαύομαι), to lie down, to rest with (*sun*,
with, and No. 1 in the Middle Voice), is used metaphorically of being
refreshed in spirit with others, in Rom. 15 : 32, A.V., " may with (you)
be refreshed " (R.V., " . . . find rest ").¶ In the Sept., Isa. 11 : 6.¶

3. ANAPSUCHŌ (ἀναψύχω), to make cool, refresh (*ana*, back,
psuchō, to cool), is used in 2 Tim. 1 : 16 (cp. B).¶ In the papyri it is
used of taking relaxation.

Note : In Acts 27 : 3, the verb *tunchanō*, to obtain or receive, with
the object *epimeleia*, care, is translated " to refresh himself " (R.V., marg.,
" to receive attention," i.e., to enjoy the kind attention of his friends).

B. Noun.

ANAPSUXIS (ἀνάψυξις), a refreshing (akin to A, No. 3), occurs
in Acts 3 : 19.¶ In the Sept., Ex. 8 : 15.¶ In the papyri it is used of
obtaining relief.

For REFUGE see FLEE, No. 3

REFUSE (Verb)

1. ARNEOMAI (ἀρνέομαι), to deny, renounce, reject, in late Greek
came to signify to refuse to acknowledge, to disown, and is translated
to refuse in Acts 7 : 35 ; Heb. 11 : 24. See DENY, No. 1.

2. PARAITEOMAI (παραιτέομαι), for the various meanings of which

see Avoid, No. 3, denotes to refuse in Acts 25 : 11 ; 1 Tim. 4 : 7 ; 5 : 11 ; 2 Tim. 2 : 23, R.V. (A.V., " avoid ") ; Tit. 3 : 10, R.V. (marg., " avoid ; " A.V., " reject ") ; Heb. 12 : 25 (twice), perhaps in the sense of begging off. See Excuse, Intreat, Reject.

3. DOKIMAZŌ (δοκιμάζω), to prove, to approve, used with a negative in Rom. 1 : 28, is translated " they refused," R.V. (A.V., " they did not like ") ; R.V. marg., " did not approve." See Approve, No. 1.

Notes : (1) For *parakouō*, to refuse to hear, R.V. in Matt. 18 : 17 (twice), see Hear, A, No. 7. (2) In 1 Tim. 4 : 4, A.V., *apoblētos*, " rejected " (R.V.), is translated " refused." See Reject.

REGARD

1. BLEPŌ (βλέπω), to behold, look, perceive, see, has the sense of regarding by way of partiality, in Matt. 22 : 16 and Mark 12 : 14. See Behold, No. 2.

2. ENTREPŌ (ἐντρέπω), to turn about (*en*, in, *trepō*, to turn), is metaphorically used of putting to shame, e.g., 1 Cor. 4 : 14 ; in the Middle Voice, to reverence, regard, translated " regard " in Luke 18 : 2, 4. See Ashamed, Reverence, Shame.

3. PHRONEŌ (φρονέω), to think, set the mind on, implying moral interest and reflection, is translated to regard in Rom. 14 : 6 (twice) ; the second part in the A.V. represents an interpolation and is not part of the original. The Scripture does not speak of not regarding a day. See Care, B, No. 6, Mind, Savour, Think, Understand.

4. EPIBLEPŌ (ἐπιβλέπω), to look upon (*epi*, upon, and No. 1), in the N.T. to look on with favour, is used in Luke 1 : 48, A.V., " hath regarded " (R.V., " hath looked upon ") ; in Jas. 2 : 3, R.V., " ye have regard to " (A.V., " ye have respect to "). See Look, No. 6, Respect.

5. OLIGŌREŌ (ὀλιγωρέω) denotes to think little of (*oligos*, little, *ōra*, care), to regard lightly, Heb. 12 : 5, R.V. (A.V., " despise "). See Despise, Note (3).¶ In the Sept., Prov. 3 : 11.¶

6. PROSECHŌ (προσέχω), to take or give heed, is translated " they had regard " in Acts 8 : 11, A.V. (R.V., " they gave heed "). See Attend, No. 1.

7. AMELEŌ (ἀμελέω), not to care, is translated " I regarded . . . not " in Heb. 8 : 9. See Neglect.

Notes : (1) In Gal. 6 : 4, R.V., *eis*, into, is translated " in regard of (himself)," A.V., " in ; " so in 2 Cor. 10 : 16 ; Eph. 5 : 32. (2) In Rom. 6 : 20, the dative case of *dikaiosunē*, righteousness, signifies, not " from righteousness," A.V., but " in regard of righteousness," R.V., lit., ' free to righteousness ; ' i.e., righteousness laid no sort of bond upon them, they had no relation to it in any way. (3) In 2 Cor. 8 : 4 the accusative case of *charis* and *koinōnia* is, in the best texts, used absolutely, i.e., not as the objects of an expressed verb ; hence the R.V., " in regard to " (A.V., " that we would receive," where the verb is the result of a supplementary gloss). (4) For "not regarding" in Phil. 2 : 30, A.V. (R.V., "hazarding "), see HAZARD, No. 2.

REGENERATION

PALINGENESIA (παλιγγενεσία), new birth (*palin*, again, *genesis*, birth), is used of spiritual regeneration, Tit. 3 : 5, involving the communication of a new life, the two operating powers to produce which are "the word of truth," Jas. 1 : 18 ; 1 Pet. 1 : 23, and the Holy Spirit, John 3 : 5, 6 ; the *loutron*, the laver, the washing, is explained in Eph. 5 : 26, "having cleansed it by the washing (*loutron*) of water with the word."

The new birth and regeneration do not represent successive stages in spiritual experience, they refer to the same event but view it in different aspects. The new birth stresses the communication of spiritual life in contrast to antecedent spiritual death ; regeneration stresses the inception of a new state of things in contrast with the old ; hence the connection of the use of the word with its application to Israel, in Matt. 19 : 28. Some regard the *kai* in Tit. 3 : 5 as epexegetic, ' even ; ' but, as Scripture marks two distinct yet associated operating powers, there is not sufficient ground for this interpretation. See under EVEN.

In Matt. 19 : 28 the word is used, in the Lord's discourse, in the wider sense, of the "restoration of all things" (Acts 3 : 21, R.V.), when, as a result of the Second Advent of Christ, Jehovah ' sets His King upon His holy hill of Zion ' (Ps. 2 : 6), and Israel, now in apostasy, is restored to its destined status, in the recognition and under the benign sovereignty of its Messiah. Thereby will be accomplished the deliverance of the world from the power and deception of Satan and from the despotic and antichristian rulers of the nations. This restitution will not in the coming Millennial age be universally a return to the pristine condition of Edenic innocence previous to the Fall, but it will fulfil the establishment of God's Covenant with Abraham concerning his descendants, a veritable re-birth of the nation, involving the peace and prosperity of the Gentiles. That the worldwide subjection to the authority of Christ will not mean the entire banishment of evil, is clear from Rev. 20 : 7, 8. Only in the new heavens and earth, "wherein dwelleth righteousness," will sin and evil be entirely absent.¶

REGION

1. CHŌRA (χώρα), a space lying between two limits, a country, land, is translated "region" in Matt. 4 : 16 ; Luke 3 : 1 ; Acts 8 : 1 ; 13 : 49 ; 16 : 6 ; 18 : 23, R.V. In the last three passages it has the technical sense of a subdivision of a Roman Province, Lat. *regio ;* as also No. 2 in Acts 14 : 6. See COUNTRY, No. 3.

2. PERICHŌROS (περίχωρος), a country or region round about (*peri*), is translated "region round about " in Matt. 3 : 5 ; 14 : 35, R.V. ; Mark

1 : 28 (in some mss. Mark 6 : 55); Luke 3 : 3, R.V.; 4 : 14; 4 : 37, R.V.; 7 : 17; Acts 14 : 6 (see No. 1). See COUNTRY, No. 4.

3. KLIMA (κλίμα), an inclination, slope, is translated "regions" in Rom. 15 : 23, R.V.; 2 Cor. 11 : 10; Gal. 1 : 21. See PART, A, No. 3.¶

Note : For "*regions* beyond," 2 Cor. 10 : 16, A.V., see PART, A. Note (9).

REGRET
A. Verb.

METAMELOMAI (μεταμέλομαι), to regret, to repent one, is translated to regret in 2 Cor. 7 : 8, R.V. (twice), A.V., "repent." See REPENT.

B. Adjective.

AMETAMELĒTOS (ἀμεταμέλητος), not repented of (*a*, negative, and A), is translated "which bringeth no regret" in 2 Cor. 7 : 10, R.V., said of repentance (A.V., "not to be repented of"); elsewhere, in Rom. 11 : 29. See REPENT.¶

For REGULAR, Acts 19 : 39, R.V., see LAW, C, No. 2

REHEARSE

1. ANANGELLŌ (ἀναγγέλλω), to bring back word (*ana*, back, *angellō*, to announce), is translated to rehearse in Acts 14 : 27; 15 : 4, R.V. See ANNOUNCE.

2. EXĒGEOMAI (ἐξηγέομαι), primarily, to lead, show the way, is used metaphorically with the meaning to unfold, declare, narrate, and is translated to rehearse in the R.V. of Luke 24 : 35; Acts 10 : 8; 15 : 12, and 14, R.V. See DECLARE, No. 8.

Note : In Acts 11 : 4, the A.V. translates the middle Voice of *archō*, to begin, "rehearsed . . . from the beginning," R.V., "began, (and)."

REIGN (Verb and Noun)

1. BASILEUŌ (βασιλεύω), to reign, is used (I) literally, (*a*) of God, Rev. 11 : 17; 19 : 6, in each of which the aorist tense (in the latter, translated "reigneth") is "ingressive," stressing the point of entrance; (*b*) of Christ, Luke 1 : 33; 1 Cor. 15 : 25; Rev. 11 : 15; as rejected by the Jews, Luke 19 : 14, 27; (*c*) of the saints, hereafter, 1 Cor. 4 : 8 (2nd part), where the Apostle, casting a reflection upon the untimely exercise of authority on the part of the church at Corinth, anticipates the due time for it in the future (see No. 2); Rev. 5 : 10; 20 : 4, where the aorist tense is not simply of a "point" character, but "constative," that is, regarding a whole action as having occurred, without distinguishing any steps in its progress (in this instance the aspect is future); ver. 6; 22 : 5; (*d*) of earthly potentates, Matt. 2 : 22; 1 Tim. 6 : 15, where "kings" is, lit., 'them that reign;' (II) metaphorically, (*a*) of believers, Rom. 5 : 17,

where " shall reign in life " indicates the activity of life in fellowship with Christ in His sovereign power, reaching its fulness hereafter ; 1 Cor. 4 : 8 (1st part), of the carnal pride that laid claim to a power not to be exercised until hereafter ; (b) of Divine grace, Rom. 5 : 21 ; (c) of sin, Rom. 5 : 21 ; 6 : 12 ; (d) of death, Rom. 5 : 14, 17.¶

2. SUMBASILEUŌ (συμβασιλεύω), to reign together with (sun, with, and No. 1), is used of the future reign of believers together and with Christ in the Kingdom of God in manifestation, 1 Cor. 4 : 8 (3rd part); of those who endure 2 Tim. 2 : 12, cp. Rev. 20 : 6.¶

Notes : (1) In Rom. 15 : 12, A.V., *archō*, to rule (R.V., is translated " to reign." (2) In Rev. 17 : 18, *echō*, to have, with *basileia*, a kingdom, is translated " reigneth," lit., ' hath a kingdom,' suggestive of a distinction between the sovereignty of mystic Babylon and that of ordinary sovereigns. (3) In Luke 3 : 1, *hēgemonia*, rule, is rendered " reign."¶

REINS

NEPHROS (νεφρός), a kidney (Eng., nephritis, etc.), usually in the plural, is used metaphorically of the will and the affections, Rev. 2 : 23, " reins " (cp. Ps. 7 : 9 ; Jer. 11 : 20 ; 17 : 10 ; 20 : 12). The feelings and emotions were regarded as having their seat in the kidneys.¶

REJECT
A. Verbs.

1. APODOKIMAZŌ (ἀποδοκιμάζω), to reject as the result of examination and disapproval (*apo*, away from, *dokimazō*, to approve), is used (a) of the rejection of Christ by the elders and chief priests of the Jews, Matt. 21 : 42 ; Mark 8 : 31 ; 12 : 10 ; Luke 9 : 22 ; 20 : 17 ; 1 Pet. 2 : 4, 7 (A.V., " disallowed ") ; by the Jewish people, Luke 17 : 25 ; (b) of the rejection of Esau from inheriting " the blessing," Heb. 12 : 17. See DISALLOW.¶ Cp. and contrast *exoutheneō*, Acts 4 : 11. See DESPISE.

2. ATHETEŌ (ἀθετέω), properly, to do away with what has been laid down, to make *atheton* (i.e., without place, *a*, negative, *tithēmi*, to place), hence, besides its meanings to set aside, make void, nullify, disannul, signifies to reject ; in Mark 6 : 26, regarding Herod's pledge to Salome, it almost certainly has the meaning ' to break faith with ' (cp. the Sept. of Jer. 12 : 6, and Lam. 1 : 2, " dealt treacherously "). Moulton and Milligan illustrate this meaning from the papyri. Field suggests ' disappoint." In Mark 7 : 9 " ye reject (the commandment) " means ' ye set aside ; ' in Luke 7 : 30, " ye reject " may have the meaning of nullifying or making void the counsel of God ; in Luke 10 : 16 (four times), " rejecteth," R.V. (A.V., " despiseth ") ; " rejecteth " in John 12 : 48 ; " reject " in 1 Cor. 1 : 19 (A.V., " bring to nothing ") ; 1 Thess. 4 : 8, to despise, where the reference is to the charges in ver. 2 ; in 1 Tim. 5 : 12, R.V., " have rejected " (A.V., " have cast off "). See DESPISE, Notes (1), DISANNUL, No. 1.

3. EKPTUŌ (ἐκπτύω), to spit out (*ek*, out, and *ptuō*, to spit), i.e., to abominate, loathe, is used in Gal. 4 : 14, " rejected " (marg., " spat out "), where the sentence is elliptical : ' although my disease repelled you, you did not refuse to hear my message.'¶

4. PARAITEOMAI (παραιτέομαι), besides the meanings to beg from another, Mark 15 : 6 (in the best texts) ; to entreat that . . . not, Heb. 12 : 19 ; to beg off, ask to be excused, Luke 14 : 18, 19 ; 12 : 25 (see REFUSE, No. 2), is translated to reject in Tit. 3 : 10, A.V. See EXCUSE, INTREAT, REFUSE.

B. Adjectives.

1. ADOKIMOS (ἀδόκιμος), not standing the test (see CAST, C), is translated " rejected " in 1 Cor. 9 : 27, R.V. ; Heb. 6 : 8, A.V. and R.V. See REPROBATE.

2. APOBLĒTOS (ἀπόβλητος), lit., cast away (*apo*, from, *ballō*, to throw), occurs in 1 Tim. 4 : 4, R.V., " rejected " (A.V., " refused "). See REFUSE.¶

REJOICE

1. CHAIRŌ (χαίρω), to rejoice, is most frequently so translated. As to this verb, the following are grounds and occasions for rejoicing, on the part of believers: in the Lord, Phil. 3 : 1 ; 4 : 4 ; His Incarnation, Luke 1 : 14 ; His power, Luke 13 : 17 ; His presence with the Father, John 14 : 28 ; His presence with them, John 16 : 22 ; 20 : 20 ; His ultimate triumph, 8 : 56 ; hearing the gospel, Acts 13 : 48 ; their salvation, Acts 8 : 39 ; receiving the Lord, Luke 19 : 6 ; their enrolment in Heaven, Luke 10 : 20 ; their liberty in Christ, Acts 15 : 31 ; their hope, Rom. 12 : 12 (cp. Rom. 5 : 2 ; Rev. 19 : 7) ; their prospect of reward, Matt. 5 : 12 ; the obedience and godly conduct of fellow-believers, Rom. 16 : 19, R.V., " I rejoice " (A.V., " I am glad ") ; 2 Cor. 7 : 7, 9 ; 13 : 9 ; Col. 2 : 5 ; 1 Thess. 3 : 9 ; 2 John 4 ; 3 John 3 ; the proclamation of Christ, Phil. 1 : 18 ; the gospel harvest, John 4 : 36 ; suffering with Christ, Acts 5 : 41 ; 1 Pet. 4 : 13 ; suffering in the cause of the gospel, 2 Cor. 13 : 9 (1st part) ; Phil. 2 : 17 (1st part) ; Col. 1 : 24 ; in persecutions, trials and afflictions, Matt. 5 : 12 ; Luke 6 : 23 ; 2 Cor. 6 : 10 ; the manifestation of grace, Acts 11 : 23 ; meeting with fellow-believers, 1 Cor. 16 : 17, R.V., " I rejoice ;" Phil. 2 : 28 ; receiving tokens of love and fellowship, Phil. 4 : 10 ; the rejoicing of others, Rom. 12 : 15 ; 2 Cor. 7 : 13 ; learning of the well-being of others, 2 Cor. 7 : 16. See FAREWELL, GLAD, GREETING, etc.

2. SUNCHAIRŌ (συγχαίρω), to rejoice with (*sun*, and No. 1), is used of rejoicing together in the recovery of what was lost, Luke 15 : 6, 9 ; in suffering in the cause of the gospel, Phil. 2 : 17 (2nd part), 18 ; in the joy of another, Luke 1 : 58 ; in the honour of fellow-believers, 1 Cor. 12 : 26 ; in the triumph of the truth, 1 Cor. 13 : 6, R.V., " rejoiceth with."¶

3. AGALLIAŌ (ἀγαλλιάω), to rejoice greatly, to exult, is used, (I) in

the Active Voice, of rejoicing in God, Luke 1 : 47 ; in faith in Christ, 1 Pet. 1 : 8, R.V. (Middle V. in some mss.), " ye rejoice greatly ; " in the event of the marriage of the Lamb, Rev. 19 : 7, " be exceeding glad," R.V.; (II) in the Middle Voice, (a) of rejoicing in persecutions, Matt. 5 : 12 (2nd part) ; in the light of testimony for God, John 5 : 35 ; in salvation received through the gospel, Acts 16 : 34, " he rejoiced greatly," R.V. ; in salvation ready to be revealed, 1 Pet. 1 : 6 ; at the revelation of His glory, 1 Pet. 4 : 13, " with exceeding joy," lit., ' ye may rejoice (see No. 1) exulting ; ' (b) of Christ's rejoicing (greatly) " in the Holy Spirit," Luke 10 : 21, R.V. ; said of His praise, as foretold in Ps. 16 : 9, quoted in Acts 2 : 26 (which follows the Sept., " My tongue ") ; (c) of Abraham's rejoicing, by faith, to see Christ's day, John 8 : 56.¶

4. EUPHRAINŌ (εὐφραίνω), in the Active Voice, to cheer, gladden (eu, well, phrēn, the mind), signifies in the Passive Voice to rejoice, make merry ; it is translated to rejoice in Acts 2 : 26, R.V., " was glad," A.V., " did . . . rejoice," of the heart of Christ as foretold in Ps. 16 : 9 [cp. No. 3, II (b)] ; in Acts 7 : 41, of Israel's idolatry ; in Rom. 15 : 10 (quoted from the Sept. of Deut. 32 : 43, where it is a command to the Gentiles to rejoice with the Jews in their future deliverance by Christ from all their foes, at the establishment of the Messianic Kingdom) the Apostle applies it to the effects of the gospel ; in Gal. 4 : 27 (touching the barrenness of Sarah as referred to in Is. 54 : 1, and there pointing to the ultimate restoration of Israel to God's favour, cp. 51 : 2), the word is applied to the effects of the gospel, in that the progeny of grace would greatly exceed the number of those who had acknowledged allegiance to the Law ; grace and faith are fruitful, law and works are barren as a means of salvation ; in Rev. 12 : 12, it is used in a call to the heavens to rejoice at the casting out of Satan and the inauguration of the Kingdom of God in manifestation and the authority of His Christ ; in 18 : 20, of a call to heaven, saints, apostles, prophets, to rejoice in the destruction of Babylon. See GLAD, No. 3, MERRY, No. 1.

5. KAUCHAOMAI (καυχάομαι), to boast, to glory, is rendered to rejoice, (a) Rom. 5 : 2, in hope of the glory of God ; (b) 5 : 3, R.V. (A.V. " glory "), in tribulation ; (c) 5 : 11, R.V. (A.V., " we joy "), in God ; (d) Phil. 3 : 3, R.V., " glory " (A.V., " rejoice ") in Christ Jesus ; (e) Jas. 1 : 9 (R.V., " glory," A.V., " rejoice "), the brother of low degree in his high estate ; the rich brother in being made low ; (f) Jas. 4 : 16, of evil glorying. See GLORY (to boast).

Notes : (1) In Jas. 2 : 13, A.V., katakauchaomai, to glory, boast against, is translated " rejoiceth against "' (R.V., " glorieth against "). See GLORY (to boast), A, No. 2. (2) The nouns kauchēma, kauchēsis, signifying glorying, boasting, are always so rendered in the R.V., where the A.V. has " rejoicing," the former in 2 Cor. 1 : 14 ; Gal. 6 : 4 ; Phil. 1 : 26 ; 2 : 16 ; Heb. 3 : 6 ; the latter in 1 Cor. 15 : 31 ; 2 Cor. 1 : 12 ; 1 Thess. 2 : 19 ; Jas. 4 : 16. See GLORY, B, Nos. 1 and 2.

RELEASE

APOLUŌ (ἀπολύω), to loose from, is translated to release in Matt. 18 : 27, R.V. (A.V., " loosed ") ; 27 : 15, 17, 21, 26 ; Mark 15 : 6, 9, 11, 15 ; Luke 6 : 37 (twice), R.V. (A.V., " forgive " and " ye shall be forgiven ") ; 23 : 16 (ver. 17, in some mss.), 18, 20, 25 ; 23 : 22, R.V. (A.V., " let . . . go ") ; John 18 : 39 (twice) ; 19 : 10 ; in 19 : 12, in the 1st part, A.V. and R.V. ; in the 2nd part, R.V., " release " (A.V., " let . . . go ") ; so in Acts 3 : 13. See DEPART, DISMISS.

Note : For *aphesis*, "release," Luke 4 : 18, R.V., see DELIVERANCE.

RELIEF

1. DIAKONIA (διακονία), ministry, is translated " relief " in Acts 11 : 29 [R.V., marg., " for (*eis*) ministry "].

2. ANESIS (ἄνεσις), a loosening, relaxation (akin to *aniēmi*, to send away, let go, loosen), is translated " relief " in 2 Cor. 2 : 13 and 7 : 5 (A.V., " rest "). See REST.

RELIEVE

EPARKEŌ (ἐπαρκέω) signifies to be strong enough for, and so either to ward off, or to aid, to relieve (a strengthened form of *arkeo*, which has the same three meanings, *epi* being intensive) ; it is used in 1 Tim. 5 : 10, 16 (twice).¶

RELIGION

1. THRĒSKEIA (θρησκεία) signifies religion in its external aspect (akin to *thrēskos*, see below), religious worship, especially the ceremonial service of religion ; it is used of the religion of the Jews, Acts 26 : 5 ; of the " worshipping " of angels, Col. 2 : 18, which they themselves repudiate (Rev. 22 : 8, 9) ; " there was an officious parade of humility in selecting these lower beings as intercessors rather than appealing directly to the Throne of Grace " (Lightfoot) ; in Jas. 1 : 26, 27 the writer purposely uses the word to set in contrast that which is unreal and deceptive, and the " pure religion " which consists in visiting " the fatherless and widows in their affliction," and in keeping oneself " unspotted from the world." He is " not herein affirming . . . these offices to be the sum total, nor yet the great essentials, of true religion, but declares them to be the body, the *thrēskeia*, of which godliness, or the love of God, is the informing soul " (Trench).¶

2. DEISIDAIMONIA (δεισιδαιμονία) primarily denotes fear of the gods (from *deidō*, to fear, *daimōn*, a pagan deity, Eng., demon), regarded whether as a religious attitude, or, in its usual meaning, with a condemnatory or contemptuous significance, superstition. That is how Festus regarded the Jews' religion, Acts 25 : 19, A.V. and R.V. marg., " superstition " (R.V., " religion "). See RELIGIOUS, Note (1), and under SUPERSTITIOUS.¶

Notes : (1) *Thrēskeia* is external, *theosebeia* is the reverential worship of God (see GODLINESS), *eusebeia* is piety (see GODLINESS), *eulabeia* the devotedness arising from godly fear (see FEAR). (2) For " the Jews' religion," Gal. 1 : 13, 14, see JEWS, B.

RELIGIOUS

THRĒSKOS (θρῆσκος), religious, careful of the externals of divine service, akin to *thrēskeia* (see above), is used in Jas. 1 : 26.¶

Notes : (1) For *deisidaimōn*, Acts 17 : 22, R.V., marg., " religious," see SUPERSTITIOUS. (2) For " religious (proselytes)," A.V. in Acts 13 : 43, see DEVOUT, No. 3.

REMAIN

1. MENŌ (μένω), to stay, abide, is frequently rendered to remain, e.g., Matt. 11 : 23 ; Luke 10 : 7 ; John 1 : 33, A.V. (R.V., " abiding ") ; 9 : 41 (in 15 : 11, the best texts have the verb to be, see R.V.) ; 15 : 16, A.V. (R.V., " abide ") ; 19 : 31 ; Acts 5 : 4 (twice), R.V., " whiles it remained, did it (not) remain (thine own) ? ; " 27 : 41 ; 1 Cor. 7 : 11 ; 15 : 6 ; 2 Cor. 3 : 11, 14 ; 9 : 9, A.V. (R.V., " abideth "); Heb. 12 : 27 ; 1 John 3 : 9. See ABIDE.

2. DIAMENŌ (διαμένω), to remain throughout (*dia*, through, and No. 1), is translated to remain in Luke 1 : 22 ; Heb. 1 : 11, A.V. (R.V., " Thou continuest "). See CONTINUE, No. 4.

3. APOLEIPŌ (ἀπολείπω), in the Passive Voice, to be reserved, to remain, is translated " remaineth " in Heb. 4 : 6, 9 ; 10 : 26. See LEAVE, No. 4.

4. PERILEIPŌ (περιλείπω), to leave over, used in the Middle Voice, is translated " remain " in 1 Thess. 4 : 15, 17, A.V. (R.V., " are left "), where it stands for the living believers at the coming (the beginning of the Parousia) of Christ.¶

5. PERISSEUŌ (περισσεύω), to abound, to be over and above, to remain over, is rendered " (that which) remained over " in Matt. 14 : 20, R.V. ; and Luke 9 : 17, R.V. (A.V., " remained ") ; John 6 : 12, 13 (A.V., " . . . over and above "). See ABUNDANCE, B, No. 1.

Notes : (1) In Mark 8 : 8, *perisseuma*, an abundance, is used in the plural, R.V., " (of broken pieces) that remained over " (A.V. " that was left "). (2) In 1 Cor. 7 : 29, A.V., *to loipon*, lit., ' (as to) what is left,' ' (as for) the rest,' is translated " it remaineth " (R.V., " henceforth ") ; in Rev. 3 : 2, *ta loipa*, the plural, " the things that remain."

REMEMBER, REMEMBRANCE, REMINDED
A. Verbs.

1. MIMNĒSKŌ (μιμνήσκω), from the older form *mnaomai*, in the Active Voice signifies to remind ; in the Middle Voice, to remind oneself of, hence, to remember, to be mindful of ; the later form is found only

in the present tense, in Heb. 2 : 6, " are mindful of," and 13 : 3, " remember ; " the perfect tense in 1 Cor. 11 : 2 and in 2 Tim. 1 : 4 (R.V., " remembering," A.V., " being mindful of "), is used with a present meaning. R.V. variations from the A.V. are, in Luke 1 : 54, R.V., " that He might remember " (A.V., " in remembrance of ") ; 2 Pet. 3 : 2, " remember " (A.V., " be mindful of ") ; Rev. 16 : 19 (Passive Voice), " was remembered " (A.V., " came in remembrance "). The Passive Voice is used also in Acts 10 : 31, A.V. and R.V., " are had in remembrance." See MINDFUL OF (to be).

2. MNĒMONEUŌ (μνημονεύω) signifies to call to mind, remember ; it is used absolutely in Mark 8 : 18 ; everywhere else it has an object, (a) persons, Luke 17 : 32 ; Gal. 2 : 10 ; 2 Tim. 2 : 8, where the R.V. rightly has " remember Jesus Christ, risen from the dead ; " Paul was not reminding Timothy (nor did he need to) that Christ was raised from the dead (A.V.), what was needful for him was to remember (to keep in mind) the One who rose, the Source and Supplier of all his requirements ; (b) things, e.g., Matt. 16 : 9 ; John 15 : 20 ; 16 : 21 ; Acts 20 : 35 ; Col. 4 : 18 ; 1 Thess. 1 : 3 ; 2 : 9 ; Heb. 11 : 15, " had been mindful of ; " 13 : 7 ; Rev. 18 : 5 ; (c) a clause, representing a circumstance etc., John 16 : 4 ; Acts 20 : 31 ; Eph. 2 : 11 ; 2 Thess. 2 : 5 ; Rev. 2 : 5 ; 3 : 3 ; in Heb. 11 : 22 it signifies to make mention of. See MENTION.¶

3. ANAMIMNĒSKŌ (ἀναμιμνήσκω), ana, back, and No. 1, signifies in the Active Voice to remind, call to one's mind, 1 Cor. 4 : 17, " put (A.V., bring) . . . into remembrance ; " so 2 Tim. 1 : 6 ; in the Passive Voice, to remember, call to (one's own) mind, Mark 11 : 21, " calling to remembrance ; " 14 : 72, " called to mind ; " 2 Cor. 7 : 15, " remembereth ; " Heb. 10 : 32, " call to remembrance."¶

4. HUPOMIMNĒSKŌ (ὑπομιμνήσκω) signifies to cause one to remember, put one in mind of (hupo, under, often implying suggestion, and No. 1), John 14 : 26, " shall . . . bring . . . to (your) remembrance ; " 2 Tim. 2 : 14, " put . . . in remembrance ; " Tit. 3 : 1, " put . . . in mind ; " 3 John 10, R.V., " I will bring to remembrance " (A.V., " I will remember ") ; Jude 5, " to put . . . in remembrance." In Luke 22 : 61 it is used in the Passive Voice, " (Peter) remembered," lit., ' was put in mind.'¶

5. EPANAMIMNĒSKŌ (ἐπαναμιμνήσκω), to remind again (epi, upon, and No. 3), is used in Rom. 15 : 15, R.V., " putting (you) again in remembrance," A.V., " putting (you) in mind." See MIND.¶

Note : In 1 Tim. 4 : 6, A.V., hupotithēmi, to lay under, to suggest, is translated " put . . . in remembrance " (R.V., " put . . . in mind "). See MIND.

B. Nouns.

1. ANAMNĒSIS (ἀνάμνησις), a remembrance (ana, up, or again, and A, No. 1), is used (a) in Christ's command in the institution of the Lord's Supper, Luke 22 : 19 ; 1 Cor. 11 : 24, 25, not ' in memory of ' but in an

affectionate calling of the Person Himself to mind ; (b) of the remembrance of sins, Heb. 10 : 3, R.V., " a remembrance " (A.V., " a remembrance again ;" but the prefix *ana* does not here signify again) ; what is indicated, in regard to the sacrifices under the law, is not simply an external bringing to remembrance, but an awakening of mind.¶   In the Sept., Lev. 24 : 7 ; Numb. 10 : 10 ; Pss. 38 and 70, Titles.¶

2. HUPOMNĒSIS (ὑπόμνησις) denotes a reminding, a reminder; in 2 Tim. 1 : 5 it is used with *lambanō*, to receive, lit., ' having received a reminder,' R.V., " having been reminded " (A.V., " when I call to remembrance ") ; in 2 Pet. 1 : 13 and 3 : 1, " remembrance."¶

Note : A distinction has been drawn between Nos. 1 and 2, in that *anamnēsis* indicates an unassisted recalling, *hupomnēsis*, a remembrance prompted by another.

3. MNEIA (μνεία) denotes a remembrance, or a mention.   See MENTION.

4. MNĒMĒ (μνήμη) denotes a memory (akin to *mnaomai*, A, No. 1), remembrance, mention, 2 Pet. 1 : 15, " remembrance ; " here, however, it is used with *poieō*, to make (Middle Voice), and some suggest that the meaning is ' to make mention.'¶

REMISSION, REMIT
A. Nouns.

1. APHESIS (ἄφεσις), a dismissal, release (from *aphiēmi*, B), is used of the forgiveness of sins and translated " remission " in Matt. 26 : 28 ; Mark 1 : 4; Luke 1 : 77; 3 : 3; 24 : 47; Acts 2 : 38; 5 : 31 (A.V., " forgiveness ") ; 10 : 43 ; 13 : 38, R.V. (A.V., " forgiveness ") ; 26 : 18 (ditto); Heb. 9 : 22 ; 10 : 18.   See FORGIVE, B, and A, No. 1.

2. PARESIS (πάρεσις), a passing by of debt or sin, Rom. 3 : 25, A.V., " remission " (R.V. and A.V. marg., " passing over "). See PASSING OVER.¶

Note : No. 2 is a matter of forbearance, No. 1 a matter of grace.

B. Verb.

APHIĒMI (ἀφίημι), to send away (akin to A, No. 1), is translated to remit in John 20 : 23 (twice), A.V. (R.V., to forgive). Scripture makes clear that the Lord's words could not have been intended to bestow the exercise of absolution, which Scripture declares is the prerogative of God alone. There is no instance in the N.T. of this act on the part of the Apostles. The words are to be understood in a " declarative " sense ; the statement has regard to the effects of their ministry of the gospel, with its twofold effects of remission or retention. They could not, nor could anyone subsequently, forgive sins, any more than that Joseph actually restored the butler to his office and hanged the baker (Gen. 41 : 13), or any more than that the prophets actually accomplished things when they declared that they were about to be done (Jer. 1 : 10 ; Ezek. 43 : 3).   See FORGIVE, No. 1.

REMNANT

1. LOIPOS (λοιπός), an adjective (akin to *leipō*, to leave) signifying remaining, is used as a noun and translated " the rest " in the R.V., where the A.V. has " the remnant," Matt. 22 : 6 ; Rev. 11 : 13 ; 12 : 17 ; 19 : 21. See OTHER, RESIDUE, REST (the).

2. LEIMMA (λεῖμμα), that which is left (akin to *leipō*, to leave), a remnant, is used in Rom. 11 : 5, " there is a remnant," more lit., ' there has come to be a remnant,' i.e., there is a spiritual remnant saved by the gospel from the midst of apostate Israel. While in one sense there has been and is a considerable number, yet, compared with the whole nation, past and present, the remnant is small, and as such is an evidence of God's electing grace (see ver. 4).¶ In the Sept., 2 Kings 19 : 4.¶

3. HUPOLEIMMA (ὑπόλειμμα), *hupo*, under, signifying diminution, and No. 2, is used in Rom. 9 : 27 : some mss. have *kataleimma*, which has virtually the same meaning (*kata*, down, behind), a remnant, where the contrast is drawn between the number of Israel as a whole, and the small number in it of those who are saved through the Gospel. The quotation is chiefly from the Sept. of Isa. 10 : 22, 23, with a modification recalling Hosea 1 : 10, especially with regard to the word " number." The return of the remnant is indicated in the name " Shear-Jashub," see Isa. 7 : 3, marg. The primary reference was to the return of a remnant from captivity to their own land and to God Himself ; here the application is to the effects of the gospel. There is stress on the word " remnant." ¶

REMOVE, REMOVING
A. Verbs.

1. METABAINŌ (μεταβαίνω), to pass over from one place to another (*meta*, implying change, and *bainō*, to go), is translated to remove in Matt. 17 : 20 (twice). See PASS, No. 7.

2. METHISTĒMI (μεθίστημι) is used transitively in the sense of causing to remove, in Acts 13 : 22, of the removing of King Saul, by bringing about his death ; in 1 Cor. 13 : 2, of removing mountains. See PUT, No. 23, TRANSLATE, TURN.

3. METATITHĒMI (μετατίθημι), to remove a person or thing from one place to another (*meta*, implying change, *tithēmi*, to put), e.g., Acts 7 : 16, " were carried over," signifies, in the Middle Voice, to change oneself, and is so used in Gal. 1 : 6 "(I marvel that) ye are . . . removing," R.V. (not as A.V., " removed ") ; the present tense suggests that the defection of the Galatians from the truth was not yet complete and would continue unless they changed their views. The Middle Voice indicates that they were themselves responsible for their declension, rather than the Judaizers who had influenced them. See CARRY, No. 5.

4. PARAPHERŌ (παραφέρω), lit., to bring to or before (*para*, beside, *pherō*, to carry), to take or carry away, is translated " remove " in the

Lord's prayer in Gethsemane, Mark 14 : 36, R.V. (A.V., " take away ") ;
Luke 22 : 42. See TAKE. In the Sept., 1 Sam. 21 : 13.¶

5. METOIKIZŌ (μετοικίζω), to remove to a new abode, cause to
migrate (meta, implying change, oikos, a dwelling place), is translated
" removed " in Acts 7 : 4 ; " I will carry . . . away " (ver. 43). See
CARRYING AWAY, B.

6. APOCHŌRIZŌ (ἀποχωρίζω), to separate, part asunder, is used in
the Passive Voice in Rev. 6 : 14, "(the heaven) was removed," R.V.
(A.V., " departed "). See DEPART, No. 14.

Notes : (1) In Matt. 21 : 21 and Mark 11 : 23, *airō*, to lift, take up, is
translated " be thou removed " (R.V., " be thou taken up "). (2) In
Rev. 2 : 5, A.V., *kineō*, to move (R.V.), is translated " will remove."
See MOVE.

B. Noun.

METATHESIS (μετάθεσις), change of position (transliterated in Eng.,
metathesis, a transposition of the letter of a word), from *meta*, implying
change, and *tithēmi*, to place, is used only in Hebrews and translated
" removing " in 12 : 27 ; " translation " in 11 : 5 ; " change " in 7 : 12.
See CHANGE, A.¶

REND, RENT (Verb and Noun)
A. Verbs.

1. RHĒGNUMI (ῥήγνυμι), to tear, rend, is translated to rend in
Matt. 7 : 6, of swine. See BREAK, A, No. 6.

2. DIARRHĒSSŌ, or DIARĒSSŌ (διαρήσσω), a late form of *diarrhēgnumi*, to break asunder, rend (*dia*, through, and No. 1), is used of
rending one's garments, Matt. 26 : 65 ; Mark 14 : 63 ; Acts 14 : 14.
See BREAK, A, No. 7.

3. PERIRRHĒGNUMI, or PERIRĒGNUMI (περιρήγνυμι), to tear
off all round (*peri*, around), is said of garments in Acts 16 : 22.¶

4. SCHIZŌ (σχίζω), to split, rend open, translated to rend in Matt.
27 : 51 (twice) ; Mark 1 : 10, R.V., " rent asunder " (A.V., " open ") ;
15 : 38 ; Luke 5 : 36, R.V., " rendeth (from) ; " the A.V. follows the mss.
which omit it in the 1st part of this verse ; 23 : 45 ; John 19 : 24 ; 21 : 11,
R.V., " rent " (A.V., " broken "), of a net. See BREAK, A, No. 12.

5. DIASPAŌ (διασπάω), to tear asunder, is translated " rent asunder "
in Mark 5 : 4, R.V. (A.V., " plucked asunder ") ; for Acts 23 : 10, see
TEAR.¶

Note : In Mark 9 : 26, A.V., *sparassō*, to tear (R.V.), is rendered
" rent." See TEAR.

B. Noun.

SCHISMA (σχίσμα), a rent, division (akin to A, No. 4), signifies a rent
in wineskins in Matt. 9 : 16 ; Mark 2 : 21. See DIVISION, No. 3.

RENDER
1. APODIDŌMI (ἀποδίδωμι), to give up or back, is translated to

render, (*a*) of righteous acts, (1) human, Matt. 21 : 41 ; 22 : 21 ; Mark 12 : 17 ; Luke 16 : 2, R.V. (A.V., " give ") ; Luke 20 : 25 ; Rom. 13 : 7 ; 1 Cor. 7 : 3 ; (2) Divine, Matt. 16 : 27, R.V., " shall render " (A.V., " shall reward "), an important R.V. change ; Rom. 2 : 6 ; 2 Tim. 4 : 14, R.V. (A.V., " reward ") ; Rev. 18 : 6 (ditto) ; 22 : 12, R.V. (A.V., " give ") ; (*b*) of unrighteous acts, Rom. 12 : 17, R.V. (A.V., " recompense ") ; 1 Thess. 5 : 15 ; 1 Pet. 3 : 9. See DELIVER, A, No. 3, RECOMPENSE, B, No. 2.

2. ANTAPODIDŌMI (ἀνταποδίδωμι), to give in return for, is translated " render " in 1 Thess. 3 : 9. See RECOMPENSE, REPAY.

3. PARECHŌ (παρέχω), to furnish, provide, supply, is translated " render " in Col. 4 : 1, R.V. (A.V., " give "), of what is due from masters to servants. See GIVE, No. 8.

4. DIDŌMI (δίδωμι), to give, is translated " rendering " in 2 Thess. 1 : 8, R.V. (A.V., " taking "), of the Divine execution of vengeance at the revelation of Christ from Heaven hereafter. See GIVE, No. 1.

RENEW, RENEWING (Verb and Noun)
A. Verbs.

1. ANAKAINOŌ (ἀνακαινόω), to make new (*ana*, back or again, *kainos*, new, not recent but different), to renew, is used in the Passive Voice in 2 Cor. 4 : 16, of the daily renewal of " the inward man " (in contrast to the physical frame), i.e., of the renewal of spiritual power ; in Col. 3 : 10, of " the new man " (in contrast to the old unregenerate nature), which " is being renewed unto knowledge," R.V. (cp. No. 3 in Eph. 4 : 23), i.e., the true knowledge in Christ, as opposed to heretical teachings.¶

Note : This word has not been found elsewhere in Greek writings as yet, though No. 2 is, which would prevent the supposition that the Apostle coined a new word.

2. ANAKAINIZŌ (ἀνακαινίζω) is a variant form of No. 1, used in Heb. 6 : 6, of the impossibility of renewing to repentance those Jews who professedly adhered to the Christian faith, if, after their experiences of it (not actual possession of its regenerating effects), they apostatized into their former Judaism.¶ In the Sept., 2 Chron. 15 : 8 ; Ps. 39 : 2 ; 103 : 5 ; 104 : 30 ; Lam. 5 : 21.¶

3. ANANEOŌ (ἀνανεόω), to renew, make young (*ana*, as in No. 1, and *neos*, recent, not different), is used in Eph. 4 : 23, " be renewed (in the spirit of your mind)." The renewal here mentioned is not that of the mind itself in its natural powers of memory, judgment and perception, but ' the spirit of the mind,' which, under the controlling power of the indwelling Holy Spirit, directs its bent and energies Godward in the enjoyment of " fellowship with the Father and with His Son, Jesus Christ," and of the fulfilment of the will of God.¶ The word is frequent in inscriptions and in the papyri.

B. Noun.

ANAKAINŌSIS (ἀνακαίνωσις), akin to A, No. 1, a renewal, is used in Rom. 12 : 2, " the renewing (of your mind)," i.e., the adjustment of the moral and spiritual vision and thinking to the mind of God, which is designed to have a transforming effect upon the life ; in Tit. 3 : 5, where " the renewing of the Holy Spirit " is not a fresh bestowment of the Spirit, but a revival of His power, developing the Christian life ; this passage stresses the continual operation of the indwelling Spirit of God ; the Romans passage stresses the willing response on the part of the believer.¶

RENOUNCE

1. APEIPON (ἀπεῖπον), lit., to tell from (apo, from, eipon, an aorist form used to supply parts of legō, to say), signifies to renounce, 2 Cor. 4 : 2 (Middle Voice), of disowning " the hidden things of shame."¶ In the Sept. of 1 Kings 11 : 2 it signifies to forbid, a meaning found in the papyri. The meaning to renounce may therefore carry with it the thought of forbidding the approach of the things disowned.

2. APOTASSŌ (ἀποτάσσω), to set apart, to appoint, a meaning found in the papyri (apo, from, tassō, to arrange), is used in the Middle Voice in the sense either of taking leave of, e.g., Acts 18 : 18, or forsaking, Luke 14 : 33, R.V., " renounceth " (A.V. " forsaketh "). See FORSAKE, LEAVE.

REPAY

1. APODIDŌMI (ἀποδίδωμι), to give back, is translated " I will repay " in Luke 10 : 35. See DELIVER, A, No. 3, RECOMPENSE, B, No. 2, RENDER, No. 1.

2. ANTAPODIDŌMI (ἀνταποδίδωμι), to give in return for, is translated " I will repay " in Rom. 12 : 19, A.V. (R.V., " I will recompense "). See RECOMPENSE, B, No. 1, RENDER, No. 2.

3. APOTINŌ or APOTIŌ (ἀποτίνω), signifying to pay off (apo, off, tinō, to pay a fine), is used in Philm. 19, of Paul's promise to repay whatever Onesimus owed Philemon, or to whatever extent the runaway slave had wronged his master.¶ The verb is very common in the papyri, e.g., in a contract of apprenticeship the father has to pay a forfeit for each day of the son's absence from work. Moulton and Milligan, who draw this and other illustrations in the way of repayment, point out that " this verb is stronger than apodidōmi (No. 1), and carries with it the idea of repayment by way of a fine or punishment, a fact which lends emphasis to its use in Philm. 19."

REPENT, REPENTANCE
A. Verbs.

1. METANOEŌ (μετανοέω), lit., to perceive afterwards (meta, after, implying change, noeō, to perceive ; nous, the mind, the seat of moral

reflection), in contrast to *pronoeō*, to perceive beforehand, hence signifies to change one's mind or purpose, always, in the N.T., involving a change for the better, an amendment, and always, except in Luke 17 : 3, 4, of repentance from sin. The word is found in the Synoptic Gospels (in Luke, nine times), in Acts five times, in the Apocalypse twelve times, eight in the messages to the churches, 2 : 5 (twice), 16, 21 (twice), R.V., " she willeth not to repent " (2nd part) ; 3 : 3, 19 (the only churches in those chapters which contain no exhortation in this respect are those at Smyrna and Philadelphia) ; elsewhere only in 2 Cor. 12 : 21. See also the general Note below.

2. METAMELOMAI (μεταμέλομαι), *meta*, as in No. 1, and *melō*, to care for, is used in the Passive Voice with Middle Voice sense, signifying to regret, to repent oneself, Matt. 21 : 29, R.V., " repented himself ; " ver. 32, R.V., " ye did (not) repent yourselves " (A.V., " ye repented not ") ; 27 : 3, " repented himself ; " 2 Cor. 7 : 8 (twice), R.V., " regret " in each case ; Heb. 7 : 21, where alone in the N.T. it is said (negatively) of God.¶

B. Adjective.

AMETAMELĒTOS (ἀμεταμέλητος), not repented of, unregretted (*a*, negative, and a verbal adjective of A, No. 2), signifies ' without change of purpose ; ' it is said (*a*) of God in regard to his " gifts and calling," Rom. 11 : 29 ; (*b*) of man, 2 Cor. 7 : 10, R.V., "[repentance (*metanoia*, see C)] . . . which bringeth no regret " (A.V., " not to be repented of ") ; the difference between *metanoia* and *metamelomai*, illustrated here, is briefly expressed in the contrast between repentance and regret.¶

C. Noun.

METANOIA (μετάνοια), after-thought, change of mind, repentance, corresponds in meaning to A, No. 1, and is used of repentance from sin or evil, except in Heb. 12 : 17, where the word " repentance " seems to mean, not simply a change of Isaac's mind, but such a change as would reverse the effects of his own previous state of mind. Esau's birthright-bargain could not be recalled, it involved an irretrievable loss.

As regards repentance from sin, (*a*) the requirement by God on man's part is set forth, e.g., in Matt. 3 : 8 ; Luke 3 : 8 ; Acts 20 : 21 ; 26 : 20 ; (*b*) the mercy of God in giving repentance or leading men to it is set forth, e.g., in Acts 5 : 31 ; 11 : 18 ; Rom. 2 : 4 ; 2 Tim. 2 : 25. The most authentic mss. omit the word in Matt. 9 : 13 and Mark 2 : 17, as in the R.V.

Note : In the O.T., repentance with reference to sin is not so prominent as that change of mind or purpose, out of pity for those who have been affected by one's action, or in whom the results of the action have not fulfilled expectations, a repentance attributed both to God and to man, e.g., Gen. 6 : 6 ; Ex. 32 : 14 (that this does not imply anything contrary to God's immutability, but that the aspect of His mind is changed toward an object that has itself changed, see under RECONCILE).

In the N.T. the subject chiefly has reference to repentance from sin, and this change of mind involves both a turning from sin and a turning to God.   The parable of the prodigal son is an outstanding illustration of this.   Christ began His ministry with a call to repentance, Matt. 4 : 17, but the call is addressed, not as in the O.T. to the nation, but to the individual.   In the Gospel of John, as distinct from the Synoptic Gospels, referred to above, repentance is not mentioned, even in connection with John the Baptist's preaching ; in John's Gospel and 1st Epistle the effects are stressed, e.g., in the new birth, and, generally, in the active turning from sin to God by the exercise of faith (John 3 : 3 ; 9 : 38 ; 1 John 1 : 9), as in the N.T. in general.

REPETITIONS (use vain)

BATTALOGEŌ or BATTOLOGEŌ (βατταλογέω), to repeat idly, is used in Matt. 6 : 7, " use (not) vain repetitions ; " the meaning to stammer is scarcely to be associated with this word.   The word is probably from an Aramaic phrase and onomatopoeic in character.   The rendering of the Sinaitic Syriac is " Do not be saying *battalatha*, idle things," i.e., meaning-less and mechanically repeated phrases, the reference being to pagan (not Jewish) modes of prayer.   *Battalos*, " the Gabbler," was a nickname for Demosthenes, the great orator, assigned to him by his rivals.¶

REPLY

ANTAPOKRINOMAI (ἀνταποκρίνομαι) is translated " repliest against " in Rom. 9 : 20 (*anti*, against, *apokrinomai*, to answer) ; in Luke 14 : 6, " answer again."   See ANSWER, B, No. 2.¶

REPORT (Noun and Verb)
A. Nouns.

1. AKOĒ (ἀκοή), a hearing, is translated " report " in John 12 : 38 and Rom. 10 : 16, and in the R.V. of Matt. 4 : 24 ; 14 : 1 ; Mark 1 : 28. See HEARING, B, No. 1.

2. EUPHĒMIA (εὐφημία), a good report, good reputation (*eu*, well, *phēmē*, a saying or report), is used in 2 Cor. 6 : 8.   Contrast No. 3.¶

3. DUSPHĒMIA (δυσφημία), evil-speaking, defamation (*dus-*, an inseparable prefix, the opposite to *eu*, well, see No. 2), is used in 2 Cor. 6 : 8.¶

4. LOGOS (λόγος), a word, is translated " report," i.e., a story, narra-tive ; in Luke 5 : 15 (A.V., " fame ") ; 7 : 17 (A.V., " rumour ") ; Acts 11 : 22 (A.V., " tidings ").   See WORD.

Note : For *marturia*, rendered " report " in 1 Tim. 3 : 7, A.V., see TESTIMONY, WITNESS.

B. Adjective.

EUPHĒMOS (εὔφημος), akin to A, No. 2, primarily, uttering words or sounds of good omen, then, avoiding ill-omened words, and hence fair-sounding, " of good report," is so rendered in Phil. 4 : 8.¶

C. Verbs.

1. MARTUREŌ (μαρτυρέω), to be a witness, bear witness, testify, signifies, in the Passive Voice, to be well testified of, to have a good report, Acts 6 : 3, " of good (A.V., honest) report," lit., ' being well testified of ; ' 10 : 22 ; 16 : 2 ; 22 : 12 ; 1 Tim. 5 : 10 ; in Heb. 11 : 2, 39, A.V., " obtained a good report " (R.V., " had witness borne to them ") ; in 3 John 12, A.V., " hath good report " (R.V., " hath the witness "), lit., ' witness hath been borne.' See TESTIFY, WITNESS.

2. APANGELLŌ (ἀπαγγέλλω), to report (apo, from, angellō, to give a message), announce, declare (by a messenger, speaker, or writer), is translated " reported " in Acts 4 : 23 ; 16 : 36, R.V. (A.V., " told ") ; ver. 38 (some mss. have No. 3 ; A.V., " told ") ; " report " in 1 Cor. 14 : 25, A.V. (R.V., " declaring ") ; 1 Thess. 1 : 9, R.V., " report " (A.V., " shew ") ; so Acts 28 : 21. See DECLARE, No. 2.

3. ANANGELLŌ (ἀναγγέλλω), to bring back word, in later Greek came to have the same meaning as No. 2, to announce, declare ; it is translated " are reported " in 1 Pet. 1 : 12, A.V. (R.V., " have been announced "). See DECLARE, No. 1.

4. AKOUŌ (ἀκούω), to hear, is used in the Passive Voice, impersonally, in 1 Cor. 5 : 1, lit., ' it is heard ' or ' there is heard,' translated " it is reported." See HEAR.

5. BLASPHĒMEŌ (βλασφημέω), to speak slanderously, impiously, profanely (blaptō, to injure, and phēmē, a saying), is translated " we be slanderously reported " in Rom. 3 : 8 (Passive Voice). See BLASPHEME, B.

Note : In Matt. 28 : 15, A.V., diaphēmizō, to spread abroad (dia, throughout, phēmē, a saying, report), is translated " is commonly reported " (R.V., " was spread abroad "). See BLAZE ABROAD.

REPROACH (Noun and Verb), REPROACHFULLY

A. Nouns.

1. ONEIDISMOS (ὀνειδισμός), a reproach, defamation, is used in Rom. 15 : 3 ; 1 Tim. 3 : 7 ; Heb. 10 : 33 ; 11 : 26 ; 13 : 13.¶

2. ONEIDOS (ὄνειδος), akin to No. 1, is used in Luke 1 : 25 in the concrete sense of a matter of reproach, a disgrace.¶ To have no children was, in the Jewish mind, more than a misfortune, it might carry the implication that this was a Divine punishment for some secret sin. Cp. Gen. 30 : 1 ; 1 Sam. 1 : 6–10.

3. ATIMIA (ἀτιμία), dishonour, is translated " reproach " in 2 Cor. 11 : 21, A.V. (R.V., " disparagement "). See DISHONOUR, SHAME, VILE.

Note : In 2 Cor. 12 : 10, A.V., hubris, insolence, injury, is translated " reproaches " (R.V., " injuries "). See HARM.

B. Verbs.

1. ONEIDIZŌ (ὀνειδίζω), akin to A, Nos. 1 and 2, signifies (a), in the Active Voice, to reproach, upbraid, Matt. 5 : 11, R.V., " shall reproach " (A.V., " shall revile ") ; 11 : 20, " to upbraid ; " 27 : 44, R.V., " cast

. . . reproach" [A.V., "cast . . . in (His) teeth"]; Mark 15 : 32, R.V., "reproached" (A.V., "reviled"); 16 : 14, "upbraided;" Luke 6 : 22, "shall reproach;" Rom. 15 : 3; Jas. 1 : 5, "upbraideth;" (b) in the Passive Voice, to suffer reproach, be reproached, 1 Tim. 4 : 10 (in some mss. in the 2nd part); 1 Pet. 4 : 14.¶

2. HUBRIZŌ (ὑβρίζω), akin to *hubris* (see A, Note), used transitively, denotes to outrage, insult, treat insolently; it is translated "Thou reproachest" in Luke 11 : 45. The word is much stronger than to reproach; the significance is 'Thou insultest (even us),' i.e., who are superior to ordinary Pharisees. The lawyer's imputation was unjust; Christ's rebuke was not *hubris*, insult. What He actually said was by way of reproach (*oneidizō*). See DESPITEFULLY.

Notes : (1) For *anepilēptos*, "without reproach," R.V., in 1 Tim. 3 : 2; 5 : 7; 6 : 14, see BLAMELESS, B, No. 5. (2) In 1 Tim. 5 : 14, A.V., *loidoria*, reviling (R.V.), used in the genitive case with *charin*, in respect of, "for," is translated "reproachfully" (R.V., "for reviling"). Cp. *loidoreō*, to revile. See RAILING.

REPROBATE

ADOKIMOS (ἀδόκιμος), signifying 'not standing the test,' rejected (*a*, negative, *dokimos*, approved), was primarily applied to metals (cp. Is. 1 : 22); it is used always in the N.T. in a Passive sense, (a) of things, Heb. 6 : 8, "rejected," of land that bears thorns and thistles; (b) of persons, Rom. 1 : 28, of a " reprobate mind," a mind of which God cannot approve, and which must be rejected by Him, the effect of refusing "to have God in *their* knowledge;" in 1 Cor. 9 : 27 (for which see CAST, REJECTED); 2 Cor. 13 : 5, 6, 7, where the R.V. rightly translates the adjective " reprobate " (A.V., " reprobates "), here the reference is to the great test as to whether Christ is in a person; in 2 Tim. 3 : 8 of those " reprobate concerning the faith," i.e., men whose moral sense is perverted and whose minds are beclouded with their own speculations; in Tit. 1 : 16, of the defiled, who are " unto every good work reprobate," i.e., if they are put to the test in regard to any good work (in contrast to their profession), they can only be rejected.¶ In the Sept., Prov. 25 : 4; Isa. 1 : 22.¶

REPROOF, REPROVE

A. Noun.

ELEGMOS (ἐλεγμός), a reproof (akin to B), is found in the best texts in 2 Tim. 3 : 16 (some mss. have *elenchos*, which denotes a proof, proving, test, as in Heb. 11 : 1, "proving," R.V. marg., "test").¶ Cp. *elenxis*, rebuke, 2 Pet. 2 : 16 (lit., ' had rebuke ').¶

B. Verb.

ELENCHŌ (ἐλέγχω), to convict, rebuke, reprove, is translated to reprove in Luke 3 : 19; John 3 : 20, R.V. marg., " convicted;" the real meaning here is "exposed" (A.V. marg., "discovered"); Eph. 5 : 11, 13, where to expose is again the significance; in John 16 : 8, A.V., "will reprove" (R.V., "will convict"); in 1 Cor. 14 : 24, R.V., "reproved" (A.V., "convinced"); in the following the R.V. has 'to reprove,' for A.V., 'to rebuke,' 1 Tim. 5 : 20; Tit. 2 : 15; Heb. 12 : 5; Rev. 3 : 19; for synonymous words see CONVICT and REBUKE.

REPUTATION, REPUTE

DOKEŌ (δοκέω) signifies (a) to be of opinion (akin to *doxa*, an opinion), to suppose, e.g., Luke 12 : 51; 13 : 2 (see SUPPOSE); (b) to seem, to be reputed; in Gal. 2 : 2, R.V., "who were of repute" (A.V., "which were of reputation"); in 2 : 6 (twice), and 9, R.V., "were reputed" and "were of repute" (A.V., "seemed"); in each case the present participle of the verb with the article is used, lit., '(well) thought of' by them, persons held in consideration; in ver. 6, R.V., "(those) who were reputed to be somewhat" (A.V., "who seemed to be somewhat"); so ver. 9, where there is no irony [cp. the rendering "are accounted" in Mark 10 : 42 (i.e., not rulers nominally)], Paul recognized that James, Cephas, and John were, as they were reputed by the church at Jerusalem, its responsible guides; (c) impersonally, to think, to seem good. See SEEM and THINK.

The first meaning, to suppose, implies a subjective opinion based on thought; the second meaning, exemplified in the Galatians passages, expresses, from the standpoint of the observer, his own judgment about a matter (Trench, Syn., § lxxx).

Notes: (1) In Acts 5 : 34, A.V., *timios*, honoured, had in honour (R.V.), is translated "had in reputation." (2) In Phil. 2 : 29, A.V., *entimos*, honourable, with *echō*, to have, i.e., to hold in honour, is translated "hold . . . in reputation" (R.V., "hold . . . in honour"). (3) For *kenoō*, in Phil. 2 : 7, A.V., "made (Himself) of no reputation," see EMPTY.

REQUEST (Noun and Verb)
A. Nouns.

1. AITĒMA (αἴτημα) denotes that which has been asked for (akin to *aiteō*, to ask); in Luke 23 : 24, R.V., "what they asked for" (A.V., "as they required"), lit., 'their request (should be done, *ginomai*);' in Phil. 4 : 6, "requests;" in 1 John 5 : 15, "petitions." See PETITION, REQUIRE.¶

2. DEĒSIS (δέησις), an asking, entreaty, supplication, is translated "request" in Phil. 1 : 4, A.V. (R.V., "supplication"). See PRAYER, SUPPLICATION.

B. Verbs.

1. DEOMAI (δέομαι), akin to A, No. 2, to beseech, pray, request, is translated to make request in Rom. 1 : 10. See BESEECH, No. 3.

2. AITEŌ (αἰτέω), to ask, is translated to make request in Col. 1 : 9, R.V. (A.V., " to desire "). See ASK, No. 1.

3. ERŌTAŌ (ἐρωτάω), to ask, is translated to make request in 1 John 5 : 16. See ASK, No. 2 and remarks on the difference between Nos. 1 and 2.

REQUIRE

1. ZĒTEŌ (ζητέω), to seek, seek after, also signifies to require, demand, " shall be required," Luke 12 : 48 ; in 1 Cor. 4 : 2, " it is required (in stewards)." See DESIRE, Note (2), ENDEAVOUR, GO, Note (2) (a), SEEK.

2. EKZĒTEŌ (ἐκζητέω), to seek out (ek, out, and No. 1), also denotes to demand, require, Luke 11 : 50, 51, of executing vengeance for the slaughter of the prophets (cp. 2 Sam. 4 : 11 ; Ezek. 3 : 18). See SEEK.

3. APAITEŌ (ἀπαιτέω), to ask back, demand back (apo, from, or back, aiteō, to ask), is translated " shall be required " in Luke 12 : 20, lit. ' do they require,' in the impersonal sense ; elsewhere, Luke 6 : 30, to ask again.¶ It is used in the papyri frequently in the sense of demanding, making demands.

4. PRASSŌ (πράσσω), to do, practise, perform, is used financially in the sense of exacting payment, in Luke 19 : 23. See EXTORT, A.

Notes : (1) In Luke 23 : 23, A.V., aiteō, to ask (Middle Voice) is translated " requiring " (R.V., " asking ") ; so in 1 Cor. 1 : 22 (Active Voice), A.V., " require " (R.V., " ask "). (2) In Luke 23 : 24, A.V., the noun aitēma (see REQUEST), that which is asked for, is translated " as they required " (R.V., " what they asked for "). (3) In 1 Cor. 7 : 36 the rendering " need so requireth " (R.V.) represents the phrase houtōs (thus) opheilei (it ought) genesthai (to become, i.e., to be done).

REQUITE

AMOIBĒ (ἀμοιβή), a requital, recompence (akin to ameibomai, to repay, not found in the N.T.), is used with the verb apodidōmi, to render, in 1 Tim. 5 : 4, and translated " to requite."¶ This use is illustrated in the papyri by way of making a return, conferring a benefaction in return for something (Moulton and Milligan).

RESCUE

EXAIREŌ (ἐξαιρέω), to take out (ek, from, haireō, to take), is used of delivering from persons and circumstances, and translated " rescued " in Acts 23 : 27. See DELIVER, No. 8, PLUCK.

For RESEMBLE, Luke 13 : 18, A.V., see LIKEN, B, No. 1

RESERVE

TĒREŌ (τηρέω), to guard, keep, preserve, give heed to, is translated to reserve, (a) with a happy issue, 1 Pet. 1 : 4 ; (b) with a retributive issue, 2 Pet. 2 : 4 ; ver. 9, A.V. (R.V., " keep ") ; 2 : 17 ; 3 : 7 ; Jude 6, A.V. (R.V., " hath kept ") ; ver. 13 ; (c) with the possibility either of deliverance or execution, Acts 25 : 21, A.V. (R.V., " kept "). See KEEP.

Note : In Rom. 11 : 4, A.V., *kataleipō*, to leave behind, leave remaining, is translated " I have reserved " (R.V., " I have left "). See LEAVE.

RESIDUE

KATALOIPOS (κατάλοιπος), an adjective denoting ' left remaining ' (*kata*, after, behind, *leipō*, to leave), akin to the verb in the Note above, is translated " residue " in Acts 15 : 17, from the Sept. of Amos 9 : 12.¶

Note : In Mark 16 : 13, A.V., the plural of *loipos*, left, is translated " residue " (R.V., " rest ").

RESIST

1. ANTHISTĒMI (ἀνθίστημι), to set against (*anti*, against, *histēmi*, to cause to stand), used in the Middle (or Passive) Voice and in the intransitive 2nd aorist and perfect Active, signifying to withstand, oppose, resist, is translated to resist in Matt. 5 : 39 ; Acts 6 : 10, A.V. (R.V., " withstand ") ; Rom. 9 : 19, A.V. (R.V., " withstandeth ") ; 13 : 2 (2nd and 3rd parts ; for 1st part, see No. 3), A.V. (R.V., " withstandeth " and " withstand ") ; Gal. 2 : 11, R.V. (A.V., " withstood ") ; 2 Tim. 3 : 8 (2nd part), A.V. (R.V., " withstand ") ; Jas. 4 : 7 ; 1 Pet. 5 : 9, A.V. (R.V., " withstand ") ; to withstand in Acts 13 : 8 ; Eph. 6 : 13 ; 2 Tim. 3 : 8 (1st part) ; 4 : 15.¶

2. ANTIKATHISTĒMI (ἀντικαθίστημι), to stand firm against (*anti*, against, *kathistēmi*, to set down, *kata*), is translated " ye have (not) resisted " in Heb. 12 : 4.¶ In the Sept., Deut. 31 : 21 ; Josh. 5 : 7 ; Mic. 2 : 8.¶

3. ANTITASSŌ (ἀντιτάσσω), *anti*, against, *tassō*, to arrange, originally a military term, to range in battle against, and frequently so found in the papyri, is used in the Middle Voice signifying to set oneself against, resist, (a) of men, Acts 18 : 6, " opposed themselves ; " elsewhere to resist, of resisting human potentates, Rom. 13 : 2 ; (b) of God, Jas. 4 : 6 ; 5 : 6, negatively, of leaving persistent evildoers to pursue their self-determined course, with eventual retribution ; 1 Pet. 5 : 5. See OPPOSE.¶

4. ANTIPIPTŌ (ἀντιπίπτω), lit., and primarily, to fall against or upon (*anti*, against, *piptō*, to fall), then, to strive against, resist, is used in Acts 7 : 51 of resisting the Holy Spirit.¶

RESOLVE

GINŌSKŌ (γινώσκω), to come to know, perceive, realize, is used in the 2nd aorist tense in Luke 16 : 4. " I am resolved," expressing the definiteness of the steward's realization, and his consequent determination of his course of action. See KNOW.

RESORT

1. ERCHOMAI (ἔρχομαι), to come, is translated "resorted" in Mark 2 : 13 ; in John 10 : 41 (R.V., " came "). See COME, No. 1.

2. EPIPOREUOMAI (ἐπιπορεύομαι), to travel or journey to a place (*epi*, to, *poreuomai*, to go), is translated "resorted" in Luke 8 : 4, R.V. (A.V., " were come ").¶

3. SUNAGŌ (συνάγω), to gather or bring together (*sun*, with, *agō*, to bring), in the Passive Voice, to be gathered or come together, is translated "resorted" in John 18 : 2 (the aorist tense expressing repeated action viewed cumulatively). See ASSEMBLE, GATHER, LEAD, Note (1).

Notes : (1) In the A.V. of John 18 : 20 and Acts 16 : 13, *sunerchomai*, to come together (R.V.), is translated to resort. (2) In Mark 10 : 1, A.V., *sumporeuomai*, to come together (R.V.), is translated "resort."

RESPECT (Noun and Verb)

A. Noun.

MEROS (μέρος), a part, has occasionally the meaning of a class or category, and, used in the dative case with *en*, in, signifies ' in respect of,' 2 Cor. 3 : 10, " in (this) respect ; " 9 : 3, R.V., A.V., " in (this) behalf ; " Col. 2 : 16, " in respect of (a feast day)."

B. Verbs.

1. APOBLEPŌ (ἀποβλέπω), to look away from all else at one object (*apo*, from), hence, to look stedfastly, is translated " he had respect " in Heb. 11 : 26, A.V. (R.V., " looked "). See LOOK.

2. EPIBLEPŌ (ἐπιβλέπω), to look upon (*epi*), is translated " have respect " in Jas. 2 : 3 (R.V. " regard ") ; see LOOK, No. 6.

Notes : (1) The following prepositions are translated " in respect of : " *peri*, concerning, in John 16 : 8, R.V. ; *epi*, upon, over, in Heb. 11 : 4, R.V. ; marg., ' over (his gifts) ; ' *kata*, in regard to, in Phil. 4 : 11. (2) For " respect of persons " and " respecter of persons " see PERSON.

REST (Noun and Verb)

A. Nouns.

1. ANAPAUSIS (ἀνάπαυσις), cessation, refreshment, rest (*ana*, up, *pauō*, to make to cease), the constant word in the Sept. for the Sabbath rest, is used in Matt. 11 : 29 ; here the contrast seems to be to the burdens imposed by the Pharisees. Christ's rest is not a rest from work, but in work, " not the rest of inactivity but of the harmonious working of all the faculties and affections—of will, heart, imagination, conscience—because each has found in God the ideal sphere for its satisfaction and development " (J. Patrick, in Hastings' Bib. Dic.) ; it occurs also in Matt. 12 : 43 ; Luke 11 : 24 ; Rev. 4 : 8, R.V., " (they have no) rest " [A.V., " (they) rest (not) "], where the noun is the object of the verb *echō*, to have ; so in 14 : 11.¶

2. KATAPAUSIS (κατάπαυσις), in classical Greek, denotes a causing to cease or putting to rest ; in the N.T., rest, repose ; it is used (a) of God's rest, Acts 7 : 49 ; Heb. 3 : 11, 18 ; 4 : 1, 3 (twice), R.V. (1st part), "that rest " (the A.V., " rest," is ambiguous), 5, 11 ; (b) in a general statement, applicable to God and man, 4 : 10.¶

3. ANESIS (ἄνεσις), for the significance of which see Ease, B, is translated " rest " in 2 Cor. 2 : 13, A.V. (R.V., " relief ") ; 7 : 5 (ditto) ; in 2 Thess. 1 : 7, the subject is not the rest to be granted to the saints, but the Divine retribution on their persecutors; hence the phrase " and to you that are afflicted rest with us," is an incidental extension of the idea of recompense, and to be read parenthetically. The time is not that at which the saints will be relieved of persecution, as in 1 Thess. 4 : 15–17, when the Parousia of Christ begins, but that at which the persecutors will be punished, namely, at the epiphany (or out-shining) of His Parousia (2 Thess. 2 : 8). For similar parentheses characteristic of epistolary writings see ver. 10 ; 1 Thess. 1 : 6 ; 2 : 15, 16.

4. SABBATISMOS (σαββατισμός), a Sabbath-keeping, is used in Heb. 4 : 9, R.V., " a sabbath rest," A.V. marg., " a keeping of a sabbath " (akin to sabbatizō, to keep the sabbath, used, e.g., in Ex. 16 : 30, not in the N.T.) ; here the sabbath-keeping is the perpetual sabbath rest to be enjoyed uninterruptedly by believers in their fellowship with the Father and the Son, in contrast to the weekly Sabbath under the Law. Because this sabbath rest is the rest of God Himself, 4 : 10, its full fruition is yet future, though believers now enter into it. In whatever way they enter into Divine rest, that which they enjoy is involved in an indissoluble relation with God.¶

5. KOIMESIS (κοίμησις), a resting, reclining (akin to keimai, to lie), is used in John 11 : 13, of natural sleep, translated " taking rest," R.V.¶

Note : In Acts 9 : 31, A.V., eirēnē, peace (R.V.), is translated " rest."

B. Verbs.

1. ANAPAUO (ἀναπαύω), akin to A, No. 1, in the Active Voice, signifies to give intermission from labour, to give rest, to refresh, Matt. 11 : 28 ; 1 Cor. 16 : 18, "have refreshed ;" Philm. 20, "refresh ;" Passive Voice, to be rested, refreshed, 2 Cor. 7 : 13, " was refreshed ; " Philm. 7, " are refreshed ; " in the Middle Voice, to take or enjoy rest, Matt. 26 : 45 ; Mark 6 : 31 ; 14 : 41 ; Luke 12 : 19, " take thine ease ; " 1 Pet. 4 : 14 ; Rev. 6 : 11 ; 14 : 13. See Refresh.¶ In the papyri it is found as an agricultural term, e.g., of giving land rest by sowing light crops upon it. In inscriptions it is found on gravestones of Christians, followed by the date of death (Moulton and Milligan).

2. KATAPAUO (καταπαύω), akin to A, No. 2, used transitively, signifies to cause to cease, restrain, Acts 14 : 18 ; to cause to rest, Heb. 4 : 8 ; intransitively, to rest, Heb. 4 : 4, 10. See Cease, A, No. 6, Restrain.¶

3. EPISKENOO (ἐπισκηνόω), to spread a tabernacle over (epi, upon,

skēnē, a tent), is used metaphorically in 2 Cor. 12 : 9, " may rest upon (me)," R.V., marg., " cover," " spread a tabernacle over."¶

4. KATASKĒNOŌ (κατασκηνόω), to pitch one's tent, lodge, is translated " shall rest," in Acts 2 : 26, A.V. (R.V., " shall dwell "). See LODGE.

5. HĒSUCHAZŌ (ἡσυχάζω), to be still, to rest from labour, is translated " they rested " in Luke 23 : 56. See PEACE hold one's), No. 3.

6. EPANAPAUŌ (ἐπαναπαύω), to cause to rest, is used in the Middle Voice, metaphorically, signifying to rest upon (*epi*, upon, and No. 1), in Luke 10 : 6 and Rom. 2 : 17.¶

Note : For " find rest," Rom. 15 : 32, R.V., see REFRESH, No. 2.

REST (the)

1. LOIPOS (λοιπός), remaining (for which see REMNANT), is frequently used to mean " the rest," and is generally so translated in the R.V. (A.V., " others " in Luke 8 : 10 ; Acts 28 : 9 ; Eph. 2 : 3 ; 1 Thess. 4 : 13; 5 : 6 ; 1 Tim. 5 : 20 ; A.V., " other " in Luke 18 : 11 ; Acts 17 : 9 ; Rom. 1 : 13 ; 2 Cor. 12 : 13 ; 13 : 2 ; Gal. 2 : 13 ; Phil. 1 : 13 ; 4 : 3) ; the neut. plur., lit., ' remaining things,' is used in Luke 12 : 26 ; 1 Cor. 11 : 34.

2. EPILOIPOS (ἐπίλοιπος), signifying still left, left over (*epi*, over, and No. 1), is used in the neuter with the article in 1 Pet. 4 : 2, " the rest (of your time)."¶

For RESTITUTION see RESTORATION

RESTLESS

AKATASTATOS (ἀκατάστατος), unsettled, unstable, disorderly (*a*, negative, *kathistēmi*, to set in order), is translated " unstable " in Jas. 1 : 8 ; " restless " in 3 : 8, R.V. [in the latter, the A.V. " unruly " represents the word *akataschetos*, signifying ' that cannot be restrained ' (*a*, negative, *katechō*, to hold down, restrain). In the Sept., Job 31 : 11¶]. See UNRULY, UNSTABLE.¶ In the Sept., Isa. 54 : 11.¶

RESTORATION

APOKATASTASIS (ἀποκατάστασις), from *apo*, back, again, *kathistēmi*, to set in order, is used in Acts 3 : 21, R.V., " restoration " (A.V., " restitution "). See under REGENERATION, concerning Israel in its regenerated state hereafter. In the papyri it is used of a temple cell of a goddess, a repair of a public way, the restoration of estates to rightful owners, a balancing of accounts. Apart from papyri illustrations the word is found in an Egyptian reference to a consummating agreement of the world's cyclical periods, an idea somewhat similar to that in the Acts passage (Moulton and Milligan).¶

RESTORE

1. APODIDŌMI (ἀποδίδωμι), to give back, is translated " I restore " in Luke 19 : 8. See DELIVER, A, No. 3.

2. APOKATHISTĒMI or the alternative form APOKATHISTANŌ (ἀποκαθίστημι) is used (a) of restoration to a former condition of health, Matt. 12 : 13 ; Mark 3 : 5 ; 8 : 25 ; Luke 6 : 10 ; (b) of the Divine restoration of Israel and conditions affected by it, including the renewal of the Covenant broken by them, Matt. 17 : 11 ; Mark 9 : 12 ; Acts 1 : 6 ; (c) of giving or bringing a person back, Heb. 13 : 19.¶ In the papyri it is used of financial restitution, of making good the breaking of a stone by a workman by his substituting another, of the reclamation of land, etc. (Moulton and Milligan).

3. KATARTIZŌ (καταρτίζω), to mend, to furnish completely, is translated "restore" in Gal. 6 : 1, metaphorically, of the restoration, by those who are spiritual, of one overtaken in a trespass, such a one being as a dislocated member of the spiritual body. The tense is the continuous present, suggesting the necessity for patience and perseverance in the process. See FIT, MEND, PERFECT.

RESTRAIN

1. KATAPAUŌ (καταπαύω) ; see REST, B, No. 2.

2. KATECHŌ (κατέχω), to hold fast or down, is translated "restraineth" in 2 Thess. 2 : 6 and 7. In ver. 6 lawlessness is spoken of as being restrained in its development : in ver. 7 " one that restraineth " is, lit., ' the restrainer ' (the article with the present participle, ' the restraining one ') ; this may refer to an individual, as in the similar construction in 1 Thess. 3 : 5, " the tempter " (cp. 1 : 10, lit., ' the Deliverer ') ; or to a number of persons presenting the same characteristics, just as ' the believer ' stands for all believers, e.g., Rom. 9 : 33 ; 1 John 5 : 10. Ver. 6 speaks of a principle, ver. 7 of the principle as embodied in a person or series of persons ; cp. what is said of " the power " in Rom. 13 : 3, 4, a phrase representing all such rulers. Probably such powers, i.e., ' constituted governments,' are the restraining influence here intimated (specifications being designedly withheld). For an extended exposition see Notes on Thessalonians, by Hogg and Vine, pp. 254–261.

RESURRECTION

1. ANASTASIS (ἀνάστασις) denotes (I) a raising up, or rising (ana, up, and histēmi, to cause to stand), Luke 2 : 34, " the rising up ; " the A.V. " again " obscures the meaning ; the Child would be like a stone against which many in Israel would stumble while many others would find in its strength and firmness a means of their salvation and spiritual life ; (II) of resurrection from the dead, (a) of Christ, Acts 1 : 22 ; 2 : 31 ; 4 : 33 ; Rom. 1 : 4 ; 6 : 5 ; Phil. 3 : 10 ; 1 Pet. 1 : 3 ; 3 : 21 ; by metonymy, of Christ as the Author of resurrection, John 11 : 25 ; (b) of those who are Christ's at His Parousia (see COMING), Luke 14 : 14, " the resurrection of the just ; " Luke 20 : 33, 35, 36 ; John 5 : 29 (1st part), " the resurrection of life ; " 11 : 24 ; Acts 23 : 6 ; 24 : 15 (1st part) ;

1 Cor. 15 : 21, 42 ; 2 Tim. 2 : 18 ; Heb. 11 : 35 (2nd part), see RAISE, Note (3) ; Rev. 20 : 5, " the first resurrection ; " hence the insertion of " is " stands for the completion of this resurrection, of which Christ was " the firstfruits ; " 20 : 6 ; (c) of " the rest of the dead," after the Millennium (cp. Rev. 20 : 5) ; John 5 : 29 (2nd part), " the resurrection of judgment ; " Acts 24 : 15 (2nd part), " of the unjust ; " (d) of those who were raised in more immediate connection with Christ's resurrection, and thus had part already in the first resurrection, Acts 26 : 23 and Rom. 1 : 4 (in each of which " dead " is plural ; see Matt. 27 : 52) ; (e) of the resurrection spoken of in general terms, Matt. 22 : 23 ; Mark 12 : 18 ; Luke 20 : 27 ; Acts 4 : 2 ; 17 : 18 ; 23 : 8 ; 24 : 21 ; 1 Cor. 15 : 12, 13 ; Heb. 6 : 2 ; (f) of those who were raised in O.T. times, to die again, Heb. 11 : 35 (1st part), lit., ' out of resurrection.'¶

2. EXANASTASIS (ἐξανάστασις), ek, from or out of, and No. 1, Phil. 3 : 11, followed by ek, lit., ' the out-resurrection from among the dead.' For the significance of this see ATTAIN, No. 1.¶

3. EGERSIS (ἔγερσις), a rousing (akin to egeirō, to arouse, to raise), is used of the resurrection of Christ, in Matt. 27 : 53.¶

RETAIN

KRATEŌ (κρατέω), to be strong, obtain, hold, hold fast, is translated to retain, of sins, John 20 : 23 (twice) ; see on REMIT. See HOLD, KEEP, OBTAIN, TAKE.

Notes : (1) In Philm. 13, A.V., katechō, to hold fast, hold back, detain, is translated to retain (R.V., to keep). (2) In Rom. 1 : 28, A.V., echō, " to have " (R.V.), is translated " to retain."

RETURN

1. ANALUŌ (ἀναλύω), to depart in Phil. 1 : 23, signifies to return in Luke 12 : 36, used in a simile of the return of a lord for his servants after a marriage feast (R.V.). See DEPART, No. 16.¶

2. ANASTREPHŌ (ἀναστρέφω), to turn back, is translated to return in Acts 5 : 22 and 15 : 16. See ABIDE, BEHAVE.

3. EPISTREPHŌ (ἐπιστρέφω), to turn about, or towards, is translated to return in Matt. 12 : 44 ; 24 : 18 ; Mark 13 : 16, R.V. (A.V., " turn back again ") ; Luke 2 : 39 ; 8 : 55, R.V. (A.V., " came again ") ; 17 : 31 ; Acts 15 : 36, R.V. (A.V., " go again "). See CONVERT, A, No. 2, TURN.

4. HUPOSTREPHŌ (ὑποστρέφω), to turn behind, or back (hupo, under), is translated to return (in some texts in Mark 14 : 40) in Luke 1 : 56 ; 2 : 20, 43 ; ver. 45, R.V. (A.V., " turned back again ") ; 4 : 1, 14 ; 7 : 10 ; 8 : 37 ; 10 : 17 ; 11 : 24, A.V. (R.V., " I will turn back ") ; 17 : 18 ; 19 : 12 ; 23 : 48, 56 ; Acts 1 : 12 ; 12 : 25 ; 13 : 13 ; 13 : 34 ; 20 : 3 ; 21 : 6 ; 22 : 17, R.V. (A.V., " was come again ") ; 23 : 32 ; Gal. 1 : 17 ; Heb. 7 : 1. See TURN (back).

5. ANAKAMPTŌ (ἀνακάμπτω), to turn or bend back, occurs in Matt. 2 : 12 ; Luke 10 : 6 (i.e., as if it was unsaid) ; Acts 18 : 21 ; Heb. 11 : 15.¶

5. EPANAGŌ (ἐπανάγω), to bring up or back (primarily a nautical term for putting to sea ; see LAUNCH, PUT), is used intransitively, in Matt. 21 : 18, " He returned."

Note : In Luke 19 : 15, A.V., *epanerchomai*, to come back again (R.V.) is translated " returned." See COME, No. 4.

REVEAL

1. APOKALUPTŌ (ἀποκαλύπτω) signifies to uncover, unveil (*apo*, from, *kaluptō*, to cover) ; both verbs are used in Matt. 10 : 26 ; in Luke 12 : 2, *apokaluptō* is set in contrast to *sunkaluptō*, to cover up, cover completely. " The N.T. occurrences of this word fall under two heads, subjective and objective. The subjective use is that in which something is presented to the mind directly, as, (*a*) the meaning of the acts of God, Matt. 11 : 25 ; Luke 10 : 21 ; (*b*) the secret of the Person of the Lord Jesus, Matt. 16 : 17 ; John 12 : 38 ; (*c*) the character of God as Father, Matt. 11 : 27 ; Luke 10 : 22 ; (*d*) the will of God for the conduct of His children, Phil. 3 : 15 ; (*e*) the mind of God to the prophets of Israel, 1 Pet. 1 : 12, and of the Church, 1 Cor. 14 : 30 ; Eph. 3 : 5.

" The objective use is that in which something is presented to the senses, sight or hearing, as, referring to the past , (*f*) the truth declared to men in the gospel, Rom. 1 : 17 ; 1 Cor. 2 : 10 ; Gal. 3 : 23 ; (*g*) the Person of Christ to Paul on the way to Damascus, Gal. 1 : 16 ; (*h*) thoughts before hidden in the heart, Luke 2 : 35 ; referring to the future, (*i*) the coming in glory of the Lord Jesus, Luke 17 : 30 ; (*j*) the salvation and glory that await the believer, Rom. 8 : 18 ; 1 Pet. 1 : 5 ; 5 : 1 ; (*k*) the true value of service, 1 Cor. 3 : 13 ; (*l*) the wrath of God (at the Cross, against sin, and, at the revelation of the Lord Jesus, against the sinner), Rom. 1 : 18 ; (*m*) the Lawless One, 2 Thess. 2 : 3, 6, 8."* ¶

2. CHRĒMATIZŌ (χρηματίζω), to give Divine admonition, instruction, revelation, is translated " it had been revealed," in Luke 2 : 26. See ADMONITION, B, No. 3, CALL.

REVELATION

APOKALUPSIS (ἀποκάλυψις), an uncovering (akin to *apokaluptō;* see above), " is used in the N.T. of (*a*) the drawing away by Christ of the veil of darkness covering the Gentiles, Luke 2 : 32 ; cp. Isa. 25 : 7 ; (*b*) ' the mystery,' the purpose of God in this age, Rom. 16 : 25 ; Eph. 3 : 3 ; (*c*) the communication of the knowledge of God to the soul, Eph. 1 : 17 ; (*d*) an expression of the mind of God for the instruction of the church, 1 Cor. 14 : 6, 26, for the instruction of the Apostle Paul, 2 Cor. 12 : 1, 7 ; Gal. 1 : 12, and for his guidance, Gal. 2 : 2 ; (*e*) the Lord Jesus Christ, to the saints at His Parousia, 1 Cor. 1 : 7, R.V. (A.V., ' coming ') ; 1 Pet. 1 : 7, R.V. (A.V., ' appearing '), 13 ; 4 : 13 ; (*f*) the

---

* From Notes on Galatians by Hogg and Vine, pp. 41, 42.

Lord Jesus Christ when He comes to dispense the judgments of God,
2 Thess. 1 : 7 ; cp. Rom. 2 : 5 ; (g) the saints, to the creation, in association
with Christ in His glorious reign, Rom. 8 : 19, R.V., 'revealing' (A.V.,
'manifestation') ; (h) the symbolic forecast of the final judgments of
God, Rev. 1 : 1 (hence the Greek title of the book, transliterated 'Apocalypse' and translated 'Revelation')."* See APPEARING, COMING,
LIGHTEN, B, Note, MANIFESTATION.¶

REVEL, REVELLING

1. TRUPHĒ (τρυφή), luxuriousness, daintiness, revelling, is translated
freely by the verb "to revel" in 2 Pet. 2 : 13, R.V. (A.V., "to riot"), lit.,
'counting revelling in the daytime a pleasure.' In Luke 7 : 25 it is used
with en, in, and translated "delicately." See DELICATELY, RIOT.¶

2. KÓMOS (κῶμος), a revel, carousal, the concomitant and consequence of drunkenness, is used in the plural, Rom. 13 : 13, translated by
the singular, R.V., "revelling" (A.V., "rioting") ; Gal. 5 : 21 and 1
Pet. 4 : 3, "revellings." See RIOT.¶

Note : For entruphaō, 2 Pet. 2 : 13, R.V., "to revel," see SPORTING.

For REVENGE and REVENGER see AVENGE and AVENGER

REVERENCE (Noun and Verb)
A. Verbs.

1. ENTREPŌ (ἐντρέπω), lit., to turn in (i.e., upon oneself), to put to
shame, denotes, when used in the Passive Voice, to feel respect for, to show
deference to, to reverence, Matt. 21 : 37 ; Mark 12 : 6 ; Luke 20 : 13 ;
Heb. 12 : 9. See ASHAMED, A, No. 4, REGARD.

2. PHOBEŌ (φοβέω), to fear, is used in the Passive Voice in the
N.T. ; in Eph. 5 : 33 of reverential fear on the part of a wife for a husband,
A.V., "reverence" (R.V., "fear"). See FEAR, D, No. 1.

B. Noun.

EULABEIA (εὐλάβεια), caution, reverence, is translated "reverence"
in Heb. 12 : 28 (1st part in the best mss ; some have aidōs). See FEAR.

REVERENT

HIEROPREPĒS (ἱεροπρεπής), suited to a sacred character, reverend
(hieros, sacred, prepō, to be fitting), is translated "reverent" in Tit.
2 : 3, R.V. (A.V., "as becometh holiness"). See BECOME, B.¶

REVILE, REVILING, REVILER
A. Verbs.

1. LOIDOREŌ (λοιδορέω) denotes to abuse, revile, John 9 : 28 ; Acts
23 : 4 ; 1 Cor. 4 : 12 ; 1 Pet. 2 : 23 (1st clause).¶

---

* From Notes on Thessalonians by Hogg and Vine, pp. 228, 229.

2. ONEIDIZŌ (ὀνειδίζω), to reproach, upbraid, is translated to revile in Matt. 5 : 11, A.V., and Mark 15 : 32 (R.V., " reproach "). See REPROACH.

3. BLASPHĒMEŌ (βλασφημέω), to speak profanely, rail at, is translated " reviled " in Matt. 27 : 39, A.V. (R.V., " railed on ") ; Luke 22 : 65, R.V., " reviling " (A.V., " blasphemously ").

4. ANTILOIDOREŌ (ἀντιλοιδορέω), to revile back or again (anti, and No. 1), is found in 1 Pet. 2 : 23 (2nd clause).¶

Note : For *epēreazō*, 1 Pet. 3 : 16, R.V., " revile," see ACCUSE, B, No. 3.

B. Adjective.

LOIDOROS (λοίδορος), akin to A, No. 1, abusive, railing, reviling, is used as a noun, 1 Cor. 5 : 11, R.V., " a reviler " (A.V. " a railer ") ; 6 : 10, " revilers."¶ In the Sept., Prov. 25 : 24 ; 26 : 21 ; 27 : 15.¶

C. Noun.

LOIDORIA (λοιδορία), akin to A, No. 1, and B, abuse, railing, is used in 1 Tim. 5 : 14, R.V., " for (*charin*, for the sake of) reviling " (A.V., " to speak reproachfully "—a paraphrase) ; 1 Pet. 3 : 9 (twice), R.V., " reviling " (A.V., " railing "). See RAIL, B.¶

REVIVE

1. ANATHALLŌ (ἀναθάλλω), to flourish anew (*ana*, again, anew, *thallō*, to flourish or blossom), hence, to revive, is used metaphorically in Phil. 4 : 10, R.V., " ye have revived (your thought for me)," A.V., " (your care of me) hath flourished again."¶ In the Sept., Psa. 28 : 7 ; Ezek. 17 : 24 ; Hos. 8 : 9.¶

2. ANAZAŌ (ἀναζάω), to live again (*ana*, and *zaō*, to live), to regain life, is used of moral revival, Luke 15 : 24, " is alive again ; " (*b*) of sin, Rom. 7 : 9, " revived," lit., ' lived again ' i.e., it sprang into activity, manifesting the evil inherent in it ; here sin is personified, by way of contrast to the man himself. Some mss. have it in Rom. 14 : 9, for *zaō*, as in the R.V., which italicises " *again*."¶

REWARD (Noun and Verb)

A. Noun.

MISTHOS (μισθός), primarily wages, hire, and then, generally, reward, (*a*) received in this life, Matt. 5 : 46 ; 6 : 2, 5, 16 ; Rom. 4 : 4 ; 1 Cor. 9 : 17, 18 ; of evil rewards, Acts 1 : 18 ; see also HIRE ; (*b*) to be received hereafter, Matt. 5 : 12 ; 10 : 41 (twice), 42 ; Mark 9 : 41 ; Luke 6 : 23, 35 ; 1 Cor. 3 : 8, 14 ; 2 John 8 ; Rev. 11 : 18 ; 22 : 12. See WAGES.

Notes : (1) In Luke 23 : 41, *axios*, worthy, befitting, used in the plur., is rendered " the due reward," lit., ' things worthy.' (2) For *antapodosis*, rendered " reward " in Col. 3 : 24, A.V., see RECOMPENSE. (3) For *katabrabeuō*, to rob of a reward, Col. 2 : 18, see BEGUILE, Note, and ROB.

B. Verb.

APODIDŌMI (ἀποδίδωμι), to give back, is nowhere translated to reward in the R.V.; A.V., Matt. 6 : 4, 6, 18 (see RECOMPENSE, B, No. 2); Matt. 16 : 27; 2 Tim. 4 : 14; Rev. 18 : 6 (see RENDER).

REWARDER

MISTHAPODOTĒS (μισθαποδότης), one who pays wages (misthos, wages, apo, back, didōmi, to give), is used by metonymy in Heb. 11 : 6, of God, as the " Rewarder " of those who " seek after Him " (R.V.).¶ Cp. misthapodosia, recompence.

RICH, RICHES, RICHLY, RICH MAN
A. Adjective.

PLOUSIOS (πλούσιος), akin to B, C, No. 1, rich, wealthy, is used (I) literally, (a) adjectivally (with a noun expressed separately) in Matt. 27 : 57; Luke 12 : 16; 14 : 12; 16 : 1, 19; (without a noun), 18 : 23; 19 : 2; (b) as a noun, singular, a rich man (the noun not being expressed), Matt. 19 : 23, 24; Mark 10 : 25; 12 : 41; Luke 16 : 21, 22; 18 : 25; Jas. 1 : 10, 11, " the rich," " the rich (man) ; " plural, Mark 12 : 41, lit., ' rich (ones) ; ' Luke 6 : 24 (ditto); 21 : 1; 1 Tim. 6 : 17, " (them that are) rich," lit., ' (the) rich ; ' Jas. 2 : 6, R.V., " the rich ; " 5 : 1, R.V., " ye rich ; " Rev. 6 : 15 and 13 : 16, R.V., " the rich ; " (II) metaphorically, of God, Eph. 2 : 4 (" in mercy "); of Christ, 2 Cor. 8 : 9; of believers, Jas. 2 : 5, R.V., " (to be) rich (in faith) ; " Rev. 2 : 9, of spiritual enrichment generally; 3 : 17, of a false sense of enrichment.¶

B. Verbs.

1. PLOUTEŌ (πλουτέω), to be rich, in the aorist or point tense, to become rich, is used (a) literally, Luke 1 : 53, " the rich," present participle, lit., ' (ones or those) being rich ; ' 1 Tim. 6 : 9, 18; Rev. 18 : 3, 15, 19 (all three in the aorist tense) ; (b) metaphorically, of Christ, Rom. 10 : 12 (the passage stresses the fact that Christ is Lord ; see ver. 9, and the R.V.) ; of the enrichment of believers through His poverty, 2 Cor. 8 : 9 (the aorist tense expressing completeness, with permanent results) ; so in Rev. 3 : 18, where the spiritual enrichment is conditional upon righteousness of life and conduct (see GOLD, No. 2) ; of a false sense of enrichment, 1 Cor. 4 : 8 (aorist), R.V., " ye are become rich " (A.V., " ye are rich "); Rev. 3 : 17 (perfect tense, R.V., " I . . . have gotten riches," A.V., " I am . . . increased with goods "), see GOODS, Note (3) ; of not being rich toward God, Luke 12 : 21.¶

2. PLOUTIZŌ (πλουτίζω), to make rich, enrich, is rendered " making (many) rich " in 2 Cor. 6 : 10 (metaphorical of enriching spiritually). See ENRICH.

C. Nouns.

1. PLOUTOS (πλοῦτος) is used in the singular (I) of material riches, used evilly, Matt. 13 : 22; Mark 4 : 19; Luke 8 : 14; 1 Tim. 6 : 17; Jas. 5 : 2; Rev. 18 : 17; (II) of spiritual and moral riches, (a) possessed

by God and exercised towards men, Rom. 2 : 4, " of His goodness and forbearance and longsuffering ; " 9 : 23 and Eph. 3 : 16, " of His glory " (i.e., of its manifestation in grace towards believers) ; Rom. 11 : 33, of His wisdom and knowledge ; Eph. 1 : 7 and 2 : 7, " of His grace ; " 1 : 18, " of the glory of His inheritance in the saints ; " 3 : 8, " of Christ ; " Phil. 4 : 19, " in glory in Christ Jesus," R.V. ; Col. 1 : 27, " of the glory of this mystery . . . Christ in you, the hope of glory ; " (b) to be ascribed to Christ, Rev, 5 : 12 ; (c) of the effects of the gospel upon the Gentiles, Rom. 11 : 12 (twice) ; (d) of the full assurance of understanding in regard to the mystery of God, even Christ, Col. 2 : 2, R.V. ; (e) of the liberality of the churches of Macedonia, 2 Cor. 8 : 2 (where " the riches " stands for the spiritual and moral value of their liberality) ; (f) of " the reproach of Christ " in contrast to this world's treasures, Heb. 11 : 26.¶

2. CHRĒMA (χρῆμα), what one uses or needs (chraomai, to use), a matter, business, hence denotes riches, Mark 10 : 23, 24 ; Luke 18 : 24 ; see MONEY, No. 2.

D. Adverb.

PLOUSIŌS (πλουσίως), richly, abundantly, akin to A, is used in Col. 3 : 16 ; 1 Tim. 6 : 17 ; Tit. 3 : 6, R.V.," richly " (A.V., " abundantly ") ; 2 Pet. 1 : 11 (ditto).¶

For RID see CARE, A, No. 1, Note

RIDE

EPIBAINŌ (ἐπιβαίνω), to go upon (epi, upon, bainō, to go), is used of Christ's riding into Jerusalem, Matt. 21 : 5, R.V., " riding " (A.V., " sitting "). See COME, No. 16.

RIGHT (opp. to left), RIGHT HAND, RIGHT SIDE

DEXIOS (δεξιός), an adjective, used (a) of the right as opposite to the left, e.g., Matt. 5 : 29, 30 ; Rev. 10 : 5, R.V., " right hand ; " in connection with armour (figuratively), 2 Cor. 6 : 7 ; with en, followed by the dative plural, Mark 16 : 5 ; with ek, and the genitive plural, e.g., Matt. 25 : 33, 34 ; Luke 1 : 11 ; (b) of giving the right hand of fellowship, Gal. 2 : 9, betokening the public expression of approval by leaders at Jerusalem of the course pursued by Paul and Barnabas among the Gentiles ; the act was often the sign of a pledge, e.g., 2 Kings 10 : 15 ; 1 Chron. 29 : 24, marg.; Ezra 10 : 19 ; Ezek. 17 : 18 ; figuratively Lam. 5 : 6 ; it is often so used in the papyri ; (c) metaphorically of power or authority, Acts 2 : 33 ; with ek, signifying " on," followed by the genitive plural, Matt. 26 : 64 ; Mark 14 : 62 ; Heb. 1 : 13 ; (d) similarly of a place of honour in the Messianic Kingdom, Matt. 20 : 21 ; Mark 10 : 37.

RIGHT (not wrong—Noun and Adjective), RIGHTLY
A. Noun.

EXOUSIA (ἐξουσία), authority power, is translated " right " in the

R.V., for A.V., " power," in John 1 : 12 ; Rom. 9 : 21 ; 1 Cor. 9 : 4, 5, 6, 12 (twice), 18 ; 2 Thess. 3 : 9, where the right is that of being maintained by those among whom the ministers of the gospel had laboured, a right possessed in virtue of the ' authority ' given them by Christ, Heb. 13 : 10 ; Rev. 22 : 14.

Exousia first denotes freedom to act and then authority for the action. This is first true of God, Acts 1 : 7. It was exercised by the Son of God, as from, and in conjunction with, the Father when the Lord was upon earth, in the days of His flesh, Matt. 9 : 6 ; John 10 : 18, as well as in resurrection, Matt. 28 : 18 ; John 17 : 2. All others hold their freedom to act from God (though some of them have abused it), whether angels, Eph. 1 : 21, or human potentates, Rom. 13 : 1. Satan offered to delegate his authority over earthly kingdoms to Christ, Luke 4 : 6, who, though conscious of His right to it, refused, awaiting the Divinely appointed time. See AUTHORITY, No. 1, and for various synonyms see DOMINION, No. 1, Note.

B. Adjectives.

1. DIKAIOS (δίκαιος), just, righteous, that which is in accordance with *dikē*, rule, right, justice, is translated " right " in Matt. 20 : 4 ; ver. 7, A.V. only (R.V. omits, according to the most authentic mss., the clause having been inserted from ver. 4, to the detriment of the narrative) ; Luke 12 : 57 ; Acts 4 : 19 ; Eph. 6 : 1 ; Phil. 1 : 7, R.V. (A.V., " meet ") ; 2 Pet. 1 : 13 (A.V., " meet "). See JUST, RIGHTEOUS.

2. EUTHUS (εὐθύς), straight, hence, metaphorically, right, is so rendered in Acts 8 : 21, of the heart ; 13 : 10, of the ways of the Lord ; 2 Pet. 2 : 15. See STRAIGHT.

C. Adverb.

ORTHŌS (ὀρθῶς), rightly (akin to *orthos*, straight, direct), is translated " plain " in Mark 7 : 35 ; in Luke 7 : 43 and 20 : 21, " rightly ; " in Luke 10 : 28, " right."¶

Notes : (1) For " right mind " see MIND, B, No. 5. (2) For the A.V., " rightly " in 2 Tim. 2 : 15, see DIVIDE, A, No. 8.

RIGHTEOUS, RIGHTEOUSLY

A. Adjective.

DIKAIOS (δίκαιος) signifies ' just,' without prejudice or partiality, e.g., of the judgment of God, 2 Thess. 1 : 5, 6 ; of His judgments, Rev. 16 : 7 ; 19 : 2 ; of His character as Judge, 2 Tim. 4 : 8 ; Rev. 16 : 5 ; of His ways and doings, Rev. 15 : 3. See further under JUST, A, No. 1, RIGHT, B, No. 1.

In the following the R.V. substitutes " righteous " for the A.V. " just ; " Matt. 1 : 19 ; 13 : 49 ; 27 : 19, 24 ; Mark 6 : 20 ; Luke 2 : 25 ; 15 : 7 ; 20 : 20 ; 23 : 50 ; John 5 : 30 ; Acts 3 : 14 ; 7 : 52 ; 10 : 22 ; 22 : 14 ; Rom. 1 : 17 ; 7 : 12 ; Gal. 3 : 11 ; Heb. 10 : 38 ; Jas. 5 : 6 ; 1 Pet. 3 : 18 ; 2 Pet. 2 : 7 ; 1 John 1 : 9 ; Rev. 15 : 3.

B. Adverb.

DIKAIŌS (δικαίως) is translated "righteously" in 1 Cor. 15 : 34, R.V., " (awake up) righteously," A.V., " (awake to) righteousness ; " 1 Thess. 2 : 10, R.V. (A.V., "justly ") ; Tit. 2 : 12 ; 1 Pet. 2 : 23. See JUSTLY.

Notes : (1) In Rev. 22 : 11 the best texts have *dikaiosunē*, righteousness, with *poieō*, to do, R.V., "let him do righteousness ; " the A.V. follows those which have the Passive Voice of *dikaioō* and renders it "let him be righteous," lit., 'let him be made righteous.' (2) *Dikaiokrisia*, "righteous judgment" (*dikaios*, and *krisis*), occurs in Rom. 2 : 5.¶

RIGHTEOUSNESS

1. DIKAIOSUNĒ (δικαιοσύνη) is the character or quality of being right or just ; it was formerly spelled ' rightwiseness,' which clearly expresses the meaning. It is used to denote an attribute of God, e.g., Rom. 3 : 5, the context of which shews that "the righteousness of God" means essentially the same as His faithfulness, or truthfulness, that which is consistent with His own nature and promises ; Rom. 3 : 25, 26 speaks of His righteousness as exhibited in the Death of Christ, which is sufficient to shew men that God is neither indifferent to sin nor regards it lightly. On the contrary, it demonstrates that quality of holiness in Him which must find expression in His condemnation of sin.

" *Dikaiosunē* is found in the sayings of the Lord Jesus, (a) of whatever is right or just in itself, whatever conforms to the revealed will of God, Matt. 5 : 6, 10, 20 ; John 16 : 8, 10 ; (b) whatever has been appointed by God to be acknowledged and obeyed by man, Matt. 3 : 15 ; 21 : 32 ; (c) the sum total of the requirements of God, Matt. 6 : 33 ; (d) religious duties, Matt. 6 : 1 (distinguished as almsgiving, man's duty to his neighbour, vv. 2–4, prayer, his duty to God, vv. 5–15, fasting, the duty of self-control, vv. 16–18).

" In the preaching of the Apostles recorded in Acts the word has the same general meaning. So also in Jas. 1 : 20 ; 3 : 18, in both Epp. of Peter, 1st John and the Revelation. In 2 Pet. 1 : 1, ' the righteousness of our God and Saviour Jesus Christ,' is the righteous dealing of God with sin and with sinners on the ground of the Death of Christ. ' Word of righteousness,' Heb. 5 : 13, is probably the gospel, and the Scriptures as containing the gospel, wherein is declared the righteousness of God in all its aspects.

" This meaning of *dikaiosunē*, right action, is frequent also in Paul's writings, as in all five of its occurrences in Rom. 6 ; Eph. 6 : 14, etc. But for the most part he uses it of that gracious gift of God to men whereby all who believe on the Lord Jesus Christ are brought into right relationship with God. This righteousness is unattainable by obedience to any law, or by any merit of man's own, or any other condition than that of faith in Christ. . . . The man who trusts in Christ becomes ' the righteousness of

God in Him,' 2 Cor. 5 : 21, i.e., becomes in Christ all that God requires a man to be, all that he could never be in himself. Because Abraham accepted the Word of God, making it his own by that act of the mind and spirit which is called faith, and, as the sequel showed, submitting himself to its control, therefore God accepted him as one who fulfilled the whole of His requirements, Rom. 4 : 3. . . .

" Righteousness is not said to be imputed to the believer save in the sense that faith is imputed (' reckoned ' is the better word) for righteous-ness.   It is clear that in Rom. 4 : 6, 11, ' righteousness reckoned ' must be understood in the light of the context, ' faith reckoned for righteousness,' vv. 3, 5, 9, 22.   ' For ' in these places is *eis*, which does not mean ' instead of,' but ' with a view to.'   The faith thus exercised brings the soul into vital union with God in Christ, and inevitably produces righteousness of life, that is, conformity to the will of God."*

2. DIKAIŌMA (δικαίωμα) is the concrete expression of righteousness : see JUSTIFICATION, A, No. 2.

Note : In Heb. 1 : 8, A.V., *euthutēs*, straightness, uprightness (akin to *euthus*, straight, right), is translated " righteousness " (R.V., " upright-ness ; " A.V., marg., " rightness, or straightness ").

RING

DAKTULIOS (δακτύλιος), a finger-ring, occurs in Luke 15 : 22.¶

Note : Chrusodaktulios, an adjective signifying " with a gold ring," a gold-ringed (person), from *chrusos,* gold, and *daktulos,* a finger, occurs in Jas. 2 : 2.¶

RINGLEADER

PRŌTOSTATĒS (πρωτοστάτης), one who stands first (*prōtos,* first, *histēmi,* to cause to stand), was used of soldiers, one who stands in the front rank ;   hence, metaphorically, a leader, Acts 24 : 5.¶

RIOT, RIOTING, RIOTOUS, RIOTOUSLY
A. Nouns.

1. ASOTIA (ἀσωτία), prodigality, a wastefulness, profligacy (*a,* negative, *sōzō,* to save), is rendered " riot " in Eph. 5 : 18, R.V. (A.V., " excess ") ; Tit. 1 : 6 and 1 Pet. 4 : 4 (A.V. and R.V., " riot ").   The corresponding verb is found in a papyrus writing, telling of ' riotous living ' (like the adverb *asōtōs,* see B).¶   In the Sept., Prov. 28 : 7.¶   Cp. the synonymous word *aselgeia* (under LASCIVIOUSNESS).

2. KŌMOS (κῶμος), a revel, is rendered " rioting " in Rom. 13 : 13, A.V. ;   see REVEL.

3. TRUPHĒ (τρυφή), luxuriousness, is rendered " riot " in 2 Pet. 2 : 13, A.V. ;   see DELICATELY, REVEL.

4. STASIS (στάσις), primarily a standing (akin to *histēmi,* to cause to

---

* From Notes on Galatians by Hogg and Vine, pp. 246, 247.

stand), then an insurrection, is translated " riot " in Acts 19 : 40, R.V.
(A.V., " uproar "). See DISSENSION, INSURRECTION, SEDITION, UPROAR.

B. Adverb.

ASŌTŌS (ἀσώτως), wastefully (akin to A, No. 1), is translated " with
riotous living " in Luke 15 : 13 ; though the word does not necessarily
signify ' dissolutely,' the parable narrative makes clear that this is the
meaning here.¶   In the Sept., Prov. 7 : 11.¶

Note : The verb *ekchunō*, a Hellenistic form of *ekcheo* (though the form
actually used is the regular classical aorist passive of *ekcheō*), to pour out,
shed, is translated " ran riotously " in Jude 11, R.V. (A.V., " ran
greedily ") ; see POUR, SHED.

RIPE (to be fully)

1. AKMAZŌ (ἀκμάζω), to be at the prime (akin to *akmē*, a point),
to be ripe, is translated " are fully ripe " in Rev. 14 : 18.¶

2. XĒRAINŌ (ξηραίνω), to dry up, wither, is used of ripened crops in
Rev. 14 : 15, R.V., " over-ripe," A.V., " ripe " (marg., " dried "). See
DRY, B, OVER-RIPE, WITHER.

3. PARADIDŌMI (παραδίδωμι), to give over, commit, deliver, etc.,
also signifies to permit ; in Mark 4 : 29, of the ripe condition of corn,
R.V., and A.V. marg., " is ripe ; " R.V. marg., " alloweth " (the nearest
rendering) ; A.V., " is brought forth."

RISE, RISING

Notes : (1) For the various verbs *anistēmi, exanistēmi, egeirō, anabainō,
anatellō, sunephistēmi*, see under ARISE.   (2) For the A.V., " should rise "
in Acts 26 : 23, see RESURRECTION.   (3) *Exanistēmi*, transitively, to raise
up (*ek*, out, from, out of), is used intransitively in Acts 15 : 5, " there rose
up," i.e., from the midst of a gathered company. See RAISE.   (4) For
the A.V. and R.V. of *sunegeirō*, to raise together with, and in the Passive
Voice in Col. 2 : 12 ; 3 : 1, see RAISE.   (5) For the word " rising," which
is used to translate the verbs *anatellō* in Mark 16 : 2, and *anistēmi*, in
Mark 9 : 10, see under ARISE, Nos. 9 and 1 respectively. (6) For *katephistēmi*, Acts 18 : 12, R.V., see INSURRECTION, B. (7) *Epanistamai*, to rise
up against, occurs in Matt. 10 : 21 ; Mark 13 : 12.¶ (8) *Anastasis*, is
rendered " rising up " in Luke 2 : 34, R.V.

RIVER

POTAMOS (ποταμός) denotes (*a*) a stream, Luke 6 : 48, 49 ; (*b*) a
flood or floods, Matt. 7 : 25, 27 ; (*c*) a river, natural, Matt. 3 : 6, R.V. ;
Mark 1 : 5 ; Acts 16 : 13 ; 2 Cor. 11 : 26, R.V. (A.V., " waters ") ; Rev.
8 : 10 ; 9 : 14 ; 16 : 4, 12 ; symbolical, Rev. 12 : 15 (1st part), R.V.,
" river " (A.V., " flood ") ; so ver. 16 ; 22 : 1, 2 (cp. Gen. 2 : 10 ; Ezek. 47) ;
figuratively, John 7 : 38, the effects of the operation of the Holy Spirit in
and through the believer. See FLOOD, WATER.¶

Note : For *potamophorētos* in Rev. 12 : 15, see FLOOD, B.

ROAR, ROARING
A. Verbs.

1. MUKAOMAI (μυκάομαι), properly of oxen, an onomatopœic word, to low, bellow, is used of a lion, Rev. 10 : 3.¶

2. ŌRUOMAI (ὠρύομαι), to howl or roar, onomatopœic, of animals or men, is used of a lion, 1 Pet. 5 : 8, as a simile of Satan.¶

B. Noun.

ĒCHOS (ἦχος), a noise or sound (Eng., echo), is used of the roaring of the sea in Luke 21 : 25, in the best mss., " for the roaring (of the sea and the billows)," R.V. ; some mss. have the present participle of *ēcheō*, to sound, A.V., " (the sea and the waves) roaring." See RUMOUR, SOUND.

ROB

1. SULAŌ (συλάω), to plunder, spoil, is translated " I robbed " in 2 Cor. 11 : 8.¶ Cp. *sulagōgeō*, to make spoil of, Col. 2 : 8.¶

2. KATABRABEUŌ (καταβραβεύω), to give judgment against, to condemn (*kata*, against, and *brabeus*, an umpire ; cp. *brabeion*, a prize in the games, 1 Cor. 9 : 24 ; Phil. 3 : 14, and *brabeuō*, to act as an umpire, arbitrate, Col. 3 : 15), occurs in Col. 2 : 18, R.V., " let (no man) rob (you) of your prize " (A.V., " . . . beguile . . . of your reward "), said of false teachers who would frustrate the faithful adherence of the believers to the truth, causing them to lose their reward. Another rendering, closer to the proper meaning of the word, as given above, is ' let no man decide for or against you ' (i.e., without any notion of a prize) ; this suitably follows the word " judge " in ver. 16, i.e., ' do not give yourselves up to the judgment and decision of any man ' (A.V., marg., " judge against ").¶

ROBBER

1. LĒSTĒS (λῃστής), a robber, brigand (akin to *leia*, booty), one who plunders openly and by violence (in contrast to *kleptēs*, a thief, see below), is always translated " robber " or " robbers " in the R.V., as the A.V. in John 10 : 1, 8 ; 18 : 40 ; 2 Cor. 11 : 26 ; the A.V. has " thief " or " thieves " in Matt. 21 : 13, and parallel passages ; 26 : 55, and parallel passages ; 27 : 38, 44 and Mark 15 : 27 ; Luke 10 : 30, 36 ; but " thief " is the meaning of *kleptēs*. See THIEF.

2. HIEROSULOS (ἱερόσυλος), an adjective signifying robbing temples (*hieron*, a temple, and *sulaō*, to rob), is found in Acts 19 : 37.¶ Cp. *hierosuleō*, to rob a temple, Rom. 2 : 22, A.V., " commit sacrilege."¶

For ROBBERY see PRIZE

ROBE

1. STOLĒ (στολή), for which see CLOTHING, No. 8, is translated " robe " in Mark 16 : 5, R.V. (A.V., " garment ") ; " long robes " in Luke 20 : 46.

2. CHLAMUS (χλαμύς), a cloak, is translated "robe" in Matt. 27 : 28, 31. See CLOTHING, Note (4).¶

3. HIMATION (ἱμάτιον) is translated "robe" in the A.V. of John 19 : 2, 5 (R.V., "garment"). See APPAREL, No. 2, CLOTHING, No. 2, GARMENT.

4. ESTHĒS (ἐσθής), apparel, is translated "robe" in Luke 23 : 11 (R.V., "apparel"). See APPAREL, No. 1.

ROCK

1. PETRA (πέτρα) denotes a mass of rock, as distinct from *petros*, a detached stone or boulder, or a stone that might be thrown or easily moved. For the nature of *petra*, see Matt. 7 : 24, 25 ; 27 : 51, 60 ; Mark 15 : 46 ; Luke 6 : 48 (twice), a type of a sure foundation (here the true reading is as in the R.V., "because it had been well builded") ; Rev. 6 : 15, 16 (cp. Is. 2 : 19, ff. ; Hos. 10 : 8) ; Luke 8 : 6, 13, used illustratively ; 1 Cor. 10 : 4 (twice), figuratively, of Christ ; in Rom. 9 : 33 and 1 Pet. 2 : 8, metaphorically, of Christ ; in Matt. 16 : 18, metaphorically, of Christ and the testimony concerning Him ; here the distinction between *petra*, concerning the Lord Himself, and *Petros*, the Apostle, is clear (see above).¶

2. SPILAS (σπιλάς), a rock or reef, over which the sea dashes, is used in Jude 12, "hidden rocks," R.V., metaphorical of men whose conduct is a danger to others.¶ A late meaning ascribed to it is that of "spots," (A.V.), but that rendering seems to have been influenced by the parallel passage in 2 Pet. 2 : 13, where *spiloi*, "spots," occurs.

ROCKY

PETRŌDĒS (πετρώδης), rock-like (*petra*, a rock, *eidos*, a form, appearance), is used of rock underlying shallow soil, Matt. 13 : 5, 20, R.V., "the rocky places" (A.V., "stony places") ; Mark 4 : 5, R.V., "the rocky ground" (A.V., "stony ground") ; ver. 16, R.V., "rocky places" (A.V., "stony ground").¶

Note : In Acts 27 : 29, A.V., the phrase *tracheis topoi*, lit., 'rough places,' is translated "rocks" (R.V., "rocky ground").

ROD
A. Noun.

RHABDOS (ῥάβδος), a staff, rod, sceptre, is used (*a*) of Aaron's rod, Heb. 9 : 4 ; (*b*) a staff used on a journey, Matt. 10 : 10, R.V., "staff" (A.V., "staves") ; so Luke 9 : 3 ; Mark 6 : 8, "staff;" Heb. 11 : 21, "staff ; " (*c*) a ruler's staff, a "sceptre," Heb. 1 : 8 (twice) ; elsewhere a rod, Rev. 2 : 27 ; 12 : 5 ; 19 : 15 ; (*d*) a rod for chastisement (figuratively), 1 Cor. 4 : 21 ; (*e*) a measuring rod, Rev. 11 : 1. See STAFF.¶

B. Verb.

RHABDIZŌ (ῥαβδίζω), to beat with a rod, is used in Acts 16 : 22, R.V., "to beat . . . with rods ; " 2 Cor. 11 : 25. The rods were those of the Roman lictors or " serjeants " (*rhabdouchoi*, lit., rod-bearers) ; the Roman beating with rods is distinct from the Jewish infliction of stripes.¶ In the Sept., Judg., 6 : 11 ; Ruth 2 : 17.¶ Cp. Matt. 26 : 67, R.V. marg.; John 18 : 22 (A.V. marg., and R.V. marg.) ; 19 : 3, R.V. marg. ; see SMITE.

ROLL (Noun and Verb)
A. Verbs.

1. APOKULIŌ or APOKULIZŌ (ἀποκυλίω), to roll away (*apo*, from, *kuliō*, to roll ; cp. Eng., cylinder, etc.), is used of the sepulchre-stone, Matt. 28 : 2 ; Mark 16 : 3 (ver. 4 in some mss. ; see No. 2) ; Luke 24 : 2.¶ In the Sept., Gen. 29 : 3, 8, 10.¶

2. ANAKULIŌ (ἀνακυλίω), to roll up or back (*ana*), is found in the best texts, in Mark 16 : 4 (see No. 1).¶

3. PROSKULIŌ (προσκυλίω), to roll up or to (*pros*), is used in Matt. 27 : 60 ; Mark 15 : 46, of the sepulchre-stone.¶

4. HEILISSŌ, or HELISSŌ (ἑλίσσω), to roll, or roll up, is used (*a*) of the rolling up of a mantle, illustratively of the heavens, Heb. 1 : 12, R.V. ; (*b*) of the rolling up of a scroll, Rev. 6 : 14, illustratively of the removing of the heaven.¶

5. ENTULISSŌ (ἐντυλίσσω), to wrap up, roll round or about, is translated "rolled up" in John 20 : 7, R.V., of the cloth or "napkin" that had been wrapped around the head of the Lord before burial. Both the R.V. and the A.V., " wrapped together," might suggest that this cloth had been rolled or wrapped up and put in a certain part of the tomb at the Lord's resurrection, whereas, as with the body wrappings, the head cloth was lying as it had been rolled round His head, an evidence, to those who looked into the tomb, of the fact of His resurrection without any disturbance of the wrappings either by friend or foe or when the change took place. It is followed by *en*, in, and translated "wrapped" in Matt. 27 : 59, a meaning and construction which Moulton and Milligan illustrate from the papyri ; in Luke 23 : 53 it is followed by the dative of the noun *sindōn*, linen cloth, used instrumentally. See WRAP.¶

B. Noun.

KEPHALIS (κεφαλίς), lit., a little head (a diminutive of *kephalē*, a head ; Lat., *capitulum*, a diminutive of *caput*), hence, a capital of a column, then, a roll (of a book), occurs in Heb. 10 : 7, R.V., " in the roll " (A.V., " in the volume "), lit., ' in the heading of the scroll ' (from Ps. 40 : 7).¶

ROMAN
RHŌMAIOS ('Ρωμαῖος) occurs in John 11 : 48 ; Acts 2 : 10, R.V., "from Rome " (A.V., " of Rome ") ; 16 : 21, 37, 38 ; 22 : 25, 26, 27, 29 ; 23 : 27 ; 25 : 16 ; 28 : 17.¶ For a note on Roman citizenship see CITIZEN, No. 3.

ROOF

STEGĒ (στέγη), a covering (stegō, to cover), denotes a roof, Mark 2 : 4 ; said of entering a house, Matt. 8 : 8 ; Luke 7 : 6.¶

ROOM
A. Nouns.

1. TOPOS (τόπος), a place, is translated " room " in Luke 2 : 7 and 14 : 22, i.e., place ; in the A.V. in Luke 14 : 9, 10, R.V., " place " (of a couch at a feast) ; of a position or condition which a person occupies, 1 Cor. 14 : 16 (R.V., " place "). See OPPORTUNITY, PLACE.

2. PRŌTOKLISIA (πρωτοκλισία), the chief reclining place at table, is rendered " uppermost rooms," in Matt. 23 : 6, A.V. (R.V., " chief place ") ; in Mark 12 : 39, " uppermost rooms," A.V. (R.V., " chief places ") ; in Luke 14 : 7, " chief rooms," A.V. (R.V., " chief seats ") ; in ver. 8, A.V., " highest room " (R.V., " chief seat ") ; in 20 : 46, A.V., " highest seats " (R.V., " chief seats "). See CHIEF, B, No. 7, PLACE, No. 5.¶

3. ANAGAION or ANŌGEON (ἀνάγαιον), an upper room (ana, above, gē, ground), occurs in Mark 14 : 15 ; Luke 22 : 12, a chamber, often over a porch, or connected with the roof, where meals were taken and privacy obtained.¶

4. HUPERŌON (ὑπερῷον), the neuter of the adjective huperōos, upper (from huper, above), used as a noun, denoted in classical Greek an upper storey or room where the women resided ; in the Sept. and the N.T., an upper chamber, a roof-chamber, built on the flat roof of the house, Acts 1 : 13, R.V., " upper chamber " (A.V. " upper room ") ; see CHAMBER, No. 2.

B. Verb.

CHŌREŌ (χωρέω), to make room, is translated " there was . . . room " in Mark 2 : 2. See CONTAIN, No. 1.

C. Preposition.

ANTI (ἀντί), in place of, instead of, is translated " in the room of " in Matt. 2 : 22.

Notes : (1) In Luke 12 : 17, A.V., pou, anywhere or where, with a negative, is translated " no room " (R.V., " not where "). (2) In Acts 24 : 27, A.V., diadochos, a successor, with lambanō, to receive, is translated " came into (Felix') room," R.V., " (Felix) was succeeded by." Diadochos often meant a deputy, a temporary successor.¶

ROOT
A. Noun.

RHIZA (ῥίζα) is used (a) in the natural sense, Matt. 3 : 10 ; 13 : 6, 21 ; Mark 4 : 6, 17 ; 11 : 20 ; Luke 3 : 9 ; 8 : 13 ; (b) metaphorically (1) of cause, origin, source, said of persons, ancestors, Rom. 11 : 16, 17, 18 (twice) ; of things, evils, 1 Tim. 6 : 10, R.V., of the love of money as a root of all "kinds of evil" (marg., "evils;" A.V., "evil"); bitterness, Heb. 12 : 15; (2) of that which springs from a root, a shoot, said of offspring, Rom. 15 : 12; Rev. 5 : 5; 22 : 16.¶

B. Verbs.

1. RHIZOŌ (ῥιζόω), to cause to take root, is used metaphorically in the Passive Voice in Eph. 3 : 17, of being rooted in love ; Col. 2 : 7, in Christ, i.e., in the sense of being firmly planted, or established.¶ In the Sept., Is. 40 : 24; Jer. 12 : 2.¶

2. EKRIZOŌ (ἐκριζόω), to root out or up (ek, out, and No. 1), is rendered to root up in Matt. 13 : 29; 15 : 13; see PLUCK.

ROPE

SCHOINION (σχοινίον), a diminutive of schoinos, a rush, is used of the small cords of which Christ made a scourge, John 2 : 15; of the ropes of a boat, Acts 27 : 32. See CORD.¶

For ROSE see RISE

ROUGH

1. SKLĒROS (σκληρός), hard, is translated "rough" in Jas. 3 : 4, R.V., of winds (A.V., "fierce"). See AUSTERE, FIERCE, Note (1).

2. TRACHUS (τραχύς), rough, uneven, is used of paths, Luke 3 : 5; of rocky places, Acts 27 : 29. See ROCKY.¶

ROUND, ROUND ABOUT

1. KUKLOTHEN (κυκλόθεν), from kuklos, a circle, ring (Eng., cycle, etc.), occurs in Rev. 4 : 3, 4; in ver. 8, R.V., "round about," with reference to the eyes.¶

2. PANTOTHEN (πάντοθεν), on all sides (from pas, all), is translated "round about" in Heb. 9 : 4. See EVERYWHERE, No. 3.

3. PERIX (πέριξ), from the preposition peri, around, occurs in Acts 5 : 16, "round about" (of cities).¶

4. KUKLŌ (κύκλῳ), the dative case of the noun kuklos, a ring, is used as an adverb, and translated "round about" in Mark 3 : 34, A.V. (R.V., "round"); 6 : 6, 36; Luke 9 : 12; Rom. 15 : 19; Rev. 4 : 6; 7 : 11.¶

Note: For combinations with other words see, e.g., COME, No. 38, COUNTRY, A, No. 6, A, No. 4, DWELL, No. 5, GO, No. 9, HEDGE, LOOK, A, No. 3, REGION, SHINE, STAND, B, No. 5.

ROUSE

EXUPNOS (ἔξυπνος), roused out of sleep (ek, out of, hupnos, sleep), occurs in Acts 16 : 27.¶ Cp. exupnizō, AWAKE, No. 4.

ROW (Verb)

ELAUNŌ (ἐλαύνω), to drive, is used of rowing or sailing a boat, Mark 6 : 48; John 6 : 19. See DRIVE.

ROYAL

1. BASILEIOS (βασίλειος), from *basileus*, a king, is used in 1 Pet. 2 : 9 of the priesthood consisting of all believers.¶ Cp. Luke 7 : 25, for which see COURT, No. 3. In the Sept., Ex. 19 : 6 ; 23 : 22 ; Deut. 3 : 10¶.

2. BASILIKOS (βασιλικός), belonging to a king, is translated " royal " in Acts 12 : 21 ; Jas. 2 : 8. See KING B, No. 2 NOBLEMAN.

RUB

PSŌCHŌ (ψώχω), to rub, to rub to pieces, is used in Luke 6 : 1.¶

RUDDER

PĒDALION (πηδάλιον), a rudder (akin to *pēdos*, the blade of an oar), occurs in Jas. 3 : 4, R.V., " rudder " (A.V., " helm "), and Acts 27 : 40, plural, R.V.," (the bands of) the rudders," A.V., " the rudder (bands)."¶

The *pēdalia* were actually steering-paddles, two of which were used as rudders in ancient ships.

RUDE

IDIŌTĒS (ἰδιώτης), for which see IGNORANT, No. 4, is translated " rude " in 2 Cor. 11 : 6.

RUDIMENTS

STOICHEION (στοιχεῖον), one of a row or series, is translated " rudiments " in the R.V. of Gal. 4 : 3, 9 ; Heb. 5 : 12, and the A.V. and R.V. of Col. 2 : 8, 20. See ELEMENTS.

RUE

PĒGANON (πήγανον), a shrubby plant with yellow flowers and a heavy smell, cultivated for medicinal purposes, is mentioned in Luke 11 : 42.¶

RUIN

1. RHĒGMA (ῥῆγμα), akin to *rhēgnumi*, to break, denotes a cleavage, fracture (so in the Sept., e.g., 1 Kings 11 : 30, 31) ; by metonymy, that which is broken, a ruin, Luke 6 : 49.¶

2. KATESTRAMMENA (κατεστραμμένα), the neuter plural, perfect participle, Passive, of *katastrephō*, to overturn, is translated " ruins " in Acts 15 : 16 ; cp. DIG, No. 3. See OVERTHROW.

RULE (Noun and Verb)

A. Nouns.

1. ARCHĒ (ἀρχή), a beginning etc., denotes rule, Luke 20 : 20, R.V., "rule" (A.V., "power") ; 1 Cor. 15 : 24 ; Eph. 1 : 21, R.V., "rule" (A.V., "principality"). See BEGINNING, B.

2. KANŌN (κανών) is translated "rule" in the A.V. of 2 Cor. 10 : 13, 15 ; in Gal. 6 : 16, A.V. and R.V. ; in Phil. 3 : 16, A.V. (R.V., in italics) : see PROVINCE, No. 2.

B. Verbs.

1. ARCHŌ (ἄρχω), (akin to A, No. 1), in the Active Voice denotes to rule, Mark 10 : 42 and Rom. 15 : 12, R.V., " to rule " (A.V., " to reign "). See BEGIN, A, No. 1.

2. OIKODESPOTEŌ (οἰκοδεσποτέω), from oikos, a house, and despotēs, a master, signifies to rule the household ; so the R.V. in 1 Tim. 5 : 14 (A.V., " guide the house "). See GUIDE, B, Note (1).¶ Cp. oikodespotēs, a householder.

3. PROISTĒMI (προίστημι), lit., ' to stand before,' hence, to lead, attend to (indicating care and diligence), is translated to rule (Middle Voice), with reference to a local church, in Rom. 12 : 8; perfect Active in 1 Tim. 5 : 17 ; with reference to a family, 1 Tim. 3 : 4 and 12 (Middle Voice) ; ver. 5 (2nd aorist, Active). See MAINTAIN.

4. HĒGEOMAI (ἡγέομαι), to lead, is translated to rule in Heb. 13 : 7, 17, 24 (A.V. marg., in the first two, " are the guides " and " guide."

5. POIMAINO (ποιμαίνω), to act as a shepherd, tend flocks, is translated to rule in Rev. 2 : 27 ; 12 : 5 ; 19 : 15, all indicating that the governing power exercised by the Shepherd is to be of a firm character ; in Matt. 2 : 6, A.V., " shall rule " (R.V., " shall be shepherd of "). See FEED.

6. BRABEUŌ (βραβεύω), properly, to act as an umpire (brabeus), hence, generally, to arbitrate, decide, Col. 3 : 15, " rule " (R.V., marg., " arbitrate "), representing " the peace of Christ " (R.V.) as deciding all matters in the hearts of believers; some regard the meaning as that of simply directing, controlling, ruling.¶ Cp. katabrabeuō ; see ROB.

RULER

1. ARCHŌN (ἄρχων), a ruler, chief, prince, is translated " rulers," e.g., in 1 Cor. 2 : 6, 8, R.V. (A.V., " princes ") ; " ruler," Rev. 1 : 5 (A.V., " prince "). See MAGISTRATE, PRINCE, No. 2.

2. ARCHĒ (ἀρχή), a rule, sovereignty, is rendered " rulers " in Luke 12 : 11, R.V. (A.V., " magistrates "). See BEGINNING.

3. KOSMOKRATŌR (κοσμοκράτωρ) denotes a ruler of this world (contrast pantokratōr, almighty). In Greek literature, in Orphic hymns, etc., and in Rabbinic writings, it signifies a ruler of the whole world, a world-lord. In the N.T. it is used in Eph. 6 : 12, " the world-rulers (of this darkness)," R.V., A.V., " the rulers (of the darkness) of this world." The context (" not against flesh and blood ") shows that not earthly potentates are indicated, but spirit powers, who, under the permissive will of God, and in consequence of human sin, exercise Satanic and therefore antagonistic authority over the world in its present condition of spiritual darkness and alienation from God. The suggested rendering ' the rulers of this dark world ' is ambiguous and not phraseologically requisite. Cp. John 12 : 31 ; 14 : 30 ; 16 : 11 ; 2 Cor. 4 : 4.¶

4. POLITARCHĒS (πολιτάρχης), a ruler of a city (polis, a city, archō,

to rule), a politarch, is used in Acts 17 : 6, 8, of the magistrates in Thessalonica, before whom the Jews, with a mob of market idlers, dragged Jason and other converts, under the charge of showing hospitality to Paul and Silas, and of treasonable designs against the Emperor. Thessalonica was a " free " city and the citizens could choose their own politarchs. The accuracy of Luke has been vindicated by the use of the term, for while classical authors use the terms *poliarchos* and *politarchos* of similar rulers, the form used by Luke is supported by inscriptions discovered at Thessalonica, one of which mentions Sosipater, Secundus, and Gaius among the politarchs, names occurring as those of Paul's companions. Prof. Burton of Chicago, in a paper on " The Politarchs," has recorded 17 inscriptions which attest their existence, thirteen of which belong to Macedonia and five presumably to Thessalonica itself, illustrating the influence of Rome in the municipal organization of the place.¶

5. ARCHITRIKLINOS (ἀρχιτρίκλινος) denotes the superintendent of a banquet, whose duty lay in arranging the tables and food (*archē*, ruler, *triklinos*, lit., a room with three couches), John 2 : 8, 9.¶

Notes : (1) In Mark 13 : 9 and Luke 21 : 12, A.V., *hēgemōn*, a leader, a governor of a Province, is translated " ruler " (R.V., " governor "). See GOVERNOR, PRINCE, No. 3. (2) For ruler of the synagogue, see SYNAGOGUE. (3) In Matt. 24 : 45, A.V., *kathistēmi*, to appoint, is translated " hath made ruler " (R.V., " hath set ") ; so in ver. 47 ; 25 : 21, 23 ; Luke 12 : 42, 44.

RUMOUR

1. AKOĒ (ἀκοή), a hearing, is translated " rumour " in Matt. 24 : 6 ; Mark 13 : 7. See HEARING, B, No. 1.

2. ĒCHOS (ἦχος), a noise, sound, is translated " rumour " in Luke 4 : 37, R.V. (A.V., " fame "). See ROAR, SOUND.

Note : In Luke 7 : 17, A.V., *logos*, a word, is translated " rumour " (R.V., " report ").

RUN, RAN

1. TRECHŌ (τρέχω), to run, is used (*a*) literally, e.g., Matt. 27 : 48 (*dramōn*, an aorist participle, from an obsolete verb *dramō*, but supplying certain forms absent from *trechō*, lit., ' having run,' ' running,' expressive of the decisiveness of the act) ; the same form in the indicative mood is used, e.g., in Matt. 28 : 8 ; in the Gospels the literal meaning alone is used ; elsewhere in 1 Cor. 9 : 24 (twice in 1st part) ; Rev. 9 : 9, A.V., " running " (R.V., " rushing ") ; (*b*) metaphorically, from the illustration of runners in a race, of either swiftness or effort to attain an end, Rom. 9 : 16, indicating that salvation is not due to human effort, but to God's sovereign right to exercise mercy ; 1 Cor. 9 : 24 (2nd part), and ver. 26, of persevering activity in the Christian course with a view to obtaining the reward ; so Heb. 12 : 1 ; in Gal. 2 : 2 (1st part), R.V., " (lest) I should be

running," continuous present tense, referring to the activity of the special service of his mission to Jerusalem ; (2nd part), " had run," aorist tense, expressive of the continuous past, referring to the activity of his antagonism to the Judaizing teachers at Antioch, and his consent to submit the case to the judgment of the church in Jerusalem ; in 5 : 7 of the erstwhile faithful course doctrinally of the Galatian believers ; in Phil. 2 : 16, of the Apostle's manner of life among the Philippian believers ; in 2 Thess. 3 : 1, of the free and rapid progress of " the word of the Lord."

2. PROSTRECHŌ (προστρέχω), to run to (*pros*, to, and No. 1), is used in Mark 9 : 15 ; 10 : 17 ; Acts 8 : 30.¶

3. PERITRECHŌ (περιτρέχω), to run about (*peri*, around, and No. 1), is used in Mark 6 : 55, R.V., " ran round about " (A.V., " ran through ").¶

4. SUNTRECHŌ (συντρέχω), to run together with (*sun*, with), is used (*a*) literally, Mark 6 : 33 ; Acts 3 : 11 ; (*b*) metaphorically, 1 Pet. 4 : 4, of running a course of evil with others.¶ In the Sept., Psa. 50 : 18.¶

5. PROTRECHŌ (προτρέχω), to run before, Luke 19 : 4 : see OUTRUN.

6. EISTRECHŌ (εἰστρέχω), to run in (*eis*, in), occurs in Acts 12 : 14.¶

7. HUPOTRECHŌ (ὑποτρέχω), to run under (*hupo*, under), is used nautically in Acts 27 : 16.¶

8. EPISUNTRECHŌ (ἐπισυντρέχω), to run together again (*epi*, upon, or again, and No. 4), occurs in Mark 9 : 25.¶

9. EKCHUNNŌ or EKCHUNŌ (ἐκχύννω), to shed, is translated " ran riotously " in Jude 11, R.V. (A.V., " ran greedily "). See RIOTOUSLY, Note. See SHED, SPILL.

10. HUPEREKCHUNNŌ (ὑπερεκχύννω), a late form of *huperekcheō*, to overflow, is rendered " running over " in Luke 6 : 38.¶

11. EPIKELLŌ or EPOKELLŌ (ἐπικέλλω), to drive upon, is used in Acts 27 : 41 of running a ship ashore.¶

Notes : (1) *Hormaō*, to set in motion, urge on, but intransitively, to hasten on, rush, is always translated to rush in the R.V. ; A.V., " ran violently," Matt. 8 : 32 ; Mark 5 : 13 ; Luke 8 : 33 ; " ran," Acts 7 : 57 ; " rushed ", 19 : 29. See RUSH.¶ (2) In Acts 21 : 30, *sundromē*, a running together, with *ginomai*, to become, take place, is translated " ran together," lit., ' a running together took place.' (3) In Matt. 9 : 17, A.V., *ekcheō*, to pour out, used in the Passive Voice (R.V., " is spilled "), is translated " runneth out." (4) In Acts 14 : 14, R.V., *ekpēdaō*, to spring forth, is translated " sprang forth " (this verb is found in the papyri) ; the A.V., " ran in " translates the mss. which have *eispēdaō*, to spring in. (5) *Katatrechō*, to run down, occurs in Acts 21 : 32.¶

RUSH, RUSHING

1. HORMAŌ (ὁρμάω), for which see RUN, Note (1), with refs., is akin to *hormē* (see ASSAULT) and *hormēma*, a rushing (see VIOLENCE).

2. PHERŌ (φέρω), to bear, is used in the present participle, Passive Voice, in Acts 2 : 2, and translated " rushing," R.V., " the rushing (of

a mighty wind)," A.V., "a rushing (mighty wind)," lit., 'a violent wind borne (along).'

3. TRECHŌ (τρέχω), to run, is translated " rushing (to war) " in Rev. 9 : 9, R.V., A.V., " running (to battle)."

RUST (Noun and Verb)
A. Nouns.

1. BRŌSIS (βρῶσις), an eating (akin to bibrōskō, to eat), is used metaphorically to denote " rust " in Matt. 6 : 19, 20. See EAT, B, No. 1, FOOD, MEAT, MORSEL.

2. IOS (ἰός), poison, denotes rust in Jas. 5 : 3. See POISON.

B. Verb.

KATIOŌ (κατιόω), an intensive form of ioō, to poison (akin to A, No. 2), strengthened by kata, down, to rust over, and in the Passive Voice, to become rusted over, occurs in Jas. 5 : 3, R.V., " are rusted " (A.V., " are cankered ").¶ Cp. gangraina, a gangrene, 2 Tim. 2 : 17, R.V.¶

S

SABACHTHANI

SABACHTHANEI (σαβαχθανεί), an Aramaic word signifying ' Thou hast forsaken Me,' is recorded as part of the utterance of Christ on the Cross, Matt. 27 : 46 ; Mark 15 : 34, a quotation from Ps. 22 : 1. Recently proposed renderings which differ from those of the A.V. and R.V. have not been sufficiently established to require acceptance.

SABAOTH

SABAÕTH (σαβαώθ) is the transliteration of a Hebrew word which denotes hosts or armies, Rom. 9 : 29 ; Jas. 5 : 4.¶ While the word " hosts " probably had special reference to angels, the title " the LORD of hosts " became used to designate Him as the One who is supreme over all the innumerable hosts of spiritual agencies, or of what are described as " the armies of heaven." Eventually it was used as equivalent to ' the LORD all-sovereign.' In the prophetical books of the O.T. the Sept. sometimes has *Kurios Sabaõth* as the equivalent of " the LORD of hosts," sometimes *Kurios Pantokratõr ;* in Job, it uses *Pantokratõr* to render the Hebrew Divine title *Shadday* (see ALMIGHTY).

SABBATH

1. SABBATON (σάββατον) or SABBATA : the latter, the plural form, was transliterated from the Aramaic word, which was mistaken for a plural ; hence the singular, *sabbaton*, was formed from it. The root means to cease, desist (Heb., *shābath ;* cp. Arab., *sabata*, to intercept, interrupt) ; the doubled *b* has an intensive force, implying a complete cessation or a making to cease, probably the former. The idea is not that of relaxation or refreshment, but cessation from activity.

The observation of the seventh day of the week, enjoined upon Israel, was ' a sign ' between God and His earthly people, based upon the fact that after the six days of creative operations He rested, Ex. 31 : 16, 17, with 20 : 8–11. The O.T. regulations were developed and systematized to such an extent that they became a burden upon the people (who otherwise rejoiced in the rest provided) and a byword for absurd extravagance. Two treatises of the Mishna (the *Shabbāth* and '*Ērūbin*) are entirely occupied with regulations for the observance ; so with the discussions in the Gemara, on Rabbinical opinions. The effect upon current opinion explains the antagonism roused by the Lord's cures wrought on the Sabbath, e.g., Matt. 12 : 9–13 ; John 5 : 5–16, and explains the fact that on a Sabbath the sick were brought to be healed after sunset, e.g., Mark 1 : 32. According to Rabbinical ideas, the disciples, by plucking ears of corn (Matt. 12 : 1 ; Mark 2 : 23), and rubbing them (Luke 6 : 1), broke the sabbath in two respects ; for to pluck was to reap, and to rub was to thresh. The Lord's attitude towards the sabbath was by way of freeing it from these vexatious traditional accretions by which it was made an end in itself, instead of a means to an end (Mark 2 : 27).

In the Epistles the only direct mentions are in Col. 2 : 16, " a sabbath day," R.V. (which rightly has the singular, see 1st parag., above), where it is listed among things that were " a shadow of the things to come " (i.e., of the age introduced at Pentecost), and in Heb. 4 : 4–11, where the perpetual *sabbatismos* is appointed for believers (see REST) ; inferential references are in Rom. 14 : 5 and Gal. 4 : 9–11. For the first three centuries of the Christian era the first day of the week was never confounded with the sabbath ; the confusion of the Jewish and Christian institutions was due to declension from apostolic teaching.

Notes : (1) In Matt. 12 : 1 and 11, where the plural is used, the A.V. (as the R.V.) rightly has the singular, " the sabbath day ; " in ver. 5 the A.V. has the plural (see above). Where the singular is used the R.V. omits the word " day," ver. 2 ; 24 : 20 ; Mark 6 : 2 ; Luke 6 : 1 (" on a sabbath ") ; 14 : 3 ; John 9 : 14 (" it was the sabbath on the day when . . . "). As to the use or omission of the article the omission does not always require the rendering ' a sabbath ; ' it is absent, e.g., in Matt. 12 : 2. (2) In Acts 16 : 13, " on the sabbath day," is, lit., ' on the day of the sabbath ' (plural). (3) For Matt. 28 : 1, see LATE. (4) For " the first day of the week " see ONE, A, (5).

2. PROSABBATON (προσάββατον) signifies " the day before the sabbath " (*pro*, before, and No. 1), Mark 15 : 42 ; some mss. have *prin*, before, with *sabbaton* separately).¶

SACKCLOTH

SAKKOS (σάκκος), a warm material woven from goat's or camel's hair, and hence of a dark colour, Rev. 6 : 12 ; Jerome renders it *saccus cilicinus* (being made from the hair of the black goat of Cilicia, the Romans called it *cilicium*) ; cp. Isa. 50 : 3 ; it was also used for saddle-cloths, Jos. 9 : 4 ; also for making sacks, e.g., Gen. 42 : 25, and for garments worn as expressing mourning or penitence, Matt. 11 : 21 ; Luke 10 : 13, or for purposes of prophetic testimony, Rev. 11 : 3.¶

SACRED

HIEROS (ἱερός) denotes consecrated to God, e.g., the Scriptures, 2 Tim. 3 : 15, R.V., " sacred " (A.V. " holy ") ; it is used as a noun in the neuter plural in 1 Cor. 9 : 13, R.V., " sacred things " (A.V., " holy things ").¶ The neuter singular, *hieron*, denotes a temple. See TEMPLE. For a comparison of this and synonymous terms see HOLY, B, No. 1 (*b*) and Note (2).

SACRIFICE (Noun and Verb)
A. Noun.

THUSIA (θυσία) primarily denotes the act of offering ; then, objectively, that which is offered (*a*) of idolatrous sacrifice, Acts 7 : 41 ; (*b*) of animal or other sacrifices, as offered under the Law, Matt. 9 : 13 ; 12 : 7 ; Mark 9 : 49 ; 12 : 33 ; Luke 2 : 24 ; 13 : 1 ; Acts 7 : 42 ; 1 Cor. 10 : 18 ; Heb. 5 : 1 ; 7 : 27 (R.V., plural) ; 8 : 3 ; 9 : 9 ; 10 : 1, 5, 8 (R.V., plural), 11 ; 11 : 4 ; (*c*) of Christ, in His sacrifice on the Cross, Eph. 5 : 2 ; Heb. 9 : 23, where the plural antitypically comprehends the various forms of Levitical sacrifices in their typical character ; 9 : 26 ; 10 : 12, 26 ; (*d*) metaphorically, (1) of the body of the believer, presented to God as a living sacrifice, Rom. 12 : 1 ; (2) of faith, Phil. 2 : 17 ; (3) of material assistance rendered to servants of God, Phil. 4 : 18 ; (4) of praise, Heb. 13 : 15 ; (5) of doing good to others and communicating with their needs, Heb. 13 : 16 ; (6) of spiritual sacrifices in general, offered by believers as a holy priesthood, 1 Pet. 2 : 5.¶

B. Verb.

THUŌ (θύω) is used of sacrificing by slaying a victim, (*a*) of the sacrifice of Christ, 1 Cor. 5 : 7, R.V., " hath been sacrificed " (A.V., " is sacrificed ") ; (*b*) of the Passover sacrifice, Mark 14 : 12, R.V., " they sacrificed " (A.V., " they killed ") ; Luke 22 : 7, R.V., " (must) be sacrificed," A.V., " (must) be killed ; " (*c*) of idolatrous sacrifices, Acts 14 : 13, 18 ; 1 Cor. 10 : 20 (twice). See KILL, No. 3.

Note : For *eidōlothutos*, sacrificed to idols, see IDOLS (offered to), No. 1.

For SACRILEGE see ROBBER, No. 2, Rom. 2 : 22

For SAD see COUNTENANCE

For SADDUCEES see under PHARISEES

SAFE, SAFELY, SAFETY
A. Adjective.

ASPHALĒS (ἀσφαλής), certain, secure, safe (from *a*, negative, and *sphallō*, to trip up), is translated " safe " in Phil. 3 : 1. See CERTAIN, B.

B. Nouns.

1. ASPHALEIA (ἀσφάλεια), certainty, safety (akin to A), is translated " safety " in Acts 5 : 23 ; 1 Thess. 5 : 3. See CERTAIN, A.

2. SŌTĒRIA (σωτηρία), salvation, is translated " safety " in Acts 27 : 34, R.V. (A.V., " health "). See HEALTH, Note.

C. Adverb.

ASPHALŌS (ἀσφαλῶς), safely (akin to A, and B, No. 1), is so rendered in Mark 14 : 44 and Acts 16 : 23. See ASSURANCE, C. In the Sept., Gen. 34 : 25.¶

D. Verbs.

1. DIASŌZŌ (διασώζω), to bring safely through danger, and, in the Passive Voice, to come safe through (dia, through, sōzō, to save), is translated "bring safe" in Acts 23 : 24; "escaped safe" in 27 : 44. See ESCAPE, HEAL, SAVE, WHOLE.

2. HUGIAINŌ (ὑγιαίνω), to be sound, healthy (Eng., hygiene, etc.), is translated "safe and sound" in Luke 15 : 27, lit., 'being healthy.' See HEALTH, SOUND, WHOLE.

For SAIL (Noun, Acts 27 : 17, A.V.) see GEAR

SAIL (Verb)

1. PLEŌ (πλέω), to sail, occurs in Luke 8 : 23 ; Acts 21 : 3 ; 27 : 2, 6, 24 ; Rev. 18 : 17, R.V., "saileth" (for the A.V. see COMPANY, A, No. 7).¶

2. APOPLEŌ (ἀποπλέω), to sail away (apo, from, and No. 1), occurs in Acts 13 : 4 ; 14 : 26 ; 20 : 15 ; 27 : 1.¶

3. EKPLEŌ (ἐκπλέω), to sail from, or thence (ek, from), occurs in Acts 15 : 39 ; 18 : 18 ; 20 : 6.¶

4. PARAPLEŌ (παραπλέω), to sail by (para), occurs in Acts 20 : 16.¶

5. DIAPLEŌ (διαπλέω), to sail across (dia, through), occurs in Acts 27 : 5.¶

6. HUPOPLEŌ (ὑποπλέω), to sail under (hupo), i.e., under the lee of, occurs in Acts 27 : 4, 7.¶

7. ANAGŌ (ἀνάγω), to lead up, is used of putting to sea, Acts 13 : 13 ; 16 : 11 ; 18 : 21 ; 20 : 3, 13 ; 21 : 1 ; 27 : 21 ; 28 : 10, 11 ; see LAUNCH.

8. PARALEGŌ (παραλέγω), to lay beside (para), is used in the Middle Voice, of sailing past in Acts 27 : 8, R.V., "coasting along" (A.V., "passing ") ; ver. 13, R.V., "sailed along" (A.V., "sailed ").¶

9. DIAPERAŌ (διαπεράω), to cross over, is translated "sailing over" in Acts 21 : 2, A.V. (R.V., "crossing over "). See PASS.

10. BRADUPLOEŌ (βραδυπλοέω), to sail slowly (bradus, slow, plous, a voyage), occurs in Acts 27 : 7.¶

For SAILING see VOYAGE

For SAILORS see MARINERS

SAINT(S)

HAGIOS (ἅγιος), for the meaning and use of which see HOLY, B, No. 1, is used as a noun in the singular in Phil. 4 : 21, where pas, "every," is used with it.   In the plural, as used of believers, it designates all such and is not applied merely to persons of exceptional holiness, or to those who, having died, were characterized by exceptional acts of saintliness. See especially 2 Thess. 1 : 10, where " His saints " are also described as " them that believed," i.e., the whole number of the redeemed.   They are called " holy ones " in Jude 14, R.V.   For the term as applied to the Holy Spirit see HOLY SPIRIT.   See also SANCTIFY.

Notes : (1) In Rev. 15 : 3 the R.V. follows those texts which have *aiōnōn,* " ages," and assigns the reading *ethnōn,* " nations," to the margin ; the A.V. translates those which have the inferior reading *hagiōn,* " saints," and puts " nations " and " ages " in the margin.   (2) In Rev. 18 : 20, the best texts have *hagioi* and *apostoloi,* each with the article, each being preceeded by *kai,* " and," R.V., " and ye saints, and ye apostles ; " the A.V., " and ye holy apostles " follows those mss. from which the 2nd *kai* and the article are absent.   (3) In Rev. 22 : 21, the R.V. follows those mss. which have *hagiōn,* with the article," (with) the saints ; " the A.V. those which simply have *pantōn,* all, but adds " you " (R.V., marg., " with all ").

SAKE (for the) : see † p. 9

SALT (Noun, Adjective and Verb), SALTNESS
A. Noun.

HALAS (ἅλας), a late form of *hals* (found in some mss. in Mark 9 : 49), is used (*a*) literally in Matt. 5 : 13 (2nd part) ; Mark 9 : 50 (1st part, twice) ; Luke 14 : 34 (twice) ; (*b*) metaphorically, of believers, Matt. 5 : 13 (1st part) ; of their character and condition, Mark 9 : 50 (2nd part) ; of wisdom exhibited in their speech, Col. 4 : 6.¶

Being possessed of purifying, perpetuating and antiseptic qualities, salt became emblematic of fidelity and friendship among eastern nations. To eat of a person's salt and so to share his hospitality is still regarded thus among the Arabs.   So in Scripture, it is an emblem of the covenant between God and His people, Num. 18 : 19 ; 2 Chron. 13 : 5 ; so again when the Lord says " Have salt in yourselves, and be at peace one with another " (Mark 9 : 50).   In the Lord's teaching it is also symbolic of that spiritual health and vigour essential to Christian virtue and counteractive of the corruption that is in the world, e.g., Matt. 5 : 13, see (*b*) above. Food is seasoned with salt (see B) ; every meal offering was to contain it, and it was to be offered with all offerings presented by Israelites, as emblematic of the holiness of Christ, and as betokening the reconciliation provided for man by God on the ground of the Death of Christ, Lev. 2 : 13. To refuse God's provision in Christ and the efficacy of His expiatory sacrifice is to expose oneself to the doom of being " salted with fire," Mark 9 : 49.

While salt is used to fertilize soil, excess of it on the ground produces sterility (e.g., Deut. 29 : 23 ; Judg. 9 : 45 ; Jer. 17 : 6 ; Zeph. 2 : 9).

B. Verb.

HALIZŌ (ἁλίζω), akin to A, signifies to sprinkle or to season with salt, Matt. 5 : 13 ; Mark 9 : 49 (see under A).¶ Cp. SAVOUR, B.

C. Adjectives.

1. HALUKOS (ἁλυκός) occurs in Jas. 3 : 12, " salt (water)."¶

2. ANALOS (ἄναλος) denotes saltless (a, negative, n, euphonic, and A), insipid, Mark 9 : 50, " have lost its saltness," lit., ' have become (ginomai) saltless (analos) ; " cp. mōrainō in Luke 14 : 34 (see SAVOUR, B).

For SALUTATION and SALUTE see GREET

SALVATION
A. Nouns.

1. SŌTĒRIA (σωτηρία) denotes deliverance, preservation, salvation. Salvation is used in the N.T. (a) of material and temporal deliverance from danger and apprehension, (1) national, Luke 1 : 69, 71 ; Acts 7 : 25, R.V. marg., " salvation " (text, " deliverance ") ; (2) personal, as from the sea, Acts 27 : 34 ; R.V., " safety " (A.V., " health ") ; prison, Phil. 1 : 19 ; the flood, Heb. 11 : 7 ; (b) of the spiritual and eternal deliverance granted immediately by God to those who accept His conditions of repentance and faith in the Lord Jesus, in whom alone it is to be obtained, Acts 4 : 12, and upon confession of Him as Lord, Rom. 10 : 10 ; for this purpose the gospel is the saving instrument, Rom. 1 : 16 ; Eph. 1 : 13 (see further under SAVE) ; (c) of the present experience of God's power to deliver from the bondage of sin, e.g., Phil. 2 : 12, where the special, though not the entire, reference is to the maintenance of peace and harmony ; 1 Pet. 1 : 9 ; this present experience on the part of believers is virtually equivalent to sanctification ; for this purpose, God is able to make them wise, 2 Tim. 3 : 15 ; they are not to neglect it, Heb. 2 : 3 ; (d) of the future deliverance of believers at the Parousia of Christ for His saints, a salvation which is the object of their confident hope, e.g., Rom. 13 : 11 ; 1 Thess. 5 : 8, and ver. 9, where salvation is assured to them, as being deliverance from the wrath of God destined to be executed upon the ungodly at the end of this age (see 1 Thess. 1 : 10) ; 2 Thess. 2 : 13 ; Heb. 1 : 14 ; 9 : 28 ; 1 Pet. 1 : 5 ; 2 Pet. 3 : 15 ; (e) of the deliverance of the nation of Israel at the Second Advent of Christ at the time of ' the epiphany (or shining forth) of His Parousia ' (2 Thess. 2 : 8) ; Luke 1 : 71 ; Rev. 12 : 10 ; (f) inclusively, to sum up all the blessings bestowed by God on men in Christ through the Holy Spirit, e.g., 2 Cor. 6 : 2 ; Heb. 5 : 9 ; 1 Pet. 1 : 9, 10 ; Jude 3 ; (g) occasionally, as standing virtually for the Saviour, e.g., Luke 19 : 9 ; cp. John 4 : 22 (see SAVIOUR) ; (h) in ascriptions of praise to God, Rev. 7 : 10, and as that which it is His prerogative to bestow, 19 : 1 (R.V.).

2. SŌTĒRION (σωτήριον), the neuter of the adjective (see B), is used as a noun in Luke 2 : 30 ; 3 : 6, in each of which it virtually stands for the Saviour, as in No. 1 (g) ; in Acts 28 : 28, as in No. 1 (b) ; in Eph. 6 : 17, where the hope of salvation [see No. 1 (d)] is metaphorically described as a helmet.¶

B. Adjective.

SŌTĒRIOS (σωτήριος), saving, bringing salvation, describes the grace of God, in Tit. 2 : 11.¶

SAME

1. AUTOS (αὐτός) denotes ' the same ' when preceded by the article, and either with a noun following, e.g., Mark 14 : 39 ; Phil 1 : 30 ; 1 Cor. 12 : 4, or without, e.g., Matt. 5 : 46, 47 ; Rom. 2 : 1 ; Phil. 2 : 2 ; 3 : 1 ; Heb. 1 : 12 ; 13 : 8. It is thus to be distinguished from uses as a personal and a reflexive pronoun.

2. HOUTOS (οὗτος), this (person or thing), or he (and the feminine and neuter forms), is sometimes translated " the same," e.g., John 3 : 2, 26 ; 7 : 18 ; Jas. 3 : 2 ; sometimes the R.V. translates it by " this " or " these," e.g., John 12 : 21, " these " (A.V., " the same ") ; 2 Cor. 8 : 6, " this " (A.V., " the same ").

SANCTIFICATION, SANCTIFY

A. Noun.

HAGIASMOS (ἁγιασμός), sanctification, is used of (a) separation to God, 1 Cor. 1 : 30 ; 2 Thess. 2 : 13 ; 1 Pet. 1 : 2 ; (b) the course of life befitting those so separated, 1 Thess. 4 : 3, 4, 7 ; Rom. 6 : 19, 22 ; 1 Tim. 2 : 15 ; Heb. 12 : 14.¶ " Sanctification is that relationship with God into which men enter by faith in Christ, Acts 26 : 18 ; 1 Cor. 6 : 11, and to which their sole title is the death of Christ, Eph. 5 : 25, 26 ; Col. 1 : 22 ; Heb. 10 : 10, 29 ; 13 : 12.

" Sanctification is also used in N.T. of the separation of the believer from evil things and ways. This sanctification is God's will for the believer, 1 Thess. 4 : 3, and His purpose in calling him by the gospel, ver. 7 ; it must be learned from God, ver. 4, as He teaches it by His Word, John 17 : 17, 19 ; cp. Ps. 17 : 4 ; 119 : 9, and it must be pursued by the believer, earnestly and undeviatingly, 1 Tim. 2 : 15 ; Heb. 12 : 14. For the holy character, hagiōsunē, 1 Thess. 3 : 13, is not vicarious, i.e., it cannot be transferred or imputed, it is an individual possession, built up, little by little, as the result of obedience to the Word of God, and of following the example of Christ, Matt. 11 : 29 ; John 13 : 15 ; Eph. 4 : 20 ; Phil. 2 : 5, in the power of the Holy Spirit, Rom. 8 : 13 ; Eph. 3 : 16.

" The Holy Spirit is the Agent in sanctification, Rom. 15 : 16 ; 2 Thess. 2 : 13 ; 1 Pet. 1 : 2 ; cp. 1 Cor. 6 : 11. . . . The sanctification of the Spirit is associated with the choice, or election, of God ; it is a Divine

act preceding the acceptance of the Gospel by the individual."*
For synonymous words see HOLINESS.

B. Verb.

HAGIAZŌ (ἁγιάζω), to sanctify, "is used of (a) the gold adorning the
Temple and of the gift laid on the altar, Matt. 23 : 17, 19 ; (b) food,
1 Tim. 4 : 5 ; (c) the unbelieving spouse of a believer, 1 Cor. 7 : 14 ;
(d) the ceremonial cleansing of the Israelites, Heb. 9 : 13 ; (e) the Father's
Name, Luke 11 : 2 ; (f) the consecration of the Son by the Father,
John 10 : 36 ; (g) the Lord Jesus devoting Himself to the redemption
of His people, John 17 : 19 ; (h) the setting apart of the believer for God,
Acts 20 : 32 ; cp. Rom. 15 : 16 ; (i) the effect on the believer of the Death
of Christ, Heb. 10 : 10, said of God, and 2 : 11 ; 13 : 12, said of the Lord
Jesus ; (j) the separation of the believer from the world in his behaviour—
by the Father through the Word, John 17 : 17, 19 ; (k) the believer who
turns away from such things as dishonour God and His gospel, 2 Tim.
2 : 21 ; (l) the acknowledgment of the Lordship of Christ, 1 Pet. 3 : 15.
"Since every believer is sanctified in Christ Jesus, 1 Cor. 1 : 2, cp.
Heb. 10 : 10, a common N.T. designation of all believers is 'saints,'
hagioi, i.e., 'sanctified' or 'holy ones.' Thus sainthood, or sanctification,
is not an attainment, it is the state into which God, in grace, calls sinful
men, and in which they begin their course as Christians, Col. 3 : 12 ;
Heb. 3 : 1."†

SANCTUARY

1. HAGION (ἅγιον), the neuter of the adjective hagios, holy, is used
of those structures which are set apart to God, (a) of the Tabernacle in the
wilderness, Heb. 9 : 1, R.V., " its sanctuary, *a sanctuary* of this world "
(A.V., " a worldly sanctuary ") ; in ver. 2 the outer part is called " the
Holy place," R.V. (A.V., " the sanctuary ") ; here the neuter plural
hagia is used, as in verse 3.
Speaking of the absence of the article, Westcott says " The anarthrous
form Ἅγια (literally *Holies*) in this sense appears to be unique, as also
ἅγια ἁγίων below, if indeed the reading is correct. Perhaps it is chosen to
fix attention on the character of the sanctuary as in other cases. The
plural suggests the idea of the sanctuary with all its parts : cp. Moulton-
Winer, p. 220." In their margin, Westcott and Hort prefix the article
ta to *hagia* in vv. 2 and 3. In ver. 3 the inner part is called " the Holy
of holies," R.V. (A.V., " the holiest of all ") ; in ver. 8, " the holy place "
(A.V., " the holiest of all "), lit., ' (the way) of the holiest ; ' in ver. 24
" a holy place," R.V. (A.V., " the holy places "), neuter plural ; so in
ver. 25, " the holy place " (A.V. and R.V.), and in 13 : 11, R.V., " the

---

* From Notes on Thessalonians by Hogg and Vine, pp. 115, 271.
† From Notes on Thessalonians by Hogg and Vine, pp. 113, 114.

holy place " (A.V., " the sanctuary ") ; in all these there is no separate word *topos*, place, as of the Temple in Matt. 24 : 15 ; (*b*) of " Heaven itself," i.e., the immediate presence of God and His Throne, Heb. 8 : 2, " the sanctuary " (R.V., marg., " holy th·ngs ") ; the neut. plur. with the article points to the text as being right, in view of 9 : 24, 25 and 13 : 11 (see above), exegetically designated " the true tabernacle ; " neut. plur. in 9 : 12, " the holy place ; " so 10 : 19, R.V. (A.V., " the holiest ; " there are no separate compartments in the antitypical and Heavenly sanctuary), into which believers have " boldness to enter " by faith.¶

2. NAOS (*vaós*) is used of the inner part of the Temple in Jerusalem, in Matt. 23 : 35, R.V., " sanctuary." See TEMPLE.

SAND

AMMOS (*ἄμμος*), sand or sandy ground, describes (*a*) an insecure foundation, Matt. 7 : 26 ; (*b*) numberlessness, vastness, Rom. 9 : 27 ; Heb. 11 : 12 ; Rev. 20 : 8 ; (*c*) symbolically in Rev. 13 : 1, R.V., the position taken up by the Dragon (not, as in the A.V., by John), in view of the rising of the Beast out of the sea (emblematic of the restless condition of nations ; see SEA).¶

SANDAL

SANDALION (*σανδάλιον*), a diminutive of *sandalon*, probably a Persian word, Mark 6 : 9 ; Acts 12 : 8. The sandal usually had a wooden sole bound on by straps round the instep and ankle.¶

SAPPHIRE

SAPPHEIROS (*σάπφειρος*) is mentioned in Rev. 21 : 19 (R.V., marg., " *lapis lazuli* ") as the second of the foundations of the wall of the heavenly Jerusalem (cp. Is. 54 : 11).¶ It was one of the stones in the high priest's breastplate, Ex. 28 : 18 ; 39 : 11 ; as an intimation of its value see Job 28 : 16 ; Ezek. 28 : 13. See also Ex. 24 : 10 ; Ezek. 1 : 26 ; 10 : 1. The sapphire has various shades of blue, and ranks next in hardness to the diamond.

SARDIUS, SARDINE (A.V.)

SARDION or SARDINOS (*σάρδιον*) denotes the sardian stone. *Sardius* is the word in the best texts in Rev. 4 : 3 (R.V., " a sardius "), where it formed part of the symbolic appearance of the Lord on His Throne, setting forth His glory and majesty in view of the judgment to follow. There are two special varieties, one a yellowish brown, the other a transparent red (like a cornelian). The beauty of the stone, its transparent brilliance, the high polish of which it is susceptible, made it a favourite among the ancients. It forms the sixth foundation of the wall of the heavenly Jerusalem, Rev. 21 : 20.¶

SARDONYX

SARDONUX (σαρδόνυξ), a name which indicates the formation of the gem, a layer of sard, and a layer of onyx, marked by the red of the sard and the white of the onyx. It was used among the Romans both for cameos and for signets. It forms the fifth foundation of the wall of the heavenly Jerusalem, Rev. 21 : 20.¶

SATAN

SATANAS (Σατανᾶς), a Greek form derived from the Aramaic (Heb., *Sātān*), an adversary, is used (*a*) of an angel of Jehovah in Num. 22 : 22 (the first occurrence of the word in the O.T.) ; (*b*) of men, e.g., 1 Sam. 29 : 4 ; Psa. 38 : 20 ; 71 : 13 ; four in Ps. 109 ; (*c*) of Satan, the Devil, some seventeen or eighteen times in the O.T. ; in Zech. 3 : 1, where the name receives its interpretation, "to be (his) adversary," R.V. (see marg. ; A.V., "to resist him").

In the N.T. the word is always used of Satan, the adversary (*a*) of God and Christ, e.g., Matt. 4 : 10 ; 12 : 26 ; Mark 1 : 13 ; 3 : 23, 26 ; 4 : 15 ; Luke 4 : 8 (in some mss.) ; 11 : 18 ; 22 : 3 ; John 13 : 27 ; (*b*) of His people, e.g., Luke 22 : 31 ; Acts 5 : 3 ; Rom. 16 : 20 ; 1 Cor. 5 : 5 ; 7 : 5 ; 2 Cor. 2 : 11 ; 11 : 14 ; 12 : 7 ; 1 Thess. 2 : 18 ; 1 Tim. 1 : 20 ; 5 : 15 ; Rev. 2 : 9, 13 (twice), 24 ; 3 : 9 ; (*c*) of mankind, Luke 13 : 16 ; Acts 26 : 18 ; 2 Thess. 2 : 9 ; Rev. 12 : 9 ; 20 : 7.

His doom, sealed at the Cross, is foretold in its stages in Luke 10 : 18 ; Rev. 20 : 2, 10. Believers are assured of victory over him, Rom. 16 : 20.

The appellation was given by the Lord to Peter, as a Satan-like man, on the occasion when he endeavoured to dissuade Him from death, Matt. 16 : 23 ; Mark 8 : 33.¶

Satan is not simply the personification of evil influences in the heart, for he tempted Christ, in whose heart no evil thought could ever have arisen (John 14 : 30 ; 2 Cor. 5 : 21 ; Heb. 4 : 15) ; moreover his personality is asserted in both the O.T. and the N.T., and especially in the latter, whereas if the O.T. language was intended to be figurative, the N.T. would have made this evident. See DEVIL.

SATISFY

1. CHORTAZO (χορτάζω), to fill or satisfy with food, is translated "satisfy" in Mark 8 : 4, A.V. (R.V., "to fill"). See FILL, No. 8.

2. EMPIPLEMI or EMPLETHO (ἐμπίπλημι), to fill up, fill full, satisfy (*en*, in, *pimplēmi* or *plēthō*, to fill), is used metaphorically in Rom. 15 : 24, of taking one's fill of the company of others, R.V., "I shall have been satisfied" (A.V., "I be . . . filled"). See FILL, No. 6.

For SATISFYING, Col. 2 : 23, A.V., see INDULGENCE

For SAVE (Preposition) see † p. 9

SAVE, SAVING

A. Verbs.

1. SŌZŌ (σώζω), to save, is used (as with the noun *sōtēria*, salvation) (*a*) of material and temporal deliverance from danger, suffering, etc., e.g., Matt. 8 : 25 ; Mark 13 : 20 ; Luke 23 : 35 ; John 12 : 27 ; 1 Tim. 2 : 15 ; 2 Tim. 4 : 18 (A.V., " preserve ") ; Jude 5 ; from sickness, Matt. 9 : 22, " made . . . whole " (R.V., marg., " saved ") ; so Mark 5 : 34 ; Luke 8 : 48 ; Jas. 5 : 15 ; (*b*) of the spiritual and eternal salvation granted immediately by God to those who believe on the Lord Jesus Christ, e.g., Acts 2 : 47, R.V. " (those that) were being saved ; " 16 : 31 ; Rom. 8 : 24, R.V., " were we saved ; " Eph. 2 : 5, 8 ; 1 Tim. 2 : 4 ; 2 Tim. 1 : 9 ; Tit. 3 : 5 ; of human agency in this, Rom. 11 : 14 ; 1 Cor. 7 : 16 ; 9 : 22 ; (*c*) of the present experiences of God's power to deliver from the bondage of sin, e.g., Matt. 1 : 21 ; Rom. 5 : 10 ; 1 Cor. 15 : 2 ; Heb. 7 : 25 ; Jas. 1 : 21 ; 1 Pet. 3 : 21 ; of human agency in this, 1 Tim. 4 : 16 ; (*d*) of the future deliverance of believers at the Second Coming of Christ for His saints, being deliverance from the wrath of God to be executed upon the ungodly at the close of this age and from eternal doom, e.g., Rom. 5 : 9 ; (*e*) of the deliverance of the nation of Israel at the Second Advent of Christ, e.g., Rom. 11 : 26 ; (*f*) inclusively for all the blessings bestowed by God on men in Christ, e.g., Luke 19 : 10 ; John 10 : 9 ; 1 Cor. 10 : 33 ; 1 Tim. 1 : 15 ; (*g*) of those who endure to the end of the time of the great tribulation, Matt. 10 : 22 ; Mark 13 : 13 ; (*h*) of the individual believer, who, though losing his reward at the Judgment-Seat of Christ hereafter, will not lose his salvation, 1 Cor. 3 : 15 ; 5 : 5 ; (*i*) of the deliverance of the nations at the Millennium, Rev. 21 : 24 (in some mss.). See SALVATION.

2. DIASŌZŌ (διασώζω), to bring safely through (*dia*, through, and No. 1), is used (*a*) of the healing of the sick by the Lord, Matt. 14 : 36, R.V., " were made whole " (A.V. adds " perfectly ") ; Luke 7 : 3 ; (*b*) of bringing safe to a destination, Acts 23 : 24 ; (*c*) of keeping a person safe, 27 : 43 ; (*d*) of escaping through the perils of shipwreck, 27 : 44 ; 28 : 1, 4, Passive Voice ; (*e*) through the Flood, 1 Pet. 3 : 20. See ESCAPE, WHOLE.¶

Note : In 2 Pet. 2 : 5, A.V., *phulassō*, to guard, keep, preserve, is translated " saved " (R.V., " preserved "). In Luke 17 : 33 some mss. have *sōzō* (A.V., " save "), for the R.V. : see GAIN, B, No. 3. For " save alive," Luke 17 : 33, R.V., see LIVE, No. 6.

B. Noun.

PERIPOIĒSIS (περιποίησις), (*a*) preservation, (*b*) acquiring or gaining something, is used in this latter sense in Heb. 10 : 39, translated " saving " (R.V. marg., " gaining ") ; the reference here is to salvation in its completeness. See OBTAIN, POSSESSION.

Note : In Heb. 11 : 7 *sōtēria* is rendered " saving." See SALVATION.

SAVING (Preposition)

PAREKTOS (παρεκτός), used as a preposition, denotes "saving," Matt. 5 : 32 (in some mss., 19 : 9). See EXCEPT.¶

Note : In Luke 4 : 27 and Rev. 2 : 17, A.V., *ei mē* (lit., 'if not'), is translated "saving" (R.V., "but only" and "but").

SAVIOUR

SŌTĒR (σωτήρ), a saviour, deliverer, preserver, is used (*a*) of God, Luke 1 : 47 ; 1 Tim. 1 : 1 ; 2 : 3 ; 4 : 10 (in the sense of Preserver, since He gives "to all life and breath and all things ") ; Tit. 1 : 3 ; 2 : 10 ; 3 : 4 ; Jude 25 ; (*b*) of Christ, Luke 2 : 11 ; John 4 : 42 ; Acts 5 : 31 ; 13 : 23 (of Israel) ; Eph. 5 : 23 (the Sustainer and Preserver of the Church, His "body ") ; Phil. 3 : 20 (at His return to receive the Church to Himself) ; 2 Tim. 1 : 10 (with reference to His Incarnation, "the days of His flesh ") ; Tit. 1 : 4 (a title shared, in the context, with God the Father) ; 2 : 13, R.V., "our great God and Saviour Jesus Christ," the pronoun "our," at the beginning of the whole clause, includes all the titles ; Tit. 3 : 6 ; 2 Pet. 1 : 1, "our God and Saviour Jesus Christ," R.V., where the pronoun "our," coming immediately in connection with "God," involves the inclusion of both titles as referring to Christ, just as in the parallel in ver. 11, "our Lord and Saviour Jesus Christ " (A.V. and R.V.) ; these passages are therefore a testimony to His Deity ; 2 Pet. 2 : 20 ; 3 : 2, 18 ; 1 John 4 : 14.¶

SAVOUR (Noun and Verb)
A. Nouns.

1. EUŌDIA (εὐωδία), fragrance (*eu*, well, *ozō*, to smell), is used metaphorically (*a*) of those who in the testimony of the gospel are to God "a sweet savour of Christ," 2 Cor. 2 : 15 ; (*b*) of the giving up of His life by Christ for us, an offering and a sacrifice to God for an odour (*osmē*, see No. 2) of "a sweet smell," Eph. 5 : 2, R.V. [A.V., "a sweet smelling (savour) "] ; (*c*) of material assistance sent to Paul from the church at Philippi " (an odour) of a sweet smell," Phil. 4 : 18. In all three instances the fragrance is that which ascends to God through the Person, and as a result of the Sacrifice, of Christ.¶

2. OSMĒ (ὀσμή), a smell, odour (from *ozō*, to smell ; Eng., ozone), is translated "odour " in John 12 : 3 ; it is used elsewhere in connection with No. 1, in the three passages mentioned, as of an odour accompanying an acceptable sacrifice ; in 2 Cor. 2 : 14, 16 (twice), of the "savour " of the knowledge of Christ through Gospel testimony, in the case of the perishing "a savour from death unto death," as of that which arises from what is dead (the spiritual condition of the unregenerate) ; in the case of the saved "a savour from life unto life," as from that which arises from what is instinct with life (the spiritual condition of the regenerate) ; in

Eph. 5 : 2, " a (sweetsmelling) savour ; " in Phil. 4 : 18, "an odour (of a sweet smell) ; " cp. No. 1. See ODOUR.¶

B. Verb.

MŌRAINŌ (μωραίνω), primarily, to be foolish, is used of salt that has lost its savour, Matt. 5 : 13 ; Luke 14 : 34. See FOOLISH, B, No. 1.

Note : In the A.V. of Matt. 16 : 23 and Mark 8 : 33, *phroneō*, to think, to mind, is translated " thou savourest " (R.V., " thou mindest ").

SAW ASUNDER

PRIZŌ or PRIŌ (πρίζω), to saw asunder, occurs in Heb. 11 : 37. Some have seen here a reference to the tradition of Isaiah's martyrdom under Manasseh.¶ In the Sept., Amos 1 : 3.¶ Cp. *diapriō*, .to cut to the heart, Acts 5 : 33 ; 7 : 54.¶

SAY

1. LEGŌ (λέγω), primarily, to pick out, gather, chiefly denotes to say, speak, affirm, whether of actual speech, e.g., Matt. 11 : 17, or of unspoken thought, e.g., Matt. 3 : 9, or of a message in writing, e.g., 2 Cor. 8 : 8. The 2nd aorist form *eipon* is used to supply that tense, which is lacking in *legō*.

Concerning the phrase " he answered and said," it is a well known peculiarity of Hebrew narrative style that a speech is introduced, not simply by ' and he said,' but by prefixing " and he answered " (*apokrinomai*, with *eipon*). In Matt. 14 : 27, " saying," and Mark 6 : 50, " and saith," emphasis is perhaps laid on the fact that the Lord, hitherto silent as He moved over the lake, then addressed His disciples. That the phrase sometimes occurs where no explicit question has preceded (e.g., Matt. 11 : 25 ; 17 : 4 ; 28 : 5 ; Mark 11 : 14 ; 12 : 35 ; Luke 13 : 15 ; 14 : 3 ; John 5 : 17, 19), illustrates the use of the Hebrew idiom.

Note : A characteristic of *legō* is that it refers to the purport or sentiment of what is said as well as the connection of the words ; this is illustrated in Heb. 8 : 1, R.V., " (in the things which) we are saying," A.V., " (which) we have spoken." In comparison with *laleō* (No. 2), *legō* refers especially to the substance of what is said, *laleō*, to the words conveying the utterance ; see, e.g., John 12 : 49, " what I should say (*legō*, in the 2nd aorist subjunctive form *eipō*), and what I should speak (*laleō*) ; " ver. 50, " even as the Father hath said (*legō*, in the perfect form *eirēke*) unto Me, so I speak " (*laleō*) ; cp. 1 Cor. 14 : 34, " saith (*legō*) the law ; " ver. 35, " to speak " (*laleō*). Sometimes *laleō* signifies the utterance, as opposed to silence, *legō* declares what is said ; e.g., Rom. 3 : 19, " what things soever the law saith (*legō*), it speaketh (*laleō*) to them that are under the law ; " see also Mark 6 : 50 ; Luke 24 : 6. In the N.T. *laleō* never has the meaning to chatter.

2. LALEŌ (λαλέω), to speak, is sometimes translated to say ; in the following where the A.V. renders it thus, the R.V. alters it to the verb to

speak, e.g., John 8 : 25 (3rd part), 26 ; 16 : 6 ; 18 : 20 (2nd part), 21 (1st part) ; Acts 3 : 22 (2nd part) ; 1 Cor. 9 : 8 (1st part) ; Heb. 5 : 5 ; in the following the R.V. uses the verb to say, John 16 : 18 ; Acts 23 : 18 (2nd part) ; 26 : 22 (2nd part) ; Heb. 11 : 18. See Note above, and SPEAK, TALK, TELL, UTTER.

3. PHĒMI (φημί), to declare, say, (a) is frequently used in quoting the words of another, e.g., Matt. 13 : 29 ; 26 : 61 ; (b) is interjected into the recorded words, e.g., Acts 23 : 35 ; (c) is used impersonally, 2 Cor. 10 : 10.

4. EIRŌ (εἴρω), an obsolete verb, has the future tense ereō, used, e.g., in Matt. 7 : 4 ; Luke 4 : 23 (2nd part) ; 13 : 25 (last part) ; Rom. 3 : 5 ; 4 : 1 ; 6 : 1 ; 7 : 7 (1st part) ; 8 : 31 ; 9 : 14, 19, 20, 30 ; 11 : 19 ; 1 Cor. 15 : 35 ; 2 Cor. 12 : 6 ; Jas. 2 : 18. The perfect is used, e.g., in John 12 : 50 ; see No. 1, Note. The 1st aorist passive, " it was said," is used in Rom. 9 : 12, 26 ; Rev. 6 : 11. See SPEAK, No. 13.

5. PROEIPON (προεῖπον) and proereō, to say before, used as aorist and future respectively of prolegō (pro, before, and No. 1), is used (a) of prophecy, e.g., Rom. 9 : 29 ; ' to tell before,' Matt. 24 : 25 ; Mark 13 : 23 ; " were spoken before," 2 Pet. 3 : 2 ; Jude 17 ; (b) of saying before, 2 Cor. 7 : 3 ; 13 : 2, R.V. (A.V., to tell before and foretell) ; Gal. 1 : 9 ; 5 : 21 ; in 1 Thess. 4 : 6, " we forewarned," R.V. See FORETELL, FOREWARN, TELL.

6. ANTEIPON (ἀντεῖπον), to say against (anti, against, and No. 1), is so rendered in Acts 4 : 14. See GAINSAY.

Notes : (1) Phaskō, to affirm, assert, is translated " saying " in Acts 24 : 9, A.V. (R.V., " affirming "), and Rev. 2 : 2 in some mss. (A.V.). See AFFIRM, No. 3. (2) In Acts 2 : 14, A.V., apophthengomai, to speak forth (R.V.), is rendered " said." (3) The phrase tout 'esti (i.e., touto esti), " that is," is so translated in Matt. 27 : 46, R.V. (A.V., " that is to say ") ; so Acts 1 : 19 ; in Heb. 9 : 11 and 10 : 20, A.V. and R.V., " that is to say ; " in Mark 7 : 11 the phrase is ho esti, lit., ' which is ; ' the phrase ho legetai, lit., ' which is said,' John 1 : 38 and 20 : 16, is rendered " which is to say." (4) In Luke 7 : 40 and Acts 13 : 15, the imperative mood of eipon and legō, respectively, is rendered " say on." (5) In Mark 6 : 22, A.V., autēs, " herself," R.V., is rendered " the said." (6) In Heb. 5 : 11, " we have many things to say " is, lit., ' much (polus) is the word (or discourse, logos) for us.'

SAYING

1. LOGOS (λόγος), a word, as embodying a conception or idea, denotes among its various meanings, a saying, statement or declaration, uttered (a) by God ; R.V., " word " or " words " (A.V., " saying "), e.g., in John 8 : 55 ; Rom. 3 : 4 ; Rev. 19 : 9 ; 22 : 6, 7, 9, 10 ; (b) by Christ, e.g., Mark 8 : 32 ; 9 : 10 ; 10 : 22 ; Luke 9 : 28 ; John 6 : 60 ; 21 : 23 ; the R.V. appropriately substitutes " word " or " words " for A.V.,

" saying " or " sayings," especially in John's Gospel, e.g., 7 : 36, 40 ; 8 : 51, 52 ;   10 : 19 ;   14 : 24 ;   15 : 20 ;   18 : 9, 32 ;   19 : 13 ;   (c) by an angel, Luke 1 : 29 ;   (d) by O.T. prophets, John 12 : 38 (R.V., " word ") ; Rom. 13 : 9 (ditto) ; 1 Cor. 15 : 54 ; (e) by the Apostle Paul in the Pastoral Epp., 1 Tim. 1 : 15 ;   3 : 1 ;   4 : 9 ;   2 Tim. 2 : 11 ;   Tit. 3 : 8 ;   (f) by other men, Mark 7 : 29 ; Acts 7 : 29 ; John 4 : 37 (in general).   See ACCOUNT, and especially WORD.

2. RHĒMA (ῥῆμα), that which is said, a word, is rendered " saying " or " sayings " in Mark 9 : 32 ; Luke 1 : 65 ;   2 : 17, 50, 51 ;   7 : 1 ;   9 : 45 (twice) ;   18 : 34.   See WORD.

Note : In Acts 14 : 18, "with these sayings" is, lit., 'saying (legō) these things.'   For *lalia*, " saying," John 4 : 42, A.V., see SPEECH, No. 2.

SCALE

LEPIS (λεπίς), from *lepō*, to peel, occurs in Acts 9 : 18.¶

For SCARCE, SCARCELY see DIFFICULTY

SCARLET

KOKKINOS (κόκκινος) is derived from *kokkos*, used of the ' berries ' (clusters of the eggs of an insect) collected from the *ilex coccifera* ; the colour, however, is obtained from the cochineal insect, which attaches itself to the leaves and twigs of the coccifera oak ; another species is raised on the leaves of the *cactus ficus*.   The Arabic name for this insect is *qirmiz*, whence the word crimson.   It is used (a) of scarlet wool, Heb. 9 : 19 ; cp., in connection with the cleansing of a leper, Lev. 14 : 4, 6, " scarlet ; " with the offering of the red heifer, Numb. 19 : 6 ; (b) of the robe put on Christ by the soldiers, Matt. 27 : 28 ; (c) of the " beast " seen in symbolic vision in Rev. 17 : 3, " scarlet-coloured ; " (d) of the clothing of the " woman " as seen sitting on the " beast," 17 : 4 ; (e) of part of the merchandise of Babylon, 18 : 12 ; (f) figuratively, of the glory of the city itself, 18 : 16 ;   the neuter is used in the last three instances.¶

SCATTER

A. Verbs.

1. SKORPIZŌ (σκορπίζω) is used in Matt. 12 : 30 ; Luke 11 : 23 ; John 10 : 12 ;   16 : 32 ;   2 Cor. 9 : 9, R.V.   See DISPERSE, No. 2.¶

2. DIASKORPIZŌ (διασκορπίζω), to scatter abroad, is rendered to scatter in Matt. 25 : 24, 26, R.V. (A.V., " strawed ") ;   26 : 31 ;   Mark 14 : 27 ;   Luke 1 : 51 ;   John 11 : 52 ;   Acts 5 : 37, R.V.   See DISPERSE, No. 3.

3. DIASPEIRŌ (διασπείρω), to scatter abroad (*dia*, throughout, *speirō*, to sow seed), is used in Acts 8 : 1, 4 ;   11 : 19, all of the church in Jerusalem scattered through persecution ;   the word in general is

suggestive of the effects of the scattering in the sowing of the spiritual seed of the Word of life. See DISPERSE, No. 4.¶

4. RHIPTŌ (ῥίπτω), to throw, cast, hurl, to be cast down, prostrate, is used in Matt. 9 : 36 of people who were scattered as sheep without a shepherd. See CAST, No. 2, THROW.

5. LIKMAŌ (λικμάω), to winnow (*likmos*, a winnowing-fan), is rendered "will scatter . . . as dust" in Matt. 21 : 44 and Luke 20 : 18, R.V. (A.V., "will grind . . . to powder"). See GRIND, Note.¶

6. DIALUŌ (διαλύω), to dissolve, is translated "scattered" in Acts 5 : 36, A.V. ; see DISPERSE, No. 1.¶

B. Noun.

DIASPORA (διασπορά), a dispersion, is rendered "scattered abroad" in Jas. 1 : 1, A.V. ; "scattered" in 1 Pet. 1 : 1, A.V. ; see DISPERSION, B.

For SCEPTRE see ROD

SCHISM

SCHISMA (σχίσμα), a rent, division, is translated "schism" in 1 Cor. 12 : 25, metaphorically of the contrary condition to that which God has designed for a local church in 'tempering the body together' (ver. 24), the members having "the same care one for another" ("the same" being emphatic). See DIVISION, No. 3, RENT.

SCHOOL

SCHOLĒ (σχολή) (whence Eng., school) primarily denotes leisure, then, that for which leisure was employed, a disputation, lecture ; hence, by metonymy, the place where lectures are delivered, a school, Acts 19 : 9.¶

For SCHOOLMASTER, Gal. 3 : 24, 25, see INSTRUCTOR, B, No. 1

SCIENCE

GNŌSIS (γνῶσις) is translated "science" in the A.V. of 1 Tim. 6 : 20 ; the word simply means "knowledge" (R.V.), where the reference is to the teaching of the Gnostics (lit., the knowers) 'falsely called knowledge.' Science in the modern sense of the word, viz., the investigation, discovery and classification of secondary laws, is unknown in Scripture. See KNOW, C, No. 1.

SCOFF

EKMUKTĒRIZŌ (ἐκμυκτηρίζω), to hold up the nose in derision at (*ek*, from, used intensively, *muktērizo*, to mock ; from *muktēr*, the nose), is translated "scoffed at" in Luke 16 : 14, R.V. (A.V., "derided"), of the Pharisees in their derision of Christ on account of His teaching ; in 23 : 35 (ditto), of the mockery of Christ on the Cross by the rulers of the people.¶ In the Sept., Ps. 2 : 4 ; 22 : 7 ; 35 : 16.¶

For SCOFFERS, 2 Pet. 3 : 3, A.V., see MOCKERS

SCORCH, SCORCHING
A. Verb.

KAUMATIZŌ (καυματίζω), to scorch (from *kauma*, heat), is used (a) of seed that had not much earth, Matt. 13 : 6 ; Mark 4 : 6 ; (b) of men, stricken retributively by the sun's heat, Rev. 16 : 8, 9.¶

B. Noun.

KAUSŌN (καύσων), burning heat (akin to *kaiō*, to burn), is translated " scorching heat " in Matt. 20 : 12 (A.V., " heat ") ; Luke 12 : 55 (ditto) ; in Jas. 1 : 11, R.V., " scorching wind " (A.V., " burning heat "), here the reference is to a hot wind from the east (cp. Job 1 : 19). See HEAT.¶ In the Sept., Job 27 : 21 ; Jer. 18 : 17 ; 51 : 1 ; Ezek. 17 : 10 ; 19 : 12 ; Hos. 12 : 1 ; 13 : 15 ; Jonah 4 : 8.¶

For SCORN see LAUGH

SCORPION

SKORPIOS (σκορπίος), akin to *skorpizō*, to scatter (which see), is a small animal (the largest of the several species is 6 in. long) like a lobster, but with a long tail, at the end of which is its venomous sting ; the pain, the position of the sting and the effect are mentioned in Rev. 9 : 3, 5, 10. The Lord's rhetorical question as to the provision of a scorpion instead of an egg, Luke 11 : 12, is, firstly, an allusion to the egg-like shape of the creature when at rest ; secondly, an indication of the abhorrence with which it is regarded.   In Luke 10 : 19, the Lord's assurance to the disciples of the authority given them by Him to tread upon serpents and scorpions conveys the thought of victory over spiritually antagonistic forces, the powers of darkness, as is shown by His reference to the " power of the enemy " and by the context in vv. 17, 20.¶

SCOURGE (Noun and Verb)
A. Noun.

PHRAGELLION (φραγέλλιον), a whip (from Latin, *flagellum*), is used of the scourge of small cords which the Lord made and employed before cleansing the Temple, John 2 : 15.   However He actually used it, the whip was in itself a sign of authority and judgment.¶

B. Verbs.

1. PHRAGELLOŌ (φραγελλόω) (akin to A : Latin, *flagello ;* Eng., flagellate), is the word used in Matt. 27 : 26, and Mark 15 : 15, of the scourging endured by Christ and administered by the order of Pilate. Under the Roman method of scourging, the person was stripped and tied in a bending posture to a pillar, or stretched on a frame.   The scourge was made of leathern thongs, weighted with sharp pieces of bone or lead, which tore the flesh of both the back and the breast (cp. Psa. 22 : 17).

Eusebius (*Chron.*) records his having witnessed the suffering of martyrs who died under this treatment.¶

Note : In John ,19 : 1 the scourging of Christ is described by Verb No. 2, as also in His prophecy of His sufferings, Matt. 20 : 19 ; Mark 10 : 34 ; Luke 18 : 33. In Acts 22 : 25 the similar punishment about to be administered to Paul is described by Verb No. 3 (the scourging of Roman citizens was prohibited by the Porcian law of 197, B.C.).

2. MASTIGOŌ (μαστιγόω), akin to *mastix* (see below), is used (*a*) as mentioned under No. 1 ; (*b*) of Jewish scourgings, Matt. 10 : 17 and 23 : 34 ; (*c*) metaphorically, in Heb. 12 : 6, of the chastening by the Lord administered in love to His spiritual sons.¶

Note : The Jewish method of scourging, as described in the Mishna, was by the use of three thongs of leather, the offender receiving thirteen stripes on the bare breast and thirteen on each shoulder, the "forty stripes save one," as administered to Paul five times (2 Cor. 11 : 24). See also SCOURGINGS (below).

3. MASTIZŌ (μαστίζω), akin to No. 2, occurs in Acts 22 : 25 (see No. 1, above).¶　In the Sept., Numb. 22 : 25.¶

SCOURGING (-S)

MASTIX (μάστιξ), a whip, scourge, is used (*a*) with the meaning scourging, in Acts 22 : 24, of the Roman method (see above, B, No. 1, Note) ; (*b*) in Heb. 11 : 36, of the sufferings of saints in the O.T. times. Among the Hebrews the usual mode, legal and domestic, was that of beating with a rod (see 2 Cor. 11 : 25) ; (*c*) metaphorically, of disease or suffering : see PLAGUE, No. 1.

SCRIBE (-S)

GRAMMATEUS (γραμματεύς), from *gramma*, a writing, denotes a scribe, a man of letters, a teacher of the law ; the scribes are mentioned frequently in the Synoptists, especially in connection with the Pharisees, with whom they virtually formed one party (see Luke 5 : 21), sometimes with the chief priests, e.g., Matt. 2 : 4 ; Mark 8 : 31 ; 10 : 33 ; 11 : 18, 27 ; Luke 9 : 22. They are mentioned only once in John's Gospel, 8 : 3, three times in the Acts, 4 : 5 ; 6 : 12 ; 23 : 9 ; elsewhere only in 1 Cor. 1 : 20, in the singular. They were considered naturally qualified to teach in the Synagogues, Mark 1 : 22. They were ambitious of honour, e.g., Matt. 23 : 5–11, which they demanded especially from their pupils, and which was readily granted them, as well as by the people generally. Like Ezra (Ezra 7 : 12), the scribes were found originally among the priests and Levites. The priests being the official interpreters of the Law, the scribes ere long became an independent company ; though they never held political power, they became leaders of the people.

Their functions regarding the Law were to teach it, develop it, and use it in connection with the Sanhedrin and various local courts. They also occupied themselves with the sacred writings both historical and didactic. They attached the utmost importance to ascetic elements, by which the nation was especially separated from the Gentiles. In their régime piety was reduced to external formalism. Only that was of value which was governed by external precept. Life under them became a burden ; they themselves sought to evade certain of their own precepts, Matt. 23 : 16, ff. ; Luke 11 : 46 ; by their traditions the Law, instead of being a help in moral and spiritual life, became an instrument for preventing true access to God, Luke 11 : 52. Hence the Lord's stern denunciations of them and the Pharisees (see PHARISEES).

  Note : The word *grammateus* is used of the town clerk in Ephesus, Acts 19 : 35.

For SCRIP see WALLET

SCRIPTURE

  1. GRAPHĒ (γραφή), akin to *graphō*, to write (Eng., graph, graphic, etc.), primarily denotes a drawing, painting ; then a writing, (a) of the O.T. Scriptures, (1) in the plural, the whole, e.g., Matt. 21 : 42 ; 22 : 29 ; John 5 : 39 ; Acts 17 : 11 ; 18 : 24 ; Rom. 1 : 2, where "the prophets" comprises the O.T. writers in general ; 15 : 4 ; 16 : 26, lit., ' prophetic writings,' expressing the character of all the Scriptures ; (2) in the singular in reference to a particular passage, e.g., Mark 12 : 10 ; Luke 4 : 21 ; John 2 : 22 ; 10 : 35 (though applicable to all) ; 19 : 24, 28, 36, 37 ; 20 : 9 ; Acts 1 : 16 ; 8 : 32, 35 ; Rom. 4 : 3 ; 9 : 17 ; 10 : 11 ; 11 : 2 ; Gal. 3 : 8, 22 ; 4 : 30 ; 1 Tim. 5 : 18, where the 2nd quotation is from Luke 10 : 7, from which it may be inferred that the Apostle included Luke's Gospel as " Scripture " alike with Deuteronomy, from which the first quotation is taken ; in reference to the whole, e.g. Jas. 4 : 5 (see R.V., a separate rhetorical question from the one which follows) ; in 2 Pet. 1 : 20, "no prophecy of Scripture," a description of all, with special application to the O.T. in the next verse ; (b) of the O.T. Scriptures (those accepted by the Jews as canonical) and all those of the N.T. which were to be accepted by Christians as authoritative, 2 Tim. 3 : 16 ; these latter were to be discriminated from the many forged epistles and other religious writings already produced and circulated in Timothy's time. Such discrimination would be directed by the fact that " every Scripture," characterized by inspiration of God, would be profitable for the purposes mentioned ; so the R.V. The A.V. states truth concerning the completed Canon of Scripture, but that was not complete when the Apostle wrote to Timothy.

  The Scriptures are frequently personified by the N.T. writers (as by the Jews, John 7 : 42), (a) as speaking with Divine authority, e.g., John 19 : 37 ; Rom. 4 : 3 ; 9 : 17, where the Scripture is said to speak to Pharaoh, giving the message actually sent previously by God to him through Moses ; Jas. 4 : 5 (see above) ; (b) as possessed of the sentient quality of foresight, and the active power of preaching, Gal. 3 : 8, where the Scripture mentioned was written more than four centuries after the words were spoken. The Scripture, in such a case, stands for its Divine Author with an intimation that it remains perpetually characterized as the living voice of God. This Divine agency is again illustrated in Gal. 3 : 22 (cp. ver. 10 and Matt. 11 : 13).

2. GRAMMA (γράμμα), a letter of the alphabet, etc. is used of the Holy Scriptures in 2 Tim. 3 : 15. For the various uses of this word see LETTER.

SCROLL

BIBLION (βιβλίον), the diminutive of *biblos*, a book, is used in Rev. 6 : 14, of a scroll, the rolling up of which illustrates the removal of the heaven. See BOOK, No. 2.

SEA

A. Nouns.

1. THALASSA (θάλασσα) is used (a) chiefly literally, e.g., the Red Sea, Acts 7 : 36 ; 1 Cor. 10 : 1 ; Heb. 11 : 29 ; the sea of Galilee or Tiberias, Matt. 4 : 18 ; 15 : 29 ; Mark 6 : 48, 49, where the acts of Christ testified to His Deity ; John 6 : 1 ; 21 : 1 ; in general, e.g., Luke 17 : 2 ; Acts 4 : 24 ; Rom. 9 : 27 ; Rev. 16 : 3 ; 18 : 17 ; 20 : 8, 13 ; 21 : 1 ; in combination with No. 2, Matt. 18 : 6 ; (b) metaphorically, of the ungodly men described in Jude 13 (cp. Is. 57 : 20) ; (c) symbolically, in the apocalyptic vision of " a glassy sea like unto crystal," Rev. 4 : 6, emblematic of the fixed purity and holiness of all that appertains to the authority and judicial dealings of God ; in 15 : 2, the same, " mingled with fire," and, standing by it (R.V.) or on it (A.V. and R.V. marg.), those who had " come victorious from the beast " (chapt. 13) ; of the wild and restless condition of nations, Rev. 13 : 1 (see 17 : 1, 15), where " he stood " (R.V.) refers to the dragon, not John (A.V.) ; from the midst of this state arises the beast, symbolic of the final Gentile power dominating the federated nations of the Roman world (see Dan., chapts. 2, 7, etc.).

Note : For the change from " the sea " in Deut. 30 : 13, to " the abyss " in Rom. 10 : 7, see BOTTOM, B.

2. PELAGOS (πέλαγος), the deep sea, the deep, is translated " the depth " in Matt. 18 : 6, and is used of the Sea of Cilicia in Acts 27 : 5. See DEPTH, No. 2.¶ *Pelagos* signifies " the vast expanse of open water," *thalassa*, " the sea as contrasted with the land " (Trench, Syn., § xiii).

B. Adjectives.

1. ENALIOS (ἐνάλιος), " in the sea," lit., of, or belonging to, the salt water (from *hals*, salt), occurs in Jas. 3 : 7.¶

2. PARALIOS (παράλιος), by the sea, Luke 6 : 17 : see COAST.¶

3. PARATHALASSIOS (παραθαλάσσιος), by the sea, Matt. 4 : 13, see COAST, Note 2.¶

4. DITHALASSOS (διθάλασσος) primarily signifies divided into two

seas (*dis*, twice, and *thalassa*) ; then, dividing the sea, as of a reef or rocky projection running out into the sea, Acts 27 : 41.¶

SEAL (Noun and Verb)
A. Noun.

SPHRAGIS (σφραγίς) denotes (*a*) a seal or signet, Rev. 7 : 2, " the seal of the living God," an emblem of ownership and security, here combined with that of destination (as in Ezek. 9 : 4), the persons to be sealed being secured from destruction and marked for reward ; (*b*) the impression of a seal or signet, (1) literal, a seal on a book or roll, combining with the ideas of security and destination those of secrecy and postponement of disclosures, Rev. 5 : 1, 2, 5, 9 ; 6 : 1, 3, 5, 7, 9, 12 ; 8 : 1 ; (2) metaphorical, Rom. 4 : 11, said of circumcision, as an authentication of the righteousness of Abraham's faith, and an external attestation of the covenant made with him by God ; the Rabbis called circumcision " the seal of Abraham ; " in 1 Cor. 9 : 2, of converts as a seal or authentication of Paul's apostleship ; in 2 Tim. 2 : 19, " the firm foundation of God standeth, having this seal, The Lord knoweth them that are His," R.V., indicating ownership, authentication, security and destination, " and, Let every one that nameth the Name of the Lord depart from unrighteousness," indicating a ratification on the part of the believer of the determining counsel of God concerning him ; Rev. 9 : 4 distinguishes those who will be found without the seal of God on their foreheads [see (*a*) above and B, No. 1].¶

B. Verbs.

1. SPHRAGIZŌ (σφραγίζω), to seal (akin to A), is used to indicate (*a*) security and permanency (attempted but impossible), Matt. 27 : 66 ; on the contrary, of the doom of Satan, fixed and certain, Rev. 20 : 3, R.V., " sealed it over ; " (*b*) in Rom. 15 : 28, " when . . . I have . . . sealed to them this fruit," the formal ratification of the ministry of the churches of the Gentiles in Greece and Galatia to needy saints in Judæa, by Paul's faithful delivery of the gifts to them ; this material help was the fruit of his spiritual ministry to the Gentiles, who on their part were bringing forth the fruit of their having shared with them in spiritual things ; the metaphor stresses the sacred formalities of the transaction (Deissmann illustrates this from the papyri of Fayyum, in which the sealing of sacks guarantees the full complement of the contents) ; (*c*) secrecy and security and the postponement of disclosure, Rev. 10 : 4 ; in a negative command, 22 : 10 ; (*d*) ownership and security, together with destination, Rev. 7 : 3, 4, 5 (as with the noun in ver. 2 ; see A) ; the same three indications are conveyed in Eph. 1 : 13, in the metaphor of the sealing of believers by the gift of the Holy Spirit, upon believing (i.e., at the time of their regeneration, not after a lapse of time in their spiritual life, " having also believed "—not as A.V., " after that ye believed "— ; the aorist-participle marks the definiteness and completeness of the act of faith) ; the idea of destination is stressed by the phrase " the Holy Spirit of

promise" (see also ver. 14) ; so 4 : 30, " ye were sealed unto the day of redemption ; " so in 2 Cor. 1 : 22, where the Middle Voice intimates the special interest of the Sealer in His act ; (e) authentication by the believer (by receiving the witness of the Son) of the fact that " God is true," John 3 : 33 ; authentication by God in sealing the Son as the Giver of eternal life (with perhaps a figurative allusion to the impress of a mark upon loaves), 6 : 27.¶

Note : In Rev. 7, after the 5th verse (first part) the original does not repeat the mention of the sealing except in ver. 8 (last part) (hence the omission in the R.V.).

2. KATASPHRAGIZŌ (κατασφραγίζω), No. 1, strengthened by *kata*, intensive, is used of the book seen in the vision in Rev. 5 : 1, R.V., " close sealed (with seven seals)," the successive opening of which discloses the events destined to take place throughout the period covered by chapters 6 to 19.¶ In the Sept., Job 9 : 7 ; 37 : 7.¶

SEAM (without)

ARAPHOS or ARRHAPHOS (ἄραφος) denotes " without seam " (*a*, negative, and *rhaptō*, to sew), John 19 : 23.¶

SEARCH

1. ERAUNAŌ or EREUNAŌ, an earlier form, (ἐραυνάω), to search, examine, is used (a) of God, as searching the heart, Rom. 8 : 27 ; (b) of Christ, similarly, Rev. 2 : 23 ; (c) of the Holy Spirit, as searching all things, 1 Cor. 2 : 10, acting in the spirit of the believer ; (d) of the O.T. prophets, as searching their own writings concerning matters foretold of Christ, testified by the Spirit of Christ in them, 1 Pet. 1 : 11 (cp. No. 2) ; (e) of the Jews, as commanded by the Lord to search the Scriptures, John 5 : 39, A.V., and R.V. marg., " search," R.V. text, " ye search," either is possible grammatically ; (f) of Nicodemus as commanded similarly by the chief priests and Pharisees, John 7 : 52.¶

2. EXERAUNAŌ (ἐξεραυνάω), a strengthened form of No. 1 (ek, or ex, out), to search out, is used in 1 Pet. 1 : 10, " searched diligently ; " cp. No. 1 (d).¶

3. EXETAZŌ (ἐξετάζω), to examine closely, inquire carefully (from *etazō*, to examine), occurs in Matt. 2 : 8, R.V., " search out ; " so Matt. 10 : 11, R.V. : see INQUIRE, No. 4.

Note: For *anakrinō*, rendered " searched " in Acts 17 : 11, A.V., see EXAMINE.

For SEARED see BRANDED

SEASON (Noun)
A. Nouns.

1. KAIROS (καιρός), primarily, due measure, fitness, proportion, is used in the N.T. to signify a season, a time, a period possessed of certain

characteristics, frequently rendered " time " or " times ; " in the following the R.V. substitutes " season " for the A.V. " time," thus distinguishing the meaning from *chronos* (see No. 2) : Matt. 11 : 25 ; 12 : 1 ; 14 : 1 ; 21 : 34 ; Mark 11 : 13 ; Acts 3 : 19 ; 7 : 20 ; 17 : 26 ; Rom. 3 : 26 ; 5 : 6 ; 9 : 9 ; 13 : 11 ; 1 Cor. 7 : 5 ; Gal. 4 : 10 ; 1 Thess. 2 : 17, lit., ' for a season (of an hour) ; ' 2 Thess. 2 : 6 ; in Eph. 6 : 18, " at all seasons " (A.V., " always ") ; in Tit. 1 : 3, " His own seasons " (marg., " its ; " A.V., " in due times ") ; in the preceding clause *chronos* is used.

The characteristics of a period are exemplified in the use of the term with regard, e.g., to harvest, Matt. 13 : 30 ; reaping, Gal. 6 : 9 ; punishment, Matt. 8 : 29 ; discharging duties, Luke 12 : 42 ; opportunity for doing anything, whether good, e.g., Matt. 26 : 18 ; Gal. 6 : 10 (" opportunity ") ; Eph. 5 : 16 ; or evil, e.g., Rev. 12 : 12 ; the fulfilment of prophecy, Luke 1 : 20 ; Acts 3 : 19 ; 1 Pet. 1 : 11 ; a time suitable for a purpose, Luke 4 : 13, lit., ' until a season ; ' 2 Cor. 6 : 2 ; see further under No. 2. See ALWAYS, Note, OPPORTUNITY, TIME, WHILE.

2. CHRONOS (χρόνος), whence Eng. words beginning with chron—, denotes a space of time, whether long or short : (*a*) it implies duration, whether longer, e.g., Acts 1 : 21, " (all the) time ; " Acts 13 : 18 ; 20 : 18, R.V., " (all the) time " (A.V., " at all seasons ") ; or shorter, e.g., Luke 4 : 5 ; (*b*) it sometimes refers to the date of an occurrence, whether past, e.g., Matt. 2 : 7, or future, e.g., Acts 3 : 21 ; 7 : 17.

Broadly speaking, *chronos* expresses the duration of a period, *kairos* stresses it as marked by certain features ; thus in Acts 1 : 7, " the Father has set within His own authority " both the times (*chronos*), the lengths of the periods, and the seasons (*kairos*), epochs characterized by certain events ; in 1 Thess. 5 : 1, " times " refers to the length of the interval before the Parousia takes place (the presence of Christ with the saints when He comes to receive them to Himself at the Rapture), and to the length of time the Parousia will occupy ; " seasons " refers to the special features of the period before, during, and after the Parousia.

Chronos marks quantity, *kairos*, quality. Sometimes the distinction between the two words is not sharply defined as, e.g., in 2 Tim. 4 : 6, though even here the Apostle's " departure " signalizes the time (*kairos*). The words occur together in the Sept. only in Dan. 2 : 21 and Eccl. 3 : 1. *Chronos* is rendered " season " in Acts 19 : 22, A.V. (R.V., " a while ") ; 20 : 18 (R.V., "all the time," see above); Rev. 6 : 11, A.V. (R.V., " time ") ; so 20 : 3. In Luke 23 : 8 it is used with *hikanos* in the plural, R.V., " (of a long) time," more lit., ' (for a sufficient number) of times.'

In Rev. 10 : 6 *chronos* has the meaning " delay " (R.V., marg.), an important rendering for the understanding of the passage (the word being akin to *chronizō*, to take time, to linger, delay, Matt. 24 : 48 ; Luke 12 : 45). See DELAY, B, Note, SPACE, TIME, WHILE.

3. HŌRA (ὥρα), an hour, is translated " season " in John 5 : 35 ; 2 Cor. 7 : 8 ; Philm. 15 : see HOUR.

B. Adjective.

PROSKAIROS (πρόσκαιρος), temporary, transient, is rendered "for a season" in Heb. 11 : 25. See TEMPORAL, TIME, WHILE.

C. Adverbs.

1. AKAIROS (ἀκαίρως) denotes "out of season," unseasonably (akin to *akairos*, unseasonable, *a*, negative, and A, No. 1), 2 Tim. 4 : 2.¶

2. EUKAIROS (εὐκαίρως), "in season" (*eu*, well), 2 Tim. 4 : 2; it occurs also in Mark 14 : 11, "conveniently."¶

Note : For *oligon*, 1 Pet. 1 : 6, A.V., "for a season," see WHILE.

SEASON (Verb)

ARTUO (ἀρτύω), to arrange, make ready (cp. *artios*, fitted), is used of seasoning, Mark 9 : 50; Luke 14 : 34; Col. 4 : 6.¶

SEAT (Noun and Verb)
A. Nouns.

1. KATHEDRA (καθέδρα), from *kata*, down, and *hedra*, a seat, denotes a seat (Eng., cathedral), a chair, Matt. 21 : 12; Mark 11 : 15; of teachers, Matt. 23 : 2.¶

2. PROTOKATHEDRIA (πρωτοκαθεδρία), the first seat, Matt. 23 : 6; Mark 12 : 39; Luke 11 : 43; 20 : 46; see CHIEF, No. 6. Cp. ROOM.¶

Note : For *thronos*, sometimes translated "seat" in the A.V., see THRONE.

B. Verb.

KATHEMAI (κάθημαι), to sit, be seated, is translated "shall . . . be seated" in Luke 22 : 69, R.V.; "is seated," Col. 3 : 1, R.V. (A.V., "shall . . . sit" and "sitteth"). See SIT.

SECOND, SECONDARILY, SECONDLY

1. DEUTEROS (δεύτερος) denotes second in order with or without the idea of time, e.g., Matt. 22 : 26, 39; 2 Cor. 1 : 15; Rev. 2 : 11; in Rev. 14 : 8, R.V. only ("a second angel"); it is used in the neuter, *deuteron*, adverbially, signifying a second time, e.g., John 3 : 4; 21 : 16; Acts 7 : 13; Rev. 19 : 3, R.V. (A.V., "again"); Jude 5, "afterward" (R.V., marg., "the second time"); used with *ek* (of) idiomatically, the preposition signifying "for (the second time)," Mark 14 : 72; John 9 : 24 and Acts 11 : 9, R.V. (A.V., "again"); Heb. 9 : 28; in 1 Cor. 12 : 28, A.V., "secondarily," R.V., "secondly."

Note : In Acts 13 : 33 some mss. have *prōtos*, "(in the) first (psalm);" the 1st and 2nd Psalms were originally one, forming a prologue to the whole book; hence the numbering in the Sept.

2. DEUTERAIOS (δευτεραῖος), an adjective with an adverbial sense (from No. 1), is used in Acts 28 : 13, R.V., "on the second day" (A.V., "the next day"), lit., 'second day (persons we came).'¶

Note : In Luke 6 : 1, the A.V. translates those mss. which have *deuteroprōtos*, lit., 'second-first,' said of a sabbath (see R.V. marg.).¶

SECRET, SECRETLY
A. Adjectives.

1. KRUPTOS (κρυπτός), secret, hidden (akin to *kruptō*, to hide), Eng., crypt, cryptic etc., is used as an adjective and rendered " secret " in Luke 8 : 17, A.V. (R.V., " hid ") ; in the neuter, with *en*, in, as an adverbial phrase, " in secret," with the article, Matt. 6 : 4, 6 (twice in each ver.) ; without the article, John 7 : 4, 10 ; 18 : 20 ; in the neuter plural, with the article, " the secrets (of men)," Rom. 2 : 16 ; of the heart, 1 Cor. 14 : 25 ; in Luke 11 : 33, A.V., " a secret place " (R.V., " cellar "). See CELLAR, HIDDEN, INWARDLY.

2. APOKRUPHOS (ἀπόκρυφος) (whence Apocrypha), hidden, is translated " kept secret " in Mark 4 : 22, A.V. (R.V., " made secret ") ; " secret " in Luke 8 : 17, R.V. (A.V., " hid "). See HIDE, B, No. 2.

3. KRUPHAIOS (κρυφαῖος) occurs in the best mss. in Matt. 6 : 18 (twice ; some have No. 1).¶

B. Adverbs.

1. KRUPHĒ (κρυφῇ), akin to A, No. 1, secretly, in secret, is used in Eph. 5 : 12.¶

2. LATHRA (λάθρα̣), akin to *lanthanō*, to escape notice, be hidden, is translated " secretly " in John 11 : 28. See PRIVILY.

C. Verb.

KRUPTŌ (κρύπτω), to hide, is translated " secretly " in John 19 : 38 [perfect participle, Passive Voice, lit., ' (but) having been hidden '], referring to Nicodemus as having been a secret disciple of Christ ; in Matt. 13 : 35, A.V., it is translated " kept secret " (R.V., " hidden ").

Notes : (1) For *tameion*, translated " secret chambers " in Matt. 24 : 26, see CHAMBER, No. 1. (2) For the A.V. rendering of *sigaō*, in Rom. 16 : 25, " kept secret," see PEACE (hold one's), No. 2, and SILENCE. (3) For " I have learned the secret," see LEARN, No. 4.

SECT

HAIRESIS (αἵρεσις), a choosing, is translated " sect " throughout the Acts, except in 24 : 14, A.V., " heresy " (R.V., " sect ") ; it properly denotes a predilection either for a particular truth, or for a perversion of one, generally with the expectation of personal advantage ; hence, a division and the formation of a party or sect in contrast to the uniting power of " the truth," held *in toto ;* a sect is a division developed and brought to an issue ; the order " divisions, heresies " (marg. " parties ") in " the works of the flesh " in Gal. 5 : 19-21 is suggestive of this. See HERESY.

SECURE (Verb)

PERIKRATĒS (περικρατής), an adjective, signifies ' having full command of ' (*peri*, around, about, *krateō*, to be strong, to rule) ; it is used with *ginomai*, to become, in Acts 27 : 16, R.V., " to secure (the boat)," A.V., " to come by."¶

Note: In Matt. 28 : 14, A.V., *amerimnos*, without anxiety, with *poieō*, to make, is translated " we will . . . secure (you)," R.V., " we will . . . rid (you) of care." The Eng. " secure " is derived from the Latin *se*, free from, and *cura*, care. See CARE.

SECURITY

HIKANOS (*ἱκανός*), sufficient, is used in its neuter form with the article, as a noun, in Acts 17 : 9, " (when they had taken) security," i.e., satisfaction, lit., ' the sufficient.' The use of *hikanos* in this construction is a Latinism in Greek. See Moulton, Proleg., p. 20. Probably the bond given to the authorities by Jason and his friends included an undertaking that Paul would not return to Thessalonica. Any efforts to have the bond cancelled were unsuccessful ; hence the reference to the hindrance by Satan (1 Thess. 2 : 18). See ABLE, C, No. 2.

SEDITION
A. Nouns.

1. STASIS (*στάσις*), a dissension, an insurrection, is translated " sedition " in Acts 24 : 5, A.V. (R.V., " insurrections "). See DISSENSION, INSURRECTION.

2. DICHOSTASIA (*διχοστασία*), lit., a standing apart (*dicha*, asunder, apart, *stasis*, a standing), hence a dissension, division, is translated " seditions " in Gal. 5 : 20, A.V. See DIVISION, No. 2.

B. Verb.

ANASTATOŌ (*ἀναστατόω*), to excite, unsettle, ' to stir up to sedition,' is so translated in Acts 21 : 38, R.V. (A.V., " madest an uproar ") ; in 17 : 6, " have turned (the world) upside down," i.e., causing tumults ; in Gal. 5 : 12, R.V., " unsettle " (A.V., " trouble "), i.e., by false teaching (here in the continuous present tense, lit., ' those who are unsettling you '). The word was supposed not to have been used in profane authors. It has been found, however, in several of the papyri writings. See TURN, UNSETTLE.¶

SEDUCE, SEDUCING
A. Verbs.

1. PLANAŌ (*πλανάω*), to cause to wander, lead astray, is translated to seduce in 1 John 2 : 26, A.V. (R.V., " lead . . . astray ") ; in Rev. 2 : 20, to seduce. See DECEIT, C, No. 6.

2. APOPLANAŌ (*ἀποπλανάω*) is translated " seduce " in Mark 13 : 22 (R.V., " lead astray ") ; see LEAD, No. 13.

B. Adjective.

PLANOS (*πλάνος*), akin to A, lit., wandering, then, deceiving, is translated " seducing " in 1 Tim. 4 : 1. See DECEIVER, No. 1.

For SEDUCERS see IMPOSTORS

SEE, SEEING
A. Verbs.

1. BLEPŌ (βλέπω), to have sight, is used of bodily vision, e.g., Matt. 11 : 4 ; and mental, e.g., Matt. 13 : 13, 14 ; it is said of God the Father in Matt. 6 : 4, 6, 18 ; of Christ as seeing what the Father doeth, John 5 : 19. It especially stresses the thought of the person who sees.   For the various uses see BEHOLD, No. 2 ; see Note below.

2. HORAŌ (ὁράω), with the form *eidon*, serving for its aorist tense, and *opsomai*, for its future tense (Middle Voice), denotes to see, of bodily vision, e.g., John 6 : 36 ; and mental, e.g., Matt. 8 : 4 ; it is said of Christ as seeing the Father, John 6 : 46, and of what He had seen with the Father, 8 : 38.   It especially indicates the direction of the thought to the object seen.   See BEHOLD, No. 1.

Note : " *Horaō* and *blepō* both denote the physical act : *horaō*, in general, *blepō*, the single look ; *horaō* gives prominence to the discerning mind, *blepō* to the particular mood or point.   When the physical side recedes, *horaō* denotes perception in general (as resulting principally from vision) . . . *Blepō*, on the other hand, when its physical side recedes, gets a purely outward sense, look (open, incline) towards [as of a situation] " (Schmidt, Grimm-Thayer).

3. APHORAŌ (ἀφοράω), with *apeidon* serving as the aorist tense, to look away from one thing so as to see another (*apo*, from, and No. 2), as in Heb. 12 : 2, simply means to see in Phil. 2 : 23.¶

4. KATHORAŌ (καθοράω), lit., to look down (*kata*, and No. 2), denotes to discern clearly, Rom. 1 : 20, " are clearly seen."¶   In the Sept., Numb. 24 : 2 ; Job 10 : 4 ; 39 : 26.¶

5. DIABLEPŌ (διαβλέπω), to see clearly (*dia*, through, and No. 1), is used in Matt. 7 : 5 ; Luke 6 : 42 ; in Mark 8 : 25, R.V., " he looked stedfastly " (No. 6 is used in the next clause ; No. 1 in ver. 24, and No. 2 in the last part).¶

6. EMBLEPŌ (ἐμβλέπω), to look at (*en*, in, and No. 1), used of earnestly looking, is translated " saw " in Mark 8 : 25 (last part) ; " could (not) see " in Acts 22 : 11.   See BEHOLD, No. 3.

7. ANABLEPŌ (ἀναβλέπω), to look up, is translated " see," of the blind, in Luke 7 : 22, A.V. (R.V., " receive their sight ").   See SIGHT.

8. THEAOMAI (θεάομαι), to view attentively, to see with admiration, desire, or regard, stresses more especially the action of the person beholding, as with No. 1, in contrast to No 2 ; it is used in Matt. 11 : 7 (R.V., " to behold "), while *idein*, the infinitive of *eidon* (see under No. 2), is used in the questions in the next two verses ; in verse 7 the interest in the onlooker is stressed, in vv. 8, 9, the attention is especially directed to the object seen. The verb is translated to see in the A.V. and R.V. of Matt. 6 : 1 ; Mark 16 : 11, 14 ; John 6 : 5 ; Acts 8 : 18 (in some mss.) ; 21 : 27 ; Rom. 15 : 24 ; elsewhere, for the A.V., to see, the R.V. uses the verb to behold, bringing out its force more suitably.   See BEHOLD, No. 8.

9. THEŌREŌ (θεωρέω) denotes to be a spectator of, indicating the careful perusal of details in the object ; it points especially, as in No. 1, to the action of the person beholding, e.g., Matt. 28 : 1 ; the R.V. frequently renders it by to behold, for the A.V., to see, e.g., John 14 : 17, 19 ; 16 : 10, 16, 17, 19.   The difference between this verb and Nos. 1 and 2 is brought out in John 20 : 5, 6, 8 ; in ver. 5 *blepō* is used of John's sight of the linen cloths in the tomb, without his entering in ; he saw at a glance the Lord was not there ; in ver. 6 the closer contemplation by Peter is expressed in the verb *theōreō*.   But in ver. 8 the grasping by John of the significance of the undisturbed cloths is denoted by *eidon* (see No. 2, and see WRAP).

10. MUŌPAZŌ (μυωπάζω), to be short-sighted (*muō*, to shut, *ōps*, the eye ; cp. Eng., myopy, myopic : the root *mu* signifies a sound made with closed lips, e.g., in the words mutter, mute), occurs in 2 Pet. 1 : 9, R.V., " seeing only what is near " (A.V., " and cannot see afar off ") ; this does not contradict the preceding word " blind," it qualifies it ; he of whom it is true is blind in that he cannot discern spiritual things, he is near-sighted in that he is occupied in regarding worldly affairs.¶

11. PHAINŌ (φαίνω), to cause to appear, and in the Passive Voice, to appear, be manifest, is rendered " (that) they may be seen " in Matt. 6 : 5 ; " it was (never so) seen," 9 : 33.   See APPEAR.

Notes : (1) For *ide* and *idou*, regularly rendered " behold " in the R.V., see BEHOLD, No. 4.   (2) For *optanō*, in Acts 1 : 3, A.V., " being seen," see APPEAR, A, No. 7.   (3) For *historeō*, in Gal. 1 : 18, A.V., to see, see VISIT.   (4) For *prooraō*, and *proeidon*, to see before, see FORESEE. (5) For " make . . . see " see ENLIGHTEN.

B. Noun.

BLEMMA (βλέμμα), primarily, a look, a glance (akin to A, No. 1), denotes sight, 2 Pet. 2 : 8, rendered " seeing ; " some interpret it as meaning " look ; " Moulton and Milligan illustrate it thus from the papyri ; it seems difficult, however to take the next word " hearing " (in the similar construction) in this way.¶

SEED

1. SPERMA (σπέρμα), akin to *speirō*, to sow (Eng., sperm, spermatic etc.), has the following usages, (*a*) agricultural and botanical, e.g., Matt. 13 : 24, 27, 32 (for the A.V. of vv. 19, 20, 22, 23, see SOW, as in the R.V.) ; 1 Cor. 15 : 38 ; 2 Cor. 9 : 10 ; (*b*) physiological, Heb. 11 : 11 ; (*c*) metaphorical and by metonymy for offspring, posterity, (1) of natural offspring, e.g., Matt. 22 : 24, 25, R.V., " seed " (A.V., " issue ") ; John 7 : 42 ; 8 : 33, 37 ; Acts 3 : 25 ; Rom. 1 : 3 ; 4 : 13, 16, 18 ; 9 : 7 (twice), 8, 29 ; 11 : 1 ; 2 Cor. 11 : 22 ; Heb. 2 : 16 ; 11 : 18 ; Rev. 12 : 17 ; Gal. 3 : 16, 19, 29 ; in the 16th ver., " He saith not, And to seeds, as of many ; but as of one, And to thy seed, which is Christ," quoted from the Sept. of Gen. 13 : 15 and 17 : 7, 8, there is especial stress on the word " seed," as

referring to an individual (here, Christ) in fulfilment of the promises to Abraham—a unique use of the singular. While the plural form " seeds," neither in Hebrew nor in Greek, would have been natural any more than in English (it is not so used in Scripture of human offspring ; its plural occurrence is in 1 Sam. 8 : 15, of crops), yet if the Divine intention had been to refer to Abraham's natural descendants, another word could have been chosen in the plural, such as ' children ; ' all such words were, however, set aside, ' seed ' being selected as one that could be used in the singular, with the purpose of showing that the " seed " was Messiah. Some of the Rabbis had even regarded " seed," e.g., in Gen. 4 : 25 and Is. 53 : 10, as referring to the Coming One. Descendants were given to Abraham by other than natural means, so that through him Messiah might come, and the point of the Apostle's argument is that since the fulfilment of the promises of God is secured alone by Christ, they only who are " in Christ " can receive them ; (2) of spiritual offspring, Rom. 4 : 16, 18 ; 9 : 8 ; here " the children of the promise are reckoned for a seed " points, firstly, to Isaac's birth as being not according to the ordinary course of nature but by Divine promise, and, secondly, by analogy, to the fact that all believers are children of God by spiritual birth ; Gal. 3 : 29.

As to 1 John 3 : 9, " his seed abideth in him," it is possible to understand this as meaning that children of God (His seed) abide in Him, and do not go on doing (practising) sin (the verb to commit does not represent the original in this passage). Alternatively, the seed signifies the principle of spiritual life as imparted to the believer, which abides in him without possibility of removal or extinction ; the child of God remains eternally related to Christ, he who lives in sin has never become so related, he has not the principle of life in him. This meaning suits the context and the general tenor of the Epistle.

2. SPOROS (σπόρος), akin to No. 1, properly a sowing, denotes seed sown, (a) natural, Mark 4 : 26, 27 ; Luke 8 : 5, 11 (the natural being figuratively applied to the Word of God) ; 2 Cor. 9 : 10 (1st part) ; (b) metaphorically of material help to the needy, 2 Cor. 9 : 10 (2nd part), R.V., " (your) seed for sowing " (A.V., " seed sown ").¶

3. SPORA (σπορά), akin to No. 1, and like No. 2, a sowing, seedtime, denotes seed sown, 1 Pet. 1 : 23, of human offspring.¶ In the Sept., 2 Kings 19 : 29.¶

SEEING, SEEING THAT (conjunction), see † p. 9.

SEEK

1. ZĒTEŌ (ζητέω) signifies (a) to seek, to seek for, e.g., Matt. 7 : 7, 8 ; 13 : 45 ; Luke 24 : 5 ; John 6 : 24 ; of plotting against a person's life, Matt. 2 : 20 ; Acts 21 : 31 ; Rom. 11 : 3 ; metaphorically, to seek by thinking, to seek how to do something, or what to obtain, e.g., Mark 11 : 18 ; Luke 12 : 29 ; to seek to ascertain a meaning, John 16 : 19, " do

ye inquire ; " to seek God, Acts 17 : 27, R.V. ; Rom. 10 : 20 ; (b) to seek or strive after, endeavour, to desire, e.g., Matt. 12 : 46, 47, R.V., " seeking " (A.V., " desiring ") ; Luke 9 : 9, R.V., " sought " (A.V., " desired ") ; John 7 : 19, R.V., " seek ye " (A.V., " go ye about ") ; so ver. 20 ; Rom. 10 : 3, R.V., " seeking " (A.V., " going about ") ; of seeking the kingdom of God and His righteousness, in the sense of coveting earnestly, striving after, Matt. 6 : 33 ; " the things that are above," Col. 3 : 1 ; peace, 1 Pet. 3 : 11 ; (c) to require or demand, e.g., Mark 8 : 12 ; Luke 11 : 29 (some mss. have No. 4) ; 1 Cor. 4 : 2, " it is required ; " 2 Cor. 13 : 3, " ye seek." See ABOUT, B, Note, DESIRE, B, Note (2), ENDEAVOUR, GO, Note (2) (a), INQUIRE, REQUIRE.

2. ANAZĒTEŌ (ἀναζητέω), to seek carefully (ana, up, used intensively, and No. 1), is used of searching for human beings, difficulty in the effort being implied, Luke 2 : 44, 45 (some mss. have No. 1 in the latter ver.) ; Acts 11 : 25 ; numerous illustrations of this particular meaning in the papyri are given by Moulton and Milligan.¶ In the Sept., Job 3 : 4 ; 10 : 6.¶

3. EKZĒTEŌ (ἐκζητέω) signifies (a) to seek out (ek) or after, to search for ; e.g., God, Rom. 3 : 11 ; the Lord, Acts 15 : 17 ; in Heb. 11 : 6, R.V., " seek after " (A.V., " diligently seek ") ; 12 : 17, R.V., " sought diligently " (A.V., " sought carefully ") ; 1 Pet. 1 : 10, R.V., " sought " (A.V., " have inquired "), followed by exeraunaō, to search diligently ; (b) to require or demand, Luke 11 : 50, 51. See INQUIRE, Note (3), REQUIRE.¶

4. EPIZĒTEŌ (ἐπιζητέω), to seek after (directive, epi, towards), is always rendered in the R.V., by some form of the verb to seek, Acts 13 : 7, " sought " (A.V., " desired ") ; 19 : 39, " seek " (A.V., " inquire ") ; Phil. 4 : 17, " seek for " (A.V., " desire "), twice ; elsewhere, Matt. 6 : 32 ; 12 : 39 ; 16 : 4 ; Mark 8 : 12 (in some texts) ; Luke 12 : 30 ; Acts 12 : 19 ; Rom. 11 : 7 ; Heb. 11 : 14 ; 13 : 14. See DESIRE, INQUIRE.¶

5. OREGŌ (ὀρέγω), to reach out, or after, used in the Middle Voice is translated " seeketh " in 1 Tim. 3 : 1, R.V., of ' seeking overseership ' (A.V., " desireth "). See DESIRE, No. 5.

Note : For the R.V. renderings of zēloō, in Gal. 4 : 17, 18, " they zealously seek," " ye may seek," " to be zealously sought," see AFFECT, Note, and ZEALOUS.

SEEM

DOKEŌ (δοκέω) denotes (a) to be of opinion (akin to doxa, opinion), e.g., Luke 8 : 18, R.V., " thinketh " (A.V., " seemeth ") ; so 1 Cor. 3 : 18 ; to think, suppose, Jas. 1 : 26, R.V., " thinketh himself " (A.V., " seem ") ; see SUPPOSE, THINK ; (b) to seem, to be reputed, e.g., Acts 17 : 18 ; 1 Cor. 11 : 16 ; 12 : 22 ; 2 Cor. 10 : 9 ; Heb. 4 : 1 ; 12 : 11 ; for Gal. 2 : 2, 6, 9, see REPUTE ; (c) impersonally (1) to think (see THINK), (2) to seem good, Luke 1 : 3 ; Acts 15 : 22, R.V., " it seemed good " (A.V., " it pleased ") ;

15 : 25, 28 (ver. 34 in some mss.) ; in Heb. 12 : 10, the neuter of the present participle is used with the article, lit., ' the (thing) seeming good,' R.V., " (as) seemed good," A.V., " after (their own) pleasure." See ACCOUNT No. 1.

Notes : In Matt. 11 : 26 and Luke 10 : 21, *eudokia*, good pleasure, satisfaction (*eu*, well, and *dokeō*), is used with *ginomai*, to become, and translated " it seemed good," A.V. (R.V., " it was well-pleasing "). (2) In Luke 24 : 11, A.V., *phainō*, to appear (Passive Voice), is translated " seemed " (R.V., " appeared ").

For SEEMLY, R.V., see COMELY, B, and Note (2)

Note : In 1 Pet. 2 : 12, R.V., *kalos*, good, fair, is rendered " seemly."

SEIZE

1. SULLAMBANŌ (συλλαμβάνω), lit., to take together (*sun*, with, *lambanō*, to take or lay hold of), chiefly signifies to seize as a prisoner ; in the following the R.V. substitutes the more suitable and forceful verb, to seize, for A.V., to take : Matt. 26 : 55 ; Mark 14 : 48 ; Luke 22 : 54 ; John 18 : 12 ; Acts 12 : 3 ; 23 : 27 ; 26 : 21 ; in Acts 1 : 16, R.V. and A.V., " took." See CATCH, No. 8, CONCEIVE, HELP.

2. SUNARPAZŌ (συναρπάζω) is translated " seized " in the R.V. of Luke 8 : 29 ; Acts 6 : 12 ; 19 : 29 ; see CATCH, No. 7.

Note : In Matt. 21 : 38, the best texts have *echō*, to have (to take, R.V.) ; some have *katechō*, to lay hold of (A.V., " seize on ").

SELF, SELVES

1. AUTOMATOS (αὐτόματος), of oneself (Eng., automatic, automaton, etc.), is used in Mark 4 : 28 ; Acts 12 : 10. See ACCORD, B, No. 2.¶

2. AUTOS (αὐτός), he, also means self, in the reflexive pronouns myself, thyself, himself, etc. (see, e.g., HE), expressing distinction, exclusion, etc. ; it is usually emphatic in the nominative case, e.g., Luke 6 : 42 ; 11 : 4 ; John 18 : 28 ; Rom. 8 : 16, R.V., " Himself."

Note : In John 16 : 27, " the Father Himself (*autos*)," Field (*Notes on the Translation of the N.T.*) remarks that *autos* stands for *automatos*.

For SELF-CONDEMNED see CONDEMN, C, No. 1

SELF-CONTROL (without)

AKRATĒS (ἀκρατής), powerless (*a*, negative, *kratos*, strength), is rendered " without self-control," in 2 Tim. 3 : 3, R.V. ; see INCONTINENT.¶

SELFSAME

Notes : (1) In 2 Cor. 5 : 5, A.V., *auto touto*, this thing itself, " this very thing," R.V., is rendered " the selfsame ; " in 2 Cor. 7 : 11, R.V. and A.V., " this selfsame thing." (2) In Matt. 8 : 13, A.V., *ekeinos*, with the article, " that," R.V., is rendered "that selfsame." (3) In 1 Cor. 12 : 11, A.V., the article with *autos*, " the same," R.V., is rendered " the selfsame."

SELF-WILLED

AUTHADĒS (αὐθάδης), self-pleasing (*autos*, self, *hēdomai*, to please), denotes one who, dominated by self-interest, and inconsiderate of others, arrogantly asserts his own will, " self-willed," Tit. 1 : 7 ; 2 Pet. 2 : 10 (the opposite of *epieikēs*, gentle, e.g., 1 Tim. 3 : 3), " one so far overvaluing any determination at which he has himself once arrived that he will not be removed from it " (Trench, who compares and contrasts *philautos*, loving self, selfish ; Syn. §xciii).¶ In the Sept., Gen. 49 : 3, 7 ; Prov. 21 : 24.¶

SELL

1. PŌLEŌ (πωλέω), to exchange or barter, to sell, is used in the latter sense in the N.T., six times in Matthew, three in Mark, six in Luke ; in John only in connection with the cleansing of the Temple by the Lord, 2 : 14, 16 ; in Acts only in connection with the disposing of property for distribution among the community of believers, 4 : 34, 37 ; 5 : 1 ; elsewhere, 1 Cor. 10 : 25 ; Rev. 13 : 17.

2. PIPRASKŌ (πιπράσκω), from an earlier form, *peraō*, to carry across the sea for the purpose of selling or to export, is used (*a*) literally, Matt. 13 : 46 ; 18 : 25 ; 26 : 9 ; Mark 14 : 5 ; John 12 : 5 ; Acts 2 : 45 ; 4 : 34 ; 5 : 4 ; (*b*) metaphorically, Rom. 7 : 14, " sold under sin," i.e., as fully under the domination of sin as a slave is under his master ; the statement evinces an utter dissatisfaction with such a condition ; it expresses, not the condemnation of the unregenerate state, but the evil of bondage to a corrupt nature, involving the futility of making use of the Law as a means of deliverance.¶

3. APODIDŌMI (ἀποδίδωμι), to give up or back, also means, in the Middle Voice, to give up of one's own will ; hence, to sell ; it is so used in Peter's question to Sapphira as to selling the land, Acts 5 : 8 ; of the act of Joseph's brothers, 7 : 9 ; of Esau's act in selling his birthright, Heb. 12 : 16.

Note : In Jas. 4 : 13, A.V., *emporeuomai*, to trade (R.V.), is rendered " buy and sell."

For SELLER see PURPLE

SENATE

GEROUSIA (γερουσία), a council of elders (from *gerōn*, an old man, a term which early assumed a political sense among the Greeks, the notion of age being merged in that of dignity), is used in Acts 5 : 21, apparently epexegetically of the preceding word *sunedrion*, " council," the Sanhedrin.¶

SEND

1. APOSTELLŌ (ἀποστέλλω), lit., to send forth (apo, from), akin to apostolos, an apostle, denotes (a) to send on service, or with a commission, (1) of persons ; Christ, sent by the Father, Matt. 10 : 40 ; 15 : 24 ; 21 : 37 ; Mark 9 : 37 ; 12 : 6 ; Luke 4 : 18, 43 ; 9 : 48 ; 10 : 16 ; John 3 : 17 ; 5 : 36, 38 ; 6 : 29, 57 ; 7 : 29 ; 8 : 42 ; 10 : 36 ; 11 : 42 ; 17 : 3, 8, 18 (1st part), 21, 23, 25 ; 20 : 21 ; Acts 3 : 20 (future) ; 3 : 26 ; 1 John 4 : 9, 10, 14 ; the Holy Spirit, Luke 24 : 49 (in some texts ; see No. 3) ; 1 Pet. 1 : 12 ; Rev. 5 : 6 ; Moses, Acts 7 : 35 ; John the Baptist, John 1 : 6 ; 3 : 28 ; disciples and apostles, e.g., Matt. 10 : 16 ; Mark 11 : 1 ; Luke 22 : 8 ; John 4 : 38 ; 17 : 18 (2nd part) ; Acts 26 : 17 ; servants, e.g., Matt. 21 : 34 ; Luke 20 : 10 ; officers and officials, Mark 6 : 27 ; John 7 : 32 ; Acts 16 : 35 ; messengers, e.g., Acts 10 : 8, 17, 20 ; 15 : 27 ; evangelists, Rom. 10 : 15 ; angels, e.g., Matt. 24 : 31 ; Mark 13 : 27 ; Luke 1 : 19, 26 ; Heb. 1 : 14 ; Rev. 1 : 1 ; 22 : 6 ; demons, Mark 5 : 10 ; (2) of things, e.g., Matt. 21 : 3 ; Mark 4 : 29, R.V., marg., " sendeth forth," text," putteth forth " (A.V., " . . . in ") ; Acts 10 : 36 ; 11 : 30 ; 28 : 28 ; (b) to send away, dismiss, e.g., Mark 8 : 26 ; 12 : 3 ; Luke 4 : 18, " to set (at liberty)." See Note below, No. 2.

2. PEMPŌ (πέμπω), to send, is used (a) of persons : Christ, by the Father, Luke 20 : 13 ; John 4 : 34 ; 5 : 23, 24, 30, 37 ; 6 : 38, 39, (40), 44 ; 7 : 16, 18, 28, 33 ; 8 : 16, 18, 26, 29 ; 9 : 4 ; 12 : 44, 45, 49 ; 13 : 20 (2nd part) ; 14 : 24 ; 15 : 21 ; 16 : 5 ; Rom. 8 : 3 ; the Holy Spirit, John 14 : 26 ; 15 : 26 ; 16 : 7 ; Elijah, Luke 4 : 26 ; John the Baptist, John 1 : 33 ; disciples and apostles, e.g., Matt. 11 : 2 ; John 20 : 21 ; servants, e.g., Luke 20 : 11, 12 ; officials, Matt. 14 : 10 ; messengers, e.g., Acts 10 : 5, 32, 33 ; 15 : 22, 25 ; 2 Cor. 9 : 3 ; Eph. 6 : 22 ; Phil. 2 : 19, 23, 25 ; 1 Thess. 3 : 2, 5 ; Tit. 3 : 12 ; a prisoner, Acts 25 : 25, 27 ; potentates, by God, 1 Pet. 2 : 14 ; an angel, Rev. 22 : 16 ; demons, Mark 5 : 12 ; (b) of things, Acts 11 : 29 ; Phil. 4 : 16 ; 2 Thess. 2 : 11 ; Rev. 1 : 11 ; 11 : 10 ; 14 : 15, 18, R.V., " send forth " (A.V., " thrust in ").

Notes : (1) *Pempō* is a more general term than *apostellō ; apostellō* usually " suggests official or authoritative sending " (Thayer). A comparison of the usages mentioned above shows how nearly (in some cases practically quite) interchangeably they are used, and yet on close consideration the distinction just mentioned is discernible ; in the Gospel of John, cp. *pempō* in 5 . 23, 24, 30, 37, *apostellō* in 5 : 33, 36, 38 ; *pempō* in 6 : 38, 39, 44, *apostellō* in 6 : 29, 57 ; the two are not used simply for the sake of variety of expression. *Pempō* is not used in the Lord's prayer in chapt. 17, whereas *apostellō* is used six times.

(2) The sending of the Son by the Father was from the glory which He had with the Father into the world, by way of the Incarnation, not a sending out into the world after His birth, as if denoting His mission among and His manifestation to the people. " Hofmann, in support of his view that Jesus is called the Son of God only in virtue of His being

born of man, vainly urges that the simple accusative after *apostellō*
also denotes what the Person is or becomes by being sent. What he
states is true but only when the name of the object spoken of is chosen
to correspond with the purposed mission, as e.g., in Mark 1 : 2 ;
Luke 14 : 32 ; 19 : 14. We can no more say, ' God sent Jesus that He
should be His Son ' than we can render ' he sent his servants,' Matt.
21 : 34, in this manner. That the Sonship of Christ is anterior to His
mission to the world . . . is clear from John 16 : 28 ; cp. especially also
the double accusative in 1 John 4 : 14, ' the Father sent the Son the
Saviour of the world.' The expression that Jesus is sent by God denotes
the mission which He has to fulfil and the authority which backs Him "
(Cremer, *Lexicon of N.T. Greek*).

　　3. EXAPOSTELLŌ (ἐξαποστέλλω) denotes (*a*) to send forth : of the
Son by God the Father, Gal. 4 : 4 ; of the Holy Spirit, 4 : 6 ; Luke 24 : 49
in the best texts (some have No. 1) ; an angel, Acts 12 : 11 ; the ancestors
of Israel, Acts 7 : 12 ; Paul to the Gentiles, 22 : 21 ; of the word of
salvation, 13 : 26 (some mss. have No. 1) ; (*b*) to send away, Luke 1 : 53 ;
20 : 10, 11 ; Acts 9.: 30 ; 11 : 22 ; 17 : 14.¶

　　4. ANAPEMPŌ (ἀναπέμπω) denotes (*a*) to send up (*ana*, up, and No. 2),
to a higher authority, Luke 23 : 7, 15 ; Acts 25 : 21 (in the best texts ;
some have No. 2) ; this meaning is confirmed by examples from the
papyri (Moulton and Milligan), by Deissmann (*Bible Studies*, p. 229) ;
see also Field, *Notes on the Trans. of the N.T. ;* (*b*) to send back, Luke
23 : 11 ; Philm. 12.¶

　　5. EKPEMPŌ (ἐκπέμπω) denotes to send forth (*ek*, out of), Acts 13 : 4,
" being sent forth " ; 17 : 10, " sent away."¶

　　6. BALLŌ (βάλλω), to cast, throw, is translated " to send (peace) "
in Matt. 10 : 34 (twice), (R.V., marg., " cast "). See CAST.

　　7. EKBALLŌ (ἐκβάλλω), to cast out, or send out, is translated " sent
out " in Mark 1 : 43, R.V. (A.V., " sent away "), and in A.V. and R.V.
in Jas. 2 : 25. See CAST, No. 5.

　　8. APOLUŌ (ἀπολύω), to set free, to let go, is translated to send
away in Matt. 14 : 15, 22, 23 ; Mark 6 : 36, 45 ; 8 : 3, 9 ; Luke 8 : 38 ;
Acts 13 : 3, where the sending is not that of commissioning, but of letting
go, intimating that they would gladly have retained them (contrast
ekpempō, the act of commissioning by the Holy Spirit in ver. 4).

　　9. METAPEMPŌ (μεταπέμπω), to send after or for, fetch (*meta*, after),
is used only in the Acts ; in the Middle Voice, translated to send for in
10 : 22, 29 (2nd part : Passive Voice in the 1st part) ; 20 : 1, R.V. only
(some texts have *proskaleō*) ; 24 : 24, 26 ; 25 : 3 ; in 10 : 5 and 11 : 13,
R.V., " fetch." See FETCH.¶

　　10. BRUŌ (βρύω), to be full to bursting, was used of the earth in
producing vegetation, of plants in putting forth buds ; in Jas. 3 : 11 it
is said of springs gushing with water, " (doth the fountain) send
forth . . . ? "¶

11. SUNAPOSTELLŌ (συναποστέλλω), to send along with, is used in 2 Cor. 12 : 18.¶ In the Sept., Ex. 33 : 2, 12.¶

12. SUNPEMPŌ (συνπέμπω), to send along with, is used in 2 Cor. 8 : 18, 22.¶

Notes : (1) In Matt. 13 : 36, A.V., *aphiēmi*, to leave, is translated " He sent . . . away " (R.V., " He left ") ; so in Mark 4 : 36, A.V., " they had sent away," R.V., " leaving." (2) In Mark 6 : 46, *apotassomai*, to take leave of (R.V.) is translated " He had sent . . . away." (3) In John 13 : 16 *apostolos* is rendered " one (A.V., he) that is sent," R.V. marg., " an apostle ". (4) *Paristēmi* is rendered " send " in Matt. 26 : 53, R.V.

For SENSELESS see FOOLISH, No. 4

SENSES

AISTHĒTĒRION (αἰσθητήριον), sense, the faculty of perception, the organ of sense (akin to *aisthanomai*, to perceive), is used in Heb. 5 : 14, " senses," the capacities for spiritual apprehension.¶ In the Sept., Jer. 4 : 19, ' (I am pained . . . in the) sensitive powers (of my heart).'¶

For SENSUAL see NATURAL, A, No. 2

SENTENCE
A. Nouns.

1. KRIMA (κρίμα), a judgment, a decision passed on the faults of others, is used especially of God's judgment upon men, and translated " sentence" in 2 Pet. 2 : 3, R.V. (A.V., " judgment "). See JUDGMENT, No. 2.

2. KATADIKĒ (καταδίκη), a judicial sentence, condemnation, is translated " sentence " in Acts 25 : 15, R.V. (A.V., " judgment ") ; some mss. have *dikē*.¶

3. APOKRIMA (ἀπόκριμα) is translated " sentence " in 2 Cor. 1 : 9, A.V. (R.V., " answer "). See ANSWER, No. 2.¶

B. Verbs.

1. KRINŌ (κρίνω), to judge, to adjudge, is translated " (my) sentence is" in Acts 15 : 19, A.V., R.V., " (my) judgment is," lit., ' I (*ego*, emphatic) judge,' introducing the substance or draft of a resolution. See JUDGE, B, No. 1.

2. EPIKRINŌ (ἐπικρινω), to give sentence, is used in Luke 23 : 24.¶

SEPARATE
A. Verbs.

1. APHORIZŌ (ἀφορίζω), to mark off by bounds (*apo*, from, *horizō*, to determine ; *horos*, a limit), to separate, is used of " (*a*) the Divine action in setting men apart for the work of the gospel, Rom. 1 : 1 ; Gal. 1 : 15 ; (*b*) the Divine judgment upon men, Matt. 13 : 49 ; 25 : 32 ; (*c*) the

separation of Christians from unbelievers, Acts 19 : 9 ; 2 Cor. 6 : 17 ; (d) the separation of believers by unbelievers, Luke 6 : 22 ; (e) the withdrawal of Christians from their brethren, Gal. 2 : 12. In (c) is described what the Christian must do, in (d) what he must be prepared to suffer, and in (e) what he must avoid."¶*

2. CHŌRIZŌ (χωρίζω), to put asunder, separate, is translated to separate in Rom. 8 : 35, 39 ; in the Middle Voice, to separate oneself, depart (see DEPART) ; in the Passive Voice in Heb. 7 : 26, R.V., " separated·" (A.V., " separate "), the verb here relates to the resurrection of Christ, not, as A.V. indicates, to the fact of His holiness in the days of His flesh ; the list is progressive in this respect that the first three qualities apply to His sinlessness, the next to His Resurrection, the last to His Ascension. See PUT, No. 14.

3. APODIORIZŌ (ἀποδιορίζω), to mark off (apo, from, dia, asunder, horizō, to limit), hence denotes metaphorically to make separations, Jude 19, R.V. (A.V., " separate themselves "), of persons who make divisions (in contrast with ver. 20) ; there is no pronoun in the original representing " themselves."¶

B. Preposition.

CHŌRIS (χωρίς), apart from, without (cp. aneu, without, a rarer word than this), is translated " separate from " in Eph. 2 : 12 (A.V., " without "). See APART, BESIDE, WITHOUT.

For SEPARATIONS see No. 3, above

SEPULCHRE

1. TAPHOS (τάφος), akin to thaptō, to bury, originally a burial, then, a place for burial, a tomb, occurs in Matt. 23 : 27 ; ver. 29, R.V. (A.V., " tombs ") ; 27 : 61, 64, 66 ; 28 : 1 ; metaphorically, Rom. 3 : 13.¶

2 and 3. MNĒMA (μνῆμα) and MNĒMEION (μνημεῖον) : see GRAVE.

SERJEANT (-S)

RHABDOUCHOS (ῥαβδοῦχος), a rod-bearer (rhabdos, a rod, echō, to hold), one who carries a staff of office, was, firstly, an umpire or judge, later, a Roman lictor, Acts 16 : 35, 38. The duty of these officials was to attend Roman magistrates to execute their orders, especially administering punishment by scourging or beheading ; they carried as their sign of office the fasces (whence " Fascist "), a bundle of rods with an axe inserted. At Philippi they acted under the stratēgoi or prætors (see MAGISTRATF, No. 1.)¶

SERPENT

1. OPHIS (ὄφις) : the characteristics of the serpent as alluded to in

---

* From Notes on Galatians by Hogg and Vine, p. 83.

Scripture are mostly evil (though Matt. 10 : 16 refers to its caution in avoiding danger) ; its treachery, Gen. 49 : 17 ; 2 Cor. 11 : 3 ; its venom, Psa. 58 : 4 ; 1 Cor. 10 : 9 ; Rev. 9 : 19 ; its skulking, Job 26 : 13 ; its murderous proclivities, e.g., Psa. 58 : 4 ; Prov. 23 : 32 ; Eccl. 10 : 8, 11 ; Amos 5 : 19 ; Mark 16 : 18 ; Luke 10 : 19 ; the Lord used the word metaphorically of the Scribes and Pharisees, Matt. 23 : 33 (cp. *echidna*, viper, in Matt. 3 : 7 ; 12 : 34). The general aspects of its evil character are intimated in the Lord's rhetorical question in Matt. 7 : 10 and Luke 11 : 11. Its characteristics are concentrated in the arch-adversary of God and man, the Devil, metaphorically described as the serpent, 2 Cor. 11 : 3 ; Rev. 12 : 9, 14, 15 ; 20 : 2. The brazen serpent lifted up by Moses was symbolical of the means of salvation provided by God, in Christ and His vicarious death under the Divine judgment upon sin, John 3 : 14. While the living serpent symbolizes sin in its origin, hatefulness and deadly effect, the brazen serpent symbolized the bearing away of the curse and the judgment of sin ; the metal was itself figurative of the righteousness of God's judgment.¶

2. HERPETON (ἑρπετόν), a creeping thing (from *herpō*, to creep), a reptile, is rendered " serpents " in Jas. 3 : 7, A.V. (R.V., " creeping things," as elsewhere). See CREEP, B.

SERVANT
A. Nouns.

1. DOULOS (δοῦλος), an adjective, signifying ' in bondage,' Rom. 6 : 19 (neuter plural, agreeing with *melē*, members), is used as a noun, and as the most common and general word for " servant ", frequently indicating subjection without the idea of bondage ; it is used (*a*) of natural conditions, e.g., Matt. 8 : 9 ; 1 Cor. 7 : 21, 22 (1st part) ; Eph. 6 : 5 ; Col. 4 : 1 ; 1 Tim. 6 : 1 ; frequently in the four Gospels ; (*b*) metaphorically of spiritual, moral and ethical conditions : servants (1) of God, e.g., Acts 16 : 17 ; Tit. 1 : 1 ; 1 Pet. 2 : 16 ; Rev. 7 : 3 ; 15 : 3 ; the perfect example being Christ Himself, Phil. 2 : 7 ; (2) of Christ, e.g., Rom. 1 : 1 ; 1 Cor. 7 : 22 (2nd part) ; Gal. 1 : 10 ; Eph. 6 : 6 ; Phil. 1 : 1 ; Col. 4 : 12 ; Jas. 1 : 1 ; 2 Pet. 1 : 1 ; Jude 1 ; (3) of sin, John 8 : 34 (R.V., " bond-servants ") ; Rom. 6 : 17, 20 ; (4) of corruption, 2 Pet. 2 : 19 (R.V., " bondservants ") ; cp. the verb *douloō* (see B). See BONDMAN.

2. DIAKONOS (διάκονος), for which see DEACON and Note there on synonymous words, is translated " servant " or " servants " in Matt. 22 : 13 (R.V. marg., " ministers ") ; 23 : 11 (R.V. marg., ditto) ; Mark 9 : 35, A.V. (R.V., " minister ") ; John 2 : 5, 9 ; 12 : 26 ; Rom. 16 : 1.

3. PAIS (παῖς), for which see CHILD, No. 4, also denotes an attendant ; it is translated " servant " (*a*) of natural conditions, in Matt. 8 : 6, 8, 13 ; 14 : 2 ; Luke 7 : 7 (" menservants " in 12 : 45) ; 15 : 26 ; (*b*) of spiritual relation to God, (1) of Israel, Luke 1 : 54 ; (2) of David, Luke 1 : 69 ; Acts 4 : 25 ; (3) of Christ, so declared by God the Father, Matt.

12 : 18 ; spoken of in prayer, Acts 4 : 27, 30, R.V. (A.V., " child ") ; the argument advanced by Dalman for the rendering " Child " in these passages, is not sufficiently valid as against the R.V., " Servant " in Acts 4, and the A.V. and R.V. in Matt. 12 (cp., e.g., the use of *pais* in the Sept. of Gen. 41 : 38 ; Jer. 36 : 24). The Matt. 12 passage by direct quotation, and the Acts 4 passages by implication, refer to the ideal " Servant of Jehovah " (Sept., *pais Kuriou*), of Is. 42 : 1 and following passages, thus identifying the Servant with the Lord Jesus ; for the same identification, cp. Acts 8 : 35.

4. OIKETĒS (οἰκέτης), a house-servant (*oikeō*, to dwell, *oikos*, a house), is translated " servant " in Luke 16 : 13 (R.V. marg., " household-servant ") ; so Rom. 14 : 4 and 1 Pet. 2 : 18 ; in Acts 10 : 7, A.V. and R.V., " household-servants."¶

5. HUPĒRETĒS (ὑπηρέτης), for which see MINISTER, No. 3, and OFFICER, is translated " servants " in the A.V. of Matt. 26 : 58 ; Mark 14 : 65 (R.V., " officers ") ; in John 18 : 36, A.V. and R.V. (R.V., marg., " officers ").

6. THERAPŌN (θεράπων), akin to *therapeuō*, to serve, to heal, an attendant, servant, is a term of dignity and freedom, used of Moses in Heb. 3 : 5.¶

7. SUNDOULOS (σύνδουλος), a fellow-servant, is used (*a*) of natural conditions, Matt. 18 : 28, 29, 31, 33 ; 24 : 49 ; (*b*) of servants of the same Divine Lord, Col. 1 : 7 ; 4 : 7 ; Rev. 6 : 11 ; of angels, Rev. 19 : 10 ; 22 : 9.¶

Note : For *misthios* and *misthōtos*, see HIRED SERVANT.

B. Verb.

DOULOŌ (δουλόω), to enslave, to bring into bondage (akin to A, No. 1), e.g., 1 Cor. 9 : 19, R.V., " I brought (myself) under bondage (to all)," A.V., " I made myself servant," denotes in the Passive Voice, to be brought into bondage, to become a slave or servant, rendered " ye became servants (of righteousness) " in Rom. 6 : 18 ; " being . . . become servants (to God)," ver. 22. See BONDAGE, B, No. 2.

SERVE

1. DIAKONEŌ (διακονέω), to minister (akin to *diakonos*, No. 2, above), to render any kind of service, is translated to serve, e.g., in Luke 10 : 40 ; 12 : 37 ; 17 : 8 ; 22 : 26, 27 (twice) ; see MINISTER, B, No. 1.

2. DOULEUŌ (δουλεύω), to serve as a *doulos* (No. 1, above), is used (*a*) of serving God (and the impossibility of serving mammon also), Matt. 6 : 24 and Luke 16 : 13 ; Rom. 7 : 6 ; in the gospel, Phil. 2 : 22 ; (*b*) Christ, Acts 20 : 19 ; Rom. 12 : 11 ; 14 : 18 ; 16 : 18 ; Eph. 6 : 7 ; Col. 3 : 24 ; (*c*) the Law of God, Rom. 7 : 25 ; (*d*) one another, Gal. 5 : 13, R.V., " be servants to " (A.V., " serve ") ; (*e*) a father, Luke 15 : 29 (with a suggestion of acting as a slave) ; (*f*) earthly masters, Matt. 6 : 24 ;

Luke 16 : 13 ; 1 Tim. 6 : 2, R.V., " serve ; " (g) the younger by the elder,
Rom. 9 : 12 ; (h) of being in bondage to a nation, Acts 7 : 7 ; Gal. 4 : 25,
to the Romans, actually, though also spiritually to Judaizers ; (i) to idols,
Gal. 4 : 8, R.V., " were in bondage " (A.V., " did service ") ; (j) to " the
weak and beggarly rudiments," ver. 9 (R.V.), " to be in bondage "
(aorist tense in the best texts, suggesting ' to enter into bondage '), i.e.,
to the religion of the Gentiles (" rudiments " being used in ver. 3 of the
religion of the Jews) ; (k) sin, Rom. 6 : 6, R.V., " be in bondage " (A.V.,
" serve ") ; (l) " divers lusts and pleasures," Tit. 3 : 3 ; (m) negatively,
to any man—a proud and thoughtless denial by the Jews, John 8 : 33.¶

3. LATREUŌ (λατρεύω), primarily to work for hire (akin to *latris*, a
hired servant), signifies (1) to worship, (2) to serve ; in the latter sense it
is used of service (a) to God, Matt. 4 : 10 ; Luke 1 : 74 (" without fear ") ;
4 : 8 ; Acts 7 : 7 ; 24 : 14, R.V., " serve " (A.V., " worship ") ; 26 : 7 ;
27 : 23 ; Rom. 1 : 9 (" with my spirit ") ; 2 Tim. 1 : 3 ; Heb. 9 : 14 ;
12 : 28, A.V., " we may serve," R.V., " we may offer service ; " Rev.
7 : 15 ; (b) to God and Christ (" the Lamb "), Rev. 22 : 3 ; (c) in the
tabernacle, Heb. 8 : 5, R.V. ; 13 : 10 ; (d) to " the host of heaven,"
Acts 7 : 42, R.V., " to serve " (A.V., " to worship ") ; (e) to " the
creature," instead of the Creator, Rom. 1 : 25, of idolatry : see WORSHIP.

Note : In Luke 2 : 37 the R.V. has " worshipping," for A.V.,
" served ; " in Heb. 9 : 9, " the worshipper," for A.V., " that did the
service."

4. HUPĒRETEŌ (ὑπηρετέω), for which see MINISTER, B, No. 3, is
translated to serve in Acts 13 : 36 ; there is a contrast intimated between
the service of David, lasting for only a generation, and the eternal character
of Christ's ministry as the One who not having seen corruption was
raised from the dead.

SERVICE, SERVING

1. DIAKONIA (διακονία) is rendered " service " in Rom. 15 : 31,
A.V. ; " serving " in Luke 10 : 40. See MINISTRY, A, No. 1.

2. LEITOURGIA (λειτουργία) is rendered " service " in 2 Cor. 9 : 12 ;
Phil. 2 : 17, 30. See MINISTRY, A, No. 2.

3. LATREIA (λατρεία), akin to *latreuō* (see No. 3, above), primarily
hired service, is used (a) of the service of God in connection with the
Tabernacle, Rom. 9 : 4 ; Heb. 9 : 1, " Divine service ; " ver. 6, plural,
R.V., " services " (A.V., " service ", and, in italics, " *of God* ") ; (b) of
the intelligent service of believers in presenting their bodies to God, a
living sacrifice, Rom. 12 : 1, R.V. marg., " worship ; " (c) of imagined
service to God by persecutors of Christ's followers, John 16 : 2.¶

Note : For " soldier on service," 2 Tim. 2 : 3, R.V., see SOLDIER, B.

S

SET
A. Verbs.

1. HISTĒMI (ἵστημι), to cause to stand, is translated to set in Matt. 4 : 5 (aorist tense in the best texts ; some have the present, as in A.V.) ; 18 : 2 ; 25 : 33 ; Mark 9 : 36 ; Luke 4 : 9 ; 9 : 47 ; John 8 : 3 : Acts 4 : 7 ; 5 : 27 ; 6 : 6 ; ver. 13, "set up ;" 22 : 30 ; in Jude 24, R.V., "to set" (A.V., "to present"). See ABIDE, No. 10.

2. KATHISTĒMI (καθίστημι), lit., to set down (kata, down, and No. 1), to appoint, constitute, is translated to set in Matt. 24 : 45, 47 ; 25 : 21, 23, R.V. (A.V., "made ") ; so Luke 12 : 42, 44 ; it is found in some mss. in Heb. 2 : 7, and translated "set over" (A.V.). See APPOINT, No. 2.

3. TITHĒMI (τίθημι), to put, to place, is translated to set in Acts 1 : 7, of times and seasons (A.V., "put ") ; Acts 13 : 47 ; Rev. 10 : 2 ; "setteth on" (of wine) in John 2 : 10, R.V. (A.V., "doth set forth ") ; in the A.V. of Mark 4 : 21 (2nd part) and in Luke 8 : 16 it is rendered "set" (R.V., "put "), of a lamp (some texts have No. 6 in both). In Mark 4 : 30 it is used of setting forth by parable the teaching concerning the Kingdom of God, R.V., "shall we set (it) forth" (A.V., "compare "). See APPOINT, No. 3.

4. PARATITHĒMI (παρατίθημι), to place beside (para, beside, and No. 3), to set forth, of a parable, Matt. 13 : 24, R.V. (A.V., "put forth ") ; to set before, of food, Mark 6 : 41 ; 8 : 6 (twice), 7 ; Luke 9 : 16 ; 10 : 8 ; 11 : 6 ; Acts 16 : 34 ; 1 Cor. 10 : 27. See ALLEGE, No. 1, PUT, No. 3.

5. PERITITHĒMI (περιτίθημι), to place or put around (peri, around, and No. 3), is translated to set about (of a hedge) in Mark 12 : 1. See BESTOW, No. 5, PUT.

6. EPITITHĒMI (ἐπιτίθημι), to put, set or lay upon, is used of the placing over the head of Christ on the Cross "His accusation," Matt. 27 : 37, "set up ;" of attacking a person, Acts 18 : 10, "shall set on." See ADD, No. 1.

7. PROTITHĒMI (προτίθημι), to set before (pro, before, and No. 3), is used in the Middle Voice, translated "set forth," of Christ, in Rom. 3 : 25 (R.V. marg., "purposed "). See PURPOSE, B, No. 3.

8. DIDŌMI (δίδωμι), to give, is translated "I have set before" in Rev. 3 : 8 (R.V. marg., "given "). See GIVE.

In the following pages † indicates that the word referred to (preposition, conjunction, or particle) is not dealt with in this volume.

¶ indicates that all the N.T. occurrences of the Greek word under consideration are mentioned under the heading or sub-heading.

9. KATHIZŌ (καθίζω), used transitively, signifies to cause to sit down, set, appoint, translated to set in Acts 2 : 30, R.V. (A.V., incorrectly, "to sit "); in 1 Cor. 6 : 4, of appointing, i.e., obtaining the services of, judges in lawcourts; in Eph. 1 : 20, R.V., "made (Him) to sit " (A.V., "set ").

Note : In Heb. 8 : 1, *kathizō* is used intransitively, R.V., "sat down " (A.V., "is set "); so in 12 : 2, R.V., "hath sat down " (A.V., "is set down "); Rev. 3 : 21, R.V., " I . . . sat down " (A.V., "am set down "). So *epikathizō* in Matt. 21 : 7 (last part), R.V., "He sat " [some mss. have the plural in a transitive sense, A.V., "they set (Him)]." See SIT, No. 8.

10. TASSŌ (τάσσω), to arrange, assign, order, is translated "set (under authority) " in Luke 7 : 8. In 1 Cor. 16 : 15, R.V., "have set (themselves)," A.V., "addicted." See APPOINT, No. 5.

11. ANATASSOMAI (ἀνατάσσομαι), to arrange in order, draw up in order (*ana*, up, and the Middle Voice of No. 10), occurs in Luke 1 : 1, A.V., "to set forth in order," R.V., "to draw up." See DRAW, No. 9.¶

12. DUNŌ (δύνω), to sink into, is used of the setting of the sun, Mark 1 : 32, "did set;" Luke 4 : 40, "was setting." The sun, moon and stars were conceived of as sinking into the sea when they set.¶

13. SUNALLASSŌ (συναλλάσσω), to reconcile (*sun*, together, *allassō*, to change or exchange), is translated " he . . . would have set (them at one, lit., ' into peace ') again " in Acts 7 : 26 (the imperfect tense being conative, expressing an attempt); some mss. have *sunelaunō*, to drive together, force together.¶

14. KATANGELLŌ (καταγγέλλω), to declare, proclaim, is translated "set forth " in Acts 16 : 21, R.V. (A.V., "teach "); "set I forth " in Acts 17 : 23, R.V. (A.V., "declare I "). See DECLARE, No. 4.

15. ENECHŌ (ἐνέχω), to hold in, has a secondary significance of setting oneself against a person, being urgent against, Mark 6 : 19; Luke 11 : 53 (R.V., marg.). See ENTANGLE, No. 3, QUARREL, URGE.

16. PROPEMPŌ (προπέμπω), lit., to send forward (*pro*, forward, *pempō*, to send), is translated "set forward " in Tit. 3 : 13, R.V. (A.V., "bring ") and in 3 John 6, R.V. (A.V., "bring forward "), of practical assistance to servants of God in their journeys. See ACCOMPANY, No. 4.

17. APODEIKNUMI (ἀποδείκνυμι), to show forth, declare, is translated "set forth " in 1 Cor. 4 : 9, here, a technical term, used for exhibiting gladiators in an arena, "last of all " referring to the grand finale, to make the most thrilling sport for the spectators (cp. 15 : 32); prophets and others had preceded the apostles in the spectacle; in 2 Thess. 2 : 4 it is used of the man of sin, who will "set (himself) forth (as God)," A.V., "shewing." Elsewhere Acts 2 : 22; 25 : 7. See APPROVE, PROVE.¶ The word is frequently used in the papyri of the proclamation of the accession of a king or the appointment of an official. Cp. *apodeixis*, "demonstration," 1 Cor. 2 : 4.¶

18. EPIBIBAZŌ (ἐπιβιβάζω), to place upon, is used of causing persons

to mount animals for riding, Luke 10 : 34 ; 19 : 35 ; Acts 23 : 24.¶

19. STĒRIZŌ (στηρίζω), to fix, establish, is rendered " He stedfastly set (His face) " in Luke 9 : 51. See ESTABLISH, No. 1.

20. ANORTHOŌ (ἀνορθόω), to set straight, set up (ana, up, orthos, straight), is used in Acts 15 : 16 in God's promise to set up the fallen tabernacle (skēnē, tent) of David. The word is used in the papyri of rearing buildings again. See LIFT, No. 6, STRAIGHT.

21. KEIMAI (κεῖμαι), to lie, to be laid (used as the Passive Voice of tithēmi, No. 3), is translated to be set, e.g., in Matt. 5 : 14 (of a city) ; Luke 2 : 34 (of Christ) ; John 2 : 6 (of waterpots) ; 19 : 29 (of a vessel of vinegar) ; Phil. 1 : 16, R.V. (ver. 17, A.V.) (of the Apostle Paul) ; Rev. 4 : 2 (of the Throne in Heaven). See APPOINT, LAY, LIE.

22. ANAKEIMAI (ἀνάκειμαι), to be laid up (ana, up), to recline at a meal, is so used in John 6 : 11, " (to them) that were set down." See LEAN, LIE, Note (1) SIT, No. 3.

23. PROKEIMAI (πρόκειμαι) signifies (a) to be set before (pro, before, and No. 21), and is so rendered in Heb. 6 : 18 of the hope of the believer ; 12 : 1, of the Christian race ; ver. 2, of the joy set before Christ in the days of His flesh and at His death ; (b) to be set forth, said of Sodom and Gomorrah, in Jude 7. It is used elsewhere in 2 Cor. 8 : 12, for which see FIRST, D, Note (2).¶

24. PROGRAPHŌ (προγράφω), to write before, is translated " were set forth (unto this condemnation) " in Jude 4, R.V. (A.V., " ordained ") ; the evil teachers were ' designated of old for this judgment ' (cp. 2 Pet. 2 : 3). For the meaning of this verb in Gal. 3 : 1, R.V., " openly set forth," see OPENLY, No. 2, Note. See WRITE.

B. Adjective.

TAKTOS (τακτός), an adjective (from tassō, A, No. 10), ordered, fixed, " set," is said of an appointed day, in Acts 12 : 21.¶ In the Sept., Job 12 : 5.¶ ·

Notes : (1) For " to set at liberty " (apoluō and apostellō), see LIBERTY. (2) In Acts 21 : 2, A.V., anagō, to set sail (R.V.), is translated " set forth ; " see LAUNCH. (3) In Luke 22 : 55, A.V., sunkathizō, to sit down together (R.V.), is translated " were set down together." See SIT, No. 10. (4) For Acts 7 : 5, " to set his foot on," see FOOT, A, No. 1, Note. (5) In Acts 13 : 9, A.V., atenizō, to look fixedly, gaze, is rendered " set his eyes on " (R.V., " fastened his eyes on "). See FASTEN, No. 1. (6) In Matt. 27 : 19, A.V., kathēmai, to sit, is rendered " he was set down " (R.V., " he was sitting "). See SIT, No. 1. (7) In John 13 : 12, A.V., anapiptō, to recline at table, is translated " was set down " (R.V., " sat down ; " marg., " reclined "). See RECLINE. (8) In Matt. 27 : 66 there is no word in the Greek representing the A.V. " setting ; " the R.V. has " the guard being with them," lit., ' with (meta) the guard.' (9) The verb is combined with other words, e.g., AFFECTION, FIRE, MIND, NOUGHT, ORDER, SEAL, UPROAR, VARIANCE.

SETTER FORTH

KATANGELEUS (καταγγελεύς), a proclaimer, herald (akin to *katangellō*, to proclaim), is used in Acts 17 : 18, " a setter forth (of strange gods)." It is found in Inscriptions in connection with proclamations made in public places.¶

SETTLE

TITHĒMI (τίθημι), to put, place, is translated " settle (it therefore in your hearts) " in Luke 21 : 14, Active Voice in the best texts (some have the Middle), the aorist tense signifying complete decision, i.e., ' resolve ' (not ' consider ') ; cp. Acts 5 : 4, to conceive in the heart, and contrast Luke 1 : 66, ' to lay up ' (both have aorist tense, Middle Voice). See APPOINT, No. 3.

Notes : (1) In 1 Pet. 5 : 10, some texts have *themelioō*, to lay a foundation, used metaphorically, and translated " settle," A.V. (2) In Col. 1 : 23, A.V., *hedraios*, lit., seated (*hedra*, a seat), is translated " settled " (R.V., " stedfast "). (3) For *epiluō* see DETERMINE, No. 4.

SEVEN

HEPTA (ἑπτά), whence Eng. words beginning with hept —, corresponds to the Heb. *sheba'* (which is akin to *sāba'*, signifying to be full, abundant), sometimes used as an expression of fulness, e.g., Ruth 4 : 15 : it generally expresses completeness, and is used most frequently in the Apocalypse ; it is not found in the Gospel of John, nor between the Acts and the Apocalypse, except in Heb. 11 : 30 (in Rom. 11 : 4 the numeral is *heptakischilioi*, seven thousand) ; in Matt. 22 : 26 it is translated " seventh " (marg., " seven ").

Note : In 2 Pet. 2 : 5, R.V., " Noah with seven others " is a translation into idiomatic English of the Greek idiom " Noah the eighth *person* " (so A.V., translating literally). See EIGHTH.

SEVENTH

HEBDOMOS (ἕβδομος) occurs in John 4 : 52 ; Heb. 4 : 4 (twice) ; Jude 14 ; Rev. 8 : 1 ; 10 : 7 ; 11 : 15 ; 16 : 17 ; 21 : 20.¶

SEVEN TIMES

HEPTAKIS (ἑπτάκις) occurs in Matt. 18 : 21, 22 ; Luke 17 : 4 (twice).¶

SEVENTY

HEBDOMĒKONTA (ἑβδομήκοντα) occurs in Luke 10 : 1, 17 ; in Acts 7 : 14 it precedes *pente*, five, lit., ' seventy-five,' rendered " threescore and fifteen ; " for the details see FIFTEEN, Note (1) ; in 23 : 23 it is translated " threescore and ten ; " in 27 : 37 it precedes *hex*, six, lit., ' seventy-six,' rendered " threescore and sixteen."¶

SEVENTY TIMES

HEBDOMĒKONTAKIS (ἑβδομηκοντάκις) occurs in Matt. 18 : 22, where it is followed by *hepta*, seven, " seventy times seven ;" R.V. marg. has " seventy times and seven," which many have regarded as the meaning ; cp. Gen. 4 : 24 (Winer, in Winer-Moulton, Gram., p. 314, remarks that while this would be the strict meaning, it " would not suit the passage ; " his translator, W. F. Moulton, in a footnote, expresses the opinion that it would. So also J. H. Moulton, Prol., p. 98, says : " A definite *allusion* to the Genesis story is highly probable : Jesus pointedly sets against the natural man's craving for seventy-sevenfold revenge the spiritual man's ambition to exercise the privilege of seventy-sevenfold forgiveness ").

The Lord's reply " until seventy times seven " was indicative of completeness, the absence of any limit, and was designed to turn away Peter's mind from a merely numerical standard. God's forgiveness is limitless ; so should man's be.¶

SEVER

1. KATARGEŌ (καταργέω), lit., to reduce to inactivity (see ABOLISH, where all the occurrences are given), is rendered " ye are severed (from Christ) " in Gal. 5 : 4, R.V. ; the aorist tense indicates that point of time at which there was an acceptance of the Judaistic doctrines ; to those who accepted these Christ would be of no profit, they were as branches severed from the tree.

2. APHORIZŌ (ἀφορίζω), to separate from, is used of the work of the angels at the end of this age, in severing the wicked from among the righteous, Matt. 13 : 49, a pre-millennial act quite distinct from the Rapture of the Church as set forth in 1 Thess. 4. See DIVIDE, No. 1.

SEVERAL

IDIOS (ἴδιος), one's own, is translated " several (ability)," in Matt. 25 : 15.

Note : For Rev. 21 : 21, " the several gates," R.V., see EVERY, No. 3.

SEVERALLY

IDIĀ (ἰδίᾳ), the dative case, feminine, of *idios* (see above), is used adverbially, signifying " severally," in 1 Cor. 12 : 11.

Notes : (1) In Rom. 12 : 5, *kata* (*kath'*) followed by the numeral *heis*, one, and preceded by the article, signifies " severally," R.V. (A.V., " every one "). Cp. EVERY, Note (1). (2) In 1 Cor. 12 : 27, R.V., the phrase *ek merous*, lit., out of a part (*meros*), is rendered " severally " (A.V., " in particular "). (3) In Heb. 9 : 5, R.V., the phrase *kata meros*, lit., according to a part, is rendered " severally." (4) For Eph. 5 : 33, R.V., " severally," see EVERY, No. 3.

SEVERITY

1. APOTOMIA (ἀποτομία), steepness, sharpness (apo, off, temnō, to cut ; tomē, a cutting), is used metaphorically in Rom. 11 : 22 (twice) of " the severity of God," which lies in His temporary retributive dealings with Israel.¶ In the papyri it is used of exacting to the full the provisions of a statute. Cp. the adverb apotomōs, sharply (which see).

2. APHEIDIA (ἀφειδία), primarily extravagance (a, negative, pheidomai, to spare), hence, unsparing treatment, severity, is used in Col. 2 : 23, R.V., " severity (to the body)," A.V., " neglecting of " (marg., " punishing, not sparing ") ; here it refers to ascetic discipline ; it was often used among the Greeks of courageous exposure to hardship and danger.¶

SEW

EPIRAPTŌ or EPIRRHAPTŌ (ἐπιράπτω) (epi, upon, rhaptō, to sew or stitch), is used in Mark 2 : 21.¶

SHADOW (Noun)

1. SKIA (σκιά) is used (a) of a shadow, caused by the interception of light, Mark 4 : 32, Acts 5 : 15 ; metaphorically of the darkness and spiritual death of ignorance, Matt. 4 : 16 ; Luke 1 : 79 ; (b) of the image or outline cast by an object, Col. 2 : 17, of ceremonies under the Law ; of the Tabernacle and its appurtenances and offerings, Heb. 8 : 5 ; of these as appointed under the Law, Heb. 10 : 1.¶

2. APOSKIASMA (ἀποσκίασμα), a shadow, is rendered " shadow that is cast " in Jas. 1 : 17, R.V. ; the A.V. makes no distinction between this and No. 1. The probable significance of this word is overshadowing or shadowing-over (which apo may indicate), and this with the genitive case of tropē, " turning," yields the meaning ' shadowing-over of mutability ' implying an alternation of shadow and light ; of this there are two alternative explanations, namely, overshadowing (1) not caused by mutability in God, or (2) caused by change in others, i.e., " no changes in this lower world can cast a shadow on the unchanging Fount of light " [Mayor, who further remarks, " The meaning of the passage will then be, ' God is alike incapable of change (parallagē) and incapable of being changed by the action of others ' "].

For SHADOWING, Heb. 9 : 5, A.V., see OVERSHADOW

SHAKE

1. SALEUŌ (σαλεύω), to agitate, shake, primarily of the action of stormy winds, waves, etc., is used (a) literally, of a reed, Matt. 11 : 7 ; Luke 7 : 24 ; a vessel, shaken in filling, Luke 6 : 38 ; a building, Luke 6 : 48 ; Acts 4 : 31 ; 16 : 26 ; the natural forces of the heavens and heavenly bodies, Matt. 24 : 29 ; Mark 13 : 25 ; Luke 21 : 26 ; the

earth, Heb. 12 : 26, "shook;" (*b*) metaphorically, (1) of shaking so as to make insecure, Heb. 12 : 27 (twice) ; (2) of casting down from a sense of security, Acts 2 : 25, "I should (not) be moved ; " (3) to stir up (a crowd), Acts 17 : 13 ; (4) to unsettle, 2 Thess. 2 : 2, "(to the end that) ye be not (quickly) shaken (from your mind)," i.e., from their settled conviction and the purpose of heart begotten by it, as to the return of Christ before the Day of the Lord begins ; the metaphor may be taken from the loosening of a ship from its moorings by a storm. See MOVE, STIR.¶

2. SEIŌ (σείω), to shake to and fro, is rendered to shake in Matt. 28 : 4, A.V. ; Heb. 12 : 26, A.V. ; Rev. 6 : 13, A.V. and R.V. ; see MOVE, No. 3.

3. APOTINASSŌ (ἀποτινάσσω), to shake off (*apo*, from, *tinassō*, to shake), is used in Luke 9 : 5, of dust from the feet ; Acts 28 : 5, of a viper from the hand.¶ In the Sept., Judg. 16 : 20 ; 1 Sam 10 : 2 ; Lam. 2 : 7.¶

4. EKTINASSŌ (ἐκτινάσσω), to shake out, is used of shaking off the dust from the feet, Matt. 10 : 14 ; Mark 6 : 11 ; Acts 13 : 51 ; of shaking out one's raiment, Acts 18 : 6.¶

SHALL

MELLŌ (μέλλω), to be about (to be or do), is used of purpose, certainty, compulsion or necessity. It is rendered simply by " shall " or " should " (which frequently represent elsewhere part of the future tense of the verb) in the following (the R.V. sometimes translates differently, as noted): Matt. 16 : 27 (1st part), lit., ' is about to come ; ' 17 : 12, 22 ; 20 : 22, R.V., " am about ; " 24 : 6 ; Mark 13 : 4 (2nd part), R.V., " are about ;" Luke 9 : 44 ; 21 : 7 (2nd part), R.V., " are about ; " ver. 36 ; Acts 23 : 3 ; 24 : 15 ; 26 : 2, R.V., " I am (to) ; " Rom. 4 : 24 ; 8 : 13 (1st part), R.V., " must ; " ver. 18 ; 2 Tim. 4 : 1 ; Heb. 1 : 14 ; 10 : 27 ; Jas. 2 : 12, R.V., " are to ; " 1 Pet. 5 : 1 ; Rev. 1 : 19 ; 2 : 10 (1st and 2nd parts), R.V., " art about," " is about ; " 3 : 10, R.V., " is (to) ; " 17 : 8 (1st part), R.V., " is about." See ABOUT, B.

Notes: (1) The use of shall, shalt, is frequently part of the rendering of a future tense of a verb. (2) The phrase " it shall come to pass " is the rendering of the future tense of *eimi*, to be, in Acts 2 : 17, 21 ; 3 : 23 ; Rom. 9 : 26.

SHAMBLES

MAKELLON (μάκελλον), a term of late Greek borrowed from the Latin *macellum*, denotes a meat-market, translated " shambles " in 1 Cor. 10 : 25. The word is found in the *koinē*, or vernacular Greek covering the time of the N.T., illustrating this passage (see Deissmann, *Light from the Ancient East*, 274). A plan, drawn by Lietzmann, of a forum in Pompeii, shows both the slaughter-house and the meat-shop next to the chapel of Cæsar. Some of the meat which had been used for sacrificial purposes was afterwards sold in the markets. The Apostle enjoins upon the believer to enter into no enquiry, so as to avoid the troubling of conscience (contrast ver. 28).¶

SHAME (Noun, and Verb)
A. Nouns.

1. ATIMIA (ἀτιμία) signifies (a) shame, disgrace, Rom 1 : 26, " vile (passions)," R.V., lit., ' (passions) of shame ; ' 1 Cor. 11 : 14 ; (b) dishonour, e.g., 2 Tim. 2 : 20, where the idea of disgrace or shame does not attach to the use of the word ; the meaning is that while in a great house some vessels are designed for purposes of honour, others have no particular honour (timē) attached to their use (the prefix a simply negatives the idea of honour). See DISHONOUR.

2. AISCHUNE (αἰσχύνη) : see ASHAMED, B, No. 1.

3. ENTROPE (ἐντροπή), 1 Cor. 6 : 5 and 15 : 34. See ASHAMED, B, No. 2.¶

4. ASCHEMOSUNE (ἀσχημοσύνη) denotes (a) " unseemliness," Rom. 1 : 27, R.V. (A.V., " that which is unseemly ") ; (b) shame, nakedness, Rev. 16 : 15, a euphemism for No. 2.¶

B. Adjective.

AISCHROS (αἰσχρός), base, shameful (akin to aischos, shame), of that which is opposed to modesty or purity, is translated as a noun in 1 Cor. 11 : 6 ; 14 : 35, A.V. (R.V., " shameful ") ; Eph. 5 : 12 ; in Tit. 1 : 11, " filthy (lucre)," lit., ' shameful (gain).' See FILTHY. ¶

C. Verbs.

1. ATIMAZO (ἀτιμάζω), to dishonour, put to shame (akin to A, No. 1) : see DISHONOUR, C, No. 1.

2. ENTREPO (ἐντρέπω), lit., to turn in upon, to put to shame (akin to A, No. 3), is translated " to shame (you) " in 1 Cor. 4 : 14. See ASHAMED, A, No. 4.

3. KATAISCHUNO (καταισχύνω), to put to shame (kata, perhaps signifying utterly), is translated " ye . . . shame (them) " in 1 Cor. 11 : 22, A.V., R.V., " ye . . . put (them) to shame." See ASHAMED, A, No. 3.

4. PARADEIGMATIZO (παραδειγματίζω) signifies to set forth as an example (para, beside, deiknumi, to show), and is used in Heb. 6 : 6 of those Jews, who, though attracted to, and closely associated with, the Christian faith, without having experienced more than a tasting of the heavenly gift and partaking of the Holy Ghost (not actually receiving Him), were tempted to apostatize to Judaism, and, thereby crucifying the Son of God a second time, would " put Him to an open shame." So were criminals exposed.¶ In the Sept., Numb. 25 : 4 ; Jer. 13 : 22 ; Ezek. 28 : 17.¶

SHAMEFASTNESS (A.V., SHAMEFACEDNESS)

AIDŌS (αἰδώς), a sense of shame, modesty, is used regarding the demeanour of women in the church, 1 Tim. 2 : 9 (some mss. have it in Heb. 12 : 28 for *deos*, "awe :" here only in N.T.). "Shamefastness is that modesty which is ' fast ' or rooted in the character . . . The change to ' shamefacedness ' is the more to be regretted because shamefacedness . . . has come rather to describe an awkward diffidence, such as we sometimes call sheepishness " (Davies ; *Bible English*, p. 12).

As to *aidōs* and *aischunē* (see ASHAMED, B, No. 1), *aidōs* is more objective, having regard to others ; it is the stronger word. "*Aidōs* would always restrain a good man from an unworthy act, *aischunē* would sometimes restrain a bad one " (Trench, Syn. § § xix, xx).

SHAMEFULLY (ENTREAT)

Note : This forms part of the rendering of (*a*) *atimazō*, Mark 12 : 4, Luke 20 : 11, see DISHONOUR, C, No. 1, ENTREAT, Note, HANDLE, No. 4 ; (*b*) *hubrizō*, to insult, Acts 14 : 5, R.V. ; 1 Thess. 2 : 2, " were (R.V., having been) shamefully entreated." See SPITEFULLY.

SHAPE

1. EIDOS (εἶδος), rendered "shape" in the A.V. of Luke 3 : 22 and John 5 : 37 : see FORM, No. 4.

2. HOMOIŌMA (ὁμοίωμα), rendered "shapes" in Rev. 9 : 7 : see LIKENESS, No. 1.

For SHARERS (Heb. 2 : 14) see PARTAKE, B, No. 1.

SHARP, SHARPER, SHARPLY, SHARPNESS

A. Adjectives.

1. OXUS (ὀξύς) denotes (*a*) sharp (Eng., *oxy*—), said of a sword, Rev. 1 : 16 ; 2 : 12 ; 19 : 15 ; of a sickle, 14 : 14, 17, 18 (twice) ; (*b*) of motion, swift, Rom. 3 : 15. See SWIFT.¶

2. TOMOS (τομός), akin to *temnō*, to cut [Eng., (ana)tomy, etc.], is used metaphorically in the comparative degree, *tomōteros*, in Heb. 4 : 12, of the Word of God.¶

B. Adverb.

APOTOMŌS (ἀποτόμως) signifies abruptly, curtly, lit., in a manner that cuts (*apo*, from, *temnō*, to cut), hence sharply, severely, 2 Cor. 13 : 10, R.V., " (that I may not . . . deal) sharply," A.V., " (use) sharpness ; " the pronoun " you " is to be understood, i.e., ' that I may not use (or deal with) . . . sharply ; ' Tit. 1 : 13, of rebuking.¶ Cp. *apotomia*, severity.

SHAVE

XURAŌ (ξυράω), a late form of *xureō*, or *xurō*, from *xuron*, a razor, occurs in Acts 21 : 24 (Middle Voice), in connection with a vow (Numb.

6 : 2–18 ; cp. Acts 18 : 18 : see Shear) ; 1 Cor. 11 : 5, 6 (2nd part in each).¶

SHE

Note : The words under HE in their feminine forms are used for this pronoun.

SHEAR, SHEARER, SHORN

KEIRŌ (κείρω) is used (a) of shearing sheep, Acts 8 : 32, " shearer," lit., ' the (one) shearing : ' (b) in the Middle Voice, to have one's hair cut off, be shorn, Acts 18 : 18 ; 1 Cor. 11 : 6 (twice ; cp. *xuraō*, to shave ; see above).¶

SHEATH

THĒKĒ (θήκη), a place to put something in (akin to *tithēmi*, to put), a receptacle, chest, case, is used of the sheath of a sword, John 18 : 11.¶

SHED

1. EKCHEŌ (ἐκχέω), to pour out, is translated to shed or to shed forth in Acts 2 : 33 ; Tit. 3 : 6, A.V. ; of shedding blood in murder, Rom. 3 : 15. See Pour, No. 3.

2. EKCHUNŌ, or EKCHUNNŌ (ἐκχύνω), a later form of No. 1, is used of the voluntary giving up of His life by Christ through the shedding of His blood in crucifixion as an atoning sacrifice, Matt. 26 : 28 ; Mark 14 : 24 ; Luke 22 : 20, A.V., "is shed," R.V., "is poured out ; " these passages do not refer to the effect of the piercing of His side (which took place after His Death) ; of the murder of servants of God, Matt. 23 : 35 ; Luke 11 : 50 ; Acts 22 : 20 (in the best texts ; others have No. 1) ; of the love of God in the hearts of believers through the Holy Spirit, Rom. 5 : 5. For the ' pouring out ' of the Holy Spirit, Acts 10 : 45, see Pour, No. 4. (The form in the last two passages might equally well come from No. 1, above.) See Gush out, Run, Spill.

SHEEP

1. PROBATON (πρόβατον), from *probainō*, to go forward, i.e., of the movement of quadrupeds, was used among the Greeks of small cattle, sheep and goats ; in the N.T., of sheep only (a) naturally, e.g., Matt. 12 : 11, 12 ; (b) metaphorically, of those who belong to the Lord, the lost ones of the house of Israel, Matt. 10 : 6 ; of those who are under the care of the Good Shepherd, e.g., Matt. 26 : 31 ; John 10 : 1, lit., ' the fold of the sheep,' and vv. 2–27 ; 21 : 16, 17 in some texts ; Heb. 13 : 20 ; of those who in a future day, at the introduction of the Millennial Kingdom, have shewn kindness to His persecuted earthly people in their great tribula-tion, Matt. 25 : 33 ; of the clothing of false shepherds, Matt. 7 : 15 ; (c) figuratively, by way of simile, of Christ, Acts 8 : 32 ; of the disciples, e.g., Matt. 10 : 16 ; of true followers of Christ in general, Rom. 8 : 36 ;

of the former wayward condition of those who had come under His Shepherd care, 1 Pet. 2 : 25 ; of the multitudes who sought the help of Christ in the days of His flesh, Matt. 9 : 36 ; Mark 6 : 34.

2. PROBATION (προβάτιον), a diminutive of No. 1, a little sheep, is found in the best texts in John 21 : 16, 17 (some have No. 1) ; distinct from *arnia*, lambs (ver. 15), but used as a term of endearment.¶

Note: For " keeping sheep," Luke 17 : 7, R.V., see CATTLE.

For SHEEPFOLD see FOLD

SHEEP *GATE*, SHEEP *MARKET*

PROBATIKOS (προβατικός), an adjective, used in the grammatically feminine form, in John 5 : 2, to agree with *pulē*, a gate, understood, R.V., "sheep *gate*" (not with *agora*, a market, A.V., "sheep *market*").¶ In the Sept., Neh. 3 : 1, 32 ; 12 : 39.¶ This sheep gate was near the Temple ; the sacrifices for the Temple probably entered by it.

SHEEPSKIN

MĒLŌTĒ (μηλωτή), from *mēlon*, a sheep or goat, occurs in Heb. 11 : 37.¶ In the Sept., 1 Kings 19 : 13, 19 ; 2 Kings 2 : 8, 13, 14.¶

SHEET

OTHONĒ (ὀθόνη) primarily denoted fine linen, later, a sheet, Acts 10 : 11 ; 11 : 5.¶ Cp. *othonion*, linen.

SHEKEL, HALF SHEKEL

1. STATĒR (στατήρ), a *tetradrachmon* or four *drachmae*, originally 224 grains, in Tyrian currency, but reduced in weight somewhat by the time recorded in Matt. 17 : 24 ; the value was about three shillings, and would pay the Temple tax for two persons, Matt. 17 : 27, R.V., " shekel " (A.V., " a piece of money ") ; in some mss., 26 : 16 ; see MONEY, Note.¶

2. DIDRACHMON (δίδραχμον), a half-shekel (i.e., *dis*, twice, *drachmē*, a drachma, the coin mentioned in Luke 15 : 8, 9), was the amount of the tribute in the 1st cent., A.D., due from every adult Jew for the maintenance of the Temple services, Matt. 17 : 24 (twice).¶ This was based on Ex. 30 : 13, 24 (see also 38 : 24–26 ; Lev. 5 : 15 ; 27 : 3, 25 ; Numb. 3 : 47, 50 ; 7 : 13 ff. ; 18 : 16).

SHEPHERD

POIMĒN (ποιμήν) is used (*a*) in its natural significance, Matt. 9 : 36 ; 25 : 32 ; Mark 6 : 34 ; Luke 2 : 8, 15, 18, 20 ; John 10 : 2, 12 ; (*b*) metaphorically of Christ, Matt. 26 : 31 ; Mark 14 : 27 ; John 10 : 11, 14, 16 ; Heb. 13 : 20 ; 1 Pet. 2 : 25 ; (*c*) metaphorically of those who act as pastors in the churches, Eph. 4 : 11.¶ See PASTOR.

For CHIEF SHEPHERD see CHIEF, B, No. 3

SHEW (SHOW)

1. DEIKNUMI, or DEIKNUŌ, (δείκνυμι) denotes (a) to shew, exhibit, e.g., Matt. 4 : 8 ; 8 : 4 ; John 5 : 20 ; 20 : 20 ; 1 Tim. 6 : 15 ; (b) to shew by making known, Matt. 16 : 21 ; Luke 24 : 40 ; John 14 : 8, 9 ; Acts 10 : 28 ; 1 Cor. 12 : 31 ; Rev. 1 : 1 ; 4 : 1 ; 22 : 6 ; (c) to shew by way of proving, Jas. 2 : 18 ; 3 : 13.

2. ANADEIKNUMI (ἀναδείκνυμι) signifies (a) to lift up and shew, shew forth, declare (ana, up, and No. 1), Acts 1 : 24 ; (b) to appoint, Luke 10 : 1. See APPOINT, No. 14.¶

3. ENDEIKNUMI (ἐνδείκνυμι) signifies (1) to shew forth, prove (Middle Voice), said (a) of God as to His power, Rom. 9 : 17 ; His wrath, 9 : 22 ; the exceeding riches of His grace, Eph. 2 : 7 ; (b) of Christ, as to His longsuffering, 1 Tim. 1 : 16 ; (c) of Gentiles, as to " the work of the Law written in their hearts," Rom. 2 : 15 ; (d) of believers, as to the proof of their love, 2 Cor. 8 : 24 ; all good fidelity, Tit. 2 : 10 ; meekness, 3 : 2 ; love toward God's Name, Heb. 6 : 10 ; diligence in ministering to the saints, ver. 11 ; (2) to manifest by evil acts, 2 Tim. 4 : 14, " did (me much evil)," marg., " shewed."¶

4. EPIDEIKNUMI (ἐπιδείκνυμι), epi, upon, intensive, and No. 1, signifies (a) to exhibit, display, Matt. 16 : 1 ; 22 : 19 ; 24 : 1 ; Luke 17 : 14 (in some mss. 24 : 40 ; No. 1 in the best texts) ; in the Middle Voice, to display, with a special interest in one's own action, Acts 9 : 39 ; (b) to point out, prove, demonstrate, Acts 18 : 28 ; Heb. 6 : 17.¶

5. HUPODEIKNUMI (ὑποδείκνυμι), primarily, to shew secretly (hupo, under), or by tracing out, hence, to make known, warn, is translated to shew in Luke 6 : 47 ; Acts 9 : 16 ; in 20 : 35, A.V. (R.V., " I gave . . . an example "). See EXAMPLE, WARN.

6. POIEŌ (ποιέω), to make, to do, is translated " He hath shewed " in Luke 1 : 51 ; " to shew (mercy)," ver. 72, R.V. (A.V., " perform ") ; " shewed (mercy)," 10 : 37 ; John 6 : 30, A.V., " shewest Thou," R.V., " doest Thou (for a sign) ; " Acts 7 : 36, A.V., " shewed," R.V., " wrought ; " Jas. 2 : 13, " shewed (no mercy) ; " in Mark 13 : 22 in the best texts (some have didōmi), " shall shew (signs)." See Do, No. 1.

7. MĒNUŌ (μηνύω), to disclose, make known (what was secret), is rendered to shew in Luke 20 : 37 ; 1 Cor. 10 : 28 ; in a forensic sense, John 11 : 57 ; Acts 23 : 30, R.V. (A.V., " it was told "). See TELL.¶

8. PARISTĒMI (παρίστημι), to shew, in Acts 1 : 3 ; 2 Tim. 2 : 15 (A.V.) : see PRESENT, No. 1.

9. PARECHŌ (παρέχω), to afford, give, shew, etc., in the Active Voice, is translated " shewed " in Acts 28 : 2 ; in the Middle Voice, " shewing " in Tit. 2 : 7 (1st part). See BRING, No. 21.

10. EXANGELLŌ (ἐξαγγέλλω), to tell out, proclaim abroad, to publish completely (ek, or ex, out, angellō, to proclaim), is rendered " shew forth " in 1 Pet. 2 : 9 ; it indicates a complete proclamation (verbs compounded with ek often suggest what is to be done fully).¶

11. DIDŌMI (δίδωμι), to give, is rendered to shew in Matt. 24 : 24.
See also No. 6.

Notes : The A.V. translates the following words by the verb to shew
in the passages indicated. The R.V. gives the better renderings : (1)
apodeiknumi (to demonstrate), 2 Thess. 2 : 4, "setting (himself) forth,"
see SET, No. 17 ; (2) *anangellō* (to declare), Matt. 11 : 4, "tell ;" John
16 : 13–15, "declare ; " 16 : 25, "shall tell ; " Acts 19 : 18 and 20 : 20,
"declaring ; " (3) *katangellō*, Acts 16 : 17 ; 26 : 23 ; 1 Cor. 11 : 26, "proclaim ; " in the last passage the partaking of the elements at the Lord's
Supper is not a showing forth of His death, but a proclamation of it ;
(4) *phaneroō*, John 7 : 4 ; 21 : 1 (twice), 14 ; Rom. 1 : 19, to manifest ;
(5) *dēloō*, (to make plain), 2 Pet. 1 : 14, "signify ; " (6) *diēgeomai* (to
recount), Luke 8 : 39, "declare ; " (7) *emphanizō* (to manifest), Acts
23 : 22, "hast signified ; " (8) *euangelizō*, Luke 1 : 19, "to bring glad
tidings ; " (9) *katatithēmi* (to lay up), Acts 24 : 27, "to gain ; " (10) *legō*
(to tell), 1 Cor. 15 : 51, "I tell ; " (11) *energeō*, Matt. 14 : 2 and Mark 6 : 14,
"work ; " (12) *ōphthē* (lit., ' was seen '), Acts 7 : 26, "He appeared ; "
(13) *ginomai* (to become), Acts 4 : 22, "was wrought ; " (14) in Acts
10 : 40, *emphanēs*, manifest, with *didōmi* to give, and *ginomai*, to become,
"gave . . . to be made manifest " (A.V. "shewed . . . openly ") ;
(15) *apangellō* (to announce), Matt. 11 : 4, "tell ; " 12 : 18, "declare ; "
28 : 11, "told ; " Luke 14 : 21, "told ; " Acts 26 : 20, "declared ; "
28 : 21, "report ; " 1 Thess. 1 : 9, "report ; " 1 John 1 : 2, "declare ; "
(16) In Luke 1 : 58, A.V., *megalunō*, to magnify (R.V.), is rendered
"shewed great." (17) See also SHEWING.

For SHEW BEFORE see FORESHEW

SHEWBREAD

Note : The phrase rendered "the shewbread" is formed by the
combination of the nouns *prothesis*, a setting forth (*pro*, before, *tithēmi*,
to place) and *artos*, a loaf (in the plural), each with the article, Matt. 12 : 4 ;
Mark 2 : 26 and Luke 6 : 4, lit., ' the loaves of the setting forth ; ' in
Heb. 9 : 2, lit., ' the setting forth of the loaves.'¶ The corresponding
O.T. phrases are lit., ' bread of the face,' Ex. 25 : 30, i.e., the presence,
referring to the Presence of God (cp. Isa. 63 : 9 with Ex. 33 : 14, 15) ;
' the bread of ordering,' 1 Chron. 9 : 32, marg. In Numb. 4 : 7 it is
called "the continual bread ; " in 1 Sam. 21 : 4, 6, "holy bread"
(A.V., "hallowed "). In the Sept. of 1 Kings 7 : 48, it is called "the
bread of the offering " (*prosphora*, a bearing towards). The twelve loaves,
representing the tribes of Israel, were set in order every Sabbath day
before the Lord, "on the behalf of the children," Lev. 24 : 8, R.V. (marg.,
and A.V., "from "), "an everlasting covenant." The loaves symbolized
the fact that on the basis of the sacrificial atonement of the Cross,
believers are accepted before God, and nourished by Him in the Person

of Christ. The shewbread was partaken of by the priests, as representatives of the nation. Priesthood now being co-extensive with all who belong to Christ, 1 Pet. 2 : 5, 9, He, the Living Bread, is the nourishment of all, and where He is, there, representatively, they are.

SHEWING

ANADEIXIS (ἀνάδειξις), a shewing forth (ana, up or forth, and deiknumi, to show), is translated " shewing " in Luke 1 : 80.¶

Note : For " shewing," Rom. 3 : 25, 26, R.V., see DECLARE, B.

SHIELD

THUREOS (θυρεός) formerly meant a stone for closing the entrance of a cave ; then, a shield, large and oblong, protecting every part of the soldier ; the word is used metaphorically of faith, Eph. 6 : 16, which the believer is to take up ' in (en in the original) all ' (all that has just been mentioned), i.e., as affecting the whole of his activities.¶

SHINE, SHINING
A. Verbs.

1. PHAINŌ (φαίνω), to cause to appear, denotes, in the Active Voice, to give light, shine, John 1 : 5 ; 5 : 35 ; in Matt. 24 : 27, Passive Voice ; so Phil. 2 : 15, R.V.," ye are seen " (for A.V., " ye shine ") ; 2 Pet. 1 : 19 (Active) ; so 1 John 2 : 8 ; Rev. 1 : 16 ; in 8 : 12 and 18 : 23 (Passive) ; 21 : 23 (Active). See APPEAR.

2. EPIPHAINŌ (ἐπιφαίνω), to shine upon (epi, upon, and No. 1), is so translated in Luke 1 : 79, R.V. (A.V., " to give light "). See APPEAR, No. 2.

3. LAMPŌ (λάμπω), to shine as a torch, occurs in Matt. 5 : 15, 16 ; 17 : 2 ; Luke 17 : 24 ; Acts 12 : 7 ; 2 Cor. 4 : 6 (twice).¶ : see LIGHT, B, No. 3.

4. STILBŌ (στίλβω), to shine, glisten, is used in Mark 9 : 3 of the garments of Christ at His Transfiguration, R.V., " glistering," A.V., " shining."¶ Cp. exastraptō, " dazzling," in Luke 9 : 29, R.V.

5. EKLAMPŌ (ἐκλάμπω), to shine forth (ek, out, and No. 3), is used in Matt. 13 : 43, of the future shining forth of the righteous " in the Kingdom of their Father."¶

6. PERILAMPŌ (περιλάμπω), to shine around (peri, around, and No. 3), is used in Luke 2 : 9, " shone round about," of the glory of the Lord ; so in Acts 26 : 13, of the light from Heaven upon Saul of Tarsus.¶

7. PERIASTRAPTŌ (περιαστράπτω), to flash around, shine round about (peri, and astrapē, shining brightness), is used in Acts 9 : 3 and 22 : 6 of the same circumstance as in 26 : 13 (No. 6).¶

8. EPIPHAUSKŌ or EPIPHAUŌ (ἐπιφαύσκω), to shine forth, is used figuratively of Christ upon the slumbering believer who awakes and arises from among the dead, Eph. 5 : 14, R.V., " shall shine upon thee " (A.V., " shall give thee light ").¶

B. Noun.

ASTRAPĒ (ἀστραπή) denotes (a) lightning, (b) bright shining, of a lamp, Luke 11 : 36. See LIGHTNING. Cp. No. 7, above, and Note (1) below.

Notes : (1) In Luke 24 : 4, A.V., *astraptō*, to lighten, is translated "shining" (R.V., "dazzling"). (2) In 2 Cor. 4 : 4, A.V., *augazō*, to shine forth, is translated "shine" (R.V., "dawn").¶

SHIP, SHIPPING

1. PLOION (πλοῖον), akin to *pleō*, to sail, a boat or a ship, always rendered appropriately "boat" in the R.V. in the Gospels; "ship" in the Acts; elsewhere, Jas. 3 : 4 ; Rev. 8 : 9 ; 18 : 17 (in some mss.), 19. See BOAT, No. 2.

2. PLOIARION (πλοιάριον), a diminutive form of No. 1, is translated "ship" in the A.V. of Mark 3 : 9 ; 4 : 36 and John 21 : 8 ; "(took) shipping" in John 6 : 24, A.V., R.V. "(got into the) boats." See BOAT, No. 1.

3. NAUS (ναῦς) denotes a ship (Lat. *navis*, Eng. nautical, naval, etc.), Acts 27 : 41.¶ *Naus*, in classical Greek the ordinary word for a ship, survived in Hellenistic Greek only as a literary word, but disappeared from popular speech (Moulton, Proleg., p. 25). Blass (*Philology of the Gospels*, p. 186) thinks the solitary Lucan use of *naus* was due to a reminiscence of the Homeric phrase for beaching a ship.

Note : For *epibainō*, Acts 21 : 6, "we took ship," see TAKE, Note (16).

For OWNER OF THE SHIP see OWNER, No. 2

For SHIPMEN see MARINERS

For SHIPMASTER see MASTER, A, No. 7

SHIPWRECK

NAUAGEŌ (ναυαγέω) signifies (a) literally, to suffer shipwreck (*naus*, a ship, *agnumi*, to break), 2 Cor. 11 : 25 ; (b) metaphorically, to make shipwreck, 1 Tim. 1 : 19, "concerning the faith," as the result of thrusting away a good conscience (both verbs in this ver. are in the aorist tense, signifying the definiteness of the acts).¶

For SHIVERS (Rev. 2 : 27) see BREAK, A, No. 5

For SHOD see BIND, No. 3

SHOE

HUPODĒMA (ὑπόδημα) denotes a sole bound under the foot (*hupo*, under, *deō*, to bind ; cp. *hupodeō*, to bind under), a sandal, always translated "shoes," e.g., Matt. 3 : 11 ; 10 : 10 ; Mark 1 : 7.

SHOOT FORTH

PROBALLŌ (προβάλλω), lit., to throw before, is used of the putting forth of leaves, blossom, fruit, said of trees in general, Luke 21 : 30, " shoot forth." See PUT (forward), Acts 19 : 33.¶

Note : In Mark 4 : 32, A.V., *poieō*, to do, make, is rendered " shooteth out," R.V., " putteth out."

For SHORE see BEACH and LIP

For SHORT (Adjective and Adverb) see LITTLE, A, No 2 and B, No. 2

Note : In 1 Thess. 2 : 17, " a short season," is lit., ' a season of an hour ' (*hōra* ; see HOUR, SEASON, No. 1.

SHORT (come, cut), SHORTEN

1. KOLOBOŌ (κολοβόω) denotes to cut off, amputate (*kolobos*, docked) ; hence, to curtail, shorten, said of the shortening by God of the time of the great tribulation, Matt. 24 : 22 (twice) ; Mark 13 : 20 (twice).¶ In the Sept., 2 Sam. 4 : 12.¶

2. SUSTELLŌ (ουστέλλω) denotes (*a*) to draw together (*sun*, together, *stellō*, to bring, gather), to contract, shorten, 1 Cor. 7 : 29, R.V., " (the time) is shortened " (A.V., " . . . is short ") ; the coming of the Lord is always to be regarded as nigh for the believer, who is to be in constant expectation of His return, and thus is to keep himself from being the slave of earthly conditions and life's relationships ; (*b*) to wrap up, of enshrouding a body for burial, Acts 5 : 6, R.V., " they wrapped (A.V., wound) . . . up."¶

3. SUNTEMNŌ (ουντέμνω), primarily, to cut in pieces (*sun*, together, *temnō*, to cut), then, to cut down, cut short, is used metaphorically in Rom. 9 : 28 (twice in some texts), " the Lord will execute His word (*logos*, not work, as A.V.) upon the earth, finishing it and cutting it short," i.e., in the fulfilment of His judgments pronounced upon Israel, a remnant only being saved ; the cutting short of His word is suggestive of the summary and decisive character of the Divine act.¶

Note : For *hustereō*, to come short, fall short, see FALL, No. 10.

SHORTLY

1. EUTHEŌS (εὐθέως), straightway, directly, is translated " shortly " in 3 John 14. The general use of the word suggests something sooner than " shortly." See FORTHWITH, STRAIGHTWAY.

2. TACHEŌS (ταχέως) : see QUICKLY, No. 3.

3. TACHEION (τάχειον) : see QUICKLY, No. 2.

4. EN TACHEI (ἐν τάχει) : see QUICKLY, No. 4.

Note : In 2 Pet. 1 : 14, A.V., *tachinos*, an adjective denoting swift (akin to the above), is translated " shortly " (R.V., " swiftly "), lit., ' the putting off of my tabernacle is swift ' (i.e., in its approach). Cp. 2 : 1.

SHOULD

Note : This is frequently part of the translation of the tense of a verb. Otherwise it translates the following :

1. MELLŌ (μέλλω), to be about to (for the significance of which see SHALL), e.g., Mark 10 : 32, R.V., " were to ; " Luke 19 : 11, R.V., " was to ; " " should " in 22 : 23 ; 24 : 21 ; John 6 : 71 ; 7 : 39, R.V., " were to ; " 11 : 51 ; 12 : 4, 33 ; 18 : 32 ; Acts 11 : 28 ; 23 : 27, R.V., " was about (to be slain) ; " 1 Thess. 3 : 4, R.V., " are to ; " Rev. 6 : 11. See ABOUT, B.

2. DEI (δεῖ), it needs, it should, e.g., Matt. 18 : 33 ; Acts 27 : 21 : see MUST.

Note : In 1 Cor. 9 : 10, A.V., *opheilō*, to owe, is rendered " should " (R.V., " ought to ").

SHOULDER

ŌMOS (ὦμος) occurs in Matt. 23 : 4 and Luke 15 : 5, and is suggestive (as in the latter passage) of strength and safety.¶

SHOUT (Noun and Verb)

A. Noun.

KELEUSMA (κέλευσμα), a call, summons, shout of command (akin to *keleuō*, to command), is used in 1 Thess. 4 : 16 of the shout with which (*en*, in, denoting the attendant circumstances) the Lord will descend from heaven at the time of the Rapture of the saints (those who have fallen asleep, and the living) to meet Him in the air. The shout is not here said to be His actual voice, though this indeed will be so (John 5 : 28).¶ In the Sept., Prov. 30 : 27, " (the locusts . . . at the) word of command (march in rank)."¶

B. Verb.

EPIPHŌNEŌ (ἐπιφωνέω), to call out (*epi*, upon, *phōneō*, to utter a sound), is translated " shouted " in Acts 12 : 22, R.V. (A.V., " gave a shout "). See CRY, B, No. 8.

SHOW (Noun)

LOGOS (λόγος), a word, is sometimes used of mere talk, the talk which one occasions ; hence, repute, reputation ; this seems to be the meaning in Col. 2 : 23, translated " a show (A.V. 'shew') of wisdom," i.e., 'a reputation for wisdom,' rather than ' appearance,' ' reason ' etc. See WORD.

Note : In Luke 20 : 47, A.V., *prophasis*, a pretence (R.V.), is translated " shew." See CLOKE (Pretence), No. 2.

SHOW (make a)

1. DEIGMATIZŌ (δειγματίζω), to make a show of, expose, is used in Col. 2 : 15 of Christ's act regarding the principalities and powers, displaying them " as a victor displays his captives or trophies in a

triumphal procession" (Lightfoot). Some regard the meaning as being that He showed the angelic beings in their true inferiority (see under TRIUMPH). For its other occurrence, Matt. 1 : 19, see EXAMPLE, B, No. 1.¶

2. EUPROSŌPEŌ (εὐπροσωπέω) denotes to look well, make a fair show (*eu*, well, *prosōpon*, a face), and is used in Gal. 6 : 12, " to make a fair show (in the flesh)," i.e., to make a display of religious zeal. Deissmann illustrates the metaphorical use of this word from the papyri in *Light from the Ancient East*, p. 96.¶

Note : For *paratērēsis*, A.V. marg. in Luke 17 : 20, " outward shew," see OBSERVATION.¶

SHOWER

OMBROS (ὄμβρος) denotes a heavy shower, a storm of rain, Luke 12 : 54.¶

For SHRANK and SHRINK see DRAW (*B*), No. 4

SHRINE

NAOS (ναός), the inmost part of a temple, a shrine, is used in the plural in Acts 19 : 24, of the silver models of the pagan shrine in which the image of Diana (Greek Artemis) was preserved. The models were large or small, and were signs of wealth and devotion on the part of purchasers. The variety of forms connected with the embellishment of the image provided "no little business" for the silversmiths. See TEMPLE.

SHUDDER

PHRISSŌ (φρίσσω), primarily, to be rough, to bristle, then, to shiver, shudder, tremble, is said of demons, Jas. 2 : 19, R.V., " shudder " (A.V., " tremble ").¶ Cp. Matt. 8 : 29, indicating a cognizance of their appointed doom.

For SHUN see AVOID, No. 4, and DRAW, (*B*),No. 4

SHUT, SHUT UP

1. KLEIŌ (κλείω) is used (*a*) of things material, Matt. 6:6 ; 25:10 ; Luke 11 : 7 ; John 20 : 19, 26 ; Acts 5 : 23 ; 21 : 30 ; Rev. 20 : 3 ; figuratively, 21 : 25 ; (*b*) metaphorically, of the Kingdom of Heaven, Matt. 23 : 13 ; of heaven, with consequences of famine, Luke 4 : 25 ; Rev. 11 : 6 ; of compassion, 1 John 3 : 17, R.V. (A.V., " bowels *of compassion* ") ; of the blessings accruing from the promises of God regarding David, Rev. 3 : 7 ; of a door for testimony, 3 : 8.¶

2. APOKLEIŌ (ἀποκλείω), to shut fast (*apo*, away from, and No. 1), is used in Luke 13 : 25, expressing the impossibility of entrance after the closing.¶

3. KATAKLEIŌ (κατακλείω), lit., to shut down (the *kata* has, however, an intensive use), signifies to shut up in confinement, Luke 3 : 20 ; Acts 26 : 10.¶ In the Sept., Jer. 32 : 3.¶

4. SUNKLEIŌ (συγκλείω) : see INCLOSE.

SICK, SICKLY, SICKNESS
A. Verbs.

1. ASTHENEŌ (ἀσθενέω), lit., to be weak, feeble (*a*, negative, *sthenos*, strength), is translated to be sick, e.g., in Matt. 10 : 8, " (the) sick ; " 25 : 36 ; ver. 39 in the best texts (some have B, No. 1) ; Mark 6 : 56 ; Luke 4 : 40 ; 7 : 10 (R.V. omits the word) ; 9 : 2 ; John 4 : 46 ; 5 : 3, R.V. (A.V., " impotent folk ") ; ver. 7 ; 6 : 2, R.V. (A.V., " were diseased ") ; 11 : 1-3, 6 ; Acts 9 : 37 ; 19 : 12 ; Phil. 2 : 26, 27 ; 2 Tim. 4 : 20 ; Jas. 5 : 14. See DISEASED, B, No. 1, IMPOTENT, and, especially, WEAK.

2. KAMNŌ (κάμνω), primarily, to work, hence, from the effect of constant work, to be weary, Heb. 12 : 3, is rendered " (him) that is sick," in Jas. 5 : 15, R.V., A.V. " (the) sick." The choice of this verb instead of the repetition of No. 1 (ver. 14, see above), is suggestive of the common accompaniment of sickness, weariness of mind (which is the meaning of this verb), which not infrequently hinders physical recovery ; hence this special cause is here intimated in the general idea of sickness. In some mss. it occurs in Rev. 2 : 3.¶ In the Sept., Job 10 : 1 ; 17 : 2.¶

3. SUNECHŌ (συνέχω), to hold in, hold fast, is used, in the Passive Voice, of being seized or afflicted by ills, Acts 28 : 8, " sick " (of the father of Publius, cp. Matt. 4 : 24 ; Luke 4 : 38, " taken with "). See CONSTRAIN, No. 3.

Notes : (1) *Noseō*, to be sick, is used metaphorically of mental ailment, in 1 Tim. 6 : 4, " doting " (marg., " sick "). (2) The adverb *kakōs*, evilly, ill, with *echō*, to hold, to have, is rendered to be sick, in Matt. 4 : 24, R.V., " that were sick ; " 8 : 16 ; 9 : 12 ; 14 : 35 and Mark 1 : 32, R.V. (A.V., " diseased ") ; 1 : 34 ; 2 : 17 ; 6 : 55 ; Luke 5 : 31 ; 7 : 2. (3) For " sick of the palsy," Luke 5 : 24 ; Acts 9 : 33, see PALSY (sick of).

B. Adjectives.

1. ASTHENĒS (ἀσθενής), lit., without strength, hence, feeble, weak, is used of bodily debility, Matt. 25 : 43 (for ver. 39, see A, No. 1), 44 ; some texts have it in Luke 9 : 2 (the best omit it, the meaning being to heal in general) ; 10 : 9 ; Acts 5 : 15, 16 ; in 4 : 9 it is rendered " impotent." See FEEBLE, IMPOTENT, WEAK.

2. ARRHŌSTOS (ἄρρωστος), feeble, sickly (*a*, negative, *rhōnnumi*, to be strong), is translated " sick " in Matt. 14 : 14 ; Mark 16 : 18 ; " sick folk " in Mark 6 : 5 ; " that were sick " in 6 : 13 ; " sickly " in 1 Cor. 11 : 30, here also of the physical state.¶ In the Sept., 1 Kings 14 : 5 ; Mal. 1 : 8.¶

C. Nouns.

1. ASTHENEIA (ἀσθένεια), weakness, sickness (akin to A, No. 1 and B, No. 1), is translated "sickness" in John 11 : 4. See DISEASE, No. 1, INFIRMITY, WEAKNESS.

2. NOSOS (νόσος) : see DISEASE, No. 3.

SICKLE

DREPANON (δρέπανον), a pruning-hook, a sickle (akin to *drepō*, to pluck), occurs in Mark 4 : 29 ; Rev. 14 : 14, 15, 16, 17, 18 (twice), 19.¶

SIDE
A. Noun.

PLEURA (πλευρά), a side (cp. Eng., pleurisy), is used of the side of Christ, into which the spear was thrust, John 19 : 34 ; 20 : 20, 25, 27 (some mss. have it in Matt. 27 : 49 ; see R.V. marg.) ; elsewhere, in Acts 12 : 7.¶

B. Adverb.

PERAN (πέραν), an adverb, signifying beyond, on the other side, is used (*a*) as a preposition and translated "on the other side of," e.g., in Mark 5 : 1 ; Luke 8 : 22 ; John 6 : 1, R.V. ; 6 : 22, 25 ; (*b*) as a noun with the article, e.g., Matt. 8 : 18, 28 ; 14 : 22 ; 16 : 5. See BEYOND, No. 2.

Notes : (1) In Luke 9 : 47, the preposition *para*, by the side of, with the dative case of the pronoun *heautou*, is rendered "by His side," R.V. (A.V., "by Him"). (2) See also EITHER, EVERYWHERE, No. 3, HIGHWAY, RIGHT.

SIFT

SINIAZŌ (σινιάζω), to winnow, sift (*sinion*, a sieve), is used figuratively in Luke 22 : 31.¶

SIGH

1. STENAZŌ (στενάζω), to groan, is translated "He sighed" in Mark 7 : 34. See GRIEF, GROAN.

2. ANASTENAZŌ (ἀναστενάζω), to sigh deeply (*ana*, up, suggesting 'deep drawn,' and No. 1), occurs in Mark 8 : 12.¶ In the Sept., Lam. 1 : 4.¶

SIGHT
A. Nouns.

1. EIDOS (εἶδος) is translated "sight" in 2 Cor. 5 : 7 ; see APPEARANCE, No. 1.

2. THEŌRIA (θεωρία) denotes a spectacle, a sight (akin to *theōreō*, to gaze, behold ; see BEHOLD), in Luke 23 : 48.¶

3. HORAMA (ὅραμα), that which is seen (akin to *horaō*, to see), besides its meaning, a vision, appearance, denotes a sight, in Acts 7 : 31. See VISION.

4. OPHTHALMOS (ὀφθαλμός), an eye (Eng., ophthalmic, etc.), in Acts 1 : 9 is translated " sight " (plur., lit.. ' eyes '). See EYE.

5. ANABLEPSIS (ἀνάβλεψις) denotes " recovering of sight " (ana, again, blepō, to see), Luke 4 : 18.¶ In the Sept., Isa. 61 : 1.¶

Notes : (1) For *horasis* (akin to No. 3), translated " in sight " in Rev. 4 : 3, A.V. (R.V., " to look upon "), see LOOK, B. (2) In Luke 7 : 21, the infinitive mood of *blepō*, to see, is used as a noun, " (He bestowed, A.V., ' gave ') sight." In Acts 9 : 9 it is used in the present participle with *mē*, not, "without sight" (lit., ' not seeing '). (3) In Heb. 12 : 21 *phantazomai*, to make visible, is used in the present participle as a noun, with the article, " (the) sight."¶ (4) In Luke 21 : 11, A.V., *phobētron* (or *phobēthron*), plur., is translated " fearful sights " (R.V., " terrors ").¶

B. Verb.

ANABLEPŌ (ἀναβλέπω), to look up, also denotes to receive or recover sight (akin to A, No. 5), e.g., Matt. 11 : 5 ; 20 : 34 ; Mark 10 : 51, 52 ; Luke 18 : 41-43 ; John 9 : 11, 15, 18 (twice) ; Acts 9 : 12, 17, 18 ; 22 : 13.

SIGHT OF (in the)

1. ENŌPION (ἐνώπιον), for which see BEFORE, No. 9, is translated ' in the sight of ' in the R.V. (for A.V., " before ") in Luke 12 : 6 ; 15 : 18 ; 16 : 15 ; Acts 7 : 46 ; 10 : 33 ; 19 : 19 ; 1 Tim. 5 : 4, 21 ; 2 Tim. 2 : 14 ; 4 : 1 ; Rev. 13 : 12. The R.V. is more appropriate in most passages, as giving the real significance of the word.

2. KATENŌPION (κατενώπιον), see BEFORE, No. 10, is translated " in the sight of " in 2 Cor. 2 : 17 (in some texts) ; Col. 1 : 22, A.V.

3. EMPROSTHEN (ἔμπροσθεν), see BEFORE, No. 4, is translated " in the sight of " in Matt. 11 : 26 ; Luke 10 : 21 ; 1 Thess. 1 : 3, A.V.

4. ENANTION (ἐναντίον), see BEFORE, No. 5, is translated " in the sight of " in Acts 7 : 10.

5. ENANTI (ἔναντι), see BEFORE, No. 6, is translated " in the sight of " in Acts 8 : 21, A.V.

6. KATENANTI (κατέναντι), see BEFORE, No. 8, is found in the best texts in 2 Cor. 12 : 19, " in the sight of," R.V., and in 2 : 17.

SIGN

1. SĒMEION (σημεῖον), a sign, mark, indication, token, is used (*a*) of that which distinguished a person or thing from others, e.g., Matt. 26 : 48 ; Luke 2 : 12 ; Rom. 4 : 11 ; 2 Cor. 12 : 12 (1st part) ; 2 Thess. 3 : 17, " token," i.e., his autograph attesting the authenticity of his letters ; (*b*) of a sign as a warning or admonition, e.g., Matt. 12 : 39, " the sign of (i.e., consisting of) the prophet Jonas ; " 16 : 4 ; Luke 2 : 34 ; 11 : 29, 30 ; (*c*) of miraculous acts (1) as tokens of Divine authority and power, e.g., Matt. 12 : 38, 39 (1st part) ; John 2 : 11, R.V., " signs ; " 3 : 2 (ditto) ; 4 : 54, " (the second) sign," R.V. ; 10 : 41 (ditto) ; 20 : 30 ;

in 1 Cor. 1 : 22, " the Jews ask for signs," R.V., indicates that the Apostles were met with the same demand from Jews as Christ had been : " signs were vouchsafed in plenty, signs of God's power and love, but these were not the signs which they sought. . . . They wanted signs of an outward Messianic Kingdom, of temporal triumph, of material greatness for the chosen people. . . . With such cravings the Gospel of a ' crucified Messiah ' was to them a stumblingblock indeed " (Lightfoot) ; 1 Cor. 14 : 22 ; (2) by demons, Rev. 16 : 14 ; (3) by false teachers or prophets, indications of assumed authority, e.g., Matt. 24 : 24 ; Mark 13 : 22 ; (4) by Satan through his special agents, 2 Thess. 2 : 9 ; Rev. 13 : 13, 14 ; 19 : 20 ; (d) of tokens portending future events, e.g., Matt. 24 : 3, where " the sign of the Son of Man " signifies, subjectively, that the Son of Man is Himself the sign of what He is about to do ; Mark 13 : 4 ; Luke 21 : 7, 11, 25 ; Acts 2 : 19 ; Rev. 12 : 1, R.V. ; 12 : 3, R.V. ; 15 : 1.

Signs confirmatory of what God had accomplished in the atoning sacrifice of Christ, His resurrection and ascension, and of the sending of the Holy Spirit, were given to the Jews for their recognition, as at Pentecost, and supernatural acts by apostolic ministry, as well as by the supernatural operations in the churches, such as the gift of tongues and prophesyings ; there is no record of the continuance of these latter after the circumstances recorded in Acts 19 : 1–20.

2. PARASĒMOS (παράσημος), an adjective meaning ' marked at the side ' (para, beside, sēma, a mark), is used in Acts 28 : 11 as a noun denoting the figure-head of a vessel.¶

SIGNS (to make)

ENNEUŌ (ἐννεύω), to nod to (en, in, neuō, to nod), denotes to make a sign to in Luke 1 : 62.¶ In the Sept., Prov. 6 : 13 ; 10 : 10.¶

Note : For dianeuō, Luke 1 : 22, R.V., see BECKON, No. 2.

For SIGNIFICATION, 1 Cor. 14 : 10, see DUMB, No. 2

SIGNIFY

1. SĒMAINŌ (σημαίνω), to give a sign, indicate (sēma, a sign : cp. SIGN, No. 1), to signify, is so translated in John 12 : 33 ; 18 : 32 ; 21 : 19 ; Acts 11 : 28 ; 25 : 27 ; Rev. 1 : 1, where perhaps the suggestion is that of expressing by signs.¶

2. DĒLOŌ (δηλόω), to make plain (dēlos, evident), is translated to signify in 1 Cor. 1 : 11, R.V., " it hath been signified " (A.V., " declared ") ; Heb. 9 : 8 ; 12 : 27 ; 1 Pet. 1 : 11, A.V. (R.V., " point unto ") ; 2 Pet. 1 : 14, R.V., " signified " (A.V., " hath shewed "). See POINT (unto).

3. EMPHANIZŌ (ἐμφανίζω), to manifest, make known, is translated " signify " in Acts 23 : 15 ; ver. 22, R.V. (A.V., " hath shewed "). See APPEAR, No. 5.

Note : In Acts 21 : 26, A.V., diangellō, to announce, is rendered " to signify " (R.V., " declaring ").

SILENCE
A. Noun.

SIGĒ (σιγή) occurs in Acts 21 : 40 ; Rev. 8 : 1, where the silence is introductory to the judgments following the opening of the seventh seal.¶

Note : For *hēsuchia*, A.V., " silence," in Acts 22 : 2 and 1 Tim. 2 : 11, 12, see QUIETNESS.

B. Verbs.

1. PHIMOŌ (φιμόω), to muzzle, is rendered " to put to silence " in Matt. 22 : 34 ; 1 Pet. 2 : 15. See MUZZLE, PEACE (hold), SPEECHLESS, STILL.

2. SIGAŌ (σιγάω), to be silent : see PEACE (hold), No. 1.

For SILENT, Luke 1 : 20, R.V., see DUMB, B

SILK

SĒRIKOS or SIRIKOS (σιρικός), silken, an adjective derived from the *Sēres*, a people of India, who seem to have produced silk originally as a marketable commodity, is used as a noun with the article, denoting silken fabric, Rev. 18 : 12.¶

For SILLY, 2 Tim. 3 : 6, see WOMAN, No. 2

SILVER
A. Nouns.

1. ARGURION (ἀργύριον) is rendered " silver " in Acts 3 : 6 ; 8 : 20, R.V. (A.V., "money") ; 20 : 33 ; 1 Cor. 3 : 12 (metaphorical) ; 1 Pet. 1 : 18. See MONEY, PIECE.

2. ARGUROS (ἄργυρος), akin to *argos*, shining, denotes silver. In each occurrence in the N.T. it follows the mention of gold, Matt. 10 : 9 ; Acts 17 : 29 ; Jas. 5 : 3 ; Rev. 18 : 12.¶

Note : For *drachmē*, Luke 15 : 8, see PIECE.

B. Adjective.

ARGUREOS (ἀργύρεος) signifies made of silver, Acts 19 : 24 ; 2 Tim. 2 : 20 ; Rev. 9 : 20.¶

SILVERSMITH

ARGUROKOPOS (ἀργυροκόπος), from *arguros* (see above) and *koptō*, to beat, occurs in Acts 19 : 24.¶ In the Sept., Judg. 17 : 4 ; Jer. 6 : 29.¶

SIMILITUDE

Note : For *homoiōma*, rendered " similitude " in Rom. 5 : 14, A.V., see LIKENESS, No. 1. For *homoiotēs*, " similitude " in Heb. 7 : 15 A.V., see LIKE, C, Note (1), and LIKENESS, No. 3. For *homoiōsis*, " similitude " in Jas. 3 : 9, A.V., see LIKENESS, No. 2.

For SIMPLE see GUILELESS, No. 2, and HARMLESS

For SIMPLICITY see LIBERALITY

SIN (Noun and Verb)
A. Nouns.

1. HAMARTIA (ἁμαρτία) is, lit., a missing of the mark, but this etymological meaning is largely lost sight of in the N.T. It is the most comprehensive term for moral obliquity. It is used of sin as (*a*) a principle or source of action, or an inward element producing acts, e.g., Rom. 3 : 9 ; 5 : 12, 13, 20 ; 6 : 1, 2 ; 7 : 7 (abstract for concrete) ; 7 : 8 (twice), 9, 11, 13, " sin, that it might be shewn to be sin," i.e., ' sin became death to me, that it might be exposed in its heinous character : ' in the last clause, " sin might become exceeding sinful," i.e., through the holiness of the Law, the true nature of sin was designed to be manifested to the conscience ;

(*b*) a governing principle or power, e.g., Rom. 6 : 6, " (the body) of sin ", here sin is spoken of as an organized power, acting through the members of the body, though the seat of sin is in the will (the body is the organic instrument) ; in the next clause, and in other passages, as follows, this governing principle is personified, e.g., Rom. 5 : 21 ; 6 : 12, 14, 17 ; 7 : 11, 14, 17, 20, 23, 25 ; 8 : 2 ; 1 Cor. 15 : 56 ; Heb. 3 : 13 ; 11 : 25 ; 12 : 4 ; Jas. 1 : 15 (2nd part) ;

(*c*) a generic term (distinct from specific terms such as No. 2, yet sometimes inclusive of concrete wrong doing, e.g., John 8 : 21, 34, 46 ; 9 : 41 ; 15 : 22, 24 ; 19 : 11) ; in Rom. 8 : 3, " God, sending His own Son in the likeness of sinful flesh," lit., ' flesh of sin,' the flesh stands for the body, the instrument of indwelling sin [Christ, pre-existently the Son of God, assumed human flesh, " of the substance of the Virgin Mary ; " the reality of incarnation was His, without taint of sin (for *homoiōma*, likeness, see LIKENESS)], " and *as an offering* for sin," i.e., ' a sin-offering ' (so the Sept., e.g., in Lev. 4 : 32 ; 5 : 6, 7, 8, 9), " condemned sin in the flesh," i.e., Christ, having taken human nature, sin apart (Heb. 4 : 15), and having lived a sinless life, died under the condemnation and judgment due to our sin ; for the generic sense see further, e.g., Heb. 9 : 26 ; 10 : 6, 8, 18 ; 13 : 11 ; 1 John 1 : 7, 8 ; 3 : 4 (1st part ; in the 2nd part, sin is defined as " lawlessness," R.V.), 8, 9 ; in these verses the A.V. use of the verb to commit is misleading ; not the committal of an act is in view, but a continuous course of sin, as indicated by the R.V., " doeth." The Apostle's use of the present tense of *poieō*, to do, virtually expresses the meaning of *prassō*, to practise, which John does not use (it is not infrequent in this sense in Paul's Epp., e.g., Rom. 1 : 32, R.V. ; 2 : 1 ; Gal. 5 : 21 ; Phil. 4 : 9) ; 1 Pet. 4 : 1 (singular in the best texts), lit., ' has been made to cease from sin,' i.e., as a result of suffering in the flesh, the mortifying of our members, and of obedience to a Saviour who suffered in flesh. Such no longer lives in the flesh, " to the lusts of men, but to the will of God ; " sometimes the word is used as virtually

equivalent to a condition of sin, e.g., John 1 : 29, " the sin (not sins) of
the world ; " 1 Cor. 15 : 17 ; or a course of sin, characterized by continuous acts, e.g., 1 Thess. 2 : 16 ; in 1 John 5 : 16 (2nd part) the R.V.
marg., is probably to be preferred, " there is sin unto death," not a special
act of sin, but the state or condition producing acts ; in ver. 17, " all
unrighteousness is sin " is not a definition of sin (as in 3 : 4), it gives a
specification of the term in its generic sense ;

(d) a sinful deed, an act of sin, e.g., Matt. 12 : 31 ; Acts 7 : 60 ; Jas.
1 : 15 (1st part) ; 2 : 9 ; 4 : 17 ; 5 : 15, 20 ; 1 John 5 : 16 (1st part).

Notes : (1) Christ is predicated as having been without sin in every
respect, e.g., (a), (b), (c) above, 2 Cor. 5 : 21 (1st part) ; 1 John 3 : 5 ;
John 14 : 30 ; (d) John 8 : 46 ; Heb. 4 : 15 ; 1 Pet. 2 : 22. (2) In Heb.
9 : 28 (2nd part) the reference is to a sin offering. (3) In 2 Cor. 5 : 21,
" Him . . . He made to be sin " indicates that God dealt with Him
as He must deal with sin, and that Christ fulfilled what was typified
in the guilt offering. (4) For the phrase " man of sin " in 2 Thess. 2 : 3,
see INIQUITY, No. 1.

2. HAMARTĒMA (ἁμάρτημα), akin to No. 1, denotes an act of disobedience to Divine law [as distinct from No. 1 (a), (b), (c)] ; plural in
Mark 3 : 28 ; Rom. 3 : 25 ; 2 Pet. 1 : 9, in some texts ; sing. in Mark
3 : 29 (some mss. have *krisis*, A.V., " damnation ") ; 1 Cor. 6 : 18.¶

Notes : (1) For *paraptōma*, rendered " sins " in the A.V. in Eph. 1 : 7 ;
2 : 5 ; Col. 2 : 13 (R.V., " trespass "), see TRESPASS. In Jas. 5 : 16, the
best texts have No. 1 (R.V., " sins "). (2) For synonymous terms see
DISOBEDIENCE, ERROR, FAULT, INIQUITY, TRANSGRESSION, UNGODLINESS.

B. Adjective.

ANAMARTĒTOS (ἀναμάρτητος), without sin (a, negative, n, euphonic,
and C, No. 1), is found in John 8 : 7.¶ In the Sept., Deut. 29 : 19.¶

C. Verbs.

1. HAMARTANŌ (ἁμαρτάνω), lit., to miss the mark, is used in the
N.T. (a) of sinning against God, (1) by angels, 2 Pet. 2 : 4 ; (2) by man,
Matt. 27 : 4 ; Luke 15 : 18, 21 (Heaven standing, by metonymy, for God) ;
John 5 : 14 ; 8 : 11 ; 9 : 2, 3 ; Rom. 2 : 12 (twice) ; 3 : 23 ; 5 : 12, 14, 16 ;
6 : 15 ; 1 Cor. 7 : 28 (twice), 36 ; 15 : 34 ; Eph. 4 : 26 ; 1 Tim. 5 : 20 ;
Tit. 3 : 11 ; Heb. 3 : 17 ; 10 : 26 ; 1 John 1 : 10 ; in 2 : 1 (twice), the
aorist tense in each place, referring to an act of sin ; on the contrary, in
3 : 6 (twice), 8, 9, the present tense indicates, not the committal of an act,
but the continuous practice of sin [see on A, No. 1 (c)] ; in 5 : 16 (twice)
the present tense indicates the condition resulting from an act, " unto
death " signifying ' tending towards death ; ' (b) against Christ, 1 Cor.
8 : 12 ; (c) against man, (1) a brother, Matt. 18 : 15, R.V., " sin " (A.V.,
" trespass ") ; ver. 21 ; Luke 17 : 3, 4, R.V., " sin " (A.V., " trespass ") ;
1 Cor. 8 : 12 ; (2) in Luke 15 : 18, 21, against the father by the prodigal
son, " in thy sight " being suggestive of befitting reverence ; (d) against
Jewish law, the Temple, and Cæsar, Acts 25 : 8, R.V., " sinned " (A.V.,

" offended ") ; (e) against one's own body, by fornication, 1 Cor. 6 : 18 ; (f) against earthly masters by servants, 1 Pet. 2 : 20, R.V., " (when) ye sin (and are buffeted for it)," A.V.," (when ye be buffeted) for your faults," lit., ' having sinned.'¶

2. PROAMARTANŌ (προαμαρτάνω), to sin previously (pro, before, and No. 1), occurs in 2 Cor. 12 : 21 ; 13 : 2, R.V. in each place, " have sinned heretofore " (so A.V. in the 2nd ; in the 1st, " have sinned already ").¶

SINCE: see † p. 9.

SINCERE, SINCERELY, SINCERITY
A. Adjectives.

1. ADOLOS (ἄδολος), guileless, pure, is translated " sincere " in 1 Pet. 2 : 2, A.V., " without guile," R.V. See GUILELESS, No. 1.

2. GNĒSIOS (γνήσιος), true, genuine, sincere, is used in the neuter, as a noun, with the article, signifying " sincerity," 2 Cor. 8 : 8 (of love). See OWN, TRUE.

3. EILIKRINĒS (εἰλικρινής) . see PURE, A, No. 3.
B. Adverb.

HAGNŌS (ἁγνῶς) denotes with pure motives, akin to words under PURE, A, No. 1, and B, Nos. 1 and 2, and is rendered " sincerely " in Phil. 1 : 17, R.V. (ver. 16, A.V.).¶
C. Noun.

EILIKRINIA (or —EIA) (εἰλικρινία), akin to A, No. 3, denotes sincerity, purity ; it is described metaphorically in 1 Cor. 5 : 8 as " un-leavened (bread) ; " in 2 Cor. 1 : 12, " sincerity (of God)," R.V., A.V., " (godly) sincerity," it describes a quality possessed by God, as that which is to characterize the conduct of believers ; in 2 Cor. 2 : 17 it is used of the rightful ministry of the Scriptures.¶

Notes : (1) For 2 Cor. 8 : 8, see A, No. 2. (2) In Eph. 6 : 24, A.V., *aphtharsia*, incorruption, is translated " sincerity " (R.V., " uncorrupt-ness," A.V. marg., " incorruption") ; some inferior mss. have it in Tit. 2 : 7, A.V. ; the R.V. follows those in which it is absent.

SINFUL

HAMARTŌLOS (ἁμαρτωλός), an adjective, akin to *hamartanō*, to sin, is used as an adjective, " sinful " in Mark 8 : 38 ; Luke 5 : 8 ; 19 : 7 (lit., ' a sinful man ') ; 24 : 7 ; John 9 : 16, and 24 (lit., ' a man sinful ') ; Rom. 7 : 13, for which see SIN, A, No. 1 (a). Elsewhere it is used as a noun : see SINNER. The noun is frequently found in a common phrase in sepulchral epitaphs in the S.W. of Asia Minor, with the threat against any desecrator of the tomb, ' let him be as a sinner before the subterranean gods ' (Moulton and Milligan).

Notes : (1) In Rom. 8 : 3, " sinful flesh " is, lit., ' flesh of sin ' (R.V.

marg.) : see SIN, No. 1 (c). (2) For the R.V. of Rom. 7 : 5, " sinful passions," see PASSION, No. 1.

SING, SINGING

1. ADŌ (ᾀδω) is used always of praise to God, (a) intransitively, Eph. 5 : 19 ; Col. 3 : 16 ; (b) transitively, Rev. 5 : 9 ; 14 : 3 ; 15 : 3.¶

2. PSALLŌ (ψάλλω) : see MELODY.

3. HUMNEŌ (ὑμνέω) : see HYMN, B.

SINGLE

HAPLOUS (ἁπλοῦς), simple, single, is used in a moral sense in Matt. 6 : 22 and Luke 11 : 34, said of the eye ; singleness of purpose keeps us from the snare of having a double treasure and consequently a divided heart.¶ The papyri provide instances of its use in other than the moral sense, e.g., of a marriage dowry, to be repaid pure and simple by a husband (Moulton and Milligan). In the Sept., Prov. 11 : 25.¶

SINGLENESS

1. APHELOTĒS (ἀφελότης) denotes simplicity, Acts 2 : 46, " singleness," for which Moulton and Milligan, from papyri examples, suggest " unworldly simplicity ; " the idea here is that of an unalloyed benevolence expressed in act.¶

2. HAPLOTĒS (ἁπλότης) : see BOUNTY, No. 2.

SINK

1. BUTHIZŌ (βυθίζω) is used literally in Luke 5 : 7. See DROWN, No. 1.

2. KATAPONTIZŌ (καταποντίζω) is translated to sink in Matt. 14 : 30 (Passive Voice). See DROWN, No. 3.

3. TITHĒMI (τίθημι), to put, is rendered " let . . . sink " in Luke 9 : 44, R.V. (" let . . . sink down," A.V.). See APPOINT, LAY.

Note : In Acts 20 : 9 (2nd part), A.V., katapherō, to bear down, is translated " he sunk down " (R.V., " being borne down ") ; in the 1st part it is rendered " being fallen," A.V., " borne down," R.V.

SINNER

HAMARTŌLOS (ἁμαρτωλός), lit., one who misses the mark (a meaning not to be pressed), is an adjective, most frequently used as a noun (see SINFUL) ; it is the most usual term to describe the fallen condition of men ; it is applicable to all men, Rom. 5 : 8, 19. In the Synoptic Gospels the word is used not infrequently, by the Pharisees, of publicans (tax-collectors) and women of ill repute, e.g., " a woman which was in the city, a sinner," Luke 7 : 37 ; " a man that is a sinner," 19 : 7. In Gal. 2 : 15, in the clause " not sinners of the Gentiles," the Apostle is taking the Judaizers on their own ground, ironically reminding them of their claim to moral superiority over Gentiles ; he proceeds to show that the Jews are equally sinners with Gentiles.

Note : In Luke 13 : 4, A.V., *opheiletēs*, a debtor, is translated " sinners " (R.V., " offenders ; " R.V. and A.V. marg., " debtors ").

SIR(-S)

1. KURIOS (κύριος) : see LORD.

2. ANĒR (ἀνήρ), a man, is translated " sirs " in Acts 7 : 26 ; 14 : 15 ; 19 : 25 ; 27 : 10, 21, 25. See MAN.

Note : In John 21 : 5 the A.V. marg. has " sirs " for *paidia,* " children."

SISTER

ADELPHĒ (ἀδελφή) is used (*a*) of natural relationship, e.g., Matt. 19 : 29 ; of the sisters of Christ, the children of Joseph and Mary after the Virgin Birth of Christ, e.g., Matt. 13 : 56 ; (*b*) of spiritual kinship with Christ, an affinity marked by the fulfilment of the will of the Father, Matt. 12 : 50 ; Mark 3 : 35 ; of spiritual relationship based upon faith in Christ, Rom. 16 : 1 ; 1 Cor. 7 : 15 ; 9 : 5, A.V. and R.V. marg. ; Jas. 2 : 15 ; Philm. 2, R.V.

Note : In Col. 4 : 10, A.V., *anepsios* (cp. Lat., *nepos*, whence Eng., nephew), a cousin (so, R.V.), is translated " sister's son." See COUSIN.¶

SIT

1. KATHĒMAI (κάθημαι) is used (*a*) of the natural posture, e.g., Matt. 9 : 9, most frequently in the Apocalypse, some 32 times ; frequently in the Gospels and Acts ; elsewhere only in 1 Cor. 14 : 30 ; Jas. 2 : 3 (twice) ; and of Christ's position of authority on the throne of God, Col. 3 : 1, A.V., " sitteth " (R.V., " is, seated ") ; Heb. 1 : 13 (cp. Matt. 22 : 44 ; 26 : 64 and parallel passages in Mark and Luke, and Acts 2 : 34) ; often as antecedent or successive to, or accompanying, another act (in no case a superfluous expression), e.g., Matt. 15 : 29 ; 27 : 36 ; Mark 2 : 14 ; 4 : 1 ; (*b*) metaphorically in Matt. 4 : 16 (twice) ; Luke 1 : 79 ; of inhabiting a place (translated " dwell "), Luke 21 : 35 ; Rev. 14 : 6, R.V. marg., " sit " (in the best texts : some have *katoikeō*, to dwell). See DWELL.

2. SUNKATHĒMAI (συγκάθημαι), to sit with (*sun*, with, and No. 1), occurs in Mark 14 : 54 ; Acts 26 : 30.¶ In the Sept., Ps. 101 : 6, " dwell."¶

3. ANAKEIMAI (ἀνάκειμαι), to recline at table (*ana*, up, *keimai*, to lie), is rendered to sit at meat in Matt. 9 : 10 (R.V., marg., " reclined ") ; 26 : 7 ; 26 : 20, R.V., " He was sitting at meat " (A.V., " He sat down ") ; Mark 16 : 14 ; in some mss. Luke 7 : 37 (see No. 5) ; 22 : 27 (twice) ; in Mark 14 : 18, " sat ; " in John 6 : 11, " were set down ; " John 12 : 2 in the best texts (see No. 4). See GUEST, LEAN, LIE, Note (1), SET, No. 22, TABLE (at the).

4. SUNANAKEIMAI (συνανάκειμαι), to recline at table with or

together (*sun*, and No. 3), to sit at meat or at table with, occurs in Matt. 9 : 10, "sat down ; " 14 : 9 ; Mark 2 : 15, R.V., "sat down with " (A.V., " sat . . . together with ") ; 6 : 22 ; Luke 7 : 49 ; 14 : 10, 15 ; John 12 : 2 (in some texts).¶

5. KATAKEIMAI (κατάκειμαι), to lie down (*kata*, down, and *keimai*, cp. No. 3), is used of reclining at a meal, Mark 2 : 15 ; 14 : 3 ; Luke 5 : 29, R.V., "were sitting at meat " (A.V., " sat down ") ; 7 : 37 (in the best texts) ; 1 Cor. 8 : 10. See KEEP, LIE.

6. ANAKLINŌ (ἀνακλίνω), to cause to recline, make to sit down, is used in the Active Voice, in Luke 12 : 37 (also in 2 : 7, of 'laying' the infant Christ in the manger) ; in the Passive, Matt. 8 : 11 ; 14 : 19 ; Mark 6 : 39 (in the best texts) ; in some texts, Luke 7 : 36 and 9 : 15 (see No. 7) ; 13 : 29. See LAY.¶

7. KATAKLINŌ (κατακλίνω) is used only in connection with meals, (*a*) in the Active Voice, to make recline, Luke 9 : 14, 15 (in the best texts) ; in the Passive Voice, to recline, Luke 7 : 36 (in the best texts), " sat down to meat ; " 14 : 8 ; 24 : 30 (R.V., " had sat down . . . to meat ").¶

8. KATHIZŌ (καθίζω) is used (*a*) transitively, to make sit down, Acts 2 : 30 (see also SET, No. 9) ; (*b*) intransitively, to sit down, e.g., Matt. 5 : 1, R.V., "when (He) had sat down " (A.V., " was set ") ; 19 : 28 ; 20 : 21, 23 ; 23 : 2 ; 25 : 31 ; 26 : 36 ; Mark 11 : 2, 7 ; 12 : 41 ; Luke 14 : 28, 31 ; 16 : 6 ; John 19 : 13 ; Acts 2 : 3 (of the tongues of fire) ; 8 : 31 ; 1 Cor. 10 : 7 ; 2 Thess. 2 : 4, " he sitteth," aorist tense, i.e., 'he takes his seat' (as, e.g., in Mark 16 : 19) ; Rev. 3 : 21 (twice), R.V., " to sit down " and " sat down ; " 20 : 4.

9. PARAKATHEZOMAI (παρακαθέζομαι), to sit down beside (*para*), in a Passive Voice form, occurs in the best mss. in Luke 10 : 39.¶ Some texts have the verb *parakathizō*, to set beside, Active form in Middle sense.

10. SUNKATHIZŌ (συγκαθίζω) denotes (*a*) transitively, to make to sit together, Eph. 2 : 6 ; (*b*) intransitively, Luke 22 : 55, R.V., " had sat down together " (A.V., " were set down ").¶

11. ANAKATHIZŌ (ἀνακαθίζω), to set up, is used intransitively, to sit up, of two who were raised from the dead, Luke 7 : 15 ; Acts 9 : 40.¶

12. ANAPIPTŌ (ἀναπίπτω), to fall back (*ana*, back, *piptō*, to fall), denotes, in the N.T., to recline for a repast, Matt. 15 : 35 ; Mark 6 : 40 ; 8 : 6 ; Luke 11 : 37 ; 14 : 10 ; 17 : 7 ; 22 : 14 ; John 6 : 10 (twice) ; 13 : 12 ; in John 13 : 25 and 21 : 20 it is used of leaning on the bosom of Christ. See LEAN.¶ In the Sept., Gen. 49 : 9.¶

13. KATHEZOMAI (καθέζομαι), to sit (down), is used in Matt. 26 : 55 ; Luke 2 : 46 ; John 4 : 6 ; 11 : 20 ; 20 : 12 ; Acts 6 : 15.¶

Note : For *epibainō*, " sitting upon," Matt. 21 : 5, A.V., see RIDE.

SIX

HEX (ἕξ), whence Eng. prefix, *hex*-, is used separately from other numerals in Matt. 17 : 1 ; Mark 9 : 2 ; Luke 4 : 25 ; 13 : 14 ; John 2 : 6 ;

12 : 1 ; Acts 11 : 12 ; 18 : 11 ; Jas. 5 : 17 ; Rev. 4 : 8. It sometimes suggests incompleteness, in comparison with the perfect number seven.

Notes : (1) In combination with *tessarakonta*, forty, it occurs in John 2 : 20 ; with *hebdomēkonta*, seventy, Acts 27 : 37, " (two hundred) three-score and sixteen." (2) It forms the first syllable of *hexēkonta*, sixty (see below), and *hexakosioi*, six hundred, Rev. 13 : 18 (see SIXTY, Note) ; 14 : 20.

SIXTH

HEKTOS (ἕκτος) is used (*a*) of a month, Luke 1 : 26, 36 ; (*b*) an hour, Matt. 20 : 5 ; 27 : 45 and parallel passages ; John 4 : 6 ; (*c*) an angel, Rev. 9 : 13, 14 ; 16 : 12 ; (*d*) a seal of a roll, in vision, Rev. 6 : 12 ; (*e*) of the sixth precious stone, the sardius, in the foundations of the wall of the heavenly Jerusalem, Rev. 21 : 20.

SIXTY, SIXTYFOLD

HEXĒKONTA (ἑξήκοντα) occurs in Matt. 13 : 8, R.V. (A.V., " sixty-fold ") ; 13 : 23 ; Mark 4 : 8, where the R.V. and A.V. reverse the trans-lation, as in Matt. 13 : 8, while in Mark 4 : 20 the R.V. has " sixtyfold ", A.V., " sixty " ; in Rev. 13 : 18, R.V., " sixty " (A.V., " threescore "). It is rendered " threescore " in Luke 24 : 13 ; 1 Tim. 5 : 9 ; Rev. 11 : 3 ; 12 : 6.¶

Note : In Rev. 13 : 18, the number of the " Beast," the human poten-tate destined to rule with Satanic power the ten-kingdom league at the end of this age, is given as " six hundred and sixty and six " (R.V.), and described as " the number of (a) man." The number is suggestive of the acme of the pride of fallen man, the fullest development of man under direct Satanic control, and standing in contrast to seven as the number of completeness and perfection.

SKIN

ASKOS (ἀσκός), a leather bottle, wineskin, occurs in Matt. 9 : 17 (four times) ; Mark 2 : 22 (four times) ; Luke 5 : 37 (three times), 38 ; in each place, R.V., " wineskins " or " skins," for A.V., " bottles." A whole goatskin, for example, would be used with the apertures bound up, and when filled, tied at the neck. They were tanned with acacia bark and left hairy on the outside. New wines, by fermenting, would rend old skins (cp. Josh. 9 : 13 ; Job 32 : 19). Hung in the smoke to dry, the skin-bottles become shrivelled (see Ps. 119 : 83).¶

Note : For " (a girdle) of a skin," Mark 1 : 6, see LEATHERN.

SKULL

KRANION (κρανίον), Lat., *cranium* (akin to *kara*, the head), is used of the scene of the Crucifixion, Matt. 27 : 33 ; Mark 15 : 22 ; John 19 : 17 ; in Luke 23 : 33, R.V., " (the place which is called) The skull," A.V.,

" Calvary " (from Latin *calvaria*, a skull : marg., " the place of a skull "). The locality has been identified by the traces of the resemblance of the hill to a skull.¶   In the Sept., Judg. 9 : 53 ;   2 Kings 9 : 35.¶

For SKY see HEAVEN

SLACK (Verb), SLACKNESS
A. Verb.

BRADUNŌ (βραδύνω), used intransitively signifies to be slow, to tarry (*bradus*, slow), said negatively of God, 2 Pet. 3 : 9, " is (not) slack ; " in 1 Tim. 3 : 15, translated " (if) I tarry."   See TARRY.¶   In the Sept., Gen. 43 : 10 ;   Deut. 7 : 10 ;   Isa. 46 : 13.¶

B. Noun.

BRADUTĒS (βραδυτής), slowness (akin to A), is rendered " slackness " in 2 Pet. 3 : 9.¶

SLANDERER

DIABOLOS (διάβολος), an adjective, slanderous, accusing falsely, is used as a noun, translated " slanderers " in 1 Tim. 3 : 11, where the reference is to those who are given to finding fault with the demeanour and conduct of others, and spreading their innuendos and criticisms in the church ; in 2 Tim. 3 : 3, R.V. (A.V., " false accusers ") ; Tit. 2 : 3 (ditto) : see ACCUSER, DEVIL.

For SLANDEROUSLY see REPORT, C, No. 5

SLAUGHTER

1. SPHAGĒ (σφαγή) is used in two quotations from the Sept., Acts 8 : 32 from Isa. 53 : 7, and Rom. 8 : 36 from Psa. 44 : 22 ; in the latter the quotation is set in a strain of triumph, the passage quoted being an utterance of sorrow. In Jas. 5 : 5 there is an allusion to Jer. 12 : 3, the luxurious rich, getting wealth by injustice, spending it on their pleasures, are " fattening themselves like sheep unconscious of their doom."¶

2. KOPĒ (κοπή), a stroke (akin to *koptō*, to strike, to cut), signifies a smiting in battle, in Heb. 7 : 1.¶   In the Sept., Gen. 14 : 17 ;   Deut. 28 : 25 ;   Josh. 10 : 20.¶

3. PHONOS (φόνος), a killing, murder, is rendered " slaughter " in Acts 9 : 1 ;   see MURDER.

SLAVE

SŌMA (σῶμα), a body, is translated " slaves " in Rev. 18 : 13 (R.V. and A.V. marg., " bodies "), an intimation of the unrighteous control over the bodily activities of slaves ; the next word " souls " stands for the whole being. See BODY.

SLAY, SLAIN, SLEW

I. APOKTEINŌ (ἀποκτείνω), the usual word for to kill, is so translated in the R.V. wherever possible (e.g., for A.V., to slay, in Luke 11 : 49 ; Acts 7 : 52 ; Rev. 2 : 13 ; 9 : 15 ; 11 : 13 ; 19 : 21) ; in the following the verb to kill would not be appropriate, Rom. 7 : 11, " slew," metaphorically of sin, as using the commandment ; Eph. 2 : 16, " having slain," said metaphorically of the enmity between Jew and Gentile. See KILL, No. 1.

Note : Some mss. have it in John 5 : 16 (A.V., " to slay ").

2. ANAIREŌ (ἀναιρέω), to take away, destroy, kill, is rendered to slay in Matt. 2 : 16 ; Acts 2 : 23 ; 5 : 33, 36 ; 9 : 29, A.V. (R.V., to kill) ; 10 : 39 ; 13 : 28 ; 22 : 20 ; 23 : 15, R.V. ; in 2 Thess. 2 : 8 the best texts have this verb (for *analiskō*, to consume, A.V. and R.V. marg.) ; hence the R.V., "·shall slay," of the destruction of the man of sin. See KILL, No. 2.

3. SPHAZŌ or SPHATTŌ (σφάττω), to slay, especially of victims for sacrifice (akin to *sphagē :* see SLAUGHTER), is used (*a*) of taking human life, 1 John 3 : 12 (twice) ; Rev. 6 : 4, R.V., " slay " (A.V., " kill ") ; in 13 : 3, probably of assassination, R.V., " smitten (unto death)," A.V., " wounded (to death)," R.V. marg., "slain ;" 18 : 24 ; (*b*) of Christ, as the Lamb of sacrifice, Rev. 5 : 6, 9, 12 ; 6 : 9 ; 13 : 8. See KILL, No. 7.¶

4. KATASPHAZŌ (κατασφάζω), to kill off (*kata*, used intensively, and No. 3), is used in Luke 19 : 27.¶. In the Sept., Ezek. 16 : 40 ; Zech. 11 : 5.¶

5. DIACHEIRIZŌ (διαχειρίζω), to lay hands on, kill, is translated " slew " in Acts 5 : 30. See KILL, No. 6.

6. PHONEUŌ (φονεύω), to kill, to murder, is rendered " ye slew " in Matt. 23 : 35. See KILL, No. 4.

Note : For *thuō*, Acts 11 : 7, A.V., " slay " (R.V., " kill "), see KILL, No. 3.

For SLAIN BEASTS see BEAST, No. 5

For SLEEP see ASLEEP

SLEIGHT

KUBIA (or -EIA) (κυβία) denotes dice-playing (from *kubos*, a cube, a die as used in gaming) ; hence, metaphorically, trickery, sleight, Eph. 4 : 14. The Eng. word is connected with 'sly' (not with slight).¶

For SLIP see DRIFT

SLOTHFUL

I. NŌTHROS (νωθρός), indolent, sluggish, is rendered " slothful " in Heb. 6 : 12, A.V. See DULL, and synonymous words there, and SLUGGISH.

2. OKNĒROS (ὀκνηρός), shrinking, irksome, is translated " slothful " in Matt. 25 : 26, and Rom. 12 : 11, where " in diligence not slothful," R.V., might be rendered ' not flagging in zeal.' See GRIEVOUS, Note (2).

SLOW

BRADUS (βραδύς) is used twice in Jas. 1 : 19, in an exhortation to be slow to speak and slow to wrath ; in Luke 24 : 25, metaphorically of the understanding.¶

Note : For " slow " (*argos*) in Tit. 1 : 12, see IDLE.

For SLOWLY (sailed) see SAIL, No. 10

SLUGGISH

NŌTHROS (νωθρός), for which see SLOTHFUL, is translated " sluggish " in Heb. 6 : 12, R.V. ; here it is set in contrast to confident and constant hope ; in 5 : 11 (" dull ") to vigorous growth in knowledge. See DULL.¶

For SLUMBER (Noun) see STUPOR

SLUMBER (Verb)

NUSTAZŌ (νυστάζω) denotes to nod in sleep (akin to *neuō*, to nod), fall asleep, and is used (*a*) of natural slumber, Matt. 25 : 5 ; (*b*) metaphorically in 2 Pet. 2 : 3, negatively, of the destruction awaiting false teachers.¶

SMALL

1. MIKROS (μικρός), little, small (of age, quantity, size, space), is translated " small " in Acts 26 : 22 ; Rev. 11 : 18 ; 13 : 16 ; 19 : 5, 18 ; 20 : 12. See LITTLE.

2. OLIGOS (ὀλίγος), little, small (of amount, number, time), is translated " small " in Acts 12 : 18 ; 15 : 2 ; 19 : 23 ; ver. 24, A.V. (R.V., " little ") ; 27 : 20.

Notes : (1) For " very small " and " smallest " see LEAST. (2) For combinations with other words, see CORD, FISH, ISLAND.

For SMELL see SAVOUR

SMELLING

OSPHRĒSIS (ὄσφρησις) denotes the sense of smell, 1 Cor. 12 : 17, " smelling."¶

SMITE

1. PATASSŌ (πατάσσω), to strike, smite, is used (I) literally, of giving a blow with the hand, or fist or a weapon, Matt. 26 : 51, R.V., " smote " (A.V., " struck ") ; Luke 22 : 49, 50 ; Acts 7 : 24 ; 12 : 7 ; (II) metaphorically, (*a*) of judgment meted out to Christ, Matt. 26 : 31 ; Mark 14 : 27 ; (*b*) of the infliction of disease, by an angel, Acts 12 : 23 ; of plagues to be inflicted upon men by two Divinely appointed witnesses, Rev. 11 : 6 ; (*c*) of judgment to be executed by Christ upon the nations,

Rev. 19 : 15, the instrument being His Word, described as a sword.¶

2. TUPTŌ (τύπτω), to strike, smite, beat, is rendered to smite in Matt. 24 : 49, A.V. (R.V., " beat ") ; 27 : 30 ; Mark 15 : 19 ; Luke 6 : 29 ; 18 : 13 ; in some texts in 22 : 64 (1st part : R.V. omits ; for the 2nd part see No. 3) ; 23 : 48 ; Acts 23 : 2, 3 (twice). See BEAT, No. 2.

3. PAIŌ (παίω) signifies to strike or smite (a) with the hand or fist, Matt. 26 : 68 ; Luke 22 : 64 (see No. 2) ; (b) with a sword, Mark 14 : 47 ; John 18 : 10, A.V. (R.V., " struck ") ; (c) with a sting, Rev. 9 : 5, " striketh."¶

4. DERŌ (δέρω), to flay, to beat, akin to derma, skin, is translated to smite in Luke 22 : 63, A.V. (R.V., " beat ") ; John 18 : 23 ; 2 Cor. 11 : 20. See BEAT, No. 1.

5. PLĒSSŌ (πλήσσω), akin to plēgē, a plague, stripe, wound, is used figuratively of the effect upon sun, moon and stars, after the sounding of the trumpet by the fourth angel, in the series of Divine judgments upon the world hereafter, Rev. 8 : 12.¶

6. RHAPIZŌ (ῥαπίζω), primarily to strike with a rod (rhapis, a rod), then, to strike the face with the palm of the hand or the clenched fist, is used in Matt. 5 : 39 ; 26 : 67, where the marg. of A.V. and R.V. has " with rods." Cp. rhapisma, Note (2), below.¶

7. KATABALLŌ (καταβάλλω), to cast down, is translated " smitten down " in 2 Cor. 4 : 9, R.V. See CAST, No. 8.

8. PROSKOPTŌ (προσκόπτω), to beat upon, is translated " smote upon " in Matt. 7 : 27. See BEAT, No. 6.

9. SPHAZŌ (σφάζω), to slay, is translated " smitten unto death " in Rev. 13 : 3 ; see KILL, SLAY.

Notes : (1) In Matt. 26 : 51, A.V., aphaireō, to take away, take off, is translated " smote off " (R.V., " struck off "). (2) The noun rhapisma, a blow, in the plural, as the object of didōmi, to give, in John 19 : 3 is translated " smote (Him) with their hands " (R.V., " struck etc."), lit., ' gave . . . blows' (R.V. marg., " with rods ") ; in 18 : 22 (where the phrase is used with the singular of the noun) the R.V. renders it " struck . . . with his hand " (A.V., " struck . . . with the palm of his hand "), marg. of both, " with a rod."

The same word is used in Mark 14 : 65, " (received Him) with blows (of their hands) ", R.V. [A.V., " did strike Him with the palms (of their hands)," R.V. margin, " strokes of rods "]. See BLOW (Noun).¶ Cp. No. 6, above, re Matt. 26 : 67.

SMOKE (Noun and Verb)
A. Noun.

KAPNOS (καπνός), smoke, occurs in Acts 2 : 19 and 12 times in the Apocalypse.¶

B. Verb.

TUPHŌ (τύφω), to raise a smoke [akin to tuphos, smoke (not in the

N.T.), and *tuphoō*, to puff up with pride, see HIGH-MINDED], is used in the Passive Voice in Matt. 12 : 20, " smoking (flax)," lit., ' caused to smoke,' of the wick of a lamp which has ceased to burn clearly, figurative of mere nominal religiousness without the Spirit's power.¶ The Sept. uses the verb *kapnizō* (akin to A).

SMOOTH

LEIOS (λεῖος), smooth, occurs in Luke 3 : 5, figurative of the change in Israel from self-righteousness, pride and other forms of evil, to repentance, humility and submission.¶ In the Sept., Gen. 27 : 11 ; 1 Sam. 17 : 40 ; Prov. 2 : 20 ; 12 : 13 ; 26 : 23 ; Isa. 40 : 4.¶

Note : *Chrēstologia* (*chrēstos*, good, *legō*, to speak) is rendered "smooth . . . (speech)," in Rom. 16 : 18, R.V. (A.V., "good words ").¶

SNARE

1. PAGIS (παγίς), a trap, a snare (akin to *pēgnumi*, to fix, and *pagideuō*, to ensnare, which see), is used metaphorically of (*a*) the allurements to evil by which the Devil ensnares one, 1 Tim. 3 : 7 ; 2 Tim. 2 : 26 ; (*b*) seductions to evil, which ensnare those who " desire to be rich," 1 Tim. 6 : 9 ; (*c*) the evil brought by Israel upon themselves by which the special privileges Divinely granted them and centring in Christ, became a snare to them, their rejection of Christ and the Gospel being the retributive effect of their apostasy, Rom. 11 : 9 ; (*d*) of the sudden judgments of God to come upon those whose hearts are " overcharged with surfeiting, and drunkenness, and cares of this life," Luke 21 : 34 (ver. 35 in A.V.).¶

2. BROCHOS (βρόχος), a noose, slip-knot, halter, is used metaphorically in 1 Cor. 7 : 35, " a snare " (R.V., marg., " constraint," " noose ").¶ In the Sept., Prov. 6 : 5 ; 7 : 21 ; 22 : 25.¶

SNATCH

HARPAZŌ (ἀρπάζω), to snatch, is translated to snatch in the R.V. only, in Matt. 13 : 19, A.V., " catcheth away ; " John 10 : 12, A.V., " catcheth ; " 10 : 28, 29, A.V., " pluck ; " Jude 23, A.V., " pulling." See CATCH, No. 1.

SNOW

CHIŌN (χιών) occurs in Matt. 28 : 3 ; Rev. 1 : 14. Some mss. have it in Mark 9 : 3 (A.V.).¶

SO

Notes : (1) *Houtōs* or *houtō*, thus, is the usual word (see THUS). (2) Some form of *houtos*, this, is sometimes rendered " so," e.g., Acts 23 : 7 ; Rom. 12 : 20. (3) It translates *homoiōs*, likewise, e.g., in Luke 5 : 10 ; *oun*, therefore, e.g., John 4 : 40, 53. (4) For " so many as," see MANY ; for " so much as," see MUCH. (5) *Sumbainō*, when used of events, signifies to come to pass, happen; in Acts 21 : 35 it is rendered "so it was." See BEFALL, HAPPEN. (6) In 1 Pet. 3 : 17, *thelō*, to will, is translated "should so will," lit., 'willeth.' (7) In 2 Cor. 12 : 16, the imperative mood, 3rd person singular, of *eimi*, to be, is used impersonally, and signifies "be it so." (8) In Heb. 7 : 9 *epos*, a word, is used in a phrase rendered "so to say;" see WORD, Note (1). (9) In 1 Tim. 3 : 11, *hōsautōs*, likewise, is translated "even so." (10) *Hōs*, as, is rendered "so" in Heb. 3 : 11 (R.V., "as"). For association with other words see † p. 9.

SOBER, SOBERLY, SOBERMINDED
A. Adjective.

SŌPHRŌN (σώφρων) denotes of sound mind (*sōzō*, to save, *phrēn*, the mind); hence, self-controlled, soberminded, always rendered "soberminded" in the R.V.; in 1 Tim. 3 : 2 and Tit. 1 : 8, A.V., "sober;" in Tit. 2 : 2, A.V., "temperate;" in 2 : 5, A.V., "discreet."¶

Note: For *nēphalios* (akin to B, No. 1), translated "sober" in 1 Tim. 3 : 11; Tit. 2 : 2, see TEMPERATE.

B. Verbs.

1. NĒPHŌ (νήφω) signifies to be free from the influence of intoxicants; in the N.T., metaphorically, it does not in itself imply watchfulness, but is used in association with it, 1 Thess. 5 : 6, 8; 2 Tim. 4 : 5; 1 Pet. 1 : 13; 4 : 7, R.V. (A.V., "watch"); 5 : 8.¶ Cp. *eknēphō* and *ananēphō*, under AWAKE, No. 3 and Note.

2. SŌPHRONEŌ (σωφρονέω), akin to A, is rendered to think soberly, Rom. 12 : 3; to be sober, 2 Cor. 5 : 13; to be soberminded, Tit. 2 : 6; in 1 Pet. 4 : 7, A.V. "be ye sober" (R.V., "of sound mind"); see MIND, B, No. 5.

3. SŌPHRONIZŌ (σωφρονίζω) denotes to cause to be of sound mind, to recall to one's senses; in Tit. 2 : 4, R.V., it is rendered "they may train" (A.V., "they may teach . . . to be sober," marg., "wise"); "train" expresses the meaning more adequately; the training would involve the cultivation of sound judgment and prudence.¶

C. Adverb.

SŌPHRONŌS (σωφρόνως), akin to A and B, Nos. 2 and 3, soberly, occurs in Tit. 2 : 12; it suggests the exercise of that self-restraint that governs all passions and desires, enabling the believer to be conformed to the mind of Christ.¶

Note: For the phrase to think soberly, see B, No. 2.

SOBERNESS, SOBRIETY

SŌPHROSUNĒ (σωφροσύνη) denotes soundness of mind (see SOBER, A), Acts 26 : 25, "soberness;" 1 Tim. 2 : 9, 15, "sobriety;" 'sound judgment' practically expresses the meaning; "it is that habitual inner self-government, with its constant rein on all the passions and desires, which would hinder the temptation to these from arising, or at all events from arising in such strength as would overbear the checks and barriers which *aidōs* (shamefastness) opposed to it" (Trench Syn. § xx, end).¶

For SOFT see EFFEMINATE

For SOFTLY see BLOW (Verb), No. 2

SOJOURN, SOJOURNER, SOJOURNING
A. Verbs.

1. PAROIKEŌ (παροικέω) denotes to dwell beside, among or by (*para*, beside, *oikeō*, to dwell) ; then, to dwell in a place as a *paroikos*, a stranger (see below), Luke 24 : 18, R.V., " Dost thou (alone) sojourn . . . ? " [marg.," Dost thou sojourn (alone) " is preferable], A.V., " art thou (only) a stranger ? " (*monos*, alone, is an adjective, not an adverb) ; in Heb. 11 : 9, R.V., " he became a sojourner " (A.V., " he sojourned "), the R.V. gives the force of the aorist tense.¶

2. EPIDĒMEŌ (ἐπιδημέω) is rendered to sojourn in Acts 17 : 21, R.V.

B. Adjectives.

1. PAROIKOS (πάροικος), an adjective, akin to A, No. 1, lit., dwelling near (see above), then, foreign, alien (found with this meaning in Inscriptions), hence, as a noun, a sojourner, is used with *eimi*, to be, in Acts 7 : 6, " should sojourn," lit., ' should be a sojourner ; ' in 7 : 29, R.V., " sojourner " (A.V., " stranger ") ; in Eph. 2 : 19, R.V., " sojourners " (A.V., " foreigners "), the preceding word rendered " strangers " is *xenos* ; in 1 Pet. 2 : 11, R.V., ditto (A.V., " strangers ").¶

2. APODĒMOS (ἀπόδημος), gone abroad (*apo*, from, *dēmos*, people), signifies " sojourning in another country," Mark 13 : 34, R.V. (A.V., " taking a far journey ").¶

3. PAREPIDĒMOS (παρεπίδημος), sojourning in a strange place, is used as a noun, denoting a sojourner, an exile, 1 Pet. 1 : 1, R.V., " sojourners " (A.V., " strangers "). See PILGRIM.¶

C. Noun.

PAROIKIA (παροικία), a sojourning (akin to A and B, Nos. 1), occurs in Acts 13 : 17, rendered " they sojourned," R.V., A.V., " dwelt as strangers," lit., ' in the sojourning ; ' in 1 Pet. 1 : 17, " sojourning."¶

SOLDIER
A. Nouns.

1. STRATIŌTĒS (στρατιώτης), a soldier, is used (*a*) in the natural sense, e.g., Matt. 8 : 9 ; 27 : 27 ; 28 : 12 ; Mark 15 : 16 ; Luke 7 : 8 ; 23 : 36 ; six times in John ; thirteen times in Acts ; not again in the N.T. ; (*b*) metaphorically of one who endures hardship in the cause of Christ, 2 Tim. 2 : 3.

2. STRATEUMA (στράτευμα), an army, is used to denote a company of soldiers in Acts 23 : 10 ; in ver. 27, R.V., " the soldiers," A.V., " an army ; " in Luke 23 : 11 (plural), R.V., " soldiers," A.V., " men of war." See ARMY.

3. SUSTRATIŌTĒS (συστρατιώτης), a fellow-soldier (sun, with, and No. 1), is used metaphorically in Phil. 2 : 25 and Philm. 2, of fellowship in Christian service.¶

B. Verb.

STRATEUŌ (στρατεύω), always in the Middle Voice in the N.T., is used (a) literally of serving as a soldier, Luke 3 : 14, " soldiers " (R.V., marg., " soldiers on service," present participle) ; 1 Cor. 9 : 7, R.V., "; (what) soldier . . . serveth," A.V., " (who) goeth a warfare ; " 2 Tim. 2 : 4, R.V., " soldier on service," A.V., " man that warreth," lit., ' serving as a soldier ; ' (b) metaphorically, of spiritual conflict : see WAR.

Notes : (1) For *spekoulatōr*, Mark 6 : 27, R.V., " soldier of his guard," see GUARD.¶ (2) In 2 Tim. 2 : 4 *stratologeō* is rendered " hath chosen (him) to be a soldier," A.V. (R.V., " enrolled (him) as a soldier ").¶

SOLID

STEREOS (στερεός), for which see FIRM, No. 2, has the meaning " solid " in Heb. 5 : 12, 14, of food (A.V., " strong "). As solid food requires more powerful digestive organs than are possessed by a babe, so a fuller knowledge of Christ (especially here with reference to His Melchizedek priesthood) required that exercise of spiritual intelligence which is derived from the practical appropriation of what had already been received.

For SOLITARY, Mark 1 : 35, A.V., see DESERT, B

SOME, SOMEONE, SOMETHING, SOMEWHAT

Notes : (1) Various forms of the article and certain pronouns, followed by the particles *men* and *de* denote " some." These are not enumerated here. (2) The indefinite pronoun *tis* in its singular or plural forms, frequently means " some," " some one " (translated " some man," in the A.V., e.g., of Acts 8 : 31 ; 1 Cor. 15 : 35), or " somebody," Luke 8 : 46 ; the neuter plural denotes " some things " in 2 Pet. 3 : 16 ; the singular denotes " something," e.g., Luke 11 : 54 ; John 13 : 29 (2nd part) ; Acts 3 : 5 ; 23 : 18 ; Gal. 6 : 3, where the meaning is ' anything,' as in 2 : 6, " somewhat." It is translated " somewhat," in the more indefinite sense, in Luke 7 : 40 ; Acts 23 : 20 ; 25 : 26 ; 2 Cor. 10 : 8 ; Heb. 8 : 3. See also ONE, B, No. 1. (3) *Meros*, a part, a measure, preceded by the preposition *apo*, from, is translated " in some measure " in Rom. 15 : 15, R.V. (A.V., " in some sort "), and ver. 24 (A.V., " somewhat "). (4) In the following *alloi*, others (" some " in the A.V.), is translated " others " in the R.V., Matt. 13 : 5, 7 ; Mark 4 : 7 (" other ") ; 8 : 28 ; Luke 9 : 19 ;

John 9 : 9. Followed by a correlative expression it denotes "some," e.g., Acts 19 : 32 ; 21 : 34 ; see OTHER, No. 1.

For SOMETIMES see TIME

SOMEWHERE

POU (ποῦ), a particle, signifies "somewhere" in Heb. 2 : 6 and 4 : 4, R.V. (A.V., "in a certain place"); the writer avoids mentioning the place to add stress to his testimony. See HAPLY, No. 5, VERILY.

SON

HUIOS (υἱός) primarily signifies the relation of offspring to parent (see John 9 : 18–20 ; Gal. 4 : 30). It is often used metaphorically of prominent moral characteristics (see below). "It is used in the N.T. of (a) male offspring, Gal. 4 : 30 ; (b) legitimate, as opposed to illegitimate offspring, Heb. 12 : 8 ; (c) descendants, without reference to sex, Rom. 9 : 27 ; (d) friends attending a wedding, Matt. 9 : 15 ; (e) those who enjoy certain privileges, Acts 3 : 25 ; (f) those who act in a certain way, whether evil, Matt. 23 : 31, or good, Gal. 3 : 7 ; (g) those who manifest a certain character, whether evil, Acts 13 : 10 ; Eph. 2 : 2, or good, Luke 6 : 35 ; Acts 4 : 36 ; Rom. 8 : 14 ; (h) the destiny that corresponds with the character, whether evil, Matt. 23 : 15 ; John 17 : 12 ; 2 Thess. 2 : 3, or good, Luke 20 : 36 ; (i) the dignity of the relationship with God whereinto men are brought by the Holy Spirit when they believe on the Lord Jesus Christ, Rom. 8 : 19 ; Gal. 3 : 26. . . .

" The Apostle John does not use huios, ' son,' of the believer, he reserves that title for the Lord ; but he does use teknon, ' child,' as in his Gospel, 1 : 12 ; 1 John 3 : 1, 2: Rev. 21 : 7 (huios) is a quotation from 2 Sam. 7 : 14.

" The Lord Jesus used huios in a very significant way, as in Matt. 5 : 9, ' Blessed are the peacemakers, for they shall be called the sons of God,' and vv. 44, 45, ' Love your enemies, and pray for them that persecute you ; that ye may be (become) sons of your Father which is in heaven.' The disciples were to do these things, not in order that they might become children of God, but that, being children (note ' your Father ' throughout), they might make the fact manifest in their character, might ' become sons.' See also 2 Cor. 6 : 17, 18.

" As to moral characteristics, the following phrases are used : (a) sons of God, Matt. 5 : 9, 45 ; Luke 6 : 35 ; (b) sons of the light, Luke 16 : 8 ; John 12 : 36 ; (c) sons of the day, 1 Thess. 5 : 5 ; (d) sons of peace, Luke 10 : 6 ; (e) sons of this world, Luke 16 : 8 ; (f) sons of disobedience, Eph. 2 : 2 ; (g) sons of the evil one, Matt. 13 : 38, cp. ' of the Devil,' Acts 13 : 10 ; (h) son of perdition, John 17 : 12 ; 2 Thess. 2 : 3. It is also used to describe characteristics other than moral, as : (i) sons of the resurrection, Luke 20 : 36 ; (j) sons of the Kingdom, Matt. 8 : 12 ; 13 : 38 ;

(*k*) sons of the bridechamber, Mark 2 : 19 ; (*l*) sons of exhortation, Acts 4 : 36 ; (*m*) sons of thunder, Boanerges, Mark 3 : 17."*

Notes : (1) For the synonyms *teknon* and *teknion* see under CHILD. The difference between believers as ' children of God ' and as ' sons of God ' is brought out in Rom. 8 : 14–21. The Spirit bears witness with their spirit that they are " children of God," and, as such, they are His heirs and joint-heirs with Christ. This stresses the fact of their spiritual birth (vv. 16, 17). On the other hand, " as many as are led by the Spirit of God, these are sons of God," i.e., ' these and no other.' Their conduct gives evidence of the dignity of their relationship and their likeness to His character. (2) *Pais* is rendered "son" in John 4 : 51. For Acts 13 : 13, 26 see below.

The Son of God

In this title the word Son is used sometimes (*a*) of relationship, sometimes (*b*) of the expression of character. " Thus, e.g., when the disciples so addressed Him, Matt. 14 : 33 ; 16 : 16 ; John 1 : 49, when the centurion so spoke of Him, Matt. 27 : 54, they probably meant that (*b*) He was a manifestation of God in human form. But in such passages as Luke 1 : 32, 35 ; Acts 13 : 33, which refer to the humanity of the Lord Jesus, . . . the word is used in sense (*a*).

" The Lord Jesus Himself used the full title on occasion, John 5 : 25 ; 9 : 35 [some mss. have ' the Son of man ; ' see R.V. marg.] ; 11 : 4, and on the more frequent occasions on which He spoke of Himself as ' the Son,' the words are to be understood as an abbreviation of ' the Son of God,' not of ' the Son of Man ; ' this latter He always expressed in full ; see Luke 10 : 22 ; John 5 : 19, etc.

" John uses both the longer and shorter forms of the title in his Gospel, see 3 : 16–18 ; 20 : 31, e.g., and in his Epistles ; cp. Rev. 2 : 18. So does the writer of Hebrews, 1 : 2 ; 4 : 14 ; 6 : 6, etc. An eternal relation subsisting between the Son and the Father in the Godhead is to be understood. That is to say, the Son of God, in His eternal relationship with the Father, is not so entitled because He at any time began to derive His being from the Father (in which case He could not be co-eternal with the Father), but because He is and ever has been the expression of what the Father is ; cp. John 14 : 9, ' he that hath seen Me hath seen the Father.' The words of Heb. 1 : 3, ' Who being the effulgence of His (God's) glory, and the very image of His (God's) substance ' are a definition of what is meant by ' Son of God.' Thus absolute Godhead, not Godhead in a secondary or derived sense, is intended in the title."†

Other titles of Christ as the Son of God are : " His Son," 1 Thess. 1 : 10 (in Acts 13 : 13, 26, R.V., *pais* is rendered "servant ") ; " His own Son ", Rom. 8 : 32 ; " My beloved Son," Matt. 3 : 17 ; " His Only Begotten Son," John 3 : 16 ; " the Son of His love," Col. 1 : 13.

---

* From Notes on Galatians, by Hogg and Vine, pp. 167–169, and on Thessalonians, pp. 158, 159. † From Notes on Galatians by Hogg and Vine, pp. 99, 100.

" The Son is the eternal object of the Father's love, John 17 : 24, and the sole Revealer of the Father's character, John 1 : 14 ; Heb. 1 : 3. The words, ' Father ' and ' Son,' are never in the N.T. so used as to suggest that the Father existed before the Son ; the Prologue to the Gospel according to John distinctly asserts that the Word existed ' in the beginning,' and that this Word is the Son, Who ' became flesh and dwelt among us.' "*

In addressing the Father in His prayer in John 17 He says, " Thou lovedst Me before the foundation of the world." Accordingly in the timeless past the Father and the Son existed in that relationship, a relationship of love, as well as of absolute Deity. In this passage the Son gives evidence that there was no more powerful plea in the Father's estimation than that co-eternal love existing between the Father and Himself.

The declaration " Thou art My Son, this day have I begotten Thee," Psa. 2 : 7, quoted in Acts 13 : 33 ; Heb. 1 : 5 ; 5 : 5, refers to the birth of Christ, not to His resurrection. In Acts 13 : 33 the verb " raise up " is used of the raising up of a person to occupy a special position in the nation, as of David in verse 22 (so of Christ as a Prophet in 3 : 22 and 7 : 37). The word " again " in the A.V. in ver. 33 represents nothing in the original. The R.V. rightly omits it. In ver. 34 the statement as to the resurrection of Christ receives the greater stress in this respect through the emphatic contrast to that in ver. 33 as to His being raised up in the nation, a stress imparted by the added words " from the dead." Accordingly ver. 33 speaks of His Incarnation, ver. 34 of His resurrection.

In Heb. 1 : 5, that the declaration refers to the Birth is confirmed by the contrast in verse 6. Here the word " again " is rightly placed in the R.V., " when He again bringeth in the Firstborn into the world." This points on to His Second Advent, which is set in contrast to His first Advent, when God brought His Firstborn into the world the first time (see FIRSTBORN).†

So again in Heb. 5 : 5, where the High Priesthood of Christ is shown to fulfil all that was foreshadowed in the Levitical priesthood, the passage stresses the facts of His humanity, the days of His flesh, His perfect obedience and His sufferings.

Son of Man

In the N.T. this is a designation of Christ, almost entirely confined to the Gospels. Elsewhere it is found in Acts 7 : 56, the only occasion where a disciple applied it to the Lord and in Rev. 1 : 13 ; 14 : 14 (see below).

---

* From Notes on Thessalonians by Hogg and Vine, pp. 46, 47.
† The Western text of Luke 3 : 22 reads " Thou art My Son, this day have I begotten Thee," instead of " Thou art My beloved Son, in Thee I am well pleased." There is probably some connection between this and those early heresies which taught that our Lord's Deity began at His Baptism.

" Son of Man " is the title Christ used of Himself ; John 12 : 34 is not an exception, for the quotation by the multitude was from His own statement. The title is found especially in the Synoptic Gospels. The occurrences in John's Gospel, 1 : 51 ; 3 : 13, 14 ; 5 : 27 ; 6 : 27, 53, 62 ; 8 : 28 (9 : 35 in some texts) ; 12 : 23, 34 (twice) ; 13 : 31, are not parallel to those in the Synoptic Gospels. In the latter the use of the title falls into two groups, (a) those in which it refers to Christ's humanity, His earthly work, sufferings and death, e.g., Matt. 8 : 20 ; 11 : 19 ; 12 : 40 ; 26 : 2, 24 ; (b) those which refer to His glory in resurrection and to that of His future Advent, e.g., Matt. 10 : 23 ; 13 : 41 ; 16 : 27, 28 ; 17 : 9 ; 24 : 27, 30 (twice), 37, 39, 44.

While it is a Messianic title it is evident that the Lord applied it to Himself in a distinctive way, for it indicates more than Messiahship, even universal headship on the part of One who is Man. It therefore stresses His manhood, manhood of a unique order in comparison with all other men, for He is declared to be of heaven, 1 Cor. 15 : 47, and even while here below, was " the Son of Man, which is in Heaven," John 3 : 13. As the Son of Man He must be appropriated spiritually as a condition of possessing eternal life, John 6 : 53. In His death, as in His life, the glory of His Manhood was displayed in the absolute obedience and submission to the will of the Father (12 : 23 ; 13 : 31), and, in view of this, all judgment has been committed to Him, who will judge in full understanding experimentally of human conditions, sin apart, and will exercise the judgment as sharing the nature of those judged, John 5 : 22, 27. Not only is He man, but He is " Son of man," not by human generation but, according to the Semitic usage of the expression, partaking of the characteristics (sin apart) of manhood belonging to the category of mankind. Twice in the Apocalypse, 1 : 13 and 14 : 14, He is described as " One like unto a Son of man," R.V. (A.V., " . . . the Son of Man "), cp. Dan. 7 : 13. He who was thus seen was indeed the Son of Man, but the absence of the article in the original serves to stress what morally characterizes Him as such. Accordingly in these passages He is revealed, not as the Person known by the title, but as the One who is qualified to act as the Judge of all men. He is the same Person as in the days of His flesh, still continuing His humanity with His Deity. The phrase " like unto " serves to distinguish Him as there seen in His glory and majesty in contrast to the days of His humiliation.

SONG

ODĒ (ᾠδή), an ode, song, is always used in the N.T. (as in the Sept.), in praise of God or Christ ; in Eph. 5 : 19 and Col. 3 : 16 the adjective " spiritual " is added, because the word in itself is generic and might be used of songs anything but spiritual ; in Rev. 5 : 9 and 14 : 3 (1st part) the descriptive word is " new " (kainos, new in reference to character and form : see NEW), a song, the significance of which was confined to those mentioned (ver. 3, and 2nd part) ; in 15 : 3 (twice), " the song of Moses . . . and the song of the Lamb," the former as celebrating the deliverance of God's people by His power, the latter as celebrating redemption by atoning sacrifice.¶

For SOON see IMMEDIATELY, No. 1 and QUICKLY, No. 3.

AS SOON AS : see † p. 9

For SOONER see QUICKLY, No. 2

SOOTHSAYING

MANTEUOMAI (μαντεύομαι), to divine, practise divination (from *mantis*, a seer, diviner), occurs in Acts 16 : 16.¶ The word is allied to *mainomai*, to rave, and *mania*, fury displayed by those who were possessed by the evil spirit (represented by the pagan god or goddess) while delivering their oracular messages. Trench (Syn. §vi) draws a distinction between this verb and *prophēteuō*, not only as to their meanings, but as to the fact of the single occurrence of *manteuomai* in the N.T., contrasted with the frequency of *prophēteuō*, exemplifying the avoidance by N.T. writers of words the employment of which " would tend to break down the distinction between heathenism and revealed religion."

SOP

PSŌMION (ψωμίον), a diminutive of *psōmos*, a morsel, denotes a fragment, a sop (akin to *psōmizō ;* see FEED), John 13 : 26 (twice), 27, 30. It had no connection with the modern meaning of sop, something given to pacify (as in the classical expression ' a sop to Cerberus ').¶

SORCERER

1. MAGOS (μάγος), (*a*) one of a Median caste, a magician : see WISE ; (*b*) a wizard, sorcerer, a pretender to magic powers, a professor of the arts of witchcraft, Acts 13 : 6, 8, where Bar-Jesus was the Jewish name, Elymas, an Arabic word meaning " wise." Hence the name Magus, " the magician," originally applied to Persian priests. In the Sept., only in Dan. 2 : 2, 10, of the " enchanters," R.V. (A.V., " astrologers "), of Babylon. The superior Greek version of Daniel by Theodotion has it also at 1 : 20 ; 2 : 27 ; 4 : 7 ; 5 : 7, 11, 15.¶

2. PHARMAKOS (φαρμακός), an adjective signifying ' devoted to magical arts,' is used as a noun, a sorcerer, especially one who uses drugs, potions, spells, enchantments, Rev. 21 : 8, in the best texts (some have *pharmakeus*), and 22 : 15.¶

SORCERY
A. Nouns.

1. PHARMAKIA (or -EIA) (φαρμακία) (Eng., pharmacy etc.) primarily signified the use of medicine, drugs, spells ; then, poisoning ; then,

sorcery, Gal. 5 : 20, R.V., " sorcery " (A.V., " witchcraft "), mentioned as one of " the works of the flesh." See also Rev. 9 : 21 ; 18 : 23.¶ In the Sept., Ex. 7 : 11, 22 ; 8 : 7, 18 ; Isa. 47 : 9, 12.¶ In sorcery, the use of drugs, whether simple or potent, was·generally accompanied by incantations and appeals to occult powers, with the provision of various charms, amulets, etc., professedly designed to keep the applicant or patient from the attention and power of demons, but actually to impress the applicant with the mysterious resources and powers of the sorcerer.

2. MAGIA (or -EIA) (μαγία), the magic art, is used in the plural in Acts 8 : 11, " sorceries" (see SORCERER, No. 1).¶

B. Verb.

MAGEUŌ (μαγεύω), akin to A, No. 2, to practise magic, Acts 8 : 9, " used sorcery," is used as in A, No. 2, of Simon Magnus.¶

SORE (Noun, Adjective, Adverb), SORER
A. Noun.

HELKOS (ἕλκος), a sore or ulcer (primarily a wound), occurs in Luke 16 : 21 ; Rev. 16 : 2, 11.¶

B. Verb.

HELKOŌ (ἑλκόω), to wound, to ulcerate, is used in the Passive Voice, signifying to suffer from sores, to be " full of sores," Luke 16 : 20 (perfect participle).¶

C. Adjectives.

1. HIKANOS (ἱκανός), used of things, occasionally denotes " much," translated " sore " in Acts 20 : 37, lit., ' there was much weeping of all.' See ABLE, C, No. 2.

2. CHEIRŌN (χείρων), worse (used as a comparative degree of kakos, evil), occurs in Heb. 10 : 29, " sorer." See WORSE.

D. Adverbs.

1. LIAN (λίαν), very, exceedingly, is translated " sore " in Mark 6 : 51 (of amazement). See EXCEED, B, No. 1.

2. SPHODRA (σφόδρα), very, very much, is translated " sore " in Matt. 17 : 6 (of fear). See GREATLY, Note (1).

Notes : (1) For the A.V., " sore vexed " in Matt. 17 : 15, see GRIEVOUSLY, B, No. 2, Note (2). (2) In Luke 2 : 9 megas, great, is used with phobos, fear, as the object of the verb to fear, " (they were) sore (afraid)," lit., ' (they feared) a great (fear).' (3) In Mark 9 : 26, A.V., polla, much (R.V.), the neuter plur. of polus, used as an adverb, is translated " sore." (4) In Matt. 21 : 15, aganakteō, to be moved with indignation (R.V.), is translated " they were sore displeased." (5) For the R.V., " sore troubled," Matt. 26 : 37 and Mark 14 : 33 (A.V., " very heavy "), see TROUBLE, B, No. 12. (6) For A.V., " were sore amazed " in Mark 14 : 33, see AMAZE, B, No. 4. (7) In Luke 9 : 39, R.V., suntribō, to break, bruise, is rendered " bruiseth sorely." See BREAK, A, No. 5. (8) In Mark 9 : 6, ekphobos is rendered " sore afraid."

SORROW (Noun and Verb), SORROWFUL
A. Nouns.

1. LUPĒ (λύπη), grief, sorrow, is translated " sorrow " in Luke 22 : 45 ; John 16 : 6, 20–22 ; Rom. 9 : 2, R.V. (A.V., " heaviness ") ; 2 Cor. 2 : 1, R.V. ; 2 : 3, 7 ; 7 : 10 (twice) ; Phil. 2 : 27 (twice). See GRIEF.

2. ODUNĒ (ὀδύνη), pain, consuming grief, distress, whether of body or mind, is used of the latter, Rom. 9 : 2, R.V., " pain ; " 1 Tim. 6 : 10.¶

3. ŌDIN (ὠδίν), a birth-pang, travail, pain, " sorrows," Matt. 24 : 8 ; Mark 13 : 8 ; see PAIN, A, No. 2.

4. PENTHOS (πένθος), mourning, " sorrow," Rev. 18 : 7 (twice) ; 21 : 4 : see MOURN.

B. Verbs.

1. LUPEŌ (λυπέω), akin to A, No. 1 : see GRIEF, B, No. 1, SORRY, A (below).

2. ODUNAŌ (ὀδυνάω), to cause pain (akin to A, No. 2), is used in the Middle Voice in Luke 2 : 48 ; Acts 20 : 38 : see ANGUISH, B, No. 3.

C. Adjectives.

1. PERILUPOS (περίλυπος), very sad, deeply grieved (peri,. intensive), is used in Matt. 26 : 38 and Mark 14 : 34, " exceeding sorrowful ; " Mark 6 : 26 ; Luke 18 : 23 (ver. 24 in some mss.).¶

2. ALUPOS (ἄλυπος) denotes free from grief (a, negative, lupē, grief), comparative degree in Phil. 2 : 28, " less sorrowful," their joy would mean the removal of a burden from his heart.¶

SORRY
A. Verb.

LUPEŌ (λυπέω) is rendered to be sorry (Passive Voice) in Matt. 14 : 9, A.V. (R.V., " grieved ") ; 17 : 23 ; 18 : 31 ; 2 Cor. 2 : 2 [1st part, Active V., " make sorry " (as in 7 : 8, twice) ; 2nd part, Passive] ; 2 : 4, R.V., " made sorry ; " 9 : 9 and 11, R.V., " ye were made sorry." See GRIEVE, B, No. 1.

B. Adjective.

PERILUPOS (περίλυπος) is translated " exceeding sorry " in Mark 6 : 26 : see SORROWFUL, C, No. 1.

SORT
A. Adjective.

HOPOIOS (ὁποῖος), of what sort, is so rendered in 1 Cor. 3 : 13. See MANNER, SUCH AS. WHAT.

B. Noun.

MEROS (μέρος), a part, is used with apo, from, in Rom. 15 : 15 and rendered " (in some) sort," A.V. (R.V., " . . . measure "). See BEHALF.

Note : See BASE, No. 3, GODLY, C, Notes (2) and (3).

For SOUGHT see SEEK

SOUL

PSUCHĒ (ψυχή) denotes the breath, the breath of life, then the soul, in its various meanings. The N.T. uses " may be analysed approximately as follows :

(*a*) the natural life of the body, Matt. 2 : 20 ; Luke 12 : 22 ; Acts 20 : 10 ; Rev. 8 : 9 ; 12 : 11 ; cp. Lev. 17 : 11 ; 2 Sam. 14 : 7 ; Esth. 8 : 11 ; (*b*) the immaterial, invisible part of man, Matt. 10 : 28 ; Acts 2 : 27 ; cp. 1 Kings 17 : 21 ; (*c*) the disembodied (or ' unclothed ' or ' naked,' 2 Cor. 5 : 3, 4) man, Rev. 6 : 9 ; (*d*) the seat of personality, Luke 9 : 24, explained as = ' own self,' ver. 25 ; Heb. 6 : 19 ; 10 : 39 ; cp. Isa. 53 : 10 with 1 Tim. 2 : 6 ; (*e*) the seat of the sentient element in man, that by which he perceives, reflects, feels, desires, Matt. 11 : 29 ; Luke 1 : 46 ; 2 : 35 ; Acts 14 : 2, 22 ; cp. Ps. 84 : 2 ; 139 : 14 ; Isa. 26 : 9 ; (*f*) the seat of will and purpose, Matt. 22 : 37 ; Acts 4 : 32 ; Eph. 6 : 6 ; Phil. 1 : 27 ; Heb. 12 : 3 ; cp. Num. 21 : 4 ; Deut. 11 : 13 ; (*g*) the seat of appetite, Rev. 18 : 14 ; cp. Ps. 107 : 9 ; Prov. 6 : 30 ; Isa. 5 : 14 (' desire ') ; 29 : 8 ; (*h*) persons, individuals, Acts 2 : 41, 43 ; Rom. 2 : 9 ; Jas. 5 : 20 ; 1 Pet. 3 : 20 ; 2 Pet. 2 : 14 ; cp. Gen. 12 : 5 ; 14 : 21 (' persons ') ; Lev. 4 : 2 (' any one ') ; Ezek. 27 : 13 ; of dead bodies, Num. 6 : 6, lit., ' dead soul ; ' and of animals, Lev. 24 : 18, lit., ' soul for soul ' ; (*i*) the equivalent of the personal pronoun, used for emphasis and effect :— 1st person, John 10 : 24 (' us ') ; Heb. 10 : 38 ; cp. Gen. 12 : 13 ; Num. 23 : 10 ; Jud. 16 : 30 ; Ps. 120 : 2 (' me ') ; 2nd person, 2 Cor. 12 : 15 ; Heb. 13 : 17 ; Jas. 1 : 21 ; 1 Pet. 1 : 9 ; 2 : 25 ; cp. Lev. 17 : 11 ; 26 : 15 ; 1 Sam. 1 : 26 ; 3rd person, 1 Pet. 4 : 19 ; 2 Pet. 2 : 8 ; cp. Ex. 30 : 12 ; Job 32 : 2, Heb. ' soul,' Sept. ' self ' ; (*j*) an animate creature, human or other, 1 Cor. 15 : 45 ; Rev. 16 : 3 ; cp. Gen. 1 : 24 ; 2 : 7, 19 ; (*k*) ' the inward man,' the seat of the new life, Luke 21 : 19 (cp. Matt. 10 : 39) ; 1 Pet. 2 : 11 ; 3 John 2.

" With (*j*) compare *a-psuchos*, soulless, inanimate, 1 Cor. 14 : 7.¶

" With (*f*) compare *di-psuchos*, two-souled, Jas. 1 : 8 ; 4 : 8 ;¶ *oligo-psuchos*, feeble-souled, 1 Thess. 5 : 14 ;¶ *iso-psuchos*, like-souled, Phil. 2 : 20 ;¶ *sum-psuchos*, joint-souled (' with one accord '), Phil. 2 : 2.¶

" The language of Heb. 4 : 12 suggests the extreme difficulty of distinguishing between the soul and the spirit, alike in their nature and in their activities. Generally speaking the spirit is the higher, the soul the lower element. The spirit may be recognised as the life principle bestowed on man by God, the soul as the resulting life constituted in the individual, the body being the material organism animated by soul and spirit. . . .

" Body and soul are the constituents of the man according to Matt. 6 : 25 ; 10 : 28 ; Luke 12 : 20 ; Acts 20 : 10 ; body and spirit according to Luke 8 : 55 ; 1 Cor. 5 : 3 ; 7 : 34 ; Jas. 2 : 26. In Matt. 26 : 38 the emotions are associated with the soul, in John 13 : 21 with the spirit ; cp. also Ps. 42 : 11 with 1 Kings 21 : 5. In Ps. 35 : 9 the soul rejoices in God, in Luke 1 : 47 the spirit.

"Apparently, then, the relationships may be thus summed up, ' Sōma, body, and *pneuma*, spirit, may be separated, *pneuma* and *psuchē*, soul, can only be distinguished' (Cremer)."*

SOUND (Noun and Verb)
A. Nouns.

1. PHŌNĒ (φωνή), most frequently "a voice," is translated "sound" in Matt. 24 : 31 (A.V. marg., " voice ") ; John 3 : 8, A.V. (R.V., " voice ") ; so 1 Cor. 14 : 7 (1st part), 8 ; Rev. 1 : 15 ; 18 : 22 (2nd part, R.V., " voice ") ; A.V. and R.V. in 9 : 9 (twice) ; in Acts 2 : 6, R.V., " (this) sound (was heard)," A.V., " (this) was noised abroad."

2. ECHOS (ἦχος), a noise, a sound of any sort (Eng., echo), is translated "sound" in Acts 2 : 2 ; Heb. 12 : 19. See ROARING, B, RUMOUR.

3. PHTHONGOS (φθόγγος), akin to *phthengomai*, to utter a voice, occurs in Rom. 10 : 18 ; 1 Cor. 14 : 7.¶ In the Sept., Psa. 19 : 4.¶

B. Verbs.

1. ĒCHEŌ (ἠχέω), akin to A, No. 2, occurs in 1 Cor. 13 : 1, " sounding (brass) ; " in some mss., Luke 21 : 25. See ROARING.¶

2. EXĒCHEŌ (ἐξηχέω), to sound forth as a trumpet or thunder (*ex*, out, and No. 1), is used in 1 Thess. 1 : 8, " sounded forth," Passive Voice, lit., ' has been sounded out.'¶ In the Sept., Joel 3 : 14.¶

3. SALPIZŌ (σαλπίζω), to sound a trumpet (*salpinx*), occurs in Matt. 6 : 2 ; 1 Cor. 15 : 52, " the trumpet shall sound ; " Rev. 8 : 6–8, 10, 12, 13 ; 9 : 1, 13 ; 10 : 7 ; 11 : 15.¶

4. BOLIZŌ (βολίζω), to heave the lead (*bolis*, that which is thrown or hurled, akin to *ballō*, to throw ; sounding-lead), to take soundings, occurs in Acts 27 : 28 (twice).¶

Note : In Luke 1 : 44, A.V., *ginomai*, to become, is rendered " sounded " (R.V., " came ").

SOUND (Adjective), BE SOUND
A. Adjective.

HUGIĒS (ὑγιής), whole, healthy, is used metaphorically of " sound speech," Tit. 2 : 8. See WHOLE.

B. Verb.

HUGIAINŌ (ὑγιαίνω), to be healthy, sound in health (Eng., hygiene etc.), translated " safe and sound " in Luke 15 : 27, is used metaphorically of doctrine, 1 Tim. 1 : 10 ; 2 Tim. 4 : 3 ; Tit. 1 : 9 ; 2 : 1 ; of words, 1 Tim. 6 : 3, R.V. (A.V., " wholesome," R.V. marg., " healthful ") ; 2 Tim. 1 : 13 ; " in the faith," Tit. 1 : 13 (R.V. marg., " healthy ") ; " in faith," Tit. 2 : 2 (R.V. marg., ditto).

Note : For " sound mind " in 2 Tim. 1 : 7, A.V., see DISCIPLINE ; in 1 Pet. 4 : 7 (A.V., " sober "), see MIND, B, No. 5.

---

* From Notes on Thessalonians by Hogg and Vine, pp. 205–207.

SOUNDNESS

HOLOKLĒRIA (ὁλοκληρία), completeness, soundness (akin to *holoklēros*, see ENTIRE), occurs in Acts 3 : 16.¶ In the Sept., Isa. 1 : 6.¶

SOUTH, SOUTH WIND

NOTOS (νότος) denotes (a) the south wind, Luke 12 : 55 ; Acts 27 : 13 ; 28 : 13 ; (b) south, as a direction, Luke 13 : 29 ; Rev. 21 : 13 ; (c) the South, as a region, Matt. 12 : 42 ; Luke 11 : 31.¶

Note : For *mesēmbria*, Acts 8 : 26, see NOON.

SOUTH WEST

LIPS (λίψ), lit., Libyan, denotes the S.W. wind, Acts 27 : 12, " (looking) north-east (and south-east)," R.V., lit., ' (looking down) the south-west wind (and down the north-west wind) ; ' to look down a wind was to look in the direction in which it blows. A S.W. wind blows towards the N.E. ; the aspect of the haven answers to this. See also under NORTH EAST, NORTH WEST.¶

SOW (Noun)

HUS (ὗς), swine (masc. or fem.), is used in the fem. in 2 Pet. 2 : 22.¶

SOW (Verb), SOWER

SPEIRŌ (σπείρω), to sow seed, is used (1) literally, especially in the Synoptic Gospels ; elsewhere, 1 Cor. 15 : 36, 37 ; 2 Cor. 9 : 10, " the sower ; " (2) metaphorically, (a) in proverbial sayings, e.g., Matt. 13 : 3, 4 ; Luke 19 : 21, 22 ; John 4 : 37 ; 2 Cor. 9 : 6 ; (b) in the interpretation of parables, e.g., Matt. 13 : 19–23 (in these vv., R.V., " was sown," for A.V., " received seed ") ; (c) otherwise as follows : of sowing " spiritual things " in preaching and teaching, 1 Cor. 9 : 11 ; of the interment of the bodies of deceased believers, 1 Cor. 15 : 42–44 ; of ministering to the necessities of others in things temporal (the harvest being proportionate to the sowing), 2 Cor. 9 : 6, 10 (see above) ; of sowing to the flesh, Gal. 6 : 7, 8 (" that " in ver. 7 is emphatic, ' that and that only,' what was actually sown) ; in ver. 8, *eis*, " unto," signifies ' in the interests of ' ; of the " fruit of righteousness " by peacemakers, Jas. 3 : 18.

SPACE

A. Noun.

DIASTĒMA (διάστημα), an interval, space (akin to B), is used of time in Acts 5 : 7.¶

B. Verb.

DIISTĒMI (διίστημι), to set apart, separate (*dia*, apart, *histēmi*, to cause to stand), see A, is rendered " after the space of " in Luke 22 : 59 ; in Acts 27 : 28, with *brachu*, a little, R.V., " after a little space " (A.V., " when they had gone a little further "). See PART.

Notes : (1) In Acts 15 : 33 and Rev. 2 : 21, A.V., *chronos*, time (R.V.), is translated " space." (2) In Acts 19 : 8 and 10, *epi*, for or during (of time), is translated " for the space of ; " in 19 : 34, " about the space of." (3) In Acts 5 : 34, A.V., *brachu* (the neuter of *brachus*, short), used adverbially, is translated " a little space " (R.V. " . . . while "). (4) In Gal. 2 : 1, *dia*, through, is rendered " after the space of," R.V., stressing the length of the period mentioned (A.V., " after," which would represent the preposition *meta*). (5) In Jas. 5 : 17 there is no word in the original representing the phrase " by the space of," A.V. (R.V., " for "). (6) In Rev. 14 : 20, A.V., *apo*, away from, is translated " by the space of " (R.V., " as far as "). (7) In Rev. 17 : 10, A.V., *oligon*, " a little while " (R.V.), is rendered " a short space."

SPARE, SPARINGLY
A. Verbs.
PHEIDOMAI (φείδομαι), to spare, i.e., to forego the infliction of that evil or retribution which was designed, is used with a negative in Acts 20 : 29 ; Rom. 8 : 32 ; 11 : 21 (twice) ; 2 Cor. 13 : 2 ; 2 Pet. 2 : 4, 5 ; positively, in 1 Cor. 7 : 28 ; 2 Cor. 1 : 3 ; rendered " forbear " in 2 Cor. 12 : 6. See FORBEAR.¶

Note : In Luke 15 : 17, *perisseuō*, to abound, have abundance, is translated " have enough and to spare."
B. Adverb.
PHEIDOMENŌS (φειδομένως), akin to A, " sparingly," occurs in 2 Cor. 9 : 6 (twice), of sowing and reaping.¶

SPARROW
STROUTHION (στρουθίον), a diminutive of *strouthos*, a sparrow, occurs in Matt. 10 : 29, 31 ; Luke 12 : 6, 7.¶

SPEAK
1. LEGŌ (λέγω), to say, speak : see SAY, No. 1.

2. LALEŌ (λαλέω), for which see SAY, No. 2, is used several times in 1 Cor. 14 ; the command prohibiting women from speaking in a church gathering, vv. 34, 35, is regarded by some as an injunction against chattering, a meaning which is absent from the use of the verb everywhere else in the N.T. ; it is to be understood in the same sense as in vv. 2, 3–6, 9, 11, 13, 18, 19, 21, 23, 27–29, 39.

3. PROSLALEŌ (προσλαλέω), to speak to or with (*pros*, to, and No. 2), is used in Acts 13 : 43 and 28 : 20.¶

4. PHTHENGOMAI (φθέγγομαι), to utter a sound or voice, is translated to speak in Acts 4 : 18 : 2 Pet. 2 : 16 ; in 2 : 18, A.V., " speak " (R.V., " utter ").

5. APOPHTHENGOMAI (ἀποφθέγγομαι), to speak forth (*apo*, forth, and No. 4), is so rendered in Acts 2 : 14, R.V. (A.V., " said "),and 26 : 25 ; in 2 : 2 it denotes to give utterance.¶

6. ANTILEGŌ (ἀντιλέγω), to speak against, is so rendered in Luke 2 : 34 ; John 19 : 12 ; Acts 13 : 45, A.V. (R.V., " contradicted ") ; 28 : 19, 22. See CONTRADICT, GAINSAY.

7. KATALALEŌ (καταλαλέω), synonymous with No. 6 (kata, against, and No. 2), is always translated to speak against in the R.V. See BACKBITER, Note.

8. KAKOLOGEŌ (κακολογέω), to speak evil : see CURSE, B, No. 4.

9. SULLALEŌ (συλλαλέω), to speak together (sun, with, and No. 2), is rendered " spake together " in Luke 4 : 36, R.V. See COMMUNE, No. 3, CONFER, No. 2, TALK.

10. PROEIPON (προεῖπον), to speak or say before (a 2nd aorist tense from an obsolete present), is rendered to speak before in Acts 1 : 16 ; 2 Pet. 3 : 2 ; Jude 17. See FORETELL.

11. PROPHTHANŌ (προφθάνω), to anticipate (an extension, by pro, before, of phthanō, which has the same meaning), is rendered " spake first " in Matt. 17 : 25, R.V. (A.V., " prevented ").¶

12. PROSPHŌNEŌ (προσφωνέω), to address, call to, is rendered " spake unto " (or " to ") in Luke 23 : 20 ; Acts 21 : 40 ; 22 : 2 ; ' to call unto ' (or ' to ') in Matt. 11 : 16 ; Luke 6 : 13 ; 7 : 32 ; 13 : 12.¶

13. EIRŌ (εἴρω), for which see SAY, No. 4, has a 1st aorist, passive participle rhēthen, " spoken " or " spoken of," used in Matt. 1 : 22 ; 2 : 15, 17, 23 ; 3 : 3 ; 4 : 14 ; 8 : 17 ; 12 : 17 ; 13 : 35 ; 21 : 4 ; 22 : 31 ; 24 : 15 ; 27 ! 9 (in some texts in 27 : 35 and Mark 13 : 14).

Notes : (1) In Heb. 12 : 5, A.V., dialegomai, to discuss, to reason , is translated " speaketh " (R.V., " reasoneth "). (2) In Heb. 12 : 25, A.V. chrēmatizō, to warn, instruct, is translated " spake " (R.V., " warned ") : see ADMONISH. (3) In Eph. 4 : 31, A.V., blasphēmia is translated " evil speaking : " see RAILING. (4) In Heb. 12 : 19, prostithēmi, to put to, add, used with logos, a word, is rendered " (that no word) more should be spoken," R.V. [A.V., " (that) the word should (not) be spoken (to them) any more "]. (5) In Acts 26 : 24, A.V., apologeomai, to make a defence (R.V.), is rendered " spake for himself." See ANSWER, B, No. 4. (6) In Rom. 15 : 21. A.V., anangellō, to bring back word (R.V., " tidings . . . came "), is translated " he was . . . spoken of." (7) For " is spoken of " in Rom. 1 : 8, A.V., see PROCLAIM, No. 2. (8) For " spake out " in Luke 1 42, A.V., see VOICE, Note. (9) In Gal. 4 : 15, there is no verb in the original for the A.V., " ye spake of " (see R.V.). (10) For " spoken against " in Acts 19 : 36 see GAINSAY, C. (11) For " speak reproachfully," 1 Tim. 5 : 14, see REVILE, C. (12) In Acts 21 : 3. A.V., ginōskō is translated " speak," R.V., " know."

SPEAKER (chief)

Note : In Acts 14 : 12 the verb hēgeomai, to lead the way, be the chief, is used in the present participle with the article (together equivalent to a noun), followed by the genitive case of logos, speech, with the article, the phrase being rendered " the chief speaker," lit., ' the leader of the dis course.' See CHIEF, C.

SPEAKING (evil, much)

POLULOGIA (πολυλογία), loquacity, " much speaking " (*polus*, much, *logos*, speech), is used in Matt. 6 : 7.¶ In the Sept., Prov. 10 : 19.¶

Note : For " evil speaking(s)," in Eph. 4 : 31, see RAILING ; in 1 Pet. 2 : 1, see BACKBITING. For " shameful speaking " see COMMUNICATION, B, Note.

SPEAR

LONCHĒ (λόγχη), primarily a spear-head, then, a lance or spear, occurs in John 19 : 34 ; some texts have it in Matt. 27 : 49 ¶ As to John 19 : 29, there is an old conjecture, mentioned by Field (*Notes on the Trans. of the N.T.*), to the effect that the sponge was put on a spear (*hussos*, a javelin, the Roman *pilum*, instead of *hussōpos*, hyssop).

SPEARMAN

DEXIOLABOS (δεξιολάβος), from *dexios*, the right (hand), and *lambanō*, to lay hold of, is used in the plural in Acts 23 : 23, " spearmen." Some texts have *dexiobolos*, one who throws with his right hand (*ballō*, to throw), ' right-handed slingers.'¶

SPECIAL

Note : Tuchōn, the 2nd aorist participle of *tunchanō*, to happen, meet with, chance, is used with a negative signifying ' not common or ordinary,' special, Acts 19 : 11 ; so in 28 : 2. See COMMON, B, Note (3).

For SPECIALLY see ESPECIALLY

SPECTACLE

THEATRON (θέατρον), akin to *theaomai*, to behold, denotes (*a*) a theatre (used also as a place of assembly), Acts 19 : 29, 31 ; (*b*) a spectacle, a show, metaphorically in 1 Cor. 4 : 9. See THEATRE.¶

SPEECH

1. LOGOS (λόγος), akin to *legō* (SPEAK, No. 1), most frequently rendered ' word ' (for an analysis see WORD), signifies speech, as follows : (*a*) discourse, e.g., Luke 20 : 20, R.V., " speech " (A.V., " words ") ; Acts 14 : 12 (see SPEAKER) ; 20 : 7 ; 1 Cor. 2 : 1, 4 ; 4 : 19, A.V. (R.V., " word ") ; 2 Cor. 10 : 10 ; (*b*) the faculty of speech, e.g., 2 Cor. 11 : 6 ; (*c*) the manner of speech, e.g., Matt. 5 : 37, R.V., " speech " (A.V., " communication ") ; Col. 4 : 6 ; (*d*) manner of instruction, Tit. 2 : 8 ; 1 Cor. 14 : 9, R.V. (A.V., " words ") ; Eph. 4 : 29, R.V. (A.V., " communication "). See SAYING.

2. LALIA (λαλιά), akin to *laleō* (SPEAK, No. 2), denotes talk, speech,

(*a*) of a dialect, Matt. 26 : 73 ; Mark 14 : 70 ; (*b*) utterances, John 4 : 42, R.V., " speaking " (A.V., " saying ") ; 8 : 43.¶

3. EULOGIA (εὐλογία) has the meaning fair speaking, flattering speech in Rom. 16 : 18, R.V., " fair speech " (A.V., " fair speeches "). See BLESSING, C, No. 1.

4. CHRĒSTOLOGIA (χρηστολογία), which has a similar meaning to No. 3, occurs with it in Rom. 16 : 18 [R.V., " smooth . . . (speech)"]. See SMOOTH, Note.¶

Notes : (1) For " persuasiveness of speech," Col. 2 : 4, R.V., see PERSUASIVE, B. (2) In Acts 14 : 11 " the speech of Lycaonia " translates the adverb *Lukaonisti*. Lycaonia was a large country in the centre and south of the plateau of Asia Minor ; the villages retained the native language, but cities like Lystra probably had a Seleucid tone in their laws and customs (Ramsay on Galatians).

SPEECHLESS

1. ENEOS (or ENNEOS) (ἐνεός), dumb, speechless, occurs in Acts 9 : 7.¶ In the Sept., Prov. 17 : 28 ; Isa. 56 : 10.¶

2. KŌPHOS (κωφός), which means either deaf or dumb (see DEAF), is translated " speechless " in Luke 1 : 22.

Note : For *phimoō*, translated " he was speechless " in Matt. 22 : 12, see MUZZLE, SILENCE.

SPEED, SPEEDILY

Notes : (1) In Acts 17 : 15 " with all speed " is the rendering of the phrase *hōs*, as, *tachista*, most speedily (the superlative of *tachu*, speedily), i.e., as speedily as possible. (2) For " speedily," *en tachei*, in Luke 18 : 8, see QUICKLY, No. 4. (3) For " God speed " see GREETING, A, No. 2.

SPEND, SPENT

1. DAPANAŌ (δαπανάω) denotes (*a*) to expend, spend, Mark 5 : 26 [for Acts 21 : 24 see CHARGE, Note (5)] : 2 Cor. 12 : 15 (1st part : for " be spent," see No. 2) ; (*b*) to consume, squander, Luke 15 : 14 ; Jas. 4 : 3. See CONSUME, Note.¶

2. EKDAPANAŌ (ἐκδαπανάω), lit., to spend out (*ek*), an intensive form of No. 1, to spend entirely, is used in 2 Cor. 12 : 15, in the Passive Voice, with reflexive significance, to spend oneself out (for others), " will . . . be spent," R.V. marg., " spent out " (see No. 1).¶

3. PROSDAPANAŌ (προσδαπανάω), to spend besides (*pros*, and No. 1), is used in Luke 10 : 35, " thou spendest more."¶

4. PROSANALISKŌ (προσαναλίσκω), to spend besides, a strengthened form of *analiskō*, to expend, consume (see CONSUME, No. 1), occurs in most texts in Luke 8 : 43.¶

5. DIAGINOMAI (διαγίνομαι), used of time, to intervene, elapse, is rendered " was spent " in Acts 27 : 9. See PAST.

6. PROKOPTŌ (προκόπτω), to cut forward a way, advance, is translated " is far spent," in Rom. 13 : 12, said metaphorically of " the night," the whole period of man's alienation from God. Though the tense is the aorist, it must not be rendered ' was far spent,' as if it referred, e.g., to Christ's first Advent. The aorist is here perfective. See ADVANCE.

7. KLINŌ (κλίνω), to lean, decline, is said of the decline of day in Luke 24 : 29, " is (now) far spent," lit., ' has declined.' See Bow (Verb).

8. GINOMAI (γίνομαι), to become, occur, is rendered " was far spent " in Mark 6 : 35, lit., ' much hour (i.e., many an hour) having taken place.'

9. POIEŌ (ποιέω), to do, is translated " have spent (*but* one hour)," in Matt. 20 : 12, R.V. (A.V., " have wrought ") lit., as in the Eng. idiom, ' have done one hour ; ' so in Acts 20 : 3, R.V., " when he had spent (lit., ' had done ') three months " (A.V., " abode ").

10. EUKAIREŌ (εὐκαιρέω). to have leisure or devote one's leisure to, is translated " spent their time," in Acts 17 : 21. See LEISURE.

11. CHRONOTRIBEŌ (χρονοτριβέω), to spend time (*chronos*, time, *tribō*, to rub, to wear out), occurs in Acts 20 : 16.¶

Note : Polus, much, is rendered " far spent " twice in Mark 6 : 35, R.V.

SPEW (A.V., SPUE)

EMEŌ (ἐμέω), to vomit (cp. Eng., emetic), is used in Rev. 3 : 16, figuratively of the Lord's utter abhorrence of the condition of the church at Laodicea.¶ In the Sept., Isa. 19 : 14.¶

SPICE(S)

1. ARŌMA (ἄρωμα), spice, occurs in Mark 16 : 1, R.V. " spices " (A.V., " sweet sp."); Luke 23 : 56 ; 24 : 1 ; John 19 : 40.¶ A papyrus document has it in a list of articles for a sacrifice.

2. AMŌMON (ἄμωμον), *amomum*, probably a word of Semitic origin, a fragrant plant of India, is translated " spice " in Rev. 18 : 13, R.V. (A.V., " odours ").¶

SPIKENARD

NARDOS (νάρδος) is derived, through the Semitic languages (Heb. *nērd*, Syriac *nardin*), from the Sanskrit *nalada*, a fragrant oil, procured from the stem of an Indian plant. The Arabs call it the Indian spike. The adjective *pistikos* is attached to it in the N.T., Mark 14 : 3 ; John 12 : 3 ; *pistikos*, if taken as an ordinary Greek word, would signify ' genuine.' There is evidence, however, that it was regarded as a technical term. It has been suggested that the original reading was *pistakēs*, i.e., the *Pistacia Terebinthus*, which grows in Cyprus, Syria, Palestine, etc., and yields a resin of very fragrant odour, and in such inconsiderable quantities as to be very costly. " Nard was frequently mixed with aromatic ingredients . . . so when scented with the fragrant resin of the *pistakē* it would quite well be called *nardos pistakēs* " (E. N. Bennett, in the *Classical Review* for 1890, Vol. iv, p. 319). The oil used for the anointing of the Lord's head was worth about £12, and must have been of the most valuable kind.¶   In the Sept., S. of Sol. 1 : 12 ;   4 : 13, 14.¶

SPILL

EKCHUNNŌ (or EKCHUNŌ) (ἐκχύννω), to pour out, shed, is rendered " be spilled " in Luke 5 : 37.   See POUR, SHED.

Note : Some texts have *ekcheō* in Mark 2 : 22 (so A.V.).   The form in Luke 5 : 37 might also come from *ekcheō*.

SPIN

NĒTHŌ (νήθω), to spin, is found in Matt. 6 : 28 and Luke 12 : 27, of the lilies of the field (see LILY).¶

SPIRIT

PNEUMA (πνεῦμα) primarily denotes the wind (akin to *pneō*, to breathe, blow) ; also breath ; then, especially the spirit, which, like the wind, is invisible, immaterial and powerful.   The N.T. uses of the word may be analysed approximately as follows :

" (a) the wind, John 3 : 8 (where marg. is, perhaps, to be preferred) ; Heb. 1 : 7 ; cp. Amos 4 : 13, Sept. ;   (b) the breath, 2 Thess. 2 : 8 ;   Rev. 11 : 11 ;   13 : 15 ;   cp. Job 12 : 10, Sept. ;   (c) the immaterial, invisible part of man, Luke 8 : 55 ;   Acts 7 : 59 ;   1 Cor. 5 : 5 ;   Jas. 2 : 26 ;   cp. Ecc. 12 : 7, Sept. ;   (d) the disembodied (or ' unclothed,' or ' naked,' 2 Cor. 5 : 3, 4) man, Luke 24 : 37, 39 ;   Heb. 12 : 23 ;   1 Pet. 4 : 6 ;   (e) the resurrection body, 1 Cor. 15 : 45 ;   1 Tim. 3 : 16 ;   1 Pet. 3 : 18 ;   (f) the sentient element in man, that by which he perceives, reflects, feels, desires, Matt. 5 : 3 ;   26 : 41 ;   Mark 2 : 8 ;   Luke 1 : 47, 80 ;   Acts 17 : 16 ;   20 : 22 ; 1 Cor. 2 : 11 ;   5 : 3, 4 ;   14 : 4, 15 ;   2 Cor. 7 : 1 ;   cp. Gen. 26 : 35 ;   Isa. 26 : 9 ;   Ezek. 13 : 3 ;   Dan. 7 : 15 ;   (g) purpose, aim, 2 Cor. 12 : 18 ; Phil. 1 : 27 ;   Eph. 4 : 23 ;   Rev. 19 : 10 ;   cp. Ezra 1 : 5 ;   Ps. 78 : 8 ; Dan. 5 : 12 ;   (h) the equivalent of the personal pronoun, used for emphasis and effect : 1st person, 1 Cor. 16 : 18 ;   cp. Gen. 6 : 3 ;   2nd person, 2 Tim. 4 : 22 ;   Philm. 25 ;   cp. Ps. 139 : 7 ;   3rd person, 2 Cor. 7 : 13 ;   cp. Isa. 40 : 13 ;   (i) character, Luke 1 : 17 ;   Rom. 1 : 4 ;   cp. Num. 14 : 24 ; (j) moral qualities and activities :   bad, as of bondage, as of a slave, Rom. 8 : 15 ;   cp. Isa. 61 : 3 ;   stupor, Rom. 11 : 8 ;   cp. Isa. 29 : 10 ; timidity, 2 Tim. 1 : 7 ;   cp. Josh. 5 : 1 ;   good, as of adoption, i.e., liberty as of a son, Rom. 8 : 15 ;   cp. Ps. 51 : 12 ;   meekness, 1 Cor. 4 : 21 ;   cp. Prov. 16 : 19 ;   faith, 2 Cor. 4 : 13 ;   quietness, 1 Pet. 3 : 4 ;   cp. Prov. 14 : 29 ;   (k) the Holy Spirit, e.g., Matt. 4 : 1 (see below) ;   Luke 4 : 18 ; (l) ' the inward man ' (an expression used only of the believer, Rom. 7 : 22 ;   2 Cor. 4 : 16 ;   Eph. 3 : 16) ;   the new life, Rom. 8 : 4-6, 10, 16 ; Heb. 12 : 9 ;   cp. Psa. 51 : 10 ;   (m) unclean spirits, demons, Matt. 8 : 16 ; Luke 4 : 33 ;   1 Pet. 3 : 19 ;   cp. 1 Sam. 18 : 10 ;   (n) angels, Heb. 1 : 14 ;

cp. Acts 12 : 15 ; (*o*) divine gift for service, 1 Cor. 14 : 12, 32 ; (*p*) by metonymy, those who claim to be depositories of these gifts, 2 Thess. 2 : 2 ; 1 John 4 : 1–3 ; (*q*) the significance, as contrasted with the form, of words, or of a rite, John 6 : 63 ; Rom. 2 : 29 ; 7 : 6 ; 2 Cor. 3 : 6 ; (*r*) a vision, Rev. 1 : 10 ; 4 : 2 ; 17 : 3 ; 21 : 10."*

Notes : (1) For *phantasma*, rendered " spirit," Matt. 14 : 26 ; Mark 6 : 49, A.V., see APPARITION. (2) For the distinction between spirit and soul, see under SOUL, last three paragraphs.

The Holy Spirit

The Holy Spirit is spoken of under various titles in the N.T. (' Spirit ' and ' Ghost ' are renderings of the same word *pneuma ;* the advantage of the rendering ' Spirit ' is that it can always be used, whereas ' Ghost ' always requires the word ' Holy ' prefixed.) In the following list the omission of the definite article marks its omission in the original (concerning this see below) : " Spirit, Matt. 22 : 43 ; Eternal Spirit, Heb. 9 : 14 ; the Spirit, Matt. 4 : 1 ; Holy Spirit, Matt. 1 : 18 ; the Holy Spirit, Matt. 28 : 19 ; the Spirit, the Holy, Matt. 12 : 32 ; the Spirit of promise, the Holy, Eph. 1 : 13 ; Spirit of God, Rom. 8 : 9 ; Spirit of (the) living God, 2 Cor. 3 : 3 ; the Spirit of God, 1 Cor. 2 : 11 ; the Spirit of our God, 1 Cor. 6 : 11 ; the Spirit of God, the Holy, Eph. 4 : 30 ; the Spirit of glory and of God, 1 Pet. 4 : 14 ; the Spirit of Him that raised up Jesus from the dead (i.e., God), Rom. 8 : 11 ; the Spirit of your Father, Matt. 10 : 20 ; the Spirit of His Son, Gal. 4 : 6 ; Spirit of (the) Lord, Acts 8 : 39 ; the Spirit of (the) Lord, Acts 5 : 9 ; (the) Lord, (the) Spirit, 2 Cor. 3 : 18 ; the Spirit of Jesus, Acts 16 : 7 ; Spirit of Christ, Rom. 8 : 9 ; the Spirit of Jesus Christ, Phil. 1 : 19 ; Spirit of adoption, Rom. 8 : 15 ; the Spirit of truth, John 14 : 17 ; the Spirit of life, Rom. 8 : 2 ; the Spirit of grace, Heb. 10 : 29."†

The use or absence of the article in the original where the Holy Spirit is spoken of cannot always be decided by grammatical rules, nor can the presence or absence of the article alone determine whether the reference is to the Holy Spirit. Examples where the Person is meant when the article is absent are Matt. 22 : 43 (the article is used in Mark 12 : 36) ; Acts 4 : 25, R.V. (absent in some texts) ; 19 : 2, 6 ; Rom. 14 : 17 ; 1 Cor. 2 : 4 ; Gal. 5 : 25 (twice) ; 1 Pet. 1 : 2. Sometimes the absence is to be accounted for by the fact that *Pneuma* (like *Theos*) is substantially a proper name, e.g., in John 7 : 39. As a general rule the article is present where the subject of the teaching is the Personality of the Holy Spirit, e.g., John 14 : 26, where He is spoken of in distinction from the Father and the Son. See also 15 : 26 and cp. Luke 3 : 22.

In Gal. 3 : 3, in the phrase " having begun in the Spirit," it is difficult to say whether the reference is to the Holy Spirit or to the quickened spirit of the believer ; that it possibly refers to the latter is not to be

---

* From Notes on Thessalonians by Hogg and Vine, pp. 204, 205
† From Notes on Galatians by Hogg and Vine, p. 193.

determined by the absence of the article, but by the contrast with "the flesh ; " on the other hand, the contrast may be between the Holy Spirit who in the believer sets His seal on the perfect work of Christ, and the flesh which seeks to better itself by works of its own. There is no preposition before either noun, and if the reference is to the quickened spirit it cannot be dissociated from the operation of the Holy Spirit. In Gal. 4 : 29 the phrase " after the Spirit " signifies ' by supernatural power,' in contrast to " after the flesh," i.e., ' by natural power,' and the reference must be to the Holy Spirit ; so in 5 : 17.

The full title with the article before both *pneuma* and *hagios* (the " resumptive " use of the article), lit., ' the Spirit the Holy,' stresses the character of the Person, e.g., Matt. 12 : 32 ; Mark 3 : 29 ; 12 : 36 ; 13 : 11 ; Luke 2 : 26 ; 10 : 21 (R.V.) ; John 14 : 26 ; Acts 1 : 16 ; 5 : 3 ; 7 : 51 ; 10 : 44, 47 ; 13 : 2 ; 15 : 28 ; 19 : 6 ; 20 : 23, 28 ; 21 : 11 ; 28 : 25 ; Eph. 4 : 30 ; Heb. 3 : 7 ; 9 : 8 ; 10 : 15.

The Personality of the Spirit is emphasized at the expense of strict grammatical procedure in John 14 : 26 ; 15 : 26 ; 16 : 8, 13, 14, where the emphatic pronoun *ekeinos*, " He," is used of Him in the masculine, whereas the noun *pneuma* is neuter in Greek, while the corresponding word in Aramaic, the language in which our Lord probably spoke, is feminine (*rûchâ*, cf. Heb. *rûach*). The rendering " itself " in Rom. 8 : 16, 26, due to the Greek gender, is corrected to " Himself " in the R.V.

The subject of the Holy Spirit in the N.T. may be considered as to His Divine attributes ; His distinct Personality in the Godhead ; His operation in connection with the Lord Jesus in His Birth, His life, His baptism, His Death ; His operations in the world ; in the Church ; His having been sent at Pentecost by the Father and by Christ ; His operations in the individual believer ; in local churches ; His operations in the production of Holy Scripture ; His work in the world, etc.

SPIRITUAL
A. Adjective

PNEUMATIKOS (πνευματικός) " always connotes the ideas of invisibility and of power. It does not occur in the Sept. nor in the Gospels ; it is in fact an after-Pentecost word. In the N.T. it is used as follows : (a) the angelic hosts, lower than God but higher in the scale of being than man in his natural state, are ' spiritual hosts,' Eph. 6 : 12 ; (b) things that have their origin with God, and which, therefore, are in harmony with His character, as His law is, are ' spiritual,' Rom. 7 : 14 ; (c) ' spiritual ' is prefixed to the material type in order to indicate that what the type sets forth, not the type itself, is intended, 1 Cor. 10 : 3, 4 ; (d) the purposes of God revealed in the gospel by the Holy Spirit, 1 Cor. 2 : 13a, and the words in which that revelation is expressed, are ' spiritual,' 13b, matching, or combining, spiritual things with spiritual words [or, alternatively, ' interpreting spiritual things to spiritual men,' see (e) below] ; ' spiritual songs ' are songs of which the burden is the things revealed by the Spirit, Eph. 5 : 19 ; Col. 3 : 16 ; ' spiritual wisdom and understanding' is wisdom in, and understanding of, those things, Col. 1 : 9 ; (e) men in Christ who walk so as to please God are ' spiritual,' Gal. 6 : 1 ; 1 Cor. 2 : 13b [but see (d) above], 15 ; 3 : 1 ; 14 : 37 ; (f) the whole company of those who believe in Christ is a ' spiritual house,' 1 Pet. 2 : 5a ; (g) the blessings that accrue to regenerate men at this present time are called ' spiritualities,' Rom. 15 : 27 ; 1 Cor. 9 : 11 ; ' spiritual blessings,' Eph. 1 : 3 ; ' spiritual gifts,' Rom. 1 : 11 ; (h) the activities Godward of regenerate men are ' spiritual sacrifices,' 1 Pet. 2 : 5b ; their appointed activities in the churches are also called ' spiritual gifts,' lit., ' spiritualities,' 1 Cor. 12 : 1 ; 14 : 1 ; (i) the resurrection body of the dead in Christ is ' spiritual,' i.e., such as is suited to the heavenly environment, 1 Cor. 15 : 44 ; (j) all that is produced and maintained among men by the operations of the Spirit of God is ' spiritual,' 1 Cor. 15 : 46. . . .

" The spiritual man is one who walks by the Spirit both in the sense of Gal. 5 : 16 and in that of 5 : 25, and who himself manifests the fruit of the Spirit in his own ways. . . .

" According to the Scriptures, the ' spiritual ' state of soul is normal for the believer, but to this state all believers do not attain, nor when it is attained is it always maintained. Thus the Apostle, in 1 Cor. 3 : 1–3, suggests a contrast between this spiritual state and that of the babe in Christ, i.e., of the man who because of immaturity and inexperience has not yet reached spirituality, and that of the man who by permitting jealousy, and the strife to which jealousy always leads, has lost it. The spiritual state is reached by diligence in the Word of God and in prayer ; it is maintained by obedience and self-judgment. Such as are led by the Spirit are spiritual, but, of course, spirituality is not a fixed or absolute condition, it admits of growth ; indeed growth in ' the grace and knowledge of our Lord and Saviour Jesus Christ,' 2 Pet. 3 : 18, is evidence of true spirituality."*

B. Adverb.

PNEUMATIKŌS (πνευματικῶς), spiritually, occurs in 1 Cor. 2 : 14, with the meaning as (j) above, and Rev. 11 : 8, with the meaning as in (c). Some mss. have it in 1 Cor. 2 : 13.¶

Notes : (1) In Rom. 8 : 6, the R.V. rightly renders the noun *pneuma* " (the mind) of the spirit," A.V., " spiritual (mind)." (2) In 1 Cor. 14 : 12 the plural of *pneuma*, " spirits," R.V., marg., stands for " spiritual *gifts* " (text). (3) In 1 Pet. 2 : 2, the R.V. renders *iogikos* " spiritual."

SPIT

1. PTUŌ (πτύω), to spit, occurs in Mark 7 : 33 ; 8 : 23 ; John 9 : 6.¶ In the Sept., Numb. 12 : 14.¶

---

* From Notes on Galatians by Hogg and Vine, pp. 308–310.

2. EMPTUŌ (ἐμπτύω), to spit upon (*en*, in, and No. 1), occurs in Matt. 26:67; 27:30; Mark 10:34; 14:65; 15:19; Luke 18:32.¶ In the Sept., Numb. 12:14, in some texts; Deut. 25:9.¶

SPITEFULLY (ENTREAT)

HUBRIZŌ (ὑβρίζω), used transitively, denotes to outrage, treat insolently; to entreat shamefully in Matt. 22:6, R.V. (A.V., "spitefully"); so in Luke 18:32, R.V.; in Acts 14:5 (A.V., "use despitefully"); in 1 Thess. 2:2, A.V. and R.V.; in Luke 11:45, "reproachest." See DESPITEFULLY, ENTREAT, REPROACH, SHAMEFULLY.¶

SPITTLE

PTUSMA (πτύσμα), akin to *ptuō*, to spit, occurs in John 9:6.¶

SPOIL (Noun and Verb), SPOILING

A. Nouns.

1. SKULON (σκῦλον), used in the plural, denotes arms stripped from a foe; "spoils" in Luke 11:22.¶

2. AKROTHINION (ἀκροθίνιον), primarily the top of a heap (*akros*, highest, top, and *this*, a heap), hence firstfruit offerings, and in war the choicest spoils, Heb. 7:4.¶

3. HARPAGĒ (ἁρπαγή), pillage, is rendered "spoiling" in Heb. 10:34. See EXTORT, B, No. 1.

B. Verbs.

1. DIARPAZŌ (διαρπάζω), to plunder, is found in Matt. 12:29, 2nd part (the 1st has *harpazo*, in the best texts), lit., '(then) he will completely (*dia*, intensive) spoil (his house);' Mark 3:27 (twice).¶

2. HARPAZŌ (ἁρπάζω), to seize, snatch away, is rendered "spoil" in Matt. 12:29a (see No. 1). See CATCH, No. 1.

3. SULAGŌGEŌ (συλαγωγέω), to carry off as spoil, lead captive (*sulē*, spoil, *ago*, to lead), is rendered "maketh spoil of" in Col. 2:8, R.V. (A.V., "spoil"), rather 'carry you off as spoil.' The false teacher, through his "philosophy and vain deceit," would carry them off as so much booty.¶

4. APEKDUŌ (ἀπεκδύω), in the Middle Voice is translated "having spoiled" in Col. 2:15, A.V., R.V., "having put off from Himself (the principalities and the powers)." These are regarded by some as the unsinning angels, because they are mentioned twice before in the Epistle (1:16; 2:10). It is also argued that the verb *apekduō*, rendered "having put off from Himself," in 2:15, is used in a somewhat different sense in 3:9. Such representations do not form a sufficiently cogent reason for regarding the principalities and the powers here mentioned as those of light, rather than those of darkness.

Others think that the reference is to the holy angels, which were in attendance at the giving of the Law (Acts 7:53; Gal. 3:19), and that

Christ wrought His work on the Cross, without any such attendance ; or, again, that, even apart from the Law and its circumstances, the Lord stripped Himself of those who usually ministered to Him, as, e.g., in the wilderness and in the Garden of Gethsemane.

The exposition given by Lightfoot and others seems to be the right one. There is no doubt that Satan and his hosts gathered together to attack the soul of Christ, while He was enduring, in propitiatory sacrifice, the judgment due to our sins, and fulfilling the great work of redemption. There is an intimation of this in Psa. 22 : 21, " Save Me from the lion's mouth ; yea, from the horns of the wild-oxen " (cp. vv. 12, 13). Doubtless the powers of darkness gathered against the Lord at that time, fiercely assaulting Him to the utmost of their power. He Himself had said, " This is your hour, and the power of darkness " (Luke 22 : 53). The metaphor of putting off from Himself these powers need not be pressed to the extent of regarding them as a garment clinging about Him. It seems to stand simply as a vivid description of His repulsion of their attack and of the power by which He completely overthrew them.

SPONGE
SPONGOS (σπόγγος) was the medium by which vinegar was carried to the mouth of Christ on the Cross, Matt. 27 : 48 ; Mark 15 : 36 ; John 19 : 29.¶

SPORTING
ENTRUPHAŌ (ἐντρυφάω) occurs in 2 Pet. 2 : 13 (R.V., " revel ").

SPOT (Noun and Verb)
A. Nouns.
1. SPILOS (σπῖλος), a spot or stain, is used metaphorically (a) of moral blemish, Eph. 5 : 27 ; (b) of lascivious and riotous persons, 2 Pet. 2 : 13.¶

2. SPILAS (σπιλάς) is rendered " spots " in Jude 12, A.V. : see ROCK, No. 2.

B. Verb.
SPILOŌ (σπιλόω), akin to A, No. 1, is used in Jude 23, in the clause " hating even the garment spotted by the flesh," the garment representing that which, being brought into contact with the polluting element of the flesh, becomes defiled : see CLOTHING, No. 3 (last par.). See DEFILE, No. 4.

C. Adjective.
ASPILOS (ἄσπιλος), unspotted, unstained (a, negative, and A), is used of a lamb, 1 Pet. 1 : 19 ; metaphorically, of keeping a commandment without alteration and in the fulfilment of it, 1 Tim. 6 : 14 ; of the believer in regard to the world, Jas. 1 : 27, and free from all defilement in the sight of God, 2 Pet. 3 : 14.¶

Note : For *amōmos*, in Heb. 9 : 14, A.V., see BLEMISH, B.

SPREAD

1. STRŌNNUŌ or STRŌNNUMI (στρωννύω), to spread, is so rendered in Matt. 21 : 8, R.V., twice ; Mark 11 : 8, R.V., once. See FURNISH.

2. HUPOSTRŌNNUŌ (ὑποστρωννύω), to spread under (hupo), of clothes, is used in Luke 19 : 36.¶

3. DIANEMŌ (διανέμω), to distribute, is used in the Passive Voice in Acts 4 : 17, "spread," lit., ' be spread about ' (dia).¶ In the Sept., Deut. 29 : 26, to assign or divide (concerning the worship of other gods).¶

4. DIAPHERŌ (διαφέρω), to carry about, spread abroad : see PUBLISH, No. 2 ; for other meanings of the word see BETTER (be), No. 1.

5. EKPETANNUMI (ἐκπετάννυμι), to spread out (as a sail), is rendered " did I spread out " in Rom. 10 : 21, R.V. (A.V., " I have stretched forth ").¶

Notes : (1) In Mark 1 : 28 and 1 Thess. 1 : 8, A.V., *exerchomai*, to go out or forth (R.V.), is rendered to spread abroad. (2) In Mark 6 : 14, A.V., *ginomai*, to become, with *phaneros*, manifest, is translated " had spread abroad " (R.V., " had become known "). (3) In 2 Cor. 8 : 18, the R.V. " *is spread* " (A.V., " *is* ") represents nothing in the original. (4) For R.V., " spread His tabernacle over," Rev. 7 : 15, see DWELL, No. 9. (5) For Mark 1 : 45, see BLAZE ABROAD.

SPRING (Noun and Verb)
A. Verbs.

1. GINOMAI (γίνομαι), to become, is used in the best texts in Heb. 11 : 12, " sprang " (some have *gennaō*, in the Passive Voice, rendered in the same way).

2. ANATELLŌ (ἀνατέλλω), to arise, is rendered by the verb to spring, or spring up, in Matt. 4 : 16 and Heb. 7 : 14. See ARISE, No. 9.

3. EXANATELLŌ (ἐξανατέλλω), *ek* or *ex*, out, and No. 2, is used of the springing up of seeds, Matt. 13 : 5 ; Mark 4 : 5 (No. 7 in ver. 8).¶

4. PHUŌ (φύω), used transitively, to bring forth, produce, denotes, in the Passive Voice, to spring up, grow, of seed, Luke 8 : 6, 8, A.V., " was sprung up " and " sprang up " (R.V., " grew ") ; in the Active Voice, intransitively, in Heb. 12 : 15, of a root of bitterness. See GROW.¶

5. SUMPHUŌ (συμφύω), to cause to grow together (*sun*, with, and No. 4), occurs in Luke 8 : 7, R.V., " grew with," A.V., " sprang up with."¶

6. BLASTANŌ (βλαστάνω), to sprout, is rendered to spring up in Matt. 13 : 26, of tare-blades, and Mark 4 : 27, of seed. See BRING, A, No. 26, BUD.

7. ANABAINŌ (ἀναβαίνω), to go up, is rendered " sprang up " in Matt. 13 : 7, A.V., of thorns, and Mark 4 : 8, of seed (R.V., " grew up "). See GROW, No. 4.

8. HALLOMAI (ἅλλομαι), to leap, spring, is rendered " springing

up," of well-water, in John 4 : 14, figurative of the Holy Spirit in the believer. See LEAP.

9. EISPĒDAŌ (εἰσπηδάω), to spring or leap in, occurs in Acts 16 : 29, " sprang in."¶ In the Sept., Amos 5 : 19.¶

10. EKPĒDAŌ (ἐκπηδάω), to spring forth, occurs in Acts 14 : 14, in the best texts. See RUN, Note (4).

B. Noun.

PĒGĒ (πηγή) is rendered " springs " in 2 Pet. 2 : 17, R.V. : see FOUNTAIN.

Note : For *epiginomai,* Acts 28 : 13, see BLOW (verb).

SPRINKLE, SPRINKLING
A. Verb.

RHANTIZŌ (ῥαντίζω), to sprinkle (a later form of *rhainō*), is used in the Active Voice in Heb. 9 : 13, of sprinkling with blood the unclean, a token of the efficacy of the expiatory sacrifice of Christ, His blood signifying the giving up of His life in the shedding of His blood (cp. 9 : 22) under Divine judgment upon sin (the voluntary act to be distinguished from that which took place after His death in the piercing of His side) ; so again in vv. 19, 21 (see B) ; in Heb. 10 : 22, Passive Voice, of the purging (on the ground of the same efficacy) of the hearts of believers from an evil conscience. This application of the blood of Christ is necessary for believers, in respect of their committal of sins, which on that ground receive forgiveness, 1 John 1 : 9. In Mark 7 : 4, the verb is found in the Middle Voice " in some ancient authorities " (R.V. marg.) instead of *baptizō.* In Rev. 19 : 13, the R.V., " sprinkled " follows those texts which have *rhantizō* (marg., " some anc. auth. read ' dipped in,' " *baptō* ; so Nestle's text).¶ This requires mention as a variant text in Rev. 19 : 13 under DIP.

B. Nouns.

1. RHANTISMOS (ῥαντισμός), sprinkling, akin to A, is used of the sprinkling of the blood of Christ, in Heb. 12 : 24 and 1 Pet. 1 : 2, an allusion to the use of the blood of sacrifices, appointed for Israel, typical of the sacrifice of Christ (see under A).¶

2. PROSCHUSIS (πρόσχυσις), a pouring or sprinkling upon, occurs in Heb. 11 : 28, of the sprinkling of the blood of the Passover lamb.¶

For SPUE see SPEW

SPY (Noun and Verb)
A. Nouns.

1. ENKATHETOS (ἐγκάθετος), an adjective denoting suborned to lie in wait (*en,* in, *kathiēmi,* to send down), is used as a noun in Luke 20 : 20, " spies."¶ In the Sept., Job. 19 : 12 ; 31 : 9.¶

2. KATASKOPOS (κατάσκοπος) denotes a spy (kata, down, signifying closely, and skopeō, to view), Heb. 11 : 31.¶

B. Verb.

KATASKOPEŌ (κατασκοπέω), to view closely (akin to A, No. 2), spy out, search out with a view to overthrowing, is used in Gal. 2 : 4.¶ In the Sept., 2 Sam. 10 : 3 ; 1 Chron. 19 : 3.¶

For STABLISH see ESTABLISH

STAFF, STAVES

1. RHABDOS (ῥάβδος), rendered " staff " or " staves " in Matt. 10 : 10, parallel passages, and Heb. 11 : 21 : see ROD.

2. XULON (ξύλον), wood, then, anything made of wood, e.g., a cudgel or staff, is rendered " staves " in Matt. 26 : 47, 55 and parallel passages. See STOCKS, TREE, WOOD.

For STAGGER see WAVER

STAIR

ANABATHMOS (ἀναβαθμός), an ascent (akin to anabainō, to go up), denotes a flight of stairs, Acts 21 : 35, 40. These were probably the steps leading down from the castle of Antonia to the Temple. (See Josephus, B.J., v., 5, 8.)¶ In the Sept., it is used, e.g., in the titles of the Songs of Ascents, Psa. 120–134.

For STALL see MANGER

STANCH

HISTĒMI (ἵστημι), transitively, to cause to stand, is used intransitively (to stand still) in Luke 8 : 44, translated " stanched." See STAND.

STAND (Noun and Verb), STANDING, STOOD

A. Noun.

LUCHNIA (λυχνία), a lampstand, is translated " stand " in Matt. 5 : 15 and parallel passages (A.V., " candlestick "). See LAMPSTAND.

B. Verbs.

1. HISTĒMI (ἵστημι), (a) transitively, denotes to cause to stand, to set ; in the Passive Voice, to be made to stand, e.g., Matt. 2 : 9, lit., ' was made to stand ; ' so Luke 11 : 18 ; 19 : 8 (Col. 4 : 12 in some mss.) ; in Rev. 13 : 1 the R.V. follows the best texts, " he stood " (not as A.V., " I stood ") ; the reference is to the Dragon. In the Middle Voice, to take one's stand, place oneself, e.g., Rev. 18 : 15 ; (b) intransitively, in the 2nd aorist and perfect Active, to stand, stand by, stand still, e.g., Matt. 6 : 5 ; 20 : 32, " stood still ; " in Luke 6 : 8, " stand forth " and " stood forth ; " metaphorically, to stand firm, John 8 : 44 (negatively),

in the truth (see No. 7) ; Rom. 5 : 2, in grace ; 1 Cor. 15 : 1, in the gospel ; Rom. 11 : 20, " by thy faith," R.V. ; 2 Cor. 1 : 24, " by faith " (marg., " by your faith ") ; of stedfastness, 1 Cor. 7 : 37 ; Eph. 6 : 11, 13, 14 ; Col. 4 : 12 [some mss. have the Passive, see (a)]. See APPOINT, ESTABLISH, SET.

2. ANISTĒMI (ἀνίστημι), to raise, intransitively, to rise, is translated to stand up in Matt. 12 : 41, R.V. ; Mark 14 : 60 ; Luke 4 : 16 ; 10 : 25 ; Acts 1 : 15 ;   5 : 34 ;   10 : 26 ;   11 : 28 ;   13 : 16 ;   in 14 : 10, " stand upright." See ARISE, No. 1.

3. EPHISTĒMI (ἐφίστημι) (epi, upon, and No. 1), used intransitively, denotes to stand upon or by, be present, Luke 2 : 9 and Acts 12 : 7, " stood by," R.V. (A.V., " came upon ") ; Luke 4 : 39, " stood over ; " 24 : 4 and Acts 23 : 11, " stood by ; " Acts 10 : 17, " stood ; " 22 : 13, " standing by (me)," R.V. ; so ver. 20, A.V. and R.V.   See ASSAULT, COME, No. 27, HAND (AT), B, Note (2), INSTANT, PRESENT.

4. PARISTĒMI (παρίστημι), intransitively, denotes to stand by or beside (para, by, and No. 1), Mark 14 : 47, 69, 70 ; 15 : 35, 39 (R.V., " stood by ") ; Luke 19 : 24 ; John 18 : 22 ; 19 : 26 ; Acts 1 : 10 ; 9 : 39 ; 23 : 2, 4 ;   27 : 23 ;   in 27 : 24, " stand before ; " in 4 : 10, " doth . . . stand here ; " in Luke 1 : 19, " stand ; " Rom. 14 : 10, " we shall . . . stand before " (Middle Voice) ; 2 Tim. 4 : 17, R.V., " stood by " (A.V., " . . . with "). See COMMEND, No. 4.

5. PERIISTĒMI (περιίστημι), intransitively, to stand around (peri), is so used in John 11 : 42 ; Acts 25 : 7. See AVOID, No. 4.

6. SUNISTĒMI (συνίστημι), intransitively, denotes to stand with (sun), Luke 9 : 32 ; for 2 Pet. 3 : 5, A.V., " standing," see COMPACTED, No. 1 : for other meanings see APPROVE, A, No. 2.

7. STĒKŌ (στήκω), a late present tense from hestēka, the perfect of histēmi, is used (a) literally, Mark 3 : 31 ;   11 : 25 ; John 1 : 26, in the best texts (in some texts Rev. 12 : 4) ;   (b) figuratively, Rom. 14 : 4, where the context indicates the meaning ' standeth upright ' rather than that of acquittal ; of standing fast, 1 Cor. 16 : 13, " in the faith," i.e., by adherence to it ; Gal. 5 : 1, in freedom from legal bondage ; Phil. 1 : 27, " in one spirit ; " Phil. 4 : 1 and 1 Thess. 3 : 8, " in the Lord," i.e., in the willing subjection to His authority ; 2 Thess. 2 : 15, in the Apostle's teaching ; some mss. have it in John 8 : 44, the most authentic have histēmi, R.V., " stood " (A.V., " abode ").¶

8. MENŌ (μένω), to abide, remain, is rendered " might stand," in Rom. 9 : 11, of the purpose of God, i.e., might abide for the permanent recognition of its true character. See ABIDE, No. 1.

9. KUKLOŌ (κυκλόω), " stood round about," Acts 14 : 20 : see COMPASS, No. 2.

Notes : (1) In Mark 3 : 3, egeirō, to raise, followed by the phrase eis to meson, ' into the midst,' is translated " stand forth." (2) In 2 Tim. 4 : 16, A.V., paraginomai (in some texts, sumparaginomai), to come up to assist, is rendered " stood with (me),'' R.V., " took (my) part."   (3) In Heb. 9 : 8, R.V., " is . . . standing " (A.V., " was . . . standing ") represents the phrase *echō*, to have, *stasis*, a standing, lit., ' has a standing.' (4) For " stand . . . in jeopardy " see DANGER.

STAR

1. ASTĒR (ἀστήρ), a star, Matt. 2 : 2–10 ; 24 : 29 ; Mk. 13 : 25 ; 1 Cor. 15 : 41 ; Rev. 6 : 13 ; 8 : 10–12 ; 9 : 1 ; 12 : 1, 4, is used metaphorically, (*a*) of Christ, as " the morning star," figurative of the approach of the day when He will appear as the " sun of righteousness," to govern the earth in peace, an event to be preceded by the Rapture of the Church, Rev. 2 : 28 ; 22 : 16, the promise of the former to the overcomer being suggestive of some special personal interest in Himself and His authority ; (*b*) of the angels of the seven churches, Rev. 1 : 16, 20 ; 2 : 1 ; 3 : 1 ; (*c*) of certain false teachers, described as " wandering stars," Jude 13, as if the stars, intended for light and guidance, became the means of deceit by irregular movements.¶

2. ASTRON (ἄστρον), practically the same as No. 1, is used (*a*) in the sing. in Acts 7 : 43, " the star of the god Rephan," R.V., the symbol or " figure," probably of Saturn, worshipped as a god, apparently the same as Chiun in Amos 5 : 26 (Rephan being the Egyptian deity corresponding to Saturn, Chiun the Assyrian) ; (*b*) in the plur., Luke 21 : 25 ; Acts 27 : 20 ; Heb. 11 : 12.¶

For STATE see ESTATE, Notes

For STATURE see AGE, A, No. 3

For STAVES see STAFF

STAY

1. KATECHŌ (κατέχω), to hold fast, hold back, is used in the sense of detaining in Luke 4 : 42, " would have stayed (Him)," R.V. See HOLD.

2. EPECHŌ (ἐπέχω) has the meaning to wait in a place, to stay, in Acts 19 : 22. See HEED, HOLD, MARK.

3. KŌLUŌ (κωλύω), to hinder, is rendered " stayed " in Acts 27 : 43, R.V. (A.V., " kept ") ; so in 2 Pet. 2 : 16, R.V. (A.V., " forbad "). See HINDER.

For STEADFAST see STEDFAST

STEAL

KLEPTŌ (κλέπτω), to steal, akin to *kleptēs*, a thief (cp. Eng., klepto-mania), occurs in Matt. 6 : 19, 20 ; 19 : 18 ; 27 : 64 ; 28 : 13 ; Mark

10 : 19 ; Luke 18 : 20 ; John 10 : 10 ; Rom. 2 : 21 (twice) ; 13 : 9 ;
Eph. 4 : 28 (twice).¶

STEDFAST, STEDFASTLY, STEDFASTNESS
A. Adjectives.

1. BEBAIOS (βέβαιος), firm, secure (akin to *bainō*, to go), is translated
"stedfast" in 2 Cor. 1 : 7 ; Heb. 2 : 2 ; 3 : 14, A.V. (R.V., "firm") ;
6 : 19. See FIRM, FORCE, SURE.

2. HEDRAIOS (ἑδραῖος) primarily denotes seated (*hedra*, a seat) ;
hence, stedfast, metaphorical of moral fixity, 1 Cor. 7 : 37 ; 15 : 58 ;
Col. 1 : 23, R.V. (A.V., "settled").¶

3. STEREOS (στερεός), firm, is rendered "stedfast" in 1 Pet. 5 : 9.
See FIRM, No. 2.

B. Nouns.

1. STEREŌMA (στερέωμα), primarily a support, foundation, denotes
strength, stedfastness, Col. 2 : 5.¶ In the Sept., in Gen. 1 : 6, and
Ezek. 1 : 22, it is used of the firmament, which was believed to be a solid
canopy. The corresponding Heb. word *rāqîa'* means 'expanse,' from
rāqa', to spread out.

2. STĒRIGMOS (στηριγμός), a setting firmly, supporting, then
fixedness, stedfastness (akin to *stērizō*, to establish), is used in 2 Pet.
3 : 17.¶

Note : For STEDFASTLY see BEHOLD, No. 10, CONTINUE, No. 9,
FASTEN, No. 1, LOOK, No. 15, SET, No. 19.

STEEP

KRĒMNOS (κρημνός), a steep bank (akin to *kremannumi*, to hang),
occurs in Matt. 8 : 32 ; Mark 5 : 13 ; Luke 8 : 33, R.V., "the steep"
(A.V., "a steep place").¶ In the Sept., 2 Chron. 25 : 12.¶

For STEERSMAN see GOVERNOR, B, Note

STEP (Noun and Verb)
A. Noun.

ICHNOS (ἴχνος), a footstep, a track, is used metaphorically of the
steps (*a*) of Christ's conduct, 1 Pet. 2 : 21 ; (*b*) of Abraham's faith, Rom.
4 : 12 ; (*c*) of identical conduct in carrying on the work of the Gospel,
2 Cor. 12 : 18.¶

B. Verb.

KATABAINŌ (καταβαίνω), to go, or come, down, is translated
"steppeth down" in John 5 : 7. See COME, No. 19.

Note : Many ancient authorities have the passage in the A.V. in
John 5 : 4, which contains *embainō*, rendered "stepped in." See COME,
No. 21.

STERN

PRUMNA (πρύμνα), the feminine form of the adjective *prumnos*, hindmost, is rendered "stern" in Acts 27 : 29 ; and in the R.V. in ver. 41 and Mark 4 : 38. See PART, A, Note (2).¶

STEWARD, STEWARDSHIP
A. Nouns.

1. OIKONOMOS (οἰκονόμος) primarily denoted the manager of a household or estate (*oikos*, a house, *nemō*, to arrange), a steward (such were usually slaves or freedmen), Luke 12 : 42 ; 16 : 1, 3, 8 ; 1 Cor. 4 : 2 ; Gal. 4 : 2, R.V. (A.V., " governors ") ; in Rom. 16 : 23, the " treasurer " (R.V.) of a city (see CHAMBERLAIN, Note) ; it is used metaphorically, in the wider sense, of a steward in general, (*a*) of preachers of the Gospel and teachers of the Word of God, 1 Cor. 4 : 1 ; (*b*) of elders or bishops in churches, Tit. 1 : 7 ; (*c*) of believers generally, 1 Pet. 4 : 10.¶

2. EPITROPOS (ἐπίτροπος) is rendered "steward" in Matt. 20 : 8 ; Luke 8 : 3 : see GUARDIAN.

3. OIKONOMIA (οἰκονομία) is rendered "stewardship" in Luke 16 : 2, 3, 4, and in the R.V. in 1 Cor. 9 : 17 : see DISPENSATION.

B. Verb.

OIKONOMEŌ (οἰκονομέω), akin to A, Nos. 1 and 3, signifies to be a house steward, Luke 16 : 2.¶ In the Sept., Psa. 112 : 5.¶

STICK

PHRUGANON (φρύγανον) denotes a dry stick (from *phrugō*, to parch) ; in the plural, brushwood, Acts 28 : 3.¶

STICK FAST

EREIDŌ (ἐρείδω), primarily to prop, fix firmly, is used intransitively in Acts 27 : 41 of a ship driving ashore, R.V., " struck."¶

STIFFNECKED

SKLĒROTRACHĒLOS (σκληροτράχηλος), from *sklēros*, harsh, hard, *trachēlos*, a neck, is used metaphorically in Acts 7 : 51.¶

STILL (Verb)

PHIMOŌ (φιμόω), in the Passive Voice, is rendered "be still" in Mark 4 : 39 : see MUZZLE.

STILL (Adverb)

ETI (ἔτι), yet, as yet, still, is translated " still " in the R.V. in 1 Cor. 12 : 31 ; 2 Cor. 1 : 10 ; Gal. 1 : 10 and 5 : 11 ; A.V. and R.V. in Rev. 22 : 11 (four times), where the word indicates the permanent character, condition and destiny of the unrighteous and the filthy, the righteous and the holy (for the verbs see the R.V.); in John 11 : 30, the best mss. have the word; so R.V. (A.V. omits).

Note : For combinations see ABIDE, IGNORANCE, B, No. 1, STAND.

For STING see GOAD

STINK

OZŌ (ὄζω), to emit a smell (cp. Eng., ozone), occurs in John 11 : 39.¶ In the Sept., Ex. 8 : 14.¶

STIR, STIR UP (Noun and Verb)

A. Noun.

TARACHOS (τάραχος), akin to *tarachē*, trouble, and *tarassō*, to trouble, is rendered " stir " in Acts 12 : 18; 19 : 23.¶

B. Verbs.

1. ANAZŌPUREŌ (ἀναζωπυρέω) denotes to kindle afresh, or keep in full flame (*ana*, up, or again, *zōos*, alive, *pur*, fire), and is used metaphorically in 2 Tim. 1 : 6, where " the gift of God " is regarded as a fire capable of dying out through neglect.¶ The verb was in common use in the vernacular of the time.

2. EPEGEIRŌ (ἐπεγείρω), " stirred up " in Acts 14 : 2. See RAISE.

3. DIEGEIRŌ (διεγείρω), " stir up " in 2 Pet. 1 : 13; 3 : 1 : see ARISE, No. 4.

4. SEIŌ (σείω), to move to and fro, is rendered "was stirred" in Matt. 21 : 10, R.V. (A.V., " was moved "). See MOVE, QUAKE, SHAKE.

5. ANASEIŌ (ἀνασείω) primarily denotes to shake back or out, move to and fro; then, to stir up, used metaphorically in Mark 15 : 11, R.V., " stirred . . . up " (A.V., " moved "), and Luke 3 : 14; 23 : 5.¶

6. SALEUŌ (σαλεύω), " stirred up " in Acts 17 : 13 : see SHAKE.

7. PAROTRUNŌ (παροτρύνω), from *para*, used intensively, beyond measure, and *otrunō*, to urge on, rouse, occurs in Acts 13 : 50, " stirred up."¶

8. SUNKINEŌ (συγκινέω), to move together (*sun*, together, *kineō*, to move), to stir up, excite, is used metaphorically in Acts 6 : 12.¶

9. SUNCHEŌ (συγχέω), to pour together, is used metaphorically in Acts 21 : 27, " stirred up." See CONFOUND, B, No. 1.

10. PAROXUNŌ (παροξύνω), " stirred " in Acts 17 : 16 : see PROVOKE, No. 2.

11. ERETHIZŌ (ἐρεθίζω), " hath stirred " in 2 Cor. 9 : 2, R.V. See PROVOKE, No. 3.

12. ANASTATOŌ (ἀναστατόω), to excite, unsettle (akin to *anistēmi*, to raise up, and *anastasis*, a raising), is used (*a*) of stirring up to sedition, and tumult, Acts 17 : 6, " turned . . . upside down; " 21 : 38, R.V., " stirred up to sedition," A.V., " madest an uproar; " (*b*) to upset by false teaching, Gal. 5 : 12, R.V., " unsettle " (A.V., " trouble ").¶

Note : In Acts 24 : 12, *poieō*, to make, with *epistasis*, a stopping (in some texts *episustasis*), signifies to collect (a crowd), A.V., " raising up (the people)," R.V., " stirring up (a crowd)." See COME, Note (9).

For STOCK see KIND

STOCKS

XULON (ξύλον), wood, is used of stocks in Acts 16 : 24. See STAFF, TREE, WOOD.

STOMACH

STOMACHOS (στόμαχος), properly a mouth, an opening, akin to *stoma*, a mouth, denotes the stomach in 1 Tim. 5 : 23.¶

STONE (Noun, Verb, and Adjective)
A. Nouns.

1. LITHOS (λίθος) is used (I) literally, of (*a*) the stones of the ground, e.g., Matt. 4 : 3, 6 ; 7 : 9 ; (*b*) tombstones, e.g., Matt. 27 : 60, 66 ; (*c*) building stones, e.g., Matt. 21 : 42 ; (*d*) a millstone, Luke 17 : 2 ; cp. Rev. 18 : 21 (see MILLSTONE) ; (*e*) the tables (or tablets) of the Law, 2 Cor. 3 : 7 ; (*f*) idol images, Acts 17 : 29 ; (*g*) the treasures of commercial Babylon, Rev. 18 : 12, 16 ; (II) metaphorically, of (*a*) Christ, Rom. 9 : 33 ; 1 Pet. 2 : 4, 6, 8 ; (*b*) believers, 1 Pet. 2 : 5 ; (*c*) spiritual edification by Scriptural teaching, 1 Cor. 3 : 12 ; (*d*) the adornment of the foundations of the wall of the spiritual and heavenly Jerusalem, Rev. 21 : 19 ; (*e*) the adornment of the seven angels in Rev. 15 : 6, R.V. (so the best texts ; some have *linon*, linen, A.V.) ; (*f*) the adornment of religious Babylon, Rev. 17 : 4 ; (III) figuratively, of Christ, Rev. 4 : 3 ; 21 : 11, where " light " stands for ' Light-giver ' (*phōstēr*).

2. PSĒPHOS (ψῆφος), a smooth stone, a pebble, worn smooth as by water, or polished (akin to *psaō*, to rub), denotes (*a*) by metonymy, a vote (from the use of pebbles for this purpose ; cp. *psēphizō*, to count), Acts 26 : 10, R.V. (A.V., " voice ") ; (*b*) a (white) stone to be given to the overcomer in the church at Pergamum, Rev. 2 : 17 (twice) ; a white stone was often used in the social life and judicial customs of the ancients ; festal days were noted by a white stone, days of calamity by a black ; in the courts a white stone indicated acquittal, a black condemnation. A host's appreciation of a special guest was indicated by a white stone with the name or a message written on it ; this is probably the allusion here.¶

Note : In John 1 : 42 *petros* stands for the proper name, Peter, as the R.V. (A.V., " a stone " ; marg., " Peter ") ; *petros* denotes a piece of a rock, a detached stone or boulder, in contrast to *petra*, a mass of rock. See ROCK.

B. Verbs.

1. LITHOBOLEŌ (λιθοβολέω), to pelt with stones (A, No. 1, and *ballō*, to throw), to stone to death, occurs in Matt. 21 : 35 ; 23 : 37 ; Luke 13 : 34 (John 8 : 5 in some mss. : see No. 2) ; Acts 7 : 58, 59 ; 14 : 5 ; Heb. 12 : 20.¶

2. LITHAZŌ (λιθάζω), to stone, virtually equivalent to No. 1, but not stressing the casting, occurs in John 8 : 5 (in the most authentic mss.) ; 10 : 31-33 ; 11 : 8 ; Acts 5 : 26 ; 14 : 19 ; 2 Cor. 11 : 25 ; Heb. 11 : 37.¶

3. KATALITHAZŌ (καταλιθάζω), an intensive form of No. 2, to cast stones at, occurs in Luke 20 : 6.¶

C. Adjective.

LITHINOS (λίθινος), of stone (akin to A, No. 1), occurs in John 2 : 6 ; 2 Cor. 3 : 3 ; Rev. 9 : 20.¶

For STONY see ROCKY

STOOP

1. KUPTŌ (κύπτω), to bow the head, stoop down, occurs in Mark 1 : 7 ; John 8 : 6, 8.¶

2. PARAKUPTŌ (παρακύπτω) is rendered to stoop down in Luke 24 : 12 ; John 20 : 5, 11, R.V., " stooping and looking in " : see Look, No. 10.

STOP

1. PHRASSŌ (φράσσω), to fence in (akin to *phragmos*, a fence), close, stop, is used (*a*) metaphorically, in Rom. 3 : 19, of preventing all excuse from Jew and Gentile, as sinners ; in 2 Cor. 11 : 10, lit., ' this boasting shall not be stopped to me ; ' Passive Voice in both ; (*b*) physically, of the mouths of lions, Heb. 11 : 33 (Active Voice).¶

2. SUNECHŌ (συνέχω), to hold together, is rendered " stopped (their ears) " in Acts 7 : 57. See Hold.

3. EPISTOMIZŌ (ἐπιστομίζω), to stop the mouth, Tit. 1 : 11 : see Mouth, B.¶

STORE (Verb)

1. THĒSAURIZŌ (θησαυρίζω), to lay up, store up, is rendered " in store " (lit., ' storing '), with a view to help a special case of need, 1 Cor. 16 : 2 ; said of the heavens and earth in 2 Pet. 3 : 7, R.V., " have been stored up (for fire)," marg., " stored (with fire)," A.V., " kept in store (reserved unto fire)." See Lay, No. 17, Treasure.

2. APOTHĒSAURIZŌ (ἀποθησαυρίζω), to treasure up, store away (*apo*), is used in 1 Tim. 6 : 19, of " laying up in store " a good foundation for the hereafter by being rich in good works.¶

For STORE-HOUSE, STORE-CHAMBER, see CHAMBER

STORM

LAILAPS (λαῖλαψ), a hurricane, whirlwind, is rendered " storm " in Mark 4 : 37 ; Luke 8 : 23 ; 2 Pet. 2 : 17, R.V. (A.V., " tempest "). See TEMPEST.¶

STORY

TRISTEGOS (τρίστεγος), an adjective denoting of three stories (*treis*, three, *stegē*, a roof), occurs in Acts 20 : 9 (with *oikēma*, a dwelling, understood), R.V., " the third story " (A.V., " the third loft ").¶

STRAIGHT
A. Adjectives.

1. EUTHUS (εὐθύς), direct, straight, right, is translated " straight," figuratively, of the paths of the Lord, Matt. 3 : 3 ; Mark 1 : 3 ; Luke 3 : 4 ; in ver. 5 of the rectification of the crooked, with reference to moral transformation ; in Acts 9 : 11, the name of a street in Damascus, still one of the principal thoroughfares. See RIGHT.

2. ORTHOS (ὀρθός), used of height, denotes " upright," Acts 14 : 10 ; of line of direction, figuratively, said of paths of righteousness, Heb. 12 : 13.¶

B. Verbs.

1. EUTHUNŌ (εὐθύνω), akin to A, No. 1, is used of the directing of a ship by the steersman, Jas. 3 : 4 (see GOVERNOR, B, Note) ; metaphorically, of making straight the way of the Lord, John 1 : 23.¶

2. ANORTHOŌ (ἀνορθόω), to set up, make straight : see LIFT, No. 6.

For STRAIGHT COURSE, see COURSE, B, Note (1)

For STRAIGHTWAY see FORTHWITH, Nos. 1, 2, 3, and IMMEDIATELY, No. 1

STRAIN OUT

DIŬLIZŌ (διϋλίζω), primarily denotes to strain thoroughly (*dia*, through, intensive, *hulizō*, to strain), then, to strain out, as through a sieve or strainer, as in the case of wine, so as to remove the unclean midge, Matt. 23 : 24, R.V. (A.V., " strain at ").¶ In the Sept., Amos 6 : 6.¶

For the Adjective STRAIT see NARROW

STRAIT (be in a), STRAITENED

1. SUNECHŌ (συνέχω), to hold together, constrain, is translated " I am in a strait " in Phil. 1 : 23 (Passive Voice), i.e., being restricted on both sides, under a pressure which prevents a definite choice ; so in Luke 12 : 50, " (how) am I straitened," i.e., pressed in. See CONSTRAIN, A, No. 3.

2. STENOCHŌREŌ (στενοχωρέω), to be pressed for room (*stenos*, narrow, *chōros*, a space), is rendered to be straitened in 2 Cor. 4 : 8, R.V. (A.V., " distressed ") ; 6 : 12 (twice). See ANGUISH, B, No. 1.¶

3. THLIBŌ (θλίβω), for which see AFFLICT, No. 4, is used in the perfect participle Passive of a narrowed way, in Matt. 7 : 14, R.V., " straitened," A.V., " narrow," of the way " that leadeth unto life," i.e., hemmed in like a narrow gorge between rocks.

STRAITEST

AKRIBESTATOS (ἀκριβέστατος), the superlative degree of *akribēs*, accurate, exact (cp. *akribōs*, see ACCURATELY and associated words there), occurs in Acts 26 : 5, " the straitest (sect)," R.V. (A.V., " most straitest ").¶

STRAITLY

Notes : (1) For *polla*, A.V., " straitly " in Mark 3 : 12 ; 5 : 43, see MUCH (R.V.). (2) In Acts 4 : 17 some mss. have *apeilē*, a threat, with *apeileō* (Middle Voice), lit., ' let us threaten them with a threat,' A.V., " let us straitly threaten ; " the best texts omit the noun (so R.V.). Moulton and Milligan (Vocab.), arguing for the presence of the noun, consider that it " clearly reflects the literal rendering of a Semitic original reported to Luke from an eye-witness—was it Paul ? " (3) A similar construction, *parangellō* with the noun *parangelia*, occurs in Acts 5 : 28, " we straitly charged you," lit., ' we charged you with a charge.' See CHARGE, A, No. 6. (4) For *embrimaomai*, A.V., " charge straitly " (R.V., " strictly ") in Matt. 9 : 30 ; Mark 1 : 43, see CHARGE, C, No. 4.

For STRAKE, Acts 27 : 17, A.V. (R.V., "lowered"), see LET DOWN, No. 2.

STRANGE

A. Adjectives.

1. XENOS (ξένος) denotes (*a*) foreign, alien, Acts 17 : 18, of gods ; Heb. 13 : 9, of doctrines ; (*b*) unusual, 1 Pet. 4 : 12, 2nd part, of the fiery trial of persecution (for 1st part, see B). See STRANGER.

2. ALLOTRIOS (ἀλλότριος) denotes (*a*) belonging to another (*allos*), see MAN'S, Note (1) ; (*b*) alien, foreign, strange, Acts 7 : 6 ; Heb. 11 : 9, A.V., R.V.," (a *land*) not his own." See ALIEN, STRANGER.

3. PARADOXOS (παράδοξος), contrary to received opinion (*para*, beside, *doxa*, opinion ; Eng. paradox, – ical), is rendered " strange things " in Luke 5 : 26.¶

4. EXŌ (ἔξω), outside, is rendered " strange " in Acts 26 : 11, A.V. : see FOREIGN.

Note : In 1 Cor. 14 : 21 (1st part), R.V., *heteroglōssos*, signifying of a different tongue (*heteros*, another, *glōssa*, a tongue) is translated " of strange (A.V., other) tongues."¶

B. Verb.

XENIZŌ (ξενίζω) denotes to think something strange, 1 Pet. 4 : 4, 12, Passive Voice, i.e., ' they are surprised,' and ' be (not) surprised ; ' in Acts 17 : 20, the present participle, Active, is rendered " strange," i.e., ' surprising.' See ENTERTAIN, LODGE.

STRANGER

A. Adjectives (used as nouns).

1. XENOS (ξένος), strange (see No. 1 above), denotes a stranger, foreigner, Matt. 25 : 35, 38, 43, 44 ; 27 : 7 ; Acts 17 : 21 ; Eph. 2 : 12, 19 ; Heb. 11 : 13 ; 3 John 5.

2. ALLOTRIOS (ἀλλότριος), " strangers," Matt. 17 : 25, 26 ; John 10 : 5 (twice) : see No. 2, above.

3. ALLOGENĒS (ἀλλογενής) (allos, another, genos, a race) occurs in Luke 17 : 18, of a Samaritan. Moulton and Milligan illustrate the use of the word by the inscription on the Temple barrier, " let no foreigner enter within the screen and enclosure surrounding the sanctuary ; " according to Mommsen this inscription was cut by the Romans : cp. PARTITION.¶

Notes : (1) For *paroikos*, in A.V., see SOJOURN, B, No. 1. For *parepidēmos*, in A.V., see PILGRIM. (2) The pronoun *heteros*, other, is translated " strangers " in 1 Cor. 14 : 21 (2nd part), R.V. (A.V., " other ") ; cp. STRANGE, A, Note.

B. Verb.

XENODOCHEŌ (ξενοδοχέω), to receive strangers (*xenos*, No. 1, above, and *dechomai*, to receive), occurs in 1 Tim. 5 : 10, R.V., " (if) she hath used hospitality to strangers," A.V., " (if) she have lodged strangers."¶

Note : For *epidēmeō*, in A.V., see SOJOURNER, A, No. 2. For *paroikeō*, in A.V., see SOJOURN, A, No. 1.

C. Noun.

PHILOXENIA (φιλοξενία), love of strangers, occurs in Rom. 12 : 13, " hospitality," and Heb. 13 : 2, R.V., " to shew love unto strangers," A.V., " to entertain strangers." See ENTERTAIN, Note.¶

Note : For *paroikia* in Acts 13 : 17, see SOJOURN, C.

STRANGLED

PNIKTOS (πνικτός), from *pnigō*, to choke, occurs in Acts 15 : 20, 29 ; 21 : 25, of the flesh of animals killed by strangling, without shedding their blood (see, e.g., Lev. 17 : 13, 14).¶

For STRAWED see FURNISH and SCATTER, No. 2

For STREAM see RIVER

STREET

1. PLATEIA (πλατεῖα), grammatically the feminine of *platus*, broad, is used as a noun (*hodos*, a way, being understood, i.e., a broad way), a street, Matt. 6 : 5 ; 12 : 19 (in some texts, Mark 6 : 56) ; Luke 10 : 10 ; 13 : 26 ; 14 : 21 ; Acts 5 : 15 ; Rev. 11 : 8 ; 21 : 21 ; 22 : 2.¶

2. AMPHODON (ἄμφοδον), properly a way around (*amphi*, around, *hodos*, a way), occurs in Mark 11 : 4, R.V., " the open street " (A.V., " where two ways met ").¶

Note : For *rhumē*, see LANE. For *agora*, see MARKET.

STRENGTH, STRENGTHEN
A. Nouns.

1. DUNAMIS (δύναμις) is rendered " strength " in the R.V. and A.V. of Rev. 1 : 16 ; elsewhere the R.V. gives the word its more appropriate meaning " power," for A.V., " strength," 1 Cor. 15 : 56 ; 2 Cor. 1 : 8 ; 12 : 9 ; Heb. 11 : 11 ; Rev. 3 : 8 ; 12 : 10. See ABILITY, No. 1, POWER, No. 1.

2. ISCHUS (ἰσχύς), ability, strength, is rendered " strength " in Mark 12 : 30, 33 ; Luke 10 : 27 ; in Rev. 5 : 12, A.V. (R.V., " might "). See ABILITY, No. 2, MIGHT.

3. KRATOS (κράτος), force, might, is rendered " strength " in Luke 1 : 51, R.V. and A.V. ; R.V.," strength " (A.V.," power ") in Eph. 1 : 19 and 6 : 10. See DOMINION, No. 1, POWER, No. 4.

Note : In Rev. 17 : 13, A.V., *exousia*, freedom of action, is rendered " strength " (R.V., " authority ").

B. Verbs.

1. DUNAMOŌ (δυναμόω), to strengthen, occurs in Col. 1 : 11, and in the best texts in Heb. 11 : 34, " were made strong " (some have No. 2) ; some have it in Eph. 6 : 10 (the best have No. 2).¶ In the Sept., Psa. 52 : 7 ; 68 : 28 ; Eccl. 10 : 10 ; Dan. 9 : 27.¶

2. ENDUNAMOŌ (ἐνδυναμόω), to make strong, is rendered " increased . . . in strength " in Acts 9 : 22 ; to strengthen in Phil. 4 : 13 ; 2 Tim. 2 : 1, R.V., " be strengthened ; " 4 : 17. See ENABLE, STRONG, B.

3. ISCHUŌ (ἰσχύω), akin to A, No. 2, to have strength, is so rendered in Mark 5 : 4, R.V. (A.V., " could ") ; in Luke 16 : 3, R.V., " I have not strength to " (A.V., " I cannot "). See AVAIL.

4. ENISCHUŌ (ἐνισχύω), akin to A, No. 2, a strengthened form of No. 3, is used in Luke 22 : 43 and Acts 9 : 19.¶

5. KRATAIOŌ (κραταιόω), to strengthen, is rendered " to be strengthened " in Eph. 3 : 16. See STRONG, B.

6. STHENOŌ (σθενόω), from *sthenos*, strength, occurs in 1 Pet. 5 : 10, in a series of future tenses, according to the best texts, thus constituting Divine promises.¶

Notes : (1) For *ischuō*, Heb. 9 : 17, see AVAIL. (2) For *stērizō*, Luke 22 : 32, see ESTABLISH, No. 1. (3) For *stereoō*, Acts 3 : 7, see ESTABLISH,

No. 2. (4) *Epistērizō* is found in some texts in Acts 18 : 23, A.V.,
" strengthening." See CONFIRM, A, No. 2, ESTABLISH, No. 1. (5) For
" without strength," Rom. 5 : 6, A.V., see WEAK.

STRETCH

1. EKTEINŌ (ἐκτείνω), to stretch out or forth, is so rendered in Matt.
12 : 13 (twice), 49 ; 14 : 31 ; 26 : 51 ; Mark 3 : 5 (twice) ; Luke 6 : 10 ;
in Matt. 8 : 3 ; Mark 1 : 41 and Luke 5 : 13, R.V. (A.V., " put forth ") ;
Luke 22 : 53 ; John 21 : 18 ; Acts 4 : 30 ; 26 : 1. For Acts 27 : 30 see
LAY, No. 13.¶

2. EPEKTEINŌ (ἐπεκτείνω), an intensive form of No. 1 (*epi*, forth),
is used in Phil. 3 : 13, R.V., " stretching forward " (A.V., " reaching
forth "), a metaphor probably from the foot race (rather than the chariot
race), so Lightfoot, who quotes Bengel's paraphrase, ' the eye goes before
and draws on the hand, the hand goes before and draws on the foot.'¶

3. HUPEREKTEINŌ (ὑπερεκτείνω), to stretch out beyond (*huper*,
over, and No. 1), occurs in 2 Cor. 10 : 14, R.V., " we stretch (not) . . .
overmuch " (A.V., " . . . beyond *our measure* ").¶

Note : For *ekpetannumi*, Rom. 10 : 21, see SPREAD, No. 5. For
epiballō, Acts 12 : 1, see PUT, No. 8.

STRICKEN (in years)

PROBAINŌ (προβαίνω), to go forward, is used metaphorically of age,
in Luke 1 : 7, 18, with the phrases " in their (her) days," translated " well
stricken in years " (see marg.) ; in 2 : 36, " of a great age " (marg.,
" advanced in many days "). See GO, No. 20.

For STRICT, R.V., see MANNER, A, No. 5. For STRICTLY,
R.V., see STRAITLY

STRIFE

1. ERIS (ἔρις), strife, contention, is the expression of enmity, Rom.
1 : 29, R.V., " strife " (A.V., " debate ") ; 13 : 13 ; 1 Cor. 1 : 11,
" contentions " (R.V. and A.V.) ; 3 : 3 ; 2 Cor. 12 : 20, R.V., " strife "
(A.V., " debates ") ; Gal. 5 : 20, R.V., " strife " (A.V., " variance ") ;
Phil. 1 : 15 ; 1 Tim. 6 : 4 ; Tit. 3 : 9, R.V., " strifes " (A.V., " contentions "). See CONTENTION, A, No. 1.¶

2. ERITHIA (or -EIA) (ἐριθία) : see FACTION.

3. ANTILOGIA (ἀντιλογία), " strife," Heb. 6 : 16, A.V. : see DISPUTE,
A, No. 4.

4. MACHĒ (μάχη), " strifes," 2 Tim. 2 : 23 : see FIGHTING, A.

5. PHILONEIKIA (φιλονεικία), " strife," Luke 22 : 24, A.V. : see
CONTENTION, A, No. 3.¶

6. LOGOMACHIA (λογομαχία), " strife of words," 1 Tim. 6 : 4 : see
DISPUTE, A, No. 2.¶

STRIKE

Notes : (1) In Rev. 7 : 16, *piptō*, to fall, is rendered " strike " in the R.V., A.V., " light (on)."   (2) In Acts 27 : 41, *ereidō*, to fix firmly, is used of a ship driving ashore, R.V., " struck " (A.V., " stuck fast ").¶   (3) For *paiō*, to smite, Rev. 9 : 5, A.V., " striketh," see SMITE, No. 3.   (4) For *patassō*, to smite, Matt. 26 : 51, A.V., " struck," see SMITE, No. 1.   (5) For *chalaō*, to let go, Acts 27 : 17, A.V., " strake," see LET DOWN, No. 2. (6) In Luke 22 : 64 some mss. have *tuptō*, to beat, imperfect tense, ' they were beating.'   (7) For *rhapizō*, Matt. 26 : 67, and *rhapisma*, Mark 14 : 65, see BLOW, SMITE, No. 6 and Note (2).   Some mss. have *ballō*, " struck."

STRIKER

PLĒKTĒS (πλήκτης), a striker, a brawler (akin to *plēssō*, to strike, smite), occurs in 1 Tim. 3 : 3 ; Tit. 1 : 7.¶

For STRING see BOND, No. 1

STRIP

EKDUŌ (ἐκδύω), to take off, strip off, is used especially of clothes, and rendered to strip in Matt. 27 : 28 (some mss. have *enduō*, to clothe), and Luke 10 : 30 ; to take off, Matt. 27 : 31 ; Mark 15 : 20 ; figuratively, 2 Cor. 5 : 4, " unclothed " (Middle Voice), of putting off the body at death (the believer's state of being unclothed does not refer to the body in the grave but to the spirit, which awaits the " body of glory " at the resurrection).¶

STRIPE

1. MŌLŌPS (μώλωψ), a bruise, a wound from a stripe, is used in 1 Pet. 2 : 24 (from the Sept. of Is. 53 : 5), lit., in the original, ' by whose bruise,' not referring to Christ's scourging, but figurative of the stroke of Divine judgment administered vicariously to Him on the Cross (a comforting reminder to these Christian servants, who were not infrequently buffeted, ver. 20, by their masters).¶

2. PLĒGĒ (πληγή), a blow, stripe, wound (akin to *plēssō*, to strike, and *plēktēs*, a striker), is rendered " stripes " in Luke 12 : 48 (the noun is omitted in the original in ver. 47 and the 2nd part of ver. 48) ; Acts 16 : 23, 33 ; 2 Cor. 6 : 5 ; 11 : 23.   See PLAGUE, WOUND.

STRIVE

1. AGŌNIZOMAI (ἀγωνίζομαι), to contend (Eng., agonize), is rendered to strive in Luke 13 : 24 ; 1 Cor. 9 : 25 ; Col. 1 : 29 ; 4 : 12, R.V. (A.V., " labouring fervently ").   In 1 Tim. 4 : 10, the best texts have this verb (R.V., " strive ") for *oneidizomai*, to suffer reproach, A.V. ; see FIGHT, B, No. 1.

2. MACHOMAI (μάχομαι), to fight, to quarrel, dispute, is rendered

to strive in John 6 : 52 ; Acts 7 : 26 ; 2 Tim. 2 : 24. See FIGHT, B, No. 3.

3. DIAMACHOMAI (διαμάχομαι), to struggle against (dia, intensive, and No. 2), is used of contending in an argument, Acts 23 : 9, " strove."¶

4. ERIZŌ (ἐρίζω), to wrangle, strive (eris, strife), is used in Matt. 12 : 19.¶

5. LOGOMACHEŌ (λογομαχέω), to strive about words (logos, a word, and No. 2), is used in 2 Tim. 2 : 14.¶

6. ANTAGŌNIZOMAI (ἀνταγωνίζομαι), to struggle against (anti), is used in Heb. 12 : 4, " striving against."¶

7. SUNAGŌNIZOMAI (συναγωνίζομαι), to strive together with (sun), is used in Rom. 15 : 30.¶

8. SUNATHLEŌ (συναθλέω), to strive together, Phil. 1 : 27 : see LABOUR, B, No. 3.

Notes : (1) In 2 Tim. 2 : 5, A.V., athleō, to contend in games, wrestle (athlos, a contest), is rendered " strive." See CONTEND. (2) For philotimeomai, Rom. 15 : 20, see AIM.

For STRIVINGS, Tit. 3 : 9, A.V., see FIGHTING

STROLLING

PERIERCHOMAI (περιέρχομαι), to go about, as an itinerant (peri, around, erchomai, to go), is used of certain Jews in Acts 19 : 13, R.V., " strolling " (A.V., " vagabond "). See COMPASS, No. 6, WANDER.

STRONG, STRONGER
A. Adjectives.

1. DUNATOS (δυνατός), powerful, mighty, is translated " strong," in Rom. 15 : 1, where the " strong " are those referred to in ch. 14, in contrast to " the weak in faith," those who have scruples in regard to eating meat and the observance of days ; 2 Cor. 12 : 10, where the strength lies in bearing sufferings in the realization that the endurance is for Christ's sake ; 2 Cor. 13 : 9, where " ye are strong " implies the good spiritual condition which the Apostle desires for the church at Corinth in having nothing requiring his exercise of discipline (contrast No. 2 in 1 Cor. 4 : 10). See ABLE, C, No. 1, MIGHTY, POSSIBLE, POWER.

2. ISCHUROS (ἰσχυρός), strong, mighty, is used of (a) persons : (1) God, Rev. 18 : 8 ; (2) angels, Rev. 5 : 2 ; 10 : 1 ; 18 : 21 ; (3) men, Matt. 12 : 29 (twice) and parallel passages ; Heb. 11 : 34, A.V., " valiant " (R.V., " mighty ") ; Rev. 6 : 15 (in the best texts ; some have No. 1) ; 19 : 18, " mighty ; " metaphorically, (4) the church at Corinth, 1 Cor. 4 : 10, where the Apostle reproaches them ironically with their unspiritual and self-complacent condition ; (5) of young men in Christ spiritually strong, through the Word of God, to overcome the evil one, 1 John 2 : 14 ; of (b) things : (1) wind, Matt. 14 : 30 (in some mss.),

" boisterous ; " (2) famine, Luke 15 : 14 ; (3) things in the mere human estimate, 1 Cor. 1 : 27 ; (4) Paul's letters, 2 Cor. 10 : 10 ; (5) the Lord's crying and tears, Heb. 5 : 7 ; (6) consolation, 6 : 18 ; (7) the voice of an angel, Rev. 18 : 2 (in the best texts ; some have *megas*, " great ") ; (8) Babylon, Rev. 18 : 10 ; (9) thunderings, Rev. 19 : 6. See BOISTEROUS, MIGHTY.

3. ISCHUROTEROS (ἰσχυρότερος), the comparative degree of No. 2, is used (*a*) of Christ, Matt. 3 : 11 ; Mark 1 : 7 ; Luke 3 : 16 ; (*b*) of " the weakness of God," as men without understanding regard it, 1 Cor. 1 : 25 ; (*c*) of a man of superior physical strength, Luke 11 : 22 ; (*d*) in 1 Cor. 10 : 22, in a rhetorical question, implying the impossibility of escaping the jealousy of God when it is kindled.¶

Notes : (1) For " strong delusion," 2 Thess. 2 : 11, A.V., see ERROR, No. 1. (2) For " strong (meat)," Heb. 5 : 12, 14, A.V., see SOLID.

B. Verbs.

1. ENDUNAMOŌ (ἐνδυναμόω), to make strong (*en*, in, *dunamis*, power), to strengthen, is rendered " waxed strong " in Rom. 4 : 20, R.V. (A.V., " was strong ") ; " be strong," Eph. 6 : 10 ; " were made strong," Heb. 11 : 34. See ENABLE, STRENGTH, B, No. 2.

2. KRATAIOŌ (κραταιόω), to strengthen (akin to *kratos*, strength), is rendered (a) to wax strong, Luke 1 : 80 ; 2 : 40 ; " be strong," 1 Cor. 16 : 13, lit., ' be strengthened ; ' " to be strengthened," Eph. 3 : 16 (Passive Voice in each place). See STRENGTHEN.¶

3. STEREOŌ (στερεόω) : see ESTABLISH, No. 2.

STRONGHOLDS

OCHURŌMA (ὀχύρωμα), a stronghold, fortress (akin to *ochuroō*, to make firm), is used metaphorically in 2 Cor. 10 : 4, of those things in which mere human confidence is imposed.¶

STUBBLE

KALAMĒ (καλάμη), a stalk of corn, denotes straw or stubble ; in 1 Cor. 3 : 12, metaphorically of the effect of the most worthless form of unprofitable doctrine, in the lives and conduct of those in a church who are the subjects of such teaching ; the teachings received and the persons who receive them are associated ; the latter are " the doctrine exhibited in concrete form " (Lightfoot).¶

For STUCK see STICK

STUDY

Notes : For *philotimeomai*, " study," 1 Thess. 4 : 11, see AIM. For *spoudazō*, 2 Tim. 2 : 15, A.V., see DILIGENCE, B, No. 1.

For STUFF, Luke 17 : 31, A.V., see GOODS, No. 4

STUMBLE

1. PROSKOPTŌ (προσκόπτω), to strike against, is used of stumbling, (a) physically, John 11 : 9, 10 ; (b) metaphorically, (1) of Israel in regard to Christ, whose Person, teaching, and atoning Death, and the Gospel relating thereto, were contrary to all their ideas as to the means of righteousness before God, Rom. 9 : 32 ; 1 Pet. 2 : 8 ; (2) of a brother in the Lord in acting against the dictates of his conscience, Rom. 14 : 21. See BEAT, No. 6.

2. PTAIŌ (πταίω), to cause to stumble, signifies, intransitively, to stumble, used metaphorically in Rom. 11 : 11, in the sense (b) (1) in No. 1 ; with moral significance in Jas. 2 : 10 and 3 : 2 (twice), R.V., " stumble " (A.V., " offend ") ; in 2 Pet. 1 : 10, R.V., " stumble " (A.V., " fall ").¶

Note : For *aptaistos*, " from stumbling," Jude 24, R.V., see FALL, B, Note (6).

For STUMBLING, STUMBLING BLOCK, STUMBLING-STONE, see OFFENCE, A, Nos. 1, 2, 3 and B

STUPOR

KATANUXIS (κατάνυξις), a pricking (akin to *katanussō*, to strike or prick violently, Acts 2 : 37), is used in Rom. 11 : 8, R.V., " stupor " (A.V., " slumber "). It is suggested that this meaning arose from the influence of the verb *katanustazō*, to nod or fall asleep (Field, *Notes on the Translation of the N.T.*). Evidently what is signified is the dulling of the spiritual sense.¶ In the Sept., Psa. 60 : 3 ; Isa. 29 : 10.¶

SUBDUE

KATAGŌNIZOMAI (καταγωνίζομαι), primarily, to struggle against (*kata*, against, *agōn*, a contest), came to signify to conquer, Heb. 11 : 33, " subdued."¶

Note : For *hupotassō*, A.V., to subdue, in 1 Cor. 15 : 28 and Phil. 3 : 21, see SUBJECT.

SUBJECT, SUBJECTION (Verb, Adjective, Noun)

A. Verb.

HUPOTASSŌ (ὑποτάσσω), primarily a military term, to rank under (*hupo*, under, *tassō*, to arrange), denotes (a) to put in subjection, to subject, Rom. 8 : 20 (twice) ; in the following, the R.V., has to subject for A.V., to put under, 1 Cor. 15 : 27 (thrice), 28 (3rd clause) ; Eph. 1 : 22 ; Heb. 2 : 8 (4th clause) ; in 1 Cor. 15 : 28 (1st clause), for A.V. " be subdued ; " in Phil. 3 : 21, for A.V., " subdue ; " in Heb. 2 : 5, A.V., " hath . . . put in subjection ; " (b) in the Middle or Passive Voice, to subject oneself, to obey, be subject to, Luke 2 : 51 ; 10 : 17, 20 ; Rom. 8 : 7 ; 10 : 3, R.V., " did (not) subject themselves " [A.V., " have (not) submitted themselves "] ; 13 : 1, 5 ; 1 Cor. 14 : 34, R.V., " be in subjection " (A.V., " be under obedience ") ; 15 : 28 (2nd clause) ; 16 : 16, R.V., " be in subjection " (A.V., " submit, etc."); so Col. 3 : 18; Eph. 5 : 21, R.V., " subjecting yourselves " (A.V., " submitting, etc. ") ; ver. 22, R.V. in italics, according to the best texts ; ver. 24, " is subject ; " Tit. 2 : 5, 9, R.V., " be in subjection " (A.V., " be obedient ") ; 3 : 1, R.V., " to be in subjection " (A.V., " to be subject ") ; Heb. 12 : 9, " be in subjection ; " Jas. 4 : 7, R.V., " be subject " (A.V., " submit your-selves ") ; so 1 Pet. 2 : 13 ; ver. 18, R.V., " be in subjection ; " so 3 : 1, A.V. and R.V. ; ver. 5, similarly ; 3 : 22, " being made subject ; " 5 : 5, R.V., " be subject " (A.V., " submit yourselves ") ; in some texts in the 2nd part, as A.V. See OBEDIENT, SUBMIT.

Note : For *doulagōgeō*, 1 Cor. 9 : 27, A.V., " bring into subjection," see BONDAGE, B, No. 3. For *anupotaktos*, " not subject," Heb. 2 : 8, see DISOBEDIENT, B, Note.

B. Adjective.

ENOCHOS (ἔνοχος), held in, bound by, in Heb. 2 : 15, " subject to : " see DANGER, B, No. 1.

Note : For " subject to like passions," Jas. 5 : 17, A.V., see PASSION.

C. Noun.

HUPOTAGĒ (ὑποταγή), subjection, occurs in 2 Cor. 9 : 13 ; Gal. 2 : 5 ; 1 Tim. 2 : 11 ; 3 : 4.¶

SUBMIT

HUPEIKŌ (ὑπείκω), to retire, withdraw (*hupo*, under, *eikō*, to yield), hence, to yield, submit, is used metaphorically in Heb. 13 : 17, of sub-mitting to spiritual guides in the churches.¶

Note : For *hupotassō*, see SUBJECT, A.

SUBORN

HUPOBALLŌ (ὑποβάλλω), to throw or put under, to subject, denoted to suggest, whisper, prompt ; hence, to instigate, translated " suborned " in Acts 6 : 11. To suborn in the legal sense is to procure a person who will take a false oath. The idea of making suggestions is probably present in this use of the word.¶

SUBSTANCE

1. OUSIA (οὐσία), derived from a present participial form of *eimi*, to be, denotes substance, property, Luke 15 : 12, 13, R.V., " substance," A.V., " goods " and " substance."¶

2. HUPARCHONTA (ὑπάρχοντα), the neuter plural of the present participle of *huparchō*, to be in existence, is used as a noun with the article, signifying one's goods, and translated " substance " in Luke 8 : 3. See GOODS, POSSESS, A, No. 3.

3. HUPARXIS (ὕπαρξις), existence (akin to No. 2), possession : see POSSESS, B, No. 4.

4. HUPOSTASIS (ὑπόστασις), for which see CONFIDENCE, A, No. 2, is translated " substance " (a) in Heb. 1 : 3, of Christ as " the very image " of God's " substance ; " here the word has the meaning of the real nature of that to which reference is made in contrast to the outward manifestation (see the preceding clause) ; it speaks of the Divine essence of God existent and expressed in the revelation of His Son. The A.V., " person " is an anachronism ; the word was not so rendered till the 4th cent. Most of the earlier Eng. Versions have " substance ; " (b) in Heb. 11 : 1 it has the meaning of confidence, " assurance " (R.V.), marg., " the giving substance to," A.V., " substance," something that could not equally be expressed by *elpis*, hope.

SUBTILLY

KATASOPHIZOMAI (κατασοφίζομαι), to deal subtilly (from *kata*, against, under, *sophos*, wise, subtle, used in the Sept. in 2 Sam. 13 : 3, of Jonadab), occurs in Acts 7 : 19.¶ In the Sept., Ex. 1 : 10.¶

SUBTILTY

Note : For *dolos*, Matt. 26 : 4 ; Acts 13 : 10, see GUILE. For *panourgia*, 2 Cor. 11 : 3, see CRAFTINESS.

SUBVERT, SUBVERTING
A. Verb.

ANASKEUAZŌ (ἀνασκευάζω), primarily, to pack up baggage (*ana*, up, *skeuos*, a vessel), hence, from a military point of view, to dismantle a town, to plunder, is used metaphorically in Acts 15 : 24, of unsettling or subverting the souls of believers. In the papyri it is used of going bankrupt.¶
Note : For *anatrepō*, Tit. 1 : 11, see OVERTHROW, B, No. 3. For *ekstrephō*, Tit. 3 : 11, see PERVERT, No. 4.
B. Noun.

KATASTROPHĒ (καταστροφή), an overthrow, 2 Pet. 2 : 6 (Eng., catastrophe), is rendered " subverting " in 2 Tim. 2 : 14. See OVER-THROW.¶

For SUCCEED, Acts 24 : 27, R.V., see ROOM, Note (2)

For SUCCOUR see HELP, B, No. 4

SUCCOURER

PROSTATIS (προστάτις), a feminine form of *prostatēs*, denotes a protectress, patroness ; it is used metaphorically of Phœbe in Rom. 16 : 2. It is a word of dignity, evidently chosen instead of others which might have been used (see, e.g., under HELPER), and indicates the high esteem with which she was regarded, as one who had been a protectress of many.

Prostatēs was the title of a citizen in Athens, who had the responsibility of seeing to the welfare of resident aliens who were without civic rights. Among the Jews it signified a wealthy patron of the community.¶

For SUCH see † p. 9.

SUCH AS

Notes : (1) In Acts 2 : 47, A.V., the article with the present participle, Passive, of *sōzō*, to save, lit., the (ones), i.e., those, being saved, is translated " such as (should be saved) ; " the R.V., " those that (were being saved)," gives the correct meaning, marking the kind of persons who were added to the company ; (2) " such as " is a rendering of certain relative pronouns : *hoios*, what sort of, e.g., Matt. 24 : 21 ; 2 Cor. 12 : 20 (twice) ; Rev. 16 : 18 ; *hostis*, whoever, e.g., Mark 4 : 20 ; *hopoios*, of what sort, preceded by *toioutos*, of such a sort, Acts 26 : 29 ; (3) *deina*, Matt. 26 : 18, denotes such a one (whom one cannot, or will not, name).¶ (4) In Heb. 13 : 5, " such things as ye have " represents the phrase *ta paronta*,‘ the (things) present’ (present participle of *pareimi*) ; (5) in Luke 11 : 41, *ta enonta*, A.V., " such things as ye have," lit., ‘ the (things) within’ (*eneimi*, to be in), R.V., " those things which are within " (A.V. marg., " as you are able," R.V., marg., " ye can "), perhaps signifying not outward things such as lustrations, but ‘ what things ye have within your cups and platters,’ i.e., your possessions.

SUCK (GIVE SUCK), SUCKLING

THĒLAZŌ (θηλάζω), from *thēlē*, a breast, is used (*a*) of the mother, to suckle, Matt. 24 : 19 ; Mark 13 : 17 ; Luke 21 : 23 ; in some texts in 23 : 29 (the best have *trephō*) ; (*b*) of the young, to suck, Matt. 21 : 16, " sucklings ; " Luke 11 : 27.¶

SUDDEN, SUDDENLY
A. Adjective.

AIPHNIDIOS (αἰφνίδιος), sudden, occurs in 1 Thess. 5 : 3, where it has the place of emphasis at the beginning of the sentence, as *olethros*, destruction, which the adjective qualifies, has at the end ; in Luke 21 : 34, it is used adverbially, R.V., " suddenly " (A.V., " unawares "). See Unawares.¶

B. Adverbs.

1. APHNŌ (ἄφνω), suddenly, occurs in Acts 2 : 2 ; 16 : 26 ; 28 : 6.¶

2. EXAIPHNĒS (ἐξαίφνης), a strengthened form, akin to No. 1, occurs in Mark 13 : 36 ; Luke 2 : 13 ; 9 : 39 ; Acts 9 : 3 ; 22 : 6.¶

3. EXAPINA (ἐξάπινα), a later form of No. 2, occurs in Mark 9 : 8.¶

Note : For *tacheōs* in 1 Tim. 5 : 22, A.V., " suddenly," R.V., " hastily," see Quickly, No. 3.

For SUE see LAW, B, No. 2

SUFFER
A. Verbs.
(a) *to permit*

1. EAŌ (ἐάω), to let, permit, is translated to suffer in Matt. 24 : 43 ; Luke 4 : 41 ; 22 : 51 ; Acts 14 : 16 ; 16 : 7 ; 19 : 30 ; 28 : 4 ; 1 Cor. 10 : 13. See LEAVE (a) No. 9, LET, No. 4.

2. PROSEAŌ (προσεάω), to permit further (*pros*, and No. 1), occurs in Acts 27 : 7.¶

3. EPITREPŌ (ἐπιτρέπω), for which see LEAVE, (b), is rendered to suffer in A.V. and R.V. in Matt. 8 : 21 ; Mark 10 : 4 ; Luke 9 : 59 ; Acts 28 : 16 ; R.V. only, Luke 9 : 61 (A.V., " let ") ; A.V. only, Acts 21 : 39 ; in some texts, Matt. 8 : 31, A.V. only. See LIBERTY, C, Note, PERMIT.

4. APHIĒMI (ἀφίημι), to send away, signifies to permit, suffer, in Matt. 3 : 15 (twice) ; Matt. 19 : 14 ; 23 : 13 ; Mark 1 : 34 ; 5 : 19, 37 ; 10 : 14 ; 11 : 16 ; Luke 8 : 51 ; 12 : 39, A.V. (R.V., " left ") ; 18 : 16 ; John 12 : 7, R.V., A.V. and R.V. marg., " let (her) alone " ; Rev. 11 : 9. See FORGIVE.

Notes : (1) In Acts 2 : 27 and 13 : 35, A.V., *didōmi*, to give (R.V.), is rendered to suffer. (2) In 1 Cor. 6 : 7, A.V., *apostereō*, in the Passive Voice, is rendered " *suffer yourselves to* be defrauded " (R.V., " be defrauded "). (3) For *kōluō* in Heb. 7 : 23, A.V., " were not suffered," see HINDER.

(b) *to endure suffering*

1. ANECHŌ (ἀνέχω), in the Middle Voice, to bear with, is rendered to suffer in Matt. 17 : 17 and parallel passages ; A.V. only, 1 Cor. 4 : 12 (R.V., " endure ") ; 2 Cor. 11 : 19, 20 and Heb. 13 : 22 (R.V., " bear with "). See BEAR, ENDURE.

2. PASCHŌ (πάσχω), to suffer, is used (I) of the sufferings of Christ (a) at the hands of men, e.g., Matt. 16 : 21 ; 17 : 12 ; 1 Pet. 2 : 23 ; (b) in His expiatory and vicarious sacrifice for sin, Heb. 9 : 26 ; 13 : 12 ; 1 Pet. 2 : 21 ; 3 : 18 ; 4 : 1 ; (c) including both (a) and (b), Luke 22 : 15 ; 24 : 26, 46 ; Acts 1 : 3, " passion ; " 3 : 18 ; 17 : 3 ; Heb. 5 : 8 ; (d) by the antagonism of the evil one, Heb. 2 : 18 ; (II) of human suffering, (a) of followers of Christ, Acts 9 : 16 ; 2 Cor. 1 : 6 ; Gal. 3 : 4 ; Phil. 1 : 29 ; 1 Thess. 2 : 14 ; 2 Thess. 1 : 5 ; 2 Tim. 1 : 12 ; 1 Pet. 3 : 14, 17 ; 5 : 10 ; Rev. 2 : 10 ; in identification with Christ in His crucifixion, as the spiritual ideal to be realized, 1 Pet. 4 : 1 ; in a wrong way, 4 : 15 ; (b) of others, physically, as the result of demoniacal power, Matt. 17 : 15, R.V., " suffereth (grievously)," A.V., " is (sore) vexed ; " cp. Mark 5 : 26 ; in a dream, Matt. 27 : 19 ; through maltreatment, Luke 13 : 2 ; 1 Pet. 2 : 19, 20 ; by a serpent (negatively), Acts 28 : 5, R.V., " took " (A.V., " felt : " see FEEL, Note) ; (c) of the effect upon the whole body through

the suffering of one member, 1 Cor. 12 : 26, with application to a church.

3. PROPASCHŌ (προπάσχω), to suffer before (*pro*, and No. 2), occurs in 1 Thess. 2 : 2.¶

4. SUMPASCHŌ (συμπάσχω), to suffer with (*sun*, and No. 2), is used in Rom. 8 : 17 of suffering with Christ ; in 1 Cor. 12 : 26 of joint suffering in the members of the body.¶

5. HUPECHŌ (ὑπέχω), to hold under (*hupo*, under, *echō*, to have or hold), is used metaphorically in Jude 7 of suffering punishment.¶ In the Sept., Ps. 89 : 50 ; Lam. 5 : 7.¶

6. KAKOUCHEŌ (κακουχέω), to ill-treat (*kakos*, evil, and *echō*, to have), is used in the Passive Voice in Heb. 11 : 37, R.V., " evil entreated " (A.V., " tormented ") ; in 13 : 3, R.V., " are evil entreated " (A.V., " suffer adversity ").¶

7. SUNKAKOUCHEOMAI (συγκακουχέομαι), to endure adversity with, is used in Heb. 11 : 25 (*sun*, with, and No. 6), R.V., " to be evil entreated with," A.V., " to suffer affliction with."¶

8. MAKROTHUMEŌ (μακροθυμέω) ·is rendered " suffereth long " in 1 Cor. 13 : 4. See PATIENCE.

9. ADIKEŌ (ἀδικέω), to do wrong, injustice (*a*, negative, *dikē*, right), is used in the Passive Voice in 2 Pet. 2 : 13, R.V., " suffering wrong " (some texts have *komizō*, to receive, A.V.) ; there is a play upon words here which may be brought out thus, ' being defrauded (of the wages of fraud),' a use of the verb illustrated in the papyri. See HURT.

Notes : (1) In 1 Cor. 9 : 12, A.V., *stegō*, to bear up under, is translated " suffer " (R.V., " bear ") ; see BEAR, No. 11. (2) For *hupomenō*, rendered to suffer in 2 Tim. 2 : 12, see ENDURE, No. 2. (3) For suffer hardship, suffer trouble, see HARDSHIP, Nos. 1 and 2. (4) For suffer need, Phil. 4 : 12, see WANT. (5) For suffer loss, 2 Cor. 7 : 9, R.V., see LOSE, No. 2. (6) For suffer persecution, see PERSECUTION. (7) For suffer shipwreck, see SHIPWRECK. (8) For *tropophoreō* in Acts 13 : 18, " suffered . . . manners," see MANNER, E. (9) For " suffereth violence," *biazō*, see FORCE, B, No. 1, VIOLENCE, B, No. 2. (10) In 2 Thess. 1 : 9, R.V., *tinō*, to pay a penalty, is rendered " shall suffer (punishment)."¶

B. Adjective.

PATHĒTOS (παθητός), akin to *paschō*, denotes one who has suffered, or subject to suffering, or destined to suffer ; it is used in the last sense of the suffering of Christ, Acts 26 : 23.¶

SUFFERING

PATHĒMA (πάθημα) is rendered " sufferings " in the R.V. (A.V., " afflictions ") in 2 Tim. 3 : 11 ; Heb. 10 : 32 ; 1 Pet. 5 : 9 ; in Gal. 5 : 24, " passions " (A.V., " affections "). See AFFLICTION, B, No. 3.

Note : For *kakopatheia*, Jas. 5 : 10, R.V., " suffering," see AFFLICTION, B, No. 1.

SUFFICE, SUFFICIENT
A. Verbs.

1. ARKEŌ (ἀρκέω), to suffice, is rendered "is sufficient" in John 6 : 7; 2 Cor. 12 : 9; "it sufficeth" in John 14 : 8. See CONTENT, ENOUGH.

Note : For 1 Pet. 4 : 3, see B, No. 2.

2. HIKANOŌ (ἱκανόω), to make sufficient, render fit, is translated "made (us) sufficient" in 2 Cor. 3 : 6, R.V. (A.V., "hath made . . . able "). See ABLE, B, No. 6, Note.

B. Adjectives.

1. HIKANOS (ἱκανός), akin to A, No. 2, enough, sufficient, fit, etc. is translated " sufficient " in 2 Cor. 2 : 6, 16 ; 3 : 5. See ABLE, C, No. 2.

2. ARKETOS (ἀρκετός), akin to A, No. 1, used with *eimi*, to be, is translated " may suffice " in 1 Pet. 4 : 3. See ENOUGH, A, No. 1.

SUFFICIENCY

1. AUTARKEIA (αὐτάρκεια) (*autos*, self, *arkeō*, see A, above ; Eng., autarchy), " contentment," 1 Tim. 6 : 6, is rendered " sufficiency " in 2 Cor. 9 : 8.¶

2. HIKANOTĒS (ἱκανότης) is rendered " sufficiency " in 2 Cor. 3 : 5.¶

For SUIT (make), Acts 25 : 24, R.V., see DEAL WITH, Note (1)

SUM (Noun), SUM UP
A. Noun.

Note : For *kephalaion*, Acts 22 : 28 ; Heb. 8 : 1, see POINT, B.¶ For *timē*, Acts 7 : 16, see PRICE, A.

B. Verb.

ANAKEPHALAIOŌ (ἀνακεφαλαιόω), to sum up, gather up (*ana*, up, *kephalē*, a head), to present as a whole, is used in the Passive Voice in Rom. 13 : 9, R.V., "summed up" (A.V., "briefly comprehended"), i.e., the one commandment expresses all that the Law enjoins, and to obey this one is to fulfil the Law (cp. Gal. 5 : 14) ; Middle Voice in Eph. 1 : 10, R.V., "sum up" (A.V., "gather together"), of God's purpose to sum up all things in the heavens and on the earth in Christ, a consummation extending beyond the limits of the Church, though the latter is to be a factor in its realization.¶

SUMMER

THEROS (θέρος), akin to *therō*, to heat, occurs in Matt. 24 : 32 ; Mark 13 : 28 ; Luke 21 : 30.¶

SUMPTUOUS, SUMPTUOUSLY
A. Adjective.

LAMPROS (λαμπρός), bright, is rendered "sumptuous" in Rev. 18 : 14, R.V. See BRIGHT, GOODLY, Note.

B. Adverb.

LAMPRŌS (λαμπρῶς), the corresponding adverb, is used in Luke 16 : 19, " sumptuously."¶

SUN

HĒLIOS (ἥλιος), whence Eng. prefix helio—, is used (a) as a means of the natural benefits of light and heat, e.g., Matt. 5 : 45, and power, Rev. 1 : 16 ; (b) of its qualities of brightness and glory, e.g., Matt. 13 : 43 ; 17 : 2 ; Acts 26 : 13 ; 1 Cor. 15 : 41 ; Rev. 10 : 1 ; 12 : 1 ; (c) as a means of destruction, e.g., Matt. 13 : 6 ; Jas. 1 : 11 ; of physical misery, Rev. 7 : 16 ; (d) as a means of judgment, e.g., Matt. 24 : 29 ; Mark 13 : 24 ; Luke 21 : 25 ; 23 : 45 ; Acts 2 : 20 ; Rev. 6 : 12 ; 8 : 12 ; 9 : 2 ; 16 : 8.

Note : In Rev. 7 : 2 and 16 : 12, *anatolē*, rising, used with *hēlios*, is translated " sunrising," R.V. (A.V., " east ").

For SUNDER (Asunder) see CUT, No. 6

For SUNDRY see PORTION, C

SUP

DEIPNEŌ (δειπνέω), to sup (said of taking the chief meal of the day), occurs in Luke 17 : 8 ; 22 : 20 (in the best texts), lit., ' (the) supping ; ' so 1 Cor. 11 : 25 ; metaphorically in Rev. 3 : 20, of spiritual communion between Christ and the faithful believer.¶

For SUPERFLUITY see ABUNDANCE, A, No. 2, B, No. 1

SUPERFLUOUS

PERISSOS (περισσός), abundant, more than sufficient, is translated " superfluous " in 2 Cor. 9 : 1. See ABUNDANT, C, No. 1, ADVANTAGE, MORE, B, No. 2.

SUPERSCRIPTION

EPIGRAPHĒ (ἐπιγραφή), lit., an over-writing (*epi*, over, *graphō*, to write) (the meaning of the anglicized Latin word " superscription "), denotes an inscription, a title. On Roman coins the Emperor's name was inscribed, Matt. 22 : 20 ; Mark 12 : 16 ; Luke 20 : 24. In the Roman Empire, in the case of a criminal on his way to execution, a board on which was inscribed the cause of his condemnation, was carried before him or hung round his neck ; the inscription was termed a title (*titlos*). The four Evangelists state that at the crucifixion of Christ the title was affixed to the cross, Mark (15 : 26) and Luke (23 : 38) call it a " superscription ; " Mark says it was " written over " (*epigraphō*, the corresponding verb). Matthew calls it " His accusation ; " John calls it " a title " (a technical term). The wording varies : the essential words are the same, and the variation serves to authenticate the narratives, shewing that there was no consultation leading to an agreement as to the details. See further under TITLE.¶

For SUPERSTITION see RELIGION

SUPERSTITIOUS

DEISIDAIMŌN (δεισιδαίμων), reverent to the deity (deidō, to fear ; daimōn, a demon, or pagan god), occurs in Acts 17 : 22 in the comparative degree, rendered "somewhat superstitious," R.V. (A.V., "too s."), a meaning which the word sometimes has ; others, according to its comparative form, advocate the meaning 'more religious (than others),' 'quite religious' (cp. the noun in 25 : 19). This is supported by Ramsay, who renders it 'more than others respectful of what is divine ;' so Deissmann in Light from the Ancient East, and others. It also agrees with the meaning found in Greek writers ; the context too suggests that the adjective is used in a good sense ; perhaps, after all, with kindly ambiguity (Grimm-Thayer). An ancient epitaph has it in the sense of 'reverent' (Moulton and Milligan).¶

SUPPER

DEIPNON (δεῖπνον) denotes a supper or feast (for an analysis of the uses see FEAST, No. 2). In John 13 : 2 the R.V., following certain texts, has "during supper" (A.V., "supper being ended").

Note : For "supper" in Luke 22 : 20 see SUP.

SUPPLICATION

1. DEĒSIS (δέησις) is always translated "supplication," or the plural, in the R.V. See PRAYER, B, No. 3.

2. HIKETĒRIA (ἱκετηρία) is the feminine form of the adjective hiketērios, denoting 'of a suppliant,' and used as a noun, formerly an olive-branch carried by a suppliant (hiketēs), then later, a supplication, used with No. 1 in Heb. 5 : 7.¶ In the Sept., Job 40 : 22 (Eng. Vers. 41 : 3).¶

SUPPLY (Noun and Verb)
A. Verbs.

1. CHORĒGEŌ (χορηγέω) primarily, among the Greeks, signified to lead a stage chorus or dance (choros, and hēgeomai, to lead), then, to defray the expenses of a chorus ; hence, later, metaphorically, to supply, 2 Cor. 9 : 10 (2nd part ; see also No. 2), R.V., "supply" (A.V. "minister ") ; 1 Pet. 4 : 11, R.V., "supplieth" (A.V., "giveth "). See GIVE, Note (4), MINISTER, B, Note (1).¶

2. EPICHORĒGEŌ (ἐπιχορηγέω), to supply fully, abundantly (a strengthened form of No. 1), is rendered to supply in the R.V. of 2 Cor.

9 : 10 (1st part) and Gal. 3 : 5 (for A.V., to minister), where the present continuous tense speaks of the work of the Holy Spirit in all His ministrations to believers individually and collectively ; in Col. 2 : 19, R.V., " being supplied " (A.V., " having nourishment ministered "), of the work of Christ as the Head of the Church His body ; in 2 Pet. 1 : 5, " supply " (A.V., " add ") ; in ver. 11, " shall be . . . supplied " (A.V., " shall be ministered "), of the reward hereafter which those are to receive, in regard to positions in the Kingdom of God, for their fulfilment here of the conditions mentioned.¶

Note : In 2 Cor. 9 : 10 (see Nos. 1 and 2 above) the stronger verb No. 2 is used where the will and capacity to receive are in view.

3. ANAPLĒROŌ (ἀναπληρόω), to fill up, fulfil, is rendered to supply in 1 Cor. 16 : 17 and Phil. 2 : 30. See FILL, FULFIL, OCCUPY.

4. PROSANAPLĒROŌ (προσαναπληρόω), to fill up by adding to, to supply fully (*pros*, to, and No. 3), is translated " supplieth " in 2 Cor. 9 : 12, A.V. (R.V., " filleth up the measure of ") ; in 11 : 9, R.V. and A.V., " supplied."¶

Note : In Phil. 4 : 19, A.V., *plēroō*, to fulfil (R.V.), is rendered " shall supply."

B. Noun.

EPICHORĒGIA (ἐπιχορηγία), a full supply, occurs in Eph. 4 : 16, " supplieth," lit., ' by the supply of every joint,' metaphorically of the members of the Church, the Body of which Christ is the Head, and Phil. 1 : 19, " the supply (of the Spirit of Jesus Christ) ", i.e., ' the bountiful supply ; ' here " of the Spirit " may be taken either in the subjective sense, the Giver, or the objective, the Gift.¶

SUPPORT

Notes : (1) In Acts 20 : 35, A.V., *antilambanomai*, to help (R.V.), is translated " support." See HELP, B, No. 1. (2) In 1 Thess. 5 : 14, *antechomai* signifies to support : see HOLD, No. 3.

SUPPOSE

1. NOMIZŌ (νομίζω), to consider, suppose, think, is rendered to suppose in Matt. 20 : 10 ; Luke 2 : 34 ; 3 : 23 ; Acts 7 : 25 ; 14 : 19 ; 16 : 27 ; 21 : 29 ; 1 Tim. 6 : 5 ; in 1 Cor. 7 : 26, A.V. (R.V., " I think ") ; in Acts 16 : 13, the R.V. adheres to the meaning " to suppose," " (where) we supposed (there was a place of prayer) ; " this word also signifies ' to practise a custom ' (*nomos*) and is commonly so used by Greek writers. Hence the A.V., " was wont (to be made) ; " it is rendered to think in Matt. 5 : 17 ; 10 : 34 ; Acts 8 : 20 ; 17 : 29 ; 1 Cor. 7 : 36. See THINK.¶

2. DOKEŌ (δοκέω), to be of opinion, is translated to suppose in Mark 6 : 49 ; Luke 24 : 37 ; John 20 : 15 ; Acts 27 : 13 ; in the following, A.V. " suppose," R.V., " think," Luke 12 : 51 ; 13 : 2 ; Heb. 10 : 29. It is most frequently rendered to think, always in Matthew ; always in

John, except 11 : 31, "supposing," R.V. [where the best texts have this verb (for *lego*, A.V., "saying")], and 20 : 15 (see above).

3. HUPOLAMBANŌ (ὑπολαμβάνω), when used of mental action, signifies to suppose, Luke 7 : 43, and Acts 2 : 15. See ANSWER, RECEIVE.

4. HUPONOEŌ (ὑπονοέω), to suspect, to conjecture, is translated "suppose ye" in Acts 13 : 25, R.V. (A.V., "think ye"); "I supposed" in 25 : 18. See DEEM.

5. OIOMAI or OIMAI (οἴομαι) signifies to expect, imagine, suppose; it is rendered to suppose in John 21 : 25; Phil. 1 : 17, R.V. (A.V., ver. 16, "thinking"); "think" in Jas. 1 : 7. See THINK.¶

Notes: (1) In 2 Cor. 11 : 5, A.V., *logizomai*, to reckon (R.V.), is rendered "I suppose;" so in 1 Pet. 5 : 12, A.V., R.V., "(as) I account (him);" Silvanus was not supposed by Peter to be faithful, he was reckoned or regarded so. (2) In Phil. 2 : 25, A.V., *hēgeomai*, to reckon, deem, is rendered "I supposed" (R.V., "I counted").

SUPREME

HUPERECHŌ (ὑπερέχω), to be superior, to excel, is translated "supreme" in 1 Pet. 2 : 13 : see EXCEL, No. 3.

SURE

A. Adjectives.

1. ASPHALĒS (ἀσφαλής), safe, is translated "sure" in Heb. 6 : 19. See CERTAIN, B.

2. BEBAIOS (βέβαιος), firm, stedfast, is used of (*a*) God's promise to Abraham, Rom. 4 : 16; (*b*) the believer's hope, Heb. 6 : 19, "stedfast;" (*c*) the hope of spiritual leaders regarding the welfare of converts, 2 Cor. 1 : 7, "stedfast;" (*d*) the glorying of the hope, Heb. 3 : 6, "firm;" (*e*) the beginning of our confidence, 3 : 14, R.V., "firm" (A.V., "stedfast"); (*f*) the Law given at Sinai, Heb. 2 : 2, "stedfast;" (*g*) the testament (or covenant) fulfilled after a death, 9 : 17, "of force;" (*h*) the calling and election of believers, 2 Pet. 1 : 10, to be made "sure" by the fulfilment of the injunctions in vv. 5–7; (*i*) the word of prophecy, "*made* more sure," 2 Pet. 1 : 19, R.V., A.V., "a more sure (word of prophecy);" what is meant is not a comparison between the prophecies of the O.T. and N.T., but that the former have been confirmed in the Person of Christ (vv. 16–18). See FIRM.¶

3. PISTOS (πιστός), faithful, is translated "sure" in Acts 13 : 34. See FAITHFUL.

Note: In 2 Tim. 2 : 19, A.V., *stereos*, firm, is translated "sure," and connected with "standeth," R.V., "the firm (foundation of God standeth)," i.e., 'however much the faith may be misrepresented or denied, the firm foundation of God's knowledge and truth, with its separating power, remains.'

B. Verb.

ASPHALIZŌ (ἀσφαλίζω), to make safe or sure (akin to A, No. 1), is rendered to make sure in Matt. 27 : 64, 65, 66, of the sepulchre of Christ ; elsewhere, Acts 16 : 24, of making feet fast in the stocks. See FAST.¶

Note : In the A.V. of John 16 : 30 ; Rom. 2 : 2 and 15 : 29, the verb *oida*, to know, is translated to be sure (R.V., in each place, to know). So with *ginōskō*, to know, in John 6 : 69. For the difference between the verbs see KNOW.

SURELY

Notes : (1) In the A.V. of Matt. 26 : 73 ; Mark 14 : 70 ; John 17 : 8, *alēthōs*, truly, is rendered " surely " (R.V., " of a truth ") ; so *pantōs*, at all events, altogether, in Luke 4 : 23 (R.V., " doubtless "), and *nai*, yea, in Rev. 22 : 20 (R.V., " yea "). (2) In Heb. 6 : 14, " surely " represents the phrase *ei mēn* (so the best texts ; some have *ē mēn*). (3) For Luke 1 : 1, A.V., see BELIEVE, C, Note (4). (4) For " surely " in 2 Pet. 2 : 12, R.V., see CORRUPT, A, No. 2 (*b*).

SURETY (Noun)

ENGUOS (ἔγγυος) primarily signifies bail, the bail who personally answers for anyone, whether with his life or his property (to be distinguished from *mesitēs*, a mediator) ; it is used in Heb. 7 : 22, " (by so much also hath Jesus become) the Surety (of a better covenant)," referring to the abiding and unchanging character of His Melchizedek priesthood, by reason of which His suretyship is established by God's oath (vv. 20, 21). As the Surety, He is the Personal guarantee of the terms of the new and better covenant, secured on the ground of His perfect sacrifice (ver. 27).¶

For SURETY (of a), Acts 12 : 11, A.V., see TRUE, D, No. 1

SURFEITING

KRAIPALĒ (κραιπάλη) signifies the giddiness and headache resulting from excessive wine-bibbing, a drunken nausea, " surfeiting," Luke 21 : 34.¶ Trench (Syn. § lxi) distinguishes this and the synonymous words, *methē*, drunkenness, *oinophlugia*, wine-bibbing (A.V., " excess of wine," 1 Pet. 4 : 3), *kōmos*, revelling.

For SURGE, Jas. 1 : 6, R V., see RAGE and WAVE

For SURMISE, SURMISINGS, see DEEM

SURNAME

EPIKALEŌ (ἐπικαλέω), to put a name upon (*epi*, upon, *kaleō*, to call), to surname, is used in this sense in the Passive Voice, in some texts in

Matt. 10 : 3 (it is absent in the best) ; in Luke 22 : 3, in some texts (the best have *kaleō*, to call) ; Acts 1 : 23 ; 4 : 36 ; 10 : 5, 18, 32 ; 11 : 13 ; 12 : 12, 25 ; in some texts, 15 : 22 (the best have *kaleō*).

Notes : (1) In Mark 3 : 16, 17, " He surnamed " is a translation of *epitithēmi*, to put upon, to add to, with *onoma*, a name, as the object. (2) In Acts 15 : 37, A.V., *kaleō*, to call (R.V., " called "), is rendered " whose surname was." (3) The verb *eponomazō*, translated " bearest the name " in Rom. 2 : 17, R.V., finds a literal correspondence in the word ' surname ' (*epi*, upon, = *sur*), and had this significance in Classical Greek.¶

For SURPASS, 2 Cor. 3 : 10, see EXCEED, A, No. 1

For SUSPENSE (hold in) see DOUBT, No. 6

SUSTENANCE

CHORTASMA (χόρτασμα), fodder (akin to *chortazō*, to feed, fill, see FEED, No. 4), is used in the plural in Acts 7 : 11, " sustenance."¶ In the Sept., Gen. 24 : 25, 32 ; 42 : 27 ; 43 : 24 ; Deut. 11 : 15 ; Judg. 19 : 19.¶

SWADDLING-CLOTHES

SPARGANOŌ (σπαργανόω), to swathe (from *sparganon*, a swathing-band), signifies to wrap in swaddling-clothes in Luke 2 : 7, 12. The idea that the word means ' rags ' is without foundation.¶ In the Sept., Job 38 : 9 ; Ezek. 16 : 4.¶

SWALLOW (Verb)

KATAPINŌ (καταπίνω), to drink down (*kata*, and *pinō*, to drink), to swallow, is used with this meaning (*a*) physically, but figuratively, Matt. 23 : 24 ; Rev. 12 : 16 ; (*b*) metaphorically, in the Passive Voice, of death (by victory), 1 Cor. 15 : 54 ; of being overwhelmed by sorrow, 2 Cor. 2 : 7 ; of the mortal body (by life), 5 : 4. See DEVOUR, No. 3, DROWN, No. 2.

SWEAR, SWORN

OMNUMI (ὄμνυμι) or OMNUŌ (ὀμνύω) is used of affirming or denying by an oath, e.g., Matt. 26 : 74 ; Mark 6 : 23 ; Luke 1 : 73 ; Heb. 3 : 11, 18 ; 4 : 3 ; 7 : 21 ; accompanied by that by which one swears, e.g., Matt. 5 : 34, 36 ; 23 : 16 ; Heb. 6 : 13, 16 ; Jas. 5 : 12 ; Rev. 10 : 6. Cp. ADJURE.

Note : For " false swearers," 1 Tim. 1 : 10, see FORSWEAR.

SWEAT

HIDRŌS (ἱδρώς) is used in Luke 22 : 44.¶ In the Sept., Gen. 3 : 19.¶

SWEEP

SAROŌ (σαρόω) occurs in Matt. 12 : 44 ; Luke 11 : 25 ; 15 : 8.¶

SWEET

GLUKUS (γλυκύς) (cp. Eng., glycerine, glucose), occurs in Jas. 3 : 11, 12 (A.V., " fresh " in this verse) ; Rev. 10 : 9, 10.¶

For SWEET SMELLING see SAVOUR, No. 1

SWELL, SWOLLEN

PIMPRĒMI (πίμπρημι), primarily, to blow, to burn, later came to denote to cause to swell, and, in the Middle Voice, to become swollen, Acts 28 : 6.¶ In the Sept., Numb. 5 : 21, 22, 27.¶

Note : Some, connecting the word *prēnēs* in Acts 1 : 18 with *pimprēmi*, give it the meaning ' swelling up : ' see HEADLONG.

SWELLING

1. PHUSIŌSIS (φυσίωσις) denotes a puffing up, swelling with pride (akin to *phusioō*, to puff up), 2 Cor. 12 : 20, " swellings."¶

2. HUPERONKOS (ὑπέρογκος), an adjective denoting of excessive weight or size, is used metaphorically in the sense of immoderate, especially of arrogant speech, in the neuter plural, virtually as a noun, 2 Pet. 2 : 18 ; Jude 16, " great swelling words," doubtless with reference to Gnostic phraseology.¶

SWERVE

ASTOCHEŌ (ἀστοχέω), to miss the mark, is translated " having swerved " in 1 Tim. 1 : 6. See ERR, No. 3. Moulton and Milligan illustrate the use of the verb from the papyri, e.g., of a man in extravagant terms bewailing the loss of a pet fighting-cock, " (I am distraught, for my cock) has failed (me)."

SWIFT, SWIFTLY

1. OXUS (ὀξύς) denotes " swift " in Rom. 3 : 15. See SHARP.

2. TACHUS (ταχύς), swift, speedy, is used in Jas. 1 : 19.¶ Cp. *tacheōs*, *tachu* and *tacheion*, quickly, *tachos*, quickness, speed.

3. TACHINOS (ταχινός), a poetical and late form of No. 2, of swift approach, is used in 2 Pet. 1 : 14, R.V., " swiftly " (A.V., " shortly "), lit., ' (the putting off of my tabernacle is) swift,' i.e., imminent ; in 2 : 1, " swift (destruction)."¶ In the Sept., Prov. 1 : 16 ; Is. 59 : 7 ; Hab. 1 : 6.¶

SWIM

1. KOLUMBAŌ (κολυμβάω), to dive, plunge, into the sea, hence, to swim, occurs in Acts 27 : 43.¶ Cp. *kolumbēthra*, a pool.

2. EKKOLUMBAŌ (ἐκκολυμβάω), to swim out of (ek), occurs in Acts 27 : 42.¶

SWINE

CHOIROS (χοῖρος), a swine, is used in the plural, in the Synoptic Gospels only, Matt. 7 : 6 ; 8 : 30, 31, 32 ; Mark 5 : 11–13, 16 ; Luke 8 : 32, 33 ; Luke 15 : 15, 16. It does not occur in the O.T.¶

SWORD

1. MACHAIRA (μάχαιρα), a short sword or dagger (distinct from No. 2), e.g., Matt. 26 : 47, 51, 52 and parallel passages ; Luke 21 : 24 ; 22 : 38, possibly a knife (Field, *Notes on the Translation of the N.T.*) ; Heb. 4 : 12 (see TWO-EDGED) ; metaphorically and by metonymy, (a) for ordinary violence, or dissensions, that destroy peace, Matt. 10 : 34 ; (b) as the instrument of a magistrate or judge, e.g., Rom. 13 : 4 ; (c) of the Word of God, " the sword of the Spirit," probing the conscience, subduing the impulses to sin, Eph. 6 : 17.

2. RHOMPHAIA (ῥομφαία), a word of somewhat doubtful origin, denoted a Thracian weapon of large size, whether a sword or spear is not certain, but usually longer than No. 1 ; it occurs (a) literally in Rev. 6 : 8 ; (b) metaphorically, as the instrument of anguish, Luke 2 : 35 ; of judgment, Rev. 1 : 16 ; 2 : 12, 16 ; 19 : 15, 21, probably figurative of the Lord's judicial utterances.¶

SYCAMINE

SUKAMINOS (συκάμινος) occurs in Luke 17 : 6.¶ It is generally recognized as the Black Mulberry, with fruit like blackberries. The leaves are too tough for silkworms and thus are unlike the White Mulberry. Neither kind is the same as the Mulberry of 2 Sam. 5 : 23, 24, etc. The town Haifa was called Sycaminopolis, from the name of the tree.

SYCAMORE

SUKOMOREA (συκομορέα) occurs in Luke 19 : 4.¶ This tree is of the fig species, with leaves like the mulberry and fruit like the fig. It is somewhat less in height than the sycamine and spreads to cover an area from 60 to 80 feet in diameter. It is often planted by the roadside, and was suitable for the purpose of Zacchæus. Seated on the lowest branch he was easily within speaking distance of Christ.

SYNAGOGUE

SUNAGŌGĒ (συναγωγή), properly a bringing together (*sun*, together, *agō*, to bring), denoted (a) a gathering of things, a collection, then, of persons, an assembling, of Jewish religious gatherings, e.g., Acts 9 : 2 ; an assembly of Christian Jews, Jas. 2 : 2, R.V., " synagogue " (A.V., marg. ; text, " assembly ") ; a company dominated by the power and activity of Satan, Rev. 2 : 9 ; 3 : 9 ; (b) by metonymy, the building in which the gathering is held, e.g. Matt. 6 : 2 ; Mark 1 : 21. The origin of the Jewish synagogue is probably to be assigned to the time of the Babylonish exile. Having no Temple, the Jews assembled on the sabbath to hear the Law read, and the practice continued in various buildings after the return. Cp. Ps. 74.: 8.

SYNAGOGUE (put out of the)

APOSUNAGŌGOS (ἀποσυνάγωγος), an adjective denoting 'expelled from the congregation,' excommunicated, is used (a) with *ginomai*, to become, be made, John 9 : 22 ; 12 : 42 ; (b) with *poieō*, to make, John 16 : 2. This excommunication involved prohibition not only from attendance at the synagogue, but from all fellowship with Israelites.¶

SYNAGOGUE (ruler of the)

ARCHISUNAGŌGOS (ἀρχισυνάγωγος) denotes the administrative official, with the duty of preserving order and inviting persons to read or speak in the assembly, Mark 5 : 22, 35, 36, 38 ; Luke 8 : 49 ; 13 : 14 ; Acts 13 : 15 ; " chief ruler " (A.V.) in Acts 18 : 8, 17.¶

Note : In Luke 8 : 41, " ruler of the synagogue " represents *archōn*, ruler, followed by the genitive case of the article and *sunagōgē*.

SYROPHŒNICIAN

SUROPHOINIKISSA or SUROPHUNISSA (Συροφοινίκισσα) occurs in Mark 7 : 26 as the national name of a woman called " a Canaanitish woman " in Matt. 15 : 22, i.e., not a Jewess but a descendant of the early inhabitants of the coast-land of Phœnicia. The word probably denoted a Syrian residing in Phœnicia proper.¶ There is a tradition that the woman's name was Justa and her daughter Bernice (*Clementine Homilies*, ii : 19 ; iii : 73). In Acts 21 : 2, 3, the two parts of the term are used interchangeably.

TAB   1115   TAB

T

TABERNACLE

1. SKĒNĒ (σκηνή), a tent, booth, tabernacle, is used of (a) tents as dwellings, Matt. 17 : 4 ; Mark 9 : 5 ; Luke 9 : 33 ; Heb. 11 : 9, A.V., "tabernacles" (R.V., " tents ") ; (b) the Mosaic Tabernacle, Acts 7 : 44 ; Heb. 8 : 5 ; 9 : 1 (in some mss.) ; 9 : 8, 21, termed " the tent of meeting," R.V. (i.e., where the people were called to meet God), a preferable description to " the tabernacle of the congregation," as in the A.V. in the O.T. ; the outer part, 9 : 2, 6 ; the inner sanctuary, 9 : 3 ; (c) the Heavenly prototype, Heb. 8 : 2 ; 9 : 11 ; Rev. 13 : 6 ; 15 : 5 ; 21 : 3 (of its future descent) ; (d) the eternal abodes of the saints, Luke 16 : 9, R.V., " tabernacles " (A.V., " habitations ") ; (e) the temple in Jerusalem, as continuing the service of the tabernacle, Heb. 13 : 10 ; (f) the house of David, i.e., metaphorically of his people, Acts 15 : 16 ; (g) the portable shrine of the god Moloch, Acts 7 : 43.¶

2. SKĒNOS (σκῆνος), the equivalent of No. 1, is used metaphorically of the body as the tabernacle of the soul, 2 Cor. 5 : 1, 4.¶

3. SKĒNŌMA (σκήνωμα) occurs in Acts 7 : 46 ; 2 Pet. 1 : 13, 14 ; see HABITATION, No. 6.¶

4. SKĒNOPĒGIA (σκηνοπηγία), properly the setting up of tents or dwellings (No. 1, and pēgnumi, to fix), represents the word " tabernacles " in " the feast of tabernacles," John 7 : 2.¶ This feast, one of the three Pilgrimage Feasts in Israel, is called " the feast of ingathering " in Ex. 23 : 16 ; 34 : 22 ; it took place at the end of the year, and all males were to attend at the tabernacle with their offerings. In Lev. 23 : 34 ; Deut. 16 : 13, 16 ; 31 : 10 ; 2 Chron. 8 : 13 ; Ezra 3 : 4 (cp. Neh. 8 : 14–18), it is called " the feast of tabernacles " (or booths, sukkôth), and was appointed for seven days at Jerusalem from the 15th to the 22nd Tishri (approximately October), to remind the people that their fathers dwelt in these in the wilderness journeys. Cp. Num. 29 : 15–38, especially vers. 35–38, for the regulations of the eighth or " last day, the great day of the feast " (John 7 : 37).

Note : For skēnoō, to spread a tabernacle over, Rev. 7 : 15, R.V., see DWELL, No. 9.

TABLE

1. TRAPEZA (τράπεζα) is used of (a) a dining-table, Matt. 15 : 27 ; Mark 7 : 28 ; Luke 16 : 21 ; 22 : 21, 30 ; (b) the table of shewbread, Heb. 9 : 2 ; (c) by metonymy, of what is provided on the table (the word

TAB 1116 TAK

being used of that with which it is associated), Acts 16 : 34 ; Rom. 11 : 9 (figurative of the special privileges granted to Israel and centring in Christ) ; 1 Cor. 10 : 21 (twice), " the Lord's table," denoting all that is provided for believers in Christ on the ground of His Death (and thus expressing something more comprehensive than the Lord's Supper) ; " the table of demons," denoting all that is partaken of by idolaters as the result of the influence of demons in connection with their sacrifices ; (*d*) a money-changer's table, Matt. 21 : 12 ; Mark 11 : 15 ; John 2 : 15 ; (*e*) a bank, Luke 19 : 23 (cp. *trapezitēs* : see BANKERS) ; (*f*) by metonymy for the distribution of money, Acts 6 : 2. See BANK.¶

2. PLAX (πλάξ) primarily denotes anything flat and broad, hence, a flat stone, a tablet, 2 Cor. 3 : 3 (twice) ; Heb. 9 : 4.¶

Note : Some texts have the word *klinē*, a couch, in Mark 7 : 4 (A.V., " tables ").

TABLE (at the)

ANAKEIMAI (ἀνάκειμαι), to recline at a meal table, is rendered " sat at the table " in John 12 : 2, A.V., R.V., " sat at meat " (some texts have *sunanakeimai*) ; " sat," of course does not express the actual attitude ; in John 13 : 23, R.V., " at the table reclining ; " A.V., " leaning ; " in 13 : 28, " at the table " (A.V. and R.V.), lit., ' of (those) reclining.'

For TABLET see WRITING TABLET

TACKLING

SKEUĒ (σκευή) denotes gear, equipment, tackling (of a ship), Acts 27 : 19.¶

TAIL

OURA (οὐρά), the tail of an animal, occurs in Rev. 9 : 10 (twice), 19 ; 12 : 4.¶

TAKE

1. LAMBANŌ (λαμβάνω), to take, lay hold of, besides its literal sense, e.g., Matt. 5 : 40 ; 26 : 26, 27, is used metaphorically, of fear, in taking hold of people, Luke 7 : 16, R.V. (A.V., " came . . . on ") ; of sin in " finding (occasion)," R.V. (A.V., " taking "), Rom. 7 : 8, 11, where sin is viewed as the corrupt source of action, an inward element using the commandment to produce evil effects ; of the power of temptation, 1 Cor. 10 : 13 ; of taking an example, Jas. 5 : 10 ; of taking peace from the earth, Rev. 6 : 4 ; of Christ in taking the form of a servant, Phil. 2 : 7 ; of taking rightful power (by the Lord, hereafter), Rev. 11 : 17. See ACCEPT, No. 4.

2. ANALAMBANŌ (ἀναλαμβάνω) signifies (*a*) to take up (*ana*),

e.g., Acts 1 : 2, 11, 22 (R.V., " received ") ; (b) to take to oneself, **Acts** 7 : 43 ; or to one's company, 20 : 13, 14 ; 23 : 31 ; 2 Tim. 4 : 11 ; **of** taking up spiritual armour, Eph. 6 : 13, 16. See RECEIVE.

3. APOLAMBANŌ (ἀπολαμβάνω), besides its common meaning, **to** receive, denotes to take apart or aside, Mark 7 : 33, Middle Voice. It is frequent in the papyri, and, in the sense of separation or drawing aside, is illustrated in a message of sorrow, concerning the non-arrival of one who with others had been ' shut up ' as recluses in a temple (Moulton and Milligan, Vocab.). See RECEIVE.

4. EPILAMBANŌ (ἐπιλαμβάνω), in the Middle Voice, to lay hold of, take hold of, is used literally, e.g., Mark 8 : 23 ; Luke 9 : 47 ; 14 : 4 ; metaphorically, e.g., Heb. 8 : 9, " (I) took them (by the hand) : " for other instances in each respect see HOLD, No. 7.

5. KATALAMBANŌ (καταλαμβάνω), to lay hold of, is rendered to take, in Mark 9 : 18 ; John 8 : 3, 4. See APPREHEND.

6. METALAMBANŌ (μεταλαμβάνω), to get, or have, a share of, is rendered " to take (food) " in Acts 2 : 46, R.V. (A.V., " did eat," see EAT, Note) ; 27 : 33, i.e., to share it together. See HAVE, PARTAKE, RECEIVE.

7. PARALAMBANŌ (παραλαμβάνω), besides its meaning to receive, denotes to take to (or with) oneself, of taking a wife, e.g., Matt. 1 : 20, 24 ; of taking a person or persons with one, e.g., Matt. 2 : 13, 14, 20, 21 ; 4 : 5, 8 ; of demons, 12 : 45 ; of Christ and His disciples, 17 : 1 ; 20 : 17 ; Mark 9 : 2 ; 10 : 32 ; 14 : 33 ; of witnesses, Matt. 18 : 16 ; of the removal of persons from the earth in judgment, when " the Son of Man is revealed," Matt. 24 : 40, 41 ; Luke 17 : 34, 35 (cp. the means of the removal of corruption, in ver. 37) ; of the taking of Christ by the soldiers for scourging, Matt. 27 : 27, R.V., and to crucifixion, John 19 : 16 ; see also Acts 15 : 39 ; 16 : 33 ; 21 : 24, 26, 32 ; 23 : 18. See RECEIVE.

8. SUMPARALAMBANŌ (συμπαραλαμβάνω), sun, with, and No. 7, denotes to take along with oneself, as a companion, Acts 12 : 25 ; 15 : 37, 38 ; Gal. 2 : 1.¶

9. PROSLAMBANŌ (προσλαμβάνω), to take to oneself (pros), is used of food, Acts 27 : 33–36 ; of persons, of Peter's act toward Christ, Matt. 16 : 22 ; Mark 8 : 32 ; for evil purposes, Acts 17 : 5 ; for good purposes, 18 : 26. See RECEIVE.

10. PROLAMBANŌ (προλαμβάνω) is rendered to take before in 1 Cor. 11 : 21. See COME, Note (2) at end, OVERTAKE.

11. SULLAMBANŌ (συλλαμβάνω), to seize, take, is rendered to take in Matt. 26 : 55 and Mark 14 : 48, A.V. (R.V., " seize ") ; Luke 5 : 9 ; Acts 1 : 16 ; in 12 : 3 and 23 : 27, A.V. (R.V., " seize "). See CATCH, CONCEIVE, HELP.

12. AIRŌ (αἴρω), to lift, carry, take up or away, occurs very frequently with its literal meanings. In John 1 : 29 it is used of Christ as " the Lamb of God, which taketh away the sin of the world," not the sins, but sin,

that which has existed from the time of the Fall, and in regard to which God has had judicial dealings with the world; through the expiatory sacrifice of Christ the sin of the world will be replaced by everlasting righteousness; cp. the plural, "sins", in 1 John 3 : 5. Righteous judgment was "taken away" from Christ at human tribunals, and His life, while voluntarily given by Himself (John 10 : 17, 18), was "taken (from the earth)," Acts 8 : 33 (quoted from the Sept. of Isa. 53 : 8). In John 15 : 2 it is used in the Lord's statement "Every branch in Me that beareth not fruit, He taketh it away." This does not contemplate members of the "body" of Christ, but those who (just as a graft which being inserted, does not "abide" or "strike") are merely professed followers, giving only the appearance of being joined to the parent stem.

The Law described in Col. 2 : 14 as "the bond written in ordinances that was against us," Christ "took" out of the way at His Cross. In 1 Cor. 5 : 2, *airō* is used in the best texts (some have No. 14), of the Divine judgment which would have been exercised in ' taking away ' from the church the incestuous delinquent, had they mourned before God. See AWAY, BEAR, No. 9, etc.

13. APAIRŌ (ἀπαίρω), to lift off (*apo*, from, and No. 12), is used, in the Passive Voice, of Christ, metaphorically as the Bridegroom of His followers, Matt. 9 : 15; Mark 2 : 20; Luke 5 : 35.¶

14. EXAIRŌ (ἐξαίρω), to take away, is used of putting away a person in church discipline, 1 Cor. 5 : 13; for this verb as a variant reading in ver. 2, see No. 12.¶

15. EPAIRŌ (ἐπαίρω), to lift, raise, is used in the Passive Voice and rendered "He was taken up" in Acts 1 : 9. See EXALT, HOIST, LIFT.

16. ANAIREŌ (ἀναιρέω), to take up (*ana*, up, and *haireō*, to take), is used of Pharaoh's daughter in taking up the infant Moses, Acts 7 : 21; of God's act in taking away the typical animal sacrifices under the Law, Heb. 10 : 9. See DEATH, C, No. 2, KILL, SLAY.

17. APHAIREŌ (ἀφαιρέω), to take away (*apo*), is used with this meaning in Luke 1 : 25; 10 : 42; 16 : 3; Rom. 11 : 27, of the removal of the sins of Israel; Heb. 10 : 4, of the impossibility of the removal of sins by offerings under the Law; in Rev. 22 : 19 (twice). See CUT, No. 8.

18. KATHAIREŌ (καθαιρέω), to take down (*kata*), besides its meaning of putting down by force, was the technical term for the removal of the body after crucifixion, Mark 15 : 36, 46; Luke 23 : 53; Acts 13 : 29. See CAST, No. 14.

19. PERIAIREŌ (περιαιρέω), to take away that which surrounds (*peri*, around), is used (*a*) literally, of casting off anchors, Acts 27 : 40, R.V. (A.V., "having taken up"); 28 : 13 in some texts, for *perierchomai*, to make a circuit; (*b*) metaphorically, of taking away the veil off the hearts of Israel, 2 Cor. 3 : 16; of hope of rescue, Acts 27 : 20; of sins (negatively), Heb. 10 : 11.¶

20. DECHOMAI (δέχομαι), to receive, is rendered " take (thy bond, R.V., A.V., bill) " in Luke 16 : 6, 7 ; " take (the helmet of salvation)," Eph. 6 : 17, suggesting a heartiness in the taking. See ACCEPT, No. 1, RECEIVE.

21. PROSDECHOMAI (προσδέχομαι), to receive favourably, is rendered " took " in Heb. 10 : 34. See ACCEPT, No. 3.

22. KRATEŌ (κρατέω), to take hold of, get possession of, is translated to take in Matt. 9 : 25 ; 22 : 6 ; 26 : 4 ; Mark 1 : 31 ; 5 : 41 ; 9 : 27 ; 14 : 1, 44, 46, 49 ; Luke 8 : 54 ; Acts 24 : 6. See HOLD, No. 6.

23. DRASSOMAI (δράσσομαι), to grasp with the hand, take hold of, is used metaphorically in 1 Cor. 3 : 19, " taketh (the wise in their craftiness)."¶

24. DIDŌMI (δίδωμι), to give, found in the best texts in Mark 3 : 6, is rendered " took (counsel) ; " some have poieō, to make.

25. KATECHŌ (κατέχω), to hold, is rendered " to take (the lowest place) " in Luke 14 : 9. See HOLD.

26. PIAZŌ (πιάζω), to lay or take hold of forcefully, is always rendered to take in the R.V. See APPREHEND, No. 2.

27. PARAPHERŌ (παραφέρω), to bear away (para, aside, pherō, to bear), remove, is rendered " take away " in Mark 14 : 36, A.V., R.V., " remove," as in Luke 22 : 42. See REMOVE.¶

28. ECHŌ (ἔχω), to have, to hold, is used in Matt. 21 : 46 in the sense of regarding a person as something, " they took (Him) for (a prophet)." See HAVE.

29. SUNAGŌ (συνάγω), to bring together, is used of taking a person into one's house receiving hospitality, " took . . . in," Matt. 25 : 35, 38, 43 ; so in Acts 11 : 26, R.V., " were gathered together," A.V., " assembled ; " perhaps the meaning is ' they were entertained.' See ASSEMBLE, BESTOW, GATHER.

30. EKDUŌ (ἐκδύω), to take off a garment from a person, is so rendered with reference to the soldiers' treatment of Christ, Matt. 27 : 31 ; Mark 15 : 20. See STRIP.

31. EKBALLŌ (ἐκβάλλω) has the meaning to bring or take out in Luke 10 : 35, " took out (two pence)," a word perhaps chosen to express the wholeheartedness of the act (lit., to throw out). See CAST, No. 5.

32. BASTAZŌ (βαστάζω), to bear, lift, is used of taking up stones, John 10 : 31. As to Matt. 3 : 11, Moulton and Milligan supply evidences from the vernacular that the word signified to take off (the sandals), which confirms Mark's word luō, to unloose (1 : 7). See BEAR, No. 1.

33. EPICHEIREŌ (ἐπιχειρέω), to take in hand (epi, upon, cheir, the hand), to attempt, take upon oneself, is rendered " have taken in hand," Luke 1 : 1 ; " took upon (them)," Acts 19 : 13. See GO, No. 30.

34. GINOMAI (γίνομαι), to become, to come to be, is rendered " he be taken " in 2 Thess. 2 : 7, lit., ' (until) he, or it, become ' (for a treatment of the whole passage see Notes on Thess. by Hogg and Vine).

Notes : (1) For *sunairō* in Matt. 18 : 23, see RECKON. (2) Some texts have *apagō*, to take away, in Acts 24 : 7. (3) In John 6 : 24, A.V., *embainō*, to enter, is rendered " took (shipping)," R.V., " got into (the boats)." (4) In 2 Thess. 1 : 8, A.V., *didōmi*, to give (R.V. " rendering "), is translated " taking." (5) In Rom. 3 : 5, A.V., *epipherō*, to bring against, is rendered " taketh (vengeance)," R.V., " visiteth (with wrath)." (6) In Luke 4 : 5, A.V., *anagō*, to lead up (R.V., " led "), is rendered " took up." (7) In Acts 10 : 26, A.V., *egeirō*, to raise (R.V.), is rendered " took . . . up." (8) For taking up baggage, Acts 21 : 15, see BAGGAGE. (9) For " taken from " in 1 Thess. 2 : 17, A.V., see BEREAVED, No. 1. (10) *Sunechō* is translated " taken with " in Matt. 4 : 24 ; Luke 4 : 38 ; 8 : 37. See HOLDEN. (11) In 2 Pet. 2 : 12 " to be taken " translates the phrase *eis halōsin*, lit., ' for capture ' (*halōsis*, a taking). (12) In 1 Pet. 2 : 20, *hupomenō*, to endure, is rendered " ye take . . . patiently." (13) In Matt. 11 : 12 ; John 6 : 15 ; Acts 23 : 10 *harpazō* (see CATCH) is rendered " take . . . by force." (14) For *apotassomai*, to take leave of, see LEAVE, (*c*) No. 1. (15) For *apaspazomai*, rendered to take leave of in Acts 21 : 6, A.V., see LEAVE, (*c*) No. 2. (16) In Acts 21 : 6 some mss. have *epibainō*, A.V., " we took ship " (R.V., *embainō*, " we went on board ") : cp. Note (3), above. (17) For " untaken " in 2 Cor. 3 : 14 see UNLIFTED. (18) In 1 Tim. 5 : 9, A.V., *katalegō* is rendered to take into the number (R.V., " be enrolled ").¶ (19) For " take . . . to record " see TESTIFY. See also CARE, HEED, JOURNEY, THOUGHT (to take).

TALENT

A. Noun.

TALANTON (τάλαντον), originally a balance, then, a talent in weight, was hence a sum of money in gold or silver equivalent to a talent. The Jewish talent contained 3,000 shekels of the sanctuary, e.g., Ex. 30 : 13 (about 114 lbs.). In N.T. times the talent was not a weight of silver, but the Roman-Attic talent, comprising 6,000 denarii or drachms, and equal to about £240. It is mentioned in Matthew only, 18 : 24 ; 25 : 15, 16, 20 (twice in the best texts), 22 (thrice), 24, 25, 28 (twice). In 18 : 24 the vastness of the sum, 10,000 talents (£2,400,000), indicates the impossibility of man's clearing himself, by his own efforts, of the guilt which lies upon him before God.¶

Note : That the talent denoted something weighed has provided the meaning of the Eng. word as a gift or ability, especially under the influence of the Parable of the Talents (Matt. 25 : 14–30).

B. Adjective

TALANTIAIOS (ταλαντιαῖος) denotes ' of a talent's weight,' Rev. 16 : 21.¶

For TALES see TALK

TALITHA

TALEITHA or TALITHA (ταλειθά), an Aramaic feminine meaning
' maiden,' Mark 5 : 41, has been variously transliterated in the N.T.
Greek mss. *Koumi* or *Koum* (Heb. and Aram.,*qûm*, arise), which follows,
is interpreted by " I say unto thee, arise." *Koum* is the better attested
word ; so in the Talmud, where this imperative occurs " seven times
in one page " (Edersheim, *Life and Times of Jesus*, i, p. 631).¶

TALK (Noun and Verb)
A. Nouns.

  1. LOGOS (λόγος), a word, is translated "talk" in Matt. 22 : 15 ;
Mark 12 : 13. See ACCOUNT, B.

  2. LĒROS (λῆρος) denotes foolish talk, nonsense, Luke 24 : 11, R.V.,
" idle talk " (A.V., " idle tales ").¶

B. Verbs.

  1. LALEŌ (λαλέω), to speak, say, is always translated to speak in the
R.V., where the A.V. renders it by to talk, Matt. 12 : 46 ; Mark 6 : 50 ;
Luke 24 : 32 ; John 4 : 27 (twice) ; 9 : 37 ; 14 : 30 ; Acts 26 : 31 ; Rev.
4 : 1 ; 17 : 1 ; 21 : 9, 15. The R.V. rendering is preferable ; the idea of chat
or chatter is entirely foreign to the N.T., and should never be regarded
as the meaning in 1 Cor. 14 : 34, 35. See COMMUNE, Note, SAY, No. 1,
Note, and No. 2, SPEAK.

  2. SULLALEŌ (συλλαλέω), to speak with (*sun*), is translated to talk
with, Matt. 17 : 3 ; Mark 9 : 4 ; Luke 9 : 30. See CONFER, No. 2.

  3. HOMILEŌ (ὁμιλέω), to be in company with, consort with (*homilos*,
a throng ; *homilia*, company), hence, to converse with, is rendered to
talk with, Acts 20 : 11. See COMMUNE, No. 2.

  4. SUNOMILEŌ (συνομιλέω), to converse, talk with, occurs in Acts
10 : 27.¶

TALKERS (vain)

MATAIOLOGOS (ματαιολόγος), an adjective denoting talking idly
(*mataios*, vain, idle, *legō*, to speak), is used as a noun (plural) in Tit. 1 : 10.¶

TALKING (vain, foolish)

  1. MATAIOLOGIA (ματαιολογία), a noun corresponding to the above,
is used in 1 Tim. 1 : 6, R.V., " vain talking " (A.V., " vain jangling ").¶

  2. MŌROLOGIA (μωρολογία), from *mōros*, foolish, dull, stupid, and
legō, is used in Eph. 5 : 4 ; it denotes more than mere idle talk.   Trench
describes it as " that ' talk of fools ' which is foolishness and sin together "
(Syn. § xxxiv).¶

TAME

DAMAZŌ (δαμάζω), to subdue, tame, is used (*a*) naturally in Mark
5 : 4 and Jas. 3 : 7 (twice) ; (*b*) metaphorically, of the tongue, in Jas.
3 : 8.¶ In the Sept., Dan. 2 : 40.¶

TANNER

BURSEUS (βυρσεύς), a tanner (from *bursa*, a hide), occurs in Acts 9 : 43 ; 10 : 6, 32.¶

For TARE (Verb) see TEAR

TARES

ZIZANION (ζιζάνιον) is a kind of darnel, the commonest of the four species, being the bearded, growing in the grain fields, as tall as wheat and barley, and resembling wheat in appearance. It was credited among the Jews with being degenerate wheat. The Rabbis called it "bastard." The seeds are poisonous to man and herbivorous animals, producing sleepiness, nausea, convulsions and even death (they are harmless to poultry). The plants can be separated out, but the custom, as in the parable, is to leave the cleaning out till near the time of harvest, Matt. 13 : 25–27, 29, 30, 36, 38, 40.¶ The Lord describes the tares as "the sons of the evil *one*;" false teachings are indissociable from their propagandists. For the Lord's reference to the Kingdom see KINGDOM.

TARRY

1. MENŌ (μένω), to abide, is translated by the verb to abide, in the R.V., for A.V., to tarry, in Matt. 26 : 38 ; Mark 14 : 34 ; Luke 24 : 29 ; John 4 : 40 ; Acts 9 : 43 ; 18 : 20 ; the R.V. retains the verb to tarry in John 21 : 22, 23 ; in Acts 20 : 5, A.V., "tarried" (R.V., "were waiting"). Some mss. have it in Acts 20 : 15 (A.V., "tarried"). See ABIDE.

2. EPIMENŌ (ἐπιμένω), to abide, continue, a strengthened form of No. 1, is translated to tarry in Acts 10 : 48 ; 21 : 4, 10 ; 28 : 12, 14 ; 1 Cor. 16 : 7, 8 ; Gal. 1 : 18, R.V. (A.V., "abode"). See ABIDE, No. 2.

3. HUPOMENŌ (ὑπομένω), to endure, is rendered "tarried behind" in Luke 2 : 43. See ENDURE, No. 2.

4. PROSMENŌ (προσμένω), to abide still, continue, is translated "tarried" in Acts 18 : 18, suggesting patience and stedfastness in remaining after the circumstances which preceded ; in 1 Tim. 1 : 3, R.V., "to tarry" (A.V., "to abide still"). See ABIDE, No. 6.

5. DIATRIBŌ (διατρίβω), for which see ABIDE, No. 7, is invariably rendered to tarry, in the R.V. ; A.V., twice, John 3 : 22 ; Acts 25 : 6 ; "continued" in John 11 : 54 ; Acts 15 : 35 ; "abode," Acts 12 : 19 ; 14 : 3, 28 ; 20 : 6 ; "abiding," 16 : 12 ; "had been," 25 : 14.¶

6. CHRONIZŌ (χρονίζω), to spend or while away time ; to tarry, Matt. 25 : 5 ; Luke 1 : 21 ; Heb. 10 : 37. See DELAY, No. 2.

7. BRADUNŌ (βραδύνω), to be slow (*bradus*, slow), is rendered "I tarry long," 1 Tim. 3 : 15 ; "is . . . slack," 2 Pet. 3 : 9.¶

8. KATHIZŌ (καθίζω), to make to sit down, or, intransitively, to sit down, is translated "tarry ye" in Luke 24 : 49. See SIT.

9. MELLŌ (μέλλω), to be about to, is rendered " (why) tarriest thou ? " in Acts 22 : 16. See ABOUT, B.

10. EKDECHOMAI (ἐκδέχομαι), to expect, await (ek, from, dechomai, to receive), is translated " tarry " in 1 Cor. 11 : 33, A.V. (R.V., " wait "). See EXPECT, LOOK, WAIT.

Notes: (1) In Acts 27 : 33, A.V., *prosdokaō*, to wait, look for, is translated " have tarried " (R.V., " wait "). (2) In Acts 15 : 33, *poieō*, to make or do, is used with *chronos*, time, A.V., " they had tarried a space," R.V., " they had spent some time."

TASTE

GEUŌ (γεύω), to make to taste, is used in the Middle Voice, signifying to taste (a) naturally, Matt. 27 : 34 ; Luke 14 : 24 ; John 2 : 9 ; Col. 2 : 21 ; (b) metaphorically, of Christ's tasting death, implying His Personal experience in voluntarily undergoing death, Heb. 2 : 9 ; of believers (negatively) as to tasting of death, Matt. 16 : 28 ; Mark 9 : 1 ; Luke 9 : 27 ; John 8 : 52 ; of tasting the heavenly gift (different from receiving it), Heb. 6 : 4 ; " the good word of God, and the powers of the age to come," 6 : 5 ; " that the Lord is gracious," 1 Pet. 2 : 3. See EAT.

TATTLER

PHLUAROS (φλύαρος), babbling, garrulous (from *phluō*, to babble : cp. *phluareō*, to prate against), is translated " tattlers " in 1 Tim. 5 : 13.¶

TAUGHT (Adjective)

1. DIDAKTOS (διδακτός), primarily what can be taught, then, taught, is used (a) of persons, John 6 : 45 ; (b) of things, 1 Cor. 2 : 13 (twice), " (not in words which man's wisdom) teacheth, (but which the Spirit) teacheth," lit., ' (not in words) taught (of man's wisdom, but) taught (of the Spirit).'¶

2. THEODIDAKTOS (θεοδίδακτος), God-taught (*Theos*, God, and No. 1), occurs in 1 Thess. 4 : 9, lit., ' God-taught (persons) ; ' while the missionaries had taught the converts to love one another, God had Himself been their Teacher. Cp. John 6 : 45 (see No. 1).¶

For TAXED, TAXING see ENROL, ENROLMENT

TEACH

A. Verbs.

1. DIDASKŌ (διδάσκω) is used (a) absolutely, to give instruction, e.g., Matt. 4 : 23 ; 9 : 35 ; Rom. 12 : 7 ; 1 Cor. 4 : 17 ; 1 Tim. 2 : 12 ; 4 : 11 ; (b) transitively, with an object, whether persons, e.g., Matt. 5 : 2 ; 7 : 29, and frequently in the Gospels and Acts, or things taught, e.g., Matt. 15 : 9 ; 22 : 16 ; Acts 15 : 35 ; 18 : 11 ; both persons and things, e.g., John 14 : 26 ; Rev. 2 : 14, 20.

2. PAIDEUŌ (παιδεύω), to instruct and train : see INSTRUCT, No. 2.

3. KATĒCHEŌ (κατηχέω), for which see INFORM, No. 2, INSTRUCT, No. 1, is rendered to teach in 1 Cor. 14 : 19, A.V. (R.V., " instruct ") ; Gal. 6 : 6 (twice).

4. HETERODIDASKALEŌ (ἑτεροδιδασκαλέω), to teach a different doctrine (heteros, " different," to be distinguished from allos, another of the same kind : see ANOTHER), is used in 1 Tim. 1 : 3 ; 6 : 3, R.V., A.V., " teach (no) other d." and " teach otherwise," of what is contrary to the faith.¶

Notes : (1) For mathēteuō, to teach, in the A.V. of Matt. 28 : 19 ; Acts 14 : 21, see DISCIPLE, B.   (2) In Acts 16 : 21, A.V., katangellō, to declare, preach, is rendered " teach " (R.V., " set forth ").   (3) For " teacheth " in 1 Cor. 2 : 13, see TAUGHT, No. 1 (b).

B. Adjective.

DIDAKTIKOS (διδακτικός), skilled in teaching (akin to No. 1 above : Eng., didactic), is translated " apt to teach " in 1 Tim. 3 : 2 ; 2 Tim. 2 : 24.¶

TEACHER, FALSE TEACHERS

1. DIDASKALOS (διδάσκαλος) is rendered " teacher " or " teachers " in Matt. 23 : 8, by Christ, of Himself ; in John 3 : 2 of Christ ; of Nicodemus in Israel, 3 : 10, R.V. ; of teachers of the truth in the churches, Acts 13 : 1 ; 1 Cor. 12 : 28, 29 ; Eph. 4 : 11 ; Heb. 5 : 12 ; Jas. 3 : 1, R.V. ; by Paul of his work among the churches, 1 Tim. 2 : 7 ; 2 Tim. 1 : 11 ; of teachers, wrongfully chosen by those who have " itching ears," 2 Tim. 4 : 3. See MASTER, RABBI.

2. KALODIDASKALOS (καλοδιδάσκαλος) denotes a teacher of what is good (kalos), Tit. 2 : 3.¶

3. PSEUDODIDASKALOS (ψευδοδιδάσκαλος), a false teacher, occurs in the plural in 2 Pet. 2 : 1.¶

For TEACHING (Noun) see DOCTRINE, Nos. 1 and 2

TEARS

DAKRUON or DAKRU (δάκρυον), akin to dakruō, to weep, is used in the plural, Mark 9 : 24 ; Luke 7 : 38, 44 (with the sense of washing therewith the Lord's feet) ; Acts 20 : 19, 31 ; 2 Cor. 2 : 4 ; 2 Tim. 1 : 4 ; Heb. 5 : 7 ; 12 : 17 ; Rev. 7 : 17 ; 21 : 4.¶

TEAR, TORN

1. SPARASSŌ (σπαράσσω), denotes to tear, rend, convulse, Mark 1 : 26 ; 9 : 20 (in some mss.), 26, R.V., " having . . . torn " (A.V., " rent ") ; Luke 9 : 39.¶ In the Sept., 2 Sam. 22 : 8, of the foundations of heaven ; Jer. 4 : 18, of the heart.¶

2. SUSPARASSŌ (συσπαράσσω), to tear violently (sun, with, intensive),

convulse completely, a strengthened form of No. 1, is used in Mark 9 : 20, in the best texts (some have No. 1) ; Luke 9 : 42.¶

3. DIASPAŌ (διασπάω), to break or tear asunder, is translated " should be torn in pieces " in Acts 23 : 10, R.V. (A.V., " . . . pulled . . . "). See REND, No. 5.

4. RHĒGNUMI (ῥήγνυμι), to break, is rendered " teareth " in Mark 9 : 18, A.V. (R.V., " dasheth . . . down "). See HINDER, No. 1.

TEDIOUS (to be)

ENKOPTŌ (ἐνκόπτω), to hinder, is rendered to be tedious in Acts 24 : 4, of detaining a person unnecessarily. See HINDER, No. 1.

For TEETH see TOOTH

TELL

1. LEGŌ (λέγω) and the 2nd aorist form *eipon*, used to supply this tense in *lego*, are frequently translated to tell, e.g., Matt. 2 : 13, R.V., " I tell," A.V., " I bring (thee) word " ; 10 : 27. See SAY, No. 1.

2. LALEŌ (λαλέω), for which see SAY, No. 2, is usually rendered to speak, in the R.V. (for A.V., to tell), e.g., Matt. 26 : 13 ; Luke 1 : 45 ; 2 : 17, 18, 20 ; Acts 11 : 14 ; 27 : 25 ; but R.V. and A.V., to tell in John 8 : 40 ; Acts 9 : 6 ; 22 : 10.

3. EKLALEŌ (ἐκλαλέω), to speak out (*ek*), is translated " tell " in Acts 23 : 22.¶

4. EIRŌ (εἴρω), for which see SAY, No. 4, is rendered to tell in Matt. 21 : 24 ; Mark 11 : 29 ; John 14 : 29 ; Rev. 17 : 7.

5. APANGELLŌ (ἀπαγγέλλω), to announce, declare, report (usually as a messenger), is frequently rendered to tell, e.g., Matt. 8 : 33 ; 14 : 12. See BRING, No. 36.

6. ANANGELLŌ (ἀναγγέλλω), to bring back word, announce, is sometimes rendered to tell, e.g., John 5 : 15 ; 2 Cor. 7 : 7. See DECLARE, No. 1.

7. DIĒGEOMAI (διηγέομαι), for which see DECLARE, No. 6, is rendered to tell, in the A.V. and R.V., in Mark 9 : 9 ; Heb. 11 : 32.

8. EXĒGEOMAI (ἐξηγέομαι), for which see DECLARE, No. 8, is translated " told " in Luke 24 : 35, A.V. (R.V., " rehearsed ").

9. DIASAPHEŌ (διασαφέω), to make clear (*dia*, throughout, *saphēs*, clear), explain fully, is translated " told " in Matt. 18 : 31. See EXPLAIN.

10. MĒNUŌ (μηνύω) is rendered " told " in Acts 23 : 30, A.V. : see SHEW, No. 7.

11. PROEIRŌ (PROLEGŌ) (προείρω), to tell before, is so rendered in Matt. 24 : 25 : see FORETELL, FOREWARN.

Note : In the following, *oida*, to know, is translated " tell " in the A.V. (R.V., " know "), Matt. 21 : 27 ; Mark 11 : 33 ; Luke 20 : 7 ; John 3 : 8 ; 8 : 14 ; 16 : 18 ; 2 Cor. 12 : 2.

TEMPER TOGETHER

SUNKERANNUMI (συγκεράννυμι), to mix or blend together, is used in 1 Cor. 12 : 24, of the combining of the members of the human body into an organic structure, as illustrative of the members of a local church (see ver. 27, where there is no definite article in the original). See MIXED (with).

TEMPERANCE, TEMPERATE
A. Noun.

ENKRATEIA (ἐγκράτεια), from *kratos*, strength, occurs in Acts 24 : 25 ; Gal. 5 : 23 ; 2 Pet. 1 : 6 (twice), in all of which it is rendered " temperance ; " the R.V. marg., " self-control " is the preferable rendering, as temperance is now limited to one form of self-control ; the various powers bestowed by God upon man are capable of abuse ; the right use demands the controlling power of the will under the operation of the Spirit of God ; in Acts 24 : 25 the word follows " righteousness," which represents God's claims, self-control being man's response thereto ; in 2 Pet. 1 : 6, it follows " knowledge," suggesting that what is learnt requires to be put into practice.¶

B. Adjectives.

1. ENKRATĒS (ἐγκρατής), akin to A, denotes exercising self-control, rendered " temperate " in Tit. 1 : 8.¶

2. NĒPHALIOS (νηφάλιος), for which see SOBER, is translated " temperate " in 1 Tim. 3 : 2, R.V. (A.V., " vigilant ") ; in 3 : 11 and Tit. 2 : 2, R.V. (A.V., " sober ").¶

Note : In Tit. 2 : 2, A.V., *sōphrōn*, sober, is rendered " temperate " (R.V., " soberminded ").

C. Verb.

ENKRATEUOMAI (ἐγκρατεύομαι), akin to A and B, No. 1, rendered " is temperate " in 1 Cor. 9 : 25, is used figuratively of the rigid self-control practised by athletes with a view to gaining the prize. See CONTINENCY.

TEMPEST

1. THUELLA (θύελλα), a hurricane, cyclone, whirlwind (akin to *thuō*, to slay, and *thumos*, wrath), is used in Heb. 12 : 18.¶ In the Sept., Ex. 10 : 22 ; Deut. 4 : 11 ; 5 : 22.¶

2. SEISMOS (σεισμός), a shaking (Eng., seismic, etc.), is used of a tempest in Matt. 8 : 24. See EARTHQUAKE.

3. CHEIMŌN (χειμών), winter, a winter storm, hence, in general, a tempest, is so rendered in Acts 27 : 20. See WEATHER, WINTER.

4. LAILAPS (λαῖλαψ), " a tempest," 2 Pet. 2 : 17, A.V. : see STORM.

Note : For " tossed with a tempest," Acts 27 : 18, A.V., see LABOUR, B, No. 2.

TEMPESTUOUS

TUPHŌNIKOS (τυφωνικός), from *tuphōn*, a hurricane, typhoon, is translated " tempestuous " in Acts 27 : 14.¶

TEMPLE

1. HIERON (ἱερόν), the neuter of the adjective *hieros*, sacred, is used as a noun denoting a sacred place, a temple, that of Artemis (Diana), Acts 19 : 27 ; that in Jerusalem, Mark 11 : 11, signifying the entire building with its precincts, or some part thereof, as distinct from the *naos*, the inner sanctuary (see No. 2) ; apart from the Gospels and Acts, it is mentioned only in 1 Cor. 9 : 13. Christ taught in one of the courts, to which all the people had access. *Hieron* is never used figuratively. The Temple mentioned in the Gospels and Acts was begun by Herod in B.C. 20, and destroyed by the Romans in A.D. 70.

2. NAOS (ναός), a shrine or sanctuary, was used (*a*) among the heathen, to denote the shrine containing the idol, Acts 17 : 24 ; 19 : 24 (in the latter, miniatures) ; (*b*) among the Jews, the sanctuary in the Temple, into which only the priests could lawfully enter, e.g., Luke 1 : 9, 21, 22 ; Christ, as being of the tribe of Judah, and thus not being a priest while upon the earth (Heb. 7 : 13, 14 ; 8 : 4), did not enter the *naos* ; for 2 Thess. 2 : 4 see Note (below) ; (*c*) by Christ metaphorically, of His own physical body, John 2 : 19, 21 ; (*d*) in apostolic teaching, metaphorically, (1) of the Church, the mystical Body of Christ, Eph. 2 : 21 ; (2) of a local church, 1 Cor. 3 : 16, 17 ; 2 Cor. 6 : 16 ; (3) of the present body of the individual believer, 1 Cor. 6 : 19 ; (4) of the Temple seen in visions in the Apocalypse, 3 : 12 ; 7 : 15 ; 11 : 19 ; 14 : 15, 17 ; 15 : 5, 6, 8 ; 16 : 1, 17 ; (5) of the Lord God Almighty and the Lamb, as the Temple of the New and Heavenly Jerusalem, Rev. 21 : 22. See SANCTUARY and HOLY, B (*b*), par. 4.

Notes: (1) The temple mentioned in 2 Thess. 2 : 4 (*naos*), as the seat of the Man of Sin, has been regarded in different ways. The weight of Scripture evidence is in favour of the view that it refers to a literal temple in Jerusalem, to be reconstructed in the future (cp. Dan. 11 : 31 and 12 : 11, with Matt. 24 : 15). For a fuller examination of the passage, see Notes on Thessalonians by Hogg and Vine, pp. 250–252. (2) For *oikos*, rendered "temple," Luke 11 : 51, A.V., see HOUSE, No. 1.

TEMPLE-KEEPER

NEŌKOROS (νεωκόρος), Acts 19 : 35, R.V., and A.V. marg., " temple-keeper " (A.V., " worshipper "), is used in profane Greek of one who has charge of a temple. Coin inscriptions show that it was an honorary title given to certain cities, especially in Asia Minor, where the cult of some god or of a deified human potentate had been established, here to Ephesus in respect of the goddess Artemis. Apparently the Imperial cult also existed at Ephesus.   Josephus applies the word to Jews as worshippers, but this is not the meaning in Acts 19.¶

TEMPORAL

PROSKAIROS (πρόσκαιρος), for a season (pros, for, kairos, a season), is rendered " temporal " in 2 Cor. 4 : 18.   See SEASON, WHILE.

TEMPT
A. Verbs.

1. PEIRAZŌ (πειράζω) signifies (1) to try, attempt, assay (see TRY) ; (2) to test, try, prove, in a good sense, said of Christ and of believers, Heb. 2 : 18, where the context shows that the temptation was the cause of suffering to Him, and only suffering, not a drawing away to sin, so that believers have the sympathy of Christ as their High Priest in the suffering which sin occasions to those who are in the enjoyment of communion with God ; so in the similar passage in 4 : 15 ; in all the temptations which Christ endured, there was nothing within Him that answered to sin.   There was no sinful infirmity in Him.   While He was truly man, and His Divine nature was not in any way inconsistent with His Manhood, there was nothing in Him such as is produced in us by the sinful nature which belongs to us ; in Heb. 11 : 37, of the testing of O.T. saints ; in 1 Cor. 10 : 13, where the meaning has a wide scope, the verb is used of testing as permitted by God, and of the believer as one who should be in the realization of his own helplessness and his dependence upon God (see PROVE, TRY) ; in a bad sense, to tempt (a) of attempts to ensnare Christ in His speech, e.g., Matt. 16 : 1 ; 19 : 3 ; 22 : 18, 35, and parallel passages ; John 8 : 6 ; (b) of temptations to sin, e.g., Gal. 6 : 1, where one who would restore an erring brother is not to act as his judge, but as being one with him in liability to sin, with the possibility of finding himself in similar circumstances, Jas. 1 : 13, 14 (see note below) ; of temptations mentioned as coming from the Devil, Matt. 4 : 1, and parallel passages ; 1 Cor. 7 : 5 ; 1 Thess. 3 : 5 (see TEMPTER) ; (c) of trying or challenging God, Acts 15 : 10 ; 1 Cor. 10 : 9 (2nd part) ; Heb. 3 : 9 ; the Holy Spirit, Acts 5 : 9 : cp. No. 2.

Note : *" James 1 : 13–15 seems to contradict other statements of Scripture in two respects, saying (a) that ' God cannot be tempted with evil,' and (b) that ' He Himself tempteth no man.'   But God tempted, or tried, Abraham, Heb. 11 : 17, and the Israelites tempted, or tried, God, 1 Cor. 10 : 9.   Ver. 14, however, makes it plain that, whereas in these cases the temptation or trial, came from without, James refers to temptation, or trial, arising within, from uncontrolled appetites and from evil passions, cp. Mark 7 : 20–23.   But though such temptation does not proceed from God, yet does God regard His people while they endure it, and by it tests and approves them."

---

* From Notes on Thessalonians by Hogg and Vine, p. 97.

2. EKPEIRAZŌ (ἐκπειράζω), an intensive form of the foregoing, is used in much the same way as No. 1 (2) (c), in Christ's quotation from Deut. 6 : 16, in reply to the Devil, Matt. 4 : 7 ; Luke 4 : 12 ; so in 1 Cor. 10 : 9, R.V., " the Lord " (A.V., " Christ ") ; of the lawyer who tempted Christ, Luke 10 : 25.¶ In the Sept., Deut. 6 : 16 ; 8 : 2, 16 ; Ps. 78 : 18.¶ Cp. *dokimazō* (see PROVE).

B. Adjective.

APEIRASTOS (ἀπείραστος), untempted, untried (*a*, negative, and A, No. 1), occurs in Jas. 1 : 13, with *eimi*, to be, " cannot be tempted," ' untemptable ' (Mayor).¶

TEMPTATION

PEIRASMOS (πειρασμός), akin to A, above, is used of (1) trials with a beneficial purpose and effect, (*a*) of trials or temptations, Divinely permitted or sent, Luke 22 : 28 ; Acts 20 : 19 ; Jas. 1 : 2 ; 1 Pet. 1 : 6 ; 4 : 12, R.V., " to prove," A.V., " to try ; " 2 Pet. 2 : 9 (singular) ; Rev. 3 : 10, R.V., " trial " (A.V., " temptation ") ; in Jas. 1 : 12, " temptation " apparently has meanings (1) and (2) combined (see below), and is used in the widest sense ; (*b*) with a good or neutral significance, Gal. 4 : 14, of Paul's physical infirmity, " a temptation " to the Galatian converts, of such a kind as to arouse feelings of natural repugnance ; (*c*) of trials of a varied character, Matt. 6 : 13 and Luke 11 : 4, where believers are commanded to pray not to be led into such by forces beyond their own control ; Matt. 26 : 41 ; Mark 14 : 38 ; Luke 22 : 40, 46, where they are commanded to watch and pray against entering into temptations by their own carelessness or disobedience ; in all such cases God provides " the way of escape," 1 Cor. 10 : 13 (where *peirasmos* occurs twice). (2) Of trial definitely designed to lead to wrong doing, temptation, Luke 4 : 13 ; 8 : 13 ; 1 Tim. 6 : 9 ; (3) of trying or challenging God, by men, Heb. 3 : 8.¶

TEMPTER

Note : The present participle of *peirazō*, to tempt, preceded by the article, lit., ' the (one) tempting,' is used as a noun, describing the Devil in this character, Matt. 4 : 3 ; 1 Thess. 3 : 5.¶

TEN

DEKA (δέκα), whence the Eng. prefix *deca-*, is regarded by some as the measure of human responsibility, e.g., Luke 19 : 13, 17 ; Rev. 2 : 10 ; it is used in a figurative setting in Rev. 12 : 3 ; 13 : 1 ; 17 : 3, 7, 12, 16.

Notes : (1) In Acts 23 : 23, *hebdomēkonta*, seventy, is translated " threescore and ten." (2) For " ten thousand " see THOUSAND.

For TEND, John 21 : 16 ; 1 Pet. 5 : 2, R.V., see FEED, No. 2

TENDER

HAPALOS (ἁπαλός), soft, tender, is used of the branch of a tree, Matt. 24 : 32 ; Mark 13 : 28.¶

Note : For Luke 1 : 78, " tender mercy ; " Phil. 1 : 8 ; 2 : 1, " tender mercies," see BOWELS.

For TENDER-HEARTED see PITIFUL, No. 2

TENTH

1. DEKATOS (δέκατος), an adjective from *deka*, ten, occurs in John 1 : 39 ; Rev. 11 : 13 ; 21 : 20.¶

2. DEKATĒ (δεκάτη), grammatically the feminine form of No. 1, with *meris*, a part, understood, is used as a noun, translated " a tenth part " in Heb. 7 : 2, " a tenth," ver. 4 ; " tithes " in vv. 8, 9.¶

For TENTS see TABERNACLE, No. 1

TENT-MAKERS

SKĒNOPOIOS (σκηνοποιός), an adjective, ' tent-making ' (*skēnē*, a tent, *poieō*, to make), is used as a noun in Acts 18 : 3.¶

TERM (appointed)

PROTHESMIOS (προθέσμιος), an adjective denoting appointed beforehand (*pro*, before, *tithēmi*, to put, appoint : see APPOINT, No. 3, Note), is used as a noun, *prothesmia* (grammatically feminine, with *hēmera*, a day, understood), as in Greek law, a day appointed before, Gal. 4 : 2, R.V., " the term appointed," i.e., ' a stipulated date ' (A.V., " the time appointed ").¶

TERRESTRIAL

EPIGEIOS (ἐπίγειος), on earth, earthly (*epi*, on, *gē*, the earth), is rendered " terrestrial " in 1 Cor. 15 : 40 (twice), in contrast to *epouranios*, heavenly. See EARTHLY, No. 2.

For TERRIBLE, Heb. 12 : 21, see FEARFUL, B, No. 1

TERRIFY
A. Verbs.

1. PTOEŌ (πτοέω), to terrify, is used in the Passive Voice, Luke 21 : 9 ; 24 : 37.¶

2. EKPHOBEŌ (ἐκφοβέω), to frighten away (*ek*, out, *phobos*, fear), occurs in 2 Cor. 10 : 9.¶

3. PTURŌ (πτύρω), to scare, Phil. 1 : 28 : see AFFRIGHTED, B, No. 1.¶

B. Adjective.

EMPHOBOS (ἔμφοβος), terrified. is so rendered in the R.V. of Acts 24 : 25. See TREMBLE.

TERROR

1. PHOBOS (φόβος), fear, is rendered "terror" in Rom. 13 : 3; in 2 Cor. 5 : 11 and 1 Pet. 3 : 14, A.V. (R.V., " fear "). See FEAR, No. 1.

2. PHOBĒTRON (φόβητρον), that which causes fright, a terror, is translated "terrors" in Luke 21 : 11, R.V. (A.V., " fearful sights ").¶ See FEAR, A, Note. For *ptoēsis*, see AMAZEMENT.

For TESTAMENT see COVENANT

TESTATOR

DIATITHĒMI (διατίθημι), to arrange, dispose, is used only in the Middle Voice in the N.T. ; in Heb. 9 : 16, 17, the present participle with the article, lit., 'the (one) making a testament (or covenant),' virtually a noun, " the testator " (the covenanting one) ; it is used of making a covenant in 8 : 10 and 10 : 16 and Acts 3 : 25. In covenant-making, the sacrifice of a victim was customary (Gen. 15 : 10 ; Jer. 34 : 18, 19). He who made a covenant did so at the cost of a life. While the terminology in Heb. 9 : 16, 17 has the appearance of being appropriate to the circumstances of making a will, there is excellent reason for adhering to the meaning ' covenant-making.' The rendering " the death of the testator " would make Christ a Testator, which He was not. He did not die simply that the terms of a testamentary disposition might be fulfilled for the heirs. Here He who is " the Mediator of a new covenant " (ver. 15) is Himself the Victim whose death was necessary. The idea of making a will destroys the argument of ver. 18. In spite of various advocacies of the idea of a will, the weight of evidence is confirmatory of what Hatch, in *Essays in Biblical Greek*, p. 48, says : " There can be little doubt that the word (*diathēkē*) must be invariably taken in this sense of ' covenant ' in the N.T., and especially in a book . . . so impregnated with the language of the Sept. as the Epistle to the Hebrews " (see also Westcott, and W. F. Moulton). We may render somewhat literally thus : ' For where a covenant (is), a death (is) necessary to be brought in of the one covenanting ; for a covenant over dead ones (victims) is sure, since never has it force when the one covenanting lives ' [Christ being especially in view]. The writer is speaking from a Jewish point of view, not from that of the Greeks. " To adduce the fact that in the case of wills the death of the testator is the condition of validity, is, of course, no proof at all that a death is necessary to make a covenant valid. . . . To support his argument, proving the necessity of Christ's death, the writer adduces the general law that he who makes a covenant does so at the expense of life " (Marcus Dods). See APPOINT, MAKE.

TESTIFY

1. MARTUREŌ (μαρτυρέω), for which see WITNESS, is frequently rendered to bear witness, to witness, in the R.V., where A.V. renders it to testify, John 2 : 25 ; 3 : 11, 32 ; 5 : 39 ; 15 : 26 ; 21 : 24 ; 1 Cor. 15 : 15 ; Heb. 7 : 17 ; 11 : 4 ; 1 John 4 : 14 ; 5 : 9 ; 3 John 3. In the following, however, the R.V., like the A.V., has the rendering to testify, John 4 : 39, 44 ; 7 : 7 ; 13 : 21 ; Acts 26 : 5 ; Rev. 22 : 16, 18, 20.

2. EPIMARTUREŌ (ἐπιμαρτυρέω), to bear witness to (a strengthened form of No. 1), is rendered " testifying " in 1 Pet. 5 : 12.¶

3. MARTUROMAI (μαρτύρομαι), primarily, to summon as witness, then, to bear witness (sometimes with the suggestion of solemn protestation), is rendered to testify in Acts 20 : 26, R.V. (A.V., " I take . . . to record ") ; 26 : 22, in the best texts (some have No. 1), R.V. ; Gal. 5 : 3 ; Eph. 4 : 17 ; 1 Thess. 2 : 11, in the best texts (some have No. 1), R.V., " testifying " (A.V., " charged ").¶

4. DIAMARTUROMAI (διαμαρτύρομαι), to testify or protest solemnly, an intensive form of No. 3, is translated to testify in Luke 16 : 28 ; Acts 2 : 40 ; 8 : 25 ; 10 : 42 ; 18 : 5 ; 20 : 21, 23, 24 ; 23 : 11 ; 28 : 23 ; 1 Thess. 4 : 6 ; Heb. 2 : 6 ; to charge in 1 Tim. 5 : 21 ; 2 Tim. 2 : 14 ; 4 : 1.¶

5. PROMARTUROMAI (προμαρτύρομαι), to testify beforehand, occurs in 1 Pet. 1 : 11, where the pronoun " it " should be " He " (the " it " being due to the grammatically neuter form of *pneuma* ; the Personality of the Holy Spirit requires the masculine pronoun).¶

Note : In Rev. 22 : 18 some texts have *summartureō*, to bear witness with. See WITNESS.

TESTIMONY

1. MARTURION (μαρτύριον), a testimony, witness, is almost entirely translated " testimony " in both A.V. and R.V. The only place where both have " witness " is Acts 4 : 33. In Acts 7 : 44 and Jas. 5 : 3, the R.V. has " testimony " (A.V., " witness ").

In 2 Thess. 1 : 10, " our testimony unto you," R.V., refers to the fact that the missionaries, besides proclaiming the truths of the gospel, had borne witness to the power of these truths. *Kērugma*, the thing preached, the message, is objective, having especially to do with the effect on the hearers ; *marturion* is mainly subjective, having to do especially with the preacher's personal experience. In 1 Tim. 2 : 6 the R.V. is important, " the testimony (i.e., of the gospel) *to be borne* in its own times," i.e., in the times Divinely appointed for it, namely, the present age, from Pentecost till the Church is complete. In Rev. 15 : 5, in the phrase, " the temple of the tabernacle of the testimony in Heaven," the testimony is the witness to the rights of God, denied and refused on earth, but about to be vindicated by the exercise of the judgments under the pouring forth of the seven bowls or vials of Divine retribution. See WITNESS.

2. MARTURIA (μαρτυρία), witness, evidence, testimony, is almost always rendered " witness " in the R.V. (for A.V., " testimony " in John 3 : 32, 33 ; 5 : 34 ; 8 : 17 ; 21 : 24, and always for A.V., " record," e.g., I John 5 : 10, 11), except in Acts 22 : 18 and in the Apocalypse, where both, with one exception, have " testimony," 1 : 2, 9 ; 6 : 9 ; 11 : 7 ; 12 : 11, 17 ; 19 : 10 (twice) ; 20 : 4 (A.V., " witness "). In 19 : 10, " the testimony of Jesus " is objective, the testimony or witness given to Him (cp. 1 : 2, 9 ; as to those who will bear it, see Rev. 12 : 17, R.V.).' The statement " the testimony of Jesus is the spirit of prophecy," is to be understood in the light, e.g., of the testimony concerning Christ and Israel in the Psalms, which will be used by the godly Jewish remnant in the coming time of " Jacob's Trouble." All such testimony centres in and points to Christ. See WITNESS.

TETRARCH
A. Noun.
TETRAARCHĒS or TETRARCHĒS (τετραάρχης) denotes one of four rulers (tetra, four, archē, rule), properly, the governor of the fourth part of a region ; hence, a dependent princeling, or any petty ruler subordinate to kings or ethnarchs ; in the N.T., Herod Antipas, Matt. 14 : 1 ; Luke 3 : 19 ; 9 : 7 ; Acts 13 : 1.¶

B. Verb.
TETRAARCHEŌ or TETRARCHEŌ (τετρααρχέω), to be a tetrarch, occurs in Luke 3 : 1 (thrice), of Herod Antipas, his brother Philip and Lysanias. Antipas and Philip each inherited a fourth part of his father's dominions. Inscriptions bear witness to the accuracy of Luke's details.¶

THAN : see † p. 9

THANK, THANKS (Noun and Verb), THANKFUL, THANKFULNESS, THANKSGIVING, THANKWORTHY
A. Nouns.
1. CHARIS (χάρις), for the meanings of which see GRACE, No. 1, is rendered " thank " in Luke 6 : 32, 33, 34 ; in 17 : 9, " doth he thank " is lit., ' hath he thanks to ; ' it is rendered " thanks (be to God) " in Rom. 6 : 17, R.V. (A.V., " God be thanked ") ; " thanks " in 1 Cor. 15 : 57 ; in 1 Tim. 1 : 12 and 2 Tim. 1 : 3, " I thank " is, lit., ' I have thanks;' " thankworthy," 1 Pet. 2 : 19, A.V. (R.V., " acceptable "). See ACCEPT, D, No. 2.

2. EUCHARISTIA (εὐχαριστία), eu, well, charizomai, to give freely (Eng., eucharist), denotes (a) gratitude, " thankfulness," Acts 24 : 3 ; (b) giving of thanks, thanksgiving, 1 Cor. 14 : 16 ; 2 Cor. 4 : 15 ; 9 : 11, 12 (plur.) ; Eph. 5 : 4 ; Phil. 4 : 6 ; Col. 2 : 7 ; 4 : 2 ; 1 Thess. 3 : 9 (" thanks ") ; 1 Tim. 2 : 1 (plur.) ; 4 : 3, 4 ; Rev. 4 : 9, " thanks ; " 7 : 12.¶

B. Verbs.

1. EUCHARISTEŌ (εὐχαριστέω), akin to A, No. 2, to give thanks, (a) is said of Christ, Matt. 15 : 36 ; 26 : 27 ; Mark 8 : 6 ; 14 : 23 ; Luke 22 : 17, 19 ; John 6 : 11, 23 ; 11 : 41 ; 1 Cor. 11 : 24 ; (b) of the Pharisee in Luke 18 : 11 in his self-complacent prayer ; (c) is used by Paul at the beginning of all his Epistles, except 2 Cor. (see, however, eulogētos in 1 : 3), Gal., 1 Tim., 2 Tim. (see, however, charin echō, 1 : 3), and Tit., (1) for his readers, Rom. 1 : 8 ; Eph. 1 : 16 ; Col. 1 : 3 ; 1 Thess. 1 : 2 ; 2 Thess. 1 : 3 (cp. 2 : 13) ; virtually so in Philm. 4 ; (2) for fellowship shown, Phil. 1 : 3 ; (3) for God's gifts to them, 1 Cor. 1 : 4 ; (d) is recorded (1) of Paul elsewhere, Acts 27 : 35 ; 28 : 15 ; Rom. 7 : 25 ; 1 Cor. 1 : 14 ; 14 : 18 ; (2) of Paul and others, Rom. 16 : 4 ; 1 Thess. 2 : 13 ; of himself, representatively, as a practice, 1 Cor. 10 : 30 ; (3) of others, Luke 17 : 16 ; Rom. 14 : 6 (twice) ; 1 Cor. 14 : 17 ; Rev. 11 : 17 ; (e) is used in admonitions to the saints, the Name of the Lord Jesus suggesting His character and example, Eph. 5 : 20 ; Col. 1 : 12 ; 3 : 17 ; 1 Thess. 5 : 18 ; (f) as the expression of a purpose, 2 Cor. 1 : 11, R.V. ; (g) negatively of the ungodly, Rom. 1 : 21.¶ Thanksgiving is the expression of joy Godward, and is therefore the fruit of the Spirit (Gal. 5 : 22) ; believers are encouraged to abound in it (e.g., Col. 2 : 7, and see C, below).

2. EXOMOLOGEŌ (ἐξομολογέω), in the Middle Voice, signifies to make acknowledgment, whether of sins (to confess), or in the honour of a person, as in Rom. 14 : 11 ; 15 : 9 (in some mss. in Rev. 3 : 5) ; this is the significance in the Lord's address to the Father, " I thank (Thee)," in Matt. 11 : 25 and Luke 10 : 21, the meaning being 'I make thankful confession' or 'I make acknowledgment with praise.' See CONFESS, No. 2, CONSENT, PROMISE.

3. ANTHOMOLOGEOMAI (ἀνθομολογέομαι), to acknowledge fully, to celebrate fully (anti) in praise with thanksgiving, is used of Anna in Luke 2 : 38.¶

Note : For homologeō, rendered " giving thanks " in Heb. 13 : 15 (R.V., " make confession "), see CONFESS, A, No. 1 (d).

C. Adjective.

EUCHARISTOS (εὐχάριστος), primarily, gracious, agreeable (as in the Sept., Prov. 11 : 16, of a wife, who brings glory to her husband¶), then grateful, thankful, is so used in Col. 3 : 15.¶

THAT (Conjunction, etc.) : see † p. 9

For THAT (Demonstrative Pronoun), see THIS

THEATRE

THEATRON (θέατρον), a theatre, was used also as a place of assembly, Acts 19 : 29, 31 ; in 1 Cor. 4 : 9 it is used of a show or spectacle. See SPECTACLE.¶

THEE

Note : This translates the oblique forms of the pronoun *su*, thou. In 2 Tim. 4 : 11, it translates the reflexive pronoun *seautou*, thyself.

THEFT

1. KLOPĒ (κλοπή), akin to *kleptō*, to steal, is used in the plural in Matt. 15 : 19 ; Mark 7 : 22.¶

2. KLEMMA (κλέμμα), a thing stolen, and so, a theft, is used in the plural in Rev. 9 : 21.¶ In the Sept., Gen. 31 : 39 ; Ex. 22 : 3, 4.¶

THEIR, THEIRS

Note : These pronouns are the rendering of (1) *autōn*, the genitive plur. of *autos*, he, e.g., Matt. 2 : 12 ; (2) *heautōn*, of themselves, the genitive plur. of *heautou*, of himself, e.g., Matt. 8: 22 ; Rom. 16 : 4, 18, " their own ; " or the accusative plur. *heautous*, e.g., 2 Cor. 8 : 5, " their own selves " (for John 20 : 10, see HOME, A, No. 3) ; (3) *idious*, the accusative plur. of *idios*, one's own, e.g., 1 Cor. 14 : 35, " their own ;" (4) *toutōn*, lit., ' of these,' the gen. plur. of *houtos*, this, Rom. 11 : 30, " their (disobedience) ; " (5) *ekeinōn*, the gen. plur. of *ekeinos*, that one (emphatic), e.g., 2 Cor. 8 : 14 (twice), " their," lit., ' of those ; ' 2 Tim. 3 : 9, " theirs."

THEM, THEMSELVES

Note : These translate the plural, in various forms, of (1) *autos* [see (1) above], e.g., Matt. 3 : 7 ; (2) *heatou* [see (2) above], e.g., Matt. 15 : 30 ; (3) *houtos* (*toutous*) [see (4) above], e.g., Acts 21 : 24 ; (4) *ekeinos* [see (5) above], e.g., Matt. 13 : 11. Regarding *allēlōn*, of one another, and its other forms, the R.V. substitutes " one another " for the A.V. " themselves " in Mark 8 : 16 ; 9 : 34 ; Luke 4 : 36 ; John 6 : 52 ; 11 : 56 ; 16 : 17 ; 19 : 24 ; Acts 26 : 31 ; 28 : 4 ; Rom. 2 : 15, but adheres to the rendering " themselves " in Mark 15 : 31 ; Acts 4 : 15 ; 28 : 25.

THEN

1. TOTE (τότε), a demonstrative adverb of time, denoting at that time, is used (*a*) of concurrent events, e.g., Matt. 2 : 17 ; Gal. 4 : 8, " at that time ; " ver. 29, " then ; " 2 Pet. 3 : 6, "(the world) that then was," lit., ' (the) then (world) ;' (*b*) of consequent events, then, thereupon, e.g., Matt. 2 : 7 ; Luke 11 : 26 ; 16 : 16, " [from (A.V., since)] that time ; " John 11 : 14 ; Acts 17 : 14 ; (*c*) of things future, e.g., Matt. 7 : 23 ; 24 : 30 (twice), 40 ; eight times in ch. 25 ; 1 Cor. 4 : 5 ; Gal. 6 : 4 ; 1 Thess. 5 : 3 ; 2 Thess. 2 : 8. It occurs 90 times in Matthew, more than in all the rest of the N.T. together.

2. EITA (εἶτα) denotes sequence (*a*) of time, then, next, Mark 4 : 17, R.V., " then ;" 4 : 28, in some texts ; 8 : 25, R.V., " then " (A.V., " after that ") ; Luke 8 : 12 ; John 13 : 5 ; 19 : 27 ; 20 : 27 ; in some texts

in 1 Cor. 12 : 28 ; 1 Cor. 15 : 5, 7, 24 ; 1 Tim. 2 : 13 ; 3 : 10 ; Jas. 1 : 15 ; (b) in argument, Heb. 12 : 9, " furthermore."¶

3. EPEITA (ἔπειτα) is used only of sequence, thereupon, thereafter, then (in some texts, Mark 7 : 5 ; kai, " and," in the best) ; Luke 16 : 7 ; John 11 : 7 ; 1 Cor. 12 : 28, R.V., " then " (A.V., " after that ") ; 15 : 6 and 7 (ditto) ; ver. 23, R.V., A.V., " afterward " (No. 2 in ver. 24) ; ver. 46 (ditto) ; Gal. 1 : 18 ; ver. 21, R.V. (A.V., " afterwards ") ; 2 : 1 ; 1 Thess. 4 : 17 ; Heb. 7 : 2, R.V. (A.V., " after that ") ; ver. 27, Jas. 3 : 17 ; 4 : 14. See AFTER.¶

4. LOIPON (λοιπόν), finally, for the rest, the neuter of loipos, (the) rest, used adverbially, is rendered " then " in Acts 27 : 20, A.V. (R.V., " now.").

5. OUN (οὖν), a particle expressing sequence or consequence, is rendered " then," e.g., Matt. 22 : 43 ; 27 : 22 ; Luke 11 : 13.

6. OUKOUN (οὐκοῦν), an adverb formed from ouk, not, oun, therefore, with the negative element dropped, meaning ' so then,' is used in John 18 : 37.¶

Notes : (1) In James 2 : 24, where in some texts the inferential particle toinun, therefore, occurs, the A.V. renders it by " then " (R.V. follows the superior mss. which omit it). (2) For conjunctions (ara, so ; de, but ; gar, for ; kai, and ; te, and), sometimes translated "then," see † p. 9.

THENCE (from)

EKEITHEN (ἐκεῖθεν) is used (a) of place, e.g., Matt. 4 : 21, " from thence ;"   5 : 26 ; in Acts 20 : 13, " there ;" often preceded by kai, written kàkeithen, e.g., Mark 9 : 30 and Luke 11 : 53 (in the best texts) ; Acts 7 : 4 ; 14 : 26 ; (b) of time, Acts 13 : 21, " and afterward." See AFTER.

Note : In Acts 28 : 13, hothen, from whence, is translated " from thence."

THENCEFORTH

ETI (ἔτι), yet, still, further, is rendered " thenceforth " in Matt. 5 : 13.

Notes : (1) In Luke 13 : 9, R.V., the phrase eis to mellon, lit., ' unto the about to be ' (mellō, to be about to), is translated " thenceforth " (A.V., " after that "). (2) In John 19 : 12, A.V., ek toutou, from this, is translated " from thenceforth " (R.V., " upon this ").

THERE, THITHER

1. EKEI (ἐκεῖ) signifies (a) there, e.g., Matt. 2 : 13, frequently in the Gospels ; (b) thither, e.g., Luke 17 : 37 ; in Rom. 15 : 24, " thitherward."

2. EKEISE (ἐκεῖσε), properly, ' thither,' signifies " there " in Acts 21 : 3 ; 22 : 5.¶ In the Sept., Job 39 : 29.¶

3. EKEITHEN (ἐκεῖθεν), thence, is rendered " there " in Acts 20 : 13. See THENCE.

4. ENTHADE (ἐνθάδε), here, hither, is rendered " there " in Acts 10 : 18. See HERE, HITHER.

5. AUTOU (αὐτοῦ), the genitive case, neuter, of *autos*, he, lit., ' of it,' is used as an adverb, " there," in Acts 18 : 19 ; 21 : 4 (in some texts in 15 : 34). See HERE.

Notes : (1) In Luke 24 : 18 and Acts 9 : 38, " there " translates the phrase *en autē,* ' in it.' (2) In John 21 : 9, " there " is used to translate the verb *keimai.* (3) In Matt. 24 : 23 (2nd part), A.V., *hōde,* " here " (R.V.), is translated " there." (4) In Acts 17 : 21, " there " forms part of the translation of *epidēmeō,* to sojourn, " sojourning there," R.V. (" which were there," A.V.).

THEREABOUT

Note : The phrase *peri toutou,* ' concerning this,' is rendered " thereabout " in Luke 24 : 4.

THEREAT

Note : The phrase *di'autēs,* lit., ' by (*dia*) it,' is rendered "thereat" in Matt. 7 : 13, A.V. (R.V., " thereby ").

THEREBY

Notes : (1) *Di'autēs* (see above) occurs in Matt. 7 : 13 ; John 11 : 4 ; Heb. 12 : 11. (2) *Dia tautēs,* by means of this, " thereby," occurs in Heb. 12 : 15 ; 13 : 2. (3) *En autē,* in, or by, it, is rendered " thereby " in Rom. 10 : 5 ; *en autō* in Eph. 2 : 16 (some texts have *en heautō,* ' in Himself ') ; 1 Pet. 2 : 2.

THEREFORE, † p. 9

THEREIN, THEREINTO, THEREOF, THEREON, THEREOUT, THERETO, THEREUNTO, THEREUPON, THEREWITH

Note : These translate various phrases consisting of a preposition with forms of either the personal pronoun *autos,* he, or the demonstrative *houtos,* this.

For THESE see THIS

THEY, THEY THEMSELVES

Note : When not forming part of the translation of the 3rd pers., plur. of a verb, (1) these translate the plural of the pronouns under HE, in their various forms, *autos, houtos, ekeinos, heautou.* (2) In Acts 5 : 16, *hoitines,* the plural of *hostis,* anyone who, is translated " they ; " so in 23 : 14, translated " and they ; " in 17 : 11, " in that they " (some texts have it in Matt. 25 : 3). (3) Sometimes the plural of the article is rendered " they," e.g., Phil. 4 : 22 ; Heb. 13 : 24 ; in 1 Cor. 11 : 19, " they which are (approved) " is, lit., ' the approved ;' in Gal. 2 : 6, " they . . . (who were of repute)," R.V.

For THICK see GATHER, A, No. 8

THIEF, THIEVES

1. KLEPTES (κλέπτης) is used (a) literally, Matt. 6 : 19, 20 ; 24 : 43 ; Luke 12 : 33, 39 ; John 10 : 1, 10 ; 12 : 6 ; 1 Cor. 6 : 10 ; 1 Pet. 4 : 15 ; (b) metaphorically of false teachers, John 10 : 8 ; (c) figuratively, (1) of the Personal coming of Christ, in a warning to a local church, with most of its members possessed of mere outward profession and defiled by the world, Rev. 3 : 3 ; in retributive intervention to overthrow the foes of God, 16 : 15 ; (2) of the Day of the Lord, in Divine judgment upon the world, 2 Pet. 3 : 10 and 1 Thess. 5 : 2, 4 ; in ver. 2, according to the order in the original " the word ' night ' is not to be read with ' the day of the Lord,' but with ' thief,' i.e., there is no reference to the time of the coming, only to the manner of it. To avoid ambiguity the phrase may be paraphrased, ' so comes as a thief in the night comes.' The use of the present tense instead of the future emphasises the certainty of the coming. . . . The unexpectedness of the coming of the thief, and the unpreparedness of those to whom he comes, are the essential elements in the figure ; cp. the entirely different figure used in Matt. 25 : 1–13."¶*

2. LESTES (λῃστής) is frequently rendered "thieves" in the A.V., e.g., Matt. 21 : 13. See ROBBER.

THIGH

MEROS (μηρός) occurs in Rev. 19 : 16 ; Christ appears there in the manifestation of His judicial capacity and action hereafter as the Executor of Divine vengeance upon the foes of God ; His Name is spoken of figuratively as being upon His thigh (where the sword would be worn ; cp. Ps. 45 : 3), emblematic of His strength to tread down His foes, His action being the exhibition of His Divine attributes of righteousness and power.¶

For THINE see THY

THING(S)

1. LOGOS (λόγος), a word, an account, etc., is translated "thing" in Matt. 21 : 24, A.V. (1st part), and Luke 20 : 3, A.V., R.V., " question " (in Matt. 21 : 24, 2nd part, " these things " translates tauta, the neut. plur. of houtos, this) ; Luke 1 : 4 ; Acts 5 : 24, A.V. (R.V., " words ") See ACCOUNT.

2. PRAGMA (πρᾶγμα), for which see MATTER, No. 2, is translated " thing " in Matt. 18 : 19, as part of the word "anything," lit., 'every thing ;' Luke 1 : 1, A.V. only ; Acts 5 : 4 ; in Heb. 6 : 18 ; 10 : 1, and 11 : 1, " things." See BUSINESS, MATTER, WORK.

3. RHEMA (ῥῆμα), a saying, word, is translated " thing " in Luke

---

* From Notes on Thessalonians by Hogg and Vine, pp. 153, 154.

2 : 15 ; ver. 19, A.V. (R.V., " saying ") ; in Acts 5 : 32, " things." See SAYING.

Notes : (1) The neuter sing. and plur. of the article are frequently rendered " the thing " and " the things ; " so with *tauta,* " these things," the neut. plur. of *houtos,* this. (2) So in the case of the neut. plur. of certain pronouns and adjectives without nouns, e.g., all, base, heavenly, which. (3) When " thing " represents a separate word in the original, it is a translation of one or other of Nos. 1, 2, 3, above. (4) In Phil. 2 : 10, " *things* " is added in italics to express the meaning of the three adjectives.

THINK

1. DOKEŌ (δοκέω), to suppose, to think, to form an opinion, which may be either right or wrong, is sometimes rendered to think, e.g., Matt. 3 : 9 ; 6 : 7 ; see ACCOUNT, No. 1, SUPPOSE, No. 2.

2. HĒGEOMAI (ἡγέομαι), for which see ACCOUNT, No. 3, is rendered to think in Acts 26 : 2 ; 2 Cor. 9 : 5, " I thought ; " Phil. 2 : 6, A.V. (R.V., " counted ") ; 2 Pet. 1 : 13.

3. NOEŌ (νοέω), to perceive, understand, apprehend, is rendered " think " in Eph. 3 : 20. See PERCEIVE, UNDERSTAND.

4. HUPONOEŌ (ὑπονοέω), to suppose, surmise (*hupo*, under, and No. 3), is rendered to think in Acts 13 : 25, A.V. (R.V., " suppose "). See DEEM.

5. LOGIZOMAI (λογίζομαι), to reckon, is rendered to think, in Rom. 2 : 3, A.V. (R.V., " reckonest "); 1 Cor. 13 : 5, A.V., R.V., " taketh (not) account of," i.e., love does not reckon up or calculatingly consider the evil done to it (something more than refraining from imputing motives) ; 13 : 11, " I thought ; " in the following, for the A.V., to think, in 2 Cor. 3 : 5, R.V., " to account ; " 10 : 2 (twice), " count ; " 10 : 7, " consider ; " 10 : 11, " reckon ; " 12 : 6, " account." In Phil. 4 : 8, " think on (these things)," it signifies ' make those things the subjects of your thoughtful consideration,' or ' carefully reflect on them ' (R.V. marg., " take account of "). See ACCOUNT, A, No. 4.

6. NOMIZŌ (νομίζω), to suppose, is sometimes rendered to think, e.g., Matt. 5 : 17. See SUPPOSE, No. 1.

7. PHRONEŌ (φρονέω), to be minded in a certain way (*phrēn*, the mind), is rendered to think, in Rom. 12 : 3 (2nd and 3rd occurrences), R.V., " not to think of himself more highly (*huperphroneō*, see No. 13) than he ought to think (*phroneō*) ; but so to think (*phroneō*) as to think soberly [*sōphroneō*, see Note (3)] ; " the play on words may be expressed by a literal rendering somewhat as follows : ' not to over-think beyond what it behoves him to think, but to think unto sober-thinking ; ' in 1 Cor. 4 : 6, some inferior texts have this verb, hence the A.V. " to think ; " in the best texts, it is absent, hence the R.V., puts " *go* " in italics ; lit., the sentence is ' that ye might learn the (i.e., the rule) not beyond what

things have been written.' The saying appears to be proverbial, perhaps a Rabbinical adage. Since, however, *graphō*, to write, was a current term for framing a law or an agreement (so Deissmann, *Bible Studies*, and Moulton and Milligan, *Vocab*.), it is quite possible that the Apostle's meaning is 'not to go beyond the terms of a teacher's commission, thinking more of himself than the character of his commission allows ;' this accords with the context and the whole passage, 3 : 1–4 : 5. In Phil. 1 : 7, A.V., "to think" (R.V., "to be . . . minded"). See AFFECTION, B, Note (1) and list there.

8. OIOMAI or OIMAI (*οἴομαι*), to imagine, is rendered "I suppose" in John 21 : 25 ; "thinking" in Phil. 1 : 17, R.V. (ver. 16, A.V., "supposing") ; "let (not that man) think," Jas. 1 : 7. See SUPPOSE.¶

9. PHAINŌ (*φαίνω*), in the Passive Voice, to appear, is rendered "(what) think (ye)" in Mark 14 : 64, lit., 'what does it appear to you ?' See APPEAR, No. 1.

10. EUDOKEŌ (*εὐδοκέω*), to be well-pleasing, is rendered "we thought it good" in 1 Thess. 3 : 1. See PLEASE.

11. AXIOŌ (*ἀξιόω*), to regard as worthy (*axios*), to deem it suitable, is rendered "thought (not) good" in Acts 15 : 38. See WORTHY, B.

12. ENTHUMEOMAI (*ἐνθυμέομαι*), to reflect on, ponder, is used in Matt. 1 : 20 ; 9 : 4 : see No. 14. Cp. *enthumēsis*, consideration (see THOUGHT).¶

13. HUPERPHRONEŌ (*ὑπερφρονέω*), to be overproud, high-minded, occurs in Rom. 12 : 3, rendered "to think of himself more highly." See No. 7.¶

14. DIENTHUMEOMAI (*διενθυμέομαι*), to consider deeply (*dia*, through, and No. 12), is used of Peter in Acts 10 : 19, in the best texts (some have No. 12).¶

15. EPIBALLŌ (*ἐπιβάλλω*), to throw oneself upon, is used metaphorically in Mark 14 : 72, "when he thought thereon (he wept)," lit., 'thinking thereon,' but to think is an exceptional sense of the word (see BEAT, CAST, LAY, PUT) ; hence various suggestions have been made. Field, following others, adopts the meaning 'putting (his garment) over (his head),' as an expression of grief. Others regard it as having here the same meaning as *archomai*, to begin (at an early period, indeed, *archomai* was substituted in the text for the authentic *epiballō*) ; Moulton confirms this from a papyrus writing. Another suggestion is to understand it as with *dianoian*, mind, i.e., 'casting his mind thereon.'

Notes : (1) In Acts 26 : 8, A.V., *krinō*, to judge, reckon, is translated "should it be thought" (R.V., "is it judged"). (2) In Luke 12 : 17, A.V., *dialogizomai*, to reason (R.V., "reasoned"), is translated "thought." (3) In Rom. 12 : 3, *sōphroneō*, "to think soberly," R.V., is, lit., 'unto sober-thinking,' the infinitive mood of the verb being used as a noun (A.V. marg., "to sobriety") : cp. No. 7. See SOBER, B, No. 2.

THIRD, THIRDLY

TRITOS (τρίτος) is used (a) as a noun, e.g., Luke 20 : 12, 31 ; in Rev. 8 : 7–12 and 9 : 15, 18, " the third part," lit., ' the third ; ' (b) as an adverb, with the article, " the third time," e.g., Mark 14 : 41 ; John 21 : 17 (twice) ; without the article, lit., ' a third time,' e.g., John 21 : 14 ; 2 Cor. 12 : 14 ; 13 : 1 ; in enumerations, in Matt. 26 : 44, with ek, from, lit., ' from the third time ' (the ek indicates the point of departure, especially in a succession of events, cp. John 9 : 24 ; 2 .Pet. 2 : 8) ; absolutely, in the accusative neuter, in 1 Cor. 12 : 28, " thirdly ; " (c) as an adjective (its primary use), e.g., in the phrase " the third heaven," 2 Cor. 12 : 2 [cp. HEAVEN, A, No. 1 (c), PARADISE] ; in the phrase " the third hour," Matt. 20 : 3 ; Mark 15 : 25 ; Acts 2 : 15 (" . . . of the day ") ; 23 : 23 (" . . . of the night ") ; in a phrase with hēmera, a day, " on the third day " (i.e., ' the next day but one '), e.g., Matt. 16 : 21 ; Luke 24 : 46 ; Acts 10 : 40 ; in this connection the idiom " three days and three nights," Matt. 12 : 40, is explained by ref. to 1 Sam. 30 : 12, 13, and Esth. 4 : 16 with 5 : 1 ; in Mark 9 : 31 and 10 : 34, the R.V., " after three days," follows the texts which have this phrase, the A.V., " the third day," those which have the same phrase as in Matt. 16 : 21, etc.

Note : For " third story," Acts 20 : 9, R.V., see STORY.

THIRST (Noun and Verb), THIRSTY (to be), ATHIRST
A. Noun.

DIPSOS (δίψος), thirst (cp. Eng., dipsomania), occurs in 2 Cor. 11 : 27.¶
B. Verb.

DIPSAŌ (διψάω) is used (a) in the natural sense, e.g., Matt. 25 : 35, 37, 42 ; in ver. 44, " athirst " (lit., ' thirsting ') ; John 4 : 13, 15 ; 19 : 28 ; Rom. 12 : 20 ; 1 Cor. 4 : 11 ; Rev. 7 : 16 ; (b) figuratively, of spiritual thirst, Matt. 5 : 6 ; John 4 : 14 ; 6 : 35 ; 7 : 37 ; in Rev. 21 : 6 and 22 : 17, " that is athirst."

THIRTY, THIRTYFOLD

TRIAKONTA (τριάκοντα) is usually rendered " thirty," e.g., Matt. 13 : 23 ; " thirtyfold," in Matt. 13 : 8, A.V. only ; in Mark 4 : 8, R.V. only ; in Mark 4 : 20, A.V. and R.V.

THIS, THESE

Note : The singular and plural translate various forms of the following : (1) houtos, which is used (a) as a noun, this one, followed by no noun, e.g., Matt. 3: 17 ; translated in Luke 2 : 34, " this *child* ; " in 1 Cor. 5 : 3, R.V., " this thing " (A.V., " this deed ") ; for " this fellow " see FELLOW, Note (3) ; in Acts 17 : 32 the R.V. rightly omits " *matter* ; " in Heb. 4 : 5 " *place* " is italicized ; it is frequently rendered " this man," e.g., Matt. 9 : 3 ; John 6 : 52 ; " of this sort," 2 Tim. 3 : 6, A.V. (R.V., " of these ") ; (b) as an adjective with a noun, either with the article and before it, e.g.,

Matt. 12 : 32, or after the noun (which is preceded by the article), e.g., Matt. 3 : 9 and 4 : 3, " these stones ; " or without the article often forming a predicate, e.g., John 2 : 11 ; 2 Cor. 13 : 1 ; (2) *ekeinos*, that one, rendered " this " in Matt. 24 : 43 ; (3) *autos*, he, rendered " this " in Matt. 11 : 14, lit., ' he ; ' in John 12 : 7, A.V. (R.V., " it ") ; in the feminine, Luke 13 : 16 ; (4) the article *ho*, Matt. 21 : 21 (*to*, the neuter), A.V. (R.V., " what ") ; in Rom. 13 : 9 (1st part) ; Gal. 5 : 14 ; Heb. 12 : 27, the article *to* is virtually equivalent to ' the following.'

The demonstrative pronouns THAT and the plural THOSE translate the same pronouns (1), (2), (3) mentioned above. In Heb. 7 : 21, A.V., " those " translates the article, which requires the R.V., " they."

THISTLE

TRIBOLOS (τρίβολος) occurs in Matt. 7 : 16 and Heb. 6 : 8 (A.V., " briers ").¶ In the Sept., Gen. 3 : 18 ; 2 Sam. 12 : 31 ; Prov. 22 : 5 ; Hos. 10 : 8.¶ Cp. THORNS.

For THITHER, THITHERWARD see THERE

Note : In John 7 : 34, 36, A.V., *hopou*, " where " (R.V.), is amplified by the italicized word " *thither*."

For THONG see LATCHET

THORN, THORNS (of)
A. Nouns.

1. AKANTHA (ἄκανθα), a brier, a thorn (from *akē*, a point), is always used in the plural in the N.T., Matt. 7 : 16 and parallel passage in Luke 6 : 44 ; Matt. 13 : 7 (twice), 22 and parallels in Mark and Luke ; in Matt. 27 : 29 and John 19 : 2, of the crown of thorns placed on Christ's head (see also B) in mock imitation of the garlands worn by emperors. They were the effects of the Divine curse on the ground (Gen. 3 : 18 ; contrast Is. 55 : 13). The thorns of the crown plaited by the soldiers, are usually identified with those of the *Zizyphus spina Christi*, some 20 feet high or more, fringing the Jordan and abundant in Palestine ; its twigs are flexible. Another species, however, the Arabian *qundaul*, crowns of which are plaited and sold in Jerusalem as representatives of Christ's crown, seems likely to be the· one referred to. The branches are easily woven and adapted to the torture intended. The word *akantha* occurs also in Heb. 6 : 8.¶

2. SKOLOPS (σκόλοψ) originally denoted anything pointed, e.g., a stake ; in Hellenistic vernacular, a thorn (so the Sept., in Numb. 33 : 55 ; Ezek. 28 : 24 ; Hos. 2 : 6¶), 2 Cor. 12 : 7, of the Apostle's " thorn in the flesh ; " his language indicates that it was physical, painful, humiliating ; it was also the effect of Divinely permitted Satanic antagonism ; the verbs rendered " that I should (not) be exalted overmuch " (R.V.) and " to

bu...
consta...
through ...
adhere to the ...ent tense, signifying recurrent action, indicating a
Alexandrine use ...k. Lightfoot interprets it as " a stake driven
meaning of ' stak...msay agrees with this. Most commentators
metaphorical size, b...n." Field says " there is no doubt that the
Attempts to connect th...rn is here intended, and that the ordinary
Gal. 4 : 13 are speculative....jected." What is stressed is not the
...ess of the suffering and its effects.
...circumstances of Acts 14 : 19 and

AKANTHINOS (ἀκάνθινος), o...
Mark 15 : 17 and John 19 : 5. ¶ In ...(from A, No. 1), is used in
Isa. 34 : 13. ¶

THOROUGHLY (THR...Y)

Note : This is usually part of the translatio... ...verb, e.g., CLEANSE,
FURNISH, PURGE. In 2 Cor. 11 : 6, the phrase *en* ... " in everything,"
R.V., is translated " throughly " in the A.V.

For THOSE see THIS (last part of Note)

THOU

Note : Frequently this forms part of the translation of a verb in the
2nd person, singular. Otherwise it translates (*a*) the pronoun *su*, used
for emphasis or contrast, e.g., John 1 : 19, 21 (twice), 25, 42 (twice) ;
8 : 5, 13, 25, 33, 48, 52, 53 ; Acts 9 : 5 ; in addressing a person or place,
e.g., Matt. 2 : 6 ; Luke 1 : 76 ; John 17 : 5 ; perhaps also in the phrase
su eipas, " thou hast said," e.g., Matt. 26 : 64 (sometimes without
emphasis, e.g., Acts 13 : 33) ; (*b*) in the oblique cases, e.g., the dative *soi*,
lit., to thee, e.g., Matt. 17 : 25, " what thinkest thou ? " (lit., ' what does
it seem to thee ? ') ; (*c*) *autos*, self, e.g., Luke 6 : 42 ; Acts 21 : 24, " thou
thyself ; " (*d*) the reflexive pronoun, *seauton*, Rom. 2 : 19, " thou thyself."

THOUGH : see † p. 9

For THOUGHT (Verb) see THINK

THOUGHT (Noun)

1. EPINOIA (ἐπίνοια), a thought by way of a design (akin to *epinoeō*,
to contrive, *epi*, intensive, *noeō*, to consider), is used in Acts 8 : 22. ¶ In
the Sept., Jer. 20 : 10. ¶

2. NOĒMA (νόημα), a purpose, device of the mind (akin to *noeō*, see
No. 1), is rendered " thought " in 2 Cor. 10 : 5, " thoughts " in Phil.
4 : 7, R.V. : see DEVICE, No. 2.

3. DIANOĒMA (διανόημα), a thought, occurs in Luke 11 : 17, where
the sense is that of machinations. ¶

4. ENTHUMĒSIS (ἐνθύμησις), is transla____ ____ in Rom. 2 : 15 :
2 : 25 ; Heb. 4 : 12 : see DEVICE, No. ____ in Matt. 9 : 4 ;

5. LOGISMOS (λογισμός) is transla____ translated " thoughts "
see IMAGINATION, No. I.

6. DIALOGISMOS (διαλογισμός) ____ng," and 24 : 38, A.V., R.V.,
in Matt. 15 : 19 ; Mark 7 : 21 ; L__ Luke 9 : 46, A.V. and R.V.,
" reasonings ; " in 9 : 47, A.V., R. 4, A.V. and R.V. See DISPUTE,
" reasonings ; " so I Cor. 3____
" reasoning ; " " thoughts "____
IMAGINATION, REASONING

___UGHT (to take)

1. MERIMNAŌ ____ω) denotes to be anxious, careful. For the
A.V., to take tho__ the R.V. substitutes to be anxious in Matt.
6 : 25, 27, 28, 3__ 10 : 19 ; Luke 12 : 11, 22, 25, 26. See CARE,
B, No. 1.

2. PROM___MNAŌ (προμεριμνάω), to be anxious beforehand, occurs
in Mark 13 ____.

3. PH__NEŌ (φρονέω) : for Phil. 4 : 10, R.V., " ye did take thought,"
see CARE, B, No. 6.

4. PRONOEŌ (προνοέω), to provide, is rendered to take thought in
Rom. 12 : 17 and 2 Cor. 8 : 21. See PROVIDE.

THOUSAND (–S)

1. CHILIOI (χίλιοι), a thousand, occurs in 2 Pet. 3 : 8 ; Rev. 11 : 3 ;
12 : 6 ; 14 : 20 ; 20 : 2-7.¶

2. CHILIAS (χιλιάς), one thousand, is always used in the plural,
chiliades, but translated in the sing. everywhere, except in the phrase
" thousands of thousands," Rev. 5 : 11.

Notes : (1) The following compounds of No. 1 represent different
multiples of a thousand : dischilioi, 2,000, Mark 5 : 13 ;¶ trischilioi,
3,000, Acts 2 : 41 ;¶ tetrakischilioi, 4,000, Matt. 15 : 38 ; 16 : 10 ;
Mark 8 : 9, 20 ; Acts 21 : 38 ;¶ pentakischilioi, 5,000, Matt. 14 : 21 ;
16 : 9 ; Mark 6 : 44 ; 8 : 19 ; Luke 9 : 14 ; John 6 : 10 ;¶ heptakischilioi,
7,000, Rom. 11 : 4.¶ (2) Murias, a myriad, a vast number, " many
thousands," Luke 12 : 1, R.V. ; Acts 21 : 20 ; it also denotes 10,000, Acts
19 : 19, lit., ' five ten-thousands ; ' Jude 14, " ten thousands ; " in Rev.
5 : 11 " ten thousand times ten thousand " is, lit., ' myriads of myriads ; '
in Rev. 9 : 16 in the best texts, dismuriades muriadōn, " twice ten thousand
times ten thousand " R.V. (A.V., " two hundred thousand thousand ") :
see INNUMERABLE. (3) Murioi (the plur. of murios), an adjective
signifying numberless, is used in this indefinite sense in 1 Cor. 4 : 15 and
14 : 19 ; it also denotes the definite number " ten thousand," Matt.
18 : 24.¶

THREATEN

1. APEILEŌ (ἀπειλέω) is used of Christ, negatively, in 1 Pet. 2 : 23 ; in the Middle Voice, Acts 4 : 17, where some texts have the noun *apeilē* in addition, hence the A.V., " let us straitly threaten," lit., ' let us threaten . . . with threatening' (see THREATENING).¶ (See also STRAITLY.)

2. PROSAPEILEŌ (προσαπειλέω), to threaten further (*pros*, and No. 1), occurs in the Middle Voice in Acts 4 : 21.¶

THREATENING

APEILĒ (ἀπειλή), akin to *apeileō* (see above), occurs in Acts 4 : 29 (in some mss. ver. 17) ; 9 : 1 ; Eph. 6 : 9.¶

THREE

TREIS (τρεῖς) is regarded by many as a number sometimes symbolically indicating fulness of testimony or manifestation, as in the Three Persons in the Godhead, cp. 1 Tim. 5 : 19 ; Heb. 10 : 28 ; the mention in 1 John 5 : 7 is in a verse which forms no part of the original ; no Greek ms. earlier than the 14th century contained it ; no version earlier than the 5th cent. in any other language contains it, nor is it quoted by any of the Greek or Latin " Fathers " in their writings on the Trinity. That there are those who bear witness in Heaven is not borne out by any other Scripture. It must be regarded as the interpolation of a copyist.

In Mark 9 : 31 and 10 : 34 the best texts have *meta treis hemeras*, " after three days," which idiomatica'ly expresses the same thing as *tē tritē hēmera*, " on the third day," which some texts have here, as, e.g., the phrase " the third day " in Matt. 17 : 23 ; 20 : 19 ; Luke 9 : 22 ; 18 : 33, where the repetition of the article lends stress to the number, lit., ' the day the third ; ' 24 : 7, 46 ; Acts 10 : 40. For THREE TIMES see THRICE.

THREE HUNDRED

TRIAKOSIOI (τριακόσιοι) occurs in Mark 14 : 5 and John 12 : 5.¶

For THREESCORE see SIXTY and SEVENTY

For THREE THOUSAND see THOUSAND

THRESH

ALOAŌ (ἀλοάω), to thresh, is so rendered in 1 Cor. 9 : 10 ; in ver. 9 and 1 Tim. 5 : 18, " that treadeth out the corn."¶

THRESHING-FLOOR

HALŌN (ἅλων), a threshing-floor, is so translated in Matt. 3 : 12, and Luke 3 : 17, R.V. (A.V., " floor "), perhaps by metonymy for the grain.¶

For THREW see THROW

THRICE

TRIS (τρίς) occurs in Matt. 26 : 34, 75 and parallel passages ; in Acts 10 : 16 and 11 : 10, preceded by *epi*, up to ; 2 Cor. 11 : 25 (twice) ; 12 : 8.

THROAT (Noun), to take by the (Verb)

A. Noun.

LARUNX (λάρυγξ), a throat (Eng., larynx), is used metaphorically of speech in Rom. 3 : 13.¶

B. Verb.

PNIGŌ (πνίγω), to choke, is rendered "took . . . by the throat" in Matt. 18 : 28. See CHOKE, No. 1.

THRONE

1. THRONOS (θρόνος), a throne, a seat of authority, is used of the throne (*a*) of God, e.g., Heb. 4 : 16, "the throne of grace," i.e., from which grace proceeds ; 8 : 1 ; 12 : 2 ; Rev. 1 : 4 ; 3 : 21 (2nd part) ; 4 : 2 (twice) ; 5 : 1 ; frequently in Rev. ; in 20 : 12, in the best texts, "the throne" (some have *Theos*, "God," A.V.) ; cp. 21 : 3 ; Matt. 5 : 34; 23 : 22 ; Acts 7 : 49 ; (*b*) of Christ, e.g., Heb. 1 : 8 ; Rev. 3 : 21 (1st part) ; 22 : 3 ; His seat of authority in the Millennium, Matt. 19 : 28 (1st part) ; (*c*) by metonymy for angelic powers, Col. 1 : 16 ; (*d*) of the Apostles in Millennial authority, Matt. 19 : 28 (2nd part) ; Luke 22 : 30 ; (*e*) of the elders in the Heavenly vision, Rev. 4 : 4 (2nd and 3rd parts), R.V., "thrones" (A.V., "seats") ; so 11 : 16 ; (*f*) of David, Luke 1 : 32 ; Acts 2 : 30 ; (*g*) of Satan, Rev. 2 : 13, R.V., "throne" (A.V., "seat") ; (*h*) of "the beast," the final and federal head of the revived Roman Empire, Rev. 13 : 2 ; 16 : 10.

2. BĒMA (βῆμα), for which see JUDGMENT-SEAT, is used of the throne or tribunal of Herod, Acts 12 : 21.

THRONG (Verb)

1. THLIBŌ (θλίβω), to press, is rendered "throng," Mark 3 : 9. See AFFLICT, No. 4.

2. SUNTHLIBŌ (συνθλίβω), to press together, on all sides (*sun*, together, and No. 1), a strengthened form, is used in Mark 5 : 24, 31.¶

3. SUMPNIGŌ (συμπνίγω), to choke, is used of thronging by a crowd, Luke 8 : 42. See CHOKE, No. 3.

Note : For *sunechō*, to hold together, press together, Luke 8 : 45 (A.V., "throng"), see PRESS.

THROUGH and THROUGHOUT : see † p. 9

For THROUGHLY see THOROUGHLY

THROW

1. BALLŌ (βάλλω), to cast, to throw, is rendered to throw in Mark 12 : 42, A.V. (R.V., "cast"); so Acts 22 : 23 (2nd part); to throw down, Rev. 18 : 21 (2nd part), A.V. (R.V., "cast down"). See CAST, No. 1.

2. RHIPTŌ (ρίπτω), to hurl, throw, throw off, is rendered "had thrown . . . down" in Luke 4 : 35, R.V. (A.V., "had thrown"). See CAST, No. 2.

3. KATAKRĒMNIZŌ (κατακρημνίζω), to throw over a precipice (krēmnos), cast down headlong, is rendered "throw . . . down" in Luke 4 : 29 (A.V., "cast . . . down headlong").¶

4. KATALUŌ (καταλύω), lit., to loosen down, is rendered to throw down (of the stones of the Temple) in Matt. 24 : 2 and parallel passages. See DESTROY, No. 5.

THRUST

1. BALLŌ (βάλλω), for which cp. THROW, No. 1, is rendered to thrust in John 20 : 25, 27, A.V. (R.V., "put"); Acts 16 : 24, A.V. (R.V., "cast"); so Rev. 14 : 16, 19. See CAST, No. 1.

2. EKBALLŌ (ἐκβάλλω), to cast out, is rendered "thrust . . . out" in Luke 4 : 29, A.V. (R.V., "cast . . . forth"); so 13 : 28 and Acts 16 : 37. See CAST, No. 5.

3. APŌTHEŌ (ἀπωθέω), to thrust away, is used in the Middle Voice, to thrust away from oneself, and translated "thrust away" in Acts 7 : 27, 39; "thrust . . . from," 13 : 46, R.V. (A.V., "put . . . from"); "having thrust from them," 1 Tim. 1 : 19, R.V. (A.V., "having put away"). See CAST, No. 13.

4. KATATOXEUŌ (κατατοξεύω), to strike down with an arrow, shoot dead, occurs in Heb. 12 : 20 in some mss. (in a quotation from Ex. 19 : 13, Sept.).¶

Notes: (1) In Matt. 11 : 23 and Luke 10 : 15 the best texts have *katabainō*, to go down (R.V.), instead of *katabibazō*, in the Passive Voice, to be thrust down or brought down (A.V.). (2) In Acts 27 : 39, A.V., *exōtheō*, to drive out, is rendered "to thrust in," R.V., "drive (the ship) upon (it [i.e., the beach])." (3) In Rev. 14 : 15, 18, A.V., *pempō*, to send (R.V., "send forth"), is translated "thrust in." (4) For Luke 5 : 3, A.V., see LAUNCH, No. 2.

THUNDER, THUNDERING

BRONTĒ (βροντή): in Mark 3 : 17 "sons of thunder" is the interpretation of Boanērges, the name applied by the Lord to James and John; their fiery disposition is seen in 9 : 38 and Luke 9 : 54; perhaps in the case of James it led to his execution. The name and its interpretation have caused much difficulty; some suggest the meaning ' the twins.' It is however most probably the equivalent of the Aramaic *benê regesh*, ' sons of tumult ; ' the latter of the two words was no doubt used of thunder in Palestinian Aramaic ; hence the meaning " the sons of thunder ; " the cognate Hebrew word *ragash*, to rage, is used in Ps. 2 : 1 and there only. In John 12 : 29 *brontē* is used with *ginomai*, to take place, and rendered " it had thundered ; " lit., ' there was thunder ; ' elsewhere, Rev. 4 : 5 ; 6 : 1 ; 8 : 5 ; 10 : 3, 4 ; 11 : 19 ; 14 : 2 ; 16 : 18 ; 19 : 6.¶

THUS

HOUTŌS or HOUTŌ (οὕτως), in this way, so, thus, is used (*a*) with reference to what precedes, e.g., Luke 1 : 25 ; 2 : 48 ; (*b*) with reference to what follows, e.g., Luke 19 : 31, rendered " on this wise," in Matt. 1 : 18 ; John 21 : 1, and before quotations, Acts 7 : 6 ; 13 : 34 ; Rom. 10 : 6, A.V. (R.V., " thus ") ; Heb. 4 : 4 ; (*c*) marking intensity, rendered " so," e.g., Gal. 1 : 6 ; Heb. 12 : 21 ; Rev. 16 : 18 ; (*d*) in comparisons, rendered " so," e.g., Luke 11 : 30 ; Rom. 5 : 15. See FASHION, B, LIKEWISE, Note (1), MANNER, C, No. 2, So, Note (1).

Notes : (1) *Touto*, the neuter of *houtos*, this, is translated " thus " in 2 Cor. 1 : 17 ; 5 : 14 ; Phil. 3 : 15 ; the neuter plural, *tauta*, these things, e.g., in Luke 18 : 11 ; 19 : 28 ; John 9 : 6 ; 11 : 43 ; 13 : 21 ; 20 : 14 ; Acts 19 : 41. (2) *Tade*, these things (the neuter plural of *hode*, this), is translated " thus " in Acts 21 : 11. (3) In Luke 17 : 30, A.V., *kata tauta*, lit., ' according to these things,' is rendered " thus " (R.V., " after the same manner," follows the reading *kata ta auta*, lit., ' according to the same things ').

THY, THINE, THINE OWN, THYSELF

Note : These are translations of (1) the possessive pronoun *sos*, and its inflections, e.g., Matt. 7 : 3 (1st part) ; it is used as a noun with the article, in the phrases *to son*, " that which is thine," Matt. 20 : 14 ; 25 : 25, " thine own ; " *hoi soi*, " thy friends," Mark 5 : 19 ; *ta sa*, " thy goods," Luke 6 : 30, lit., ' the thine ; ' (2) one of the oblique cases of *su*, thou ; *sou*, of thee, e.g., Matt. 1 : 20 ; 7 : 3 (2nd part), " thine own ; " *soi*, to thee, e.g., Mark 5 : 9 ; with *menō*, to remain, Acts 5 : 4 (1st part), " thine own," lit., ' remain to thee ; ' in Matt. 26 : 18, *pros se*, " at thy house," lit., ' with thee ; ' (3) *seauton*, " (as) thyself," Rom. 13 : 9 ; *seautou*, of thyself, e.g., Matt. 4 : 6 ; *seautō*, to thyself, Acts 16 : 28 ; (4) *heautou* (with *apo*, from), John 18 : 34, " of thyself," lit., ' from thyself ; ' (5) *autos*, self, is sometimes used for " thyself," e.g., Luke 6 : 42.

THYINE (WOOD)

THUÏNOS (θύϊνος) is akin to *thuia*, or *thua*, an African aromatic and coniferous tree ; in Rev. 18 : 12 it describes a wood which formed part of the merchandise of Babylon ; it was valued by Greeks and Romans for tables, being hard, durable and fragrant (A.V. marg., " sweet ").¶

TIDINGS
A. Noun.

PHASIS (φάσις), akin to *phēmi*, to speak, denotes information, especially against fraud or other delinquency, and is rendered "tidings" in Acts 21 : 31.¶

Note: In Acts 11 : 22, A.V., *logos*, a word, a "report" (R.V.), is rendered "tidings."

B. Verbs.

1. EUANGELIZŌ (εὐαγγελίζω) is used of any message designed to cheer those who receive it ; it is rendered to bring, declare, preach, or show good or glad tidings, e.g., Luke 1 : 19 ; 2 : 10 ; 3 : 18, R.V. ; 4 : 43, R.V. ; 7 : 22, R.V. ; 8 : 1 ; Acts 8 : 12 and 10 : 36, R.V. ; 14 : 15, R.V. ; in 1 Thess. 3 : 6, " brought us glad (A.V., good) tidings ; " in Heb. 4 : 2, R.V., " we have had good tidings preached ; " similarly, 4 : 6 ; in 1 Pet. 1 : 25 *rhēma*, a word, is coupled with this verb, " the word of good tidings which was preached," R.V. (A.V., " the word which by the gospel is preached "). See PREACH, A, No. 1.

2. ANANGELLŌ (ἀναγγέλλω), to announce, declare, is rendered " (no) tidings . . . came," in Rom. 15 : 21, R.V., A.V., " was (not) spoken of." See TELL.

TIE

1. DEŌ (δέω), to bind, is rendered to tie in Matt. 21 : 2 ; Mark 11 : 2, 4 ; Luke 19 : 30. See BIND.

2. PROTEINŌ (προτείνω), to stretch out or forth, is used of preparations for scourging, Acts 22 : 25, R.V., " had tied (him) up " (A.V., " bound ").¶

TILES, TILING

KERAMOS (κέραμος), potter's clay, or an earthen vessel, denotes in the plural " tiles " in Luke 5 : 19, R.V., A.V., " tiling."¶ In the Sept., 2 Sam. 17 : 28.¶

For TILL (Conjunction) see † p. 9

TILL (Verb)

GEŌRGEŌ (γεωργέω), to till the ground, is used in the Passive Voice in Heb. 6 : 7, R.V., " it is tilled " (A.V., " . . . dressed ").¶ Moulton and Milligan point out that, agriculture being the principal industry in Egypt, this word and its cognates (*geōrgion*, see HUSBANDRY, and *geōrgos*, see HUSBANDMAN) are very common in the papyri with reference to the cultivation of private allotments and the crown lands.

TIME
A. Nouns.

1. CHRONOS (χρόνος) denotes a space of time, whether short, e.g.,

Matt. 2 : 7 ; Luke 4 : 5, or long, e.g., Luke 8 : 27 ; 20 : 9 ; or a succession of times, shorter, e.g., Acts 20 : 18, or longer, e.g., Rom. 16 : 25, R.V., "times eternal ; " or duration of time, e.g., Mark 2 : 19, 2nd part, R.V., " while " (A.V., " as long as "), lit., ' for whatever time.' For a fuller treatment see SEASON, A, No. 2.

2. KAIROS (καιρός), primarily due measure, due proportion, when used of time, signified a fixed or definite period, a season, sometimes an opportune or seasonable time, e.g., Rom. 5 : 6, R.V., " season " ; Gal. 6 : 10, " opportunity." In Mark 10 : 30 and Luke 18 : 30, " this time " (kairos), i.e., in this lifetime, is contrasted with ' the coming age.' In I Thess. 5 : 1, " the times and the seasons," " times " (chronos) refers to the duration of the interval previous to the Parousia of Christ and the length of time it will occupy (see COMING, No. 3, Vol. I, top of p. 209), as well as other periods ; " seasons " refers to the characteristics of these periods. See SEASON, A, No. 1, and the contrasts between chronos and kairos under SEASON, A, No. 2.

3. HŌRA (ὥρα), primarily, any time or period fixed by nature, is translated " time " in Matt. 14 : 15 ; Luke 14 : 17 ; Rom. 13 : 11, " high time ; " in the following the R.V. renders it " hour," for A.V., " time," Matt. 18 : 1 ; Luke 1 : 10 ; John 16 : 2, 4, 25 ; I John 2 : 18 (twice) ; Rev. 14 : 15 ; in Mark 6 : 35, R.V., " day ; " in I Thess. 2 : 17, R.V., " a short (season)," lit., ' (the season, A.V., time) of an hour.' See HOUR.

B. Adverbs.

1. PŌPOTE (πώποτε), ever yet, is rendered " at any time " in John 1 : 18 ; 5 : 37 ; I John 4 : 12. For Luke 15 : 29 see Note (14) below. See NEVER.

2. ĒDĒ (ἤδη), already, now, is translated " by this time " in John 11 : 39. See ALREADY.

3. PALAI (πάλαι), long ago, of old, is rendered " of old time " in Heb. 1 : 1 (A.V., " in time past "). See OLD.

Notes : (1) In Luke 9 : 51 and Acts 8 : 1, A.V., hēmera, a day, is translated " time," in the former, plural, R.V., " the days ; " in Luke 23 : 7 (plural), R.V. " (in these) days," A.V., " (at that) time." (2) In I Tim. 6 : 19 the phrase eis to mellon, lit., ' unto the about-to-be,' i.e., ' for the impending (time),' is rendered " against the time to come." (3) In I Cor. 16 : 12, A.V., nun, " now " (R.V.), is rendered " at this time ; " in Acts 24 : 25, the phrase to nun echon, lit., ' the now having,' is rendered " at this time " (the verb is adjectival) ; the phrase is more expressive than the simple " now." Cp. heōs tou nun, " until now," Matt. 24 : 21 and Mark 13 : 19, R.V., A.V., " unto (this time)." (4) For polumerōs, strangely rendered " at sundry times," in Heb. 1 : 1, A.V., see PORTION, C. (5) For " long time," see LONG. (6) For " nothing . . . at any time," see NOTHING, Note (3). (7) For proskairos, rendered " for a time " in Mark 4 : 17, A.V., see SEASON, WHILE. (8) In Matt., apo tote, " from that time," lit., ' from then,' occurs thrice, 4 : 17 ; 16 : 21 ; 26 : 16 ; in Luke

16 : 16, R.V. (A.V., " since that time ") ; in John 6 : 66, A.V., " from that time " translates *ek toutou*, lit., ' from, or out of, this,' R.V., " upon this." (9) In Luke 4 : 27, the preposition *epi* signifies " in the time of." (10) For *genea*, rendered "times" in Acts 14 : 16, "time" in 15 : 21, see AGE, No. 2 (R.V., "generations"). (11) For "at every time," 2 Pet. 1 : 15, R.V., see ALWAYS, No. 2. (12) For " in time of need," Heb. 4 : 16, see CONVENIENT, and NEED, C, Note. (13) In Heb. 2 : 1, *pote* signifies " at any time ; " in 1 Pet. 3 : 5, " in the old time ; " in 2 Pet. 1 : 21, " in old time." See PAST. In the following where the A.V. has " sometimes " the R.V. has " once " in Eph. 2 : 13 and 5 : 8 ; " aforetime " in Tit. 3 : 3. (14) In Luke 15 : 29, A.V., " *oudepote* ," never, is rendered " neither . . . at any time " (R.V., " never "). (15) For *eukaireō*, to spend time, Acts 17 : 21, see SPEND, No. 10. (16) For *chronotribeō*, to spend time, see SPEND, No. 11. (17) For *prolegō*, rendered " told . . . in time past," in Gal. 5 : 21, A.V., see FOREWARN. (18) In Luke 12 : 1, " in the mean time " is a rendering of the phrase *en hois*, lit., ' in which (things or circumstances).' (19) In Rev. 5 : 11 there is no word representing " times : " see THOUSAND, Note (2). (20) In Gal. 4 : 2 *prothesmios* (in its feminine form, with *hēmera*, day, understood) is rendered " time appointed " (see APPOINT, No. 3 and Note, TERM).

For TINKLING see CLANGING

TIP

AKRON (ἄκρον), the top, an extremity, is translated " tip " in Luke 16 : 24. See END, C, Note (6), TOP.

For TITHES (Noun) see TENTH, No. 2

TITHE (Verb)

1. DEKATOŌ (δεκατόω), from *dekatos*, tenth, in the Active Voice denotes to take tithes of, Heb. 7:6, R.V., "hath taken (A.V., received) tithes;" in the Passive, to pay tithes, 7:9, R.V., "hath paid (A.V., payed) tithes."¶ In the Sept., Neh. 10:37.¶

2. APODEKATOŌ (ἀποδεκατόω) denotes (*a*) to tithe (*apo*, from, *dekatos*, tenth), Matt. 23:23 (A.V., "pay tithe of"); Luke 11:42; in Luke 18:12 (where the best texts have the alternative form *apodekateuō*), "I give tithes;" (*b*) to exact tithes from Heb. 7:5.¶

3. APODEKATEUŌ (ἀποδεκατεύω), to give tithes, in Luke 18:12 (some texts have No. 2).¶

Note: Heb. 7:4–9 shows the superiority of the Melchizedek priesthood to the Levitical, in that (1) Abraham, the ancestor of the Levites, paid tithes to Melchizedek (Gen. 14:20) ; (2) Melchizedek, whose genealogy is outside that of the Levites, took tithes of Abraham, the recipient himself of the Devine promises; (3) whereas death is the natural lot of those who receive tithes, the death of Melchizedek is not recorded ; (4) the Levites who received tithes virtually paid them through Abraham to Melchizedek.

TITLE

TITLOS (τίτλος), from Latin *titulus*, is used of the inscription above the Cross of Christ, John 19 : 19, 20. See SUPERSCRIPTION.¶

TITTLE

KERAIA or KEREA (κεραία), a little horn (*keras*, a horn), was used to denote the small stroke distinguishing one Hebrew letter from another. The Rabbis attached great importance to these ; hence the significance of the Lord's statements in Matt. 5 : 18 and Luke 16 : 17, charging the Pharisees with hypocrisy, because, while professing the most scrupulous reverence to the Law, they violated its spirit.

Grammarians used the word to denote the accents in Greek words.¶

For TO see † p. 9

TO-DAY, THIS DAY

SĒMERON (σήμερον), an adverb (the Attic form is *tēmeron*), akin to *hēmera*, a day, with the prefix *t* originally representing a pronoun. It is used frequently in Matthew, Luke and Acts ; in the last it is always rendered " this day ; " also in Heb. 1 : 5, and the R.V. of 5 : 5 (A.V., " to day ") in the same quotation ; "to-day" in 3 : 7, 13, 15 ; 4 : 7 (twice) ; 13 : 8 ; also Jas. 4 : 13.

The clause containing *sēmeron* is sometimes introduced by the conjunction *hoti*, ' that,' e.g., Mark 14 : 30 ; Luke 4 : 21 ; 19 : 9 ; sometimes without the conjunction, e.g., Luke 22 : 34 ; 23 : 43, where " today " is to be attached to the next statement, " shalt thou be with Me ; " there are no grammatical reasons for the insistence that the connection must be with the statement " Verily I say unto thee," nor is such an idea necessitated by examples from either the Sept. or the N.T. ; the connection given in the A.V. and R.V. is right.

In Rom. 11:8 and 2 Cor. 3:14, 15, the lit. rendering is 'unto the to-day day,' the emphasis being brought out by the R.V.," unto (until) this very day."

In Heb. 4:7, the "to-day" of Ps. 95:7 is evidently designed to extend to the present period of the Christian faith.

TOGETHER

1. HOMOU (ὁμοῦ), used in connection with place, in John 21:2; Acts 2:1 (in the best texts), R.V., "together" (A.V., "with one accord," translating the inferior reading *homothumadon*: see ACCORD, A), is used without the idea of place in John 4:36; 20:4.¶

2. HAMA (ἅμα), at once, is translated "together" in Rom. 3:12; 1 Thess. 4:17; 5:10. See EARLY, Note, WITHAL.

Notes: (1) For *pamplēthei*, Luke 23:18, R.V., see ONCE, Note. (2) In 1 Thess. 5:11, A.V., *allēlous*, "one another" (R.V.), is rendered

" yourselves together ; " in Luke 23 : 12, A.V., *meta allēlōn*, lit., with one another, is rendered " together " (R.V., " with each other ") ; so in Luke 24 : 14, A.V., *pros allēlous*, R.V., " with each other." (3) In the following, " together " translates the phrase *epi to auto*, lit., ' to (upon, or for) the same,' Matt. 22 : 34 ; Luke 17 : 35 ; Acts 1 : 15 ; 2 : 44 (3 : 1, in some texts) ; 4 : 26 ; 1 Cor. 7 : 5 ; 14 : 23, R.V. : see PLACE, A, Note (7). (4) In Acts 14 : 1, it translates *kata to auto*, ' at the same ; ' it may mean ' in the same way ' (i.e., as they had entered the synagogue at Pisidian Antioch). (5) In many cases " together " forms part of another word.

TOIL (Verb and Noun)
A. Verbs.

1. KOPIAŌ (κοπιάω), to be weary, to labour, is rendered to toil in Matt. 6 : 28 ; Luke 5 : 5 (12 : 27, in some mss.) ; in 1 Cor. 4 : 12, R.V. (A.V., " we labour "). See LABOUR.

2. BASANIZŌ (βασανίζω), primarily, to rub on the touchstone, to put to the test, then, to examine by torture (*basanos*, touchstone, torment), hence denotes to torture, torment, distress ; in the Passive Voice it is rendered " toiling " in Mark 6 : 48, A.V. (R.V., " distressed "). See PAIN, TORMENT, VEX.

B. Noun.

KOPOS (κόπος), labour, trouble, is rendered " toil " in Rev. 2 : 2, R.V. (A.V., " labour "). See LABOUR.

TOKEN

1. SĒMEION (σημεῖον), a sign, token or indication, is translated " token " in 2 Thess. 3 : 17, of writing of the closing salutations, the Apostle using the pen himself instead of his amanuensis, his autograph attesting the authenticity of his Epistles. See MIRACLE, SIGN.

2. SUSSĒMON (σύσσημον), a fixed sign or signal, agreed upon with others (*sun*, with), is used in Mark 14 : 44, " a token."¶ In the Sept., Judg. 20 : 38, 40 ; Is. 5 : 26 ; 49 : 22 ; 62 : 10.¶

3. ENDEIGMA (ἔνδειγμα), a plain token, a proof (akin to *endeiknumi*, to point out, prove), is used in. 2 Thess. 1 : 5, " a manifest token," said of the patient endurance and faith of the persecuted saints at Thessalonica, affording proof to themselves of their new life, and a guarantee of the vindication by God of both Himself and them (see No. 4, Note).¶

4. ENDEIXIS (ἔνδειξις), a pointing out, showing forth, is rendered " evident token " in Phil. 1 : 28. See DECLARE, B, PROOF. Cp. *apodeixis*, 1 Cor. 2 : 4.

Note : No. 4 refers to the act or process of proving, No. 3 to the thing proved. While the two passages, Phil. 1 : 28 and 2 Thess. 1 : 5, contain similar ideas, *endeigma* indicates the token as acknowledged by those referred to ; *endeixis* points more especially to the inherent veracity of the token.

TOLERABLE

ANEKTOS (ἀνεκτός) (akin to *anechō*, in the Middle Voice, to endure, see ENDURE, No. 5) is used in its comparative form, *anektoteros*, in Matt. 10 : 15 ; 11 : 22, 24 ; Luke 10 : 12, 14 ; some texts have it in Mark 6 : 11.¶

For TOLL see CUSTOM (Toll)

TOMB

1. MNĒMEION (μνημεῖον) is almost invariably rendered " tomb " or "tombs" in the R.V., never "grave," sometimes "sepulchre ; " in the A.V., "tomb" in Matt. 8 : 28 ; 27 : 60 ; Mark 5 : 2 ; 6 : 29. See GRAVE, No. 1, SEPULCHRE.

2. MNĒMA (μνῆμα), rendered "tombs" in Mark 5 : 3, 5 ; Luke 8 : 27 : see GRAVE, No. 2, SEPULCHRE.

3. TAPHOS (τάφος), akin to *thaptō*, to bury, is translated "tombs" in Matt. 23 : 29 ; elsewhere "sepulchre." See SEPULCHRE.

TO-MORROW

AURION (αὔριον) is used either without the article, e.g., Matt. 6 : 30 ; 1 Cor. 15 : 32 ; Jas. 4 : 13 ; or with the article in the feminine form, to agree with *hēmera*, day, e.g., Matt. 6 : 34 ; Acts 4 : 3, R.V., " the morrow " (A.V., " next day ") ; Jas. 4 : 14 ; preceded by *epi*, on, e.g., Luke 10 : 35 ; Acts 4 : 5.

TONGUE (–S)

A. Nouns.

1. GLŌSSA (γλῶσσα) is used of (1) the " tongues . . . like as of fire " which appeared at Pentecost ; (2) the tongue, as an organ of speech, e.g., Mark 7 : 33 ; Rom. 3 : 13 ; 14 : 11 ; 1 Cor. 14 : 9 ; Phil. 2 : 11 ; Jas. 1 : 26 ; 3 : 5, 6, 8 ; 1 Pet. 3 : 10 ; 1 John 3 : 18 ; Rev. 16 : 10 ; (3) (*a*) a language, coupled with *phulē*, a tribe, *laos*, a people, *ethnos*, a nation, seven times in the Apocalypse, 5 : 9 ; 7 : 9 ; 10 : 11 ; 11 : 9 ; 13 : 7 ; 14 : 6 ; 17 : 15 ; (*b*) the supernatural gift of speaking in another language without its having been learnt ; in Acts 2 : 4–13 the circumstances are recorded from the view-point of the hearers ; to those in whose language the utterances were made it appeared as a supernatural phenomenon ; to others, the stammering of drunkards ; what was uttered was not addressed primarily to the audience but consisted in recounting " the mighty works of God ; " cp. 2 : 46 ; in 1 Cor., chapters 12 and 14, the use of the gift of tongues is mentioned as exercised in the gatherings of local churches ; 12 : 10 speaks of the gift in general terms, and couples with it that of " the interpretation of tongues ; " chapt. 14 gives instruction concerning the use of the gift, the paramount object being the edification

of the church ; unless the tongue was interpreted the speaker would speak " not unto men, but unto God," ver. 2 ; he would edify himself alone, ver. 4, unless he interpreted, ver. 5, in which case his interpretation would be of the same value as the superior gift of prophesying, as he would edify the church, vv. 4–6 ; he must pray that he may interpret, ver. 13 ; if there were no interpreter, he must keep silence, ver. 28, for all things were to be done " unto edifying," ver. 26. " If I come . . . speaking with tongues, what shall I profit you," says the Apostle (expressing the great object in all oral ministry), " unless I speak to you either by way of revelation, or of knowledge, or of prophesying, or of teaching ? " (ver. 6). Tongues were for a sign, not to believers, but to unbelievers, ver. 22, and especially to unbelieving Jews (see ver. 21) : cp. the passages in the Acts.

There is no evidence of the continuance of this gift after Apostolic times nor indeed in the later times of the Apostles themselves ; this provides confirmation of the fulfilment in this way of 1 Cor. 13 : 8, that this gift would cease in the churches, just as would " prophecies " and " knowledge " in the sense of knowledge received by immediate super-natural power (cp. 14 : 6). The completion of the Holy Scriptures has provided the churches with all that is necessary for individual and collective guidance, instruction, and edification.

2. DIALEKTOS (διάλεκτος), language (Eng., dialect), is rendered " tongue " in the A.V. of Acts 1 : 19 ; 2 : 6, 8 ; 21 : 40 ; 22 : 2 ; 26 : 14. See LANGUAGE.¶

B. Adjective.

HETEROGLŌSSOS (ἑτερόγλωσσος) is rendered " strange tongues " in 1 Cor. 14 : 21, R.V. (heteros, another of a different sort—see ANOTHER— and A, No. 1), A.V., " other tongues."¶

C. Adverb.

HEBRAISTI (or EBRAISTI, Westcott and Hort) (Ἑβραϊστί) denotes (a) " in Hebrew," Rev. 9 : 11, R.V. (A.V., " in the Hebrew tongue ") ; so 16 : 16 ; (b) in the Aramaic vernacular of Palestine, John 5 : 2, A.V., " in the Hebrew tongue " (R.V., " in Hebrew ") ; in 19 : 13, 17, A.V., " in the Hebrew " (R.V., " in Hebrew ") ; in ver. 20, A.V. and R.V., " in Hebrew ; " in 20 : 16, R.V. only, " in Hebrew (Rabboni)."¶

Note : Cp. Hellēnisti, " in Greek," John 19 : 20, R.V. ; Acts 21 : 37, " Greek."¶ See also Rhōmaisti, under LATIN.

TOOTH, TEETH

ODOUS (ὀδούς) is used in the sing. in Matt. 5 : 38 (twice) ; elsewhere in the plural, of the gnashing of teeth, the gnashing being expressive of anguish and indignation, Matt. 8 : 12 ; 13 : 42, 50 ; 22 : 13 ; 24 : 51 ; 25 : 30 ; Mark 9 : 18 ; Luke 13 : 28 ; Acts 7 : 54 ; in Rev. 9 : 8, of the beings seen in a vision and described as locusts.¶

TOP
A. Noun.

AKRON (ἄκρον), for which see TIP, is used of Jacob's staff, Heb. 11 : 21.

B. Phrases.

Note : In Matt. 27 : 51 and Mark 15 : 38, *apo anōthen*, " from the top " (lit., ' from above '), is used of the upper part of the Temple veil. In John 19 : 23, the different phrase *ek tōn anōthen* is used of the weaving of the Lord's garment (the *chitōn* : see CLOTHING), lit., ' from the parts above.'

TOPAZ

TOPAZION (τοπάζιον) is mentioned in Rev. 21 : 20, as the ninth of the foundation stones of the wall of the Heavenly Jerusalem ; the stone is of a yellow colour (though there are topazes of other colours) and is almost as hard as the diamond. It has the power of double refraction, and when heated or rubbed becomes electric.¶ In the Sept., Ex. 28 : 17 ; 39 : 10 ; Job 28 : 19 ; Ps. 119 : 127, " (gold and) topaz " ; Ezek. 28 : 13.¶

TORCH

LAMPAS (λαμπάς), a torch, is used in the plur. and translated "torches" in John 18 : 3 ; in Rev. 8 : 10, R.V., " torch " (A.V., " lamp "). See LAMP.

TORMENT (Noun and Verb)
A. Nouns.

1. BASANISMOS (βασανισμός), akin to *basanizō* (see TOIL, No. 2), is used of Divine judgments in Rev. 9 : 5 ; 14 : 11 ; 18 : 7, 10, 15.¶

2. BASANOS (βάσανος), primarily a touchstone, employed in testing metals, hence, torment, is used (*a*) of physical diseases, Matt. 4 : 24 ; (*b*) of a condition of retribution in Hades, Luke 16 : 23, 28.¶

Note : In 1 John 4 : 18, A.V., *kolasis*, " punishment " (R.V.), is rendered "torment." See PUNISHMENT, No. 3.

B. Verbs.

1. BASANIZŌ (βασανίζω), for which see TOIL, No. 2, is translated to torment, (*a*) of sickness, Matt. 8 : 6 ; (*b*) of the doom of evil spirits, Mark 5 : 7 ; Luke 8 : 28 ; (*c*) of retributive judgments upon impenitent mankind at the close of this age, Rev. 9 : 5 ; 11 : 10 ; (*d*) upon those who worship the Beast and his image and receive the mark of his name, 14 : 10 ; (*e*) of the doom of Satan and his agents, 20 : 10.

2. KAKOUCHEŌ (κακουχέω), to treat evilly, in the Passive Voice is translated " tormented " in Heb. 11 : 37, A.V. (R.V., " evil entreated "). See SUFFER, No. 6.

3. ODUNAŌ (ὀδυνάω), for which see ANGUISH, B, No. 3, in the Passive Voice is rendered " I am (thou art) tormented " in Luke 16 : 24, 25, A.V.

TORMENTOR

BASANISTĒS (βασανιστής), properly, a torturer (akin to *basanizō*, see TORMENT, B), one who elicits information by torture, is used of jailors, Matt. 18 : 34.¶

TORTURE (Verb)

TUMPANIZŌ (τυμπανίζω) primarily denotes to beat a drum (*tumpanon*, a kettle-drum, Eng., tympanal, tympanitis, tympanum), hence, to torture by beating, to beat to death, Heb. 11 : 35.¶ In the Sept., 1 Sam. 21 : 13, "(David) drummed (upon the doors of the city)."¶ The tympanum as an instrument of torture seems to have been a wheel-shaped frame upon which criminals were stretched and beaten with clubs or thongs.

TOSS

1. RHIPIZŌ (ῥιπίζω), primarily to fan a fire (*rhipis*, a fan, cp. *rhipē*, twinkling), then, to make a breeze, is used in the Passive Voice in Jas. 1 : 6, " tossed," of the raising of waves by the wind.¶

2. KLUDŌNIZOMAI (κλυδωνίζομαι) signifies to be tossed by billows (*kludōn*, a billow) ; metaphorically, in Eph. 4 : 14, of an unsettled condition of mind influenced and agitated by one false teaching and another, and characterized by that immaturity which lacks the firm conviction begotten by the truth.¶ In the Sept., Isa. 57 : 20.¶

Note : For " being . . . tossed," Acts 27 : 18, see LABOUR, B, No. 2.

TOUCH (Verb)

1. HAPTŌ (ἅπτω), primarily, to fasten to, hence, of fire, to kindle, denotes, in the Middle Voice (*a*) to touch, e.g., Matt. 8 : 3, 15 ; 9 : 20, 21, 29 ; (*b*) to cling to, lay hold of, John 20 : 17 ; here the Lord's prohibition as to clinging to Him was indicative of the fact that communion with Him would, after His ascension, be by faith, through the Spirit ; (*c*) to have carnal intercourse with a woman, 1 Cor. 7 : 1 ; (*d*) to have fellowship and association with unbelievers, 2 Cor. 6 : 17 ; (*e*) (negatively) to adhere to certain Levitical and ceremonial ordinances, in order to avoid contracting external defilement, or to practise rigorous asceticism, all such abstentions being of " no value against the indulgence of the flesh," Col. 2 : 21, A.V. (R.V., " handle ") ; (*f*) to assault, in order to sever the vital union between Christ and the believer, said of the attack of the Evil One, 1 John 5 : 18. See HANDLE, No. 2, KINDLE, LIGHT.

2. THINGANŌ (θιγγάνω), to touch, a lighter term than No. 1, though Heb. 11 : 28 approximates to it, in expressing the action of the Destroyer of the Egyptian firstborn ; in Heb. 12 : 20 it signifies to touch, and is not to be interpreted by Ps. 104 : 32, " He toucheth (No. 1 in the Sept.) the hills and they smoke ; " in Col. 2 : 21, R.V. (A.V., " handle "). See HANDLE, No. 2.¶

3. PROSPSAUŌ (προσψαύω), to touch upon, to touch slightly, occurs in Luke 11 : 46.¶

4. PSĒLAPHAŌ (ψηλαφάω), to feel, to handle, is rendered " that might be touched " in Heb. 12 : 18. See FEEL, No. 3, HANDLE, No. 1.

5 KATAGŌ (κατάγω), to bring down, is used of bringing a ship to land in Acts 27 3. See BRING No. 16.

6. SUMPAΓHEŌ συμπαθέω), for which see COMPASSION, A, No. 3, is rendered   be touched with " in Heb. 4 : 15.

7. PARABALLŌ (παραβάλλω), for which see ARRIVE, No. 4, COMPARE, No. 2, is rendered " touched at " in Acts 20 : 15, R.V.

For TOUCHING (Preposition) see † p. 9

For TOWARD (Preposition), see † p. 9

TOWEL

LENTION (λέντιον) denotes a linen cloth or towel (Lat., *linteum*), as used by the Lord, John 13 : 4, 5 ; it was commonly used by servants in a household.¶

TOWER

PURGOS (πύργος) is used of a watch-tower in a vineyard, Matt. 21 : 33 ; Mark 12 : 1 ; probably, too, in Luke 14 : 28 (cp. Is. 5 : 2) ; in Luke 13 : 4, of the tower in Siloam, the modern Silwan, which is built on a steep escarpment of rock.¶

TOWN

1. KŌMOPOLIS (κωμόπολις) denotes a country town, Mark 1 : 38, a large village usually without walls.¶

2. KŌMĒ (κώμη), a village, or country town without walls. The R.V. always renders this " village " or " villages," A.V., " town " or " towns," Matt. 10 : 11 ; Mark 8 : 23, 26 (twice), 27 ; Luke 5 : 17; 9 : 6, 12 ; John 7 : 42 ; 11 : 1, 30. See VILLAGE.

TOWNCLERK

GRAMMATEUS (γραμματεύς), a writer, scribe, is used in Acts 19 : 35 of a state clerk, an important official, variously designated, according to inscriptions found in Græco-Asiatic cities. He was responsible for the form of decrees first approved by the Senate, then sent for approval in the popular assembly, in which he often presided. The decrees having been passed, he sealed them with the public seal in the presence of witnesses. Such an assembly frequently met in the theatre. The Roman administration viewed any irregular or unruly assembly as a grave and even capital offence, as tending to strengthen among the people the consciousness of their power and the desire to exercise it. In the circumstances at Ephesus the townclerk feared that he might himself be held responsible for the irregular gathering. See SCRIBE.

TRACE
A. Verb.

PARAKOLOUTHEŌ (παρακολουθέω), to follow up, is used of investigating or tracing a course of events, Luke 1 : 3, where the writer, humbly differentiating himself from those who possessed an essential apostolic qualification, declares that he " traced the course of all things " (R.V.) about which he was writing (A.V., " having had . . . understanding, etc."). See FOLLOW, No. 5.

B. Adjective.

ANEXICHNIASTOS (ἀνεξιχνίαστος) signifies ' that cannot be traced out' (a, negative, ex, for ek, out, ichnos, a track), is rendered " past tracing out " in Rom. 11 : 33, R.V. (A.V., " past finding out "); in Eph. 3 : 8, " unsearchable." See FIND, Note (3), UNSEARCHABLE.¶ In the Sept., Job 5 : 9; 9 : 10; 34 : 24.¶

TRADE (Noun and Verb)
A. Verbs.

1. ERGAZOMAI (ἐργάζομαι), to work, is rendered " traded " in Matt. 25 : 16; in Rev. 18 : 17, A.V., " trade," R.V., " gain their living." See COMMIT, DO, LABOUR, B, Note (1), MINISTER, WORK.

2. PRAGMATEUOMAI (πραγματεύομαι) is rendered " trade ye " in Luke 19 : 13, R.V., which adds " *herewith* : " see OCCUPY.¶

3. DIAPRAGMATEUOMAI (διαπραγματεύομαι), to accomplish by traffic, to gain by trading, occurs in Luke 19 : 15.¶

4. EMPOREUOMAI (ἐμπορεύομαι) is rendered " trade " in Jas. 4 : 13, R.V.: see BUY, Note, MERCHANDISE, B.

B. Nouns.

1. TECHNĒ (τέχνη), an art (Eng., technique, technical), is used in Acts 18 : 3 (2nd part) of a " trade," R.V. (A.V., " occupation "). For the 1st part see Note below. See ART.

2. MEROS (μέρος), a portion, is used of a trade in Acts 19 : 27. See CRAFT, No. 5.

Note : For the adjective *homotechnos*, " of the same trade," Acts 18 : 3, 1st part, R.V., see CRAFT, No. 4.¶

TRADITION

PARADOSIS (παράδοσις), a handing down or on (akin to *paradidōmi*, to hand over, deliver), denotes a tradition, and hence, by metonymy, (a) the teachings of the Rabbis, interpretations of the Law, which was thereby made void in practice, Matt. 15 : 2, 3, 6; Mark 7 : 3, 5, 8, 9, 13; Gal. 1 : 14; Col. 2 : 8; (b) of apostolic teaching, 1 Cor. 11 : 2, R.V., " traditions " (A.V., " ordinances "), of instructions concerning the gatherings of believers (instructions of wider scope than ordinances in the limited sense) ; in 2 Thess. 2 : 15, of Christian doctrine in general, where the Apostle's use of the word constitutes a denial that what he preached originated with himself, and a claim for its Divine authority (cp. *paralambanō*, to receive, I Cor. 11 : 23 ; 15 : 3) ; in 2 Thess. 3 : 6, it is used of instructions concerning everyday conduct.¶

For TRAIN, Tit. 2 : 4, R.V., see SOBER, B, No. 3

TRAITOR

PRODOTĒS (προδότης) denotes a betrayer, traitor ; the latter term is assigned to Judas, virtually as a title, in Luke 6 : 16 ; in 2 Tim. 3 : 4 it occurs in a list of evil characters, foretold as abounding in the last days. See BETRAY, B.

TRAMPLE

KATAPATEŌ (καταπατέω), to tread down, trample under foot, is rendered "trample" in Matt. 7 : 6. See TREAD, No. 2.

TRANCE

EKSTASIS (ἔκστασις), for which see AMAZE, A, No. I, denotes a trance in Acts 10 : 10 ; 11 : 5 ; 22 : 17, a condition in which ordinary consciousness and the perception of natural circumstances were withheld, and the soul was susceptible only to the vision imparted by God.

For TRANQUIL, I Tim. 2 : 2, R.V., see QUIET, No. I

For TRANSFER (in a figure) see FASHION, C, No. I, and FIGURE, Note (2).

TRANSFIGURE

METAMORPHOŌ (μεταμορφόω), to change into another form (*meta*, implying change, and *morphē*, form : see FORM, No. I), is used in the Passive Voice (*a*) of Christ's transfiguration, Matt. 17 : 2 ; Mark 9 : 2 ; Luke (in 9 : 29) avoids this term, which might have suggested to Gentile readers the metamorphoses of heathen gods, and uses the phrase *egeneto heteron*, "was altered", lit., 'became (*ginomai*) different (*heteros*) ;' (*b*) of believers, Rom. 12 : 2, "be ye transformed," the obligation being to undergo a complete change which, under the power of God, will find expression in character and conduct ; *morphē* lays stress on the inward change, *schēma* (see the preceding verb in that verse, *suschēmatizō*) lays stress on the outward (see FASHION, No. 3, FORM, No. 2) ; the present continuous tenses indicate a process ; 2 Cor. 3 : 18 describes believers as being "transformed (R.V.) into the same image" (i.e., of Christ in all His moral excellencies), the change being effected by the Holy Spirit.¶

TRANSFORM

1. METAMORPHOŌ (μεταμορφόω) is rendered "transformed" in Rom. 12 : 2 : see TRANSFIGURE.

2. METASCHĒMATIZŌ (μετασχηματίζω) in the Passive Voice is rendered to be transformed in the A.V. of 2 Cor. 11 : 13, 14, 15 : see FASHION, C, No. 1.

TRANSGRESS, TRANSGRESSION
A. Verbs.

1. PARABAINŌ (παραβαίνω), lit., to go aside (*para*), hence to go beyond, is chiefly used metaphorically of transgressing the tradition of the elders, Matt. 15 : 2 ; the commandment of God, 15 : 3 ; in Acts 1 : 25, of Judas, A.V., " by transgression fell " (R.V., " fell away ") ; in 2 John 9 some texts have this verb (A.V., " transgresseth "), the best have *proagō* (see GO, No. 10).¶

2. HUPERBAINŌ (ὑπερβαίνω), lit., to go over (*huper*), used metaphorically and rendered " transgress " in 1 Thess. 4 : 6 (A.V., " go beyond "), i.e., of overstepping the limits separating chastity from licentiousness, sanctification from sin.¶.

3. PARERCHOMAI (παρέρχομαι), to come by (*para*, by, *erchomai*, to come), pass over, and hence, metaphorically, to transgress, is so used in Luke 15 : 29. See COME, No. 9, PASS.

B. Nouns.

1. PARABASIS (παράβασις), akin to A, No. 1, primarily a going aside, then, an overstepping, is used metaphorically to denote transgression (always of a breach of law) : (*a*) of Adam, Rom. 5 : 14 ; (*b*) of Eve, 1 Tim. 2 : 14 ; (*c*) negatively, where there is no law, since transgression implies the violation of law, none having been enacted between Adam's transgression and those under the Law, Rom. 4 : 15 ; (*d*) of transgressions of the Law, Gal. 3 : 19, where the statement " it was added because of transgressions " is best understood according to Rom. 4 : 15 ; 5 : 13 and 5 : 20 ; the Law does not make men sinners, but makes them transgressors ; hence sin becomes " exceeding sinful," Rom. 7 : 7, 13. Conscience thus had a standard external to itself ; by the Law men are taught their inability to yield complete obedience to God, that thereby they may become convinced of their need of a Saviour ; in Rom. 2 : 23, R.V., " transgréssion (of the Law)," A.V., " breaking (the Law) ; " Heb. 2 : 2 ; 9 : 15.¶

2. PARANOMIA (παρανομία), law-breaking (*para*, contrary to, *nomos*, law), is rendered " transgression " in 2 Pet. 2 : 16, R.V. (A.V., " iniquity ").¶

Note : In 1 John 3 : 4 (1st part), A.V., *poieō*, to do, with *anomia*, lawlessness, is rendered " transgresseth . . . the law " (R.V., " doeth . . . lawlessness ") ; in the 2nd part *anomia* alone is rendered " transgression of the law," A.V. (R.V., " lawlessness ").

TRANSGRESSOR

1. PARABATĒS (παραβάτης), lit. and primarily, one who stands beside, then, one who oversteps the prescribed limit, a transgressor (akin to *parabainō*, to transgress, see above) ; so Rom. 2 : 25, R.V. (A.V., " a breaker ") ; ver. 27, R.V., " a transgressor " (A.V., " dost transgress ") ; Gal. 2 : 18 ; Jas. 2 : 9, 11.¶

Note : *Hamartōlos,* a sinner, one who misses the mark, is applicable to all men without distinction ; *parabatēs* stresses the positive side of sin, and is applicable to those who received the Law.

2. ANOMOS (ἄνομος), without law (*a* –, negative), is translated " transgressors " in Luke 22 : 37 (in some texts, Mark 15 : 28), in a quotation from Isa. 53 : 12. See LAW, C, No. 3, LAWLESS, A.

TRANSLATE, TRANSLATION
A. Verbs.

1. METHISTĒMI or METHISTANŌ (μεθίστημι), to change, remove (*meta,* implying change, *histēmi,* to cause to stand), is rendered " hath translated " in Col. 1 : 13. See PUT, REMOVE, TURN (away).

2. METATITHĒMI (μετατίθημι), to transfer to another place (*meta,* see above, *tithēmi,* to put), is rendered to translate in Heb. 11 . 5 (twice). See CARRY, CHANGE, REMOVE, TURN.

B. Noun.

METATHESIS (μετάθεσις), a change of position (akin to A, No. 2), is rendered " translation " in Heb. 11 : 5. See CHANGE, REMOVING.

For TRANSPARENT, Rev. 21 : 21, see DAWN, A, No. 2, Note

TRAP

THĒRA (θήρα) denotes a hunting, chase, then, a prey ; hence, figuratively, of preparing destruction by a net or " trap," Rom. 11 : 9.¶

TRAVAIL (Noun and Verb)
A. Nouns.

1. MOCHTHOS (μόχθος), labour, involving painful effort, is rendered " travail " in 2 Cor. 11 : 27, R.V. (A.V., " painfulness ") ; in 1 Thess. 2 : 9 and 2 Thess. 3 : 8 it stresses the toil involved in the work.¶

2. ŌDIN (ὠδίν), a birth pang, travail pain, is used illustratively in 1 Thess. 5 : 3 of the calamities which are to come upon men at the beginning of the Day of the Lord ; the figure used suggests the inevitableness of the catastrophe. See PAIN, No. 2, SORROW.

B. Verbs.

1. ŌDINŌ (ὠδίνω), akin to A, No. 2, is used negatively in Gal. 4 : 27, " (thou) that travailest (not)," quoted from Isa. 54 : 1 ; the Apostle applies the circumstances of Sarah and Hagar (which doubtless Isaiah **was** recalling) to show that, whereas the promise by grace had temporarily

been replaced by the works of the Law (see Gal. 3 : 17), this was now reversed, and, in the fulfilment of the promise to Abraham, the number of those saved by the Gospel would far exceed those who owned allegiance to the Law. Isa. 54 has primary reference to the future prosperity of Israel restored to God's favour, but frequently the principles underlying events recorded in the O.T. extend beyond their immediate application.

In 4 : 19 the Apostle uses it metaphorically of a second travailing on his part regarding the churches of Galatia ; his first was for their deliverance from idolatry (ver. 8), now it was for their deliverance from bondage to Judaism. There is no suggestion here of a second re-generation necessitated by defection. There is a hint of reproach, as if he was enquiring whether they had ever heard of a mother experiencing second birthpangs for her children.

In Rev. 12 : 2 the woman is figurative of Israel ; the circumstances of her birth-pangs are mentioned in Isa. 66 : 7 (see also Micah 5 : 2, 3). Historically the natural order is reversed. The Man-child, Christ, was brought forth at His first Advent ; the travail is destined to take place in " the time of Jacob's trouble," the " great tribulation," Matt. 24 : 21 ; Rev. 7 : 14. The object in 12 : 2 in referring to the Birth of Christ is to connect Him with His earthly people Israel in their future time of trouble, from which the godly remnant, the nucleus of the restored nation, is to be delivered (Jer. 30 : 7).¶

2. SUNŌDINŌ (συνωδίνω), to be in travail together, is used meta-phorically in Rom. 8 : 22, of the whole creation.¶

3. TIKTO (τίκτω), to beget, is rendered " travail " in John 16 : 21.

For TRAVEL (companions in), Acts 19 : 29, and TRAVEL WITH, 2 Cor. 8 : 19, see COMPANION, No. 1.

TRAVEL

DIERCHOMAI (διέρχομαι), to go or pass through, is translated " travelled " in Acts 11 : 19. See COME, No. 5.

Note : For *apodēmeō*, rendered " travelling " in Matt. 25 : 14, A.V., see GO, No. 27.

TREAD, TRODE, TRODDEN

1. PATEŌ (πατέω) is used (*a*) intransitively and figuratively, of treading upon serpents, Luke 10 : 19 ; (*b*) transitively, of treading on, down or under, of the desecration of Jerusalem by its foes, Luke 21 : 24 ; Rev. 11 : 2 ; of the avenging, by the Lord in Person hereafter, of this desecration and of the persecution of the Jews, in Divine retribution, metaphorically spoken of as the treading of the winepress of God's wrath, Rev. 14 : 20 ; 19 : 15 (cp. Isa. 63 : 2, 3).¶

2. KATAPATEŌ (καταπατέω), to tread down, trample under foot, is used (*a*) literally, Matt. 5 : 13 ; 7 : 6 ; Luke 8 : 5 ; 12 : 1 ; (*b*) meta

phorically, of 'treading under foot' the Son of God, Heb. 10 : 29, i.e., turning away from Him, to indulge in wilful sin.¶

For TREADING out the corn, see THRESH

TREASURE (Noun and Verb)
A. Nouns.

1. THĒSAUROS (θησαυρός) denotes (1) a place of safe keeping (possibly akin to *tithēmi*, to put), (*a*) a casket, Matt. 2 : 11 ; (*b*) a store-house, Matt. 13 : 52 ; used metaphorically of the heart, Matt. 12 : 35, twice (R.V., "out of his treasure") ; Luke 6 : 45 ; (2) a treasure, Matt. 6 : 19, 20, 21 ; 13 : 44 ; Luke 12 : 33, 34 ; Heb. 11 : 26 ; treasure (in heaven or the heavens), Matt. 19 : 21 ; Mark 10 : 21 ; Luke 18 : 22 ; in these expressions (which are virtually equivalent to that in Matt. 6 : 1, "with your Father which is in Heaven") the promise does not simply refer to the present life, but looks likewise to the hereafter ; in 2 Cor. 4 : 7 it is used of "the light of the knowledge of the glory of God in the face of Jesus Christ," descriptive of the Gospel, as deposited in the earthen vessels of the persons who proclaim it (cp. ver. 4) ; in Col. 2 : 3, of the wisdom and knowledge hidden in Christ.¶

2. GAZA (γάζα), a Persian word, signifying royal treasure, occurs in Acts 8 : 27.¶

B. Verb.

THĒSAURIZŌ (θησαυρίζω), akin to A, No. 1, is used metaphorically in Rom. 2 : 5 of treasuring up wrath. See LAY, No. 17.

For TREASURER see CHAMBERLAIN, Note

TREASURY

1. GAZOPHULAKION (γαζοφυλάκιον), from *gaza*, a treasure, *phulakē*, a guard, is used by Josephus for a special room in the women's court in the Temple in which gold and silver bullion was kept. This seems to be referred to in John 8 : 20 ; in Mark 12 : 41 (twice), 43 and Luke 21 : 1 it is used of the trumpet-shaped or ram's-horn-shaped chests, into which the temple-offerings of the people were cast. There were 13 chests, six for such gifts in general, seven for distinct purposes.¶

2. KORBANAS (κορβανᾶς), signifying the place of gifts, denoted the Temple treasury, Matt. 27 : 6. See CORBAN.¶

For TREATED, Acts 27 : 3, R.V., see ENTREAT (to deal with)

TREATISE

LOGOS (λόγος), a word, denotes a treatise or written narrative in Acts 1 : 1. See WORD.

TREE

1. DENDRON (δένδρον), a living, growing tree (cp. Eng., rhodo-dendron, lit., rose-tree), known by the fruit it produces, Matt. 12 : 33 ; Luke 6 : 44 ; certain qualities are mentioned in the N.T. ; " a good tree," Matt. 7 : 17, 18 ; 12 : 33 ; Luke 6 : 43 ; " a corrupt tree " (ditto) ; in Jude 12, metaphorically, of evil teachers, " autumn trees (A.V., trees whose fruit withereth) without fruit, twice dead, plucked up by the roots," R.V. ; in Luke 13 : 19 in some texts, " a great tree," A.V. (R.V., " a tree ") ; for this and Matt. 13 : 32 see MUSTARD ; in Luke 21 : 29 the fig tree is illustrative of Israel, " all the trees " indicating Gentile nations.

2. XULON (ξύλον) wood, a piece of wood, anything made of wood (see STAFF, STOCKS), is used, with the rendering " tree," (a) in Luke 23 : 31, where " the green tree " refers either to Christ, figuratively of all His living power and excellencies, or to the life of the Jewish people while still inhabiting their land, in contrast to " the dry," a figure fulfilled in the horrors of the Roman massacre and devastation in A.D. 70 (cp. the Lord's parable in Luke 13 : 6-9 ; see Ezek. 20 : 47, and cp. 21 : 3) ; (b) of the Cross, the tree being the *stauros*, the upright pale or stake to which Romans nailed those who were thus to be executed, Acts 5 : 30 ; 10 : 39 ; 13 : 29 ; Gal. 3 : 13 ; 1 Pet. 2 : 24 ; (c) of the tree of life, Rev. 2 : 7 ; 22 : 2 (twice), 14, 19, R.V., A.V., " book." See WOOD.

TREMBLE, TREMBLING
A. Verbs.

1. TREMŌ (τρέμω), to tremble, especially with fear, is used in Mark 5 : 33 ; Luke 8 : 47 (Acts 9 : 6, in some mss.) ; 2 Pet. 2 : 10, R.V.," they tremble (not)," A.V., " they are (not) afraid."¶

2. SEIŌ (σείω), to move to and fro, shake, is rendered " will I make to tremble " in Heb. 12 : 26, R.V. (A.V., " I shake "). See QUAKE, SHAKE.

Notes : (1) For *phrissō* in Jas. 2 : 19, A.V., " tremble," see SHUDDER. (2) For the adjective *entromos*, trembling, Acts 7 : 32 ; 16 : 29, R.V., " trembling for fear," see QUAKE, No. 1. (3) The adjective *emphobos*, used with *ginomai*, to become, is rendered " trembled " in Acts 24 : 25 (R.V., " was terrified ") ; in Luke 24 : 5, R.V., " they were affrighted," A.V., " they were afraid." See AFFRIGHTED, A.

B. Noun.

TROMOS (τρόμος), a trembling (akin to A, No. 1), occurs in Mark 16 : 8, R.V., " trembling (. . . had come upon them) ;" 1 Cor. 2 : 3 ; 2 Cor. 7 : 15 ; Eph. 6 : 5 ; Phil. 2 : 12.¶

TRENCH

CHARAX (χάραξ), primarily a pointed stake, hence, a palisade or rampart, is rendered " trench " in Luke 19 : 43, A.V. (R.V., " bank," marg., " palisade "). In A.D. 70, Titus, the Roman general, surrounded Jerusalem with a palisaded mound (Tyndale, *l.c.*, renders it " mound ").

The Jews in one of their sorties destroyed this *charax*, after which Titus surrounded the city with a wall of masonry.¶

TRESPASS (Noun and Verb)
A. Noun.

PARAPTŌMA (παράπτωμα), primarily a false step, a blunder (akin to *parapiptō*, to fall away, Heb. 6 : 6), lit., 'a fall beside,' used ethically, denotes a trespass, a deviation, from uprightness and truth, Matt. 6 : 14, 15 (twice) ; 18 : 35, in some mss. ; Mark 11 : 25, 26 ; in Romans the R.V. substitutes " trespass " and " trespasses " for A.V., " offence " and " offences," 4 : 25, " for (i.e., because of) our trespasses ; " 5 : 15 (twice), where the trespass is that of Adam (in contrast to the free gift of righteousness, ver. 17, a contrast in the nature and the effects) ; 5 : 16, where " of many trespasses " expresses a contrast of quantity ; the condemnation resulted from one trespass, the free gift is " of (*ek*, expressing the origin, and throwing stress upon God's justifying grace in Christ) many trespasses ; " ver. 17, introducing a contrast between legal effects and those of Divine grace ; ver. 18, where the R.V., " through one trespass," is contrasted with " one act of righteousness ; " this is important, the difference is not between one man's trespass and Christ's righteousness (as A.V.), but between two acts, that of Adam's trespass and the vicarious Death of Christ ; ver. 20 [cp. TRANSGRESSION, B, No. 1 (*d*)] ; in 2 Cor. 5 : 19, A.V. and R.V., " trespasses ; " in Eph. 1 : 7, R.V., " trespasses " (A.V., " sins ") ; in 2 : 1, R.V., " (dead through your) trespasses," A.V., " (dead in) trespasses ; " 2 : 5, R.V., " (dead through our) trespasses," A.V., " (dead in) sins ; " so Col 2 : 13 (1st part) ; in the 2nd part, A.V. and R.V., " trespasses."

In Gal. 6 : 1, R.V., " (in any) trespass " (A.V., " fault "), the reference is to " the works of the flesh " (5 : 19), and the thought is that of the believer's being found off his guard, the trespass taking advantage of him ; in Jas. 5 : 16, A.V., " faults " (R.V., " sins " translates the word *hamartias*, which is found in the best texts), auricular confession to a priest is not in view here or anywhere else in Scripture ; the command is comprehensive, and speaks either of the acknowledgment of sin where one has wronged another, or of the unburdening of a troubled conscience to a godly brother whose prayers will be efficacious, or of open confession before the church.

In Rom. 11 : 11, 12, the word is used of Israel's " fall," i.e., their deviation from obedience to God and from the fulfilment of His will (to be distinguished from the verb *ptaiō*, " fall," in the 1st part of ver. 11, which indicates the impossibility of recovery). See FALL, A, No. 2.¶

B. Verb.

HAMARTANŌ (ἁμαρτάνω) to sin, is translated to trespass, in the A.V. of Matt. 18 : 15, and Luke 17 : 3, 4 (R.V., to sin).

Note : For the different meanings of words describing sin, see SIN.

Paraptōma, and *hamartēma* (a sinful deed) are closely associated, with regard to their primary meanings : *parabasis* seems to be a stronger term, as the breach of a known law (see TRANSGRESSION).

TRIAL

1. DOKIMĒ (δοκιμή), for which see EXPERIENCE, No. 2, is rendered " trial " in 2 Cor. 8 : 2, A.V. (R.V., " proof ").

2. PEIRA (πεῖρα), a making trial, an experiment, is used with *lambanō*, to receive or take, in Heb. 11 : 29, rendered " assaying," and ver. 36, in the sense of ' having experience of ' (akin to *peiraō*, to assay, to try), " had trial."¶ In the Sept., Deut. 28 : 56.¶

3. PEIRASMOS (πειρασμός), akin to No. 2, is rendered " trials " in Acts 20 : 19, R.V. See TEMPTATION.

4. PURŌSIS (πύρωσις), akin to *puroō*, to set on fire, signifies (*a*) a burning ; (*b*) a refining, metaphorically in 1 Pet. 4 : 12, " fiery trial," or rather ' trial by fire,' referring to the refining of gold (1 : 7). See BURNING.

Note : For *dokimion*, rendered " trial " in 1 Pet. 1 : 7, A.V., see PROOF, No. 2.

TRIBE (–S)

1. PHULĒ (φυλή), a company of people united by kinship or habitation, a clan, tribe, is used (*a*) of the peoples of the earth, Matt. 24 : 30 ; in the following the R.V. has " tribe(–s) " for A.V., " kindred(–s)," Rev. 1 : 7 ; 5 : 9 ; 7 : 9 ; 11 : 9 ; 13 : 7 ; 14 : 6 ; (*b*) of the tribes of Israel, Matt. 19 : 28 ; Luke 2 : 36 ; 22 : 30 ; Acts 13 : 21 ; Rom. 11 : 1 ; Phil. 3 : 5 ; Heb. 7 : 13, 14 ; Jas. 1 : 1 ; Rev. 5 : 5 ; 7 : 4–8 ; 21 : 12.¶

2. DŌDEKAPHULOS (δωδεκάφυλος), an adjective signifying ' of twelve tribes ' (*dōdeka*, twelve, and No. 1), used as a noun in the neuter, occurs in Acts 26 : 7.¶

TRIBULATION

THLIPSIS (θλῖψις), for which see AFFLICTION, B, No. 4, is translated " tribulation " in the R.V. (for A.V., " affliction ") in Mark 4 : 17 ; 13 : 19 ; plural in 2 Thess. 1 : 4, A.V., " tribulations," R.V., " afflictions " ; in Acts 14 : 22 " many tribulations " (A.V., " much tribulation ") ; in Matt. 24 : 9, " unto tribulation " (A.V., " to be afflicted ") ; in 2 Cor. 1 : 4 ; 7 : 4 ; 2 Thess. 1 : 6, A.V., " tribulation " for R.V., " affliction ; " R.V. and A.V., " tribulation(–s)," e.g., in Rom. 2 : 9 ; 5 : 3 (twice) ; 8 : 35 ; 12 : 12 ; Eph. 3 : 13 ; Rev. 1 : 9 ; 2 : 9, 10, 22.¶

In Rev. 7 : 14, " the great tribulation," R.V., lit., ' the tribulation, the great one ' (not as A.V., without the article), is not that in which all saints share ; it indicates a definite period spoken of by the Lord in Matt. 24 : 21, 29 ; Mark 13 : 19, 24, where the time is mentioned as preceding His Second Advent, and as a period in which the Jewish nation, restored to Palestine in unbelief by Gentile instrumentality, will suffer an unprecedented outburst of fury on the part of the antichristian powers confederate under the Man of Sin (2 Thess. 2 : 10–12 ; cp. Rev. 12 : 13–17) ; in this tribulation Gentile witnesses for God will share (Rev. 7 : 9), but it will be distinctly " the time of Jacob's trouble " (Jer. 30 : 7) ; its beginning is signalized by the setting up of the " abomination of desolation " (Matt. 24 : 15 ; Mark 13 : 14, with Dan. 11 : 31 ; 12 : 11).

Note : For the verb *thlibō,* in the Passive Voice rendered " suffer tribulation " in 1 Thess. 3 : 4, A.V. (R.V., " suffer affliction "), see AFFLICT, No. 4.

TRIBUTE

1. PHOROS (φόρος), akin to *pherō,* to bring, denotes tribute paid by a subjugated nation, Luke 20 : 22 ; 23 : 2 ; Rom. 13 : 6, 7.¶

2. KĒNSOS (κῆνσος), Lat. and Eng., census, denotes a poll tax, Matt. 17 : 25 ; 22 : 17, 19 ; Mark. 12 : 14.¶

3. DIDRACHMON (δίδραχμον), the half-shekel, is rendered " tribute " in Matt. 17 : 24 (twice) : see SHEKEL, No. 2.¶

TRIM

KOSMEŌ (κοσμέω), to arrange, adorn, is used of trimming lamps, Matt. 25 : 7. See ADORN, GARNISH.

TRIUMPH

THRIAMBEUŌ (θριαμβεύω) denotes (a) to lead in triumph, used of a conqueror with reference to the vanquished, 2 Cor. 2 : 14. Theodoret paraphrases it ' He leads us about here and there and displays us to all the world.' This is in agreement with evidences from various sources. Those who are led are not captives exposed to humiliation, but are displayed as the glory and devoted subjects of Him who leads (see the context). This is so even if there is a reference to a Roman " triumph." On such occasions the general's sons, with various officers, rode behind his chariot (Livy, xlv. 40). But there is no necessary reference here to a Roman " triumph " (Field, in *Notes on the Trans. of the N.T.*). The main thought is that of the display, " in Christ " being the sphere ; its evidences are the effects of gospel testimony.

In Col. 2 : 15 the circumstances and subjects are quite different, and relate to Christ's victory over spiritual foes at the time of His Death ; accordingly the reference may be to the triumphant display of the defeated.¶

For TRODE see TREAD

TROUBLE (Noun and Verb)
A. Noun.

THLIPSIS (θλῖψις), for which see AFFLICTION, No. 4, and TRIBULATION, is rendered " trouble " in the A.V. of 1 Cor. 7 : 28 (R.V., " tribulation ") ; 2 Cor. 1 : 4 (2nd clause), 8 (R.V., " affliction ").

Note : In some mss. *tarachē*, an agitation, disturbance, trouble, is found in Mark 13 : 8 (plur.) and John 5 : 4 (R.V. omits).¶

B. Verbs.

1. TARASSŌ (ταράσσω), akin to *tarachē* (A, Note), is used (1) in a physical sense, John 5 : 7 (in some mss. ver. 4), (2) metaphorically, (a) of the soul and spirit of the Lord, John 11 : 33, where the true rendering is ' He troubled Himself ; ' (b) of the hearts of disciples, 14 : 1, 27 ; (c) of the minds of those in fear or perplexity, Matt. 2 : 3 ; 14 : 26 ; Mark 6 : 50 ; Luke 1 : 12 ; 24 : 38 ; 1 Pet. 3 : 14 ; (d) of subverting the souls of believers, by evil doctrine, Acts 15 : 24 ; Gal. 1 : 7 ; 5 : 10 ; (e) of stirring up a crowd, Acts 17 : 8 ; ver. 13 in the best texts, " troubling (the multitudes)," R.V.¶

2. DIATARASSŌ (διαταράσσω), to agitate greatly (*dia*, throughout, and No. 1), is used of the Virgin Mary, Luke 1 : 29.¶

3. EKTARASSŌ (ἐκταράσσω), to throw into great trouble, agitate, is used in Acts 16 : 20, " do exceedingly trouble (our city)."¶ In the Sept., Psa. 18 : 4 ; 88 : 16.¶

4. THLIBŌ (θλίβω), to afflict, is rendered to trouble in the A.V., e.g., 2 Cor. 4 : 8 (R.V., " pressed ") ; 7 : 5, but never in the R.V. : see AFFLICT, No. 4, PRESS, STRAITENED, TRIBULATION.

5. ENOCHLEŌ (ἐνοχλέω), from *en*, in, *ochlos*, a throng, crowd, is used in Heb. 12 : 15 of a root of bitterness ; in Luke 6 : 18 (in the best texts ; some have *ochleō*), R.V., " were troubled " (A.V., " were vexed ").¶

6. PARENOCHLEŌ (παρενοχλέω), to annoy concerning anything (*para*, and No. 5), occurs in Acts 15 : 19, " we trouble (not them)."¶

7. SKULLŌ (σκύλλω), primarily to flay, hence, to vex, annoy (" there was a time when the Greek, in thus speaking, compared his trouble to the pains of flaying alive," Moulton, *Proleg.*, p. 89), is used in the Active Voice in Mark 5 : 35 ; Luke 8 : 49 ; in the Passive Voice, Matt. 9 : 36, in the best texts, R.V., " they were distressed " (some have *ekluō*, A.V., " they fainted ") ; in the Middle Voice, Luke 7 : 6, " trouble (not thyself)."¶ The word is frequent in the papyri.

8. ANASTATOŌ (ἀναστατόω) is rendered " trouble " in Gal. 5 : 12, A.V. : see STIR, No. 12, TURN, No. 15, UPROAR.

9. THORUBEŌ (θορυβέω), akin to *thorubos*, a tumult, in the Middle Voice, to make an uproar, is rendered " trouble not yourselves " in Acts 20 : 10, A.V. See ADO, TUMULT.

10. THROEŌ (θροέω), to make an outcry (*throos*, a tumult), is used in the Passive Voice, Matt. 24 : 6 ; Mark 13 : 7 ; Luke 24 : 37 ; 2 Thess. 2 : 2.¶ In the Sept., S. of Sol. 5 : 4.¶

11. THORUBAZŌ (θορυβάζω), to disturb, to trouble (akin to No. 9), is used in Luke 10 : 41, in the best texts (in some, *turbazō*, with the same meaning).¶

12. ADĒMONEŌ (ἀδημονέω), to be much troubled, distressed (perhaps from *a*, negative, and *dēmōn*, knowing, the compound therefore originally suggesting bewilderment), is translated " sore troubled " in Matt. 26 : 37 and Mark 14 : 33, R.V. (A.V., " very heavy ") ; so the R.V. in Phil. 2 : 26 (A.V., " full of heaviness ") ; Lightfoot renders it " distressed," a meaning borne out in the papyri. See HEAVY.¶

13. DIAPONEŌ (διαπονέω) denotes to work out with toil, hence, to be " sore troubled ; " so the R.V. in Acts 4 : 2 and 16 : 18 (A.V., " grieved ") ; Mark 14 : 4 in some texts.¶

Notes : (1) The noun *kopos*, a striking, beating, then, laborious toil, trouble, used with *parechō*, to furnish, to supply, is rendered to trouble (lit., to give trouble to), in Matt. 26 : 10 ; Mark 14 : 6 ; Luke 11 : 7 ; 18 : 5 ; Gal. 6 : 17 ; the meaning is to embarrass a person by distracting his attention, or to give occasion for anxiety. In the last passage the Apostle expresses his determination not to allow the Judaizing teachers to distract him any further. See LABOUR, A. No. 1. (2) For " suffer trouble " in 2 Tim. 2 : 9, see HARDSHIP.

TROW

Note : Some mss. have *dokeō*, to think, in Luke 17 : 9, A.V., " I trow (not)."

For TRUCE-BREAKERS see IMPLACABLE

TRUE, TRULY, TRUTH
A. Adjectives.

1. ALĒTHĒS (ἀληθής), primarily, unconcealed, manifest (*a*, negative, *lēthō*, to forget,= *lanthanō*, to escape notice), hence, actual, true to fact, is used (*a*) of persons, truthful, Matt. 22 : 16 ; Mark 12 : 14 ; John 3 : 33 ; 7 : 18 ; 8 : 26 ; Rom. 3 : 4 ; 2 Cor. 6 : 8 ; (*b*) of things, true, conforming to reality, John 4 : 18, " truly," lit., ' true ; ' 5 : 31, 32 ; in the best texts, 6 : 55 (twice), " indeed ; " 8 : 13, 14 (ver. 16 in some texts : see No. 2), 17 ; 10 : 41 ; 19 : 35 ; 21 : 24 ; Acts 12 : 9 ; Phil. 4 : 8 ; Tit. 1 : 13 ; 1 Pet. 5 : 12 ; 2 Pet. 2 : 22 ; 1 John 2 : 8, 27 ; 3 John 12.¶

2. ALĒTHINOS (ἀληθινός), akin to No. 1, denotes true in the sense of real, ideal, genuine ; it is used (*a*) of God, John 7 : 28 (cp. No. 1 in 7 : 18, above) ; 17 : 3 ; 1 Thess. 1 : 9 ; Rev. 6 : 10 ; these declare that God fulfils the meaning of His Name, He is " very God," in distinction from all other gods, false gods (*alēthēs*, see John 3 : 33 in No. 1, signifies that He is veracious, true to His utterances, He cannot lie) ; (*b*) of Christ, John 1 : 9 ; 6 : 32 ; 15 : 1 ; 1 John 2 : 8 ; 5 : 20 (thrice) ; Rev. 3 : 7, 14 ; 19 : 11 ; His judgment, John 8 : 16 (in the best texts, instead of No. 1) ; (*c*) God's words, John 4 : 37 ; Rev. 19 : 9 ; 21 : 5 ; 22 : 6 ; the last three

are equivalent to No. 1 ; (d) His ways, Rev. 15 : 3 ; (e) His judgments, Rev. 16 : 7 ; 19 : 2 ; (f) His riches, Luke 16 : 11 ; (g) His worshippers, John 4 : 23 ; (h) their hearts, Heb. 10 : 22 ; (i) the witness of the Apostle John, John 19 : 35 ; (j) the spiritual, antitypical Tabernacle, Heb. 8 : 2 ; 9 : 24, not that the wilderness Tabernacle was false, but that it was a weak and earthly copy of the Heavenly.¶

Note : " *Alēthinos* is related to *alēthēs* as form to contents or substances ; *alēthēs* denotes the reality of the thing, *alēthinos* defines the relation of the conception to the thing to which it corresponds=genuine " (Cremer).

3. GNĒSIOS (γνήσιος), primarily lawfully begotten (akin to *ginomai*, to become), hence, true, genuine, sincere, is used in the Apostle's exhortation to his " true yoke-fellow " in Phil. 4 : 3. See OWN, SINCERITY.

Note : In the A.V. of 2 Cor. 1 : 18 and 1 Tim. 3 : 1, *pistos*, " faithful " (R.V.), is translated " true."

B. Verb.

ALĒTHEUŌ (ἀληθεύω) signifies to deal faithfully or truly with anyone (cp. Gen. 42 : 16, Sept., " whether ye deal truly or no "), Eph. 4 : 15, " speaking the truth ; " Gal. 3 : 16, " I tell (you) the truth," where probably the Apostle is referring to the contents of his Epistle.¶

C. Noun.

ALĒTHEIA (ἀλήθεια), truth, is used (a) objectively, signifying " the reality lying at the basis of an appearance ; the manifested, veritable essence of a matter " (Cremer), e.g., Rom. 9 : 1 ; 2 Cor. 11 : 10 ; especially of Christian doctrine, e.g., Gal. 2 : 5, where " the truth of the Gospel " denotes the true teaching of the Gospel, in contrast to perversions of it ; Rom. 1 : 25, where " the truth of God " may be ' the truth concerning God ' or ' God whose existence is a verity ; ' but in Rom 15 : 8 " the truth of God " is indicative of His faithfulness in the fulfilment of His promises as exhibited in Christ ; the word has an absolute force in John 14 : 6 ; 17 : 17 ; 18 : 37, 38 ; in Eph. 4 : 21, where the R.V., " even as truth is in Jesus," gives the correct rendering, the meaning is not merely ethical truth, but truth in all its fulness and scope, as embodied in Him ; He was the perfect expression of the truth ; this is virtually equivalent to His statement in John 14 : 6 ; (b) subjectively, truthfulness, truth, not merely verbal, but sincerity and integrity of character, John 8 : 44 ; 3 John 3, R.V. ; (c) in phrases, e.g., " in truth " (*epi*, on the basis of), Mark 12 : 14 ; Luke 20 : 21 ; with *en*, in, 2 Cor. 6 : 7 ; Col. 1 : 6 ; 1 Tim. 2 : 7, R.V. (A.V., " in . . . verity ") ; 1 John 3 : 18 ; 2 John 1, 3, 4.

Note : In Matt. 15 : 27, A.V., *nai*, " yea " (R.V.), is translated " truth."

D. Adverbs.

1. ALĒTHŌS (ἀληθῶς), truly, surely, is rendered " of a truth " in Matt. 14 : 33 ; 26 : 73 and Mark 14 : 70, R.V. (A.V., " surely ") ; Luke

9 : 27 ; 12 : 44 ; 21 : 3 ; John 6 : 14 ; 7 : 40 ; 17 : 8, R.V., " of a truth " (A.V., " surely ") ; Acts 12 : 11, R.V. (A.V., " of a surety ") ; " in truth," 1 Thess. 2 : 13 ; " truly," Matt. 27 : 54 ; Mark 15 : 39. See INDEED, No. 3.

2. GNĒSIOS (γνησίως), sincerely, honourably (akin to A, No. 3), is rendered " truly " (marg., " genuinely ") in Phil. 2 : 20 (A.V., " naturally ").¶

Notes : (1) The particles *ara*, *men*, and *de* are sometimes rendered " truly " in the A.V., but are differently rendered in the R.V. (2) In 1 Cor. 14 : 25, A.V., *ontōs* (R.V., " indeed ") is rendered " of a truth." See CERTAIN, C, No. 1, INDEED, No. 4. (3) In John 20 : 30, A.V., the particle *oun*, therefore (R.V.), is rendered " truly."

TRUMP, TRUMPET
A. Noun.

SALPINX (σάλπιγξ) is used (1) of the natural instrument, 1 Cor. 14 : 8 ; (2) of the supernatural accompaniment of Divine interpositions, (*a*) at Sinai, Heb. 12 : 19 ; (*b*) of the acts of angels at the Second Advent of Christ, Matt. 24 : 31 ; (*c*) of their acts in the period of Divine judgments preceding this, Rev. 8 : 2, 6, 13 ; 9 : 14 ; (*d*) of a summons to John to the presence of God, Rev. 1 : 10 ; 4 : 1 ; (*e*) of the act of the Lord in raising from the dead the saints who have fallen asleep and changing the bodies of those who are living, at the Rapture of all to meet Him in the air, 1 Cor. 15 : 52, where " the last trump " is a military allusion, familiar to Greek readers, and has no connection with the series in Rev. 8 : 6 to 11 : 15 ; there is a possible allusion to Num. 10 : 2–6, with reference to the same event, 1 Thess. 4 : 16, " the (lit., a) trump of God " (the absence of the article suggests the meaning ' a trumpet such as is used in God's service ').¶

B. Verb.

SALPIZŌ (σαλπίζω), to sound a trumpet, Matt. 6 : 2 ; as in (2) (*c*) above, Rev. 8 : 6, 7, 8, 10, 12, 13 ; 9 : 1, 13 ; 10 : 7 ; 11 : 15 ; as in (2) (*e*), 1 Cor. 15 : 52.¶

TRUMPETER
SALPISTĒS (σαλπιστής) occurs in Rev. 18 : 22.¶

TRUST (Noun and Verb)
A. Noun.

PEPOITHĒSIS (πεποίθησις) is rendered " trust " in 2 Cor. 3 : 4, A.V. ; see CONFIDENCE, No. 1.

B. Verbs.

1. PEITHŌ (πείθω), intransitively, in the perfect and pluperfect Active, to have confidence, trust, is rendered to trust in Matt. 27 : 43 ; Mark 10 : 24 ; Luke 11 : 22 ; 18 : 9 ; 2 Cor. 1 : 9 ; 10 : 7 ; Phil. 2 : 24 ; 3 : 4, A.V. (R.V., " to have confidence ") ; Heb. 2 : 13 ; in the present

Middle, Heb. 13 : 18, A.V. (R.V., " are persuaded "). See AGREE, No. 5, PERSUADE.

2. PISTEUŌ (πιστεύω), to entrust, or, in the Passive Voice, to be entrusted with, is rendered to commit to one's trust, in Luke 16 : 11 ; 1 Tim. 1 : 11 ; to be put in trust with, 1 Thess. 2 : 4, A.V. (R.V., " to be intrusted ").

Note : Wherever *elpizō*, to hope, is translated to trust in .the A.V., the R.V. substitutes to hope. So *proelpizō*, to hope before. See HOPE.

For TRUTH see TRUE

TRY, TRIED

1. DOKIMAZŌ (δοκιμάζω) is rendered to try in the A.V. in 1 Cor. 3 : 13 ; 1 Thess. 2 : 4 ; 1 Pet. 1 : 7 ; 1 John 4 : 1 : see PROVE, No. 1.

2. PEIRAZŌ (πειράζω) is rendered to try in Heb. 11 : 17 ; Rev. 2 : 2, 10 ; 3 : 10. In Acts 16 : 7 it is rendered "assayed ;" in 24 : 6, R.V., " assayed " (A.V., " hath gone about ") : see GO, Note (2) (b). See EXAMINE, PROVE, TEMPT. Cp. *peiraō* in Acts 26 : 21, R.V., " assayed " (A.V., " went about ") ; see GO, Note (2) (c).

Notes : (1) In Rev. 3 : 18, A.V., *puroō*, in the Passive Voice, to be purified by fire (R.V., " refined "), is rendered " tried." (2) For *dokimion*, Jas. 1 : 3, A.V., " trying," see PROOF. (3) For *dokimos*, Jas. 1 : 12, A.V., " tried," see APPROVED. (4) In 1 Pet. 4 : 12, A.V., the phrase *pros peirasmon*, lit., ' for trial,' i.e., for testing, is rendered " to try (you) ", R.V., " to prove (you)."

TUMULT

1. AKATASTASIA (ἀκαταστασία) is rendered " tumults " in Luke 21 : 9, R.V. ; 2 Cor. 6 : 5 ; 12 : 20. See CONFOUND, A, No. 1.

2. THORUBOS (θόρυβος), a noise, uproar, tumult, is rendered " tumult " in Matt. 27 : 24 and Mark 5 : 38 ; in Matt. 26 : 5, R.V. (A.V., " uproar "), so in Mark 14 : 2 ; in Acts 20 : 1, " uproar," A.V. and R.V. ; in 24 : 18, " tumult ;" in 21 : 34, A.V., " tumult " (R.V., " uproar ").¶

Note : For *thorubeō*, R.V., to make a tumult, see NOISE, *Note* (2).

TURN

1. STREPHŌ (στρέφω) denotes (1) in the Active Voice, (a) to turn (something), Matt. 5 : 39 ; (b) to bring back, Matt. 27 : 3 (in the best texts ; some have No. 2) ; (c) reflexively, to turn oneself, to turn the back to people, said of God, Acts 7 : 42 ; (d) to turn one thing into another, Rev. 11 : 6 (the only place where this word occurs after the Acts) ; (2) in the Passive Voice, (a) used reflexively, to turn oneself, e.g. Matt. 7 : 6 ; John 20 : 14, 16 ; (b) metaphorically, Matt. 18 : 3, R.V., " (except) ye tur n " (A.V., ". . . be converted ") ; John 12 : 40 (in the best texts ; some have No. 4). See CONVERT, A, No. 1.

2. APOSTREPHŌ (ἀποστρέφω) denotes (a) to cause to turn away

(*apo*), to remove, Rom. 11 : 26 ; 2 Tim. 4 : 4 (1st clause) ; metaphorically, to turn away from allegiance, pervert, Luke 23 : 14 ; (*b*) to make to return, put back, Matt. 26 : 52 ; (*c*) in the Passive Voice, used reflexively, to turn oneself away from, Matt. 5 : 42 ; 2 Tim. 1 : 15 ; Tit. 1 : 14 ; Heb. 12 : 25 ; in the Active Voice, Acts 3 : 26. See PERVERT, PUT.¶

3. DIASTREPHŌ (διαστρέφω), to distort (*dia*, asunder), is rendered " to turn aside," R.V. (A.V., " . . . away "), in Acts 13 : 8. See PERVERT, No. 2.

4. EPISTREPHŌ (ἐπιστρέφω) is used (*a*) transitively, to make to turn towards (*epi*), Luke 1 : 16, 17 ; Jas 5 : 19, 20 (to convert) ; (*b*) intransitively, to turn oneself round, e.g., in the Passive Voice, Mark 5 : 30 (see RETURN) ; in the Active Voice, Matt. 13 : 15, R.V., " turn again " (A.V., " be converted ") ; Acts 11 : 21 ; 14 : 15 ; 15 : 19 ; 1 Thess. 1 : 9, " ye turned," the aorist tense indicating an immediate and decisive change, consequent upon a deliberate choice ; conversion is a voluntary act in response to the presentation of truth. See CONVERT.

5. METASTREPHŌ (μεταστρέφω) signifies, in the Passive Voice, to be turned (of a change into something different, *meta*) in Acts 2 : 20 and Jas. 4 : 9 : see PERVERT, No. 3.

6. HUPOSTREPHŌ (ὑποστρέφω) is used intransitively of turning back, behind (*hupo*), e.g., Luke 17 : 15, " turned back ; " in 2 : 45, R.V., " returned : " see RETURN.

7. APOBAINŌ (ἀποβαίνω), to go from, is used metaphorically of events, to issue, turn out, Luke 21 : 13 ; Phil. 1 : 19. See Go, No. 21.

8. METAGŌ (μετάγω), to move from one side to another, is rendered to turn about in Jas. 3 : 3, 4.¶

9. METATITHĒMI (μετατίθημι), to change, is translated " turning (the grace of God) " in Jude 4. See CARRY, CHANGE, REMOVE, TRANSLATE.

10. ANAKAMPTŌ (ἀνακάμπτω), *ana*, back, *kamptō*, to bend, is rendered " shall turn . . . again," in Luke 10 : 6. See RETURN.

11. EKTREPŌ (ἐκτρέπω), to cause to turn aside (*ek*, from, *trepō*, to turn), is used in the Passive Voice, with Middle sense, in 1 Tim. 1 : 6 ; 5 : 15 ; 6 : 20, R.V., " turning away " (A.V., " avoiding ") ; 2 Tim. 4 : 4 (2nd clause) ; Heb. 12 : 13, " be (not) turned out of the way " (R.V., marg., " put out of joint ") ; some adhere to the meaning to turn aside, go astray ; the interpretation depends on the antithesis which follows, " but rather be healed " (R.V.), which is not the antithesis to turning aside or being turned out of the way ; accordingly the marg. is to be preferred (the verb is often used medically).¶ In the Sept., Amos 5 : 8.¶

12. APOTREPŌ (ἀποτρέπω), to cause to turn away (*apo*), is used in the Middle Voice in 2 Tim. 3 : 5.¶

13. PERITREPŌ (περιτρέπω), to turn about (*peri*), is rendered " doth turn (thee to madness) " in Acts 26 : 24, R.V., A.V., " doth make (thee mad)."¶

14. METHISTĒMI (μεθίστημι) is used metaphorically in Acts 19 : 26,

" turned away (much people)." See PUT, REMOVE, TRANSLATE.

15. ANASTATOŌ (ἀναστατόω), to stir up, excite, unsettle (*ana*, up, *histēmi*, to cause to stand), is rendered " have turned (the world) upside down " in Acts 17 : 6. See TROUBLE, UPROAR.

16. GINOMAI (γίνομαι), to become, is rendered " shall be turned " in John 16 : 20 (of sorrow into joy).

17. EKKLINŌ (ἐκκλίνω), to turn aside (*ek*, from, *klinō*, to lean), is rendered " have . . . turned aside " in Rom. 3 : 12 (A.V., " are . . . gone out of the way ") ; 16 : 17, R.V., " turn away " (A.V., " avoid ") ; 1 Pet. 3 : 11, R.V., ditto (A.V., " eschew ").¶

18. DIADECHOMAI (διαδέχομαι), to receive through another, to receive in turn (*dia*, through, *dechomai*, to receive), occurs in Acts 7 : 45, R.V., " in their turn . . . when they entered " (A.V., " that came after ") ; the meaning here is ' having received (it) after,' i.e., as from Moses under Joshua's leadership. In the papyri the word is used similarly of visiting as deputy (see also Field, *Notes on the Trans. of the N.T.*, 116).¶

Notes : (1) In Matt. 2 : 22, A.V., *anachōreō*, to retire, withdraw, is rendered " turned aside " (R.V., " withdrew "). (2) For " turned to flight," *klinō*, Heb. 11 : 34, see FLIGHT, B. (3) For the phrase " by turn " in 1 Cor. 14 : 27 see COURSE, B, Note (3).

TURNING

TROPĒ (τροπή), used especially of the revolution of the heavenly orbs (akin to *trepō*, to turn), occurs in Jas. 1 : 17, " (neither shadow) that is cast by turning," R.V. (A.V., " of turning "). For a more detailed treatment of the passage, see SHADOW, No. 2.¶

For TURTLE-DOVE see DOVE

For TUTOR see GUARDIAN and INSTRUCTOR, No. 1.

TWAIN, TWO

DUO (δύο) is rendered " twain " in Matt. 5 : 41 ; 19 : 5, 6 ; 21 : 31 ; 27 : 21, 51 ; Mark 10 : 8 (twice) ; 15 : 38 ; in 1 Cor. 6 : 16 and Eph. 5 : 31, R.V. (A.V., " two ") ; Eph. 2 : 15 ; in Rev. 19 : 20, R.V. (A.V., " both ").

Notes : (1) In the following phrases the numeral is used distributively : (*a*) *ana duo*, " two apiece," John 2 : 6 (in some mss., Luke 9 : 3) ; in Luke 10 : 1, " two and two " (' by twos ') ; (*b*) *kata duo*, " by two," 1 Cor. 14 : 27 ; (*c*) *duo duo*, " by two and two," lit., ' two (and) two,' Mark 6 : 7 (not a Hebraism ; the form of expression is used in the papyri) ; (*d*) *eis duo*, ' into two,' " in twain," Matt. 27 : 51 and Mark 15 : 38 (see above). (2) In Luke 17 : 34 *duo* stands for " two men ; " in ver. 35 for " two women."

TWELFTH

DŌDEKATOS (δωδέκατος) occurs in Rev. 21 : 20.¶

TWELVE

DŌDEKA (δώδεκα) is used frequently in the Gospels for the twelve Apostles, and in Acts 6 : 2 ; 1 Cor. 15 : 5 ; Rev. 21 : 14b ; of the tribes of Israel, Matt. 19 : 28 ; Luke 22 : 30 ; Jas. 1 : 1 ; Rev. 21 : 12c (cp. 7 : 5–8 ; 12 : 1) ; in various details relating to the Heavenly Jerusalem, Rev. 21 : 12–21 ; 22 : 2. The number in general is regarded as suggestive of Divine administration.

TWENTY

EIKOSI (εἴκοσι) occurs in Luke 14 : 31 ; John 6 : 19 ; Acts 1 : 15 ; 27 : 28 ; 1 Cor. 10 : 8 ; of the four and twenty elders, in Rev. 4 : 4 (twice), 10 ; 5 : 8 ; 11 : 16 ; 19 : 4 (combined in one numeral with *tessares*, four, in some mss.).¶

TWICE

DIS (δίς) occurs in Mark 14 : 30, 72 ; Luke 18 : 12 ; Jude 12 ; combined with *muriades*, ten thousand, in Rev. 9 : 16 ; rendered "again" in Phil. 4 : 16 and 1 Thess. 2 : 18. See AGAIN.¶

TWINKLING

RHIPĒ (ῥιπή), akin to *rhiptō*, to hurl, was used of any rapid movement, e.g., the throw of a javelin, the rush of wind or flame ; in 1 Cor. 15 : 52 of the twinkling of an eye.¶

For TWO see TWAIN

TWO-EDGED

DISTOMOS (δίστομος), lit., 'two-mouthed' (*dis*, and *stoma*, a mouth), was used of rivers and branching roads ; in the N.T. of swords, Heb. 4 : 12 ; Rev. 1 : 16 ; 2 : 12, R.V., "two-edged" (A.V., "with two edges").¶ In the Sept., Judg. 3 : 16 ; Psa. 149 : 6 ; Prov. 5 : 4.¶

For TWOFOLD MORE see DOUBLE

TWO HUNDRED

DIAKOSIOI (διακόσιοι) occurs in Mark 6 : 37 ; John 6 : 7 ; 21 : 8 ; Acts 23 : 23 (twice) ; 27 : 37, "two hundred (threescore and sixteen) ; " Rev. 11 : 3, "(a thousand) two hundred (and threescore) ; " so 12 : 6.¶

Note : In Acts 27 : 37, some ancient authorities read "about threescore and sixteen souls " (R.V., margin). The confusion was quite natural when the word *diakosioi* was not written in full but represented by one Greek letter. The larger number is by no means improbable : Josephus sailed for Rome in A.D. 63 in a ship which had 600 on board (*Life*, ch. 3).

For TWO THOUSAND see THOUSAND, Note (1)

U

For UNAPPROACHABLE, 1 Tim. 6 : 16, R.V., see APPROACH, B

UNAWARES

Notes : (1) In Heb. 13 : 2, *lanthanō*, to escape notice, is used with the aorist participle of *xenizō*, to entertain, signifying "entertained . . . unawares" (an idiomatic usage common in classical Greek). (2) For *aiphnidios*, "unawares," in Luke 21 : 34, A.V., see SUDDENLY. (3) In Gal. 2 : 4, A.V., *pareisaktos*, brought in secretly, is rendered "unawares brought in." See PRIVILY, *Note :* cp. BRING, No. 17.¶ (4) In Jude 4, A.V., *pareisdunō*, to slip in secretly, is rendered "crept in unawares." See CREEP, A, No. 2.¶.

UNBELIEF

1. APISTIA (ἀπιστία), "unbelief" 12 times, but see BELIEF, C, Note (2) for references.

2. APEITHEIA (ἀπείθεια) is always rendered "disobedience" in the R.V. ; in Rom. 11 : 30, 32 and Heb. 4 : 6, 11, A.V., "unbelief." See DISOBEDIENCE, A, No. 1.

UNBELIEVER

APISTOS (ἄπιστος), an adjective, is used as a noun, rendered "unbeliever" in 2 Cor. 6 : 15 and 1 Tim. 5 : 8, R.V. ; plural in 1 Cor. 6 : 6 and 2 Cor. 6 : 14 ; A.V. only, Luke 12 : 46 (R.V., "unfaithful"). See BELIEF, C, Note (3), FAITHLESS, INCREDIBLE.

UNBELIEVING
A. Adjective.
APISTOS (ἄπιστος) : see BELIEF, C, Note (3).
B. Verb.
APEITHEŌ (ἀπειθέω) : see DISBELIEVE, DISOBEDIENT, C.

UNBLAMEABLE, UNBLAMEABLY
A. Adjectives.
1. AMEMPTOS (ἄμεμπτος), "unblameable" (from *a*, negative, and *memphomai*, to find fault), is so rendered in 1 Thess. 3 : 13, i.e., free from all valid charge. See BLAME, B, No. 3.

2. AMŌMOS (ἄμωμος) : see BLEMISH, B.

B. Adverb.

AMEMPTŌS (ἀμέμπτως) is used in 1 Thess. 2 : 10, " unblameably," signifying that no charge could be maintained, whatever charges might be made. See BLAME, C.

___

For UNCEASING see CEASE, B.   For UNCEASINGLY, R.V., in Rom. 1 : 9, see CEASE, C

___

UNCERTAIN, UNCERTAINLY, UNCERTAINTY
A. Adjective.

ADĒLOS (ἄδηλος) denotes (a) unseen ; with the article, translated " which appear not " (a, negative, dēlos, evident), Luke 11 : 44 ; (b) " uncertain," indistinct, 1 Cor. 14 : 8.¶   In the Sept., Ps. 51 : 6.¶

B. Adverb.

ADĒLŌS (ἀδήλως), uncertainly (akin to A), occurs in 1 Cor. 9 : 26.¶

C. Noun.

ADĒLOTĒS (ἀδηλότης), uncertainty (akin to A and B), occurs in 1 Tim. 6 : 17, " (the) uncertainty (of riches)," R.V. (the A.V. translates it as an adjective, " uncertain "), i.e., riches the special character of which is their uncertainty ; the Greek phrase is a rhetorical way of stressing the noun " riches ; " when a genitive (here " of riches ") precedes the governing noun (here " uncertainty ") the genitive receives emphasis.¶

___

UNCHANGEABLE

APARABATOS (ἀπαράβατος) is used of the priesthood of Christ, in Heb. 7 : 24, " unchangeable," unalterable, inviolable, R.V., marg. (a meaning found in the papyri) ; the more literal meaning in A.V. and R.V. margins, " that doth not pass from one to another," is not to be preferred.   This active meaning is not only untenable, and contrary to the constant usage of the word, but does not adequately fit with either the preceding or the succeeding context.¶

___

For UNCIRCUMCISED and UNCIRCUMCISION see CIRCUMCISION

___

UNCLEAN
A. Adjectives.

1. AKATHARTOS (ἀκάθαρτος), unclean, impure (a, negative, kathairō, to purify), is used (a) of unclean spirits, frequently in the Synoptists, not in John's Gospel ; in Acts 5 : 16 ; 8 : 7 ; Rev. 16 : 13 ; 18 : 2a (in the 2nd clause the birds are apparently figurative of destructive Satanic agencies) ; (b) ceremonially, Acts 10 : 14, 28 ; 11 : 8 ; 1 Cor. 7 : 14 ; (c) morally, 2 Cor. 6 : 17, including (b), R.V.; " no unclean thing ; " Eph. 5 : 5 ; Rev. 17 : 4, R.V., " the unclean things " (A.V. follows the texts which have the noun akatharēs, " the filthiness ").

2. KOINOS (κοινός), common, is translated " unclean " in Rom. 14 : 14 (thrice) ; in Rev. 21 : 27, R.V. (A.V., " that defileth," follows the inferior

texts which have the verb *koinoō :* see B).   See COMMON, DEFILE, C, UNHOLY, No. 2.

B. Verb.

KOINOŌ (κοινόω), to make *koinos*, to defile, is translated " unclean " in Heb. 9 : 13, A.V., where the perfect participle, Passive, is used with the article, hence the R.V., " them that have been defiled."   See DEFILE, A, No. 1.

C. Noun.

AKATHARSIA (ἀκαθαρσία), akin to A, No. 1, denotes uncleanness, (*a*) physical, Matt. 23 : 27 (instances in the papyri speak of tenants keeping houses in good condition) ;   (*b*) moral, Rom. 1 : 24 ;   6 : 19 ;   2 Cor. 12 : 21 ; Gal. 5 : 19 ;   Eph. 4 : 19 ;   5 : 3 ;   Col. 3 : 5 ;   1 Thess. 2 : 3 (suggestive of the fact that sensuality and evil doctrine are frequently associated) ; 4 : 7.¶

Note : In 2 Pet. 2 : 10, A.V., *miasmos*, a defilement, is rendered " uncleanness ; " see DEFILEMENT, B, No. 2.¶

For UNCLOTHED see STRIP

UNCOMELY

ASCHĒMŌN (ἀσχήμων), shapeless (*a*, negative, *schēma*, a form), the opposite of *euschēmōn*, comely, is used in 1 Cor. 12 : 23.¶   In the Sept., Gen. 34 : 7 ;   Deut. 24 : 3.¶

Note : For the verb *aschēmoneō*, rendered to behave oneself uncomely in 1 Cor. 7 : 36, A.V., see BEHAVE, No. 4.

UNCONDEMNED

AKATAKRITOS (ἀκατάκριτος), rendered " uncondemned " in Acts 16 : 37 ;   22 : 25 (*a*, negative, *katakrinō*, to condemn), properly means ' without trial,' not yet tried.   Sir W. M. Ramsay points out that the Apostle, in claiming his rights, would probably use the Roman phrase *re incognita*, i.e., ' without investigating our case ' (*The Cities of St. Paul*, p. 225).¶

For UNCORRUPTIBLE see CORRUPT, C, No. 2.   For UNCORRUPT-
NESS, see CORRUPT, B, No. 4

UNCOVER

APOSTEGAZO (ἀποστεγάζω) signifies to unroof (*apo*, from, *stegē*, a roof), Mark 2 : 4.¶

For UNCOVERED, 1 Cor. 11 : 5, 13, see UNVEILED

For UNCTION see ANOINT, B

UNDEFILED

AMIANTOS (ἀμίαντος), undefiled, free from contamination (*a*, negative, *miainō*, to defile), is used (*a*) of Christ, Heb. 7 : 26 ; (*b*) of pure religion, Jas. 1 : 27 ; (*c*) of the eternal inheritance of believers, 1 Pet. 1 : 4 ; (*d*) of the marriage bed as requiring to be free from unlawful sexual intercourse, Heb. 13 : 4.¶

UNDER, UNDERNEATH

1. HUPOKATŌ (ὑποκάτω), an adverb signifying under, is used as a preposition and rendered " under " in Mark 6 : 11 ; 7 : 28 ; Luke 8 : 16 ; Heb. 2 : 8 ; Rev. 5 : 3, 13 ; 6 : 9 ; 12 : 1 ; " underneath " in Matt. 22 : 44, R.V. (Mark 12 : 36 in some mss.) ; John 1 : 50, R.V. (A.V., "under").¶

2. KATŌTERŌ (κατωτέρω), the comparative degree of *katō*, below, beneath, occurs in Matt. 2 : 16, " under."

3. ELASSON (ἔλασσον), the neuter of the adjective *elassōn*, less, is used adverbially in 1 Tim. 5 : 9, " under " (or ' less than '). See LESS.

Notes : (1) The preposition *epi*, upon, is rendered " under " in Heb. 7 : 11 ; 9 : 15 ; 10 : 28, A.V. (R.V., "on *the word of*"). (2) The preposition *en*, in, is rendered " under " in Matt. 7 : 6 ; Rom. 3 : 19 (1st part). (3) The usual preposition is *hupo*.

UNDERGIRD

HUPOZŌNNUMI (ὑποζώννυμι), *hupo*, under, *zōnnumi*, to gird, is used of frapping a ship, Acts 27 : 17, bracing the timbers of a vessel by means of strong ropes.¶

UNDERSTAND, UNDERSTOOD
A. Verbs.

1. SUNIĒMI (συνίημι), primarily, to bring or set together, is used metaphorically of perceiving, understanding, uniting (*sun*), so to speak, the perception with what is perceived, e.g., Matt. 13 : 13-15, 19, 23, 51 ; 15 : 10 ; 16 : 12 ; 17 : 13, and similar passages in Mark and Luke ; Acts 7 : 25 (twice) ; 28 : 26, 27 ; in Rom. 3 : 11, the present participle, with the article, is used as a noun, lit., ' there is not the understanding (one),' in a moral and spiritual sense ; Rom. 15 : 21 ; 2 Cor. 10 : 12, R.V., " are (without) understanding," A.V., " are (not) wise ; " Eph. 5 : 17, R.V., " understand." See CONSIDER, Note (2).

2. NOEŌ (νοέω), to perceive with the mind, as distinct from perception by feeling, is so used in Matt. 15 : 17, A.V., " understand," R.V., " perceive ; " 16 : 9, 11 ; 24 : 15 (here rather perhaps in the sense of considering) and parallels in Mark (not in Luke) ; John 12 : 40 ; Rom. 1 : 20 ; 1 Tim. 1 : 7 ; Heb. 11 : 3 ; in Eph. 3 : 4, A.V., " may understand " (R.V., " can perceive ") ; 3 : 20, " think ; " 2 Tim. 2 : 7, " consider." See CONSIDER, No. 4.¶

3. GINŌSKŌ (γινώσκω), to know, to come to know, is translated to

understand in the A.V. in Matt. 26 : 10 and John 8 : 27 (R.V., to perceive) ;
A.V. and R.V. in John 8 : 43 ; 10 : 6 ; in 10 : 38, R.V. (in some texts
pisteuō, A.V., " believe ") ; A.V. and R.V. in 12 : 16 ; 13 : 7, R.V., A.V.,
" know " (see Note under KNOW, No. 2) ; Acts 8 : 30 ; in Phil. 1 : 12,
A.V., R.V., " know " (in some texts, Acts 24 : 11, A.V.). See KNOW,
No. 1.

4. EPISTAMAI (ἐπίσταμαι), to know well, is rendered to understand
in Mark 14 : 68 ; Jude 10, R.V., 2nd clause (A.V., " know "). See
KNOW, No. 5.

5. PUNTHANOMAI (πυνθάνομαι), to inquire, is rendered to understand in Acts 23 : 34. See INQUIRE.

6. GNŌRIZŌ (γνωρίζω), to make known, is rendered " I give . . . to
understand " in 1 Cor. 12 : 3. See KNOW, No. 8.

7. AGNOEŌ (ἀγνοέω), to be ignorant, is rendered " they understood
not " in Mark 9 : 32 ; Luke 9 : 45 ; in 2 Pet. 2 : 12, A.V., R.V., " they
are ignorant of." See IGNORANT, B, No. 1.

Notes : (1) In 1 Cor. 13 : 2, A.V., *oida*, to know, to perceive, is rendered
" understand " (R.V., " know ") ; so in 14 : 16. (2) For *manthanō*,
rendered " understand " in Acts 23 : 27, A.V., see LEARN, No. 1. (3)
In 1 Cor. 13 : 11, A.V., *phroneō*, to be minded, is rendered "I understood "
(R.V., " I felt "). (4) For *parakoloutheō*, Luke 1 : 3, A.V., " have perfect
understanding of," see TRACE.

B. Adjectives.

1 EUSĒMOS (εὔσημος) primarily denotes conspicuous or glorious (as
in Ps. 81 : 3, Sept. ; E.V., " solemn "¶), then, distinct, clear to understanding, 1 Cor. 14 : 9, " easy to be understood " (A.V., marg., " significant ").¶

2. DUSNOĒTOS (δυσνόητος), hard to be understood (*dus*, a prefix
like Eng., *mis-* or *un-*, and A, No. 2), occurs in 2 Pet. 3 : 16.¶

UNDERSTANDING
A. Nouns.

1. NOUS (νοῦς), for which see MIND, No. 1, is translated " understanding " in Luke 24 : 45, A.V. (R.V., " mind ") ; 1 Cor. 14 : 14, 15
(twice), 19 ; Phil. 4 : 7 ; Rev. 13 : 18.

2. SUNESIS (σύνεσις), akin to *suniēmi*, to set together, to understand,
denotes (*a*) the understanding, the mind or intelligence, Mark 12 : 33 ;
(*b*) understanding, reflective thought, Luke 2 : 47 ; 1 Cor. 1 : 19, R.V.,
" prudence ;" Eph. 3 : 4, R.V. (A.V., " knowledge ") ; Col. 1 : 9 ; 2 : 2 ;
2 Tim. 2 : 7 ¶ See PRUDENCE, No. 2.

3. DIANOIA (διάνοια), for which see MIND, No. 2, is rendered " understanding " in Eph. 4 : 18 ; 1 John 5 : 20 (in some texts, Eph. 1 : 18, A.V.,
for *kardia*, " heart," R.V.).

B. Adjective.

ASUNETOS (ἀσύνετος), without understanding or discernment (*a*, negative, *sunetos*, intelligent, understanding), is translated "without understanding" in Matt. 15 : 16 ; Mark 7 : 18 ; Rom. 1 : 31 ; 10 : 19, R.V., " void of understanding " (A.V., " foolish ") ; in Rom. 1 : 21, R.V., " senseless " (A.V., " foolish ").¶

Note : In 1 Cor. 14 : 20, A.V., *phrēn*, the mind, is translated " understanding " (twice), R.V., " mind."

For UNDONE (leave) see LEAVE, No. 1

UNDRESSED

AGNAPHOS (ἄγναφος), uncarded (*a*, negative, *knaptō*, to card wool), is rendered " undressed," of cloth, in Matt. 9 : 16 and Mark 2 : 21, R.V. (A.V., " new ").¶

For UNEQUALLY see YOKED

UNFAITHFUL

APISTOS (ἄπιστος), unbelieving, faithless, is translated " unfaithful " in Luke 12 : 46, R.V. (A.V., " unbelievers "). See BELIEF, C, Note (3), FAITHLESS, INCREDIBLE.

For UNFEIGNED see DISSIMULATION, C

For UNFRUITFUL see FRUIT, B, No. 2

UNGODLINESS, UNGODLY
A. Noun.

ASEBEIA (ἀσέβεια), impiety, ungodliness, is used of (*a*) general impiety, Rom. 1 : 18 ; 11 : 26 ; 2 Tim. 2 : 16 ; Tit. 2 : 12 ; (*b*) ungodly deeds, Jude 15, R.V., " works of ungodliness " ; (*c*) of lusts or desires after evil things, Jude 18. It is the opposite of *eusebeia*, godliness.¶

Note : Anomia is disregard for, or defiance of, God's laws ; *asebeia* is the same attitude towards God's Person.

B. Adjective.

ASEBĒS (ἀσεβής), impious, ungodly (akin to A), without reverence for God, not merely irreligious, but acting in contravention of God's demands, Rom. 4 : 5 ; 5 : 6 ; 1 Tim. 1 : 9 ; 1 Pet. 4 : 18 ; 2 Pet. 2 : 5 (v. 6 in some mss.) ; 3 : 7 ; Jude 4, 15 (twice).¶

C. Verb.

ASEBEŌ (ἀσεβέω), akin to A and B, signifies (*a*) to be or live ungodly, 2 Pet. 2 : 6 ; (*b*) to commit ungodly deeds, Jude 15.¶

UNHOLY

1. ANOSIOS (ἀνόσιος) (*a*, negative, *n*, euphonic, *hosios*, holy), unholy, profane, occurs in 1 Tim. 1 : 9 ; 2 Tim. 3 : 2.¶ Cp. HOLY. In the Sept., Ezek. 22 : 9.¶

2. KOINON (κοινόν), the neut. of *koinos*, common, is translated " an unholy thing " in Heb. 10 : 29. See COMMON, DEFILE, C, UNCLEAN, A, No. 2.

For UNITED, Rom. 6 : 5, R.V., see PLANT, C ; in Heb. 4 : 2, see MIXED (with), Note

---

UNITY

HENOTĒS (ἑνότης), from *hen*, the neuter of *heis*, one, is used in Eph. 4 : 3, 13.¶

UNJUST

ADIKOS (ἄδικος), not in conformity with *dikē*, right, is rendered " unjust " in the A.V. and R.V. in Matt. 5 : 45 ; Luke 18 : 11 ; Acts 24 : 15 ; elsewhere for the A.V. " unjust " the R.V. has " unrighteous." See UNRIGHTEOUS.

Note : For *adikeō*, to be unrighteous, or do unrighteousness, Rev. 22 : 11, R.V., and *adikia*, " unrighteous," Luke 16 : 8 and 18 : 6, R.V., see UNRIGHTEOUSNESS.

For UNKNOWN see IGNORANCE, B, No. 1, and KNOW, B, No. 4

UNLADE

APOPHORTIZŌ (ἀποφορτίζω), to discharge a cargo (*apo*, from, *phortizō*, to load), is used in Acts 21 : 3.¶

UNLAWFUL

ATHEMITOS (ἀθέμιτος), a late form for *athemistos* (*themis*, custom, right ; in classical Greek, divine law), contrary to what is right, is rendered " an unlawful thing " (neuter) in Acts 10 : 28 ; in 1 Pet. 4 : 3, " abominable."¶

Note : For 2 Pet. 2 : 8, A.V., see LAWLESS.

UNLEARNED

1. AGRAMMATOS (ἀγράμματος), lit., unlettered (*grammata*, letters : *graphō*, to write), Acts 4 : 13, is explained by Grimm-Thayer as meaning " unversed in the learning of the Jewish schools ; " in the papyri, however, it occurs very frequently in a formula used by one who signs for another who cannot write, which suggests that the rulers, elders and scribes regarded the Apostles as " unlettered " (Moulton and Milligan).¶

2. AMATHĒS (ἀμαθής), unlearned (*manthanō*, to learn), is translated " unlearned " in 2 Pet. 3 : 16, A.V. (R.V., " ignorant ").¶

3. APAIDEUTOS (ἀπαίδευτος), uninstructed (*paideuō*, to train, teach), is translated " unlearned " in 2 Tim. 2 : 23, A.V. (R.V., " ignorant ").¶

Note : For *idiōtēs*, rendered " unlearned " in 1 Cor. 14 : 16, 23, 24, see IGNORANT, No. 4.

For UNLEAVENED see BREAD, No. 2

For UNLESS see EXCEPT

UNLIFTED

ANAKALUPTŌ (ἀνακαλύπτω), to uncover, unveil, used in 2 Cor. 3 : 14 with the negative *mē*, not, is rendered " unlifted," R.V., A.V., " untaken away " (a paraphrase rather than translation) ; the R.V. marg., " remaineth, it not being revealed that it is done away," is not to be preferred. The best rendering seems to be, ' the veil remains unlifted (for it is in Christ that it is done away).' Judaism does not recognise the vanishing of the glory of the Law as a means of life, under God's grace in Christ. In 3 : 18 the R.V., " unveiled (face) " (A.V., " open "), continues the metaphor of the veil (vv. 13–17), referring to hindrances to the perception of spiritual realities, hindrances removed in the unveiling.¶

UNLOOSE

LUŌ (λύω), to loose, is rendered to unloose in Mark 1 : 7 ; Luke 3 : 16 ; John 1 : 27 ; in Acts 13 : 25, R.V. : see LOOSE.

UNMARRIED

AGAMOS (ἄγαμος), *a*, negative, *gameō*, to marry, occurs in 1 Cor. 7 : 8, 11, 32, 34.¶

UNMERCIFUL

ANELEĒMŌN (ἀνελεήμων), without mercy (*a*, negative, *n*, euphonic, *eleēmōn*, merciful), occurs in Rom. 1 : 21.¶

For UNMIXED, Rev. 14 : 10, R.V., see MIXTURE, Note

For UNMOVEABLE, Acts 27 : 41, see MOVE, B, No. 1 ; in 1 Cor. 15 : 58, MOVE, B, No. 2

UNPREPARED

APARASKEUASTOS (ἀπαρασκεύαστος), from *a*, negative, and *paraskeuazō* (see PREPARE, B, No. 4), occurs in 2 Cor. 9 : 4.¶

UNPROFITABLE, UNPROFITABLENESS
A. Adjectives.

1. ACHREIOS (ἀχρεῖος), useless (*chreia*, use), unprofitable, occurs in Matt. 25 : 30 and Luke 17 : 10.¶ In the Sept., 2 Sam. 6 : 22.¶

2. ACHRĒSTOS (ἄχρηστος), unprofitable, unserviceable (*chrēstos*, serviceable), is said of Onesimus, Philm. 11, antithetically to *euchrēstos*, profitable, with a play on the name of the converted slave (from *onēsis*, profit).¶

Note : *Achreios* is more distinctly negative than *achrēstos*, which suggests positively hurtful.

3. ALUSITELĒS (ἀλυσιτελής), not advantageous, not making good the expense involved (*lusitelēs*, useful), occurs in Heb. 13 : 17.¶

4. ANŌPHELĒS (ἀνωφελής), not beneficial or serviceable (*a*, negative, *n*, euphonic, *ōpheleō*, to do good, to benefit), is rendered " unprofitable " in Tit. 3 : 9 ; in the neuter, used as a noun, " unprofitableness," Heb. 7 : 18, said of the Law as not accomplishing that which the " better hope " could alone bring.¶   In the Sept., Prov. 28 : 3 ; Isa. 44 : 10 ; Jer. 2 : 8.¶

B. Verb.

ACHREOŌ, or ACHREIOŌ (ἀχρεόω), akin to A, No. 1, to make useless, occurs in Rom. 3 : 12, in the Passive Voice, rendered " they have . . . become unprofitable."¶

For UNQUENCHABLE see QUENCH

UNREASONABLE

1. ALOGOS (ἄλογος), without reason, irrational, is rendered " unreasonable " in Acts 25 : 27. See Brute.

2. ATOPOS (ἄτοπος), lit., ' out of place ' (*topos*, a place), is translated " unreasonable " in 2 Thess. 3 : 2, where the meaning intended seems to be ' perverse,' ' truculent.' See Amiss.

For UNREBUKEABLE see BLAME, B, No. 5

UNRIGHTEOUS

ADIKOS (ἄδικος), not conforming to *dikē*, right, is translated " unrighteous " in Luke 16 : 10 (twice), R.V., 11 ; Rom. 3 : 5 ; 1 Cor. 6 : 1, R.V. ; 6 : 9 ; Heb. 6 : 10 ; 1 Pet. 3 : 18, R.V. ; 2 Pet. 2 : 9, R.V. : see Unjust.

UNRIGHTEOUSNESS
A. Noun.

ADIKIA (ἀδικία) denotes (*a*) injustice, Luke 18 : 6, lit., ' the judge of injustice ; ' Rom. 9 : 14 ; (*b*) unrighteousness, iniquity, e.g., Luke 16 : 8, lit., " the steward of unrighteousness," R.V. marg., i.e., characterized by unrighteousness ; Rom. 1 : 18, 29 ; 2 : 8 ; 3 : 5 ; 6 : 13 ; 1 Cor. 13 : 6, R.V., " unrighteousness ; " 2 Thess. 2 : 10, " [with all (lit., in every) deceit] of unrighteousness," i.e., deceit such as unrighteousness uses, and that in every variety ; Antichrist and his ministers will not be restrained by any scruple from words or deeds calculated to deceive ; 2 Thess. 2 : 12, of those who have pleasure in it, not an intellectual but a moral evil ; distaste for truth is the precursor of the rejection of it ; 2 Tim. 2 : 19, R.V. ; 1 John 1 : 9, which includes (*c*) ; (*c*) a deed or deeds violating law and justice (virtually the same as *adikēma*, an unrighteous act), e.g., Luke 13 : 27, " iniquity ; " 2 Cor. 12 : 13, " wrong," the wrong of depriving another of what is his own, here ironically of a favour ; Heb. 8 : 12, 1st clause, " iniquities," lit., ' unrighteousnesses' (plural, not as A.V.) ; 2 Pet. 2 : 13, 15, R.V., " wrong doing," A.V., " unrighteousness ; " 1 John 5 : 17. See INIQUITY.

Notes : (1) In 2 Cor. 6 : 14, A.V., *anomia,* lawlessness, is translated " unrighteousness " (R.V., " iniquity "). (2) *Adikia* is the comprehensive term for wrong, or wrong-doing, as between persons ; *anomia,* lawlessness, is the rejection of Divine law, or wrong committed against it.

B. Verb.

ADIKEŌ (ἀδικέω), to do wrong, is rendered in Rev. 22 : 11, R.V., firstly, " he that is unrighteous," lit., ' the doer of unrighteousness' (present participle of the verb, with the article), secondly, " let him do unrighteousness (still)," the retributive and permanent effect of a persistent course of unrighteous-doing (A.V., " he that is unjust, let him be unjust "). See HURT, OFFENDER, Note, WRONG.

For UNRIPE, UNTIMELY, see FIG, No. 2

UNRULY

1. ANUPOTAKTOS (ἀνυπότακτος), not subject to rule (*a*, negative, *n*, euphonic, *hupotassō*, to put in subjection), is used (*a*) of things, Heb. 2 : 8, R.V., " not subject " (A.V., " not put under ") ; (*b*) of persons, " unruly," 1 Tim. 1 : 9, R.V. (A.V., " disobedient ") ; Tit. 1 : 6, 10. See DISOBEDIENT, B, Note.¶

2. ATAKTOS (ἄτακτος) is rendered " unruly " in 1 Thess. 5 : 14, A.V. (marg. and R.V., " disorderly "). See DISORDERLY, A.¶

Note : In Jas. 3 : 8, some texts have *akataschetos,* ' that cannot be restrained,' A.V., " unruly : " see RESTLESS.¶

UNSEARCHABLE

1. ANEXERAUNĒTOS, or ANEXEREUNĒTOS (ἀνεξεραύνητος), *a*, negative, *n*, euphonic, *ex* (*ek*), out, *eraunaō*, to search, examine, is used in Rom. 11 : 33, of the judgments of God.¶

2. ANEXICHNIASTOS (ἀνεξιχνίαστος), with the same prefixes as in No. 1, and an adjectival form akin to *ichneuō*, to trace out (*ichnos*, a footprint, a track), is translated " unsearchable " in Eph. 3 : 8, of the riches of Christ ; in Rom. 11 : 33, " past tracing out," of the ways of the Lord (cp. No. 1, in the same verse). The ways of God are the outworkings of His judgment. Of the two questions in ver. 34, the first seems to have reference to No. 1, the second to No. 2. See FIND, Note (3), TRACE.¶

UNSEEMLINESS, UNSEEMLY

ASCHĒMOSUNĒ (ἀσχημοσύνη), from *aschēmōn*, unseemly, is rendered " unseemliness " in Rom. 1 : 27, R.V. : see SHAME, No. 4.

Note : For " behave . . . unseemly " see BEHAVE, No. 4.

For UNSETTLE, Gal. 5 : 12, R.V., see STIR, No. 12

For UNSKILFUL, Heb. 5 : 13, see EXPERIENCE, No. 1

UNSPEAKABLE

1. ANEKDIĒGĒTOS (ἀνεκδιήγητος) denotes inexpressible (*a*, negative, *n*, euphonic, *ekdiēgeomai*, to declare, relate), 2 Cor. 9 : 15, " unspeakable " (of the gift of God) ; regarding the various explanations of the gift, it seems most suitable to view it as the gift of His Son.¶

2. ANEKLALĒTOS (ἀνεκλάλητος) denotes unable to be told out (*eklaleō*, to speak out), 1 Pet. 1 : 8, of the believer's joy.¶

3. ARRHĒTOS (ἄρρητος), primarily, unspoken (*a*, negative, *rhētos*, spoken), denotes unspeakable, 2 Cor. 12 : 4, of the words heard by Paul when caught up into Paradise.¶ The word is common in sacred inscriptions especially in connection with the Greek Mysteries ; hence Moulton and Milligan suggest the meaning ' words too sacred to be uttered.'

For UNSPOTTED see SPOT, C

UNSTABLE, UNSTEDFAST

1. ASTĒRIKTOS (ἀστήρικτος), *a*, negative, *stērizō*, to fix, is used in 2 Pet. 2 : 14 ; 3 : 16, A.V., " unstable," R.V., " unstedfast."¶

2. AKATASTATOS (ἀκατάστατος), from *kathistēmi*, to set in order, is rendered " unstable " in Jas. 1 : 8 : see RESTLESS.

For UNTAKEN AWAY, 2 Cor. 3 : 14, A.V., see UNLIFTED

UNTHANKFUL

ACHARISTOS (ἀχάριστος) denotes ungrateful, thankless (*charis*, thanks), Luke 6 : 35 ; 2 Tim. 3 : 2.¶

UNTIL and UNTO : see † p. 9

For UNTIMELY see FIG, No. 2

For UNTOWARD see CROOKED

UNVEILED

AKATAKALUPTOS (ἀκατακάλυπτος), uncovered (*a*, negative, *katakaluptō*, to cover), is used in 1 Cor. 11 : 5, 13, R.V., " unveiled," with reference to the injunction forbidding women to be unveiled in a church gathering.¶ Whatever the character of the covering, it is to be on her head as " a sign of authority " (ver. 10), R.V., the meaning of which is indicated in ver. 3 in the matter of headships, and the reasons for which are given in vv. 7–9, and in the phrase " because of the angels," intimating their witness of, and interest in, that which betokens the headship of Christ. The injunctions were neither Jewish, which required men to be veiled in prayer, nor Greek, by which men and women were alike unveiled. The Apostle's instructions were " the commandment of the Lord " (14 : 37) and were for all the churches (vv. 33, 34).

Note : For the verb *anakaluptō,* rendered " unveiled " in 2 Cor. 3 : 18, R.V., see UNLIFTED (2nd ref.).

UNWASHEN

ANIPTOS (ἄνιπτος), unwashed (*a*, negative, *niptō*, to wash), occurs in Matt. 15 : 20 ; Mark 7 : 2 (ver. 5 in some mss.).¶

UNWILLING

Note : " I am unwilling " is the R.V. rendering of *thelō,* to will, with the negative *ou*, in 3 John 13 (A.V., " I will not ").

UNWISE

1. ANOĒTOS (ἀνόητος) is translated " unwise " in Rom. 1 : 14, A.V. ; see FOOLISH, No. 2.

2. APHRŌN (ἄφρων) is translated " unwise " in Eph. 5 : 17, A.V. ; see FOOLISH, No. 1.

3. ASOPHOS (ἄσοφος), *a*, negative, is rendered " unwise " in Eph. 5 : 15, R.V. (A.V., " fools ").¶

UNWORTHILY, UNWORTHY
A. Adverb.

ANAXIŌS (ἀναξίως) is used in 1 Cor. 11 : 27, of partaking of the Lord's Supper unworthily, i.e., treating it as a common meal, the bread and cup as common things, not apprehending their solemn symbolic import. In the best texts the word is not found in ver. 29 (see R.V.).¶

B. Adjective.

ANAXIOS (ἀνάξιος), *a*, negative, *n*, euphonic, *axios*, worthy, is used in 1 Cor. 6 : 2. In modern Greek it signifies " incapable."¶

Note : In Acts 13 : 46, " unworthy " represents the adjective *axios,* preceded by the negative *ouk.*

UP

Notes : (1) In Matt. 13 : 6 and Mark 4 : 6, A.V., *anatellō,* to rise (of the sun), is rendered " was up." See RISE. (2) The adverb is used with numerous Eng. verbs to translate single Greek verbs. In John 11 : 41 and Heb. 12 : 15, however, the adverb *anō,* up, is used separately : see ABOVE, BRIM, HIGH.

For UPBRAID see REPROACH, B, No. 1

UPHOLD

PHERŌ (φέρω), to bear, carry, uphold, is rendered "upholding" in Heb. 1 : 3. See BEAR.

UPON : see † p. 9

For UPPER see CHAMBER, COUNTRY, B, No. 1, ROOM

UPPERMOST

Note: In Luke 11 : 43 *prōtokathedria*, a chief seat, is translated "uppermost seats," A.V. (R.V., "chief seats"). In Matt. 23 : 6 and Mark 12 : 39, A.V., *prōtoklisia*, a chief place, is translated "uppermost rooms" (R.V., "chief place" and "chief places"). See CHIEF, B, Nos. 6 and 7.

UPRIGHT : see STRAIGHT, No. 2 ; UPRIGHTLY : see WALK, No. 6

UPRIGHTNESS

EUTHUTĒS (εὐθύτης), from *euthus*, straight, is rendered "uprightness" in Heb. 1 : 8, R.V., A.V., "righteousness," marg., "rightness," or, "straightness."¶

For UPROAR (Noun), *thorubos*, see TUMULT, and for *stasis* see RIOT

UPROAR (Verbs)

THORUBEŌ (θορυβέω), used in the Middle Voice, denotes to make a noise or uproar, or, transitively, in the Active Voice, to trouble, throw into confusion, Acts 17 : 5. See ADO, NOISE, TROUBLE.

Note: For *suncheō*, to confuse, Acts 21 : 31 (A.V., "was in an uproar"), see CONFUSION ; for *anastatoō*, Acts 21 : 38 (A.V., "madest an uproar"), see STIR UP.

For UPSIDE DOWN see TURN, No. 15

URGE

Notes: (1) In Acts 13 : 50, A.V., *parotrunō*, to urge on (R.V.), is rendered "stirred up".¶ (2) In Acts 13 : 43, *peithō*, to persuade, is rendered "urged," R.V. (A.V., "persuaded"). (3) For *enechō*, rendered "to urge" in Luke 11 : 53, A.V., see ENTANGLE, No. 3.

US

The oblique cases of *hēmeis*, we, are the genitive *hēmōn*, of us, the dative *hēmin*, to us, the accusative *hēmas*, us. When the nominative *hēmeis* is used, it is always emphatic, e.g., John 11 : 16, " (let) us (go);" lit., ' we, let us go ; ' 1 Thess. 5 : 8, " let us . . . be sober," lit., ' we . . . let us be sober.' Sometimes the oblique cases are governed by prepositions.

USE (Noun), USEFUL

1. HEXIS (ἕξις), akin to *echō*, to have, denotes habit, experience, " use," Heb. 5 : 14.¶

2. CHREIA (χρεία), need, is translated " uses " in Tit. 3 : 14 ; in Eph. 4 : 29, A.V., " (for the) use (of edifying)," R.V., " (as the) need (may be)." See NECESSITY, NEED.

3. CHRĒSIS (χρῆσις), use (akin to *chraomai*, to use), occurs in Rom. 1 : 26, 27.¶

Notes : (1) In 2 Tim. 2 : 21, the adjective *euchrēstos*, useful, serviceable (*eu*, well, *chraomai*, to use), is translated " meet for . . . use ; " in 4 : 11, " useful," R.V. (A.V., " profitable ") ; in Philm. 11, " profitable." See PROFITABLE, B, No. 2.¶ (2) In 1 Cor. 8 : 7 the best texts have the noun *sunētheia*, R.V., " being used," lit., ' by the custom (of the idol) ', i.e., by being associated. See CUSTOM. In the Sept., Prov. 31 : 13.¶ Contrast *achrēstos*, unprofitable, Philm. 11.¶

USE (Verb)

1. CHRAOMAI (χράομαι), from *chrē*, it is necessary, denotes (*a*) to use, Acts 27 : 17 ; 1 Cor. 7 : 21, where " use it rather " means ' use your bondservice rather ; ' 7 : 31, where " they that use (this world) " is followed by the strengthened form *katachraomai*, rendered " abusing," or " using to the full " (R.V., marg.) ; 9 : 12, 15 ; 2 Cor. 1 : 17 ; 3 : 12 ; 13 : 10 ; 1 Tim. 1 : 8, of using the Law lawfully, i.e., agreeably to its designs ; 1 Tim. 5 : 23 ; (*b*) deal with, Acts 27 : 3. See ENTREAT (to treat). Cp. the Active *chraō* (or *kichrēmi*), to lend, Luke 11 : 5. See LEND.¶

2. ECHŌ (ἔχω), to have, is rendered " using " in 1 Pet. 2 : 16 (marg., " having ") ; see HAVE.

3. ANASTREPHŌ (ἀναστρέφω) chiefly denotes to behave, to live in a certain manner, rendered " (were so) used " in Heb. 10 : 33 (Passive Voice) ; the verb, however, does not mean to treat or use ; here it has the significance of living amidst sufferings, reproaches etc. See ABIDE, BEHAVE, LIVE, OVERTHROW, PASS, RETURN.

Notes : (1) In Acts 19 : 19, A.V., *prassō*, to practise (R.V.), is rendered " used." (2) For Heb. 5 : 13, A.V., " useth (milk)," see PARTAKE, B, No. 3. (3) In 1 Thess. 2 : 5, " were we found using " is the rendering of the verb *ginomai*, to become, with the preposition *en*, in, governing the noun, " words (or speech) [of flattery] ; " this idiomatic phrase signifies to be engaged in, to resort to. A rendering close to the meaning of the Greek is ' for neither at any time did we fall into the use of flattering speech ; ' cp. 1 Tim. 2 : 14, " fallen into transgression." (4) To use is combined in Eng. with other words, e.g., DECEIT, DESPITEFULLY, HOSPITALITY, REPETITIONS.

USING

APOCHRĒSIS (ἀπόχρησις), a strengthened form of *chrēsis*, a using, and signifying a misuse (akin to *apochraomai*, to use to the full, abuse), is translated "using" in Col. 2 : 22 ; the clause may be rendered ' by their using up.' "The unusual word was chosen for its expressiveness ; the *chrēsis* here was an *apochrēsis* ; the things could not be used without rendering them unfit for further use" (Lightfoot).¶

For USURP see AUTHORITY, B, No. 3

USURY

Note: The R.V., "interest," Matt. 25 : 27 ; Luke 19 : 23, is the preferable rendering of *tokos* here. See INTEREST.¶

For UTMOST PART see END, A, No. 3

UTTER

1. LALEŌ (λαλέω), to speak, is rendered to utter in 2 Cor. 12 : 4 and Rev. 10 : 3, 4 (twice). See PREACH, SAY, SPEAK, TALK, TELL.

2. EREUGOMAI (ἐρεύγομαι), primarily, to spit or spue out, or, of oxen, to bellow, roar, hence, to speak aloud, utter, occurs in Matt. 13 : 35.¶ This affords an example of the tendency for certain words to become softened in force in late Greek.

3. APHIĒMI (ἀφίημι), to send forth, is used of uttering a cry, Mark 15 : 37, of Christ's final utterance on the Cross, R.V., "uttered" (A.V., "cried"). See FORGIVE, LAY, Note (2), LEAVE, LET, OMITTED, PUT, REMIT, SUFFER, YIELD.

4. DIDŌMI (δίδωμι), to give, is translated "utter" in 1 Cor. 14 : 9. See GIVE.

5. PHTHENGOMAI (φθέγγομαι), to utter a sound or voice, is translated "uttering" in 2 Pet. 2 : 18, R.V.: see SPEAK, No. 4.

Notes: (1) In Rom. 8 : 26, *alalētos*, inexpressible (*a*, negative, *laleō*, to speak), is rendered "which cannot be uttered."¶ (2) In Heb. 5 : 11, A.V., *dusermēneutos*, followed by *legō*, to speak, [translated "hard of interpretation" (R.V.), *dus* (whence *dys-* in Eng., dyspeptic, etc.), a prefix like Eng., un-, or mis-, and *hermēneuō*, to interpret], is rendered "hard to be uttered."¶

UTTERANCE

LOGOS (λόγος), a word, is translated "utterance" in 1 Cor. 1 : 5 ; 2 Cor. 8 : 7 ; Eph. 6 : 19. See WORD.

Notes: (1) In Col. 4 : 3, A.V., *logos* is rendered " (a door) of utterance." (2) For *apophthengomai*, rendered "utterance" in Acts 2 : 4, see SPEAK, No. 5.

For UTTERLY, 1 Cor. 6 : 7, see ACTUALLY ; 2 Pet. 2 : 12, see CORRUPT, A, No. 2 (*b*)

UTTERMOST

1. PANTELES (παντελές), the neuter of the adjèctive *pantelēs*, complete, perfect, used with *eis to* ('unto the'), is translated "to the uttermost" in Heb. 7 : 25, where the meaning may be 'finally;' in Luke 13 : 11 (negatively), "in no wise."¶

2. TELOS (τέλος), an end, is rendered "the uttermost" in 1 Thess. 2 : 16, said of Divine wrath upon the Jews, referring to the prophecy of Deut. 28 : 15–68; the nation as such, will yet, however, be delivered (Rom. 11 : 26; cp. Jer. 30 : 4–11). The full phrase is *eis telos*, to the uttermost, which is probably the meaning in John 13 : 1, "to the end."

Notes : (1) For "uttermost (farthing)," Matt. 5 : 26, A.V., see LAST. For "uttermost" in Acts 24 : 22, see DETERMINE, No. 5. (2) For "uttermost part (-s)", see END, A, No. 3 (*a*) and C (*b*).

V

For VAGABOND see STROLLING

For VAIL see VEIL

VAIN, IN VAIN, VAINLY
A. Adjectives.

1. KENOS (κενός), empty, with special reference to quality, is translated " vain " (as an adjective) in Acts 4 : 25 ; 1 Cor. 15 : 10, 14 (twice) ; Eph. 5 : 6 ; Col. 2 : 8 ; Jas. 2 : 20 ; in the following the neuter, *kenon*, follows the preposition *eis*, in, and denotes " in vain," 2 Cor. 6 : 1 ; Gal. 2 : 2 ; Phil. 2 : 16 (twice) ; 1 Thess. 3 : 5. See EMPTY, B, where the applications are enumerated.

2. MATAIOS (μάταιος), void of result, is used of (*a*) idolatrous practices, Acts 14 : 15, R.V., " vain things " (A.V., " vanities ") ; (*b*) the thoughts of the wise, 1 Cor. 3 : 20 ; (*c*) faith, if Christ is not risen, 1 Cor. 15 : 17 ; (*d*) questionings, strifes, etc., Tit. 3 : 9 ; (*e*) religion, with an unbridled tongue, Jas. 1 : 26 ; (*f*) manner of life, 1 Pet. 1 : 18.¶ For the contrast between No. 1 and No. 2 see EMPTY.

Note : For *mataiologoi*, Tit. 1 : 10, see TALKERS (vain).¶

B. Verbs.

1. MATAIOŌ (ματαιόω), to make vain, or foolish, corresponding in meaning to A, No. 2, occurs in Rom. 1 : 21, " became vain."¶

2. KENOŌ (κενόω), to empty, corresponding to A, No. 1, is translated " should be in vain " in 2 Cor. 9 : 3, A.V. See EFFECT, EMPTY, VOID.

C. Adverbs.

1. MATĒN (μάτην), properly the accusative case of *matē*, a fault, a folly, signifies in vain, to no purpose, Matt. 15 : 9 ; Mark 7 : 7.¶

2. DŌREAN (δωρεάν), the accusative of *dōrea*, a gift, is used adverbially, denoting (*a*) freely (see FREE, D) ; (*b*) uselessly, " in vain," Gal. 2 : 21, A.V. (R.V., " for nought "). See CAUSE, A, under " *without a cause.*"

3. EIKĒ (εἰκῆ) denotes (*a*) without cause, " vainly," Col. 2 : 18 ; (*b*) to no purpose, " in vain," Rom. 13 : 4 ; Gal. 3 : 4 (twice) ; 4 : 11. See CAUSE, A, Note (1), under " *without a cause.*"

VAINGLORY, VAINGLORIOUS
A. Nouns.

1. KENODOXIA (κενοδοξία), from *kenos*, vain, empty, *doxa*, glory, is used in Phil. 2 : 3.¶

2. ALAZONEIA, or –IA (ἀλαζονεία) denotes boastfulness, vaunting, translated " vainglory " in 1 John 2 : 16, R.V. (A.V., " pride ") ; in Jas. 4 : 16, R.V., " vauntings " (A.V., " boastings "). Cp. *alazōn*, a boaster.¶

B. Adjective.

KENODOXOS (κενόδοξος), akin to A, No. 1, is rendered " vainglorious " in Gal. 5 : 26, R.V. (A.V., " desirous of vain glory ").¶

For VALIANT see MIGHTY, B, No. 2, STRONG, No. 2 (a) (3)

VALLEY

PHARANX (φάραγξ) denotes a ravine or valley, sometimes figurative of a condition of loneliness and danger (cp. Psa. 23 : 4) ; the word occurs in Luke 3 : 5 (from the Sept. of Isa. 40 : 4).¶

VALUE
A. Verb.

DIAPHERŌ (διαφέρω), used intransitively, means to differ, to excel, hence to be of more value, Matt. 6 : 26, R.V., " are (not) ye of (much) more value " (A.V., " better ") ; 12 : 12 and Luke 12 : 24, ditto ; Matt. 10 : 31 ; Luke 12 : 7. See BETTER (be), CARRY, No. 4, DIFFER, DRIVE, No. 7, EXCELLENT, MATTER, Note (1), PUBLISH, No. 2.

Note : For *timaō*, rendered to value in Matt. 27 : 9 (twice), A.V., see PRICE.

B. Noun.

TIMĒ (τιμή) denotes a valuing, a price, honour ; in Col. 2 : 23, R.V., " (not of any) value (against the indulgence of the flesh) " [A.V., " (not in any) honour . . ."], i.e., the ordinances enjoined by human tradition are not of any value to prevent (*pros*, against ; cp. Acts 26 : 14) indulgence of the flesh. See HONOUR, PRECIOUS, PRICE, SUM.

VANISH, VANISHING
A. Verb.

APHANIZŌ (ἀφανίζω), to render unseen, is translated " vanisheth away " in Jas. 4 : 14 (Passive Voice, lit., ' is made to disappear '). See CONSUME, DISFIGURE, PERISH.

Note : In 1 Cor. 13 : 8, A.V., *katargeō*, to abolish, is rendered " it shall vanish away " (R.V., ". . . be done away "). See ABOLISH.

B. Noun.

APHANISMOS (ἀφανισμός), *a*, negative, *phainō*, to cause to appear (akin to A), occurs in Heb. 8 : 13, R.V., " (nigh unto) vanishing away ; " the word is suggestive of abolition.¶

Note : In Luke 24 : 31, the adjective *aphantos* (akin to A and B), invisible, used with *ginomai*, to become, and followed by *apo*, from, with the plural personal pronoun, is rendered " He vanished out of their sight " (A.V., marg., " He ceased to be seen of them "), lit., ' He became invisible from them.'¶

VANITY

MATAIOTĒS (ματαιότης), emptiness as to results, akin to *mataios* (see EMPTY, VAIN), is used (*a*) of the creation, Rom. 8 : 20, as failing of the results designed, owing to sin ; (*b*) of the mind which governs the manner of life of the Gentiles, Eph. 4 : 17 ; (*c*) of the " great swelling *words* " of false teachers, 2 Pet. 2 : 18.¶

Note : For *mataios*, in the neut. plur. in Acts 14 : 15, " vanities," see VAIN, A, No. 2 (*a*).

VAPOUR

ATMIS (ἀτμίς) is used of smoke, Acts 2 : 19 ; figuratively of human life, Jas. 4 : 14.¶

VARIABLENESS, VARIATION

PARALLAGĒ (παραλλαγή) denotes, in general, a change (Eng., *parallax*, the difference between the directions of a body as seen from two different points), a transmission from one condition to another ; it occurs in Jas. 1 : 17, R.V., " variation " (A.V., " variableness ") ; the reference may be to the sun, which varies its position in the sky.¶ In the Sept., 2 Kings 9 : 20.¶

VARIANCE

DICHAZŌ (διχάζω), to cut apart, divide in two, is used metaphorically in Matt. 10 : 35, " to set at variance."¶

Notes : (1) In Gal. 5 : 20, A.V., *eris*, strife (R.V.), is rendered " variance." (2) For *adiakritos*, Jas. 3 : 17, R.V., " without variance " (marg., " doubtfulness, or partiality "), A.V., " without partiality " (marg., " without wrangling "), see PARTIAL.¶

VAUNT (ONESELF)

PERPEREUOMAI (περπερεύομαι), to boast or vaunt oneself (from *perperos*, vainglorious, braggart, not in the N.T.), is used in 1 Cor. 13 : 4, negatively of love.¶

For VAUNTINGS see VAINGLORY

For VEHEMENT see DESIRE, A, No. 3

VEHEMENTLY

1. DEINŌS (δεινῶς), for which see GRIEVOUS, B, No. 1, is rendered " vehemently " in Luke 11 : 53.

2. EUTONŌS (εὐτόνως), vigorously, is translated " vehemently " in Luke 23 : 10, of accusations against Christ. See MIGHTY, D.

3. EKPERISSŌS (ἐκπερισσῶς), formed from *ek*, out of, and the adverb *perissōs*, exceedingly, the more, is found in Mark 14 : 31, in the best texts (some have *ek perissou*, the genitive case of the adjective *perissos*, more), R.V., " exceeding vehemently " (A.V., " the more vehemently "), of Peter's protestation of loyalty ; the R.V. gives the better rendering.¶

Note : For " brake (A.V., beat) vehemently," Luke 6 : 48, 49, see BEAT, No. 8.

VEIL

1. KATAPETASMA (καταπέτασμα), lit., that which is spread out (*petannumi*) before (*kata*), hence, a veil, is used (*a*) of the inner veil of the Tabernacle, Heb. 6 : 19 ; 9 : 3 ; (*b*) of the corresponding veil in the Temple, Matt. 27 : 51 ; Mark 15 : 38 ; Luke 23 : 45 ; (*c*) metaphorically of the " flesh " of Christ, Heb. 10 : 20, i.e., His body which He gave up to be crucified, thus by His expiatory Death providing a means of the spiritual access of believers, the " new and living way," into the presence of God.¶

2. KALUMMA (κάλυμμα), a covering, is used (*a*) of the veil which Moses put over his face when descending Mount Sinai, thus preventing Israel from beholding the glory, 2 Cor. 3 : 13 ; (*b*) metaphorically of the spiritually darkened vision suffered retributively by Israel, until the conversion of the nation to their Messiah takes place, vv. 14, 15, 16. See under UNLIFTED.¶

3. PERIBOLAION (περιβόλαιον), rendered " a veil " in the A.V. marg. of 1 Cor. 11 : 15 : see COVER, B, No. 1, VESTURE.¶

VENGEANCE

EKDIKĒSIS (ἐκδίκησις), lit., ' (that which proceeds) out of justice,' not, as often with human vengeance, out of a sense of injury or merely out of a feeling of indignation. The word is most frequently used of Divine vengeance, e.g., Rom. 12 : 19 ; Heb. 10 : 30. For a complete list see AVENGE, B, No. 2. The judgments of God are holy and right (Rev. 16 : 7), and free from any element of self-gratification or vindictiveness.

Notes : (1) *Dikē*, justice, is translated " vengeance " in the A.V. of Acts 28 : 4 and Jude 7 : see JUSTICE. (2) In Rom. 3 : 5, A.V., *orgē*, wrath (R.V.), is rendered " vengeance " : see ANGER, WRATH

For VENOMOUS see BEAST, No. 2

VERILY

1. ALĒTHŌS (ἀληθῶς), truly (akin to *alētheia*, truth), is translated "verily" in 1 John 2 : 5. See INDEED, No. 3, SURELY, TRULY.

2. AMĒN (ἀμήν), the transliteration of a Heb. word = 'truth,' is usually translated "verily" in the four Gospels ; in John's Gospel the Lord introduces a solemn pronouncement by the repeated word "verily, verily" twenty-five times. See AMEN.

3. ONTŌS (ὄντως), really (connected with *eimi*, to be), is rendered "verily" in Mark 11 : 32, R.V., and Gal. 3 : 21. See INDEED, No. 4.

Notes : (1) In Acts 16 : 37, *gar*, for, is translated "verily." (2) In Heb. 2 : 16, *dēpou* (in some texts *dē pou*), a particle meaning of course, we know, is rendered "verily."¶ (3) In Luke 11 : 51, A.V., *nai*, yea (R.V.), is translated "verily." (4) The particle *men* (see INDEED, No. 1) is rendered "verily," e.g., in 1 Cor. 5 : 3 ; 14 : 17 ; Heb. 12 : 10 ; in the A.V., Heb. 3 : 5 ; 7 : 5, 18 ; 1 Pet. 1 : 20 ; in Acts 26 : 9 it is combined with *oun* (therefore) : see YEA, No. 4.

For VERITY, 1 Tim. 2 : 7, A.V., see TRUTH

VERY

Notes : (1) When "very" forms part of the translation of numerous other words (e.g., act, bold, many, precious, sorrowful, well), there is no separate word in the original. (2) For *sphodra*, exceedingly, sometimes rendered "very" in the A.V., see EXCEEDING, B, No. 2. (3) Occasionally one of the forms of the pronoun *autos*, self, same, is translated "very ;" the R.V. rendering is sometimes "himself" etc., e.g., 1 Thess. 5 : 23, "(The God of peace) Himself ;" see, however, John 14 : 11, "(the) very (works) ;" Rom. 13 : 6 and Phil. 1 : 6, "(this) very (thing) ;" Heb. 10 : 1, "(the) very (image) ; "and the R.V., " very " (A.V., " same ") in Luke 12 : 12 ; 20 : 19 ; 24 : 13, 33 ; Acts 16 : 18 ; Rom. 9 : 17 ; Eph. 6 : 22. (4) Sometimes it translates the conjunction *kai*, in the sense of " even," e.g., Matt. 10 : 30 ; in 24 : 24, A.V., " very " (R.V., " even ") ; Luke 12 : 59. (5) In Philm. 12, R.V., " my very " translates the possessive pronoun *emos* (in the neuter plural, *ema*) used with emphasis. (6) In Mark 8 : 1 some texts have *pampollou*, " very great," A.V. (from *pas*, all, *polus*, much), R.V., "a great (*pollou*) multitude " (after *palin*, again). (7) For " very great " in Matt. 21 : 8 see GREAT, Note (6). (8) The adverb *lian* is translated "very" in Mark 16 : 2 ; 2 Cor. 11 : 5 ; 12 : 11. See EXCEEDING, B, No. 1.

VESSEL

1. SKEUOS (σκεῦος) is used (*a*) of a vessel or implement of various kinds, Mark 11 : 16 ; Luke 8 : 16 ; John 19 : 29 ; Acts 10 : 11, 16 ; 11 : 5 ; 27 : 17 (a sail) ; Rom. 9 : 21 ; 2 Tim. 2 : 20 ; Heb. 9 : 21 ; Rev. 2 : 27 ; 18 : 12 ; (*b*) of goods or household stuff, Matt. 12 : 29 and Mark 3 : 27,

"goods;" Luke 17 : 31, R.V., "goods" (A.V., "stuff"); (c) of persons, (1) for the service of God, Acts 9 : 15, "a (chosen) vessel;" 2 Tim. 2 : 21, "a vessel (unto honour);" (2) the subjects of Divine wrath, Rom. 9 : 22; (3) the subjects of Divine mercy, Rom. 9 : 23; (4) the human frame, 2 Cor. 4 : 7; perhaps 1 Thess. 4 : 4; (5) a husband and wife, 1 Pet. 3 : 7; of the wife, probably, 1 Thess. 4 : 4; while the exhortation to each one "to possess himself of his own vessel in sanctification and honour" is regarded by some as referring to the believer's body [cp. Rom. 6 : 13; 1 Cor. 9 : 27; see No. (4)], the view that the "vessel" signifies the wife, and that the reference is to the sanctified maintenance of the married state, is supported by the facts that in 1 Pet. 3 : 7 the same word *timē*, honour, is used with regard to the wife; again in Heb. 13 : 4, *timios*, honourable (R.V., "in honour") is used in regard to marriage; further, the preceding command in 1 Thess. 4 is against fornication, and the succeeding one (ver. 6) is against adultery.¶ In Ruth 4 : 10, Sept., *ktaomai*, to possess, is used of a wife.

2. ANGOS (ἄγγος) denotes a jar or pail, Matt. 13 : 48, in the best texts (some have No. 3). It is used, in an inscription, of a cinerary urn.¶

3. ANGEION (ἀγγεῖον) denotes a small vessel (a diminutive of No. 2), e.g., for carrying oil, Matt. 25 : 4.¶

Note : For *phaulos*, Jas. 3 : 16, R.V., see EVIL, A, No. 3.

VESTURE

1. HIMATION (ἱμάτιον), an outer garment, is rendered "vesture" in Rev. 19 : 13, 16, A.V. (R.V., "garment"). See APPAREL, No. 2.

2. HIMATISMOS (ἱματισμός), used of clothing in general, is translated "vesture" in Matt. 27 : 35, A.V., in a quotation from Ps. 22 : 18 (R.V., following the better texts, omits the quotation); in John 19 : 24, A.V. and R.V.; see CLOTHING, No. 4.

3. PERIBOLAION (περιβόλαιον) is translated "vesture" in Heb. 1 : 12, A.V. (R.V., "mantle"). See COVER, B, No. 1.

VEX

1. OCHLEŌ (ὀχλέω), to disturb, trouble, is used in the Passive Voice, of being troubled by evil spirits, Acts 5 : 16.¶

2. BASANIZŌ (βασανίζω), to torment, is translated "vexed" in 2 Pet. 2 : 8. See TORMENT.

Notes : (1) In Luke 6 : 18, the best texts have *enochleō*, R.V., "troubled." See TROUBLE, B, No. 5. (2) In 2 Pet. 2 : 7, A.V., *kataponeō*, to wear down with toil, is translated "vexed." See DISTRESS, B, No. 4. (3) In Acts 12 : 1, A.V., *kakoō*, to afflict (R.V.), is translated "to vex." See AFFLICT, No. 1. (4) For Matt. 17 : 15, A.V., "vexed," see GRIEVOUSLY, B, Note (2).

For VIAL see BOWL

VICTORY, VICTORIOUS
A. Nouns.

1. NIKĒ (νίκη), victory, is used in 1 John 5 : 4.¶
2. NIKOS (νῖκος), a later form of No. 1, is used in Matt. 12 : 20 ; 1 Cor. 15 : 54, 55, 57.¶

B. Verb.

NIKAŌ (νικάω), to conquer, overcome, is translated " (them) that come victorious (from) " in Rev. 15 : 2, R.V. (A.V., " that had gotten the victory "). See CONQUER, OVERCOME, PREVAIL.

VICTUALS

EPISITISMOS (ἐπισιτισμός), provisions, food (epi, upon, sitizō, to feed, nourish ; sitos, food), is translated " victuals " in Luke 9 : 12.¶

Note : In Matt. 14 : 15, A.V., brōma, food, meat, is translated " victuals " (R.V., " food "). See MEAT.

For VIGILANT, 1 Tim. 3 : 2, see TEMPERATE ; 1 Pet. 5 : 8, see WATCHFUL

VILE
A. Noun.

ATIMIA (ἀτιμία), dishonour, is translated " vile " in Rom. 1 : 26, R.V., marg., " (passions) of dishonour." See DISHONOUR.

B. Adjectives.

1. RHUPAROS (ῥυπαρός), filthy, dirty, is used (a) literally, of old shabby clothing, Jas. 2 : 2, " vile ;" (b) metaphorically, of moral defilement, Rev. 22 : 11 (in the best texts).¶ In the Sept., Zech. 3 : 3, 4.¶
2. PONĒROS (πονηρός), evil, is translated " vile " in Acts 17 : 5, R.V. (A.V., " lewd "). See BAD, EVIL.

Note : For " vile " in the A.V. of Phil. 3 : 21, see HUMILIATION.

VILLAGE

KŌMĒ (κώμη), a village, or country town, primarily as distinct from a walled town, occurs in the Gospels ; elsewhere only in Acts 8 : 25. The difference between polis, a city, and kōmē, is maintained in the N.T., as in Josephus. Among the Greeks the point of the distinction was not that of size or fortification, but of constitution and land. In the O.T. the city and the village are regularly distinguished. The Mishna makes the three distinctions, a large city, a city and a village.

The R.V. always substitutes " village(-s) " for A.V., " town(-s)," Matt. 10 : 11 ; Mark 8 : 23, 26, 27 ; Luke 5 : 17 ; 9 : 6, 12 ; John 7 : 42 ; 11 : 1, 30. See TOWN.

VILLANY

1. RHADIOURGIA (ῥᾳδιουργία) lit. and primarily denotes ease in working (rhadios, easy, ergon, work), easiness, laziness ; hence recklessness,

wickedness, Acts 13 : 10, R.V., " villany," A.V., " mischief."¶   In the papyri it is used of theft.

2. RHADIOURGĒMA (ῥᾳδιούργημα), a reckless act (akin to No. 1), occurs in Acts 18 : 14, R.V., " villany " (A.V., " lewdness ").¶

VINE, VINTAGE

AMPELOS (ἄμπελος) is used (a) lit., e.g., Matt. 26 : 29 and parallel passages ; Jas. 3 : 12 ; (b) figuratively, (1) of Christ, John 15 : 1, 4, 5 ; (2) of His enemies, Rev. 14 : 18, 19, " the vine of the earth " (R.V., " vintage " in v. 19), probably figurative of the remaining mass of apostate Christendom.¶

VINEDRESSER

AMPELOURGOS (ἀμπελουργός), a worker in a vineyard (from ampelos, a vine, and ergon), is rendered " vine-dresser " in Luke 13 : 7, R.V. (A.V., " dresser of the vineyard ").¶

VINEGAR

OXOS (ὄξος), akin to oxus, sharp, denotes sour wine, the ordinary drink of labourers and common soldiers ; it is used in the four Gospels of the vinegar offered to the Lord at His crucifixion.   In Matt. 27 : 34 the best texts have oinos, " wine " (R.V.). Some have oxos (A.V., vinegar), but Mark 15 : 23 (A.V. and R.V.) confirms the R.V. in the passage in Matthew.   This, which the soldiers offered before crucifying, was refused by Him, as it was designed to alleviate His sufferings ; the vinegar is mentioned in Mark 15 : 36 ; so Luke 23 : 36, and John 19 : 29, 30.¶   In the Sept., Numb. 6 : 3 ; Ruth 2 : 14 ; Ps. 69 : 21 ; Prov. 25 : 20.¶

VINEYARD

AMPELŌN (ἀμπελών) is used 22 times in the Synoptic Gospels ; elsewhere in 1 Cor. 9 : 7.

VIOLENCE, VIOLENT, VIOLENTLY
A. Nouns.

1. BIA (βία) denotes force, violence, said of men, Acts 5 : 26 ; 21 : 35 ; 24 : 7 ; of waves, 27 : 41.¶

2. HORMĒMA (ὅρμημα), a rush (akin to hormaō, to urge on, to rush), is used of the fall of Babylon, Rev. 18 : 21, A.V., " violence," R.V., " mighty fall."¶

3. BIASTĒS (βιαστής), a forceful or violent man, is used in Matt. 11 : 12. See FORCE, B, No. 1, Note.¶

Note : In Heb. 11 : 34, A.V., dunamis, power (R.V.), is rendered " violence."

B. Verbs.

1. DIASEIŌ (διασείω), to shake violently, is used in Luke 3 : 14, " do violence," including intimidation.¶   In the Sept., Job 4 : 14.¶

2. BIAZŌ (βιάζω), in the Passive Voice, is rendered "suffereth violence" in Matt. 11 : 12 ; see FORCE, B, Nos. 1 and 2. Some, e.g., Cremer (Lexicon) and Dalman (*Words of Jesus*, pp. 139, ff.), hold that the reference is to the antagonism of the enemies of the Kingdom, but Luke 16 : 16 (Middle Voice : R.V., " entereth violently ") indicates the meaning as referring to those who make an effort to enter the Kingdom in spite of violent opposition : see PRESS, A, No. 3.¶

Note : For *hormaō*, rendered "ran violently," in Matt. 8 : 32 and parallels, see RUN, RUSH.

VIPER

ECHIDNA (ἔχιδνα) is probably a generic term for poisonous snakes. It is rendered " viper " in the N.T., (*a*) of the actual creature, Acts 28 : 3 ; (*b*) metaphorically in Matt. 3 : 7 ; 12 : 34 ; 23 : 33 ; Luke 3 : 7.¶

VIRGIN

PARTHENOS (παρθένος) is used (*a*) of the Virgin Mary, Matt. 1 : 23 ; Luke 1 : 27 ; (*b*) of the ten virgins in the parable, Matt. 25 : 1, 7, 11 ; (*c*) of the daughters of Philip the evangelist, Acts 21 : 9 ; (*d*) those concerning whom the Apostle Paul gives instructions regarding marriage, 1 Cor. 7 : 25, 28, 34 ; in vv. 36, 37, 38, the subject passes to that of 'virgin *daughters*' (R.V.), which almost certainly formed one of the subjects upon which the church at Corinth sent for instructions from the Apostle ; one difficulty was relative to the discredit which might be brought upon a father (or guardian), if he allowed his daughter or ward to grow old unmarried. The interpretation that this passage refers to a man and woman already in some kind of relation by way of a spiritual marriage and living together in a vow of virginity and celibacy, is untenable if only in view of the phraseology of the passage ; (*e*) figuratively, of a local church in its relation to Christ, 2 Cor. 11 : 2 ; (*f*) metaphorically, of chaste persons, Rev. 14 : 4.¶

VIRGINITY

PARTHENIA (παρθενία), akin to the above, occurs in Luke 2 : 36.¶ In the Sept., Jer. 3 : 4.¶

VIRTUE

ARETĒ (ἀρετή) properly denotes whatever procures pre-eminent estimation for a person or thing ; hence, intrinsic eminence, moral goodness, virtue, (*a*) of God, 1 Pet. 2 : 9, " excellencies " (A.V., " praises ") ; here the original and general sense seems to be blended with the impression made on others, i.e., renown, excellence or praise (Hort) ; in 2 Pet. 1 : 3, " (by His own glory and) virtue," R.V. (instrumental dative), i.e., the manifestation of His divine power ; this significance is frequently illustrated in the papyri and was evidently common in current Greek speech ; (b) of any particular moral excellence, Phil. 4 : 8 ; 2 Pet. 1 : 5 (twice), where virtue is enjoined as an essential quality in the exercise of faith, R.V., " (in your faith supply) virtue."¶

Note : In the A.V. of Mark 5 : 30 ; Luke 6 : 19 ; 8 : 46, *dunamis*, " power " (R.V.), is rendered " virtue."

VISIBLE

HORATOS (ὁρατός), from *horaō*, to see, occurs in Col. 1 : 16.¶

VISION

1. HORAMA (ὅραμα), that which is seen (*horaō*), denotes (a) a spectacle, sight, Matt. 17 : 9 ; Acts 7 : 31 (" sight ") ; (b) an appearance, vision, Acts 9 : 10 (ver. 12 in some mss.) ; 10 : 3, 17, 19 ; 11 : 5 ; 12 : 9 ; 16 : 9, 10 ; 18 : 9.¶

2. HORASIS (ὅρασις), sense of sight, is rendered " visions " in Acts 2 : 17 ; Rev. 9 : 17. See Look, B.

3. OPTASIA (ὀπτασία) (a late form of *opsis*, the act of seeing), from *optanō*, to see, a coming into view, denotes a vision in Luke 1 : 22 ; 24 : 23 ; Acts 26 : 19 ; 2 Cor. 12 : 1.¶

VISIT

1. EPISKEPTOMAI (ἐπισκέπτομαι), primarily, to inspect (a late form of *episkopeō*, to look upon, care for, exercise oversight), signifies (a) to visit with help, of the act of God, Luke 1 : 68, 78 ; 7 : 16 ; Acts 15 : 14 ; Heb. 2 : 6 ; (b) to visit the sick and afflicted, Matt. 25 : 36, 43 ; Jas. 1 : 27 ; (c) to go and see, pay a visit to, Acts 7 : 23 ; 15 : 36 ; (d) to look out certain men for a purpose, Acts 6 : 3. See Look.¶

Note : In the Sept., to visit with punishment, e.g., Psa. 89 : 32 ; Jer. 9 : 25.

2. HISTOREO (ἱστορέω), from *histōr*, one learned in anything, denotes to visit in order to become acquainted with, Gal. 1 : 18, R.V., " visit " (A.V., " see "), R.V. marg., " become acquainted with."¶

3. EPIPHERO (ἐπιφέρω), for which see Bring, No. 6, is rendered " visiteth (with wrath) " in Rom. 3 : 5, R.V., A.V., " taketh (vengeance)."

VISITATION

EPISKOPE (ἐπισκοπή), for which see Bishop, No. 2, denotes a visitation, whether in mercy, Luke 19 : 44, or in judgment, 1 Pet. 2 : 12.

For VOCATION, Eph. 4 : 1, see CALL, B

VOICE

PHONE (φωνή), a sound, is used of the voice (a) of God, Matt. 3 : 17 ; John 5 : 37 ; 12 : 28, 30 ; Acts 7 : 31 ; 10 : 13, 15 ; 11 : 7, 9 ; Heb. 3 : 7, 15 ; 4 : 7 ; 12 : 19, 26 ; 2 Pet. 1 : 17, 18 ; Rev. 18 : 4 ; 21 : 3 ; (b) of Christ,

(1) in the days of His flesh, Matt. 12 : 19 (negatively) ; John 3 : 29 ; 5 : 25 ; 10 : 3, 4, 16, 27 ; 11 : 43 ; 18 : 37 ; (2) on the Cross, Matt. 27 : 46, and parallel passages ; (3) from heaven, Acts 9 : 4, 7 ; 22 : 7, 9, 14 ; 26 : 14 ; Rev. 1 : 10, 12 (here, by metonymy, of the speaker), 15 ; 3 : 20 ; (4) at the resurrection " to life ", John 5 : 28 ; 1 Thess. 4 : 16, where " the voice of the archangel " is, lit., ' a voice of an archangel,' and probably refers to the Lord's voice as being of an archangelic character ; (5) at the resurrection to judgment, John 5 : 28 [not the same event as (4)] ; (c) of human beings on earth, e.g., Matt. 2 : 18 ; 3 : 3 ; Luke 1 : 42, in some texts, A.V., " voice ", and frequently in the Synoptists ; (d) of angels, Rev. 5 : 11, and frequently in the Apocalypse ; (e) of the redeemed in heaven, e.g., Rev. 6 : 10 ; 18 : 22 ; 19 : 1, 5 ; (f) of a pagan god, Acts 12 : 22 ; (g) of things, e.g., wind, John 3 : 8, R.V., " voice " (A.V., " sound "). See SOUND.

Notes : (1) In Luke 1 : 42 (1st part), A.V., *anaphōneō,* to lift up one's voice, is rendered " spake out," R.V., " lifted up (her) voice." (2) In Acts 26 : 10, A.V., " I gave my voice " (R.V., " . . . vote ") : see STONE, No. 2.

VOID

1. KENOŌ (κενόω), to empty, make of no effect, is rendered to make void, in Rom. 4 : 14 ; 1 Cor. 1 : 17, R.V. ; 9 : 15 ; 2 Cor. 9 : 3, R.V. See EFFECT (of none), No. 3, EMPTY, VAIN, B, No. 2.

2. ATHETEŌ (ἀθετέω), for which see DISANNUL, No. 1, is rendered to make void in Gal. 2 : 21, R.V. (A.V., " frustrate "); 3 : 15, R.V.

3. AKUROŌ (ἀκυρόω), for which see DISANNUL, No. 2, is rendered to make void in Matt. 15 : 6 ; Mark 7 : 13, R.V.

Notes : (1) In Rom. 3 : 31, A.V., *katargeō* is translated to make void. See ABOLISH, EFFECT (of none), No. 2. (2) See also IMPOSSIBLE, B, OFFENCE, UNDERSTANDING.

For VOLUME see ROLL, B

VOLUNTARY

Note : In Col. 2 : 18, *thelō* (for which see DESIRE, B, No. 6) is rendered " (in a) voluntary (humility)," present participle, i.e., " being a voluntary (in humility)," A.V. marg., R.V. marg., " of his own mere will (by humility)," *en,* in, being rendered as instrumental; what was of one's own mere will, with the speciousness of humility, would mean his being robbed of his prize.

VOMIT

EXERAMA (ἐξέραμα), a vomit (from *exeraō,* to disgorge), occurs in 2 Pet. 2 : 22. ¶

For VOTE, Acts 26 : 10, R.V., see STONE, No. 2

VOUCHSAFE

HOMOLOGEŌ (ὁμολογέω), to agree, is found in the best texts in Acts 7 : 17, and rendered " vouchsafed," R.V., with reference to God's promise to Abraham ; some mss. have ōmosen, " swore " (omnumi, to swear), as in A.V. See CONFESS, PROFESS, PROMISE, THANKS, B, Note.

VOW

EUCHĒ (εὐχή) denotes also a vow, Acts 18 : 18 ; 21 : 23, with reference to the vow of the Nazirite (wrongly spelt Nazarite), see Numb. 6, R.V. ; in Jas. 5 : 15, " prayer." See PRAYER.¶

VOYAGE

PLOOS or PLOUS (πλόος) is rendered a voyage (pleō, to sail) in Acts 27 : 10 (A.V. and R.V.) ; in 21 : 7, R.V. (A.V., " course ") ; in 27 : 9, R.V. (A.V., " sailing "). See COURSE, B, Note (4).¶

W

WAG

KINEŌ (κινέω), to move, is used of those who mocked the Lord at His crucifixion, nodding their heads in the direction of the Cross as if sneering at this supposed ending of His career, Matt. 27 : 39 ; Mark 15 : 29. Cp. 2 Kings 19 : 21 ; Job 16 : 4 ; Psa. 22 : 7 ; 109 : 25 ; Is. 37 : 22. See MOVE, No. 1.

WAGES

1. OPSŌNION (ὀψώνιον), for which see CHARGE, A, No. 5, denotes (a) soldiers' pay, Luke 3 : 14 ; 1 Cor. 9 : 7 (" charges ") ; (b) in general, hire, wages of any sort, used metaphorically, Rom. 6 : 23, of sin ; 2 Cor. 11 : 8, of material support which Paul received from some of the churches which he had established and to which he ministered in spiritual things ; their support partly maintained him at Corinth, where he forebore to receive such assistance (vv. 9, 10).¶

2. MISTHOS (μισθός), hire, is rendered " wages " in John 4 : 36 ; in 2 Pet. 2 : 15, A.V. (R.V., " hire "). See HIRE, A.

WAIL, WAILING

Notes : (1) For *alalazō*, rendered to wail in Mark 5 : 38, see CLANGING. (2) For *koptō*, rendered to wail in Rev. 1 : 7, A.V. (R.V., " shall mourn ") and 18 : 9, R.V., " wail " (A.V., " lament "), see BEWAIL. (3) For *pentheō*, rendered to wail in Rev. 18 : 15, 19, A.V., see MOURN. (4) For *klauthmos*, rendered " wailing " in Matt. 13 : 42, 50, A.V., see WEEP. (5) In Matt. 11 : 17 and Luke 7 : 32, A.V.,*thrēneō*, to wail (R.V.), is rendered to mourn. See BEWAIL, Note (1), MOURN.

WAIT

1. EKDECHOMAI (ἐκδέχομαι), for which see EXPECT, No. 1, is rendered to wait in John 5 : 3, A.V. ; Acts 17 : 16 ; 1 Cor. 11 : 33, R.V.

2. APEKDECHOMAI (ἀπεκδέχομαι), to await or expect eagerly, is rendered to wait for in Rom. 8 : 19, 23, 25 ; 1 Cor. 1 : 7 ; Gal. 5 : 5 ; Phil. 3 : 20, R.V. (A.V., " look for ") ; Heb. 9 : 28, R.V. (A.V., " look for "), here " them that wait " represents believers in general, not a section of them ; 1 Pet. 3 : 20 (in the best texts ; some have No. 1). See LOOK (for), Note (1).¶

3. PROSDECHOMAI (προσδέχομαι), to look for with a view to

favourable reception, is rendered to wait for in Mark 15 : 43 ; Luke 2 : 25 ; 12 : 36 ; 23 : 51. See LOOK (for), No. 2.

4. PROSDOKAŌ (προσδοκάω), to await, is rendered to wait for in Luke 1 : 21 ; 8 : 40 ; Acts 10 : 24 ; in 27 : 33, R.V., " ye wait " (A.V., " have tarried "). See LOOK (for), No. 1.

5. ANAMENŌ (ἀναμένω), to wait for (ana, up, used intensively, and menō, to abide), is used in 1 Thess. 1 : 10, of waiting for the Son of God from Heaven ; the word carries with it the suggestion of waiting with patience and confident expectancy.¶

6. PERIMENŌ (περιμένω), to await an event, is used in Acts 1 : 4, of waiting for the Holy Spirit, " the promise of the Father."¶ In the Sept., Gen. 49 : 18.¶

7. PROSKARTEREŌ (προσκαρτερέω), to continue stedfastly, is rendered to wait on, in Mark 3 : 9 and Acts 10 : 7. See CONTINUE, No. 9 (in the Sept., Numb. 13 : 21¶).

8. PAREDREUŌ (παρεδρεύω), to sit constantly beside (para, beside, hedra, a seat), is used in the best texts in 1 Cor. 9 : 13, R.V., " wait upon (A.V., at) (the altar)."¶ In the Sept., Prov. 1 : 21 ; 8 : 3.¶

Notes : (1) In 2 Thess. 3 : 5, A.V., *hupomonē*, patience (so R.V.), is rendered " patient waiting " (marg., " patience "). See PATIENCE. (2) For " lie in wait " in Eph. 4 : 14, A.V., see WILES. (3) For " lying in wait," Acts 20 : 19, A.V., and " laid wait," 20 : 3 ; 23 : 30, see PLOT.

WAKE

GRĒGOREŌ (γρηγορέω), translated " wake " in 1 Thess. 5 : 10, is rendered " watch " in the R.V. marg., as in the text in ver. 6, and the R.V. in the twenty-one other places in which it occurs in the N.T. (save 1 Pet. 5 : 8, " be watchful "). It is not used in the metaphorical sense of ' to be alive ; ' here it is set in contrast with *katheudō*, ' to sleep,' which is never used by the Apostle with the meaning ' to be dead ' (it has this meaning only in the case of Jairus' daughter). Accordingly the meaning here is that of vigilance and expectancy as contrasted with laxity and indifference. All believers will live together with Christ from the time of the Rapture described in chap. 4 ; for all have spiritual life now, though their spiritual condition and attainment vary considerably. Those who are lax and fail to be watchful will suffer loss (1 Cor. 3 : 15 ; 9 : 27 ; 2 Cor. 5 : 10, e.g.), but the Apostle is not here dealing with that aspect of the subject. What he does make clear is that the Rapture of believers at the Second Coming of Christ will depend solely on the Death of Christ for them, and not upon their spiritual condition. The Rapture is not a matter of reward, but of salvation. See WATCH.

WALK

1. PERIPATEŌ (περιπατέω) is used (a) physically, in the Synoptic Gospels (except Mark 7 : 5) ; always in the Acts except in 21 : 21 ; never in

the Pauline Epistles, nor in those of John ; (b) figuratively, " signifying the whole round of the activities of the individual life, whether of the unregenerate, Eph. 4 : 17, or of the believer, 1 Cor. 7 : 17 ; Col. 2 : 6. It is applied to the observance of religious ordinances, Acts 21 : 21 ; Heb. 13 : 9, marg., as well as to moral conduct. The Christian is to walk in newness of life, Rom. 6 : 4, after the spirit, 8 : 4, in honesty, 13 : 13, by faith, 2 Cor. 5 : 7, in good works, Eph. 2 : 10, in love, 5 : 2, in wisdom, Col. 4 : 5, in truth, 2 John 4, after the commandments of the Lord, v. 6. And, negatively, not after the flesh, Rom. 8 : 4 ; not after the manner of men, 1 Cor. 3 : 3 ; not in craftiness, 2 Cor. 4 : 2 ; not by sight, 5 : 7 ; not in the vanity of the mind, Eph. 4 : 17 ; not disorderly, 2 Thess. 3 : 6."* See Go, Note (2) (r).

2. POREUŌ (πορεύω), for which see DEPART, No. 8, and GO, No. 1, is used in the Middle Voice and rendered to walk in Luke 1 : 6, of the general activities of life ; so in Luke 13 : 33, A.V.," walk " (R.V., " go on My way ") ; Acts 9 : 31 ; 14 : 16 ; 1 Pet. 4 : 3 ; 2 Pet. 2 : 10 ; Jude, 16, 18.

3. EMPERIPATEŌ (ἐμπεριπατέω), to walk about in, or among (en, in, and No. 1), is used in 2 Cor. 6 : 16, of the activities of God in the lives of believers.¶

4. STOICHEŌ (στοιχέω), from stoichos, a row, signifies to walk in line, and is used metaphorically of walking in relation to others (No. 1 is used more especially of the individual walk) ; in Acts 21 : 24, it is translated " walkest orderly ; " in Rom. 4 : 12, " walk (in . . . steps) ; " in Gal. 5 : 25 it is used of walking " by the Spirit," R.V., in an exhortation to keep step with one another in submission of heart to the Holy Spirit, and therefore of keeping step with Christ, the great means of unity and harmony in a church (contrast No. 1 in ver. 16 ; ver. 25 begins a new section which extends to 6 : 10) ; in 6 : 16 it is used of walking by the rule expressed in vv. 14, 15 ; in Phil. 3 : 16 the reference is to the course pursued by the believer who makes " the prize of the high calling " the object of his ambition.¶   In the Sept., Eccl. 11 : 6.¶

5. DIERCHOMAI (διέρχομαι), to go through (dia), is rendered to walk through in the A.V. of Matt. 12 : 43 and Luke 11 : 24 (R.V., " passeth through "). See COME, No. 5, PASS, No. 2.

6. ORTHOPODEŌ (ὀρθοποδέω), to walk in a straight path (orthos, straight, pous, a foot), is used metaphorically in Gal. 2 : 14, signifying a course of conduct by which one leaves a straight track for others to follow (" walked . . . uprightly ").¶

Note : In Mark 1 : 16, A.V., paragō, to pass along (R.V., " passing along "), is translated " walked."

WALL

1. TEICHOS (τεῖχος), a wall, especially one around a town, is used

---

* From Notes on Thessalonians by Hogg and Vine, p. 67.

(a) literally, Acts 9 : 25 ; 2 Cor. 11 : 33 ; Heb. 11 : 30 ; (b) figuratively, of the wall of the Heavenly city, Rev. 21 : 12, 14, 15, 17, 18, 19.¶

2. TOICHOS (τοῖχος), a wall, especially of a house, is used figuratively in Acts 23 : 3, " (thou whited) wall."¶

3. MESOTOICHON (μεσότοιχον), a partition wall (mesos, middle, and No. 2), occurs in Eph. 2 : 14, figuratively of the separation of Gentile from Jew in their unregenerate state, a partition demolished by the Cross for both on acceptance of the Gospel. Cp. PARTITION.¶

WALLET

PĒRA (πήρα), a traveller's leathern bag or pouch for holding provisions, is translated " wallet " in the R.V. (A.V., " scrip "), Matt. 10 : 10 ; Mark 6 : 8 ; Luke 9 : 3 ; 10 : 4 ; 22 : 35, 36.¶ Deissmann (*Light from the Ancient East*) regards it as an alms-bag.

WALLOW (Verb and Noun)
A. Verb.

KULIŌ (κυλίω) in the Active Voice denotes to roll, roll along ; in the Middle Voice in Mark 9 : 20, rendered " wallowed."¶

B. Noun.

KULISMOS (κυλισμός), a rolling, wallowing, akin to A (some texts have *kulisma*), is used in 2 Pet. 2 : 22, of the proverbial sow that had been washed.¶

WANDER
A. Verb.

PLANAŌ (πλανάω), for which see DECEIT, C, No. 6, is translated to wander in Heb. 11 : 38, Passive Voice, lit., ' were made to wander.'

Note : In the A.V. of 1 Tim. 5 : 13 and Heb. 11 : 37, *perierchomai*, to go about or around, is translated to wander about. See Go, No. 29.

B. Noun.

PLANĒTĒS (πλανήτης), a wanderer (Eng., planet), is used metaphorically in Jude 13, of the evil teachers there mentioned as " wandering (stars)."¶ In the Sept., Hos. 9 : 17.¶

WANT (Noun and Verb)
A. Nouns.

1. HUSTERĒSIS (ὑστέρησις), akin to B, No. 1 (below), occurs in Mark 12 : 14 and Phil. 4 : 11.¶

2. HUSTERĒMA (ὑστέρημα) denotes (more concretely than No. 1) (a) that which is lacking (see LACK) ; (b) need, poverty, want, rendered " want " in Luke 21 : 4 (A.V., " penury ") ; 2 Cor. 8 : 14 (twice) ; 9 : 12 ; 11 : 9 (2nd occurrence), R.V., " want " (A.V., " that which was lacking ").

3. CHREIA (χρεία) is rendered " want " in Phil. 2 : 25, A.V. (R.V., " need "). See BUSINESS.

B. Verbs.

1. HUSTEREŌ (ὑστερέω) signifies to be in want, Luke 15 : 14 ; 2 Cor. 11 : 9 (1st occurrence) ; Phil. 4 : 12, R.V. (A.V. " to suffer need ") ; in John 2 : 3, A.V., " wanted " (R.V., " failed "). See BEHIND, B, No. 1.

2. LEIPŌ (λείπω), to leave, is rendered ' to be wanting ' in Tit. 1 : 5 and 3 : 13, and in the A.V. in Jas. 1 : 4. See LACK, C, No. 3.

WANTONNESS, WANTON, WANTONLY
A. Nouns.

1. ASELGEIA (ἀσέλγεια), lasciviousness, licentiousness, is rendered " wantonness " in 2 Pet. 2 : 18, A.V. ; see LASCIVIOUSNESS.

2. STRĒNOS (στρῆνος), insolent luxury, is rendered " wantonness " in Rev. 18 : 3, R.V. (marg., " luxury ; " A.V., " delicacies," not a sufficiently strong rendering).¶

B. Verbs.

1. STRĒNIAŌ (στρηνιάω), akin to A, No. 2, to run riot, is rendered " waxed wanton " in Rev. 18 : 7, R.V., and " lived wantonly " in ver. 8. See DELICATELY, Note (1). The root of the verb is seen in the Latin strenuus.¶

2. KATASTRĒNIAŌ (καταστρηνιάω), an intensive form of No. 1, to wax wanton against, occurs in 1 Tim. 5 : 11.¶

WAR (Verb and Noun)
A. Verbs.

1. POLEMEŌ (πολεμέω) (Eng., polemics), to fight, to make war, is used (a) literally, Rev. 12 : 7 (twice), R.V. ; 13 : 4 ; 17 : 14 ; 19 : 11 ; (b) metaphorically, Rev. 2 : 16, R.V. ; (c) hyperbolically, Jas. 4 : 2. See FIGHT, B, Note (1).¶

2. STRATEUŌ (στρατεύω), used in the Middle Voice, to make war (from stratos, an encamped army), is translated to war in 2 Cor. 10 : 3 ; metaphorically, of spiritual conflict, 1 Tim. 1 : 18 ; 2 Tim. 2 : 3, A.V. ; Jas. 4 : 1 ; 1 Pet. 2 : 11. See SOLDIER, B.

3. ANTISTRATEUOMAI (ἀντιστρατεύομαι), not found in the Active Voice antistrateuō, to make war against (anti), occurs in Rom. 7 : 23.¶

Note : For " men of war," Luke 23 : 11, A.V., see SOLDIER, No. 2.

B. Noun.

POLEMOS (πόλεμος), war (akin to A, No. 1), is so translated in the R.V., for A.V., " battle," 1 Cor. 14 : 8 ; Rev. 9 : 7, 9 ; 16 : 14 ; 20 : 8 ; for A.V., " fight," Heb. 11 : 34 ; A.V. and R.V. in Jas. 4 : 1, hyperbolically of private quarrels ; elsewhere, literally, e.g., Matt. 24 : 6 ; Rev. 11 : 7. See BATTLE.

WARD

1. PHULAKĒ (φυλακή), a guard, is used of the place where persons are kept under guard (akin to phulax, a keeper), and translated " ward "

in Acts 12 : 10. See CAGE, HOLD (Noun), IMPRISONMENT, PRISON, WATCH.

2. TĒRĒSIS (τήρησις) primarily denotes a watching (tēreō, to watch) ; hence imprisonment, ward, Acts 4 : 3 (A.V., " hold ") ; 5 : 18, R.V., " (public) ward" [A.V., "(common) prison"]. See HOLD (Noun), KEEPING, B, PRISON.

Note : For " were kept in ward," Gal. 3 : 23, see GUARD, B, No. 3, KEEP, No. 6.

WARE OF

PHULASSŌ (φυλάσσω) denotes to guard, watch ; in 2 Tim. 4 : 15, " of (whom) be thou ware " (Middle Voice) : see BEWARE, No. 3.

Note : For *sunoida*, translated "were ware " in Acts 14 : 6, A.V. (R.V., " became aware of it "), see KNOW, A, No. 6.

WARFARE

STRATEIA, or -TIA (στρατεία), primarily a host or army, came to denote a warfare, and is used of spiritual conflict in 2 Cor. 10 : 4 ; 1 Tim. 1 : 18.¶

Note : For the verb to go a warfare, 1 Cor. 9 : 7, A.V., see SOLDIER, B, No. 1.

WARM (Verb)

THERMAINŌ (θερμαίνω), to warm, heat (Eng. thermal etc.), when used in the Middle Voice, signifies to warm oneself, Mark 14 : 54, 67 ; John 18 : 18 (twice), 25 ; Jas. 2 : 16.¶

WARN

1. NOUTHETEŌ (νουθετέω), to put in mind, warn, is translated to warn in the A.V., in the passages mentioned under ADMONISH, B, No. 1 (which see) ; the R.V. always translates this word by the verb to admonish.

2. HUPODEIKNUMI (ὑποδείκνυμι), primarily, to show secretly (*hupo*, under, *deiknumi*, to show), hence, generally, to teach, make known, is translated to warn in Matt. 3 : 7 ; Luke 3 : 7 ; 12 : 5, R.V. (A.V., " forewarn "). See FOREWARN, Note, SHEW.

3. CHRĒMATIZŌ (χρηματίζω), for which see ADMONISH, B, No. 3, is translated to warn in Matt. 2 : 12, 22 ; Acts 10 : 22 ; Heb. 8 : 5, R.V. (A.V., " admonished ") ; 11 : 7 ; 12 : 25, R.V. (A.V., " spake ").

WAS, WAST, WERE, WERT

Note : When not part of another verb, or phrase, these translate *eimi*, to be, e.g., Matt. 1 : 18, or the following : (*a*) *ginomai*, to become, e.g., Matt. 8 : 26 ; (*b*) *huparchō*, to exist, especially when referring to an already existing condition, e.g., Luke 8 : 41 ; Acts 5 : 4 (2nd part) ; 16 : 3 ; 27 : 12 ; Rom. 4 : 19, A.V., " when he was " (R.V., " he being ") ; (*c*) *cchō*, to have, e.g., Acts 12 : 15 ; (*d*) *apechō*, to be away, to be distant, e.g.,

Luke 7 : 6 ; 24 : 13 ; (e) *mellō,* to be about to, e.g., Luke 19 : 4 ; Acts 21 : 27, 37, A.V. (R.V., " was about to ") ; (f) *sumbainō,* to come to pass, happen, e.g., Acts 21 : 35 ; (g) in Gal. 4 : 28, the preposition *kata,* according to, is rendered " was," in the phrase " as Isaac was," lit., ' like Isaac ; ' as Isaac's birth came by Divine interposition, so does the spiritual birth of every believer.

WASH

1. NIPTŌ (νίπτω) is chiefly used of washing part of the body, John 13 : 5, 6, 8 (twice, figuratively in 2nd clause), 12, 14 (twice) ; in 1 Tim. 5 : 10, including the figurative sense ; in the Middle Voice, to wash oneself, Matt. 6 : 17 ; 15 : 2 ; Mark 7 : 3 ; John 9 : 7, 11, 15 ; 13 : 10.¶ For the corresponding noun see BASON.

2. APONIPTŌ (ἀπονίπτω), to wash off, is used in the Middle Voice, in Matt. 27 : 24.¶

3. LOUŌ (λούω) signifies to bathe, to wash the body, (a) Active Voice, Acts 9 : 37 ; 16 : 33 ; (b) Passive Voice, John 13 : 10, R.V., " bathed " (A.V., " washed ") ; Heb. 10 : 22, lit., ' having been washed as to the body,' metaphorical of the effect of the Word of God upon the activities of the believer ; (c) Middle Voice, 2 Pet. 2 : 22. Some inferior mss. have it instead of *luō,* to loose, in Rev. 1 : 5 (see R.V.).¶

4. APOLOUŌ (ἀπολούω), to wash off or away, is used in the Middle Voice, metaphorically, to wash oneself, in Acts 22 : 16, where the command to Saul of Tarsus to wash away his sins indicates that by his public confession, he would testify to the removal of his sins, and to the complete change from his past life ; this ' washing away ' was not in itself the actual remission of his sins, which had taken place at his conversion ; the Middle Voice implies his own particular interest in the act (as with the preceding verb " baptize," lit., ' baptize thyself,' i.e., ' get thyself baptized ') ; the aorist tenses mark the decisiveness of the acts ; in 1 Cor. 6 : 11, lit., ' ye washed yourselves clean ; ' here the Middle Voice (rendered in the Passive in A.V. and R.V., which do not distinguish between this and the next two Passives ; see R.V. marg.) again indicates that the converts at Corinth, by their obedience to the faith, voluntarily gave testimony to the complete spiritual change Divinely wrought in them.¶ In the Sept., Job 9 : 30.¶

5. PLUNŌ (πλύνω) is used of washing inanimate objects, e.g., nets, Luke 5 : 2 (some texts have *apoplunō*) ; of garments, figuratively, Rev. 7 : 14 ; 22 : 14 (in the best texts ; the A.V. translates those which have the verb *poieō,* to do, followed by *tas entolas autou,* " His commandments ").¶

6. RHANTIZŌ (ῥαντίζω), to sprinkle, is used in the Middle Voice in Mark 7 : 4, in some ancient texts, of the acts of the Pharisees in their assiduous attention to the cleansing of themselves after coming from the market place (some texts have *baptizō* here). See SPRINKLE.

7. BRECHŌ (βρέχω), to wet, is translated to wash in Luke 7 : 38, 44, A.V. ; the R.V., " to wet " and " hath wetted," gives the correct rendering. See RAIN, B.

8. BAPTIZŌ (βαπτίζω) is rendered "washed " in Luke 11 : 38. See BAPTIZE.

Note : With regard to Nos. 1, 3, 5, the Sept. of Lev. 15 : 11 contains all three with their distinguishing characteristics, No. 1 being used of the hands, No. 3 of the whole body, No. 5 of the garments.

WASHING

1. BAPTISMOS (βαπτισμός) denotes the act of washing, ablution, with special reference to purification, Mark 7 : 4 (in some texts, ver. 8) ; Heb. 6 : 2, " baptisms ; " 9 : 10, " washings." See BAPTISM.¶

2. LOUTRON (λουτρόν), a bath, a laver (akin to *louō*, see above), is used metaphorically of the Word of God, as the instrument of spiritual cleansing, Eph. 5 : 26; in Tit. 3 : 5, of "the washing of regeneration " (see REGENERATION).¶ In the Sept., S. of Sol. 4 : 2 ; 6 : 6.¶

WASTE (Noun and Verb)
A. Noun.

APŌLEIA (ἀπώλεια), destruction, is translated " waste " in Matt. 26 : 8 ; Mark 14 : 4. See DESTRUCTION, B, II, No. 1.
B. Verbs.

1. DIASKORPIZŌ (διασκορπίζω), to scatter abroad, is used metaphorically of squandering property, Luke 15 : 13 ; 16 : 1. See DISPERSE, SCATTER.

2. PORTHEŌ (πορθέω), to ravage, is rendered " wasted " in Gal. 1 : 13, A.V. ; see DESTROY, Note, HAVOCK.

3. LUMAINŌ (λυμαίνω), to outrage, maltreat, is used in the Middle Voice in Acts 8 : 3, of Saul's treatment of the church, R.V., " laid waste " (A.V., " made havock of ").¶

WATCH (Noun and Verb), WATCHERS, WATCHFUL, WATCHINGS
A. Nouns.

1. PHULAKĒ (φυλακή) is used (*a*) with the meaning ' a watch,' actively, a guarding, Luke 2 : 8, lit., ' (keeping, *phulassō*) watches ; ' (*b*) of the time during which guard was kept by night, a watch of the night, Matt. 14 : 25 ; 24 : 43 ; Mark 6 : 48 ; Luke 12 : 38. See CAGE, HOLD, IMPRISONMENT, PRISON.

Note : Among the Jews the night was divided into three watches (see, e.g., Ex. 14 : 24 ; Judg. 7 : 19), and this continued on through Roman times. The Romans divided the night into four watches ; this was recognized among the Jews (see Mark 13 : 35).

2. KOUSTŌDIA (κουστωδία), from Lat., *custodia* (cp. Eng., custody), is rendered " watch " in Matt. 27 : 65, 66 and 28 : 11, A.V. : see GUARD.¶

3. AGRUPNIA (ἀγρυπνία), sleeplessness (akin to B, No. 4), is rendered "watchings" in 2 Cor. 6 : 5 ; 11 : 27.¶

B. Verbs.

1. GRĒGOREŌ (γρηγορέω), to watch, is used (a) of keeping awake, e.g., Matt. 24 : 43 ; 26 : 38, 40, 41 ; (b) of spiritual alertness, e.g., Acts 20 : 31 ; 1 Cor. 16 : 13 ; Col. 4 : 2 ; 1 Thess. 5 : 6, 10 (for which see WAKE) ; 1 Pet. 5 : 8, R.V., "be watchful" (A.V., "be vigilant") ; Rev. 3 : 2, 3 ; 16 : 15.

2. TĒREŌ (τηρέω), to keep, is rendered to watch, of those who kept guard at the Cross, Matt. 27 : 36, 54 ; 28 : 4, R.V., "watchers" (A.V., "keepers"), lit., 'the watching ones.' See HOLD, No. 8, KEEP, OBSERVE, PRESERVE, RESERVE.

3. PARATĒREŌ (παρατηρέω), to observe, especially with sinister intent (para, near, and No. 2), is rendered to watch in Mark 3 : 2 ; Luke 6 : 7 ; 14 : 1 ; 20 : 20 ; Acts 9 : 24. See OBSERVE.

4. AGRUPNEŌ (ἀγρυπνέω), to be sleepless (from agreuō, to chase, and hupnos, sleep), is used metaphorically, to be watchful, in Mark 13 : 33 ; Luke 21 : 36 ; Eph. 6 : 18 ; Heb. 13 : 17. The word expresses not mere wakefulness, but the watchfulness of those who are intent upon a thing.¶

5. NĒPHŌ (νήφω), to abstain from wine, is used metaphorically of moral alertness, and translated to watch, in the A.V. of 2 Tim. 4 : 5. See SOBER.

WATER (Noun and Verb), WATERING, WATERLESS
A. Noun.

HUDŌR (ὕδωρ), whence Eng. prefix, hydro-, is used (a) of the natural element, frequently in the Gospels ; in the plural especially in the Apocalypse ; elsewhere, e.g., Heb. 9 : 19 ; Jas. 3 : 12 ; in 1 John 5 : 6, that Christ "came by water and blood," may refer either (1) to the elements that flowed from His side on the Cross after His Death, or, in view of the order of the words and the prepositions here used, (2) to His baptism in Jordan and His Death on the Cross. As to (1), the water would symbolize the moral and practical cleansing effected by the removal of defilement by our taking heed to the Word of God in heart, life and habit ; cp. Lev. 14, as to the cleansing of the leper. As to (2), Jesus the Son of God came on His mission by, or through, water and blood, namely, at His baptism, when He publicly entered upon His mission and was declared to be the Son of God by the witness of the Father, and at the Cross, when He publicly closed His witness ; the Apostle's statement thus counteracts the doctrine of the Gnostics that the Divine Logos united Himself with the Man Jesus at His baptism, and left him at Gethsemane. On the contrary, He who was baptized and He who was crucified was the Son of God throughout in His combined Deity and humanity.

The word water is used symbolically in John 3 : 5, either (1) of the Word of God, as in 1 Pet. 1 : 23 (cp. the symbolic use in Eph. 5 : 26), or, in view of the preposition *ek*, out of, (2) of the truth conveyed by baptism, this being the expression, not the medium, the symbol, not the cause, of the believer's identification with Christ in His Death, Burial and Resurrection. So the new birth is, in one sense, the setting aside of all that the believer was according to the flesh, for it is evident that there must be an entirely new beginning. Some regard the *kai*, " and," in John 3 : 5, as epexegetic, = ' even,' in which case the water would be emblematic of the Spirit, as in John 7 : 38 (cp. 4 : 10, 14), but not in 1 John 5 : 8, where the Spirit and the water are distinguished. " The water of life," Rev. 21 : 6 and 22 : 1, 17, is emblematic of the maintenance of spiritual life in perpetuity. In Rev. 17 : 1 the waters are symbolic of nations, peoples, etc.

Note : For *potamos*, rendered " waters " in 2 Cor. 11 : 26, see RIVER.

B. Verb.

POTIZŌ (ποτίζω), to give to drink, is used (*a*) naturally in Luke 13 : 15, " watering," with reference to animals ; (*b*) figuratively, with reference to spiritual ministry to converts, 1 Cor. 3 : 6–8. See DRINK, B, No. 3.

Notes : (1) For *hudropoteō*, to drink water, 1 Tim. 5 : 23, see DRINK, B, No. 5.   (2) For the adjective *anudros*, waterless (R.V.), without water, see DRY, No. 2.

WATERPOT

HUDRIA (ὑδρία) occurs in John 2 : 6, 7 ; 4 : 28.¶

WAVE

1. KUMA (κῦμα), from *kuō*, to be pregnant, to swell, is used (*a*) literally in the plural, Matt. 8 : 24 ; 14 : 24 ; Mark 4 : 37 (Acts 27 : 41, in some mss.) ; (*b*) figuratively, Jude 13.¶

2. SALOS (σάλος) denotes a tossing, especially the rolling swell of the sea, Luke 21 : 25, A.V., " waves " (R.V., " billows ").¶

3. KLUDŌN (κλύδων), a billow, is translated " wave " in Jas. 1 : 6, A.V. (R.V., " surge ") ; in Luke 8 : 24 it is translated " raging (of the water)."   See RAGE, B.¶

WAVER, WAVERING
A. Adjective.

AKLINĒS (ἀκλινής), without bending (*a*, negative, *klinō*, to bend), occurs in Heb. 10 : 23, A.V., " without wavering," R.V., " that it waver not."¶

B. Verb.

DIAKRINŌ (διακρίνω) is rendered to waver in Rom. 4 : 20, R.V. (A.V., " staggered ") ; in Jas. 1 : 6 (twice).   See DOUBT, No. 3.

WAX

1. PROKOPTŌ (προκόπτω), for which see ADVANCE, is rendered to wax in 2 Tim. 3 : 13.

2. GINOMAI (γίνομαι), to become, is translated "waxed" in **Luke** 13 : 19, A.V. (R.V., "became"); in Heb. 11 : 34, A.V. and R.V., "waxed :" see COME, No. 12, etc.

Note : This verb forms part of the translation of certain tenses of other verbs ; see, e.g., BOLD, A, No. 2, COLD, C, CONFIDENT, B, No. 1, CORRUPT, A, No. 2, GROSS, OLD, D, No. 2, STRONG, B, No. 2, WANTON, B, Nos. 1 and 2, WEARY, No. 2, WROTH, No. 1.

WAY

1. HODOS (ὁδός) denotes (*a*) a natural path, road, way, frequent in the Synoptic Gospels ; elsewhere, e.g., Acts 8 : 26 ; 1 Thess. 3 : 11 ; Jas. 2 : 25 ; Rev. 16 : 12 ; (*b*) a traveller's way (see JOURNEY) ; (*c*) metaphorically, of a course of conduct, or way of thinking, e.g., of righteousness, Matt. 21 : 32 ; 2 Pet. 2 : 21 ; of God, Matt. 22 : 16, and parallels, i.e., the way instructed and approved by God ; so Acts 18 : 26 and Heb. 3 : 10, " My ways " (cp. Rev. 15 : 3) ; of the Lord, Acts 18 : 25 ; " that leadeth to destruction," Matt. 7 : 13 ; ". . . unto life," 7 : 14 ; of peace, Luke 1 : 79 ; Rom. 3 : 17 ; of Paul's ways in Christ, 1 Cor. 4 : 17 (plural) ; " more excellent " (of love), 1 Cor. 12 : 31 ; of truth, 2 Pet. 2 : 2 ; of the right way, 2 : 15 ; of Balaam (*id.*) ; of Cain, Jude 11 ; of a way consisting in what is from God, e.g., of life, Acts 2 : 28 (plural) ; of salvation, Acts 16 : 17 ; personified, of Christ as the means of access to the Father, John 14 : 6 ; of the course followed and characterized by the followers of Christ, Acts 9 : 2 ; 19 : 9, 23 ; 24 : 22. See HIGHWAY.

Note : In Luke 5 : 19 and 19 : 4 the noun is not expressed in the original, but is understood.

2. PARODOS (πάροδος), a passing or passage, is used with *en*, in, 1 Cor. 16 : 7, " by the way " (lit, ' in passing ').¶

3. TROPOS (τρόπος), a turning, a manner, is translated " way " in Rom. 3 : 2, " (every) way ;" Phil. 1 : 18, " (in every) way." See CONVERSATION, MANNER, MEANS.

Notes: (1) In Jas. 1:11, A.V., *poreia*, a journey, a going, is rendered "ways" (R.V., "goings"). (2) In Heb. 12:17, *topos*, a place, is rendered in A.V. marg., "way (to change his mind)." (3) For the A.V. rendering of *makran*, a good (or great) way off, Matt. 8:30; Luke 15:20, see FAR, B, No. 1. (4) In Luke 14:32, *porrō* is rendered "a great way off." (5) In Heb. 5:2, A.V., *planaō*, Middle Voice, to wander, is rendered "(them) that are out of the way," R.V., "(the) erring." (6) In Col. 2:14 and 2 Thess. 2:7, *ek mesou*, is translated "out of the way;" see MIDST, Note (1) (*e*). (7) For "two ways" in Mark 11:4, A.V., see STREET. (8) In John 10:1, the adverb *allachothen*, from some other place (from *allos*, another), is translated "some other way". (9) In 2 Pet. 3:1, the A.V. translates *en* "by way of" ("by, R.V.). (10) In Gal. 2:5, the renderings "by," A.V., "in the way of," R.V., serve to express the dative case of *hupotagē*, subjection. (11) For *propempō*, to bring on one's way, Acts 15:3; 21:5, and the A.V. of 2 Cor. 1 : 16 (R.V., " to be set forward on my journey "), see BRING, No. 25. (12) *Aperchomai*, to go away, is rendered to go one's way, e.g., Matt. 13 : 25 ; 20 : 4 ; Mark 11 : 4 ; 12 : 12 ; Luke 19 : 32 ; John 11 : 46 ; Acts 9 : 17 ; Jas. 1 : 24 : see GO, No. 14. (13) In Luke 8 : 14, A.V., *poreuomai*, to go on one's way (R.V.), is rendered " go forth ; " in 13 : 33, A.V., " walk " (R.V., " go on my way ") ; in Matt. 24 : 1, A.V., it is rendered " departed " (R.V., " was going on his way ") : see DEPART, No. 8. (14) In Acts 24 : 3, *pantē* is rendered " in all ways " (A.V., " always ").¶ (15) In Rom. 3 : 12, A.V., *ekklinō*, to turn aside (R.V.), is rendered " are gone out of the way." (16) See also ESCAPE, B, LASCIVIOUS.

WE

Note : When this is not part of the translation of a verb or phrase, it stands for some case of *hēmeis*, the plural of *egō*, I ; this separate use of the pronoun is always emphatic. For " we ourselves," see OURSELVES.

WEAK, WEAKENED, WEAKER, WEAKNESS
A. Adjectives.

1. ASTHENĒS (ἀσθενής), lit., strengthless (see IMPOTENT), is translated " weak," (*a*) of physical weakness, Matt. 26 : 41 ; Mark 14 : 38 ; 1 Cor. 1 : 27 ; 4 : 10 ; 11 : 30 (a judgment upon spiritual laxity in a church) ; 2 Cor. 10 : 10 ; 1 Pet. 3 : 7 (comparative degree) ; (*b*) in the spiritual sense, said of the rudiments of Jewish religion, in their inability to justify anyone, Gal. 4 : 9 ; of the Law, Heb. 7 : 18 ; in Rom. 5 : 6, R.V., " weak " (A.V., " without strength "), of the inability of man to accomplish his salvation ; (*c*) morally or ethically, 1 Cor. 8 : 7, 10 ; 9 : 22 ; (*d*) rhetorically, of God's actions according to the human estimate, 1 Cor. 1 : 25, " weakness," lit., ' the weak things of God.' See FEEBLE, SICK.

2. ADUNATOS (ἀδύνατος), lit., not powerful, is translated " weak " in Rom. 15 : 1, of the infirmities of those whose scruples arise through lack of faith (see 14 : 22, 23), in the same sense as No. 1 (*c*) ; the change in the adjective (cp. 14 : 1) is due to the contrast with *dunatoi*, the " strong," who have not been specifically mentioned as such in chap. 14. See IMPOSSIBLE.

B. Verb.

ASTHENEŌ (ἀσθενέω), to lack strength, is used in much the same way as A, No. 1, and translated "being . . . weak" in Rom. 4:19, A.V. (R.V., "being weakened") ; 8:3; 14:1, 2 (in some texts, 1 Cor. 8:9) ; 2 Cor. 11:21, 29 (twice) ; 12:10; 13:3, 4, 9. See DISEASED, IMPOTENT, SICK.

C. Noun.

ASTHENEIA (ἀσθένεια), for which see INFIRMITY, is rendered " weakness," of the body, 1 Cor. 2 : 3 ; 15 : 43 ; 2 Cor. 11 : 30, R.V. ; 12 : 5 (plural, R.V.), 9, 10, R.V. ; Heb. 11 : 34 ; in 2 Cor. 13 : 4, " He was crucified through weakness " is said in respect of the physical sufferings to which Christ voluntarily submitted in giving Himself up to the death of the Cross.

WEALTH

EUPORIA (εὐπορία), primarily facility (eu, well, poros, a passage), hence plenty, wealth, occurs in Acts 19 : 25.¶ Cp. euporeō, to be well provided for, to prosper, Acts 11 : 29.¶

Note : In 1 Cor. 10 : 24, the A.V., " *wealth*," R.V., " *good*," is, lit., ' the (thing) of the other.'

WEAPONS

HOPLON (ὅπλον), always in the plur., is translated " weapons " in John 18 : 3 and 2 Cor. 10 : 4, the latter metaphorically of those used in spiritual warfare. See ARMOUR, INSTRUMENTS.

WEAR, WEARING
A. Verbs.

1. PHOREŌ (φορέω), a frequentative form of *pherō*, to bear, and denoting repeated or habitual action, is chiefly used of clothing, weapons, etc., of soft raiment, Matt. 11 : 8 ; fine clothing,. Jas. 2 : 3 ; the crown of thorns, John 19 : 5. See BEAR, No. 7.

2. ENDIDUSKŌ (ἐνδιδύσκω), to put on, is used in the Active Voice in Mark 15 : 17 (in good mss. ; some have No. 3) ; in Luke 8 : 27 (Middle Voice), in some texts ; the best have No. 3. For Luke 16 : 19, see CLOTHE, No. 3.¶

3. ENDUŌ (ἐνδύω) is rendered to wear in Luke 8 : 27 (Middle Voice ; see No. 2). See CLOTHE, No. 2, PUT, No. 26.

4. KLINŌ (κλίνω), to bend, decline, is used of a day, wearing away, Luke 9 : 12 (in 24 : 29, " is far spent "). See Bow, No. 4, FLIGHT, B, LAY, No. 6, SPEND.

5. HUPŌPIAZŌ (ὑπωπιάζω) is translated " wear (me) out " in Luke 18 : 5, R.V. (A.V., " weary "). For this and the somewhat different application in 1 Cor. 9 : 27, see BUFFET, No. 2.¶
B. Noun.

PERITHESIS (περίθεσις), a putting around or on (*peri*, around, *tithēmi*, to put), is used in 1 Pet. 3 : 3 of wearing jewels of gold (R.V.).¶

For WEARINESS, 2 Cor. 11 : 27, R.V., see LABOUR, No. 1

WEARY

1. KOPIAŌ (κοπιάω), to grow weary, be beaten out (*kopos*, a beating, toil), is used of the Lord in John 4 : 6 (used in His own word " labour " in Matt. 11 : 28), in Rev. 2 : 3, R.V. See, LABOUR, TOIL.

2. KAMNŌ (κάμνω), to be weary, is rendered to wax weary in Heb.

12 : 3, R.V. See Faint, No. 3, Sick.

3. EKKAKEŌ or ENKAKEŌ (ἐκκακέω), for which see Faint, No. 2, is rendered to be weary in Gal. 6 : 9 ; 2 Thess. 3 : 13.

Note : For *hupōpiazō,* rendered to weary in Luke 18 : 5, A.V., see Wear, A, No. 5.

WEATHER

1. EUDIA (εὐδία), akin to *eudios,* calm, denotes " fair weather," Matt. 16 : 2.¶

2. CHEIMŌN (χειμών), winter, also a winter storm, is translated " foul weather " in Matt. 16 : 3. See Tempest, Winter.

For WEDDING see MARRIAGE

WEEK

SABBATON (σάββατον) is used (*a*) in the plural in the phrase " the first day of the week," Matt. 28 : 1 ; Mark 16 : 2, 9 ; Luke 24 : 1 ; John 20 : 1, 19 ; Acts 20 : 7 ; 1 Cor. 16 : 2. For this idiomatic use of the word see One, A, (5) ; (*b*) in the singular, Luke 18 : 12, " twice in the week," lit., ' twice of the sabbath,' i.e., twice in the days after the sabbath. See Sabbath.

WEEP, WEEPING
A. Verbs.

1. KLAIŌ (κλαίω) is used of any loud expression of grief, especially in mourning for the dead, Matt. 2 : 18 ; Mark 5 : 38, 39 ; 16 : 10 ; Luke 7 : 13 ; 8 : 52 (twice) ; John 11 : 31, 33 (twice) ; 20 : 11 (twice), 13, 15 ; Acts 9 : 39 ; otherwise, e.g., in exhortations, Luke 23 : 28 ; Rom. 12 : 15 ; Jas. 4 : 9 ; 5 : 1 ; negatively, " weep not," Luke 7 : 13 ; 8 : 52 ; 23 : 28 ; Rev. 5 : 5 (cp. Acts 21 : 13) ; in 18 : 9, R.V., " shall weep " (A.V., " bewail "). See Bewail.

2. DAKRUŌ (δακρύω), to shed tears (*dakruon,* a tear), is used only of the Lord Jesus, John 11 : 35.¶

Note : Other synonymous verbs are *thrēneō,* to mourn, of formal lamentation : see Bewail, Note (1) ; *alalazō,* to wail ; *stenazō,* to groan (*oduromai,* to lament audibly, is not used in N.T. ; see the noun *odurmos,* mourning).

B. Noun.

KLAUTHMOS (κλαυθμός), akin to A, No. 1, denotes weeping, crying, Matt. 2 : 18 ; 8 : 12 ; 13 : 42, 50, R.V. (A.V., " wailing ") ; 22 : 13 ; 24 : 51 ; 25 : 30 ; Luke 13 : 28 ; Acts 20 : 37.¶

WEIGH, WEIGHT, WEIGHTY, WEIGHTIER
A. Verbs.

1. BAREŌ (βαρέω), to weigh down, is so rendered in 2 Cor. 1 : 8, R.V. ; see Burden, B, No. 1.

2. HISTĒMI (ἴστημι), to cause to stand, is used in Matt. 26 : 15, R.V., " they weighed (unto) " (of pieces of silver), A.V., metaphorically, " covenanted (with)."

B. Nouns.

1. BAROS (βάρος), akin to A, is rendered " weight " in 2 Cor. 4 : 17. See BURDEN, A, No. 1.

2. ONKOS (ὄγκος) denotes a bulk or mass ; hence, metaphorically, an encumbrance, weight, Heb. 12 : 1.¶

C. Adjective.

BARUS (βαρύς), heavy (akin to A and B, No. 1), is rendered " weighty " in 2 Cor. 10 : 10, of Paul's letters. The comparative degree is used in the neuter plural in Matt. 23 : 23, " (the) weightier matters (of the Law)." See GRIEVOUS, HEAVY.

WELCOME

1. APODECHOMAI (ἀποδέχομαι), to receive gladly, is rendered to welcome in the R.V. of Luke 8 : 40 ; 9 : 11. See RECEIVE.

2. HUPOLAMBANŌ (ὑπολαμβάνω), to take up, to entertain, is rendered " to welcome " in 3 John 8, R.V., of a hearty welcome to servants of God. See RECEIVE.

WELL (Noun)

PHREAR (φρέαρ), a pit, is translated a " well " in John 4 : 11, 12. See PIT.

Note : For *pēgē*, translated " well " in John 4 : 6 (twice), 14 ; 2 Pet. 2 : 17, see FOUNTAIN.

WELL (Adverb)

1. KALŌS (καλῶς), finely (akin to *kalos*, good, fair), is usually trans-lated " well," indicating what is done rightly ; in the Epistles it is most frequent in 1 Tim. (3 : 4, 12, 13 ; 5 : 17) ; twice it is used as an exclamation of approval, Mark 12 : 32 ; Rom. 11 : 20 ; the comparative degree *kallion*, " very well," occurs in Acts 25 : 10. See GOOD, C, No. 1.

Note : The neuter form of the adjective *kalos*, with the article and the present participle of *poieō*, to do, is translated " well-doing " in Gal. 6 : 9.

2. EU (εὖ), primarily the neuter of an old word, *eus*, noble, good, is used (*a*) with verbs, e.g., Mark 14 : 7, " do (*poieō*) . . . good ; " Acts 15 : 29 (*prassō*) ; Eph. 6 : 3 (*ginomai*, to be) ; (*b*) in replies, good, " well done," Matt. 25 : 21, 23 ; in Luke 19 : 17, *eu ge* (in the best texts). The word is the opposite of *kakos*, evilly. See GOOD, C, No. 2.¶

Notes : (1) In 2 Tim. 1 : 18, *beltion*, the neuter form of what is used as the comparative degree of *agathos*, good, is used adverbially and trans-lated " very well."¶ (2) For John 2 : 10, " have well drunk " (R.V., " freely "), see DRINK, B, No. 2. (3) *Hōs*, as, with *kai*, also (and), is rendered " as well as " in Acts 10 : 47 (*kathōs* in some mss.) and 1 Cor.

9 : 5.   (4) In Heb 4 : 2 *kathaper*, even as, with *kai*, is translated " as well as : " see EVEN, No. 8.

WELL (do), WELL-DOING
A. Verbs.

1. AGATHOPOIEŌ (ἀγαθοποιέω), to do good (*agathos*, good, *poieō*, to do), is used (*a*) of such activity in general, 1 Pet. 2 : 15, " well-doing ; " ver. 20, " do well ; " 3 : 6, 17 ; 3 John 11, " doeth good ; " (*b*) of acting for another's benefit, Mark 3 : 4 ; Luke 6 : 9, 33, 35.¶

2. KALOPOIEŌ (καλοποιέω), to do well, excellently, act honourably (*kalos*, good, *poieō*, to do), occurs in 2 Thess. 3 : 13.¶ The two parts of the word occur separately in Rom. 7 : 21 ; 2 Cor. 13 : 7 ; Gal. 6 : 9 ; Jas. 4 : 17.

Notes : (1) The distinction between Nos. 1 and 2 follows that between *agathos* and *kalos* (see GOOD).   (2) In John 11 : 12, A.V., *sōzō* (Passive Voice, to be saved), is rendered " he shall do well " (R.V., " he will recover ").

B. Noun.

AGATHOPOIIA (ἀγαθοποιία), well-doing (akin to A, No. 1), occurs in 1 Pet. 4 : 19.¶

C. Adjective.

AGATHOPOIOS (ἀγαθοποιός), doing good, beneficent, is translated " them that do well " in 1 Pet. 2 : 14, lit., ' well-doing (ones).'¶

For WELL-BELOVED see BELOVED

WELL-NIGH

Note : This forms part of the translation of *sumplēroō*, to fulfil, in Luke 9 : 51, " were well-nigh " come (see COME, No. 36), and *plēroō*, to fulfil, in Acts 7 : 23, " was well-nigh . . .," lit., ' a time (of forty years) was fulfilled (to him) ' (see FULFIL, A, No. 1).

WELL PLEASED
A. Noun.

EUDOKIA (εὐδοκία), good pleasure, occurs in the genitive case in Luke 2 : 14, lit., " (men) of good pleasure " (so R.V. marg.), R.V., " (men) in whom He is well pleased " (the genitive is objective) ; the A.V., " good will (toward men)," follows the inferior texts which have the nominative. See DESIRE, PLEASURE, SEEM, WELL-PLEASING, WILL.

B. Verb.

EUDOKEŌ (εὐδοκέω), to be well pleased : see PLEASE, A, No. 3, WILLING, B, No. 3.

WELL-PLEASING
A. Adjective.

EUARESTOS (εὐάρεστος) is used in Rom. 12 : 1, 2, translated

" acceptable " (R.V. marg., " well-pleasing ") ; in the following the R.V. has " well-pleasing," Rom. 14 : 18 ; 2 Cor. 5 : 9 ; Eph. 5 : 10 ; in Phil. 4 : 18 and Col. 3 : 20 (R.V. and A.V.) ; in Tit. 2 : 9, R.V., " well-pleasing " (A.V., " please . . . well ") ; in Heb. 13 : 21, R.V. and A.V. See ACCEPTABLE.¶

B. Verb.

EUARESTEŌ (εὐαρεστέω), akin to A, is rendered to be well-pleasing in Heb. 11 : 5, 6, R.V. (A.V., " please ") ; in Heb. 13 : 16, " is well pleased."¶

C. Noun.

EUDOKIA (εὐδοκία), lit., ' good pleasure,' is rendered " well-pleasing " in Matt. 11 : 26 and Luke 10 : 21. See DESIRE, PLEASURE, SEEM, WELL PLEASED, WILL.

For WENT see GO

WEST

DUSMĒ (δυσμή), the quarter of the sun-setting (dusis, a sinking, setting ; dunō, to sink), hence, the west, occurs in Matt. 8 : 11 ; 24 : 27 ; Luke 12 : 54 (some regard this as the sunset) ; 13 : 29 ; Rev. 21 : 13.¶

For WET, Luke 7 : 38, 44, R.V., see WASH, No. 7

WHALE

KĒTOS (κῆτος) denotes a huge fish, a sea-monster, Matt. 12 : 40.¶ In the Sept., Gen. 1 : 21 ; Job 3 : 8 ; 9 : 13 ; 26 : 12 ; Jonah 1 : 17 (twice) ; 2 : 1, 10.¶

WHAT

Notes : (1) Most frequently this is a translation of some form of the relative pronoun *hos* or the interrogative *tis.* (2) Other words are (a) *hoios*, of what kind, e.g., 2 Cor. 10 : 11, R.V. (A.V., " such as ") ; 1 Thess. 1 : 5, " what manner of men ; " 2 Tim. 3 : 11 (twice), lit., ' what sorts of things,' ' what sorts of persecutions ; ' (b) *poios*, what sort of, e.g., Matt. 21 : 23, 24, 27 ; 24 : 42, 43 ; Luke 5 : 19 ; 6 : 32–34 ; 20 : 2, 8 ; 24 : 19 ; John 12 : 33, " what manner of ; " so in 18 : 32 ; 21 : 19 ; Rom. 3 : 27 ; 1 Cor. 15 : 35 ; in Jas. 4 : 14, " what ; " 1 Pet. 2 : 20 and Rev. 3 : 3 (ditto) ; 1 Pet. 1 : 11, " what manner of ; " (c) *hopoios*, " what sort of," 1 Cor. 3 : 13 ; " what manner of," 1 Thess. 1 : 9 ; (d) *hosos*, how great, Mark 6 : 30 (twice), R.V., " whatsoever ; " Acts 15 : 12 ; Rom. 3 : 19, " what things soever ; " Jude 10 (1st part), " what soever things," R.V. ; (2nd part) " what ; " (e) *posos*, how great, how much, 2 Cor. 7 : 11, " what (earnest care)," R.V. (*posos* here stands for the repeated words in the Eng. Versions, the adjective not being repeated in the original) ; (f) *hostis*, " what (things)," Phil. 3 : 7 ; (g) in Matt. 26 : 40, *houtōs*, thus, so, is used as an exclamatory expression, translated " What " (in a word immediately addressed by the Lord to Peter), lit., ' So ; ' (h) for *potapos*, rendered " what " in Mark 13 : 1 (2nd part), A.V., see MANNER ; (*i*) in 1 Cor. 6 : 16, 19, A.V., the particle *ē*, " or " (R.V.), is rendered " What ? " ; in 1 Cor. 14 : 36, A.V. and R.V., " what ? " (*j*) in 1 Cor. 11 : 22, *gar*, in truth, indeed, has its exclamatory use " What ? ".   (3) In John 5 : 19 " but what " translates a phrase, lit., ' if not anything.'   (4) In Matt. 8 : 33 " what " is, lit., ' the things ' (neuter plural of the article).

WHATSOEVER

Note : For this see Notes on words under WHAT. Frequently by the addition of the particle *an*, or the conjunction *ean*, if, the phrase has the more general idea of " whatsoever," e.g., with *hos*, Matt. 10 : 11 ; with *hosos*, Matt. 17 : 12 ; with *hostis*, neuter form, Luke 10 : 35.

For WHEAT see CORN

For WHEEL, Jas. 3 : 6, R.V., see COURSE, A, No. 4

For WHEN, WHENCE, WHENSOEVER, WHERE, etc., see † p. 9

WHEREFORE

Note : This represents (1) some phrases introduced by the preposition *dia*, on account of, *dia touto*, on account of this, e.g., Matt. 12 : 31 ; Rom. 5 : 12 ; Eph. 1 : 15 ; 3 John 10 ; *dia hēn* (the accusative feminine of *hos*, who), on account of which (*aitia*, a cause, being understood), e.g., Acts 10 : 21 (with *aitia*, expressed, Tit. 1 : 13 ; Heb. 2 : 11) ; *dia ti* on account of what ? (sometimes as one word, *diati*), e.g., Luke 19 : 23 ; Rom. 9 : 32 ; 2 Cor. 11 : 11 ; Rev. 17 : 7 ; (2) *dio = dia ho* (the neuter of the relative pronoun *hos*), on account of which (thing), e.g., Matt. 27 : 8 ; Acts 15 : 19 ; 20 : 31 ; 24 : 26 ; 25 : 26 ; 27 : 25, 34 ; Rom. 1 : 24 ; 15 : 7 ; 1 Cor. 12 : 3 ; 2 Cor. 2 : 8 ; 5 : 9 ; 6 : 17 ; Eph. 2 : 11 ; 3 : 13 ; 4 : 8, 25 ; 5 : 14 ; Phil. 2 : 9 ; 1 Thess. 5 : 11 ; Philm. 8 ; Heb. 3 : 7, 10 ; 10 : 5 ; 11 : 16 ; 12 : 12, 28 ; 13 : 12 ; Jas. 1 : 21 ; 4 : 6 ; 1 Pet. 1 : 13 ; 2 Pet. 1 : 10, 12 ; 3 : 14 ; (3) *dioper*, for which very reason (a strengthened form of the preceding), 1 Cor. 8 : 13 ; 10 : 14 (14 : 13 in some mss.) ;¶ (4) *hothen* (which denotes ' whence ', when used of direction or source, e.g., Matt. 12 : 44), used of cause and denoting ' wherefore ' in Heb. 2 : 17 ; 3 : 1 ; 7 : 25 ; 8 : 3 ; (5) *ti*, what, why, John 9 : 27 ; Acts 22 : 30 ; Gal. 3 : 19, A.V. (R.V., " what ") ; (6) *heneka* with *tinos* (the genitive case of *ti*), because of what, Acts 19 : 32 ; (7) *charin* with *hou*, the genitive case, neuter of *hos*, for the sake of what, Luke 7 : 47 ; (8) *eis*, unto, with *ti*, what, Matt. 14 : 31 ; with *ho*, which (the accusative neuter of *hos*), 2 Thess. 1 : 11, A.V. (R.V., " to which end ") ; (9) *ara*, so, 2 Cor. 7 : 12, A.V. (R.V., " so ") ; with *ge*, at least, Matt. 7 : 20, A.V. (R.V., " therefore ") ; (10)

hina, in order that, with *ti*, what, Matt. 9 : 4 ; (11) *toigaroun*, therefore, rendered "wherefore" in Heb. 12 : 1, A.V. ; (12) in Matt. 26 : 50, *epi*, unto, with *ho*, as in No. (8) above, A.V., "wherefore (art thou come) ?" R.V., "(*do* that) for which (thou art come) ;" (13) *oun*, a particle expressing sequence or consequence, e.g., Matt. 24 : 26 ; Acts 6 : 3 ; (14) *hōste*, so that, "wherefore," e.g., Rom. 7 : 12, 13 ; 1 Cor. 10 : 12 ; 11 : 27, 33 ; 14 : 22, 39 ; 2 Cor. 5 : 16 ; Gal. 3 : 24 ; 4 : 7 ; Phil. 4 : 1 ; 1 Thess. 4 : 18 ; 1 Pet. 4 : 19.

WHETHER : see † p. 9

WHICH

Notes : (1) This is the translation of (*a*) the article with nouns, adjectives, numerals, participles, etc., e.g., "that which" etc. ; (*b*) the relative pronoun *hos*, "who," in one of its forms (a frequent use) ; (*c*) *hostis*, whoever, differing from *hos* by referring to a subject in general, as one of a class, e.g., Rom. 2 : 15 ; Gal. 4 : 24 (twice) ; 5 : 19 ; Rev. 2 : 24 ; 20 : 4 ; (*d*) the interrogative pronoun *tis*, who ? which ?, e.g., Matt. 6 : 27 ; John 8 : 46 ; (*e*) *hoios*, of what kind, e.g., Phil. 1 : 30 ; (*f*) *poios*, the interrogative of (*e*), e.g., John 10 : 32 ; (*g*) *hosos*, whatsoever, etc. ; plural, how many, translated "which" in Acts 9 : 39. (2) In Acts 8 : 26, A.V., *hautē* (the feminine of *houtos*, this), "the same" (R.V.), is translated "which." (3) In the triple title of God in Rev. 1 : 4, 8 ; 4 : 8, "which" is the translation, firstly, of the article with the present participle of *eimi*, to be, lit., 'the (One) being,' secondly, of the article with the imperfect tense of *eimi* (impossible of lit. translation, the title not being subject to grammatical change), thirdly, of the article with the present participle of *erchomai*, to come, lit., 'the coming (One) ;' in 11 : 17 and 16 : 5 the wording of the A.V. and R.V. differs ; in 11 : 17 the A.V. follows the inferior mss. by adding "and art to come" (R.V. omits) ; in 16 : 5, the A.V., "and shalt be," represents *kai* (and) followed by the article and the future participle of *eimi*, to be, lit., 'and the (One) about to be ;' the R.V. substitutes the superior reading "Thou Holy One," lit., 'the holy (One) :' see HOLY, B, No. 2. (4) In Phil. 2 : 21, A.V., "the things of Jesus Christ" (R.V.), is rendered "the things which are Jesus Christ's.

WHILE, WHILES, WHILST

Notes : (1) See LITTLE, B, No. 1. (2) In Matt. 13 : 21, *proskairos estin*, lit., 'is for a season,' is rendered "dureth (R.V., endureth) for a while." (3) *Chronos*, time, is rendered "while" in Luke 18 : 4 ; John 7 : 33 ; 12 : 35 (1st part) ; 1 Cor. 16 : 7 ; *kairos*, a season, "a while," Luke 8 : 13 ; in Acts 19 : 22, R.V., "while" (A.V., "season ") ; for the different meanings of these words see SEASON. (4) In Acts 18 : 18, A.V., "a good while," is, lit., 'sufficient days,' R.V., "many days."

(5) In Acts 28 : 6, A.V., *epi polu*, lit., ' upon much,' is rendered " a great while " (R.V., " long "). (6) For Mark 1 : 35 see DAY, B. (7) In Mark 15 : 44 *palai*, long ago, is rendered " any while." (8) In Acts 27 : 33 and Heb. 3 : 13 *achri* (or *achris*) followed by *hou*, the genitive case of the relative pronoun *hos*, lit., ' until which,' is rendered " while ; " cp. *en hō*, in Mark 2 : 19 ; Luke 5 : 34 ; John 5 : 7 ; *en tō*, in Luke 1 : 21, R.V., " while ; " in Heb. 3 : 15, " while it is said," is, lit., ' in the being said ' (*en*, with the article and the pres. infin., Passive of *legō*) ; so, e.g., in Matt. 13 : 25 (9) In Heb. 10 : 33, AV., " whilst ye were made," partly translating the present participle of *theatrizomai*, to become a gazing-stock, R.V., " being made ; " in the 2nd part, *ginomai*, to become, is translated " whilst ye became," A.V. (R.V., " becoming ").¶ (10) The conjunction *heōs*, until, etc., has the meaning " while " in Matt. 14 : 22 ; Mark 6 : 45 ; 14 : 32 ; in some texts, John 9 : 4 ; 12 : 35, 36 ; with *hotou*, whatever (an oblique case, neuter, of *hostis*, whoever), " whiles," Matt. 5 : 25. (11) In Acts 20 : 11 *hikanos*, sufficient, is rendered " a long while." (12) *Hōs*, as, " while " in Luke 24 : 32 (twice) ; John 12 : 35, 36 ; Acts 1 : 10 ; 10 : 17. (13) *Hotan*, when, is rendered " while " in 1 Cor. 3 : 4, A.V. (R.V., " when "). (14) *Hote*, when, is rendered " while " in John 17 : 12 ; Heb. 9 : 17. (15) In John 4 : 31 *metaxu*, between, used with *en tō*, ' in the,' is rendered " meanwhile ; " in Rom. 2 : 15 *metaxu* is itself rendered " the mean while " (R.V., " between "). (16) In Acts 18 : 18, R.V., *hikanos* is rendered " many " (A.V., " good "). (17) In 1 Pet. 1 : 6, R.V., *oligon*, a little, is rendered " for a little while " (A.V., " for a season ").

WHISPERER, WHISPERING

1. PSITHURISTĒS (ψιθυριστής), a whisperer, occurs in an evil sense in Rom. 1 : 29.¶

2. PSITHURISMOS (ψιθυρισμός), a whispering, is used of secret slander in 2 Cor. 12 : 20.¶ In the Sept., Eccl. 10 : 11, of a murmured enchantment.¶

Note : Synonymous with No. 1 is *katalalos*, a backbiter (Rom. 1 : 30¶), the distinction being that this denotes one guilty of open calumny, *psithuristēs*, one who does it clandestinely.

For WHIT see EVERY WHIT and NOTHING, No. 2

WHITE (Adjective and Verb)
A. Adjective.

LEUKOS (λευκός) is used of (*a*) clothing (sometimes in the sense of bright), Matt. 17 : 2 ; 28 : 3 ; Mark 9 : 3 ; 16 : 5 ; Luke 9 : 29 ; John 20 : 12 ; Acts 1 : 10 ; symbolically, Rev. 3 : 4, 5, 18 ; 4 : 4 ; 6 : 11 ; 7 : 9, 13 ; 19 : 14 (2nd part) ; (*b*) hair, Matt. 5 : 36 ; Christ's head and hair (in a vision ; cp. Dan. 7 : 9), Rev. 1 : 14 (twice) ; ripened grain, John 4 : 35 ; a stone, Rev. 2 : 17, an expression of the Lord's special delight in the overcomer, the new name on it being indicative of a secret communication of love and joy ; a horse (in a vision), 6 : 2 ; 19 : 11, 14 (1st part) ; a cloud, 14 : 14 ; the throne of God, 20 : 11.¶

Note : Lampros, bright, clear, is rendered " white " in Rev. 15 : 6, A.V., of " white (linen) " (R.V., " bright," following those mss. which have *lithon*, stone) ; in 19 : 8 (R.V., " bright "). See BRIGHT, CLEAR, GOODLY, Note, GORGEOUS.

B. Verbs.

1. LEUKAINŌ (λευκαίνω), to whiten, make white (akin to A), is used in Mark 9 : 3 ; figuratively in Rev. 7 : 14.¶

2. KONIAŌ (κονιάω), from *konia*, dust, lime, denotes to whiten, whitewash, of tombs, Matt. 23 : 27 ; figuratively of a hypocrite, Acts 23 : 3.¶ In the Sept., Deut. 27 : 2, 4 ; Prov. 21 : 9.¶

WHITHER, WHITHERSOEVER, see † p. 9.

WHO, WHOM, WHOSE

Notes : These are usually the translations of forms of the relative pronoun *hos*, or of the interrogative pronoun *tis* ; otherwise of *hostis*, whoever, usually of a more general subject than *hos*, e.g., Mark 15 : 7 ; Luke 23 : 19 ; Gal. 2 : 4 ; *hosos*, as many as, Heb. 2 : 15 ; in Acts 13 : 7, A.V., *houtos*, this (man), is translated " who," R.V., " the same."

WHOLE (made), WHOLLY, WHOLESOME
A. Adjectives.

1. HOLOS (ὅλος), for which see ALL, A, No. 3, and ALTOGETHER, signifies " whole," (a) with a noun, e.g., Matt. 5 : 29, 30 ; Mark 8 : 36 ; 15 : 1, 16, 33 ; Luke 11 : 36 (1st part), though *holon* may here be used adverbially with *phōteinon*, ' wholly light ' [as in the 2nd part, R.V., " wholly (full of light) "] ; John 11 : 50 ; 1 Cor. 12 : 17 (1st part) ; 1 John 2 : 2 ; 5 : 19 ; (b) absolutely, as a noun, e.g., Matt. 13 : 33 ; 1 Cor. 12 : 17 (2nd part).

2. PAS (πᾶς), for which see ALL, A, No. 1, is sometimes translated " the whole " when used with the article, e.g., Matt. 8 : 32, 34 ; Rom. 8 : 22.

3. HAPAS (ἅπας), for which see ALL, A, No. 2, is rendered " the whole," e.g., in Luke 19 : 37 ; 23 : 1.

4. HOLOKLĒROS (ὁλόκληρος), from No. 1 and *klēros*, a lot, is rendered " whole " in 1 Thess. 5 : 23 : see ENTIRE.

5. HUGIĒS (ὑγιής) (cp. Eng., hygiene) is used especially in the Gospels of making sick folk " whole," Matt. 12 : 13 ; 15 : 31 ; Mark 3 : 5 ; 5 : 34 ; Luke 6 : 10 ; John 5 : 4, 6, 9, 11, 14, 15 ; 7 : 23 ; also Acts 4 : 10 ; of " sound (speech)," Tit. 2 : 8. See SOUND.¶

6. HOLOTELĒS (ὁλοτελής), " wholly," 1 Thess. 5 : 23, is lit., ' whole-complete ' (A, No. 1, and *telos*, an end), i.e., ' through and through ; '

the Apostle's desire is that the sanctification of the believer may extend to every part of his being. The word is similar in meaning to No. 4; *holokleros* draws attention to the person as a whole, *holoteles* to the several parts which constitute him.¶

Note: In 1 Tim. 4 : 15, the sentence freely rendered " give thyself wholly to them " is, lit., ' be in these (things) '.

B. Verbs.

1. HUGIAINŌ (ὑγιαίνω), to be in good health, akin to A, No. 5, is rendered " they that are whole " in Luke 5 : 31 ; " whole " in 7 : 10 (present participle) ; " wholesome " in 1 Tim. 6 : 3, A.V. (R.V., " sound ; " marg., " healthful "). See HEALTH, SOUND.

2. SŌZŌ (σώζω), to save, is sometimes rendered to make whole, and, in the Passive Voice, to be made whole, or to be whole, e.g., Matt. 9 : 21, 22 (twice), and parallel passages ; Acts 4 : 9. See HEAL, SAVE.

3. IAOMAI (ἰάομαι), to heal, is rendered to make whole, Matt. 15 : 28 ; Acts 9 : 34, A.V. (R.V., " healeth "). See HEAL.

4. ISCHUŌ (ἰσχύω), to be strong, is rendered " they that are whole " in Matt. 9 : 12 and Mark 2 : 17. See ABLE, B, No. 4.

5. DIASŌZŌ (διασώζω), to save thoroughly (*dia*), is used in the Passive Voice and rendered " were made whole " in Matt. 14 : 36, R.V. (A.V., " were made perfectly whole "). See ESCAPE, HEAL, SAVE.

For WHORE, WHOREMONGER see FORNICATION, HARLOT

WHOSO, WHOSOEVER

Note: The same pronouns as those under WHO are used for the above, often with the addition of the particle *an* and a change of construction when a generalisation is expressed. Some texts in Mark 15 : 6 have *hosper*, a strengthened form of *hos*, A.V., " whomsoever." For sentences introduced by the conjunction *ei* or *ean*, if, see † p. 9.

WHY : see † p. 9

WICKED

1. PONĒROS (πονηρός), for which see BAD, No. 2, EVIL, A and B, No. 2, is translated " wicked " in the A.V. and R.V. in Matt. 13 : 49 ; 18 : 32 ; 25 : 26 ; Luke 19 : 22 ; Acts 18 : 14 ; 1 Cor. 5 : 13 ; in the following the R.V. substitutes " evil " for A.V., " wicked : " Matt. 12 : 45 (twice) ; 13 : 19 ; 16 : 4 ; Luke 11 : 26 ; Col. 1 : 21 ; 2 Thess. 3 : 2 ; and in the following, where Satan is mentioned as " the (or that) evil one : " Matt. 13 : 38 ; Eph. 6 : 16 ; 1 John 2 : 13, 14 ; 3 : 12 (1st part) ; 5 : 18 ; in ver. 19 for A.V., " wickedness ; " he is so called also in A.V. and R.V. in John 17 : 15 ; 2 Thess. 3 : 3 ; A.V. only in Luke 11 : 4 ; in 3 John 10, A.V., the word is translated " malicious," R.V., " wicked."

2. ATHESMOS (ἄθεσμος), lawless (a, negative, *thesmos*, law, custom), " wicked," occurs in 2 Pet. 2 : 7 ; 3 : 17.¶ An instance of the use of the word is found in the papyri, where a father breaks off his daughter's engagement because he learnt that her fiancé was giving himself over to lawless deeds (Moulton and Milligan, Vocab.).

Notes : (1) In Matt. 21 : 41, A.V., *kakos* (for which see BAD, No. 1, EVIL, A, No. 1), is translated " wicked " (R.V., " miserable "). (2) In Acts 2 : 23 and 2 Thess 2 : 8, A.V., *anomos*, " lawless " (R.V.), is translated " wicked."

WICKEDNESS

1. PONĒRIA (πονηρία), akin to *ponēros* (see above, No. 1), is always rendered " wickedness " save in Acts 3 : 26 : see INIQUITY, No. 4.

2. KAKIA (κακία), evil, is rendered " wickedness " in Acts 8 : 22 ; R.V. in Jas. 1 : 21, A.V., " naughtiness." See EVIL, B, No. 1, MALICE.

Notes : (1) For the A.V. of 1 John 5 : 19 see WICKED, No. 1. (2) In Acts 25 : 5, A.V., the word *atopos* (R.V., " amiss ") is incorrectly rendered " wickedness."

For WIDE see BROAD

WIDOW

CHĒRA (χήρα), Matt. 28 : 13 (in some texts) ; Mark 12 : 40, 42, 43 ; Luke 2 : 37 ; 4 : 25, 26, lit., ' a woman a widow ; ' 7 : 12 ; 18 : 3, 5 ; 20 : 47 ; 21 : 2, 3 ; Acts 6 : 1 ; 9 : 39, 41 ; 1 Tim. 5 : 3 (twice), 4, 5, 11, 16 (twice) ; Jas. 1 : 27 ; 1 Tim. 5 : 9 refers to elderly widows (not an ecclesiastical " order "), recognized, for relief or maintenance by the church (cp. vv. 3, 16), as those who had fulfilled the conditions mentioned ; where relief could be ministered by those who had relatives that were widows (a likely circumstance in large families), the church was not to be responsible ; there is an intimation of the tendency to shelve individual responsibility at the expense of church funds. In Rev. 18 : 7, it is used figuratively of a city forsaken.¶

WIFE, WIVES

1. GUNĒ (γυνή) denotes (1) a woman, married or unmarried (see WOMAN) ; (2) a wife, e.g., Matt. 1 : 20 ; 1 Cor. 7 : 3, 4 ; in 1 Tim. 3 : 11, R.V., " women," the reference may be to the wives of deacons, as the A.V. takes it.

2. GUNAIKEIOS (γυναικεῖος), an adjective denoting womanly, female, is used as a noun in 1 Pet. 3 : 7, A.V., " wife," R.V., " woman."¶

Note : In John 19 : 25 the article stands idiomatically for " the *wife* (of) ; " in Matt. 1 : 6, the article is rendered " her *that had been the wife* (of).'

WIFE'S MOTHER

PENTHERA (πενθερά) denotes a mother-in-law, Matt. 8 : 14 ; 10 : 35 ; Mark 1 : 30 ; Luke 4 : 38 ; 12 : 53 (twice).¶

WILD

AGRIOS (ἄγριος) denotes (a) of or in fields (agros, a field), hence, not domestic, said of honey, Matt. 3 : 4 ; Mark 1 : 6 ; (b) savage, fierce, Jude 13, R.V., metaphorically, " wild (waves)," A.V., " raging."¶ It is used in the papyri of a malignant wound.

Note : In Rev. 6 : 8 the R.V. renders *thērion* (plural) " wild beasts " (A.V., " beasts ").

WILDERNESS

1. ERĒMIA (ἐρημία), an uninhabited place, is translated " wilderness " in the A.V. of Matt. 15 : 33 and Mark 8 : 4 (R.V., " a desert place ") ; R.V. and A.V., " wilderness " in 2 Cor. 11 : 26. See DESERT, A. (In the Sept., Is. 60 : 20 ; Ezek. 35 : 4, 9.¶)

2. ERĒMOS (ἔρημος), an adjective signifying desolate, deserted, lonely, is used as a noun, and rendered " wilderness " 32 times in the A.V. ; in Matt. 24 : 26 and John 6 : 31, R.V., " wilderness " (A.V., " desert "). For the R.V., " deserts " in Luke 5 : 16 and 8 : 29 see DESERT, B.

WILES

METHODIA, or –EIA (μεθοδία) denotes craft, deceit (*meta*, after, *hodos*, a way), a cunning device, a wile, and is translated " wiles (of error) " in Eph. 4 : 14, R.V. [A.V. paraphrases it, " they lie in wait (to deceive) "], lit., ' (with a view to) the craft (singular) of deceit ; ' in 6 : 11, " the wiles (plural) (of the Devil.)"¶

WILFULLY

A. Adverb.

HEKOUSIŌS (ἐκουσίως) denotes voluntarily, willingly, Heb. 10 : 26, (of sinning) " wilfully ; " in 1 Pet. 5 : 2, " willingly " (of exercising oversight over the flock of God).¶

B. Verb.

THELŌ (θέλω), to will, used in the present participle in 2 Pet. 3 : 5, is rendered " wilfully (forget) " in the R.V., A.V., " willingly (are ignorant of)," lit., ' this escapes them (i.e., their notice) willing (i.e. of their own will).' See WILL, C, No. 1, WILLING, B, No. 1.

WILL, WOULD

A. Nouns.

1. THELĒMA (θέλημα) signifies (a) objectively, that which is willed, of the will of God, e.g., Matt. 18 : 14 ; Mark 3 : 35, the fulfilling being a sign of spiritual relationship to the Lord ; John 4 : 34 ; 5 : 30 ; 6 : 39, 40 ; Acts 13 : 22, plural, ' my desires ; ' Rom. 2 : 18 ; 12 : 2, lit., ' the will

of God, the good and perfect and acceptable ; ' here the repeated article is probably resumptive, the adjectives describing the will, as in the Eng. Versions ; Gal. 1 : 4 ; Eph. 1 : 9 ; 5 : 17, " of the Lord ; " Col. 1 : 9 ; 4 : 12 ; 1 Thess. 4 : 3 ; 5 : 18, where it means ' the gracious design,' rather than ' the determined resolve ; ' 2 Tim. 2 : 26, which should read ' which have been taken captive by him [(*autou*), i.e., by the Devil; the R.V., " by the Lord's servant " is an interpretation, it does not correspond to the Greek] unto His (*ekeinou*) will ' (i.e., God's will ; the different pronoun refers back to the subject of the sentence, viz., God) ; Heb. 10 : 10 ; Rev. 4 : 11, R.V., " because of Thy will ; " of human will, e.g., 1 Cor. 7 : 37 ; (*b*) subjectively, the will being spoken of as the emotion of being desirous, rather than as the thing willed ; of the will of God, e.g., Rom. 1 : 10 ; 1 Cor. 1 : 1 ; 2 Cor. 1 : 1 ; 8 : 5 ; Eph. 1 : 1, 5, 11 ; Col. 1 : 1 ; 2 Tim. 1 : 1 ; Heb. 10 : 7, 9, 36 ; 1 John 2 : 17 ; 5 : 14 ; of human will, e.g., John 1 : 13 ; Eph. 2 : 3, " the desires of the flesh ; " 1 Pet. 4 : 3 (in some texts) ; 2 Pet. 1 : 21. See DESIRE, A, No. 5, PLEASURE, Note (1).

2. THELĒSIS (θέλησις) denotes a willing, a wishing [similar to No. 1 (*b*)], Heb. 2 : 4.¶

3. BOULĒMA (βούλημα), a deliberate design, that which is purposed, Rom. 9 : 19 ; 1 Pet. 4 : 3 (in the best texts). See PURPOSE, A, No. 1.

4. EUDOKIA (εὐδοκία) (*eu*, well, *dokeō*, to think) is rendered " good will " in Luke 2 : 14, A.V. (see WELL PLEASED) ; Phil. 1 : 15 : see DESIRE, PLEASURE, SEEM, WELL-PLEASING.

5. EUNOIA (εὔνοια), good will (*eu*, well, *nous*, the mind), occurs in Eph. 6 : 7 (in some texts, 1 Cor. 7 : 3).¶ ·

Notes : (1) In Acts 13 : 36, A.V., *boulē*, " counsel " (R.V.), is translated " will." (2) In Rev. 17 : 17, A.V., *gnōmē*, an opinion, R.V., " mind," is translated " will." (3) For " will-worship," Col. 2 : 23, see WORSHIP, B, No. 2.

B. Adjectives.

1. HEKŌN (ἑκών), of free will, willingly, occurs in Rom. 8 : 20, R.V., " of its own will " (A.V., " willingly ") ; 1 Cor. 9 : 17, R.V., " of my own will " (A.V., " willingly ").¶ In the Sept., Ex. 21 : 13 ; Job 36 : 19.¶

2. AKŌN (ἄκων), *a*, negative, and No. 1, unwillingly, occurs in 1 Cor. 9 : 17, R.V., " not of mine own will " (A.V., " against my will ").¶ In the Sept., Job 14 : 17.¶

C. Verbs.

When " will " is not part of the translation of the future tense of verbs, it represents one of the following :

1. THELŌ (θέλω), for the force of which see DESIRE, B, No. 6, usually expresses desire or design ; it is most frequently translated by " will " or " would ; " see especially Rom. 7 : 15, 16, 18–21. In 1 Tim. 2 : 4, R.V., " willeth " signifies the gracious desire of God for all men to be saved ; not all are willing to accept His condition, depriving themselves either by the self-established criterion of their perverted reason, or

because of their self-indulgent preference for sin. In John 6 : 21, the A.V. renders the verb " willingly " (R.V., " they were willing ") ; in 2 Pet. 3 : 5, A.V., the present participle is translated " willingly " (R.V., " wilfully ").

The following are R.V. renderings for the A.V., ' will : ' Matt. 16 : 24, 25, " would ; " " wouldest," 19 : 21 and 20 : 21 ; " would," 20 : 26, 27 ; Mark 8 : 34, 35 ; 10 : 43, 44 ; " would fain," Luke 13 : 31 ; " would," John 6 : 67 ; " willeth," 7 : 17 ; in 8 : 44, " it is your will (to do) ; " " wouldest," Rom. 13 : 3 ; " would," 1 Cor. 14 : 35 and 1 Pet. 3 : 10.

2. BOULOMAI (βούλομαι), for the force of which see DESIRE, B, No. 7, usually expresses the deliberate exercise of volition more strongly than No. 1, and is rendered as follows in the R.V., where the A.V. has " will : " Matt. 11 : 27 and Luke 10 : 22, " willeth ; " Jas. 4 : 4, " would ; " in Jas. 3 : 4, R.V., " willeth " (A.V., " listeth "). In Jas. 1 : 18 the perfect participle is translated " of His own will," lit. ' having willed.'

3. MELLŌ (μέλλω), to be about to, is translated " will " in Matt. 2 : 13 and John 7 : 35 (twice) ; " wilt," John 14 : 22 ; " will," Acts 17 : 31 ; " wouldest," 23 : 20 ; " will," 27 : 10 and Rev. 3 : 16. See ABOUT, B.

WILLING (Adjective and Verb)

A. Adjectives.

1. PROTHUMOS (πρόθυμος) is rendered " willing " in Matt. 26 : 41 ; Mark 14 : 38, R.V. See READY, No. 2.

2. HEKOUSIOS (ἐκούσιος), willing, is used with kata in Philm. 14, lit., ' according to willing,' R.V., " of free will " (A.V., " willingly ").¶

B. Verbs.

1. THELŌ (θέλω) is rendered " ye were willing " in John 5 : 35. See WILL, C, No. 1.

2. BOULOMAI (βούλομαι) is rendered " (if) Thou be willing " in Luke 22 : 42 ; in 2 Pet. 3 : 9, A.V. (R.V., " wishing "). See WILL, C, No. 2.

3. EUDOKEŌ (εὐδοκέω), to be well pleased, to think it good, is rendered " we are willing " in 2 Cor. 5 : 8 ; in 1 Thess. 2 : 8, A.V., " we were willing " (R.V., " we were well pleased "). See PLEASE, PLEASURE.

Notes : (1) In 2 Cor. 8 : 3, A.V., *authairetos*, of one's own accord (R.V.), is rendered " willing of themselves ; " in ver. 17, " of his own accord." See ACCORD.¶ (2) For " willing to communicate," 1 Tim. 6 : 18, see COMMUNICATE, C.

For WILLING MIND see READINESS

WILLINGLY

Notes : (1) For *hekōn* see WILL, B, No. 1. (2) For *hekousiōs*, see WILFULLY. (3) For Philm. 14 see WILLING, A, No. 2. (4) For 2 Pet. 3 : 5 see WILL, C, No. 1.

For WIN see POSSESS, A, No. 2

WIND (Noun)

1. ANEMOS (ἄνεμος), besides its literal meaning, is used metaphorically in Eph. 4 : 14, of variable teaching. In Matt. 24 : 31 and Mark 13 : 27 the four winds stand for the four cardinal points of the compass ; so in Rev. 7 : 1, " the four winds of the earth " (cp. Jer. 49 : 36 ; Dan. 7 : 2) ; the contexts indicate that these are connected with the execution of Divine judgments. Deissmann (*Bible Studies*) and Moulton and Milligan (Vocab.) illustrate the phrase from the papyri.

2. PNOĒ (πνοή), a blowing, blast (akin to *pneō*, to blow), is used of the rushing wind at Pentecost, Acts 2 : 2. See BREATH.

3. PNEUMA (πνεῦμα) is translated " wind " in John 3 : 8 (R.V., marg., " the Spirit breatheth," the probable meaning) ; in Heb. 1 : 7 the R.V. has " winds " for A.V., " spirits." See SPIRIT.

Notes : (1) For *pneō*, to blow ("wind" in Acts 27 : 40), see BLOW, No. 1. (2) For *anemizō*, Jas. 1 : 6, " driven by the wind," see DRIVE, No. 8.¶

WIND (Verb)

1. DEŌ (δέω), to bind, is translated " wound (it in linen clothes)," John 19 : 40, A.V., of the body of Christ (R.V., " bound "). See BIND, No. 1, TIE.

2. SUSTELLŌ (συστέλλω) is translated " wound . . . up " in Acts 5 : 6 (R.V., " wrapped . . . round "). See SHORTEN, No. 2, WRAP.

3. ENEILEŌ (ἐνειλέω), to roll in, wind in, is used in Mark 15 : 46, of winding the cloth around the Lord's body, R.V., " wound " (A.V., " wrapped ").¶

WINDOW

THURIS (θυρίς), a diminutive of *thura*, a door, occurs in Acts 20 : 9 ; 2 Cor. 11 : 33.¶

WINE

1. OINOS (οἶνος) is the general word for wine. The mention of the bursting of the wineskins, Matt. 9 : 17 ; Mark 2 : 22 ; Luke 5 : 37, implies fermentation. See also Eph. 5 : 18 (cp. John 2 : 10 ; 1 Tim. 3 : 8 ; Tit. 2 : 3). In Matt. 27 : 34, the R.V. has " wine " (A.V., " vinegar," translating the inferior reading *oxos*).

The drinking of wine could be a stumbling-block and the Apostle enjoins abstinence in this respect, as in others, so as to avoid giving an occasion of stumbling to a brother, Rom. 14 : 21. Contrast 1 Tim. 5 : 23, which has an entirely different connection. The word is used metaphorically (*a*) of the evils ministered to the nations by religious Babylon, 14 : 8 ; 17 : 2 ; 18 : 3 ; (*b*) of the contents of the cup of Divine wrath upon the nations and Babylon, Rev. 14 : 10 ; 16 : 19 ; 19 : 15.

2. GLEUKOS (γλεῦκος) denotes sweet " new wine," or must, Acts

2 : 13, where the accusation shows that it was intoxicant and must have been undergoing fermentation some time.¶ In the Sept., Job 32 : 19.¶

Note : In instituting the Lord's Supper He speaks of the contents of the cup as the "fruit of the vine." So Mark 14 : 25.

For GIVEN TO WINE see BRAWLER, No. 1

WINE-BIBBER

OINOPOTĒS (οἰνοπότης), a wine-drinker (*oinos*, and *potēs*, a drinker), is used in Matt. 11 : 19 ; Luke 7 : 34.¶ In the Sept., Prov. 23 : 20.¶

For WINEBIBBINGS see EXCESS, Note (2)

WINEPRESS, WINE-FAT

1. LĒNOS (ληνός) denotes a trough or vat, used especially for the treading of grapes, Matt. 21 : 33. Not infrequently they were dug out in the soil or excavated in a rock, as in the rock-vats in Palestine to-day. In Rev. 14 : 19, 20 (twice) and 19 : 15 (where *oinos* is added, lit., ' the winepress of the wine ') the word is used metaphorically with reference to the execution of Divine judgment upon the gathered foes of the Jews at the close of this age preliminary to the establishment of the Millennial kingdom.¶

2. HUPOLĒNION (ὑπολήνιον) was a vessel or trough beneath the press itself (*hupo*, beneath, and No. 1), for receiving the juice, Mark 12 : 1, R.V., " a pit for the winepress."¶ In the Sept., Isa. 16 : 10 ; Joel 3 : 13 ; Hag. 2 : 16 ; Zech. 14 : 10.¶

For WINE-SKINS see SKIN

WING

PTERUX (πτέρυξ) is used of birds, Matt. 23 : 37 ; Luke 13 : 34 ; symbolically in Rev. 12 : 14, R.V., " the two wings of the great eagle " (A.V., " two wings of a great eagle "), suggesting the definiteness of the action, the wings indicating rapidity and protection, an allusion, perhaps, to Ex. 19 : 4 and Deut. 32 : 11, 12 ; of the " living creatures " in a vision, Rev. 4 : 8 ; 9 : 9.¶ Cp. *pterugion*, a pinnacle.

For WINK AT see OVERLOOK

WINTER (Noun and Verb)
A. Noun.

CHEIMŌN (χειμών) denotes winter, in Matt. 24 : 20 ; Mark 13 : 18 ; John 10 : 22 ; 2 Tim. 4 : 21. See TEMPEST.

B. Verb.

PARACHEIMAZŌ (παραχειμάζω) denotes to winter at a place (*para*, at, and A), Acts 27 : 12 (2nd part) ; 28 : 11 ; 1 Cor. 16 : 6 ; Tit. 3 : 12.¶

Note : In Acts 27 : 12 (1st part) *paracheimasia,* a wintering, is rendered " (to) winter in."¶

WIPE

1. APOMASSŌ (ἀπομάσσω), to wipe off, wipe clean (*apo,* from, *massō,* to touch, handle), is used in the Middle Voice, of wiping dust from the feet, Luke 10 : 11.¶

2. EKMASSŌ (ἐκμάσσω), to wipe out (*ek*), wipe dry, is used of wiping tears from Christ's feet, Luke 7 : 38, 44 ; John 11 : 2 ; 12 : 3 ; of Christ's wiping the disciples' feet, John 13 : 5.¶

3. EXALEIPHŌ (ἐξαλείφω), to wipe out or away (*ek,* or *ex,* out, *aleiphō,* to anoint), is used metaphorically of wiping away tears from the eyes, Rev. 7 : 17 ; 21 : 4. See BLOT OUT.

WISDOM

1. SOPHIA (σοφία) is used with reference to (*a*) God, Rom. 11 : 33 ; 1 Cor. 1 : 21, 24 ; 2 : 7 ; Eph. 3 : 10 ; Rev. 7 : 12 ; (*b*) Christ, Matt. 13 : 54 ; Mark 6 : 2 ; Luke 2 : 40, 52 ; 1 Cor. 1 : 30 ; Col. 2 : 3 ; Rev. 5 : 12 ; (*c*) wisdom personified, Matt. 11 : 19 ; Luke 7 : 35 ; 11 : 49 ; (*d*) human wisdom (1) in spiritual things, Luke 21 : 15 ; Acts 6 : 3, 10 ; 7 : 10 ; 1 Cor. 2 : 6 (1st part) ; 12 : 8 ; Eph. 1 : 8, 17 ; Col. 1 : 9, R.V., " (spiritual) wisdom," 28 ; 3 : 16 ; 4 : 5 ; Jas. 1 : 5 ; 3 : 13, 17 ; 2 Pet. 3 : 15 ; Rev. 13 : 18 ; 17 : 9 ; (2) in the natural sphere, Matt. 12 : 42 ; Luke 11 : 31 ; Acts 7 : 22 ; 1 Cor. 1 : 17, 19, 20, 21 (twice), 22 ; 2 : 1, 4, 5, 6 (2nd part), 13 ; 3 : 19 ; 2 Cor. 1 : 12 ; Col. 2 : 23 ; (3) in its most debased form, Jas. 3 : 15, " earthly, sensual, devilish " (marg., " demoniacal ").¶

2. PHRONĒSIS (φρόνησις), understanding, prudence, i.e., a right use of *phrēn,* the mind, is translated " wisdom " in Luke 1 : 17. See PRUDENCE.

Note : " While *sophia* is the insight into the true nature of things, *phronēsis* is the ability to discern modes of action with a view to their results ; while *sophia* is theoretical, *phronēsis* is practical " (Lightfoot). *Sunesis,* understanding, intelligence, is the critical faculty ; this and *phronēsis* are particular applications of *sophia.*

WISE, WISER, WISELY
A. Adjectives.

1. SOPHOS (σοφός) is used of (*a*) God, Rom. 16 : 27 ; in 1 Tim. 1 : 17 and Jude 25 *sophos* is absent, in the best mss. (see the R.V.), the comparative degree, *sophōteros,* occurs in 1 Cor. 1 : 25, where " foolishness " is simply in the human estimate ; (*b*) spiritual teachers in Israel, Matt. 23 : 34 ; (*c*) believers endowed with spiritual and practical wisdom, Rom. 16 : 19 ; 1 Cor. 3 : 10 ; 6 : 5 ; Eph. 5 : 15 ; Jas. 3 : 13 ; (*d*) Jewish teachers in the time of Christ, Matt. 11 : 25 ; Luke 10 : 21 ; (*e*) the

naturally learned, Rom. 1 : 14, 22 ; 1 Cor. 1 : 19, 20, 26, 27 ; 3 : 18–20.¶

2. PHRONIMOS (φρόνιμος), prudent, sensible, practically wise, Matt. 7 : 24 ; 10 : 16 ; 24 : 45 ; 25 : 2, 4, 8, 9 ; Luke 12 : 42 ; 16 : 8 (comparative degree, *phronimōteros*) ; 1 Cor. 10 : 15 ; in an evil sense, " wise (in your own conceits)," lit., ' wise (in yourselves),' i.e., ' judged by the standard of your self-complacency,' Rom. 11 : 25 ; 12 : 16 ; ironically, 1 Cor. 4 : 10 ; 2 Cor. 11 : 19.¶

B. Noun.

MAGOS (μάγος) denotes a Magian, one of a sacred caste, originally Median, who apparently conformed to the Persian religion while retaining their old beliefs ; it is used in the plural, Matt. 2 : 1, 7, 16 (twice), " wise men." See also Sorcerer.

C. Verbs.

1. SOPHIZŌ (σοφίζω) is rendered to make wise in 2 Tim. 3 : 15 : see Devised.

2. SUNIĒMI or SUNIŌ (συνίημι), to perceive, understand, is used negatively in 2 Cor. 10 : 12, A.V., " are not wise " (R.V., " are without understanding "). See Understand.

D. Adverbs.

PHRONIMŌS (φρονίμως), wisely (akin to A, No. 2), occurs in Luke 16 : 8.¶

WISE (IN NO)

1. OU MĒ (οὐ μή), a double negative, expressing an emphatic negation, ' by no means,' is rendered " in no wise " in Matt. 10 : 42 ; Luke 18 : 17 ; John 6 : 37 ; Acts 13 : 41 ; Rev. 21 : 27.

2. PANTŌS (πάντως), altogether, by all means, is used with the negative *ou* (not) in Rom. 3 : 9, stating a complete denial, rendered " No, in no wise." See All, B, 3, Altogether, B, 1.

3. PANTELES (παντελές), the neuter of *panteles*, is used with the negative *mē*, and with *eis to*, ' unto the,' in Luke 13 : 11, and translated " in no wise," lit., ' not to the uttermost : ' see Uttermost, No. 1.

For WISE (ON THIS) see THUS

WISH

1. EUCHOMAI (εὔχομαι) is rendered to wish in Acts 27 : 29 (R.V. marg., " prayed ") ; so Rom. 9 : 3 ; in 2 Cor. 13 : 9 and 3 John 2, R.V., " pray : " see Pray.

2. BOULOMAI (βούλομαι), in Mark 15 : 15, R.V., is translated " wishing " (A.V., " willing ") ; so 2 Pet. 3 : 9 ; in Acts 25 : 22, R.V., " could wish " (A.V., " would "). See Will, C, No. 2.

3. THELŌ (θέλω), in 1 Cor. 16 : 7, R.V., is translated " wish " (A.V., " will ") ; Gal. 4 : 20, " I could wish " (A.V. " I desire "). See Will, C, No. 1.

WIST

OIDA (οἶδα), to know, in the pluperfect tense (with imperfect meaning) is rendered " wist " (the past tense of the verb to wit : cp. WOT) in Mark 9 : 6 ; 14 : 40 ; Luke 2 : 49 ; John 5 : 13 ; Acts 12 : 9 ; 23 : 5. See KNOW, No. 2.

WIT (TO)
A. Adverb.

HŌS (ὡς), a relative adverb signifying ' as,' or ' how,' is used in 2 Cor. 5 : 19 to introduce the statement " that God was . . .," and rendered " to wit," lit., ' how.'

B. Verb.

GNŌRIZŌ (γνωρίζω), to know, to make known, is rendered " we do (you) to wit " in 2 Cor. 8 : 1, A.V., R.V., " we make known (to you)." See KNOW, No. 8.

Note : In Rom. 8 : 23 the italicized words *" to wit "* are added to specify the particular meaning of " adoption " there mentioned.

For WITCHCRAFT see SORCERY

WITH : see † p. 9

WITHAL

HAMA (ἅμα), at the same time, is rendered " withal " in Acts 24 : 26, R.V. (A.V., " also ") ; 1 Tim. 5 : 13 (with *kai*, ' also ') ; Philm. 22.

Notes : (1) In Eph. 6 : 16, R.V., the phrase *en pasin* (*en*, in, and the dative plural of *pas*, all) is rightly rendered " withal " (A.V., " above all ") ; the shield of faith is to accompany the use of all the other parts of the spiritual equipment. (2) In 1 Cor. 12 : 7 *sumpherō* is rendered " profit withal." See EXPEDIENT, PROFIT, B, No. 1. (3) In Acts 25 : 27, *kai*, also, is rendered " withal."

WITHDRAW

1. HUPOSTELLŌ (ὑποστέλλω) is translated " withdraw " in Gal. 2 : 12 : see DRAW (B), No. 4.

2. APOSPAŌ (ἀποσπάω), in the Passive Voice, is translated " was withdrawn " in Luke 22 : 41, A.V. : see PART (Verb), No. 3.

3. ANACHŌREŌ (ἀναχωρέω) is translated to withdraw in the R.V. of Matt. 2 : 22 and John 6 : 15 ; R.V. and A.V. in Matt. 12 : 15 and Mark 3 : 7. See DEPART, No. 10.

4. HUPOCHŌREŌ (ὑποχωρέω), to retire, is translated " withdrew Himself " in Luke 5 : 16 ; elsewhere in 9 : 10, R.V., " withdrew apart " (A.V., " went aside "). See GO, No. 16.¶

5. STELLŌ (στέλλω), to bring together, gather up (used of furling sails), hence, in the Middle Voice, signifies to shrink from a person or

thing, 2 Thess. 3 : 6, " withdraw ; " elsewhere, 2 Cor. 8 : 20, " avoiding."
See AVOID.¶ Cp. No. 1.

Note : In 1 Tim. 6 : 5, some texts have *aphistēmi*, rendered " withdraw
thyself," A.V.

WITHER (away)

XĒRAINŌ (ξηραίνω), to dry up, parch, wither, is translated to
wither, (a) of plants, Matt. 13 : 6 ; 21 : 19, 20 ; Mark 4 : 6 ; 11 : 20,
R.V. (A.V., " dried up "), 21 ; Luke 8 : 6 ; John 15 : 6 ; Jas. 1 : 11 ;
1 Pet. 1 : 24 ; (b) of members of the body, Mark 3 : 1, and, in some
texts, 3. See DRY, B, OVER-RIPE, PINE AWAY, RIPE.

Notes : (1) For the adjective *xēros*, dry, withered, see DRY, A, No. 1.
(2) For " whose fruit withereth," Jude 12, A.V., see AUTUMN.

WITHHOLD

KŌLUŌ (κωλύω), to hinder, restrain, is translated " withhold (not) "
in Luke 6 : 29, R.V., A.V., " forbid (not) to take." See FORBID, HINDER,
KEEP, Note (7), SUFFER, WITHSTAND.

Note : For " withholdeth " in 2 Thess. 2 : 6 see RESTRAIN.

WITHIN

Note : This is a translation of (a) *entos* : see INSIDE, No. 1 ; in Luke
17 : 21 the R.V. marg., " in the midst of," is to be preferred ; the Kingdom
of God was not in the hearts of the Pharisees ; (b) *en*, of thinking or saying
within oneself, e.g., Luke 7 : 39, 49 (marg., " among ") ; locally, e.g.,
Luke 19 : 44 ; (c) *esōthen*, 2 Cor. 7 : 5 ; Rev. 4 : 8 ; 5 : 1 ; " from within,"
Mark 7 : 21, 23 ; Luke 11 : 7 ; " within ", Matt. 23 : 25 ; Luke 11 : 40,
R.V., " inside ; " in Matt. 23 : 27, 28, R.V., " inwardly ; " (d) *esō*, John
20 : 26 ; Acts 5 : 23 ; 1 Cor. 5 : 12 (i.e., within the church) ; (e) *pros*,
to, or with, in Mark 14 : 4, A.V., " within " (R.V., " among ") ; (f)
dia, through, rendered " within (three days) " in Mark 14 : 58, A.V. (R.V.,
" in," looking through the time to the event, and in keeping with the
metaphor of building) ; (g) *esōteros*, Heb. 6 : 19, the comparative degree
of *esō*, used with the article translated " that within," lit., ' the inner
(part of the veil) ', i.e., inside : see INNER, No. 2 ; (h) in Luke 11 : 41,
R.V., *eneimi*, to be in, is rendered " are within " (A.V., " ye have ").

WITHOUT

Notes : (1) This is a translation of (a) *exō*, outside, e.g., Matt. 12 : 46,
47 ; " (them that are) without," 1 Cor. 5 : 12, 13 ; Col. 4 : 5 ; 1 Thess.
4 : 12 (the unregenerate) ; Heb. 13 : 11–13 ; (b) *exōthen*, from without,
or without, e.g., Mark 7 : 15, 18 ; Luke 11 : 40 ; 2 Cor. 7 : 5 ; 1 Tim. 3 : 7 ;
as a preposition, Rev. 11 : 2 ; (c) *chōris*, apart from, frequently used as a
preposition, especially in Hebrews [4 : 15 ; 7 : 7, 20, 21 ; 9 : 7, 18, 22,
28 ; 11 : 6 ; in 11 : 40, R.V., " apart from " (A.V., " without ") ; 12 : 8,
14] ; (d) *aneu*, like *chōris*, but rarer, Matt. 10 : 29 ; Mark 13 : 2 ;

1 Pet. 3 : 1 ; 4 : 9 ; ¶   (e) *ater*, Luke 22 : 6, marg., "without (tumult) ;" ver. 35 ; ¶   (f) *ektos*, out of, outside, 1 Cor. 6 : 18 : see OTHER, OUT, OUTSIDE ;   (g) *parektos*, besides, in addition, 2 Cor. 11 : 28, " (those things that are) without," R.V., marg., " (the things which) I omit," or " (the things that come) out of course." (2) In Acts 5 : 26, *ou*, not, *meta*, with, is rendered " without (violence)." (3) In Acts 25 : 17, A.V., " without (any delay) " represents *poieō*, to make, and *mēdemian*, no, R.V., " I made no (delay)." (4) For " without ceasing," Acts 12 : 5, A.V., see EARNESTLY, C, No. 1. (5) In many nouns the negative prefix *a* forms part of the word and is translated " without."

WITHSTAND

1. KŌLUŌ (κωλύω), to hinder, is rendered " withstand " in Acts 11 : 17. See FORBID, HINDER.

2. ANTHISTĒMI (ἀνθίστημι), to set against, is translated to withstand in Acts 13 : 8 (Middle Voice) ; in the intransitive 2nd aorist, Active Voice, Eph. 6 : 13 ; 2 Tim. 3 : 8 (1st part ; Middle Voice in 2nd part) ; 4 : 15. See RESIST.

WITNESS (Noun and Verb)
A. Nouns.

1. MARTUS or MARTUR (μάρτυς) (whence Eng., martyr, one who bears witness by his death) denotes one who can or does aver what he has seen or heard or knows ; it is used (a) of God, Rom. 1 : 9 ; 2 Cor. 1 : 23 ; Phil. 1 : 8 ; 1 Thess. 2 : 5, 10 (2nd part) ; (b) of Christ, Rev. 1 : 5 ; 3 : 14 ; (c) of those who witness for Christ by their death, Acts 22 : 20 ; Rev. 2 : 13 ; Rev. 17 : 6 ; (d) of the interpreters of God's counsels, yet to witness in Jerusalem in the times of the Antichrist, Rev. 11 : 3 ; (e) in a forensic sense, Matt. 18 : 16 ; 26 : 65 ; Mark 14 : 63 ; Acts 6 : 13 ; 7 : 58 ; 2 Cor. 13 : 1 ; 1 Tim. 5 : 19 ; Heb. 10 : 28 ; (f) in a historical sense, Luke 11 : 48 ; 24 : 48 ; Acts 1 : 8, 22 ; 2 : 32 ; 3 : 15 ; 5 : 32 ; 10 : 39, 41 ; 13 : 31 ; 22 : 15 ; 26 : 16 ; 1 Thess. 2 : 10 (1st part) ; 1 Tim. 6 : 12 ; 2 Tim. 2 : 2 ; Heb. 12 : 1, " (a cloud) of witnesses," here of those mentioned in chapt. 11, those whose lives and actions testified to the worth and effect of faith, and whose faith received witness in Scripture ; 1 Pet. 5 : 1.¶

2. MARTURIA (μαρτυρία), testimony, a bearing witness, is translated " witness " in Mark 14 : 55, 56, 59 ; Luke 22 : 71 ; John 1 : 7, 19 (R.V.) ; 3 : 11, 32 and 33 (R.V.) ; 5 : 31, 32, 34 (R.V.), 36 ; R.V. in 8 : 13, 14, 17 ; 19 : 35 ; 21 : 24 ; A.V. in Tit. 1 : 13 ; A.V. and R.V. in 1 John 5 : 9 (thrice), 10a ; R.V. in 10b, 11 ; 3 John 12 : see TESTIMONY, No. 2.

3. MARTURION (μαρτύριον), testimony or witness as borne, a declaration of facts, is translated " witness " in Matt. 24 : 14, A.V. ; Acts 4 : 33 ; 7 : 44 (A.V.) ; Jas. 5 : 3 (A.V.) : see TESTIMONY, No. 1.

4. PSEUDOMARTUS or –TUR (ψευδομάρτυς) denotes a false witness, Matt. 26 : 60 ; 1 Cor. 15 : 15.¶

5. PSEUDOMARTURIA (ψευδομαρτυρία), false witness, occurs in Matt. 15 : 19 ; 26 : 59.¶

B. Verbs.

1. MARTUREŌ (μαρτυρέω) denotes (I) to be a *martus* (see A, No. 1), or to bear witness to, sometimes rendered to testify (see TESTIFY, No. 1) ; it is used of the witness (*a*) of God the Father to Christ, John 5 : 32, 37 ; 8 : 18 (2nd part) ; 1 John 5 : 9, 10 ; to others, Acts 13 : 22 ; 15 : 8 ; Heb. 11 : 2, 4 (twice), 5, 39 ; (*b*) of Christ, John 3 : 11, 32 ; 4 : 44 ; 5 : 31 ; 7 : 7 ; 8 : 13, 14, 18 (1st part) ; 13 : 21 ; 18 : 37 ; Acts 14 : 3 ; 1 Tim. 6 : 13 ; Rev. 22 : 18, 20 ; of the Holy Spirit, to Christ, John 15 : 26 ; Heb. 10 : 15 ; 1 John 5 : 7, 8, R.V., which rightly omits the latter part of ver. 7 (it was a marginal gloss which crept into the original text : see THREE) ; it finds no support in Scripture ; (*c*) of the Scriptures, to Christ, John 5 : 39 ; Heb. 7 : 8, 17 ; (*d*) of the works of Christ, to Himself, and of the circumstances connected with His Death, John 5 : 36 ; 10 : 25 ; 1 John 5 : 8 ; (*e*) of prophets and apostles, to the righteousness of God, Rom. 3 : 21 ; to Christ, John 1 : 7, 8, 15, 32, 34 ; 3 : 26 ; 5 : 33, R.V. ; 15 : 27 ; 19 : 35 ; 21 : 24 ; Acts 10 : 43 ; 23 : 11 ; 1 Cor. 15 : 15 ; 1 John 1 : 2 ; 4 : 14 ; Rev. 1 : 2 ; to doctrine, Acts 26 : 22 (in some texts, so A.V. ; see No. 2) ; to the Word of God, Rev. 1 : 2 ; (*f*) of others, concerning Christ, Luke 4 : 22 ; John 4 : 39 ; 12 : 17 ; (*g*) of believers to one another, John 3 : 28 ; 2 Cor. 8 : 3 ; Gal. 4 : 15 ; Col. 4 : 13 ; 1 Thess. 2 : 11 (in some texts : see No. 2) ; 3 John 3, 6, 12 (2nd part) ; (*h*) of the Apostle Paul concerning Israel, Rom. 10 : 2 ; (*i*) of an angel, to the churches, Rev. 22 : 16 ; (*j*) of unbelievers, concerning themselves, Matt. 23 : 31 ; concerning Christ, John 18 : 23 ; concerning others, John 2 : 25 ; Acts 22 : 5 ; 26 : 5 ; (II) to give a good report, to approve of, Acts 6 : 3 ; 10 : 22 ; 16 : 2 ; 22 : 12 ; 1 Tim. 5 : 10 ; 3 John 12 (1st part) ; some would put Luke 4 : 22 here.¶

2. MARTUROMAI (μαρτύρομαι), strictly meaning to summon as a witness, signifies to affirm solemnly, adjure, and is used in the Middle Voice only, rendered to testify in Acts 20 : 26, R.V. (A.V., " I take . . . to record ") ; 26 : 22, R.V., in the best texts [see No. 1 (*e*)] ; Gal. 5 : 3 ; Eph. 4 : 17 ; 1 Thess. 2 : 11, in the best texts [see No. 1 (*g*)].¶

3. SUMMARTUREŌ (συμμαρτυρέω) denotes to bear witness with (*sun*), Rom. 2 : 15 ; 8 : 16 ; 9 : 1.¶

4. SUNEPIMARTUREŌ (συνεπιμαρτυρέω) denotes to join in bearing witness with others, Heb. 2 : 4.¶

5. KATAMARTUREŌ (καταμαρτυρέω) denotes to witness against (*kata*), Matt. 26 : 62 ; 27 : 13 ; Mark 14 : 60 (in some mss., 15 : 4, for *katēgoreō*, to accuse, R.V.).¶

6. PSEUDOMARTUREŌ (ψευδομαρτυρέω), to bear false witness (*pseudēs*, false), occurs in Matt. 19 : 18 ; Mark 10 : 19 ; 14 : 56, 57 ; Luke 18 : 20 ; in some texts, Rom. 13 : 9.¶

C. Adjectives.

AMARTUROS (ἀμάρτυρος) denotes without witness (a, negative, and martus), Acts 14 : 17.¶

WOE

OUAI (οὐαί), an interjection, is used (a) in denunciation, Matt. 11 : 21 ; 18 : 7 (twice) ; eight times in ch. 23 ; 24 : 19 ; 26 : 24 ; Mark 13 : 17 ; 14 : 21 ; Luke 6 : 24, 25 (twice), 26 ; 10 : 13 ; six times in ch. 11 ; 17 : 1 ; 21 : 23 ; 22 : 22 ; 1 Cor. 9 : 16 ; Jude 11 ; Rev. 8 : 13 (thrice) ; 12 : 12 ; as a noun, Rev. 9 : 12 (twice) ; 11 : 14 (twice) ; (b) in grief, " alas," Rev. 18 : 10, 16, 19 (twice in each).¶

WOLF

LUKOS (λύκος) occurs in Matt. 10 : 16 ; Luke 10 : 3 ; John 10 : 12 (twice) ; metaphorically, Matt. 7 : 15 ; Acts 20 : 29.¶

WOMAN

1. GUNĒ (γυνή), for which see also WIFE, is used of a woman unmarried or married, e.g., Matt. 11 : 11 ; 14 : 21 ; Luke 4 : 26, of a widow ; Rom. 7 : 2 ; in the vocative case, used in addressing a woman, it is a term not of reproof or severity, but of endearment or respect, Matt. 15 : 28 ; John 2 : 4, where the Lord's words to His mother at the wedding in Cana, are neither rebuff nor rebuke. The question is, lit., ' What to Me and to thee ? ' and the word "woman," the term of endearment, follows this. The meaning is ' There is no obligation on Me or you, but love will supply the need.' She confides in Him, He responds to her faith. There was lovingkindness in both hearts. His next words about ' His hour ' suit this ; they were not unfamiliar to her. Cana is in the path to Calvary ; Calvary was not yet, but it made the beginning of signs possible. See also 4 : 21 ; 19 : 26.

In Gal. 4 : 4 the phrase " born of a woman " is in accordance with the subject there, viz., the real humanity of the Lord Jesus ; this the words attest. They declare the method of His Incarnation and " suggest the means whereby that humanity was made free from the taint of sin consequent upon the Fall, viz., that He was not born through the natural process of ordinary generation, but was conceived by the power of the Holy Spirit . . . To have written ' born of a virgin ' would have carried the argument in a wrong direction . . . Since that man is born of woman is a universal fact, the statement would be superfluous if the Lord Jesus were no more than man " (Notes on Galatians, by Hogg and Vine, pp. 184 f.).

2. GUNAIKARION (γυναικάριον), a diminutive of No. 1, a little woman, is used contemptuously in 2 Tim. 3 : 6, a silly woman.¶

3. PRESBUTEROS (πρεσβύτερος), elder, older, in the feminine plural, denotes " elder women " in 1 Tim. 5 : 2. See ELDER, A, No. 1.

4. PRESBUTIS (πρεσβῦτις), the feminine of *presbutēs*, aged, is used in the plural and translated " aged women " in Tit. 2 : 3.¶

5. THĒLEIA (θήλεια), the feminine of the adjective *thēlus*, denotes female, and is used as a noun, Rom. 1 : 26, 27. See FEMALE.

WOMB

1. KOILIA (κοιλία) denotes the womb, Matt. 19 : 12 ; Luke 1 : 15, 41, 42, 44 ; 2 : 21 ; 11 : 27 ; 23 : 29 ; John 3 : 4 ; Acts 3 : 2 ; 14 : 8 ; Gal. 1 : 15. See BELLY, No. 1.

2. GASTĒR (γαστήρ), is rendered " womb" in Luke 1 : 31. See BELLY, No. 2.

3. MĒTRA (μήτρα), the matrix (akin to *mētēr*, a mother), occurs in Luke 2 : 23 ; Rom. 4 : 19.¶

WONDER (Noun and Verb)

A. Nouns.

1. TERAS (τέρας), something strange, causing the beholder to marvel, is always used in the plural, always rendered " wonders," and generally follows *sēmeia*, " signs ; " the opposite order occurs in Acts 2 : 22, 43 ; 6 : 8, R.V. ; 7 : 36 ; in Acts 2 : 19 " wonders " occurs alone. A sign is intended to appeal to the understanding, a wonder appeals to the imagination, a power (*dunamis*) indicates its source as supernatural. " Wonders " are manifested as Divine operations in thirteen occurrences (9 times in Acts) ; three times they are ascribed to the work of Satan through human agents, Matt. 24 : 24 ; Mark 13 : 22 and 2 Thess. 2 : 9.

2. THAMBOS (θάμβος), amazement, is rendered " wonder " in Acts 3 : 10. See AMAZE, A, No. 2.

Notes : (1) For *thauma*, a wonder (rendered " admiration " in Rev. 17 : 6, A.V.), see MARVEL. (2) In Rev. 12 : 1, 3 and 13 : 13 *sēmeion*, a sign, is translated in the A.V., " wonder(s)," R.V., " sign(s)." (3) In Acts 3 : 11 *ekthambos* (*ek*, intensive, and No. 2) is translated " greatly wondering."¶ (4) For *pseudos*, 2 Thess. 2 : 9, " lying wonders," see FALSE, B. Cp. AMAZE, B, Nos. 3 and 4.

B. Verbs.

Note : For *thaumazō*, see MARVEL ; for *existēmi*, Acts 8 : 13, A.V., see AMAZE, B, No. 1.

WONDERFUL (THING, WORK)

Notes : (1) In Matt. 7 : 22, A.V., *dunamis* (in the plural) is rendered " wonderful works " (R.V., " mighty works," marg., " powers "). See POWER. (2) In Acts 2 : 11, A.V., the adjective *megaleios*, magnificent, in the neuter plural with the article, is rendered " the wonderful works " (R.V., " the mighty works ").¶ (3) In Matt. 21 : 15, the neuter plural of the adjective *thaumasios*, wonderful, is used as a noun, " wonderful things," lit., ' wonders.'

WONT

ETHŌ (ἔθω), to be accustomed, is used in the pluperfect te‿se (with imperfect meaning), *eiōtha*, rendered " was wont " in Matt. 27 : 15 ; Mark 10 : 1.   See CUSTOM, B, No. 2, MANNER, A, Note (1).

Notes : (1) In Mark 15 : 8, " he was wont to do," R.V., represents the imperfect tense of *poieō*, to do (A.V., " he had ever done ").   (2) In Luke 22 : 39, A.V., *ethos*, a custom, preceded by *kata* and the article, lit., ' according to the (i.e., His) custom ', is translated " as He was wont " (R.V., " as His custom was ") : see CUSTOM, A, No. 1.   (3) In Acts 16 : 13 the A.V., " was wont ", translates the texts which have the Passive Voice of *nomizō* with its meaning to hold by custom ; the R.V., " we supposed," translates the texts which have the imperfect tense, Active, with the meaning to consider, suppose.

WOOD

1. XULON (ξύλον) denotes timber, wood for any use 1 Cor. 3 : 12 ; Rev. 18 : 12 (twice).   See STAFF, STOCKS, TREE.

2. HULĒ (ὕλη) denotes a wood, a forest, Jas. 3 : 5 (A.V., " matter ", marg., " wood ").¶   See MATTER, Note (3).

WOOL

ERION (ἔριον) occurs in Heb. 9 : 19 ; Rev. 1 : 14.¶

WORD

1. LOGOS (λόγος) denotes (I) the expression of thought—not the mere name of an object—(a) as embodying a conception or idea, e.g., Luke 7 : 7 ; 1 Cor. 14 : 9, 19 ; (b) a saying or statement, (1) by God, e.g., John 15 : 25 ; Rom. 9 : 9 ; 9 : 28, R.V., " word " (A.V., " work ") ; Gal. 5 : 14 ; Heb. 4 : 12 ; (2) by Christ, e.g., Matt. 24 : 35 (plur.) ; John 2 : 22 ; 4 : 41 ; 14 : 23 (plur.) ; 15 : 20.   In connection with (1) and (2) the phrase " the word of the Lord," i.e., the revealed will of God (very frequent in the O.T.), is used of a direct revelation given by Christ, 1 Thess. 4 : 15 ; of the gospel, Acts 8 : 25 ; 13 : 49 ; 15 : 35, 36 ; 16 : 32 ; 19 : 10 ; 1 Thess. 1 : 8 ; 2 Thess. 3 : 1 ; in this respect it is the message from the Lord, delivered with His authority and made effective by His power (cp. Acts 10 : 36) ; for other instances relating to the gospel see Acts 13 : 26 ; 14 : 3 ; 15 : 7 ; 1 Cor. 1 : 18, R.V. ; 2 Cor. 2 : 17 ; 4 : 2 ; 5 : 19 ; 6 : 7 ; Gal. 6 : 6 ; Eph. 1 : 13 ; Phil. 2 : 16 ; Col. 1 : 5 ; Heb. 5 : 13 ; sometimes it is used as the sum of God's utterances, e.g., Mark 7 : 13 ; John 10 : 35 ; Rev. 1 : 2, 9 ; (c) discourse, speech, of instruction etc., e.g., Acts 2 : 40 ; 1 Cor. 2 : 13 ; 12 : 8 ; 2 Cor. 1 : 18 ; 1 Thess. 1 : 5 ; 2 Thess. 2 : 15 ; Heb. 6 : 1, R.V., marg. ; doctrine, e.g., Matt. 13 : 20 ; Col. 3 : 16 ; 1 Tim. 4 : 6 ; 2 Tim. 1 : 13 ; Tit. 1 : 9 ; 1 John 2 : 7 ;

(II) The Personal Word, a title of the Son of God ; this identification is substantiated by the statements of doctrine in John 1 : 1-18, declaring in verses 1 and 2 (1) His distinct and superfinite Personality, (2) His relation in the Godhead (*pros*, with, not mere company, but the most intimate communion), (3) His Deity ; in ver. 3 His creative power ; in ver. 14 His Incarnation (" became flesh," expressing His voluntary act ; not as A.V., " was made "), the reality and totality of His human nature, and His glory " as of the only begotten from the Father," R.V. (marg., " an only begotten from a father "), the absence of the article in each place lending stress to the nature and character of the relationship ; His was the Shekinah glory in open manifestation ; ver. 18 consummates the identification : " the only-begotten Son (R.V. marg., many ancient authorities read ' God only begotten,'), which is in the bosom of the Father, He hath declared Him," thus fulfilling the significance of the title " *Logos*," the Word, the personal manifestation, not of a part of the Divine nature, but of the whole Deity (see IMAGE).

The title is used also in 1 John 1, " the Word of life " combining the two declarations in John 1 : 1 and 4 and Rev. 19 : 13 (for 1 John 5 : 7 see THREE).

2. RHĒMA (ῥῆμα) denotes that which is spoken, what is uttered in speech or writing ; in the singular, a word, e.g., Matt. 12 : 36 ; 27 : 14 ; 2 Cor. 12 : 4 ; 13 : 1 ; Heb. 12 : 19 ; in the plural, speech, discourse, e.g., John 3 : 34 ; 8 : 20 ; Acts 2 : 14 ; 6 : 11, 13 ; 11 : 14 ; 13 : 42 ; 26 : 25 ; Rom. 10 : 18 ; 2 Pet. 3 : 2 ; Jude 17 ; it is used of the gospel in Rom. 10 : 8 (twice), 17, R.V., " the word of Christ " (i.e., the word which preaches Christ) ; 10 : 18 ; 1 Pet. 1 : 25 (twice) ; of a statement, command, instruction, e.g., Matt. 26 : 75 ; Luke 1 : 37, R.V., " (no) word (from God shall be void of power) ; " ver. 38 ; Acts 11 : 16 ; Heb. 11 : 3.

The significance of *rhēma* (as distinct from *logos*) is exemplified in the injunction to take " the sword of the Spirit, which is the word of God," Eph. 6 : 17 ; here the reference is not to the whole Bible as such, but to the individual scripture which the Spirit brings to our remembrance for use in time of need, a prerequisite being the regular storing of the mind with Scripture.

Notes : (1) *Epos*, a word, is used in a phrase in Heb. 7 : 9, lit., ' (as to say) a word,' R.V., " (so to) say," A.V., " (as I may so) say ; " *logos* is reasoned speech, *rhēma*, an utterance, *epos*, " the articulated expression of a thought " (Abbott-Smith). (2) In Rom. 16 : 18, A.V., *chrēstologia*, useful discourse (*chrēstos*, beneficial), is rendered " good words " [R.V., " smooth ... (speech) "].¶ (3) For *logikos*, 1 Pet. 2 : 2 (R.V., "spiritual "), rendered " of the word," A.V., see MILK. (4) For the verb *apangellō*, rendered to bring word, see BRING, No. 36. (5) In Matt. 2 : 13, A.V., *eipon*, to tell (R.V.), is rendered " bring . . . word." (6) For " enticing words," Col. 2 : 4, see ENTICE and PERSUASIVENESS. (7) For " strifes of words," 1 Tim. 6 : 4, A.V., and " strive . . . about words," 2 Tim. 2 : 14, see STRIFE, STRIVE. (8) For *suntomōs*, Acts 24 : 4, " a few words," see FEW, B.¶ For the same phrase see FEW, A, Nos. 1 and 2.

WORK (Noun and Verb), WROUGHT
A. Nouns.

1. ERGON (ἔργον) denotes (I) work, employment, task, e.g., Mark 13 : 34; John 4 : 34; 17 : 4; Acts 13 : 2; Phil. 2 : 30; 1 Thess. 5 : 13; in Acts 5 : 38 with the idea of enterprise; (II) a deed, act, (a) of God, e.g., John 6 : 28, 29; 9 : 3; 10 : 37; 14 : 10; Acts 13 : 41; Rom. 14 : 20; Heb. 1 : 10; 2 : 7; 3 : 9; 4 : 3, 4, 10; Rev. 15 : 3; (b) of Christ, e.g., Matt. 11 : 2; especially in John, 5 : 36; 7 : 3, 21; 10 : 25, 32, 33, 38; 14 : 11, 12; 15 : 24; Rev. 2 : 26; (c) of believers, e.g., Matt. 5 : 16; Mark 14 : 6; Acts 9 : 36; Rom. 13 : 3; Col. 1 : 10; 1 Thess. 1 : 3, " work of faith," here the initial act of faith at conversion (turning to God, ver. 9); in 2 Thess. 1 : 11, " *every* work of faith," R.V., denotes every activity undertaken for Christ's sake; 2 : 17; 1 Tim. 2 : 10; 5 : 10; 6 : 18; 2 Tim. 2 : 21; 3 : 17; Tit. 2 : 7, 14; 3 : 1, 8, 14; Heb. 10 : 24; 13 : 21; frequent in James, as the effect of faith [in 1 : 25, A.V., " (a doer) of the work," R.V., " (a doer) that worketh"]; 1 Pet. 2 : 12; Rev. 2 : 2 and in several other places in chapts. 2 and 3; 14 : 13; (d) of unbelievers, e.g., Matt. 23 : 3, 5; John 7 : 7; Acts 7 : 41 (for idols); Rom. 13 : 12; Eph. 5 : 11; Col. 1 : 21; Tit. 1 : 16 (1st part); 1 John 3 : 12; Jude 15, R.V.; Rev. 2 : 6, R.V.; of those who seek justification by works, e.g., Rom. 9 : 32; Gal. 3 : 10; Eph. 2 : 9; described as the works of the law, e.g., Gal. 2 : 16; 3 : 2, 5; dead works, Heb. 6 : 1; 9 : 14; (e) of Babylon, Rev. 18 : 6; (f) of the Devil, John 8 : 41; 1 John 3 : 8. See DEED.

2. ERGASIA (ἐργασία) denotes a work or business, also a working, performance, Eph. 4 : 19, where preceded by *eis*, to, it is rendered " to work " (marg., " to make a trade of "). See DILIGENCE, GAIN.

Notes: (1) In Rom. 9 : 28, A.V., *logos*, a word (R.V.), is rendered " work." (2) For *pragma*, Jas. 3 : 16, rendered " work " in A.V., the R.V. has " deed." (3) For *praxis*, a doing, Matt. 16 : 27, R.V. marg., A.V., " works," see DEED. (4) For the A.V., " much work," Acts 27 : 16, see DIFFICULTY. (5) For " workfellow," Rom. 16 : 21, A.V., see WORKER, No. 2. (6) In Matt. 14 : 2 and Mark 6 : 14, A.V., *dunameis*, " powers," R.V., is translated " mighty works;" in Acts 2 : 22, R.V., " mighty works," A.V., " miracles." (7) For " wonderful works " see WONDERFUL, Note (2).

B. Verbs.

1. ERGAZOMAI (ἐργάζομαι) is used (I) intransitively, e.g., Matt. 21 : 28; John 5 : 17; 9 : 4 (2nd part); Rom. 4 : 4, 5; 1 Cor. 4 : 12; 9 : 6; 1 Thess. 2 : 9; 4 : 11; 2 Thess. 3 : 8, 10–12 (for the play upon words in ver. 11 see BUSYBODY, A); (II) transitively, (a) to work something, produce, perform, e.g., Matt. 26 : 10, " she hath wrought;" John 6 : 28, 30; 9 : 4 (1st part); Acts 10 : 35; 13 : 41; Rom. 2 : 10; 13 : 10; 1 Cor. 16 : 10; 2 Cor. 7 : 10a, in the best texts, some have No. 2; Gal. 6 : 10, R.V., " let us work;" Eph. 4 : 28; Heb. 11 : 33; 2 John 8; (b) to earn

by working, work for, John 6 : 27, R.V., " work " (A.V., " labour ").
See COMMIT, DO, LABOUR, MINISTER, TRADE.

2. KATERGAZOMAI (κατεργάζομαι), an emphatic form of No. 1,
signifies to work out, achieve, effect by toil, rendered to work (past tense,
wrought) in Rom. 1 : 27 ; 2 : 9, R.V. ; 4 : 15 (the Law brings men under
condemnation and so renders them subject to Divine wrath) ; 5 : 3 ;
7 : 8, 13 ; 15 : 18 ; 2 Cor. 4 : 17 ; 5 : 5 ; 7 : 10 (see No. 1), 11 ; 12 : 12 ;
Phil. 2 : 12, where " your own salvation " refers especially to freedom
from strife and vainglory ; Jas. 1 : 3, 20 ; 1 Pet. 4 : 3. See DO, No. 5.

3. ENERGEŌ (ἐνεργέω), lit., to work in (en, and A, No. 1), to be
active, operative, is used of " (a) God, 1 Cor. 12 : 6 ; Gal. 2 : 8 ; 3 : 5 ;
Eph. 1 : 11, 20 ; 3 : 20 ; Phil. 2 : 13a ; Col. 1 : 29 ; (b) the Holy Spirit,
1 Cor. 12 : 11 ; (c) the Word of God, 1 Thess. 2 : 13 (Middle Voice ; A.V.,
'effectually worketh') ; (d) supernatural power, undefined, Matt. 14 : 2 ;
Mark 6 : 14 ; (e) faith, as the energizer of love, Gal. 5 : 6 ; (f) the
example of patience in suffering, 2 Cor. 1 : 6 ; (g) death (physical) and
life (spiritual), 2 Cor. 4 : 12 ; (h) sinful passions, Rom. 7 : 5 ; (i) the spirit
of the Evil One, Eph. 2 : 2 ; (j) the mystery of iniquity, 2 Thess. 2 : 7."*

To these may be added (k) the active response of believers to the
inworking of God, Phil. 2 : 13b, R.V., " to work (for)," A.V., " to do
(of) ; " (l) the supplication of the righteous, Jas. 5 : 16, R.V., " in its
working " (A.V., " effectual fervent ").

4. POIEŌ (ποιέω), to do, is rendered to work in Matt. 20 : 12, A.V.
(R.V., " spent ") ; Acts 15 : 12, " had wrought ; " 19 : 11 ; 21 : 19 ;
Heb. 13 : 21 ; Rev. 16 : 14 ; 19 : 20 ; 21 : 27, A.V. (R.V., " maketh ; "
marg., " doeth "). See DO.

5. SUNERGEŌ (συνεργέω), to work with or together (sun), occurs
in Mark 16 : 20 ; Rom. 8 : 28, " work together ; " 1 Cor. 16 : 16, " helpeth
with ; " 2 Cor. 6 : 1, " workers together," present participle, ' working
together ; ' the " with Him " represents nothing in the Greek ; Jas. 2 : 22,
" wrought with." See HELP.¶

6. GINOMAI (γίνομαι), to become, take place, is rendered " wrought "
in Mark 6 : 2 ; Acts 5 : 12, " were . . . wrought."

WORKER, WORKFELLOW, FELLOW-WORKERS, WORKMAN

1. ERGATĒS (ἐργάτης) is translated " workers " in Luke 13 : 27
(" of iniquity ") ; 2 Cor. 11 : 13 (" deceitful ") ; Phil. 3 : 2 (" evil ") ;
" workman," Matt. 10 : 10, A.V. (R.V., " labourer ") ; " workman,"
2 Tim. 2 : 15 ; " workmen," Acts 19 : 25. See LABOURER.

2. SUNERGOS (συνεργός) denotes a worker with, and is rendered
" workfellow " in Rom. 16 : 21, A.V., R.V., " fellow-worker ; " in Col.
4 : 11, " fellow-workers " (see R.V.). See the R.V., " God's fellow-workers," in 1 Cor. 3 : 9. See COMPANION, HELPER, LABOURER, Note.

Note : For " workers at home," Tit. 2 : 5, see HOME, B.

---

* From Notes on Galatians by Hogg and Vine, pp. 114, 115.

WORKING

1. ENERGEIA (ἐνέργεια) (Eng., energy) is used (1) of the power of God, (a) in the resurrection of Christ, Eph. 1 : 19 ; Col. 2 : 12, R.V., " working " (A.V., " operation ") ; (b) in the call and enduement of Paul, Eph. 3 : 7 ; Col. 1 : 29 ; (c) in His retributive dealings in sending " a working of error " (A.V., " strong delusion ") upon those under the rule of the Man of Sin who receive not the love of the truth, but have pleasure in unrighteousness, 2 Thess. 2 : 11 ; (2) of the power of Christ (a) generally, Phil. 3 : 21 ; (b) in the Church, individually, Eph. 4 : 16 ; (3) of the power of Satan in energising the Man of Sin in his ' parousia,' 2 Thess. 2 : 9, " coming."¶

2. ENERGĒMA (ἐνέργημα), what is wrought, the effect produced by No. 1, occurs in 1 Cor. 12 : 6, R.V., " workings " (A.V., " operations ") ; ver. 10.¶

For WORKMANSHIP see MADE, B

WORLD

1. KOSMOS (κόσμος), primarily order, arrangement, ornament, adornment (1 Pet. 3 : 3, see ADORN, B), is used to denote (a) the earth, e.g., Matt. 13 : 35 ; John 21 : 25 ; Acts 17 : 24 ; Rom. 1 : 20 (probably here the universe : it had this meaning among the Greeks, owing to the order observable in it) ; 1 Tim. 6 : 7 ; Heb. 4 : 3 ; 9 : 26 ; (b) the earth in contrast with Heaven, 1 John 3 : 17 (perhaps also Rom. 4 : 13) ; (c) by metonymy, the human race, mankind, e.g., Matt. 5 : 14 ; John 1 : 9 [here " that cometh (R.V., coming) into the world " is said of Christ, not of " every man ; " by His coming into the world He was the light for all men] ; ver. 10 ; 3 : 16, 17 (thrice), 19 ; 4 : 42, and frequently in Rom., 1 Cor. and 1 John ; (d) Gentiles as distinguished from Jews, e.g., Rom. 11 : 12, 15, where the meaning is that all who will may be reconciled (cp. 2 Cor. 5 : 19) ; (e) the present condition of human affairs, in alienation from and opposition to God, e.g., John 7 : 7 ; 8 : 23 ; 14 : 30 ; 1 Cor. 2 : 12 ; Gal. 4 : 3 ; 6 : 14 ; Col. 2 : 8 ; Jas. 1 : 27 ; 1 John 4 : 5 (thrice) ; 5 : 19 ; (f) the sum of temporal possessions, Matt. 16 : 26 ; 1 Cor. 7 : 31 (1st part) ; (g) metaphorically, of the tongue as " a world (of iniquity)," Jas. 3 : 6, expressive of magnitude and variety.

2. AIŌN (αἰών), an age, a period of time, marked in the N.T. usage by spiritual or moral characteristics, is sometimes translated " world ; " the R.V. marg. always has " age." The following are details concerning the world in this respect ; its cares, Matt. 13 : 22 ; its sons, Luke 16 : 8 ; 20 : 34 ; its rulers, 1 Cor. 2 : 6, 8 ; its wisdom, 1 Cor. 1 : 20 ; 2 : 6 ; 3 : 18 ; its fashion, Rom. 12 : 2 ; its character, Gal. 1 : 4 ; its god, 2 Cor. 4 : 4. The phrase " the end of the world " should be rendered " the end of the age," in most places (see END, A, No. 2) ; in 1 Cor. 10 : 11, A.V., " the ends (telē) of the world," R.V., " the ends of the ages," probably signifies

the fulfilment of the Divine purposes concerning the ages, in regard to the Church [this would come under END, A, No. 1, (c)]. In Heb. 11 : 3 [lit., ' the ages (have been prepared) '] the word indicates all that the successive periods contain ; cp. 1 : 2.

Aiōn is always to be distinguished from *kosmos*, even where the two seem to express the same idea, e.g., 1 Cor. 3 : 18, *aiōn*, ver. 19, *kosmos* ; the two are used together in Eph. 2 : 2, lit., ' the age of this world.' For a list of phrases containing *aiōn*, with their respective meanings, see EVER, B.

3. OIKOUMENĒ (οἰκουμένη), the inhabited earth (see EARTH, No. 2), is used (a) of the whole inhabited world, Matt. 24 : 14 ; Luke 4 : 5 ; 21 : 26 ; Rom. 10 : 18 ; Heb. 1 : 6 ; Rev. 3 : 10 ; 16 : 14 ; by metonymy, of its inhabitants, Acts 17 : 31 ; Rev. 12 : 9 ; (b) of the Roman Empire, the world as viewed by the writer or speaker, Luke 2 : 1 ; Acts 11 : 28 ; 24 : 5 ; by metonymy, of its inhabitants, Acts 17 : 6 ; 19 : 27 ; (c) the inhabited world in a coming age, Heb. 2 : 5.¶

Notes : (1) In Rev. 13 : 3, A.V., *gē*, the earth (R.V.), is translated " world." (2) For phrases containing *aiōnios*, e.g., Rom. 16 : 25 ; 2 Tim. 1 : 9 ; Tit. 1 : 2, see ETERNAL, No. 2.

WORLDLY

KOSMIKOS (κοσμικός), pertaining to this world, is used (a) in Heb. 9 : 1, of the tabernacle, A.V., " worldly," R.V., " of this world " (i.e., made of mundane materials, adapted to this visible world, local and transitory) ; (b) in Tit. 2 : 12, ethically, of " worldly lusts," or desires.¶

For WORLD-RULERS, Eph. 6 : 12, R.V., see RULER, No. 3

WORM

1. SKŌLĒX (σκώληξ), a worm which preys upon dead bodies, is used metaphorically by the Lord in Mark 9 : 48 ; in some mss. vv. 44, 46, cp. Is. 66 : 24. The statement signifies the exclusion of the hope of restoration, the punishment being eternal.¶

2. SKŌLĒKOBRŌTOS (σκωληκόβρωτος) denotes devoured by worms (*skōlēx*, and *bibrōskō*, to eat), Acts 12 : 23.¶

WORMWOOD

APSINTHOS (ἄψινθος) (Eng., absinth), a plant both bitter and deleterious, and growing in desolate places, figuratively suggestive of calamity (Lam. 3 : 15) and injustice (Amos 5 : 7), is used in Rev. 8 : 11 (twice ; in the 1st part as a proper name).¶

WORSE
A. Adjectives.

1. CHEIRŌN (χείρων), used as the comparative degree of *kakos*,

evil, describes (a) the condition of certain men, Matt. 12 : 45 ; Luke 11 : 26 ; 2 Pet. 2 : 20 ; (b) evil men themselves and seducers, 2 Tim. 3 : 13 ; (c) indolent men who refuse to provide for their own households, and are worse than unbelievers, 1 Tim. 5 : 8, R.V. ; (d) a rent in a garment, Matt. 9 : 16 ; Mark 2 : 21 ; (e) an error, Matt. 27 : 64 ; (f) a person suffering from a malady, Mark 5 : 26 ; (g) a possible physical affliction, John 5 : 14 ; (h) a punishment, Heb. 10 : 29, " sorer." See Sore. ¶

2. ELASSŌN or ELATTŌN (ἐλάσσων) is said of wine in John 2 : 10. See Less.

3. HĒSSŌN or HĒTTŌN (ἥσσων), less, inferior, used in the neuter, after epi, for, is translated " worse " in 1 Cor. 11 : 17 ; in 2 Cor. 12 : 15 the neuter, used adverbially, is translated " the less." ¶

B. Verbs.

1. HUSTEREŌ (ὑστερέω) is rendered " are we the worse " in 1 Cor. 8 : 8.   See Behind, B, No. 1, Come, No. 39, Destitute, Fail, Note (2), Lack, Want.

2. PROECHŌ (προέχω), to hold before, promote, is rendered " are we better " in Rom. 3 : 9, A.V. (Passive Voice) ; R.V., " are we in worse case."   See Better (be), Note (1). ¶

WORSHIP (Verb and Noun), WORSHIPPING
A. Verbs.

1. PROSKUNEŌ (προσκυνέω), to make obeisance, do reverence to (from pros, towards, and kuneō, to kiss), is the most frequent word rendered to worship.   It is used of an act of homage or reverence (a) to God, e.g., Matt. 4 : 10 ; John 4 : 21-24 ; 1 Cor. 14 : 25 ; Rev. 4 : 10 ; 5 : 14 ; 7 : 11 ; 11 : 16 ; 19 : 10 (2nd part) and 22 : 9 ; (b) to Christ, e.g., Matt. 2 : 2, 8, 11 ; 8 : 2 ; 9 : 18 ; 14 : 33 ; 15 : 25 ; 20 : 20 ; 28 : 9, 17 ; John 9 : 38 ; Heb. 1 : 6, in a quotation from the Sept. of Deut. 32 : 43, referring to Christ's Second Advent ; (c) to a man, Matt. 18 : 26 ; (d) to the Dragon, by men, Rev. 13 : 4 ; (e) to the Beast, his human instrument, Rev. 13 : 4, 8, 12 ; 14 : 9, 11 ; (f) the image of the Beast, 13 : 15 ; 14 : 11 ; 16 : 2 ; (g) to demons, Rev. 9 : 20 ; (h) to idols, Acts 7 : 43.

Note : As to Matt. 18 : 26, this is mentioned as follows, in the " List of readings and renderings preferred by the American Committee " (see R.V. Classes of Passages, IV) : " At the word ' worship ' in Matt. 2 : 2, etc., add the marginal note ' The Greek word denotes an act of reverence, whether paid to man (see chap. 18 : 26) or to God (see chap. 4 : 10) '."   The Note to John 9 : 38 in the American Standard Version in this connection is most unsound ; it implies that Christ was a creature. J. N. Darby renders the verb ' do homage ' [see the Revised Preface to the Second Edition (1871) of his New Translation].

2. SEBOMAI (σέβομαι), to revere, stressing the feeling of awe or

devotion, is used of worship (*a*) to God, Matt. 15 : 9 ; Mark 7 : 7 ; Acts 16 : 14 ; 18 : 7, 13 ; (*b*) to a goddess, Acts 19 : 27. See DEVOUT, No. 3.

3. SEBAZOMAI (σεβάζομαι), akin to No. 2, to honour religiously, is used in Rom. 1 : 25.¶

4. LATREUŌ (λατρεύω), to serve, to render religious service or homage, is translated to worship in Phil. 3 : 3, " (who) worship (by the Spirit of God)," R.V., A.V., " (which) worship (God in the spirit) " ; the R.V. renders it to serve (for A.V., to worship) in Acts 7 : 42 ; 24 : 14 ; A.V. and R.V., " (the) worshippers " in Heb. 10 : 2, present participle, lit., ' (the ones) worshipping.' See SERVE.

5. EUSEBEŌ (εὐσεβέω), to act piously towards, is translated " ye worship " in Acts 17 : 23. See PIETY (to shew).

Notes : (1) The worship of God is nowhere defined in Scripture. A consideration of the above verbs shows that it is not confined to praise ; broadly it may be regarded as the direct acknowledgement to God, of His nature, attributes, ways and claims, whether by the outgoing of the heart in praise and thanksgiving or by deed done in such acknowledgment. (2) In Acts 17 : 25 *therapeuō*, to serve, do service to (so R.V.), is rendered " is worshipped." See CURE, HEAL.

B. Nouns.

1. SEBASMA (σέβασμα) denotes an object of worship (akin to A, No. 3) ; Acts 17 : 23 (see DEVOTION) ; in 2 Thess. 2 : 4, " that is worshipped ; " every object of worship, whether the true God or pagan idols, will come under the ban of the Man of Sin.¶

2. ETHELOTHRĒSKEIA (or -IA) (ἐθελοθρησκεία), will-worship (*ethelō*, to will, *thrēskeia*, worship), occurs in Col. 2 : 23, voluntarily adopted worship, whether unbidden or forbidden, not that which is imposed by others, but which one affects.¶

3. THRĒSKEIA (θρησκεία), for which see RELIGION, is translated " worshipping " in Col. 2 : 18.

Note : In Luke 14 : 10, A.V., *doxa*, " glory " (R.V.), is translated " worship."

WORSHIPPER

1. PROSKUNĒTĒS (προσκυνητής), akin to *proskuneō* (see WORSHIP, A, No. 1), occurs in John 4 : 23.¶

2. NEŌKOROS (νεωκόρος) is translated " worshipper " in Acts 19 : 35, A.V. : see TEMPLE-KEEPER.¶

3. THEOSEBĒS (θεοσεβής) denotes ' reverencing God ' (*theos*, God, *sebomai*, see WORSHIP, A, No. 2), and is rendered " a worshipper of God " in John 9 : 31.¶ Cp. *theosebeia*, godliness, 1 Tim. 2 : 10.¶

Note : For Heb. 10 : 2, see WORSHIP, A, No. 4.

WORTHY, WORTHILY
A. Adjectives.

1. AXIOS (ἄξιος), of weight, worth, worthy, is said of persons and their deeds : (a) in a good sense, e.g., Matt. 10 : 10, 11, 13 (twice), 37 (twice), 38 ; 22 : 8 ; Luke 7 : 4 ; 10 : 7 ; 15 : 19, 21 ; John 1 : 27 ; Acts 13 : 25 ; 1 Tim. 5 : 18 ; 6 : 1 ; Heb. 11 : 38 ; Rev. 3 : 4 ; 4 : 11 ; 5 : 2, 4, 9, 12 ; (b) in a bad sense, Luke 12 : 48 ; 23 : 15 ; Acts 23 : 29 ; 25 : 11, 25 ; 26 : 31 ; Rom. 1 : 32 ; Rev. 16 : 6. See MEET, REWARD.

2. HIKANOS (ἱκανός), sufficient, is translated " worthy " in this sense in Matt. 3 : 11 (marg., " sufficient ") ; so 8 : 8 ; Mark 1 : 7 ; Luke 3 : 16 ; 7 : 6. See ABILITY, C, No. 2, etc.

3. ENOCHOS (ἔνοχος), held in, bound by, is translated " worthy (of death) " in Matt. 26 : 66 and Mark 14 : 64, R.V. (marg., " liable to ; " A.V., " guilty "). See DANGER.

Notes : (1) In Jas. 2 : 7, A.V., *kalos*, good, fair, is translated " worthy " (R.V., " honourable "). (2) For the A.V. of Eph. 4 : 1 ; Col. 1 : 10 ; 1 Thess. 2 : 12, see C, below.

B. Verbs.

1. AXIOŌ (ἀξιόω), to think or count worthy, is used (1) of the estimation formed by God (a) favourably, 2 Thess. 1 : 11, " may count (you) worthy (of your calling)," suggestive of grace (it does not say ' may make you worthy ') ; Heb. 3 : 3, " of more glory," of Christ in comparison with Moses ; (b) unfavourably, 10 : 29, " of how much sorer punishment ; " (2) by a centurion (negatively) concerning himself, Luke 7 : 7 ; (3) by a church, regarding its elders, 1 Tim. 5 : 17, where " honour " stands probably for ' honorarium,' i.e., material support. See also DESIRE, B, No. 1 (Acts 28 : 22), THINK (Acts 15 : 38).¶

2. KATAXIOŌ (καταξιόω), a strengthened form of No. 1, occurs in Luke 20 : 35 ; 21 : 36, in some texts ; Acts 5 : 41 ; 2 Thess. 1 : 5.¶ See ACCOUNT, A, No. 5.

C. Adverb.

AXIŌS (ἀξίως), worthily, so translated in the R.V. [with one exception, see (c)], for A.V., " worthy " and other renderings, (a) " worthily of God," 1 Thess. 2 : 12, of the Christian walk as it should be ; 3 John 6, R.V., of assisting servants of God in a way which reflects God's character and thoughts ; (b) " worthily of the Lord," Col. 1 : 10 ; of the calling of believers, Eph. 4 : 1, in regard to their " walk " or manner of life ; (c) " worthy of the gospel of Christ," Phil. 1 : 27, of a manner of life in accordance with what the gospel declares ; (d) " worthily of the saints," R.V., of receiving a fellow-believer, Rom. 16 : 2, in such a manner as befits those who bear the name of " saints."¶ Deissmann (*Bible Studies*, pp. 248 ff.) shows from various inscriptions that the phrase " worthily of the god " was very popular at Pergamum.

For WORTHY DEEDS, Acts 24 : 2, A.V., see CORRECTION

WOT

Note : This form, the 1st person singular and the plural of the present tense of an Anglo-Saxon verb *witan*, to see or to know (for the past tense cp. WIST), is a rendering of (1) *oida*, to know, in Acts 3 : 17 ; 7 : 40 ; Rom. 11 : 2 (see KNOW, No. 2) ; (2) *gnōrizō*, to come to know, in Phil. 1 : 22 (see KNOW, No. 8).

WOULD

Notes : (1) This is often a translation of various inflections of a Greek verb. When it represents a separate word, it is always emphatic, and is a translation of one or other of the verbs mentioned under WILL. (2) *Ophelon* (the 2nd aorist tense of *opheilō*, to owe) expresses a wish, " I would that," either impracticable, 1 Cor. 4 : 8, R.V. (A.V., " would to God ") ; or possible, 2 Cor. 11 : 1 ; Gal. 5 : 12 ; Rev. 3 : 15.   (3) *Euchomai*, to pray, with the particle *an*, expressing a strong desire with a remote possibility of fulfilment, is used in Acts 26 : 29, " I would (to God, that)."

WOUND (Noun and Verb)
A. Nouns.
TRAUMA (*τραῦμα*), a wound, occurs in Luke 10 : 34.¶
Note: *Plēgē*, a blow, a stroke, is used in Luke 10 : 30 with *epitithēmi*, to lay on, lit., ' laid on blows,' R.V., " beat " (A.V., " wounded "). In Rev. 13 : 3, 12, *plēgē* is used with the genitive case of *thanatos*, death, lit., ' stroke of death,' R.V., " death-stroke " (A.V., " deadly wound ") ; the rendering " wound " does not accurately give the meaning ; in ver. 14, with the genitive of *machaira*, a sword, A.V., " wound " (R.V., " stroke ").

B. Verbs.
TRAUMATIZŌ ·(*τραυματίζω*), to wound (from A), occurs in Luke 20 : 12 and Acts 19 : 16.¶
Note : In Rev. 13 : 3, A.V., *sphazō*, to slay, is translated " wounded," R.V., " smitten " (A.V. and R.V. marg., " slain ").

For WOUND (wrapped) see WIND (Verb)

WOVEN

HUPHANTOS (*ὑφαντός*), from *huphainō*, to weave (found in good mss. in Luke 12 : 27), is used of Christ's garment, John 19 : 23.¶

WRANGLINGS

DIAPARATRIBĒ (*διαπαρατριβή*), found in 1 Tim. 6 : 5, denotes constant strife, ' obstinate contests ' (Ellicott), ' mutual irritations ' (Field), A.V., " perverse disputings " (marg., " gallings one of another "),

R.V. "wranglings.'"° Some texts have *paradiatribē*. The preposition *dia-* is used intensively, indicating thoroughness, completeness.¶ The simple word *paratribē* (not found in the N.T.), denotes hostility, enmity. See DISPUTE, No. 3.

WRAP

1. ENEILEŌ (ἐνειλέω), to roll in, wind in, occurs in Mark 15 : 46 ; see WIND (Verb), No. 3.¶

2. ENTULISSŌ (ἐντυλίσσω), to roll in, occurs in Matt. 27 : 59 ; Luke 23 : 53 ; John 20 : 7 : see ROLL, No. 5.¶

3. SUSTELLŌ (συστέλλω), to wrap or wind up, Acts 5 : 6 ; see WIND, No. 2 ; 1 Cor. 7 : 29, see SHORTEN, No. 2.¶

WRATH

1. ORGĒ (ὀργή) : see ANGER and Notes (1) and (2).

2. THUMOS (θυμός), hot anger, passion, for which see ANGER, Notes (1) and (2), is translated " wrath " in Luke 4 : 28 ; Acts 19 : 28 ; Rom. 2 : 8, R.V. ; Gal. 5 : 20 ; Eph. 4 : 31 ; Col. 3 : 8 ; Heb. 11 : 27 ; Rev. 12 : 12 ; 14 : 8, 10, 19 ; 15 : 1, 7 ; 16 : 1 ; 18 : 3 ; " wraths " in 2 Cor. 12 : 20 ; " fierceness " in Rev. 16 : 19 ; 19 : 15 (followed by No. 1).¶

3. PARORGISMOS (παροργισμός) occurs in Eph. 4 : 26 : see ANGER, A, Note (2).¶

Note : For the verb *parorgizō*, to provoke to wrath, Eph. 6 : 4, A.V., see ANGER, B, No. 2.

WREST

STREBLOŌ (στρεβλόω), to twist, to torture (from *streblē*, a winch or instrument of torture, and akin to *strephō*, to turn), is used metaphorically in 2 Pet. 3 : 16, of wresting the Scriptures on the part of the ignorant and unstedfast.¶ In the Sept., 2 Sam. 22 : 27.¶

WRESTLE, WRESTLING

PALĒ (πάλη), a wrestling (akin to *pallō*, to sway, vibrate), is used figuratively in Eph. 6 : 12, of the spiritual conflict engaged in by believers, R.V., " (our) wrestling," A.V., " (we) wrestle."¶

WRETCHED

TALAIPŌROS (ταλαίπωρος), distressed, miserable, wretched, is used in Rom. 7 : 24 and Rev. 3 : 17.¶ Cp. *talaipōria*, misery, and *talaipōreō* (see AFFLICT).

WRINKLE

RHUTIS (ῥυτίς), from an obsolete verb *rhuō*, signifying to draw together, occurs in Eph. 5 : 27, describing the flawlessness of the complete Church, as the result of the love of Christ in giving Himself up for it, with the purpose of presenting it to Himself hereafter.¶

WRITE, WROTE, WRITTEN
A. Verbs.

1. GRAPHŌ (γράφω) is used (a) of forming letters on a surface or writing material, John 8 : 6 ; Gal. 6 : 11, where the Apostle speaks of his having written with large letters in his own hand, which not improbably means that at this point he took the pen from his amanuensis and finished the Epistle himself ; this is not negatived by the fact that the verb is in the aorist or past definite tense, lit., ' I wrote,' for in Greek idiom the writer of a letter put himself beside the reader and spoke of it as having been written in the past ; in Eng. we should say ' I am writing,' taking our point of view from the time at which we are doing it ; cp. Philm. 19 (this Ep. is undoubtedly a holograph), where again the equivalent English translation is in the present tense (see also Acts 15 : 23 ; Rom. 15 : 15) ; possibly the Apostle, in Galatians, was referring to his having written the body of the Epistle but the former alternative seems the more likely ; in 2 Thess. 3 : 17 he says that the closing salutation is written by his own hand and speaks of it as " the token in every Epistle " which some understand as a purpose for the future rather than a custom ; see, however, 1 Cor. 16 : 21 and Col. 4 : 18. The absence of the token from the other Epistles of Paul can be explained differently, their authenticity not being dependent upon this ; (b) to commit to writing, to record, e.g., Luke 1 : 63 ; John 19 : 21, 22 ; it is used of Scripture as a standing authority, " it is written," e.g., Mark 1 : 2 ; Rom. 1 : 17 (cp. 2 Cor. 4 : 13) ; (c) of writing directions or giving information, e.g., Rom. 10 : 5, " (Moses) writeth," R.V. (A.V., "describeth") ; 15 : 15 ; 2 Cor. 7 : 12 ; (d) of that which contained a record or message, e.g., Mark 10 : 4, 5 ; John 19 : 19 ; 21 : 25 ; Acts 23 : 25.

2. EPISTELLŌ (ἐπιστέλλω) denotes to send a message by letter, to write word (stellō, to send ; Eng., epistle), Acts 15 : 20 ; 21 : 25 (some mss. have apostellō, to send) ; Heb. 13 : 22.¶

3. PROGRAPHŌ (προγράφω) denotes to write before, Rom. 15 : 4 (in the best texts ; some have graphō) ; Eph. 3 : 3. See SET (forth).

4. ENGRAPHŌ (ἐγγράφω) denotes to write in, Luke 10 : 20 ; 2 Cor. 3 : 2, 3.¶

5. EPIGRAPHŌ (ἐπιγράφω) is rendered to write over or upon (epi) in Mark 15 : 26 ; figuratively, on the heart, Heb. 8 : 10 ; 10 : 16 ; on the gates of the Heavenly Jerusalem, Rev. 21 : 12. See INSCRIPTION.

Notes : (1) For *apographō*, Heb. 12 : 23, A.V., " written," see ENROL. (2) In 2 Cor. 3 : 7 " written " is a translation of *en*, in, with the dative plural of *gramma*, a letter, lit., ' in letters.'

B. Adjective.

GRAPTOS (γραπτός), from A, No. 1, written, occurs in Rom. 2 : 15.¶

WRITING

GRAMMA (γράμμα), from *graphō*, to write, is rendered " writings " in John 5 : 47. See LETTER, No. 1.

Notes : (1) For *biblion*, " writing," A.V. in Matt. 19 : 7, see BILL, No. 1. (2) In John 19 : 19, A.V., " the writing (was) " is a translation of the perfect participle, Passive Voice, of *graphō*, R.V., " (there was) written."

WRITING TABLET (A.V., WRITING TABLE)

PINAKIDION (πινακίδιον) occurs in Luke 1 : 63, a diminutive of *pinakis*, a tablet, which is a variant reading here.¶

WRONG (Noun and Verb), WRONG-DOER, WRONG-DOING
A. Nouns.

1. ADIKIA (ἀδικία), *a*, negative, *dikē*, right, is translated " wrong " in 2 Pet. 2 : 13 (2nd part), 15, R.V., " wrong-doing " (A.V., unrighteousness) ; in 2 Cor. 12 : 13, it is used ironically. See INIQUITY, UNJUST, UNRIGHTEOUSNESS.

2. ADIKĒMA (ἀδίκημα) denotes a misdeed, injury, in the concrete sense (in contrast to No. 1), Acts 18 : 14, " a matter of wrong ; " 24 : 20, R.V., " wrong-doing " (A.V., " evil doing "). See INIQUITY.

B. Verb.

ADIKEŌ (ἀδικέω), to do wrong, is used (*a*) intransitively, to act unrighteously, Acts 25 : 11, R.V., " I am a wrong-doer " (A.V., " . . . an offender ") ; 1 Cor. 6 : 8 ; 2 Cor. 7 : 12 (1st part) ; Col. 3 : 25 (1st part) ; cp. Rev. 22 : 11 (see UNRIGHTEOUSNESS, B) ; (*b*) transitively, to wrong, Matt. 20 : 13 ; Acts 7 : 24 (Passive Voice), 26, 27 ; 25 : 10 ; 2 Cor. 7 : 2, ver. 12 (2nd part ; Passive Voice) ; Gal. 4 : 12, " ye did (me no) wrong," anticipating a possible suggestion that his vigorous language was due to some personal grievance ; the occasion referred to was that of his first visit ; Col. 3 : 25 (2nd part), lit., ' what he did wrong,' which brings consequences both in this life and at the Judgment-Seat of Christ ; Philm. 18 ; 2 Pet. 2 : 13 (1st part) ; in the Middle or Passive Voice, to take or suffer wrong, to suffer (oneself) to be wronged, 1 Cor. 6 : 7. See HURT, OFFENDER, UNJUST.

WRONGFULLY

ADIKŌS (ἀδίκως), akin to the above, occurs in 1 Pet. 2 : 19.¶

Note : For "exact wrongfully," Luke 3 : 14, R.V., see ACCUSE, B, No. 5.

WROTH (be)

1. ORGIZŌ (ὀργίζω), always in the Middle or Passive Voice in the

N.T., is rendered "was (were) wroth" in Matt. 18 : 34 ; 22 : 7 ; Rev. 11 : 18, R.V., (A.V., "were angry ") ; 12 : 17, R.V., "waxed wroth." See ANGER, B, No. 1.

2. THUMOŌ (θυμόω) signifies to be very angry (from *thumos*, wrath, hot anger), to be stirred into passion, Matt. 2 : 16, of Herod (Passive Voice).¶

3. CHOLAŌ (χολάω), primarily, to be melancholy (*cholē*, gall), signifies to be angry, John 7 : 23, R.V., "are ye wroth " (A.V., ". . . angry ").¶

For WROUGHT see WORK

Y

YE, YOU, YOURSELVES, YOUR OWN SELVES

Notes : (1) These are most frequently the translations of various inflections of a verb ; sometimes of the article before a nominative used as a vocative, e.g., Rev. 18 : 20, " ye saints, and ye apostles, and ye prophets " (lit., ' the saints, etc.'). When the 2nd person plural pronouns are used separately from a verb, they are usually one or other of the forms of *humeis*, the plural of *su*, " thou," and are frequently emphatic, especially when they are subjects of the verb, an emphasis always to be noticed, e.g., Matt. 5 : 13, 14, 48 ; 6 : 9, 19, 20 ; Mark 6 : 31, 37 ; John 15 : 27a ; Rom. 1 : 6 ; 1 Cor. 3 : 17, 23 ; Gal. 3 : 28, 29a ; Eph. 1 : 13a ; 2 : 8 ; 2 : 11, 13 ; Phil. 2 : 18 ; Col. 3 : 4, 7a ; 4 : 1 ; 1 Thess. 1 : 6 ; 2 : 10, 19, 20 ; 3 : 8 ; 2 Thess. 3 : 13 ; Jas. 5 : 8 ; 1 Pet. 2 : 9a ; 1 John 2 : 20, 24 (1st and 3rd occurrences), 27a ; 4 : 4 ; Jude 17, 20. (2) The addition of *autoi*, yourselves, to the pronoun marks especial emphasis, e.g., Mark 6 : 31 ; John 3 : 28 ; 1 Cor. 11 : 13 ; 1 Thess. 4 : 9. Sometimes *autoi* is used without the pronoun, e.g., Luke 11 : 46, 52 ; Acts 2 : 22 ; 20 : 34 ; 1 Thess. 2 : 1 ; 3 : 3 ; 5 : 2 ; 2 Thess. 3 : 7 ; Heb. 13 : 3. (3) The reflexive pronoun " yourselves " represents the various plural forms of the reflexive pronoun *heautou* (frequently governed by some preposition), e.g., Matt. 3 : 9 ; 16 : 8 ; 23 : 31 ; 25 : 9 ; Mark 9 : 50 ; Luke 3 : 8 ; 12 : 33, 57 ; 16 : 9 ; 21 : 30, " of your own selves ;" 21 : 34 ; Acts 5 : 35 ; in Rom. 11 : 25, " in your own (conceits)," lit., ' in (*en* ; some texts have *para*, among) yourselves ;' so 12 : 16 (with *para*) ; 1 Pet. 4 : 8 ; Jude 20, 21 ; in Eph. 5 : 19, R.V., " one to another " (A.V., and R.V. marg., " to yourselves ").

Note : In 1 Thess. 5 : 11, A.V., *allēlous*, " one another " (R.V.), is rendered " yourselves together."

YEA, YES

1. NAI (*vai*), a particle of affirmation, is used (*a*) in answer to a question, Matt. 9 : 28 ; 11 : 9 ; 13 : 51 ; 17 : 25 ; 21 : 16 ; Luke 7 : 26 ; John 11 : 27 ; 21 : 15, 16 ; Acts 5 : 8 ; 22 : 27 ; Rom. 3 : 29 ; (*b*) in assent to an assertion, Matt. 15 : 27, R.V. (A.V., " truth ") ; Mark 7 : 28 ; Rev. 14 : 13 ; 16 : 7, R.V. (A.V., " even so ") ; (*c*) in confirmation of an assertion, Matt. 11 : 26 and Luke 10 : 21, R.V. (A.V., " even so ") ; Luke 11 : 51, R.V. (A.V., " verily ") ; 12 : 5 ; Phil. 4 : 3 (in the best texts) ; Philm. 20 ; (*d*) in solemn asseveration, Rev. 1 : 7 (A.V. and R.V., " even

so ") ; 22 : 20, R.V. (A.V., " surely ") ; (e) in repetition for emphasis, Matt. 5 : 37 ; 2 Cor. 1 : 17 ; Jas. 5 : 12 ; (f) singly in contrast to *ou*, " nay," 2 Cor. 1 : 18, 19 (twice), 20, " (the) yea," R.V.¶

2. ALLA (ἀλλά), but, is translated " yea " in John 16 : 2 ; Rom. 3 : 31, A.V. (R.V., " nay ") ; 1 Cor. 4 : 3 ; 2 Cor. 7 : 11 (six times) ; Gal. 4 : 17, A.V. (R.V., " nay ") ; Phil. 1 : 18 ; 2 : 17 ; 3 : 8 ; Jas. 2 : 18.

3. KAI (καί), and, even, is rendered " yea," e.g., Luke 2 : 35 ; John 16 : 32 ; 1 Cor. 2 : 10 ; 2 Cor. 8 : 3 ; in Acts 7 : 43, A.V. (R.V., " and ").

4. MEN OUN (μὲν οὖν), in some texts *menounge*, i.e., *men-oun-ge*, " yea rather," occurs, e.g., in Luke 11 : 28 ; in Rom. 10 : 18, " yea (A.V., yes) verily ; " in Phil. 3 : 8, R.V., " yea verily " (A.V., " yea doubtless ").

Notes : (1) In 1 Cor. 15 : 15 the R.V. translates *kai* by " and " (A.V., " yea "). (2) In Luke 24 : 22 the R.V. translates *alla kai* " moreover " (A.V., " yea . . . and "). (3) In 1 Cor. 16 : 6, A.V., *ē kai*, " or even " (R.V.), is translated " yea, and." (4) In 2 Cor. 5 : 16, A.V., the phrase *ei kai* (some texts have *ei de kai*) is translated " yea, though " (R.V., " even though "). (5) In Phil. 2 : 8, R.V., the particle *de*, but, is translated " yea " (A.V., " even ").

YEAR
A. Nouns.

1. ETOS (ἔτος) is used (a) to mark a point of time at or from which events take place, e.g., Luke 3 : 1 (dates were frequently reckoned from the time when a monarch began to reign) ; in Gal. 3 : 17 the time of the giving of the Law is stated as 430 years after the covenant of promise given to Abraham ; there is no real discrepancy between this and Ex. 12 : 40 ; the Apostle is not concerned with the exact duration of the interval ; it certainly was not less than 430 years ; the point of the argument is that the period was very considerable ; Gal. 1 : 18 and 2 : 1 mark events in Paul's life ; as to the former the point is that three years elapsed before he saw any of the Apostles ; in 2 : 1 the 14 years may date either from his conversion or from his visit to Peter mentioned in 1 : 18 ; the latter seems the more natural (for a full discussion of the subject see Notes on Galatians by Hogg and Vine, pp. 55 ff.) ; (b) to mark a space of time, e.g., Matt. 9 : 20 ; Luke 12 : 19 ; 13 : 11 ; John 2 : 20 ; Acts 7 : 6, where the 400 years mark not merely the time that Israel was in bondage in Egypt, but the time that they sojourned or were strangers there (the R.V. puts a comma after the word " evil ") ; the Genevan Version renders Gen. 15 : 13 " thy posterity shall inhabit a strange land for 400 years ; " Heb. 3 : 17 ; Rev. 20 : 2–7 ; (c) to date an event from one's birth, e.g., Mark 5 : 42 ; Luke 2 : 42 ; 3 : 23 ; John 8 : 57 ; Acts 4 : 22 ; 1 Tim. 5 : 9 ; (d) to mark recurring events, Luke 2 : 41 (with *kata*, used distributively) ; 13 : 7 ; (e) of an unlimited number, Heb. 1 : 12.

2. ENIAUTOS (ἐνιαυτός), originally a cycle of time, is used (a) of a particular time marked by an event, e.g., Luke 4 : 19 ; John 11 : 49, 51 ;

18 : 13 ; Gal. 4 : 10 ; Rev. 9 : 15 ; (*b*) to mark a space of time, Acts 11 : 26 ; 18 : 11 ; Jas. 4 : 13 ; 5 : 17 ; (*c*) of that which takes place every year, Heb. 9 : 7 ; with *kata* [cp. (*d*) above], Heb. 9 : 25 ; 10 : 1, 3.¶

3. DIETIA (διετία) denotes a space of two years (*dis*, twice, and No. 1), Acts 24 : 27 ; 28 : 30.¶

4. TRIETIA (τριετία) denotes a space of three years (*treis*, three, and No. 1), Acts 20 : 31.¶

Note : In Luke 1 : 7, 18, *hēmera*, a day, is rendered "years."

B. Adjectives.

1. DIETĒS (διετής), akin to A, No. 3, denotes lasting two years, two years old, Matt. 2 : 16.¶

2. HEKATONTAETĒS (ἑκατονταετής) denotes a hundred years old, Rom. 4 : 19.¶

C. Adverb.

PERUSI (πέρυσι), last year, a year ago (from *pera*, beyond), is used with *apo*, from 2 Cor. 8 : 10 ; 9 : 2.¶

Note : In Heb. 11 : 24, A.V., *ginomai*, to become, with *megas*, great, is rendered "when he was come to years" (R.V., "when he was grown up ").

For YES, see YEA

YESTERDAY

ECHTHES or CHTHES (ἐχθές) occurs in John 4 : 52 ; Acts 7 : 28 ; Heb. 13 : 8.¶

YET

Notes : This represents (1) the adverb *eti*, implying addition or duration, e.g., Matt. 12 : 40 ; Rom. 3 : 7 ; 5 : 6, 8 ; 9 : 19 ; in Heb. 12 : 26, 27, "yet . . . more ;" (2) *alla*, but, marking antithesis or transition, e.g., Mark 14 : 29 ; 1 Cor. 4 : 4, 15 ; 9 : 2 ; (3) *mentoi*, nevertheless, John 4 : 27 ; 20 : 5 ; (4) *akmēn*, even to this point of time (the accusative case of *akmē*, a point), Matt. 15 : 16 ; ¶ (5) *ouketi*, no longer, Mark 15 : 5, A.V., "yet . . . nothing " (R.V., "no more . . . anything ") ; 2 Cor. 1 : 23, A.V., "not as yet ;" " yet not," e.g. Gal. 2 : 20, A.V. ; (6) *oupō*, "not yet," John 7 : 39 and 1 Cor. 8 : 2 (*oudepō*, in some mss., A.V., " nothing yet ") ; *oudepō*, John 19 : 41, " never yet ;" 20 : 9, " as yet . . . not ;" (7) *mēpō*, not yet, Rom. 9 : 11 ; Heb. 9 : 8 ;¶ (8) *kai*, and, even, also, " yet " in Luke 3 : 20 ; in Gal. 3 : 4, *ei ge kai*, A.V., "if . . . yet " (R.V., " if . . . indeed ") ; (9) *ge*, a particle meaning 'indeed,' " yet," Luke 11 : 8 ; (10) *oudeis pōpote*, 19 : 30, R.V., " no man ever yet," A.V., " yet never man," lit., ' no one at any time (yet) ;' (11) the following, in which the R.V. gives the correct meaning for the A.V., " yet :" *ēdē*, " now," Mark 13 : 28 ; *pote*, " ever," Eph. 5 : 29 (A.V., " ever yet ") ; *kai . . . de*, John 8 : 16, " yea and " (A.V., " and yet ") ; *ou pleious*, Acts 24 : 11, "not more;" (12) *mellō*, to be about to, "are yet," Rev. 8:13; (13) other combinations with AND, AS, NOR, NOT.

YIELD

1. DIDŌMI (δίδωμι), to give, is translated to yield, i.e., to produce, in Matt. 13:8, R.V. (A.V., "brought forth"); Mark 4:7, 8. See GIVE.

2. APODIDŌMI (ἀποδίδωμι), to give up or back, is translated to yield in Heb. 12:11; Rev. 22:2 (in each case, of bearing fruit). See DELIVER, A, No. 3, etc.

3. PARISTĒMI or PARISTANŌ (παρίστημι), to present, is translated to yield in Rom. 6:13 (twice), 16, 19 (twice), R.V., to present, in each place. See COMMEND, etc.

4. POIEŌ (ποιέω), to make, to do, is translated "yield" in Jas. 3:12. See DO.

5. APHIĒMI (ἀφίημι), to send away, is translated "yielded up (His spirit)" in Matt. 27:50 (cp. *paratithēmi*, "I commend," Luke 23:46, and *paradidōmi*, "He gave up," John 19:30). See FORGIVE, etc.

6. PEITHŌ (πείθω), to persuade, in the Passive Voice, to be persuaded, is translated "do (not) thou yield," Acts 23:21. See PERSUADE.

Note: In Acts 5:10, A.V., *ekpsuchō*, to breathe one's last, expire (*ek*, out, *psuchē*, the life), is translated "yielded up (R.V., gave up) the ghost." See GHOST (give up the), No. 2.

YOKE, YOKED

A. Noun.

1. ZUGOS (ζυγός), a yoke, serving to couple two things together, is used (1) metaphorically, (*a*) of submission to authority, Matt. 11:29, 30, of Christ's yoke, not simply imparted by Him but shared with Him; (*b*) of bondage, Acts 15:10 and Gal. 5:1, of bondage to the Law as a supposed means of salvation; (*c*) of bondservice to masters, 1 Tim. 6:1; (2) to denote a balance, Rev. 6:5. See BALANCE.¶

2. ZEUGOS (ζεῦγος), a pair of animals, Luke 14:19. See PAIR.

B. Verb.

HETEROZUGEŌ (ἑτεροζυγέω), to be unequally yoked (*heteros*, another of a different sort, and A, No. 1), is used metaphorically in 2 Cor. 6:14.¶

YOKE-FELLOW

SUNZUGOS or SUZUGOS (σύνζυγος), an adjective denoting yoked together, is used as a noun in Phil. 4:3, a yoke-fellow, fellow-labourer; probably here it is a proper name, Synzygus, addressed as "true," or genuine (*gnēsios*), i.e., properly so-called.¶

YONDER

EKEI (ἐκεῖ), there, is rendered "yonder" in Matt. 26:36; "to yonder place," 17:20. See THERE, THITHER.

For YOU see YE

YOUNG, YOUNG (children, daughter, man, men, woman, women)

1. NEŌTEROS (νεώτερος), the comparative degree of *neos*, new, youthful, is translated " young " in John 21 : 18 ; in the plural, Acts 5 : 6, " young men " (marg., " younger ") ; Tit. 2 : 6, A.V., R.V., " younger men." See YOUNGER.

2. NEOS (νέος), in the feminine plural, denotes " young women," Tit. 2 : 4. See NEW, No. 2.

3. NEANIAS (νεανίας), a young man, occurs in Acts 7 : 58 ; 20 : 9 ; 23 : 17, 18 (in some texts).¶

4. NEANISKOS (νεανίσκος), a diminutive of No. 3, a youth, a young man, occurs in Matt. 19 : 20, 22 ; Mark 14 : 51 (1st part ; R.V. omits in 2nd part) ; 16 : 5 ; Luke 7 : 14 ; Acts 2 : 17 ; 5 : 10 (i.e., attendants) ; 23 : 18 (in the best texts), 22 ; 1 John 2 : 13, 14, of the second branch of the spiritual family.¶

5. NOSSOS or NEOSSOS (νοσσός), a young bird (akin to No. 2), is translated " young " in Luke 2 : 24.¶ Cp. *nossia*, a brood, Luke 13 : 34, and the noun *nossion*, used in the neuter plural, *nossia*, in Matt. 23 : 37, " chickens ; " *nossion* is the diminutive of *nossos*.¶

Notes : (1) In Acts 20 : 12, A.V., *pais*, a " lad " (R.V.), is translated " young man." (2) In Mark 7 : 25, A.V., *thugatrion*, a diminutive of *thugatēr*, a daughter, is rendered " young (R.V., little) daughter." (3) In Mark 10 : 13, A.V., *paidion*, in the neuter plural, is rendered " young (R.V., little) children." (4) In Acts 7 : 19, A.V., *brephos*, in the neuter plural, is rendered " young children," R.V., " babes." See BABE, No. 1.

YOUNGER

1. NEŌTEROS (νεώτερος), for which see No. 1, above, occurs in Luke 15 : 12, 13 ; 22 : 26 ; 1 Tim. 5 : 1 (" younger men ") ; 5 : 2, feminine ; ver. 11, " younger (widows) ; " ver. 14, " younger (*widows*)," R.V., marg. and A.V., " younger (women) " (see WIDOW) ; 1 Pet. 5 : 5. For Tit. 2 : 6 see YOUNG, No. 1.¶

2. ELASSŌN (ἐλάσσων) is rendered " younger " in Rom. 9 : 12 : see LESS.

YOUR, YOURS

Notes : (1) " Your " is most frequently the translation of *humōn*, lit., of you, the genitive plural of *su*, thou, you ; it is translated " yours " in 1 Cor. 3 : 21, 22 ; in 8 : 9, " of yours ; " 16 : 18 ; 2 Cor. 12 : 14. In the following the dative plural, *humin*, lit., ' to you,' is translated " your ; " Luke 16 : 11, lit., ' (who will entrust) to you ; ' in 21 : 15 " your adversaries " is, lit., ' (those opposed) to you ; ' in 1 Cor. 6 : 5 and 15 : 34, A.V., " (I speak to) your (shame)," R.V., " (I say *this* to move) you (to shame)," is, lit., ' (I speak unto a shame) to you.' The accusative plural, *humas*, preceded by *kata*, according to, is rendered in Acts 18 : 15 " your own (law)," R.V., A.V., " your (law)," lit., ' (of the law) according to you,' with emphasis and scorn ; in Eph. 1 : 15 the same construction is used of faith, but *kata* here means " among," as in the R.V., " (the faith . . . which is) among you," A.V., " your (faith) ; " in John 14 : 26 " He shall . . . bring to your remembrance " is, lit., ' He shall . . . put you in mind of.' (2) The possessive pronoun, *humeteros*, your, is used in Luke 6 : 20 ; John 7 : 6 ; 8 : 17 ; 15 : 20 ; Acts 27 : 34 ; Rom. 11 : 31 ; 1 Cor. 15 : 31 ; 16 : 17 ; 2 Cor. 8 : 8 ; Gal. 6 : 13 ; in Luke 16 : 12, " your own."¶ (3) In Rom. 16 : 19, A.V., the phrase *to epi humin*, lit., ' the (matter) over you,' is rendered " on your behalf " (R.V., " over you," following the mss. which omit the neuter article *to*).

YOUTH

NEOTĒS (νεότης), from *neos*, new, occurs in Mark 10 : 20 ; Luke 18 : 21 ; Acts 26 : 4 ; 1 Tim. 4 : 12 (in some mss., Matt. 19 : 20).¶

YOUTHFUL

NEŌTERIKOS (νεωτερικός), from *neōteros*, the comparative degree of *neos*, new, is used especially of qualities, of lusts, 2 Tim. 2 : 22.¶

Z

ZEAL

ZĒLOS (ζῆλος) denotes zeal in the following passages : John 2 : 17, with objective genitive, i.e., ' zeal for Thine house ; ' so in Rom. 10 : 2, "a zeal for God;" in 2 Cor. 7 : 7, R.V., " (your) zeal (for me)," A.V., " (your) fervent mind (toward me) ; " used absolutely in 7 : 11 ; 9 : 2 ; Phil. 3 : 6 (in Col. 4 : 13 in some texts ; the best have *ponos*, " labour," R.V.). See Envy, Note, Fervent, C, Note (2), Indignation, A, Note (3), Jealousy.

ZEALOUS
A. Noun.

ZĒLŌTĒS (ζηλωτής) is used adjectivally, of being zealous (a) " of the Law," Acts 21 : 20 ; (b) " toward God," lit., ' of God,' 22 : 3, R.V., " for God;" (c) " of spiritual gifts," 1 Cor. 14 : 12, i.e., for exercise of spiritual gifts (lit., ' of spirits,' but not to be interpreted literally) ; (d) " for (A.V., of) the traditions of my fathers," Gal. 1 : 14, of Paul's loyalty to Judaism before his conversion ; (e) " of good works," Tit. 2 : 14.

The word is, lit., ' a zealot,' i.e., an uncompromising partisan. The " Zealots " was a name applied to an extreme section of the Pharisees, bitterly antagonistic to the Romans. Josephus (*Antiq.* xviii. 1. 1, 6 ; *B.J.* ii. 8. 1) refers to them as the " fourth sect of Jewish philosophy " (i.e., in addition to the Pharisees, Sadducees, and Essenes), founded by Judas of Galilee (cp. Acts 5 : 37). After his rebellion in A.D. 6, the Zealots nursed the fires of revolt, which, bursting out afresh in A.D. 66, led to the destruction of Jerusalem in 70. To this sect Simon, one of the Apostles, had belonged, Luke 6 : 15 ; Acts 1 : 13. The equivalent Hebrew and Aramaic term was " Cananæan " (Matt. 10 : 4) ; this is not connected with Canaan, as the A.V. " Canaanite " would suggest, but is derived from Heb. *qannâ*, jealous.¶

B. Verbs.

1. ZĒLOŌ (ζηλόω), to be jealous, also signifies to seek or desire eagerly ; in Gal. 4 : 17, R.V., " they zealously seek (you)," in the sense of taking a very warm interest in ; so in ver. 18, Passive Voice, " to be zealously sought " (A.V., " to be zealously affected "), i.e., to be the object of warm interest on the part of others ; some texts have this verb in Rev. 3 : 19 (see No. 2). See Affect, Note, Covet, Desire, Envy, Jealous.

2. ZĒLEUŌ (ζηλεύω), a late and rare form of No. 1, is found in the best texts in Rev. 3 : 19, " be zealous."¶

Note : For *spoudazō*, Gal. 2 : 10, R.V., see Diligent, B, No. 1.

ADDITIONAL NOTES.

(1) On the Particle KAI (καί).

(a) The particle *kai*, " and," chiefly used for connecting words, clauses and sentences (the copulative or connective use), not infrequently signifies " also." This is the *adjunctive*, or *amplificatory*, use, and it is to be distinguished from the purely copulative significance " and." A good illustration is provided in Matt. 8 : 9, in the words of the centurion, " I also am a man under authority." Other instances are Matt. 5 : 39, 40 ; 8 : 9 ; 10 : 18 ; 18 : 33 ; 20 : 4 ; Luke 11 : 49 ; 12 : 41, 54, 57 ; 20 : 3 ; John 5 : 26, " the Son also," R.V. ; 7 : 3 ; 12 : 10 ; 14 : 1, 3, 7, 19 ; 15 : 9, 27 ; 17 : 24 ; Acts 11 : 17 ; Rom. 1 : 13 ; 6 : 11 ; 1 Cor. 7 : 3 ; 11 : 25 ; 15 : 30 ; Gal. 6 : 1 ; Phil. 4 : 12, " I know also," R.V. ; 1 Thess. 3 : 12. In 1 Cor. 2 : 13 the *kai* phrase signifies ' which are the very things we speak, with the like power of the Holy Spirit.'

This use includes the meanings " so," or " just so," by way of comparison, as in Matt. 6 : 10, and " so also," e.g., John 13 : 33 ; cp. Rom. 11 : 16. In Heb. 7 : 26 the most authentic mss. have *kai* in the first sentence, which may be rendered ' for such a High Priest also became us.' Here it virtually has the meaning " precisely."

(b) Occasionally *kai* tends towards an *adversative* meaning, expressing a contrast, " yet," almost the equivalent of *alla*, " but ; " see, e.g., Mark 12 : 12, ' yet they feared ; ' Luke 20 : 19 ; John 18 : 28, ' yet they themselves entered not.' Some take it in this sense in Rom. 1 : 13, where, however, it may be simply parenthetic. Sometimes in the English Versions the " yet " has been added in italics, as in 2 Cor. 6 : 8, 9, 10.

(c) In some passages *kai* has the meaning " and yet," e.g., Matt. 3 : 14, ' and yet comest Thou to me ? ; ' 6 : 26, ' and yet (R.V. " and," A.V., " yet ") your Heavenly Father feedeth them ; ' Luke 18 : 7, ' and yet He is longsuffering ; ' John 3 : 19, ' and yet men loved the darkness ; ' 4 : 20, ' and yet we say ; ' 6 : 49, ' and yet they died ; ' 1 Cor. 5 : 2, ' and yet ye are puffed up ; ' 1 John 2 : 9, ' and yet hateth his brother.' The same is probably the case in John 7 : 30, ' and yet no man laid hands on Him ; ' some rule this and similar cases out because of the negative in the sentence following the *kai*, but that seems hardly tenable.

(d) In some passages it has a *temporal* significance, " then." In Luke 7 : 12 the *kai*, which is untranslated in the English Versions, provides the meaning ' then, behold, there was carried out ; ' so Acts 1 : 10, ' then, behold, two men stood.' This use is perhaps due to the influence of the Septuagint, reflecting the Hebrew idiom, especially when *idou*, " behold " follows the *kai*.

(*e*) There is also the *inferential* use before a question, e.g., Mark 10 : 26, " then who can be saved ? " R.V. This is commonly expressed by the English " and," as in Luke 10 : 29 ; John 9 : 36.

(*f*) Occasionally it has almost the sense of *hoti*, " that," e.g., Matt. 26 : 15 (first part) ; Mark 14 : 40 (last part) ; Luke 5 : 12, 17, where, if the *kai* had been translated, the clause might be rendered ' that, behold, a man . . . ,' lit., ' and behold . . . ; ' so ver. 17 ; see also 9 : 51, where *kai*, ' that,' comes before " He stedfastly set ; " in 12 : 15, ' take heed that ye keep.' What is said under (*d*), regarding the influence of the Septuagint, is applicable also to this significance.

(*g*) Sometimes it has the consecutive meaning of " and so : " e.g., Matt. 5 : 15, ' and so it shineth ; ' Phil. 4 : 7, ' and so the peace . . . ; ' Heb. 3 : 19, ' and so we see.'

(*h*) The *epexegetic* or *explanatory* use. This may be represented by the expressions ' namely, ' ' again ,' ' and indeed,' ' that is to say ; ' it is usually translated by ' and. ' In such cases not merely an addition is in view. In Matt. 21 : 5, ' and upon a colt ' means ' that is to say, upon a colt.' In John 1 : 16 the clause " and grace for grace " is explanatory of the " fulness." In John 12 : 48, " and receiveth not My sayings," is not simply an addition to " that rejecteth Me," it explains what the rejection involves, as the preceding verse shows. In Mark 14 : 1, " and the unleavened bread " is perhaps an instance, since the Passover feast is so defined in Luke 22 : 1. In Acts 23 : 6 the meaning is ' the hope, namely, the resurrection of the dead.' In Rom. 1 : 5 " grace and apostleship " may signify ' grace expressed in apostleship.' In Eph. 1 : 1 " and the faithful " does not mark a distinct class of believers, it defines " the saints ; " but in this case it goes a little further than what is merely epexegetical, it adds a more distinctive epithet than the preceding and may be taken as meaning ' yes indeed.'

For the suggestion as to the epexegetic use of *kai* in John 3 : 5, ' water, even the Spirit,' see Vol. IV, p. 202, ll. 6–9.

In regard to Titus 3 : 5, " the renewing of the Holy Ghost " is co-ordinate with " the washing of regeneration," and some would regard it as precisely explanatory of that phrase, taking the *kai* as signifying ' namely. ' Certainly the " renewing " is not an additional and separate impartation of the Holy Spirit ; but the scope of the renewal is surely not limited to regeneration ; the second clause goes further than what is merely epexegetic of the first. Just so in Rom. 12 : 2, " the renewing of your mind " is not a single act, accomplished once and for all, as in re-generation. See under RENEW, B. The Holy Ghost, as having been ' shed on us,' continues to act in renewing us, in order to maintain by His power the enjoyment of the relationship into which He has brought us. " The man is cleansed in connection with the new order of things ; but the Holy Ghost is a source of an entirely new life, entirely new thoughts ; **not** only of a new moral being, but of the communication of all that in which this new being develops itself . . . He ever communicates more and more of the things of this new world into which He has brought us . . . ' the renewing of the Holy Ghost ' embraces all this . . . so that it is not only that we are born of Him, but that He works in us, communicating to us all that is ours in Christ " (J. N. Darby). Both the washing and the renewing are His work.

(i) The *ascensive* use. This is somewhat similar to the epexegetic significance. It represents, however, an advance in thought upon what precedes and has the meaning " even." The context alone can determine the occurrences of this use. The following are some instances. In Matt. 5 : 46, 47, the phrases " even the publicans " and " even the Gentiles " represent an extension of thought in regard to the manner of reciprocity exhibited by those referred to, in comparison with those who, like the Pharisees, were considered superior to them. In Mark 1 : 27, " even the unclean spirits " represents an advance in the minds of the people concerning Christ's miraculous power, in comparison with the authority exercised by the Lord in less remarkable ways. So in Luke 10 : 17. In Acts 10 : 45, the *kai*, rendered " also," in the phrase " on the Gentiles also," seems necessary to be regarded in the same way, in view of the amazement manifested by those of the circumcision, and thus the rendering will be ' even on the Gentiles was poured out the gift ; ' cp. 11 : 1.

In Rom. 13 : 5, the clause " but also for conscience sake " should probably be taken in this sense. In Gal. 2 : 13, the phrase " even Barnabas " represents an advance of thought in comparison with the waywardness of others ; as much as to say, ' the Apostle's closest associate, from whom something different might be expected, was surprisingly carried away.' In Phil. 4 : 16 there are three occurrences of *kai*, the first ascensive, " even " ; the second (untranslated) meaning " both," before the word " once ; " the third meaning " and. " In 1 Thess. 1 : 5, in the cause " and in the Holy Ghost," the *kai* rendered " and," is ascensive, conveying an extension of thought beyond " power ; " that is to say, ' power indeed, but the power of the Holy Spirit.' In 1 Pet. 4 : 14 " the Spirit of God " is " the Spirit of glory." Here there is an advance in idea from the abstract to the Personal. The phrase " the Spirit of God " does more than define " the Spirit of glory ; " it is explanatory but ascensive also.

When preceded or followed by the conjunction *ei*, " if," the phrase signifies " even if," or " if even," e.g., Mark 14 : 29 ; Phil. 2 : 17 ; 1 Pet. 3 : 1.

ON THE PARTICLE DE (δέ)

The particle *de* has two chief uses, (*a*) *continuative* or *copulative*, signifying ' and,' or ' in the next place,' (*b*) *adversative*, signifying ' but,' or ' on the other hand.' The first of these, (*a*), is well illustrated in the genealogy in Matt. 1 : 2–16, the line being simply reckoned from Abraham to Christ. So in 2 Cor. 6 : 15, 16, where the *de* anticipates a negative more precisely than would be the case if *kai* had been used. In 1 Cor. 15 : 35 ; Heb. 12 : 6, e.g., the *de* " and (scourgeth) " is purely copulative.

(*b*) The adversative use distinguishes a word or clause from that which precedes. This is exemplified, for instance, in Matt. 5 : 22, 28, 32, 34, 39, 44, in each of which the *egō*, " I," stands out with pronounced stress by way of contrast. This use is very common. In Matt. 23 : 4 the first *de* is copulative, " Yea, they bind heavy burdens " (R.V.), the second is adversative, " but they themselves will not . . . "

In John 3 : 1, R.V., it may not at first sight seem clear whether the *de*, " Now," is copulative, introducing an illustration of Christ's absolute knowledge, or adversative, signifying ' But.' In the former case the significance would be that, however fair the exterior might be, as exemplified in Nicodemus, he needs to be born again. In the latter case it introduces a contrast, in regard to Nicodemus, to what has just been stated, that " Jesus did not trust Himself " (2 : 24) to those mentioned in v. 23. And, inasmuch as He certainly did afford to Nicodemus the opportunity of learning the truths of the new birth and the Kingdom of God, as a result of which he became a disciple (" secret " though he was), he may be introduced in the Apostle's narrative as an exception to those who believed simply through seeing the signs accomplished by the Lord (2 : 23).

In Rom. 3 : 22, in the clause " even the righteousness," the *de* serves to annexe not only an explanation, defining " a righteousness of God " (v. 21, R.V.), but an extension of the thought ; so in 9 : 30, " even the righteousness which is of faith."

In 1 Cor. 2 : 6, in the clause " yet a wisdom," an exception (not an addition) is made to what precedes ; some would regard this as belonging to (*a*) ; it seems, however, clearly adversative. In 4 : 7 the first *de* is copulative, " and what hast thou . . . ? ; " the second is adversative, " but if thou didst receive . . . "

In 1 Thess. 5 : 21 " many ancient authorities insert ' but ' " (see R.V. marg.), so translating *de*, between the two injunctions " despise not prophesyings " and " prove all things," and this is almost certainly the correct reading. In any case the injunctions are probably thus contrastingly to be connected.

In 2 Pet. 1 : 5–7, after the first *de*, which has the meaning " yea," the six which follow, in the phrases giving virtues to be supplied, suggest the thought ' but there is something further to be done.' These are not merely connective, as expressed by the English " and," but adversative, as indicating a contrast to the possible idea that to add virtue to our faith is sufficient for the moral purpose in view.

De, in combination with the negatives *ou* and *mē* (*oude* and *mēde*, usually " but not," " and not," " neither ", " nor,"), sometimes has the force of " even," e.g., *oude* in Matt. 6 : 29, " even Solomon . . . was not arrayed . . . ; " Mark 6 : 31, lit., ' (they had) not even leisure to eat ; ' Luke 7 : 9, lit., ' not even in Israel have I found such faith ; ' John 7 : 5, " For even His brethren did not believe on Him ; " Acts 4 : 32, lit., ' not even one of them ; ' 1 Cor. 5 : 1, " not even among the Gentiles ; " *mēde*, in Mark 2 : 2, " not even about the door ; " 1 Cor 5 : 11, lit., "with such a one not even to eat.'

On the Prepositions ANTI (ἀντί) and HUPER (ὑπέρ).

The basic idea of *anti* is " facing." This may be a matter of opposition, unfriendliness or antagonism, or of agreement. These meanings are exemplified in compounds of the preposition with verbs, and in nouns. The following are instances : *antiparerchomai* in Luke 10 : 31, 32, where the verb is rendered " passed by on the other side," i.e., of the road, but facing the wounded man ; *antiballō* in Luke 24 : 17, where the *anti* suggests that the two disciples, in exchanging words (see R.V. marg.), turned to face one another, indicating the earnest nature of their conversation. The idea of antagonism is seen in *antidikos*, an adversary, Matt. 5 : 25, *antichristos*, antichrist, 1 John 4 : 3, etc.

There is no instance of the uncompounded preposition signifying " against." Arising from the basic significance, however, there are several other meanings attaching to the separate use of the preposition. In the majority of the occurrences in the N.T., the idea is that of " in the place of," " instead of," or of exchange ; e.g., Matt. 5 : 38, " an eye for (*anti*) an eye ; " Rom. 12 : 17, " evil for evil ; " so 1 Thess, 5 : 15 ; 1 Pet. 3 : 9, and, in the same verse, " reviling for reviling." The ideas of substitution and exchange are combined, e.g., in Luke 11 : 11, " for a fish . . . a serpent ; " Heb. 12 : 16, " for one mess of meat . . his own birthright." So in Matt. 17 : 27, " a shekel (*statēr*) . . . for thee and Me," where the phrase is condensed ; that is to say, the exchange is that of the coin for the tax demanded from Christ and Peter, rather than for the persons themselves. So in 1 Cor. 11 : 15, where the hair is a substitute for the covering.

Of special doctrinal importance are Matt. 20 : 28 ; Mark 10 : 45, " to give His life a ransom (*lutron*) for (*anti*) many." Here the substitutionary significance, " instead of," is clear, as also with the compound *antilutron* in 1 Tim. 2 : 6, " who gave Himself a ransom (*antilutron*) for (*huper*) all ; " here the use of *huper*, " on behalf of," is noticeable. Christ gave Himself as a ransom (of a substitutionary character), not instead of all men, but on behalf of *all*. The actual substitution, as in the passages in Matthew and Mark, is expressed by the *anti*, instead of, " *many*." The unrepentant man should not be told that Christ was his substitute, for in that case the exchange would hold good for him and though unregenerate he would not be in the place of death, a condition in which, however, he exists while unconverted. Accordingly the " many " are those who, through faith, are delivered from that condition. The substitutionary meaning is exemplified in Jas. 4 : 15, where the A.V. and R.V. render the *anti* " for that " (R.V., marg., " instead of ").

In Heb. 12 : 2, " for (*anti*) the joy that was set before Him endured the cross," neither the thought of exchange nor that of substitution is conveyed ; here the basic idea of facing is present. The cross and the joy faced each other in the mind of Christ and He chose the one with the other in view.

In John 1 : 16 the phrase " grace for grace " is used. The idea of ' following upon ' has been suggested, as wave follows wave. Is not the meaning that the grace we receive corresponds to the grace inherent in Christ, out of whose fulness we receive it ?

The primary meaning of *huper* is " over," " above." Hence, metaphorically, with the accusative case, it is used of superiority, e.g., Matt. 10 : 24, " above his master " (or teacher) ; or of measure in excess, in the sense of beyond, e.g., 1 Cor. 4 : 6, " beyond the things that are written ; " or " than ", after a comparative, e.g., Luke 16 : 8 ; Heb. 4 : 12 ; or " more than," after a verb, e.g., Matt. 10 : 37. With the genitive it means (1) on behalf of, in the interests of, e.g., of prayer, Matt. 5 : 44 ; of giving up one's life, and especially of Christ's so doing for man's redemption, e.g., John 10 : 15 ; 1 Tim. 2 : 6, ' on behalf of all ' (see under *Anti*) ; 2 Thess. 2 : 1, ' in the interest of (i.e., ' with a view to correcting your thoughts about ') the Coming.' The difficult passage, 1 Cor. 15 : 29, possibly comes here. With an alteration of the punctuation (feasible from the ms. point of view), the reference may be to baptism as taught elsewhere in the N.T., and the verse may read thus : ' Else what shall they do which are being baptized ? (i.e., what purpose can they serve ?) ; (it is) in the interest of the dead, if the dead are not raised at all. Why then are they baptized in the interest of them ? ' That is to say, they fulfil the ordinance in the interest of a Christ who is dead and in joint witness with (and therefore, in the interest of) believers who never will be raised, whereas an essential element in baptism is its testimony to the resurrection of Christ and of the believer.

In some passages *huper* may be used in the substitutionary sense, e.g., John 10 : 11, 15 ; Rom. 8 : 32 ; but it cannot be so taken in the majority of instances. Cp. 2 Cor. 5 : 15, in regard to which, while it might be said that Christ died in place of us, it cannot be said that Christ rose again in the place of us.

On the Prepositions APO (ἀπό) and EK (ἐκ).

The primary meaning of *apo* is " off ; " this is illustrated in such compounds as *apokaluptō*, to take the veil off, to reveal ; *apokoptō*, to cut off ; hence there are different shades of meaning, the chief of which is " from " or " away from," e.g., Matt. 5 : 29, 30 ; 9 : 22 ; Luke 24 : 31, lit., ' He became invisible from them ; ' Rom. 9 : 3.

The primary meaning of *ek* is " out of," e.g., Matt. 3 : 17, " a voice out of the heavens " (R.V.) ; 2 Cor. 9 : 7, lit., ' out of necessity.' Omitting such significances of *ek* as origin, source, cause, occasion, etc., our consideration will here be confined to a certain similarity between *apo* and *ek*. Since *apo* and *ek* are both frequently to be translated by " from " they often approximate closely in meaning. The distinction is largely seen in this, that *apo* suggests a starting point from without, *ek* from within ; this meaning is often involved in *apo*, but *apo* does not give prominence to the " within-ness," as *ek* usually does. For instance, *apo* is used in Matt. 3 : 16, where the R.V. rightly reads " Jesus . . . went up straightway from the water ; " in Mark 1 : 10 *ek* is used, " coming up out of the water ; " *ek* (which stands in contrast to *eis* in v. 9) stresses more emphatically than *apo* the fact of His having been baptized in the water. In all instances where these prepositions appear to be used alternately this distinction is to be observed.

The literal meaning " out of " cannot be attached to *ek* in a considerable number of passages. In several instances *ek* obviously has the significance of ' away from ; ' and where either meaning seems possible, the context, or some other passage, affords guidance. The following are examples in which *ek* does not mean ' out of the midst of ' or ' out from within,' but has much the same significance as *apo* : John 17 : 15, " that Thou shouldest keep them from the evil one ; " 1 Cor. 9 : 19, " though I was free from all men ; " 2 Cor. 1 : 10, " who delivered us from so great a death " (A.V.) ; 2 Pet. 2 : 21, " to turn back from the holy commandment ; " Rev. 15 : 2, " them that had come victorious from the beast, and from his image, and from the number of his name " (*ek* in each case).

Concerning the use of *ek*, in 1 Thess. 1 : 10, " Jesus, which delivereth (the present tense, as in the R.V., is important) us from the wrath to come " [or, more closely to the original, ' our Deliverer (cp. the same phrase in Rom. 11 : 26) from the coming wrath '], the passage makes clear that the wrath signifies the calamities to be visited by God upon men when the present period of grace is closed. As to whether the *ek* here denotes ' out of the midst of ' or ' preservation from,' this is determined by the statement in 5 : 9, that " God appointed us not unto wrath, but unto the obtaining of salvation ; " the context there shows that the salvation is from the wrath just referred to. Accordingly the *ek* signifies ' preservation from ' in the same sense as *apo*, and not ' out from the midst of.'

ON THE PREPOSITION EN (ἐν).

En, " in," is the most common preposition. It has several meanings, e.g., of place (e.g., Heb. 1 : 3, lit., ' on the right hand,' i.e., in that position), and time, e.g., in 1 Thess. 2 : 19 ; 3 : 13 ; 1 John 2 : 28, in each of which the phrase " at His coming " (inadequately so rendered, and lit., ' in His Parousia ') combines place and time ; the noun, while denoting a period, also signifies a presence involving accompanying circumstances, e.g., 1 Thess. 4 : 15.

Further consideration must here be confined to the instrumental use, often rendered " with " (though *en* in itself does not mean " with "), e.g., Matt. 5 : 13, " wherewith " (lit., ' in what,' i.e., by what means) shall it be salted ; " 7 : 2, " with what measure ye mete." Sometimes the instrumental is associated with the locative significance (which indeed attaches to most of its uses), e.g., Luke 22 : 49, " shall we smite with the sword ? " the smiting being viewed as located in the sword ; so in Matt. 26 : 52, " shall perish with the sword ; " cp. Rev. 2 : 16 ; 6 : 8 ; 13 : 10. In Matt. 12 : 24, " by (marg., ' in ') Beelzebub," indicates that the casting out is located in Beelzebub. Cp. Luke 1 : 51, " with His arm." In Heb. 11 : 37, the statement " they were slain with the sword " is, lit., ' they died by (*en*) slaughter of the sword.' There is a noticeable change in Rom. 12 : 21, from *hupo*, by, to *en*, with, in this instrumental and locative sense ; the lit. rendering is ' be not overcome by (*hupo*) evil, but overcome evil with (*en*) good,' *en* expressing both means and circumstances. A very important instance of the instrumental *en* is in Rom. 3 : 25, where the R.V., " faith, by His blood," corrects the A.V., " faith in His blood," and the commas which the R.V. inserts are necessary. Thus the statement reads " whom God set forth to be a propitiation, through faith, by His blood." Christ is a propitiation, by means of His blood, i.e., His expiatory death. Faith is exercised in the living God, not in the blood, which provides the basis of faith.

INDEX

Note: The English words in the Index are not necessarily the meanings of the Greek words which are found under the English headings.

A

ABARĒS
burdensome

ABBA
abba

ABUSSOS
abyss
bottom
deep
pit

ACHARISTOS
unthankful

ACHEIROPOIĒTOS
hands (not made with)

ACHLUS
mist

ACHRE(I)OŌ
unprofitable

ACHREIOS
unprofitable

ACHRĒSTOS
unprofitable

ACHRI(S)
until

ACHURON
chaff

ADAPANOS
charge

ADĒLOS
appear (not)
uncertain

ADĒLŌS
uncertainly

ADĒLOTĒS
uncertain
uncertainly

ADELPHĒ
believer
sister

ADELPHOS
brother

ADELPHOTĒS
brotherhood

ADĒMONEŌ
heaviness
heavy
trouble

ADIAKRITOS
partiality
variance

ADIALEIPTOS
cease
continual
unceasing

ADIALEIPTŌS
cease
unceasingly

ADIAPHTHORIA
uncorruptness

ADIKĒMA
evil
iniquity
wrong

ADIKEŌ
hurt
injure
offender
suffer
unjust
unrighteousness
wrong
wrong-doer

ADIKIA
iniquity
unjust
unrighteousness
wrong

ADIKOS
unjust
unrighteous

ADIKŌS
wrongfully

ADŌ
sing

ADOKIMOS
cast
reject
reprobate

ADOLOS
guileless
sincere

ADUNATEŌ
impossible

ADUNATOS
impossible
impotent
weak

AEI
always
ever

AĒR
air

AETOS
eagle

AGALLIAŌ
glad
joy
rejoice

AGALLIASIS
gladness
joy

AGAMOS
unmarried

AGANAKTEŌ
displeased
indignation

AGANAKTĒSIS
indignation

AGAPAŌ
beloved
love

AGAPĒ
charity
dear
feast
love

AGAPĒTOS
beloved
dear

AGATHOPOIEŌ
good (to do)
well
well-doing

AGATHOPOIIA
well-doing

AGATHOPOIOS
well (do)

AGATHOS
benefit
good
goods
kind

AGATHŌSUNĒ
goodness

AGATHOURGEŌ
good (to do)

AGELĒ
herd

AGENEALOGĒTOS
genealogy

AGENĒS
base

AGNAPHOS
new
undressed

AGNOĒMA
error
ignorance

AGNOEŌ
ignorant
ignorantly
know
understand

AGNOIA
ignorance

AGNŌSIA
ignorance

AGNŌSTOS
known
unknown

AGŌ
bring
carry
go
keep
lead
open

AGŌGĒ
conduct
life
manner

AGŌN
conflict
contention
fight
race

AGŌNIA
agony

AGŌNIZOMAI
fervently
fight
labour
strive

AGORA
market

AGORA—*contd.*
market-place
street

AGORAIOS
baser
court

AGORAZŌ
buy
purchase
redeem

AGRA
draught

AGRAMMATOS
unlearned

AGRAULEŌ
abide

AGREUŌ
catch

AGRIELAIOS
olive tree (*wild*)

AGRIOS
raging
wild

AGROS
country
farm
field
ground
land
piece

AGRUPNEŌ
watch

AGRUPNIA
watching

AICHMALŌSIA
captivity

AICHMALŌTEUŌ
captive

AICHMALŌTIZŌ
captive
captivity

AICHMALŌTOS
captive

AÏDIOS
eternal
everlasting

AIDŌS
ashamed
reverence
shamefastness

AIGEIOS
goat (skin)

AIGIALOS
beach
shore

AINEŌ
praise

AINESIS
praise

AINIGMA
darkly

AINOS
praise

AIŌN
age

AIŌN—contd.
 course
 eternal
 ever
 evermore
 world
AIŌNIOS
 eternal
 everlasting
AIPHNIDIOS
 sudden
 unawares
AIRŌ
 away
 bear
 carry
 doubt (make to)
 hoise up
 hoist up
 lift
 loose
 put
 remove
 suspense
 take
AISCHROKERDĒS
 filthy
 lucre
AISCHROKERDŌS
 filthy
 lucre
AISCHROLOGIA
 communication
 filthy
AISCHROS
 filthy
 shame
AISCHROTĒS
 filthiness
AISCHUNĒ
 dishonesty
 shame
AISCHUNŌ
 ashamed
AISTHANOMAI
 perceive
AISTHĒSIS
 judgment
AISTHĒTĒRION
 sense
AITĒMA
 ask
 petition
 request
 require
AITEŌ
 ask
 beg
 call
 crave
 desire
 request
 require
AITIA
 accusation
 case
 cause
 charge
 crime
 fault
AITIŌMA
 charge
 complaint
AITION
 cause
 fault

AITIOS
 author
AKAIREOMAI
 opportunity (lack)
AKAIRŌS
 season
AKAKOS
 guileless
 harmless
 innocent
 simple
AKANTHA
 thorn(s) (of)
AKANTHINOS
 thorns (of)
AKARPOS
 fruit
 unfruitful
AKATAGNŌSTOS
 condemn
AKATAKALUPTOS
 uncovered
 unveiled
AKATAKRITOS
 uncondemned
AKATALUTOS
 endless
AKATAPAUSTOS
 cease
AKATASCHETOS
 unruly
AKATASTASIA
 commotion
 confusion
 tumult
AKATASTATOS
 restless
 unstable
AKATHARSIA
 uncleanness
AKATHARTĒS
 foul
 unclean
AKATHARTOS
 filthy
 foul
 unclean
AKERAIOS
 harmless
 simple
AKLINĒS
 waver
AKMAZŌ
 ripe (to be fully)
AKMĒN
 yet
AKOĒ
 ear
 fame
 hear
 hearing
 message
 report
 rumour
AKOLOUTHEŌ
 follow
 reach
AKŌLUTŌS
 forbid
AKŌN
 will
AKOUŌ
 audience

AKOUŌ—contd.
 ear
 hear
 hearer
 hearing
 hearken
 noise
 report
AKRASIA
 excess
 incontinency
AKRATĒS
 incontinent
 self-control (without)
AKRATOS
 mixture
 unmixed
AKRIBEIA
 manner
 strict
AKRIBĒS
 straitest
AKRIBESTERON
 carefully
 exact
 exactly
 perfectly
AKRIBESTATOS
 straitest
AKRIBOŌ
 inquire
 learn
AKRIBŌS
 accurately
 carefully
 circumspectly
 diligently
 perfectly
AKRIS
 locust
AKROATĒRION
 hearing
 place
AKROATĒS
 hearer
AKROBUSTIA
 uncircumcision
AKROGŌNIAIOS
 chief
 corner
AKRON
 end
 tip
 top
 uttermost part
AKROTHINION
 spoil
AKUROŌ
 disannul
 effect
 void
ALABASTRON
 box
 cruse
ALALAZŌ
 clanging
 tinkle
 wail
ALALĒTOS
 utter
ALALOS
 dumb
ALAZŌN
 boast
 boastful

ALAZON(E)IA
 boast
 pride
 vainglory
 vaunt
ALEIPHŌ
 anoint
ALEKTŌR
 cock
ALEKTOROPHŌNIA
 cock-crowing
ALĒTHEIA
 true
 truth
 verity
ALĒTHĒS
 indeed
 true
 truly
 truth
ALĒTHEUŌ
 truth
ALĒTHINOS
 true
ALĒTHŌ
 grind
ALĒTHŌS
 indeed
 surely
 truth
 true
 truly
 verily
ALEURON
 meal
ALISGĒMA
 pollution
ALLA
 nay
 notwithstanding
 rather
 yea
 yet
ALLACHOTHEN
 way
ALLACHOU
 elsewhere
ALLASSŌ
 change
ALLĒGOREŌ
 allegory
 contain
ALLĒLŌN
 each other
 mutual
 one another
 other
 themselves
 together
 yourselves
ALLOGENĒS
 stranger
ALLOPHULOS
 nation
ALLOS
 another
 more
 one
 other (-s)
 otherwise
 some
ALLŌS
 otherwise
ALLOTRIOEPISKOPOS
 busybody

ALLOTRIOEPISKOPOS—
contd.
  meddler
ALLOTRIOS
  alien
  man's (another)
  other
  strange
  stranger
ALOAŌ
  corn
  thresh
  tread
ALOĒ
  aloes
ALOGOS
  brute
  unreasonable
ALŌPĒX
  fox
ALUPOS (-OTEROS)
  sorrowful (less)
ALUSITELĒS
  unprofitable
AMACHOS
  brawler
AMAŌ
  mow
  reap down
AMARANTINOS
  fade
AMARANTOS
  fade
AMARTUROS
  witness
AMATHĒS
  unlearned
AMELEŌ
  light of (make)
  neglect
  negligent
  regard
AMEMPTOS
  blameless
  faultless
  unblameable
AMEMPTŌS
  blame (without)
  blameless
  unblameably
AMĒN
  amen
  verily
AMERIMNOS
  care
  carefulness
  rid
  secure
AMETAKINĒTOS
  move
  unmoveable
AMETAMELĒTOS
  regret
  repent
  repentance
AMETANOĒTOS
  impenitent
AMETATHETOS
  immutable
  immutability
AMETHUSTOS
  amethyst
AMĒTŌR
  mother
AMETROS
  measure

AMIANTOS
  undefiled
AMMOS
  sand
AMNOS
  lamb
AMOIBĒ
  requite
AMŌMĒTOS
  blameless
  rebuke
AMŌMON
  odour
  spice
AMŌMOS
  blame (without)
  blemish
  faultless
  unblameable
AMPELŌN
  vineyard
AMPELOS
  vine
AMPELOURGOS
  vinedresser
AMPHIBALLŌ
  cast
AMPHIBLĒSTRON
  net
AMPHIENNUMI
  clothe
AMPHODON
  place
  street
AMPHOTEROI
  master
AMUNŌ
  defend
ANA
  apiece
  each
  every
ANABAINŌ
  arise
  ascend
  climb up
  come
  enter
  go
  grow
  rise
  spring
ANABALLŌ
  defer
ANABATHMOS
  stair
ANABIBAZŌ
  draw
ANABLEPŌ
  look
  receive
  see
  sight
ANABLEPSIS
  sight
ANABOAŌ
  cry
ANABOLĒ
  delay
ANACHŌREŌ
  depart
  go
  place
  turn

ANACHŌREŌ—contd.
  withdraw
ANACHUSIS
  excess
ANADECHOMAI
  receive
ANADEIKNUMI
  appoint
  shew
ANADEIXIS
  shewing
ANADIDŌMI
  deliver
ANAGAION,
  (see ANŌGEON)
ANAGENNAŌ
  beget
  born
ANAGINŌSKŌ
  read
ANAGNŌRIZŌ
  known
ANAGNŌSIS
  reading
ANAGŌ
  bring
  depart
  launch
  lead
  loose
  offer
  put
  sail
  set
  take
ANAID(E)IA
  importunity
ANAIREŌ
  death
  kill
  slay
  take
ANAIRESIS
  death
ANAITIOS
  blameless
  guiltless
ANAKAINIZŌ
  renew
ANAKAINOŌ
  renew
ANAKAINŌSIS
  renewing
ANAKALUPTŌ
  open
  unlifted
  untaken
  unveiled
ANAKAMPTŌ
  return
  turn
ANAKATHIZŌ
  sit
ANAKEIMAI
  guest
  lean
  lie
  recline
  set
  sit
  table (at the)
ANAKEPHALAIOŌ
  comprehend
  gather

ANAKEPHALAIOŌ—
contd.
  sum up
ANAKLINŌ
  lay
  sit
ANAKOPTŌ
  hinder
ANAKRAZŌ
  cry
ANAKRINŌ
  ask
  discern
  examine
  judge
  search
ANAKRISIS
  examination
ANAKULIŌ
  roll
ANAKUPTŌ
  lift
  look
ANALAMBANŌ
  receive
  take
ANALĒPSIS
  receive
ANALISKŌ
  consume
ANALOGIA
  proportion
ANALOGIZOMAI
  consider
ANALOS
  saltness
ANALUŌ
  depart
  return
ANALUSIS
  departure
ANAMARTĒTOS
  sin
ANAMENŌ
  wait
ANAMIMNĒSKŌ
  mind
  remember
  remembrance
ANAMNĒSIS
  remembrance
ANANEOŌ
  renew
ANANĒPHŌ
  awake
  recover
  sober
ANANGELLŌ
  announce
  declare
  rehearse
  report
  shew
  speak
  tell
  tidings
ANANKAIOS
  near
  necessary
ANANKAIOTEROS
  needful
ANANKASTŌS
  constraint
ANANKAZŌ
  compel

ANANKAZŌ—*contd.*
constrain
ANANKĒ
distress
necessary
necessity
needs
ANANTIRRHĒTOS
gainsay
speak
ANANTIRRHĒTŌS
gainsay
ANAPAUŌ
ease
refresh
rest
ANAPAUSIS
rest
ANAPEITHŌ
persuade
ANAPEMPŌ
send
ANAPĒ(I)ROS
maimed
ANAPHAINŌ
appear
discover
ANAPHERŌ
bear
bring
carry
lead
offer
ANAPHŌNEŌ
voice
ANAPIPTŌ
lean
set
sit
ANAPLĒROŌ
fill
fulfil
supply
ANAPOLOGĒTOS
excuse
inexcusable
ANAPSUCHŌ
refresh
ANAPSUXIS
refreshing
ANAPTŌ
kindle
ANAPTUSSŌ
open
ANARITHMĒTOS
innumerable
ANASEIŌ
move
stir
ANASKEUAZŌ
subvert
ANASPAŌ
draw
pull
ANASTASIS
raise
resurrection
rising
ANASTATOŌ
sedition
stir
trouble
turn
uproar

ANASTAUROŌ
crucify
ANASTENAZŌ
sigh
ANASTREPHŌ
abide
behave
conversation
live
overthrow
pass
return
use
ANASTROPHĒ
behaviour
conversation
life
living
manner
ANATASSOMAI
draw
order
set (forth)
ANATELLŌ
arise
rise
rising
spring
up
ANATHALLŌ
flourish
revive
ANATHEMA
curse
anathema
ANATHĒMA
gift
offering
ANATHEMATIZŌ
curse
oath
ANATHEŌREŌ
behold
consider
observe
ANATITHĒMI
communicate
declare
lay
ANATOLĒ
dayspring
east
ANATREPHŌ
bring
nourish
ANATREPŌ
overthrow
subvert
ANAXIOS
unworthy
ANAXIŌS
unworthily
ANAZAŌ
alive
live
revive
ANAZĒTEŌ
seek
ANAZŌNNUMI
gird
ANAZŌPUREŌ
stir
ANDRAPODISTĒS
men-stealers

ANDRIZŌ
men
quit
ANDROPHONOS
manslayer
ANECHOMAI (or -CHŌ)
bear
endure
forbear
suffer
ANEKDIĒGĒTOS
unspeakable
ANEKLALĒTOS
unspeakable
ANEKLEIPTOS
fail
ANĒKŌ
befit
convenient
fit
ANEKTOS
ANEKTOTEROS
tolerable
ANELEĒMŌN
unmerciful
ANELEOS (or ANIL-)
mercy
ANĒMEROS
fierce
ANEMIZŌ
drive
wind
ANEMOS
wind
ANENDEKTOS
impossible
ANENKLĒTOS
blameless
unreprovable
ANEPAISCHUNTOS
ashamed
ANEPILĒPTOS
blameless
reproach
unrebukeable
ANEPSIOS
cousin
sister
ANĒR
fellow
husband
man
sir
ANERCHOMAI
go
ANESIS
eased
indulgence
liberty
relief
rest
ANETAZŌ
examine
ANĒTHON
anise
ANEU
without
ANEURISKŌ
find
ANEUTHETOS
commodious

ANEXERAUNĒTOS
(or -REU-)
unsearchable
ANEXICHNIASTOS
find
trace
unsearchable
ANEXIKAKOS
forbearing
patient
ANGAREUŌ
compel
ANGEION
vessel
ANGELIA
message
ANGELOS
angel
messenger
ANGOS
vessel
ANIĒMI
forbear
leave
loose
ANIPTOS
unwashen
ANISTĒMI
arise
lift
raise (up)
rise
stand
ANKALĒ
arm
ANKISTRON
hook
ANKURA
anchor
ANŌ
above
brim
high
up
ANOCHĒ
forbearance
ANOĒTOS
fool
foolish
unwise
ANŌGEON
room
ANOIA
folly
madness
ANOIGŌ
open
ANOIKODOMEŌ
build
ANOIXIS
open
opening
ANOMIA
iniquity
lawlessness
transgression
unrighteousness
ANOMOS
law
lawless
transgressor
unlawful
wicked
ANOMŌS
law

ANŌPHELĒS
  unprofitable
ANORTHOŌ
  lift
  set
  straight
ANOSIOS
  unholy
ANŌTERIKOS
  upper
ANŌTERON
  above
  higher
ANŌTHEN
  above
  again
  anew
  first
  top
ANTAGŌNIZOMAI
  strive
ANTALLAGMA
  exchange
ANTANAPLĒROŌ
  fill
ANTAPODIDŌMI
  recompense
  render
  repay
ANTAPODOMA
  recompense
ANTAPODOSIS
  recompense
  reward
ANTAPOKRINOMAI
  answer
  reply
ANTECHŌ (-OMAI)
  hold
  support
ANTEIPON
  gainsay
  say
ANTHISTĒMI
  resist
  withstand
ANTHOMOLOGEOMAI
  thanks
ANTHOS
  flower
ANTHRAKIA
  coals
ANTHRAX
  coal
ANTHRŌPARESKOS
  men-pleasers
ANTHRŌPINOS
  man's
  men
ANTHRŌPOKTONOS
  murderer
ANTHRŌPOS
  man
  people
  person
ANTHUPATEUŌ
  proconsul
ANTHUPATOS
  deputy
  proconsul
ANTI
  room
ANTIBALLŌ
  have

ANTICHRISTOS
  Antichrist
ANTIDIATITHĒMI
  oppose
ANTIDIKOS
  adversary
ANTIKALEŌ
  bid
ANTIKATHISTĒMI
  resist
ANTIKEIMAI
  adversary
  contrary
  oppose
ANTILAMBANŌ
  (-OMAI)
  help
  partake
  partaker
  support
ANTILEGŌ
  answer
  contradict
  deny
  gainsay
  gainsayer
  speak
ANTILĒ(M)PSIS
  help
ANTILOGIA
  contradiction
  dispute
  gainsaying
  strife
ANTILOIDOREŌ
  revile
ANTILUTRON
  ransom
ANTIMETREŌ
  measure
ANTIMISTHIA
  recompense
ANTIPARERCHOMAI
  pass
ANTIPIPTŌ
  resist
ANTISTRATEUOMAI
  war
ANTITASSŌ
  oppose
  resist
ANTITHESIS
  opposition
ANTITUPOS (-ON)
  figure
  likeness
  pattern
ANTLĒMA
  draw
ANTLEŌ
  draw
ANTOPHTHALMEŌ
  bear
  face
ANUDROS
  dry
  water
ANUPOKRITOS
  dissimulation
  hypocrisy
  unfeigned
ANUPOTAKTOS
  disobedient
  put

ANUPOTAKTOS—*contd.*
  subject
  unruly
AORATOS
  invisible
APAGŌ
  bring
  carry
  death
  lead
  take
APAIDEUTOS
  unlearned
APAIRŌ
  take
APAITEŌ
  require
APALGEŌ
  feel
APALLASSŌ
  deliver
  depart
  quit
APALLOTRIŌ
  alien
  alienated
APANCHŌ
  hang
APANGELLŌ
  bring
  declare
  go
  report
  shew
  tell
  word
APANTAŌ
  meet
APANTĒSIS
  meet
APARABATOS
  unchangeable
APARASKEUASTOS
  unprepared
APARCHĒ
  firstfruit(s)
APARNEOMAI
  deny
APARTI
  henceforth
  now (from)
APARTISMOS
  complete
  finish
APASPAZOMAI
  bid farewell
  leave
  take
APATAŌ
  beguile
  deceive
APATĒ
  deceit
  deceitful
  deceitfulness
  deceivableness
APATŌR
  father
APAUGASMA
  brightness
  effulgence
APECHŌ
  abstain
  enough

APECHO—*contd.*
  have
  receive
  was, etc.
APEIDON
  (*see* APHORAŌ)
APEILĒ
  straitly
  threaten
  threatening
APEILEŌ
  threaten
APEIMI
  absent
APEIMI
  go
APEIPON
  renounce
APEIRASTOS
  tempt
APEIROS
  experience (without)
  unskilful
APEITHEIA
  disobedience
  unbelief
APEITHEŌ
  believe
  disobedient
  obey
  unbelieving
APEITHĒS
  disobedient
APEKDECHOMAI
  look
  wait
APEKDUŌ
  put
  spoil
APEKDUSIS
  putting
APELAUNŌ
  drive
APELEGMOS
  disrepute
  nought
APELEUTHEROS
  freedman
APELPIZŌ
  despair
  hope
APENANTI
  before
  contrary
  presence
APERANTOS
  endless
APERCHOMAI
  come
  depart
  go
  pass
  way
APERISPASTŌS
  distraction
APERITMĒTOS
  uncircumcised
APHAIREŌ
  cut
  smite
  take
APHANĒS
  manifest

APHANISMOS
vanishing

APHANIZŌ
consume
corrupt
disfigure
perish
vanish

APHANTOS
vanish

APHEDRŌN
draught

APHEIDIA
neglecting
severity

APHELOTĒS
singleness

APHEŌ
(see APHIĒMI)

APHESIS
deliverance
forgiveness
liberty
release
remission

APHIĒMI
alone
cease
cry
forgive
forsake
lay
leave
let
put
remit
send
suffer
utter
yield

APHIKNEOMAI
come

APHILAGATHOS
despiser
lover

APHILARGUROS
covetous
covetousness
free
lover

APHISTĒMI
depart
draw
fall
refrain
withdraw

APHIXIS
departing

APHNŌ
suddenly

APHOBŌS
fear

APHOMOIOŌ
like

APHŌNOS
dumb
signification

APHORAŌ (APHEIDON)
look
see

APHORIZŌ
divide
separate
sever

APHORMĒ
occasion

APHRIZŌ
foam

APHRŌN
foolish
unwise

APHROS
foam

APHROSUNĒ
folly
foolishness
foolishly

APHTHARSIA
immortality
incorruption
sincerity

APHTHARTOS
immortal
incorruptible

APHTHORIA
uncorruptness

APHUPNOŌ
asleep

APHUSTEREŌ
fraud

APISTEŌ
believe
disbelieve
faith

APISTIA
belief
faith
unbelief

APISTOS
believe
faithless
incredible
infidel
unbeliever
unbelieving
unfaithful

APO
far
space

APOBAINŌ
come
get
go
turn

APOBALLŌ
cast

APOBLEPŌ
look
respect

APOBLĒTOS
refuse
reject

APOBOLĒ
cast
loss

APOCHŌREŌ
depart

APOCHŌRIZŌ
depart
part
remove

APOCHRĒSIS
using

APODECHOMAI
accept
receive
welcome

APODEIKNUMI
approve
prove
set

APODEIKNUMI—contd.
shew

APODEIXIS
demonstration

APODEKATEUŌ
tithe

APODEKATOŌ
pay
tithe

APODEKTOS
acceptable

APODĒMEŌ
country
far
go
journey
travel

APODĒMOS
far
journey
sojourn

APODIDŌMI
deliver
give
pay
perform
recompense
render
repay
restore
reward
sell
yield

APODIORIZŌ
separate

APODOCHĒ
acceptation

APODOKIMAZŌ
disallow
reject

APOGINOMAI
die

APOGRAPHĒ
enrolment
taxing

APOGRAPHŌ
enrol
tax
write

APOKALUPSIS
appearing
coming
lighten
manifestation
revelation

APOKALUPTŌ
reveal

APOKARADOKIA
expectation

APOKATALLASSŌ
reconcile

APOKASTATASIS
restitution
restoration

APOKATHISTĒMI
(or APOKATHISTANŌ)
restore

APOKEIMAI
appoint
lay

APOKEPHALIZŌ
behead

APOKLEIŌ
shut

APOKOPTO
cut

APOKRIMA
answer
sentence

APOKRINOMAI
answer

APOKRISIS
answer

APOKRUPHOS
hid
hidden
secret

APOKRUPTŌ
hide

APOKTEINŌ
death
kill
put
slay

APOKUEŌ
beget
bring

APOKULIŌ (or -IZŌ)
roll

APOLAMBANŌ
receive
take

APOLAUSIS
enjoy
pleasure

APŌLEIA
destruction
perdition
perish
pernicious
waste

APOLEICHŌ
lick

APOLEIPŌ
leave
remain

APOLLUMI
destroy
destroyer
die
fall
lose
marred
perish

APOLOGEOMAI
answer
defence
excuse
speak

APOLOGIA
answer
clearing
defence

APOLOUŌ
wash

APOLUŌ
depart
dismiss
divorce
forgive
go
let
liberty
loose
put
release
send

APOLUTRŌSIS
deliverance
redemption

APOMASSŌ
wipe

APONEMŌ
give

APONIPTŌ
wash

APOPHERŌ
bring
carry

APOPHEUGŌ
escape

APOPHORTIZŌ
unlade

APOPHTHENGOMAI
say
speak
utterance

APOPIPTŌ
fall

APOPLANAŌ
err
lead
seduce

APOPLEŌ
sail

APOPLUNŌ
wash

APOPNIGŌ
choke

APOPSUCHŌ
fail

APOREŌ
doubt
perplex

APORIA
perplexity

APORPHANIZOMAI
bereave

APORIPTŌ
cast

APOSKEUAZŌ
baggage
carriage

APOSKIASMA
cast
shadow

APOSPAŌ
draw
get
part
withdraw

APOSTASIA
falling
forsake

APOSTASION
divorcement

APOSTEGAZŌ
uncover

APOSTELLŌ
liberty
put
send
set

APOSTEREŌ
bereft
defraud
destitute
fraud
suffer

APOSTOLĒ
apostleship

APOSTOLOS
apostle
messenger
send

APOSTOMATIZŌ
provoke

APOSTREPHŌ
bring
pervert
put
turn

APOSTUGEŌ
abhor

APOSUNAGŌGOS
synagogue
(put out of the)

APOTASSŌ (-OMAI)
bid farewell
farewell
forsake
leave
renounce
send
take

APOTELEŌ
do
finish
perform

APOTHĒKĒ
barn
garner

APŌTHEŌ
cast
put
thrust

APOTHĒSAURIZŌ
store

APOTHESIS
putting

APOTHLIBŌ
crush
press

APOTHNĒSKŌ
die
perish

APOTINASSŌ
shake

APOTINŌ (or -TIŌ)
repay

APOTITHĒMI
cast
lay
put

APOTOLMAŌ
bold

APOTOMIA
severity

APOTOMŌS
sharply
sharpness

APOTREPŌ
turn

APOUSIA
absence

APROSITOS
approach

APROSKOPOS
offence
stumbling

APROSŌPOLĒMPTŌS
persons (respect of)

APSEUDĒS
lie

APSINTHOS
wormwood

APSUCHOS
life

APTAISTOS
falling

APTAISTOS—*contd.*
stumbling

ARA
curse

ARA
doubt (no)
haply
manner
perhaps
then
truly

ARAGE
haply

ARCHANGELOS
archangel

ARCHAIOS
old

ARCHĒ
beginning
corner
estate
first
magistrate
power
principality
principles
rule
ruler

ARCHĒGOS
author
captain
prince

ARCHIERATIKOS
priest

ARCHIEREUS
chief
priest

ARCHIPOIMĒN
chief
shepherd

ARCHISUNAGŌGOS
chief
synagogue
(ruler of the)

ARCHITEKTŌN
masterbuilder

ARCHITELŌNĒS
chief
publican

ARCHITRIKLINOS
governor
ruler

ARCHŌ (-OMAI)
begin
beginning
rehearse
reign
rule

ARCHŌN
chief
magistrate
prince
ruler

ARĒN
lamb

ARESKEIA
pleasing

ARESKŌ
please

ARESTOS
fit
please
reason

ARETĒ
excellence
praise

ARETĒ—*contd.*
virtue

ARGEŌ
linger

ARGOS
barren
idle
slow

ARGURION
money
piece
silver

ARGUROKOPOS
silversmith

ARGUREOS
silver

ARGUROS
silver

ARISTAŌ
dine

ARISTEROS
left

ARISTON
dinner

ARITHMEŌ
number

ARITHMOS
number

ARKEŌ
content
enough
suffice
sufficient

ARKETOS
enough
suffice
sufficient

ARK(T)OS
bear

ARNEOMAI
deny
refuse

ARNION
lamb

ARŌMA
spice(s)

AROTRIAŌ
plough (plow)

AROTRON
plough (plow)

ARRABŌN
earnest

AR(RH)APHOS
seam (without)

ARRĒN (or ARSĒN)
male
man

ARRHĒTOS
unspeakable

ARRHŌSTOS
sick

ARSENOKOITĒS
abuser

ARTEMŌN
foresail
mainsail

ARTI
henceforth
hitherto
now
present

ARTIGENNĒTOS
newborn

ARTIOS
  complete
  perfect
ARTOS
  bread
  loaf
  shewbread
ARTUŌ
  season
ASALEUTOS
  move
  unmoveable
ABESTOS
  quench
  unquenchable
ASCHĒMŌN
  uncomely
ASCHĒMONEŌ
  behave
  uncomely
ASCHĒMOSUNĒ
  shame
  unseemliness
  unseemly
ASEBEIA
  ungodliness
  ungodly
ASEBEŌ
  ungodly
ASEBĒS
  ungodly
ASELGEIA
  filthy
  lasciviousness
  wantonness
ASĒMOS
  mean
ASIARCHĒS
  chief
ASITIA
  abstinence
  food
ASITOS
  fasting
ASKEŌ
  exercise
ASKOS
  bottle
  skin
ASMENŌS
  gladly
ASOPHOS
  unwise
ASŌTIA
  excess
  riot
ASŌTŌS
  riotous
ASPASMOS
  greeting
  salutation
ASPAZOMAI
  embrace
  farewell
  greet
  leave
  salute
ASPHALEIA
  certainty
  safety
ASPHALĒS
  certain
  certainty
  safe
  sure

ASPHALIZŌ
  fast (to make)
  sure
ASPHALŌS
  assuredly
  safely
ASPILOS
  spot
  unspotted
ASPIS
  asp
ASPONDOS
  implacable
  truce-breaker
ASSARION
  farthing
ASSON
  close
ASTATEŌ
  certain
  dwelling (place)
ASTEIOS
  beautiful
  fair
  goodly
  proper
ASTĒR
  star
ASTĔRIKTOS
  unstable
ASTHENEIA
  disease
  infirmity
  sickness
  weakness
ASTHENĒMA
  infirmity
ASTHENEŌ
  diseased
  impotent
  sick
  weak
ASTHENĒS
  feeble
  impotent
  sick
  weak
ASTOCHEŌ
  err
  swerve
ASTORGOS
  affection
ASTRAPĒ
  lightning
  shining
ASTRAPTŌ
  dazzling
  lighten
  shine
ASTRON
  star
ASUMPHŌNOS
  agree
ASUNETOS
  foolish
  senseless
  understanding
ASUNTHETOS
  covenant-breakers
ATAKTEŌ
  behave
  disorderly
ATAKTOS
  disorderly
  unruly

ATAKTŌS
  disorderly
ATEKNOS
  childless
ATENIZŌ
  behold
  earnestly
  fasten
  look
  set
ATER
  absence
  without
ATHANASIA
  immortality
ATHEMITOS
  abominable
  unlawful
ATHEOS
  God (without)
ATHESMOS
  wicked
ATHETEŌ
  bring
  cast
  despise
  disannul
  frustrate
  nothing
  nought
  reject
  void
ATHETĒSIS
  disannuling
  put
ATHLEŌ
  contend
  strive
ATHLĒSIS
  conflict
  fight
ATHŌOS
  innocent
ATHROIZŌ
  gather
ATHUMEŌ
  discourage
ATIMAŌ
  handle
ATIMAZŌ
  despise
  dishonour
  entreat
  handle
  shame
  shamefully
ATIMIA
  dishonour
  disparagement
  reproach
  shame
  vile
ATIMOS
  despised
  dishonour
  honour (without)
ATIMOTEROS
  honourable
ATMIS
  vapour
ATOMOS
  moment
ATOPOS
  amiss
  harm
  unreasonable

ATOPOS—contd.
  wickedness
AUCHMĒROS
  dark
AUGAZŌ
  dawn
  shine
AUGĒ
  day
AULĒ
  court
  fold
  hall
  palace
  prætorium
AULEŌ
  pipe
AULĒTĒS
  flute-players
  piper
AULIZOMAI
  abide
  lodge
AULOS
  pipe
AURION
  morrow
  next day
  to-morrow
AUSTĒROS
  austere
AUTARKEIA
  contentment
  sufficiency
AUTARKĒS
  content
AUTHADĒS
  self-willed
AUTHAIRETOS
  accord
  willing
AUTHENTEŌ
  authority
  dominion
AUTOCHEIR
  hand (with one's own)
AUTOKATAKRITOS
  condemn
AUTOMATOS
  accord
  self
AUTOPTĒS
  eye-witness
AUTOS
  company
  halt
  he
  here
  myself
  ourselves
  same
  say
  self
  their
  them
  themselves
  there
  they
  this
  thou
  thyself
  very
AUTOU
  here
  there

AUXANŌ
grow
increase

AUXĒSIS
increase

AXINĒ
axe

AXIOŌ
desire
think
worthy
worthily

AXIOS
due
meet
reward
worthy

AXIŌS
become
godly
worthy

AZUMOS
bread

B

BAION
branch

BALLANTION
bag

BALLŌ
arise
beat
cast
dung
lay
lie
pour
put
send
throw
thrust

BAPTISMA
baptism

BAPTISMOS
baptism
washing

BAPTISTĒS
Baptist

BAPTIZŌ
baptize

BAPTŌ
dip

BARBAROS
barbarian
barbarous

BAREŌ
charge
burden
heavy
overcharge
press
weigh

BAREŌS
dull

BAROS
burden
weight

BARUNŌ
overcharge

BARUS
grievous
heavy
weighty

BARUTIMOS
precious

BASANISMOS
torment

BASANISTĒS
tormentor

BASANIZŌ
distress
pain
toil
torment
vex

BASANOS
torment

BASILEIA
kingdom

BASILEION
court

BASILEIOS
king
royal

BASILEUŌ
king
reign

BASILEUS
king

BASILIKOS
king
nobleman
royal

BASILISSA
queen

BASIS
foot

BASKAINŌ
bewitch

BASTAZŌ
bear
carry
take

BATHEŌS
deeply
early

BATHMOS
degree

BATHOS
deep
deepness
depth

BATHUNŌ
deep

BATHUS
deep

BATOS
bramble
bush

BATOS
measure

BATRACHOS
frog

BATTOLOGEŌ
repetitions

BDELUGMA
abomination

BDELUKTOS
abominable

BDELUSSŌ
abhor
abominable

BEBAIOŌ
confirm
establish
stablish

BEBAIOS
firm
force
stedfast
sure

BEBAIŌSIS
confirmation

BEBĒLOŌ
profane

BEBĒLOS
profane

BELIAL, –AR
Belial

BELONĒ
needle

BELOS
dart

BELTION
well (Adverb)

BĒMA
judgment-seat
throne

BĒRULLOS
beryl

BIA
violence

BIAIOS
mighty

BIASTĒS
violence
violent

BIAZŌ
enter
force
press
suffer
violence

BIBLARIDION
book

BIBLION
bill
book
scroll
writing

BIBLOS
book

BIBRŌSKŌ
eat

BIOŌ
live

BIOS
good(s)
life
living

BIŌSIS
life

BIŌTIKOS
life

BLABEROS
hurtful

BLAPTŌ
hurt

BLASPHĒMEŌ
blaspheme
defame
rail
report
revile

BLASPHĒMIA
blasphemy
evil speaking
railing
speak

BLASPHĒMOS
blasphemous
railing (-ers)

BLASTANŌ
bring
bud
spring

BLEMMA
seeing

BLEPŌ
behold
beware
heed (take)
lie
look
perceive
regard
see
sight

BLĒTEOS
put

BOAŌ
cry

BOĒ
cry

BOĒTHEIA
help

BOĒTHEŌ
help
succour

BOĒTHOS
helper

BOLĒ
cast
dart

BOLIS
dart

BOLIZŌ
dart
sound

BŌMOS
altar

BORBOROS
mire

BORRAS
north

BOSKŌ
feed
keep

BOTANĒ
herb

BOTHUNOS
ditch
pit

BOTRUS
cluster

BOULĒ
advise
counsel
will

BOULĒMA
desire
purpose
will

BOULEUTĒS
counsellor

BOULEUŌ
consult
counsel
minded
purpose

BOULOMAI
desire

BOULOMAI—*contd.*
determine
disposed
fain
intend
list
minded
will
willing
wish

BOUNOS
hill

BOUS
ox

BRABEION
prize

BRABEUŌ
rule

BRACHIŌN
arm

BRACHUS
few
further
little
space
while
words

BRADUNŌ
slack
tarry

BRADUPLOEŌ
sail

BRADUS
slow

BRADUTĒS
slackness

BRECHŌ
rain
wash

BREPHOS
babe
child
infant
young

BROCHĒ
rain

BROCHOS
snare

BRŌMA
food
meat
victuals

BRONTĒ
thunder

BRŌSIMOS
eat
meat

BRŌSIS
eating
food
meat
rust

BRUCHŌ
gnash

BRUGMOS
gnashing

BRUŌ
send

BURSEUS
tanner

BUSSINOS
linen (fine)

BUSSOS
linen (fine)

BUTHIZŌ
drown
sink

BUTHOS
deep

C

CHAIRŌ
farewell
glad
God-speed
greeting
hail
joy
rejoice

CHALAŌ
let down
lower
strake
strike

CHALAZA
hail

CHALEPOS
fierce
grievous
perilous

CHALINAGŌGEŌ
bridle

CHALINOS
bit
bridle

CHALKĒDŌN
chalcedony

CHALKEOS
brass

CHALKEUS
coppersmith

CHALKION
brazen

CHALKOLIBANON
brass

CHALKOS
brass
money

CHAMAI
ground

CHARA
gladness
greatly
joy
joyfulness

CHARAGMA
graven
mark

CHARAKTĒR
image

CHARAX
trench

CHARIN
cause

CHARIS
acceptable
benefit
bounty
favour
gift
grace
gracious
liberality
pleasure
thank(s)
thankworthy

CHARISMA
free
gift

CHARITOŌ
accepted
favour

CHARIZOMAI
bestow
deliver
forgive
frankly
freely
give
grant

CHARTĒS
paper

CHASMA
gulf

CHEILOS
lip
shore

CHEIMARRHOS
brook

CHEIMAZŌ
labour

CHEIMŌN
tempest
weather
winter

CHEIR
hand

CHEIRAGŌGEŌ
hand (lead by the)

CHEIRAGŌGOS
hand (lead by the)

CHEIROGRAPHOS
bond
handwriting

CHEIRŌN
sorer
worse

CHEIROPOIĒTOS
hands (made by)

CHEIROTONEŌ
appoint
choose
ordain

CHEROUBIM
cherubim

CHĒRA
widow

CHILIARCHOS
captain

CHILIAS
thousand

CHILIOT
thousands

CHIŌN
snow

CHITŌN
clothes
coat
garment

CHLAMUS
robe

CHLEUAZŌ
mock

CHLIAROS
lukewarm

CHLŌROS
green
pale

CHOÏKOS
earthy

CHOINIX
measure

CHOIROS
swine

CHOLAŌ
angry
wroth (be)

CHOLĒ
gall

CHŌLOS
cripple
halt
lame

CHOOS (CHOUS)
dust

CHŌRA
coast
country
field
ground
land
region

CHORĒGEŌ
give
minister
supply

CHŌREŌ
come
contain
go
heart
pass
place
receive
room

CHŌRION
field
ground
land
parcel
pass
place
possession

CHŌRIS
apart
beside
separate
without

CHŌRIZŌ
depart
put
separate

CHOROS
dancing

CHŌROS
north-west

CHORTASMA
sustenance

CHORTAZŌ
feed
fill
satisfy

CHORTOS
blade
grass
hay

CHRAŌ (-AOMAI)
deal with
entreat
lend
treat
use

CHRĒ
ought

CHREIA
business
lack
necessary

CHR

CHREIA—*contd.*
necessity
need
needful
use
want

CHRĒMA
money
riches

CHRĒMATISMOS
answer

CHRĒMATIZŌ
admonish
call
reveal
speak
warn

CHREŌPHEILETĒS
debtor

CHRĒSIMOS
profit

CHRĒSIS
use

CHRĒSTEUOMAI
kind (be)

CHRĒSTOLOGIA
word

CHRĒSTOS
better
easy
good
goodness
gracious
kind

CHRĒSTOTĒS
gentleness
good
goodness
kindness

CHRĒZŌ
need

CHRIŌ
anoint

CHRISMA
anointing
unction

CHRISTOS
Christ

CHRISTIANOS
Christian

CHRONIZŌ
delay
tarry

CHRONOS
delay
season
space
time
while

CHRONOTRIBEŌ
spend
time

CHRŌS
body

CHRUSEOS
gold
golden

CHRUSION
gold
jewels

CHRUSODAKTULIOS
gold ring
ring

CHRUSOLITHOS
chrysolite

CHRUSOŌ
deck

CHRUSOPRASOS
chrysoprasus

CHRUSOS
gold

CHTHES (or ECH-)
yesterday

D

DAIMŌN
demon
devil

DAIMONIŌDĒS
devilish

DAIMONION
demon

DAIMONIZOMAI
demon
possess

DAKNŌ
bite

DAKRU (or -UON)
tear

DAKRUŌ
weep

DAKTULIOS
ring

DAKTULOS
finger

DAMALIS
heifer

DAMAZŌ
tame

DANEION
debt

DAN(E)ISTĒS
creditor
lender

DANEIZŌ
borrow
lend

DAPANAŌ
charges
consume
spend

DAPANĒ
cost

DE
even
moreover
now
truly

DĒ
now

DECHOMAI
accept
receive
take

DEĒSIS
prayer
request
supplication

DEI
behove
due
meet
must
needful
needs
ought
should

DEIGMA
example

DEIGMATIZŌ
example
show (make a)

DEIKNUMI (or -NUŌ)
shew

DEILIA
fear
fearfulness

DEILIAŌ
afraid
fearful

DEILOS
fearful

DEINA
such as

DEINŌS
grievously
vehemently

DEIPNEŌ
sup

DEIPNON
feast
supper

DEISIDAIMŌN
superstitious

DEISIDAIMONIA
religion
superstition

DEKA
ten

DEKADUO
twelve

DEKAPENTE
fifteen

DEKATĒ
tenth
tithe

DEKATESSARES
fourteen

DEKATOŌ
pay
tithe

DEKATOS
tenth

DEKTOS
acceptable

DĒLAUGŌS
clearly

DELEAZŌ
beguile
entice

DĒLOŌ
declare
point
shew
signify

DĒLOS
bewray
certain
evident
manifest

DĒMĒGOREŌ
oration

DĒMIOURGOS
maker

DĒMOS
people

DĒMOSIOS
common
openly

DĒMOSIOS—*contd.*
public
publicly

DĒNARION
pence
penny
pennyworth

DENDRON
tree

DEŌ
bind
knit
tie
wind

DEOMAI
beseech
pray
request

DEOS
awe

DEON
need

DĒPOU
verily

DERMA
goatskin

DERMATINOS
leathern

DERŌ
beat
smite

DESMĒ
bundle

DESMEŌ (or -EUŌ)
bind

DESMIOS
bond
prisoner

DESMOPHULAX
jailor
prison-keeper

DESMOS
band
bond
chain
string

DESMŌTĒRION
prison
prison-house

DESMŌTĒS
prisoner

DESPOTĒS
lord
master

DEURO
come
hither
hitherto

DEUTE
come

DEUTERAIOS
next day
second

DEUTEROPRŌTOS
second

DEUTEROS
again
second
secondarily

DEXIOLABOS
spearman

DEXIOS
  right
  right hand
  right side
DIA
  means (by)
  occasion
  space
  within
DIABAINŌ
  come
  pass
DIABALLŌ
  accuse
DIABEBAIOOMAI
  affirm
DIABLEPŌ
  clearly
  see
DIABOLOS
  accuser
  devil
  slanderer
DIACHEIRIZŌ
  kill
  slay
DIACHŌRIZŌ
  depart
DIACHLEUAZŌ
  mock
DIADECHOMAI
  come
  turn
DIADĒMA
  crown
DIADIDŌMI
  distribute
  divide
  give
DIADOCHOS
  room
DIAGINOMAI
  past
  spent
DIAGINŌSKŌ
  determine
  inquire
  know
DIAGNŌRIZŌ
  known
DIAGNŌSIS
  decision
  hearing
DIAGŌ
  lead
  live
DIAGONGUZŌ
  murmur
DIAGRĒGOREŌ
  awake
DIAIREŌ
  divide
DIAIRESIS
  difference
  diversity
DIAKATELENCHOMAI
  confute
  convince
DIAKATHAIRŌ
  purge
DIAKATHARIZŌ
  cleanse
  purge
DIAKŌLUŌ
  forbid

DIAKŌLUŌ—contd.
  hinder
DIAKONEŌ
  administer
  minister
  office
  serve
DIAKONIA
  administration
  minister
  ministration
  ministering
  ministry
  office
  relief
  service
  serving
DIAKONOS
  deacon
  minister
  servant
DIAKOSIOI
  two hundred
DIAKOUŌ
  hear
DIAKRINŌ
  contend
  decide
  difference
  discern
  doubt
  judge
  partial
  put
  stagger
  waver
DIAKRISIS
  decision
  discern
DIALALEŌ
  commune
  noise
DIALEGOMAI
  discourse
  dispute
  preach
  reason
  speak
DIALEIPŌ
  cease
DIALEKTOS
  language
  tongue
DIALLASSŌ
  reconcile
DIALOGISMOS
  disputation
  disputing
  doubting
  imagination
  reasoning
  thought
DIALOGIZOMAI
  cast
  consider
  dispute
  musing
  reason
  think
DIALUŌ
  disperse
  scatter
DIAMACHOMAI
  strive
DIAMARTUROMAI
  charge
  testify

DIAMARTUROMAI—contd.
  witness
DIAMENŌ
  continue
  remain
DIAMERISMOS
  division
DIAMERIZŌ
  cloven
  divide
  part
DIANGELLŌ
  declare
  preach
  publish
  signify
DIANEMŌ
  spread
DIANEUŌ
  beckon
  signs (to make)
DIANOĒMA
  thought
DIANOIA
  imagination
  mind
  understanding
DIANOIGŌ
  open
DIANUKTEREUŌ
  continue
DIANUŌ
  finish
DIA PANTOS
  always
  continually
DIAPARATRIBĒ
  disputing
  wrangling
DIAPERAŌ
  cross
  go
  pass
  sail
DIAPHANĒS
  transparent
DIAPHĒMIZŌ
  blaze abroad
  commonly
  fame
  report
DIAPHERŌ
  better
  carry
  differ
  drive
  excellent
  matter
  publish
  spread
  value
DIAPHEUGŌ
  escape
DIAPHOROS
  differing
  divers
  excellent
DIAPHORŌTEROS
  excellent
DIAPHTHEIRŌ
  corrupt
  decay
  destroy
  perish

DIAPHTHORA
  corruption
DIAPHULÁSSŌ
  guard
  keep
DIAPLEŌ
  sail
DIAPONEŌ
  grieve
  trouble
DIAPOREŌ
  doubt
  perplex
DIAPOREUŌ (-OMAI)
  go
  journey
  pass
DIAPRAGMATEUOMAI
  gain
  trade
DIAPRIŌ
  cut
DIARPAZŌ
  spoil
DIARRHĒGNUMI
  (or DIARRHĒSSŌ)
  break
  rend
DIASAPHEŌ
  explain
  tell
DIASEIŌ
  fear
  violence
DIASKORPIZŌ
  disperse
  scatter
  strawed
  waste
DIASŌZŌ
  escape
  heal
  safe
  save
  whole
DIASPAŌ
  pluck
  pull
  rend
  tear
DIASPEIRŌ
  scatter
DIASPORA
  disperse
  scatter
DIASTELLŌ (-OMAI)
  charge
  command
DIASTĒMA
  space
DIASTOLĒ
  difference
  distinction
DIASTREPHŌ
  perverse
  pervert
  turn
DIATAGĒ
  disposition
  ordinance
DIATAGMA
  commandment
DIATARASSŌ
  trouble

DIATASSŌ
appoint
command
ordain
order

DIATELEŌ
continue

DIATĒREŌ
keep

DIATHĒKĒ
covenant
testament

DIATI
wherefore

DIATITHĒMI
appoint
make
testator

DIATRIBŌ
abide
continue
tarry

DIATROPHĒ
food

DIAUGAZŌ
dawn

DIAZŌNNUMI
gird

DICHAZŌ
variance

DICHOSTASIA
division
sedition

DICHOTOMEŌ
cut

DIDACHĒ
doctrine
teaching

DIDAKTIKOS
teach

DIDAKTOS
taught
teach

DIDASKALIA
doctrine
learning
teaching

DIDASKALOS
doctor
master
teacher

DIDASKŌ
teach

DIDŌMI
add
adventure
bestow
cause
commit
deliver
give
grant
make
minister
offer
power
put
receive
render
set
shew
smite
suffer
take
utter
yield

DIDRACHMON
half-shekel
tribute

DIEGEIRŌ
arise
awake
raise
stir up

DIĒGEOMAI
declare
shew
tell

DIĒGĒSIS
declaration
narrative

DIĒNEKĒS
continually
ever

DIENTHUMEOMAI
think

DIERCHOMAI
come
depart
go
pass
pierce
travel
walk

DIERMĒNEUŌ
expound
interpret
interpretation

DIERMĒNEUTĒS
interpreter

DIERŌTAŌ
inquiry

DIETĒS
year

DIETIA
year

DIEXODOS
highway

DIIKNEOMAI
pierce

DIISCHURIZOMAI
affirm

DIISTĒMI
go
part
space

DIKAIOKRISIA
judgment
righteous

DIKAIŌMA
act
judgment
justification
ordinance
righteousness

DIKAIOŌ
free
justify
justifier
righteous

DIKAIOS
just
meet
right
righteous

DIKAIŌS
justly
righteously
righteousness

DIKAIŌSIS
justification

DIKAIOSUNĒ
righteousness

DIKASTĒS
judge

DIKĒ
judgment
justice
punishment
vengeance

DIKTUON
net

DILOGOS
double-tongued

DIO
wherefore

DIODEUŌ
go
pass

DIŌGMOS
persecution

DIŌKŌ
ensue
follow
give
persecute
persecution
press
pursue

DIŌKTĒS
persecutor

DIOPER
wherefore

DIOPETĒS
fall

DIORTHŌMA
correction
deed

DIORTHŌSIS
reformation

DIORUSSŌ
break

DIPLOŌ
double

DIPLOUS
double
twofold

DIPSAŌ
thirst

DIPSOS
thirst

DIPSUCHOS
double-minded

DIS
again
twice

DISCHILIOI
thousand

DISMURIADES
thousand

DISTAZŌ
doubt

DISTOMOS
edge
two-edged

DITHALASSOS
sea

DIULIZŌ
strain out

DOCHĒ
feast

DŌDEKA
twelve

DŌDEKAPHULOS
tribes

DŌDEKATOS
twelfth

DOGMA
decree
ordinance

DOGMATIZŌ
ordinance

DOKEŌ
account
please
pleasure
reputation
repute
seem
suppose
think
trow

DOKIMAZŌ
allow
approve
discern
examine
prove
refuse
try

DOKIMĒ
experience
experiment
probation
proof
trial

DOKIMION
proof
trial
try

DOKIMOS
approved
tried

DOKOS
beam

DOLIOŌ
deceit

DOLIOS
deceitful

DOLOŌ
deceitfully
handle

DOLOS
craft
deceit
guile
subtilty

DOMA
gift

DŌMA
housetop

DŌREA
gift

DŌREAN
cause
freely
nought
vain

DŌRĒMA
boon
gift

DŌREŌ
give

DŌRON
gift
offering

DOSIS
gift

DOTĒS
giver

DOULAGŌGEŎ
bondage
subjection

DOULĒ
handmaid

DOULEIA
bondage

DOULEUŌ
bondage
serve

DOULOŎ
bondage
enslaved
give
servant

DOULOS
bondman
bondservant
servant

DOXA
dignity
glory
honour
praise
worship

DOXAZŌ
glorify
honour
magnify

DRACHMĒ
piece

DRAKŌN
dragon

DRASSOMAI
take

DREPANON
sickle

DROMOS
course

DUNAMAI
able
can
may
possible
power

DUNAMIS
ability
abundance
deed
meaning
might
miracle
power
strength
violence
virtue
wonderful (work)
work

DUNAMOŌ
strengthen

DUNASTĒS
authority
mighty
potentate

DUNATEŌ
able
mighty

DUNATOS (-ON)
able
mighty
possible
power
strong

DUNŌ
set

DUO
twain
two

DUSBASTAKTOS
grievous

DUSENTERION
dysentery

DUSERMĒNEUTOS
utter

DUSKOLOS
hard

DUSKOLŌS
hardly

DUSMĒ
west

DUSNOĒTOS
understood

DUSPHĒMEŎ
defame

DUSPHĒMIA
report

E

Ē
either

Ē
what
yea

EA
ah!
alone

EAŌ
commit
leave
let
suffer

ĒCHEŌ
roar
sound

ECHIDNA
viper

ECHŌ
ability
able
accompany
can
case
count
do
fare
follow
have
hold
keep
lie
next
old
possess
retain
take
use

ĒCHOS
fame
roar
rumour
sound

ECHTHES
yesterday

ECHTHRA
enmity
hatred

ECHTHROS
enemy

ECHTHROS—*contd.*
foe

EDAPHIZŌ
dash
ground

EDAPHOS
ground

ĒDĒ
already
now
time
yet

EGEIRŌ
arise
awake
lift
raise (up)
rear
stand
take

EGERSIS
resurrection

EGŌ
I

EIDEA (or IDEA)
countenance

EIDŌLION
idol's temple

EIDŌLOLATREIA
idolatry

EIDŌLOLATRĒS
idolater

EIDŌLON
idol

EIDŌLOTHUTON
idols (offered to)
meat
offer
sacrifice

EIDON
(*see* HORAŌ)

EIDOS
appearance
fashion
form
shape
sight

EIKĒ
cause
vain (in)
vainly

EIKŌ
place

EIKŌN
image

EIKOSI
twenty

EILIKRIN(E)IA
sincerity

EILIKRINĒS
pure
sincere

EIMI (to be)
come
have
hold
make
mean
might
pass
possible
was etc.

EIPON

EIPON—*contd.*
bid
call
command
say
speak
tell
word

EIRĒNĒ
peace
quietness
rest

EIRĒNEUŌ
peace
peaceably

EIRĒNIKOS
peaceable

EIRĒNOPOIEŌ
peace

EIRĒNOPOIOS
peacemaker

EIRŌ
(ERŌ)
make
say
speak
tell

EIS
regard (in . . . to)

EISAGŌ
bring
lead

EISAKOUŌ
hear

EISDECHOMAI
receive

EISEIMI
enter
go

EISERCHOMAI
arise
come
enter
go

EISKALEŌ
call

EISODOS
coming
enter
entering
entrance

EISPĒDAŌ
run
spring

EISPHERŌ
bring
lead

EISPOREUOMAI
come
enter
go

EISTRECHŌ
run

EITA
afterward
furthermore
then

EK
means (by)
of
out
out of

EKBAINŌ
come

EKBAINŌ—contd.
  go
EKBALLŌ
  bring
  cast
  drive
  expel
  leave
  pluck (out)
  pull
  put
  send
  take
  thrust
EKBASIS
  end
  escape
  issue
EKBOLĒ
  freight
EKCHEŌ
  pour
  run
  shed
  spill
EKCHŌREŌ
  depart
EKCHUN(N)Ō
  gush out
  pour
  riotously
  run
  shed
  spill
EKDAPANAOMAI
  spend
EKDECHOMAI
  expect
  look
  tarry
  wait
EKDĒLOS
  manifest
EKDĒMEŌ
  absent
EKDIDŌMI
  let out
EKDIĒGEOMAI
  declare
EKDIKEŌ
  avenge
  revenge
EKDIKĒSIS
avenge
  punishment
  revenge
  vengeance
EKDIKOS
  avenger
  revenger
EKDIŌKŌ
  drive
  persecute
EKDOCHĒ
  expectation
  looking
EKDOTOS
  deliver
EKDUŌ
  strip
  take
  unclothed
EKEI
  there
  thither
  yonder

EKEINOS
  he
  it
  other
  she
  that
  their
  them
  they
  this
EKEISE
  there
EKEITHEN
  afterward
  place
  thence (from)
  there
EKGAMISKŌ
  marriage (give in)
EKGAMIZŌ
  marriage (give in)
EKGONOS
  grandchildren
  nephews
EKKAIŌ
  burn
EKKAKEŌ
  (see ENKAKEŌ)
EKKATHAIRŌ
  purge
EKKENTEŌ
  pierce
EKKLAŌ
  break
EKKLEIŌ
  exclude
EKKLĒSIA
  assembly
  church
EKKLINŌ
  avoid
  eschew
  go
  turn
  way
EKKOLUMBAŌ
  swim
EKKOMIZŌ
  carry (out)
EKKOPTŌ
  cut
  hew
  hinder
EKKREMANNUMI
  attentive
  hang
EKLALEŌ
  tell
EKLAMPŌ
  shine
EKLANTHANOMAI
  forget
EKLEGŌ
  choice
  choose
EKLEIPŌ
  fail
EKLEKTOS
  chosen
  elect
EKLOGĒ
  chosen
  election
EKLUŌ
  faint

EKMASSŌ
  wipe
EKMUKTĒRIZŌ
  deride
  scoff
EKNĒPHŌ
  awake
EKNEUŌ
  convey
EKPALAI
  long
  old
EKPēDAŌ
  run
  spring
EKPEIRAZŌ
  tempt
EKPEMPŌ
  send
EKPERISSŌS
  vehemently
EKPETANNUMI
  spread
  stretch
EKPHERŌ
  bear
  bring
  carry
EKPHEUGŌ
  escape
  flee
EKPHOBEŌ
  terrify
EKPHOBOS
  fear
EKPHUŌ
  put
EKPIPTŌ
  cast
  effect
  fail
  fall
  nought
EKPLEŌ
  sail
EKPLĒROŌ
  fulfil
EKPLĒRŌSIS
  accomplishment
EKPLĒSSŌ
  amaze
  astonish
EKPNEŌ
  ghost (give up the)
EKPOREUŌ
  come
  depart
  go
  issue
  proceed
EKPORNEUŌ
  fornication
EKPSUCHŌ
  ghost (give up the)
  yield
EKPTUŌ
  reject
EKRIZOŌ
  pluck
  root
EKSTASIS
  amazement
  astonishment
  trance

EKSTREPHŌ
  pervert
  subvert
EKTARASSŌ
  trouble
EKTEINŌ
  cast
  lay
  put
  stretch
EKTELEŌ
  finish
EKTENEIA
  earnestly
  instantly
EKTENĒS
  cease
  fervent
EKTENESTERON
  earnestly
EKTENŌS
  earnestly
  fervently
EKTHAMBEŌ
  affright
  amaze
EKTHAMBOS
  wonder
EKTHAUMAZŌ
  wonder
EKTHETOS
  cast
EKTINASSŌ
  shake
EKTITHĒMI
  cast
  expound
EKTOS
  except
  other
  out of
  outside
  unless
  without
EKTREPHŌ
  bring
  nourish
EKTREPŌ
  avoid
  turn
EKTRŌMA
  beget
EKTROMOS
  fear
EKZĒTEŌ
  inquire
  require
  seek
EKZĒTĒSIS
  questioning
ELACHISTOS
  least
  little
  small
ELACHISTOTEROS
  least
ELAIA
  olive (berry)
  olive tree
ELAION
  oil
ELAIŌN
  Olives
  Olivet

ELAPHRIA
  fickleness
  lightness
ELAPHROS
  light
ELASSŌN
  less
  under
  worse
  younger
ELATTONEŌ
  lack
ELATTOŌ
  decrease
  lower
ELAUNŌ
  carry
  drive
  row
ELEEINOS
  miserable
ELEEINOTEROS
  miserable
  pitiable (most)
ELEĒMŌN
  merciful
ELEĒMOUSNĒ
  alms
  almsdeeds
ELEEŌ
  compassion
  mercy
  obtain
  receive
ELEGMOS
  reproof
ELENCHŌ
  convict
  fault
  rebuke
  reprove
ELENCHOS
  reproof
ELENXIS
  rebuke
ELEOS
  mercy
ELEPHANTINOS
  ivory
ELEUSIS
  coming
ELEUTHERIA
  freedom
  liberty
ELEUTHEROŌ
  deliver
  free
ELEUTHEROS
  free
  freeman
  freewoman
  liberty
ELLOGEŌ (or -AŌ)
  account
  impute
ELPIS
  faith
  hope
ELPIZŌ
  hope
  trust
EMAUTOU
  me
  myself

EMBAINŌ
  come
  enter
  get
  go
  step
  take
EMBALLŌ
  cast
EMBAPTŌ
  dip
EMBATEUŌ
  dwell
EMBIBAZŌ
  put
EMBLEPŌ
  behold
  gaze
  look
  see
EMBRIMAOMAI
  charge
  groan
  murmur
  straitly
EME, EMOI
  me
EMEŌ
  spue
EMMAINOMAI
  mad
EMMENŌ
  continue
EMOS
  me
  my (mine)
  very
EMPAIGMONĒ
  mockery
EMPAIGMOS
  mocking
EMPAIKTĒS
  mocker
  scoffer
EMPAIZŌ
  mock
EMPERIPATEŌ
  walk
EMPHANĒS
  manifest
  openly
  shew
EMPHANIZŌ
  appear
  declare
  inform
  manifest
  shew
  signify
EMPHOBOS
  affrighted
  terrify
  tremble
EMPHUSAŌ
  breathe
EMPHUTOS
  engrafted
  implanted
EMPIPLAŌ
  fill
EMPIPLĒMI
  fill
  satisfy

EMPIPRĒMI or
EMPRĒTHŌ
  burn
EMPIPTŌ
  fall
EMPLEKŌ
  entangle
EMPLOKĒ
  plaiting
EMPNEŌ
  breathe
EMPOREUOMAI
  buy
  merchandise
  sell
  trade
EMPORIA
  merchandise
EMPIRION
  merchandise
EMPOROS
  merchant
EMPROSTHEN
  before
  presence
  sight of (in the)
EMPTUŌ
  spit
EN
  under
  way (by . . . of)
  within
ENALIOS
  sea
ENANKALIZOMAI
  arm (physical)
ENANTI
  before
  sight of (in the)
ENANTION
  before
  contrariwise
  sight of (in the)
ENANTIOS
  contrary
ENARCHOMAI
  begin
ENCHRIŌ
  anoint
ENDECHOMAI
  can
ENDEĒS
  lack
ENDEIGMA
  token
ENDEIKNUMI
  shew
ENDEIXIS
  declare
  proof
  shew
  token
ENDĒMEŌ
  home
  present
ENDIDUSKŌ
  clothe
  wear
ENDIKOS
  just
ENDOMĒSIS
  buliding

ENDOXAZŌ
  glorify
ENDOXOS
  glorious
  glory
  gorgeously
  honourable
ENDUMA
  clothing
  garment
  raiment
ENDUNAMOŌ
  enable
  strength
  strengthen
  strong
ENDUNŌ
  creep
ENDUŌ
  clothe
  endue
  have
  put
EUDUSIS
  putting
ENECHŌ
  entangle
  press
  quarrel
  set
  urge
ENEDRA (or -DRON)
  lie in wait
ENEDREUŌ
  lie in wait
ENEILEŌ
  wrap
ENEIMI
  have
  within
ENENĒKONTA-
  ninety
ENEOS
  (see ENNEOS)
ENERGEIA
  effectual
  operation
  strong
  working
ENERGĒMA
  operation
  working
ENERGEŌ
  do
  effectual
  mighty
  shew
  work
ENERGĒS
  active
  effectual
  powerful
ENEULOGEOMAI
  bless
ENGIZŌ
  approach
  come
  draw
  hand (at)
  near
  nigh
ENGRAPHŌ
  write in

ENGUOS
surety

ENGUS
hand (at)
near
nigh
ready

ENGUTERON
nearer

ENIAUTOS
year

ENISCHUŌ
strengthen

ENISTĒMI
come
hand (at)
now
present

ENKAINIA
dedication

ENKAINIZŌ
consecrate
dedicate

ENKAKEŌ
faint
weary

ENKALEŌ
accuse
call
charge
implead
question

ENKATALEIPŌ
forsake
leave

ENKATHETOS
spy

ENKATOIKEŌ
dwell

ENKAUCHAOMAI
glory

ENKENTRIZŌ
graff
graft

ENKLĒMA
charge
crime
matter

ENKOMBOOMAI
clothe

ENKOPĒ
hinder
hindrance

ENKOPTŌ
hinder
tedious (to be)

ENKRATEIA
temperance

ENKRATĒS
temperate

ENKRATEUOMAI
contain
continency
temperate

ENKRINŌ
number

ENKRUPTŌ
hide

ENKUOS
child

ENNATOS
ninth

ENNEA
nine

ENNEOS
speechless

ENNEUŌ
signs (to make)

ENNOIA
intent
mind

ENNOMOS
law
lawful
regular

ENNUCHA
day

ENOCHLEŌ
trouble

ENOCHOS
danger
guilty
subject
worthy

ENOIKEŌ
dwell

ENŌPION
before
presence
sight of (in the)

ENORKIZŌ
adjure
charge

ENŌTIZOMAI
hearken

ENTALMA
commandment
precept

ENTAPHIASMOS
burying

ENTAPHIAZŌ
bury
burial

ENTELLŌ (-OMAI)
charge
command
enjoined

ENTEUTHEN
either
hence

ENTEUXIS
intercessions
prayer

ENTHADE
here
hither
there

ENTHEN
hence

ENTHUMEOMAI
think

ENTHUMĒSIS
device
thought

ENTIMOS
dear
honour
precious
reputation

ENTIMOTEROS
honourable

ENTOLĒ
commandment
precept

ENTOPIOS
place

ENTOS
inside
within

ENTREPHŌ
nourish

ENTREPŌ
ashamed
regard
reverence
shame

ENTROMOS
fear
quake
trembling

ENTROPĒ
shame

ENTRUPHAŌ
revel
sport

ENTULISSŌ
roll
wrap

ENTUNCHANŌ
deal with
intercessions
plead
suit

ENTUPOŌ
engrave

ENUBRIZŌ
despite

ENUPNIAZŌ
dream
dreamer

ENUPNION
dream

EOIKA
like

EPAGŌ
bring

EPAGŌNIZOMAI
contend
earnestly

EPAINEŌ
commend
praise

EPAINOS
praise

EPAIRŌ
exalt
hoist up
lift
take

EPAISCHUNOMAI
ashamed

EPAITEŌ
beg

EPAKOLOUTHEŌ
follow

EPAKOUŌ
hear

EPAKROAOMAI
hear

EPANAGŌ
launch
put
return
thrust

EPANAMIMNĒSKŌ
mind
remembrance

EPANANKĒS
necessary

EPANAPAUŌ
rest

EPANERCHOMAI
come

EPANERCHOMAI—contd.
return

EPANGELIA
message
promise

EPANGELLŌ
profess
promise

EPANGELMA
promise

EPANISTAMAI
rise

EPANŌ
above
more

EPANORTHŌSIS
correction

EPAPHRIZŌ
foam

EPARATOS
accursed

EPARCH(E)IA
province

EPARKEŌ
relieve

EPATHROIZŌ
gather

EPAULIS
habitation

EPAURION
follow
morrow
next day

EPAUTOPHŌRŌ
act

EPECHŌ
heed
hold
mark
stay

EPEGEIRŌ
raise
stir

EPEI
else
otherwise

EPEIDON
look

EPEIMI
follow
next
next day

EPEISAGŌGĒ
bringing

EPEITA
afterward(s)
then

EPEKEINA
beyond

EPEKTEINŌ
reach
stretch

EPENDUŌ
clothe

EPENDUTĒS
clothing

EPERCHOMAI
come

EPĒREAZŌ
accuse
despitefully
revile

EPERŌTAŌ
ask

EPERŌTAŌ—*contd.*
demand
desire
question

EPERŌTĒMA
answer
interrogation

EPHALLOMAI
leap

EPHAPAX
once

EPHĒMERIA
course

EPHĒMEROS
daily

EPHEURETĒS
inventor

EPHIKNEOMAI
reach

EPHISTĒMI
assault
come
hand (at)
instant
present
stand

EPHPHATHA
ephphatha
open

EPI
of
respect
space
time
under

EPIBAINŌ
aboard
come
embark
enter
foot
go
ride
ship
sit
take

EPIBALLŌ
beat
cast
fall
lay
put
stretch
think

EPIBAREŌ
burden
chargeable
overcharge
press

EPIBIBAZŌ
set

EPIBLĒMA
piece

EPIBLEPŌ
look
regard
respect

EPIBOAŌ
cry

EPIBOULĒ
plot

EPICHEIREŌ
go
hand (take in)
take

EPICHEŌ
pour

EPICHORĒGEŌ
add
minister
supply

EPICHORĒGIA
supply

EPICHRIŌ
anoint

EPIDE
behold

EPIDECHOMAI
receive

EPIDEIKNUMI
shew

EPIDĒMEŌ
stranger
there

EPIDIATASSŌ
add

EPIDIDŌMI
deliver
give
offer

EPIDIORTHOŌ
order

EPIDUŌ
go

EPIEIKEIA
clemency
gentleness

EPIEIKĒS
forbearance
gentle
moderation
patient

EPIGAMBREUŌ
marry

EPIGEIOS
earth
earthly
terrestrial

EPIGINOMAI
blow

EPIGINŌSKŌ
acknowledge
know
knowledge
perceive

EPIGNŌSIS
acknowledgement
know
knowledge

EPIGRAPHĒ
superscription

EPIGRAPHŌ
inscription
write

EPIKALEŌ
appeal
call
surname

EPIKALUMMA
cloke

EPIKALUPTŌ
cover

EPIKATARATOS
cursed

EPIKATHIZŌ
set

EPIKEIMAI
imposed

EPIKEIMAI—*contd.*
instant
lay
lie

EPIKELLŌ (or EPOK-)
run

EPIKOURIA
help

EPIKRINŌ
give
sentence

EPILAMBANŌ
catch
hold
lay
take

EPILANTHANOMAI
forget
forgetful

EPILEGŌ
call
choose

EPILEICHŌ
lick

EPILEIPŌ
fail

EPILĒSMONĒ
forget
forgetful

EPILOIPOS
rest (the)

EPILUŌ
determine
expound
settle

EPILUSIS
interpretation

EPIMARTUREŌ
testify

EPIMELEIA
refresh

EPIMELEOMAI
care

EPIMELŌS
diligently

EPIMENŌ
abide
continue
tarry

EPINEUŌ
consent

EPINOIA
thought

EPIORKEŌ
forswear

EPIORKOS
perjured person

ĒPIOS
gentle

EPIOUSIOS
daily

EPIPHAINŌ
appear
light

EPIPHANEIA
appearing
brightness

EPIPHANĒS
notable

**EPIPHAUŌ
(or -AUSKŌ)**
light
shine

EPIPHERŌ
bring
take
visit

EPIPHŌNEŌ
cry
shout

EPIPHŌSKŌ
dawn
draw

EPIPIPTŌ
fall
lie
press

EPIPLĒSSŌ
rebuke

EPIPOREUOMAI
come
resort

EPIPOTHEŌ
desire
long
lust

EPIPOTHĒSIS
desire
longing

EPIPOTHĒTOS
long (*verb*)

EPIPOTHIA
desire
longing

EPIRRHAPTŌ
sew

EPIRIPTŌ
cast

EPISCHUŌ
fierce

EPISĒMOS
notable
note

EPISITISMOS
victuals

EPISKĒNOŌ
rest

EPISKEPTOMAI
look
visit

EPISKEUAZŌ
baggage
carriage

EPISKIAZŌ
overshadow

EPISKOPĒ
bishop
bishoprick
office
visitation

EPISKOPEŌ
carefully
exercise
look
oversight

EPISKOPOS
bishop
overseer

EPISŌREUŌ
heap

EPISPAOMAI
uncircumcised

EPISPHALĒS
dangerous

EPISTAMAI
know
understand

EPISTASIS
  come
  press
  raise
  stir
EPISTATĒS
  master
EPISTELLŌ
  write
EPISTĒMŌN
  endue
  knowledge
  understanding
EPISTĒRIZŌ
  confirm
  strengthen
EPISTOLĒ
  epistle
  letter
EPISTOMIZŌ
  mouth
  stop
EPISTREPHŌ
  come
  convert
  go
  return
  turn
EPISTROPHĒ
  conversion
EPISUNAGŌ
  gather
EPISUNAGŌGĒ
  assembling
  gathering
EPISUNTRECHŌ
  come
  run
EPISUSTASIS
  come
  press
  raise
EPITAGĒ
  authority
  commandment
EPITASSŌ
  charge
  command
  enjoin
EPITĒDEIOS
  needful
EPITELEŌ
  accomplish
  complete
  do
  finish
  make
  perfect
  perform
EPITHANATIOS
  appointed
  death
  doomed
EPITHESIS
  laying on
  putting
EPITHUMEŌ
  covert
  desire
  fain
  lust
EPITHUMĒTĒS
  lust
EPITHUMIA
  concupiscence
  coveting

EPITHUMIA—contd.
  desire
  lust
EPITIMAŌ
  charge
  rebuke
EPITIMIA
  punishment
EPITITHĒMI
  add
  lade
  lay
  put
  set
  surname
EPITREPŌ
  leave
  let
  liberty
  licence
  permit
  suffer
EPITROPĒ
  commission
EPITROPOS
  guardian
  steward
  tutor
EPITUNCHANŌ
  obtain
EPIZĒTEŌ
  desire
  inquire
  seek
EPOIKODOMEŌ
  build
EPONOMAZŌ
  call
  name
EPOPTĒS
  eye-witness
EPOPTEUŌ
  behold
EPOS
  so
  word
EPOURANIOS
  celestial
  heavenly
ERCHOMAI
  bring
  come
  enter
  fall
  go
  grow
  light (to . . . upon)
  next
  pass
  resort
ERAUNAŌ
(or EREU-)
  search
EREIDŌ
  stick fast
  strike
ERĒMIA
  desert
  place
  wilderness
ERĒMOŌ
  desolation
  desolate
  nought
ERĒMOS
  desert

ERĒMOS—contd.
  desolate
  solitary
  wilderness
ĒREMOS
  quiet
  tranquil
ERĒMŌSIS
  desolation
ERETHIZŌ
  anger
  provoke
  stir
EREUGOMAI
  utter
ERGASIA
  business
  craft
  diligence
  gain
  work
ERGATĒS
  labourer
  worker
  workman
ERGAZOMAI
  commit
  do
  gain
  labour
  minister
  trade
  work
  working
ERGON
  deed
  labour
  work
ERION
  wool
ERIPHION
  goat
ERIPHOS
  goat
  kid
ERIS
  contention
  debate
  strife
  variance
ERITH(E)IA
  contention
  contentious
  faction
  strife
ERIZŌ
  strive
ERŌ (see EIRŌ)
ERŌTAŌ
  ask
  beseech
  desire
  intreat
  pray
  request
ERUTHROS
  red
ESCHATOS
  end
  last
  lowest
  part
  uttermost
ESCHATŌS
  death

ESŌ
  inner
  inward
  within
ESOPTRON
  glass
  mirror
ESŌTEROS
  inner
  within
ESŌTHEN
  inside
  inward
  inwardly
  within
ESTHĒS
  apparel
  clothing
  raiment
  robe
ESTHĒSIS
  apparel
  garment
ESTHIŌ
  devour
  eat
  live
ETHELOTHRĒSK(E)IA
  worship
ETHIZŌ
  custom
ETHNARCHĒS
  governor
ETHNIKOS
  Gentile(s)
  heathen
ETHNIKŌS
  Gentiles
  manner
ETHNOS
  Gentiles
  heathen
  nation
  people
ETHŌ
  custom
  manner
  wont
ETHOS
  custom
  manner
  wont
ĒTHOS
  manner
ETI
  also
  even
  further
  longer
  more
  moreover
  still
  thenceforth
  yet
ETOS
  year
EU
  good
  well
EUANGELION
  gospel
EUANGELISTĒS
  evangelist
EUANGELIZŌ
  gospel
  preach

EUANGELIZŌ—contd.
shew
tidings

EUARESTEŌ
please
well-pleasing

EUARESTOS
acceptable
well-pleasing

EUARESTŌS
acceptably

EUCHARISTEŌ
thank
thankful

EUCHARISTIA
thanks
thankfulness
thanksgiving

EUCHARISTOS
thankful

EUCHĒ
prayer
vow

EUCHOMAI
pray
wish
would

EUCHRĒSTOS
profitable
use

EUDIA
fair
weather

EUDOKEŌ
please
pleasure
think
willing

EUDOKIA
desire
pleasure
seem
well-pleasing
will
willing

EUERGESIA
benefit
deed

EUERGETEŌ
good (to do)

EUERGETĒS
benefactor

EUGENĒS
noble
nobleman

EUGENESTEROS
noble

EUKAIREŌ
leisure
opportunity
spend
time

EUKAIRIA
opportunity

EUKAIROS
convenient
need

EUKAIRŌS
conveniently
season

EUKOPŌTEROS
easier

EULABEIA
fear
godly

EULABEIA—contd.
reverence

EULABEOMAI
fear
godly
moved

EULABĒS
devout

EULOGEŌ
bless
praise

EULOGĒTOS
blessed

EULOGIA
blessing
bounty
fair
speech

EUMETADOTOS
distribute

EUNOEŌ
agree

EUNOIA
benevolence
will

EUNOUCHIZŌ
eunuch

EUNOUCHOS
eunuch

EUŌDIA
savour
smell

EUODOŌ
journey
prosper

EUŌNUMOS
left

EUPAREDROS
attend

EUPEITHĒS
intreat

EUPERISTATOS
beset
easily

EUPHĒMIA
report

EUPHĒMOS
report

EUPHOREŌ
bring
plentifully

EUPHRAINŌ
fare
glad
merry
rejoice

EUPHROSUNĒ
gladness
joy

EUPOIEŌ
good (to do)

EUPOIIA
good

EUPOREŌ
ability

EUPORIA
wealth

EUPREPEIA
grace

EUPROSDEKTOS
acceptable
accepted

EUPROSEDROS
attend

EUPROSŌPEŌ
fair
show (make a)

EUPSUCHEŌ
comfort

EURUCHŌROS
broad

EUSCHĒMŌN
comely
estate
honourable

EUSCHĒMONŌS
decently
honestly

EUSCHĒMOSUNĒ
comeliness

EUSEBEIA
godliness
holiness

EUSEBEŌ
piety (to shew)
worship

EUSEBĒS
devout
godly

EUSEBŌS
godly

EUSĒMOS
understood

EUSPLANCHNOS
pitiful
tenderhearted

EUTHEŌS
forthwith
immediately
shortly
straightway

EUTHETOS
fit
meet

EUTHUDROMEŌ
course

EUTHUMEŌ
cheer
cheerful
merry

EUTHUMOS
cheer

EUTHUMŌS
cheerfully

EUTHUMOTERON
cheerfully

EUTHUNŌ
governor
straight
steersman

EUTHUS (adj.)
right
straight

EUTHUS (adv.)
anon
forthwith
immediately
straightway

EUTHUTĒS
righteousness
uprightness

EUTONŌS
mightily
powerfully
vehemently

EUTRAPELIA
jesting

EXAGŌ
bring

EXAGŌ—contd.
fetch
lead

EXAGORAZŌ
redeem

EXAIPHNĒS
suddenly

EXAIREŌ
deliver
pluck
rescue

EXAIRŌ
put
take

EXAITEŌ
ask
desire

EXAKOLOUTHEŌ
follow

EXALEIPHŌ
blot
wipe

EXALLOMAI
leap

EXANASTASIS
resurrection

EXANATELLŌ
spring

EXANGELLŌ
shew

EXANISTĒMI
raise (up)
rise
(see ARISE)

EXAPATAŌ
beguile
deceive

EXAPINA
suddenly

EXAPOREŌ
despair

EXAPOSTELLŌ
send

EXARTIZŌ
accomplish
furnish

EXASTRAPTŌ
dazzling
glister

EXAUTĒS
forthwith
immediately
presently
straightway

EXECHEŌ
sound

EXEGEIRŌ
raise (up)

EXĒGEOMAI
declare
rehearse
tell

EXEIMI
depart
get
go

EXELENCHŌ
convict

EXELKŌ
draw

EXERAMA
vomit

EXERAUNAŌ
search

EXERCHOMAI
come
depart
escape
get
go
proceed
spread

EXESTI
lawful
let
may

EXETAZŌ
ask
inquire
search

EXISCHUŌ
able

EXISTĒMI
amaze
beside oneself
bewitch
wonder

EXŌ
foreign
forth
outward
strange
without

EXOCHĒ
principal

EXODOS
decease
departure

EXOLOTHREUŌ
destroy

EXOMOLOGEŌ
confess
consent
praise
promise
thank

EXORKISTĒS
exorcist

EXORKIZŌ
adjure

EXORUSSŌ
break
pluck

EXŌTEROS
outer

EXŌTHEN
outside
outward
outwardly
without

EXŌTHEŌ
drive
thrust

EXOUDENOŌ
nought

EXOUSIA
authority
jurisdiction
liberty
power
right
strength

EXOUSIAZŌ
authority
exercise
power

EXOUTHENEŌ
account
contemptible
despise

EXOUTHENEŌ—contd.
esteem
least
nought

EXUPNIZŌ
awake
sleep

EXUPNOS
rouse
sleep

G

GALA
milk

GALĒNĒ
calm

GAMEŌ
marry

GAMISKŌ
marriage (give in)

GAMIZŌ
marriage (give in)

GAMOS
feast
marriage
marriage feast
wedding

GANGRAINA
canker
gangrene

GAR
doubt (no)
indeed
moreover
verily
what
why
yea
yet

GASTĒR
belly
glutton
womb

GAZA
treasure

GAZOPHULAKION
treasury

GE
yet

GĒ
country
earth
ground
land
world

GEENNA
hell

GEITŌN
neighbour

GELAŌ
laugh

GELŌS
laughter

GEMIZŌ
fill
full

GEMŌ
full
laden

GENEA
age
generation
nation

GENEA—contd.
time

GENEALOGEŌ
descent
genealogy

GENEALOGIA
genealogy

GENĒMA
fruit

GENESIA
birthday

GENESIS
generation
nature
natural

GENETĒ
birth

GENNAŌ
bear
beget
bring forth
conceive
deliver
gender
made (be)
spring

GENNĒMA
fruit
generation
offspring

GENNĒSIS
birth

GENNĒTOS
beget

GENOS
beget
country
countrymen
diversity
generation
kind
kindred
nation
offspring
stock

GEŌRGEŌ
dress
till

GEŌRGION
husbandry

GEŌRGOS
husbandman

GĒRAS
aged
old

GĒRASKŌ
aged
old

GERŌN
old

GEROUSIA
senate

GEUŌ
eat
taste

GINOMAI
arise
assemble
become
befall
behave
bring
come
continue
divide

GINOMAI—contd.
do
end
fall
far
finish
follow
forbid
grow
have
keep
marry
means (by . . . of)
ordain
pass
past
perform
place (take)
prefer
prove
publish
shew
sound
spent
spring
take
turn
use
was etc.
wax
work

GINŌSKŌ
allow
can
feel
know
knowledge
perceive
resolve
speak
sure
understand

GLEUKOS
wine

GLŌSSA
tongue

GLŌSSOKOMON
bag

GLUKUS
fresh
sweet

GNAPHEUS
fuller

GNĒSIOS
own
sincerity
true

GNĒSIŌS
naturally
truly

GNŌMĒ
advice
agree
judgment
mind
purpose
will

GNOPHOS
blackness

GNŌRIZŌ
certify
declare
know
understand
wit
wot

GNŌSIS
knowledge
science

GNŌSTĒS
expert

GNŌSTOS
acquaintance
known
notable

GOĒS
impostor
seducer

GOMOS
burden
merchandise

GONEUS
parents

GONGUSMOS
grudging
murmuring

GONGUSTĒS
murmurer

GONGUZŌ
murmur

GŌNIA
corner
quarter

GONU
knee
kneel

GONUPETEŌ
bow
kneel

GRAMMA
bill
learning
letter
scripture
writing

GRAMMATEUS
scribe
townclerk

GRAŌDĒS
old wives

GRAPHĒ
scripture

GRAPHŌ
describe
write
writing

GRAPTOS
written

GRĒGOREŌ
vigilant
wake
watch
watchful

GUMNASIA
exercise

GUMNAZŌ
exercise

GUMNITEUŌ
naked

GUMNOS
bare
naked

GUMNOTĒS
nakedness

GUNAIKARION
woman

GUNAIKEIOS
wife

GUNĒ
wife
woman

H

HADĒS
Hades
hell

HADROTĒS
abundance
bounty

HAGIASMOS
holiness
sanctification

HAGIAZO
beloved
hallow
holy
sanctify

HAGION
sanctuary

HAGIOS
holy
saint
sanctuary

HAGIŌSUNĒ
holiness

HAGIOTĒS
holiness

HAGNEIA
purity

HAGNISMOS
purification

HAGNIZŌ
purify

HAGNOS
chaste
clear
pure

HAGNŌS
sincerely

HAGNOTĒS
pureness
purity

HAIMA
blood

HAIMATEKCHUSIA
blood

HAIMORRHOEŌ
blood

HAIREŌ
choose

HAIRESIS
heresy
sect

HAIRETIKOS
heretical

HAIRETIZŌ
choose

HALIEUŌ
fish

HALIEUS
fisher
fisherman

HALIZŌ
salt

HALLĒLOUIA
Hallelujah

HALLOMAI
leap
spring

HALŌN
threshing-floor

HALŌSIS
take

HAL(A)S
salt

HALUKOS
salt

HALUSIS
bond
chain

HAMA
early
together
withal

HAMARTANŌ
fault
offend
sin
trespass

HAMARTĒMA
sin

HAMARTIA
offence
sin
sinful

HAMARTŌLOS
sinful
sinner

HAPALOS
tender

HAPAS
all
every
whole

HAPAX
once

HAPHĒ
joint

HAPLOUS
single

HAPLŌS
liberally

HAPLOTĒS
bountifulness
liberal
liberality
simplicity
singleness

HAPTŌ
handle
kindle
light
touch

HARMA
chariot

HARMOS
joint

HARMOZŌ
espouse

HARPAGĒ
extortion
ravening
spoiling

HARPAGMOS
prize
robbery

HARPAX
extortioner
ravening

HARPAZŌ
catch
force
pluck
pull
snatch
spoil
take

HEAUTOU (etc.)
herself
himself
his

his own
itself
one . . . another
our own
ourselves
own
their
them
themselves
thyself
yourselves
(see conceits)

HEBDOMĒKONTA
seventy
ten

HEBDOMĒKONTAKIS
seventy times

HEBDOMOS
seventh

HEBRAÏSTI (or EBR-)
tongue
(*in Hebrew*)
(*in the Hebrew*)

HĒDEŌS
gladly

HĒDISTA
gladly

HĒDONĒ
lust
pleasure

HEDRAIŌMA
ground

HEDRAIOS
settled
stedfast

HĒDUOSMON
mint

HĒGEMŌN
governor
prince
ruler

HĒGEMONEUŌ
governor

HĒGEMONIA
reign

HĒGEOMAI
account
chief
count
esteem
governor
judge
rule
suppose
think

HEILISSŌ (or HEL-)
fold
roll

HEIS
first
one
only
other

HEKASTOS
each
every

HEKASTOTE
always
time

HEKATON
hundred
hundredfold

HEKATONTAETĒS
year

HEKATONTAPLASIŌN
hundredfold

HEKATONTARCHĒS centurion **HEKATONTARCHOS** centurion **HĒKŌ** come **HEKŌN** will willingly **HEKOUSIOS** will willingly **HEKOUSIŌS** wilfully willingly **HEKTOS** sixth **HĒLIKIA** age stature **HĒLIKOS** great **HĒLIOS** sun **HELKŌ** drag draw **HELKOŌ** sore **HELKOS** sore **HELKUŌ** drag draw **HELLĒN** Gentiles **HĒLOS** nail **HĒMEIS (etc.)** company our ourselves us we **HĒMERA** age daily day ever judgment time year **HĒMETEROS** our ours **HĒMIŌRON** hour **HĒMISUS** half **HĒMITHANĒS** (half) dead **HENDEKA** eleven **HENDEKATOS** eleventh **HENEKA** cause **HENOTĒS** unity **HEORTAZŌ** feast **HEORTĒ** feast holy day	**HEŌS** far much (as) **HEPTA** seven seventh **HEPTAKIS** seven times **HEPTAKISCHILIOI** seven thousand **HERMĒNEIA** interpretation **HERMĒNEUŌ** interpret interpretation **HERPETON** creeping serpent **HESPERA** evening eventide **HESPERINOS** evening **HĒSSŌN** (see HĒTTŌN) **HĒSUCHAZŌ** cease peace (hold one's) quiet rest **HĒSUCHIA** quietness silence **HĒSUCHIOS** peaceable quiet **HETAIROS** fellow friend **HETERODIDASKALEŌ** teach **HETEROGLŌSSOS** strange tongue **HETEROS** another neighbour next day other strange stranger **HETERŌS** otherwise **HETEROZUGEŌ** another yoke **HETOIMASIA** preparation **HETOIMAZŌ** hold prepare provide ready **HETOIMOS** prepared readiness ready **HETOIMŌS** ready **HĒTTAOMAI** inferior overcome **HĒTTĒMA** defect	**HĒTTĒMA**—*contd.* diminishing fault loss **HĒTTŌN** less worse **HEURISKŌ** find get obtain perceive **HEX** six **HEXAKOSIOI** six hundred **HEXĒKONTA** sixty sixtyfold **HEXĒS** afterwards follow morrow next **HEXIS** use **HIDRŌS** sweat **HIERATEIA** office priesthood priest's office **HIERATEUMA** priesthood **HIERATEUŌ** execute office priest's office **HIERATIKOS** priest **HIEREUS** priest **HIERON** temple **HIEROPREPĒS** become holiness reverent **HIEROS** holy sacred **HIEROSULEŌ** commit sacrilege **HIEROSULOS** robber **HIERŌSUNĒ** priesthood **HIEROURGEŌ** minister **HIKANOŌ** able meet sufficient **HIKANOS** able content enough good great large long many meet much	**HIKANOS**—*contd.* security sore sufficient worthy **HIKANOTĒS** sufficiency **HIKETĒRIA** supplication **HILAROS** cheerful **HILAROTĒS** cheerfulness **HILASKOMAI** merciful propitiation reconciliation **HILASMOS** propitiation **HILASTĒRION** mercy-seat propitiation **HILEŌS** far merciful **HIMAS** latchet thong **HIMATION** apparel clothes garment raiment robe vesture **HIMATISMOS** apparel array clothing raiment vesture **HIMATIZŌ** clothe **HIMEIROMAI** affection desire **HINA** albeit end intent lest must wherefore **HIPPEUS** horsemen **HIPPIKOS** horsemen **HIPPOS** horse **HISTĒMI** abide appoint bring charge continue covenant establish holden present set stand stanch weigh **HISTOREŌ** see visit

HO (1)
one (the)
this

HO (2)
which

HODE (TODE)
manner
these
thus

HŌDE
here
hither
place
there

HODĒGEŌ
guide
lead

HODĒGOS
guide
leader

HODEUŌ
journey

HODOIPOREŌ
go
journey

HODOIPORIA
journey
journeyings

HODOS
highway
highwayside
journey
way

HOIOS
manner
such as
what
which

HOLOKAUTŌMA
burnt (offering)
offering

HOLOKLĒRIA
soundness

HOLOKLĒROS
entire
whole

HOLOS
all
altogether
every whit
whole

HOLŌS
actually
all
altogether
commonly
utterly

HOLOTELĒS
wholly

HOMEIROMAI
(see HIMEIROMAI)

HOMICHLĒ
mist

HOMILEŌ
commune
talk

HOMILIA
communication
company

HOMILOS
company

HOMOIAZŌ
agree

HOMOIŌMA
like (made)

HOMOIŌMA—contd.
likeness
shape
similitude

HOMOIOŌ
like (make)
liken
resemble

HOMOIOPATHĒS
passions

HOMOIOS
like

HOMOIŌS
likewise
manner
so

HOMOIŌSIS
likeness
similitude

HOMOIOTĒS
like as
similitude

HOMOLOGEŌ
acknowledge
confess
profess
promise
thanks
vouchsafe

HOMOLOGIA
confession
profession
professed

HOMOLOGOUMENŌS
controversy (without)

HOMOPHRŌN
likeminded
mind
one

HOMŌS
even
yet

HOMOTECHNOS
craft
trade

HOMOTHUMADON
accord
mind

HOMOU
accord
together

HOPLIZŌ
arm

HOPLON
armour
instruments
weapons

HOPOIOS
manner
sort
such as
what

HŌRA
day
hour
instant
season
short
time

HŌRAIOS
beautiful

HORAMA
sight
vision

HORAŌ (with EIDON and OPTOMAI)
appear
behold
consider
heed (take)
look
look (to)
perceive
see
shew

HORASIS
look
sight
vision

HORATOS
visible

HORION
border
coast

HORIZŌ
declare
define
determine
determinate
limit
ordain

HORKIZŌ
adjure
charge

HORKŌMOSIA
oath

HORKOS
oath

HORMAŌ
run
rush
violently

HORMĒ
assault
impulse

HORMĒMA
violence

HOROTHESIA
bound

HOS
he that
one . . . another
what
whatsoever
which
who
whosoever

HŌS
about
even as
like
wit (to)
while

HOSAKIS
oft
often

HŌSANNA
Hosanna

HŌSAUTŌS
even so
likewise
manner
so

HŌSEI
about
like

HOSGE
he that

HOSIOS
blessing
holy
mercy

HOSIŌS
holily

HOSIOTĒS
holiness

HOSOS
all
great
long
many
more
much (as)
what
whatsoever
which
who
whosoever

HOSPER
whosoever

HŌSPER
even as
like as

HŌSTE
insomuch that, as
wherefore

HOSTIS
he that
such as
they
what
which
who
whosoever

HOTAN
while

HOTHEN
thence (from)
wherefore

HOUTOS
fellow
he
one
same
she
so
that
their
them
they
this
which
who

HOUTŌ (-S)
even so
fashion
like
likewise
manner
so
thus
what

HUAKINTHINOS
jacinth

HUAKINTHOS
jacinth

HUALINOS
glass

HUALOS
glass

HUBRIS
harm
hurt

HUBRIS—*contd.*
  reproach
HUBRISTĒS
  despiteful
  injurious
  insolent
HUBRIZŌ
  despitefully
  entreat
  reproach
  shamefully
  spitefully
HUDŌR
  water
HUDRIA
  waterpot
HUDRŌPIKOS
  dropsy
HUDROPOTEŌ
  drink
  water
HUETOS
  rain
HUGIAINŌ
  health
  safe
  sound (be)
  sound
  whole
  wholesome
HUGIĒS
  sound
  whole
HUGROS
  green
HUIOS
  child
  foal
  son
HUIOTHESIA
  adoption
HULĒ
  matter
  wood
HUMEIS
  ye
  you
  your
HUMETEROS
  your
  yours
HUMNEŌ
  hymn
  praise
  sing
HUMNOS
  hymn
HUPAGŌ
  depart
  get
  go
HUPAKOĒ
  obedience
  obedient
  obey
HUPAKOUŌ
  answer
  hearken
  obedient
  obey
HUPANDROS
  husband
HUPANTAŌ
  meet

HUPANTĒSIS
  meet
HUPARCHŌ
  exist
  goods
  have
  live
  possess
  was (etc.)
HUPARCHONTA
  substance
HUPARXIS
  goods
  possession
  substance
HUPECHŌ
  suffer
HUPEIKŌ
  submit
HUPĒKOOS
  obedient
HUPENANTIOS
  adversary
  contrary
HUPER
  behalf
  more
  of
  part
HUPERAIRŌ
  exalt
  overmuch
HUPERAKMOS
  age
  flower
  pass
HUPERAUXANŌ
  grow
HUPERBAINŌ
  go
  transgress
HUPERBALLŌ
  exceed
  excel
  pass
  surpass
HUPERBALLONTŌS
  measure
HUPERBOLĒ
  abundance
  exceeding
  excel
  excellency
  excellent
  greatness
  measure
HUPERECHŌ
  better
  excellency
  higher
  pass
  supreme
HUPEREIDON
  overlook
  wink
HUPEREKCHU(N)NŌ
  run
HUPEREKEINA
  beyond
HUPEREKPERISSOU
  abundantly
  exceeding
  exceedingly
HUPEREKTEINŌ
  measure

HUPEREKTEINŌ—*contd.*
  overmuch
  stretch
HUPERENTUNCHANŌ
  intercession
HUPERĒPHANIA
  pride
HUPERĒPHANOS
  haughty
  proud
HUPĒRETEŌ
  minister
  serve
HUPĒRETĒS
  attendant
  minister
  officer
  servant
HUPERLIAN
  chiefest
HUPERNIKAŌ
  conquer
HUPEROCHĒ
  authority
  excellency
  place
HUPERONKOS
  swelling
HUPERŌON
  chamber
  room
HUPERPERISSEUŌ
  abound
  joyful
  overflow
HUPERPERISSŌS
  measure
HUPERPHRONEŌ
  think
HUPERPLEONAZŌ
  abundant
HUPERUPSOŌ
  exalt
HUPHANTOS
  woven
HUPNOS
  sleep
HUPO
  under
HUPOBALLŌ
  suborn
HUPOCHŌREŌ
  go
  withdraw
HUPODECHOMAI
  receive
HUPODEIGMA
  copy
  ensample
  example
  pattern
HUPODEIKNUMI
  example
  forewarn
  shew
  warn
HUPODĒMA
  shoe
HUPODEŌ
  bind
  shod
HUPODIKOS
  guilty
  judgment

HUPOGRAMMOS
  copy
  example
HUPOKATŌ
  under
  underneath
HUPOKRINOMAI
  feign
HUPOKRISIS
  dissimulation
  hypocrisy
HUPOKRITĒS
  hypocrite
HUPOLAMBANŌ
  answer
  receive
  suppose
  welcome
HUPOLEIMMA
  remnant
HUPOLEIPŌ
  leave
HUPOLĒNION
  wine-fat
  pit
HUPOLIMPANŌ
  leave
HUPOMENŌ
  abide
  behind
  endure
  patient
  patiently
  suffer
  take
  tarry
HUPOMIMNĒSKŌ
  mind
  remember
  remembrance
HUPOMNĒSIS
  remembrance
HUPOMONĒ
  continuance
  enduring
  patience
  patient
  wait
HUPONOEŌ
  deem
  suppose
  surmise
  think
HUPONOIA
  surmising
HUPOPHERŌ
  bear
  endure
HUPŌPIAZŌ
  buffet
  wear
  weary
HUPOPLEŌ
  lee
  sail
HUPOPNEŌ
  blow
HUPOPODION
  footstool
HUPOSTASIS
  assurance
  confidence
  person
  substance

HUP

HUPOSTELLŌ
draw (back)
keep
shrink
shun
withdraw

HUPOSTOLĒ
draw (back)

HUPOSTREPHŌ
come
return
turn

HUPOSTRŌNNUŌ
spread

HUPOTAGĒ
obedience
subjection

HUPOTASSŌ
obedience
obedient
put
subdue
subject
subjection

HUPOTITHĒMI
lay
remembrance

HUPOTRECHŌ
lee
run

HUPOTUPŌSIS
ensample
form
pattern

HUPOZŌNNUMI
undergird

HUPOZUGION
ass

HUPSĒLOPHRONEŌ
high-minded

HUPSĒLOS
high
highly

HUPSISTOS
high
highest

HUPSŌMA
height
high

HUPSOŌ
exalt
lift

HUPSOS
estate
height
high

HUS
sow

HUSSŌPOS
hyssop

HUSTERĒMA
behind
lacking
penury
want

HUSTEREŌ
behind
come
destitute
fail
fall
lack
need
short (come)
want
worse

HUSTERĒSIS
want

HUSTERON
afterward(-s)
last

HUSTEROS
later
latter

I

IAMA
healing

IAOMAI
heal
whole

IASIS
cure
heal
healing

IASPIS
jasper

IATROS
physician

ICHNOS
step

ICHTHUDION
fish

ICHTHUS
fish

IDE : IDOU
behold
lo
see

IDEA (*see* EIDEA)

IDIOS
acquaintance
alone
business
company
due
his
his own
home
our own
own
private(-ly)
proper
several
severally
their

IDIŌTĒS
ignorant
rude
unlearned

IĒSOUS
Jesus

IKMAS
moisture

IOS
poison
rust

IŌTA
jot

IOUDAÏKOS
Jewish

IOUDAÏKŌS
Jew (as do the)

IOUDAIOS
Jew(s)
Jewess
Jewish
Jewry

IOUDAÏSMOS
Jews' religion

IOUDAÏZŌ
Jews (live as do the)

IRIS
rainbow

ISANGELOS
angel

ISCHUŌ
able
avail
can
do
good
may
might
prevail
strength
whole
work

ISCHUROS
boisterous
mighty
powerful
strong
valiant

ISCHUROTEROS
mightier
stronger

ISCHUS
ability
might
power
strength

ISOPSUCHOS
likeminded

ISOS
agree
equal
like
much (as)

ISŌS
may

ISOTĒS
equal
equality

ISOTIMOS
precious

K

KAI
also
even
indeed
likewise
manner
moreover
very
yea
yet

KAIGE
(at) least

KAINOS
new

KAINOTĒS
newness

KAIŌ
burn
light

KAIPER
yet

KAIROS
always
opportunity
season
time
while

KAL

KAKIA
evil
malice
maliciousness
naughtiness
wickedness

KAKOĒTHEIA
malignity

KAKOLOGEŌ
curse
evil
speak

KAKOŌ
affect
afflict
entreat
evil
harm
hurt
vex

KAKOPATHEIA
affliction
suffering

KAKOPATHEŌ
afflict
endure
hardship
suffer

KAKOPOIEŌ
evil
harm

KAKOPOIOS
evil-doer
malefactor

KAKOS
bad
evil
harm
ill
miserable
noisome
wicked

KAKŌS
amiss
diseased
evil
grievously
miserably
sick
sore

KAKŌSIS
affliction

KAKOUCHEŌ
afflict
entreat
evil
suffer
torment

KAKOURGOS
evil-doer
malefactor

KALAMĒ
stubble

KALAMOS
pen
reed

KALEŌ
bid
call
name
surname

KALLIELAIOS
olive tree

KALLION
well

KALODIDASKALOS
teacher
KALOPOIEŌ
well-doing
KALOS
better
fair
good
goodly
honest
honourable
meet .
seemly
worthy
KALŌS
good
honestly
place
well
KALUMMA
veil
KALUPTŌ
cover
hide
KAMĒLOS
camel
KAMINOS
furnace
KAMMUŌ
close
KAMNŌ
faint
sick
weary
KAMPTŌ
bow
KANŌN
line
province
rule
KAPĒLEUŌ
corrupt
KAPNOS
smoke
KARDIA
heart
KARDIOGNŌSTĒS
heart (knowing the)
knowing
KARPHOS
mote
KARPOPHOROS
fruitful
KARPOPHOREŌ
bear
fruit
fruitful
KARPOS
fruit
KARTEREŌ
endure
KATA
every
happen
manner
out of
pertain to
points
respect
was
KATABAINŌ
come
descend
fall
get
go

KATABAINŌ—*contd.*
step
KATABALLŌ
cast
lay
smite
KATABAREŌ
burden
KATABASIS
descent
KATABIBAZŌ
bring
thrust
KATABOLĒ
conceive
foundation
KATABRABEUŌ
beguile
prize
reward
rob
KATACHEŌ
pour
KATACHRAOMAI
abuse
KATACHTHONIOS
earth
KATADĒLOS
evident
KATADEŌ
bind
KATADIKAZŌ
condemn
KATADIKĒ
judgment
sentence
KATADIŌKŌ
follow
KATADOULOŌ
bondage
KATADUNASTEUŌ
oppress
KATAGELAŌ
laugh to scorn
KATAGINŌSKŌ
blame
condemn
KATAGNUMI
break
KATAGŌ
bring
land
touch
KATAGŌNIZOMAI
subdue
KATAISCHUNŌ
ashamed
confound
dishonour
shame
KATAKAIŌ
burn
KATAKALUPTŌ
cover
KATAKAUCHAOMAI
boast
glory
rejoice
KATAKEIMAI
keep
lie
sit
KATAKLAŌ
break

KATAKLEIŌ
shut
KATAKLĒRODOTEŌ
divide
KATAKLINŌ
meat
sit
KATAKLUSMOS
flood
KATAKLUZŌ
overflow
KATAKOLOUTHEŌ
follow
KATAKOPTŌ
cut
KATAKRĒMNIZŌ
cast
headlong
throw
KATAKRIMA
condemnation
KATAKRINŌ
condemn
KATAKRISIS
condemn
condemnation
KATAKURIEUŌ
dominion
exercise
lord
master
overcome
KATALALEŌ
speak
KATALALIA
backbiting
evil speaking
KATALALOS
backbiter
KATALAMBANŌ
apprehend
attain
come
find
obtain
overtake
perceive
take
KATALEGŌ
enrol
number
KATALEIMMA
remnant
KATALEIPŌ
behind
forsake
leave
reserve
KATALITHAZŌ
stone
KATALLAGĒ
atonement
reconciliation
KATALLASSŌ
reconcile
KATALOIPOS
residue
KATALUMA
guest-chamber
inn
KATALUŌ
come
destroy
dissolve
guest

KATALUŌ—*contd.*
lodge
nought
overthrow
throw
KATAMANTHANŌ
consider
KATAMARTUREŌ
witness
KATAMENŌ
abide
KATA MONAS
alone
KATANALISKŌ
consume
KATANARKAŌ
burdensome
chargeable
KAT(AN)ATHEMA
curse
KATANATHEMATIZŌ
curse
KATANEUŌ
beckon
KATANGELEUS
setter forth
KATANGELLŌ
declare
preach
proclaim
set
shew
teach
KATANOEŌ
behold
consider
discover
perceive
KATANTAŌ
arrive
attain
come
reach
KATANUSSŌ
prick
KATANUXIS
stupor
KATAPATEO
foot
trample
tread
KATAPAUŌ
cease
rest
restrain
KATAPAUSIS
rest
KATAPETASMA
veil
KATAPHAGŌ
devour
eat
KATAPHERŌ
bear down
fall
give
sink
KATAPHEUGŌ
flee
KATAPHILEŌ
kiss
KATAPHRONEŌ
despise
KATAPHRONĒTĒS
despiser

KATAPHTHEIRŌ
corrupt

KATAPINŌ
devour
drown
swallow

KATAPIPTŌ
fall

KATAPLEŌ
arrive

KATAPONEŌ
distress
oppress
vex

KATAPONTIZŌ
drown
sink

KATAPSUCHŌ
cool

KATARA
curse
cursing

KATARAOMAI
curse

KATARGEŌ
abolish
cease
cumber
destroy
do
effect
fail
loose
nought
pass
put
sever
vanish
void

KATARITHMEŌ
number

KATARTISIS
perfection

KATARTISMOS
perfecting

KATARTIZŌ
fit
frame
join
mend
perfect
prepare
restore

KATASCHESIS
possession

KATASEIŌ
beckon

KATASKAPTŌ
dig
overthrow
ruin

KATASKĒNOŌ
dwell
lodge
rest

KATASKĒNŌSIS
nest

KATASKEUAZŌ
build
make
ordain
prepare

KATASKIAZŌ
overshadow

KATASKOPEŌ
spy

KATASKOPOS
spy

KATASOPHIZOMAI
deal with
subtilly

KATASPHAZŌ
slay

KATASPHRAGIZŌ
seal

KATASTELLŌ
appease
quiet

KATASTĒMA
behaviour
demeanour

KATASTOLĒ
apparel
clothing

KATASTREPHŌ
dig
overthrow
ruin

KATASTRĒNIAŌ
wanton

KATASTRŌNNUMI
overthrow

KATASTROPHĒ
overthrow
subverting

KATASURŌ
hale

KATATITHĒMI
do
gain
lay
shew

KATATOMĒ
concision

KATATOXEUŌ
thrust

KATATRECHŌ
run

KATAXIOŌ
account
count
worthy

KATĒCHEŌ
inform
instruct
teach

KATECHŌ
have
hold
keep
make
possess
restrain
retain
seize
stay
take
withhold

KATĒGOREŌ
accuse
witness

KATĒGORIA
accusation

KATĒGOROS
accuser

KATEIDŌLOS
idols (full of)

KATENANTI
before
sight of (in the)

KATENŌPION
before
presence
sight of (in the)

KATĒPHEIA
heaviness

KATEPHISTEMI
insurrection
rise

KATERCHOMAI
come
depart
descend
go
land

KATERGAZOMAI
cause
do
perform
work

KATESTHIŌ
devour
eat

KATESTRAMMENA
ruin

KATEUTHUNŌ
direct
guide

KATEXOUSIAZŌ
authority
exercise

KATHAIREŌ
cast
depose
destroy
pull (down)
put
take

KATHAIRESIS
cast
destruction
pull

KATHAIRŌ
clean
purge

KATHAPER
even as

KATHAPTŌ
fasten

KATHARISMOS
cleansing
purge
purfiication
purifying

KATHARIZŌ
clean
cleanse
purge
purify

KATHAROS
clean
clear
pure

KATHAROTĒS
cleanness
purifying

KATHEDRA
seat

KATHĒGĒTĒS
master

KATHĒKŌ
convenient
fit
fitting

KATHĒMAI
dwell

KATHEMAI—*contd.*
seat
set
sit

KATHĒMERINOS
daily

KATHEUDŌ
asleep

KATHEXĒS
afterward
follow
order

KATHEZOMAI
sit

KATHIĒMI
let down

KATHISTĒMI
appoint
conduct
make
ordain
ruler
set

KATHIZŌ
continue
dwell
set
sit
tarry

KATHO
according as
inasmuch as
insomuch as

KATHOLOU
all

KATHOPLIZŌ
arm

KATHORAŌ
see

KATHŌS
according as
even as

KATHOTI
according as
inasmuch as

KATIOŌ
rust

KATISCHUŌ
prevail

KATŌ
beneath
bottom

KATOIKEŌ
dwell
dweller

KATOIKĒSIS
dwelling

KATOIKĒTĒRION
habitation

KATOIKIA
habitation

KATOIKIZŌ
dwell

KATOPTRIZŌ
behold
mirror

KATORTHŌMA
correction
deed

KATŌTERŌ
under

KATŌTEROS
lower

KAUCHAOMAI
boast
glory
joy
rejoice

KAUCHEMA
boasting
glory
glorying
rejoice

KAUCHESIS
boasting
glory
glorying
rejoice

KAUMA
heat

KAUMATIZŌ
scorch

KAUSIS
burning

KAUSŌN
burning
heat
scorching

KAUSOŌ
heat

KAUSTĒRIAZŌ
(or KAUTĒR—)
branded

KEIMAI
appoint
lay
lie
made (be)
set
there

KEIRIA
grave-clothes

KEIRŌ
shear
shearer

KELEUŌ
bid
command

KELEUSMA
shout

KENODOXIA
vainglory

KENODOXOS
vainglory

KENOŌ
effect (of none)
empty
reputation
vain
void

KENOPHŌNIA
babblings

KENOS
empty
vain

KENŌS
vain (in)

KĒNSOS
tribute

KENTRON
goad

KENTURIŌN
centurion

KEPHALAION
chief
point
sum

KEPHAL(A)IOŌ
head (to wound in the)

KEPHALĒ
head

KEPHALIS
roll

KĒPOS
garden

KĒPOUROS
gardener

KERAIA (KEREA)
tittle

KERAMEUS
potter

KERAMIKOS
potter

KERAMION
pitcher

KERAMOS
tiling

KERANNUMI
fill
mingle

KERAS
horn

KERATION
husks

KERDAINŌ
gain
get

KERDOS
gain
lucre

KĒRION
honey-comb

KERMA
money

KERMATISTĒS
changer

KĒRUGMA
message
preaching

KĒRUSSŌ
preach
preacher
preaching
proclaim
publish

KĒRUX
preacher

KĒTOS
whale

KIBŌTOS
ark

KICHRĒMI (or CHRAŌ)
lend

KINDUNEUŌ
danger

KINDUNOS
peril

KINEŌ
move
mover
remove
wag

KINĒSIS
moving

KINNAMŌMON
cinnamon

KITHARA
harp

KITHARIZŌ
harp

KITHARŌDOS
harper

KLADOS
branch

KLAIŌ
bewail
weep

KLAŌ (KLAZŌ)
break

KLASIS
breaking

KLASMA
break
meat
piece

KLAUTHMOS
wailing
weeping

KLEIŌ
shut

KLEIS
key

KLĒMA
branch

KLEMMA
theft

KLEOS
glory

KLEPTĒS
thief

KLEPTŌ
steal

KLĒRONOMEŌ
heir
inherit

KLĒRONOMIA
inheritance

KLĒRONOMOS
heir

KLĒROŌ
heritage
inheritance

KLĒROS
charge
inheritance
lot
part
portion

KLĒSIS
call
calling

KLĒTOS
called

KLIBANOS
oven

KLIMA
part
region

KLINARION
bed

KLINĒ
bed
table

KLINIDION
couch

KLINŌ
bow
flight
lay
spent
wear

KLISIA
company

KLOPĒ
theft

KLUDŌN
raging
wave

KLUDŌNIZOMAI
toss

KNĒTHŌ
itching

KODRANTĒS
farthing

KOILIA
belly
womb

KOIMAŌ (-OMAI)
asleep
dead (to be: see DIE)
fall

KOIMĒSIS
rest

KOINŌNEŌ
communicate
distribute
fellowship
partake
partaker

KOINŌNIA
communication
communion
contribution
distribution
fellowship

KOINŌNIKOS
communicate

KOINŌNOS
companion
fellowship
partaker
partner

KOINOŌ
call
common
defile
unclean

KOINOS
common
defiled
unclean
unholy

KOITĒ
bed
chambering

KOITŌN
chamberlain

KOKKINOS
scarlet

KOKKOS
corn
grain

KOLAK(E)IA
flattery
flattering

KOLAPHIZŌ
buffet

KOLASIS
punishment
torment

KOLAZŌ
punish

KOLLAŌ
cleave
company

KOLLAŌ—*contd.*
 join
KOLLOURION
 eye-salve
KOLLUBISTĒS
 changer
KOLOBOŌ
 shorten
KŌLON
 carcase
KOLŌNIA
 colony
KOLPOS
 bay
 bosom
KOLUMBAŌ
 swim
KOLUMBĒTHRA
 pool
KŌLUŌ
 forbid
 hinder
 keep
 stay
 suffer
 withhold
 withstand
KOMAŌ
 hair
KOMĒ
 hair
KŌMĒ
 town
 village
KOMIZŌ
 bring
 receive
KŌMOPOLIS
 town
KŌMOS
 revelling
 rioting
KOMPSOTERON
 amend
KONIAŌ
 white
KONIORTOS
 dust
KOPAZŌ
 cease
KŌNŌPS
 gnat
KOPĒ
 slaughter
KOPETOS
 bewail
KOPHINOS
 basket
 basketful
KŌPHOS
 deaf
 dumb
 speechless
KOPIAŌ
 bestow
 labour
 toil
 weary
KOPOS
 labour
 toil
 trouble
 weariness

KOPRIA
 dung
 dunghill
KOPRION
 dung
KOPTŌ
 bewail
 cut
 mourn
 wail
KORASION
 damsel
 maid
KORAX
 raven
KORBAN
 Corban
KORBANAS
 treasury
KORENNUMI
 eat
 enough
 fill
KOROS
 measure
KOSMEŌ
 adorn
 garnish
 trim
KOSMIKOS
 worldly
KOSMIOS
 behaviour
 modest
 orderly
KOSMOKRATŌR
 ruler
KOSMOS
 adorning
 world
KOUM (I)
 talitha
KOUPHIZŌ
 lighten
KOUSTŌDIA
 guard
 watch
KRABBATOS
 bed
 couch
KRAIPALĒ
 surfeiting
KRANION
 Calvary
 skull
KRASPEDON
 border
KRATAIOŌ
 strengthen
 strong
KRATAIOS
 mighty
KRATEŌ
 hands on (lay)
 hold
 holden
 keep
 obtain
 retain
 take
KRATISTOS
 excellent
 noble

KRATOS
 dominion
 power
 strength
KRAUGAZŌ
 cry
KRAUGE
 clamour
 cry
 crying
KRAZŌ
 cry
KREAS
 flesh
KREISSŌN (or -TT-)
 better
KREMANNUMI
 hang
 steep
KRĒMNOS
 steep
KRIMA
 condemnation
 judgment
 sentence
KRINŌ
 call
 conclude
 condemn
 decree
 determine
 esteem
 judge
 judgment
 law
 ordain
 sentence
 think
KRINON
 lily
KRISIS
 accusation
 condemnation
 judgment
KRITĒRION
 judge
 judgment
 judgment-seat
KRITĒS
 judge
KRITHĒ
 barley
KRITHINOS
 barley
KRITIKOS
 discerner
KROUŌ
 knock
KRUPHAIOS
 secret
KRUPHĒ
 secret
KRUPTĒ
 cellar
KRUPTŌ
 hide
 secretly
KRUPTOS
 hid
 hidden
 inwardly
 secret
KRUSTALLIZŌ
 clear

KRUSTALLIZŌ—*contd.*
 crystal
KRUSTALLOS
 crystal
KTAOMAI
 get
 obtain
 possess
 provide
 purchase
 win
KTĒMA
 possession
KTĒNOS
 beast
 cattle
KTĒTŌR
 possessor
KTISIS
 building
 creation
 creature
 ordinance
KTISMA
 creature
KTISTĒS
 Creator
KTIZŌ
 create
 Creator
 make
KUBEIA or -BIA
 sleight
KUBERNĒSIS
 government
KUBERNĒTĒS
 master
KUKLEUŌ
 compass
KUKLOŌ
 come
 compass
 stand
KUKLŌ
 about
 round about
KUKLOTHEN
 about
 round about
KULIŌ
 wallow
KULISMOS
 wallowing
KULLOS
 maimed
KUMA
 wave
KUMBALON
 cymbal
KUMINON
 cummin
KUNARION
 dog
KUŌN
 dog
KUPTŌ
 stoop
KURIA
 lady
KURIAKOS
 Lord
KURIEUŌ
 dominion

KURIEUŌ—*contd.*
exercise
lord
lordship
KURIOS
lord
master
owner
sir
KURIOTĒS
dominion
government
KUROŌ
confirm

L

LACHANON
herb
LAILAPS
storm
tempest
LAKEŌ or **LASKŌ**
burst
LAKTIZŌ
kick
LALEŌ
preach
say
speak
talk
tell
utter
LALIA
saying
speech
LAMA
lama
LAMBANŌ
accept
attain
bring
call
catch
find
have
hold
obtain
receive
take
LAMPAS
lamp
light
torch
LAMPŌ
light
shine
LAMPROS
bright
clear
fine
gay
goodly
gorgeous
sumptuous
white
LAMPRŌS
sumptuously
LAMPROTĒS
brightness
LANCHANŌ
lot
obtain
receive
LANTHANŌ
forget

LANTHANŌ—*contd.*
hide
ignorant
unawares
LAOS
people
LARUNX
throat
LATHRA
privily
secretly
LATOMEŌ
hew
LATREIA
divine
service
LATREUŌ
serve
service
worship
LAXEUTOS
hewn
LEGEŌN or **LEGIŌN**
legion
LEGŌ
ask
bid
boast
call
describe
give
mean
name
pronounce
put
reckon
say
speak
tell
utter
LEIMMA
remnant
LEIOS
smooth
LEIPŌ
destitute
lack
want
LEITOURGEŌ
minister
LEITOURGIA
ministration
ministry
service
LEITOURGIKOS
ministering
LEITOURGOS
minister
LĒ(M)PSIS
receiving
LĒNOS
wine-press
LENTION
towel
LEŌN
lion
LEPIS
scale
LEPRA
leprosy
LEPROS
leper
LEPTON
mite

LĒROS
talk
LĒSTĒS
robber
thief
LĒTHĒ
forget
LEUKAINŌ
white
LEUKOS
very
LIAN
exceeding
greatly
sore
while
LIBANOS
frankincense
LIBANŌTOS
censer
LIKMAŌ
dust
grind
scatter
LIMĒN
haven
LIMNĒ
lake
LIMOS
famine
hunger
LINON
flax
linen
LIPAROS
dainty
LIPS
north-east
south-west
LITHAZŌ
stone
LITHINOS
stone
LITHOBOLEŌ
stone
LITHOS
stone
LITHOSTRŌTOS
pavement
LĪTRA
pound
LOGIA
collection
gathering
LOGIKOS
milk
reasonable
spiritual
word
LOGION
oracle
LOGIOS
eloquent
LOGISMOS
imagination
thought
LOGIZOMAI
account
charge
conclude
count
esteem
impute
number

LOGIZOMAI—*contd.*
reason
reckon
suppose
think
LOGOMACHEŌ
strive
LOGOMACHIA
dispute
strife
LOGOS
account
cause
communication
do
doctrine
fame
intent
matter
mouth
preaching
question
reason
reckon
report
rumour
saying
show
speech
talk
thing
tidings
treatise
utterance
word
work
LOIDOREŌ
revile
LOIDORIA
railing
reproachfully
reviling
LOIDOROS
railer
reviler
LOIMOS
fellow
pestilence
pestilent fellow
LOIPON
besides
finally
furthermore
henceforth
moreover
now
then
LOIPOS
other
remain
remnant
residue
rest (the)
LONCHĒ
spear
LOUŌ
bathed
wash
LOUTRON
washing
LUCHNIA
lampstand
LUCHNOS
lamp
light
LUKOS
wolf

LUMAINŌ (-OMAI)
havock
lay waste
waste

LUŌ
break
destroy
dissolve
loose
melt
put
unloose

LUPĒ
grief
grievous
grudingly
heaviness
sorrow

LUPEŌ
grief
grieve
heaviness
sorrow
sorrowful
sorry

LUSIS
loose

LUSITELEŌ
better (be)

LUTRON
ransom

LUTROŌ
redeem

LUTRŌSIS
redeem
redemption

LUTRŌTĒS
deliverer

M

MACHAIRA
sword

MACHĒ
fighting
strife

MACHOMAI
fight
strive

MAG(E)IA
sorcery

MAGEUŌ
sorcery

MAGOS
sorcerer
wise

MAINOMAI
beside oneself
mad

MAKARIOS
blessed
happy

MAKARISMOS
blessedness
blessing
gratulation

MAKARIZŌ
bless
happy

MAKELLON
shambles

MAKRAN
afar
far
hence
way

MAKROCHRONIOS
live long

MAKROS
far
long

MAKROTHEN
afar
far

MAKROTHUMEŌ
bear
endure
longsuffering
patient
patience
suffer

MAKROTHUMIA
longsuffering
patience

MAKROTHUMŌS
patiently

MALAKIA
disease

MALAKOS
effeminate

MALISTA
chiefly
especially
most

MALLON
more
rather

MAMMĒ
grandmother

**MAMŌNAS
(or MAMMON-)**
mammon

MANIA
mad
madness

MANNA
manna

MANTEUOMAI
soothsaying

MANTHANŌ
learn
learned (be)
understand

MARINŌ
fade

MARAN-ATHA
Maran-atha

MARGARITĒS
pearl

MARMAROS
marble

MARTUREŌ
charge
give
obtain
report
testify
testimony
witness

MARTURIA
report
testimony
witness

MARTURION
testimony
witness

MARTUROMAI
testify

MARTUS (or MARTUR)
witness

MAS(S)AOMAI
gnaw

MASTIGOŌ
scourge

MASTIX
plague
scourging

MASTIZŌ
scourge

MASTOS
breast

MATAIOLOGIA
talking (vain)

MATAIOLOGOS
talkers (vain)

MATAIOŌ
vain

MATAIOS
vain
vanity

MATAIOTĒS
vanity

MATĒN
vain

MATHĒTĒS
disciple

MATHĒTEUŌ
disciple
instruct
teach

MATHĒTRIA
disciple

MĒ
lest
never
no one
nothing

MĒDE
much (as)

MĒDEIS (-DEN)
no man
no one
nothing

MĒDEPOTE
never

MEGALAUCHEŌ
boast

MEGALEIOS
great
mighty
wonderful (work)

MEGALEIOTĒS
magnificence
majesty
mighty

MEGALOPREPES
excellent

MEGALOS
greatly

MEGALŌSUNĒ
majesty

MEGALUNŌ
enlarge
great
magnify
shew

MEGAS
great
greatest
high
large
loud
matter
mighty
strong

MEGAS—contd.
years

MEGETHOS
greatness

MEGISTAN
great
lord
prince

MEGISTOS
great

MEIZŌN
best
elder
greater
greatest
more

MEIZOTEROS
greater

MĒKETI
henceforth
henceforward
no longer
no more

MĒKOS
length

MĒKUNOMAI
grow

MELAN
ink

MELAS
black

MELEI
care

MELETAŌ
diligent
imagine
meditate
premeditate

MELI
honey

MELISSOS
honey-comb

MELLŌ
about
almost
begin
come
hereafter
intend
mean
mind
point
ready
shall
should
tarry
was (etc.)
will
yet

MELŌ
care

MELOS
member

MĒLŌTĒ
sheepskin

MEMBRANA
parchment

MEMPHOMAI
blame
fault

MEMPSIMOIROS
complainer

MEN
even
indeed

MEN—*contd.*
truly
verily

MĒN
indeed

MĒN
month

MENŌ
abide
continue
dwell
endure
own
present
remain
stand
tarry

MENOUN, or
MENOUNGE
nay
yea

MENTOI
yet

MĒNUŌ
shew
tell

MĒPŌ
yet

MĒPŌS
haply
lest

MĒPOTE
haply
lest
peradventure

MĒPOU
haply
lest

MERIMNA
care

MERIMNAŌ
care
careful
thought (to take)

MERIS
district
part
portion

MERISMOS
dividing
gift

MERISTĒS
divider

MERIZŌ
deal
difference
distribute
divide
give
part

MĒROS
thigh

MEROS
behalf
coast
country
course
craft
measure
part
piece
portion
respect
somewhat
sort
trade

MESĒMBRIA
noon
south

MESITĒS
mediator

MESITEUŌ
confirm
interposed

MESONUKTION
midnight

MESOŌ
midst

MESOS
between
midday
midnight
midst
way

MESOTOICHON
wall

MESOURANĒMA
heaven

MESTOŌ
fill

MESTOS
full

META
hence

METABAINŌ
depart
go
pass
remove

METABALLŌ
change

METADIDŌMI
give
impart

METAGŌ
turn

METAIRŌ
depart

METAKALEŌ
call

METAKINEŌ
move

METALAMBANŌ
eat
have
partake
receive
take

METALĒPSIS
receive

METALLASSŌ
change
exchange

METAMELOMAI
regret
repent

METAMORPHOŌ
change
transfigure
transform

METANOEŌ
repent

METANOIA
repentance

METAPEMPŌ
call
fetch
send

METASCHĒMATIZŌ
change

METASCHEMATIZŌ—
contd.
fashion
figure
transform

METASTREPHŌ
pervert
turn

METATHESIS
change
removing
translation

METATITHĒMI
carry
change
remove
translate
turn

METAXU
between
next
while

MĒTE
much as

METECHŌ
belong
part
partake
partaker
pertain

METEŌRIZŌ
doubtful

METEPEITA
afterward

MĒTĒR
mother

METHĒ
drunkenness

METHERMĒNEUŌ
interpret
interpretation

METHISTĒMI
(or **METHISTANŌ**)
put
remove
translate
turn

METHOD(E)IA
wiles

METHORION
border

METHUŌ
drunk
drunken

METHUSKŌ
drunk
drunken

METHUSOS
drunkard

METOCHĒ
fellowship

METOCHOS
fellow
partaker
partner

METOIKESIA
bring
carrying away

METOIKIZŌ
carry away
remove

METŌPON
forehead

METRA
womb

MĒTRALŌAS
(or **METROL-**)
mother

METREŌ
measure
mete

METRĒTĒS
firkin

METRIOPATHEŌ
bear
compassion
gently
little

METRIŌS

METRON
measure

MIA
first
one

MIAINŌ
defile

MIASMA
defilement
pollution

MIASMOS
defilement
uncleanness

MIGMA
mixture

MIGNUMI
mingle

MIKROS(-ON)
least
less
little
small
while

MIKROTEROS
least
less
little

MILION
mile

MIMEOMAI
follow
imitate

MIMĒTĒS
follower
imitator

MIMNĒSKŌ
mindful
remember
remembrance

MISEŌ
hate

MISTHAPODOSIA
recompence

MISTHAPODOTĒS
rewarder

MISTHIOS
hired servant

MISTHŌMA
dwelling
hired house

MISTHOŌ
hire

MISTHOS
hire
reward
wages

MISTHŌTOS
  hired servant
  hireling
MNA
  pound
MNEIA
  mention
  remembrance
MNĒMA
  grave
  sepulchre
  tomb
MNĒMĒ
  remembrance
MNĒMEION
  grave
  sepulchre
  tomb
MNĒMONEUŌ
  mention
  mindful
  remember
MNĒMOSUNON
  memorial
MNĒSTEUŌ
  betroth
  espoused
MOCHTHOS
  travail
MODIOS
  bushel
MOGILALOS
  impediment
MOGIS
  hardly
MOICHALIS
  adulteress
  adulterous
MOICHAŌ
  adultery
MOICHEIA
  adultery
MOICHEUŌ
  adultery
MOICHOS
  adulterer
MOLIS
  difficulty
  hardly
MŌLŌPS
  stripe
MOLUNŌ
  defile
MOLUSMOS
  defilement
  filthiness
MŌMAOMAI
  blame
MŌMOS
  blemish
MOMPHĒ
  complaint
MONĒ
  abode
  mansion
MONOGENĒS
  child
  only
  only begotten
MONOŌ
  desolate
MONOPHTHALMOS
  eye (with one)

MONOS (-ON)
  alone
  only
MŌRAINŌ
  foolish
  savour
MŌRIA
  foolishness
MŌROLOGIA
  foolish
  talking (foolish)
MŌROS
  fool
  foolish
  foolishness
MORPHĒ
  form
MORPHOŌ
  formed
MORPHŌSIS
  form
MOSCHOPOIEŌ
  calf
MOSCHOS
  calf
MOUSIKOS
  minstrel
MUELOS
  marrow
MUEŌ
  instruct
  learn
MUKAOMAI
  roar
MUKTĒRIZŌ
  mock
MULIKOS
  millstone
MULINOS
  millstone
MULŌN
  mill
MULOS
  millstone
MUŌPAZŌ
  afar
  see
MURIAS
  company
  innumerable
  thousand(s)
MURIOI
  ten thousand
MURIZŌ
  anoint
MURON
  ointment
MUSTĒRION
  mystery
MUTHOS
  fable

N

NAI
  even so
  surely
  truth
  verily
  yea
NAOS
  sanctuary
  shrine

NAOS—*contd.*
  temple
NARDOS
  spikenard
NAUAGEŌ
  shipwreck
NAUKLĒROS
  owner
NAUS
  ship
NAUTĒS
  mariners
NĒ
  protest
NEANIAS
  young (man)
NEANISKOS
  young (man)
NEKROŌ
  dead
  mortify
NEKROS
  dead
NEKRŌSIS
  deadness
NEŌKOROS
  temple-keeper
  worshipper
NEOMĒNIA
(or NOUM-)
  moon
NEOPHUTOS
  novice
NEOS
  fresh
  new
  young
N(E)OSSOS
  young
NEŌTERIKOS
  youthful
NEŌTEROS
  young
  young (man)
  younger
NEOTĒS
  youth
NĒPHALIOS
  sober
  temperate
NEPHELĒ
  cloud
NĒPHŌ
  sober
  watch
NEPHOS
  cloud
NEPHROS
  reins
NĒPIAZŌ
  babe
  child
NĒPIOS
  babe
  child
NĒSION
  island
NĒSOS
  island
  isle
NĒSTEIA
  fast

NĒSTEIA—*contd.*
  fasting
NĒSTEUŌ
  fast
NĒSTIS
  fasting
NĒTHŌ
  spin
NEUŌ
  beckon
NIKAŌ
  conquer
  overcome
  prevail
  victorious
  victory
NIKE
  victory
NIKOS
  victory
NIPTĒR
  bason
NIPTŌ
  wash
NOĒMA
  device
  mind
  thought
NOEŌ
  consider
  perceive
  think
  understand
NOMĒ
  eat
  pasture
NOMIKOS
  law
  lawyer
NOMIMŌS
  lawfully
NOMISMA
  money
NOMIZŌ
  suppose
  think
  wont
NOMODIDASKALOS
  doctor
  teacher
NOMOS
  law
NOMOTHESIA
  law
NOMOTHETEŌ
  enact
  establish
  law
NOMOTHETĒS
  lawgiver
NOSĒMA
  disease
NOSEŌ
  dote
  sick
NOSOS
  disease
  infirmity
  sickness
NOSPHIZŌ
  keep
  purloin
NOSSIA
  brood

NOSSION
  brood
NOTHOS
  bastard
NŌTHROS
  dull
  slothful
  sluggish
NOTOS
  south
  south wind
NŌTOS
  back
NOUNECHŌS
  discreetly
NOUS
  mind
  understanding
NOUTHESIA
  admonition
NOUTHETEŌ
  admonish
  warn
NUCHTHĒMEROS
  night and a day (a)
NUMPHĒ
  bride
  daughter-in-law
NUMPHIOS
  bridegroom
NUMPHŌN
  bride-chamber
  wedding
NUN
  henceforth
  late
  now
  present
  time
NUNI
  now
NUSSŌ
  pierce
NUSTAZŌ
  slumber
NUX
  night

O

OCHLEŌ
  vex
OCHLOPOIEŌ
  company
  crowd
OCHLOS
  common
  company
  crowd
  multitude
  number
  people
OCHURŌMA
  strongholds
ŌDĒ
  song
ŌDIN
  pain
  sorrow
  travail
ŌDINŌ
  birth
  travail
ODOUS
  tooth

ODUNAŌ
  anguish
  sorrow
  torment
ODUNĒ
  sorrow
ODURMOS
  mourning
OGDOĒKONTA
  fourscore
OGDOOS
  eighth
OIDA
  can
  know
  sure
  tell
  wist
OIKEIOS
  house
  household
OIKĒMA
  cell
  prison
OIKEŌ
  dwell
OIKETEIA
  household
OIKĒTĒRION
  habitation
  house
OIKETĒS
  household-servant
  servant
OIKIA
  home
  house
  household
OIKIAKOS
  household
OIKODESPOTEŌ
  guide
  householder
  rule
OIKODESPOTĒS
  goodman
  householder
  master
OIKODOMĒ
  building
  edification
  edify
OIKODOMEŌ
  build
  builder
  edify
  embolden
(OIKODOMIA)
  dispensation
OIKONOMEŌ
  steward
OIKONOMIA
  dispensation
  stewardship
OIKONOMOS
  chamberlain
  governor
  steward
OIKOS
  family
  home
  house
  household
  temple

OIKOUMENĒ
  earth
  world
OIKOUR(G)OS
  home
OIKTEIRŌ
  compassion
  mercy
OIKTIRMŌN
  merciful
  mercy
OIKTIRMOS
  compassion
  mercy
OINOPHLUGIA
  excess
  wine
  winebibbings
OINOPOTĒS
  wine-bibber
OINOS
  wine
OIOMAI (OIMAI)
  suppose
  think
OKNEŌ
  delay
OKNĒROS
  grievous
  irksome
  slothful
OKTAĒMEROS
  eighth
OKTŌ
  eight
OLETHROS
  destruction
OLIGOPISTOS
  faith (of little)
OLIGOPSUCHOS
  fainthearted
OLIGŌREŌ
  despise
  regard
OLIGOS (-ON)
  few
  little
  season
  small
  space
  while
OLOLUZŌ
  howl
OLOTHREUŌ
  destroy
OLOTHREUTĒS
  destroyer
OLUNTHOS
  fig
OMBROS
  shower
OMMA
  eye
OMNUMI (or OMNUŌ)
  swear
ŌMOS
  shoulder
ONAR
  dream
ONARION
  ass
ONEIDISMOS
  reproach

ONEIDIZŌ
  cast
  reproach
  revile
ONEIDOS
  reproach
ŌNEOMAI
  buy
ONIKOS
  millstone
ONINĒMI
  joy
ONKOS
  weight
ONOMA
  call
  name
ONOMAZŌ
  call
  name
ONOS
  ass
ONTŌS
  certainly
  clean
  indeed
  truth
  verily
ŌON
  egg
OPĒ
  cave
  hole
  opening
  place
OPHEILĒ
  debt
  due
OPHEILĒMA
  debt
OPHEILETĒS
  debtor
  offender
  owe
  sinner
OPHEILŌ
  behove
  bound (to be)
  debt
  debtor
  due
  duty
  guilty
  indebted
  must
  needs
  ought
  owe
  require
  should
ŌPHELEIA
  advantage
  profit
ŌPHELEŌ
  advantage
  bettered
  prevail
  profit
ŌPHELIMOS
  profit
  profitable
OPHELON
  would
OPHELOS
  advantage
  profit

OPHIS
serpent
OPHRUS
brow
OPHTHALMODOULIA
eye-service
OPHTHALMOS
eye
sight
OPISŌ
back
backward
behind
OPISTHEN
backside
behind
OPŌRA
fruits
OPSARION
fish
OPSE
even
end
late
OPSIA
even
evening
OPSIMOS
latter
OPSIS
appearance
countenance
face
OPSŌNION
charges
wages
OPTANŌ
appearing
see
OPTASIA
vision
OPTOMAI,
see HORAŌ
OPTOS
broiled
ORCHEŌ
dance
OREGŌ
covet
desire
reach
seek
OREINOS
country
hill
OREXIS
lust
ORGĒ
anger
indignation
vengeance
wrath
ORGILOS
angry
ORGIZŌ
angry
wroth (be)
ORGUIA
fathom
ORNEON
bird
ORNIS
hen

OROS
hill
mount
mountain
ORPHANOS
comfortless
desolate
fatherless
ORTHOPODEŌ
walk
ORTHOS
even
straight
ORTHŌS
plain
right
rightly
ORTHOTOMEŌ
divide
handle
ORTHRINOS
dawn
early
morning
ORTHRIOS
early
ORTHRIZŌ
morning
ORTHROS
dawn
early
morning
ŌRUOMAI
roar
ORUSSŌ
dig
OSMĒ
odour
savour
OSPHRĒSIS
smelling
OSPHUS
loins
OSTEON
bone
OSTRAKINOS
earthen
ŌTARION
ear
OTHONĒ
sheet
OTHONION
linen
ŌTION
ear
OU (OUK)
nay
never
no man
nothing
OUA
ah
OUAI
woe
OUCHI
nay
OUDAMŌS
no wise (in)
OUDE
much (as)
OUDEIS (-DEN)
never
no man

OUDEIS (-DEN)—contd.
no one
nothing
nought
OUDEPŌ
never
yet
OUDEPOTE
never
nothing
OUKETI
henceforth
hereafter
no longer
no more
now
yet
OUKOUN
then
OUN
now
so
then
verily
OUPŌ
hitherto
yet
OURA
tail
OURANIOS
heavenly
OURANOS
air
heaven(s)
OURANOTHEN
heaven
OUS
ear
OUSIA
substance
OUTHEN
nothing
OXOS
vinegar
OXUS
sharp
swift
OZŌ
stink

P

PACHUNŌ
gross (to wax)
PAGIDEUŌ
ensnare
entangle
PAGIS
snare
PAGOS
hill
PAIDAGŌGOS
instructor
tutor
PAIDARION
child
PAIDEIA
chastening
chastisement
instruction
PAIDEUŌ
chasten
chastise

PAIDEUŌ—contd.
correcting
instruct
learn
learned
teach
PAIDEUTĒS
correct
instructor
PAIDION
child
damsel
young
PAIDIOTHEN
child
PAIDISKĒ
bondmaid
damsel
maid
maiden
PAIŌ
smite
strike
PAIS
boy
child
maid
maiden
manservant
servant
son
young man
PAIZŌ
play
PALAI
great
long
old
time
while
PALAIOŌ
decay
old
PALAIOS
old
PALAIOTĒS
oldness
PALĒ
wrestle
wrestling
PALIN
again
PALINGENESIA
regeneration
PAMPLĒTHEI
once
together
PAMPOLUS
very
PANDOCHEION
inn
PANDOCHEUS
host
PANĒGURIS
assembly
PANOIKEI
house
PANOPLIA
armour
PANOURGIA
craftiness
subtilty
PANOURGOS
crafty

PANTACHĒ
everywhere
PANTACHOTHEN
every quarter
PANTACHOU
everywhere
place
PANTĒ
always
way
PANTELES
uttermost
PANTOKRATŎR
almighty
PANTŎS
all
altogether
certainly
doubt (no)
means (by all)
surely
wise (in no)
PANTOTE
always
ever
evermore
PANTOTHEN
every side
quarter
round about
PARA
contrary
more
nigh
of
rather
side
PARABAINŌ
fall
transgress
transgression
PARABALLŌ
arrive
compare
touch
PARABASIS
breaking
transgression
PARABATĒS
breaker
transgressor
PARABIAZOMAI
constrain
PARABOLĒ
comparison
figure
parable
PARABO(U)LEUOMAI
hazard
PARACHEIMASIA
winter
PARACHEIMAZŌ
winter
PARACHRĒMA
forthwith
immediately
PARADECHOMAI
receive
PARADEIGMATIZŌ
example
put
shame
PARADEISOS
paradise
PARADIATRIBĒ
disputing

PARADIATRIBĒ—
contd.
wrangling
PARADIDŌMI
betray
bring
cast
commend
commit
deliver
give
hazard
prison
put
ripe
PARADOSIS
ordinance
tradition
PARADOXOS
strange
PARAGINOMAI
arrive
come
go
part
present
stand
PARAGŌ
depart
pass
walk
PARAINEŌ
admonish
exhort
PARAITEOMAI
avoid
excuse
intreat
refuse
reject
PARAKALEŌ
beseech
call
comfort
desire
exhort
intreat
pray
PARAKALUPTŌ
conceal
hide
PARAKATATHĒKĒ
commit
PARAKATHEZOMAI
sit
PARAKATHIZŌ
sit
PARAKEIMAI
present (to be)
PARAKLĒSIS
comfort
consolation
encouragement
exhortation
intreaty
PARAKLĒTOS
Comforter
PARAKOĒ
disobedience
PARAKOLOUTHEŌ
attain
follow
know
trace
understand
PARAKOUŌ
hear

PARAKUPTŌ
look
stoop
PARALAMBANŌ
receive
take
PARALEGŌ
coasting
sail
PARALIOS
coast
sea
PARALLAGĒ
variableness
PARALOGIZOMAI
beguile
deceive
delude
PARALUŌ
feeble
palsy (sick of)
PARALUTIKOS
palsy (sick of)
PARAMENŌ
abide
continue
PARAMUTHEOMAI
comfort
console
encourage
PARAMUTHIA
comfort
PARAMUTHION
comfort
consolation
PARANGELIA
charge
commandment
straitly
PARANGELLŌ
charge
command
declare
PARANOMEŌ
law
PARANOMIA
iniquity
transgression
PARAPHERŌ
remove
take
PARAPHRONEŌ
fool
beside oneself (to be)
PARAPHRONIA
madness
PARAIKRAINŌ
provoke
PARAPIKRASMOS
provocation
PARAPIPTŌ
fall
PARAPLEŌ
sail
PARAPLĒSION
nigh
PARAPLĒSIŌS
likewise
manner
PARAPOREUOMAI
go
pass
PARAPTŌMA
fall
fault

PARAPTŌMA—contd.:
offence
sin
trespass
PARARHEŌ
drift
PARASĒMOS
sign
PARASKEUAZŌ
prepare
ready
PARASKEUĒ
preparation
PARATEINŌ
continue
prolong
PARATĒREŌ
observe
watch
PARATĒRĒSIS
observation
show
PARATHALASSIOS
coast
sea
PARATHĒKĒ
commit
PARATHEŌREŌ
neglect
PARATITHĒMI
allege
commend
commit
keeping
put
set
PARATUNCHANŌ
meet (verb)
PARAUTIKA
moment
PARAZĒLOŌ
jealousy
provoke
PARDALIS
leopard
PARECHŌ
bring
do
give
keep
minister
offer
render
shew
trouble
PAREDREUŌ
wait
PARĒGORIA
comfort
PAREIMI
come
have
here (to be)
lack
present (to be)
PAREISAGŌ
bring
PAREISAKTOS
privily
unawares
PAREISDU(N)Ō
creep
privily
PAREISERCHOMAI
come
enter

PAREISERCHOMAI—
contd.
  privily
PAREISPHERŌ
  add
  give
PAREKTOS
  except
  saving
  without
PAREMBOLĒ
  army
PARENOCHLEŌ
  trouble
PAREPIDĒMOS
  pilgrim
  sojourner
  stranger
PARERCHOMAI
  come
  go
  pass
  transgress
PARESIS
  passing over
  remission
PARIĒMI
  hang
PARISTANŌ
  present (verb)
  yield
PARISTĒMI
  bring
  come
  commend
  give
  present (verb)
  prove
  provide
  send
  shew
  stand
  yield
PARODOS
  way
PAROICHOMAI
  pass
PAROIKEŌ
  sojourn
  stranger
PAROIKIA
  dwell
  strangers
  sojourning
PAROIKOS
  foreigner
  sojourner
  stranger
PAROIMIA
  parable
PAROINOS
  brawler
  wine
PAROMOIAZŌ
  like
PAROMOIOS
  like
PAROPSIS
  platter
PARORGISMOS
  wrath
PARORGIZŌ
  anger
  provoke
  wrath

PAROTRUNŌ
  stir
  urge
PAROUSIA
  coming
  presence
PAROXUNŌ
  provoke
  stir
PAROXUSMOS
  contention
  provoke
PARRHĒSIA
  boldness
  confidence
  freely
  openly
  plainly
  plainness
PARRHĒSIAZOMAI
  bold
  freely
  preach
PARTHENIA
  virginity
PARTHENOS
  virgin
PAS
  all
  every
  everything
  manner
  many
  one
  whatsoever
  whole
  whosoever
PASCHA
  Easter
  passover
PASCHŌ
  feel
  passion
  suffer
PATASSŌ
  smite
  strike
PATEŌ
  tread
PATĒR
  father
  parent
PATHĒMA
  affection
  affliction
  passion
  suffering
PATHĒTOS
  suffer
PATHOS
  affection
  lust
  passion
PATROLŌAS
  (or PATRAL-)
  murderer
PATRIA
  family
  kindred
PATRIARCHĒS
  patriarch
PATRIKOS
  father
PATRIS
  country

PATRŌOS
  father
PATROPARADOTOS
  father
  handed down
  receive
PAUŌ
  cease
  leave
  refrain
PĒCHUS
  cubit
PĒDALION
  rudder
PEDĒ
  fetter
PEDINOS
  place
PĒGANON
  rue
PĒGĒ
  fountain
  spring
  well
PĒGNUMI
  pitch
PEINAŌ
  hunger
  hungry
PEIRA
  trial
PEIRAŌ
  go
  try
PEIRASMOS
  temptation
  trial
  try
PEIRAZŌ
  examine
  go
  prove
  tempt
  tempter
  try
PEISMONĒ
  persuasion
PEITHARCHEŌ
  hearken
  obey
PEITHŌ
  agree
  assure
  believe
  confident
  friend
  obey
  persuade
  trust
  urge
  yield
PEITHOS
  enticing
  persuasive
PELAGOS
  depth
  sea
PELEKIZŌ
  behead
PĒLIKOS
  great
  large
PĒLOS
  clay
PEMPŌ

PEMPŌ—contd.
  send
  thrust
PEMPTOS
  fifth
PENĒS
  poor
PENICHROS
  poor
PENTAKIS
  five times
PENTAKISCHILIOI
  five
  thousand
PENTAKOSIOI
  five (hundred)
PENTE
  five
PENTEKAIDEKATOS
  fifteenth
PENTĒKONTA
  fifty
PENTĒKOSTOS
  Pentecost
PENTHEŌ
  bewail
  mourn
  wail
PENTHERA
  mother-in-law
  wife's mother
PENTHEROS
  father-in-law
PENTHOS
  mourning
  sorrow
PEPOITHĒSIS
  confidence
  trust
PĒRA
  wallet
PERAN
  beyond
  side
PERAS
  end
  final
  part
PERI
  of
  pertain to
  respect
PERIAGŌ
  compass
  go
  lead
PERIAIREŌ
  cast
  take
PERIAPTŌ
  kindle
PERIASTRAPTŌ
  shine
PERIBALLŌ
  cast
  clothe
  put
PERIBLEPŌ
  look
PERIBOLAION
  covering
  mantle
  veil
  vesture

PERICHŎROS
country
region
PERIDEŌ
bind
PERIECHŌ
contain
PERIERCHOMAI
circuit
compass
go
strolling
wander
PERIERGAZOMAI
busybody
PERIERGOS
arts
busybody
curious
PERIÏSTĒMI
avoid
stand
PERIKALUPTŌ
blindfold
cover
overlay
PERIKATHARMA
filth
PERIKEMAI
bound (to be)
compass
hang
PERIKEPHALAIA
helmet
PERIKRATĒS
secure
PERIKRUPTŌ
hide
PERIKUKLOŌ
compass
PERILAMPŌ
shine
PERILEIPŌ
leave
remain
PERILUPOS
sorrowful
sorry
PERIMENŌ
wait
PERIOCHĒ
place
PERIOIKEŌ
dwell
PERIOIKOS
neighbour
PERIOUSIOS
possession
PERIPATEŌ
go
occupy
walk
PERIPEIRŌ
pierce
PERIPHERŌ
bear
carry
PERIPHRONEŌ
despise
PERIPIPTŌ
fall
PERIPOIEŌ
gain
purchase

PERIPOIĒSIS
obtaining
possession
purchase
saving
PERIPSĒMA
offscouring
PERIRRHĒGNUMI
rend
PERISPAŌ
cumber
PERISSEIA
abundance
overflowing
PERISSEUMA
abundance
leave
remain
PERISSEUŌ
abound
abundance
better (be)
enough
exceed
excel
increase
leave
remain
spare
PERISSOS
abundant
advantage
measure
more
superfluous
PERISSŌS
abundantly
exceedingly
measure
more
PERISSOTEROS (-ON)
abundant
far
greater
more
overmuch
PERISSOTERŌS
abundantly
earnest
exceedingly
more
rather
PERISTERA
dove
PERITEMNŌ
circumcise
PERITHESIS
wearing
PERITITHĒMI
bestow
put
set
PERITOMĒ
circumcision
PERITRECHŌ
run
PERITREPŌ
turn
PERIX
round about
PERIZŌNNUMI
gird
PERPEREUOMAI
vaunt

PERUSI—
contd.
year
PETAOMAI
fly
PETEINON
bird
PETOMAI
fly
PETRA
rock
PETRŌDĒS
ground
rocky
PETROS
stone
PEZEUŌ
foot
land
PEZOS
foot
PHAGŌ
eat
meat
PHAGOS
gluttonous
PHAILONĒS
clothing
PHAINŌ
appear
see
seem
shine
think
PHANEROŌ
appear
declare
manifest
shew
PHANEROS
appear
known
manifest
openly
outwardly
PHANERŌS
evidently
openly
publicly
PHANERŌSIS
manifestation
PHANOS
lantern
PHANTASIA
pomp
PHANTASMA
apparition
spirit
PHANTAZŌ
appearance
sight
PHARANX
valley
PHARISAIOS
Pharisees
PHARMAK(E)IA
sorcery
witchcraft
PHARMAKOS
(or -KEUS)
sorcerer
PHASIS
tidings

PHASKŌ
affirm
profess
say
PHATNĒ
manger
PHAULOS
evil
ill
vessel
PHEIDOMAI
forbear
spare
PHEIDOMENŌS
sparingly
PHELONĒS
clothing
PHĒMĒ
fame
PHĒMI
affirm
say
PHENGOS
light
PHERŌ
bear
bring
carry
come
drive
endure
go
lay
lead
move
press
reach
rushing
uphold
PHEUGŌ
escape
flee
PHIALĒ
bowl
PHILADELPHIA
brother
PHILADELPHOS
brethren
PHILAGATHOS
lover
PHILANDROS
husband
PHILANTHRŌPIA
kindness
love
PHILANTHRŌPŌS
courteously
kindly
PHILARGURIA
money (love of)
PHILARGUROS
covetous
lover
PHILAUTOS
lover
PHILĒDONOS
lover
pleasure
PHILĒMA
kiss
PHILEŌ
kiss
love

PHILIA
friendship
PHILONEIKIA
contention
strife
PHILONEIKOS
contentious
PHILOPHRŌN
courteous
PHILOPHRONŌS
courteously
PHILOPRŌTEUŌ
pre-eminence
PHILOS (PHILĒ)
friend
PHILOSOPHIA
philosophy
PHILOSOPHOS
philosopher
PHILOSTORGOS
affection
PHILOTEKNOS
children
PHILOTHEOS
lover
PHILOTIMEOMAI
aim
labour
strive
study
PHILOXENIA
entertain
hospitality
stranger
PHILOXENOS
hospitality
lover
PHIMOŌ
muzzle
peace (hold one's)
put
silence
speechless
still
PHLOGIZŌ
fire
PHLOX
flame
flaming
PHLUAREŌ
prate
PHLUAROS
tattler
PHOBEŌ
fear
marvel
reverence
PHOBEROS
fearful
PHOBĒTRON
fearful
sight
terror
PHOBOS
fear
terror
PHOINIX
palm (tree)
PHŌLEOS
hole
PHŌNĒ
noise
sound
voice

PHŌNEŌ
call
cry
PHONEUŌ
kill
murder
slay
PHONEUS
murderer
PHONOS
murder
slaughter
PHOREŌ
bear
wear
PHOROS
tribute
PHORTION
burden
lading
PHORTIZŌ
lade
PHORTOS
lading
PHŌS
light
PHŌSPHOROS
day-star
PHŌSTĒR
light
PHŌTEINOS
bright
light
PHŌTISMOS
light
PHŌTIZŌ
enlighten
light
lighten
PHRAGELLION
scourge
PHRAGELLOŌ
scourge
PHRAGMOS
hedge
partition
PHRASSŌ
stop
PHRAZŌ
declare
explain
PHREAR
pit
well
PHRĒN
understanding
PHRENAPATAŌ
deceive
PHRENAPATĒS
deceiver
PHRISSŌ
shudder
tremble
PHRONĒMA
mind
minded
PHRONEŌ
affection
careful
feel
mind
minded
observe
regard

PHRONEŌ—contd.
savour
think
thought (to take)
understand
PHRONĒSIS
prudence
wisdom
PHRONIMOS
wise
PHRONIMŌS
wisely
PHRONTIZŌ
careful
PHROUREŌ
guard
keep
PHRUASSŌ
rage
PHRUGANON
stick
PHTHANŌ
arrive
attain
come
precede
PHTHARTOS
corruptible
PHTHENGOMAI
speak
utter
PHTHEIRŌ
corrupt
defile
destroy
PHTHINOPŌRINOS
autumn
fruit
PHTHONEŌ
envy
PHTHONGOS
sound
PHTHONOS
envy
envying
PHTHORA
corruption
destroy
perish
PHUGĒ
flight
PHULAKĒ
cage
hold (noun)
imprisonment
prison
ward
watch
PHULAKIZŌ
imprison
PHULAKTĒRION
phylactery
PHULASSŌ
beware
guard
keep
observe
preserve
save
ware of
PHULAX
guard
keeper

PHULĒ
kindred
tribe
PHULLON
leaf
PHUŌ
grow
spring
PHURAMA
lump
PHUSIKOS
natural
PHUSIKŌS
naturally
PHUSIOŌ
puff (up)
PHUSIŌSIS
swelling
PHUSIS
kind (noun)
nature
natural
PHUTEIA
plant
PHUTEUŌ
plant
PIAZŌ
apprehend
catch
hands (lay . . . on)
take
PIEZŌ
press
PIKRAINŌ
bitter
PIKRIA
bitterness
PIKROS
bitter
PIKRŌS
bitterly
PIMPLĒMI (PLĒTHŌ)
accomplish
fill
furnish
PIMPRĒMI
swell
PINAKIDION
writing-tablet
PINAX
charger
platter
PINŌ
drink
PIOTĒS
fatness
PIPRASKŌ
sell
PIPTŌ
fail
fall
light (to . . . upon)
strike
PISTEUŌ
believe
believer
commit
intrust
trust
PISTIKOS
spikenard
PISTIS
assurance

PISTIS—contd.
belief
faith
faithfulness
fidelity
PISTOŌ
assured
PISTOS
believer
believing
faithful
faithfully
sure
true
PITHANOLOGIA
enticing
persuasiveness
PLANAŌ
deceive
err
lead
seduce
wander
way
PLANĒ
deceit
delusion
error
PLANĒTĒS
wandering
PLANOS
deceiver
seducing
PLASMA
formed
PLASSŌ
formed
PLASTOS
feigned
PLATEIA
street
PLATOS
broad
PLATUNŌ
broad
enlarge
PLATUS
wide
PLAX
table
PLĒGĒ
plague
stripe
wound
PLEGMA
braided
PLEIŌN (-ON)
above
excellent
greater
long
longer
many
more
most
number
yet
PLEISTOS
great
most
PLEKŌ
plait
PLĒKTĒS
striker
PLĒMMURA
flood

PLĒN
except
notwithstanding
rather
PLEŌ
sail
PLEONAZŌ
abundant
increase
multiply
over
PLEONEKTEŌ
advantage
defraud
gain
wrong
PLEONEKTĒS
covetous
PLEONEXIA
covetousness
extortion
PLĒRĒS
full
PLĒRŌMA
fill up
fulfilling
fulness
put
PLĒROŌ
accomplish
complete
end
expire
fill
fulfil
preach
supply
well-nigh
PLĒROPHOREŌ
assure
believe
fulfil
know
persuade
proclaim
proof
PLĒROPHORIA
assurance
PLĒSION
near
neighbour
PLĒSMONĒ
indulgence
PLĒSSŌ
smite
PLĒTHŌ
(see PIMPLĒMI)
PLĒTHOS
assembly
bundle
company
multitude
PLĒTHUNŌ
abound
multiply
PLEURA
side
PLOIARION
boat
ship
PLOION
boat
ship
shipping
PLOOS
course

PLOOS—contd.
voyage
PLOUSIOS
rich
rich man
PLOUSIŌS
abundantly
richly
PLOUTEŌ
get
goods
rich
PLOUTIZŌ
enrich
rich
PLOUTOS
riches
PLUNŌ
wash
PNEŌ
blow
wind
PNEUMA
breath
life
spirit
Spirit
spiritual
wind
PNEUMATIKOS
spiritual
PNEUMATIKŌS
spiritually
PNIGŌ
choke
throat (take by the)
PNIKTOS
strangled
PNOE
breath
wind
PODĒRĒS
clothing
foot
POIĒMA
made (be)
workmanship
POIEŌ
abide
appoint
bear
bring
cause
commit
continue
deal with
do
execute
exercise
fulfil
gain
give
hold
keep
make
mean
observe
ordain
perform
provide
purpose
put
shew
shoot forth
spend
take
tarry

POIEŌ—contd.
work
yield
POIĒSIS
deed
POIĒTĒS
doer
poet
POIKILOS
divers
manifold
POIMAINŌ
cattle
feed
rule
POIMĒN
pastor
shepherd
POIMNĒ
flock
fold
POIMNION
flock
POIOS
manner
what
which
POLEMEŌ
fight
war
POLEMOS
battle
fight
war
PŌLEŌ
sell
POLIS
city
POLITARCHĒS
ruler
POLITEIA
citizenship
commonwealth
freedom
POLITĒS
citizen
POLITEUMA
citizenship
commonwealth
conversation
POLITEUŌ
citizen
conversation
live
POLLAKIS
oft
often
oftentimes
oft-times
POLLAPLASIŌN
manifold
PŌLOS
colt
POLULOGIA
speaking (much)
POLUMERŌS
portion
time
POLUPOIKILOS
manifold
POLUS
abundant
common
great

POLUS—*contd.*
greatly
long
many
much
oft
plenteous
sore
straitly

POLUSPLANCHNOS
pitiful

POLUTELĒS
costly
precious
price

POLUTIMOS
costly
precious
price

POLUTROPŌS
divers
manners

POMA
drink

PONĒRIA
iniquity
wickedness

PONĒROS
bad
evil
grievous
harm
malicious
person
vile
wicked

PONOS
labour
pain

PŌPOTE
never
time

POREIA
journey
way

POREUŌ (-OMAI)
depart
go
journey
walk
way

PORISMOS
gain

PORNĒ
harlot
whore

PORNEIA
fornication

PORNEUŌ
fornication

PORNOS
fornicator
whoremonger

PŌROŌ
blind
harden

PŌRŌSIS
blindness
hardening
hardness

PORPHURA
purple

PORPHUREOS
purple

PORPHUROPŌLIS
purple (seller of)

PORRŌ
far
way

PORRŌTERON
further

PORRŌTHEN
afar

PORTHEŌ
destroy
havock
waste

PŌS (1)
haply
means (by any, etc.)
perhaps

PŌS (2)
manner
means

POSAKIS
oft
often

POSIS
drink

POSOS
great
long
many
what

POTAMOPHORĒTOS
flood
river

POTAMOS
flood
river
water

POTAPOS
manner
what

POTE (1)
aforetime
haply
last
length (at)
never
old
once
past
sometimes
time
time (some)
(ever) yet

POTE (2)
long

POTĒRION
cup

POTIZŌ
drink
feed
water

POTOS
carousings

POU
about
haply
place
room
somewhere

POUS
foot

PRAGMA
business
matter
thing
work

PRAGMATEIA
affair

PRAGMATEUOMAI
trade

PRAITŌRION
guard
hall
palace

PRAKTŌR
officer

PRASIA
ranks

PRASSŌ
commit
deeds
do
exact
extort
keep
practise
require
use

PRAÜPATHIA
meekness

PRAÜS (or -OS)
meek

PRAÜTES (or -OTĒS)
meekness

PRAXIS
deed
office
work

PRĒNĒS
fall
headlong
swell

PREPŌ
become
befit
comely

PRESBEIA
ambassage
message

PRESBEUŌ
ambassador

PRESBUTERION
elder
estate

PRESBUTEROS
elder
eldest
old

PRESBUTĒS
aged
old

PRESBUTIS
aged

PRIN
before

PRIZŌ (or PRIŌ)
saw asunder

PROAGŌ
bring
foregoing
go

PROAIREŌ
purpose

PROAITIAOMAI
charge
prove

PROAKOUŌ
hear

PROAMARTANŌ
sin

PROAULION
porch

PROBAINŌ
go
stricken (in years)

PROBALLŌ
put
shoot forth

PROBATIKOS
sheep *gate*
sheep *market*

PROBATION
sheep

PROBATON
sheep

PROBIBAZŌ
draw
instruct
put

PROBLEPŌ
foresee
provide

PROCHEIRIZŌ
appoint
choose
make

PROCHEIROTONEŌ
choose

PRODĒLOS
evident
manifest

PRODIDŌMI
give

PRODOTĒS
betrayer
traitor

PRODROMOS
forerunner

PROECHŌ
better (be)
case
worse

PROĒGEOMAI
prefer

PROEIDON
foresee
see

PROEIPON
(PROLEGŌ)
foretell
forewarn
say
speak

PROEIRŌ
tell

PROELPIZŌ
hope
trust

PROENARCHOMAI
begin

PROEPANGELLŌ
(-OMAI)
aforepromised
promise

PROERCHOMAI
go
outgo
pass

PROETOIMAZŌ
ordain
prepare

PROEUANGELIZO-
MAI
preach

PROGINOMAI
past

PROGINŌSKŌ
  foreknow
  foreordain
  know
PROGNŌSIS
  foreknowledge
PROGONOS
  forefather
  parents
PROGRAPHŌ
  openly
  ordain
  set
  write
PROÏ
  early
  morning
PRŌÏMOS
  early
PRŌÏNOS
  morning
PRŌÏOS
  day
  early
  morning
PROÏSTĒMI
  maintain
  over (to be)
  rule
PROKALEŌ
  provoke
PROKATANGELLŌ
  foreshew
  foretell
  shew
PROKATARTIZŌ
  make
PROKEIMAI
  first
  set
PROKĒRUSSŌ
  preach
PROKOPĒ
  furtherance
  profiting
  progress
PROKOPTŌ
  advance
  increase
  proceed
  profit
  spent
  wax
PROKRIMA
  prefer
  prejudice
PROKUROŌ
  confirm
PROLAMBANŌ
  come
  overtake
  take
PROLEGŌ
  (see PROEIPON)
PROMARTUROMAI
  testify
PROMELETAŌ
  meditate
PROMERIMNAŌ
  thought (to take)
PRONOEŌ
  provide
  thought (to take)

PRONOIA
  providence
  provision
PROORAŌ
  foresee
  see
PROORIZŌ
  determine
  ordain
  predestinate
PROORMIZŌ
  draw
PROPASCHŌ
  suffer
PROPATŌR
  forefather
PROPEMPŌ
  accompany
  bring
  conduct
  journey
  set
  way
PROPETĒS
  heady
  headstrong
PROPHASIS
  cloke (pretence)
  excuse
  pretence
  show (noun)
PROPHERŌ
  bring
PROPHĒTEIA
  prophecy
  prophesying
PROPHĒTĒS
  prophet
PROPHĒTEUŌ
  prophesy
PROPHĒTIKOS
  prophecy
PROPHĒTIS
  prophetess
PROPHTHANŌ
  speak
PROPOREUOMAI
  go
PRŌRA
  foreship
PROS
  belong
  compare
  nigh
  pertain to
PROSABBATON
  sabbath
PROSAGŌ
  bring
  draw
PROSAGŌGĒ
  access
PROSAGOREUŌ
  call
  name
PROSAITEŌ
  beg
PROSANABAINŌ
  go
PROSANALISKŌ
  spend
PROSANAPLĒROŌ

PROSANAPLĒROŌ—
contd.
  measure
  supply
PROSANATITHĒMI
  add
  confer
  impart
PROSAPEILEŌ
  threaten
PROSCHUSIS
  sprinkling
PROSDAPANAŌ
  spend
PROSDECMOMAI
  accept
  allow
  look (for)
  receive
  take
  wait
PROSDEOMAI
  need
PROSDOKAŌ
  expect
  expectation
  look (for)
  tarry
  wait
PROSDOKIA
  expectation
  looking (after)
PROSEAŌ
  suffer
PROSECHŌ
  attend
  attendance
  beware
  give
  heed
  regard
PROSEDREUŌ
  wait
PROSENGIZŌ
  come
PROSĒLOŌ
  nail
PROSĒLUTOS
  proselyte
PROSERCHOMAI
  come
  consent
  draw
  go
PROSERGAZOMAI
  gain
PROSEUCHĒ
  earnestly
  fervently
  prayer
PROSEUCHOMAI
  pray
  prayer
PROSKAIROS
  season
  temporal
  time
  while
PROSKALEŌ
  call
PROSKARTEREŌ
  attend
  continue

PROSKARTEREŌ—
contd.
  give
  instant
  wait
PROSKARTERĒSIS
  perseverance
PROSKEPHALAION
  pillow
PROSKLĒROŌ
  consort
PROSKLISIS
  partiality
PROSKOLLAŌ
  cleave
  join
PROSKOMMA
  offence
PROSKOPĒ
  offence
PROSKOPTŌ
  beat
  dash
  smite
  stumble
PROSKULIŌ
  roll
PROSKUNEŌ
  beseech
  worship
PROSKUNĒTĒS
  worshipper
PROSLALEŌ
  speak
PROSLAMBANŌ
  receive
  take
PROSLĒ(M)PSIS
  receiving
PROSMENŌ
  abide
  cleave
  continue
  tarry
PROSOCHTHIZŌ
  displease
  grieve
PROSŌPOLĒ(M)PSIA
  persons (respect of)
  receive
PROSŌPOLĒ(M)PTEŌ
  persons (respect of)
  receive
PROSŌPOLĒ(M)PTĒS
  persons (respect of)
  receive
PROSŌPON
  appearance
  countenance
  face
  fashion
  person
  presence
PROSORMIZŌ
  draw
  moor
PROSOPHEILŌ
  owe
PROSPĒGNUMI
  crucify
PROSPEINOS
  hungry

PROSPHAGION
  eat
  meat
PROSPHATOS
  new
PROSPHATŌS
  lately
PROSPHERŌ
  bring
  deal with
  do
  offer
  present (verb)
  put
PROSPHILĒS
  lovely
PROSPHŌNEŌ
  call
  speak
PROSPHORA
  offering
PROSPIPTŌ
  beat
  fall
PROSPOIEŌ
  make
PROSPOREUOMAI
  come
PROSPSAUŌ
  touch
PROSRĒGNUMI
  beat
  break
PROSTASSŌ
  bid
  command
PROSTATIS
  succourer
PROSTITHĒMI
  add
  give
  increase
  lay
  proceed
  speak
PROSTRECHŌ
  run
PROTASSŌ
  appoint
PROTEINŌ
  bind
  tie
PROTEROS (-ON)
  aforetime
  before
  first
  former
PRŌTEUŌ
  pre-eminence
PROTHESIS
  purpose
  shewbread
PROTHESMIOS
  appoint
  term
  time
PROTHUMIA
  forwardness
  readiness
  willing
PROTHUMOS
  ready
  willing

PROTHUMŌS
  ready
PROTITHĒMI
  purpose
  set
PRŌTOKATHEDRIA
  chief
  seat
  uppermost
PRŌTOKLISIA
  chief
  place
  room
  uppermost
PRŌTON
  before
  beginning
  chiefly
  first
PRŌTOS
  best
  chief
  chiefest
  estate
  first
  former
  principal
PRŌTŌS
  first
PRŌTOSTATĒS
  ringleader
PRŌTOTOKIA
  birthright
PRŌTOTOKOS
  first-begotten
  firstborn
PROTRECHŌ
  outrun
  run
PROTREPŌ
  encourage
  exhort
PROÜPARCHŌ
  before
  beforetime
PRUMNA
  stern
PSALLŌ
  melody
  praise
  psalm
  sing
PSALMOS
  psalm
PSĒLAPHAŌ
  feel
  handle
  touch
PSĒPHIZŌ
  count
PSĒPHOS
  stone
PSEUDADELPHOS
  brethren
PSEUDAPOSTOLOS
  apostle
PSEUDĒS
  false
  liar
PSEUDOCHRISTOS
  false Christs
    (see Christ)
PSEUDODIDASKALOS
  teacher, false teachers

PSEUDOLOGOS
  lie
PSEUDŌ
  falsely
  lie
PSEUDOMARTUREŌ
  witness
PSEUDOMARTURIA
  witness
PSEUDOMARTUS
  witness
PSEUDŌNUMOS
  falsely
PSEUDOPROPHĒTĒS
  prophet
PSEUDOS
  falsehood
  lie
  lying
PSEUSMA
  lie
PSEUSTĒS
  liar
PSICHION
  crumb
PSITHURISMOS
  whispering
PSITHURISTĒS
  whisperer
PSŌCHŌ
  rub
PSŌMION
  sop
PSŌMIZŌ
  bestow
  feed
PSUCHĒ
  heart
  heartily
  life
  mind
  soul
PSUCHIKOS
  natural
PSUCHŌ
  cold
PSUCHOS
  cold
PSUCHROS
  cold
PTAIŌ
  fall
  offend
  stumble
PTĒNON
  bird
PTERNA
  heel
PTERUGION
  pinnacle
PTERUX
  wing
PTŌCHEIA
  poverty
PTŌCHEUŌ
  poor
PTŌCHOS
  beggar
  beggarly
  poor
PTOEŌ
  terrify

PTOĒSIS
  amazement
  terror
PTŌMA
  body
  carcase
  corpse
PTŌSIS
  fall
PTUŌ
  spit
PTUON
  fan
PTURŌ
  affrighted
  terrify
PTUSMA
  spittle
PTUSSŌ
  close (verb)
PUGMĒ
  diligently
PUKNOS (-NA)
  often
PUKNOTERON
  oftener
PUKTEUŌ
  fight
PULĒ
  city
  gate
PULŌN
  gate
  porch
PUNTHANOMAI
  ask
  inquire
  understand
PUR
  fire
PURA
  fire
PURESSŌ
  fever (be sick of)
PURETOS
  fever
PURGOS
  tower
PURINOS
  fire
PUROOMAI (-OŌ)
  burn
  fiery
  fire
  refined
  try
PURŌSIS
  burning
  fiery
  trial
PURRHAZŌ
  red
PURRHOS
  red
PUTHŌN
  divination

R

RABBI (-EI)
  master
  Rabbi

RABBŌNI (or -OUNEI)
 lord
 Rabboni
RHABDIZŌ
 beat
 rod
RHABDOS
 rod
 staff
RHABDOUCHOS
 serjeant
RHADIOURGĒMA
 villany
RHADIOURGIA
 villany
RHAKA
 raca
RHAKOS
 cloth
RHANTISMOS
 sprinkling
RHANTIZŌ
 sprinkle
 wash
RHAPHIS
 needle
RHAPISMA
 blow (noun)
 smite
 strike
RHAPIZŌ
 palm
 smite
 strike
RHEDĒ
 chariot
RHĒGMA
 ruin
RHĒGNUMI
 break
 burst
 dash
 rend
 tear
RHĒMA
 saying
 thing
 word
RHEŌ
 flow
RHEŌ (see EIRŌ)
 command
RHĒTŌR
 orator
RHĒTŌS
 expressly
RHIPĒ
 twinkling
RHIPIZŌ
 toss
RHIPTŌ
(or RHIPTEŌ)
 cast
 scatter
 throw
RHIZA
 root
RHIZOŌ
 root
RHOIZĒDON
 noise
RHŌMAIOS
 Roman

RHŌMAÏSTI
 Latin
RHŌMAÏKOS
 Latin
RHOMPHAIA
 sword
RHŌNNUMI
 farewell
RHUMĒ
 lane
 street
RHUOMAI
 deliver
 deliverer
RHUPAINŌ
 filthy (to make)
RHUPARIA
 filthiness
RHUPAROS
 filthy
 vile
RHUPAREUOMAI
 filthy
RHUPOS
 filth
RHUSIS
 issue
RHUTIS
 wrinkle

S

SABACHTHANEI
 sabachthani
SABAŌTH
 sabaoth
SABBATISMOS
 rest
 sabbath
SABBATON
 sabbath
 week
SAGĒNĒ
 net
SAINŌ
 move
SAKKOS
 sackcloth
SALEUŌ
 move
 shake
 stir
SALOS
 wave
SALPINX
 trump
 trumpet
SALPISTĒS
 trumpeter
SALPIZŌ
 sound
 trumpet
SANDALION
 sandal
SANIS
 board
SAPPHEIROS
 sapphire
SAPROS
 bad
 corrupt

SARDINOS
 sardine
SARDIOS (-ON)
 sardius
SARDONUX
 sardonyx
SARGANĒ
 basket
SARKIKOS
 carnal
 flesh
 fleshly
SARKINOS
 carnal
 flesh
 fleshy
SAROŌ
 sweep
SARX
 flesh
SATANAS
 Satan
SATON
 measure
SBENNUMI
 go
 quench
SCHEDON
 almost
SCHĒMA
 fashion
SCHISMA
 division
 rent
 schism
SCHIZŌ
 break
 divide
 open
 rend
 rent
SCHOINION
 cord
 rope
SCHOLAZŌ
 empty
 give
SCHOLĒ
 school
SEAUTOU
 thee
 thyself
SEBASMA
 devotion
 worship
SEBASTOS
 emperor
SEBAZOMAI
 worship
SEBŌ (-OMAI)
 devout
 worship
SEIŌ
 move
 quake
 shake
 stir
 tremble
SEIRA
 chain
SEIROS
 pits

SEISMOS
 earthquake
 tempest
SELĒNĒ
 moon
SELĒNIAZŌ
 epileptic
SĒMAINŌ
 signify
SĒMEION
 miracle
 sign
 token
 wonder
SEMEIOŌ
 note (verb)
SĒMERON
 to-day
 this day
SEMIDALIS
 flour
SEMNOS
 grave (Adjective)
 honest
SEMNOTĒS
 gravity
 honesty
 honourable
SĒPŌ
 corrupt
SĒRIKOS (or SIR-)
 silk
SĒS
 moth
SĒTOBRŌTOS
 moth-eaten
SIAGŌN
 cheek
SIDĒREOS
 iron
SIDĒROS
 iron
SIGAŌ
 close (verb)
 peace (hold one's)
 secret
 silence
SIGĒ
 silence
SIKARIOS
 assassin
 murderer
SIKERA
 drink
SIMIKINTHION
 apron
SINAPI
 mustard
SINDŌN
 linen
SINIAZŌ
 sift
SIOPAŌ
 dumb
 peace (hold one's)
SITEUTOS
 fatted
SITION
 corn
SITISTOS
 fatling

SITOMETRION
food
meat

SITOS
corn
wheat

SKANDALIZŌ
offend

SKANDALON
fall
falling
offence

SKAPHĒ
boat

SKAPTŌ
dig

SKELOS
leg

SKĒNĒ
habitation
tabernacle

SKĒNŌMA
habitation
tabernacle

SKĒNOŌ
dwell
tabernacle

SKĒNOPĒGIA
tabernacle

SKĒNOPOIOS
tent-maker

SKĒNOS
tabernacle

SKEPASMA
covering
raiment

SKEUĒ
tackling

SKEUOS
gear
goods
vessel

SKIA
shadow

SKIRTAŌ
leap

SKLĒROKARDIA
heart (hardness of)

SKLĒROS
fierce
hard
rough

SKLĒROTĒS
hardness

SKLĒROTRACHĒLOS
stiffnecked

SKLĒRUNŌ
harden

SKŌLĒKOBRŌTOS
worm

SKŌLĒX
worm

SKOLIOS
crooked

SKOLOPS
thorn

SKOPEŌ
consider
heed (to take)
look
mark

SKOPOS
goal
mark

SKORPIOS
scorpion

SKORPIZŌ
disperse
scatter

SKOTEINOS
dark
darkness

SKOTIA
dark
darkness

SKOTIZŌ
darken

SKOTOŌ
darken
darkness

SKOTOS
darkness

SKUBALON
dung

SKULLŌ
distress
trouble

SKULON
spoil

SKUTHRŌPOS
countenance

SMARAGDINOS
emerald

SMARAGDOS
emerald

SMURNA
myrrh

SMURNIZŌ
mingle
myrrh

SŌMA
body
slave

SŌMATIKOS
bodily

SŌMATIKŌS
bodily

SOPHIA
wisdom

SOPHIZŌ
devised (cunningly)
wise

SOPHOS
wise

SŌPHRŌN
discreet
sober
soberminded
temperate

SŌPHRONEŌ
mind
sober
soberminded
think
watch

SŌPHRONISMOS
discipline
mind

SŌPHRONIZŌ
soberminded

SŌPHRONŌS
soberly

SŌPHROSUNĒ
soberness
sobriety

SŌREUŌ
heap
lade

SOROS
bier

SOS
thine
thy

SŌTĒR
saviour

SŌTĒRIA
health
safety
salvation
saving

SŌTĒRION
salvation

SŌTĒRIOS
salvation

SOUDARION
handkerchief
napkin

SŌZŌ
heal
recover
save
whole

SPAŌ
draw

SPARASSŌ
rend
tear

SPARGANOŌ
swaddling-clothes

SPATALAŌ
delicately
live
pleasure
wanton

SPEIRA
band

SPEIRŌ
receive
sow
sower

SPEKOULATŌR
guard
soldier

SPĒLAION
cave
den

SPENDŌ
offer

SPERMA
issue
seed

SPERMOLOGOS
babbler

SPEUDŌ
desire
earnestly
haste

SPHAGĒ
slaughter

SPHAGION
beast

SPHAZŌ (or -TTŌ)
kill
slay
smite

SPHAZO (or -TTŌ—
contd.
wound

SPHODRA
exceeding
exceedingly
greatly
sore
very

SPHODRŌS
exceedingly

SPHRAGIS
seal

SPHRAGIZŌ
seal

SPHURON
ankle-bones

SPILAS
rock
spot

SPILOŌ
defile
spot

SPILOS
spot

SPLANCHNON (-NA)
affection
bowels
compassion
mercy

SPLANCHNIZOMAI
compassion

SPODOS
ashes

SPONGOS
sponge

SPORA
seed

SPORIMOS
corn
cornfield
field

SPOROS
seed

SPOUDAIOS
careful
diligent
earnest
forward

SPOUDAIŌS
diligently
earnestly
instantly

SPOUDAIOTEROS
diligent
earnest

SPOUDAIOTERŌS
carefully
diligently

SPOUDAZŌ
diligence
diligent
endeavour
forward
labour
study
zealous

SPOUDĒ
business
care
carefulness
diligence
earnestness
forwardness
haste

SPURIS
  basket
STACHUS
  corn
  ear (of corn)
STADION
  furlong
  race
STAMNOS
  pot
STAPHULĒ
  grape
STASIASTĒS
  insurrection
STASIS
  dissension
  insurrection
  riot
  sedition
  standing
  uproar
STATĒR
  money
  piece
  shekel
STAUROŌ
  crucify
STAUROS
  cross
STEGĒ
  roof
STEGŌ
  bear
  forbear
  suffer
STEIROS
  barren
STĒKŌ
  stand
STELLŌ
  avoid
  withdraw
STEMMA
  garland
STENAGMOS
  groaning
STENAZŌ
  grief
  groan
  murmur
  sigh
STENOCHŌREO
  anguish
  distress
  straitened
STENOCHŌRIA
  anguish
  distress
STENOS
  narrow
STEPHANOŌ
  crown
STEPHANOS
  crown
STEREŌMA
  stedfastness
STEREOŌ
  establish
  strength
  strengthen
  strong
STEREOS
  firm
  solid
  stedfast

STEREOS—contd.
  strong
  sure
STĒRIGMOS
  stedfastness
STĒRIZŌ
  establish
  fix
  set
  strengthen
STĒTHOS
  breast
STHENOŌ
  strengthen
STIGMA
  mark
STIGMĒ
  moment
STILBŌ
  shine
STOA
  porch
STOIBAS
  branch
STOICHEION
  elements
  principles
  rudiments
STOICHEŌ
  walk
STOLĒ
  clothing
  robe
STOMA
  edge
  face
  mouth
STOMACHOS
  stomach
STRATĒGOS
  captain
  magistrate
STRATEIA
  warfare
STRATEUMA
  army
  soldier
STRATEUŌ
  go
  soldier
  war
  warfare
STRATIA (or -EIA)
  host (of angels, etc.)
  warfare
STRATIŌTĒS
  soldier
STRATOLOGEŌ
  choose
  enrol
  soldier
STRATOPEDARCHĒS
  captain
  guard
STRATOPEDON
  army
STREBLOŌ
  wrest
STRĒNIAŌ
  deliciously
  wanton
STRĒNOS
  delicacies
  wantonness

STREPHŌ
  convert
  turn
STRŌNNUMI
or STRŌNNUŌ
  furnish
  spread
STROUTHION
  sparrow
STUGĒTOS
  hateful
STUGNAZŌ
  countenance
  lowring (to be)
STULOS
  pillar
SU
  thee
  thine
  thou
  thy
SUKAMINOS
  sycamine
SUKĒ (or SUKEA)
  fig tree
SUKOMŌREA
  sycamore
SUKON
  fig
SUKOPHANTEŌ
  accuse
  exact (verb)
SULAGŌGEŌ
  spoil
SULAŌ
  rob
SULLALEŌ
  commune
  confer
  speak
  talk
SULLAMBANŌ
  catch
  conceive
  help
  seize
  take
SULLEGŌ
  gather
SULLOGIZOMAI
  reason
SULLUPEŌ
  (see SUNL–)
SUMBAINŌ
  befall
  happen
  so
  was etc.
SUMBALLŌ
  confer
  encounter
  help
  make
  meet
  ponder
SUMBASILEUŌ
  reign
SUMBIBAZŌ
  assuredly
  bring
  compacted
  conclude
  instruct
  knit together
  prove

SUMBOULEUŌ
  consult
  counsel
SUMBOULION
  consultation
  council
SUMBOULOS
  counsellor
SUMMARTUREŌ
  testify
  witness
SUMMATHĒTĒS
  disciple
SUMMERIZŌ
  partaker
  portion
SUMMETOCHOS
  partaker
SUMMIMĒTĒS
  follower
  imitator
SUMMORPHIZŌ
  conformed
SUMMORPHOŌ
  conformable
SUMMORPHOS
  conformed
  fashion
SUMPARAGINOMAI
  come
  stand
SUMPARAKALEŌ
  comfort
SUMPARALAMBANŌ
  take
SUMPARAMENŌ
  continue
SUMPAREIMI
  present (to be)
SUMPASCHŌ
  suffer
SUMPATHEŌ
  compassion
  feeling
  touch
SUMPATHĒS
  compassion
  compassionate
SUMPEMPŌ (or SUNP-)
  send
SUMPERILAMBANŌ
  embrace
SUMPHĒMI
  consent
SUMPHERŌ
  better (be)
  bring
  expedient
  good (to be)
  profitable
SUMPHERON
  profit
SUMPHŌNEŌ
  agree
SUMPHŌNĒSIS
  concord
SUMPHŌNIA
  music
SUMPHŌNOS
  consent
SUMPHOROS
  profitable

SUMPHULETĒS
countryman
SUMPHUŌ
grow
spring
SUMPHUTOS
plant
SUMPINŌ
drink
SUMPLĒROŌ
come
fill
well-nigh
SUMPNIGŌ
choke
throng
SUMPOLITĒS
citizen
SUMPOREUOMAI
go
resort
SUMPOSION
company
SUMPRESBUTEROS
elder
SUMPSĒPHIZŌ
count
SUMPSUCHOS
accord
SUNAGŌ
assemble
bestow
come
gather
lead
resort
take
SUNAGŌGĒ
assembly
congregation
synagogue
SUNAGŌNIZOMAI
strive
SUNAICHMALŌTOS
prisoner
SUNAIRŌ
reckon
take
SUNAKOLOUTHEŌ
follow
SUNALIZŌ
assemble
SUNALLASSŌ
set
SUNANABAINŌ
come
SUNANAKEIMAI
meat
sit
table (at the)
SUNANAMIGNUMI
company
SUNANAPAUOMAI
find
refresh
SUNANTAŌ
befall
meet
SUNANTĒSIS
meet
SUNANTILAMBANŌ
help
SUNAPAGŌ
carry

SUNAPAGŌ—*contd.*
condescend
lead
SUNAPOLLUMI
perish
SUNAPOSTELLŌ
send
SUNAPOTHNĒSKŌ
die
SUNARMOLOGEŌ
fitly
frame
join
SUNARPAZŌ
catch
seize
SUNATHLEŌ
labour
strive
SUNATHROIZŌ
call
gather
SUNAUXANŌ
grow
SUNCHAIRŌ
rejoice
SUNCHEŌ
or **SUNCHUN(N)Ō**
confound
confuse
stir
uproar
SUNCHRAOMAI
dealings with
SUNCHUSIS
confusion
SUNDEŌ
bind
SUNDESMOS
band
bond
SUNDOULOS
servant
SUNDOXAZŌ
glorify
SUNDROMĒ
run
SUNECHŌ
anguish
constrain
hold
keep
press
sick
stop
strait
straiten
take
throng
SUNĒDOMAI
delight in
SUNEDRION
council
SUNEGEIRŌ
raise
rise
SUNEIDĒSIS
conscience
SUNEIDON
(or **SUNOIDA**)
consider
know
privy
ware

SUNEIMI
gather
SUNEISERCHOMAI
enter
go
SUNEKDĒMOS
companion
SUNEKLEKTOS
elect
SUNELAUNŌ
set
SUNĒLIKIŌTĒS
equal
own
SUNEPHISTĒMI
rise (*see ARISE*)
SUNEPIMARTUREŌ
witness
SUNEPOMAI
accompany
SUNERCHOMAI
accompany
appear
assemble
come
company
go
resort
SUNERGEŌ
help
work
worker
SUNERGOS
companion
helper
labourer
worker
work-fellow
SUNESIS
knowledge
prudence
understanding
SUNESTHIŌ
eat
SUNĒTHEIA
custom
SUNETOS
prudent
understanding
SUNEUDOKEŌ
allow
consent
content
please
SUNEUŌCHEŌ
feast
SUNGENEIA
kindred
SUNGENĒS
cousins
kin
kinsfolk
kinsman
SUNGENEUS
kin
kinsfolk
SUNGENIS
cousin
kinswoman
SUNGNŌMĒ
permission
SUNIĒMI (or **SUNIŌ**)
consider
understand
wise

SUNISTĒMI
approve
commend
compacted
consist
make
prove
stand
SUNKAKOPATHEŌ
hardship
SUNKAKOUCHEOMAI
affliction
entreat
suffer
SUNKALEŌ
call
SUNKALUPTŌ
cover
SUNKAMPTŌ
bow
SUNKATABAINŌ
go
SUNKATAPSĒPHIZŌ
number
SUNKATATHESIS
agreement
SUNKATATITHĒMI
agree
consent
SUNKATHĒMAI
sit
SUNKATHIZŌ
set
sit
SUNKERANNUMI
mixed (with)
temper together
SUNKINEŌ
stir
SUNKLEIŌ
conclude
inclose
shut
SUNKLĒRONOMOS
heir
SUNKOINŌNEŌ
communicate
fellowship
partake(r)
SUNKOINŌNOS
companion
partake
partaker
SUNKOMIZŌ
carry
SUNKRINŌ
compare
SUNKUPTŌ
bow
SUNKURIA
chance
SUNLUPEŌ (or **SULL-**
grieve
SUNOCHĒ
anguish
distress
SUNODEUŌ
journey
SUNODIA
company
SUNŌDINŌ
travail
SUNOIDA
consider

SUNOIDA—*contd.*
  know
  privy
  ware
SUNOIKEŌ
  dwell
SUNOIKODOMEŌ
  build
SUNOMILEŌ
  talk
SUNOMOREŌ
  join
SUNŌMOSIA
  conspiracy
SUNTASSŌ
  appoint
SUNTELEIA
  end
SUNTELEŌ
  complete
  end
  finish
  fulfil
  make
SUNTEMNŌ
  cut
  short
SUNTĒREŌ
  keep
  observe
  preserve
SUNTHAPTŌ
  bury
SUNTHALŌ
  break
SUNTHLIBŌ
  throng
SUNTHRUPTŌ
  break
SUNTITHĒMI
  agree
  covenant
SUNTOMŌS
  few
SUNTRECHŌ
  run
SUNTRIBŌ
  break
  bruise
SUNTRIMMA
  destruction
SUNTROPHOS
  bring
  foster-brother
SUNTUNCHANŌ
  come
SUNUPOKRINOMAI
  dissemble
SUNUPOURGEŌ
  help
SURŌ
  drag
  draw
  hale
SUROPHOINIKISSA
  (or SUROPHUNISSA)
  Syrophœnician
SURTIS
  quicksands
SUSCHĒMATIZŌ
  conform
  fashion
SUSPARASSŌ
  grievously
  tear

SUSSĒMON
  token
SUSSŌMOS
  body
SUSTASIASTĒS
  insurrection
SUSTATIKOS
  commendation
SUSTAUROŌ
  crucify
SUSTELLŌ
  short
  wind
  wrap
SUSTENAZŌ
  groan
SUSTOICHEŌ
  answer
SUSTRATIŌTĒS
  soldier
SUSTREPHŌ
  gather
SUSTROPHĒ (or SUN-)
  banded
  concourse
SU(N)ZAŌ
  live
SU(N)ZĒTEŌ
  dispute
  inquire
  question
  reason
SUZĒTĒSIS
  disputation
  reasoning
SUZĒTĒTĒS
  disputer
SU(N)ZEUGNUMI
  join
SU(N)ZŌOPOIEŌ
  quicken
SU(N)ZUGOS
  yoke-fellow

T

TACHA
  peradventure
  perhaps
TACHEI (EN)
  quickly
  shortly
  speedily
TACHEION
  quickly
  shortly
TACHEŌS
  hastily
  quickly
  shortly
  suddenly
TACHINOS
  shortly
  swift
  swiftly
TACHISTA
  speed
TACHU
  lightly
  quickly
TACHUS
  swift
TAGMA
  order

TAKTOS
  set
TALAIPŌREŌ
  afflict
TALAIPŌRIA
  misery
TALAIPŌROS
  wretched
TALANTIAIOS
  talent
TALANTON
  talent
TAL(E)ITHA
  talitha
TAMEION
  chamber
TAPEINOŌ
  abase
  humble
  low
TAPEINOPHRŌN
  courteous
  humble-minded
TAPEINOPHROSUNĒ
  humbleness
  humility
  lowliness
TAPEINOS
  base
  cast
  degree
  estate
  humble
  low
  lowly
TAPEINŌSIS
  estate
  humiliation
  low (estate)
TAPHĒ
  burial
TAPHOS
  sepulchre
  tomb
TARACHĒ
  trouble
TARACHOS
  stir
TARASSŌ
  trouble
TARTAROŌ
  hell
TASSŌ
  appoint
  determine
  ordain
  set
TAUROS
  ox
TAXIS
  order
TECHNĒ
  art
  craft
  trade
TECHNITĒS
  builder
  craftsman
TEICHOS
  wall
TEKMĒRION
  proof
TEKNION
  child

TEKNOGONEŌ
  children
TEKNOGONIA
  child-bearing
TEKNON
  child
  daughter
  son
TEKNOTROPHEŌ
  children
TĒKŌ
  melt
TEKTŌN
  carpenter
TĒLAUGŌS
  clearly
TELEIOŌ
  accomplish
  consecrate
  do
  finish
  fulfil
  perfect
TELEIOS
  age
  man
  perfect
TELEIŌS
  end
  perfectly
TELEIŌSIS
  fulfilment
  perfection
TELEIOTEROS
  perfect
TELEIOTĒS
  perfection
  perfectness
TELEIŌTĒS
  finisher
TELEŌ
  accomplish
  end
  expire
  fill
  finish
  fulfil
  go
  pay
  perform
TELESPHOREŌ
  perfection
TELEUTAŌ
  decease
  die
TELEUTĒ
  death
TĒLIKOUTOS
  great
  mighty
TELŌNĒS
  publican
TELŌNION
  custom (toll)
TELOS
  continual
  custom (toll)
  end
  ending
  finally
  uttermost
TEPHROŌ
  ashes
TERAS
  wonder

TĒREŌ
charge
hold
keep
keeper
observe
preserve
reserve
watch

TĒRĒSIS
hold
keeping
prison
ward

TESSARAKONTA
forty

TESSARAKO NTAETĒS
forty (years)

TESSARES
four

TESSARESKAI-
DEKATOS
fourteenth

TETARTAIOS
four

TETARTOS
four
fourth

TETRA(A)RCHEŌ
tetrarch

TETRA(A)RCHĒS
tetrarch

TETRADION
quaternion

TETRAGŌNOS
foursquare

TETRAKISCHILIOI
thousand

TETRAKOSIA
four hundred

TETRAMENOS
months

TETRAPLOOS
fourfold

TETRAPOUS
beast
fourfooted

THALASSA
sea

THALPŌ
cherish

THAMBEŌ
amaze

THAMBOS
amazement
wonder

THANASIMOS
deadly

THANATĒPHOROS
deadly

THANATOŌ
dead
death
kill
mortify

THANATOS
death

THAPTŌ
bury

THARREŌ
bold
boldly
confident
confidence

THARREŌ—contd.
courage

THARSEŌ
cheer
comfort

THARSOS
courage

THAUMA
marvel
wonder

THAUMASIOS
wonderful (thing)

THAUMASTOS
marvel
marvellous

THAUMAZŌ
marvel
wonder

THEA
goddess

THEAOMAI
behold
look
see

THEATRIZŌ
gazingstock

THEATRON
spectacle
theatre

THEIŌDĒS
brimstone

THEION
brimstone

THEIOS
divine

THEIOTĒS
Divinity

THĒKĒ
sheath

THĒLAZŌ
suck
suckling

THĒLEIA
woman

THELĒMA
desire
pleasure
will

THELĒSIS
will

THELŌ
desire
disposed
fain
forward (be)
intend
list
love
pleased
rather
unwilling
voluntary
will
willing
wish
would

THĒLUS
female
woman

THEMELIOŌ
found
grounded
settle

THEMELIOS
foundation

THEODIDAKTOS
taught

THEOMACHEŌ
fight

THEOMACHOS
fighting

THEOPNEUSTOS
inspiration

THEŌREŌ
behold
consider
look
perceive
see

THEORIA
sight

THEOS
God
godly

THEOSEBEIA
godliness

THEOSEBĒS
worshipper

THEOSTUGĒS
hateful
hater

THEOTĒS
Divinity

THĒRA
trap

THERAPEIA
healing
household

THERAPEUŌ
cure
heal
worship

THERAPŌN
servant

THĒREUŌ
catch

THĒRIOMACHEŌ
fight

THĒRION
beast

THERISMOS
harvest

THERISTĒS
reaper

THERIZŌ
reap

THERMAINŌ
warm

THERMĒ
heat

THEROS
summer

THĒSAURIZŌ
lay
store
treasure

THĒSAUROS
treasure

THINGANŌ
handle
touch

THLIBŌ
afflict
narrow
press
straitened
throng
tribulation

THLIBŌ—contd.
trouble

THLIPSIS
afflict
affliction
anguish
burdened
distress
persecution
tribulation
trouble

THNĒSKŌ
die

THNĒTOS
mortal
mortality

THŌRAX
breastplate

THORUBAZŌ
trouble

THORUBEŌ
ado
noise
trouble
tumult
uproar

THORUBOS
tumult
uproar

THRAUŌ
bruise

THREMMA
cattle

THRĒNEŌ
bewail
mourn
wail

THRĒNOS
lamentation

THRĒSKEIA
religion
worship

THRĒSKOS
religious

THRIAMBEUŌ
cause
lead
triumph

THRIX
hair

THROEŌ
trouble

THROMBOS
drop

THRONOS
seat
throne

THUELLA
tempest

THUGATĒR
daughter

THUGATRION
daughter

THUÏNOS
thyine (word)

THUMIAMA
incense
odour

THUMIAŌ
incense

THUMIATĒRION
censer

THUMOMACHEŌ
displease

THUMOŌ
wroth (be)

THUMOS
anger
fierceness
indignation
wrath

THUŌ
kill
sacrifice
slay

THURA
door
gate

THUREOS
shield

THURIS
window

THURŌROS
door
porter

THUSIA
sacrifice

THUSIASTĒRION
altar

TIKTŌ
beget, bear
bring
deliver
travail
usury

TILLŌ
pluck

TIMAŌ
esteem
honour
price
value

TIMĒ
honour
precious
price
sum
value

TIMIOS
costly
dear
honourable
precious
reputation

TIMIOTĒS
costliness

TIMŌREŌ
punish

TIMŌRIA
punishment

TINŌ
punish

TIS, TI (1)
certain
every
he
kind
man
manner
one
some
somebody
someone
something
somewhat

TIS, TI (2)
what
whatever
which
who

TIS, TI (2)—*contd.*
whom

TITHĒMI
appoint
bow (Verb)
commit
conceive
give
lay
make
ordain
purpose
put
set
settle
sink

TITLOS
superscription
title

TOICHOS
wall

TOIGAROUN
wherefore

TOINUN
then

TOIOUTOS
fellow
such as

TOKOS
interest
usury

TOLMAŌ
bold
dare

TOLMĒROTERŌS (–ON)
boldly

TOLMĒTĒS
daring

TOMOS
sharp

TOMŌTEROS
sharper

TOPAZION
topaz

TOPOS
everywhere
opportunity
place
quarter
rocky
room
way

TOSOUTOS
great
long
many
much

TOTE
then
time

TOUNANTION
contrariwise

TOXON
bow (noun)

TRACHĒLIZŌ
lay

TRACHĒLOS
neck

TRACHUS
rocky
rough

TRAGOS
goat

TRAPEZA
bank

TRAPEZA—*contd.*
meat
table

TRAPEZITĒS
banker

TRAUMA
wound

TRAUMATIZŌ
wound

TRECHŌ
course
run
rush

TREIS
three

TREMŌ
tremble

TREPHŌ
bring
feed
nourish

TRIAKONTA
thirty
thirtyfold

TRIAKOSIOI
three hundred

TRIBOLOS
thistle

TRIBOS
path

TRICHINOS
hair

TRIETIA
year

TRIMĒNOS
months

TRIS
thrice

TRISCHILIOI
thousand

TRISTEGOS
story

TRITOS
third
thirdly

TRIZŌ
gnash
grind

TROCHIA
path

TROCHOS
course
wheel

TRŌGŌ
eat

TROMOS
trembling

TROPĒ
turning

TROPHĒ
food
meat

TROPHOS
nurse

TROPOPHOREŌ
bear
manner
suffer

TROPOS
conversation
even as
manner
means
way

TRUBLION
dish

TRUGAŌ
gather

TRUGŌN
dove

TRUMALIA
eye

TRUPĒMA
eye

TRUPHAŌ
delicately (live)
pleasure

TRUPHĒ
delicately
revel
riot

TUCHŌN
special

TUMPANIZŌ
torture

TUNCHANŌ
attain
chance
common
enjoy
may
obtain

TUPHLOŌ
blind

TUPHLOS
blind

TUPHŌ
smoke

TUPHŌNIKOS
tempestuous

TUPHOŌ
high minded
pride
proud
puff (up)
smoke

TUPOS
ensample
example
fashion
figure
form
manner
pattern
print

TUPTŌ
beat
smite
strike
wound

TURBAZŌ
trouble

X

XENIA
lodging

XENIZŌ
entertain
lodge
strange

XENODOCHEŌ
stranger

XENOS
host (of guests)
strange
stranger

XĒRAINŌ
dry

XĒRAINŌ—*contd.*
over-ripe
pine away
ripe
wither

XĒROS
dry
land
withered

XESTĒS
pot

XULINOS
wood

XULON
staff
stocks
tree
wood

XURAŌ
shave

Z

ZAŌ
lifetime
live
lively
living

ZĒLOŌ
affect
covet
desire
earnestly
envy
jealous
seek
zealously

ZĒLOS
envy
fervent
fierceness
indignation
jealousy
zeal

ZĒLŌTĒS
zealous

ZĒMIA
loss

ZĒMIOŌ
cast
forfeit
lose
loss
receive

ZEŌ
fervent

ZESTOS
hot

ZĒTĒMA
question

ZĒTEŌ
about
desire
endeavour
go
inquire
require
seek

ZĒTĒSIS
disputation
inquire
question

ZEUGOS
pair
yoke

ZEUKTĒRIA
band

ZIZANION
tares

ZŌĒ
life

ZŌGREŌ
captive
catch

ZŌNĒ
bag
girdle

ZŌNNUMI
gird

ZŌOGONEŌ
live
preserve
quicken

ZŌON
beast
creature

ZŌOPOIEŌ
life
quicken

ZOPHOS
blackness
darkness
mist

ZUGOS
balance
pair
yoke

ZUMĒ
leaven

ZUMOŌ
leaven